CASES AND MATERIALS ON

LEGISLATION AND REGULATION

STATUTES AND THE CREATION OF PUBLIC POLICY

Fifth Edition

■ ■ ■

by

William N. Eskridge Jr.
John A. Garver Professor of Jurisprudence
Yale University

Philip P. Frickey
Late Alexander F. & May T. Morrison Professor of Law
University of California at Berkeley

Elizabeth Garrett
Frances R. and John J. Duggan Professor of Law, Political Science,
Finance and Business Economics, and Public Policy
University of Southern California

James J. Brudney
Professor of Law
Fordham University

AMERICAN CASEBOOK SERIES®

Mat #41666833

COPYRIGHT © 1988, 1995 WEST PUBLISHING CO.
© West, a Thomson business, 2001, 2007
© 2014 LEG, Inc. d/b/a West Academic
    444 Cedar Street, Suite 700
    St. Paul, MN 55101
    1-877-888-1330

West, West Academic Publishing, and West Academic are trademarks of West Publishing Corporation, used under license.

Printed in the United States of America

ISBN: 978-1-62810-173-7

In Memory of Our Friend and the Parent of These Materials

Philip P. Frickey

1953–2010

PREFACE TO FIFTH EDITION

The Fifth Edition addresses the regulatory process in greater depth than previous editions, as indicated by the expanded title for the Casebook. This edition includes extensive new treatment on the different kinds of agencies; the range of regulatory mechanisms and strategies potentially available for implementing statutory schemes; and White House oversight of agency rulemaking. It also presents considerable new material addressing judicial review of agency rulemaking, adjudication, and informal guidance under the Administrative Procedure Act, as well as the various regimes requiring judicial deference to agency interpretations of statutes. The new treatment, evident in chapters 1, 8, and 9, reflects the fact that law school Legislation courses increasingly emphasize regulatory implementation as part of the lawmaking enterprise.

Updating the book's longstanding coverage, the new edition also describes important recent developments in scholarship and caselaw addressed to the legislative process, lobbying, campaign finance, and direct democracy. This expanded discussion and analysis is presented in chapters 2, 3, and 4.

In addition, the Fifth Edition continues its in-depth examination of the theory and practice of statutory interpretation. In chapters 5, 6, and 7, we present new judicial and scholarly discussion on the deployment of dictionaries and textual canons in statutory interpretation, the canon avoiding interpretations that pose constitutional difficulties, and state-level developments including useful surveys of state court statutory interpretation practices,

We are grateful for the suggestions and comments of many colleagues in preparing this new edition. While listing them inevitably risks omitting some who also deserve mention, we would single out Abbe Gluck, Jennifer Gordon, Steve Huefner, Clare Huntington, Ethan Leib, John Manning, Victoria Nourse, Kimani Paul-Emile, Aaron Saiger, Kevin Stack, Matthew Stephenson, Peter Strauss, Olivier Sylvain, and Dan Tokaji for especially helpful insights.

We thank Yale, the University of Southern California, and Fordham law schools for generous research support. In preparing the Fifth Edition, we have benefitted from the contributions of many outstanding research assistants: Steve Della Fera (Fordham Class of 2014), Alexander Fullman (USC Class of 2013), Erika Nyborg-Burch (Yale Class of 2016), Chris Pagliarella (Yale Class of 2016), Anthony Piccirillo (Fordham Class of 2013), Lise Rahdert (Yale Class of 2015), Marissa Roy (USC Class of 2014), Eliza Simon (Yale Class of 2013), Amanda Shami (Fordham Class of 2015), Sam Thypin-Bermeo (Yale Class of 2015), Natalie Turchi (Fordham Class of 2016), and Ben Wallace (Yale Class of 2016). We also appreciate the excellent copy editing performed by Susan Wampler.

Finally, we continue to benefit enormously from the talents and insights of our departed colleague and friend Phil Frickey, whose pathfinding work and a great deal of his original writing remain foundational to this expanded Fifth Edition. We cannot repay that debt but we remain ever mindful of its magnitude.

WILLIAM N. ESKRIDGE JR.
NEW HAVEN, CONNECTICUT

ELIZABETH GARRETT
LOS ANGELES, CALIFORNIA

JAMES J. BRUDNEY
NEW YORK, NY

September 2014

SUMMARY OF CONTENTS

———

TABLE OF CONTENTS

674-690

TABLE OF CASES

The principal cases are in bold type.

CASES AND MATERIALS ON

LEGISLATION AND REGULATION

STATUTES AND THE CREATION OF PUBLIC POLICY

Fifth Edition

CHAPTER 1

AN INTRODUCTION TO STATUTES

∎ ∎ ∎

We introduce the study of statutory interpretation through a case study, followed by descriptions of several theoretical frameworks for understanding that story. Section 1 of this chapter tells the story of the Civil Rights Act of 1964, Pub. L. No. 88–352, 78 Stat. 241 (codified as amended in scattered sections of 42 U.S.C.). We have chosen this law, in part, because it is a dramatic example of how statutes can and do make a significant difference in our society and our lives. The principles set forth in *Brown v. Board of Education*, 347 U.S. 483 (1954), would have been left largely unfulfilled were it not for the statute, which amplified and implemented the principles in ways that the Court was not able, or willing, to do. Also, the story of the law's enactment is itself a case study of the legislative process and of the unpredictable path followed by the official as well as private implementers of the statute. In fairness, the path of the 1964 Civil Rights Act was and remains atypical of the federal legislative process; major legislation increasingly travels paths that diverge from the textbook descriptions of Congress.

The Civil Rights Act is also a useful starting point for a theoretical discussion of the legislative process in the United States. In Section 2, we offer three types of theories: pluralist theories, which focus on the role of social and economic groups in policymaking; public choice theories, which treat legislation as a transaction between buyers (interest groups) and sellers (legislators); and proceduralist theories, which emphasize the many obstacles a bill must pass through before it becomes a law. Each theory has a descriptive dimension (this is how the legislative process *does* work) and a normative dimension (this is how the legislative process *should* work).

In Section 3, we trace the dynamic interpretation of Title VII (the employment discrimination title) of the Civil Rights Act. We start with the implementation of the 1964 Act by the Equal Employment Opportunity Commission (EEOC). Although Congress purposely structured the EEOC as a weak agency, it developed important legal rules that gave teeth to the statutory scheme—more teeth than some of the law's supporters probably thought they were enacting into law. We also introduce you to theories of statutory interpretation through examination of an important case, *United Steelworkers v. Weber*, in which the Court interpreted the Act to allow voluntary affirmative action plans.

1

1. THE STORY OF THE CIVIL RIGHTS ACT OF 1964 AND THE PROCEDURES OF STATUTE-CREATION[1]

Brown v. Board of Education declared a great principle—non-discrimination and racial equality—but the principle did little to change the day-to-day lives of most African Americans in the 1950s. *Brown* applied only to public institutions, leaving private hotels, restaurants, swimming pools, and employers free to continue racially discriminatory practices. Even public institutions (mainly schools) were only required to desegregate "with all deliberate speed." The pace of official desegregation was slothlike. In 1961, seven years after *Brown*, it required a bevy of federal marshals to escort James Meredith through the doors of the University of Mississippi as its first African-American student.

On February 1, 1960, four black students from North Carolina A & T University sat down to order at a "whites only" lunch counter at a Woolworth's store in Greensboro, North Carolina. The store's manager refused to serve them. They remained seated, silently demanding equal treatment. Hundreds of similar "sit-ins" followed in other Southern locales.

In April 1963, the Reverend Dr. Martin Luther King, Jr. launched a nonviolent offensive to protest and boycott the segregated shops, churches, and restaurants of Birmingham, Alabama. When Dr. King defied an injunction and led a protest march, the Birmingham Commissioner of Public Safety, T. Eugene "Bull" Connor, had him and 54 others arrested and jailed. In May 1963, Connor and his cohorts brutally attacked hundreds of black schoolchildren marching and singing the anthem "We Shall Overcome." Front-page photos of Connor's hounds attacking African-American youths, of fire hose water pressing back the waves of black bodies, and of burly policemen sitting on a prostrate woman, aroused the national conscience (Harvey 55).

African-American leaders saw this as their historic moment. Dr. King wrote from his Birmingham jail cell:

> For years now I have heard the word "Wait!" It rings in the ear of every Negro with piercing familiarity. This "wait" has almost always meant "never." * * * We have waited for more than 340 years for our constitutional and God-given rights. * * * [W]hen you take a cross-country drive and find it necessary to sleep night after night in the uncomfortable

---

[1] The most informative source for our account of the 1964 Act was Charles Whalen & Barbara Whalen, *The Longest Debate: A Legislative History of the 1964 Civil Rights Act* (1985) (cited in text as "Whalens," with page numbers). Quotations from *The Longest Debate* are reprinted with the permission of Charles Whalen, Barbara Whalen, and the publisher, Seven Locks Press, Inc., P.O. Box 27, Cabin John, Maryland 20818. Other useful sources were Carl Brauer, *John F. Kennedy and the Second Reconstruction* (1977) ("Brauer"); Robert Caro, *The Passage of Power: The Years of Lyndon Johnson* (2012) ("Caro"); Hugh Davis Graham, *The Civil Rights Era: Origins and Development of National Policy, 1960–1972* (1990) ("Graham"); Cynthia Harrison, *On Account of Sex: The Politics of Women's Issues, 1945–1968* (1988) ("Harrison"); James Harvey, *Civil Rights During the Kennedy Administration* (1971) ("Harvey"); Hubert Humphrey, *Beyond Civil Rights: A New Day of Equality* (1968) ("Humphrey"); Neil MacNeil, *Dirksen: Portrait of a Public Man* (1970) ("MacNeil"); John Martin, *Civil Rights and the Crisis of Liberalism: The Democratic Party, 1945–1976* (1979) ("Martin"); Merle Miller, *Lyndon: An Oral Biography* (1980) ("Miller"); Edward Schapsmeier & Frederick Schapsmeier, *Dirksen of Illinois: Senatorial Statesman* (1985) ("Schapsmeiers"); Bernard Schwartz, ed., *Statutory History of the United States: Civil Rights* (1970) ("Schwartz"); and Francis Vaas, *Title VII: Legislative History,* 7 B.C. Indus. & Com. L. Rev. 431 (1966) ("Vaas").

corners of your automobile because no motel will accept you; when you are humiliated day in and day out by nagging signs reading "white" and "colored"; when your first name becomes "nigger," your middle name becomes "boy" (however old you are) and your last name becomes "John," and your wife and mother are never given the respected title of "Mrs."; when you are harried by day and haunted by night by the fact that you are a Negro, living constantly at tiptoe stance, never quite knowing what to expect next, and are plagued with inner fears and outer resentments; when you are forever fighting a degenerating sense of "no-bodiness"—then you will understand why we find it difficult to wait.

National media attention and outrage helped ensure the success of Dr. King's Birmingham campaign. On May 10, 1963, the city's businesses entered into a settlement in which the African-American community agreed to cease their boycott and the white-owned businesses agreed to hire blacks as clerks and salespeople, and to establish training programs in job categories previously closed to African Americans.

The Kennedy Administration was listening. Attorney General Robert Kennedy hailed the Birmingham settlement. On June 11, 1963, President John Kennedy addressed the country on national television and announced his intention to propose a comprehensive civil rights bill to address the burning issue, "whether all Americans are to be afforded equal rights and equal opportunities, whether we are going to treat our fellow Americans as we want to be treated." Although President Lincoln's Emancipation Proclamation (freeing the slaves) had been issued exactly one hundred years earlier, the descendants of those men and women "are not yet freed from the bonds of injustice. They are not yet freed from social and economic oppression. And this Nation, for all its hopes and all its boasts, will not be fully free until all its citizens are free."

OBSTACLES TO CIVIL RIGHTS LEGISLATION

Title II of the President's proposed legislation, the public accommodations provision, would guarantee equal access to all hotels, restaurants, places of amusement, and retail establishments. Title III covered school desegregation. It would give the federal government, particularly the Attorney General, greater authority to implement the *Brown* decision. Employment discrimination was treated in Title V of the President's bill, which expanded the powers of the Civil Rights Commission, and in Title VII, which would have established a Committee on Equal Employment to monitor the conduct of federal contractors. While not addressing private discrimination, the President reaffirmed his support for legislation addressing employment discrimination in the private sector. Finally, in Title VI, the President proposed that recipients of federal assistance be prohibited from discriminating on the basis of race. The events of 1963 suggested the need for such legislation. But there was good reason to doubt that the President's bill would ever become law.

1. *The Ambivalence of Both Political Parties.* On the issue of civil rights, the Democratic Party could be described as two parties. Southern Democrats normally controlled as many as half of the party's votes in the Senate, and systematically

killed civil rights bills through parliamentary maneuvers (Martin 157). In 1948, the Democratic Party split when adoption of a civil rights plank at the national convention caused a walkout by segregationists. Efforts to heal those wounds led the Democrats to downplay civil rights in the 1952 and 1956 platforms. In contrast, the Republicans—the Party of Lincoln—showed renewed interest in civil rights. In 1957, President Eisenhower introduced a civil rights bill—but a filibuster by Senate Democrats forced supporters to propose changes that made it an essentially toothless law. A similar presidential initiative in 1960 yielded a weak voting rights law, after Senate Democrats deleted school desegregation, employment, and housing discrimination provisions from the bill.

As the 1960 election approached, black leaders wondered which—if either—of the major parties was capable of delivering civil rights legislation. The Republicans had pushed for moderate civil rights laws in the 1950s but had been unable to deliver them. Democrats had both supported and torpedoed civil rights initiatives. The platforms of both parties called for civil rights legislation, but the support seemed increasingly rhetorical as the campaign wore on (Harvey 13). Because the Democrat (Kennedy) took stronger stands on the civil rights issue than did the Republican (Nixon), he won the black vote, which was probably critical to his election, given the narrowness of his margin of victory.

2.   *The Uncertain Commitment of the Administration.* Although President Kennedy opposed discrimination, he had no deep emotional concern for the issue. Some have suggested that Kennedy was primarily concerned with foreign affairs and economic issues and thought of African Americans only in terms of votes (Harvey 19). As a senator in 1957, Kennedy had voted with the Democratic majority to weaken the Republicans' civil rights bill (Martin 167). Thus it was hardly surprising that, after the 1960 election, President Kennedy disregarded his campaign rhetoric and decided not to seek civil rights legislation. He reasoned that such an effort would not only fail, but it would also delay enactment of important economic legislation (Harvey 19–20).

Kennedy did, gradually, use his powers as chief executive to appoint African Americans to important positions and to establish equal opportunity in federal employment. In November 1962, he issued the order prohibiting racial discrimination in federally financed housing, the same order he had, as a candidate in 1960, chastised Eisenhower for not issuing with a "stroke of his pen" (Martin 177). It was not until he was faced with blatant defiance by Governors Ross Barnett (D–MS) and George Wallace (D–AL) that Kennedy, as Commander-in-Chief, used federal troops to enforce judicial desegregation orders.

Although he was opposed to discrimination as a matter of private conscience, Vice-President Johnson was not known as a force for civil rights either. In his 1948 campaign for the Senate, Lyndon Johnson had called President Truman's civil rights program (repeal of the poll tax; anti-lynching law; nondiscrimination in employment) "an effort to set up a police state in the guise of liberty" (Miller 118). Through his friendship with powerful Senator Richard Russell (D–GA), Johnson became the Democrats' Senate leader in 1953. In 1957, LBJ persuaded the Senate to pass the first civil rights statute since 1874—but liberals were disappointed that the law had virtually no legal effect.

3. *Obstacles in Congress.* Over 90% of bills introduced in Congress die in the legislative labyrinth. Though a senator for eight years and representative for six years before that, Kennedy was not a skilled legislative strategist. It was unlikely that he could move a civil rights bill through Congress.

Virtually all bills introduced in Congress are referred initially to a committee for consideration and cannot be voted on until the committee has reported them out.[2] Because a committee's chair controls the committee's staff and agenda, he or she has the power to effectively kill a bill by preventing the committee from considering it. Committee chairmanships have generally been awarded on the basis of seniority—and in 1963 many powerful chairs were Southern Democrats such as Senator James Eastland (D–MS), chair of the Senate Judiciary Committee, and Representative Howard "Judge" Smith (D–VA), chair of the House Rules Committee. In 1957, Smith stalled consideration of the civil rights bill simply by leaving Washington; he claimed that he needed to attend to his barn in Virginia that had recently burned down. Speaker of the House Sam Rayburn (D–TX) replied that he knew Smith was opposed to civil rights, but he never suspected that the Chairman would resort to arson (Martin 166).

Even if the civil rights bill were to survive the committee process, it faced a certain *filibuster* on the floor of the Senate. Senate rules allow unlimited debate of a question before voting, and civil rights opponents had successfully used this tactic in 1957 and 1960 to prevent consideration of civil rights bills, allowing a vote only after they had exacted tremendous concessions from the bills' supporters. The only ways to break a filibuster are by permitting it to continue until the filibusterers are physically exhausted or by invoking *cloture* (a two-thirds vote to end discussion).[3] The former had been tried and had failed in 1957, while the latter had been successfully invoked only five times in the history of the Senate and never to end debate on a civil rights bill (Whalens 126).

PASSAGE IN THE HOUSE

The President's civil rights bill was introduced in both houses of Congress on June 19, 1963, but its supporters pushed for immediate consideration only in the House of Representatives. If they could develop a strong record and publicity for the bill in the House, supporters hoped that political momentum would improve the bill's chances in the Senate.

---

[2] Current House Rule X, clause 1 and Senate Rule XXV, clause 1 identify the standing (permanent) committees in the two chambers and define the jurisdiction (area of exclusive authority) for each standing committee. House Rule XII, clause 2 and Senate Rule XVII, clause 3 govern referral to committees by the Speaker of the House and the Senate Majority Leader.

[3] Under current Senate Rule XXII, clause 2, cloture can be invoked in most cases by the vote of 60 of the 100 senators, but in 1963–64, Rule XXII provided for cloture of debate only by two-thirds of the senators voting on the question. Since important cloture votes could be expected to command all 100 senators, 67 votes were usually needed to close off debate. Even now, a two-thirds vote is required to end debate on any measure amending the Senate Rules, including the rule governing cloture.

1. *Writing a Bill the Hard Way—The Judiciary Committee*. House Speaker John McCormack (D–MA) referred H.R. 7152[4] to the House Judiciary Committee, which had jurisdiction over civil rights bills. Chairman Emanuel Celler (D–NY) referred the bill to Subcommittee No. 5. The Chairman referred the bill to this subcommittee, which normally handled antitrust matters, because it was dominated by civil rights advocates: its Chairman was Celler himself, the ranking Republican was William McCulloch (R–OH), and it had no senior Southern member (Harvey 60).

A longtime representative from Brooklyn, Celler had become one of Congress's leading civil rights advocates. His co-sponsor was the ranking Republican on the Judiciary Committee, Bill McCulloch, whose district in rural Ohio was a universe away from Brooklyn. Although there was little interest in civil rights legislation at home, McCulloch's popularity allowed him latitude to pursue a personal agenda to align the federal government with the anti-discrimination principle (Whalens 7–11). Indeed, he introduced a GOP civil rights measure in 1961. McCulloch's support, and the Republican votes he might bring with him, were essential to success in the House where, because of the split in the Democratic ranks, the Republicans held the balance of power (Harvey 59).

Celler scheduled subcommittee hearings to start before the Fourth of July recess. The free ride that the bill was expected to get through the subcommittee hit a snag with the first witness, Attorney General Robert Kennedy. The Attorney General was unaware of McCulloch's earlier bill, as well as a bill introduced by John Lindsay (R–NY), and his failure to acknowledge Republican civil rights efforts was interpreted as a Democratic attempt to take partisan advantage of the civil rights issue. The Republican members of the subcommittee threatened to scuttle H.R. 7152 if it became a partisan measure. To repair the nascent bipartisan coalition, the Administration dispatched Assistant Attorney General Burke Marshall to negotiate a deal with McCulloch during the recess (Whalens 5–11).

Marshall found McCulloch supportive of civil rights, but he was also unwilling to allow the Democrats to hog the issue (particularly since the Democrats heading the Administration had undermined his own efforts in 1957 and 1960). Marshall brokered a deal whereby McCulloch pledged his support in exchange for the Administration's promise to publicize the initiative as bipartisan and not to allow the Senate to water down the bill, as it had done in 1957 (Whalens 10–14). This meant that McCulloch would be consulted on all changes to H.R. 7152 that the Administration wanted to accept after the bill passed the House.

During the congressional hearings, the Administration engaged in a campaign to build public support for H.R. 7152, meeting with over 1,600 members of interest groups in June and July. Representatives of labor, the clergy, and civil rights groups received special attention (Brauer 273–74). The President was especially interested in a vigorous clerical lobby because it provided a means of influencing legislators from states where the impact of blacks and labor was minimal (Brauer

---

⁴ Bills introduced in the House and Senate are assigned identifying numbers—"H.R. ___" and "S. ___"— just as cases filed in U.S. courts are assigned a docket number.

275). On the other hand, the Administration cautioned civil rights allies not to expect a really ambitious law, given all the obstacles to any legislation.

By August 2, the subcommittee had held 22 days of hearings on H.R. 7152 and was ready to *mark up* the bill. A mark-up is a committee's drafting session where members consider amendments and rewrite bills. The Administration had asked Celler to stall final consideration on the bill until his tax reform proposal was voted out of the House Ways and Means Committee, where it had been languishing since January. The highly controversial tax cut was a cornerstone in the President's economic program, and Kennedy feared that Southerners on Ways and Means might use the bill as a target for retaliation if the civil rights bill cleared Subcommittee No. 5 first. Therefore, Celler delayed substantive mark-up of H.R. 7152 until September (Whalens 22–23). Meanwhile, public pressure for legislation mounted.[5]

On September 10, the Ways and Means Committee approved the tax bill, and Celler prepared for the mark-up of H.R. 7152. Deputy Attorney General Nicholas Katzenbach had written Celler a letter setting forth the "tactics" that the Administration expected him to follow, pursuant to its deal with McCulloch. But Celler chose to pursue a more aggressive approach. He remembered that the Senate had watered down the moderate civil rights bills passed by the House in 1957 and 1960. Why not start with a very strong bill this time, so that a compromise version would still be acceptable? Moreover, by publicly pushing a strong bill, Celler would be a hero to civil rights groups and would still be able to preserve his friendship with the conservatives by allowing them to score points with their constituents when the bill was inevitably weakened (Whalens 30–31).

Bill McCulloch watched in disbelief as Manny Celler and the liberal Democrats on the subcommittee proceeded to strengthen almost every title of the Administration's bill, betraying the President's agreement with the Republican leadership in the process. For example, Bob Kastenmeier (D–WI) offered an amendment to broaden Title II, the public accommodations provision, to include every private business—law firms, medical associations, and private schools— except rooming houses with five units or less (Whalens 34–35; Harvey 60). On September 25, the subcommittee replaced H.R. 7152's weak equal employment provisions with a new title, embodied in a 30–page amendment offered by Peter Rodino (D–NJ). The new title would create an Equal Employment Opportunity Commission (EEOC) with authority to investigate employment discrimination on account of race, religion, or national origin and to issue enforceable cease-and-desist orders (Vaas 435; Whalens 35).

---

[5] On August 28, 1963, as Congress prepared to adjourn for the Labor Day recess, almost a quarter of a million people converged on Washington, D.C., in a peaceful demonstration for equal rights—the March on Washington for Jobs and Freedom (Martin 176–77). In his address to the crowd that afternoon, Dr. King argued that, one hundred years after the Emancipation Proclamation, African Americans were still not free. "One hundred years later, the life of the Negro is still sadly crippled by the manacles and the chains of discrimination. * * * One hundred years later, the Negro is still languishing in the corners of American society and finds himself an exile in his own land." Dr. King concluded: "I have a dream today that my four little children will one day live in a nation where they will not be judged by the color of their skin but by the content of their character. I have a dream today."

On October 2, Subcommittee No. 5 reported the new H.R. 7152 to the full Judiciary Committee. Civil rights leaders, who had received virtually every provision they had lobbied for, called the bill a triumph. But McCulloch labeled the bill "a pail of garbage" with no chance of passage on the floor of the House (Whalens 38). Southern members of the Judiciary Committee who hoped to derail the bill apparently agreed, for they joined the liberals to vote H.R. 7152 as amended out of subcommittee (Harvey 60).

House Minority Leader Charles Halleck (R–IN) met with Deputy Attorney General Katzenbach and Speaker McCormack on October 8 to tell them that the Republicans would allow the strengthened bill to go to the House floor, where it would probably die—unless the liberal Democrats themselves cooperated in weakening the bill. The Administration agreed to the GOP proposal and persuaded Celler to go along (Whalens 42–44). On October 15, the Attorney General testified before the Committee to recommend weakening changes (Brauer 304). On October 22, the amendments were to be offered, the first by Roland Libonati (D–IL). At the last moment Libonati backed out, leaving the Republicans feeling betrayed again. A Republican member moved to report the subcommittee bill to the full House. The motion would have easily passed had Celler not adjourned the Committee for the day. The situation was a mess.

Administration officials met with Halleck and McCulloch to work out a compromise bill that would satisfy the Republicans (Whalens 52–53). The President agreed to Republican demands that the bill should be revised. The new bill reconciled a Republican redraft and the original Administration bill. The President and Republican leadership agreed that the compromise bill would be offered as a substitute for the subcommittee bill (Harvey 61). All that remained was to defeat the motion to report out the unacceptable subcommittee version of H.R. 7152. Halleck and McCulloch agreed to provide seven Republican votes if the Democrats would provide ten votes. The President twisted arms and Celler invoked loyalty to party and the chairman to meet their quota (Whalens 59–64).

Now uneasy with Chairman Celler's ability to run the Judiciary Committee, the Administration prepared a "six-point script" for him to follow on October 29, describing precisely the manner in which to proceed. For once, events went as planned (Whalens 64–66). (1) A roll call vote was taken on the pending motion to report the subcommittee bill. Democratic members were called first, according to tradition, allowing Halleck and McCulloch to see if the Democrats could deliver their share of the votes to defeat the motion before having to commit themselves. Celler delivered ten Democratic votes, and the Republicans provided nine votes (more than promised) to defeat the motion. (2) Celler moved to strike all but the first sentence of the subcommittee bill and to insert the compromise bill as an amendment. (3) Celler and McCulloch explained the substitute, and Celler brushed aside a *point of order* challenge. (4) Once the compromise was read in its entirety, Representative Rodino moved the *previous question*, cutting off any debate on the proposed amendment. The Committee voted 20–12 in favor of the previous question. (5) The Judiciary Committee passed the compromise substitute by a vote of 20–14. (6) The Committee reported H.R. 7152 to the House.

Although civil rights leaders criticized the Administration for favoring cutbacks in the subcommittee substitute, the committee version was stronger than the Administration's original bill. For example, Title II (public accommodations) broadly prohibited discrimination in places of lodging, sports stadiums and arenas, theaters, restaurants, cafeterias, lunch counters, and gas stations. Title VII (equal employment) retained the main features of Rodino's substitute for the Administration's weak monitoring provisions, though the EEOC's adjudicatory powers were limited. The President praised the bill as "comprehensive and fair," and the Administration evenly distributed credit among Democrats and Republicans (Whalens 66).

2. *Surviving the Rules Committee.* On November 21, H.R. 7152 and the Judiciary Committee's report were conveyed to the Clerk of the House and then to the Rules Committee. Each bill reported out of committee passes through the Rules Committee, where a resolution (the *rule*) governing floor debate is prepared.[6] In addition to providing that high priority bills receive expedited consideration, the Rules Committee determines the amount of time to be allowed for debate, how the time for debate will be allocated, and the scope of permissible amendments.

The Rules Committee stage often constitutes a substantive consideration of the bill, and it presents an opportunity to derail a bill before the House itself has a chance to consider it. Unfortunately, the chairman of the Rules Committee, 80-year-old Howard ("Judge") Smith, had spent 33 years in the House killing or eviscerating progressive legislation in the areas of labor, public housing, education, medical care and, of course, civil rights. His effectiveness had brought him a reputation as one of the most powerful members of the House.[7]

President Kennedy's assassination on November 22 meant that the task of getting H.R. 7152 through the Rules Committee fell to Lyndon Johnson. In an effort to seize the moral leadership of the nation, President Johnson addressed a joint session of Congress soon after Kennedy's death: "[N]o memorial oration or eulogy could more eloquently honor President Kennedy's memory than the earliest possible passage of the civil rights bill for which he fought so long." Apparently, popular support for the bill was increasing—but to no effect on Judge Smith, who had a firm grip on the fate of H.R. 7152. Following the Southern strategy of delay, he declined even to hold hearings on the bill.

There were three procedural options for dislodging Smith's stranglehold on H.R. 7152, and each was tried by the bill's supporters (Whalens 84–85). First,

---

[6] Current House Rule XIII, clause 2 provides that all committee reports, including the views of the minority, shall be delivered to the Clerk for printing and reference to the proper *calendar* (described *infra*). Because House calendars contain many bills, and bills are to be considered in their order on the calendars, there is no assurance that the bill will be considered at all. The Rules Committee has the power to recommend a rule to expedite consideration of any bill—ahead of those previously placed on the calendars.

[7] In an effort to curtail Judge Smith's ability to bury the Administration's progressive legislative agenda, President Kennedy had worked prior to the 1961 session with then-Speaker of the House, Sam Rayburn, to enlarge the Rules Committee from ten to fifteen members (ten Democrats and five Republicans). The appointment of five new committee members allowed Rayburn and the Administration to create an 8–7 liberal majority on the Rules Committee and to increase the control of party leaders over it. While the enlargement improved prospects for the President's legislative agenda, highly controversial bills—like civil rights proposals—still faced unfavorable odds in Judge Smith's lair (Harvey 15–16).

under House Rule XV, a petition signed by a majority of the House's members (218 when there are no vacancies) can remove any bill from committee, including the Rules Committee, after it has been in committee for 30 days. On December 9, Celler began circulating such a *discharge petition*, but McCulloch and Halleck refused to deliver the needed Republican signatures, on the ground that such a course was antithetical to the committee process (Whalens 84). Only a handful of discharge petitions have been successful in the last fifty years.

On December 11, the Republicans announced their intent to use a second device, *Calendar Wednesday*, to call up H.R. 7152. House Rule XXV allows the Speaker on each Wednesday to call the standing committees in alphabetical order to inquire whether the chairman wishes the House to consider any bill previously reported out of that committee. But with eleven committees coming alphabetically before the Judiciary Committee, including six chaired by Southerners, the bill's opponents could easily defeat the tactic by calling up other bills to exhaust the available time. To prevent an embarrassing display of intraparty divisions, the Democratic leadership simply adjourned the House before the Calendar Wednesday maneuver could be tried (Whalens 85).

The third mechanism was to be the key. House Rule XI permits any three members of a committee to request the chairman to call a meeting to consider a bill; if the meeting is not scheduled within three days, a majority of the committee may schedule one. Liberal Democrats numbered five on the Rules Committee, so three Republican votes were needed. The pivotal votes were controlled by Clarence Brown (R–OH), the ranking minority member on the Rules Committee (Whalens 85). The conservative Ohio Republican shared the commitment to civil rights of his friend Bill McCulloch.[8] Brown gently informed Judge Smith of his plans to lead a mutiny, so to head off a confrontation, Smith announced that hearings would begin on January 9, 1964 (Whalens 86).

Between January 9 and January 30, the House Rules Committee heard testimony from 40 different members of Congress (Vaas 438). No one expected the hearings to have any effect on the outcome, but they provided Southern Democrats a forum for airing their opposition to the bill. On January 30, 1964, the Rules Committee approved House Resolution 616, governing debate on H.R. 7152, by a vote of 11–4 (Whalens 99). The bill had not only survived the Rules Committee, it had survived without a single amendment (Vaas 438).

3. *Bipartisan House Victory.* The House of Representatives follows a six-step process in considering a bill called up from the floor. First, the House debates and votes on the bill's rule. If the rule is accepted, the body will resolve into the *Committee of the Whole House on the State of the Union*, which is simply the full House following simplified procedures for purposes of debate. Next, pursuant to the rule, members offer amendments, which are debated and then accepted or rejected by unrecorded votes. The members will then resume sitting formally as the House and, if requested by one-fifth of the members, take recorded votes on any accepted

---

[8]   Two major black universities (Wilberforce and Central State) were situated in Brown's district. The town of Xenia in his district was one of the major links in the Underground Railway, used by slaves to escape to Canada in the nineteenth century (Whalens 86).

amendments. A minority party member will be recognized to offer a motion to recommit the bill to committee. Finally, the House will vote on the bill, as amended by the Committee of the Whole (Whalens 101).

On January 3, 1964, Speaker John McCormack recognized a Rules Committee member to call up House Resolution 616 (the special rule) for immediate consideration. Under the rules of the House, debate on the resolution was limited to one hour, divided equally between each party. In a voice vote, the House approved the rule (Whalens 102–03). The House then resolved itself into the Committee of the Whole, and Speaker McCormack stepped down and handed the gavel to Eugene Keogh (D–NY), who assumed his position as Chairman of the Committee of the Whole.

The rule approved for H.R. 7152 specified that general debate would be limited to ten hours, divided equally between the two parties and between opponents and supporters, after which amendments would be offered, title by title, in accordance with *the five minute rule*. Under this rule, all speakers—the amendment's sponsor, its proponents, and its opponents—were limited to five minutes of remarks each. Furthermore, in exchange for the bill's supporters' pledge not to limit debate on any amendment, the bill's opponents agreed not to bog down the proceedings with redundant quorum calls. This was to be a battle, but it would be a genteel one (Whalens 108).

Celler and McCulloch delivered the opening statements. Manny Celler chose to describe the bill in broad dramatic terms:

> The legislation before you seeks only to honor the constitutional guarantees of equality under the law for all. It bestows no preferences on any one group; what it does is to place into balance the scales of justice so that the living force of our Constitution shall apply to all people, not only to those who by accident of birth were born with white skins.

Bill McCulloch discussed H.R. 7152 more simply, explaining the need for federal legislation and its validity under the Constitution. He argued that "this bill is comprehensive in scope, but moderate in application."

Southern Congressmen cast the bill in a different light. Edwin Willis (D–LA), for example, characterized the bill as "the most drastic and far-reaching proposal and grab for power ever to be reported out of a committee of Congress in the history of our Republic." Congressman Thomas Abernethy (D–MS) went even further:

> If this bill is enacted, I predict it will precipitate upheaval that will make the sit-ins, kneel-ins, lie-ins, stand-ins, mass picketing, chanting, the march on Washington, and all the other elements of the so-called Negro revolution, all of these—I predict—will look like kindergarten play in comparison with the counter-revolution that is bound to arise and continue to grow and grow and grow.

After ten hours of such general debate, H.R. 7152 was ready to meet its ultimate test in the House—the amendment process on the floor.

McCulloch and Celler had prepared carefully for this stage of the process. They and other supporters had at hand a detailed manual created by the Justice Department. The manual, containing a section-by-section defense of the bill, responded to the opposing views expressed by the Southern minority in the Judiciary Committee's report. The floor leaders had also assigned a member of the Judiciary Committee to each title with responsibility for becoming an expert on that particular area. Finally, there were eight Justice Department attorneys—one for each title of the bill—standing by for additional assistance (Whalens 103).

An important concern was the coalition's ability to keep sufficient members on the floor to defeat weakening amendments. Because votes taken in the Committee of the Whole were unrecorded, constituents were not likely to find out how (or even if) their representatives had voted, and so marginally interested members often skipped those votes. Thus it was not unusual to find a determined minority passing substantial amendments to bills by simply waiting until enough of the bill's supporters left the floor. If such a situation arose, Celler and McCulloch planned to stall a final vote for ten minutes while they attempted to get their forces together. By objecting to the chair's call for a voice vote, they could force a standing vote. Then, with 20 members objecting to the standing vote, they could force a teller vote—a head count as the "yeas" and "nays" walked down the center aisle. During this delaying process, supporters could be rounded up.[9]

The amendment process began at noon on Monday, February 3, and continued, title-by-title and section-by-section, until 7:00 p.m. on February 10. Over the course of that week, 124 amendments were offered, debated, and voted on, but only 34 were accepted by the Committee of the Whole. Most were technical corrections, including 12 offered by Celler.

The most significant amendment expanded the scope of Title VII and was sponsored by none other than Judge Smith. Alice Paul and the National Women's Party had asked Judge Smith, a long-time ally and supporter of the Equal Rights Amendment, to offer an amendment protecting women against job discrimination. On February 8, 1964, the Rules Committee Chairman proposed the addition of the word "sex" to Title VII's list of impermissible bases for employment decisions (Vaas 441–42; Whalens 115–16). Judge Smith explained that his amendment was necessary to "prevent discrimination against another minority group, the women," and that "it is indisputable fact that all throughout industry women are discriminated against in that just generally speaking they do not get as high compensation." He then read a letter from a female citizen complaining "that women currently outnumber men, that Congress and the President have made the situation worse by engaging in wars that further the imbalance, and that the

---

[9]   Celler and McCulloch relied on a three-level organization. First, 17 members of the Democratic Study Group, each with responsibility for six to eight colleagues, would be responsible for directly contacting their respective Congressmen whenever a vote was about to occur. Second, a group of 25 volunteers under the direction of labor lobbyist Jane O'Grady, known as O'Grady's Raiders, would patrol the halls of the congressional office buildings, making sure that representatives knew when a vote was coming up. Finally, in an effort to coerce some public accountability, hundreds of volunteers from the Leadership Conference on Civil Rights in the House gallery watched who voted and how. Because writing is forbidden in the galleries, members had to memorize the face of a particular member and then remember how he or she voted (Whalens 108–09).

imbalance prevents women from obtaining their 'right to happiness.'" Smith's comments evoked laughter among his male colleagues.

A mildly flustered Manny Celler opposed the amendment. While McCulloch sat on the sidelines, several liberal representatives joined Celler in ridiculing the amendment. The tone of good-ole-boy jocularity changed as eleven of the House's twelve female legislators rose to address Judge Smith's proposal. "I feel as a white woman when this bill has passed this House and the Senate and has been signed by the President that white women will be the last at the hiring gate," said Representative Martha W. Griffiths (D–MI). Representative Katharine Price Collier St. George (R–NY), joined Griffiths in favor of the amendment. "Why should women be denied equality of opportunity? Why should women be denied equal pay for equal work? That is all we are asking." Representatives Frances Bolton (R–OH), Catherine May (R–WA), and Edna Kelly (D–NY) also spoke in favor of the Smith Amendment. Opponents of the amendment responded that sex discrimination should have its own legislation, because of the physical differences between men and women; a letter from Esther Peterson, the head of the Women's Bureau in the Department of Labor, endorsed this approach. Ultimately, the Smith Amendment passed, 168–133. The votes of individual members were not recorded; apparently the amendment was supported by Southern opponents of the civil rights bill as well as many supporters of the bill, while most of the negative votes came from supporters of the bill (Vaas 442).

At the close of amendments on February 10, the Committee of the Whole dissolved, John McCormack reclaimed the Speaker's chair, and the members resumed sitting as the House. Chairman Keogh reported H.R. 7152, as amended, back to the House, and the Speaker prepared to complete the final three steps in the process. It was 7:00 p.m., and few were interested in prolonging the affair. Attempts to obtain recorded votes on certain substantive amendments failed to receive sufficient support, and the motion to recommit the bill to the Judiciary Committee failed on a voice vote. Finally it was time for the vote—up or down—on H.R. 7152. When the roll call was over, there were 152 Democratic votes and 138 Republican votes in favor, 96 Democratic votes and 34 Republican votes against. The civil rights bill passed overwhelmingly, 290–130 (Whalens 120–21). Now it was on to the Senate.

PASSAGE IN THE SENATE

The euphoria that accompanied passage in the House of Representatives was short-lived. H.R. 7152 next had to face the Senate, the body that had diluted civil rights bills in 1957 and 1960. Senator Eastland's Judiciary Committee had essentially ignored the Senate version of the Administration's bill (introduced in June 1963), holding only perfunctory hearings and calling only one witness: Attorney General Robert Kennedy.[10]

---

[10] The Attorney General had opened his testimony by quoting from a couple of tourist guidebooks covering the South. According to the guides, there was only one hotel serving African Americans in the city of Montgomery, Alabama and none in Danville, Virginia. However, a dog, if traveling with a white person, would have his choice of five places in Montgomery and four in Danville (Brauer 279).

At that time, consideration of a typical bill in the Senate usually followed an eight-step process. (1) The bill was read for the first time. (2) If no objections were heard, the bill would immediately be read for the second time. (3) After the second reading, the bill was generally referred to committee, unless a majority voted to place the bill directly on the Senate calendar. (4) The next step was committee consideration where, as in the House, the bill could be amended or killed. (5) If the bill survived committee action, it was placed on the Senate calendar. (6) The supporters would then call up the bill for consideration, (7) and the actual debate of the bill would proceed, subject to the Senate's unlimited debate rules. (8) The final step was the third reading, followed by a vote on the bill, as amended by the committee and during floor debate (Whalens 131–32). The big obstacle to the civil rights bill, however, was the expected Southern filibuster.

1.   *The Longest Debate Begins.* H.R. 7152 arrived in the Senate from the House on Monday, February 17, 1964. On Senator Mike Mansfield's motion, the bill was read for the first time. However, Mansfield objected to a second reading of the bill because he wanted to delay a filibuster until the Senate had completed work on the tax bill. Through a deft combination of flattery and budgetary logrolling, President Johnson persuaded his old friend Senator Harry Byrd to move forward on the tax cut bill just before the civil rights bill arrived in the Senate (Caro 466–83, 552–57).

When the tax bill was completed on February 26, Mansfield called up the civil rights bill for its second reading. Mansfield then moved to have the bill placed directly on the Senate calendar, thereby bypassing the Judiciary Committee. Senator Richard Russell (D–GA), leader of the Southern senators, objected and was joined by Minority Leader Everett Dirksen (R–IL). Although Dirksen shared Mansfield's concern about referring a civil rights bill to Eastland's committee, he felt that a bill of this importance deserved the full legislative history that only committee consideration could provide. Mansfield persuaded 20 Republicans to join him and was able to place H.R. 7152 on the Senate calendar of pending bills (Whalens 132–35).

Mansfield delayed his next motion—to call up H.R. 7152 for debate—until after the Senate voted on a pending farm bill. This two-week hiatus provided an opportunity for the Senate leadership to organize for the coming battle. Although the chairman of the committee having jurisdiction over a bill is usually chosen to act as the primary floor leader during debate, Mansfield was not going to select Eastland. Instead he selected Hubert Horatio Humphrey (D–MN), the Democrats' Senate Whip. No one was more committed to civil rights legislation than Humphrey. In 1948, it was he who led the battle for a strong civil rights plank in the Democratic platform.[11] The Republican floor manager was Thomas Kuchel (R–CA), that party's Senate Whip (Whalens 137–38). Dirksen appointed seven other Republicans to assist Kuchel (MacNeil 232). Senators Joseph Clark (D–PA) and

---

[11]   Hubert Humphrey's interest in the 1964 civil rights bill was not completely philosophical; he was a politically ambitious man who correctly saw the bill as an opportunity to establish himself a leader in the Democratic Party. Lyndon Johnson was conceded the presidential nomination in 1964, and if Humphrey could lead the Democrats to a solid legislative accomplishment on civil rights, he would solidify his position as front-runner for the vice presidency.

Clifford Case (R–NJ) were the senators responsible for handling issues involving Title VII, the equal employment title (Vaas 445).

One of Mansfield's chief concerns was to maintain discipline throughout the ordeal of getting H.R. 7152 through the Senate. The liberals' disorganization had contributed to the success of the last two civil rights filibusters. President Johnson challenged Humphrey to keep the troops together this time. "You have this great opportunity now, Hubert, but you liberals will never deliver. You don't know the rules of the Senate, and your liberal friends will be off making speeches when they ought to be present. You've got a great opportunity here, but I'm afraid it's going to fall between the boards" (Miller 368). Humphrey accepted the challenge. He organized a daily bipartisan newsletter, designed to inform members of the status of the debate, to refute arguments made on the floor by the bill's opponents, and to maintain a united front (Humphrey 86–87). The Democratic floor leader also set up a "quorum duty" system to ensure that there would always be sufficient senators on the floor to prevent the Southerners from adjourning the Senate. Finally, Humphrey scheduled regular strategy sessions with the bill's supporters (Humphrey 90).

On March 9, after the important farm legislation had been passed, Mansfield moved to make H.R. 7152 the pending business of the Senate, a motion he knew would draw a filibuster by the Southern conservatives (Vaas 444).[12] For fourteen days the Senate debated this issue—not whether to pass H.R. 7152, but simply whether to consider the bill at all. Prior to moving for immediate consideration of the bill, Mansfield had met with the Southerners and had been assured that the filibuster on this preliminary issue would not last longer than four or five days. It became apparent, though, as debate dragged on, that the Southerners had merely been maneuvering to convince Mansfield not to call all-night sessions.[13] On March 23, Humphrey kept the Senate in session until 10:15 p.m.—not all night, but long enough to give the filibusterers a taste of what was to come. The next day, supporters announced that they would object to the holding of any committee hearings before the Senate had finished with the civil rights bill. Southern opponents finally decided to allow a vote on Mansfield's motion. On March 26, 1964, the motion to take up H.R. 7152 passed 67–17, with only Southern Democrats opposing (Whalens 146–47).

On March 30, 1964, the Senate began debate on the merits of H.R. 7152. Humphrey delivered the opening statement, treating the half-dozen senators

---

[12] Unlike the House, the Senate does not have a Rules Committee that recommends to the full chamber a rule allowing expedited consideration of important bills. Instead, the Majority Leader normally expedites consideration by negotiating a *unanimous consent agreement*, in which all interested senators agree to consider the bill on a stated date, sometimes with limitations on debate and amendments (like a House rule). But if even a single senator objects to this arrangement, it is nullified. Obviously, the Southern senators in 1964 were not going to agree readily to expedited consideration of the civil rights bill.

[13] Mansfield was not inclined to hold all-night sessions in any event. Round-the-clock sessions had not worked in 1960 or in 1957, when Strom Thurmond (D–SC) had set the all-time filibuster record of 24 hours and 18 minutes of uninterrupted talk. Mansfield thought the tactic was demeaning to the Senate. "This is not a circus or a sideshow. We are not operating in a pit with spectators coming into the galleries late at night to see senators of the republic come out in bedroom slippers without neckties, with their hair uncombed, and pajama tops sticking out of their necks." Also, Mansfield feared that some older senators would not survive the tactic (MacNeil 23).

present to a 55–page, three and one-half hour speech. Tom Kuchel followed with an opening of a mere one and three-quarter hours (Whalens 150–51). Rather than let the Southerners monopolize debate, Humphrey and his team decided to take the offensive early, presenting a detailed, title-by-title defense of the bill over a period of twelve days. Senators were sent to appear on television and radio talk shows and were encouraged to send regular newsletters back to their constituents in an effort to maintain support for the bill in the press and public at large (Humphrey 89–90). Supporters of the civil rights bill emphasized the moral importance of the bill, attempting to elevate the issue above politics and appeal to a broad concept of justice (Humphrey 91–92).[14]

2. *Wooing the Wizard of Ooze.* Southern filibusterers dominated debate after early April and seemed capable of talking the year away. Could Humphrey and Kuchel muster the 67 votes needed to invoke cloture? A block of about 20 Southern Democrats were certain to vote against cloture, and about 30 liberal Democrats and 12 liberal Republicans were equally certain to vote for it. To reach the 67 votes needed for cloture, Humphrey and Kuchel needed to win the votes of 25 senators from two groups: 21 conservative Republicans who were opposed to big government programs and 17 moderate Democrats from Western and Border states that had traditionally relied upon the filibuster to protect themselves from more populous states (Miller 370). Since 1917, when the procedure was formally codified in the Senate's standing rules, cloture had been invoked successfully only once (Vaas 446).

Although some conservative Republicans were willing to support cloture, the bill needed them to vote as a virtual block—which seemed unlikely unless the Minority Leader himself became an enthusiastic supporter of the bill. Although he led the minority party, with only 33 of the 100 senators, Everett Dirksen ruled the Senate along with Majority Leader Mike Mansfield (MacNeil 230–31). Dirksen had risen to his position of power on the strength of an oratorical prowess that combined flowery language with a throatily mellifluous voice, and an uncanny ability to turn the most difficult political situations into personal triumphs. The former earned him the sobriquet "Wizard of Ooze"; the latter, "Old Doctor Snake Oil" (Whalens 151).

Publicly, Dirksen struck a Delphic pose in his attitude toward the civil rights bill. When the Administration's bill was introduced in June 1963, Dirksen expressed doubts about either a public accommodations provision or a fair employment practices section (Humphrey 85), and as late as August he told representatives of the NAACP that a public accommodations title was not acceptable (MacNeil 223). The momentum created by House passage and increasing public support for the bill led him to soften his position. In early November he assured Katzenbach that a civil rights bill would make it to a vote in the Senate (Brauer 308). The bill's strong support from McCulloch and Halleck in the House

---

[14] As a consequence, Humphrey realized that among all the groups lobbying for passage, the religious lobby would be crucial, because it reinforced the moral importance of the issue and provided a means of reaching senators not otherwise influenced by the labor and black lobbying efforts. Humphrey met with religious leaders and actively planned high-profile events to emphasize the interdenominational support for civil rights, including a silent, 24–hour vigil maintained by Protestant, Catholic, and Jewish seminarians on the Capitol grounds throughout the Senate debate (Humphrey 93–94).

put further pressure on Dirksen to play a leadership role—a role that Humphrey urged upon him. One of Humphrey's key strategies for collecting the support of GOP conservatives was to cast Dirksen in the starring role of this battle (Humphrey 85–86).

By the time the filibuster began in earnest, Dirksen was in all probability going to support some kind of strong civil rights bill. But his support carried a price tag—namely Dirksen's own conservative stamp on the final product (MacNeil 232–33). The day after the Senate took up consideration of the bill, Dirksen met with the Senate Republican Policy Committee to discuss the amendments he wanted to propose, and the next day he met with the Republican caucus. A week later he unveiled a package of 40 weakening amendments to Title VII. The amendments pleased conservative Republicans but created great concern among the party's influential liberals, including Senators George Aiken (VT), John Sherman Cooper (KY), Jacob Javits (NY), Tom Kuchel (CA), Leverett Saltonstall (MA), Hugh Scott (PA), and Margaret Chase Smith (ME). The liberals' opposition forced Dirksen to trim the package to ten. On April 16, Dirksen introduced his ten amendments, but did not seek a vote on the package (Whalens 159–64).

As April stretched on and Dirksen was unable to muster sufficient support for his amendments, he decided to approach the President in an effort to reach a compromise. He met with Johnson on April 29 and offered to deliver 22 to 25 Republican votes for cloture if the Administration would go along with weakening the bill. By one account, Johnson and Humphrey refused to compromise because they thought Dirksen had little choice but to support the civil rights bill (Whalens, 171–72). Another account, however, posits that Dirksen was in a stronger bargaining position. When he met with Mansfield, Humphrey, and the Attorney General to hammer out a compromise on May 4, Dirksen achieved much of what he wanted to gain for the small businesses that were his primary concern. Thus, he procured the Administration's support for provisions in the jobs title limiting the authority of the EEOC, protecting employers against government-required quota programs, and expanding employer defenses.[15]

Dirksen spent the next week selling his deal to the Republican caucus. He presented his package—the most he thought he could get the Democrats to go along with—to the Republican senators (MacNeil 234–35). Just as his earlier amendments had been attacked by his party's liberals as going too far, Dirksen's latest proposal was attacked by some conservatives as not going nearly far enough. His response was to go public, with a *fait accompli* challenging his Republicans to follow their Minority Leader. Following the caucus, Dirksen announced to stunned reporters that the time for action had arrived, that passage of the civil rights bill had become a moral imperative and that he was resolved to see it happen. Quoting Victor Hugo, Dirksen proclaimed, "No army is stronger than an idea whose time has come" (Whalens 185).

---

[15] For sharply contrasting views as to the meaning and scope of the Dirksen amendments, compare Daniel Rodriguez & Barry Weingast, *The Positive Political Theory of Legislative History: New Perspectives on the 1964 Civil Rights Act and Its Interpretation*, 151 U. Pa. L. Rev. 1417 (2003), with Victoria Nourse, *Misunderstanding Congress: Statutory Interpretation, the Supermajoritarian Difficulty, and the Separation of Powers*, 99 Geo. L.J. 1119 (2011).

On May 26, Dirksen presented Amendment No. 656 to the Senate, an amendment in the nature of a substitute for H.R. 7152, known as the "Mansfield-Dirksen Amendment" (Vaas 445).[16] Although the Democrats and liberal Republicans were ultimately satisfied that the anti-discrimination goal of the civil rights bill had not been significantly undermined (Whalens 188–89), the jobs title of the Mansfield-Dirksen substitute was somewhat more business-friendly and less regulatory than the earlier version of the bill (Rodriguez & Weingast 1487–96). Dirksen characteristically termed his bill "infinitely better than what came to us from the House" (Whalens 188), but Humphrey had little trouble concluding that he had kept his promise to Bill McCulloch not to support a bill that significantly departed from the House bill (Humphrey 85), probably in part because Dirksen's changes benefitted small businesses that were important constituents for any Midwestern Republican such as McCulloch.

With cloture now a tangible possibility, the bill's supporters spent the next two weeks stumping for votes. President Johnson used a combination of arm-twisting and inducements to lobby Senate Democrats. He spoke with Howard Cannon (D–NV), whom Majority Leader Johnson had appointed to critical Senate committees, and J. Howard Edmondson (D–OK), whom President Johnson had supported during the state's Democratic primary. While Johnson only stressed the principles in the bill, his personal involvement indicated that he was calling in markers (Whalens 187–88). Both senators would vote for cloture. A devastating earthquake had struck Alaska on March 27, and Johnson had responded promptly, making Air Force Two available to Senators Bartlett and Gruening (both D–AS) and moving to free up $77.5 million in relief for the state. Although both senators had been considered questionable votes for cloture, the President's timely political favor pulled them into line (Whalens 200).

Mansfield and Humphrey concentrated on Democratic senators from the key Western states, attempting to disrupt a traditional understanding between Southern and Western senators involving the exchange of votes on water projects for Western votes against civil rights (Whalens 201). Meanwhile, Everett Dirksen worked to pull in the 11 or more conservative Republicans he would need for cloture. In shifting H.R. 7152's focus toward federal intervention as a secondary, rather than primary, enforcement alternative, Dirksen argued to conservative colleagues from states with antidiscrimination laws that the federal legislation would have only a small incremental effect in their states. He complemented this approach by pointing to the Republican Party's heritage as the "Party of Lincoln." Conservatives were also influenced by the moral fervor of religious leaders who supported the bill. Finally, the effects of the filibuster itself were beginning to create pressure for cloture. The Senate had devoted twelve weeks to ducking the civil rights issue, and many senators were beginning to feel the embarrassment that came with public recognition of that fact (Whalens 202–03).

    3. *Cloture and Victory in the Senate.* One by one, the necessary commitments fell into place. On June 8, Mansfield and Dirksen moved for cloture: "We the

---

[16] An *amendment in the nature of a substitute* proposes a whole new bill to replace the bill under consideration. We will briefly discuss the various kinds of amendments in the "Note on How a Bill Becomes a Federal Law," *infra.*

undersigned Senators [27 Democrats, 11 Republicans], in accordance with the provisions of Rule XXII of the Standing Rules of the Senate, hereby move to bring to a close the debate on the bill * * *." After the required two-day wait, the time came to vote. Mansfield explained the importance of the cloture motion and then listened as a weary Richard Russell denounced the bill as contrary to both the spirit and the letter of the Constitution. After an uncharacteristically brief statement by Humphrey, Dirksen rose to make the final speech. He introduced Senate Amendment No. 1052, a second substitute for the entire bill to replace his earlier substitute amendment. Dirksen argued: "The time has come for equality of opportunity in sharing in government, in education, and in employment. It will not be stayed or denied."

The obligatory quorum call was a true formality on June 10, 1964: all 100 senators were present, including Clair Engle (D–CA), suffering from a brain tumor and unable to speak (Humphrey 91). The roll was called alphabetically by each senator's last name. Senator Engle cast his vote from his wheelchair by feebly lifting his left hand toward his eye. John Williams (R–DE) cast the 67th vote for cloture. Hubert Humphrey raised his arms over his head in jubilation (Whalens 199). The final vote was 71–29, four votes more than required.

After over 534 hours of continuous debate, spanning 58 days, the longest filibuster in the history of the Senate had been broken—the first time ever that cloture had been achieved on a civil rights bill (Miller 368). The final breakdown was 44 Democrats and 27 Republicans in favor and 23 Democrats and 6 Republicans against. Johnson and Humphrey had succeeded in capturing the votes of 19 of the 21 Democrats from Western states, and Dirksen had convinced 16 of the 17 Republican senators from states with public accommodations and equal employment laws on the books (as well as eight of the ten senators from states with one or the other) to vote for cloture.

Even though cloture limited senators to sixty minutes of remarks—on both the bill and proposed amendments—the Southern opponents of H.R. 7152 continued to delay the bill's progress. They attempted to bog down the proceedings by calling up countless amendments, even though they knew their proposals had no chance of adoption. They slowed things down further by insisting on long roll-call votes (including a record 34 in one day) on virtually every question (Schwartz 1091).[17] But they succeeded only in delaying the inevitable for another eight days (Vaas 446). In all, 115 different amendments were defeated, 106 on roll-call votes (Miller 371), with only two amendments of substance being accepted (Schwartz 1091).

On June 19, 1964—one year after President Kennedy had sent his civil rights bill to Congress—the Senate finally voted on H.R. 7152, having accepted the second Mansfield-Dirksen substitute two days earlier by an overwhelming 76–18 margin.

---

[17] This phenomenon—the *post-cloture filibuster*—is made possible by the collegial Senate rules. During this period, absent a unanimous consent agreement, a Senator could propose any number of amendments, including those unrelated to the subject matter of the bill. (House Rule XVI, in contrast, limits amendments to those which are *germane* to the subject of the bill.) Moreover, any Senator could demand roll-call votes, not only on the amendments, but also on the normally routine motion to reconsider, and could seek repeated quorum calls. In 1979, the Senate amended Rule XXII, clause 2 to limit each Senator to calling up two amendments and to impose an overall 100 hour limit on post-cloture consideration.

The bill was read for the third time and the Clerk called the roll (Vaas 446). At 7:40 p.m., to the applause of the observers in the gallery, the Clerk of the Senate announced the final vote: 73–27 in favor of H.R. 7152, as amended by the Mansfield-Dirksen substitute. The bill received the support of 46 Democrats and 27 Republicans, including four senators who had opposed cloture. Twenty-one Democrats and six Republicans voted nay (Whalens 215).

Most important, the bill approved by the Senate was in substance almost as broad as the bill approved by the House in February (Miller 371). For example, of the 24 amendments to Title VII that were offered from the floor, only five were accepted. Even considering Dirksen's important changes, the title was not vastly weaker than the version delivered from the House in February.[18]

THE CIVIL RIGHTS BILL BECOMES LAW

A bill does not become a law unless both chambers of Congress agree to identical legislative language. Because the Senate had made a number of changes in H.R. 7152, it returned the bill to the House on June 27, 1964, together with a message asking for acquiescence in the Senate's changes. In a joint press release, Manny Celler and Bill McCulloch said that "none of the amendments do serious violence to the purpose of the bill. We are of a mind that a conference could fatally delay enactment of this measure" (Whalens 218). Celler and McCulloch knew that if the House refused to accept all of the Senate changes and a conference committee were called, the Senate conferees would be selected by Judiciary Chairman Eastland, guaranteeing further delay. Even if the conference committee did report out a bill, the Southerners would have another opportunity to filibuster in the Senate. On balance, the best strategy was simply to accept the Senate's changes (Whalens 218–19).

The revised H.R. 7152 returned to Judge Smith's Rules Committee. This time, with the national conventions of both parties approaching, supporters would tolerate no stalling by the Chairman. After a single day of hearings, the Rules Committee voted to report House Resolution 789, expressing the House's concurrence with the Senate's amendments to H.R. 7152. The Rules Committee also voted to limit debate to one hour prior to the final vote.

On July 2, the House took up consideration of House Resolution 789. Judge Smith spoke for 15 minutes, denouncing the Rules Committee's "exercise of raw, brutal power" in limiting debate to a single hour. But he conceded that "the bell has tolled. In a few minutes you will vote this monstrous instrument of oppression upon all of the American people." As he yielded the floor, Smith received applause from his Southern colleagues and a handshake from Manny Celler. Bill McCulloch, in his usual restrained manner, recommended approval of the Senate version of H.R.

---

[18] See Rodriguez & Weingast, 1487–96. A new provision specified that preferential hiring practices to correct racial imbalances in the workforce (*affirmative action*) would not be required. The authority of the EEOC to sue in court was eliminated and replaced with a provision authorizing the Commission, when conciliation efforts failed, to refer a case to the Attorney General for possible civil suit or to authorize private suit. However, the reduction in EEOC authority was agreed to only in exchange for the inclusion of provisions allowing the courts to appoint attorneys to represent private Title VII plaintiffs and providing for an award of attorney's fees to successful plaintiffs. The new version also allowed local authorities to retain jurisdiction over cases for a short time, to attempt conciliation, before the EEOC could step in (Vaas 447–56).

7152 as a comprehensive, fair, and moderate statute. As he sat down, the House rose in a rare standing ovation. Finally, Manny Celler claimed the floor to use the remaining six minutes of the allotted hour. When he finished, the House rose once again in a standing ovation, this time led by the redoubtable Judge Smith (Whalens 224–26).

The House vote on House Resolution 789 was 289–126. After the House accepted the Senate bill, Speaker McCormack signed the official copy of H.R. 7152 and handed it to the House Clerk for return to the Senate. When the bill arrived in the other chamber, business was suspended so that Carl Hayden, the Senate's President pro tempore, could place his signature alongside McCormack's. H.R. 7152, as amended, was now ready to be signed into law by the President. At 6:00 that evening, July 2, 1964, members of Congress and civil rights leaders arrived at the White House and, after brief remarks by President Johnson, witnessed the presidential signing of H.R. 7152 into law. H.R. 7152 had finally become "The Civil Rights Act of 1964."

Within days, Lyndon Johnson met with Nicholas Katzenbach, the new Attorney General, to discuss the President's plans for the next civil rights bill: "I want you to write me the goddamndest, toughest voting rights act that you can devise." As he had told Hubert Humphrey during the battle for the 1964 Act, "Yes, yes, Hubert, I want all of those other things—buses, restaurants, all of that—but the right to vote with no ifs, ands, or buts, that's the key. When the Negroes get that, they'll have every politician, north and south, east and west, kissing their ass, begging for their support" (Miller 371).[19] Johnson may have been overly optimistic (and typically crude), but he was astute enough to realize that the Civil Rights Act of 1964 was merely a start toward true equality and the end of discrimination.

NOTE ON HOW A BILL BECOMES A FEDERAL LAW[20]

The Civil Rights Act illuminates the important features of the federal legislative process. The Constitution and its amendments set forth the basic structure: laws will be enacted by elected representatives, not by the people directly or by some authoritarian person or group. "All legislative powers herein granted shall be vested in a Congress of the United States, which shall consist of a Senate and House of Representatives." U.S. Const. art. I, § 1. House members are "chosen every second Year by the People of the several states," *id.* art. I, § 2, and each state has two Senators, "elected by the people thereof," *id.* amend. XVII. Laws must be approved by two legislative chambers (the *bicameralism* requirement) and the chief executive (the *presentment* requirement). If the President signs it, the "Bill" is "Law"; if he returns it without signature, it is not law unless two-thirds majorities of each chamber vote to override his *veto. Id.* art. I, § 7. If the President does not sign or return the bill within ten days and the Congress remains

---

[19] Johnson was successful. In 1965, Congress adopted a strong Voting Rights Act, which was reenacted in 1970, 1975, 1982, and 2006 and remains a major component of federal civil rights law.

[20] Among the best scholarly sources on legislative procedures are Barbara Sinclair, *Unorthodox Lawmaking: New Legislative Processes in the U.S. Congress* (4th ed. 2011), as well as William Keefe & Morris Ogul, *The American Legislative Process: Congress and the States* (10th ed. 2000); Burdett Loomis & Wendy Schiller, *The Contemporary Congress* (5th ed. 2005); Walter Oleszek, *Congressional Procedures and the Policy Process* (9th ed. 2014); Gregory J. Wawro & Eric Schickler, *Filibuster: Obstruction and Lawmaking in the U.S. Senate* (2007).

in session, the bill becomes law as though he had signed it. If Congress adjourns during the ten-day period, the bill does not become law, and the President has *pocket vetoed* the proposal.

Most of the procedures followed in Congress are the products of history and custom, rather than constitutional mandate. It may be helpful to think about congressional rules as lying along a spectrum, with constitutional requirements such as bicameralism and presentment as the strongest and most durable. Each house also has a series of formal rules that bind it.[21] As the Story of the Civil Rights Act demonstrates, there are many such rules affecting legislation, including committee consideration, scheduling procedures, and Senate rules allowing filibusters. All of these requirements are less durable than constitutional ones because, in most cases, they can be changed by a majority vote of the relevant house. Moreover, if the House or Senate violates the rules, there is often no effective enforcement mechanism to void the action. Courts have been reluctant to enforce congressional rules when they are ignored, holding instead that rulemaking and enforcement are committed by the Constitution to the discretion of each house. Finally, the least durable procedures are those that are matters of informal norms and practices, sometimes called the *folkways* of Congress. See Donald Matthews, *U.S. Senators and Their World* 151 (1960). One norm that played a role in the enactment of the Civil Rights Act was the seniority norm, which allocates power and position to members with long tenure and allows senior legislators and committee chairs to block bills they do not like even when a majority of the chamber or committee favors the legislation. The seniority norm is now weaker than it was at the time of our case study, perhaps because of higher turnover rates and an influx of junior members.

The discussion that follows focuses on the traditional or "textbook" federal legislative process, which is presented in Chart 1–1. State legislatures usually follow similar procedures. In recent years, major federal legislation has often followed paths previously considered unorthodox. For example, Congress now enacts many major laws as part of complex omnibus legislation that is considered by several committees, may involve congressional party leaders and organizations in nontraditional ways, and provides challenges for congressional rules. Barbara Sinclair defines *omnibus legislation* as "[l]egislation that addresses numerous and not necessarily related subjects, issues, and programs, and therefore is usually highly complex and long." Sinclair, *Unorthodox Lawmaking: New Legislative Processes in the U.S. Congress* 71 (4th ed. 2011). In a few instances, party leaders appoint special task forces of sympathetic members to draft and negotiate important legislation, either bypassing committees entirely or reducing their role substantially. The Civil Rights Act is an early example of unorthodox lawmaking; as the case study reveals, party leaders were unusually influential in determining the path of enactment, and several strategies were used to bypass particular committees and undermine the power of senior lawmakers.

---

[21] The Senate has permanent rules that can be amended. See *Standing Rules of the Senate*, in *Senate Manual*, S. Doc. No. 112–1 (2011). The House adopts "new" rules in every Congress. See *Rules of the House of Representatives*, 113th Congress (Jan 3, 2013), for the current (2013–14) House Rules.

Chart 1–1: How a Federal Bill Becomes a Law—Simplified Overview

HOUSE OF REPRESENTATIVES   SENATE

Drafting of Bill or Resolution
(e.g., by legislative staff, government
agency, interest group, academic)
↓
Introduction of Bill by Member
(revenue bills originate in House,
see U.S. Const., art. I, § 7, cl. 1;
customarily, appropriations bills
do also)
↓
Referral to Standing Committee
↓
Committee Action
−can be referred to subcommittee
−hearings held on major bills
−committee resolution: take no action,
    defeat, accept or amend and report
↓
Major Calendars
−Union (appropriations and revenue)
−House (public)
−Discharge (extract bills from
    committee)
↓
Rules Committee (major bills)
(closed rules possible but generally
modified open or open rules)
↓
Floor Action (passage or defeat) ────

Referred to standing committee
↓
Committee action (similar to House)
↓
Floor action (similar to House except
that there is filibuster option in Senate;
overriding filibuster requires 60 votes)
↓
CONFERENCE COMMITTEE
(if House and Senate pass differing
versions, a conference committee
can be created with members from
each house; each House must agree
to the conference report)
↓
BILL SIGNED BY SPEAKER AND
VICE PRESIDENT
↓
PRESENTMENT TO PRESIDENT
(may sign, veto, or permit bill to
become law without his/her signature;
also possibility of "pocket veto"
after adjournment)

1. *Introduction of Bills.* More than 200,000 bills are introduced in the 50 state legislatures each biennium, and around 10,000 in each Congress. Only legislators can introduce bills, although in some states the governor is required to submit budget bills to the legislature. See, e.g., Ill. Const. art. VIII, § 2. The legislators themselves do not always come up with the ideas for major bills or draft them. The chief executive proposes or drafts much of the important legislation considered by the legislature. See Vasan Kesavan & Gregory Sidak, *The Legislator-in-Chief*, 44 Wm. & Mary L. Rev. 1, 48–55 (2002). As chief executive and head of one of the political parties, the President may be the country's chief law-initiator. For example, the Celler, Lindsay, and McCulloch civil rights bills went nowhere until President Kennedy publicized the issue; his Justice Department drafted the civil rights bill introduced in both the House and

Senate in 1963. Private groups also present draft bills to members of the legislature or advise them about amendments to bills proposed by the executive. The NAACP, for example, probably helped draft the liberalizing amendments adopted by Subcommittee No. 5.

Whether legislation is enacted depends in large part on the nation's political agenda. John Kingdon defines *agenda* as "the list of subjects or problems to which governmental officials, and people outside of government closely associated with those officials, are paying some serious attention at any given time." Kingdon, *Agendas, Alternatives, and Public Policies* 3 (2d ed. 1995). Getting an issue on the agenda is a prerequisite to adopting a policy to address it. Kingdon identifies four aspects to policymaking: setting the agenda; specifying alternatives from which a policy choice is to be made; choosing among the alternatives; and implementing the decision. His work focuses on the first two processes and attempts to explain why some subjects and not others become salient to policymakers and the public, and why some alternatives receive serious consideration and others do not. With respect to the first, agenda setting, the President is the most influential political actor. "No other single actor in the political system has quite the capability of the president to set agendas in given policy areas for all who deal with those policies." *Id.* at 23. As suggested by our case study, the President has much more power to press an issue onto the legislative agenda than to determine the policy tradeoffs and compromises needed to pass the final legislation.

State legislators are often even more dependent upon the offices of state attorneys general and private groups to draft legislation than members of Congress are, because state legislators do not have the staff support enjoyed by federal lawmakers. The staff situation in state legislatures has improved somewhat in the last 35 years, however. Typically, states now provide full-time staff to individual legislators and additional staff during legislative sessions. Since 1979, the size of permanent state legislative staff has almost doubled; the combination of part-time and permanent staff available to legislators during legislative sessions has increased by more than one quarter. See National Conference of State Legislatures, *Size of State Legislative Staff* (2009).

2.   *Committee Consideration.* The presiding officer of the legislative chamber refers bills to standing committees. House Rule XII, clause 2 requires the Speaker to refer a bill to the committee(s) having jurisdiction over its subject matter. Clause 2 was amended in 1975 to give the Speaker the power to send parts of the same bill to more than one committee, to send the whole bill to more than one committee, and/or to create an "ad hoc committee" to consider a bill. In 1995, the House modified the process for referring legislation to committee by abolishing joint referrals and mandating instead that the Speaker designate a committee of "primary" jurisdiction upon initial referral. Senate Rule XVII and the rules in many state legislatures do not require referral of bills to the appropriate committees, but the practice is to do so.

Committee jurisdiction is akin to a property right over political issues, so lawmakers work hard to place important legislation within the jurisdiction of committees on which they serve. The parliamentarian, a relatively nonpartisan player, makes referral decisions using a "weight of the bill" test to assign a proposal to the committee or committees with the most compatible jurisdiction. In his study of changes in committee jurisdiction over time, David King argues that such change is incremental, resembling legal change in the courts.[22] Parliamentarians rely on

---

[22]   See David King, *Turf Wars: How Congressional Committees Claim Jurisdiction* (1997).

congressional rules (a sort of *statutory jurisdiction*) and precedent (a sort of *common law jurisdiction*) to determine the appropriate referral. For example, congressional rules specify that tax legislation must be referred to the House Ways and Means and the Senate Finance Committees, but the rules provide only a partial list of all possible subject matter of federal legislation. When the rules are silent, the parliamentarian follows past practice to make the referral. This common law of jurisdiction is substantial; King estimates that more than two-thirds of the House Commerce Committee's activity focuses on issues assigned to it through common law means. Politicians work to frame bills so they fall within jurisdictionally ambiguous areas and then to convince the parliamentarian to assign them to a committee on which the framers have influence. Once a precedent is established, the same committee will prevail on referrals of bills in related areas through the common law reasoning so familiar to lawyers.

Probably the most important power of committees is the *power of negation*; the vast majority of bills referred to committees never emerge for consideration by the full body. In a typical Congress, fewer than one-sixth of the bills introduced survive committee consideration and actually make it to the floor of either chamber.[23] The key player is the chair of the committee. If the chair refuses to schedule hearings for a bill or refer the bill to subcommittee, or refers the bill to a hostile subcommittee, the bill will usually die—even if most of the committee members favor the bill. House Rule XI and Senate Rule XXVI permit a majority of the committee to compel the chair to place a bill on the agenda, as Representative Brown threatened to do in the House Rules Committee's consideration of the civil rights bill. This is a maneuver rarely threatened and almost never attempted.

In addition, a majority of the House can bypass a committee by filing a *discharge petition* calling for a measure to be brought to the floor. When half of the House members have signed the petition, the bill is taken away from the committee and brought to the full House. Before 1993, the names of members signing a discharge petition were kept confidential until 218 people had signed. Now, the list of signers is public from the first signature, making it easier for supporters to pressure members to sign and to check if those who promised to sign actually have. Although the discharge petition route is seldom successful, committees have been bypassed more frequently in recent Congresses than, for example, during the time of our case study, when the path of the Civil Rights Act was truly anomalous. See Sinclair, *Unorthodox Lawmaking*, 93–94. In the Senate, circumventing committees is easier, because bills languishing in committees can be added as nongermane amendments to most bills as they are considered on the floor.

The committee process is also crucial for bills that have a good chance of being enacted. The committee can iron out difficulties and build a consensus in favor of the bill. The chair is again the critical person when a bill is actively considered. The committee or subcommittee chair schedules hearings, determines who will testify at the hearings, and asks most of the questions. Recall Representative Celler's power to manipulate both the committee and subcommittee consideration of the civil rights bill. The power of the committee chair has waned in recent years, as more power has been

---

[23] See Steven Smith, Jason Roberts & Ryan Vander Wielen, *The American Congress* (7th ed. 2011).

claimed by party organizations[24] and as recent Congresses have adopted rules diminishing the influence of chairs. For example, in 1995 as part of the Republicans' "Contract with America," the House voted to limit the terms of committee and subcommittee chairs (except for the chair of the Rules Committee) to "three consecutive Congresses" (i.e., six years) and abolished several subcommittees, thereby reducing the power of these positions and some of the more senior members of the body. Even as power has changed hands in the House, term limits for committee chairs have remained in effect (as of 2014).

In short, committees are congressional players with great influence over the agenda and legislative outcomes. Unlike some other constitutions, the U.S. Constitution does not require that Congress establish committees; instead, this organizational pattern is entirely a matter of lawmaker preference. The description of committee activities suggests several reasons legislators might prefer to do work through committees, even though such an organization transfers power from floor majorities to small groups of lawmakers and to committee chairs in particular.

First, committees allow members to specialize and accumulate expertise in a substantive area. Other members defer to the specialists, thereby avoiding the costly prospect of becoming experts in every matter raised for a vote. This *informational role* suggests that committees are part of an efficient congressional organization, particularly necessary in an increasingly complex world.[25] Members must monitor committees to ensure that they are faithful agents of the full body and that the information and recommendations they put forth are consistent with the wishes of the majority. As long as monitoring is less costly than developing expertise on all matters and allows members to detect divergence between committee activities and majority preferences, a committee structure is sensible.

Another theory of legislative organization, the *distributive theory*, describes committees as the engine of *rent-seeking*, or the distribution of unjustified benefits to interest groups. Members partly self-select their committee assignments, so they seek appointment to committees with jurisdiction over areas about which they and their constituents have particularly intense preferences. At least some committees are composed of preference outliers.[26] In most cases, lawmakers specialize in areas that allow them to send benefits back to their constituents or to key special interests in order to improve their reelection chances. In other cases, they may seek committee assignments that allow them to capture personal benefits from interest groups. For example, the Senate Commerce Committee has wide jurisdiction over the

---

[24] Since the mid-1990s, more legislative work has been done in informal task forces or leadership committees, entirely controlled by the majority party and often followed by perfunctory or no formal hearings. Because these are not governed by open meeting rules, lobbyists and interest groups can have substantial influence. See Roger Davidson, *Building the Republican Regime: Leaders and Committees*, in *New Majority or Old Minority? The Impact of Republicans on Congress* 69, 79–80 (Nicol Rae & Colton Campbell eds., 1999).

[25] See Keith Krehbiel, *Information and Legislative Organization* (1991); Arthur Lupia & Mathew McCubbins, *Who Controls? Information and the Structure of Legislative Decision Making*, 19 Legis. Stud. Q. 361 (1994).

[26] See Glenn Parker, *Congress and the Rent-Seeking Society* 74–81 (1996); Kenneth A. Shepsle, *The Giant Jigsaw Puzzle: Democratic Committee Assignments in the Modern House* (1978); Barry Weingast & William Marshall, *The Industrial Organization of Congress; or, Why Legislatures, Like Firms, Are Not Organized as Markets*, 96 J. Pol. Econ. 132 (1988). See also Scott Adler, *Why Congressional Reforms Fail: Reelection and the House Committee System* (2002) (explaining the durability of committee structure and jurisdiction using the distributive theory).

telecommunications industry, full of wealthy interest groups willing to compensate their legislative friends.[27]

These two explanations for committees are not necessarily exclusive.[28] Members may be willing to invest time and resources in developing expertise and producing helpful information for the full body because they have special interest in the issues that fall within the jurisdiction of a particular committee. A member from a largely urban state may be unwilling to specialize in agriculture topics because she and her constituents have no special interest in farm policy. Members from farm states, on the other hand, who want to channel public benefits to their farmer-constituents and may have extensive knowledge of agriculture before coming to the legislature, will actively seek membership on the Agriculture Committee. The more likely it is that committees consist of preference outliers, however, the more diligence is required of the other members to monitor committee activity and ensure that extreme policies are not enacted.

A third theory posits that committees are primarily the *tools of the majority party*.[29] Majority-party committee members exclude members of the other party from decisionmaking and cooperate among themselves to further the majority party's collective goals. Again, consider the Agriculture Committee. Although most members of the majority party are likely to support only modest agriculture subsidies, there are some members whose reelection prospects are substantially affected by enactment of generous subsidies. Committees provide a mechanism for members of the majority party to defer to the wishes of the few with intense preferences and to ensure that those lawmakers in turn defer in the future on other issues vital to the reelection of their colleagues. This process allows the majority party to remain in power by enhancing the reelection prospects of its members; party dominance is a goal shared by all party members who want to continue to receive the benefits of majority control.

Once a committee marks up the bill and votes to send it to the full legislative chamber, the committee staff drafts a report on the bill that will be circulated to the other legislators. This is mandatory in both chambers of Congress (House Rule XIII; Senate Rule XXVI) and is the practice in some state legislatures as well. Committee reports in Congress set forth the procedural and substantive background of the reported bill, the exact language of the bill, and a section-by-section analysis of the bill. Such reports in state legislatures are often shorter, more general descriptions of reported bills; thus, they are often less helpful to interpreters than the more extensive federal legislative history.[30] Committee reports, or distillations of them prepared by party organizations, are frequently the only documents that most legislators and their staffs read before a vote is taken on the bill. Reports are not only the principal means of communicating committee decisions to the chamber, but they are also persuasive briefs setting forth the factual and policy reasons justifying the proposed legislation.

---

[27] See also Christopher Deering & Steven Smith, *Committees in Congress* 63–77 (3d ed. 1997) (discussing committees in terms of their primary benefits to lawmakers and providing tripartite classification: constituency, policy, and influence committees).

[28] See Forrest Maltzman, *Competing Principals: Committees, Parties, and the Organization of Congress* (1997) (offering sophisticated theory of committee formation).

[29] See Gary Cox & Mathew McCubbins, *Legislative Leviathan: Party Government in the House* (2d ed. 2007); Jeffrey Stonecash, ed., *New Directions in American Political Parties* (2010).

[30] See, e.g., Eric Lane, *How to Read a Statute in New York: A Response to Judge Kaye and Some More*, 28 Hofstra L. Rev. 85, 118–19 (1999) (describing committee reports in New York).

Committee members dissenting from all or part of the report are entitled to set forth their views as well. Finally, provisions in several laws require committees to include certain information about bills in committee reports.

3. *Scheduling Legislative Consideration.* Bills reported by committee are placed on a calendar of the legislative chamber. The U.S. House's calendar arrangement is especially complex. It has three primary calendars. The most important calendar is the *Union Calendar*, or the "Calendar of the Committee of the Whole House on the State of the Union." Virtually all bills are placed on this calendar. Second is the *House Calendar*, which now contains few bills, mostly special rules from the Rules Committee, changes in House rules, ethics resolutions, and some constitutional amendments. Third, private bills, such as those for the relief of individual noncitizens seeking to remain in the country, are placed on the *Private Calendar*. In addition, there are two calendars to which bills on the three main ones may move. The *Consent Calendar* consists of bills involving spending of less than $1 million on the Union or House Calendar that a member anticipates will be passed by unanimous consent. Minor bills on the Consent Calendar are considered by the House twice a month. The *Discharge Calendar* lists motions to discharge bills that are pending in committee.[31] Additionally, bills may be called up and considered by the House under a process called *suspension of the rules*. Suspension of the rules allows the House, with the consent of the Speaker, to consider a bill in an expedited fashion with no amendments or motions, but it requires that the bill be passed by a two-thirds vote. The U.S. Senate has only two calendars, the *Calendar of General Orders* and the *Executive Calendar* for treaties and executive nominations.

Simply being on the appropriate calendar does not assure that the chamber will consider the bill. Salient or time-sensitive bills usually will be considered before other bills ahead of them on the calendar. In the House, major legislation moves to the floor from committees in two ways. Budget and appropriations bills are privileged matters and can be brought to the floor at virtually any time. For other major bills, and often for budget and appropriations bills when supporters want to structure deliberation in a particular way, the reporting committee will request a special order, or *rule*, from the Rules Committee to advance the bill for expedited floor consideration. The Rules Committee, which is essentially an arm of the majority party, then decides whether it will propose a rule for the bill (its refusal to grant a rule effectively kills the bill for that session); what kind of rule to grant (an *open rule* permitting amendments, a *closed rule* prohibiting all floor amendments, or a *modified closed rule* permitting specified floor amendments and structuring the order of their introduction); when a bill is to be considered; and how much time for debate. The full House votes on the proposed rule; such rules are almost always passed by party-line votes. Control of the legislative agenda, facilitated through the use of special rules, is an important tactical advantage that accrues to the majority party.[32]

There is no Rules Committee in the Senate, and expedited consideration is usually accomplished by a *unanimous consent agreement* (Senate Rule V). Like a House rule, a unanimous consent agreement is a roadmap for the bill's consideration: when it may be brought up, what amendments may be proposed, and how much time may be spent on

---

[31] See Charles Tiefer, *Congressional Practice and Procedure: A Reference, Research, and Legislative Guide* 245–46 (1989).

[32] Gary Cox & Mathew McCubbins, *Setting the Agenda: Responsible Party Government in the U.S. House of Representatives* (2005).

it. Unlike a House rule, a Senate unanimous consent agreement must be acceptable to all senators; the objection of a single senator kills it. Recall that the civil rights bill languished for weeks in a pre-consideration filibuster, during which Southern senators objected to any expedition at all. Under current Senate rules, most bills are still susceptible to two filibuster threats: on the motion to proceed to consider the bill and on final passage.[33] Most filibusters now are virtual ones, which may explain the recent increase in threatened and actual filibusters. Members threaten to engage in extended debate, placing a *hold* on the bill until floor leaders can work out a compromise. For years, holds were largely anonymous, but their widespread use has prompted cries for reforms, and now the names of members blocking consideration of legislation or nominations are sometimes revealed.

In 2013, Senate Majority Leader Harry Reid challenged the Senate filibuster-and-cloture rules as applied to confirmation of nominations to executive branch and lower court positions. Fifty-three Democratic senators voted to support his challenge, which set a new Senate precedent. As of 2014, this new precedent leaves the filibuster in place as a mechanism for a 41–senator minority to block substantive legislation, as well as nominations to the Supreme Court. A formal change to Senate Rule XXII (cloture) would require a two-thirds vote, but this procedural challenge enabled the Majority Leader to alter the rule by a simple majority (albeit over the strong objections of Republican senators).

Most state legislatures use only a single calendar on which they list all pending bills ready for floor action. As in Congress, the order of listing is not a reliable indication of when the bill will actually be considered; priority items of consequence are mixed with unimportant bills. Oversimplifying a little, one can say that the actual order of consideration is determined in one of two ways, parallel to the two methods used in Congress. State legislatures with strong party caucus systems tend to have their agendas set by the majority leader and/or the majority party caucus. State legislatures in which parties are weak typically vest agenda control in calendar committees, rules committees, or informal but less partisan mechanisms. In some states, the two methods effectively merge. For instance, where the presiding officer of the legislative chamber is also the chair of the rules committee, there is little functional difference between the two methods.

4. *Floor Consideration: Debate, Amendment, Voting.* Once a bill has been placed on the agenda by the relevant committee and advanced for consideration by the full legislative chamber, the process is mostly automatic. Most legislators routinely vote "yes," and the bill is passed. In the Senate, for example, dozens of routine bills are adopted through unanimous consent agreements read quickly at the end of a day's session. Consistent with the informational theory of legislative organization, the chamber as a whole usually ratifies the decisions and compromises reached in the smaller, more expert groups (committees). Of course, much important legislation, such as the Civil Rights Act, is controversial and has to run the further gauntlet of floor

---

[33] See generally Gregory Koger, *Filibustering: A Political History of Obstructionism in the House and Senate* (2010); Gregory Wawro & Eric Schickler, *Filibuster: Obstruction and Lawmaking in the U.S. Senate* (2006); Barbara Sinclair, *The '60 Vote Senate': Strategies, Process, and Outcomes,* in *U.S. Senate Exceptionalism* 241–61 (Bruce Oppenheimer ed. 2002). Some forms of budget legislation cannot be filibustered because the Senate has adopted strict time limits on the consideration of these important legislative vehicles. See Sarah Binder & Steven Smith, *Politics or Principle? Filibustering in the United States Senate* 192–94 (1997) (contrasting budget rules from traditional rules allowing filibuster).

consideration. Three important aspects of congressional decisionmaking occur during such floor consideration: debate, amendment, and vote.

In the U.S. House and most state chambers, debate is severely limited by general or special rules. (Indeed, because many state legislatures still only meet for several months each year, there is simply not enough time for extended public debate on more than a few issues.) Even where debate is not formally limited, as in the U.S. Senate, it normally consists of "set" speeches read by members to virtually empty chambers (although many staffers and some lawmakers will watch the floor proceedings on closed circuit television) or of *colloquies*, rehearsed questions posed to the bill's sponsor in order to build a legislative record on some issue. Frequently, members of Congress simply submit statements for printing in the *Congressional Record*, and the statements are never uttered on the floor. The *Record* is supposed to identify such a statement by either a "bullet" (·) preceding it or by a different typeface.

Relatively few votes are altered by floor debates; instead members often use them to publish their positions, and sometimes to include in legislative history remarks supporting an interpretation of the proposal that they favor. Members may make floor speeches to publicize their positions or to pack the legislative history with remarks supporting an interpretation of the proposal that they favor. In the modern era of televised floor proceedings, members know that their constituents and lobbyists can monitor their activity and their positions. In addition, debate can be manipulated by organized minorities to delay passage of legislation that they oppose. For example, the filibuster used in the U.S. Senate enables a determined group of senators to kill a bill or force concessions from the majority by extended debate. Cloture (cutting off the debate) required a two-thirds vote of the Senators voting in 1964; under amended Senate Rule XXII, it now requires 60 votes except with respect to changes in the rules themselves.

More important than debate is amendment. Once they have been reported by committee, bills can be amended on "second reading," sometimes in the legislature sitting as a committee of the whole, or on "third reading" (just before the final up or down vote is taken on the bill). Amendment on third reading is rare and may require unanimous consent or some other special dispensation. Most legislative chambers do not follow the U.S. House practice of dissolving into a Committee of the Whole to consider amendments.

Major bills on controversial subjects will attract numerous proposed amendments. A first-degree amendment changing the text of the bill is a *perfecting amendment*, which can strike language, insert language, or do both. The reporting committee (through the chair or a sponsor) will sometimes propose perfecting amendments to correct minor problems with the bill or to attract more support for the bill through *saving amendments*. Perfecting amendments from the floor may include minor amendments addressed to a narrow problem with the bill; *riders*, or amendments seeking to add irrelevant matter to the bill (riders are prohibited by House Rule XVI and the rules of some state legislatures); and hostile amendments. Some floor amendments, called *killer amendments*, ostensibly strengthen the bill but are designed to antagonize the bill's more moderate supporters. In the story of the Civil Rights Act, Judge Smith's amendment adding "sex" to the list of impermissible bases for employment decisions prompted the opposition of floor leaders worried that expanding the legislation would prove fatal.

Amendments in the nature of a substitute seek to replace the entire bill, striking all after the enacting clause and inserting entirely new text. They can represent radically different approaches to the problem addressed by the bill, and adoption of such an amendment may spell the end of the bill either by ensuring its ultimate defeat or by impairing the operation of the bill, making passage useless. In other cases, the managers of the bill will propose an amendment in the nature of a substitute that reflects the results of negotiations on the proposal following committee action. Not to be confused with amendments in the nature of a substitute are *substitute amendments*. These are offered when another amendment is pending, and it changes part of the proposed amendment. This second-degree amendment can be minor—replacing only one word or phrase—or significant—proposing an entirely new text but in a way different from the pending amendment in the nature of a substitute. In the latter case, the amendment is both a substitute amendment and an amendment in the nature of a substitute.

Both opponents and proponents of legislation use amendments strategically, seeking to fill up the complex *amendment tree* to foreclose other changes in the bill or to obtain a special rule in the House that favors a particular sequence of voting on amendments. In some cases, bill managers will accept floor amendments in order to move debate forward and ensure final passage, but they do not intend to support the amendment in the conference committee. Lawmakers often observe that amendments can be "lost" in the Capitol building when conferees walk across the Rotunda to the other chamber to begin negotiations on the final legislation.

The vote on an amendment or a bill may be taken in one of four ways: voice vote, roll calls (increasingly by use of electronic devices), division of the house, and tellers. The first two methods do not leave a record of how each member of the legislative chamber voted, but division (where the yeas and nays rise to be counted) and tellers (where the yeas pass down the aisle to be counted, then the nays) permit observers to record how each member voted. The U.S. House of Representatives uses all four methods, and the Senate uses all but tellers. One-fifth of a quorum may demand a roll-call vote in either chamber, except when the House committee of the whole is in session. Moreover, congressional rules can often require roll call votes on particular matters; for example, House Rule XX requires roll call votes on all tax rate increases and appropriations bills.

The number of votes needed to adopt an amendment or pass a bill is normally a majority of those voting in each house of Congress, assuming a quorum is present. Some state legislatures, in contrast, require the votes of a majority of the members elected; thus, members not wanting to commit themselves against a measure may help defeat it simply by staying away when the vote is taken. Two-thirds supermajorities are needed for Congress to propose a constitutional amendment, to override a presidential veto, to expel a member, or for the Senate to concur in a treaty. In states, supermajorities can be required to override gubernatorial vetoes, to pass emergency legislation or special appropriation bills, or to enact new tax legislation.

5.   *Conference Committees and Summits.* In the prevailing system of bicameral legislatures, there must be a "meeting of the minds" of the two legislative chambers to enact statutes. If the version passed by the U.S. House differs in any respect from that passed by the U.S. Senate, there is no enactment—unless one chamber recedes from its differences and joins the version of the other (as was the case for the Civil Rights Act).

Sometimes the House and Senate send bills back and forth several times, acceding to part of the other chamber's alterations each time, in an effort to reconcile the two versions.

After both chambers have voted themselves into a state of disagreement, the last chamber to disagree may request a conference. The Speaker of the House and the Presiding Officer of the Senate formally appoint the conferees, but in practice the chair and ranking minority member of each relevant committee will submit a list of proposed conferees, who are then appointed. Note that this involvement in the final conference committee allows congressional committees influence over legislation both before and after the main floor consideration. Knowing that they will have this ex post influence will affect the interaction of committee leaders and floor managers with rank-and-file members. There can be any number of conferees from either chamber, and modern conference committees vary in size from more than 200 members to only a handful of party leaders. Any compromise adopted in conference must be approved by a majority of the conferees from each chamber.

The objectives of the conferees are, first, to preserve the provisions most important to their respective chambers and, second, to achieve an overall result acceptable to a majority in each chamber. In Congress and most state legislatures, conferees are only authorized to consider matters about which the bills passed by the two chambers are in disagreement. Thus, they may not strike or amend any part of the bill that is identical in both versions, nor may they insert new matter not germane to the differences, nor may they expand any provision beyond that found in either version. In practice, because congressional conference committees do much of their work in private, it is difficult for other members, interest groups, and the public to monitor conferees' behavior. Lengthy omnibus bills that have been the product of long negotiations often emerge from conference with provisions never considered by either house or by any substantive committee. If the bill is nevertheless enacted, the rule against new provisions in conference is considered waived. When the conferees have reached agreement, they set forth their recommendations in a conference report, which will be printed in both chambers and will include a statement explaining the effect of the amendments or propositions agreed upon by the conferees on the measure.

In recent years, the textbook version of the legislative process has, increasingly, been supplemented or replaced by various techniques of "unorthodox lawmaking." Sinclair, *Unorthodox Lawmaking*. In recent decades, for example, a significant number of bills are referred to at least two House committees, while some major proposals bypass committees altogether.[34] Increased partisanship and committee as well as chamber gridlock are factors that have encouraged lawmakers to use unorthodox lawmaking techniques for significant legislation. Through an increased use of amendments in the nature of a substitute, committee leaders and floor managers often make substantial changes in bills after they leave committee but before floor consideration. In the last two decades, major legislation, which is more often subject to unorthodox lawmaking than ordinary legislation, has considerably better chances of enactment. An important institution of unorthodox lawmaking is the use of *summits*, "relatively formal negotiations between congressional leaders and high-ranking administration officials representing the president directly." Sinclair, *Unorthodox*

---

[34] See Sinclair, *Unorthodox Lawmaking,* 15, 37. See also Oleszek, 107–09 (providing reasons for trend); Don Wolfensberger, *Have House-Senate Conferences Gone the Way of the Dodo?*, Roll Call, April 28, 2008.

Lawmaking, 111. Summits may disrupt the traditional legislative dynamics and may even trump or render conference committees perfunctory or irrelevant. Indeed, Sinclair points to the 2009 economic stimulus legislation as an example of *hyper-unorthodox lawmaking.* "In circumstances that might well have led to what have been labeled a summit in the recent past, the negotiating group consisted only of the Speaker of the House, the House minority leader, and the Secretary of the Treasury, a group too small seemingly for the media to label it a summit." *Id.* at 183. Thus, summits might involve the top officials in the House and Senate but not committee leaders—or the House or Senate leaders might task committee chairs and ranking minority members to negotiate legislation, as occurred during the healthcare reform deliberations of 2009–10. *See id.* at 231.

Summitry is a rational legislative response to the threat that hyperpartisan division poses to urgent needs for legislative action, such as passing budgets. See John Gilmour, *Strategic Disagreement: Stalemate in American Politics* (1995); Sinclair, *Unorthodox Lawmaking,* 111, 183. Increasingly, polarized partisan politics has threatened congressional stalemate. When gridlock would be disastrous, lawmakers try to find a way to reach a balanced compromise. Summit negotiations provide a nonpublic environment where compromise can occur in a way that will bind all the necessary parties in both branches of government to the agreement. Furthermore, the results of summits, which often come to the Congress as a legislative package not easily amended from the floor, present rank-and-file members with a palatable vote in a politically charged context. Much as with complex and large omnibus measures, a form many products of summits take, a lawmaker can explain to interest groups opposing particular provisions or compromises that she had no option other than to vote for the large negotiated deal. This explanation is more convincing when offered by House members, because special rules may foreclose amendments and changes to legislation on the floor, and less persuasive in the context of the Senate, where members can unravel deals by offering amendments and threatening filibusters.

In the normal course of events in which a bill goes to a conference committee rather than a summit, the chamber that did not request the conference acts first on the conference bill, because that chamber has the "papers" (the bill as originally introduced and the amendments to it). That chamber has three options—adopt the conference bill, reject it, or recommit it to conference (which is tantamount to killing the bill). If the first chamber adopts the conference bill, the conference committee is dissolved, and the other chamber is faced with a straight up-or-down vote on the bill. If the bill is agreed to by both chambers, a copy of the bill is enrolled for presentment to the President or the Governor for signature.

6.   *Presentment for the Presidential or Gubernatorial Signature.* Under Article I, § 7 of the U.S. Constitution, once an enrolled bill is presented to the President, the President has ten days (not including Sundays) to sign it or veto it. If the President vetoes the bill, it is returned to Congress, where the veto can be overridden by two-thirds of those voting in each chamber. If the veto is overridden, the bill then becomes law without the President's signature. In most cases, if no action is taken within the constitutional ten-day period, the bill also becomes law without the President's signature. The exception to this last rule is that if Congress adjourns before the end of the ten-day period and the President fails to sign the bill, it is killed by a *pocket veto.*

Many major bills are passed in the waning days of each Congress, and so the President often has ample discretion to kill legislation without immediate congressional override.

The U.S. President must accept or reject the entire bill; if there are several provisions the President dislikes in the bill, the only formal option is to veto (or pocket veto) the entire bill. State Governors typically have more options, because they can veto individual provisions called *items* in bills presented to them. Congress attempted to delegate a similar power to the President in the Line Item Veto Act of 1996, Pub. L. No. 104–130, 110 Stat. 1200, codified at 2 U.S.C. §§ 691–92, but the Supreme Court struck down the federal act in *Clinton v. City of New York*, 524 U.S. 417 (1998).

NOTE ON TITLE VII OF THE CIVIL RIGHTS ACT OF 1964

The most complex, and most often litigated, portion of the Civil Rights Act has been Title VII, 78 Stat. 241, 253–66 (1964), codified as amended at 42 U.S.C. § 2000e *et seq.*, which prohibits job discrimination on the basis of race, sex, religion, or national origin. We shall now introduce you to the main provisions of the 1964 Act, before its amendments in 1972 and 1991. *The prime directive of Title VII is found in § 703(a), 42 U.S.C. § 2000e–2(a):*

It shall be an unlawful employment practice for an employer—

(1) to fail or refuse to hire or to discharge any individual, or otherwise to discriminate against any individual with respect to his compensation, terms, conditions, or privileges of employment, because of such individual's race, color, religion, sex, or national origin; or

(2) to limit, segregate, or classify his employees or applicants for employment in any way which would deprive or tend to deprive any individual of employment opportunities or otherwise adversely affect his status as an employee, because of such individual's race, color, religion, sex, or national origin.

Section 703(b)–(c), *id.* § 2000e–2(b)–(c), sets forth similar prohibitions of "unlawful employment practices" by employment agencies and labor organizations (unions). Section 703(d), *id.* § 2000e–2(d), applies the antidiscrimination principle specifically to apprenticeship or training programs.

The exact scope of this anti-discrimination rule (i.e., how broadly does the rule apply?) is provided by § 701's definitions of key terms. Thus "employer" is defined in § 701(b), *id.* § 2000e(b):

The term "employer" means a person engaged in an industry affecting commerce who has twenty-five or more employees for each working day in each of twenty or more calendar weeks in the current or preceding calendar year, and any agent of such a person, but such term does not include (1) the United States, a corporation wholly owned by the Government of the United States, an Indian tribe, or a State or political subdivision thereof, (2) a bona fide private membership club (other than a labor organization) which is exempt from taxation under section 501(c) of the Internal Revenue Code of 1954 * * *.

Section 701(h), *id.* § 2000e(h), defines "an industry affecting commerce" as "any activity, business, or industry in commerce or in which a labor dispute would hinder or obstruct commerce or the free flow of commerce and includes any activity or industry 'affecting commerce' within the meaning of the Labor-Management Reporting and Disclosure Act of 1959, and further includes any governmental industry, business, or activity." Section 701(g), *id.* § 2000e(g), defines "commerce" as "trade, traffic, commerce, transportation, transmission, or communication among the several States; or between a State and any place outside thereof; or within the District of Columbia, or a possession of the United States; or between points in the same State but through a point outside thereof." Section 701(i), *id.* § 2000e(i), defines "State" to include "a State of the United States, the District of Columbia, Puerto Rico, the Virgin Islands, American Samoa, Guam, Wake Island, the Canal Zone, and Outer Continental Shelf lands defined in the Outer Continental Shelf Lands Act." Definitions for "employment agency" and "labor organization" are set forth in § 701(c)–(e), *id.* § 2000e(c)–(e). There is no definition of "discriminate" or "discrimination" in Title VII.

There are various "exemptions" or "defenses" to the charge of unlawful employment practices under Title VII. Section 702, *id.* § 2000e–1, for example, exempts employment of aliens outside any State or employment of persons by religious groups from Title VII's application. But the main defenses are those which qualify the meaning of "unlawful employment practice" in § 703. Section 703(e), *id.* § 2000e–2(e), presents a defense for practices based on bona fide occupational qualifications:

> Notwithstanding any other provision of this subchapter, (1) it shall not be an unlawful employment practice for an employer to hire and employ employees, for an employment agency to classify, or refer for employment any individual, for a labor organization to classify its membership or to classify or refer for employment any individual, or for an employer, labor organization, or joint labor-management committee controlling apprenticeship or other training or retraining programs to admit or employ any individual in any such program, on the basis of his religion, sex, or national origin in those certain instances where religion, sex, or national origin is a bona fide occupational qualification reasonably necessary to the normal operation of that particular business or enterprise, and (2) it shall not be an unlawful employment practice for a school, college, university, or other educational institution or institution of learning to hire and employ employees of a particular religion if such school, college, university, or other educational institution or institution of learning is, in whole or in substantial part, owned, supported, controlled, or managed by a particular religion or by a particular religious corporation, association, or society, or if the curriculum of such school, college, university, or other educational institution or institution of learning is directed toward the propagation of a particular religion.

Section 703(f)–(g), *id.* § 2000e–2(f)–(g), relates to employment decisions based upon Communist Party membership and national security reasons.

Section 703(h), id. § 2000e–2(h), protects employment decisions based upon "a bona fide seniority or merit system, * * * provided that such differences are not the result of an intention to discriminate because of race, color, religion, sex, or national origin, nor shall it be an unlawful employment practice for an employer to give and to act upon the results of any professionally developed ability test provided that such test, its administration or action upon the results is not designed, intended, or used to discriminate because of race, color, religion, sex or national origin." Section 703(i), id. § 2000e–2(i), stipulates Title

VII's inapplicability "to any business or enterprise on or near an Indian reservation with respect to any publicly announced employment practice of such business or enterprise under which a preferential treatment is given to any individual because he is an Indian living on or near a reservation." *Section 703(j), id. § 2000e–2(j), deals with affirmative action under Title VII*:

> Nothing contained in this subchapter shall be interpreted to require any employer, employment agency, labor organization, or joint labor-management committee subject to this subchapter to grant preferential treatment to any individual or to any group because of the race, color, religion, sex, or national origin of such individual or group on account of an imbalance which may exist with respect to the total number or percentage of persons of any race, color, religion, sex, or national origin employed by any employer, referred or classified for employment by any employment agency or labor organization, admitted to membership or classified by any labor organization, or admitted to, or employed in, any apprenticeship or other training program, in comparison with the total number or percentage of persons of such race, color, religion, sex, or national origin in any community, State, section, or other area, or in the available work force in any community, State, section, or other area.

Section 713(b)(1), *id.* § 2000e–12(b)(1), provides a defense to a person charged with violating Title VII "if he pleads and proves that the act or omission complained of was in good faith, in conformity with, and in reliance on any written interpretation or opinion of the Commission."

A person "claiming to be aggrieved" may not file suit herself, but should file a "charge" with the EEOC asserting violation of the substantive norms of Title VII, pursuant to § 706(a), *id.* § 2000e–5(a). (Note that § 706(b), (d) sets forth time requirements within which the charge must be filed with the EEOC; the schedule depends in part on whether the state has a remedy for the violation.) Once the aggrieved person has filed a timely charge, the EEOC determines whether there is "reasonable cause to believe that the charge is true," and if so it will try to eliminate the unlawful practice informally through "conference, conciliation, and persuasion" (§ 706(a)). If the EEOC is unable to obtain voluntary compliance with Title VII, it notifies the aggrieved person and informs her that she may bring a lawsuit in federal court within thirty days (§ 706(e), *id.* § 2000e–5(e)). To remedy an unlawful employment practice, a court may enjoin the practice and order "such affirmative action as may be appropriate, which may include reinstatement or hiring of employees, with or without back pay" (§ 706(g), *id.* § 2000e–5(g)).

PROBLEMS APPLYING TITLE VII TO EMPLOYMENT POLICIES HAVING A DISPARATE RACIAL IMPACT

Problem 1–1. Duke Power Company's electrical generating plant at Dan River Stream Station in Draper, North Carolina has ninety-five employees in 1966, including fourteen African Americans. Employees are divided into five departments: (1) Operations (responsible for the day-to-day operation of the plant's generating equipment); (2) Maintenance (fixing and maintaining equipment); (3) Laboratory and Testing (analysis of water and coal used in the plant's operation); (4) Coal Handling (unloading and handling coal); and (5) Labor (janitorial services). Workers in the Labor

Department received the lowest hourly wage ($1.565), which was lower than any other department's minimum hourly wage ($1.705) and less than half the amount of other departments' maximum hourly wages ($3.18 to $3.65).

In 1955, Duke Power began requiring that every employee, except those in the Labor Department, had to have a high school diploma. The company also made the diploma a prerequisite for promotion of workers from the Labor Department into any of the others. Before 1955, the company's policy had been to limit African-American workers to the Labor Department. Under the 1955 policy, every African-American employee in the Dan River plant continued to work in Labor, and none was promoted. In 1965, when Title VII went into effect, the company instituted a new policy under which employees could be promoted out of Labor by passing one of two high school equivalency tests. Duke promoted Jesse Martin, a black man, from Labor to Coal Handling in 1966. Two other African-American workers were promoted in 1968. All had high school degrees.

After exhausting their administrative remedies with the EEOC, 13 of the 14 African-American employees at Dan River sued Duke Power for job discrimination in violation of Title VII. Six of the plaintiffs had no high school diplomas and were hired in Labor before 1955—when Duke had no high school diploma requirement for promotion but when it refused to promote African Americans as a matter of company policy. Four plaintiffs had no high school diplomas but were hired after the company instituted the diploma requirement in 1955. The plaintiffs sought an injunction requiring Duke to discontinue its diploma and testing requirements for promotion.

You are the General Counsel for Duke Power. The company wants to retain its diploma and testing requirements, and you believe that company policy is no longer to exclude African Americans from higher positions simply because of their race. Do the diploma and testing requirements violate Title VII? There is no precedent on this issue in the court system in early 1966, when the lawsuits are brought. You understand that the EEOC is going to issue guidelines on the subject of testing later in 1966. Can you predict what the EEOC guidelines will say? Should they make a difference in your advice to Duke Power? We shall return to this issue in Section 3, which examines the structure of implementation for statutes, starting with administrative measures by the EEOC and other agencies.

Problem 1–2. You are still General Counsel for Duke Power, which in 1966 is concerned that its diploma-and-test policy will be rejected by the EEOC and the liberal Warren Court. Its concerns are shared by the Chamber of Commerce, the nation's premier association of small businesses and a potent lobbying group in Washington DC. Both Duke and the Chamber are interested in seeking legislation amending Title VII to insulate policies like Duke's from liability. You are in charge of this effort.

First, suggest statutory language that could be added to Title VII in order to confirm Duke's immunity from liability. **Second,** suggest a legislative strategy for passing this amendment through all the vetogates that are characteristic of the congressional process outlined above. (Assume that Congress in 1966 has pretty much the same key players as it had in 1964; the main exception is that Senator Humphrey is now Vice-President.) **Third,** figure out what obstacles might thwart the client's agenda and how those obstacles might be surmounted. You might read the materials in Section 2 before jotting down your thoughts.

2. DESCRIPTIVE AND NORMATIVE THEORIES OF LEGISLATION

Congress launched Title VII in 1964; in the following decades, the statute has evolved in ways scarcely imaginable to its enactors. To understand the statute's enactment as well as evolution (explored in Section 3), it is useful to consider both theories of how the legislative process actually works (*descriptive* theories) and of how it should work (*normative* theories).

Pluralist theories (Part A) consider the legislature a forum where social and economic groups work through their often-conflicting visions of what policies government ought to be following. Interest group or public choice theories (Part B) focus on the influence and behavior of organized groups in the political process. And proceduralist or vetogate theories (Part C) focus on the procedures by which a bill becomes law. Each theory attempts to describe the congressional process, and each one also contains explicit or implicit assumptions about how that process should function. No one theory fully describes the rich and complex world of legislatures, lawmakers, interest groups, and constituents. Scholars often draw insights from several of the perspectives. Each approach highlights important aspects of the legislative process for students, judges, legislators, and lawyers seeking to influence Congress and state legislatures or to understand the legislative product.

A. PLURALIST THEORIES OF LEGISLATION

Many modern theories of the legislative process claim their genesis in the political thought of James Madison. As he worked to construct institutions of governance, Madison started with the propensity of human society to contain "factions" of citizens "who are united and actuated by some common impulse of passion, or of interest, adverse to the rights of other citizens, or to the permanent and aggregate interests of the community." *Federalist* No. 10. Like the Anti-Federalists (who opposed adoption of the Constitution), Madison believed factions must be controlled. However, Madison rejected the Anti-Federalist view that government could educate people to avoid faction and petty self-interest. "The latent causes of faction are thus sown in the nature of man," and hence cannot be eliminated short of unacceptable limitations on liberty. Madison viewed institutions of government as ways to contain the effects of faction and to channel them in socially productive ways.

Madison wrote that factions are driven by common interests that are "adverse" to the public good. A group of modern American theorists of democratic institutions who have emphasized the role of organized interests have a more positive view of "factions." These thinkers write in the *pluralist* tradition, exemplified by Robert Dahl, *A Preface to Democratic Theory* (1956). For them, an interest group is "any group that, on the basis of one or more shared attitudes, makes certain claims upon other groups in the society for the establishment, maintenance, or enhancement of forms of behavior that are implied by the shared attitudes." David Truman, *The Governmental Process* 33 (1951). Under some definitions, political parties would be interest groups; other theorists distinguish between the major political parties and other organized groups.

Pluralism entails a number of interrelated propositions. (1) *Citizens organize into groups for political action.* Citizens have different opinions and different economic interests, which leads to the formation of "interest groups." (2) *Interest group politics results in "pluralism"—the spreading of political power across many political actors.* "Actual authority tends to be dispersed and exercised not solely by governmental officials but also by private individuals and groups within the society. Moreover, the power structure tends to be segmented; authority over one question rests here and over another there. All this contrasts with the model of a clear and rigid hierarchical pattern of power." V.O. Key Jr., *Politics, Parties, and Pressure Groups* 9 (1958). Strong interest groups, many of which are private or voluntary organizations, protect individuals against oppressive and tyrannical government. In a way, a decentralized pluralist system expands one of Madison's checks on self-serving factions, as the ambition of one group checks the ambition of others and of government actors. See *Federalist* No. 10. (3) *Politics can be conceptualized as the process by which conflicting interest-group desires are resolved.* Because the objectives of one interest group can often be obtained only at the expense of others, the groups will come into conflict. The state regulates that conflict, and indeed the political system might be seen as nothing more than the arena in which interest group conflict is played out.

This third assumption might be stated more normatively. Although some pluralist theories posit a mechanical understanding of politics, whereby rubber-stamp legislators simply enact into law whatever interest groups want, theorists such as Dahl and Truman maintain that pluralist politics is good for the country. Some maintain that a political environment with many groups actively competing will tend to produce moderate and well-considered policies. Others emphasize that pluralist politics produces benefits beyond the virtues of specific policies—namely, the systemwide legitimacy and stability resulting from the participation of most groups. "Because constant negotiations among different centers of power are necessary in order to make decisions, citizens and leaders will perfect the precious art of dealing peacefully with their conflicts, and not merely to the benefit of one partisan but to the mutual benefit of all the parties to a conflict." Robert Dahl, *Pluralist Democracy in the United States: Conflict and Consent* 24 (1967).

Our pluralist system aspires to be a marketplace of ideas, where all perspectives are articulated forcefully and persuasively. The best ideas succeed, while the worst are discarded. Pluralists argue that groups have a degree of power proportionate to their numbers—the larger, more general interest will prevail over the smaller, special interest. In addition, they have a degree of power proportionate to the intensity with which they hold their views, a factor which can increase the influence of smaller groups. " '[I]nterests' are not all equal: some are intensely felt, others only weakly so. 'Democracy' is more than a math problem. The *number* of people favoring a particular candidate or proposition is only one factor for which [a governance] system needs to account. The intensity of preferences also must weigh in the balance." Nathaniel Persily, *Toward a Functional Defense of Political Party Autonomy*, 76 N.Y.U. L. Rev. 750 (2001).[35] In short, bargaining among interest

---

[35] See also Robert Dahl, *Democracy and Its Critics* 150 (1989) (arguing that our system is one of "minorities rule" rather than of "majority rule"); Sidney Verba, Kay Lehman Schlozman & Henry Brady, *Voice*

groups allows the system to reach a long-term equilibrium providing many interest groups one or a few policy objectives they care deeply about because they are willing to give up on issues about which they care much less. For a useful empirical survey of the breadth of interest group activity, see Frank R. Baumgartner, Jeffrey M. Berry, Marjorie Hojnacki, David C. Kimball & Beth L. Leech, *Lobbying and Policy Change: Who Wins, Who Loses, and Why* (2009).

Pluralist theory, grounded in empirical work that supplements and often confirms the aspirations of normative theorists, is perhaps the most useful way to understand the operation of the legislative process. But it is also important to understand the forces that threaten to clog or distort that process. Public choice theories of interest group formation (Part B) and vetogates theories of the legislative process (Part C) are two such theories.

B. INTEREST GROUP (PUBLIC CHOICE) THEORIES OF LEGISLATION

1. Patterns of Interest Group Formation (Free Rider Problems)

A crucial assumption underlying the most optimistic pluralist theories is that all views and interests are represented. Early critics of interest-group liberalism noted pervasive disparities of access to the political process. One prominent skeptic, Elmer Schattschneider, in *The Semisovereign People: A Realist's View of Democracy in America* (1960), argued that interest groups are not broad-based or representative of all societal interests. "The flaw in the pluralist heaven is that the heavenly chorus sings with a strong upper-class accent. Probably about 90 percent of the people cannot get into the pressure system. * * * Pressure politics is a selective process ill designed to serve diffuse interests," such as the interests of consumers and other ordinary people. *Id.* at 34–35.

Schattschneider based his observation in part on his study of the Smoot-Hawley Tariff, which he found to have been enacted as a result of deals struck by well-heeled special interest groups rather than any deliberative consideration of the public interest. See Elmer Schattschneider, *Politics, Pressures and the Tariff: A Study of Free Private Enterprise in Pressure Politics, as Shown in the 1929–1930 Revision of the Tariff* (1935). Accord, Kay Lehman Schlozman & John Tierney, *Organized Interests and American Democracy* 68 (1986). On the other hand, Baumgartner et al., *Lobbying and Policy Change,* found that, although consumer groups represented a small percentage of the filings required under the Lobbying Disclosure Act of 1992, their presence was much larger in the overall picture of grass-roots lobbying, congressional testimony, and survey data. Accord, Jeffrey Berry, *The New Liberalism: The Rising Power of Citizen Groups* 21–22 (1999).

In *The Logic of Collective Action* (1965), Mancur Olson provided a theory to explain why some groups form and work to influence politics and why some do not. Legislation is a *public good*; once the state has decided to provide clean waterways or safe highways, for example, all in society will benefit. Yet any individual effort to

---

and Equality: Civic Voluntarism in American Politics 179–82 (1995) (explaining the importance of intensity of preference for pluralist democratic theory).

pass such laws will have only an infinitesimal effect on the probability of its enactment. Therefore, a rational person will not participate in the political process at all, preferring instead to *free-ride* on the efforts of others. As long as the free-rider cannot be excluded from enjoying the public goods that legislation and the efforts of groups lobbying in favor of new laws provide, she will have no incentive to join the group or to expend time and resources. If all citizens follow this rational course, then none will work to influence her representative to pass legislation providing diffuse benefits to the public at large.

Olson's theory predicts, therefore, that groups will form most often when there are a few interested members. In that case, each member has a large enough stake in the sought-after law to justify its participation. Furthermore, in small groups, members can monitor the behavior of others, detect and punish shirking, and ensure collective action. In other cases, a group will form because one member will receive such a large fraction of the governmental benefit that it would work to obtain the legislation even if it had to internalize all the costs of political activity. Indeed, the interested party may expend significant resources forming an interest "group" as part of its political strategy. It may fare better in the political process if the policy it advocates appears to elicit broader support. For example, a great deal of modern grassroots activity is financed, and to some extent manufactured, by well-funded, relatively small groups that hope to lend populist credentials to their policy proposals.[36] Under both of these scenarios of group formation, small groups have the advantage over larger ones, and they will work to obtain targeted benefits at the expense of the diffuse and unorganized public. As Olson concludes: "[T]here is a surprising tendency for the 'exploitation' of the great by the small." *Logic of Collective Action,* 35 (emphasis omitted). Other groups form because they can successfully coerce members to participate. For example, some have argued that labor unions' legislative and electoral clout results in part from their ability essentially to require workers to belong and to participate in their activities.

Olson's theory suggests that minority interests might threaten the public good. In a democracy, Madison feared the tyranny of majority factions that could adopt policies oppressing minorities and dismissed concerns about minority factions in *Federalist* No. 10: "If a faction consists of less than a majority, relief is supplied by the republican principle, which enables a majority to defeat its sinister views by regular vote." Contrary to Madison, however, minority factions sometimes possess organizational advantages over majority factions, and they may also be adept in using aspects of the political process to dominate the discussion of policy alternatives, the selection of a particular course of action, and the implementation of the policy.

How serious is the problem of minority "rent-seeking" legislation? Some studies suggest that the problem may be less serious than Olson predicted. As the 2009 empirical study by Baumgartner and his colleagues documents, large groups do form and influence political outcomes. Interest groups representing larger, more diffuse groups of citizens can exist and exercise influence even under Olson's model.

---

[36] See Richard Davis, *The Web of Politics: The Internet's Impact on the American Political System* 81–83 (1999).

For example, some groups formally organize for nonpolitical reasons and then turn to political activity as a *byproduct*. For these groups, the initial costs of organizing, often the greatest hurdle facing those who seek to influence governmental policies, have already been met. Examples include unions, farmers' cooperatives, and trade and business associations. Perhaps most important, agency officials, often representing the general public, are also important interest groups that exercise systematic, pervasive influence on the legislative process. Baumgartner et al., *Lobbying and Policy Change,* 208.

Large groups can also form if they offer desirable *selective benefits* only to their members. For example, groups may offer life insurance, discounts on travel, dinners and events, and other goodies only to their members. The AARP offers members discounts on drugs; the NRA offers members discounts on bullets. To explain large political groups on the basis of this sort of selective benefit seems rather unpersuasive, however. Why pay dues that fund the Sierra Club's political activity just to get the calendar when one can buy a nature calendar for much less money? The kind of selective benefit that prompts people to join large groups must relate to the political activity itself. Accordingly, some public choice theorists argue that participation in group activity provides members with purposive or solidary benefits that justify any costs they incur.[37] *Purposive benefits* accrue to members who seek ideological or issue-oriented goals and find pursuit of those objectives more meaningful as part of an organized group.[38] *Solidary benefits* provide members social rewards, including the satisfaction of the desire to be politically motivated.

It is also possible that the Internet offers new ways to overcome the free-rider problem, allowing large numbers of dispersed citizens to organize and exert political influence. Thus, the Internet facilitates the sharing of information, allows like-minded people to connect at lower cost, and reduces the cost of mobilizing like-minded people and institutions to act in political capacities. See Bruce Bimber et al., *Technological Change and the Shifting Nature of Political Organization,* in *Handbook of Internet Politics* 72–85 (Andrew Chadwick & Philip Howard eds., 2009). Indeed, the Internet has fueled the most "fecund" period of political group activity and organization since the Progressive era. *Id.* at 73–74. The Internet played a major role Barack Obama's 2008 and 2012 presidential races, and its influence is apparent in the green politics of global warming and other environmental issues. But it remains to be seen how important the Internet will prove to be in the politics of ordinary legislation. For a skeptical view, see Mathew Hindman, *The Myth of the Digital Democracy* (2009).

In *The Logic of Congressional Action* (1990), a book designed to expand on Olson's seminal work, R. Douglas Arnold explains why legislators respond to the general public, which he calls the *inattentive public,* and do not spend all their time legislating in favor of organized groups that comprise the *attentive public.* The

---

[37] See Paul Johnson, *Interest Group Recruiting: Finding Members and Keeping Them,* in *Interest Group Politics* 35 (Allan Cigler & Burdett Loomis eds., 5th ed. 1998).

[38] See Edward Rubin, *Getting Past Democracy,* 149 U. Pa. L. Rev. 711, 745–746 (2001) (describing social movement theorists and noting that "meaning, not self-interest, * * * motivated many citizens' participation.").

simple explanation is the electoral connection between lawmakers and the public. Members of Congress want to be reelected, and they know that the inattentive public, many of whom will vote in the next election, can be roused into action on particular issues under certain conditions. To avoid reprisals at election time, legislators will consider the potential preferences of the inattentive public and the likelihood that voters will focus on these preferences at election time. Given their limited attention, however, the inattentive public may be satisfied with legislation that is largely symbolic, effecting no real change in policy.

2. A Transactional View of the Legislative Process

Based on the theories of classical market economics, *public choice theorists* seek to explain the operation of the processes by which legislators are selected, take action and positions, and make collective decisions.[39] Public choice scholars treat politicians and voters as rational utility-maximizers operating in a competitive electoral market. One prominent aspect of public choice theory has been the creation of models treating the legislative process as a microeconomic system in which "actual political choices are determined by the efforts of individuals and groups to further their own interests." Gary Becker, *A Theory of Competition Among Pressure Groups for Political Influence*, 98 Q.J. Econ. 371, 371 (1983). "The basic assumption is that taxes, subsidies, regulations, and other political instruments are used to raise the welfare of more influential pressure groups." *Id.* at 373–74. Compared to most pluralist thinkers, public choice theorists claim to be less normative and more descriptive in their methods and objectives. They are not wholly descriptive, however; for example, they often criticize existing institutional arrangements and propose changes based on their assumptions about individual and group behavior.

True to their perspective as economists, public choice scholars model the legislative environment as a political market. Interest groups, and to a lesser extent the public, are the demanders of legislation. They send benefits to legislators, who can supply them with governmental largesse. Legislators can respond to demand by refusing to pass a bill, by avoiding a clear choice through delegation of broad decisionmaking authority to an agency in the executive branch, or by explicitly allocating tangible benefits. Based on Olson's *Logic of Collective Action* and James Wilson's *Political Organizations* (1973), Michael Hayes posits a transactional theory of legislation in *Lobbyists and Legislators: A Theory of Political Markets* (1981). Inspired by the idea that political markets are analogous to economic markets, Hayes outlines the demand and supply patterns for several different categories of political issues.

a.   *Demand Patterns in Political Markets.* On the demand side (what interest groups want out of the legislature), legislators are often faced with a myriad of interest groups on any given issue, and these groups may either agree (consensual pattern) or disagree (conflictual pattern) with each other. A consensual demand pattern is similar to a non-zero-sum situation, while a conflictual demand pattern

---

[39] In addition to Olson's book, other prominent works of public choice theory include James Buchanan & Gordon Tullock, *The Calculus of Consent* (1962); Anthony Downs, *An Economic Theory of Democracy* (1957); William Riker, *Liberalism Against Populism* (1982).

is basically zero sum. If an issue is consensual, then everyone who is aware of and actively interested in the issue can come out a winner, while if it is conflictual, then the resolution of the conflict will necessarily result in immediately identifiable winners and losers. In a way, this dichotomy is unrealistic; in a world of limited resources, all policies are zero sum because someone, either now or later, has to pay for them. In the short run, however, government decisions can be relatively unconstrained by resource limitations if policymakers can push the costs onto an inattentive group or a group that does not vote in the next election. For example, government benefits funded through deficit financing places the costs on future generations of taxpayers, some of whom have not yet been born. See Daniel Shaviro, *Do Deficits Matter?* (1997). Living voters may be harmed by higher interest rates as the government competes for credit or by inflation if the government just prints more money, but those costs can be hard for citizens to trace back to particular legislative decisions. In these essentially consensual circumstances, interest groups may cooperate, making deals among themselves to obtain benefits at the expense of the general public. This type of interest group behavior is often called *logrolling* as minority interests work together to enact a bill, providing goodies to the organized constituents of a majority of lawmakers. Examples of these kinds of bills include tax bills that enact tax benefits for hundreds of interest groups, military construction bills that send money to projects in hundreds of congressional districts, or tariff bills like the Smoot-Hawley Act that Schattschneider studied.

The extent to which an interest group is formally organized is one key to its effectiveness in demanding legislation. Organized groups provide useful information to political actors and tend to frame the issues more clearly and precisely for legislators. Increasingly, the demand side of the market is characterized by interest groups working in coalitions in which several groups with shared interests work together typically for a limited time.[40] Coordination among groups can reveal to lawmakers that a policy's advocates span numerous congressional districts, and coalitions are often nonpartisan, giving them the advantage of bipartisan support. Of course, coalitions are not invincible. The larger and broader a coalition, the more susceptible it may be to tactics that divide members and dissipate its strength.

James Wilson maintains that the degree and nature of interest group organization is determined by the perceived incidence of costs and benefits from a specified policy. Costs of a policy may be broadly *distributed*, such as a sales tax paid by all consumers, or may be *concentrated* on a small group, such as a license fee. Similarly, benefits may be widely distributed or shared by all, such as the benefits of national security, or they may be concentrated in the hands of a few, such as state subsidies to tobacco farmers. When Wilson's typology is combined with the insights of Olson's theory, a transactional theorist might surmise that because bills providing concentrated costs or benefits will affect smaller groups,

---

[40]   See Kevin Hula, *Lobbying Together: Interest Group Coalitions in Legislative Politics* (2000).

they will *on average* stimulate more organizational activity than measures with distributed costs and benefits.[41] Table 1–1 sets forth this model.

Each of these quadrants produces a particular kind of political climate. Quadrant I is best described as *majoritarian politics*. Although there is little group activity on either side, some large groups of citizens will weigh in both in favor of distributed benefits (for example, environmental groups will favor clean air legislation) and against distributed costs (Citizens for a Sound Economy will oppose tax increases or the Concord Coalition will oppose deficit spending). Quadrant II fits the model of *entrepreneurial politics*. Organized interests will form to derail the legislation; support is likely only if a policy entrepreneur is willing to push the proposal, rouse the inattentive public, and perhaps take the initiative in forming citizen groups offering purposive or solidary benefits to participants. *Client politics* describes the consensual interest group activity in Quadrant III, where logrolling dominates the essentially non-zero sum game that interest groups play. Finally, Quadrant IV is the area of conflictual *interest group politics* where the process produces identifiable and short-term winners and losers, and both sides are organized and active.

Table 1–1
Taxonomy of Demand for Legislation Based on Benefits/Costs

I *Distributed benefits/distributed costs*	II *Distributed benefits/concentrated costs*
A general benefit-general taxation case that usually involves public goods. Little group activity on either side of most cases.	A general benefit-specific taxation case in which the majority imposes its will on the minority up to the capacity of the minority to pay. Opposition will tend to be well organized.
III *Concentrated benefits/distributed costs*	IV *Concentrated benefits/concentrated costs*
Tends to have strong interest group support and weak, if any, organized opposition because of the free-rider problem. The benefit to an individual of having the policy changed is simply too immaterial.	Results in continuous organized conflict over payment of benefits and distribution costs. A prime example is the NLRB and the conflicts between labor and management.

b.   *Supply Patterns in Legislative Markets.* Public choice theorists tend to discount legislators' statements that they vote "for the public interest." Morris Fiorina, *Congress: Keystone of the Washington Establishment* (2d ed. 1989), and David Mayhew, *Congress: The Electoral Connection* (1974), posit that legislative behavior can best be explained by the assumption that the primary goal of legislators is to be reelected. Of course, regardless of the ultimate motivation for

---

[41] Note the textual emphasis, *on average*; this is only a generalization, not an iron rule. Due to the free-rider problem, the formation of even small groups cannot be assumed. Extremely large groups sometimes organize. In addition, as our analysis of proceduralism will demonstrate, numerous advantages exist for groups in a defensive posture, which means that such groups are perhaps more likely to form. Also, an effective demand pattern is not limited to interest groups—the existence of an inattentive public can and does exert influence in certain situations. Finally, the work of interest groups can all be for naught due to the countervailing power of the latitude possessed by legislators.

legislative behavior, the desire for reelection is a good focus of study because, as long as lawmakers do not face term limits, reelection is a prerequisite to achieving any other goals. To put it differently, legislators may ultimately want to enact particular policies that they believe benefit the country, or to receive benefits from interest groups, or to gain publicity because of their positions. But to achieve any of these goals, they must remain in office; thus, the electoral connection is a paramount concern.

A large majority of legislators respond to this electoral incentive effectively and are reelected time after time. Although the advantage of incumbency has declined slightly, it is still one of the strongest predictors of electoral success.[42] How can a politician ensure that she will remain undefeated if her elected position demands that she take public stands on controversial issues? Fiorina has suggested that *abstention* (the legislator does not take sides) or *casework* (the legislator dollops out individual, nonlegislative favors, such as intervention in agency decisionmaking, to the groups voted against) can ameliorate the harmful effects of conflicting constituent demands. Other transactional theorists argue that the most effective response is for the legislator to act so that each of the conflicting groups will believe it has won something. Thus, the legislator's best strategies for dealing with conflictual demand patterns are to persuade the conflicting groups to reach a compromise which the legislator will then support *or* to pass an ambiguous bill which delegates policy responsibility to an administrative agency which is even more prone to interest group manipulation. The capture theory has gained wide currency in administrative law: agencies charged with regulating an industry or making political value choices regarding a cluster of issues become tools of the interests they are supposed to be ruling.[43]

Again, Wilson's typology may be useful. If a policy imposes concentrated costs, legislators will want to avoid responsibility as much as possible, perhaps by delegating the cost-imposition to a regulatory agency, such as the Food and Drug Administration or the Environmental Protection Agency. The regulated interest may accept this outcome, hoping that its superior organization will allow it to capture the regulating agency and subvert the policy.[44] Even if the costs are distributed, such as in majoritarian politics, legislators may be wary of acting directly and decisively. Take, for example, the case of a clean air act funded through a general tax rate hike. The inattentive public is more likely to trace the immediate and somewhat costly increase in taxes back to lawmakers and vote against them than voters are apt to notice slight increases in air quality and to make the connection between cleaner air and a particular piece of legislation. In cases of concentrated benefits and distributed costs, however, legislators may risk the wrath of the electorate to gain the gratitude of the attentive and organized public, particularly if they believe that the cost-bearers will remain unaware of the

---

[42] See Bruce Cain, *The American Electoral System,* in *Developments in American Politics* 37, 43–46 (Gillian Peele, Christopher Bailey & Bruce Cain eds., 1992).

[43] See, e.g., Thomas Merrill, *Capture Theory and the Courts: 1967–1983,* 72 Chi.–Kent L. Rev. 1039, 1050–52 (1997).

[44] See Peter Aranson, Ernest Gellhorn, & Glen Robinson, *A Theory of Legislative Delegation,* 69 Cornell L. Rev. 1 (1982).

costs or can be deceived by public-regarding half-truths about the statutory purposes. Thus, in the arena of client politics, legislators often reward friendly interest groups with self-regulation or distributive benefits.

Table 1–2 illustrates the transactional supply model. As you study the interest group dynamics in the various quadrants, ask yourself where the Civil Rights Act of 1964 fits. Businesses required to change their hiring and promotion practices may have believed they were subject to concentrated costs. On the other hand, businesses in the South that wanted to expand their client base or expand their pool of potential workers may have preferred legislation that would allow them to integrate without violating ingrained racist norms in those regions.[45] What about the interest groups on the other side? As we have noted, the religious organizations favoring the bill were already organized; their political activity was a relatively cheap byproduct since the initial costs of organization had been defrayed and mechanisms of collecting financial support and harnessing human resources were well established. Policy entrepreneurs inside and outside of government abound, all with varying personal interests. And while blacks and other groups facing discrimination were relatively powerless in society, they had the potential to organize and affect electoral outcomes, particularly after President Johnson succeeded in meeting his subsequent objective of enacting strong voting rights laws.

Table 1–2
Taxonomy of Supply of Legislation Based on Benefits/Costs

I *Distributed benefits/distributed costs*	II *Distributed benefits/concentrated*
Because there is no strong pressure from organized interests, legislature will favor *no bill or symbolic action*. Sometimes delegation to agency regulation will occur.	Because the proposal will be opposed by organized interests, the best legislative solution is to draft an ambiguous bill and *delegate to agency regulation*, so all sides can claim victory. Regulatory capture can result.
III *Concentrated benefits/distributed costs*	IV *Concentrated benefits/concentrated costs*
Because the costs can be allocated to an uninformed public, legislature will follow a policy of *distribution* of subsidies and power to the organized beneficiaries. Often *self-regulation* is the chosen policy.	Because any policy choice will incur the wrath of opposing interests groups, legislators will favor *no bill* or delegation to *agency regulation*.

c. *The Implications of a Transactional Model of Legislation: Madison's Nightmare.*[46] The transactional model developed in Tables 1–1 and 1–2 suggests considerable pessimism regarding the results of imperfect political markets. On the one hand, the public sector will tend to spend too much money on statutes that concentrate benefits on special interests while distributing their costs to the general, and often unsuspecting, public. There is an obvious tendency to logroll in a

---

[45] But see Richard Epstein, *Forbidden Grounds: The Case Against Employment Discrimination Laws* 127–28 (1992) (contesting this prisoner's dilemma view and the conclusion that it justified regulation).

[46] Compare the different governance problem examined in Peter Shane, *Madison's Nightmare: How Executive Power Threatens American Democracy* (2009).

specific benefit-general taxation scheme such as ours, because legislators can please important groups with tax subsidies, while avoiding blame for the overspending that results.

On the other hand, the public sector will tend to supply too few statutes that are likely to be public-regarding, namely, statutes that distribute benefits broadly (e.g., infrastructure programs, commercial codes, effective criminal laws). Legislators often have little interest in such statutes, because they do not as reliably generate votes in the next election. And even if the populace were appreciative of these statutes, it is possible that in many cases Congress would be unaware of the demand, because the free-rider problem precludes effective organization. This problem is particularly acute in Quadrant II because a statute that provides distributed benefits through enacting concentrated costs will face strong and organized opposition that is likely to prevail over the shallow support that a policy entrepreneur can create. Some of these laws, notably federal criminal laws when violence and crime are salient for voters, may produce political payoffs attractive enough to encourage lawmakers to spend some time on these proposals and to pass legislation that is often primarily symbolic.

This taxonomy may suggest reforms that are likely to improve the legislative process because it helps to identify the equivalents of market failures. For example, if legislation in the majoritarian and entrepreneurial arenas tends to be more consistent with the public good but is underproduced because of interest group dynamics, reforms might emphasize empowering people whose interests are not well represented by organized groups. Alternatively, it might suggest that we should identify proxy groups with related interests that can serve as champions for the unorganized. Criminals are, for the most part, not well-organized politically, but lawyers are well-organized and usually serve as virtual representatives for the interests of those accused of crimes.

If we notice that inefficient, private-regarding legislation is less likely when interest group behavior is conflictual and not cooperative, we might seek to structure the legislative process to force interest groups to compete for limited resources. Structuring legislative processes so that losers are more clearly identified will make such legislation more difficult to pass.[47] It is also worth considering how changing technology may affect the dynamics of the transactional model. As noted above, the Internet may be a resource for consumers and other large and dispersed social groups to organize themselves into a more potent lobbying force. See generally Bruce Bimber, *Information and American Democracy: Technology in the Evolution of Power* (2003).

3. Criticisms of the Public Choice Vision

Public choice models of the legislative process have come under increasing attack in the last two decades for their oversimplification of the political process

---

[47] See Elizabeth Garrett, *Rethinking the Structures of Decisionmaking in the Federal Budget Process*, 35 Harv. J. Legis. 387 (1998).

and their failure to recognize its institutional richness.[48] Even some scholars writing in the public choice tradition have criticized the transactional model because it treats legislators as ciphers, merely implementing the deals that interest groups reach. For example, Fred McChesney observes that those who posit the economic theory of legislation and legal regulation largely ignore the ways in which politicians obtain benefits from their office other than by sending legislative goodies to interest groups. He argues that campaign contributions, gifts, post-tenure employment, and other payments to politicians are often made, "not for particular political favors, but to avoid particular political disfavor, that is, as part of a system of political extortion or 'rent extraction.' * * * Because the state, quite legally, can (and does) take money and other forms of wealth from its citizens, politicians can extort from private parties payments *not* to expropriate private wealth." Fred McChesney, *Money for Nothing: Politicians, Rent Extraction, and Political Extortion* 2–3 (1997).

Rent extraction is theoretically possible in any field of legislation because lawmakers always have the capacity to repeal existing beneficial laws or to enact new taxes or fees burdening particular activities or industries. Practically, however, the threat to burden an interest group must be credible for successful rent extraction. In other words, the threatened group must believe that the chances are good that lawmakers will actually pass harmful legislation. One arena of particularly credible threats is the tax legislative arena, because Congress frequently passes new tax laws decreasing some tax subsidies and increasing taxes on particular groups. This behavior produces enough uncertainty that current beneficiaries of tax subsidies are regularly worried that their provisions will be scaled back or modified and are willing to pay protection money to lawmakers.[49] Like other public choice accounts, McChesney's rent-extraction theory is limited by its thin understanding of legislators as one-dimensional seekers of financial rewards from interest groups.

Empirical studies also provide a basis for a critique of public choice, revealing that money and organization do not always translate into clout. See Baumgartner et al., *Lobbying and Policy Change,* 208–09, 223–24; Berry, *Interest Group Society,* 226–33. Instead, an interest group's influence depends upon the context. First, interest groups are more successful at blocking legislation than enacting a new policy. See Schlozman & Tierney, *Organized Interests,* 314–15. Groups defending the status quo need to prevail at only one stage in the convoluted legislative process. Proponents of new legislation must successfully navigate all of the

---

[48] For commentary, see, e.g., Daniel Farber & Philip Frickey, *Law and Public Choice: A Critical Introduction* (1991); *The Rational Choice Controversy* (Jeffrey Friedman ed., 1996); Donald Green & Ian Shapiro, *Pathologies of Rational Choice Theory* (1994); Jerry Mashaw, *Greed, Chaos, and Governance: Using Public Choice To Improve Public Law* (1997); Maxwell Stearns, *Public Choice and Public Law: Readings and Commentary* (1997); Frank Cross, *The Judiciary and Public Choice,* 50 Hastings L. J. 355 (1999); Einer Elhauge, *Does Interest Group Theory Justify More Intensive Judicial Review?,* 101 Yale L.J. 31 (1991); Colin Hay, *Theory, Stylized Heuristic or Self-Fulfilling Prophecy? The Status of Rational Choice Theory in Public Administration,* 82 Pub. Admin. 39 (2004); Thomas Merrill, *Does Public Choice Justify Judicial Activism After All?,* 21 Harv. J. L. & Pub. Pol. 219 (1997); *Symposium: Getting Beyond Cynicism: New Theories of the Regulatory State,* 87 Cornell L. Rev. 267 (2002).

[49] See, e.g., Richard Doernberg & Fred McChesney, *Doing Good or Doing Well?: Congress and the Tax Reform Act of 1986,* 62 N.Y.U. L. Rev. 891 (1987); Edward McCaffery & Linda Cohen, *Shakedown at Gucci Gulch: The New Logic of Collective Action,* 84 N.C. L. Rev. 1159 (2006).

procedural obstacles. In addition, cognitive psychology suggests that people work harder to preserve what they have than to gain a new benefit. This finding is confirmed by leaders of interest groups who report it is easier to ward off an attack than to mount one. Second, interest groups succeed more frequently on issues that are not salient to the larger public and that are perceived as narrow, technical, nonpartisan issues. *Id.* at 314. Client politics is easier when it occurs outside the glare of publicity, and members are willing to trade support on minor issues in backroom deals. Indeed, Baumgartner and his colleagues found that, on salient policy issues, the financial clout of pro-business interests did not translate into policy success at all. *Lobbying and Policy Change*, 208–09, 223–24. Finally, groups work to locate the decisionmaking in institutions that are sympathetic to their position or have procedures they can use to their advantage.[50]

Just as empirical studies have given us a more complex explanation than that provided by public choice theory for the demand side of legislation (interest group behavior), case studies of Congress by institutional political scientists have questioned the public choice explanation for the supply side (behavior of legislators). Richard Fenno's classic case study, *Congressmen in Committees* (1973), argues that legislators are interested in more than simply being reelected, contrary to the assumptions of public choice theory. While reelection is certainly a powerful motivating factor and a necessary intermediate goal, legislators also want to have "status" within government and to make some positive contribution to what they consider good public policy. Especially when an issue involves moral questions and is publicly visible, the legislator's vote depends on something more than her calculations about reelection.[51] Recall the behavior of the legislators in our story of the Civil Rights Act; can it all be explained solely in terms of interest group influence, or were other factors at work?

Not only may public choice theory oversimplify legislator motivations, it may also misconceive the legislative process by viewing it statically and disregarding institutional changes that affect behavior. For example, political parties exercise pervasive influence over the operation of the legislative process, relative to committees and rank-and-file members, allowing lawmakers to coordinate their efforts more effectively and resist the urge to act in ways that benefit only narrow special interests or small constituencies. Lawmakers who serve in party leadership roles tend to come from relatively safe districts and therefore to be insulated from narrow constituent pressures. Thus, they can survive the electoral heat of authoring a compromise bill that offends the sensibilities of extremists or particular interest groups, and they may have more leeway in pursuing their vision of the public good without fearing electoral reprisals.[52] Counterbalancing this, however, is their desire to remain in the majority and an awareness that the reelection of some of their members may depend on legislation benefitting special interests.

---

[50] See Neil Komesar, *Imperfect Alternatives: Choosing Institutions in Law, Economics, and Public Policy* (1994).

[51] See also Keith Poole & Howard Rosenthal, *Congress: A Political-Economic History of Roll Call Voting* (1997) (finding ideology was largest influence on roll call voting behavior).

[52] See John Aldrich, *Why Parties? The Origin and Transformation of Political Parties in America* 205 (1995).

Another institution that affects legislative behavior—the executive branch—was long slighted by traditional public choice theory. It has recently been receiving more attention.[53] The President may be the dominant influence in the national legislative process. As a unitary office backed by a more cohesive coalition than the multi-membered Congress, the Presidency is in a better position to develop coherent policies and, consequently, often initiates and propels controversial bills through the legislative labyrinth. As our nation's most visible public figure, the President is ideally situated to stimulate publicity about a public problem. As the chief of the executive branch, the President has access to an impressive brain trust (such as the Office of Management and Budget, the Treasury Department's Office of Tax Policy, and other prestigious executive branch entities), which can think creatively about a problem and draft proposed legislation. As the head of one of the political parties, representative of a uniquely national constituency, and someone who controls a number of desirable benefits, the President can be the best possible lobbyist a bill can have.[54]

Also modeling the dynamic nature of the legislative process, John Kingdon, in *Agenda, Alternatives, and Public Policies* (2d ed. 1995), de-emphasizes the role of interest groups and argues that public officials (the President, the Cabinet appointed by the President, Congress, as well as leaders of political parties) play the key roles in setting the nation's political agenda. The role of interest groups is usually to formulate and debate policy alternatives, a role they share with other less visible (but perhaps more public-regarding) participants, such as civil servants, academics and experts, the media, and legislative staff. Kingdon's model of the legislative process is drawn from the "garbage can model of organizational choice," described in Michael Cohen, James March & Johan Olsen, *A Garbage Can Model of Organizational Choice*, 17 Ad. Sci. Q. 1 (March 1972). Under this conceptualization, Congress operates through an "organized anarchy," in which there is no linear process for identifying a problem, defining alternative solutions, and reaching a decision. See also Charles Lindblom & Edward Woodhouse, *The Policy-Making Process* Chapters 1 & 2 (3d ed. 1993).

Under Kingdon's model, salient problems, possible solutions, and choice opportunities will coexist as separate "streams" in the "garbage can" (the system). Sometimes problems are resolved; sometimes they go away; sometimes the system despairs of solving them. The outcome depends on the "coupling of the streams": a problem becomes salient at the same time a solution becomes well-regarded and participants favoring the solution can seize the legislative process for that end. To change policy, groups must have more than just political clout; they must draw attention to their proposal when the political environment is receptive to it. Activists need a focusing event, preferably after they have laid the groundwork necessary to increase the chances that the event will lead to movement in a direction they support. Sometimes streams connect and issues become prominent

---

[53] See, e.g., *The Presidency and the Political System* (Michael Nelson ed., 8th ed. 2006); Terry Moe & Scott Wilson, *Presidents and the Politics of Structure*, 57 Law & Contemp. Probs. 1 (Spring 1994).

[54] But see Benjamin Ginsberg, Walter Mebane & Martin Shefter, *The President and "Interests": Why the White House Cannot Govern*, in *The Presidency and the Political System* 361 (Michael Nelson ed., 6th ed. 2000); Michael Fitts, *The Paradox of Power in the Modern State: Why a Unitary, Centralized Presidency May Not Exhibit Effective or Legitimate Leadership*, 144 U. Pa. L. Rev. 827 (1996).

on the political agenda because of chance. Airline safety becomes a topic of national concern and attention after a tragic plane accident, for example. Political entrepreneurs, whether inside or outside of government, need not leave matters completely to the vagaries of fate, however; they can manipulate the policy environment to increase receptivity to their objectives. When focusing events do not occur fortuitously, they can be created, much as Greenpeace has done in the environmental area when it confronts hunters and polluters on the high seas.

Moreover, administrative agencies are important players in the legislative process. Agency experts not only provide relatively neutral and fact-based arguments for and against policy initiatives, but they also form personal relationships with Members of Congress and their staff that render them important and sometimes essential coalition partners for successful legislation. Indeed, the most thorough empirical analysis of lobbying effectiveness found that established interest groups, including big business, have had little success persuading Congress to enact legislation *unless* they found support for their positions with public officials and agencies. See Baumgartner et al., *Lobbying and Policy Change,* 208.

Another way of criticizing the static perspective is to question the public choice assumption that preferences are independent of and prior to political activity. To use economic terminology, pluralism, particularly public choice, tends to view preferences as *exogenous* rather than *endogenous*. This assumption is clearly unrealistic; we all know that participating in decisionmaking, whether in the political realm or elsewhere, significantly affects the way we think and feel about a particular issue.[55] As the members of Congress deliberated about the Civil Rights Act of 1964 and discussed their views with their colleagues and constituents, their conclusions about integration and racism surely developed and changed. As we turn to theories of the legislative process that focus on the procedures shaping it, we will consider how the structures of deliberation affect our preferences about outcomes.

One can reject the public choice description of the legislative process in favor of one of the institutional political descriptions, yet still believe that some form of pluralism is and should be characteristic of our political system. But this normative vision has also become controversial. Typically, defenders of pluralism will now concede that interest group government sacrifices elements of fairness, rational policy, or other values but will argue that pluralism is justified by its facilitation of stability, moderation, and broad satisfaction with the political system. This may not be a persuasive justification for those who consider social justice more important than stability.[56] Furthermore, by defining "politics" as the relatively narrow conflict among professional groups, pluralism implicitly denies the existence or feasibility of other forms of political struggle as mechanisms to change existing institutions and to organize around broader lines of cleavage (such as class). Because most of the political activity under pluralism is by and among elites, pluralist democracy may tend to reinforce already-existing social and economic inequalities.[57]

---

[55] See Amartya Sen, *Behavior and the Concept of Preference,* 40 Economica 241 (1973).

[56] See, e.g., Stuart Hampshire, *Justice Is Conflict* (2000); Thomas Simon, *Democracy and Social Injustice: Law, Politics, and Philosophy* 151–71 (1995).

[57] See C. Wright Mills, *The Power Elite* (1959).

C. VETOGATES AND OTHER PROCEDURALIST THEORIES OF LEGISLATION

Proceduralists also claim James Madison as their founding father, largely because his solution to the problem of faction lay in government design. Because the causes of faction cannot be eradicated except by destroying liberty or by forcing all people to share identical opinions, Madison reasoned the best strategy is to contain the effects of faction. Where the faction remains a minority, popular government is sufficient to contain it, because its views will not command the necessary majority. But, noted Madison, sometimes a faction will temporarily command majority support because of inflamed passions, deception, and so forth. In that circumstance, a direct democracy would be little protection against oppression. In contrast, a representative government has the structural ability "to refine and enlarge the public views, by passing them through the medium of a chosen body of citizens, whose wisdom may best discern the true interest of their country * * *. The public voice, pronounced by the representatives of the people, will be more consonant to the public good than if pronounced by the people themselves, convened for the purpose." *Federalist* No. 10. Madison admitted the possibility of corruption of representatives but argued that republics of great size (such as the United States) would have a large enough number of representatives and a broad enough constituency for each so as to minimize the possibility of corruption of a majority of the elected representatives.

In *Federalist* No. 51, Madison explained another protective strategy, the theory of *checks and balances* among the departments of government. If ill-motivated officials control one or more of the branches of the government, they are countered by those officials in the other branches—even when they, too, are not public-spirited. "Ambition," said Madison, "must be made to counteract ambition." Bicameralism is particularly important, not only because it provides a double review of proposed legislation and essentially requires supermajority support for any legislative proposal, but also because the two chambers perform complementary tasks. With its representatives being from smaller districts and subject to electoral scrutiny every two years, the House of Representatives would have an "immediate dependence on, and an intimate sympathy with, the people." *Federalist* No. 52. The Senate, whose members were originally elected by state legislatures for six-year terms, would have a stabilizing influence. Its members would have greater leisure to acquaint themselves with the issues and to discuss the issues deliberatively. *Federalist* No. 62.

1. Vetogates: Procedural Doors That Bills Must Pass Through

The most obvious feature of the legislative process described in the "Note on How a Bill Becomes a Federal Law," *supra*, is that any legislative proposal has to surmount a series of hurdles before it becomes a law. Most basically, Article I, § 7 of the Constitution requires endorsement of the proposal in identical form by both the House and Senate and then presentment to the President. Hence any of these bodies, and not just the President, can "veto" a proposal. The congressional process itself creates most of the "gates" that a bill must pass through and where it can be killed rather than moved along to the next stage of the process. Because of the nature of each of these obstacles, scholars have coined the term *vetogates*[58] to apply to the choke points in the process, some with the durability of constitutional requirements, others matters of congressional rule or norm. Opponents of a bill have many vetogates to exploit: (1) kill the bill in committee; (2) if committee approval cannot be avoided, stop the bill before full chamber consideration; (3) if full chamber consideration occurs, kill the bill there by filibustering it in the Senate, by amending it to death, or by outright defeating it on the chamber floor; (4) if one chamber has approved the bill, exploit the veto opportunities in the other chamber to prevent it from passing an identical measure; (5) if the other chamber produces a similar but not identical bill, amend or defeat it at the conference committee stage or in an interbranch summit; (6) if all else fails, persuade the President to veto it and then work against any congressional effort to override the veto.

Descriptively, the existence of vetogates means that determined minorities can often kill legislation or, in the alternative, maim legislation they cannot kill. Southern opponents of civil rights legislation were able to stop or to dilute such bills until 1964 because they controlled pivotal vetogates (the House Rules Committee, the Senate Judiciary Committee). Rather than killing a measure, a minority controlling a vetogate may extract concessions from the enacting coalition by a threat to stall it or change it significantly. This was the approach taken by Senator Dirksen. Indeed, one way a small faction "exploits" majority factions, is the former's ability to influence those who control various vetogates. Interest groups spend time forming and maintaining connections with members of Congress and other participants in federal lawmaking. In this process, a group seeking to block legislation rather than to pass it has a tremendous advantage. Because legislation can be stopped at many points along the legislative path, groups need to secure the assistance of only one key player to succeed. The electoral strength of incumbents, combined with a strong seniority system that significantly influences committee assignments, gives organized groups great certainty about which legislator will occupy a strategic position in the system.

Normatively, the existence of vetogates may tell statutory interpreters (courts, administrative agencies, lawyers advising clients) whom they should pay attention to if they consult legislative history. Legislative statements are most important when they reflect assurances by the enacting coalition—especially promises to or by gatekeepers—to enable the bill to pass through a vetogate. Thus committee reports are conventionally referred to, both because they reflect the understanding of the key gatekeepers (the committee), and also because they are important representations by the floor managers of the bill (almost always leading members of the committee) to attract votes on the floor. Thus, they reflect the expertise of the specialists in the area who act as the agents of the full body. Moreover, their statements are credible; if non-committee members discover that committee reports contain inaccurate statements (perhaps because preference outliers dominate the

---

[58] McNollgast (short for Mathew McCubbins, Roger Noll & Barry Weingast), *Legislative Intent: The Use of Positive Political Theory in Statutory Interpretation*, 57 Law & Contemp. Probs. 3 (1994). See also William Eskridge Jr., *Vetogates, Preemption,* Chevron, 83 Notre Dame L. Rev. 1441 (2008).

drafting), then they will no longer trust the committee members' assurances and will be less likely to defer to them. To the extent that those who control vetogates are repeat players, they must maintain their reputations for honesty to assure their continuing influence.[59]

Vetogates have always created roadblocks for federal (and state) legislation, yet Congress and state legislatures continue to pass many statutes, including broad, ambitious "super-statutes" such as the Civil Rights Act of 1964 or the Patient Protection and Affordable Care Act of 2010. To be sure, the 112th Congress (2011–13) was hopelessly gridlocked, with the situation even worse in the 113th Congress (2013–14). The same vetogates are in place as before—but the operation of the congressional process has been stymied by partisan hyper-polarization: as the Democratic Party has become more monolithically liberal, the Republican Party has become more monolithically conservative. See Richard Hasen, *End of the Dialogue? Political Polarization, the Supreme Court, and Congress*, 86 S. Cal. L. Rev. 205, 233–38 (2013). Divided government often produces significant legislation, as we saw during the Reagan and Clinton Administrations, but divided government during the Obama Administration has yielded paralysis. Indeed, we have seen the rise of another important vetogate: Speakers of the House presumptively decline to bring bills to the floor that do not enjoy support from a majority of the majority party caucus. This has been an informal practice that during the 112th and 113th Congresses has become a more prominent roadblock to legislation with majority legislator support, because the majority Republican caucus is more intensely divided than has been the case in decades. (In the 1950s and early 1960s, the majority Democrat caucus was also strongly divided, which gummed up the legislative process until the Speaker took firmer control during the Kennedy-Johnson Administration.)

2. Liberal (Libertarian) Theory: Statutes Should Be Hard to Enact

The Framers believed that the Constitution's requirements of bicameral approval and presentment to the President (with the possibility of a veto) would assure that most social and economic problems would not generate legislation at all, because the two bodies would have different views about what should be done. *Federalist* No. 73. Hamilton saw proceduralism as "an additional security against the [enactment] of improper laws." However, he admitted that "the power of preventing bad laws includes that of preventing good ones; and may be used to the one purpose as well as to the other. * * * The injury which may possibly be done by defeating a few good laws will be amply compensated by the advantage of preventing a number of bad ones." As Nelson Polsby observed even before the current congressional paralysis, we should not be surprised that periods of stalemate are longer than periods of innovation, because collective action is difficult "when formal power and autonomy are as dispersed as they are in the United States and it is necessary legislatively to mobilize the consent of majorities over

---

[59] See Victoria Nourse, *Misunderstanding Congress: Statutory Interpretation, the Supermajoritarian Difficulty, and the Separation of Powers*, 99 Geo. L.J. 1119 (2011); Daniel Rodriguez & Barry Weingast, *The Positive Political Theory of Legislative History: New Perspectives on the 1964 Civil Rights Act and its Interpretation*, 151 U. Pa. L. Rev. 1417, 1442–51 (2003).

and over—successively first in subcommittees, then in committees, the on the floors of the two legislative chambers, and finally behind the occupant of the White House." Polsby, *How Congress Evolves: Social Bases of Institutional Change* 147 (2004).

These consequences are consistent with libertarian versions of *liberal theory*,[60] which favors private autonomy and free economic markets and thus generally disfavors government regulation. To what extent do these assumptions remain robust today? Perhaps they are outdated: the post-New Deal regulatory state may assume that governmental regulation is the norm and indeed is perhaps even essential for the proper functioning of the private market.[61] Common law ordering is not the natural order of things; instead, it is just another kind of regulatory regime. Thus, to the extent that proceduralism protects one vision of regulation—a particular liberal vision—and reduces the ability of lawmakers to adopt different regulatory systems, it must be defended on that basis. It is not a neutral decision.

Although recent experience suggests the possibilities of legislative paralysis to which vetogates might contribute, vetogates do not necessarily protect libertarian values. For one thing, the baseline today is either federal or state regulation, not a market-based libertarian regime. If vetogates make legislation harder to enact, they also make it harder for Congress to deregulate. More important, vetogates may not retard legislation at all under some circumstances. Legislation may still be possible when the enacting coalition is willing to *compromise* its policy objectives and *logroll* (i.e., support other legislative proposals) with competing groups. Indeed, the process of logrolling, which vetogates encourage, may open Congress to *more* rather than *less* legislative activity.

3. Civic Republican Theory: The Deliberative Value of Process

Rather than blocking enactment of most legislation, procedures can be seen as the way to shape public deliberation on legislative proposals so that they better serve the public good. This view of proceduralism is consistent with *civic republican theory*, and such theorists also lay claim to *The Federalist Papers* as inspiration.[62] Thus, Madison's *Federalist* No. 10 addresses the republican concern about corruption of the common good (focusing on factions) and creatively argues that republican virtue might best be preserved through a national political structure with checks and balances, not through local government. A republican form of government, shaped by a variety of countermajoritarian or supermajoritarian procedures, would allow for deliberation among lawmakers, communication with constituents, and informed decisionmaking. For example, Madison justified the arguably duplicative role of the Senate as useful "to check the misguided career" of bills inspired by temporary passions or deception "and to suspend the blow

---

[60] Here the term "liberal" is being used in its classic sense, see, e.g., John Stuart Mill, *On Liberty* (1857), and not in the contemporary American sense in which it is associated with a wing of the Democratic Party.

[61] See Cass Sunstein, *After the Rights Revolution: Reconceiving the Regulatory State 19–20 (1990);* Bruce Ackerman, *Constitutional Law/Constitutional Politics,* 99 Yale L.J. 453 (1989).

[62] See David Epstein, *The Political Theory of the Federalist* (1984); Robert Morgan, *Madison's Theory of Representation in the Tenth Federalist,* 36 J. Pol. 852 (1974). See also Larry Kramer, *Madison's Audience,* 112 Harv. L. Rev. 611 (1999).

mediated by the people against themselves, until reason, justice, and truth can regain their authority over the public mind." *Federalist* No. 63.

Republican theorists, both past and current, emphasize the importance of deliberation to a normatively attractive legislative process. Deliberation shapes and changes public preferences on issues; it allows lawmakers to modify, amend, or discard proposals on the basis of new thinking and information; and it facilitates the development of civic virtue in citizens. Deliberation thus is not just an end in itself, for it serves the larger instrumental purpose of improving public policy. Madisonian deliberation remains a robust theory today as a justification for the procedurally complex legislative process. Henry Hart and Albert Sacks, in their classic *legal process* materials, argued for the "vitally important relationship between procedure and substance. A procedure which is soundly adapted to the type of power to be exercised is conducive to well-informed and wise decisions. An unsound procedure invites ill-informed and unwise ones." Hart and Sacks reported a "general agreement" that "the best criterion of sound legislation is * * * whether it is the product of a sound process of enactment," namely, a process that is informed, deliberative, and efficient. Henry Hart Jr. & Albert Sacks, *The Legal Process: Basic Problems in the Making and Application of Law* 154, 695 (William Eskridge Jr. & Philip Frickey eds., 1994) (from the 1958 "tentative edition").

Notice that this formulation attempts to defend the process of deliberation on the ground that it will improve the substance of legislation.[63] Many scholars educated under the aegis of the legal process materials emphasize deliberation as an achievable ideal in our representative democracy. Theories of "neo-republicanism" integrate earlier theories of politics with this legal process heritage.[64] Their essential point is that the legitimacy of government rests not just upon its democratic pedigree, but also upon the commitment of its officials to engage in a process of practical reasoning, deliberating for the common good.[65]

The effect of proceduralism on deliberation and, in turn, the effect of deliberation on legislative outcomes are difficult to understand completely. Procedures cannot guarantee that deliberation will occur at all, or that any deliberation will be enlightened and positive. At the most, rules and structure provide an opportunity for deliberation and an environment conducive to public dialogue. For example, the Civil Rights Act of 1964 was delayed for years by

---

[63] Joseph Bessette, *The Mild Voice of Reason: Deliberative Democracy and American National Government* 48 (1994). See also Larry Alexander, *Are Procedural Rights Derivative of Substantive Rights?*, 17 Law & Phil. 19, 36–42 (1998). But see Mathew McCubbins & Daniel Rodriguez, *When Does Deliberating Improve Decisionmaking?*, 15 J. Contemp. Legal Iss. 9 (2006) (providing results from experiments suggesting that deliberation does not improve social welfare and "in all but rare circumstances, may decrease it").

[64] For important analyses of republican theory, see Frank Michelman, *The Supreme Court, 1985 Term— Foreword: Traces of Self-Government*, 100 Harv. L. Rev. 4 (1986), as well as Philip Pettit, *Republicanism: A Theory of Freedom and Government* (1997); Michael Sandel, *Liberalism and the Limits of Justice* (2d ed. 1998); Mark Seidenfeld, *A Civic Republican Justification for the Bureaucratic State,* 105 Harv. L. Rev. 1511 (1992); Suzanna Sherry, *Responsible Republicanism: Educating for Citizenship*, 62 U. Chi. L. Rev. 131 (1995); Symposium: *The Republican Civic Tradition*, 97 Yale L.J. 1043 (1988). The historical discussion in these legal materials should be supplemented by reference to the historiographical literature, especially Daniel Rodgers, *Republicanism: The Career of a Concept*, 79 J. Am. Hist. 11 (1992).

[65] See John Rawls, *Political Liberalism* 212–54 (1993) (classic statement of what constitutes acceptable public reason). See also Amy Gutmann & Dennis Thompson, *Democracy and Disagreement* (1996) (formulation of a principled framework for deliberation).

congressional vetogates controlled by Southern Democrats. Did the extended process also yield useful deliberation?

Some political scientists are dubious about the value of deliberation as a feature of the legislative process. John Hibbing and Elizabeth Theiss-Morse used a series of in-depth interviews with citizens and several focus groups to determine why the public is so dissatisfied with Congress as an institution. They summarize their findings: "Congress embodies practically everything Americans dislike about politics. It is large and ponderous; * * * it is open and therefore disputes are played out for all to see; it is based on compromise and therefore reminds people of the disturbing fact that most issues do not have right answers. * * * [T]he public does not like overly deliberative politics. They would like to see something done quickly when in fact legislatures * * * are not well-equipped for rapid action." Hibbing & Theiss-Morse, *Congress as Public Enemy: Public Attitudes Toward American Political Institutions* 60–61 (1995).[66]

Hibbing and Theiss-Morse are deeply skeptical of the value of deliberation per se. In practice, they found that "deliberation can fan emotion unproductively, can exacerbate rather than diminish power differentials among those deliberating, can make people feel frustrated with the system that made them deliberative, is ill-suited to many issues and can lead to worse decisions than would have occurred if no deliberation had taken place." Hibbing & Theiss-Morse, *Stealth Democracy: Americans' Beliefs About How Government Should Work* 191 (2002). See also Dennis Thompson, *Deliberative Democratic Theory and Empirical Political Science,* 2008 Ann. Rev. Pol. Sci. 497–520 (reviewing the literature raising these and other problems with public deliberation).

Theorists of deliberative democracy respond that improving the conditions of deliberation and educating the public will enable the populace to appreciate the benefits of public consideration of alternatives by representatives. See Dennis Thompson & Amy Gutmann, *Why Deliberative Democracy?* (2004). Psychologists suggest that some amount of public participation and deliberation in decisionmaking is necessary for citizens to view outcomes as legitimate and just.[67] At least part of law's legitimacy and authority comes from the fact that multi-member assemblies pass statutes through collective decisionmaking after some discussion that allows for an airing of diverse viewpoints. The "dignity of legislation" is a result of the ability of a legislature to act in concert in what philosopher Jeremy Waldron terms the "circumstances of politics"; such collective action in the face of disagreement is a significant achievement that deserves our respect. See Waldron, *The Dignity of Legislation* 156–57 (1999).

Consider a related line of academic inquiry responsive to public choice (or social choice) scholars who argue that the democratic process is inherently arbitrary and irrational. These social choice scholars draw from Kenneth Arrow, *Social Choice and Individual Values* (2d ed. 1963), the following paradox of

---

[66] See also Carolyn Funk, *Process Performance: Public Reaction to Legislative Policy Debate,* in *What Is It About Government that Americans Dislike?* 193 (John Hibbing & Elizabeth Theiss-Morse eds., 2001).

[67] See, e.g., Tom Tyler, *Why People Obey the Law* (rev. ed. 2006); Heather Smith & Tom Tyler, *Justice and Power: When Will Justice Concerns Encourage the Advantaged to Support Policies Which Redistribute Economic Resources and the Disadvantaged to Willingly Obey the Law?,* 26 Eur. J. Soc. Psych. 171 (1996).

majority-voting systems, similar to those used to determine state and federal legislative outcomes.[68] In some circumstances, majority rule may not resolve the choice among three or more mutually exclusive alternatives that are voted on in pairs. For a simple example, assume that three children—Alice, Bobby, and Cindy—have been pestering their parents for a pet. The parents agree that the children may vote on having a dog, a parrot, or a cat. Each child's order of pet preferences is as follows:

Alice: dog, parrot, cat

Bobby: parrot, cat, dog

Cindy: cat, dog, parrot.

If these are the voters' preferences and pairwise voting is required, then majority voting cannot resolve their dilemma. A majority (Alice and Cindy) will vote for a dog rather than a parrot; a majority (Alice and Bobby) will vote for a parrot rather than a cat; and a majority (Bobby and Cindy) will vote for a cat rather than a dog. Even if the children form coalitions to attempt to reach a lasting decision, each coalition will be unstable. For example if Alice and Cindy decide to vote for the dog to defeat Bobby's top choice of parrot, Bobby can convince Cindy to move to his camp if he promises to vote for the cat (a better outcome for him than dog).

One way to stop this phenomenon of *majority cycling* is to establish procedures to limit pure majority rule, such as allowing only one set of pair-wise votes under a set agenda. For example, if the parents define the decisional agenda as (1) dog versus parrot [dog wins]; then (2) dog versus cat [cat wins], the children will have a cat. But note that if the parents structure the decisional agenda differently and still allow only one set of pair-wise votes, a parrot can win ((1) cat versus dog [cat wins]; (2) cat versus parrot [parrot wins]) or a dog can win ((1) parrot versus cat [parrot wins]; (2) parrot versus dog [dog wins]). If, instead of three children, we hypothesize three legislative factions and, instead of three pets, we suppose three legislative alternatives, it is obvious that cycling can occur in a legislative setting. Legislative rules (for example, that allow a committee chair to structure a decisional agenda or that require the status quo to be included in the last pair-wise vote) may result in the selection of one alternative by virtue of the order of voting, even though it has no more legitimate claim to majority support than the others.

In the simple example above we assumed that each child would vote sincerely in each pair-wise contest. But one child with complete information can prevent the cycle—and substantially satisfy her desires—by *strategic* rather than *sincere* voting. For example, assume that Alice, who likes parrots almost as much as dogs but hates cats, has discovered the preferences of her siblings. If the first pair-wise contest is dog versus parrot, sincere voting on her part will eventually lead to the selection of a cat. If she casts a strategic vote for a parrot rather than a dog, however, a parrot will win. Similar strategic behavior in a legislature—for example, sophisticated voting rules for amending, vote trading, and logrolling—can affect

---

[68] The paradox is also closely associated with Duncan Black, *The Theory of Committees and Elections* (1958). The core idea was conceptualized in the late eighteenth century by the Marquis de Condorcet. See also Dennis Mueller, 2 *Public Choice* 384–99 (1989) (summarizing Arrow's Theorem and its proof).

legislative outcomes. What examples of strategic behavior occurred during the consideration of the Civil Rights Act of 1964? Do the incoherence and susceptibility to strategic behavior of majority voting schemes suggest that there may be no significant correlation between what laws a legislature passes (or fails to pass) and the preferences of the majority of legislators? Is our legislative process a "rational" way to decide issues of public policy?

The prevalence of strategic voting as a response to cycling has led some social choice scholars to be very pessimistic about democracy. William Riker, for example, concludes from Arrow's work that all methods of aggregating preferences are prone to irrationality and chaos, and therefore meaningless, or that they will be manipulated by those in power, and are therefore arbitrary and undemocratic. Riker, *Liberalism Against Populism: A Confrontation Between the Theory of Democracy and the Theory of Public Choice* 137 (1982). This conclusion is too pessimistic because it assumes that the procedures and decision rules chosen to avoid chaotic outcomes will be unfair and undemocratic. Certainly, that will not inevitably be the case, but the observation underscores the importance of designing rules and institutions that structure legislative choices in transparent and defensible ways.

In short, one crucial consideration in political decisionmaking is to identify the mechanisms of stability, often found in institutional design. Thus, Arrow's work leads us to focus on institutions and proceduralism and what some political scientists term *structure-induced equilibrium*. See Kenneth Shepsle & Barry Weingast, *Positive Theories of Congressional Institutions* 8–9 (1995). Deliberation and the procedures that shape it may be structures that counteract cycling. Bernard Grofman identifies two norms of public discourse which enhance stability: the *idea of benefit of the doubt* means that voters will decide to shift from the status quo only when the alternative is clearly superior, and the *no-quibbling norm* means that voters disregard alternatives that are only trivially different from one another. Grofman, *Public Choice, Civic Republicanism, and American Politics: Perspectives of a "Reasonable Choice" Modeler*, 71 Tex. L. Rev. 1541, 1563–64 (1993). Other scholars argue that stability comes not just from institutional arrangements, which themselves can be subject to instability if chosen by strategic players, but stability also results from exogenous factors that are not easily manipulated. For example, an institution cannot cycle through alternatives without cost; thus, a group may meaningfully choose to stick with a policy and achieve stability.[69] Perhaps not surprisingly given these forces pushing toward stability in decisionmaking, Gerry Mackie's analysis of case studies of cycling calls into question virtually all "published and developed example[s]" of cycling and manipulation," finding alternative explanations or consequences of "little practical importance." Mackie, *Democracy Defended* 21 (2003).

---

[69] See Jerry Mashaw, *Greed, Chaos, and Governance: Using Public Choice to Improve Public Law* 13 (1997); Richard Pildes & Elizabeth Anderson, *Slinging Arrows at Democracy: Social Choice Theory, Value Pluralism, and Democratic Politics*, 90 Colum. L. Rev. 2121, 2200 (1990).

3. TITLE VII AS APPLIED: AN INTRODUCTION TO STATUTORY IMPLEMENTATION AND INTERPRETATION

The enactment of a statute is just the beginning, and not the end, of lawmaking, for the statute will invariably evolve as it is implemented and interpreted. See William Eskridge Jr., *Dynamic Statutory Interpretation* chs. 1–2 (1994). This section will introduce you to important themes of statutory implementation and will suggest that issues of legal theory and political theory are inextricably intertwined. The starting point for most statutory implementation and interpretation is agency action. As a case study of agency interpretation, we shall explore the EEOC's guidelines relating to employment policies having a disparate impact on employees based upon race (Part A). The EEOC's position, rejected by the Fourth Circuit, ultimately prevailed with the Supreme Court—but the Supreme Court's decision raised new problems. The most notable is whether Title VII permits employers to engage in "affirmative action" to rectify underrepresentation of minority employees. Again, the EEOC tackled the issue first, and the Supreme Court followed the agency once again in the fascinating case of *Steelworkers v. Weber,* examined in Part B. Part C reveals that the Supreme Court's understanding of its own precedents has been just as dynamic as its reading of Title VII.

A. AGENCY IMPLEMENTATION OF TITLE VII: DISPARATE IMPACT LIABILITY

1. Introduction to "Independent" and "Executive" Agencies

When Congress enacts a statute, a primary concern is how it will be administered. Some statutes, such as the Sherman Antitrust Act of 1890 as well as most criminal laws, vest administration in the judiciary. The Department of Justice or (in the case of antitrust) private enforcers bring lawsuits against alleged violators, with courts and juries as principal arbiters of whether the statute has been violated. Congress rarely follows such a model anymore, except for criminal liability. Instead, Congress vests primary administration in one or more agencies, with various powers and authorities to pursue the statutory goals. Agency enforcement has the advantages of creating expertise over time by those specializing in administration and of vesting authority in officials who will be more responsive to Congress. Chapter 8, § 1 introduces you to the large variety of agencies (including the EEOC) that Congress has created in the last 150 years.

In Title VII, Congress followed something of a hybrid approach. As the liberals like Humphrey wanted, Title VII created a new agency, the EEOC, which supporters expected would attract civil rights advocates who would work zealously and creatively to advance and elaborate on the statutory antidiscrimination norm. As conservatives like Dirksen wanted, however, the EEOC was not given authority to make legislative rules or deliver adjudicated orders having the force of law. In that respect, the EEOC was a weaker agency than the Interstate Commerce Commission ("ICC" created in 1887) or the Federal Communications Commission ("FCC" created in 1934), which had both rulemaking and adjudication authority. Our "Note on Different Agency Tools for Implementing Statutes," below, examines the different mechanisms agencies have for administering statutes. Because the EEOC did not have lawmaking authority under Title VII, a great deal of potential enforcement was left to private and sometimes public litigation in court.

Another kind of choice Congress made in 1964 was *not* to place the EEOC within the Department of Labor, where the Women's Bureau was located. Because the Secretary of Labor is appointed by the President and can be discharged by the President at any time (see Chapter 8, § 1C), the Department of Labor is considered an *executive* department under the direct supervision of the White House. In contrast, the National Labor Relations Board ("NLRB" created in 1935), which adjudicates labor-management disputes is an *independent* agency outside of the Department of Labor. The EEOC is more like the NLRB in this respect. The FCC is another independent agency along these lines.

We do not know exactly why Congress constructed the EEOC as an independent rather than executive agency. A potential advantage of an independent agency is that it may administer the law more neutrally, because its officials will not be subject to as much presidential and even partisan pressure. There are several possible indicia of functional independence possessed by the EEOC based on how Congress created the agency. One is its multimember structure: there are five commissioners rather than simply one agency head. Another is its partisan balance: no more than three of the five may be members of the same political party. A third is fixed-term tenure: each commissioner is appointed to a five-year term. A fourth indicator is litigation authority: the EEOC General Counsel (appointed for a four-year term) is responsible for conducting litigation under specific provisions of Title VII. See generally Kirti Datla & Richard Revesz, *Deconstructing Independent Agencies (and Executive Agencies)*, 98 Cornell L. Rev. 769 (2013).

At the same time, the EEOC is Exhibit "A" for the proposition that a highly independent agency can also be a very weak agency. Moreover, the EEOC got off to a delayed start because President Johnson was slow to name commissioners and Congress was stingy in funding the agency. Notwithstanding these many obstacles, the EEOC's early history was one of innovation and some degree of regulatory achievement, to which we now turn.

2. The Tools by Which Agencies "Regulate"

Recall Duke Power's diploma or testing requirement for promotion beyond its Labor Department (Problem 1–1). An employer that once explicitly discriminated because of race had, by 1965, abandoned de jure (as a matter of rule) segregation in its workforce. But Duke Power's workforce remained de facto (as a matter of practice) segregated even after Title VII took effect: almost all the black employees were relegated to the Labor Department, and almost all the white employees were in the better-paying departments of the company. Did this violate the statute?

On the one hand, the statute that was enacted in 1964 focused on intentional de jure discrimination: under § 703(a)(1), it was unlawful for Duke Power to set a race-based condition for employment opportunities—and in fact there was no such condition by 1965. What kept most blacks out of the better-paying jobs was the diploma or testing requirement, which was not explicitly race-based. On the other hand, the diploma or testing requirement had a dramatic race-based effect. It kept the black employees in the Labor Department and benefited white employees. Who was to say that this was not the "intent" of the executives running Duke Power? In any event, the perpetuation of workplace segregation surely undermined the overall point of the statute. As President Johnson put it in 1965, Title VII's goal was "not just equality as a right and a theory but equality as a fact and equality as a result."[70]

From its first year in operation, key players in the EEOC believed that racial inequality in employment was the result of structural factors, not just intentional discrimination, and that the statutory mission was actual integration of workplaces.[71] Based upon her labor law experience, Sonia Pressman of the General Counsel's Office argued that it would be impractical to expect direct evidence of discriminatory intent in most cases where workers of color continued to be absent. Just as litigants challenging racial discrimination in jury selection could rely on underrepresentation of minorities to prove an equal protection violation, Pressman urged that plaintiffs and the agency be permitted to make out a claim of employment discrimination based upon the statistical underrepresentation of minorities in the workplace. Memorandum from Sonia Pressman to EEOC General Counsel Charles Duncan, "Use of Statistics in Title VII Proceedings" (31 May 1966) (reprinted in the 2011 Documents Supplement for this casebook, 97–105).

The EEOC legal staff were candid about the tension between their views and the apparent compromises adopted in the 1964 statute, but they urged their approach as the most practical way to implement the statutory goal. By the end of the Johnson Administration, the EEOC Commissioners publicly interpreted the statute to bar employer practices "which prove to have a demonstrable racial effect." EEOC Commissioner Samuel Jackson, *EEOC vs. Discrimination, Inc.*, The Crisis, Jan. 1968, 16–17. For the student of legislation, an important question then becomes this one: Given the understanding EEOC's officials came to have about their statutory mission, namely, to discourage employment policies with discriminatory effects, how might the agency have sought to implement its understanding? Each agency has a mix of means by which it might seek to "enforce" its understanding of the statute, and the following note will explore the possibilities, as applied (or not) to the EEOC.

---

[70] 2 *Public Papers: Lyndon B. Johnson, 1965*, at 636 (1966) (June 1965 speech by President Johnson at Howard University). The story that follows is drawn from the records in the main cases and from recent archival research set forth in Hugh Davis Graham, *The Civil Rights Era: Origins and Development of National Policy, 1962–1971* (1990), reviewed and supplemented by Neal Devins, *The Civil Rights Hydra*, 89 Mich. L. Rev. 1723 (1991). See also Herman Belz, *Equality Transformed: A Quarter-Century of Affirmative Action* (1991).

[71] See White House Conference on Equal Educational Opportunity (EEOC, 1965). Several key agency players published explanations and defenses of this approach. See EEOC Executive Director Herman Edelsberg, *Title VII of the Civil Rights Act: The First Year*, 19 N.Y.U. Conf. on Labor 289–295 (1967), and EEOC staff member Alfred Blumrosen, *Black Employment and the Law* (1971).

NOTE ON DIFFERENT AGENCY TOOLS FOR IMPLEMENTING STATUTES

Agencies always have a choice of instruments by which to seek compliance with statutes and to influence (and often dominate) the evolving interpretation of statutes.[72] We introduce here a continuum of mechanisms that agencies *might* use in order to implement their understanding of the statute they are charged with administering. Some of the mechanisms require authorization from Congress. The main reason the EEOC is considered a weak agency is that Congress vested it with few formal powers, and so the EEOC has had to rely on more informal mechanisms to press its vision for Title VII.

Substantive/Legislative Rulemaking. Substantive, or legislative, rules are like statutes, for they not only announce policy but give it legal force; typically, violations of substantive rules can be subject to sanctions. This is theoretically the most powerful tool for agency regulation, because legislative rules can set forth statutory requirements in greater detail and violators may be subject to direct sanctions. Under most circumstances, people and corporations want to avoid even the possibility of legal sanctions, and part of your job as a lawyer is to advise clients (whether the agency itself or a regulated entity) as to what "the law" (including agency rules) requires and what the penalties are for noncompliance. Thus, if the EEOC had been able to promulgate a legislative rule requiring employers like Duke Power to justify requirements having significant race-based effects, the EEOC could have supplemented the Title VII protections in an important way, for victims of "disparate impact" discrimination could have invoked the rule in proceedings before the EEOC or before a court.

The EEOC never issued such a disparate impact rule, because Congress has never vested the EEOC with substantive rulemaking authority to enforce Title VII, cf. 42 U.S.C. § 2000e–12(a) (granting the EEOC only authority to make rules for its internal process), though the EEOC does have substantive rulemaking authority in administering the Age Discrimination in Employment Act of 1967 and part of the Americans with Disabilities Act of 1990. Other agencies rely on rulemaking as their primary mode of regulation, especially the Environmental Protection Agency ("EPA"), as well as the Securities and Exchange Commission ("SEC"), the National Highway Traffic Safety Administration ("NHTSA"), and the Occupational Safety & Health Administration ("OSHA"). Because Congress has vested each of these agencies with legislative rulemaking authority, which each has deployed sometimes aggressively, they are considered to be more powerhouse agencies (i.e., more feared and respected) than the EEOC.

Even when Congress has delegated legislative rulemaking authority to an agency, this powerful tool has its limitations, examined in Chapter 8. Most important, the Administrative Procedure Act of 1946 ("APA") sets forth an arduous process for even "informal" rulemaking. In this process, the agency must publish notice of proposed rules in the Federal Register, 5 U.S.C. § 553(b), followed by the opportunity for interested persons to submit (usually written) comments on the proposed rules, 5 U.S.C. § 553(c), which may be followed by judicial review at the behest of affected persons or companies. *Id.* §§ 701–706. (The APA is excerpted in Appendix B to this casebook and is examined in detail in Chapter 8, § 2.)

---

[72] For useful analyses, see M. Elizabeth Magill, *Agency Choice of Policymaking Form*, 71 U. Chi. L. Rev. 1383 (2004); Peter Strauss, *The Rulemaking Continuum*, 41 Duke L. J. 1463 (1992).

Agency Adjudication. Agency enforcement through administrative adjudication, resulting in orders that either have the force of law or can be enforced judicially, also requires congressional authorization. An agency may charge a person or company with a statutory violation; if the administrative law judge finds culpability, she may direct sanctions. This is a retail approach (identifying particular lawbreakers) that might complement the wholesale approach of legislative rulemaking. Note that the possibility of adjudication is also a powerful regulatory tool: the agency can build a case against an apparent lawbreaker, present some or all of its evidence to its attorneys or officers, and usually exact an agreement between the agency and the lawbreaker where the latter agrees to some kind of restitution and commitment to not violate the statute again.

Again, there are limitations. For adjudication to be most effective, Congress must delegate the ability to issue adjudicative orders having the force of law to the agency. Persons complaining of job discrimination violating Title VII must seek resolution of their grievances from the EEOC, but the agency has no power to order employers to remedy policies or actions the agency believes to have violated the statute without going to court to seek enforcement. In this way, the EEOC offers aggrieved Title VII complainants the worst of both worlds: it imposes a burdensome procedure upon complainants, but without much hope that the agency procedure will promptly motivate employers to remedy unlawful actions.

Although Congress has not delegated formal adjudication authority to the EEOC, it has done so for other important agencies, usually in tandem with a delegation of legislative rulemaking. The NLRB has adjudication authority, though it must go to court to enforce its orders. The Board also has rulemaking authority but has chosen to enforce the labor statute mainly through adjudication—a choice within the agency's discretion. In this respect, the NLRB is something of a relic from times past. In the 1950s, agency enforcement was primarily through adjudication, but since the 1970s it has been overwhelmingly through legislative rulemaking, especially by newer agencies such as the EPA, OSHA, and NHTSA. See Chapter 8, § 2.

Initiation of Litigation in Court. Agencies can bring their own lawsuits to enforce the statute they are charged with implementing if Congress has given them litigation authority. *See generally* Office of Legal Counsel, *The Attorney General's Role as Chief Litigator for the United States,* 6 Op. O.L.C. 47, 48 (1982) (opining that the Attorney General has, by statute and custom, plenary authority over litigation by the United States, "absent clear legislative directives to the contrary"). The main advantage of this authority is that it gives the agency a path toward powerful judicial remedies—preliminary injunctions (often swiftly granted) to preserve the status quo, injunctive relief (including perhaps structural injunctions), civil and possibly criminal monetary sanctions, and so forth. During the New Deal and Great Society eras, the Antitrust Division of the Department of Justice asserted a great deal of regulatory authority by bringing Sherman Act lawsuits against large companies or alliances of firms; even the threat of suit typically brought significant changes in the way whole industries did business. Since the Reagan Administration, the Antitrust Division has been less regulatory, but has used its *amicus* brief power to continue to dominate the evolution of antitrust law.

Likewise, the EEOC has authority to bring federal lawsuits against private employers to seek preliminary relief during an employment discrimination investigation or, more commonly, to remedy a probable discrimination that conciliation has been unable to remedy. Title VII § 706(f), 42 U.S.C. § 2000e–5(f); see also § 705(g)(6), 42 U.S.C. § 2000e–4(g)(6) (authorizing the EEOC to intervene in a lawsuit brought to enforce Title VII against nongovernmental employers). Pursuant to an executive order, the EEOC has authority to bring lawsuits to remedy a "pattern or practice" of statutory violations by private employers. *Id.* § 2000e–6. The Attorney General alone makes such decisions for lawsuits against public employers.

The main drawback to agency lawsuits is that they are an expensive way to enforce the statute. Like agency rulemaking and agency adjudication, this form of enforcement rests upon the very old "command and control" model of government regulation and for some agencies on the less old, but even more controversial, "structural injunction" approach to regulation. These forms of regulation are "hard shoves"; economists are skeptical of hard shoves and tend to favor "gentle nudges." *See* Dan Kahan, *Gentle Nudges vs. Hard Shoves: Solving the Sticky Norms Problem*, 67 U. Chi. L. Rev. 607 (2000). Nudges include government inducements or incentives for companies to engage in socially productive conduct, information about best practices that employers might follow, and default rules that can be contracted around (perhaps with some expense) if companies find them inefficient. Lawsuits are often a clunky way of nudging regulated parties, but the next three items in the regulatory toolkit will often be useful in that regard.

Informal Guidances, Policy Statements, Etc. Agencies have a default authority to offer their opinion about what the law requires. Agencies do so through a broad range of mechanisms, including published guidances or policy statements, agency website announcements, speeches by agency heads or commissioners at conferences or other public forums, media press releases, question-and-answer portions of the agency's website, and *amicus* briefs filed with the Supreme Court. (*Amicus* briefs almost always have to be submitted by the Solicitor General, who consults with the agency but is not bound by its interpretations of law.)

Without legislative rulemaking authority, the EEOC has relied extensively on these informal mechanisms for enforcing its understanding of Title VII. Many of its guidances have been pathbreaking. Shortly after Sonia Pressman's May 1966 memorandum, the EEOC issued Guidelines on Employment Testing Procedures that suggested legal problems with tests that had a demonstrated "adverse impact" upon racial minorities. In 1970, the EEOC promulgated detailed "Guidelines on Employee Selection Procedures," 35 Fed. Reg. 12333–36 (July 21, 1970) (2011 Documents Supplement 106–09), which provided that employer tests and other job prerequisites that had a significant disparate impact on different racial groups had to be justified by job-related criteria. Thus, not only would an employer violate Title VII by imposing diploma requirements only on black and not white employees (the old regime of de jure segregation), but an employer might *also* violate the statute by imposing diploma requirements that excluded most blacks from desirable jobs, unless the requirements were needed for a person to do the job well. In Problem 1–1, Duke Power's diploma or testing requirement for the job of Coal Handler was not *disparate treatment* discrimination—but it may have been *disparate impact* discrimination. (Did you really need a high school degree to be a Coal Handler?)

Unlike a legislative rule, the 1970 guidelines did not have the force of law. The biggest problem with these informal mechanisms for statutory enforcement is that they carry no penalties for disobedience by the regulated parties. Why should a company follow EEOC guidelines? There are actually several reasons they might do so. One is that the guidelines tell the company what issues the EEOC actually might bring a lawsuit to enforce, and so the EEOC's litigation authority backs up its guidance. A company openly flouting the agency's guidelines is asking for trouble. Additionally, guidelines give the EEOC a first-mover advantage: the agency can canvass regulated firms as well as civil rights groups to come up with instructions that are well-linked to the statute and its goals, are easy to understand, and are reasonably comprehensive. They instantly become focal points for further discussion. Employees and their lawyers will plan complaints around such guidelines and firms will tend to avoid clashing with them.

Advice-Giving and Conciliation. Agencies spend a lot of time giving advice. The advice-giving function of an agency helps it enforce the statute, often in combination with public guidances and policy statements. The best example of this strategy is the Internal Revenue Service ("IRS"), which dispenses advice to millions of Americans through its instructions book mailed to taxpayers, its website, its telephone operators, and the local offices where IRS agents answer questions and help people with their taxes in the months before April 15 (the date on which most of us have to file our tax returns or request extensions). Although taxpayers have a natural incentive to minimize their income taxes, they form a remarkably cooperative relationship with the tax collector because of the IRS's advice-giving culture. Some have argued that tax compliance is as high as it is in the United States for mostly normative reasons,[73] but our compliance also owes something to the agency's detailed advice to taxpayers. Most taxpayers pay their share of taxes more because they follow the agency's advice than because they fear a lawsuit or penalties.

Especially in its early days, the EEOC spent a lot of time answering employer inquiries about how the statute applied to common policies, such as Duke Power's diploma and testing requirement. Indeed, Sonia Pressman's 1966 memorandum was partly in response to questions the EEOC was getting from employers wanting to know what their responsibilities were under Title VII. After the EEOC suggested the invalidity of tests having a racially significant impact, the agency figured out what such a rule might look like through exchanges of letters with employers wanting to know what the agency's views were. For example, the Commission opined that requiring a sixth-grade education for a labor position was unlawful when it excluded many black workers from jobs they were perfectly qualified to fill.

Moreover, Congress vested the EEOC with conciliation authority: persons complaining of employer discrimination in violation of Title VII must file a "charge" with the EEOC, which in turn makes an evaluation of its merits and tries to persuade employers to rectify policies and actions that violate Title VII. Because the agency is not able to impose legal sanctions on employers, the conciliation process is not coercive in the same way a lawsuit process would be. (In the latter, the defendant has an incentive to accommodate complainants who have plausible claims that might result in monetary liability or intrusive injunctions.) But the agency's forced dialogue with the employer's officials and supervisors can lead to some form of relief for the employee and altered personnel policies. For example, employers required to explain their policies will

---

[73] See Michael Wenzel, *Misperceptions of Social Norms About Tax Compliance: From Theory to Intervention*, 26 J. Econ. Psychol. 862 (2005) (providing an overview of academic explanations for tax compliance).

sometimes reconsider those policies in the face of an agency's questions and the complainant's story.

As is often true for regular individuals, companies may simply want to know what the law requires of them—and agency advice-giving is a potentially useful way to induce compliance in those cases. But if a firm or an individual believes that following the law is too expensive or distasteful, advice-giving or conciliation might be of little use. Put another way, the law often assumes the "bad person" standard: make rules that even bad, law-avoiding people will have to follow. Bad people and companies might listen attentively to agency advice and even solicit it (just to see how secretive they have to be), but then they will ignore the advice, cheat, and make extra profits compared to more law-abiding competitors. The existence of even a few bad apples might trigger a cascade of disobedience, as persons or companies inclined to obey the law do not want the sucker's payoff.

On the other hand, the cascade might fall the other way, because of network power. See David Grewal, *Network Power: The Social Dynamics of Globalization* (2008). That is, bad actors might still obey the law articulated by agencies without sanctioning power, because other firms follow the law, internalize its norms, and exclude bad actors from the benefits of their networks on the basis of a reputation for not following norms. In other words, if an agency can tie its efforts into widespread social or economic networks, the impulse to conform to collective norms can do much of the enforcement. For example, after 1964 almost no company would openly admit to discriminating on the basis of race; the EEOC played little role in that overnight success, which owed its authority to the normative revolution led by the civil rights movement and the network power of the nondiscrimination idea. The EEOC proved very useful, however, in developing evidence that employers were still discriminating and bad numbers could reveal patterns of discrimination. It has taken decades for that idea to permeate American culture, but it has done so. Even the worst firm today thinks twice before hiring that tenth white guy for an executive position filled by nine white guys.

Investigation, Information-Gathering and Promulgation, Publicity. Another tool available to agencies is informational. Congress often assigns agencies particular informational tasks, and agencies have broad discretion to gather and promulgate information they consider useful to the public. Many kinds of information have a regulatory value. For example, the EEOC gathers information about the race and sex composition of workforces, by state and by region; this information can be very useful to target companies that may be secretly or unconsciously discriminating, because their numbers will be out of line with aggregate numbers. Publishing this information has the further regulatory value of placing local employers on notice as to the "normal" numbers and encouraging concern if their numbers are not within the normal range.

Agencies can exercise great power through promulgation of information, through their websites, informational booklets, and other forms of publicity. For example, the famous "food pyramid" suggesting a healthful balance of food groups for a day's meal, has shaped the thinking of two generations of Americans. (The federal government has recently abandoned the pyramid and has changed its mind about the most healthful balance of foods, as it turns out.) One of the most powerful regulatory tools is *normalization,* where an institution simply promulgates a standard as normal and people follow that standard because they do not want to deviate from that norm.

Federal agencies have no monopoly on normalizing strategies (think about church-supported and media-publicized norms), but by collecting data and publicizing trends, agencies can contribute powerfully to social normalization.

Finally, agencies can regulate by creating systematic arrays of regimes, through menus, for example. In family law and corporate law, to take two different areas, menus can be useful channeling devices even when people and companies are not required to follow the regimes listed in the menus.

PROBLEM APPLYING THE EEOC'S 1970 GUIDELINES TO THE DUKE POWER CASE

Problem 1–3. Recall the Duke Power policy described in Problem 1–1. Assume that three categories of workers file unfair employment practice charges with the EEOC:

(a)   Black employees with the company before 1955, who were disallowed from anything but the Labor Department until 1955 but did not have the diploma needed to advance;

(b)   Black employees hired between 1955 and 1965, who were subject to the same diploma requirements as white employees but were generally unable to advance beyond the Labor Department because most black men in North Carolina did not receive high school diplomas from schools that remained segregated by race;

(c)   Black employees hired after 1965, who were subject to the same diploma and testing requirements as white employees but whose education and testing lagged significantly behind white workers.

For which employees should the EEOC conclude that a violation of the statute has occurred? What legal analysis should the EEOC provide to Duke Power? What might motivate Duke Power to provide a remedy for one or more categories of workers? Think more broadly, and engage in the following thought experiment: If you were the Chair of the EEOC and wanted to entrench the disparate impact standard reflected in the 1970 Guidelines, what strategies might you follow?

3.   Interaction of Agency Administration and Judicial Authority

That an agency administers a statute does not mean that courts are irrelevant, even when Congress has vested the agency with legislative rulemaking and adjudication authority. As we shall explore in Chapter 8, § 2, the APA subjects agency rules and orders to judicial review, mainly to determine whether they are consistent with the statute and are not "arbitrary and capricious." 5 U.S.C. § 706. More informal mechanisms of agency administration, such as guidelines and conciliation (two important regulatory tools used by the EEOC), may be trumped by judicial opinions. Because agency guidelines, opinion letters, press releases, and the like do not have the force of law, they are not binding authority on courts interpreting the statute. Indeed, Title VII vests ultimate interpretive authority in the federal judiciary.

On the other hand, should the agency's interpretation of a statute not "inform" the court's determination of what the law requires with regard to an issue where the agency has considerable experience and deliberation? Judge John Minor

Wisdom, for example, deferred to the EEOC's 1970 guidelines when his court ruled that seniority rules having a disparate impact upon racial minorities violated Title VII if they were not justified by business necessity. *Local 189, United Paper Makers,* 416 F.2d 980, 988–89 (5th Cir. 1969). Consider the following judgment by the Fourth Circuit in the Duke Power Case. (We shall give detailed attention to the issue of judicial deference to agency guidances as well as rules in Chapter 9.)

GRIGGS V. DUKE POWER COMPANY

United States Court of Appeals for the Fourth Circuit, 1970.
420 F.2d 1225.

BOREMAN, CIRCUIT JUDGE.

[Writing for the panel majority, Judge Boreman ruled that the claims of three of the Duke Power plaintiffs were moot, because the plaintiffs had been promoted. Further, his opinion held that Duke's application of the diploma or testing requirement to six pre-1955 employees violated Title VII, because these employees had been treated differently from white employees of the same period. That is, prior to 1955 whites were sometimes hired or promoted into the other departments without high school diplomas. But Judge Boreman rejected the claims of four employees hired after 1955 and held that Duke's diploma or testing requirements were not discriminatory within the meaning of Title VII.]

Pointing out that it uses an intra-company promotion system to train its own employees for supervisory positions inside the company rather than hire supervisory personnel from outside, Duke claims that it initiated the high school education requirement, at least partially, so that it would have some reasonable assurance that its employees could advance into supervisory positions; further, that its educational and testing requirements are valid because they have a legitimate business purpose, and because the tests are professionally developed ability tests, as sanctioned under § 703(h) of the Act, 42 U.S.C. § 2000e–2(h).

* * * [I]t seems reasonably clear that this requirement did have a genuine business purpose and that the company initiated the policy with no intention to discriminate against Negro employees who might be hired after the adoption of the educational requirement. This conclusion would appear to be not merely supported, but actually compelled by the following facts:

(1) Duke had long ago established the practice of training its own employees for supervisory positions rather than bringing in supervisory personnel from outside.

(2) Duke instituted its educational requirement in 1955, nine years prior to the passage of the Civil Rights Act of 1964 and well before the civil rights movement had gathered enough momentum to indicate the inevitability of the passage of such an act.

(3) Duke has, by plaintiffs' own admission, discontinued the use of discriminatory tactics in employment, promotions and transfers.

(4) The company's expert witness, Dr. Moffie, testified that he had observed the Dan River operation * * * and he concluded that a high school education would provide the training, ability and judgment to perform tasks in the higher skilled classifications. This testimony is uncontroverted in the record.

(5) When the educational requirement was adopted it adversely affected the advancement and transfer of white employees who were Watchmen [a miscellaneous category] or were in the Coal Handling Department as well as Negro employees in the Labor Department.

(6) Duke has a policy of paying the major portion of the expenses incurred by an employee who secures a high school education or its equivalent. In fact, one of the plaintiffs recently obtained such equivalent, the company paying seventy-five percent of the cost.

[Having found the diploma requirement acceptable under Title VII, Judge Boreman then examined the testing requirement, which he found to be "professionally developed" and presumptively acceptable under § 703(h).]

The plaintiffs claim that tests must be *job-related* in order to be valid under § 703(h). The Equal Employment Opportunity Commission * * * supports plaintiffs' view. The EEOC has ruled that tests are unlawful " * * * in the absence of evidence that the tests are properly related to specific jobs and have been properly validated * * *." Decision of EEOC, December 2, 1966, reprinted in CCH Employment Practices Guide, ¶ 17,304.53. * * *

[Judge Boreman conceded that courts should give "great weight" to agency interpretations of statutes they administer, citing *Udall v. Tallman*, 380 U.S. 1, 15 (1965). But such interpretations are not binding on courts.] We cannot agree with plaintiffs' contention that such an interpretation by [the] EEOC should be upheld where, as here, it is clearly contrary to compelling legislative history * * *.

The amendment which incorporated the testing provision of § 703(h) was proposed in a modified form by Senator Tower, who was concerned about a then-recent finding by a hearing examiner for the Illinois Fair Employment Practices Commission in a case involving Motorola, Inc. The examiner had found that a pre-employment general intelligence test which Motorola had given to a Negro applicant for a job had denied the applicant an equal employment opportunity because Negroes were a culturally deprived or disadvantaged group. In proposing his original amendment, essentially the same as the version later unanimously accepted by the Senate, Senator Tower stated:

"It [the amendment] is an effort to protect the system whereby employers give *general ability and intelligence tests to determine the trainability of prospective employees*. The amendment arises from my concern about what happened in the Motorola FEPC case * * *.

"*If we should fail to adopt language of this kind, there could be an Equal Employment Opportunity Commission ruling which would in effect invalidate tests of various kinds of employees by both private business and Government to determine the professional competence or ability or trainability or suitability of a person to do a job.*" (Emphasis added.) 110 Congressional Record 13492, June 11, 1964.

The discussion which ensued among members of the Senate reveals that proponents and opponents of the Act agreed that general intelligence and ability tests, if fairly administered and acted upon, were not invalidated by the Civil Rights Act of 1964. See 110 Congressional Record 13503–13505, June 11, 1964.

The "Clark-Case" interpretive memorandum pertaining to Title VII fortifies the conclusion that Congress did not intend to invalidate an employer's use of bona fide general intelligence and ability tests. It was stated in said memorandum:

"There is no requirement in Title VII that employers abandon bona fide qualification tests *where, because of differences in background and education, members of some groups are able to perform better on these tests than members of other groups.* An employer may set his qualifications as high as he likes, he may test to determine which applicants have these qualifications, and he may hire, assign, and promote on the basis of test performance." (Emphasis added.) 110 Congressional Record 7213, April 8, 1964.

[When the Tower amendment was called up for a vote, Judge Boreman observed that Senator Humphrey urged its adoption, and it passed without dissent.]

SOBELOFF, CIRCUIT JUDGE [concurring in granting injunctive relief to the six pre-1955 employees and dissenting in refusing relief to the four post-1955 employees].

The pattern of racial discrimination in employment parallels that which we have witnessed in other areas. Overt bias, when prohibited, has oft-times been supplanted by more cunning devices designed to impart the appearance of neutrality, but to operate with the same invidious effect as before. Illustrative is the use of the Grandfather Clause in voter registration—a scheme that was condemned by the Supreme Court without dissent over a half century ago. *Guinn v. United States*, 238 U.S. 347 (1915). Another illustration is the resort to pupil transfer plans to nullify rezoning which would otherwise serve to desegregate school districts. Again, the illusory even-handedness did not shield the artifice from attack; the Supreme Court unanimously repudiated the plan. *Goss v. Bd. of Education*, 373 U.S. 683 (1963). It is long-recognized constitutional doctrine that "sophisticated as well as simple-minded modes of discrimination" are prohibited. *Lane v. Wilson*, 307 U.S. 268, 275 (1938) (Frankfurter, J.). We should approach enforcement of the Civil Rights Act in much the same spirit. * * *

The statute is unambiguous. Overt racial discrimination in hiring and promotion is banned [by § 703(a)(1)]. So too, the statute [presumably § 703(a)(2)] interdicts practices that are fair in form but discriminatory in substance. Thus it has become well settled that "objective" or "neutral" standards that favor whites but do not serve business needs are indubitably unlawful employment practices. * * * For example, a requirement that all applicants for employment shall have attended a particular type of school would seem racially neutral. But what if it develops that the specified schools were open only to whites, and if, moreover, they taught nothing of particular significance to the employer's needs? No one can doubt that the requirement would be invalid. It is the position of the Equal Employment Opportunities Commission (EEOC) that educational or test requirements which are irrelevant to job qualifications and which put blacks at a disadvantage are similarly forbidden. * * *

Whites fare overwhelmingly better than blacks on all the criteria [imposed by Duke Power for promotion],[6] as evidenced by the relatively small promotion rate from the Labor Department since 1965. Therefore, the EEOC contends that use of the standards as conditions for transfer, unless they have significant relation to performance on the job, is improper. The requirements, to withstand attack, must be shown to appraise accurately those characteristics (and only those) necessary for the job or jobs an employee will be expected to perform. In other words, the standards must be "job-related."

[Judge Sobeloff urged deference to the EEOC interpretation of § 703(h). He further maintained that the EEOC's interpretation was not only "not unreasonable, but it makes eminent common sense," especially compared with Duke Power's lenient approach, which only required tests to be "professionally developed" to assure protection under the statutory exemption.] But, what is professionally developed for one purpose is not necessarily so for another. * * * [A] test that is adequately designed to determine academic ability, such as a college entrance examination, may be grossly wide of the mark when used in hiring a machine operator. * * * [M]y brethren's resolution of the issue contains a built-in invitation to evade the mandate of the statute. To continue his discriminatory practices an employer need only choose any test that favors whites and is irrelevant to actual job qualifications. * * *

[Judge Sobeloff then examined the legislative response to *Motorola*.] That case went to the extreme of suggesting that standardized tests on which whites performed better than Negroes could never be used. The decision was generally taken to mean that such tests could never be justified *even if the needs of the business required them.*

Understandably, there was an outcry in Congress that Title VII might produce a *Motorola* decision. [Judge Sobeloff analyzed the language from the Clark-Case memorandum quoted above by Judge Boreman.] Read against the context of the *Motorola* controversy, the import of the Clark-Case statement plainly appears: employers were not to be prohibited from using tests that determine *qualifications.* "Qualification" implies qualification *for* something. A reasonable interpretation of what the Senators meant, in light of the events, was that nothing in the Act prevents employers from requiring that applicants be fit for the job. * * *

---

6   * * * *High School Education.* In North Carolina, census statistics show, as of 1960, while 34% of white males had completed high school, only 12% of Negro males had done so. On a gross level, then, use of the high school diploma requirement would favor whites by a ratio of approximately 3 to 1.

Standardized Tests. * * * Since for generations blacks have been afforded inadequate educational opportunities and have been culturally segregated from white society, it is no more surprising that their performance on "intelligence" tests is significantly different than whites' than it is that fewer blacks have high school diplomas. In one instance, for example, it was found that 58% of whites could pass a battery of standardized tests, as compared with only 6% of the blacks. Included among those tests were the Wonderlic and Bennett tests.

[Judge Sobeloff quoted Senator Tower's amendment as targeted only to protect tests "designed to determine or predict whether such individual is suitable or trainable with respect to his employment in the particular business or enterprise involved." 110 Cong. Rec. 13492 (1964) (text of original Tower amendment). Senators Humphrey and Case opposed the amendment as redundant, and Senator Case feared it was too broad: "If this amendment were enacted, it * * * would give an absolute right to an employer to state as a fact that he had given a test to all applicants, whether it was a good test or not, so long as it was professionally designed." *Id.* at 13504. The original Tower amendment was then defeated. *Id.* at 13724. Tower revised his amendment to render it acceptable to Humphrey and Case, and as revised the amendment passed.]

[Judge Sobeloff concluded that the EEOC interpretation, that employment tests must be job-related, was consistent with the legislative history. The District Court had found the tests not to be job-related, and Duke Power did not produce evidence showing that a high school education was necessary for jobs such as coal handling. He rejected Duke's argument that the tests were designed to identify future prospects rather than immediate promotion.] [T]he Company's criteria unfairly apply only to outsiders seeking entrance to the inside departments. This policy disadvantages those who were not favored with the lax criteria used for whites before 1955. * * * [T]his when juxtaposed with the history and racial composition of the Dan River plant, is itself sufficient to constitute a violation of Title VII. * * *

[While Duke's] practice does not constitute forthright racial discrimination, the policy disfavoring the outside employees has primary impact upon blacks. This effect is possible only because a history of overt bias caused the departments to become so imbalanced in the first place. The result is that in 1969, four years after the passage of Title VII, Dan River looks substantially like it did before 1965. The Labor Department is all black; the rest is virtually lily-white.

There no longer is room for doubt that a neutral superstructure built upon racial patterns that were discriminatorily erected in the past comes within the Title VII ban. * * *

A remedy for this kind of wrong is not without precedent. The "freezing" principle (more properly, the anti-freezing principle) developed by the Fifth Circuit in voting cases is analogous. In those cases a pattern and practice of discrimination excluded almost all eligible Negroes from the voting lists but enrolled the vast majority of whites. Faced with judicial attack, the authorities found that they could no longer avowedly employ discriminatory practices. They invented and put into effect instead new, unquestionably even-handed, but onerous voting requirements which had the effect of excluding new applicants of both races, but, as was to be expected, primarily affected Negroes, who in the main were the unlisted ones. [For this reason, the Fifth Circuit struck down the new rules, and the Supreme Court agreed. *Louisiana v. United States*, 380 U.S. 145 (1965).]

Title VII bars "freeze-outs" as well as pure discrimination, where the freeze is achieved by requirements that are arbitrary and have no real business justification. Thus Duke Power's discrimination against *all* those who did not benefit from the pre-1955 rule for whites operates as an illegal "freeze-out" of blacks from the inside departments.

NOTE ON GRIGGS AND BACKGROUND AGAINST WHICH STATUTES ARE READ

The NAACP Legal Defense & Education, Inc. Fund (the "Inc. Fund"), which represented the plaintiffs, appealed this decision's denial of relief for the post-1955 plaintiffs to the Supreme Court. Should defendant cross-appeal the Court's granting relief to the pre-1955 plaintiffs? Should the EEOC join in plaintiffs' appeal? How ought the Supreme Court rule on this issue?

As you ponder this last query, consider the issues that divided Judges Boreman and Sobeloff. Some are technical issues, such as how to read §§ 703(a), (h) and what to make of the legislative history of the Tower Amendment (§ 703(h)). Sympathetic to Judge Boreman's account, Daniel Rodriguez and Barry Weingast focus on the pivotal legislators—conservative Republicans who were needed to break the Senate filibuster—and claim that those members had a narrower vision of civil rights, namely, one focusing on equality of opportunity, with minimal "meddling" from the EEOC. They cite the history of the Tower Amendment as evidence that the liberal sponsors of Title VII needed the support of conservative Republicans and, for that reason, made a costly concession by ultimately going along with the Tower Amendment. See Rodriguez & Weingast, *The Positive Political Theory of Legislative History: New Perspectives on the 1964 Civil Rights Act and Its Interpretation*, 151 U. Pa. L. Rev. 1417, 1501–10 (2003).

Disputing this account is Victoria Nourse, *Misunderstanding Congress: Statutory Interpretation, the Supermajoritarian Difficulty, and the Separation of Powers*, 99 Geo. L.J. 1119 (2011). Nourse observes that Senator Tower, from segregated Texas, was *not* a possible vote for the civil rights bill, and so his statements about the proposed legislation are precisely the sort of cheap talk that interpreters should not rely on. Moreover, the Tower Amendment, ultimately accepted by the Senate, was a *post-cloture* amendment; in other words, it came *after* the pivotal legislators (especially Senator Dirksen) had signed onto the civil rights bill, with the changes reflected in the Mansfield-Dirksen substitute.

There are also larger issues that separate the two opinions, including different visions of racial justice, different degrees of deference to the EEOC, and different visions of the role of courts in implementing Title VII. Indeed, reading the legislative record may reflect different approaches. Nourse's account focuses on the majority coalition of liberal Democrats and moderate Republicans, whose project was racial integration of our country's segregated workforces. In contrast, Rodriguez and Weingast's account focuses on legislators they consider pivotal, such as the conservative Republicans whose votes were needed to break the Senate filibuster.[74]

---

[74] See also James Brudney, *Intentionalism's Revival*, 44 San Diego L. Rev. 1001, 1022–24 (2007) (suggesting that ardent supporters such as the majority coalition may be more important than short-term pivotal participants when determining legislative intent, because the former group's continuity in leadership and oversight roles means that ardent legislators are more likely to follow closely how agencies and courts implement the statutory commands).

NOTE ON THE *EEOC*, THE *SOLICITOR GENERAL*, AND THE *SUPREME COURT'S DECISION IN* GRIGGS V. DUKE POWER

The EEOC's rationale for an effects-based approach was that such an interpretation better served the statutory purpose. This position was shared by the Inc. Fund and other civil rights litigation groups. Directly encouraged by the EEOC, which filed helpful *amicus* briefs, civil rights litigation groups challenged employer testing and union seniority arrangements which had disproportionate and negative effects upon African Americans. These groups sometimes found a receptive audience in Eisenhower- and Johnson-appointed federal judges who were struggling with similar issues of racially discriminatory effects of arguably "neutral" state policies in the areas of education, voting, and jury selection. See, e.g., Judge Butzner's opinion in *Quarles v. Philip Morris, Inc.*, 279 F. Supp. 505 (E.D. Va. 1968), and Judge Wisdom's opinion in *Local 189, United Papermakers v. United States*, 416 F.2d 980 (5th Cir. 1969). Judge Sobeloff, dissenting in *Griggs*, relied on *Quarles* and *Local 189* to argue for a results-oriented rather than just intent-focused inquiry in Title VII.

The Inc. Fund appealed its loss in *Griggs*, with the support of the EEOC and the Nixon Administration's Solicitor General, Erwin Griswold. To the surprise of many pundits, the Supreme Court not only unanimously reversed in *Griggs v. Duke Power Co.*, 401 U.S. 424 (1971), but it expanded upon Judge Sobeloff's opinion. The Court held that a facially neutral employment practice that is not openly or intentionally discriminatory is nonetheless unlawful if it has the effect of excluding a group on the basis of race and without a strict showing of business necessity. Query: What provision of Title VII would such an employer be violating if it could not make a cogent showing of business necessity?

Although the Court reaffirmed the colorblindness of Title VII, its rationale stressed that "Congress directed the thrust of the Act to the *consequences* of employment practices." This appeared to be a recognition that, while § 703(a) speaks in terms of individuals, the problems addressed by Title VII might include institutionalized societal practices that systematically exclude minority groups from employment opportunities. The lower courts viewed *Griggs* as a mandate to use Title VII to reform group employment practices in entire companies, based upon the disparate impact idea.[75] *Cf.* Exec. Order No. 11,246 (1965) (2011 Documents Supp. 111–17) (imposing nondiscrimination duties onto federal government contractors and their subcontractors, which created administrative pressure for those private firms to have more racially balanced workplaces).

---

[75] Thus the Fifth Circuit sustained affirmative action remedies, finding that "[i]t is the collective interest, governmental as well as social, in effectively ending unconstitutional racial discrimination that justifies temporary, carefully circumscribed resort to racial criteria, whenever the chancellor determines that it represents the only rational, nonarbitrary means of eradicating past evils." *NAACP v. Allen*, 493 F.2d 614, 619 (5th Cir. 1974). "By reasonable affirmative action programs, courts can order employers to use ratios, percentages and quotas to ensure that members of minority groups traditionally discriminated against have reasonable opportunities to be hired." 2 Chester Antieau, *Federal Civil Rights Act: Civil Practice* § 528, at 237 (1980) (citing cases). Additional pressures for preferential hiring were generated by Executive Order 11,246, which required government contracts to include an affirmative action clause. 3 C.F.R. page 339 (1964–65). As elaborated in 1970, the Order required government contractors to establish "a set of specific and result-oriented procedures" to yield "equal employment opportunity." 35 Fed. Reg. 2586, 2587 (1970). For a discussion of the role of executive orders to expand civil rights, perhaps beyond what Congress would enact, see Kenneth Mayer, *With the Stroke of a Pen: Executive Orders and Presidential Power* ch. 6 (2001).

Some commentators (such as Rodriguez and Weingast, discussed above) have criticized disparate impact liability as inconsistent with the original "deal" needed to get Title VII's protections through the vetogates, specifically, past the Senate filibuster. Assume that they are right. What, then, explains *Griggs*?

Judge Sobeloff's opinion in the lower court suggests one way of explaining an effects-based inquiry: it is needed to fulfill the statute's purpose. Congress in 1964 did not focus on the possibility that pre-1964 discrimination would have continuing effects, but once that became clear to the EEOC and the courts, they had a responsibility to apply the statute to new circumstances in a way that carried out the original purpose. One might understand such an approach as a *translation* of the statute, moving it away from its apparent textual mandates on the ground that a liberal reading is required to fulfill the statutory objectives. In other words, an interpretation that departs from the terms of the deal, as reflected in the text of the statute, is actually more faithful to legislative intent than a more literal interpretation. This sort of dynamic statutory interpretation is controversial, because it concedes the existence of discretionary power in the unelected judiciary. On the other hand, at least in theory, it requires judges to be the faithful and careful agents of the legislative drafters, modifying or enhancing statutory provisions only when necessary to avoid undermining legislative purpose and intent.

Another way of explaining *Griggs* is that the liberal EEOC and Supreme Court were moving statutory policy in a leftward direction away from original legislative intent. This can be expressed in the game-theoretic terms familiar to us from our study of institutional theories of the legislative process. *See* Lee Epstein & Jack Knight, *The Choices Justices Make* (1999); William Eskridge Jr. & John Ferejohn, *The Article I, Section 7 Game,* 70 Geo. L.J. 523 (1992). Strategic theories of institutional behavior emphasize the importance of all the players in the policymaking game, including the executive branch agencies that will implement the statute and the judges who will interpret it. If their preferences diverge from the legislature's, they may try to move policy closer to their ideal point, realizing that the Congress will monitor them and try to avert any substantial change in the outcome.

Thus, the experience the EEOC and the Supreme Court had with rooting out covert or even unconscious race discrimination gave those institutions a more liberal viewpoint about how broadly Title VII ought to be applied than Senator Dirksen and Representative McCulloch might have had in 1964. Moreover, even if it were true that the 1964 Congress would have disapproved the result in *Griggs,* by 1971 Congress itself had changed in response to the evolving norms of the country. Especially after citizens of color gained greater access to the ballot box in the wake of the Voting Rights Act of 1965, Congress gradually shed its most ardent segregationists, who were replaced with pro-integration or neutral representatives. Overall, a Congress more sympathetic to actual workplace integration was a Congress that would have been okay with the EEOC's and the Supreme Court's approach in *Griggs*.

To be sure, any shift in legislative preferences between 1964 and 1971 was modest,[76] and it is not clear that Congress in 1971 would have *enacted* a policy like *Griggs*. But here is where the third political dynamic comes into play: once the agency or a court has authoritatively and dynamically interpreted a statute, that

---

[76] See Barbara Sinclair, *Agenda, Policy, and Alignment Change from Coolidge to Reagan*, in *Congress Reconsidered* 291, 306–07 (Lawrence Dodd & Bruce Oppenheimer eds., 3d ed. 1985).

interpretation prevails unless Congress can affirmatively *override* it. See Matthew Christiansen & William Eskridge Jr., *Congressional Overrides of Supreme Court Statutory Interpretation Decisions, 1967–2011,* 92 Tex. L. Rev. 1317 (2014). But to override the interpretation, a proposal must surmount all the vetogates that the original enactment did. In 1972, Congress passed the Equal Employment Opportunity Act, 86 Stat. 103, increasing enforcement authority for the EEOC and otherwise broadening protections available under Title VII. The Court decided *Griggs* while the bill was being considered in committee. Both the House and Senate committee reports accompanying the 1972 Act discussed and expressly approved the holding and reasoning of *Griggs.* The reports emphasized that testing programs should be reexamined to assure compliance with *Griggs* by public and private employers. In addition, each report cited *Griggs* to support its conclusion that because employment discrimination was more complex and pervasive than had previously been believed—characterized "in terms of 'systems' and 'effects' rather than simply intentional wrongs"—the EEOC needed broad and meaningful enforcement powers. *See* H.R. Rep. No. 238, 92d Cong., 1st Sess. 8–9, 20–22 (1971), reprinted in 1972 U.S.C.C.A.N. 2137, 2144–45, 2155–57; Sen. Rep. No. 415, 92d Cong., 1st Sess. 5 & n.1, 14–15 [14] (1971). Because those committees exercised gatekeeping power over issues on the legislative agenda, they had substantial ability to head off overrides of agency policies or judicial decisions, especially when they were supported by the majority party leadership, which was similarly liberal on civil rights issues and exerted great control over the congressional agenda and floor politics.

Under the foregoing analysis, the EEOC and the Supreme Court have a certain amount of slack in setting statutory policy—and in moving statutory policy away from original congressional deals. Note that under the preceding analysis, the EEOC and the Court can be more strongly influenced by the preferences of members of the *current* Congress than they are by the preferences of the *enacting* Congress. This thought experiment reveals that the notion of legislative intent has a temporal element. Although many think of courts and executive branch officials as the agents of the enacting Congress, subsequent Congresses can exert substantial influence over policies even when (unlike the 1972 setting) they do not revisit the substantive statutory provisions, because they control the budget and have close connections with agency personnel with day-to-day oversight of federal programs. Indeed, one scholar has argued that enacting legislators may rationally prefer interpreters to track current legislative preferences, which he calls "enactable preferences," because that allows the enacting legislators to influence not only the legislation they pass but all legislation being interpreted while they are in office. Einer Elhauge, *Preference-Estimating Statutory Default Rules,* 102 Colum. L. Rev. 2027 (2002).

Under an analysis focused on strategy, however, *Griggs* itself might be subject to reinterpretation. After Justices Lewis Powell and William Rehnquist took their seats in 1972, the Burger Court became much more ambivalent about aggressively pressing for racial integration in schools as well as workplaces. In constitutional cases, where the Court is better protected against political overrides, the Burger Court rejected the *Griggs* approach and held that race-based or gender-based effects do not amount to unlawful discrimination, unless complainants can demonstrate a discriminatory "intent." *See Washington v. Davis,* 426 U.S. 229 (1976); *Personnel Administrator of Massachusetts v. Feeney,* 442 U.S. 256 (1979); *see also* Jeffrey Segal & Albert Cover, *Ideological Values and the Votes of U.S. Supreme Court Justices,* 83 Am. Pol. Sci. Rev.

557, 560 (1989) (Table 1). The Burger Court narrowed *Griggs* itself by tightening up proof burdens on plaintiffs but did not directly attack the decision—perhaps because the relevant congressional committees had embraced it in 1971, and Congress as a whole moved further to the left on civil rights issues in the 1970s.[77] Any open retreat from *Griggs* would have generated immediate controversy because the civil rights community, the EEOC, and the gatekeeping (labor) committees would have mobilized for an override. In fact, this is precisely what happened when the Court retreated from *Griggs* by refusing to treat pregnancy discrimination as sex discrimination under Title VII: the Court suffered a firestorm of protest and was promptly overridden.[78]

B. THE NEXT BIG ISSUE: RACE-BASED AFFIRMATIVE ACTION

If you were counsel to a big company or a labor union in the 1970s, you would probably be very concerned about the representation of people of color in your company's workforce. Under *Griggs*, your company or union might be subject to a disparate impact lawsuit if bad numbers were not justified. And if your company did business with the federal government, the Johnson and Nixon Administrations had implemented a policy under which such companies had to improve their numbers or lose their lucrative contracts. *See* Executive Order 11246, "Equal Employment Opportunity," (Sept. 24, 1965) (2011 Documents Supplement 111–17); "Affirmative Action Programs," 35 Fed. Reg. 2568 (Feb. 2, 1970) (2011 Documents Supplement 118–22). In short, companies faced the loss of government contracts and judicially imposed back-pay awards and quota systems if their hiring efforts did not produce concrete results.

Although the EEOC also supported affirmative action, the primary federal government impetus behind it was the Johnson and Nixon Administration's executive orders—which were politically controversial. When Congress revisited Title VII in 1971–72, proposals to overturn the executive orders were advanced and rejected in both chambers (2011 Documents Supplement 123–28). At the same time, *Griggs* escaped controversy; the EEOC-Supreme Court approach to disparate impact liability was endorsed in the House committee report and not challenged on the floor as the executive orders were.

Consistent with *Griggs*, the Supreme Court encouraged companies to adopt their own plans to integrate their workforces. For example, in *Albemarle Paper Co. v. Moody*, 422 U.S. 405, 417–18 (1975), the Court approved broad EEOC guidelines out of an announced desire to provide the "spur or catalyst which causes employers and unions to self-examine and to self-evaluate their employment practices and to endeavor to eliminate, so far as possible, the last vestiges of an unfortunate and ignominious page in this country's history." *See also Franks v. Bowman Transp. Co.*, 424 U.S. 747, 778 (1976) (upholding retroactive award of seniority to African-American victims of discrimination and saying that "a collective bargaining

---

[77] Sinclair, *Agenda, Policy, and Alignment Change, supra*, at 307 (big jump in civil liberties scores for House members, 1973–1976).

[78] The Pregnancy Discrimination Act of 1978, Pub. L. No. 95–555, 92 Stat. 2076 (1978), overriding *General Electric Co. v. Gilbert*, 429 U.S. 125 (1976); see William Eskridge Jr., *Reneging on History? Playing the Court/Congress/President Civil Rights Game*, 79 Calif. L. Rev. 613 (1991).

agreement may go further, enhancing the seniority status of certain employees for purposes of furthering public policy interests beyond what is required by statute").

As a result of these developments, companies like Kaiser Aluminum and Chemical Corp. and labor unions like the United Steelworkers of America had incentives to adopt their own preferential hiring programs, with the hope that they could avoid having one thrust upon them by a court. In *McDonald v. Santa Fe Trail Transp. Co.*, 427 U.S. 273 (1976), however, the Court held that Title VII prohibits racial discrimination against whites as well as African Americans. The upshot of that case was that displaced white employees like Brian Weber had a colorable argument that voluntary affirmative action programs were unlawfully discriminatory against them as well—and that they had a cause of action under Title VII. That clash of different statutory purposes, different legally protected civil rights, and different Supreme Court signals generated the following case.

UNITED STEELWORKERS OF AMERICA V. WEBER
Supreme Court of the United States, 1979.
443 U.S. 193, 99 S.Ct. 2721, 61 L.Ed.2d 480.

MR. JUSTICE BRENNAN delivered the opinion of the Court. * * *

In 1974, petitioner United Steelworkers of America (USWA) and petitioner Kaiser Aluminum & Chemical Corp. (Kaiser) entered into a master collective-bargaining agreement covering terms and conditions of employment at 15 Kaiser plants. The agreement contained, *inter alia*, an affirmative action plan designed to eliminate conspicuous racial imbalances in Kaiser's then almost exclusively white craft-work forces. Black craft-hiring goals were set for each Kaiser plant equal to the percentage of blacks in the respective local labor forces. To enable plants to meet these goals, on-the-job training programs were established to teach unskilled production workers—black and white—the skills necessary to become craftworkers. The plan reserved for black employees 50% of the openings in these newly created in-plant training programs.

This case arose from the operation of the plan at Kaiser's plant in Gramercy, La. Until 1974, Kaiser hired as craftworkers for that plant only persons who had had prior craft experience. Because blacks had long been excluded from craft unions, few were able to present such credentials. As a consequence, prior to 1974 only 1.83% (5 out of 273) of the skilled craftworkers at the Gramercy plant were black, even though the work force in the Gramercy area was approximately 39% black.

Pursuant to the national agreement Kaiser altered its craft-hiring practice in the Gramercy plant. Rather than hiring already trained outsiders, Kaiser established a training program to train its production workers to fill craft openings. Selection of craft trainees was made on the basis of seniority, with the proviso that at least 50% of the new trainees were to be black until the percentage of black skilled craftworkers in the Gramercy plant approximated the percentage of blacks in the local labor force.

During 1974, the first year of the operation of the Kaiser-USWA affirmative action plan, 13 craft trainees were selected from Gramercy's production work force. Of these, seven were black and six white. The most senior black selected into the program had less seniority than several white production workers whose bids for admission were rejected. Thereafter one of those white production workers, respondent Brian Weber (hereafter respondent), instituted this class action in the United States District Court for the Eastern District of Louisiana.

The complaint alleged that the filling of craft trainee positions at the Gramercy plant pursuant to the affirmative action program had resulted in junior black employees' receiving training in preference to senior white employees, thus discriminating against respondent and other similarly situated white employees in violation of §§ 703(a)[2] and (d)[3] of Title VII. The District Court held that the plan violated Title VII, entered a judgment in favor of the plaintiff class, and granted a permanent injunction prohibiting Kaiser and the USWA "from denying plaintiffs, Brian F. Weber and all other members of the class, access to on-the-job training programs on the basis of race." A divided panel of the Court of Appeals for the Fifth Circuit affirmed, holding that all employment preferences based upon race, including those preferences incidental to bona fide affirmative action plans, violated Title VII's prohibition against racial discrimination in employment. * * * We reverse.

We emphasize at the outset the narrowness of our inquiry. * * * [S]ince the Kaiser-USWA plan was adopted voluntarily, we are not concerned with what Title VII requires or with what a court might order to remedy a past proved violation of the Act. The only question before us is the narrow statutory issue of whether Title VII *forbids* private employers and unions from voluntarily agreeing upon bona fide affirmative action plans that accord racial preferences in the manner and for the purpose provided in the Kaiser-USWA plan. * * *

Respondent argues that Congress intended in Title VII to prohibit all race conscious affirmative action plans. Respondent's argument rests upon a literal interpretation of §§ 703(a) and (d) of the Act. Those sections make it unlawful to "discriminate * * * because of * * * race" in hiring and in the selection of apprentices for training programs. Since, the argument runs, *McDonald v. Santa Fe Trail Transp. Co.,* [427 U.S. 273, 281 n.8 (1976)], settled that Title VII forbids

---

[2] Section 703(a), 78 Stat. 255, as amended, 86 Stat. 109, 42 U.S.C. § 2000e–2(a), provides:

"(a)   * * * It shall be an unlawful employment practice for an employer—

(1) to fail or refuse to hire or to discharge any individual, or otherwise to discriminate against any individual with respect to his compensation, terms, conditions, or privileges of employment, because of such individual's race, color, religion, sex, or national origin; or

(2) to limit, segregate, or classify his employees or applicants for employment in any way which would deprive or tend to deprive any individual of employment opportunities or otherwise adversely affect his status as an employee, because of such individual's race, color, religion, sex, or national origin."

[3] Section 703(d), 78 Stat. 256, 42 U.S.C. § 2000e–2(d), provides:

"It shall be an unlawful employment practice for any employer, labor organization, or joint labor-management committee controlling apprenticeship or other training or retraining, including on-the-job training programs to discriminate against any individual because of his race, color, religion, sex, or national origin in admission to, or employment in, any program established to provide apprenticeship or other training."

discrimination against whites as well as blacks, and since the Kaiser-USWA affirmative action plan operates to discriminate against white employees solely because they are white, it follows that the Kaiser-USWA plan violates Title VII.

Respondent's argument is not without force. But it overlooks the significance of the fact that the Kaiser-USWA plan is an affirmative action plan voluntarily adopted by private parties to eliminate traditional patterns of racial segregation. In this context respondent's reliance upon a literal construction of §§ 703(a) and (d) and upon *McDonald* is misplaced. It is a "familiar rule, that a thing may be within the letter of the statute and yet not within the statute, because not within its spirit, nor within the intention of its makers." *Holy Trinity Church v. United States*, 143 U.S. 457, 459 (1892). The prohibition against racial discrimination in §§ 703(a) and (d) of Title VII must therefore be read against the background of the legislative history of Title VII and the historical context from which the Act arose. Examination of those sources makes clear that an interpretation of the sections that forbade all race-conscious affirmative action would "bring about an end completely at variance with the purpose of the statute" and must be rejected. *United States v. Public Utilities Comm'n*, 345 U.S. 295, 315 (1953).

Congress's primary concern in enacting the prohibition against racial discrimination in Title VII of the Civil Rights Act of 1964 was with "the plight of the Negro in our economy." 110 Cong. Rec. 6548 (1964) (remarks of Sen. Humphrey). Before 1964, blacks were largely relegated to "unskilled and semiskilled jobs." *Ibid.* (remarks of Sen. Humphrey); *id.*, at 7204 (remarks of Sen. Clark); *id.*, at 7379–7380 (remarks of Sen. Kennedy). Because of automation the number of such jobs was rapidly decreasing. See *id.*, at 6548 (remarks of Sen. Humphrey); *id.*, at 7204 (remarks of Sen. Clark). As a consequence, "the relative position of the Negro worker [was] steadily worsening." * * *

Congress feared that the goals of the Civil Rights Act—the integration of blacks into the mainstream of American society—could not be achieved unless this trend were reversed. And Congress recognized that that would not be possible unless blacks were able to secure jobs "which have a future." *Id.*, at 7204 (remarks of Sen. Clark). See also *id.*, at 7379–7380 (remarks of Sen. Kennedy). As Senator Humphrey explained to the Senate:

"What good does it do a Negro to be able to eat in a fine restaurant if he cannot afford to pay the bill? What good does it do him to be accepted in a hotel that is too expensive for his modest income? How can a Negro child be motivated to take full advantage of integrated educational facilities if he has no hope of getting a job where he can use that education?" *Id.*, at 6547. * * *

Accordingly, it was clear to Congress that "[t]he crux of the problem [was] to open employment opportunities for Negroes in occupations which have been traditionally closed to them," 110 Cong. Rec. 6548 (1964) (remarks of Sen. Humphrey), and it was to this problem that Title VII's prohibition against racial discrimination in employment was primarily addressed.

It plainly appears from the House Report accompanying the Civil Rights Act that Congress did not intend wholly to prohibit private and voluntary affirmative action efforts as one method of solving this problem. The Report provides:

> "No bill can or should lay claim to eliminating all of the causes and consequences of racial and other types of discrimination against minorities. There is reason to believe, however, that national leadership provided by the enactment of Federal legislation dealing with the most troublesome problems *will create an atmosphere conducive to voluntary or local resolution of other forms of discrimination.*" H.R. Rep. No. 914, 88th Cong., 1st Sess., pt. 1, p. 18 (1963). (Emphasis supplied.) * * *

Given this legislative history, we cannot agree with respondent that Congress intended to prohibit the private sector from taking effective steps to accomplish the goal that Congress designed Title VII to achieve. * * * It would be ironic indeed if a law triggered by a Nation's concern over centuries of racial injustice and intended to improve the lot of those who had "been excluded from the American dream for so long," 110 Cong. Rec. 6552 (1964) (remarks of Sen. Humphrey), constituted the first legislative prohibition of all voluntary, private, race-conscious efforts to abolish traditional patterns of racial segregation and hierarchy.

Our conclusion is further reinforced by examination of the language and legislative history of § 703(j) of Title VII.[5] Opponents of Title VII raised two related arguments against the bill. First, they argued that the Act would be interpreted to *require* employers with racially imbalanced work forces to grant preferential treatment to racial minorities in order to integrate. Second, they argued that employers with racially imbalanced work forces would grant preferential treatment to racial minorities, even if not required to do so by the Act. See 110 Cong. Rec. 8618–8619 (1964) (remarks of Sen. Sparkman). Had Congress meant to prohibit all race-conscious affirmative action, as respondent urges, it easily could have answered both objections by providing that Title VII would not require or *permit* racially preferential integration efforts. But Congress did not choose such a course. Rather, Congress added § 703(j) which addresses only the first objection. The section provides that nothing contained in Title VII "shall be interpreted to *require* any employer * * * to grant preferential treatment * * * to any group because of the race * * * of such * * * group on account of" a *de facto* racial imbalance in the employer's work force. The section does *not* state that "nothing in Title VII shall be

---

[5]   Section 703(j) of Title VII, 78 Stat. 257, 42 U.S.C. § 2000e–2(j), provides:

"Nothing contained in this title shall be interpreted to require any employer, employment agency, labor organization, or joint labor-management committee subject to this title to grant preferential treatment to any individual or to any group because of the race, color, religion, sex, or national origin of such individual or group on account of an imbalance which may exist with respect to the total number or percentage of persons of any race, color, religion, sex, or national origin employed by any employer, referred or classified for employment by any employment agency or labor organization, admitted to membership or classified by any labor organization, or admitted to, or employed in, any apprenticeship or other training program, in comparison with the total number or percentage of persons of such race, color, religion, sex, or national origin in any community, State, section, or other area, or in the available work force in any community, State, section, or other area."

Section 703(j) speaks to substantive liability under Title VII, but it does not preclude courts from considering racial imbalance as evidence of a Title VII violation. * * * Remedies for substantive violations are governed by § 706(g), 42 U.S.C. § 2000e–5(g).

interpreted to *permit*" voluntary affirmative efforts to correct racial imbalances. The natural inference is that Congress chose not to forbid all voluntary race-conscious affirmative action.

The reasons for this choice are evident from the legislative record. Title VII could not have been enacted into law without substantial support from legislators in both Houses who traditionally resisted federal regulation of private business. Those legislators demanded as a price for their support that "management prerogatives, and union freedoms * * * be left undisturbed to the greatest extent possible." H.R. Rep. No. 914, 88th Cong., 1st Sess., pt. 2, p. 29 (1963). Section 703(j) was proposed by Senator Dirksen to allay any fears that the Act might be interpreted in such a way as to upset this compromise. The section was designed to prevent § 703 of Title VII from being interpreted in such a way as to lead to undue "Federal Government interference with private businesses because of some Federal employee's ideas about racial balance or racial imbalance." 110 Cong. Rec. 14314 (1964) (remarks of Sen. Miller). See also *id.*, at 9881 (remarks of Sen. Allott); *id.*, at 10520 (remarks of Sen. Carlson); *id.*, at 11471 (remarks of Sen. Javits); *id.*, at 12817 (remarks of Sen. Dirksen). Clearly, a prohibition against all voluntary, race-conscious, affirmative action efforts would disserve these ends. Such a prohibition would augment the powers of the Federal Government and diminish traditional management prerogatives while at the same time impeding attainment of the ultimate statutory goals. In view of this legislative history and in view of Congress's desire to avoid undue federal regulation of private businesses, use of the word "require" rather than the phrase "require or permit" in § 703(j) fortifies the conclusion that Congress did not intend to limit traditional business freedom to such a degree as to prohibit all voluntary, race-conscious affirmative action.[7]

We therefore hold that Title VII's prohibition in §§ 703(a) and (d) against racial discrimination does not condemn all private, voluntary, race-conscious affirmative action plans. * * * [The Court held that the Kaiser plan was lawful under Title VII because both its purpose and effect were permissible: it was "designed to eliminate conspicuous racial imbalance in traditionally segregated job categories," and it did

---

[7]   Respondent argues that our construction of § 703 conflicts with various remarks in the legislative record. See, *e.g.*, 110 Cong. Rec. 7213 (1964) (Sens. Clark and Case); *id.*, at 7218 (Sens. Clark and Case); *id.*, at 6549 (Sen. Humphrey); *id.*, at 8921 (Sen. Williams). We do not agree. In Senator Humphrey's words, these comments were intended as assurances that Title VII would not allow establishment of systems "to *maintain* racial balance in employment." *Id.*, at 11848 (emphasis added). They were not addressed to temporary, voluntary, affirmative action measures undertaken to eliminate manifest racial imbalance in traditionally segregated job categories. Moreover, the comments referred to by respondent all preceded the adoption of § 703(j), 42 U.S.C. § 2000e–2(j). After § 703(j) was adopted, congressional comments were all to the effect that employers would not be *required* to institute preferential quotas to avoid Title VII liability, see, *e.g.*, 110 Cong. Rec. 12819 (1964) (remarks of Sen. Dirksen); *id.*, at 13079–13080 (remarks of Sen. Clark); *id.*, at 15876 (remarks of Rep. Lindsay). There was no suggestion after the adoption of § 703(j) that wholly voluntary, race-conscious, affirmative action efforts would in themselves constitute a violation of Title VII. On the contrary, as Representative MacGregor told the House shortly before the final vote on Title VII:

"Important as the scope and extent of this bill is, it is also vitally important that all Americans understand what this bill does not cover.

"Your mail and mine, your contacts and mine with our constituents, indicates a great degree of misunderstanding about this bill. People complain about * * * preferential treatment or quotas in employment. There is a mistaken belief that Congress is legislating in these areas in this bill. When we drafted this bill we excluded these issues largely because the problems raised by these controversial questions are more properly handled at a governmental level closer to the American people and by communities and individuals themselves." 110 Cong. Rec. 15893 (1964).

not unnecessarily trammel the interests of white employees, because no white employees lost their jobs, half of those trained in the program would be white, and it was a temporary measure ending when "the percentage of black skilled craftworkers in the Gramercy plant approximates the percentage of blacks in the local labor force."]

MR. JUSTICE POWELL and MR. JUSTICE STEVENS took no part in the consideration or decision of these cases.

MR. JUSTICE BLACKMUN, concurring.

While I share some of the misgivings expressed in MR. JUSTICE REHNQUIST's dissent concerning the extent to which the legislative history of Title VII clearly supports the result the Court reaches today, I believe that additional considerations, practical and equitable, only partially perceived, if perceived at all, by the 88th Congress, support the conclusion reached by the Court today, and I therefore join its opinion as well as its judgment.

In his dissent from the decision of the United States Court of Appeals for the Fifth Circuit, Judge Wisdom pointed out that this litigation arises from a practical problem in the administration of Title VII. The broad prohibition against discrimination places the employer and the union on what he accurately described as a "high tightrope without a net beneath them." 563 F.2d 216, 230. If Title VII is read literally, on the one hand they face liability for past discrimination against blacks, and on the other they face liability to whites for any voluntary preferences adopted to mitigate the effects of prior discrimination against blacks.

In this litigation, Kaiser denies prior discrimination but concedes that its past hiring practices may be subject to question. Although the labor force in the Gramercy area was proximately 39% black, Kaiser's work force was less than 15% black, and its craftwork force was less than 2% black. Kaiser had made some effort to recruit black painters, carpenters, insulators, and other craftsmen, but it continued to insist that those hired have five years' prior industrial experience, a requirement that arguably was not sufficiently job related to justify under Title VII any discriminatory impact it may have had. * * * The parties dispute the extent to which black craftsmen were available in the local labor market. They agree, however, that after critical reviews from the Office of Federal Contract Compliance, Kaiser and the Steelworkers established the training program in question here and modeled it along the lines of a Title VII consent decree later entered for the steel industry. * * * Yet when they did this, respondent Weber sued, alleging that Title VII prohibited the program because it discriminated against him as a white person and it was not supported by a prior judicial finding of discrimination against blacks.

Respondent Weber's reading of Title VII, endorsed by the Court of Appeals, places voluntary compliance with Title VII in profound jeopardy. The only way for the employer and the union to keep their footing on the "tightrope" it creates would be to eschew all forms of voluntary affirmative action. Even a whisper of emphasis on minority recruiting would be forbidden. Because Congress intended to encourage private efforts to come into compliance with Title VII, see *Alexander v. Gardner-*

Denver Co., 415 U.S. 36, 44 (1974), Judge Wisdom concluded that employers and unions who had committed "arguable violations" of Title VII should be free to make reasonable responses without fear of liability to whites. Preferential hiring along the lines of the Kaiser program is a reasonable response for the employer, whether or not a court, on these facts, could order the same step as a remedy. The company is able to avoid identifying victims of past discrimination, and so avoids claims for backpay that would inevitably follow a response limited to such victims. If past victims should be benefited by the program, however, the company mitigates its liability to those persons. Also, to the extent that Title VII liability is predicated on the "disparate effect" of an employer's past hiring practices, the program makes it less likely that such an effect could be demonstrated. And the Court has recently held that work-force statistics resulting from private affirmative action were probative of benign intent in a "disparate treatment" case. *Furnco Construction Corp. v. Waters*, 438 U.S. 567 (1978).

The "arguable violation" theory has a number of advantages. It responds to a practical problem in the administration of Title VII not anticipated by Congress. It draws predictability from the outline of present law and closely effectuates the purpose of the Act. Both Kaiser and the United States urge its adoption here. Because I agree that it is the soundest way to approach this case, my preference would be to resolve this litigation by applying it and holding that Kaiser's craft training program meets the requirement that voluntary affirmative action be a reasonable response to an "arguable violation" of Title VII. * * *

MR. JUSTICE REHNQUIST, with whom THE CHIEF JUSTICE joins, dissenting.

In a very real sense, the Court's opinion is ahead of its time: it could more appropriately have been handed down five years from now, in 1984, a year coinciding with the title of a book from which the Court's opinion borrows, perhaps subconsciously, at least one idea. Orwell describes in his book a governmental official of Oceania, one of the three great world powers, denouncing the current enemy, Eurasia, to an assembled crowd:

> "It was almost impossible to listen to him without being first convinced and then maddened. * * * The speech had been proceeding for perhaps twenty minutes when a messenger hurried onto the platform and a scrap of paper was slipped into the speaker's hand. He unrolled and read it without pausing in his speech. Nothing altered in his voice or manner, or in the content of what he was saying, but suddenly the names were different. Without words said, a wave of understanding rippled through the crowd. Oceania was at war with Eastasia! * * * The banners and posters with which the square was decorated were all wrong! * * *

> "[T]he speaker had switched from one line to the other actually in mid-sentence, not only without a pause, but without even breaking the syntax."—G. Orwell, Nineteen Eighty-Four 181–182 (1949).

Today's decision represents an equally dramatic and equally unremarked switch in this Court's interpretation of Title VII. * * *

[II] Were Congress to act today specifically to prohibit the type of racial discrimination suffered by Weber, it would be hard pressed to draft language better tailored to the task than that found in § 703(d) of Title VII:

> "It shall be an unlawful employment practice for any employer, labor organization, or joint labor-management committee controlling apprenticeship or other training or retraining, including on-the-job training programs to discriminate against any individual because of his race, color, religion, sex, or national origin in admission to, or employment in, any program established to provide apprenticeship or other training." 78 Stat. 256, 42 U.S.C. § 2000e–2(d).

Equally suited to the task would be § 703(a)(2), which makes it unlawful for an employer to classify his employees "in any way which would deprive or tend to deprive any individual of employment opportunities or otherwise adversely affect his status as an employee, because of such individual's race, color, religion, sex, or national origin." 78 Stat. 255, 42 U.S.C. § 2000e–2(a)(2).

Entirely consistent with these two express prohibitions is the language of § 703(j) of Title VII, which provides that the Act is not to be interpreted "to require any employer * * * to grant preferential treatment to any individual or to any group because of the race * * * of such individual or group" to correct a racial imbalance in the employer's work force. 42 U.S.C. § 2000e–2(j). Seizing on the word "require," the Court infers that Congress must have intended to "permit" this type of racial discrimination. Not only is this reading of § 703(j) outlandish in the light of the flat prohibitions of §§ 703(a) and (d), but also, as explained in Part III, it is totally belied by the Act's legislative history.

Quite simply, Kaiser's racially discriminatory admission quota is flatly prohibited by the plain language of Title VII. This normally dispositive fact, however, gives the Court only momentary pause. An "interpretation" of the statute upholding Weber's claim would, according to the Court, " 'bring about an end completely at variance with the purpose of the statute.' " To support this conclusion, the Court calls upon the "spirit" of the Act, which it divines from passages in Title VII's legislative history indicating that enactment of the statute was prompted by Congress's desire " 'to open employment opportunities for Negroes in occupations which [had] been traditionally closed to them.' " But the legislative history invoked by the Court to avoid the plain language of §§ 703(a) and (d) simply misses the point. To be sure, the reality of employment discrimination against Negroes provided the primary impetus for passage of Title VII. But this fact by no means supports the proposition that Congress intended to leave employers free to discriminate against white persons. In most cases, "[l]egislative history . . . is more vague than the statute we are called upon to interpret." [*United States v. Public Utilities Comm'n*, 345 U.S. 295, 320 (1953) (Jackson, J., concurring).] Here, however, the legislative history of Title VII is as clear as the language of §§ 703(a) and (d), and it irrefutably demonstrates that Congress meant precisely what it said in §§ 703(a) and (d)—that *no* racial discrimination in employment is permissible under Title VII, not even preferential treatment of minorities to correct racial imbalance.

[III] In undertaking to review the legislative history of Title VII, I am mindful that the topic hardly makes for light reading, but I am also fearful that nothing short of a thorough examination of the congressional debates will fully expose the magnitude of the Court's misinterpretation of Congress's intent.

[A] Introduced on the floor of the House of Representatives on June 20, 1963, the bill—H.R. 7152—that ultimately became the Civil Rights Act of 1964 contained no compulsory provisions directed at private discrimination in employment. The bill was promptly referred to the Committee on the Judiciary, where it was amended to include Title VII. With two exceptions, the bill reported by the House Judiciary Committee contained §§ 703(a) and (d) as they were ultimately enacted. Amendments subsequently adopted on the House floor added § 703's prohibition against sex discrimination and § 703(d)'s coverage of "on-the-job training."

After noting that "[t]he purpose of [Title VII] is to eliminate * * * discrimination in employment based on race, color, religion, or national origin," the Judiciary Committee's Report simply paraphrased the provisions of Title VII without elaboration. H.R. Rep., pt. 1, p. 26. In a separate Minority Report, however, opponents of the measure on the Committee advanced a line of attack which was reiterated throughout the debates in both the House and Senate and which ultimately led to passage of § 703(j). Noting that the word "discrimination" was nowhere defined in H.R. 7152, the Minority Report charged that the absence from Title VII of any reference to "racial imbalance" was a "public relations" ruse and that "the administration intends to rely upon its own construction of 'discrimination' as including the lack of racial balance. . . ." H.R. Rep., pt. 1, pp. 67–68. To demonstrate how the bill would operate in practice, the Minority Report posited a number of hypothetical employment situations, concluding in each example that the employer *may be forced to hire according to race*, to 'racially balance' those who work for him *in every job classification* or be in violation of Federal law." *Id.*, at 69 (emphasis in original).

When H.R. 7152 reached the House floor, the opening speech in support of its passage was delivered by Representative Celler, Chairman of the House Judiciary Committee and the Congressman responsible for introducing the legislation. A portion of that speech responded to criticism "seriously misrepresent[ing] what the bill would do and grossly distort[ing] its effects":

"[T]he charge has been made that the Equal Employment Opportunity Commission to be established by title VII of the bill would have the power to prevent a business from employing and promoting the people it wished, and that a 'Federal inspector' could then order the hiring and promotion only of employees of certain races or religious groups. This description of the bill is entirely wrong. * * *

"Even [a] court could not order that any preference be given to any particular race, religion or other group, but would be limited to ordering an end of discrimination. The statement that a Federal inspector could order the employment and promotion only of members of a specific racial or religious group is therefore patently erroneous. * * *

" * * * The Bill would do no more than prevent * * * employers from discriminating against *or in favor* of workers because of their race, religion, or national origin.

"It is likewise not true that the Equal Employment Opportunity Commission would have power to rectify existing 'racial or religious imbalance' in employment by requiring the hiring of certain people without regard to their qualifications simply because they are of a given race or religion. Only actual discrimination could be stopped." 110 Cong. Rec. 1518 (1964) (emphasis added).

Representative Celler's construction of Title VII was repeated by several other supporters during the House debate.

Thus, the battle lines were drawn early in the legislative struggle over Title VII, with opponents of the measure charging that agencies of the Federal Government such as the Equal Employment Opportunity Commission (EEOC), by interpreting the word "discrimination" to mean the existence of "racial imbalance," would "require" employers to grant preferential treatment to minorities, and supporters responding that the EEOC would be granted no such power and that, indeed, Title VII prohibits discrimination "in favor of workers because of their race." Supporters of H.R. 7152 in the House ultimately prevailed by a vote of 290 to 130, and the measure was sent to the Senate to begin what became the longest debate in that body's history.

[B] The Senate debate was broken into three phases: the debate on sending the bill to Committee, the general debate on the bill prior to invocation of cloture, and the debate following cloture. * * *

Formal debate on the merits of H.R. 7152 began on March 30, 1964. Supporters of the bill in the Senate had made elaborate preparations for this second round. Senator Humphrey, the majority whip, and Senator Kuchel, the minority whip, were selected as the bipartisan floor managers on the entire civil rights bill. Responsibility for explaining and defending each important title of the bill was placed on bipartisan "captains." Senators Clark and Case were selected as the bipartisan captains responsible for Title VII. Vaas, Title VII: Legislative History, 7 B.C. Ind. & Com. L. Rev. 431, 444–445 (1966) (hereinafter Title VII: Legislative History).

In the opening speech of the formal Senate debate on the bill, Senator Humphrey addressed the main concern of Title VII's opponents, advising that not only does Title VII not require use of racial quotas, *it does not permit* their use. "The truth," stated the floor leader of the bill, "is that this title forbids discriminating against anyone on account of race. This is the simple and complete truth about title VII." 110 Cong. Rec. 6549 (1964). Senator Humphrey continued:

"Contrary to the allegations of some opponents of this title, there is nothing in it that will give any power to the Commission or to any court to require hiring, firing, or promotion of employees in order to meet a racial 'quota' or to achieve a certain racial balance.

"That bugaboo has been brought up a dozen times; but it is nonexistent. In fact, *the very opposite is true. Title VII prohibits discrimination.* In effect, it says that race, religion and national origin are not to be used as the basis for hiring and firing. Title VII is designed to encourage hiring on the basis of ability and qualifications, not race or religion." *Ibid.* (emphasis added).

At the close of his speech, Senator Humphrey returned briefly to the subject of employment quotas: "It is claimed that the bill would require racial quotas for all hiring, when in fact it provides that race shall not be a basis for making personnel decisions." *Id.*, at 6553. * * *

A few days later the Senate's attention focused exclusively on Title VII, as Senators Clark and Case rose to discuss the title of H.R. 7152 on which they shared floor "captain" responsibilities. In an interpretative memorandum submitted jointly to the Senate, Senators Clark and Case took pains to refute the opposition's charge that Title VII would result in preferential treatment for minorities. * * * Of particular relevance to the instant litigation were their observations regarding seniority rights. As if directing their comments at Brian Weber, the Senators said:

"Title VII would have no effect on established seniority rights. Its effect is prospective and not retrospective. Thus, for example, if a business has been discriminating in the past and as a result has an all-white working force, when the title comes into effect the employer's obligation would be simply to fill future vacancies on a nondiscriminatory basis. He would not be obliged—*or indeed permitted*—to fire whites in order to hire Negroes, *or to prefer Negroes for future vacancies, or, once Negroes are hired, to give them special seniority rights at the expense of the white workers hired earlier.*" *Id.*, at 7213 (emphasis added).

[In addition, Senator Kuchel made similar comments. Southern opponents to the bill were still not satisfied, though. Senator Robertson (D–VA) argued that the bill would mandate quotas. Senator Harrison Williams (D–NJ) responded:]

"Those opposed to H.R. 7152 should realize that to hire a Negro solely because he is a Negro is racial discrimination, just as much as a 'white only' employment policy. Both forms of discrimination are prohibited by title VII of this bill. The language of that title simply states that race is not a qualification for employment. . . . Some people charge that H.R. 7152 favors the Negro, at the expense of the white majority. But how can the language of equality favor one race or one religion over another? Equality can have only one meaning, and that meaning is self-evident to reasonable men. Those who say that equality means favoritism do violence to common sense." *Id.*, at 8921. * * *

While the debate in the Senate raged, a bipartisan coalition under the leadership of Senators Dirksen, Mansfield, Humphrey, and Kuchel was working with House leaders and representatives of the Johnson administration on a number of amendments to H.R. 7152 designed to enhance its prospects of passage. The so-called "Dirksen-Mansfield" amendment was introduced on May 26 by Senator Dirksen as a substitute for the entire House-passed bill. The substitute bill, which ultimately became law, left unchanged the basic prohibitory language of §§ 703(a) and (d), as well as the remedial provisions in § 706(g). It added, however, several provisions defining and clarifying the scope of Title VII's substantive prohibitions. One of those clarifying amendments, § 703(j), was specifically directed at the opposition's concerns regarding racial balancing and preferential treatment of minorities, providing in pertinent part: "Nothing contained in [Title VII] shall be interpreted to require any employer . . . to grant preferential treatment to any individual or to any group because of the race . . . of such individual or group on account of" a racial imbalance in the employer's work force. 42 U.S.C. § 2000e–2(j). * * *

Contrary to the Court's analysis, the language of § 703(j) is precisely tailored to the objection voiced time and again by Title VII's opponents. Not once during the 83 days of debate in the Senate did a speaker, proponent or opponent, suggest that the bill would allow employers *voluntarily* to prefer racial minorities over white persons. In light of Title VII's flat prohibition on discrimination "against any individual . . . because of such individual's race," § 703(a), 42 U.S.C. § 2000e–2(a), such a contention would have been, in any event, too preposterous to warrant response. Indeed, speakers on both sides of the issue, as the legislative history makes clear, recognized that Title VII would tolerate no *voluntary* racial preference, whether in favor of blacks or whites. The complaint consistently voiced by the opponents was that Title VII, particularly the word "discrimination," would be *interpreted* by federal agencies such as the EEOC to *require* the correction of racial imbalance through the granting of preferential treatment to minorities. Verbal assurances that Title VII would not require—indeed, would not permit—preferential treatment of blacks having failed, supporters of H.R. 7152 responded by proposing an amendment carefully worded to meet, and put to rest, the opposition's charge. Indeed, unlike §§ 703(a) and (d), which are by their terms directed at entities—*e.g.*, employers, labor unions—whose actions are restricted by Title VII's prohibitions, the language of § 703(j) is specifically directed at entities—federal agencies and courts—charged with the responsibility of interpreting Title VII's provisions.

In light of the background and purpose of § 703(j), the irony of invoking the section to justify the result in this case is obvious. The Court's frequent references to the "voluntary" nature of Kaiser's racially discriminatory admission quota bear no relationship to the facts of this case. Kaiser and the Steelworkers acted under pressure from an agency of the Federal Government, the Office of Federal Contract Compliance, which found that minorities were being "underutilized" at Kaiser's plants. That is, Kaiser's work force was racially imbalanced. Bowing to that pressure, Kaiser instituted an admissions quota preferring blacks over whites, thus confirming that the fears of Title VII's opponents were well founded. Today, § 703(j), adopted to allay those fears, is invoked by the Court to uphold imposition of a racial quota under the very circumstances that the section was intended to prevent. * * *

[Justice Rehnquist also pointed to Senator Ervin's June 9 amendment to delete Title VII. Responding for the sponsors, Senator Clark emphasized that the bill "establishes no quotas." Senator Cotton (R–NH) offered an amendment to limit

Title VII to firms having more than 100 employees. He opined that Title VII would forbid quotas. Although his amendment was defeated, Justice Rehnquist observed that the sponsors did not dispute the Cotton view.

[When cloture was invoked June 10, 1964, debate was limited, but several post-cloture statements by the bill's supporters reinforced the earlier view that Title VII imposed no quotas. The substitute bill was passed June 19. In final form, the bill was passed by the House on July 2 and signed by the President the same day.]

[V] Our task in this case, like any other case involving the construction of a statute, is to give effect to the intent of Congress. To divine that intent, we traditionally look first to the words of the statute and, if they are unclear, then to the statute's legislative history. Finding the desired result hopelessly foreclosed by these conventional sources, the Court turns to a third source—the "spirit" of the Act. But close examination of what the Court proffers as the spirit of the Act reveals it as the spirit animating the present majority, not the 88th Congress. For if the spirit of the Act eludes the cold words of the statute itself, it rings out with unmistakable clarity in the words of the elected representatives who made the Act law. It is *equality*. Senator Dirksen, I think, captured that spirit in a speech delivered on the floor of the Senate just moments before the bill was passed:

> " * * * [T]oday we come to grips finally with a bill that advances the enjoyment of living; but, more than that, it advances the equality of opportunity.

> "I do not emphasize the word 'equality' standing by itself. It means equality of opportunity in the field of education. It means equality of opportunity in the field of employment. It means equality of opportunity in the field of participation in the affairs of government * * *.

> "That is it.

> "Equality of opportunity, if we are going to talk about conscience, is the mass conscience of mankind that speaks in every generation, and it will continue to speak long after we are dead and gone." 110 Cong. Rec. 14510 (1964).

There is perhaps no device more destructive to the notion of equality than the *numerus clausus*—the quota. Whether described as "benign discrimination" or "affirmative action," the racial quota is nonetheless a creator of castes, a two-edged sword that must demean one in order to prefer another. In passing Title VII, Congress outlawed *all* racial discrimination, recognizing that no discrimination based on race is benign, that no action disadvantaging a person because of his color is affirmative. With today's holding, the Court introduces into Title VII a tolerance for the very evil that the law was intended to eradicate, without offering even a clue as to what the limits on that tolerance may be. We are told simply that Kaiser's racially discriminatory admission quota "falls on the permissible side of the line." By going not merely *beyond*, but directly *against* Title VII's language and legislative history, the Court has sown the wind. Later courts will face the impossible task of reaping the whirlwind.

NOTES ON WEBER AND MODES OF INTERPRETATION

The three opinions in this case present strikingly different normative visions of the Court's role in statutory interpretation. See William Eskridge Jr., *Dynamic Statutory Interpretation* 13–31, 35–44 (1994); Philip Frickey, *Wisdom on* Weber, 74 Tulane L. Rev. 1169 (2000). Each vision is beset with practical problems of evidence, however.

1. *Divining the "Intent" of Congress: Did the Court Invalidate the Original Legislative "Deal"?* One way to look at the role of the interpreter of a statute is to say that she is seeking the original intent of the author (the enacting Congress). Justices Brennan and Rehnquist both purported to perform this interpretive role, with four Justices agreeing with Justice Brennan and only the Chief Justice agreeing with Justice Rehnquist. Many of the commentators agree with Rehnquist that the Court "changed" the meaning of the statute by judicial fiat, and "[t]hat change goes to the roots of the bargain struck by the 88th Congress, and the roots of our color-blind aspiration." Bernard Meltzer, *The* Weber *Case: The Judicial Abrogation of the Antidiscrimination Standard in Employment*, 47 U. Chi. L. Rev. 423, 456 (1980).[79] Do you agree?

Was Justice Rehnquist right to charge that Congress would have been "hard pressed" to have chosen language more clearly protecting Brian Weber than that of § 703(d), which makes it an unlawful practice for an employer "to discriminate against any individual because of his race * * * in admission to, or employment in, any program established to provide apprenticeship or other training"? What about the following:

> It shall be an unlawful employment practice for the employer * * * not to include any individual in any program established to provide apprenticeship or other training as a result of prohibited criteria, namely race * * *.

Did Justice Rehnquist overstate the clarity of § 703(d)?

Justice Rehnquist's dissent assumed, as many dictionaries say, that an employer *discriminates* on the basis of race if it makes a race-based *differentiation*. In a dictionary sense, it is a correct use of the term to say "I discriminate against peaches," if I prefer pears to peaches. But that is not the way we usually use the word *discriminate*, which connotes an *invidious* differentiation. Consider the definition of *discriminate* found in a desk dictionary published in 1968, soon after Congress enacted Title VII. In this dictionary, the "prejudice" meaning is the first definition given. Is there a single "plain meaning" of "discriminate"? Are there other text-based arguments that Justice Rehnquist should have emphasized? *See* Eskridge, *Dynamic Statutory Interpretation*, 42–43 (laying out arguments for Justice Rehnquist's position based on the structure of § 703).

Perhaps it is not so clear that the "deal" described by Justice Rehnquist is inscribed in the language of the statute. For that reason, statutory interpreters often look to the legislative history to figure out the "intent" of Congress. As a rule, the most authoritative legislative history is the House and Senate committee reports, but Justice Rehnquist did not rely on them. Instead, like Justice Brennan, he relied on the colloquies between the bill's sponsors and the bill's opponents. Does this tell us

---

[79] See also Nelson Lund, *The Law of Affirmative Action In and After the Civil Rights Act of 1991: Congress Invites Judicial Reform*, 6 Geo. Mason L. Rev. 87, 90–101 (1997); Daniel Rodriguez & Barry Weingast, *The Positive Political Theory of Legislative History: New Perspectives on the 1964 Civil Rights Act and Its Interpretation*, 151 U. Pa. L. Rev. 1417 (2003).

anything about the "intent" of the 73 Senators and 290 Representatives who voted for the bill? Suppose that the statements of the sponsors are binding on everyone. Did anyone say: "We never want preferences for whites or blacks. By that we mean either governmentally required preferences, or preferences voluntarily agreed to by an employer or union to redress past discrimination." Did Justice Rehnquist discover such a "smoking gun" in the Clark-Case memorandum's passage that he claimed spoke directly to Brian Weber's situation?

Finally, note that most of Justice Rehnquist's evidence comes from legislative discussions *before* the final deal was reached, namely, the Mansfield-Dirksen substitute. Participants in the congressional process point out that anything that happens *before* the final deal is irrelevant if inconsistent with the final deal. The Mansfield-Dirksen substitute added § 703(j), which provides some support to Justice Brennan's position, and none to Justice Rehnquist's. To be sure, the latter would vehemently object that Senator Dirksen (a conservative Republican like Rehnquist) would *never* have read § 703(j) that way—but Rehnquist cited nothing to support his view, while Brennan cited Representative MacGregor (also a conservative Republican), who defended the Mansfield-Dirksen substitute precisely along the give-business-discretion lines that Justice Brennan did. See Victoria Nourse, *A Decision Theory of Statutory Interpretation: Legislative History by the Rules*, 122 Yale L.J. 70, 104–09 (2012).

2.   *Pitfalls of a Purpose-Oriented Interpretation.* Supporting the "spirit" approach taken by Justice Brennan, Burt Neuborne (ACLU counsel in *Weber*) argues:

> At best, the concept of legislative intent is discernible primarily by the judges who claim to have deciphered it. The truth of the matter is that a legislature, especially in the civil rights area, generally enacts a statute aimed at a broad philosophical concept—in this case, equality in employment. It does not and cannot foresee, much less resolve, the myriad questions which must arise whenever a broad philosophical proposition is applied to the protean complexity of everyday life * * *.

Neuborne, *Observations on* Weber, 54 N.Y.U. L. Rev. 546, 553 (1979). Is this a more realistic way of looking at the Civil Rights Act than Meltzer's specific bargain idea?

But who was right about the "spirit" of the Act? There is much to be said for Justice Rehnquist's position that when you read the committee report and the debate, you come away with the impression that the statute was mainly intended to eradicate racial criteria in hiring. Supporting Justice Brennan, Ronald Dworkin argues that the judge should interpret the statute to advance the policy that furnishes "the best political justification for the statute," because the "intent" of Congress on this issue is indeterminate. Dworkin, *How to Read the Civil Rights Act*, in *A Matter of Principle* 316, 327 (1985). Upon what model of the legislative process might this suggestion rest? Even if it is a valid approach, there seem to be two purposes in the Act—jobs for African Americans and creation of a color-blind society. How does the judge choose one politically coherent purpose over the other?

If we decide to interpret Title VII in light of its equal-results spirit, will encouraging unions and companies to set up their own affirmative action programs (effectively shifting the costs of past discrimination from them onto white employees) really contribute to this purpose? For example, will the kind of "quota" programs approved in *Weber* undermine mainstream political support for Title VII? Would such programs "create incentives for employers to locate jobs away from black labor," so that they can avoid high black quotas? Edmund Kitch, *The Return of Color Consciousness to the Constitution:* Weber, Dayton, *and* Columbus, 1979 Sup. Ct. Rev. 1, 12–13. Indeed, in 1979 African-American unemployment was no less a problem than it had been in 1964.

Judge Wisdom's dissenting opinion in the court below recognized several purposes for the statute—integration, color-blindness, and flexible voluntary remedies—and concluded that the "arguable violation" approach best balanced these competing purposes. See Philip Frickey & William Eskridge Jr., *The Story of* Steelworkers v. Weber *(1979): Statutory Text, Spirit, and Practical Reasoning,* in *Statutory Interpretation Stories* 92, 112–14 (Eskridge, Frickey & Garrett eds., 2011). Yet only Justice Blackmun accepted that argument. Why did it not have more traction among the Court majority?

3. *Reading Statutes Dynamically.* Both Justices Brennan and Rehnquist purported to be interpreting the "will" of Congress on this issue as of 1964, when the statute was enacted. The implicit argument of each opinion is that on the day Title VII became law, this is the answer the interpreter as well as the representative would have given to the *Weber* question. Does that make sense to you? For purposes of statutory interpretation, the *Weber* issue is so important because it represents a tension that did not really exist in the statute as enacted, as Justice Blackmun's concurring opinion suggests. In a functional sense, the Title VII of 1964 was not the same statute as the Title VII of 1979, not just because the statute was formally amended (in 1972), but also because the ongoing process of interpretation and elaboration altered the statute in response to evolving circumstances. *Griggs* as well as other decisions changed not only the statute, but the society on which the statute operated. For this reason, Justice Blackmun urged that the interpretation of Title VII reflect the unanticipated tension created by the ongoing application and interpretation process and permit the affirmative action plan in *Weber.* Upon what model of legislation was Justice Blackmun operating?

Two of us have argued that the most persuasive approach to *Weber* is Justice Blackmun's pragmatic appeal to current problems of statutory fairness and workability, not just the historical choices allegedly made in 1964.[80] The argument is that statutes start with gaps and ambiguities (including the precise meaning of "discriminate," a term that is not self-defining), which the EEOC and the Court had to interpret in light of factual settings they faced, and their interpretations went "beyond" Congress's original expectations. The gaps and ambiguities proliferated as the world changed— often in response to the statute and its applications—and offered more radical variations, including repeated fact patterns like *Weber,* where past discrimination continued to have present effects. Moreover, Title VII changed, often "against" the original legislative expectations, because the EEOC and the Court had their own values and "spin" on the statute, because the Congress with power to discipline these interpreters was the current rather than the enacting Congress (and the latter had a different spin on the statute than the former), and because the legal and social context changed over time. This is a description of what interpreters do with the statute. Do

---

[80] See Eskridge, *Dynamic Statutory Interpretation,* 24–25; Philip Frickey, *From the Big Sleep to the Big Heat: The Revival of Theory in Statutory Interpretation,* 77 Minn. L. Rev. 241, 245–47, 259 (1992); Frickey & Eskridge, *Story of* Weber.

you find it normatively acceptable? Is it appropriate for the judiciary to undertake this task of updating the statute and filling gaps with new policies, or should Congress have the sole responsibility for amending old statutes to account for new social and economic developments? Does the answer change when the new conditions have resulted in large part from prior judicial opinions interpreting the act in unexpected ways?

Liberals have no monopoly on dynamic interpretation. The conservative Justices on the Burger Court had their own spin on affirmative action, and the cases after *Weber* were harder on affirmative action plans. See *Sheet Metal Workers v. EEOC*, 478 U.S. 421 (1986); *Local No. 93, Int'l Ass'n of Firefighters v. Cleveland*, 478 U.S. 501 (1986); *Local Union No. 1784 Firefighters v. Stotts*, 467 U.S. 561 (1984). The Supreme Court drifted further to the right when Justice Rehnquist became Chief Justice and yielded his seat to Judge Antonin Scalia, a devout foe of affirmative action. Would the new Court move Title VII policy in a more conservative direction?

An argument *against* such a move is *stare decisis*: the Court is obliged to follow its own precedents, with a narrow exception: the precedent was wrongly decided *and* there is positive harm in continuing its error. Indeed, in statutory cases, the Court says it follows a super-strong form of *stare decisis*, where courts should leave correction of its own errors to Congress (see Chapter 5). Does this precept make sense to you? Should it save *Weber*? If you think it should save *Weber*, should it save precedents you think are very wrong?

JOHNSON V. TRANSPORTATION AGENCY, SANTA CLARA COUNTY

Supreme Court of the United States, 1987.
480 U.S. 616, 107 S.Ct. 1442, 94 L.Ed.2d 613.

JUSTICE BRENNAN delivered the opinion of the Court.

[The Transportation Agency of Santa Clara County, California promulgated an Affirmative Action Plan to remedy historic patterns of discrimination against women and minorities in some job categories. The Plan provided that, in making promotions to positions within a traditionally segregated job classification in which women had been significantly underrepresented, the Agency was authorized to consider as one factor the sex of a qualified applicant. The Agency found women significantly underrepresented in its work force generally, and virtually unrepresented in the 238 Skilled Craft Worker positions. Pursuant to the Plan, the Agency promoted Diane Joyce to the position of road dispatcher in the Agency's Roads Division. Dispatchers assign road crews, equipment, and materials, and maintain records pertaining to road maintenance jobs. One of the applicants passed over was Paul Johnson, who had a slightly higher score than Joyce based upon his paper credentials and an oral interview. Johnson filed a complaint with the EEOC, and subsequently a federal lawsuit. The district court granted Johnson relief, based upon its finding that Johnson was more qualified for the position than Joyce, and that sex was the "determining factor" in Joyce's selection. The Ninth Circuit reversed.]

[*Weber*] upheld the employer's decision to select less senior black applicants over the white respondent, for we found that taking race into account was consistent with Title VII's objective of "break[ing] down old patterns of racial segregation and hierarchy." As we stated:

> "It would be ironic indeed if a law triggered by a Nation's concern over centuries of racial injustice and intended to improve the lot of those who had 'been excluded from the American dream for so long' constituted the first legislative prohibition of all voluntary, private, race-conscious efforts to abolish traditional patterns of racial segregation and hierarchy." *Id.* (quoting remarks of Sen. Humphrey).[7]

* * * As JUSTICE BLACKMUN'S concurrence made clear, *Weber* held that an employer seeking to justify the adoption of a plan need not point to its own prior discriminatory practices, nor even to evidence of an "arguable violation" on its part. Rather, it need point only to a "conspicuous . . . imbalance in traditionally segregated job categories." * * *

In reviewing the employment decision at issue in this case, we must first examine whether that decision was made pursuant to a plan prompted by concerns similar to those of the employer in *Weber*. Next, we must determine whether the effect of the Plan on males and nonminorities is comparable to the effect of the Plan in that case.

The first issue is therefore whether consideration of the sex of applicants for skilled craft jobs was justified by the existence of a "manifest imbalance" that reflected underrepresentation of women in "traditionally segregated job categories." In determining whether an imbalance exists that would justify taking sex or race into account, a comparison of the percentage of minorities or women in the

---

[7] JUSTICE SCALIA's dissent maintains that *Weber*'s conclusion that Title VII does not prohibit voluntary affirmative action programs "rewrote the statute it purported to construe." *Weber*'s decisive rejection of the argument that the "plain language" of the statute prohibits affirmative action rested on (1) legislative history indicating Congress' clear intention that employers play a major role in eliminating the vestiges of discrimination, and (2) the language and legislative history of section 703(j) of the statute, which reflect a strong desire to preserve managerial prerogatives so that they might be utilized for this purpose. As JUSTICE BLACKMUN said in his concurrence in *Weber*, "[I]f the Court has misconceived the political will, it has the assurance that because the question is statutory Congress may set a different course if it so chooses." Congress has not amended the statute to reject our construction, nor have any such amendments even been proposed, and we therefore may assume that our interpretation was correct.

JUSTICE SCALIA's dissent faults the fact that we take note of the absence of Congressional efforts to amend the statute to nullify *Weber*. It suggests that Congressional inaction cannot be regarded as acquiescence under all circumstances, but then draws from that unexceptional point the conclusion that *any* reliance on Congressional failure to act is necessarily a "canard." The fact that inaction may not always provide crystalline revelation, however, should not obscure the fact that it may be probative to varying degrees. *Weber*, for instance, was a widely-publicized decision that addressed a prominent issue of public debate. Legislative inattention thus is not a plausible explanation for Congressional inaction. Furthermore, Congress not only passed no contrary legislation in the wake of *Weber*, but not one legislator even proposed a bill to do so. The barriers of the legislative process therefore also seem a poor explanation for failure to act. By contrast, when Congress has been displeased with our interpretation of Title VII, it has not hesitated to amend the statute to tell us so. For instance, when Congress passed the Pregnancy Discrimination Act of 1978, 42 U.S.C. section 2000e(k), "it unambiguously expressed its disapproval of both the holding and the reasoning of the Court in [*General Electric v. Gilbert*, 429 U.S. 125 (1976)]." *Newport News Shipbuilding & Dry Dock v. EEOC*, 462 U.S. 669, 678 (1983). Surely, it is appropriate to find some probative value in such radically different Congressional reactions to this Court's interpretations of the same statute.

As one scholar has put it, "When a court says to a legislature: 'You (or your predecessor) meant X,' it almost invites the legislature to answer: 'We did not.'" G. Calabresi, A Common Law for the Age of Statutes 31–32 (1982). Any belief in the notion of a dialogue between the judiciary and the legislature must acknowledge that on occasion an invitation declined is as significant as one accepted.

employer's work force with the percentage in the area labor market or general population is appropriate in analyzing jobs that require no special expertise, or training programs designed to provide expertise. Where a job requires special training, however, the comparison should be with those in the labor force who possess the relevant qualifications. The requirement that the "manifest imbalance" relate to a "traditionally segregated job category" provides assurance both that sex or race will be taken into account in a manner consistent with Title VII's purpose of eliminating the effects of employment discrimination, and that the interests of those employees not benefitting from the plan will not be unduly infringed.

A manifest imbalance need not be such that it would support a prima facie case against the employer, as suggested in Justice O'Connor's concurrence, since we do not regard as identical the constraints of Title VII and the Federal Constitution on voluntarily adopted affirmative action plans. Application of the "prima facie" standard in Title VII cases would be inconsistent with *Weber*'s focus on statistical imbalance, and could inappropriately create a significant disincentive for employers to adopt an affirmative action plan. A corporation concerned with maximizing return on investment, for instance, is hardly likely to adopt a plan if in order to do so it must compile evidence that could be used to subject it to a colorable Title VII suit.

It is clear that the decision to hire Joyce was made pursuant to an Agency plan that directed that sex or race be taken into account for the purpose of remedying underrepresentation. The Agency Plan acknowledged the "limited opportunities that have existed in the past" for women to find employment in certain job classifications "where women have not been traditionally employed in significant numbers." As a result, observed the Plan, women were concentrated in traditionally female jobs in the Agency, and represented a lower percentage in other job classifications than would be expected if such traditional segregation had not occurred. Specifically, 9 of the 10 Para-Professionals and 110 of the 145 Office and Clerical Workers were women. By contrast, women were only 2 of the 28 Officials and Administrators, 5 of the 58 Professionals, 12 of the 124 Technicians, none of the Skilled Craft Workers, and 1—who was Joyce—of the 110 Road Maintenance Workers. The Plan sought to remedy these imbalances through "hiring, training and promotion of . . . women throughout the Agency in all major job classifications where they are underrepresented." * * *

We next consider whether the Agency Plan unnecessarily trammeled the rights of male employees or created an absolute bar to their advancement. In contrast to the plan in *Weber*, which provided that 50% of the positions in the craft training program were exclusively for blacks, and to the consent decree upheld last term in *Firefighters v. Cleveland*, 478 U.S. 501 (1986), which required the promotion of specific numbers of minorities, the Plan sets aside no positions for women. The Plan expressly states that "[t]he 'goals' established for each Division should not be construed as 'quotas' that must be met." Rather, the Plan merely authorizes that consideration be given to affirmative action concerns when evaluating qualified applicants. As the Agency Director testified, the sex of Joyce was but one of numerous factors he took into account in arriving at his decision. The Plan thus resembles the "Harvard Plan" approvingly noted by Justice Powell in *University of*

California Regents v. Bakke, 438 U.S. 265, 316–319 (1978), which considers race along with other criteria in determining admission to the college. As Justice Powell observed: "In such an admissions program, race or ethnic background may be deemed a 'plus' in a particular applicant's file, yet it does not insulate the individual from comparison with all other candidates for the available seats." Similarly, the Agency Plan requires women to compete with all other qualified applicants. *No* persons are automatically excluded from consideration; *all* are able to have their qualifications weighed against those of other applicants. * * *

We therefore hold that the Agency appropriately took into account as one factor the sex of Diane Joyce in determining that she should be promoted to the road dispatcher position. The decision to do so was made pursuant to an affirmative action plan that represents a moderate, flexible, case-by-case approach to effecting a gradual improvement in the representation of minorities and women in the Agency's work force. Such a plan is fully consistent with Title VII, for it embodies the contribution that voluntary employer action can make in eliminating the vestiges of discrimination in the workplace. * * *

JUSTICE STEVENS, concurring. * * *

Prior to 1978 the Court construed the Civil Rights Act of 1964 as an absolute blanket prohibition against discrimination which neither required nor permitted discriminatory preferences for any group, minority or majority. * * * As I explained in my separate opinion in *Bakke*, and as the Court forcefully stated in *McDonald v. Santa Fe Trail Transportation Co.*, Congress intended " 'to eliminate all practices which operate to disadvantage the employment opportunities of any group protected by Title VII including Caucasians.' " If the Court had adhered to that construction of the Act, petitioner would unquestionably prevail in this case. But it has not done so.

In the *Bakke* case in 1978 and again in *Weber*, a majority of the Court interpreted the antidiscriminatory strategy of the statute in a fundamentally different way. * * * [T]he only problem for me is whether to adhere to an authoritative construction of the Act that is at odds with my understanding of the actual intent of the authors of the legislation. I conclude without hesitation that I must answer that question in the affirmative[.]

Bakke and *Weber* have been decided and are now an important part of the fabric of our law. This consideration is sufficiently compelling for me to adhere to the basic construction of this legislation that the Court adopted in *Bakke* and in *Weber*. There is an undoubted public interest in "stability and orderly development of the law."

The logic of antidiscrimination legislation requires that judicial constructions of Title VII leave "breathing room" for employer initiatives to benefit members of minority groups. If Title VII had never been enacted, a private employer would be free to hire members of minority groups for any reason that might seem sensible from a business or a social point of view. The Court's opinion in *Weber* reflects the same approach; the opinion relied heavily on legislative history indicating that

Congress intended that traditional management prerogatives be left undisturbed to the greatest extent possible. * * *

As construed in *Weber* * * * the statute does not absolutely prohibit preferential hiring in favor of minorities; it was merely intended to protect historically disadvantaged groups *against* discrimination and not to hamper managerial efforts to benefit members of disadvantaged groups that are consistent with that paramount purpose. The preference granted by respondent in this case does not violate the statute as so construed; the record amply supports the conclusion that the challenged employment decision served the legitimate purpose of creating diversity in a category of employment that had been almost an exclusive province of males in the past. Respondent's voluntary decision is surely not prohibited by Title VII as construed in *Weber*.

Whether a voluntary decision of the kind made by respondent would ever be prohibited by Title VII is a question we need not answer until it is squarely presented. Given the interpretation of the statute the Court adopted in *Weber*, I see no reason why the employer has any duty, prior to granting a preference to a qualified minority employee, to determine whether his past conduct might constitute an arguable violation of Title VII. Indeed, in some instances the employer may find it more helpful to focus on the future. Instead of retroactively scrutinizing his own or society's possible exclusions of minorities in the past to determine the outer limits of a valid affirmative-action program—or indeed, any particular affirmative-action decision—in many cases the employer will find it more appropriate to consider other legitimate reasons to give preferences to members of underrepresented groups. Statutes enacted for the benefit of minority groups should not block these forward-looking considerations. * * *

JUSTICE O'CONNOR, concurring in the judgment. * * *

In my view, the proper initial inquiry in evaluating the legality of an affirmative action plan by a public employer under Title VII is no different from that required by the Equal Protection Clause. In either case, consistent with the congressional intent to provide some measure of protection to the interests of the employer's nonminority employees, the employer must have had a firm basis for believing that remedial action was required. An employer would have such a firm basis if it can point to a statistical disparity sufficient to support a prima facie claim under Title VII by the employee beneficiaries of the affirmative action plan of a pattern or practice claim of discrimination.

[Justice O'Connor argued that the constitutional standard for public employer affirmative action plans is consistent with the *Weber* standard for private employer affirmative action plans. In both cases, the Court has required that the employer have a "firm basis" for concluding that action be necessary to remedy past discrimination. In neither case has the Court required an employer to prove or admit that it "actually discriminated against women or minorities." Hence, evidence sufficient for a prima facie case under Title VII would justify an employer's adoption of voluntary affirmative action.]

* * * At the time the plan was adopted, not one woman was employed in respondents' 238 skilled craft positions, and the plan recognized that women "are not strongly motivated to seek employment in job classifications where they have not been traditionally employed because of the limited opportunities that have existed in the past for them to work in such classifications." Additionally, the plan stated that respondents "recognize[d] that mere prohibition of discriminatory practices is not enough to remedy the effects of past practices and to permit attainment of an equitable representation of minorities, women and handicapped persons," and that "the selection and appointment processes are areas where hidden discrimination frequently occurs." Thus, the respondents had the expectation that the plan "should result in improved personnel practices that will benefit all Agency employees who may have been subjected to discriminatory personnel practices in the past." * * *

[Justice O'Connor rejected Justice Scalia's characterization of the decision as resting upon a single factor, sex. She credited the Director's testimony that he looked at the "whole picture," and chose Joyce for a variety of reasons, one of which was her sex.] While I agree * * * that an affirmative action program that automatically and blindly promotes those marginally qualified candidates falling within a preferred race or gender category, or that can be equated with a permanent plan of "proportionate representation by race and sex," would violate Title VII, I cannot agree that this was such a case. Rather, as the Court demonstrates, Joyce's sex was simply used as a "plus" factor.

In this case, I am also satisfied that the respondent had a firm basis for adopting an affirmative action program. Although the District Court found no discrimination against women in fact, at the time the affirmative action plan was adopted, there were *no* women in its skilled craft positions. Petitioner concedes that women constituted approximately 5% of the local labor pool of skilled craft workers in 1970. Thus, when compared to the percentage of women in the qualified work force, the statistical disparity would have been sufficient for a prima facie Title VII case brought by unsuccessful women job applicants. * * *

[JUSTICE WHITE's dissenting opinion urged his colleagues to overrule *Weber* (an opinion he joined in 1979), because the Court's reinterpretation of it was "a perversion of Title VII."]

JUSTICE SCALIA, with whom THE CHIEF JUSTICE [REHNQUIST] joins and with whom JUSTICE WHITE joins in Parts I and II, dissenting.

With a clarity which, had it not proved so unavailing, one might well recommend as a model of statutory draftsmanship, Title VII of the Civil Rights Act of 1964 declares:

"It shall be an unlawful employment practice for an employer—

"(1) to fail or refuse to hire or to discharge any individual, or otherwise to discriminate against any individual with respect to his compensation, terms, conditions, or privileges of employment, because of such individual's race, color, religion, sex, or national origin; or

"(2) to limit, segregate, or classify his employees or applicants for employment in any way which would deprive or tend to deprive any individual of employment opportunities or otherwise adversely affect his status as an employee, because of such individual's race, color, religion, sex, or national origin."

The Court today completes the process of converting this from a guarantee that race or sex will *not* be the basis for employment determinations, to a guarantee that it often *will*. Ever so subtly, without even alluding to the last obstacles preserved by earlier opinions that we now push out of our path, we effectively replace the goal of a discrimination-free society with the quite incompatible goal of proportionate representation by race and by sex in the workplace. * * *

[In Part I of his dissent, Justice Scalia argued that the Court and Justice O'Connor wrongly ignored the District Court's finding of fact that "if the Affirmative Action Coordinator had not intervened, 'the decision as to whom to promote . . . would have been made by [the Road Operations Division Director],' who had recommended that Johnson be appointed to the position"; and the further findings of fact that Johnson was "more qualified for the position" and that Joyce's gender was "the determining factor" in her selection. Justice Scalia maintained in Part II that the Court's opinion sanctioned affirmative action plans to remedy societal rather than employer discrimination, a holding contrary to *Wygant* and in tension with *Bakke*.]

[III] I have omitted from the foregoing discussion the most obvious respect in which today's decision o'erleaps, without analysis, a barrier that was thought still to be overcome. In *Weber*, this Court held that a private-sector affirmative action training program that overtly discriminated against white applicants did not violate Title VII. However, although the majority does not advert to the fact, until today the applicability of *Weber* to public employers remained an open question. In *Weber* itself, and in later decisions, this Court has repeatedly emphasized that *Weber* involved only a private employer. This distinction between public and private employers has several possible justifications. *Weber* rested in part on the assertion that the 88th Congress did not wish to intrude too deeply into private employment decisions. Whatever validity that assertion may have with respect to private employers (and I think it negligible), it has none with respect to public employers or to the 92d Congress that brought them within Title VII. Another reason for limiting *Weber* to private employers is that state agencies, unlike private actors, are subject to the Fourteenth Amendment. As noted earlier, it would be strange to construe Title VII to permit discrimination by public actors that the Constitution forbids.

In truth, however, the language of 42 U.S.C. § 2000e–2 draws no distinction between private and public employers, and the only good reason for creating such a distinction would be to limit the damage of *Weber*. It would be better, in my view, to acknowledge that case as fully applicable precedent, and to use the Fourteenth Amendment ramifications—which *Weber* did not address and which are implicated for the first time here—as the occasion for reconsidering and overruling it. It is well to keep in mind just how thoroughly *Weber* rewrote the statute it purported to construe. The language of that statute, as quoted at the outset of this dissent, is unambiguous[.] *Weber* disregarded the text of the statute, invoking instead its " 'spirit,' " and "practical and equitable [considerations] only partially perceived, if perceived at all, by the 88th Congress" (Blackmun, J., concurring). It concluded, on the basis of these intangible guides, that Title VII's prohibition of intentional discrimination on the basis of race and sex does not prohibit intentional discrimination on the basis of race and sex, so long as it is "designed to break down old patterns of racial [or sexual] segregation and hierarchy," "does not unnecessarily trammel the interests of the white [or male] employees," "does not require the discharge of white [or male] workers and their replacement with new black [or female] hirees," "does [not] create an absolute bar to the advancement of white [or male] employees," and "is a temporary measure . . . not intended to maintain racial [or sexual] balance, but simply to eliminate a manifest racial [or sexual] imbalance." In effect, *Weber* held that the legality of intentional discrimination by private employers against certain disfavored groups or individuals is to be judged not by Title VII but by a judicially crafted code of conduct, the contours of which are determined by no discernible standard, aside from (as the dissent convincingly demonstrated) the divination of congressional "purposes" belied by the face of the statute and by its legislative history. We have been recasting that self-promulgated code of conduct ever since—and what it has led us to today adds to the reasons for abandoning it.

The majority's response to this criticism of *Weber* [see note 7 of the majority opinion] asserts that, since "Congress has not amended the statute to reject our construction, . . . we . . . may assume that our interpretation was correct." This assumption, which frequently haunts our opinions, should be put to rest. It is based, to begin with, on the patently false premise that the correctness of statutory construction is to be measured by what the current Congress desires, rather than by what the law as enacted meant. To make matters worse, it assays the current Congress's desires *with respect to the particular provision in isolation*, rather than (the way the provision was originally enacted) as part of a total legislative package containing many *quids pro quo*. Whereas the statute as originally proposed may have presented to the enacting Congress a question such as "Should hospitals be required to provide medical care for indigent patients, with federal subsidies to offset the cost?," the question theoretically asked of the later Congress, in order to establish the "correctness" of a judicial interpretation that the statute provides no subsidies, is simply "Should the medical care that hospitals are required to provide for indigent patients be federally subsidized?" Hardly the same question—and many of those legislators who accepted the subsidy provisions in order to gain the votes necessary for enactment of the care requirement would not vote for the subsidy in isolation, now that an unsubsidized care requirement is, thanks to the judicial opinion, safely on the books. But even accepting the flawed premise that the intent of the current Congress, with respect to the provision in isolation, is determinative, one must ignore rudimentary principles of political science to draw any conclusions regarding that intent from the *failure* to enact legislation. The "complicated check on legislation," The Federalist No. 62, p. 378 C. Rossiter ed. 1961), erected by our Constitution creates an inertia that makes it impossible to assert with any degree of assurance that congressional failure to act represents (1) approval of the status quo, as opposed to (2) inability to agree upon how to alter the status quo, (3) unawareness of the status quo, (4) indifference to the status quo, or even (5) political cowardice * * *. I think we should admit that vindication by congressional inaction is a canard.

Justice Stevens' concurring opinion emphasizes "the undoubted public interest in 'stability and orderly development of the law' " that often requires adherence to an erroneous decision. As I have described above, however, today's decision is a demonstration not of stability and order but of the instability and unpredictable expansion which the substitution of judicial improvisation for statutory text has produced. For a number of reasons, *stare decisis* ought not to save *Weber*. First, this Court has applied the doctrine of *stare decisis* to civil rights statutes less rigorously than to other laws. See *Maine v. Thiboutot*, 448 U.S. 1, 33 (1980) (Powell, J., dissenting); *Monroe v. Pape*, [365 U.S. 167, 221–22 (1961)] (Frankfurter, J., dissenting in part). Second, * * * *Weber* was itself a dramatic departure from the Court's prior Title VII precedents, and can scarcely be said to be "so consistent with the warp and woof of civil rights law as to be beyond question." Third, *Weber* was decided a mere seven years ago, and has provided little guidance to persons seeking to conform their conduct to the law, beyond the proposition that Title VII does not mean what it says. Finally, "even under the most stringent test for the propriety of overruling a statutory decision . . .—'that it appear beyond doubt . . . that [the decision] misapprehended the meaning of the controlling provision,' " *Weber* should be overruled.

In addition to complying with the commands of the statute, abandoning *Weber* would have the desirable side effect of eliminating the requirement of willing suspension of disbelief that is currently a credential for reading our opinions in the affirmative action field—from *Weber* itself, which demanded belief that the corporate employer adopted the affirmative action program "voluntarily," rather than under practical compulsion from government contracting agencies, to *Bakke*, a Title VI case cited as authority by the majority here, which demanded belief that the University of California took race into account as merely one of the many diversities to which it felt it was educationally important to expose its medical students, to today's opinion, which—in the face of a plan obviously designed to force promoting officials to prefer candidates from the favored racial and sexual classes, warning them that their "personal commitment" will be determined by how successfully they "attain" certain numerical goals, and in the face of a particular promotion awarded to the less qualified applicant by an official who "did little or nothing" to inquire into sources "critical" to determining the final candidates' relative qualifications other than their sex—in the face of all this, demands belief that we are dealing here with no more than a program that "merely authorizes that consideration be given to affirmative action concerns when evaluating qualified applicants." Any line of decisions rooted so firmly in naiveté must be wrong. * * *

Today's decision does more, however, than merely reaffirm *Weber*, and more than merely extend it to public actors. It is impossible not to be aware that the practical effect of our holding is to accomplish *de facto* what the law—in language even plainer than that ignored in *Weber*, see 42 U.S.C. § 2000e–2(j)—forbids anyone from accomplishing *de jure*: in many contexts it effectively *requires* employers, public as well as private, to engage in intentional discrimination on the basis of race or sex. This Court's prior interpretations of Title VII, especially the decision in *Griggs*, subject employers to a potential Title VII suit whenever there is a noticeable imbalance in the representation of minorities or women in the employer's work force. * * * If, however, employers are free to discriminate through affirmative action, without fear of "reverse discrimination" suits by their nonminority or male victims, they are offered a threshold defense against Title VII liability premised on numerical disparities. Thus, after today's decision the *failure* to engage in reverse discrimination is economic folly, and arguably a breach of duty to shareholders or taxpayers, wherever the cost of anticipated Title VII litigation exceeds the cost of hiring less capable (though still minimally capable) workers. (This situation is more likely to obtain, of course, with respect to the least skilled jobs—perversely creating an incentive to discriminate against precisely those members of the nonfavored groups *least* likely to have profited from societal discrimination in the past.) It is predictable, moreover, that this incentive will be greatly magnified by economic pressures brought to bear by government contracting agencies upon employers who refuse to discriminate in the fashion we have now approved. A statute designed to establish a color-blind and gender-blind workplace has thus been converted into a powerful engine of racism and sexism, not merely *permitting* intentional race- and sex-based discrimination, but often making it, through operation of the legal system, practically compelled.

It is unlikely that today's result will be displeasing to politically elected officials, to whom it provides the means of quickly accommodating the demands of organized groups to achieve concrete, numerical improvement in the economic status of particular constituencies. Nor will it displease the world of corporate and governmental employers (many of whom have filed briefs as *amici* in the present case, all on the side of Santa Clara) for whom the cost of hiring less qualified workers is often substantially less—and infinitely more predictable—than the cost of litigating Title VII cases and of seeking to convince federal agencies by nonnumerical means that no discrimination exists. In fact, the only losers in the process are the Johnsons of the country, for whom Title VII has been not merely repealed but actually inverted. The irony is that these individuals—predominantly unknown, unaffluent, unorganized—suffer this injustice at the hands of a Court fond of thinking itself the champion of the politically impotent. I dissent.

NOTES ON JOHNSON

1. *What Happened to* Weber? The debate in *Weber* is hardly recognizable in *Johnson*, not only because there are two new players (Justices O'Connor and Scalia), but also because the old players changed their positions. Justice White switched from the *Weber* majority to overruling the decision, Justice Stevens switched from probable dissent from *Weber* (a case where he did not actually vote) to an aggressive approval of affirmative action, and Justice Powell joined the Brennan opinion that went much further than his opinion in *Regents of the University of California v. Bakke*, 438 U.S. 265 (1978). (Like Stevens, Powell did not vote in *Weber* but, according to an internal memorandum, leaned against the Brennan approach.) Almost as dramatic is Justice

Brennan's new rationale for affirmative action, which ignored his *Weber* reasoning that Title VII was mainly aimed at bringing racial minorities into the workplace. Recall the origins of Title VII's prohibition of sex discrimination, namely, Judge Smith's killer amendment. Note, too, that the dissenting Justices in *Johnson* pretty much ignored the legislative history of the 1964 statute.

2. *Congressional Acquiescence?* Footnote 7 of the Court's opinion is a classically dynamic move: whatever the original validity of *Weber* as implementing the intent or purpose of the 1964 Congress, it should not be reconsidered because Congress in the 1980s approved of the decision. Justice Scalia considered this argument a "canard," but the end of his opinion suggests why Justice Brennan may have been right. The powerful political forces inside the Beltway—labor unions, civil rights groups, and business interests—were satisfied with *Weber*, because it allowed them to advance their own goals (such as avoiding *Griggs* lawsuits) relatively cheaply, at least to them. The cost-payers were the diffuse group of blue-collar males like Paul Johnson and Brian Weber, unorganized and ill-represented on Capitol Hill. This point seems accurate, and it suggests that Congress in the 1980s was also happy with *Weber*. (By the way, and contrary to the Court's footnote 7, hearings were held in 1981 on a constitutional amendment introduced in Congress to override *Weber* and other affirmative action cases; none of the political powerhouses showed up, demonstrating the absence of interest among the powerful lobbies to override *Weber*.)

Justice Scalia's main point is a normative one, of course. He considers it objectionable for the Court to pay any attention to what goes on, or doesn't go on, in Congress short of formal bicameral approval mandated by Article I, § 7. And he also seems to have sympathy for the downtrodden, politically powerless, blue-collar white men who pay the price for affirmative action. Is this an appropriate factor to consider in statutory interpretation? Should statutory ambiguities be resolved *against* the more politically potent interests?

3. *The Court/Congress/President Civil Rights Game.* Recall that the blue-collar men whom Justice Scalia claims are politically "impotent" elected President Reagan twice, based upon a platform hostile to affirmative action—and Reagan delivered on his platform by appointing Rehnquist Chief Justice, elevating Scalia to the Court, and trying to elevate Judge Robert Bork to the Court (after *Johnson*). Although Bork was defeated, Reagan ended up appointing Judge Anthony Kennedy, a conservative on issues of race discrimination. Because Kennedy replaced Powell—Brennan's critical fifth vote in *Johnson*—the Court in 1988 was poised to shift civil rights policy rightward. Four Justices (Rehnquist, White, Scalia, Kennedy) were openly opposed to affirmative action, and one Justice (O'Connor) was skeptical. The Court had a great deal of room to maneuver, as a rightward shift in policy could be protected against congressional override by a presidential veto (by Reagan or his successor, George H.W. Bush).

C. THE COURT'S RETREAT FROM *GRIGGS*, CONGRESS'S RESPONSE, AND NEW DIRECTIONS FOR AFFIRMATIVE ACTION DOCTRINE

The 1988–89 Term included several employment discrimination cases that bitterly divided the Court. The most important was *Wards Cove Packing Co. v. Atonio*, 490 U.S. 642 (1989), rejecting a Title VII claim against the operation of two salmon canneries in Alaska. Unskilled positions at the canneries were staffed almost entirely by Pacific Americans, while about half of the skilled office positions were filled by whites, usually hired through personal references. A cannery employee could not be promoted to an office position. The cannery jobs paid a lot less than the office jobs. Cannery employees ate and lived in separate areas from the office employees. This arrangement may be viewed as a classic "plantation" set-up, and the cannery employees sued Wards Cove for discriminating against them in making its office hires. The Ninth Circuit held that plaintiffs made out a prima facie case of disparate impact employment discrimination under *Griggs*. The Supreme Court reversed. The majority opinion was written by Justice White and was joined by Chief Justice Rehnquist and Justices O'Connor, Scalia, and Kennedy, none of whom had joined Justice Brennan's *Johnson* opinion.

The majority held that the lower court's approach would impose excessive burdens on employers to get good numbers, and would encourage such employers to adopt quotas—actions in tension with § 703(j). Thus, a prima facie case of disparate impact discrimination is not made out unless the plaintiffs demonstrate that the bad numbers are out of line with the number of "qualified" minority applicants for the positions in question. "As long as there are no barriers or practices deterring qualified nonwhites from applying for noncannery positions, if the percentage of selected applicants who are nonwhite is not significantly less than the percentage of qualified applicants who are nonwhite, the employer's selection mechanism probably does not operate with a disparate impact upon minorities." The Court disapproved the Ninth Circuit's focus on the substantial disparity between the overwhelming minority composition of cannery workers and their trivial representation among office workers. To make out a prima facie case, the plaintiffs would have to show that the poor minority representation among office workers is disproportionate to the percentage of qualified minority applicants for those positions.

The Court remanded the case to the lower courts to reevaluate the disparate impact claim, but also set forth some guidelines for the lower courts to follow. Plaintiffs' burden of proof in disparate impact cases includes the burden of identifying not only a statistical disparity in light of qualified applicants, but also the specific employment practice that caused the disparity. The *Wards Cove* plaintiffs argued that a variety of practices contributed to the bad numbers— nepotism in hiring for office positions, the firm's refusal to advertise such positions locally, and its failure to consider cannery employees for promotions. The Court admonished the plaintiffs "to demonstrate that the disparity they complain of is the result of one or more of the employment practices that they are attacking here, specifically showing that each challenged practice has a significantly disparate impact on employment opportunities for whites and nonwhites." In response to plaintiffs' argument that such a burden is unfair, the Court noted that "liberal civil discovery rules give plaintiffs access to employers' records in an effort to document their claims," and that most employers are required to keep impact-related employment records as a matter of federal law. If plaintiffs were to succeed in establishing a prima facie disparate impact case, the Court further stated that the employer would have the burden of producing some evidence that the challenged practices were justified business practices. The burden of persuasion would remain with the plaintiffs.

According to the *Wards Cove* majority, disparate impact plaintiffs would have to persuade the finder of fact (1) that there was a statistical disparity, (2) that the disparity could be linked to specific employment practices, and (3) that those practices did not have a substantial business justification. Dissenting were the four Justices remaining from the *Johnson* majority (Brennan, Marshall, Blackmun, and Stevens). The dissenters argued that the Court's opinion, especially its dicta about plaintiffs' burden of persuasion on the business justification defense, represented a striking departure from existing law and a partial renunciation of *Griggs*.

At about the same time it was deciding *Wards Cove* (June 5, 1989), the Supreme Court handed down five other decisions that gave a narrow construction to Title VII and related statutes. In *Martin v. Wilks*, 490 U.S. 755 (June 12, 1989), the same 5–4 majority held that white employees who were not parties to original job discrimination litigation could challenge court-approved consent decrees providing for affirmative action. In *McLean Credit Union v. Patterson,* 491 U.S. 164 (June 15, 1989), the same majority narrowly interpreted the Civil Rights Act of 1866, to deprive employees of contract claims based upon race-based workplace harassment. In *Lorance v. AT & T Technologies*, 490 U.S. 900 (June 12, 1989), the Court in a 5–3 vote held that Title VII's statute of limitations for challenging seniority plans begins to run when the plan is adopted, not when the plan is applied to specific individuals. In *Independent Federation of Flight Attendants v. Zipes*, 491 U.S. 754 (June 22, 1989), a 5–2 Court held that Title VII does not provide for the statutory award of counsel fees against intervening defendants unless the intervenors' action is frivolous. And in *Price Waterhouse v. Hopkins*, 490 U.S. 228 (May 1, 1989), a Court divided on other issues unanimously held that employment decisions motivated in part by prejudice do not violate Title VII if the employer can show after the fact that the same decision would have been made irrespective of the intentional discrimination.

These decisions created a number of practical difficulties for litigants challenging discriminatory employment practices. More generally, they signaled a determination by five Justices to close off the expansion of older civil rights statutes to help modern litigants (*Patterson*), to provide more procedural advantages for defendants in Title VII cases (*Wards Cove, Price Waterhouse, Lorance*), and, most important, to discourage employers from adopting affirmative action programs (*Wards Cove, Martin*). As to the last item, the Court earlier in the Term had struck down the Richmond municipal program for setting aside business for minority-owned enterprises in *City of Richmond v. J.A. Croson Co.*, 488 U.S. 469 (1989).

These six statutory job-discrimination decisions shocked the nation's civil rights community, which immediately sought to override them legislatively. On February 27, 1990, Senator Kennedy (D–MA) and 33 co-sponsors introduced S. 2104, the Civil Rights Act of 1990. A similar House bill, H.R. 4000, was introduced by Representative Augustus Hawkins (D–CA) at the same time. The bill's purpose was "to respond to the Supreme Court's recent decisions by restoring the civil rights protections that were dramatically limited by those decisions." The substantive sections of the bill then amended Title VII and § 1981 to override one or more of the six offending Supreme Court cases, plus three earlier ones as well. The sponsors of the bill roundly condemned the Supreme Court's performance. "I believe the Supreme Court's recent rulings represent an effort to renege on history," said Senator Jeffords (R–VT). 136 Cong. Rec. S1022 (daily ed. Feb. 7, 1990).

The George H.W. Bush Administration agreed that *Patterson* and *Lorance* should be overridden, but opposed the overrides of *Wards Cove* and *Martin v. Wilks* on the ground that the overrides as drafted encouraged employers to adopt racial quotas, in violation of § 703(j). See Letter from Attorney General Richard Thornburgh to Senator Kennedy, Apr. 3, 1990. The sponsors realized that they did not have enough votes to override a presidential veto, and the result was a series of negotiations to work out a compromise bill. Between June and October 1990, rotating groups representing liberal Democrats, moderate Republicans, and the Administration engaged in such negotiations—which continued after the Senate passed a revised bill on July 18 (by a vote of 65–34) and the House passed its own bill on August 3 (by a vote of 272–154), and after the submission of conference reports on September 26 and October 12.

The final conference bill made a number of changes in the controversial *Wards Cove* provision in a final effort to appease the White House and/or to obtain Republican support for the bill. Specifically, the bill included a more liberal definition of the business necessity defense in disparate impact cases, required that plaintiffs prove which employer practices caused the disparate impact alleged, confirmed that bad numbers alone do not violate Title VII, and reiterated that Title VII does not require quotas. 136 Cong. Rec. S15,327 (daily ed. Oct. 16, 1990) (statement of Sen. Kennedy). Nonetheless, the President vetoed the bill, and the Senate failed to override the veto by one vote (66–34).

The *Wards Cove* issue was a minor theme of the 1990 off-year elections, which yielded a net gain to the Democrats of one senator and about a dozen House members. On January 3, 1991, the bill that had come so close in 1990 was reintroduced as the Civil Rights and Women's Equity in Employment Act of 1991, H.R. 1, 102d Cong., 1st Sess. (1991). Hearings were held before the Education & Labor and the Judiciary Committees in February and March 1991, the Committees reported a very liberal bill, and the House passed H.R. 1 on June 5, 1991. 137 Cong. Rec. H3924–25 (daily ed. June 5, 1991). It was a bill likely to be vetoed.

Again, once the bill reached the Senate floor, bipartisan negotiations intensified. Negotiations yielded a new compromise bill, the Danforth-Kennedy substitute, S. 1745, which significantly rewrote the House bill, just as the Senate had done in 1990. On the *Wards Cove* issues, S. 1745 simplified the burdens of proof in disparate impact cases (by adding new § 703(k)(1)(A)), generally required that plaintiffs link specific employer practices to their claimed disparate impact (see new § 703(k)(1)(B)), and abandoned prior efforts to define "business necessity" and left the definition to pre-*Wards Cove* case law (see § 3(2) of the Act). Importantly, new § 703(k) represented a clear congressional ratification of *Griggs* in the text of the job discrimination law, but a ratification setting limits on disparate impact lawsuits. According to some inside-the-beltway accounts, at a meeting with President Bush in mid-October, several GOP senators told the President that they wanted to vote for a civil rights bill and would vote to override a veto. After the meeting, President Bush dramatically announced his support for broad override legislation, after a few more changes.

The final language of the bill (with much focus on § 703(k)) was hammered out during the week of October 21. During the Senate's debate upon the compromise bill, between October 25 and 30, numerous amendments were accepted and rejected and—perhaps not surprisingly given the tools of interpretation used by the courts— a flurry of "interpretive statements" or "memoranda" were inserted into the Congressional Record to "explain" what the bill now "meant." Senator Danforth (R–MO), a key architect of the compromise, offered his own interpretive memorandum, as well as the following wisdom, in response to attempts to amend the bill to forbid courts from using legislative history to interpret provisions of the 1991 Act (137 Cong. Rec. S15325 (daily ed. Oct. 29, 1991)):

> It is very common for Members of the Senate to try to affect the way in which a court will interpret a statute by putting things into the Congressional Record. * * * [A] court would be well advised to take with a large grain of salt floor debate and statements placed into the Congressional Record which purport to create an interpretation for the legislation that is before us. * * * [A]ny judge who tries to make legislative history out of the free-for-all that takes place on the floor of the Senate is on very dangerous grounds.

The Senate passed S. 1745 on October 30, and the House passed it on November 7, 1991, in both cases by overwhelming margins (reflecting the new bipartisan consensus). The President signed the bill on November 21, 1991, as the "Civil Rights Act of 1991," Pub. L. No. 102–166, 105 Stat. 1071. See 1991 U.S. Code Cong. & Admin. News 768, for the President's signing statement.

PROBLEM ON THE CIVIL RIGHTS
ACT OF 1991 AND AFFIRMATIVE ACTION

Problem 1–4. You are a law clerk to *Weber*-hating Justice Scalia. The Civil Rights Act of 1991 has been enacted, and a new race-based affirmative action case comes before the Supreme Court, where a city has rejected promotions of municipal firefighters awarded on the basis of professionally developed tests, allegedly because there were not enough Latino- and African-American candidates awarded promotions. Does Justice Scalia have any *legal* basis for overruling *Weber* in, say, 2009? Does he have any *legal* basis for finding that Caucasian-American fire-fighters should have a Title VII claim for relief? Consider the text of the 1991 act. New § 703(m), added in 1991, says this:

> (m) Except as otherwise provided in this title, an unlawful employment practice is established when the complaining party demonstrates that race, color, religion, sex, or national origin was a motivating factor for any employment practice, even though other factors also motivated the practice.

Should Justice Scalia rely on new § 703(m) as a reason to overrule *Weber*? Would it make a difference if you told him § 703(m) was added to override *Hopkins* and to provide a more plaintiff-friendly burden of proof in "mixed motive" cases?

Section 116 of the Civil Rights Act of 1991 said this: "Nothing in the amendments made by this title shall be construed to affect court-ordered remedies, affirmative action, or conciliation agreements, that are in accordance with the law." Jot down your answer and consider the most recent case.

Ricci v. DeStefano
557 U.S. 557 (2009).

In 2003, 118 New Haven firefighters took examinations to qualify for promotion to the rank of lieutenant or captain. The results would determine which firefighters would be considered for promotions during the next two years, and the order in which they would be considered. The City contracted with Industrial/Organizational Solutions, Inc. (IOS), a well-regarded job-testing firm for police and fire departments, to develop and administer the examinations. IOS representatives worked with officials and firefighters (including minority firefighters) within the department to develop written and oral tests that would be related to the job requirements and would be fair to all groups.

Seventy-seven candidates completed the lieutenant examination—43 persons of European ancestry, 19 of African ancestry, and 15 of Latino ancestry. Of those, 34 candidates passed—25 European Americans, 6 African Americans, and 3 Latino Americans. Eight lieutenant positions were vacant at the time of the examination; the top 10 candidates were eligible for an immediate promotion to lieutenant, and all were of European ancestry. Subsequent vacancies would have allowed at least three African-American candidates to be considered for promotion to lieutenant. Forty-one candidates completed the captain examination—25 European Americans, 8 African Americans, and 8 Latino Americans. Of those, 22 candidates passed—16 European Americans, 3 African Americans, and 3 Latino Americans. Seven captain positions were vacant at the time of the examination; 9 candidates were eligible for an immediate promotion to captain—7 European Americans and 2 Latino Americans.

When the examination results showed that white candidates had outperformed minority candidates, Mayor DeStefano and other local politicians opened a public debate that turned rancorous. Some firefighters argued the tests should be discarded because the results showed the tests to be discriminatory. They threatened a discrimination lawsuit if the City made promotions based on the tests. Other firefighters said the exams were neutral, and they threatened a discrimination lawsuit if the City, relying on the statistical racial disparity, ignored the test results and denied promotions to the candidates who had performed well. In the end, New Haven threw out the examinations.

White and Latino firefighters who likely would have been promoted based on their test performances sued the City and some of its officials. They alleged that, by discarding the test results, the City and its officials discriminated against them based on their race, in violation of Title VII and the Equal Protection Clause. New Haven defended its actions, arguing that, if officials had certified the results, they could have faced liability under Title VII for adopting a practice that had a disparate impact on the minority firefighters.

The District Court granted summary judgment for the City, and the Court of Appeals (in a panel that included Judge, now Justice, Sonia Sotomayor) affirmed. Joined by Chief Justice Roberts and Justices Scalia, Thomas, and Alito, **Justice Kennedy**'s opinion for the Court ruled that "race-based action like the City's in this case is impermissible under Title VII unless the employer can demonstrate a strong basis in evidence that, had it not taken the action, it would have been liable under the disparate-impact statute. The respondents, we further determine, cannot meet that threshold standard. As a result, the City's action in discarding the tests was a violation of Title VII." Because New Haven's action violated Title VII, the Court did not reach the constitutional (equal protection) challenge.

Justice Kennedy's opinion rejected the firefighters' arguments that New Haven's disparate treatment of them (because of their white race) could not be justified by the threat of disparate impact lawsuits if the City had followed the test results. Reading the 1964 and 1991 Acts together, the Court held that an employer may adopt voluntary race-based remedies for apparent violations of the disparate impact provision of the 1991 Act, without violating the disparate treatment provision of the 1964 Act. The opinion also rejected the City's argument that a "good faith" belief that the tests violated the disparate impact provision would justify race-based remedies; such a lenient standard would, Justice Kennedy feared, open the door to a "*de facto* quota system," inconsistent with the premises of § 703(j).

"In searching for a standard that strikes a more appropriate balance, we note that this Court has considered cases similar to this one, albeit in the context of the Equal Protection Clause of the Fourteenth Amendment. The Court has held that certain government actions to remedy past racial discrimination—actions that are themselves based on race—are constitutional only where there is a 'strong basis in evidence' that the remedial actions were necessary." *Richmond v. J.A. Croson Co.*, 488 U.S. 469, 500 (1989) (O'Connor, J., for a majority), quoting *Wygant v. Jackson Bd. of Educ.*, 476 U.S. 267, 277 (1986) (Powell, J., for a plurality).

"The standard leaves ample room for employers' voluntary compliance efforts, which are essential to the statutory scheme and to Congress's efforts to eradicate workplace discrimination. And the standard appropriately constrains employers' discretion in making race-based decisions: It limits that discretion to cases in which there is a strong basis in evidence of disparate-impact liability, but it is not so restrictive that it allows employers to act only when there is a provable, actual violation." Was there a "strong basis in evidence" for New Haven to conclude that it would face disparate impact liability if it followed the test results? The disparate racial impact of the tests made out a prima facie case for liability under the 1991 Act, but Justice Kennedy ruled that the City had no "strong basis" to believe that its business necessity defense would not prevail in potential lawsuits.

Writing also for Justices Stevens, Souter, and Breyer, **Justice Ginsburg** dissented. She started with a broader context, namely, the long history of exclusion for African- and Latino-American citizens from municipal police and firefighting jobs, including near-total exclusion for most of New Haven's history. In light of this history of exclusion, especially in the officer ranks, New Haven had a great deal of discretion to question the results of a test that statistically favored persons of European descent. At public meetings (before the test results had been released), several observers claimed that the test had several questions not relevant to firefighting duties or command;

others pointed out that some firefighters had earlier access to study materials than others did; one participant pointed out that a neighboring city had a racially imbalanced force until it abandoned the use of standardized tests such as this one. Experts told the City that a more problem-oriented approach would have been practical and would probably have had a less racially discriminatory impact.

"Congress [has] declared unambiguously that selection criteria operating to the disadvantage of minority group members can be retained only if justified by business necessity. In keeping with Congress's design, employers who reject such criteria due to reasonable doubts about their reliability can hardly be held to have engaged in discrimination 'because of' race. A reasonable endeavor to comply with the law and to ensure that qualified candidates of all races have a fair opportunity to compete is simply not what Congress meant to interdict. I would therefore hold that an employer who jettisons a selection device when its disproportionate racial impact becomes apparent does not violate Title VII's disparate-treatment bar automatically or at all, subject to this key condition: The employer must have good cause to believe the device would not withstand examination for business necessity."

Justice Ginsburg maintained that her approach was more consistent with the EEOC's longstanding guidance on remedial race-based affirmative action permissible under Title VII and with the Court's precedents, specifically *Johnson*. She also argued that equal protection precedents were of "limited utility" because the Equal Protection Clause does *not* regulate state rules that only have a disparate race-based impact; there is no equal protection parallel to either *Griggs* or to the 1991 Act's provision for disparate impact liability. Even under the Court's announced standard, Justice Ginsburg maintained that the City had a "strong basis in evidence" to question whether the IOS-developed test really met the business necessity requirement of the 1991 Act. So many questions were raised about the test, and the City had followed it simply because the union insisted on such a test.

Writing also for Justices Scalia and Thomas, **Justice Alito** wrote a concurring opinion responding to Justice Ginsburg's factual points. Justice Alito's understanding was that the City's volte-face was politically motivated. "Almost as soon as the City disclosed the racial makeup of the list of firefighters who scored the highest on the exam, the City administration was lobbied by an influential community leader to scrap the test results, and the City administration decided on that course of action before making any real assessment of the possibility of a disparate-impact violation. To achieve that end, the City administration concealed its internal decision but worked— as things turned out, successfully—to persuade the [review board] that acceptance of the test results would be illegal and would expose the City to disparate-impact liability. But in the event that the [review board] was not persuaded, the Mayor, wielding ultimate decisionmaking authority, was prepared to overrule the [board] immediately. Taking this view of the evidence, a reasonable jury could easily find that the City's real reason for scrapping the test results was not a concern about violating the disparate-impact provision of Title VII but a simple desire to please a politically important racial constituency."

Justice Ginsburg replied that she would be in favor of a remand to see precisely what various options a "reasonable" jury would have accepted. Moreover, Justice Alito's understanding of the decisionmaking ignored the fact that the reviewing board—an unelected, politically insulated group of experts—made the actual decision, and the

Mayor did not. Finally, are all "political considerations" tantamount to race discrimination itself? "The real issue, then, is not whether the mayor and his staff were politically motivated; it is whether their attempt to score political points was legitimate (*i.e.,* nondiscriminatory). Were they seeking to exclude white firefighters from promotion (unlikely, as a fair test would undoubtedly result in the addition of white firefighters to the officer ranks), or did they realize, at least belatedly, that their tests could be toppled in a disparate-impact suit? In the latter case, there is no disparate-treatment violation. Justice Alito, I recognize, would disagree. In his view, an employer's action to avoid Title VII disparate-impact liability qualifies as a presumptively improper race-based employment decision. I reject that construction of Title VII. As I see it, when employers endeavor to avoid exposure to disparate-impact liability, they do not thereby encounter liability for disparate treatment."

NOTES ON THE NEW HAVEN FIREFIGHTERS CASE: WHAT IS THE STATUS OF WEBER?

1. *Have* Weber *and* Johnson *Been Overruled?* At no point did Justice Kennedy cite *Weber*, and his opinion made only a perfunctory reference to *Johnson*. Has *Weber* been overruled? Has *Johnson* been overruled? If these statutory precedents have been overruled, what might be the *legal* justification? And why did the *Ricci* majority not mention that it was overruling these precedents?

2. *What Is the Law Now?* Presumably, current Title VII law is the interpretation rendered by the Court majority in *Ricci*—but what is a "strong basis in evidence" for the existence of a *Griggs* violation? For example, would the *Ricci* Court have followed Justice O'Connor in *Johnson*, where she found that the employer had a "firm basis" for remedying prior discrimination? Recall that Justice Scalia (now part of the Court majority) rejected Justice O'Connor's reading of the record, in part because the District Court had found, as a matter of fact, that there had been "no discrimination" against women in *Johnson*. How can the "strong basis in evidence" standard be administered? Should the EEOC issue a guidance along these lines? If so, what should it say?

3. *Continuing the Court/Congress/President Civil Rights Game.* Notice how *Ricci* reflects the dynamic potential of the law-implementation process. Soon after the 1964 Act was adopted, the EEOC and the Court pushed Title VII to the left through liberal construction of the disparate impact claim for relief. Congress rejected proposals to trim back Title VII in the 1972 Amendments, and *Weber-Johnson* confirmed the evolution of Title VII toward a more strongly integrationist stance than Congress had probably assumed in 1964. But the Supreme Court pushed the statute in a more conservative direction—and Congress pushed back with the 1991 Amendments. As *Ricci* dramatically illustrates, the 1989 Supreme Court decisions did not push Title VII back to 1964—nor did the 1991 Amendments push Title VII back to the heyday of liberal interpretation in the 1970s. Instead, Title VII's text represents a pretty detailed compromise between the Brennan-Ginsburg vision for workplace diversity and the Rehnquist-Scalia-Alito vision for employer color-blindness.

A TRANSITIONAL NOTE

This chapter introduced you to the legislative lawmaking process, warts and all. The empirical generalizations and models of the political process presented in this chapter are worth considering as you study the rest of this book. For example, Chapters

5 and 6 consider public law theory—the jurisprudence of the common law and constitutional law, which are both overtly made by judges, and the jurisprudence of statutory interpretation, where the judge's discretion in construing a statute requires theoretical underpinnings as well. The chapter you have just completed is important for your approach to public law theory because that theory cannot be divorced from some conception of the legislative process.

Someone who accepts the pluralist conception of what the political process looks like has several options for normative theories of public law. One option would be to accept normatively what is assumed to happen empirically. Under this approach, there should be little outside (judicial) interference with the legislative process—let the market operate freely. In contrast, theorists who accept the pluralist conception empirically but not normatively would probably adopt a different, interventionist, judicial strategy. They might seek to create constitutional rights protecting individuals from certain legislative intrusions and might attempt to break down barriers preventing politically powerless groups from bargaining effectively in the legislative arena. To some of these theorists, techniques of forcing legislative reconsideration of an issue or otherwise promoting legislative deliberation are of no utility, since the mechanistic process of legislation allows no thoughtful, independent deliberation to occur. A third approach emphasizes the importance of administrative procedures and argues that they work to ameliorate negative consequences of interest group behavior. See, e.g., Steven Croley, *Public Interested Regulation*, 28 Fla. St. U. L. Rev. 7 (2000). Administrative process, one focus of Chapter 8, may be the most pervasive framework affecting policy outcomes because agencies implement the laws enacted by Congress and many administrative decisions are never challenged in court.

Alternatively, those who believe that legislators can operate somewhat autonomously from private political interests have a different set of theoretical possibilities available. For those who find a common weal that is different from the equilibrium of interest group power either incapable of formulation or a tyrannical imposition upon those with dissenting views unless it is a result of some democratic process, the proper response might include techniques strengthening the electoral connection between average voters and their agents, the legislators. Those who have greater faith in the capacity of legislators to formulate and promote a beneficent public interest might urge restructuring of the processes of representation to encourage legislative insulation from powerful private interests. Of course, it is sometimes difficult to determine which mechanisms facilitate which visions of the legislative process.

As you proceed through the rest of this book, ask yourself the following questions: (1) What assumptions about the political process are animating the judicial behavior under consideration? Are those conceptions realistic? How would public law theory change, in a given situation, if the judicial understanding of the political process were altered? Should judges modify public law theory in light of what social scientists or public choice theorists suggest about the nature of the political process? (2) What role, if any, should be played by the understandings of the constitutional framers? Should Madisonian theory be rejected in light of modern circumstances? Or should the courts attempt to develop public law theory that would encourage the representative process to act more in accord with Madison's vision? (3) In the modern world of interest group politics, is the legislature a truly legitimate entity to make important public policies largely unchallenged by judicial review? Conversely, in the modern world in which the meaning of the federal Constitution has strayed far from the original intent of the framers, does a court have a legitimate basis for interfering with legislative outcomes? Does democracy simply mean that voters have periodic opportunities to replace representatives, or should it mean more than that—and if so, do courts have any role in promoting enhanced democracy?

Modern American public law is the result of a complex, contentious lawmaking partnership among legislatures, administrative agencies, the courts, and the citizenry. The remainder of this book continues the inquiry about how this law is made.

CHAPTER 2

REPRESENTATIONAL STRUCTURES

■ ■ ■

Public policy, even in a modern democracy, is not created directly by the people but by their representatives. Hanna Pitkin, in *The Concept of Representation* (1967), analyzes political theories conceptualizing the ideal role of the representative. First, a representative body may be viewed as *descriptive* of the larger group, a microcosm of the collective. John Adams, for example, argued that a legislature "should be an exact portrait, in miniature, of the people at large, as it should think, feel, reason and act like them." Letter to John Penn, in 4 *The Works of John Adams* 205 (1851). Descriptive theory retains a robust constituency today, particularly in thinking about the representation of minority groups.

Second, the representative may be viewed as the *agent* of the people who selected her. In the most extreme form, the representative's every action must be explicitly authorized by her constituency, but a moderate position would urge the representative to act as she thinks her constituents would have her act if the constituency were in her position and knew all that she knows. Pluralist theories of democracy today tend to rely on a moderate version of such an agency theory.

Third, the representative may be viewed as the *trustee* of the interests of her constituents. She should exercise her own conscientious judgment on issues. As Madison put it, the role of representatives as trustees of the public good is to "refine and enlarge the public views" through the exercise of their wisdom, which "may best discern the true interest of their country, and whose patriotism and love of justice will be least likely to sacrifice it to temporary or partial considerations." *The Federalist #10.* Republican theories of government usually envision legislators as trustees charged with deliberating among themselves for the common good.

These three views of the representative are not mutually exclusive. Perhaps the ideal representative democracy would be one in which the legislative representatives broadly resemble the entire citizenry and thus naturally reflect the informed preferences of the majority, which happen to coincide with the best course of action for the society as a whole. In practice, however, these visions of representation lead in different directions. In connection with the choice of representatives, descriptive theory could favor proportionate representation, in which each important segment of society is represented in the legislature; agency theory could favor frequent elections, so that the representative's votes could be periodically reviewed by her constituents; trusteeship theory could tend to eschew frequent elections and strict proportionality in favor of a system that would choose wise people and (perhaps) keep them in office for long periods of time.

Section 1 of this chapter explores the constitutional structures that shape the way we choose our legislative representatives. We outline the electoral structures laid out in the Constitution and then explore the further limitations that the

Supreme Court has drawn from the constitutional norm of equal participation (a norm found in the Equal Protection Clause, the First Amendment, the Fifteenth Amendment, and elsewhere in the Constitution). Equality values include the principle of one person, one vote; a rule against racial vote dilution; and jurisprudence attempting to address gerrymandering, the political manipulation of district lines to produce a particular electoral result.

In § 2, we introduce several ways in which the eligibility to serve as a representative is restricted. The first vehicle for discussion is the case involving Representative Adam Clayton Powell, whom the people kept reelecting notwithstanding criminal and contempt charges against him. The Supreme Court in *Powell v. McCormack*, 395 U.S. 486 (1969), struck down the decision of the House of Representatives to exclude Powell. The Court's reasoning disallowing congressionally imposed qualifications in addition to those set forth in the Constitution served as the foundation for the Court's subsequent decision striking down state-imposed term limitations on federal lawmakers. We will discuss term limitations, which are a common feature of state legislatures and apply to most governors and to the President. Finally, we will focus on laws regulating candidate access to ballots because these laws significantly limit the choices voters can make on Election Day.

Section 3 examines the complex campaign finance system. Money has always been the lifeblood of elections, and how a polity regulates the use of money speaks loudly about its political self-image. Is money in politics "corrupting," and in what ways? How would each theory of representation provide a different answer to that question? Whatever the political theory of campaign finance, the First Amendment may be an impediment to extensive regulation of campaign finance, and this last part of the chapter introduces the debate within the First Amendment tradition.

1. ELECTORAL STRUCTURES AND EQUALITY VALUES

The Constitution, in Article I, specifies the broad outlines of our national representative legislature, the Congress. "All legislative Powers herein granted shall be vested in a Congress of the United States, which shall consist of a Senate and House of Representatives." U.S. Const. Art. I, § 1. From the outset, House members have been elected for two-year terms and apportioned among the states according to their population. *Id.* § 2, cl. 1 & 3. In 1911, Congress fixed House membership at 435. 37 Stat. 13, 14. The Constitution originally stated that each state would be represented by two senators elected to six-year terms by the state legislature. U.S. Const. Art. I, § 3, cl. 1. The Seventeenth Amendment, ratified in 1913, now provides that senators are directly elected.

The Constitution also specifies the framework for congressional elections. "The Times, Places and Manner of holding Elections for Senators and Representatives, shall be prescribed in each State by the Legislature thereof; but the Congress may at any time by Law make or alter such Regulations." *Id.* Art. I, § 4, cl. 1. Congress has exercised this authority in 2 U.S.C. §§ 1–9, providing, *inter alia*, for the date of each regular election; the number, apportionment, and reapportionment of representatives; and the manner in which to fill a vacancy. Persons qualified to vote for representatives "of the most numerous Branch of the State Legislature" are likewise qualified to vote for representatives and senators. U.S. Const. Art. I, § 2, cl. 1; *id.* amend. XVII, cl. 1. Pursuant to the authority of "[e]ach House [to] * * * Judge * * * the Elections, Returns and Qualifications of its own Members," *id.* Art. I, § 5, cl. 1, Congress has enacted a rather thorough code of provisions governing the resolution of contested elections. 2 U.S.C. §§ 381–396.

Every state has a bicameral legislative system with competing political parties except Nebraska, which has a nonpartisan unicameral legislature. The size of the state legislatures varies greatly.[1] For example, the lower house of the New Hampshire legislature contains 400 members, almost 17 times the number of its upper house. A member of the New Hampshire lower house represents around 3,000 people. In contrast, each of California's 80 members of its lower house represents a constituency about 140 times larger. Alaska has the smallest lower house, with 40 members. The number of members of the upper houses varies substantially as well, with Minnesota the largest with 67 and Alaska the smallest with 20.[2]

In most states, members of the upper house serve four-year terms; in 12 states such officeholders serve two-year terms. Lower-house members generally serve two-year terms. As of 2013, 15 states limit the number of terms their state legislators can serve (see § 2B of this chapter). Most states have annual rather than biennial legislative sessions, but in a majority of states the length of the session is limited, often to no more than 60 or 90 calendar days. In 34 states, either the governor or the legislature can call a special session.[3]

In this century, the composition of state and local legislatures, as well as of Congress, has been subject to various constitutional challenges, and the resulting jurisprudence has illuminated that the "right to vote" encompasses several different kinds of rights. Most basically, there is a right of *participation*. Outright exclusion from the vote—through such devices as the white primary, the poll tax, and durational residency requirements—is subject to searching judicial review.[4] The point of voting is to combine individual desires into a collective choice, however, so the right to participate, standing alone, is insufficient. Therefore, a second conception of the right to vote involves a right to a fair rule of *aggregation*. At its simplest level, this right encompasses the notion that legislators should represent

---

[1]   See National Conference of State Legislatures, *2010 Constituents Per State Legislative District Table*, http://www.ncsl.org/research/about-state-legislatures/2010–constituents-per-state-legislative-district.aspx.

[2]   The size of the legislature is important for many reasons. It affects, among other things, the costs and difficulty of campaigning for office, the visibility and prestige of members, the difficulty of managing and administering the work of the legislature, and perhaps the degree to which a constituent feels represented. Yet policymakers and scholars have given little attention to the relationship between state population and land area on the one hand and legislative size on the other.

[3]   For information on the makeup of state legislatures, see various websites provided by the National Conference of State Legislatures, such as http://www.ncsl.org/legislatures-elections/legisdata/number-of-legislators-and-length-of-terms.aspx (providing length of legislative terms for both houses) and http://www.ncsl.org/legislatures-elections/legislatures/legislative-session-length.aspx (providing length of session).

[4]   See, e.g., *Terry v. Adams,* 345 U.S. 461 (1953) (invalidating white primary as violating the Fifteenth Amendment); *Harper v. Virginia State Bd. of Elections*, 383 U.S. 663 (1966) (invalidating poll tax as violating Equal Protection Clause); *Dunn v. Blumstein*, 405 U.S. 330 (1972) (invalidating one-year residency requirement under Equal Protection Clause).

roughly an equal number of persons, the so-called "one person, one vote" requirement. More complex controversies involving aggregation include how to draw districts of equal population so that distinctive communities of interest are not split among different districts or otherwise have their political power submerged. As this chapter will explain, this problem of the *vote dilution* of distinctive communities—whether they are racial minorities or the minority political party—has generated complex litigation and confusing judicial responses.[5]

Constitutional constraints on aggregation frequently attack the practice of gerrymandering, the drawing of electoral district lines for political advantage. Consider the following gerrymandering techniques. *Cracking* occurs when a geographically concentrated political or racial group that is large enough to constitute a dominant force in a district is broken up by district lines and dispersed throughout two or more districts. It is therefore denied a realistic chance of being a majority in any of the districts. *Stacking* occurs when a large political or racial group is not split up, but rather is combined with and dominated by a larger opposition group that constitutes a supermajority. A classic example of stacking in the context of racial politics would be creating one large multimember district for the state legislature by combining two majority-black counties with four majority-white counties. *Packing* occurs when the majority finds itself unable completely to deny representation to a minority, but minimizes minority representation by concentrating the minority into as few districts as possible—for example, creating one 97% black district rather than two 60% black districts.

Although political or racial gerrymandering would usually be easier to accomplish if population equality among districts were not required, a requirement of population equality will not prevent any of these tactics. As you review the discussion that follows, consider whether the constitutional and statutory regulations of gerrymandering serve a coherent theory of representation, or perhaps are motivated by several theories.

A. ONE PERSON, ONE VOTE:
FORMAL EQUALITY IN REPRESENTATION

Numerical equality in representation (one person, one vote) now seems fundamental to our polity. For most of this country's history this was only an aspirational goal, however, because the issue was considered "nonjusticiable," an essentially "political question" unsuited to federal adjudication under Article III of the Constitution, which limits the federal judicial power to resolving "cases" and "controversies." The federal judicial reluctance to intervene in state and local legislative apportionment stemmed from concerns about federalism, from the notion that other government institutions were better suited to deal with essentially political issues, from the sense that no judicially administrable standard

---

[5] Pamela Karlan also posits a third conception of voting rights, as an integral part of *governance*. In this sense, voting involves not simply selecting a particular legislator, but being satisfied with the overall composition and operation of the legislative body in question. See *The Rights to Vote: Some Pessimism About Formalism*, 71 Tex. L. Rev. 1705, 1716–19 (1993). Her thesis is that the Supreme Court's decisions on voting rights are doctrinally incoherent because they fail to differentiate among the three interconnected features of a "right to vote."

could be created to decide when there was too much population deviation across legislative districts, and from the concern that federal injunctions to remedy the problem would be too difficult to define and administer, inappropriately embroiling the federal courts in local and state politics. The most famous catchphrase capturing these concerns is found in Justice Frankfurter's plurality opinion in *Colegrove v. Green*, 328 U.S. 549, 556 (1946): "Courts ought not to enter this political thicket." But when demographic shifts after World War II exacerbated population disparities in local, state, and federal electoral districts, with booming urban and suburban areas greatly underrepresented and rural areas overrepresented, the Supreme Court changed direction (over the strident objection of Justice Frankfurter). *Baker v. Carr*, 369 U.S. 186 (1962), reversed the longstanding judicial avoidance and held that equal protection attacks on legislative apportionment are justiciable.

Baker is still the leading case setting out the political question doctrine. Justice Brennan's opinion for the Court reasoned that the doctrine stems from the separation of powers within the national government. The Court's survey of its precedents concluded that decisions finding nonjusticiable political questions did so for one or more of the following reasons:

> a textually demonstrable constitutional commitment of the issue to a coordinate political department; or a lack of judicially discoverable and manageable standards for resolving it; or the impossibility of deciding without an initial policy determination of a kind clearly for nonjudicial discretion; or the impossibility of a court's undertaking independent resolution without expressing lack of the respect due coordinate branches of government; or an unusual need for unquestioning adherence to a political decision already made; or the potentiality of embarrassment from multifarious pronouncements by various departments on one question.

Since *Baker*, the Court has developed equal representation rules for the U.S. House of Representatives and state legislatures. The national Senate flouts rules of formal equality, of course. The state with the smallest population has as many senators as the one with the largest population. And this inequality is particularly entrenched in the Constitution; Article V provides that no state can be deprived of its "equal Suffrage in the Senate" without its consent. In part this is the result of the historic compromise at the Convention of 1787: the small states, fearing domination by the large states, were given the Senate to make them more secure. See Gordon Wood, *The Creation of the American Republic 1776–1787*, 553–62 (1998 ed.). In part, too, the Senate, with its six-year terms and larger geographic units of representation, reflects the Framers' desire that one body be insulated somewhat from "democratic" fluctuations, thus protecting property interests against "numbers." Under what theory of representation can this be justified?[6]

---

[6] It has been suggested that the structure of the Senate systematically redistributes wealth from large population states to small ones and dilutes the influence of racial minorities in Congress. See Lynn Baker & Samuel Dinkin, *The Senate: An Institution Whose Time Has Gone?*, 13 J.L. & Pol. 21 (1997); Frances Lee & Bruce Oppenheimer, *Sizing Up the Senate: The Unequal Consequence of Equal Representation* (1999). For overviews of objections to Senate structure, see Scott Bowman, *Wild Political Dreaming: Constitutional*

1. The House of Representatives

Article I, § 2 of the Constitution requires that the members of the House of Representatives be "chosen every second Year by the People of the several States" and "apportioned among the several States * * * according to their respective Numbers." The task of drawing congressional district lines is left to the state legislatures. In *Wesberry v. Sanders*, 376 U.S. 1 (1964), the Court struck down a Georgia congressional districting scheme in which some districts had more than twice the population of others, and stated that Article I, § 2 requires that "as nearly as is practicable one [person's] vote in a congressional election is to be worth as much as another's." Does the text of § 2 support such a holding? Justice Harlan's dissent in *Wesberry* argued that before the Civil War the text of § 2 specifically mandated inequality, for it excluded "Indians not taxed" from those counted for districting purposes and included only "three-fifths of all other Persons," that is, slaves. Hence it was most improbable that this provision of the Constitution protects against disproportionate districts within a state, he argued.

After *Wesberry*, the Court was faced with a series of cases in which it defined and applied the one person, one vote standard. In these cases, the Court first inquired whether there was a statistical disparity between the largest and smallest districts, and then it required the plaintiffs to show that disparities could have been reduced or eliminated by a "good faith effort to draw districts of equal population." If plaintiffs carried that burden of persuasion, then the state bore a burden of justifying the remediable disparities by reference to a "legitimate state goal." Under this approach, the Court struck down almost all the deviations that it examined.[7]

In *Karcher v. Daggett*, 462 U.S. 725 (1983), the Court struck down the New Jersey legislature's reapportionment of the state's congressional districts in response to the 1980 census, even though the population of the largest and smallest districts differed by only 0.6984%. In a 5–4 vote, the Court rejected a *de minimis* exception to Article I, § 2 and swore fidelity to "absolute population equality" as "the paramount objective." Applying the test described above, the Court concluded that the New Jersey plan failed under the first requirement because it could have achieved greater population equality "merely by shifting a handful of municipalities from one district to another." Nor did the state bear its burden of proving that the population variances were necessary to achieve some legitimate state objective, such as making districts compact, respecting municipal boundaries, preserving the cores of prior districts, or avoiding contests between incumbent representatives. The one justification presented by the state—the preservation of the voting strength of racial minority groups—was found to be factually unsupported.

Writing for four dissenters, Justice White argued that the Court's precedents did not require strict scrutiny of a "minuscule" deviation, and that good policy did not require such mathematical exactitude. The critical fifth vote in the case was

---

Reformation of the United States Senate, 72 Fordham L. Rev. 1017 (2004) (student note); Misha Tseytlin, *The United States Senate and the Problem of Equal State Suffrage*, 94 Geo. L.J. 859 (2006) (student note).

    7   See, e.g., *Kirkpatrick v. Preisler*, 394 U.S. 526, 530–31 (1969) (striking down redistricting plan leaving deviation of 5.97% between most and least populous congressional districts); *White v. Weiser*, 412 U.S. 783 (1973) (striking down plan leaving deviation of 4.13%).

that of Justice Stevens, who rejected the formalist approach of the majority opinion of Justice Brennan and embraced a more functional approach. "In evaluating * * * challenges to districting plans * * * I would consider whether the plan has a significant adverse impact on an identifiable political group, whether the plan has objective indicia of irregularity, and then, whether the State is able to produce convincing evidence that the plan nevertheless serves neutral, legitimate interests of the community as a whole." (We shall return to Stevens' concurring opinion below, in § 1C.) In response to Justices White and Stevens, Justice Brennan's opinion for the Court noted that exactitude in redistricting is now possible with the aid of computers, and that reality may explain why there was not a plethora of *Karcher* challenges after subsequent censuses.

Other issues have arisen, however. First, consider the obvious but difficult problem of allocating the seats in the House of Representatives. Allocating the 435 seats among 50 states of differing populations is made especially difficult because the Constitution guarantees each state at least one seat. The average size of a congressional district after the 1990 census was 572,466. The census found that Montana had 803,655 people, and under 2 U.S.C. § 2a(a), Montana was entitled to only one representative (it had two before the 1990 census), because its population was less than 150% the size of the average district. Montana complained that this "method of equal proportions" violates Article I, § 2: If Montana had retained its two districts, each would have varied from the average congressional district by — 170,638; with just one district, Montana varies from the average district by +231,189.[8] The District Court agreed that the principle of equal representation for equal numbers applied to intrastate districting in *Wesberry* should also be applied to interstate districting. Invoking *Baker v. Carr*, the Supreme Court rejected the government's argument on appeal that this is a nonjusticiable political question and reached the merits of Montana's claim. See *United States Dep't of Commerce v. Montana*, 503 U.S. 442 (1992). It unanimously upheld the apportionment, concluding that Congress had considered a variety of mathematical methods for House apportionment with the guidance of experts. Each method could be said to implement a norm of equal representation plausibly, but none could be said to be clearly superior based on simple equality principles. Thus, the mathematical precision required by *Wesberry* for intrastate congressional districts could not be required in making interstate comparisons.

Second, the census method of asking persons to identify themselves and then having census counters attempt to enumerate any others obviously produces an undercount of the total number of persons. Racial minorities are probably the group most prone to undercounting under the usual method.[9] By the use of statistical sampling, demographers can make a good faith estimate of the undercount. Is the Secretary of Commerce required by equality principles to revise the census based on such statistical sampling? No, held the unanimous Court in *Wisconsin v. City of*

---

[8]   After the 2010 census, Montana remained the largest district in the country with 994,416 voters in its one district, compared to 710,767 voters in an average congressional district.

[9]   See, e.g., Samuel Issacharoff & Allan Lichtman, *The Census Undercount and Minority Representation: The Constitutional Obligation of the States to Guarantee Equal Representation*, 13 Rev. Litig. 1 (1993); Nathaniel Persily, *The Law of the Census: How to Count, What to Count, Whom to Count, and Where to Count Them*, 32 Cardozo L. Rev. 755 (2011).

New York, 517 U.S. 1 (1996). Under the Constitution, Congress is charged with implementing an "actual Enumeration . . . in such Manner as [it] shall by Law direct," U.S. Const. Art. I, § 2, cl. 3, and has delegated the authority to do so to the Secretary of Commerce. The Secretary's exercise of discretion was not subject to heightened judicial scrutiny under either *Wesberry* (because, under *Montana*, it involved national rather than intrastate questions) or the Court's equal protection cases protecting racial minorities from discrimination (because the decision was not motivated by a desire to harm minorities). Applying a reasonableness standard, the Court deferred to the Secretary's decision to use traditional methods of census taking.

Third, even if the Secretary is not required to use statistical sampling to modify the final census results, may the Secretary choose to do so if he or she wishes? The Clinton Administration attempted to change policy on this question and factor in statistical sampling for the 2000 census. Here the Court's unanimity in census disputes evaporated. In *Dep't of Commerce v. U.S. House of Representatives*, 525 U.S. 316 (1999) (see Chapter 7, Problem 7–3), by a 5–4 vote, the Court held that the Census Act did not authorize the Secretary to use statistical sampling to modify the count obtained through traditional means. Although the decision turns on an interpretation of the federal statutes, such that presumably Congress could amend them to authorize or require statistical sampling, Justice Scalia, writing separately, suggested that statistically rooted revisions might even be unconstitutional as inconsistent with the Constitution's text (requiring an "actual Enumeration") and our longstanding tradition of how to conduct the census.[10]

2. State Legislatures

The Supreme Court in *Reynolds v. Sims*, 377 U.S. 533 (1964), held that apportionment in state legislatures must conform to the one person, one vote rule. The Court thereby reached the issue not considered in *Wesberry* (that holding rested upon Article I, § 2) and held that the Equal Protection Clause of the Fourteenth Amendment also ensures equality of representation. Chief Justice Warren's opinion for the Court reasoned:

> Legislators represent people, not trees or acres. Legislators are elected by voters, not farms or cities or economic interests. As long as ours is a representative form of government, * * * the right to elect legislators in a free and unimpaired fashion is a bedrock of our political system. It could hardly be gainsaid that a constitutional claim had been asserted by an allegation that certain otherwise qualified voters had been entirely prohibited from voting for members of their state legislature. And, if a State should provide that the votes of citizens in one part of the State

---

[10] Cf. *Utah v. Evans*, 536 U.S. 452 (2002), in which the Court held that the census technique of "hot-deck imputation"—whereby a housing unit with unknown population characteristics is assumed to have the same characteristics as its closest neighbor of the same type—may be used for purposes of apportionment of the House of Representatives. Justice O'Connor dissented on the ground that this technique was outlawed by the Census Act. Justice Thomas, joined by Justice Kennedy, dissented on constitutional grounds. Justice Scalia did not reach the merits, as he concluded that the appellants lacked standing.

should be given two times, or five times, or 10 times the weight of votes of citizens in another part of the State, it could hardly be contended that the right to vote of those residing in the disfavored areas had not been effectively diluted. * * * Of course, the effect of state legislative districting schemes which give the same number of representatives to unequal numbers of constituents is identical. * * *

Logically, in a society ostensibly grounded on representative government, it would seem reasonable that a majority of the people of a State could elect a majority of that State's legislators. To conclude differently, and to sanction minority control of state legislative bodies, would appear to deny majority rights in a way that far surpasses any possible denial of minority rights that might otherwise be thought to result. * * *

Does this reasoning provide a better explanation for *Wesberry*? (Justice Clark's concurring opinion in *Wesberry* in fact relied on the Equal Protection Clause, as did Justice Stevens' concurring opinion in *Karcher*.) Under what theory of representation is this point of view operating?

The equal representation assured in state legislatures is both broader and narrower than that assured in the federal legislature. It is broader because the precept applies to both houses of bicameral state legislatures, and not just the lower house. Chief Justice Warren explained why the *Reynolds* Court found the analogy to the U.S. Senate (which flouts the equal representation precept) unpersuasive at the state level:

> The system of representation in the two Houses of the Federal Congress is one ingrained in our Constitution, as part of the law of the land. It is one conceived out of compromise and concession indispensable to the establishment of our federal republic. Arising from unique historical circumstances, it is based on the consideration that in establishing our type of federalism a group of formerly independent States bound themselves together under one national government. * * *
>
> * * * The right of a citizen to equal representation and to have [his or her] vote weighted equally with those of all other citizens in the election of members of one house of a bicameral state legislature would amount to little if States could effectively submerge the equal-population principle in the apportionment of seats in the other house. * * * Deadlock between the two bodies might result in compromise and concession on some issues. But in all too many cases the more probable result would be frustration of the majority will through minority veto in the house not apportioned on a population basis[.]

Do you agree with this reasoning? Isn't the sort of "deadlock" suggested by the Chief Justice pretty much inherent in all the other blocking devices of legislatures, such as the committee system, expanded or unlimited debate, the amendment process, and so forth?

The equal representation guarantee for state legislatures is also narrower than that for the national legislature. Unlike apportionment of congressional districts under Article I, § 2, demonstrable population deviation among districts has been upheld in the context of state legislatures. For example, deviations under 10% have been routinely upheld.[11] Even an apportionment plan that contains a higher deviation may be upheld if it is deemed necessary to the achievement of legitimate state interests.[12] Why does the Court require near perfection for U.S. House seat apportionment, while only general approximation for state legislatures?

B. RACE AND ELECTORAL STRUCTURES

Even under the regime of *Colegrove v. Green* (p. 121, *supra*), when the Supreme Court, led by Justice Frankfurter, generally refused to entertain claims concerning the distribution of political power, Frankfurter himself sometimes led the way in addressing claims that electoral structures were tainted by racial discrimination. *Gomillion v. Lightfoot*, 364 U.S. 339 (1960), involved an Alabama statute that allegedly altered the boundaries of the City of Tuskegee from the shape of a square to an irregular 28–sided figure, thereby removing from the city all but a few of its 400 African-American voters while not removing a single white voter or resident. Justice Frankfurter's unanimous opinion for the Court concluded that these allegations stated a Fifteenth Amendment claim. He explained:

> [*Colegrove*] involved a complaint of discriminatory apportionment of congressional districts. The appellants in *Colegrove* complained only of a dilution of the strength of their votes as a result of legislative inaction over a course of many years. The petitioners here complain that affirmative legislative action deprives them of their votes and the consequent advantages that the ballot affords. When a legislature thus singles out a readily isolated segment of a racial minority for special discriminatory treatment, it violates the Fifteenth Amendment. In no case involving unequal weight in voting distribution that has come before the Court did the decision sanction a differentiation on racial lines whereby approval was given to unequivocal withdrawal of the vote solely from colored citizens. Apart from all else, these considerations lift this controversy out of the so-called "political" arena and into the conventional sphere of constitutional litigation.

A separate problem from the formal equality of one person, one vote and from protection against intentional discrimination against racial minorities in drawing district lines is the tendency of majoritarian elections in the United States, by their very nature, to deprive minorities of "effective" voting strength. For example, even the most perfect numerical equality will often not yield districts where African Americans will have a good chance of election, especially if whites tend to vote *en bloc*, because of the winner-take-all character of Senate elections and the geographic concentration of African-American voters in big states.

---

[11] See *Connor v. Finch*, 431 U.S. 407 (1977); *White v. Regester*, 412 U.S. 755 (1973).

[12] See, e.g., *Brown v. Thomson*, 462 U.S. 835 (1983) (5–4 decision upholding reapportionment of Wyoming's lower house that included the allocation of one of its 64 seats to the state's least populous county, which created an average deviation from population equality of 16% and a maximum deviation of 89%).

These concerns generated legal efforts to secure increased minority legislative representation.[13] The relevant constitutional provisions are the Equal Protection Clause of the Fourteenth Amendment and § 1 of the Fifteenth Amendment, which provides that "[t]he right of citizens of the United States to vote shall not be denied or abridged by the United States or by any State on account of race, color, or previous condition of servitude." The first cases we analyze in this part are constitutional cases. The protections against vote dilution in these cases have been supplemented by statutory protections in the Voting Rights Act of 1965, as amended. In more recent years, efforts to comply with the Voting Rights Act have sometimes produced a reverse dynamic, in which state legislatures have reapportioned seats with an eye toward ensuring minority representation through the use of "majority-minority" districts. The remainder of this part addresses these complex subjects.

1.   The Constitutionality of At-Large Electoral Schemes

The Progressive movement of the late 19th and early 20th centuries sought to eliminate the corruption and inefficiency purportedly endemic in the then-commonplace mayor-council form of municipal government, in which the mayor's powers are predominant and council members are elected on a district basis. The Progressives were "structural" reformers: they believed that a different format of municipal government, rather than just better officeholders, was the appropriate solution. The movement reached its zenith with the development of the "Galveston-Des Moines Plan." This proposal replaced the mayor-council structure with a city commission, in which legislative and executive functions are combined. Usual features included (1) centralized authority and responsibility; (2) a small number of commissioners; (3) the election of commissioners from the city at large and not by wards or districts; and (4) each commissioner serving as the head of a single executive and administrative department. By 1917, nearly 500 cities had adopted the commission system. By 1976, only 215 cities, including 163 (or 4%) of those with populations of more than 5,000, had retained the plan. Well over five million people resided in cities that retained the plan, however, and its direct historical successor, the council-manager system, was found in more than 2,400 cities, including 70 that contained populations greater than 100,000.[14]

The traditional view that the resulting Progressive reforms were beneficial has been questioned by scholars asserting that " '[t]he movement for reform in municipal government * * * constituted an attempt by upper-class, advanced professional and large business groups to take formal political power from the previously dominant lower- and middle-class elements so that they might advance their own conceptions of desirable public policy.' "[15] Moreover, some of the "reforms"

---

[13] See generally *Quiet Revolution in the South* (Chandler Davidson & Bernard Grofman eds., 1994); Peyton McCrary, *How the Voting Rights Act Works: Implementation of a Civil Rights Policy, 1965–2005*, 57 S.C. L. Rev. 785 (2006); Richard Pildes, *The Politics of Race*, 108 Harv. L. Rev. 1359 (1995) (reviewing Davidson & Grofman).

[14] See Bradley Rice, *Progressive Cities* xi–xiv, xviii–xix (1977).

[15] *Id.* at xvi (quoting Samuel Hays, *The Politics of Reform in Municipal Government in the Progressive Era*, 55 Pac. Nw. Q. 157, 162 (1964)). See also Chandler Davidson & George Korbel, *At-Large Elections and Minority-Group Representation: A Reexamination of Historical and Contemporary Evidence*, 43 J. of Pol. 982 (1981).

were part of a larger historical process by which state and local governments ensured that African Americans would not be well represented in their legislatures. To marginalize racial minorities, state and local governments imposed literacy tests and other exclusionary requirements, enforced those requirements in a discriminatory way, and gerrymandered electoral districts to ensure white-only representation. One way to gerrymander was to elect all representatives "at large." If whites held a voting majority (as sometimes ensured by the other tactics just noted) and voted as a bloc, people of color could be denied any representation in the legislature. Consider the legitimacy of such practices under the various theories of representation (descriptive, agency, trustee). Now consider their constitutional legality. The following case provides an important starting point for current regulation.

City of Mobile v. Bolden
446 U.S. 55 (1980).

African-American citizens of Mobile, Alabama, challenged the constitutionality of at-large elections for the city commission. The at-large scheme had been adopted in 1911, when African Americans in Alabama were effectively disenfranchised by the state's 1901 constitution. Although African Americans made up about one-third of the city's population, none had ever been elected to the city commission. The lower courts invalidated the electoral scheme, but a plurality of the Supreme Court reversed, because the lower courts had not required a proper showing of discriminatory intent. The plurality decision, written by **Justice Stewart**, noted that a state action that "is racially neutral on its face violated the Fifteenth Amendment only if motivated by a discriminatory purpose." Similarly, the Court has recognized that multimember legislative districts may violate the Equal Protection Clause of the Fourteenth Amendment "if their purpose were invidiously to minimize or cancel out the voting potential of racial or ethnic minorities."

In reaching the conclusion that an invidious purpose is required to prevail, the plurality discussed *White v. Regester*, 412 U.S. 755 (1973), the case that had found that multimember legislative districts diluted the voting strength of discrete racial groups. In its holding that the political processes were not equally open to participation by African Americans and Mexican Americans in Texas, "the Court relied upon evidence in the record that included a long history of official discrimination against minorities as well as indifference to their needs and interests on the part of white elected officials. The Court also found in each county additional factors that restricted the access of minority groups to the political process. In one county, Negroes effectively were excluded from the process of slating candidates for the Democratic Party, while the plaintiffs in the other county were Mexican-Americans who 'suffer[ed] a cultural and language barrier' that made 'participation in community processes extremely difficult, particularly * * * with respect to the political life' of the county. * * * The Court stated the constitutional question in *White* to be whether the 'multimember districts [were] *being used invidiously* to cancel out or minimize the voting strength of racial groups,' strongly indicating that only a purposeful dilution of the plaintiffs' vote would offend the Equal Protection Clause."

Justice Stevens concurred in the judgment. He noted two kinds of fundamentally distinct cases: state action that inhibits a person's right to vote and state action that affects the political strength of various groups competing for leadership in a democracy. The first type of cases include those challenging poll taxes or literacy tests that are used to deny people the right to vote. *Bolden* is not that type of case; instead, "this case draws into question a political structure that treats all individuals as equals but adversely affects the political strength of a racially identifiable group."

Justice Stevens argued that the same standards of review should be applied to any allegation of gerrymandering, whether aimed at racial minorities or other groups. "By definition, gerrymandering involves drawing district boundaries * * * in order to maximize the voting strength of those loyal to the dominant political faction and to minimize the strength of those opposed to it. In seeking the desired result, legislators necessarily make judgments about the probability that the members of certain identifiable groups, whether racial, ethnic, economic, or religious, will vote in the same way. * * * A prediction based on a racial characteristic is not necessarily more reliable than a prediction based on some other group characteristic. Nor, since a legislator's ultimate purpose in making the prediction is political in character, is it necessarily more invidious or benign than a prediction based on other group characteristics. In the line-drawing process, racial, religious, ethnic, and economic gerrymanders are all species of political gerrymanders."

Justice Stevens then reasoned that the proper test in these cases should focus "on the objective effects of the political decision rather than the subjective motivation of the decisionmaker." That standard means that "a political decision that affects group voting rights may be valid even if it can be proved that irrational or invidious factors have played some part in its enactment or retention. The standard for testing the acceptability of such a decision must take into account the fact that the responsibility for drawing political boundaries is generally committed to the legislative process and that the process inevitably involves a series of compromises among different group interests. * * * The standard cannot, therefore, be so strict that any evidence of a purpose to disadvantage a bloc of voters will justify a finding of 'invidious discrimination'; otherwise, the facts of political life would deny legislatures the right to perform the districting function. Accordingly, a political decision that is supported by valid and articulable justifications cannot be invalid simply because some participants in the decisionmaking process were motivated by a purpose to disadvantage a minority group." For Justice Stevens, the decision by Mobile was such a decision: although supported by some in order to make it more difficult to elect African Americans, "I do not believe otherwise legitimate political choices can be invalidated simply because an irrational or invidious purpose played some role in the decisionmaking process."

Like Justice Stevens, **Justice Marshall**, in dissent, rejected the requirement of discriminatory intent as necessary to hold multimember districting unconstitutional. "*Reynolds v. Sims* and its progeny focused solely on the discriminatory *effects* of malapportionment. They recognize that, when population figures for the representational districts of a legislature are not similar, the votes of citizens in larger districts do not carry as much weight in the legislature as do votes cast by citizens in smaller districts. The equal protection problem attacked by the 'one person, one vote' principle is, then, one of vote dilution: under *Reynolds*, each citizen must have an 'equally effective voice' in the election of representatives. In the present cases, the alleged vote dilution, though caused by the combined effects of the electoral structure and social and historical factors rather than by unequal population distribution, is analytically the same concept: the unjustified abridgment of a fundamental right." Justice Marshall rejected the idea that the Constitution requires proportional representation and opined that for the Court to impose such a requirement would transform it into a "super-legislature." Instead, "[t]o prove unconstitutional vote dilution, the group is also required to carry the far more onerous burden of demonstrating that it has been effectively fenced out of the political process."

Marshall's dissent then went on to describe the situation in Mobile. "[N]o Negro had ever been elected to the Mobile City Commission, despite the fact that Negroes constitute about one-third of the electorate, and that the persistence of severe racial bloc voting made it highly unlikely that any Negro could be elected at large in the foreseeable future. * * * The plaintiffs convinced the District Court that Mobile Negroes were unable to use alternative avenues of political influence. They showed that Mobile Negroes still suffered pervasive present effects of massive historical, official and private discrimination, and that the City Commission had been quite unresponsive to the needs of the minority community. The City of Mobile has been guilty of such pervasive racial discrimination in hiring employees that extensive intervention by the Federal District Court has been required. Negroes are grossly underrepresented on city boards and committees. The city's distribution of public services is racially discriminatory. City officials and police were largely unmoved by Negro complaints about police brutality and a 'mock lynching.'"

Marshall concluded: "The Fifteenth Amendment cannot tolerate [a decision regarding electoral processes that has a discriminatory effect upon the minority's vote], even if made in good faith, because the Amendment grants racial minorities the full enjoyment of the right to vote, not simply protection against the unfairness of intentional vote dilution along racial lines."

NOTES ON BOLDEN AND CONSTITUTIONAL ATTACKS ON MINORITY VOTE DILUTION

1. *Discriminatory Intent. Bolden* says that legislative discrimination under the Fifteenth Amendment does not exist without proof of "intent" to discriminate. As the Court notes, a similar requirement of intentional legislative action was established for Fourteenth Amendment cases such as *Washington v. Davis*, 426 U.S. 229 (1976). These cases contemplate adjudication of legislative motivations. But consider the cautionary words of Chief Justice John Marshall in *Fletcher v. Peck*, 10 U.S. (6 Cranch) 87 (1810):

That * * * impure motives should contribute to the passage of a law * * * [is a circumstance] most deeply to be deplored. * * * [Nonetheless, it] may well be doubted how far the validity of a law depends upon the motives of its framers * * *. If the principle be conceded, that an act of the supreme sovereign power might be declared null by a court, in consequence of the means which procured it, still would there be much difficulty in saying to what extent those means must be applied to produce this effect. * * * Must the vitiating cause operate on a majority, or on what number of its members? Would the act be null, whatever might be the wish of the nation, or would its * * * nullity depend upon the public sentiment?

If the majority of the legislature be corrupted, it may well be doubted, whether it be within the province of the judiciary to control their conduct, and, if less than a majority act from impure motives, the principle by which judicial interference would be regulated, is not clearly discerned.

Why has the Court rejected the reasoning of Chief Justice Marshall?

2. *Proving Discriminatory Intent (Fourteenth Amendment). Personnel Adm'r of Massachusetts v. Feeney*, 442 U.S. 256 (1979), upheld a state statute granting veterans a preference in being hired for state civil service positions. Although the obvious effect of the law was to discriminate against women, the Court rejected the Fourteenth Amendment challenge because there was no proof of discriminatory intent. In footnote 25, the Court stated:

> This is not to say that the inevitability or foreseeability of consequences of a neutral rule has no bearing upon the existence of discriminatory intent. Certainly, when the adverse consequences of a law upon an identifiable group are [plainly] inevitable * * * a strong inference that the adverse effects were desired can reasonably be drawn. But in this inquiry * * * an inference is a working tool, not a synonym for proof. When * * * the impact is essentially an unavoidable consequence of legislative policy that has in itself always been deemed to be legitimate, and when * * * the statutory history and all of the available evidence effectively demonstrate the opposite, the inference simply fails to ripen into proof.

Would creating a rebuttable presumption that the decisionmaker intended the natural and foreseeable consequences of her act (a common concept in tort law) be a good idea, because the decisionmaker has far better access to the true reasons for a decision and should be required to articulate a credible explanation? Should that be the Fifteenth Amendment standard?

3. *Proof of Discriminatory Intent (Fifteenth Amendment): The Subsequent History of* Bolden. In 1982, the federal District Court on remand in *Bolden* held that the city's form of government had been adopted in 1911 for discriminatory purposes, even though blacks were already disenfranchised at the time by the Alabama Constitution of 1901, because the 1911 scheme was "adopted in substantial part to reinforce the 1901 Constitution as a buttress against the possibility of black office holding." 542 F. Supp. 1050, 1075 (S.D. Ala. 1982). The parties settled the case soon after this decision. In a companion case involving the School Commission of Mobile County, the District Court also found that the adoption in 1876 of an at-large election plan for the school board was motivated by discriminatory animus. See *Brown v. Bd. of Sch. Comm'rs*, 542 F. Supp. 1078 (S.D. Ala. 1982).

While *Brown* was pending on appeal to the Eleventh Circuit, the Supreme Court in *Rogers v. Lodge*, 458 U.S. 613 (1982), upheld a lower court's finding that the system of at-large election of county commissioners of Burke County, Georgia, had been maintained for racially discriminatory purposes. Justice Powell, joined by Justice Rehnquist, protested in dissent that the evidence relied upon by the District Court—the presence of racial bloc voting, the failure of any African American to be elected despite the fact that African Americans made up a majority of the county's citizens, the present impact upon Burke County blacks of past racial discrimination, and the county elected officials' unresponsiveness and insensitivity to the needs of African Americans—was no different in any relevant respect from that presented in *Bolden*, which in Justice Powell's view held that "this *kind* of evidence was not enough." Following *Rogers v.*

Lodge, the Eleventh Circuit affirmed *Brown* in all respects, 706 F.2d 1103 (1983), and the Supreme Court summarily affirmed, 464 U.S. 1005 (1983). Do *Rogers* and *Brown* effectively nullify the thrust of *Bolden*?

2. The Voting Rights Act and Racial Vote Dilution

(a) *Section 5 Preclearance.* Although the Fifteenth Amendment was adopted in 1870 and provides Congress the "power to enforce this article by appropriate legislation" (§ 2), it was not until 1965 that "Congress found that racial discrimination in voting was an 'insidious and pervasive evil which had been perpetuated in certain parts of our country through unremitting and ingenious defiance of the Constitution.'" *City of Rome v. United States*, 446 U.S. 156, 182 (1980) (quoting *South Carolina v. Katzenbach*, 383 U.S. 301, 309 (1966)). Congress found that case-by-case litigation had failed to enforce compliance with the Amendment because it had proved to be too slow, too expensive, and too cumbersome, and because a decree outlawing a discriminatory device could easily be circumvented simply by adopting a different method of discrimination.

Congress responded by adopting the Voting Rights Act of 1965 (VRA), 42 U.S.C. § 1971 *et seq.* The Act outlawed "tests and devices" required in order to register to vote, such as literacy tests, which had earlier been found constitutional in *Lassiter v. Northampton County Bd. of Elections*, 360 U.S. 45 (1959). To prevent circumvention of the Act by the adoption of other discriminatory methods, § 5 of the Act required that no change in voting qualifications or procedures may be implemented without the prior determination of either the attorney general or the United States District Court for the District of Columbia that the change "neither has the purpose nor will have the effect of denying or abridging the right to vote on account of race or color." 42 U.S.C. § 1973c. The 1965 Act did not apply nationwide: through its coverage formula in § 4(b), it reached only those jurisdictions that on November 1, 1964, (1) maintained any "test or device" and (2) had less than 50% of the voting-age population registered or in which less than 50% of such persons voted in the presidential election of 1964. Although the coverage formula was written in these neutral terms, the Act was designed to have, and has had, the effect of bringing the Deep South within its coverage.

The 1965 Act provided that its preclearance requirement would lapse in five years. In 1970, the Act was renewed for another five years, and in 1975 the Act was renewed for another seven years. In 1982, the Act was renewed again, but this time it was extensively amended to terminate the Act's coverage in 25 years and to allow covered jurisdictions more opportunity to bail out of its coverage. In 2006, the Act was extended for another 25 years. Although the 2006 legislation passed by votes of 98–0 in the Senate and 390–33 in the House, there was considerable backroom grumbling from Southern legislators chafing at its continuation of preclearance coverage and from a spectrum of legislators concerning the requirement of bilingual ballots.[16] The Act was substantially unchanged from the 1982 Act with the

---

[16] On the conflictual legislative history behind the seeming consensus, see Nathaniel Persily, *The Promise and Pitfalls of the New Voting Rights Act*, 117 Yale L.J. 174 (2007); James Tucker, *The Politics of Persuasion: Passage of the Voting Rights Reauthorization Act of 2006*, 33 J. Legis. 205 (2007). In addition, see generally, *The Future of the Voting Rights Act* (David Epstein, Richard Pildes, Rodolfo de al Garza & Sharyn

exception of an alteration to the standard for what constitutes discriminatory purpose and discriminatory effect. Congress effectively overturned *Reno v. Bossier Parish Sch. Bd.*, 528 U.S. 341 (2000), and made it clear that mere discriminatory purpose, regardless of the effect on minorities, is grounds for a denial of preclearance. Furthermore, by overturning *Georgia v. Ashcroft*, 539 U.S. 461 (2003), the Act required the denial of preclearance when the voting laws effectively diminish the ability of minorities to elect their preferred candidates.

Section 5's coverage formula, which was reenacted without change in 2006, was immediately criticized as being simultaneously overinclusive and underinclusive. For example, in states that do not have substantial histories of racial discrimination, such as Michigan and New Hampshire, certain jurisdictions were still covered. Jurisdictions in Ohio and Florida, where there had been more recent and well-publicized instances of serious voting rights violations, were not covered. The shortcomings of the coverage formula were acknowledged during the congressional debates on reenactment, but "[w]hat became clear throughout the reauthorization process was that a debate over the coverage formula would turn into a debate about the purpose and utility of section 5 itself. Such a debate likely would have led to the complete unraveling of the bill." Nathaniel Persily, *The Promise and Pitfalls of the New Voting Rights Act*, 117 Yale L.J. 174, 208–09 (2007). Moreover, the political concerns about partisan and regional backlash dissuaded Congress from changing the coverage criteria: Ohio and Florida are large and powerful, and the jurisdictions that would be targeted for coverage were controlled by Republicans whose votes were needed to ensure bipartisan support for the extension of the Act.

The question of the constitutionality of the coverage formula and the preclearance requirement was brought to the Supreme Court in the following case.

Shelby County v. Holder
133 S.Ct. 2612 (2013).

Shelby County, Alabama, a covered jurisdiction, sued for a declaratory judgment on two grounds. First, both the coverage formula in § 6 and the preclearance provisions in § 5 were facially unconstitutional because they were no longer justified by current conditions in the covered jurisdictions. Second, Congress' decision to retain the decades-old coverage formula for another 25 years was not sufficiently supported by evidence of intentional discrimination in those states. The constitutional claim related to the structure of the federal government: the VRA, the petitioners argued, represents a "sharp depart[ure]" from the "basic principles" of our system in which states are allocated substantial (but not unlimited) authority to regulate elections and in which states enjoy equal "power, dignity and authority."

The 5–4 majority opinion, written by **Chief Justice Roberts**, reiterated the constitutional framework that had been established in a previous VRA case that had avoided the constitutional challenge to preclearance. *Northwest Austin Mun. Util. Dist. No. One v. Holder (NAMUDNO)*, 557 U.S. 193 (2009). That opinion had emphasized

---

O'Halloran eds., 2006); *Voting Rights Act Reauthorization of 2006: Perspectives on Democracy, Participation, and Power* (Ana Henderson ed., 2007); Michael Kang, *Race and Democratic Contestation*, 117 Yale L.J. 734 (2008).

that the VRA "imposes current burdens and must be justified by current needs." More sweepingly—and with implications beyond this law—the Court reaffirmed *NAMUDNO*'s conclusion that "a departure from the fundamental principle of equal sovereignty requires a showing that a statute's disparate geographic coverage is sufficiently related to the problem that it targets." This approach is influenced by the Court's federalism jurisprudence over the past two decades and requires not only an appreciation that states retain sovereignty through the Tenth Amendment and the constitutional structure, but also that the relationship between states and the federal government is further characterized by a "fundamental principle of *equal* sovereignty" (emphasis by Court). The VRA undermines that principle, applying preclearance to only nine states, and some additional counties, and thus the Court viewed it as "extraordinary legislation otherwise unfamiliar to our federal system" (quoting *NAMUDNO*). Thus, it requires justification by "exceptional circumstances."

The Court believed that the coverage formula of the VRA satisfied that stringent test when it was first enacted because Congress limited its scope "to the geographic areas where immediate action seemed necessary" given the longstanding, pervasive, and systematic practices designed to deny black citizens the right to vote. The majority acknowledged that the significant improvement in African-American voter turnout and minority representation in the covered areas were no doubt "in large part *because of* the Voting Rights Act." Justice Roberts then observed that, notwithstanding these improvements, "the Act has not eased the restrictions in § 5 or narrowed the scope of the coverage formula in § 4(b) along the way. Those extraordinary and unprecedented features were reauthorized—as if nothing had changed." The dissent, written by **Justice Ginsburg**, took a dim view of this approach: "In the Court's view, the very success of § 5 of the Voting Rights Act demands its dormancy."

Although the majority acknowledged that Congress in 2006 had compiled an extensive record of intentional discrimination that resulted in vote dilution, rather than of the existence of the barriers to actual voting that had existed in 1965, it did not find that record sufficient to justify the scope of the coverage formula. "Viewing the preclearance requirements as targeting such efforts simply highlights the irrationality of continued reliance on the § 4 coverage formula, which is based on voting tests and access to the ballot, not vote dilution. We cannot pretend that we are reviewing an updated statute, or try our hand at updating the statute ourselves, based on the new record compiled by Congress. * * * [W]e are not ignoring the record; we are simply recognizing that it played no role in shaping the statutory formula before us today." The majority concluded: "If Congress had started from scratch in 2006, it plainly could not have enacted the present coverage formula. It would have been irrational for Congress to distinguish between states in such a fundamental way based on 40-year-old data, when today's statistics tell an entirely different story. And it would have been irrational to base coverage on the use of voting tests 40 years ago, when such tests have been illegal since that time."

Accordingly, the Court struck down § 4(b)'s coverage formula, noting that it did not rule on § 5, nor did its ruling affect the "permanent, nation-wide ban on racial discrimination found in § 2." The majority concluded: "Congress may draft another [coverage] formula based on current conditions. * * * Our country has changed, and while any racial discrimination in voting is too much, Congress must ensure that the legislation it passes to remedy that problem speaks to current condition." Only **Justice Thomas** wrote separately that he would also have struck down § 5.

In her impassioned and lengthy dissent, Justice Ginsburg would have deferred to Congress' determination, "based on a voluminous record, that the scourge of discrimination was not yet extirpated." She argued that Congress, which passed the Act by overwhelming bipartisan margins in both houses, should be allowed to determine whether continuance of preclearance and the coverage formula "would facilitate completion of the impressive gains thus far made; and * * * would guard against backsliding." The dissent questioned the view of the federal system adopted by the majority, noting that the Civil War Amendments, at issue in voting rights cases, "authorized transformative new federal statutes designed to uproot all vestiges of unfreedom and inequality" and included "sweeping enforcement powers * * * to enact 'appropriate' legislation targeting state abuses" (quoting Akhil Amar, *America's Constitution: A Biography* 361, 363, 399 (2005)). The dissent described the scrutiny it thought should be applied: "This Court has repeatedly reaffirmed Congress' prerogative to use any rational means in exercise of its power [in the area of protecting the right to vote]. And both precedent and logic dictate that the rational-means test should be easier to satisfy, and the burden on the statute's challenger should be higher, when what is at issue is the reauthorization of a remedy that the Court has previously affirmed, and that Congress has found, from contemporary evidence, to be working to advance the legislature's legitimate objective."

The dissenters were particularly dismayed that the Court would support a facial challenge by a county in Alabama, a state with a well-known history of intentional and often flagrant discrimination designed to discourage its African-American citizens from voting, including examples of purposeful discrimination that had supported recent successful legal challenges. The dissent accused the majority of "hubris" for allowing a facial challenge by a political subdivision that probably could not have succeeded in an as-applied challenge. Moreover, the Court erred "egregiously" in refusing to defer to Congress' judgment based on a record that the dissent viewed as "replete with examples of denial or abridgement of a paramount federal right." The dissent described the record as demonstrating a current need for the coverage formula, citing, among other evidence, a disproportionate number of § 2 lawsuits, which also had a greater chance of success, and greater racial polarization in the covered jurisdictions.

In conclusion, Justice Ginsburg wrote: "The Court appears to believe that the VRA's success in eliminating the specific devices extant in 1965 means that preclearance is no longer needed. With that belief, and the argument derived from it, history repeats itself. The same assumption—that the problem could be solved when particular methods of voting discrimination are identified and eliminated—was indulged and proved wrong repeatedly prior to the VRA's enactments. * * * In truth, the evolution of voting discrimination into more subtle second-generation barriers is powerful evidence that a remedy as effective as preclearance remains vital to protect minority voting rights and prevent backsliding. Beyond question, the VRA is no ordinary legislation. It is extraordinary because Congress embarked on a mission long delayed and of extraordinary importance: to realize the purpose and promise of the Fifteenth Amendment. For half a century, a concerted effort has been made to end racial discrimination in voting. Thanks to the Voting Rights Act, progress once the subject of a dream has been achieved and continues to be made."

NOTES ON SHELBY COUNTY *AND THE FUTURE OF PRECLEARANCE*

1. *Is Congressional Reaction to* Shelby County *Likely?* It might seem that, by avoiding a decision on § 5, the Court left open the possibility that Congress could more appropriately tailor the coverage formula to current realities. How realistic is it, however, to expect that the current Congress, which seems gridlocked on virtually every important issue before it, will be able to respond to this judicial invitation? Remember the description of the 2006 legislative process to reauthorize the Act: testimony from scholars and others highlighted the possible constitutional problems that would likely arise if a 40-year-old coverage formula were reenacted unchanged. Richard Hasen, Shelby County *and the Illusion of Minimalism*, 22 Wm. & Mary Bill Rts. J. 713 (2014). The main reason for congressional reluctance to revisit the coverage formula is that any changes will likely effect the partisan balance. Samuel Issacharoff notes "that current voting controversies, unlike the concerns of racial exclusion under Jim Crow, are likely motivated by partisan zeal and emerge in contested partisan environments." *Beyond the Discrimination Model of Voting*, 127 Harv. L. Rev. 95, 100 (2013). He observes, for example, that the likelihood that a state will adopt a restrictive voter identification law "turns on one variable: Republican control of the state legislature." *Id.* at 103.

One possible avenue for congressional action would be for lawmakers to craft a "grand bargain" in this arena. Such a comprehensive approach would take advantage of the Constitution's Elections Clause, which allows federal action to supersede state laws setting the "Times, Places and Manner of holding Elections for Senators and Representatives." Art. I, § 4. Daniel Tokaji suggests pairing expansion of voter registration with a reasonable federal voter identification requirement, legislation that could also include an updated coverage formula.[17] Another proposal, offered by social scientists, would be to craft a new coverage formula using certain factors that suggest a climate leading to racial discrimination in voting laws.[18] They identify the existence of racially polarized voting and minority population size as two unsurprising factors; they also find that evidence of "worse-than-ordinary racial stereotyping would be a necessary condition for coverage." To calibrate coverage to current conditions over time, the authors recommend delegating to the Department of Justice or an independent agency the authority to update the coverage formula prospectively. Interestingly, using these factors in 2014, particularly the measure of racial stereotyping, would lead to similar coverage as that mandated by § 4, which was overturned by the Court in *Shelby County.*

2. *Do the States Now Deserve Equal Dignity in the Arena of Voting Rights?* In oral argument, Justice Roberts asked the Solicitor General: "Is it the government's submission that the citizens of the South are more racist than citizens of the North?" Certainly, the rejected coverage formula of the VRA "holds that the states with the worst histories of Jim Crow disenfranchisement from the middle part of the twentieth century remain, even today, under a cloud of suspicion that other states are not under.

---

[17] Daniel Tokaji, *Responding to* Shelby County: *A Grand Election Bargain*, 8 Harvard L. & Pol'y Rev. 71 (2014). See also Bruce Cain, *Moving Past Section 5: More Fingers or a New Dike?*, 12 Election L.J. 338 (2013) (also identifying the need for national standardization of voting rules and the possibility of a tradeoff between "easier paths to voting and registration [and] ballot security").

[18] Christopher Elmendorf & Douglas Spencer, *The Geography of Racial Stereotyping: Evidence and Implications for VRA Preclearance after* Shelby County, 102 Cal. L. Rev. ___ (forthcoming 2014). See also David Kimball, *Judges Are Not Social Scientists (Yet)*, 12 Election L.J. 324 (2013) (also arguing for a new coverage formula linked to social science evidence).

* * * Section 5 thus places the Southern states under a regime of regional federal oversight that is a faint echo, especially in its geographic outline, of Reconstruction itself." Joseph Fishkin, *Dignity of the South*, 123 Yale L.J. Online 175, 178 (2013). Referring to the social science work discussed above, Fishkin notes that there may be empirical evidence that the covered Southern states still suffer disproportionately from racial prejudice, perhaps not surprising given the history of the region.

The sense that this particular petitioner, Shelby County, lies in a state that does not merit being treated with "equal dignity" as most other states in this realm motivated an extensive passage in Justice Ginsburg's dissent. Not only does Alabama have one of the highest rates of successful § 2 lawsuits in the nation, but it has also given rise to several successful Supreme Court cases concerning purposeful discrimination with respect to voting rights. Finally, the dissent quoted extensively from FBI wiretaps in 2010 that recorded "shocking" conversations filled with racial epithets and plans to adopt strategies to discourage African Americans from coming to the polls. Quoting the District Court judge who presided over the subsequent criminal trial, the dissent noted that "[r]acist sentiments * * * 'remain regrettably entrenched in the high echelons of state government.' " Fishkin observes in his essay that the Chief Justice would not likely be moved by such evidence because "[h]e was not asking whether the citizens of the South are, as a factual matter, 'more racist' than the citizens of the North. Rather, he was asking whether the United States was making a *claim* that would amount to an insult, a dignitary harm, to the South as a region and to its people." *Supra*, at 191. How can we understand this notion of dignitary harm to states (and presumably their people), and how should it be balanced against the current harm of vote dilution? Does history play an appropriate role here?

3. *The Immediate Aftermath of* Shelby County *and the Possibility of "Bail In" Actions*. Within hours of the Court's decision, five states previously covered by § 5 announced plans to proceed with pending voter identification laws that many had argued would discourage particular racial groups of voters from coming to the polls. A month after *Shelby County* was decided, the Department of Justice announced it would use § 3 to bring one of those states, Texas, back into the preclearance regime by arguing that the state had intentionally discriminated against Hispanics in the last redistricting process. This "bail in" provision requires evidence of intentional racial discrimination in voting on the part of state actors. It also allows judges significant discretion to tailor the remedy; for example, the judge might require only certain types of changes in voting procedures to be precleared, and she will determine the duration of the oversight. Litigation under § 3 can also result in a consent decree, which involves targeted preclearance and continued monitoring by the court. This provision has been used rarely since its enactment as part of the original VRA: two states (New Mexico and Arkansas) and about a dozen counties and cities have been bailed in. Because it applies nationwide, some of these regions have been outside the traditional area of concern for the VRA, including counties in South Dakota and Nebraska and the city of Los Angeles. See Travis Crum, *The Voting Rights Act's Secret Weapon: Pocket Trigger Litigation and Dynamic Preclearance*, 119 Yale L.J. 1992 (2010) (one of the few law review analyses of this previously obscure section of the VRA).

Of course, after *Shelby County*, other avenues of challenging laws on the grounds of racial discrimination remain, including § 2 of the VRA described in more detail below. Voting rights advocates are already at work determining alternative legal avenues to attack practices and policies designed to suppress or dilute the right to vote, including those aimed at or affecting racial minorities. Issacharoff identifies an emerging line of cases in the lower courts using language in *Bush v. Gore*, 531 U.S. 98 (2000) (see Chapter 9, § 2C), to apply equal protection guarantees to the manner in which people vote. This equal protection principle has been invoked in cases involving different, and arguably inferior, voting machines and different methods of counting provisional ballots within the same state. This jurisprudence, unlike the VRA, targets more than racial discrimination; it "helps insulate the right to vote from naked efforts at partisan manipulation." *Supra*, at 106.

Section 2 Protection Against Racial Vote Dilution. African-American plaintiffs prevailed in *Rogers* and in *Bolden* on remand by satisfactorily proving that the at-large electoral schemes at issue in those cases had been adopted or maintained for discriminatory purposes. In the ordinary case, however, this burden of proof is hard to surmount: proof of discriminatory reasons for the adoption of an electoral scheme many years ago is usually unavailable because of the passage of time, and discriminatory maintenance of such a scheme cannot be shown without either overtly discriminatory actions or overwhelming circumstantial evidence. Moreover, to some extent the *Bolden* approach asks the wrong question, for it is the present discriminatory impact of the electoral scheme, and not the motivations of present or past officials, that unfairly skews the political process.

The *Bolden* result in the Supreme Court triggered a firestorm of protest from civil rights advocates and members of Congress. A bipartisan coalition voted to amend the VRA in 1982 to override the *Bolden* decision. The operative provision is revised § 2 of the Act, 42 U.S.C. § 1973, which provides a permanent, nationwide ban on electoral procedures with discriminatory "results":

> (a) No voting qualification or prerequisite to voting or standard, practice, or procedure shall be imposed or applied by any State or political subdivision in a manner which results in a denial or abridgement of the right of any citizen of the United States to vote on account of race or color, or in contravention of the guarantees set forth in section 1973b(f)(2) of this title [dealing with language-minority groups], as provided in subsection (b) of this section.

> (b) A violation of subsection (a) of this section is established if, based on the totality of circumstances, it is shown that the political processes leading to nomination or election in the State or political subdivision are not equally open to participation by members of a class of citizens protected by subsection (a) of this section in that its members have less opportunity than other members of the electorate to participate in the political process and to elect representatives of their choice. The extent to which members of a protected class have been elected to office in the State or political subdivision is one circumstance which may be considered: *Provided*, That nothing in this section establishes a right to have members of a protected class elected in numbers equal to their proportion in the population.

The Senate committee report explaining § 2 (S. Rep. 97–417, 97th Cong., 2d Sess. 28–29, reprinted in 1982 U.S. Code Cong. & Admin. News 206–07) cited these "typical factors," gleaned from pre-*Bolden* cases, as illustrative of the vote dilution Congress intended to outlaw by amending the statute:

   1.   the extent of any history of official discrimination in the state or political subdivision that touched the right of the members of the minority group to register, to vote, or otherwise to participate in the democratic process;

   2.   the extent to which voting in the elections of the state or political subdivision is racially polarized;

   3.   the extent to which the state or political subdivision has used unusually large election districts, majority vote requirements, anti-single shot provisions, or other voting practices or procedures that may enhance the opportunity for discrimination against the minority group;

      * * *

   5.   the extent to which members of the minority group in the state or political subdivision bear the effects of discrimination in such areas as education, employment and health, which hinder their ability to participate effectively in the political process;

   6.   whether political campaigns have been characterized by overt or subtle racial appeals;

   7.   the extent to which members of the minority group have been elected to public office in the jurisdiction.

Other factors mentioned in the Senate report were:

   whether there is a significant lack of responsiveness on the part of elected officials to the particularized needs of the members of the minority group.

   whether the policy underlying the state or political subdivision's use of such voting qualification, prerequisite to voting, or standard, practice or procedure is tenuous.

Thornburg v. Gingles
478 U.S. 30 (1986).

In this case, the Supreme Court construed the "totality of the circumstances" test of new § 2. **Justice Brennan's** opinion for a five-justice Court concluded that the factors identified in the Senate report were probative, but neither comprehensive nor exclusive. For multimember districting to violate § 2, the Court held, three elements must be shown: (1) "[T]he minority group must be able to demonstrate that it is sufficiently large and geographically compact to constitute a majority in a single-member district." (2) "[T]he minority group must be able to show that it is politically cohesive." (3) "[T]he minority must be able to demonstrate that the white majority votes sufficiently as a bloc to enable it—in the absence of special circumstances, such as the minority candidate running unopposed—usually to defeat the minority's preferred candidate."

The Court "observe[d] that the usual predictability of the majority's success distinguishes structural dilution from the mere loss of an occasional election." Thus, "a pattern of racial bloc voting that extends over a period of time is more probative of a claim that a district experiences legally significant polarization than are the results of a single election." Moreover, "in a district where elections are shown usually to be polarized, the fact that racially polarized voting is not present in one or a few individual elections [or] the success of a minority candidate in a particular election does not necessarily prove" that § 2 has not been violated. The District Court's ultimate finding of the presence or absence of vote dilution is subject only to the clearly erroneous test in appellate review. The Court majority held that the occasional election of minority candidates does not, by itself, defeat a § 2 claim, but two Justices (Brennan and **White**) concluded that "persistent proportional representation" will do so unless the plaintiffs can show that this "sustained success does not accurately reflect the minority group's ability to elect its preferred representatives."

Justice O'Connor (writing also for **Chief Justice Burger** and **Justices Powell** and **Rehnquist**) concurred only in the judgment. Her opinion conceded that the 1982 Act overrode *Bolden*'s "intent" test and adopted the "results" test of *White v. Regester*, but she also noted that § 2 "unequivocally disclaims the creation of a right of proportional representation. This disclaimer was essential to the compromise that resulted in passage of the amendment," she argued, citing the views of Senator Dole in the Senate committee report. Note that in 1982 Dole was the Senate Majority Leader, and no bill opposed by the Republicans could have been enacted, either because they controlled the Senate or (most likely, given liberal Republican defections) because their opposition could sustain a presidential veto.

In *Gingles*, Justice O'Connor argued that the Court's approach would press enforcement of the VRA toward proportional representation. Consider her hypothetical: a 1,000–person town has an African-American population of 30%, concentrated in one section of town. If the town council has four members, the configuration of districts could determine the number of African-American councilmembers (assuming racial bloc voting). Single-member districts could yield results ranging from two African-American representatives (if two of the districts had 60% African Americans in each, while the other two districts had none) to none (if the 30% African-American vote were evenly distributed through all four districts). At-large elections would likely yield no minority representation. Justice O'Connor agreed that the last two options might be challenged under the 1982 Act but posed the question: if the Act prohibits minority "vote dilution," what would an "undiluted" minority representation look like? Would it be proportional representation, as the Court suggested, or a variety of results, including an all-white council whose members competed for the African-American vote and catered to minority group desires? Justice O'Connor argued for a more variegated approach than the relatively more bright-line approach adopted by the Court majority. She would have disallowed claims in three districts where African Americans had enjoyed some electoral success since the 1970s and would have reversed the trial court as to those three districts.[19]

---

[19] In *Holder v. Hall*, 512 U.S. 874 (1994), the Court held that § 2 provides no basis for a claim of racial vote dilution based on changing the size of a legislative body (e.g., whether a commission is made up of a single member or multiple members). Justice Thomas, joined by Justice Scalia, concurred in the judgment in *Holder* and launched a full-scale attack upon *Gingles*, arguing that its test is inconsistent with the text of § 2 and encourages racial gerrymandering. Justices Thomas and Scalia would have overruled *Gingles* and held that § 2 applies only to claims of discriminatory denial of the ballot or discriminatory processing of ballots, and not to vote dilution claims. In *League of United Latin Am. Citizens v. Perry*, 548 U.S. 399 (2006), a

A VOTING RIGHTS ACT PROBLEM

Problem 2–1. After the 1990 census, the state of North Carolina gained an additional seat in the House of Representatives (up from 11 to 12). The racial composition of the state is 78% white, 20% black, 1% Indian, and 1% predominantly Asian. The African-American population is relatively dispersed through the state, constituting a majority in only five of the state's 100 counties (all located in the Coastal Plain in the eastern part of the state). As of 1992, no African American had been elected to the House from North Carolina in this century.

(a) Assume that North Carolina redistricts after the 1990 census by creating a new Republican district and strengthening incumbents in surrounding districts. (Even though Democrats control the legislature, there was a Republican governor, and population growth had been in Republican areas.) Under this configuration, 12 whites will be elected in 1992. What are the odds that North Carolina could be successfully sued for violating § 2 of the VRA, as amended in 1982 and as interpreted in *Gingles*?

(b) Assume that North Carolina redistricts after the 1990 census by creating a new "majority-minority" district (namely, a district where a majority of the population consists of racial minorities) in the Coastal Plain. If there were racial bloc voting, an African American would probably be elected in 1992, the first in that century. African-American plaintiffs challenge the plan under § 2, nonetheless. Their argument is that there should have been two rather than one majority-minority district and that a second district could have been created in the central part of the state by using boundary lines no more irregular than those found elsewhere. Does this lawsuit have a chance under § 2?

(c) North Carolina had 40 counties covered by § 5 of the VRA, and, until *Shelby County*, any redistricting had to be precleared by the Department of Justice or approved by the D.C. Circuit. Assume that the Department of Justice insists on two rather than one majority-minority district, for the reasons suggested in part (b) of this problem. The North Carolina General Assembly goes along with the suggestion and creates two such districts. The majority-minority districts are Districts 1 and 12. To create the second district (#12), the legislature snakes the district lines along Interstate 85; the district passes through 10 counties, cutting most of them in half, as it also does many towns and cities. It is contiguous but only barely so. In the 1992 elections, eight Democrats and four Republicans are elected, with the Democrats picking up the extra seat. Two of the eight Democrats are African American—from districts 1 and 12.

Republicans challenge this plan on the ground that it is a partisan gerrymander designed to minimize their representation. Population growth occurred in GOP areas, yet the Democratic legislature captured the extra seat for themselves. In another lawsuit, white voters in the odd-shaped District 12 challenge the plan because it "dilutes" their votes on racial grounds. Should either of these lawsuits succeed? Write down your answers, and then read on.

---

fractured Court applied the *Gingles* factors and concluded that at least one redrawn Texas congressional district violated § 2 by diluting the voting power of the Latino community.

3. Redistricting Designed to Ensure Minority Representation

SHAW V. RENO
United States Supreme Court, 1993.
509 U.S. 630, 113 S.Ct. 2816, 125 L.Ed. 2d 511.

JUSTICE O'CONNOR delivered the opinion of the Court.

[The North Carolina General Assembly's reapportionment of the state's 12 seats in the federal House of Representatives based on the 1990 census included one majority-black congressional district. After the federal Attorney General objected to the plan pursuant to § 5 of the VRA, the General Assembly revised the plan and created a second majority-black district. Plaintiffs challenged the revised plan as involving an unconstitutional racial gerrymander.]

The first of the two majority-black districts contained in the revised plan, District 1, is somewhat hook shaped. Centered in the northeast portion of the State, it moves southward until it tapers to a narrow band; then, with finger-like extensions, it reaches far into the southern-most part of the State near the South Carolina border. District 1 has been compared to a "Rorschach ink-blot test" and a "bug splattered on a windshield."

The second majority-black district, District 12, is even more unusually shaped. It is approximately 160 miles long and, for much of its length, no wider than the I–85 corridor. It winds in snake-like fashion through tobacco country, financial centers, and manufacturing areas "until it gobbles in enough enclaves of black neighborhoods." Northbound and southbound drivers on I–85 sometimes find themselves in separate districts in one county, only to "trade" districts when they enter the next county. Of the 10 counties through which District 12 passes, five are cut into three different districts; even towns are divided. At one point the district remains contiguous only because it intersects at a single point with two other districts before crossing over them. * * *

[Appellants, five residents of Durham County, two of whom live in District 12 and three of whom live in neighboring District 2,] alleged that the General Assembly deliberately "create[d] two Congressional Districts in which a majority of black voters was concentrated arbitrarily—without regard to any other considerations, such as compactness, contiguousness, geographical boundaries, or political subdivisions" with the purpose "to create Congressional Districts along racial lines" and to assure the election of two black representatives to Congress. [The lower courts denied relief.]

[IIB]   * * * [A]ppellants' claim that the State engaged in unconstitutional racial gerrymandering * * * strikes a powerful historical chord: It is unsettling how closely the North Carolina plan resembles the most egregious racial gerrymanders of the past. [Earlier, the Court had described such past racial gerrymandering, citing *Gomillion v. Lightfoot* and Alabama's change in Tuskegee's boundaries "from a square to an uncouth twenty-eight-sided figure." Plaintiffs' complaint alleging that gerrymandering voters into districts that are "so extremely irregular" that they can only be understood as "an effort to segregate the races for purposes of voting" presents a claim for which relief can be granted under the Equal Protection Clause.]

[IIIA]   * * * The * * * central purpose [of the Equal Protection Clause] is to prevent the States from purposefully discriminating between individuals on the basis of race. *Washington v. Davis*, 426 U.S. 229 (1976). Laws that explicitly distinguish between individuals on racial grounds fall within the core of that prohibition.

No inquiry into legislative purpose is necessary when the racial classification appears on the face of the statute. Express racial classifications are immediately suspect because, "[a]bsent searching judicial inquiry . . ., there is simply no way of determining what classifications are 'benign' or 'remedial' and what classifications are in fact motivated by illegitimate notions of racial inferiority or simple racial politics." *Richmond v. J.A. Croson Co.*, 488 U.S. 469, 493 (1989) (plurality opinion); *id.* (Scalia, J., concurring in the judgment).

Classifications of citizens solely on the basis of race "are by their very nature odious to a free people whose institutions are founded upon the doctrine of equality." *Hirabayashi v. United States*, 320 U.S. 81, 100 (1943). They threaten to stigmatize individuals by reason of their membership in a racial group and to incite racial hostility. Accordingly, we have held that the Fourteenth Amendment requires state legislation that expressly distinguishes among citizens because of their race to be narrowly tailored to further a compelling governmental interest.

These principles apply not only to legislation that contains explicit racial distinctions, but also to those "rare" statutes that, although race-neutral, are, on their face, "unexplainable on grounds other than race." *Village of Arlington Heights v. Metropolitan Housing Development Corp.*, 429 U.S. 252, 266 (1977). * * *

[IIIB]   Appellants contend that redistricting legislation that is so bizarre on its face that it is "unexplainable on grounds other than race" demands the same close scrutiny that we give other state laws that classify citizens by race. Our voting rights precedents support that conclusion.

[In *Guinn v. United States*, 238 U. S. 347 (1915), the Court found a Fifteenth Amendment violation when a state adopted a literacy requirement with a " 'grandfather clause' applicable to individuals and their lineal descendants" entitled to vote on January 1, 1866. Although facially neutral, the Court concluded that the law "was invalid because, on its face, it could not be explained on grounds other than race."]

The Court applied the same reasoning to the "uncouth twenty-eight-sided" municipal boundary line at issue in *Gomillion*. Although the statute that redrew the city limits of Tuskegee was race-neutral on its face, plaintiffs alleged that its effect was impermissibly to remove from the city virtually all black voters and no white voters. The Court reasoned:

"If these allegations upon a trial remained uncontradicted or unqualified, the conclusion would be irresistible, tantamount for all practical purposes to a mathematical demonstration, that the legislation is solely concerned with segregating white and colored voters by fencing Negro citizens out of town so as to deprive them of their pre-existing municipal vote." * * *

The Court extended the reasoning of *Gomillion* to congressional districting in *Wright v. Rockefeller*, 376 U.S. 52 (1964). At issue in *Wright* were four districts contained in a New York apportionment statute. The plaintiffs alleged that the statute excluded nonwhites from one district and concentrated them in the other three. Every member of the Court assumed that the plaintiffs' allegation that the statute "segregate[d] eligible voters by race and place of origin" stated a constitutional claim. The Justices disagreed only as to whether the plaintiffs had carried their burden of proof at trial. The dissenters thought the unusual shape of the district lines could "be explained only in racial terms." The majority, however, accepted the District Court's finding that the plaintiffs had failed to establish that the districts were in fact drawn on racial lines. Although the boundary lines were somewhat irregular, the majority reasoned, they were not so bizarre as to permit of no other conclusion. Indeed, because most of the nonwhite voters lived together in one area, it would have been difficult to construct voting districts without concentrations of nonwhite voters.

Wright illustrates the difficulty of determining from the face of a single-member districting plan that it purposefully distinguishes between voters on the basis of race. A reapportionment statute typically does not classify persons at all; it classifies tracts of land, or addresses. Moreover, redistricting differs from other kinds of state decisionmaking in that the legislature always is *aware* of race when it draws district lines, just as it is aware of age, economic status, religious and political persuasion, and a variety of other demographic factors. That sort of race consciousness does not lead inevitably to impermissible race discrimination. As *Wright* demonstrates, when members of a racial group live together in one community, a reapportionment plan that concentrates members of the group in one district and excludes them from others may reflect wholly legitimate purposes. The district lines may be drawn, for example, to provide for compact districts of contiguous territory, or to maintain the integrity of political subdivisions.

The difficulty of proof, of course, does not mean that a racial gerrymander, once established, should receive less scrutiny under the Equal Protection Clause than other state legislation classifying citizens by race. * * * In some exceptional cases, a reapportionment plan may be so highly irregular that, on its face, it rationally cannot be understood as anything other than an effort to "segregat[e] . . . voters" on the basis of race. *Gomillion*. *Gomillion*, in which a tortured municipal boundary line was drawn to exclude black voters, was such a case. So, too, would be a case in which a State concentrated a dispersed minority population in a single district by disregarding traditional districting principles such as compactness, contiguity, and respect for political subdivisions. We emphasize that these criteria are important not because they are constitutionally required—they are not—but because they are objective factors that may serve to defeat a claim that a district has been gerrymandered on racial lines.

Put differently, we believe that reapportionment is one area in which appearances do matter. A reapportionment plan that includes in one district individuals who belong to the same race, but who are otherwise widely separated by geographical and political boundaries, and who may have little in common with one another but the color of their skin, bears an uncomfortable resemblance to political apartheid. It reinforces the perception that members of the same racial group—regardless of their age, education, economic status, or the community in which they live—think alike, share the same political interests, and will prefer the same candidates at the polls. * * * By perpetuating such notions, a racial gerrymander may exacerbate the very patterns of racial bloc voting that majority-minority districting is sometimes said to counteract.

The message that such districting sends to elected representatives is equally pernicious. When a district obviously is created solely to effectuate the perceived common interests of one racial group, elected officials are more likely to believe that their primary obligation is to represent only the members of that group, rather than their constituency as a whole. This is altogether antithetical to our system of representative democracy. * * *

For these reasons, we conclude that a plaintiff challenging a reapportionment statute under the Equal Protection Clause may state a claim by alleging that the legislation, though race-neutral on its face, rationally cannot be understood as anything other than an effort to separate voters into different districts on the basis of race, and that the separation lacks sufficient justification. It is unnecessary for us to decide whether or how a reapportionment plan that, on its face, can be explained in nonracial terms successfully could be challenged. Thus, we express no view as to whether "the intentional creation of majority-minority districts, without more" always gives rise to an equal protection claim. * * *

[IIIC]   The dissenters make two * * * arguments that cannot be reconciled with our precedents. First, they suggest that a racial gerrymander of the sort alleged here is functionally equivalent to gerrymanders for nonracial purposes, such as political gerrymanders. * * * But nothing in our case law compels the conclusion that racial and political gerrymanders are subject to precisely the same constitutional scrutiny. In fact, our country's long and persistent history of racial discrimination in voting—as well as our Fourteenth Amendment jurisprudence, which always has reserved the strictest scrutiny for discrimination on the basis of race—would seem to compel the opposite conclusion.

Second, Justice Stevens argues that racial gerrymandering poses no constitutional difficulties when district lines are drawn to favor the minority, rather than the majority. We have made clear, however, that equal protection analysis "is not dependent on the race of those burdened or benefited by a particular classification." *Croson.* * * *

[IV] Justice Souter contends that exacting scrutiny of racial gerrymanders under the Fourteenth Amendment is inappropriate because reapportionment "nearly always require[s] some consideration of race for legitimate reasons." "As long as members of racial groups have [a] commonality of interest" and "racial bloc voting takes place," he argues, "legislators will have to take race into account" in order to comply with the Voting Rights Act. Justice Souter's reasoning is flawed.

* * * That racial bloc voting or minority political cohesion may be found to exist in *some* cases, of course, is no reason to treat *all* racial gerrymanders differently from other kinds of racial classification. Justice Souter apparently views racial gerrymandering of the type presented here as a special category of "benign" racial discrimination that should be subject to relaxed judicial review. As we have said, however, the very reason that the Equal Protection Clause demands strict scrutiny of all racial classifications is because without it, a court cannot determine whether or not the discrimination truly is "benign." Thus, if appellants' allegations of a racial gerrymander are not contradicted on remand, the District Court must determine whether the General Assembly's reapportionment plan satisfies strict scrutiny. We therefore consider what that level of scrutiny requires in the reapportionment context.

The state appellees suggest that a covered jurisdiction may have a compelling interest in creating majority-minority districts in order to comply with the Voting Rights Act. * * *

[For example,] the state appellees contend that the General Assembly's revised plan was necessary * * * to avoid dilution of black voting strength in violation of § 2, as construed in *Thornburg v. Gingles*. In *Gingles* the Court considered a multimember redistricting plan for the North Carolina State Legislature. The Court held that members of a racial minority group claiming § 2 vote dilution through the use of multimember districts must prove three threshold conditions: that the minority group "is sufficiently large and geographically compact to constitute a majority in a single-member district," that the minority group is "politically cohesive," and that "the white majority votes sufficiently as a bloc to enable it . . . usually to defeat the minority's preferred candidate." * * *

Appellants maintain that the General Assembly's revised plan could not have been required by § 2. They contend that the State's black population is too dispersed to support two geographically compact majority-black districts, as the bizarre shape of District 12 demonstrates, and that there is no evidence of black political cohesion. They also contend that recent black electoral successes demonstrate the willingness of white voters in North Carolina to vote for black candidates. Appellants point out that blacks currently hold the positions of State Auditor, Speaker of the North Carolina House of Representatives, and chair of the North Carolina State Board of Elections. They also point out that in 1990 a black candidate defeated a white opponent in the Democratic Party run-off for a United States Senate seat before being defeated narrowly by the Republican incumbent in the general election. Appellants further argue that if § 2 did require adoption of North Carolina's revised plan, § 2 is to that extent unconstitutional. These arguments were not developed below, and the issues remain open for consideration on remand.

* * *

[V] Racial classifications of any sort pose the risk of lasting harm to our society. They reinforce the belief, held by too many for too much of our history, that individuals should be judged by the color of their skin. Racial classifications with respect to voting carry particular dangers. Racial gerrymandering, even for remedial purposes, may balkanize us into competing racial factions; it threatens to carry us further from the goal of a political system in which race no longer matters—a goal that the Fourteenth and Fifteenth Amendments embody, and to which the Nation continues to aspire. It is for these reasons that race-based districting by our state legislatures demands close judicial scrutiny.

In this case, the Attorney General suggested that North Carolina could have created a reasonably compact second majority-minority district in the south-central to southeastern part of the State. We express no view as to whether appellants successfully could have challenged such a district under the Fourteenth Amendment. * * * Today we hold only that appellants have stated a claim under the Equal Protection Clause by alleging that the North Carolina General Assembly adopted a reapportionment scheme so irrational on its face that it can be understood only as an effort to segregate voters into separate voting districts because of their race, and that the separation lacks sufficient justification. If the allegation of racial gerrymandering remains uncontradicted, the District Court further must determine whether the North Carolina plan is narrowly tailored to further a compelling governmental interest. * * *

JUSTICE WHITE, with whom JUSTICE BLACKMUN and JUSTICE STEVENS join, dissenting.

* * * [IA] The grounds for my disagreement with the majority are simply stated: Appellants have not presented a cognizable claim, because they have not alleged a cognizable injury. [Justice White asserted that in no prior voting case alleging unfair districting had relief been granted without a showing that the state action in question had both been intended to dilute the complaining group's power and had such a substantial discriminatory effect that the group was essentially "shut out of the political process." This requirement of substantial discriminatory impact was justified by "the nature of the redistricting process," which is inherently partisan and in which politically salient factors such as race are inevitably taken into account.]

[I]t strains credulity to suggest that North Carolina's purpose in creating a second majority-minority district was to discriminate against members of the majority group by "impair[ing] or burden[ing their] opportunity . . . to participate in the political process." The State has made no mystery of its intent, which was to respond to the Attorney General's objections by improving the minority group's prospects of electing a candidate of its choice. I doubt that this constitutes a discriminatory purpose as defined in the Court's equal protection cases—i.e., an intent to aggravate "the unequal distribution of electoral power." But even assuming that it does, there is no question that appellants have not alleged the requisite discriminatory effects. Whites constitute roughly 76 percent of the total population and 79 percent of the voting age population in North Carolina. Yet, under the State's plan, they still constitute a voting majority in 10 (or 83 percent) of the 12 congressional districts. Though they might be dissatisfied at the prospect of casting a vote for a losing candidate—a lot shared by many, including a disproportionate number of minority voters—surely they cannot complain of discriminatory treatment.

[IB] * * * As I understand the [majority's theory], a redistricting plan that uses race to "segregate" voters by drawing "uncouth" lines is harmful in a way that a plan that uses race to distribute voters differently is not, for the former "bears an uncomfortable resemblance to political apartheid." The distinction is untenable.

Racial gerrymanders come in various shades: At-large voting schemes; the fragmentation of a minority group among various districts "so that it is a majority in none," otherwise known as "cracking"; the "stacking" of "a large minority population concentration . . . with a larger white population"; and, finally, the "concentration of [minority voters] into districts where they constitute an excessive majority," also called "packing." In each instance, race is consciously utilized by the legislature for electoral purposes; in each instance, we have put the plaintiff challenging the district lines to the burden of demonstrating that the plan was meant to, and did in fact, exclude an identifiable racial group from participation in the political process.

Not so, apparently, when the districting "segregates" by drawing odd-shaped lines.[7] In that case, we are told, such proof no longer is needed. Instead, it is the *State* that must rebut the allegation that race was taken into account, a fact that, together with the legislators' consideration of ethnic, religious, and other group characteristics, I had thought we practically took for granted. Part of the explanation for the majority's approach has to do, perhaps, with the emotions stirred by words such as "segregation" and "political apartheid." But their loose and imprecise use by today's majority has, I fear, led it astray. The consideration of race in "segregation" cases is no different than in other race-conscious districting; from the standpoint of the affected groups, moreover, the line-drawings all act in similar fashion. A plan that "segregates" being functionally indistinguishable from any of the other varieties of gerrymandering, we should be consistent in what we require from a claimant: Proof of discriminatory purpose and effect.

The other part of the majority's explanation of its holding is related to its simultaneous discomfort and fascination with irregularly shaped districts. * * *

[While] district irregularities may provide strong indicia of a potential gerrymander, they do no more than that. * * * Given two districts drawn on similar, race-based grounds, the one does not become more injurious than the other simply by virtue of being snake-like * * *. The majority's contrary view is perplexing in light of its concession that "compactness or attractiveness has never been held to constitute an independent federal constitutional requirement for state legislative districts." It is shortsighted as well, for a regularly shaped district can just as effectively effectuate racially discriminatory gerrymandering as an odd-shaped one. * * *

---

[7]   I borrow the term "segregate" from the majority, but, given its historical connotation, believe that its use is ill-advised. Nor is it a particularly accurate description of what has occurred. The majority-minority district that is at the center of the controversy is, according to the State, 54.71% African-American. Even if racial distribution was a factor, no racial group can be said to have been "segregated"—i.e., "set apart" or "isolate[d]." Webster's Collegiate Dictionary 1063 (9th ed. 1983).

Limited by its own terms to cases involving unusually-shaped districts, the Court's approach nonetheless will unnecessarily hinder to some extent a State's voluntary effort to ensure a modicum of minority representation. This will be true in areas where the minority population is geographically dispersed. It also will be true where the minority population is not scattered but, for reasons unrelated to race—for example, incumbency protection—the State would rather not create the majority-minority district in its most "obvious" location[.] * * *

[III] * * * [T]he Court's discussion of the level of scrutiny it requires warrants a few comments. I have no doubt that a State's compliance with the Voting Rights Act clearly constitutes a compelling interest. * * *

The Court * * * warns that the State's redistricting effort must be "narrowly tailored" to further its interest in complying with the law. It is evident to me, however, that what North Carolina did was precisely tailored to meet the objection of the Attorney General to its prior plan. Hence, I see no need for a remand at all, even accepting the majority's basic approach to this case.

* * * To the extent that no other racial group is injured, remedying a Voting Rights Act violation does not involve preferential treatment. It involves, instead, an attempt to *equalize* treatment, and to provide minority voters with an effective voice in the political process. * * *

[The dissent of JUSTICE BLACKMUN is omitted.]

JUSTICE STEVENS, dissenting.

* * * [T]wo critical facts in this case are undisputed: first, the shape of District 12 is so bizarre that it must have been drawn for the purpose of either advantaging or disadvantaging a cognizable group of voters; and, second, regardless of that shape, it *was* drawn for the purpose of facilitating the election of a second black representative from North Carolina.

These unarguable facts, which the Court devotes most of its opinion to proving, give rise to three constitutional questions: Does the Constitution impose a requirement of contiguity or compactness on how the States may draw their electoral districts? Does the Equal Protection Clause prevent a State from drawing district boundaries for the purpose of facilitating the election of a member of an identifiable group of voters? And, finally, if the answer to the second question is generally "No," should it be different when the favored group is defined by race? * * *

The first question is easy. There is no independent constitutional requirement of compactness or contiguity, and the Court's opinion (despite its many references to the shape of District 12) does not suggest otherwise. The existence of bizarre and uncouth district boundaries is powerful evidence of an ulterior purpose behind the shaping of those boundaries—usually a purpose to advantage the political party in control of the districting process. Such evidence will always be useful in cases that lack other evidence of invidious intent. In this case, however, we know what the legislators' purpose was: The North Carolina Legislature drew District 12 to include a majority of African-American voters. Evidence of the district's shape is therefore convincing, but it is also cumulative, and, for our purposes, irrelevant.

As for the second question, I believe that the Equal Protection Clause is violated when the State creates * * * uncouth district boundaries * * * for the sole purpose of making it more difficult for members of a minority group to win an election. The duty to govern impartially is abused when a group with power over the electoral process defines electoral boundaries solely to enhance its own political strength at the expense of any weaker group. That duty, however, is not violated when the majority acts to facilitate the election of a member of a group that lacks such power because it remains underrepresented in the state legislature—whether that group is defined by political affiliation, by common economic interests, or by religious, ethnic, or racial characteristics. The difference between constitutional and unconstitutional gerrymanders has nothing to do with whether they are based on assumptions about the groups they affect, but whether their purpose is to enhance the power of the group in control of the districting process at the expense of any minority group, and thereby to strengthen the unequal distribution of electoral power. When an assumption that people in a particular minority group (whether they are defined by the political party, religion, ethnic group, or race to which they belong) will vote in a particular way is used to benefit that group, no constitutional violation occurs. Politicians have always relied on assumptions that people in particular groups are likely to vote in a particular way when they draw new district lines, and I cannot believe that anything in today's opinion will stop them from doing so in the future.

Finally, we must ask whether otherwise permissible redistricting to benefit an underrepresented minority group becomes impermissible when the minority group is defined by its race. The Court today answers this question in the affirmative, and its answer is wrong. If it is permissible to draw boundaries to provide adequate representation for rural voters, for union members, for Hasidic Jews, for Polish Americans, or for Republicans, it necessarily follows that it is permissible to do the same thing for members of the very minority group whose history in the United States gave birth to the Equal Protection Clause. A contrary conclusion could only be described as perverse.

JUSTICE SOUTER, dissenting.

[I] * * * Unlike other contexts in which we have addressed the State's conscious use of race, see, e.g., *Croson* (city contracting), electoral districting calls for decisions that nearly always require some consideration of race for legitimate reasons where there is a racially mixed population. As long as members of racial groups have the commonality of interest implicit in our ability to talk about concepts like "minority voting strength," and "dilution of minority votes," cf. *Thornburg v. Gingles*, and as long as racial bloc voting takes place, legislators will have to take race into account in order to avoid dilution of minority voting strength in the districting plans they adopt. One need look no further than the Voting Rights Act to understand that this may be required * * *.

A second distinction between districting and most other governmental decisions in which race has figured is that those other decisions using racial criteria characteristically occur in circumstances in which the use of race to the advantage of one person is necessarily at the obvious expense of a member of a different race.

Thus, for example, awarding government contracts on a racial basis excludes certain firms from competition on racial grounds. * * *

In districting, by contrast, the mere placement of an individual in one district instead of another denies no one a right or benefit provided to others. All citizens may register, vote, and be represented. In whatever district, the individual voter has a right to vote in each election, and the election will result in the voter's representation. As we have held, one's constitutional rights are not violated merely because the candidate one supports loses the election or because a group (including a racial group) to which one belongs winds up with a representative from outside that group. It is true, of course, that one's vote may be more or less effective depending on the interests of the other individuals who are in one's district, and our cases recognize the reality that members of the same race often have shared interests. "Dilution" thus refers to the effects of districting decisions not on an individual's political power viewed in isolation, but on the political power of a group. This is the reason that the placement of given voters in a given district, even on the basis of race, does not, without more, diminish the effectiveness of the individual as a voter.

[II] Our different approaches to equal protection in electoral districting and nondistricting cases reflect these differences. There is a characteristic coincidence of disadvantageous effect and illegitimate purpose associated with the State's use of race in those situations in which it has immediately triggered at least heightened scrutiny (which every Member of the Court to address the issue has agreed must be applied even to race-based classifications designed to serve some permissible state interest). Presumably because the legitimate consideration of race in a districting decision is usually inevitable under the Voting Rights Act when communities are racially mixed, however, and because, without more, it does not result in diminished political effectiveness for anyone, we have not taken the approach of applying the usual standard of such heightened "scrutiny" to race-based districting decisions. * * *

[III] The Court offers no adequate justification for treating the narrow category of bizarrely shaped district claims differently from other districting claims.[9] The only justification I can imagine would be the preservation of "sound districting principles" such as compactness and contiguity. But * * * as the Court acknowledges, we have held that such principles are not constitutionally required, with the consequence that their absence cannot justify the distinct constitutional regime put in place by the Court today. * * * I would not respond to the seeming

---

[9]   The Court says its new cause of action is justified by what I understand to be some ingredients of stigmatic harm and by a "threa[t] . . . to our system of representative democracy," both caused by the mere adoption of a districting plan with the elements I have described in the text. To begin with, the complaint nowhere alleges any type of stigmatic harm. Putting that to one side, it seems utterly implausible to me to presume, as the Court does, that North Carolina's creation of this strangely-shaped majority-minority district "generates" within the white plaintiffs here anything comparable to "a feeling of inferiority as to their status in the community that may affect their hearts and minds in a way unlikely ever to be undone." *Brown v. Board of Education*, 347 U.S. 483 (1954). As for representative democracy, I have difficulty seeing how it is threatened (indeed why it is not, rather, enhanced) by districts that are not even alleged to dilute anyone's vote.

egregiousness of the redistricting now before us by untethering the concept of racial gerrymander in such a case from the concept of harm exemplified by dilution. * * *

NOTES ON SHAW *AND THE*
CONUNDRUM OF REPRESENTATION AND RACE

1. *What, Exactly, Did North Carolina Do Wrong?* Justice O'Connor creates a new cause of action: even if there is no dilution of the vote of a group nor any exclusion from the ballot, the Equal Protection Clause is violated if district lines are drawn with *too much* consideration of race and *not enough* consideration of traditional line-drawing practices. The opinion takes a sort of "Goldilocks" approach to the districting porridge— not too hot, not too cold, just right—that has bedeviled commentators and lower courts in trying to figure out how to apply it.[20] Her opinion is made all the more opaque by her apparent rejection of more judicially administrable approaches to intent (such as forbidding all consideration of race or allowing the consideration of race consistent with the purposes of the VRA) or to traditional districting practices (note that she does not hold that practices such as maintaining contiguity and compactness are constitutionally required).

Suggesting that only majority-majority districts with uncouth lines and excessive considerations of race are vulnerable begs a number of questions. Surely the intentions of the redistricting would be just as clear to white voters in a nice square-shaped district drawn to be majority-minority as it was to the plaintiffs in *Shaw*. If the basis of *Shaw* is stigmatization and dignitary harm, are not the white voters in the square district injured in precisely the same way as the plaintiffs in *Shaw*? If the basis of *Shaw* is the pernicious effects upon the political process of the elected representative being beholden to a racial group, aren't those effects the same regardless of whether the district's shape is couth or uncouth?

In the wake of *Shaw*, Richard Pildes and Richard Niemi wrote: "In resisting the use of race *in this specific way*, *Shaw* requires that redistricting continue to be understood—and, perhaps more important, perceived—as implicating multiple values. Public officials must maintain this commitment to value pluralism, even when they legitimately and intentionally take race into account." *Expressive Harms, "Bizarre Districts," and Voting Rights: Evaluating Election-District Appearances after* Shaw v. Reno, 92 Mich. L. Rev. 483, 501 (1993). If that is so, however, why does the Court emphasize "couthness"? Isn't that a pretty crude marker for value pluralism? Also, it appears that the "uncouthness" of District 12 was the result not only of the state's effort to create a majority-minority district, but also the Democrats' desire to protect their incumbents. In that event, it appears that race did not completely dominate the redistricting process. Pildes and Niemi draw from Niemi's earlier work quantifying criteria to determine relative compactness of districts (considering their geographic dispersion, perimeter, and population distribution). One finding of their study is that on

---

[20] Scholarship analyzing *Shaw* and its aftermath has become its own cottage industry. For a small sampling of some of the literature, see, in addition to other sources cited in these notes, J. Morgan Kousser, *Colorblind Injustice: Minority Voting Rights and the Undoing of the Second Reconstruction* 366–455 (1999); W. Mark Crain, *The Constitutionality of Race-Conscious Redistricting: An Empirical Analysis*, 30 J. Leg. Stud. 193 (2001); Heather Gerken, *Understanding the Right to an Undiluted Vote*, 114 Harv. L. Rev. 1663 (2001); Grant Hayden, *Resolving the Dilemma of Minority Representation*, 92 Cal. L. Rev. 1589 (2004); Daniel Lowenstein, *You Don't Have to Be Liberal to Hate the Racial Gerrymandering Cases*, 50 Stan. L. Rev. 779 (1998).

a quantitative compactness scale, North Carolina's District 12 was the least compact district in the country. Would it have been preferable for the Court to adopt some statistical requirements for compactness, contiguity, and other factors, much like it has used the one person, one vote principle to implement geographical redistricting?

2. *Questions Left Open by* Shaw. *Miller v. Johnson*, 515 U.S. 900 (1995), and *United States v. Hays*, 515 U.S. 737 (1995), resolved some of the issues opened up in *Shaw*, as to a lesser extent did *Bush v. Vera*, 517 U.S. 952 (1996), *Shaw v. Hunt*, 517 U.S. 899 (1996), and *Bartlett v. Strickland*, 556 U.S. 1 (2009).

(a) *Who may challenge majority-minority districting?* In *Hays*, the Court held that white Louisianans who did not live in the challenged majority-minority Louisiana district lacked standing to bring the case because they had not shown that they had been subjected to a racial classification.

(b) *What is the nature of the harm involved?* Justice O'Connor, in her plurality opinion in *Bush v. Vera*, wrote that some majority-minority districts "cause constitutional harm insofar as they convey the message that political identity is, or should be, predominantly racial." She labeled this an "expressive harm," which Justice Souter, in dissent, defined as "one that 'results from the idea or attitudes expressed through a governmental action, rather than from the more tangible or material consequences the action brings about'" (quoting Pildes & Niemi, *supra*). Why is expressive harm, rather than more concrete harm, sufficient in this context to constitute a constitutional claim?

(c) *To be subject to challenge, must the challenged majority-minority district have a bizarre shape?* In *Miller*, Justice Kennedy's majority opinion for a Court that remained closely divided answered this question in the negative: "Shape is relevant not because bizarreness is a necessary element of the constitutional wrong or a threshold requirement of proof, but because it may be persuasive circumstantial evidence that race for its own sake, and not other districting principles, was the legislature's dominant and controlling rationale in drawing its district lines. The logical implication * * * is that parties may rely on evidence other than bizarreness to establish race-based districting."

(d) *If bizarre shape is not a requirement, what identifies presumptively unconstitutional majority-minority districts?* Recall the debate in *Shaw* about how the consideration of demographics, including race, is an inherent part of the redistricting process. If, as *Miller* held, there is no threshold requirement of bizarre configuration, what stops the *Shaw* cause of action from invalidating not only all majority-minority districts, but any district (regardless of demographics) that was designed in part because of racial considerations? *Miller* announced a potentially important qualification:

> Federal court review of districting legislation represents a serious intrusion on the most vital of local functions. It is well settled that "reapportionment is primarily the duty and responsibility of the State." Electoral districting is a most difficult subject for legislatures, and so the States must have discretion to exercise the political judgment necessary to balance competing interests. Although race-based decisionmaking is inherently suspect, until a claimant makes a showing sufficient to support that allegation the good faith of a state legislature must be presumed. The courts, in assessing the sufficiency of a

challenge to a districting plan, must be sensitive to the complex interplay of forces that enter a legislature's redistricting calculus. Redistricting legislatures will, for example, almost always be aware of racial demographics; but it does not follow that race predominates in the redistricting process. *Shaw.* The distinction between being aware of racial considerations and being motivated by them may be difficult to make. This evidentiary difficulty, together with the sensitive nature of redistricting and the presumption of good faith that must be accorded legislative enactments, requires courts to exercise extraordinary caution in adjudicating claims that a state has drawn district lines on the basis of race. The plaintiff's burden is to show, either through circumstantial evidence of a district's shape and demographics or more direct evidence going to legislative purpose, that race was the predominant factor motivating the legislature's decision to place a significant number of voters within or without a particular district. To make this showing, a plaintiff must prove that the legislature subordinated traditional race-neutral districting principles, including but not limited to compactness, contiguity, respect for political subdivisions or communities defined by actual shared interests, to racial considerations. Where these or other race-neutral considerations are the basis for redistricting legislation, and are not subordinated to race, a state can "defeat a claim that a district has been gerrymandered on racial lines." *Shaw.*

Is this consistent with the Court's general approach to proving discriminatory intent under the Equal Protection Clause (see notes following *Mobile v. Bolden, supra*)? Will it not require intensive case-by-case review of every majority-minority district? If, as is commonly asserted, redistricting involves a host of complex and interactive questions, including potentially hundreds of small decisions about precisely where to draw each little segment of the lines, is it likely that one "predominant" motive can be isolated after the fact? Moreover, if the harm in these cases concerns social messages and perceptions arising from redistricting lines, shouldn't liability turn on the public processes and outcomes (i.e., maps) of redistricting rather than whether, at the end of litigation some years later, a judge decides race was, or was not, the predominant motive? Consider Richard Pildes, *Principled Limitations on Racial and Partisan Redistricting*, 106 Yale L.J. 2505, 2540 (1997): "Judicial opinions in these cases, as well as editorial pages, reprint maps of the districts, not transcripts of political processes, for a reason. Social perceptions about the 'excessive' role of race are more likely attuned to objective characteristics of districts, such as their shapes, rather than the mysteries of intent."

(e)   *What constitutes a compelling governmental interest sufficient to save majority-minority districting that would otherwise be unconstitutional? Miller* interpreted the VRA narrowly to avoid any conflict between the statute and the equal protection principle announced in *Shaw.* In *Miller,* Georgia had adopted the challenged majority-minority district after pressure from the federal Department of Justice, which had refused to preclear earlier Georgia reapportionment plans under § 5 of the Act. Justice Kennedy's opinion interpreted the VRA as authorizing the Department of Justice to withhold preclearance only when a redistricting plan constitutes a "retrogression" in minority voting power—that is, a showing of reduced minority voting strength relative to the appropriate benchmark year. Thus, because earlier Georgia redistricting plans following the 1990 census had increased minority voting power over the scheme used to elect Georgia Congress members in the 1980s, the Department had wrongly withheld preclearance, and compliance with the Department's demands could not be justified as being required to comply with federal law. Justice Kennedy then suggested that, had the Department been correct in its interpretation of the VRA, the Act might have been unconstitutional.[21] In *Bush v. Vera* and *Shaw v. Hunt*, which also both struck down majority-minority congressional districting, the Court again did not resolve whether compliance with the Act would constitute a compelling governmental interest.

It seems that the issue here is not so much whether compliance with the Act constitutes a compelling governmental interest—the Justices seem to assume that it does—as it is what the Act actually requires of the states. If the Act broadly requires race-conscious districting, then the Act itself may well be unconstitutional. If the Act is considerably narrower, then compliance with it presumably should suffice as a compelling governmental interest.

(f) *How large must the minority population be to be considered "sufficiently large and geographically compact to constitute a majority in a single-member district"?* In *Bartlett v. Strickland*, the minority voters argued that crossover majority voters could provide them the support they needed to elect their preferred candidate so they could attack a new districting plan that split African-American voters into two districts even though their numbers had fallen below 50% in the previous district. A plurality of the Court, led by Justice Kennedy, held that a party asserting a claim under § 2 must show that the minority population in the potential district is greater than 50%.

(g) *Nonjusticiability redux.* Recall that under the regime of *Colegrove v. Green*, federal courts were generally to stay out of "political thickets" involving state legislative apportionment—with an exception for cases involving intentional discrimination against racial minorities, who could invoke the specific protections of the Fifteenth Amendment (rather than merely the general protection of the Equal Protection Clause of the Fourteenth Amendment) and, at least in some cases, could plausibly claim they have been singled out as identified individuals, not simply as members of a group (*Gomillion*). *Baker v. Carr* and *Reynolds v. Sims* changed all that—or did they? Could *Baker* and *Reynolds* simply be understood as allowing federal courts to hear state apportionment cases invoking equal protection only in the context where a simple, administrable standard—one person, one vote—was available? Contrast *Shaw v. Reno*'s allowance of race to be taken into account in ensuring minority representation so long as it is not taken into account too much. Should the Supreme Court's willingness to consider open-ended equality claims to state apportionment decisions be limited to unequal population claims (*Reynolds*) and race claims (*Gomillion* and *Shaw*)? What

---

[21] Justice Kennedy wrote:

In *South Carolina v. Katzenbach*, we upheld § 5 as a necessary and constitutional response to some states' "extraordinary stratagem[s] of contriving new rules of various kinds for the sole purpose of perpetuating voting discrimination in the face of adverse federal court decrees." But our belief in *Katzenbach* that the federalism costs exacted by § 5 preclearance could be justified by those extraordinary circumstances does not mean they can be justified in the circumstances of this case. And the Justice Department's implicit command that States engage in presumptively unconstitutional race-based districting brings the Voting Rights Act, once upheld as a proper exercise of Congress' authority under § 2 of the Fifteenth Amendment, into tension with the Fourteenth Amendment. As we recalled in *Katzenbach* itself, Congress' exercise of its Fifteenth Amendment authority even when otherwise proper still must " 'consist with the letter and spirit of the Constitution.' " We need not, however, resolve these troubling and difficult constitutional questions today. There is no indication Congress intended such a far-reaching application of § 5, so we reject the Justice Department's interpretation of the statute and avoid the constitutional problems that interpretation raises.

about apportionment designed to ensure the continued success of the political party currently in power, an even thicker political thicket and the topic of our next subsection?

C. POLITICAL GERRYMANDERING

In *Karcher v. Daggett*, 462 U.S. 725 (1983) (discussed above in § 1(A)(1)), the plaintiffs who challenged the New Jersey congressional districting included all the Republican members of the House from New Jersey. They argued that "the bizarre configuration of New Jersey's congressional districts is sufficient to demonstrate that the plan was not adopted in 'good faith.' This argument * * * is a claim that the district boundaries are unconstitutional because they are the product of political gerrymandering." *Id.* at 744 (Stevens, J., concurring). Invoking the Equal Protection Clause, Justice Stevens was willing to strike down the redistricting based solely upon the taking of partisan advantage and to consider the noncompact shape of district configurations and "extensive deviation from established political boundaries" as evidence of illicit political gerrymandering. He explained:

> A procedural standard * * * may also be enlightening. If the process for formulating and adopting a plan excluded divergent viewpoints, openly reflected the use of partisan criteria, and provided no explanation of the reasons for selecting one plan over another, it would seem appropriate to conclude that an adversely affected plaintiff group is entitled to have the majority explain its action. On the other hand, if neutral decisionmakers developed the plan on the basis of neutral criteria, if there was an adequate opportunity for the presentation and consideration of differing points of view, and if the guidelines used in selecting a plan were explained, a strong presumption of validity should attach to whatever plan such a process produced. * * *

> A glance at the [districting] map * * * shows district configurations well deserving the kind of descriptive adjectives—"uncouth" and "bizarre"— that have traditionally been used to describe acknowledged gerrymanders. * * * In addition [to] disregarding geographical compactness, the redistricting scheme wantonly disregards county boundaries. For example, in the words of a commentator, "In a flight of cartographic fancy, the Legislature packed New Jersey Republicans into a new district many call 'the Swan.' Its long neck and twisted body stretch from the New York suburbs to the rural upper reaches of the Delaware River." That district, the Fifth, contains segments of at least seven counties. The same commentator described the Seventh District, comprised of parts of five counties, as tracing "a curving partisan path through industrial Elizabeth, liberal academic Princeton and largely Jewish Marlboro in Monmouth County. The resulting monstrosity was called 'the Fishhook' by detractors."

Such a map prompts an inquiry into the process that led to its adoption. The plan was sponsored by the leadership in the Democratic Party, which controlled both houses of the state legislature as well as the Governor's office, and was signed into law the day before the inauguration of a Republican Governor. The legislators never formally explained the guidelines used in formulating their plan or in selecting it over other available plans. Several [other plans] contained districts that were more nearly equal in population, more compact, and more consistent with subdivision boundaries[.]   * * *   [T]he record indicates that the decisionmaking process leading to adoption of the challenged plan was far from neutral. It was designed to increase the number of Democrats, and to decrease the number of Republicans, that New Jersey's voters would send to Congress in future years. * * *

Consider the full Court's various responses to political gerrymandering in the cases following *Karcher*.

Davis v. Bandemer
478 U.S. 109 (1986).

Democrats challenged the reapportionment of the Indiana legislature carried out in response to the 1980 census by the Republican majorities in both legislative houses and approved by the Republican governor. The three-judge District Court invalidated the reapportionment on equal protection grounds, and the state appealed. The plurality opinion of **Justice White**, joined by **Justices Brennan**, **Marshall**, and **Blackmun**, first rejected the contention that the issue was a nonjusticiable political question. Justice White noted that, since *Baker v. Carr*, the Court has adjudicated claims based on population inequality among districts, racial gerrymandering, and racial vote dilution allegedly resulting from multimember districting. None of *Baker*'s five "identifying characteristics" of a political question was present in this case, just as none had been present in *Baker*, *Reynolds*, and other reapportionment cases.

The plurality then endorsed a narrow cause of action under the Equal Protection Clause, by analogy to the approach taken in *Bolden*. "[U]nconstitutional discrimination occurs only when the electoral system is arranged in a manner that will consistently degrade a voter's or a group of voters' influence on the political process as a whole. * * * [T]he question is whether a particular group has been unconstitutionally denied its chance to effectively influence the political process. * * * Statewide, * * * the inquiry centers on the voters' direct or indirect influence on the elections of the state legislature as a whole." Thus, "[r]elying on a single election to prove unconstitutional discrimination is unsatisfactory." Because the District Court's findings did not satisfy this test, the Court reversed.

Justice O'Connor, joined by **Chief Justice Burger** and **Justice Rehnquist**, concurred in the judgment of reversal, but on the ground that political gerrymandering raises only a nonjusticiable political question. The issue was certainly "political" in the classic sense of the term. In her view, legislatively controlled reapportionment was a "critical and traditional part of politics in the United States" that was generally self-correcting over time. Political (as opposed to racial) groups should have no constitutional protection against losses in the political process. The plurality's test for an equal protection violation provided no judicially manageable standard. "[T]his standard will over time either prove unmanageable and arbitrary or else evolve towards some loose form of proportionality."

Justice Powell, joined by **Justice Stevens**, dissented. They agreed with the plurality that the issue was justiciable but strongly disagreed with the plurality's constitutional test. Starting with the precept that "[t]he Equal Protection Clause guarantees citizens that their State will govern them impartially," Justice Powell drew two further precepts from the Court's prior cases on voting rights. First, those cases recognize that "equal protection encompasses a guarantee of equal *representation,* requiring a State to seek to achieve through redistricting 'fair and effective representation of all citizens.'" (Quoting *Reynolds.*) Second, those cases recognized that "redistricting should be based on a number of neutral criteria, of which districts of equal population was only one." In light of these precepts, the plurality opinion was "seriously flawed" by its formalistic, and unrealistic, focus on mathematical standards of representation and by its failure to announce any workable standard for review.

Relying upon Justice Stevens' concurring opinion in *Karcher,* Justice Powell proposed that judicial review should investigate such neutral criteria as "the shapes of voting districts and adherence to established political subdivision boundaries. Other relevant considerations include the nature of the legislative procedures by which the apportionment law was adopted and legislative history reflecting contemporaneous legislative goals. To make out a case of unconstitutional partisan gerrymandering, the plaintiff should be required to offer proof concerning these factors, which bear directly on the fairness of a redistricting plan, as well as evidence concerning population disparities and statistics tending to show vote dilution. No one factor should be dispositive." Tracing the history of the Indiana reapportionment, Justice Powell concluded that "[t]he legislative process consisted of nothing more than the majority party's private application of computer technology to map-making." The maps ignored traditional political subdivisions and communities of interest and appeared rooted solely in partisan considerations. He concluded that appellants "failed to justify the discriminatory impact of the plan by showing that the plan had a rational basis in permissible neutral criteria." Responding to this approach for the plurality, Justice White argued that the Powell-Stevens approach was inconsistent with *Bolden* and would tend to promote judicially imposed proportional representation.

By finding political gerrymandering a justiciable issue, *Bandemer* fostered litigation in the lower courts. But because the plurality defined the cause of action so narrowly (as well as so vaguely), virtually no redress for political gerrymandering resulted. When given an opportunity to reconsider *Bandemer* in the following case, however, the Court could reach no definitive conclusion.

VIETH V. JUBELIRER

Supreme Court of the United States, 2004.
541 U.S. 267, 124 S.Ct. 1769, 158 L.Ed.2d 546.

JUSTICE SCALIA announced the judgment of the Court and delivered an opinion, in which THE CHIEF JUSTICE [REHNQUIST], JUSTICE O'CONNOR, and JUSTICE THOMAS join.

[I] The facts, as alleged by the plaintiffs, are as follows. The population figures derived from the 2000 census showed that Pennsylvania was entitled to only 19 Representatives in Congress, a decrease in 2 from the Commonwealth's previous delegation. Pennsylvania's General Assembly took up the task of drawing a new districting map. At the time, the Republican Party controlled a majority of both state Houses and held the Governor's office. Prominent national figures in the Republican Party pressured the General Assembly to adopt a partisan redistricting plan as a punitive measure against Democrats for having enacted pro-Democrat redistricting plans elsewhere. The Republican members of Pennsylvania's House and Senate worked together on such a plan. On January 3, 2002, the General Assembly passed its plan, which was signed into law by Governor Schweiker * * *.

[The lawsuit filed by registered Democrats who vote in Pennsylvania alleged that the legislation created malapportioned districts, in violation of the one person, one vote requirement. Moreover, the plaintiffs argued that the redistricting plan constituted a political gerrymander, because the districts were "meandering and irregular" and "ignor[ed] all traditional redistricting criteria, including the preservation of local government boundaries, solely for the sake of partisan advantage." The plaintiffs initially won before a three-judge District Court panel, Pennsylvania passed a remedial plan to cure the apportionment problems identified by the court, and the District Court panel denied the plaintiffs' claim that the remedial proposal was also an impermissible political gerrymander.]

[III] [The plurality provided the *Baker v. Carr* tests for the existence of a political question (p. 121, *supra*). It stated that "there is no doubt" of the applicability of the second test to this case: the lack of "judicially discoverable and manageable standards" to resolve the claim.]

Over the dissent of three Justices, the Court held in *Davis v. Bandemer* that, since it was "not persuaded that there are no judicially discernible and manageable standards by which political gerrymander cases are to be decided," such cases *were* justiciable. The clumsy shifting of the burden of proof for the premise (the Court was "not persuaded" that standards do not exist, rather than "persuaded" that they do) was necessitated by the uncomfortable fact that the six-Justice majority could not discern what the judicially discernable standards might be. * * * The lower courts have lived with that assurance of a standard (or more precisely, lack of assurance that there is no standard), coupled with that inability to specify a standard, for the past 18 years. In that time, they have considered numerous political gerrymandering claims; this Court has never revisited the unanswered question of what standard governs.

[T]he lower courts have [not], over 18 years, succeeded in shaping the standard that this Court was initially unable to enunciate. They have simply applied the standard set forth in *Bandemer*'s four–Justice plurality opinion. This might be thought to prove that the four–Justice plurality standard has met the test of time— but for the fact that its application has almost invariably produced the same result (except for the incurring of attorney's fees) as would have obtained if the question were nonjusticiable: Judicial intervention has been refused. As one commentary has put it, "[t]hroughout its subsequent history, *Bandemer* has served almost exclusively as an invitation to litigation without much prospect of redress." S. Issacharoff, P. Karlan & R. Pildes, *The Law of Democracy* 886 (rev. 2d ed. 2002). * * *

Eighteen years of judicial effort with virtually nothing to show for it justify us in revisiting the question whether the standard promised by *Bandemer* exists. As the following discussion reveals, no judicially discernible and manageable standards for adjudicating political gerrymandering claims have emerged. Lacking them, we must conclude that political gerrymandering claims are nonjusticiable and that *Bandemer* was wrongly decided.

[IIIB]   Appellants take a run at enunciating their own workable standard based on Article I, § 2, and the Equal Protection Clause. * * * Appellants' proposed standard retains the two-pronged framework of the *Bandemer* plurality—intent plus effect—but modifies the type of showing sufficient to satisfy each.

To satisfy appellants' intent standard, a plaintiff must "show that the mapmakers acted with a *predominant intent* to achieve partisan advantage," which can be shown "by direct evidence or by circumstantial evidence that other neutral and legitimate redistricting criteria were subordinated to the goal of achieving partisan advantage." (Emphasis added). As compared with the *Bandemer* plurality's test of mere intent to disadvantage the plaintiff's group, this proposal seemingly makes the standard more difficult to meet—but only at the expense of making the standard more indeterminate.

"Predominant intent" to disadvantage the plaintiff political group refers to the relative importance of that goal as compared with all the other goals that the map seeks to pursue—contiguity of districts, compactness of districts, observance of the lines of political subdivision, protection of incumbents of all parties, cohesion of natural racial and ethnic neighborhoods, compliance with requirements of the Voting Rights Act of 1965 regarding racial distribution, etc. Appellants contend that their intent test *must* be discernible and manageable because it has been borrowed from our racial gerrymandering cases. To begin with, in a very important respect that is not so. In the racial gerrymandering context, the predominant intent test has been applied to the challenged district in which the plaintiffs voted. Here, however, appellants do not assert that an apportionment fails their intent test if any single district does so. Since "it would be quixotic to attempt to bar state legislatures from considering politics as they redraw district lines," appellants propose a test that is satisfied only when "partisan advantage was the predominant motivation *behind the entire statewide plan*." (Emphasis added). Vague as the "predominant motivation" test might be when used to evaluate single districts, it all but evaporates when applied statewide. Does it mean, for instance, that partisan intent must outweigh all other goals—contiguity, compactness, preservation of neighborhoods, etc.—*statewide*? And how is the statewide "outweighing" to be determined? If three-fifths of the map's districts forgo the pursuit of partisan ends in favor of strictly observing political-subdivision lines, and only two-fifths ignore those lines to disadvantage the plaintiffs, is the observance of political subdivisions the "predominant" goal between those two? We are sure appellants do not think so.

Even within the narrower compass of challenges to a single district, applying a "predominant intent" test to *racial* gerrymandering is easier and less disruptive. The Constitution clearly contemplates districting by political entities, and unsurprisingly that turns out to be root-and-branch a matter of politics. By contrast, the purpose of segregating voters on the basis of race is not a lawful one, and is much more rarely encountered. Determining whether the shape of a particular district is so substantially affected by the presence of a rare and constitutionally suspect motive as to invalidate it is quite different from determining whether it is so substantially affected by the excess of an ordinary and lawful motive as to invalidate it. Moreover, the fact that partisan districting is a lawful and common practice means that there is almost *always* room for an election-impeding lawsuit contending that partisan advantage was the predominant motivation; not so for claims of racial gerrymandering. * * *

The effects prong of appellants' proposal replaces the *Bandemer* plurality's vague test of "denied its chance to effectively influence the political process" with criteria that are seemingly more specific. The requisite effect is established when "(1) the plaintiffs show that the districts systematically 'pack' and 'crack' the rival party's voters, *and* (2) the court's examination of the 'totality of circumstances' confirms that the map can thwart the plaintiffs' ability to translate a majority of votes into a majority of seats." (Emphasis added.) This test is loosely based on our cases applying § 2 of the Voting Rights Act to discrimination by race. But a person's politics is rarely as readily discernible—and *never* as permanently discernible—as a person's race. Political affiliation is not an immutable characteristic, but may shift from one election to the next; and even within a given election, not all voters follow the party line. We dare say (and hope) that the political party which puts forward an utterly incompetent candidate will lose even in its registration stronghold. These facts make it impossible to assess the effects of partisan gerrymandering, to fashion a standard for evaluating a violation, and finally to craft a remedy.

Assuming, however, that the effects of partisan gerrymandering can be determined, appellants' test would invalidate the districting only when it prevents a majority of the electorate from electing a majority of representatives. Before considering whether this particular standard is judicially manageable we question whether it is judicially discernible in the sense of being relevant to some constitutional violation. Deny it as appellants may (and do), this standard rests upon the principle that groups (or at least political-action groups) have a right to proportional representation. But the Constitution contains no such principle. It guarantees equal protection of the law to persons, not equal representation in government to equivalently sized groups. It nowhere says that farmers or urban dwellers, Christian fundamentalists or Jews, Republicans or Democrats, must be accorded political strength proportionate to their numbers.

Even if the standard were relevant, however, it is not judicially manageable. To begin with, how is a party's majority status to be established? Appellants propose using the results of statewide races as the benchmark of party support. But as their own complaint describes, in the 2000 Pennsylvania statewide elections some Republicans won and some Democrats won. Moreover, to think that majority status in statewide races establishes majority status for district contests, one would have to believe that the only factor determining voting behavior at all levels is political affiliation. That is assuredly not true. * * *

But if we could identify a majority party, we would find it impossible to assure that that party wins a majority of seats—unless we radically revise the States' traditional structure for elections. In any winner-take-all district system, there can be no guarantee, no matter how the district lines are drawn, that a majority of party votes statewide will produce a majority of seats for that party. * * * Consider, for example, a legislature that draws district lines with no objectives in mind except compactness and respect for the lines of political subdivisions. Under that system, political groups that tend to cluster (as is the case with Democratic voters in cities) would be systematically affected by what might be called a "natural" packing effect.

[In Part IV, the plurality responded to the contentions of the separate opinions; this discussion is summarized in the Notes following the case.]

JUSTICE KENNEDY, concurring in the judgment.

* * * When presented with a claim of injury from partisan gerrymandering, courts confront two obstacles. First is the lack of comprehensive and neutral principles for drawing electoral boundaries. No substantive definition of fairness in districting seems to command general assent. Second is the absence of rules to limit and confine judicial intervention. * * *

There are, then, weighty arguments for holding cases like these to be nonjusticiable; and those arguments may prevail in the long run. In my view, however, the arguments are not so compelling that they require us now to bar all future claims of injury from a partisan gerrymander. It is not in our tradition to foreclose the judicial process from the attempt to define standards and remedies where it is alleged that a constitutional right is burdened or denied. * * *

That no [judicially manageable] standard [for partisan gerrymandering claims] has emerged in this case should not be taken to prove that none will emerge in the future. Where important rights are involved, the impossibility of full analytical satisfaction is reason to err on the side of caution. * * *

* * * [T]he rapid evolution of technologies in the apportionment field suggests yet unexplored possibilities. Computer assisted districting has become so routine and sophisticated that legislatures, experts, and courts can use databases to map electoral districts in a matter of hours, not months. Technology is both a threat and a promise. On the one hand, if courts refuse to entertain any claims of partisan gerrymandering, the temptation to use partisan favoritism in districting in an unconstitutional manner will grow. On the other hand, these new technologies may

produce new methods of analysis that make more evident the precise nature of the burdens gerrymanders impose on the representational rights of voters and parties. That would facilitate court efforts to identify and remedy the burdens, with judicial intervention limited by the derived standards. * * *

JUSTICE STEVENS, dissenting.

* * * [W]hile political considerations may properly influence the decisions of our elected officials, when such decisions disadvantage members of a minority group—whether the minority is defined by its members' race, religion, or political affiliation—they must rest on a neutral predicate. * * * [T]he Equal Protection Clause implements a duty to govern impartially that requires, at the very least, that every decision by the sovereign serve some nonpartisan public purpose.

In evaluating a claim that a governmental decision violates the Equal Protection Clause, we have long required a showing of discriminatory purpose. That requirement applies with full force to districting decisions. The line that divides a racial or ethnic minority unevenly between school districts can be entirely legitimate if chosen on the basis of neutral factors—county lines, for example, or a natural boundary such as a river or major thoroughfare. But if the district lines were chosen for the purpose of limiting the number of minority students in the school, or the number of families holding unpopular religious or political views, that invidious purpose surely would invalidate the district.

Consistent with that principle, our recent racial gerrymandering cases have examined the shape of the district and the purpose of the districting body to determine whether race, above all other criteria, predominated in the line-drawing process. [Justice Stevens summarized *Shaw v. Reno* and its progeny.] Under the *Shaw* cases, * * * the use of race as a criterion in redistricting is not *per se* impermissible, but when race is elevated to paramount status—when it is the be-all and end-all of the redistricting process—the legislature has gone too far. * * *

Just as irrational shape can serve as an objective indicator of an impermissible legislative purpose, other objective features of a districting map can save the plan from invalidation. We have explained that "traditional districting principles," which include "compactness, contiguity, and respect for political subdivisions," are "important not because they are constitutionally required . . . but because they are objective factors that may serve to defeat a claim that a district has been gerrymandered on racial lines." * * *

In my view, the same standards should apply to claims of political gerrymandering, for the essence of a gerrymander is the same regardless of whether the group is identified as political or racial. Gerrymandering always involves the drawing of district boundaries to maximize the voting strength of the dominant political faction and to minimize the strength of one or more groups of opponents. In seeking the desired result, legislators necessarily make judgments about the probability that the members of identifiable groups—whether economic, religious, ethnic, or racial—will vote in a certain way. The overriding purpose of those predictions is political. It follows that the standards that enable courts to identify and redress a racial gerrymander could also perform the same function for other species of gerrymanders. * * *

In sum, in evaluating a challenge to a specific district, I would apply the standard set forth in the [racial gerrymandering] cases and ask whether the legislature allowed partisan considerations to dominate and control the lines drawn, forsaking all neutral principles. Under my analysis, if no neutral criterion can be identified to justify the lines drawn, and if the only possible explanation for a district's bizarre shape is a naked desire to increase partisan strength, then no rational basis exists to save the district from an equal protection challenge. Such a narrow test would cover only a few meritorious claims, but it would preclude extreme abuses, * * * and it would perhaps shorten the time period in which the pernicious effects of such a gerrymander are felt. * * *

[JUSTICE SOUTER'S dissent, joined by JUSTICE GINSBURG, set out a five-part test. A plaintiff would be required to show (1) that he is a member of a "cohesive political group"; (2) that the district he lived in paid no or little attention to traditional districting principles; (3) that there were "specific correlations between the district's deviations from traditional districting principles and the distribution of the population of his group"; (4) that a hypothetical district exists that includes the plaintiff's residence, remedies the packing or cracking of the plaintiff's group, and deviates less from traditional districting principles; and (5) that "the defendants acted intentionally to manipulate the shape of the district in order to pack or crack his group." When a plaintiff made such showings, the burden would shift to the defendants to justify the district by reference to goals other than "naked partisan advantage."

[In response to the plurality's argument that his test was unworkable, he wrote: "It is common sense * * * to break down a large and intractable issue into discrete fragments as a way to get a handle on the larger one, and the elements I propose are not only tractable in theory, but the very subjects that judges already deal with in practice. The plurality asks, for example, '[w]hat . . . a lower court [is] to do when, as will often be the case, the district adheres to some traditional criteria but not others?' This question already arises in cases under § 2 of the Voting Rights Act of 1965, and the district courts have not had the same sort of difficulty answering it as they have in applying the *Davis v. Bandemer* plurality. The enquiries I am proposing are not, to be sure, as hard-edged as I wish they could be, but neither do they have a degree of subjectivity inconsistent with the judicial function."]

JUSTICE BREYER, dissenting.

The use of purely political considerations in drawing district boundaries is not a "necessary evil" that, for lack of judicially manageable standards, the Constitution inevitably must tolerate. Rather, pure politics often helps to secure constitutionally important democratic objectives. But sometimes it does not. Sometimes purely political "gerrymandering" will fail to advance any plausible democratic objective while simultaneously threatening serious democratic harm. And sometimes when that is so, courts can identify an equal protection violation and provide a remedy. Because the plaintiffs could claim (but have not yet proved) that such circumstances exist here, I would reverse the District Court's dismissal of their complaint. * * *

[I]   * * * [T]he workable democracy that the Constitution foresees must mean more than a guaranteed opportunity to elect legislators representing equally populous electoral districts. There must also be a method for transforming the will of the majority into effective government.

This Court has explained that political parties play a necessary role in that transformation. At a minimum, they help voters assign responsibility for current circumstances, thereby enabling those voters, through their votes for individual candidates, to express satisfaction or dissatisfaction with the political status quo. Those voters can either vote to support that status quo or vote to "throw the rascals out." A party-based political system that satisfies this minimal condition encourages democratic responsibility. It facilitates the transformation of the voters' will into a government that reflects that will.

Why do I refer to these elementary constitutional principles? Because I believe they can help courts identify at least one abuse at issue in this case. To understand how that is so, one should begin by asking why single-member electoral districts are the norm, why the Constitution does not insist that the membership of legislatures better reflect different political views held by different groups of voters. History, of course, is part of the answer, but it does not tell the entire story. The answer also lies in the fact that a single-member-district system helps to assure certain democratic objectives better than many "more representative" (*i.e.*, proportional) electoral systems. Of course, single-member districts mean that only parties with candidates who finish "first past the post" will elect legislators. That fact means in turn that a party with a bare majority of votes or even a plurality of votes will often obtain a large legislative majority, perhaps freezing out smaller parties. But single-member districts thereby diminish the need for coalition governments. And that fact makes it easier for voters to identify which party is responsible for government decisionmaking (and which rascals to throw out), while simultaneously providing greater legislative stability. This is not to say that single-member districts are preferable; it is simply to say that single-member-district systems and more-directly-representational systems reflect different conclusions about the proper balance of different elements of a workable democratic government.

If single-member districts are the norm, however, then political considerations will likely play an important, and proper, role in the drawing of district boundaries. In part, that is because politicians, unlike nonpartisan observers, normally understand how "the location and shape of districts" determine "the political complexion of the area." It is precisely *because* politicians are best able to predict the effects of boundary changes that the districts they design usually make some political sense.

More important for present purposes, the role of political considerations reflects a surprising mathematical fact. Given a fairly large state population with a fairly large congressional delegation, districts assigned so as to be perfectly random in respect to politics would translate a small shift in political sentiment, say a shift from 51% Republican to 49% Republican, into a seismic shift in the makeup of the legislative delegation, say from 100% Republican to 100% Democrat. Any such exaggeration of tiny electoral changes—virtually wiping out legislative representation of the minority party—would itself seem highly undemocratic.

Given the resulting need for single-member districts with nonrandom boundaries, it is not surprising that "traditional" districting principles have rarely, if ever, been politically neutral. Rather, because, in recent political memory, Democrats have often been concentrated in cities while Republicans have often been concentrated in suburbs and sometimes rural areas, geographically drawn boundaries have tended to "pac[k]" the former. Neighborhood or community-based boundaries, seeking to group Irish, Jewish, or African-American voters, often did the same. All this is well known to politicians, who use their knowledge about the effects of the "neutral" criteria to partisan advantage when drawing electoral maps. * * *

* * * [R]eference back to these underlying considerations helps to explain why the legislature's use of political boundary drawing considerations ordinarily does *not* violate the Constitution's Equal Protection Clause. The reason lies not simply in the difficulty of identifying abuse or finding an appropriate judicial remedy. The reason is more fundamental: Ordinarily, there simply is no abuse. The use of purely political boundary-drawing factors, even where harmful to the members of one party, will often nonetheless find justification in other desirable democratic ends, such as maintaining relatively stable legislatures in which a minority party retains significant representation.

[II] At the same time, these considerations can help identify at least one circumstance where use of purely political boundary-drawing factors can amount to a serious, and remediable, abuse, namely the *unjustified* use of political factors to entrench a minority in power. By entrenchment I mean a situation in which a party that enjoys only minority support among the populace has nonetheless contrived to take, and hold, legislative power. By *unjustified* entrenchment I mean that the minority's hold on power is purely the result of partisan manipulation and not other factors. These "other" factors that could lead to "justified" (albeit temporary) minority entrenchment include sheer happenstance, the existence of more than two major parties, the unique constitutional requirements of certain representational bodies such as the Senate, or reliance on traditional (geographic, communities of interest, etc.) districting criteria. * * *

[III] Courts need not intervene often to prevent the kind of abuse I have described, because those harmed constitute a political majority, and a majority normally can work its political will. Where a State has improperly gerrymandered legislative or congressional districts to the majority's disadvantage, the majority should be able to elect officials in statewide races—particularly the Governor—who may help to undo the harm that districting has caused the majority's party, in the next round of districting if not sooner. And where a State has improperly gerrymandered congressional districts, Congress retains the power to revise the State's districting determinations.

Moreover, voters in some States, perhaps tiring of the political boundary-drawing rivalry, have found a procedural solution, confiding the task to a commission that is limited in the extent to which it may base districts on partisan concerns. According to the National Conference of State Legislatures, 12 States currently give "first and final authority for [state] legislative redistricting to a group other than the legislature." A number of States use a commission for congressional redistricting: Arizona, Hawaii, Idaho, Montana, New Jersey, and Washington, with Indiana using a commission if the legislature cannot pass a plan and Iowa requiring the district-drawing body not to consider political data. Indeed, where state governments have been unwilling or unable to act, "an informed, civically militant electorate" has occasionally taken matters into its own hands, through ballot initiatives or referendums. Arizona voters, for example, passed Proposition 106, which amended the State's Constitution and created an independent redistricting commission to draw legislative and congressional districts. * * *

But we cannot always count on a severely gerrymandered legislature itself to find and implement a remedy. The party that controls the process has no incentive to change it. And the political advantages of a gerrymander may become ever greater in the future. The availability of enhanced computer technology allows the parties to redraw boundaries in ways that target individual neighborhoods and homes, carving out safe but slim victory margins in the maximum number of districts, with little risk of cutting their margins too thin. By redrawing districts every 2 years, rather than every 10 years, a party might preserve its political advantages notwithstanding population shifts in the State. The combination of increasingly precise map-drawing technology and increasingly frequent map drawing means that a party may be able to bring about a gerrymander that is not only precise, but virtually impossible to dislodge. Thus, court action may prove necessary. * * *

[IV] I do not claim that the problem of identification and separation is easily solved, even in extreme instances. But courts can identify a number of strong indicia of abuse. The presence of actual entrenchment, while not always unjustified (being perhaps a chance occurrence), is such a sign, particularly when accompanied by the use of partisan boundary drawing criteria * * * that both departs from traditional criteria and cannot be explained other than by efforts to achieve partisan advantage. Below, I set forth several sets of circumstances that lay out the indicia of abuse I have in mind. The scenarios fall along a continuum: The more permanently entrenched the minority's hold on power becomes, the less evidence courts will need that the minority engaged in gerrymandering to achieve the desired result.

Consider, for example, the following sets of circumstances. First, suppose that the legislature has proceeded to redraw boundaries in what seem to be ordinary ways, but the entrenchment harm has become obvious. E.g., (a) the legislature has not redrawn district boundaries more than once within the traditional 10–year period; and (b) no radical departure from traditional districting criteria is alleged; but (c) a majority party (as measured by the votes actually cast for all candidates who identify themselves as members of that party in the relevant set of elections;

i.e., in congressional elections if a congressional map is being challenged) has *twice* failed to obtain a majority of the relevant legislative seats in elections; and (d) the failure cannot be explained by the existence of multiple parties or in other neutral ways. In my view, these circumstances would be sufficient to support a claim of unconstitutional entrenchment.

Second, suppose that plaintiffs could point to more serious departures from redistricting norms. *E.g.*, (a) the legislature has not redrawn district boundaries more than once within the traditional 10-year period; but (b) the boundary-drawing criteria depart radically from previous or traditional criteria; (c) the departure cannot be justified or explained other than by reference to an effort to obtain partisan political advantage; and (d) a majority party (as defined above) has once failed to obtain a majority of the relevant seats in election using the challenged map (which fact cannot be explained by the existence of multiple parties or in other neutral ways). These circumstances could also add up to unconstitutional gerrymandering.

Third, suppose that the legislature clearly departs from ordinary districting norms, but the entrenchment harm, while seriously threatened, has not yet occurred. *E.g.*, (a) the legislature has redrawn district boundaries more than once within the traditional 10-year census-related period—either, as here, at the behest of a court that struck down an initial plan as unlawful, or of its own accord; (b) the boundary-drawing criteria depart radically from previous traditional boundary-drawing criteria; (c) strong, objective, unrefuted statistical evidence demonstrates that a party with a minority of the popular vote within the State in all likelihood will obtain a majority of the seats in the relevant representative delegation; and (d) the jettisoning of traditional districting criteria cannot be justified or explained other than by reference to an effort to obtain partisan political advantage. To my mind, such circumstances could also support a claim, because the presence of midcycle redistricting, for any reason, raises a fair inference that partisan machinations played a major role in the map-drawing process. Where such an inference is accompanied by statistical evidence that entrenchment will be the likely result, a court may conclude that the map crosses the constitutional line we are describing.* * *

NOTES ON JUDICIAL REVIEW OF POLITICAL GERRYMANDERING

1. *The Plurality's Response to the Separate Opinions in* Vieth. Justice Scalia responded:

(a) Justice Stevens' approach failed to appreciate the differences between the racial gerrymandering cases and the political gerrymandering cases.

(b) Justice Souter's five-part test was unworkable because it provided no guidance on "[h]ow *much* disregard of traditional districting principles? *How many* correlations between deviations and distribution? *How much* remedying of packing or cracking by the hypothetical district? *How many legislators* must have had the intent to pack and crack—and *how efficacious* must that intent have been (must it have been, for example, a *sine qua non* cause of the districting, or a *predominant* cause)? * * * The central problem is determining when political gerrymandering has gone too far. It does not solve that problem to break down the original unanswerable question (How much political motivation and effect is too much?) into four more discrete but equally unanswerable questions."

(c) Justice Breyer's opinion similarly lacked specification of what constitutes a constitutional violation and also failed to appreciate the costs of interposing judicial review (uncertainty, delay, expense) when the benefits seem minimal ("[h]e gives no instance (and we know none) of permanent frustration of majority will" through political gerrymandering).

(d) Justice Kennedy's preferred approach—to continue to allow litigation so that a justiciable standard might emerge—"is not legally available. The District Court in this case considered the plaintiffs' claims *justiciable* but dismissed them because the standard for unconstitutionality had not been met. It is logically impossible to affirm that dismissal without either (1) finding that the unconstitutional-districting standard applied by the District Court, or some other standard that it *should* have applied, has not been met, or (2) finding (as we have) that the claim is nonjusticiable. Justice Kennedy seeks to affirm '[b]ecause, in the case before us, we have no standard.' But it is *our* job, not the plaintiffs', to explicate the standard that makes the facts alleged by the plaintiffs adequate or inadequate to state a claim. We cannot nonsuit *them* for our failure to do so. * * * Reduced to its essence, Justice Kennedy's opinion boils down to this: 'As presently advised, I know of no discernible and manageable standard that can render this claim justiciable. I am unhappy about that, and hope that I will be able to change my opinion in the future.' What are the lower courts to make of this pronouncement? We suggest that they must treat it as a reluctant fifth vote against justiciability at district and statewide levels—a vote that may change in some future case but that holds, for the time being, that this matter is nonjusticiable."

2. *Another Case, Another Indeterminacy.* Two years after *Vieth*, in *League of United Latin Am. Citizens v. Perry*, 548 U.S. 399 (2006), the Court considered a challenge, on gerrymandering and VRA grounds, to the Texas Legislature's mid-decade redistricting of the Texas congressional seats. Although the Court granted relief on a VRA claim under § 2, it denied the political gerrymandering contention. Justice Scalia, joined by Justice Thomas, reiterated that such claims should be nonjusticiable. The other Justices left for another day the final resolution of that issue. Justice Kennedy again concluded that appellants had not proffered a workable approach to political gerrymandering claims in this case; the two new Justices, Chief Justice Roberts and Justice Alito, agreed. Justice Souter, joined by Justice Ginsburg, treated the political gerrymandering claim as one that the Court had, for all practical purposes, ducked, as if it had determined that certiorari had been improvidently granted. Justice Stevens, joined by Justice Breyer, argued that the political gerrymandering was unconstitutional.

3. *Coherence Across the Cases?* Precisely why is it that a majority of Justices are confident they can hear *Shaw v. Reno* sorts of cases, but not political gerrymandering cases? How persuasive is it to say that the difference is that race, unlike politics, is a constitutionally forbidden factor—when *Shaw* itself says that race may be taken into account in ensuring minority representation, so long as it is not taken into account too much? Why not say, similarly, that entrenching the current political majority may be taken into account, but not too much? Could it be the case that courts are better at figuring out when racial considerations have gone too far than when political

considerations have? Or perhaps there is a stronger dignitary harm in the former situation—though that still begs the question of how the courts draw the line. Is a more salient difference that the VRA requires state legislatures to consider race?

What of the possibility that, even if political gerrymandering claims will be largely immune to judicial review, cases that involve egregious political gerrymandering will provoke especially vigorous judicial enforcement of claims that are justiciable, such as one person, one vote claims? Consider *Larios v. Cox*, 300 F. Supp. 2d 1320 (N.D. Ga. 2004) (three-judge court), which dismissed a political gerrymandering claim but nonetheless invalidated the Georgia state legislative apportionment scheme on one person, one vote grounds. It was not lost on the district judges that the deviations from population equality were the result of partisan considerations. Interestingly, the Supreme Court summarily affirmed. *Cox v. Larios*, 542 U.S. 947 (2004). Only Justice Scalia noted a dissent. Justice Stevens, joined by Justice Breyer, wrote a short concurring statement squarely indicating that deviations from one person, one vote should be allowed to stand only if they are motivated by a neutral justification—even if the deviations are not substantial. Unsurprisingly, Justice Stevens left no doubt that, in his view, political entrenchment was not a sufficient justification. Note that three of the Justices who in *Vieth* would have held political gerrymandering nonjusticiable (Chief Justice Rehnquist and Justices O'Connor and Thomas) voted to affirm in the *Cox* litigation.[22]

4. *Removing Politics Through Independent Redistricting Commissions*. As Justice Breyer noted in his concurring opinion in *Vieth*, some states have created redistricting commissions in an attempt to remove state legislators from the process, thereby reducing partisan considerations. In 2008, California passed Proposition 11, creating the California Citizens Redistricting Commission of five Democrats, five Republicans, and four other commissioners outside of the two major parties, which would draw borders for the state legislature. Commissioners are selected through an extensive and complicated process, whereby eight commissioners are randomly chosen by the California Bureau of State Audits from a list of citizen applicants culled by state legislative leadership, with the final six commissioners selected by the original eight. In 2010, California voters passed Proposition 20, which extended the Commission's role to redrawing California's congressional boundaries. As a result of these initiatives, California became the "largest and most diverse jurisdiction" to have removed redistricting authority from the state legislature in favor of an independent commission.[23]

---

[22] On the political gerrymandering debate, see, e.g., Guy-Uriel Charles, *Democracy and Distortion*, 92 Cornell L. Rev. 601 (2007); Bernard Grofman & Gary King, *The Future of Partisan Symmetry as a Judicial Test for Partisan Gerrymandering after* LULAC v. Perry, 6 Election L.J. 2 (2007). For commentary seeking to place the partisan gerrymandering cases into this broader context of the judicial regulation of politics (e.g., one person, one vote; judicial regulation of political parties; campaign finance), see, e.g., James Gardner, *How to Do Things with Boundaries: Redistricting and the Construction of Politics*, 11 Election L.J. 399 (2012); Samuel Issacharoff & Pamela Karlan, *Where to Draw the Line?: Judicial Review of Political Gerrymanders*, 153 U. Pa. L. Rev. 541 (2004).

[23] Justin Levitt, *Democracy on the High Wire: Citizen Commission Implementation of the Voting Rights Act*, 46 U.C. Davis L. Rev. 1041, 1044 (2013); Vladimir Kogan & Thad Kousser, *Great Expectations and the California Citizens Redistricting Commission*, in *Reapportionment and Redistricting in the West* 219 (Gary Moncrief ed., 2011). For discussions of independent redistricting commissions, see Bruce Cain, *Redistricting Commissions: A Better Political Buffer?*, 121 Yale L.J. 1808 (2012); Dennis Thompson, *Just Elections: Creating a Fair Electoral Process in the United States* 173–79 (2002).

Proponents of the Commission envisioned that removing state legislators from the redistricting process would produce more competitive races and result in fewer incumbent victories. The 2012 congressional elections, the first in which the Commission's maps were in force, did not appear to have fully achieved these objectives. One analysis suggests that most California districts remain lopsided, with only four out of 53 California districts having a partisan balance providing a possibility of regular electoral competitiveness. For House races, the average margin of victory for incumbents was no different from the past 10 years. Additionally, at the state level, the Democrats gained a two-thirds supermajority in both houses of the legislature, a feat not seen since 1976. However, others noted some limited successes: the number of safe congressional seats was reduced by nine, and the new map included a new Asian-American majority district.[24] And while 10 congressional incumbents lost in 2010, with a handful more choosing not to run for reelection, only time will tell whether the Commission's efforts have produced a new normal for incumbency reelection rates or whether 2012 was an anomaly in the first election with new congressional borders. After you read the material on partisan lockups later in this chapter in § 2C, consider the need for independent redistricting commissions and other mechanisms that remove self-interested politicians from this crucial process.

2. ELIGIBILITY TO SERVE IN THE LEGISLATURE

Shift your attention from the process of voting for legislators to the process of serving in the legislature. Theoretically, most people are eligible to serve in the legislature because state and federal laws place few substantive restrictions on service. Article I, § 2 only requires that members of the House of Representatives be at least 25 years of age, U.S. citizens for seven years or more, and inhabitants of the states from which they are elected. Article I, § 3 requires that senators be at least 30 years of age, U.S. citizens for nine years or more, and inhabitants of the states from which they are elected. What theory or concept of representation inspires these particular limitations? What requirements would you impose, based upon your preferred theory of representation?

Some extra-constitutional limitations on eligibility to serve in Congress have given rise to interesting constitutional litigation. We will first consider the case of Representative Adam Clayton Powell, in which Congress attempted to exclude Powell from the federal legislature notwithstanding his election to the position. We will then turn to the effort through popular initiatives to impose term limitations on federal lawmakers, an effort that was halted abruptly when the Supreme Court ruled such limitations unconstitutional. We will conclude with a less obvious way of restricting eligibility to serve in public office: state laws regulating access to the ballot. These laws, which are routinely upheld by courts, present the biggest

---

[24] See Rob Richie & Devin McCarthy, FairVote: The Center for Voting and Democracy, *California and the Limits of Independent Redistricting Commissions with Winner-Take-All* (Feb. 15, 2013), http://www.fairvote.org/california-and-the-limits-of-independent-redistricting-commissions-with-winner-take-all#.UdBkn-ubC_G; Raphael Sonenshein, *When the People Draw the Lines: An Examination of the California Citizens Redistricting Commission* 71–73 (2013), http://cavotes.org/sites/default/files/jobs/RedistrictingCommission %20Report6122013.pdf. For a more positive view of the changes, but giving most of the credit to reforms other than redistricting, see Eric McGhee & Daniel Krimm, *California's New Electoral Reforms: The Fall Election* (Nov. 8, 2012), http://www.ppic.org/main/publication_show.asp?i=1039.

hurdles to election. After all, we may all be eligible to serve in Congress, but our chances of election are nonexistent if our names never appear on the ballot.

A. CONGRESSIONALLY IMPOSED QUALIFICATIONS

POWELL V. MCCORMACK

Supreme Court of the United States, 1969.
395 U.S. 486, 89 S.Ct. 1944, 23 L.Ed.2d 491.

MR. CHIEF JUSTICE WARREN delivered the opinion of the Court.

In November 1966, petitioner Adam Clayton Powell, Jr., was duly elected from the 18th Congressional District of New York to serve in the United States House of Representatives for the 90th Congress. However, pursuant to a House resolution, he was not permitted to take his seat. Powell (and some of the voters of his district) then filed suit in Federal District Court, claiming that the House could exclude him only if it found he failed to meet the standing requirements of age, citizenship, and residence contained in Art. I, § 2, of the Constitution—requirements the House specifically found Powell met—and thus had excluded him unconstitutionally. The District Court dismissed petitioners' complaint "for want of jurisdiction of the subject matter." A panel of the Court of Appeals affirmed the dismissal, although on somewhat different grounds, each judge filing a separate opinion. We have determined that it was error to dismiss the complaint and that petitioner Powell is entitled to a declaratory judgment that he was unlawfully excluded from the 90th Congress.

[I.] During the 89th Congress, a Special Subcommittee on Contracts of the Committee on House Administration conducted an investigation into the expenditures of the Committee on Education and Labor, of which petitioner Adam Clayton Powell, Jr., was chairman. The Special Subcommittee issued a report concluding that Powell and certain staff employees had deceived the House authorities as to travel expenses. The report also indicated there was strong evidence that certain illegal salary payments had been made to Powell's wife at his direction. No formal action was taken during the 89th Congress. However, prior to the organization of the 90th Congress, the Democratic members-elect met in caucus and voted to remove Powell as chairman of the Committee on Education and Labor.

When the 90th Congress met to organize in January 1967, Powell was asked to step aside while the oath was administered to the other members-elect. Following the administration of the oath to the remaining members, the House discussed the procedure to be followed in determining whether Powell was eligible to take his seat. After some debate, by a vote of 363 to 65 the House adopted House Resolution No. 1, which provided that the Speaker appoint a Select Committee to determine Powell's eligibility. Although the resolution prohibited Powell from taking his seat until the House acted on the Select Committee's report, it did provide that he should receive all the pay and allowances due a member during the period.

The Select Committee, composed of nine lawyer-members, issued an invitation to Powell to testify before the Committee. The invitation letter stated that the scope of the testimony and investigation would include Powell's qualifications as to age, citizenship, and residency; his involvement in a civil suit (in which he had been held in contempt); and "[m]atters of * * * alleged official misconduct since January 3, 1961." Powell appeared at the Committee hearing held on February 8, 1967. After the Committee denied in part Powell's request that certain adversary-type procedures be followed, Powell testified. He would, however, give information relating only to his age, citizenship, and residency; upon the advice of counsel, he refused to answer other questions.

On February 10, 1967, the Select Committee issued another invitation to Powell. In the letter, the Select Committee informed Powell that its responsibility under the House Resolution extended to determining not only whether he met the standing qualifications of Art. I, § 2, but also to "inquir[ing] into the question of whether you should be punished or expelled pursuant to the powers granted * * * the House under Article I, § 5, * * * of the Constitution. In other words, the Select Committee is of the opinion that at the conclusion of the present inquiry, it has authority to report back to the House recommendations with respect to * * * seating, expulsion or other punishment." Powell did not appear at the next hearing, held February 14, 1967. However, his attorneys were present, and they informed the Committee that Powell would not testify about matters other than his eligibility under the standing qualifications of Art. I, § 2. Powell's attorneys reasserted Powell's contention that the standing qualifications were the exclusive requirements for membership, and they further urged that punishment or expulsion was not possible until a member had been seated.

The Committee held one further hearing at which neither Powell nor his attorneys were present. Then, on February 23, 1967, the Committee issued its report, finding that Powell met the standing qualifications of Art. I, § 2. However, the Committee further reported that Powell had asserted an unwarranted privilege and immunity from the processes of the courts of New York; that he had wrongfully diverted House funds for the use of others and himself; and that he had made false reports on expenditures of foreign currency to the Committee on House Administration. The Committee recommended that Powell be sworn and seated as a member of the 90th Congress but that he be censured by the House, fined $40,000, and be deprived of his seniority.

The report was presented to the House on March 1, 1967, and the House debated the Select Committee's proposed resolution. At the conclusion of the debate, by a vote of 222 to 202 the House rejected a motion to bring the resolution to a vote. An amendment to the resolution was then offered; it called for the exclusion of Powell and a declaration that his seat was vacant. The Speaker ruled that a majority vote of the House would be sufficient to pass the resolution if it were so amended. 113 Cong. Rec. 5020. After further debate, the amendment was adopted by a vote of 248 to 176. Then the House adopted by a vote of 307 to 116 House Resolution No. 278 in its amended form, thereby excluding Powell and directing that the Speaker notify the Governor of New York that the seat was vacant.

[Powell and 13 voters in his district brought suit against five members of the House seeking a declaratory judgment that he had been improperly excluded. Chief

Justice Warren first decided that the controversy was not mooted by the seating of Powell by the 91st Congress and then held that the Speech or Debate Clause (examined in Chapter 3, § 2C) did not bar the lawsuit.]

[IV. *Exclusion or Expulsion*] The resolution excluding petitioner Powell was adopted by a vote in excess of two-thirds of the 434 Members of Congress—307 to 116. Article I, § 5, grants the House authority to expel a member "with the Concurrence of two thirds."[27] Respondents assert that the House may expel a member for any reason whatsoever and that, since a two-thirds vote was obtained, the procedure by which Powell was denied his seat in the 90th Congress should be regarded as an expulsion, not an exclusion. Cautioning us not to exalt form over substance, respondents quote from the concurring opinion of Judge McGowan in the court below:

"Appellant Powell's cause of action for a judicially compelled seating thus boils down, in my view, to the narrow issue of whether a member found by his colleagues * * * to have engaged in official misconduct must, because of the accidents of timing, be formally admitted before he can be either investigated or expelled. The sponsor of the motion to exclude stated on the floor that he was proceeding on the theory that the power to expel included the power to exclude, provided a 2/3 vote was forthcoming. It was. Therefore, success for Mr. Powell on the merits would mean that the District Court must admonish the House that it is form, not substance, that should govern in great affairs, and accordingly command the House members to act out a charade."

Although respondents repeatedly urge this Court not to speculate as to the reasons for Powell's exclusion, their attempt to equate exclusion with expulsion would require a similar speculation that the House would have voted to expel Powell had it been faced with that question. Powell had not been seated at the time House Resolution No. 278 was debated and passed. After a motion to bring the Select Committee's proposed resolution to an immediate vote had been defeated, an amendment was offered which mandated Powell's exclusion. Mr. Celler, chairman of the Select Committee, then posed a parliamentary inquiry to determine whether a two-thirds vote was necessary to pass the resolution if so amended "in the sense that it might amount to an expulsion." The Speaker replied that "action by a majority vote would be in accordance with the rules." Had the amendment been regarded as an attempt to expel Powell, a two-thirds vote would have been constitutionally required. The Speaker ruled that the House was voting to exclude Powell, and we will not speculate what the result might have been if Powell had been seated and expulsion proceedings subsequently instituted.

Nor is the distinction between exclusion and expulsion merely one of form. The misconduct for which Powell was charged occurred prior to the convening of the 90th Congress. On several occasions the House has debated whether a member can

[27] Powell was "excluded" from the 90th Congress, *i.e.*, he was not administered the oath of office and was prevented from taking his seat. If he had been allowed to take the oath and subsequently had been required to surrender his seat, the House's action would have constituted an "expulsion." Since we conclude that Powell was excluded from the 90th Congress, we express no view on what limitations may exist on Congress' power to expel or otherwise punish a member once he has been seated.

be expelled for actions taken during a prior Congress and the House's own manual of procedure applicable in the 90th Congress states that "both Houses have distrusted their power to punish in such cases." * * * Members of the House having expressed a belief that such strictures apply to its own power to expel, we will not assume that two-thirds of its members would have expelled Powell for his prior conduct had the Speaker announced that House Resolution No. 278 was for expulsion rather than exclusion.[30]

Finally, the proceedings which culminated in Powell's exclusion cast considerable doubt upon respondents' assumption that the two-thirds vote necessary to expel would have been mustered. These proceedings have been succinctly described by Congressman Eckhardt:

> "The House voted 202 votes for the previous question leading toward the adoption of the [Select] Committee report. It voted 222 votes against the previous question, opening the floor for the Curtis Amendment which ultimately excluded Powell.

> "Upon adoption of the Curtis Amendment, the vote again fell short of two-thirds, being 248 yeas to 176 nays. Only on the final vote, adopting the Resolution as amended, was more than a two-thirds vote obtained, the vote being 307 yeas to 116 nays. On this last vote, as a practical matter, members who would not have denied Powell a seat if they were given the choice to punish him had to cast an aye vote or else record themselves as opposed to the only punishment that was likely to come before the House. Had the matter come up through the processes of expulsion, it appears that the two-thirds vote would have failed, and then members would have been able to apply a lesser penalty."[32]

We need express no opinion as to the accuracy of Congressman Eckhardt's prediction that expulsion proceedings would have produced a different result. However, the House's own views of the extent of its power to expel combined with the Congressman's analysis counsel that exclusion and expulsion are not fungible proceedings. The Speaker ruled that House Resolution No. 278 contemplated an

---

[30] We express no view as to whether such a ruling would have been proper. A further distinction between expulsion and exclusion inheres in the fact that a member whose expulsion is contemplated may as a matter of right address the House and participate fully in debate while a member-elect apparently does not have a similar right. In prior cases the member whose expulsion was under debate has been allowed to make a long and often impassioned defense. On at least one occasion the member has been allowed to cross-examine other members during the expulsion debate.

[32] Eckhardt, *The Adam Clayton Powell Case*, 45 Texas L. Rev. 1205, 1209 (1967). The views of Congressman Eckhardt were echoed during the exclusion proceedings. Congressman Cleveland stated that, although he voted in favor of and supported the Select Committee's recommendation, if the exclusion amendment received a favorable vote on the motion for the previous question, then he would support the amendment "on final passage." Congressman Gubser was even more explicit:

> "I shall vote against the previous question on the Curtis amendment simply because I believe future and perfecting amendments should be allowed. But if the previous question is ordered, then I will be placed on the horns of an impossible dilemma.

> "Mr. Speaker, I want to expel Adam Clayton Powell, by seating him first, but that will not be my choice when the Curtis amendment is before us. I will be forced to vote for exclusion, about which I have great constitutional doubts, or to vote for no punishment at all. Given this raw and isolated issue, the only alternative I can follow is to vote for the Curtis amendment. I shall do so, Mr. Speaker, with great reservation."

exclusion proceeding. We must reject respondents' suggestion that we overrule the Speaker and hold that, although the House manifested an intent to exclude Powell, its action should be tested by whatever standards may govern an expulsion.

[VI. *Justiciability.*] [Justiciability implicates two determinations: (1) whether the claims presented and the relief sought are of the type that admit of judicial resolution, and (2) whether the structure of the federal government renders the issue a "political question" that is not justiciable because of the separation of powers provided by the Constitution. The Court found that the claims and relief did admit of judicial resolution and then turned to the second issue.]

[*VIB.   Political Question Doctrine—1. Textually Demonstrable Constitutional Commitment.*] [The opinion quoted the criteria for political question cases found in *Baker v. Carr.*]

Respondents' first contention is that this case presents a political question because under Art. I, § 5, there has been a "textually demonstrable constitutional commitment" to the House of the "adjudicatory power" to determine Powell's qualifications. Thus it is argued that the House, and the House alone, has power to determine who is qualified to be a member.

In order to determine whether there has been a textual commitment to a coordinate department of the Government, we must interpret the Constitution. In other words, we must first determine what power the Constitution confers upon the House through Art. I, § 5, before we can determine to what extent, if any, the exercise of that power is subject to judicial review. Respondents maintain that the House has broad power under § 5, and, they argue, the House may determine which are the qualifications necessary for membership. On the other hand, petitioners allege that the Constitution provides that an elected representative may be denied his seat only if the House finds he does not meet one of the standing qualifications expressly prescribed by the Constitution.

If examination of § 5 disclosed that the Constitution gives the House judicially unreviewable power to set qualifications for membership and to judge whether prospective members meet those qualifications, further review of the House determination might well be barred by the political question doctrine. On the other hand, if the Constitution gives the House power to judge only whether elected members possess the three standing qualifications set forth in the Constitution, further consideration would be necessary to determine whether any of the other formulations of the political question doctrine are "inextricable from the case at bar." *Baker v. Carr.* * * *

In order to determine the scope of any "textual commitment" under Art. I, § 5, we necessarily must determine the meaning of the phrase to "be the Judge of the Qualifications of its own Members." Petitioners argue that the records of the debates during the Constitutional Convention; available commentary from the post-Convention, pre-ratification period; and early congressional applications of Art. I, § 5, support their construction of the section. Respondents insist, however, that a careful examination of the pre-Convention practices of the English Parliament and American colonial assemblies demonstrates that by 1787, a legislature's power to judge the qualifications of its members was generally understood to encompass exclusion or expulsion on the ground that an individual's character or past conduct rendered him unfit to serve. When the Constitution and the debates over its adoption are thus viewed in historical perspective, argue respondents, it becomes clear that the "qualifications" expressly set forth in the Constitution were not meant to limit the long-recognized legislative power to exclude or expel at will, but merely to establish "standing incapacities," which could be altered only by a constitutional amendment. Our examination of the relevant historical materials leads us to the conclusion that petitioners are correct and that the Constitution leaves the House without authority to *exclude* any person, duly elected by his constituents, who meets all the requirements for membership expressly prescribed in the Constitution.

[*a. The Pre-Convention Precedents*] [The Court's opinion examined historical evidence of exclusion of members from the English Parliament. The English Parliament in the 18th century had excluded members, most notoriously Robert Walpole in 1712 and John Wilkes in the 1760s and 1770s. Wilkes was elected and reelected to Parliament several times during that period, and repeatedly excluded because of his 1763 published attack on the Treaty of Paris ending the Seven Years' War (the French and Indian War in the colonies). This repeated exclusion generated popular outrage in both England and the colonies because it denied the voters their elected representative. The House of Commons in 1782 expunged from the record Wilkes' prior exclusions and a resolution declaring him incapable of reelection; the 1782 resolution found the earlier actions "subversive of the rights of the whole body of electors of this kingdom." The 1782 resolution was important because it repudiated prior practice, and it was this resolution rather than the prior English practice that was celebrated in the colonies on the eve of their revolt.]

[*b. Convention Debates*] The Convention opened in late May 1787. By the end of July, the delegates adopted, with a minimum of debate, age requirements for membership in both the Senate and the House. The Convention then appointed a Committee of Detail to draft a constitution incorporating these and other resolutions adopted during the preceding months. Two days after the Committee was appointed, George Mason, of Virginia, moved that the Committee consider a clause " 'requiring certain qualifications of landed property & citizenship' " and disqualifying from membership in Congress persons who had unsettled accounts or who were indebted to the United States. A vigorous debate ensued. * * * John Dickinson, of Delaware, opposed the inclusion of any statement of qualifications in the Constitution. He argued that it would be "impossible to make a compleat one, and a partial one would by implication tie up the hands of the Legislature from supplying the omissions." Dickinson's argument was rejected; and, after eliminating the disqualification of debtors and the limitation to "landed" property, the Convention adopted Mason's proposal to instruct the Committee of Detail to draft a property qualification.

The Committee reported in early August, proposing no change in the age requirement; however, it did recommend adding citizenship and residency requirements for membership. After first debating what the precise requirements should be, on August 8, 1787, the delegates unanimously adopted the three qualifications embodied in Art. I, § 2.

On August 10, the Convention considered the Committee of Detail's proposal that the "Legislature of the United States shall have authority to establish such uniform qualifications of the members of each House, with regard to property, as to the said Legislature shall seem expedient." * * * James Madison urged its rejection, stating that the proposal would vest

> "an improper & dangerous power in the Legislature. The qualifications of electors and elected were fundamental articles in a Republican Govt. and ought to be fixed by the Constitution. If the Legislature could regulate those of either, it can by degrees subvert the Constitution. * * * It was a power also, which might be made subservient to the views of one faction agst. another. Qualifications founded on artificial distinctions may be devised, by the stronger in order to keep out partizans of [a weaker] faction." * * *

In view of what followed Madison's speech, it appears that on this critical day the Framers were facing and then rejecting the possibility that the legislature would have the power to usurp the "indisputable right [of the people] to return whom they thought proper" to the legislature. * * * Gouverneur Morris then moved to strike "with regard to property" from the Committee's proposal. His intention was "to leave the Legislature entirely at large." * * * Madison then referred to the British Parliament's assumption of the power to regulate the qualifications of both electors and the elected and noted that "the abuse they had made of it was a lesson worthy of our attention. They had made the changes in both cases subservient to their own views, or to the views of political or Religious parties." Shortly thereafter, the Convention rejected both Gouverneur Morris' motion and the Committee's proposal. Later the same day, the Convention adopted without debate the provision authorizing each House to be "the judge of the * * * qualifications of its own members."

[On the same day, the Convention considered the Committee of Detail's provision empowering each house to expel members and adopted Madison's amendment that expulsion could only be accomplished "with the concurrence of two-thirds" of the chamber. Thus, the Convention's decision to increase the vote required to expel—because that power was "too important to be exercised by a bare majority"—while at the same time not restricting the power to judge qualifications, is compelling evidence that they considered the latter already limited to the standing qualifications previously adopted.]

[c. *Post-Ratification*] [The opinion emphasized that, until the Civil War, Congress was unwilling to exclude duly elected members. In 1807, the House agreed to seat William McCreery. Its Committee on Elections found that he met the constitutional requirements, and operated under the assumption that "neither the State nor the Federal Legislatures are vested with authority to add to those qualifications, so as to change them." In 1868, the House did exclude two members on the ground that they gave aid and comfort to the Confederacy during the Civil War. The last person to be excluded from the House before Powell was Victor

Berger, a Socialist who was excluded after World War I for giving aid and comfort to the enemy in that war. The Court concluded that Congress' early understanding was the correct one, and that these subsequent exclusions had not changed the proper constitutional rule.]

[*d. Conclusion*] Had the intent of the Framers emerged from these materials with less clarity, we would nevertheless have been compelled to resolve any ambiguity in favor of a narrow construction of the scope of Congress' power to exclude members-elect. A fundamental principle of our representative democracy is, in Hamilton's words, "that the people should choose whom they please to govern them." As Madison pointed out at the Convention, this principle is undermined as much by limiting whom the people can select as by limiting the franchise itself. In apparent agreement with this basic philosophy, the Convention adopted his suggestion limiting the power to expel. To allow essentially that same power to be exercised under the guise of judging qualifications, would be to ignore Madison's warning, borne out in the Wilkes case and some of Congress' own post-Civil War exclusion cases, against "vesting an improper & dangerous power in the Legislature." Moreover, it would effectively nullify the Convention's decision to require a two-thirds vote for expulsion. Unquestionably, Congress has an interest in preserving its institutional integrity, but in most cases that interest can be sufficiently safeguarded by the exercise of its power to punish its members for disorderly behavior and, in extreme cases, to expel a member with the concurrence of two-thirds. In short, both the intention of the Framers, to the extent it can be determined, and an examination of the basic principles of our democratic system persuade us that the Constitution does not vest in the Congress a discretionary power to deny membership by a majority vote.

For these reasons, we have concluded that Art. I, § 5, is at most a "textually demonstrable commitment" to Congress to judge only the qualifications expressly set forth in the Constitution. Therefore, the "textual commitment" formulation of the political question doctrine does not bar federal courts from adjudicating petitioners' claims.

[*2. Other Considerations*] Respondents' alternate contention is that the case presents a political question because judicial resolution of petitioners' claim would produce a "potentially embarrassing confrontation between coordinate branches" of the Federal Government. But, as our interpretation of Art. I, § 5, discloses, a determination of petitioner Powell's right to sit would require no more than an interpretation of the Constitution. Such a determination falls within the traditional role accorded courts to interpret the law, and does not involve a "lack of the respect due [a] coordinate [branch] of government," nor does it involve an "initial policy determination of a kind clearly for nonjudicial discretion." *Baker.* * * * [Thus, the Court concluded that the case was justiciable.]

[VII.   *Conclusion*] To summarize, we have determined the following: (1) This case has not been mooted by Powell's seating in the 91st Congress. (2) Although this action should be dismissed against respondent Congressmen, it may be sustained against their agents. (3) The 90th Congress' denial of membership to

Powell cannot be treated as an expulsion. (4) We have jurisdiction over the subject matter of this controversy. (5) The case is justiciable.

Further, analysis of the "textual commitment" under Art. I, § 5 (see Part VI, B(l)), has demonstrated that in judging the qualifications of its members Congress is limited to the standing qualifications prescribed in the Constitution. Respondents concede that Powell met these. Thus, there is no need to remand this case to determine whether he was entitled to be seated in the 90th Congress. Therefore, we hold that, since Adam Clayton Powell, Jr., was duly elected by the voters of the 18th Congressional District of New York and was not ineligible to serve under any provision of the Constitution, the House was without power to exclude him from its membership.

[The concurring opinion of JUSTICE DOUGLAS and the dissenting opinion of JUSTICE STEWART have been omitted.]

NOTES ON POWELL AND THE LEGISLATURE'S AUTHORITY TO REGULATE ITS MEMBERSHIP

1.   *Rationale for* Powell. The general rule before *Powell* was that Congress and state legislatures have unreviewable authority to determine the qualifications of their members. Why was that rule not followed in *Powell*? Justice Douglas' concurring opinion asserts that the root concern in *Powell* "is the basic integrity of the electoral process. Today we proclaim the constitutional principle of 'one [person], one vote.' When the principle is followed and the electors choose a person who is repulsive to the Establishment in Congress, by what constitutional authority can that group of electors be disenfranchised?" What view or theory of representation does this embody? Justice Douglas admits that the House could have expelled Powell, probably for the same reasons it excluded him. Is there a policy supporting the exclusion-expulsion distinction?

The institutional theories we discussed in Chapter 1, § 2C, provide support for the Court's refusal to equate a two-thirds vote to exclude Powell with a two-thirds vote to expel him. Understanding the order of voting illuminates the decision. The Committee that investigated the allegations against Powell recommended that he be seated and censured. After debate, the House rejected a motion that would have forced an immediate vote on the recommendation, thereby signaling that the Committee's proposal was in trouble. The resolution was then amended so that it required exclusion; that amendment passed by a simple majority of 248–176. In a pivotal ruling, the Chair determined that the final vote required to exclude Powell was also a simple majority; only expulsion required a two-thirds majority under the Constitution. Why was this ruling so important to the final vote margin? Think about the 59 members who changed their votes to support passage of the amended resolution even though they had opposed the amendment. Had they been convinced to change their positions because of persuasive debate by their colleagues? Probably not. These members voted strategically. They realized that the resolution of exclusion was going to pass because a simple majority had already voted in favor of it. Perhaps they changed their votes because they thought some punishment appropriate and this resolution was the only option, or perhaps they did not want their votes to become controversial issues in their next reelection campaigns. The Supreme Court was entirely right, under this analysis, to refuse to equate the exclusion motion with a decision to expel, given the difference in the voting rule applied to each.

2. *Exclusion and the First Amendment.* In *Bond v. Floyd*, 385 U.S. 116 (1966), the Supreme Court held that the Georgia House of Representatives had violated Julian Bond's First Amendment rights (as secured by the Due Process Clause of the Fourteenth Amendment) when it excluded him from membership, though he had been duly elected, because of his criticism of the Vietnam War and of the federal draft laws. Georgia argued that (1) the exclusion was proper because the Georgia Constitution requires representatives to take an oath pledging to support the constitutions of Georgia and the United States; (2) this requirement is clearly constitutional because the United States Constitution itself (Article VI, cl. 3) requires members of state legislatures to take an oath to support the federal Constitution; and (3) the state legislature has the power to determine whether a given representative can take the oath with sincerity. Georgia conceded that Bond stood ready to take the oath, but insisted on its legislature's right to withhold office because Bond's criticism of federal policy showed that he could not take the oath with sincerity.

The Court agreed that the Georgia oath requirement was constitutional, but held that neither Article VI, cl. 3, on its own force, nor the Georgia oath requirement in light of the First Amendment, can "authorize a majority of state legislators to test the sincerity with which another duly elected legislator can swear to uphold the Constitution. * * * [W]hile the State has an interest in requiring its legislators to swear to a belief in constitutional processes of government, surely the oath gives it no interest in limiting its legislators' capacity to discuss their views of local or national policy. The manifest function of the First Amendment in a representative government requires that legislators be given the widest latitude to express their views on issues of policy."

3. *Exclusion and Race.* Julian Bond was an African-American representative; Powell was a black Congressman from Harlem, one of the few African Americans then in the U.S. House. Justice Douglas adverted to the "racist overtones" of Powell's exclusion. During the debate on the exclusion, members who opposed the exclusion as unconstitutional noted that Congress had excluded members on the grounds of extra-constitutional qualifications only three times before "in rare instances of extreme political tension. * * * These deviations occurred in three categories of cases reflecting anti-Mormon[,] anti-Confederate[,] and antiradical * * * feeling." 113 Cong. Rec. 5023 (Mar. 1, 1967) (statement of Rep. Celler). Should these factors have led the Court to investigate the motives of the Georgia legislature in Bond's case or of Congress in Powell's? If so, what records should the Court have used to determine the legislature's motivation—only public records of deliberations or also affidavits from legislators detailing private conversations or internal reasoning? What about evidence of constituent communications and views that might have influenced the outcome?

Some state constitutions use an additional method to guard against self-interested or improper expulsion from the legislature. They allow a state house to expel a member "only once for the same offense." See, e.g., Ill. Const. Art. IV, § 6(d); see also Conn. Const. III, § 13. Adrian Vermeule explains the advantages of this sort of protection. Not only does it allow the voters to override the legislature's decision by reelecting a member who has been expelled, but it also provides "outside review [that] is, as a matter of institutional design, superior to any of the alternatives, either the supermajority requirement or the hypothetical alternatives that would vest review of expulsion decisions in the other house or in the president." *The Constitutional Law of Congressional Procedure*, 71 U. Chi. L. Rev. 361, 396 (2004).

PROBLEMS OF CONGRESSIONAL EXCLUSION AND EXPULSION

Problem 2–2. Representative Powell was reelected and seated before the Supreme Court's decision, and he was not later excluded from Congress. But assume that after Powell's next reelection, the House voted by a two-thirds majority to expel him. Powell sues on the ground that his expulsion was racially motivated. Is that controversy justiciable? Has Powell stated a claim for which relief can be granted, if he can prove racially discriminatory intent? If Congress does not expel him but continues to deny him seniority, can he return to court to obtain an injunction restoring his status and placing him at the head of a subcommittee on which he is the most senior member? Or do matters of seniority and committee assignments present political questions that the courts should avoid? What if Powell sues for any back pay that was withheld during his unlawful exclusion?

Problem 2–3. When Barack Obama became President of the United States, he left his Senate seat from Illinois vacant. State law allowed the Governor, Democrat Rod Blagojevich, to appoint the successor to serve until the 2010 election. It soon became apparent through federal wiretaps and other evidence that the Governor, who was already under investigation for corruption, was seeking favors from people he was considering for the position. As this controversy raged, Blagojevich announced that he would appoint Roland Burris, a Democrat who had been elected Illinois' first African-American State Comptroller and Attorney General. Soon there were allegations that Burris had discussed a *quid pro quo* with the venal Blagojevich, and his appointment became controversial. Although Burris received appointment papers from the Governor, the Illinois Secretary of State refused to sign them. When Burris arrived in Washington to take his seat, the Secretary of the Senate rejected his credentials because Senate Rule 2, part of the Senate rules since 1884, requires that an appointment include the signatures of both the Governor and Secretary of State. Senate Majority Leader Harry Reid (D–Nev.) and the senior Senator from Illinois, Dick Durbin (D), declared that Burris should not be seated; Reid cited Article I, § 5, of the Constitution that "each House shall be the Judge of the Elections, Returns, and Qualifications of its own Members." Does *Powell v. McCormack* provide guidance as to the Senate's power in this case to scrutinize this appointment and possibly to refuse to seat Burris? What is the appropriate venue to determine Burris' suitability to serve, or is it sufficient that the sitting Governor appointed him, notwithstanding the circumstances of the appointment? To the extent that charges of corruption accompanied Blagojevich's decision, are there any facts that might support a decision by the Senate not to seat his appointee? To seat and then expel him by a two-thirds vote?

In the end, Burris went to state court, which ruled that state law did not require the Secretary of State's signature for the appointment to be valid, and the Illinois Secretary of State signed a second document acknowledging the appointment to be legally valid. Accordingly, the Secretary of the Senate accepted his credentials, ending the possibility that the case might reach federal court on that ground. But in another twist to the case, the Seventh Circuit ruled that the Seventeenth Amendment requires a special election to fill a Senate vacancy, with any appointment serving temporarily until the election can be held. See *Judge v. Quinn*, 624 F.3d 352 (7th Cir. 2010). The new Governor of Illinois, Pat Quinn, set the vote to fill the remaining weeks of Obama's Senate term in a special election that was held on November 2, 2010—the same date as the regular Senate election for the seat's next full term. Following the Seventh Circuit's ruling, a U.S. District Court judge ruled that only candidates on the ballot for the general election would be eligible for the special election. Burris, who had publicly expressed an interest in running to finish out the term, filed an emergency appeal with the Supreme Court arguing that the order violated voters' rights to due process and unfettered access to the ballot. In June 2011—months after Republican Mark Kirk won both the special election and the general election and assumed his Senate seat—the Court denied the appeal. Later that year, former Governor Blagojevich was convicted of 18 counts of corruption and sentenced to a 14–year prison term.

B. QUALIFICATIONS IMPOSED BY STATES: TERM LIMITATIONS FOR FEDERAL LEGISLATORS

By the end of the 1994 elections, 22 states had amended their constitutions or passed legislation limiting the terms of office of their U.S. representatives and senators. Fourteen of these provisions, including the Arkansas limitation at issue in *U.S. Term Limits, Inc. v. Thornton*, were designed as ballot access measures, allowing long-term incumbents to run, but only as write-in candidates. We will discuss ballot access regulations, and the willingness of the courts to tolerate such restrictions, in Part C of this section. Term-limit advocates hope to rid Congress of professional politicians because they believe that such lawmakers inevitably act in ways that are contrary to the public interest. They seek to replace the professionals with amateurs who, like the legendary Cincinnatus,[25] have little experience in politics but a great deal of experience as ordinary citizens. They believe that this reform will weaken the power of special interests and eliminate unseemly, close relationships between elected officials and lobbyists.[26]

Others, including many political scientists, have remained skeptical of term limits.[27] Some dispute that term limits will usher in the era of the citizen-legislator, noting that political careers remain possible with term limits, although a careerist will be forced to adopt a strategy of *progressive* political ambition by moving periodically to a new office or political job.[28] Many object to term limits because they will deprive legislatures of their most experienced members, thereby reducing the ability of Congress to pass legislation to deal with controversial or difficult problems without corresponding advantages in deliberativeness or public spiritedness. Reduced legislator effectiveness also may shift the balance of power between the branches of government. Longtime federal bureaucrats will represent

---

[25] In 458 B.C., Cincinnatus was appointed dictator of Rome in order to rescue a besieged army. At the time of his appointment, he was a farmer; after defeating the enemy, he is said to have resigned and returned to his plow.

[26] See, e.g., George Will, *Restoration: Congress, Term Limits, and the Recovery of Deliberative Democracy* (1992) (arguing that term limits would enhance deliberation and representative democracy).

[27] See *Legislative Term Limits: Public Choice Perspectives* (Bernard Grofman ed., 1996) (containing views of scholars on both sides of the debate); Thad Kousser, *Term Limits and the Dismantling of State Legislative Professionalism* (2005); Peter Schrag, *Paradise Lost: California's Experience, America's Future* (2004) (blaming term limits as well as direct democracy for California's recurring political problems).

[28] See Elizabeth Garrett, *Term Limitations and the Myth of the Citizen-Legislator*, 81 Cornell L. Rev. 623 (1996).

a source of expertise for congressional amateurs, a situation that will strengthen the President and executive branch relative to Congress. Similarly, term-limited politicians may rely more heavily on unelected, professional congressional staff or on lobbyists with congressional experience. Finally, some opponents argue that interest groups will continue to influence representatives disproportionately by giving campaign money either to the representative or to political parties. Moreover, term limits will provide special interests with an even more powerful tool for influence: post-service jobs for term-limited representatives.

As the debate about the effect of state-imposed term limitations on federal legislators heated up, the Supreme Court considered the constitutionality of such measures in the following case.

U.S. TERM LIMITS, INC. v. THORNTON
Supreme Court of the United States, 1995.
514 U.S. 779, 115 S.Ct. 1842, 131 L.Ed.2d 881.

JUSTICE STEVENS delivered the opinion of the Court.

* * * Today's cases present a challenge to an amendment to the Arkansas State Constitution that prohibits the name of an otherwise-eligible candidate for Congress from appearing on the general election ballot if that candidate has already served three terms in the House of Representatives or two terms in the Senate. The Arkansas Supreme Court held that the amendment violates the Federal Constitution. We agree with that holding. Such a state-imposed restriction is contrary to the "fundamental principle of our representative democracy," embodied in the Constitution, that "the people should choose whom they please to govern them." *Powell v. McCormack.* Allowing individual States to adopt their own qualifications for congressional service would be inconsistent with the Framers' vision of a uniform National Legislature representing the people of the United States. If the qualifications set forth in the text of the Constitution are to be changed, that text must be amended.

[I] At the general election on November 3, 1992, the voters of Arkansas adopted Amendment 73 to their State Constitution. Proposed as a "Term Limitation Amendment," its preamble stated:

> "The people of Arkansas find and declare that elected officials who remain in office too long become preoccupied with reelection and ignore their duties as representatives of the people. Entrenched incumbency has reduced voter participation and has led to an electoral system that is less free, less competitive, and less representative than the system established by the Founding Fathers. Therefore, the people of Arkansas, exercising their reserved powers, herein limit the terms of the elected officials."

[Section 3 prohibited any person who had served for three or more terms in the House of Representatives from appearing on the ballot. A similar restriction applied to persons who had served in the Senate for two or more terms. Bobbie Hill, a voter and citizen of Arkansas, brought suit in state court for a declaratory judgment that § 3 was unconstitutional. The Arkansas Supreme Court held that the provision violated the federal Constitution because a state has no authority to change the qualifications for congressional office enumerated in Article I, § 5.]

[II] As the opinions of the Arkansas Supreme Court suggest, the constitutionality of Amendment 73 depends critically on the resolution of two distinct issues. The first is whether the Constitution forbids States to add or alter the qualifications specifically enumerated in the Constitution. The second is, if the Constitution does so forbid, whether the fact that Amendment 73 is formulated as a ballot access restriction rather than as an outright disqualification is of constitutional significance. [Based on *Powell*, Justice Stevens "reaffirm[ed] that the qualifications for service in Congress set forth in the text of the Constitution are 'fixed,' at least in the sense that they may not be supplemented by Congress."]

[III] Our reaffirmation of *Powell* does not necessarily resolve the specific questions presented in these cases. For petitioners argue that whatever the constitutionality of additional qualifications for membership imposed by Congress, the historical and textual materials discussed in *Powell* do not support the conclusion that the Constitution prohibits additional qualifications imposed by States. In the absence of such a constitutional prohibition, petitioners argue, the Tenth Amendment and the principle of reserved powers require that States be allowed to add such qualifications.

* * * We disagree for two independent reasons. First, we conclude that the power to add qualifications is not within the "original powers" of the States, and thus is not reserved to the States by the Tenth Amendment. Second, even if States possessed some original power in this area, we conclude that the Framers intended the Constitution to be the exclusive source of qualifications for members of Congress, and that the Framers thereby "divested" States of any power to add qualifications.

[Relying heavily on Justice Story's treatise on constitutional law, the Court determined that the only powers reserved to the states under the Tenth Amendment were those that they had possessed before the Constitution was ratified and that had not been transferred to the national government. The states did not have an "original power" to appoint a national official; thus, the power to set qualifications for such offices cannot be a reserved power. "Instead, any state power to set the qualifications for membership in Congress must derive not from the reserved powers of state sovereignty, but rather from the delegated powers of national sovereignty."]

Even if we believed that States possessed as part of their original powers some control over congressional qualifications, the text and structure of the Constitution, the relevant historical materials, and, most importantly, the "basic principles of our democratic system" all demonstrate that the Qualifications Clauses were intended to preclude the States from exercising any such power and to fix as exclusive the qualifications in the Constitution.

[The Court began its analysis by reviewing the historical evidence that the Constitution did not delegate to the states the power to add qualifications. Constitutional provisions that minimize the possibility of state interference in national elections[29] and the ratification debates reveal the Framers' fear that the states would undermine the national legislature. For example, the Framers did not leave to the states the determination of congressional salaries because of fears of "improper dependence."]

The dissent nevertheless contends that the Framers' distrust of the States with respect to elections does not preclude the people of the States from adopting eligibility requirements to help narrow their own choices. As the dissent concedes, however, the Framers were unquestionably concerned that the States would simply not hold elections for federal officers, and therefore the Framers gave Congress the power to "make or alter" state election regulations. Yet under the dissent's approach, the States could achieve exactly the same result by simply setting qualifications for federal office sufficiently high that no one could meet those qualifications. In our view, it is inconceivable that the Framers would provide a specific constitutional provision to ensure that federal elections would be held while at the same time allowing States to render those elections meaningless by simply ensuring that no candidate could be qualified for office. * * *

We also find compelling the complete absence in the ratification debates of any assertion that States had the power to add qualifications. In those debates, the question whether to require term limits, or "rotation," was a major source of controversy. The draft of the Constitution that was submitted for ratification contained no provision for rotation. In arguments that echo in the preamble to Arkansas' Amendment 73, opponents of ratification condemned the absence of a rotation requirement, noting that "there is no doubt that senators will hold their office perpetually; and in this situation, they must of necessity lose their dependence, and their attachments to the people." Even proponents of ratification expressed concern about the "abandonment in every instance of the necessity of rotation in office." At several ratification conventions, participants proposed amendments that would have required rotation.

The Federalists' responses to those criticisms and proposals addressed the merits of the issue, arguing that rotation was incompatible with the people's right to choose. * * * Robert Livingston argued:

> "The people are the best judges who ought to represent them. To dictate and control them, to tell them whom they shall not elect, is to abridge their natural rights. This rotation is an absurd species of ostracism."

Similarly, Hamilton argued that the representatives' need for reelection rather than mandatory rotation was the more effective way to keep representatives responsive to the people, because "[w]hen a man knows he must quit his station, let his merit be what it may, he will turn his attention chiefly to his own emolument."

Regardless of which side has the better of the debate over rotation, it is most striking that nowhere in the extensive ratification debates have we found any

---

[29] *Editors' note*: Justice Stevens referred to Art. I, § 2, cl. 1 (qualifications for federal electors to be same as those for state electors); Art. I, § 4, cl. 1 (giving states the freedom to regulate the "Times, Places and Manner of holding Elections," but giving Congress the power "by Law [to] make or alter such Regulations"); Art I, § 6 (Congress sets its own compensation); Art. I, § 5, cl. 1 ("Each House shall be the Judge of the Elections, Returns and Qualifications of its own Members").

statement by either a proponent or an opponent of rotation that the draft constitution would permit States to require rotation for the representatives of their own citizens. If the participants in the debate had believed that the States retained the authority to impose term limits, it is inconceivable that the Federalists would not have made this obvious response to the arguments of the pro-rotation forces. The absence in an otherwise freewheeling debate of any suggestion that States had the power to impose additional qualifications unquestionably reflects the Framers' common understanding that States lacked that power. * * *

Our conclusion that States lack the power to impose qualifications vindicates the same "fundamental principle of our representative democracy" that we recognized in *Powell*, namely, that "the people should choose whom they please to govern them." [The Court noted that *Powell*'s fundamental principle included two ideas. First, *Powell* "emphasized the egalitarian concept that the opportunity to be elected was open to all." Second, the Court recognized that "sovereignty confers on the people the right to choose freely their representatives to the National Government." State-imposed qualifications, the Court argued, are inconsistent with both these concepts: "the source of the qualification is of little moment in assessing the qualification's restrictive impact."]

Finally, state-imposed restrictions, unlike the congressionally imposed restrictions at issue in *Powell*, violate a third idea central to this basic principle: that the right to choose representatives belongs not to the States, but to the people. From the start, the Framers recognized that the "great and radical vice" of the Articles of Confederation was "the principle of LEGISLATION for STATES or GOVERNMENTS, in their CORPORATE or COLLECTIVE CAPACITIES, and as contradistinguished from the INDIVIDUALS of whom they consist." [The *Federalist No. 15* (Hamilton).] Thus the Framers, in perhaps their most important contribution, conceived of a Federal Government directly responsible to the people, possessed of direct power over the people, and chosen directly, not by States, but by the people. * * *

Consistent with these views, the constitutional structure provides for a uniform salary to be paid from the national treasury, allows the States but a limited role in federal elections, and maintains strict checks on state interference with the federal election process. The Constitution also provides that the qualifications of the representatives of each State will be judged by the representatives of the entire Nation. The Constitution thus creates a uniform national body representing the interests of a single people.

Permitting individual States to formulate diverse qualifications for their representatives would result in a patchwork of state qualifications, undermining the uniformity and the national character that the Framers envisioned and sought to ensure. Such a patchwork would also sever the direct link that the Framers found so critical between the National Government and the people of the United States.[32] * * *

---

[32] There is little significance to the fact that Amendment 73 was adopted by a popular vote, rather than as an act of the state legislature. In fact, none of the petitioners argues that the constitutionality of a state law would depend on the method of its adoption. This is proper, because the voters of Arkansas, in adopting

[IV] Petitioners argue that, even if States may not add qualifications, Amendment 73 is constitutional because it is not such a qualification, and because Amendment 73 is a permissible exercise of state power to regulate the "Times, Places and Manner of Holding Elections." We reject these contentions.

* * * [Section 3 of Amendment 73] provides that certain Senators and Representatives shall not be certified as candidates and shall not have their names appear on the ballot. They may run as write-in candidates and, if elected, they may serve. Petitioners contend that only a legal bar to service creates an impermissible qualification, and that Amendment 73 is therefore consistent with the Constitution.

Petitioners support their restrictive definition of qualifications with language from *Storer v. Brown*, 415 U.S. 724 (1974), in which we faced a constitutional challenge to provisions of the California Elections Code that regulated the procedures by which both independent candidates and candidates affiliated with qualified political parties could obtain ballot position in general elections. The Code required candidates affiliated with a qualified party to win a primary election, and required independents to make timely filing of nomination papers signed by at least 5% of the entire vote cast in the last general election. The Code also denied ballot position to independents who had voted in the most recent primary election or who had registered their affiliation with a qualified party during the previous year.

In *Storer*, we rejected the argument that the challenged procedures created additional qualifications as "wholly without merit." We noted that petitioners "would not have been disqualified had they been nominated at a party primary or by an adequately supported independent petition and then elected at the general election." We concluded that the California Code "no more establishes an additional requirement for the office of Representative than the requirement that the candidate win the primary to secure a place on the general ballot or otherwise demonstrate substantial community support." Petitioners maintain that, under *Storer*, Amendment 73 is not a qualification.

We need not decide whether petitioners' narrow understanding of qualifications is correct because, even if it is, Amendment 73 may not stand. * * * In our view, Amendment 73 is an indirect attempt to accomplish what the Constitution prohibits Arkansas from accomplishing directly. As the plurality opinion of the Arkansas Supreme Court recognized, Amendment 73 is an "effort to dress eligibility to stand for Congress in ballot access clothing," because the "intent and the effect of Amendment 73 are to disqualify congressional incumbents from further service." We must, of course, accept the State Court's view of the purpose of its own law: we are thus authoritatively informed that the sole purpose of § 3 of Amendment 73 was to attempt to achieve a result that is forbidden by the Federal Constitution. Indeed, it cannot be seriously contended that the intent behind Amendment 73 is other than to prevent the election of incumbents. The preamble of Amendment 73 states explicitly: "[T]he people of Arkansas . . . herein limit the terms of elected officials." * * *

Amendment 73, were acting as citizens of the State of Arkansas, and not as citizens of the National Government. The people of the State of Arkansas have no more power than does the Arkansas Legislature to supplement the qualifications for service in Congress. * * *

* * * In our view, an amendment with the avowed purpose and obvious effect of evading the requirements of the Qualifications Clauses by handicapping a class of candidates cannot stand. To argue otherwise is to suggest that the Framers spent significant time and energy in debating and crafting Clauses that could be easily evaded. More importantly, allowing States to evade the Qualifications Clauses by "dress[ing] eligibility to stand for Congress in ballot access clothing" trivializes the basic principles of our democracy that underlie those Clauses. Petitioners' argument treats the Qualifications Clauses not as the embodiment of a grand principle, but rather as empty formalism. * * *

Petitioners make the related argument that Amendment 73 merely regulates the "Manner" of elections, and that the Amendment is therefore a permissible exercise of state power under Article I, § 4, cl. 1 (the Elections Clause), to regulate the "Times, Places and Manner" of elections. We cannot agree. * * * The Framers intended the Elections Clause to grant States authority to create procedural regulations, not to provide States with license to exclude classes of candidates from federal office. * * *

The provisions at issue in *Storer* and our other Elections Clause cases were thus constitutional because they regulated election *procedures* and did not even arguably impose any substantive qualification rendering a class of potential candidates ineligible for ballot position. They served the state interest in protecting the integrity and regularity of the election process, an interest independent of any attempt to evade the constitutional prohibition against the imposition of additional qualifications for service in Congress. And they did not involve measures that exclude candidates from the ballot without reference to the candidates' support in the electoral process. Our cases upholding state regulations of election procedures thus provide little support for the contention that a state-imposed ballot access restriction is constitutional when it is undertaken for the twin goals of disadvantaging a particular class of candidates and evading the dictates of the Qualifications Clauses.

[V] The merits of term limits, or "rotation," have been the subject of debate since the formation of our Constitution, when the Framers unanimously rejected a proposal to add such limits to the Constitution. The cogent arguments on both sides of the question that were articulated during the process of ratification largely retain their force today. Over half the States have adopted measures that impose such limits on some offices either directly or indirectly, and the Nation as a whole, notably by constitutional amendment, has imposed a limit on the number of terms that the President may serve. Term limits, like any other qualification for office, unquestionably restrict the ability of voters to vote for whom they wish. On the other hand, such limits may provide for the infusion of fresh ideas and new perspectives, and may decrease the likelihood that representatives will lose touch with their constituents. It is not our province to resolve this longstanding debate.

We are, however, firmly convinced that allowing the several States to adopt term limits for congressional service would effect a fundamental change in the constitutional framework. Any such change must come not by legislation adopted either by Congress or by an individual State, but rather—as have other important changes in the electoral process—through the Amendment procedures set forth in Article V. The Framers decided that the qualifications for service in the Congress of the United States be fixed in the Constitution and be uniform throughout the Nation. * * * In the absence of a properly passed constitutional amendment, allowing individual States to craft their own qualifications for Congress would thus erode the structure envisioned by the Framers, a structure that was designed, in the words of the Preamble to our Constitution, to form a "more perfect Union."

[JUSTICE KENNEDY concurred in the opinion for the Court and wrote a separate opinion responding to Justice Thomas' theory of federal/state sovereignty. "Federalism was our Nation's own discovery. The Framers split the atom of sovereignty. It was the genius of their idea that our citizens would have two political capacities, one state and one federal, each protected from incursion by the other. The resulting Constitution created a legal system unprecedented in form and design, establishing two orders of government, each with its own direct relationship, its own privity, its own set of mutual rights and obligations to the people who sustain it and are governed by it." *McCulloch v. Maryland*, 4 Wheat. 316 (1819). Because the Arkansas amendment directly affected the unique federal right to vote, a right also implicating the First Amendment, Justice Kennedy believed it crossed the line. But his concurring opinion emphasized that the states must be equally well protected against federal incursions.]

JUSTICE THOMAS, with whom THE CHIEF JUSTICE [REHNQUIST], JUSTICE O'CONNOR, and JUSTICE SCALIA join, dissenting.

It is ironic that the Court bases today's decision on the right of the people to "choose whom they please to govern them." Under our Constitution, there is only one State whose people have the right to "choose whom they please" to represent Arkansas in Congress. The Court holds, however, that neither the elected legislature of that State nor the people themselves (acting by ballot initiative) may prescribe any qualifications for those representatives. The majority therefore defends the right of the people of Arkansas to "choose whom they please to govern them" by invalidating a provision that won nearly 60% of the votes cast in a direct election and that carried every congressional district in the State.

I dissent. Nothing in the Constitution deprives the people of each State of the power to prescribe eligibility requirements for the candidates who seek to represent them in Congress. The Constitution is simply silent on this question. And where the Constitution is silent, it raises no bar to action by the States or the people.

[Justice Thomas first discussed the idea of "reserved powers" in the federal system. He argued that the States "can exercise all powers that the Constitution does not withhold from them." Whether the states enjoyed those powers before the adoption of the Constitution is not relevant.]

[I] The majority's essential logic is that the state governments could not "reserve" any powers that they did not control at the time the Constitution was drafted. * * * The Tenth Amendment's use of the word "reserved" does not help the majority's position. If someone says that the power to use a particular facility is reserved to some group, he is not saying anything about whether that group has previously used the facility. He is merely saying that the people who control the facility have designated that group as the entity with authority to use it. The Tenth Amendment is similar: The people of the States, from whom all governmental powers stem, have specified that all powers not prohibited to the States by the Federal Constitution are reserved "to the States respectively, or to the people." * * *

In a final effort to deny that the people of the States enjoy "reserved" powers over the selection of their representatives in Congress, the majority suggests that the Constitution expressly delegates to the States certain powers over congressional elections. Such delegations of power, the majority argues, would be superfluous if the people of the States enjoyed reserved powers in this area.

Only one constitutional provision—the Times, Places and Manner Clause of Article I, § 4—even arguably supports the majority's suggestion. * * * Contrary to the majority's assumption, however, this Clause does not delegate any authority to the States. Instead, it simply imposes a duty upon them. * * * This command meshes with one of the principal purposes of Congress' "make or alter" power: to ensure that the States hold congressional elections in the first place, so that Congress continues to exist. * * *

[II] I take it to be established, then, that the people of Arkansas do enjoy "reserved" powers over the selection of their representatives in Congress. Purporting to exercise those reserved powers, they have agreed among themselves that the candidates covered by § 3 of Amendment 73—those whom they have already elected to three or more terms in the House of Representatives or to two or more terms in the Senate—should not be eligible to appear on the ballot for reelection, but should nonetheless be returned to Congress if enough voters are sufficiently enthusiastic about their candidacy to write in their names. Whatever one might think of the wisdom of this arrangement, we may not override the decision of the people of Arkansas unless something in the Federal Constitution deprives them of the power to enact such measures. * * *

The people of other States could legitimately complain if the people of Arkansas decide, in a particular election, to send a 6-year-old to Congress. But the Constitution gives the people of other States no basis to complain if the people of Arkansas elect a freshman representative in preference to a long-term incumbent. That being the case, it is hard to see why the rights of the people of other States have been violated when the people of Arkansas decide to enact a more general disqualification of long-term incumbents. * * *

The majority responds that "a patchwork of state qualifications" would "undermin[e] the uniformity and the national character that the Framers envisioned and sought to ensure." Yet the Framers thought it perfectly consistent with the "national character" of Congress for the Senators and Representatives from each State to be chosen by the legislature or the people of that State. The majority never explains why Congress' fundamental character permits this state-centered system, but nonetheless prohibits the people of the States and their state legislatures from setting any eligibility requirements for the candidates who seek to represent them. * * *

The fact that the Framers did not grant a qualification-setting power to Congress does not imply that they wanted to bar its exercise at the state level. One reason why the Framers decided not to let Congress prescribe the qualifications of its own members was that incumbents could have used this power to perpetuate themselves or their ilk in office. As Madison pointed out at the Philadelphia Convention, Members of Congress would have an obvious conflict of interest if they could determine who may run against them. But neither the people of the States nor the state legislatures would labor under the same conflict of interest when prescribing qualifications for Members of Congress, and so the Framers would have had to use a different calculus in determining whether to deprive them of this power.

* * * There is a world of difference between a self-imposed constraint and a constraint imposed from above. * * * Congressional power over qualifications would have enabled the representatives from some States, acting collectively in the National Legislature, to prevent the people of another State from electing their preferred candidates. * * *

* * * The majority never identifies the democratic principles that would have been violated if a state legislature, in the days before the Constitution was amended to provide for the direct election of Senators, had imposed some limits of its own on the field of candidates that it would consider for appointment. Likewise, the majority does not explain why democratic principles forbid the people of a State from adopting additional eligibility requirements to help narrow their choices among candidates seeking to represent them in the House of Representatives. Indeed, the invocation of democratic principles to invalidate Amendment 73 seems particularly difficult in the present case, because Amendment 73 remains fully within the control of the people of Arkansas. If they wanted to repeal it (despite the 20–point margin by which they enacted it less than three years ago), they could do so by a simple majority vote.

The majority appears to believe that restrictions on eligibility for office are inherently undemocratic. * * * [But] the authority to narrow the field of candidates [as Amendment 73 does] may be part and parcel of the right to elect Members of Congress. That is, the right to choose may include the right to winnow.

* * * Amendment 73 is not the act of a state legislature; it is the act of the people of Arkansas, adopted at a direct election and inserted into the state constitution. The majority never explains why giving effect to the people's decision would violate the "democratic principles" that undergird the Constitution. Instead, the majority's discussion of democratic principles is directed entirely to attacking eligibility requirements imposed on the people of a State by an entity other than themselves.

[Justice Thomas exhaustively analyzed the historical evidence of the Framers' intentions, the ratification debates, state practice around the time the Constitution was adopted, and the congressional practice over time. He concluded that "the historical evidence is simply inadequate to warrant the majority's conclusion that the Qualifications Clauses mean anything more than what they say."]

[III] In order to invalidate § 3 of Amendment 73, however, the majority must go farther [than presenting analysis under the Qualifications Clause.] * * * Amendment 73 does not actually create this kind of disqualification. It does not say that covered candidates may not serve any more terms in Congress if reelected, and it does not indirectly achieve the same result by barring those candidates from seeking reelection. It says only that if they are to win reelection, they must do so by write-in votes. * * *

The majority suggests that this does not matter, because Amendment 73 itself says that it has the purpose of "evading the requirements of the Qualifications Clauses." The majority bases this assertion on the Amendment's preamble, which speaks of "limit[ing] the terms of elected officials." [But this statement may] simply reflect the limiting effects that the drafters of the preamble expected to flow from what they perceived as the restoration of electoral competition to congressional races. In any event, inquiries into legislative intent are even more difficult than usual when the legislative body whose unified intent must be determined consists of 825,162 Arkansas voters. * * * One of petitioners' central arguments is that congressionally conferred advantages have artificially inflated the pre-existing electoral chances of the covered candidates, and that Amendment 73 is merely designed to level the playing field on which challengers compete with them.

To understand this argument requires some background. Current federal law (enacted, of course, by congressional incumbents) confers numerous advantages on incumbents, and these advantages are widely thought to make it "significantly more difficult" for challengers to defeat them. For instance, federal law gives incumbents enormous advantages in building name recognition and good will in their home districts. See, e.g., 39 U.S.C. § 3210 (permitting Members of Congress to send "franked" mail free of charge); 2 U.S.C. §§ 61–1, 72a, 332 (permitting Members to have sizable taxpayer-funded staffs); 2 U.S.C. § 123b (establishing the House Recording Studio and the Senate Recording and Photographic Studios). At the same time that incumbent Members of Congress enjoy these in-kind benefits, Congress imposes spending and contribution limits in congressional campaigns that "can prevent challengers from spending more . . . to overcome their disadvantage in name recognition." Many observers believe that the campaign-finance laws also give incumbents an "enormous fund-raising edge" over their challengers by giving a large financing role to entities with incentives to curry favor with incumbents. In addition, the internal rules of Congress put a substantial premium on seniority, with the result that each Member's already plentiful opportunities to distribute benefits to his constituents increase with the length of his tenure. In this manner, Congress effectively "fines" the electorate for voting against incumbents. * * *

At the same time that incumbents enjoy the electoral advantages that they have conferred upon themselves, they also enjoy astonishingly high reelection rates. * * * Even in the November 1994 elections, which are widely considered to have effected the most sweeping change in Congress in recent memory, 90% of the incumbents who sought reelection to the House were successful, and nearly half of the losers were completing only their first terms. Only 2 of the 26 Senate incumbents seeking reelection were defeated, and one of them had been elected for the first time in a special election only a few years earlier.

The voters of Arkansas evidently believe that incumbents would not enjoy such overwhelming success if electoral contests were truly fair—that is, if the government did not put its thumb on either side of the scale. The majority offers no reason to question the accuracy of this belief. * * *

To be sure, the offset is only rough and approximate; no one knows exactly how large an electoral benefit comes with having been a long-term Member of Congress, and no one knows exactly how large an electoral disadvantage comes from forcing a well-funded candidate with high name recognition to run a write-in campaign. But the majority does not base its holding on the premise that Arkansas has struck the wrong balance. Instead, the majority holds that the Qualifications Clauses preclude Arkansas from trying to strike any balance at all; the majority simply says that "an amendment with the avowed purpose and obvious effect of evading the requirements of the Qualifications Clauses by handicapping a class of candidates cannot stand." Thus, the majority apparently would reach the same result even if one could demonstrate at trial that the electoral advantage conferred by Amendment 73 upon challengers precisely counterbalances the electoral advantages conferred by federal law upon long-term Members of Congress.

For me, this suggests only two possibilities. Either the majority's holding is wrong and Amendment 73 does not violate the Qualifications Clauses, or (assuming the accuracy of petitioners' factual claims) the electoral system that exists without Amendment 73 is no less unconstitutional than the electoral system that exists with Amendment 73.

* * * [L]aws that allegedly have the purpose and effect of handicapping a particular class of candidates traditionally are reviewed under the First and Fourteenth Amendments rather than the Qualifications Clauses. * * * To analyze such laws under the Qualifications Clauses may open up whole new vistas for courts. If it is true that "the current congressional campaign finance system . . . has created an electoral system so stacked against challengers that in many elections voters have no real choices," are the Federal Election Campaign Act Amendments of 1974 unconstitutional under (of all things) the Qualifications Clauses? Cf. *Buckley v. Valeo* [*infra*, § 3A] (upholding the current system against First Amendment challenge). If it can be shown that nonminorities are at a significant disadvantage when they seek election in districts dominated by minority voters, would the intentional creation of "majority-minority districts" violate the Qualifications Clauses even if it were to survive scrutiny under the Fourteenth Amendment? Cf. *Shaw v. Reno* ("we express no view as to whether [the intentional creation of such districts] always gives rise to an equal protection claim"). * * *

NOTES ON U.S. TERM LIMITS AND SUBSEQUENT DEVELOPMENTS

1.   *Were the Voters Irrational?* At the same time that voters passed ballot initiatives imposing term limits on federal legislators, they also voted in most cases to return their senior incumbents to office. How can these seemingly inconsistent choices be reconciled? Einer Elhauge argues that this paradox disappears when we understand the collective-action problems that faced voters. "Incumbents by definition have more seniority than challengers, and this seniority gives them more legislative clout. Any

individual district that ousts its incumbent is thus penalized by a smaller share of legislative power and governmental benefits unless the other districts also oust their incumbents." *Are Term Limits Undemocratic?*, 64 U. Chi. L. Rev. 83, 85 (1997). Elhauge argues that voters might prefer less senior representatives with ideological views closer to theirs, but, on balance, voters will prefer a more influential representative, who can send her constituency a greater share of governmental benefits. If, however, voters can be sure that no district can vote for a more senior lawmaker because of term limits, the penalty for electing a challenger is reduced. In addition, term limits allow voters to get rid of the senior representatives from other districts, a result that cannot be obtained through regular voting. In some cases, the benefits of removing these lawmakers from office may exceed any costs to voters of losing the ability to elect their own incumbent to an unlimited number of terms.

Elhauge's explanation suggests why rational voters might simultaneously support term limits for all federal lawmakers and yet still vote for their own incumbent in the absence of such restrictions. It does not explain, however, why voters in a particular state would limit the terms of their representatives without an assurance that other states would also adopt term limitations. Again, however, voters may have been wiser than they appear at first glance. It is no coincidence that groups of states adopted term limits at the same time through a coordinated national effort led by a few organized interest groups. For example, 13 states adopted term limits in 1992. Some of the state constitutional amendments specified that the limitation would not go into effect until 21 or more states had also adopted limitations on the terms of federal lawmakers. Moreover, many of the provisions had delayed effective dates, allowing time for the states that moved quickly to repeal term limits if voters from other states declined to follow their lead.[30] Once a critical mass of states had adopted federal term limits, their representatives would command the votes to change congressional rules to weaken the power of the seniority system and reduce the relative advantage of longtime incumbents over junior members.

2.   *Limitations on State Officials.* Term limitations are common in state and local government. Fifteen states place term limits on state legislators, 36 states limit the number of terms their governors can serve, and many local officials face term limits after a few years of public service. Although term limits on state legislators have been challenged as violating both state and federal constitutional requirements, they have generally been upheld. The leading case is *Legislature of the State of California v. Eu*, 816 P.2d 1309 (Cal. 1991), which balanced the interest of incumbents in retaining office and the interest of voters in having the choice of reelecting them against the state's interest in unclogging the political system and ending the "incumbent's advantage" in elections. The court found that no fundamental rights had been critically burdened (voters have no "right" to vote for a particular candidate) and the state's interest was considerable.[31]

In some states, term limits have had very little effect on political dynamics because legislators did not tend to serve for long periods of time even when their terms were unlimited. In states like California, however, where legislatures were full of career

---

[30]   See John Carey, *Term Limits and Legislative Representation* 12–13 (1996) (detailing provisions of the state amendments).

[31]   See also *Bates v. Jones*, 131 F.3d 843 (9th Cir. 1997) (en banc) (holding that voters could constitutionally adopt lifetime bans on incumbents after a limited period of service "as a means to promote democracy by opening up the political process and restoring competitive elections").

politicians, term limits have caused significant, and sometimes complete, turnover, helped bring to power new leaders, and may have decreased the ability of legislators to pass controversial or significant laws. Term limits are also often associated with demographic changes in legislatures. In 2010, more than one out of four California state lawmakers was a woman, up from 13% in the Senate and 20% in the Assembly 20 years before when voters imposed limits. However, the non-term-limited federal delegation also saw a significant increase in the number of women during this period, suggesting that the change may have been inevitable. Ava Alexander, *Citizen Legislators or Political Musical Chairs?: Term Limits in California* 16–18 (2011). The same study found that Latino representation increased more in the state legislature than in the federal delegation, although low turnout of Latino voters kept numbers in both much lower than the representation of this racial group in the state's population. Most analysts have concluded that term limitations merely sped up the gender and racial diversification of the legislature that was already under way because of demographic and other changes. Bruce Cain & Thad Kousser, *Adapting to Term Limits: Recent Experiences and New Directions* (2004).

Supporters of term limits argued that elections would become more competitive because there would inevitably be more elections for open seats. Kousser reveals, however, that that has not occurred because "the increase in number of open seats has been outweighed by the decrease in the competitiveness of both open seats and races with incumbents." *Term Limits and State Legislatures*, in *Democracy in the States: Experiments in Election Reform* 117, 119 (Bruce Cain, Todd Donovan & Caroline Tolbert eds., 2008). Open-seat races now occur regularly, including in districts that are drawn to be dominated by one party, and strong challengers now wait until the incumbent is termed out, making the interim races less competitive. Moreover, a national survey of state legislators demonstrates that the world of term limits has not ushered in the rise of the citizen-legislator. The overwhelming majority of lawmakers facing the end of their terms intend to run for another office, become a lobbyist, or vie for an appointed role. Only 18% of those in the lower house and 28% of those in the upper house plan to return to private life. *Id.* at 120–21.

Term limits' most significant effects are institutional ones. Term limits appear to weaken legislative party leaders and to strengthen the influence of governors, who, although term limited themselves, have access to more professional staff and the substantial resources of the executive branch. In several state legislatures, term limits have weakened the seniority norm and increased the involvement of junior members in key decisions. Although opponents of term limits predicted they would increase the influence of lobbyists, some commentators have observed that lobbyists find the change a "mixed bag," as they have to establish relationships with new people and educate them about their issues.[32]

Some states with term limitations on state legislators subsequently witnessed efforts to roll back or repeal the limits. In February 2002, the Idaho legislature became the first to repeal term limits, a reform that had been enacted nearly eight years earlier

---

[32] Alan Greenblatt, *The Truth About Term Limits*, Governing Mag., Jan. 2006, at 2; Thomas Little & Rick Farmer, *Legislative Leadership*, in *The Case of Term Limits* 55, 58–64 (Karl Kurtz, Bruce Cain & Richard Niemi eds., 2007). See also Christopher Mooney, *Lobbyists and Interest Groups*, in *Institutional Change in American Politics: The Case of Term Limits, supra*, at 119 (finding mixed evidence of increased influence of lobbyists in term-limited states but finding considerable effect on lobbyist behavior and legislator perceptions of lobbyists).

through a ballot initiative. The Governor vetoed the legislation on the ground that the "will of the voters * * * must be protected," but the legislature overrode his veto with a two-thirds vote in both houses. A study of the vote to overturn term limits reveals that support came primarily from Republican legislators, who wanted to retain their party's control over the legislature, and from representatives of rural areas.[33] Legislators from rural districts argued that term limits would deprive their constituents in sparsely populated areas of experienced leaders, particularly in local offices that are traditionally hard to fill. The reaction following the legislature's decision was swift but not extraordinary. A few incumbents were defeated in the 2002 primary elections, but it appears that other issues played a large role in those elections. A popular referendum to "repeal the repeal" and reinstate term limits ended in a narrow victory for anti-term-limits forces.

Only a few states with term limitations passed them in legislative form that would allow state legislators to repeal or modify them; in the other states, a popular vote would be required to repeal provisions in state constitutions imposing term limits on legislators. So far, voters have been unwilling to reject their decision to adopt legislative term limits. Recently, an initiative to make term limits more flexible was adopted by the voters in California. Proposition 28, adopted in 2012, reduced the total number of years allowed to a state legislator from 14 to 12, but it allowed a legislator to serve that entire period in one house (rather than limiting a politician to three two-year terms in the state house and two four-year terms in the state senate). Legislators have also challenged term limits through litigation. Term limits adopted in 1992 in Wyoming were overturned in May 2004 by the state supreme court, which ruled in *Cathcart v. Meyer*, 88 P.3d 1050 (Wyo. 2004), that they should have been enacted as a constitutional amendment, not through a statutory ballot initiative. This holding substantially increased the obstacles for term-limit supporters in Wyoming because constitutional amendments must be first approved by two-thirds of each legislative house before they can be placed on the ballot.

3.   *Developments in Congress Since* U.S. *Term Limits.* The majority in *U.S. Term Limits* made clear that the adoption of federal term limits requires a constitutional amendment. Shortly after the decision, Congress considered such an amendment to impose 12–year limits on service in each house. Although the proposal received majority support, it lacked the two-thirds vote required for a constitutional amendment. (The Senate did not actually vote on the amendment because supporters lacked two votes to cut off a filibuster.) In 1995, as part of the Republican "Contract with America," the House of Representatives limited committee chairmanships to six years. The effect of the rule was significant. Four senior Republican members, including the Chair of the powerful Ways and Means Committee, retired in 2000 because they could not retain their powerful positions. In January 2002, the House eliminated the eight-year limit on holding the position as Speaker. Critics argue that these term limits make it more difficult for Congress to oversee the executive branch effectively, although defenders maintain that any loss is balanced by an increase in innovative ideas. Since 2000, House members have tended not to include term limits on committee chairs in the rules when Democrats control the body, and to reinstate them when Republicans return to power.

---

[33] See Daniel Smith, *Overturning Term Limits: The Legislature's Own Private Idaho?*, 36 PS 215 (2003).

In recent years, the issue of term limits for members of Congress has again gained some traction, largely because of the support of "Tea Party" Republicans. Keith Larson argues that this new movement is not likely to succeed in convincing a supermajority of federal lawmakers to support a term-limit amendment because one of two necessary conditions for legislators to act against their electoral self-interest is not present. *Republican Revolutionaries and Tea Party Patriots: A Public Choice Analysis of Congressional Term Limits*, 86 St. John's L. Rev. 761 (2012). The two conditions he identifies as necessary to convince strategic lawmakers to apply term limits to themselves are, first, that the lawmakers are members "of an historically underrepresented ideological political faction," *id.* at 765, and, second, that voter dissatisfaction with Congress is strong. "[L]egislators will take public positions in favor of term limits to signal to voters that they are not part of the problem in Congress; rather, that they are attempting to fix the institution." *Id.* at 766. Although public opinion of Congress is currently at a modern all-time low, conservatives no longer suffer the sense of chronic underrepresentation given their recent power in Congress and the states. Thus, he concludes that this current push for federal term limits will be no more successful than the one a decade ago. Are there any other conditions necessary or conducive for lawmaker support of a reform so distant from their interest in reelection? Can you imagine any scenario under which a term-limit constitutional amendment is sent to the states for ratification? If it were, what position would strategic state lawmakers likely take?

4. *Distinguishing Between Indirect Qualifications and Legitimate Ballot Access Provisions.* Remember that the Arkansas provision in *U.S. Term Limits* was phrased as a ballot access provision, denying a place on the ballot to lawmakers who had served a certain period of time in the House or Senate. The Court rejected the argument that the Arkansas amendment merely restricted incumbents' access to the ballot and found that it imposed an additional qualification on federal legislative offices. The Court looked to both the effect and the intent of the provision in reaching the conclusion that the state was trying to do indirectly what it was prohibited from doing directly. Although the Court indicated that empirical evidence was not required to determine the likely effect of a provision, it believed that the ballot restriction "will make it significantly more difficult for the barred candidate to win the election." It supported this conclusion with the following evidence: "[I]n over 1,300 Senate elections since the passage of the Seventeenth Amendment in 1913, only one has been won by a write-in candidate. In over 20,000 House elections since the turn of the century, only five have been won by write-in candidates."

Justice Thomas responded that this empirical data would not describe the state of affairs in a world with term limits. He argued that most write-in candidates in the past had been fringe candidates with virtually no name recognition or financial backing, while write-in candidates under the Arkansas amendment would be well-known incumbents. In the past, only twice had *incumbent* Congress members sought reelection as write-in candidates; one of them won with 83% of the vote, and the other managed a respectable showing of 23% support. Which prediction is likely to have been more accurate? Should the determination of the effect of such an amendment rest on this kind of empirical analysis?

In the *U.S. Term Limits* case, the Court relied on the state supreme court's finding that the intent of the amendment was to impose term limits on federal lawmakers. The opinion, therefore, says little about how a court is to discern the intent behind such a provision, particularly one that was enacted by hundreds of thousands of voters. The majority mentioned the initiative's preamble, which stated explicitly that "the people of Arkansas * * * herein limit the terms of elected officials." Also, the name of the primary group supporting the amendment and participating in the lawsuit—U.S. Term Limits, Inc.—led one judge on the state supreme court to conclude that the ballot access provision was actually a qualification. Are these legitimate ways to discern the intent of those enacting this provision? As the dissent noted, the preamble also evidenced a concern with entrenched incumbency that results in a system offering voters very little real choice among candidates. Given the electoral advantages that Justice Thomas lists in his dissent, term limits may provide challengers—who lack the same access to the media, lists of donors and volunteers, and the ability to correspond with constituents using franked mail—a fair chance to unseat incumbents. Would an intent to level the political playing field be acceptable under the majority's test, allowing a court to uphold a provision similar to the Arkansas amendment as a permissible ballot access regulation?

Determining whether a law imposes qualifications on candidates or only restricts their access to the ballot is more than merely a matter of semantics. As we will see in the next section, the Court tends to apply less exacting constitutional tests to ballot access regulations, even though *U.S. Term Limits* suggests that imposing explicit qualifications on candidates for the federal legislature may not be relevantly different from restricting access to the ballot for certain categories of people.

C. BALLOT ACCESS PROVISIONS

Article I, § 4 of the Constitution, the Elections Clause, allows the states to regulate the "Times, Places and Manner of holding Elections for Senators and Representatives," although Congress can pass legislation to make or alter state electoral regulations. Before 1900, concerns about ballot access restrictions were nonexistent. There were no official ballots; instead, political parties provided voters with ballots listing only their candidates for office. Because party ballots were printed in distinctive colors, keeping one's vote secret was difficult, and voters were often bribed or intimidated into voting a particular way. Only with the adoption of the secret, uniform, and government-printed ballot did the question of ballot access become important for policymakers and the courts.[34] Ballot access implicates the interests of many players in the political system: voters, who realistically can only elect candidates who appear on the ballot; candidates; and political parties, the groups that largely determine who will be listed on the ballot.

Although states have the constitutional power to regulate elections, their authority is limited because restrictions implicate constitutional guarantees. Most obviously, ballot access laws affect the right to vote. In addition, laws that impair the right of minor-party or independent candidates to obtain a spot on the ballot undermine the right to associate for political purposes. Balanced against these constitutional concerns is the states' legitimate interest in regulating elections to reduce voter confusion, disorder, and fraud. The Court has applied a sliding-scale approach, calibrating the level of scrutiny to the burden imposed by the ballot

---

[34] See Marjorie Hershey, *Party Politics in America* 151 (15th ed. 2013).

access provision. In *Williams v. Rhodes*, 393 U.S. 23 (1968), the Court struck down a law requiring new political parties to obtain signatures equal to 15% of the ballots cast in the last election and to file the petitions long before the election. It required that regulations imposing serious burdens on rights—in this case, essentially making it impossible for new parties to obtain ballot access—be narrowly tailored to achieve a compelling state interest. Laws that do not operate as prohibitions on access trigger less exacting scrutiny, allowing legitimate state regulatory interests to support reasonable and nondiscriminatory burdens. The choice of the standard of review—strict scrutiny versus some lesser scrutiny—often determines the outcome of the judicial analysis. See, e.g., *Lee v. Keith*, 463 F.3d 763 (7th Cir. 2006) (applying strict scrutiny to Illinois requirements that independent candidates file 323 days before the general election, the earliest filing deadline in the country, as well as meet stringent petition requirements, and holding statute unconstitutional); *Libertarian Party of Ohio v. Blackwell*, 462 F.3d 579 (6th Cir. 2006) (using strict scrutiny, invalidating Ohio deadlines for minor parties that required filing petitions more than a year before the general election).

Permissible state interests are linked to the Court's belief that "there must be a substantial regulation of elections if they are to be fair and honest and if some sort of order, rather than chaos, is to accompany the democratic processes." *Storer v. Brown*, 415 U.S. 724, 730 (1974). Consider the state interests identified in the following decision upholding a law that prohibits a candidate from appearing on the ballot as a candidate of more than one party. Such multiparty candidacies are called *fusion candidacies*. Is a ban on fusion candidacies designed to reduce voter confusion and protect the integrity of the electoral process, or is it a prohibition adopted by the two major parties to eliminate any threat from emerging political parties?

Timmons v. Twin Cities Area New Party
520 U.S. 351 (1997).

State Representative Andy Dawkins was running unopposed in the Democratic-Farmer-Labor (DFL) Party's primary. The Minnesota chapter of the national New Party also chose him as their candidate for the state legislature. Because Dawkins had already filed as a candidate for the DFL's nomination, local election officials refused to accept the New Party's nominating petition, citing state laws that prohibit fusion candidacies. The New Party sued, contending that the laws violate their members' associational rights under the federal Constitution. Although noting that the First Amendment "protects the right of citizens to associate and to form political parties for the advancement of common political goals and ideas," **Chief Justice Rehnquist** for the six-justice majority held that the antifusion law is a reasonable regulation of parties, elections, and ballots designed to reduce "election- and campaign-related disorder."

The Court reasoned that this burden on the New Party is a minor one. Although it cannot nominate the candidates of other parties, a political party "remains free to endorse whom it likes, to ally itself with others, to nominate candidates for office, and to spread its message to all who will listen." The state prohibition closes off one avenue of communication with the voters (i.e., the ballot), but "[b]allots serve primarily to elect candidates, not as forums for political expression." Because the burden on the New Party is slight, the state's interest in avoiding voter confusion and political chaos is sufficient to justify the law. As in previous ballot access cases, the majority did not require any empirical proof of voter confusion. Instead, it used the following worst-case scenario to support its conclusion that voters might be misled: "[M]embers of a major party could decide that a powerful way of 'sending a message' via the ballot would be for various factions of that party to nominate the major party's candidate as the candidate for the newly-formed 'No New Taxes,' 'Conserve Our Environment,' and 'Stop Crime Now' parties." Such tactics would transform the ballot "from a means of choosing candidates to a billboard for political advertising." This hypothetical implicated a second legitimate state interest: protecting the integrity of the electoral process and thus avoiding increased voter alienation and dissatisfaction.

Dissenting **Justice Stevens**, joined by **Justice Ginsburg**, thought fusion candidacies are "the best marriage of the virtues of minor party challenge to entrenched viewpoints and the political stability that the two-party system provides. * * * [They provide] a means by which voters with viewpoints not adequately represented by platforms of the two major parties can indicate to a particular candidate that—in addition to his support for the major party views—he should be responsive to the views of the minor party whose support for him was demonstrated where political parties demonstrate support—on the ballot." The majority, however, dismissed the argument that, without fusion-based alliances, minor parties would be unable to thrive, reasoning that the existence of benefits for minor parties does not mean that the state must permit fusion candidacies. "Many features of our political system—e.g., single-member districts, 'first past the post' elections, and the high costs of campaigning—make it difficult for third parties to succeed in American politics. But the Constitution does not require States to permit fusion any more than it requires them to move to proportional-representation elections or public financing of campaigns."

Justice Stevens' dissent took particular issue with the majority's suggestion that the interest in maintaining a stable two-party system might be an acceptable state concern to justify ballot restrictions. "In most States, perhaps in all, there are two and only two major political parties. It is not surprising, therefore, that most States have enacted election laws that impose burdens on the development and growth of third parties. * * * The fact that the law was both intended to disadvantage minor parties and has had that effect is a matter that should weigh against, rather than in favor of, its constitutionality." He concluded: "It demeans the strength of the two-party system to assume that the major parties need to rely on laws that discriminate against independent voters and minor parties in order to preserve their positions of power. Indeed, it is a central theme of our jurisprudence that the entire electorate, which necessarily includes the members of major parties, will benefit from robust competition in ideas and governmental policies * * *."

NOTES ON TIMMONS AND THE IDEA OF A PARTISAN LOCKUP

1. *Voter Confusion.* As in previous cases, the *Timmons* Court deferred to the state's allegation of voter confusion without requiring empirical proof. In *Munro v. Socialist Workers Party*, 479 U.S. 189, 195–96 (1986), the Court stated: "To require States to prove actual voter confusion, ballot overcrowding, or the presence of frivolous

candidacies as a predicate to the imposition of reasonable ballot access restrictions would invariably lead to endless court battles over the sufficiency of the 'evidence' marshaled by a State to prove the predicate. Such a requirement would necessitate that a State's political system sustain some level of damage before the legislature could take corrective action. Legislatures, we think, should be permitted to respond to potential deficiencies in the electoral process with foresight rather than reactively, provided that the response is reasonable and does not significantly impinge on constitutionally protected rights." Criticizing this kind of approach, Justice Stevens noted in *Timmons* that the only empirical data from a state with vibrant fusion politics, New York, revealed that the majority's "parade of horribles is fantastical."

Should courts require some showing that long ballots, fusion candidates, or multi-candidate races actually confuse voters rather than provide them with information or allow them more choices? With respect to fusion candidacies, is it not at least theoretically possible that the additional ballot information improves voters' ability to vote competently? Few voters are willing to invest significant time and energy to find and understand information about candidates for public office. Given their limited attention to political matters, most people vote on the basis of voting cues or shortcuts, such as party affiliation, that will allow them to vote in the same way that they would if they had full information about the candidates and their positions. Helpful voting cues allow them to vote competently even with limited information.[35] The strongest voting cues—party affiliation and incumbency—are usually apparent from the ballot; indeed, party affiliation is provided for most elections.

But the major-party cue may not sufficiently allow voters to distinguish among candidates. One result of a two-party system combined with single-member electoral districts is a convergence of the parties with respect to their positions on the issues.[36] Third-party endorsements, however, can provide a more particularized cue about a candidate's positions on the issues. Third parties that endorse candidates of major parties tend to be issue-oriented or ideologically driven; for example, knowing that the Republican candidate is supported by the Right-to-Life Party or the Libertarian Party reveals more completely her ideology than the Republican nomination alone. Can you make an argument that fusion candidacies actually help voters cast their ballots more competently, rather than add to their confusion?

Our discussion of ballot access rules demonstrates the profound importance of political parties in the organization of our electoral system. Political parties are challenging entities for the state to regulate. In a sense they organize government, and thus they are both the regulated and the regulators. They are fairly fragmented

---

[35] See Elisabeth Gerber & Arthur Lupia, *Voter Competence in Direct Legislation Elections*, in *Citizen Competence and Democratic Institutions* 147 (Stephen Elkin & Karol Soltan eds., 1999); Christopher Elmendorf & David Schleicher, *Informing Consent: Voter Ignorance, Political Parties, and Election Law*, 2013 U. Ill. L. Rev. 363 (discussing ways to improve the partisan cue and improve voter competence).

[36] See Jeffrey Berry & Clyde Wilcox, *The Interest Group Society* 64 (5th ed. 2009); Anthony Downs, *An Economic Theory of Democracy* 136 (1957). But see John Aldrich, *Why Parties? The Origin and Transformation of Political Parties in America* 169–74 (1995) (providing data to suggest that the public perceives parties as distinct and arguing that the "perception has a plausible basis"); Morris Fiorina, *Divided Government* 121–22 (2d ed. 1996) (suggesting that the two major parties are further apart ideologically than in the past, largely because of internal party politics).

organizations, with local, state, and national organizations, and with arms in the government and outside it.[37]

2. *The State Interest in Protecting the Two-Party System.* In some ballot access cases, the Court has accepted state claims that regulation was required to promote political stability, to avoid splintered parties, and to restrain factionalism. This concern may be merely an interest in avoiding intraparty disputes by, for example, limiting the ability of people who have previously run in party primaries to appear on the ballot as independent candidates.[38] See *Storer v. Brown, supra.* Framed in this manner, the interest is not sufficient to support restrictions that are applied to independent candidates not recently associated with political parties. See *Anderson v. Celebrezze,* 460 U.S. 780 (1983). In *Clingman v. Beaver,* 544 U.S. 581 (2005), the Court upheld Oklahoma's law limiting participation in party primaries to only that party's members and independents, thereby forbidding, for example, a Republican from voting in the Libertarian Party's primary even if the Libertarian Party wished to open its primary fully. One of the state interests accepted to justify this law was the goal of preserving political parties as clearly identifiable groups with particular ideologies, and therefore ensuring that party affiliation sends a meaningful signal to voters who rely on party cue in casting ballots.

Increasingly, courts such as *Timmons* are also willing to consider the state's interest in maintaining a stable, two-party electoral system. Even though he dissented in *Timmons,* Justice Souter agreed with the majority that "[i]f it could be shown that the disappearance of the two-party system would undermine" the state's interest in preserving a political system capable of governing effectively, it might justify certain restrictions. Unlike state interests tied to intraparty tension, this state interest can support broader ballot access regulations affecting independents, write-in candidates, and minor parties. In contrast, Stevens' dissent draws on *Williams v. Rhodes, supra,* in which the Court seemed dubious about the legitimacy of a state interest to protect the two-party system. Very clearly, the Court in *Williams* rejected the notion that laws could favor two particular parties, giving them a duopoly over ballot access. Instead, "[c]ompetition in ideas and governmental policies is at the core of our electoral process and of the First Amendment freedoms."

Several scholars have been sympathetic to Justice Stevens' concern in *Timmons* and have argued that courts should not apply very deferential review to ballot access provisions. Instead, they argue that the Court should be particularly aggressive in its review of such laws because they are enacted by incumbents who are members of established political parties and who are hostile to strong minor parties or independent candidacies.[39] Michael Klarman, for example, cites ballot access laws as examples of

---

[37] See V.O. Key, Jr., *Politics, Parties, and Pressure Groups* 163–65 (5th ed. 1964) (differentiating among the party-in-government, the party-organization, and the party-in-the-electorate). For additional analysis of the regulation of political parties, see Samuel Issacharoff, Pamela Karlan & Richard Pildes, *The Law of Democracy: Legal Structure of the Political Process,* chap. 4 (4th ed. 2012); David Ryden, *Representation in Crisis: The Constitution, Interest Groups, and Political Parties* (1996); Daniel Lowenstein, *Associational Rights of Major Political Parties: A Skeptical Inquiry,* 71 Tex. L. Rev. 1741 (1993); Symposium, *Law and Political Parties,* 100 Colum. L. Rev. 593–899 (2000).

[38] For a sophisticated analysis of these "sore loser laws" and their effects on intraparty competition, see Michael Kang, *Sore Loser Laws and Democratic Contestation,* 99 Geo. L.J. 1013 (2011).

[39] See, e.g., Richard Hasen, *Entrenching the Duopoly: Why the Supreme Court Should Not Allow the States to Protect the Democrats and Republicans from Political Competition,* 1997 Sup. Ct. Rev. 331; Samuel Issacharoff & Richard Pildes, *Politics as Markets: Partisan Lockups of the Democratic Process,* 50 Stan. L. Rev. 643 (1998).

legislative entrenchment that foreclose for voters the option of expressing discontent with the two major parties. Incumbents have little to lose by passing restrictive ballot access laws because the laws themselves operate to keep candidates who might change the system off the ballot. *Majoritarian Judicial Review: The Entrenchment Problem*, 85 Geo. L.J. 491 (1997). These scholars not only do not accept protection of the current two-party system as a legitimate state interest, but they also argue that it should serve as a red flag to courts to view ballot access restrictions with great skepticism.[40]

Under the *partisan lockup theory*, are many well-established features of our electoral system subject to constitutional attack? Many aspects of our electoral system, including single-member districts and a simple plurality system, work to favor the development and entrenchment of two major parties.[41] Where should we draw the line between rigorous judicial scrutiny of laws that entrench the current political duopoly and more deferential review of choices made by the political branches? Are courts institutionally suited to draw such a line or to determine which laws fall on either side?

3. *The Other Side of the Balance: The First Amendment Rights Infringed by Ballot Access Restrictions.* Not only are courts willing to accept a variety of rationales as legitimate state interests justifying regulation, but they also tend to discount some of the interests of voters and political groups that are burdened by the restrictions. For example, the right to vote is viewed by the Court purely in instrumental terms. Similarly, as *Timmons* and the following case suggest, the Court has viewed the role of minor parties in our political system as a narrow one: to elect their own candidates. Is this an accurate vision of the influence of third parties?[42]

Munro v. Socialist Workers Party
479 U.S. 189 (1986).

The state of Washington used a blanket primary to select candidates for the general election.[43] There are three types of primaries: *closed*, in which only a voter who

---

[40] But see David Dulio & James Thurber, *America's Two-Party System: Friend or Foe?*, 52 Admin. L. Rev. 769 (2000) (defending the two-party system as "the natural and most effective system" for the United States' ballot access cases from the perspective of "firm believers in the utility and value of the two-party system for American politics").

[41] See Maurice Duverger, *Political Parties: Their Organization and Activity in the Modern State* (1954) (classic formulation of this "true sociological law"); Gary Cox, *Making Votes Count: Strategic Coordination in the World's Electoral Systems* (1997) (evaluating Duverger's law).

[42] See Steven Rosenstone, Roy Behr & Edward Lazarus, *Third Parties in America: Citizen Response to Major Party Failure* (2d ed. 1996).

[43] Washington's blanket primary has since been ruled unconstitutional. *Democratic Party of Washington v. Reed*, 343 F.3d 1198 (9th Cir. 2003) (relying on *California Democratic Party v. Jones*, 530 U.S. 567 (2000), which struck down a California law enacted by popular vote to require blanket primaries on the ground that it interfered with the associational rights of political parties, which had internal rules limiting participation in their primaries to members). The Supreme Court upheld the similar nonpartisan, or "top-two," primary that voters adopted to replace the blanket primary, but it left open the possibility of an as-applied challenge if the ballot design and text do not sufficiently alert voters that the party preference expressed by candidates is not the same as the parties endorsing those candidates. *Washington State Grange v. Washington State Republican Party*, 552 U.S. 442 (2008). The ballot provides a statement next to a candidate's name noting which party she prefers, or that she prefers no party, and a candidate is not limited to naming a qualified party. For example, in 2008, some candidates indicated a preference for the "Salmon Yoga Party," the "No Gas Taxes (R) Party," and similar labels, as well as the more traditional political parties. In the subsequent as-applied challenge, the appellate court ruled that the design of the ballot and other voter information materials made clear that a candidate's party preference was not an endorsement by the party and that there was no evidence of voter confusion. *Washington State Republican Party v. Washington State Grange*, 676 F.3d

has declared her party affiliation can vote in the party's primary; *open*, in which a voter can participate in any party's primary, regardless of her partisan affiliation, but can vote in only one party's primary; and *blanket*, in which a voter not only does not have to declare a party affiliation, but may also vote in the primary of more than one party. In a blanket primary, for example, a voter can choose among Democrats for governor and then among Republicans for lieutenant governor. In Washington's system, minor-party candidates could appear on the ballot for the general election only if they had been nominated at their parties' conventions and had received at least 1% of all the votes cast in the primary election. Before the ballot access law was adopted in 1977, minor-party candidates regularly appeared on the ballot (12 appeared in 1976); after the law was passed, only one in 12 minor-party candidates had qualified for the ballot for statewide office.

Dean Peoples was the nominee of the Socialist Workers Party, but received only nine one-hundredths of 1% of the total votes cast in the blanket primary. Accordingly, his name did not appear on the general ballot. Peoples, the party, and two voters argued that the ballot access law violated their rights under the First and Fourteenth Amendments. **Justice White** accepted as legitimate the state's interest in reducing ballot overcrowding and adopting reasonable regulations to ensure that candidates on the ballot had sufficient community support. Such regulations reduce voter confusion, avoid deception, and mitigate frustration of the democratic process. "We think that the State can properly reserve the general election ballot 'for major struggles,' " the Court wrote, citing *Storer*. The Court acknowledged that the restriction substantially burdened minor-party candidates and was a relatively greater burden than a requirement to gather signatures on a petition prior to the election, an alternative way of ensuring a modicum of support before a candidate appeared on the ballot. It noted, however, that in a blanket primary, minor-party candidates can campaign among the entire pool of electorates to garner their 1%.

Although the majority realized that many minor parties only use a campaign as a platform to discuss issues, "[i]t can hardly be said that Washington's voters are denied freedom of association because they must channel their expressive activity into a campaign at the primary as opposed to the general election." Quoting *Storer*, the majority held that the foremost goal of the electoral process is "to winnow out and finally reject all but the chosen candidates." In dissent, **Justice Marshall** took vigorous exception to this cursory treatment of the associational rights of members of minor parties. "The minor party's often unconventional positions broaden political debate, expand the range of issues with which the electorate is concerned, and influence the positions of the majority, in some instances ultimately becoming majority positions. And its very existence provides an outlet for voters to express dissatisfaction with the candidates or platforms of the major parties." Marshall emphasized that minor parties' primary role is to affect political debate, not to elect their own candidates. To play a meaningful role in the process, minor-party candidates need to be included in the phase of the electoral process in which voters are most seriously considering their choices: the general election.

---

784 (9th Cir. 2012). But see Mathew Manweller, *The Very Partisan Nonpartisan Top-Two Primary: Understanding What Voters Don't Understand*, 10 Election L.J. 255 (2011) (finding significant voter confusion about the relationship of candidates to parties in the Washington system). In June 2010, California adopted a similar top-two primary system through the initiative process.

BALLOT ACCESS PROBLEMS

Problem 2–4. Hawaii's election law requires a candidate to participate in a new-party, established party, or nonpartisan primary election to obtain a position on the general election ballot. Primaries in Hawaii are open. The state does not allow write-in voting, and a voter who notified state officials that he intended to vote for a write-in candidate in the Democratic primary was told that such a vote would be ignored. The voter filed suit, claiming that the ban on write-in voting violates his freedom of expression and association under the First Amendment. How should this claim be analyzed? Remember the statistics marshaled by the majority and dissent in *U.S. Term Limits* about the success (or, more accurately, the lack of success) of write-in candidates for major offices. Also consider these facts about Hawaii's electoral system: its election laws date to the 1890s when Hawaii was still a monarchy. Hawaii is for all practical purposes a one-party Democratic state, so that the winner of the Democratic primary invariably wins the general election. The rules for new-party primaries and partisan primaries discourage independent voters or candidates from using these avenues to challenge the established political structure. A new political party can be organized through a petition drive to obtain signatures of 1% of registered voters; independents can run in a nonpartisan primary, but to advance to the general election, they need 10% of the total primary vote or votes equal to the minimum number required to nominate a partisan candidate to the general election ballot. The real disincentive to serious rivals to the Democratic candidates is the price voters pay for voting in a primary other than the Democratic. Since the Democratic primary essentially determines the winner, a voter who chooses to vote in another primary will have no effect on the outcome. As Issacharoff and Pildes conclude: "[T]he cumulative structure of Hawaii's laws eviscerates any nascent resistance to the Democratic monopoly." Issacharoff & Pildes, *supra*, at 671. After thinking about this problem, look at *Burdick v. Takushi*, 504 U.S. 428 (1992), for the Supreme Court's approach. See also *Clingman v. Beaver*, 544 U.S. at 607 (O'Connor, concurring in part and concurring in the judgment) (expressing concern that the statutory framework governing elections—particularly provisions affecting party registration and affiliation—as a whole might impermissibly burden voters, but noting that the question of the "*cumulative* burdens imposed by the *overall* scheme of electoral regulation upon the rights of voters and parties to associate" had not been properly raised).

Problem 2–5. The main problem identified by partisan lockup theorists is that, in the realm of election law, there is an inherent conflict of interest. This conflict leads to ballot access provisions favoring major parties and penalizing minor parties and independent candidates, to partisan gerrymandering, and, as we will see, to certain kinds of campaign finance and other ethics laws. Are courts the only way to guard against the self-interest of politicians in this arena? Some countries, including Australia, Canada, and the United Kingdom, rely on nonpartisan electoral administration entities to take the lead in regulating campaigns and elections. For example, the U.K.'s Electoral Commission supervises elections and oversees the regulatory structure, and it also provides reports and recommendations to Parliament on issues affecting campaign finance laws, districting, and political advertising. See Christopher Elmendorf, *Representation Reinforcement through Advisory Commissions: The Case of Election Law*, 80 N.Y.U. L. Rev. 1366 (2005) (describing these entities and proposing such a commission for the U.S.). Wisconsin has adopted a nonpartisan model, creating in 2007 a Government Accountability Board that oversees election administration and enforcement of campaign finances, ethics, and lobbying laws. Daniel Tokaji, *America's Top Model: The Wisconsin Government Accountability Board*, 3 UCI L. Rev. 576 (2013).

Could a nonpartisan, independent election commission work in the United States at the federal level? What are the constitutional, political, and logistical challenges for such a reform? How successful have nonpartisan redistricting commissions been in drawing legislative district boundaries without undue political influence? What other solutions to partisan lockup, besides aggressive judicial review, are possible? See, e.g., Dennis Thompson, *Just Elections* 156–57 (2002) (discussing the appropriate role for direct democracy in decisions affecting the design of democratic institutions).

3. STRUCTURES OF CAMPAIGN FINANCE

Concerns about the influence of money in electoral outcomes are not new, and they have led to a century of federal regulation. The Tillman Act of 1907, 34 Stat. 864 (1907), prohibited all corporations and national banks from making "money contribution[s]" in connection with federal elections. The prohibition was extended to *all* contributions by the Federal Corrupt Practices Act of 1925, 43 Stat. 1074 (1925) (later repealed). The Smith-Connally Act, 57 Stat. 163 (1943) (expired 1945), and then the Taft-Hartley Act, 61 Stat. 159 (1947), prohibited unions from making contributions in connection with federal elections. Because of the vagueness of these early laws, however, unions and corporations were able to make contributions virtually at will. Comprehensive reform was triggered by concern over the $60 million raised by President Nixon's 1972 reelection campaign. When it was discovered that some of this money was illegally diverted to finance the Watergate break-in, concern stimulated passage of significant reform. The Federal Election Campaign Act Amendments of 1974 (FECA), Pub. L. No. 93–443, 88 Stat. 1263, codified at 2 U.S.C. § 431 *et seq.*, set limits on campaign contributions and expenditures in presidential and congressional election campaigns and established the Federal Election Commission (FEC) to administer and enforce the law.

Decades of experience with FECA demonstrated that serious challenges remained to effective federal campaign finance regulation, but Congress seemed unable to respond. The bankruptcy of Enron Corporation, an energy trading company, in late 2001, provided the momentum for reformers to get their proposal out of committee. Enron and its officers had contributed millions of dollars in largely unregulated money, and thus the company's collapse made these contributions and the political clout they might have bought more salient to voters and lawmakers. Primary Senate supporters John McCain (R–Ariz.) and Russ Feingold (D–Wisc.), together with their House counterparts Christopher Shays (R–Conn.) and Martin Meehan (D–Mass.), overcame all the procedural hurdles, and the Bipartisan Campaign Reform Act of 2002 (BCRA), Pub. L. No. 107–55, 116 Stat. 81, went into effect the day after the 2002 midterm elections. BCRA remains the primary law regulating federal campaigns, although some of its provisions have been struck down by the Supreme Court, just as occurred with FECA.

Some pluralist theorists object to regulating campaign finance. First, they argue that such regulation is counterproductive because money can be used to express political views that need to be heard and reflected by the representative. Indeed, the amount of the contribution can signal the intensity of those political views. Second, they view most regulation of money in politics as inconsistent with the Constitution. Whatever the outer limits of the sphere of the Free Speech Clause of the First Amendment, it is clear that at its core it protects "political speech." The Supreme Court has recognized "a profound national commitment to the principle that debate on public issues should be uninhibited, robust, and wide-open." *New York Times Co. v. Sullivan*, 376 U.S. 254 (1964). Is political speech involved when someone contributes money to a candidate? The contribution helps the candidate spread her message, and thus perhaps amounts to "indirect speech," or speech by proxy. Is this different from the situation in which someone uses her money to engage in political speech independent of the candidate—for example, by directly purchasing an advertisement supporting the candidate or attacking her opponent? Which kind of expenditure poses the greater threat to corrupt the representational process? Does the answer to this question depend upon how "corruption" is defined?

Republican and critical theorists, however, tend to consider the political advantages of wealth in an unregulated political system to be corrupting in ways similar to outright bribery. "The American system is rooted in the assumption of political equality: 'one person, one vote.' But money, which candidates need to harvest votes, is not distributed equally. The substantial inequities of campaign financing have hindered the quest for political equality and have worried concerned Americans since the beginning of the twentieth century."[44] More skeptical observers of electoral politics respond to those who advocate far-reaching regulation with a pragmatic argument. They note that regulations and limitations merely change the form of the expenditure, diverting the money into unregulated channels and rendering campaign finance laws largely futile.[45]

We will begin our analysis of campaign finance by assessing FECA, and the Supreme Court case that reshaped that law (*Buckley v. Valeo*, 424 U.S. 1 (1976) (per curiam)), and then BCRA, and the first major Supreme Court case that left it largely intact (*McConnell v. Fed. Election Comm'n*, 540 U.S. 93 (2003)). After *McConnell*, a change in Supreme Court personnel shifted the judicial approach to campaign finance. We will accordingly next consider *Citizens United v. Fed. Election Comm'n*, 558 U.S. 310 (2010), which struck down key provisions of BCRA, and discuss the federal landscape in the wake of that decision. Finally, we will conclude by describing some key features of state regulatory systems, including public financing.

---

[44]   Herbert Alexander, *Financing Politics: Money, Elections, and Political Reform* 3 (4th ed. 1992).

[45]   See, e.g., Samuel Issacharoff & Pamela Karlan, *The Hydraulics of Campaign Finance Reform*, 77 Tex. L. Rev. 1705 (1999).

A. THE CONSTITUTIONAL FOUNDATION FOR REGULATING CAMPAIGNS

1. Providing the First Amendment Framework: *Buckley v. Valeo*

In *Buckley v. Valeo*, 424 U.S. 1 (1976) (per curiam), the Supreme Court addressed the constitutionality of the Federal Election Campaign Act (FECA) as amended in 1974 and Subtitle H of the Internal Revenue Code, which provides for the public financing of presidential elections. *Buckley* remains the foundational case in the constitutional jurisprudence affecting campaign finance laws, as well as other regulation of political speech and activity.

Perhaps the most important aspect of *Buckley* is the Court's decision to assess campaign regulation through the lens of the First Amendment, equating spending in campaigns with political expression and political association. The Court has never afforded these fundamental rights absolute protection but, under traditional First Amendment jurisprudence, has required the government to show a "compelling" or "sufficiently important" state interest, depending on the extent of the burden on expression, and to demonstrate that the regulation of political speech is "narrowly" or "closely" tailored to serve that interest. *Buckley* also identified the state interest that the Court continues to view as the primary justification for campaign regulation: the actuality and appearance of *quid pro quo* corruption. As it set forth in *Buckley*:

> To the extent that large contributions are given to secure a political *quid pro quo* from current and potential office holders, the integrity of our system of representative democracy is undermined. Although the scope of such pernicious practices can never be reliably ascertained, the deeply disturbing examples surfacing after the 1972 election demonstrate that the problem is not an illusory one.

> Of almost equal concern as the danger of actual *quid pro quo* arrangements is the impact of the appearance of corruption stemming from public awareness of the opportunities for abuse inherent in a regime of large individual financial contributions. * * *

Limitations on Political Contributions. FECA prohibited individuals and most groups from contributing more than $1,000 per candidate for each primary election, and more than $1,000 per candidate for each runoff or general election. In addition, individuals could not contribute more than a total of $25,000 per year. (These thresholds have since been increased and indexed for inflation; the aggregate limit on contributions was held unconstitutional in *McCutcheon v. Fed. Election Comm'n*, 134 S.Ct. 1434 (2014).) Certain "political committees"—those registered as political committees with the FEC for not less than six months that have received contributions from more than 50 persons and, except for state political-party organizations, have contributed to five or more candidates for federal office—could contribute up to $5,000 to any candidate for federal office. (This threshold has not changed and is not indexed.) The Court in *Buckley* upheld these provisions. Although the Court stated that contribution limitations significantly interfered with the First Amendment right of political association, the Court found that these provisions passed constitutional muster because they limited "the actuality and appearance of corruption resulting from large * * * financial contributions."

Limitations on Political Expenditures. The Act (a) limited expenditures by individuals and groups "relative to a clearly identified candidate during a calendar year" to $1,000. Other provisions (b) limited spending by candidates from their personal or family funds and (c) limited overall expenditures by candidates to differing amounts depending upon the federal office sought. The Court in *Buckley* struck down these provisions, establishing a bifurcated constitutional regime for contributions and expenditures that continues to shape regulatory policy today.[46] The Court first held that expenditure limits operated as a substantial restriction on First Amendment freedoms because "[a] restriction on the amount of money a person or group can spend on political communication during a campaign necessarily reduces the quantity of expression by restricting the number of issues discussed, the depth of their exploration and the size of the audience reached."

The Court determined that these restrictions were more severe than the limitations on contributions because "[a] contribution serves as a general expression of support for the candidate and his views, but does not communicate the underlying basis for the support. The quantity of communication by the contributor does not increase perceptibly with the size of his contribution, since the expression rests solely on the undifferentiated, symbolic act of contributing." In contrast, the Court said, "a primary effect of these expenditure limitations is to restrict the quantity of campaign speech by individuals, groups and candidates. The restrictions, while neutral as to the ideas expressed, limit political expression 'at the core of our electoral process and of the First Amendment freedoms.'" Accordingly, their "constitutionality * * * turns on whether the governmental interests advanced [to] support [them] satisfy the exacting scrutiny applicable to limitations on core First Amendment rights of political expression."

The limitations on individual and group expenditures independent of a particular candidate did not survive this exacting scrutiny because, the Court held, they did not substantially serve the governmental interest in stemming actual or apparent corruption. Such expenditures are made independent of any candidates, alleviating the danger that expenditures will be given as a *quid pro quo* for improper commitments from the candidate. Furthermore, in response to the argument that the expenditure limitations serve a government interest "in equalizing the relative ability of individuals and groups to influence the outcome of elections," the Court stated:

> [T]he concept that government may restrict the speech of some elements of our society in order to enhance the relative voice of others is wholly foreign to the First Amendment, which was designed "to secure 'the widest possible dissemination of information from diverse and antagonistic sources,'" and "to assure unfettered interchange of ideas for the bringing about of political and social changes desired by the people." The First Amendment's protection against governmental abridgement of free

---

[46] See Kathleen Sullivan, *Against Campaign Finance Reform*, 1998 Utah L. Rev. 311 (noting the instability of a system that restricts the supply of money while leaving the demand for it unregulated).

expression cannot properly be made to depend on a person's financial ability to engage in public discussion.

Assuming that the only legitimate government purpose can be prevention of *quid pro quo* corruption or the appearance of corruption, is the Court's rationale persuasive? Isn't it more realistic to assume that candidates will be aware of independent expenditures and be grateful if they play a role in their electoral success? Certainly, in a world where direct contributions are limited but independent expenditures are not, wouldn't we expect groups wanting to influence lawmakers to take advantage of the unregulated route in order to circumvent the statute's limitations?

The limitations on expenditures from the funds of the candidate and the candidate's family were also inconsistent with the First Amendment. Most fundamentally, it is hard to see how a candidate spending on her own campaign could amount to *quid pro quo* corruption of that candidate. Moreover,

> [t]he * * * interest in equalizing the relative financial resources of candidates competing for elective office * * * provides the sole relevant rationale for [this] expenditure ceiling. That interest is clearly not sufficient to justify the provision's infringement of fundamental First Amendment rights. [T]he limitation may fail to promote financial equality among candidates. A candidate who spends less of his personal resources on his campaign may nonetheless outspend his rival as a result of more successful fundraising efforts. Indeed, a candidate's personal wealth may impede his efforts to persuade others that he needs their financial contributions or volunteer efforts to conduct an effective campaign.

Reporting and Disclosure Requirements. FECA required political committees to keep records of contributions and expenditures, including the names and addresses of contributors who gave them more than $10. Such committees were required to disclose to the FEC the source of every contribution of more than $100 and the payee and purpose of every expenditure of more than $100. (The current threshold for reporting is set at more than $200.) Moreover, the Act also mandated that individuals and groups, other than candidates and political committees, making contributions or expenditures exceeding $100 (now $250) "other than by contribution to a political committee or candidate" file reports with the Commission. The Court construed this disclosure requirement applying to independent political expenditures to reach only individuals and groups "when they make contributions earmarked for political purposes" and "when they make expenditures for communications that expressly advocate the election or defeat of a clearly identified candidate."

The Court in *Buckley* upheld these provisions. It noted that compelled disclosure, in itself, can seriously infringe on privacy of association and belief guaranteed by the First Amendment, but held that the governmental interests sought to be advanced by the required disclosures were sufficiently important to outweigh the possibility of infringement of First Amendment rights. The Court identified these governmental interests:

First, disclosure provides the electorate with information "as to where political campaign money comes from and how it is spent by the candidate" in order to aid the voters in evaluating those who seek federal office. * * *

Second, disclosure requirements deter actual corruption and avoid the appearance of corruption by exposing large contributions and expenditures to the light of publicity. * * *

Third, * * * recordkeeping, reporting, and disclosure requirements are an essential means of gathering the data necessary to detect violations of the contribution limitations described above.

In response to the contention that disclosure would infringe upon the First Amendment rights of contributors to minor parties and independent candidates, see *NAACP v. Alabama*, 357 U.S. 449 (1958) (disclosure required by state law of NAACP members is unconstitutional if it exposed those persons to physical or economic retaliation), the Court stated:

> * * * [T]he damage done by disclosure to the associational interests of the minor parties and their members and to supporters of independents could be significant. These movements are less likely to have a sound financial base and thus are more vulnerable to falloffs in contributions. In some instances fears of reprisal may deter contributions to the point where the movement cannot survive. The public interest also suffers if that result comes to pass, for there is a consequent reduction in the free circulation of ideas both within and without the political arena.

> There could well be a case * * * where the threat to the exercise of First Amendment rights is so serious and the state interest furthered by disclosure so insubstantial that the Act's requirements cannot be constitutionally applied. But no appellant in this case has tendered record evidence of the sort proffered in *NAACP v. Alabama*. Instead, appellants primarily rely on "the clearly articulated fears of individuals, well experienced in the political process." At best they offer the testimony of several minor-party officials that one or two persons refused to make contributions because of the possibility of disclosure. On this record, the substantial public interest in disclosure identified by the legislative history of this Act outweighs the harm generally alleged.

Public Financing of Presidential Election Campaigns. At the time of *Buckley*, Subtitle H of the Internal Revenue Code provided that taxpayers could authorize payment to a Presidential Election Campaign Fund of one dollar of their tax liability in the case of an individual return and two dollars in the case of a joint return. The Fund provides money to finance party nominating conventions, primary campaigns, and general election campaigns. In 1993, Congress raised the tax check-off amount to three dollars for single returns and six dollars for joint returns.

Subtitle H distinguishes among *major parties* (parties whose candidates for President in the most recent election received 25% or more of the popular vote), *minor parties* (parties whose candidates received at least 5% but less than 25% of the vote in the most recent election), and *new parties* (all others). With respect to expenses of general election campaigns, each major-party candidate is entitled to $20 million, adjusted for inflation, and is required to pledge not to incur expenses in excess of this amount and not to accept private contributions except to the extent that the public fund is insufficient to provide the full amount to which the candidate is entitled. In 2012, the major-party candidates each were eligible in the general election for $91.2 million in federal funds. Minor-party candidates, if they meet certain prerequisites, are entitled to a percentage of the amount available to major-party candidates; new-party candidates receive nothing. Subtitle H also created the Presidential Primary Matching Payment Account, which provides funds to candidates running in presidential primary elections who, *inter alia*, raise at least $5,000 in each of 20 states. Funds are provided through a matching formula based on the amount of private contributions received by the candidate. In return for federal money during the primaries, candidates must agree to abide by limitations applied to aggregate and state-by-state expenditures.

In recent years, this public financing system has become essentially irrelevant because major candidates have opted out during the campaign primaries in order to avoid expenditure limits during that period, and recently they have opted out as well in the general election. In 2000 and 2004, George W. Bush did not accept public funds during the primaries because he knew he could raise sufficient funds for a competitive campaign and he wanted the flexibility to spend large amounts of money in early races to lock in the nomination quickly. In 2008, President Obama became the first major-party presidential candidate to opt out of matching funds in both the primary and general elections (a practice he continued in his reelection campaign), and in 2012, Mitt Romney, the Republican nominee, did the same. Ironically, only because major candidates have opted out has the Presidential Election Campaign Fund managed to avoid insolvency, as the number of taxpayers participating in the check-off has declined.[47]

The Supreme Court in *Buckley* upheld the constitutionality of this system of partial public financing. The Court generally held that the important public interest in limiting "the improper influence of large private contributions" outweighed any First Amendment concerns, and that the distinctions among major parties, minor parties, and new parties did not violate the equal protection component of the Due Process Clause of the Fifth Amendment. Doesn't the Act, and the Supreme Court's decision upholding it, tend to ossify American politics by presumptively reinforcing the status quo? If the Court is correct that the First Amendment generally favors *more* variety, how could the Court justify such a heavy financial benefit to already-established political parties? Is this yet another instance of partisan lockup that we discussed in the context of ballot access laws?

---

[47] For discussion of the challenges facing the presidential system of public financing, see Task Force on Presidential Nomination Finance, Campaign Finance Institute, *Participation, Competition, Engagement: How to Revive and Improve Public Funding for Presidential Nomination Politics* (2003), http://www.cfinst.org/pdf/federal/president/TaskForce1_Fullreport.pdf. For a discussion of possible reforms, see John Green & Anthony Corrado, *The Impact of BCRA on Presidential Campaign Finance*, in *Life After Reform: When the Bipartisan Campaign Reform Act Meets Politics* 175, 180–86 (Michael Malbin ed., 2003).

As this description of *Buckley* reveals, the traditional justification for campaign finance regulation is connected to notions of corruption of the political system. Corruption, however, is an ambiguous term; it means different things to different people. Moreover, the extent and shape of regulation that one finds acceptable depends on one's vision of the corruption that must be combated. Let's think about various kinds of corruption that may occur in the election process and determine whether regulation should target each of them—and whether regulation can effectively control them.

Quid Pro Quo *Corruption*. The traditional justification for campaign finance regulation provided by the Court in *Buckley* is to combat *quid pro quo* corruption or the appearance of such arrangements. A system dominated by large contributions from wealthy individuals and interest groups clearly seeking influence, access, and favorable legislation appears to be corrupt to ordinary voters. This notion of corruption can be a rather limited one, focused on activity that appears virtually indistinguishable from bribery, or a more expansive vision of corruption. In *Nixon v. Shrink Missouri Gov't PAC*, 528 U.S. 377, 389 (2000), the Court rejected an especially narrow notion. "In speaking [in *Buckley*] of 'improper influence' and 'opportunities for abuse' in addition to '*quid pro quo* arrangements,' we recognized a concern not confined to bribery of public officials, but extending to the broader threat from politicians too compliant with the wishes of large contributors." The Court worried that the "cynical assumption that large donors call the tune" jeopardizes public faith in the democratic system. *Id.* at 390. In recent years, the Roberts Court has embraced the narrower version of *quid pro quo* corruption—using contributions to secure political favors from individual politicians—and rejected a formulation of the corruption interest that aimed to limit "the appearance of mere influence or access" derived from large contributions. *McCutcheon*, 134 S.Ct. at 1451 (plurality opinion).

Are the parameters of this more expansive notion of corruption clear? When is a lawmaker *too* compliant with the wishes of large donors, and when is the lawmaker merely representing constituents who supported her? Perhaps large contributions provide accurate signals of the intensity with which some constituents hold particular views. In a system where votes are equalized, campaign contributions and other electoral support can provide valuable information about the strength of voter preferences, certainly relevant information as lawmakers compromise and create policy. Theorists from a liberal tradition might be wary of the Court's apparent willingness to broaden its definition of *quid pro quo* corruption.

Bradley Smith (a professor who served as a commissioner on the FEC) attacks the *Buckley* formulation of political corruption on two grounds.[48] First, he points to empirical studies suggesting that money seldom buys votes or particular outcomes. Rather, "the dominant forces in legislative voting [are] personal ideology, party affiliation and agenda, and constituency views." To the extent that money influences lawmaking, it affects the legislative agenda, the timing and subjects of lawmakers' speeches, and legislative drafting in the early stages. Second, Smith

---

[48] *Money Talks: Speech, Corruption, Equality, and Campaign Finance*, 86 Geo. L.J. 45, 58–59 (1997).

argues that "there are intuitive and logical reasons to believe that the problem [of *quid pro quo* corruption] is not as serious as it is made out to be. Most obviously, people who are attracted to electoral politics tend to have strong views on issues. Party support can be just as important to re-election efforts, if not more important, than private contributions. * * * And, of course, elected officials ultimately need votes, not cash." Are Smith's arguments persuasive? At the least, are they sufficient to encourage courts to demand persuasive empirical proof of the existence of *quid pro quo* corruption more subtle than outright bribery? Or does Smith ignore the corruption inherent in a system in which large donors can set the political agenda for the rest of us?

Finally, scholars who have attempted to discern whether adoption of campaign finance regulation actually causes voters to have more confidence in the integrity of the political system have generally found no effect on public perception. In *The Limits of Electoral Reform* (2013), Shaun Bowler and Todd Donovan compare public attitudes across U.S. states and among Western democracies and find virtually no impact of reforms on citizens' attitudes toward politics. They suggest several reasons for this null finding, including the possibility that politicians respond strategically to any reform and undermine real change. Moreover, reform may spark an unintended consequence of more public cynicism as better disclosure increases the awareness of the strong influence of money in politics. *Id.* at 94–95. Does this empirical result undermine *Buckley*'s state interest justifying regulation of campaign spending as combating the deleterious effects of the appearance of *quid pro quo* corruption on the public's confidence in our electoral system?

Increasing Voter Competence. A political system is corrupt if it systematically undermines voters' ability to vote competently. A competent voter is one who votes the same way on the basis of the limited information available to her as she would have voted if she had had complete information about candidates and their proposals.[49] Voters rely on numerous cues to improve their competence, including party affiliation and incumbency. Knowing who supports the candidate and with how much enthusiasm can also improve voter competence. Moreover, allowing all candidates—challengers and incumbents—the resources to participate in vigorous political debate may enrich the political environment for voters. An outsider watching our campaigns and listening to our political debates is unlikely to conclude that we have too much meaningful political dialogue, but rather that our political debate is often repetitive and devoid of substance.

The *Buckley* Court identified such an interest as an important justification for FECA's disclosure system. That might be the most significant interest supporting disclosure in campaigns on ballot initiatives in which the threat of *quid pro quo* corruption is reduced. (See Chapter 4, § 1B.) The kinds of regulation that would promote voter competence may turn on one's notion of what can realistically be expected of voters. Daniel Ortiz identifies two groups of voters: engaged citizens and civic slackers. *The Democratic Paradox of Campaign Finance Reform*, 50 Stan. L. Rev. 893, 895 (1998). He argues that most democratic theory assumes that

---

[49] See Elisabeth Gerber & Arthur Lupia, *Voter Competence in Direct Legislation Elections*, in *Citizen Competence and Democratic Institutions* 147 (Stephen Elkin & Karol Soltan eds., 1999).

citizens are "engaged, informed voters who carefully reason through political arguments." Much of campaign finance reform, however, implicitly questions voters' ability or interest in spending the time required to develop civic virtue. Instead, most of us focus our attention on other aspects of life—our families, jobs, or leisure activities—and thus are susceptible to manipulation by slick advertisements funded by well-heeled interests and overflowing political coffers. To be successful, campaign finance reform efforts should be directed toward helping people make political decisions in light of their limited attention and scanty information. "[I]f reformers are to make their case, they must force us to recognize our civic failings. For only by recognizing our failings can we ever hope to grapple with and perhaps eventually overcome them." *Id* at 914. What kind of information should be provided to civic slackers to improve their competence? What is the role of regulation in this process?

Electoral Competitiveness. Richard Briffault has argued that the Court should consider another important state interest in assessing the constitutionality of campaign finance restrictions. He contends that "[f]air and vigorous competition among candidates and parties is critical for the legitimacy of our elections and of the government those elections produce. Campaign finance law, in turn, can have a direct effect on the competitiveness of elections. In constructing a new campaign finance doctrine—or in revamping current doctrine—the Court should give greater weight to the effect of campaign finance rules on electoral competition." Nixon v. Shrink Missouri Government PAC: *The Beginning of the End of the* Buckley *Era?*, 85 Minn. L. Rev. 1729, 1731–32 (2001). If competitiveness were a compelling interest, what sort of regulation of campaign finance spending is permissible under the Constitution? What reform is best suited to improve electoral competition? How should courts measure the level of competition and determine what features of the regulatory landscape are hindering more robust competition?

At least some studies suggest that spending by political parties is an important factor contributing to competitive races, both in the context of open seats and, more importantly, in the context of candidates challenging entrenched incumbents.[50] Should the Court be especially leery of restrictions on expenditures by political parties? Or is it the province of the legislature to make the policy choices that will affect electoral competitiveness, at least in cases where reasonable people could disagree about the right answer? On the other hand, does the partisan lockup scholarship suggest that campaign finance regulation devised by incumbent politicians is more likely to work to their advantage than to herald the resurgence of competitiveness in legislative elections?

Equality Concerns and Corruption. Republican thinkers, along with many critical theorists, have argued that a system is corrupt if wealthy special interests and individuals have more political influence solely because of their wealth.[51] Equal

---

[50] See, e.g., Gary Jacobson, *The Politics of Congressional Elections* 81–85 (8th ed. 2013). See also Richard Briffault, *The Political Parties and Campaign Finance Reform*, 100 Colum. L. Rev. 620, 661 (2000) (although favoring more stringent regulation of party campaign expenditures, acknowledging that parties "are more likely to support promising challengers. * * * Thus, far more than PAC money or donations by wealthy individuals, party money promotes the value of electoral competition.").

[51] See Symposium: *Money, Politics, and Equality*, 77 Tex. L. Rev. 1603–2021 (1999); John Rawls, *The Idea of Public Reason Revisited*, 64 U. Chi. L. Rev. 765 (1997).

opportunity to influence political outcomes is undermined if that opportunity is tied to wealth and if economic resources are not equally distributed. This situation is even more disturbing because there is no reason to believe that the distribution of economic resources is related in any way to people's ability or desire to participate in the political realm. In other words, a poor voter and a rich one may have very intensely held and well-reasoned views, but only the latter will be able to affect the political agenda, participate in debate, and influence lawmakers. There is a "donor class" of people wealthy enough to contribute money to candidates and parties and thus obtain special access to policymakers that ordinary Americans are denied. See Spencer Overton, *The Donor Class: Campaign Finance, Democracy, and Participation*, 153 U. Pa. L. Rev. 73 (2004). Such a system is corrupt if political equality is an important democratic ideal.

Buckley rejected egalitarian justifications for campaign finance reform, holding clearly that "the concept that government may restrict the speech of some elements of our society in order to enhance the relative voice of others is wholly foreign to the First Amendment, which was designed 'to secure "the widest possible dissemination of information from diverse and antagonistic sources," ' and 'to assure unfettered interchange of ideas for the bringing about of political and social changes desired by the people.'" 424 U.S. at 48–49. *Buckley* was thus consistent with a libertarian notion of the First Amendment, a view that the Amendment protects only *negative liberty* because it only prohibits government intervention. Judge Guido Calabresi, among others, argues that the Supreme Court's jurisprudence is "impoverished" because it does not deal explicitly with egalitarian concerns, which are "at least as important as [*quid pro quo* corruption], and, perhaps, at the very heart of the problem."[52] Does the following case provide some indication that the Court might be (or was once) willing to accept some equality-based notion of corruption? (Note: This case was overruled by *Citizens United v. Fed. Election Comm'n* in an opinion written by Justice Kennedy, so we will return to these themes later in the chapter.)

Austin v. Michigan Chamber of Commerce
494 U.S. 652 (1990).

The Michigan Campaign Finance Act prohibited corporations from making contributions or independent expenditures in connection with state-candidate elections. Corporations could only use segregated funds to spend money in candidate elections; money for the segregated funds was solicited explicitly for political purposes. The Michigan Chamber of Commerce was a nonprofit corporation with 8,000 members, three-quarters of which were for-profit corporations. It used its general treasury funds to place an advertisement in a local paper supporting a particular candidate. Because such an expenditure was punishable as a felony, the Chamber brought suit for injunctive relief, arguing that the restriction on independent expenditures was unconstitutional. The Court upheld the statute.

---

[52] *Landell v. Sorrell*, 406 F.3d 159, 163 (2d Cir. 2005) (Calabresi, J., concurring in the denial of rehearing en banc), *rev'd sub nom.*, *Randall v. Sorrell*, 548 U.S. 230 (2006). See also Ronald Dworkin, *The Curse of American Politics*, N.Y. Rev. of Books, Oct. 17, 1996, at 19, 21 ("It is another premise of democracy that citizens must be able, as individuals, to participate on equal terms in both formal politics and in the informal cultural life that creates the moral environment of the community.").

Justice Marshall, writing for the majority, applied strict scrutiny as required by *Buckley* for regulation of independent expenditures. The Court acknowledged that, although corporations could spend money from special segregated funds, the prohibition on the use of general treasury funds and the requirements surrounding the segregated funds were burdens on political speech. The Court then looked for a compelling state interest to justify the burden. "State law grants corporations special advantages—such as limited liability, perpetual life, and favorable treatment of the accumulation and distribution of assets—that enhance their ability to attract capital and to deploy their resources in ways that maximize the return on their shareholders' investments. These state-created advantages not only allow corporations to play a dominant role in the Nation's economy, but also permit them to use 'resources amassed in the economic marketplace' to obtain 'an unfair advantage in the political marketplace.' *Federal Election Comm'n v. Massachusetts Citizens for Life*, 479 U.S. 238, 257 (1986) (*MCFL*). As the Court explained in *MCFL*, the political advantage of corporations is unfair because '[t]he resources in the treasury of a business corporation . . . are not an indication of popular support for the corporation's political ideas. They reflect instead the economically motivated decisions of investors and customers. The availability of these resources may make a corporation a formidable political presence, even though the power of the corporation may be no reflection of the power of its ideas.' "

The Court differentiated the corruption that justified the Michigan statute from the *quid pro quo* corruption in *Buckley* that justified limitations on contributions. "Michigan's regulation aims at a different type of corruption in the political arena: the corrosive and distorting effects of immense aggregations of wealth that are accumulated with the help of the corporate form and that have little or no correlation to the public's support for the corporation's political ideas. The Act does not attempt 'to equalize the relative influence of speakers on elections'; rather, it ensures that expenditures reflect actual public support for the political ideas espoused by corporations. We emphasize that the mere fact that corporations may accumulate large amounts of wealth is not the justification for [the Michigan statute]; rather, the unique state-conferred corporate structure that facilitates the amassing of large treasuries warrants the limit on independent expenditures. Corporate wealth can unfairly influence elections when it is deployed in the form of independent expenditures, just as it can when it assumes the guise of political contributions."

The Court also rejected the argument that the restriction could not be constitutionally applied to a nonprofit corporation such as the Chamber of Commerce. In the previous case concerning Massachusetts Citizens for Life, a nonprofit focused on pursuing a clear ideological agenda, the Court had struck down similar restrictions on independent expenditures. Justice Marshall found that the Chamber of Commerce was more like a traditional corporation than the right-to-life group. The Chamber was primarily engaged in nonpolitical activities; its members might be reluctant to resign even if they disagreed with the Chamber's political stands because they wished to benefit from the Chamber's nonpolitical programs (unlike MCFL's members, who presumably strongly supported the entity's political activities opposing abortion); and the Chamber could easily serve as a conduit for corporate independent expenditures, allowing circumvention of the Act. Accordingly, the restrictions could be applied to the Chamber of Commerce in the same way they applied to for-profit corporations.

Justice Scalia's dissent attacked the majority as engaged in "Orwellian" censorship on the "principle that too much speech is an evil that the democratic majority can proscribe." He challenged the majority's argument that limits on political speech can be justified because corporations have special advantages under state law and can amass great wealth. He pointed out that many individuals and private associations, not just corporations, receive special breaks under state law, and that in any event the government cannot condition the receipt of these benefits on the waiver of First Amendment rights. Great wealth alone does not render anyone or anything susceptible to lesser First Amendment rights, and Justice Scalia argued that the majority provided no reason to assume that corporate expenditures promoting candidates pose any substantial risk of corruption. He also argued that, even accepting the majority's assumptions, the Michigan statute was subject to attack because it was not narrowly tailored to reach only wealthy corporations.

Justice Kennedy's dissent complained of two censorships of speech: first, a "content-based law which decrees it a crime for a nonprofit corporate speaker to endorse or oppose candidates for [office]"; and, second, a censorship scheme created by the Court "that permits some nonprofit corporate groups but not others to engage in political speech. After failing to disguise its animosity and distrust for a particular kind of political speech here at issue—the qualifications of a candidate to understand economic matters—the Court adopts a rule that allows Michigan to stifle the voices of some of the most respected groups in public life, on subjects central to the integrity of our democratic system." According to this dissent, the majority's notion that the state may combat the "corrosive and distorting effects of immense aggregations of wealth" accumulated in corporate form deals not with fighting corruption, but with "altering political debate by muting the impact of certain speakers."

Austin prompted a great deal of scholarly debate, in part because it appeared to resurrect an egalitarian justification for campaign finance regulations, although perhaps only in the case of certain corporations.[53] Arguably, the equality concern sounded in *Austin* is relatively narrow and limited to the distortion of the political environment when money raised for business purposes has been spent for political expression. The rationale in *Austin* may be related to an interest in democratizing the political process and increasing public participation in campaigns. Justice Breyer has articulated a First Amendment principle of participatory self-government that could be seen as a way to include some element of equality concerns into the campaign finance jurisprudence without expressly overruling *Buckley*. See *Active Liberty: Interpreting Our Democratic Constitution* 43–50 (2005). See also *McCutcheon*, 134 S.Ct. at 1467–68 (Breyer, dissenting) ("Where enough money calls the tune, the general public will not be heard. * * * That is one reason why the Court has stressed the constitutional importance of Congress' concern that a few large donations not drown out the voices of the many.").

---

[53] See, e.g., Gerald Ashdown, *Controlling Campaign Spending and the "New Corruption": Waiting for the Court*, 44 Vand. L. Rev. 767 (1991); Julian Eule, *Promoting Speaker Diversity:* Austin *and* Metro Broadcasting, 1990 Sup. Ct. Rev. 105; Adam Winkler, *The Corporation in Election Law*, 32 Loy. L.A. L. Rev. 1243 (1999).

The unprecedented involvement of small donors in Barack Obama's successful campaign for the presidency seemed a sign that a political system with more participation by ordinary citizens, and therefore less influence by well-heeled interests, was within reach. President Obama raised nearly $782 million in the 2012 presidential election; more than $216 million—28% of donations to Obama— came from donors who contributed $200 or less.[54] The campaign's sophisticated use of the Internet was primarily responsible for the widespread grassroots involvement, not only in contributing but also in organizing meetings and volunteering. My.BarackObama.com used social networking sites to build a close online relationship with Obama supporters; it encouraged repeated small donations using techniques such as matching the small donation with another new donor or charging small recurring donations monthly to supporters' credit cards. Anthony Corrado, Michael Malbin, Thomas Mann & Norman Ornstein, *Reform in an Age of Networked Campaigns: How to Foster Citizen Participation Through Small Donors and Volunteers* 12–14 (2010).

Reform advocates have begun to reformulate campaign finance proposals given the potential of the Internet to broaden the group of people participating in campaigns. For example, some have proposed an overhaul of the presidential public financing system so that small contributions would receive more generous matching funds (such as a match of three- or four-to-one for contributions of $200 or less) and candidates would not be subject to expenditure limits as long as they were spending funds raised from small donations. See Spencer Overton, *The Participation Interest*, 100 Geo. L.J. 1259, 1296–98 (2012) (discussing such systems used at the local level and linking them to a Breyer-like participation interest).

Some commentators have counseled that the claims of a new era of the small donor are overstated. Although small donors played an important role in Obama's success, he still received most of his sizable campaign war chest from wealthy individuals. The Campaign Finance Institute study revealed that in 2012 Obama received 40% more money from people giving at least $1,000 than from small donors. In light of the expense of running a federal campaign for the presidency or Congress, is it reasonable to expect that small donations can drown out the influence of rich and connected individuals who deliver substantial amounts of money to campaigns? Can the Internet really transform political campaigns, serving as the engine of equalization that *Buckley* rules out for legal change? What challenges does the Internet pose for political campaigns—and what new avenues of reform does it open up? For one state's analysis of appropriate regulation of the Internet, including broad principles to guide reform, see California Fair Political Practices Commission, *Internet Political Activity and the Political Reform Act* (August 2010).

Are contribution and expenditure limitations the best way to ensure political equality in a world where financial resources are distributed unevenly? Even if they successfully reduce the amount of political spending by the wealthy, how can such regulations provide resources to the poor who wish to be politically active?

[54] Campaign Finance Institute, *Money vs. Money-Plus: Post-Election Reports Reveal Two Different Campaign Strategies* (Jan. 2013), http://www.cfinst.org/Press/PReleases/13–01–11/Money_vs_Money-Plus_Post-Election_Reports_Reveal_Two_Different_Campaign_Strategies.aspx.

Some theorists have suggested a more radical egalitarian reform: allowing people to spend only special money—"red-white-and-blue" dollars in Bruce Ackerman's proposal—for election-related activities.[55] All citizens would receive an equal amount of this special money; it could not be sold for green money, but it could be contributed to candidate campaigns, used to fund independent advertisements, or accumulated by PACs to signal the support of a group of voters for an idea or candidate. These proposals advocate a sort of public financing system, albeit a decentralized one in which the voters determine how to channel the money. Just as all citizens have an equal number of votes, so would they all have equal amounts of political resources to deploy. Of course, these proposals do not claim to impose absolute equality among citizens; there would remain inequality of talents, ability to communicate persuasively, appearance, and access to people with free time to volunteer. Perhaps in a world where financial resources were equalized, the distribution of these other qualities would become more important. Or, perhaps, inequality along these dimensions is less pernicious.

PROBLEM RELATING TO CAMPAIGN FINANCE PROPOSALS

Problem 2–6. Some scholars have argued that, instead of mandating disclosure of all campaign contributions, we should instead consider mandating that all contributions be anonymous. Ian Ayres & Jeremy Bulow, *The Donation Booth: Mandating Donor Anonymity to Disrupt the Market for Political Influence*, 50 Stan. L. Rev. 837 (1998). Just as the secret ballot makes it more difficult for candidates to buy votes, requiring anonymity of contributors would make it more difficult for candidates to sell access or influence. They suggest setting up blind trusts that would receive all campaign contributions. This structure would eliminate *quid pro quo* corruption because candidates would not know who had wanted to pay the price for beneficial legislation or official actions. In a world of anonymous donors, anyone could claim to have contributed to the blind trust, just as anyone can claim to have voted for a certain candidate. Is such a proposal constitutional? Is it sensible policy?

In *Voting with Dollars: A New Paradigm for Campaign Finance* (2002), Ian Ayres and Bruce Ackerman combine the proposal mandating anonymous private giving with the decentralized public financing plan described above. In this detailed, comprehensive proposal, each voter would receive 50 "Patriot dollars" that could be used only to support political campaigns. This influx of substantial public resources—directed by individual citizens to the candidates they support—would increase the overall resources spent on political activity, allow public funds to dominate private funds (they hope), and increase participation. They explain: "We refuse * * * to view the problem of campaign finance as if it represents the all-or-nothing choice of suppressing private contributions or leaving them unregulated. Our new paradigm uses anonymity to cleanse private giving of its worst abuses while allowing it to serve as a valuable supplementary support to the robust public debate fostered by billions of Patriot dollars allocated by millions of concerned citizens." *Id.* at 9. What are the likely effects of such a campaign finance system if adopted by a state or the federal government? Have the developments,

---

[55] See Bruce Ackerman, *Crediting the Voters: A New Beginning for Campaign Finance*, 13 Am. Prospect 71 (1993). In addition, see Edward Foley, *Equal-Dollars-Per-Voter: A Constitutional Principle of Campaign Finance*, 94 Colum. L. Rev. 1204 (1994); Richard Hasen, *Clipping Coupons for Democracy: An Egalitarian/Public Choice Defense of Campaign Finance Vouchers*, 84 Cal. L. Rev. 1 (1996).

both judicial and political, in the decade since Ayres and Ackerman put forward this proposal undermined its likelihood of meeting their goals or increased the urgency to consider a sweeping reform like this? Why has no jurisdiction considered a decentralized public financing program like this that allows citizens to channel public support to candidates, rather than directly subsidizing qualifying candidates? How would this proposal affect established political players such as major parties and incumbents? Are there other ways to expand the resources available to campaigns so that participation is broadened and the threat of undue influence by wealthy individuals, groups, and corporations is diluted?

2.   The Experience After *Buckley* and the Need for Further Reform

Decades of experience with FECA demonstrated that serious challenges remained to effective campaign finance regulation. The Bipartisan Campaign Reform Act of 2002 (BCRA) sought to address these issues, so understanding them is fundamental to understanding BCRA and the jurisprudence that followed.

Political Action Committees. Political action committees (PACs) are not creatures of FECA, and the term does not appear in the Act, which uses instead "multicandidate political committee." Generally speaking, a PAC is a political committee, other than a political party, that receives contributions from more than 50 people and makes contributions to at least five candidates for federal office. PACs are required to register with and report information to the FEC. 1976 amendments to FECA limited PAC contributions to a candidate to $5,000 per election and limited PAC contributions to a national committee of a political party to $15,000. By creating limitations that at the time were more generous than those applying to individuals, FECA encouraged the formation and growth of PACs. The first PAC was established in 1943 by a national labor union. In 1974, the number of registered PACs stood at 608; 10 years later, 4,009 were registered; and in 2012 there were 7,311 registered PACs. The largest category consists of corporate PACs; in 2012, 1,851 registered PACs were characterized as corporate, and they donated more money in absolute terms to campaigns than labor or membership organizations.[56]

In the years immediately following *Buckley*, the issue of the influence of corporate and business PACs on the electoral process was the primary focus for reformers. For example, Judge J. Skelly Wright of the D.C. Circuit wrote in *Money and the Pollution of Politics: Is the First Amendment an Obstacle to Political Equality?*, 82 Colum. L. Rev. 609, 616, 618–19 (1982), that PACs have a malign effect on legislative policymaking: "When wealth of this magnitude is injected into the political bloodstream, the legislative process itself is affected. PAC contributions are given with a legislative purpose and it is a telling fact that they are most numerous in the more highly regulated industries, such as oil, transportation, utilities, drugs, health care, and government contracting. * * * Whatever the cause and effect relationship, studies of issue after issue demonstrate that a much higher percentage of legislators who voted with a PAC's position

---

[56] See Federal Election Commission, *Summary of PAC Activity* (Dec. 2012), http://www.fec.gov/press/summaries/2012/tables/pac/PAC1_2012_24m.pdf; Federal Election Commission, *PAC Count: 1974 to Present* (January 2014), http://www.fec.gov/press/summaries/2011/2011paccount.shtml.

received money from the PAC in the previous campaign than those who voted the other way, and among the beneficiaries of PAC money those supporting the PAC position had received a substantially higher average contribution."

Empirical research, however, tends to show that PAC contributions influence legislative votes less than the legislator's personal philosophy, political party, and constituent views and interests.[57] Moreover, most of the money contributed to federal candidates comes from individuals, not PACs. One study of contributions to federal candidates in the 1999–2000 election cycle concluded that only around 22% of all money contributed to those campaigns could be considered special-interest money (e.g., from corporations, unions, other associations, or PACs). Stephen Ansolabehere, John de Figueiredo & James Snyder, Jr., *Why Is There So Little Money in U.S. Politics?*, 17 J. Econ. Persp. 105 (2003). Critics of PACs reply that PACs overwhelmingly contribute to incumbents, thereby further entrenching the status quo. In the 2012 election cycle, corporate PACs gave mainly to incumbents—with many, including those affiliated with energy, finance, health, and transportation, directing more than 85% of their funds to incumbents—and labor PACs sent 64% of their money to incumbents.[58]

Although they are often described as pernicious influences on the electoral process, PACs also empower individuals, who can increase their political influence by working collectively. If various and diverse interests use this type of political organization to wield electoral influence, then PACs can be seen as a positive political force. For example, EMILY's List contributes money to female candidates and promotes a moderately feminist agenda. Critics of PACs argue that EMILY's List is notable because it is so rare; they maintain that corporate and business PACs exert a disproportionate influence compared to labor PACs or public-interest PACs. Opponents of further restrictions on PAC spending counter with a pragmatic argument, contending that any limitations will be easily circumvented. They point to the practice of *bundling*, in which individual contributions are presented as a group to a candidate in a way that makes it clear that the contributions were organized through a collective effort. Because the contributions are individual, the bundles of money do not count against the PAC contribution limit, although no single check can exceed the ceiling for individual contributions.

Until 2007, candidates were aware of the forces behind bundling and the interests that the contributions sought to advance, but they were not disclosed to the public unless the organizers voluntarily provided the information. As part of

---

[57] See, e.g., Stephen Bronars & John Lott, Jr., *Do Campaign Contributions Alter How a Politician Votes? Or, Do Donors Support Candidates Who Value the Same Things That They Do?*, 40 J.L. & Econ. 317 (1997). See also Jeffrey Milyo, David Primo & Timothy Groseclose, *Corporate PAC Campaign Contributions in Perspective*, 2 Bus. & Pol. 75 (2000) (arguing that corporate PAC contributions have little influence on policymakers and that other routes to influence, such as lobbying and soft-money contributions, are preferred by corporations); Note: *The Ass Atop the Castle: Competing Strategies for Using Campaign Donations to Influence Lawmaking*, 116 Harv. L. Rev. 2610, 2615–16 & n.24 (2003) (canvassing literature).

[58] Center for Responsive Politics, *PAC Dollars to Incumbents, Challengers, and Open Seat Candidates*, 2012 table, http://www.opensecrets.org/bigpicture/pac2cands.php?cycle=2012 & display=. See also Paul Herrnson & Stephanie Perry Curtis, *Financing the 2008 Congressional Elections*, in *Financing the 2008 Election* 166, 187 (David Magleby & Anthony Corrado eds., 2011) (corporate PACs directed 93% of their funds to House incumbents in 2008 elections); Randall Kroszner & Thomas Stratmann, *Corporate Campaign Contributions, Repeat Giving, and the Rewards to Legislator Reputation*, 48 J.L. & Econ. 41 (2005).

the Honest Leadership and Open Government Act of 2007, disclosure is required of any registered lobbyist providing bundled contributions to federal candidates or their committees that exceed $15,000 in any six-month period. Section 204, Pub. L. No. 110–81, 121 Stat. 735 (2007). The Act defines a bundled contribution as any contribution forwarded to the candidate by the person or any contribution "credited [by the candidate] to the person through records, designations, or other means of recognizing that a certain amount of money has been raised by the person."

Concerns about *stealth PACs* or *Section 527 organizations* (named for the section of the tax code under which such groups were organized) prompted a congressional response a few years before passage of the more comprehensive BCRA. In the late 1990s, political entrepreneurs began to use tax-exempt entities to evade campaign finance disclosure laws and contribution limitations. Section 527 groups took advantage of a tax provision designed to protect most income of political parties from taxation. Section 527 organizations are nonprofit groups organized for the "function of influencing or attempting to influence the selection, nomination, election, or appointment of any individual to any Federal, State, or local public office." Internal Revenue Code § 527(e)(2). As is often the case in this area of unintended consequences, the drafters of Section 527 never envisioned its use as a blueprint for stealth PACs.[59] In the summer of 2000, President Clinton signed a bill requiring Section 527 organizations to disclose their donors and their expenditures. Pub. L. No. 106–230, 114 Stat. 477 (2000). Within one month, nearly 5,000 organizations had filed disclosure forms with the IRS, which was then required to post the information on its website.

Soft Money. Money spent in connection with federal candidates, and therefore regulated by FECA, is hard money. *Soft money*, then, became the term used for any money left unregulated by FECA (although in 1990, the FEC required limited disclosure of soft-money expenditures). Soft money is spent on activities to benefit state candidates, to build infrastructure, and to fund voter mobilization programs, including direct-mail campaigns. Political parties also use soft money to fund issue advertisements that do not expressly advocate the election or defeat of a particular candidate. Although soft-money expenditures cannot be connected with a particular candidate, in fact they contribute significantly to the success of parties' nominees and are often intertwined with candidates' campaigns.

The use of soft money to evade federal restrictions, particularly in a presidential election in which candidates must comply with expenditure limitations in order to qualify for federal matching funds, increased substantially in the 1990s. The *McConnell* Court described the process through which parties and candidates exploited this loophole: "The evidence in the record shows that candidates and donors alike have in fact exploited the soft-money loophole, the former to increase their prospects of election and the latter to create debt on the part of officeholders, with the national parties serving as willing intermediaries. * * * Parties kept tallies of the amounts of soft money raised by each officeholder, and 'the amount of money a Member of Congress raise[d] for the national political committees often affect[ed]

---

[59] See Donald Tobin, *Anonymous Speech and Section 527 of the Internal Revenue Code*, 37 Ga. L. Rev. 611, 623 (2003).

the amount the committees g[a]ve to assist the Member's campaign.' Donors often asked that their contributions be credited to particular candidates, and the parties obliged, irrespective of whether the funds were hard or soft. National party committees often teamed with individual candidates' campaign committees to create joint fundraising committees, which enabled the candidates to take advantage of the party's higher contribution limits while still allowing donors to give to their preferred candidate. Even when not participating directly in the fundraising, federal officeholders were well aware of the identities of the donors: National party committees would distribute lists of potential or actual donors, or donors themselves would report their generosity to officeholders." 540 U.S. at 146–47.

The pace of soft-money fundraising escalated immediately before passage of BCRA, so this phenomenon became a target of reformers. A study of the 1998 congressional elections revealed that soft money spent by party committees and raised from a few large donors played an important role in competitive congressional elections.[60] Soft-money expenditures in this midterm election were more than double the spending in 1994. From January 1999 through the end of November 2000, a time period that included a presidential campaign, the national party committees raised more than $487 million in soft money. Not surprisingly given these figures, reformers argued that soft-money donations directly resulted in favorable legislation for the groups providing funds. For example, Common Cause published a report linking large soft-money donations to particular tax breaks in the 1997 Budget Act. *Return on Investment: The Hidden Story of Soft Money, Corporate Welfare and the 1997 Budget & Tax Deal* (1997). Do such allegations provide support under any of the justifications described previously for laws regulating soft-money contributions?

Issue Advocacy. Adopting a narrow interpretation of FECA to avoid constitutional problems, the Court in *Buckley* upheld disclosure requirements only with respect to independent expenditures used for communications that expressly advocate the election or defeat of a clearly identified federal candidate. In a footnote, the Court indicated that the following terms would meet the express advocacy test: "vote for," "elect," "support," "cast your ballot for," "Smith for Congress," "vote against," "defeat," or "reject." 424 U.S. at 44 n.52. Although the footnote does not state that using these words is the only way to meet the express advocacy test, they became known as the *magic words* distinguishing regulated communications from unregulated ones. See also *Fed. Election Comm'n v. Massachusetts Citizens for Life, Inc.*, 479 U.S. 238 (1986) (indicating some flexibility in the "magic words" formulation by noting that a communication of support "marginally less direct than 'Vote for Smith' does not change its essential nature"). The Court in *Buckley* rejected any test for express advocacy that would depend on the speaker's purpose or the audience's understanding because such a subjective test would chill political speech.

---

[60] See *Outside Money: Soft Money and Issue Ads in Competitive 1998 Congressional Elections* (David Magleby & Marianne Holt eds., 1999).

The absence of federal regulation after *Buckley* resulted in an explosion in the use of issue advocacy—political speech that did not meet the test for express advocacy but that often mentioned specific candidates or political parties. The Annenberg Public Policy Center estimated that political parties and various interest groups spent between $135 million and $150 million for issue ads in the 1996 election cycle. Deborah Beck, Paul Taylor, Jeffrey Stranger & Douglas Rivlin, *Issue Advocacy Advertising During the 1996 Campaign* (1997). Although issue advertisements were supposedly designed only to further the discussion of particular issues, the Annenberg Center found that nearly 87% mentioned a candidate for office by name and 59% of them pictured a candidate. Furthermore, issue ads appeared to be more negative in tone than other political advertising, perhaps because candidates tried to avoid being associated in the voters' minds with negative campaigning but understood how effective such communication could be. Of the issue ads, 41% were purely negative in tone, whereas only 24% of the advertisements directly paid for by presidential candidates criticized their opponents.

A Brennan Center for Justice study of more than 2,100 separate commercials run over 300,000 times in the top 75 media markets in the 1998 elections provided additional information about issue advertisements. Jonathan Krasno & Daniel Seltz, *Buying Time: Television Advertising in the 1998 Congressional Elections* (2000). Most (65%) issue ads were sponsored by political parties, rather than by interest groups, corporations, or labor unions. Perhaps surprisingly, candidate ads, which can include express advocacy, seldom used the magic words. Only 9% of candidate ads in the final week of the campaign included any of the magic words. This conclusion cast doubt on the efficacy of the magic words test as a way to separate express advocacy from other political communication. While none of the issue ads contained the key phrases required by *Buckley*'s footnote, 87% of them urged viewers to take some concrete action such as calling an elected official or candidate, although the ads rarely provided a phone number to assist motivated citizens. Just as with soft money, so-called "sham issue" ads became a focus for the authors of BCRA.

Finally, some of the issue ads were financed by groups designed to conceal their major donors. The Court in *McConnell v. Fed. Election Comm'n* noted two such examples: " 'Citizens for Better Medicare,' for instance, was not a grassroots organization of citizens, as its name might suggest, but was instead a platform for an association of drug manufacturers. And 'Republicans for Clean Air,' which ran ads in the 2000 Republican Presidential primary, was actually an organization consisting of just two individuals—brothers who together spent $25 million on ads supporting their favored candidate." 540 U.S. at 128. This increased use of veiled political actors suggested the need for more effective disclosure, beyond even what had been adopted in 2000 aimed at Section 527 groups.

3. The Bipartisan Campaign Reform Act of 2002 and *McConnell v. Federal Election Commission*

The key provisions of the Bipartisan Campaign Reform Act of 2002[61] include the following:

A Ban on Soft Money. The national committees of a political party can neither receive nor spend soft money. BCRA also prohibits federal-candidate-controlled PACs from raising or spending soft money. Local and state committees of political parties cannot spend soft money on federal election activities, although they can still spend such money solely to influence state or local races. "Federal election activity" is defined to include voter registration drives within 120 days of an election; get-out-the-vote drives conducted in connection with a federal election; any work by state or local campaign employees who spend more than 25% of their time on federal election activities; and advertisements specific to federal candidates. There is an exception to this ban that applies only to state and local party committees: they may use soft money to fund generic voter registration and get-out-the-vote drives that relate to federal elections, but they are limited to using contributions of no more than $10,000 per source.

A Ban on Candidate Solicitation of Soft Money. Federal office seekers and officeholders and their agents can neither solicit nor spend soft money. They may engage in soft-money fundraising efforts by nonprofit organizations for voter registration and get-out-the-vote drives, but they may only solicit up to $20,000 per individual and only from individuals.

Provisions Affecting Hard Money. The new law raised most of the hard-money limits, and it indexes for inflation the limits on individuals' contributions to candidates and national parties. The aggregate limit for an individual's contributions to candidates was raised from $25,000 to $37,500 per election cycle. Individuals could contribute $25,000 per year per national party committee, with an aggregate contribution limit of $20,000 to $57,500 per election cycle for donations to all national party committees, depending on how much money the individual contributes to PACs. (The aggregate contribution limits were ruled unconstitutional by the Supreme Court in *McCutcheon v. Fed. Election Comm'n*, 134 S.Ct. 1434 (2014).) The limit on contributions that an individual can give to a federal candidate per election doubled to $2,000. Although BCRA would have allowed higher contribution limits to apply to candidates facing self-financed opponents who spend substantial amounts of their own money in their campaigns—

---

[61] For an excellent description and analysis of BCRA, see the Campaign Finance Institute's E-Guide on the Web: http://www.cfinst.org/legacy/eguide. The Campaign Legal Center's website, http://www.campaignlegalcenter.org, provides helpful information, particularly about litigation and administrative proceedings related to BCRA implementation. Stanford Law School's library maintains a website with materials relating to BCRA and the judicial challenges. See http://campaignfinance.law.stanford.edu. Other useful websites include http://www.publicintegrity.org (Center for Public Integrity); http://www.fec.gov (Federal Election Commission); http://www.jamesmadisoncenter.org (James Madison Center for Free Speech); http://www.citizen.org/congress/campaign/index.cfm (Public Citizen); and http://www.opensecrets.org (Center for Responsive Politics). Among the best books on BCRA are *The New Campaign Finance Sourcebook* (Anthony Corrado, Thomas Mann, Daniel Ortiz & Trevor Potter eds., 2005), and *The Election After Reform: Money, Politics, and the Bipartisan Campaign Reform Act* (Michael Malbin ed., 2006).

a provision called the "millionaire opponent" provision—the Supreme Court struck this down as unconstitutional because it did not further the state's interest in deterring *quid pro quo* corruption. *Davis v. Fed. Election Comm'n*, 554 U.S. 724 (2008). The justification that the provision was required to "equalize the playing field" for candidates who were not personally wealthy was rejected as a revival of the equalization rationale rejected in *Buckley*.

Limitation on Expenditures for Electioneering Communications. The Act defines "electioneering communication" to include broadcast, cable, or satellite advertisements that refer to a clearly identified candidate; that are run within 30 days of a primary election and 60 days of a general election; and that are "targeted" in that they can be received by 50,000 or more persons in the congressional district or state where the election is being held. Political parties and candidates may spend only hard money to fund such advertisements. Corporations and unions were prohibited from funding such communication directly; instead, they were required to fund these broadcast advertisements through PACs that raise and use regulated hard money. This provision was challenged in *Citizens United v. Fed. Election Comm'n*, 558 U.S. 310 (2010), and we will consider its fate in the next section. Individuals and unincorporated entities can fund electioneering communication directly, but they must disclose within 24 hours the sources of contributions of $1,000 or more, once an aggregate of $10,000 has been spent.

Within hours of its passage, opponents of the law filed suit claiming the BCRA was facially unconstitutional in several respects. The case consolidated the challenges of nearly 80 plaintiffs, led by Senator Mitch McConnell (R–Ky.) and the National Rifle Association, and it generated 100,000 pages of evidence and testimony from more than 200 witnesses. A special District Court panel of three judges first heard the case. The judges issued four separate opinions totaling more than 1,600 typewritten pages that struck down parts of BCRA, upheld others, and even rewrote a few. *McConnell v. Fed. Election Comm'n*, 251 F. Supp. 2d 176 (D.D.C. 2003) (three-judge panel). BCRA required the Supreme Court to review the case following a decision by the special panel, so the case immediately went to the Supreme Court, which expedited the process and held oral arguments in September before the regular term began. With the campaigns for the 2004 federal elections well under way, the Supreme Court issued its opinion on the constitutionality of BCRA, upholding virtually all of it and certainly all of its key provisions—at least for the time being.

McConnell v. Federal Election Commission
540 U.S. 93 (2003).

The majority opinion, written by **Justice Stevens** and **Justice O'Connor**, noted the problems that Congress hoped to solve by enacting BCRA: the increasing use of soft money and the explosion of issue ads. Section 323(a) is the main weapon used to regulate soft money; this section prohibits national party committees or their agents from soliciting, receiving, directing, or spending any soft-money contributions, thereby "tak[ing] national parties out of the soft-money business." Sections 201 and 203 are the provisions designed to more effectively regulate certain issue ads, called "electioneering communication" by the Act. The regulations both increased disclosure requirements and mandated the use of segregated funds by corporations and unions to fund that communication.

The Court first determined the appropriate First Amendment standard of review for Section 323, holding that a contribution limit that interferes with First Amendment rights is constitutional if it satisfies the "lesser demand" of being "closely drawn" to match a "sufficiently important interest." This test, rather than strict scrutiny, is used because "contribution limits, like other measures aimed at protecting the integrity of the process, tangibly benefit public participation in political debate. * * * The less rigorous standard of review we have applied to contribution limits (*Buckley*'s 'closely drawn' scrutiny) shows proper deference to Congress' ability to weigh competing constitutional interests in an area in which it enjoys particular expertise. It also provides Congress with sufficient room to anticipate and respond to concerns about circumvention of regulations designed to protect the integrity of the political process."

Applying this test, the majority believed combating *quid pro quo* corruption or its appearance provided ample justification for Congress' decision to close the soft-money loophole through § 323. "The evidence connects soft money to manipulations of the legislative calendar, leading to Congress' failure to enact, among other things, generic drug legislation, tort reform, and tobacco legislation. To claim that such actions do not change legislative outcomes surely misunderstands the legislative process. * * * More importantly, plaintiffs conceive of corruption too narrowly. * * * Many of the 'deeply disturbing examples' of corruption cited by this Court in *Buckley* to justify FECA's contribution limits were not episodes of vote buying, but evidence that various corporate interests had given substantial donations to gain access to high-level government officials. Even if that access did not secure actual influence, it certainly gave the 'appearance of such influence.' "

Justice Kennedy's dissent took vigorous issue with what he saw as an expansion of the traditional corruption rationale to include "any conduct that wins goodwill from or influences a Member of Congress. * * * [The majority] concludes that access, without more, proves influence is undue. Access, in the Court's view, has the same legal ramifications as actual or apparent corruption of officeholders. This new definition of corruption sweeps away all protections for speech that lie in its path. * * *Access in itself, however, shows only that in a general sense an officeholder favors someone or that someone has influence on the officeholder. There is no basis, in law or in fact, to say favoritism or influence in general is the same as corrupt favoritism or influence in particular." He went on: "Favoritism and influence are not, as the Government's theory suggests, avoidable in representative politics. It is in the nature of an elected representative to favor certain policies, and, by necessary corollary, to favor the voters and contributors who support those policies. It is well understood that a substantial and legitimate reason, if not the only reason, to cast a vote for, or to make a contribution to, one candidate over another is that the candidate will respond by producing those political outcomes the supporter favors. Democracy is premised on responsiveness."

Section 323(b) limits the ability of state and local parties to accept soft-money contributions, even though the congressional record contained little evidence that these entities presented the same problems for the federal campaign system. This was justified, the majority held, to prevent the possibility that political actors would circumvent the other provisions restricting soft money. "Having been taught the hard lesson of circumvention by the entire history of campaign finance regulation, Congress knew that soft-money donors would react to § 323(a) by scrambling to find another way to purchase influence. It was 'neither novel nor implausible,' *Nixon v. Shrink Missouri Gov't PAC*, 528 U.S. at 391, for Congress to conclude that political parties would react to § 323(a) by directing soft-money contributors to the state committees, and that federal candidates would be just as indebted to these contributors as they had been to those who had formerly contributed to the national parties." The Court concluded that it should defer to Congress' prediction of future political behavior, "particularly when, as here, those predictions are so firmly rooted in relevant history and common sense."

Justices Stevens and O'Connor next turned to the provisions aimed at issue ads. The parties challenging BCRA had interpreted *Buckley* as drawing "a constitutionally mandated line between express advocacy and so-called issue advocacy, and that speakers possess an inviolable First Amendment right to engage in the latter category of speech. * * * [However,] a plain reading of *Buckley* makes clear that the express advocacy limitation, in both the expenditure and the disclosure contexts, was the product of statutory interpretation rather than a constitutional command." The Court determined that no "rigid barrier" is required by the First Amendment between express advocacy and so-called issue advocacy. "That notion cannot be squared with our longstanding recognition that the presence or absence of magic words cannot meaningfully distinguish electioneering speech from a true issue ad. Indeed, the unmistakable lesson from the record in this litigation, as all three judges on the District Court agreed, is that *Buckley*'s magic-words requirement is functionally meaningless." It concluded that the Act's definition of electioneering communication was not impermissibly vague, but clearly applied "(1) to a broadcast (2) clearly identifying a candidate for federal office, (3) aired within a specific time period, and (4) targeted to an identified audience of at least 50,000 viewers or listeners. These components are both easily understood and objectively determinable."

It then analyzed the various regulations applying to electioneering communication. First, BCRA imposed more sweeping disclosure requirements, all of which were upheld by the majority and most of the dissenting justices. The state interests articulated in *Buckley* relating to disclosure—providing the electorate with information, deterring actual corruption and avoiding any appearance thereof, and aiding in the enforcement of the more substantive electioneering restrictions—were relevant here. The Court was particularly concerned with the evidence that showed groups and individuals running ads while "hiding behind dubious and misleading names." The Court worried that public debate was significantly harmed when organizations producing political communications could avoid the scrutiny of voters. Finally, although the Court rejected the facial attack in this lawsuit, it allowed for the possibility of future lawsuits brought by organizations with credible evidence that their members had been exposed to "economic reprisals or physical threats as a result of the compelled disclosures."

Second, BCRA § 203 extended a segregated-fund requirement to include payments for any electioneering communication: corporations and unions could not use their general treasury funds to finance electioneering communication, but they could organize and administer segregated funds, or PACs, for that purpose. In its analysis, the Court noted that § 203 was not a "complete ban" on political expression, as those challenging it argued, because regulated entities could still use a segregated fund to pay for electioneering communication. With regard to the state interest justifying this regulation, the majority cited *Austin v. Michigan Chamber of Commerce*: "We have repeatedly sustained legislation aimed at 'the corrosive and distorting effects of immense aggregations of wealth that are accumulated with the help of the corporate form and that have little or no correlation to the public's support for the corporation's political ideas.'" The Court thus sustained § 203 because it regulated issue ads during a certain period of time that "are the functional equivalent of express advocacy * * * intended to influence the voters' decisions and [that] have that effect."

The majority concluded: "Many years ago we observed that '[t]o say that Congress is without power to pass appropriate legislation to safeguard . . . an election from the improper use of money to influence the result is to deny to the nation in a vital particular the power of self protection.' *Burroughs v. United States*, 290 U.S. [534,] 545 [1934]. We abide by that conviction in considering Congress' most recent effort to confine the ill effects of aggregated wealth on our political system. We are under no illusion that BCRA will be the last congressional statement on the matter. Money, like water, will always find an outlet. What problems will arise, and how Congress will respond, are concerns for another day."

In a separate opinion by **Chief Justice Rehnquist**, the Court held the challenge to the increased contribution limits, such as the increase from $1,000 to $2,000 in the amount that individuals can contribute to candidates per election cycle, to be nonjusticiable because the plaintiffs lacked standing to bring such a challenge. The Court struck down as unconstitutional the provision that prohibited minors from making contributions to candidates or political parties because it violates their First Amendment rights.

Justice Scalia began his dissent: "This is a sad day for the freedom of speech. Who could have imagined that the same Court which, within the past four years, has sternly disapproved of restrictions upon such inconsequential forms of expression as virtual child pornography, tobacco advertising, dissemination of illegally intercepted communications, and sexually explicit cable programming, would smile with favor upon a law that cuts to the heart of what the First Amendment is meant to protect: the right to criticize the government." He alluded to a partisan lockup issue when he noted that, although the restrictions applied in an evenhanded way to all who ran for federal office, "[i]f *all* electioneering were evenhandedly prohibited, incumbents would have an enormous advantage. Likewise, if incumbents and challengers are limited to the same quantity of electioneering, incumbents are favored. * * * Beyond that, however, the present legislation *targets* for prohibition certain categories of campaign speech that are particularly harmful to incumbents. Is it accidental, do you think, that incumbents raise about three times as much 'hard money'—the sort of funding generally *not* restricted by this legislation—as do their challengers? * * * And is it mere happenstance, do you estimate, that national-party funding, which is severely limited by the Act, is more likely to assist cash-strapped challengers than flush-with-hard-money incumbents?"

Justice Scalia's main concern with the majority opinion concerned its view of corporations within the First Amendment jurisprudence of campaign finance, a view he traced to *Austin v. Michigan Chamber of Commerce*. "People who associate—who pool their financial resources—for purposes of economic enterprise overwhelmingly do so in the corporate form; and with increasing frequency, incorporation is chosen by those who associate to defend and promote particular ideas—such as the American Civil Liberties Union and the National Rifle Association, parties to these cases. Imagine, then, a government that wished to suppress nuclear power—or oil and gas exploration, or automobile manufacturing, or gun ownership, or civil liberties—and that had the power to prohibit corporate advertising against its proposals. To be sure, the individuals involved in, or benefited by, those industries, or interested in those causes, could (given enough time) form political action committees or other associations to make their case. But the organizational form in which those enterprises already *exist*, and in which they can most quickly and most effectively get their message across, is the corporate form. The First Amendment does not in my view permit the restriction of that political speech. And the same holds true for corporate electoral speech: A candidate should not be insulated from the most effective speech that the major participants in the economy and major incorporated interest groups can generate."

He also noted that disclosure statutes eliminated the risk that the political dialogue would be "distorted" by corporate spending because voters would know who is behind the speech. "The premise of the First Amendment is that the American people are neither sheep nor fools, and hence fully capable of considering both the substance of the speech presented to them and its proximate and ultimate source. If that premise is wrong, our democracy has a much greater problem to overcome than merely the influence of amassed wealth."

Justice Thomas argued that the appropriate standard of review is strict scrutiny, and that bribery laws and disclosure statutes would be less restrictive means of curtailing corruption. However, unlike all the other Justices, Justice Thomas would have invalidated BCRA's disclosure requirements because they allowed "the established right to anonymous speech to be stripped away based on the flimsiest of justifications." He rejected the notion that the interest of voters in knowing the source of political speech could support disclosure statutes because this interest was outweighed by the First Amendment right to engage in anonymous political speech.

Justice Kennedy's lengthy dissent took on the majority's reasoning with respect to § 203, the segregated-fund requirement imposed on corporations and unions that spend money on electioneering communication in the weeks before an election. He stated that he would have overruled *Austin*, rather than relying on it or "extending" it. He noted that the communications targeted by § 203 are "the ads speakers find most effective. Unlike express ads that leave nothing to the imagination, the record shows that issues ads are preferred by almost all candidates, even though politicians, unlike corporations, can lawfully broadcast express ads if they so choose." "The Government's use of the pejorative label [of 'sham issue' ad] should not obscure § 203's practical effect: It prohibits a mass communication technique favored in the modern political process for the very reason that it is the most potent." He also noted that that the burden on entities regulated by § 203 was not trivial. "These [segregated-fund] regulations are more than minor clerical requirements. Rather, they create major disincentives for speech, with the effect falling most heavily on smaller entities that often have the most difficulty bearing the costs of compliance."

Justice Kennedy next addressed the definition of "electioneering communication." He provided a hypothetical to prove his point: "[S]uppose a few Senators want to show their constituents in the logging industry how much they care about working families and propose a law, 60 days before the election, that would harm the environment by allowing logging in national forests. Under [BCRA], a nonprofit environmental group would be unable to run an ad referring to these Senators in their districts. The suggestion that the group could form and fund a PAC in the short time required for effective participation in the political debate is fanciful. * * * The group would want to refer to these Senators, either by name or by photograph, not necessarily because an election is at stake. * * * The ability to refer to candidates and officeholders is important because it allows the public to communicate with them on issues of common concern. [BCRA's] sweeping approach fails to take into account this significant free speech interest. Under any conventional definition of overbreadth, it fails to meet strict scrutiny standards. It forces electioneering communications sponsored by an environmental group to contend with faceless and nameless opponents and consign their broadcast * * * to a world where politicians who threaten the environment must be referred to as 'He Whose Name Cannot Be Spoken.' "

The Justice concluded his example: "We are supposed to find comfort in the knowledge that the ad is banned under § 203 only if it 'is targeted to the relevant electorate,' defined as communications that can be received by 50,000 or more persons in the candidate's district. This Orwellian criterion, however, is analogous to a law, unconstitutional under any known First Amendment theory, that would allow a speaker to say anything he chooses, so long as his intended audience could not hear him. A central purpose of issue ads is to urge the public to pay close attention to the candidate's platform on the featured issues. By banning broadcast in the very district where the candidate is standing for election, § 203 shields information at the heart of the First Amendment from precisely those citizens who most value the right to make a responsible judgment at the voting booth."

NOTE ON MCCONNELL V. FEDERAL ELECTION COMMISSION

Corruption and the Standard of Review. In this facial challenge to BCRA, *McConnell* clarifies that the standard of review for restrictions on campaign contributions is less rigorous than strict scrutiny, and it is less stringent than judicial review of expenditure limitations. In addition, the majority demonstrates a willingness to defer to Congress throughout its analysis. For example, it notes that Congress had enacted a comprehensive response to problems in the campaign fundraising system and thus judges should consider BCRA an integrated approach to regulation. The implication of this language is that judges should be hesitant to strike down part of the statute and leave other parts in place because such a piecemeal approach could lead to unintended consequences. The majority ends the main opinion by underscoring the primary role Congress plays in designing campaign finance laws and predicting that it will need to formulate new approaches as money begins to find new outlets.

McConnell also continues to develop the notion of "corruption" by highlighting one aspect of corruption: the "special access" to politicians that large contributions appear to buy. As Richard Briffault writes: "Although the Court had previously made clear that corruption was not limited to outright vote-buying, the Court's language of undue influence had nonetheless focused on the effects of large contributions on government decision-making. By focusing on special access, *McConnell* reframed the corruption analysis from the consideration of the impact of contributions on formal decisions to their effect on the *opportunity to influence* government actions." McConnell v. FEC *and the Transformation of Campaign Finance Law,* 3 Election L.J. 147, 162–63 (2004). Much of Justice Kennedy's dissent argues against this expansion of the corruption rationale, contending that access to lawmakers is not inherently harmful but is instead an inevitable part of representative government. What do you think about this formulation of corruption? Does this state interest in preventing special access bought with large contributions, as the majority articulates it, have a limiting principle? What sorts of additional regulation of the electoral process would it support?

Problem 2–7. Remember the other state interests that have been put forth in the campaign finance context, although not all have been embraced by the Court: increasing voter competence, enhancing electoral competitiveness, equality concerns, and encouraging a more participatory democracy. Would the judicial analysis of BCRA's provisions be different if those state interests were considered as compelling or important? Would they support more aggressive regulation than Congress adopted in 2002?

———

The 2004 presidential and congressional campaigns were the first conducted under BCRA. Perhaps the biggest change was the increased importance of hard money both because of BCRA's soft-money restrictions and because of larger contribution limits for hard money. Thus, people who could bundle many $2,000 contributions from individuals were particularly important to candidates and political parties. Initially, the new emphasis on hard money was thought to provide a significant advantage to the Republican Party because it has a larger base of hard-money donors, many of whom could give amounts up to the new limits. Before enactment of BCRA, the two political parties were roughly equal in their ability to raise soft money, but the Republicans have always substantially outpaced the Democrats for hard money. In the 2002 election cycle, the GOP had raised $289 million in hard money compared to the Democrats' $127 million, while the GOP had garnered $222 million in soft money compared to the Democrats' $200 million. As the 2004 election cycle developed, however, both parties were able to replace soft money with new hard money, and any Republican advantage was clearly not long-lived. Anthony Corrado found that "[b]y the end of the 2004 election, the national party committees had raised more money in hard dollars *alone* than they raised in hard and soft dollars *combined* in any previous election cycle." *Party Finance in the Wake of BCRA: An Overview*, in *The Election After Reform, supra*, at 19, 25.

With the closing of the soft-money spigot for political parties, 527 organizations, discussed above, became increasingly crucial political players in the 2004 elections. Although all PACs are also 527 organizations, not all 527s involved in politics at the federal level were considered PACs before BCRA and *McConnell.* These groups argued that, as long as they did not engage in express advocacy (as defined by the *Buckley* "magic words") and did not directly contribute to federal candidates' campaigns, they could raise unlimited amounts of soft money. Taking advantage of this loophole, federally active 527 groups spent approximately $424 million in the 2004 election cycle immediately following *McConnell.*[62] Although some of the top 527s, such as Progress for America, were politically conservative, most of the 527s with significant resources in 2004—such as Americans Coming Together, supported by liberal financier George Soros, and the Media Fund, run by

---

[62] Michael Malbin, *Assessing the Bipartisan Campaign Reform Act*, in *The Election After Reform, supra*, at 1, 11.

former Clinton aide Harold Ickes—supported Kerry and the Democrats. Many of the 527s worked informally with the political parties; leading political consultants affiliated with parties in the past helped them raise money, and party officials signaled their support for certain 527s. See Stephen Weissman & Ruth Hassan, *BCRA and the 527 Groups*, in *The Election After Reform*, *supra*, at 79. Through the activities of a group called Swift Boat Veterans for Truth—which ran a series of ads effectively tarnishing Kerry's image as a Vietnam War hero—527 groups gained notoriety; this group was bankrolled by several politically active conservatives who had long supported Bush. The episode ushered a new word into the political parlance: "swift boating" has come to mean using a smear campaign to impugn a candidate's patriotism and veracity.

The *McConnell* opinions noted that evasion of BCRA was likely to center on the use of nonprofit organizations, which would include not only 527 organizations but also nonprofit organizations created under Sections 501(c)(3) and 501(c)(4) of the tax code. Chief Justice Rehnquist, in dissent, stated that "[n]onprofit organizations are currently able to accept, without disclosing [in the case of nonprofits other than 527 organizations], unlimited donations for voter registration, voter identification, and get-out-the-vote activities, and the record indicates that such organizations already receive large donations, sometimes in the millions of dollars, for these activities." Indeed, the next major campaign finance cases that reshaped the jurisprudential landscape focused on nonprofit corporations primarily engaged in political activity.

B. THE ROBERTS COURT'S CHANGE OF COURSE: *CITIZENS UNITED V. FEDERAL ELECTION COMMISSION*

Although *McConnell* left some questions open, it initially appeared that the issues would be resolved within the *Buckley*/*McConnell* framework and that the courts would be relatively deferential to legislative decisions regarding the appropriate regulation of campaign contributions. However, two changes in Supreme Court personnel unsettled the jurisprudential landscape. John Roberts replaced Chief Justice Rehnquist, and Samuel Alito replaced Justice Sandra Day O'Connor, one of the authors of the majority opinion in *McConnell*.

In 2007, Wisconsin Right to Life, Inc. (WRTL), a nonprofit ideological advocacy 501(c)(4) corporation, brought an as-applied challenge to BCRA's rules concerning electioneering communication.[63] During the 30–day period before Wisconsin's 2004 primary election, WRTL planned to run broadcast advertisements telling viewers to contact Senators Feingold and Kohl to urge them to oppose a filibuster of conservative judicial nominees. Because WRTL accepted some contributions from for-profit corporations and the ads it proposed to air met the requirements of § 203, BCRA required that WRTL set up a segregated fund and use that money to pay for the ads.

---

[63] For an examination of the Roberts Court's use of as-applied challenges to determine broad questions of election law, see Nathaniel Persily & Jennifer Rosenberg, *Defacing Democracy?: The Changing Nature and Rising Importance of As-Applied Challenges in the Supreme Court's Recent Election Law Decisions*, 93 Minn. L. Rev. 1644 (2009).

In *Fed. Election Comm'n v. Wisconsin Right to Life, Inc.*, 551 U.S. 449 (2007), a majority of the Court agreed with WRTL that BCRA was unconstitutional as applied to these ads. Chief Justice Roberts and Justice Alito noted that *McConnell* allowed regulation of issue ads under § 203 only when they are the "functional equivalent" of express advocacy. They held that "a court should find that an ad is the functional equivalent of express advocacy only if the ad is susceptible of no reasonable interpretation other than as an appeal to vote for or against a specific candidate." Noting that strict scrutiny demands that a "compelling state interest supports *each application* of a statute restricting speech," the Justices found that BCRA could not be applied in this instance because the concern about *quid pro quo* corruption was not implicated by "genuine" issue ads that are not the functional equivalent of express advocacy. Thus, WRTL could fund them directly with general treasury funds.

A few years later, *McConnell* came under even more serious attack. Citizens United, another ideological nonprofit that accepted a small amount of contributions from for-profit corporations, produced a 90–minute documentary called *Hillary: The Movie*, which it proposed to release on cable video-on-demand channels. The movie was a critical assessment of then-Senator Hillary Clinton (D–N.Y.) and her run for the presidency in 2008. The movie, as well as the ads produced to publicize it, seemed to trigger § 203's requirement that Citizens United use a segregated fund to produce the movie and the ads because all would have been aired within 30 days of the 2008 primary elections. Citizens United had funded the movie directly and thus faced civil and criminal penalties, so it brought an action for declaratory and injunctive relief, arguing that § 203, as well as BCRA's disclosure and disclaimer provisions applying to independent expenditures used for electioneering communication, were unconstitutional as applied to *Hillary* and the surrounding publicity for it.

After losing in federal court, Citizens United appealed to the Supreme Court, which asked for a second round of arguments in an unusual September 2009 sitting. The Supreme Court had a new member: Justice Sonia Sotomayor had replaced Justice Souter. The reargument was also noteworthy because it was Solicitor General Elena Kagan's first appearance before the Court; less than a year later, she replaced retiring Justice Stevens. When the Court ordered reargument, it requested supplemental briefs addressing whether it should overrule *Austin v. Michigan Chamber of Commerce* and the part of *McConnell* dealing with the regulation of electioneering communication. It thus signaled a willingness to revisit the holding of *McConnell* that § 203 was facially constitutional, and not limit its consideration to the as-applied challenge before it. (Note: Section 203 of BCRA amended 2 U.S.C. § 441b, which regulates corporate contributions and independent expenditures for express advocacy. Accordingly, the majority opinion in *Citizens United* refers to § 441b when it considers the regulation of corporate independent expenditures for electioneering communication.)

CITIZENS UNITED V. FEDERAL ELECTION COMMISSION
Supreme Court of the United States, 2010.
558 U.S. 310, 130 S.Ct. 876, 175 L.Ed.2d 753.

JUSTICE KENNEDY delivered the opinion of the Court, in which THE CHIEF JUSTICE, and JUSTICE SCALIA and JUSTICE ALITO, joined, in which JUSTICE THOMAS joined as to all but Part IV, and in which JUSTICES STEVENS, GINSBURG, BREYER, and SOTOMAYOR joined as to Part IV.

Federal law prohibits corporations and unions from using their general treasury funds to make independent expenditures for speech defined as an "electioneering communication" or for speech expressly advocating the election or defeat of a candidate. Limits on electioneering communications were upheld in *McConnell v. Federal Election Comm'n.* The holding of *McConnell* rested to a large extent on an earlier case, *Austin v. Michigan Chamber of Commerce. Austin* had held that political speech may be banned based on the speaker's corporate identity.

In this case we are asked to reconsider *Austin* and, in effect, *McConnell.* * * * [We] hold that *stare decisis* does not compel the continued acceptance of *Austin.* The Government may regulate corporate political speech through disclaimer and disclosure requirements, but it may not suppress that speech altogether. * * *

[The Court noted that federal law has long prohibited corporations and unions from using general treasury funds to make direct contributions to candidates or independent expenditures that expressly advocate the election or defeat of a federal candidate. The Court first considered several narrower ways in which it could have decided the case without overruling precedent or reaching the constitutional issues. For example, it had been argued that Citizens United might not meet the test in *WRTL* because *Hillary* should not be considered express advocacy or its functional equivalent; the test provided by *WRTL* was whether the communication is "susceptible of no reasonable interpretation other than as an appeal to vote for or against a specific candidate." But the Court concluded that *Hillary* was equivalent to express advocacy: "The movie, in essence, is a feature-length negative advertisement that urges viewers to vote against Senator Clinton for President." Thus, because it could not resolve the case on a narrower ground, the Court concluded that "full consideration of the continuing effect of the speech suppression upheld in *Austin*" was required.]

[II] * * * In the exercise of its judicial responsibility, it is necessary then for the Court to consider the facial validity of § 441b. Any other course of decision would prolong the substantial, nation-wide chilling effect caused by § 441b's prohibitions on corporate expenditures. * * *

[S]ubstantial time would be required to bring clarity to the application of the statutory provision on these points in order to avoid any chilling effect caused by some improper interpretation. It is well known that the public begins to concentrate on elections only in the weeks immediately before they are held. There are short timeframes in which speech can have influence. * * * A speaker's ability to engage in political speech that could have a chance of persuading voters is stifled if the speaker must first commence a protracted lawsuit. By the time the lawsuit concludes, the election will be over and the litigants in most cases will have neither the incentive nor, perhaps, the resources to carry on, even if they could establish that the case is not moot because the issue is "capable of repetition, yet evading review." Here, Citizens United decided to litigate its case to the end. Today, Citizens United finally learns, two years after the fact, whether it could have spoken during the 2008 Presidential primary—long after the opportunity to persuade primary voters has passed.

[An additional factor] is the primary importance of speech itself to the integrity of the election process. As additional rules are created for regulating political speech, any speech arguably within their reach is chilled. Campaign finance regulations now impose "unique and complex rules" on "71 distinct entities." Brief for Seven Former Chairmen of FEC et al. as *Amici Curiae* 11–12. These entities are subject to separate rules for 33 different types of political speech. The FEC has adopted 568 pages of regulations, 1,278 pages of explanations and justifications for those regulations, and 1,771 advisory opinions since 1975. In fact, after this Court in *WRTL* adopted an objective "appeal to vote" test for determining whether a communication was the functional equivalent of express advocacy, the FEC adopted a two-part, 11–factor balancing test to implement *WRTL*'s ruling.

This regulatory scheme may not be a prior restraint on speech in the strict sense of that term, for prospective speakers are not compelled by law to seek an advisory opinion from the FEC before the speech takes place. As a practical matter, however, given the complexity of the regulations and the deference courts show to administrative determinations, a speaker who wants to avoid threats of criminal liability and the heavy costs of defending against FEC enforcement must ask a governmental agency for prior permission to speak. * * *

The ongoing chill upon speech that is beyond all doubt protected makes it necessary in this case to invoke the earlier precedents that a statute which chills speech can and must be invalidated where its facial invalidity has been demonstrated. For these reasons we find it necessary to reconsider *Austin*.

[III] * * * The law before us is an outright ban [of political speech], backed by criminal sanctions. Section 441b makes it a felony for all corporations—including nonprofit advocacy corporations—either to expressly advocate the election or defeat of candidates or to broadcast electioneering communications within 30 days of a primary election and 60 days of a general election. Thus, the following acts would all be felonies under § 441b: The Sierra Club runs an ad, within the crucial phase of 60 days before the general election, that exhorts the public to disapprove of a Congressman who favors logging in national forests; the National Rifle Association publishes a book urging the public to vote for the challenger because the incumbent U.S. Senator supports a handgun ban; and the American Civil Liberties Union creates a Web site telling the public to vote for a Presidential candidate in light of that candidate's defense of free speech. These prohibitions are classic examples of censorship.

Section 441b is a ban on corporate speech notwithstanding the fact that a PAC created by a corporation can still speak. A PAC is a separate association from the corporation. So the PAC exemption from § 441b's expenditure ban does not allow corporations to speak. Even if a PAC could somehow allow a corporation to speak—and it does not—the option to form PACs does not alleviate the First Amendment problems with § 441b. PACs are burdensome alternatives; they are expensive to administer and subject to extensive regulations. * * *

Premised on mistrust of governmental power, the First Amendment stands against attempts to disfavor certain subjects or viewpoints. Prohibited, too, are restrictions distinguishing among different speakers, allowing speech by some but not others. As instruments to censor, these categories are interrelated: Speech restrictions based on the identity of the speaker are all too often simply a means to control content. * * *

[The Court cited a long line of precedents holding that corporations are protected by the First Amendment and that the protection extends to political speech. Nonetheless, direct contributions to candidates by corporations have been banned since the latter part of the 19th century, and in 1947 Congress prohibited independent expenditures in candidate elections by corporations and unions. After the Court in *Buckley* invalidated FECA's restriction on independent expenditures in federal elections, Congress enacted a prohibition on the use of the general treasury funds of corporations or unions for independent expenditures funding express advocacy. Subsequent Supreme Court cases dealt with corporate expenditures in state ballot measure campaigns. In *First Nat'l Bank of Boston v. Bellotti*, 435 U.S. 765 (1978), the Court struck down a state ban on the use of corporate treasury funds for such expenditures, resting on "the principle that the Government lacks the power to ban corporations from speaking." The next time the Court considered corporate political speech was in *Austin*. "To bypass *Buckley* and *Bellotti*, the *Austin* Court identified a new governmental interest in limiting political speech: an antidistortion interest."]

[III.B]   The Court is thus confronted with conflicting lines of precedent: a pre-*Austin* line that forbids restrictions on political speech based on the speaker's corporate identity and a post-*Austin* line that permits them. * * *

In its defense of the corporate-speech restrictions in § 441b, the Government notes the antidistortion rationale on which *Austin* and its progeny rest in part, yet it all but abandons reliance upon it. It argues instead that two other compelling interests support *Austin*'s holding that corporate expenditure restrictions are constitutional: an anticorruption interest, and a shareholder-protection interest. We consider the three points in turn.

* * * [First,] *Austin* sought to defend the antidistortion rationale as a means to prevent corporations from obtaining "an unfair advantage in the political marketplace" by using "resources amassed in the economic marketplace." But *Buckley* rejected the premise that the Government has an interest "in equalizing the relative ability of individuals and groups to influence the outcome of elections." * * * The rule that political speech cannot be limited based on a speaker's wealth is a necessary consequence of the premise that the First Amendment generally prohibits the suppression of political speech based on the speaker's identity. * * *

[The Court turned then to the argument that § 441b was designed to prevent corruption and its appearance. It relied on the analysis in *Buckley* that independent expenditures, not coordinated or arranged with a candidate, do not sufficiently implicate concerns about *quid pro quo* corruption to allow the restriction at issue in *Citizens United*. The majority definitively stated: "[W]e now conclude that independent expenditures, including those made by corporations, do not give rise to corruption or the appearance of corruption." Finally, it addressed the argument that corporate independent expenditures can be limited because of a state interest "in protecting dissenting shareholders from being compelled to fund corporate political speech."]

[With regard to this interest of shareholder protection,] the statute is both underinclusive and overinclusive. As to the first, if Congress had been seeking to protect dissenting shareholders, it would not have banned corporate speech in only certain media within 30 or 60 days before an election. A dissenting shareholder's interests would be implicated by speech in any media at any time. As to the second, the statute is overinclusive because it covers all corporations, including nonprofit corporations and for-profit corporations with only single shareholders. * * *

[III.C]   * * * For the reasons above, it must be concluded that *Austin* was not well reasoned. The Government defends *Austin*, relying almost entirely on "the quid pro quo interest, the corruption interest or the shareholder interest," and not *Austin*'s expressed antidistortion rationale. When neither party defends the reasoning of a precedent, the principle of adhering to that precedent through *stare decisis* is diminished. * * *

No serious reliance interests are at stake. As the Court stated in *Payne v. Tennessee,* 501 U.S. 808, 828 (1991), reliance interests are important considerations in property and contract cases, where parties may have acted in conformance with existing legal rules in order to conduct transactions. Here, though, parties have been prevented from acting—corporations have been banned from making independent expenditures. Legislatures may have enacted bans on corporate expenditures believing that those bans were constitutional. This is not a compelling interest for *stare decisis*. If it were, legislative acts could prevent us from overruling our own precedents, thereby interfering with our duty "to say what the law is." *Marbury v. Madison*, 5 U.S. 137, 1 Cranch 137, 177 (1803).

Due consideration leads to this conclusion: *Austin* should be and now is overruled. We return to the principle established in *Buckley* and *Bellotti* that the Government may not suppress political speech on the basis of the speaker's corporate identity. No sufficient governmental interest justifies limits on the political speech of nonprofit or for-profit corporations. * * *

Given our conclusion we are further required to overrule the part of *McConnell* that upheld BCRA § 203's extension of § 441b's restrictions on corporate independent expenditures. The *McConnell* Court relied on the antidistortion interest recognized in *Austin* to uphold a greater restriction on speech than the restriction upheld in *Austin*, and we have found this interest unconvincing and insufficient. This part of *McConnell* is now overruled.

[In Part IV, joined by all the Justices except Justice Thomas, the Court upheld BCRA's disclosure and disclaimer provisions as applied to *Hillary* and the ads for the movie. BCRA requires that electioneering communications funded by entities other than candidates include a disclaimer identifying the person or group responsible for the content of the communication, and that any entity spending more than $10,000 on electioneering communications within a calendar year must file a disclosure statement with the FEC. The Court found that disclosure served the compelling state interest of providing the electorate with the information necessary to evaluate the arguments and to avoid confusion about who is behind the communications. It approved of applying disclosure provisions to a wide array of political communication, not just express advocacy and its functional equivalent. It found that "the informational interest alone is sufficient to justify" applying BCRA's disclosure provisions to the movie and ads produced by Citizens United. It rejected Citizens United's argument that disclosure could subject its donors to threats or harassment because there was no such evidence of retaliation even though Citizens United has disclosed it donors publicly for years.]

[V] When word concerning the plot of the movie *Mr. Smith Goes to Washington* reached the circles of Government, some officials sought, by persuasion, to discourage its distribution. Under *Austin*, though, officials could have done more than discourage its distribution—they could have banned the film. After all, it, like *Hillary*, was speech funded by a corporation that was critical of Members of Congress. *Mr. Smith Goes to Washington* may be fiction and caricature; but fiction and caricature can be a powerful force. * * *

Some members of the public might consider *Hillary* to be insightful and instructive; some might find it to be neither high art nor a fair discussion on how to set the Nation's course; still others simply might suspend judgment on these points but decide to think more about issues and candidates. Those choices and assessments, however, are not for the Government to make. "The First Amendment underwrites the freedom to experiment and to create in the realm of thought and speech. Citizens must be free to use new forms, and new forums, for the expression of ideas. The civic discourse belongs to the people, and the Government may not prescribe the means used to conduct it." *McConnell* (opinion of KENNEDY, J.).

[The concurrences of CHIEF JUSTICE ROBERTS and JUSTICE SCALIA are omitted.]

JUSTICE STEVENS, with whom JUSTICE GINSBURG, JUSTICE BREYER, and JUSTICE SOTOMAYOR join, concurring in part [with respect to the disclosure provisions] and dissenting in part.

The real issue in this case concerns how, not if, the appellant may finance its electioneering. Citizens United is a wealthy nonprofit corporation that runs a political action committee (PAC) with millions of dollars in assets. Under the Bipartisan Campaign Reform Act of 2002 (BCRA), it could have used those assets to televise and promote *Hillary: The Movie* wherever and whenever it wanted to. It also could have spent unrestricted sums to broadcast *Hillary* at any time other than the 30 days before the last primary election. Neither Citizens United's nor any other corporation's speech has been "banned." All that the parties dispute is whether Citizens United had a right to use the funds in its general treasury to pay for broadcasts during the 30–day period. The notion that the First Amendment dictates an affirmative answer to that question is, in my judgment, profoundly misguided. Even more misguided is the notion that the Court must rewrite the law relating to campaign expenditures by *for-profit* corporations and unions to decide this case.

The basic premise underlying the Court's ruling is its iteration, and constant reiteration, of the proposition that the First Amendment bars regulatory distinctions based on a speaker's identity, including its "identity" as a corporation. * * *

In the context of election to public office, the distinction between corporate and human speakers is significant. Although they make enormous contributions to our society, corporations are not actually members of it. They cannot vote or run for office. Because they may be managed and controlled by nonresidents, their interests may conflict in fundamental respects with the interests of eligible voters. The financial resources, legal structure, and instrumental orientation of corporations raise legitimate concerns about their role in the electoral process. Our lawmakers have a compelling constitutional basis, if not also a democratic duty, to take measures designed to guard against the potentially deleterious effects of corporate spending in local and national races.

[The dissent takes strong issue with the decision of the Court to overrule its precedents, thereby deciding the case "on a basis relinquished below, not included in the questions presented to us by the litigants, and argued here only in response to the Court's invitation. * * * Our colleagues' suggestion that 'we are asked to reconsider *Austin* and, in effect, *McConnell*,' would be more accurate if rephrased to state that 'we have asked ourselves' to reconsider those cases."]

[II] * * * We have recognized that "*[s]tare decisis* has special force when legislators or citizens 'have acted in reliance on a previous decision, for in this instance overruling the decision would dislodge settled rights and expectations or require an extensive legislative response.' " *Hubbard v. United States*, 514 U.S. 695, 714 (1995). *Stare decisis* protects not only personal rights involving property or contract but also the ability of the elected branches to shape their laws in an effective and coherent fashion. Today's decision takes away a power that we have long permitted these branches to exercise. State legislatures have relied on their authority to regulate corporate electioneering, confirmed in *Austin*, for more than a century. The Federal Congress has relied on this authority for a comparable stretch of time, and it specifically relied on *Austin* throughout the years it spent developing and debating BCRA. The total record it compiled was *100,000 pages* long. Pulling out the rug beneath Congress after affirming the constitutionality of § 203 six years ago shows great disrespect for a coequal branch. * * *

[III] The novelty of the Court's procedural dereliction and its approach to *stare decisis* is matched by the novelty of its ruling on the merits. The ruling rests on several premises. First, the Court claims that *Austin* and *McConnell* have "banned" corporate speech. Second, it claims that the First Amendment precludes regulatory distinctions based on speaker identity, including the speaker's identity as a corporation. Third, it claims that *Austin* and *McConnell* were radical outliers in our First Amendment tradition and our campaign finance jurisprudence. Each of these claims is wrong.

The So-Called "Ban"

Pervading the Court's analysis is the ominous image of a "categorical ba[n]" on corporate speech. Indeed, the majority invokes the specter of a "ban" on nearly every page of its opinion. This characterization is highly misleading, and needs to be corrected.

* * * "The ability to form and administer separate segregated funds," we observed in *McConnell*, "has provided corporations and unions with a constitutionally sufficient opportunity to engage in express advocacy. That has been this Court's unanimous view."

* * * Administering a PAC entails some administrative burden, but so does complying with the disclaimer, disclosure, and reporting requirements that the Court today upholds, and no one has suggested that the burden is severe for a sophisticated for-profit corporation. To the extent the majority is worried about this issue, it is important to keep in mind that we have no record to show how substantial the burden really is, just the majority's own unsupported factfinding. * * *

So let us be clear: Neither *Austin* nor *McConnell* held or implied that corporations may be silenced; the FEC is not a "censor"; and in the years since these cases were decided, corporations have continued to play a major role in the national dialogue. Laws such as § 203 target a class of communications that is especially likely to corrupt the political process, that is at least one degree removed from the views of individual citizens, and that may not even reflect the views of those who pay for it. Such laws burden political speech, and that is always a serious matter, demanding careful scrutiny. But the majority's incessant talk of a "ban" aims at a straw man.

Identity-Based Distinctions

The second pillar of the Court's opinion is its assertion that "the Government cannot restrict political speech based on the speaker's . . . identity." * * * Like its paeans to unfettered discourse, the Court's denunciation of identity-based distinctions may have rhetorical appeal but it obscures reality. * * *

* * * As we have unanimously observed, legislatures are entitled to decide "that the special characteristics of the corporate structure require particularly careful regulation" in an electoral context. *Federal Election Commission v. National Right to Work Committee*, 459 U.S. 197, 209–10 (1982). Not only has the distinctive potential of corporations to corrupt the electoral process long been recognized, but * * * [c]ampaign finance distinctions based on corporate identity tend to be less worrisome, * * * because the "speakers" are not natural persons, much less members of our political community, and the governmental interests are of the highest order. * * *

Our First Amendment Tradition

A third fulcrum of the Court's opinion is the idea that *Austin* and *McConnell* are radical outliers, "aberration[s]," in our First Amendment tradition. The Court has it exactly backwards. It is today's holding that is the radical departure from what had been settled First Amendment law. * * *

By the time Congress passed FECA in 1971, the bar on corporate contributions and expenditures had become such an accepted part of federal campaign finance regulation that when a large number of plaintiffs, including several nonprofit corporations, challenged virtually every aspect of the Act in *Buckley,* no one even bothered to argue that the bar as such was unconstitutional. *Buckley* famously (or infamously) distinguished direct contributions from independent expenditures, but its silence on corporations only reinforced the understanding that corporate expenditures could be treated differently from individual expenditures. * * *

[IV] Having explained why this is not an appropriate case in which to revisit *Austin* and *McConnell* and why these decisions sit perfectly well with "First Amendment principles," I come at last to the interests that are at stake. The majority recognizes that *Austin* and *McConnell* may be defended on anticorruption, antidistortion, and shareholder protection rationales. * * *

The Anticorruption Interest

Undergirding the majority's approach to the merits is the claim that the only "sufficiently important governmental interest in preventing corruption or the appearance of corruption" is one that is "limited to *quid pro quo* corruption." This is the same "crabbed view of corruption" that was * * * squarely rejected by the Court in [*McConnell*]. * * *

Quid Pro Quo *Corruption*

* * * Even in the cases that have construed the anticorruption interest most narrowly, we have never suggested that such *quid pro quo* debts must take the form of outright vote buying or bribes, which have long been distinct crimes. Rather, they encompass the myriad ways in which outside parties may induce an officeholder to confer a legislative benefit in direct response to, or anticipation of, some outlay of money the parties have made or will make on behalf of the officeholder. * * * A democracy cannot function effectively when its constituent members believe laws are being bought and sold. * * *

Austin *and Corporate Expenditures*

* * * The majority fails to appreciate that *Austin*'s antidistortion rationale is itself an anticorruption rationale, tied to the special concerns raised by corporations. Understood properly, "antidistortion" is simply a variant on the classic governmental interest in protecting against improper influences on officeholders that debilitate the democratic process. It is manifestly not just an "equalizing" ideal in disguise.

1. *Antidistortion*

* * * Corporate speech * * * is derivative speech, speech by proxy. A regulation such as BCRA § 203 may affect the way in which individuals disseminate certain messages through the corporate form, but it does not prevent anyone from speaking in his or her own voice. * * *

It is an interesting question "who" is even speaking when a business corporation places an advertisement that endorses or attacks a particular candidate. Presumably it is not the customers or employees, who typically have no say in such matters. It cannot realistically be said to be the shareholders, who tend to be far removed from the day-to-day decisions of the firm and whose political preferences may be opaque to management. Perhaps the officers or directors of the corporation have the best claim to be the ones speaking, except their fiduciary duties generally prohibit them from using corporate funds for personal ends. Some individuals associated with the corporation must make the decision to place the ad, but the idea that these individuals are thereby fostering their self-expression or cultivating their critical faculties is fanciful. It is entirely possible that the corporation's electoral message will *conflict* with their personal convictions. Take away the ability to use general treasury funds for some of those ads, and no one's autonomy, dignity, or political equality has been impinged upon in the least. * * *

* * * When citizens turn on their televisions and radios before an election and hear only corporate electioneering, they may lose faith in their capacity, as citizens, to influence public policy. A Government captured by corporate interests, they may come to believe, will be neither responsive to their needs nor willing to give their views a fair hearing. The predictable result is cynicism and disenchantment: an increased perception that large spenders "call the tune" and a reduced "willingness of voters to take part in democratic governance." *McConnell.* To the extent that corporations are allowed to exert undue influence in electoral races, the speech of the eventual winners of those races may also be chilled. Politicians who fear that a certain corporation can make or break their reelection chances may be cowed into silence about that corporation. * * * At the least, I stress again, a legislature is entitled to credit these concerns and to take tailored measures in response. * * *

2. *Shareholder Protection*

* * * Interwoven with *Austin*'s concern to protect the integrity of the electoral process is a concern to protect the rights of shareholders from a kind of coerced speech: electioneering expenditures that do not "reflec[t] [their] support." When corporations use general treasury funds to praise or attack a particular candidate for office, it is the shareholders, as the residual claimants, who are effectively footing the bill. Those shareholders who disagree with the corporation's electoral message may find their financial investments being used to undermine their political convictions.

The PAC mechanism, by contrast, helps assure that those who pay for an electioneering communication actually support its content and that managers do not use general treasuries to advance personal agendas. * * *

[V] In a democratic society, the longstanding consensus on the need to limit corporate campaign spending should outweigh the wooden application of judge-made rules. The majority's rejection of this principle "elevate[s] corporations to a level of deference which has not been seen at least since the days when substantive due process was regularly used to invalidate regulatory legislation thought to unfairly impinge upon established economic interests." *Bellotti* (White, J., dissenting). At bottom, the Court's opinion is thus a rejection of the common sense of the American people, who have recognized a need to prevent corporations from undermining self-government since the founding, and who have fought against the distinctive corrupting potential of corporate electioneering since the days of Theodore Roosevelt. It is a strange time to repudiate that common sense. While American democracy is imperfect, few outside the majority of this Court would have thought its flaws included a dearth of corporate money in politics.

I would affirm the judgment of the District Court.

[The dissent by JUSTICE THOMAS, arguing that BCRA's disclosure provisions are unconstitutional, is omitted.]

NOTES ON CITIZENS UNITED AND ITS AFTERMATH

1. *The Corruption Interest After* Citizens United. The idea of *quid pro quo* corruption has evolved since *Buckley*, as the Court has worked to define what constitutes this sort of corruption, in actuality and appearance. Remember that *McConnell* had expanded *quid pro quo* corruption to encompass the "special access" that large donors obtain, or that ordinary voters worry these donors might have obtained. Justice Kennedy, the author of the majority in *Citizens United*, took issue with this formulation in his separate opinion in *McConnell*, arguing that access is part of the democratic process. Perhaps not surprisingly then, Justice Kennedy cited his *McConnell* opinion on this issue at length in *Citizens United*, and noted that "[t]he fact that speakers may have influence over or access to elected officials does not mean that these officials are corrupt." 558 U.S. at 359. The Roberts Court has continued to move away from the expansive notion of *quid pro quo* corruption articulated by *McConnell*, rejecting in a recent plurality opinion the idea that the state is justified in regulating large contributions to combat "the appearance of mere influence or access." *McCutcheon*, 134 S.Ct. at 1451. The *McCutcheon* opinion cited *Citizens United* for the proposition that "ingratiation and access * * * are not corruption." This narrower vision of *quid pro quo* corruption will likely now guide the Court's jurisprudence because the fifth vote in *McCutcheon* was cast by Justice Thomas, who argued that all limits on campaign contributions are unconstitutional restrictions on political speech. *Id.* at 1462–63 (Thomas, concurring in the judgment and arguing to overrule *Buckley v. Valeo* entirely).

In *Citizens United*, Justice Kennedy also questioned the evidence in *McConnell* that the Court then had found sufficient to uphold the regulation, observing that there were no direct examples of votes being exchanged for political expenditures. Considered together with the language rejecting special access as an indication of corruption that might undermine the integrity of democratic institutions, this discussion seems to increase the quantity and quality of evidence required to provide a foundation for regulation. How realistic is it to expect lawmakers to produce a record with specific examples of votes changed on account of financial support in campaigns? Wasn't that difficulty the reason that *Buckley* included the "appearance" of such corruption that exists when the political system allows large contributions from wealthy interests, rather than limiting the state interest to one supported by proof of actual corruption? Does the *Citizens United* majority reduce the governmental interest of *quid pro quo* corruption back to bribery-like behavior, moving away from the expansive view the Court had developed in *McConnell* and other cases?

One state supreme court read the outcome in *Citizens United* to depend on the nature of the evidence of corruption and determined that a more extensive evidentiary record proving a century-long history of electoral corruption could support a state law limiting direct corporate spending for independent expenditures relating to candidates. *Western Tradition P'ship, Inc. v. Attorney General*, 271 P.3d 1 (Mont. 2011). The Montana Supreme Court canvassed the history of state elections, and allegations of improper behavior by corporate interests, since the enactment of its campaign laws in the early 20th century. It also relied on evidence that direct political spending by corporations could significantly affect the outcomes of current races because of the lower cost of campaigns in Montana relative to other states and the federal system. It finally held that the administrative burdens of establishing separate political committees were relatively minimal. It therefore distinguished the case from *Citizens United* by finding that the differences in historical and modern contexts provided Montana a compelling state interest to require corporations to fund independent expenditures through separate political committees. The U.S. Supreme Court put a stop to this creative approach, reversing the Montana decision in a terse decision that stated there can be "no serious doubt" that the outcome was controlled by *Citizens United Am. Tradition P'ship, Inc. v. Bullock*, 132 S.Ct. 2490 (2012).

2. *Regulation of Corporate Political Activity After* Citizens United. *Citizens United* considered only independent expenditures by corporations for electioneering communications; it did not change the longstanding rules requiring corporations to set up PACs to make contributions directly to federal candidates for office and to political parties. Federal law includes a series of limitations on contributions made by corporate PACs, all of which still apply. For example, a PAC can contribute only $5,000 to a federal congressional candidate during an election cycle and only $15,000 to a political party per year. (These were not raised or indexed by BCRA, unlike many other limitations on campaign contributions.) The *Citizens United* Court attempted to distinguish contribution limits, calling them "an accepted means to prevent *quid pro quo* corruption," but opponents of campaign finance limitations immediately mounted challenges, arguing that the reasoning of the opinion could not be limited to independent expenditures.

A district court in Virginia was persuaded that there is no difference, and that the ban on direct corporate contributions to candidates is unconstitutional. *United States v. Danielczyk*, 791 F. Supp. 2d 513 (E.D. Va. 2011). Judge Cacheris ruled that "[t]aken seriously, *Citizens United* requires that corporations and individuals be afforded equal rights to political speech, unqualified. * * * [I]ndividuals and corporations must have equal rights to engage in *both* independent expenditures *and* direct contributions." He noted that corporations would be governed by the contribution limitations that restrict individuals, and so any contributions would be limited and disclosed. The appellate court reversed this decision, holding that nothing in Supreme Court jurisprudence signaled a change in the treatment of contributions made by corporations. 683 F.3d 611 (4th Cir. 2012).[64]

Citizens United was an ideological nonprofit, so political spending relating to candidates and political parties lay at the heart of its mission. In contrast, some—perhaps many—for-profit corporations are not eager to take advantage of the ability to use general treasury funds for independent expenditures. Traditionally, corporate managers have preferred to spend money on lobbying members of Congress rather than on campaign activity because they have viewed lobbying as a more successful and direct means of influencing policy and accomplishing a company's political objectives. See Samuel Issacharoff, *On Political Corruption*, 124 Harv. L. Rev. 118, 131–32 (2010). Some corporations have also found that taking political positions in a public way can cause backlash from consumers or employees. Following the Court's decision in *Citizens United*, Target donated $150,000 in 2010 to a conservative pro-business organization, which spent funds to pay for television ads in Minnesota supporting Republican gubernatorial candidate Tom Emmer, who believes that same-sex marriage should be banned. When Target's contribution was disclosed, Target came under fire from gay-rights groups, and their calls for a nationwide boycott attracted media attention and hurt Target's image nationally.[65]

Which corporations do you expect will take advantage of the more liberal rules governing independent expenditures? Is their spending likely to be of greater help to incumbents or to challengers? In an early analysis of the effect of *Citizens United* on corporate spending during the 2010 and 2012 state legislative races, social scientists measured the change in the level of corporate political activity caused by *Citizens United* through sophisticated statistical techniques that take advantage of the fact that only a subset of all states were affected by the Supreme Court's decision because some states had never banned direct corporate expenditures. Tilman Klumpp, Hugo Mialon & Michael Williams, *The Business of American Democracy:* Citizens United, *Independent Spending, and Elections* (Feb. 3, 2014), SSRN Working Paper, http://papers.ssrn.com/sol3/papers.cfm?abstract_id=2312519. They found that the additional corporate spending tended to benefit Republican candidates more than Democrats, increasing by four percentage points the likelihood of a Republican winner in state legislative races. In some states, the impact was even greater, with 11 states witnessing a seven or more percentage increase in Republican election probabilities. One open question is whether this is a short-term consequence of the Supreme Court's decision, or whether opposing political forces will regroup to take advantage of the new rules.

With corporations now able to spend significantly more money on independent political expenditures, will businesses face pressure from legislators to play more active roles in federal campaigns? In an analysis of the corruption rationale in campaign finance cases published well before *Citizens United*, Professor David Strauss identified an element of extortion in a system "in which campaign contributions are freely exchanged for official action." Under these conditions, "there is a danger that

---

[64] For a discussion of the tension between *Citizens United* and case law allowing restrictions on corporate contributions to candidates, see Richard Hasen, Citizens United *and the Illusion of Coherence*, 109 Mich. L. Rev. 581, 615–17 (2011).

[65] See Taren Kingser & Patrick Schmidt, *Business in the Bulls-Eye? Target Corp. and the Limits of Campaign Finance Disclosure*, 11 Election L.J. 21 (2012) (describing the Target situation and drawing conclusions about the efficacy of disclosure laws).

representatives may coerce potential contributors, in effect extorting contributions by the threat that they will act against the contributor's interests." *Corruption, Equality, and Campaign Finance Reform*, 94 Colum. L. Rev. 1369, 1380 (1994). Are particular industries more likely to be the target of this manipulation by lawmakers seeking reelection? Is the possibility of such "extortion" reduced because *Citizens United* applies only to independent expenditures by corporations and unions, or can pressure still be applied? Is this kind of corruption likely to persuade the Supreme Court to uphold some restrictions on corporate political spending?

Some reform proposals that respond to *Citizens United* have centered on corporate law. For example, the Brennan Center for Justice proposed a Shareholder's Rights Act to require that shareholders vote at a public corporation's annual meeting to authorize the use of general treasury funds for political expenditures.[66] It would amend the Securities Exchange Act of 1934 to require periodic public disclosure of corporate political activities. If a public corporation made political expenditures without first obtaining shareholder approval, then the directors would be forced to repay the corporation, with interest. Several states began to consider similar changes in their corporate law codes. Is this a promising avenue for regulation of corporate political speech? For an intriguing proposal, see Lucian Bebchuk & Robert Jackson, *Corporate Political Speech: Who Decides?*, 124 Harv. L. Rev. 83 (2010) (arguing for different corporate rules to govern corporate political speech decisions than other business decisions, including shareholder participation, oversight by independent directors, and disclosure).[67]

3. *Developments Affecting Independent Expenditures and the Rise of "Super PACs."* The change ushered in by *Citizens United* receiving the most attention in recent elections is the rise of "Super PACs," nonprofit organizations that can receive unlimited amounts of money from donors to deploy in independent expenditures. Justice Kennedy's majority opinion stated, without equivocation, that independent expenditures do not give rise to corruption. "The appearance of influence or access * * * will not cause the electorate to lose faith in our democracy. * * * In fact, there is only scant evidence that independent expenditures even ingratiate. * * * Ingratiation and access, in any event, are not corruption." 558 U.S. at 360. This language may be more consequential for campaign finance regulation than the Court's decision to treat corporations like human beings with respect to independent expenditures. If such expenditures categorically cannot give rise to *quid pro quo* corruption, and that is the only acceptable state interest to justify regulation other than disclosure, then a great deal of the regulatory structure is open to challenge.

Not surprisingly, then, the D.C. Court of Appeals found no acceptable state interest limiting contributions to entities making independent expenditures in federal campaigns in a case immediately following the *Citizens United* decision. *SpeechNow.org v. Fed. Election Comm'n*, 599 F.3d 686 (D.C. Cir. 2010) (en banc). SpeechNow.org is an unincorporated nonprofit organization that promotes its view of the First Amendment in a variety of ways, including through advertisements supporting federal candidates who share its views and opposing those it believes are not sufficiently committed to the

---

[66] Ciara Torres-Spelliscy, *Corporate Campaign Spending: Giving Shareholders a Voice* 25–26 (2010).

[67] These efforts may be strengthened by scholarship finding that politically connected firms have lower firm value and poor corporate governance quality. Ashley Newton & Vahap Uysal, *The Impact of Political Connectedness on Firm Value and Corporate Policies: Evidence from* Citizens United (June 3, 2013), http://www.ou.edu/content/dam/price/Finance/CFS/paper/pdf/Newton%20and%20Uysal%20-%20Paper.pdf.

First Amendment. Donors wanted to contribute more than the $5,000 PAC limit to the nonprofit so that SpeechNow.org could produce ads attacking two incumbent lawmakers in the 2010 election cycle. Judge Sentelle wrote in a unanimous decision: "[B]ecause *Citizens United* holds that independent expenditures do not corrupt or give the appearance of corruption as a matter of law, then the government can have no anti-corruption interest in limiting contributions to independent expenditure-only organizations." *Id.* at 696. Consistent with *Citizens United*, the court allowed application of disclosure requirements and other administrative regulations to this organization. These rulings mean that independent-expenditure-only organizations are unconstrained by any limitations on contributions to them or any restrictions on their independent campaign expenditures advocating for the victory or defeat of federal candidates.

In response, the FEC released guidance on October 5, 2011, that freed independent PACs (those not associated with a company or union) from the $5,000 limit on individual contributions to them, including from corporations and unions.[68] If a PAC wishes to take advantage of this decision, it need not limit itself solely to independent expenditures, but it will have to maintain two accounts: one that can be used to make contributions to federal candidates and is subject to contribution limitations, and another that can be used solely for independent expenditures and is not subject to any limitations. These accounts join the independent-expenditure-only PACs that sprang up after *Citizens United*—around 150 by fall 2011, and 1,310 as of June 2013—and first earned the title "Super PAC."

Beginning with the 2010 congressional elections, the newly permissive regulatory environment for corporate spending has unleashed a torrent of money into the federal system, directed by ideological nonprofits and funded by wealthy Americans who can contribute unlimited amounts. Although both ends of the political spectrum can take advantage of the Super PAC structure, conservative groups initially have been more successful in raising money through these vehicles. In the 2012 election, nearly $1 billion in independent expenditures was spent in federal elections, with money coming from corporations, unions, and individuals.[69] Many of the Super PACs, although formally independent, are run by political operatives with close ties to candidates and parties. Richard Briffault, *Super PACs*, 96 Minn. L. Rev. 1644, 1674–82 (2012). However, political party leaders, especially in the Republican Party, are increasingly concerned that the power of Super PACs to deploy substantial sums of money may undermine larger party objectives.[70] Where ideological purity on a hot-button issue diverges from considerations of electability, for example, party leaders and some PAC leaders (those, for example, who are more sympathetic to the "Tea Party" agenda) may not have aligned interests. What does this factionalism within major parties mean for elections, including primary elections? Did *Citizens United* weaken political parties in ways that will undermine governance at the federal level? How will parties evolve to account for this change in the campaign finance landscape?

---

[68] Federal Election Commission, FEC Statement on *Carey v. FEC*: Reporting Guidance for Political Committees that Maintain a Non-Contribution Account, Oct. 6, 2011, http://www.fec.gov/press/press2011/20111006postcarey.shtml.

[69] Reity O'Brien & Andrea Fuller, Citizen United *Ruling Opened Door to $933 Million in New Election Spending*, NBCNews.com, Jan. 16, 2013, http://investigations.nbcnews.com/_news/2013/01/16/16530772–citizen-united-ruling-opened-door-to–933–million-in-new-election-spending?lite.

[70] Eliza Newlin Carney, *Who Owns the GOP?*, Cong. Q., May 6, 2013, at 804.

Justice Stevens predicted in his dissent that political parties would be harmed by *Citizens United*: "By removing one of its central components, today's ruling makes a hash out of BCRA's 'delicate and interconnected regulatory scheme.' *McConnell.* Consider just one example of the distortions that will follow: Political parties are barred under BCRA from soliciting or spending 'soft money,' funds that are not subject to the statute's disclosure requirements or its source and amount limitations. Going forward, corporations and unions will be free to spend as much general treasury money as they wish on ads that support or attack specific candidates, whereas national parties will not be able to spend a dime of soft money on ads of any kind. The Court's ruling thus dramatically enhances the role of corporations and unions—and the narrow interests they represent—vis-à-vis the role of political parties—and the broad coalitions they represent—in determining who will hold public office." 558 U.S. at 412. Nathaniel Persily agreed that "political parties as institutions were probably the losers," but then wondered whether that would improve campaigns or affect them negatively. "[T]he extreme cohesiveness and polarization of the political parties might be countered by independent, non-party bases of support that influence candidates. At the same time (and more likely from my view), the decision might polarize the parties even further, because independent spenders tend to come from and support extreme positions."[71] Of course, after BCRA was passed, drastically limiting soft-money contributions to political parties, many predicted that parties would be significantly weakened, while groups that often focused on only one issue would disproportionately influence federal elections. That did not happen as a result of BCRA or *McConnell.* Are the new developments in the regulatory landscape likely to be more destructive of political parties?

One change in the jurisprudential landscape after *Citizens United* was the Court's decision in 2014 to strike down aggregate limits on federal campaign contributions. *McCutcheon v. Fed. Election Comm'n*, 134 S.Ct. 1434 (2014). The plurality opinion reasoned that, because aggregate limits did not directly combat the narrowed notion of *quid pro quo* corruption, they impermissibly burdened political speech. Even without an overall limit, the limit on the amount of a contribution that can be made to any particular candidate sufficiently protects against *quid pro quo* corruption and its appearance. To the extent that one donor might give the maximum contribution to many candidates and organizations in one political party and thus lead party leaders to appreciate that level of support, "[t]hat gratitude stems from the basic nature of the party system." Moreover, such contributions, all within the base limit to each candidate or organization, do not allow a donor to control a particular officeholder's official duties—the system has determined that contributions below the limit do not implicate *quid pro quo* corruption.

With the new opportunity for the wealthy to donate broadly to many candidates and committees supporting those candidates, will the influence of Super PACs be reduced? The Chief Justice in *McCutcheon* suggested it might: "The existing aggregate limits may in fact encourage the movement of money away from entities subject to disclosure. Because individuals' direct contributions are limited, would-be donors may turn to other avenues for political speech. * * * Individuals can, for example, contribute unlimited amounts to 501(c) organizations, which are not required to publicly disclose their donors. * * * Such organizations spent some $300 million on independent

---

[71] Nathaniel Persily, Citizens United: *Qui Bono and Que Sera*, Balkinization blog (Jan. 25, 2010), http:// balkin.blogspot.com/2010/01/citizens-united-qui-bono-and-que-sera.html.

expenditures in the 2012 election cycle." Similarly, the ability of donors to directly and substantially support a political party through its many committees, candidates, and subsidiaries may rejuvenate these flexible political actors and again prove wrong those who predicted the decline of political parties in elections after *Citizens United*.

The role of corporations in politics, especially nonprofit corporations that seem wholly focused now on influencing elections, will continue to be the subject of scrutiny and regulatory efforts as the new post-*Citizens United* world evolves. The most recent proposal came from the Internal Revenue Service, which issued for comment proposed new guidelines regarding the political activity of nonprofits organized under Section 501(c)(4) of the Internal Revenue Code. *Guidance for Tax-Exempt Social Welfare Organizations on Candidate-Related Political Activities*, 78 Fed. Reg. 71535 (Nov. 29, 2013). If new guidelines are adopted, it will be the first time since 1959 that the IRS has amended the regulations for Section 501(c)(4) organizations, which are civic and social welfare organizations that promote the "common good and general welfare." These proposed amendments would significantly restrict the ability of such groups to engage in certain candidate-related political activity because such activity would not count toward the "social welfare" efforts that justify their tax-exempt status. Other aspects of the rules might actually increase certain kinds of political activity, for example, by clarifying that some issue ads aired well before an election would not be considered candidate-related political activity, and providing more certainty in an arena previously governed by nebulous "facts and circumstances" tests. The proposal will be altered, likely substantially, during the notice-and-comment period because it has been greeted with concern by groups across the political spectrum. Any final guidance will doubtlessly spawn litigation, so any change will occur well after the 2014 elections.

4.   *Challenges to Disclosure and the Rise of "Dark Money."* For many, after *Citizens United*, disclosure appears to be the least problematic form of regulation from a constitutional perspective (only Justice Thomas has objected to disclosure) and perhaps the only kind of law that is likely to work. Far-reaching disclosure statutes will raise constitutional issues; ironically, the more a law succeeds in revealing the identities of supporters and opponents, the more serious the constitutional concern. Disclosure certainly chills some kinds of political speech, especially when it links the speaker to disfavored groups or ideas, and some individuals and organizations may be less likely to participate in political debate if their involvement will be publicized. In other contexts, the Court has held that the First Amendment protects anonymous political speech. See *McIntyre v. Ohio Elections Comm'n*, 514 U.S. 334 (1995) (protecting a person's decision to remain anonymous while distributing campaign literature for issue-based election).

In *Buckley*, the Supreme Court held that FECA's provisions requiring the disclosure of contributors to a political group were constitutional on their face but might conceivably be unconstitutional as applied to a given group; *McConnell* echoed that with respect to BCRA. Given "the extensive body of state and federal legislation subjecting Communist Party members to civil disability and criminal liability, * * * the history of governmental surveillance and harassment of Communist Party members, as well as * * * the desire of contributors to the [Communist Party] to remain anonymous," are disclosure requirements invalid as applied to the Communist Party?[72] What other kinds of groups could make the required showing to avoid disclosure?

Disclosure poses a practical problem as well. The more complex the reporting requirements, the more costly the burden placed on those who must provide information to the state. Moreover, this burden affects grassroots groups with few monetary resources and less access to consultants more severely than it does well-funded groups and sophisticated political players. See Dick Carpenter & Jeffrey Milyo, *The Public's Right to Know Versus Compelled Speech: What Does Social Science Research Tell Us About the Benefits and Costs of Campaign Finance Disclosure in Non-Candidate Elections?*, 40 Fordham Urb. L.J. 603 (2012) (identifying costs and burdens in ballot measure campaigns, some of which would also apply to groups active in candidate elections through independent expenditures). Although exemptions or reduced reporting requirements for small groups or individuals spending little money can reduce some of the burden, exemptions also increase the complexity of the regulatory regime.

Clearly, enhanced disclosure statutes are required for voters to have full information about the sources of funding in the post-*Citizens United* world. Although Section 527 groups are required to disclose their donors, more money is being injected into the federal political system anonymously now than in previous recent elections because of less rigorous disclosure requirements for other types of affiliated nonprofits and lax enforcement by federal regulatory bodies. Increasingly, political groups, including Super PACs, are using other nonprofit structures, such as 501(c)(4) social welfare organizations. One advantage of the 501(c)(4) structure is that, unlike Section 527 groups, they are under no legal requirement to disclose their individual donors, although such donors do not receive a tax deduction. So a Super PAC can set up an associated 501(c)(4) to engage in educational activities and keep the sources of funding for that closely related activity shrouded from scrutiny.

The organization of political groups can be stunningly complex, as one group may use various nonprofit structures—including, to a limited extent, charitable 501(c)(3) organizations—to arrange its political activities to provide the most flexibility, the desired level of protection against disclosure, and the greatest ability to raise funds. A study by the Center for Responsive Politics concludes that 48.8% of non-party, independent political spending was fully disclosed publicly in 2010[73]; the rest has been called "dark money." The Center concluded that, in the 2012 federal elections, more than $310 million of campaign money was spent in ways that evaded disclosure, the vast majority from conservative groups.[74] Even 527 organizations manage to evade or significantly delay disclosure by receiving contributions from nonprofits not subject to disclosure themselves or from corporations that do not disclose their owners or go out of business soon after the donation.

Inspired by the Court's strong affirmation of disclosure provisions, Democrats in the Senate and the House introduced the Democracy Is Strengthened by Casting Light

---

[72] See *Fed. Election Comm'n v. Hall-Tyner Election Campaign Comm.*, 678 F.2d 416, 419 (2d Cir. 1982). See also *Brown v. Socialist Workers '74 Campaign Comm.*, 459 U.S. 87 (1982), in which the Court struck down an Ohio statute requiring disclosure of contributors.

[73] See Center for Responsive Politics, *Outside Spending by Disclosure, Excluding Party Committees*, http://www.opensecrets.org/outsidespending/disclosure.php (visited Jan. 29, 2012).

[74] Thomas Edsall, *Dark Money Politics*, N.Y. Times, June 12, 2013.

On Spending in Elections (DISCLOSE) Act in 2010. The Act provided for enhanced disclosure provisions for nonprofit and for-profit corporations, as well as unions. These included requirements that a CEO or organization leader appear at the end of a broadcast advertisement to affirm that she "approves this message"; that the top five contributors to the organization be listed on the screen; and that groups inform their shareholders and members about political spending. It would also have banned spending by corporations with substantial foreign ownership or control, and political spending by government contractors and recipients of federal bailout funds for banks and other financial institutions. Are any of these provisions constitutionally problematic? What state interests justify the proposed regulations?

The DISCLOSE Act faced significant opposition when it reached the floor of the House—opposition that extended beyond the expected disapproval of most Republicans. First, conservative Democrats were concerned about the opposition of groups such as the U.S. Chamber of Commerce, the National Federation of Independent Business, and the National Association of Realtors. Most importantly, however, these Democrats, facing reelection battles in the fall in conservative states, demanded that congressional leadership and the White House agree to exempt the National Rifle Association (NRA) from the bill's coverage.[75] An exemption was drafted that applied to organizations with more than one million members, with members in all 50 states, that had been in existence for more than 10 years, and that raised 15% or less of their funds from corporations. When it turned out that only the NRA met these requirements, the exemption was amended to cover organizations with more than 500,000 members, thereby also exempting the Sierra Club, the Humane Society, and the American Association of Retired Persons. Not only did this exemption call into question the constitutionality of the bill—because it is difficult to construct a justification (other than sheer political power) for treating these organizations differently from all others seeking to exercise their First Amendment rights—but it also provoked a backlash from liberal Democrats. The bill, containing the exemption, managed to pass the House by a vote of 219–206 in June 2010, but faced united Republican opposition in the Senate. The final Senate vote was 59–39, one vote short of the votes required to cut off a filibuster.

In the absence of meaningful federal action to shine the light on dark money, some states have adopted aggressive stances to disclosure of political activity in state elections. For example, in October 2012, $11 million—perhaps the largest sum given in a statewide contest without its source being revealed—was injected into a California ballot measure campaign through a committee actively opposing the Governor's proposal to increase taxes and provide money for higher education. Another $4 million from a separate source was also sent to a California campaign committee from an out-of-state nonprofit. California's election law watchdog, the Fair Political Practices Commission (FPPC), worked to track down the donor behind the contribution, which is not subject to contribution limits because its support related to a ballot measure. The FPPC worked through layers of nonprofit organizations both in and outside the state, ultimately tracing the money to a Virginia-based nonprofit group, Americans for Job Security, associated with operatives who have been affiliated with the conservative

---

[75] For a description of this legislative saga, see Kenneth Vogel, Jonathan Allen & John Bresnahan, *How Dems' NRA Loophole Backfired*, Politico.com (June 18, 2010), http://www.politico.com/news/stories/0610/38713.html. See also Richard Briffault, *Updating Disclosure for the New Era of Independent Spending*, 27 J.L. & Pol. 683 (2012).

Koch brothers.[76] In the end, California imposed a record $16 million in penalties on two California campaign committees and two Arizona nonprofits for failing to appropriately report their campaign activities. At the same time, the FPPC adopted new regulations designed to pierce through the veil of the nonprofit form to determine the ultimate source behind funding being deployed in state elections; other states are enacting or considering enhanced disclosure statutes aimed at independent spending.[77] These developments at the state level are only part of the regulatory picture at the subnational level, our final topic in this chapter.

C. STATE REFORMS AND PUBLIC FINANCING

The past two decades have witnessed significant state activity regarding campaign finance. In 1980, 29 states placed no limits on individual contributions to candidates running for the state legislature; today, only four states place no limits on contributions, although another seven states impose only minimal restrictions.[78] Several states have adopted sweeping campaign finance reforms, often through ballot initiatives. State contribution limits can be significantly lower than the federal limits, with a few as low as $500 per candidate from an individual. See *Randall v. Sorrell*, 548 U.S. 230 (2006) (plurality opinion striking down very stringent statewide limits in Vermont). Some empirical studies suggest that the state reforms may fall victim to the hydraulic quality of political money. Evidence from Oregon, for example, indicates that, after the people passed a measure imposing a cap of $100 for contributions in statewide races, independent expenditures increased sharply in the next election.[79]

The other innovative state reform, largely a result of ballot initiatives, is public financing. Until recently, most state public financing systems had withstood significant judicial challenge; now their fate—at least as comprehensive systems designed to encourage robust participation by many serious candidates—is uncertain. Consistent with the presidential system upheld in *Buckley*, state public financing systems are all voluntary, providing public money to candidates who agree either not to accept any private money (see Me. Rev. Stat. Ann. tit. 21–A, § 1121 *et seq.*) or to abide by strict spending limits (see Vt. Stat. Ann. tit. 17, § 2853 *et seq.*).[80] In Maine, for, example, candidates qualify for public funds by raising seed

---

[76] Peter Stone, *California Officials Turn Up the Heat on Secretive "Dark Money" Groups*, Huffington Post, March 25, 2013; Chris Megerian & Anthony York, *California Probe of Campaign Donations Sheds Light on "Dark Money,"* L.A. Times, Nov. 3, 2013.

[77] See Elizabeth Garrett, *Campaign Finance in the Hybrid Realm of Recall Elections*, 97 Minn. L. Rev. 1654, 1696–97 (2013) (discussing California regulations and approaches to disclosure with respect to nonprofit groups); Matea Gold, Chris Megerian & Mark Barabak, *States Try to Tackle "Secret Money" in Politics*, L.A. Times, May 2, 2013 (describing efforts in Maryland and New York).

[78] National Conference of State Legislatures, *Contribution Limits: An Overview*, Oct. 3, 2011, http://www.ncsl.org/legislatures-elections/elections/campaign-contribution-limits-overview.aspx.

[79] See Eliza Newlin Carney, *Taking on the Fat Cats*, Nat'l J., Jan. 18, 1997, at 110. Oregon's stringent limits were struck down by the state supreme court in 1997. *Vannatta v. Keisling*, 931 P.2d 770, 773–74 (Or. 1997). See also David Schultz, *Money, Politics, and Campaign Finance Reform Law in the States* 20–21 (2002) (finding rise in soft-money and independent expenditures in some states with restrictions on individual contributions).

[80] See Elizabeth Daniel, *Subsidizing Political Campaigns: The Varieties and Values of Public Financing* (2000) (a report by the Brennan Center for Justice describing various kinds of public financing); Jason Frasco, *Full Public Funding: An Effective and Legally Viable Model for Campaign Finance Reform in the States*, 92 Cornell L. Rev. 733 (2007) (student note) (describing laws and legal challenges).

money from voters making small contributions; this threshold ensures that recipients demonstrate a level of popular support.

The Arizona Citizens Clean Elections Act was adopted by initiative in 1998, and created a voluntary public financing system available to candidates for statewide office. Candidates who opt in to the system and receive public money must accept certain restrictions, such as limiting expenditures of their own funds to $500, participating in at least one public debate, and adhering to an expenditure cap (which differs according to the office sought). Publicly financed candidates receive a specified grant of money from the state and, under some circumstances, qualify for additional "matching funds." Payment of this additional grant of public money is triggered if the expenditures of a privately financed opponent, combined with independent expenditures in support of that privately financed opponent, exceed the initial public grant to the publicly financed candidate. After that trigger, the state would provide the publicly financed candidate essentially a dollar-for-dollar match of the amount spent by her opponent. It was this matching funds provision that was ruled unconstitutional by the Supreme Court in the following case.

Arizona Free Enterprise Club's Freedom Club PAC v. Bennett
131 S.Ct. 2806 (2011).

In a 5–4 decision written by **Chief Justice Roberts**, the Court held that the matching funds provision triggered by the expenditures relating to a privately financed candidate unconstitutionally burdened political speech without serving a permissible compelling state interest. The plaintiffs were candidates who did not opt in to the public financing system and independent groups that wanted to support such candidates. In holding in favor of plaintiffs' position, the Court found *Davis v. Fed. Election Comm'n*, 554 U.S. 724 (2008), the case striking down BCRA's "millionaire opponent" amendment, to control the analysis. Although neither BCRA nor the Arizona law imposed a cap on any candidate's expenditures without her consent, both imposed a burden on certain kinds of spending by a privately financed candidate by offering her publicly financed opponent a substantial financial benefit. In the case of BCRA, the benefit was higher contribution limits for candidates facing opponents who spent significant personal resources; in the case of the Arizona law, the benefit was additional public money to candidates who were facing privately financed candidates spending over a certain threshold. The Court found the Arizona law especially problematic. With respect to BCRA, "[t]he candidate who benefited from the increased [contribution] limits still had to go out and raise the funds. He may or may not have been able to do so. * * * Here [in the Arizona law] the benefit to the publicly financed candidate is the direct and automatic release of public money. That is a far heavier burden than in *Davis*." There might even be a multiplier effect for the privately financed candidate facing several publicly financed opponents, all of whom would benefit from the additional subsidies.

Furthermore, the additional grant of public money could be triggered not only by the opponent's expenditures but also by the spending of independent groups to support that candidate. "That disparity in control—giving money directly to a publicly financed candidate, in response to independent expenditures that cannot be coordinated with the privately funded candidate—is a substantial advantage for the publicly financed candidate." Once the triggering amount of expenditures was reached, an independent group would be faced with a choice that the Court found unacceptable. "The group can either opt to change its message from one addressing the merits of the candidates to one addressing the merits of an issue, or refrain from speaking altogether." Taking these effects of the statute into account, the majority found a substantial burden on political speech that would reduce the amount of speech by privately funded candidates and groups supporting them.

The Court then turned to the state interest advanced to support the trigger mechanism and found a dispute as to whether it was the permissible interest of preventing *quid pro quo* corruption or the desire to equalize candidate resources and thereby level the political playing field. The Chief Justice was persuaded that the latter motive was the sole support for this aspect of Arizona's public financing statute. Not only did the provision operate explicitly to equalize resources, but the statutory section setting it out also was entitled "Equal funding of candidates." Since *Buckley*, the Court has rejected regulating campaign speech to serve an equalization rationale, and *Davis* warned that "[l]eveling electoral opportunities means making and implementing judgments about which strengths should be permitted to contribute to the outcome of an election." The Court concluded: " 'Leveling the playing field' can sound like a good thing. But in a democracy, campaigning for office is not a game. It is a critically important form of speech."

Finally, the majority dismissed the argument that a corruption justification might be served by the trigger mechanism. First, burdening the candidate's expenditures of her own funds is completely unrelated to a concern about *quid pro quo* corruption because use of personal funds actually reduces the appearance of corruption by special interests. In *Citizens United*, the Court similarly held that independent expenditures cannot lead to corruption or the appearance of corruption, so burdening that speech could not be linked to the asserted state interest. Finally, the Court noted that Arizona has "ascetic" contribution limits of $840 for statewide candidates and $410 for legislative candidates. Combined with strict disclosure laws, these low contribution limits eliminate the threat of influence by large donors. Therefore, "it is hard to imagine what marginal corruption deterrence could be generated by the matching funds provision."

Justice Kagan issued a blistering dissent. She looked at the Arizona system as a comprehensive regulatory scheme, with the matching funds provision as a key component that ensured the willingness of candidates to opt in to public financing. "[C]andidates will choose to sign up only if the subsidy provided enables them to run competitive races." The state faces a dilemma in crafting a system that meets this essential goal: if the grant of public money is too low, no candidate will participate and the anticorruption interest that public financing serves generally will not be vindicated; if the subsidy is too high, the fiscal demands of the program may be unsustainable. The trigger provision that Arizona constructed solves that dilemma by allowing adjustments only in certain races, and it assures candidates considering public financing that they will not be placed in an untenable situation should they face a well-heeled opponent.

The dissent also took issue with the majority's characterization of the provision as restricting or burdening speech. "The law has quite the opposite effect: It subsidizes and so produces *more* political speech. * * * Except in a world gone topsy-turvy, additional campaign speech and electoral competition is not a First Amendment injury." Justice Kagan noted that all candidates are eligible to participate in public financing so the law does not discriminate against any particular set of ideas or ideological positions. No one is denied access to the state's subsidy unless she chooses not to participate in the system. "[W]hat petitioners demand is essentially a right to quash others' speech through the prohibition of a (universally available) subsidy program. Petitioners are able to convey their ideas without public financing—and they would prefer the field to themselves, so that they can speak free from response." In sharply worded language, the dissent observed that, after refusing the state's offer of public financing, the petitioners "are making a novel argument: that Arizona violated *their* First Amendment rights by disbursing funds to *other* speakers even though they could have received (but chose to spurn) the same financial assistance. Some people might call that *chutzpah*."

The majority and dissent fundamentally disagreed about whether to consider the matching funds provision separately from the rest of the regulatory structure. For the majority, the provision was assessed as a stand-alone feature of the law and therefore had only a marginal effect on reducing corruption. When viewed in isolation from the rest of the statute, the matching funds device seemed solely focused on providing equal resources for candidates, whether they opted in to the state system or chose to remain outside of it. For Justice Kagan, the provision was critical to the success of the Act: although serving as "no more than a disbursement mechanism * * * it is also the thing that makes the whole Clean Elections Act work." To the extent that there was ample evidence that a primary motivation for adopting the Clean Elections Act was to combat corruption and the influence of special interests in state politics, the entire Act could withstand First Amendment scrutiny.

The dissent concluded in the more deferential tone of the pre-*Citizens United* case law: "This case arose because Arizonans wanted their government to work on behalf of all the State's people. On the heels of a political scandal involving the near-routine purchase of legislators' votes, Arizonans passed a law designed to sever political candidates' dependence on large contributors. * * * The legislation that Arizona's voters enacted was the product of deep thought and care. It put into effect a public financing system that attracted large numbers of candidates at a sustainable cost to the State's taxpayers. The system discriminated against no ideas and prevented no speech. * * * No fundamental principle of our Constitution backs the Court's ruling; to the contrary, it is the law struck down today that fostered both the vigorous competition of ideas and its ultimate object—a government responsive to the will of the people."

The Chief Justice ended his majority opinion by limiting the breadth of the holding. "We do not today call into question the wisdom of public financing as a means of funding political candidacy. That is not our business." The Court reaffirmed its view in *Buckley* that public financing systems designed to serve the anticorruption rationale would be consistent with the First Amendment. Arizona went too far with its matching funds provision because it "inhibit[s] robust and wide-open political debate without sufficient justification." Thus, the fate of other state public financing systems that do not include the matching funds provision struck down by the Supreme Court was not determined by *Arizona Free Enterprise*. (Matching funds provisions in other states were immediately placed in jeopardy and suffered the fate of Arizona's. For example, the matching funds provision in Maine was declared unconstitutional by a stipulated agreement less than one month after *Arizona Free Enterprise* was issued.) The decision will surely spur more legal attacks on public financing and has injected uncertainty into an aspect of campaign finance regulation that had been seen as relatively unproblematic from a constitutional perspective.[81] Review some of the public financing laws—perhaps one in your state—and consider how parts of them would fare if scrutinized by the Roberts Court. What mechanisms are still available to tailor the amount of any public subsidy to the features of a particular race to ensure that serious candidates will opt to participate at the outset and that competitive races will ensue?[82]

* * *

One question facing advocates of public financing is whether the reform has the intended effects on elections. Interestingly, a study of the effect of the trigger mechanism ruled unconstitutional in *Arizona Free Enterprise* had revealed that publicly financed candidates continued to feel at a disadvantage in campaigns. They were often forced into defensive positions, with their opponents withholding expenditures in excess of the threshold until the last days of the campaign, giving the subsidized candidates little time to deploy additional resources effectively. Had that part of the law remained in effect, it would have been interesting to see the effect of later expenditures of money on voter mobilization and other aspects of the campaign. Michael Miller, *Gaming Arizona: Public Money and Shifting Candidate Strategies*, 41 PS 527 (2008).

In 2010, the Government Accountability Office (GAO) released a study of the effects of full public financing in Maine and Arizona since 2000 (pre-*Arizona Free Enterprise*, which struck down the matching funds provision found in both systems). *Campaign Finance Reform: Experiences of Two States That Offered Full Public Funding for Political Candidates* (2010). In both states, the GAO found that more candidates participated in public financing over time. In Maine, participating candidates were more likely to win, while in Arizona nonparticipating candidates were more successful. Differences might be a result of incumbency, partisan affiliation, or other characteristics not evident from the data. Changes in interest group participation and citizens' confidence in government after adoption of the Clean Elections Laws were not statistically significant, nor were measures of competition, except for a reduced margin of victory for winners, which might have been caused by other factors. Independent expenditures increased from 2000 to 2008 in both states, although that may have been influenced in Maine by a change in what counted as an independent expenditure.

Problem 2–8. You are a staff member of a state senator who seeks to adopt comprehensive campaign finance reform. In light of the Roberts Court precedents, provide your recommendation of the most aggressive legislation that is likely to withstand constitutional challenge. The senator has asked you to concentrate on the design of disclosure statutes; assessing the efficacy of contribution limits in the context of unlimited independent expenditures; and the promise, and challenges, of electioneering through the Internet and social media. Are there any provisions you would recommend that might give your boss—an incumbent in a relatively competitive district—pause as likely to make reelection more difficult? Even if she is willing to go forward because of her commitment to reform, such provisions could make legislative enactment unlikely. Would you recommend that the senator consider the avenue of

---

[81] See Stephen Ansolabehere, Arizona Free Enterprise v. Bennett *and the Problem of Campaign Finance*, 2011 Sup. Ct. Rev. 39 (concluding that the only options after *Arizona Free Enterprise* and other Roberts Court cases is either full public financing or full private financing of elections).

[82] See Nicholas Bamman, *Campaign Financing: Public Funding after* Bennett, 27 J.L. & Pol. 323 (2012) (providing some ideas for systems that could pass constitutional muster).

direct democracy, assuming it is available in your state? We will return to this mechanism for reform in Chapter 4.

CHAPTER 3

STRUCTURES OF LEGISLATIVE DELIBERATION

■ ■ ■

Chapter 2 discussed different theories of representation, describing Hanna Pitkin's argument that representatives can be viewed in three different ways: as a microcosm of the larger electorate, as agents of the voters who elect them, or as trustees for the public interest. In this chapter, we consider the implications each theory might have for decisions that legislators make once elected.

In connection with the legislative deliberations of representatives, agency theorists suggest that the representative should mirror the views of her constituents, while trusteeship theorists direct the representative to use her judgment to advance the common good. Pitkin argues that the tension between these two views is largely a false one. First, a representative necessarily acts in a dual capacity most of the time: she is acting for her constituents, but on matters about which they have given little informed thought. Second, what the representative thinks is right and what the people want "normally * * * will coincide, and * * * when they fail to coincide there is a reason." The duty is to do what serves the "objective interest" of the people—so when the representative acts against the apparent desires of the constituents, she must be able to justify that action in terms of the long-range interests of society. Overall, Pitkin argues, representative government is most legitimate when it both promotes the public interest and responds to the people's desires over time.

Pitkin's general position that representative government should be broadly responsive to, but not specifically directed by, private preferences is widely accepted. Her more specific position, that representative government should sometimes seek to further the "public interest" and transform private preferences, is appealing to a republican vision of government. It seems consistent with, and surely is inspired by, Madison's argument in *Federalist #10* that "the public voice, pronounced by the representatives of the people, will be more consonant to the public good than if pronounced by the people themselves, convened for the purpose." Nonetheless, the Madison-Pitkin position is subject to a pluralist critique. Much pluralist political theory questions whether there is such a thing as the "public interest" separate from aggregated private interests. Even if there is a public interest, how can it reliably be determined? When Congressman Howard Smith (D–Va.) opposed the Civil Rights Act in 1963–64, most of his constituents probably agreed with him. Was his vote in the public interest of Virginia? In retrospect, we think it was not, because over time the principles of that statute have made Virginia a "better" place. We believe that Smith was a poor and shortsighted representative. He might have responded that a vote for the bill would have killed his reelection chances, denying him the opportunity to work for other policies and depriving Virginians of a senior and powerful representative.[1]

Both pluralist (agency) and republican (trusteeship) theorists emphasize the importance of legislative deliberation, although they view the process differently. Pluralism requires representatives to aggregate the preferences of various interests and work out compromises to satisfy as many interests as possible and perhaps also to satisfy the most intense preferences of each relevant group. To do this, the representatives must deliberate, both with their constituents and supporting groups, and with their colleagues in the legislature. As we discussed in Chapter 1, deliberation may help to solve some of the pathologies of majority rule (like cycling), thereby allowing legislatures to reach rational and relatively stable outcomes. Consistent with republican theory, deliberation seeks out useful information and points of view that advance the collective understanding of common goals and that perhaps also transform the preferences of political citizens.

Both pluralist and republican theorists consider legislative deliberation illegitimate if it is corrupt. The theorists differ, however, in their view of what unacceptably warps the deliberative process, as we saw in the discussion of corruption and campaign finance reform in the previous chapter. Virtually everyone agrees that a deliberative process is corrupt if it is tainted by monetary bribes, physical coercion or threats, or other cheating by forces outside the legislature. Section 1 of this chapter explores issues associated with a relatively straightforward conception of corruption in the legislative process, especially as it relates to laws governing bribery, extortion, and conflicts of interest. As we will see, however, even uncontroversial notions of corruption become fuzzy when we move away from the obvious examples of bribery and extortion. In that regard, we turn to lobbying, which is expressly protected by the First Amendment but is also a possible source of corruption in the legislative process, at least according to republican theory. We also provide the current legal regime regulating lobbying contacts, a regime shaped since 1995 by the Lobbying Disclosure Act (LDA), Pub. L. 104–65, 109 Stat. 691 (codified at 2 U.S.C. §§ 1601–1607). In 2007, LDA was strengthened as part of a larger ethics reform effort in the wake of several corruption scandals involving members of Congress and lobbyists.

Section 2 sets forth some of the substantive constitutional rules designed to decrease interest group pressure on lawmakers and to impede legislative deal-making that often leads to omnibus legislation full of provisions that individually could garner only minority support. We will discuss the item vetoes provided to governors in most states and assess a federal law that purported to give the same kind of power to the President. This section also suggests some tensions between legislative immunities that are designed to preserve the independence of lawmakers and efforts to keep the legislative process free from bribery, extortion, and other forms of obvious and unhealthy corruption.

Finally, Section 3 identifies several constitutional rules that require particular processes be followed to enact laws. In a few cases, courts have required that some decisions be made by Congress, rather than other governmental institutions,

---

[1]   Smith was defeated in the Democratic primary in 1966, notwithstanding his opposition to civil rights.

because the legislature's institutional features better ensure the democratic pedigree of the decision. These mandates are not focused on the kind of corruption we have discussed in the preceding sections, but are designed to "improve" the legislative process. This material introduces an influential concept first articulated by a former justice of the Oregon Supreme Court: *due process of lawmaking.* Justice Linde argued in *Due Process of Lawmaking*, 55 Neb. L. Rev. 197 (1976), that the legislative process should be designed to produce "rational lawmaking," which he described as follows: "It would obligate legislators to inform themselves in some fashion about the existing conditions on which the proposed law would operate, and about the likelihood that the proposal would in fact further the intended purpose. In order to weigh the anticipated benefits for some against the burdens the law would impose on others, legislators must inform themselves about those burdens. * * * The projections and assessments of conditions and consequences must presumably take some account of evidence, at least in committee sessions. * * * The committee must explain its factual and value premises to the full body. Surely there is no place for a vote on final passage by members who have never read even a summary of the bill, let alone a committee report or a resume of the factual documentation." *Id.* at 223–24. Can we devise procedures that facilitate due process of lawmaking, and should it be a constitutional principle that courts use to review statutes?

1. REGULATING DELIBERATION TO COMBAT "CORRUPTION"

The Anglo-American tradition has a rich history of regulating corrupt legislators through laws regulating behavior falling into such categories as bribery, extortion, and conflicts of interest—all of which have received considerable elaboration in recent years. What is properly prohibited under these categories? Consider the following conduct:

- Senator Doris Soaper agrees to support a bill exempting labor unions from certain tax liabilities in return for a promise by union leaders in her state that they will support her reelection bid.

- Senator Soaper and her husband attend a lavish cruise on the Potomac, hosted by the AFL-CIO. Pending labor legislation is discussed over drinks and a lobster dinner. The next day, Senator Soaper votes for a bill exempting labor unions from certain tax liabilities.

- Senator Soaper's law firm represents labor unions in matters before the National Labor Relations Board and derives substantial revenue from that activity. Senator Soaper introduces and supports a bill to exempt labor unions from certain tax liabilities.

- Senator Soaper has established a legal defense fund to raise money to pay lawyers representing her in an investigation of her legislative activities related to the AFL-CIO's agenda. All the high-ranking officials of that union contribute $50,000 each to her fund, which is run by a group of her supporters.

Should any of this conduct be regulated? Prohibited?

This section will briefly consider these broad questions. We shall proceed in three parts: Part A will examine laws prohibiting bribery and accepting gratuities. It will also examine federal law prohibiting extortion, including obtaining property under color of official right. Part B will set forth various conflict of interest rules prompted by concerns of legislative corruption. Part C will analyze legislation passed at the federal level to regulate the activity of lobbying, which is essential for a well-functioning democracy but sometimes seems to veer into the realm of corruption.

As you read these materials, consider whether it makes sense as a policy matter or as a constitutional matter to regulate political conduct as extensively as we do. Glenn Parker argues that the most effective mechanism to constrain corrupt behavior is a lawmaker's interest in maintaining a reputation for ethical behavior because, at least in the House, it increases the length of the lawmaker's career and enhances his chances of attractive post-elective employment. *Self-Policing in Politics: The Political Economy of Reputational Controls on Politicians* (2004). How do ethics codes benefit lawmakers who want to establish a reputation for trustworthiness? Are reputational controls sufficient given the temptations of elective office?

A. BRIBERY AND EXTORTION

Anti-bribery statutes might serve three different purposes: (1) to protect the integrity of the public servant's decisionmaking process, so that decisions are made to advance the public interest and not the decisionmaker's private agenda; (2) to avoid the appearance of unfairness and abuse of office; and (3) to assure equal access of all citizens to the services of public servants.[2] For such reasons, the United States and all the states have anti-bribery laws.

The federal bribery statute, 18 U.S.C. § 201(b)–(c) (as amended), provides in part:

(b) Whoever—

(1) directly or indirectly, corruptly gives, offers or promises anything of value to any public official or person who has been selected to be a public official, or offers or promises any public official or any person who has been selected to be a public official to give anything of value to any other person or entity, with intent—

(A) to influence any official act; or

---

[2] See John Noonan, Jr., *Bribes* 704 (1984); Beth Nolan, *Public Interest, Private Income: Conflicts and Control Limits on the Outside Income of Government Officials*, 87 Nw. U.L. Rev. 57, 71–80 (1992). For an analysis of the federal statute with citations to relevant case law, see Nicholas Jarcho & Neal Shechter, *Public Corruption*, 49 Am. Crim. L. Rev. 1107 (2012).

(B) to influence such public official or person who has been selected to be a public official to commit or aid in committing, or collude in, or allow, any fraud * * * on the United States; or

(C) to induce such public official or such person who has been selected to be a public official to do or omit to do any act in violation of the lawful duty of such official or person;

(2) being a public official or person selected to be a public official, directly or indirectly, corruptly demands, seeks, receives, accepts, or agrees to receive or accept anything of value personally or for any other person or entity, in return for:

(A) being influenced in the performance of any official act;

(B) being influenced to commit or aid in committing, or to collude in, or allow, any fraud, or make opportunity for the commission of any fraud, on the United States; or

(C) being induced to do or omit to do any act in violation of the official duty of such official or person; * * *

shall be fined under this title or not more than three times the monetary equivalent of the thing of value, whichever is greater, or imprisoned for not more than fifteen years, or both, and may be disqualified from holding any office of honor, trust, or profit under the United States.

(c) Whoever—

(1) otherwise than as provided by law for the proper discharge of official duty—

(A) directly or indirectly, gives, offers, or promises anything of value to any public official, former public official, or person selected to be a public official, for or because of any official act performed or to be performed by such public official, former public official, or person selected to be a public official; or

(B) being a public official, former public official, or person selected to be a public official, otherwise than as provided by law for the proper discharge of official duty, directly or indirectly demands, seeks, receives, accepts, or agrees to receive or accept anything of value personally for or because of any official act performed or to be performed by such official or person; * * *

shall be fined under this title or imprisoned for not more than two years, or both.

"Public official" is defined in § 201(a)(1) as "Member of Congress, Delegate, or Resident Commissioner, either before or after such official has qualified, or an officer or employee or person acting for or on behalf of the United States, or any department, agency or branch of Government thereof, including the District of Columbia, in any official function, under or by authority of any such department, agency, or branch of Government, or a juror." Section 201(a)(3) defines "official act" as any "decision or action on any question, matter, cause, suit, proceeding or controversy, which may at any time be pending, or which may by law be brought before any public official, in such official's official capacity, or in such official's place of trust or profit."

This federal statute covers conduct that state statutes traditionally have divided into categories of "bribery" (§ 201(b)) and "unlawful gratuities" (§ 201(c)). Section 201(b) has been interpreted to impose requirements similar to those of most state bribery statutes, namely, that a public official (1) obtains anything of value (2) in return for performing an official act, committing fraud on the U.S., or violating a lawful duty, and (3) the defendant public official or private person acted with "corrupt intent." The last element is the primary distinction between bribery and unlawful gratuity offenses. Payments to a public official for acts that would have occurred in any event are in most circumstances probably unlawful gratuities and not bribes. See *United States v. Campbell*, 684 F.2d 141 (D.C. Cir. 1982).

Section 201 and analogous state laws are phrased generally and might be interpreted to reach far beyond the prototype of bribery (the selling of one's legislative influence for money or a valuable thing). How far should these statutes reach? Should they include Senator Soaper's agreement to support a bill exempting labor unions from certain tax liabilities in return for a promise by union leaders in her state that they will support her reelection bid? Should they cover campaign contributions to the Senator's campaign, based upon the mutual expectation that Soaper will continue to support labor legislation?

Daniel Lowenstein, *Political Bribery and the Intermediate Theory of Politics*, 32 UCLA L. Rev. 784 (1985), argues that the answers to these questions typically depend upon one's definition of "corrupt intent," which in turn depends upon one's theory of politics. If you view a legislative representative as a trustee for the public good, you might be inclined to criminalize campaign contributions that carry a commitment by the legislator to vote in specified ways on future issues. On the other hand, if you view the legislator as nothing more than an agent for popular desires, you might want to limit bribery prosecutions to those cases in which the representative benefits personally (she fattens her bank account or acquires a new yacht). You might not want to prosecute those cases in which the representative is merely making political tradeoffs resulting in legislation that, on balance, serves the interests of her constituents. Obviously, most cases fall somewhere along the spectrum between clearly legitimate arrangements and patently corrupt deals—but where?

In light of this background, consider the following case, notes, and problem.

PEOPLE EX REL. DICKINSON V. VAN DE CARR

Supreme Court of New York, Appellate Division, First Department, 1903.
87 App. Div. 386, 84 N.Y.S. 461.

LAUGHLIN, J.

The relator is an alderman of the city of New York. He has been held to bail, and to appear at the Court of General Sessions, upon a charge of violating section 72 of the Penal Code, which relates to bribery, by Justice Wyatt, of the Court of

Special Sessions, sitting as magistrate. The warden returned the commitment of the magistrate under which he held the relator. It is in due form, and appears to be valid. The relator traversed the return, claiming that the evidence upon which commitment was based does not show that any crime has been committed; and he annexed to his traverse the exhibits and testimony, which were conceded to be correct. The testimony showed that John McGaw Woodbury, the commissioner of street cleaning of the city of New York, wrote a letter to the relator on the 23d day of September, 1902, saying:

> "In reply to your letter of September 20th, I would say that the Department is so short of horses, particularly in the Borough of Brooklyn, that we have been very strict with the drivers during the warm weather to prevent any possibility of over-heating or damaging the stock. We are many behind our complement. Should, however, the Honorable Board grant me the moneys for new stock and plant, this would give employment to more drivers, and as the heavy season comes on, having made a note of your favorable recommendation, the case of Covino will be reconsidered."

—That on the 30th day of the same month the relator wrote and mailed a letter to Commissioner Woodbury in reply, saying:

> "If you will reinstate Antonio Covino, who I think was too severely punished by being dismissed from your Department, I will vote and otherwise help you to obtain the money needed for a new plant in Brooklyn."

And at this time there was pending in the board of aldermen a bill to authorize an issue of corporate stock "for new stock or plant for the Department of Street Cleaning, Borough of Brooklyn."

There is no question but that the magistrate has jurisdiction to inquire into a violation of section 72 of the Penal Code, and thereafter, upon proper proof, to hold a person to answer for the crime. The relator has not been convicted. He has been merely held to answer. We are therefore not concerned with the weight of evidence. Our inquiry is limited to whether there was any evidence tending to show his guilt. This is the single question presented by the appeal. Section 72 of the Penal Code provides as follows:

> "Officer Accepting Bribe. A judicial officer, a person who executes any of the functions of a public office not designated in titles VI and VII of this Code, or a person employed by or acting for the state, or for any public officer in the business of the state, who asks, receives, or agrees to receive a bribe, or any money, property, or value of any kind, or any promise or agreement therefor, upon any agreement or understanding that his vote, opinion, judgment, action, decision, or any other official proceeding, shall be influenced thereby, or that he will do or omit any act or proceeding, or in any way neglect or violate any official duty, is punishable by imprisonment for not more than ten years, or by a fine of not more than five thousand dollars, or both. A conviction also forfeits any office held by

the offender, and forever disqualifies him from holding any public office under the state."

It will be observed that the clause, "asks, receives or agrees to receive a bribe, or any money, property, or value of any kind, or any promise or agreement therefor," is disjunctive. It first specifically includes certain officers who ask, receive, or agree to receive a bribe. In the absence of any statute defining a bribe, we must have recourse to the decisions and text-writers to determine what was embraced in that term at common law. Bribery was an indictable offense at common law, and, although in the early days it was limited to judicial officers and those engaged in the administration of justice, it was later extended to all public officers. It was variously defined as taking or offering an "undue reward" or a "reward" to influence official action. Bribery is defined in 4 Am. & Eng. Enc. of Law, p. 907, to be "the giving, offering, or receiving of anything of value, or any valuable service, intended to influence one in the discharge of legal duty." The cases of bribery that have been before the courts of this state, so far as brought to our attention, have related to the offering or giving of property or something of intrinsic value. The relator claims that, as no money or property was asked or agreed to be received by him to influence the official action of the street commissioner, he has not violated this statute. In view of the circumstances disclosed, his letter is open to the inference that he desired to obtain a political or other personal advantage from or by securing Covino's reinstatement in the public service, and that he took advantage of the known desire on the part of the street commissioner to obtain this appropriation of public moneys to improperly influence the action of the street commissioner on the application of Covino for reinstatement, by offering, in case that were done, to vote for and further the desired appropriation, and impliedly threatening in case of refusal to withhold his support therefrom. The interests of the public service require that public officers shall act honestly and fairly upon propositions laid before them for consideration, and shall neither be influenced by, nor receive pecuniary benefit from, their official acts, or enter into bargains with their fellow legislators or officers or with others for the giving or withholding of their votes, conditioned upon their receiving any valuable favor, political or otherwise, for themselves or for others. It was the duty of the relator to act fairly and honestly and according to his judgment upon the proposition of the street commissioner. It does not appear to have been the mandatory duty of the board of aldermen to favor the recommendation of Commissioner Woodbury. In these circumstances, it was the duty of the relator to favor or oppose the recommendation according to its merits or demerits. If, in his judgment, it should have been disapproved, he should have opposed it, and he should not bargain to vote for it upon obtaining an agreement from the street commissioner to reinstate Covino. It is quite as demoralizing to the public service, and as much against the spirit and intent of the statute, for a legislator or other public official to bargain to sell his vote or official action for a political or other favor or reward as for money. Either is a bribe, and they only differ in degree. Nor should he, by holding out this inducement, have tempted the commissioner to act favorably upon Covino's application for reinstatement. This was undue influence, and would be detrimental to the public service. In addition to the word "bribe" in section 72 of the Penal Code, other words are employed sufficiently broad to reach this case. It is a violation of the statute for a public officer to ask, receive, or agree to receive "property or value of any kind, or any promise or agreement therefor," upon any agreement or understanding that his vote or official action shall be influenced thereby. It is clear that words "value of any kind," as here used, are more comprehensive than "property." The benefit which the relator expected to receive from the reinstatement of his constituent would, we think, be embraced in the meaning of this clause, and would also constitute a bribe. We are therefore of the opinion that the facts tend to show that the relator has offended against the provisions of section 72 of the Penal Code, and that he was properly held to answer upon the charge.

It follows that the order should be affirmed. All concur.

NOTES ON BRIBERY PROSECUTIONS AND THEORIES OF REPRESENTATION

1.   *Is This Prosecution Supportable by Any Theory?* Wisconsin explicitly prohibits logrolling by legislators in a law that dates back to the Progressive Era. Section 13.05 of the Wisconsin statutes makes it a felony for a legislator to give, offer, or promise his vote on a bill "in consideration or upon condition that any other person elected to the same legislature will give or will promise or agree to give his or her vote or influence in favor of or against any other measure or proposition" in the legislature. Similarly, a lawmaker cannot promise to vote in a particular way on a bill in return for a promise by the governor to sign, veto, or line item veto any other legislation. Wisc. Stat., § 13.06. Wisconsin statutes further specify that these provisions shall not "be construed as prohibiting free discussion and deliberation upon any question pending before the legislature by members thereof, privately or publicly, nor as prohibiting agreements by members to support any single measure pending, on condition that certain changes be made in such measure, nor as prohibiting agreements to compromise conflicting provisions of different measures." *Id.* § 13.07.

Consider *Van de Carr* and the Wisconsin statutes in light of the different theories of representation developed in this and the preceding chapter. They might be consistent with a theory that considers the representative to be a trustee for the people, using her independent judgment to figure out what is best for the people. But even under a republican or trusteeship approach, shouldn't the representative be able to make deals with other officials, to ensure that her constituents receive needed services? Would *Van de Carr* and Wisconsin law outlaw most forms of cooperative behavior to construct majority support for bills? Does the rationale of *Van de Carr* criminalize any voting or legislative action for strategic reasons and require that the representative always sincerely believe in the merits of the positions she takes? Can a legislature effectively work under such constraints? See generally Dennis Thompson, *Ethics in Congress: From Individual to Institutional Corruption* (1995) (arguing that a concern of modern ethics rules should be institutional corruption, where the gains are political rather than personal, the service offered by the lawmaker is procedurally improper, and the connection between gain and service damages either the legislature or the democratic process).

2.   *The Sweep of* Van de Carr. This case may be a product of its times. It was written during a period in New York politics in which reformers in and out of

government were working to eliminate rampant corruption and to break the power of party bosses. Leaders like Theodore Roosevelt came to national attention because of their efforts to clean up the sewers of local politics. Thus, Judge Laughlin may well have known about aspects of this case that made the political deal more dubious than it appears from the facts he gives, or he may have been a reform-minded judge hoping his opinion would get the attention of graft-addicted politicos.[3] If the *Van de Carr* facts had occurred in Congress today, would § 201 apply? Recall that § 201(b) and (c) use the same "anything of value" language that the New York bribery statute did, and that most bribery laws use.

3. *The Connection Between an Unlawful Gratuity and the Official's Position.* The Supreme Court construed the unlawful gratuities portion of § 201 in a case that grew out of an independent prosecutor's investigation of President Bill Clinton's Secretary of Agriculture Mike Espy. *United States v. Sun-Diamond Growers of California*, 526 U.S. 398 (1999). Sun-Diamond Growers was a trade association for businesses that grew raisins, figs, walnuts, prunes, and hazelnuts. The independent prosecutor alleged that the association had given Espy tickets to the U.S. Open, luggage, meals, and a crystal bowl, which had a total value of less than $6,000. The trade organization had several matters before the Secretary. For example, it wanted to be designated as a representative of "small-sized entities" so that it would continue to receive federal funds for overseas marketing plans for its members' commodities. It also wanted the Department of Agriculture to oppose plans by the Environmental Protection Agency to ban a particular kind of pesticide. The indictment of Sun-Diamond Growers described these matters, but it did not allege a direct nexus between them and the gratuities conferred on Espy. The government argued that it need not show a link to a particular official act, but only that the gratuity was motivated more generally by "the recipient's capacity to exercise governmental power or influence in the donor's favor." Justice Scalia's opinion for the Court rejected that interpretation, arguing that § 201(c)(1)(A)'s explicit provision that the gift be made "for or because of any official act" requires that some official act be identified and proved. Thus, the unlawful gratuity statute does not criminalize gifts given merely because the recipient holds a powerful office; instead, laws and ethics rules prohibiting or limiting gift giving to officials are designed to cover such situations. Scalia's opinion underscores the relationship among the laws regulating corruption: "[T]his regulation, and the numerous other regulations and statutes littering this field, demonstrate that this is an area where precisely targeted prohibitions are commonplace, and where more general prohibitions have been qualified by numerous exceptions. Given that reality, a statute in this field that can linguistically be interpreted to be either a meat axe or a scalpel should reasonably be taken to be the latter."

A BRIBERY PROBLEM

Problem 3–1. Robert McCormick is a member of the West Virginia House of Delegates in 1984, representing a district with a severe shortage of doctors. McCormick supports a state program that allows nonlicensed doctors, often from overseas, to practice in the state. During his campaign for reelection in 1984, McCormick informs the lobbyist for the foreign doctors association that his campaign is short of money and

---

[3]   For discussion of this era in New York and reform efforts, see Louis Eisenstein & Elliot Rosenberg, *A Stripe of Tammany's Tiger* (1966); Jerome Mushkat, *Tammany: The Evolution of a Political Machine, 1789–1865* (1971).

"we haven't heard anything from your association this year." The lobbyist gives McCormick $2,000 in cash, which McCormick pockets. McCormick wins reelection and subsequently sponsors legislation permitting experienced doctors to be licensed in West Virginia without passing the state licensing exams. Two weeks after the bill is enacted, McCormick receives more cash from the foreign doctors association. Consider the following. Decide your answer to each question before moving on to the next:

(a) Can McCormick be convicted of violating 18 U.S.C. § 201?

(b) Can McCormick be convicted of violating a West Virginia analogue to § 201?

(c) Would your answer to (a) or (b) change if McCormick had not pocketed the money but, instead, treated it as a campaign contribution reported under state law?

* * *

Another type of public crime is *extortion*, which at common law consisted of a public official's use of official position to exact money or other benefits from private persons. 4 William Blackstone, *Commentaries* 141, defined extortion as "an abuse of public justice, which consists in an officer's unlawfully taking, by colour of his office, from any man, any money or thing of value, that is not due to him, or more than is due, or before it is due." Common law extortion was, apparently, very similar to modern bribery.[4] Why have two crimes that overlap so much?

The federal Hobbs Act, 18 U.S.C. § 1951, criminalizes extortion:

(a) Whoever in any way or degree obstructs, delays, or affects commerce or the movement of any article or commodity in commerce, by robbery or extortion or attempts or conspires so to do, or commits or threatens physical violence to any person or property in furtherance of a plan or purpose to do anything in violation of this section shall be fined under this title or imprisoned not more than twenty years, or both.

(b) As used in this section—* * *

(2) The term "extortion" means the obtaining of property from another, with his consent, induced by wrongful use of actual or threatened force, violence, or fear, or under color of official right.

Note that, unlike § 201, which criminalizes bribery and unlawful gratuities by federal "public officials," the federal Hobbs Act might apply to official misconduct at either the federal or state level.[5]

Would the Hobbs Act cover the conduct of McCormick described in Problem 3–1? A line of lower court cases decided in the 1970s and 1980s held that the Hobbs Act can be applied to public officials who receive a stream of benefits from people under their jurisdiction.[6] But the Supreme Court, in the context of campaign contributions,

---

[4] See James Lindgren, *The Elusive Distinction between Bribery and Extortion: From the Common Law to the Hobbs Act*, 35 UCLA L. Rev. 815 (1988).

[5] A number of other federal criminal statutes might be used against official legislative misconduct at either the federal or state level, including the mail fraud statute, 18 U.S.C. § 1341, and the wire fraud statute, § 1343. See Chapter 7, § 2A (rule of lenity cases involving application of mail and wire fraud statutes to state officials, political bosses and others).

[6] See Herbert Stern, *Prosecutions of Local Political Corruption under the Hobbs Act: The Unnecessary Distinction Between Bribery and Extortion*, 3 Seton Hall L. Rev. 1 (1971) (important article by former U.S. Attorney for New Jersey, who pressed for this use of the Hobbs Act).

interpreted the Hobbs Act to require a *quid pro quo* by a public official who receives money from someone under his jurisdiction; a politician cannot be convicted of Hobbs Act extortion unless there is an explicit exchange of money for an official act. *McCormick v. United States*, 500 U.S. 257 (1991). Should an explicit *quid pro quo* be required if the money provided to the politician cannot be characterized as a campaign contribution? See *Evans v. United States*, 504 U.S. 255 (1992) (providing a different formulation in the non-campaign contribution context, requiring the government to "only show that a public official has obtained a payment to which he was not entitled, knowing the payment was made in return for official acts"); *United States v. Ganim*, 510 F.3d 134 (2d Cir. 2007) (making a distinction in an opinion written by then-Judge Sotomayor).[7]

B. CONFLICTS OF INTEREST

The criminal sanctions found in laws prohibiting bribery, unlawful gratuities, and extortion have not inspired complete confidence in politicians and the government in the wake of Watergate; ethics scandals that dogged the Clinton Administration; the successful prosecution of lobbyist Jack Abramoff for influence peddling, including bribing Rep. Bob Ney (R–Ohio); the resignation of House Majority Leader Tom DeLay (R–Tex.) in 2006 amid allegations of corruption; and other episodes that occur regularly. As a result, both state and federal legislatures have enacted statutes or adopted procedural rules designed to mitigate conflicts of interest, namely, any financial incentive that might affect a legislator's deliberations. As you review the various prescriptions and proscriptions, ask: Do the rules address important conflicts that would impair members' judgment or their ability to deliberate about the public good? Do the rules go further than necessary? Which rules could be most usefully pruned? Which strengthened?

The responses to the overall problem of conflicted interest have been twofold: the disinfectant of full disclosure of financial interests and the adoption of prophylactic rules to prevent even the potential for certain types of financial incentives to slant public deliberations. At the national level, Title I of the Ethics in Government Act of 1978, Pub. L. No. 95–521, 92 Stat. 1824 (codified as amended at 5 U.S.C. App. § 101 (2012)), sets forth comprehensive "Financial Disclosure Requirements of Federal Personnel." The requirements apply to Congress members, designated officers and employees of the legislative branch, and candidates seeking to become Congress members (§ 101(c)). Members of Congress, as well as the designated officers and employees, must file on or before May 15 of each year "full and complete statements" of income, gifts, honoraria, interest in property, liabilities owed to creditors, sales or exchanges of property or stocks, officership on corporate boards, and so forth (§ 102(a)). An exception from the reporting requirements is created in the Act for holdings of or the source of income

---

[7] For helpful discussions, see Daniel Lowenstein, *When Is a Campaign Contribution a Bribe?* in *Private and Public Corruption* 127 (William Heffernan & John Kleinig eds., 2004) (excellent analysis of statutes and cases, with application to hypotheticals); Ilissa Gold, Note, *Explicit, Express, and Everything in Between: The Quid Pro Quo Requirement for Bribery and Hobbs Act Prosecutions in the 2000s*, 36 Wash. U. J.L. & Pol'y 261 (2011).

from any holdings in "qualified blind trusts" and trusts not created by the regulated individual or the individual's spouse or dependent child (§ 102(f)).[8]

In addition to disclosure requirements, Congress has adopted various substantive prohibitions to head off potential conflicts of interest. The relevant provisions are a rich array of statutory and legislative rules, which the following introduces.[9] It appears that the state's ability to regulate conflicts of interest is robust, and limited primarily by political will. For example, the Supreme Court recently considered a state conflict of interest rule that requires public officials, including legislators, to recuse themselves from voting on or advocating the passage or defeat of any matter in which they might have a conflict of interest. *Nevada Comm'n on Ethics v. Carrigan*, 131 S.Ct. 2343 (2011). A legislator who failed to abstain from voting to approve a construction project that used his campaign manager as a paid consultant argued that the conflict of interest rule violated the First Amendment by burdening his freedom of expression. Writing for the Court, Justice Scalia upheld the law, holding first that a legislator's vote is "not personal to the legislator but belongs to the people; the legislator has no personal right to it." It is not a constitutionally protected expression of a particular political view, but a "commitment of his apportioned share of the legislature's power to the passage or defeat of a particular proposal" and could reflect various motivations from a deeply held personal view to the reflection of constituents' views to the influence of a major contributor. Because the state has the power to exclude a lawmaker with a conflict of interest from voting, the prohibition on advocating a position on the matter during the legislative session is a reasonable time, place, and manner limitation. In the Court's view, such laws reflect a venerable and universal tradition of legislative recusal rules: virtually every state has such a rule; federal conflict of interest rules have applied to the federal judiciary since the founding; and Thomas Jefferson adopted such a rule when he was President of the Senate.

The rules governing members of Congress regulate the following:

1.   *Gifts Are Severely Limited*. The Ethics Reform Act of 1989, Pub. L. 101–194, 103 Stat. 1716, substantially amended federal law pertaining to gifts, bribes, honoraria, and other activities presenting potential conflicts of interest. In particular, it prohibits members of Congress from seeking or accepting "anything of value" from any person "whose interests may be substantially affected by the performance or nonperformance of the individual's official duties." 5 U.S.C. § 7353(a). The ethics offices of the House and Senate are empowered to devise reasonable exemptions to this rule. § 7353(b). Senate Rule XXXV and House Rule XXV, clause 5, set forth the gift rules of the respective chambers, which add further

---

[8]   Candidates seeking to become members of Congress must file a similar report (with fewer disclosures) within 30 days of becoming a candidate or by May 15 of that year (whichever is later) and in every successive year until the election (§§ 101(d), 102(b)). See also Thomas Little & David Ogle, *The Legislative Branch of State Government: People, Process, and Politics* 113–14 (2006) (providing overview of ethics and conflict of interest rules and state-by-state descriptions); Alan Rosenthal, *The Decline of Representative Democracy: Process, Participation, and Power in State Legislatures* 94–100 (1998) (detailing ethics laws and codes in various states).

[9]   For a clear description of congressional ethics rules, see Robert Bauer & Rebecca Gordon, *Congressional Ethics: Gifts, Travel, Income, and Post-Employment Restrictions*, in *The Lobbying Manual: A Complete Guide to Federal Lobbying Law and Practice* 477 (William Luneberg, Thomas Susman & Rebecca Gordon eds., 4th ed. 2009).

limitations on the receipt of gifts by members. These rules were substantially strengthened in 2007, largely as a response to corruption scandals involving high-profile lawmakers.

No member, employee, or officer of the House of Representatives or the Senate may accept gifts or meals from lobbyists unless they fit into certain exceptions, such as a meal that is served at a reception (sometimes called the "toothpick rule") or at a "widely attended" event on a particular issue that attracts many people other than just congressional aides. Furthermore, both chambers have adopted stringent restrictions on the kinds of travel for which private parties can reimburse members and their staff, and lobbyists are entirely banned from paying for member travel. Because Congress has now prohibited much of the travel, entertainment, and gifts previously allowed, the major arena excepted from regulation through ethics rules—campaign fundraisers in Washington and in a lawmaker's state or district—has become an increasingly important way for lobbyists to interact with legislators and their aides. In the past, congressional gift and travel rules were regularly evaded as lawmakers took advantage of loopholes; evasion is more difficult with the current rules but still occurs.[10]

One major change in the congressional gift rules occurred in 2007 when Congress amended the Lobbying Disclosure Act to require that lobbyists certify twice a year that no one covered in their disclosure filings (which may include other employees of the firm who engage in lobbying activities) has provided gifts or offered travel to senators or representatives that would violate the rules. Section 203 of the Honest Leadership and Open Government Act of 2007 (HLOGA), Pub. L. No. 110–81, 121 Stat. 735 (2007). Violations of this provision can be punished by up to $200,000 in fines and, for knowing and corrupt violations, up to five years in prison. Prior to this, House and Senate rules could only be enforced against members and staff, although gifts that were part of a scheme to bribe legislators could always form the basis of a criminal prosecution.

An Oregon Supreme Court case dealt with a First Amendment challenge to that state's gift restrictions. *Vannatta v. Oregon Gov't Ethics Comm'n*, 222 P.3d 1077 (Ore. 2009). A registered lobbyist attacked the gift ban and the restriction on the offering of gifts to lawmakers as an unconstitutional burden on expression protected by the First Amendment. The plaintiff argued that the law, by prohibiting gifts to lawmakers that exceeded $50 in value in a calendar year, banned "expenditures designed to facilitate dialogue and obtain goodwill with public officials." He also contended that the restrictions on communicating offers of gifts discriminated among speech on the basis of conduct and interfered with the constitutionally protected right to petition government for redress of grievances. The court rejected the attack on the provisions dealing with receipt of gifts because this action is not expressive conduct. Lawmakers and citizens, including lobbyists, can communicate and engage in the range of official conduct without also providing gifts to the public officials. It ruled, however, that the ban on offering gifts above the threshold did impermissibly burden speech and noted that the restrictions on

---

[10] See Fredreka Schouten, *Despite Ethics Rules, Congress' Travel Junkets Creep Back Up*, USA Today, Nov. 1, 2011 (noting that travel is now funded by nonprofits, which is allowed by the rules).

offering gifts were not intended to curtail invidious behavior but were focused on the mere "utterance of an offer" without regard to its effects or intended behavior. Are the federal gift restrictions subject to similar First Amendment attack, either as political expression or as an intrinsic part of petitioning the government for policy change?

2.   *Outside Earned Income Is Limited.* The Ethics Reform Act, as amended in 1990, provides that Congress members can have "outside earned income" no greater than 15% of level II of the executive pay schedule under 5 U.S.C. § 5313 for each calendar year. 5 U.S.C. App. § 501(a)(1) (2012). Members may not serve in firms providing professional services with a fiduciary duty, receive compensation for practicing such a profession, serve on corporate boards of directors, or be paid for teaching (without the consent of the ethics body). § 502(a). Senate Rule XXXVII(2) provides: "No Member * * * shall engage in any outside business or professional activity or employment for compensation which is inconsistent or in conflict with the conscientious performance of official duties." House Rule XXV(2) provides: "A Member * * * may not receive compensation for affiliating with or being employed by a firm, partnership, association, corporation, or other entity that provides professional services involving a fiduciary relationship except for the practice of medicine." These rules go beyond the statutory requirements and are enforceable by the chambers themselves.

3.   *Post-Employment Lobbying Is Restricted.* The number of former members who become highly compensated lobbyists continues to rankle the public, and there have been calls for reform to address the revolving door between government service and lobbying. As revised by the Ethics Reform Act, 18 U.S.C. § 207(e)(1) prohibits members of the House of Representatives, within a year of leaving office, from lobbying current members or employees of either House. In 2007, HLOGA extended the ban on lobbying that applies to former senators to two years. Unlike some of the other prohibitions, this one is found in the Criminal Code and is enforceable through criminal sanctions. Opponents of longer waiting periods argue that they make public service less attractive. It is too much, they contend, to ask that public servants not only forego large salaries while they work for Congress or the executive branch, but then also to expect them to refrain from using their expertise and skills for a substantial time after they leave government. See David Zaring, *Against Being Against the Revolving Door*, 2013 U. Ill. L. Rev. 507 (arguing that stints in the government and in the private sector can enhance the work done in both and foster citizen participation in government, but focusing mainly on law enforcement jobs).

Former lawmakers also enjoy perks that provide them special access to current legislators, including the use of the members' dining rooms and floor privileges. In the ethics reform bill that Congress enacted in 2007, these privileges were curtailed or eliminated for lawmakers-turned-lobbyists. For example, the Senate denied floor privileges, special parking spaces, and access to the Senate athletic facilities to former members who are currently registered lobbyists. Senate Rule XXIII.

4. *Honoraria Are Banned.* The Ethics Reform Act of 1989, as amended at 5 U.S.C. App. §§ 501, 505, prohibits members of Congress from receiving honoraria. The scope of this law was the subject of the following case:

United States v. National Treasury Employees Union
513 U.S. 454 (1995).

The honoraria ban applied not only to members of Congress and top-level executive branch officials, but it also broadly prohibited federal employees from accepting any compensation for making speeches or writing articles. This class action brought on behalf of executive branch employees below grade GS–16 (employees with salaries in 1994 between $11,903 and $86,589, with a mean salary between $28,000 and $36,000) challenged the prohibition on First Amendment grounds. A mail handler employed by the Postal Service in Arlington, Virginia, had given lectures on the Quaker religion for which he received small payments that were "not much, but enough to supplement my income in a way that makes a difference." An aerospace engineer employed at the Goddard Space Flight Center in Greenbelt, Maryland, had lectured on black history for a fee of $100 per lecture. A microbiologist at the Food and Drug Administration had earned almost $3,000 per year writing articles and making radio and television appearances reviewing dance performances. An Internal Revenue Service tax examiner in Ogden, Utah, had received comparable pay for articles about the environment. The Act defined "honorarium" to mean "a payment of money or any thing of value for an appearance, speech, or article (including a series of appearances, speeches, or articles if the subject matter is directly related to the individual's status with the Government)." Thus, the ban applied even without a nexus between the employee's work for the government and her speech, article, or appearance. The text of the statute added the nexus requirement only in relation to a series of activities. Accordingly, all the individual plaintiffs had violated the Ethics in Government law.

Justice Stevens, writing for the majority, held that the law as applied to the class of lower-level federal employees was unconstitutional. Although the Court's jurisprudence allows Congress to impose restraints on the job-related speech of public employees that would be unconstitutional if applied to the public at large, see *Pickering v. Board of Educ.*, 391 U.S. 563 (1968), the government does not have unfettered discretion. The interests of the employee in commenting on matters of public concern are balanced with the interests of the state, as an employer, in promoting efficiency of the public services it performs. Stevens noted that the broad sweep of the law worked a substantial burden on the expressive rights of federal employees. Several of the federal workers testified that the inability to receive compensation for their activities meant that they would no longer engage in them.

The government's interest was "that federal officers not misuse or appear to misuse power by accepting compensation for their unofficial and nonpolitical writing and speaking activities." Stevens acknowledged that this interest is a powerful one, but he noted that there was no evidence that employees below grade GS–16 were engaged in this sort of misconduct. Indeed, the report of a special Commission on Executive, Legislative and Judicial Salaries that was the catalyst for the enactment of the law talked only about the honoraria practices of top government officials. The lawmakers who enacted the ban did so in part as a tradeoff for higher salaries for members of Congress, federal judges, and executive branch employees above the GS–15 level. "[T]he Government has based its defense of the ban on abuses of honoraria by members of

Congress. Congress reasonably could assume that payments of honoraria to judges or high-ranking officials in the Executive Branch might generate a similar appearance of improper influence. Congress could not, however, reasonably extend that assumption to all federal employees below grade GS–16, an immense class of workers with negligible power to confer favors on those who might pay to hear them speak or to read their articles. A federal employee, such as a supervisor of mechanics at the mint, might impair efficiency and morale by using political criteria to judge the performance of his or her staff. But one can envision scant harm, or appearance of harm, resulting from the same employee's accepting pay to lecture on the Quaker religion or to write dance reviews."

Stevens also rejected the government's argument that a wholesale prophylactic rule, rather than a rule that banned only activities with a nexus to the employee's work for the government, was justified on ease of administration grounds. "The nexus limitation for series, however, unambiguously reflects a congressional judgment that agency ethics officials and the [Office of Government Ethics] can enforce the statute when it includes a nexus test. A blanket burden on the speech of nearly 1.7 million federal employees requires a much stronger justification than the Government's dubious claim of administrative convenience."

Justice O'Connor agreed that the law violated the First Amendment, but she proposed remedying the violation by interpreting the statute to require a nexus not only for a series of speeches but also for single appearances. She argued that the statute could be easily fixed by moving the end of the parentheses forward several words in the definition of "honorarium." The majority rejected this approach. "We cannot be sure that our attempt to redraft the statute to limit its coverage to cases involving an undesirable nexus between the speaker's official duties and either the subject matter of the speaker's expression or the identity of the payor would correctly identify the nexus Congress would have adopted in a more limited honoraria ban. We cannot know whether Congress accurately reflected its sense of an appropriate nexus in the terse, 33–word parenthetical statement with which it exempted series of speeches and articles from the definition of honoraria in the 1992 amendment; in an elaborate, nearly 600–word provision with which it later exempted Department of Defense military school faculty and students from the ban; or in neither."

Finally, **Chief Justice Rehnquist** dissented. "The Court concedes that in light of the abuses of honoraria by its Members, Congress could reasonably assume that 'payments of honoraria to judges or high-ranking officials in the Executive Branch might generate a similar appearance of improper influence,' but it concludes that Congress could not extend this presumption to federal employees below grade GS–16. The theory underlying the Court's distinction—that federal employees below grade GS–16 have negligible power to confer favors on those who might pay to hear them speak or to read their articles—is seriously flawed. Tax examiners, bank examiners, enforcement officials, or any number of federal employees have substantial power to confer favors even though their compensation level is below grade GS–16."

The honoraria ban for higher-level executive branch officials, members of Congress, and federal judges is controversial.[11] In the fiscal year 2001 appropriations

---

[11] See George Brown, *Putting Watergate Behind Us*—Salinas, Sun-Diamond, *and Two Views of the Anticorruption Model*, 74 Tul. L. Rev. 747 (2000) (analyzing the honoraria case as well as others discussed previously to discern the Supreme Court's view of corruption); Daniel Koffsky, *Coming to Terms with*

process, Senator McConnell (R–Ky.) inserted a provision into the appropriations bill for the Justice Department that would have lifted the ban as it applied to federal judges. Following the advice of Chief Justice Rehnquist, he argued that federal judges made less than first-year associates in major law firms so that more liberal rules for outside income are necessary to attract the best lawyers to the federal bench. The provision would have also required the Judicial Conference to promulgate regulations to avoid conflicts and impropriety before the ban was lifted. After the proposal received substantial negative publicity, the appropriations rider was dropped and not enacted.

CONFLICT OF INTEREST PROBLEMS

Problem 3–2. Consider the following findings of the Senate Ethics Committee: from April 1987 to April 1989, Senator Alan Cranston (D–Cal.) personally or through his staff contacted the Federal Home Loan Bank Board (FHLBB) on behalf of Lincoln Savings & Loan, during a period when Cranston was soliciting and accepting large campaign contributions from Charles Keating, who ran Lincoln. On at least four occasions, these contacts were made in close connection with the solicitation or receipt of contributions. For example, in January 1988 Keating offered to make an additional contribution and also asked Cranston to set up a meeting for him with Danny Wall, the Chair of the FHLBB. Cranston did so on January 20; Wall and Keating met eight days later. On February 10, Cranston personally collected checks from Keating for $500,000 for voter registration groups. (If not reported, does this violate federal campaign finance law, as described in Chapter 2, § 3?)

Joy Jacobson, Cranston's chief fundraiser but not a member of his Senate staff, sometimes solicited contributions from Keating for Cranston. She repeatedly scheduled meetings between the Senator and contributors (especially Keating) at which regulatory issues were discussed. She was often the intermediary whom Keating or his assistant called when they could not reach the Senator or his legislative aides. Jacobson wrote memoranda to the Senator indicating her belief that contributors were entitled to special attention and special services. Cranston never told her that this was incorrect.

Lincoln went bankrupt, and cleaning up the insolvent thrift cost taxpayers around $2 billion. The committee found no evidence that Cranston's interventions directly contributed to regulatory lapses that cost the taxpayers this money. In your view, has Cranston behaved corruptly or unethically? Has he violated any of the laws or rules noted above? See Dennis Thompson, *Mediated Corruption: The Case of the Keating Five*, 87 Am. Pol. Sci. Rev. 369 (1993) (arguing that this case is an example of "mediated corruption," which is the use of public office for private purposes in a way that subverts the democratic process; the public official's contribution to "the corruption is filtered through various practices that are otherwise legitimate and may even be duties of office. As a result, both the official and citizens are less likely to recognize that the official has done anything wrong."). See also Ronald Levin, *Congressional Ethics and Constituent Advocacy in an Age of Mistrust*, 95 Mich. L. Rev. 1 (1996) (discussing this example and other examples of allegations of corruption in the context of casework).

Problem 3–3. Jack Abramoff was a registered lobbyist whose clients included numerous Indian tribes and Foxcom, an Israeli telecommunications start-up. He formed

---

Bureaucratic Ethics, 11 J.L. & Pol. 235 (1995) (discussing ethics bureaucracies established to deal with conflict of interest problems and how consultation with these entities affects the judicial approach).

an unofficial business partnership with Michael Scanlon, who ran a lobbying and grassroots public relations firm. Among his many dubious business practices, Abramoff would refer clients to Scanlon's firm for grassroots and public relations services without revealing that he received 50% of the profits from these deals. Abramoff also requested that some clients pay a nonprofit he set up, the Capital Athletic Foundation, rather than his law firm, and then used the money from the nonprofit to underwrite golf trips for himself and members of Congress. Abramoff had a particularly close relationship with Rep. Bob Ney (R–Ohio), in part because a former Ney staffer joined Abramoff's firm after he left government employment. Neil Volz, Ney's former Chief of Staff, acted as an intermediary between the lobbyist and the Congressman beginning just months after Volz left Capitol Hill.

Among the items of value given to Ney were all-expense-paid trips to the Super Bowl in Florida and golf courses in Scotland, numerous tickets to concerts and sporting events (including tickets to classical and rock concerts worth more than $1,100), tens of thousands of dollars of campaign contributions, and regular meals and drinks at Abramoff's restaurant. In return, Ney agreed to enter certain statements into the *Congressional Record* supporting Abramoff's clients or their positions; to endorse as Chair of the House Administration Committee Foxcom's bid to provide wireless telephone service to the House; and to work as the Co-chair of the relevant conference committee to enact gaming legislation that would benefit Abramoff's tribal clients and to ensure that the government transferred property to a religious school founded by Abramoff. Ney also met with several of Abramoff's clients and promised them his help on matters or indicated to them that Abramoff was an effective lobbyist. Finally, Ney contacted executive branch officials to influence decisions in ways that benefited Abramoff's clients.

What laws or ethical rules have each of these four men violated? Which particular acts violated which law or rule? Would Abramoff's payment for travel and gifts to Ney be treated differently from the campaign contributions that he provided to Ney? Should there be different treatment? How would each violation be punished? As you read through the Lobbying Disclosure Act, amended in the wake of the Abramoff scandal and discussed in the next subsection, consider how it might apply to these interactions and what it would require be disclosed.

Problem 3–4. Is it corrupt for a politician to break a promise made during a campaign? Take, for example, Representative Marty Meehan (D–Mass.), who in 1995 filed a letter with the clerk of the House of Representatives stating: "Should I be elected to serve more than two additional terms of office in the U.S. House of Representatives following the 104th Congress, by this letter I hereby resign and direct you to remove my name permanently from the Roll of Members." When Meehan announced that he was running for the 107th Congress (an election he ultimately won), the Massachusetts Republican Party began to investigate legal remedies to enforce the resignation letter. Are there other ways to ensure that candidates tell the truth during campaigns?[12] Is this sort of corruption policed effectively by requiring members of Congress to stand for frequent reelection, thereby holding members accountable for their promises? Or is the electoral tie insufficient in a world where incumbents are usually reelected despite disappointing records on campaign promises? Is it even corrupt to break a campaign

---

[12]   See Saul Levmore, *Precommitment Politics*, 82 Va. L. Rev. 567 (1996) (presenting creative approaches to this question).

promise when everyone understands that campaign themes are often aspirational (or pandering), rather than realistic? For a case concerning whether a campaign promise made generally to all voters could itself be corrupt, see *Brown v. Hartlage*, 456 U.S. 45 (1982) (candidate who promised to accept a lower salary, a promise that violated state law, prosecuted under state corrupt practices act as the equivalent of a bribe; prosecution held unconstitutional under the First Amendment).

C. LOBBYING

The First Amendment to the U.S. Constitution provides that "Congress shall make no law * * * abridging the freedom of speech, or of the press; or the right of the people peaceably to assemble, and to petition the Government for a redress of grievances." The Speech Clause recognizes the general precept that speech, especially about political matters, presumptively cannot be limited by the government. The Petition Clause recognizes the general precept that legislative representatives in a democracy should be open to the viewpoints of their constituents, and the latter in turn should be encouraged to present their proposals and ideas to their representatives. But should "the people" be free to use any means to persuade their representatives to press their views in the legislature?

In the 19th century, lobbying was often thinly disguised bribery. But most modern lobbying is, at least formally, a rather ordinary affair. Almost all organized lobbying before Congress is aimed at getting the group's point of view across to the legislators and influencing legislative decisions.[13] According to H.R. Mahood, *Interest Groups in American National Politics: An Overview* 54 (2000), methods of lobbying fall into two main categories:

- *Direct Lobbying* is the presentation of a group's point of view by the lobbyist to the legislator or the staff. The most common means of direct lobbying are testimony at legislative hearings; contacting legislators by letter, phone, or email; presenting research results; submitting drafts of proposed legislation; and making contributions to legislators' reelection campaigns. Interest groups focus not only on the legislature but also on the executive branch, seeking to influence agency outcomes, the position the executive branch takes on legislation, and other decisions of implementation or agenda setting. Direct lobbying has also long included *social lobbying*, a less substantive and more controversial method of influence. Social interactions lay the groundwork for the future when the lobbyists and the interests they represent will seek access to the legislator and to influence policy outcomes. One variation of social lobbying is to offer legislators gifts, trips, or fees for speaking engagements. One can consider the involvement of lobbyists in raising campaign funds a form of social lobbying when it is not accompanied by any substantive discussion of the issues. Generally, social lobbying is on the decline, in large part

---

[13] See John Wright, *Interest Groups and Congress: Lobbying, Contributions, and Influence* chap. 4 (2003); Richard Hasen, *Lobbying, Rent-Seeking, and the Constitution*, 64 Stan. L. Rev. 191, 219–25 (2012).

because of the new gift, travel, and other conflict of interest rules discussed in the previous section.

- *Indirect Lobbying* involves efforts by interest groups and their lobbyists to stir up outside forces, primarily constituents, to bring pressure to bear. Increasingly, interest groups are using indirect methods, including "stealth campaigns with other organizations, alliances under positive-sounding names such as Citizens for Reform, or sponsorship of research studies or public opinion polls through independent organizations such as think tanks."[14] The most important kind of indirect lobbying is *grassroots lobbying* or "any type of action that attempts to influence inside-the-beltway inhabitants by influencing the attitudes or behavior of outside-the-beltway inhabitants."[15] An interest group stimulates constituent interest by mobilizing its own members, talking with media representatives to ensure that its point of view is presented favorably, conducting a public relations campaign to inspire letter writing, phone calls, and emails by constituents, and publicizing the legislator's voting record or "scorecard" on relevant votes.[16] Although there is concern that some of this activity produces "astroturf" lobbying based on false information or misrepresenting the breadth of public support, grassroots lobbying generally communicates substantive and relevant content about public opinion to policymakers and represents one of the most vibrant forms of mass political participation.

William Keefe & Morris Ogul, *The American Legislative Process: Congress and the States* 366–70 (10th ed. 2001), observe that interest groups and their lobbying techniques vary greatly as to effectiveness. Access (presenting the group's point of view) does not ensure success, and organization is not necessarily synonymous with clout. In fact, the term *access* can encompass a variety of concepts: "(1) convincing a policy maker to listen to arguments; (2) establishing a 'regular relationship' with a policy maker for the exchange of information; (3) becoming 'institutionalized' into the policy process, for example, acquiring formal representation on governing boards of agencies; and (4) gaining influence."[17] The most effective groups are those that have large, cohesive, and dispersed memberships, are considered prestigious, have skillful leaders who seem to have the support of the group's members and can rally them on an issue, and have a lot of money to spend. We would add other

---

[14] Darrell West & Burdett Loomis, *The Sound of Money: How Political Interests Get What They Want* 207 (1999). See also Mark Smith, *American Business and Political Power: Public Opinion, Elections, and Democracy* (2000).

[15] Kenneth Goldstein, *Interest Groups, Lobbying, and Participation in America* 3 (1999).

[16] See William Browne, *Lobbying the Public: All-Directional Advocacy*, in *Interest Group Politics* 343 (Allan Cigler & Burdett Loomis eds., 5th ed. 1998). See also Richard Davis, *The Web of Politics: The Internet's Impact on the American Political System* chap. 3 (1999) (analyzing electronic methods of grassroots lobbying and arguing that the new technology merely reinforces past patterns); Jonathan Zellner, Note, *Artificial Grassroots Advocacy and the Constitutionality of Legislative Identification and Control Measures*, 43 Conn. L. Rev. 357, 360–61 (2010) (describing "astroturf" lobbying and its increased use).

[17] Wright, *supra,* at 77 (citing S.J. Makielski, *Pressure Politics in America* (1980)). See Lloyd Mayer, *What Is This "Lobbying" that We Are All So Worried About?*, 26 Yale L. & Pol'y Rev. 485, 534–39 (2008) (discussing factors that influence clout and access).

factors, such as the ability of the groups to form alliances and the value of the group in supplying information (and any monopoly it might have on information).[18]

Lobbyists can play a positive role in the legislative process by providing information to elected officials, who then can focus their energies, and those of their staff, on assessing the credibility of the information and on producing data about aspects of policy that may have escaped the notice of interest groups. Lobbyists produce three different but related kinds of information: information about the status and prospects of pending legislation; information about the electoral ramifications of the legislator's position on proposals; and analyses of the economic, social, and other substantive consequences of bills.[19] Although an interest group and its lobbyists will usually present arguments in a light most favorable to its position, lobbyists suffer reputational sanctions for lying, and competing interest groups have an incentive to point out the flaws in arguments or any inaccuracies. See Bruce Wolpe & Bertram Levine, *Lobbying Congress: How the System Works* 13–19 (2d ed. 1996) (including in the "Five Commandments" of lobbying "Tell the Truth" and "Spring No Surprises"). Thus, the information can be accurate and useful, and the government benefits because it has externalized some of its information costs.

Most lobbying activity consists of speech and written communications that are protected by the First Amendment. Very little lobbying involves clearly corrupt activity, and that sort of lobbying (or *influence peddling*) can probably be prosecuted under state or federal bribery, extortion, or gratuity statutes. Think back to the broad wording of § 201, the federal law criminalizing bribery and extortion. What sorts of lobbying activities fall within the plain meaning of those provisions? How should courts distinguish corrupt attempts to influence legislators from ordinary politics? Is more regulation needed of behavior that is not quite corrupt but disturbing nonetheless? How would you describe that behavior?

Some pluralist theorists might oppose any additional regulation. Viewing government officials, and especially legislators, as the accommodators of interest group pressures who register the strength of the conflicting pressures and reach an appropriate middle position, pluralists might consider lobbying as simply part of the process itself.[20] This would suggest a relatively *laissez-faire* approach to the political process, although even some pluralist thinkers recoil from such an extreme position. David Truman, for example, did not view legislators as utterly passive objects of interest group pressures, and he argued that there were certain basic

---

[18] For a discussion of the factors, including access, that seem to allow interest groups to influence political outcomes, see Matt Grossmann, *The Not-So-Special Interests: Interest Groups, Public Representation, and American Governance* 86–90 (2012). On forming alliances, see Kevin Hula, *Lobbying Together: Interest Group Coalitions in Legislative Politics* (1999); on the role of interest groups in providing information and expertise, see Frank Baumgartner, Jeffrey Berry, Marie Hojnacki, David Kimball & Beth Leech, *Lobbying and Policy Change: Who Wins, Who Loses, and Why* 122–27 (2009).

[19] See Wright, *supra*, at 88–89.

[20] See Earl Latham, *The Group Basis of Politics: A Study in Basing-Point Legislation* 35–36 (1952); Nelson Polsby, *Money Gains Access. So What?*, N.Y. Times, August 13, 1997, at A23.

"rules of the game" (mainly, to avoid the appearance of corruption that would undermine confidence in the legislature) that must be obeyed.[21]

The rules of the game advocated by Truman and others primarily involved disclosure of lobbying activities because secrecy can allow corruption that the light of public scrutiny can destroy. One of the most influential early works indicting lobbying practices that seemed to thrive when sheltered from public scrutiny was Elmer Schattschneider's *Politics, Pressures and the Tariff: A Study of Free Private Enterprise in Pressure Politics, as Shown in the 1929–1930 Revision of the Tariff* (1935). The study focused on the 1929 House and Senate hearings that crafted what was to become the notorious Smoot-Hawley Tariff of 1930. Schattschneider found that the deliberative process was essentially controlled by lobbyists for American businesses (every business facing actual or potential foreign competition was represented in Washington, D.C., during these hearings). "Indeed, the language of the hearings often was not what one might expect to find in communications between a sovereign state and its citizens, nor was it, in many instances, that of an inquiry by a governmental body into the merits of a public policy. It was, rather, in the style and manner of equals engaged in negotiation." *Id.* at 43–44. The most striking consequences were that Congress acted with skewed and often inaccurate information, and that overall policy was dramatically tilted.

At the same time Schattschneider's book was published, Senate hearings revealed similar patterns of conduct (misleading information, pressure, "inside" access) by public utility lobbyists. Responding to the Senate hearings, Senator Hugo Black (D–Ala.) championed lobbying reform in the mid–1930s. But the compromise bill that was crafted by a conference committee was rejected decisively by the House, defeated by a 3–1 majority. Lobbying reform was a dead issue in Congress for the next ten years, although Congress did enact the Foreign Agents Registration Act (FARA) in 1938 to expose Nazi propaganda efforts. FARA, as amended in 1966 and 1995, imposes substantial registration and disclosure obligations on representatives of a "foreign principal" before Congress, agencies, and the executive. 22 U.S.C. § 611 et seq. (2012).

The Joint Committee on the Organization of Congress proposed the Legislative Reorganization Act of 1946, which included a lobbying reform title as a minor part of its overall package of reforms.[22] Congressional consideration of the lobbying title was perfunctory, confused, and skeptical—but the whole package passed intact and became the Federal Regulation of Lobbying Act (FRLA), §§ 302–305, 307–308 & 310, 60 Stat. 839 (codified at 2 U.S.C. §§ 261–270 (1994)). FRLA was aimed primarily at disclosure of both contributions to a person who lobbied the Congress and the expenditures made by lobbyists. The Act clearly encompassed more than natural persons; it defined "person" to include not only individuals but also partnerships, committees, associations, corporations, and other organizations or groups. Because the bill had been cobbled together from past proposals, and

---

[21] David Truman, *The Governmental Process: Political Interests and Public Opinion* 114–15, 159, 512 (1951).

[22] See Belle Zeller, *American Government and Politics: The Federal Regulation of Lobbying Act*, 42 Am. Pol. Sci. Rev. 239 (1948) (providing detailed legislative history of Act).

received little consideration during enactment, however, other aspects of its scope were not entirely clear.

Section 305 required that "[e]very person receiving any contributions or expending any money" for the principal purpose of influencing "directly or indirectly" the "passage or defeat of any legislation" must report the sources of contributions of $500 or greater and the recipients of expenditures of $10 or more. (The "principal purpose" language was not included in § 305, but was incorporated by a reference to § 307.) Section 307, which was labeled "Persons to Whom Applicable" and appeared to apply to the entire Act, described the class of persons regulated as "any person * * * who by himself, or through any agent or employee or other persons in any manner whatsoever, directly or indirectly, solicits, collects, or receives money or any other thing of value to be used principally to aid" in influencing "directly or indirectly" the "passage or defeat of any legislation." Thus, while § 305 seemed to include in the regulatory ambit anyone who spent money on lobbying, regardless of the source of that money, the provision that explicitly defined the group of people subject to disclosure limited the Act's effect only to those who received contributions from others that were then used for lobbying expenses. To make things more confusing, § 305 referred to § 307, but only to incorporate certain language regarding the purpose of actions, not specifically to include the limitation to persons receiving contributions.

In addition, § 308 of FRLA required that persons "engage[d] for pay or for any consideration for the purpose of attempting to influence the passage or defeat of any legislation by the Congress of the United States shall * * * register with the Clerk of the House of Representatives and the Secretary of the Senate." Violations of FRLA were punishable by a fine of up to $5,000 or imprisonment up to a year. The constitutionality of FRLA was challenged in the following case, which remains the foundational case with respect to the constitutional validity of lobbying regulations.

UNITED STATES V. HARRISS
Supreme Court of the United States, 1954.
347 U.S. 612, 74 S.Ct. 808, 98 L. Ed. 989.

CHIEF JUSTICE WARREN delivered the opinion of the Court.

[The plaintiffs in this case were Robert Harriss, a commodity broker; Tom Linder, Commissioner of Agriculture for the State of Georgia; Ralph Moore, a trader of commodity futures; and the National Farm Committee (NFC), of which Harriss, Linder, and Moore were directors. Harriss funneled money to Moore ($50,000 in the last three months of 1946 alone), who would host dinners for members of Congress in the name of NFC and other farmer groups. It is not clear what subjects were discussed at these social gatherings. None of the individuals, nor NFC, registered or delivered reports under FRLA. The Justice Department secured indictments against Harriss for failure to report expenditure of his own monies to influence legislation; Linder and Moore for seeking to influence Congress for pay without registering; and NFC for failing to report the solicitation and receipt of contributions to influence the enactment of legislation. The District Court judge dismissed the indictment against Harriss, Linder, Moore, and NFC, on the ground that FRLA as enacted was unconstitutional, a decision appealed to the Supreme Court.]

[I] The constitutional requirement of definiteness is violated by a criminal statute that fails to give a person of ordinary intelligence fair notice that his contemplated conduct is forbidden by the statute. The underlying principle is that no man shall be held criminally responsible for conduct which he could not reasonably understand to be proscribed. * * *

* * * The key section of the Lobbying Act is § 307, entitled "Persons to Whom Applicable." This section modifies the substantive provisions of the Act, including § 305 and § 308. In other words, unless a "person" falls within the category established by § 307, the disclosure requirements of § 305 and § 308 are inapplicable. Thus coverage under the Act is limited to those persons (except for the specified political committees) who solicit, collect, or receive contributions of money or other thing of value, and then only if "the principal purpose" of either the persons or the contributions is to aid in the accomplishment of the aims set forth in § 307(a) and (b). [These sections describe two purposes: "The passage or defeat of any legislation by the Congress of the United States" and "To influence, directly or indirectly, the passage or defeat of any legislation by the Congress of the United States."] In any event, the solicitation, collection, or receipt of money or other thing of value is a prerequisite to coverage under the Act.

The Government urges a much broader construction—namely, that under § 305 a person must report his expenditures to influence legislation even though he does not solicit, collect, or receive contributions as provided in § 307.[8] Such a construction, we believe, would do violence to the title and language of § 307 as well as its legislative history. If the construction urged by the Government is to become law, that is for Congress to accomplish by further legislation.

We now turn to the alleged vagueness of the purposes set forth in § 307(a) and (b). As in *United States v. Rumely*, 345 U.S. 41 (1953), which involved the interpretation of similar language, we believe this language should be construed to refer only to "lobbying in its commonly accepted sense"—to direct communication with members of Congress on pending or proposed federal legislation. The legislative history of the Act makes clear that, at the very least, Congress sought disclosure of such direct pressures, exerted by the lobbyists themselves or through their hirelings or through an artificially stimulated letter campaign.[10] It is likewise

---

[8] The Government's view is based on a variance between the language of § 307 and the language of § 305. Section 307 refers to any person who "solicits, collects, or receives" contributions; § 305, however, refers not only to "receiving any contributions" but also to "expending any money." It is apparently the Government's contention that § 307—since it makes no reference to expenditures—is inapplicable to the expenditure provisions of § 305. Section 307, however, limits the application of § 305 as a whole, not merely a part of it.

[10] The Lobbying Act was enacted as Title III of the Legislative Reorganization Act of 1946, which was reported to Congress by the Joint Committee on the Organization of Congress. The Senate and House reports accompanying the bill were identical with respect to Title III. Both declared that the Lobbying Act applies "chiefly to three distinct classes of so-called lobbyists:

"First. Those who do not visit the Capitol but initiate propaganda from all over the country in the form of letters and telegrams, many of which have been based entirely upon misinformation as to facts. This class of persons and organizations will be required under the title, not to cease or curtail

clear that Congress would have intended the Act to operate on this narrower basis, even if a broader application to organizations seeking to propagandize the general public were not permissible.

There remains for our consideration the meaning of "the principal purpose" and "to be used principally to aid." The legislative history of the Act indicates that the term "principal" was adopted merely to exclude from the scope of § 307 those contributions and persons having only an "incidental" purpose of influencing legislation. Conversely, the "principal purpose" requirement does not exclude a contribution which in substantial part is to be used to influence legislation through direct communication with Congress or a person whose activities in substantial part are directed to influencing legislation through direct communication with Congress. If it were otherwise—if an organization, for example, were exempted because lobbying was only one of its main activities—the Act would in large measure be reduced to a mere exhortation against abuse of the legislative process. In construing the Act narrowly to avoid constitutional doubts, we must also avoid a construction that would seriously impair the effectiveness of the Act in coping with the problem it was designed to alleviate.

To summarize, therefore, there are three prerequisites to coverage under § 307: (1) the "person" must have solicited, collected, or received contributions; (2) one of the main purposes of such "person," or one of the main purposes of such contributions, must have been to influence the passage or defeat of legislation by Congress; (3) the intended method of accomplishing this purpose must have been through direct communication with members of Congress. And since § 307 modifies the substantive provisions of the Act, our construction of § 307 will of necessity also narrow the scope of § 305 and § 308, the substantive provisions underlying the information in this case. Thus § 305 is limited to those persons who are covered by § 307; and when so covered, they must report all contributions and expenditures having the purpose of attempting to influence legislation through direct communication with Congress. Similarly, § 308 is limited to those persons (with the stated exceptions) who are covered by § 307 and who, in addition, engage themselves for pay or for any other valuable consideration for the purpose of attempting to influence legislation through direct communication with Congress.

---

their activities in any respect, but merely to disclose the sources of their collections and the methods in which they are disbursed.

"Second. The second class of lobbyists are those who are employed to come to the Capitol under the false impression that they exert some powerful influence over Members of Congress. These individuals spend their time in Washington presumably exerting some mysterious influence with respect to the legislation in which their employers are interested, but carefully conceal from Members of Congress whom they happen to contact the purpose of their presence. The title in no wise prohibits or curtails their activities. It merely requires that they shall register and disclose the sources and purposes of their employment and the amount of their compensation.

"Third. There is a third class of entirely honest and respectable representatives of business, professional, and philanthropic organizations who come to Washington openly and frankly to express their views for or against legislation, many of whom serve a useful and perfectly legitimate purpose in expressing the views and interpretations of their employers with respect to legislation which concerns them. They will likewise be required to register and state their compensation and the sources of their employment."

S. Rep. No. 1400, 79th Cong., 2d Sess., p. 27; Committee Print, July 22, 1946, statement by Representative Monroney on Legislative Reorganization Act of 1946, 79th Cong., 2d Sess., pp. 32–33. See also the statement in the Senate by Senator La Follette, who was Chairman of the Joint Committee, at 92 Cong. Rec. 6367–6368.

Construed in this way, the Lobbying Act meets the constitutional requirement of definiteness.

[II] Thus construed, §§ 305 and 308 also do not violate the freedoms guaranteed by the First Amendment—freedom to speak, publish, and petition the Government.

Present-day legislative complexities are such that individual members of Congress cannot be expected to explore the myriad pressures to which they are regularly subjected. Yet full realization of the American ideal of government by elected representatives depends to no small extent on their ability to properly evaluate such pressures. Otherwise the voice of the people may all too easily be drowned out by the voice of special interest groups seeking favored treatment while masquerading as proponents of the public weal. This is the evil which the Lobbying Act was designed to help prevent.

Toward that end, Congress has not sought to prohibit these pressures. It has merely provided for a modicum of information from those who for hire attempt to influence legislation or who collect or spend funds for that purpose. It wants only to know who is being hired, who is putting up the money, and how much. * * *

The judgment below is reversed and the cause is remanded to the District Court for further proceedings not inconsistent with this opinion.

MR. JUSTICE DOUGLAS, with whom MR. JUSTICE BLACK concurs, dissenting. * * *

I am now convinced that the formula adopted to save this Act is too dangerous for use. It can easily ensnare people who have done no more than exercise their constitutional rights of speech, assembly, and press. * * *

It is contended that the Act plainly applies:

—to persons who pay others to present views to Congress either in committee hearings or by letters or other communications to Congress or Congressmen and

—to persons who spend money to induce others to communicate with Congress.

The Court adopts that view, with one minor limitation which the Court places on the Act—that only persons who solicit, collect, or receive money are included.

The difficulty is that the Act has to be rewritten and words actually added and subtracted to produce that result. * * *

What contributions might be used "principally to aid" in influencing "directly or indirectly, the passage or defeat" of any such measure by Congress? When is one retained for the purpose of influencing the "passage or defeat of any legislation"?

(1)   One who addresses a trade union for repeal of a labor law certainly hopes to influence legislation.

(2)   So does a manufacturers' association which runs ads in newspapers for a sales tax.

(3) So does a farm group which undertakes to raise money for an educational program to be conducted in newspapers, magazines, and on radio and television, showing the need for revision of our attitude on world trade.

(4) So does a group of oil companies which puts agents in the Nation's capital to sound the alarm at hostile legislation, to exert influence on Congressmen to defeat it, to work on the Hill for the passage of laws favorable to the oil interests.

(5) So does a business, labor, farm, religious, social, racial, or other group which raises money to contact people with the request that they write their Congressman to get a law repealed or modified, to get a proposed law passed, or themselves to propose a law.

Are all of these activities covered by the Act? If one is included why are not the others? The Court apparently excludes the kind of activities listed in categories (1), (2), and (3) and includes part of the activities in (4) and (5)—those which entail contacts with the Congress.

There is, however, difficulty in that course, a difficulty which seems to me to be insuperable. I find no warrant in the Act for drawing the line, as the Court does, between "direct communication with Congress" and other pressures on Congress. The Act is as much concerned with one as with the other.

The words "direct communication with Congress" are not in the Act. Congress was concerned with the raising of money to aid in the passage or defeat of legislation, whatever tactics were used. But the Court not only strikes out one whole group of activities—to influence "indirectly"—but substitutes a new concept for the remaining group—to influence "directly." To influence "directly" the passage or defeat of legislation includes any number of methods—for example, nationwide radio, television or advertising programs promoting a particular measure, as well as the "buttonholing" of Congressmen. To include the latter while excluding the former is to rewrite the Act. * * *

[We have omitted the dissenting opinion of JUSTICE JACKSON, who believed that FRLA infringed on the Petition Clause of the First Amendment. "[O]ur constitutional system is to allow the greatest freedom of access to Congress, so that the people may press for their selfish interests, with Congress acting as arbiter of their demands and conflicts."]

NOTES ON THE AFTERMATH OF HARRISS

1. *The Court's Analysis.* One irony of *Harriss* is that the Court essentially rewrote the statute (judicial activism) in order to save its constitutionality (judicial restraint). Was the Court on firm ground in reading § 307's "principal purpose" requirement into §§ 305 and 308? Where does the Court find the "direct communication" requirement? In its desire to trim back a "vague" statute, has the Court instead created a confusing one?

Consider whether the Court was doing the statute a "favor" by rewriting rather than just invalidating it. Justice Jackson thought not. Instead, he made an institutional argument for striking down the law, rather than redrafting it. "Congress has power to regulate lobbying for hire as a business or profession and to require such agents to disclose their principals, their activities, and their receipts. However, to reach the real evils of lobbying without cutting into the constitutional right of petition is a difficult and delicate task for which the Court's action today gives little guidance. I am in doubt whether the Act as construed does not permit applications which would abridge the right of petition, for which clear, safe and workable channels must be maintained. I think we should point out the defects and limitations which condemn this Act so clearly that the Court cannot sustain it as written, and leave its rewriting to Congress. After all, it is Congress that should know from experience both the good in the right of petition and the evils of professional lobbying." Is he right? Think about his observation again after you read about the aftermath of *Harriss*, and again later in this chapter when we turn to the concept of due process of lawmaking.

2.   *The Impact of* Harriss. The Supreme Court's decision remanded *Harriss* to Judge Holtzoff for further proceedings. The Justice Department not only abandoned the Harriss prosecutions (the last indictment, against Moore, was dropped on November 2, 1955), but essentially also abandoned any serious effort to enforce the statute, after having been fairly active between 1947 and 1954. Only a handful of indictments were returned under the Act after 1955, and the Justice Department testified in 1979 that the statute was a dead letter.

Congress itself expressed dissatisfaction with the statute as reconstructed. In the wake of the Watergate scandal and with a heightened sensitivity to ethics issues, the Senate Committee on Government Operations reported the following defects:

- Groups that used their own funds in an attempt to influence legislation were not required to register unless they solicited, collected, or received funds from others for that purpose.

- FRLA did not apply to organizations or individuals unless lobbying was their principal purpose. Due to the vagueness of the definition, many organizations did not register at all, concluding that lobbying was not their "principal purpose."

- FRLA did not clearly cover efforts by a lobbyist that did not involve direct contact with Congress. Thus, lobbyists who attempted to influence Congress by soliciting others to communicate with Congress did not report these grassroots lobbying efforts.

- FRLA did not clearly include lobbying communications with staff employees of Congress members.

- FRLA's reporting requirements were so vague and ambiguous that the lobbyists who did report often filed incomplete information or interpreted the requirements differently. Some groups considered more kinds of expenses to be related to lobbying than others. As a result, it was difficult to make a meaningful comparison between the reports filed by any two lobbyists.

See Senate Report No. 94–763 on S. 2477, 94th Cong., 2d Sess. (1976).

* * *

After years of dissatisfaction with FRLA and increasing public concern about lobbying excesses, Congress finally became serious about revising the lobbying laws when Senator Carl Levin (D–Mich.) held hearings on the topic in 1991 in the Senate Governmental Affairs Subcommittee on Oversight of Government Management. In the 103rd Congress, the bill passed the Senate by a vote of 95–2; the House of Representatives also passed a version of a comprehensive lobbying disclosure bill in 1993. The conference committee managed to draft a compromise proposal, but opposition to the proposal had developed since floor consideration.

Most significantly, a coalition of interests had come together to oppose disclosure of grassroots lobbying. This coalition included a number of unusual political bedfellows, including the Christian Coalition and the American Civil Liberties Union. They argued that the reform proposal would violate the First Amendment by requiring them to open their membership lists to public scrutiny. Although the conference report passed the House, it was killed in the Senate by a filibuster led by the perennial opponent of campaign finance reform laws as well as this particular lobbying reform bill, Mitch McConnell (R–Ky.). In the next Congress, proponents dropped this controversial provision and made other concessions, and the Lobbying Disclosure Act of 1995 (LDA) passed unanimously.

Lobbying and ethics reform became a salient issue again in the 110th Congress in the wake of several scandals involving lobbyists and members of Congress. For example, as part of the scandal involving lobbyist Jack Abramoff (detailed in Problem 3–3, *supra*), Representative Bob Ney (R–Ohio) pled guilty to conspiracy to commit, among other things, defrauding his constituents of their right to his honest service and making false statements about the items he received from Abramoff and others. Representative Randall "Duke" Cunningham (R–Calif.) pled guilty in 2005 to various charges stemming from his accepting at least $2.4 million in bribes. Cunningham, a member of the Defense Appropriations Subcommittee, provided a "menu" to defense contractors from which the contractor could determine how many millions of dollars in defense and intelligence contracts would be awarded to the contractor based upon the value of the bribe. Cunningham's dealings were more closely scrutinized, and eventually led to his arrest, when he sold his house to a defense contractor for substantially more than market value. Other bribes he admitted receiving included a used Rolls-Royce, antique furniture, jewelry, and money for his daughter's graduation party.

As with the 1995 LDA, original ethics reform proposals were more far reaching than the bill that ultimately passed in 2007. Again, for example, attempts to extend the Act's provisions to some grassroots lobbying were quickly abandoned after facing stiff opposition from many groups active in the legislative realm. The compromise reached was passed overwhelmingly by both houses (411–8 in the House, and 83–14 in the Senate) in identical form to avoid a conference committee, and the Act was sent to the President just days before Congress left on its August break. With two former lawmakers serving prison time, others in trouble, and campaign promises of cleaning up Congress' act in danger of remaining unfulfilled, legislators did not want to return to their districts and states without having taken action on anti-corruption legislation.

As you read the following excerpts from LDA, as amended in 2007 by HLOGA, determine whether it remedies the defects in the old law identified in Senate Committee Report No. 94–763, *supra*.

LOBBYING DISCLOSURE ACT OF 1995

Pub. L. 104–65, 109 Stat. 691; codified as amended at 2 U.S.C.A. §§ 1601–1607.

SEC. 2. FINDINGS.

The Congress finds that—

(1) responsible representative Government requires public awareness of the efforts of paid lobbyists to influence the public decisionmaking process in both the legislative and executive branches of the Federal Government;

(2) existing lobbying disclosure statutes have been ineffective because of unclear statutory language, weak administrative and enforcement provisions, and an absence of clear guidance as to who is required to register and what they are required to disclose; and

(3) the effective public disclosure of the identity and extent of the efforts of paid lobbyists to influence Federal officials in the conduct of Government actions will increase public confidence in the integrity of Government.

SEC. 3. DEFINITIONS. * * *

(2) CLIENT.—The term "client" means any person or entity that employs or retains another person for financial or other compensation to conduct lobbying activities on behalf of that person or entity. A person or entity whose employees act as lobbyists on its own behalf is both a client and an employer of such employees. In the case of a coalition or association that employs or retains other persons to conduct lobbying activities, the client is the coalition or association and not its individual members.

(3) COVERED EXECUTIVE BRANCH OFFICIAL.—The term "covered executive branch official" means—

(A) the President;

(B) the Vice President;

(C) any officer or employee, or any other individual functioning in the capacity of such an officer or employee, in the Executive Office of the President;

(D) any officer or employee serving in a [senior position in the executive branch.] * * *

(4) COVERED LEGISLATIVE BRANCH OFFICIAL.—The term "covered legislative branch official" means—

(A) a Member of Congress;

(B) an elected officer of either House of Congress;

(C) any employee of, or any other individual functioning in the capacity of an employee of—(i) a Member of Congress; (ii) a committee of either House of Congress; (iii) the leadership staff of the House of Representatives or the leadership staff of the Senate; (iv) a joint committee of Congress; and (v) a working group or caucus organized to provide legislative services or other assistance to Members of Congress[.] * * *

(5) EMPLOYEE.—The term "employee" means any individual who is an officer, employee, partner, director, or proprietor of a person or entity, but does not include [independent contractors or volunteers]. * * *

(7) LOBBYING ACTIVITIES.—The term "lobbying activities" means lobbying contacts and efforts in support of such contacts, including preparation and planning activities, research and other background work that is intended, at the time it is performed, for use in contacts, and coordination with the lobbying activities of others.

(8) LOBBYING CONTACT.—

(A) DEFINITION.—The term "lobbying contact" means any oral or written communication (including an electronic communication) to a covered executive branch official or a covered legislative branch official that is made on behalf of a client with regard to—

(i) the formulation, modification, or adoption of Federal legislation (including legislative proposals);

(ii) the formulation, modification, or adoption of a Federal rule, regulation, Executive order, or any other program, policy, or position of the United States Government;

(iii) the administration or execution of a Federal program or policy (including the negotiation, award, or administration of a Federal contract, grant, loan, permit, or license); or

(iv) the nomination or confirmation of a person for a position subject to confirmation by the Senate.

(B) EXCEPTIONS.—The term "lobbying contact" does not include a communication that is—

(i) made by a public official acting in the public official's official capacity; * * *

(iii) made in a speech, article, publication or other material that is distributed and made available to the public, or through radio, television, cable television, or other medium of mass communication;

(iv) made on behalf of a government of a foreign country or a foreign political party and disclosed under the Foreign Agents Registration Act of 1938 (22 U.S.C. 611 et seq.);

(v) a request for a meeting, a request for the status of an action, or any other similar administrative request, if the request does not include an attempt to influence a covered executive branch official or a covered legislative branch official; * * *

(vii) testimony given before a committee, subcommittee, or task force of the Congress, or submitted for inclusion in the public record of a hearing conducted by such committee, subcommittee, or task force; * * *

(ix) required by subpoena, civil investigative demand, or otherwise compelled by statute, regulation, or other action of the Congress or an agency; * * *

(xi) not possible to report without disclosing information, the unauthorized disclosure of which is prohibited by law;

(xii) made to an official in an agency with regard to—(I) a judicial proceeding or a criminal or civil law enforcement inquiry, investigation, or proceeding; or (II) a filing or proceeding that the Government is specifically required by statute or regulation to maintain or conduct on a confidential basis, if that agency is charged with responsibility for such proceeding, inquiry, investigation, or filing; * * *

(xiv) a written comment filed in the course of a public proceeding or any other communication that is made on the record in a public proceeding;

(xv) a petition for agency action made in writing and required to be a matter of public record pursuant to established agency procedures;

(xvi) made on behalf of an individual with regard to that individual's benefits, employment, or other personal matters involving only that individual, except that this clause does not apply to any communication with—(I) a covered executive branch official, or (II) a covered legislative branch official (other than the individual's elected Members of Congress or employees who work under such Members' direct supervision), with respect to the formulation, modification, or adoption of private legislation for the relief of that individual;

(xvii)   a disclosure by an individual that is protected under the amendments made by the Whistleblower Protection Act of 1989 [5 U.S.C. § 1211 et seq.], under the Inspector General Act of 1978 [5 U.S.C. app.] or under another provision of law;

(xviii)   made by [a church, an association of churches, or a religious order]. * * *

(9) LOBBYING FIRM.—The term "lobbying firm" means a person or entity that has 1 or more employees who are lobbyists on behalf of a client other than that person or entity. The term also includes a self-employed individual who is a lobbyist.

(10) LOBBYIST.—The term "lobbyist" means any individual who is employed or retained by a client for financial or other compensation for

services that include more than one lobbying contact, other than an individual whose lobbying activities constitute less than 20 percent of the time engaged in the services provided by such individual to that client over a 3–month period. * * *

(13) ORGANIZATION.—The term "organization" means a person or entity other than an individual.

(14) PERSON OR ENTITY.—The term "person or entity" means any individual, corporation, company, foundation, association, labor organization, firm, partnership, society, joint stock company, group of organizations, or State or local government. * * *

SEC. 4. REGISTRATION OF LOBBYISTS.

(a)   REGISTRATION.—

(1)   GENERAL RULE.—No later than 45 days after a lobbyist first makes a lobbying contact or is employed or retained to make a lobbying contact, whichever is earlier, * * * such lobbyist (or, as provided under paragraph (2), the organization employing such lobbyist), shall register with the Secretary of the Senate and the Clerk of the House of Representatives.

(2)   EMPLOYER FILING.—Any organization that has 1 or more employees who are lobbyists shall file a single registration under this section on behalf of such employees for each client on whose behalf the employees act as lobbyists.

(3)   EXEMPTION.—* * * Notwithstanding paragraphs (1) and (2), a person or entity whose—

(i)   total income for matters related to lobbying activities on behalf of a particular client (in the case of a lobbying firm) does not exceed and is not expected to exceed $2,500 [adjusted for inflation]; or

(ii)   total expenses in connection with lobbying activities (in the case of an organization whose employees engage in lobbying activities on its own behalf) do not exceed or are not expected to exceed $10,000 [adjusted for inflation],

(as estimated under section 5 [of this title]) in the quarterly period described in section 5(a) [of this title] during which the registration would be made is not required to register under this subsection with respect to such client. * * *

(b)   CONTENTS OF REGISTRATION.—Each registration * * * shall contain—

(1)   the name, address, business telephone number, and principal place of business of the registrant, and a general description of its business or activities;

(2)   the name, address, and principal place of business of the registrant's client, and a general description of its business or activities (if different from paragraph (1));

(3) the name, address, and principal place of business of any organization, other than the client, that—

(A) contributes more than $5,000 to the registrant or the client in the quarterly period to fund the lobbying activities of the registrant; and

(B) actively participates in the planning, supervision, or control of such lobbying activities * * *.

(5) a statement of—

(A) the general issue areas in which the registrant expects to engage in lobbying activities on behalf of the client; and

(B) to the extent practicable, specific issues that have (as of the date of the registration) already been addressed or are likely to be addressed in lobbying activities; and

(6) the name of each employee of the registrant who has acted or whom the registrant expects to act as a lobbyist on behalf of the client and, if any such employee has served as a covered executive branch official or a covered legislative branch official in the 20 years before the date on which the employee first acted as a lobbbyist. * * *

No disclosure is required under paragraph (3)(B) if the organization that would be identified as affiliated with the client is listed on the client's publicly accessible Internet website as being a member of or contributor to the client, unless the organization in whole or in major part plans, supervises, or controls such lobbying activities. If a registrant relies upon the preceding sentence, the registrant must disclose the specific Internet address of the web page containing the information relied upon. Nothing in paragraph (3)(B) shall be construed to require the disclosure of any information about individuals who are members of, or donors to, an entity treated as a client by this Act or an organization identified under that paragraph.

SEC. 5. REPORTS BY REGISTERED LOBBYISTS.

(a) QUARTERLY REPORT.—No later than 20 days after the end of the quarterly period beginning on the first day of January, April, July, and October of each year in which a registrant is registered under section 4, * * * each registrant shall file a report with the Secretary of the Senate and the Clerk of the House of Representatives on its lobbying activities during such quarterly period. A separate report shall be filed for each client of the registrant.

(b) CONTENTS OF REPORT.—Each quarterly report filed under subsection (a) of this section shall contain—

(1) the name of the registrant, the name of the client, and any changes or updates to the information provided in the initial registration * * *;

(2) for each general issue area in which the registrant engaged in lobbying activities on behalf of the client during the quarterly period—

(A) a list of the specific issues upon which a lobbyist employed by the registrant engaged in lobbying activities, including, to the maximum extent practicable, a list of bill numbers and references to specific executive branch actions;

(B) a statement of the Houses of Congress and the Federal agencies contacted by lobbyists employed by the registrant on behalf of the client; [and]

(C) a list of the employees of the registrant who acted as lobbyists on behalf of the client * * *[.]

(3) in the case of a lobbying firm, a good faith estimate of the total amount of all income from the client (including any payments to the registrant by any other person for lobbying activities on behalf of the client) during the quarterly period, other than income for matters that are unrelated to lobbying activities;

(4) in the case of a registrant engaged in lobbying activities on its own behalf, a good faith estimate of the total expenses that the registrant and its employees incurred in connection with lobbying activities during the quarterly period * * *.

(c) ESTIMATES OF INCOME OR EXPENSES.—For purposes of this section, estimates of income or expenses shall be made as follows:

(1) Estimates of amounts in excess of $5,000 shall be rounded to the nearest $10,000.

(2) In the event income or expenses do not exceed $5,000, the registrant shall include a statement that income or expenses totaled less than $5,000 for the reporting period. * * *

(e) ELECTRONIC FILING REQUIRED.—A report required to be filed under this section shall be filed in electronic form, in addition to any other form that the Secretary of the Senate or the Clerk of the House of Representatives may require or allow. * * *

SEC. 6. DISCLOSURE AND ENFORCEMENT.

(a) IN GENERAL.—The Secretary of the Senate and the Clerk of the House of Representatives shall—

(1) provide guidance and assistance on the registration and reporting requirements of this chapter and develop common standards, rules, and procedures for compliance with this chapter;

(2) review, and, where necessary, verify and inquire to ensure the accuracy, completeness, and timeliness of registration and reports;

(3) develop filing, coding, and cross-indexing systems to carry out the purpose of this chapter, including—

(A) a publicly available list of all registered lobbyists, lobbying firms, and their clients; and

(B) computerized systems designed to minimize the burden of filing and maximize public access to materials filed under this chapter;

(4) make available for public inspection and copying at reasonable times the registrations and reports filed under this chapter and, in the case of a report filed in electronic form under section 5(e), make such report available for public inspection over the Internet as soon as technically practicable after the report is so filed; * * *

(7) notify any lobbyist or lobbying firm in writing that may be in noncompliance with this chapter;

(8) notify the United States Attorney for the District of Columbia that a lobbyist or lobbying firm may be in noncompliance with this chapter, if the registrant has been notified in writing and has failed to provide an appropriate response within 60 days after notice was given under paragraph (7); and

(9) maintain all registrations and reports filed under this Act, and make them available to the public over the Internet, without a fee or other access charge, in a searchable, sortable, and downloadable manner, to the extent technically practicable, that—

> (A) includes the information contained in the registration and reports;
>
> (B) is searchable and sortable to the maximum extent practicable, including searchable and sortable by each of the categories of information described in section 4(b) or 5(b); and
>
> (C) provides electronic links or other appropriate mechanisms to allow users to obtain relevant information in the database of the Federal Election Commission * * *.

SEC. 7. PENALTIES.

(a) CIVIL PENALTY.—Whoever knowingly fails to—

(1) remedy a defective filing within 60 days after notice of such a defect by the Secretary of the Senate or the Clerk of the House of Representatives; or

(2) comply with any other provision of this chapter;

shall, upon proof of such knowing violation by a preponderance of the evidence, be subject to a civil fine of not more than $200,000, depending on the extent and gravity of the violation.

(b) CRIMINAL PENALTY.—Whoever knowingly and corruptly fails to comply with any provision of this Act shall be imprisoned for not more than 5 years or fined under title 18, United States Code, or both.

SEC. 8. RULES OF CONSTRUCTION.

(a) CONSTITUTIONAL RIGHTS.—Nothing in this Act shall be construed to prohibit or interfere with—(1) the right to petition the government for the redress of grievances; (2) the right to express a personal opinion; or (3) the

right of association, protected by the first amendment to the Constitution.
* * *

NOTES ON THE LOBBYING DISCLOSURE ACT[23]

1. *Lobbying Contacts and Lobbying Activities.* The Act distinguishes between *lobbying contacts* and *lobbying activities*. The Act's requirements are triggered when an individual makes a lobbying contact, which is a certain kind of communication to a covered official. Once such a contact has occurred, the individual must report on all her lobbying activities, which, among other things, include planning and preparing for the contact. An individual who makes such a contact is considered a lobbyist unless her lobbying activities constitute less than 20% of the services she provides a client during a three-month period. As you can see, the definitions of *lobbying contact*, *lobbying activities*, and *lobbyist* work together to determine when the Act's registration and disclosure provisions are triggered. In addition, it is clear that the definitions of these terms were drafted to address some of the problems in FRLA. For example, the 20% threshold provides a concrete way to determine whether someone's activities before the government are significant enough to make her a lobbyist. Furthermore, a communication need merely relate to legislation, executive branch rules, federal policies, nominations, and the like; it need not be intended to influence the passage or defeat of legislation.

Interestingly, the definition of *lobbying contact* depends in large part on a series of exceptions. Perhaps drafters believed it was easier to state what kinds of communication are *not* lobbying and thus sought to define the term accordingly. The exceptions fall into four general categories: (1) ministerial or de minimis activities (e.g., a request for a meeting as long as there is no attempt to influence a covered official); (2) information that other laws require people to disclose (e.g., disclosure pursuant to the Foreign Agents Registration Act of 1938) or that is otherwise a part of the public record (e.g., testimony before a congressional committee); (3) contacts that are required by other laws or court order (e.g., disclosure compelled by a subpoena); and (4) hardship cases (e.g., disclosure protected under the Whistleblower Protection Act and, perhaps, disclosure by churches).

Is LDA specific enough to withstand constitutional challenge, a case that would be governed by *Harriss*, as well as other First Amendment precedents in the realm of political speech? As in those cases, a court considering a challenge to the Act would apply strict scrutiny to this law that burdens fundamental political rights such as the right to petition the federal government and the right of free speech.

2. *Effects of LDA.* LDA has been in effect since January 1, 1996, and significantly more information about lobbying at the federal level is now available to the press and the public. For example, more people and organizations are registering. Before 1996, the Government Accountability Office found that only 6,000 individuals and organizations had registered with Congress. As of 2010, the number of lobbyists registered with the Senate stood at 17,695, with 6,260 lobbying organizations filing. (Remember that a lobbying firm can file one registration listing all its employees.)

---

[23] For a comprehensive explanation and analysis of LDA and HLOGA, as well as other rules applying to lobbyists at the federal level, see William Luneberg, Thomas Susman & Rebecca Gordon, eds., *The Lobbying Manual: A Complete Guide to Federal Lobbying Law and Practice* (4th ed. 2009 & Supp. 2011).

Lobbying the federal government is now a more than two-billion-dollar-a-year industry. The Center for Responsive Politics reported that spending on federal lobbying in 2012 exceeded $3.3 billion. During 2012, the top industries with regard to lobbying expenses were pharmaceutical businesses ($236 million), business associations ($173 million), the insurance industry ($151 million), electric utilities ($146 million), oil and gas companies ($141 million), and computers and the Internet industry ($133 million). The Chamber of Commerce (and its affiliates) topped the list with respect to individual companies and trade organizations that are active in Washington, shelling out more than $136 million on in-house lobbyists and hired firms in 2012. The second-highest spender, the National Association of Realtors, spent less than half that amount, coming in at more than $41 million.[24] Trade organizations representing corporate and business interests are extremely active in Washington, a phenomenon that merits study because membership in such organizations requires individual interests to cooperate and compromise. Participation in coalitions not only enhances the interests' clout on the Hill, but companies also participate to influence the trade organizations' positions so that they are consistent with their own interests.[25]

The Obama Administration took a very hard line with respect to the ability of registered lobbyists to work in the administration and imposed significant post-employment restrictions on officials. On his first day in office, the President issued an executive order laying out an ethics pledge required of all executive branch appointees. Exec. Order No. 13490, 74 Fed. Reg. 4673 (Jan. 26, 2009). The teeth of the pledge is a provision that bans any appointed official who is a registered lobbyist from participating in any matter on which she lobbied within the last two years or "in any specific issue areas in which that particular matter falls." In other words, someone who was a registered lobbyist for an environmental group advocating for a green energy bill could not work on policy relating to energy issues, climate change proposals, or environmental policy relating to energy. In addition, the ethics pledge requires that a registered lobbyist cannot seek employment with any executive branch agency that she lobbied in the past two years. This has essentially kept lobbyists out of the executive branch—not just lobbyists from corporate America, but also people involved in nonprofits who registered as lobbyists because of their contacts with legislative and executive branch officials on their policy reform issues. Waivers have been allowed in a few instances, including for a former Raytheon lobbyist to become Deputy Secretary of Defense and a former lobbyist for Goldman Sachs to become the Secretary of the Treasury's Chief of Staff. The bad press surrounding these exceptions soon convinced the administration to grant even fewer, including with respect to people who came from the reform sector.

Finally, the ethics pledge also contains a provision aimed broadly at the "revolving door" between government and lobbying. It restricts outgoing appointees from lobbying any covered executive branch official anywhere in the federal government during the entirety of the Obama Administration's tenure in office. The Obama Administration also announced that it plans to reduce the number of registered lobbyists serving on the

---

[24] See Center for Responsive Politics, *Lobbying Database*, http://www.opensecrets.org/lobby/index.php; *Top Spenders in 2012*, http://www.opensecrets.org/lobby/top.php?indexType=s & showYear=2012; and *Top Industries in 2012*, http://www.opensecrets.org/lobby/top.php?indexType=i & showYear=2012 (visited November 28, 2013).

[25] Lee Drutman, *Trade Associations, the Collective Action Dilemma, and the Problem of Cohesion*, in *Interest Group Politics* 74 (Allen Cigler & Burdett Loomis eds., 8th ed. 2012).

nearly 1,000 federal advisory panels, which have more than 60,000 members. The White House Ethics Adviser defended this position because lobbyists "traffic in relationships, working both the Congress and federal agencies to bend legislation and policies on behalf of their clients."[26] The ban on lobbyists serving on the Industry Trade Advisory Committees currently faces a constitutional attack in federal district court, which has been instructed by the appellate court to consider First and Fifth Amendment arguments raised by the lobbyists denied membership on the committees. *Autor v. Pritzker*, 740 F.3d 176 (D.C. Cir. 2014). The district court will be balancing the burden placed on lobbyists' First Amendment right to petition against the government's interest in choosing to whom to listen on particular issues. This is a particularly interesting question in the context of advisory panels where members often serve as representatives of an industry in the private sector, although presumably there are industry representatives who are not also lobbyists. The Fifth Amendment argument raises an equal protection claim, as the plaintiffs contend they are being denied a benefit because of their exercise of a fundamental right. How do you think this case should come out?

One effect of the Obama rules, as well as of the anti-lobbyist rhetoric that characterized his campaigns and continued into the President's terms of office, has been a demand for formal methods of de-registering as a lobbyist. Before the new rules, some would register even when they might not clearly meet the requirements or would continue to be registered after ceasing lobbying activities because there was no perceived disadvantage to registration and disclosure. Instead, people were counseled to register and remain registered when in doubt: better safe than sorry. As soon as the status of lobbyist resulted in concrete negative consequences, the Secretary of the Senate and the Clerk of the House—the officials responsible for the registration system—began to receive questions about de-registering. In June 2009, they released guidance about terminating registrations if a currently registered lobbyist "reasonably" expects that she will not be making lobbying contacts on behalf of a client at any time in the future, or if she spends less than 20% of her time lobbying over the current or upcoming six-month period.[27] The guidance does not allow retroactive de-registering, something some lobbyists had sought so that they could qualify to serve in the Obama Administration. The Center for Responsive Politics reports that 1,732 lobbyists deactivated their registrations in 2012, slightly fewer than have taken this step each year since the Obama rules took effect. Interestingly, the passage in 2007 of the more stringent HLOGA seems to have precipitated many more deactivations than the Obama rules: more than 3,400 lobbyists declined to re-register in 2008.[28] Anecdotally, some observers note that many who might have been willing to register as lobbyists before President Obama was elected have avoided that process and portray themselves as "senior advisors" on policy, giving rise to fears that the administration's policies may have actually reduced transparency.

3. *Increasing the Amount and Relevance of Disclosure.* The information provided by the registration and disclosure forms has been made publicly available by news organizations and public interest groups. Both House and Senate offices now have registration reports available on their respective websites, although it is ironic that the

---

[26] Anna Palmer, *Lobby League Pressures White House on Advisory Boards*, Roll Call, Oct. 28, 2009.

[27] See Lobbying Disclosure Act Guidance (rev. June 2010).

[28] Center for Responsive Politics, *Lobbyists 2012: Out of the Game or Under the Radar?* 6–7 (2013).

government was slow to take advantage of electronic communication while lobbyists quickly adopted (and embraced as an integral part of their lobbying activities) new technology. The 2007 amendments required Congress to make the information disclosed by lobbyists available on the Internet in a searchable, sortable, and downloadable format, and to link to related information provided by the Federal Election Commission.

HLOGA closed or reduced some of the loopholes in LDA's coverage, but did not eliminate all gaps. A crucial improvement made in 2007 was to lower LDA's thresholds for reporting and to require quarterly, rather than semiannual, reports on lobbying activities. Now lobbyists must disclose income from each client in increments of $10,000 (rather than $20,000 as required by the 1995 Act). Another major change in 2007, in provisions not included above, is the requirement that persons covered by LDA file semiannual reports detailing their campaign contributions exceeding $200. Although this information has been available through Federal Election Commission filings, the new semiannual reports will bring more transparency to the campaign activities of lobbyists. In addition, HLOGA requires that federal candidates and political committees associated with officeholders and parties disclose contributions exceeding $15,000 (indexed for inflation, so $17,300 in 2014) that have been bundled by lobbyists registered under LDA. See Trevor Potter & Matthew Sanderson, *Federal Campaign-Finance Law: A Primer for the Lobbyist* and *Lobbyist Bundling of Campaign Contributions*, in *The Lobbying Manual, supra,* at 429 and 471.

Before the 2007 amendments, LDA did not require that lobbyists reveal all the members of coalitions that hired them; only the names of organizational members that contributed more than $10,000 in a six-month period and that planned, supervised, or controlled, *in whole or in major part*, lobbying activities had to be listed in registration forms. (Emphasis added.) Because interest groups work increasingly through coalitions to enhance their clout and broaden their base of support, this gap in the disclosure law was a target of reformers. The new law increases the disclosure relating to coalitions to include any organization that contributes more than $5,000 in any quarter and that "actively participates" in the planning, supervision, or control of lobbying activities. In other words, the organization need not be the major force behind the coalition; it will be disclosed as long as it is actively participating in the group. Balancing this more aggressive disclosure is language that protects individuals from disclosure and that allows a coalition to meet some of the disclosure requirements by posting information on its website.

4.   *Enforcing LDA.* Before the 2007 amendments, LDA was enforced through civil fines that could be calibrated up to $50,000 to reflect the "extent and gravity of the violation." (This was an approach different from the criminal sanctions in FRLA.) In the hearings on the 2007 Act, a House committee noted that there was substantial noncompliance with LDA's disclosure provisions, with more than 2,000 late submissions, failure to file certain forms by virtually all the top lobbying firms, and "almost 300 individuals, companies or associates [who] have lobbied without being registered." H.R. Rep. No. 110–161, 110th Cong., 1st Sess., at 10 (2007) (citing study by the Center for Public Integrity of activity since 1998). Firms realized that they could understate their expenses or fail to report certain lobbying contacts without much risk of a sanction. By 2005, the Department of Justice had pursued only thirteen cases of the

possible LDA violations referred to it by Congress. Six cases had been resolved; three resulted in total fines of $47,000.[29]

Accordingly, HLOGA increased the possible civil fines to $200,000 and authorized criminal prosecutions for knowing and corrupt violations of the Act. In criminal cases, offenders can be sentenced to up to five years in prison, as well as fined. In addition, the Attorney General is required to submit semiannual reports on the aggregate number of enforcement actions and the sentences imposed. The Government Accountability Office reported in 2013 that enforcement has increased, with more than 2,000 referrals for noncompliance sent from Congress to the U.S. Attorney's office in 2009 through 2012. The U.S. Attorney was focusing its efforts on a handful of lobbyists identified as repeat nonfilers. *2012 Lobbying Disclosure: Observations on Lobbyists' Compliance with Disclosure Requirements* 1722–19 (April 2013).[30] Should we expect enforcement to be more vigorous after the increase of the penalties? Why was disclosure up so significantly after passage of the 1995 Act, notwithstanding the absence of aggressive enforcement? What changes in behavior on the part of lobbyists and lawmakers are likely given the expansion of enforcement options?

5. *Constitutional Objections to LDA.* The first challenge to LDA was brought in 2008 after HLOGA changed the rules affecting disclosure of members of a coalition engaged in lobbying. The provision at issue was Section 4(b)(3), requiring any registrant under LDA to provide information about any organization (but not individuals) that contributes more than $5,000 to fund its lobbying activities and that "actively participates" in the "planning, supervision, or control" of the activities. The National Association of Manufacturers (NAM), the country's largest trade organization with more than 11,000 corporate members, challenged this provision under the First Amendment. NAM argued that disclosure of its organizational members would chill them from participating in the political process for fear of the consequences of such publicity. It also contended that the provisions were unconstitutionally vague.

The appellate court unanimously sustained the law against the attack in *Nat'l Ass'n of Mfrs. v. Taylor*, 582 F.3d 1 (D.C. Cir. 2009). In applying a strict scrutiny standard, the court identified the compelling state interest behind the disclosure statute as revealing to the public the interests behind coalitions of organizations, including, but not limited to, so-called "stealth coalitions." It relied on the long line of cases affirming disclosure statutes in a variety of political contexts—lobbying and campaign-finance regulation—to demonstrate the legitimacy of the congressional objective of providing information to the public about the effect of paid lobbying on federal policy. It held that the provision was appropriately tailored to vindicate the state's interest in transparency. The court also found that LDA was not impermissibly vague; for example, other laws that did even more than require disclosure of political activity using a standard such as "actively participates" had been upheld. See, e.g., *U.S. Civil Service Comm'n v. Nat'l Ass'n of Letter Carriers*, 413 U.S. 548 (1973) (rejecting a similar attack on the Hatch Act, which bars federal employees from taking "an active part" in managing political campaigns). Moreover, LDA had been in effect since 1995

---

[29]   Kenneth Doyle, *Love It or Hate It, Lobbying, Ethics Bill Seen as Sea Change for Industry*, BNA Money & Politics Report (Aug. 20, 2007).

[30]   For criticism of enforcement since HLOGA, see William Luneberg, *The Evolution of Federal Lobbying Regulation: Where We Are Now and Where We Should be Going*, 41 McGeorge L. Rev. 85, 123–25 (2009).

with no reported problems of registrants not understanding what constituted "lobbying activities."

The court also considered NAM's argument that, even if the provision is facially constitutional, it was nonetheless problematic as applied to NAM's members. The organization provided examples of some of the consequences its members feared from disclosure: "[M]ob violence has been directed at firms targeted by anti-globalization forces. * * * Firms that are identified as actively lobbying on issues relating to on-going litigation, e.g., asbestos, risk becoming litigation targets. Taking policy positions that are unpopular with some groups may lead to boycotts, shareholder suits, demands for political contributions or support, and other forms of harassment." There was, however, no evidence of the kind of serious harm or retaliation suffered by the members of the NAACP or the Socialist Workers Party that had led courts to exempt those organizations from disclosing their members in the campaign finance realm. See *NAACP v. Alabama*, 357 U.S. 449 (1958); *Brown v. Socialist Workers 74 Campaign Comm. (Ohio)*, 459 U.S. 87 (1982). Indeed, the court noted that NAM's website already identified more than 250 members, and none had produced evidence of adverse consequences from that publicity.

6.   *Further Federal Lobbying Reform Efforts*. Many believe that the federal law, even with the 2007 amendments, needs further refinement. The American Bar Association (ABA) embarked on an extensive effort to propose improvements to LDA, resulting in a January 2011 document, *Lobbying Law in the Spotlight: Challenges and Proposed Improvements*, Report of the Task Force on Federal Lobbying Laws, Section of Administrative Law and Regulatory Practice, 63 Admin. L. Rev. 419 (2011). The ABA's House of Delegates recommended many of the improvements, including:

- Refining the threshold that triggers the lobbying registration requirement, while also avoiding imposing unduly burdensome requirements on small entities. The Task Force recommended, for example, that a firm be required to register if employees make two or more lobbying contacts on behalf of a client and it expects to receive at least $3,000 as compensation for those activities during a quarter. This recommendation would eliminate the 20% threshold in the current law.

- Requiring LDA registrants to disclose lobbying support activities, including strategy, polling, coalition building, and public relations activities. Disclosure should include such activities performed by firms retained by the registrants. This recommendation would result in disclosure of some grassroots lobbying efforts but only by those entities required to register because of direct lobbying contacts; grassroots activities alone would not trigger registration.

- Requiring disclosure of all congressional offices and committees and federal agencies and offices contacted by lobbyists. **Query:** What is the optimal level of additional disclosure? Identifying a committee? A particular congressional office or agency subdivision? An individual staff member or agency bureaucrat? If congressional offices are identified whenever a member or key staff person meets with lobbyists from "the other side" (e.g., a conservative Republican House member or staffer meets with the AFL-CIO or Planned Parenthood; a liberal Democratic Senator or staffer meets with the Chamber of Commerce or the National Rifle Association), might this chill or prevent responsible efforts at information sharing and policy compromise? What constitutional issues might arise with more specific disclosure?

- Prohibiting registered lobbyists from lobbying a member of Congress for whom she engaged in fundraising in the past two years; from fundraising for a member of Congress whom she lobbied in the past two years; or making or soliciting a campaign contribution to a reelection committee for a member of Congress whom the lobbyist has approached for an earmark or narrow benefit. This proposal responded to the Task Force's recommendation that lobbying and campaign participation be separated to the extent possible.

- Transferring authority to enforce LDA to an appropriate administrative authority with sufficient power and resources to effectively enforce the Act. The Task Force suggested the Civil Division of the Department of Justice as a reasonable candidate for this responsibility.

LOBBYING DISCLOSURE ACT PROBLEMS

Problem 3–5. How would the amended LDA affect Robert Harriss, Tom Linder, and Ralph Moore, the people involved in the *Harriss* case? Who would be required to register under the Act, and what information would they be required to disclose? Does it matter if the conversations at the dinners with the members of Congress focused on a possible nominee for the Secretary of Agriculture, whose name had not yet been sent to the Senate for its advice and consent? What if those attending the dinners talked only generally about the country's agricultural policy, including the future of price supports? Would your answer change if the people that Linder and Moore entertained were congressional staff working on the House Appropriations Committee? What if they were high-level appointees in the Department of Commerce?

Problem 3–6. You are a practitioner at a Washington, D.C., law firm in 1990. The following clients come to you for advice about their compliance with LDA in connection with activity concerning a proposed amendment to Title VII of the Civil Rights Act of 1964, the purpose of which would be to overturn the Supreme Court's decision in *United Steelworkers v. Weber* (found in Chapter 1, § 3). At the time, federal lobbying was regulated by FRLA, so first determine what the registration and reporting requirements under that statute would have been. To get a sense of how the landscape has changed, then apply the current regulatory regime of LDA to the facts and note the differences. Are there still gaps in coverage? If so, how would you amend LDA to close those loopholes?

(a)   Jeff Martin is the general counsel of Kaiser Aluminum, one of the defendants in the *Weber* case (which was delighted that it won the case). He spends three days in Washington, D.C., during which he speaks with several members of Congress; Martin then returns home and never makes a subsequent appearance before Congress.

(b)   Kaiser Aluminum itself has a permanent office in D.C., and for several months in 1980 the office staff spends virtually all of its time working to defeat the proposed legislation. Its activities include consultations with legislative staff, writing articles for newspapers throughout the country defending the *Weber* decision, and direct contact with members of Congress.

(c)   United Steelworkers hires Nancy Shea to be a full-time lobbyist on this issue, and she spends several months contacting members of Congress and legislative staff to arouse them to oppose the proposed legislation. United Steelworkers assesses a special fee of $5 per member from each local union so it can pay Shea for her efforts.

Problem 3–7. Okarche Corporation is very concerned with a proposal in Congress to repeal the tax provision allowing small businesses to deduct immediately ("expense") their purchases of some capital equipment. The proposal would require them to depreciate the cost of business assets, i.e., deduct only part of the purchase price each year, over a five-year period. The President of Okarche, Sarah Roberts, asks her assistant to call their Representative to discover the status of the proposal, the date and time of the committee hearings on it, and the timetable for consideration by Congress. Roberts discovers that the proposal has been included in a major tax proposal that seems to be on a fast track for enactment. She then schedules meetings with her Representative and Senator and their staffs; she flies to Washington for these discussions. Her Senator is too busy to see her, but she spends an hour with his legislative assistant, who is responsible for tax matters.

While she is in Washington, she hires Sam Williams, a self-employed consultant specializing in federal tax and budget legislation. Williams accompanies Roberts on the visits to the Hill. He also arranges for Roberts to meet tax lawyers in the Department of Treasury who support this proposal. Finally, he convinces Okarche to join the Coalition to Preserve Small Businesses in America, which is coordinating a nationwide effort to oppose this legislation. Following Williams' advice, Roberts includes a note (that Williams has written) in Okarche's monthly bills explaining the reasons to oppose this tax proposal and urging Okarche's customers to write or call their federal representative.

In the end, Roberts spends about 10% of her time for three months working to oppose the tax proposal. Her company spends approximately $30,000, most of which is paid to Williams for his help. Roberts also pays $3,000 in dues to the Coalition to Preserve Small Businesses in America. (The Coalition pays Williams more than $80,000 for his work as its leader.) Two months after the tax proposal is defeated (in small part due to Roberts' crusade), she puts Williams on a $20,000 annual retainer to keep Okarche informed about developments in Washington relating to small business and to advise her of strategies that Okarche can adopt to influence such matters. Under LDA, as amended in 2007, must either Roberts or Williams register with the Senate and the House? What information must be disclosed in any registration?

Now, suppose Okarche Corporation is a large multistate corporation lobbying in favor of the enactment of an investment tax credit. Roberts follows a similar strategy to the one described above (except this time, she follows Williams' advice and joins the Invest in America Coalition, a group of large corporations hoping to benefit from a new investment tax credit). Although she spends only 10% of her time on the matter, her vice president for legislative affairs, Rachel Alexander, devotes nearly all her time to this matter during a three-month period. Okarche pays Williams about $40,000, spends $5,000 in dues to the coalition, and spends almost $25,000 on its in-house effort, including the letters to its customers. Who must register with the Senate and House? What information must be disclosed?

Problem 3–8. All states have enacted statutes requiring lobbying disclosure (with Pennsylvania being the last state to adopt such a law, in 2007), and the Center for Public Integrity found 47 states to have more effective lobbying-regulation laws than does the federal government.[31] Six states have a two-year waiting period affecting lawmakers who become lobbyists, and 19 states have a one-year ban to combat the problem of the revolving door. Twenty-seven states have independent agencies to oversee lobbying disclosure, with 18 states delegating that authority to the secretary of state. Like the federal government, 37 states include lobbying of the executive branch within the scope of their regulatory structure. Some of the state regulation goes beyond disclosure, however. Some states, including California, Kentucky, South Carolina, and Tennessee, prohibit lobbyists from making contributions to candidates for state offices; Alaska prohibits lobbyist contributions except to candidates in the district where the lobbyist votes; and other states prohibit any contributions while the legislature is in session (e.g., Arizona, Colorado, Connecticut, Iowa, Kansas, Louisiana, Maine, Minnesota, Oklahoma, Vermont, and Wisconsin).[32] Is this prohibition constitutional? How would a court assess it? Compare *Preston v. Leake*, 660 F.3d 726 (4th Cir. 2011) (upholding North Carolina's ban on lobbyists contributing to state legislators, passed in 2006), with *Green Party of Connecticut v. Garfield*, 616 F.3d 189 (2d Cir. 2010) (striking down such a ban because of insufficient evidence of actual corruption, while sustaining a more targeted ban on contributions by federal contractors). Finally, a few states adopt a more aggressive regulatory stance toward disclosure of grassroots lobbying than does the federal government, and some courts have upheld these laws against First Amendment challenge. Compare *Minn. State Ethical Practices Bd. v. Nat'l Rifle Ass'n of America*, 761 F.2d 509 (8th Cir. 1985) ("extensive letter-writing campaign for the purpose of influencing specific legislation" may be regulated as lobbying), with *New Jersey State Chamber of Commerce v. New Jersey Election Law Enforcement Comm'n*, 411 A.2d 168 (N.J. 1980) (reading *Harriss* limitations into ambiguous state statute). How would you analyze the constitutionality of these differing approaches? Are they wise policy even if constitutional?[33]

2. RULES FACILITATING LEGISLATIVE DELIBERATION

At both the state and federal levels there are rules that structure and facilitate deliberation in the legislature. These rules are found in state and federal constitutions, in statutes, at common law, and in customs and regulations of specific legislative chambers. For analytical convenience, we shall organize our discussion around two kinds of rules: first, substantive constitutional requirements affecting legislation, primarily at the state level, including the single-subject rule and generality requirements; and, second, line item veto provisions that allow the executive to influence substance. We follow with an analysis of legislative

---

[31] Leah Rush & David Jimenez, *States Outpace Congress in Upgrading Lobbying Laws*, The Center for Public Integrity, updated Nov. 17, 2011, http://www.publicintegrity.org/2001/03/01/6544/states-outpace-congress-upgrading-lobbying-laws (analysis does not include new Pennsylvania law, 65 Pa.C.S. § 1301–A et seq.).

[32] See National Conference of State Legislatures, *Prohibited Donors*, http://www.ncsl.org/legislatures-elections/elections/prohibited-donors.aspx (visited Dec. 6, 2011).

[33] For an argument that regulation of grassroots lobbying is unconstitutional, see Jay Sekulow & Erik Zimmerman, *Weeding Them Out by the Roots: The Unconstitutionality of Regulating Grassroots Issue Advocacy*, 19 Stan. L. & Pol'y Rev. 164 (2008).

immunities, which can affect the ability to enforce all the rules discussed in this chapter.

A. SUBSTANTIVE LIMITATIONS ON THE LEGISLATIVE PROCESS: SINGLE-SUBJECT RULES AND GENERALITY REQUIREMENTS

Federal and, even more frequently, state constitutions contain a variety of limitations on legislation and the legislative process. Some are substantive limits on the nature of legislation.[34] Generally, the substantive constitutional protections found at the state level are aimed at various forms of rent-seeking by private groups at the public's expense. Why do state constitutions seem more concerned about this problem than the U.S. Constitution seems to be? Perhaps part of the answer lies in the smaller geographic areas of the states relative to the entire United States. James Madison in *Federalist #10* argued that a benefit of a large country was the reduced likelihood that government would be captured by one faction. "[I]t is this circumstance [the greater extent of territory permitted by a representative government] principally which renders factious combinations less to be dreaded[.] * * * Extend the sphere [of territory] and you take in a greater variety of parties and interests; you make it less probable that a majority of the whole will have a common motive to invade the rights of other citizens; or if such a common motive exists, it will be more difficult for all who feel it to discover their own strength and act in unison with each other." Is Madison's argument persuasive? Can you think of other reasons why state constitutions might be more concerned with rent-seeking?

Interestingly, there have been proposals to import some of the state limitations into the federal sphere,[35] if not by constitutional amendment then by congressional rule. For example, the tax-law-writing committees in Congress adopted a policy in the late 1980s against *rifleshot provisions*, or tax provisions that benefit only one or a very few taxpayers. This was a self-imposed generality requirement of sorts.

Generality Requirements. Most state constitutions have provisions regulating the tendency of government to distribute benefits to special interests or private parties, at the state's expense. See Adrian Vermeule, *Veil of Ignorance Rules in Constitutional Law*, 111 Yale L.J. 399, 411–15 (2001) (describing how constitutional provisions requiring generality adopted behind a "partial veil of ignorance" can dampen self-interested behavior). Such "anti-rent-seeking" provisions include the following:

1. *Public Purpose Requirements.* Most state constitutions have general clauses requiring legislation (especially appropriations) to serve public rather than private purposes, and some state codes include general admonitions for courts to interpret statutes as though they were adopted for public rather than private

---

[34] For a good analysis, see Robert Williams, *State Constitutional Limits on Legislative Procedure: Legislative Compliance and Judicial Enforcement*, 48 U. Pitt. L. Rev. 797 (1987).

[35] See Brannon Denning & Brooks Smith, *Uneasy Riders: The Case for a Truth-in-Legislation Amendment*, 1999 Utah L. Rev. 957; Nancy Townsend, Comment, *Single Subject Restrictions as an Alternative to the Line-Item Veto*, 1 Notre Dame J. L. Ethics & Pub. Pol'y 227 (1985) (both arguing for a single-subject requirement at the federal level).

purposes.[36] Theoretically (but usually not in practice) such requirements would require courts to invalidate or to construe rent-seeking legislation narrowly.

2. *Rules Against Special Legislation.* Some state constitutions prohibit *special legislation*, others list subjects on which such legislation is not permitted, while others forbid special statutes when more general ones exist or might be drafted instead. Article 3, § 32, cl. 5–6 of the Pennsylvania Constitution combines these approaches, prohibiting special laws relating to specific subjects (for example, remission of fines, property tax exemptions, or labor regulations) or displacing general laws. Other state constitutions prohibit the government from making gifts, subsidies, or grants to private individuals.[37] For example, Article IV, § 13 of the Illinois Constitution states: "The General Assembly shall pass no special or local law when a general law is or can be made applicable. Whether a general law is or can be made applicable shall be a matter for judicial determination." Courts have not often found that targeted laws are so narrow as to violate the constitutional prohibition against special legislation.[38]

3. *Uniformity.* Many state constitutions require that laws (especially tax laws) be uniform. Compare U.S. Const. Art. I, § 8, cl. 1 (federal "Taxes, Duties, Imposts and Excises * * * shall be uniform throughout the United States") with *id.* Amend. XVI (allowing federal income tax without apportionment among the several states, overruling the Supreme Court's interpretation of § 8, clause 1). State constitutions often require that state laws apply generally and uniformly across the state—an effort to prevent the legislature from providing special benefits to one region or locality. See, e.g., Wis. Const. Art. VIII, § 1 (amended 1974) ("The rule of taxation shall be uniform but the legislature may empower cities, villages or towns to collect and return taxes on real estate located therein by optional methods."); N.J. Const. Art. VIII, § 1 ("Property shall be assessed for taxation under general laws and by uniform rules."); Pa. Const. Art. VIII, § 1 ("All taxes shall be uniform,

---

[36] See Donald Kochan, *"Public Use" and the Independent Judiciary: Condemnation in an Interest-Group Perspective,* 3 Tex. Rev. L. & Pol. 49 (1998) (noting that all states except North Carolina require that any takings of property by the government be only for public use); compare U.S. Const. Amend. V (takings of property must be for a "public use").

[37] The U.S. Constitution has no general prohibition or limitation on special legislation. During each Congress various *private bills* are enacted; one common type consists of a waiver of immigration requirements for particular individuals, and another common type allows compensation to persons whose claims against the federal government fall outside the scope of the Federal Tort Claims Act and other claims statutes. Although, theoretically, federal legislation that is special in character might violate the equal protection component of the Due Process Clause of the Fifth Amendment, we know of no case so holding. See generally Matthew Mantel, *Private Bills and Private Laws,* 99 Law Libr. J. 87 (2007) (providing short history of private bills and reasons for declining use); Note, *Private Bills in Congress,* 79 Harv. L. Rev. 1684 (1966). See also Bernadette Maguire, *Immigration: Public Legislation and Private Bills* (1997) (studying private bills in the immigration context through a series of case studies).

[38] See, e.g., *Cutinello v. Whitley,* 641 N.E.2d 360 (Ill. 1994) (statute allowing that specified counties that impose tax on individuals who sell fuel at retail in respective counties does not violate special legislation provision of state constitution); *Village of Schaumburg v. Doyle,* 661 N.E.2d 496 (Ill. App. 1996) (amendment to Pesticide Act prohibiting regulation of pesticides by any political subdivisions except for counties and municipalities with populations of more than 2 million does not violate the state constitution's special legislation provision). See also Thomas Palisi, Comment, Town of Secaucus v. Hudson County Board of Taxation: *An Analysis of the Special Legislation and Tax Uniformity Clauses of the New Jersey Constitution,* 47 Rutgers L. Rev. 1229 (1995).

upon the same class of subjects, within the territorial limits of the authority of levying the tax, and shall be levied and collected under general law.").[39]

Tax legislation is also increasingly the subject of state constitutional amendments, not all of which are substantive. For example, according to the National Conference of State Legislatures, fifteen states now require supermajority votes to pass certain kinds of tax-rate increases. Six states have either a legislative or constitutional tax-limitation provision that requires the state to return to the taxpayers amounts of tax collected that exceed a certain threshold.[40] All these provisions are designed to make it harder for legislators and organized interests to construct special-interest tax breaks paid for by general tax revenues.

The Single-Subject Rule. Forty-one state constitutions have requirements that limit bills to one subject.[41] Under the majority of these provisions, the single subject of the bill must be expressed in its title. The requirement that the title explain what is in the bill historically predates the single-subject requirement; it apparently resulted from the notorious Yazoo Act of the Georgia Legislature in 1795.[42]

The major purpose of single-subject provisions is to minimize logrolling, derogatorily described by one court as the "practice of jumbling together in one act inconsistent subjects in order to force passage by uniting minorities with different interests when the particular provisions could not pass on their own separate merits."[43] The fear is the following: proposals A, B, and C are bad measures, each benefiting a special interest and each favored by only a minority of legislators. Thus, none could be enacted as a stand-alone bill. But if the three factions can assemble a "Christmas tree" bill—i.e., a bill that, like a Christmas tree, is available for supporting each legislator's pet "ornament"—containing A, B, and C, a majority may well adopt the bill. This runs the risk of creating bad public policy and—if A, B, and C are spending proposals—state overspending.

Several states have single-subject and title requirements for popular initiatives. These provisions are justified not only on the ground that they reduce logrolling, but also that they reduce voter confusion that might arise with

---

[39] See also J. Anthony Coughlan, *Land Value Taxation and Constitutional Uniformity*, 7 Geo. Mason L. Rev. 261 (1999); Jack Stark, *The Uniformity Clause of the Wisconsin Constitution*, 76 Marq. L. Rev. 577 (1993).

[40] Bert Waisanen, *State Tax and Expenditure Limits—2010*, http://www.ncsl.org/research/fiscal-policy/state-tax-and-expenditure-limits-2010.aspx (visited May 12, 2013).

[41] National Conference of State Legislatures, *Single Subject Rules*, http://www.ncsl.org/legislatures-elections/elections/single-subject-rules.aspx (updated May 8, 2009). For the classic study, see Millard Ruud, *No Law Shall Embrace More than One Subject*, 42 Minn. L. Rev. 389 (1958).

[42] The Yazoo Act was entitled "An act supplementary to an act for appropriating part of the unlocated territory of this state, for the payment of the late state troops, and for other purposes therein mentioned, and declaring the right of this state to the unappropriated territory thereof, for the protection and support of the frontiers of this state, and for other purposes." In fact, the Act ordered the sale of a considerable portion of state land to certain companies. Later, in 1796, the Georgia legislature passed a statute declaring the Yazoo Act null and void because of undue influence and fraud in its enactment. In *Fletcher v. Peck*, 10 U.S. (6 Cranch.) 87 (1810), the Supreme Court held that the 1796 Act could not divest title to land sold to an innocent purchaser under the earlier Act.

[43] *State ex rel. Martin v. Zimmerman*, 289 N.W. 662, 664 (Wis. 1940); see *Simpson v. Tobin*, 367 N.W.2d 757, 767 (S.D. 1985).

complicated and intricate legislative proposals. We will return to the single-subject requirement in the context of direct democracy in Chapter 4, § 1B.

Consider the following case concerning the single-subject requirement for laws passed by a state legislature.

DEPARTMENT OF EDUCATION V. LEWIS

Supreme Court of Florida, 1982.
416 So.2d 455.

BOYD, JUSTICE.

House Bill No. 30–B was the general appropriations bill adopted by the 1981 Legislature[.] The appropriations for the Department of Education and the Commissioner of Education was prefaced by the following proviso:

> No funds appropriated herein shall be used to finance any state-supported public or private postsecondary educational institution that charters or gives official recognition or knowingly gives assistance to or provides meeting facilities for any group or organization that recommends or advocates sexual relations between persons not married to each other.

> Sexual relations means contact with sexual organs of one person by the body of another person for sexual gratification.

> Any postsecondary educational institution found in violation of this provision shall have all state funds withheld until that institution is again in compliance with the law.

> No state financial aid shall be given to students enrolled at any postsecondary educational institution located in Florida which is in violation of this provision. * * *

Article III, section 12, Florida Constitution, provides:

> Laws making appropriations for salaries of public officers and other current expenses of the state shall contain provisions on no other subject.

This provision is a corollary of Article III, section 6, which requires that all laws be limited to a single subject and matters properly related to that subject. An extensive body of constitutional law teaches that the purpose of article III, section 6 is to ensure that every proposed enactment is considered with deliberation and on its own merits. A lawmaker must not be placed in the position of having to accept a repugnant provision in order to achieve adoption of a desired one.

Through a number of cases decided over many years this Court has attempted to make clear to the Legislature that under our constitutional plan for the lawful exercise of governmental powers an appropriations act is not the proper place for the enactment of general public policies on matters other than appropriations. In *Brown v. Firestone*, [382 So.2d 654 (Fla. 1980)], the Court said:

> * * * Provisions on substantive topics should not be ensconced in an appropriations bill in order to logroll or to circumvent the legislative process normally applicable to such action. Similarly, general

appropriations bills should not be cluttered with extraneous matters which might cloud the legislative mind when it should be focused solely upon appropriations matters.

* * * *[Brown]* establish[ed] two principles[.] * * * First, if a provision in an appropriations bill changes existing law on any subject other than appropriations, it is invalid. Second, a qualification or restriction must directly and rationally relate to the purpose of the appropriation to which it applies. * * *

* * * The proviso [in question] attempts to make substantive policy on the governance of postsecondary educational institutions. Thus it amends a whole host of statutes pertaining to the operation of public colleges and universities and the regulation of private colleges and universities, [thereby failing the first test of *Brown*].

* * * The proviso is not directly and rationally related to the appropriation of state funds to postsecondary institutions and students. It is, rather, designed to further a legislative objective unrelated to such funding [and thereby fails the second test as well].

NOTES ON ENFORCEMENT OF STATE RESTRICTIONS ON LEGISLATION AND LEGISLATIVE PROCEDURES

1. *Enforcing the Single-Subject Rule.* State constitutions do not define what they mean by a "single subject" and "strict adherence to [the rule's] letter would seriously interfere with the practical business of legislation."[44] Thus, many state courts have articulated liberal tests that are easy for legislatures to meet. "[I]f, from the standpoint of legislative treatment, there is any reasonable basis for the grouping together in one 'act' of various matters, this court cannot say that such matters constitute more than one subject."[45] The remedy for a violation of the single subject varies among the states. Some state constitutions explicitly provide the remedy; in Iowa, for example, the Constitution states that any provision that is not consistent with the subject of an Act may be severed and declared void, while the rest of the provisions remain in effect. Iowa Const. Art. III, § 29. Where constitutions are silent, courts must determine whether to sever the offending provisions or to strike down the entire law because the unconstitutional procedure of enactment tainted the entire bill. See Martha Dragich, *State Constitutional Restrictions on Legislative Procedure: Rethinking the Analysis of Original Purpose, Single Subject, and Clear Title Challenges*, 38 Harv. J. Legis. 103, 154–63 (2001) (arguing that severance tends to be the better remedy and providing severance analysis).

Illinois has more aggressively enforced the single-subject requirement than most other states, and, in some instances, it has used the rule to throw out entire statutes, not just the offending provisions. In *Johnson v. Edgar*, No. 95 CH 12004 (Ill. Circ. Ct. May 7, 1996), *aff'd*, 680 N.E.2d 1372 (Ill. 1997), the Illinois Circuit Court was faced with a challenge to a crime bill. The bill had begun its legislative life as "An act in relation to prisoners' reimbursement to the Department of Corrections for the expenses incurred by their incarcerations," but by the end of House consideration it was known merely as

---

[44] *Bernstein v. Comm'r of Public Safety*, 351 N.W.2d 24, 25 (Minn. App. 1984).

[45] *Dague v. Piper Aircraft Corp.*, 418 N.E.2d 207, 214–15 (Ind. 1981).

"An act in relation to crime" because so many provisions had been added. These amendments included provisions dealing with pupil expulsion for bringing a weapon to school, competitive selection procedures on contracts in the State Public Defender's office, and permission for the Attorney General to bring a civil action against organizations engaging in international terrorism. By the end of the second conference committee, the proposal was "An act in relation to public safety" because it now included provisions dealing with fees for motor fuels, regulations for underground storage tanks, and exemptions for businesses from the wiretapping statute. (The judicial challenge to the bill was brought by opponents of this last provision.) The bill had grown from eight pages to 243 pages.

In striking the entire law down, the judge described some of the rationales justifying the constitutional rule: "The Act is a textbook case of the type of situation that Article IV of the Illinois Constitution was enacted to prevent—attaching an unpopular bill to a popular one to circumvent legislative input or scrutiny. Imagine the public rebuke that would be directed at a legislator who did not vote for a bill that sought to protect children from the horrid abuses at the hand of sex offenders [one of the many provisions in the Act]. At the same time these legislators are drafting in a measure in the very same Act that would allow employers to, in effect, eavesdrop on their own workforce. It is a reprehensible measure to ride a potentially unpassable piece of legislation on the backs of abused children." The court objected not only to the violation of the single-subject requirement, but also to the extensive revisions made by a conference committee without public hearings or deliberation. See also *People v. Olender*, 854 N.E.2d 593 (2005) (striking down a law in its entirety and detailing how it grew from a bill amending three criminal laws to a more than 100–page act "in relation to government regulation").

The Illinois courts will sometimes pull back, however, when the effect of invalidating a statute seems particularly disruptive. In *Arangold Corp. v. Zehnder,* 718 N.E.2d 191 (Ill. 1999), the Illinois Supreme Court found that an act implementing the fiscal year 1996 budget, and including provisions that began their legislative life as the Tobacco Products Tax Act, did not violate the single-subject rule. The supreme court held that all the provisions of the budget act, which amended more than 20 other laws, related to the implementation of the state's budget. Unlike *Johnson*, where the court rejected the legislature's attempt to unite disparate provisions under the rubric of "public safety," the challenged legislation included "all the means reasonably necessary to accomplish" the purpose of implementing the state budget and thus covered only a single subject. The court held that all the provisions need not be related to each other, but only to the single subject identified by the legislature. Perhaps the law at issue in *Arangold Corp.* was different from the previous act in relation to public safety. Or, perhaps the court shied away from striking down the act that implemented Illinois' budget for an entire fiscal year. If the court had been able merely to invalidate the challenged portion of the bill, here the provisions taxing tobacco products, do you think the outcome would have been different?

2. *Public Choice Arguments.* The insights of public choice theory suggest that more rigorous enforcement of the single-subject rule might well limit logrolling and help foster legislative deliberation. For example, consider how the proviso held unconstitutional in *Lewis* might have been attached to the appropriations bill. What

group was the likely target of the proviso in question? Are there not scenarios in which a conscientious legislator could get trapped into voting for the bill, proviso and all?

But public choice theory also might suggest the following normative argument for a narrow view of the single-subject rule: the overall political satisfaction of groups with their political system might be enhanced if each group receives the legislation that it most intensely desires. Hence, even though proposals A, B, and C reflect minority preferences, the groups favoring them might have very strong preferences for those policies (e.g., anti-smoking regulations, anti-discrimination protections, and stricter penalties for drunk driving). In a simple majority-vote model, these groups could not satisfy their strongest preferences. With logrolling, the groups can express the intensity of their preferences by their willingness to trade votes for their favored proposals, in return for supporting proposals they would otherwise oppose.[46] Furthermore, logrolling allows legislatures to assemble majority support for proposals and provides the necessary lubrication to allow multi-member bodies to overcome collective-action problems and enact laws.

Michael Gilbert adopts this approach—arguing that logrolling is often beneficial and a court cannot easily distinguish a "bad" logroll from a "good" one—to provide a procedurally based definition of "subject" for enforcement of the requirement. *Single Subject Rules and the Legislative Process*, 67 U. Pitt. L. Rev. 803 (2006). He contends that the more troublesome legislative phenomenon is the addition of riders, or unpopular substantive provisions attached to popular bills. Whereas logrolling leaves a majority of legislators better off through exchange, riders are a product of "manipulation of legislative procedures. Well-placed legislators can attach self-serving measures to otherwise popular bills, and they need not offer anything to the measures' opponents." Courts should therefore enforce the single-subject rule against riders but not against the product of legislative logrolls. How can a court distinguish one from the other? Gilbert suggests that any provisions added on the floor of the legislature are more likely to be logrolls; whereas provisions attached in committee are often riders. Courts should be less deferential when a bill is considered under a relatively closed rule on the floor, and "[i]n general, more floor debate should correspond to less judicial scrutiny." He advises courts to look carefully at legislative history, "voting records, political affiliation, and even poll data to hypothesize how legislators would vote on a truncated bill." Is this test realistic? Can courts differentiate between logrolls that should be encouraged and riders that reflect manipulation of the political process? Isn't this analysis especially challenging in the context of state legislatures, which produce less legislative history than the federal House or Senate? Is Gilbert's approach an improvement over the *Lewis* court's analysis?

      3.   *Substantive Legislation Through Riders to Appropriations Legislation.* As *Lewis* demonstrates, appropriations bills are popular targets for riders. Appropriations riders short-circuit the ordinary committee process because they emerge from a committee without primary jurisdiction over the legislative proposal, thereby depriving the legislature of the value of expert-committee deliberation. However, many states exempt appropriations measures from their single-subject rules, presumably so that omnibus budgets can be enacted. For jurisdictions having no single-subject rule for appropriations measures, courts can protect deliberative processes by relying on devices

---

[46] See James Buchanan & Gordon Tullock, *The Calculus of Consent: Logical Foundations of Constitutional Democracy* 131–45 (1962).

such as the canon of statutory interpretation that presumes against legislative amendment of substantive law through appropriations measures.[47] The leading federal case is *TVA v. Hill*, 437 U.S. 153 (1978), Chapter 7, § 2C (Endangered Species Act of 1973 required halting $100+ million dam whose construction threatened endangered snail darter, notwithstanding continued post-1973 congressional appropriations for the dam and evidence that appropriations committees knew of the Act and believed it inapplicable). The federal House and Senate also usually have internal rules that prohibit members from adding riders to appropriations bills, although these rules can be waived or ignored without substantial political cost.

B. THE LINE ITEM VETO AND OTHER RULES TO ENFORCE BUDGET LIMITATIONS

Extensive logrolling in budgetary measures yields a deeper problem than just biased law; it also produces budget deficits that might be debilitating to government. Unlike the U.S. Constitution, three-fourths of the state constitutions require state budgets to be balanced every year. All but one state, Vermont, have either constitutional or statutory balanced budget requirements.[48] Forty-three states also provide that the state governor may veto "items" in appropriations bills; a few of those states extend the power to all bills. In such states, the line item veto is often a complement to single-subject rules that may not apply to appropriations bills. In other words, the traditional veto coupled with a single-subject rule protects the governor from take-it-or-leave-it proposals in most contexts, and the line item veto empowers him to unravel such deals with respect to omnibus appropriations laws. For 38 states with item vetoes, the veto can be overridden only by supermajority votes (two-thirds of legislators present, two-thirds of legislators elected, or three-fifths of legislators elected); for the other states, an override requires only simple majorities or elected majorities in each legislative chamber.[49]

The main purpose of the item veto is to supplement state balanced budgets, but the broader purpose of both the item veto and balanced budget requirements is to ameliorate logrolling. In that regard, the item veto may be more effective than the single-subject rule because it is focused on the most serious logrolling problem (spending money) and because it is vested in the governor, who bears responsibility for balancing the budget.[50] Some scholars have argued that spending constraints such as balanced budget rules will be ineffective in changing legislative behavior without the threat of third-party enforcement, a threat provided by an item veto.[51] In fact, most studies of the state item veto find that its availability does not push spending levels downward, although it does allow the executive more influence over

---

[47] See Sandra Beth Zellmer, *Sacrificing Legislative Integrity at the Altar of Appropriations Riders: A Constitutional Crisis*, 21 Harv. Envtl. L. Rev. 457 (1997). For a critique of the appropriations canon, see Mathew McCubbins & Daniel Rodriguez, *Canonical Construction and Statutory Revisionism: The Strange Case of the Appropriations Canon*, 14 J. Contemp. Legal Issues 669 (2005).

[48] See Tracy Gordon, *The Calculus of Constraint: A Critical Review of State Fiscal Institutions*, in *Fiscal Challenges: An Interdisciplinary Approach to Budget Policy* 271, 275 (Elizabeth Garrett, Elizabeth Graddy & Howell Jackson eds. 2008).

[49] *The Book of the States 2012* Table 3.16, at 156–57.

[50] See Richard Briffault, *The Item Veto in State Courts*, 66 Temple L. Rev. 1171, 1178–79 (1993) (excellent article on item veto generally).

[51] See, e.g., Lawrence Lessig, *Lessons from a Line Item Veto Law*, 47 Case W. Res. L. Rev. 1659 (1997).

budgetary decisions. In other words, the final budget will reflect more of the governor's preferences if she wields the item veto weapon; thus, the tool affects the mix of spending programs rather than the level of spending.[52]

Maxwell Stearns argues that the item veto will necessarily change the kinds of deals legislators reach and the bargaining dynamics. *The Public Choice Case Against the Item Veto,* in *Public Choice and Public Law: Reading and Commentary* 11 (1997). Legislators will attempt to protect legislation from the governor's item veto through sophisticated drafting techniques and by reaching bargains with the governor. The latter strategy may actually increase the amount of spending if the price for the governor's forbearance is enactment of programs that she favors along with the legislative spending items. With respect to what Stearns calls *length bargains*, relatively unrelated riders added to proposals to attract majority support, a line item veto does not eliminate these deals; instead, it merely requires the executive's approval to assure bargainers that the item veto will not be used to eliminate goodies. In contrast, legislators can work unimpeded by the threat of an item veto to assemble majority support for bills by negotiating *substantive bargains* embedded in provisions to reduce any adverse effect on minority interests. Such changes do not produce new items and so are immune from the governor's item veto. Finally, legislative resistance to the item veto often kicks the issues into the courts, whose resolution will then affect subsequent interactions between the governor and the legislature in the veto game.

RUSH V. RAY
Supreme Court of Iowa, 1985.
362 N.W.2d 479.

SCHULTZ, JUSTICE.

[The Iowa General Assembly enacted five separate appropriation bills, each of which contained a provision that either provided "notwithstanding section eight point thirty-nine (8.39) of the Code, funds appropriated by this Act shall not be subject to transfer or expenditure for any purpose other than the purposes specified" or recited a phrase similar in language and content. Governor Robert D. Ray exercised his item veto power to excise the quoted and similar phrases from each act. The issue was whether use of the governor's item veto power to eliminate a provision in an appropriation bill that prohibits the expenditure or transfer of appropriated funds from one department of state government to another is proper.]

The constitutional provision which gives the governor item veto authority provides in pertinent part:

> The governor may approve appropriation bills in whole or in part and may disapprove any item of an appropriation bill; and the part approved shall

---

[52] For some of the best studies of the line item veto power in the states, see George Abney & Thomas Lauth, *The Line-Item Veto in the States: An Instrument for Fiscal Restraint or Partnership?*, 45 Pub. Admin. Rev. 372 (1985); James Dearden & Thomas Husted, *Do Governors Get What They Want?: An Alternative Examination of the Line-Item Veto*, 77 Pub. Choice 707 (1993); Rui de Figueiredo, Jr., *Budget Institutions and Political Insulation: Why States Adopt the Item Veto*, 87 J. Pub. Econ. 2677 (2003); Douglas Holtz-Eakin, *The Line Item Veto and Public Sector Budgets: Evidence from the States*, 36 J. Pub. Econ. 269 (1988); Glen Robinson, *Public Choice Speculations on the Item Veto*, 74 Va. L. Rev. 403 (1988).

become a law. Any item of an appropriation bill disapproved by the governor shall be returned, . . . Any such item of an appropriation bill may be enacted into law notwithstanding the governor's objections, in the same manner as provided for other bills.

Iowa Const. Art. III, § 16 (1857, amended 1968).

Appellant [State Senator Robert Rush] asserts that the vetoed portions of these five acts are provisos or limitations, not items; thus, they were not subject to the governor's item veto power. On the other hand, the Governor asserts that the language stricken from the five appropriation bills constituted distinct, severable "items" within the meaning of article III, section 16 of the Iowa Constitution, that could be removed from the appropriation bills by the use of the item veto.

We have twice passed on the legality of the governor's exercise of the item veto power. * * * *Welden v. Ray*, 229 N.W.2d 706 (Iowa 1975); *State ex rel. Turner v. Iowa State Highway Commission*, 186 N.W.2d 141 (Iowa 1971). * * *

The problem presented in *Turner* arose when the legislature appropriated funds to the primary road fund, and the governor vetoed a portion of the bill that additionally prohibited removing certain established offices from their present location. When this item veto was challenged, we upheld the veto. We established certain principles to be used in interpreting the term "item" and distinguished items, which are subject to veto, from provisos or conditions inseparably connected to an appropriation, which are not subject to veto. We approved another court's statement that an "item" is "something that may be taken out of a bill without affecting its other purposes and provisions. It is something that can be lifted bodily from it rather than cut out. No damage can be done to the surrounding legislative tissue, nor should any scar tissue result therefrom." * * * While we surmised that the legislature may have intended to make the challenged language a limitation or proviso on the expenditure of funds, we held the act as drawn and enacted did not restrict the use of the appropriated funds for the purposes and uses referred to in the deleted language. We held the deleted language was an item rather than a qualification.

When the governor's authority to exercise his item veto power was challenged in *Welden*, we reached a different result than in *Turner*, holding that the attempted vetoes by the governor were beyond the scope of his constitutional power. The vetoed items in the appropriation bills provided limitations on how the money appropriated for each department was to be spent. Specifically, these provisions included limitations on the number of employees in a department, limitations on the percent of the appropriation that could be used for salaries, prohibition against construction of buildings, prohibition against spending beyond budget, and elimination of matching fund grants if the federal funds were discontinued—with the further provision that unused state matching funds would revert to the general fund. We held that these clauses were lawful qualifications upon the respective appropriations rather than separate, severable provisions.

In *Welden* we * * * quoted a New Mexico ruling that stated:

The power of partial veto is the power to disapprove. This is a negative power, or a power to delete or destroy a part or item, and is not a positive power, or a power to alter, enlarge or increase the effect of the remaining parts or items. . . . Thus, a partial veto must be so exercised that it eliminates or destroys the whole of an item or part and does not distort the legislative intent, and in effect create legislation inconsistent with that enacted by the Legislature, by the careful striking of words, phrases, clauses or sentences.

Id. (quoting *State ex rel. Sego v. Kirkpatrick*, 86 N.M. 359, 524 P.2d 975 (1974)). * * * The message of these cases and others reviewed in *Welden* is that the governor's power is a negative one that does not allow him to legislate by striking qualifications in a manner which distorts legislative intent. Thus, he cannot strike a provision that would divert money appropriated by the legislature for one purpose so that it may be used for another. Finally, we held in *Welden* that the governor's veto of a legislatively-imposed qualification upon an appropriation must also include a veto of the appropriation.

In the present case the trial court determined that the vetoed portion of each appropriation bill did not change the basic purpose of the legislation; thus, the provision is properly considered a severable item rather than a legislatively-imposed condition. We agree with appellant's contention that "the effect of this veto was to make money from the treasury available for purposes not authorized by the legislation as it was originally written, contrary to the clear intent of the legislature." The Governor has used the item veto power affirmatively to create funds not authorized by the legislature. The vetoed language created conditions, restricting use of the money to the stated purpose. It is not severable, because upon excision of this language, the rest of the legislation is affected. The appropriated money is no longer required to be used only for the stated purpose; it could be used for other purposes. Thus, these are not items which are subject to veto.

This case is unlike *Turner* in which the deletion of directions concerning office changes had no effect on the appropriation of funds. We find it closer akin to *Welden* in which the governor had deleted provisions which dictated how and for what purposes the appropriated funds were to be expended. In the present case the legislature clearly limited the expenditure of the appropriated funds to specified purposes. The veto distorted the obvious legislative intent that the funds only be spent for the appropriated purposes and created additional ways the funds might be spent. This was use of the veto power to create rather than negate. We hold that the language vetoed constituted qualifications on the appropriations rather than separate items subject to veto. * * *

HARRIS, JUSTICE (dissenting [for three dissenting justices]).

The experience in other states shows that, at best, there tends to be a blurred line between an "item" (which can be vetoed from an appropriation bill) and a proviso or condition on how the funds are to be spent (which cannot). It does however seem clear that the line, no matter how blurred, is crossed when legislation (even if labeled a proviso or condition) is appended to an appropriation bill in violation of the single subject provision of a state constitution.

The cases recognize a difficulty faced by governors when presented with appropriation bills which have been infused with legislation, going beyond the appropriation, which impacts either on existing statutes or upon purely executive functions. Some governors are unprotected even by a single-subject constitutional provision. It is quite common to find provisions such as Art III, § 29 of the Iowa Constitution which provide that "every act shall embrace but one subject. . . ." Single subject provisions offer some protection but it is limited. If a provision is attached to an appropriation bill in violation of the single-subject provision the whole act could be challenged as void. But a governor is usually in a poor position to ask for an appropriation bill to be declared void. This would be the case when the government could not continue to function without the funds from the appropriation. Legislation attached by means of proviso or condition labels to crucial appropriation bills might thus become impervious to veto. The upshot was a liberal definition of an item, mentioned by the majority, which we adopted in *Turner*. We said: ". . . should the . . . [l]egislature attempt to coerce the [g]overnor into approving a lump sum appropriation by combining purposes and amount the court [will] interpret the term 'item' liberally to preserve the purpose of the item veto amendment."

[Both *Turner* and *Welden* applied the "scar tissue" test, treating as vetoable "something that may be taken out of a bill without affecting its other purposes and provisions. It is something which can be lifted bodily from it rather than cut out. No damage can be done to the surrounding legislative tissue, nor should any scar tissue result therefrom." Senator Rush and the other plaintiffs object to that test.] But courts elsewhere commonly apply it. [Justice Harris cited decisions from nine other states.]

The majority recites, and seems to acknowledge the validity of, the "scar tissue test," but does not follow it. Under the test the provisions in question here were proper subjects of item vetoes. Each appropriation was earmarked to a department of government which could use the funds only for the purpose specified by the legislature. The vetoes here in no way modified the legislative plan of how the department could use the funds. The vetoed provisions related only to funds which might remain unused. The power of the governor to transfer unused funds under section 8.39, acting after notice to and "review and comment by" appropriate legislative chairpersons, has been statutorily provided for more than forty years. All branches of Iowa government have become quite used to it. It is, to put it in simple terms, the way our state government works.

If the legislature were to pass an act calling for the repeal or suspension of section 8.39 the act would be subject to an executive veto. Under the scar tissue rule the governor should not be robbed of this veto power by the simple process of attaching the repeal or suspension of this existing statute to an appropriation bill. This is a textbook example of why we and states elsewhere adopted the scar tissue rule. The trial court should be affirmed.

NOTES ON DIFFERENT APPROACHES TO THE ITEM VETO

1. *Situating the Iowa Approach.* We have chosen this Iowa case in part because item vetoes have been rather frequently litigated in Iowa (see the next note) and in part because this approach is a fairly moderate one. Some state courts basically let the legislature define a vetoable "item," e.g., *Washington State Motorcycle Dealers Ass'n v. State*, 763 P.2d 442 (Wash. 1988). In his article *The Item Veto in State Court*, *supra*, Richard Briffault argues that these courts enable the legislature to evade the purposes of the item veto by clever drafting. On the other hand, Wisconsin courts have very expansively interpreted that state's item veto to allow the governor to veto words and phrases even when the veto completely changes the meaning of the statute. In *State ex rel. Wisconsin Senate v. Thompson*, 424 N.W.2d 385 (Wis. 1988), a divided court allowed the governor to veto word fragments, individual letters from words, and even individual digits from numbers as long as the resulting law made grammatical sense.[53] The reaction to this "Vanna White veto" was swift, with the voters in 1990 prohibiting the governor from deleting individual letters or numerical characters to change the intent of the legislature. Another referendum was passed by Wisconsin voters in 2008 to further limit the governor's line item veto, which had become known as the "Frankenstein veto" because he could still, through strategic editing, stitch two sentences together to form a new sentence with a different meaning. The new law prohibits the governor from creating "a new sentence by combining parts of two or more sentences," but still allows the governor the power to veto parts of appropriations bills and other provisions that are considered "items." See Wis. Const. Art. V, § 10 (c) (2010).

The Iowa approach is an effort to find a middle way between approaches too deferential to the legislature and those too empowering of the governor. This approach seeks to limit item vetoes in a way that will not negate them altogether. It originates in the old "affirmative-negative" test that prevents the governor from creating "affirmative" or new legislation, e.g., *Colorado General Assembly v. Lamm*, 704 P.2d 1371, 1382–83 (Colo. 1985), but then elaborates upon that test. Does *Rush* create an appropriate balance (as the court thought), or does it open up the item veto to evasion (as the dissenters thought)?

2. *Subsequent Iowa Cases.* In *Colton v. Branstad*, 372 N.W.2d 184 (Iowa 1985), the court upheld an item veto of a condition attached to an appropriations bill that the court characterized as a *rider*, a non-germane attachment to the bill. What the court saw as a rider was language in the appropriation for the State Department of Health that directed the Department to relinquish authority over certain grants to the State Family Planning Council. "The Governor's constitutional power to veto bills of general legislation cannot be abridged by the careful placement of such measures in a general appropriation bill, thereby forcing the Governor to choose between approving unacceptable substantive legislation or vetoing 'items' of expenditure essential to the operation of government." Isn't this more in the spirit of the *Rush* dissent than of the majority opinion?

You might wonder, what is a *rider*? What is *non-germane* to an appropriations bill? Recall *Lewis*, the Florida single-subject case, which involved a "substantive" provision added onto an appropriations measure, and the distinction between logrolls and riders

---

[53] See Mary Burke, Comment, *The Wisconsin Partial Veto: Past, Present and Future*, 1989 Wis. L. Rev. 1395; Winston Holliday, Jr., Comment, *Tipping the Balance of Power: A Critical Survey of the Gubernatorial Line Item Veto*, 50 S.C. L. Rev. 503 (1999) (focusing on Wisconsin, Iowa, and Virginia).

for a procedural perspective; one of our notes to the case described a widely accepted policy of preventing substantive legislation through the appropriations process, presumably because riders of this sort do not receive the deliberative scrutiny of committees expert on the matter and often "slip by" the legislature without careful debate or focus.

ITEM VETO PROBLEMS

Problem 3–9. The governor of Iowa vetoes language attached to an appropriation for tourism and export trade promotion, which provided "as a condition, limitation, and qualification, any official Iowa trade delegation led by the governor which receives financial or other support from the appropriation in this subsection shall be represented by a bipartisan delegation." Under the Iowa precedents, could the governor veto this "condition"? Or was it really a "rider"? See *Welsh v. Branstad*, 470 N.W.2d 644 (Iowa 1991).

Problem 3–10. The legislature enacts a statewide sales tax of 6%. A clause in the bill sets a ceiling of $500 on the amount of tax that can be charged per product or service. The legislature apparently is concerned that the sales tax might discourage purchases of "big ticket" items, such as cars, boats, and appliances. The governor uses the item veto to delete the $500 ceiling, arguing that the state needs the revenue and that the exemption favors the wealthy, who purchase luxury goods. How would this exercise of the item veto be analyzed under the tests discussed above? How could the legislature draft the sales tax provision to insulate the ceiling from the item veto? See Antony Petrilla, *The Role of the Line-Item Veto in the Federal Balance of Power*, 31 Harv. J. Legis. 469 (1994) (providing this example and analyzing under various tests).

NOTE ON THE FEDERAL LINE ITEM VETO ACT

In 1996, Congress passed the Line Item Veto Act (LIVA), Pub. L. 104–130, 110 Stat. 1200, which granted the President the power to cancel certain spending programs. Despite its name, the Act did not give the President the same kind of power enjoyed by governors. Governors can veto particular items in legislation while enacting only the rest of the bill into law; the vetoed items are never enacted. In contrast, before the President could exercise his power under the federal Act, he was required to sign, and thereby enact, the entirety of the bill that contained provisions subject to the cancellation authority. However, the President's cancellation power was broader than that of most governors. Although he was limited to canceling spending items in their entirety (like most governors, he could not reduce spending for a program), he could use his power to eliminate certain tax provisions (those that provided benefits to 100 or fewer entities). In this way, the drafters of the Act recognized that spending programs can be found in the tax code as well as in appropriations bills. For example, Congress can subsidize homeowners through grants of federal money or through tax provisions allowing deductions for the payment of mortgage interest or eliminating tax on gains from the sales of homes. These sorts of tax provisions are often called *tax expenditures* because of their similarity to other kinds of government expenditures.

In the first year the Act was effective, President Clinton canceled 82 items in 11 laws. Congress reinstated 38 of the provisions over the President's veto, and a court case challenging another cancellation resulted in a settlement that required the executive branch to spend the funds. In the end, the savings to the federal government amounted to less than $600 million over five years. Notwithstanding the relatively trivial amounts involved, the Court reached the merits of the constitutional challenge in the summer of 1998.

Clinton v. City of New York
524 U.S. 417 (1998).

In the District Court, the appellees had challenged two of the President's exercises of the cancellation power under LIVA. First, he canceled a "direct spending" (or entitlement) provision in the Balanced Budget Act of 1997 that gave New York preferential treatment under the Medicaid law. Second, President Clinton canceled a tax provision in the Taxpayer Relief Act of 1997 that allowed owners of certain food refineries and processors to defer paying tax on the gain from the sale of their stock if they sold to eligible farmers' cooperatives. Because very few taxpayers could take advantage of the tax expenditure, it was a limited tax benefit eligible for cancellation. In canceling these provisions, all parties agreed that the President had adhered to the requirements of LIVA, including determining that cancellation would "(i) reduce the Federal budget deficit; (ii) not impair any essential Government functions; and (iii) not harm the national interest." LIVA provided that a cancellation of items such as these prevented them "from having legal force or effect," even as the remainder of the provisions in the acts continued to be effective and binding law.

Justice Stevens, writing for the majority, held that these cancellations had allowed the President unilaterally to amend two acts of Congress by repealing a part of each. While the Constitution allows the President to veto an entire bill before signing it, he was not given the authority to enact parts and effectively repeal, after signing, other parts. Quoting *INS v. Chadha*, 462 U.S. 919 (1985) [Chapter 8, § 3A], he noted that "[t]he procedures governing the enactment of statutes set forth in the text of Article I were the product of the great debates and compromises that produced the Constitution itself. Familiar historical materials provide abundant support for the conclusion that the power to enact statutes may only 'be exercised in accord with a single, finely wrought and exhaustively considered, procedure.' * * * What has emerged in these cases from the President's exercise of his statutory cancellation powers, however, are truncated versions of two bills that passed both Houses of Congress. They are not the product of the 'finely wrought' procedure that the Framers designed." * * *

Stevens rejected two arguments made by the government to defend the Act. First, relying primarily on *Field v. Clark*, 143 U.S. 649 (1892) [*infra*, § 3A], the government contended that the cancellations were merely exercises of discretionary authority delegated to the President, like the power delegated by the Tariff Act of 1890 that allowed the President to suspend the exemption from import duties on some products when he determined that another country was imposing duties on U.S. products that were "reciprocally unequal and unreasonable." The majority opinion disagreed, noting several differences between the power under the Tariff Act and under LIVA. Perhaps most importantly, "whenever the President suspended an exemption under the Tariff Act, he was executing the policy that Congress had embodied in the statute. In contrast, whenever the President cancels an item of new direct spending or a limited tax benefit he is rejecting the policy judgment made by Congress and relying on his own policy judgment."

Second, the government argued that the cancellation power under LIVA was merely the power to "decline to spend" certain money or to "decline to implement" certain tax rules, a power that the executive had long enjoyed in other contexts. "The critical difference between this statute and all of its predecessors, however," the majority held, "is that unlike any of them, this Act gives the President the unilateral power to change the text of duly enacted statutes. None of the Act's predecessors could even arguably have been construed to authorize such a change."

The majority concluded that it was not making a judgment about the wisdom of providing the President with a line item veto, but clearly holding that such a change would require constitutional amendment. This conclusion was met by two vigorous dissents. First, **Justice Scalia** rejected the notion that the constitutional requirements for lawmaking had been violated; instead, the appropriate frame was to determine whether the cancellation power was a permissible delegation of authority to the executive branch. "Insofar as the degree of political, 'law-making' power conferred upon the Executive is concerned, there is not a dime's worth of difference between Congress's authorizing the President to *cancel* a spending item, and Congress's authorizing money to be spent on a particular item at the President's discretion. And the latter has been done since the Founding of the Nation. From 1789–1791, the First Congress made lump-sum appropriations for the entire Government—'sum[s] not exceeding' specified amounts for broad purposes. From a very early date Congress also made permissive individual appropriations, leaving the decision whether to spend the money to the President's unfettered discretion. * * * The constitutionality of such appropriations has never seriously been questioned." He concluded, "The title of the Line Item Veto Act, which was perhaps designed to simplify for public comprehension, or perhaps merely to comply with the terms of a campaign pledge, has succeeded in faking out the Supreme Court. The President's action it authorizes in fact is not a line-item veto and thus does not offend Art. I, § 7; and insofar as the substance of that action is concerned, it is no different from what Congress has permitted the President to do since the formation of the Union."

Similarly, **Justice Breyer** also viewed the case as one raising the question of whether Congress had permissibly delegated power to the President and rejected the notion that the President had repealed parts of an enacted law. "When the President 'canceled' the two appropriation measures now before us, he did not *repeal* any law nor did he *amend* any law. He simply *followed* the law, leaving the statutes, as they are literally written, intact. To understand why one cannot say, *literally speaking*, that the President has repealed or amended any law, imagine how the provisions of law before us might have been, but were not, written. Imagine that the canceled New York [Medicaid] provision at issue here had instead said the following:

> Section One. Taxes . . . that were collected by the State of New York from a health care provider before June 1, 1997 and for which a waiver of provisions [requiring payment] have been sought . . . are deemed to be permissible health care related taxes . . . *provided however that the President may prevent the just-mentioned provision from having legal force or effect if he determines x, y and z.* (Assume x, y and z to be the same determinations required by the Line Item Veto Act).

"Whatever a person might say, or think, about the constitutionality of this imaginary law, there is one thing the English language would prevent one from saying. One could not say that a President who 'prevent[s]' the deeming language from 'having legal force or effect' has either *repealed* or *amended* this particular hypothetical statute. Rather, the President has *followed* that law to the letter. He has exercised the power it explicitly delegates to him. He has executed the law, not repealed it." Breyer then argued that the only difference in this case is that the discretionary power provided to the President by Congress occurred in one act, LIVA, and it was applied under the terms Congress envisioned in a subsequent act.

Thus, the dissenters had to determine whether such a delegation of powers was constitutional or whether the authority provided to the President was "legislative" in nature so that it encroached on Congress' constitutional role. Justice Breyer concluded that the delegation was permissible. "Viewed conceptually, the power the Act conveys is the right kind of power. It is 'executive.' * * * Conceptually speaking, it closely resembles the kind of delegated authority—to spend or not to spend appropriations, to change or not to change tariff rates—that Congress has frequently granted the President, any differences being differences in degree, not kind." Moreover, LIVA does not encroach on congressional legislative power because "Congress retained the power to insert, by simple majority, into any future appropriations bill, into any section of any such bill, or into any phrase of any section, a provision that says the Act will not apply. Congress also retained the power to 'disapprov[e],' and thereby reinstate, any of the President's cancellations. And it is Congress that drafts and enacts the appropriations statutes that are subject to the Act in the first place—and thereby defines the outer limits of the President's cancellation authority."

Constitutional law shaping the delegation doctrine has long required that Congress provide "an intelligible principle" that directs the exercise of the delegated authority. *J.W. Hampton, Jr., & Co. v. United States*, 276 U.S. 394 (1928) [Chapter 8, § 1B]. Justice Breyer found such a principle in LIVA. The purpose of the Act provided guidance; its legislative history made clear that Congress ought to promote "greater fiscal accountability" and to "eliminate wasteful federal spending and . . . special tax breaks." The President also had to make the three determinations listed above: that the canceled item will reduce the federal budget deficit, not impair any essential governmental function, and not harm the national interest. Although broad, these guidelines are no less confining than other provisions upheld against delegation attacks. See, e.g., *Nat'l Broadcasting Co. v. United States*, 319 U.S. 190, 225–26 (1943) (upholding delegation to Federal Communications Commission to regulate broadcast licensing as "public interest, convenience, or necessity" require); *FPC v. Hope Natural Gas Co.*, 320 U.S. 591, 600–03 (1944) (upholding delegation to Federal Power Commission to determine "just and reasonable" rates).

Justice Breyer concluded: "In sum, I recognize that the Act before us is novel. In a sense, it skirts a constitutional edge. But that edge has to do with means, not ends. The means chosen do not amount literally to the enactment, repeal, or amendment of a law. Nor, for that matter, do they amount literally to the 'line item veto' that the Act's title announces. Those means * * * represent an experiment that may, or may not, help representative government work better. The Constitution, in my view, authorizes Congress and the President to try novel methods in this way."

1. *Is the Line Item Veto Act Dead?* The cancellations before the Court concerned a tax provision and a provision affecting an entitlement program, Medicaid. As the dissents noted, presidents have long used a power functionally indistinguishable from cancellation—the impoundment authority—to withhold funds that Congress had allocated to government programs in the annual appropriations process. Presidents have considered congressional appropriations to be permissive, allowing them to spend up to the amount appropriated but not requiring them to spend all the money. Congress has frequently expressly given the President the power to decline to spend federal funds, sometimes in cases in which congressional objectives can be met with fewer resources and sometimes as a tool to enforce spending ceilings and deficit targets. Indeed, even the majority in *Clinton v. City of New York* distinguished the cancellations before it from the President's "traditional authority to decline to spend appropriated funds."

Is the cancellation power relating to discretionary spending, which consists of appropriated funds that have been the traditional target of presidential impoundments, unconstitutional after this case? Seventy-nine of the 82 cancellations related to this kind of spending; the President canceled only two tax provisions and one entitlement provision. Notice that LIVA's definition of *cancel* was different in the context of discretionary spending through annual appropriations laws. Rather than rendering a provision of law without "legal force and effect," the President "rescinds" an item of discretionary spending when he cancels it. In budget parlance, a rescission is a congressionally authorized impoundment. Since 1974, federal law has allowed the President to propose to rescind federal spending, but his rescission proposal does not go into effect unless approved by Congress within 45 days. One way to view LIVA's provisions affecting appropriated money is as merely a change in the way Congress authorizes rescissions. Rather than requiring ex post congressional approval, LIVA delegates a continuing power to rescind spending, as long as the President complies with the standards set forth in the Act. In short, LIVA amended the portion of the budget law relating to rescissions by changing the effect of congressional inaction—now Congress' failure to act after an impoundment means that the money will not be spent.

On the day that the Court decided *Clinton v. City of New York*, members of Congress announced plans to re-establish the President's power in a constitutional form. Although some worked to draft and ratify a constitutional amendment giving the President a true line item veto, others in Congress hoped to find a less difficult path to success. One option is called *separate enrollment*. Using this procedure, Congress would divide an omnibus spending bill, formally enrolling each provision allocating funds to particular programs as a separate bill. The group of bills would be passed by Congress (probably using a procedure that would require only one vote to enact the bundle of bills). The President would then have the ability to use his constitutional veto to cancel as many of the programs as he wishes; Congress would have the opportunity to override any veto with a supermajority vote. For example, rather than one bill with 950 sections, Congress would pass 950 bills, and the President would sign only the bills that provided money to programs he supported. Justice Breyer seemed to believe that separate enrollment is too unwieldy a procedure to work in the modern era; however, during the negotiations that led to the passage of LIVA, the Senate proposed separate enrollment as the best way to adopt a cancellation process that would survive constitutional review. Do you agree with the Senate's assessment? Are the political dynamics of separate enrollment different from those that resulted from LIVA? Would you expect members of Congress to be willing to pass as separate bills provisions that they had been willing to support as parts of one large bill? Does the state experience illustrated by *Rush v. Ray* suggest that Congress will divide omnibus bills in a way to minimize the effect of the President's veto?

In his 2006 State of the Union address, President Bush asked Congress to enact a new line item veto, but his proposal was different from the 1996 Act. He proposed an *expedited rescission* process whereby he would send cancellations to Congress, and Congress would be required, through internal rules, to consider his recommendations quickly and vote on them as a package without further amendment. In addition, the Senate would not be allowed to filibuster. This approach was considered by Congress in 1996, and it is generally considered to be constitutional because the decision not to spend money or enforce tax provisions is left to the Congress, albeit under streamlined procedures.[54] President Obama has stated that he supports a similar expedited rescission process. How effective would expedited rescission be in reducing federal spending? Should Congress avoid using the words "line item veto" in the name of any bill it enacts? How binding are internal congressional procedures that purport to restrain congressional power to amend the President's proposal?

2. *Federal Earmark Rules.* Earmarks, which have received increased public scrutiny as a result of the lobbying scandals of the mid-2000s and notorious projects such as the "Bridge to Nowhere" in Alaska, are similar to the kinds of items that LIVA targeted or that governors excise from state bills through their line item veto powers. Rebecca Kysar defines the "elusive" concept of an earmark as "funds bestowed by Congress upon projects or programs by specifying a narrow location or recipient, or without a competitive allocation process." *Listening to Congress: Earmark Rules and Statutory Interpretation*, 94 Cornell L. Rev. 519, 534 (2009). Rule XXI of the House of Representatives defines "congressional earmark" in similar terms: "a provision or report language included primarily at the request of a Member * * * or Senator providing, authorizing, or recommending a specific amount of discretionary budget authority, credit authority, or other spending authority for a contract, loan, loan guarantee, grant, loan authority, or other expenditure with or to an entity, or targeted to a specific State, locality, or Congressional district, other than through a statutory or administrative formula-driven or competitive award process."

The House Rules mandate disclosure of all earmarks as part of committee reports: "It shall not be in order to consider a bill or joint resolution reported by a committee unless the report includes a list of congressional earmarks, limited tax benefits, and limited tariff benefits in the bill or in the report (and the name of any Member * * * who submitted a request to the committee for each respective item included in such list) or a statement that the proposition contains no congressional earmarks, limited tax benefits, or limited tariff benefits." See also Senate Rule XLIV.

How should courts review challenges brought against earmarks? Professor Kysar argues that, in cases of ambiguous text, "courts should construe narrowly, against special benefits, statutory benefits that were not disclosed in accordance with the earmark disclosure rules but that would fall within the ambit of the rules if the statute

---

[54] See Elizabeth Garrett, *The Story of* Clinton v. City of New York*: Congress Can Take Care of Itself*, in *Administrative Law Stories* 47 (Peter Strauss ed., 2006) (providing legislative history of 1996 Act); Aaron-Andrew Bruhl, *The New Line Item Veto Proposal: This Time It's Constitutional (Mostly)*, 116 Yale L.J. Pocket Part 84 (2006) (discussing constitutionality of expedited rescission).

were construed in the manner urged by the special interest." Do you see any problems with this approach? To what extent should courts defer to Congress' internal rules on what constitutes an earmark? Or on what constitutes adequate disclosure? See also Victoria Nourse, *A Decision Theory of Statutory Interpretation: Legislative History by the Rules*, 122 Yale L.J. 70 (2102) (arguing more broadly that interpreters should consider congressional rules when faced with ambiguous language). Kysar suggests that special-interest deals will often be concealed in more public-regarding terms. If this is true, how is a court to decide whether the text is ambiguous? And what approach should a court take if the statute is unambiguously a special-interest deal? We will return to some of these issues in the chapters following on statutory interpretation, especially Chapter 6, § B2.

In addition to disclosure-oriented rules, Congress has adopted what amounts to a moratorium on earmarks since the 112th Congress. The House Republican majority agreed to an earmark ban, and the Senate Appropriations Committee prohibited earmarks in appropriations bills. Moreover, President Obama threatened to veto any legislation including earmarks.[55] Although this ban has been successful in reducing earmarks an estimated 98%,[56] there is evidence that members of Congress have been employing other methods to steer spending toward pet projects. For example, in a recent budget for the Army Corps of Engineers, Congress included $507 million for special projects not included in the President's budget request, and directed the agency to use specific criteria when selecting those projects. In 2010, Senator Lindsay Graham (R–S.C.) threatened to block presidential appointees in the Senate if a South Carolina harbor-dredging project did not receive federal funds.[57]

Although critics of earmarks argue that they improperly direct government funds to special interests and result in wasteful spending, not all members of Congress are opposed to them. Both Democrat and Republican members have argued that earmarks preserve congressional control over the appropriations process and appropriately help advance the interests of constituents. Senate Majority Leader Harry Reid (D–Nev.) has argued that legislators have a "constitutional duty to dole out congressionally directed spending" and eliminating earmarks would improperly increase presidential power over spending.[58] One scholar has mounted a limited defense of earmarks, noting that some are substantively justifiable and that earmarks represent a relatively transparent mechanism of making political deals necessary to enact compromises.[59] Would a member of Congress who refused to request earmarks for her district shirk her responsibilities as a representative? To what extent does the answer to this question depend on your conception of the proper role of representatives laid out at the beginning of this chapter—as agents or trustees?

How persuasive is the Senators' argument that earmarks help preserve Congress' Article I authority to appropriate funds? Apart from the text and spirit of the Constitution, would it make better sense as a matter of policy for politically insulated agencies rather than legislators to dole out federal funds? On the other hand, how politically insulated are agencies from intense interest group pressures? If such

[55] Carl Hulse, *Senate Spending Panel Bans Earmarks for Two Years*, N.Y. Times, Feb. 2, 2011.

[56] *Outrageous Bills*, The Economist, Nov. 23, 2013, at 32.

[57] Ron Nixon, *Congress Appears to Be Trying to Get Around Earmark Ban*, N.Y. Times, Feb. 5, 2012.

[58] Shira Toeplitz, *Harry Reid Defends Earmarks in Omnibus*, Politico, Dec. 16, 2010.

[59] Mariano-Florentino Cuellar, *Earmarking Earmarking*, 49 Harv. J. on Legis. 249, 284–85 (2012).

pressures are to be brought, is it preferable that any exchanges and deals occur with elected representatives rather than unelected bureaucrats?

3.   *Broader Applicability of* Clinton v. City of New York. The Supreme Court's decision in the LIVA case has not been particularly influential in subsequent separation-of-powers challenges, but R. Craig Kitchen argues that the analysis is relevant to provisions in federal laws allowing the executive branch to waive aspects of a law as it applies to states or individuals. *Negative Lawmaking Delegations: Constitutional Structure and Delegations to the Executive of Discretionary Authority to Amend, Waive, and Cancel Statutory Text*, 50 Hastings Const. L.Q. 525 (2013). The issue was made salient by Republican presidential candidate Mitt Romney's pledge in 2011 to waive through executive order all the provisions in the Patient Protection and Affordable Care Act of 2010 (ACA or "Obamacare") so that states would not have to provide health insurance. He said he would resort to this action if he could not convince Congress to repeal the ACA. Although this would have been a broad use of the waiver power in the Act, the law expressly contemplates some waivers of various provisions, and other federal laws routinely include sections delegating waiver authority to the executive branch. Kitchen differentiates such "negative" delegations of authority from the more typical "positive" delegation to an agency to fill gaps or extend a law through rulemaking. The cancellation power in LIVA was just such a negative delegation.

Kitchen argues that a negative power is more problematic than positive delegations because the former allows the executive branch to undermine "specific compromises in the negated statutory text [that were] likely integral to the statute clearing the hurdles of bicameralism and presentment in the first place." *Id.* at 590. Romney's campaign pledge was extreme and would have "unravel[ed] the near-entirety of a comprehensive statute," serving "in effect, [as] a promise to partially repeal the ACA." *Id.* at 601. However, Kitchen argues that courts should apply some of the lessons of *Clinton v. City of New York* in assessing even less sweeping negative delegations. Such provisions should "provide express, specific criteria as requirements for the executive negation of the legal force or effect of statutory text," *id.* at 606, a requirement he concludes that LIVA lacked. Second, "judicial review of the exercise of [negative] delegated authority is critical." *Id.* at 607. Finally, in the process used to negate statutory provisions, political minorities, often the beneficiaries of political compromise, should be "given a voice." *Id.*

Does Kitchen's distinction between negative and positive delegations remind you of the tests used by state courts to analyze the traditional state constitutional line item veto authority? What kinds of federal provisions can be characterized as negative? Do they implicate heightened judicial scrutiny in all cases, or only when used as Governor Romney threatened: to circumvent Congress entirely and effectively repeal a comprehensive regulatory scheme?

C. LEGISLATIVE IMMUNITIES

1. Federal Protection for Members of Congress (Speech or Debate Clause)

Article I, § 6, clause 1 of the U.S. Constitution provides that "for any Speech or Debate in either House, [Members of Congress] shall not be questioned in any other place." The purpose of the clause was "to prevent intimidation [of legislators] by the executive and accountability before a possibly hostile judiciary." *United States v. Johnson*, 383 U.S. 169 (1966); see also *Kilbourn v. Thompson*, 103 U.S. 168 (1881) (the germinal case). "It insures that legislators are free to represent the interests of their constituents without fear that they will be later called to task in the courts for that representation." *Powell v. McCormack*, 395 U.S. 486 (1969). The clause encompasses speeches on the floor of Congress, voting on bills, conduct at committee hearings, preparation of committee reports, authorization of committee publications and their internal distribution, circulation of information to other members, and participation in committee investigations. *Eastland v. United States' Servicemen's Fund*, 421 U.S. 491 (1975); *Doe v. McMillan*, 412 U.S. 306 (1973); *Dombrowski v. Pfister*, 387 U.S. 82 (1967) (per curiam).

The Speech or Debate Clause is rooted in English history. In the sixteenth and seventeenth centuries, when Parliament was slowly wresting power from the Crown, the Tudor and Stuart monarchs would arrest Members of Parliament and question them about their legislative activities and try to coerce them into changing their policies. The Framers of the Constitution, therefore, felt it important to insulate Members of Congress from such harassment. Without the Speech or Debate Clause, Members of Congress could be vulnerable to persecution from one of the other branches. The clause is a cornerstone of the separation of powers.

There is a tension in the Speech or Debate Clause between the desire to protect the independence of the legislative process and the desire not to create congressional "super-citizens." *United States v. Brewster*, 408 U.S. 501, 516 (1972). Thus, defining the scope of the clause is crucial and subject to much discussion in the case law. The next case implicates at least two questions relevant to scope. First, what activities fall under the protection of the Speech or Debate Clause? The Court in *Brewster* distinguishes between acts that involve the legislative process per se and acts that are mere "legislative errands," such as constituent services and newsletters. Is this distinction realistic? Second, who besides members of Congress should receive the protection? Are legislative aides immunized and, if so, is the immunity co-extensive with that accorded to legislators?

GRAVEL V. UNITED STATES

Supreme Court of the United States, 1972.
408 U.S. 606, 92 S.Ct. 2614, 33 L.Ed.2d 583.

Opinion of the Court by MR. JUSTICE WHITE, announced by MR. JUSTICE BLACKMUN.

These cases arise out of the investigation by a federal grand jury into possible criminal conduct with respect to the release and publication of a classified Defense Department study entitled History of the United States Decision-Making Process on Viet Nam Policy. This document, popularly known as the Pentagon Papers, bore a Defense security classification of Top Secret-Sensitive. The crimes being investigated included the retention of public property or records with intent to convert (18 U.S.C. § 641), the gathering and transmitting of national defense information (18 U.S.C. § 793), the concealment or removal of public records or documents (18 U.S.C. § 2071), and conspiracy to commit such offenses and to defraud the United States (18 U.S.C. § 371).

Among the witnesses subpoenaed were Leonard S. Rodberg, an assistant to Senator Mike Gravel of Alaska and a resident fellow at the Institute of Policy Studies, and Howard Webber, Director of M.I.T. Press. Senator Gravel, as intervenor, filed motions to quash the subpoenas and to require the Government to specify the particular questions to be addressed to Rodberg. He asserted that requiring these witnesses to appear and testify would violate his privilege under the Speech or Debate Clause of the United States Constitution, Art. I, § 6, cl. 1.

It appeared that on the night of June 29, 1971, Senator Gravel, as Chairman of the Subcommittee on Buildings and Grounds of the Senate Public Works Committee, convened a meeting of the subcommittee and there read extensively from a copy of the Pentagon Papers. He then placed the entire 47 volumes of the study in the public record. Rodberg had been added to the Senator's staff earlier in the day and assisted Gravel in preparing for and conducting the hearing. Some weeks later there were press reports that Gravel had arranged for the papers to be published by Beacon Press, and that members of Gravel's staff had talked with Webber as editor of M.I.T. Press.

[The District Court overruled the motions to quash but prohibited the asking of certain questions. The Court of Appeals held that (a) neither the Senator nor his aide could be questioned about the episode on the Senate floor because of the Speech or Debate Clause, (b) third parties could be questioned about the episode, and (c) republication with Beacon Press was protected by a common law immunity but not by the Speech or Debate Clause. Although agreeing with much of its analysis, the Supreme Court vacated the Court of Appeals opinion.]

[I]   * * * [T]he United States strongly urges that because the Speech or Debate Clause confers a privilege only upon "Senators and Representatives," Rodberg himself has no valid claim to constitutional immunity from grand jury inquiry. * * * We agree with the Court of Appeals that for the purpose of construing the privilege a Member and his aide are to be "treated as one," or, as the District Court put it: the "Speech or Debate Clause prohibits inquiry into things done by Dr. Rodberg as the Senator's agent or assistant which would have been legislative acts, and therefore privileged, if performed by the Senator personally." Both courts recognized what the Senate of the United States urgently presses here: that it is literally impossible, in view of the complexities of the modern legislative process, with Congress almost constantly in session and matters of legislative concern constantly proliferating, for Members of Congress to perform their legislative tasks without the help of aides and assistants; that the day-to-day work of such aides is so critical to the Members' performance that they must be treated as the latter's alter egos; and that if they are not so recognized, the central role of the Speech or Debate Clause—to prevent intimidation of legislators by the Executive and accountability before a possibly hostile judiciary—will inevitably be diminished and frustrated. * * *

It is true that the Clause itself mentions only "Senators and Representatives," but prior cases have plainly not taken a literalistic approach in applying the privilege. The Clause also speaks only of "Speech or Debate," but the Court's consistent approach has been that to confine the protection of the Speech or Debate Clause to words spoken in debate would be an unacceptably narrow view. Committee reports, resolutions, and the act of voting are equally covered; "[i]n short, . . . things generally done in a session of the House by one of its members in relation to the business before it." *Kilbourn.* Rather than giving the clause a cramped construction, the Court has sought to implement its fundamental purpose of freeing the legislator from executive and judicial oversight that realistically threatens to control his conduct as a legislator. We have little doubt that we are neither exceeding our judicial powers nor mistakenly construing the Constitution by holding that the Speech or Debate Clause applies not only to a Member but also to his aides insofar as the conduct of the latter would be a protected legislative act if performed by the Member himself.

Nor can we agree with the United States that our conclusion is foreclosed by *Kilbourn*, *Dombrowski*, and *Powell*, where the speech or debate privilege was held unavailable to certain House and committee employees. Those cases do not hold that persons other than Members of Congress are beyond the protection of the Clause when they perform or aid in the performance of legislative acts. In *Kilbourn*, the Speech or Debate Clause protected House Members who had adopted a resolution authorizing Kilbourn's arrest; that act was clearly legislative in nature. But the resolution was subject to judicial review insofar as its execution impinged on a citizen's rights as it did there. That the House could with impunity order an unconstitutional arrest afforded no protection for those who made the arrest. * * *

Dombrowski v. Eastland is little different in principle. The Speech or Debate Clause there protected a Senator, who was also a subcommittee chairman, but not the subcommittee counsel. The record contained no evidence of the Senator's involvement in any activity that could result in liability, whereas the committee counsel was charged with conspiring with state officials to carry out an illegal seizure of records that the committee sought for its own proceedings. The committee counsel was deemed protected to some extent by legislative privilege, but it did not shield him from answering as yet unproved charges of conspiring to violate the constitutional rights of private parties. Unlawful conduct of this kind the Speech or Debate Clause simply did not immunize.

Powell v. McCormack reasserted judicial power to determine the validity of legislative actions impinging on individual rights—there the illegal exclusion of a representative-elect—and to afford relief against House aides seeking to implement the invalid resolutions. The Members themselves were dismissed from the case because shielded by the Speech or Debate Clause both from liability for their illegal legislative act and from having to defend themselves with respect to it. * * *

* * * The three cases reflect a decidedly jaundiced view towards extending the Clause so as to privilege illegal or unconstitutional conduct beyond that essential to foreclose executive control of legislative speech or debate and associated matters such as voting and committee reports and proceedings. In *Kilbourn*, the Sergeant-at-Arms was executing a legislative order, the issuance of which fell within the Speech or Debate Clause; in *Eastland*, the committee counsel was gathering

information for a hearing; and in *Powell*, the Clerk and Doorkeeper were merely carrying out directions that were protected by the Speech or Debate Clause. In each case, protecting the rights of others may have to some extent frustrated a planned or completed legislative act; but relief could be afforded without proof of a legislative act or the motives or purposes underlying such an act. No threat to legislative independence was posed, and Speech or Debate Clause protection did not attach.

None of this, as we see it, involves distinguishing between a Senator and his personal aides with respect to legislative immunity. In *Kilbourn*-type situations, both aide and Member should be immune with respect to committee and House action leading to the illegal resolution. So, too, in *Eastland*, as in this litigation, senatorial aides should enjoy immunity for helping a Member conduct committee hearings. On the other hand, no prior case has held that Members of Congress would be immune if they executed an invalid resolution by themselves carrying out an illegal arrest, or if, in order to secure information for a hearing, themselves seized the property or invaded the privacy of a citizen. Neither they nor their aides should be immune from liability or questioning in such circumstances. * * *

[II] We are convinced also that the Court of Appeals correctly determined that Senator Gravel's alleged arrangement with Beacon Press to publish the Pentagon Papers was not protected speech or debate within the meaning of Art. I, § 6, cl. 1, of the Constitution.

Historically, the English legislative privilege was not viewed as protecting republication of an otherwise immune libel on the floor of the House. *Stockdale v. Hansard*, 9 Ad. & E., at 114, 112 Eng. Rep., at 1156 (1839), recognized that "[f]or speeches made in Parliament by a member to the prejudice of any other person, or hazardous to the public peace, that member enjoys complete impunity." But it was clearly stated that "if the calumnious or inflammatory speeches should be reported and published, the law will attach responsibility on the publisher." This was accepted in *Kilbourn v. Thompson* as a "sound statement of the legal effect of the Bill of Rights and of the parliamentary law of England" and as a reasonable basis for inferring "that the framers of the Constitution meant the same thing by the use of language borrowed from that source."

Prior cases have read the Speech or Debate Clause "broadly to effectuate its purposes," *Johnson*, and have included within its reach anything "generally done in a session of the House by one of its members in relation to the business before it." *Kilbourn*. Thus, voting by Members and committee reports are protected; and we recognize today * * * that a Member's conduct at legislative committee hearings, although subject to judicial review in various circumstances, as is legislation itself, may not be made the basis for a civil or criminal judgment against a Member because that conduct is within the "sphere of legitimate legislative activity."

But the Clause has not been extended beyond the legislative sphere. That Senators generally perform certain acts in their official capacity as Senators does not necessarily make all such acts legislative in nature. Members of Congress are constantly in touch with the Executive Branch of the Government and with administrative agencies—they may cajole, and exhort with respect to the administration of a federal statute—but such conduct, though generally done, is not protected legislative activity. *United States v. Johnson* decided at least this much. "No argument is made, nor do we think that it could be successfully contended, that the Speech or Debate Clause reaches conduct, such as was involved in the attempt to influence the Department of Justice, that is in no wise related to the due functioning of the legislative process."

Legislative acts are not all-encompassing. The heart of the Clause is speech or debate in either House. Insofar as the Clause is construed to reach other matters, they must be an integral part of the deliberative and communicative processes by which Members participate in committee and House proceedings with respect to the consideration and passage or rejection of proposed legislation or with respect to other matters which the Constitution places within the jurisdiction of either House. As the Court of Appeals put it, the courts have extended the privilege to matters beyond pure speech or debate in either House, but "only when necessary to prevent indirect impairment of such deliberations."

Here, private publication by Senator Gravel through the cooperation of Beacon Press was in no way essential to the deliberations of the Senate; nor does questioning as to private publication threaten the integrity or independence of the Senate by impermissibly exposing its deliberations to executive influence. The Senator had conducted his hearings; the record and any report that was forthcoming were available both to his committee and the Senate. Insofar as we are advised, neither Congress nor the full committee ordered or authorized the publication. We cannot but conclude that the Senator's arrangements with Beacon Press were not part and parcel of the legislative process. * * *

[III] Similar considerations lead us to disagree with the Court of Appeals insofar as it fashioned, tentatively at least, a nonconstitutional testimonial privilege protecting Rodberg from any questioning by the grand jury concerning the matter of republication of the Pentagon Papers. This privilege, thought to be similar to that protecting executive officials from liability for libel, see *Barr v. Matteo*, 360 U.S. 564 (1959), was considered advisable "[t]o the extent that a congressman has responsibility to inform his constituents. . . ." But we cannot carry a judicially fashioned privilege so far as to immunize criminal conduct proscribed by an Act of Congress or to frustrate the grand jury's inquiry into whether publication of these classified documents violated a federal criminal statute. The so-called executive privilege has never been applied to shield executive officers from prosecution for crime, the Court of Appeals was quite sure that third parties were neither immune from liability nor from testifying about the republication matter, and we perceive no basis for conferring a testimonial privilege on Rodberg as the Court of Appeals seemed to do.

[Part IV of the Court's opinion defined the appropriate remedial order in the case to allow the grand jury to interrogate Rodberg about the arrangements for republication of the papers and about "the source of obviously highly classified documents that came into the Senator's possession and are the basic subject matter of inquiry in this case, as long as no legislative act is implicated by the questions." The Court prohibited questions "(1) concerning the Senator's conduct, or the conduct of his aides, at the June 29, 1971, meeting of the subcommittee; (2) concerning the motives and purposes behind the Senator's conduct, or that of his aides, at that meeting; (3) concerning communications between the Senator and his aides during the term of their employment and related to said meeting or any other legislative act of the Senator; (4) except as it proves relevant to investigating possible third-party crime, concerning any act, in itself not criminal, performed by the Senator, or by his aides in the course of their employment, in preparation for the subcommittee hearing."]

MR. JUSTICE DOUGLAS, dissenting.

I would construe the Speech or Debate Clause to insulate Senator Gravel and his aides from inquiry concerning the Pentagon Papers, and Beacon Press from inquiry concerning publication of them, for that publication was but another way of informing the public as to what had gone on in the privacy of the Executive Branch concerning the conception and pursuit of the so-called "war" in Vietnam. Alternatively, I would hold that Beacon Press is protected by the First Amendment from prosecution or investigations for publishing or undertaking to publish the Pentagon Papers. * * *

As to Senator Gravel's efforts to publish the Subcommittee record's contents, wide dissemination of this material as an educational service is as much a part of the Speech or Debate Clause philosophy as mailing under a frank a Senator's or a Congressman's speech across the Nation. * * * "[I]t is the proper duty of a representative body to look diligently into every affair of government and to talk much about what it sees. . . . The informing function of Congress should be preferred even to its legislative function." W. Wilson, *Congressional Government* 303 (1885). "From the earliest times in its history, the Congress has assiduously performed an 'informing function.' " *Watkins v. United States*, 354 U.S. 178, 200 n.3. "Legislators have an obligation to take positions on controversial political questions so that their constituents can be fully informed by them." *Bond v. Floyd*, 356 U.S. 116, 136.

We said in *Johnson* that the Speech or Debate Clause established a "legislative privilege" that protected a member of Congress against prosecution "by an unfriendly executive and conviction by a hostile judiciary" in order, as Mr. Justice Harlan put it, to ensure "the independence of the legislature." That hostility emanates from every stage of the present proceedings. It emphasizes the need to construe the Speech or Debate Clause generously, not niggardly. If republication of a Senator's speech in a newspaper carries the privilege, as it doubtless does, then republication of the exhibits introduced at a hearing before Congress must also do so. That means that republication by Beacon Press is within the ambit of the Speech or Debate Clause and that the confidences of the Senator in arranging it are not subject to inquiry "in any other Place" than the Congress.

[We have omitted the dissenting opinion of MR. JUSTICE BRENNAN, with whom MR. JUSTICE DOUGLAS and MR. JUSTICE MARSHALL joined. These Justices agreed that the Speech and Debate Clause protects legislative aides but dissented from the Court's refusal to protect republication.]

NOTES ON THE SPEECH OR DEBATE CLAUSE AFTER GRAVEL

1. *Analytical Conundrums Presented by the Court's Decision.* Why should the Speech or Debate Clause be construed very liberally to include staff, but then narrowly to exclude republication? The Court distinguishes *Kilbourn*, *Eastland*, and *Powell* because the officials in those cases committed illegal acts, but wasn't Rodberg's alleged conspiracy to disclose classified documents equally illegal? And what about Gravel: could he be prosecuted for participating in a breach of national secrecy?

In *Kilbourn*, an 1881 case, the Supreme Court held that Thompson, the Sergeant-at-Arms of the House, was liable for his wrongful arrest of Kilbourn, who had refused to comply with a House subpoena *duces tecum*. Thompson made the arrest pursuant to the order of a House committee that was investigating Kilbourn's bankrupt company. The Court held that the members of the committee were protected by the Speech or Debate Clause for their actions and deliberation, but that the Sergeant-at-Arms was not for his actions. After *Gravel*, would the House Sergeant-at-Arms (a House staff member) still be liable? How can *Gravel* be reconciled with *Kilbourn*? And would the result in *Kilbourn* have been different if the wrongful arrest had been carried out by a member of Congress?

Gravel holds that the Speech or Debate Clause applies to Members of Congress and their aides who are their "alter egos." Is that a qualification of the Court's holding? If so, which staff qualify? All of them? The Sergeant-at-Arms in *Kilbourn*? How about the staff of the General Accounting Office, who work for the Congress but are not the aides of any one member? Should they have the same immunity as someone on a member's personal staff? See *Campaign for Fiscal Equity v. New York*, 687 N.Y.S. 2d 227 (N.Y. Sup. Ct), *aff'd* 265 A.D. 2d 277 (N.Y. App. 1999) (interpreting parallel state constitutional provision as extending Speech or Debate Clause protection to employee of the State Education Department who assisted legislators in analyzing budget legislation).

2. *Whistleblowing Versus Blacklisting.* The dissenters appeal to the value of whistleblowing: Members of Congress ought to be able to "blow the whistle" on government skullduggery by exposing documents that reveal valuable information to the American people. Leaking classified documents has become a widely imitated practice on Capitol Hill, and in many instances the public finds the ventilation of state secrets informative and useful. On the other hand, republication of legislative reports may also chill freedom. During the Cold War, members of Congress sometimes made lavish allegations about the loyalty of Americans who criticized our government, and their accusations would be republished, often to the ruin of those accused. Judge Gerhard Gesell enjoined the publication of a report of the Committee on Internal Security of the House of Representatives on the ground that it served no "legitimate" public purpose and was little more than an effort to "blacklist" and smear people who held different points of view from the conservative House Committee. *Hentoff v. Ichord*, 318 F. Supp. 1175 (D.D.C. 1970). In 1970, he drew the same conclusion from the Court's precedents that Justice White drew in 1972: the Speech or Debate Clause does not protect republication.

3. *Balancing Legislative Independence Against Individual Rights.* Sometimes, as in *Hentoff*, recognizing legislative immunity would mean denial of rights to citizens that otherwise would be enforced in a court of law. Chief Justice Burger forcefully described

this difficulty: "The immunities of the Speech or Debate Clause were not written into the Constitution simply for the personal or private benefit of Members of Congress, but to protect the integrity of the legislative process by insuring the independence of individual legislators." *Brewster*, 408 U.S. at 507. The tension is presented by cases in which congressional staff seek to sue members of Congress for some form of employment discrimination. The Court of Appeals for the D.C. Circuit wrestled with this issue in several cases, and it initially ruled that members were insulated from liability only with respect to employees whose duties were integral to the legislative process. *Browning v. Clerk, U.S. House of Representatives*, 789 F.2d 923 (D.C. Cir 1986). Thus, a female manager of the House of Representatives' restaurant could sue representatives who oversaw food services in the House on the ground that she was fired because she was female. *Walker v. Jones*, 733 F.2d 923 (D.C. Cir. 1984). In *Fields v. Office of Eddie Bernice Johnson*, 459 F.3d 1 (D.C. Cir. 2006) (en banc), the D.C. Circuit rejected a broad reading of *Browning* and barred review only when the claim "question[s] the conduct of official Senate legislative business." *Id.* at 8 (relying on *Bastien v. Office of Sen. Ben Nighthorse Campbell*, 390 F.3d 1301 (10th Cir. 2004)). Therefore, the plaintiffs, one of whom was fired after telling a senator he needed heart surgery and the other after objecting to a hiring decision, could maintain their suits, although they might be hindered in presenting arguments that turned on the motivation behind any legislative acts.

The Congressional Accountability Act of 1995, P.L. 104–1, 109 Stat. 3, *codified at* 2 U.S.C. § 1301 *et seq.*, adds a new wrinkle to this aspect of Speech or Debate Clause jurisprudence. The Act allows congressional employees to sue their employing office for wrongful discharge, but it also states that the Act is not a waiver of the Speech or Debate Clause privileges of any member. Members of Congress are not personally liable under the act for damages; instead, awards are paid by a contingent fund of the United States.[60]

4.   *Statements by a Member of Congress to a Congressional Ethics Committee.* Is a member of Congress immune for statements he or she makes to a Congressional Ethics Committee? The District of Columbia Circuit wrestled with this question in *In re Grand Jury Subpoenas*, 571 F.3d 1200 (D.C. Cir. 2009). The case arose out of a House Ethics Committee investigation into Rep. Tom Feeney's (R–Fla.) 2003 golf trip to Scotland, funded by infamous lobbyist Jack Abramoff. Although Feeney claimed he had embarked on a legitimate legislative fact-finding trip, the House Ethics Committee determined that Feeney had violated House Ethics rules and he agreed to pay the cost of the trip to the U.S. Treasury. Judge Douglas Ginsburg, writing for the unanimous three-judge panel, held that the Government could not subpoena Feeney's statements to the House Ethics Committee. The court noted that, under D.C. Circuit precedent, the Speech or Debate Clause gives a member of Congress immunity when an ethics investigation is connected to an act that is claimed to have been performed in the legislative capacity. Inquiries into ethical violations for non-legislative activities, however, are not covered by the Speech or Debate Clause. The court held that, because Feeney claimed he was

---

[60] See Christina Deneka, *Congressional Anti-Accountability and the Separation of Powers: A Survey of the Congressional Accountability Act's Problems*, 52 Rutgers L. Rev. 855 (2000) (discussing structural concerns with the Act); James Brudney, *Congressional Accountability and Denial: Speech or Debate Clause and Conflict of Interest Challenges to Unionization of Congressional Employees*, 36 Harv. J. on Legis. 1 (1999); David Frederick, *Commentary on the Congressional Accountability Act of 1995: A Section-by-Section Analysis*, in *Lobbying the New Congress* (Thomas Susman & Barbara Timmer eds., 1995).

engaging in legislative factfinding when he traveled to Scotland, and the Ethics Committee was trying to resolve whether the trip was in fact for legislative or recreational purposes, the Government could not subpoena his statements to the Ethics Committee.

In a concurring opinion, Judge Kavanaugh criticized the D.C. Circuit's focus on the subject matter of the underlying congressional investigation. This approach, Judge Kavanaugh noted, "creates great uncertainty. After all, it can be quite difficult to determine whether an allegation of wrongdoing involves official or personal acts because the categories often overlap—for example, when a Member is alleged to have abused his or her official position for personal gain." Judge Kavanaugh contended that *all* statements by members of Congress to congressional ethics committees should be immune under the Speech or Debate Clause. Regardless of the subject of the investigation, "[a] Member's statement to a congressional ethics committee is speech in an official congressional proceeding."

Should Speech or Debate Clause protection hinge on whether conduct being examined by the Ethics Committee is characterized as personal or official? Should it matter whether the Ethics Committee or the member of Congress does the characterizing? For further discussion, see Case Note, *Constitutional Law—Speech or Debate Clause—D.C. Circuit Quashes Subpoena for Congressman's Testimony to the House Ethics Committee—In re Grand Jury Subpoenas, 571 F.3d 1200 (D.C. Cir. 2009)*, 123 Harv. L. Rev. 564 (2009).

SPEECH OR DEBATE CLAUSE PROBLEMS

Problem 3–11. Senator William Proxmire (D–Wis.) in the 1970s started a practice of awarding a "Golden Fleece of the Month Award" for egregiously wasteful governmental spending. The award went to federal agencies that funded projects that Proxmire felt accomplished little for their cost. The second such award, made in April 1975, went to the National Science Foundation and NASA for spending almost $500,000 to fund research by Ronald Hutchinson, a behavioral scientist who studied tension and aggressive behavior under conditions of stress. He studied the behavior of animals, focusing on their clenching of teeth when they were exposed to stressful stimuli.

Senator Proxmire found this wasteful and made the award to Hutchinson in a speech on the floor of the Senate, preceded by a press release to 275 members of the news media. The speech and release said:

> The funding of this nonsense makes me almost angry enough to scream and kick or even clench my jaws. It seems to me it is outrageous.

> Dr. Hutchinson's studies should make the taxpayers as well as his monkeys grind their teeth. In fact, the good doctor has made a fortune from his monkeys and in the process made a monkey out of the American taxpayer.

In May 1975 Proxmire referred to this Fleece Award and quoted the above language from his speech in a newsletter to approximately 100,000 constituents. Later in 1975, Proxmire appeared on a television interview program and repeated the charge of waste.

Hutchinson sues Proxmire and Morton Schwartz (the aide who researched the matter and worked on the speech) for defamation. Assuming that he has made out a claim under state law (and a claim that is permissible under the First Amendment), should the court accept Proxmire's defense under the Speech or Debate Clause to immunize him from liability for his speech on the Senate floor? What about his press release? Is the republication in the constituent newsletter immunized? If there is a difference in treatment, what is the justification? Does Schwartz have a good defense? See *Hutchinson v. Proxmire*, 443 U.S. 111 (1979). Assume that Schwartz called the agency after the award had been given to discover whether it had changed its decision or altered the way it dispensed federal money. During those phone calls with National Science Foundation staff, Schwartz made allegedly defamatory remarks about Dr. Hutchinson. Can he be sued, or is he protected under the Speech or Debate Clause? What if his calls had been prompted initially by a constituent concerned about the way the agencies awarded federal money? See *Chastain v. Sundquist*, 833 F.2d 311 (D.C. Cir. 1987) (allowing defamation suit against congressman relating to casework concerning the activities of attorneys in the Memphis Area Legal Services office).

Problem 3–12. The chairman of the Senate Judiciary Committee replaces his assistant committee counsel, Martin, with a comparably qualified woman, Marianne, based on the chairman's stated desire for more diversity in committee policymaking positions. When Martin asks whether his termination is due to poor performance, the chairman responds: "No, you have been doing a fine job. But I want a qualified woman in this position to develop a cross-section of perspectives among my inner circle of advisors. In addition, the Committee is facing a series of gender-related criminal and civil rights issues, and a woman's perspective will be valuable to me." Assuming arguendo that this personnel decision raises a red flag on sex discrimination, should the Senator's decision be protected under the Speech or Debate Clause? *See Davis v. Passman*, 442 U.S. 228 (1979) (declining to address the question because the circuit court had not done so); *id.* at 249–54 (noting views of four dissenting justices).

Problem 3–13. In the summer of 2013, Edward Snowden, a contract employee who had worked for the National Security Agency (NSA), leaked classified documents exposing the NSA's massive and longstanding surveillance program. In addition to igniting domestic and foreign outrage, the leaks led members of Congress to admit that they had known of the surveillance program for years but they felt restricted from bringing it into the public light. Senators Ron Wyden (D–Ore.) and Mark Udall (D–Colo.), members of the Senate Intelligence Committee who had been briefed on the surveillance program at secret sessions, chose not to raise it on the Senate floor despite their grave concerns. In an August 2013 interview with *Rolling Stone* magazine, Senator Wyden stated that when he first learned of the surveillance in early 2007, he and one other senator wrote classified letters to senior officials urging them to disclose their interpretation that the 2001 Patriot Act authorized this level of data collection. Asked whether he regretted not having exposed the program well before the Snowden leaks, Senator Wyden stated that there are "very significant limits" on what a person can and cannot say, and "[i]f you want to play a watchdog role, you try to work within the rules."

Would the Speech or Debate Clause have protected Senator Wyden from prosecution for reading the classified material into the public record? Could such a public reading by a member of Congress on the Senate floor qualify as "treason," which the Constitution defines in relevant part (Art. III, Sec. 3) as "giving [enemies of the United States] aid and comfort."? *See Cramer v. United States*, 325 U.S. 1 (1945). What penalties might Senator Wyden face from Congress itself? Are any such penalties relevant to whether he should be protected under the Speech or Debate Clause?[61]

SPEECH OR DEBATE AND BRIBERY PROSECUTIONS

Do prosecutions for corruption, like that in *Van de Carr* (Section 1A of this chapter), undermine the independence of the legislature? If so, the decision might trigger concern under the speech or debate provision of the applicable constitution. The 1938 New York Constitution (Art. III, § 11) provided: "for any speech or debate in either house of the legislature, the members shall not be questioned in any other place." Would this change the result in *Van de Carr* if the defendant had been a state legislator? Would the federal Speech or Debate Clause preclude such a prosecution under the federal bribery statute, 18 U.S.C. § 201? Consider the following case.

UNITED STATES V. HELSTOSKI

Supreme Court of the United States, 1979.
442 U.S. 477, 99 S.Ct. 2432, 61 L.Ed.2d 12.

MR. CHIEF JUSTICE BURGER delivered the opinion of the Court.

[Henry Helstoski, a former Member of the House of Representatives from New Jersey, was indicted under § 201 for receiving money from noncitizens in return for introducing private bills in Congress that would suspend the application of U.S. immigration laws so that they could remain in the United States. The lower courts ruled that the Government could not introduce "evidence of the performance of a past legislative act on the part of the defendant * * * derived from any source and for any purpose." The Government appealed this ruling, arguing that it was not required by the Speech or Debate Clause.]

The Court's holdings in *United States v. Johnson*, 383 U.S. 169 (1966), and *United States v. Brewster*, 408 U.S. 501 (1972), leave no doubt that evidence of a legislative act of a Member may not be introduced by the Government in a prosecution under § 201. In *Johnson* there had been extensive questioning of both Johnson, a former Congressman, and others about a speech which Johnson had delivered in the House of Representatives and the motive for the speech. The Court's conclusion was unequivocal:

> "We see no escape from the conclusion that such an intensive judicial inquiry, made in the course of a prosecution by the Executive Branch under a general conspiracy statute, violates the express language of the Constitution and the policies which underlie it."

In *Brewster*, we explained the holding of *Johnson* in this way:

---

[61] See generally Bruce Ackerman, *Breach or Debate,* Foreign Policy, August 1, 2013, http://www.foreign policy.com/articles/2013/08/1/breach_or_debate_congress_snowden_prism; Emma Roller, *What's the Worst That Could Happen to a Member of Congress Who Reveals Secret Information?*, Slate.com, June 14, 2013, http://www.slate.com/articles/news_and_politics/explainer/2013/06/senate_intelligence_hints_at_prism_can_ members_of_congress_be_tried_for.html.

"*Johnson* thus stands as a unanimous holding that a Member of Congress may be prosecuted under a criminal statute provided that the Government's case does not rely on legislative acts or the motivation for legislative acts. A legislative act has consistently been defined as an act generally done in Congress in relation to the business before it. In sum, the Speech or Debate Clause prohibits inquiry only into those things generally said or done in the House or the Senate in the performance of official duties and into the motivation for those acts."

The Government, however, argues that exclusion of references to past legislative acts will make prosecutions more difficult because such references are essential to show the motive for taking money. In addition, the Government argues that the exclusion of references to past acts is not logically consistent. In its view, if jurors are told of promises to perform legislative acts they will infer that the acts were performed, thereby calling the acts themselves into question.

We do not accept the Government's arguments; without doubt the exclusion of such evidence will make prosecutions more difficult. Indeed, the Speech or Debate Clause was designed to preclude prosecution of Members for legislative acts. The Clause protects "against inquiry into acts that occur in the regular course of the legislative process and into the motivation for those acts." It "precludes any showing of how [a legislator] acted, voted, or decided." *Brewster*. Promises by a Member to perform an act in the future are not legislative acts. *Brewster* makes clear that the "compact" may be shown without impinging on the legislative function.

We therefore agree with the Court of Appeals that references to past legislative acts of a Member cannot be admitted without undermining the values protected by the Clause. We implied as much in *Brewster* when we explained: "To make a prima facie case under [the] indictment, the Government need not show any act of [Brewster] *subsequent* to the corrupt promise for payment, for it is taking the bribe, not performance of the illicit compact, that is a criminal act." A similar inference is appropriate from *Johnson* where we held that the Clause was violated by questions about motive addressed to others than Johnson himself. That holding would have been unnecessary if the Clause did not afford protection beyond legislative acts themselves.

MR. JUSTICE STEVENS misconstrues our holdings on the Speech or Debate Clause in urging: "The admissibility line should be based on the purpose of the offer rather than the specificity of the reference." The Speech or Debate Clause does not refer to the prosecutor's purpose in offering evidence. The Clause does not simply state, "No proof of a legislative act shall be offered"; the prohibition of the Clause is far broader. It provides that Members "shall not be questioned in any other Place." Indeed, as MR. JUSTICE STEVENS recognizes, the admission of evidence of legislative acts "may reveal [to the jury] some information about the performance of legislative acts and the legislator's motivation in conducting official duties." Revealing information as to a legislative act—speaking or debating—to a jury would subject a Member to being "questioned" in a place other than the House or Senate, thereby violating the explicit prohibition of the Speech or Debate Clause.

As to what restrictions the Clause places on the admission of evidence, our concern is not with the "specificity" of the reference. Instead, our concern is whether there is mention of a legislative act. To effectuate the intent of the Clause, the Court has construed it to protect other "legislative acts" such as utterances in committee hearings and reports. E.g., *Doe v. McMillan*, 412 U.S. 306 (1973). But it is clear from the language of the Clause that protection extends only to an act that has already been performed. A promise to deliver a speech, to vote, or to solicit other votes at some future date is not "speech or debate." Likewise, a promise to introduce a bill is not a legislative act. Thus, in light of the strictures of *Johnson* and *Brewster*, the District Court order prohibiting the introduction of evidence "of the performance of a past legislative act" was redundant.

[The Government also argued that the Speech or Debate Clause had been waived, either by (a) Helstoski's testimony before the grand jury in which he produced documentary evidence of his legislative acts or (b) the enactment of § 201 by Congress. The Court did not decide whether waiver was ever possible by the defendant, but held that any possible waiver would have to be an "explicit and unequivocal renunciation of the protection," which Helstoski's actions were not.]

The Speech or Debate Clause was designed neither to assure fair trials nor to avoid coercion. Rather, its purpose was to preserve the constitutional structure of separate, coequal, and independent branches of government. The English and American history of the privilege suggests that any lesser standard would risk intrusion by the Executive and the Judiciary into the sphere of protected legislative activities. The importance of the principle was recognized as early as 1808 in *Coffin v. Coffin*, 4 Mass. 1, 27, where the court said that the purpose of the principle was to secure to every member "*exemption* from prosecution, for every thing said or done by him, as a representative, in the exercise of the functions of that office."

This Court has reiterated the central importance of the Clause for preventing intrusion by Executive and Judiciary into the legislative sphere.

> [I]t is apparent from the history of the clause that the privilege was not born primarily of a desire to avoid private suits . . . but rather to prevent intimidation by the executive and accountability before a possibly hostile judiciary. * * *

> There is little doubt that the instigation of criminal charges against critical or disfavored legislators by the executive in a judicial forum was the chief fear prompting the long struggle for parliamentary privilege in England and, in the context of the American system of separation of powers, is the predominate thrust of the Speech or Debate Clause. *Johnson*. * * *

We recognize that an argument can be made from precedent and history that Congress, as a body, should not be free to strip individual Members of the protection guaranteed by the Clause from being "questioned" by the Executive in the courts. The controversy over the Alien and Sedition Acts reminds us how one political party in control of both the Legislative and the Executive Branches sought to use the courts to destroy political opponents.

The Supreme Judicial Court of Massachusetts noted in *Coffin* that "the privilege secured . . . is not so much the privilege of the house as an organized body, as of each individual member composing it, who is entitled to this privilege, *even against the declared will of the house*." In a similar vein in *Brewster* we stated:

> "The immunities of the Speech or Debate Clause were not written into the Constitution simply for the personal or private benefit of Members of Congress, but to protect the integrity of the legislative process *by insuring the independence of individual legislators*."

We perceive no reason to undertake, in this case, consideration of the Clause in terms of separating the Members' rights from the rights of the body.

[*Affirmed.*]

MR. JUSTICE POWELL took no part in the consideration or decision of this case.

MR. JUSTICE STEVENS, with whom MR. JUSTICE STEWART joins, concurring in part and dissenting in part. * * *

In *Brewster*, the Court held that the Speech or Debate Clause did not bar prosecution of a former Senator for receiving money in return for being influenced in the performance of a legislative act. The Court read *Johnson* as allowing a prosecution of a Member of Congress so long as the Government's case does not rely on legislative acts or the motivation for such acts. It reasoned that Brewster was not being prosecuted for the performance of a legislative act, but rather for soliciting or agreeing to take money with knowledge that the donor intended to compensate him for an official act. Whether the Senator ever performed the official act was irrelevant.

As a practical matter, of course, it is clear that evidence relating to a legislator's motivation for accepting a bribe will also be probative of his intent in committing the official act for which the bribe was solicited or paid. Nonetheless, the Court made clear in *Brewster* that inquiries into the legislator's motivation in accepting payment are not barred by *Johnson*'s proscription against inquiry into legislative motivation. "[A]n inquiry into the purpose of a bribe," the *Brewster* Court held, " 'does not draw in question the legislative acts of the defendant member of Congress or his motives for performing them.' " Thus, so long as the Government's case does not depend upon the legislator's motivation in committing an official act, inquiries into his motivation in accepting a bribe—which obviously may be revealing as to both the existence of legislative acts and the motivation for them— are permissible under the Speech or Debate Clause, as interpreted in *Brewster*.

* * * Here, the Government is seeking to introduce written and testimonial evidence as to Helstoski's motivation in soliciting and accepting bribes. Some of this evidence makes reference to past or future legislative acts for which payment is being sought or given. Obviously, this evidence, to the extent it is probative of Helstoski's intent in accepting payment, is an important and legitimate part of the Government's case against the former Congressman. Whether or not he ever committed the legislative acts is wholly irrelevant to the Government's proof, and inquiry into that subject is prohibited by *Johnson* and *Brewster*. But the mere fact that legislative acts are mentioned does not, in my view, require that otherwise

relevant and admissible evidence be excluded. * * * The admissibility line should be based on the purpose of the offer rather than the specificity of the reference. So long as the jury is instructed that it should not consider the references as proof of legislative acts, and so long as no inquiry is made with respect to the motivations for such acts, *Brewster* does not bar the introduction of evidence simply because reference is made to legislative acts.

Indeed, I think it important to emphasize that the majority today does not read *Brewster* to foreclose the introduction of any evidence making reference to legislative acts. The Court holds that evidence referring only to acts to be performed in the future may be admitted into evidence. The Court explains this holding by noting that a promise to perform a legislative act in the future is not itself a legislative act. But it is equally true that the solicitation of a bribe which contains a self-laudatory reference to past performance is not itself a legislative act. Whether the legislator refers to past or to future performance, his statement will be probative of his intent in accepting payment and, in either event, may incidentally shed light on the performance and motivation of legislative acts. The proper remedy, in my judgment, is not automatic inadmissibility for past references and automatic admissibility for future references. Rather, drawing on the language of the Constitution itself, the test should require the trial court to analyze the purpose of the prosecutor's questioning. If the evidentiary references to legislative acts are merely incidental to a proper purpose, the judge should admit the evidence and instruct the jury as to its limited relevance. The Constitution mandates that legislative acts "shall not be questioned"; it does not say they shall not be mentioned.

[The dissenting opinion of MR. JUSTICE BRENNAN has been omitted. The dissent argued that the indictment should have been dismissed. " '[P]roof of an agreement to be "influenced" in the performance of legislative acts is by definition an inquiry into their motives, whether or not the acts themselves or the circumstances surrounding them are questioned at trial.' " Quoting *Brewster*, 408 U.S. at 536 (Brennan, J., dissenting).]

NOTE ON BRIBERY PROSECUTIONS AFTER HELSTOSKI

In *United States v. Myers*, 635 F.2d 932 (2d Cir. 1980), former Congressman Myers (D–Pa.) argued that his indictment for bribery in violation of § 201 as part of the Abscam investigation was subject to dismissal under the Speech or Debate Clause because it required or contemplated that the prosecutor present evidence protected by the Clause. In rejecting this argument, the Second Circuit noted that the indictment alleged a *promise* to perform a legislative act (introduction of a private bill to allow foreign businessmen to remain in the United States), not the performance of the act. See also *United States v. Murphy*, 642 F.2d 699 (2d Cir. 1980), where the court stated that, under *Brewster*, acceptance of bribes in return for corrupt promises to take official action is not protected by the Clause.

In *United States v. Williams*, 644 F.2d 950 (2d Cir. 1981), the court held that the Speech or Debate Clause was not violated when the indicting grand jury was shown a videotape of defendant, former Senator Harrison Williams (D–N.J.), discussing a proposed immigration bill, because this discussion involved only possible future performance of legislative functions. And in *United States v. Myers, supra,* the Second Circuit rejected the contention of a co-defendant, former Congressman Frank Thompson (D–N.J.), that the trial court had erred in allowing into evidence proof of his private conversations on the floor of the House of Representatives in which he invited a second Congressman to join the ranks of those accepting bribes. The court said that "[o]ne would think that a Congressman, even when grasping for objections to a criminal conviction, would understand that the Speech or Debate Clause accords immunity to what is said on the House floor in the course of the legislative process, * * * not to whispered solicitations to commit a crime."

These cases reflect the difficulty of applying the Court's test for Speech or Debate Clause immunity to instances of allegedly corrupt behavior. Inquiry into the lawmaker's decision to accept a bribe, which seems to be allowed, may well shed light on the motives in performing any subsequent related legislative act. And how should courts treat self-laudatory references to past legislative acts designed to convince listeners to participate in the corrupt scheme? Under the Court's jurisprudence, these statements would probably be excluded from the courtroom, even though the accuracy of the statements is arguably not relevant to the prosecution. Should we worry that the clause is too expansive in its coverage, immunizing from prosecution corrupt politicians who should be held to answer for their perfidy? See also *Kansas v. Neufeld,* 926 P.2d 1325 (Kan. 1996) (using the state speech or debate provision to exclude evidence of a particularly squalid blackmail threat from one lawmaker to another on the floor of the legislature to coerce a vote, a result in tension with *Myers,* above). Remember that the Clause protects a member only from questioning "in any other Place," thereby allowing the legislature the power to investigate and discipline its members.

Problem 3–14. The House of Representatives was nearing a vote on the President's health reform proposal. The vote was going to be close, and the Republican Party leadership wanted to maintain party discipline to ensure passage. Representative Alex Noah, a Republican on the committee with jurisdiction over the bill, opposed the bill and announced his intention to vote no on the floor. A week before, Noah had announced that he was retiring from Congress, and his daughter Samantha had declared that she would run for her father's now-open seat in the next election.

On the floor of the House, during the voting period on the health care bill, the Speaker of the House told Noah that "a yes vote on this bill will help you and help your daughter because it will be a popular vote with the President and your Party." Minutes later, Noah was called off the floor into the cloakroom (a room right off the House floor where only representatives can enter and that has phones and comfortable chairs) to take a phone call from the Secretary of Health and Human Services. The Secretary told Noah that it was important that he end his distinguished career on a high note of support for the President. The Secretary added that he was sure Noah's expertise would be crucial to several blue-ribbon panels being established to study the challenges facing the health care system, and that he hoped the President would be in a position to nominate Noah for such positions after he retired. When Noah returned to the floor, the Republican Majority Leader told him that the state's Chamber of Commerce had decided to raise $100,000 for Samantha's campaign, but that a no vote would likely discourage the Chamber from helping Samantha's election effort. Representative Jane Skye, another Republican from Noah's state, told Noah on his way up to vote that if he voted no, she and other Republicans would make sure Samantha never came to Congress and that Samantha would be political "dead meat."

Noah voted no. Noah is willing to testify about the events in any criminal prosecutions that may be brought or in any other forum. What crimes may have been committed? What obstacles would stand in the way of any prosecutions? What arguments would you expect to be made by possible defendants? Are avenues available for an investigation into the events that Representative Noah has described other than criminal prosecutions in court?

Problem 3–15. In 2006, the FBI conducted an investigation of bribery and other allegations concerning Rep. William Jefferson (D–La.). It was alleged that Jefferson used his position to influence some African nations to buy telecommunications equipment and services from a Louisiana-based firm in return for substantial cash and stock. One of his former staffers and the president of the firm pleaded guilty to bribing and conspiring to bribe the Congressman. Pursuant to a search warrant but without alerting congressional leadership, the FBI searched Jefferson's congressional office in Washington, D.C.—apparently the first time that federal law enforcement officials had searched the office of a representative or senator. The FBI seized computer hard drives and boxes of paper records, which it agreed to review using a "Filter Team" to remove any irrelevant documents or any material protected by the Speech or Debate Clause or any other privilege. (The FBI also searched Jefferson's home, where agents found $90,000 wrapped in aluminum foil and hidden in the freezer.) Lawmakers from both parties objected to the search as a violation of legislative privilege. Can congressional offices be searched consistent with the Speech or Debate Clause? Can law enforcement use the documents that agents find there? How would the case against Representative Jefferson be affected by the constitutional privilege and the cases interpreting it? See *United States v. Rayburn House Office Building*, 497 F.3d 654 (D.C. Cir. 2007) (holding that the execution of the search warrant violated the Speech or Debate Clause, that all privileged documents (originals and copies) must be returned, that the FBI officers who participated in the search cannot reveal contents of privileged documents or be involved in pending prosecution, but that non-privileged documents need not be returned). As you consider this case, are you surprised that Jefferson was reelected after the raid of his home and office but before he was indicted for racketeering, soliciting bribes, and money laundering?

## 2.	State Protection of State Legislators (Speech or Debate Clauses in State Constitutions)

Just as New York did at the time of the *Van de Carr* prosecution (a provision that remains unchanged today), 43 state constitutions contain clauses similar to the U.S. Constitution's Speech or Debate Clause. State courts often interpret these clauses as having a similar meaning to the federal clause.[62] Some state constitutional provisions are much more narrowly phrased, however. Article 4, § 11 of the Michigan Constitution protects state legislators "from civil arrest and civil process during sessions of the legislature and for five days next before the commencement and after the termination thereof." The scope of these provisions is

---

[62] See, e.g., *Romer v. Colorado General Assembly*, 810 P.2d 215 (Colo. 1991); *People v. Ohrenstein*, 565 N.E.2d 493, 501 (N.Y. 1990); *Harristown Dev. Corp. v. Comm'r*, 580 A.2d 1174 (Pa. 1990).

usually interpreted to be equivalent to the federal protection, notwithstanding the difference in formulation.

Thus, the Michigan provision immunizes lawmakers in their legislative activities, but it does not extend to casework or informing activities. See, e.g., *Wilkins v. Gagliardi*, 556 N.W.2d 171 (Mich. App. 1996). Michigan courts have had to determine the scope of the time period in which legislators are protected by the state immunity. In *Bishop v. Montante*, 237 N.W. 2d 465 (Mich. 1976), the Michigan Supreme Court was asked to interpret the word "sessions" in its state speech or debate clause. It found that the immunity continued even during a legislative recess, when the legislature was formally in session because it had not adjourned. The court reasoned that legislators continue to perform legislative business such as "[c]onstituent contact, research, [and] committee assignments" even when the body is not sitting. Is this expansive view of the constitutional protection consistent with courts' understanding of the scope of the clause to cover only legislative activities, and not casework, newsletters, or other interactions with constituents? For a comprehensive examination of state privileges and a list of all the provisions, see Steven Huefner, *The Neglected Value of the Legislative Privilege in State Legislatures*, 45 Wm. & Mary L. Rev. 221 (2003).

In *Iron v. Rhode Island Ethics Comm'n*, 973 A.2d 1124 (R.I. 2009), the Rhode Island Supreme Court held that the state's constitutional "speech in debate clause" prohibited the Rhode Island Ethics Commission from prosecuting Rhode Island State Senator William V. Irons for alleged violations of the Rhode Island Code of Ethics. The Ethics Commission accused Senator Irons of improperly participating in debate and voting on legislation impacting entities with which he had business ties. Neither party disputed that Senator Irons' allegedly improper activities were core legislative activities ordinarily covered by the "speech in debate" clause. However, the Ethics Commission, which was created by an amendment to the Rhode Island Constitution stating that "All elected and appointed officials * * * shall be subject to the code of ethics," argued that this more recent constitutional provision effected a "narrow repeal" of the Rhode Island Constitution's "speech in debate clause." The state supreme court rejected the argument and held that the Ethics Commission can only investigate and prosecute legislators for non-core legislative activities. The court further noted that while the "speech in debate" clause is an absolute immunity, it does not protect: "speeches delivered outside the legislature; political activities of legislators; undertakings for constituents; assistance in securing government contracts; republication of defamatory material in press releases and newsletters; solicitation and acceptance of bribes; and criminal activities, even those committed to further legislative activity." For further discussion see James Mure, *Case Note, Speech in Debate Clause—The Rhode Island Supreme Court Refuses to Read an Implied Exception into the Speech in Debate Clause:* Irons v. Rhode Island Ethics Comm'n, 973 A.2d 1124 (R.I. 2009), 41 Rutgers L.J. 1099 (2010).

3.   Federal Protection of State Legislators

The Court addressed whether the policies of the Speech or Debate Clause protected state legislators in *United States v. Gillock*, 445 U.S. 360 (1980). In that case, a Tennessee state legislator was indicted on federal charges stemming from allegations that he had accepted money in return for using his office to block extradition of criminal defendants and for introducing legislation that would have enabled four persons to obtain electrician's licenses that they had been unable to obtain by way of examination. The District Court had granted Gillock's motion to suppress all evidence relating to his legislative activities, on the ground that the Federal Rules of Evidence should recognize a privilege to protect the integrity of the state legislative process. After the Court of Appeals affirmed, the Supreme Court reversed. The Court noted that the Speech or Debate Clause technically protects only federal legislators and rejected arguments that the policy considerations underlying the Speech or Debate Clause counsel recognition of a comparable evidentiary privilege for state legislators in federal prosecutions. The Court stated:

> Two interrelated rationales underlie the Speech or Debate Clause: first, the need to avoid intrusion by the Executive or Judiciary into the affairs of a coequal branch, and second, the desire to protect legislative independence. * * *

> The first rationale, resting solely on the separation of powers doctrine, gives no support to the grant of a privilege to state legislators in federal criminal prosecutions. * * * [I]n those areas where the Constitution grants the Federal Government the power to act, the Supremacy Clause dictates that federal enactments will prevail over competing state exercises of power. * * *

> [As to the second rationale,] we believe that recognition of an evidentiary privilege for state legislators for their legislative acts would impair the legitimate interest of the Federal Government in enforcing its criminal statutes with only speculative benefit to the state legislative process.

Compare *Tenney v. Brandhove*, 341 U.S. 367 (1951) (recognizing a federal common law immunity for state legislators against civil lawsuits brought under § 1983 for violations of federal constitutional or statutory rights).

3. STRUCTURAL DUE PROCESS OF LAWMAKING

In an article proposing an alternative method of judicial review to replace the deferential rational basis review accorded to many statutes, former Justice of the Oregon Supreme Court Hans Linde articulated a theory of due process of lawmaking. *Due Process of Lawmaking*, 55 Neb. L. Rev. 197 (1976). He argued that the Due Process Clauses of the Constitution "instruct government itself to act by due process of law, not simply to legislate subject to later judicial second-guessing." *Id.* at 222. Legislative process should be designed, he argued, to produce "rational lawmaking," which we described at the outset of this chapter: legislators should be well informed about legislative proposals before they vote on them; decisions by committees and on the floor should be based on evidence about the problems in the status quo, the purpose of the bill, and the likely consequences of the new legal framework; and the committee's report should provide full explanations to members.

Linde acknowledged that his description did not accurately depict reality, but he argued that courts should adopt methods of adjudication and statutory review designed to promote this type of lawmaking by legislative bodies. Courts could work toward this objective by scrutinizing the rationale articulated by lawmakers to justify their choices of legislative ends and the means to reach those ends. Justices on the Supreme Court have only infrequently pursued this strategy of judicial review, however. One example is *Fullilove v. Klutznick*, 448 U.S. 448 (1980), a case in which the majority upheld a federal statute requiring that a certain percentage of federal contracting money go to minority business enterprises. Justice Stevens, in dissent, would have required a reasoned explanation for a congressional decision to provide preferential treatment for some racial and ethnic minorities. See Ittai Bar-Siman-Tov, *Semiprocedural Judicial Review*, 6 Legisprudence 271 (2012) (describing this as a growing approach internationally and providing principles for application).

More recently, the Supreme Court has adopted a similar technique in assessing the constitutionality of federal laws passed pursuant to Congress' interstate commerce authority and its authority to enforce the Reconstruction Amendments. In cases such as *Board of Trustees of the Univ. of Alabama v. Garrett*, 531 U.S. 356 (2001) (concerning the Americans with Disabilities Act) and *United States v. Morrison*, 529 U.S. 598 (2000) (concerning the Violence Against Women Act), the Court has reviewed the state of the legislative record to determine whether the empirical basis on which Congress legislated was sufficient. Many commentators have criticized this approach as an unacceptably intrusive encroachment on the prerogatives of the most politically accountable branch and as unsophisticated in its determination of what documents make up the legislative record. Ruth Colker and James Brudney, in their article *Dissing Congress*, argued that the Court "has treated the federal legislative process as akin to agency or lower court decisionmaking; in doing so, the Court has undermined Congress's ability to decide for itself how and whether to create a record in support of pending legislation." 100 Mich. L. Rev. 80, 83 (2001). Similarly, Philip Frickey and Steven Smith have suggested that the Court has placed unrealistic record-developing obligations upon Congress and failed to respect that, in circumstances of political conflict, legislatures decide by majority vote rather than by consensual deliberation. See *Judicial Review, the Congressional Process, and the Federalism Cases: An Interdisciplinary Critique*, 111 Yale L.J. 1707 (2002).[63]

In *Fullilove*, Stevens justified his departure from the norm because laws making distinctions on racial grounds are reviewed with strict scrutiny; it is unlikely he would be willing to require proof of rational lawmaking in cases challenging other kinds of laws. Linde was dubious about the merits of the more aggressive judicial approach. "Candor in giving reasons for a policy can be a mixed blessing. It may result in invalidating a policy for faulty premises even though it

---

[63] See also William Araiza, *Deference to Congressional Fact-Finding in Rights-Enforcing and Rights-Limiting Legislation*, 88 N.Y.U. L. Rev. 878 (2013) (providing factors to determine level of judicial deference in certain contexts); William Buzbee & Robert Schapiro, *Legislative Record Review*, 54 Stan. L. Rev. 87 (2001). But see John McGinnis & Charles Mulaney, *Judging Facts Like Law*, 25 Const. Comm. 69 (2008) (arguing for an independent judicial role in assessing "social fact-finding" by Congress).

would be quite desirable if based on different reasons. * * * Pursued into the legislative process [past the context of administrative agencies], the hope for candor is more likely to produce hypocrisy. Recitals of findings and purposes are the task of anonymous draftsmen, committee staffs, and counsel for interested parties, not legislators." 448 U.S., at 230–31.

Accordingly, Linde focused on the process of lawmaking, its rules and structural arrangements that are designed to facilitate reasoned deliberation and rational decisionmaking. Due process of lawmaking focuses in part on the "structures through which policies are both formed and applied." Laurence Tribe, *Structural Due Process*, 10 Harv. C.R.–C.L. L. Rev. 269, 269 (1975). This notion suggests that some kinds of actions should be taken only by entities with particular institutional features that enhance their special democratic legitimacy. After we assess requirements in the federal Constitution and in state constitutions setting forth procedural requirements for lawmaking,[64] we will turn to *Hampton v. Mow Sun Wong*, 426 U.S. 88 (1976), where the Court adopted a due process of lawmaking approach.

A. FEDERAL STRUCTURAL DUE PROCESS

The Bicameralism and Presentment Requirements. Article I, § 7, clauses 2–3 of the U.S. Constitution provide that a bill becomes a law only if it is enacted in the same form by both the House and Senate, and then presented to the President. If the President vetoes the bill, the House and Senate can override the veto by a two-thirds vote in each chamber. State constitutions have similar provisions, with one exception (Nebraska only has one legislative chamber) and one interesting twist (most states allow their governors to veto specific items in some bills, discussed in Chapter 3, § 3B). The Court in *Clinton v. City of New York* emphasized that bicameralism and presentment are mandatory requirements of the legislative process: "The procedures governing the enactment of statutes set forth in the text of Article I were the product of the great debates and compromises that produced the Constitution itself. Familiar historical materials provide abundant support for the conclusion that the power to enact statutes may only 'be exercised in accord with a single, finely wrought and exhaustively considered, procedure.' " 524 U.S. 417, at 439–40 (quoting *INS v. Chadha*, Chapter 8, § 3A).

One justification for the bicameralism and presentment requirements is to ensure the sustained consideration of different points of view. In *Federalist #51*, James Madison defended the bicameralism requirement on the ground that it mandates consent of two bodies elected in different ways, representing different interests and electorates, and developing different internal customs. Moreover, requiring two heterogeneous bodies to agree on legislation ensures that factious and partial laws would not be adopted.[65] In *Federalist #62*, Madison argued that the Senate, with its longer terms and smaller membership, is a cooling-off chamber, preventing the enactment of hasty legislation. Alexander Hamilton argued in

---

[64] See also Adrian Vermeule, *The Constitutional Law of Congressional Procedure*, 71 U. Chi. L. Rev. 361 (2004).

[65] For a formal proof of Madison's proposition, see James Buchanan & Gordon Tullock, *The Calculus of Consent* (1962).

Federalist #73 that the executive veto is likewise "calculated to guard the community against the effects of faction, precipitancy, or of any impulse unfriendly to the public good, which may happen to influence a majority" of Congress.

Saul Levmore has offered a modern analysis of bicameralism in *Bicameralism: When Are Two Decisions Better than One?*, 12 Int'l Rev. L. & Econ. 145 (1992). He first considers the possibility that bicameralism reduces the "manipulative power of the agenda setter" because one cannot control outcomes as well in a bicameral system as in a unicameral process. Levmore concludes, however, that "only a very careful and difficult empirical inquiry would establish that a convener's power to influence committee and conference-committee membership does not offset the fact that bicameralism diminishes the convener's ability to manipulate the order in which alternative proposals are considered." *Id.* at 151. He acknowledges the Buchanan and Tullock argument that bicameralism protects the status quo by making it more difficult to enact legislation. Levmore argues that although supermajority voting requirements could achieve the same purpose, "supermajoritarianism [likely] encourages more wasteful rent-seeking and corruption than does bicameralism. The simple fact that in a bicameral system a proposal must be openly considered in two forums may work to expose misbehavior. And if the problems of corruption and inefficient rent-seeking are in part functions of a legislator's ability to promise and deliver results, then it is surely the case that with supermajoritarianism a legislator, or small group of legislators, is more likely to be in a position to block legislation on behalf of some interest group than is a legislator likely to be able to block or promote legislation in a bicameral system with simple-majority voting." *Id.* at 155.

Bicameralism on the federal level requires that two legislative institutions that are constituted in very different ways each have a say in the enactment of laws. These differences were more pronounced before passage of the Seventeenth Amendment, which ended the practice of having state legislatures select senators and required their direct election.[66] The most obvious remaining difference between the two institutions is the Senate's unique apportionment scheme in which each state is equally represented. This feature of the Senate is almost certainly a permanent one; Article V of the Constitution provides that "no State, without its Consent, shall be deprived of its equal Suffrage in the Senate."[67] In contrast, both houses of bicameral state legislatures are subject to the principle of one person, one vote, although courts may accept greater population deviations in state districting than in the context of districting for the House of Representatives. See, e.g., *Connor v. Finch*, 431 U.S. 407 (1977).

Frances Lee and Bruce Oppenheimer have raised several fairness concerns in their study of the Senate, *Sizing Up the Senate: The Unequal Consequences of Equal Representation* (1999). They find first that state population "dramatically affects both the quantity of contact that constituents have with their senators and

---

[66] See Vikram Amar, *Indirect Effects of Direct Election: A Structural Examination of the Seventeenth Amendment*, 49 Vand. L. Rev. 1347 (1996).

[67] For a critique of the Senate as an institution that violates the one person, one vote principle, see Lynn Baker & Samuel Dinkin, *The Senate: An Institution Whose Time Has Gone?*, 13 J. L. & Pol. 21 (1997); William Eskridge Jr., *The One Senator, One Vote Clause*, 12 Const. Comment. 159 (1995).

the perceived quality of those interactions." *Id.* at 12. Constituents from less populous states have more contact with their senators and are more likely to ask them for help with their problems, rather than just registering their opinion on some policy matter. This reality causes a disparity of access for both individuals and interest groups to influence members of Congress. Another troubling disparity that Lee and Oppenheimer link to the malapportionment of the Senate affects partisan control of the institution. "[E]qual representation of states often means that one political party wins Senate seats disproportionate to its share of the national popular vote, owing to its success in small-state elections." *Id.* at 226.[68] Small-state senators tend to spend more time pursuing particularized benefits for their constituents, whereas large-state senators spend relatively more time pursuing policy activism, which appeals more to the media and thus furthers their reelection goal in states where personal campaigning is logistically impossible.

One way that small-state senators enhance their ability to obtain benefits for their constituents is that they often cast the decisive votes on closely fought legislation. "[C]oalition leaders tend to seek out senators from small states to find needed votes and * * * these senators—who know that their demands are less costly and thus more likely to be accommodated—delay committing themselves to a side, expecting to be courted by coalition leaders." *Id.* at 14. Not surprisingly given their disproportionate influence in the Senate, small-state senators are able to force the Senate to adopt funding formulas in government programs that systematically favor small states and distribute resources away from populous ones. Lee and Oppenheimer find that neither the House nor the President exerts "sufficient influence to counterbalance the effects of equal representation of states in the Senate in distributive policymaking." *Id.* at 14–15.

What is the sanction if a bill is passed in violation of either the bicameralism or presentment requirements? The main check is institutional. The *enrolled bill* is signed by the presiding officers of the House and Senate; if it is then approved by the President, it is sent to the Secretary of State, who furnishes a correct copy to the Congressional Printer for publication in the Statutes at Large. What if a mistake is made? That was the argument in *Marshall Field & Co. v. Clark*, 143 U.S. 649 (1892). Because § 30 of the bill that passed by both chambers of Congress was omitted from the enrolled bill, the appellants argued that the law was null and void. The Court agreed with the general proposition but still refused the relief requested; the Court refused to look at the extrinsic evidence offered by the appellants to question the enrolled bill:

> It is said that * * * it becomes possible for the Speaker of the House of Representatives and the President of the Senate to impose upon the people as a law a bill that was never passed by Congress. But this possibility is too remote to be seriously considered in the present inquiry. It suggests a deliberate conspiracy to which the presiding officers, the committees on enrolled bills and the clerks of the two houses must necessarily be parties, all acting with a common purpose to defeat an expression of the popular

---

[68] But see Franco Mattei, *Senate Apportionment and Partisan Advantage: A Second Look*, 26 Legis. Stud. Q. 391 (2001) (finding smaller apportionment bias than Lee & Oppenheimer).

will in the mode prescribed by the Constitution. Judicial action based upon such a suggestion is forbidden by the respect due to a coordinate branch of the government. The evils that may result from the recognition of the principle that an enrolled act, in the custody of the Secretary of State, attested by the signatures of the presiding officers of the two houses of Congress, and the approval of the President, is conclusive evidence that it was passed by Congress, according to the forms of the Constitution, would be far less than those that would certainly result from a rule making the validity of Congressional enactments depend upon the manner in which the journals of the respective houses are kept by the subordinate officers charged with the duty of keeping them.

Later that same year, however, in *United States v. Ballin*, 144 U.S. 1 (1892), the Court examined the Journal of the House of Representatives to conclude that a quorum had been present when a bill was passed. See Ittai Bar-Siman-Tov, *Legislative Supremacy in the United States?: Rethinking the "Enrolled Bill" Doctrine*, 97 Geo. L.J. 323 (2009) (arguing that the federal doctrine is inconsistent with the Constitution and allows too much power to the legislature without judicial check).

Is the enrolled bill rule still a good one more than a century after *Field v. Clark*? Would differences in modern congressional recordkeeping impact the viability of this rule? Think about this issue in connection with our discussion of the political question doctrine in Chapter 2, § 1A. You might reconsider your answer after reading the discussion of the enrolled bill rule in state courts found later in this section.

FEDERAL ENROLLED BILL PROBLEM

Problem 3–16. The Deficit Reduction Act of 2005 (DRA) contained ten titles and 181 pages dealing with subjects such as deposit insurance for federal financial institutions, the allocation of the spectrum for commercial wireless users, student loans, filing fees in the federal courts, and assistance to people affected by Hurricane Katrina. It included provisions making substantial changes to the Medicare and Medicaid programs. The version of DRA signed by the President provided that the duration of Medicare payments for certain medical equipment would be 13 months. That version passed the Senate (thanks to a tie-breaking vote by the Vice President), but, apparently because of an error by the Secretary of the Senate, the version of DRA sent to the House, and voted on by that chamber, provided for a payment duration of 36 months. The enrolled bill, signed by the Speaker of the House and President pro tempore of the Senate, specified thirteen months. Should *Field v. Clark* control the outcome, meaning that the court would not look past the enrolled bill to determine whether the constitutional requirements for lawmaking were followed? Does it matter that the difference between the two versions of the bill amounts to $2 billion in additional Medicare spending? If a court decides to look beyond the enrolled bill's language and determines that different versions of the bill passed the House and Senate, what is the appropriate remedy? Should the entire bill be void because of a failure to comply with bicameralism, or should the problematic provision be severed? See *Public Citizen v.*

United States Dist. Court for the Dist. of Columbia, 486 F.3d 1342 (D.C. Cir. 2007) (applying the enrolled bill rule of *Field v. Clark* and dismissing challenge to the DRA).

Special Procedures for Revenue Measures. Article I, § 7, clause 1 requires that "[a]ll Bills for raising Revenue shall originate in the House of Representatives." The purpose of this rule is to assure that the representatives "closest" to the people (House members, who are up for reelection every two years) bear responsibility for initiating measures (taxes) that have the greatest potential for oppressing the citizenry.[69] Some state constitutions have similar requirements.

The provision prompts several questions: when does a bill not "originate" in the House? If a bill does not so originate, but the House and Senate enact the bill and the President signs it, do we have a "law" under Article I, § 7? Consider the following case.

United States v. Munoz-Flores
495 U.S. 385 (1990).

Munoz-Flores challenged his conviction and fines pursuant to 18 U.S.C. § 3013 on the ground that the statute is a revenue measure that had not originated in the House of Representatives. **Justice Marshall**'s opinion for the Court first held that Origination Clause issues are justiciable under the standards set by *Baker v. Carr* (discussed and applied in Chapter 2, § 1A). Considering the merits, the Court held that § 3013 did not violate the Origination Clause. In *Twin City Bank v. Nebeker*, 167 U.S. 196, 202 (1897), the Court had earlier ruled that "revenue bills are those that levy taxes in the strict sense of the word, and are not bills for other purposes which may incidentally create revenue." The Victims of Crime Act of 1984 established a Crime Victims Fund, 42 U.S.C. § 10601(a) (as amended), as a federal source of funds for programs that compensate and assist crime victims. The scheme established by the Act included mechanisms to provide money for the Fund, including § 3013. Although the statute provided that if the total income to the Fund from all sources exceeded $100 million in any one year, the excess would be deposited in the general fund of the Treasury, that happened only once, in fiscal year 1989. Any revenue for the general Treasury generated by § 3013 was thus found to be "incidenta[l]" to the regulatory purposes of the statute. In footnote 7, the Court reserved judgment on whether it would apply the *Nebeker* rule to a funded program that was entirely unrelated to the persons paying for the program.

Justice Stevens (joined by **Justice O'Connor**), concurring in the judgment, argued from the structure of Article I, § 7 that improperly "originated" bills become "law" so long as they are passed by both the House and Senate and presented to the President. Read Article I, § 7, which says that "[e]very" bill passed by both Houses and presented to the President "shall become a Law." Also, compare the consequences of improper origination (no explicit consequence) with failure of bicameralism (no law) or presentment (also no law). Justice Stevens agreed with the Court that the Origination Clause is an important means by which the most popularly accountable institution (the

---

[69] See Michael Evans, *"A Source of Frequent and Obstinate Altercations": The History and Application of the Origination Clause*, Tax Notes, Nov. 29, 2004, at 1215; J. Michael Medina, *The Origination Clause in the American Constitution: A Comparative Survey*, 23 Tulsa L.J. 165 (1987).

House) is to monitor efforts to tax the people, but Stevens argued that the House itself—rather than the Court—is in the best position to enforce and effectuate this goal.

Justice Scalia concurred in the judgment as well. Relying on *Field v. Clark*, he argued that the Court cannot look behind the "enrolled bill" as it was presented to the President. The enrolled bill that became the Victims of Crime Act of 1984, 98 Stat. 2170, bore the indication "H.J. Res. 648." The designation "H.J. Res." ("House Joint Resolution") conclusively attested that the legislation originated in the House.

ORIGINATION CLAUSE PROBLEMS

Problem 3–17. The Senate passes S. 93, which might fairly be characterized as a revenue bill. The House then passes a similar bill of its own, H.R. 617. The Senate requests a conference, and the bill that ultimately emerges is called H.R. 617, but its provisions are more like those in S. 93. The President signs the bill into law. Has the Origination Clause been violated? If so, what remedy (if any) is available?

Problem 3–18. One problem not present in *Munoz-Flores* is that of standing. The Supreme Court has disapproved of broad "taxpayer" standing. Assuming a general revenue measure, as in the preceding problem, would members of Congress have standing to bring suit for violation of the Origination Clause? For a pre-*Munoz-Flores* decision, see *Moore v. United States House of Representatives*, 733 F.2d 946 (D.C. Cir. 1984). What about nonjudicial ways to enforce the requirements of the Origination Clause? In the House of Representatives, members have the right to object to consideration of a bill because it violates the Origination Clause; a majority must vote against the constitutional point of order for deliberation to continue. The House also uses a "blue slip" procedure to notify the Senate when it believes that a Senate bill or amendment violates the Origination Clause. The blue slip informs the Senate that the House will not consider the proposal. Is this sufficient protection? See *Raines v. Byrd*, 521 U.S. 811 (1997) (severely limiting legislator standing in the context of a challenge to the federal Line Item Veto Act).

B. THE ENROLLED BILL RULE IN STATE CONSTITUTIONAL PRACTICE

State constitutions often include more procedural requirements for the enactment of laws than the relatively spare federal Constitution. Many state constitutions, for example, require that a bill be read a certain number of times before it can be passed and set specific time limits for legislative sessions. However, a bill that has been passed without receiving the requisite number of readings will not reveal that defect on its face; the same is true if, as is sometimes done, a bill has been passed after the legislature was supposed to have adjourned, but the legislative clock had been covered before the time for adjournment and the legislature pretended that time was standing still. How could one prove such a defect or any other violation of constitutionally prescribed procedures?

In many states, the enrolled bill rule severely restricts judicial review of legislative procedural errors. Just as on the federal level, an enrolled bill is a bill that purports to have passed both houses of the legislature and that has been signed by the presiding officers of both houses. In some states, the process of enrollment also involves the signature of the governor and filing with the secretary of state. Courts following the enrolled bill rule conclusively presume that the enrolled bill was validly enacted according to the prescribed procedures and refuse to entertain evidence purporting to demonstrate the contrary. One commentator has noted that:

> the rule has been supported by several theories. Traditionally the doctrine of separation of powers was the underlying support for the rule. Under this doctrine the courts are kept from being placed in the position of reviewing the work of a supposedly equal branch of government. Other practical considerations have been advanced in support of the rule. Certain defects are apparent on the face of the enrolled bill itself, but other judicial attacks on the status of legislation could undermine stability in the law and would confuse the trial of substantive issues. * * * Flagrant disregard for constitutional duties is better remedied by internal legislative procedures or by the electorate. The enrolled bill rule is further justified by the argument that legislative journals are subject to error and fraud, whereas enrollment includes "certification by the presiding officers * * * witnessed by other present members * * * [furnishing] adequate protection against the risk of error in the process of certification itself.

Elizabeth Cobb, Comment, *Judicial Review of the Legislative Enactment Process: Louisiana's "Journal Entry" Rule*, 41 La. L. Rev. 1187, 1190 (1981). Are these arguments persuasive? Consider the responsive argument of Linde in *Due Process of Lawmaking, supra*, at 243:

> Neither [respect for a co-equal branch nor evidentiary difficulties] keeps courts from insisting on [adherence to procedural rules] by executive officers or by local lawmakers, and those who oppose judicial review of faulty lawmaking on evidentiary grounds will equally oppose it on uncontested pleadings or stipulations. Fear of legislative resentment at judicial interference is not borne out by experience where procedural review exists, any more than it was after the Supreme Court told Congress that it had used faulty procedure in unseating Representative Adam Clayton Powell. It is far more cause for resentment to invalidate the substance of a policy that the politically accountable branches and their constituents support than to invalidate a lawmaking procedure that can be repeated correctly, yet we take substantive judicial review for granted.

As Linde's analysis suggests, the enrolled bill rule at the state level has long been under sustained academic attack, and many state courts have responded favorably. See the useful discussion in Robert Williams, *State Constitutional Limits on Legislative Procedure: Legislative Compliance and Judicial Enforcement*, 48 U. Pitt. L. Rev. 797 (1987). Some courts have adopted special exceptions to the rule. In many cases, these exceptions are based on evidence found in the journals of legislative proceedings that all state constitutions require state legislatures to keep. (Article I, § 5, cl. 3 of the U.S. Constitution similarly requires that "[e]ach House shall keep a Journal of its Proceedings, and from time to time publish the same.") State constitutions differ on the timing and manner of publication, the number of members necessary to have roll call votes recorded in the journal, and whether dissenting comments or protests must be recorded. Courts seeking to modify the enrolled bill rule have often relied on information found in these official journals. As explained in Cobb's comment, *supra*, at 1191–92:

> [Two] general categories have been delineated: 1) the "pure" journal entry rule, a conclusive presumption that the enrolled bill is valid only if it is in accordance with procedures recorded in the journal and the constitution; 2) the "affirmative contradiction" rule, a determination that the enrolled bill is valid unless the journals affirmatively show a statement that there has not been compliance with constitutional requirements * * *.

South Dakota, for example, finds the enrolled bill conclusive evidence of proper enactment, except when the asserted impropriety concerns a provision for which the constitution requires a journal entry. *Barnsdall Refining Corp. v. Welsh*, 269 N.W. 853 (S.D. 1936); cf. *Indep. Community Bankers Ass'n v. South Dakota*, 346 N.W.2d 737 (S.D. 1984) (reaffirming modified enrolled bill rule, over dissent arguing for abandonment of enrolled bill rule). For other examples of the journal entry rule, see *State v. Kaufman*, 430 So. 2d 904 (Fla. 1983); *People v. Dunigan*, 650 N.E.2d 1026 (Ill. 1995). See also *Fumo v. Pa. Public Utility Comm'n*, 719 A.2d 10 (Pa. Commw. Ct. 1998); *League of Women Voters of Pa. v. Commonwealth*, 692 A.2d 263 (Pa. Commw. Ct. 1996) (describing Pennsylvania's modified enrolled bill rule that allows courts some discretion when there is a clear violation of the state constitution).

Finally, some states follow an *extrinsic evidence rule*, in which they will entertain evidence beyond legislative journals. This rule was adopted in *D & W Auto Supply v. Dep't of Revenue*, 602 S.W.2d 420 (Ky. 1980), to invalidate a statute violating the constitution's requirement that appropriations measures be adopted by an absolute majority of the legislators in each chamber of the legislature. In contrast, see *Ass'n of Texas Prof. Educators v. Kirby*, 788 S.W.2d 827 (Tex. 1990) (under the enrolled bill rule, no extrinsic evidence may be considered to contradict the enrolled version of the bill). Even if commentators are generally right that extrinsic evidence should be considered, how far should courts carry that precept? Consider the problem of the legislature's "stopping the clock" and remaining in session past the time limit specified in the state constitution. In *State ex rel. Heck's Discount Ctrs. v. Winters*, 132 S.E.2d 374 (W. Va. 1963), the court concluded from the legislative journal and extrinsic evidence that the bill in question had been passed a few minutes into the early morning of March 10, 1963, when under the state constitution the legislative term had expired at midnight on March 9. The court noted the common legislative practice of "staying the hands of the clock to enable the Legislature to effect an adjournment apparently within the time fixed by the Constitution for the expiration of the term," and it concluded that "[d]oubtless it is a fact that the legislature of this state is not unique in having indulged in that practice." Nonetheless, the court held that when the legislative term expires the legislature "ceases to have the legislative power accorded to it while in lawful, constitutional session." Accordingly, it invalidated the legislation.

Consider the evidence in *Winters*. An affidavit by the clerk of the West Virginia House of Delegates stated that on March 9 "he was directed by the Speaker of the

House of Delegates * * * to stop * * * the official clock of the House of Delegates," and that the legislation in question "was passed when the official clock was stopped at 11:28 P.M., but that the actual time was 12:15 or 12:18 A.M. March 10, 1963." The journal of the House contained comments such as these:

Mr. Nuzum. Mr. Watson, do you have a watch?

Mr. Watson. Yes, sir.

Mr. Nuzum. What time does your watch show?

Mr. Watson. I've got nine after one. * * *

Mr. Nuzum. Mr. Simonton, do you have a watch?

Mr. Simonton. Yes, sir.

Mr. Nuzum. What time does your watch show?

Mr. Simonton. My watch shows six after one. * * *

Mr. Nuzum. Mr. Myles, do you have a watch?

Mr. Myles. Yes, sir.

Mr. Nuzum. What time does your watch say?

Mr. Myles. I can't see it but the clock on the wall says four minutes till twelve on March 9, 1963.

Mr. Nuzum. You can't see your watch?

Mr. Myles. No, sir. It's covered up with my shirt sleeve.

If you were on a state supreme court, how would you react to this evidence? Can the enrolled bill rule be defended in these circumstances? See *Dillon v. King*, 529 P.2d 745 (N. Mex. 1974), where the court held prospectively that the enrolled bill rule would no longer be applied to an allegation that the bill under review was adopted after the legislative term had expired.

C. REQUIRING LAWMAKING BY THE MOST INSTITUTIONALLY COMPETENT BRANCH OF GOVERNMENT

The structures of lawmaking put in place by constitutions, statutes, and legislative rules are designed to ensure that legislatures discharge their responsibilities as the most democratically accountable governance entities in a rational and transparent way. Because of these features of institutional design, a due process of lawmaking perspective suggests that the legislature may be uniquely suited to make particular important decisions. Thus, perhaps some decisions made by administrative agencies should be subject to judicial invalidation and, in effect, remanded to the legislature (or perhaps the politically accountable chief executive) for reconsideration. Consider the following example of structural due process.

HAMPTON V. MOW SUN WONG

Supreme Court of the United States, 1976.
426 U.S. 88, 96 S.Ct. 1895, 48 L.Ed.2d 495.

JUSTICE STEVENS delivered the opinion of the Court.

[Respondents, five permanent resident aliens, had been denied employment by the General Services Administration, the Department of Health, Education, and Welfare, and the Postal Department. They filed this action challenging a Civil Service Commission rule barring noncitizens, including lawfully admitted resident aliens, from employment in the federal civil service on the ground that the rule violated the equal protection component of the Due Process Clause of the Fifth Amendment. Justice Stevens' opinion began with recognition of the "paramount federal power over immigration and naturalization," thereby distinguishing the case from *Sugarman v. Dougall*, 413 U.S. 634 (1973), in which the Court had invalidated a section of the New York civil service law providing that only U.S. citizens could hold permanent positions in the state's civil service.]

When the Federal Government asserts an overriding national interest as justification for a discriminatory rule which would violate the Equal Protection Clause if adopted by a State, due process requires that there be a legitimate basis for presuming that the rule was actually intended to serve that interest. If the agency which promulgates the rule has direct responsibility for fostering or protecting that interest, it may reasonably be presumed that the asserted interest was the actual predicate for the rule. That presumption would, of course, be fortified by an appropriate statement of reasons identifying the relevant interest. Alternatively, if the rule were expressly mandated by the Congress or the President, we might presume that any interest which might rationally be served by the rule did in fact give rise to its adoption.

In this case the petitioners have identified several interests which the Congress or the President might deem sufficient to justify the exclusion of noncitizens from the federal service. They argue, for example, that the broad exclusion may facilitate the President's negotiation of treaties with foreign powers by enabling him to offer employment opportunities to citizens of a given foreign country in exchange for reciprocal concessions—an offer he could not make if those aliens were already eligible for federal jobs. Alternatively, the petitioners argue that reserving the federal service for citizens provides an appropriate incentive to aliens to qualify for naturalization and thereby to participate more effectively in our society. They also point out that the citizenship requirement has been imposed in the United States with substantial consistency for over 100 years and accords with international law and the practice of most foreign countries. Finally, they correctly state that the need for undivided loyalty in certain sensitive positions clearly justifies a citizenship requirement in at least some parts of the federal service, and that the broad exclusion serves the valid administrative purpose of avoiding the trouble and expense of classifying those positions which properly belong in executive or sensitive categories.

The difficulty with all of these arguments except the last is that they do not identify any interest which can reasonably be assumed to have influenced the Civil

Service Commission, the Postal Service, the General Services Administration, or the Department of Health, Education, and Welfare in the administration of their respective responsibilities or, specifically, in the decision to deny employment to the respondents in this litigation. We may assume with the petitioners that if the Congress or the President had expressly imposed the citizenship requirement, it would be justified by the national interest in providing an incentive for aliens to become naturalized, or possibly even as providing the President with an expendable token for treaty negotiating purposes; but we are not willing to presume that the Chairman of the Civil Service Commission, or any of the other original defendants, was deliberately fostering an interest so far removed from his normal responsibilities. Consequently, before evaluating the sufficiency of the asserted justification for the rule, it is important to know whether we are reviewing a policy decision made by Congress and the President or a question of personnel administration determined by the Civil Service Commission.

It is perfectly clear that neither the Congress nor the President has ever *required* the Civil Service Commission to adopt the citizenship requirement as a condition to eligibility for employment in the federal civil service. On the other hand, in view of the fact that the policy has been in effect since the Commission was created in 1883, it is fair to infer that both the Legislature and the Executive have been aware of the policy and have acquiesced in it. In order to decide whether such acquiescence should give the Commission rule the same support as an express statutory or Presidential command, it is appropriate to review the extent to which the policy has been given consideration by Congress or the President, and the nature of the authority specifically delegated to the Commission. * * *

[The Court concluded that the Commission had the statutory authority to retain or modify the citizenship requirement without further authorization from Congress or the President. But "[e]ven if this conclusion were doubtful," the Court added in a footnote, "in view of the consequences of the rule it would be appropriate to require a much more explicit directive from either Congress or the President before accepting the conclusion that the political branches of Government would consciously adopt a policy raising the constitutional questions presented by this rule." The Court then turned to the question of whether the rule was valid, assuming (without deciding) that Congress and the President have the constitutional power to impose the requirement that the Commission adopted.]

It is the business of the Civil Service Commission to adopt and enforce regulations which will best promote the efficiency of the federal civil service. That agency has no responsibility for foreign affairs, for treaty negotiations, for establishing immigration quotas or conditions of entry, or for naturalization policies. Indeed, it is not even within the responsibility of the Commission to be concerned with the economic consequences of permitting or prohibiting the participation by aliens in employment opportunities in different parts of the national market. On the contrary, the Commission performs a limited and specific function.

The only concern of the Civil Service Commission is the promotion of an efficient federal service. In general it is fair to assume that its goal would be best served by removing unnecessary restrictions on the eligibility of qualified applicants for employment. With only one exception, the interests which the petitioners have put forth as supporting the Commission regulation at issue in this case are not matters which are properly the business of the Commission. That one exception is the administrative desirability of having one simple rule excluding all noncitizens when it is manifest that citizenship is an appropriate and legitimate requirement for some important and sensitive positions. Arguably, therefore, administrative convenience may provide a rational basis for the general rule.

For several reasons that justification is unacceptable in this case. The Civil Service Commission, like other administrative agencies, has an obligation to perform its responsibilities with some degree of expertise, and to make known the reasons for its important decisions. There is nothing in the record before us, or in matter of which we may properly take judicial notice, to indicate that the Commission actually made any considered evaluation of the relative desirability of a simple exclusionary rule on the one hand, or the value to the service of enlarging the pool of eligible employees on the other. Nor can we reasonably infer that the administrative burden of establishing the job classifications for which citizenship is an appropriate requirement would be a particularly onerous task for an expert in personnel matters. * * * Of greater significance, however, is the quality of the interest at stake. Any fair balancing of the public interest in avoiding the wholesale deprivation of employment opportunities caused by the Commission's indiscriminate policy, as opposed to what may be nothing more than a hypothetical justification, requires rejection of the argument of administrative convenience in this case.

In sum, assuming without deciding that the national interests identified by the petitioners would adequately support an explicit determination by Congress or the President to exclude all noncitizens from the federal service, we conclude that those interests cannot provide an acceptable rationalization for such a determination by the Civil Service Commission. The impact of the rule on the millions of lawfully admitted resident aliens is precisely the same as the aggregate impact of comparable state rules which were invalidated by our decision in *Sugarman*. By broadly denying this class substantial opportunities for employment, the Civil Service Commission rule deprives its members of an aspect of liberty. Since these residents were admitted as a result of decisions made by the Congress and the President, implemented by the Immigration and Naturalization Service acting under the Attorney General of the United States, due process requires that the decision to impose that deprivation of an important liberty be made either at a comparable level of government or, if it is to be permitted to be made by the Civil Service Commission, that it be justified by reasons which are properly the concern of that agency. We hold that § 338.101(a) of the Civil Service Commission Regulations has deprived these respondents of liberty without due process of law and is therefore invalid.

JUSTICE BRENNAN, with whom JUSTICE MARSHALL joins, concurring.

I join the Court's opinion with the understanding that there are reserved the equal protection questions that would be raised by congressional or Presidential enactment of a bar on employment of aliens by the Federal Government.

[The dissenting opinion of JUSTICE REHNQUIST, joined by CHIEF JUSTICE BURGER and JUSTICES WHITE and BLACKMUN, is omitted.]

NOTES ON MOW SUN WONG AND INSTITUTIONAL COMPETENCE

1.   *Aftermath of* Mow Sun Wong. Three months after the Supreme Court decided *Mow Sun Wong*, President Ford issued Executive Order 11935, which barred almost all noncitizens from employment in the federal civil service. In a letter to the Speaker of the House and the President of the Senate, President Ford stated that it was in the national interest to preserve the longstanding policy of exclusion, at least pending thorough reconsideration of the matter. He also stated that "a recognition of the specific constitutional authority vested in the Congress prompts me to urge that the Congress promptly address these issues." See 41 Fed. Reg. 37,303–04 (1976). The lower courts upheld the constitutionality of the order. See *Mow Sun Wong v. Hampton*, 435 F. Supp. 37 (N.D. Cal. 1977), aff'd, 626 F.2d 739 (9th Cir. 1980), cert. denied, 450 U.S. 959 (1981) (Justices Brennan, White, and Marshall voted to grant certiorari). Congress has never modified President Ford's order.

Did President Ford's action demonstrate that the Court's decision in *Mow Sun Wong* was futile? Alexander Aleinikoff has uncovered some internal government documents that shed light upon whether the Court's "remand for reconsideration" of the issue in *Mow Sun Wong* actually stimulated any thoughtful reconsideration. According to these documents, the impetus for President Ford's executive order came from the Civil Service Commission (CSC), which drafted the proposal to overturn the Court's decision. Several governmental departments, asked to comment on the proposal by the Office of Management and Budget (OMB), voiced support for the proposal without identifying any underlying reasons for their views; the U.S. Postal Service indicated that it had no difficulty with admitting resident aliens to nonsensitive and nonpolicymaking positions; the Department of Housing and Urban Development suggested a more narrowly drawn prohibition that would limit employment to resident aliens in nonpolicymaking positions; and the Department of State expressed doubts about the wisdom of a total prohibition. When the matter came before President Ford, accompanying it was a memorandum from the general counsel of the OMB that stated:

> * * * CSC suggested various reasons related to the national interest which might serve as justification for the issuance of [the] order. Agency comments, although generally favoring or having no objection to such an order, indicate that CSC's suggested justifications (*e.g.*, need for undivided loyalty; consistency with the practices of foreign states) are more apparent than real. Further, the Postal Service advises that its recent practice of employing aliens in nonsensitive and nonpolicymaking positions has not presented any policy difficulties. Nevertheless, there is a widespread visceral feeling that Government jobs should be reserved for citizens, at least where there are qualified citizen-applicants.

The Department of Justice is of the opinion that the Congress, pursuant to its constitutional authority over immigration, has the authority to broadly prohibit aliens from employment in the competitive civil service. Although the Supreme Court left open the question whether the President could exclude aliens from the competitive service, there are Presidential concerns (*e.g.*, foreign policy) which would lend some support to Presidential order barring aliens from government employment. The Department of Justice concludes, based on the *Wong* decision, that an executive order barring aliens would probably be upheld by a divided Supreme Court.[70]

What do you make of this? Consider this view (which was written without the benefit of the internal documents noted above):

If the Court's goal in *Mow Sun Wong* was * * * to force either the executive or legislative branch to face up to the underlying policy questions and accept political responsibility for the rule, the goal was plainly not achieved. * * * The whole point of [President Ford's] order, as his letter makes clear, was to preserve the status quo pending congressional rethinking of the problem. * * * But Congress may well prefer to stay clear of the issue and allow the present policy to remain in operation by default. * * * [W]e are left precisely where we were before the decision in *Mow Sun Wong*: Aliens are still barred from employment in the civil service, although neither of the political branches has taken clear responsibility for the formulation of the policy.[71]

2. *Precedential Value of* Mow Sun Wong. *Mow Sun Wong* and another case decided the same day were Justice Stevens' first opinions for the Supreme Court. It has been suggested that the other four Justices in the majority had voted to strike down the civil service regulation on the traditional equal protection ground that it discriminated against aliens, and that Stevens initially stood alone in proposing a due process of lawmaking solution to the case. The Chief Justice assigned the case to Justice Stevens, who wrote a proposed majority opinion in line with his personal views, and the other four Justices went along with it. See Bob Woodward & Scott Armstrong, *The Brethren: Inside the Supreme Court* 402 (1979). We do not know whether this is accurate, but assume for purposes of discussion that it is. Assume also that the other four Justices voted with Stevens at least in part to avoid friction over his first opinion (which is a plausible assumption, if the other assertions made above are accurate). Does this mean that *Mow Sun Wong* is of little precedential value? So far as we can ascertain, *Mow Sun Wong* has never directly controlled the result in any subsequent Supreme Court decision, although it has been cited a number of times.

3. *The Passport Case: A More Successful Suspensive Veto?* In *Kent v. Dulles*, 357 U.S. 116 (1958), the Secretary of State denied a passport to Kent because he was allegedly a Communist or Communist sympathizer. The Court avoided the question of the constitutionality of this decision by interpreting the relevant statutes narrowly: "Congress has made no such provision [of authority to the Secretary to withhold passports to citizens because of their beliefs or associations] in explicit terms; and absent one, the Secretary may not employ that standard to restrict the citizens' right of

---

[70] Memorandum from William N. Nichols, General Counsel, OMB, to Robert D. Linden, White House Chief Executive Clerk, Aug. 30, 1976 (on file in Gerald R. Ford Library, Ann Arbor, MI).

[71] Gerald Rosberg, *The Protection of Aliens from Discriminatory Treatment by the National Government*, 1977 Sup. Ct. Rev. 275, 280–81.

free movement." *Id.* at 130. Despite President Eisenhower's urgent message to Congress calling for legislative action, continued pressure from the White House, and strong support for it from many members of Congress, Congress did not enact even a limited form of the legislation the President sought. Apparently, the Senate leadership killed all such proposals.[72] At the least, this episode shows the potential impact of judicial decisions shifting the burden of inertia through a suspensive veto. But does it indicate that Congress "deliberated"? *Kent v. Dulles* and *Mow Sun Wong* demonstrate that many of the techniques of due process of lawmaking provide an opportunity for Congress to address particular issues with focused deliberation and thoughtful legislation, but they do not guarantee that Congress will take advantage of that opportunity.

4. *Scholarly Interpretation.* Although it may not have influenced much jurisprudence, scholars have spent a great deal of time considering the ramifications of the Court's approach in *Mow Sun Wong*. First, consider Lawrence Sager, *Insular Majorities Unabated:* Warth v. Seldin *and* City of Eastlake v. Forest City Enterprises, Inc., 91 Harv. L. Rev. 1373, 1414, 1417 (1978):

> *Mow Sun Wong* posits a right to procedural due process which requires that some legislative actions be undertaken only by a governmental entity which is so structured and so charged as to make possible a reflective determination that the action contemplated is fair, reasonable, and not at odds with specific prohibitions in the Constitution. * * *

> * * * In *Mow Sun Wong* * * * the Court refused to consider two justifications offered for the policy of alien exclusion: the fact that the policy effected a reservation of a "token" for foreign affairs bargaining, and the fact that the exclusion operated to encourage aliens to become naturalized citizens. These interests can be viewed as beyond accurate judicial assessment for two reasons. First, consideration of their importance involves technical judgments informed by a range of material to which the judiciary does not have full access; and second, the interests, though potentially quite weighty, are discretionary in the sense that they depend for their importance on prior decisions of policy or strategy made by the President or Congress. These factors combine to result in a judiciary largely dependent upon the judgment of either the President or Congress as to whether there are "overriding national interests" which justify the exclusion policy; thus, when the judiciary is confronted with the enactment of such an exclusion by either of these two entities, it will defer broadly to the judgment thus manifested.

> In contrast, when a body—like the Civil Service Commission in *Mow Sun Wong*—which lacks the information, expertise, and discretion as to policy and strategy enacts such a rule, the courts face a dilemma. Either they sustain the enactment, thus endorsing a transgression of constitutional principles without any assurance that it is justified by weighty national interests; or they invalidate it and thus jeopardize what may indeed be weighty national interests. In such a circumstance, a decision like that in *Mow Sun Wong* seems entirely appropriate: it in effect constitutes a remand to the decisionmaking

---

[72] See Daniel Farber, *National Security, The Right to Travel, and the Court*, 1981 Sup. Ct. Rev. 263, 278–81. See also Philip Frickey, *Getting from Joe to Gene (McCarthy): The Avoidance Canon, Legal Process Theory, and Narrowing Statutory Interpretation in the Early Warren Court*, 93 Cal. L. Rev. 397, 425–26 (2005) (assessing this "aggressive understanding of the passive virtues").

body able to make appropriate policy judgments for an initial assessment of the validity of the enactment.

5. *Judicial Minimalism and Congressional Consideration of Constitutional Issues.* Cass Sunstein has described *Mow Sun Wong* and *Kent v. Dulles* as examples of judicial minimalism that reinforces democratic institutions. *One Case at a Time: Judicial Minimalism on the Supreme Court* (1999). He defines this "phenomenon of saying no more than necessary to justify an outcome, and leaving as much as possible undecided, as 'decisional minimalism.' Decisional minimalism has * * * attractive features. * * * [M]inimalism is likely to make judicial errors less frequent and (above all) less damaging. A court that leaves things open will not foreclose options in a way that may do a great deal of harm. * * * A court that decides relatively little will also reduce the risks that come from intervening in complex systems, where a single-shot intervention can have a range of unanticipated bad consequences. There is a relationship between judicial minimalism and democratic deliberation. Of course minimalist rulings increase the space for further reflection and debate at the local, state, and national levels, simply because they do not foreclose subsequent decisions." *Id.* at 3–4. Sunstein's work essentially updates the "passive virtues" philosophy of Alexander Bickel, most notably articulated in *The Least Dangerous Branch: The Supreme Court at the Bar of Politics* (1962). Sunstein argues that *Kent v. Dulles* and *Mow Sun Wong*, where the Court avoided deciding the constitutional issues presented, are "conspicuously" democracy-forcing because "in both cases the Court's judgment was expressly founded on the idea that publicly accountable bodies should make the decision that was challenged in the case." *Supra*, at 35. What do you think of this judicial strategy? Can we rely on legislators to take seriously an increased responsibility to consider constitutional issues?

Consider the following episode from the "gays in the military" debate in the first year of Clinton's presidency. As you know from Chapter 2, § 1B, a statute that is facially neutral but disproportionally disadvantages a suspect (i.e., racial minorities) or semi-suspect (e.g., women) class of persons violates the Equal Protection Clause only if it is motivated by animus against the disadvantaged class. In reaching this conclusion, the Supreme Court refused to adopt a "discriminatory effects" approach under which such legislation would be unconstitutional in some circumstances even if it were not improperly motivated. May a legislator adopt a "discriminatory effects" approach to her own review of pending legislation? If she does, is that decision motivated by what her views are likely to be as a matter of policy? And would that be inappropriate? Must a legislator vote against legislation that she supports if she is aware that other legislators support it for discriminatory reasons? If that law is enacted due to the votes of illicitly motivated legislators, and if the conscientious legislator is aware of that, must she "blow the whistle" on that discriminatory intent in later litigation challenging the constitutionality of the law?[73]

Immediately after President Clinton announced his version of a "don't ask, don't tell" policy concerning lesbians, bisexuals, and gay men in the armed forces, a subcommittee of the House Armed Services Committee held hearings exploring the

---

[73] On these issues, see Stephen Ross, *Legislative Enforcement of Equal Protection*, 72 Minn. L. Rev. 311 (1987). See also Neal Katyal, *Impeachment as Congressional Constitutional Interpretation*, 63 Law & Contemp. Probs. 169 (2000) (arguing that the style of constitutional interpretation used by the legislature should be different from the judicial approach).

constitutionality of the new policy.[74] Three academics testified on this topic. David Schleuter testified that on the whole the new policy probably passed constitutional muster for the same reasons (mainly deference to the military) the old policy did. William Woodruff testified that the new policy raised additional constitutional problems because it seemed to penalize people simply because of what they said (the "don't tell" part of the new policy). Cass Sunstein's written statement contained two different constitutional analyses. As a matter of predicting what the Supreme Court would do, Sunstein testified that invalidation of the new policy was "unlikely." Relying on *Bowers v. Hardwick*, 478 U.S. 186 (1986), he testified that the military's interest in morale would justify any discrimination against gay men, lesbians, and bisexuals, and that its interest in suppressing sodomy would justify its penalization of speech (because the speech would be "evidence" of illegal conduct). At the end of his statement, Sunstein testified that Congress can make its own independent judgment of what is required by the Constitution. Specifically, he suggested that discrimination against "homosexuals" would require more justification if Congress concluded that sexual orientation were a suspect criterion or if Congress found such discrimination related to sex discrimination.

There is no evidence from the transcript of the hearing that Sunstein's latter analysis was of controlling interest to any member of the Subcommittee. What did seem important to all concerned was simply whether Congress and the President could do what they wanted on the issue. Perhaps because of these and other examples, some have expressed doubts that members of Congress can play a productive role in deliberating about constitutional issues. One problem is that in most instances constitutional debate appears to change very few votes. Those opposed to proposed legislation on the merits tend also to be the ones who accept arguments that it would be unconstitutional.

Those who strategically raise constitutional arguments may spark serious deliberation of the issues, however, and at least the "civilizing force of hypocrisy"[75] in congressional debates may produce arguments that constrain what Congress can do without prompting public dismay. Elizabeth Garrett and Adrian Vermeule suggest:

> Even a wholly self-interested legislator cannot afford to take positions in constitutional argument that are too transparently favorable to his own interests. So legislators who want to invest in credibility will have to adjust their positions to disfavor or disguise their own interests to some degree. Likewise, the pressure to maintain a reputation for consistency will, to some degree, cause even self-interested legislators to adhere to a previously established constitutional position when, in changed circumstances, that position works to a legislator's disadvantage.[76]

Similarly, Hanah Volokh has assessed the increasingly used constitutional authority statements and argues that the practice, especially if changed in certain ways, can "trigger further discussions about constitutionality within Congress, which could help

---

[74] *Assessment of the Plan to Lift the Ban on Homosexuals in the Military: Hearings Before the Subcomm. on Military Forces and Personnel of the House Comm. on the Armed Services*, 103d Cong., 1st Sess. (July 21–23, 1993).

[75] See Jon Elster, *Alchemies of the Mind: Transmutation and Misrepresentation*, 3 Legal Theory 133 (1997) (discussing the role of such "hypocrisy" in legitimate deliberation).

[76] *Institutional Design of a Thayerian Congress*, 50 Duke L.J. 1277, 1289 (2001).

legislators make more robust and considered decisions." *Constitutional Authority Statements in Congress*, 65 Fla. L. Rev. 173, 177 (2013).

Former representative and federal judge Abner Mikva has been very critical of Congress' performance when considering constitutional issues. "Both institutionally and politically, Congress is designed to pass over the constitutional questions, leaving the hard decisions to the courts. * * * The paucity of constitutional dialogue in Congress is due to many factors. Structurally, both houses are large, making the process of engaging in complex arguments during a floor debate difficult. For the most part, the speeches made on the floor are designed to get a member's position on the record rather than to initiate a dialogue. Because of the volume of legislation, the time spent with constituents, and the technical knowledge required to understand the background of every piece of legislation, it is infrequent that a member considers the individual merits of a particular bill."[77]

Are Mikva's criticisms fair? As a former representative, he must be aware that most of Congress' work is done in committees, where specialized staff and more involved members consider issues and produce committee reports and other documents to inform the body and enhance deliberation. Moreover, as Garrett and Vermeule argue, additional structures can be put in place to enhance congressional capacity in this area, providing more expertise to Congress, ensuring that focused deliberation on constitutional issues will occur in committee and on the floor, and providing information to interest groups so that they present arguments relevant to Congress' decisions. See also Hanah Volokh, *supra* (arguing that constitutional authority statements would increase congressional deliberations about constitutional issues).

Congress' role in constitutional interpretation has been hotly contested at least since 1892, when James Bradley Thayer delivered his address, *The Origin and Scope of the American Doctrine of Constitutional Law*, at the Chicago World's Fair. Thayer argued that judges should employ a rational-basis standard for reviewing congressional determinations of constitutional questions, largely for two reasons. First, many constitutional questions raise significant issues of policy and politics that legislators are better suited to decide than judges. Second, more aggressive judicial review would encourage Congress to shift its constitutional responsibilities onto the courts, weakening representative democracy.[78] Even without changes in institutional arrangements and expectations, Congress will play a significant role in constitutional interpretation because the courts do not decide every issue. If that is inevitably the case, then we must continue to pay close attention to the process through which the legislature enacts laws and to the structure of due process of lawmaking.

---

[77] *How Well Does Congress Support and Defend the Constitution?*, 61 N.C. L. Rev. 587, 609 (1983).

[78] For modern reactions to Thayer's influential work, see *Congress and the Constitution* (Neal Devins & Keith Whittington eds., 2005); *One Hundred Years of Judicial Review: The Thayer Centennial Symposium*, 88 Nw. U. L. Rev. 1–468 (1993). See also Larry Alexander & Frederick Schauer, *On Extrajudicial Constitutional Interpretation*, 110 Harv. L. Rev. 1359 (1997) (defending the proposition that Congress should always accept the Constitution to mean whatever the Supreme Court says it means).

CHAPTER 4

DIRECT DEMOCRACY

■ ■ ■

No examination of lawmaking in the United States is complete without a discussion of the instruments of direct democracy: the initiative, the popular referendum, and the recall. Direct democracy is a consequential form of lawmaking in its own right; more than 70% of Americans live in a state, locality, or both that provide access to the initiative.[1] It also influences the behavior of elected and appointed officials, affects election results across the ballot, and elevates issues on the policy agenda. Understanding how direct democracy differs from representative processes also provides new insight into the latter, from lawmaking to agency implementation to judicial interpretation. In this chapter, we will first provide an overview of the tools of direct democracy, focusing particularly on the initiative. In § 2, we will discuss methods of statutory interpretation applied to laws adopted by the people. Finally, we will end with an assessment of the recall, which has gained new attention with two high-profile recall efforts directed at state governors in the last few years.

As you read these materials, ask yourself: is governance improved by some sort of *hybrid democracy* in which representative government operates alongside forms of popular lawmaking, rather than the relatively pure system of representative government that we have at the federal level? And, if it is a better system, what is the right mix of direct democracy and representative institutions? The reality is that subnational governance is typified by hybrid democracy—a mix of representative and direct democracy, in which both kinds of institutions influence the other. How do we ensure that both lead to accountability in government and effective policymaking?

1. OVERVIEW OF DIRECT DEMOCRACY

Doubts about the capacity of legislatures to address social problems, as well as fears that legislatures were often captured by powerful business interests and were subject to corruption, led the Populists (circa 1890) and their political successors, the Progressives, to propose a "return of the government to the people." The two major mechanisms they adopted to provide the people with lawmaking authority are the initiative and the referendum. In addition, a third device, recall, allows voters to remove elected officials from office before the expiration of their terms.

The *initiative* allows a certain percentage of the electorate to petition to have a proposed statute or amendment to the state constitution put on the ballot for a vote of the electorate. There are two common forms. The *direct initiative* refers to the method in which the issue goes on the ballot automatically after the requisite

---

[1] John Matsusaka, *Direct Democracy Works*, 19 J. Econ. Persp. 185, 185–86 (2005).

signatures of voters are collected. In contrast, under the less prevalent format of the *indirect initiative*, after the collection of the requisite signatures, the proposed statute is submitted to the legislature, which is given a period of time to act on the measure. If the legislature fails to pass the proposal, or if it adopts a significantly amended version, the proposed statute in its original form is placed on the ballot, sometimes along with any legislatively approved variation.

The *referendum* is direct democracy from the other end of the telescope: a method whereby the electorate may approve or disapprove of a law proposed or already enacted by the legislature. One form, called the *popular referendum*, provides that, upon the collection of the requisite signatures, a law passed by the legislature is subject to approval or rejection by the electorate. Under the other form, referred to as the *legislative* or *submitted referendum*, the legislature places before the electorate a proposed law for approval or disapproval (a *binding legislative referendum*) or for the electorate's advice (an *advisory legislative referendum*).

The United States is one of the few major democracies not to have held a national referendum. However, 27 states provide for initiative, popular referendum, or both. Eighteen of those states have a constitutional initiative process, through which the people can directly initiate a constitutional change; 21 have a statutory initiative process; and 23 allow for popular referendum. A popular vote is required in every state except Delaware for adoption of constitutional amendments.[2] Moreover, state or local law often requires that certain questions—e.g., whether to issue bonds for construction of public facilities—must be submitted as referendums as well. From 1904, when the first statewide initiative appeared on Oregon's ballot, until 2012, there have been 2,421 statewide initiatives across the United States, with 984 (41%) being approved.[3] According to the *Initiative and Referendum Almanac*, "over 60% of all initiative activity has taken place in just six states—Arizona, California, Colorado, North Dakota, Oregon and Washington."[4]

Since the 1970s, when California passed the property-tax-cutting Proposition 13, ballot propositions have grown in importance and addressed such controversial subjects as tax or governmental spending limitations, same-sex marriage and civil unions, the death penalty, and educational policy—including charter schools and affirmative action. The 1990s saw the greatest number of initiatives on the ballot, with more than 377 proposed, and the first decade of the 21st century nearly matched that record with 373 initiatives.

---

[2] See M. Dane Waters, *Initiative and Referendum Almanac* 12 (2003) (still the most comprehensive printed guide to the initiative and referendum process in the United States). The Initiative and Referendum Institute (IRI) at the University of Southern California maintains a database of statewide initiatives and referendums and provides links to information by each state about its initiative process. See http://www.iandrinstitute.org/ballotwatch.htm (for the Ballotwatch database) and http://www.iandrinstitute.org/statewide_i%26r.htm (for information on states and links). In addition, the National Conference of State Legislatures has developed extensive information on state-level direct democracy. See, e.g., Initiative and Referendum States, www.ncsl.org/legislatures-elections/elections/chart-of-the-initiative-states.aspx (visited Sept. 2012).

[3] Initiative and Referendum Institute, *Overview of Initiative Use, 1904–2012* 1 (Jan. 2013).

[4] Waters, *supra*, at 7. Oregon has had the most initiatives on the ballot, with 363 through 2012, and California is a close second with 352 during the same time period.

The *recall* has a different relationship to representative government. Using this mechanism, a certain percentage of the electorate, by petition, may force the continued service of an elected official to be put to a vote. Nineteen states have statewide recall provisions[5]; recall is more frequently used on the local level in at least 29 states to target school board members, city councilmembers, and other local officials. Is recall a good way to "throw the bums out"? Or does it inhibit elected officials from adopting policies that are wise in the long run but painful in the short run? Does recall have an important impact upon the concept of representation?

Direct democracy may be in tension with the conception of representative government embraced by the Framers of the American Constitution. The Constitution includes a provision requiring the United States to "guarantee to every State in this Union a Republican Form of Government." U.S. Const., art. IV, § 4. Challenges to direct democracy in the states on the theory that it is inconsistent with this provision have, however, been held to be nonjusticiable political questions. See *Pacific States Tel. & Tel. Co. v. Oregon*, 223 U.S. 118 (1912).[6] Does it make a difference to the analysis that direct democracy always exists together with representative institutions? Does the Guarantee Clause suggest a constitutional reason to prefer methods of popular lawmaking that include some meaningful role for elected officials, such as the indirect initiative or the popular referendum?[7]

Think back to the discussion in Chapter 2, § 2C, about theories of partisan lockup: the concern that elected officials will not pass certain reforms of the electoral system that voters might prefer because the changes are not in the self-interest of lawmakers. Could that theory provide an argument that representative government might actually work better if some avenues of direct lawmaking were incorporated?[8] The early proponents of direct democracy saw it as a way to circumvent state legislators and political parties that would block governance reforms like the direct primary and anti-corruption laws. Many modern initiatives deal with electoral reforms such as changes in the primary system, lobbying and campaign finance laws, term limits for legislators, and less partisan redistricting commissions. The evidence that states with hybrid democracy design their representative institutions differently from states without any form of direct democracy, however, is mixed. States with vibrant initiative processes are more

---

[5] National Conference of State Legislatures, *Recall of State Officials* (June 6, 2012), http://www.ncsl.org/legislatures-elections/elections/recall-of-state-officials.aspx.

[6] On the Guarantee Clause generally, see James Fischer, *Plebiscites, the Guaranty Clause, and the Role of the Judiciary*, 41 Santa Clara L. Rev. 973 (2001). For the argument that state courts should enforce the Guarantee Clause in the context of direct democracy, see Hans Linde, *Who Is Responsible for Republican Government?*, 65 U. Colo. L. Rev. 709, 710 (1994) ("[T]he Guarantee Clause precludes misuse of initiatives for * * * measures of popular passion or self-interest * * * [and the use] of initiatives to enact ordinary laws * * * in the form of constitutional text so as to insulate a law from change by elected lawmakers as well as from review of its constitutionality.").

[7] For a proposal to reform the direct initiative process to provide opportunities for legislative involvement and to allow flexibility to amend the language of proposals before they are placed on the ballot, see Elizabeth Garrett & Mathew McCubbins, *The Dual Path Initiative Framework*, 80 S. Cal. L. Rev. 299 (2007).

[8] See Dennis Thompson, *The Role of Theorists and Citizens in* Just Elections: *A Response to Professors Cain, Garrett, and Sabl,* 4 Election L.J. 153, 158–60 (2005).

likely, Caroline Tolbert has found, to have legislative term limits, tax and expenditure limitations, and supermajority voting requirements for tax increases.[9] Although Nathaniel Persily and Melissa Anderson determined that only the enactment of term limits would be "unimaginable" without the outlet of direct democracy, the presence of the initiative process has also influenced the adoption of public financing for legislative elections and redistricting commissions.[10]

Is this too rosy a view of hybrid democracy? Critics argue that the ballot measures proposed and passed by the people tend to weaken representative institutions and undermine the ability of lawmakers to govern. They point to term limits and tax limitations as examples. They contend that because people turn to initiatives out of frustration with their elected representatives, they will mostly enact legislation in the arena of electoral reform that reduces the power of elected officials. Certainly, there is some validity to this argument. Even the "good government" reforms, such as campaign finance legislation and nonpartisan redistricting commissions, work to reduce the discretion of elected officials. The issue is whether the policies adopted through popular means tend to reduce legislative discretion in ways that improve or harm representative institutions.

In addition, critics of direct democracy worry that initiatives are a tool for the majority of voters to enact laws that target ethnic, racial, and other minority groups. In such cases, those affected by the laws can turn to the courts to invalidate all or part of a statute or state constitutional amendment that violates federal constitutional protections. Courts do tend to be active in oversight of direct legislation. Between 1960 and 1999, for example, more than half (52%) of 163 statewide initiatives approved by voters in California, Oregon, Washington, and Colorado were challenged in court after the vote, and courts nullified, in part or in their entirety, more than half (55%) of those challenged, for a total invalidation rate of 28%.[11]

Even with this level of judicial review, however, direct democracy would be open to significant criticism if the evidence demonstrated a systematic tendency to enact discriminatory and oppressive legislation. Studies have come to mixed conclusions, but they do give rise to concerns. A study of all initiatives in California revealed that Latinos are more likely than other racial minorities to be targeted in anti-minority initiatives and are less likely than others to be on the winning side of initiatives targeting minority groups.[12] Other studies focused on initiatives

---

[9] *Changing Rules for State Legislatures: Direct Democracy and Governance Policies*, in *Citizens as Legislators: Direct Democracy in the United States* 171 (Shaun Bowler, Todd Donovan & Caroline Tolbert eds., 1998).

[10] *Regulating Democracy Through Democracy: The Use of Direct Legislation in Election Law Reform*, 78 S. Cal. L. Rev. 997 (2005). Matsusaka studied 14 different kinds of laws related to electoral reform and concluded that the initiative process has been essential only for legislative term limits. *Direct Democracy and Electoral Reform*, in *The Marketplace of Democracy: Electoral Competition and American Politics* 151 (Michael McDonald & John Samples eds., 2006).

[11] Kenneth Miller, *The Davis Recall and the Courts*, 33 Am. Pol. Res. 135, 155–6 (2005) (some invalidations on grounds other than violation of federal constitutional guarantees).

[12] Zoltan Hajnal, Elisabeth Gerber & Hugh Louch, *Minorities and Direct Legislation: Evidence from California Ballot Propositions*, 64 J. of Pol. 154 (2002). But see Barbara Gamble, *Putting Civil Rights to a Popular Vote*, 41 Am. J. Pol. Sci. 245 (1997) (finding that voters pass three-quarters of initiatives limiting civil rights for minority groups, while only passing one-third of all popular initiatives).

targeting the rights of gays and lesbians have reached differing conclusions. Donovan and Bowler found that only 18% of such ballot measures passed between 1972 and 1996, and most of those were later invalidated by courts. A more recent study, however, found that gays and lesbians fare much better in the legislative process than in direct democracy, and that 71% of 143 ballot measures that would reduce their civil rights passed between 1972 and 2005.[13]

More study of the impact of initiatives on the rights of minority groups—including the role of courts in review and the impact of inflammatory rhetoric during campaigns—is required. Donovan recently analyzed the campaigns and advertisements surrounding initiatives that seek to prohibit same-sex marriages. He noted that these campaigns take advantage of the "politics of backlash" and that the side seeking to deny gays and lesbians marriage equality often engages in rhetoric that stigmatizes the minority group and causes the community to become less sympathetic to them.[14] As you remember from Chapter 1, § 2A, Madison and the Founders favored representative democracy and rejected direct democracy at the national level in part because of their concern that the latter process allows impassioned majorities to threaten the rights of minorities.

The issues raised by the increasing use of the popular initiative and referendum are many. In this section, we will discuss three of the most important ones for assessing the initiative process and crafting reform: the role of money in both ballot access and outcomes of initiative elections; the ability of voters to make decisions competently when they go to the polls and the importance of disclosure rules; and the interaction between direct democracy and representative institutions. As you read through these materials, keep in mind that one must evaluate the mechanisms of direct democracy by comparing them realistically to representative institutions. For example, money plays a role in both issue and candidate campaigns, and voters are often not fully informed about all the candidates on the ballot. Moreover, reforms of direct democracy might involve structures that include representative bodies in the process, and reforms of the legislative process might be possible because of the initiative process. Hybrid democracy allows opportunities for a wide array of responses to problems that arise in democratic structures.

A. THE IMPORTANCE OF MONEY IN DIRECT DEMOCRACY

Progressive-era reformers who advocated in favor of direct democracy characterized the initiative process as a way to take power away from special interests with disproportionate influence over elected officials and empower ordinary citizens to determine the direction of policy. The modern concern is that the initiative process is merely another avenue for the wealthy to influence public policy unduly. In just the 11 ballot-measure campaigns in California in 2012, groups and individuals spent more than $370 million, and in the campaign in 2008

---

[13] Compare Todd Donovan & Shaun Bowler, *Direct Democracy and Minority Rights: An Extension*, 42 Am. J. Pol. Sci. 1020, 1022 (1998) and Todd Donovan & Shaun Bowler, *Reforming the Republic* 140 (2004), with Donald Haider-Markel, Alana Querze & Kara Lindaman, *Lose, Win, or Draw? A Reexamination of Direct Democracy and Minority Rights*, 60 Pol. Res. Q. 304 (2007).

[14] Todd Donovan, *Direct Democracy and Campaigns Against Minorities*, 97 Minn. L. Rev. 1730 (2013).

surrounding Proposition 8 in that state—the referendum prohibiting same-sex marriage that was ruled unconstitutional—both sides spent a total of $83 million, making it the most expensive race in that election other than the presidential contest.[15]

One substantial expense for initiative proponents is money spent to qualify a question for the ballot. It often requires hundreds of thousands of signatures to trigger a vote on a direct initiative or popular referendum. Well-funded interests have a great advantage at this stage because states may not prohibit them from paying petition circulators.[16] In California, circulating petitions can cost $2–$3 million per ballot proposition,[17] and, if they are paid enough, some firms will offer money-back guarantees ensuring a successful outcome. In short, money is a sufficient condition for ballot access. Even if the outcome of any vote on a ballot question mirrors the preference of the majority of voters, the dominance of money at the qualification stage means that groups with funds will determine which issues are placed before the people. As we discussed in Chapter 1, control of the political agenda is a valuable asset.

Although the Supreme Court has ruled out laws prohibiting paid petition circulators, states continue seeking to regulate this process. The following case involves a challenge to Colorado's law. Are these restrictions apt to reduce the role of money in the initiative process, while retaining it as an outlet for expression of the popular will, or is the statute mainly an attempt to muzzle direct democracy? Are there other ways to encourage true grassroots petition drives? Will the Internet provide a mechanism to gather signatures at a lower cost, and would that development cause other problems? Consider as well what information should be provided to those asked to sign petitions at the beginning stages of the initiative process. Should they be informed of the interests bankrolling the petition drive, for example?

Buckley v. American Constitutional Law Foundation
525 U.S. 182 (1999).

Colorado's statute controlling the initiative petition process included three provisions at issue in this case: petition circulators were required to be registered voters; circulators were required to wear name badges; and initiative backers had to report the names and addresses of paid circulators and how much each was paid. **Justice Ginsburg** began with the proposition that petition circulation is "core political speech" that involves "interactive communication concerning political change"; therefore, First Amendment protection is "at its zenith." On the other hand, citing the ballot access cases (Chapter 2, § 2C), she noted that states can regulate elections to

---

[15] See MapLight, *California Ballot Measure Funding Tops $372 Million*, Nov. 5, 2012, http://maplight. org/content/73144; *Proposition 8: Who Gave in the Gay Marriage Battle?*, L.A. Times, http://projects.latimes. com/prop8/ (visited Jan. 8, 2013).

[16] See *Meyer v. Grant*, 486 U.S. 414 (1988) (First Amendment violation to prohibit paid petition circulators).

[17] Andrew Gloger, *Initiative and Referendum Institute Report 2006–1: Paid Petitioners after Prete 2* (May 2006).

avoid chaos and to ensure fairness. The Court concluded that "the First Amendment requires us to be vigilant in making * * * judgments [about the constitutionality of electoral regulations], to guard against undue hindrances to political conversations and the exchange of ideas."

The Court struck down the requirement that circulators be registered voters, noting that it burdened political speech by reducing the number of potential speakers, i.e., the number of people who could engage in discourse about initiatives as they gathered signatures. **Justice Thomas**, concurring, noted the "anecdotal evidence" that petition circulators do not actually engage in much political speech, working to gather as many signatures as possible as quickly as possible because often their pay is tied to the number of signatures. He concluded, however, that "the level of scrutiny cannot turn on the content or sophistication of a political message."

The Court acknowledged the argument, made by **Justice O'Connor** in dissent, that it is relatively easy for a circulator to register to vote and that this law is not a severe burden. However, it contended that some who wished to circulate petitions did not register as a form of protest against the system or because they were alienated from the political process. The state's primary justification for the provision, to police illegal activity among circulators, was adequately served by the requirement that signature gatherers be residents of the state, and it would be better served by requiring that circulators be eligible to vote, rather than actually registered. **Chief Justice Rehnquist** was scornful in his dissent on this point, noting that the majority held that "a State is constitutionally required to instead allow those who make no effort to register to vote—political dropouts—and convicted drug dealers to engage in this electoral activity."

The majority also struck down the requirement that circulators wear name badges, which the state had justified as necessary to help it combat fraudulent practices by signature gatherers seeking to increase their compensation. The Court worried that those circulating petitions on unpopular issues might face harassment in face-to-face conversations with passersby; requiring them to provide their names would therefore chill political speech. Unlike the constitutional requirement that each petition submitted to the state include the circulator's name and address, the badge required identification "at the precise moment when the circulator's interest in anonymity is greatest." See also *McIntyre v. Ohio Elections Comm'n*, 514 U.S. 334 (1995) (protecting right of leafleter to distribute campaign literature anonymously).

The Court also trimmed the disclosure provisions relating to the information provided by initiative proponents to the state. It struck down requirements that information specific to each circulator be provided (e.g., the name, address, and total amount paid), but it left unchanged the requirement that proponents report how much they paid circulators per signature, which effectively discloses the entire amount spent in the petition drive. Justice Ginsburg was sympathetic to the notion that some disclosure was necessary as "a control or check on domination of the initiative process by affluent special interest groups" and to inform voters "of the source and amount of money spent" on ballot access.

In dissent, Justice O'Connor was willing to be much more deferential to the state's determination of what information it needed to regulate the electoral process effectively, particularly with regard to information disclosed to a state official rather than information disclosed during the signature-gathering stage to citizens in one-on-

one discussions. She was not concerned that Colorado applied the more burdensome disclosure only to paid circulators because "the record suggests that paid circulators are more likely to commit fraud and gather false signatures than other circulators."

Query: The Court did not address the related issue of whether a badge could identify a circulator as either *PAID* or *VOLUNTEER* without also including a name, a provision currently included in several state systems, including Colorado's. Is that provision constitutional? Would it influence voter behavior?

———————

Money also plays a role in the outcomes of ballot contests, but the picture here is more complicated than that of the influence of wealth in ballot access.[18] Studies suggest that money spent to defeat initiatives and referendums is more effective than money spent to pass them. In an early influential study, Daniel Lowenstein found that between 1968 and 1980 in California, in elections in which spending levels exceeded $250,000 and one side had a 2–1 spending advantage, opposition committees defeated 90% of the measures they opposed, and proponent committees won 64% of the time. *Campaign Spending and Ballot Propositions: Recent Experience, Public Choice Theory, and the First Amendment*, 29 UCLA L. Rev. 505 (1982). Subsequent studies have similarly found that money has a greater effect when spent to defeat an initiative, although increasingly sophisticated analyses of ballot campaigns may begin to reveal the influence of well-funded campaigns supporting ballot measures.[19] For example, Elisabeth Gerber has assessed whether spending by certain groups is particularly influential, finding that contributions from citizen groups have greater success in passing initiatives than do contributions from economic groups.[20]

The Supreme Court has consistently held that the First Amendment forbids states from limiting the amount of money spent or contributions made in support of or in opposition to a ballot measure because there is no possibility of *quid pro quo* corruption in the absence of candidates. See *Citizens Against Rent Control v. Berkeley*, 454 U.S. 290 (1981). Just as in the candidate-election context, the Court has been unwilling to accept egalitarian arguments to justify restrictions on spending in initiative contests. As more candidates take advantage of hybrid democracy and use initiatives to serve their own electoral and political goals, there are increasing discussions of the possibility of limiting contributions to campaign committees in initiative campaigns that are controlled by candidates or elected officials.[21] In these cases, the traditional *quid pro quo* argument could arguably support contribution limits. If such restrictions are constitutional, are they

---

[18] For discussion of the studies on the role of money in ballot campaigns, see Elizabeth Garrett & Elisabeth Gerber, *Money in the Initiative and Referendum Process: Evidence of Its Effects and Prospects for Reform*, in *The Battle Over Citizen Lawmaking* 73 (M. Dane Waters ed., 2001).

[19] See Thomas Stratmann, *The Effectiveness of Money in Ballot Measure Campaigns*, 78 S. Cal. L. Rev. 1041 (2005).

[20] See *The Populist Paradox: Interest Group Influence and the Promise of Direct Legislation* 101–20 (1999).

[21] See Richard Hasen, *Rethinking the Unconstitutionality of Contribution and Expenditures Limits in Ballot Measure Campaigns*, 78 S. Cal. L. Rev. 885 (2005); Hank Dempsey, *The "Overlooked Hermaphrodite" of Campaign Finance: Candidate-Controlled Ballot Measure Committees in California Politics*, 95 Cal. L. Rev. 123 (2007) (student comment).

desirable? Is it wise policy to restrict contributions to candidate-controlled ballot-measure committees if the courts won't allow restrictions on contributions to independent committees involved in the same election? How would you expect politicians to try to evade such regulations? We return to this question in the context of recalls later in this chapter.

B. VOTER COMPETENCE, VOTER CONFUSION, AND VOTING CUES

Whatever one concludes about the wisdom of a system with elements of direct democracy, it seems likely that the initiative process will endure in states that have it because voters like popular lawmaking. When asked what they thought about the initiative process in 2010, Californians had more trust in their fellow voters with respect to policymaking than in state elected officials (44% had at least a fair amount of trust in other voters compared to 33% in elected officials). Moreover, 66% of Californians were at least somewhat satisfied with the initiative process, although 42% of them supported unspecified "major changes" to the process.[22] One important question to ask in assessing whether those opinions are accurate—that is, whether the policies adopted at the voting booth are actually better than those formulated by legislators—is whether voters are sufficiently informed about the issues they are asked to decide.

If decisionmaking at the polls requires voters to be well versed in all the issues surrounding every contest, then very few voters will meet that standard. Of course, very few lawmakers casting their votes in a state legislature or Congress meet that standard for more than a handful of crucial bills. A more reasonable standard is voter competence. Voters are competent "if they cast the same votes they would have cast had they possessed all available knowledge about the policy consequences of their decision."[23] They need not have encyclopedic knowledge about every choice, but they need reliable shortcuts—voting cues or heuristics—that can allow them to vote in the same way that they would have with more complete information. Thinking back to the theories of politics discussed in Chapter 1 § 2, how would republican thinkers react to this notion of voter competence? Is it consistent with the ideal of civic virtue?

Scholars continue to work to determine which cues are helpful to voters, when they make a difference, and how to structure disclosure rules so that they provide information voters need at the time they can use it most effectively. In candidate elections, voters can use the strong voting cue of partisan affiliation, and they may also be able to use the cue of incumbency. But the information environment for ballot measures is much less rich; even though political parties and candidates now often associate themselves with one side or the other of an initiative, this information is not available on the ballot itself. Interestingly, the hybrid nature of democracy provides information to voters through the interaction of candidate and issue elections: candidates seek to use initiatives to demonstrate their commitment

---

[22] Mark Baldassare, Dean Bonner, Sonja Petek & Nicole Willcoxon (Public Policy Institute of California), *PPIC Statewide Survey: Californians and Their Government* 18–20 (Dec. 2010).

[23] Elisabeth Gerber & Arthur Lupia, *Voter Competence in Direct Legislation Elections*, in *Citizen Competence and Democratic Institutions* 147, 149 (Stephen Elkin & Karol Soltan eds., 1999).

to certain issues, and the information environment surrounding ballot measures is enriched by the support or opposition of elected officials with a political "brand name."

Another helpful cue in direct democracy is knowing the groups—economic and ideological—that support and oppose an initiative. For example, in a study of voting on insurance-related ballot initiatives, Arthur Lupia compared voters who knew nothing about the initiatives' details but knew the insurance industry's preference, with voters who were "model citizens" in that they consistently gave correct answers to detailed questions about ballot measures. His study also included a third group who knew nothing about the ballot measures or the insurance industry's views. The first two groups of voters voted similarly, while the third group had completely different voting patterns. *Shortcuts versus Encyclopedias: Information and Voting Behavior in California Insurance Reform Elections*, 88 Am. Pol. Sci. Rev. 63 (1994). This finding suggests that, under certain circumstances, just knowing which group supports an initiative (or opposes it) may be enough to vote competently. Here, Californians could ascertain the economic interests of the insurance industry, determine if their interests differed from those companies, and vote accordingly.

The most recent empirical work questions how often voters currently use cues, however, finding relatively infrequent use of cues that could be effective heuristics in some ballot-measure campaigns.[24] These results reinforce the need to provide effective cues in ways that voters can access them in appropriate campaigns. Some states send voters pamphlets with explanations of each ballot measure and arguments submitted by proponents and opponents (examples of which are included in Problem 4–5) but it is not clear whether voters use those regularly. It seems likely that information provided on the ballot itself at the crucial moment of voting might be more influential, and some states are considering reforms along these lines. There is also persuasive evidence that voters protect themselves when they are confused. The "defensive no" is the typical reaction by voters who are unsure about initiatives. See Shaun Bowler & Todd Donovan, *Demanding Choices: Opinion, Voting, and Direct Democracy* 47 (2000).

What information other than the identity of groups with political brand names, such as parties or politicians, might provide voters shortcuts to enable them to vote competently? Knowing the amount of money that a group spends to support or oppose a ballot measure might give voters a sense of the intensity of the group's preferences. Knowing how much money out-of-state interests contributed to an issue committee might be important. Having a sense of the percentage of small donations to a campaign might allow a voter to determine whether this issue elicits widespread grassroots appeal or is being bankrolled by only a few well-heeled individuals or groups. As you think about the kind of information most necessary for voter competence, consider also how to ensure that the information reaches citizens in a timely way, as well as how to structure the information so that they

---

[24] See Craig Burnett, Elizabeth Garrett & Mathew McCubbins, *The Dilemma of Direct Democracy*, 9 Election L.J. 305 (2010); Craig Burnett & Mathew McCubbins, *When Common Wisdom Is Neither Common Nor Wisdom: Exploring Voters' Limited Use of Endorsements on Three Ballot Measures*, 97 Minn. L. Rev. 1557 (2013).

can use it. Does this interest in voter competence justify fairly aggressive disclosure laws about campaign spending in direct elections? What groups would you expect to try to avoid disclosure, and how would they do so? Could laws be drafted to pierce through such veiled political actors to discern the true parties in interest?

Disclosure Statutes in Direct Democracy. Generally, disclosure statutes in both candidate and ballot-measure elections have been upheld by courts as constitutional under the First Amendment. For example, in *First Nat'l Bank of Boston v. Belloti*, 435 U.S. 765 (1978), in which the Supreme Court struck down prohibitions on corporate expenditures in issue campaigns, the Court noted that "[i]dentification of the source of advertising may be required as a means of disclosure, so that people will be able to evaluate the arguments to which they are being subjected." *Id.* at 792 n.32. Similarly, when the Court struck down contribution limits in direct democracy, it observed that "[t]he integrity of the political system will be adequately protected if contributors are identified in a public filing revealing the amounts contributed; if it is thought wise, legislation can outlaw anonymous contributions." *Citizens Against Rent Control v. City of Berkeley*, 454 U.S. 290, 299–300 (1981). Disclosure statutes sometimes have gone too far to withstand the Court's "exacting scrutiny," such as the Ohio disclosure law that was applied to Mrs. McIntyre, who was disseminating anonymous leaflets in a campaign concerning a school board referendum. *McIntyre v. Ohio Elections Comm'n*, 514 U.S. 334 (1995). But *McIntyre* involved an ordinary citizen engaging in small-scale political speech; it has not generally been extended to laws requiring that information about political expenditures be reported to a government agency.

The growth of the Internet—together with the ease with which people can access information disclosed to state agencies and made available on public websites—may have changed the balance under the First Amendment, particularly when it comes to disclosure of the identity of people making relatively small contributions to a committee involved in a ballot-measure campaign. The issues have been raised clearly in two cases. First, in June 2010, the Supreme Court considered disclosure in the context of a request to reveal the names of those signing a petition regarding a ballot measure seeking to overturn a state law providing certain rights to same-sex couples.

Doe v. Reed
561 U.S. 186 (2010).

The Washington Public Records Act (PRA) requires disclosure of all public records, including referendum petitions. Petitions include the names and addresses of the people who sign them. In 2009, Protect Marriage Washington, a politically active nonprofit group organized to protect what it calls "traditional marriage," circulated a petition to overturn a state law that provided substantial rights to domestic partners. When the petition was turned in to the Secretary of State, several pro-gay-rights groups sought to obtain the documents under the PRA so they could post the names and addresses of signatories on websites. Protect Marriage Washington and individuals who signed the petition moved to enjoin the public release of the documents, claiming disclosure burdened their constitutional rights and chilled political speech.

The Supreme Court ruled that the PRA was not facially unconstitutional with respect to the disclosure of referendum petitions, but it left open the possibility of as-applied challenges in the future. Although eight members of the Court agreed with the judgment, there were seven opinions. The concurring opinions mainly provided views about the standard to be applied in any subsequent as-applied challenges raised by these plaintiffs or others concerned about the consequences of releasing referendum petitions. In the opinion for the Court, **Chief Justice Roberts** characterized signing a petition as an expression of a political view, thus implicating the First Amendment. He found that disclosure of petitions met the "exacting scrutiny" required by the First Amendment because it assists state officials in discovering fraud and in verifying the accuracy of the signatures. The Secretary of State can only check a small fraction of signatures; disclosure "can help cure the inadequacies of the verification and canvassing process [and help] prevent certain types of petition fraud otherwise difficult to detect, such as outright forgery." He concluded that "[p]ublic disclosure also promotes transparency and accountability in the electoral process to an extent other measures cannot."

Although the Chief Justice acknowledged that these plaintiffs might be able to demonstrate a reasonable probability of threats, reprisals, and harassment—and thus avoid disclosure in this particular case—he rejected the argument that most ballot measures would give rise to such harm. He suggested that the subject matter of this measure was especially "controversial," in contrast to the typical fodder for direct democracy: tax policy, revenue and budget issues, property rights laws, and utility regulation. In his concurrence, **Justice Stevens** took issue with any distinction based on the subject matter of initiatives, noting that "[d]ebates about tax policy and regulation of private property can become just as heated as debates about domestic partnerships." And **Justice Thomas**, the only justice who dissented, argued that the nature of direct democracy, which operates as a "safety valve" for interests that have not succeeded in the legislature, means that many ballot measures will often be controversial.

Applying strict scrutiny to the PRA and finding it constitutionally objectionable as it affected referendum petitions, Justice Thomas argued that the state had many other, less burdensome approaches available to detect and combat fraud in the signature-gathering process. He characterized the Washington statute as a "blunderbuss approach," noting alternatives such as an electronic referendum database that could detect multiple references to a single voter and that could allow voters to search for their names to discover outright fraud. On the other side of the balance, he was concerned that as-applied challenges would not offer sufficient protection to petition signers. For example, if petition sponsors must seek an injunction before circulating petitions, how could they present sufficient evidence of a reasonable probability of threats, reprisals, and harassment? Do they have to wait until such retaliation occurs and then seek protection? Moreover, Thomas argued, "the state of technology today creates at least *some* probability that signers of every referendum will be subjected to threats, harassment, or reprisals if their personal information is disclosed."

Most of the other opinions focused on providing guidance for future as-applied challenges in the age of the Internet, and the justices disagreed about the showing that would be required for such a challenge to succeed. **Justice Alito** contended that First Amendment rights are appropriately protected only if an as-applied challenge could be brought "sufficiently far in advance" to avoid any political chill and "the showing necessary to obtain the exemption is not overly burdensome." Justice Alito went further to opine that the plaintiffs in *Doe v. Reed* had a strong case for an exemption. He rejected the notion that it was permissible to provide information to allow voters to contact signers and discuss the matter with them. In this case, the groups seeking names were intent on having "uncomfortable conversation[s]" with the supporters of the petition, so "disclosure becomes a means of facilitating harassment."

In contrast, **Justice Sotomayor** and **Justice Stevens** both wrote separately to underscore their views that the standard of proof to obtain a judicial exemption from disclosure should be rigorous. Disclosure is a long-accepted mechanism to protect the integrity of the electoral process; citizens signing petitions do so in public without a guarantee of confidentiality; and there is little, if any, evidence that disclosing the names of signers causes people to be less willing to sign a petition. Justice Sotomayor counseled that "courts * * * should be deeply skeptical of any assertion that the Constitution, which embraces political transparency, compels States to conceal the identity of persons who seek to participate in lawmaking through a state-created referendum process." Justice Stevens put it differently: for a successful as-applied challenge, "there would have to be a significant threat of harassment directed at those who sign the petition that cannot be mitigated by law enforcement measures."

Justice Scalia took a unique approach to the case, rejecting the initial conclusion that signing a petition implicated the First Amendment. His originalist approach included discussion of the history of voting in the U.S., which was not done by secret ballot until the late 19th century and was not justified then as a move compelled by the Constitution. He also noted that the initiative process grew out of town hall meetings and the right to petition the government for change—both of these activities occur in public. He viewed direct democracy as lawmaking, and "[t]he public nature of federal lawmaking is constitutionally required" by, among other things, Article I, § 5, cl. 3 of the Constitution that mandates each house of Congress to keep a Journal of Proceedings. He concluded: "There are laws against threats and intimidation; and harsh criticism, short of unlawful action, is a price our people have traditionally been willing to pay for self-governance. Requiring people to stand up in public for their political acts fosters civic courage, without which democracy is doomed."

———

The second case dealing with disclosure and the Internet presents the as-applied challenge that the Supreme Court left open in *Doe v. Reed*. It grew out of Proposition 8 in California, the 2008 ballot measure that amended the state constitution to deny marriage to same-sex couples and was later declared unconstitutional. After opponents of same-sex marriage won in a tight contest, supporters of same-sex marriage created a website that provided the names of the donors to the winning side, their addresses, the amount they contributed, and their occupations. The format through which the information was conveyed—a "mash-up" of Google maps and Prop 8 donor data posted by the Secretary of State— enabled people to easily check whether their neighbors, co-workers, and acquaintances had supported the controversial ballot measure. Gay-rights activists urged people who supported same-sex marriage to boycott businesses owned or run by those contributors.

After the election, several ballot committees that had been formed to support the passage of Prop 8, and thereby to end same-sex marriage, sought an exemption from the state's disclosure provisions. *ProtectMarriage.com v. Bowen*, 830 F. Supp. 2d 914 (E.D. Cal. 2011). They alleged that, because personal information about donors was available on the Secretary of State's website, Prop 8 supporters and their businesses had been subject to threats, reprisals, and harassment. Among other allegations, they claimed that Fresno Mayor Alan Autry and a local pastor, both Prop 8 supporters, had received death threats. The plaintiffs also claimed that some supporters had been forced to resign from their jobs; others had property vandalized. Their arguments focused in particular on the $100 threshold for disclosure. ProtectMarriage.com contended that the state had no compelling interest in revealing personal information about individuals whose contributions were so small.

The District Court granted the Secretary of State's motion for summary judgment, affirming the constitutionality of the disclosure regime. The judge did not view the contributors to Prop 8 as facing the same threats that the Socialist Workers Party demonstrated with respect to its members in the case that exempted it from federal campaign disclosure laws. See *Brown v. Socialist Workers '74 Campaign Comm. (Ohio)*, 459 U.S. 87 (1982). The 60 members of the Socialist Workers Party experienced destruction of their property, hate mail and threatening phone calls, harassment by the police, and shots fired into the Party's offices. In contrast, the donors to Prop 8 are not part of a "fringe organization" out of step with the views of the majority. They were able to win in a statewide election, receiving more than seven million votes supporting their position. They did not face government persecution or widespread vilification; rather, they "sought to legislate a concept steeped in tradition and history." The judge noted that the decision in *Doe v. Reed* had not explicitly changed the threshold required to merit an exemption from disclosure, even though at least one of the concurring opinions (Justice Alito) expressed a willingness to provide an exemption on the basis of a substantially lower showing of retaliation. Finally, while decrying any illegal actions taken against Prop 8 supporters, the court also noted that the First Amendment allows dissent through speech, debate, and even economic boycotts.

Perhaps the most difficult issue posed by this case is whether the state interest justifying disclosure of contributors in a ballot-measure campaign—the interest in providing important information to voters—is really implicated with regard to small donations of $100 by individuals. The judge described the state's informational interest in the language of voting cues. He concluded that voters "often base their decisions to vote for or against [a ballot measure] on cognitive cues such as the names of individuals supporting or opposing a measure." But can voters use the name of an individual donating $100 to a ballot committee as a credible voting cue? And if there is a chance that small donors may face some retaliation, even if it does not reach the level of harassment and threats faced by the Socialist Workers Party, won't that discourage some from participating in the political process? The threat of such political chill, made more serious by broad and immediate disclosure through user-friendly websites, might be sufficient to cause a court to question low disclosure thresholds that do not produce informational benefits.

However, the District Court judge in *ProtectMarriage.com* held that the $100 threshold in California is constitutionally permissible. He noted that to hold otherwise would draw into question "scores of statutes in which the legislature or the people have sought to draw similar lines." The judge also observed that only six states have higher thresholds and that laws range from no threshold to $300. While it may be constitutional to require disclosure of contributions to ballot measures or candidates as low as $100, is it good policy? What helpful information to voters does this level of detail provide? Does it threaten instead to deluge voters with so much information that they cannot distinguish credible voting cues from mere "noise"? As lawmakers consider the optimal design of a new disclosure regime, they should keep in mind that distinctions can be made between information provided to government regulators, justified by the need to enforce other campaign regulations, and information disseminated broadly. Thresholds triggering requirements that information be provided to regulators might be lower than those triggering wider disclosure. See Richard Briffault, *Campaign Finance Disclosure 2.0*, 9 Election L.J. 273 (2010).

What is the right standard for a court to apply when asked for an as-applied exemption from disclosure in cases like these? Think about the subsequent as-applied challenge to Washington's release of the names and addresses of petition signers. How would you analyze that case? For the lower court's analysis, see *Doe v. Reed*, 823 F. Supp. 2d 1195 (W.D. Wash. 2011), *appeal dismissed as moot*, 697 F.3d 1235 (9th Cir. 2012) (court allowed disclosure, relying on reasoning in *ProtectMarriage.com* about the nature of the group; holding that exemption from disclosure is available only to minor parties and fringe organizations; and finding no evidence of serious and widespread threats or harassment); see also *Doe v. Reed*, 132 S.Ct. 449 (2011) (Alito, J., dissenting from the denial of an application for an injunction during the appeal).

PROBLEM ON DISCLOSURE AND DIRECT DEMOCRACY

Problem 4–1. How would you design a disclosure statute to apply to campaigns for ballot measures? What information would you seek to disclose? How would you provide it to voters? How would you take account of technology, both in what is subject to disclosure and how disclosure is made most effectively? How would you pierce the veils that political actors sometimes throw up to avoid disclosure by creating groups with innocuous-sounding names that mask the economic and ideological forces driving them?[25]

Single-Subject Rules. Some features of the initiative process are designed to reduce voter confusion. For example, some states restrict the subject matter of initiatives, prohibiting revenue or appropriations measures from being proposed through the

---

[25] For discussion of such tactics of evasion, see Elizabeth Garrett & Daniel Smith, *Veiled Political Actors and Campaign Disclosure Laws in Direct Democracy*, 4 Election L.J. 295 (2005).

initiative process.[26] Perhaps the most important such restriction is the single-subject rule that, as applied to ballot measures, is designed to ensure voters are presented with a proposal on a single subject that they can accept or reject. Of course, ballot measures on one topic can be extremely complicated, just as an initiative that combines two straightforward proposals can be relatively easily understood. Thus, it is not clear that the single-subject rule is tailored appropriately to fit the objective. Another rationale given for the single-subject rule in direct democracy mirrors the justification offered in the legislative context discussed in Chapter 3, § 2A: "The purpose of the single-subject requirement is to allow the citizens to vote on singular changes in our government that are identified in the proposal and to avoid voters having to accept parts of a proposal which they oppose in order to obtain a change which they support." *Fine v. Firestone*, 448 So. 2d 984, 993 (Fla. 1984).

The California Constitution has a single-subject rule specifically designed for direct democracy. It provides: "An initiative measure embracing more than one subject may not be submitted to the electors or have any effect." Cal. Const., art. II, § 8(d). The California Supreme Court has construed it identically with the state constitution's single-subject rule regarding legislation, applying to both a standard under which the rule is construed " 'liberally to uphold proper legislation, all parts of which are reasonably germane.' " *Perry v. Jordan*, 207 P.2d 47 (Cal. 1949) (quoting *Evans v. Superior Court of Los Angeles Cnty.*, 8 P.2d 467 (Cal. 1932)). Several justices have suggested, however, that a more stringent standard should apply in the context of direct democracy, under which the parts of an initiative must be "functionally related in furtherance of a common underlying purpose." *Schmitz v. Younger*, 577 P.2d 652 (Cal. 1978) (Manuel, J., dissenting). What policies support adoption of a stricter standard? Compare Marilyn Minger, Comment, *Putting the "Single" Back in the Single-Subject Rule: A Proposal for Initiative Reform in California*, 24 U.C. Davis L. Rev. 879 (1991) (proposing an amendment to encourage the court to engage in vigorous single-subject review), with Richard Hasen, *Ending Court Protection of Voters from the Initiative Process*, 116 Yale L.J. Pocket Part 115 (2006) (arguing that justifications for aggressive enforcement of the single-subject rule are unpersuasive and that the rule should be repealed).

An invigoration of the single-subject rule for ballot propositions seems to be occurring in some states. Florida has had a reputation for applying the single-subject rule aggressively; interestingly, the state is a relative newcomer to the initiative process, adopting it in 1968 for constitutional changes. Although deferential until the mid-1980s, Florida courts began to wield the single-subject rule so enthusiastically to strike down initiatives or keep them off the ballot that a 1994 ballot measure exempted initiatives limiting government revenues from the single-subject requirement.[27] A study by Daniel Lowenstein reveals that Florida is no longer the only state with a judiciary willing to enforce the single-subject rule aggressively in the context of initiatives. *Initiatives and the New Single Subject Rule*, 1 Election L.J. 35 (2002). Between 1998 and 1999, the supreme courts of California, Oregon, and Montana applied the single-subject doctrine "with surprising strictness," and Oklahoma, Missouri, and Colorado have inconsistently adopted a strict approach. Lowenstein concludes: "Whether the[se] decisions * * * really set a new course or will turn out to be aberrations is impossible to

---

[26] See Waters, *supra*, at 18 (listing subject-matter restrictions).

[27] See Philip Dubois & Floyd Feeney, *Lawmaking by Initiative: Issues, Options and Comparisons* 136–38 (1998).

say. * * * [But] even in states that have not so far been affected by the trend toward restrictive review, the developments in the states reviewed above may provide a strong temptation to supreme court justices who are personally hostile to an initiative that comes before them." *Id.* at 44.

One challenge in the context of direct democracy, just as it was with traditional legislation, is the definition of subject. Review the discussion of what constitutes a subject in Chapter 3, § 2A. Should the inquiry be different when the people, rather than representative bodies, enact the law? Scholars have argued that the malleability of the tests allows judges to mask their political preferences in deciding cases they claim are determined on procedural grounds.[28] Robert Cooter and Michael Gilbert have developed a test to determine what constitutes a "subject" based on their conception of the democratic process. *A Theory of Direct Democracy and the Single Subject Rule*, 110 Colum. L. Rev. 687 (2010). They argue that the test should turn on whether voters have "sufficiently separable preferences" with respect to the two policy proposals—that is, whether they can decide how to vote on each without knowing the other will become law. A voter has insufficiently separable preferences when either the two are "strong complements, such that the voter only votes for one if she is certain also to get the other" or "strong substitutes, such that the voter only votes for one if she is certain not to get the other." *Id.* at 714. Consider this theory, as well as the judicially applied tests as you work through the following problems. How is a court to determine what voters' preferences are and how closely related they are? Would such a test really avoid the problems that exist in the current system? For questions about the Cooter/Gilbert proposal, see Richard Hasen & John Matsusaka, *Some Skepticism about the "Separable Preferences" Approach to the Single Subject Rule: A Comment on Cooter & Gilbert*, 110 Colum. L. Rev. Sidebar 35 (2010).

PROBLEMS ON DIRECT DEMOCRACY AND THE SINGLE-SUBJECT RULE

Problem 4–2. Citizens in Florida petition to add the following to Article I, § 10 of the Florida Constitution:

> The state, political subdivisions of the state, municipalities or any other governmental entity shall not enact or adopt any law regarding discrimination against persons which creates, establishes or recognizes any right, privilege or protection for any person based upon any characteristic, trait, status, or condition other than race, color, sex, national origin, age, handicap, ethnic background, marital status, or familial status. * * *

As we noted in Chapter 3, § 2A, Florida has a single-subject rule: Any revision to the Florida Constitution by initiative "shall embrace but one subject and matter directly connected therewith." The Florida Supreme Court has stated that the rule is "designed to insulate Florida's organic law from precipitous and cataclysmic change."

As is often done now, groups opposing this initiative bring suit to knock it off the ballot. Should the Florida Supreme Court hear such preliminary challenges? If so, how should it rule? See *In re Advisory Opinion to the Attorney General—Restricts Laws Related to Discrimination*, 632 So. 2d 1018 (Fla. 1994).

---

[28]   John Matsusaka & Richard Hasen, *Aggressive Enforcement of the Single Subject Rule*, 9 Election L.J. 399 (2010).

Problem 4–3. A proposed amendment to the Arizona state constitution provides:

> To preserve and protect marriage in this state, only a union between one man and one woman shall be valid or recognized as a marriage by this state or its political subdivisions and no legal status for unmarried persons shall be created or recognized by this state or its political subdivisions that is similar to that of marriage.

Does this measure contain a single subject? Consider the formal argument that it (1) defines marriage, (2) prohibits same-sex marriages, (3) might prohibit civil unions and domestic partnerships, and (4) might even prohibit the state and its subdivisions from conferring any benefits upon persons in same-sex relationships, whether that status is recognized by law or not (e.g., it might prohibit the University of Arizona from extending health insurance coverage to partners of its employees). In addition, consider the functional argument that common sense and public opinion polls alike indicate that many voters who support (1) and (2) will not understand that (3) and (4) might also be involved—and at least a good number of them might oppose either or both (3) and (4) if they could vote separately on them. See *Arizona Together v. Brewer*, 214 Ariz. 118, 149 P.3d 742 (Ariz. 2007); see also *McConkey v. Van Hollen*, 326 Wis. 2d 1, 783 N.W. 2d 855 (Wisc. 2010) (more recent case, reaching similar result).

C. INTERACTION BETWEEN DIRECT DEMOCRACY AND REPRESENTATIVE INSTITUTIONS

Effect on the Lawmaking Agenda. The term "hybrid democracy" makes salient the reality that the presence of a robust initiative process affects the legislative branch in several ways. First, the presence of an initiative on the ballot will affect turnout generally, which in turn influences the results of candidate elections. Daniel Smith and Caroline Tolbert found that, in presidential elections, each ballot measure boosts turnout by half a percentage, and in midterm elections, each ballot measure increases turnout by 1.2%.[29] Of course, turnout is not increased randomly; rather, the subject matter of the initiative motivates different groups of people to vote, and the shape of that turnout may determine who is elected to serve at the state and federal levels. The initiatives prohibiting same-sex marriage on the ballot in 11 states in 2004 certainly affected the outcome of Senate and other legislative races, and they may even have played a role in President George W. Bush's reelection by encouraging the turnout of conservative voters in Ohio, the key state for his victory.

Perhaps one of the most interesting findings by political scientists who focus on the interaction between the two sides of hybrid democracy is that the mere possibility of an initiative influences the outcomes in the state legislature. Gerber describes the *indirect effect* of direct democracy, which she describes as political actors using initiatives to pressure state lawmakers to pass a new law. *The Populist Paradox: Interest Group Influence and the Promise of Direct Democracy* 23–28 (1999). Sometimes the pressure can be overt. For example, in 1998, Silicon Valley entrepreneur Reed Hastings led a group frustrated by the California Assembly's

---

[29] *Educated by Initiative: The Effects of Direct Democracy on Citizens and Political Organizations in the American States* 42 (2004) (also finding that, at a certain point, each additional measure does not further increase turnout).

refusal to expand the charter school program. They believed that an entrenched special interest, the teachers' union, was blocking meaningful reform through the traditional legislative process. Accordingly, they spent $3.5 million to pay petition circulators and obtained 1.2 million signatures for a proposal to institute their vision of charter schools, twice the number of required signatures. In addition, they threatened to spend another $12 million to pass the initiative. Hastings made it clear, however, that his group would halt the petition drive if representatives increased the number of charter schools and addressed other concerns. Within a short time, a compromise bill had passed the state legislature; once Governor Pete Wilson signed the bill, the initiative drive stopped.

Not all groups can enter into this sort of bargaining game with politicians. Under what conditions will such a threat be successful? Gerber identifies three conditions. First, "the group has sufficient resources to attract the legislature's attention." Second, "the group must have something legislators want," such as the ability to provide future campaign contributions. Third, "legislators must be electorally vulnerable."

Often the indirect influence of direct democracy is not as overt as in the charter schools example in California. For example, political scientists have found that legislative outcomes in states with the possibility of initiatives are different in meaningful ways from the outcomes in states without robust popular democracy. In *For the Many or the Few* (2004), John Matsusaka focuses his attention on fiscal policies. He finds that initiative states have lower overall spending by state and local governments; that spending in these states has shifted from the state to local governments; and that broad-based taxes in initiative states are reduced and replaced with more user fees. Using opinion polls, he determines that a majority of voters in those states favor such fiscal policies, leading him to conclude that, at least in this realm, direct democracy favors the majority, rather than special interests. Importantly, these policies are not all adopted through the initiative; rather, it is the pressure of the possibility of direct democracy that may be responsible for these systematic differences.[30] The existence of the initiative process may therefore empower the median voter in all policymaking realms, under some conditions. Of course, this may lead to other concerns, such as the tyranny of the majority undermining the rights of the minority.

In addition, political actors may turn to the initiative, or the threat of one, to enact policies that they cannot pass through the regular legislative channels. Former California Governor Arnold Schwarzenegger successfully wielded the threat of direct democracy early in his first term to pressure the legislature into adopting workers' compensation reform that had been stymied in the legislature,

---

[30] See also Elisabeth Gerber, *Legislative Response to the Threat of Popular Initiatives*, 40 Am. J. Pol. Sci. 99 (1996) (finding that parental consent laws in initiative states are closer to the median voter's preference than such laws in states without the initiative process); John Matsusaka & Nolan McCarty, *Political Resource Allocation: Benefits and Costs of Voter Initiatives*, 17 J. Law, Econ. & Org. 413 (2001) (detailing conditions under which outcomes are closer to median voter's preference in initiative states). One study has even found that initiatives affect congressional voting behavior, particularly in the House. Joshua Huder, Jordan Ragusa & Daniel Smith, *Shirking the Initiative: The Effects of Statewide Ballot Measures on Congressional Roll Call Behavior*, 39 Am. Pol. Res. 582 (2011).

blocked by powerful interest groups representing labor.[31] In Minnesota, the structure of the ballot-measure process allows a majority of the legislature to propose a constitutional amendment for a vote of the people without any involvement by the Governor. Accordingly, in 2012 when the Republican-dominated legislature was blocked by the Democratic Governor from enacting a voter ID law, it bypassed the executive by placing the issue on the ballot (where it ultimately lost). The legislature also avoided having a Democratic Secretary of State provide a ballot title that might not have been as favorable as supporters desired by requiring particular wording for the title, and then defeating a judicial challenge to its end run around the regular process of titling and an examination of the accuracy of the title.[32]

The Implementation Problem. Another interaction between direct democracy and representative institutions occurs after an initiative is passed. Once enacted, many initiatives must be implemented by elected and appointed officials—people who often resisted the policy in the first place. After all, the people resort to enacting laws themselves when their representatives have been insufficiently attentive. This leads to the "implementation problem" in direct democracy. For example, a ballot measure might enact sweeping reform of the state's school system, which then must be implemented by the Department of Education, school administrators, and unions. Or the initiative might enact public financing for campaigns, but the legislature has to appropriate the money. Of course, some initiatives are struck down by courts holding that they are unconstitutional or legally flawed in some way. Here the people cannot get what they want because their preferences conflict with larger principles and values, such as the protection of individual rights guaranteed in the Constitution. But when state officials block initiatives by surreptitiously undermining them, they ignore the will of the majority in a way that reduces accountability.

In *Stealing the Initiative: How State Government Responds to Direct Democracy* (2001), Gerber, Lupia, McCubbins, and Kiewiet identify several conditions that allow government officials to ignore or undermine initiatives more easily. First, substantial technical or political costs will lead to lower levels of compliance because the net value of implementation is reduced. Technical costs might include the effort involved in writing and adopting legislation or regulations to implement the initiative. Political costs might be incurred if legislators have to make promises to enact legislation or take steps that will be opposed by powerful organized interests. Or money to implement the initiative might reduce the resources available for other important legislative goals. Second, if implementers face significant sanctions for noncompliance, they are more likely to work to implement the initiative. Third, and related to the second factor, when it is easier for the public or others who support the initiative to observe compliance, it is more likely that officials will comply. Finally, the more people required for full compliance, the lower the chances of implementation.

---

[31] Elizabeth Garrett, *Democracy in the Wake of the California Recall*, 153 U. Penn. L. Rev. 239, 280 (2004).

[32] *Limmer v. Ritchie*, 819 N.W. 2d 622 (Minn. 2012) (see dissent by Justice Anderson describing the "end run" aspect of the legislative decision to propose the voter ID requirement as a constitutional amendment).

One aspect of the implementation problem reached the Supreme Court as part of the litigation surrounding Prop 8, the referendum preventing same-sex marriage in California. When supporters of same-sex marriage attacked Prop 8 in federal District Court, no state official named as a defendant—including the Governor and Attorney General—was willing to defend it. The District Court allowed the proponents of the initiative to intervene and defend the law; ultimately, the judge found Prop 8 to violate the constitutional guarantee of equal protection. *Perry v. Schwarzenegger*, 704 F. Supp. 2d 921 (N.D. Cal. 2010), *aff'd sub nom. Perry v. Brown*, 671 F.3d 1052 (2012). The Supreme Court did not address the merits of that decision, finding instead that the initiative proponents did not have standing to defend the ballot measure. *Hollingsworth v. Perry*, 113 S.Ct. 2652 (2013). Without some specific authorization from the state that would allow proponents to act as agents of the people of California, these citizens had only a generalized grievance insufficient to confer standing under Article III. As the Supreme Court explained, "Their only interest in having the District Court order reversed was to vindicate the constitutional validity of a generally applicable California law." Their unique role in the initiative process is limited to the process of enacting the law; once the ballot measure is passed, the proponents become simply what the majority called "concerned bystanders." Four justices dissented and supported the approach of the California Supreme Court, which had concluded that the initiative's primary purpose "is undermined if the very officials the initiative process seeks to circumvent are the only parties who can defend an enacted initiative when it is challenged in a legal proceeding." The dissent noted the irony of the Court's decision that resulted in "litigation conducted by state officials whose preference is to lose the case."

After *Hollingsworth,* can a state enable initiative proponents—or some group other than elected officials who likely do not support the measure—to defend it in court? How would you construct a system that would provide some authority to such groups (and which groups would you choose?), but also provide some oversight of their decisions and actions? See Elizabeth Garrett & Mathew McCubbins, *The Dual Path Initiative Framework*, 80 S. Cal. L. Rev. 299, 332–42 (2007) (proposing an independent Citizens Initiative Implementation Oversight Commission, with members appointed in provisions in successful ballot measures).

Problem 4–4. Consider some of the policies we have already studied that have often been implemented as a result of direct democracy: term limits for legislators, public financing of campaigns, ethics rules, changes in party primaries, supermajority voting requirements for tax increases, and redistricting commissions. Why do groups resort to direct democracy to enact these policies? What hurdles will each face in the effort to gain ballot access? Which interest groups are likely to be active as proponents and opponents, and how successfully can they raise money? Are political candidates likely to align themselves with either side to increase their chances at the polls? Which face significant implementation problems? If you are a proponent of the initiative, how can you minimize the implementation problems when you draft the initiative? See Gerber, Lupia, McCubbins & Kiewiet, *supra* (providing case studies, including term limits and open primaries).

2. STATUTORY INTERPRETATION OF INITIATIVES

In subsequent chapters of this casebook, we will consider at length how courts interpret statutes enacted through traditional means, and we introduced some of these concepts in Chapter 1 in the context of judicial interpretation of provisions of the Civil Rights Act. Consider what different issues and difficulties might arise when interpreting laws that originate and are adopted outside the normal legislative process. Should interpretive techniques for ballot measures parallel those for legislative enactments, or should the fundamental differences in the two enactment procedures result in differing approaches to interpretation?

In *The Pursuit of "Popular Intent": Interpretive Dilemmas in Direct Democracy*, 105 Yale L.J. 107 (1995), a comprehensive treatment of these issues, Jane Schacter demonstrates that state courts routinely purport to use the same interpretive techniques regardless of statutory enactment process, usually stating that the linchpin of statutory meaning is the "intent" of the enacting authority. Schacter criticizes this approach on empirical grounds. How can the people, at the polls, have some determinate intent about non-obvious issues that could arise under the measure? She suggests that any serious effort to understand voter intent would require an examination of the media coverage and advertising surrounding a ballot campaign, which social science research demonstrates affect the voters much more than formal sources such as the text of the ballot proposition and the official voter pamphlet distributed by the state. Yet state courts routinely refuse to consider the informal materials and counterfactually assume that voter intent coheres with the text of the ballot and pamphlet.

An example of this phenomenon is the Michigan marriage initiative, which added new Article 25, § 11 to the Michigan Constitution in 2004: "To secure and preserve the benefits of marriage for our society and for future generations of children, the union of one man and one woman in marriage shall be the only agreement recognized as a marriage or similar union for any purpose." The Michigan Attorney General and the state's Court of Appeals have interpreted that language to bar public employers from giving health care benefits to the "domestic partners" of lesbian and gay employees. *Nat'l Pride at Work, Inc. v. Governor*, 274 Mich. App. 147, 732 N.W. 2d 139 (2007), *aff'd*, 481 Mich. 56, 784 N.W. 2d 524 (2008). The court ruled that the statutory language plainly applied to even the most limited domestic-partnership benefits and refused to consider background materials—which demonstrated that the sponsors repeatedly assured voters that their marriage initiative would *not* affect domestic-partnership benefits. See also Glen Staszewski, *The Bait-and-Switch in Direct Democracy*, 2006 Wis. L. Rev. 17, 21–32 (discussing the proposition and its text). Staszewski argues that initiative proponents should be treated as sponsors accountable for their representations to the electorate, especially ones that appeal to popular prejudices (for purposes of judicial review) or that claim a narrow effect of their proposals if enacted (for purposes of statutory interpretation). *Rejecting the Myth of Popular Sovereignty and Applying an Agency Model to Direct Democracy*, 56 Vand. L. Rev. 395 (2003).

Sensitive to the issues Staszewski identifies, Schacter rejects a more capacious judicial consideration of informal materials on the grounds that they are unlikely to assist judges in choosing among the plausible interpretations surrounding ambiguous ballot measures and that judicial receptivity to arguments based on such materials will only encourage interest groups to manipulate media accounts and advertising for post-enactment judicial consumption. Schacter argues that, in place of an illusory search for voter intent, courts should craft principles of statutory interpretation specifically for the context of direct democracy. She proposes that ballot propositions disadvantaging groups subject to the hostility of the majority—such as antigay measures like the Michigan marriage initiative—should be interpreted narrowly. On the other hand, initiatives that break through self-interested legislative gridlocks and seek to enhance the legitimacy of government processes—such as campaign finance restrictions or perhaps term limits—might be interpreted more liberally.

Other scholars have also developed coherent interpretive regimes for ballot measures. Philip Frickey begins with the notion that direct democracy is in tension with the federal constitutional principle of republican government. *Interpretation on the Borderline: Constitution, Canons, Direct Democracy*, 1996 N.Y.U. Ann. Surv. Am. L. 477 (1996). Because the Supreme Court has refused to invalidate state ballot measures on this ground, the voters must be given their due: ballot measures should be interpreted consistent with the plain meaning of their text and the obvious understandings of the voters concerning the core purposes of the measure. As to ambiguities, however, such measures should be interpreted narrowly, to limit their effects in displacing prior law enacted in republican fashion (i.e., by the legislature).

Frickey's argument is premised on the notion that republican lawmaking is an underenforced constitutional norm. Courts do not void statutes on the basis of this constitutional principle, but it is nonetheless worthy of some protection through rules, or canons, of statutory interpretation. (The Supreme Court has followed this approach with respect to another less underenforced constitutional norm: federalism. See *Gregory v. Ashcroft*, 501 U.S. 452 (1991), discussed in Chapter 7, § 2C) In addition to privileging republican enactments, this approach suggests that longstanding substantive canons on construction should be more strongly applied in the context of ballot propositions. For example, because voters are less capable than a legislature in evaluating whether a proposal satisfies constitutional norms, ballot propositions should be subjected more aggressively than legislatively adopted laws to the canon concerning the avoidance of serious constitutional issues. (This canon is discussed in Chapter 7, § 2B.) Consider this argument in light of the following case.

Evangelatos v. Superior Court
44 Cal.3d 1188, 246 Cal. Rptr. 629, 753 P.2d 585 (1988).

The voters of California approved Proposition 51, the "Fair Responsibility Act of 1986," which "modified the traditional, common law 'joint and several liability' doctrine by limiting an individual tortfeasor's liability for noneconomic damages to a proportion of such damages equal to the tortfeasor's own percentage of fault." Under the California

Constitution, the measure took effect the day after the election. The proposition was silent on whether it applied to pending cases. A sharply divided California Supreme Court held that the measure did not apply to causes of action that accrued prior to the effective date.

Justice Arguelles, for the majority, noted that it would have been simple enough for the proponents of the measure to have drafted it expressly to apply to pending cases and that they should have been on notice that, in the absence of a retroactivity provision, courts were likely to apply it only prospectively. (See Chapter 5, § 3.) The majority embraced a strong nonretroactivity principle, concluding that "in the absence of an express retroactivity provision, a statute will not be applied retroactively unless it is very clear from extrinsic sources that the Legislature or the voters must have intended a retroactive application." The majority stressed that nothing in the proposition's "findings and declaration of purpose" or in the ballot pamphlet distributed to the voters indicated that the retroactivity question "was actually consciously considered during the enactment process." The majority contended that a retroactive application could interfere with the reasonable expectations of plaintiffs in pending cases (who might have decided whom to sue and not to sue based on the law existing at the time suit was filed) and could result in a windfall to insurance companies.

In dissent, **Justice Kaufman**, joined by two colleagues, disputed whether California precedents required such a strong canon against retroactivity and whether retroactivity would produce unfairness in pending cases or an insurance windfall. He argued that the presumption of prospectivity should apply "only after, considering *all pertinent factors*, it is determined that it is impossible to ascertain the legislative intent." Two pertinent factors, the context surrounding the enactment of the bill and the perceived evils to be remedied by the measure, strongly supported retroactive application. Proposition 51, a "tort reform" measure, was a response to the widely perceived "liability crisis" facing government agencies and private businesses. Section 3 of Proposition 51 stated:

Findings and Declaration of Purpose

The People of the State of California find and declare as follows:

(a)　The legal doctrine of joint and several liability, also known as "the deep pocket rule," has resulted in a system of inequity and injustice that has threatened financial bankruptcy of local governments, other public agencies, private individuals and businesses and has resulted in higher prices for goods and services to the public and in higher taxes to the taxpayers.

(b)　Some governmental and private defendants are perceived to have substantial financial resources or insurance coverage and have thus been included in lawsuits even though there was little or no basis for finding them at fault. Under joint and several liability, if they are found to share even a fraction of the fault, they often are held financially liable for all the damage. The People—taxpayers and consumers alike—ultimately pay for these lawsuits in the form of higher taxes, higher prices and higher insurance premiums.

(c)　Local governments have been forced to curtail some essential police, fire and other protections because of the soaring costs of lawsuits and insurance premiums.

Therefore, the People of the State of California declare that to remedy these inequities, defendants in tort actions shall be held financially liable in closer proportion to their degree of fault. To treat them differently is unfair and inequitable.

The People of the State of California further declare that reforms in the liability laws in tort actions are necessary and proper to avoid catastrophic economic consequences for state and local governmental bodies as well as private individuals and businesses.

Justice Kaufman concluded that, in light of both the text of § 3 and the spirit of the overall provision, "the inference is virtually inescapable that the electorate intended Proposition 51 to apply as soon and as broadly as possible. When the electorate voted to reform a system perceived as 'inequitable and unjust,' they obviously voted to change that system *now*, not in five or ten years when causes of action that accrued prior to Proposition 51 finally come to trial. * * * A crisis does not call for *future* action. It calls for action *now*, action across the board, action as broad and as comprehensive as the Constitution will allow. It is clear that the purposes of Proposition 51 will be fully served only if it is applied to all cases not tried prior to its effective date."

Query: How would Professors Schacter, Staszewski, and Frickey decide this case, based upon their different theories? The most recent attempt to formulate a theory of statutory interpretation for popular enactments draws from the principle that direct democracy is "a fundamentally majoritarian" institution, and therefore initiatives are to be interpreted to reflect the will of the "median" voter. Michael Gilbert, *Interpreting Initiatives*, 97 Minn. L. Rev. 1621 (2013). Social choice teaches that, in certain circumstances, which Gilbert argues often obtain in an initiative election, the Condorcet winner among a set of policies can be considered to reflect majoritarian social choice. The Condorcet winner is that policy that would defeat all others in a head-to-head vote in a system of majority rule. Using that as the guide, judges should consider the views of all voters—not just those voting for the initiative, and certainly not just the drafters—to ascertain the median voter's view on the question presented. Gilbert also posits that elected state judges, often the interpreters in these cases, may be particularly well situated to determine the median voter's likely view. Does this approach to interpretation provide a clearer answer in *Evangelatos?* To the same-sex marriage provision's scope in Problem 4–3? Consider the application of all the theories in the next problem.

PROBLEM INVOLVING POPULAR LAWMAKING AND INTERPRETATION

Problem 4–5. In 1990, California voters adopted Proposition 140, "The Political Reform Act of 1990," which imposed term limits on state elected officials and limited expenditures funding the state legislature. You have been asked to provide advice to several former state legislators who fear that this measure imposes on them a lifetime ban on ever seeking election to the legislature again. They are hoping that you will figure out a persuasive argument for construing the proposition as allowing them to seek office in the future. In addition, they have asked you to investigate whether the proposition might be invalidated as inconsistent with either the federal or state constitution. (Remember that California has a single-subject rule for initiatives.)

Each registered voter in California is mailed an official voter pamphlet. The pamphlet contains the text of each ballot measure, an official summary of it, and arguments for and against it prepared by proponents and opponents. The California pamphlet for the November 1990 election contained the following (which has been edited only slightly to give you a sense of the entirety of the official materials that inform voters):[33]

PROPOSITION 140: TEXT OF PROPOSED LAW

This initiative measure expressly amends the Constitution by amending and combining sections thereof; therefore, new provisions proposed to be inserted or added are printed in *italic type* to indicate they are new.

PROPOSED LAW

Section 1.   This measure shall be known and may be cited as "The Political Reform Act of 1990."

Section 2.   Section 1.5 is added to Article IV of the California Constitution, to read:

SEC 1.5. The people find and declare that the Founding Fathers established a system of representative government based upon free, fair and competitive elections. The increased concentration of political power in the hands of incumbent representatives has made our electoral system less free, less competitive and less representative.

The ability of legislators to serve unlimited number of terms, to establish their own retirement system, and to pay for staff and support services at state expense contribute heavily to the extremely high number of incumbents who are elected. These unfair incumbent advantages discourage qualified candidates from seeking public office and create a class of career politicians, instead of the citizen representatives envisioned by the Founding Fathers. These career politicians become representatives of the bureaucracy, rather than of the people whom they are elected to represent.

To restore a free and democratic system of fair elections, and to encourage qualified candidates to seek public office, the people find and declare that the powers of incumbency must be limited. Retirement benefits must be restricted, state-financed incumbent staff and support services limited, and limitations placed upon the number of terms which may be served.

SEC. 3. Section 2 of Article IV of the California Constitution is amended to read:

SEC. 2. (a) The Senate has a membership of 40 Senators elected for 4–year terms, 20 to begin every 2 years. *No Senator may serve more than 2 terms.* The Assembly has a membership of 80 members elected for 2–year terms. *No member of the Assembly may serve more than 3 terms.* Their terms shall commence on the first Monday in December next following their election.

[33] We thank Einer Elhauge, who served as counsel for the Secretary of State of California, and Thomas Gede, then Special Assistant Attorney General of California, for providing us with these materials.

* * *

SEC. 4. Section 4.5 is added to Article IV of the California Constitution, to read:

SEC. 4.5.   Notwithstanding any other provision of this Constitution or existing law, a person elected to or serving in the Legislature on or after November 1, 1990, shall participate in the Federal Social Security (Retirement, Disability, Health Insurance) Program and the State shall pay only the employer's share of the contribution necessary to such participation. No other pension or retirement benefit shall accrue as a result of service in the Legislature, such service not being intended as a career occupation. This Section shall not be construed to abrogate or diminish any vested pension or retirement benefit which may have accrued under an existing law to a person holding or having held office in the Legislature, but upon adoption of this Act no further entitlement to nor vesting in any existing program shall accrue to any such person, other than Social Security to the extent herein provided.

SEC. 5. Section 7.5 is added to Article IV of the California Constitution to read:

SEC. 7.5.   In the fiscal year immediately following the adoption of this Act, the total aggregate expenditures of the Legislature for the compensation of members and employees of, and the operating expenses and equipment for, the Legislature may not exceed an amount equal to nine hundred fifty thousand dollars ($950,000) per member for that fiscal year or 80 percent of the amount of money expended for those purposes in the preceding fiscal year, whichever is less. For each fiscal year thereafter, the total aggregate expenditures may not exceed an amount equal to that expended for those purposes in the preceding fiscal year, adjusted and compounded by an amount equal to the percentage increase in the appropriations limit for the state established pursuant to Article XIII B.

SEC. 6. Section 2 of Article V of the California Constitution is amended to read:

SEC. 2. The Governor shall be elected every fourth year at the same time and places as members of the Assembly and hold office from the Monday after January 1 following the election until a successor qualifies. The Governor shall be an elector who has been a citizen of the United States and a resident of this State for 5 years immediately preceding the Governor's election. The Governor may not hold other public office. *No Governor may serve more than 2 terms.*

SEC. 7. Section 11 of Article V of the California Constitution is amended to read:

SEC. 11. The Lieutenant Governor, Attorney General, Controller, Secretary of State, and Treasurer shall be elected at the same time and places and for the same term as the Governor. *No Lieutenant Governor, Attorney General, Controller, Secretary of State, or Treasurer may serve in the same office for more than 2 terms.*

SEC. 8. Section 2 of Article IX of the California Constitution is amended to read:

SEC. 2. A Superintendent of Public Instruction shall be elected by the qualified electors of the State at each gubernatorial election. The Superintendent of Public Instruction shall enter upon the duties of the office on the first Monday after the first day of January next succeeding each gubernatorial election. *No Superintendent of Public Instruction may serve more than 2 terms.*

SEC. 9. Section 17 of Article XIII of the California Constitution is amended to read:

SEC. 17. The Board of Equalization consists of 5 voting members: the Controller and 4 members elected for 4–year terms at gubernatorial elections. The state shall be divided into four Board of Equalization districts with the voters of each district electing one member. *No member may serve more than 2 terms.*

SEC. 10. Section 7 is added to Article XX of the California Constitution to read:

SEC. 7. The limitations on the number of terms prescribed by Section 2 of Article IV, Sections 2 and 11 of Article V, Section 2 of Article IX, and Section 17 of Article XIII apply only to terms to which persons are elected or appointed on or after November 6, 1990, except that an incumbent Senator whose office is not on the ballot for general election on that date may serve only one additional term. Those limitations shall not apply to any unexpired term to which a person is elected or appointed if the remainder of the term is less than half of the full term.

SEC. 11. Section 11 (d) is added to Article VII of the California Constitution to read:

(d) If any part of this measure or the application to any person or circumstance is held invalid, the invalidity shall not affect other provisions or applications which reasonably can be given effect without the invalid provision or application.

Official Title and Summary:

LIMITS ON TERMS OF OFFICE, LEGISLATORS'
RETIREMENT, LEGISLATIVE OPERATING COSTS.
INITIATIVE CONSTITUTIONAL AMENDMENT

- Persons elected or appointed after November 5, 1990, holding offices of Governor, Lieutenant Governor, Attorney General, Controller, Secretary of State, Treasurer, Superintendent of Public Instruction, Board of Equalization members, and State Senators, limited to two terms; members of the Assembly limited to three terms.

- Requires legislators elected or serving after November 1, 1990, to participate in federal Social Security program; precludes accrual of other pension and retirement benefits resulting from legislative service, except vested rights.

- Limits expenditures of Legislature for compensation and operating costs and equipment, to specified amount.

Summary of Legislative Analyst's Estimate of Net State and Local Government Fiscal Impact:

- The limitation on terms will have no fiscal effect.
- The restrictions on the legislative retirement benefits would reduce state costs by approximately $750,000 a year. * * *
- Legislative expenditures in 1991–92 would be reduced by about 38 percent, or $70 million.
- In subsequent years, the measure would limit growth in these expenditures to the changes in the state's appropriations limit.

Analysis by the Legislative Analyst

Background

There are 132 elected state officials in California. This includes 120 legislators and 12 other state officials, including the Governor, Lieutenant Governor, and Attorney General. Currently, there is no limit on the number of terms that these officials can serve. Proposition 112, passed by the voters in June 1990, requires the annual salaries and benefits (excluding retirement) of these state officials to be set by a commission. Most of these officials participate in the federal Social Security system, and all have the option of participating in the Legislators' Retirement System. The vast majority of the 132 elected state officials participate in this retirement system. The system is supported by contributions from participating officials and the state. * * *

Proposal

This initiative makes three major changes to the California Constitution. First, it limits the number of terms that an elected state official can serve in the *same office* (the new office of Insurance Commissioner is not affected by this measure). Second, it prohibits legislators from earning state retirement benefits from their future service in the Legislature. Third, it limits the total amount of expenditures by the Legislature for salaries and operating expenses.

The specific provisions of this measure are:

Limits on the Terms of Elected State Officials

- The following state elected officials would be limited to no more than two four-year terms in the same office: Governor, Lieutenant Governor, Attorney General, Controller, Secretary of State, Superintendent of Public Instruction, Treasurer, members of the Board of Equalization, and State Senators.
- Members of the State Assembly would be limited to no more than three two-year terms in the same office.
- These limits apply to a state official who is elected on or after November 6, 1990. However, State Senators whose offices are *not* on the November 6, 1990 ballot may serve only one additional term.

Restrictions on Legislative Retirement Benefits

- This measure prohibits current and future legislators from earning state retirement benefits from their service in the Legislature on or after November 7, 1990. This restriction would not eliminate retirement benefits earned prior to that time.

- This measure requires a legislator serving in the Legislature on or after November 7, 1990 to participate in the federal Social Security system. (However, federal law may permit only current legislators who are presently participating in the federal Social Security system to continue to participate in the system. It may also prohibit future legislators from participating in the federal Society Security system.)

- This measure does not change the Social Security coverage or the state retirement benefits of other state elected officials such as the Governor, Lieutenant Governor, and Attorney General.

Limits on Expenditures by the Legislature

- This measure limits the amount of expenditures by the Legislature for salaries and operating expenses, beginning in the 1991–92 fiscal year.

- In 1991–92, these expenditures are limited to the *lower* of two amounts: (1) a total of $950,000 per Member or (2) 80 percent of the total amount of money expended in the previous year for these purposes. In future years, the measure limits expenditure growth to an amount equal to the percentage change in the state's appropriations limit.

Fiscal Effect

Limits on the Terms of Elected State Officials. This provision would not have any fiscal effect.

Restrictions on Legislative Retirement Benefits. The provision which prohibits current and future Members of the Legislature from earning state retirement benefits from legislative service on or after November 7, 1990 would reduce state costs by about $750,000 a year.

To the extent that future legislators do not participate in the federal Social Security system, the measure would result in unknown future savings to the state.

Limits on Expenditures by the Legislature. In 1991–92, expenditures by the Legislature would be reduced by about 38 percent, or $70 million. In subsequent years, this measure would limit growth in these expenditures to the changes in the state's appropriations limit.

Argument in Favor of Proposition 140

Proposition 140 will for the first time ever place a limit on the number of times a State official may serve in office.

A Yes Vote on Proposition 140 will reform a political system that has created a legislature of career politicians in California. It is a system that has given a tiny elite (only 120 people out of 30 million) almost limitless power over the lives of California's taxpayers and consumers.

Proposition 140 will limit State Senators to two terms (8 years); will limit Assembly members to three terms (6 years); and limit the Governor and other elected constitutional officers to two terms (8 years).

By reducing the amount they can spend on their personal office expenses, Proposition 140, will cut back on the 3,000 political staffers who serve the legislature in Sacramento. In the first year alone, according to the legislative analyst, it will save taxpayers $60 million.

Proposition 140, will end extravagant pensions for legislators. While most Californians have to depend on Social Security and their own savings, the legislative pension system often pays more than the legislator received while in office. In fact, 50 former officials receive $2,000.00 per month or more from the Legislative retirement fund.

Limiting Terms, will create more competitive elections, so good legislators will always have the opportunity to move up the ladder. Term limitation will end the ingrown, political nature of both houses—to the benefit of every man, woman and child in California.

Proposition 140 will remove the grip that vested interests have over the legislature and remove the huge political slush funds at the disposal of Senate and Assembly leaders.

Proposition 140 will put an end to the life-time legislators, who have developed cozy relationships with special interests. We all remember the saying, "Power corrupts and absolute power corrupts absolutely." But limit the terms of Legislative members, remove the Speaker's cronies, and we will also put an end to the Sacramento web of special favors and patronage.

Proposition 140 will end the reign of the Legislature's powerful officers—the Assembly Speaker (first elected a quarter of a century ago) and the Senate Leader (now into his third decade in the Legislature). Lobbyists and power brokers pay homage to these legislative dictators, for they control the fate of bills, parcel out money to the camp followers and hangers-on, and pull strings behind the scenes to decide election outcomes.

Incumbent legislators seldom lose. In the 1988 election, 100% of incumbent state senators and 96% of incumbent members of the assembly were re-elected. The British House of Lords—even the Soviet Legislature—has a higher turnover rate. Enough is Enough! It's time to put an end to a system that makes incumbents a special class of citizen and pays them a guaranteed annual wage from first election to the grave. Let's restore that form of government of citizens representing their fellow citizens.

VOTE YES ON PROPOSITION 140 TO *LIMIT STATE OFFICIALS TERM OF OFFICE!*

PETER E. SCHABARUM *Chairman, Los Angeles County Board of Supervisors*

LEWIS K. UHLER *President, National Tax-Limitation Committee*

J.G. FORD, JR. *President, Marin United Taxpayers Association*

Rebuttal to Argument in Favor of Proposition 140

Proposition 140 is a proposal by a downtown Los Angeles politician to take away your right to choose your legislators. He has a history of taking away voting rights. He and two political cronies voted to spend $500,000.00 in tax dollars to hire a personal lawyer to defend him against Voting Rights Act violations in Federal Court. Newspapers call it an "outrageous back room deal."

His "Big Bucks" friends, including high-priced lobbyists, have lined his pockets with campaign contributions to help control who *you* can vote for.

- IF 140 PASSES, LOBBYISTS COULD SUBSTITUTE THEIR OWN PAID EMPLOYEES FOR THE INDEPENDENT STAFF RESEARCHERS OF THE LEGISLATURE ELIMINATED BY THIS MEASURE.
- 140 MISLEADS YOU ABOUT THE SO-CALLED "HIGH" COST OF THE LEGISLATURE—THE COST IS LESS THAN ½ PENNY PER TAX DOLLAR.
- THE BIGGEST LIE IS THE FACT THAT THEY DON'T TELL YOU THAT 140 IS A *LIFETIME BAN*.

This is a blatant power grab by Los Angeles contributors and lobbyists who have been wining and dining "Mr. Downtown Los Angeles" in government for SEVEN TERMS—OVER TWENTY YEARS.

Practice what you preach, "Mr. Downtown Los Angeles," Peter Schabarum. Cut *your own* budget and limit *your own* terms. Don't be a piggy and take away the people's rights after you have fully eaten at the table.

There is no need for 140. The vast majority of the Legislature *already* serves less than 10 years.

That's *your* choice. * * *

ED FOGLIA *President, California Teachers Association*

DAN TERRY *President, California Professional Firefighters*

LINDA M. TANGREN *State Chair, California National Women's Political Caucus*

Argument Against Proposition 140

Proposition 140 claims to mandate term limits. But in fact, it limits our voting rights.

This measure takes away the cherished constitutional right to freely cast a ballot for candidates of our choice.

We are asked to forfeit *our* right to decide *who our* individual representatives will be.

PROPOSITION 140'S LIFETIME BAN

140 does *not* limit *consecutive* terms of office. Instead 140 says:

- After serving six years in the Assembly, individuals will be constitutionally *banned for life* from ever serving in the Assembly.
- After serving eight years in the Senate, individuals will be constitutionally *banned for life* from ever serving in the Senate.
- Similar lifetime bans will be imposed on the Superintendent of Public Instruction and other statewide offices.

  There are no exceptions—not for merit, not for statewide emergencies, not for the overwhelming will of the people.

  Once banned, always banned.

PROPOSITION 140 IS UNFAIR

It treats everyone—good and bad, competent and incompetent—the same.

No matter how good a job someone does in office, they will be *banned for life*.

You won't even be able to write-in their names on your ballot. If you do, your vote won't count.

That's just not fair.

LIMITS OUR RIGHT TO CHOOSE

The backers of 140 don't trust us, the people, to choose our elected officials. So instead of promoting thoughtful reforms that help us weed out bad legislators, they impose a lifetime ban that eliminates good legislators and bad ones alike at the expense of our constitutional rights.

No eligible citizen should be *permanently banned* for life from seeking any office in a free society. And we should not be *permanently banned* from voting freely for the candidate of our choice.

Resist the rhetoric. Proposition 140 is not about restricting the powers of incumbency. It's about taking away our powers to choose.

PHONY PENSION REFORM

Proposition 140's retirement provisions are also misdirected and counterproductive.

140 does not eliminate the real abuses: double and triple dipping—the practice of taking multiple pensions.

Instead it raises new barriers to public office by banning our future representatives from earning *any* retirement except their current social security.

140's retirement ban won't hurt rich candidates. It will hurt qualified, ordinary citizens who are not rich and have to work hard to provide economic security for themselves and their families.

PROPOSITION 140 GOES TOO FAR

It upsets our system of constitutional checks and balances, forcing our representatives to become even more dependent on entrenched bureaucrats and shrewd lobbyists.

VOTE NO ON PROPOSITION 140

STOP THIS RADICAL AND DANGEROUS SCHEME! PROTECT OUR CONSTITUTIONAL RIGHTS. VOTE NO ON PROPOSITION 140'S LIFETIME BAN.

DR. REGENE L. MITCHELL *President, Consumer Federation of California*

LUCY BLAKE *Executive Director, California League of Conservation Voters*

DAN TERRY *President, California Professional Firefighters*

Rebuttal to Argument Against Proposition 140

Proposition 140 restores *true* democracy, gives you *real* choices of candidates, protects *your* rights to be represented by someone who knows and cares about *your* wishes. It opens up the political system so *everyone*—not just the entrenched career politicians—can participate.

Proposition 140 will bring new ideas, workable policies and fresh cleansing air to Sacramento. All are needed badly. A stench of greed and vote-selling hangs over Sacramento because lifetime-in-office incumbents think it's *their* government, not yours.

Californians polled by the state's largest newspaper say "most politicians are for sale," and "taking bribes is a relatively common practice" among lawmakers. Proposition 140 cuts the ties between corrupting special interest money and long-term legislators.

Why don't more people vote? Because incumbents have rigged the system in their favor so much, elections are meaningless. Even the worst of legislators get reelected 98% of the time. Honest, ethical, *truly* representative people who want to run for office don't stand a chance.

Who really opposes Proposition 140? It isn't ordinary people who have to work for a living. It's incumbent legislators and their camp followers. * * *

VOTE "YES!" ON PROPOSITION 140. ENOUGH, IS ENOUGH!

W. BRUCE LEE, II *Executive Director, California Business League*

LEE A. PHELPS *Chairman, Alliance of California Taxpayers*

ART PAGDAN, M.D. *National 1st V.P., Filipino-American Political Association*

A final note from your casebook editors: As is customary in California, the November 1990 ballot did not reprint the text of Proposition 140 or any of the pro and con arguments. Instead, the voters were given this question:

TERMS OF OFFICE. LEGISLATURE. INITIATIVE CONSTITUTIONAL AMENDMENT. Limits: terms of specified state elected officials, legislators' retirement, pensions. [The text continued to describe briefly the predicted financial impact of the proposal, as required by state law].

Yes ___ No ___

The measure passed by a margin of 52.17% to 47.83%. When you have finished your analysis, compare your conclusions with the published judicial opinions. See *Bates v. Jones*, 131 F.3d 843 (9th Cir. 1997) (en banc), reversing the panel opinion of *Jones v. Bates*, 127 F.3d 839 (9th Cir. 1997); *Legislature v. Eu*, 54 Cal.3d 492, 286 Cal. Rptr. 283, 816 P.2d 1309 (1991).

3. RECALL

CHANDLER V. OTTO
Supreme Court of Washington, 1984.
103 Wash. 2d 268, 693 P.2d 71.

[*Editors' note:* In considering this case, the reader may find useful the language of the Washington Constitution governing recall:

Recall of Elective Officers. Every elective public officer in the state of Washington except judges of courts of record is subject to recall and discharge by the legal voters of the state, or of the political subdivision of the state, from which he was elected whenever a petition demanding his recall, reciting that such officer has committed some act or acts of malfeasance or misfeasance while in office, or who has violated his oath of office, stating the matters complained of, signed by the percentages of the qualified electors thereof, hereinafter provided, the percentage required to be computed from the total number of votes cast for all candidates for his said office to which he was elected at the preceding election, is filed with the officer with whom a petition for nomination, or certificate for nomination, to such office must be filed under the laws of this state, and the same officer shall call a special election as provided by the general election laws of this state, and the result determined as therein provided. Wash. Const. Art. I, § 33 (amendment 8).

Same. The legislature shall pass the necessary laws to carry out the provisions of section thirty-three (33) of this article, and to facilitate its operation and effect without delay: Provided, That the authority hereby conferred upon the legislature shall not be construed to grant to the legislature any exclusive power of lawmaking nor in any way limit the initiative and referendum powers reserved by the people. * * * Wash. Const. Art. I, § 34 (also adopted as amendment 8).]

PEARSON, JUSTICE.

This case involves a recall petition filed against members of the Moses Lake City Council. The issue presented is whether the charges propounded in the petition allege sufficient grounds for recall. The trial court, pursuant to RCW 29.82.010, as amended by Laws of 1984, ch. 170, conducted a hearing to determine the sufficiency of the charges and adequacy of the ballot synopsis and concluded that the charges were sufficient. We hold that the recall charges were legally insufficient to serve as the basis for a recall election. Accordingly, we reverse the decision of the trial court.

The salient facts are as follows. In early 1984 the City of Moses Lake invited bids from interested persons desiring to contract with the City for the handling of the City's solid waste. The invitations for bids called for a bid opening on April 27, 1984. The bids were opened on that date and there were seven bidders. Superior Refuse Removal submitted the lowest bid. Shortly after the opening it was discovered that Superior's bid failed to fully comply with the invitation in that some of the pages were not signed as required. Similarly, the second lowest bidder, Western Refuse, had also failed to sign all the pages of its bid. The third lowest bidder was Lakeside Disposal. Lakeside had complied with the invitation and signed each proposal page.

At its regular meeting on May 22, 1984, the City Council considered the seven bids. After some discussion about whether the Council could waive the irregularities in the bids submitted by Superior Refuse and Western Refuse, the Council voted 4–3 not to waive the irregularities and awarded the contract to Lakeside Disposal as the lowest responsible bidder. Thereafter on July 12, 1984, a petition for recall was filed against each of the four councilmen who had voted to award the contract to Lakeside. The petition alleged the foregoing facts and contended that the actions of the councilmen were an abuse of discretion, done in contravention of the public interest, and would result in increased costs to the citizens of Moses Lake.

* * * On August 9, 1984, a hearing was held in the Superior Court for Grant County wherein the judge determined that the allegations contained in the recall petitions were sufficient to warrant proceeding with the recall election. The councilmen immediately appealed this decision.

Recall is the electoral process by which an elected officer is removed before the expiration of the term of office. Provisions for the recall of public officers did not appear in the Washington Constitution until 1912 when a constitutional recall referendum proposed by the State House of Representatives was passed by the voters. This amendment is the only constitutional recall provision that requires a showing of cause before recall will be allowed. In addition, Washington is one of only a few states that requires a recall petition to allege acts of malfeasance, misfeasance or a violation of the oath of office. These requirements indicate that the drafters of Washington's recall provision wanted to prevent recall elections from reflecting on the popularity of the political decisions made by elected officers.

In 1913 the Legislature passed the necessary laws to carry out the provisions of the new constitutional amendment. *See* RCW 29.82. The Legislature did not, however, define misfeasance, malfeasance, or violation of the oath of office. Nor did the Legislature suggest what might constitute cause. Because of this, interpretation of the unique requirements of Washington's recall provision has been the focus of over half the recall cases at the appellate level. These cases, in trying to interpret the right of recall, developed a narrow scope of review based on the court's traditional role of nonintervention in political controversies. *Cudihee v. Phelps*, 136 P. 367 (Wash. 1913); *McCormick v. Okanogan Cy.*, 578 P.2d 1303 (Wash. 1978). This scope of review has in most instances allowed the court to uphold nearly every recall petition. Such a narrow scope of review, however, disregards the apparent intent of the framers of the recall provision to limit the scope of the recall right to recall for cause. Furthermore, it has encouraged two abuses:

> (1)　The charges, though adequate on their face as cause for recall, may lack any factual basis whatsoever,
>
> (2)　The charge may be entirely unrelated to the dispute; the real political issue or dispute between the recall petitioners and the elective officer may be submerged beneath the rhetoric of the charge.

Cohen, [*Recall in Washington: A Time for Reform,*] 50 Wash. L. Rev. [29,] 30 [(1974)].

The narrow scope of review dictated by the vagueness of the enabling legislation has until recently prevented the courts from dealing with these abuses. Recent amendments to RCW 29.82, however, indicate that the Legislature has finally followed the suggestions of members of this court and has provided safeguards to protect an elected official from being subjected to the financial and personal burden of a recall election grounded on false or frivolous charges.

In 1976 * * * the specificity requirements were changed by adding the portions italicized below.

> Whenever any legal voter . . . shall desire to demand the recall and discharge of any elective public officer * * * under the provisions of sections 33 and 34 of Article 1 of the Constitution, he . . . shall prepare a typewritten charge, reciting that such officer . . . has committed an act or acts of malfeasance, or an act or acts of misfeasance while in office, or has violated his oath of office * * * which charge shall state the act or acts complained of in concise language, *giving a detailed description including the approximate date, location, and nature of each act complained of* . . .

(Italics ours.) RCW 29.82.010 (as amended by Laws of 1975, 2d Ex. Sess., ch. 47, § 1, p. 199).

RCW 29.82 was amended for a second time in 1984. First, in addition to believing a charge to be true, a petitioner must now *verify under oath that he or she has knowledge of the alleged facts upon which the stated grounds for recall are based.* (Italics ours.) Laws of 1984, ch. 170, § 1, p. 821. Second, the amendments codify the definitions of misfeasance, malfeasance, or violation of the oath of office in accordance with case law definitions:

(1) "Misfeasance" or "malfeasance" in office means any wrongful conduct that affects, interrupts, or interferes with the performance of official duty;

(a) Additionally, "misfeasance" in office means the performance of a duty in an improper manner, and

(b) Additionally, "malfeasance" in office means the commission of an unlawful act;

(2) "Violation of the oath of office" means the wilful neglect or failure by an elective public officer to perform faithfully a duty imposed by law.

Laws of 1984, ch. 170, § 1, p. 821. Third, a new section requires the recall petitioner to file the petition with a specified officer who will formulate a ballot synopsis. The preparer shall additionally certify and transmit the charges and the ballot synopsis to the superior court and shall petition the superior court to approve the synopsis and to determine the sufficiency of the charges. Hence, under the new statute the superior courts, rather than the prosecuting attorney, attorney general or Chief Justice of the Supreme Court, are entrusted with initially determining whether the charges are sufficient. A fourth section outlines the duties of the superior court.

Within fifteen days after receiving the petition, the superior court shall have conducted a hearing on and shall have determined, without cost to any party, (1) whether or not the acts stated in the charge satisfy the criteria for which a recall petition may be filed, and (2) the adequacy of the ballot synopsis. The clerk of the superior court shall notify the person subject to recall and the person demanding recall of the hearing date. Both persons may appear with counsel. The court may hear arguments as to the sufficiency of the charges and the adequacy of the ballot synopsis. *The court shall not consider the truth of the charges, but only their sufficiency.* An appeal of a sufficiency decision shall be filed in the supreme court as specified by RCW 29.82.160. The superior court shall correct any ballot synopsis it deems inadequate. Any decision regarding the ballot synopsis by the superior court is final. * * *

(Italics ours.) Laws of 1984, ch. 170, § 4, p. 823.

Our obligation in interpreting the foregoing amendments is to ascertain and give effect to the intent of the Legislature. The changes to RCW 29.82 are presumed to indicate a change in the legislative purpose behind recall petitions. We believe the changes indicate a legislative intent to place limits on the recall right, *i.e.,* to allow recall for cause yet free public officials from the harassment of recall elections grounded on frivolous charges or mere insinuations. We perceive the legislative amendments to mean that a recall petition must be both legally and factually sufficient.

Factually sufficient means the petition must comply with the specificity requirements of RCW 29.82.010. As noted [in a previous decision], "these statutory requirements ensure that both the public electorate and the challenged elective official will make informed decisions in the recall process." Factually sufficient indicates that although the charges may contain some conclusions, taken as a whole they do state sufficient facts to identify to the electors and to the official being recalled acts or failure to act which without justification would constitute a prima facie showing of misfeasance, malfeasance, or a violation of the oath of office.

Legally sufficient means that an elected official cannot be recalled for appropriately exercising the discretion granted him or her by law. To be legally sufficient, the petition must state with specificity substantial conduct clearly amounting to misfeasance, malfeasance or violation of the oath of office. 4 E. McQuillin, *Municipal Corporations* § 12.251b, at 334 (3d rev. ed. 1979).

In analyzing the recall petition in the instant case, we conclude that it is not legally sufficient. Pursuant to RCW 35.23.352–.353, members of Moses Lake City Council have the authority to let contracts, such as the one in question here, to the "lowest responsible bidder." This authority is well analyzed in 10 E. McQuillin, *Municipal Corporations* § 29.73, at 398 (3d rev. ed. 1981):

> Concerning the inquiry, how the responsibility is to be determined, "the authorities speak with practically one voice," namely, that the officers in whom the power is vested "must determine the fact, and such determination cannot be set aside unless the action of the tribunal is arbitrary, oppressive or fraudulent. The determination of the question of who is the lowest responsible bidder does not rest in the exercise of an arbitrary and unlimited discretion, but upon a bona fide judgment, based upon facts tending to support the determination." This view has in general been supported by the authorities. The determination of the municipal officials concerning the lowest responsible bidder will not be disturbed by the courts, unless it is shown to have been influenced by fraud, or unless it is an arbitrary, unreasonable misuse of discretion. When the officers have exercised their discretion in the award of the contract, the presumption obtains that such action was regular and lawful, and such presumption can be overcome only by proof that the officers acted without justification or fraudulently.

(Footnotes omitted.)

Respondent's recall petition fails to allege any fraud or arbitrary, unreasonable misuse of discretion. There is no evidence that the appellants exercised their discretion inappropriately. The petition merely attacks the judgment of the councilmen. The exercise of judgment is not grounds for recall. Hence, the petition does not state with specificity substantial conduct clearly amounting to misfeasance, malfeasance, or violation of the oath of office.

Accordingly, we reverse the decision of the trial court and direct a dismissal of the recall charges.

[A concurring opinion is omitted.]

DORE, JUSTICE (dissenting).

The majority affirms the action of the Moses Lake City Council in refusing to award a 5–year garbage contract to the lowest bidder but instead awarded it to the third lowest bidder, at an additional cost to the Moses Lake taxpayers of $3,000 a month, or $180,000 over the life of the contract. It is undisputed that both are competent contractors. The majority affirms the holding that the Council properly exercised its discretion. I disagree and would hold that the Moses Lake Council's actions were a manifest abuse of discretion, and I believe the citizens of Moses Lake, who have to pay the bill, would agree with me.

From the time this court first decided a case dealing with the recall right promulgated in Const. art. 1, §§ 33 and 34, to as recently as last year, we have always interpreted the recall provision broadly so as to allow the people to exercise their right of self-governance.

Only last year, we reaffirmed the principle that

> our constitution establishes a very broad right of the electorate to recall elective public officials. * * * The rights of initiative, referendum, and recall form a weighty triumvirate intended to preserve the people's most basic right of self-governance and any interference with these rights requires strong justification.

Pederson v. Moser, [662 P.2d 866 (Wash. 1983)]. This broad right of recall has manifested itself by providing the foundation for many of the rules which protect this basic right:

> First, in determining the validity of recall charges, courts are limited to examination of the charges stated and cannot inquire into factual matters extraneous to the allegations. Second, courts must assume the truth of the charges in determining whether legally sufficient grounds for recall have been stated. Third, just as there can be no inquiry into the truth or falsity of the charges, there can be no inquiry into the motives of those filing the charges. Fourth, recall charges are sufficiently specific if they are definite enough to allow the charged official to meet them before the tribunal of the people. Finally, any one sufficient charge requires the holding of a recall election.

State ex rel. Citizens Against Mandatory Bussing v. Brooks, [492 P.2d 536 (Wash. 1972)]. The majority now restricts this fundamental right. The majority provides two arguments to justify narrowing the recall right. First, it cites our constitutional requirement that a recall petition allege an act of malfeasance, or a violation of the oath of office. Not once, however, in the past 72 years has this court ever interpreted these requirements to mean that the right of recall should be narrowly construed. Indeed, in the past 72 years this court has always held that the constitution establishes a very broad right of recall. The majority fails to explain what prompted it to decide that over 70 years of case law interpreting the recall provision was wrong. Instead, it meekly states that our constitution requires that cause be shown for a recall election[3] and concludes, without providing any reasoning, that our right of recall has been construed too broadly in the past.

The second justification the majority narrates for its surprising interpretation of the recall provision is that the Legislature, in 1976 and 1984, amended the enabling legislation to the recall provision. The majority asserts that the amendments show that the Legislature intended to narrow the right of recall.[4] As to the 1976 amendment, the majority points to two changes that it asserts show that the Legislature intended to narrow the right of recall. First, it points out that the statute was amended to require that the official who is the subject of the recall receive a copy of the ballot synopsis. RCW 29.82.015. This provision, however, can hardly be characterized as narrowing the recall right. Secondly, the statute was amended to require the petitioner to give a detailed description of the changes, including the approximate date, location and nature of each act complained of. RCW 29.82.010. This provision is a procedural clarification and does not restrict the electorate's right of recall. Instead, it merely ensures that both the public and the challenged official will make an informed decision in the recall process.

* * *

The majority asserts that there was no abuse of discretion when the Moses Lake City Council refused to accept the lowest bid and, instead, accepted the third lowest bid. * * * It does not cite any cases to support its position; instead, it cites a treatise on municipal corporations which discusses *judicial review* of bid acceptances. The standard a court uses for reviewing an official's conduct is different from the standard the electorate uses for review. The majority may not feel that accepting a higher bid is an abuse of discretion but the voters of Moses Lake might find that the Council's award of a contract, for an additional windfall of $180,000 to the third bidder, was an abuse of discretion, especially when an equally competent contractor (low bidder) admittedly was available for $180,000 less.

* * *

---

[3] The majority erroneously asserts that our constitution is the only one in the nation that requires a showing of cause before recall will be allowed. That is simply untrue. West Virginia's constitution provides that

> All officers elected or appointed under this Constitution, may, unless in cases herein otherwise provided for, be removed from office for *official misconduct, incompetence, neglect of duty, or gross immorality, in such manner as may be prescribed by general laws,* . . .

(Italics mine.) W.Va. Const. art. 4, § 6. Moreover, while some state constitutions do not explicitly state that cause must be shown, their courts have construed their constitutional recall provisions to require that cause must be shown. *See, e.g., Amberg v. Welsh,* [38 N.W.2d 304 (Mich. 1949)]. Consequently, contrary to what the majority concludes, the drafters of our recall provision did not intend the recall right to be narrowly construed.

[4] The Legislature's authority to enact enabling legislation is limited and cannot be used to change the scope of recall right.

> The legislature shall pass the necessary laws to carry out the provisions of section thirty-three (33) of this article, and to facilitate its operation and effect without delay: *Provided, That the authority hereby conferred upon the legislature shall not be construed to grant to the legislature any exclusive power of lawmaking nor in any way limit the initiative and referendum powers reserved by the people.*

(Italics mine.) Const. art. 1, § 34.

I believe that the average person in Moses Lake, if allowed to vote, would find that the Council members who voted for the garbage "windfall" abused their discretion. The majority, by depriving such person of his constitutional right to recall public officials, unfortunately prohibits this.

I would affirm the trial court.

NOTES ON CHANDLER V. OTTO

1.   *The Value of Recall.* Consider R. Perry Sentell, Jr., *Remembering Recall in Local Government Law*, 10 Ga. L. Rev. 883, 886 (1976):

> [The value of recall] to the science of local government has been long debated. On the one side, the arguments are that it provides unremitting popular control over persons in public office; it permits the lengthening of terms of elective local officials with the least possible risk; it encourages principles of both responsibility and responsiveness; and it maintains public interest and confidence in the process of government. Alternative contentions are that recall engenders political demoralization; that it can be invoked to displace conscientious officials and thus discourages their participation in government; and that its operation entails prohibitive public expense. That both perspectives are persuasive is manifested by the split of jurisdictions authorizing recall, as well as the varying extent of utilization even where it is authorized.

Although the recall tool is in the news primarily because of a few salient state-level recall efforts—including one that elected movie star Arnold Schwarzenegger as Governor of California in 2003—they are much more frequently used at the local level. Recall was first adopted at the municipal level when Los Angeles enacted it in 1903; five years later, the first recall process for state legislators was adopted in Oregon.[34] Nineteen states provide for recall at the state level, and 60% of cities have charters with recall provisions, which is more than provide for local initiative or popular referendum.[35] It is estimated that there have been 4,000 to 5,000 recalls at the local level, with three-fourths of these directed at members of city councils or school boards.[36]

Thus, *Chandler v. Otto* presents a typical recall situation aimed at local officeholders. Are there any characteristics of local politics that make recalls of officials here more necessary than at the state level? If local officials tend to face less competition, or have longer terms of office, could that explain the prevalence of the use of recall by frustrated constituents? Or are local politics more likely to give rise to hot-button issues—like zoning, selection of textbooks, or corruption in contracting—that a dedicated group of opponents can use to trigger a recall? What are the dynamics of a local recall election, in terms of turnout and campaigning, particularly given that they are held at times other than general elections or even broader primary elections?

---

[34]   Floyd Feeney, *The 2003 California Gubernatorial Recall*, 41 Creighton L. Rev. 37, 39–40 (2007).

[35]   See National Conference of State Legislatures, *Recall of State Officials* (June 6, 2012), http://www.ncsl.org/legislatures-elections/elections/recall-of-state-officials.aspx (for state figures); Richard Feiock & Seung-Bum Yang, *Factors Affecting Constitutional Choice: The Case of the Recall in Municipal Charters*, 37 State & Local Gov't Rev. 40, 41 (2005).

[36]   Rachel Weinstein, *You're Fired!: The Voters' Version of "The Apprentice": An Analysis of Local Recall Elections in California*, 15 S. Cal. Interdis. L.J. 131, 138 (2005).

2.   *Grounds for a Recall.* As the dissent in *Chandler v. Otto* correctly pointed out in a footnote, Washington is not the only state with a recall process that requires certain grounds for recall, although in most states a voter can begin the process for any reason (and usually that reason seems political). Michigan's constitution expressly states that "[t]he sufficiency of any statement of reasons or grounds * * * shall be a political rather than judicial question." Mich. Const., Art. II, § 8. One explanation for the political nature of recall in most states is that there are other methods available to evict state officials from office—for example, removal by impeachment, whereby certain high state officials may be impeached by a majority of the state house of representatives for misconduct, tried by the state senate, and convicted (that is, removed from office and disqualified from holding "any office of honor, trust or profit in the state") by a vote of a supermajority of the senators. In addition, statutory procedures set out provisions for removal for misconduct of officers not subject to impeachment. The Supreme Court of Colorado has explained that these methods of defrocking contemplate removal from office for cause, but that

> [r]ecall, on the other hand, may be used for a purely political reason. The purpose underlying recall of public officials for political reasons is to provide an effective and speedy remedy to remove an official who is unsatisfactory to the public and whom the electors do not want to remain in office, regardless of whether the person is discharging his or her duties consistent with his or her abilities and conscience.

Groditsky v. Pinckney, 661 P.2d 279, 283 (Colo. 1983). The court stated that "the power of recall is a fundamental constitutional right of Colorado citizens and the reservation of this power in the people must be liberally construed," and that "[i]t is not within the purview of courts to pass upon the sufficiency of the grounds in recall petitions." Is the Colorado approach superior to the Washington approach to recall demonstrated in *Chandler*? Would it matter to your answer what percentage of voters is required to initiate a recall election?

Thomas Cronin suggests that the recall petition should contain the names of the persons or groups sponsoring the petition and state why the official should be recalled. *Direct Democracy: The Politics of Initiative, Referendum, and Recall* 245–46 (1999). Moreover, there should be a "high signature requirement" (either the higher of 25% of those voting in the last election for the particular office or 20% of registered voters in general), to deter personal vendettas ending up imposing costly elections upon the public. Furthermore, elected officials should not be subject to recall during their first six months of office; this stops "sour-grapes" attacks upon them through the recall process. Finally, if a recall election results in the retention of an official, that official should be immune from another recall effort for six months. Cronin also suggests that some neutral, public body conduct a hearing concerning the merits of the proposed recall.

3.   *Recall and Campaign Finance: Lessons from the California and Wisconsin Gubernatorial Recalls.* We began this chapter by describing hybrid democracy; recalls are explicitly hybrid, combining a ballot question about the recall of an official with, sometimes simultaneously, the election of a successor. This frame provides a way to consider the regulation of campaign spending in candidate and ballot-measure campaigns, and we will explore that briefly in the context of the two recent recall efforts

directed at governors.[37] As background, review the material in Chapter 2, § 3, describing the current jurisprudential landscape shaping campaign finance laws.

Historically low approval ratings (21%) and an historically high budget deficit (more than $38 billion) led to the recall of California's Democratic Governor Gray Davis in 2003. The recall was initially backed mostly by anti-tax crusaders who used talk radio and the Internet to make their case. Once the movement began to gain momentum, a Republican member of the U.S. House of Representatives, Darrell Issa, decided to actively support the effort, contributing more than $1 million for the petition drive. Primarily using paid petition circulators, pro-recall forces submitted petitions with 1.36 million signatures, substantially more than the nearly 900,000 signatures required to trigger a recall election.

The recall election in California was historic not only because it was the first gubernatorial recall in California to qualify for a vote, but also because it was only the second time in U.S. history that a governor was successfully recalled.[38] The California recall election received a great deal of media attention throughout the country and the world because it was so unusual, and also because the main contender to succeed Davis was movie star Arnold Schwarzenegger. Under California state law, the names of Davis' potential successors appeared on the same ballot as the recall measure, but Davis could not be listed as a candidate; thus, voters decided whether to recall Davis at the same time that they chose his replacement if the recall passed. Not all states with the recall process structure the election in this way. Some states allow the target of the recall also to appear on the ballot as a candidate in the election for a successor. Some first hold the recall vote, and only if the recall succeeds is a subsequent election held to choose a new governor. In a few states, a successful recall results in a successor being appointed, usually from the same political party as the officeholder who was recalled.

The California recall election was also noteworthy because 135 candidates appeared on the recall ballot in the election to succeed the Governor. Candidates seeking ballot access needed to obtain only 65 signatures and pay $3,500 or obtain 10,000 signatures. That opened the door for the multitude of candidates, the majority of whom ran for reasons other than winning. A few were concerned with publicizing particular political issues or concerns. Some, like former child actor Gary Coleman, porn star Mary Carey, and melon-smashing comedian Gallagher, ran to enhance their visibility in other careers. More importantly for the result of the recall, the wide-open process for getting on the ballot allowed a candidate like Schwarzenegger, who is more liberal than many in his party on some issues, to bypass the usual route to a general election—the Republican Party's closed primary—and proceed directly to a final election.

The two-part ballot and the 135 candidates not only had the potential for a great deal of voter confusion, but also the possibility of a number of troubling election outcomes.[39] For example, because the successor to Davis needed only a plurality to win

---

[37] Much of this discussion is drawn from Elizabeth Garrett, *Campaign Finance in the Hybrid Realm of Recall Elections*, 97 Minn. L. Rev. 1654 (2013).

[38] The first instance occurred in 1921, when North Dakota recalled Governor Lynn Frazier. Arizona Governor Evan Mecham probably would have been recalled in the late 1980s had he not been impeached and removed from office by the legislature, which was reacting to the recall effort.

[39] For a discussion of the voter confusion that occurred in this recall, see Michael Alvarez, Melanie Goodrich, Thad Hall, Roderick Kiewiet & Sarah Sled, *The Complexity of the California Recall Election*, 37 PS: Pol. Sci. & Pol. 23, (Jan. 2004). See also Michael Alvarez, Roderick Kiewiet & Betsy Sinclair, *Rational Voters*

the office, there was a chance that the recall would barely succeed, and the next Governor would be elected by a relatively small plurality. In such a case, there could be more "no" votes on the recall than votes for the Governor-elect, a possibility that could undermine the legitimacy of the new administration. That scenario did not come to pass in California because Schwarzenegger won decisively with 48.6% of the votes, while only 44.6% of voters cast ballots against the recall (and therefore in support of Davis).

Only a decade later, in 2012, the country witnessed the third effort to recall a governor. Wisconsin Governor Scott Walker fought successfully to complete his term in the face of a recall sparked by a reaction to his support of state legislation that weakened collective-bargaining rights for government workers. Mounting a successful petition drive in Wisconsin is more difficult than in California: the threshold for signatures is higher (a number equal to 25% of voters in the last election versus 12%) and the period for circulation is shorter (60 days versus 150). It is noteworthy that Walker's foes collected more than 900,000 valid signatures—nearly double the 540,208 required—using volunteer circulators working in the cold Wisconsin winter.

Wisconsin's recall structure is significantly different from California's. A sufficient number of valid signatures on a recall petition in Wisconsin triggers a new election for the office. There is no separate vote on the recall itself; instead, there is a recall election for the office six weeks after the certification of the petitions, and the incumbent automatically appears as a candidate in that election unless he has resigned. If there are more than two candidates for the position, then a partisan recall primary is held six weeks after the certification and the recall election occurs four weeks after that primary. Access to the ballot is governed by the rules that apply in regular elections for the position.

In an election between Walker and Milwaukee Mayor Tom Barrett, the same opponent he defeated to win office in 2010, Walker won with more than 53% of the vote. Although some of the reasons for his victory are peculiar to this election, the Wisconsin system generally favors the incumbent more than the California process because of the automatic inclusion of the incumbent on the ballot and the higher hurdles for qualifying a recall for a vote. Perhaps the most favorable structural advantage stems from the campaign finance rules, however, which allow the incumbent in Wisconsin to raise unlimited amounts of money for particular uses during the campaign, while opponents are limited by the $10,000 cap on campaign contributions throughout the process. Walker used that advantage to raise about $30 million in a record-breaking $63–million campaign. In contrast, all the candidates involved in the California recall had the capacity to raise money through unlimited contributions, and all the major candidates took advantage of that loophole in the $80–million recall campaign there.

Both states have bifurcated campaign rules that apply to recalls because of their hybrid nature. Candidates running for the office are limited by the contribution limits that apply to the office ($21,200 in California in 2003, and $10,000 in Wisconsin) with respect to their campaign committees. However, campaign activities focused only on the recall process are regulated by the rules that apply in ballot-measure campaigns and thus are wholly unaffected by contribution caps, even if the committees are associated with active candidates. To understand how these rules played out, consider their

---

and the Recall Election, in *Clicker Politics* 87 (Shawn Bowler & Bruce Cain eds., 2006) (finding that "all but a small number of voters appear able to [make sense of the recall's two-question structure], and that they appear to have cast their ballots in a manner that was consistent with their preferences").

application to three different groups: the target of the recall, candidates during the replacement election, and committees active during the election but independent from the targets or candidates.

First, while Gray Davis was essentially a candidate, seeking to defeat the recall so he could stay in office, he was not listed as a candidate and was active only with respect to the ballot-measure portion of this recall process. California law expressly exempts the target of a recall from regulations on campaign contributions, other than disclosure, and Davis took advantage of that loophole to raise nearly $18.3 million though his anti-recall committee "Californians Against the Costly Recall of the Governor." Could California apply contribution limits to the target of a recall even though the incumbent cannot appear on the second part of the ballot? Isn't there the specter of *quid pro quo* corruption, given the close connection between defeating the recall and retaining office?

The different recall structure in Wisconsin meant that the target of the recall was subject to bifurcated rules. Governor Walker could raise money from unlimited contributions only with respect to expenses related to the recall petition and incurred before the recall election was certified. Once an election is certified, the target—who appears on the ballot as a candidate—is thereafter subject to contribution limits. Of course, many of the pre-certification expenditures play a role in retaining office; Walker spent most of his anti-recall money on broadcast ads and other political communications defending his performance, as well as on setting up campaign infrastructure that he used during the entire campaign. Separating the money he could raise from unlimited contributions and money subject to the gubernatorial limits was difficult because he collected it all in one committee, further blurring the lines.

Second, the candidates running to replace the targets of the recall faced different rules in the two states. In California, the two-part ballot—with simultaneously a vote on the recall and a vote on the replacement—meant that replacement candidates could set up separate committees focused only on the recall itself and spend money from those committees in ways that also helped their campaigns to succeed Davis should he be recalled. While the candidate committees were subject to contribution limits, the candidate-controlled recall committees were governed by ballot-measure campaign rules that did not include any caps. So, for example, Arnold Schwarzenegger had two committees: his candidate committee, which was limited to accepting contributions of $21,200, and his "Total Recall" committee, which supported the recall effort and raised $4.5 million through unrestricted contributions. Both committees ran advertisements that featured the candidate and communicated essentially the same message through slightly different words: Arnold should be the next Governor of the Golden State.

In Wisconsin, none of the candidates seeking to defeat Walker had the ability to raise money in unlimited amounts during the campaign. While it seems that the rules might have allowed them to do so before any recall was certified, none of them—even those seriously considering a run at that early stage—did so, perhaps because it was uncertain until the very end that the recall effort would succeed in triggering an election.

Could current campaign finance jurisprudence support contribution limits on any campaign-related activities of declared candidates in California, including their recall committees? Isn't there the same possibility of *quid pro quo* corruption with respect to contributions to a pro-recall committee and a candidate committee controlled by the same person? Does your answer suggest that more restrictions are constitutionally possible with respect to candidate-controlled committees involved in more traditional initiative campaigns? If a candidate sees an initiative as beneficial to her electoral success—perhaps by affecting turnout or enacting policy agendas she supports—and a supporter provides substantial financial backing for that ballot measure, is there an appearance of *quid pro quo* corruption sufficient to justify more regulation? Does the Wisconsin system—which essentially restricts all candidates other than the incumbent with respect to contributions—create an unequal playing field? Or should the incumbent enjoy favorable rules, at least to fight off a recall, given the disruption a recall causes in governance?

Third, consider independent committees involved in the recall as well as the election for a replacement: can they be subject to contribution caps? Neither Wisconsin nor California applies limits to contributions to such committees, and there was significant independent expenditure spending in both states. Independent expenditures in California's recall election exceeded $10.5 million, a figure that would no doubt have been higher had there not been other avenues for all major candidates to raise money through uncapped contributions. In Wisconsin, groups spent more than $30 million in independent expenditures or issue advertisements, with unions providing significant funding to Democratic challenger Tom Barrett. This independent spending arguably counterbalanced Governor Walker's spending from unlimited contributions earlier in the process.

Review the discussion of *Citizens United v. Federal Election Comm'n*, 558 U.S. 310 (2010), in Chapter 2, § 3B, particularly the holding by the majority that independent expenditures in federal candidate elections "do not give rise to corruption." Is there any way under current constitutional precedent to regulate contributions to independent committees active in recalls, other than through disclosure statutes? The appellate courts have concluded that there is not. See *Wisconsin Right to Life State Political Action Committee v. Barland*, 664 F.3d 139 (7th Cir. 2011) (concluding "after *Citizens United* there is *no* valid governmental interest sufficient to justify imposing limits on fundraising by independent expenditure organizations" in context of groups active in the recalls mounted against nine Wisconsin state senators); *Farris v. Seabrook*, 677 F.3d 858 (9th Cir. 2012) (drawing a parallel between independent-expenditure-only committees in candidate elections, governed by *Citizens United*, and recall committees unaffiliated with candidates to strike down Washington law that limited contributions to the latter).

As you devise a system of regulation for campaign spending in recall elections, assess the following questions. Is your proposal still bifurcated in ways that give certain candidates or groups substantial advantages? Are there arguments that can be mounted in the context of direct democracy—a governance system devised to attack disproportionate political influence of monied interests in our representative institutions—that might support more robust regulation in this realm? If not, what are the alternatives for those concerned about the role of money in these elections? And what does your analysis suggest for the local ordinances that apply to recalls in this realm and that often severely restrict contributions not only to the targets of the recall and candidates, but also to independent committees active in petition drives as well as the campaigns for replacements? Are those ordinances still constitutional after *Citizens United*? See *Citizens for a Clean Gov't v. City of San Diego*, 474 F.3d 647 (9th Cir. 2007) (considering the constitutionality of such sweeping restrictions—still in place but with higher thresholds—in San Diego before *Citizens United*).

Problem 4–6. Recalls might be seen as a way to hold elected officials accountable for decisions in office. Cronin describes this as "continuous accountability" because voters do not have to wait until the next election to express their displeasure. *Direct Democracy, supra,* at 133. He also provides another argument in support of the recall mechanism: "Recall offers a safety-valve mechanism for intense feelings." *Id.* at 134. The popular referendum is another tool of direct democracy that offers both those features but allows voters to target their disapproval to a particular action by public officials and avoid any disruption of an early election with a potential change of leadership. The issue that sparked the recall against Scott Walker—limiting collective-bargaining rights of public workers—gave rise to a popular referendum in nearby Ohio in November 2011. Like the effort in Wisconsin, proponents of stronger union rights obtained many more signatures than were required to put the referendum on the ballot, and the election was characterized by heavy campaign spending with more than $30 million raised by union supporters.[40] Unlike the case with the Wisconsin recall, however, those opposing reduced collective-bargaining rights won in the Ohio referendum battle: the law was overturned by the people with 62% voting for repeal. Consider these two mechanisms that allow the voters a voice after elected officials make controversial decisions. Which is more effective at expressing displeasure, and in what cases, if any, is each one appropriate? How does each affect the politician—in both of these cases first-term Republican governors—seen as responsible for the action if he remains in power after the vote? As you analyze these different methods of allowing voters a "veto" over policy decisions, the following three aspects of the cases may be relevant:

- The President of the Wisconsin AFL-CIO said during the petition drive to place the Walker recall on the ballot: "Unlike Ohio, Wisconsin workers do not have the opportunity to put a referendum on the ballot. Thankfully we have the right to recall."[41] If Wisconsin had allowed both recall and popular referendum, which one would opponents of the Governor have used? And what would have been the factors they considered as they made their choice? Keep in mind that California has a robust state-level referendum and initiative process, and yet opponents of Governor Davis still used the recall mechanism. Were there relevant differences in the motivations behind the two gubernatorial recalls?

- Exit polls in the Wisconsin gubernatorial election revealed significant voter disapproval of the recall process, which was seen as costly and disruptive. Sixty percent said that a recall was appropriate only in cases of official misconduct, and 10% rejected the recall mechanism entirely. A significant number of people who opposed Walker's actions with regard to

---

[40] See John Celock, *Ohio SB 5 Collective Bargaining Law Follows Efforts in Wisconsin and New Jersey*, Huffington Post, Sept. 21, 2011, http://www.huffingtonpost.com/2011/09/20/ohio-sb5–referendum-collective-%1Fbargaining_n_972321.html; Alex Altman, *The Lessons of Issue 2's Defeat in Ohio*, Time, Nov. 15, 2011, http://swampland.time.com/2011/11/15/the-lessons-of-issue–2s-defeat-in-ohio.

[41] David Ariosto, *Ohio Voters Repeal Law Limiting Union Rights, CNN Projects*, CNN.com, Nov. 8, 2011, http://www.cnn.com/2011/11/08/us/ohio-collective-bargaining-vote/index.html.

public unions also opposed the use of the recall.[42] Does that provide an explanation for the difference between the two outcomes?

- Finally, could opponents of laws limiting collective-bargaining rights of public employees use the third tool of direct democracy, the initiative, to obtain their objectives proactively rather than responding to unfavorable legislation through recall or popular referendum? Under what conditions might advocates consider using the initiative, and how are the dynamics of an initiative campaign different from the campaigns surrounding the other mechanisms? For an example of this approach, consider the campaign in fall 2012 in Michigan to pass a ballot measure supported by unions to amend the state constitution to guarantee public and private-sector employees the right to organize and collectively bargain. Proposal 2 was defeated with only 42% of voters supporting the initiative in a state with some of the strongest unions in the country. Moreover, heartened by the result of the initiative, Republican lawmakers led a successful effort to enact "right to work" legislation, long opposed by organized labor, signed into law by Republican Governor Rick Snyder in December 2012.[43] Thus, the Michigan situation, like the statewide recalls in California and Wisconsin and referendum in Ohio, provides yet another example of hybrid democracy.

---

[42] E.J. Dionne, Jr., *Wisconsin's Dangerous Result*, Wash. Post, June 6, 2012, http://articles.washington post.com/2012–06–06/opinions/35460549_1_wisconsin-outcome-three-republican-state-senators-wisconsin-voters.

[43] Amanda Terkel, *Rick Snyder: Right to Work Bills Signed Into Law in Michigan*, Huff. Post, Dec. 11, 2012, http://www.huffingtonpost.com/2012/12/11/rick-snyder-right-to-work_n_2280050.html.

CHAPTER 5

STATUTES AS A SOURCE OF PUBLIC POLICY AND LEGAL PRINCIPLE

■ ■ ■

Chapters 1 through 4 introduced you to theories of legislatures—who is in them, how they are organized, what incentives legislators have. The four chapters following this one focus on theories of how the statutory product, i.e., legislation, is implemented and applied. How do courts interpret statutes when agencies are not primarily involved (Chapters 6 and 7)? How are agencies constituted and in what ways do they perform their critical role of statutory implementation (Chapter 8)? How do agencies interact with courts in statutory interpretation (Chapter 9)?

Traditional American *legisprudence*[1] was of two minds about statutes. As a formal matter, it treated statutes as a superior source of law. Our Constitution reflects this: Article I vests "[a]ll legislative Powers" in the Congress, Article II commands that the President and the executive branch "shall take Care that the Laws be faithfully executed," and Article III assures that the "judicial Power" shall be available to adjudicate cases and controversies. State constitutions either explicitly or implicitly set forth the same division. Clearly, the primary lawmaking power is vested in the legislature; the executive implements statutes, and courts exist to interpret and apply them in specific cases.

On the other hand, the formal superiority of statutes over executive and judicial decisions did not prevent traditional legisprudes from considering statutes functionally inferior to judicial decisions, which were treated as the primary source of legal reasoning and policy guidance. Several provisions of the Constitution (such as the Ex Post Facto, Bill of Attainder, and Contract Clauses) explicitly restrict the power of federal or state legislatures to enact statutes which operate retroactively, while there are no such restrictions on judicial decisions. Some state constitutions simply prohibit any and all "retrospective" laws. The reason: Statutes are "political" intrusions into the body politic and create new and unexpected rights and duties, but judicial decisions merely "declare" what the "law" (whether common law or statutory law) already was. Of course, the power of judicial review threatens statutes with invalidation if their political will falls athwart the Constitution, as interpreted by courts. Even the separation of powers precept seems to work against the functional importance of statutes. Although the legislature has the power to enact statutes, it must rely on the executive and the judiciary to enforce and apply them.

---

[1] This term describes the systematic analysis of statutes within the framework of jurisprudential philosophies about the role and nature of law. See Julius Cohen, *Towards Realism in Legisprudence*, 59 Yale L.J. 886 (1950).

The classical vision of the formal primacy but functional inferiority of statutes has become outdated in the past century, as America has transitioned from a common law polity to a *republic of statutes*.[2] There was an intellectual shift in legisprudential emphasis systematized by the so-called "legal process" scholars and jurists after World War II. Legal process theory emphasizes the duty of government institutions to operate within their realm of institutional competence but defines that realm quite flexibly; the purpose of all branches of government is to cooperate in the creation of dynamic and rational public policy. Under legal process precepts, statutes reflect the purposive and reason-centered goals of the state. Section 1 will offer a brief history of legisprudence, through the prism of a central issue: What is the relationship between statutes and the common law?

Sections 2 and 3 explore the implications of legal process theory for important doctrinal issues about the American practice of *stare decisis* in statutory cases and the differences in retroactive effect given to judicial decisions and statutes. Legal process theory may have been the most sustained intellectual accomplishment in legal theory in the twentieth century, but (as suggested in Section 1 and developed in Sections 2 and 3) legal process theory has left an ambiguous heritage. In practice, its prescriptions have not been followed; the U.S. Supreme Court and most state courts continue to follow more purely formalistic modes of thought. In theory, legal process thought has been attacked from several directions, leaving its conceptual validity in dispute.

1. STATUTES AS SOURCES OF LEGAL PRINCIPLE (LEGISPRUDENCE FROM BLACKSTONE TO LEGAL PROCESS)

A. COMMON LAW AND STATUTES, 1890–1940[3]

Legisprudence in the common law era can be understood by examining 1 William Blackstone, *Commentaries on the Laws of England* 63–92 (1765). Judges, Blackstone's "depositories of law," must and do decide cases according to objective rules—that is, rules that are known to everyone beforehand and do not arbitrarily favor one person or group over another. Judges do not "make" law; they simply "declare" the existing objective law (whether it be written statute or prior decisions). Blackstone readily admitted the preeminence of legislation. Judges apply statutes, not because they reflect principles of natural order, but because they are dictates of sovereign will; as opposed to "reasoned" judicial decisions, statutes are intrusions into the organic law. (They are "in" but not "of" the law.) They are political, not principled. Blackstone saw law as deeply reflecting as well as preserving the social order. Law rooted in the society's culture and history is stable,

---

[2]   William Eskridge Jr. & John Ferejohn, *A Republic of Statutes: The New American Constitution* (2010).

[3]   This part is adapted from William Eskridge Jr. & Philip Frickey, *Historical and Critical Introduction*, to Henry Hart Jr. & Albert Sacks, *The Legal Process: Basic Problems in the Making and Application of Law* (Eskridge & Frickey eds., 1994) (1958 tent. ed.); Neil Duxbury, *Faith in Reason: The Process Tradition in American Jurisprudence*, 15 Cardozo L. Rev. 601 (1993). We also found instructive David Rabban, *Law's History: American Legal Thought and the Transatlantic Turn to History* (2013), as well as Brian Tamanaha, *Beyond the Formalist-Realist Divide: The Role of Politics in Judging* (2009)

gives citizens advance notice of its application, and can be relied upon by private actors.

Blackstone's legisprudence contrasted reasoned, ordered, objective, eternal, principled *judicial decisions*, against willful, disorderly, subjective, contingent, changing, political *legislative decisions*. Central was the idea that statutes are formally but not functionally superior sources of law. A corollary to Blackstone's basic vision is that statutes (reflecting current political decisions) should not be treated as sources for legal reasoning, while judicial decisions (embedded in the polity's culture and history) should be. Statutes are ad hoc, while judicial decisions are part of an historical pyramid. Similarly, statutes are only effective after their enactment, while judicial decisions are effective retroactively, because they are thought to be just statements of pre-existing law.

A final corollary is that statutes should be narrowly construed. Because it was assumed that no reasoning process was involved in formulating statutes, it fell to judges to squeeze the political aims of the legislature into the interstices of the organic law; relatedly, statutes in derogation of the common law were to be narrowly construed. The latter maxim neatly encapsulates the view of late nineteenth century common law formalists that judge-made law, which Justice Holmes sarcastically described as "a brooding omnipresence in the sky," *Southern Pacific Co. v. Jensen*, 244 U.S. 205, 222 (1917) (Holmes, J., dissenting), was a relatively closed, rational, objective system which brooked minimal interference from half-baked statutory trespassers.[4] See *Swift v. Tyson*, 41 U.S. 1 (1842) (Story, J.) (applying this concept to justify federal common law applicable in diversity cases).

Nineteenth-century legal thinkers re-presented the Blackstonian understanding of law as one rooted in organic society, whose evolving needs were addressed by the common law. See David Rabban, *Law's History: American Legal Thought and the Transatlantic Turn to History* 325–80 (2013). Even as updated, this understanding was challenged in the twentieth century, as statutes swiftly displaced the common law as the source of policy, law, and even principle. See *Erie R. Co. v. Tompkins*, 304 U.S. 64 (1938) (overruling *Swift* and renouncing the notion of a "general federal common law" that displaces state positive law in diversity cases).

1. *Law as Policy.* Justice Oliver Wendell Holmes Jr. was an important critic of the Blackstonian understanding of law.[5] Holmes's articles and opinions viewed law as the product of social struggle, a view in striking contrast to the claim that law was an apolitical, neutral set of rules. This clash was best illustrated in the labor cases of the period, in which courts relied on vested rights of property and freedom of contract to justify injunctions against labor activity and invalidation of labor-protective legislation. Holmes dissented from this judicial practice, positing that the cases submerged a conflict between two legally acknowledged "rights": the

---

[4] See Grant Gilmore, *The Ages of American Law* 62–63 (1977); John Goldberg & Benjamin C. Zipursky, *Seeing Tort Law from the Internal Point of View: Holmes and Hart on Legal Duties*, 75 Fordham L. Rev. 1563 (2006).

[5] See Rabban, *Law's History*, 215–68; G. Edward White, *Justice Oliver Wendell Holmes: law and the Inner Self* (1993); Thomas Grey, *Holmes and Legal Pragmatism*, 41 Stan. L. Rev. 787 (1989).

freedom of contract right (which courts recognized) and the right to free economic competition (equally supported by precedent but suppressed in the labor cases). Notwithstanding judges' characterization of these decisions as apolitical and predetermined by precedent, Holmes insisted that prior decisional law suggested no single answer, because the new labor controversies fit into more than one category. Hence, deductive reasoning could not resolve the labor cases. Holmes argued that experience, and not logic, is the life of the law; the goal of law should be pragmatic and utilitarian rather than formal and purely historical. See Holmes, *The Path of the Law* (1899).

Holmes's analysis inspired legal scholars of all stripes for the next two generations. Specifically, sociological jurisprudence and legal realism pursued both the deconstructive and constructive features of Holmes's critique of common law formalism.[6] Critical realists like Wesley Hohfeld, Felix Cohen, and Jerome Frank delighted in showing how there was no determinate way to move from the generalities of rules and precedents to one inevitable result in particular cases, and realists such as Robert Hale argued that the results in cases were more easily traceable to a commonly held judicial ideology than to any logical consistency. Constructively, some realists studied judicial behavior to ascertain consistent patterns, while others studied social phenomena as the best starting point for their regulation. Karl Llewellyn was exemplary of the latter; his work in sales law rested upon a deep understanding of custom and practice among businessmen.

By the 1930s, many scholars actively writing in American public law agreed with the proposition that law is the creation and elaboration of social policy. The policy theorists were also forming a tentative consensus around several corollaries to that axiom. One was that law itself has social purposes that must be understood and evaluated along criteria that are not exclusively legal. Whatever its source, law should be instrumental toward some collective purpose. A further implication of the view that law is policy was that scholars questioned the judge-centered nature of Anglo-American law. Although some realists wrote mainly about common law policymaking, the sorry performance of the Supreme Court as a policymaking institution between 1894 and 1937—the era of *Lochner* and the labor injunction— made this an unattractive aspiration for law. Critics argued that the Supreme Court's statutory and constitutional decisions were both illegitimate and stupid policymaking.[7] The Court's decisions were illegitimate, because they represented policy choices by unelected judges who refused to give full effect to the policy preferences of elected legislators. The Court's choices were stupid policy as well, because the complicated social problems of industrial America were beyond the ken of common law judges; legislative policy preferences on such issues were presumptively to be preferred. The role of courts in a democratic society should be the elaboration and application of statutory policy, rather than the direct creation of public policy in the common law.

---

[6] See Laura Kalman, *Legal Realism at Yale, 1927–1960* (1986); Rabban, *Law's History*, 423–519; William Twining, *Karl Llewellyn and the Realist Movement* (2d ed. 1985); Gary Peller, *The Metaphysics of American Law*, 73 Calif. L. Rev. 1151 (1985).

[7] See, e.g., Roscoe Pound, *Mechanical Jurisprudence*, 8 Colum. L. Rev. (1908).

2.   *Institutional Responsibilities in the Modern Regulatory State.* Common law theories were superseded by theories of the regulatory state. Here, there were two seminal figures: Louis Brandeis and Felix Frankfurter.[8] They developed affirmative theories of government, especially of the institutional architecture of the modern administrative state. Brandeis was the leading intellectual force behind Woodrow Wilson's New Freedom programs for policing market abuses, and Frankfurter and his students played a similar role during the New Deal. While both had substantive theories of regulation, it was their theories of institutional architecture and process that were the more important contribution to American public law.

The difference between Holmes's law-is-policy viewpoint and Brandeis's law-is-policy-but-also-institutional-architecture viewpoint is illustrated in *International News Service v. Associated Press*, 248 U.S. 215 (1918). The issue was whether the Associated Press (AP) held a protected property interest in news stories it generated and was entitled to an injunction against theft of those stories by International News Service (INS), a rival news service. The opinion for the Court was a typical exercise in common law reasoning, deciding that AP was entitled to an injunction because its investment of time, effort, and resources in generating the news stories was analogous to other efforts treated as property. The Court's assumption of a preexisting concept of property was challenged in Holmes's concurring opinion, which argued that property is a consequence and not an antecedent of law. The issue for him was whether state policy would be advanced by recognizing rights in newsgathering; he decided that it was worth it, in order to encourage this socially productive activity.

Brandeis agreed with Holmes that there is no natural category, "property," and that the decision whether to characterize news stories in this way depends upon a balancing of the consequences of the different positions. But Brandeis dissented on the ground that the policy balancing required by Holmes was best done by the legislature and not the judiciary:

> [W]ith the increasing complexity of society * * * the problems presented by new demands for justice cease to be simple. Then the creation or recognition by courts of a new private right may work serious injury to the general public, unless the boundaries of the right are definitely established and wisely guarded. In order to reconcile the private right with the public interest, it may be necessary to prescribe limitations and rules for its enjoyment; and also to provide administrative machinery for enforcing the rules. It is largely for this reason that, in the effort to meet the many new demands for justice incident to a rapidly changing civilization, resort to legislation has latterly been had with increasing frequency. * * *

> Courts are ill-equipped to make the investigations which should precede a determination of the limitations which should be set upon any property right in news or of the circumstances under which news gathered by a private agency should be deemed affected with a public interest. Courts

---

[8]   See Leonard Baker, *Brandeis and Frankfurter: A Dual Biography* (1984); Robert Burt, *Two Jewish Justices: Outcasts in the Promised Land* (1988); Thomas McCraw, *Prophets of Regulation: Charles Francis Adams, Louis D. Brandeis, James M. Landis, Alfred E. Kahn* (1984).

would be powerless to prescribe the detailed regulations essential to full enjoyment of the rights conferred or to introduce the machinery required for enforcement of such regulations. Considerations such as these should lead us to decline to establish a new rule of law in the effort to redress a newly-disclosed wrong, although the propriety of some remedy appears to be clear.

Thus Brandeis deepened Holmes's critique of the *Lochner* judiciary: its decisions were not only analytically misleading, poor policy choices, and undemocratic, but also reflected a power grabbiness that was beyond the competence of the judiciary and indeed dangerously debilitating to the entire system of government.

Frankfurter and James Landis applied this idea of institutional specialization to develop a defense of the key feature of the modern regulatory state—lawmaking by agencies. Frankfurter maintained that government's aspiration to develop useful policies depended not only upon the enactment of good legislation and judicial deference to those legislative judgments (Holmesian points), but much more upon their elaboration and application by an expert administration. Neither the legislature nor the judiciary was competent to make all the technical, fact-bound judgments necessary for the regulatory process, tasks an agency filled with specially trained experts was particularly competent to fulfill. Expertise not only solved problems, but offered neutral criteria for the solution of problems, which obviated democratic theory concerns with broad legislative delegations to agencies. This is, of course, precisely what happened during the New Deal, which Brandeis defended within the Court, Frankfurter helped craft as an adviser to the President, and Landis (just after his appointment as Dean at Harvard) defended in Yale's 1938 Storrs Lectures on *The Administrative Process*.

3. *Statutes, Reason, and Legal Principles.* The New Deal was the death knell for the belief that law is and ought to be backward-looking. Precisely the opposite was the case: Because law structured the market and had pervasive effects on the community, the law is and ought to be forward-looking. Many of the realists, especially those who served in the New Deal, believed that law's legitimacy rested upon its instrumental value, its ability to deliver good policy. But there was another way of looking at law's legitimacy once one rejected common law formalism, and that other way was the rationalist tradition in American law.

In his Storrs Lectures, Judge Benjamin Cardozo agreed with Holmes that judges create law but maintained that "some principle, however unavowed and inarticulate and subconscious, has regulated" such creation. The judge "is not free to innovate at pleasure. * * * He is to draw his inspiration from consecrated principles." Cardozo, *The Nature of the Judicial Process* (1921). Principles emerge from the testing, retesting, and reformulation process of common law judging, in which an accepted principle "becomes a datum, a point of departure, from which new lines will be run, from which new courses will be measured" and "principles that have served their day expire, and new principles are born." Implicitly assuming that law's legitimacy is tied in some way to reason, Cardozo suggested that the effect of statutes will be tempered by principle.

Roscoe Pound had earlier suggested another consequence: Statutes in turn could be a source of principle. He argued in *Common Law and Legislation*, 21 Harv. L. Rev. 383, 385–86 (1908):

> Four ways may be conceived of in which courts in such a legal system as ours might deal with a legislative innovation. (1) They might receive it fully into the body of the law as affording not only a rule to be applied but a principle from which to reason, and hold it, as a later and more direct expression of the general will, of superior authority to judge-made rules on the same general subject; and so reason from it by analogy in preference to them. (2) They might receive it fully into the body of the law to be reasoned from by analogy the same as any other rule of law, regarding it, however, as of equal or co-ordinate authority in this respect with judge-made rules upon the same general subject. (3) They might refuse to receive it fully into the body of the law and give effect to it directly only; refusing to reason from it by analogy but giving it, nevertheless, a liberal interpretation to cover the whole field it was intended to cover. (4) They might not only refuse to reason from it by analogy and apply it directly only, but also give to it a strict and narrow interpretation, holding it down rigidly to those cases which it covers expressly. The fourth hypothesis represents the orthodox common law attitude toward legislative innovations. Probably the third hypothesis, however, represents more nearly the attitude toward which we are tending. The second and first hypotheses doubtless appeal to the common law lawyer as absurd. He can hardly conceive that a rule of statutory origin may be treated as a permanent part of the general body of the law. But it is submitted that the course of legal development upon which we have entered already must lead us to adopt the method of the second and eventually the method of the first hypothesis.

Justice Harlan Stone likewise argued that there is "no adequate reason for our failure to treat a statute much more as we treat a judicial precedent, as both a declaration and source of law, and as a premise for legal reasoning."[9]

While virtually all of the new theorists of the regulatory state accepted the proposition that law is policy creation and must be forward-looking, the role of principle was much contested in the 1930s. Many legal realists made sport of the role of principles, viewing them as simply a kind of formalism. Rationalists insisted that reason in law was what differentiated American law from, say, Nazi law (which like the realists' vision was policy-centered).[10]

Perhaps the most sophisticated analysis was Lon Fuller's Rosenthal Lectures, published as *The Law in Quest of Itself* (1940) Fuller argued against the prevailing positivism of American law. He maintained that fact could not be separated from

---

[9] Harlan Stone, *The Common Law in the United States*, 50 Harv. L. Rev. 4, 12–13 (1936). See also James Landis, *Statutes as the Sources of Law*, in *Harvard Legal Essays* 213 (1934) (urging revival of civil law concept, "equity of a statute").

[10] See Edward Purcell Jr., *The Crisis of Democratic Theory: Scientific Naturalism and the Problem of Value* (1973); David Bixby, *The Roosevelt Court, Democratic Ideology, and Minority Rights: Another Look at United States v. Classic*, 90 Yale L.J. 741 (1981).

value, and law could not be separated from moral evaluation—"in the moving world of law, the *is* and the *ought* are inseparably linked." *Id.* at 64. What facts get noticed, how they are interpreted and assembled depends upon values and is useless without integration into a normative framework, Fuller claimed; conversely, the normative framework itself is influenced by what one perceives to be possible in the world and by a variety of facts that one has collected from experience. This was an organic theory of law as "purposive." When law fails to fulfill worthy goals it falls short of being law, just as a steam engine that does not work might be junked.

Theorists in the 1930s also maintained that issues of law's relationship to democracy should be central. Again reflecting the views of his contemporaries, Fuller emphasized that a democracy had to be committed to organic principles. Indeed, what most distinguishes democratic society from a totalitarian one is the former's commitment to free exchange of ideas. See *id.* at 122–23, 126. Fuller also suggested that defining and implicitly valorizing law as nothing more than power (the realists' positivism) was corrupting of a polity, for it may induce people to behave in that way. Once a polity accepts a philosophy of "I'll obey the law only because I have to," it is encouraging its citizens to think, "I'll get away with what I can." In contrast, a polity based upon organic principle (Fuller's philosophy) vests the citizenry with responsibility for the law. That responsibility might induce the population to behave in a principled and cooperative way.

B. THE LEGAL PROCESS ERA, 1940–1973

Justices Brandeis, Cardozo, and Frankfurter were godparents to the approach to law that crystallized in the period just before World War II and dominated American law after the war. Many legal philosophers contributed to this school of thought, notably Lon Fuller, Willard Hurst, Louis Jaffe, Walter Gellhorn, and Herbert Wechsler. The most complete elaboration of its vision was in Henry Hart and Albert Sacks' teaching materials, *The Legal Process: Basic Problems in the Making and Application of Law*, which took their final mimeographed form in 1958.[11] The Hart and Sacks synthesis sought the best of each pre-war tradition, without its drawbacks. Hart and Sacks' view of law as policy tried to avoid the realists' conclusion that law is nothing but politics and whimsy. They incorporated the idea of comparative institutional competence but eschewed a conception bereft of substantive evaluation. And the materials viewed law in terms of reasons, coherence, and rationality, without lapsing into natural law modes of thought.

1. *The Reasoned Elaboration of Purposive Law.* Hart and Sacks posited a New Deal-inspired theory of society different from traditional liberal (social contract) theory. Central to society is people's recognition of "the fact of their interdependence with other human beings and the community of interest that

---

[11] The 1958 "tentative edition" has been published as Henry Hart Jr. & Albert Sacks, *The Legal Process: Basic Problems in the Making and Application of Law* (William Eskridge Jr. & Philip Frickey eds. 1994), and all citations are to this published edition. This part draws upon the *Historical and Critical Introduction* Eskridge and Frickey wrote for that edition. Other useful sources are Charles Barzun, *The Forgotten Foundations of Hart and Sacks*, 99 Va. L. Rev. 1 (2013); Duxbury, *Faith in Reason, supra*; Gary Peller, *Neutral Principles in the 1950's*, 21 U. Mich. J.L. Ref. 561 (1988); Jan Vetter, *Postwar Legal Scholarship on Judicial Decision Making*, 33 J. Legal Educ. 412 (1983).

grows out of it. So recognizing, people form themselves into groups for the protection and advancement of their common interests * * *." Hart & Sacks, *The Legal Process,* 2. The state is one of several institutions thus formed, but it is also the "overriding general purpose group" which has the greatest power, and the greatest responsibility, for "establishing, maintaining and perfecting the conditions necessary for community life to perform its role in the complete development of man." *Id.* at 102. In accord with this activist view of the state, Hart and Sacks posited: "Law is a doing of something, a purposive activity, a continuous striving to solve the basic problems of social living." *Id.* at 148.

Law's purposiveness generated Hart and Sacks' theory of "reasoned elaboration." *Id.* at 145–52. General directives often do not transparently tell officials and citizens what to do in specific situations, but Hart and Sacks sharply disputed the realist claim that this lack of easy transparency meant that the official simply imposed a political interpretation on the general directive. To the contrary, an official applying a "general directive arrangement" must "elaborate the arrangement in a way which is consistent with the other established applications of it" and "must do so in a way which best serves the principles and policies it expresses." *Id.* at 147. Hart and Sacks extended this idea to legal interpretation. A judge interpreting common law precedents has a responsibility to draw from those precedents some rule, principle, or standard, a responsibility that is only fulfilled if the judge reads the precedents, and the law generally, to figure out what purposes they serve. *Id.* at 397–403. A judge interpreting a statute must first identify the purpose of the statute, what policy or principle it embodies, and then reason toward the interpretation most consistent with that policy or principle. *Id.* at 148–50, 1149–71.

2. *Law as an Institutional System; Rules and Standards, Policies and Principles.* As a purposive system, law contains a number of "substantive understandings or arrangements" to coordinate people's conduct. But Hart and Sacks emphasized the greater importance of the "constitutive or procedural understandings or arrangements" by which the substantive arrangements are applied, interpreted, and changed. *Id.* at 3. Broad dispersion of decisionmaking is the most practical way to proceed. Because of the "boundless and unpredictable variety" of our dynamic society, they asserted that "private ordering is the primary process of social adjustment." *Id.* at 161–63. To the extent that private ordering does not work, Hart and Sacks contemplated an interaction between private and public institutions—allocated according to their relative "competence" to handle the matter. For example, although they accepted the conventional view that the common law is the "initial resort" for problems not solved privately, Hart and Sacks were concerned "as much with the shortcomings of the common law as a form of law as with its merits" and sought "to lay a foundation for an understanding of the frequent need for one of the more sophisticated types of administered regulation or non-regulatory control." *Id.* at 342.

Hart and Sacks then explored the ways in which legislated policy choices and implementational discretion interact. One way is through the choice of rules versus standards. *Id.* at 138–41. If the legislature decides to deal with a social problem through specific rules, it is expressing its confidence that it has sufficient information to solve the social problem. If the legislature is unsure of how to proceed, it will adopt a standard, essentially delegating rulemaking responsibilities to courts, agencies, or private institutions. Even when a statute simply sets forth a policy or objective, official discretion is usually limited by more specific statements of a policy or by an underlying "principle," or a policy supported by reasons it will be good for society. If underlying statutory policy is ambiguous, "the official should interpret it in the way which best harmonizes with more basic principles and policies of law." *Id.* at 147. Thus, basic principles and policies form the basis for extending a rule or statute to a novel context, *id.* at 362–83; reformulating old rules or provisions, *id.* at 383–403; and even replacing prior rules or practices with new ones. *Id.* at 545–70.

3. *The Centrality of Process.* In a government of dispersed power and diverse views about substantive issues, frequently "the substance of decision cannot be planned in advance in the form of rules and standards," but "the procedure of decision commonly can be." *Id.* at 154. Procedure is practically important in three different ways. To begin, a procedure "which is soundly adapted to the type of power to be exercised is conducive to well-informed and wise decisions. An unsound procedure invites ill-informed and unwise ones." The procedures that facilitate good policy decisions by the legislature, for example, are (1) openness to the views of all affected persons and groups, (2) focus on factual information subjected to expert and critical scrutiny, and (3) public deliberation through which the pros and cons are thoroughly discussed. *Id.* at 694–95. The suggestion that "the best criterion of sound legislation is the test of whether it is the product of a sound process of enactment" epitomized the legal process philosophy. *Id.* at 695.

Additionally, procedure is the means by which the interconnected institutional system works smoothly. Process also provides mechanisms for controlling discretion and for self-correction. For the administrative process, such safeguards include "the arrangements which prescribe the procedure to be followed in exercising * * * power; the information which must be secured; the people whose views must be listened to; the findings and justification of the decision which must be made; and the formal requisites of action which must be observed." *Id.* at 153–54. For the legislative process, the safeguards include the constitutional requirements of bicameralism and presentment, plus the rules and safeguards adopted voluntarily by Congress, and the "ultimate check" of the ballot box. *Id.* at 153–54, 157–58. For the judicial process, safeguards include the due process guarantees of notice, an impartial decisionmaker, and a right to appeal, as well as prudential limitations on the types of cases or controversies that courts will hear.

Last, process is critical to law's legitimacy. The "principle of institutional settlement" was, for Hart and Sacks, "the central idea of law" (*id.* at 4–5):

> The alternative to disintegrating resort to violence is the establishment of regularized and peaceable methods of decision. The principle of institutional settlement expresses the judgment that decisions which are the duly arrived at result of duly established procedures [for making decisions] of this kind ought to be accepted as binding upon the whole society unless and until they are changed. * * *

* * * When the principle of institutional settlement is plainly applicable, we say that the law "is" thus and so, and brush aside further discussion of what it "ought" to be. Yet the "is" is not really an "is" but a special kind of "ought"—a statement that, for the reasons just reviewed, a decision which is the duly arrived at result of a duly established procedure for making decisions of that kind "ought" to be accepted as binding upon the whole society unless and until it has been duly changed.

The philosophy laid out in *The Legal Process* has important implications for thinking about the relationship between the common law and statutes. Consider its application in the following opinion.

MORAGNE V. STATES MARINE LINES, INC.

Supreme Court of the United States, 1970.
398 U.S. 375, 90 S.Ct. 1772, 26 L.Ed.2d 339.

MR. JUSTICE HARLAN delivered the opinion of the Court.

[Edward Moragne, a longshoreman, was killed while working aboard the vessel *Palmetto State* in Florida's navigable waters. His surviving spouse sued the owner of the vessel for wrongful death, relying on theories of negligence and unseaworthiness. (Unseaworthiness is akin to strict liability: If the vessel is unseaworthy, the owner is liable even if it took reasonable precautions.) Moragne's widow was unlucky. Under virtually any other circumstance, she would have had an unseaworthiness claim. If her husband had died a league or more from Florida's shores, her claim would have been covered by the Death on the High Seas Act, 46 U.S.C. §§ 761–768, which permitted claims based on unseaworthiness. If her husband had died within the state's territorial waters as a result of the owner's negligence, she would have had a state law negligence claim in all state jurisdictions. And in the overwhelming majority of states, the wrongful death laws were construed to include unseaworthiness claims. That was not the case in Florida, however; its supreme court held that its wrongful death statute, originally enacted in 1833, before the federal courts established the tort of unseaworthiness, encompassed only traditional common law torts requiring a showing of fault, and that it was up to the legislature to make the changes in Florida law required to expand the statute beyond that.

[Federal maritime law overlaps with state tort law in a good many instances. Thus it would be entirely appropriate to sue for state law negligence and federal law unseaworthiness. But the U.S. Supreme Court held in *The Harrisburg*, 119 U.S. 199 (1886), that federal maritime law does not afford a cause of action for wrongful death.]

[I] The Court's opinion in *The Harrisburg* acknowledged that the result reached had little justification except in primitive English legal history—a history far removed from the American law of remedies for maritime deaths. That case, like this, was a suit on behalf of the family of a maritime worker for his death on the navigable waters of a State. [The lower courts afforded damages relief.] This Court, in reversing, relied primarily on * * * *Insurance Co. v. Brame*, 95 U.S. 754

(1878), in which it had held that in American common law, as in English, "no civil action lies for an injury which results in * * * death." In *The Harrisburg*, as in *Brame*, the Court did not examine the justifications for this common-law rule; rather, it simply noted that "we know of no country that has adopted a different rule on this subject for the sea from that which it maintains on the land," and concluded, despite contrary decisions of the lower federal courts both before and after *Brame*, that the rule of *Brame* should apply equally to maritime deaths. * * *

One would expect, upon an inquiry into the sources of the common-law rule, to find a clear and compelling justification for what seems a striking departure from the result dictated by elementary principles in the law of remedies. Where existing law imposes a primary duty, violations of which are compensable if they cause injury, nothing in ordinary notions of justice suggests that a violation should be nonactionable simply because it was serious enough to cause death. On the contrary, that rule has been criticized ever since its inception, and described in such terms as "barbarous." *E.g., Osborn v. Gilliett*, L.R. 8 Ex. 88, 94 (1873) (Lord Bramwell, dissenting); F. Pollock, Law of Torts 55 (Landon ed. 1951); 3 W. Holdsworth, History of English Law 676–677 (3d ed. 1927). Because the primary duty already exists, the decision whether to allow recovery for violations causing death is entirely a remedial matter. * * * One expects, therefore, to find a persuasive, independent justification for this apparent legal anomaly.

Legal historians have concluded that the sole substantial basis for the rule at common law is a feature of the early English law that did not survive into this century—the felony-merger doctrine. According to this doctrine, the common law did not allow civil recovery for an act that constituted both a tort and a felony. The tort was treated as less important than the offense against the Crown, and was merged into, or pre-empted by, the felony. The doctrine found practical justification in the fact that the punishment for the felony was the death of the felon and the forfeiture of his property to the Crown; thus, after the crime had been punished, nothing remained of the felon or his property on which to base a civil action. Since all intentional or negligent homicide was felonious, there could be no civil suit for wrongful death.

The first explicit statement of the common-law rule against recovery for wrongful death came in the opinion of Lord Ellenborough, sitting at *nisi prius*, in *Baker v. Bolton*, 1 Camp. 493, 170 Eng.Rep. 1033(1808). That opinion did not cite authority, or give supporting reasoning, or refer to the felony-merger doctrine in announcing that "[i]n a Civil court, the death of a human being could not be complained of as an injury." Nor had the felony-merger doctrine seemingly been cited as the basis for the denial of recovery in any of the other reported wrongful-death cases since the earliest ones, in the 17th century. However, it seems clear from those first cases that the rule *of Baker v. Bolton* did derive from the felony-merger doctrine, and that there was no other ground on which it might be supported even at the time of its inception. * * *

The historical justification marshaled for the rule in England never existed in this country. In limited instances American law did adopt a vestige of the felony-merger doctrine, to the effect that a civil action was delayed until after the criminal trial. However, in this country the felony punishment did not include forfeiture of property; therefore, there was nothing, even in those limited instances, to bar a subsequent civil suit. Nevertheless, * * * American courts generally adopted the English rule as the common law of this country as well. Throughout the period of this adoption, culminating in this Court's decision in *Brame*, the courts failed to produce any satisfactory justification for applying the rule in this country. * * *

The most likely reason that the English rule was adopted in this country without much question is simply that it had the blessing of age. That was the thrust of this Court's opinion in *Brame*, as well as many of the lower court opinions. Such nearly automatic adoption seems at odds with the general principle, widely accepted during the early years of our Nation, that while "[o]ur ancestors brought with them [the] general principles [of the common law] and claimed it as their birthright[,] * * * they brought with them and adopted only that portion which was applicable to their situation." *Van Ness v. Pacard*, 2 Pet. 137, 144 (1829) (Story, J.); *The Lottawanna*, 21 Wall. 558, 571–574 (1875); see R. Pound, The Formative Era of American Law 93–97 (1938); H. Hart & A. Sacks, The Legal Process 450 (tent. ed. 1958). The American courts never made the inquiry whether this particular English rule, bitterly criticized in England, "was applicable to their situation," and it is difficult to imagine on what basis they might have concluded that it was. * * *

[II] We need not, however, pronounce a verdict on whether *The Harrisburg*, when decided, was a correct extrapolation of the principles of decisional law then in existence. A development of major significance has intervened, making clear that the rule against recovery for wrongful death is sharply out of keeping with the policies of modern American maritime law. This development is the wholesale abandonment of the rule in most of the areas where it once held sway, quite evidently prompted by the same sense of the rule's injustice that generated so much criticism of its original promulgation. * * *

* * * The legislatures both here and in England began to evidence unanimous disapproval of the rule against recovery for wrongful death. The first statute partially abrogating the rule was Lord Campbell's Act, 9 & 10 Vict., c. 93 (1846), which granted recovery to the families of persons killed by tortious conduct, "although the Death shall have been caused under such Circumstances as amount in Law to Felony."

In the United States, every State today has enacted a wrongful-death statute. The Congress has created actions for wrongful deaths of railroad employees, Federal Employers' Liability Act, 45 U.S.C. §§ 51–59; of merchant seamen, Jones Act, 46 U.S.C. § 688; and of persons on the high seas, Death on the High Seas Act, 46 U.S.C. §§ 761, 762. Congress has also, in the Federal Tort Claims Act, 28 U.S.C. § 1346(b), made the United States subject to liability in certain circumstances for negligently caused wrongful death to the same extent as a private person.

These numerous and broadly applicable statutes, taken as a whole, make it clear that there is no present public policy against allowing recovery for wrongful death. The statutes evidence a wide rejection by the legislatures of whatever justifications may once have existed for a general refusal to allow such recovery. This legislative establishment of policy carries significance beyond the particular scope of each of the statutes involved. The policy thus established has become itself a part of our law, to be given its appropriate weight not only in matters of statutory construction but also in those of decisional law. See Landis, Statutes and the Sources of Law, in Harvard Legal Essays 213, 226–227 (1934). Mr. Justice Holmes, speaking also for Chief Justice Taft and Justices Brandeis and McKenna, stated on the very topic of remedies for wrongful death:

> "[I]t seems to me that courts in dealing with statutes sometimes have been too slow to recognize that statutes even when in terms covering only particular cases may imply a policy different from that of the common law, and therefore may exclude a reference to the common law for the purpose of limiting their scope. Without going into the reasons for the notion that an action (other than an appeal) does not lie for causing the death of a human being, it is enough to say that they have disappeared. The policy that forbade such an action, if it was more profound than the absence of a remedy when a man's body was hanged and his goods confiscated for the felony, has been shown not to be the policy of present law by statutes of the United States and of most if not all of the States." *Panama R. Co. v. Rock*, 266 U.S. 209, 216 (1924) (dissenting opinion).

Dean Pound subsequently echoed this observation, concluding that: "Today we should be thinking of the death statutes as part of the general law." Pound, Comment on State Death Statutes—Application to Death in Admiralty, 13 NACCA L.J. 188, 189 (1954).

This appreciation of the broader role played by legislation in the development of the law reflects the practices of common-law courts from the most ancient times. As Professor Landis has said, "much of what is ordinarily regarded as 'common law' finds its source in legislative enactment." Landis, *supra.* It has always been the duty of the common-law court to perceive the impact of major legislative innovations and to interweave the new legislative policies with the inherited body of common-law principles—many of them deriving from earlier legislative exertions.

The legislature does not, of course, merely enact general policies. By the terms of a statute, it also indicates its conception of the sphere within which the policy is to have effect. In many cases the scope of a statute may reflect nothing more than the dimensions of the particular problem that came to the attention of the legislature, inviting the conclusion that the legislative policy is equally applicable to other situations in which the mischief is identical. This conclusion is reinforced where there exists not one enactment but a course of legislation dealing with a series of situations, and where the generality of the underlying principle is attested by the legislation of other jurisdictions. On the other hand, the legislature may, in order to promote other, conflicting interests, prescribe with particularity the compass of the legislative aim, erecting a strong inference that territories beyond the boundaries so drawn are not to feel the impact of the new legislative dispensation. We must, therefore, analyze with care the congressional enactments that have abrogated the common-law rule in the maritime field, to determine the impact of the fact that none applies in terms to the situation of this case. See Part

III, *infra*. However, it is sufficient at this point to conclude, as Mr. Justice Holmes did 45 years ago, that the work of the legislatures has made the allowance of recovery for wrongful death the general rule of American law, and its denial the exception. Where death is caused by the breach of a duty imposed by federal maritime law, Congress has established a policy favoring recovery in the absence of a legislative direction to except a particular class of cases.

[III] Our undertaking, therefore, is to determine whether Congress has given such a direction in its legislation granting remedies for wrongful deaths in portions of the maritime domain. We find that Congress has given no affirmative indication of an intent to preclude the judicial allowance of a remedy for wrongful death to persons in the situation of this petitioner.

From the date of *The Harrisburg* until 1920, there was no remedy for death on the high seas caused by breach of one of the duties imposed by federal maritime law. For deaths within state territorial waters, the federal law accommodated the humane policies of state wrongful-death statutes by allowing recovery whenever an applicable state statute favored such recovery. Congress acted in 1920 to furnish the remedy denied by the courts for deaths beyond the jurisdiction of any State, by passing two landmark statutes. The first of these was the Death on the High Seas Act, 41 Stat. 537, 46 U.S.C. § 761 *et seq.* Section 1 of that Act provides that:

> "Whenever the death of a person shall be caused by wrongful act, neglect, or default occurring on the high seas beyond a marine league from the shore of any State, * * * the personal representative of the decedent may maintain a suit for damages in the district courts of the United States, in admiralty, for the exclusive benefit of the decedent's wife, husband, parent, child or dependent relative against the vessel, person, or corporation which would have been liable if death had not ensued."

Section 7 of the Act further provides:

> "The provisions of any State statute giving or regulating rights of action or remedies for death shall not be affected by this [Act]. Nor shall this [Act] apply to the Great Lakes or to any waters within the territorial limits of any State * * *."

The second statute was the Jones Act, 41 Stat. 1007, 46 U.S.C. § 688, which, by extending to seamen the protections of the Federal Employers' Liability Act, provided a right of recovery against their employers for negligence resulting in injury or death. This right follows from the seaman's employment status and is not limited to injury or death occurring on the high seas.

The United States, participating as *amicus curiae*, contended at oral argument that these statutes, if construed to forbid recognition of a general maritime remedy for wrongful death within territorial waters, would perpetuate three anomalies of present law. The first of these is simply the discrepancy produced whenever the rule of *The Harrisburg* holds sway: within territorial waters, identical conduct violating federal law (here the furnishing of an unseaworthy vessel) produces liability if the victim is merely injured, but frequently not if he is killed. As we have concluded, such a distinction is not compatible with the general policies of federal maritime law.

The second incongruity is that identical breaches of the duty to provide a seaworthy ship, resulting in death, produce liability outside the three-mile limit— since a claim under the Death on the High Seas Act may be founded on unseaworthiness, see *Kernan v. American Dredging Co.*, 355 U.S. 426, 430 n.4 (1958)—but not within the territorial waters of a State whose local statute excludes unseaworthiness claims. The United States argues that since the substantive duty is federal, and federal maritime jurisdiction covers navigable waters within and without the three-mile limit, no rational policy supports this distinction in the availability of a remedy.

The third, and assertedly the "strangest" anomaly is that a true seaman—that is, a member of a ship's company, covered by the Jones Act—is provided no remedy for death caused by unseaworthiness within territorial waters, while a longshoreman, to whom the duty of seaworthiness was extended only because he performs work traditionally done by seamen, does have such a remedy when allowed by a state statute.

There is much force to the United States' argument that these distinctions are so lacking in any apparent justification that we should not, in the absence of compelling evidence, presume that Congress affirmatively intended to freeze them into maritime law. There should be no presumption that Congress has removed this Court's traditional responsibility to vindicate the policies of maritime law by ceding that function exclusively to the States. However, respondents argue that an intent to do just that is manifested by the portions of the Death on the High Seas Act quoted above.

The legislative history of the Act suggests that respondents misconceive the thrust of the congressional concern. Both the Senate and House Reports consist primarily of quoted remarks by supporters of the proposed Act. Those supporters stated that the rule of *The Harrisburg*, which had been rejected by "[e]very country of western Europe," was a "disgrace to a civilized people." "There is no reason why the admiralty law of the United States should longer depend on the statute laws of the States. * * * Congress can now bring our maritime law into line with the laws of those enlightened nations which confer a right of action for death at sea." The Act would accomplish that result "for deaths on the high seas, leaving unimpaired the rights under State statutes as to deaths on waters within the territorial jurisdiction of the States. * * * This is for the purpose of uniformity, as the States can not properly legislate for the high seas." S. Rep. No. 216, 66th Cong., 1st Sess., 3, 4, (1919); H.R. Rep. No. 674, 66th Cong., 2d Sess., 3, 4 (1920). The discussion of the bill on the floor of the House evidenced the same concern that a cause of action be provided "in cases where there is now no remedy," 59 Cong.Rec. 4486, and at the same time that "the power of the States to create actions for wrongful death in no way be affected by enactment of the federal law." *The Tungus v. Skovgaard*, 358 U.S., at 593.

Read in light of the state of maritime law in 1920, we believe this legislative history indicates that Congress intended to ensure the continued availability of a remedy, historically provided by the States, for deaths in territorial waters; its failure to extend the Act to cover such deaths primarily reflected the lack of necessity for coverage by a federal statute, rather than an affirmative desire to insulate such deaths from the benefits of any federal remedy that might be available independently of the Act. The void that existed in maritime law up until 1920 was the absence of any remedy for wrongful death on the high seas. Congress, in acting to fill that void, legislated only to the three-mile limit because that was the extent of the problem. The express provision that state remedies in territorial waters were not disturbed by the Act ensured that Congress' solution of one problem would not create another by inviting the courts to find that the Act pre-empted the entire field, destroying the state remedies that had previously existed. * * *

To put it another way, the message of the Act is that it does not by its own force abrogate available state remedies; no intention appears that the Act have the effect of foreclosing any nonstatutory federal remedies that might be found appropriate to effectuate the policies of general maritime law.

That our conclusion is wholly consistent with the congressional purpose is confirmed by the passage of the Jones Act almost simultaneously with the Death on the High Seas Act. As we observed in *Gillespie v. United States Steel Corp.*, 379 U.S. 148, 155 (1964), the Jones Act was intended to achieve "uniformity in the exercise of admiralty jurisdiction" by giving seamen a federal right to recover from their employers for negligence regardless of the location of the injury or death. That strong concern for uniformity is scarcely consistent with a conclusion that Congress intended to *require* the present nonuniformity in the effectuation of the duty to provide a seaworthy ship. Our recognition of a right to recover for wrongful death under general maritime law will assure uniform vindication of federal policies, removing the tensions and discrepancies that have resulted from the necessity to accommodate state remedial statutes to exclusively maritime substantive concepts. Such uniformity not only will further the concerns of both of the 1920 Acts but also will give effect to the constitutionally based principle that federal admiralty law should be "a system of law coextensive with, and operating uniformly in, the whole country." *The Lottawanna*, 21 Wall. 558, 575 (1875).

We conclude that the Death on the High Seas Act was not intended to preclude the availability of a remedy for wrongful death under general maritime law in situations not covered by the Act. Because the refusal of maritime law to provide such a remedy appears to be jurisprudentially unsound and to have produced serious confusion and hardship, that refusal should cease unless there are substantial countervailing factors that dictate adherence to *The Harrisburg* simply as a matter of *stare decisis*. We now turn to a consideration of those factors.

[IV] Very weighty considerations underlie the principle that courts should not lightly overrule past decisions. Among these are the desirability that the law furnish a clear guide for the conduct of individuals, to enable them to plan their affairs with assurance against untoward surprise; the importance of furthering fair and expeditious adjudication by eliminating the need to relitigate every relevant proposition in every case; and the necessity of maintaining public faith in the judiciary as a source of impersonal and reasoned judgments. The reasons for rejecting any established rule must always be weighed against these factors.

The first factor, often considered the mainstay of *stare decisis*, is singularly absent in this case. The confidence of people in their ability to predict the legal consequences of their actions is vitally necessary to facilitate the planning of primary activity and to encourage the settlement of disputes without resort to the courts. However, that confidence is threatened least by the announcement of a new remedial rule to effectuate well-established primary rules of behavior. There is no question in this case of any change in the duties owed by shipowners to those who work aboard their vessels. Shipowners well understand that breach of the duty to provide a seaworthy ship may subject them to liability for injury regardless of where it occurs, and for death occurring on the high seas or in the territorial waters of most States. It can hardly be said that shipowners have molded their conduct around the possibility that in a few special circumstances they may escape liability for such a breach. Rather, the established expectations of both those who own ships and those who work on them are that there is a duty to make the ship seaworthy and that a breach of that federally imposed duty will generally provide a basis for recovery. It is the exceptional denial of recovery that disturbs these expectations. "If the new remedial doctrine serves simply to reenforce and make more effectual well-understood primary obligations, the net result of innovation may be to strengthen rather than to disturb the general sense of security." Hart & Sacks, *supra*, at 577; *id.*, at 485, 574–577, 585–595, 606–607; Pound, Some Thoughts About Stare Decisis, 13 NACCA L.J. 19 (1954).

Nor do either of the other relevant strands of *stare decisis* counsel persuasively against the overruling of *The Harrisburg*. Certainly the courts could not provide expeditious resolution of disputes if every rule were fair game for *de novo* reconsideration in every case. However, the situation we face is far removed from any such consequence as that. We do not regard the rule of *The Harrisburg* as a closely arguable proposition—it rested on a most dubious foundation when announced, has become an increasingly unjustifiable anomaly as the law over the years has left it behind, and, in conjunction with its corollary, *The Tungus*, has produced litigation-spawning confusion in an area that should be easily susceptible of more workable solutions. The rule has had a long opportunity to prove its acceptability, and instead has suffered universal criticism and wide repudiation. To supplant the present disarray in this area with a rule both simpler and more just will further, not impede, efficiency in adjudication. Finally, a judicious reconsideration of precedent cannot be as threatening to public faith in the judiciary as continued adherence to a rule unjustified in reason, which produces different results for breaches of duty in situations that cannot be differentiated in policy. Respect for the process of adjudication should be enhanced, not diminished, by our ruling today.

[V] Respondents argue that overruling *The Harrisburg* will necessitate a long course of decisions to spell out the elements of the new "cause of action." We believe these fears are exaggerated, because our decision does not require the fashioning of a whole new body of federal law, but merely removes a bar to access to the existing general maritime law. In most respects the law applied in personal-injury cases will answer all questions that arise in death cases. * * *

In sum, in contrast to the torrent of difficult litigation that has swirled about *The Harrisburg, The Tungus,* which followed upon it, and the problems of federal-state accommodation they occasioned, the recognition of a remedy for wrongful death under general maritime law can be expected to bring more placid waters. That prospect indeed makes for, and not against, the discarding of *The Harrisburg.*

We accordingly overrule *The Harrisburg,* and hold that an action does lie under general maritime law for death caused by violation of maritime duties. * * *

MR. JUSTICE BLACKMUN took no part in the consideration or decision of this case.

NOTES ON STATUTORY GAPFILLING AND MORAGNE

1. *Pre-*Moragne *Common Law Examples of Creating Norms by Analogy from Statutes.* Justice Harlan cites the Hart and Sacks materials, and their endorsement of the purposive, principled nature of statutes certainly anticipated *Moragne.* Other legal process scholars and jurists anticipated the *Moragne* approach in other contexts. Chief Justice Traynor of the California Supreme Court suggested prior to *Moragne* that "it has long since been normal procedure for judges, even those who resist reading up on any law outside that inscribed in their own caves, to consult the richly worked relevant statutes when they come upon problems of the marketplace." Roger Traynor, *Statutes Revolving in Common-Law Orbits,* 17 Cath. U.L. Rev. 401, 421 (1968). Consider the following pre-*Moragne* examples. Is Justice Harlan's use of statutes similar or different?

(a) *Criminal or Mandatory Statutes Creating Tort Standards.* Although criminal statutes do not usually stipulate civil liability, state common law courts have used such statutes (i) as setting forth a standard for negligence per se in tort actions, (ii) as a declaration of public policy justifying a judicial finding that a contract is void or unenforceable, and (iii) as a standard for a new cause of action for damages.[12] An early leading decision is *Martin v. Herzog,* 126 N.E. 814, 815 (N.Y. 1920), in which Judge Cardozo found contributory negligence as a matter of law in plaintiff's failure to have lights on his car, as required by New York's Highway Law. "We think the unexcused omission of the statutory signals is more than some evidence of negligence. It *is* negligence in itself. * * * By the very terms of the hypothesis, to omit, willfully or heedlessly, the safeguards prescribed by law for the benefit of another that he may be preserved in life or limb, is to fall short of the standard of diligence to which those who live in organized society are under a duty to conform."

In *Clinkscales v. Carver,* 136 P.2d 777 (Cal. 1943), defendant ran a stop sign and crashed into plaintiff. The defendant could not have been prosecuted criminally, because the stop sign had been set up under an ordinance which had never become effective since it was not properly published. Justice Traynor still upheld per se negligence. The significance of the statute lay, not in its legal force, but in its

---

[12] Jeffrey Pojanowski, *Private Law in the Gaps,* 82 Fordham L. Rev. 1689, 1723–24 (2014); Robert Williams, *Statutes as Sources of Law Beyond Their Terms in Common-Law Cases,* 50 Geo. Wash. L. Rev. 554, 570–80 (1982); Note, *The Use of Criminal Statutes in the Creation of New Torts,* 48 Colum. L. Rev. 456 (1948).

"formulation of a standard of conduct which the court adopts in the determination of [civil] liability. * * * When a legislative body has generalized a standard from the experience of the community and prohibits conduct that is likely to cause harm, the court accepts the formulated standards and applies them."

Federal courts generally do not create common law in the same way state courts do, but they have grappled with the question of creating standards of conduct from criminal or mandatory statutes. In *Texas and Pacific Ry. v. Rigsby*, 241 U.S. 33, 39 (1916), the Court held that an employee switchman could sue the defendant railroad for injuries sustained when he fell off a train due to defects in the "grab irons" (handholds) on the side of the train. Federal relief was based on the railroad's violation of the Safety Appliance Act of 1893, as amended in 1910. Although the Act itself did not provide the worker with a cause of action, the Court inferred one from the statutory purpose to promote the safety of employees. "A disregard of the command of the statute is a wrongful act, and where it results in damage to one of the class for whose especial benefit the statute was enacted, the right to recover damages from the party in default is implied," reasoned the Court. How is *Rigsby*'s treatment of the federal statute different from Judge Cardozo's treatment of the state statute in *Herzog*?

(b) *The Uniform Commercial Code (UCC).* The UCC encourages decisionmakers to apply its policies by analogy to unprovided for situations and to apply the Code liberally according to its rationale, see U.C.C. §§ 1–102, Comment 1; 2–313, Comment 2, and legal scholars have eagerly urged this civil law approach.[13] For example, the Third Circuit in *Vitex Mfg. Corp. v. Caribtex Corp.*, 311 F.2d 795, 799 (3d Cir. 1967), relied on the damages provisions of Article Two to set the recovery for breach of a service contract (not covered by the Code), "because it embodies the foremost modern legal thought concerning commercial transactions." The UCC expressly refuses to cover service contracts—should that be reason not to follow its principles in such cases? Consider Chief Justice Traynor's position that the Code's "authority" derives from its being "the culmination of years of scholarly work," drafted by impartial experts beholden to no one, criticized at open meetings of the ALI and elsewhere, and closely checked against existing law and commercial customs. Traynor, *Statutes in Common-Law Orbits*, 423–24.

The Code has had a particularly enthusiastic reception at the federal level, particularly in molding the law of government contracts, one aspect of federal common law. A leading opinion is that of Judge Friendly, in *United States v. Wegematic Corp.*, 360 F.2d 674, 676 (2d Cir. 1966), which applied § 2–615 (the impracticability section) to government contracts:

> We find persuasive the defendant's suggestion of looking to the Uniform Commercial Code as a source for the "federal" law of sales. The Code has been adopted by Congress for the District of Columbia, has been enacted in over forty states, and is thus well on its way to becoming a truly national law of commerce, which, as Judge L. Hand said of the Negotiable Instruments Law, is "more complete and more certain, than any other which can conceivably be drawn from those sources of 'general law' to which we were accustomed to

---

[13] See, e.g., Bruce Frier, *Interpreting Codes,* 89 Mich. L. Rev. 2201 (1991); Mitchell Franklin, *On the Legal Method of the Uniform Commercial Code,* 16 Law & Contemp. Prob. 330 (1951); Note, *The Uniform Commercial Code as a Premise for Judicial Reasoning,* 65 Colum. L. Rev. 880 (1965). See also Pojanowski, *Private Law in the Gaps,* 1723 (recent discussion of this approach).

resort in the days of *Swift v. Tyson*." When the states have gone so far in achieving the desirable goal of a uniform law governing commercial transactions, it would be a distinct disservice to insist on a different one for the segment of commerce, important but still small in relation to the total, consisting of transactions with the United States.

See *In re Yale Express Sys., Inc.*, 370 F.2d 433, 437–38 (2d Cir. 1966) (applying UCC as a source for the formulation of analogous rules for federal bankruptcy law).

(c)   *Property Matters.* "In matters involving property, statutory rules have been adopted by analogy as principles of common law and equity. Among them are the adoption by analogy of statutes which apply to realty, in cases which involve personalty," and so forth. William Page, *Statutes as Common Law Principles,* 1944 Wis. L. Rev. 175, 208; accord, Traynor, *Statutes in Common-Law Orbits,* 425. Consider *Karr v. Robinson*, 173 A. 584 (Md. 1934), which involved a testator who failed to change his will after the birth of his child. Although Maryland made no provision for this situation, almost all other English-speaking jurisdictions provided for the child to inherit (by treating the child's birth as a revocation of the will or by imputing new terms into the will). The Maryland Court of Appeals followed the principle underlying the legislation of the other states, and the child inherited. How is this case like *Moragne*? Consider the next note.

2.   *Equal Protection Analysis Applied to* Moragne. Given Moragne's unique predicament—under almost any other circumstances and in any other state she would have had an unseaworthiness cause of action—would it have been an unconstitutional denial of equal protection if the law denied her a wrongful death recovery? Consider the following analysis:

> Under our traditional [equal protection] view, underinclusive legislation will be invalidated unless some reasonable justification can be perceived for the legislature's failure to extend the benefits or burdens of that legislation to others who would appear to be similarly situated with respect to the legislation's purpose. But under civil law methodology, the benefits or burdens of a particular piece or course of legislation will be extended to those similarly situated, unless it can be shown that there is no justification for analogous treatment because no sound analogy itself exists.

Note, *The Legitimacy of Civil Law Reasoning in the Common Law: Justice Harlan's Contribution*, 82 Yale L.J. 258, 273 (1972). This commentary argues that there is a difference of presumption. Common law courts will presume that the legislature excluded the class for a valid reason and the court will try to figure out a valid reason so that the exclusion can be upheld, whereas a civil law court will presume that the legislature intended all the logical consequences following from the specific legislative formulation.

Does equal protection analysis support the result in *Moragne*? If the decedent had been a truck driver, the surviving spouse would only have received worker's compensation damages (at most), since assumedly no one was negligent under the facts of the case. Viewed this way, isn't *Moragne* itself anachronistic in rendering maritime employers strictly liable for full wrongful death damages in situations where most employer liability would be defined by worker's compensation laws?

Based on *Moragne* and similar cases, some states will look at statutes not only as specific mandates, but also as sources of policy which "carr[y] significance beyond the particular scope of each of the statutes involved." *Boston Housing Auth. v. Hemingway*, 293 N.E.2d 831, 840 (Mass. 1973).[14] Other states, such as California, had already moved in this direction before *Moragne*. Nonetheless, we know of no flood of decisions following the methodology of *Moragne*. Are there good reasons to expect that in most instances a limited statutory ambit should preclude courts from applying the statute in analogous circumstances? Could it be that many attorneys miss the argument that statutes may be sources of principles beyond their terms?

3.   *Stare de Statute*. In *Moragne*, the Supreme Court used statutory developments as authority for overruling a prior decision. Similarly, legislatures may use prior statutes as the basis for drafting new ones. Frank Horack, *The Common Law of Legislation*, 23 Iowa L. Rev. 41, 41–43 (1937), describes this process as "Stare de Statute" and explains:

> The function of precedent in judge-made law has been discussed elaborately; its similar function in legislation has been ignored. Nevertheless, legislation, like judge-made law, follows precedent. * * *

> Statutory precedent grows as case-precedent grows. First, someone bolder than the rest marks a new course. If the course appears satisfactory, others follow. Legal science calls this doctrine *stare decisis*. Legislative process is similar. For example, the common-law rule prior to legislative change was that the operator of an automobile owed a duty to an invited guest to exercise due care to protect the guest from unreasonable danger of injury. A few states limited the operator's liability to "gross negligence." When this seemed to provide an undesirable stimulus to hitchhiking and to assist collusion between guest and host for the recovery of insurance, legislative change was thought to be desirable. Connecticut adopted a statute relieving the operator from liability to a guest, except for "wilful or wanton conduct." Twenty-three states followed that lead. Described in juristic language, the legislatures have followed the rules of precedent. In popular language, the statute has been copied. The result is the same.

PROBLEMS IN THE WAKE OF MORAGNE

"Over the past three decades, Justice Harlan's opinion in *Moragne* has come to occupy an important place within the Supreme Court's canon. Generations of law students have studied *Moragne* for its scholarly discussion of legal process and the role of precedent. But before those students reach these abstract questions, their professors have no doubt tormented them by asking a seemingly simple question that defies a simple answer: What, precisely, is the holding of *Moragne?*" *Garris* v. *Norfolk Shipbuilding & Drydock Corporation*, 210 F.3d 209, 222–23 (4th Cir. 2000) (Hall, J., concurring in the judgment), *aff'd*, 532 U.S. 811 (2001); accord, Jeffrey Pojanowski,

---

[14] Examples of post-*Moragne* modification of the common law in light of principles reflected in statutes include the decisions of state courts to abolish the common law cause of action for alienation of affections in light of the statutes in other states that have done away with the tort. See Eugene Volokh, *The Mechanisms of the Slippery Slope*, 116 Harv. L. Rev. 1026, 1083 & n. 167 (2003). For a discussion of recent developments in New Zealand common law using statutes as sources of principles, see Gehan Gunasekara & Alexandra Sims, *Statutory Trends and the 'Genetic Modification' of the Common Law: Company Law as a Paradigm*, 26 Statute L. Rev. 82 (2005).

Private Law in the Gaps, 82 Fordham L. Rev. 1689, 1718–25 (2014) (examining different approaches to the *Moragne* problem).

Problem 5–1. A longshoreman dies as a result of injuries suffered while working aboard a vessel in state territorial waters. In a *Moragne* wrongful death action based on unseaworthiness, may decedent's dependents recover for their loss of society (that is, their loss of decedent's love, companionship, etc.)? The Death on the High Seas Act (DOHSA) limits recovery to "a fair and just compensation for the *pecuniary* loss sustained by the persons for whose benefit the suit is brought," 46 U.S.C. § 762 (emphasis added), and longstanding precedent holds that DOHSA does not allow recovery for loss of society. Should recovery in a *Moragne* action for unseaworthiness within the territorial waters be similarly limited? See *Sea-Land Services v. Gaudet,* 414 U.S. 573 (1974).

Problem 5–2. Assume that the Court in *Gaudet,* discussed in Problem 5–1, holds that loss of society is recoverable because that element of damages is recoverable in the clear majority of the states and because recovery is favored by "the humanitarian policy of the maritime law." Assume that the Court refuses to allow recovery for the dependents' mental grief or anguish, however. In an action brought for a wrongful death that occurred in territorial waters, may decedent's dependents recover for mental anguish and grief if the state wrongful death statute generally allows such recovery, or is the state statute preempted by the general federal law under *Moragne,* in which case under *Gaudet* there can be no recovery for mental anguish and grief? See *In re S/S Helena,* 529 F.2d 744 (5th Cir. 1976) (Wisdom, J.).

Problem 5–3. After *Gaudet,* assume that an action is brought for a wrongful death that occurred on the High Seas. Should the court conceptualize the wrongful death action as a *Moragne* action (and thus allow recovery for loss of society under *Gaudet*), or should it conceptualize it as a DOHSA action (and therefore deny recovery for loss of society)? See *Mobil Oil Co. v. Higginbotham,* 436 U.S. 618 (1978). Cf. *Dooley v. Korean Air Lines,* 524 U.S. 116 (1998) (declining to create, under general maritime law, a survival action for pre-death pain and suffering of victims of airline tragedies and limiting recovery to the terms of DOHSA).

Problem 5–4. Assume that the Court in *Higginbotham,* discussed in Problem 5–3, holds that loss of society is not recoverable in that case. After this decision, in an action for wrongful death in the territorial waters resulting from negligence that is brought under the Jones Act, may decedent's dependents recover loss of society? Prior to *Moragne, Gaudet,* and *Higginbotham,* it was settled that only pecuniary loss was recoverable in a Jones Act death action. How should a lower court rule in this new case? See *Ivy v. Security Barge Lines, Inc.,* 606 F.2d 524 (5th Cir. 1979) (en banc) (Rubin, J.).

Problem 5–5. Assume that the Court in *Higginbotham,* discussed in Problem 5–3, holds that loss of society is not recoverable. After this decision, in an action for wrongful death on the High Seas, may decedent's dependents bring their action under a state wrongful death statute that allows recovery for nonpecuniary loss, or are such state statutes preempted by DOHSA? In answering this question, note that § 7 of DOHSA provides that "[t]he provisions of any state statute giving or regulating rights of action or remedies for death shall not be affected by this chapter." See *Offshore Logistics v. Tallentire,* 477 U.S. 207 (1986), reversing 754 F.2d 1274 (5th Cir. 1985).

Problem 5–6. Assume that (a) the Court in *Higginbotham*, discussed in Problem 5–3, holds that there is no *Moragne* cause of action for death on the high seas; (b) the court of appeals in *Ivy*, discussed in Problem 5–4, holds that the survivors of a *seaman* who died within territorial waters do not have a *Moragne-Gaudet* cause of action for loss of society; and (c) Congress amends the Longshore and Harbor Workers' Compensation Act to bar any recovery from shipowners for the death or injury to a *longshore* or *harbor worker* resulting from breach of the duty of seaworthiness (see 86 Stat. 1251, codified at 33 U.S.C. §§ 901–950). After all this occurs, the estate of a *seaman* killed within territorial waters brings a *Moragne-Gaudet* action for wrongful death due to breach of the duty of unseaworthiness and seeks recovery for loss of society. Will the Court allow this cause of action? If so, should damages for loss of society be recoverable? See *Miles v. Apex Marine Corp.*, 498 U.S. 19 (1990).

Problem 5–7. Assume that the Court in *Tallentire* and in *Miles* refuses to allow the recovery of nonpecuniary loss, in part on the rationale that the common law recovery under *Moragne* should not exceed the amount of recovery that would be available under the express terms of DOHSA and the Jones Act if those statutes applied. Now suppose a *nonseaworker* is killed in state waters. In this case, a 12-year-old child was killed in a jet ski accident in state waters, and her family sues the manufacturer, seeking to apply state wrongful death and survival statutes. As *Moragne* indicated, historically the federal courts routinely applied these statutes to deaths in territorial waters to soften the harshness of *The Harrisburg* rule, and this approach worked fairly well until the creation of unseaworthiness claims, which some state courts (as the Florida courts did in *Moragne*) held were not within the scope of their wrongful death and survival statutes. The manufacturer argues that *Moragne* created a uniform federal approach to wrongful death on the waters that preempts the application of state law; thus, the family cannot recover nonpecuniary loss. What should the family argue? Who should win? See *Yamaha Motor Corp., U.S.A. v. Calhoun*, 516 U.S. 199 (1996).

Problem 5–8. A case arises with facts similar to *Moragne* except that the survivors of the person who died as the result of injuries in state territorial waters wish to state a claim in general federal maritime law for negligence, not unseaworthiness. (The decedent had been repairing a ship when injured, and thus was not a seaman, and so the Jones Act does not apply.) Because this is not a hard problem, we will give you the answer: Had the worker lived, he would have had a general maritime law cause of action for negligence; had he died, his survivors would have had a cause of action for unseaworthiness (*Moragne*), and so it only made sense to allow his survivors a cause of action for wrongful death negligence. See *Norfolk Shipbuilding & Drydock Corp. v. Garris*, 532 U.S. 811 (2001) (unanimous holding).

We call *Garris* to your attention because Justice Scalia's opinion for the Court states: "Because of Congress's extensive involvement in legislating causes of action for maritime personal injuries, it will be the better course, in many cases that assert new claims beyond what those statutes . . . allow, to leave further development to Congress." Concurring in part, Justice Ginsburg, joined by Justices Souter and Breyer, objects to this language on the ground that *Moragne* "tugs in the opposite direction. Inspecting the relevant legislation, the Court in *Moragne* found no measures counseling against the judicial elaboration of general maritime law there advanced." Justice Ginsburg views the "development of the law in admiralty as a shared venture in which 'federal common lawmaking' does not stand still, but 'harmonize[s] with the enactments of Congress in the field.' " (Quoting *Moragne*.)

Is Justice Ginsburg correct in her sense of *Moragne*? Even if so, is the majority's language truer to the more recent cases cited in these Problems? When filling in gaps in statutes written against a common law background, courts must decide "whether legislative silence precludes judicial elaboration of law within the gaps and, if it does not, whether they should fill the gaps with background private law principles, statutory policy, or some accommodation between the two." Pojanowksi, *Private Law in the Gaps*, 1725; see *id.* at 1725–38 (applying this analysis to the post-*Moragne* cases). Justice Ginsburg's *Garris* dissent suggests that the approach to this issue taken in *Moragne* (filling in the DOSHA gap with legislative judgments) is not the one that the Court is now taking in cases like *Garris*. Consider one final problem.

Problem 5–9. Atlantic Sounding Co. allegedly refused to pay maintenance and cure to a seaman for injuries he suffered while working on its tugboat. The seaman sues to enforce his admiralty law rights of maintenance and cure, and (consistent with traditional admiralty common law) receives punitive damages for Atlantic's intentional withholding of maintenance and cure. On appeal, the company argues that punitive damages for injured seamen are inconsistent with the Jones Act, which does not provide such damages for seamen injured by their employer's negligence. The company relies on *Miles*: Is that precedent distinguishable, or should its reasoning control? Would a common law admiralty court retain punitive damages as an award here? See *Atlantic Sounding Co. v. Townsend,* 557 U.S. 404 (2009) (divided Court).

C. THE NEW LEGAL PROCESS: POSITIVISM, PRAGMATISM, PRINCIPLES

Legal process theory remains important in American law, but for recent generations of lawyers, process theory has taken on new meanings and nuances. One group (and by far the largest group among judges) emphasizes the positivist features of process theory: its commitment to neutrality and neutral principles, the principle of institutional settlement, and the importance of vertical continuity (precedent, tradition) in law. This group of thinkers is on the whole preservationist and relatively formalist in its approach to law—seeking to preserve the New Deal regulatory status quo and protecting formal values through procedural requirements (standing, mootness, clear statement rules).[15] Legal process formalists would be tempted to quarrel with *Moragne*, which after all did edit "High" out of the Death on the High Seas Act. Although Justice Scalia expanded upon *Moragne* in *Atlantic Sounding Co. v. Townsend,* 557 U.S. 404 (2009), he also sounded a note of caution, that the Court should generally avoid filling in statutory details and leave that job to Congress.

At the other extreme, but still within the legal process tradition, are the progressives, who emphasize law's purposivism, the fidelity owed by officials to

---

[15]   E.g., Martin Redish, *The Federal Courts in the Political Order* (1991); Jeremy Waldron, *The Dignity of Legislation* (1999); Antonin Scalia, *The Rule of Law as a Law of Rules*, 56 U. Chi. L. Rev. 1775 (1989); John Manning, *The New Purposivism,* 2011 S.Ct.Rev. 113.

reason, and the central role of principle.[16] Common themes tie together these process progressives. One is anti-pluralist: Legislation must be more than the accommodation of exogenously defined interests; lawmaking is a process of value creation that should be informed by theories of justice and fairness. Another theme is that legislation too often fails to achieve this aspiration and that creative lawmaking by courts and agencies is needed to ensure rationality and justice in law. A final theme is the importance of dialogue or conversation as the means by which innovative lawmaking can be validated in a democratic polity and by which the rule of law can best be defended against charges of unfairness or illegitimacy. Progressive legal process thinkers love *Moragne*.

The distinction between formalist and progressive process theorists may be (crudely) captured in Ronald Dworkin's distinction between a pluralist "rulebook community," in which citizens generally agree to obey rules created by the government, and a "community of principle," in which citizens see themselves governed by basic principles, not just political compromises. The latter is a worthier sense of community, Dworkin argues, and legislation as well as adjudication must be evaluated by its contribution to the principled integrity of the community. Thus, in Dworkin's ideal community of principle, "integrity in legislation" requires lawmakers to try to make the total set of laws morally coherent. Like justice and fairness, integrity in the law contributes to the sorority/fraternity of the body politic, the moral community that bonds the nation together. The role of courts is to interpret authoritative statements of law in light of the underlying principles of the community. In the "hard cases" of statutory interpretation, for example, the best interpretation is the one that is most consonant with the underlying values of society and makes the statute the best statute it can be (within the limitations imposed by the statutory language).

In between the process formalists and the progressives lies a centrist group, one which travels under the broad banner of "pragmatism."[17] These thinkers emphasize the eclectic and instrumental features of the process tradition. Legal reasoning is a grab bag of different techniques, including not just textual analysis, but also sophisticated appreciation of the goals underlying the legal text and the consequences of adopting different interpretations. Law involves a balance between form and substance, tradition and innovation, text and context. Pragmatists tend to agree with *Moragne* as sound and practical.

---

[16] See generally Stephen Breyer, *Active Liberty: Interpreting Our Democratic Constitution* (2005); Ronald Dworkin, *Law's Empire* (1986); William Eskridge Jr., *Dynamic Statutory Interpretation* (1994); Richard Posner, *The Problems of Jurisprudence* (1990); Owen Fiss, *The Supreme Court, 1978 Term—Foreword: The Forms of Justice*, 93 Harv. L. Rev. 1 (1978). For a neat essay appreciating the new legal process by a critic, see John Manning, *Justice Ginsburg and the New Legal Process*, 127 Harv. L. Rev. 455 (2013).

[17] See generally Stephen Breyer, *Making Our Democracy Work: A Judge's View* (2010); Richard Posner, *Overcoming Law* (1995); Scott Shapiro, *Legality* (2011); William Eskridge Jr. & Philip Frickey, *Statutory Interpretation as Practical Reasoning*, 42 Stan. L. Rev. 321 (1990); Martha Minow, *The Supreme Court, 1986 Term—Foreword: Justice Engendered*, 101 Harv. L. Rev. 10 (1987). For an argument that Hart & Sacks were themselves most deeply pragmatic, see Charles Barzun, *The Forgotten Foundations of Hart and Sacks*, 99 Va. L. Rev. 1 (2013).

2. VERTICAL VERSUS HORIZONTAL COHERENCE IN STATUTORY IMPLEMENTATION

Traditional American law emphasized vertical coherence in statutory interpretation. That is, the statutory interpreter must demonstrate that her interpretation is coherent with authoritative sources situated in the past—the original intent of the enacting legislature, previous administrative or judicial precedents interpreting the statute, and traditional or customary norms. This was important to common law formalism, for which law's legitimacy rests upon consent, either express (original text and intent) or implied (acceptance over time). The formalists also valorized vertical coherence in order to assure predictability and stability in the law.

The legal realists debunked arguments based upon vertical coherence, arguing descriptively that there is no determinate "past" to which judges can link their current interpretations (vertical sources being manipulable) and then arguing prescriptively that law ought to be future-oriented rather than archaeological. Thus, the realists suggested that statutory interpretation depends more on horizontal coherence, or "consistency with the rest of the law" today.[18] The statutory interpreter demonstrates that her interpretation is coherent with authorities or norms located in the present—the statute's contemporary purposes, other statutes now in effect and their statutory policies, and current values, perhaps even the judge's personal values. Because the realists considered law's legitimacy to be grounded upon present policy needs, they were willing to throw over historical practice.

Although the realist critique revealed the importance of horizontal coherence for law's legitimacy, its cynical attitude was not welcome within the mainstream legal academy or the federal judiciary. Mainstream scholars pragmatically sought ways to reconcile the formal legitimacy and rule of law values subserved by vertical coherence, with the functional legitimacy and efficiency values subserved by horizontal coherence. Legal process thinkers sought to mediate the tension between vertical and horizontal coherence in statutory interpretation. Their challenge was to develop theories that paid due regard to vertical sources and tradition, while serving present needs in statutory interpretation. The key to the legal process resolution was, in our view, the concept of reliance on public law. The formalists were right that law should be predictable, and the citizenry ought to be able to rely on it, but the realists were right that the public interest could override private reliance on traditional rules. Legal process theory suggests that the public interest itself involves a reliance upon those rules. During the legal process era, this idea accommodated realist policy thinking, but without requiring great shifts in public law.

Doctrinal debates about *stare decisis* for statutory precedents, the prospectivity of judicial decisions (both discussed in this section), and the retroactivity of new statutes (the next section) have largely been carried on within the legal process

---

[18]   Charles Curtis, *A Better Theory of Legal Interpretation*, 3 Vand. L. Rev. 407, 423 (1950).

philosophy, with an emphasis on public reliance as a justification for preserving a status quo bias.

NOTE ON STARE DECISIS *AND STATUTORY PRECEDENTS*

Under common law formalist theory, the role of courts is to declare the law and not to change it. The doctrine of *stare decisis* requires that a court treat prior decisions as presumptively correct. Nineteenth century theory specifically held that private law precedents, involving "vested rights" of contract or property, should almost never be overruled, although the Court had greater discretion to rethink constitutional precedents. See *Smith v. Turner*, 48 U.S. 283, 470 (1849). The same virtually absolute *stare decisis* applied to decisions interpreting at least some statutes: "After a statute has been settled by judicial construction, the construction becomes, so far as contract rights acquired under it are concerned, as much a part of the statute as the text itself, and a change of decision is to all intents and purposes the same in its effect on contracts as an amendment of the law by means of a legislative enactment," *Douglass v. Pike County*, 101 U.S. 677, 687 (1879), and hence unavailable under traditional premises.

The legal realists argued that judges are not particularly constrained by precedent and that *stare decisis* should be more of a functional rule of thumb than a formal command. A court is not, and should not be, "inexorably bound by its own precedents, but, in the interest of uniformity of treatment to litigants, and of stability and certainty in the law * * * will follow the rule of law which it has established in earlier cases unless clearly convinced that the rule was originally erroneous or is no longer sound because of changed conditions and that more good than harm would come by departing from precedent."[19]

The realists' willingness to reexamine precedents freely made the mainstream legal community very nervous. Responsive to that nervousness, legal process judges and theorists of the 1930s and 1940s suggested functional reasons for something like traditional doctrine, that the statutory precedents are entitled to extra *stare decisis* deference, because Congress and not the Court is more institutionally competent to change statutory meaning. See *Burnet v. Coronado Oil & Gas Co.*, 285 U.S. 393, 406–07 (1932) (Brandeis, J., dissenting); William Eskridge Jr., *Overruling Statutory Precedents,* 76 Geo. L.J. 1361 (1988). Also important was Edward Levi's argument that public as well as private decisionmakers rely on statutory precedents, which set a direction for the statute that ought not be unraveled unless unconstitutional. A heightened adherence to *stare decisis* "marks an essential difference between statutory interpretation on the one hand and [common] law and constitutional interpretation on the other." Edward Levi, *An Introduction to Legal Reasoning*, 15 U. Chi. L. Rev. 501, 540 (1948). Consider the rule as applied in the following case.

---

[19] J.W. Moore & R.S. Oglebay, *The Supreme Court, Stare Decisis and Law of the Case*, 21 Tex. L. Rev. 514, 539–40 (1943); accord, Justice William Douglas, *Stare Decisis*, 49 Colum. L. Rev. 735 (1949).

FLOOD V. KUHN

Supreme Court of the United States, 1972.
407 U.S. 258, 92 S.Ct. 2099, 32 L.Ed.2d 728.

MR. JUSTICE BLACKMUN delivered the opinion of the Court.

[I. *The* Game] It is a century and a quarter since the New York Nine defeated the Knickerbockers 23 to 1 on Hoboken's Elysian Fields June 19, 1846, with Alexander Jay Cartwright as the instigator and the umpire. The teams were amateur, but the contest marked a significant date in baseball's beginnings. That early game led ultimately to the development of professional baseball and its tightly organized structure.

The Cincinnati Red Stockings came into existence in 1869 upon an outpouring of local pride. With only one Cincinnatian on the payroll, this professional team traveled over 11,000 miles that summer, winning 56 games and tying one. Shortly thereafter, on St. Patrick's Day in 1871, the National Association of Professional Baseball Players was founded and the professional league was born.

The ensuing colorful days are well known. The ardent follower and the student of baseball know of General Abner Doubleday; the formation of the National League in 1876; Chicago's supremacy in the first year's competition under the leadership of Al Spalding and with Cap Anson at third base; the formation of the American Association and then of the Union Association in the 1880's; the introduction of Sunday baseball; interleague warfare with cut-rate admission prices and player raiding; the development of the reserve "clause"; the emergence in 1885 of the Brotherhood of Professional Ball Players, and in 1890 of the Players League; the appearance of the American League, or "junior circuit," in 1901, rising from the minor Western Association; the first World Series in 1903, disruption in 1904, and the Series' resumption in 1905; the short-lived Federal League on the majors' scene during World War I years; the troublesome and discouraging episode of the 1919 Series; the home run ball; the shifting of franchises; the expansion of the leagues; the installation in 1965 of the major league draft of potential new players; and the formation of the Major League Baseball Players Association in 1966.

Then there are the many names, celebrated for one reason or another, that have sparked the diamond and its environs and that have provided tinder for recaptured thrills, for reminiscence and comparisons, and for conversation and anticipation in-season and off-season: Ty Cobb, Babe Ruth, Tris Speaker, Walter Johnson, Henry Chadwick, Eddie Collins, Lou Gehrig, Grover Cleveland Alexander, Rogers Hornsby, Harry Hooper, Goose Goslin, Jackie Robinson, Honus Wagner, Joe McCarthy, John McGraw, Deacon Phillippe, Rube Marquard, Christy Mathewson, Tommy Leach, Big Ed Delahanty, Davy Jones, Germany Schaefer, King Kelly, Big Dan Brouthers, Wahoo Sam Crawford, Wee Willie Keeler, Big Ed Walsh, Jimmy Austin, Fred Snodgrass, Satchel Paige, Hugh Jennings, Fred Merkle, Iron Man McGinnity, Three-Finger Brown, Harry and Stan Coveleski, Connie Mack, Al Bridwell, Red Ruffing, Amos Rusie, Cy Young, Smokey Joe Wood, Chief Meyers, Chief Bender, Bill Klem, Hans Lobert, Johnny Evers, Joe Tinker, Roy Campanella, Miller Huggins, Rube Bressler, Dazzy Vance, Edd Roush, Bill Wambsganss, Clark Griffith, Branch Rickey, Frank Chance, Cap Anson, Nap Lajoie, Sad Sam Jones,

Bob O'Farrell, Lefty O'Doul, Bobby Veach, Willie Kamm, Heinie Groh, Lloyd and Paul Waner, Stuffy McInnis, Charles Comiskey, Roger Bresnahan, Bill Dickey, Zack Wheat, George Sisler, Charlie Gehringer, Eppa Rixey, Harry Heilmann, Fred Clarke, Dizzy Dean, Hank Greenberg, Pie Traynor, Rube Waddell, Bill Terry, Carl Hubbell, Old Hoss Radbourne, Moe Berg, Rabbit Maranville, Jimmie Foxx, Lefty Grove. The list seems endless.

And one recalls the appropriate reference to the "World Serious," attributed to Ring Lardner, Sr.; Ernest L. Thayer's "Casey at the Bat"; the ring of "Tinker to Evers to Chance"; and all the other happenings, habits, and superstitions about and around baseball that made it the "national pastime" or, depending upon the point of view, "the great American tragedy."

[Curt Flood, the petitioner, was a star center fielder with the St. Louis Cardinals. Under the "reserve clause" in his contract he was required to play for the Cardinals, the Cardinals could unilaterally assign his contract to another team, and the Cardinals could annually renew that contract so long as the minimum salary was provided. In October 1969, the Cards traded Flood to the Philadelphia Phillies. Flood refused to report to the Phillies and asked Bowie Kuhn, the Commissioner of Baseball, to be allowed to negotiate a contract with the team of his choice. Kuhn refused. Flood filed a lawsuit claiming, *inter alia*, that the reserve clause violated the antitrust laws because it prevented him from contracting with the team of his choice. Lower courts denied relief based on Supreme Court precedents holding baseball immune from the antitrust laws.]

[IVA. *The Legal Background*] *Federal Baseball Club v. National League*, 259 U.S. 200 (1922), was a suit for treble damages instituted by a member of the Federal League (Baltimore) against the National and American Leagues and others. The plaintiff obtained a verdict in the trial court, but the Court of Appeals reversed. The main brief filed by the plaintiff with this Court discloses that it was strenuously argued, among other things, that the business in which the defendants were engaged was interstate commerce; that the interstate relationship among the several clubs, located as they were in different States, was predominant; that organized baseball represented an investment of colossal wealth; that it was an engagement in moneymaking; that gate receipts were divided by agreement between the home club and the visiting club; and that the business of baseball was to be distinguished from the mere playing of the game as a sport for physical exercise and diversion.

Mr. Justice Holmes, in speaking succinctly for a unanimous Court, said:

"The business is giving exhibitions of base ball, which are purely state affairs. * * * But the fact that in order to give the exhibitions the Leagues must induce free persons to cross state lines and must arrange and pay for their doing so is not enough to change the character of the business. * * * [T]he transport is a mere incident, not the essential thing. That to which it is incident, the exhibition, although made, for money would not be called trade or commerce in the commonly accepted use of those words. As it is put by the defendant, personal effort, not related to production, is not a subject of commerce. That which in its consummation is not commerce does not become commerce among the States because the transportation that we have mentioned takes place. To repeat the illustrations given by the Court below, a firm of lawyers sending out a member to argue a case, or the Chautauqua lecture bureau sending out lecturers, does not engage in such commerce because the lawyer or lecturer goes to another State.

"If we are right the plaintiff's business is to be described in the same way and the restrictions by contract that prevented the plaintiff from getting players to break their bargains and the other conduct charged against the defendants were not an interference with commerce among the States." 259 U.S., at 208–209. * * *

In the years that followed, baseball continued to be subject to intermittent antitrust attack. The courts, however, rejected these challenges on the authority of *Federal Baseball.* In some cases stress was laid, although unsuccessfully, on new factors such as the development of radio and television with their substantial additional revenues to baseball. For the most part, however, the Holmes opinion was generally and necessarily accepted as controlling authority. And in the 1952 Report of the Subcommittee on Study of Monopoly Power of the House Committee on the Judiciary, H.R.Rep. No. 2002, 82d Cong., 2d Sess., 229, it was said, in conclusion:

> "On the other hand the overwhelming preponderance of the evidence established baseball's need for some sort of reserve clause. Baseball's history shows that chaotic conditions prevailed when there was no reserve clause. Experience points to no feasible substitute to protect the integrity of the game or to guarantee a comparatively even competitive struggle. The evidence adduced at the hearings would clearly not justify the enactment of legislation flatly condemning the reserve clause."

C.   The Court granted certiorari in [*Toolson, Kowalski,* and *Corbett*], and, by a short per curiam (Warren, C. J., and Black, Frankfurter, Douglas, Jackson, Clark, and Minton, JJ.), affirmed the judgments of the respective courts of appeals in those three cases. *Toolson v. New York Yankees, Inc.,* 346 U.S. 356 (1953). *Federal Baseball* was cited as holding "that the business of providing public baseball games for profit between clubs of professional baseball players was not within the scope of the federal antitrust laws," and:

> "Congress has had the ruling under consideration but has not seen fit to bring such business under these laws by legislation having prospective effect. The business has thus been left for thirty years to develop, on the understanding that it was not subject to existing antitrust legislation. The present cases ask us to overrule the prior decision and, with retrospective effect, hold the legislation applicable. We think that if there are evils in this field which now warrant application to it of the antitrust laws it should be by legislation. Without re-examination of the underlying issues, the judgments below are affirmed on the authority of *Federal Baseball Club of Baltimore v. National League of Professional Baseball Clubs, supra,* so far as that decision determines that Congress had no intention of

including the business of baseball within the scope of the federal antitrust laws."

This quotation reveals four reasons for the Court's affirmance of *Toolson* and its companion cases: (a) Congressional awareness for three decades of the Court's ruling in *Federal Baseball*, coupled with congressional inaction. (b) The fact that baseball was left alone to develop for that period upon the understanding that the reserve system was not subject to existing federal antitrust laws. (c) A reluctance to overrule *Federal Baseball* with consequent retroactive effect. (d) A professed desire that any needed remedy be provided by legislation rather than by court decree. The emphasis in *Toolson* was on the determination, attributed even to *Federal Baseball*, that Congress had no intention to include baseball within the reach of the federal antitrust laws. * * *

[Justice Blackmun discussed three subsequent opinions. In *United States v. Shubert*, 348 U.S. 222 (1955), the Court reversed a dismissal of an antitrust suit against defendants engaged in theatrical attractions across the country, indicating that *Federal Baseball* and *Toolson* gave no general antitrust exemption for businesses built around local exhibitions. Similarly, the Court in *United States v. International Boxing Club*, 348 U.S. 236 (1955), reversed a district court for dismissing the antitrust complaint; the Court denied that *Federal Baseball* gave sports other than baseball an exemption from the antitrust laws. Finally, in *Radovich v. National Football League*, 352 U.S. 445 (1957), the Supreme Court reversed the lower courts for dismissing another antitrust complaint against a football league. Justice Clark's opinion for the Court noted that *Toolson* upheld baseball's immunity, "because it was concluded that more harm would be done in overruling *Federal Base Ball* than in upholding a ruling which at best was of dubious validity." The opinion said:]

"All this, combined with the flood of litigation that would follow its repudiation, the harassment that would ensue, and the retroactive effect of such a decision, led the Court to the practical result that it should sustain the unequivocal line of authority reaching over many years.

"[S]ince *Toolson* and *Federal Base Ball* are still cited as controlling authority in antitrust actions involving other fields of business, we now specifically limit the rule there established to the facts there involved, *i.e.*, the business of organized professional baseball. As long as the Congress continues to acquiesce we should adhere to—but not extend—the interpretation of the Act made in those cases. * * *

"If this ruling is unrealistic, inconsistent, or illogical, it is sufficient to answer, aside from the distinctions between the businesses, that were we considering the question of baseball for the first time upon a clean slate we would have no doubts. But *Federal Base Ball* held the business of baseball outside the scope of the Act. No other business claiming the coverage of those cases has such an adjudication. We therefore, conclude that the orderly way to eliminate error or discrimination, if any there be, is by legislation and not by court decision. Congressional processes are more accommodative, affording the whole industry hearings and an opportunity to assist in the formulation of new legislation. The resulting product is therefore more likely to protect the industry and the public alike. The whole scope of congressional action would be known long in advance and effective dates for the legislation could be set in the future without the injustices of retroactivity and surprise which might follow court action."

Mr. Justice Frankfurter dissented essentially for the reasons stated in his dissent in *International Boxing*. Mr. Justice Harlan, joined by Mr. Justice Brennan, also dissented because he, too, was "unable to distinguish football from baseball." Here again the dissenting Justices did not call for the overruling of the baseball decisions. They merely could not distinguish the two sports and, out of respect for *stare decisis*, voted to affirm.

G. Finally, in *Haywood v. National Basketball Assn.*, 401 U.S. 1204 (1971), Mr. Justice Douglas, in his capacity as Circuit Justice, reinstated a District Court's injunction *pendente lite* in favor of a professional basketball player and said, "Basketball * * * does not enjoy exemption from the antitrust laws."

H. This series of decisions understandably spawned extensive commentary, some of it mildly critical and much of it not; nearly all of it looked to Congress for any remedy that might be deemed essential.

I. Legislative proposals have been numerous and persistent. Since *Toolson* more than 50 bills have been introduced in Congress relative to the applicability or nonapplicability of the antitrust laws to baseball. A few of these passed one house or the other. Those that did would have expanded, not restricted, the reserve system's exemption to other professional league sports. And the Act of Sept. 30, 1961, Pub.L. 87–331, 75 Stat. 732, and the merger addition thereto effected by the Act of Nov. 8, 1966, Pub. L. 89–800, § 6(b), 80 Stat. 1515, 15 U.S.C. §§ 1291–1295, were also expansive rather than restrictive as to antitrust exemption.

[V.] In view of all this, it seems appropriate now to say that:

1. Professional baseball is a business and it is engaged in interstate commerce.

2. With its reserve system enjoying exemption from the federal antitrust laws, baseball is, in a very distinct sense, an exception and an anomaly. *Federal Baseball* and *Toolson* have become an aberration confined to baseball.

3. Even though others might regard this as "unrealistic, inconsistent, or illogical," see *Radovich*, the aberration is an established one, and one that has been recognized not only in *Federal Baseball* and *Toolson*, but in *Shubert*, *International Boxing*, and *Radovich*, as well, a total of five consecutive cases in this Court. It is an aberration that has been with us now for half a century, one heretofore deemed fully entitled to the benefit of *stare decisis*, and one that has survived the Court's expanding concept of interstate commerce. It rests on a recognition and an acceptance of baseball's unique characteristics and needs.

4. Other professional sports operating interstate—football, boxing, basketball, and, presumably, hockey and golf—are not so exempt.

5. The advent of radio and television, with their consequent increased coverage and additional revenues, has not occasioned an overruling of *Federal Baseball* and *Toolson*.

6. The Court has emphasized that since 1922 baseball, with full and continuing congressional awareness, has been allowed to develop and to expand unhindered by federal legislative action. Remedial legislation has been introduced repeatedly in Congress but none has ever been enacted. The Court, accordingly, has concluded that Congress as yet has had no intention to subject baseball's reserve system to the reach of the antitrust statutes. This, obviously, has been deemed to be something other than mere congressional silence and passivity.

7. The Court has expressed concern about the confusion and the retroactivity problems that inevitably would result with a judicial overturning of *Federal Baseball*. It has voiced a preference that if any change is to be made, it come by legislative action that, by its nature, is only prospective in operation.

8. The Court noted in *Radovich* that the slate with respect to baseball is not clean. Indeed, it has not been clean for half a century.

This emphasis and this concern are still with us. We continue to be loath, 50 years after *Federal Baseball* and almost two decades after *Toolson*, to overturn those cases judicially when Congress, by its positive inaction, has allowed those decisions to stand for so long and, far beyond mere inference and implication, has clearly evinced a desire not to disapprove them legislatively.

Accordingly, we adhere once again to *Federal Baseball* and *Toolson* and to their application to professional baseball. We adhere also to *International Boxing* and *Radovich* and to their respective applications to professional boxing and professional football. If there is any inconsistency or illogic in all this, it is an inconsistency and illogic of long standing that is to be remedied by the Congress and not by this Court. If we were to act otherwise, we would be withdrawing from the conclusion as to congressional intent made in *Toolson* and from the concerns as to retrospectivity therein expressed. Under these circumstances, there is merit in consistency even though some might claim that beneath that consistency is a layer of inconsistency.

* * * [W]hat the Court said in *Federal Baseball* in 1922 and what it said in *Toolson* in 1953, we say again here in 1972: the remedy, if any is indicated, is for congressional, and not judicial, action.

MR. JUSTICE WHITE joins in the judgment of the Court, and in all but Part I of the Court's opinion.

MR. JUSTICE POWELL took no part in the consideration or decision of this case.

MR. CHIEF JUSTICE BURGER, concurring.

I concur in all but Part I of the Court's opinion but, like Mr. Justice Douglas, I have grave reservations as to the correctness of *Toolson*; as he notes in his dissent, he joined that holding but has "lived to regret it." The error, if such it be, is one on which the affairs of a great many people have rested for a long time. Courts are not the forum in which this tangled web ought to be unsnarled. I agree with Mr. Justice

Douglas that congressional inaction is not a solid base, but the least undesirable course now is to let the matter rest with Congress; it is time the Congress acted to solve this problem.

MR. JUSTICE DOUGLAS, with whom MR. JUSTICE BRENNAN concurs, dissenting.

This Court's decision in *Federal Baseball Club*, made in 1922, is a derelict in the stream of the law that we, its creator, should remove. Only a romantic view[1] of a rather dismal business account over the last 50 years would keep that derelict in midstream.

In 1922 the Court had a narrow, parochial view of commerce. With the demise of the old landmarks of that era, the whole concept of commerce has changed.

Under the modern [Commerce Clause] decisions, the power of Congress was recognized as broad enough to reach all phases of the vast operations of our national industrial system. An industry so dependent on radio and television as is baseball and gleaning vast interstate revenues (see H.R.Rep. No. 2002, 82d Cong., 2d Sess., 4, 5 (1952)) would be hard put today to say with the Court in the *Federal Baseball Club* case that baseball was only a local exhibition, not trade or commerce.

Baseball is today big business that is packaged with beer, with broadcasting, and with other industries. The beneficiaries of the *Federal Baseball Club* decision are not the Babe Ruths, Ty Cobbs, and Lou Gehrigs.

The owners, whose records many say reveal a proclivity for predatory practices, do not come to us with equities. The equities are with the victims of the reserve clause. I use the word "victims" in the Sherman Act sense, since a contract which forbids anyone to practice his calling is commonly called an unreasonable restraint of trade.

If congressional inaction is our guide, we should rely upon the fact that Congress has refused to enact bills broadly exempting professional sports from antitrust regulation.[3] H.R.Rep. No. 2002, 82nd Cong., 2d Sess. (1952). The only statutory exemption granted by Congress to professional sports concerns broadcasting rights. 15 U.S.C. §§ 1291–1295. I would not ascribe a broader exemption through inaction than Congress has seen fit to grant explicitly.

There can be no doubt "that were we considering the question of baseball for the first time upon a clean slate" we would hold it to be subject to federal antitrust regulation. *Radovich*. The unbroken silence of Congress should not prevent us from correcting our own mistakes.

---

[1]   While I joined the Court's opinion in *Toolson*, I have lived to regret it; and I would now correct what I believe to be its fundamental error.

[3]   The Court's reliance upon congressional inaction disregards the wisdom of *Helvering v. Hallock*, 309 U.S. 106, 119–121, where we said:

"Nor does want of specific Congressional repudiations * * * serve as an implied instruction by Congress to us not to reconsider, in the light of new experience * * * those decisions * * *. It would require very persuasive circumstances enveloping Congressional silence to debar this Court from re-examining its own doctrines. * * * Various considerations of parliamentary tactics and strategy might be suggested as reasons for the inaction of * * * Congress, but they would only be sufficient to indicate that we walk on quicksand when we try to find in the absence of corrective legislation a controlling legal principle."

MR. JUSTICE MARSHALL, with whom MR. JUSTICE BRENNAN joins, dissenting.

This is a difficult case because we are torn between the principle of *stare decisis* and the knowledge that the decisions in *Federal Baseball Club* and *Toolson* are totally at odds with more recent and better reasoned cases. * * * Has Congress acquiesced in our decisions in *Federal Baseball Club* and *Toolson*? I think not. Had the Court been consistent and treated all sports in the same way baseball was treated, Congress might have become concerned enough to take action. But, the Court was inconsistent, and baseball was isolated and distinguished from all other sports. In *Toolson* the Court refused to act because Congress had been silent. But the Court may have read too much into this legislative inaction.

Americans love baseball as they love all sports. Perhaps we become so enamored of athletics that we assume that they are foremost in the minds of legislators as well as fans. We must not forget, however, that there are only some 600 major league baseball players. Whatever muscle they might have been able to muster by combining forces with other athletes has been greatly impaired by the manner in which this Court has isolated them. It is this Court that has made them impotent, and this Court should correct its error.

We do not lightly overrule our prior constructions of federal statutes, but when our errors deny substantial federal rights, like the right to compete freely and effectively to the best of one's ability as guaranteed by the antitrust laws, we must admit our error and correct it. We have done so before and we should do so again here. See, *e.g., Blonder-Tongue Laboratories, Inc. v. University of Illinois Foundation*, 402 U.S. 313 (1971); *Boys Markets, Inc. v. Retail Clerks Union*, 398 U.S. 235, 241 (1970).[4]

To the extent that there is concern over any reliance interests that club owners may assert, they can be satisfied by making our decision prospective only. Baseball should be covered by the antitrust laws beginning with this case and henceforth, unless Congress decides otherwise.[5]

NOTES ON FLOOD AND THE "SUPER-STRONG" PRESUMPTION AGAINST OVERRULING STATUTORY PRECEDENTS

1. *Is There a Rationale for* Flood? It appears that every member of the Court thought that *Federal Baseball* was wrongly decided, yet a majority nevertheless applied the wrongheaded precedent. Is there something to Justice Blackmun's view that this is "an inconsistency and illogic of long standing" which might as well be perpetuated? One's initial reaction to Justice Blackmun's opinion might be that it is simply silly not to overrule discredited precedents. The same argument might have been made to the *Brown* Court not to overrule *Plessy v. Ferguson*, 163 U.S. 537 (1896). Justice Blackmun would respond that he would be more willing to overrule constitutional precedents, because Congress cannot easily correct such decisions. See *Burnet v. Coronado Oil and*

---

[4]   In the past this Court has not hesitated to change its view as to what constitutes interstate commerce. Compare *United States v. E. C. Knight Co.*, 156 U.S. 1 (1895), with *Mandeville Island Farms v. American Crystal Sugar Co.*, 334 U.S. 219 (1948), and *United States v. Darby*, 312 U.S. 100(1941).

[5]   We said recently that "[i]n rare cases, decisions construing federal statutes might be denied full retroactive effect, as for instance where this Court overrules its own construction of a statute * * *." *United States v. Estate of Donnelly*, 397 U.S. 286, 295 (1970).

Gas Co., 285 U.S. 393, 406–07 (1932) (Brandeis, J., dissenting). Is this reasoning persuasive? Contrast *Moragne*, in which the Court overruled a common law decision affecting a minuscule range of cases. Wouldn't the same reasons (decisive shift in the legal terrain) have justified overruling *Federal Baseball*? Does *Flood* present more compelling justifications for stare decisis?

In strictly respecting *stare decisis*, the *Flood* Court notes "retrospectivity" problems that would inhere if it were to overturn *Toolson* and *Federal Baseball*, suggesting that the Court assumed that the industry had been relying on these precedents in conducting its affairs. Justice Marshall's dissenting opinion suggests the possibility of a "prospective" overruling, to take effect after the industry has time to revamp its rules and practices (see the discussion in the next Note). Does a prospective overruling solve the reliance problem?

Could *Flood v. Kuhn* be an example of stare nostalgia? Consider Justice Blackmun's "Ode to Baseball" in Part I of the opinion. Was that an appropriate matter to be included in a judicial opinion? Even if not, were Chief Justice Burger and Justice White right in making a point of not joining Part I? (We think this is the only time in history that all of an opinion commanded a Court majority except for its statement of facts!)

The Court never returned to the *Flood* issue (maybe on the ground that, after *Federal Baseball*, *Toolson*, and *Flood*, three strikes and you're out?). Thwarted on antitrust grounds, the players' union agitated for change through interest arbitration. Five years after *Flood*, an arbitrator awarded free-agent status to two players; the collective bargaining between owners and the players' union that followed, with impasses sometimes resulting in strikes, led to labor agreements that provided players with significant freedom.

In the mid-1990s, following particularly acrimonious labor conflict, management agreed with the union to approach Congress jointly and request legislation effectively overriding *Flood*. Congress responded by enacting the Curt Flood Act of 1998, Pub. L. 105–297, 112 Stat. 2824. The statute subjects any business practices "directly relating to or affecting employment of major league baseball players * * * to the antitrust laws to the same extent such * * * practices * * * would be subject to the antitrust laws if engaged in by persons in any other professional sports business affecting interstate commerce." Drafted to avoid any application of the antitrust laws to such matters as franchise relocation and the treatment of minor-league players, it is not clear that the statute changed the law in general or, in particular, provided any rights to players that they had not already achieved through collective bargaining. Nor did the override provide solace to Curt Flood, who died of cancer in 1997.[20]

Note that congressional overrides of Supreme Court decisions have become scarce since 1998. See Matthew Christiansen & William Eskridge Jr., *Congressional Overrides of Supreme Court Statutory Interpretation Decisions, 1967–2011,* 92 Tex. L. Rev. 1317 (2014). Should Congress's inability to respond affect the Court's willingness to overrule bad precedents?

---

[20] For the full story of the case, the arbitral resolution, and the override statute, see Brad Snyder, *A Well Paid Slave: Curt Flood's Fight For Free Agency in Professional Sports* (2007); Stephen Ross, *The Story of* Flood v. Kuhn (1972): *Dynamic Statutory Interpretation, At the Time,* in *Statutory Interpretation Stories* 36–57 (Eskridge, Frickey & Garrett eds., 2011).

2.   *When Is It Appropriate to Overrule a Statutory Precedent?* As *Flood* suggests, the Supreme Court will not routinely overrule a prior interpretation of a statute. Many state courts are even more emphatic that statutory precedents should rarely, or never (in some states), be overruled, since the legislature can change the statute.[21] Is it ever appropriate to overrule a statutory precedent?

In *Monell v. Department of Social Servs.*, 436 U.S. 658 (1978), the Supreme Court held that municipal corporations were "persons" subject to suit under § 1983 for depriving people of the "rights, privileges, or immunities secured by the Constitution and laws." The Court thereby overruled *Monroe v. Pape*, 365 U.S. 167 (1961), which had inferred that Congress meant to immunize municipalities when it rejected such a provision in the bill which became the Civil Rights Act of 1871. The proposed provision would have held a municipal corporation liable for damage done to its inhabitants by private persons "riotously and tumultuously assembled" and was rejected (apparently) because the House of Representatives doubted that Congress had the constitutional power to impose that obligation.

Justice Brennan's opinion in *Monell* explained that the objection to the proposed provision was not that it imposed liability on municipal corporations, but that it held them responsible for the actions of private citizens, which carried *respondeat superior* beyond the bounds of the Constitution. Justice Brennan then made his positive case for finding municipal corporations to be persons by citing to (1) statements of Representative Bingham (a sponsor of the Act) that the statute would effectively provide a remedy in cases of unlawful municipal actions, (2) cases decided before 1871 in which municipalities were held liable to private persons, and (3) the "Dictionary Act," which defined "persons" to include "bodies politic." Justice Brennan recognized the seriousness of overruling *Monroe* and sought to justify it, as did the concurring opinion of Justice Powell. Consider the following articulated grounds for softening stare decisis and overruling *Monroe*. Does any of them suggest that *Monell* presents a better-justified case for overruling prior judicial construction of statutes than *Flood*?

(a)   Stare Decisis *Cuts Both Ways.* Justices Brennan and Powell both thought that *stare decisis* was less of a problem because *Monroe's* construction of § 1983 was inconsistent with other Supreme Court cases—earlier cases in which municipal corporations had been defendants, *e.g., Douglas v. Jeannette*, 319 U.S. 157 (1943), and post-*Monroe* cases in which school boards were found liable under § 1983. But Justice Rehnquist pointed out that three subsequent Supreme Court decisions—*Moor v. Alameda County*, 411 U.S. 693 (1973); *City of Kenosha v. Bruno*, 412 U.S. 507 (1973) (extending *Monroe* to suits for injunctive relief); *Aldinger v. Howard*, 412 U.S. 1 (1976)—had explicitly reaffirmed *Monroe*. Isn't this like *Flood*? Indeed, the Supreme Court's reaffirmance of *Monroe* had never been grudging, as its reaffirmance of the moribund *Federal Baseball* had been in the cases cited by Justice Blackmun in *Flood*.

(b)   *Congressional Nonaquiescence.* Justice Brennan argued that Congress implicitly approved of § 1983 suits against school boards and other "local bodies" when it enacted the Civil Rights Attorney's Fees Awards Act of 1976, 90 Stat. 2641, codified

---

[21] Representative of this approach are *Williams v. Ray*, 246 S.E.2d 387 (Ga. App. 1978); *Williams v. Crickman*, 405 N.E.2d 799 (Ill. 1980); *Land Comm'r v. Hutton*, 307 So.2d 415 (Miss. 1974); *Higby v. Mahoney*, 396 N.E.2d 183 (N.Y. 1979); *Fulton v. Lavallee*, 265 A.2d 655 (R.I. 1970); *James v. Vernon Calhoun Packing Co.*, 498 S.W.2d 160 (Tex. 1973). But see, e.g., *Jepson v. Department of Labor and Indus.*, 573 P.2d 10 (Wash. 1977).

at 42 U.S.C. § 1988 (1982); see S. Rep. No. 94–1011, 94th Cong., 2d Sess. 5 (1976) (noting that defendants in § 1983 cases "are often State or local bodies"). But Justice Rehnquist noted that there was nothing in the language of the Attorney's Fees Awards Act to suggest that municipal corporations were liable under § 1983, and the Senate Report cited by Justice Brennan states that liability may be imposed "whether or not the agency or government is a named party," which suggests that Congress did not view the Act as inconsistent with *Monroe*. More important, Justice Brennan's assertion of congressional nonacquiescence was inconsistent with 1978 Senate hearings on a bill to remove the municipal immunity imposed by *Monroe*. Isn't that the very same argument that prevailed in *Flood*?

(c) *The Requirements of a Dynamic Statutory Scheme.* Justice Powell's concurrence quoted Holmes, *The Path of the Law*, 10 Harv. L. Rev. 457, 469 (1897): The law recognizes the necessity of change, lest rules "simply persis[t] from blind imitation of the past." Doesn't this suggest a decent reason to overrule *Monroe*'s holding that municipalities were not subject to § 1983 suits? *Monroe* ironically had breathed new life into § 1983 in the 1960s, but it became clear over time that violations of civil rights, especially rights to free speech and nondiscriminatory treatment, were systemic at the local level: They were caused by city or county policy, and not just by individual misconduct. Whether they were named defendants or not, municipal corporations were very often the "real" defendants (for example, they regularly provided attorneys for individual defendants and/or reimbursed them for awards rendered against them). By 1978, it was painfully clear—from many of the Court's own § 1983 cases, which were brought against local agencies—that it was blinking reality not to permit direct suit against municipal corporations. That § 1983 was one means by which constitutional rights were protected made an expansive construction of § 1983 liability all the more natural. Does this explain the Court's willingness, by a 7–2 vote, to overrule *Monroe*?

3. Stare Decisis *and the Sherman Act, Revisited.* The debate over the super-strong presumption of correctness for statutory precedents has intensified in the last several years. Following Hart and Sacks, who strongly disapproved of *Toolson* for some of the reasons developed above, most legal process academics have endorsed a relaxation of the super-strong presumption, so that statutory precedents would be treated more like other precedents.[22]

In the context of the antitrust laws, consider *State Oil Co. v. Khan*, 522 U.S. 3 (1997), in which the Court unanimously overruled *Albrecht v. Herald Co.*, 390 U.S. 145 (1968), which had considered vertical maximum price fixing a per se antitrust violation, and replaced that approach with the "rule of reason." The Court dismissed any barrier created by *Toolson* and *Flood*, viewing those cases as having no import outside the peculiar context of baseball. That Congress had not reacted adversely to *Albrecht* "seems neither clearly to support nor to denounce" the holding of that case. The Court also concluded that *stare decisis* has somewhat less force in antitrust law because, "[i]n the area of antitrust law, there is a competing interest, well represented in this Court's decisions, in recognizing and adapting to changed circumstances and the lessons of

---

[22] E.g., Reed Dickerson, *The Interpretation and Application of Statutes* 252–55 (1975); Amy Coney Barrett, *Statutory Stare Decisis in the Courts of Appeals,* 73 Geo. Wash. L. Rev. 317 (2005); Frank Easterbrook, *Stability and Reliability in Judicial Decisions,* 73 Corn. L. Rev. 422 (1988); William Eskridge Jr., *Overruling Statutory Precedents*, 76 Geo. L.J. 1361 (1988); Earl Maltz, *The Nature of Precedent*, 66 N.C. L. Rev. 367 (1988). But see Lawrence Marshall, *"Let Congress Do It": The Case for an Absolute Rule of Statutory Stare Decisis*, 88 Mich. L. Rev. 177 (1989), who argues for an "absolute" rule of stare decisis in statutory cases.

accumulated experience. Thus, the general presumption that legislative changes should be left to Congress has less force with respect to the Sherman Act in light of the accepted view that Congress 'expected the courts to give shape to the statute's broad mandate by drawing on common-law tradition.' As we have explained, the term 'restraint of trade' * * * also 'invokes the common law itself, and not merely the static content that the common law had assigned to the term in 1890.'" Accord, *Leegin Creative Leather Products, Inc. v. PSKS, Inc.*, 551 U.S. 877 (2007) (invoking the idea that the Sherman Act is a common law statute).

Patterson v. McLean Credit Union
491 U.S. 164 (1989).

Brenda Patterson brought a lawsuit against her former employer for workplace racial harassment. She based her claim on 42 U.S.C. § 1981, which prohibits discrimination on the basis of race in the making and enforcement of contracts. Her complaint was dismissed by the lower courts on the ground that it did not state a claim for relief under § 1981. On its own motion after receiving briefs in the case, the Supreme Court requested the parties to brief the issue whether § 1981 affords a remedy against private, as opposed to public, employers. *Runyon v. McCrary*, 427 U.S. 160 (1976), had interpreted § 1981 to provide such a remedy against private schools excluding children on the basis of race, and so the Court invited the parties to address the question whether *Runyon* should be "reconsidered" (i.e., overruled). The Court's request stimulated a firestorm of protest from the civil rights community, the press, legal scholars, historians, and Members of Congress (who took the unusual step of submitting a brief on the issue). To some observers, the request raised the possibility that a new conservative majority on the Court would use a relaxed approach to *stare decisis* to overturn decades of Warren and Burger Court civil rights precedents.

In the end, the Court chose a somewhat more politique path. The opinion for the Court, written by **Justice Kennedy** and joined by the other four Justices (Chief Justice Rehnquist and Justices White, Scalia, and O'Connor) who had requested rehearing, declined to overrule *Runyon* but also declined to extend it to workplace harassment claims. The majority opinion essentially adopted the commentators' position that statutory precedents are subject to normal (not super-strong) *stare decisis* rules (although not the very lenient *stare decisis* of constitutional precedents). The Court's reason for preserving *Runyon* recalls the sort of analysis we saw in *Moragne*.

"We conclude * * * that no special justification has been shown for overruling *Runyon*. In cases where statutory precedents have been overruled, the primary reason for the Court's shift in position has been the intervening development of the law, through either the growth of judicial doctrine or further action taken by Congress. Where such changes have removed or weakened the conceptual underpinnings from the primary decision, or where the law has rendered the decision irreconcilable with competing legal doctrines or policies, the Court has not hesitated to overrule an earlier decision. Our decision in *Runyon* has not been undermined by subsequent changes or developments in the law.

"Another traditional justification for overruling a prior case is that a precedent may be a positive detriment to coherence and consistency in the law, either because of inherent confusion created by an unworkable decision, or because the decision poses a direct obstacle to the realization of important objectives embodied in other laws. In this regard, we do not find *Runyon* to be unworkable or confusing. * * *

"Finally, it has sometimes been said that a precedent becomes more vulnerable as it becomes outdated and after being ' "tested by experience, has been found to be inconsistent with the sense of justice or with the social welfare." ' *Runyon* (Stevens, J., concurring), quoting B. Cardozo, The Nature of the Judicial Process 149 (1921). Whatever the effect of this consideration may be in statutory cases, it offers no support for overruling *Runyon*. In recent decades, state and federal legislation has been enacted to prohibit private racial discrimination in many aspects of our society. Whether *Runyon*'s interpretation of section 1981 as prohibiting racial discrimination in the making and enforcement of private contracts is right or wrong as an original matter, it is certain that it is not inconsistent with the prevailing sense of justice in this country. To the contrary, *Runyon* is entirely consistent with our society's deep commitment to the eradication of discrimination based on a person's race or the color of his or her skin."

Although the Court reaffirmed its prior interpretation applying § 1981 to prohibit racial discrimination in the "mak[ing] and enforce[ment]" of private contracts, the five-Justice majority declined to find that racial harassment on the job is actionable. The majority reasoned that racial harassment did not impair Patterson's ability to "make" or "enforce" the employment contract and, hence, did not fall under § 1981's plain language.

Justice Brennan wrote a separate opinion concurring in the judgment, joined by Justices Marshall, Blackmun, and Stevens. The concurring Justices disagreed with the majority on the *Runyon* issue in three different ways. First, they argued that *Runyon* was correctly decided as an initial matter (a proposition not squarely addressed by the majority). Second, they argued that Congress had "ratified" *Runyon* (a) by failing to overturn the precedent even while Congress was overturning a number of other civil rights precedents in the late 1970s and 1980s, (b) by rejecting an amendment to the Civil Rights Act of 1964 inconsistent with *Runyon*, and (c) by relying on *Runyon* when it enacted an attorney's fees statute in 1976, 42 U.S.C. § 1988. Third, the concurring Justices argued that the Court's refusal to apply *Runyon* to the instant case was a failure to take the precedent's authority seriously. If the Court really believed in the current policy and other reasons for reaffirming *Runyon*, they argued, the Court would have applied the precedent to Patterson's claims of racial harassment on the job. The implications of the separate opinion are that the Court was giving lip service to *stare decisis*, while actually departing from the principles and policies it seemingly reaffirmed.

NOTE ON ABROGATING STARE DECISIS

The traditional view is that, although adhering to any given precedent is a matter of policy and is not compelled by an iron rule of law, the American practice *of stare decisis* is deeply rooted and may in some circumstances even be constitutionally compelled as inherent in the "judicial Power" granted by Article III. See Michael Dorf, *Dicta and Article III*, 142 U. Pa. L. Rev. 1997, 1997 (1994); Henry Monaghan, *Stare Decisis and Constitutional Adjudication*, 88 Colum. L. Rev. 723, 748 (1988). Could Congress by statute abrogate the practice of *stare decisis* in a given area and require the Supreme Court to overrule a constitutional precedent if the Court is persuaded that the prior case was incorrect on the merits? Arguing for such a power is Michael Paulsen, *Abrogating Stare Decisis by Statute: May Congress Remove the Precedential Effect of* Roe *and* Casey?, 109 Yale L.J. 1535 (2000). Could Congress ameliorate *stare decisis* in statutory cases, as by legislating that statutory precedents should *not* receive any additional deference?

PROBLEM ON OVERRULING STATUTORY PRECEDENTS

Problem 5–10. Recall the *Weber* issue from Chapter 1, § 3. The Court has once reaffirmed *Weber*, over a strong dissent by Justice Scalia, in *Johnson v. Transportation Agency.* Assume you are Justice Scalia's law clerk. If another challenge to voluntary affirmative action in the workplace comes up, should he mount another attack on *Weber*? Consider the following new § 703(m), added by the Civil Rights Act of 1991 (described in Chapter 1, § 3):

> (m) Except as otherwise provided in this title, an unlawful employment practice is established when the complaining party demonstrates that race, color, religion, sex, or national origin was a motivating factor for any employment practice, even though other factors also motivated the practice.

Should *Weber* be overruled? Compare *Officers for Justice v. Civil Serv. Comm'n*, 979 F.2d 721, 725 (9th Cir. 1992), with Michael Stokes Paulsen, *Reverse Discrimination and Law School Faculty Hiring: The Undiscovered Opinion*, 71 Tex. L. Rev. 993, 1005–06 (1993).

NOTE ON JUDICIAL DECISIONS WITH PROSPECTIVE EFFECT

The Blackstonian view was that judicial decisions are always retroactive. This view came under sustained attack from the legal realists. The classic argument, by Chief Justice Roger Traynor in *Quo Vadis, Prospective Overruling: A Question of Judicial Responsibility*, 28 Hastings L.J. 533 (1977), advocated "occasional exceptions to the normally retroactive operation of judicial decisions."[23] Traynor continued: "It is my opinion that however sound this prevailing rule may be in the main, it can on occasion unduly restrict the development of the law. A court usually will not overrule a precedent even if it is convinced that the precedent is unsound, when the hardship caused by a retroactive change would not be offset by its benefits. The technique of prospective overruling enables courts to solve this dilemma by changing bad law without upsetting the reasonable expectations of those who relied on it." Note the relationship between Traynor's endorsement of prospective overruling and Justice Marshall's dissenting opinion in *Flood v. Kuhn.*

The Warren Court had sometimes overruled constitutional criminal procedure precedents, with partial prospective effect, namely, granting relief to the fortunate petitioners but denying application of the new constitutional rule to pending cases. In *Griffith v. Kentucky,* 479 U.S. 314 (1987), the Rehnquist Court rejected that practice and eliminated limits on retroactivity in the criminal context. *Griffith* held that all "newly declared" rules must be applied retroactively to all "criminal cases pending on

---

[23] For other defenses of prospective overrulings, see Guido Calabresi, *A Common Law for the Age of Statutes* (1982); Beryl Harold Levy, *Realist Jurisprudence and Prospective Overruling*, 109 U. Pa. L. Rev. 1, 17–25 (1960); Note, *Prospective Overruling and Retroactive Application in the Federal Courts*, 71 Yale L.J. 907, 945 (1962).

direct review." This holding rested on two "basic norms of constitutional adjudication." First, "the nature of judicial review" strips the Court of the quintessentially "legislat[ive]" prerogative to make rules of law retroactive or prospective as the Justices see fit. Second, the Court concluded that "selective application of new rules violates the principle of treating similarly situated [parties] the same." Because it involved criminal constitutional issues, *Griffith* left open the viability of Warren Court decisions allowing selective prospectivity when the Court overruled civil precedents.

James B. Beam Distilling Co. v. Georgia
501 U.S. 529 (1991).

The Court applied a new civil constitutional precedent, *Bacchus Imports, Ltd. v. Dias*, 468 U.S. 263 (1984) (overruling prior Commerce Clause precedent) retroactively, but fractured as to rationale.

The judgment of the Court was delivered by **Justice Souter**, in an opinion joined only by Justice Stevens. Justice Souter started from the baseline that retroactivity of judicial decisions, including constitutional decisions, is "overwhelmingly the norm," because it "is in keeping with the traditional function of the courts to decide cases before them based upon their best current understanding of the law" and reflects "the declaratory theory of the law." "But in some circumstances," he continued, "retroactive application may prompt difficulties of a practical sort. However much it comports with our received notions of the judicial role, the practice has been attacked for its failure to take account of reliance on cases subsequently abandoned, a fact of life if not always one of jurisprudential recognition." For that reason, the Court has sometimes applied some constitutional decisions purely prospectively, applicable only to conduct and controversies arising after the date of the Court's decision. "But this equitable method has its own drawback: it tends to relax the force of precedent, by minimizing the costs of overruling, and thereby allows the courts to act with a freedom comparable to that of legislatures."

Justice Souter categorically rejected a third approach, selective prospectivity (retroactive as to the litigants and/or pending cases but prospective as to others similarly situated), because it "breaches the principle that litigants in similar situations should be treated the same, a fundamental component *of stare decisis* and the rule of law generally." Although selective prospectivity was used in some of the Court's criminal procedure precedents, the Court abandoned it for criminal cases in *Griffith*. Justice Souter rejected its application in civil constitutional cases as well. Because the Court in *Bacchus* applied its new rule to the litigants in that case, Justice Souter felt compelled to apply it to all similarly situated parties, including those in this case.

Justice White concurred in the judgment, generally agreeing with Justice Souter's opinion and specifically rejecting selective prospectivity in civil cases.

Justice Scalia, writing also for Justices Marshall and Blackmun, concurred in the judgment upon a broader ground, that either pure or selective prospectivity in judicial decisions is unconstitutional, as a violation of Article Ill's vesting the "judicial Power" in the federal courts. "That is the power 'to say what the law is,' *Marbury v. Madison*, 1 Cranch 137, 177 (1803), not the power to change it. I am not so naive (nor do I think our forebears were) as to be unaware that judges in a real sense 'make' law. But they make it *as judges make it*, which is to say *as though* they were 'finding' it—discerning what the law *is*, rather than decreeing what it is today *changed to*, or what it will *tomorrow* be. Of course, this mode of action poses 'difficulties of a practical sort,' when courts decide to overrule prior precedent. But those difficulties are one of the understood checks upon judicial law-making; to eliminate them is to render courts more substantially free to 'make new law,' and thus to alter in a fundamental way the assigned balance of responsibility and power among the three Branches."

Justice O'Connor, joined by Chief Justice Rehnquist and Justice Kennedy, dissented. Those Justices would have retained the Court's practice of applying some overrulings only to the parties in the case and not others similarly situated. Like Justice Souter, Justice O'Connor invoked precepts underlying *stare decisis*. "At its core, *stare decisis* allows those affected by the law to order their affairs without fear that the established law upon which they rely will suddenly be pulled out from under them. A decision *not* to apply a new rule retroactively is based upon principles of *stare decisis*. By not applying a law-changing decision retroactively, a court respects the settled expectations that have built up around the old law."

Harper v. Virginia Department of Taxation
509 U.S. 86 (1993).

The Court returned to this issue for civil cases. Writing for a Court majority, **Justice Thomas** confirmed that the point of law from *Jim Beam* is that "a rule of federal law, once announced and applied to the parties to the controversy, must be given full retroactive effect by all courts adjudicating federal law." That is, in civil as well as criminal cases, the Court cannot overrule a precedent, give the petitioning party the benefit of the new rule, and deny application of the new rule to other legally cognizable cases and controversies. "[B]oth the common law and our own decisions" have "recognized a general rule of retrospective effect for the constitutional decisions of this Court." *Robinson v. Neil,* 409 U.S. 505, 507 (1973). Nothing in the Constitution alters the fundamental rule of "retrospective operation" that has governed "[j]udicial decisions . . . for near a thousand years." *Kuhn v. Fairmont Coal Co.,* 215 U.S. 349, 372 (1910) (Holmes, J., dissenting).

Accordingly, "*Beam* controls this case, and we accordingly adopt a rule that fairly reflects the position of a majority of Justices in *Beam:* When this Court applies a rule of federal law to the parties before it, that rule is the controlling interpretation of federal law and must be given full retroactive effect in all cases still open on direct review and as to all events, regardless of whether such events predate or postdate our announcement of the rule. This rule extends *Griffith*'s ban against 'selective application of new rules.' Mindful of the 'basic norms of constitutional adjudication' that animated our view of retroactivity in the criminal context, we now prohibit the erection of selective temporal barriers to the application of federal law in noncriminal cases. In both civil and criminal cases, we can scarcely permit 'the substantive law [to] shift and spring' according to 'the particular equities of [individual parties'] claims' of actual reliance on an old rule and of harm from a retroactive application of the new rule. *Beam* (opinion of Souter, J.)."

Concurring, **Justice Scalia** maintained that "[p]rospective decisionmaking is the handmaid of judicial activism, and the born enemy of *stare decisis*. It was formulated in the heyday of legal realism and promoted as a 'techniqu[e] of judicial lawmaking' in general, and more specifically as a means of making it easier to overrule prior precedent." Justice Scalia assailed this legacy of legal realism as inconsistent with

Article III. "Th[e] original and enduring American perception of the judicial role sprang not from the philosophy of Nietzsche but from the jurisprudence of Blackstone, which viewed retroactivity as an inherent characteristic of the judicial power, a power 'not delegated to pronounce a new law, but to maintain and expound the old one.' 1 W. Blackstone, Commentaries *69 (1765). Even when a 'former determination is most evidently contrary to reason . . . [or] contrary to the divine law,' a judge overruling that decision would 'not pretend to make a new law, but to vindicate the old one from misrepresentation.' 'For if it be found that the former decision is manifestly absurd or unjust, it is declared, not that such a sentence was *bad law*, but that it was *not law.' Id.* (emphases in original). Fully retroactive decisionmaking was considered a principal distinction between the judicial and the legislative power: '[I]t is said that that which distinguishes a judicial from a legislative act is, that the one is a determination of what the existing law is in relation to some existing thing already done or happened, while the other is a predetermination of what the law shall be for the regulation of all future cases.' T. Cooley, Constitutional Limitations *91 (1868)."

Justice Kennedy (joined by Justice White) concurred in part and in the Court's judgment, based upon earlier precedents.

Justice O'Connor (joined by Chief Justice Rehnquist) dissented. Justice O'Connor understood *Jim Beam* as having invalidated "selective prospectivity" (such as applying the Court's new rule to the parties in the case) as inconsistent with Article III. She sharply criticized the intimation in Justice Thomas's opinion for the Court that "pure prospectivity" (neither the parties nor any present actor gets the advantage of the new rule of law) also violates Article III.

In *Jim Beam,* Justice Scalia had presented the argument that all forms of prospective overruling violates Article III, and it was rejected by six other Justices. Justice O'Connor would have followed the advice of Justice Frankfurter: "We should not indulge in the fiction that the law now announced has always been the law. It is much more conducive to law's self-respect to recognize candidly the considerations that give prospective content to a new pronouncement of law." *Griffin v. Illinois*, 351 U.S. 12 (1956) (opinion concurring in judgment).

After *Harper*, is there any way that the Supreme Court could have overruled *Federal Baseball, Toolson,* and *Flood v. Kuhn*, without upsetting huge reliance interests?

3. STATUTORY RETROACTIVITY

Consistent with Blackstone, the traditional view in American law is that statutes apply prospectively.[24] In the modern regulatory state, however, legislators often believe that they need to act with some retroactive effect. Is it constitutional for them to do so? Will courts give effect to their efforts? These are surprisingly complicated inquiries.

---

[24] E.g., Debra Bassett, *In the Wake of* Schooner Peggy: *Deconstructing Legislative Retroactivity Analysis*, 69 U. Cin. L. Rev. 453 (2001); Elmer Smead, *The Rule Against Retroactive Legislation: A Basic Principle of Jurisprudence*, 20 Minn. L. Rev. 775 (1936); Ann Woolhandler, *Public Rights, Private Rights, and Statutory Retroactivity*, 94 Geo. L.J. 1015, 1063 (2006).

NOTES ON CONSTITUTIONAL PROBLEMS
WITH RETROACTIVE STATUTES

1.   *Retroactive Statutes and the Regulatory State.* Sometimes, to solve a problem or to assure equal treatment, Congress would like its statute to apply retroactively, the way a judicial decision would. According to Charles Hochman, *The Supreme Court and the Constitutionality of Retroactive Legislation,* 73 Harv. L. Rev. 692, 693 (1960), there are a number of traditional objections:

> Perhaps the most fundamental reason why retroactive legislation is suspect stems from the principle that a person should be able to plan his [or her] conduct with reasonable certainty of the legal consequences. * * * Closely allied to this factor is the [person's] desire for stability with respect to past transactions. Moreover, to the extent that statutory law should serve as a guide to individual conduct, this purpose is thwarted by retroactive enactments. Still another reason underlying the hostility to retroactive legislation is that such a statute may be passed without an exact knowledge of who will benefit from it.

How weighty are these objections? Do they support a constitutional rule against retroactive legislation?

2.   Ex Post Facto *Laws and Bills of Attainder.* The Constitution prohibits both state and federal governments from enacting any "Bill of Attainder" or "*ex post facto* law." U.S. Const. art. I, §§ 9 & 10. "[A]ny statute which punishes as a crime an act previously committed, which was innocent when done; which makes more burdensome the punishment for a crime, after its commission, or which deprives one charged with a crime of any defense available according to law at the time when the act was committed, is prohibited as *ex post facto.*" *Beazell v. Ohio,* 269 U.S. 167, 169–70 (1925); see *Carmell v. Texas,* 529 U.S. 513 (2000) (laws that require less evidence to obtain conviction than was required when the alleged criminal act took place are *ex post facto* laws). Prohibited bills of attainder are "legislative acts, no matter what their form," in other words, criminal as well as civil statutes, "that apply either to named individuals or to easily ascertainable members of a group in such a way as to inflict punishment on them without a judicial trial." *United States v. Lovett,* 328 U.S. 303, 315–16 (1946).

Most cases overturning laws based upon the Bill of Attainder Clause have related to the classic situation in which certain Members of Congress hone in on persons or small groups whom they dislike, make findings that such persons have violated the law, and then penalize them. See *United States v. Brown,* 381 U.S. 437 (1965) (invalidating law making it a crime for members of the Communist Party to serve as union officers). Cf. *Nixon v. Administrator of General Servs.,* 433 U.S. 425, 475–76 (1977).

3.   *The Contract Clause.* The Contract Clause provides that "[n]o state shall * * * pass any * * * Law impairing the Obligation of Contracts." U.S. Const. art. I, § 10. It reflects the Framers' strong disapproval of widespread retroactive state laws altering private contracts during and after the Revolution and was intended as an "added * * * constitutional bulwark in favor of personal security and private rights." *The Federalist,* No. 44, at 301 (J. Cooke ed. 1961); see Benjamin Wright, *The Contract Clause of the Constitution* (1938). While the prohibition is not an absolute one, it does impose restraints on the authority of a State "to abridge existing contractual relationships, even in the exercise of its otherwise legitimate police power." *Allied Structural Steel Co.*

v. Spannaus, 438 U.S. 234, 242 (1978). Where a state law has substantially impaired a preexisting contractual relationship and cannot justify the impairment as a reasonable means to address an important social problem, the statute might be invalidated. *United States Trust Co. v. New Jersey*, 431 U.S. 1 (1977) (striking down state alteration of the terms of its debt).

4. *The Takings Clause.* Just as the Contracts Clause urges special caution with regard to retroactive laws affecting contract rights, so, too, the Takings Clause of the Fifth Amendment restricts retroactive laws unduly affecting property rights. See *United States v. Security Indus. Bank*, 459 U.S. 70 (1982); *Pennsylvania Coal Co. v. Mahon*, 260 U.S. 393 (1922) (Holmes, J.). Note that the constitutional restrictions on civil statutory retroactivity are much less stringent than those applied to monitor retroactive criminal statutes. See Harold Krent, *The Puzzling Boundary Between Criminal and Civil Retroactive Lawmaking,* 84 Geo. L.J. 2143 (1996) (noting and criticizing this strong distinction).

5. *The Due Process Clauses.* The Due Process Clauses of the Fifth and Fourteenth Amendments preclude federal and state governments from depriving persons of "life, liberty, or property, without due process of law." This requirement is easy for Congress to meet, so long as the federal interest in retroactive application is clearly articulated. E.g., *United States v. Carlton,* 512 U.S. 26 (1988). The Supreme Court has used the Fifth Amendment to extend Contract Clause precepts to federal legislation, *Lynch v. United States*, 292 U.S. 571 (1934), and Justice Kennedy relied on due process concepts in a contract-based retirement funds case, *Eastern Enterprises v. Apfel,* 524 U.S. 498 (1998).

6. *A Functional Approach to Retroactive Legislation.* Hochman, *Constitutionality of Retroactive Legislation*, argues from the cases that Congress usually has authority to enact statutes that apply retroactively. Some of the factors which tend to support retroactivity are the following:

(a) *Emergency Situation.* Unforeseen, urgent, crisis situations often call forth decisive legislative responses. Wider constitutional latitude is given when the situation calls for strong measures. Thus in *Home Building and Loan Ass'n v. Blaisdell*, 290 U.S. 398 (1934), a leading Contract Clause case, the Court approved Depression measures creating a moratorium on mortgage foreclosures. But cf. *Louisville Joint Stock Land Bank v. Radford,* 295 U.S. 555 (1935) (striking down Frazier-Lemke Act suspending mortgage default proceedings for five years).

(b) *Strong Public Interest Requiring Retroactivity.* A related justification is that if retroactivity is necessary to the success of a statutory regime aimed at some important social policy, it will typically be accepted. The Court in *Usery v. Turner Elkhorn Mining Co.,* 428 U.S. 1, 14–20 (1976), upheld provisions in the Federal Coal Mine Health and Safety Act that required employers to compensate miners having black lung disease, even when their employment had terminated before the relevant provisions were enacted. The Court reasoned that the statute was a rational way to spread the costs of an important social problem—especially since mine operators had known about the effects of black lung disease for two decades and done nothing about it. Could the operators have been criminally punished retroactively?

(c) *Limited Abrogation of the Preenactment Right.* The more limited the legislative alteration of the legal incidents of a claim arising from a pre-enactment transaction, the stronger the case for the validity of the retroactive legislation. For example, the Court in *Penn Central Transp. Co. v. New York City*, 438 U.S. 104 (1978), upheld against a Takings Clause challenge New York's restrictions on the use that could be made of Grand Central Terminal because of its designation as a historic landmark. The Court reasoned that ownership of the landmark included a complex "bundle of rights," only some of which had been taken by the retroactive regulation. The Minnesota act in *Blaisdell*, extending the period for redemption of foreclosed mortgages and permitting the mortgagor to remain in control of the property also required the mortgagor to pay a reasonable rent on the property. And the statute stated that it would expire within two years, or whenever the emergency ended (whichever came first). Thus both the duration of the statutory impairment *and the* number of legal incidents taken away may be relevant to analysis of the validity of retroactive legislation.

(d) *Reasonable Expectation of Regulation.* Fairness concerns are greatly attenuated when the persons retroactively deprived of contractual or property rights had no reasonable expectation that they would be able to keep them. In other words, retroactivity can be justified to prevent "windfalls." Thus the Court in *Energy Reserves Group, Inc. v. Kansas Power and Light Co.*, 459 U.S. 400, 419–20 (1983), upheld a state law retroactively restricting price escalator clauses in contracts for the intrastate sale of natural gas. A critical reason for the retroactivity was that due to partial federal deregulation of interstate gas, intrastate gas prices had unexpectedly gone up, which would have given energy producers a $128 million windfall, to be borne by consumers (according to the legislature). Where a law only serves to restrict a party to those gains reasonably to be expected from the contract, *City of El Paso v. Simmons*, 379 U.S. 497, 515 (1965), its retroactive application will usually be upheld.

(e) *Lack of Process Corruption.* The Court may look askance at retroactive legislation when there is self-dealing. For example, when a state tries to void or substantially alter its own contractual obligations, the Court will apply a stricter standard of scrutiny and often invalidate the regulation. E.g., *United States Trust Co. v. New Jersey*, 431 U.S. 1 (1977). One consideration in Takings Clause cases is whether the burden of regulation is "disproportionately" concentrated on a few persons, suggesting process bias. See *Goldblatt v. Hempstead*, 369 U.S. 590, 594 (1962). See generally Note, *A Process-Oriented Approach to the Contract Clause*, 89 Yale L.J. 1623, 1638–39 (1980) (judicial review should require that the political process provide all groups interested in retroactive legislation with meaningful opportunity for their objections to be heard and considered).

(f) *Retroactivity and Original Meaning.* Renewed interest in original constitutional meaning might give a boost to constitutional review, because the Founding Generation was highly skeptical of retroactive legislation. See Robert Natelson, *Statutory Retroactivity: The Founders' View,* 39 Idaho L. Rev. 489 (2003). The dispute in *Eastern Enterprises v. Apfel*, 524 U.S. 498 (1998), involved a 1992 federal statute that required a company that had left the coal mining industry in 1965 to assist in financing current health care costs for retired miners. The 1992 law was sparked by a funding crisis relating to benefit plans for retired miners. Speaking for a plurality (including Chief Justice Rehnquist and Justices Scalia and Thomas), Justice O'Connor labeled this a "taking" of the funds needed to comply with the statute. When government action "singles out certain employers to bear a burden that is substantial in amount, based on the employer's conduct far in the past, and unrelated to any commitment that the employers made or to any injury they caused, the governmental action implicates fundamental principles of fairness underlying the Takings Clause."

Concurring Justice Thomas added that he thought the statute also violated the *Ex Post Facto* Clause; he rejected the Court's longstanding doctrine limiting that clause to criminal proceedings. See Krent, *Puzzling Boundary Between Criminal and Civil Retroactive Lawmaking* (also skeptical of the Court's strong distinction between civil and criminal retroactivity). Justice Kennedy concurred in the judgment on the ground that the statute violated due process because it fell "far outside the bounds of retroactivity permissible under our law." He agreed with the dissenting Justices that the law did not effectuate a taking because no "specific property right or interest" was at stake. Dissenting Justices Stevens, Souter, Ginsburg, and Breyer thought the statute was not fundamentally unfair because it comported with long-term, if informal, expectations within the industry.

Because there was no controlling opinion for the Court, and because lower courts have been unable to craft a rule of law capturing the rationale for a majority, *Apfel* has had a limited effect on federal retroactivity jurisprudence. *Swisher Int'l Inc. v. Schafer*, 550 F.3d 1046 (11th Cir. 2008).

NOTE ON THE PRESUMPTION AGAINST STATUTORY RETROACTIVITY

Although the post-New Deal consensus is that the legislature can now make most statutory obligations retroactive to some extent, there remains substantial reluctance on the part of legislators to enact statutes that are retroactive on their face and on the part of judges to apply statutes retroactively where the statute is not clear. Scholars have generally been amenable to this approach, e.g., Hart & Sacks, *The Legal Process* 618–30, and the Supreme Court has even in the post-New Deal era stated that "[r]etroactivity is not favored in the law. * * * Congressional enactments and administrative rules will not be construed to have retroactive effect unless their language requires this result." *Bowen v. Georgetown University Hospital*, 488 U.S. 204 (1988).

On the other hand are Supreme Court decisions that require application of a change in law—whether arising from a judicial decision or from enactment of a new statute—to all pending civil cases. The germinal case is *United States v. Schooner Peggy*, 5 U.S. (1 Cranch) 103 (1800), a decision by Chief Justice Marshall. More recent precedents are *Bradley v. School Board of City of Richmond*, 416 U.S. 696 (1974), and *Thorpe v. Housing Authority of City of Durham*, 393 U.S. 268 (1969). In *Bradley*, the Court held that a change in law should apply to pending civil cases so long as the legislature or the court making the change did not clearly intend to prohibit retroactive application and manifest injustice does not result.

The Supreme Court noted in *Kaiser Aluminum and Chemical Corp. v. Bonjorno*, 494 U.S. 827 (1990), that there is a tension between the *Bradley-Thorpe* line of cases and the *Bowen* line of cases but declined to resolve the matter, because a majority of the Court thought both lines required non-retroactive application of Congress' amendment of the postjudgment interest law, 28 U.S.C. § 1961. The Civil Rights Act of 1991 provided the Court the opportunity to resolve the tension between the competing lines of cases.

LANDGRAF V. USI FILM PRODUCTS

Supreme Court of the United States, 1994.
511 U.S. 244, 114 S.Ct. 1483, 128 L.Ed.2d 229.

JUSTICE STEVENS delivered the opinion of the Court.

[From September 4, 1984, through January 17, 1986, Barbara Landgraf was employed in the USI Film Products (USI) plant in Tyler, Texas. She complained that her employer had tolerated a "hostile work environment," in violation of Title VII. The EEOC declined to pursue her complaint, because it found the employer had adequately remedied the violation. Landgraf brought a lawsuit, which was dismissed. On November 21, 1991, while petitioner's appeal was pending, the President signed into law the Civil Rights Act of 1991. The Court of Appeals rejected Landgraf's argument that her case should be remanded for a jury trial on damages pursuant to the 1991 Act.]

[II] The Civil Rights Act of 1991 is in large part a response to a series of decisions of this Court interpreting the Civil Rights Acts of 1866 and 1964. Section 3(4) expressly identifies as one of the Act's purposes "to respond to recent decisions of the Supreme Court by expanding the scope of relevant civil rights statutes in order to provide adequate protection to victims of discrimination." That section, as well as a specific finding in § 2(2), identifies *Wards Cove Packing Co. v. Atonio*, 490 U.S. 642 (1989), as a decision that gave rise to special concerns. Section 105 of the Act, entitled "Burden of Proof in Disparate Impact Cases," is a direct response to *Wards Cove*. [Other sections were drafted to override other decisions. E.g., § 101, amending 42 U.S.C. § 1981, to override *Patterson v. McLean Credit Union*, 491 U.S. 164 (1989).] A number of important provisions in the Act, however, were not responses to Supreme Court decisions. * * * Among the provisions that did not directly respond to any Supreme Court decision is the one at issue in this case, § 102.

Entitled "Damages in Cases of Intentional Discrimination," § 102 provides in relevant part:

"(a) Right of Recovery.—

"(1) Civil Rights.—In an action brought by a complaining party under section 706 or 717 of the Civil Rights Act of 1964 (42 U.S.C. 2000e–5) against a respondent who engaged in unlawful intentional discrimination (not an employment practice that is unlawful because of its disparate impact) prohibited under section 703, 704, or 717 of the Act (42 U.S.C. 2000e–2 or 2000e–3), and provided that the complaining party cannot recover under section 1977 of the Revised Statutes (42 U.S.C. 1981), the complaining party may recover compensatory and punitive damages . . . in addition to any relief authorized by section 706(g) of the Civil Rights Act of 1964, from the respondent.

"(c) Jury Trial.—If a complaining party seeks compensatory or punitive damages under this section—

"(1) any party may demand a trial by jury."

Before the enactment of the 1991 Act, Title VII afforded only "equitable" remedies. The primary form of monetary relief available was backpay. * * * [T]he new compensatory damages provision of the 1991 Act is "in addition to," and does not replace or duplicate, the backpay remedy allowed under prior law. * * *

Section 102 also allows monetary relief for some forms of workplace discrimination that would not previously have justified *any* relief under Title VII. As this case illustrates, even if unlawful discrimination was proved, under prior law a Title VII plaintiff could not recover monetary relief unless the discrimination was also found to have some concrete effect on the plaintiff's employment status, such as a denied promotion, a differential in compensation, or termination. Section 102, however, allows a plaintiff to recover in circumstances in which there has been unlawful discrimination in the "terms, conditions, or privileges of employment," 42 U.S.C. § 2000e–2(a)(l), even though the discrimination did not involve a discharge or a loss of pay. * * *

In 1990, a comprehensive civil rights bill passed both Houses of Congress. Although similar to the 1991 Act in many other respects, the 1990 bill differed in that it contained language expressly calling for application of many of its provisions, including the section providing for damages in cases of intentional employment discrimination, to cases arising before its (expected) enactment.[8] The President vetoed the 1990 legislation, however, citing the bill's "unfair retroactivity rules" as one reason for his disapproval. Congress narrowly failed to override the veto. See 136 Cong. Rec. S16589 (Oct. 24, 1990) (66–34 Senate vote in favor of override). * * *

The omission of the elaborate retroactivity provision of the 1990 bill—which was by no means the only source of political controversy over that legislation—is not dispositive because it does not tell us precisely where the compromise was struck in the 1991 Act. The Legislature might, for example, have settled in 1991 on a less expansive form of retroactivity that, unlike the 1990 bill, did not reach cases already finally decided. A decision to reach only cases still pending might explain Congress' failure to provide in the 1991 Act, as it had in 1990, that certain sections would apply to proceedings pending on specific preenactment dates. Our first question, then, is whether the statutory text on which petitioner relies manifests an intent that the 1991 Act should be applied to cases that arose and went to trial before its enactment.

[III] Petitioner's textual argument relies on three provisions of the 1991 Act: §§ 402(a), 402(b), and 109(c). Section 402(a), the only provision of the Act that speaks directly to the question before us, states:

---

8   [In this footnote, Justice Stevens quoted the retroactivity and transition provisions of the proposed Civil Rights Act of 1990, S. 2104, 101st Cong., 1st Sess. (1990). Thus, § 15(a)(1) provided that "section 4 [the provision overriding *Wards Cove*] shall apply to all proceedings pending on or commenced after June 5, 1989," the date of *Wards Cove.* Section 15(a)(2), (5)–(6) provided similarly retroactive effect for the provisions overriding *Martin v. Wilks,* 490 U.S. 755 (1989), *Lorance v. AT & T Technologies, Inc.,* 490 U.S. 900 (1989), and *Patterson.* Section 15(1)(4) provided that the provisions that would have given relief to Landgraf would "apply to all proceedings pending on or commenced after the date of enactment of this Act." Section 15(b) set forth "Transition Rules," including provisions directing courts to vacate judgments entered before the effective date of the Act.]

"Except as otherwise specifically provided, this Act and the amendments made by this Act shall take effect upon enactment."

That language does not, by itself, resolve the question before us. A statement that a statute will become effective on a certain date does not even arguably suggest that it has any application to conduct that occurred at an earlier date.[10] Petitioner does not argue otherwise. Rather, she contends that the introductory clause of § 402(a) would be superfluous unless it refers to §§ 402(b) and 109(c), which provide for prospective application in limited contexts.

The parties agree that § 402(b) was intended to exempt a single disparate impact lawsuit against the Wards Cove Packing Company. Section 402(b) provides:

"(b) CERTAIN DISPARATE IMPACT CASES.—Notwithstanding any other provision of this Act, nothing in this Act shall apply to any disparate impact case for which a complaint was filed before March 1, 1975, and for which an initial decision was rendered after October 30, 1983."

Section 109(c), part of the section extending Title VII to overseas employers, states:

"(c) APPLICATION OF AMENDMENTS.—The amendments made by this section shall not apply with respect to conduct occurring before the date of the enactment of this Act."

According to petitioner, these two subsections are the "other provisions" contemplated in the first clause of § 402(a), and together create a strong negative inference that all sections of the Act not specifically declared prospective apply to pending cases that arose before November 21, 1991.

Before addressing the particulars of petitioner's argument, we observe that she places extraordinary weight on two comparatively minor and narrow provisions in a long and complex statute. Applying the entire Act to cases arising from preenactment conduct would have important consequences, including the possibility that trials completed before its enactment would need to be retried and the possibility that employers would be liable for punitive damages for conduct antedating the Act's enactment. Purely prospective application, on the other hand, would prolong the life of a remedial scheme, and of judicial constructions of civil rights statutes, that Congress obviously found wanting. Given the high stakes of the retroactivity question, the broad coverage of the statute, and the prominent and specific retroactivity provisions in the 1990 bill, it would be surprising for Congress

---

[10] The history of prior amendments to Title VII suggests that the "effective-upon-enactment" formula would have been an especially inapt way to reach pending cases. When it amended Title VII in the Equal Employment Opportunity Act of 1972, Congress explicitly provided:

"The amendments made by this Act to section 706 of the Civil Rights Act of 1964 shall be applicable with respect to charges pending with the Commission on the date of enactment of this Act and all charges filed thereafter." Pub. L. 92–261, § 14, 86 Stat. 113.

In contrast, in amending Title VII to bar discrimination on the basis of pregnancy in 1978, Congress provided:

"Except as provided in subsection (b), the amendment made by this Act shall be effective on the date of enactment." § 2(a), 92 Stat. 2076.

The only Courts of Appeals to consider whether the 1978 amendments applied to pending cases concluded that they did not. If we assume that Congress was familiar with those decisions, cf. *Cannon v. University of Chicago*, 441 U.S. 677, 698–699 (1979), its choice of language in § 402(a) would imply non-retroactivity.

to have chosen to resolve that question through negative inferences drawn from two provisions of quite limited effect.

Petitioner, however, invokes the canon that a court should give effect to every provision of a statute and thus avoid redundancy among different provisions. Unless the word "otherwise" in § 402(a) refers to either § 402(b) or § 109(c), she contends, the first five words in § 402(a) are entirely superfluous. Moreover, relying on the canon "[e]xpressio unius est exclusio alterius," petitioner argues that because Congress provided specifically for prospectivity in two places (§§ 109(c) and 402(b)), we should infer that it intended the opposite for the remainder of the statute.

* * * Petitioner's argument has some force, but we find it most unlikely that Congress intended the introductory clause to carry the critically important meaning petitioner assigns it. Had Congress wished § 402(a) to have such a determinate meaning, it surely would have used language comparable to its reference to the predecessor Title VII damages provisions in the 1990 legislation: that the new provisions "shall apply to all proceedings pending on or commenced after the date of enactment of this Act." S. 2104, 101st Cong., 1st Sess. § 15(a)(4) (1990).

It is entirely possible that Congress inserted the "otherwise specifically provided" language not because it understood the "takes effect" clause to establish a rule of retroactivity to which only two "other specific provisions" would be exceptions, but instead to assure that any specific timing provisions in the Act would prevail over the general "take effect on enactment" command. The drafters of a complicated piece of legislation containing more than 50 separate sections may well have inserted the "except as otherwise provided" language merely to avoid the risk of an inadvertent conflict in the statute. If the introductory clause of § 402(a) was intended to refer specifically to §§ 402(b), 109(c), or both, it is difficult to understand why the drafters chose the word "otherwise" rather than either or both of the appropriate section numbers.

* * * It is entirely possible—indeed, highly probable—that, because it was unable to resolve the retroactivity issue with the clarity of the 1990 legislation, Congress viewed the matter as an open issue to be resolved by the courts. Our precedents on retroactivity left doubts about what default rule would apply in the absence of congressional guidance, and suggested that some provisions might apply to cases arising before enactment while others might not. Compare *Bowen v. Georgetown Univ. Hospital*, 488 U.S. 204 (1988) with *Bradley v. Richmond School Bd.*, 416 U.S. 696 (1974). The only matters Congress did *not* leave to the courts were set out with specificity in §§ 109(c) and 402(b). Congressional doubt concerning judicial retroactivity doctrine, coupled with the likelihood that the routine "take effect upon enactment" language would require courts to fall back upon that doctrine, provide a plausible explanation for both §§ 402(b) and 109(c) that makes neither provision redundant. * * *

The relevant legislative history of the 1991 Act reinforces our conclusion that §§ 402(a), 109(c) and 402(b) cannot bear the weight petitioner places upon them. The 1991 bill as originally introduced in the House contained explicit retroactivity provisions similar to those found in the 1990 bill. However, the Senate substitute that was agreed upon omitted those explicit retroactivity provisions. The legislative history discloses some frankly partisan statements about the meaning of the final effective date language, but those statements cannot plausibly be read as reflecting any general agreement.[15] * * *

Although the passage of the 1990 bill may indicate that a majority of the 1991 Congress also favored retroactive application, even the will of the majority does not become law unless it follows the path charted in Article I, § 7, cl. 2 of the Constitution. See *INS v. Chadha*, 462 U.S. 919, 946–951 (1983). In the absence of the kind of unambiguous directive found in § 15 of the 1990 bill, we must look elsewhere for guidance on whether § 102 applies to this case.

[IV] * * * [T]he presumption against retroactive legislation is deeply rooted in our jurisprudence, and embodies a legal doctrine centuries older than our Republic. Elementary considerations of fairness dictate that individuals should have an opportunity to know what the law is and to conform their conduct accordingly; settled expectations should not be lightly disrupted. For that reason, the "principle that the legal effect of conduct should ordinarily be assessed under the law that existed when the conduct took place has timeless and universal appeal." [*Kaiser Alum. & Chem. Corp. v. Bonjorno*, 494 U.S. 827, 855 (1990) (Scalia, J., concurring).] In a free, dynamic society, creativity in both commercial and artistic endeavors is fostered by a rule of law that gives people confidence about the legal consequences of their actions.

It is therefore not surprising that the antiretroactivity principle finds expression in several provisions of our Constitution. The *Ex Post Facto* Clause flatly prohibits retroactive application of penal legislation. Article I, § 10, cl. 1 prohibits States from passing another type of retroactive legislation, laws "impairing the Obligation of Contracts." The Fifth Amendment's Takings Clause prevents the Legislature (and other government actors) from depriving private persons of vested property rights except for a "public use" and upon payment of "just compensation." The prohibitions on "Bills of Attainder" in Art. I, §§ 9–10, prohibit legislatures from singling out disfavored persons and meting out summary punishment for past conduct. The Due Process Clause also protects the interests in fair notice and repose that may be compromised by retroactive legislation; a justification sufficient to validate a statute's prospective application under the Clause "may not suffice" to warrant its retroactive application.

These provisions demonstrate that retroactive statutes raise particular concerns. The Legislature's unmatched powers allow it to sweep away settled

---

[15] For example, in an "interpretive memorandum" introduced on behalf of seven Republican sponsors of S. 1745, the bill that became the 1991 Act, Senator Danforth stated that "[t]he bill provides that, unless otherwise specified, the provisions of this legislation shall take effect upon enactment *and shall not apply retroactively.*" 137 Cong. Rec. S15485 (Oct. 30, 1991) (emphasis added). Senator Kennedy responded that it "will be up to the courts to determine the extent to which the bill will apply to cases and claims that were pending on the date of enactment." *Ibid.* (citing *Bradley*). The legislative history reveals other partisan statements on the proper meaning of the Act's "effective date" provisions. Senator Danforth observed that such statements carry little weight as legislative history. As he put it, "a court would be well advised to take with a large grain of salt floor debate and statements placed in the Congressional Record which purport to create an interpretation for the legislation that is before us." 137 Cong. Rec. S15325 (Oct. 29, 1991).

expectations suddenly and without individualized consideration. Its responsivity to political pressures poses a risk that it may be tempted to use retroactive legislation as a means of retribution against unpopular groups or individuals. As Justice Marshall observed in his opinion for the Court in *Weaver v. Graham*, 450 U.S. 24 (1981), the *Ex Post Facto* Clause not only ensures that individuals have "fair warning" about the effect of criminal statutes, but also "restricts governmental power by restraining arbitrary and potentially vindictive legislation."

The Constitution's restrictions, of course, are of limited scope. Absent a violation of one of those specific provisions, the potential unfairness of retroactive civil legislation is not a sufficient reason for a court to fail to give a statute its intended scope. Retroactivity provisions often serve entirely benign and legitimate purposes, whether to respond to emergencies, to correct mistakes, to prevent circumvention of a new statute in the interval immediately preceding its passage, or simply to give comprehensive effect to a new law Congress considers salutary. However, a requirement that Congress first make its intention clear helps ensure that Congress itself has determined that the benefits of retroactivity outweigh the potential for disruption or unfairness. * * *

A statute does not operate "retrospectively" merely because it is applied in a case arising from conduct antedating the statute's enactment, or upsets expectations based in prior law. Rather, the court must ask whether the new provision attaches new legal consequences to events completed before its enactment. * * *

Since the early days of this Court, we have declined to give retroactive effect to statutes burdening private rights unless Congress had made clear its intent. * * *

* * * [W]hile the *constitutional* impediments to retroactive civil legislation are now modest, prospectivity remains the appropriate default rule. Because it accords with widely held intuitions about how statutes ordinarily operate, a presumption against retroactivity will generally coincide with legislative and public expectations. Requiring clear intent assures that Congress itself has affirmatively considered the potential unfairness of retroactive application and determined that it is an acceptable price to pay for the countervailing benefits. Such a requirement allocates to Congress responsibility for fundamental policy judgments concerning the proper temporal reach of statutes, and has the additional virtue of giving legislators a predictable background rule against which to legislate.

[B] Although we have long embraced a presumption against statutory retroactivity, for just as long we have recognized that, in many situations, a court should "apply the law in effect at the time it renders its decision," *Bradley*, even though that law was enacted after the events that gave rise to the suit. There is, of course, no conflict between that principle and a presumption against retroactivity when the statute in question is unambiguous. Chief Justice Marshall's opinion in *United States v. Schooner Peggy*, 1 Cranch 103 (1801), illustrates this point. Because a treaty signed on September 30, 1800, while the case was pending on appeal, unambiguously provided for the restoration of captured property "not yet *definitively* condemned," (emphasis in original), we reversed a decree entered on September 23, 1800, condemning a French vessel that had been seized in American waters. Our application of "the law in effect" at the time of our decision in *Schooner Peggy* was simply a response to the language of the statute.

Even absent specific legislative authorization, application of new statutes passed after the events in suit is unquestionably proper in many situations. When the intervening statute authorizes or affects the propriety of prospective relief, application of the new provision is not retroactive. Thus, in *American Steel Foundries v. Tri-City Central Trades Council*, 257 U.S. 184 (1921), we held that § 20 of the Clayton Act, enacted while the case was pending on appeal, governed the propriety of injunctive relief against labor picketing. * * *

Our holding in *Bradley* is * * * compatible with the line of decisions disfavoring "retroactive" application of statutes. In *Bradley*, the District Court had awarded attorney's fees and costs, upon general equitable principles, to parents who had prevailed in an action seeking to desegregate the public schools of Richmond, Virginia. While the case was pending before the Court of Appeals, Congress enacted § 718 of the Education Amendments of 1972, which authorized federal courts to award the prevailing parties in school desegregation cases a reasonable attorney's fee. The Court of Appeals held that the new fee provision did not authorize the award of fees for services rendered before the effective date of the amendments. This Court reversed. We concluded that the private parties could rely on § 718 to support their claim for attorney's fees, resting our decision "on the principle that a court is to apply the law in effect at the time it renders its decision, unless doing so would result in manifest injustice or there is statutory direction or legislative history to the contrary."

Although that language suggests a categorical presumption in favor of application of *all* new rules of law, we now make it clear that *Bradley* did not alter the well-settled presumption against application of the class of new statutes that would have genuinely "retroactive" effect. * * * [T]he attorney's fee provision at issue in *Bradley* did not resemble the cases in which we have invoked the presumption against statutory retroactivity. Attorney's fee determinations, we have observed, are "collateral to the main cause of action" and "uniquely separable from the cause of action to be proved at trial." Moreover, even before the enactment of § 718, federal courts had authority to award fees based upon equitable principles. As our opinion in *Bradley* made clear, it would be difficult to imagine a stronger equitable case for an attorney's fee award than a lawsuit in which the plaintiff parents would otherwise have to bear the costs of desegregating their children's public schools. * * *

[V] * * * The jury trial right set out in § 102(c)(1) is plainly a procedural change of the sort that would ordinarily govern in trials conducted after its effective date. If § 102 did no more than introduce a right to jury trial in Title VII cases, the provision would presumably apply to cases tried after November 21, 1991, regardless of when the underlying conduct occurred. However, because § 102(c) makes a jury trial available only "[i]f a complaining party seeks compensatory or punitive damages," the jury trial option must stand or fall with the attached damages provisions.

Section 102(b)(1) is clearly on the other side of the line. That subsection authorizes punitive damages if the plaintiff shows that the defendant "engaged in a discriminatory practice or discriminatory practices with malice or with reckless indifference to the federally protected rights of an aggrieved individual." The very labels given "punitive" or "exemplary" damages, as well as the rationales that support them, demonstrate that they share key characteristics of criminal sanctions. Retroactive imposition of punitive damages would raise a serious constitutional question. Before we entertained that question, we would have to be confronted with a statute that explicitly authorized punitive damages for preenactment conduct. The Civil Rights Act of 1991 contains no such explicit command.

The provision of § 102(a)(1) authorizing the recovery of compensatory damages is not easily classified. It does not make unlawful conduct that was lawful when it occurred; as we have noted, § 102 only reaches discriminatory conduct already prohibited by Title VII. Concerns about a lack of fair notice are further muted by the fact that such discrimination was in many cases (although not this one) already subject to monetary liability in the form of backpay. Nor could anyone seriously contend that the compensatory damages provisions smack of a "retributive" or other suspect legislative purpose. Section 102 reflects Congress' desire to afford victims of discrimination more complete redress for violations of rules established more than a generation ago in the Civil Rights Act of 1964. At least with respect to its compensatory damages provisions, then, § 102 is not in a category in which objections to retroactive application on grounds of fairness have their greatest force.

Nonetheless, the new compensatory damages provision would operate "retrospectively" if it were applied to conduct occurring before November 21, 1991. Unlike certain other forms of relief, compensatory damages are quintessentially backward-looking. Compensatory damages may be intended less to sanction wrongdoers than to make victims whole, but they do so by a mechanism that affects the liabilities of defendants. They do not "compensate" by distributing funds from the public coffers, but by requiring particular employers to pay for harms they caused. The introduction of a right to compensatory damages is also the type of legal change that would have an impact on private parties' planning. In this case, the event to which the new damages provision relates is the discriminatory conduct of respondents' agent John Williams; if applied here, that provision would attach an important new legal burden to that conduct. The new damages remedy in § 102, we conclude, is the kind of provision that does not apply to events antedating its enactment in the absence of clear congressional intent. * * *

JUSTICE BLACKMUN, dissenting. * * *

* * * The well-established presumption against retroactive legislation, which serves to protect settled expectations, is grounded in a respect for vested rights. See, e.g., Smead, *The Rule Against Retroactive Legislation: A Basic Principle of Jurisprudence*, 20 Minn. L. Rev. 774, 784 (1936) (retroactivity doctrine developed as an "inhibition against a construction which . . . would violate vested rights"). This presumption need not be applied to remedial legislation, such as § 102, that does not proscribe any conduct that was previously legal.

At no time within the last generation has an employer had a vested right to engage in or to permit sexual harassment; " 'there is no such thing as a vested right to do wrong.' " *Freeborn v. Smith*, 2 Wall. 160 (1865). Section 102 of the Act expands the remedies available for acts of intentional discrimination, but does not alter the scope of the employee's basic right to be free from discrimination or the employer's corresponding legal duty. There is nothing unjust about holding an employer responsible for injuries caused by conduct that has been illegal for almost 30 years.

[JUSTICE SCALIA, with whom JUSTICE KENNEDY and JUSTICE THOMAS joined, concurred in the judgment. The concurring Justices objected to the Court's failure to announce a "clear statement rule" against statutory retroactivity and to overrule *Bradley* and *Thorpe*. They also rejected the Court's effort to ground the antiretroactivity presumption in nineteenth century "vested rights" theory. Vested rights theory would seem to allow "procedure" rules to be retroactive, but the Court created an ad hoc exception to cover the instant case—a process that demonstrates the absurdity of the Court's approach.]

* * * The critical issue, I think, is not whether the rule affects "vested rights," or governs substance or procedure, but rather what is the relevant activity that the rule regulates. Absent clear statement otherwise, only such relevant activity which occurs *after* the effective date of the statute is covered. Most statutes are meant to regulate primary conduct, and hence will not be applied in trials involving conduct that occurred before their effective date. But other statutes have a different purpose and therefore a different relevant retroactivity event. A new rule of evidence governing expert testimony, for example, is aimed at regulating the conduct of trial, and the event relevant to retroactivity of the rule is introduction of the testimony. Even though it is a procedural rule, it would unquestionably not be applied to *testimony already taken*—reversing a case on appeal, for example, because the new rule had not been applied at a trial which antedated the statute. * * *

PROBLEMS OF STATUTORY RETROACTIVITY

Problem 5–11. Companion Case Interpreting the Civil Rights Act of 1991. The 1991 Act also overrode *Patterson*, replete with congressional findings that the Supreme Court had misinterpreted § 1981. The *Patterson* override was therefore *curative* in ways that the *Landgraf* provision was not. Although distinguishable in this way, does *Landgraf* nonetheless control the disposition of this issue as well? How would Justice Stevens analyze a curative override? Justice Blackmun? Justice Scalia? See *Rivers v. Roadway Express, Inc.,* 511 U.S. 298 (1994). For a more recent application of the presumption, see *Vartelas v. Holder,* 132 S.Ct. 1479 (2012).

Problem 5–12. Marriage and California's Proposition 8. In 2008, the California Supreme Court invalidated that state's denial of equal marriage rights to lesbian and gay couples. Immediately, there were both gay weddings and popular pushback in California. In November 2008, the voters amended the state constitution to allow the Legislature to exclude lesbian and gay couples from the institution of civil marriage. Specifically, Proposition 8 added a new Section 7.5 to Article I of the California Constitution: "Only marriage between a man and a woman is valid or recognized in California."

Between June and November, however, more than 18,000 lesbian and gay couples were legally married in California. Did Proposition 8 apply retroactively, to invalidate those marriages? To analyze this issue, consider, first, whether California should follow the strong presumption found in *Landgraf*, see *Evangelatos v. Superior Court*, 753 P.2d 585 (Cal. 1988) (leading state case); second, whether the text or background materials for Proposition 8 rebut however strong a presumption you think justified under the circumstances; and third, whether the strong presumption applies to marriages performed before Proposition 8 (namely, is the new constitutional provision even being applied "retroactively").

Recall the text of Proposition 8, augmented by this statement in the ballot materials distributed to every voter: "Your YES vote on Proposition 8 means that only marriage between a man and a woman will be valid or recognized in California, regardless of when or where performed." Do these sources justify retroactive treatment here? See *Strauss v. Horton,* 207 P.3d 48 (Cal. 2009) (unanimous court ruling on this issue).

CHAPTER 6

THEORIES OF STATUTORY INTERPRETATION

■ ■ ■

Statutes, rather than the common law or constitutional law, have created the modern structure for American governance, most of our nation's fundamental public policies, and even many of its basic norms. Notwithstanding the "statutorification" of American law, courts and agencies retain an important role, because they apply and interpret statutes to situations not clearly answered by the statutory language. Such "hard cases" are inevitable, partly because of the inherent imprecision of language and partly because of the inability of statute drafters to anticipate all problems or circumstances within the statute's ambit. A statute "is not an equation or a formula representing a clearly marked process, nor is it an expression of individual thought to which is imparted the definiteness a single authorship can give. A statute is an instrument of government partaking of its practical purposes but also of its infirmities and limitations, of its awkward and groping efforts." Felix Frankfurter, in *Some Reflections on the Reading of Statutes*, 47 Colum. L. Rev. 527, 528 (1947).

Thus, while Frankfurter, as a professor at Harvard Law School, had developed "his threefold imperative to law students: (1) Read the statute; (2) read the statute; (3) read the statute," Henry Friendly, *Mr. Justice Frankfurter and the Reading of Statutes*, in Friendly, *Benchmarks* 202 (1967), Frankfurter the judge appreciated the difficulty of understanding a statute simply by parsing its language. The following example illustrates this point: A municipal ordinance provides that "all drug shops * * * shall be closed * * * at 10 p.m. on each and every day of the week." Does this require all such shops to remain open until 10 p.m., at which time they must be closed (i.e., is "closed" used as a verb or an adjective)? If a shop is closed at 10 p.m., may it lawfully open ten minutes later? In *Rex v. Liggetts-Findlay Drug-Stores Ltd.*, [1919] 3 W.W.R. 1025, the Supreme Court of Alberta answered the latter of these questions in the negative. The judge delivering the judgment stated:

> I think no one but a lawyer—I mean a person trained in legal technicalities such as a Judge or a lawyer—would ever think of imputing such a meaning to the [ordinance]. Everyone knows what is meant by closing a shop at 10 o'clock p.m. The meaning conveyed by the words used is too obvious for doubt. The rule, of course, is that the grammatical sense must in general be adhered to but with this limitation that if it leads to an absurdity or to something meaningless an effort must be made to give some sensible reading unless the language is absolutely intractable. * * * I think we should take the words to mean what they would quite clearly mean to the ordinary person and that is that shops should be closed not only at the moment of 10 o'clock but for the rest of that day.

Under this decision, could a store lawfully open at one minute after midnight?

Most statutes do not clearly answer all the questions that might arise, and over time the number of ambiguities or unanswered questions tends to increase. This gives rise to a predicament in our constitutional system. On the one hand, it is generally assumed that "any conflict between the legislative will and the judicial will must be resolved in favor of the former." Reed Dickerson, *The Interpretation and Application of Statutes* 8 (1975). Thus, statutory interpretation is not "an opportunity for a judge to use words as 'empty vessels into which he can pour anything he will'—his caprices, fixed notions, even statesmanlike beliefs in a particular policy." Frankfurter, *Reflections*, 529. On the other hand, statutory interpretation cannot be appropriately undertaken by a mechanical application of rules or "unimaginative adherence to well-worn professional phrases." *Id.* The proper interplay among statutory language, legislative purposes, extrinsic material such as other statutes and legislative history, and the particular facts of the case at hand may not be discerned by any formula. As a consequence, statutory interpretation in the hard cases involves substantial judicial discretion and political judgment. It is very much an art and not a science.

For most of this country's history, both the theory and the practice of statutory interpretation have been "eclectic" rather than systematic. After 1900, judges and scholars began to formulate their thoughts more systematically (Section 1 of this chapter). An initial impulse was to emphasize *legislative intent* as the foundational enterprise in statutory cases. In turn, beginning in the 1930s an influential group of skeptics, the legal realists, debunked legislative intent as an indeterminate and incoherent concept for statutory interpretation. During the New Deal, American public law turned toward *purpose*-based approaches as the foundation for statutory meaning (Section 2). Purposivism was in turn criticized for slighting traditional rule-of-law values (e.g., predictability of law, limiting judicial discretion) and for engaging courts in policy analysis for which they are ill-equipped. These critiques revived interest in *plain meaning* as the lodestar for statutory interpretation (Section 3). The "new textualism" is a particularly stringent version of the plain meaning rule, although this approach has in turn been criticized as impractical and unrealistic.

Our goal in this theoretical and historical survey is to offer you different theories from which you can learn, even as you criticize each of them. We think you will find the history and the theory useful, both in developing your own analytical skills for interpreting statutes and in appreciating the doctrinal material presented in the remaining chapters.

1. FROM ECLECTICISM TO SYSTEMATIC THEORY, 1789–1938

The early history of statutory interpretation in the United States is a complicated one, with American courts employing a grab-bag variety of approaches. Following English rhetoric and practice,[1] American courts in the eighteenth and

---

[1] See Samuel Thorne, *A Discourse upon the Exposicion & Understanding of Statutes* (1942) (reprinting leading early modern English treatise developing intent as lodestar of statutory interpretation). See also Peter Tiersma, *A Message in a Bottle: Text, Autonomy, and Statutory Interpretation*, 76 Tul. L. Rev. 431 (2001) (medieval English law treated statutes as mere "evidence of law").

early nineteenth centuries generally proclaimed their fidelity to legislative "intent" but would consider as evidence of such intent the statute's text, canons of statutory construction, the common law, the circumstances of enactment, principles of equity, and so forth.[2] Indeed, the big debate at the time of the drafting of the Constitution was how much discretion a court's *equity* powers gave it to ameliorate or extend the letter of the statute.

Chief Justice John Marshall was the first great American statutory interpreter, vigorously exercising equitable powers of construction in pursuit of his nationalist understanding of the Constitution, but under the cover of rigorous and sometimes brilliant analysis of statutory text and structure, the common law, and the law of nations.[3] Consider his remarkable opinion in *Ex parte Bollman*, 8 U.S. (4 Cranch) 75 (1807). Section 14 of the Judiciary Act of 1789 provided, in its first sentence, that the Supreme Court and other federal courts "shall have power to issue writs of *scire facias, habeas corpus*, and all other writs not specially provided for by statute, which may be necessary for the exercise of their respective jurisdictions * * *." The second sentence provided that Supreme Court Justices and district judges, in their chambers, "shall have power to grant writs of *habeas corpus* for the purpose of an inquiry into the cause of commitment." The government maintained that the Supreme Court itself had no jurisdiction to inquire into the legality of Bollman's confinement, as that power was only given to individual judges.

Marshall suggested there was a grammatical objection to this excellent plain meaning argument but declined to rest the decision on linguistic niceties.[4] Instead, "the sound construction, which the court thinks it safer to adopt," was the one consistent with a central goal of the Constitution—to assure "that the privilege of the writ of *habeas corpus* should not be suspended, unless, when in cases of rebellion or invasion, the public safety might require it." *Id.* at 95. "Acting under the immediate influence of this injunction, [Congress in 1789] must have felt, with peculiar force, the obligation of providing efficient means by which this great constitutional privilege should receive life and activity." *Id.* Given the centrality of this writ to the liberty assured by the Constitution as well as the common law, the Chief Justice reasoned "that congress could never intend to give a power of this kind to one of the judges of this court, which is refused to all of them when

---

[2] See Hans Baade, *"Original Intent" in Historical Perspective: Some Critical Glosses*, 69 Tex. L. Rev. 1001, 1062–1107 (1991); Hans Baade, *The Casus Omissus: A Pre-History of Statutory Analogy*, 20 Syr. J. Int'l L. 45 (1994). See also William Popkin, *Statutes in Court: The History and Theory of Statutory Interpretation* (1999); William Blatt, *The History of Statutory Interpretation: A Study in Form and Substance*, 6 Cardozo L. Rev. 799 (1985).

[3] See G. Edward White, *The Marshall Court and Cultural Change, 1815–1835*, in 3 *Oliver Wendell Holmes Devise, History of the Supreme Court of the United States* (1988); William Eskridge Jr., *All About Words: Early Understandings of the "Judicial Power" in Statutory Interpretation, 1776–1806*, 101 Colum. L. Rev. 990 (2001); John Yoo, Note, *Marshall's Plan: The Early Supreme Court and Statutory Interpretation*, 101 Yale L.J. 1607 (1991).

[4] Marshall noted the rule of the last antecedent: because the limiting language of the first sentence followed "and all other writs etc.," it only modified that item in the list, and not the habeas corpus item. 8 U.S. at 95. As the Chief surely recognized, this was a weak argument, in part because a comma set off the qualifying phrase from the items in the list, see Lawrence Solan, *The Language of Judges* 29–38 (1993) (showing that the last antecedent rule—weak to begin with—does not apply when the modifying phrase is set off from the list by a comma), and in part because the point of the first sentence seems to be the qualification, with no apparent reason for limiting it only to the third catch-all item in the list.

assembled. * * * This is not consistent with the genius of our legislation, nor with the course of our judicial proceedings." *Id.* at 96. To make sense of this confusing statute, Marshall concluded that "the first sentence vests this power in all courts of the United States; but as those courts are not always in session, the second sentence vests it in every justice or judge of the United States." *Id.* Marshall cemented his argument with precedent: the Court had implicitly resolved the issue of its habeas jurisdiction by granting the writ in the 1795 case of *United States v. Hamilton*, 3 U.S. (3 Dall.) 17 (1795).

Note the eclectic mode of argumentation in *Bollman*: Chief Justice Marshall's opinion considered the statutory text, its purpose in light of the constitutional background, and prior precedent. Such eclecticism was characteristic of American practice throughout the nineteenth century. Treatise-writers sought to systematize Anglo-American practice by developing elaborate lists of "canons" of statutory interpretation—most of them borrowed or derived from English treatises.[5] By the end of the century, statutory interpretation was pretty settled in practice, but was theoretically chaotic. Consider the sampler of general theoretical approaches, which we have excerpted from the Hart and Sacks "Legal Process" materials, and then consider a leading case that unsettled practice—*Holy Trinity Church*.

HENRY HART JR. AND ALBERT SACKS, *THE LEGAL PROCESS: BASIC PROBLEMS IN THE MAKING AND APPLICATION OF LAW*
Pp. 1111–15 (William Eskridge Jr. & Philip Frickey eds., 1994).

A.   *The Mischief Rule*

HEYDON'S CASE

Exchequer, 1584

30 Co. 7a, 76 Eng. Rep. 637

* * * And it was resolved by them, that for the sure and true interpretation of all statutes in general (be they penal or beneficial, restrictive or enlarging of the common law,) four things are to be discerned and considered:—

1st. What was the common law before the making of the Act.

2nd. What was the mischief and defect for which the common law did not provide.

3rd. What remedy the Parliament hath resolved and appointed to cure the disease of the commonwealth.

And, 4th. The true reason of the remedy; and then the office of all the Judges is always to make such construction as shall suppress the mischief, and advance the remedy, and to suppress subtle inventions and evasions for continuance of the mischief, and *pro privato commodo*, and to add force and life to the cure and remedy, according to the true intent of the makers of the Act, *pro bono publico*.

---

[5]   See, e.g., Theodore Sedgwick, *A Treatise on the Rules Which Govern the Interpretation and Application of Statutory and Constitutional Law* (1857); J.G. Sutherland, *Statutes and Statutory Construction* (1st ed. 1891).

B. *The "Golden" Rule*

Lord Blackburn, in *River Wear Comm'rs v. Adamson*, 2 App. Cas. 743, 764 (House of Lords, 1877):

> * * * But it is to be borne in mind that the office of the Judges is not to legislate, but to declare the expressed intention of the Legislature, even if that intention appears to the Court injudicious; and I believe that it is not disputed that what *Lord Wensleydale* used to call the golden rule is right, viz., that we are to take the whole statute together, and construe it all together, giving the words their ordinary signification, unless when so applied they produce an inconsistency, or an absurdity or inconvenience so great as to convince the Court that the intention could not have been to use them in their ordinary signification, and to justify the Court in putting on them some other signification, which, though less proper, is one which the Court thinks the words will bear.

C. *The Literal Rule*

Lord Atkinson, in *Vacher & Sons, Ltd. v. London Soc'y of Compositers*, [1913] App. Cas. 107, 121–22 (House of Lords):

> If the language of a statute be plain, admitting of only one meaning, the Legislature must be taken to have meant and intended what it has plainly expressed, and whatever it has in clear terms enacted must be enforced though it should lead to absurd or mischievous results. If the language of this subsection be not controlled by some of the other provisions of the statute, it must, since its language is plain and unambiguous, be enforced, and your Lordships' House sitting judicially is not concerned with the question whether the policy it embodies is wise or unwise, or whether it leads to consequences just or unjust, beneficial or mischievous.

Lord Bramwell, in *Hill v. East and West India Dock Co.*, 9 App. Cas. 448, 464–65 (House of Lords, 1884):

> I should like to have a good definition of what is such an absurdity that you are to disregard the plain words of an Act of Parliament. It is to be remembered that what seems absurd to one man does not seem absurd to another. * * * I think it is infinitely better, although an absurdity or an injustice or other objectionable result may be evolved as the consequence of your construction, to adhere to the words of an Act of Parliament and leave the legislature to set it right than to alter those words according to one's notion of an absurdity. * * *

F. *A Second Breath of Fresh Air*

LIEBER, LEGAL AND POLITICAL HERMENEUTICS
(2d ed. St. Louis, 1880) pp. 17–20.

IV. Let us take an instance of the simplest kind, to show in what degree we are continually obliged to resort to interpretation. By and by we shall find that the same rules which common sense teaches every one to use, in order to understand his neighbor in the most trivial intercourse, are necessary likewise, although not sufficient, for the interpretation of documents or texts of the highest importance, constitutions as well as treaties between the great nations.

Suppose a housekeeper says to a domestic: "fetch some soupmeat," accompanying the act with giving some money to the latter; he will be unable to execute the order without interpretation, however easy and, consequently, rapid the performance of the process may be. Common sense and good faith tell the domestic, that the housekeeper's meaning was this: 1. He should go immediately, or as soon as his other occupations are finished; or, if he be directed to do so in the evening, that he should go next day at the *usual* hour; 2. that the money handed him by the housekeeper is intended to pay for the meat thus ordered, and not as a present to him; 3. that he should buy such meat and of such part of the animal, as, to his knowledge, has commonly been used in the house he stays at, for making soups; 4. that he buy the best meat he can obtain, for a fair price; 5. that he go to that butcher who usually provides the family, with whom the domestic resides, with meat, or to some convenient stall, and not to any unnecessarily distant place; 6. that he return the rest of the money; 7. that he bring home the meat in good faith, neither adding anything disagreeable nor injurious; 8. that he fetch the meat for the use of the family and not for himself. Suppose, on the other hand, the housekeeper, afraid of being misunderstood, had mentioned these eight specifications, she would not have obtained her object, if it were to exclude all *possibility* of misunderstanding. For, the various specifications would have required new ones. Where would be the end? We are constrained then, always, to leave a considerable part of our meaning to be found out by interpretation, which, in many cases must necessarily cause greater or less obscurity with regard to the exact meaning, which our words were intended to convey.

* * * Men have at length found out that little or nothing is gained by attempting to speak with absolute clearness and endless specifications, but that human speech is the clearer, the less we endeavor to supply by words and specifications that interpretation which common sense must give to human words. However minutely we may define, somewhere we [must] trust at last to common sense and good faith. * * *

STATUTORY PREFACE TO THE HOLY TRINITY CASE

An act to prohibit the importation and migration of foreigners and aliens under contract or agreement to perform labor in the United States, its Territories and the District of Columbia, Act of February 26, 1885, 23 Stat. 332, c. 164.

Section 1. That from and after the passage of this act it shall be unlawful for any person, company, partnership, or corporation, in any manner whatsoever, to prepay the transportation, or in any way assist or encourage the importation or migration of any alien or aliens, any foreigner or foreigners, into the United States, its Territories, or the District of Columbia, under contract or agreement, parol or special, express or implied, made previous to the importation or migration of such alien or aliens, foreigner or foreigners, to perform labor or service of any kind in the United States, its Territories, or the District of Columbia.

Section 4. That the master of any vessel who shall knowingly bring within the United States on any such vessel * * * any alien, laborer, mechanic or artisan * * * who had entered into contract or agreement * * * to perform labor or service in the United States, shall be guilty of a misdemeanor * * *.

Section 5. * * * [N]or shall the provisions of this act apply to professional actors, artists, lecturers, or singers, nor to persons employed strictly as personal or domestic servants. * * *

RECTOR, HOLY TRINITY CHURCH V. UNITED STATES
Supreme Court of the United States, 1892.
143 U.S. 457, 12 S.Ct. 511, 36 L.Ed. 226.

MR. JUSTICE BREWER delivered the opinion of the Court.

Plaintiff in error is a corporation, duly organized and incorporated as a religious society under the laws of the State of New York. E. Walpole Warren was, prior to September, 1887, an alien residing in England. In that month the plaintiff in error made a contract with him, by which he was to remove to the city of New York and enter into its service as rector and pastor; and in pursuance of such contract, Warren did so remove and enter upon such service. It is claimed by the United States that this contract on the part of the plaintiff in error was forbidden by the act of February 26, 1885, 23 Stat. 332, c. 164, and an action was commenced to recover the penalty prescribed by that act. The Circuit Court held that the contract was within the prohibition of the statute, and rendered judgment accordingly, and the single question presented for our determination is whether it erred in that conclusion.

[Justice Brewer quoted § 1 of the Act.] It must be conceded that the act of the corporation is within the letter of this section, for the relation of rector to his church is one of service, and implies labor on the one side with compensation on the other. Not only are the general words labor and service both used, but also, as it were to guard against any narrow interpretation and emphasize a breadth of meaning, to them is added "of any kind;" and, further, as noticed by the Circuit Judge in his opinion, the fifth section, which makes specific exceptions, among them professional actors, artists, lecturers, singers and domestic servants, strengthens the idea that every other kind of labor and service was intended to be reached by the first section. While there is great force to this reasoning, we cannot think Congress intended to denounce with penalties a transaction like that in the present case. It is a familiar rule, that a thing may be within the letter of the statute and yet not within the statute, because not within its spirit, nor within the intention of its makers. This has been often asserted, and the reports are full of cases illustrating its application. This is not the substitution of the will of the judge for that of the legislator, for frequently words of general meaning are used in a statute, words broad enough to include an act in question, and yet a consideration of the whole legislation, or of the circumstances surrounding its enactment, or of the absurd results which follow from giving such broad meaning to the words, makes it unreasonable to believe that the legislator intended to include the particular act. As said in Plowden, 205: "From which cases, it appears that the sages of the law heretofore have construed statutes quite contrary to the letter in some appearance, and those statutes which comprehend all things in the letter they have expounded to extend to but some things, and those which generally prohibit all people from doing such an act they have interpreted to permit some people to do it, and those which include every person in the letter, they have adjudged to reach to some persons only, which expositions have always been founded upon the intent of the legislature, which they have collected sometimes by considering the cause and necessity of making the act, sometimes by comparing one part of the act with another, and sometimes by foreign circumstances." * * *

* * * [T]he title of this act is, "An act to prohibit the importation and migration of foreigners and aliens under contract or agreement to perform labor in the United States, its Territories and the District of Columbia." Obviously the thought expressed in this reaches only to the work of the manual laborer, as distinguished from that of the professional man. No one reading such a title would suppose that Congress had in its mind any purpose of staying the coming into this country of ministers of the gospel, or, indeed, of any class whose toil is that of the brain. The common understanding of the terms labor and laborers does not include preaching and preachers; and it is to be assumed that words and phrases are used in their ordinary meaning. So whatever of light is thrown upon the statute by the language of the title indicates an exclusion from its penal provisions of all contracts for the employment of ministers, rectors and pastors.

Again, another guide to the meaning of a statute is found in the evil which it is designed to remedy; and for this the court properly looks at contemporaneous events, the situation as it existed, and as it was pressed upon the attention of the legislative body. The situation which called for this statute was briefly but fully stated by Mr. Justice Brown when, as District Judge, he decided the case of *United States v. Craig*, 28 Fed. Rep. 795, 798: "The motives and history of the act are matters of common knowledge. It had become the practice for large capitalists in this country to contract with their agents abroad for the shipment of great numbers of an ignorant and servile class of foreign laborers, under contracts, by which the employer agreed, upon the one hand, to prepay their passage, while, upon the other hand, the laborers agreed to work after their arrival for a certain time at a low rate of wages. The effect of this was to break down the labor market, and to reduce other laborers engaged in like occupations to the level of the assisted immigrant. The evil finally became so flagrant that an appeal was made to Congress for relief by the passage of the act in question, the design of which was to raise the standard of foreign immigrants, and to discountenance the migration of those who had not sufficient means in their own hands, or those of their friends, to pay their passage."

It appears, also, from the petitions, and in the testimony presented before the committees of Congress, that it was this cheap unskilled labor which was making the trouble, and the influx of which Congress sought to prevent. It was never suggested that we had in this country a surplus of brain toilers, and, least of all, that the market for the services of Christian ministers was depressed by foreign competition. Those were matters to which the attention of Congress, or of the people, was not directed. So far, then, as the evil which was sought to be remedied interprets the statute, it also guides to an exclusion of this contract from the penalties of the act.

A singular circumstance, throwing light upon the intent of Congress, is found in this extract from the report of the Senate Committee on Education and Labor, recommending the passage of the bill: "The general facts and considerations which induce the committee to recommend the passage of this bill are set forth in the Report of the Committee of the House. The committee report the bill back without amendment, although there are certain features thereof which might well be changed or modified, in the hope that the bill may not fail of passage during the present session. Especially would the committee have otherwise recommended amendments, substituting for the expression 'labor and service,' whenever it occurs in the body of the bill, the words 'manual labor' or 'manual service,' as sufficiently broad to accomplish the purposes of the bill, and that such amendments would remove objections which a sharp and perhaps unfriendly criticism may urge to the proposed legislation. The committee, however, believing that the bill in its present form will be construed as including only those whose labor or service is manual in character, and being very desirous that the bill become a law before the adjournment, have reported the bill without change." Page 6059, Congressional Record, 48th Congress. And, referring back to the report of the Committee of the House, there appears this language: "It seeks to restrain and prohibit the immigration or importation of laborers who would have never seen our shores but for the inducements and allurements of men whose only object is to obtain labor at the lowest possible rate, regardless of the social and material well-being of our own citizens and regardless of the evil consequences which result to American laborers from such immigration. This class of immigrants care nothing about our institutions, and in many instances never even heard of them; they are men whose passage is paid by the importers; they come here under contract to labor for a certain number of years; they are ignorant of our social condition, and that they may remain so they are isolated and prevented from coming into contact with Americans. They are generally from the lowest social stratum, and live upon the coarsest food and in hovels of a character before unknown to American workmen. They, as a rule, do not become citizens, and are certainly not a desirable acquisition to the body politic. The inevitable tendency of their presence among us is to degrade American labor, and to reduce it to the level of the imported pauper labor." Page 5359, Congressional Record, 48th Congress.

We find, therefore, that the title of the act, the evil which was intended to be remedied, the circumstances surrounding the appeal to Congress, the reports of the committee of each house, all concur in affirming that the intent of Congress was simply to stay the influx of this cheap unskilled labor.

But beyond all these matters no purpose of action against religion can be imputed to any legislation, state or national, because this is a religious people. This is historically true. From the discovery of this continent to the present hour, there is a single voice making this affirmation. The commission to Christopher Columbus, prior to his sail westward, is from "Ferdinand and Isabella, by the grace of God,

King and Queen of Castile," etc., and recites that "it is hoped that by God's assistance some of the continents and islands in the ocean will be discovered," etc. The first colonial grant, that made to Sir Walter Raleigh in 1584, was from "Elizabeth, by the grace of God, of England, Fraunce and Ireland, queene, defender of the faith," etc.; and the grant authorizing him to enact statutes for the government of the proposed colony provided that "they be not against the true Christian faith nowe professed in the Church of England." * * *

If we examine the constitutions of the various States we find in them a constant recognition of religious obligations. Every constitution of every one of the forty-four States contains language which either directly or by clear implication recognizes a profound reverence for religion and an assumption that its influence in all human affairs is essential to the well being of the community. This recognition may be in the preamble, such as is found in the constitution of Illinois, 1870; "We, the people of the State of Illinois, grateful to Almighty God for the civil, political and religious liberty which He hath so long permitted us to enjoy, and looking to Him for a blessing upon our endeavors to secure and transmit the same unimpaired to succeeding generations," etc. * * *

Even the Constitution of the United States, which is supposed to have little touch upon the private life of the individual, contains in the First Amendment a declaration common to the constitutions of all the States, as follows: "Congress shall make no law respecting an establishment of religion, or prohibiting the free exercise thereof," etc. And also provides in Article 1, section 7, (a provision common to many constitutions,) that the Executive shall have ten days (Sundays excepted) within which to determine whether he will approve or veto a bill. * * *

If we pass beyond these matters to a view of American life as expressed by its laws, its business, its customs and its society, we find everywhere a clear recognition of the same truth. Among other matters note the following: The form of oath universally prevailing, concluding with an appeal to the Almighty; the custom of opening sessions of all deliberative bodies and most conventions with prayer; the prefatory words of all wills, "In the name of God, amen;" the laws respecting the observance of the Sabbath, with the general cessation of all secular business, and the closing of courts, legislatures, and other similar public assemblies on that day; the churches and church organizations which abound in every city, town and hamlet; the multitude of charitable organizations existing everywhere under Christian auspices; the gigantic missionary associations, with general support, and aiming to establish Christian missions in every quarter of the globe. These, and many other matters which might be noticed, add a volume of unofficial declarations to the mass of organic utterances that this is a Christian nation. In the face of all these, shall it be believed that a Congress of the United States intended to make it a misde-meanor for a church of this country to contract for the services of a Christian minister residing in another nation? * * *

NOTES ON HOLY TRINITY AND
ECLECTICISM IN STATUTORY INTERPRETATION

1. *The Court's Eclectic Approach and the Text of the Statute.* Justice Brewer's opinion seems to follow all the theories introduced at the beginning of this section—except that it seems to violate the "literal rule" of *Vacher & Sons.* Brewer concedes that his interpretation is not "within the letter of the statute." Was this concession too quickly made?

The first definition of the term "labor" listed in the 1879 and 1886 editions of *Webster's Dictionary* was "[p]hysical toil or bodily exertion * * * hard muscular effort directed to some useful end, as agriculture, manufactures, and the like." The second definition was "[i]ntellectual exertion, mental effort." In the 1880s, judges interpreting the laws and treaties excluding Chinese "laborers" or persons brought over for "labor" held that the terms should be read in their primary popular senses, to mean "physical labor for another for wages," and therefore not to include actors, teachers, or merchants, for example. See, e.g., *In re Ho King*, 14 F. 724 (D. Or. 1883). *Webster's* (1879 and 1886) only relevant definition of "service" was the "act of serving; the occupation of a servant; the performance of labor for the benefit of another, or at another's command; the attendance of an inferior, or hired helper or slave, etc., on a superior employer, master, and the like." *Black's Law Dictionary* (1891) defined "service" as "being employed to serve another; duty or labor to be rendered by one person to another." Is it 100% clear that the letter of the law supported the prosecution?[6]

2. *The Structure of the Statute.* The prohibition is found in § 1 of the 1885 law. (Section 2 voids contracts made in violation of § 1, and § 3 provides for criminal penalties for such alien labor contracts.) Although ignored by the Court, § 4 might be relevant, holding criminally accountable the master of a ship "who shall knowingly bring within the United States * * * any alien *laborer, mechanic or artisan*" who had contracted to perform "labor or service in the United States." Should § 1 be read narrowly, to track the terms in § 4, or does the narrowness of § 4 confirm a broader reading for § 1? The marginal note in the Statutes at Large (not part of the enacted law) describes § 4 as applying to the master of a vessel who knowingly brings "such emigrant laborer" to our shores. 23 Stat. 332 (1885).

Justice Brewer mentions § 5, a list of exemptions to the liabilities imposed by §§ 1–4. Section 5 exempts "professional actors, artists, lecturers, or singers" as well as "personal or domestic servants" from the "provisions of this act." Does the omission of ministers from § 5 confirm their inclusion in § 1? In § 4, which is also subject to the § 5 exclusions? Might a minister fall under one of the exemptions? A "lecturer"? You might want to consult the *Oxford English Dictionary* or the 1879 edition of *Webster's.*

3. *Legislative History as Evidence of Legislative "Intent."* To narrow what he views as the apparent plain meaning of the law, Brewer relies on the evil (or mischief) against which the Act was aimed and the inapplicability to a "brain toiler" of a statute seeking to exclude "laborers." Brewer further cites the Senate committee report saying that the bill was only intended to exclude people engaged in "manual labor" but that it was too late in the session to amend the statute to add that precise language. Note the

---

[6] See William Eskridge Jr., *Textualism, The Unknown Ideal?*, 96 Mich. L. Rev. 1509, 1517–19, 1533, 1539–40 (1998).

two ways that Brewer deploys the idea of legislative intent: one looks to the general goal of the law and tailors the text to meet the goal ("general intent"), and the other asks what the legislators thought they were doing as to the particular issue ("specific intent"). Recall these two levels of intent at work in *Weber*, the affirmative action case in Chapter 1, § 3. Recall, too, that the *Weber* majority quoted and followed *Holy Trinity*.

The Supreme Court had essentially rewritten statutes in earlier cases, in order to avoid absurd consequences (the golden rule) or where required by common law or constitutional maxims, but both the Court and commentators followed a rule whereby legislative materials were inadmissible evidence to alter "plain" statutory meanings. *Holy Trinity Church* seems to be the first case where the Supreme Court rewrote the statute based upon evidence from the legislative record. A revised edition of the leading treatise cited it repeatedly and endorsed its proposition that courts could consider legislative records to figure out what the intent of the legislature was on a particular issue. See J.G. Sutherland, *Statutes and Statutory Construction* 879–83 (John Lewis ed., 2d ed. 1904). (The first edition of the Sutherland treatise, published in 1891, followed the English practice of excluding extrinsic legislative materials from consideration in statutory cases.) The federal courts in the twentieth century cited an increasing amount and variety of legislative history, a trend that abated only in the late 1980s.

4.   *Legislative History the Court Missed.* Independent examination by modern scholars suggests that Brewer was right about the general intent of Congress and the problem it was addressing, see Carol Chomsky, *Unlocking the Mysteries of* Holy Trinity: *Spirit, Letter, and History in Statutory Interpretation*, 100 Colum. L. Rev. 901 (2000), but missed important evidence bearing on legislators' specific intent. Contrary to Brewer's opinion, the alien contract labor bill was not enacted in 1884, as the Senate committee had hoped, but was brought up in the 1885 session of the 48th Congress, just before the Cleveland Administration took office (see 2011 Documents Supplement 180). The Senate had a lengthy debate about the bill, which was amended in minor ways. Among the amendments were those expanding the exempted classes, but no amendment was proposed to make clear that "labor" referred only to "manual labor." When pressed by an opponent of the bill, who argued that § 5 discriminated against "other classes of professional men" by granting exemptions to singers and lecturers and actors, Senator Blair, the floor manager, engaged in this exchange with the opponent:

> Mr. MORGAN: * * * [If the alien] happens to be a lawyer, an artist, a painter, an engraver, a sculptor, a great author, or what not, and he comes under employment to write for a newspaper, or to write books, or to paint pictures * * * he comes under the general provisions of the bill. * * *

> *Mr. BLAIR: If that class of people are liable to become the subject-matter of such importation, then the bill applies to them. Perhaps the bill ought to be further amended.*

> Mr. MORGAN: * * * I shall propose when we get to it to put an amendment in there. I want to associate with the lecturers and singers and actors, painters, sculptors [etc.], or any person having special skill in any business, art, trade or profession. * * *

16 Cong. Rec. 1633 (1885) (emphasis added). The House floor manager, Representative Hopkins, responded to an inquiry regarding agricultural workers by saying that the bill

"prohibits the importation under contract of all classes with the exceptions named in [§ 5]." 16 Cong. Rec. 2032 (1885). Does this more complete record undermine Brewer's conclusion? See Adrian Vermeule, *Judging Under Uncertainty* 86–117 (2006) (filling in this gap in Brewer's deployment of legislative history and concluding that the judiciary was and remains incompetent to evaluate legislative history).

There is more legislative history that both the Court and subsequent commentators also missed. What is the relationship between § 1, with seemingly broad application to "labor or service of any kind," and § 4, with narrower application only to "labor or service" by "any alien laborer, mechanic, or artisan"? Senator Blair repeatedly assured his colleagues that § 4 was aimed at "the man who knowingly brings an immigrant * * * who comes here under and by virtue of a contract such as is prohibited by [§ 1] of the bill." 16 Cong. Rec. 1630 (1885). We are not aware of any on-the-record statement to the contrary. Should this evidence influence the Court's understanding of the relationship between §§ 1 and 4? See William Eskridge Jr., *No Frills Textualism*, 119 Harv. L. Rev. 2041, 2065–70 (2006).

Similarly, there is potentially relevant legislative history for § 5, which exempted "lecturers" from the statutory coverage (2011 Documents Supplement 175). Senator Morgan, who offered the lecturer exclusion as an amendment to § 5, explained that "[p]eople who can instruct us in morals and *religion* and in every species of elevation by lectures . . . are not prohibited." 16 Cong. Rec. 1633 (1885) (emphasis added). No one spoke against his interpretation. Does this legislative history strike you as relevant? Does it alter your understanding of the statute's meaning?

5. *Subsequent Legislation.* After the federal circuit court in the Southern District of New York construed the statute to apply to Reverend Warren in the *Holy Trinity Church* litigation, Congress amended the alien contract labor law to exempt ministers and professionals generally. Reversing the lower court, the Supreme Court in *Holy Trinity* did not mention the 1891 statute, which by its terms did not apply to pending proceedings, Act of March 3, 1891, § 12, 26 Stat. 1084, 1086. Does this later statute vindicate, or undermine, the Court's holding? Cf. *United States v. Laws*, 163 U.S. 258, 265 (1896) (discussing the 1891 amendment).

6. *The "Christian Nation" Discussion: Avoiding Absurd Results and Constitutional Issues.* Students might be taken aback by *Holy Trinity*'s invocation of the "Christian nation" analysis to clinch the Court's argument. (Born of Christian missionaries in Asia Minor, Justice Brewer was an evangelical jurist.) Was this critical to the Court's opinion? Would Justice Brewer have exempted a doctor from the statute's exclusion, for example? Cf. *Laws*, 163 U.S. 258 (determining whether the 1885 law covered chemists).

A modern version of Justice Brewer's Christian nation argument might be the idea that judges should read even clear statutory texts to avoid "absurd results." *Brown v. Plata*, 131 S.Ct. 1910, 1951 (2012) (Scalia, J., dissenting) (judges should "bend every effort" to avoid "outrageous" interpretations); Glen Staszewski, *Avoiding Absurdity,* 81 Ind. L. Rev. 101 (2009). Perhaps, however, the Christian nation discussion suggests how one judge's "absurdity" might be another judge's "public value." See John Manning, *The Absurdity Doctrine,* 116 Harv. L. Rev. 2387 (2003) (strong critique of any absurd results exception to the plain meaning rule).

Another modern rendition of Justice Brewer's concerns would be through the canon that judges should construe ambiguous statutes to avoid serious constitutional difficulties (Chapter 7, § 2A). Current Supreme Court doctrine says that the First Amendment requires that anti-discrimination statutes permit religions to discriminate on the basis of faith in the hiring and firing of "ministers." *Hosanna-Tabor Evangelical Lutheran Church and School v. EEOC,* 132 S.Ct. 694 (2012).

Caminetti v. United States
242 U.S. 470 (1917).

A federal statute criminalized the transportation of, or the inducement to travel of, "any woman or girl to go from one place to another in interstate or foreign commerce, or in any territory or the District of Columbia, for the purpose of prostitution or debauchery, or for any other immoral purpose * * *." The case concerned a man who brought a woman from Sacramento, California, to Reno, Nevada, to "become his mistress and concubine." The Court, per **Justice Day**, stated that "it is elementary that the meaning of a statute must, in the first instance, be sought in the language in which the act is framed, and if that is plain, and if the law is within the constitutional authority of the lawmaking body which passed it, the sole function of the courts is to enforce it according to its terms." The majority found the statutory meaning plain—the conduct in question was for an "immoral purpose"—and held that Caminetti violated the statute. It refused to consider the title to the Act ("the White Slave Traffic Act") or legislative history suggesting that the purpose of the statute was narrower than its plain meaning (to reach only "commercialized vice").

The majority did not cite *Holy Trinity Church,* but **Justice McKenna**, joined in dissent by two other Justices, relied on it for the proposition that "the words of the statute should be construed to execute [the statutory purpose], and they may be so construed even if their literal meaning be otherwise." The dissent also argued that the statutory text was not plain: "other immoral purpose" should not be read literally and in isolation, but in light of the limiting words preceding them. As illuminated by the legislative history and by the principle that statutes should be read with "common sense" to avoid absurd applications, the statute should not reach "the occasional immoralities of men and women," but rather the "systematized and mercenary immorality epitomized in the statute's graphic phrase 'white slave traffic.'"

Although the free-wheeling approach of *Holy Trinity Church* may seem worlds apart from the mechanical approach of *Caminetti,* it appears that unarticulated judicial values played a heavy role in both cases. That is, the Court would stick with literalism (*Caminetti*), or trump literalism with the mischief approach and the golden rule (*Holy Trinity Church*), in order to reach the interpretation that better matched its sensibilities. In *Caminetti,* for example, Justice McKenna's dissent stated that "[t]here is much in the present case to tempt to a violation of the [mischief] rule. Any measure that protects the purity of women from assault or enticement to degradation finds an instant advocate in our best emotions; but the judicial function cannot yield to emotion * * *." Similarly, in *Holy Trinity Church* the Court's importation of "Christian nation" and other reasoning to rework the statute caused anxiety among progressive commentators, the same people who would later decry the Court's opinion in *Lochner v. New York,* 198 U.S. 45 (1905) (invalidating a state statute establishing the maximum hours per week certain employees could be required to work on the ground that the due process clause protects economic liberty against unjustified regulation). For progressives who favored aggressive legislation supplanting the common law, decisions like *Lochner* and *Holy Trinity Church* sent the same message of judicial reluctance to accept new statutes. Dean Roscoe Pound of Harvard, the founder of sociological jurisprudence, laid out the following theory of statutory interpretation, designed to cabin judicial willfulness. Recall his argument that statutes should be a source of principles affecting the common law (Chapter 6, § 1).

ROSCOE POUND, *SPURIOUS INTERPRETATION*
7 Colum. L. Rev. 379, 381 (1907).

The object of genuine interpretation is to discover the rule which the law-maker intended to establish; to discover the intention which the law-maker made the rule, or the sense which he attached to the words wherein the rule is expressed. Its object is to enable others to derive from the language used "the same idea which the author intended to convey." Employed for these purposes, interpretation is purely judicial in character; and so long as the ordinary means of interpretation, namely the literal meaning of the language used and the context, are resorted to, there can be no question. But when, as often happens, these primary indices to the meaning and intention of the law-maker fail to lead to a satisfactory result, and recourse must be had to the reason and spirit of the rule, or to the intrinsic merit of the several possible interpretations, the line between a genuine ascertaining of the meaning of the law, and the making over of the law under guise of interpretation, becomes more difficult. Strictly, both are means of genuine interpretation. * * * The former means of interpretation tries to find out directly what the law-maker meant by assuming his position, in the surroundings in which he acted, and endeavoring to gather from the mischiefs he had to meet and the remedy by which he sought to meet them, his intention with respect to the particular point in controversy. The latter, if the former fails to yield sufficient light, seeks to reach the intent of the law-maker indirectly. It assumes that the law-maker thought as we do on general questions of morals and policy and fair dealing. Hence it assumes that of several possible interpretations the one which appeals most to our sense of right and justice for the time being is most likely to give the meaning of those who framed the rule. If resorted to in the first instance, or without regard to the other means of interpretation, this could not be regarded as a means of genuine interpretation. But inherent difficulties of expression and want of care in drafting require continual resort to this means of interpretation for the legitimate purpose of ascertaining what the law-maker in fact meant.

On the other hand, the object of spurious interpretation is to make, unmake, or remake, and not merely to discover. It puts a meaning into the text as a juggler puts coins, or what not, into a dummy's hair, to be pulled forth presently with an air of discovery. It is essentially a legislative, not a judicial process, made necessary in formative periods by the paucity of principles, feebleness of legislation, and rigidity of rules characteristic of archaic law. * * * Spurious interpretation is an anachronism in an age of legislation. It is a fiction. * * *

* * * Rigid constitutions, difficult of amendment, * * * are presenting to modern common-law courts the same problem which the rigid formalism of archaic

procedure, and the terse obscurity of ancient codes, put before the jurists of antiquity. Cases must be decided, and they must be decided in the long run so as to accord with the moral sense of the community. This is the good side of spurious interpretation. It is this situation that provokes the general popular demand for judicial amendment of constitutions, state and federal, under the guise of interpretation.

Looking at the matter purely from the standpoint of expediency, * * * the bad features of spurious interpretation, as applied to the modern state, may be said to be three: (1) That it tends to bring law into disrepute, (2) that it subjects the courts to political pressure, (3) that it reintroduces the personal element into judicial administration. * * *

NOTES ON INTERPRETATION AS DETERMINATION OF LEGISLATIVE "INTENT"

1.   *"Genuine Interpretation" Versus "Spurious Interpretation."* Pound assumes that "genuine interpretation" means ascertaining the meaning a speaker intended to convey when uttering a statement. His approach may seem simple, but in fact it raises highly controversial questions at the core of statutory interpretation theory. On his understanding, textual meaning and authorial intent are not separable concepts: the text has no autonomous significance; it merely consists of signifiers encoding an intended message, however difficult it might be for the interpreter to decode that message. This understanding retains force for some students of interpretation today, both in law and other fields.[7]

Thus, one cannot speak about the "plain meaning" of statutory text in isolation and be engaged in "interpretation" at all. In this way, Pound denies that the "plain meaning" approach to statutory construction constitutes "interpretation"—unless the best textual meaning is simply used as good evidence of legislative intent, to be supplemented by any other evidence of legislative intent available. On this reading, his argument is a remarkable rejection of literalism in statutory interpretation. It also suggests that purposivism is "genuine interpretation," but only so long as the interpreter sticks as closely as possible to the probable purposes that animated the enacting legislature and avoids imposing her own views of appropriate public-policy purposes upon the statute. Anything beyond that is "spurious interpretation." Pound is not saying that what he calls "spurious interpretation" is always illegitimate; his point is that it should be called what it actually is—"revising to promote justice" or whatever—and debated on its own merits.

2.   *Ascertaining Legislative Intent: Actual Intent Versus Imaginative Reconstruction.* Pound proposes that interpreters follow legislative "intent," but admits that this method is frequently difficult to implement. To begin with, if the interpreter has clear evidence of the *actual intent* of the enacting legislature about what the statute should mean in the context under consideration, the interpreter should follow it. Because strong evidence of actual intent will often be absent, the interpreter usually

---

[7]   Joseph Raz, *Intention in Interpretation*, in *The Autonomy of Law: Essays on Legal Positivism* 249, 258 (Robert George ed. 1996); Lawrence Solan, *The Language of Statutes: Laws and Their Interpretation* (2010). See also Andrei Marmor, *Positive Law and Objective Values* ch. 5 (2001); Paul Campos, *That Obscure Object of Desire: Hermeneutics and the Autonomous Text,* 77 Minn. L. Rev. 1065 (1993).

must engage in a second-best inquiry, what we might call the *imaginative reconstruction of legislative intent*. This approach requires the interpreter to put herself in the position of the enacting legislature and, like a historian, examine the available historical evidence against a background of assumptions about the legislature (that it would prefer justice to injustice, for example) that are commonplace to our legal system, but can be rebutted by evidence that this enacting legislature had a different view (for example, that it defined "justice" and "injustice" differently than the interpreter would).[8] These remain the two fundamental inquiries of intentionalist interpretation today. Note that for both, the statutory text is important because it frequently will be the best evidence of legislative intent.

3. *Federal Courts and Pound's Approach.* The Supreme Court grew increasingly interested in what legislators actually expected out of their statutes, e.g., *Johnson v. Southern Pacific Company*, 196 U.S. 1 (1904), though the Court did not always follow legislative history (recall *Caminetti*). Consider *Duplex Printing Press Co. v. Deering*, 254 U.S. 443 (1921), which interpreted the Clayton Act to justify an injunction against a secondary boycott by print workers against an "unfair" employer. Although the Clayton Act contained two broad provisions exempting most labor activity from antitrust regulation, the Court held that it was not the actual intent of Congress to insulate labor boycotts from regulation. The Court relied on a statement by the Clayton Act's House floor manager that neither he nor any member of the reporting committee intended the bill to exempt boycotts from the regulation courts had imposed on them under the older Sherman Act. Justice Brandeis's dissenting opinion railed against this narrowing interpretation, also based upon the actual, subjective expectations of the enacting Congress. (Brandeis was a close adviser of President Wilson, who had proposed the Clayton Act, and hence had an "inside view" of the Act.)

The classic early practitioner of imaginative reconstruction was Judge Learned Hand of the Second Circuit, one of the judges reversed in *Duplex Printing*. See, e.g., *Lehigh Valley Coal Co. v. Yensavage*, 218 F. 547, 553 (2d Cir. 1914); Archibald Cox, *Judge Learned Hand and the Interpretation of Statutes*, 60 Harv. L. Rev. 370 (1947). Consider the following exemplar of Pound's theory.

Fishgold v. Sullivan Drydock and Repair Corporation
154 F.2d 785 (2d Cir. 1946), *aff'd*, 328 U.S. 275 (1946).

Section 8(b)(B) of the Selective Training & Service Act of 1940, 49 Stat. 888, 890, as amended in 1944, provided that the private employer of a person who had left employment for U.S. military service and then sought to return to the same position after discharge from the service "shall restore such person to such position or to a position of like seniority, status, and pay unless the employer's circumstances have so changed as to make it impossible or unreasonable to do so." Section 8(c) provided:

> Any person who is restored to a position in accordance with the provisions of paragraph (A) or (B) of subsection (b) shall be considered as having been on furlough or leave of absence during his period of training and service in the land or naval forces, shall be so restored without loss of seniority * * * and

---

[8] Pound's statement of imaginative reconstruction is taken from the commentary to *Eyston v. Studd*, (1574) 2 Plowden 459, 467, 75 Eng. Rep. 688, 699 (K.B), paraphrasing Aristotle, *The Nicomachean Ethics* bk. V, ch. 10. For a modern exposition, see Richard Posner, *The Federal Courts: Crisis and Reform* 286–93 (1985).

shall not be discharged from such position without cause within one year after such restoration.

Fishgold returned from service in the army during World War II and then was laid off within a year, while non-veteran employees who had more seniority were not laid off. Fishgold challenged the decision to lay him off, relying on § 8(c). **Judge Hand**'s opinion concluded that the layoff was legal. He avoided the thrust of § 8(c)'s protection against "discharge" by noting that its dictionary definition was a permanent termination of employment, rather than the temporary termination denoted by "layoff." This reflects the traditional labor law distinction between being terminated or fired (the employment relationship is severed) and being laid off (the employee is not employed but might be recalled to employment). Seniority typically affords virtually absolute protection against discharge or termination but only limited protection against layoffs.

"When we consider the situation at the time that the Act was passed—September, 1940—it is extremely improbable that Congress should have meant to grant any broader privilege than as we are measuring it. * * * The original act limited service to one year, and it was most improbable that within that time we should be called upon to fight upon our own soil; as indeed the event proved, for we were still at peace in September, 1941. Congress was calling young men to the colors to give them an adequate preparation for our defence, but with no forecast of the appalling experiences which they were later to undergo. Against that background it is not likely that a proposal would then have been accepted which gave industrial priority, regardless of their length of employment, to unmarried men—for the most part under thirty—over men in the thirties, forties or fifties, who had wives and children dependent upon them. Today, in the light of what has happened, the privilege then granted may appear an altogether inadequate equivalent for their services; but we have not to decide what is now proper; we are to reconstruct, as best we may, what was the purpose of Congress when it used the words in which § 8(b) and § 8(c) were cast." **Judge Chase** dissented, based upon a broader view of the statute's purpose.

MAX RADIN, *STATUTORY INTERPRETATION*
43 Harv. L. Rev. 863, 870–71 (1930).

It has frequently been declared that the most approved method is to discover the intent of the legislator. * * * On this transparent and absurd fiction it ought not to be necessary to dwell. It is clearly enough an illegitimate transference to law of concepts proper enough in literature and theology. * * *

That the intention of the legislature is undiscoverable in any real sense is almost an immediate inference from a statement of the proposition. The chances that of several hundred men each will have exactly the same determinate situations in mind as possible reductions of a given [statutory issue], are infinitesimally small. * * * In an extreme case, it might be that we could learn all that was in the mind of the draftsman, or of a committee of half a dozen men who completely approved of every word. But when this draft is submitted to the legislature and at once accepted without a dissentient voice and without debate, what have we then learned of the intentions of the four or five hundred approvers? Even if the contents of the minds of the legislature were uniform, we have no means of knowing that content except by the external utterances or behavior of these hundreds of men, and in almost every case the only external act is the extremely ambiguous one of acquiescence, which may be motivated in literally hundreds of ways, and which by itself indicates little or nothing of the pictures which the statutory descriptions imply. * * *

And if [legislative intent] were discoverable, it would be powerless to bind us. What gives the intention of the legislature obligating force? * * * [I]n law, the specific individuals who make up the legislature are men to whom a specialized function has been temporarily assigned. That function is not to impose their will even within limits on their fellow citizens, but to "pass statutes," which is a fairly precise operation. That is, they make statements in general terms of undesirable and desirable situations, from which flow certain results. * * * When the legislature has uttered the words of a statute, it is *functus officio*, not because of the Montesquieuan separation of powers, but because that is what legislating means. The legislature might also be a court and an executive, but it can never be all three things simultaneously.

And once the words are out, recorded, engrossed, registered, proclaimed, inscribed in bronze, they in turn become instrumentalities which administrators and courts must use in performing their own specialized functions. The principal use is that of "interpretation." Interpretation is an act which requires an existing determinate event—the issue to be litigated—and obviously that determinate event cannot exist until after the statute has come into force. To say that the intent of the legislature decides the interpretation is to say that the legislature interprets in advance * * * a situation which does not exist."

NOTES ON CRITIQUES OF INTENTIONALIST APPROACHES

1. *The Narrow Role of Legislatures.* Radin's last point, that legislatures exist only to pass statutes and not to impose their will on the citizenry, echoed Oliver Wendell Holmes Jr., who insisted that in a "government of laws, not men," legal standards must be external to the decisionmaker. Holmes, *The Common Law* 41, 44 (1881). "[W]e ask, not what this man meant, but what those words would mean in the mouth of a normal speaker of English, using them in the circumstances in which they were used. * * * [T]he normal speaker of English is merely a special variety, a literary form, so to speak, of our old friend the prudent man. He is external to the particular writer, and a reference to him as the criterion is simply another instance of the externality of law. * * * We do not inquire what the legislature meant; we ask only what the statute means." Holmes, *The Theory of Legal Interpretation*, 12 Harv. L. Rev. 417, 417–18, 419 (1899).

But "what the statute means" is not always clear. If the law is ambiguous, should interpreters consider the expectations of the legislators who wrote the statute?[9] If a judge were interpreting a contract, would the judge prefer an interpretation that reconstructs the intent or expectations of the parties to one that the parties did not want? Shouldn't a court pay at least as much attention to the intent of Congress, not only because Congress drafts and enacts statutes, but also because Congress-acting-

---

[9] See Frederick de Sloovère, *Textual Interpretation of Statutes*, 11 N.Y.U. L. Rev. 538 (1934); cf. *Boston Sand & Gravel Co. v. United States*, 278 U.S. 41, 48 (1928) (Holmes, J.) (consulting legislative history to figure out "what the statute means").

with-the-President (Article I, § 7) is the "supreme" lawmaking authority in our constitutional democracy?[10]

2. *The Incoherence or Indeterminacy of Collective Intent.* Radin responds that legislative intent is incoherent or undiscoverable. It is incoherent to the extent that a collective body cannot easily be charged with having an "intent." As political scientist Kenneth Shepsle subsequently put it, "Congress is a They, not an It."[11] Intent is undiscoverable because too little evidence of collective understanding finds its way into the public record, and even when reported is hard to interpret. Also, how can the different "intents" of the House, Senate, and President be aggregated?

These are logical quarrels, but there is another way of looking at this matter. If the President or the Board of Directors of a company negotiates a contract with Joan Doe, the President's or Board's representations might be taken to be those of the company itself. As linguist and legal scholar Lawrence Solan has argued, both common sense and the law routinely attribute "intent" to collective bodies based upon the purposive declarations made by subgroups or agents publicly deputized to deliberate for the whole group.[12] Political scientists make the same point about committees and sponsors in Congress.[13] In the same manner, statements by sponsors and committees might reasonably be thought to represent congressional consensus unless denied by other representatives. Arguably, this is an institutional convention that is reasonable, and that Congress can be expected to adjust to (through better monitoring) if it yields results that systematically fail to reflect legislative bargains or consensuses.[14]

3. *The Inevitability of Interpretive Discretion and Interstitial Lawmaking?* A further critique of imaginative reconstruction is that it is more "imaginative" than it is "reconstruction." Judges in the early twentieth century were considered hidebound and hostile to many legislative innovations. The enthusiasm Pound and Hand felt for imaginative reconstruction was, in part, motivated by the need to tie judges more closely to progressive developments in the legislature. This was only partially achieved at the Supreme Court level, for imaginative reconstruction could also be utilized by conservatives bending statutes their way, as in *Duplex Printing* and *Holy Trinity*, and then ignoring legislative expectations when it suited them in cases like *Caminetti*.

An underlying theme of Radin's article is that the nature of the judicial process—application of generally phrased statutes to unforeseen fact situations by an independent and co-equal branch of government—assures discretion. Cf. Benjamin Cardozo, *The Nature of the Judicial Process* 166 (1921) (judicial decisionmaking "is not discovery but creation"). This suggests the possibility that often statutory

---

[10] See Daniel A. Farber, *Statutory Interpretation and Legislative Supremacy*, 78 Geo. L.J. 281 (1989).

[11] Kenneth Shepsle, *Congress Is a "They," Not an "It": Legislative Intent as Oxymoron*, 12 Int'l Rev. L. & Econ. 239 (1992). Accord, Ronald Dworkin, *Law's Empire* 314, 335–36 (1986); Jeremy Waldron, *Law and Disagreement* (1999); Frank Easterbrook, *Text, History, and Structure in Statutory Interpretation*, 17 Harv. J.L. & Pub. Pol'y 61 (1994).

[12] Lawrence Solan, *Private Language, Public Laws: The Central Role of Legislative Intent in Statutory Interpretation*, 93 Geo. L.J. 427, 437–49 (2005); accord, Stephen Breyer, *Making Our Democracy Work: A Judge's View* (2010); Christian List & Philip Pettit, *Group Agency* (2011).

[13] Daniel Rodriguez & Barry Weingast, *The Positive Political Theory of Legislative History: New Perspectives on the 1964 Civil Rights Act and Its Interpretation*, 151 U. Pa. L. Rev. 1417 (2003).

[14] See James Landis, *A Note on "Statutory Interpretation,"* 43 Harv. L. Rev. 886, 888–90 (1930) (responding to Radin's article); McNollgast, *Positive Canons: The Role of Legislative Bargains in Statutory Interpretation*, 80 Geo. L.J. 705 (1992).

interpretation might be "spurious," to use Pound's provocative label, or at least not an easy exercise in imaginative reconstruction.

The debates over statutory interpretation took several important turns in the 1930s.[15] The unprecedented degree of statute-making during the New Deal vindicated Pound's claim that the twentieth century would be the age of legislatures rather than courts, but this statutory binge also vindicated Radin's point that there was unlikely to be a clear legislative intent (reconstructed or otherwise) on any but a handful of issues and that interpretive discretion was required. During the New Deal and right before U.S. entry into World War II, an academic consensus found a way to accept both points of view. This approach, whose outlines were clear in the period from 1938–41,[16] blossomed into "legal process" theory after World War II (Section 2).

PROBLEMS APPLYING IMAGINATIVE RECONSTRUCTION TO STATUTES

Problem 6–1. How would Judge Hand and Dean Pound have voted if they were presented with the statutory issue in *Holy Trinity Church*?

Problem 6–2. Recall the *Weber* case from Chapter 1. How would Judge Hand and Dean Pound have voted in *Weber*? What might Professor Radin have said in that case?

Problem 6–3. Williams tells her servant to "fetch me some soupmeat" from "Store X" (recall Lieber's hypothetical). The servant goes to Store X and discovers that the store only has one pound of soupmeat left, and it looks old and wormy. The servant knows that Store Y also carries soupmeat and, upon inspection, sees that Store Y's soupmeat looks pretty good. How would the following "servants" interpret the boss' command: Judge Hand? Justice Holmes? What do you think the proper interpretation is? Is statutory interpretation similar to this example?

2. LEGAL PROCESS THEORIES OF STATUTORY INTERPRETATION

A. THE LEGAL PROCESS CLASSICS, 1940s–50s

The consensus about public law issues reached by intellectuals between 1938 and 1941 was reflected, after World War II, in Supreme Court decisions, law review articles, and teaching materials dealing with statutory issues. This consensus gave rise to "legal process theory." The following materials are the two legal process classics regarding issues of statutory interpretation.

---

[15] See William Eskridge Jr. & Philip Frickey, "Historical and Critical Introduction," to Henry Hart Jr. & Albert Sacks, *The Legal Process: Basic Problems in the Making and Application of Law* (Eskridge & Frickey eds. 1994); Nicholas Parrillo, *Leviathan and Interpretive Revolution: The Administrative State, the Judiciary, and the Rise of Legislative History, 1890–1950,* 123 Yale L.J. 266 (2014).

[16] The leading precursors of legal process theory were Lon Fuller, *The Law in Quest of Itself* (1940); Harry Willmer Jones, *Statutory Doubts and Legislative Intention*, 40 Colum. L. Rev. 957 (1940); Frederick de Sloovère, *Extrinsic Aids in the Interpretation of Statutes*, 88 U. Pa. L. Rev. 527 (1940); Lloyd Garrison & Willard Hurst, "Law in Society" (1940 & 1941) (teaching materials at Wisconsin).

LON FULLER, *THE CASE OF THE SPELUNCEAN EXPLORERS*
62 Harv. L. Rev. 616, 619–21, 623–26, 628–40 (1949)[17].

TRUEPENNY, C.J. [The members of the Speluncean Society were amateur cave explorers. In May 4299, several members, including Roger Whetmore, were trapped in a cave because of a rockslide. Communication with the explorers was established on day 20 of the ordeal, and the explorers learned that they would not likely be rescued for another ten days, that they would probably die if they did not have sustenance within that period, and that they would probably not die if they cannibalized one of their number. Given this information, all of the explorers agreed that one of them must die, and that the person to die would be chosen by lots (rolls of the dice). Whetmore agreed to both propositions and suggested the method of lots, but before the dice were rolled he withdrew from the plan. The other explorers proceeded with the agreement. Whetmore was the one chosen by lots. On the 23d day, the explorers killed and ate him. After the surviving explorers were saved, they were indicted and convicted of the murder of Roger Whetmore. The defendants were sentenced to death, but both jurors and the judge requested that the chief executive commute the sentence to six months' imprisonment. The defendants appealed their convictions.]

* * * The language of our statute is well known: "Whoever shall willfully take the life of another shall be punished by death." N. C. S. A. (N. S.) § 12–A. This statute permits of no exception applicable to this case, however our sympathies may incline us to make allowance for the tragic situation in which these men found themselves.

In a case like this the principle of executive clemency seems admirably suited to mitigate the rigors of the law, and I propose to my colleagues that we follow the example of the jury and the trial judge by joining in the communications they have addressed to the Chief Executive. * * * I think we may therefore assume that some form of clemency will be extended to these defendants. If this is done, then justice will be accomplished without impairing either the letter or spirit of our statutes and without offering any encouragement for the disregard of law.

FOSTER, J. * * * If this Court declares that under our law these men have committed a crime, then our law is itself convicted in the tribunal of common sense * * *.

* * * I take the view that the enacted or positive law of this Commonwealth, including all of its statutes and precedents, is inapplicable to this case, and that the case is governed instead by what ancient writers in Europe and America called "the law of nature." [Judge Foster argued that once the reason for law disappears, so too does the law itself. As a matter of political morality, the defendants' conduct was justified by the agreement they entered into that ensured the survival of five at the expense of one. Assuming that state authority reached the spelunceans, Judge Foster announced an alternative ground for his decision.]

Now it is, of course, perfectly clear that these men did an act that violates the literal wording of the statute which declares that he who "shall willfully take the

---

[17]   Copyright 1949 by the Harvard Law Review Association. Reprinted by permission.

life of another" is a murderer. But one of the most ancient bits of legal wisdom is the saying that a man may break the letter of the law without breaking the law itself. Every proposition of positive law, whether contained in a statute or a judicial precedent, is to be interpreted reasonably, in the light of its evident purpose. * * *

The statute before us for interpretation has never been applied literally. Centuries ago it was established that a killing in self-defense is excused. There is nothing in the wording of the statute that suggests this exception. Various attempts have been made to reconcile the legal treatment of self-defense with the words of the statute, but in my opinion these are all merely ingenious sophistries. The truth is that the exception in favor of self-defense cannot be reconciled with the *words* of the statute, but only with its *purpose.*

The true reconciliation of the excuse of self-defense with the statute making it a crime to kill another is to be found in the following line of reasoning. One of the principal objects underlying any criminal legislation is that of deterring men from crime. Now it is apparent that if it were declared to be the law that a killing in self-defense is murder such a rule could not operate in a deterrent manner. A man whose life is threatened will repel his aggressor, whatever the law may say. Looking therefore to the broad purposes of criminal legislation, we may safely declare that this statute was not intended to apply to cases of self-defense. * * *

* * * [P]recisely the same reasoning is applicable to the case at bar. If in the future any group of men ever find themselves in the tragic predicament of these defendants, we may be sure that their decision whether to live or die will not be controlled by the contents of our criminal code. * * * The withdrawal of this situation from the effect of this statute is justified by precisely the same considerations that were applied by our predecessors in office centuries ago to the case of self-defense.

* * * The line of reasoning I have applied above raises no question of fidelity to enacted law, though it may possibly raise a question of the distinction between intelligent and unintelligent fidelity. No superior wants a servant who lacks the capacity to read between the lines. The stupidest housemaid knows that when she is told "to peel the soup and skim the potatoes" her mistress does not mean what she says. She also knows that when her master tells her to "drop everything and come running" he has overlooked the possibility that she is at the moment in the act of rescuing the baby from the rain barrel. Surely we have a right to expect the same modicum of intelligence from the judiciary. The correction of obvious legislative errors or oversights is not to supplant the legislative will, but to make that will effective. * * *

TATTING, J. [This jurist responds to both arguments raised by Judge Foster. At what point, exactly, did the explorers find themselves back in a state of nature? Even if they were in a state of nature, by what authority or right can the Court resolve itself into a "Court of Nature"? Isn't the propounded code of nature a "topsy-turvy and odious" one? "It is a code in which the law of contracts is more fundamental than the law of murder." Would Whetmore have had a defense if he had shot his assailants as they set upon him? For these reasons, Judge Tatting cannot join Judge Foster's first reason. Nor can he join the second.]

* * * It is true that a statute should be applied in the light of its purpose, and that *one* of the purposes of criminal legislation is recognized to be deterrence. The difficulty is that other purposes are also ascribed to the law of crimes. It has been said that one of its objects is to provide an orderly outlet for the instinctive human demand for retribution. It has also been said that its object is the rehabilitation of the wrongdoer. Other theories have been propounded. Assuming that we must interpret a statute in the light of its purpose, what are we to do when it has many purposes or when its purposes are disputed?

[These other purposes provide a different explanation for self-defense as outside the murder prohibition. The statute requires a "willful" act, but the person who acts to repel a threat to life is not acting "willfully," according to at least one precedent, *Commonwealth v. Parry*. This purpose of the statute provides no justification for the explorers, who acted willfully. Moreover, the Court's decision in *Commonwealth v. Valjean* upheld the larceny conviction of a man who stole bread to prevent his own starvation.] If hunger cannot justify the theft of wholesome and natural food, how can it justify the killing and eating of a man? Again, if we look at the thing in terms of deterrence, is it likely that a man will starve to death to avoid a jail sentence for the theft of a loaf of bread? My brother's demonstrations would compel us to overrule *Commonwealth v. Valjean* and many other precedents that have been built on that case. * * *

There is still a further difficulty in my brother Foster's proposal to read an exception into the statute to favor this case * * *. What shall be the scope of this exception? Here the men cast lots and the victim was himself originally a party to the agreement. What would we have to decide if Whetmore had refused from the beginning to participate in the plan? Would a majority be permitted to overrule him? Or, suppose that no plan were adopted at all and the others simply conspired to bring about Whetmore's death, justifying their act by saying that he was in the weakest condition. Or again, that a plan of selection was followed but one based on a different justification than the one adopted here, as if the others were atheists and insisted that Whetmore should die because he was the only one who believed in an afterlife. These illustrations could be multiplied, but enough have been suggested to reveal what a quagmire of hidden difficulties my brother's reasoning contains. * * *

Since I have been wholly unable to resolve the doubts that beset me about the law of this case, I am with regret announcing a step that is, I believe, unprecedented in the history of this tribunal. I declare my withdrawal from the decision of this case.

KEEN, J. [This jurist insists that the Court put aside the issue, raised by the Chief Justice, of whether the Chief Executive should grant clemency. This is a "confusion of government functions," and judges should not intrude into this realm of the executive.]

The second question that I wish to put to one side is that of deciding whether what these men did was "right" or "wrong," "wicked" or "good." That is also a question that is irrelevant to the discharge of my office as a judge sworn to apply, not my conceptions of morality, but the law of the land. * * *

Whence arise all the difficulties of the case, then, and the necessity for so many pages of discussion about what ought to be so obvious? The difficulties, in whatever tortured form they may present themselves, all trace back to a single source, and that is a failure to distinguish the legal from the moral aspects of this case. To put it bluntly, my brothers do not like the fact that the written law requires the conviction of these defendants. Neither do I, but unlike my brothers I respect the obligations of an office that requires me to put my personal predilections out of my mind when I come to interpret and apply the law of this Commonwealth. * * *

[After a period in which the Commonwealth's judiciary often freely interpreted statutes,] we now have a clear-cut principle, which is the supremacy of the legislative branch of our government. From that principle flows the obligation of the judiciary to enforce faithfully the written law, and to interpret that law in accordance with its plain meaning without reference to our personal desires or our individual conceptions of justice. I am not concerned with the question whether the principle that forbids the judicial revision of statutes is right or wrong, desirable or undesirable; I observe merely that this principle has become a tacit premise underlying the whole of the legal and governmental order I am sworn to administer. * * *

My brother Foster's penchant for finding holes in statutes reminds one of the story told by an ancient author about the man who ate a pair of shoes. Asked how he liked them, he replied that the part he liked best was the holes. That is the way my brother feels about statutes; the more holes they have in them the better he likes them. In short, he doesn't like statutes.

One could not wish for a better case to illustrate the specious nature of this gap-filling process than the one before us. My brother thinks he knows exactly what was sought when men made murder a crime, and that was something he calls "deterrence." My brother Tatting has already shown how much is passed over in that interpretation. But I think the trouble goes deeper. I doubt very much whether our statute making murder a crime really has a "purpose" in any ordinary sense of the term. Primarily, such a statute reflects a deeply-felt human conviction that murder is wrong and that something should be done to the man who commits it. * * *

Now I know that the line of reasoning I have developed in this opinion will not be acceptable to those who look only to the immediate effects of a decision and ignore the long-run implications of an assumption by the judiciary of a power of dispensation. A hard decision is never a popular decision. * * * Hard cases may even have a certain moral value by bringing home to the people their own responsibilities toward the law that is ultimately their creation, and by reminding them that there is no principle of personal grace that can relieve the mistakes of their representatives.

Indeed, I will go farther and say that not only are the principles I have been expounding those which are soundest for our present conditions, but that we would have inherited a better legal system from our forefathers if those principles had been observed from the beginning. For example, with respect to the excuse of self-defense, if our courts had stood steadfast on the language of the statute the result would undoubtedly have been a legislative revision of it. Such a revision would have drawn on the assistance of natural philosophers and psychologists, and the resulting regulation of the matter would have had an understandable and rational basis, instead of the hodgepodge of verbalisms and metaphysical distinctions that have emerged from the judicial and professional treatment.

HANDY, J. * * * I never cease to wonder at my colleagues' ability to throw an obscuring curtain of legalisms about every issue presented to them for decision. * * *

* * * The problem before us is what we, as officers of the government, ought to do with these defendants. That is a question of practical wisdom to be exercised in a context, not of abstract theory, but of human realities. When the case is approached in this light, it becomes, I think, one of the easiest to decide that has ever been argued before this Court. * * *

I have never been able to make my brothers see that government is a human affair, and that men are ruled, not by words on paper or by abstract theories, but by other men. They are ruled well when their rulers understand the feelings and conceptions of the masses. They are ruled badly when that understanding is lacking. * * *

* * * I believe that all government officials, including judges, will do their jobs best if they treat forms and abstract concepts as instruments. We should take as our model, I think, the good administrator, who accommodates procedures and principles to the case at hand, selecting from among the available forms those most suited to reach the proper result.

The most obvious advantage of this method of government is that it permits us to go about our daily tasks with efficiency and common sense. My adherence to this philosophy has, however, deeper roots. I believe that it is only with the insight this philosophy gives that we can preserve the flexibility essential if we are to keep our actions in reasonable accord with the sentiments of those subject to our rule. More governments have been wrecked, and more human misery caused, by the lack of this accord between ruler and ruled than by any other factor that can be discerned in history. Once drive a sufficient wedge between the mass of people and those who direct their legal, political, and economic life, and our society is ruined. Then neither Foster's law of nature nor Keen's fidelity to written law will avail us anything.

* * * One of the great newspaper chains made a poll of public opinion on the question, "What do you think the Supreme Court should do with the Speluncean explorers?" About ninety per cent expressed a belief that the defendants should be pardoned or let off with a kind of token punishment. It is perfectly clear, then, how the public feels about the case. We could have known this without the poll, of course, on the basis of common sense, or even by observing that on this Court there are apparently four-and-a-half men, or ninety per cent, who share the common opinion.

This makes it obvious, not only what we should do, but what we must do if we are to preserve between ourselves and public opinion a reasonable and decent accord. Declaring these men innocent need not involve us in any undignified quibble or trick. No principle of statutory construction is required that is not consistent with the past practices of this Court. Certainly no layman would think that in letting these men off we had stretched the statute any more than our ancestors did when they created the excuse of self-defense. If a more detailed demonstration of the method of reconciling our decision with the statute is required, I should be content to rest on the arguments developed in the second and less visionary part of my brother Foster's opinion.

HENRY HART JR. AND ALBERT SACKS, *THE LEGAL PROCESS: BASIC PROBLEMS IN THE MAKING AND APPLICATION OF LAW*
pp. 1374–80 (William Eskridge Jr. & Philip Frickey eds., 1994)[18].

Note on the Rudiments of Statutory Interpretation

A.   The General Nature of the Task of Interpretation

The function of the court in interpreting a statute is to decide what meaning ought to be given to the directions of the statute in the respects relevant to the case before it. * * *

B.   The Mood in Which the Task Should Be Done

In trying to discharge this function the court should:

1.   Respect the position of the legislature as the chief policy-determining agency of the society, subject only to the limitations of the constitution under which it exercises its powers; * * *

5.   Be mindful of the nature of law and of the fact that every statute is a part of the law and partakes of the qualities of law, and particularly of the quality of striving for even-handed justice.

C.   A Concise Statement of the Task

In interpreting a statute a court should:

1.   Decide what purpose ought to be attributed to the statute and to any subordinate provision of it which may be involved; and then

2.   Interpret the words of the statute immediately in question so as to carry out the purpose as best it can, making sure, however, that it does not give the words either—

(a)   a meaning they will not bear, or

(b)   a meaning which would violate any established policy of clear statement.

D.   The Double Role of the Words as Guides to Interpretation

* * * When the words fit with all the relevant elements of their context to convey a single meaning, as applied to the matter at hand, the mind of the interpreter moves to a confident conclusion almost instantaneously * * *.

---

[18]   Reprinted by permission of the editors of the materials.

Interpretation requires a conscious effort when the words do not fit with their context to convey any single meaning. It is in such case that the words will be seen to play a double part, first, as a factor together with relevant elements of the context in the formulation of hypotheses about possible purposes, and, second, as a separately limiting factor in checking the hypotheses.

E.   The Meaning the Words Will Bear

* * * The words of the statute are what the legislature has enacted as law, and all that it has the power to enact. Unenacted intentions or wishes cannot be given effect as law.

In deciding whether words will bear a particular meaning, a court needs to be linguistically wise and not naive. It needs to understand, especially, that meaning depends upon context. But language is a social institution. Humpty Dumpty was wrong when he said that you can make words mean whatever you want them to mean.

The language belongs to the whole society and not to the legislature in office for the time being. Courts on occasion can correct mistakes, as by inserting or striking out a negative, when it is completely clear from the context that a mistake has been made. But they cannot permit the legislative process, and all the other processes which depend upon the integrity of language, to be subverted by the misuse of words. * * *

* * * [T]he proposition that words must not be given a meaning they will not bear operates almost wholly to *prevent* rather than to *compel* expansion of the scope of statutes. The meaning of words can almost always be narrowed if the context seems to call for narrowing.

F.   Policies of Clear Statement

* * * Like the first requirement just considered that words must bear the meaning given them, these policies of clear statement may on occasion operate to defeat the actual, consciously held intention of particular legislators, or of the members of the legislature generally. * * * But the requirement should be thought of as constitutionally imposed. The policies have been judicially developed to promote objectives of the legal system which transcend the wishes of any particular session of the legislature. * * *

Two policies of clear statement call for particular mention.

The first of these * * * requires that words which mark the boundary between criminal and non-criminal conduct should speak with more than ordinary clearness. This policy has special force when the conduct on the safe side of the line is not, in the general understanding of the community, morally blameworthy.

The second forbids a court to understand the legislature as directing a departure from a generally prevailing principle or policy of the law unless it does so clearly. This policy has special force when the departure is so great as to raise a serious question of constitutional power. * * *

G.   The Attribution of Purpose

[Hart and Sacks emphasize the complexity of the task. A statute may have several purposes, and different purposes may press the interpreter in different directions. Also, the relevant "purpose" includes both the immediate policy objective as well as "a larger and subtler purpose as to how the particular statute is to be fitted into the legal system as a whole."]

In determining the more immediate purpose which ought to be attributed to a statute * * * a court should try to put itself in imagination in the position of the legislature which enacted the measure.

The court, however, should not do this in the mood of a cynical political observer, taking account of all the short-run currents of political expedience that swirl around any legislative session.

It should assume, unless the contrary unmistakably appears, that the legislature was made up of reasonable persons pursuing reasonable purposes reasonably. * * *

[The court should follow the approach of *Heydon's Case*.] Why would reasonable men, confronted with the law as it was, have enacted this new law to replace it? * * *

The most reliable guides to an answer will be found in the instances of unquestioned application of the statute. Even in the case of a new statute there almost invariably *are* such instances, in which, because of the perfect fit of words and context, the meaning seems unmistakable.

Once these points of reference are established, they throw a double light. The purposes necessarily implied in them illuminate facets of the general purpose. At the same time they provide a basis for reasoning by analogy to the disputed application in hand. * * * What is crucial here is the realization that law is being made, and that law is not supposed to be irrational. * * *

[Hart and Sacks urge that "the whole context of the statute" should be examined, including the "state of the law" both before and after enactment, "general public knowledge" of the mischief to be remedied, and published legislative history as it sheds light on the statute's general purpose.]

The judicial, administrative, and popular construction of a statute, subsequent to its enactment, are all relevant in attributing a purpose to it.

The court's own prior interpretations of a statute in related applications should be accepted, on the principle of *stare decisis*, unless they are manifestly out of accord with other indications of purpose. * * *

H.   Interpreting the Words to Carry Out the Purpose

* * * The main burden of the [interpretive] task should be carried by the institution (court or administrative agency) which has the first-line responsibility for applying the statute authoritatively.

This agency should give sympathetic attention to indications in the legislative history of the lines of contemplated growth, if the history is available. It should give weight to popular construction of self-operating elements of the statute, if that is uniform. Primarily, it should strive to develop a coherent and reasoned pattern of applications intelligibly related to the general purpose. * * *

An interpretation by an administrative agency charged with first-line responsibility for the authoritative application of the statute should be accepted by the court as conclusive, if it is consistent with the purpose properly to be attributed to the statute, and if it has been arrived at with regard to the factors which should be taken into account in elaborating it.

PROBLEMS APPLYING A PURPOSE-BASED APPROACH TO STATUTORY INTERPRETATION

Problem 6–4. If they were to join one of the opinions in *Speluncean Explorers*, which ones would the following thinkers have joined, and why: (i) Justice Holmes; (ii) Professor Radin; (iii) Professors Hart and Sacks. See William Eskridge Jr., The Case of the Speluncean Explorers: *Twentieth Century Statutory Interpretation in a Nutshell*, 61 Geo. Wash. L. Rev. 1731 (1993).

Problem 6–5. A British statute provides criminal penalties for a person who willfully, fraudulently, and with intent to affect the result in an election "personate[s] any person entitled to vote at such election." The defendant, Whiteley, is charged with having "personated" Marston, a person who had been entitled to vote at an election of guardians for the township of Bradford; Marston was a ratepayer listed in the proper book and was authorized to vote at the election. Marston had died before the election, and Whiteley delivered a vote ostensibly signed by Marston to the proper voting personnel. The dictionary defines "personate" as meaning "to act or play the part of a character in a drama or the like." There is no relevant legislative history.

How would Hart and Sacks decide such a case? Before you answer, try their suggestion of figuring out the statute's purpose by posing various situations, starting with the "core" of the statutory policy and radiating out with variations. Compare *The Legal Process* 1116–26 (1994 ed.), with *Whiteley v. Chappel*, [1868] 4 L.R.Q.B. 147.

Problem 6–6. Return to *Weber* in Chapter 1. How would Hart and Sacks have decided that case? How would their opinion have differed from those written in the case?

B. IMPLICATIONS OF AND DEBATES WITHIN LEGAL PROCESS THEORY, 1950s–1980s

The legal process methodology was the dominant mode for thinking about statutes for a generation and, in fact, remains highly relevant to issues of statutory interpretation.[19] At the very same time Lon Fuller, Henry Hart, and other scholars

---

[19] On the robustness of legal process thought for current theorizing, see, e.g., Stephen Breyer, *Making Our Democracy Work: A Judge's View* (2010); Nicholas Parrillo, *Leviathan and Interpretive Revolution: The Administrative State, the Judiciary, and the Rise of Legislative History, 1890–1950*, 123 Yale L.J. 266 (2014); Daniel Rodriguez, *The Substance of the New Legal Process*, 77 Calif. L. Rev. 919 (1989) (book review); Edward Rubin, *Legal Reasoning, Legal Process and the Judiciary as an Institution*, 85 Calif. L. Rev. 265 (1997). See also William Eskridge Jr. & Philip Frickey, *The Supreme Court, 1993 Term—Foreword: Law as Equilibrium*, 108 Harv. L. Rev. 26, 27 (1994) (alumni of the legal process class were a majority of the Court in 1994, and still number four in 2014).

were crystallizing their purposive theory, it was being written into the U.S. Reports. Consider the analysis of Justice Stanley Reed in *United States v. American Trucking Associations*, 310 U.S. 534, 543 (1940):

> There is, of course, no more persuasive evidence of the purpose of a statute than the words by which the legislature undertook to give expression to its wishes. Often these words are sufficient in and of themselves to determine the purpose of the legislation. In such cases we have followed their plain meaning. When that meaning has led to absurd or futile results, however, this Court has looked beyond the words to the purpose of the Act. Frequently, however, even when the plain meaning did not produce absurd results but merely an unreasonable one "plainly at variance with the policy of the legislation as a whole" this Court has followed that purpose, rather than the literal words. When aid to construction of the meaning of words, as used in the statute, is available, there certainly can be no "rule of law" which forbids its use, however clear the words may appear on "superficial examination."

The Supreme Court in the 1950s and 1960s generally followed this approach, but not without some debate as to how far to carry out purposive analysis. For example, *Schwegmann Bros. v. Calvert Distillers Corp.*, 341 U.S. 384 (1951), contained a debate among the Justices as to whether the Court's responsibility to apply the statute's purpose (as Justice Douglas' plurality opinion did) could trump the original legislative expectations (Justice Frankfurter's dissenting opinion argued not). Justice Jackson's concurring opinion relied solely on the statutory text: because its meaning was plain, he did not care much about the original legislative intent.

As the debate in *Schwegmann* illustrated, the two generations of judges and lawyers who have deployed legal process arguments have followed more than one path. Two contesting strains within legal process thinking that have diverged into competing schools of thought.[20] One strain, represented by Judge Foster in Speluncean Explorers, emphasizes statutory purposes and sees judges and agencies as helpful partners as well as normative updaters in the ongoing statutory enterprise. The other strain, represented by Judge Keen, emphasizes the rule-of-law virtues in following statutory plain meanings and the greater institutional competence of the legislature to make and update public policy. See how these legal process debates play out in the following cases: When, if ever, should judges or agencies correct what they consider to be legislative "mistakes"? Can courts or agencies "update" statutes or read them "dynamically"? To what extent should judges "bend" statutes in light of larger public values?

---

[20] This is the argument of William Eskridge Jr. & Gary Peller, *The New Public Law Movement: Moderation as a Postmodern Cultural Form*, 89 Mich. L. Rev. 707 (1991).

1.   Correcting Legislative "Mistakes"?

SHINE V. SHINE
United States Court of Appeals, First Circuit, 1986.
802 F.2d 583.

Before COFFIN, BOWNES and BREYER, CIRCUIT JUDGES.

BOWNES, CIRCUIT JUDGE. * * *

The plaintiff, Marguerite Shine, and the defendant, Louis Shine, were married in the District of Columbia on September 20, 1969. They did not have any children and, on October 30, 1972, they divided their property and separated without making any agreement regarding support. In December of 1972, plaintiff commenced an action for separate maintenance from defendant in the Superior Court of the District of Columbia where defendant was a resident. The Superior Court issued an order requiring defendant to pay $250 per month to plaintiff beginning in April 1973. In 1975, plaintiff, then a resident of Virginia, was granted a decree of divorce from defendant by the Circuit Court of Fairfax County, Virginia. The decree made no provision for alimony and support. [Marguerite later secured a judgment requiring Louis to pay his support arrearage. Louis still did not pay, and Marguerite brought a second lawsuit, which was stayed when Louis filed for bankruptcy.]

Plaintiff then filed a complaint in the United States Bankruptcy Court for the District of New Hampshire seeking to have the support obligation declared nondischargeable under 11 U.S.C. § 523(a)(5) (1978). Section 523(a)(5) excepted from discharge any debt "to a spouse, former spouse, or child of the debtor, for alimony to, maintenance for, or support of such spouse or child, in connection with a separation agreement, divorce decree, or property settlement agreement * * *." The Bankruptcy Court initially held that the debt was not dischargeable because it "relates to the oral separation agreement between the parties." *In re Shine*, 43 B.R. 686, 688 (Bankr. D.N.H. 1984). Upon motion for reconsideration, however, it held that the debt was dischargeable because it was not created by a "separation agreement *which itself* embodies an agreed arrangement between the parties for the obligation to make support payments." Upon appeal, the district court held that the debt was not dischargeable because "to allow the defendant's debt to be discharged would be contrary to Congressional intent and public policy." Defendant has appealed. [The courts are divided on the issue whether child or spousal support obligations ordered by a court independent of a divorce proceeding or formal agreement are dischargeable.]

These conflicting interpretations of the statute derive from the two established public policies in this area. The general bankruptcy rule of construing exceptions to discharge against the creditor and in favor of the debtor, *Gleason v. Thaw*, 236 U.S. 558, 562 (1915), supports a narrow construction of the statute. This general rule implements "[t]he overriding purpose of the bankruptcy laws * * * to provide the bankrupt with comprehensive, much needed relief from the burden of his indebtedness by releasing him from virtually all his debts." On the other hand, the long-standing policy of excepting spousal and child support from discharge in bankruptcy supports a more liberal construction:

> The bankruptcy law should receive such an interpretation as will effectuate its beneficent purposes and not make it an instrument to deprive dependent wife and children of the support and maintenance due them from the husband and father, which it has ever been the purpose of the law to enforce. * * * Unless positively required by direct enactment the courts should not presume a design upon the part of Congress in relieving the unfortunate debtor to make the law a means of avoiding enforcement of the obligation, moral and legal, devolved upon the husband to support his wife and to maintain and educate his children.

Wetmore v. Markoe, 196 U.S. 68, 77 (1904).

The exception from discharge for alimony and payments for maintenance and support has long been an accepted part of bankruptcy law. Even prior to the 1903 Amendment to § 17 of the 1898 Bankruptcy Act, which explicitly incorporated this exception, the majority of courts held that such payments constituted a nondischargeable "duty" rather than a provable "debt." In *Audubon v. Shufeldt*, 181 U.S. 575 (1901), the Supreme Court found this exception to be implied in the 1898 Act, which discharged all debts "founded * * * upon a contract, expressed or implied," Act of July 1, 1898, ch. 541, § 63(4), 30 Stat. 544, 563:

> Alimony does not arise from any business transaction but from the relation of marriage. It is not founded on a contract, express or implied, but on the natural and legal duty of the husband to support the wife. The general obligation to support is made specific by the decree of the Court of appropriate jurisdiction. * * * But its obligation in that respect does not affect its nature.

And in *Wetmore*, the Court found that the 1903 Amendment explicitly including the exception was "declaratory of the true meaning and sense of the statute," rather than indicating the exception's absence prior to 1903.

Litigation arose under amended § 17 concerning the definition of "alimony." Cases were decided on the basis of whether the payments in question constituted genuine "alimony" or, rather, dischargeable "property settlements." In making this determination courts looked at the substance, rather than the formal designation, of the payments. [Citing cases.]

Under the interpretation of the statute urged by the appellant, the 1978 Amendment would be viewed as reversing this long-standing differentiation between property settlements and alimony or payments for maintenance and support. Under appellant's interpretation, property settlements, traditionally dischargeable, would have become nondischargeable, while alimony and payments for maintenance and support, traditionally nondischargeable, would have been limited by a strictly construed "in connection" clause. We, therefore, examine the history of the 1978 Amendment to determine whether such a reversal was intended by Congress.

In 1970, the Commission on the Bankruptcy Laws of the United States was charged with recommending changes in the statute. Act of July 24, 1970, Pub.L. No. 91–354, 84 Stat. 468. The Commission proposed amending § 17(a)(7) to make nondischargeable "any liability to a spouse or child for maintenance or support, for alimony due or to become due, or under a property settlement in connection with a separation agreement or divorce decree." *Report of the Commission*, H.R. Doc. No. 93–137, 93d Cong., 1st Sess. (1973)[.] The Commission's proposal left untouched the existing broad exemption for *any* liability for maintenance or support. * * * The Commission intended to expand nondischargeable support debts beyond the support, maintenance and alimony obligations which had traditionally been nondischargeable. The proposal included property settlements in divorce or separation agreements which were in the nature of support but which did not take the form of periodic payments. The Commission did not intend to *limit* the nondischargeability of the traditionally protected categories. It sought, rather, to broaden the bankruptcy law's protection of the families of the bankrupt spouse in accordance with changing times.

The version of the Amendment that originally passed the House of Representatives, H.R. 8200, retained the traditional exception to dischargeability:

(a) A discharge * * * does not discharge an individual debtor from any debt—

* * *

(5) to a spouse, former spouse, or child of the debtor, for alimony to, maintenance for, or support of such spouse or child * * *.

H.R. 8200, § 523, 95th Cong., 1st Sess., U.S. Code Cong. & Admin. News 1978, p. 5787 (1977).

In the Senate, the original version of the Amendment substantially repeated the Commission's language, making nondischargeable "any liability to a spouse or child for maintenance or support, or for alimony due or to become due, or under a property settlement in connection with a separation agreement or divorce decree * * *." S. 2266, 95th Cong., 1st Sess. (1977). When it was reported out of committee, the Amendment read:

(a) A discharge * * * does not discharge an individual debtor from * * *—

* * *

(6) any liability to a spouse or child for maintenance or support, or for alimony due or to become due, in connection with a separation agreement or divorce decree.

S. 2266, § 523, 95th Cong., 2d Sess. (1978).

The final text of the bill was an amalgam of the Commission, House and Senate versions. The first part of the new § 523(a)(5) derived from the House language, while the "in connection" clause combines the wording of the House and Senate. The result, if construed narrowly, could convey a meaning not intended by anyone.

This final version, produced in the "harried and hurried atmosphere" in which the bill was finally enacted [at the eleventh-plus hour of the Congress ending in October 1978], should not be read to effect a reversal of the long-standing principles governing this area. Such a reversal would surely have been noted in the congressional discussions. Yet, neither the House nor Senate Committee Reports accompanying the final version make any reference to a limitation upon support debts considered nondischargeable. The Senate Report does not even mention the "in connection" language in its discussion of the section nor does it suggest that any kind of new limitation had been imposed. S.Rep. No. 989, 95th Cong., 2d Sess. 79, *reprinted in* 1978 U.S. Code Cong. & Ad. News 5787, 5865. The House Report follows the Senate Report in its general discussion, H.R.Rep. No. 595, 95th Cong., 2d Sess. 364, *reprinted in* 1978 U.S. Code Cong. & Ad. News 5963, 6320. In its section-by-section discussion of § 523(a)(5), the House Report merely restates the "in connection" language without explaining any effect it might have on dischargeability. *Id.* at 6454.

In 1984, the statute was amended again, clearly making nondischargeable the kind of court-ordered debts involved in this case. Spousal or child support debts incurred "in connection with a separation agreement, divorce decree, or other order of a court of record or property settlement agreement" are now nondischargeable. 11 U.S.C. § 523(a)(5) (Supp. II) (as amended by the Bankruptcy Amendments and Federal Judgeship Act of 1984, Pub.L. 98–353, effective July 10, 1984). [The amendment was not retroactive and so did not apply to the current controversy.] This Amendment should not be read as proof of a contrary state of the law from 1978 through 1984. Rather, as the Supreme Court, in *Wetmore*, analogously noted in relation to the 1903 Amendment, it simply declares and clarifies the "true meaning and sense" of the law, allowing it to "effectuate its beneficent purposes."

After this examination of the legislative history of § 523, as well as of the established principles in this area, we cannot agree with the Bankruptcy Court's view of the requirements for nondischargeability under the 1978 statute. Congressional policy in this area has always been to ensure that genuine support obligations would not be discharged. Interpreting the statute to require the test proposed would violate the principle that in bankruptcy law, "substance will not give way to form * * * technical considerations will not prevent substantial justice from being done." *Pepper v. Litton*, 308 U.S. 295, 305 (1939). While the wording of the statute may have given rise to some confusion, "[t]he result of an obvious mistake should not be enforced, particularly when it 'overrides common sense and evident statutory purpose.'" *In re Adamo*, 619 F.2d 216, 222 (2d Cir. 1980), *cert. denied*, 449 U.S. 843 (1980) (quoting *United States v. Brown*, 333 U.S. 18, 26 (1948)).

We hold, therefore, that this support obligation is not dischargeable in bankruptcy. * * *

NOTE ON JUDICIAL "CORRECTION"
OF STATUTORY SCRIVENER'S ERRORS

Hart and Sacks opined that "[c]ourts on occasion can correct mistakes, as by inserting or striking out a negative, when it is completely clear from the context that a mistake has been made. But they cannot permit the legislative process, and all the other processes which depend upon the integrity of language, to be subverted by the misuse of words." *The Legal Process,* 1375 (1994 ed.). Is *Shine* correctly decided under this precept? There are cases in which courts have disregarded, eliminated, transposed, or inserted words in a statute when it is clear that a drafting error or other mistake was made, or where an absurd interpretation would otherwise result. See 2A Sutherland, *Statutes and Statutory Construction,* §§ 47.35–.38. Is *Shine* really a "scrivener's error" case? Would the contrary result be "absurd"? (Hint: it appears that the statute contained a drafting mistake. See if you can figure out where that occurred.)

Consider another example. The district court entered an order denying remand back to state court of a lawsuit that had been removed by the defendant to federal court. 28 U.S.C. § 1453(c)(1) requires that any appeal from such an order must be made "not *less* than 7 days after entry of the order." Was there no time limit on appeals? The Ninth Circuit held this was a scrivener's error and interpreted the statute to require an appeal to be filed "not *more* than 7 days after entry of the order." *Amalgamated Transit Union Local 1309 v. Laidlaw Transit Servs., Inc.,* 435 F.3d 1140 (9th Cir. 2006). Dissenting from the full court's denial of en banc review, 448 F.3d 1092 (2006), Judge Bybee (joined by Judges Kozinski, O'Scannlain, Rymer, Callahan, and Bea) rejected the panel's rewrite of a statute. This kind of judging "is a trap for citizens (and their lawyers) who can no longer trust the statute as written to mean what it plainly says." Also, "[w]hen courts turn the meaning of statutes up-side-down, Congress must legislate defensively, not by enacting statutes in the plainest possible language, but by enacting statutes in the language that it predicts the courts will interpret to effectuate its intentions." For a textualist theory arguing in favor of correcting scrivener's errors, see John David Ohlendorf, *Textualism and the Problem of Scrivener's Error,* 64 Me. L. Rev. 119 (2011).[21]

For an argument that the scrivener's error problem (quite common in statutes today) is a strong reason not to adopt the plain meaning rule without exceptions, see Jonathan Siegel, *What Statutory Drafting Errors Teach Us About Statutory Interpretation,* 69 Geo. Wash. L. Rev. 309, 333–44 (2001). In scrivener's error cases, Jonathan Siegel argues that "the best reading of a statute may not be the one most consonant with the statutory text, nor even necessarily the one 'intended' by the Congress, but, rather, the one that is most in keeping with judicially discoverable background principles that undergird the relevant area of law." See also Siegel, *Textualism and Contextualism in Administrative Law,* 78 B.U.L. Rev. 1023 (1998). How would this approach resolve the issue in *Shine v. Shine?*

---

[21] For other thoughtful treatments of the scrivener's error problem, see Michael Fried, *A Theory of Scrivener's Error,* 52 Rutgers L. Rev. 589 (2000) (Constitution allows courts to deviate from words enacted by legislature and signed by executive that are absurd and can be easily fixed); Andrew Gold, *Absurd Results, Scrivener's Errors, and Statutory Interpretation,* 75 U. Cin. L. Rev. 25 (2006), and David Sollors, *The Scrivener's Error Doctrine and Textual Criticism: Confronting Errors in Statutes and Literary Texts,* 49 Santa Clara L. Rev. 459 (2009).

Shine noted that, in 1984, Congress amended the statute *prospectively* to correct the problem in that case. (Recall the same phenomenon in *Holy Trinity*, though the Court did not note it.) Which way does that cut? Does it suggest that Congress can fix its own mistakes or oversights, and thus that courts ought not roam freely about the United States Code correcting legislative imprudence? Had there been no 1984 amendment, would it be easier or harder for you to agree with *Shine*? The effect of *Shine* is to make the 1984 amendment retroactive. Should this be a concern?

United States v. Locke
471 U.S. 84 (1985).

The Federal Land Policy and Management Act (FLPMA), Pub. L. 94–579, 90 Stat. 2743, codified at 43 U.S.C. §§ 1701–1784 (1982), provided that holders of certain mining claims to federal land must, "prior to December 31" of every year, file certain documents with state officials and the federal Bureau of Land Management (BLM) or lose their claims. § 1744. Simply put, this is the quintessential trap for the unwary, for it seems wholly illogical to require someone to file something, under severe penalty for default, the day *before* the last day of the year. The Locke family had been exercising rights to mine gravel on federal land since the 1950s. Knowing they were required to file papers in order to retain these rights, they sent their daughter to the nearest BLM office, which told her that claims had to be filed by December 31. The Lockes filed on that date, and the BLM rejected the papers on the ground that they were too late.

Justice Marshall, for the Court, agreed with the BLM that the Lockes were out of luck: "While we will not allow a literal reading of a statute to produce a result 'demonstrably at odds with the intentions of its drafters,' with respect to filing deadlines a literal reading of Congress' words is generally the only proper reading of those words. To attempt to decide whether some date other than the one set out in the statute is the date actually 'intended' by Congress is to set sail on an aimless journey, for the purpose of a filing deadline would be just as well served by nearly any date a court might choose as by the date Congress has in fact set out in the statute. * * * [N]othing in the legislative history suggests why Congress chose December 30 over December 31, [b]ut '[d]eadlines are inherently arbitrary,' while fixed dates 'are often essential to accomplish necessary results.' " * * *

Justice Marshall continued: "[W]e are not insensitive to the problems posed by congressional reliance on the words 'prior to December 31.' But the fact that Congress might have acted with greater clarity or foresight does not give courts a *carte blanche* to redraft statutes in an effort to achieve that which Congress is perceived to have failed to do. 'There is a basic difference between filling a gap left by Congress' silence and rewriting rules that Congress has affirmatively and specifically enacted.' *Mobil Oil Corp. v. Higginbotham*, 436 U.S. 618, 625 (1978). * * * [D]eference to the supremacy of the legislature, as well as recognition that congressmen typically vote on the language of a bill, generally requires us to assume that 'the legislative purpose is expressed by the ordinary meaning of the words used.' * * * The phrase 'prior to' may be clumsy, but its meaning is clear."

Justice Stevens, joined by Justice Brennan, dissented. In part, he argued: (1) FLPMA contained obvious drafting errors, which "should cause us to pause before concluding that Congress commanded blind allegiance to the remainder of the literal text" of the statute; (2) the BLM's implementing regulations do not repeat the statutory language, but rather state that filing must be accomplished "on or before December 30 of each year," suggesting that the BLM itself recognized that the statutory language was unclear; (3) indeed, the BLM once made the same mistake as the claimholders in *Locke*, for the agency had issued an information pamphlet that stated that documents must be filed "on or before December 31 of each [year]," demonstrating again that the statutory language is not "plain." Had the BLM issued regulations allowing filings on December 31, the Court surely would have upheld them, which suggests the anomaly that the agency "has more power to interpret an awkwardly drafted statute in an enlightened manner consistent with Congress' intent than does this Court." Justice Stevens continued: "The statutory scheme requires periodic filings on a calendar-year basis. The end of the calendar year is, of course, correctly described either as 'prior to the close of business on December 31,' or 'on or before December 31,' but it is surely understandable that the author of [this statute] might inadvertently use the words 'prior to December 31' when he meant to refer to the end of the calendar year. * * * That it was in fact an error seems rather clear to me because no one has suggested any rational basis for omitting just one day from the period in which an annual filing may be made, and I would not presume that Congress deliberately created a trap for the unwary by such an omission." The dissent concluded: "I have no doubt that Congress would have chosen to adopt a construction of the statute that filing take place by the end of the calendar year if its attention had been focused on this precise issue." Do you agree?

Query: How would Hart and Sacks have decided *Locke*? Can you think of a policy reason for requiring filing before December 31? Think hard, for this is not an impossible task. Suppose that the Lockes had shown up at the BLM at 11:00 p.m. on December 30, "before December 31," but after the BLM had closed for the day. Would they have satisfied the statute as interpreted by the Court? Is this example at all similar to the facts of *Locke*? To the example of the ordinance governing pharmacy closing mentioned at the outset of this chapter?

2. Statutory Interpreters as Faithful Agents or Cooperative Partners of the Legislature

One important criticism of legal process theory's approach to statutory interpretation is that it represents a common law baseline, where the judge is a lawmaker and so approaches statutory interpretation as a *partner* with legislators. The criticism is that this metaphor is inconsistent with the structure of the modern regulatory state: most federal law is now made by Congress (federal courts retain some limited common-law making authority in special areas). On this view, Congress is essentially the only *valid* lawmaking institutions at the federal level, and the role of the judge is to be the *faithful agent* (not the partner) of Congress, to carry out the congressional project and not to impose her own norms and rules.[22] This more limited view of the role of federal judges remains hotly contested. Judge Katzmann, for example, has argued that statutory interpretation by judges must be situated within an institutional context, where courts cooperate with agencies as well as legislatures to create public policy and where courts make substantive contributions to the evolution of statutory policy. Robert Katzmann, *Statutes*, 87

---

[22] See, e.g., Thomas Merrill, *The Common Law Powers of Federal Courts*, 52 U. Chi. L. Rev. 1 (1985); John Manning, *What Divides Textualists from Purposivists?*, 106 Colum. L. Rev. 70 (2006).

N.Y.U.L. Rev. 637 (2012); see also Robert Katzmann, *Judging Statutes* (2014); Amy Coney Barrett, *Substantive Canons and Faithful Agency*, 90 B.U.L. Rev. 109 (2012).[23] Even assuming that federal judges are required to be "faithful agents" of the enacting Congress, does that metaphor tell you anything about what method courts should deploy when applying statutes to circumstances not contemplated by the "principal" (i.e., Congress)? Consider the following analysis.

WILLIAM N. ESKRIDGE JR., *DYNAMIC STATUTORY INTERPRETATION*
125–28 (1994)[24].

Interpretation can be viewed as an honest effort by an "agent" to apply the "principal's" directive to unforeseen circumstances. (When circumstances were foreseen and provided for by the principal, it might be said that there is no "interpretive" effort needed.) The dynamic nature of interpretation arises, in large part, out of the agent's need for practical accommodation of the directive to new circumstances. Consider the following homely example, adapted from Francis Lieber's famous "fetch me the soup meat" hypothetical, excerpted at the beginning of this section.

* * * Williams, the head of the household, retains Diamond as a relational agent to run the household while Williams is away on business. The contract is detailed, setting forth Diamond's duties to care for Williams's two children, maintain the house, prepare the meals, and do the shopping on a weekly basis. One of the more specific directives is that Diamond fetch five pounds of soup meat every Monday (the regular shopping day), so that he can prepare enough soup for the entire week. Diamond knows from talking to Williams that by "soup meat" she means a certain type of nutritious beef that is sold at several local stores. When Williams leaves, Diamond has no doubt as to what he is supposed to do. But over time his interpretation of the directive will change if the social, legal, and constitutional context changes so as to affect important assumptions made in Williams's original directive.

Changes in Social Context. There are a number of changes in the world that would justify Diamond's deviation from the directive that he fetch five pounds of soup meat each Monday. For example, suppose Diamond goes to town one Monday and discovers that none of the stores has the precise kind of soup meat he knows Williams had in mind when she gave the order. Should he drive miles to other towns in search of the proper soup meat? Not necessarily. It might be reasonable for him to purchase a suitable alternative in town, especially if it appears in his judgment to be just as good for the children. One can imagine many practical reasons why, in a given week, Diamond should not follow the apparent command.

---

[23] Accord, Stephen Breyer, *Making Our Democracy Work: A Judge's View* (2010); Richard Posner, *The Problems of Jurisprudence* ch. 7 (1990); William Eskridge Jr. & Philip Frickey, *The Supreme Court, 1993 Term—Foreword: Law as Equilibrium*, 108 Harv. L. Rev. 26 (1994); Daniel Farber, *Legislative Deals and Statutory Bequests*, 75 Minn. L. Rev. 667 (1991); Philip Frickey, *Congressional Intent, Practical Reasoning, and the Dynamic Nature of Federal Indian Law*, 78 Calif. L. Rev. 1137 (1990); Lawrence Lessig, *Fidelity in Translation*, 71 Tex. L. Rev. 1165 (1993).

[24] Reprinted by permission of the publishers, Harvard University Press, Copyright © 1994 by the President and Fellows of Harvard College.

The reasons for deviating are akin to the interpretive creation of 'exceptions' to a statute's broad mandate based on the interpreter's judgment about the statute's goals and the extent to which other goals should be sacrificed. [Recall Justice Brewer's opinion in *Holy Trinity Church* and Justice Brennan's opinion in *Weber*.]

As the reasons multiply over time, one can imagine changed circumstances that effectively nullify Williams's directive altogether[.] Suppose Diamond discovers that one of the children has an allergy to soup meat. That child can continue to eat soup, but not with meat in it. Because Diamond realizes that one of the reasons Williams directed him to fetch soup meat every Monday was to ensure the good health and nourishment of the children, and because he believes that Williams would not want him to waste money on uneaten soup meat, he henceforth purchases only three pounds of soup meat per week. If both children are allergic to the soup meat, and Diamond does not care for the soup meat himself, he might be justified in entirely forgoing his directive to fetch it. Although he would be violating the original specific intent as well as the plain meaning of Williams's orders, Diamond could argue that his actions are consistent with her general intent that he act to protect the children's health and with her meta-intent that Diamond adapt specific directives to that end.

New Legal Rules and Policies. The agent might receive inconsistent directives over time. Suppose that two months after Williams embarks on her trip, she reads in a "Wellness Letter" that if children do not eat healthy foods, they will have cholesterol problems later in life. She sends Diamond a letter instructing him to place the children on a low-cholesterol diet, which should include Wendy's Bran Muffins and fresh apples. As a faithful relational agent, Diamond complies. He also reads up on the cholesterol literature, including the "Wellness Letter," and discovers that soup meat is high in cholesterol. He discontinues the weekly fetching of soup meat and fetches chicken instead because it is lower in cholesterol. Diamond's action is akin to a court's reconciliation of conflicting statutory mandates, in which one of the statutes often is given a narrowing interpretation to accommodate the policies of a later statute. * * *

Changed circumstances might further alter Diamond's interpretation of Williams's inconsistent directives. Weeks after he has substituted chicken for soup meat, Diamond learns from the "Wellness Letter" that Wendy's Bran Muffins actually do not help lower cholesterol, and that they have been found to cause cancer in rats. Furthermore, Diamond discovers that 50 percent of the apples sold in his region have a dangerous chemical on them. Diamond thereupon switches from Wendy's Bran Muffins to Richard's Bran Muffins, recommended by the "Wellness Letter," and from fresh apples to fresh oranges. Thus, not only has Diamond overthrown Williams's earlier directive on soup meat because of the new policy in her latter directive, but he has also altered her specific choice of low-cholesterol foods in the latter directive!

New Meta-Policies. The relational agent's interpretation of his orders may well be influenced over time by changing meta-policies. The new meta-policies may be endogenous or exogenous. Endogenous meta-policies are those generated from the principal herself and are just a more dramatic form of inconsistent directives.

Suppose that, after several months, Williams writes to Diamond that financial reversals impel her to cut back on household expenses. Food costs must thereafter be limited to $100 per week. Although he has long been directed to fetch soup meat every Monday, and there are other ways to economize, Diamond cuts back on soup meat, in part because it is the most expensive item on the shopping list. This is akin to a court's modifying an original statutory policy to take account of supervening statutory policies.

Exogenous meta-policies are those generated from an authority greater than the principal. Suppose that Diamond has an unlimited food budget and no health concerns about soup meat, yet he stops fetching it on a weekly basis because the town is in a crisis period and meat of all sorts is being rationed; hence, Diamond could not lawfully fetch five pounds of soup meat per week. This is akin to a court construing a statute narrowly to avoid constitutional problems based on the legislature's meta-intent not to pass statutes of questionable constitutionality.

In all of these hypotheticals Diamond, our relational agent, has interpreted Williams's soup meat directive dynamically. Quite dynamically, in fact, because in most of the variations Diamond created substantial exceptions to or even negated the original specific meaning of the directive. Notwithstanding his dynamic interpretation of the directive, I believe that Diamond has been nothing but an honest agent.

Query: Consider how Eskridge's theory of the judge as a relational agent could explain (and defend) the result in *Weber* (Chapter 1, § 3). Does it have any bearing on *Holy Trinity*, where the Court was construing a more recent statute? Is it a persuasive justification for dynamic readings of laws in the following state cases? If so, what "circumstances" have "changed," and why do any such changes support interpretations that seem to bend statutory language, perhaps beyond its breaking point?

STATUTORY PREFACE FOR THE SECOND-PARENT ADOPTION CASE

New York's Domestic Relations Law (1995)

Section 110.   Who May Adopt * * *

An adult unmarried person or an adult husband and his adult wife together may adopt another person. An adult married person who is living separate and apart from his or her spouse pursuant to a decree or judgment of separation or pursuant to a written agreement of separation subscribed by the parties thereto * * * or an adult married person who has been living separate and apart from his or her spouse for at least three years prior to commencing an adoption proceeding may adopt another person; provided, however, that the person so adopted shall not be deemed the child or step-child of the non-adopting spouse for the purposes of inheritance or support rights or obligations or for any other purposes. An adult or minor husband and his adult or minor wife together may adopt a child of either of them born in or out of wedlock and an adult or minor husband or an adult or minor wife may adopt such a child of the other spouse. No person shall hereafter be adopted except in pursuance of this article, and in conformity with section three hundred seventy-three of the social services law. * * *

Adoption is the legal proceeding whereby a person takes another person into the relation of child and thereby acquires the rights and incurs the responsibilities of parent in respect of such other person. * * *

Section 115–b. Special provisions relating to consents in private-placement adoptions * * *

[This section sets out the rules governing private placement adoptions, especially the rules governing the consent of the birth parent(s). The consent "may be executed or acknowledged before any judge or surrogate in this state having jurisdiction over adoption proceedings" (§ 115–b(2)(a)). "[T]he judge or surrogate shall inform such parent of the consequences of such act pursuant to the provisions of this section, including informing such parent of the right to be represented by legal counsel of the parent's own choosing; of the right to obtain supportive counseling and of any rights the parent may have * * *." Where the parent's consent is extrajudicial (through a notarized statement), § 115–c(3)–(4) requires detailed notice, in writing, of the parent's rights and what she or he is giving up, as well as a 45–day revocation period.]

8.   Notwithstanding any other provision of this section, a parent having custody of a child whose adoption is sought by his or her spouse need only consent that his or her child be adopted by a named stepfather or stepmother.

Section 117.   Effect of Adoption

1.   (a) After the making of an order of adoption the birth parents of the adoptive child shall be relieved of all parental duties toward and of all responsibilities for and shall have no rights over such adoptive child or to his property by descent or succession, except as hereinafter stated.

(b) The rights of an adoptive child to inheritance and succession from and through his natural parents shall terminate upon the making of the order of adoption except as hereinafter provided.

(c) The adoptive parents or parent and the adoptive child shall sustain toward each other the legal relation of parent and child and shall have all the rights and be subject to all the duties of that relation including the rights of inheritance from and through each other and the natural and adopted kindred of the adoptive parents or parent.

(d) When a natural or adoptive parent, having lawful custody of a child, marries or remarries and consents that the stepparent may adopt such child, such consent shall not relieve the parent so consenting of any parental duty toward such child nor shall such consent or the order of adoption affect the rights of such consenting spouse and such adoptive child to inherit from and through each other and the natural and adopted kindred of such consenting spouse. * * *

(h) The consent of the parent of a child to the adoption of such child by his or her spouse shall operate to vest in the adopting spouse only the rights as distributee of a natural parent and shall leave otherwise unaffected the rights as distributee of the consenting spouse.

(i) This subdivision shall apply only to the intestate descent and distribution of real and personal property. * * *

New York's Social Services Law (1995)

§ 383–c. Guardianship and custody of children in foster care

[This section regulates adoptions through agencies, which enter into "surrender instruments" with a child's birth parent(s). Like § 115–b of the Domestic Relations Law, which regulates private placement adoptions, this section, governing agency adoptions, imposes detailed procedures and notice requirements to assure that birth parents understand their rights and what rights they are giving up.]

2. Terms. (a) Such guardianship shall be in accordance with the provisions of this article and the instrument shall be upon such terms and subject to such conditions as may be agreed upon by the parties thereto * * *.

(b) If a surrender instrument designates a particular person or persons who will adopt a child, such person or persons, the child's birth parent or parents, the authorized agency having care and custody of the child and the child's attorney, may enter into a written agreement providing for communication or contact between the child and the child's parent or parents on such terms and conditions as may be agreed to by the parties. If a surrender instrument does not designate a particular person or persons who will adopt the child, then the child's birth parent or parents, the authorized agency having care and custody of the child and the child's attorney may enter into a written agreement providing for communication or contact, on such terms and conditions as may be agreed to by the parties. * * * If the court before which the surrender instrument is presented for approval determines that the agreement concerning communication and contact is in the child's best interests, the court shall approve the agreement. If the court does not approve the agreement, the court may nonetheless approve the surrender; provided, however, that the birth parent or parents executing the surrender instrument shall be given the opportunity at that time to withdraw such instrument. * * *

IN THE MATTER OF JACOB
IN THE MATTER OF DANA

New York Court of Appeals, 1995.
86 N.Y.2d 651, 636 N.Y.S.2d 716, 660 N.E.2d 397.

KAYE, C.J. [delivered the opinion for the Court.]

Under the New York adoption statute, a single person can adopt a child (Domestic Relations Law § 110). Equally clear is the right of a single homosexual to adopt (*see,* 18 NYCRR 421.16 [h] [2] [qualified adoption agencies "shall not . . . reject[ ] [adoption petitions] solely on the basis of homosexuality"]). These appeals call upon us to decide if the unmarried partner of a child's biological mother, whether heterosexual or homosexual, who is raising the child together with the biological parent, can become the child's second parent by means of adoption. [The appeal involved two petitions for adoption. In the *Jacob* case, the cohabiting boyfriend, Stephen T.K., of the child's biological mother, Roseanne M.A., moved to adopt Jacob. In the *Dana* case, the cohabiting female partner, G.M., of the child's biological mother, P.I., petitioned to adopt Dana. In both cases, the family courts denied the petitions as not falling within New York's adoption statute. The Court of Appeals, by a 4–3 vote, reversed.]

[S]ince adoption in this State is "solely the creature of . . . statute," the adoption statute must be strictly construed. What is to be construed strictly and applied rigorously in this sensitive area of the law, however, is legislative purpose as well as legislative language. Thus, the adoption statute must be applied in harmony with the humanitarian principle that adoption is a means of securing the best possible home for a child. * * *

This policy would certainly be advanced in situations like those presented here by allowing the two adults who actually function as a child's parents to become the child's legal parents. The advantages which would result from such an adoption include Social Security and life insurance benefits in the event of a parent's death or disability, the right to sue for the wrongful death of a parent, the right to inherit under rules of intestacy and eligibility for coverage under both parents' health insurance policies. In addition, granting a second parent adoption further ensures that two adults are legally entitled to make medical decisions for the child in case of emergency and are under a legal obligation for the child's economic support *(see,* Domestic Relations Law § 32).

Even more important, however, is the emotional security of knowing that in the event of the biological parent's death or disability, the other parent will have presumptive custody, and the children's relationship with their parents, siblings and other relatives will continue should the coparents separate. Indeed, viewed from the children's perspective, permitting the adoptions allows the children to achieve a measure of permanency with both parent figures * * *.

A second, related point of overriding significance is that the various sections comprising New York's adoption statute today represent a complex and not entirely reconcilable patchwork. Amended innumerable times since its passage in 1873, the adoption statute was last consolidated nearly 60 years ago, in 1938 (L. 1938, ch. 606). Thus, after decades of piecemeal amendment upon amendment, the statute today contains language from the 1870's alongside language from the 1990's. * * *

Despite ambiguity in other sections, one thing is clear: section 110 allows appellants to become adoptive parents. Domestic Relations Law § 110, entitled "Who May Adopt," provides that an "adult unmarried person or an adult husband and his adult wife together may adopt another person" (Domestic Relations Law § 110). Under this language, both appellant G.M. in *Matter of Dana* and appellant Stephen T.K. in *Matter of Jacob,* as adult unmarried persons, have standing to adopt and appellants are correct that the Court's analysis of section 110 could appropriately end here. [Although Jacob's adoption was a joint petition, his mother already enjoyed parental rights, and so only Stephen T.K.'s rights were really at stake in the petition. Chief Judge Kaye faulted the dissenting opinion for reading too much into the word "together."]

The conclusion that appellants have standing to adopt is also supported by the history of section 110. The pattern of amendments since the end of World War II evidences a successive expansion of the categories of persons entitled to adopt regardless of their marital status or sexual orientation. [Section 110 was expanded in 1951 to allow adoptions by minors and in 1984 to allow adoptions by adults not yet divorced but living apart from their spouses pursuant to separation agreements.] Supporting [the 1984] amendment was New York's "strong policy of assuring that as many children as possible are adopted into suitable family situations" (Bill Jacket, L. 1984, ch. 218, Mem. of Dept. of Social Services, at 2 [June 19, 1984]). * * *

These amendments reflect some of the fundamental changes that have taken place in the makeup of the family. Today, for example, at least 1.2 of the 3.5 million American households which consist of an unmarried adult couple have children under 15 years old, more than a six-fold increase from 1970. Yet further recognition of this transformation is evidenced by the fact that unlike the States of New Hampshire and Florida (N.H.Rev.Stat.Annot. § 170–B:4; Fla.Stat.Ann. § 63.042[3]), New York does not prohibit adoption by homosexuals. Indeed, as noted earlier, an administrative regulation is in place in this State forbidding the denial of an agency adoption based solely on the petitioner's sexual orientation (18 NYCRR 421.16[h][2]). * * *

Appellants having standing to adopt pursuant to Domestic Relations Law § 110, the other statutory obstacle relied upon by the lower courts in denying the petitions is the provision that "[a]fter the making of an order of adoption the natural parents of the adoptive child shall be relieved of all parental duties toward and of all responsibilities for and shall have no rights over such adoptive child or to his property by descent or succession" (Domestic Relations Law § 117[l][a]). Literal application of this language would effectively prevent these adoptions since it would require the termination of the biological mothers' rights upon adoption thereby placing appellants in the "Catch–22" of having to choose one of two coparents as the child's only legal parent. * * *

Both the title of section 117 ("Effect of adoption") and its opening phrase ("After the making of an order of adoption") suggest that the section has nothing to do with the standing of an individual to adopt, an issue treated exclusively in section 110. Rather, section 117 addresses the legal effect of an adoption on the parties and their property. [This reading of section 117 is directed by the Court's precedents and commentary on the section, as well as the section's textual focus on estate law, § 117(a)(1)(i).]

[Chief Judge Kaye described a 1990 amendment to Social Services Law § 383–c, which now requires agency adoptions to follow detailed procedures to assure that parents explicitly renounce their legal rights when placing a child for adoption. Likewise, a 1986 amendment to Domestic Relations Law § 115–b[1] now requires private placements to follow similar procedures.]

The procedural safeguards contained in Social Services Law § 383–c and Domestic Relations Law § 115–b—safeguards that reflect modern sensitivities as to the level of procedural protection required for waiver of parental rights—further indicate that section 117 does not invariably mandate termination in all circumstances. Under the language of section 117 alone, a biological mother's rights could theoretically be severed unilaterally, without notice as to the consequences or other procedural protections. Though arguably adequate in 1938 when the statute was enacted, such a summary procedure would be unlikely to pass muster today *(see, e.g., Santosky v. Kramer,* 455 US 745, 768–770; *Matter of Sarah K.,* 66 NY2d 223, 237).

[E]ven though the language of section 117 still has the effect of terminating a biological parent's rights in the majority of adoptions between strangers—where there is a need to prevent unwanted intrusion by the child's former biological relatives to promote the stability of the new adoptive family—the cases before us are entirely different. As we recognized in *Matter of Seaman* (78 N.Y.2d 451, 461), "complete severance of the natural relationship is not necessary when the adopted person remains within the natural family unit as a result of an intrafamily adoption." [The Legislature has recognized this principle by amending section 117 to allow adoptions by stepparents and to allow adoptive parents in some circumstances to agree to a continuing relationship between the child and her or his biological parents, though so-called "open adoptions." N.Y. Soc. Servs. Law § 383–c.]

A year prior to the enactment of Social Services Law § 383–c, this Court declined to sanction the concept of "open adoption" because of our belief that it was inconsistent with what we perceived to be section 117's requirement that termination of parental rights was mandatory in all cases *(Matter of Gregory B.,* 74 NY2d 77, 91 [citations omitted]). Significantly, when enacting Social Services Law § 383–c the very next year, the Legislature saw no need to amend Domestic Relations Law § 117. Again, if section 117 automatically terminated parental rights in all circumstances, it would have the practical effect of overriding the conditional surrender/"open adoption" provisions of Social Services Law § 383–c. By passing Social Services Law § 383–c as it did, the Legislature thus necessarily rejected the reading of section 117 articulated in *Matter of Gregory B.*

Given the above, it is plain that an interpretation of section 117 that would limit the number of beneficial intrafamily adoptions cannot be reconciled with the legislative intent to authorize open adoptions and adoptions by minors. The coexistence of the statute's seemingly automatic termination language along with these more recent enactments creates a statutory puzzle not susceptible of ready resolution.

One conclusion that can be drawn, however, is that section 117 does not invariably require termination in the situation where the biological parent, having consented to the adoption, has agreed to retain parental rights and to raise the child together with the second parent. Despite their varying factual circumstances, each of the adoptions described above—stepparent adoptions, adoptions by minor fathers and open adoptions—share such an agreement as a common denominator.

Because the facts of the cases before us are directly analogous to these three situations, the half-century-old termination language of section 117 should not be read to preclude the adoptions here. * * *

"Where the language of a statute is susceptible of two constructions, the courts will adopt that which avoids injustice, hardship, constitutional doubts or other objectionable results" *(Kauffman & Sons Saddlery Co. v. Miller,* 298 N.Y. 38, 44 [Fuld, J.]; *see also,* McKinney's Cons. Laws of N.Y., Book 1, Statutes § 150). Given that section 117 is open to two differing interpretations as to whether it automatically terminates parental rights in all cases, a construction of the section that would deny children like Jacob and Dana the opportunity of having their two de facto parents become their legal parents, based solely on their biological mother's sexual orientation or marital status, would not only be unjust under the circumstances, but also might raise constitutional concerns in light of the adoption statute's historically consistent purpose—the best interests of the child. (*See, e.g., Gomez v. Perez,* 409 U.S. 535, 538 [Equal Protection Clause prevents unequal treatment of children whose parents are unmarried]; *Plyler v. Doe,* 457 U.S. 202, 220 [State may not direct the onus of parent's perceived "misconduct against his (or her) children"]; *Matter of Burns v. Miller Constr.,* 55 N.Y.2d 501, 507–510 [New York statute requiring child born out of wedlock to prove "acknowledgment" by deceased parent did not further legitimate State interest].)

These concerns are particularly weighty in *Matter of Dana.* Even if the Court were to rule against him on this appeal, the male petitioner in *Matter of Jacob* could still adopt by marrying Jacob's mother. Dana, however, would be irrevocably deprived of the benefits and entitlements of having as her legal parents the two individuals who have already assumed that role in her life, simply as a consequence of her mother's sexual orientation.

Any proffered justification for rejecting these petitions based on a governmental policy disapproving of homosexuality or encouraging marriage would not apply. * * * New York has not adopted a policy disfavoring adoption by either single persons or homosexuals. In fact, the most recent legislative document relating to the subject urges courts to construe section 117 in precisely the manner we have as it cautions against discrimination against "nonmarital children" and "unwed parents". An interpretation of the statute that avoids such discrimination or hardship is all the more appropriate here where a contrary ruling could jeopardize the legal status of the many New York children whose adoptions by second parents have already taken place. * * *

BELLACOSA, J., dissenting. JUDGES SIMONS, TITONE and I respectfully dissent and vote to affirm in each case. * * *

Although adoption has been practiced since ancient times, the authorization for this unique relationship derives solely from legislation. It has no common-law roots or evolution. Therefore, our Court has approved the proposition that the statutory adoption charter exclusively controls. [Judge Bellacosa also emphasized that the "transcendent societal goal in the field of domestic relations is to stabilize family relationships, particularly parent-child bonds. That State interest promotes permanency planning and provides protection for an adopted child's legally secure familial placement." The state has chosen not to recognize common-law marriages or "lesbian marriages."]

Domestic Relations Law § 110, entitled "Who May Adopt," provides at its outset that *"an adult unmarried person or an adult husband and his adult wife together* may adopt another person" (emphasis added). Married aspirants are directed to apply "together", i.e., jointly, as spouses, except under circumstances not applicable in these cases. [Appellant G.M., the lesbian co-parent in *Dana*, meets this requirement, but appellants Stephen T.K. and Roseanne M.A., the unmarried cohabitants in *Jacob*, do not.]

The legislative history of adoption laws over the last century also reveals a dynamic process with an evolving set of limitations. The original version enacted in 1873 provided: "Any minor child may be adopted *by any adult*" (L. 1873, ch 830 [emphasis added]). In 1896, the Legislature cut back by stating that "[a]n adult unmarried person, or an adult husband or wife, or an adult husband and his adult wife together, may adopt a minor" (L. 1896, ch. 272, § 60; *see also,* L. 1915, ch. 352; L. 1917, ch. 149). This language was further restricted, in 1920, when the Legislature omitted from the statute the language "or an adult husband or wife" *(see,* L. 1920, ch. 433). Since enactment of the 1920 amendment, the statute has provided that "[a]n adult unmarried person or an adult husband and his adult wife *together* may adopt" (Domestic Relations Law § 110 [emphasis added]). The words chosen by the Legislature demonstrate its conclusion that a stable familial entity is provided by either a one-parent family or a two-parent family when the concentric interrelationships enjoy a legal bond. The statute demonstrates that the Legislature, by express will and words, concluded that households that lack legally recognized bonds suffer a relatively greater risk to the stability needed for adopted children and families, because individuals can walk out of these relationships with impunity and unknown legal consequences. * * *

Domestic Relations Law § 117 provides: "After the making of an order of adoption the natural parents of the adoptive child *shall be relieved of all parental duties toward and of all responsibilities for and* shall have no rights over such adoptive child *or* to his [or her] property by descent or succession" (emphasis added). The plain and overarching language and punctuation of section 117 cannot be judicially blinked, repealed or rendered obsolete by interpretation. [Judge Bellacosa cited precedent where the Court of Appeals had refused to read equitable exceptions into the plain language of section 117 to ameliorate its harsh application.]

A careful examination of the Legislature's unaltered intent based on the entire history of the statute reveals the original purpose of section 117 was to enfold adoptees within the exclusive embrace of their new families and to sever all relational aspects with the former family. That goal still applies and especially to the lifetime and lifelong relationships of the affected individuals, not just to the effect of dying intestate.

[Judge Bellacosa faulted the majority's concern that the statute be construed to avoid constitutional problems because (1) that concern had not been briefed or even mentioned by appellants, nor did the Attorney General have an opportunity to present the state's views, (2) the presumption of constitutionality augurs against vague and speculative doubts about a statute's constitutionality, and (3) such a concern could not override the plain meaning of the statute.] Ambiguity cannot directly or indirectly create or substitute for the lack of statutory authorization to adopt. These adoption statutes are luminously clear on one unassailable feature: no express legislative authorization is discernible for what is, nevertheless, permitted by the holdings today. Nor do the statutes anywhere speak of de facto, functional or second parent adoptions. Frankly, if the Legislature had intended to alter the definitions and interplay of its plenary, detailed adoption blueprint to cover the circumstances as presented here, it has had ample and repeated opportunities, means and words to effectuate such purpose plainly and definitively as a matter of notice, guidance, stability and reliability. It has done so before (*see, e.g.*, L. 1984, ch. 218 [permitting adoption by adults not yet divorced]; L. 1951, ch. 211 [permitting adoption by a minor]).

Because the Legislature did not do so here, neither should this Court in this manner. Cobbling law together out of interpretative ambiguity that transforms fundamental, societally recognized relationships and substantive principles is neither sound statutory construction nor justifiable lawmaking. * * *

Li v. Yellow Cab of California
13 Cal. 3d 804, 119 Cal. Rptr. 858, 532 P.2d 1226 (1975).

Although the doctrine of contributory negligence (barring all recovery to a tort plaintiff whose own negligence contributes in any way to her or his injury) is of judicial origin, see *Butterfield v. Forrester* (1809) 103 Eng. Rep. 926 (K.B.), the California Supreme Court had long construed section 1714 of the Civil Code (1872) to have codified the doctrine as it stood at that date. Section 1714 provided: "Everyone is responsible, not only for the result of his willful acts, but also for an injury occasioned to another by his want of ordinary care or skill in the management of his property or person, *except so far as the latter has, willfully or by want of ordinary care, brought the injury upon himself.* The extent of liability in such cases is defined by the Title on Compensatory Relief" (emphasis added). Although the statutory language might easily be read to adopt a rule of comparative negligence (where the plaintiff's recovery is reduced according to her or his negligence but not eliminated entirely), the California Supreme Court, in an opinion by **Justice Sullivan**, reaffirmed that the 1872 code had originally codified the rule of contributory negligence.[25] Nonetheless, the Court ruled that section 1714 should be reinterpreted to codify a rule of comparative negligence—the modern trend in other states (where it had mostly been adopted by statute rather

---

[25] [Eds.] Justice Sullivan noted that comparative negligence was virtually unheard of in American law in 1872 and relied on the Code Commissioners' Note that appeared immediately following section 1714 in the 1872 code. That note provided as follows: "Code La., § 2295; Code Napoleon, § 1383; Austin vs. Hudson River R.R. Co., 25 N.Y., p. 334; Jones vs. Bird, 5 B. & Ald., p. 837; Dodd vs. Holmes, 1 Ad. & El., p. 493. *This section modifies the law heretofore existing.*—See 20 N.Y., p. 67; 10 M. & W., p. 546; 5 C.B. (N.S.), p. 573. This class of obligations imposed by law seems to be laid down in the case of Baxter vs. Roberts, July Term, 1872, Sup.Ct. Cal. Roberts employed Baxter to perform a service which he (Roberts) knew to be perilous, without giving Baxter any notice of its perilous character; Baxter was injured. Held: that Roberts was responsible in damages for the injury which Baxter sustained. (See facts of case.)" The Court construed this reference to be a legislative recognition of contributory negligence, as modified to incorporate the common-law exception of "last clear chance" (which explains the statute's "except so far as" clause).

than by judicial decision) and a practice that was apparently being informally followed by many juries in California and elsewhere.

The Court justified this updating, first, by reference to the flexible rules of construction the court has traditionally applied to the code. "The Civil Code was not designed to embody the whole law of private and civil relations, rights and duties; it is incomplete and partial; and except in those instances where its language clearly and unequivocally discloses an intention to depart from, alter, or abrogate the common-law rule concerning a particular subject matter, a section of the Code purporting to embody such doctrine or rule will be construed in light of common-law decisions on the same subject." *Estate of Elizalde* (1920) 188 P. 560, 562. Indeed, the Code itself said, "The rule of the common law, that statutes in derogation thereof are to be strictly construed, has no application to this Code. The Code establishes the law of this State respecting the subjects to which it relates, and its provisions are to be liberally construed with a view to effect its objects and to promote justice." Civ. Code [1872] § 4. Also, "[t]he provisions of this Code, so far as they are substantially the same as existing statutes or the common law, must be construed as *continuations* thereof, and not as new enactments." *Id.* § 5; emphasis added.

The Court further explained that its precedents had developed section 1714 in a common-law way. "For example, the statute by its express language speaks of causation only in terms of actual cause or cause in fact ('Every one is responsible * * * for an injury occasioned to another by his want of ordinary care.'), but this has not prevented active judicial development of the twin concepts of proximate causation and duty of care. Conversely, the presence of this statutory language has not hindered the development of rules which, in certain limited circumstances, permit a finding of liability *in the absence* of direct evidence establishing the defendant's negligence as the actual cause of damage. (See *Summers v. Tice* (1948) 199 P.2d 1, 5; *Ybarra v. Spangard* (1944) 154 P.2d 687.) By the same token we do not believe that the general language of section 1714 dealing with defensive considerations should be construed so as to stifle the orderly evolution of such considerations in light of emerging techniques and concepts. On the contrary we conclude that the rule of liberal construction made applicable to the code by its own terms (Civ. Code, § 4, discussed [above]) together with the Code's peculiar character as a continuation of the common law (see Civ. Code, § 5, also discussed [above]) permit if not require that section 1714 be interpreted so as to give dynamic expression to the fundamental precepts which it summarizes.

"The aforementioned precepts are basically two. The first is that one whose negligence has caused damage to another should be liable therefor. The second is that one whose negligence has contributed to his own injury should not be permitted to cast the burden of liability upon another." The Legislature used what common law resources that existed in 1872 (namely, contributory negligence, with a last clear chance defense) to balance these precepts. By 1975, the common law had developed a more equitable way to balance them, namely, comparative negligence. Now that such a doctrine has been developed, and adopted in most other states, the court ruled that it should be read into section 1714.

Justice Clark dissented. "First, the majority's decision deviates from settled rules of statutory construction. A cardinal rule of construction is to effect the intent of the Legislature," which the court concededly violated. "The majority decision also departs significantly from the recognized limitation upon judicial action—encroaching on the powers constitutionally entrusted to the Legislature. . . . The majority's altering the meaning of section 1714, notwithstanding the original intent of the framers and the century-old judicial interpretation of the statute, represents no less than amendment by judicial fiat." Although society has changed, the proper process to update the statute is through legislative, not judicial, amendment.

NOTES ON JACOB, LI, AND DYNAMIC READINGS OF STATE CODES

1. *Common Law Judges Interpreting Civil Codes.* Statutory interpretation of a provision (like § 1714) in a comprehensive civil (or other) code is in some ways different from interpretation of a provision in a less integrated statutory scheme.[26] Consider the treatment of civil law versus common law approaches to statutes—especially the civil law concept of the "equity of a statute," which encourages reasoning from one statute to another. *Li* illustrates another practice characteristic of civil codes—that the statute itself will set forth rules of interpretation. The Italian Civil Code, for example, provides:

> In interpreting the statute, no other meaning can be attributed to it than that made clear by the actual significance of the words * * * and by the intention of the legislature.

> If a controversy cannot be decided by a precise provision, consideration is given to provisions that regulate similar cases or analogous matters; if the case still remains in doubt, it is decided according to the general principles of the legal order of the state.

Note the similarities between this formulation and that of Hart and Sacks' general theory of statutory interpretation—and of the approach followed by Chief Judge Kaye in *Jacob*.

Likewise, the California Civil Code provisions quoted by the *Li* Court arguably mandate a "liberal" construction of the Code. Section 3510 of the California Civil Code also enacted in 1872 (not cited by the Court) is perhaps most pertinent to the Court's reworking of § 1714: "When the reason of a rule ceases, so should the rule itself." The leading commentator on the California Code, John Norton Pomeroy, argued that the Code provisions should be treated like common law precedents, to be expanded or modified as times changed. Pomeroy, *The True Method of Interpreting the Civil Code*, 4 West Coast Rptr. 109–10 (1884). *Li* seems to follow the Pomeroy precept.

Another way of understanding the dynamic interpretations in *Li* and *Jacob* is through the lens of common law judging. In contrast to federal courts, which are courts of strictly limited jurisdiction having little if any lawmaking authority, see Thomas Merrill, *The Common Law Powers of Federal Courts*, 52 U. Chi. L. Rev. 1, 32–35 (1985), state judiciaries are common law courts, with inherent lawmaking authority. See Peter Strauss, *The Common Law and Statutes*, 70 U. Colo. L. Rev. 225 (1999). Their common law authority to make law vests state judges with greater legitimacy as well as competence to update statutes to reflect new circumstances. See Judith Kaye, *State Courts at the Dawn of a New Century: Common Law Courts Reading Statutes and Constitutions*, 70 N.Y.U. L. Rev. 1 (1995); Jeffrey Pojanowski, *Statutes in Common Law*

---

[26] On statutory interpretation of civil law codes, see John Henry Merryman, *The Civil Law Tradition* 40–49 (1969); John Henry Merryman, *Interpreting Statutes: A Comparative Study* (Neil MacCormick & Robert Summers eds. 1991); Konrad Zweigert & Hans-Jurgen Puttfarken, *Statutory Interpretation—Civilian Style in Civilian Methodology*, 44 Tul. L. Rev. 673 (1970).

Courts, 91 Tex. L. Rev. 479 (2013). Additionally, most state court judges do not serve for life, and many are either initially elected by the voters or subject to retention elections. (New York Court of Appeals judges are appointed for 14–year terms, with mandatory retirement at age of 70.) As a result, such judges are also more democratically accountable, and their accountability might give them greater freedom (a freedom which we should expect such judges to exercise cautiously). See Aaron-Andrew Bruhl & Ethan Leib, *Elected Judges and Statutory Interpretation,* 79 U. Chi. L. Rev. 1215 (2012).

Do these rationales justify Chief Judge Kaye's significant recasting of the adoption statute in *Jacob?* Even by her account, the effect of the Court of Appeals' ruling is that § 117's limitation on property and inheritance rights has been expanded to include cohabiting couples. That is, the Court expanded a relatively clear statutory text that was not a scrivener's error. What is the theoretical basis for such judicial surgery? Would her rationales be a better justification for *Li,* which involved a common law area (torts), an open-textured statute, and judges appointed for 12–year terms and then subject to retention elections?

2.   *Reversing the Burden of Legislative Inertia as a Justification for Judicial Recognition of Second-Parent Adoptions.* The changed circumstance in *Jacob* is somewhat different from the one in *Li.* When New York passed its adoption law, the idea of two women raising a child in a "lesbian" household would have been inconceivable. By 1995, lesbian unions with children were not unusual. Like most other states, New York had amended its adoption law to accommodate "second-parent adoptions," but those did not include female couples whose unions were not recognized as "marriages" by the state.[27]

This legislative failure may have been due to ambivalence about lesbian and gay families—and so the New York Court of Appeals' willingness to update the statute may have been a move to *reverse the burden of legislative inertia* in these cases: second parents presumptively can adopt, until the legislature overrides that interpretation. Most state supreme courts in gay-tolerant states have followed Chief Judge Kaye's dynamic reading of state adoption statutes,[28] but some have gone the other way,[29] and some states have allowed joint lesbian or gay parenting through legislation recognizing their civil unions or domestic partnerships (Nevada and Oregon).

Is this kind of political burden-shifting justifiable—or is it yet another example of hated "judicial activism"? Drawing from representation-reinforcing theories of judicial review, William Eskridge Jr., *Dynamic Statutory Interpretation* ch. 5 (1994), argues that reversing the burden of inertia is particularly justified when the political process has traditionally been hostile to a minority group. Not only does this kind of judicial updating level the playing field a little, but it places the burden on political groups that are actually able to attract the legislature's attention. If the will of the people is to deny lesbian and gay parents these rights, a decision granting relief in *Jacob* will probably be overridden in short order. (The converse case will not be: minorities traditionally

---

[27] See Nancy Polikoff, *This Child Does Have Two Mothers: Redefining Parenthood To Meet the Needs of Children in Lesbian-Mother and Other Nontraditional Families,* 78 Geo. L.J. 459 (1990).

[28] E.g., *Sharon S. v. Superior Court,* 31 Cal.4th 417 (2003); *In re M.M.D. and B.H.M.,* 662 A.2d 837 (D.C. 1995); *Petition of K.M. and D.M.,* 653 N.E.2d 888 (Ill. App. 1995); *Adoption of Tammy,* 619 N.E.2d 315 (Mass. 1993); *Adoptions of B.L.V.B. and E.L.V.B.,* 628 A.2d 1271 (Vt. 1993).

[29] E.g., *Adoption of Baby Z,* 724 A.2d 1035 (Conn. 1999); *Adoption of Luke,* 640 N.W.2d 374 (Neb. 2002); *In re Angel Lace M.,* 516 N.W.2d 678 (Wis. 1994).

disadvantaged in the political process find it doubly hard to persuade the legislature to do anything for them, because legislators fear backlash.)

Moreover, reversing the burden of inertia gives the disadvantaged minority an opportunity to falsify stereotypes—in this case, the stereotype of gay people as incapable of forming families or, indeed, as anti-family or even predatory. By allowing lesbian and gay couples to adopt children, Chief Judge Kaye was giving New Yorkers an opportunity to see that lesbian and gay families can be nurturing and productive. The New York Legislature did not rebuke Chief Judge Kaye, and years of lesbian and gay family formation helped persuade the Legislature in 2011 to amend its family law code to recognize same-sex marriages. Now that New York allows lesbian couples to get married—and hence take advantage of the step-parent allowance in the statutory adoption law—should the Court of Appeals overrule *Jacob* and require marital commitment in order for a "second parent" to adopt?

3.   *The Female Juror Cases, a Classic Example of Judicial Updating.* State statutes have often provided that juries are to be selected from a list of the qualified "electors" (i.e., voters) of the jurisdiction. Both the legislatures of Pennsylvania and Illinois adopted such statutes at a time when women were not allowed to vote in either state. After the ratification of the Nineteenth Amendment, which guaranteed women the right to vote, were women eligible to serve as jurors in these states by virtue of these statutes? In *Commonwealth v. Maxwell*, 114 A. 825, 829 (Pa. 1921), the Supreme Court of Pennsylvania held that women were qualified to serve on juries. Because the statute required jury selection "from the whole qualified electors," and because women were "electors" after the Nineteenth Amendment, women were then eligible to serve on juries. "Statutes framed in general terms apply to new cases that arise, and to new subjects that are created from time to time, and which come within their general scope and policy."

But in *People ex rel. Fyfe v. Barnett*, 150 N.E. 290, 292 (Ill. 1925), the Supreme Court of Illinois reached the opposite result. Its jury selection law was adopted under the state's 1870 constitution, which limited the franchise to "male citizen[s]." "The legislative intent that controls in the construction of a statute has reference to the Legislature which passed the given act. * * * The word 'electors,' in the statute here in question, meant male persons, only, to the legislators who used it." Accord *Commonwealth v. Welosky*, 177 N.E. 656 (Mass. 1931).

How would Hart and Sacks analyze these cases? See Hart & Sacks, *The Legal Process*, 1172–85 (1994 ed.). What "purpose" would they "attribute" to the jury selection laws? Should the court avoid an "irrational pattern of particular applications" of the statute? *Id.* at 1125. Does a court have an obligation to enhance law's overall "coherence," rather than recognizing inconsistent rules? Should the court be reluctant to interpret the juror-selection statutes in a way that runs against a fundamental legal principle or policy? Would the exclusion of women from juries have been unconstitutional when Hart and Sacks were writing? Cf. *Hoyt v. Florida*, 368 U.S. 57 (1961) (a system where women but not men could "opt out" of jury service was constitutional in 1961). If the issue just raised difficult constitutional questions, would that provide a justification for construing the open-textured statute to include women?

3.   Coherence with Public Norms

Legal process theory maintains that judges should attribute a purpose to the statute and then apply the statute so as best to achieve the purpose—so long as that does not impose on the words a "meaning they will not bear" *and* does not violate a policy of "clear statement." See Hart & Sacks, *The Legal Process*, excerpted at the beginning of this section. As to the latter point, Hart and Sacks assume that judges operate under a duty to lend greater coherence to the body of law. This duty, they say, "forbids a court to understand the legislature as directing a departure from a generally prevailing principle or policy of the law unless it does so clearly. This policy has special force when the departure is so great as to raise a serious question of constitutional power." What is the source of that duty? And how strong should this interpretive precept operate? Ought judges rewrite clear texts to avoid a conflict between a new statute and deeply rooted principles of law, or even constitutional mandates? Ponder this for a few minutes, and then read the following cases.

STATUTORY PREFACE FOR THE BOB JONES CASE

Internal Revenue Code of 1954 (Tax Advantages for Educational Institutions)

26 U.S.C. § 170. Charitable, etc., contributions and gifts

(a) Allowance of deduction. (1) General rule.—There shall be allowed as a deduction any charitable contribution (as defined in subsection (c)) payment of which is made within the taxable year. A charitable contribution shall be allowable as a deduction only if verified under regulations prescribed by the Secretary. * * *

(c) Charitable contribution defined.—For purposes of this section, the term "charitable contribution" means a contribution or gift to or for the use of * * *

(2) A corporation, trust, or community chest, fund, or foundation * * *

   (B) organized and operated exclusively for religious, charitable, scientific, literary, or educational purposes, or to foster national or international amateur sports competition (but only if no part of its activities involve the provision of athletic facilities or equipment), or for the prevention of cruelty to children or animals; * * *

(4) In the case of a contribution or gift by an individual, a domestic fraternal society, order, or association, operating under the lodge system, but only if such contribution or gift is to be used exclusively for religious, charitable, scientific, literary, or educational purposes, or for the prevention of cruelty to children or animals. * * *

26 U.S.C. § 501. Exemption from tax on corporations, certain trusts, etc.

(a) Exemption from taxation.—An organization described in subsection (c) or (d) or section 401(a) shall be exempt from taxation under this subtitle unless such exemption is denied under section 502 or 503. * * *

(c) List of exempt organizations.—The following organizations are referred to in subsection (a): * * *

(3) Corporations, and any community chest, fund, or foundation, organized and operated exclusively for religious, charitable, scientific, testing for public safety, literary, or educational purposes, or to foster national or international amateur sports competition (but only if no part of its activities involve the provision of athletic facilities or equipment), or for the prevention of cruelty to children or animals, no part of the net earnings of which inures to the benefit of any private shareholder or individual, no substantial part of the activities of which is carrying on propaganda, or otherwise attempting, to influence legislation (except as otherwise provided in subsection (h)), and which does not participate in, or intervene in (including the publishing or distributing of statements), any political campaign on behalf of (or in opposition to) any candidate for public office.

[Also listed for exemption were (4) nonprofit "civic leagues or organizations"; (5) "labor, agricultural, or horticultural organizations"; (6) nonprofit "business leagues, chambers of commerce, boards of trade, or professional football leagues"; (7) nonprofit "[c]lubs organized for pleasure, recreation, and other nonprofitable purposes"; and (8) specified "[f]raternal beneficiary societies, orders, or associations" providing health or life insurance for its members.]

(i) Prohibition of discrimination by certain social clubs.—Notwithstanding subsection (a), an organization which is described in subsection (c)(7) shall not be exempt from taxation under subsection (a) for any taxable year if, at any time during such taxable year, the charter, bylaws, or other governing instrument, of such organization or any written policy statement of such organization contains a provision which provides for discrimination against any person on the basis of race, color, or religion. The preceding sentence to the extent it relates to discrimination on the basis of religion shall not apply to—

(1) an auxiliary of a fraternal beneficiary society if such society—

(A) is described in subsection (c)(8) and exempt from tax under subsection (a), and

(B) limits its membership to the members of a particular religion, or

(2) a club which in good faith limits its membership to the members of a particular religion in order to further the teachings or principles of that religion, and not to exclude individuals of a particular race or color. * * *

BOB JONES UNIVERSITY V. UNITED STATES
Supreme Court of the United States, 1983.
461 U.S. 574, 103 S.Ct. 2017, 76 L.Ed.2d 157.

CHIEF JUSTICE BURGER delivered the opinion of the Court.

We granted certiorari to decide whether petitioners, nonprofit private schools that prescribe and enforce racially discriminatory admissions standards on the basis of religious doctrine, qualify as tax-exempt organizations under § 501(c)(3) of the Internal Revenue Code of 1954.

[I] Until 1970, the Internal Revenue Service granted tax-exempt status to private schools, without regard to their racial admissions policies, under § 501(c)(3) of the Internal Revenue Code, 26 U.S.C. § 501(c)(3), and granted charitable deductions for contributions to such schools under § 170 of the Code, 26 U.S.C. § 170.

On January 12, 1970, a three-judge District Court for the District of Columbia issued a preliminary injunction prohibiting the IRS from according tax-exempt status to private schools in Mississippi that discriminated as to admissions on the basis of race. *Green v. Kennedy*, 309 F. Supp. 1127, *app. dismissed sub nom. Cannon v. Green*, 398 U.S. 956 (1970). Thereafter, in July 1970, the IRS concluded that it could "no longer legally justify allowing tax-exempt status [under § 501(c)(3)] to private schools which practice racial discrimination." IRS News Release July 7, 1970. At the same time, the IRS announced that it could not "treat gifts to such schools as charitable deductions for income tax purposes [under § 170]." By letter dated November 30, 1970, the IRS formally notified private schools, including those involved in this case, of this change in policy, "applicable to all private schools in the United States at all levels of education."

On June 30, 1971, the three-judge District Court issued its opinion on the merits of the Mississippi challenge. *Green v. Connally*, 330 F.Supp. 1150 (D.D.C.), *aff'd sub nom. Coit v. Green*, 404 U.S. 997 (1971). That court approved the IRS's amended construction of the Tax Code. The court also held that racially discriminatory private schools were not entitled to exemption under § 501(c)(3) and that donors were not entitled to deductions for contributions to such schools under § 170. The court permanently enjoined the Commissioner of Internal Revenue from approving tax-exempt status for any school in Mississippi that did not publicly maintain a policy of nondiscrimination.

The revised policy on discrimination was formalized in Revenue Ruling 71–447, 1971–2 Cum. Bull. 230:

> "Both the courts and the Internal Revenue Service have long recognized that the statutory requirement of being 'organized and operated exclusively for religious, charitable, . . . or educational purposes' was intended to express the basic common law concept [of 'charity']. . . . All charitable trusts, educational or otherwise, are subject to the requirement that the purpose of the trust may not be illegal or contrary to public policy."

Based on the "national policy to discourage racial discrimination in education," the IRS ruled that "a private school not having a racially nondiscriminatory policy as to students is not 'charitable' within the common law concepts reflected in sections 170 and 501(c)(3) of the Code." * * *

[II.A] In Revenue Ruling 71–447, the IRS formalized the policy, first announced in 1970, that § 170 and § 501(c)(3) embrace the common law "charity" concept. Under that view, to qualify for a tax exemption pursuant to § 501(c)(3), an institution must show, first, that it falls within one of the eight categories expressly set forth in that section, and second, that its activity is not contrary to settled public policy.

Section 501(c)(3) provides that "[c]orporations . . . organized and operated exclusively for religious, charitable . . . or educational purposes" are entitled to tax exemption. Petitioners argue that the plain language of the statute guarantees them tax-exempt status. They emphasize the absence of any language in the statute expressly requiring all exempt organizations to be "charitable" in the common-law sense, and they contend that the disjunctive "or" separating the categories in § 501(c)(3) precludes such a reading. Instead, they argue that if an institution falls within one or more of the specified categories it is automatically entitled to exemption, without regard to whether it also qualifies as "charitable." The Court of Appeals rejected that contention and concluded that petitioners' interpretation of the statute "tears section 501(c)(3) from its roots."

It is a well-established canon of statutory construction that a court should go beyond the literal language of a statute if reliance on that language would defeat the plain purpose of the statute. * * *

Section 501(c)(3) therefore must be analyzed and construed within the framework of the Internal Revenue Code and against the background of the congressional purposes. Such an examination reveals unmistakable evidence that, underlying all relevant parts of the Code, is the intent that entitlement to tax exemption depends on meeting certain common-law standards of charity—namely, that an institution seeking tax-exempt status must serve a public purpose and not be contrary to established public policy.

This "charitable" concept appears explicitly in § 170 of the Code. That section contains a list of organizations virtually identical to that contained in § 501(c)(3). It is apparent that Congress intended that list to have the same meaning in both sections.[10] In § 170, Congress used the list of organizations in defining the term "charitable contributions." On its face, therefore, § 170 reveals that Congress' intention was to provide tax benefits to organizations serving charitable purposes. The form of § 170 simply makes plain what common sense and history tell us: in enacting both § 170 and § 501(c)(3), Congress sought to provide tax benefits to charitable organizations, to encourage the development of private institutions that serve a useful public purpose or supplement or take the place of public institutions of the same kind.

Tax exemptions for certain institutions thought beneficial to the social order of the country as a whole, or to a particular community, are deeply rooted in our

---

[10]   The predecessor of § 170 originally was enacted in 1917, as part of the War Revenue Act of 1917, ch. 63, § 1201(2), 40 Stat. 300, 330 (1917), whereas the predecessor of § 501(c)(3) dates back to the income tax law of 1894, Act of Aug. 27, 1894, ch. 349, 28 Stat. 509. There are minor differences between the lists of organizations in the two sections. Nevertheless, the two sections are closely related; both seek to achieve the same basic goal of encouraging the development of certain organizations through the grant of tax benefits. The language of the two sections is in most respects identical, and the Commissioner and the courts consistently have applied many of the same standards in interpreting those sections. To the extent that § 170 "aids in ascertaining the meaning" of § 501(c)(3), therefore, it is "entitled to great weight," *United States v. Stewart*, 311 U.S. 60, 64–65 (1940).

history, as in that of England. The origins of such exemptions lie in the special privileges that have long been extended to charitable trusts.[12]

More than a century ago, this Court announced the caveat that is critical in this case:

"[I]t has now become an established principle of American law, that courts of chancery will sustain and protect . . . a gift . . . to public charitable uses, *provided the same is consistent with local laws and public policy . . . .*" *Perin v. Carey*, 24 How. 465, 501 (1861) (emphasis added).

Soon after that, in 1878, the Court commented:

"A charitable use, *where neither law nor public policy forbids*, may be applied to almost any thing *that tends to promote the well-doing and well-being of social man.*" *Ould v. Washington Hospital for Foundlings*, 95 U.S. 303, 311 (1878) (emphasis added). * * *

When the Government grants exemptions or allows deductions all taxpayers are affected; the very fact of the exemption or deduction for the donor means that other taxpayers can be said to be indirect and vicarious "donors." Charitable exemptions are justified on the basis that the exempt entity confers a public benefit—a benefit which the society or the community may not itself choose or be able to provide, or which supplements and advances the work of public institutions already supported by tax revenues. History buttresses logic to make clear that, to warrant exemption under § 501(c)(3), an institution must fall within a category specified in that section and must demonstrably serve and be in harmony with the public interest. The institution's purpose must not be so at odds with the common community conscience as to undermine any public benefit that might otherwise be conferred.

[II.B]   We are bound to approach these questions with full awareness that determinations of public benefit and public policy are sensitive matters with serious implications for the institutions affected; a declaration that a given institution is not "charitable" should be made only where there can be no doubt that the activity involved is contrary to a fundamental public policy. But there can no longer be any doubt that racial discrimination in education violates deeply and widely accepted views of elementary justice. Prior to 1954, public education in many places still was conducted under the pall of *Plessy v. Ferguson*, 163 U.S. 537 (1896); racial segregation in primary and secondary education prevailed in many parts of the country.[20] This Court's decision in *Brown v. Board of Education*, 347

---

[12] The form and history of the charitable exemption and deduction sections of the various income tax acts reveal that Congress was guided by the common law of charitable trusts. See Simon, *The Tax-Exempt Status of Racially Discriminatory Religious Schools*, 36 Tax L.Rev. 477, 485–489 (1981). Congress acknowledged as much in 1969. The House Report on the Tax Reform Act of 1969, Pub.L. 91–172, 83 Stat. 487, stated that the § 501(c)(3) exemption was available only to institutions that served "the specified charitable purposes," H.R.Rep. No. 91–413, pt. 1, p. 35 (1969), and described "charitable" as "a term that has been used in the law of trusts for hundreds of years." *Id.*, at 43. We need not consider whether Congress intended to incorporate into the Internal Revenue Code any aspects of charitable trust law other than the requirements of public benefit and a valid public purpose.

[20] In 1894, when the first charitable exemption provision was enacted, racially segregated educational institutions would not have been regarded as against public policy. Yet contemporary standards must be considered in determining whether given activities provide a public benefit and are entitled to the charitable

U.S. 483 (1954), signalled an end to that era. Over the past quarter of a century, every pronouncement of this Court and myriad Acts of Congress and Executive Orders attest a firm national policy to prohibit racial segregation and discrimination in public education.

An unbroken line of cases following *Brown v. Board of Education* establishes beyond doubt this Court's view that racial discrimination in education violates a most fundamental national public policy, as well as rights of individuals.

> "The right of a student not to be segregated on racial grounds in schools . . . is indeed so fundamental and pervasive that it is embraced in the concept of due process of law." *Cooper v. Aaron*, 358 U.S. 1, 19 (1958).

In *Norwood v. Harrison*, 413 U.S. 455, 468–469 (1973), we dealt with a nonpublic institution:

> "[A] private school—even one that discriminates—fulfills an important educational function; *however, . . . [that] legitimate educational function cannot be isolated from discriminatory practices . . . [D]iscriminatory treatment exerts a pervasive influence on the entire educational process.*" (Emphasis added.)

Congress, in Titles IV and VI of the Civil Rights Act of 1964, Pub.L. 88–352, 78 Stat. 241, 42 U.S.C. §§ 2000c et seq., 2000c–6, 2000d et seq., clearly expressed its agreement that racial discrimination in education violates a fundamental public policy. Other sections of that Act, and numerous enactments since then, testify to the public policy against racial discrimination. See, *e.g.*, the Voting Rights Act of 1965; Title VIII of the Civil Rights Act of 1968; [the Emergency School Aid Acts of 1972 and 1978].

The Executive Branch has consistently placed its support behind eradication of racial discrimination. Several years before this Court's decision in *Brown v. Board of Education*, President Truman issued Executive Orders prohibiting racial discrimination in federal employment decisions, Exec. Order No. 9980, 3 CFR 720 (1943–1948 Comp.), and in classifications for the Selective Service, Exec. Order No. 9988, 3 CFR 726, 729 (1943–1948 Comp.). In 1957, President Eisenhower employed military forces to ensure compliance with federal standards in school desegregation programs. Exec. Order No. 10730, 3 CFR 389 (1954–1958 Comp.). And in 1962, President Kennedy announced:

> "[T]he granting of Federal assistance for . . . housing and related facilities from which Americans are excluded because of their race, color, creed, or national origin is unfair, unjust, and inconsistent with the public policy of the United States as manifested in its Constitution and laws." Exec. Order No. 11063, 3 CFR 652 (1959–1963 Comp.).

---

tax exemption. In *Walz v. Tax Comm'n*, 397 U.S. 664, 673 (1970), we observed: "Qualification for tax exemption is not perpetual or immutable; some tax-exempt groups lose that status when their activities take them outside the classification and new entities can come into being and qualify for exemption." Charitable trust law also makes clear that the definition of "charity" depends upon contemporary standards. See, *e.g.*, Restatement (Second) of Trusts § 374, comment a (1959).

These are but a few of numerous Executive Orders over the past three decades demonstrating the commitment of the Executive Branch to the fundamental policy of eliminating racial discrimination.

Few social or political issues in our history have been more vigorously debated and more extensively ventilated than the issue of racial discrimination, particularly in education. Given the stress and anguish of the history of efforts to escape from the shackles of the "separate but equal" doctrine of *Plessy v. Ferguson*, it cannot be said that educational institutions that, for whatever reasons, practice racial discrimination, are institutions exercising "beneficial and stabilizing influences in community life," *Walz v. Tax Comm'n*, 397 U.S. 664, 673 (1970), or should be encouraged by having all taxpayers share in their support by way of special tax status.

There can thus be no question that the interpretation of § 170 and § 501(c)(3) announced by the IRS in 1970 was correct. That it may be seen as belated does not undermine its soundness. It would be wholly incompatible with the concepts underlying tax exemption to grant the benefit of tax-exempt status to racially discriminatory educational entities, which "exer[t] a pervasive influence on the entire educational process." *Norwood v. Harrison, supra.* Whatever may be the rationale for such private schools' policies, and however sincere the rationale may be, racial discrimination in education is contrary to public policy. Racially discriminatory educational institutions cannot be viewed as conferring a public benefit within the "charitable" concept discussed earlier, or within the Congressional intent underlying § 170 and § 501(c)(3).

[II.C]   [Chief Justice Burger rejected the argument that the IRS did not have the authority to issue the 1970 rule and that its longstanding prior policy could only be overturned by legislative amendment of the Code. He reasoned that the IRS had been given broad rulemaking power by Congress and, moreover, that the policy adopted by the IRS was fully consistent with national policy since *Brown* and the Civil Rights Act of 1964.]

[II.D]   The actions of Congress since 1970 leave no doubt that the IRS reached the correct conclusion in exercising its authority. It is, of course, not unknown for independent agencies or the Executive Branch to misconstrue the intent of a statute; Congress can and often does correct such misconceptions, if the courts have not done so. Yet for a dozen years Congress has been made aware—acutely aware—of the IRS rulings of 1970 and 1971. As we noted earlier, few issues have been the subject of more vigorous and widespread debate and discussion in and out of Congress than those related to racial segregation in education. Sincere adherents advocating contrary views have ventilated the subject for well over three decades. Failure of Congress to modify the IRS rulings of 1970 and 1971, of which Congress was, by its own studies and by public discourse, constantly reminded; and Congress' awareness of the denial of tax-exempt status for racially discriminatory schools when enacting other and related legislation make out an unusually strong case of legislative acquiescence in and ratification by implication of the 1970 and 1971 rulings.

Ordinarily, and quite appropriately, courts are slow to attribute significance to the failure of Congress to act on particular legislation. We have observed that "unsuccessful attempts at legislation are not the best of guides to legislative intent." Here, however, we do not have an ordinary claim of legislative acquiescence. Only one month after the IRS announced its position in 1970, Congress held its first hearings on this precise issue. *Equal Educational Opportunity: Hearings before the Senate Select Comm. on Equal Educational Opportunity*, 91st Cong., 2d Sess. 1991 (1970). Exhaustive hearings have been held on the issue at various times since then. These include hearings in February 1982, after we granted review in this case. *Administration's Change in Federal Policy Regarding the Tax Status of Racially Discriminatory Private Schools: Hearing before the House Comm. on Ways and Means*, 97th Cong., 2d Sess. (1982).

Non-action by Congress is not often a useful guide, but the non-action here is significant. During the past 12 years there have been no fewer than 13 bills introduced to overturn the IRS interpretation of § 501(c)(3). Not one of these bills has emerged from any committee, although Congress has enacted numerous other amendments to § 501 during this same period, including an amendment to § 501(c)(3) itself. Tax Reform Act of 1976, Pub.L. 94–455, § 1313(a), 90 Stat. 1730. It is hardly conceivable that Congress—and in this setting, any Member of Congress—was not abundantly aware of what was going on. In view of its prolonged and acute awareness of so important an issue, Congress' failure to act on the bills proposed on this subject provides added support for concluding that Congress acquiesced in the IRS rulings of 1970 and 1971.

The evidence of Congressional approval of the policy embodied in Revenue Ruling 71–447 goes well beyond the failure of Congress to act on legislative proposals. Congress affirmatively manifested its acquiescence in the IRS policy when it enacted the present § 501(i) of the Code, Act of Oct. 20, 1976, Pub.L. 94–568, 90 Stat. 2697 (1976). That provision denies tax-exempt status to social clubs whose charters or policy statements provide for "discrimination against any person on the basis of race, color, or religion." Both the House and Senate Committee Reports on that bill articulated the national policy against granting tax exemptions to racially discriminatory private clubs. S. Rep. No. 94–1318, p. 8 (1976); H.R. Rep. No. 94–1353, p. 8 (1976).

Even more significant is the fact that both reports focus on this Court's affirmance of *Green v. Connally*, 330 F.Supp. 1150 (DC 1971), as having established that "discrimination on account of race is inconsistent with an *educational institution's* tax-exempt status." S. Rep. No. 94–1318 at 7–8, and n. 5; H.R. Rep. No. 94–1353 at 8, and n. 5 (emphasis added). These references in congressional Committee Reports on an enactment denying tax exemptions to racially discriminatory private social clubs cannot be read other than as indicating approval of the standards applied to racially discriminatory private schools by the IRS subsequent to 1970, and specifically of Revenue Ruling 71–447.[27]

---

[27] Reliance is placed on scattered statements in floor debate by Congressmen critical of the IRS' adoption of Revenue Ruling 71–447. Those views did not prevail. That several Congressmen, expressing their individual views, argued that the IRS had no authority to take the action in question, is hardly a balance for the overwhelming evidence of Congressional awareness of and acquiescence in the IRS rulings of 1970 and

[In Part III, Chief Justice Burger rejected the argument that the IRS ruling violated the Free Exercise Clause of the First Amendment, and in Part IV he rejected the argument that the IRS ruling was not properly applied to the petitioners.]

JUSTICE POWELL, concurring in the judgment.

[Justice Powell found much to admire in the dissenting opinion's analysis of the statutory text but agreed with the Court's result, based upon the reasoning in Part II.B-D of the opinion for the Court. He did not agree with the reasoning in Part II.A.] I am unconvinced that the critical question in determining tax-exempt status is whether an individual organization provides a clear "public benefit" as defined by the Court. Over 106,000 organizations filed § 501(c)(3) returns in 1981. I find it impossible to believe that all or even most of those organizations could prove that they "demonstrably serve and [are] in harmony with the public interest" or that they are "beneficial and stabilizing influences in community life." Nor I am prepared to say that petitioners, because of their racially discriminatory policies, necessarily contribute nothing of benefit to the community. It is clear from the substantially secular character of the curricula and degrees offered that petitioners provide educational benefits.

Even more troubling to me is the element of conformity that appears to inform the Court's analysis. The Court asserts that an exempt organization must "demonstrably serve and be in harmony with the public interest," must have a purpose that comports with "the common community conscience," and must not act in a manner "affirmatively at odds with [the] declared position of the whole government." Taken together, these passages suggest that the primary function of a tax-exempt organization is to act on behalf of the Government in carrying out governmentally approved policies. In my opinion, such a view of § 501(c)(3) ignores the important role played by tax exemptions in encouraging diverse, indeed often sharply conflicting, activities and viewpoints. * * * [P]rivate, nonprofit groups receive tax exemptions because "each group contributes to the diversity of association, viewpoint, and enterprise essential to a vigorous, pluralistic society." [*Walz v. Tax Comm'n*, 397 U.S. 664, 689 (1970) (Brennan, J., concurring).] Far from representing an effort to reinforce any perceived "common community conscience," the provision of tax exemptions to nonprofit groups is one indispensable means of limiting the influence of governmental orthodoxy on important areas of community life. Given the importance of our tradition of pluralism, "[t]he interest in preserving

---

1971. Petitioners also argue that the Ashbrook and Dornan Amendments to the Treasury, Postal Service, and General Government Appropriations Act of 1980, Pub.L. 96–74, §§ 103, 614, 615, 93 Stat. 559, 562, 576–577 (1979), reflect Congressional opposition to the IRS policy formalized in Revenue Ruling 71–447. Those amendments, however, are directly concerned only with limiting more aggressive enforcement procedures proposed by the IRS in 1978 and 1979 and preventing the adoption of more stringent substantive standards. The Ashbrook Amendment, § 103 of the Act, applies only to procedures, guidelines, or measures adopted after August 22, 1978, and thus in no way affects the status of Revenue Ruling 71–447. In fact, both Congressman Dornan and Congressman Ashbrook explicitly stated that their amendments would have no effect on prior IRS policy, including Revenue Ruling 71–447, see 125 Cong.Rec. H5982 (1979) (Cong. Dornan: "[M]y amendment will not affect existing IRS rules which IRS has used to revoke tax exemptions of white segregated academies under Revenue Ruling 71–447 . . . ."); *id.*, at 18446 (Cong. Ashbrook: "My amendment very clearly indicates on its face that all the regulations in existence as of August 22, 1978, would not be touched"). These amendments therefore do not indicate Congressional rejection of Revenue Ruling 71–447 and the standards contained therein.

an area of untrammeled choice for private philanthropy is very great." *Jackson v. Statler Foundation*, 496 F.2d 623, 639 (CA2 1974) (Friendly, J., dissenting from denial of reconsideration en banc).

[Judgments about whether a class of institutions advances the public interest are best left to Congress, reasoned Justice Powell. The IRS has, by its own admission, no special expertise in making the kind of determinations the Court upholds in this case.] The contours of public policy should be determined by Congress, not by judges or the IRS.

JUSTICE REHNQUIST, dissenting.

The Court points out that there is a strong national policy in this country against racial discrimination. To the extent that the Court states that Congress in furtherance of this policy could deny tax-exempt status to educational institutions that promote racial discrimination, I readily agree. But, unlike the Court, I am convinced that Congress simply has failed to take this action and, as this Court has said over and over again, regardless of our view on the propriety of Congress' failure to legislate we are not constitutionally empowered to act for them.

In approaching this statutory construction question the Court quite adeptly avoids the statute it is construing. This I am sure is no accident, for there is nothing in the language of § 501(c)(3) that supports the result obtained by the Court. Section 501(c)(3) provides tax-exempt status for:

> "Corporations, and any community chest, fund, or foundation, organized and operated exclusively for religious, charitable, scientific, testing for public safety, literary, or educational purposes, or to foster national or international amateur sports competition (but only if no part of its activities involve the provision of athletic facilities or equipment), or for the prevention of cruelty to children or animals, no part of the net earnings of which inures to the benefit of any private shareholder or individual, no substantial part of the activities of which is carrying on propaganda, or otherwise attempting, to influence legislation (except as otherwise provided in subsection (h)), and which does not participate in, or intervene in (including the publishing or distributing of statements), any political campaign on behalf of any candidate for public office." 26 U.S.C. § 501(c)(3).

With undeniable clarity, Congress has explicitly defined the requirements for § 501(c)(3) status. An entity must be (1) a corporation, or community chest, fund, or foundation, (2) organized for one of the eight enumerated purposes, (3) operated on a nonprofit basis, and (4) free from involvement in lobbying activities and political campaigns. Nowhere is there to be found some additional, undefined public policy requirement.

The Court first seeks refuge from the obvious reading of § 501(c)(3) by turning to § 170 of the Internal Revenue Code which provides a tax deduction for contributions made to § 501(c)(3) organizations. In setting forth the general rule, § 170 states:

"There shall be allowed as a deduction any charitable contribution (as defined in subsection (c)) payment of which is made within the taxable year. A charitable contribution shall be allowable as a deduction only if verified under regulations prescribed by the Secretary." 26 U.S.C. § 170(a)(1).

The Court seizes the words "charitable contribution" and with little discussion concludes that "[o]n its face, therefore, § 170 reveals that Congress' intention was to provide tax benefits to organizations serving charitable purposes," intimating that this implies some unspecified common-law charitable trust requirement.

The Court would have been well advised to look to subsection (c) where, as § 170(a)(1) indicates, Congress has defined a "charitable contribution":

"For purposes of this section, the term 'charitable contribution' means a contribution or gift to or for the use of . . . [a] corporation, trust, or community chest, fund, or foundation . . . organized and operated exclusively for religious, charitable, scientific, literary, or educational purposes, or to foster national or international amateur sports competition (but only if no part of its activities involve the provision of athletic facilities or equipment), or for the prevention of cruelty to children or animals; . . . no part of the net earnings of which inures to the benefit of any private shareholder or individual; and . . . which is not disqualified for tax exemption under section 501(c)(3) by reason of attempting to influence legislation, and which does not participate in, or intervene in (including the publishing or distributing of statements), any political campaign on behalf of any candidate for public office." 26 U.S.C. § 170(c).

Plainly, § 170(c) simply tracks the requirements set forth in § 501(c)(3). Since § 170 is no more than a mirror of § 501(c)(3) and, as the Court points out, § 170 followed § 501(c)(3) by more than two decades, it is at best of little usefulness in finding the meaning of § 501(c)(3).

Making a more fruitful inquiry, the Court next turns to the legislative history of § 501(c)(3) and finds that Congress intended in that statute to offer a tax benefit to organizations that Congress believed were providing a public benefit. I certainly agree. But then the Court leaps to the conclusion that this history is proof Congress intended that an organization seeking § 501(c)(3) status "must fall within a category specified in that section *and must demonstrably serve and be in harmony with the public interest.*" (Emphasis added). To the contrary, I think that the legislative history of § 501(c)(3) unmistakably makes clear that *Congress has decided* what organizations are serving a public purpose and providing a public benefit within the meaning of § 501(c)(3) and has clearly set forth in § 501(c)(3) the characteristics of such organizations. In fact, there are few examples which better illustrate Congress' effort to define and redefine the requirements of a legislative act.

The first general income tax law was passed by Congress in the form of the Tariff Act of 1894. A provision of that Act provided an exemption for "corporations, companies, or associations organized and conducted solely for charitable, religious, or educational purposes." The income tax portion of the 1894 Act was held unconstitutional by this Court, see *Pollock v. Farmers' Loan & Trust Co.*, 158 U.S. 601 (1895), but a similar exemption appeared in the Tariff Act of 1909 which imposed a tax on corporate income. The 1909 Act provided an exemption for "any corporation or association organized and operated exclusively for religious, charitable, or educational purposes, no part of the net income of which inures to the benefit of any private stockholder or individual."

With the ratification of the Sixteenth Amendment, Congress again turned its attention to an individual income tax with the Tariff Act of 1913. And again, in the direct predecessor of § 501(c)(3), a tax exemption was provided for "any corporation or association organized and operated exclusively for religious, charitable, scientific, or educational purposes, no part of the net income of which inures to the benefit of any private stockholder or individual." In subsequent Acts Congress continued to broaden the list of exempt purposes. The Revenue Act of 1918 added an exemption for corporations or associations organized "for the prevention of cruelty to children or animals." The Revenue Act of 1921 expanded the groups to which the exemption applied to include "any community chest, fund, or foundation" and added "literary" endeavors to the list of exempt purposes. The exemption remained unchanged in the Revenue Acts of 1924, 1926, 1928, and 1932. In the Revenue Act of 1934 Congress added the requirement that no substantial part of the activities of any exempt organization can involve the carrying on of "propaganda" or "attempting to influence legislation." Again, the exemption was left unchanged by the Revenue Acts of 1936 and 1938.

The tax laws were overhauled by the Internal Revenue Code of 1939, but this exemption was left unchanged. When the 1939 Code was replaced with the Internal Revenue Code of 1954, the exemption was adopted in full in the present § 501(c)(3) with the addition of "testing for public safety" as an exempt purpose and an additional restriction that tax-exempt organizations could not "participate in, or intervene in (including the publishing or distributing of statements), any political campaign on behalf of any candidate for public office." Ch. 1, § 501(c)(3), 68A Stat. 163 (1954). Then in 1976 the statute was again amended adding to the purposes for which an exemption would be authorized, "to foster national or international amateur sports competition," provided the activities did not involve the provision of athletic facilities or equipment. Tax Reform Act of 1976, Pub. L. 94–455, § 1313(a), 90 Stat. 1520, 1730 (1976).

One way to read the opinion handed down by the Court today leads to the conclusion that this long and arduous refining process of § 501(c)(3) was certainly a waste of time, for when enacting the original 1894 statute Congress intended to adopt a common law term of art, and intended that this term of art carry with it all of the common law baggage which defines it. Such a view, however, leads also to the unsupportable idea that Congress has spent almost a century adding illustrations simply to clarify an already defined common law term. * * *

Perhaps recognizing the lack of support in the statute itself, or in its history, for the 1970 IRS change in interpretation, the Court finds that "[t]he actions of Congress since 1970 leave no doubt that the IRS reached the correct conclusion in exercising its authority," concluding that there is "an unusually strong case of legislative acquiescence in and ratification by implication of the 1970 and 1971 rulings." The Court relies first on several bills introduced to overturn the IRS interpretation of § 501(c)(3). But we have said before, and it is equally applicable here, that this type of congressional inaction is of virtually no weight in determining legislative intent. See *United States v. Wise*, 370 U.S. 405, 411 (1962); *Waterman S.S. Corp. v. United States*, 381 U.S. 252, 269 (1965). These bills and related hearings indicate little more than that a vigorous debate has existed in Congress concerning the new IRS position.

The Court next asserts that "Congress affirmatively manifested its acquiescence in the IRS policy when it enacted the present § 501(i) of the Code," a provision that "denies tax-exempt status to social clubs whose charters or policy statements provide for" racial discrimination. Quite to the contrary, it seems to me that in § 501(i) Congress showed that when it wants to add a requirement prohibiting racial discrimination to one of the tax-benefit provisions, it is fully aware of how to do it.

The Court intimates that the Ashbrook and Dornan Amendments also reflect an intent by Congress to acquiesce in the new IRS position. The amendments were passed to limit certain enforcement procedures proposed by the IRS in 1978 and 1979 for determining whether a school operated in a racially nondiscriminatory fashion. The Court points out that in proposing his amendment, Congressman Ashbrook stated: " 'My amendment very clearly indicates on its face that all the regulations in existence as of August 22, 1978, would not be touched.' " The Court fails to note that Congressman Ashbrook also said:

> "The IRS has no authority to create public policy.... So long as the Congress has not acted to set forth a national policy respecting denial of tax exemptions to private schools, it is improper for the IRS or any other branch of the Federal Government to seek denial of tax-exempt status.... There exists but a single responsibility which is proper for the Internal Revenue Service: To serve as tax collector." 125 Cong. Rec. H5879–80 (1979).

In the same debate, Congressman Grassley asserted: "Nobody argues that racial discrimination should receive preferred tax status in the United States. However, the IRS should not be making these decisions on the agency's own discretion. Congress should make these decisions." *Id.*, at 5884. The same debates are filled with other similar statements. While on the whole these debates do not show conclusively that Congress believed the IRS had exceeded its authority with the 1970 change in position, they likewise are far less than a showing of acquiescence in and ratification of the new position.

This Court continuously has been hesitant to find ratification through inaction. This is especially true where such a finding "would result in a construction of the statute which not only is at odds with the language of the section in question and the pattern of the statute taken as a whole, but also is extremely far reaching in terms of the virtually untrammeled and unreviewable power it would vest in a regulatory agency." *SEC v. Sloan*, 436 U.S. 103, 121 (1978). Few cases would call for more caution in finding ratification by acquiescence than the present one. The new IRS interpretation is not only far less than a long-standing administrative policy, it is at odds with a position maintained by the IRS, and unquestioned by Congress, for several decades prior to 1970. The interpretation is unsupported by the statutory language, it is unsupported by legislative history, the interpretation has led to considerable controversy in and out of Congress, and the interpretation gives to the IRS a broad power which until now Congress had kept for itself. Where in addition to these circumstances Congress has shown time and time again that it is ready to enact positive legislation to change the Tax Code when it desires, this Court has no business finding that Congress has adopted the new IRS position by failing to enact legislation to reverse it.

I have no disagreement with the Court's finding that there is a strong national policy in this country opposed to racial discrimination. I agree with the Court that Congress has the power to further this policy by denying § 501(c)(3) status to organizations that practice racial discrimination. But as of yet Congress has failed to do so. Whatever the reasons for the failure, this Court should not legislate for Congress. * * *

NOTES ON BOB JONES AND READING STATUTES IN LIGHT OF PUBLIC VALUES

1.   *Was There a Plain Meaning? Why Not Stop with That?* Justice Rehnquist's dissenting opinion argues that § 501(c)(3) had a plain meaning that supported Bob Jones: the statute grants an exemption to any "educational" institution, which clearly includes Bob Jones University. The Chief Justice responds that §§ 501 and 170 should be read together, and the "charitable" requirement of § 170 read into § 501(c)(3)—but § 170 defines "charitable contribution" to include contributions to "educational" institutions, again just like Bob Jones. So why should the Court not apply the statutory plain meaning? Three legal process reasons are advanced: (1) statutory purpose, (2) coherence with larger norms, and (3) congressional acquiescence. Chapter 7 will examine the acquiescence argument. Does the Chief Justice have an answer to Justice Powell's argument that the statutory purpose is to encourage diversity of institutions that offer educational and other services?

2.   *Larger Statutory and Constitutional Policy.* Chief Justice Burger invokes a wide array of sources—constitutional precedents, statutes, executive orders, etc.—to demonstrate that government subsidies to Bob Jones would violate deeply held public values. Yet none of the sources cited by Chief Justice Burger actually prohibited Bob Jones University's private race discrimination. Is there something anomalous about "expanding" these constitutional and statutory authorities beyond their well-defined ambit? For a critique, see Mayer G. Freed and Daniel D. Polsby, in *Race, Religion & Public Policy*: Bob Jones University v. United States, 1983 Sup. Ct. Rev. 1, 5.

An earlier draft of the Chief Justice's opinion did note that federal law barred private schools from discriminating on the basis of race—but Burger dropped that highly relevant reference in the final opinion. Olatunde Johnson, *The Story of* Bob Jones University v. United States (1983): *Race, Religion, and Congress's Extraordinary Acquiescence*, in *Statutory Interpretation Stories* 126, 151 (Eskridge, Frickey & Garrett eds., 2011). In fact, Bob Jones was violating 42 U.S.C. § 1981, which bars race discrimination in private contracting, and which the Supreme Court had interpreted to bar private schools from discriminating on the basis of race. Does § 1981 provide a cogent response to the Freed and Polsby concerns? Why might the Chief Justice have dropped reference to § 1981 in his opinion for the Court?

3.   *Public Values or Public Hypocrisy? Bob Jones* reads like a very high-minded opinion: How can we as a society subsidize segregated schools? We cannot! That sounds great, a ringing reaffirmation of *Brown v. Board of Education*. But the reality is a great deal less inspiring. See Johnson, *Story of* Bob Jones (detailed account from which we draw). The Carter Administration's IRS issued regulations in 1978–79 placing burdens on schools with low minority percentages to "prove" their nondiscrimination. Congress reacted with the Dornan and Ashbrook Amendments, which effectively barred the IRS from implementing the new regulations. (Justice Rehnquist relies on these amendments in objecting to the acquiescence argument. Does he have a point?) When *Bob Jones* was decided, IRS enforcement depended heavily on "self-reporting": Institutions that admitted to race discrimination were the only ones to lose their tax exemptions. In short, only those institutions that discriminated as a matter of principle—like Bob Jones—lost their tax exemption. Institutions that deceived the IRS (or themselves) did not. Is this a "public value"?

At the same time Bob Jones was suing to recover its tax-exempt status, African-American parents were suing the IRS to enforce the nondiscrimination rule more effectively. Judge Ruth Bader Ginsburg of the D.C. Circuit wrote an opinion favorable to the parents, but the Supreme Court reversed. A year after the Court decided *Bob Jones*, it held (by a 5–4 majority) that these parents lacked "standing" to sue the IRS, thereby failing to satisfy the Court's "case or controversy" requirement. *Allen v. Wright*, 468 U.S. 737 (1984). The grudging approach to standing taken in *Allen* is an ironic contrast to the expansive approach to the antidiscrimination principle taken in *Bob Jones*. The contrast is all the more striking in light of significant justiciability problems in *Bob Jones* itself. While *Bob Jones* was pending on appeal to the Supreme Court, the Reagan Administration switched sides and announced that it agreed with Bob Jones and wanted to change the regulation back to its pre-1970 status. Because the two parties in *Bob Jones University v. United States* both agreed that Bob Jones should be exempt, why was the case not moot? Was there an ongoing "case or controversy" as required by the Court's reading of Article III? As it has done in other cases, the Court kept the appeal alive by appointing William Coleman, a former Secretary of Transportation, "to brief and argue this case, as *amicus curiae*, in support of the judgments below." 456 U.S. 922 (1982) (order of Court). Coleman, who represented neither party, won the case!

After 1984, the IRS was left with few incentives to enforce *Bob Jones*: Congress in the Ashbrook Amendment had signaled that it didn't want vigorous enforcement, President Reagan had formally abandoned the policy until it was forced back upon him by the Supreme Court, and private citizens who might object to the virtual abandonment of the policy were not easily able to get into court, while any segregated school that loses its exemption of course has standing to sue the IRS. Is this a scenario likely to promote "public values"?

Consider a final historical irony. Bob Jones University in the new millennium not only revoked its race-discriminatory admissions policy, but also issued a public apology for the race discrimination it practiced for most of its history. See Johnson, *Story of* Bob Jones, 157.

Public Citizen v. United States Department of Justice
491 U.S. 440 (1989).

The question was whether the Standing Committee on the Federal Judiciary of the American Bar Association (ABA) was subject to the Federal Advisory Committee Act (FACA), 5 U.S.C. § 1 et seq., which imposes disclosure and open meeting requirements on a federal "advisory committee." Section 3(2) of the statute defines "advisory committee" as, among other things, any committee "established or utilized" by the President or by one or more agencies, "in the interest of obtaining advice or recommendations" for the President or an agency. The President, through the Justice Department, routinely seeks the advice of the ABA committee concerning the qualifications of potential federal judicial nominees.

Justice Brennan's majority opinion declined to hold that the ABA committee was within the scope of FACA § 3(2). He started with the proposition that a broad reading of "established or utilized" would impose disclosure and openness requirements on presidential consultation with political consultants, informal advisers, and an indeterminate number of other groups. "FACA was enacted to cure specific ills, above all the wasteful expenditure of public funds for worthless committee meetings and biased proposals; although its reach is extensive, we cannot believe that it was intended to cover every formal and informal consultation between the President or an Executive agency and a group rendering advice. As we said in *Church of the Holy Trinity v. United States*: '[F]requently words of general meaning are used in a statute, words broad enough to include an act in question, and yet a consideration of the whole legislation, or of the circumstances surrounding its enactment, or of the absurd results which follow from giving such broad meaning to the words, makes it unreasonable to believe that the legislator intended to include the particular act.' "

Finding some degree of ambiguity, Justice Brennan examined the background of FACA, starting with President Kennedy's 1962 executive order requiring disclosure of advisory committees; no President considered the ABA committees to fall under that previous, executive department regime. During the Nixon Administration, Congress confirmed and expanded this idea. The original House bill applied to advisory committees "established" by statute or by the Executive, whether by a federal agency or by the President himself. H.R. 4383, 92d Cong., 2d Sess. § 3(2) (1972). The House Committee Report stated that "advisory committees" would include "committees which may have been organized before their advice was sought by the President or any agency, but which are used by the President or any agency in the same way as an advisory committee formed by the President himself or the agency itself," H. R. Rep. No. 92–1017, at 4. This language was aimed at bringing into the disclosure regime quasi-public organizations receiving public funds, such as the National Academy of Sciences. Neither the report nor congressional discussions mentioned anything like these ABA Committees, namely, groups not formed by the executive branch, accepting no public funds, and assisting the President in performing constitutionally specified tasks such as judicial nominations.

The parallel Senate bill defined "advisory committee" as one "established or organized" by statute, the President, or an Executive agency. S. 3529, 92d Cong., 2d

Sess. §§ 3(1), (2) (1972). The Senate Report stated that the phrase "established or organized" was to be understood in its "most liberal sense, so that when an officer brings together a group by formal or informal means, by contract or other arrangement, and whether or not Federal money is expended, to obtain advice and information, such group is covered by the provisions of this bill." S. Rep. No. 92–1098, at 8 (1972). The Report listed as examples "the Advisory Council on Federal Reports, the National Industrial Pollution Control Council, the National Petroleum Council, advisory councils to the National Institutes of Health, and committees of the national academies where they are utilized and officially recognized as advisory to the President, to an agency, or to a Government official." Justice Brennan characterized these examples as "limited to groups organized by, or closely tied to, the Federal Government, and thus enjoying quasi-public status. Given the prominence of the ABA Committee's role and its familiarity to Members of Congress, its omission from the list of groups formed and maintained by private initiative to offer advice with respect to the President's nomination of Government officials is telling. If the examples offered by the Senate Committee on Government Operations are representative, as seems fair to surmise, then there is little reason to think that there was any support, at least at the committee stage, for going beyond the terms of Executive Order No. 11007 to regulate comprehensively the workings of the ABA Committee."

Of course, the final version of FACA employed the phrase "established or utilized," somewhat broader than the word "established" or the phrase "established or organized." The words "or utilized" were added by the Conference Committee to the definition included in the House bill. See H.R. Conf. Rep. No. 92–1403, p. 2 (1972). The Joint Explanatory Statement, however, said that the definition contained in the House bill was adopted "with modification." *Id.* at 9. Justice Brennan drew this conclusion: "The Conference Report offered no indication that the modification was significant, let alone that it would substantially broaden FACA's application by sweeping within its terms a vast number of private groups, such as the Republican National Committee, not formed at the behest of the Executive or by quasi-public organizations whose opinions the Federal Government sometimes solicits. Indeed, it appears that the House bill's initial restricted focus on advisory committees established by the Federal Government, in an expanded sense of the word 'established,' was retained rather than enlarged by the Conference Committee. In the section dealing with FACA's range of application, the Conference Report stated: 'The Act does not apply to persons or organizations which have contractual relationships with Federal agencies *nor to advisory committees not directly established by or for such agencies.' Id.,* at 10 (emphasis added). The phrase 'or utilized' therefore appears to have been added simply to clarify that FACA applies to advisory committees established by the Federal Government in a generous sense of that term, encompassing groups formed indirectly by quasi-public organizations such as the National Academy of Sciences 'for' public agencies as well as 'by' such agencies themselves."

Given the statutory ambiguity revealed by the legislative history, Justice Brennan concluded that the words ought to be given their narrower construction. He added: "[C]onstruing FACA to apply to the Justice Department's consultations with the ABA Committee would present formidable constitutional difficulties," because it might "infring[e] unduly on the President's Article II power to nominate federal judges and violat[e] the doctrine of separation of powers. * * * Where the competing arguments based on FACA's text and legislative history, though both plausible, tend to show that

Congress did not desire FACA to apply to the Justice Department's confidential solicitation of the ABA Committee's views on prospective judicial nominees, sound sense counsels adherence to our rule of caution. Our unwillingness to resolve important constitutional questions unnecessarily thus solidifies our conviction that FACA is inapplicable."

Justice Kennedy, joined by Chief Justice Rehnquist and Justice O'Connor, concurred only in the judgment. (**Justice Scalia** did not participate in this case.) "Where the language of a statute is clear in its application, the normal rule is that we are bound by it. There is, of course, a legitimate exception to this rule, which the Court invokes, citing *Holy Trinity Church*, and with which I have no quarrel. Where the plain language of the statute would lead to 'patently absurd consequences' that 'Congress could not *possibly* have intended,' we need not apply the language in such a fashion. When used in a proper manner, this narrow exception to our normal rule of statutory construction does not intrude upon the lawmaking powers of Congress, but rather demonstrates a respect for the coequal Legislative Branch, which we assume would not act in an absurd way."

Justice Kennedy concluded, however, that it would not at all be "absurd" to apply the FACA to ABA committees. "Unable to show that an application of FACA according to the plain meaning of its terms would be absurd, the Court turns instead to the task of demonstrating that a straightforward reading of the statute would be inconsistent with the congressional purposes that lay behind its passage. To the student of statutory construction, this move is a familiar one. It is, as the Court identifies it, the classic *Holy Trinity* argument. '[A] thing may be within the letter of the statute and yet not within the statute, because not within its spirit, nor within the intention of its makers.' *Holy Trinity*. I cannot embrace this principle. Where it is clear that the unambiguous language of a statute embraces certain conduct, and it would not be patently absurd to apply the statute to such conduct, it does not foster a democratic exegesis for this Court to rummage through unauthoritative materials to consult the spirit of the legislation in order to discover an alternative interpretation of the statute with which the Court is more comfortable. It comes as a surprise to no one that the result of the Court's lengthy journey through the legislative history is the discovery of a congressional intent not to include the activities of the ABA Committee within the coverage of FACA. The problem with spirits is that they tend to reflect less the views of the world whence they come than the views of those who seek their advice."

Justice Kennedy sharply criticized *Holy Trinity* for substituting judicial values for rule of law values (as evidenced by the "Christian nation" passage). So the FACA applies, by its plain meaning, to the ABA Committee—but Justice Kennedy also concluded that such an application unconstitutionally infringed on the President's Article II authority to solicit advice. Hence, Justice Kennedy concurred in the result reached by the Court, but in none of its reasoning.

NOTES ON PUBLIC CITIZEN AND COHERENCE-BASED JUSTIFICATIONS FOR "JUDICIAL SURGERY"

1.   *Did the FACA Have a Plain Meaning That Included the ABA Committees?* One wonders whether Hart and Sacks could have gone along with the majority's approach in *Public Citizen*. Has Justice Brennan given the words of FACA § 3(2) a "meaning they will not bear"? Specifically, can you come up with linguistic support for a reading of

"established or utilized" by the President or an agency that covers NAS advisory committees but not the ABA's committees?

Does the legislative history suggest that a narrow reading of "utilized" is possible? Consider these facts: (1) neither the House nor the Senate bill included the broader term "utilized," (2) the term was added by the Conference Committee, and (3) the Rules of both House and Senate say that Conference Committees *cannot expand* any provision beyond the scope set forth in either the House bill or the Senate bill (i.e., the Conference can only *reconcile* the House and Senate bills, not use them as a starting point for crafting new legislation). Do these facts about Congress and its FACA deliberations suggest a defense of the majority's approach? For illumination, consider Victoria Nourse, *A Decision Theory of Statutory Interpretation: Legislative History by the Rules,* 122 Yale L.J. 70, 92–97 (2012) (arguing for a narrow understanding of "utilized" based upon the foregoing Rules of the House and Senate). Before reaching a final conclusion, reread the House and Senate committee report language, discussing or alluding to "established" (the language used in both House and Senate bills). Does this discussion suggest a broader reading of "established" that the Conference Committee might have been trying to capture when it revised the bill language to add "or utilized"?

2.   *Can Judicial Surgery Be Defended in* Public Citizen? Assume that Justice Kennedy is right, that the FACA unequivocally includes the ABA's advisory committees, and that Justice Brennan, basically, rewrites the statute. How might the Court's decision be justified? Although a state court judge has analogized this kind of "judicial surgery" to the limited discretion afforded a musician interpreting a piece of music, Stewart Pollock, *The Art of Judging,* 71 N.Y.U. L. Rev. 591, 601–02 (1996), the strong arm given the statutory language makes the case look more like an exercise in "spurious interpretation," to use Roscoe Pound's terminology. Does the Supreme Court even have the constitutional authority (under Article III) to rewrite the statute? As Justice Kennedy observes, the Court clearly has the authority to declare the statute's plain meaning and then invalidate it as inconsistent with the Constitution.

One way to defend Justice Brennan's approach is that congressional purpose, if clear, can justify a narrowing construction of broad statutory text—precisely the holding of *Holy Trinity* and, perhaps, consistent with legal process theory. A problem with such a defense is that the FACA's purpose might be broader than the purpose identified by Justice Brennan. According to the Conference Report, the FACA was aimed at curbing the proliferation of executive branch advisory committees and rendering those committees more transparent to the public. H.R. Conf. Rep. No. 92–1403, at 1–2 (1972). A broader understanding of the statutory purpose, drawn from the same source the majority invoked, might confirm that the statute's apparent plain meaning is exactly what Congress "intended." Note, also, that Justice Kennedy rejects the *Holy Trinity* notion that a narrower congressional purpose can justify judicial constriction of plain statutory text. Would Hart and Sacks disagree? How about Judge Foster in the Case of the Speluncean Explorers?

3.   *Coherence-Based Justifications for Judicial Surgery.* Another way to defend Justice Brennan's approach might be institutionally normative: a central role of judges is to make the law relatively coherent and to assure continuity in legal rules. This is the basis for Hart and Sacks' maxim that the legislature ought to be presumed not "depart[ ] from a generally prevailing principle or policy of the law unless it does so clearly." Hart & Sacks, *The Legal Process,* 1377 (excerpted at the beginning of this

section). Amy Coney Barrett has defended this perspective, based on the original meaning of Article III, reflecting the founding era practice where courts read even relatively clear texts in light of substantive values reflected in longstanding canons of statutory construction. See Barrett, *Substantive Canons and Faithful Agency,* 90 B.U.L. Rev. 109, 11–12 (2012); Chapter 7, § 2 (examining some of the leading substantive canons, such as the rule of lenity).

Another institutional way of understanding this issue is that courts should be deliberation-forcing when legislatures are venturing into territory where fundamental values are at stake. See William Eskridge Jr. & Philip Frickey, *Quasi-Constitutional Law: Clear Statement Rules as Constitutional Lawmaking,* 45 Vand. L. Rev. 493, 529–32 (1992); Amanda Tyler, *Continuity, Coherence, and the Canons,* 99 Nw. U. L. Rev. 1389 (2005).[30] Congress is the body that ought to make major policy decisions, but courts ought to be leary of imputing to Congress any intention to alter fundamental rules of the polity, without a careful examination of the legislative deliberations as well as the statutory text (precisely the methodology followed by Justice Brennan in *Public Citizen*).

A final way to view these cases is to understand the role of judges as openly critical and normative. This does not sound like a legal process mode of thinking, but leading jurisprudes have developed precisely that idea. As you read the following note, consider the separation of powers and majoritarian difficulties with each theory.

NOTE ON LAW AS INTEGRITY AND STATUTORY INTERPRETATION AS A CHAIN NOVEL

In his book, *Law in Quest of Itself* (1940), Lon Fuller contested the positivist claim that fact is wholly independent of value—and interpretation independent of norms:

> If I attempt to retell a funny story which I have heard, the story as I tell it will be the product of two forces: (1) the story as I heard it [and] (2) my conception of the point of the story, in other words, my notion of the story *as it ought to be.* * * * If the story as I heard it was, in my opinion, badly told, I am guided largely by my conception of the story as it ought to be * * *. On the other hand, if I had the story from a master raconteur, I may exert myself to reproduce his exact words. * * * These two forces, then, supplement one another in shaping the story as I tell it. It is the product of the *is* and the *ought* working together. * * * The two are inextricably interwoven, to the point where we can say that "the story" as an entity really embraces both of them. Indeed, if we look at the story across time, its reality becomes even more complex. The "point" of the story, which furnishes its essential unity, may in the course of retelling be changed. As it is brought out more clearly through the skill of successive tellers it becomes a new point; at some indefinable juncture the story has been so improved that it has become a new story. In a sense, then, the thing we call "the story" is not something that is, but something that becomes; it is not a hard chunk of reality, but a fluid process, which is as much directed by men's creative impulses, by their conception of the story as it ought to be, as it is by

---

[30]   See also Einer Elhauge, *Preference-Eliciting Statutory Default Rules,* 102 Colum. L. Rev. 2162 (2002); Christopher Elmendorf, *Refining the Democracy Canon,* 95 Cornell L. Rev. 1051 (2010). For a critical view of this kind of roving normative authority, see John Manning, *Clear Statement Rules and the Constitution,* 110 Colum. L. Rev. 399 (2010).

the original even which unlocked those impulses. The *ought* here is just as real, as a part of human experience, as the *is*, and the line between the two melts away in the common stream of telling and retelling into which they both flow.

"Exactly the same thing may be said of a statute or a decision," Fuller continued. "The statute or decision is not a segment of being, but, like the anecdote, a process of becoming." *Id.* at 9–10.

Fuller maintained that the interconnection between law and morality is a good thing. The main argument was one of coherence. Because the "bulk of human relations find their regulation outside the field of positive law," a continuous interpenetration of law and social morality creates a more seamless web of interconnected rights and duties. *Id.* at 11–12. Fuller emphasized that such interconnection was necessary to the efficacy of law; without a link with changing social mores, law would not be able to achieve its goals or, worse, would lose the respect of the citizenry. See Lon Fuller, *Human Interaction and the Law*, in *The Principles of Social Order: The Selected Essays of Lon L. Fuller* 211–46 (Kenneth Winston ed. 1981).

Following upon Fuller's idea, Ronald Dworkin posited that law is an interpretive enterprise that seeks to "show it as the best work of art it can be." *Law as Interpretation*, 60 Tex. L. Rev. 527 (1982). Dworkin explained his vision of interpretation by reference to the idea of a "chain novel," *id.* at 541–43:

> Suppose that a group of novelists is engaged for a particular project and that they draw lots to determine the order of play. The lowest number writes the opening chapter of a novel, which he or she then sends to the next number, with the understanding that he is adding a chapter to that novel rather than beginning a new one, and then sends the two chapters to the next number, and so on. Now every novelist but the first has the dual responsibilities of interpreting and creating because each must read all that has gone before in order to establish, in the interpretivist sense, what the novel so far created is. He or she must decide what the characters are "really" like; what motives in fact guide them; what the point or theme of the developing novel is; how far some literary device or figure, consciously, or unconsciously used, contributes to these, and whether it should be extended or refined or trimmed or dropped in order to send the novel further in one direction rather than another. This must be interpretation in a non-intention-bound style because, at least for all novelists after the second, there is no single author whose intentions any interpreter can, by the rules of the project, regard as decisive. * * *

> Deciding hard cases at law is rather like this strange literary exercise. The similarity is most evident when judges consider and decide common-law cases; that is, when no statute figures centrally in the legal issue, and the argument turns on which rules or principles of law "underlie" the related decisions of other judges in the past. Each judge is then like a novelist in the chain. He or she must read through what other judges in the past have written not simply to discover what these judges have said, or their state of mind when they said it, but to reach an opinion about what these judges have collectively *done*, in the way that each of our novelists formed an opinion about the collective novel so far written.

In *Law's Empire* 313 (1986), Dworkin described how the chain novel tells judges to interpret statutes:

> He will treat Congress as an author earlier than himself in the chain of law, though an author with special powers and responsibilities different from his own [as a judge], and he will see his own role as fundamentally the creative one of a partner continuing to develop, in what he believes is the best way, the statutory scheme Congress began. He will ask himself which reading of the act * * * shows the political history including and surrounding that statute in the better light. His view of how the statute should be read will in part depend on what certain congressmen said when debating it. But it will also depend on the best answer to political questions: how far Congress should defer to public opinion in matters of this sort, for example * * *.

On the application of his theory to *Weber*, see Dworkin, *How to Read the Civil Rights Act*, in Dworkin, *A Matter of Principle* (1985). How would Dworkin's theory apply to *Public Citizen*?[31]

C. CRITIQUES OF LEGAL PROCESS PRECEPTS, 1970s–80s

Legal process theory came into focus around the time of World War II. This was a period of relative consensus in America, sustained economic growth, and burgeoning optimism about government's ability to foster economic growth by solving market failures and creating opportunities. After the mid-1960s, America was a different society, as consensus collapsed on fundamental issues of war, family, and citizenship; economic growth faltered and oil price shocks introduced stagflation; and government came to be perceived as problematic, often even as a drain on society's productivity. These developments raised inevitable questions about statutory methodology, such as the ones that follow.

1.   *A More Realistic (or Cynical) View of the Legislative Process?* Public choice and other theories of legislation establish that legislators are not entirely "reasonable," as Hart and Sacks assume, and are often acting to extract "rents" for their constituents and supportive interest groups. Moreover, even reasonable legislators will disagree, and the resulting statutes may be compromises more than easily understood purposive enactments. Some scholars argue from such theories that Hart and Sacks' purposive approach should therefore be reined back toward something like Pound's imaginative reconstruction. See Richard Posner, *The Federal Courts: Crisis and Reform* 286–93 (1985).

On the other hand, Hart and Sacks never claimed their "reasonable legislator" approach actually describes the legislature; they only said that courts should "attribute" purposes to the legislature, suggesting that theirs is a normative-based rather than a descriptive-based theory of interpretation. Why should ambiguous interest-group deals be enforced by courts if they do not serve a larger public purpose? See Jonathan Macey, *Promoting Public-Regarding Legislation Through Statutory Interpretation: An Interest Group Model*, 86 Colum. L. Rev. 223 (1986),

---

[31]   For jurisprudential connections between Dworkin's theory of law as integrity and legal process theory, see Vincent Wellman, *Dworkin and the Legal Process Tradition: The Legacy of Hart and Sacks,* 29 Ariz. L. Rev. 413 (1987), as well as William Eskridge Jr., *Nino's Nightmare: Legal Process Theory as a Jurisprudence of Toggling Between Facts and Norms,* 57 St. Louis U.L.J. 865 (2013).

who argues that the public interest requires that rent-seeking legislators should be held to their stated (public-regarding) justifications.

2. *Does the Hart and Sacks Approach Submerge Substantive Issues?* Both pragmatic and critical scholars criticize legal process theory for suppressing useful substantive discussion. Judge Posner, for example, openly inquires about the practical consequences of different interpretations. See, e.g., Richard Posner, *How Judges Think* ch. 5 (2008), and *The Problems of Jurisprudence* (1990). His practice is to figure out what is the most reasonable statutory interpretation, as applied to the facts before him, and then see if statutory text, history, and precedent foreclose the best option. This sounds a lot like Hart and Sacks, but Posner would say that he adds empirical data and systematic economic thinking that Hart and Sacks did not emphasize. Why not introduce rigorous, empirically based economic analysis into decisionmaking?

Critical scholars argue that legal process judges are making unarticulated value choices under the auspices of neutral craft. Allan Hutchinson and Derek Morgan, in *The Semiology of Statutes*, 21 Harv. J. Legis. 583, 593–94 (1984), state:

> Words do not interpret themselves. A sentence will never mean exactly the same thing to any two different people or even the same thing to one person on different occasions. Meaning is shaped by the apperceptive mass of understanding and background that an individual brings to bear on the external fact of a sound or series of marks. As words lack "self-evident reference," purpose and context are ultimately major determinants of meaning. However, as the expression of legislative intent is always more or less incomplete, it is doubtful whether any impartial method of adjudication can be fashioned in a liberal society. * * *

> The necessity of engaging in such invention requires the courts to make substantive political decisions, the very decisions that semantic, historical or counter-factual approaches *claim* to avoid. No one single "construction" is inevitable or natural. Construction means choice. And choice confers power. Of course, this is not to suggest that judicial creativity breeds constitutional anarchy. Communities of interpretation have their own bonding mechanisms, a mixture of moral values and social customs. Interpretation is inextricably bound up with values and it is nowhere seriously suggested the values do not carry ideological underpinnings. The lesson to be gathered from this realization is quite simple. Courts that shield themselves behind descriptions of law as clear, predetermined and objective norms against which they pitch their neutral decisions are worthy of suspicion. * * *

On this understanding, a virtue of Justice Brewer's opinion in *Holy Trinity Church* is that it was candid about the values it was implementing (the Christian nation idea). Hart and Sacks' approach would likely generate the same result in the hands of an evangelical jurist such as Justice Brewer, but perhaps a less candid discussion. Recall, too, Judge Handy's opinion in the Case of the Speluncean Explorers.

3. *The Appeal of Formalism.* Among judges, the most telling criticism of the legal process approach to statutory interpretation is that it neglects the virtues of a more formalist approach. Even contextualists might concede the attractions of the plain meaning rule, defended by Judge Keen in Speluncean Explorers. First, it is arguably more consistent with the structure of the U.S. Constitution (and most state constitutions), which vests political power with the legislative and executive branches and only the judicial power with the courts, and which creates formal barriers to lawmaking that are disregarded when courts make new law. See John Manning, *Textualism as a Nondelegation Doctrine*, 97 Colum. L. Rev. 673 (1997). Second, it can be argued that applying statutory plain meanings is more within the "judicial competence" than making policy or even scanning through legislative history to figure out whether the legislature "really meant" the apparent meaning of its statutory words. See Adrian Vermeule, *Legislative History and the Limits of Judicial Competence: The Untold Story of* Holy Trinity Church, 50 Stan. L. Rev. 1833 (1998).

Third, the ordinary meaning of statutory language is the common understanding of what the "rule of law" is. See Antonin Scalia, *The Rule of Law as a Law of Rules*, 56 U. Chi. L. Rev. 1175 (1989). Citizens ought to be able to open up the statute books and find out what the law requires of them. Once law is understood by the cognoscenti as purposes, spirits, and collective intents, the citizenry might lose faith in the externality of law—the objectivity of legal reasoning which provides us with some assurance that our problems are susceptible of the same rules as those of our neighbor (even if she is a rich and influential neighbor). The changes in American society since the 1960s make an external vision of the rule of law even more important than before. In a society where so many values are open to contest, language may be the main thing we share in common. In a society where "the pie" is not expanding and the economy is stagnant, dividing the pie by an objective criterion becomes ever more critical.

A less complicated approach may also be more democracy-enhancing, because it places responsibility for updating statutes on the shoulders of the people and their legislators, rather than their unelected (federal and some state) or not-often-elected (most state) judges. Recall Judge Keen's argument that hard cases generating inequitable results should trigger a popular outrage that changes statutes more usefully and more democratically than judicial updating through a Hart and Sacks purpose approach. As potential examples of this phenomenon, consider the following cases.

STATUTORY PREFACE TO *TVA V. HILL* (THE SNAIL DARTER CASE)

The Endangered Species Act of 1973, Public Law 93–205 (codified at 16 U.S.C. § 1531 et seq.)

Section 2, 16 U.S.C. § 1531. Findings, Purposes, and Policy * * *

(b) Purposes.—The purposes of this Act are to provide a means whereby the ecosystems upon which endangered species and threatened species depend may be conserved, to provide a program for the conservation of such endangered species and threatened species, and to take such steps as may be appropriate to achieve the purposes of [various species-protecting] treaties and conventions * * *.

(c) Policy.—It is further declared to be the policy of Congress that all federal departments and agencies shall seek to conserve endangered species and threatened species and shall utilize their authorities in furtherance of the purposes of this Act.

Section 4, 16 U.S.C. § 1533. Determination of Endangered Species and Threatened Species [This section delegates to the Secretary of the Interior the authority, after consultation, to designate species as either endangered or threatened. Private persons and other governmental agencies are bound by the Secretary's determination.]

Section 7, 16 U.S.C. § 1536. Interagency Cooperation

The Secretary [of the Interior] shall review other programs administered by him and utilize such programs in furtherance of the purposes of this Act. All other Federal departments and agencies shall, in consultation with and with the assistance of the Secretary, utilize their authorities in furtherance of the purposes of this Act by carrying out programs for the conservation of endangered species and threatened species listed pursuant to section 4 of this Act and by taking such action necessary to insure that actions authorized, funded, or carried out by them do not jeopardize the continued existence of such endangered species and threatened species or result in the destruction or modification of habitat of such species which is determined by the Secretary, after consultation as appropriate with the affected States, to be critical.

TENNESSEE VALLEY AUTHORITY V. HILL

United States Supreme Court, 1978.
437 U.S. 153, 98 S.Ct. 2279, 57 L.Ed.2d 117.

CHIEF JUSTICE BURGER delivered the opinion of the Court.

[Pursuant to the statute, the Secretary of the Interior declared the snail darter (*Percina tanasi*) an endangered species and designated a portion of the Little Tennessee River as the only remaining natural habitat of the snail darter. That part of the river, however, would be flooded by operation of the Tellico Dam, a $100 million Tennessee Valley Authority (TVA) project that was under way in 1973 and was almost completed by 1976, when environmentalists sought an injunction against the dam's operation, on the basis of § 7 of the new Act. The district court denied relief. It found that the dam would destroy the snail darter's critical habitat, but it noted that Congress, though fully aware of the snail darter problem, had continued to fund the Tellico Dam after 1973. The court concluded that the Act did not justify an injunction against a project initiated before enactment. The court of appeals reversed and ordered the lower court to enjoin completion of the dam.]

One would be hard pressed to find a statutory provision whose terms were any plainer than those in § 7 of the Endangered Species Act. Its very words affirmatively command all federal agencies "to *insure* that actions *authorized, funded, or carried out* by them do not *jeopardize* the continued existence" of an endangered species or "*result* in the destruction or modification of habitat of such species. . . ." 16 U.S.C. § 1536 (1976 ed.). (Emphasis added.) This language admits of no exception. Nonetheless, petitioner urges, as do the dissenters, that the Act cannot reasonably be interpreted as applying to a federal project which was well under way when Congress passed the Endangered Species Act of 1973. To sustain that position, however, we would be forced to ignore the ordinary meaning of plain language. It has not been shown, for example, how TVA can close the gates of the Tellico Dam without "carrying out" an action that has been "authorized" and "funded" by a federal agency. Nor can we understand how such action will "*insure*" that the snail darter's habitat is not disrupted. * * *

Concededly, this view of the Act will produce results requiring the sacrifice of the anticipated benefits of the project and of many millions of dollars in public funds. But examination of the language, history, and structure of the legislation under review here indicates beyond doubt that Congress intended endangered species to be afforded the highest of priorities.

[Chief Justice Burger examined statutes enacted in 1966 and 1969, which sought to discourage the taking of endangered species. Congressional hearings in 1973 revealed that strategies of encouragement had not abated the "pace of disappearance of species," which appeared to be "accelerating." H.R. Rep. No. 93–412, p. 4 (1973). The dominant theme of the hearings and debates on the 1973 Act was "the overriding need to devote whatever effort and resources were necessary to avoid further diminution of national and worldwide wildlife resources." Congressional committees expressed the "incalculable" value of lost species.]

The legislative proceedings in 1973 are, in fact, replete with expressions of concern over the risk that might lie in the loss of *any* endangered species. Typifying these sentiments is the Report of the House Committee on Merchant Marine and Fisheries on H.R. 37, a bill which contained the essential features of the subsequently enacted Act of 1973; in explaining the need for the legislation, the Report stated:

"As we homogenize the habitats in which these plants and animals evolved, and as we increase the pressure for products that they are in a position to supply (usually unwillingly) we threaten their- and our own- genetic heritage.

"The value of this genetic heritage is, quite literally, incalculable. * * *

"From the most narrow possible point of view, *it is in the best interests of mankind to minimize the losses of genetic variations*. The reason is simple: they are potential resources. They are keys to puzzles which we cannot solve, and may provide answers to questions which we have not yet learned to ask.

"To take a homely, but apt, example: one of the critical chemicals in the regulation of ovulations in humans was found in a common plant. Once discovered, and analyzed, humans could duplicate it synthetically, but had it never existed—or had it been driven out of existence before we knew its potentialities—we would never have tried to synthesize it in the first place.

"Who knows, or can say, what potential cures for <u>cancer</u> or other scourges, present or future, may lie locked up in the structures of plants which may yet be undiscovered, much less analyzed? . . . Sheer self-interest impels us to be cautious.

"*The institutionalization of that caution* lies at the heart of H.R. 37. . . ."

H.R.Rep.No.93–412, pp. 4–5 (1973) (emphasis added). As the examples cited here demonstrate, Congress was concerned about the *unknown* uses that endangered species might have and about the *unforeseeable* place such creatures may have in the chain of life on this planet. * * *

Section 7 of the Act * * * provides a particularly good gauge of congressional intent. As we have seen, this provision had its genesis in the Endangered Species Act of 1966, but that legislation qualified the obligation of federal agencies by stating that they should seek to preserve endangered species only "*insofar as is practicable and consistent with their primary purposes*. . . ." Likewise, every bill introduced in 1973 contained a qualification similar to that found in the earlier statutes. * * * This type of language did not go unnoticed by those advocating strong endangered species legislation. A representative of the Sierra Club, for example, attacked the use of the phrase "consistent with the primary purpose" in proposed H.R. 4758, cautioning that the qualification "could be construed to be a declaration of congressional policy that other agency purposes are necessarily more important than protection of endangered species and would always prevail if conflict were to occur."

What is very significant in this sequence is that the final version of the 1973 Act carefully omitted all of the reservations described above. [The Senate bill contained a practicability reservation; the House bill had no qualifications. The Conference Committee rejected the Senate version of § 7 and adopted the House language. Explaining the Conference action, Representative Dingell pointed out that under existing law the Secretary of Defense has discretion to ignore dangers its bombing missions posed to the near-extinct whooping crane. "[O]nce the bill is enacted, [the Secretary of Defense] *would be required to take the proper steps.*" Another example was the declining population of grizzly bears, whose habitats would have to be protected by the Department of Agriculture. "The purposes of the bill included the conservation of the species and of the ecosystems upon which they depend, and every agency of government is committed to see that those purposes are carried out. The agencies of Government can no longer plead that they can do nothing about it. *They can and they must. The law is clear.*" 119 Cong. Rec. 42913 (emphasis added by the Chief Justice).]

It is against this legislative background that we must measure TVA's claim that the Act was not intended to stop operation of a project which, like Tellico Dam, was near completion when an endangered species was discovered in its path. While there is no discussion of precisely this problem, the totality of congressional action makes it abundantly clear that the result we reach today is wholly in accord with both the words of the statute and the intent of Congress. The plain intent of Congress in enacting this statute was to halt and reverse the trend toward species extinction, whatever the cost. This is reflected not only in the stated provisions of the Act, but in literally every section of the statute. All persons, including federal agencies, are specifically instructed not to "take" endangered species, meaning that no one is "to harass, harm, pursue, hunt, shoot, wound, kill, trap, capture, or collect" such life forms. 16 U.S.C. §§ 1532(14), 1538(a)(1)(B) (1976 ed.). * * *

[TVA also argued that Congress's continued funding of the Dam reflected a congressional judgment, embodied in appropriations statutes, that the Dam not be shut down. Appropriations committees were aware of the effect of the Dam on the snail darter.] There is nothing in the appropriations measures, as passed, which states that the Tellico Project was to be completed irrespective of the requirements of the Endangered Species Act. * * * To find a repeal of the Endangered Species Act under these circumstances would surely do violence to the " 'cardinal rule . . . that repeals by implication are not favored.' " *Morton v. Mancari*, 417 U.S. 535, 549 (1974), quoting *Posadas v. National City Bank*, 296 U.S. 497, 503 (1936). * * *

The doctrine disfavoring repeals by implication "applies with full vigor when . . . the subsequent legislation is an *appropriations* measure." *Committee for Nuclear Responsibility v. Seaborg*, 463 F.2d 783, 785 (D.C. Cir. 1971). This is perhaps an understatement since it would be more accurate to say that the policy applies with even *greater* force when the claimed repeal rests solely with an Appropriations Act. * * * When voting on appropriations measures, legislators are entitled to operate under the assumption that the funds will be devoted to purposes which are lawful and not for any purpose forbidden. [The Chief Justice also pointed to House Rule XXI(2), which forbids amendments to appropriations bills which seeks to "chang[e] existing law." See also Senate Rule 16.4.] Thus, to sustain petitioner's position, we would be obliged to assume that Congress meant to repeal *pro tanto* § 7 of the Act by means of a procedure expressly prohibited under the rules of Congress.

[Chief Justice Burger rejected TVA's urging the Court to balance the harms of shutting down the dam against the dangers to the snail darter. Not only did the Court not consider itself competent to calibrate such a balance, but Congress had already made the judgment that no cost was too high to allow the federal government to imperil a species.] [I]n our constitutional system the commitment to the separation of powers is too fundamental for us to pre-empt congressional action by judicially decreeing what accords with "common sense and the public weal." Our Constitution vests such responsibilities in the political branches.

[JUSTICE POWELL's dissenting opinion, joined by Justice Blackmun, argued that the Court's opinion "disregards 12 years of consistently expressed congressional intent to complete the Tellico Project" and is "an extreme example of a literalist construction, not required by the language of the Act and adopted without regard to its manifest purpose." Citing *Holy Trinity Church*, Justice Powell contended that the Court ought not read the broad language of § 7 so sweepingly and, instead, ought to narrow the language so as to avoid "absurd results." He would have construed the "actions" governed by § 7 to be only those taken *after* 1973, when the statute was enacted.]

[JUSTICE REHNQUIST dissented on the ground that the legitimate debate over the statute's meaning properly informed the district court's decision not to enjoin work on the dam.]

GRIFFIN V. OCEANIC CONTRACTORS, INC.

Supreme Court of the United States, 1982.
458 U.S. 564, 102 S.Ct. 3245, 73 L.Ed.2d 973.

JUSTICE REHNQUIST delivered the opinion of the Court.

[In February 1976, Danny Griffin contracted to work as a senior pipeline welder on board vessels operated by respondent in the North Sea. The contract specified that petitioner's employment would extend "until December 15, 1976 or until Oceanic's 1976 pipeline committal in the North Sea is fulfilled, whichever shall occur first." The contract also provided that if Griffin quit the job prior to its termination date, or if his services were terminated for cause, he would be charged with the cost of transportation back to the United States. Oceanic reserved the right to withhold $137.50 from each of petitioner's first four paychecks "as a cash deposit for the payment of your return transportation in the event you should become obligated for its payment." On April 1, 1976, Griffin suffered an injury while working on the deck of the vessel readying it for sea. Oceanic refused to take responsibility for the injury or to furnish transportation back to the United States, and continued to retain $412.50 in earned wages that had been deducted from Griffin's first three paychecks for that purpose. He returned to the United States and on May 5, began working as a welder for another company operating in the North Sea.

[In 1978 Griffin brought suit against respondent under the Jones Act, § 20, 38 Stat. 1185, as amended, 46 U.S.C. § 688, and under general maritime law, seeking damages for respondent's failure to pay maintenance, cure, unearned wages, repatriation expenses, and the value of certain personal effects lost on board respondent's vessel. He also sought penalty wages under Rev. Stat. § 4529, as amended, 46 U.S.C. § 596, for respondent's failure to pay over the $412.50 in earned wages allegedly due upon discharge. The District Court found for Griffin and awarded damages totaling $23,670.40.]

In assessing penalty wages under 46 U.S.C. § 596, the court held that "[t]he period during which the penalty runs is to be determined by the sound discretion of the district court and depends on the equities of the case." It determined that the appropriate period for imposition of the penalty was from the date of discharge, April 1, 1976, through the date of petitioner's reemployment, May 5, 1976, a period of 34 days. Applying the statute, it computed a penalty of $6,881.60. Petitioner appealed the award of damages as inadequate. [The Fifth Circuit affirmed the district court judgment. The Supreme Court reversed and ruled that Oceanic owed Griffin more than $302,000 in penalty wages.]

[II.A]   The language of the statute first obligates the master or owner of any vessel making coasting or foreign voyages to pay every seaman the balance of his unpaid wages within specified periods after his discharge[6]. It then provides:

> "Every master or owner who refuses or neglects to make payments in the manner hereinbefore mentioned without sufficient cause shall pay to the seaman a sum equal to two days' pay for each and every day during which payment is delayed beyond the respective periods * * *."

The statute in straightforward terms provides for the payment of double wages, depending upon the satisfaction of two conditions. First, the master or owner must have refused or failed to pay the seaman his wages within the periods specified. Second, this failure or refusal must be "without sufficient cause." Once these conditions are satisfied, however, the unadorned language of the statute dictates that the master or owner "*shall pay* to the seaman" the sums specified "*for each and every day* during which payment is delayed." The words chosen by Congress, given their plain meaning, leave no room for the exercise of discretion either in deciding whether to exact payment or in choosing the period of days by which the payment is to be calculated. As this Court described the statute many years ago, it "affords a definite and reasonable procedure by which the seaman may establish his right to recover double pay where his wages are unreasonably withheld." Our task is to give effect to the will of Congress, and where its will has been expressed in reasonably plain terms, "that language must ordinarily be regarded as conclusive." *Consumer Product Safety Comm'n v. GTE Sylvania, Inc.*, 447 U.S. 102, 108 (1980).

The District Court found that respondent had refused to pay petitioner the balance of his earned wages promptly after discharge, and that its refusal was "without sufficient cause." Respondent challenges neither of these findings. Although the two statutory conditions were satisfied, however, the District Court obviously did not assess double wages "for each and every day" during which payment was delayed, but instead limited the assessment to the period of petitioner's unemployment. Nothing in the language of the statute vests the courts with the discretion to set such a limitation.

[B] Nevertheless, respondent urges that the legislative purpose of the statute is best served by construing it to permit some choice in determining the length of the penalty period. In respondent's view, the purpose of the statute is essentially

---

[6]   The statute reads in full:

"The master or owner of any vessel making coasting voyages shall pay to every seaman his wages within two days after the termination of the agreement under which he was shipped, or at the time such seaman is discharged, whichever first happens; and in case of vessels making foreign voyages, or from a port on the Atlantic to a port on the Pacific, or vice versa, within twenty-four hours after the cargo has been discharged, or within four days after the seaman has been discharged, whichever first happens; and in all cases the seaman shall be entitled to be paid at the time of his discharge on account of wages a sum equal to one-third part of the balance due him. Every master or owner who refuses or neglects to make payment in the manner hereinbefore mentioned without sufficient cause shall pay to the seaman a sum equal to two days' pay for each and every day during which payment is delayed beyond the respective periods, which sum shall be recoverable as wages in any claim made before the court; but this section shall not apply to masters or owners of any vessel the seamen of which are entitled to share in the profits of the cruise or voyage. This section shall not apply to fishing or whaling vessels or yachts."

remedial and compensatory, and thus it should not be interpreted literally to produce a monetary award that is so far in excess of any equitable remedy as to be punitive.

Respondent, however, is unable to support this view of legislative purpose by reference to the terms of the statute. "There is, of course, no more persuasive evidence of the purpose of a statute than the words by which the legislature undertook to give expression to its wishes." *United States v. American Trucking Assns., Inc.,* 310 U.S. 534, 543 (1940). Nevertheless, in rare cases the literal application of a statute will produce a result demonstrably at odds with the intentions of its drafters, and those intentions must be controlling. We have reserved "some 'scope for adopting a restricted rather than a literal or usual meaning of its words where acceptance of that meaning * * * would thwart the obvious purpose of the statute.'" *Commissioner v. Brown,* 380 U.S. 563, 571 (1965) (quoting *Helvering v. Hammel,* 311 U.S. 504, 510–511 (1941)). This, however, is not the exceptional case.

As the Court recognized in *Collie v. Fergusson,* 281 U.S. 52 (1930), the "evident purpose" of the statute is "to secure prompt payment of seamen's wages * * * and thus to protect them from the harsh consequences of arbitrary and unscrupulous action of their employers, to which, as a class, they are peculiarly exposed." This was to be accomplished "by the imposition of a liability which is not exclusively compensatory, but designed to prevent, by its coercive effect, arbitrary refusals to pay wages, and to induce prompt payment when payment is possible." Thus, although the sure purpose of the statute is remedial, Congress has chosen to secure that purpose through the use of potentially punitive sanctions designed to deter negligent or arbitrary delays in payment.

The legislative history of the statute leaves little if any doubt that this understanding is correct. The law owes its origins to the Act of July 20, 1790, ch. 29, § 6, 1 Stat. 133, passed by the First Congress. Although the statute as originally enacted gave every seaman the right to collect the wages due under his contract "as soon as the voyage is ended," it did not provide for the recovery of additional sums to encourage compliance. Such a provision was added by the Shipping Commissioners Act of 1872, ch. 322, § 35, 17 Stat. 269, which provided for the payment of "a sum not exceeding the amount of two days' pay for each of the days, not exceeding ten days, during which payment is delayed." The Act of 1872 obviously established a ceiling of 10 days on the period during which the penalty could be assessed and, by use of the words "not exceeding," left the courts with discretion to choose an appropriate penalty within that period.

Congress amended the law again in 1898. As amended, it read in relevant part:

"Every master or owner who refuses or neglects to make payment in manner hereinbefore mentioned without sufficient cause shall pay to the seaman a sum equal to one day's pay for each and every day during which payment is delayed beyond the respective periods." Act of Dec. 21, 1898, ch. 28, § 4, 30 Stat. 756.

The amending legislation thus effected two changes: first, it removed the discretion theretofore existing by which courts might award less than an amount calculated on the basis of each day during which payment was delayed, and, second, it removed the 10–day ceiling which theretofore limited the number of days upon which an award might be calculated. The accompanying Committee Reports identify the purpose of the legislation as "the amelioration of the condition of the American seamen," and characterize the amended wage penalty in particular as "designed to secure the promptest possible payment of wages." H.R.Rep. No. 1657, 55th Cong., 2d Sess., 2, 3 (1898). See also S.Rep. No. 832, 54th Cong., 1st Sess., 2 (1896). Nothing in the legislative history of the 1898 Act suggests that Congress intended to do anything other than what the Act's enacted language plainly demonstrates: to strengthen the deterrent effect of the statute by removing the courts' latitude in assessing the wage penalty.

The statute was amended for the last time in 1915 to increase further the severity of the penalty by doubling the wages due for each day during which payment of earned wages was delayed. Seamen's Act of 1915, ch. 153, § 3, 38 Stat. 1164. There is no suggestion in the Committee Reports or in the floor debates that, in so doing, Congress intended to reinvest the courts with the discretion it had removed in the Act of 1898. Resort to the legislative history, therefore, merely confirms that Congress intended the statute to mean exactly what its plain language says.

[III] Respondent argues, however, that a literal construction of the statute in this case would produce an absurd and unjust result which Congress could not have intended. The District Court found that the daily wage to be used in computing the penalty was $101.20. If the statute is applied literally, petitioner would receive twice this amount for each day after his discharge until September 17, 1980, when respondent satisfied the District Court's judgment.[9] Petitioner would receive over $300,000 simply because respondent improperly withheld $412.50 in wages. In respondent's view, Congress could not have intended seamen to receive windfalls of this nature without regard to the equities of the case.

It is true that interpretations of a statute which would produce absurd results are to be avoided if alternative interpretations consistent with the legislative purpose are available. See *United States v. American Trucking Assns., Inc.*, 310 U.S., at 542–543; *Haggar Co. v. Helvering*, 308 U.S. 389, 394 (1940). In refusing to nullify statutes, however hard or unexpected the particular effect, this Court has said:

> "Laws enacted with good intention, when put to the test, frequently, and to the surprise of the law maker himself, turn out to be mischievous, absurd or otherwise objectionable. But in such case the remedy lies with the law making authority, and not with the courts." *Crooks v. Harrelson*, 282 U.S. 55, 60 (1930).

---

[9]   Respondent assumes that the penalty would run until September 17, 1980, since that was the date on which it finally paid petitioner the $412.50. Brief for Respondent 17. Petitioner, on the other hand, apparently assumes that the penalty period expired on May 6, 1980, the date of the District Court's judgment. Brief for Petitioner 19. Under our construction of the statute, the District Court's entry of judgment will not toll the running of the penalty period unless delays beyond that date are explained by sufficient cause. * * *

It is highly probable that respondent is correct in its contention that a recovery in excess of $300,000 in this case greatly exceeds any actual injury suffered by petitioner as a result of respondent's delay in paying his wages. But this Court has previously recognized that awards made under this statute were not intended to be merely compensatory:

"We think the use of this language indicates a purpose to protect seamen from delayed payments of wages by the imposition of a liability which is not exclusively compensatory, but designed to prevent, by its coercive effect, arbitrary refusals to pay wages, and to induce prompt payment when payment is possible." *Collie v. Fergusson*, 281 U.S., at 55–56.

It is in the nature of punitive remedies to authorize awards that may be out of proportion to actual injury; such remedies typically are established to deter particular conduct, and the legislature not infrequently finds that harsh consequences must be visited upon those whose conduct it would deter. It is probably true that Congress did not precisely envision the grossness of the difference in this case between the actual wages withheld and the amount of the award required by the statute. But it might equally well be said that Congress did not precisely envision the trebled amount of some damages awards in private antitrust actions, see *Reiter v. Sonotone Corp.*, 442 U.S. 330, 344–345 (1979), or that, because it enacted the Endangered Species Act, "the survival of a relatively small number of three-inch fish * * * would require the permanent halting of a virtually completed dam for which Congress ha[d] expended more than $1 million," *TVA v. Hill*, 437 U.S. 153, 172 (1978). It is enough that Congress intended that the language it enacted would be applied as we have applied it. The remedy for any dissatisfaction with the results in particular cases lies with Congress and not with this Court. Congress may amend the statute; we may not. * * *

JUSTICE STEVENS, with whom JUSTICE BLACKMUN joins, dissenting.

In final analysis, any question of statutory construction requires the judge to decide how the legislature intended its enactment to apply to the case at hand. The language of the statute is usually sufficient to answer that question, but "the reports are full of cases" in which the will of the legislature is not reflected in a literal reading of the words it has chosen.[1] In my opinion this is such a case. * * *

[II.A] In fixing the amount of the award of double wages, the District Court in this case may have reasoned that respondent had sufficient cause for its delay in paying the earned wages after petitioner obtained employment with another shipmaster, but that there was not sufficient cause for its failure to make payment before that time. Although this reasoning conflicts with a literal reading of § 596, it is perfectly consistent with this Court's contemporary construction of the statute in *Pacific Mail S.S. Co. v. Schmidt*, 241 U.S. 245 (1916). The teaching of Justice Holmes' opinion for the Court in that case is that the wrongful character of the initial refusal to pay does not mean that all subsequent delay in payment is also "without sufficient cause" within the meaning of the statute.

---

[1] It is a familiar rule, that a thing may be within the letter of the statute and yet not within the statute, because not within its spirit, nor within the intention of its makers. This has been often asserted, and the reports are full of cases illustrating its application. * * * *Holy Trinity Church.*

The controversy in *Pacific Mail* arose in 1913, when the statute provided that the sum recoverable as wages was measured by one day's pay, rather than double that amount, for each day that the wages were withheld without sufficient cause; the statute was otherwise exactly as it is today. The seaman was discharged on October 1, 1913, but $30.33 was withheld from his wages because he was believed responsible for the loss of some silverware. He filed an action on October 20, 1913, and on November 5, 1913, obtained a judgment for his wages and an additional sum of $151.59, representing the sum recoverable as wages for the period between October 1 and November 5, 1913. The District Court's decree established the proposition that the vessel owner's defenses did not constitute sufficient cause for refusing to pay the wages and requiring the seaman to sue to recover them.

The vessel owner prosecuted an unsuccessful appeal. The Court of Appeals not only affirmed the decision of the District Court, but also added an additional recovery of daily wages for the period between the entry of the original judgment on November 5 and the actual payment of the disputed wages. The Court of Appeals thus read the statute literally and ordered the result that the District Court's finding seemed to dictate. This Court, however, set aside the additional recovery, reaching a conclusion that cannot be reconciled with a wooden, literal reading of the statute. Concurrent findings of the District Court and the Court of Appeals established that the refusal to make the wage payment when due was without sufficient cause. Justice Holmes and his Brethren accepted that finding for purposes of decision, but reasoned that there was sufficient cause for the owner's decision to appeal and his refusal to pay while the appeal was pending.

The curious character of this Court's conclusion that reasons insufficient to justify the refusal to pay before the trial court's decision somehow became sufficient to justify a subsequent refusal to pay is not the most significant point to Justice Holmes' opinion. The case is primarily significant because its holding cannot be squared with a literal reading of the statute. Even though the initial refusal is without sufficient cause, statutory wages are not necessarily recoverable for the entire period until payment is made either to the seaman or to a stakeholder. A subsequent event—even though not expressly mentioned in the statute itself—may foreshorten the recovery period.

In *Pacific Mail* the subsequent event was the vessel owner's decision to appeal. The finding that that event provided sufficient cause for the delay after November 5, 1913, was made *sua sponte* by this Court. In this case the subsequent event was the reemployment of petitioner in a comparable job on May 5, 1976. The finding that that event—coupled with the failure to make any additional demand for almost two years thereafter—was sufficient cause for the delay after May 5, 1976, was made by the District Court. It is true that the judge did not expressly frame his decision in these terms, but his actual decision fits precisely the mold established by *Pacific Mail*. Both cases give a flexible reading to the "sufficient cause" language in the statute. They differ with respect to the nature of the subsequent event but not with respect to their departure from the statutory text. [Justice Stevens also cited *Collie v. Fergusson*, 281 U.S. 52 (1930), in which the Court refused to read the statute to penalize an employer for failing to pay wages because of its financial difficulties. The conclusions reached by Justice Stevens's analysis "dispel any notion that the statute means exactly what it says." Indeed, the same flexibility shown by the Supreme Court in *Collie* also characterized the lower federal courts' treatment of the statute from 1896 to 1966.]

[III] The construction permitting the district court to exercise some discretion in tailoring the double-wage award to the particular equities of the case is just as consistent with the legislative history of § 596 as the Court's new literal approach to this statute. In 1872, when Congress authorized the recovery of additional wages by seamen who were not paid within five days of their discharge, it used the word "shall" to make it clear that such a recovery must be awarded, but it allowed the district courts a limited discretion in setting the amount of such recovery.[17] The judge's discretion as to amount was limited in two ways: (1) the statutory wage rate could not be more than double the amount of the seaman's daily wage; and (2) the period for which the statutory wage could be awarded could not exceed 10 days.

Subsequent amendments to the statute did not remove the requirement that some recovery "shall" be awarded, but did modify both of the limits on the judge's discretion. With respect to the wage rate, Congress first specified that it should equal the daily rate—rather than double the daily rate—and later specified that the rate should be the double rate.[18] With respect to the period for which the statutory wage was payable, the 1898 amendment simply removed the 10–day limit. This amendment is subject to two different interpretations, one that would represent a rather unremarkable change and the other that would be both drastic and dramatic.

The unremarkable change would amount to nothing more than a removal of the narrow 10–day limit on the scope of the judge's discretion. The word "shall" would continue to do nothing more than require some recovery in an amount to be fixed by the judge, but in recognition of the reality that seamen might be stranded for more than 10 days, the recovery period could extend beyond 10 days. This sort of unremarkable change is consistent with the purpose of the statute, as well as with a legislative history that fails to make any comment on its significance. As Justice Rehnquist has perceptively observed in another context, the fact that the dog did not bark can itself be significant.[20]

---

[17] The 1872 version of § 596 provided in pertinent part:

"[E]very master or owner who neglects or refuses to make payment [of a seaman's earned wages within five days after the seaman's discharge] without sufficient cause shall pay to the seaman a sum not exceeding the amount of two days' pay for each of the days, not exceeding ten days, during which payment is delayed beyond the [five-day period]; and such sum shall be recoverable as wages in any claim made before the court * * *." Act of June 7, 1872, ch. 322, § 35, 17 Stat. 269.

[18] The 1898 version of § 596 provided in pertinent part:

"Every master or owner who refuses or neglects to make payment [of a seaman's earned wages within four days of the seaman's discharge] without sufficient cause shall pay to the seaman a sum equal to one day's pay for each and every day during which payment is delayed beyond the [four-day period], which sum shall be recoverable as wages in any claim made before the court * * *." Act of Dec. 21, 1898, § 4, 30 Stat. 756.

The 1915 amendment substituted "two days' pay" for "one day's pay." See Act of Mar. 4, 1915, § 3, 38 Stat. 1164–1165.

[20] *Harrison v. PPG Industries, Inc.,* 446 U.S. 578, 602 (1980) (dissenting opinion); cf. A. Conan Doyle, Silver Blaze, in The Complete Sherlock Holmes 383 (1938).

The Court's construction of the amendment is, however, both drastic and dramatic. Instead of effecting a modest enlargement of the judge's discretion to do justice in these cases, the Court's construction effects a complete prohibition of judicial discretion. Instead of permitting recoveries for a period somewhat longer than 10 days, the amendment is construed as a command that even when the unresolved dispute persists for two or three years without any special hardship to the seaman, an automatic recovery must be ordered for the entire period regardless of the equitable considerations that may arise after the shipmaster's initial mistake has been made. Such a major change in both the potential amount of the statutory recovery and the character of the judge's authority would normally be explained in the committee reports or the debates if it had been intended. * * *

NOTES ON HILL, GRIFFIN, AND THE REVIVAL OF THE PLAIN MEANING RULE

1. *The Legislative Response in* Griffin *and in* TVA v. Hill. As the briefs in the case had suggested would occur, Chief Justice Burger's opinion in *TVA v. Hill* triggered an immediate legislative response. The Endangered Species Act Amendments of 1978, Pub. L. No. 95–632, § 7, 92 Stat. 3751, 3752–60 (1978), established an administrative mechanism for granting exemptions to the Act. When administrators revealed reluctance to apply this process to save the Tellico Dam, that project was specifically exempted by Congress in Pub. L. No. 96–69, tit. IV, 93 Stat. 437, 449 (1979). For an analysis of the complicated politics of the override process in this case, see Elizabeth Garrett, *The Story of* TVA v. Hill, in *Statutory Interpretation Stories* 58–91 (Eskridge, Frickey & Garrett eds. 2011).

Justice Rehnquist's argument for deferring to Congress to change the statute in *Griffin* had a different legislative response. In 1983, Congress revised much of 46 U.S.C. through Pub. L. No. 98–89. Section 596 was repealed and replaced in part by 46 U.S.C. § 10313(g). The new provision says: "When payment is not made as provided [by the statute] without sufficient cause, the master or owner shall pay to the seaman 2 days' wages for each day payment is delayed." See also *id.* § 10504(c). Obviously, Congress did not change the language important to the Court's result in *Griffin*. Can you speculate why not?

2. *The Supreme Court's Revival of the Plain Meaning Rule, 1976–86.* Although most commentators of the Burger Court's statutory opinions assumed that the Court was no more interested in the plain meaning rule than the Warren Court had been, e.g., Judge Patricia Wald, *Some Observations on the Use of Legislative History in the 1981 Supreme Court Term*, 68 Iowa L. Rev. 195, 195, 199 (1983), one commentator astutely observed that *Griffin*'s literalism was more characteristic of the Burger Court's statutory interpretation than the legal process purpose approach was. See Richard Pildes, Note, *Intent, Clear Statements and the Common Law: Statutory Interpretation in the Supreme Court*, 95 Harv. L. Rev. 892 (1982).

On the one hand, the Burger Court sometimes found the bare language of a statute determinative and applied it stringently, even if it yielded unreasonable results. See, e.g., *Board of Governors of the Federal Reserve System v. Dimension Financial Corp.*, 474 U.S. 361 (1986); *United Air Lines v. McMann*, 434 U.S. 192 (1977). On the other hand, the Burger Court followed a "soft" version of the plain meaning rule, for it typically (as it did in *Hill* and *Griffin*) attempted to justify harsh results in light of the legislative history and purposes of the statute. See *CPSC v. GTE Sylvania*, 447 U.S. 102 (1980). Indeed, passages in *Griffin* can be read for the proposition that legislative intent controls interpretation, and that the statutory text is given primacy in large part because it provides the best evidence of legislative intent. Moreover, sometimes the Burger Court went beyond even this understanding and interpreted statutes contrary to their apparent plain meaning, but consistent with their purposes and policies. See, e.g., *FDIC v. Philadelphia Gear Corp.*, 476 U.S. 426 (1986); *Midlantic Nat'l Bank v. New Jersey Dept. of Environmental Protection*, 474 U.S. 494 (1986).

3. *What Is a "Plain Meaning"?* An important issue underlying both *TVA* and *Griffin*, but not seriously examined by the Court's opinions, is what suggests to a judge that there is a "plain meaning" for a statutory provision? The obvious answer to that question is that a statute has a plain meaning if there is only one reasonable interpretation that an ordinary speaker/reader of English would take from the text. One might put it as Hart and Sacks did: There is one plain meaning if any other interpretation would impose on the statutory words a meaning they will not bear. E.g., *Rapanos v. United States*, 547 U.S. 715, 731–32 (2006) (Scalia, J., plurality opinion) (asserting plain meaning in precisely those terms). Do § 7 of the ESA (*TVA*) and § 596 (*Griffin*) both have plain meanings under this formulation?

The dissenting opinions in both cases argued that there is no single plain meaning when the literal meaning is so unreasonable. Thus, if I tell a subordinate to "drop everything and come here immediately," the plain meaning of my command does not require him or her to drop a $100,000 vase or arise immediately from the bathroom. The Court in both *TVA* and *Griffin* seems to concede that possibility, by checking the legislative history to make sure its reading is not unreasonable in light of the statutory purposes. (In both instances, the Court finds evidence that Congress's purpose supported the literal meaning. Why did this not satisfy the dissenters?)

Plain meaning analysis does not necessarily stop with ordinary meaning. See Miranda McGowan, *Do as I Do, Not as I Say: An Empirical Investigation of Justice Scalia's Ordinary Meaning Method of Statutory Interpretation*, 78 Miss. L.J. 129 (2008) (comparing Justice Scalia's textualist approach with that of the Court as a whole). A statute may have a "plain meaning" that would be unavailable to ordinary readers when legal authorities impose a specialized meaning on a term or phrase. Thus, a plain meaning might be different from an ordinary meaning when (a) Congress has defined the term in the statute; (b) the term has been authoritatively construed by the Court, or perhaps even just by the specialized community to which the statute applies (or experts testifying about that); or (c) the ordinary meaning is inconsistent with the whole act or with the way Congress has used the term in other statutes. See *Rapanos* (applying those exceptions).

One of these special exceptions to the presumption in favor of ordinary meaning was applied in *Griffin*: the Supreme Court *had* authoritatively construed the statutory terms in *Pacific Mail*, to cut off the running of the double wages ticker when the district court entered judgment. In footnote 9, Justice Rehnquist (or some aggressive law clerk) overruled the holding of *Pacific Mail*, without even mentioning the precedent. This is bizarre as well as anti-textualist, for the *Pacific Mail* cutoff is justified by the law of judgments: all damages are "merged" into a trial court's judgment, hence the cutting of double wages by Justice Holmes. Is there any justification for the Court's footnote-overrule?

In *Griffin,* Justice Stevens propounded another source of context: *statutory history,* namely, the formal evolution in the actual terms of the statute, as it is amended over time. Stevens demonstrates that Congress's editing of the double wages law in the two generations after the Civil War rested upon the assumption that there would be a short time between injury (the ship abandons the seaman) and lawsuit and judgment (any judgment for penalty wages would merge with the judgment). See *Pacific Mail,* where the whole matter was wrapped up in months. How would Justice Rehnquist respond to Justice Stevens?

NOTE ON THE PLAIN MEANING RULE IN STATE COURTS

In general, the plain meaning rule had greater staying power at the state level. Through most of the twentieth century, state courts were more likely to resolve issues of statutory interpretation merely by construing the apparent meaning of the statutory language, with attention to textual canons of statutory construction but without *any* examination of the statute's purpose or legislative history. See, e.g., *Bishop v. Linkway Stores, Inc.,* 655 S.W.2d 426 (Ark. 1983). The two most frequently mentioned reasons for state court textualism are the dearth of legislative history materials available for state statutes and a more restrained methodology practiced by many state judges, especially those who are elected by the people or subject to retention elections to remain in office.

This textualist practice changed during the post-World War II era in most states. For example, California courts often eschewed a plain meaning approach. See, e.g., *People v. Hallner,* 277 P.2d 393 (Cal. 1954); *McKeag v. Board of Pension Comm'rs of Los Angeles,* 132 P.2d 198 (Cal. 1942). The California Supreme Court has often used a contextual approach to interpret legislation broadly to promote liberal social policy and fairness. For instance, *County of San Diego v. Muniz,* 583 P.2d 109 (Cal. 1978), involved a statute requiring former or present welfare recipients to reimburse the state if the person "acquires property." The Supreme Court construed "property" *not* to include wages, because deprivation of wages would undermine the overall goal of the welfare law to assist recipients in becoming self-supporting and would be unfair and oppressive.

Other states have looked beyond the plain language of state statutes more and more. Written or published legislative histories of state statutes are now more readily available than at any previous point in American history, and they have wider availability now that more of the materials can be found on the internet. This phenomenon (increased availability) has given rise to a growing body of scholarship analyzing state court use of state legislative history. See generally Abbe Gluck, *States as Laboratories of Statutory Interpretation: Methodological Consensus and the New Modified Textualism,* 117 Yale L.J. 1750 (2010).[32]

---

[32] For scholarship tracing the decline of the plain meaning rule, and concomitant rise of the use of legislative history, by courts in particular states, see Shirley Abrahamson & Robert Hughes, *Shall We Dance? Steps for Legislators and Judges in Statutory Interpretation,* 75 Minn. L. Rev. 1045 (1991); Melinda Allison & James Hambleton, *Research in Texas Legislative History,* 47 Tex. B.J. 314 (1984); D.A. Divilbiss, *The Need for Comprehensive Legislative History in Missouri,* 36 J. Mo. B. 520 (1980); Kenneth Dortzbach, *Legislative History: The Philosophies of Justices Scalia and Breyer and the Use of Legislative History by the Wisconsin State Courts,* 80 Marq. L. Rev. 161 (1996); Judith Kaye, *Things Judges Do: State Statutory Interpretation,* 13 Touro L. Rev. 595 (1997); Jack Landau, *Some Observations About Statutory Construction in Oregon,* 32

3. CURRENT DEBATES IN STATUTORY INTERPRETATION

In this final section we survey the debates over appropriate method concerning statutory interpretation that began in the 1980s. The primary debate has involved the challenge of the "new textualism" against more traditional approaches relying on legislative purpose and intent. We introduce the new textualism in Part A. Part B considers the ramifications of economic approaches to statutory interpretation, and Part C does the same for pragmatic approaches.

A. THE NEW TEXTUALISM

In the 1980s, a group of judges and executive officials developed a more constrained version of the plain meaning rule than that followed in cases like *Griffin* and *TVA v. Hill.* For example, Judge Frank Easterbrook's *Statutes' Domains,* 50 U. Chi. L. Rev. 533 (1983), insisted that courts have no authority even to apply a statute to a problem unless the statute's language clearly targets that problem. Judge Easterbrook's *Legal Interpretation and the Power of the Judiciary,* 7 Harv. J.L. & Pub. Pol'y 87 (1984), argued that courts interpreting statutes have no business figuring out legislative intent, which is an incoherent concept, largely for the reasons suggested in 1930 by Professor Radin, but updated to reflect modern public choice theory. Judge Antonin Scalia delivered a series of speeches in 1985–86, urging courts to abandon virtually any reference to legislative history, especially the committee reports referred to in *Griffin* and *TVA v. Hill.* The Department of Justice's Office of Legal Policy endorsed and developed these views in a document drafted by Stephen Markman, *Using and Misusing Legislative History: A Re-Evaluation of the Status of Legislative History in Statutory Interpretation* (1989).

What we call "the new textualism"[33] is an approach to statutory interpretation developed by these judges and scholars. Although its proponents draw from legal

---

Willamette L. Rev. 1 (1996); Eric Lane, *How To Read a Statute in New York: A Response to Judge Kaye and Some More,* 28 Hofstra L. Rev. 85 (1999); Jean McKnight, *Compiling an Illinois Legislative History,* 85 Ill. B.J. 335 (1997); Maureen Bonace McMahon, *Legislative History in Ohio: Myths and Realities,* 46 Clev. St. L. Rev. 49 (1998); Michael Mullane, *Statutory Interpretation in Arkansas: How Arkansas Courts Interpret Statutes. A Rational Approach,* 2005 Ark. L. Notes 73; William Nast, *The Use of Legislative History in Construing Pennsylvania Statutes Part II,* Pa. L.J. Rep., May 25, 1981, at 18, col. 1; Donald O'Connor, *The Use of Connecticut Legislative History in Statutory Construction,* 58 Conn. B.J. 422 (1984); William Popkin, *Statutory Interpretation in State Courts—A Study of Indiana Opinions,* 24 Ind. L. Rev. 1155 (1991); Roy Pulvers & Wendy Willis, *Revolution and Evolution: What Is Going on with Statutory Interpretation in the Oregon Courts,* 56 Or. St. B. Bull. 13 (Jan. 1996); Robert Rhodes & Susan Seereiter, *The Search for Intent: Aids to Statutory Construction in Florida—An Update,* 13 Fla. St. U. L. Rev. 485 (1985); Fritz Snyder, *Researching Legislative Intent,* 51 Kan. B.A.J. 93 (1982); Adam Yoffie, *From Poritz to Rabner: The New Jersey Supreme Court's Statutory Jurisprudence, 2000–2009,* 35 Seton Hall Legis. J. 302 (2011); Matthew Hertko, Note, *Statutory Interpretation in Illinois: Abandoning the Plain Meaning Rule for an Extratextual Approach,* 2005 U. Ill. L. Rev. 377; Walter Hurst, Comment, *The Use of Extrinsic Aids in Determining Legislative Intent in California: The Need for Standardized Criteria,* 12 Pac. L.J. 189 (1981); Comment, *Legislative History in Washington,* 7 U. Puget Sound L. Rev. 571 (1984).

[33] See William Eskridge Jr., *The New Textualism,* 37 UCLA L. Rev. 621 (1990); George H. Taylor, *Structural Textualism,* 75 B.U. L. Rev. 321 (1995); Jonathan Molot, *The Rise and Fall of Textualism,* 106 Colum. L. Rev. 1 (2006); Nicholas Zeppos, *Justice Scalia's Textualism and the "New" New Legal Process,* 12 Cardozo L. Rev. 1597 (1991). For a short overview placing textualism in context with prior theories, see Philip Frickey, *From the Big Sleep to the Big Heat: The Revival of Theory in Statutory Interpretation,* 77 Minn. L. Rev. 241 (1992).

process theory for their own purposes, their approach to statutory interpretation differs from that supported by Professors Hart, Sacks, and Fuller. Also, new textualist construction is different from the "soft" plain meaning rule of *TVA v. Hill* and *Griffin*, as suggested by the exchanges in the cases that follow.

GREEN V. BOCK LAUNDRY MACHINE COMPANY

Supreme Court of the United States, 1989.
490 U.S. 504, 109 S.Ct. 1981, 104 L.Ed.2d 557.

JUSTICE STEVENS delivered the opinion of the Court.

[Paul Green, a county prisoner working at a car wash on a work-release program, reached inside a large dryer to stop it and had his arm torn off. At trial in his product liability action against the machine's manufacturer, he testified that he had been inadequately instructed about the machine's operation and dangerousness. Green admitted that he had been convicted of burglary and of conspiracy to commit burglary, both felonies, and those convictions were used by defendant to impeach his credibility. The jury returned a verdict for Bock Laundry. The Court of Appeals affirmed, rejecting Green's argument that the district court erred by denying his pretrial motion to exclude the impeaching evidence.]

[Criticism of automatic admissibility of prior felony convictions to impeach civil witnesses, particularly civil plaintiffs, has been "longstanding and widespread."] Our task in deciding this case, however, is not to fashion the rule we deem desirable but to identify the rule that Congress fashioned. * * *

[I]   Federal Rule of Evidence 609(a) provides:

"General Rule. For the purpose of attacking the credibility of a witness, evidence that the witness has been convicted of a crime shall be admitted if elicited from the witness or established by public record during cross-examination but only if the crime (1) was punishable by death or imprisonment in excess of one year under the law under which the witness was convicted, and the court determines that the probative value of admitting this evidence outweighs its prejudicial effect to the defendant, or (2) involved dishonesty or false statement, regardless of the punishment."

By its terms the Rule requires a judge to allow impeachment of any witness with prior convictions for felonies not involving dishonesty "only if" the probativeness of the evidence is greater than its prejudice "to the defendant." It follows that impeaching evidence detrimental to the prosecution in a criminal case "shall be admitted" without any such balancing.

The Rule's plain language commands weighing of prejudice to a defendant in a civil trial as well as in a criminal trial. But that literal reading would compel an odd result in a case like this. Assuming that all impeaching evidence has at least minimal probative value, and given that the evidence of plaintiff Green's convictions had some prejudicial effect on his case—but surely none on defendant Bock's—balancing according to the strict language of Rule 609(a)(1) inevitably leads to the conclusion that the evidence was admissible. In fact, under this construction of the Rule, impeachment detrimental to a civil plaintiff always would have to be admitted.

No matter how plain the text of the Rule may be, we cannot accept an interpretation that would deny a civil plaintiff the same right to impeach an adversary's testimony that it grants to a civil defendant. The Sixth Amendment to the Constitution guarantees a criminal defendant certain fair trial rights not enjoyed by the prosecution, while the Fifth Amendment lets the accused choose not to testify at trial. In contrast, civil litigants in federal court share equally the protections of the Fifth Amendment's Due Process Clause. Given liberal federal discovery rules, the inapplicability of the Fifth Amendment's protection against self-incrimination, and the need to prove their case, civil litigants almost always must testify in depositions or at trial. Denomination as a civil defendant or plaintiff, moreover, is often happenstance based on which party filed first or on the nature of the suit. Evidence that a litigant or his witness is a convicted felon tends to shift a jury's focus from the worthiness of the litigant's position to the moral worth of the litigant himself. It is unfathomable why a civil plaintiff—but not a civil defendant—should be subjected to this risk. Thus we agree with the Seventh Circuit that as far as civil trials are concerned, Rule 609(a)(1) "can't mean what it says." *Campbell v. Greer*, 831 F.2d 700, 703 (1987) [Posner, J.].

Out of this agreement flow divergent courses, each turning on the meaning of "defendant." The word might be interpreted to encompass all witnesses, civil and criminal, parties or not. It might be read to connote any party offering a witness, in which event Rule 609(a)(1)'s balance would apply to civil, as well as criminal, cases. Finally, "defendant" may refer only to the defendant in a criminal case. These choices spawn a corollary question: must a judge allow prior felony impeachment of all civil witnesses as well as all criminal prosecution witnesses, or is Rule 609(a)(1) inapplicable to civil cases, in which event Rule 403 would authorize a judge to balance in such cases?* Because the plain text does not resolve these issues, we must examine the history leading to enactment of Rule 609 as law.

[II] At common law a person who had been convicted of a felony was not competent to testify as a witness. "[T]he disqualification arose as part of the punishment for the crime, only later being rationalized on the basis that such a person was unworthy of belief." 3 J. Weinstein & M. Berger, Weinstein's Evidence paragraph 609[02], p. 609–58 (1988)[.] As the law evolved, this absolute bar gradually was replaced by a rule that allowed such witnesses to testify in both civil and criminal cases, but also to be impeached by evidence of a prior felony conviction or a *crimen falsi* misdemeanor conviction. In the face of scholarly criticism of automatic admission of such impeaching evidence, some courts moved toward a more flexible approach.

[The American Law Institute's Model Code of Evidence and the ABA's proposed Uniform Rules of Evidence recommended that trial judges be given discretion to exclude evidence of prior convictions in appropriate circumstances. In

---

* *Editors' note*: Rule 403 provides that relevant evidence may be excluded "if its probative value is substantially outweighed by the danger of unfair prejudice, confusion of the issues, or misleading the jury, or by considerations of undue delay, waste of time, or needless presentation of cumulative evidence."

1969, however, the Advisory Committee's proposed Rules of Evidence included Rule 6–09, which allowed all *crimen falsi* and felony convictions evidence without mention of judicial discretion. But the Committee's second draft of Rule 609(a)] authorized the judge to exclude either felony or *crimen falsi* evidence upon determination that its probative value was "substantially outweighed by the danger of unfair prejudice." The Committee specified that its primary concern was prejudice to the witness-accused; the "risk of unfair prejudice to a party in the use of [convictions] to impeach the ordinary witness is so minimal as scarcely to be a subject of comment." Yet the text of the proposal was broad enough to allow a judge to protect not only criminal defendants, but also civil litigants and nonparty witnesses, from unfair prejudice.

[T]he Advisory Committee's revision of Rule 609(a) met resistance. The Department of Justice urged that the Committee supplant its proposal with the strict, amended version of the District Code. Senator McClellan objected to the adoption of the *Luck* doctrine and urged reinstatement of the earlier draft.

The Advisory Committee backed off. As Senator McClellan had requested, it submitted as its third and final draft the same strict version it had proposed in March 1969. * * * This Court forwarded the Advisory Committee's final draft to Congress on November 20, 1972.

The House of Representatives did not accept the Advisory Committee's final proposal. A Subcommittee of the Judiciary Committee recommended an amended version similar to the text of the present Rule 609(a), except that it avoided the current rule's ambiguous reference to prejudice to "the defendant." Rather, in prescribing weighing of admissibility of prior felony convictions, it used the same open-ended reference to "unfair prejudice" found in the Advisory Committee's second draft.

The House Judiciary Committee departed even further from the Advisory Committee's final recommendation, preparing a draft that did not allow impeachment by evidence of prior conviction unless the crime involved dishonesty or false statement. Motivating the change were concerns about the deterrent effect upon an accused who might wish to testify and the danger of unfair prejudice, "even upon a witness who was not the accused," from allowing impeachment by prior felony convictions regardless of their relation to the witness' veracity. H.R.Rep. No. 93–650, p. 11 (1973). Although the Committee Report focused on criminal defendants and did not mention civil litigants, its express concerns encompassed all nonaccused witnesses.

Representatives who advocated the automatic admissibility approach of the Advisory Committee's draft and those who favored the intermediate approach proposed by the Subcommittee both opposed the Committee's bill on the House floor. Four Members pointed out that the Rule applied in civil as well as criminal cases. The House voted to adopt the Rule as proposed by its Judiciary Committee.

The Senate Judiciary Committee proposed an intermediate path. For criminal defendants, it would have allowed impeachment only by *crimen falsi* evidence; for other witnesses, it also would have permitted prior felony evidence only if the trial judge found that probative value outweighed "prejudicial effect against the party offering that witness." This language thus required the exercise of discretion before prior felony convictions could be admitted in civil litigation. But the full Senate, prodded by Senator McClellan, reverted to the version that the Advisory Committee had submitted. See 120 Cong. Rec. 37076, 37083 (1974).

Conflict between the House bill, allowing impeachment only by *crimen falsi* evidence, and the Senate bill, embodying the Advisory Committee's automatic admissibility approach, was resolved by a Conference Committee. The conferees' compromise—enacted as Federal Rule of Evidence 609(a)(1)—authorizes impeachment by felony convictions, "but only if" the court determines that probative value outweighs "prejudicial effect to the defendant." The Conference Committee's Report makes it perfectly clear that the balance set forth in this draft, unlike the second Advisory Committee and the Senate Judiciary Committee versions, does not protect all nonparty witnesses:

> "The danger of prejudice to a witness other than the defendant (such as injury to the witness' reputation in his community) was considered and rejected by the Conference as an element to be weighed in determining admissibility. It was the judgment of the Conference that the danger of prejudice to a nondefendant witness is outweighed by the need for the trier of fact to have as much relevant evidence on the issue of credibility as possible." H.R.Conf.Rep. No. 93–1597, pp. 9–10 (1974).

Equally clear is the conferees' intention that the rule shield the accused, but not the prosecution, in a criminal case. Impeachment by convictions, the Committee Report stated, "should only be excluded where it presents a danger of improperly influencing the outcome of the trial by persuading the trier of fact to convict the defendant on the basis of his prior criminal record."

But this emphasis on the criminal context, in the Report's use of terms such as "defendant" and "to convict" and in individual conferees' explanations of the compromise,[26] raises some doubt over the Rule's pertinence to civil litigants. The discussions suggest that only two kinds of witnesses risk prejudice—the defendant who elects to testify in a criminal case and witnesses other than the defendant in the same kind of case. Nowhere is it acknowledged that undue prejudice to a civil litigant also may improperly influence a trial's outcome. Although this omission lends support to [an] opinion that "legislative oversight" caused exclusion of civil

---

[26] Representative Dennis, who had stressed in earlier debates that the Rule would apply to both civil and criminal cases, see 120 Cong. Rec. 2377 (1974), explained the benefits of the Rule for criminal defendants and made no reference to benefits for civil litigants when he said:

> "[Y]ou can ask about all . . . felonies on cross examination, only if you can convince the court, and the burden is on the *government*, which is an important change in the law, that the probative value of the question is greater than the damage to the *defendant*; and that is damage or prejudice *to the defendant alone*." *Id.*, at 40894 (emphases supplied).

In the same debate Representative Hogan manifested awareness of the Rule's broad application. While supporting the compromise, he reiterated his preference for a rule

> "that, for the purpose of attacking the credibility of a witness, *even if the witness happens to be the defendant in a criminal case*, evidence that he has been convicted of a crime is admissible and may be used to challenge that witness' credibility if the crime is a felony or is a misdemeanor involving dishonesty of [sic] false statement." *Id.*, at 40895 (emphasis added).

parties from Rule 609(a)(1)'s balance, a number of considerations persuade us that the Rule was meant to authorize a judge to weigh prejudice against no one other than a criminal defendant.

A party contending that legislative action changed settled law has the burden of showing that the legislature intended such a change. Cf. *Midlantic National Bank v. New Jersey Department of Environmental Protection*, 474 U.S. 494, 502 (1986). The weight of authority before Rule 609's adoption accorded with the Advisory Committee's final draft, admitting all felonies without exercise of judicial discretion in either civil or criminal cases. Departures from this general rule had occurred overtly by judicial interpretation, as in *Luck*, or in evidence codes, such as the Model Code and the Uniform Rules. Rule 609 itself explicitly adds safeguards circumscribing the common-law rule. The unsubstantiated assumption that legislative oversight produced Rule 609(a)(1)'s ambiguity respecting civil trials hardly demonstrates that Congress intended silently to overhaul the law of impeachment in the civil context.

To the extent various drafts of Rule 609 distinguished civil and criminal cases, moreover, they did so only to mitigate prejudice to criminal defendants. Any prejudice that convictions impeachment might cause witnesses other than the accused was deemed "so minimal as scarcely to be a subject of comment." Advisory Committee's Note, 51 F.R.D., at 392. Far from voicing concern lest such impeachment unjustly diminish a civil witness in the eyes of the jury, Representative Hogan declared that this evidence ought to be used to measure a witness' moral value.[27] Furthermore, Representative Dennis—who in advocating a Rule limiting impeachment to *crimen falsi* convictions had recognized the impeachment Rule's applicability to civil trials—not only debated the issue on the House floor, but also took part in the conference out of which Rule 609 emerged. See 120 Cong.Rec. 2377–2380, 39942, 40894–40895 (1974). These factors indicate that Rule 609(a)(1)'s textual limitation of the prejudice balance to criminal defendants resulted from deliberation, not oversight.

Had the conferees desired to protect other parties or witnesses, they could have done so easily. Presumably they had access to all of Rule 609's precursors, particularly the drafts prepared by the House Subcommittee and the Senate Judiciary Committee, both of which protected the civil litigant as well as the criminal defendant. Alternatively, the conferees could have amended their own draft to include other parties. They did not for the simple reason that they intended that only the accused in a criminal case should be protected from unfair prejudice by the balance set out in Rule 609(a)(1).

---

[27] "Suppose some governmental body instituted a civil action for damages, and the defendant called a witness who had been previously convicted of malicious destruction of public property. Under the committee's formulation, the convictions could not be used to impeach the witness' credibility since the crimes did not involve dishonesty or false statement. Yet, in the hypothetical case, as in any case in which the government was a party, justice would seem to me to require that the jury know that the witness had been carrying on some private war against society. Should a witness with an anti-social background be allowed to stand on the same basis of believability before juries as law-abiding citizens with unblemished records? I think not. . . . Personally I am more concerned about the moral worth of individuals capable of engaging in such outrageous acts as adversely reflecting on a witness' character than I am of thieves. . . ." *Id.*, at 2376.

[Finally, the Court concluded that Rule 609, as the specific provision governing the facts of the case, controlled over the general balancing provisions of Rule 403. The Court affirmed the judgment for defendant.]

JUSTICE SCALIA, concurring in the judgment.

We are confronted here with a statute which, if interpreted literally, produces an absurd, and perhaps unconstitutional, result. Our task is to give some alternate meaning to the word "defendant" in Federal Rule of Evidence 609(a)(1) that avoids this consequence; and then to determine whether Rule 609(a)(1) excludes the operation of Federal Rule of Evidence 403.

I think it entirely appropriate to consult all public materials, including the background of Rule 609(a)(1) and the legislative history of its adoption, to verify that what seems to us an unthinkable disposition (civil defendants but not civil plaintiffs receive the benefit of weighing prejudice) was indeed unthought of, and thus to justify a departure from the ordinary meaning of the word "defendant" in the Rule. For that purpose, however, it would suffice to observe that counsel have not provided, nor have we discovered, a shred of evidence that anyone has ever proposed or assumed such a bizarre disposition. The Court's opinion, however, goes well beyond this. Approximately four-fifths of its substantive analysis is devoted to examining the evolution of Federal Rule of Evidence 609 * * * all with the evident purpose, not merely of confirming that the word "defendant" cannot have been meant literally, but of determining what, precisely, the Rule does mean.

I find no reason to believe that any more than a handful of the Members of Congress who enacted Rule 609 were aware of its interesting evolution from the 1942 Model Code; or that any more than a handful of them (if any) voted, with respect to their understanding of the word "defendant" and the relationship between Rule 609 and Rule 403, on the basis of the referenced statements in the Subcommittee, Committee, or Conference Committee Reports, or floor debates— statements so marginally relevant, to such minute details, in such relatively inconsequential legislation. The meaning of terms on the statute books ought to be determined, not on the basis of which meaning can be shown to have been understood by a larger handful of the Members of Congress; but rather on the basis of which meaning is (1) most in accord with context and ordinary usage, and thus most likely to have been understood by the *whole* Congress which voted on the words of the statute (not to mention the citizens subject to it), and (2) most compatible with the surrounding body of law into which the provision must be integrated—a compatibility which, by a benign fiction, we assume Congress always has in mind. I would not permit any of the historical and legislative material discussed by the Court, or all of it combined, to lead me to a result different from the one that these factors suggest.

I would analyze this case, in brief, as follows:

(1) The word "defendant" in Rule 609(a)(1) cannot rationally (or perhaps even constitutionally) mean to provide the benefit of prejudice-weighing to civil defendants and not civil plaintiffs. Since petitioner has not produced, and we have not ourselves discovered, even a snippet of support for this absurd result, we may

confidently assume that the word was not used (as it normally would be) to refer to all defendants and only all defendants.

(2) The available alternatives are to interpret "defendant" to mean (a) "civil plaintiff, civil defendant, prosecutor, and criminal defendant," (b) "civil plaintiff and defendant and criminal defendant," or (c) "criminal defendant." Quite obviously, the last does least violence to the text. It adds a qualification that the word "defendant" does not contain but, unlike the others, does not give the word a meaning ("plaintiff" or "prosecutor") it simply will not bear. The qualification it adds, moreover, is one that could understandably have been omitted by inadvertence—and sometimes is omitted in normal conversation ("I believe strongly in defendants' rights"). Finally, this last interpretation is consistent with the policy of the law in general and the Rules of Evidence in particular of providing special protection to defendants in criminal cases.*

(3) As well described by the Court, the "structure of the Rules" makes it clear that Rule 403 is not to be applied in addition to Rule 609(a)(1).

I am frankly not sure that, despite its lengthy discussion of ideological evolution and legislative history, the Court's reasons for both aspects of its decision are much different from mine. I respectfully decline to join that discussion, however, because it is natural for the bar to believe that the juridical importance of such material matches its prominence in our opinions—thus producing a legal culture in which, when counsel arguing before us assert that "Congress has said" something, they now frequently mean, by "Congress," a committee report; and in which it was not beyond the pale for a recent brief to say the following: "Unfortunately, the legislative debates are not helpful. Thus, we turn to the other guidepost in this difficult area, statutory language." * * *

JUSTICE BLACKMUN, with whom JUSTICE BRENNAN and JUSTICE MARSHALL join, dissenting.

* * * The majority concludes that Rule 609(a)(1) cannot mean what it says on its face. I fully agree.

I fail to see, however, why we are required to solve this riddle of statutory interpretation by reading the inadvertent word "defendant" to mean "criminal defendant." I am persuaded that a better interpretation of the Rule would allow the trial court to consider the risk of prejudice faced by any party, not just a criminal defendant. Applying the balancing provisions of Rule 609(a)(1) to all parties would have prevented the admission of unnecessary and inflammatory evidence in this case and will prevent other similar unjust results until Rule 609(a) is repaired, as it must be. The result the Court reaches today, in contrast, endorses "the irrationality and unfairness" of denying the trial court the ability to weigh the risk of prejudice

---

*   Acknowledging the statutory ambiguity, the dissent would read "defendant" to mean "any party" because, it says, this interpretation "extend[s] the protection of judicial supervision to a larger class of litigants" than the interpretation the majority and I favor, which "takes protection *away* from litigants." But neither side in this dispute can lay claim to generosity without begging the policy question whether judicial supervision is better than the automatic power to impeach. We could as well say—and with much more support in both prior law and this Court's own recommendation—that our reading "extend[s] the protection of [the right to impeach with prior felony convictions] to a larger class of litigants" than the dissent's interpretation, which "takes protection *away* from litigants."

to any party before admitting evidence of a prior felony for purposes of impeachment.

The majority's lengthy recounting of the legislative history of Rule 609 demonstrates why almost all that history is entitled to very little weight. Because the proposed rule changed so often—and finally was enacted as a compromise between the House and the Senate—much of the commentary cited by the majority concerns versions different from the Rule Congress finally enacted.

The only item of legislative history that focuses on the Rule as enacted is the Report of the Conference Committee. Admittedly, language in the Report supports the majority's position: the Report mirrors the Rule in emphasizing the prejudicial effect on the defendant, and also uses the word "convict" to describe the potential outcome. But the Report's draftsmanship is no better than the Rule's, and the Report's plain language is no more reliable an indicator of Congress' intent than is the plain language of the Rule itself.

Because the slipshod drafting of Rule 609(a)(1) demonstrates that clarity of language was not the Conference's forte, I prefer to rely on the underlying reasoning of the Report, rather than on its unfortunate choice of words, in ascertaining the Rule's proper scope. The Report's treatment of the Rule's discretionary standard consists of a single paragraph. After noting that the Conference was concerned with prejudice to a defendant, the Report states:

> "The danger of prejudice to a witness other than the defendant (such as injury to the witness' reputation in the community) was considered and rejected by the Conference as an element to be weighed in determining admissibility. It was the judgment of the Conference that the danger of prejudice to a nondefendant witness is outweighed by the need for the trier of fact to have as much relevant evidence on the issue of credibility as possible. Such evidence should only be excluded where it presents a danger of improperly influencing the outcome of the trial by persuading the trier of fact to convict the defendant on the basis of his prior criminal record."

The Report indicates that the Conference determined that any felony conviction has sufficient relevance to a witness' credibility to be admitted, even if the felony had nothing directly to do with truthfulness or honesty. In dealing with the question of undue prejudice, however, the Conference drew a line: it distinguished between two types of prejudice, only one of which it permitted the trial court to consider.

As the Conference observed, admitting a prior conviction will always "prejudice" a witness, who, of course, would prefer that the conviction not be revealed to the public. The Report makes clear, however, that this kind of prejudice to the witness' life outside the courtroom is not to be considered in the judicial balancing required by Rule 609(a)(1). Rather, the kind of prejudice the court is instructed to be concerned with is prejudice which "presents a danger of improperly influencing the outcome of the trial." Congress' solution to that kind of prejudice was to require judicial supervision: the conviction may be admitted only if "the court determines that the probative value of admitting this evidence outweighs its prejudicial effect to the defendant." Rule 609(a)(1).

Although the Conference expressed its concern in terms of the effect on a criminal defendant, the potential for prejudice to the outcome at trial exists in any type of litigation, whether criminal or civil, and threatens all parties to the litigation. The Report and the Rule are best read as expressing Congress' preference for judicial balancing whenever there is a chance that justice shall be denied a party because of the unduly prejudicial nature of a witness' past conviction for a crime that has no direct bearing on the witness' truthfulness. In short, the reasoning of the Report suggests that by "prejudice to the defendant," Congress meant "prejudice to a party," as opposed to the prejudicial effect of the revelation of a prior conviction to the witness' own reputation.

It may be correct, as Justice Scalia notes in his opinion concurring in the judgment, that interpreting "prejudicial effect to the defendant" to include only "prejudicial effect to [a] *criminal* defendant," and not prejudicial effect to other categories of litigants as well, does the "least violence to the text," if what we mean by "violence" is the interpolation of excess words or the deletion of existing words. But the reading endorsed by Justice Scalia and the majority does violence to the logic of the only rationale Members of Congress offered for the Rule they adopted.

Certainly the possibility that admission of a witness' past conviction will improperly determine the outcome at trial is troubling when the witness' testimony is in support of a criminal defendant. The potential, however, is no less real for other litigants. Unlike Justice Scalia, I do not approach the Rules of Evidence, which by their terms govern both civil and criminal proceedings, with the presumption that their general provisions should be read to "provid[e] special protection to defendants in criminal cases." Rather, the Rules themselves specify that they "shall be construed to secure fairness in administration . . . to the end that the truth may be ascertained and proceedings justly determined" in *all* cases. Rule 102. The majority's result does not achieve that end. * * *

As I see it, therefore, our choice is between two interpretations of Rule 609(a)(1), neither of which is completely consistent with the Rule's plain language. The majority's interpretation takes protection *away* from litigants—*i.e.*, civil defendants—who would have every reason to believe themselves entitled to the judicial balancing offered by the Rule. The alternative interpretation—which I favor—also departs somewhat from plain language, but does so by *extending* the protection of judicial supervision to a larger class of litigants—*i.e.*, to all parties. Neither result is compelled by the statutory language or the legislative history, but for me the choice between them is an easy one. I find it proper, as a general matter and under the dictates of Rule 102, to construe the Rule so as to avoid "unnecessary hardship," see *Burnet v. Guggenheim*, 288 U.S. 280, 285 (1933), and to produce a sensible result. * * *

NOTES ON BOCK LAUNDRY AND DIFFERENT THEORIES IN ACTION

1. *Does Textualism Work in* Bock Laundry? Note that, like the other eight Justices, textualist Justice Scalia *also* rewrote the statute, which has a perfectly "plain

meaning" in this case: The felony convictions of civil plaintiffs can always be introduced to impeach them, but those of civil defendants are subject to a balancing test. Of course, such a plain meaning is probably unconstitutional, but in that event why doesn't the textualist simply invalidate Rule 609(a)(1) (at least as far as civil cases) and apply the Rule 403 default rule, which would probably exclude Green's conviction from evidence?

Justice Scalia disregarded plain meaning in this case because he believed that Rule 609(a)(1) was absurd as written, that the absurdity was unintended, and that an unintended absurdity justifies departure from plain meaning. This is itself significant. By creating an exception to textualism when a statute requires unintended "absurd" consequences, is Justice Scalia not conceding that following statutory text is not all that is going on in statutory interpretation, and that current interpretive values have a role to play in statutory interpretation? While Justice Scalia surely believes that plain meaning can only be sacrificed in the rare absurd-result case, why not sacrifice plain meaning when it directs an "unreasonable" result that was probably unintended by Congress?

Although Justice Scalia agreed to rewrite the statute in *Bock Laundry*, his opinion dismissed the dissenting opinion's rewrite in favor of the majority's rewrite:

> The available alternatives [for rewriting the rule] are to interpret "defendant" to mean (a) "civil plaintiff, civil defendant, prosecutor and criminal defendant," (b) "civil plaintiff and defendant and criminal defendant," or (c) "criminal defendant." Quite obviously, the last does least violence to the text.

Is that so obvious? In essence, Justice Blackmun's dissent rewrote Rule 609(a)(1) to permit impeaching convictions only when "the court determines that the probative value of admitting this evidence outweighs its prejudicial effect to *a party*" (new language italicized). Does this do more "violence" to the text than Justice Scalia's rewrite to permit impeaching convictions only when "the court determines that the probative value of admitting this evidence outweighs its prejudicial effect to the *criminal* defendant"?

Indeed, from a purely textualist perspective, Justice Blackmun's rewrite may be a better version, because Justice Scalia's rewrite leaves the statute as chaotic as it was originally. Rewritten Rule 609(a)(1) still applies in a civil case like *Bock Laundry*, and Justice Scalia's version tells the judge to follow a strange rule: Allow the witness to be impeached by his prior felony convictions, but only if its probative value outweighs its prejudice to the "criminal defendant." What criminal defendant? This is a civil case, after all. While the original Rule 609(a)(1) favored civil defendants over civil plaintiffs without apparent justification, it at least set forth a rule that could be applied by the district judge in a civil case. Under the pretense of doing "least violence" to the text, does Justice Scalia's rewrite deprive the judge of an intelligible rule?

In our view, the shortest way to rewrite Rule 609(a)(1) to reflect the understanding of the majority and of Justice Scalia *and* to have it make sense as a rule applicable to civil as well as criminal cases is something like the following: Allow a witness to be impeached by his prior criminal conviction "if the crime (1) was punishable by death or imprisonment in excess of one year under the law under which the witness was convicted, and, *in a criminal case*, the court determines that the probative value of admitting this evidence outweighs its prejudicial effect to the defendant" (new language italicized). Would this flunk Justice Scalia's test of doing "least violence" to the text?

2. *Does Imaginative Reconstruction Work Any Better?* Imaginative reconstruction also may be problematic in *Bock Laundry*, for the reasons suggested by Professor Radin and revived by the new textualists. Who can really tell what the median Member of Congress thought about this issue?

Recall that the House voted for a version of Rule 609(a) that would have given Green the benefit of a balancing test, and a similar version was voted out of the Senate Judiciary Committee. On the floor of the Senate, Senator McClellan proposed an amendment making all felony convictions admissible; his amendment failed by a 35–35 vote. 120 Cong. Rec. 37080 (1974). But on immediate motion for reconsideration, his amendment was adopted, 38–34, because a couple of new senators showed up and a couple changed their votes. *Id.* at 37083. The median senator was apparently (and ironically) Senator Stevens (R–Alaska): He voted against the McClellan amendment, for reconsideration, for the McClellan amendment, and then for the final conference bill, which adopted the ambiguous compromise. Why did he vote this way? What was his "intent"?

In 2006, we posed these questions to Senator Stevens, who was still representing Alaska in the Senate. Senator Stevens told us that the voting pattern for him and several other senators was "confused" as a matter of logic, but not as a matter of political collegiality. "As a former U.S. Attorney I favored the House and Senate Judiciary Committees' version—but McClellan was a friend. He had traveled to Alaska with me—and Jackson and Stennis were sort of mentors. This was my sixth year in the Senate—I voted with McClellan to take his 'compromise' to conference."[34]

In any event, the Senate did vote for a much more limited version of Rule 609(a) than the House, and so the key question for imaginative reconstruction is: What was the conference committee "deal" that was struck on Rule 609(a)? And of course that's completely unclear as well, since the conference report doesn't even mention civil cases, and Senator Stevens does not recall any consensus on the matter when he and other senators passed the conference bill by voice vote. Justice Stevens finds great significance in the conference action, but only because of a judicially created canon of statutory construction: If the dog (here, Congress) doesn't bark, assume that "nothing happened"—no radical change was made in the fabric of the law (recall the dog-doesn't-bark canon). Thus, Justice Stevens's imaginative reconstruction boils down to the application of a judicial presumption! And one that seems flimsy at best, because the common law rule was in the process of collapsing—and did collapse within the federal system the year after *Bock Laundry*. See the next note.

3. *Why Did the Court Go Through This Exercise?* As Justice Stevens's opinion noted, there was a proposed change to Rule 609(a) pending when the Supreme Court interpreted the Rule in *Bock Laundry*.[35] In January 1990 (soon after the decision in *Bock Laundry*), the Supreme Court notified Congress that it had adopted an amendment to Federal Rule of Evidence 609 to take effect on December 1, 1990, unless Congress by statute disapproved it. As explained in the report of the advisory

---

[34] E-mail from Lily Stevens (Senator Stevens's daughter) to Philip Frickey (April 5, 2006) (incorporating an email that Senator Stevens authorized his daughter to forward to Professor Frickey).

[35] Pursuant to the Federal Rules Enabling Act, amendments to the Federal Rules of Evidence are proposed to the Supreme Court by an advisory committee established by the Judicial Conference of the United States. The Court then notifies Congress of the amendment, including any modifications made by the Court. After a waiting period, the amendment takes effect unless, in the interim, Congress has nullified it by statute.

committee, the amendment "does not disturb the special balancing test for the criminal defendant who chooses to testify, but applies the general balancing test of Rule 403 to protect all other litigants against unfair impeachment of witnesses." (Rule 403 is quoted in the editors' footnote in the majority opinion in *Bock Laundry*.) The report noted that the advisory committee had approved the proposed amendment prior to *Bock Laundry*, but had held it pending the outcome of the case. Congress never disapproved the revised Rule 609(a), and it went into effect on December 1, 1990.

After this amendment, Rule 609 provided:

a.   General rule.—For purposes of attacking the credibility of a witness,

(1)   evidence that a witness other than an accused has been convicted of a crime shall be admitted, subject to Rule 403, if the crime was punishable by death or imprisonment in excess of one year under the law under which the witness was convicted, and evidence that an accused has been convicted of such a crime shall be admitted if the court determines that the probative value of admitting this evidence outweighs its prejudicial effect to the accused; and

(2)   evidence that any witness has been convicted of a crime shall be admitted if it involved dishonesty or false statement, regardless of the punishment.

Under this rule, Paul Green would have gotten a new trial. Why did the Court not reach that result in *Bock Laundry*? If the Court was required to deny Green relief in *Bock Laundry*, why did it have the power to veto Congress's intent a year later?

ANTONIN SCALIA, *A MATTER OF INTERPRETATION*
Summary and Selected Quotations (1997)*.

In this published version of his Tanner Lectures delivered at Princeton University, Justice Antonin Scalia presents his *textualist* philosophy of legal interpretation. He contends that law students (brainwashed by the first-year indoctrination in common-law methodology) and law professors (who do the brainwashing) tend to approach statutory interpretation as an exercise in applying legal authorities to new factual settings in a manner which yields both a fair result in the case and works toward a just and efficient general rule. Such an equitable common-law approach is not appropriate for construing statutes in a democracy, Justice Scalia argues, because it is fundamentally anti-democratic (pp. 9–14). A theme of the Tanner Lectures is that the common law has its place, but in a democracy it is more important that judges be constrained by, and held to, the legislatively enacted statutory law, than that they do "justice" in the individual case.

Should the lodestar for statutory interpretation, then, be legislative *intent*? Most assuredly not! "It is the *law* that governs, not the intent of the lawgiver. That seems to me the essence of the famous American ideal set forth in the Massachusetts constitution: A government of laws, not of men. Men may intend what they will; but it is only the laws that they enact which bind us" (p. 17).

Indeed, Justice Scalia argues that judges following a legislative-intent approach usually end up finding their own preferences in the statute, because "your best shot at figuring out what the legislature meant is to ask yourself what a wise and intelligent person *should* have meant; and that will surely bring you to the conclusion that the law means what you think it *ought* to mean—which is precisely how judges decide things under the common law" (p. 18). Note the implicit criticism of Hart and Sacks' theory, *supra*.

Justice Scalia then applies this critique to *Holy Trinity Church*. The Court interpreted the alien contract law contrary to its plain meaning because the Justices believed it inconsistent with legislative intent and purpose. Justice Scalia finds such an approach no more than invalid judicial lawmaking, although he would allow courts to correct scrivener's errors. "Well of course I think that the act was within the letter of the statute, and was therefore within the statute: end of case" (p. 20). "The text is the law, and it is the text which must be observed" (p. 22), says the author, citing Justice Holmes.

The apparent plain meaning of a statutory text must be the alpha and the omega in a judge's interpretation of a statute. The apparent plain meaning is that which an ordinary speaker of the English language—twin sibling to the common law's reasonable person—would draw from the statutory text. That is what textualism *is*. What it is *not*, according to Justice Scalia, is either "strict constructionism" (p. 23), which gives statutory words their stingiest ambit, nor "nihilism" (p. 24), which reads words to mean anything and everything. "A text should not be construed strictly, and it should not be construed leniently; it should be construed reasonably, to contain all that it fairly means" (p. 23).

Nor is textualism canonical, maintains Justice Scalia. The Tanner Lectures are skeptical of "presumptions and rules of construction that load the dice for or against a particular result" (p. 27), because they "increase the unpredictability, if not the arbitrariness of judicial decisions" (p. 28). "To the honest textualist, all of these preferential rules and presumptions are a lot of trouble," says Scalia (p. 28). On the other hand, canons such as the rule of lenity (ambiguous penal statutes should be construed in favor of the defendant) might have been "validated by sheer antiquity," and other canons (such as the requirement of a clear statement for congressional abrogation of state immunity) might be defensible as rule-of-thumb presumptions about normal meaning (p. 29).

Doctrinally, the most distinctive feature of Justice Scalia's legisprudence is an insistence that judges should almost never consult, and never rely on, the legislative history of a statute (pp. 29–37). Consistent with his concurring opinion in *Bock Laundry*, the Tanner Lectures identify several kinds of reasons for rejecting the relevance of legislative history. First, to the extent that legislative history is mined to determine legislative "intent," it must be rejected as a matter of constitutional principle. Legislative intent is not the proper goal for the statutory interpreter. This is a corollary of the rule of law: law must be objective and impersonal (the "government of laws"), not subjective and intentional ("and not of men"). This reason is related to Professor Radin's critique of legislative intent—and

Justice Scalia's second objection to legislative history is very much an elaboration of Professor Radin's criticism two generations earlier.

Even if intent were a proper criterion and it were constitutional to consider the views of legislative subgroups, the debating history preceding statutory enactment would not be reliable evidence of such intent. For most issues, there was no collective understanding; if there were such an understanding, public statements would often point in different directions, as some representatives would find it in their interest to plant misleading evidence. Indeed, the more courts have relied on legislative history, the less reliable it has become! "In earlier days, it was at least genuine and not contrived—a real part of the legislation's *history*, in the sense that it was part of the *development* of the bill, part of the attempt to inform and persuade those who voted. Nowadays, however, when it is universally known and expected that judges will resort to floor debates and (especially) committee reports as authoritative expressions of 'legislative intent,' affecting the courts rather than informing the Congress has become the primary purpose of the exercise" (p. 34).

Justice Scalia also claims that legislators themselves do not read the committee reports (pp. 32–33). Critics respond that legislators do not read the statutes they enact, either. Justice Scalia replies that the claim to authority of the two sources is different: a committee report's (supposed) authority is bottomed on its being evidence of intent about the law, and so knowledge about its contents would seem critical; the statutory text, on the other hand, is law itself, whether or not anyone read or understood it before enactment (pp. 34–35).

In response to this reply, critics say that committee reports are authoritative evidence because of conventions by which Congress has delegated most of the detail work to committees, with the implication being that the committee product is presumptively the work of Congress. Unconstitutional! says Justice Scalia.[36] "The legislative power is the power to make laws, not the power to make legislators. It is nondelegable. Congress can no more authorize one committee to 'fill in the details' of a particular law in a binding fashion than it can authorize a committee to enact minor laws. * * * That is the very essence of the separation of powers [and Article I, Section 7, requiring bicameral approval and presentment to the President]. The only conceivable basis for considering committee reports authoritative, therefore, is that they are a genuine indication of the will of the entire house—which, as I have been at pains to explain, they assuredly are not" (p. 35).

Earlier thinkers—like Dean Pound and Professor Landis—had called for courts to consider legislative history, so that judges might be constrained by the legislators' preferences. This was a laudable impulse, Justice Scalia concedes, but it has not worked. Legislative history has augmented rather than ameliorated the discretion of the willful judge, and this is Justice Scalia's third major quarrel with the use of legislative history. "In any major piece of legislation, the legislative history is extensive, and there is something for everybody. As Judge Harold

---

[36] The following argument is supported and elaborated in detail by John Manning, *Textualism as a Nondelegation Doctrine*, 97 Colum. L. Rev. 673 (1997), and Manning, *Second-Generation Textualism,* 98 Calif. L. Rev. 1287 (2010).

Leventhal used to say, the trick is to look over the heads of the crowd and pick out your friends" (p. 36).

NOTES ON THE NEW TEXTUALISM AS A THEORY OF INTERPRETATION

One might say that the new textualist approach demands that the statutory interpreter consider the text, the whole text, and nothing but the text. This description leaves many important issues unaddressed and may be an oversimplification. Consider the following nuances that have been flagged by scholars and by Justice Scalia himself.

1.   *When Is Meaning Ambiguous?* Surely the obvious question for a textualist theory is this: When is the meaning "plain"? When is there ambiguity? The plain meaning is that which an ordinary speaker of the English language—twin sibling to the common law's reasonable person—would draw from the statutory text. In another context, Justice Scalia has said that ordinary meaning requires judges to ask "whether you could use the word in that sense at a cocktail party without having people look at you funny." *Johnson v. United States*, 529 U.S. 694, 718 (2000) (Scalia, J., dissenting). Does a "cocktail party textualism" render statutory meaning too dependent on the perspective of the group a judge parties with?

Many words, phrases, and sentences can have more than one meaning to the ordinary speaker of the English language (fellow partiers will not "look at you funny"). Often Justice Scalia will still find a plain meaning, based on statutory context, including the whole act or even the entire U.S. Code. Thus, if Congress has used the same language elsewhere in the statute or even in other statutes, Justice Scalia will usually presume that the same language has the same ordinary meaning. E.g., *United Sav. Ass'n v. Timbers of Inwood Forest Assocs. Ltd.*, 484 U.S. 365, 371 (1988). Consider also his point in *Bock Laundry*, that the ordinary use of "defendant" typically assumes one is talking about a criminal defendant; that takes some edge off of Justice Scalia's willingness to give Rule 609(a)(1) a narrowing construction.

If a statute is genuinely ambiguous, one might wonder what a textualist should do. For Justice Scalia himself, the answer is to follow and reason from Supreme Court precedent construing open-textured laws like the Sherman Act *or* defer to reasonable agency interpretations of statutes *or* attribute a purpose to the statute and construe it according to such purpose. See Miranda McGowan, *Do as I Do, Not as I Say: An Empirical Investigation of Justice Scalia's Ordinary Meaning Method of Statutory Interpretation,* 78 Miss. L.J. 129 (2008). In an empirical analysis of Justice Scalia's dissents, McGowan reports that the Justice followed something other than an "ordinary" or "plain" meaning in most cases and, instead, followed judicial or administrative implications of purpose as the lodestar for construing statutes. Her conclusion is that Justice Scalia's textualism (even in his dissents, less constrained by the process of collecting a majority) contains just as much judicial discretion and judgment as does the approach traditionally followed by the Court.

2.   *Should the New Textualists Ever Examine Legislative History?* All of the new textualists reject the use of legislative history for its *authoritative value*: such materials have no legal authority. This is their strongest point, but it does not preclude consultation of legislative history for other kinds of reasons. Notice that Justice Scalia was willing to have a law clerk examine the legislative history of the 1974 amendment—but simply to confirm that no one in Congress realized that rule 609(a)(1),

as written, was going to have possibly unconstitutional consequences in civil cases. This might be the *confirmatory value* of legislative history. See James Brudney, *Confirmatory Legislative History*, 76 Brooklyn L. Rev. 901 (2011). If legislative history can be examined to determine whether Members of Congress "intended" or "thought of" an absurd or probably unconstitutional interpretation, why not look at it to confirm the apparent plain meaning of a statute? See *Carr v. United States*, 560 U.S. 438 (2010), where Justice Sotomayor deployed legislative history in precisely this way—but Justice Scalia refused to join that portion of her opinion.

As a general matter, why shouldn't legislative history be consulted for its *text-illuminating value*—namely, as evidence of how language was used at the time of the statute's enactment? One would expect new textualists who follow "original meaning" to consider legislative history carefully, for the same kinds of reasons they consider *The Federalist Papers* in determining how the public would have understood the "original meaning" of the language used in the Constitution. William Eskridge Jr., *Should the Supreme Court Read the* Federalist *But Not Statutory Legislative History?*, 66 Geo. Wash. L. Rev. 1301 (1998). Such legislative history would take the edge off of Justice Scalia's blistering critique of *Holy Trinity*. Scholars have reported that the legislative debates used the terms "labor and service" to refer only to manual work, and never to pastoral or brain work, and the term "lecturers" to refer to moral and religious speakers.[37] Justice Scalia responds that he only uses *The Federalist* to suggest how "the public" understood the Constitution at the time, and only as confirmatory evidence of original meaning. Antonin Scalia & John Manning, *A Dialogue on Statutory and Constitutional Interpretation,* 80 Geo. Wash. L. Rev. 1610, 1617–18 (2012). So why does he object so strongly to the Court's use of legislative debates to confirm the original public meaning of a statutory text?

Also, should the new textualists ever consider legislative history as a means to understand the structure of a statute? In his analysis of Justice Scalia's critique of *Holy Trinity*, William Eskridge Jr., *No Frills Textualism*, 119 Harv. L. Rev. 2041, 2065–70 (2006), argues that the legislative history indicates that §§ 1 and 4 of the Alien Contract Law were *in pari materia*, namely, they were understood at the time (1885) to cover the same class of aliens. This suggests that the more general terms in § 1 (persons performing labor or service of any kind) might be limited to the more particular ones in § 4 (mechanics, artisans, and laborers). Justice Scalia's book never mentions § 4. Is there a possibility that he would consider legislative materials to reveal statutory structure?

3.   *Should the New Textualists Recognize an Absurd Results Rule?* Justice Scalia's concurring opinion in *Bock Laundry* rests on the absurdity of following Rule 609(a)(1) as written. For other examples where Justice Scalia has emphasized absurdity as a guide to statutory text, see *Brown v. Plata*, 131 S.Ct.1910, 1950–51 (2011) (Scalia, J., dissenting in part because the majority's interpretation of the statute is "absurd" and represents a "judicial travesty"); Jane Schacter, *Text or Consequences?*, 76 Brooklyn L. Rev. 1007 (2011) (collecting pre-*Plata* examples from Justice Scalia's opinions).

---

[37] Carol Chomsky, *Unlocking the Mysteries of* Holy Trinity: *Spirit, Letter, and History in Statutory Interpretation*, 100 Colum. L. Rev. 901 (2000); William Eskridge Jr., *Textualism, The Unknown Ideal?*, 96 Mich. L. Rev. 1509 (1998) (reviewing Scalia's book and examining the original meaning of "labor or service" in 1885); Victoria Nourse, *Decision Theory and Legislative Intent* (draft 2014) (examining congressional understanding of "lecturers" as speakers on moral and religious topics).

Recognizing an absurd results exception to the plain meaning rule has its risks: what is absurd to Justice Scalia might be debatable or even reasonable to Justice Kennedy and might be good policy to Justice Ginsburg. (Indeed, that was the case in *Brown v. Plata*, where five Justices approved an injunction requiring a state to reduce its prison population because it created cruel and unusual conditions for mentally and physically disabled inmates. The majority considered the injunction necessary to correct constitutional violations—while the dissenters considered it "absurd" to protect prisoners against probable harm through a "structural" injunction.)

For this reason, leading textualist theorists argue that there should *not* be an "absurd results" exception to the plain meaning rule. See John Nagle, *Textualism's Exceptions,* Issues in Legal Scholarship: Dynamic Statutory Interpretation (2002): Article 15, available at http://www.bepress.com/ils/iss3/art15; John Manning, *The Absurdity Doctrine,* 116 Harv. L. Rev. 2387 (2003). Their argument is that the normative rule of law advantages of textualism would be compromised by a subjective absurd-results exception: because "absurdity" is in the mind of the beholder, the law would lose some degree of predictability and objectivity. Should Justice Scalia abandon his support for the absurd results exception? For an argument that normative judgments pervade his statutory jurisprudence, see Schacter, *supra.*

4.   *On the Whole, Does the New Textualism "Constrain" Judicial Decisionmaking Better Than Other Methodologies?* Justice Scalia is certain that his method *does* constrain judges and produces more predictable, less ideological decisions. See Antonin Scalia & Bryan Garner, *Reading Law* (2013). Legal academics who have studied the matter empirically do not agree, finding either that textualism constrains no more than other methodologies, see Frank Cross, *The Theory and Practice of Statutory Interpretation* 177–79 (2009), or that it actually constrains *less* than methodologies that consider more context. See James Brudney & Corey Ditslear, *Liberal Justices' Reliance on Legislative History: Principle, Strategy, and the Scalia Effect*, 29 Berkeley J. Emp. & Lab. L. 117 (2008). As you read the remaining statutory decisions in this book, you will have an opportunity to decide for yourself whether the new textualism constrains interpreters. Indeed, that is the very puzzle posed in the following Problem.

PROBLEM APPLYING THE NEW TEXUALISM TO THE VOTING RIGHTS ACT, AS AMENDED 1982

Problem 6–7. From his book, we know that Justice Scalia would have dissented in *Holy Trinity Church.* There is little doubt he would have voted with the majority in *TVA* and *Griffin*—but he would have reached the same result through a different path of reasoning. Now consider the Voting Rights Act of 1965, as amended in 1982, which invalidates state electoral districts or rules that have a disparate impact on racial minorities. For example, in the South, at-large elections were an effective way of excluding candidates of color from elected office, because the majority white electorate would vote against any such candidate. In 1980, the Supreme Court had ruled that § 2 did not police electoral arrangements that were race-neutral and not motivated by racial exclusionary motives (which are hard to prove). To enable minority voters to challenge electoral arrangements, like at-large elections, that were not race-based on their face but that had questionable race-based effects, § 2 was amended in 1982 to provide as follows:

(a) No voting qualification or prerequisite to voting or standard, practice, or procedure shall be imposed or applied by any State or political subdivision in a manner which results in a denial or abridgement of the right of any citizen of the United States to vote on account of race or color, or in contravention of the guarantees set forth in section 4(f)(2), as provided in subsection (b).

(b) A violation of subsection (a) is established if, based on the totality of circumstances, it is shown that the political processes leading to nomination or election in the State or political subdivision are not equally open to participation by members of a class of citizens protected by subsection (a) in that its members have less opportunity than other members of the electorate to participate in the political process and to elect representatives of their choice. The extent to which members of a protected class have been elected to office in the State or political subdivision is one circumstance which may be considered: *Provided,* That nothing in this section establishes a right to have members of a protected class elected in numbers equal to their proportion in the population.

Does § 2 apply to state elections for judges? (Unlike the federal system, judges are popularly elected in many states.) How would a new textualist analyze the foregoing statutory text? Is there a plain meaning? If not, how should ambiguities be resolved? Would it make a difference to you if you knew that § 2 was applied to judicial elections before the Voting Rights Act was amended in 1982? Jot down your answer now.

Chisom v. Roemer
501 U.S. 380 (1991).

Five of the seven members of the Louisiana Supreme Court are elected from single-member districts, each of which consists of a number of parishes (counties). The other two are elected from one multimember district. In three of the four parishes in this multimember district, more than three-fourths of the registered voters are white. In the fourth parish in the multimember district, Orleans Parish, which contains about half of the population of the multimember district and has about half the registered voters in the district, more than one-half of the registered voters are African American. A class of African American registered voters in Orleans Parish brought this action, contending that the use of the multimember district diluted the voting strength of the minority community in violation of § 2 of the Voting Rights Act, as amended in 1982. Following circuit precedent, the lower court ruled that § 2 was inapplicable to judicial elections.

Section 2 as enacted in 1965 provided: "No voting qualification or prerequisite to voting, or standard, practice, or procedure shall be imposed or applied by any State or political subdivision to deny or abridge the right of any citizen of the United States to vote on account of race or color." In *Mobile v. Bolden*, 446 U.S. 55, 60–61 (1980), the Supreme Court interpreted § 2 to be inapplicable when a jurisdiction's voting rules are race-neutral, even if they have race-based effects. The Voting Rights Act Amendments of 1982 revised § 2, quoted in Problem 6–7, above.

Writing for the Court, **Justice Stevens** ruled that § 2 applied to judicial elections. "Section 2(a) adopts a results test, thus providing that proof of discriminatory intent is no longer necessary to establish *any* violation of the section. Section 2(b) provides guidance about how the results test is to be applied." Louisiana argued that Congress' choice of the word "representatives" in the phrase "have less opportunity than other members of the electorate to participate in the political process and to elect representatives of their choice" in § 2(b) is evidence of congressional intent to exclude vote dilution claims involving judicial elections from the coverage of § 2. The Justices were convinced that "if Congress had such an intent, Congress would have made it explicit in the statute, or at least some of the Members would have identified or mentioned it at some point in the unusually extensive legislative history of the 1982 amendment.[23]

The lower court assumed that § 2 provides two distinct types of protection for minority voters—it protects their opportunity "to participate in the political process" and their opportunity "to elect representatives of their choice." Although the majority interpreted "representatives" as a word of limitation, it assumed that the word eliminated judicial elections only from the latter protection, without affecting the former. Justice Stevens rejected the court's bifurcation: "Any abridgement of the opportunity of members of a protected class to participate in the political process inevitably impairs their ability to influence the outcome of an election. * * * The statute does not create two separate and distinct rights. Subsection (a) covers every application of a qualification, standard, practice, or procedure that results in a denial or abridgement of '*the right*' to vote. The singular form is also used in subsection (b) when referring to an injury to members of the protected class who have less 'opportunity' than others 'to participate in the political process *and* to elect representatives of their choice.' 42 U.S.C. § 1973 (emphasis added). It would distort the plain meaning of the sentence to substitute the word 'or' for the word 'and.' Such radical surgery would be required to separate the opportunity to participate from the opportunity to elect."

The lower court ruled that the term "representatives" was used to extend § 2 coverage to executive officials, but not to judges. "We think, however, that the better reading of the word 'representatives' describes the winners of representative, popular elections. If executive officers, such as prosecutors, sheriffs, state attorneys general, and state treasurers, can be considered 'representatives' simply because they are chosen by popular election, then the same reasoning should apply to elected judges.

The lower court reasoned that, ideally, judges are not "representatives" in the way governors and legislators are. The Framers of Article III certainly saw matters that way—but Louisiana has made a different choice. "The fundamental tension between the ideal character of the judicial office and the real world of electoral politics cannot be resolved by crediting judges with total indifference to the popular will while simultaneously requiring them to run for elected office. When each of several members of a court must be a resident of a separate district, and must be elected by the voters of that district, it seems both reasonable and realistic to characterize the winners as representatives of that district. * * * Louisiana could, of course, exclude its judiciary from the coverage of the Voting Rights Act by changing to a system in which judges are appointed, and in that way, it could enable its judges to be indifferent to popular opinion. The reasons why Louisiana has chosen otherwise are precisely the reasons why

---

[23] [Justice Stevens, for the Court:] Congress' silence in this regard can be likened to the dog that did not bark. See A. Doyle, Silver Blaze, in The Complete Sherlock Holmes 335 (1927). Cf. *Harrison v. PPG Industries, Inc.*, 446 U.S. 578, 602 (1980) (Rehnquist, J., dissenting) ("In a case where the construction of legislative language such as this makes so sweeping and so relatively unorthodox a change as that made here, I think judges as well as detectives may take into consideration the fact that a watchdog did not bark in the night.").

it is appropriate for § 2, as well as § 5, of the Voting Rights Act to continue to apply to its judicial elections.

"The close connection between § 2 and § 5 further undermines respondents' view that judicial elections should not be covered under § 2. Section 5 requires certain States to submit changes in their voting procedures to the District Court of the District of Columbia or to the Attorney General for preclearance. Section 5 uses language similar to that of § 2 in defining prohibited practices: 'any voting qualification or prerequisite to voting, or standard, practice, or procedure with respect to voting.' This Court has already held that § 5 applies to judicial elections. *Clark v. Roemer*, 500 U.S. 646 (1991). If § 2 did not apply to judicial elections, a State covered by § 5 would be precluded from implementing a new voting procedure having discriminatory effects with respect to judicial elections, whereas a similarly discriminatory system already in place could not be challenged under § 2. It is unlikely that Congress intended such an anomalous result."

Finally, Congress enacted the Voting Rights Act of 1965 for the broad remedial purpose of "rid[ding] the country of racial discrimination in voting." *South Carolina v. Katzenbach*, 383 U.S. 301, 315 (1966). In *Allen v. State Board of Elections*, 393 U.S. 544, 567 (1969), the Court said that the Act should be interpreted in a manner that provides "the broadest possible scope" in combatting racial discrimination. Concluded Justice Stevens: "Congress amended the Act in 1982 in order to relieve plaintiffs of the burden of proving discriminatory intent, after a plurality of this Court had concluded that the original Act, like the Fifteenth Amendment, contained such a requirement. See *Mobile v. Bolden*. Thus, Congress made clear that a violation of § 2 could be established by proof of discriminatory results alone. It is difficult to believe that Congress, in an express effort to broaden the protection afforded by the Voting Rights Act, withdrew, without comment, an important category of elections from that protection. Today we reject such an anomalous view and hold that state judicial elections are included within the ambit of § 2 as amended."

In dissent, **Justice Scalia** (joined by Chief Justice Rehnquist and Justice Kennedy) started with this: "Section 2 of the Voting Rights Act is not some all-purpose weapon for well-intentioned judges to wield as they please in the battle against discrimination. It is a statute. I thought we had adopted a regular method for interpreting the meaning of language in a statute: first, find the ordinary meaning of the language in its textual context; and second, using established canons of construction, ask whether there is any clear indication that some permissible meaning other than the ordinary one applies. If not—and especially if a good reason for the ordinary meaning appears plain—we apply that ordinary meaning.

"Today, however, the Court adopts a method quite out of accord with that usual practice. It begins not with what the statute says, but with an expectation about what the statute must mean absent particular phenomena ('*we are convinced* that if Congress had . . . an intent [to exclude judges] Congress would have made it explicit in the statute, or at least some of the Members would have identified or mentioned it at some point in the unusually extensive legislative history'); and the Court then interprets the words of the statute to fulfill its expectation. Finding nothing in the legislative history affirming that judges were excluded from the coverage of § 2, the Court gives the phrase 'to elect representatives' the quite extraordinary meaning that covers the election of judges.

"As method, this is just backwards, and however much we may be attracted by the result it produces in a particular case, we should in every case resist it. Our job begins with a text that Congress has passed and the President has signed. We are to read the words of that text as any ordinary Member of Congress would have read them, see Holmes, The Theory of Legal Interpretation, 12 Harv. L. Rev. 417 (1899), and apply the meaning so determined. In my view, that reading reveals that § 2 extends to vote dilution claims for the elections of representatives only, and judges are not representatives."

Although the 1965 VRA applied to all elections, including judicial ones, "[t]he 1982 amendments, however, radically transformed the Act. As currently written, the statute proscribes intentional discrimination only if it has a discriminatory effect, but proscribes practices with discriminatory effect whether or not intentional. This new 'results' criterion provides a powerful, albeit sometimes blunt, weapon with which to attack even the most subtle forms of discrimination. The question we confront here is how broadly the new remedy applies. The foundation of the Court's analysis, the itinerary for its journey in the wrong direction, is the following statement: 'It is difficult to believe that Congress, in an express effort to broaden the protection afforded by the Voting Rights Act, withdrew, without comment, an important category of elections from that protection.' There are two things wrong with this. First is the notion that Congress cannot be credited with having achieved anything of major importance by simply saying it, in ordinary language, in the text of a statute, 'without comment' in the legislative history. As the Court colorfully puts it, if the dog of legislative history has not barked nothing of great significance can have transpired. Apart from the questionable wisdom of assuming that dogs will bark when something important is happening, see 1 T. Livius, The History of Rome 411–413 (1892) (D. Spillan translation), we have forcefully and explicitly rejected the Conan Doyle approach to statutory construction in the past. See *Harrison v. PPG Industries, Inc.*, 446 U.S. 578, 592 (1980) ('In ascertaining the meaning of a statute, a court cannot, in the manner of Sherlock Holmes, pursue the theory of the dog that did not bark'). We are here to apply the statute, not legislative history, and certainly not the absence of legislative history. Statutes are the law though sleeping dogs lie."

Justice Scalia agreed with the lower court that § 2 created two separate rights for protected classes: (1) "to participate in the political process" and (2) "to elect representatives of their choice." On this reading, judicial elections are subject to the first right, but not the second because judges are not "representatives." The Court, petitioners, and petitioners' *amici* have labored mightily to establish that there is *a* meaning of 'representatives' that would include judges, and no doubt there is. But our job is not to scavenge the world of English usage to discover whether there is any possible meaning of 'representatives' which suits our preconception that the statute includes judges; our job is to determine whether the *ordinary* meaning includes them, and if it does not, to ask whether there is any solid indication in the text or structure of the statute that something other than ordinary meaning was intended.

"There is little doubt that the ordinary meaning of 'representatives' does not include judges, see Webster's Second New International Dictionary 2114 (1950). The Court's feeble argument to the contrary is that 'representatives' means those who 'are chosen by popular election.' On that hypothesis, the fan-elected members of the baseball All-Star teams are 'representatives'—hardly a common, if even a permissible, usage.

Surely the word 'representative' connotes one who is not only *elected by* the people, but who also, at a minimum, *acts on behalf of* the people. Judges do that in a sense—but not in the ordinary sense. As the captions of the pleadings in some States still display, it is the prosecutor who represents "the People"; the judge represents the Law—which often requires him to rule against the People. It is precisely because we do not *ordinarily* conceive of judges as representatives that we held judges not within the Fourteenth Amendment's requirement of 'one person, one vote.' *Wells v. Edwards*, 347 F.Supp. 453 (MD La.1972), aff'd, 409 U.S. 1095 (1973). The point is not that a State could not make judges in some senses representative, or that all judges must be conceived of in the Article III mold, but rather, that giving 'representatives' its ordinary meaning, the ordinary speaker in 1982 would not have applied the word to judges, see Holmes, The Theory of Legal Interpretation, 12 Harv. L. Rev. 417 (1899). It remains only to ask whether there is good indication that ordinary meaning does not apply." Justice Scalia answered "no" to that question.

Justice Scalia also observed that the principle of "one person, one vote" did not apply to the election of judges, *Wells v. Edwards*, 347 F.Supp. 453 (MD La. 1972), aff'd, 409 U.S. 1095 (1973). If Congress was making vote dilution claims available with respect to the election of judges, it was, for the first time, extending that remedy to a context in which "one person, one vote" did not apply. *That* would have been a significant change in the law, and given the need to identify some other baseline for computing "dilution," *that* is a matter which those who believe in barking dogs should be astounded to find unmentioned in the legislative history. If "representatives" is given its normal meaning, on the other hand, there is no change in the law (except elimination of the intent requirement) and the silence is entirely understandable.

"The Court transforms the meaning of § 2, not because the ordinary meaning is irrational, or inconsistent with other parts of the statute, see, *e.g., Green v. Bock Laundry; Public Citizen v. Department of Justice* (Kennedy, J., concurring in the judgment), but because it does not fit the Court's conception of what Congress must have had in mind. When we adopt a method that psychoanalyzes Congress rather than reads its laws, when we employ a tinkerer's toolbox, we do great harm. Not only do we reach the wrong result with respect to the statute at hand, but we poison the well of future legislation, depriving legislators of the assurance that ordinary terms, used in an ordinary context, will be given a predictable meaning. Our highest responsibility in the field of statutory construction is to read the laws in a consistent way, giving Congress a sure means by which it may work the people's will. We have ignored that responsibility today."

WEST VIRGINIA UNIVERSITY HOSPITALS V. CASEY

Supreme Court of the United States, 1991
499 U.S. 83, 111 S.Ct. 1138, 113 L.Ed.2d 68.

[Excerpted in Chapter 7, § 1C]

NOTES ON CHISOM, CASEY, AND THE COURT'S TEXTUALIST TRAJECTORY

1. *The Rise of the New Textualism, 1987–95, and Its Relationship to the Plain Meaning Rule.* The Court's practice changed after Justice Scalia's appointment. After

1986, the Court's statutory opinions more often found a "plain meaning," less often examined legislative history to confirm the existence of a plain meaning, and relied less often on legislative history to interpret a statute against what the Court felt was its plain meaning. The Justices' opinions also have tended to be more dogmatic about whether there is any ambiguity in statutes; the Court was more likely to find a plain meaning in the 1990s than it was before 1986.[38] As in *Casey*, Justice Scalia's own opinions set forth and defended the precepts of the new textualism, often with Justice Stevens in dissent (also as in *Casey*). E.g., *United States v. Nordic Village*, 503 U.S. 30 (1992); *Finley v. United States*, 490 U.S. 545 (1989).

The relationship between the new textualism and the old plain meaning rule is evident, but they are not the same thing. Justice Scalia's formulation of textualism at the beginning of his *Chisom* dissent, as well as his discussion in *A Matter of Interpretation*, stresses the "ordinary meaning" or "reasonable meaning" of statutory text. In his view, legislative history should never trump such ordinary meaning. In contrast, the old plain meaning rule, as exemplified by *Caminetti* (§ 1 of this chapter), operated as an exclusionary rule concerning the use of legislative history: if the statutory text was "plain," one could not consult legislative history; if the statutory text was ambiguous, legislative history was fair game. The softer approach to plain meaning in *TVA v. Hill* and *Griffin* was even less confining, stating merely that a statutory plain meaning was presumptively the interpretation to be given to the statute, but legislative history could be consulted to confirm that understanding (and in a rare case in which the legislative history conclusively demonstrated that the textual plain meaning was not the appropriate interpretation, the plain meaning could be jettisoned).

In the post-1986 period, "plain meaning" remains an ambiguous term. What we understand Justice Scalia to mean by "plain meaning" is the best (most coherent) textual understanding that emerges after close textual analysis, which then makes the result in the case plain on his terms—not merely the relatively rare "plain meaning" that leaps off the page to the experienced judge. It is regrettable that in some cases— both federal and state—judges have used the term "plain meaning" loosely, sometimes to mean a textual interpretation that is pretty obvious on the face of the statute (say, 90/10 clear) and sometimes to mean something similar to Justice Scalia's expression of the best textual understanding that emerges from close analysis of statutory provisions that, at the outset, may have seemed ambiguous, confusing, or at least complicated. The former approach to plain meaning is akin to a pretty literal approach to the face of the statute; the latter approach of Justice Scalia sees statutory interpretation to be something like a word puzzle, capable of being solved in almost all cases with a best answer emerging.

Although the Court's practice was influenced by the new textualism in the first few years of Justice Scalia's membership, the Court has never completely accepted its tenets. In *Wisconsin Public Intervenor v. Mortier*, 501 U.S. 597, 610 n.4 (1991), all of the other Justices joined a footnote explicitly rejecting Justice Scalia's insistence that legislative history is irrelevant to proper statutory interpretation. In many cases, the Court still considers legislative background to statutes and is open to understanding a statute from the perspective of the legislators who enacted it. Often such decisions are

---

[38] For empirical examinations of the Supreme Court's relatively textualist methodology, see Frank Cross, *The Theory and Practice of Statutory Interpretation* (2009) (reporting that the Court increasingly relies on textual plain meanings, which do not meaningfully constrain the Justices); David Law, *Law versus Ideology: The Supreme Court and the Use of Legislative History*, 51 Wm. & Mary L. Rev. 1653 (2010).

written by Justices Stevens or Souter, with Justice Scalia dissenting, as in *Chisom*, or concurring only in the judgment, as in *Bock Laundry*. E.g., *Landgraf v. USI Film Products*, 511 U.S. 244 (1994); *American Red Cross v. S.G.*, 505 U.S. 247 (1992). For recent examples of this phenomenon, see *Samantar v. Yousuf*, 560 U.S. 305 (2010); *Carr v. United States*, 560 U.S. 438 (2010).

2. *1995 Onward.* According to Charles Tiefer, *The Reconceptualization of Legislative History in the Supreme Court*, 2000 Wis. L. Rev. 205, the new textualism is not only past its peak, but its strong claims were rejected by the Court in the 1990s.[39] Since 1995, the Court has often followed the approach pressed by Justice Breyer in *The Uses of Legislative History*, 65 S. Cal. L. Rev. 845 (1992) and by Justice Stevens in *Chisom* and his *Casey* dissent—what Tiefer calls "institutional legislative history."

Under the institutional approach, the Court treats the legislative process as a group engaged in coordinated purposive action, in which the group relies on the guidance and judgment of committees and ratifies their publicly presented understandings when the group takes action (i.e., enacts statutes). Hence, statutory interpretation is neither an effort to imaginatively reconstruct a collective intent nor to divine the objective meaning the statutory text would have had when adopted, but instead is an effort to carry out the ongoing institutional project along the lines laid out in the public presentations of those institutional actors charged with developing the original statute. Note the close connection between the institutionalist approach espoused by Justices Stevens and Breyer, and the legal process theory of Professors Hart and Sacks.

3. *So Where Is the Court's Methodology Now?* First, and foremost, the text is now, more than it was 30 years ago, the central inquiry at the Supreme Court level and in other courts that are now following the Supreme Court's lead. A brief that starts off with, "The statute means thus-and-so because it says so in the committee report," is asking for trouble. Both advice and advocacy should start with the statutory text: "The statute means thus-and-so because that is its plain meaning," "because that is the meaning the structure of the statute supports," or "because this statute uses more narrow language than Congress purposefully used in other statutes."

Because the Court frequently uses the dictionary to provide meaning to key statutory terms, the advocate should incorporate this methodology as well. The lexicon has become a fortress for the effective advocate.[40] Although there are many theoretical problems with relying upon dictionaries to interpret statutory texts,[41] they are a fertile resource for advocates to support a particular position. In this respect, consider Justice

---

[39] In addition, see James Brudney & Corey Ditslear, *The Decline and Fall of Legislative History? Patterns of Supreme Court Reliance in the Burger and Rehnquist Eras*, 89 Judicature 220 (2006); Jonathan Molot, *The Rise and Fall of Textualism*, 106 Colum. L. Rev. 1 (2006); Lawrence Solan, *Learning Our Limits: The Decline of Textualism in Statutory Cases*, 1997 Wis. L. Rev. 235.

[40] Samuel Thumma & Jeffrey Kirchmeier, *The Lexicon Has Become a Fortress: The United States Supreme Court's Use of Dictionaries*, 47 Buff. L. Rev. 227 (1999), and *Scaling the Lexicon Fortress: The United States Supreme Court's Use of Dictionaries in the Twenty-First Century*, 94 Marq. L. Rev. 77 (2010). See also James Brudney & Lawrence Baum, *Oasis or Mirage: The Supreme Court's Thirst for Dictionaries in the Rehnquist and Roberts Eras*, 55 William & Mary L. Rev. 483 (2013).

[41] Thus, dictionaries (1) are not part of the text of a statute and might seem even further removed from it than legislative history; (2) are necessarily conservative, in the sense of reflecting past English usage rather than emerging usage; (3) usually permit judicial cherry-picking, because there are hundreds of dictionaries in print or on-line, with each dictionary offering several definitions. See Ellen Aprill, *The Law of the Word: Dictionary Shopping in the Supreme Court*, 30 Ariz. St. L.J. 275 (1998); Brudney & Baum, *Oasis or Mirage*.

Scalia's conclusion in *Chisom*, based on a dictionary, that the customary usage of "representative" excludes elected judges. Consult your own dictionary, or several: Can you find a definition of "representative" that supports the majority's holding in *Chisom*?

Second, the "contextual" evidence the Court is interested in is now statutory context more than just historical context. Arguments that your position is more consistent with other parts of the same statute are more likely to be winning arguments than those based upon legislative history. As *Casey* indicates, the Court today goes beyond the "whole act" rule to something like a "whole code" rule, searching the United States Code for guidance on the usage of key statutory terms and phrases. For an example, consider *Arlington Central School District v. Murphy*, 548 U.S. 291 (2006), where the Court narrowly construed the fee-shifting provision of a 1986 education-rights statute following the same methodology as *Casey*, over strong contrary legislative history and a powerful argument based on the statutory structure (both developed by Justice Breyer's dissenting opinion).

Third, the Court will still look at other kinds of contextual evidence, especially the public law landscape. If a statute seems to require an odd result (as in *Bock Laundry*), the Court will interrogate the background materials to find out why. If a statute overrides judicial or agency decisions (as in *Chisom*), the Court will usually be responsive to Congress's concerns. When the Justices are themselves divided as to the statute's "plain meaning" (as in *Weber*), at least some of them will examine the statute's background to figure out how the typical legislator would have read the statute—or to confirm the apparent plain meaning derived from the statutory text and structure. See *Carr v. United States*, 560 U.S. 438 (2010) (Sotomayor, J., relying on legislative history to confirm plain meaning, triggering a Scalia, J., concurring opinion rejecting that part of the Court's opinion). For these reasons, it remains important to research and brief the legislative history thoroughly. The effective advocate will appreciate that the presence of such materials in the briefs may influence the outcome more than the opinion in the case will indicate.[42]

B. ECONOMIC THEORIES OF STATUTORY INTERPRETATION

Economic theory assumes that individuals are rational actors who seek to maximize their utilities through actions reasonably designed to do so. Institutions, too, may be rational actors, with their preferences usually determined by the views of the median senator, representative, or judge. Most purely economic theorizing is descriptive, helping us predict the behavior of groups of real people. Consider a simple example of how purely descriptive economic theorizing can enrich your thinking about statutory interpretation.

---

[42] Consider the comments of Judge A. Raymond Randolph of the United States Court of Appeals for the District of Columbia Circuit, in *Dictionaries, Plain Meaning, and Context in Statutory Interpretation*, 17 Harv. J.L. & Pub. Pol'y 71, 76 (1994):

> * * * Nearly every brief I see in cases involving issues of statutory construction contains a discourse on legislative history. This is a wise precaution on the part of appellate advocates. Counsel can never be sure that the court will find the words plain, and stop there. To be safe, in the event the court takes two steps instead of one, counsel must include a backup argument addressing the meaning of the statute in light of the legislative history. Judges read those briefs from cover to cover, or at least they are supposed to. I do. Somewhere during the reading, preliminary views begin to form. When the reading is done and the case has been analyzed and argued, how can it be said that the judge turned to the legislative history only after finding the statutory language ambiguous? The judge himself often cannot identify exactly when his perception of the words actually jelled. * * *

For most of us, law is prediction of the rules that interacting government institutions will apply to your facts. We ask the IRS, read the newspaper, call a government clerk, note the posted speed limit, or just absorb it by osmosis. Law as prediction also entails evolution through sequential institutional interaction.[43] Congress enacts statutes, agencies interpret and apply those statutes, the judiciary sometimes reviews agency actions and interpretations, and Congress periodically considers legislation updating the law or overriding errant interpretations.[44] A consequence of this sequence is that each institution has trumping power. The agency can undo some legislative bargains by stingy enforcement, the Supreme Court can overturn the agency's application, and Congress can override the Court or the agency. Groups press for changes in the law by working the institution most favorable to their interests and then seeking to protect it against trumping by the next institution down the line.

Most of the time, law is in a *stable equilibrium*: none of the institutions wants to change the rule, in part because if any makes that effort it may be overridden by the next institution in the chain. As a weak political actor ("the least dangerous branch"), the Supreme Court usually locates and applies that political equilibrium on high-visibility issues of public law, as it did in the affirmative action cases (*Weber* and *Johnson*) in Chapter 1, § 3. On the other hand, the equilibrium is often potentially unstable: one actor may be able to change the rule without being overridden. This is what happened in *Griffin*, where the Supreme Court imposed its rule-of-law values on a statute that apparently was understood for decades to embody a less generous compensation rule—and the issue was too divisive (seafaring unions liking the Court's result, companies not) for Congress to override.

Political scientists maintain that judges often read their substantive values into statutes.[45] As Deborah Widiss has documented, in politicized areas of law such as workplace discrimination, the Roberts Court gives congressional overrides a narrow reading and expansively follows the Court's own repudiated "shadow precedents."[46] For example, in *Lorance v. AT & T Technologies, Inc.,* 490 U.S. 500

---

[43] The model that follows was developed in William Eskridge Jr. & Philip Frickey, *The Supreme Court, 1993 Term—Foreword: Law as Equilibrium*, 108 Harv. L. Rev. 26 (1994). For a different interactive model attempting to explain why interpretive methodology changes over time, see Adrian Vermeule, *The Cycles of Statutory Interpretation*, 68 U. Chi. L. Rev. 149 (2001). Vermeule suggests that legislators and judges develop inconsistent expectations of each other and engage in sequential interaction to affect the other's behavior—for example, judges consult legislative history; legislators notice and abuse the process by skewing the legislative history to affect interpretation; judges notice and stop using legislative history; legislators notice and stop abusing it; judges then start consulting the legislative history once again, because it seems uncontaminated.

[44] See Jeb Barnes, *Overruled? Legislative Overrides, Pluralism, and Contemporary Court-Congress Relations* (2004); Matthew Christiansen & William Eskridge Jr., *Congressional Overrides of Supreme Court Statutory Interpretation Decisions, 1967–2011*, 92 Tex. L. Rev. 1317 (2014); Richard Hasen, *End of the Dialogue? Political Polarization, the Supreme Court, and Congress*, 86 S. Cal. L. Rev. 205 (2013); Nancy Staudt et al., *Judicial Decisions as Legislation: Congressional Oversight of Supreme Court Tax Cases, 1954–2005*, 82 N.Y.U. L. Rev. 1340 (2007).

[45] E.g., Cross, *Practice of Statutory Interpretation,* 159–79; Lee Epstein & Jack Knight, *The Choices Justices Make* (1998); Jeffrey Segal & Albert Cover, *Ideological Values and the Votes of U.S. Supreme Court Justices*, 83 Am. Pol. Sci. Rev. 557 (1989); Jeffrey Segal, *Separation-of-Powers Games in the Positive Theory of Congress and Courts,* 91 Am. Pol. Sci. Rev. 28–43 (1997).

[46] See Deborah Widiss, *Shadow Precedents and the Separation of Powers: Statutory Interpretation of Congressional Overrides*, 84 Notre Dame L. Rev. 511 (2009), and Widiss, *Undermining Congressional Overrides: The Hydra Problem in Statutory Interpretation*, 90 Tex. L. Rev. 859 (2012).

(1989), the Court ruled that women complaining of seniority rules had to file complaints with the EEOC within 180 or 300 days after the rules went into effect. After concluding that the Court should have followed a more liberal line of Title VII limitations precedents, Congress overrode *Lorance* in the 1991 Civil Rights Act, Pub. L. No. 102–166, § 112, which created a more liberal limitations period for seniority claims, 42 U.S.C. § 2000e–5(e)(2). The next case involved female employees who were paid unequal salaries but did not know precisely what male employees were paid—yet the Court imposed a strict limitations period on these plaintiffs as well, in *Ledbetter v. Goodyear Tire & Rubber Co.*, 550 U.S. 618 (2007). The *Ledbetter* majority not only declined to apply the override, as it just covered seniority claims, but followed *Lorance* as binding precedent—and *relied on* the override as evidence that Congress, when it liberalized the limitations period for seniority claims, "intended" to leave strict limitations periods in place everywhere else in Title VII. *Id.* at 627 n.2. Dissenting Justices objected that the Court should have followed its more forgiving precedents and that *Ledbetter*, where the employees were highly unlikely to have known about the pay differentials, was a stronger case than *Lorance* had been. Congress angrily overrode *Ledbetter* with the Lilly Ledbetter Fair Pay Act of 2009, P.L. 111–2, but the Court continues to hand down decisions applying "shadow precedents" and narrowly construing Title VII overrides. E.g., *University of Texas Southwestern Medical Center v. Nassar*, 133 S.Ct. 2517 (2013).

Some of these descriptive points, such as the political science view that judges mainly vote their substantive preferences, are controversial. E.g., Connor Raso & William Eskridge Jr., Chevron *as a Canon, Not a Precedent: An Empirical Study of What Motivates Justices in Agency Deference Cases*, 110 Colum. L. Rev. 1727 (2010) (finding evidence that rule of law values motivate the Court at least as much as substantive preferences, even in cases like *Ledbetter*). You might maintain a healthy skepticism about the predictive claims of economics-based theories. In the hands of legal scholars and judges, economics-based thinking is more typically harnessed for some kind of normative point. In this part of the chapter, we shall explore three different kinds of normative contributions law and economics might make to statutory interpretation. They draw from economists' *ex ante* approach to rules, from public choice theory, and from cost-benefit analysis.

1. *Ex Ante* Approaches to the Debate Between Textualists and Contextualists

Most people respond to "hard cases" from an *ex post* point of view: this result is unfair to or visits needless hardship upon a sympathetic claimant. From an economics point of view, hard cases make bad law because they invite *ex post* decisionmaking, where the judge creates rules and standards that are fair in the particular case—but often have excessive social costs for a society that then has to apply the rule in future interactions and lawsuits. In law generally, and statutory interpretation particularly, economic theory would valorize an *ex ante* perspective: evaluate a decision or rule based on whether it sets up a legal directive that will be good for the average case and provides proper incentives for the citizenry—and not because you like its result in a particular case. The same kind of thinking can apply to general theories. What could be more reasonable than Hart and Sacks's notion that interpreters should apply statutes to carry out admirable public-regarding purposes? Defending the Hart and Sacks approach from an *ex ante* perspective is Jonathan Macey, *Promoting Public-Regarding Legislation Through Statutory Interpretation: An Interest Group Model*, 86 Colum. L. Rev. 223 (1986). Macey argues that interpreting statutes to carry out their *announced* public-regarding purposes is a good way for judges to maintain a minimal level of honesty in the legislative process: *knowing* that judges will take their public-regarding rhetoric seriously, legislators in the future will be more cautious, and perhaps even more honest, when they defend legislation they want to pass.

Pushing in a different direction, William Landes and Richard Posner make an *ex ante* argument for applying original legislative intent in statutory cases, even when such application leads to harsh results. William Landes & Richard Posner, *The Independent Judiciary in an Interest-Group Perspective,* 18 J.L. & Econ. 875 (1976). They argue that judges must be faithful agents reconstructing original deals, not because that is required by the Constitution, but because any other rule would undermine the conditions under which statutes are enacted. *Ex ante*, such an approach gives members of Congress and interest groups sufficient assurance that their deals will be enforced. To the extent that the enforcement of statutory deals is a good thing for our pluralist democracy, this is what judges ought to do. The Landes and Posner approach would consider legislative materials.

Frank Easterbrook agrees with Landes and Posner's *ex ante* way of thinking but rejects their approach, on the ground that the best evidence of statutory deals is the statutory text. See Frank Easterbrook, *The Supreme Court, 1993 Term— Foreword: The Court and the Economic System,* 98 Harv. L. Rev. 4 (1984), and *Statutes' Domains,* 50 Chi. L. Rev. 533 (1983). Treating statutes as contract-like deals is controversial, e.g., Mark Movesian, *Are Statutes Really "Legislative Bargains"? The Failure of the Contract Analogy in Statutory Interpretation*, 76 N.C. L. Rev. 1145 (1998), but assume that this is an apt analogy. Consider how the different "dealist" theories play out in the following case.[47] Note how the approach Judge Posner takes here is different than the theory he developed with Landes and reiterated just five years before this case, in Richard Posner, *The Federal Courts: Crisis and Reform* 286–93 (1985).

UNITED STATES V. MARSHALL

United States Court of Appeals for the Seventh Circuit (en banc), 1990.
908 F.2d 1312, *aff'd sub nom. Chapman v. United States*, 500 U.S. 453 (1991).

EASTERBROOK, CIRCUIT JUDGE.

* * * Stanley J. Marshall was convicted after a bench trial and sentenced to 20 years' imprisonment for conspiring to distribute, and distributing, more than ten grams of LSD, enough for 11,751 doses. Patrick Brumm, Richard L. Chapman, and

---

[47] Consistent with descriptive economic theory, Posner and Easterbrook, both law and economics "conservatives" appointed by President Reagan, vote the same way in the large majority of statutory cases, even if for different reasons. See Daniel Farber, *Do Theories of Statutory Interpretation Matter?*, 94 Nw. U. L. Rev. 1409 (2000).

John M. Schoenecker were convicted by a jury of selling ten sheets (1,000 doses) of paper containing LSD. Because the total weight of the paper and LSD was 5.7 grams, a five-year mandatory minimum applied. The district court sentenced Brumm to 60 months (the minimum), Schoenecker to 63 months, and Chapman to 96 months' imprisonment. All four defendants confine their arguments on appeal to questions concerning their sentences.

The three questions we must resolve are these: (1) Whether 21 U.S.C. § 841(b)(1)(A)(v) and (B)(v), which set mandatory minimum terms of imprisonment—five years for selling more than one gram of a "mixture or substance containing a detectable amount" of LSD, ten years for more than ten grams—exclude the weight of the carrier medium. (2) Whether the weight tables in the sentencing guidelines likewise exclude the weight of any carrier. (3) Whether the statute and the guidelines are unconstitutional to the extent their computations are based on anything other than the weight of the pure drug. * * *

According to the Sentencing Commission, the LSD in an average dose weighs 0.05 milligrams. Twenty thousand pure doses are a gram. But 0.05 mg is almost invisible, so LSD is distributed to retail customers in a carrier. Pure LSD is dissolved in a solvent such as alcohol and sprayed on paper or gelatin; alternatively the paper may be dipped in the solution. After the solvent evaporates, the paper or gel is cut into one-dose squares and sold by the square. Users swallow the squares or may drop them into a beverage, releasing the drug. Although the gelatin and paper are light, they weigh much more than the drug. Marshall's 11,751 doses weighed 113.32 grams; the LSD accounted for only 670.72 mg of this, not enough to activate the five-year mandatory minimum sentence, let alone the ten-year minimum. The ten sheets of blotter paper carrying the 1,000 doses Chapman and confederates sold weighed 5.7 grams; the LSD in the paper did not approach the one-gram threshold for a mandatory minimum sentence. This disparity between the weight of the pure LSD and the weight of LSD-plus-carrier underlies the defendants' arguments.

If the carrier counts in the weight of the "mixture or substance containing a detectable amount" of LSD, some odd things may happen. Weight in the hands of distributors may exceed that of manufacturers and wholesalers. Big fish then could receive paltry sentences or small fish draconian ones. Someone who sold 19, 999 doses of pure LSD (at 0.05 mg per dose) would escape the five-year mandatory minimum of § 841(b)(1)(B)(v) and be covered by § 841(b)(1)(C), which lacks a minimum term and has a maximum of "only" 20 years. Someone who sold a single hit of LSD dissolved in a tumbler of orange juice could be exposed to a ten-year mandatory minimum. Retailers could fall in or out of the mandatory terms depending not on the number of doses but on the medium: sugar cubes weigh more than paper, which weighs more than gelatin. One way to eliminate the possibility of such consequences is to say that the carrier is not a "mixture or substance containing a detectable amount" of the drug. Defendants ask us to do this.

Defendants' submission starts from the premise that the interaction of the statutory phrase "mixture or substance" with the distribution of LSD by the dose in a carrier creates a unique probability of surprise results. The premise may be unwarranted. The paper used to distribute LSD is light stuff, not the kind used to absorb ink. Chapman's 1,000 doses weighed about 0.16 ounces. More than 6,000 doses, even in blotter paper, weigh less than an ounce. Because the LSD in one dose weighs about 0.05 milligrams, the combination of LSD-plus-paper is about 110 times the weight of the LSD. The impregnated paper could be described as "0.9% LSD". * * *

This is by no means an unusual dilution rate for illegal drugs. Heroin sold on the street is 2% to 3% opiate and the rest filler. Sometimes the mixture is even more dilute, approaching the dilution rate for LSD in blotter paper. Heroin and crack cocaine, like LSD, are sold on the streets by the dose, although they are sold by weight higher in the distributional chain. * * *

It is not possible to construe the words of § 841 to make the penalty turn on the net weight of the drug rather than the gross weight of carrier and drug. The statute speaks of "mixture or substance containing a detectable amount" of a drug. "Detectable amount" is the opposite of "pure"; the point of the statute is that the "mixture" is not to be converted to an equivalent amount of pure drug.

The structure of the statute reinforces this conclusion. The 10–year minimum applies to any person who possesses, with intent to distribute, "100 grams or more of phencyclidine (PCP) or 1 kilogram or more of a mixture or substance containing a detectable amount of phencyclidine (PCP)", § 841(b)(1)(A)(iv). Congress distinguished the pure drug from a "mixture or substance containing a detectable amount of" it. All drugs other than PCP are governed exclusively by the "mixture or substance" language. Even brute force cannot turn that language into a reference to pure LSD. Congress used the same "mixture or substance" language to describe heroin, cocaine, amphetamines, and many other drugs that are sold after being cut—sometimes as much as LSD. There is no sound basis on which to treat the words "substance or mixture containing a detectable amount of", repeated verbatim for every drug mentioned in § 841 except PCP, as *different* things for LSD and cocaine although the language is identical, while treating the "mixture or substance" language as meaning the *same* as the reference to pure PCP in 21 U.S.C. § 841(b)(1)(A)(iv) and (B)(iv).

Although the "mixture or substance" language shows that the statute cannot be limited to pure LSD, it does not necessarily follow that blotter paper *is* a "mixture or substance containing" LSD. That phrase cannot include all "carriers". One gram of crystalline LSD in a heavy glass bottle is still only one gram of "statutory LSD". So is a gram of LSD being "carried" in a Boeing 747. How much mingling of the drug with something else is essential to form a "mixture or substance"? The legislative history is silent, but ordinary usage is indicative.

"Substance" may well refer to a chemical compound, or perhaps to a drug in a solvent. LSD does not react chemically with sugar, blotter paper, or gelatin, and none of these is a solvent. "Mixture" is more inclusive. Cocaine often is mixed with mannitol, quinine, or lactose. These white powders do not react, but it is common ground that a cocaine-mannitol mixture is a statutory "mixture".

LSD and blotter paper are not commingled in the same way as cocaine and lactose. What is the nature of their association? The possibility most favorable to defendants is that LSD sits on blotter paper as oil floats on water. Immiscible substances may fall outside the statutory definition of "mixture". The possibility does not assist defendants—not on this record, anyway. LSD is applied to paper in a solvent; after the solvent evaporates, a tiny quantity of LSD remains. Because the fibers absorb the alcohol, the LSD solidifies inside the paper rather than on it. You cannot pick a grain of LSD off the surface of the paper. Ordinary parlance calls the paper containing tiny crystals of LSD a mixture.

United States v. Rose, 881 F.2d 386 (7th Cir. 1989), like every other appellate decision that has addressed the question, concludes that the carrier medium for LSD, like the "cut" for heroin and cocaine, is a "mixture or substance containing a detectable amount" of the drug. Although a chemist might be able to offer evidence bearing on the question whether LSD and blotter paper "mix" any more fully than do oil and water, the record contains no such evidence. Without knowing more of the chemistry than this record reveals, we adhere to the unanimous conclusion of the other courts of appeals that blotter paper treated with LSD is a "mixture or substance containing a detectable quantity of" LSD.

Two reasons have been advanced to support a contrary conclusion: that statutes should be construed to avoid constitutional problems, and that some members of the sitting Congress are dissatisfied with basing penalties on the combined weight of LSD and carrier. Neither is persuasive.

A preference for giving statutes a constitutional meaning is a reason to construe, not to rewrite or "improve". * * * "[S]ubstance or mixture containing a detectable quantity" is not ambiguous. * * * Neither the rule of lenity nor the preference for avoiding constitutional adjudication justifies disregarding unambiguous language.

The canon about avoiding constitutional decisions, in particular, must be used with care, for it is a closer cousin to invalidation than to interpretation. It is a way to enforce the constitutional penumbra, and therefore an aspect of constitutional law proper. Constitutional decisions breed penumbras, which multiply questions. Treating each as justification to construe laws out of existence too greatly enlarges the judicial power. And heroic "construction" is unnecessary, given our conclusion [in discussion omitted here] that Congress possesses the constitutional power to set penalties on the basis of gross weight.

As for the pending legislation: subsequent debates are not a ground for avoiding the import of enactments. Although the views of a subsequent Congress are entitled to respect, ongoing debates do not represent the views of Congress. * * *

CUMMINGS, CIRCUIT JUDGE, with whom BAUER, CHIEF JUDGE, and WOOD, JR., CUDAHY, and POSNER, CIRCUIT JUDGES, join, dissenting.

[T]he United States District Court for the District of Columbia held that blotter paper was not a mixture or substance within the meaning of the statute. *United States v Healy*, 729 F.Supp. 140 (D.D.C. 1990). The court relied not only on ordinary dictionary definitions of the words mixture and substance but also on a November 30, 1988, Sentencing Commission publication, entitled "Questions Most Frequently Asked About the Sentencing Guidelines," which states that the Commission has not taken a position on whether the blotter paper should be weighed. The conclusion that the Commission has not yet resolved this question is further supported by a Sentencing Commission Notice issued on March 3, 1989, which requested public comments on whether the Commission should exclude the weight of the carrier for sentencing purposes in LSD cases.[3]

The *Healy* court also stated that Congress could have intended the words "mixture or substance" to refer to the liquid in which the pure LSD is dissolved. Finally, the *Healy* court relied on a Guidelines table designed to provide a sentencing court with an equivalent weight for sentencing purposes in cases in which the number of doses distributed is known but the actual weight is unknown. The table provides that a dose of LSD weighs .05 milligrams. Guidelines § 2D1.1, Commentary, Drug Equivalency Tables. This weight closely approximates the weight of one dose of LSD without blotter paper, but is not an accurate reflection of one dose with blotter paper. * * *

Two subsequent pieces of legislative history * * * shed some light on this question. In a letter to Senator Joseph R. Biden, Jr., dated April 26, 1989, the Chairman of the Sentencing Commission, William W. Wilkens, Jr., noted the ambiguity in the statute as it is currently written:

> With respect to LSD, it is unclear whether Congress intended the carrier to be considered as a packaging material, or, since it is commonly consumed along with the illicit drug, as a dilutant ingredient in the drug mixture. . . . The Commission suggests that Congress may wish to further consider the LSD carrier issue in order to clarify legislative intent as to whether the weight of the carrier should or should not be considered in determining the quantity of LSD mixture for punishment purposes.

Presumably acting in response to this query, Senator Biden added to the Congressional Record for October 5, 1989, an analysis of one of a series of technical corrections to 21 U.S.C. § 841 that were under consideration by the Senate that day. This analysis states that the purpose of the particular correction at issue was to remove an unintended "inequity" from Section 841 caused by the decisions of some courts to include the weight of the blotter paper for sentencing purposes in LSD cases. According to Senator Biden, the correction "remedie[d] this inequity by removing the weight of the carrier from the calculation of the weight of the mixture or substance." This correction was adopted as part of Amendment No. 976 to S. 1711. 135 Cong.Rec. S12749 (daily ed. Oct. 5, 1989). The amended bill was passed by a unanimous vote of the Senate (*id.* at S12765) and is currently pending before the House.

---

[3]   The Commission has recently adopted several amendments and sent them to Congress for approval. Among these is an amendment to Application Note 11 to Guidelines Section 2D1.1. This amendment specifically states that the typical weight per dose of LSD that is given in the Weight Per Dose Table as .05 milligrams is the weight of the LSD alone and not of the LSD combined with any carrier. 55 Fed.Reg. 19197 (May 8, 1990). * * *

Comments in more recent issues of the Congressional Record indicate that S. 1711 is not expected to pass the House of Representatives. See 136 Cong.Rec. S943 (daily ed. Feb. 7, 1990). In the meantime, however, a second attempt to clarify Congress' intent in amending 21 U.S.C. § 841 to include the words mixture or substance has now been introduced in the Senate. On April 18, 1990, Senator Kennedy introduced an amendment to S. 1970 (a bill establishing constitutional procedures for the imposition of the death penalty) seeking to clarify the language of 21 U.S.C. § 841. That amendment, Amendment No. 1716, states:

> Section 841(b)(1) of title 21, United States Code, is amended by inserting the following new subsection at the end thereof: "(E) In determining the weight of a 'mixture or substance' under this section, the court shall not include the weight of the carrier upon which the controlled substance is placed, or by which it is transported."

136 Cong.Rec. S7069 (daily ed. May 24, 1990). [Judge Cummings argued from this evidence that the draconian penalty scheme for LSD was simply a mistake never intended by Congress and that the Seventh Circuit should follow *Healy*.]

POSNER, CIRCUIT JUDGE, joined by BAUER, CHIEF JUDGE, and CUMMINGS, WOOD, JR., and CUDAHY, CIRCUIT JUDGES, dissenting.

* * * Based as it is on weight, [the § 841 sentencing scheme] works well for drugs that are sold by weight; and ordinarily the weight quoted to the buyer is the weight of the dilute form, although of course price will vary with purity. The dilute form is the product, and it is as natural to punish its purveyors according to the weight of the product as it is to punish moonshiners by the weight or volume of the moonshine they sell rather than by the weight of the alcohol contained in it. So, for example, under Florida law it is a felony to possess one or more gallons of moonshine, and a misdemeanor to possess less than one gallon, regardless of the alcoholic content. Fla.Stat. §§ 561.01, 562.451.

LSD, however, is sold to the consumer by the dose; it is not cut, diluted, or mixed with something else. Moreover, it is incredibly light. An average dose of LSD weighs .05 milligrams, which is less than two millionths of an ounce. To ingest something that small requires swallowing something much larger. Pure LSD in granular form is first diluted by being dissolved, usually in alcohol, and then a quantity of the solution containing one dose of LSD is sprayed or eyedropped on a sugar cube, or on a cube of gelatin, or, as in the cases before us, on an inch-square section of "blotter" paper. * * * After the solution is applied to the carrier medium, the alcohol or other solvent evaporates, leaving an invisible (and undiluted) spot of pure LSD on the cube or blotter paper. The consumer drops the cube or the piece of paper into a glass of water, or orange juice, or some other beverage, causing the LSD to dissolve in the beverage, which is then drunk. * * * [A] quart of orange juice containing one dose of LSD is not more, in any relevant sense, than a pint of juice containing the same one dose, and it would be loony to punish the purveyor of the quart more heavily than the purveyor of the pint. It would be like basing the punishment for selling cocaine on the combined weight of the cocaine and of the vehicle (plane, boat, automobile, or whatever) used to transport it or the syringe used to inject it or the pipe used to smoke it. The blotter paper, sugar cubes, etc. are the vehicles for conveying LSD to the consumer.

The weight of the carrier is vastly greater than that of the LSD, as well as irrelevant to its potency. There is no comparable disparity between the pure and the mixed form (if that is how we should regard LSD on blotter paper or other carrier medium) with respect to the other drugs in section 841, with the illuminating exception of PCP. There Congress specified alternative weights, for the drug itself and for the substance or mixture containing the drug. For example, the five-year minimum sentence for a seller of PCP requires the sale of either ten grams of the drug itself or one hundred grams of a substance or mixture containing the drug. 21 U.S.C. § 841(b)(1)(B)(iv).

Ten sheets of blotter paper, containing a thousand doses of LSD, weigh almost six grams. The LSD itself weighs less than a hundredth as much. If the thousand doses are on gelatin cubes instead of sheets of blotter paper, the total weight is less, but it is still more than two grams, which is forty times the weight of the LSD. In both cases, if the carrier plus the LSD constitutes the relevant "substance or mixture" (the crucial "if" in this case), the dealer is subject to the minimum mandatory sentence of five years. One of the defendants before us (Marshall) sold almost 12,000 doses of LSD on blotter paper. This subjected him to the ten-year minimum, and the Guidelines then took over and pushed him up to twenty years. Since it takes 20,000 doses of LSD to equal a gram, Marshall would not have been subject to even the five-year mandatory minimum had he sold the LSD in its pure form. And a dealer who sold fifteen times the number of doses as Marshall—180,000—would not be subject to the ten-year mandatory minimum sentence if he sold the drug in its pure form, because 180,000 doses is only nine grams.

At the other extreme, if Marshall were not a dealer at all but dropped a square of blotter paper containing a single dose of LSD into a glass of orange juice and sold it to a friend at cost (perhaps 35 cents), he would be subject to the ten-year minimum. The juice with LSD dissolved in it would be the statutory mixture or substance containing a detectable amount of the illegal drug and it would weigh more than ten grams (one ounce is about 35 grams, and the orange juice in a glass of orange juice weighs several ounces). So a person who sold one dose of LSD might be subject to the ten-year mandatory minimum sentence while a dealer who sold 199,999 doses in pure form would be subject only to the five-year minimum. Defendant Dean sold 198 doses, crowded onto one sheet of blotter paper: this subjected him to the five-year mandatory minimum, too, since the ensemble weighed slightly more than a gram. * * *

All this seems crazy but we must consider whether Congress might have had a reason for wanting to key the severity of punishment for selling LSD to the weight of the carrier rather than to the number of doses or to some reasonable proxy for dosage (as weight is, for many drugs). The only one suggested is that it might be costly to determine the weight of the LSD in the blotter paper, sugar cube, etc., because it is so light! That merely underscores the irrationality of basing the punishment for selling this drug on weight rather than on dosage. But in fact the weight is reported in every case I have seen, so apparently it can be determined readily enough; it *has* to be determined in any event, to permit a purity adjustment under the Guidelines. If the weight of the LSD is difficult to determine, the difficulty is easily overcome by basing punishment on the number of doses, which makes much more sense in any event. To base punishment on the weight of the carrier medium makes about as much sense as basing punishment on the weight of the defendant. * * *

This is a quilt the pattern whereof no one has been able to discern. The legislative history is silent, and since even the Justice Department cannot explain the why of the punishment scheme that it is defending, the most plausible inference is that Congress simply did not realize how LSD is sold. The inference is reinforced by the statutory treatment of PCP. * * *

[The] irrationality is magnified when we compare the sentences for people who sell other drugs prohibited by 21 U.S.C. § 841. Marshall, remember, sold fewer than 12,000 doses and was sentenced to twenty years. Twelve thousand doses sounds like a lot, but to receive a comparable sentence for selling heroin Marshall would have had to sell ten kilograms, which would yield between one and two million doses. To receive a comparable sentence for selling cocaine he would have had to sell fifty kilograms, which would yield anywhere from 325,000 to five million doses. While the corresponding weight is lower for crack—half a kilogram—this still translates into 50,000 doses. * * *

Well, what if anything can we judges do about this mess? The answer lies in the shadow of a jurisprudential disagreement that is not less important by virtue of being unavowed by most judges. It is the disagreement between the severely positivistic view that the content of law is exhausted in clear, explicit, and definite enactments by or under express delegation from legislatures, and the natural lawyer's or legal pragmatist's view that the practice of interpretation and the general terms of the Constitution (such as "equal protection of the laws") authorize judges to enrich positive law with the moral values and practical concerns of civilized society. Judges who in other respects have seemed quite similar, such as Holmes and Cardozo, have taken opposite sides of this issue. Neither approach is entirely satisfactory. The first buys political neutrality and a type of objectivity at the price of substantive injustice, while the second buys justice in the individual case at the price of considerable uncertainty and, not infrequently, judicial willfulness. It is no wonder that our legal system oscillates between the approaches. The positivist view, applied unflinchingly to this case, commands the affirmance of prison sentences that are exceptionally harsh by the standards of the modern Western world, dictated by an accidental, unintended scheme of punishment nevertheless implied by the words (taken one by one) of the relevant enactments. The natural law or pragmatist view leads to a freer interpretation, one influenced by norms of equal treatment; and let us explore the interpretive possibilities here. One is to interpret "mixture or substance containing a detectable amount of [LSD]" to exclude the carrier medium—the blotter paper, sugar or gelatin cubes, and orange juice or other beverage. That is the course we rejected in *United States v Rose, supra,* as have the other circuits. I wrote *Rose,* but I am no longer confident that its literal interpretation of the statute, under which the blotter paper, cubes, etc. are "substances" that "contain" LSD, is inevitable. The blotter paper, etc. are better viewed, I now think, as carriers, like the package in which a kilo of cocaine comes wrapped or the bottle in which a fifth of liquor is sold.

Interpreted to exclude the carrier, the punishment schedule for LSD would make perfectly good sense; it would not warp the statutory design. The comparison with heroin and cocaine is again illuminating. The statute imposes the five-year mandatory minimum sentence on anyone who sells a substance or mixture containing a hundred grams of heroin, equal to 10,000 to 20,000 doses. One gram of pure LSD, which also would trigger the five-year minimum, yields 20,000 doses. The comparable figures for cocaine are 3250 to 50,000 doses, placing LSD in about the middle. So Congress may have wanted to base punishment for the sale of LSD on the weight of the pure drug after all, using one and ten grams of the pure drug to trigger the five-year and ten-year minima (and corresponding maxima—twenty years and forty years). This interpretation leaves "substance or mixture containing" without a referent, so far as LSD is concerned. But we must remember that Congress used the identical term in each subsection that specifies the quantity of a drug that subjects the seller to the designated minimum and maximum punishments. In thus automatically including the same term in each subsection, Congress did not necessarily affirm that, for each and every drug covered by the statute, a substance or mixture containing the drug *must* be found.

The flexible interpretation that I am proposing is decisively strengthened by the constitutional objection to basing punishment of LSD offenders on the weight of the carrier medium rather than on the weight of the LSD. Courts often do interpretive handsprings to avoid having even to *decide* a constitutional question. In doing so they expand, very questionably in my view, the effective scope of the Constitution, creating a constitutional penumbra in which statutes wither, shrink, are deformed. A better case for flexible interpretation is presented when the alternative is to nullify Congress's action: when in other words there is not merely a constitutional question about, but a constitutional barrier to, the statute when interpreted literally. This is such a case.

[Judge Posner then argued that the sentencing scheme for LSD upheld by the majority violates the equal protection guarantee of the Fifth Amendment's due process clause, because of the "unequal treatment of people equally situated." That even the Justice Department cannot formulate a rational basis for the distinctions it has drawn from § 841 in LSD cases is persuasive evidence that Congress has to be sent back to the drawing board.]

The literal interpretation adopted by the majority is not inevitable. All interpretation is contextual. The words of the statute—interpreted against a background that includes a constitutional norm of equal treatment, a (closely related) constitutional commitment to rationality, an evident failure by both Congress and the Sentencing Commission to consider how LSD is actually produced, distributed, and sold, and an equally evident failure by the same two bodies to consider the interaction between heavy mandatory minimum sentences and the Sentencing Guidelines—will bear an interpretation that distinguishes between the carrier vehicle of the illegal drug and the substance or mixture containing a detectable amount of the drug. The punishment of the crack dealer is not determined by the weight of the glass tube in which he sells the crack; we should not lightly attribute to Congress a purpose of punishing the dealer in LSD according to the weight of the LSD carrier. We should not make Congress's handiwork an embarrassment to the members of Congress and to us.

NOTES ON THE *LSD* CASE AND EX ANTE *THINKING*

1. *Review: The New Textualism and Linguistic Meaning.* Judge Easterbrook's opinion in the LSD case is an excellent example of the distinctive features of the new textualism: (a) focus on the text of the statute, including not just the plain meaning of the provision at issue, but also how that provision fits into the "whole statute"; (b) a rejection of, and some contempt for, legislative history as a context for interpreting the statute; and (c) a relatively black-and-white vision of what words mean. Note that judges on the Seventh Circuit were in sharp disagreement about whether LSD on blotter paper is a "mixture." Should the very fact of good-faith disagreement about the law's plain meaning be evidence that the statute has no plain meaning (as Professor Stephen Ross has long suggested)?

In affirming *Marshall*, the Supreme Court was also divided as to what "mixture" meant in the LSD sentencing law. See *Chapman v. United States*, 500 U.S. 453 (1991). While Judge Easterbrook relied on "ordinary usage" to define "mixture," Chief Justice Rehnquist's opinion for the Supreme Court relied on a dictionary definition of mixture as "two substances blended together so that the particles of one are diffused among the particles of the other." Because the LSD "is diffused among the fibers of the paper," the Chief Justice found a statutory plain meaning. This might be called a denotative approach to plain meaning: Apply the dictionary definition and see if it fits.

Professional linguists don't necessarily approach meaning in this way. They are willing to expand and contract meaning beyond its dictionary denotations. Words reflect categories which are fuzzy at the margins; the necessary and sufficient conditions for membership in the category are not completely accessible to us before the fact. Lawrence Solan, a Ph.D. linguist, in *When Judges Use the Dictionary*, 68 Am. Speech 50, 54–55 (1993), analyzes the *Marshall* case in this way:

> Calling the blotter paper impregnated with LSD a mixture seems odd for the same reason that it seems odd to call a pancake soaked with syrup *a pancake-syrup mixture*; or to call a wet towel *a water-cotton mixture*; or to call a towel that one has used to dry one's face during a tennis game *a cotton-sweat mixture*, or later, after the sweat has dried, *a cotton-salt mixture*. The last two I would call *a wet towel* and *a dirty towel*, respectively. In all of these examples, both substances have kept their character in a chemical sense, but one of the substances seems to have kept too much of its character for us to feel natural using the term *mixture*. * * *

Solan criticizes *Chapman* for "taking a concept that is fuzzy at the margins and substituting for it a definition that is subject to more refined application than the concept itself." If the new textualists cannot satisfy professional linguists with their insistence that a statute has a "plain meaning," what legitimacy does their approach offer? Recall that people's personal liberty (the terms of their incarceration) depended upon this semantic debate. On the other hand, is there some necessary reason why judicial and linguistic interpreters must agree on methodology?

2.   *Liberty Versus* Ex Ante *Thinking?* Judge Easterbrook's first major article on interpretation urged that statutes not be construed beyond the "domain" clearly demarcated by their texts. He defended this approach on the basis of a libertarian presumption akin to the standard Chicago School idea that most things should not be regulated by the state and should be left to the free operation of the market:

> Those who wrote and approved the Constitution thought that most social relations would be governed by private agreements, customs, and understandings, not resolved in the halls of government. There is still at least a presumption that people's arrangements prevail unless expressly displaced by legal doctrine. All things are permitted unless there is some contrary rule. It is easier for an agency to justify the revocation of rules (or simple nonregulation) than the creation of new rules.

Easterbrook, *Statutes' Domains*, 50 U. Chi. L. Rev. 533, 549–50 (1983). Note that the libertarian position in *Marshall* is the one taken by Judges Cummings and Posner, not that of Judge Easterbrook, who sends the defendants into confinement for a long period of time. (The same is true for a new textualist approach to *Holy Trinity*, which d settled an issue of criminal liability.)

Consider an *ex ante* counterargument: a textualism that yields harsh results, as in the LSD case, sends a signal to judges that they should be careful not to make policy— and to Congress that its statutes will be interpreted "as written," and that any updating or fixing will have to be done by the legislators themselves. If they adopt the "tough love" of the new textualism, as Judge Keen argued in Speluncean Explorers, courts may enhance democracy and legislative accountability. Everyone will know that Congress, alone, is responsible for statutory applications, and voters can act accordingly.

A problem with the foregoing argument is that there is no evidence that such tough love will have any effect on Congress. One of us has argued from the nature and structure of the politics of legislation that Congress cannot enact statutes with the degree of specification the new textualists would require. See James Brudney, *Congressional Commentary on Judicial Interpretations of Statutes: Idle Chatter or Telling Response?*, 93 Mich. L. Rev. 1 (1994). An implication of Brudney's idea is that the new textualism will sometimes have a likely libertarian effect (by reducing Congress' practical capacity to regulate), bringing us back to Easterbrook's point in *Statute's Domain*. The problem is that legislative paralysis will also sometimes have an anti-libertarian effect—as in the LSD Case, when Congress could not correct what was apparently a drafting error, and Messrs. Marshall, Chapman et al. paid the price with more years in federal prison.

3.   Ex Ante *Arguments for an Approach That Considers Fairness.* Judge Posner is not a bleeding-heart liberal—the classic *ex post* position—yet he voted to overturn the conviction. And he did so for reasons that went well beyond the original legislative intent approach he once championed. Since 1990, Posner has come out of the closet as a flexible pragmatic interpreter of statutes.[48] There are some economic arguments for a more flexible approach than the one followed by the en banc majority in *Marshall*. One argument is that a relentless textualism will undermine rather than cultivate the

---

[48]   Richard Posner, *The Problems of Jurisprudence* (1990); *Overcoming Law* (1995); and *How Judges Think* (2008). See also John Manning, *Statutory Pragmatism and Constitutional Structure*, 120 Harv. L. Rev. 1161 (2007) (evaluating Posner's approach from a textualist perspective).

conditions for legislation: because deals will not be reasonably enforced, legislators will be more reluctant to make them; legislators might even lose confidence that the judiciary can be trusted to carry out statutes in a fair way. Another *ex ante* argument is that an unreasonable construction of the LSD law undermines the overall legitimacy of our system of criminal justice (the small fries like Marshall are being treated really unfairly; many of those arrested are people of color), without any discernible offsetting benefit to criminal justice (such as increased deterrence). Congress has not shown enormous wisdom in this area, and if any institution is going to act responsibly it must be the judiciary.

A NEW LSD ISSUE

Problem 6–8. In 1993, the Sentencing Commission revised the method for calculating the weight of LSD for Sentencing Guideline purposes. Abandoning its former approach of weighing the entire blotter paper containing LSD, the amended Guideline told courts to give each dose of LSD on a carrier medium a presumed weight of 0.4 mg. U.S. Sentencing Comm'n, U.S. Sentencing Guidelines Manual § 2D1.1(c), n. (H). The new method was retroactive.

Meirl Neal was sentenced to 192 months in prison for selling 11,456 doses of LSD on blotter paper. He moved to have his sentence reduced to between 70 and 87 months, the Guideline period for sale of 4.58 grams of LSD (11,456 times 0.4 mg). The Government argued that Neal should serve at least 120 months, because of the mandatory minimum sentence required by 21 U.S.C. § 841(b)(1)(A)(v), as interpreted in *Marshall/Chapman*. Neal argued that the blotter paper should now not be counted for purposes of the mandatory minimum, just as it is now not counted for purposes of setting the ordinary sentence. Should the courts have accepted Neal's argument and reduced his sentence? See *Neal v. United States*, 516 U.S. 284 (1996).

2.   Advancing Public-Regarding Goals and Minimizing Rent-Seeking

Public choice theory is the application of economic principles to actions by the state. One conclusion reached by some public choice theorists, developed in Chapter 1, § 2, is that an interest-group-driven legislative process produces too few public-regarding statutes (i.e., those broadly distributing benefits as well as costs) and too many rent-seeking statutes (i.e., those distributing benefits to a small group, at the expense of the general public, and without an efficiency justification).

Frank Easterbrook, *The Supreme Court, 1983 Term—Foreword: The Court and the Economic System*, 98 Harv. L. Rev. 4, 14–15 (1984), suggests a general interpretive strategy for the judiciary to respond to this asymmetry:

> * * * There are two basic styles of statutory construction. In one the judge starts with the statute, attributes to it certain purposes (evils to be redressed), and then brings within the statute the class of activities that produce the same or similar objectionable results. The statute's reach goes on expanding so long as there are unredressed objectionable results. The judge interprets omissions and vague terms in the statute as evidence of want of time or foresight and fills in these gaps with more in the same vein. The maxim "Remedial statutes are to be liberally construed" sums up this approach.

In the other approach the judge treats the statute as a contract. He first identifies the contracting parties and then seeks to discover what they resolved and what they left unresolved. For example, he may conclude that a statute regulating the price of fluid milk is a pact between milk producers and milk handlers designed to cut back output and raise price, to the benefit of both at the expense of consumers. A judge then implements the bargain as a faithful agent but without enthusiasm; asked to extend the scope of a back-room deal, he refuses unless the proof of the deal's scope is compelling. Omissions are evidence that no bargain was struck: some issues were left for the future, or perhaps one party was unwilling to pay the price of a resolution in its favor. Sometimes the compromise may be to toss an issue to the courts for resolution, but this too is a term of the bargain, to be demonstrated rather than presumed. What the parties did not resolve, the court should not resolve either. The maxim "Statutes in derogation of the common law are to be strictly construed" sums up this approach.

These maxims are useless as guides to construction; every remedial statute is in derogation of the common law. Yet this hopeless conflict of maxims does not justify despair. The appropriate treatment of statutes depends on how they come to be and what they are for. A judge cannot set about rearranging economic relations on the basis of an ambiguous statute without first resolving a question about the nature of legislation. If statutes generally are designed to overcome "failures" in markets and to replace the calamities produced by unguided private conduct with the ordered rationality of the public sector, then it makes sense to use the remedial approach to the construction of statutes—or at least most of them. If, on the other hand, statutes often are designed to replace the outcomes of private transactions with monopolistic ones, to transfer the profits ("rents") of productive activity to a privileged few, then judges should take the beady-eyed contractual approach. The warehouseman does not deliver the grain without seeing the receipt, and so too with goodies dispensed by judges.

See also Jonathan Macey, *Promoting Public-Regarding Legislation Through Statutory Interpretation: An Interest Group Model*, 86 Colum. L. Rev. 223 (1986), who argues that public-interest statutes ought to be liberally interpreted by reference to their announced purposes. By raising the costs of rent-seeking, judges can contribute to the public welfare.

The Table below suggests the risks entailed in various kinds of statutes, together with counter-strategies courts could follow in applying those statutes. Consider the application of this kind of thinking to cases like *Weber*, the affirmative action case in Chapter 1, § 3, and to the cases in this chapter. For example, into which quadrant would the alien contract labor law of *Holy Trinity* fit? If quadrant one, the Court's stingy construction becomes less defensible—but there is good reason to think the law was purely rent-seeking: unions were seeking to restrict the supply of labor so as to bid up wages in certain occupations. Congress has the power to enact such laws, but the Court ought not apply them beyond the original statutory target.

Table of Interpretive Strategies for Different Kinds of Laws

[1] Distributed Benefit/Distributed Cost Laws (General Interest)	**[2] Distributed Benefit/Concentrated Cost Laws**
Danger: These laws are usually in the public interest, but the legislature will often fail to update them as society and the underlying problem change.	*Danger*: Regulated groups will tend to evade their statutory duties and press to "capture" the agency created to administer the law.
Response: Courts can expand the law to new situations and develop it in common law fashion, subject to the limits imposed by the statutory text.	*Response*: Courts can monitor agency enforcement and private compliance, and open up procedures to assure excluded groups are heard. Courts can press the agency to be faithful to the stated public-regarding goal of the law.
[3] Concentrated Benefit/ Distributed Cost Laws (Rent-Seeking)	**[4] Concentrated Benefit/Concentrated Cost Laws**
Danger: Rent-seeking by special interest groups at the expense of the general public.	*Danger*: The statutory deal may grow unexpectedly lopsided over time.
Response: Courts ought to construe the law narrowly to minimize the unwarranted benefits. Hold the statute to its public-regarding justifications.	*Response*: Do not attempt much judicial updating, unless affected groups are not able to get the legislature's attention.

Source: William Eskridge Jr., *Politics Without Romance: Implications of Public Choice Theory for Statutory Interpretation*, 74 Va. L. Rev. 275, 325 (1988).

PEREZ V. WYETH LABORATORIES, INC.
New Jersey Supreme Court, 1999.
734 A.2d 1245.

O'HERN, J., writing for a majority of the Court.

[Norplant is an FDA-approved, reversible contraceptive that prevents pregnancy for up to five years. Wyeth began a massive advertising campaign for Norplant in 1991, which it directed at women rather than at their doctors. Wyeth advertised on television and in women's magazines. None of the advertisements warned of any dangers or side effects associated with Norplant, but rather praised its convenience and simplicity. In 1995, several women filed lawsuits in various New Jersey counties claiming injuries that resulted from their use of Norplant.

Their principal claim was that Wyeth failed to warn adequately about the side effects associated with the contraceptive, including weight gain, headaches, dizziness, nausea, diarrhea, acne, vomiting, fatigue, facial hair growth, numbness in the arms and legs, irregular menstruation, hair loss, leg cramps, anxiety and nervousness, vision problems, anemia, mood swings and depression, high blood pressure, and removal complications that resulted in scarring.

[Perez sought a determination of whether the "learned intermediary" doctrine applied. This doctrine generally relieves a pharmaceutical manufacturer of an independent duty to warn the ultimate user of prescription drugs, so long as it has supplied the physician with information about a drug's dangerous propensities and risks. The assumption of the doctrine is that the doctor will play the key role in informing and counseling the patient about the risks. Holding the doctrine applicable by reason of the New Jersey Products Liability Act, N.J.S.A. 2A:58C–1 to –11, the trial court dismissed those plaintiffs' complaints, concluding that even when a manufacturer advertises directly to the public, and a woman is influenced by the advertising campaign, a physician nevertheless retains the duty to weigh the benefits and risks associated with a drug before deciding whether the drug is appropriate for the patient.]

Our medical-legal jurisprudence is based on images of health care that no longer exist. At an earlier time, medical advice was received in the doctor's office from a physician who most likely made house calls if needed. The patient usually paid a small sum of money to the doctor. Neighborhood pharmacists compounded prescribed medicines. Without being pejorative, it is safe to say that the prevailing attitude of law and medicine was that the "doctor knows best."

Pharmaceutical manufacturers never advertised their products to patients, but rather directed all sales efforts at physicians. In this comforting setting, the law created an exception to the traditional duty of manufacturers to warn consumers directly of risks associated with the product as long as they warned health-care providers of those risks.

For good or ill, that has all changed. Medical services are in large measure provided by managed care organizations. Medicines are purchased in the pharmacy department of supermarkets and often paid for by third-party providers. Drug manufacturers now directly advertise products to consumers on the radio, television, the Internet, billboards on public transportation, and in magazines. [New Jersey has accepted the learned intermediary doctrine as a defense in tort suits against drug companies, e.g., *Niemiera v. Schneider*, 114 N.J. 550, 559, 555 A.2d 1112 (1989). Now that firms mass-market drugs directly to consumers, see Jon D. Hanson & Douglas A. Kysar, *Taking Behavioralism Seriously: Some Evidence of Market Manipulation*, 112 Harv. L. Rev. 1420, 1456 (1999), the court was faced with the question whether the learned intermediary doctrine should still apply to such drugs, like Norplant.]

[T]he New Jersey Products Liability Act provides:

An adequate product warning or instruction is one that a reasonably prudent person in the same or similar circumstances would have provided with respect to the danger and that communicates adequate information on the dangers and safe use of the product, taking into account the characteristics of, and the ordinary knowledge common to, the persons by whom the product is intended to be used, or in the case of prescription drugs, taking into account the characteristics of, and the ordinary knowledge common to, the prescribing physician. If the warning or instruction given in connection with a drug or device or food or food additive has been approved or prescribed by the federal Food and Drug Administration under the "Federal Food, Drug, and Cosmetic Act," 52 Stat. 1040, 21 U.S.C. § 301 et seq., . . . a rebuttable presumption shall arise that the warning or instruction is adequate. . . .

N.J.S.A. 2A:58C–4.

The Senate Judiciary Committee Statement that accompanied L. 1987, c. 197 recites: "The subsection contains a general definition of an adequate warning and a special definition for warnings that accompany prescription drugs, since, in the case of prescription drugs, the warning is owed to the physician." See N.J.S.A. 2A:58C–1 (providing the Committee Statement). At oral argument, counsel for Wyeth was candid to acknowledge that he could not "point to a sentence in the statute" that would make the learned intermediary doctrine applicable to the manufacturers' direct marketing of drugs, but rather relied on the Committee Statement. Although the statute provides a physician-based standard for determining the adequacy of the warning due to a physician, the statute does not legislate the boundaries of the doctrine. For example, the Act does not purport to repeal a holding such as *Davis v. Wyeth Labs*, [399 F.2d 121 (9th Cir. 1968)], which required that manufacturers directly warn patients in mass inoculation cases. Rather, the statute governs the content of an "adequate product warning," when required. As noted [above], in 1987, direct-to-consumer marketing of prescription drugs was in its beginning stages. The Committee Statement observes that "the warning is owed to the physician" because drugs were then marketed to the physician. We believe that the part of the provision establishing "a presumption that a warning or instruction is adequate on drug or food products if the warning has been approved or prescribed by the Food and Drug Administration," Committee Statement, *supra*, will provide the benchmark for this decision.

[The court ruled that the rationales for the learned intermediary doctrine—deference to physicians and the integrity of the doctor-patient relationship—did not apply when the drug company marketed directly to patients. Hence, the doctrine was not legally available as a defense in this case.]

POLLOCK, J., dissenting.

[Justice Pollack objected that the Court ignored statutory plain meaning.] The majority finds ambiguity in the NJPLA, stating that "although the statute provides a physician-based standard for determining the adequacy of the warning due to a physician, the statute does not legislate the boundaries of the doctrine." According to the Senate Committee statement accompanying the NJPLA, however, a drug manufacturer's duty to warn is owed to the physician, not the consumer:

A manufacturer or seller is not liable in a warning-defect case if an adequate warning is given when the product has left the control of the manufacturer or seller. . . . The subsection contains a general definition of an adequate warning and a special definition for warnings that accompany prescription drugs, since, in the case of prescription drugs, the warning is owed to the physician.

Senate Judiciary Committee, Statement to Senate Bill No. 2805 (L. 1987, c. 197), N.J.S.A. 2A:58C–1a.

The NJPLA provides that "committee statements that may be adopted or included in the legislative history of this act shall be consulted in the interpretation and construction of this act." N.J.S.A. 2A:58C–1a. Through that extraordinary mandate, the Legislature sought to preclude judicial circumvention of the plain meaning of the statute.

Today's decision demonstrates that the Legislature's efforts were unavailing. The majority has mischaracterized both the statute and the rationale for the learned intermediary doctrine. Contrary to the majority opinion, the statute directs that the warning is owed to the physician not "because drugs were then marketed to the physician," but because the physician is in the best position to make an individualized evaluation of the risks of drugs and warn the patient of those risks. The patient, moreover, cannot obtain the drugs without a prescription written by a physician.

Underlying the majority opinion is the assumption that the Legislature in 1987 could not have anticipated the mass-marketing of prescription drugs. That assumption, however, has no basis in the record. In fact, the drug companies and the Legislature, like the Federal Food and Drug Administration (FDA), were aware of such marketing. * * *

The majority's imposition of expanded duties on drug manufacturers contravenes the legislative history of the NJPLA. That history demonstrates that the statute was intended to strengthen the protections afforded manufacturers:

It is important to recognize that this bill not only conforms New Jersey product liability law to the law of the majority of states but, in some instances, changes New Jersey law in favor of the manufacturer in a way that is not currently recognized by the law of the majority of states. Thus, the effect of the enactment of this bill would be to shift the status of the law of New Jersey on certain issues from its current position of being more favorable to the injured consumer than the majority of states to being more favorable to the manufacturer than the majority of states.

Passed Bill Memorandum to Governor Thomas H. Kean on S–2805, *supra*, at 3.

Judges, although they may disagree with a legislative policy, are bound to respect it. In adapting the common law to society's needs, this Court may not have favored manufacturers, including pharmaceutical companies, as enthusiastically as has the Legislature. The issue, however, is not whether the Court shares the Legislature's enthusiasm or even whether the majority would prefer to amend the common-law learned intermediary doctrine. Because of the enactment of the

NJPLA, the issue is whether the majority should respect the learned intermediary doctrine as declared by the Legislature. * * *

NOTE ON THE NORPLANT CASE AND NARROW INTERPRETATIONS OF RENT-SEEKING STATUTES

Assume that the liability-waiver law is rent-seeking: How would the Table's analysis apply here? Presumably, Easterbrook would not apply his narrow interpretation rule, given the relative clarity of the statutory language. How would Posner vote? Because the legislative history supports the plain meaning, would he go along with Easterbrook? How about Macey: Does his theory support the majority's result? At what point should standard legal criteria trump an anti-rent-seeking rationale under economic theory?

A special case is presented by statutes regulating areas in which the common law has long been the baseline. Many law and economics scholars believe the common law is more efficient than other forms of law, because of the way it develops incrementally and relatively untainted by special interest pressure.[49] If this is true, relatively speaking, then courts might be particularly picky in applying exceptions to the common law that are pressed upon the legislative process by special interests—which is precisely the way the New Jersey Supreme Court seems to see the matter in *Perez*. The dissent sees the statute the same way but feels that it is too clearly written to support the narrowing construction. How do you arbitrate this kind of dispute? How clear does a rent-seeking statute have to be under the Easterbrook approach?

3.   Institutional Cost-Benefit Analysis

Neil Komesar, *Imperfect Alternatives: Choosing Institutions in Law, Economics, and Public Policy* (1994), argues that allocation of public law decisionmaking duties should be the result of an institutional cost-benefit analysis, much like the Kaldor-Hicks concept of efficiency. (Under Kaldor-Hicks, a move is efficient if the overall benefits to society of such a move outweigh the overall costs.) Thus, he urges courts to reconsider their constitutional activism, in some areas at least, because it is not clear that the system-wide benefits of judge-made rules outweigh their costs. The benefits of judicial activism are limited by the structure of adjudication and the constrained resources of the court system. Costs of judicial activism include third-party expenses incurred in following new judicial rules, as well as the effects of judicial activism on other institutions, such as the legislature. Komesar does not apply his institutional cost-benefit analysis to issues of statutory interpretation, but other scholars have done so.

A Komesarian skepticism about the institutional limits of courts has driven most statutory scholars to endorse the notion that it is agencies, rather than courts, that should do most of the work updating statutes to reflect new circumstances. E.g., William Eskridge Jr., *Dynamic Statutory Interpretation* ch. 5 (1994), and Eskridge, *Expanding* Chevron's *Domain: A Comparative Institutional Analysis of the Relative Competence of Courts and Agencies to Interpret Statutes*, 2013 Wis. L.

---

[49] See, e.g., William Landes & Richard Posner, *Adjudication as a Private Good*, 8 J. Legal Stud. 235 (1979). But see George Priest, *The Common Law Process and the Selection of Efficient Rules*, 6 J. Legal Stud. 65 (1977).

Rev. 411. Professional administrators have the expertise and at least some resources to follow changes in society and to adapt statutory policy so that new developments do not undermine the statutory goals. They are in a position to think about the statutory scheme holistically and to balance competing considerations in the context of the big regulatory picture. Agencies will tend to be much more responsive to current presidential and legislative policy preferences than to those of enacting Congresses. Edward Rubin, *Dynamic Statutory Interpretation in the Administrative State,* Issues in Legal Scholarship: Dynamic Statutory Interpretation (2002): Article 2, http://www.bepress.com/ils/iss3/art2, argues that agencies will interpret statutes even more dynamically than courts will, and that agency dynamism fuels ever more judicial dynamism in statutory interpretation. Accord, Kevin Stack, *Interpreting Regulations,* 111 Mich. L. Rev. 355 (2012) (urging that agency regulations be interpreted purposively, given this characteristic form of agency reasoning).

Going further than Rubin, Stack, and Eskridge, Adrian Vermeule, *Judging Under Uncertainty: An Institutional Theory of Legal Interpretation* (2006), maintains that courts are incompetent to do anything but apply statutory plain meanings—and ought to defer to agencies in statutory interpretation unless the specific statutory language is clearly contrary to the agency's rule of law. The costs of such an approach, Vermeule argues, would be relatively small, because lawyers and officials would no longer "waste" their time reading legislative histories. The main benefit would be greater agency freedom to update statutes in light of new information. But by shackling courts, might such an approach leave agencies insufficiently monitored? Would Vermeule's "no frills textualism" undermine the legitimacy of statutory rules? Or might it sharpen lines of accountability for organs within the government?[50]

Evaluate the following case. Does an institutional cost-benefit analysis support the Court's approach? Does a textualist (Easterbrook), legislative intent (old Posner), or purposive (Macey, Stack, and newer Posner) approach support the majority? Or is the majority reading its own pro-business values into a public interest health-protective statute? As we have done with other cases, we start with a digest of the most relevant statutory language.

STATUTORY PREFACE TO THE FDA TOBACCO CASE

Food, Drug & Cosmetics Act of 1938, P.L. 75–717, codified at various points in 21 U.S.C.

Section 321(g)(1): The term "drug" means (A) articles recognized in the official United States Pharmacopœia, official Homœopathic Pharmacopœia of the United States, or official National Formulary, or any supplement to any of them; and (B) articles intended for use in the diagnosis, cure, mitigation, treatment, or prevention

---

[50] On accountability and statutory methodology, consider Jane Schacter, in *Accounting for Accountability in Dynamic Statutory Interpretation and Beyond,* Issues in Legal Scholarship: Dynamic Statutory Interpretation (2002): Article 5, http://www.bepress.com/ils/iss3/art5. Cf. *Printz v. United States,* 521 U.S. 898 (1997) (relying on notions of accountability to justify limits on congressional authority to regulate state officials); *New York v. United States,* 505 U.S. 144 (1992) (similar).

of disease in man or other animals; and (C) articles (other than food) intended to affect the structure or any function of the body of man or other animals; and (D) articles intended for use as a component of any article specified in clause (A), (B), or (C). * * *

Section 321(h): The term "device" * * * means an instrument, apparatus, implement, machine, contrivance, implant, in vitro reagent, or other similar or related article, including any component, part, or accessory, which is—

> **(3)** intended to affect the structure or any function of the body of man or other animals, and which does not achieve its primary intended purposes through chemical action within or on the body of man or other animals and which is not dependent upon being metabolized for the achievement of its primary intended purposes.

Section 321(n): If an article is alleged to be misbranded because the labeling or advertising is misleading, then in determining whether the labeling or advertising is misleading there shall be taken into account (among other things) not only representations made or suggested by statement, word, design, device, or any combination thereof, but also the extent to which the labeling or advertising fails to reveal facts material in the light of such representations or material with respect to consequences which may result from the use of the article to which the labeling or advertising relates under the conditions of use prescribed in the labeling or advertising thereof or under such conditions of use as are customary or usual.

Section 352(f), (j): A drug or device shall be deemed to be misbranded—

> **(f)** Unless its labeling bears (1) adequate directions for use; and (2) such adequate warnings against use in those pathological conditions or by children where its use may be dangerous to health, or against unsafe dosage or methods or duration of administration or application, in such manner and form, as are necessary for the protection of users, * * * [or]

> **(j)** If it is dangerous to health when used in the dosage or manner, or with the frequency or duration prescribed, recommended, or suggested in the labeling thereof.

Section 355(e)(1): The Secretary shall, after due notice and opportunity for hearing to the applicant, withdraw approval of an application with respect to any drug under this section if the Secretary finds (1) that clinical or other experience, tests, or other scientific data show that such drug is unsafe for use under the conditions of use upon the basis of which the application was approved; * * *

Federal Cigarette Labeling and Advertising Act, Pub. L. No. 89–92, 79 Stat. 282 (1965), codified at 15 U.S.C. § 1331 et seq.

Section 1331. It is the policy of the Congress, and the purpose of this chapter, to establish a comprehensive Federal program to deal with cigarette labeling and advertising with respect to any relationship between smoking and health, whereby—

(1) the public may be adequately informed about any adverse health effects of cigarette smoking by inclusion of warning notices on each package of cigarettes and in each advertisement of cigarettes; and

(2) commerce and the national economy may be (A) protected to the maximum extent consistent with this declared policy and (B) not impeded by diverse, nonuniform, and confusing cigarette labeling and advertising regulations with respect to any relationship between smoking and health.

Section 1333: It shall be unlawful for any person to manufacture, import, or package for sale or distribution within the United States any cigarettes the package for which fails to bear the following statement: "Caution: Cigarette Smoking May Be Hazardous to Your Health." Such statement shall be located in a conspicuous place on every cigarette package and shall appear in conspicuous and legible type in contrast by typography, layout, or color with other printed matter on the package.

Comprehensive Smoking Education Act of 1984, P.L. 98–474 (1984), amending 15 U.S.C. § 1331.

Section 1331(a)(1). [Congress revised § 1331 and added new warnings to cigarette packages and, in other revisions to § 1331, advertisements:]

> **SURGEON GENERAL'S WARNING:** Smoking Causes Lung Cancer, Heart Disease, Emphysema, And May Complicate Pregnancy.

> **SURGEON GENERAL'S WARNING:** Quitting Smoking Now Greatly Reduces Serious Risks to Your Health.

> **SURGEON GENERAL'S WARNING:** Smoking By Pregnant Women May Result in Fetal Injury, Premature Birth, And Low Birth Weight.

> **SURGEON GENERAL'S WARNING:** Cigarette Smoke Contains Carbon Monoxide.

FDA v. BROWN & WILLIAMSON TOBACCO CORP.

Supreme Court of the United States, 2000.
529 U.S. 120, 120 S.Ct. 1291, 146 L.Ed.2d 121.

JUSTICE O'CONNOR delivered the opinion of the Court.

[The Food, Drug, and Cosmetic Act (FDCA), 21 U.S.C. § 301 et seq., grants the Food and Drug Administration (FDA) the authority to regulate, among other items, "drugs" and "devices," §§ 321(g)–(h), 393. In 1996, the FDA asserted jurisdiction to regulate tobacco products, concluding that, under the FDCA, nicotine is a "drug" and cigarettes and smokeless tobacco are "devices" that deliver nicotine to the body. Pursuant to this authority, the FDA promulgated regulations governing tobacco products' promotion, labeling, and accessibility to children and adolescents. The FDA found that tobacco use is the nation's leading cause of premature death, resulting in more than 400,000 deaths annually, and that most adult smokers begin when they are minors. The regulations therefore aim to reduce tobacco use by minors so as to substantially reduce the prevalence of addiction in future generations, and thus the incidence of tobacco-related death and disease. Respondents, a group of tobacco manufacturers, retailers, and advertisers, filed this suit challenging the FDA's regulations. The Supreme Court held that Congress has not granted the FDA jurisdiction to regulate tobacco products.]

[II] In determining whether Congress has specifically addressed the question at issue, a reviewing court should not confine itself to examining a particular statutory provision in isolation. The meaning—or ambiguity—of certain words or phrases may only become evident when placed in context. It is a "fundamental canon of statutory construction that the words of a statute must be read in their context and with a view to their place in the overall statutory scheme." *Davis v. Michigan Dept. of Treasury*, 489 U.S. 803, 809 (1989). A court must therefore interpret the statute "as a symmetrical and coherent regulatory scheme," *Gustafson v. Alloyd Co.*, 513 U.S. 561, 569 (1995), and "fit, if possible, all parts into an harmonious whole," *FTC v. Mandel Brothers, Inc.*, 359 U.S. 385, 389 (1959). Similarly, the meaning of one statute may be affected by other Acts, particularly where Congress has spoken subsequently and more specifically to the topic at hand. See *United States v. Estate of Romani*, 523 U.S. 517, 530–31 (1998); *United States v. Fausto*, 484 U.S. 439, 453 (1988). In addition, we must be guided to a degree by common sense as to the manner in which Congress is likely to delegate a policy decision of such economic and political magnitude to an administrative agency. * * *

[In Part II.A, Justice O'Connor concluded that the FDCA rests on the assumption that the FDA will not approve unsafe drugs or devices and will remove them from the market as soon as it determines they are unsafe. E.g., 21 U.S.C. § 355(e)(1)–(3). Congress has enacted six statutes that require disclosure of information regarding tobacco products but do not ban their sale. E.g., 15 U.S.C. § 1331. Given the assumption of the FDCA, these statutes disallow the agency from finding that tobacco products fall within its health and safety regime. "A fundamental precept of the FDCA is that any product regulated by the FDA—but not banned—must be safe for its intended use. * * * Consequently, if tobacco products were within the FDA's jurisdiction, the Act would require the FDA to remove them from the market entirely. But a ban would contradict Congress' clear intent as expressed in its more recent, tobacco-specific legislation. The inescapable conclusion is that there is no room for tobacco products within the FDCA's regulatory scheme."]

[II.B]   In determining whether Congress has spoken directly to the FDA's authority to regulate tobacco, we must also consider in greater detail the tobacco-specific legislation that Congress has enacted over the past 35 years. At the time a statute is enacted, it may have a range of plausible meanings. Over time, however, subsequent acts can shape or focus those meanings. The "classic judicial task of reconciling many laws enacted over time, and getting them to 'make sense' in combination, necessarily assumes that the implications of a statute may be altered by the implications of a later statute." *Fausto.* This is particularly so where the scope of the earlier statute is broad but the subsequent statutes more specifically address the topic at hand. As we recognized recently in *United States v. Estate of*

Romani, "a specific policy embodied in a later federal statute should control our construction of the earlier statute, even though it has not been expressly amended."

Congress has enacted six separate pieces of legislation since 1965 addressing the problem of tobacco use and human health. Those statutes, among other things, require that health warnings appear on all packaging and in all print and outdoor advertisements, see 15 U.S.C. §§ 1331, 1333, 4402; prohibit the advertisement of tobacco products through "any medium of electronic communication" subject to regulation by the Federal Communications Commission (FCC), see §§ 1335, 4402(f); require the Secretary of Health and Human Services (HHS) to report every three years to Congress on research findings concerning "the addictive property of tobacco," 42 U.S.C. § 290aa–2(b)(2); and make States' receipt of certain federal block grants contingent on their making it unlawful "for any manufacturer, retailer, or distributor of tobacco products to sell or distribute any such product to any individual under the age of 18," § 300x–26(a)(1).

In adopting each statute, Congress has acted against the backdrop of the FDA's consistent and repeated statements that it lacked authority under the FDCA to regulate tobacco absent claims of therapeutic benefit by the manufacturer. In fact, on several occasions over this period, and after the health consequences of tobacco use and nicotine's pharmacological effects had become well known, Congress considered and rejected bills that would have granted the FDA such jurisdiction. Under these circumstances, it is evident that Congress' tobacco-specific statutes have effectively ratified the FDA's long-held position that it lacks jurisdiction under the FDCA to regulate tobacco products. Congress has created a distinct regulatory scheme to address the problem of tobacco and health, and that scheme, as presently constructed, precludes any role for the FDA.

[In 1964 congressional hearings responding to the Surgeon General's opinion that cigarette smoking is hazardous to one's health, FDA representatives testified that the agency did not have authority to regulate cigarettes or smoking under the FDCA. This was consistent with the position taken by the FDA's predecessor agency, the Bureau of Chemistry under the Pure Food & Drug Act of 1906.] And, as the FDA admits, there is no evidence in the text of the FDCA or its legislative history that Congress in 1938 even considered the applicability of the Act to tobacco products. Given the economic and political significance of the tobacco industry at the time, it is extremely unlikely that Congress could have intended to place tobacco within the ambit of the FDCA absent any discussion of the matter. * * *

Moreover, before enacting the FCLAA [Federal Cigarette Labeling and Advertising Act] in 1965, Congress considered and rejected several proposals to give the FDA the authority to regulate tobacco. In April 1963, Representative Udall introduced a bill "to amend the Federal Food, Drug, and Cosmetic Act so as to make that Act applicable to smoking products." H. R. 5973, 88th Cong., 1st Sess., 1. Two months later, Senator Moss introduced an identical bill in the Senate. S. 1682, 88th Cong., 1st Sess. (1963). In discussing his proposal on the Senate floor, Senator Moss explained that "this amendment simply places smoking products under FDA jurisdiction, along with foods, drugs, and cosmetics." 109 Cong. Rec. 10322 (1963). In December 1963, Representative Rhodes introduced another bill that would have amended the FDCA "by striking out 'food, drug, device, or cosmetic,' each place where it appears therein and inserting in lieu thereof 'food, drug, device, cosmetic, or smoking product.' " H. R. 9512, 88th Cong., 1st Sess., § 3 (1963). And in January 1965, five months before passage of the FCLAA, Representative Udall again introduced a bill to amend the FDCA "to make that Act applicable to smoking products." H. R. 2248, 89th Cong., 1st Sess., 1. None of these proposals became law.

Congress ultimately decided in 1965 to subject tobacco products to the less extensive regulatory scheme of the FCLAA, which created a "comprehensive Federal program to deal with cigarette labeling and advertising with respect to any relationship between smoking and health." Pub. L. 89–92, § 2, 79 Stat. 282. The FCLAA rejected any regulation of advertising, but it required the warning, "Caution: Cigarette Smoking May Be Hazardous to Your Health," to appear on all cigarette packages. *Id.*, § 4, 79 Stat. 283. In the Act's "Declaration of Policy," Congress stated that its objective was to balance the goals of ensuring that "the public may be adequately informed that cigarette smoking may be hazardous to health" and protecting "commerce and the national economy . . . to the maximum extent." *Id.*, § 2, 79 Stat. 282 (codified at 15 U.S.C. § 1331). * * *

[Justice O'Connor examined in detail each of the six subsequent tobacco-regulating statutes, as well as extensive legislative history supporting those changes and rejecting other legislative proposals: In each instance, the FDA disclaimed jurisdiction over cigarettes and other tobacco products, and Congress expanded upon the disclosure regime that it had adopted in 1965.]

Taken together, these actions by Congress over the past 35 years preclude an interpretation of the FDCA that grants the FDA jurisdiction to regulate tobacco products. We do not rely on Congress' failure to act—its consideration and rejection of bills that would have given the FDA this authority—in reaching this conclusion. Indeed, this is not a case of simple inaction by Congress that purportedly represents its acquiescence in an agency's position. To the contrary, Congress has enacted several statutes addressing the particular subject of tobacco and health, creating a distinct regulatory scheme for cigarettes and smokeless tobacco. In doing so, Congress has been aware of tobacco's health hazards and its pharmacological effects. It has also enacted this legislation against the background of the FDA repeatedly and consistently asserting that it lacks jurisdiction under the FDCA to regulate tobacco products as customarily marketed. Further, Congress has persistently acted to preclude a meaningful role for *any* administrative agency in making policy on the subject of tobacco and health. Moreover, the substance of Congress' regulatory scheme is, in an important respect, incompatible with FDA jurisdiction. Although the supervision of product labeling to protect consumer health is a substantial component of the FDA's regulation of drugs and devices, see 21 U.S.C. § 352 (1994 ed. and Supp. III), the FCLAA and the CSTHEA [Comprehensive Smokeless Tobacco Health Education Act] explicitly prohibit any federal agency from imposing any health-related labeling requirements on cigarettes or smokeless tobacco products, see. 15 U. S C. §§ 1334(a), 4406(a). * * *

[II.C]   [W]e are confident that Congress could not have intended to delegate a decision of such economic and political significance to an agency in so cryptic a fashion. To find that the FDA has the authority to regulate tobacco products, one must not only adopt an extremely strained understanding of "safety" as it is used throughout the Act—a concept central to the FDCA's regulatory scheme—but also ignore the plain implication of Congress' subsequent tobacco-specific legislation. It is therefore clear, based on the FDCA's overall regulatory scheme and the subsequent tobacco legislation, that Congress has directly spoken to the question at issue and precluded the FDA from regulating tobacco products. * * *

JUSTICE BREYER, joined by JUSTICE STEVENS, JUSTICE SOUTER, and JUSTICE GINSBURG, dissenting.

The Food and Drug Administration (FDA) has the authority to regulate "articles (other than food) intended to affect the structure or any function of the body. . . ." Federal Food, Drug and Cosmetic Act (FDCA), 21 U.S.C. § 321(g)(1)(C). Unlike the majority, I believe that tobacco products fit within this statutory language.

In its own interpretation, the majority nowhere denies the following two salient points. First, tobacco products (including cigarettes) fall within the scope of this statutory definition, read literally. Cigarettes achieve their mood-stabilizing effects through the interaction of the chemical nicotine and the cells of the central nervous system. Both cigarette manufacturers and smokers alike know of, and desire, that chemically induced result. Hence, cigarettes are "intended to affect" the body's "structure" and "function," in the literal sense of these words.

Second, the statute's basic purpose—the protection of public health—supports the inclusion of cigarettes within its scope. See *United States v. Article of Drug . . . Bacto-Unidisk,* 394 U.S. 784, 798 (1969) (FDCA "is to be given *a liberal construction consistent with [its] overriding purpose to protect the public health*" (emphasis added)). Unregulated tobacco use causes "more than 400,000 people [to] die each year from tobacco-related illnesses, such as cancer, respiratory illnesses, and heart disease." 61 Fed. Reg. 44398 (1996). Indeed, tobacco products kill more people in this country every year "than . . . AIDS, car accidents, alcohol, homicides, illegal drugs, suicides, and fires, *combined.*" *Ibid.* (emphasis added).

Despite the FDCA's literal language and general purpose (both of which support the FDA's finding that cigarettes come within its statutory authority), the majority nonetheless reads the statute as *excluding* tobacco products for two basic reasons:

(1) the FDCA does not "fit" the case of tobacco because the statute requires the FDA to prohibit dangerous drugs or devices (like cigarettes) outright, and the agency concedes that simply banning the sale of cigarettes is not a proper remedy; and

(2) Congress has enacted other statutes, which, when viewed in light of the FDA's long history of denying tobacco-related jurisdiction and considered together with Congress' failure explicitly to grant the agency tobacco-specific authority, demonstrate that Congress did not intend for the FDA to exercise jurisdiction over tobacco.

In my view, neither of these propositions is valid. Rather, the FDCA does not significantly limit the FDA's remedial alternatives. And the later statutes do not tell the FDA it cannot exercise jurisdiction, but simply leave FDA jurisdictional law where Congress found it. [C]f. Food and Drug Administration Modernization Act of 1997, 111 Stat. 2380 (codified at note following 21 U.S.C. § 321 (1994 ed., Supp. III)) (statute "shall" *not* "be construed to affect the question of whether" the FDA "has any authority to regulate any tobacco product").

The bulk of the opinion that follows will explain the basis for these latter conclusions. In short, I believe that the most important indicia of statutory meaning—language and purpose—along with the FDCA's legislative history (described briefly in Part I) are sufficient to establish that the FDA has authority to regulate tobacco. The statute-specific arguments against jurisdiction that the tobacco companies and the majority rely upon (discussed in Part II) are based on erroneous assumptions and, thus, do not defeat the jurisdiction-supporting thrust of the FDCA's language and purpose. The inferences that the majority draws from later legislative history are not persuasive, since (as I point out in Part III) one can just as easily infer from the later laws that Congress did not intend to affect the FDA's tobacco-related authority at all. And the fact that the FDA changed its mind about the scope of its own jurisdiction is legally insignificant because (as Part IV establishes) the agency's reasons for changing course are fully justified. [The FDA's stated reasons for not regulating were that it did not have evidence that the cigarette manufacturers "intended" for their product to have a medical effect; by the 1990s, there was ample evidence of such intent.]

In the majority's view, laws enacted since 1965 require us to deny jurisdiction, whatever the FDCA might mean in their absence. But why? Do those laws contain language barring FDA jurisdiction? The majority must concede that they do not. Do they contain provisions that are inconsistent with the FDA's exercise of jurisdiction? With one exception, the majority points to no such provision. Do they somehow repeal the principles of law * * * that otherwise would lead to the conclusion that the FDA has jurisdiction in this area? The companies themselves deny making any such claim. See Tr. of Oral Arg. 27 (denying reliance on doctrine of "partial repeal"). Perhaps the later laws "shape" and "focus" what the 1938 Congress meant a generation earlier. But this Court has warned against using the views of a later Congress to construe a statute enacted many years before. See *Pension Benefit Guaranty Corporation v. LTV Corp.,* 496 U.S. 633, 650 (1990) (later history is " 'a hazardous basis for inferring the intent of an earlier' Congress" (quoting *United States v. Price,* 361 U.S. 304, 313 (1960)). * * * Regardless, the later statutes do not support the majority's conclusion. That is because, whatever individual Members of Congress after 1964 may have assumed about the FDA's jurisdiction, the laws they enacted did not embody any such "no jurisdiction" assumption. And one cannot automatically *infer* an antijurisdiction intent, as the majority does, for the later statutes are both (and similarly) consistent with quite a different congressional desire, namely, the intent to proceed without interfering with whatever authority the FDA otherwise may have possessed. As I demonstrate below, the subsequent legislative history is critically ambivalent, for it can be read *either* as (a) "ratifying" a no-jurisdiction assumption, *or* as (b) leaving the jurisdictional question just where Congress found it. And the fact that both inferences are "equally tenable," *Pension Benefit Guaranty Corp.*, prevents the majority from drawing from the later statutes the firm, antijurisdiction implication that it needs.

Consider, for example, Congress' failure to provide the FDA with express authority to regulate tobacco—a circumstance that the majority finds significant. In fact, Congress *both* failed to grant express authority to the FDA when the FDA denied it had jurisdiction over tobacco *and* failed to take that authority expressly away when the agency later asserted jurisdiction. See, *e.g.*, S. 1262, 104th Cong., 1st Sess., § 906 (1995) (failed bill seeking to amend FDCA to say that "nothing in this Act or any other Act shall provide the [FDA] with any authority to regulate in any manner tobacco or tobacco products"); [other examples from the 104th Congress, 1995–96]. Consequently, the defeat of various different proposed jurisdictional changes proves nothing. This history shows only that Congress could not muster the votes necessary either to grant or to deny the FDA the relevant authority. It neither favors nor disfavors the majority's position.

[We omit the remainder of Justice Breyer's lengthy opinion, but like Justice O'Connor's opinion it is worth reading in its entirety.]

NOTE ON THE *FDA TOBACCO CASE* AND THE SUPREME COURT AS A STRATEGIC ACTOR IN OUR POLITY

1. *Lawmaking as a Sequential Game.* This case might be an example of strategic behavior among legal institutions.[51] For years, the FDA had known that tobacco was a deadly drug; one reason it did not move earlier was that it knew that any regulation would be overridden by Congress, where the tobacco companies were powerfully represented. President Clinton was a relatively anti-tobacco chief executive, who supported the regulatory moves of Dr. David Kessler, the FDA Administrator, to bring tobacco within the agency's health-protective regime. Unlike Presidents Bush and Reagan, Clinton would probably have vetoed a congressional effort to override the agency. Armed with that political knowledge—as well as the medical and "intent" knowledge emphasized in Justice Breyer's dissent—the agency moved to regulate.

The FDA's problem was that the tobacco industry might be able to mobilize the judiciary to override the agency even if Congress-with-the-President would not. Affirming the Fourth Circuit (filled with North Carolina and Virginia tobacco farms as well as GOP judges appointed in the 1980s), the Supreme Court trumped the agency's initiative. Under the assumptions of rational choice theory, the Court might have been reluctant to act if it were likely to be overridden by Congress—but the Justices knew that would not happen, because relatively pro-tobacco Republicans controlled both houses of Congress in 2000. By reversing the default rule—from the FDA's regulation to the industry's nonregulation—the Court reversed the political outcome, and its resolution stuck until the Democrats secured control of both the Presidency and Congress in 2009.

---

[51] The rich history is recounted and analyzed in Theodore Ruger, *The Story of* FDA v. Brown & Williamson *(2000): The Norm of Agency Continuity*, in *Statutory Interpretation Stories* 334–65 (Eskridge, Frickey & Garrett eds. 2010).

2.   *The Judiciary as a Part of the Rent-Seeking Process?* The FDA Tobacco Case can be viewed as one kind of caution about economic theories of statutory interpretation, namely, those seeing courts as a remedy for legislative rent-seeking. The courts might be part of the interest-group process. Groups press for the appointment of friendly lawyers or ideologically compatible law professors as judges and then use the judiciary to overturn at least some of their defeats in the political process. This is easier to accomplish by "have" groups, because judges tend to be libertarian, either as a matter of philosophy or practicality (it is much easier for the courts to slow things down than to require the state to act), and "have" groups are usually trying to protect their freedom of action against government regulation.[52] So the FDA Tobacco Case can be viewed, in part, as an expression of the majority Justices' personal aversion to aggressive state regulation of private industry. The five Justices in the majority were the most conservative Republican Justices, the same jurists who formed the majority several months later in *Bush v. Gore,* 531 U.S. 98 (2000), an intervention into the 2000 election that assured the election of the GOP's candidate, Governor George W. Bush; the four dissenters in the FDA Tobacco Case were the four dissenters in *Bush v. Gore.*

3.   *The Rule of Law as a Judicial Preference.* There is another way of looking at the FDA Tobacco Case. Most judges carry or develop strong preferences for rule-of-law values, including predictability in the law, following orderly procedures, and acting within jurisdictional boundaries. The FDA Tobacco Case might be an example of the power of the rule of law: these companies may be morally squalid, but regulation of moral squalor must still follow the proper procedures under the appropriate congressional authorization. As one scholar puts it, the 1965 statute confirmed a longstanding political *deal*, that the FDCA did not regulate tobacco products, which would be subject to warning and disclosure regimes instead (the FCLAA and subsequent laws). Everything Congress did after 1965 reflected and reaffirmed that deal—until the FDA unilaterally abrogated it in 1996. Richard Merrill, *The FDA May Not Regulate Tobacco Products as "Drugs" or "Medical Devices,"* 47 Duke L.J. 1071, 1074–81 (1998).

Consistent with Merrill's argument, Justice O'Connor rested her opinion upon an equilibrium-based idea: the longstanding agreement that the FDA could not regulate smoking without fresh congressional authorization, and the reliance interests it generated, have created a stable "rule of law" not perfectly reflected in the statutory text. This kind of response (supported by lots of legislative history) is inconsistent with Justice Scalia's philosophy—but he swallowed, without a textualist whimper, Justice O'Connor's lengthy recitation of evidence from legislative hearings, reports, and debates. Why would he join that part of the opinion? A further irony: Justice O'Connor (with Justices Scalia and Thomas going along) deploys the kind of "institutional legislative history" that Justices Breyer and Stevens have championed—with Breyer and Stevens themselves in dissent based in part on the plain meaning rule.

---

[52] See also Mark Galanter, *Why the "Haves" Come Out Ahead: Speculations on the Limits of Legal Change,* 9 L. & Soc'y Rev. 95 (1974), which shows how Repeat-Player "Have" groups can deploy the litigation process to advance their goals even if judges are neutral or even hostile.

NOTE ON THE *2009* CONGRESSIONAL OVERRIDE OF THE *FDA* TOBACCO DECISION

Congress ultimately responded to *Brown & Williamson* with the Family Smoking Prevention & Tobacco Control Act of 2009, Pub. L. No. 111–31, 123 Stat. 1776 (2009). To discourage tobacco use among younger persons, Title I of the Act banned sales of tobacco products to persons under the age of 18 and authorized the FDA to develop an enforcement scheme. Title I also required the FDA to reissue the rules that had been invalidated in *Brown & Williamson*. Other provisions of the 2009 Act gave the FDA authority to set standards for the content of tobacco products (including tar and nicotine levels), to register tobacco companies, and to inspect such companies for compliance with the law. Before tobacco companies can introduce new products, they must secure FDA approval (the FDA has traditionally exercised its approval power aggressively to force changes in products and their marketing). The Act also imposed limitations on the FDA's regulatory authority. Sections 906–907 bar the FDA from banning face-to-face retail sales of tobacco products entirely or from requiring a doctor's prescription to purchase these items.

Title II of the 2009 Act imposed nine new warnings for tobacco products, 15 U.S.C. § 1333, and authorized the FDA to develop the details of these warnings. After notice and comment, the FDA in 2011 announced final rules, with detailed requirements for advertisements of tobacco products. 76 Fed. Reg. 36,628 (June 22, 2011) (final rule, codified in 21 C.F.R. Part 1141, with responses to comments). Among the most controversial were new FDA requirements that packages include not only verbal warnings but also "graphic images" of smokers ravaged by lung cancer and other smoking-related illnesses. Tobacco companies successfully challenged these rules because they forced the companies to spout the government's "ideological" message, contrary to the First Amendment. *R.J. Reynolds Tobacco Co. v. Food & Drug Administration,* 696 F.3d 1205, 1216–17 (D.C. Cir. 2012) (characterizing the FDA-required advertisements as "inflammatory" rather than purely factual disclosures).

Does the congressional override mean that *Brown & Williamson* was wrongly decided? On the one hand, the override vindicates the FDA's original rulemaking. Also relevant is the FDA's finding that the limitations and warnings imposed by its original rules would have saved thousands of lives between 1996 and 2010. On the other hand, the 2009 override statute was not only a more legitimate form of regulation (accomplished after achieving the political consensus required by the vetogate-ridden structure of Congress and bringing the tobacco industry to the table), but also went much further than the FDA had dared go in the 1990s (and remember, the Kessler FDA was a pretty daring agency). Congress was able to reconcile the various disclosure statutes with the drug-regulatory statute—and the 2009 override was an occasion for Congress to strengthen required disclosures and to authorize the FDA to create more effective disclosures than the abstract ones Congress had been imposing (with disappointing effects) since 1965. On the legitimating and policy-updating advantages of congressional overrides, see Matthew Christiansen & William Eskridge Jr., *Congressional Overrides of Supreme Court Statutory Interpretation Decisions, 1967–2011,* 92 Tex. L. Rev. 1317 (2014).

C. PRAGMATIC THEORIES OF STATUTORY INTERPRETATION

In *How Judges Think* (2008), Judge Richard Posner distinguishes between "legalistic" and "pragmatic" theories of statutory interpretation. Legalistic theories claim that law is an autonomous discipline that can reach neutral interpretations through application of plain meanings (assisted perhaps with dictionaries and linguists), following precedent, reasoning by analogy, and the like. Pragmatic theories, in contrast, openly admit that law is not (entirely) separate from politics and that interpretation carries with it discretion and policy choice. Hart and Sacks's purpose-based interpretation is, by this reading, pragmatic, and Posner's current approach, well-illustrated in the LSD Case above, is an updated or more sophisticated version of legal process theory. Similarly pragmatic is Justice Stephen Breyer, as illustrated in his dissenting opinion in the FDA Tobacco Case and in his books, *Active Liberty: Interpreting Our Democratic Constitution* (2005), and *Making Our Democracy Work: A Judge's View* (2010).

Another kind of *pragmatic* thinking is philosophical. Inspired by American pragmatic philosophers who rejected "foundationalist" thinking and urged multifocal theorizing, the following article reflects a practical approach to statutory interpretation that the authors believe best reflects what the Supreme Court (and most state courts) are actually doing in statutory cases.

WILLIAM ESKRIDGE JR. AND PHILIP FRICKEY, *STATUTORY INTERPRETATION AS PRACTICAL REASONING*
42 Stan. L. Rev. 321, 345–53 (1990).

[Eskridge and Frickey criticize each of the leading "foundationalist" theories of interpretation—textualism, original intent, purpose—and find each wanting in the same ways.] [T]he leading foundationalist theories cannot redeem their claim to follow from the very nature of majoritarian democracy, do not yield objective and determinate answers, and cannot convincingly exclude other values, including current values. *Weber* [Chapter 1, § 3] and *Griffin* illustrate our theoretical critique and suggest that the Supreme Court does not follow any one of the foundationalist theories. We now suggest that these observations form the basis for a positive theory which refuses to privilege intention, purpose, or text as the sole touchstone of interpretation, but which both explains the Supreme Court's practice in statutory interpretation and, at the same time, reflects the insights of modern theories of interpretation.

First, statutory interpretation involves creative policymaking by judges and is not just the Court's figuring out the answer that was put 'in' the statute by the enacting legislature. An essential insight of hermeneutics [the philosophy of interpretation] is that interpretation is a dynamic process, and that the interpreter is inescapably situated historically. 'Every age has to understand a transmitted text in its own way,' says Gadamer [in *Truth and Method* 263 (1965)]. * * *

Hermeneutics suggests that the text lacks meaning *until* it is interpreted. * * * [O]ne does not 'understand' a text in the abstract, without an 'application' of the text to a specific problem. American pragmatism, also influenced by Aristotle, complements this hermeneutic insight. Reasoning in human affairs does not seek abstract answers, but concretely useful results. Theories of reasoning, for [William James, in *Pragmatism* (1907)] are simply "mental modes of *adaptation* to reality, rather than revelations or gnostic answers."

Consider *Weber* in this light. The interpretive process is creative, not mechanical. Viewed in the context of the complex goals of the Civil Rights Act and subsequent difficulties in implementation, making sense of the statute's command not to 'discriminate' requires much more than finding a meaning for the term. Even if the interpretive process were viewed as retrieving the answer Congress would have reached in 1964 (had it deliberated on the issue), the inquiry involves 'imaginative' work by the judge. These lessons of *Weber* are consistent with the insights of modern literary theory, historiography, and philosophy: There is no interpretation without an interpreter, and the interpreter will interact with the text or historical event. Just as the interpreter learns from the text and history, so too does she speak to it. What was decisive in *Weber,* surely to Justice Blackmun and probably to other Justices in the majority as well, was what the interpreters learned about the statute from considering the facts of the case: More than a decade after the statute was enacted there were only 2 percent blacks in the craft workforce, contrasted with 39 percent blacks in the overall workforce.

Second, because this creation of statutory meaning is not a mechanical operation, it often involves the interpreter's choice among several competing answers. Although the interpreter's range of choices is somewhat constrained by the text, the statute's history, and the circumstances of its application, the actual choice will not be 'objectively' determinable; interpretation will often depend upon political and other assumptions held by judges. Under Gadamer's [analysis], interpretation seeks 'to make the law concrete in each specific case,' and '[t]he creative supplementing of the law that is involved is a task that is reserved to the judge.' As a practical matter, how could it be otherwise? Many statutes leave key terms ambiguous, often intentionally, and thereby delegate rulemaking authority to courts or agencies. Over time, these ambiguities and unanswered questions multiply, as society changes and background legal assumptions change with it. Hermeneutics suggests that as the interpreter's own background context—her 'tradition'—changes, so too will her interpretive choices. * * *

Third, when statutory interpreters make these choices, they are normally not driven by any single value—adhering to majoritarian commands *or* encouraging private reliance on statutory texts *or* finding the best answer according to modern policy—but are instead driven by multiple values. Both hermeneutics and pragmatism emphasize the complex nature of human reasoning. When solving a problem, we tend to test different solutions, evaluating each against a range of values and beliefs we hold as important. The pragmatic idea that captures this concept is the 'web of beliefs' metaphor. We all accept a number of different values and propositions that, taken together, constitute a web of intertwined beliefs about, for example, the role of statutes in our public law. Each of us may accord different weight to the specific values, but almost no one excludes any of the important values altogether. Decisionmaking is, therefore, polycentric, and thus cannot be linear and purely deductive. Instead, it is spiral and inductive: We consider the consistency of the evidence for each value before reaching a final decision, and even then check our decision against the values we esteem the most. Given this web of beliefs and the spiral form of decisionmaking, an individual's reasoning will depend very much on the context of the case at hand, and specifically on the relative strength of each consideration.

Consider *Griffin* from the perspective of the web metaphor. A Justice who is a thoroughgoing textualist would surely agree with the *Griffin* result, given the relative clarity of the statutory language. But so could an intentionalist Justice: Although there is no smoking gun in the legislative history, the legislative context and the strong statutory language suggest that Congress would probably have favored substantial punitive sanctions had it addressed the issue. And so could a purposivist Justice, because surely one major purpose of the statute was to deter employer misconduct, which the $302,000 award in *Griffin* would seem to do. Even a Justice concerned only with fair results might applaud the *Griffin* result. In fact, seven Justices of differing jurisprudential stripes formed the majority in *Griffin,* and Justice Rehnquist's opinion justified the result by arguing from the relatively clear statutory language, the original legislative intent, the overall statutory purpose, and (to some extent) the reasonableness of the interpretation. Whether ultimately correct, the opinion in *Griffin,* by its strategy of cumulative assessment and weighing of factors potentially relevant to interpretation, seems more persuasive than would any foundationalist avenue to the same result. * * *

In addition to the web of beliefs idea, two other metaphors, one drawn from the pragmatist tradition and one drawn from the hermeneutical tradition, suggest more precisely how a practical reasoning approach would work. First, consider [pragmatist philosopher Charles] Peirce's contrast of the chain and the cable. A chain is no stronger than its weakest link, because if any of the singly connected links should break, so too will the chain. In contrast, a cable's strength relies not on that of individual threads, but upon their cumulative strength as they are woven together. Legal arguments are often constructed as chains, but they tend to be more successful when they are cable-like. The Court's opinion in *Griffin* draws its strength from this phenomenon: The text, one probable purpose, some legislative history, and current policy each lend some—even if not unequivocal—support to the result. Each thread standing alone is subject to quarrel and objection; woven together, the threads persuaded both Justice Rehnquist *and* Justice Brennan, a not unimpressive achievement.

In many cases of statutory interpretation, of course, the threads will not all run in the same direction. The cable metaphor suggests that in these cases the result will depend upon the strongest overall combination of threads. That, in turn, depends on which values the decisionmakers find most important, and on the strength of the arguments invoking each value. For most of the Supreme Court Justices, a persuasive textual argument is a stronger thread than an otherwise equally persuasive current policy or fairness argument, because of the reliance and legislative supremacy values implicated in following the clear statutory text. And a clear and convincing textual argument obviously counts more than one beclouded with doubts and ambiguities.

Our model of practical reasoning in statutory interpretation is still not complete, for it lacks a dynamic element that is intrinsic to human reasoning in general, and interpretation in particular. The various arguments (the threads of our cable) do not exist in isolation; they interact with one another. A final metaphor that captures this interaction is the 'hermeneutical circle': A part can only be understood in the context of the whole, and the whole cannot be understood without analyzing its various parts. To interpret the statute in *Griffin,* for example, the interpreter will look at the text and the legislative history and the purpose and current values. But to evaluate the text, the interpreter will consider it in light of the whole enterprise, including the history, purpose, and current values. In other words, none of the interpretive threads can be viewed in isolation, and each will be evaluated in its relation to the other threads. * * *

The positive metaphors of our analysis—the web of beliefs idea, the cable-versus-chain contrast, and the hermeneutical circle—suggest the contours of a practical reasoning model of statutory interpretation that roughly captures the Court's practice. Our model holds that an interpreter will look at a broad range of evidence—text, historical evidence, and the text's evolution—and thus form a preliminary view of the statute. The interpreter then develops that preliminary view by testing various possible interpretations against the multiple criteria of fidelity to the text, historical accuracy, and conformity to contemporary circumstances and values. Each criterion is relevant, yet none necessarily trumps the others. Thus while an apparently clear text, for example, will create insuperable doubts for a contrary interpretation if the other evidence reinforces it *(Griffin),* an apparently clear text may yield if other considerations cut against it *(Weber).* As the interpreter comes to accept an interpretation (perhaps a confirmation of her preliminary view), she considers a congeries of supporting arguments, which may buttress her view much 'like the legs of a chair and unlike the links of a chain.' "

[As tweaked by Eskridge in light of pedagocical feedback, the pragmatic method can be diagrammed along the following lines:]

A PRACTICAL REASONING MODEL OF STATUTORY INTERPRETATION

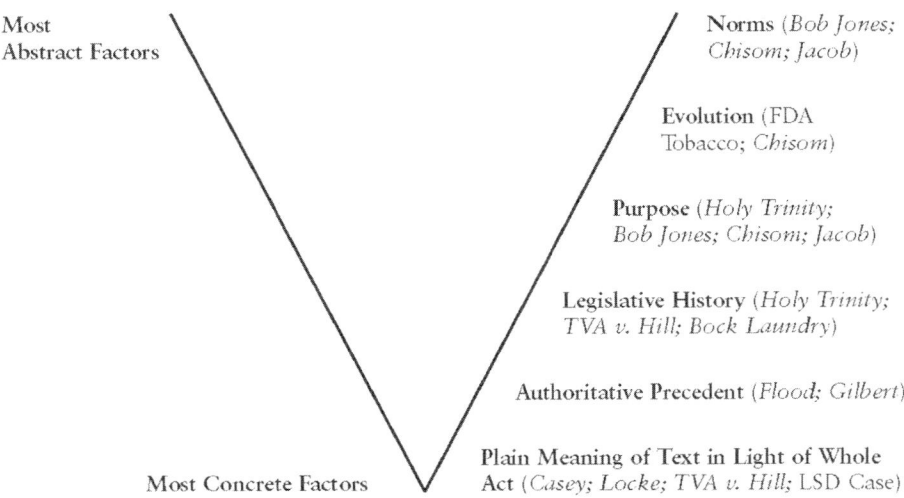

Most
Abstract Factors

Norms (*Bob Jones;
Chisom; Jacob*)

Evolution (FDA
Tobacco; *Chisom*)

Purpose (*Holy Trinity;
Bob Jones; Chisom; Jacob*)

Legislative History (*Holy Trinity;
TVA v. Hill; Bock Laundry*)

Authoritative Precedent (*Flood; Gilbert*)

Most Concrete Factors

Plain Meaning of Text in Light of Whole
Act (*Casey; Locke; TVA v. Hill;* LSD Case)

* * * [T]his model identifies the primary evidentiary inquiries in which the Court will engage. The model is, in crude imagery, a "funnel of abstraction." It is funnel-shaped for three reasons. First, the model suggests the hierarchy of sources that the Court has in fact assumed. For example, in formulating her preunderstanding of the statute *and* in testing it, the interpreter will value more highly a good argument based on the statutory text than a conflicting and equally strong argument based upon the statutory purpose. Second, the model suggests the degree of abstraction at each source. The sources at the bottom of the diagram involve more focused, concrete inquiries, typically with a more limited range of arguments. As the interpreter moves up the diagram, a broader range of arguments is available, partly because the inquiry is less concrete. Third, the model illustrates the pragmatistic and hermeneutical insights explained above: In formulating and testing her understanding of the statute, the interpreter will move up and down the diagram, evaluating and comparing the different considerations represented by each source of argumentation. * * *

NOTE ON THE FUNNEL OF ABSTRACTION

On the whole, the Funnel of Abstraction is a descriptive theory of statutory interpretation: this is how the judicial (or administrative) mind goes about deciding statutory cases, as a practical matter.[53] Its insights derive in large part from an

---

[53] For evidence suggesting that this diagram accurately displays the factors routinely taken into account in judicial opinions interpreting statutes, see Lawrence Solan, *The Language of Statutes: Laws and Their Interpretation* 50–159 (2010); Nancy Staudt et al., *Judging Statutes: Interpretive Regimes,* 38 Loy. L.A. L. Rev. 1909 (2005) (empirical analysis of tax decisions); Nicholas Zeppos, *The Use of Authority in Statutory Interpretation: An Empirical Analysis,* 70 Tex. L. Rev. 1073 (1992) (earlier and broader analysis of statutory interpretation decisions). See also Frank Cross, *The Theory and Practice of Statutory Interpretation* 24–133

application of American pragmatism to statutory interpretation. See Daniel Farber, *Practical Reason and the Scholarship of Philip P. Frickey,* 98 Calif. L. Rev. 1111 (2010); Francis Mootz III, *Ugly American Hermeneutics,* 10 Nev. L.J. 587 (2010) (fascinating account of the interplay of Americans' "ugly" understanding of hermeneutics, which is redeemed by their pragmatic application of statutes to concrete cases).

The features of the Funnel that are most important are these: **First**, judges will consider a variety of factors, including statutory text and structure, but also statutory purpose, legislative history, authoritative precedents, practical applications of the statute, and current norms. The Funnel theory is distinctive in the formal importance it attributes to *stare decisis* in statutory cases: Supreme Court precedents interpreting a particular statute, or words and phrases borrowed from other statutes (e.g., *Casey*), are always relevant and will be controlling if the statutory text is open-ended or vague. See Peter Tiersma, *The Textualization of Precedent,* 82 Notre Dame L. Rev. 1187 (2007), who describes a process where, over time, Supreme Court statutory precedents will often displace the statutory text as the most concrete authority, unless Congress frequently amends the statute and overrides and modifies those precedents.

Second, the factors have varying legal force. They are hierarchical: a good text-based argument will trump a good legislative history or purpose argument, as in *Casey*. (*Chisom* would be distinguishable on the ground that the statutory text was ambiguous and statutory structure supported the majority.) This feature, by the way, is normative as well as descriptive. The funnel authors are textualists, like Justice Rehnquist in *Griffin*, for they start with the text but do not stop with the text (as Justice Scalia would have done in *Griffin*). See also Lawrence Solan, *The Language of Statutes: Laws and Their Interpretation* (2010), a similarly pragmatic account by a text-loving scholar of linguistics as well as statutory interpretation.

Third, and most unlike more formalist theories, the Funnel of Abstraction posits that the various factors will *interact* with one another. Thus, a textual "plain meaning" will not become firm in the judicial mind until *after* the judge has considered all the evidence; the "authority" of a precedent will not be conclusive until the judge has thought about its consistency with statutory text and purpose; the good judge will not be firm about the relevance of "norms" until she has processed the weight of the textual and historical factors. And so forth.

Think about how the Funnel helps explain the decisions in this chapter, especially *Holy Trinity, Bock Laundry, Jacob, Li,* and *Chisom,* which openly follow the method, but also cases that don't seem to follow the method, like *Casey* and *Marshall*. Although Judge Easterbrook is not a "Funnel judge," the judges who went along with his decision in *Marshall* might well have been—what might have been persuasive to them? Consider the debate among the Justices in *Brown & Williamson* as a debate about how to apply the Funnel. How would the Funnel apply to the issue raised by the Case of the Speluncean Explorers? Map out your analysis and then rethink it after you read the material that immediately follows. Next, take the reasoning and see if you can devise a more complicated model for understanding the courts' decisions. Finally, rethink the

(2009); Robert John Araujo, *Method in Interpretation: Practical Wisdom and the Search for Meaning in Public Legal Texts,* 68 Miss. L.J. 225 (1998); Morrell Mullins, *Tools Not Rules: The Heuristic Nature of Statutory Interpretation,* 30 J. Legis. 1 (2003). Cf. Miranda McGowan, *Do as I Do, Not as I Say: An Empirical Investigation of Justice Scalia's Ordinary Meaning Method of Statutory Interpretation,* 78 Miss. L.J. 129 (2008) (showing that even Justice Scalia ignores statutory text that he thinks delegates lawmaking authority to federal judges).

Funnel from a normative perspective. What values should courts be pressing in statutory cases? The Funnel assumes that the rule of law values (text, original intent, precedent) are the weightiest and that process and substantive values are relevant but less weighty. Should the text be as privileged as we assume it to be? Should it be as flexible as hermeneutics suggests? And so on. See how your normative deliberation edits or changes the Funnel or your variation of it.

NOTE ON INSTITUTIONAL CONSIDERATIONS IN STATUTORY INTERPRETATION

Yet another kind of "pragmatic" consideration in statutory interpretation is *institutional*. How does the operation of an institution affect its interpretation of statutes? This is the kind of inquiry Professors Hart and Sacks (and, before them, Justices Brandeis and Frankfurter) pioneered, and that Justice Breyer represents today. Consider just a few hypotheses that such institutional thinking might generate.

1. *Supreme Court of the United States.* Often forgotten is the fact that the Supreme Court "administers" a pyramid of lower federal courts, state courts, agencies, and other governmental bodies. As a practical matter, the Court cannot operate as a court of correction, rebuking lower courts for incorrect decisions, and so the Court's approach to cases reflects its institutional incentive to "administer" the rule of law in this country. This institutional role offers a possible argument in favor of any theory that offers more predictability in statutory cases. Thus, if it were true that judges adhering closely to Justice Scalia's new textualism would produce more consistent results, that would be an excellent argument for all the Justices to adopt his approach *and* to impose it on lower courts as a matter of *stare decisis*. See Sydney Foster, *Should Courts Give* Stare Decisis *Effect to Statutory Interpretation Methodology?*, 96 Geo. L.J. 1863 (2008). Unfortunately, there is no evidence that the new textualism constrains interpreters in any manner. E.g., Cross, *Practice of Statutory Interpretation*, 177–79; James Brudney & Corey Ditslear, *Canons of Construction and the Elusive Quest for Neutral Reasoning*, 58 Vanderbilt L. Rev. 1, 57–60, 95–105 (2005).

A more modest, but perhaps also more robust, doctrinal effect of the Court's institutional role is that the Court may follow an *anti-messiness principle*. Given the choice between a complicated multi-factor approach and a simpler bright line rule, the Court prefers the latter, because it is easier to administer. See Anita Krishnakumar, *The Anti-Messiness Principle in Statutory Interpretation*, 87 Notre Dame L. Rev. 1465 (2012). The Supreme Court's decision in *TVA v. Hill* is a classic example: the anti-messiness principle was one strong reason for the Court to *reject* the dissenters' approach, whereby expensive or almost-completed projects could be carried out notwithstanding their effects on endangered species. Likewise, the principle is consistent with the Court's decisions in *Casey, Chisom, Locke,* and *Chapman* (the LSD Case). On the other hand, the points of law emerging from *Holy Trinity* and the FDA Tobacco Case, for examples, are complicated, "messy" precepts, and the Court in each case rejected a simpler bright-line rule. So, too, are the highest state court dispositions in *Jacob* and *Li*.

2. *Lower Federal Courts.* Given the foregoing analysis, one might assume that lower federal courts should behave exactly like the Supreme Court. Surely, a lower federal court, like the Seventh Circuit in *Marshall*, needs to consider the Supreme Court's preferred methodology and its precedents. But there is ample room for

divergence, and there is good reason to expect that lower court interpretive practice might differ from that followed by the Supreme Court. See Aaron-Andrew Bruhl, *Hierarchy and Heterogeneity: How to Read a Statute in a Lower Court,* 97 Cornell L. Rev. 433, 442–58 (2012). An obvious difference is that Congress regularly responds to and overrides Supreme Court statutory decisions, especially when the Justices invite overrides, but it rarely overrides lower court decisions, because they are less salient and perhaps less ripe for political response. Hence, lower courts ought to be less attentive to institutional dialogue than the Supreme Court is, and they ought to assume that their interpretations will not provoke a political response. *Id.* at 460.

Bruhl also suggests that Supreme Court review will often trigger the creation of new sources of interpretive guidance, especially in the form of *amicus* briefs. *Id.* at 464. The Solicitor General plays a major role in most Supreme Court statutory cases for this reason, and not so big a role among lower courts. Because the Solicitor General mediates, within the executive branch, purposive agency constructions, higher-level presidential policies (sometimes), and coherence and rule of law concerns, her or his advice to the Supreme Court is usually followed. But this deep and public engagement of the Solicitor General and agency inputs into statutory interpretation decisions usually does not occur in lower court cases.

Further, given the resource constraints on lower federal courts (fewer staff, poor briefing, a dearth of helpful *amicus* briefs), Bruhl maintains that their constructions of federal statutes will and ought to be less methodologically complex—hence less reliance on hard-to-research legislative history and elaborate examinations of the whole statute and other parts of the code. *Id.* at 470–6. Lower courts, Bruhl maintains, ought to hew closely to statutory plain meanings, the reasoning and even dicta of Supreme Court or binding appellate decisions, and agency interpretations. *Id.* at 477–84. Such a restricted approach to statutory interpretation might seem much less appropriate for federal circuit courts than for district courts, however. *Id.*

Do you think a system in which federal district courts, appellate courts, and the Supreme Court apply different methodological rules is workable? How would this affect Congress's incentives to draft in the shadow of legal rules? Think about the LSD case. You know how the Seventh Circuit (in *Marshall*) and the Supreme Court (in *Chapman,* affirming the Seventh Circuit) handled the issue, and the different methodologies each judge applied. You also know that the Department of Justice, including the Solicitor General, supported the stiff penalty. Do you think the trial court should have applied a different methodological approach than that applied by the Seventh Circuit? See for yourself whether it did. *United States v. Marshall,* 706 F. Supp, 650 (C.D. Ill. 1989).

3. *State High Courts, Including Elected Judges.* Recall that Chief Judge Judith Kaye maintained that state courts are common law courts—and that such a connection to common law methodology generates greater nontextual flexibility for state high courts. See Judith Kaye, *State Courts at the Dawn of a New Century: Common Law Courts Reading Statutes and Constitutions,* 70 N.Y.U. L. Rev. 1 (1995); accord, Jeffrey Pojanowski, *Statutes in Common Law Courts,* 91 Tex. L. Rev. 479 (2013). Does this institutional theory support Kaye's decision in *Jacob*—and justify a result that the U.S. Supreme Court might not have reached?

The election of many state court judges, for instance, drives a wedge between a judge's constituency and the faithful agent model for statutory interpretation. See Aaron-Andrew Bruhl & Ethan Leib, *Elected Judges and Statutory Interpretation,* 79 U.

Chi. L. Rev. 1215, 1243–46 (2012); Jed Handelsman Shugerman, *The Twist of Long Terms: Judicial Elections, Role Fidelity, and American Tort Law,* 98 Geo. L.J. 1349 (2010). Indeed, elected judges might best be understood as faithful agents of "We the People, with whom judges have the same kind of direct relationship as other "representatives." Bruhl and Leib argue, for example, that the kind of dynamic interpretation Kaye applied in the *Jacob* and *Dana* appeals would have been much more democratically legitimate if the judges of the New York Court of Appeals were elected or were subject to retention votes. Bruhl & Leib, *Elected Judges,* 1262–67.

The foregoing accounts do not exhaust current state court practice. Indeed, as the following case and notes demonstrate, state courts have pioneered newer versions of text-based as well as pragmatic approaches to statutory interpretation and have often imposed such methodologies as a matter of methodological *stare decisis* (consistent with Sydney Foster's article, noted above).

STATUTORY PREFACE TO *PORTLAND GENERAL ELECTRIC*

Oregon Revised Statutes (1992)

Section 659.360

(3) The employee seeking parental leave shall be entitled to utilize any accrued vacation leave, sick leave or other compensatory leave, paid or unpaid, during the parental leave. The employer may require the employee seeking parental leave to utilize any accrued leave during the parental leave unless otherwise provided by an agreement of the employer and the employee, by collective bargaining agreement or by employer policy.

(6) The parental leave required by subsection (1) of this section is not required to be granted with pay unless so specified by agreement of the employer and employee, by collective bargaining agreement or by employer policy.

PORTLAND GENERAL ELECTRIC CO. V. BUREAU OF LABOR AND INDUSTRIES

Supreme Court of Oregon, 1993.
317 Or. 606, 859 P.2d 1143.

VAN HOOMISSEN, J. * * *

[The issue was whether an employee taking family or medical leave could take paid sick leave even if she or he were not sick. Following the opinion of the Bureau of Labor, the Supreme Court of Oregon unanimously ruled that employees had that option, essentially converting much of the unpaid leave time into paid leave. Justice Van Hoomissen's opinion started with a statement of the interpretive approach Oregon courts are supposed to follow.] In interpreting a statute, the court's task is to discern the intent of the legislature. ORS 174.020. To do that, the court examines both the text and context of the statute. That is the first level of our analysis.

In this first level of analysis, the text of the statutory provision itself is the starting point for interpretation and is the best evidence of the legislature's intent. In trying to ascertain the meaning of a statutory provision, and thereby to inform the court's inquiry into legislative intent, the court considers rules of construction of the statutory text that bear directly on how to read the text. Some of those rules are mandated by statute, including, for example, the statutory enjoinder "not to insert what has been omitted, or to omit what has been inserted." ORS 174.010. Others are found in the case law, including, for example, the rule that words of common usage typically should be given their plain, natural, and ordinary meaning.

Also at the first level of analysis, the court considers the context of the statutory provision at issue, which includes other provisions of the same statute and other related statutes. Just as with the court's consideration of the text of a statute, the court utilizes rules of construction that bear directly on the interpretation of the statutory provision in context. Some of those rules are mandated by statute, including, for example, the principles that "where there are several provisions or particulars such construction is, if possible, to be adopted as will give effect to all," ORS 174.010, and that "a particular intent shall control a general one that is inconsistent with it," ORS 174.020. Other such rules of construction are found in case law, including, for example, the rules that use of a term in one section and not in another section of the same statute indicates a purposeful omission, and that use of the same term throughout a statute indicates that the term has the same meaning throughout the statute.

If the legislature's intent is clear from the above-described inquiry into text and context, further inquiry is unnecessary.

If, but only if, the intent of the legislature is not clear from the text and context inquiry, the court will then move to the second level, which is to consider legislative history to inform the court's inquiry into legislative intent. When the court reaches legislative history, it considers it along with text and context to determine whether all of those together make the legislative intent clear. If the legislative intent is clear, then the court's inquiry into legislative intent and the meaning of the statute is at an end and the court interprets the statute to have the meaning so determined.

If, after consideration of text, context, and legislative history, the intent of the legislature remains unclear, then the court may resort to general maxims of statutory construction to aid in resolving the remaining uncertainty. Although some of those maxims of statutory construction may be statutory, *see, e.g.,* ORS 174.030 (natural rights), others more commonly may be found in case law. Those include, for example, the maxim that, where no legislative history exists, the court will attempt to determine how the legislature would have intended the statute to be applied had it considered the issue. * * *

[Applying this structure to the issue on appeal, the Court went no further than level one.] Both of the sentences in ORS 659.360(3) are *empowerment* sentences. The second sentence *empowers* the employer to compel an employee taking parental leave "to utilize any accrued leave." Thus, if an employee has accrued leave, the employer could require the employee to utilize that accrued leave during the parental leave, "unless otherwise provided by an agreement of the employer and the employee, by collective bargaining agreement or by employer policy." ORS 659.360(3).

The reciprocal power, granted to the employee by the first sentence of ORS 659.360(3), permits the employee, at the employee's option, to do what the employer may require the employee to do. The employee may require the employer to let the employee "utilize" any accrued vacation leave, sick leave or other compensatory leave, paid or unpaid, during the parental leave. As noted, the first sentence of the statute does not contain any limitation on the employee's rights imposed under the provisions of a collective bargaining agreement.

In sum, the employer may *require* the employee seeking parental leave to utilize any accrued leave during parental leave, unless otherwise provided by an agreement of the employer and the employee, by collective bargaining agreement, or by employer policy, even if the employee is not on vacation or sick or does not wish to use accrued leave during the parental leave. Similarly, the employee may *require* the employer to let the employee utilize any accrued vacation leave, sick leave, or other compensatory leave, paid or unpaid during the parental leave, even if the employee is not on vacation or sick, and even if the employer does not want to do so. If the legislature had wanted to make the use of accrued leave during parental leave subject to any preconditions in an existing collective bargaining agreement, it easily could have done so by including in the first sentence of ORS 659.360(3) the same qualifying language that presently is found only in the second sentence of that subsection. The legislature knows how to include qualifying language in a statute when it wants to do so. It did not do so here. * * *

STATUTORY POSTSCRIPT TO *PORTLAND GENERAL ELECTRIC*

When the Oregon Legislature recodified its family and medical leave statute in 1995 and 2007, it created a new **Oregon Revsied Statutes § 659A.174, "Paid Leave":**

(1) Except as provided in subsection (2) of this section, and unless otherwise provided by the terms of an agreement between the eligible employee and the covered employer, a collective bargaining agreement or an employer policy, family leave is not required to be granted with pay.

(2) An employee taking family leave is entitled to use any paid accrued sick leave or any paid accrued vacation leave during the period of family leave, or to use any other paid leave that is offered by the employer in lieu of vacation leave during the period of family leave.

(3) Subject to the terms of any agreement between the eligible employee and the covered employer or the terms of a collective bargaining agreement, the employer may determine the particular order in which accrued leave is to be used in circumstances in which more than one type of accrued leave is available to the employee.

NOTES ON THE OREGON *PG&E* CASE AND
STATES AS LABORATORIES OF STATUTORY INTERPRETATION

1.   *A Pragmatic or Modified Textualism? A "Tiered" Funnel of Abstraction?* The Oregon Supreme Court's *PGE* opinion sets forth a pragmatic but largely textualist

approach to statutory interpretation—one that rejects the new textualist exclusion of legislative history but gives a formal primacy to textualist analysis that reflects a harder plain meaning rule than the Supreme Court has traditionally applied. In contrast to *TVA v. Hill*, for example, the *PGE* approach does not require judges to check their understanding of plain meaning by reference to legislative history. But the textualism is pragmatic insofar as it invites legislative history and normative analysis when the statute's meaning is not plain.

Note, also, how the *PGE* approach reflects but alters the Funnel of Abstraction. *PGE* retains the Funnel factors but "tiers" them. The most concrete factors in the first tier or level—statutory text, structure, and precedent—are not only primary but are also exclusive when they answer the interpretive question. So, for many cases, the Funnel is foreshortened considerably. The factors in the second tier or level—legislative history and purpose—are considered where the text is ambiguous, but note that if there is relevant legislative history it will be briefed by the parties and considered by the judges. So you can never know whether a plain meaning has been found without any reference to legislative history (for the judges have read that part of the brief). Finally, the normative canons, the most abstract considerations, are presented in the third tier or level as a last-resort tiebreaker by the *PGE* Court.

The lower court considered the following legislative history. The original draft of the family leave bill provided that "[t]he leave required by subsection (1) of this Act may be unpaid leave or any other leave the employer and employee agree upon or any leave specified or allowed by any collective bargaining agreement." *Portland Gen. Elec. Co. v. Bureau of Labor & Industries*, 842 P.2d 419, 422 (Or. App. 1992). That language was changed to say: "The leave, with preference given to accumulated sick leave and vacation leave, required by subsection (1) of this section may be paid or unpaid leave or any other leave the employer and employee agree upon or any leave specified or allowed by any collective bargaining agreement." Finally, that subsection was changed and subsection (6) added, to read essentially as it now reads. The House sponsor explained that the final change was to clarify the meaning in the second version: "The second change is * * * to clarify, * * * to make certain that any sick leave, vacation leave, that that will run concurrently with the 12 weeks. And so this 12 weeks is not added on to any vacation time or sick leave that the individual would have." Tape Recording, House Committee on Labor, March 18, 1987, Tape 61, Side B. Would this legislative history make a difference in your vote if you were a judge?

2.   Stare Decisis *for Methodological Precedents?* Perhaps the most notable feature of *PGE* is that the Oregon Supreme Court made a self-conscious decision to set forth, in clear terms, the methodology it expected lower courts to follow in statutory cases—and that its own justices committed themselves to in subsequent supreme court cases. The House of Lords in the United Kingdom gives *stare decisis* effect to methodological precedents, and Sydney Foster argues that the U.S. Supreme Court should do the same. See Sydney Foster, *Should Courts Give* Stare Decisis *Effect to Statutory Interpretation Methodology?*, 96 Geo. L.J. 1863 (2008). Consider the values of *stare decisis*: judicial economy, predictability, and reliance interests. Foster argues that consistent treatment in matters of methodology would serve those interests—so courts should follow that practice.

On the other hand, are the reliance interests so strong in matters of methodological *stare decisis*? Is *stare decisis* as desirable or even workable for legal *standards* as they are for legal *rules*? Compare Foster, Stare Decisis *Effect*, 1901–05 (on the whole, yes), with Connor Raso & William Eskridge Jr., Chevron *as a Canon, Not a Precedent: An Empirical Analysis of What Motivates Justices in Agency Deference Cases*, 110 Colum. L. Rev. 1727 (2010) (on the whole, no).

Consider Abbe Gluck, *The States as Laboratories of Statutory Interpretation: Methodological Consensus and the New Modified Textualism,* 119 Yale L.J. 1750, 1779–1781 (2010), who praises the *PGE* experiment: "Three preliminary studies, including one conducted as part of this project, have collected data on how the *PGE* regime has been implemented since its installation. One clearly observable effect of the regime is that it has reduced the number of interpretive tools employed by the Oregon Supreme Court and so made it easier to predict which tools the court will rely on to decide cases. 'The court resolves the vast majority of statutory issues at level one,' i.e., the text-based tier. Between 1993 and 1998, for example, out of 137 statutory interpretation cases, the court looked at legislative history only thirty-three times, finding it 'useless' in one third of those cases. It consequently reached tier three—nontextual canons—only eleven times during the same period. Even more strikingly, between 1999 and 2006, the court applied the *PGE* framework 150 times, and only reached tier two (legislative history) nine times. Not a single case during that period reached the other-maxims tier (tier three). And, in a study conducted as part of this project, across the thirty-five cases in which *PGE* was cited between 2006 and May 2009, legislative history was applied six times and a substantive canon only once.

"Compare the five years before *PGE* was decided. There was no single approach: more than half of the cases resorted immediately to legislative history or policy analysis without prior consideration of text alone, and without the tiered hierarchy of sources that *PGE* later imposed. One justice called the pre-*PGE* period a 'legislative history free-for-all.'

"In contrast, under *PGE*, the court is fairly consistent with respect to which interpretive tools it relies upon. Over the four-and-a-half year period ending in May 2009, the following eight types of textual tools were used in roughly half of the cases: 'plain meaning,' dictionaries, state court precedents, close readings of statutory definition sections, analysis of related statutes, analysis of the contested term's place in the statutory scheme, historical evolution of the statute itself, and textual canons. With respect to the textual canons, the court applied the same eight canons repeatedly throughout the cases in which textual canons were used. The only additional tools used in more than three cases were rules of grammar (ten cases) and legislative history (nine cases), making the list of the eight types of tools described above the fairly complete universe of Oregon statutory interpretation principles. All but six of the opinions over the five-year period were unanimous."

3.   *Oregon's Statutory Pushback.* Gluck's study of Oregon's *PGE* experiment noted that, in 2001, the Oregon Legislature enacted a statute in direct response to *PGE*: "A court may limit its consideration of legislative history to the information that the parties provide to the court. A court shall give the weight to the legislative history that the court considers to be appropriate." Although the language of the statute was hortatory, its legislative history suggested that the legislature was reacting negatively to *PGE*. Yet it was not until 2009 that the Oregon Supreme Court acknowledged the legislation. In *State v. Gaines*, 206 P.3d 1042, 1046–51 (Or. 2009), the Oregon Supreme Court held that parties are free to "proffer" legislative history as part of the level one

(textual) inquiry, and that the court will consult it regardless of ambiguity, but only "where that legislative history appears useful to the court's analysis."

As Gluck feared in 2010, *Gaines* may have been the closing curtain for the *PGE* regime of strict tiers or levels. Since *Gaines*, the Oregon Supreme Court has frequently relaxed the first level of the *PGE* approach and has considered legislative history to confirm apparent plain meanings, see, e.g., *State v. Miskell,* 351 Or. 680, 692–93 (2012); *State v. Swanson,* 266 P.3d 45, 49 (Or. 2011), *In re Marriage of Harris,* 244 P.3d 801, 809–11 (Or. 2010); *State v. Baker-Krofft,* 239 P.3d 226, 231–32 (Or. 2010), or has examined legislative history in detail before rejecting it in favor of statutory plain meanings, see, e.g., *A.G. v. Guitron,* 268 P.3d 589, 592–600 (Or. 2011), or has rested interpretation decisively on legislative history as the best means to fill in the details of a statutory provision, e.g., *Hopkins v. SAIF Corp.,* 245 P.3d 90 (Or. 2010) (seamlessly combining textual and detailed legislative history analysis).

Indeed, the Oregon Supreme Court's decisions after *Gaines* look a lot more like the complicated Funnel of Abstraction (considering text, statutory and legislative history, purpose, case law, and norms) than like the strict tiers/levels announced in *PGE*. See, e.g., *State v. Glushko,* 266 P.3d 50, 54–60 (Or. 2011) (citing only *Gaines* and not *PGE*); *Arken v. City of Portland,* 263 P.3d 975, 990–92 (Or. 2011) (citing only *Gaines* and examining a wide range of evidence, including a detailed account of the legislative history); *State v. Cloutier,* 261 P.3d 1234 (Or. 2011) (similar). Often, however, the Oregon Supreme Court simply applies statutory text and structure, without any discussion of what method it is applying. E.g., *Malan v. Tipton,* 247 P.3d 1223 (Or. 2011) (citing only *Gaines* but examining just the common law and text to interpret the statute).

What lessons might be drawn from Oregon's experiment? Abbe Gluck's article demonstrates that other states have adopted different interpretive regimes, some with rocky histories, and she argues that methodological *stare decisis* is an idea whose time has come for federal courts as well as state courts. For examples of the methodological diversity that still characterizes Supreme Court decisionmaking, see, e.g., *Adoptive Couple v. Baby Girl,* 133 S.Ct. 2552 (2013) (intense debate, where different Justices rely on statutory plain meaning as understood by the enforcing agency, the avoidance of constitutional problems, the common law rights of biological parents, and the statutory structure and congressional purpose); *Brown v. Plata,* 131 U.S. 1910 (2011) (majority opinion relying on statutory plain meaning and avoidance of Eighth Amendment problems, contrasted with dissenting views based upon the absurd results canon and avoidance of Article III problems); *Zuni Public School District No. 89 v. Department of Education,* 550 U.S. 81 (2007) (clash between pragmatic and textualist theories, and a debate between concurring and dissenting Justices over the current validity of *Holy Trinity*).

A TRANSITIONAL NOTE

The foregoing historical and theoretical introduction to statutory interpretation can, we admit, be a bit overwhelming. Between the various theories and the strong critiques that can be lodged against each of them, keeping track of everything can be difficult, and finding one's own moorings about which approach to prefer can be daunting indeed. We offer this discussion to review what we have seen and to provide a transition to the remaining, largely doctrinal, chapters in the book.

When we think of a legal theory, we often suppose a rule or method that one follows to deduce the answer to a question. In this chapter, we examined three such deductive theories. Textualism, or plain meaning, posits that the court's role is to give the statutory text its plain or best meaning. Intentionalism posits that the court's role is to give the statute the meaning most consistent with the intentions of the enacting legislature. Purposivism (admittedly, an awkward term) posits that the court's role is to attribute to the statute the meaning most consistent with the general reasons why the enacting legislature believed the statute should be adopted. Another way to articulate purposivism is to recall the "mischief approach" of *Heydon's Case, supra*, under which the court first identifies the mischief in the prior law that the legislature wished to remedy and then interprets the statute to promote that remedial purpose. Much of the history of American statutory interpretation has involved the elaboration of the fine points of these theories (e.g., the old "plain meaning" approach versus the new textualism) and the competition among them for the hearts and opinions of judges.

Recently, several commentators have proposed less deductive methods of attributing meaning to statutes. These approaches, sometimes labeled "dynamic interpretation" or "practical reasoning," are inspired by hermeneutics, the study of interpretation in general. They all see statutory interpretation as essentially a practical, rather than primarily a theoretical or deductive, inquiry. On this understanding, the interpreter's task is to mediate the important factors in a statutory case—statutory text, the original context in which the statute was adopted, and the context in which the interpreters currently find themselves—rather than privilege one or more of these factors to the exclusion of the remainder. As this chapter indicates, your casebook authors fall into this last camp. Nonetheless, we do not agree among ourselves on all matters of statutory interpretation, and we hope that you will feel free to disagree with us in any or all respects.

In assessing the utility of the theories introduced in this chapter, we suggest three approaches.

1.   Begin by engaging in empirical analysis. Which theory best describes the way American judges actually interpret statutes? We realize that this is an impossible question to answer completely, in part because you have not seen anything approaching the whole universe of American case law interpreting statutes. It may be possible at this point, however, to answer a subsidiary question: Based on the cases in this chapter, does any one theory capture the universal judicial practice? If, based on the cases we have read, it seems doubtful that a working majority on the current Supreme Court follows any one theory religiously, does that suggest that attorneys will find it impossible to advise clients about the probabilities in a hard statutory case (that is, one where the theories would produce different answers)? Or will the attorney skilled in statutory analysis (that is, you, once you complete this course and eventually graduate from law school) have the capacity to provide appropriate advice and to write strong briefs on either side of a hard statutory case?

Although we are not deductive theorists about statutory interpretation, we do believe theoretical inquiry is important in a statutory case. In our judgment, the hard cases are those in which the plausible competing theories conflict, and one role of theory (whether solely deductive or otherwise) is to develop a defensible, replicable model for resolving these conflicts. In this respect, some would say that even we are too theoretical. Some scholars, from the legal realists onward, have argued that judicial *decisionmaking*, as opposed to opinion writing, is barely theoretical at all.[54] We concede that judges reach decisions for a variety of reasons, and that pristine legal theory is not a high priority for many of them. We do reject the view, however, that theory makes no difference. Our view, expressed in the manner in which we have organized these materials, is that learning the craft of lawyering requires, among other things, the capacity to construct theoretical arguments persuasively within a given context. See Richard Posner, *The Problems of Jurisprudence* 100 (1990).

In concluding your empirical inquiry, consider whether context may affect the utility of a theory. For example, although none of us is a Scalia-type new textualist, as appellate judges we would give especially strong primacy to statutory text in some cases. Illustratively, the bankruptcy code is mammoth and complex, and none of us is much familiar with its complicated subject matter of secured financing, commercial transactions, and the like. To be sure, we might engage in flexible approaches to interpretation in uncomplicated bankruptcy cases involving obvious issues of justice, such as *Shine v. Shine*. In the complicated corporate bankruptcy case, however, we might pretty much stick with the statutory text, especially where no drafting error is apparent and policy arguments do not cut conclusively in either direction. We also might tend to defer to an interpreter with more expertise than ourselves, such as the specialized federal bankruptcy judges. Only after gaining greater familiarity and confidence with the bankruptcy code and the policy issues associated with it might we become more venturesome interpreters.[55]

---

[54] Robert Martineau, *Craft and Technique, Not Canons and Grand Theories: A Neo-Realist View of Statutory Interpretation*, 62 Geo. Wash. L. Rev. 1, 26 (1993):

> There are several key elements to the appellate process that the statutory interpretation scholar should keep in mind. First, the positions that the parties take in their arguments to a court are purely result-oriented. Their lawyers make the arguments, textual or contextual, that support their position. Second, the judges' primary concern prior to the decision conference is understanding the facts and contentions of the parties. Third, the decision conference is devoted primarily to result, not to the approach to be taken in the opinion. Fourth, the law clerk, often the person with the principal responsibility for drafting an opinion to support the decision, is not present at the decision conference. The judge assigned the opinion-writing responsibility directs the law clerk concerning the result and may instruct the clerk about the approach to be taken in the draft opinion. Finally, the other judges on the panel play some part, but not a major role, in the opinion's development.

> * * * [An appellate] opinion would justify the development of canons and grand theories of statutory construction if it either reflected the thought processes by which the judges reached the decision or was argued in the document submitted to the judges that persuaded them to decide the case in the way they did. In fact, the opinion is neither. It is, rather, a reasoned justification of the decision prepared after the decision is made. The principal purpose of the opinion is to make the decision appear consistent with the facts and the relevant statutory and judicial authority.

On whether theories and scholarship concerning statutory interpretation have affected judicial practice, see Gregory Crespi, *The Influence of a Decade of Statutory Interpretation Scholarship on Judicial Rulings: An Empirical Analysis*, 53 SMU L. Rev. 9 (2000) (identifying an explosion in such scholarship over the past decade and increasing citation of several of these articles by judges, but speculating that the citations are included more to add academic flourish than to reflect influence upon actual decisionmaking); Daniel Farber, *Do Theories of Statutory Interpretation Matter? A Case Study*, 94 Nw. U. L. Rev. 1409 (2000) (finding only rare differences in outcome between Judges Posner and Easterbrook despite their differences in interpretive approach).

[55] See generally Daniel Bussel, *Textualism's Failures: A Study of Overruled Bankruptcy Decisions*, 53 Vand. L. Rev. 887 (2000); Robert Rasmussen, *A Study of the Costs and Benefits of Textualism: The Supreme Court's Bankruptcy Cases*, 71 Wash. U. L.Q. 535 (1993). For the argument that statutes generally involve at least three interpretive communities (the policy community of specialists in government bureaucracies, the political community of elected officials, and the public) and that pragmatic interpreters should design their interpretive methodology in light of which community is the primary audience for the decision at hand, see William Blatt, *Interpretive Communities: The Missing Element in Statutory Interpretation*, 95 Nw. U. L. Rev. 629 (2001).

2. Next, engage in normative analysis. What approach to statutory interpretation strikes you as the most attractive for the American legal system? Work hard to identify those values that lead you to this conclusion. What values ought to be important: Rule of law? Regularized decisionmaking by the institutions most competent to make each kind of decision? The best rule? If the last, what is the criterion for "best"? Efficiency? A conception of justice? (Whose—Rawls? Nozick?) Are all these values relevant? If so, how do you balance them?

In making your normative assessment, note that you do not escape empirical claims. For example, if textualism strikes you as the best approach because it is good to limit judicial discretion (a normative conclusion), you must assess criticisms of your conclusion from both empirical perspectives (e.g., textualism will not, in fact, operate to limit judicial discretion) and normative ones (e.g., handcuffing judges from reaching obviously just and right results in individual cases is wrong).

3. Finally, engage in doctrinal analysis. There is really no way to assess the utility of any approach to statutory interpretation without knowing the details of American legal doctrine. For example, textualism posits that legislative history should hardly ever be examined in the interpretive process. Is that consistent with the case law? Textualism—at least as articulated by Justice Scalia in his *Chisom* dissent—also posits that "established canons of statutory interpretation" should have a strong role in guiding the meaning of statutory text. What are these canons, and, in particular, how does one distinguish an "established" one from a mere pretender? Are the legal rules or presumptions found in the canons empirically supportable? Normatively attractive? Similar "micro-level" inquiries will enrich your perspectives on the other theories as well. Last, but hardly least important, it will be your knowledge of and capacity to use these doctrinal details that will determine much about your success as an attorney, at least if you (as do most attorneys) end up practicing in an area in which statutes and administrative regulations provide much of the law. It is to these doctrines that we turn in the next several chapters.

CHAPTER 7

DOCTRINES OF STATUTORY INTERPRETATION

■ ■ ■

The previous chapter introduced you to the history of statutory interpretation in the United States and to the major theories that have been debated (textualism old and new, intentionalism and imaginative reconstruction, purposivism and dynamic theories). This chapter turns to the doctrines that underlie these theories.

Section 1 considers two major interpretive resources grounded in statutory text: *ordinary meaning rules*, including reliance on *dictionaries*; and *textual canons of statutory construction*, focusing on the language and structure of enacted words and provisions. Courts have always examined words for their ordinary meaning, but while judges rarely relied on dictionaries as an interpretive aid before 1980, they now do so on a regular basis. Language and structural canons have been a bedrock of Anglo-American interpretation for centuries. Although they were de-emphasized in federal courts after the New Deal, the canons remained critically important at the state level and have made a federal comeback since the mid-1980s. Section 1 introduces you to the ordinary meaning approach and to most of the language and structural canons.

Section 2 addresses canons of interpretation that are based on substantive policy values rather than conventional understandings of language. Unlike their linguistic counterparts, *substantive canons* generally derive from policy positions articulated by courts. Most often, they reflect presumptions regarding how statutory text should be harmonized with judicially perceived constitutional priorities, pre-enactment common law practices, or specific statutorily-based policies. For example, the "rule of lenity" is based in part on principles of fair notice; it presumes that criminal statutes do not outlaw behavior unless the activity clearly comes within the sweep of the statutes. Section 2 focuses on three principal substantive canons: the rule of lenity, constitutional avoidance, and the new federalism canons. Section 2 also examines the rather intense theoretical debates over the textual and substantive canons and provides several practical problems on their usage.

Finally, Section 3 deals with sources extrinsic to the statutory text, notably the *common law, legislative history*, and *related statutes*. These sources help place the words of the statute in an appropriate larger context, enhancing the interpreter's ability to discern statutory meaning. Legislative history—principally the record of hearings, committee reports, and floor statements preceding a bill's enactment—was not much used before 1892, when the Supreme Court decided *Holy Trinity Church* (Chapter 6, § 1). Since the late 1930s, the Court has often used legislative history, and many state courts will consider it as well. At the same time, canons such as the plain meaning rule, which severely limits the use of extrinsic evidence, especially legislative history, and the rule of deference to agency decisions have made a big comeback since the mid1980s. The revival of the canons and the corresponding decline in reliance on legislative history have generated an unusually rich discussion, and we examine what has become an intense debate over legislative history among judges and scholars.

Section 3 concludes with the Supreme Court decision in *Babbitt v. Sweet Home Chapter of Communities for a Great Oregon*, 515 U.S. 687 (1995). *Sweet Home* features Justices Stevens (majority) and Scalia (dissent) invoking many of the core interpretive doctrines in diverse and sophisticated fashion. For this reason, it is an excellent vehicle for reviewing the chapter as a whole.

1. ORDINARY MEANING RULES AND TEXTUAL CANONS

There are a good many rules of thumb for interpreting statutes. Typically, courts will assume that the legislature uses words in their ordinary sense: What would the words convey to the "ordinary" or "reasonable" reader? To answer this question, judges have often relied on their own linguistic experience or intuition to decide the most reasonable meaning of the words, given the context in which they are being used and applied. Starting in the 1980s, courts have increasingly identified ordinary meaning by invoking specific interpretive resources, especially dictionaries.[1]

In addition, courts seek to understand statutory text by relying on "maxims," "canons," or "principles" of construction—rules that are said to enable interpreters to draw inferences from the legislature's choice of certain words rather than others, or its configuration of those words in a given statutory provision, or the relationship between those words and text found in other parts of the same statute. Most of the nineteenth century English and American treatises on statutory interpretation were organized around the canons, and the leading doctrinal compilation today (a descendant of an 1891 treatise) is an exhaustive canon-by-canon tour. Sutherland, *Statutes and Statutory Construction* (7th ed., Norman Singer ed.) (hereinafter referred to as Sutherland).[2] Many states have codified the traditional canons in their state codes. See, e.g., Minn. Stat. § 645; Pennsylvania Statutory Construction Act, 1 Pa. Consol. Stat. §§ 1921–28 (hereinafter "Pa. Stat. Constr. Act"). See also 1 U.S.C. §§ 1–8 (codification of word-meaning canons).

Consider the following problem as an introduction.

---

[1] See Ellen Aprill, *The Law of the Word: Dictionary Shopping in the Supreme Court*, 30 Ariz. St. L.J. 275 (1998); Jeffrey Kirchmeier & Samuel Thumma, *Scaling the Lexicon Fortress: The United States Supreme Court's Use of Dictionaries in the Twenty-First Century*, 94 Marq. L. Rev. 77 (2010); Lawrence Solan, *When Judges Use the Dictionary*, 68 Am. Speech 50 (1993); Samuel Thumma & Jeffrey Kirchmeier, *The Lexicon Has Become a Fortress: The United States Supreme Court's Use of Dictionaries*, 47 Buff. L. Rev. 227 (1999); Note, *Looking It Up: Dictionaries and Statutory Interpretation*, 107 Harv. L. Rev. 1437 (1994).

[2] Sutherland is the leading American treatise. Also valuable as reference works are leading treatises in the United Kingdom, see P. St.J. Langan, *Maxwell on the Interpretation of Statutes* (12th ed. 1969), and F.A.R. Bennion, *Statutory Interpretation* (6th ed. 2013); Canada, see Ruth Sullivan, *Sullivan on the Construction of Statutes* (5th ed. 2008); Ruth Sullivan, *Statutory Interpretation* (2d ed. 2007); Australia, see Donald Gifford, *Statutory Interpretation* (1990), and D.C. Pearce & R.S. Geddes, *Statutory Interpretation in Australia* (7th ed. 2011); New Zealand, see Jim Evans, *Statutory Interpretation: Problems of Communication* (1988); and South Africa, see G.E. Devenish, *Interpretation of Statutes* (1992). For a compendium surveying the practice in civil law countries as well, see *Interpreting Statutes: A Comparative Study* (D. Neil MacCormick & Robert Summers eds., 1991).

PROBLEM: *THE* NO VEHICLES IN THE PARK *STATUTE*

Problem 7–1. In the wake of an accident in which a motorcycle speeding through Pierre Trudeau Park ran over and killed an elderly gentleman, the City Council enacted the following statute in 1980:

> Sec. 1.   The Council finds that vehicles create safety problems when they are operated in parks and further finds that the best solution is to ban any and all vehicles from all municipal parks.

> Sec. 2.   No vehicles of any kind shall be allowed in any municipal park. Any person who brings or drives a vehicle into one of these parks shall be guilty of a misdemeanor, which may be punished by a fine not exceeding $500 or by a two-day incarceration in the municipal jail, or both.

> Sec. 3.   "Vehicle" for purposes of this law means any mechanism for conveying a person from one place to another, including automobiles, trucks, motorcycles, and motor scooters. *Provided that*, bicycles shall be allowed in the park, so long as they are being pushed or carried and not ridden.

After a decade of spotty enforcement, a new constable, Barney Fife, adopts a strict, no-tolerance enforcement policy. In 1996, he arrests (a) a 13-year-old boy riding a skateboard through the park; (b) a mother pushing a baby carriage in the park; and (c) a 6-year-old girl riding her tricycle in the park. All three "perps" (and the parents of the child perps) challenge their arrests, on the ground that the statute does not apply to their conduct. How should the City Magistrate rule?

A. ORDINARY MEANING AND DICTIONARIES

1. Ordinary and Technical Meaning of Words

The starting point of statutory interpretation is to *read* the statute carefully. Judges often rely on their own common sense analysis to determine the ordinary meaning of statutory words. Thus, for example, in *Watson v. United States*, 552 U.S. 74 (2007), the Court held that someone who trades his drugs for a gun does not "use" a firearm "during and in relation to a drug trafficking crime" so as to qualify for a mandatory minimum sentence. 552 U.S. at 83. Justice Souter, writing for the majority, observed that absent a statutory definition, "the meaning of the verb 'use' has to turn on the language as we normally speak it," adding that "[t]he Government may say that a person 'uses' a firearm simply by receiving it in a barter transaction, but no one else would." *Id.* at 79. Typically, courts will assume that the legislature uses words in their ordinary sense: What would these words convey to the "ordinary" or "reasonable" reader? Ordinary meaning should be distinguished from literal meaning or strict construction; the latter connotes a narrow understanding of words used, while the former connotes the everyday understanding.

Linguists suggest that the interpreter start with the *prototypical* meaning of statutory words.[3] What is the core idea associated with a word or phrase? For

---

[3]   See Lawrence Solan, *Learning Our Limits: The Decline of Textualism in Statutory Cases*, 1997 Wis. L. Rev. 235, 270–75 (explaining linguists' "prototype" theory and applying it to several statutory interpretation cases).

example, this was the approach implicitly followed by Justice Brennan in *Weber*, the affirmative action case (Chapter 1, § 3B): although some dictionaries define "discriminate" broadly enough to include any kind of differentiation, the core or prototypical use of the word requires some invidious intent. Thus, we do not say we "discriminate" against pears if we prefer peaches, nor (according to Brennan) do we say we "discriminate" against a minority if we give him a helping hand to counterbalance what we believe is an inferior starting point because of preexisting prejudice or stereotyping. Ordinary meaning, therefore, might be associated with prototypical meaning. This idea usually supports cautious, or restrictive, readings of statutes. See, e.g., *Holy Trinity Church* (Chapter 6, § 1) (confining "labor or service of any kind" to manual work); *Canada (Attorney General) v. Mossop*, [1991] 1 F.C. 18, 34 (Fed. Ct.), aff'd, [1993] 1 S.C.R. 554 (Can. Sup. Ct.) (applying the "core meaning" of "family" to exclude same-sex partnerships).

What if the statute is an old one? In that event, judges sometimes consult dictionaries and other evidence from the era in which the statute was enacted. For example, the Supreme Court in *St. Francis College v. Al-Khazraji*, 481 U.S. 604 (1987), interpreted the Civil Rights Act of 1866 to apply to discrimination against a person of Arab ancestry. Defendant had argued that any discrimination against an ethnic Arab was not actionable, because the statute only required the same protections as are "enjoyed by white citizens" and Arabs are ethnographically Caucasian. The Court invoked nineteenth-century dictionaries and encyclopedias to demonstrate that defendant's conception of race was not the one held in the nineteenth century, which viewed different ethnic "stock" and family "lineage" as different "races." Thus, these sources referred to Finns, Greeks, Basques, Arabs, Norwegians, Jews, and Hungarians as identifiable "races." For another example, see *Cook County v. United States*, 538 U.S. 119, 132 (2003), interpreting the False Claims Act of 1863.

In addition to special meanings that words may have had historically, words often have meanings limited to parlance in a trade, academic discipline, or technical area. Where the statute itself deals with a technical, specialized subject, courts tend to adopt the specialized meaning of words used in the statute, unless that leads to an absurd result. For a hoary, and perhaps amusing, example of this maxim, see *Nix v. Hedden*, 149 U.S. 304, 306–07 (1893). This was an action to recover back duties on tomatoes, paid under protest by the plaintiff pursuant to the Tariff Act of 1883. The statute imposed a high duty on "[v]egetables in their natural state, or in salt or brine" while exempting "[f]ruits, green, ripe, or dried." At trial, counsel for plaintiff and defendant read into the record multiple dictionary definitions of certain words—including "fruit," "vegetables," "tomato," "eggplant," "pepper," "cucumber," "squash,", "bean," and "pea." Two expert witnesses testified that the terms "fruit" and "vegetables" did not have any special meaning in trade or commerce different from what appeared in dictionaries. The Supreme Court opted for ordinary rather than technical meaning:

> There being no evidence that the words "fruit" and "vegetables" have acquired any special meaning in trade or commerce, they must receive their ordinary meaning. Of that meaning the court is bound to take judicial notice, as it does in regard to all words in our own tongue; and

upon such a question dictionaries are admitted, not as evidence, but only as aids to the memory and understanding of the court.

Botanically speaking, tomatoes are the fruit of a vine, just as are cucumbers, squashes, beans and peas. But in the common language of the people, whether sellers or consumers of provisions, all these are vegetables, which are grown in kitchen gardens, and which, whether eaten cooked or raw, are, like potatoes, carrots, parsnips, turnips, beets, cauliflower, cabbage, celery and lettuce, usually served at dinner in, with, or after the soup, fish or meats which constitute the principal part of the repast, and not, like fruits generally, as dessert.

See also *Zuni Pub. Sch. Dist. v. Dep't of Educ.*, 550 U.S. 81, 90–93 (2007) (deferring to the experts when construing technical statutory language for determining whether a state aid program "equalizes expenditures.")

A related maxim is this: "Where Congress uses terms that have accumulated settled meaning under either equity or the common law, a court must infer, unless the statute otherwise dictates, that Congress means to incorporate the established meaning of these terms." *NLRB v. Amax Coal Co.*, 453 U.S. 322, 329 (1981); accord *Scheidler v. NOW*, 537 U.S. 393, 402 (2003); *United States v. Wells*, 519 U.S. 482, 491 (1997); *Cmty. for Creative Non-Violence v. Reid*, 490 U.S. 730, 739 (1989); § 1C of this chapter. Compare *Jodrey Estate v. Nova Scotia*, [1980] 2 S.C.R. 774 (Can. Sup. Ct.) (reflecting the Canadian preference for following ordinary rather than technical meanings).

2. The Rising Status of Dictionaries

In recent years, Supreme Court Justices have consulted dictionaries with increased regularity when construing key statutory words or phrases.[4] The Court has relied on dictionary definitions to help determine the meaning of technical legal terms such as "quorum," *New Process Steel L.P. v. NLRB*, 560 U.S. 674 (2010), and "license," *Chamber of Commerce v. Whiting*, 131 S.Ct. 1968 (2011), as well as more ordinary words or phrases like "oppose," *Crawford v. Metro. Gov't of Nashville & Davidson Co.*, 555 U.S. 271 (2009), or "because of," *Gross v. FBL Fin. Servs., Inc.*, 557 U.S. 167 (2009). In these and numerous other decisions, the justices have disagreed over which words need to be defined, which dictionary to use, which definition within a given dictionary is applicable, and whether dictionary definitions are relevant at all.

TANIGUCHI V. KAN PACIFIC SAIPAN, LTD.

Supreme Court of the United States 2012.
___ U.S. ___, 132 S.Ct. 1997, 182 L.Ed.2d 903.

JUSTICE ALITO delivered the opinion of the Court.

The costs that may be awarded to prevailing parties in lawsuits brought in federal court are set forth in 28 U.S.C. § 1920. The Court Interpreters Act amended that statute to include "compensation of interpreters." § 1920(6). The question

---

[4] See sources collected in note 1, *supra*.

presented in this case is whether "compensation of interpreters" covers the cost of translating documents. Because the ordinary meaning of the word "interpreter" is a person who translates orally from one language to another, we hold that "compensation of interpreters" is limited to the cost of oral translation and does not include the cost of document translation.

[I. Taniguchi, a professional baseball player in Japan, was injured when his leg broke through a wooden deck during a tour of respondent's resort property. In preparing its defense, respondent paid to have various documents translated from Japanese to English. The District Court granted summary judgment in respondent's favor, and subsequently awarded respondent the costs associated with these written translations under § 1920(6). The court explained that interpreter services cannot be separated into 'translation' and 'interpretation,' and that costs for document translation qualify as compensation of an interpreter.]

[II.B.] To determine whether the item "compensation of interpreters" includes costs for document translation, we must look to the meaning of "interpreter." That term is not defined in the Court Interpreters Act or in any other relevant statutory provision. When a term goes undefined in a statute, we give the term its ordinary meaning. The question here is: What is the ordinary meaning of "interpreter"?

Many dictionaries in use when Congress enacted the Court Interpreters Act in 1978 defined "interpreter" as one who translates spoken, as opposed to written, language. The American Heritage Dictionary, for instance, defined the term as "[o]ne who translates orally from one language into another." American Heritage Dictionary 685 (1978). The Scribner-Bantam English Dictionary defined the related word "interpret" as "to translate orally." Scribner-Bantam English Dictionary 476 (1977). Similarly, the Random House Dictionary defined the intransitive form of "interpret" as "to translate what is *said* in a foreign language." Random House Dictionary of the English Language 744 (1973) (emphasis added). And, notably, the Oxford English Dictionary defined "interpreter" as "[o]ne who translates languages," but then divided that definition into two senses: "a. [a] translator of books or writings," which it designated as obsolete, and "b. [o]ne who translates the communications of persons speaking different languages; *spec.* one whose office it is to do so orally in the presence of the persons; a dragoman." 5 Oxford English Dictionary 416 (1933); see also Concise Oxford Dictionary of Current English 566 (6th ed. 1976) ("One who interprets; one whose office it is to translate the words of persons speaking different languages, esp. orally in their presence"); Chambers Twentieth Century Dictionary 686 (1973) ("one who translates orally for the benefit of two or more parties speaking different languages: . . . a translator (*obs.*)").

Pre-1978 legal dictionaries also generally defined the words "interpreter" and "interpret" in terms of oral translation. The then-current edition of Black's Law Dictionary, for example, defined "interpreter" as "[a] person sworn at a trial to interpret the evidence of a foreigner . . . to the court," and it defined "interpret" in relevant part as "to translate orally from one tongue to another." Black's Law Dictionary 954, 953 (rev. 4th ed. 1968); see also W. Anderson, A Dictionary of Law 565 (1888) ("One who translates the testimony of witnesses speaking a foreign tongue, for the benefit of the court and jury"); 1 B. Abbott, Dictionary of Terms and Phrases Used in American or English Jurisprudence 639 (1878) ("one who restates the testimony of a witness testifying in a foreign tongue, to the court and jury, in their language"). But see Ballentine's Law Dictionary 655, 654 (3d ed. 1969) (defining "interpreter" as "[o]ne who interprets, particularly one who interprets words written or spoken in a foreign language," and "interpret" as "to translate from a foreign language").

Against these authorities, respondent relies almost exclusively on Webster's Third New International Dictionary (hereinafter Webster's Third). The version of that dictionary in print when Congress enacted the Court Interpreters Act defined "interpreter" as "one that translates; *esp*: a person who translates orally for parties conversing in different tongues." Webster's Third 1182 (1976).[2] The sense divider *esp* (for especially) indicates that the most common meaning of the term is one "who translates orally," but that meaning is subsumed within the more general definition "one that translates." See 12,000 Words: A Supplement to Webster's Third 15a (1986) (explaining that *esp* "is used to introduce the most common meaning included in the more general preceding definition"). For respondent, the general definition suffices to establish that the term "interpreter" ordinarily includes persons who translate the written word. Explaining that "the word 'interpreter' can reasonably encompass a 'translator,'" the Court of Appeals reached the same conclusion. We disagree.

That a definition is broad enough to encompass one sense of a word does not establish that the word is *ordinarily* understood in that sense. The fact that the definition of "interpreter" in Webster's Third has a sense divider denoting the most common usage suggests that other usages, although acceptable, might not be common or ordinary. It is telling that all the dictionaries cited above defined "interpreter" at the time of the statute's enactment as including persons who translate orally, but only a handful defined the word broadly enough to encompass translators of written material. Although the Oxford English Dictionary, one of the most authoritative on the English language, recognized that "interpreter" *can* mean one who translates writings, it expressly designated that meaning as obsolete. Were the meaning of "interpreter" that respondent advocates truly common or ordinary, we would expect to see more support for that meaning. We certainly would not expect to see it designated as obsolete in the Oxford English Dictionary. Any definition of a word that is absent from many dictionaries and is deemed obsolete in others is hardly a common or ordinary meaning.

Based on our survey of the relevant dictionaries, we conclude that the ordinary or common meaning of "interpreter" does not include those who translate writings. Instead, we find that an interpreter is normally understood as one who translates orally from one language to another. This sense of the word is far more natural. As

---

[2] A handful of other contemporaneous dictionaries used a similar formulation. See Funk & Wagnalls New Comprehensive International Dictionary of the English Language 665 (1977) ("One who interprets or translates; specifically, one who serves as oral translator between people speaking different languages"); 1 World Book Dictionary 1103 (C. Barnhart & R. Barnhart eds. 1977) ("a person whose business is translating, especially orally, from a foreign language"); Cassell's English Dictionary 617 (4th ed. 1969) ("One who interprets, esp. one employed to translate orally to persons speaking a foreign language").

the Seventh Circuit put it: "Robert Fagles made famous translations into English of the *Iliad*, the *Odyssey*, and the *Aeneid*, but no one would refer to him as an English-language 'interpreter' of these works."

To be sure, the word "interpreter" can encompass persons who translate documents, but because that is not the ordinary meaning of the word, it does not control unless the context in which the word appears indicates that it does. Nothing in the Court Interpreters Act or in § 1920, however, even hints that Congress intended to go beyond the ordinary meaning of "interpreter" and to embrace the broadest possible meaning that the definition of the word can bear. * * *

Because the ordinary meaning of "interpreter" is someone who translates orally from one language to another, we hold that the category "compensation of interpreters" in § 1920(6) does not include costs for document translation. * * *

JUSTICE GINSBURG, with whom JUSTICE BREYER and JUSTICE SOTOMAYOR join, dissenting.

To be comprehended by the parties, the witnesses, and the court, expression in foreign languages must be translated into English. Congress therefore provided, in 28 U.S.C. § 1920(6), that the prevailing party may recoup compensation paid to "interpreters." The word "interpreters," the Court emphasizes, commonly refers to translators of oral speech. But as the Court acknowledges, "interpreters" is more than occasionally used to encompass those who translate written speech as well. See Webster's Third New International Dictionary of the English Language 1182 (1976) (hereinafter Webster's) (defining "interpreter" as "one that translates; *esp*: a person who translates orally for parties conversing in different tongues"); Black's Law Dictionary 895 (9th ed. 2009) (defining "interpreter" as a "person who translates, esp. orally, from one language to another"); Ballentine's Law Dictionary 655 (3d ed. 1969) (defining "interpreter" as "[o]ne who interprets, particularly one who interprets words written or spoken in a foreign language").

In short, employing the word "interpreters" to include translators of written as well as oral speech, if not "the most common usage," is at least an "acceptable" usage. Moreover, the word "interpret" is generally understood to mean "to explain or tell the meaning of: translate into intelligible or familiar language or terms," while "translate" commonly means "to turn into one's own or another language." Webster's 1182, 2429. See also Random House Dictionary of the English Language 744, 1505 (1973) (defining the transitive verb "interpret" as, *inter alia*, "to translate," and "translate" as "to turn (something written or spoken) from one language into another").

Notably, several federal district court decisions refer to translators of written documents as "interpreters." *E.g.*, *United States v. Prado-Cervantez*, 2011 WL 4691934 (D. Kan. 2011) ("Standby counsel should also be prepared to arrange for interpreters to interpret or translate documents when necessary for defendant."); *Mendoza v. Ring*, 2008 WL 2959848 (C.D. Ill. 2008) ("The interpreter is also directed to translate filings by the plaintiff from Spanish to English. The original and translated versions will be docketed."). So do a number of state statutes. *E.g.*, Cal. Gov't. Code Ann. § 26806(a) (West 2008) ("[T]he clerk of the court may employ as many foreign language interpreters as may be necessary . . . to translate documents intended for filing in any civil or criminal action. . . ."). * * *

In practice, federal trial courts have awarded document translation costs in cases spanning several decades. See, *e.g.*, *Raffold Process Corp. v. Castanea Paper Co.*, 25 F. Supp. 593, 594 (W.D. Pa. 1938). Before the Court Interpreters Act added § 1920(6) to the taxation of costs statute in 1978, district courts awarded costs for document translation under § 1920(4), which allowed taxation of "[f]ees for exemplification and copies of papers," or under § 1920's predecessor, 28 U.S.C. § 830 (1925 ed.). Pre-1978, district courts also awarded costs for oral translation of witness testimony. See, *e.g.*, *Kaiser Indus. Corp. v. McLouth Steel Corp.*, 50 F.R.D. 5, 11 (E.D. Mich. 1970). Nothing in the Court Interpreters Act, a measure intended to expand access to interpretation services, indicates a design to eliminate the availability of costs awards for document translation. See S. Rep. No. 95–569, at 4 (1977) (hereinafter S. Rep.) ("The committee . . . feels the time has come to provide by statute for the provision of and access to qualified certified interpreters, for a broader spectrum of people than the present law allows."). Post-1978, rulings awarding document translation costs under § 1920(6) indicate the courts' understanding both that the term "interpreter" can readily encompass oral and written translation, and that Congress did not otherwise instruct. I agree that context should guide the determination whether § 1920(6) is most sensibly read to encompass persons who translate documents. But the context key for me is the practice of federal courts both before and after § 1920(6)'s enactment.

The purpose of translation, after all, is to make relevant foreign-language communication accessible to the litigants and the court. See S. Rep., at 1 (The Court Interpreters Act is intended "to insure that all participants in our Federal courts can meaningfully take part."). Documentary evidence in a foreign language, no less than oral statements, must be translated to equip the parties to present their case clearly and the court to decide the merits intelligently. And it is not extraordinary that what documents say, more than what witnesses testify, may make or break a case. * * *

In short, § 1920(6)'s prescription on "interpreters" is not so clear as to leave no room for interpretation. Given the purpose served by translation and the practice prevailing in district courts, there is no good reason to exclude from taxable costs payments for placing written words within the grasp of parties, jurors, and judges. * * *

NOTE ON DICTIONARY USE IN TANIGUCHI

A recent article examined the Court's use of dictionaries from 1986 to 2011, and found that the justices almost always rely on one or at most two dictionaries to define a particular statutory term. See James Brudney & Lawrence Baum, *Oasis or Mirage: The Supreme Court's Thirst for Dictionaries in the Rehnquist and Roberts Eras*, 55 William & Mary L. Rev. 483 (2013). Justice Alito for the majority in *Taniguchi* surveys fourteen dictionaries to settle on the ordinary meaning of "interpreter." Is this analysis more persuasive than if the majority had looked to only one or two dictionaries? Why or why not?

legal dictionary (handwritten margin note)

Consider whether "interpreter" in § 1920(6) is being used in an ordinary meaning sense or instead has a more specialized connotation. If legal dictionaries were deemed more relevant than general dictionaries, would this alter the balance of lexicographic evidence produced by the majority?

Unlike general dictionaries that rely on citation files or electronic corpora to identify word usages, legal dictionaries such as Black's rely on judicial opinions as their primary citation source. See Ellen Aprill, *The Law of the Word: Dictionary Shopping in the Supreme Court*, 30 Ariz. St. L.J. 275, 303–10 (1998) (discussing development of American law dictionaries from mid-nineteenth century to present). Justice Alito invokes the definition of "interpreter" from the fourth edition of Black's Law Dictionary, published in 1968, which referenced exclusively oral translation. The definition in Black's eighth edition (2004) is broader, referencing "a person who translates, esp. orally, from one language to another." Is it appropriate to infer that this broadening reflects an appreciation for developing district court practices, given that Black's derives its definitions from a review of court decisions?

Who is the primary intended audience for the statutory section authorizing costs that is at issue in *Taniguchi*? Is the nature of the statute's intended audience relevant to the type of dictionary a court should use when seeking to understand the ordinary meaning of "interpreter"? Also, what was Congress's evident purpose in enacting the 1978 Court Interpreters Act? How, if at all, should that purpose influence our understanding of the contested term in this case? Assuming Justice Ginsburg's dissent accurately summarizes past federal court practice, does it matter that district court judges had awarded document translation and oral translation costs for many years prior to the 1978 Act?

STATUTORY PREFACE TO THE COSTELLO CASE

Immigration Act of February 5, 1917, Pub. L. No. 64–301, ch. 29, § 8, 39 Stat. 874, 880 (repealed).

Section 8.   That any person, including the master, agent, owner, or cosignee of any vessel, who shall bring into or land in the United States, by vessel or otherwise, or shall attempt, by himself or through another, to bring into or land in the United States, by vessel or otherwise, or shall conceal or harbor, or attempt to conceal or harbor, or assist or abet another to conceal or harbor in any place, including any building, vessel, railway car, conveyance, or vehicle, any alien not duly admitted by an immigrant inspector or not lawfully entitled to enter or to reside within the United States under the terms of this Act, shall be deemed guilty of a misdemeanor, and upon conviction therefor shall be punished. . . .

Immigration and Nationality Act of June 27, 1952, Pub. L. No. 82–411, Title IV § 274(a), 66 Stat. 163, 228–29 (codified at 8 U.S.C. § 1324(a)).

Section 1324.   *Bringing in and harboring certain aliens.*

(a) Criminal penalties

(1)(A)   Any person who—* * *

(iii) knowing or in reckless disregard of the fact that an alien has come to, entered, or remains in the United States in violation of law, conceals, harbors, or shields from detection, or attempts to conceal, harbor, or shield from detection, such alien in any place, including any building or any means of transportation; * * *

(v)(I) engages in any conspiracy to commit any of the preceding acts, or

(II) aids or abets the commission of any of the preceding acts, shall be punished as provided in subparagraph (B).

United States v. Costello

United States Court of Appeals for the Seventh Circuit, 2012.
666 F.3d 1040.

Posner, Circuit Judge:

[The defendant was convicted under a federal law that punishes anyone who "knowing or in reckless disregard of the fact that an alien has come to, entered, or remains in the United States in violation of law, conceals, harbors or shields from detection [or attempts to do any of these things], such alien in any place, including any building or any means of transportation." The Government relied on dictionary definitions of the word "harbors" to argue that the defendant violated the act when she let her boyfriend live with her for seven months after he illegally reentered the United States. Judge Posner was skeptical.]

The government argues that "to harbor" just means to house a person, a meaning that it claims to derive from dictionaries that were in print in 1952 or today; surprisingly the government omits dictionaries that were current in 1917, when concealing and harboring aliens were added to the prohibition of smuggling aliens into this country. Immigration Act of February 5, 1917, Pub. L. No. 64–301, ch. 29, § 8, 39 Stat. 874, 880 (repealed). In the Immigration and Nationality Act of June 27, 1952, Pub. L. No. 82–411, Title IV, § 274(a), 66 Stat. 163, 228–29, Congress added penalties for the concealing and harboring offenses, in response to a Supreme Court decision, *United States v. Evans*, 333 U.S. 483 (1948), that had held that the 1917 Act had somehow failed to specify penalties for those offenses.

The actual definition of "to harbor" that the government has found in these dictionaries and urges us to adopt is "to shelter," which is not synonymous with "to provide a place to stay." "To shelter" has an aura of protectiveness, as in taking "shelter" from a storm. To shelter is to provide a refuge. "Sheltering" doesn't seem the right word for letting your boyfriend live with you. We have not scoured dictionaries current in 1917 or 1952, but note for what it's worth that the 1910 edition of Black's Law Dictionary defines "to harbor" as: "To receive clandestinely and without lawful authority a person for the purpose of so concealing him that another having a right to the lawful custody of such person shall be deprived of the same. A distinction has been taken, in some decisions, between 'harbor' and 'conceal.' A person may be convicted of harboring a slave, although he may not have concealed her." Henry Campbell Black, A Law Dictionary 561 (2d ed. 1910) (citations omitted).

So the government's reliance on the dictionary definition of "harboring" is mistaken, though a point of greater general importance is that dictionaries must be used as sources of statutory meaning only with great caution. "Of course it is true that the words used, even in their literal sense, are the primary, and ordinarily the most reliable, source of interpreting the meaning of any writing: be it a statute, a contract, or anything else. But it is one of the surest indexes of a mature and developed jurisprudence not to make a fortress out of the dictionary; but to remember that statutes always have some purpose or object to accomplish, whose sympathetic and imaginative discovery is the surest guide to their meaning." *Cabell v. Markham*, 148 F.2d 737, 739 (2d Cir. 1945) (L. Hand, J.). "[T]he choice among meanings [of words in statutes] must have a footing more solid than a dictionary—which is a museum of words, an historical catalog rather than a means to decode the work of legislatures." Frank H. Easterbrook, *Text, History, and Structure in Statutory Interpretation*, 17 Harv. J.L. & Public Policy 61, 67 (1994). * * *

Dictionary definitions are acontextual, whereas the meaning of sentences depends critically on context, including all sorts of background understandings. A sign in a park that says "Keep off the grass" is not properly interpreted to forbid the grounds crew to cut the grass. * * * We doubt that the government would argue that a hospital emergency room that takes in a desperately ill person whom the hospital staff knows to be an illegal alien would be guilty of harboring, although it fits the government's definition of the word.

A Google search (conducted on December 13, 2011, rather than in 1952 or 1917, but the government implies by its reliance on current dictionaries that the word means the same today as on the date of the statute's enactment, an implication consistent with Black's Law Dictionary) of several terms in which the word "harboring" appears—a search based on the supposition that the number of hits per term is a rough index of the frequency of its use—reveals the following:

"harboring fugitives": 50,800 hits

"harboring enemies": 4,730 hits

"harboring refugees": 4,820 hits

"harboring victims": 114 hits

"harboring flood victims": 0 hits

"harboring victims of disasters": 0 hits

"harboring victims of persecution": 0 hits

"harboring guests": 184 hits

"harboring friends": 256 hits (but some involve harboring Quakers—"Friends," viewed in colonial New England as dangerous heretics)

"harboring Quakers": 3,870 hits

"harboring Jews": 19,100 hits

It is apparent from these results that "harboring," as the word is actually used, has a connotation—which "sheltering," and *a fortiori* "giving a person a place to stay"—does not, of deliberately safeguarding members of a specified group from the authorities, whether through concealment, movement to a safe location, or physical protection. This connotation enables one to see that the emergency staff at the hospital may not be "harboring" an alien when it renders emergency treatment even if he stays in the emergency room overnight, that giving a lift to a gas station to an alien with a flat tire may not be harboring, that driving an alien to the local office of the Department of Homeland Security to apply for an adjustment of status to that of lawful resident may not be harboring, that inviting an alien for a "one night stand" may not be attempted harboring, that placing an illegal alien in a school may not be harboring (*cf. Plyler v. Doe*, 457 U.S. 202 (1982)), and finally that allowing your boyfriend to live with you may not be harboring, even if you know he shouldn't be in the United States.

The prohibition of concealing, shielding from detection, and harboring known illegal aliens grew out of the prohibition of smuggling aliens into the United States. Immigration Act of 1907, Pub. L. No. 59–96, 34 Stat. 898. Concealing illegal aliens in the United States and shielding them from detection in the United States are closely related to smuggling; they are active efforts to keep illegal aliens in the United States. * * *

To call this harboring would carry section 1324 far beyond smuggling, and a considerable distance as well from concealing and from shielding from detection. That considerable distance identifies a further problem with the use of dictionaries to determine statutory meaning. Legislative prohibitions are often stated in strings of closely related and overlapping terms, to plug loopholes. They do not have identical dictionary definitions (if they did, the use of multiple terms would have no point), but the overlap means that in many applications they will be redundant, so that to pick out of the dictionary, for each statutory term, a definition remote from that of the other terms may be to misunderstand why the legislature included multiple overlapping terms. We have warned that "the fact that a clause is broadly worded to stop up loopholes doesn't justify a literal interpretation that carries far beyond any purpose that can reasonably be imputed to the drafter. 'When a statute is broadly worded in order to prevent loopholes from being drilled in it by ingenious lawyers, there is a danger of its being applied to situations absurdly remote from the concerns of the statute's framers.'" * * *

Rather than contenting themselves with "simple sheltering" or its synonyms as definitions of harboring, some courts struggle for a definition that will avoid the anomalies that we've discussed at such length in this opinion. * * * Some cases, in order to refine the definition of "harboring," adopt the formula "substantial facilitation of" or "substantially to facilitate" the alien's presence, * * * A better gloss than "substantial facilitation" would be providing (or offering—for remember that the statute punishes the attempt as well as the completed act) a known illegal alien a secure haven, a refuge, a place to stay in which the authorities are unlikely to be seeking him—and thus a definition of "harboring" that differentiates it from "simple sheltering" in the sense of just providing a place to stay or just cohabiting, although as we said that is not what sheltering actually means.

Our rejection of equating harboring to providing a place to stay compels the acquittal of the defendant, for on our understanding of the offense no trier of fact could reasonably find that the defendant had "harbored" her boyfriend based on the stipulated facts, or that she had concealed him or shielded him from detection.

[The dissenting opinion of CIRCUIT JUDGE MANION is omitted].

NOTES ON COSTELLO *AND THE* ROLE *OF* DICTIONARIES *IN* GENERAL

1. *The Google Standard.* Judge Posner concludes that on the stipulated facts of this case, no trier of fact could reasonably find that Costello had "harbored" her boyfriend in the Google-search sense of safeguarding someone from the authorities through concealment or movement to a safe location. The more detailed record discloses that Costello's boyfriend lived with her for a year when he was in the U.S. without having been legally admitted. He then committed drug crimes and was convicted, imprisoned for a period, and deported. In 2006, he re-entered the country in violation of his deportation order. Later that year, Costello picked him up at the Greyhound station in St. Louis and transported him to her home in a southern Illinois town. He lived with her thereafter for extended periods although he also moved out on several occasions and stayed with his uncle or brother elsewhere in Illinois. On this evidence, is there a persuasive argument that Costello's home was a secure haven in which she concealed her boyfriend from the authorities?

2. *Some Broader Context.* In 2010, there were an estimated 10.8 million undocumented immigrants in the United States. The government conceded at oral argument in *Costello* that under its dictionary definition of "harboring" as "sheltering," there might be as many as two million violators of the relevant criminal provision. Should a reviewing court consider this prospect when deciding the meaning of "harboring"? Assume, for instance, that a U.S. citizen couple invites their daughter's immigrant friend and classmate to stay with the family for two weeks in the summer, and that the parents know their young guest is illegally in the country. How likely is it that Congress meant for these parents to be subject to criminal liability for harboring? Even if the invitation is refused, the statute criminalizes attempts: should we infer that Congress meant the criminal prohibition to extend this far? Compare *Costello*, 666 F.3d at 1047 (Posner, J.) with *id.* at 1051 (Manion, J., dissenting).

3. *Dictionaries as an Objective Source.* Is Judge Posner's skepticism about dictionaries warranted? The Supreme Court hardly used dictionaries at all before 1980. What accounts for the enormous increase in usage since that time, and especially in the last 25 years? Might the increase be related to the length or complexity of modern statutes? To the justices' inclination—subconscious or otherwise—to seek out objective and neutral proxies for ordinary meaning? To their desire to deflect or rebut charges of judicial activism? How exactly does reliance on dictionaries contribute to a better understanding of a statutory provision? Dictionaries define words removed from a larger sentence framework, whereas statutory language typically involves some context beyond a particular word or phrase. Should courts adopt any cautionary rules regarding the limitations of dictionaries for interpretive purposes?

In *Oasis or Mirage*, Brudney and Baum examined roughly 700 statutory decisions by the Supreme Court since 1986 in the areas of criminal law, labor and employment law, and commercial and business law. The Court relied on dictionaries in 117 cases, about one-sixth of its decisions. While textualist Justices Scalia, Thomas, and Alito were relatively heavy dictionary users, so too were purposivist Justices Stevens, Souter, and Breyer. See 55 William & Mary L. Rev. at 490.

The authors found that dictionary use overall was strikingly *ad hoc* and subjective, and they concluded that this inconsistent dictionary usage reflected a tendency to cherry-pick definitions in support of results reached largely on other grounds. In addition to the Court's tendency to rely on only one or two dictionaries, the justices had varied individual brand preferences (*e.g.*, Scalia favors Webster's Second International; O'Connor preferred Webster's Third; Thomas favors Black's Law Dictionary) yet they very often departed from these individual preferences. Further, the justices seemed to use general and legal dictionaries interchangeably: they invoked Black's to define traditional legal terms but also for common words like "use" or "occur"; and in seeking to define more technical law-related terms, the justices sometimes invoked legal dictionaries alone, sometimes general dictionaries alone, and sometimes both. Finally, the authors found that the justices lacked a coherent position on the choice between citing editions from the time of statutory enactment (tailored to meanings presumptively understood by the enacting Congress) or from the time the instant case was filed in court (tailored to meanings presumptively understood by citizens living under the statute today). *Id.* at 488–90, 509–10.

To what extent do these findings undermine the argument that dictionaries are an objective or neutral source for courts to use in determining ordinary meaning? Brudney and Baum contend that the Court should acknowledge it is operating with virtually unbridled discretion in the dictionary domain and take steps to reduce dictionary cherry-picking. Among the options they suggest are (a) identifying one or more dictionaries as presumptive sources and explaining the basis for their selection; (b) consulting a presumptive minimum number of dictionaries for every contested word or phrase, probably at least four; (c) developing a rationale for when it is appropriate to use a general dictionary, a legal dictionary, or both; and (d) similarly, developing a rationale for when to use enactment date, case-filing date, both, or neither. Would you endorse any or all of these suggestions? What else might the Court do to make its now-steady reliance on dictionaries a less subjective enterprise?

B. TEXTUAL CANONS

A number of rules—based either on general notions of English composition or syntax or the structure of a statute—have been stated as guides for finding meaning from the words of the statute and nothing else. These are called "intrinsic aids" or "textual canons" of interpretation. They are normally invoked by courts as conventional benchmarks for discerning the most appropriate use of language. Some judicial rhetoric to the contrary, text-based canons are decidedly not hard-and-fast rules; they are at best presumptions and might be considered most like adages. See Antonin Scalia & Bryan A. Garner, *Reading Law: The Interpretation of Legal Texts* 59–63 (2012) (discussing interrelation of canons and their non-mandatory nature); Lawrence Solan, *The Language of Judges* ch. 2 (1993) (linguistic analysis of several textual canons); Neil MacCormick, *Argumentation and Interpretation in Law*, 6 Ratio Juris 16 (1993) (discussing linguistic arguments as a category of interpretive argument).

1.   Maxims of Word Association

Noscitur a Sociis and Ejusdem Generis. Words are social creatures: they travel in packs. Several canons suggest permissible inferences from the company that words keep. "Noscitur a sociis" translates as "[i]t is known from its associates." Light may be shed on the meaning of an ambiguous word by reference to words associated with it. "Thus, when two or more words are grouped together, and ordinarily have a similar meaning, but are not equally comprehensive, the general word will be limited and qualified by the special word." 2A Sutherland § 47.16; see *Maxwell*, *supra* note 2, at 289–93 (hereinafter *Maxwell*); *Sullivan*, *supra* note 2, at 227–31 (hereinafter *Sullivan*). For example, in *Jarecki v. G. D. Searle & Co.*, 367 U.S. 303 (1961), a federal income tax statute allowed allocation to other years of income "resulting from exploration, discovery, or prospecting." A drug manufacturer and a camera manufacturer argued that they should be allowed to take advantage of the allocation statute with respect to income from the sale of patented products because by definition such a product resulted from a "discovery." The Court disagreed. When interpreted in light of the associated words "exploration" and "prospecting," the term "discovery" meant only the discovery of mineral resources.

"Ejusdem generis," a sibling of noscitur a sociis, translates as "[o]f the same kind, class, or nature." "Where general words follow specific words in a statutory enumeration, the general words are construed to embrace only objects similar in nature to those objects enumerated by the preceding specific words. Where the opposite sequence is found, i.e., specific words following general ones, the doctrine is equally applicable, and restricts application of the general term to things that are similar to those enumerated." 2A Sutherland § 47.17; see *Maxwell* 297–303; *Sullivan* 231–43. The purpose of this rule is to give effect to all the words—the particular words indicate the class and the general words extend the provisions of the statute to everything else in the class (even though not enumerated by the specific words).

Section 1 of the Federal Arbitration Act of 1926 excludes from coverage "contracts of employment of seamen, railroad employees, or any other class of workers engaged in foreign or interstate commerce." 9 U.S.C. § 1. The issue in *Circuit City Stores, Inc. v. Adams*, 532 U.S. 105 (2001), was whether the exclusion was limited to contracts involving *transportation* but not other kinds of employment contracts. Workers suing their employers generally want a court, not an arbitrator, especially for discrimination claims such as those in *Circuit City*. So the plaintiff argued that his job at a retail store, obviously engaged in "interstate commerce," fell within the exclusion: Congress, he argued, meant to exclude employment contracts generally, and used language tied to the jurisdictional basis of the FAA, the Commerce Clause. The Supreme Court rejected that reading, on the ground that *ejusdem generis* suggested that Congress meant the exclusion to be limited to contracts "like" those involving seamen and railroad workers—namely, transportation contracts.

Noscitur a sociis and ejusdem generis, like the other canons, are just aids to meaning, not ironclad rules. Thus, they have no value if the statute evidences a meaning contrary to their presumptions. See *United States v. Turkette*, 452 U.S. 576, 581 (1981). Dissenting in *Circuit City*, Justice Souter argued that the legislative purpose and specific history rebutted any presumption created by ejusdem generis. Both the labor unions that had petitioned Congress for the exemption covering contracts of employment and Secretary of Commerce Herbert Hoover, the primary architect of the law, endorsed the broader view of the exclusion. (The Court found the statute sufficiently clear in purely textual terms so that it did not need to assess this evidence of legislative history or purpose.)

Deployment of ejusdem generis involves a judgment—often a debatable one—about what it is that makes the items in the series "similar." The *Circuit City* Court found that the common denominator was "transportation contracts," while the dissenters found it to be "employment contracts within Congress's Commerce Clause power." See also *Bilski v. Kappos*, 130 S.Ct. 3218 (2010) (Justice Kennedy for majority declined to apply noscitur a sociis because the assertedly ambiguous term "process" was expressly defined in the patent statute; Justice Stevens, concurring in the judgment, found noscitur useful because the patent statute's definition of "process" included the term "process," leaving residual ambiguity). See generally 2A Sutherland § 47.17–.22 (discussing ejusdem generis and qualifications to its use); *Maxwell* 303–06. For another example of such a debatable judgment, consider the following case.

STATUTORY PREFACE TO *ALI V. FEDERAL BUREAU OF PRISONS*

Federal Tort Claims Act, 28 U.S.C. §§ 1346, 2680.

Section 1346.   *United States as Defendant*

(b)(1)   * * * the district courts * * * shall have exclusive jurisdiction of civil actions on claims against the United States, for money damages * * * for injury or loss of property, or personal injury or death caused by the negligent or wrongful act or omission of any employee of the Government while acting within the scope of his office or employment, under circumstances where the United States, if a private person, would be liable to the claimant in accordance with the law of the place where the act or omission occurred.

Section 2680.   *Exceptions.*

The provisions of this chapter and section 1346(b) of this title shall not apply to—
* * *

> **(c)** Any claim arising in respect of * * * the detention of any goods, merchandise, or other property by any officer of customs or excise or any other law enforcement officer, except that the provisions of this chapter and section 1346(b) of this title apply to any claim based on injury or loss of goods, merchandise, or other property, while in the possession of any officer of customs or excise or any other law enforcement officer, if—

(1) the property was seized for the purpose of forfeiture under any provision of Federal law providing for the forfeiture of property other than as a sentence imposed upon conviction of a criminal offense;

(2) the interest of the claimant was not forfeited;

(3) the interest of the claimant was not remitted or mitigated (if the property was subject to forfeiture); and

(4) the claimant was not convicted of a crime for which the interest of the claimant in the property was subject to forfeiture under a Federal criminal forfeiture law.

ALI V. FEDERAL BUREAU OF PRISONS

Supreme Court of the United States, 2008.
552 U.S. 214, 128 S.Ct. 831, 169 L.Ed.2d 680.

JUSTICE THOMAS delivered the opinion of the Court.

This case concerns the scope of 28 U.S.C. § 2680, which carves out certain exceptions to the United States' waiver of sovereign immunity for torts committed by federal employees. Section 2680(c) provides that the waiver of sovereign immunity does not apply to claims arising from the detention of property by "any officer of customs or excise or any other law enforcement officer." Petitioner contends that this clause applies only to law enforcement officers enforcing customs or excise laws, and thus does not affect the waiver of sovereign immunity for his property claim against officers of the Federal Bureau of Prisons (BOP). We conclude that the broad phrase "any other law enforcement officer" covers all law enforcement officers. Accordingly, we affirm the judgment of the Court of Appeals upholding the dismissal of petitioner's claim.

[I] [Upon being transferred to a new prison facility, some of petitioner Ali's personal belongings that were of personal and religious significance, such as a Qur'an and prayer rug, went missing. After petitioner's administrative claim failed, he filed a complaint alleging violations of the Federal Tort Claims Act (FTCA), 28 U.S.C. §§ 1346, 2671 et seq. The District Court held, and the Eleventh Circuit agreed, that petitioner's claim was barred by the exception in § 2680(c) for property claims against law enforcement officers.]

[II] As relevant here, the FTCA authorizes "claims against the United States, for money damages . . . for injury or loss of property . . . caused by the negligent or wrongful act or omission of any employee of the Government while acting within the scope of his office or employment." [28 U.S.C. § 1346(b)(1)]. The FTCA exempts from this waiver certain categories of claims [including] "[a]ny claim arising in respect of the assessment or collection of any tax or customs duty, or the detention of any goods, merchandise, or other property by any officer of customs or excise or any other law enforcement officer." § 2680(c).

This case turns on whether the BOP officers who allegedly lost petitioner's property qualify as "other law enforcement officer[s]" within the meaning of § 2680(c). Petitioner argues that they do not because "any other law enforcement officer" includes only law enforcement officers acting in a customs or excise capacity. Noting that Congress referenced customs and excise activities in both the language at issue and the preceding clause in § 2680(c), petitioner argues that the entire subsection is focused on preserving the United States' sovereign immunity only as to officers enforcing those laws.

Petitioner's argument is inconsistent with the statute's language. The phrase "any other law enforcement officer" suggests a broad meaning. * * * Congress' use of "any" to modify "other law enforcement officer" is most naturally read to mean law enforcement officers of whatever kind. The word "any" is repeated four times in the relevant portion of § 2680(c), and two of those instances appear in the particular phrase at issue: "any officer of customs or excise or any other law enforcement officer." (Emphasis added.) Congress inserted the word "any" immediately before "other law enforcement officer," leaving no doubt that it modifies that phrase. To be sure, the text's references to "tax or customs duty" and "officer[s] of customs or excise" indicate that Congress intended to preserve immunity for claims arising from an officer's enforcement of tax and customs laws. The text also indicates, however, that Congress intended to preserve immunity for claims arising from the detention of property, and there is no indication that Congress intended immunity for those claims to turn on the type of law being enforced.

Petitioner would require Congress to clarify its intent to cover all law enforcement officers by adding phrases such as "performing any official law enforcement function," or "without limitation." But Congress could not have chosen a more all-encompassing phrase than "any other law enforcement officer" to express that intent. We have no reason to demand that Congress write less economically and more repetitiously. * * *

Against this textual and structural evidence that "any other law enforcement officer" does in fact mean any other law enforcement officer, petitioner invokes numerous canons of statutory construction. He relies primarily on ejusdem generis, or the principle that "when a general term follows a specific one, the general term should be understood as a reference to subjects akin to the one with specific enumeration." * * * In petitioner's view, "any officer of customs or excise or any other law enforcement officer" should be read as a three-item list, and the final, catchall phrase "any other law enforcement officer" should be limited to officers of the same nature as the preceding specific phrases.

Petitioner likens his case to two recent cases in which we found the canon useful. In *Washington State Department. of Social and Health Services v. Guardianship Estate of Keffeler*, 537 U.S. 371 (2003), we considered the clause "execution, levy, attachment, garnishment, or other legal process" in 42 U.S.C. § 407(a). Applying ejusdem generis, we concluded that "other legal process" was limited to legal processes of the same nature as the specific items listed. The department's scheme for serving as a representative payee of the benefits due to children under its care, while a "legal process," did not share the common attribute of the listed items, viz., "utilization of some judicial or quasi-judicial mechanism . . . by which control over property passes from one person to another in order to discharge" a debt. Similarly, in *Dolan v. Postal Service*, 546 U.S. 481 (2006), the Court considered whether an exception to the FTCA's waiver of sovereign immunity for claims arising out of the " 'loss, miscarriage, or negligent transmission of letters or postal matter' " barred a claim that mail negligently left on the petitioner's porch caused her to slip and fall. (quoting 28 U.S.C. § 2680(b)). Noting that "loss" and "miscarriage" both addressed "failings in the postal obligation to deliver mail in a timely manner to the right address," the Court concluded that "negligent transmission" must be similarly limited, and rejected the Government's argument that the exception applied to "all torts committed in the course of mail delivery."

Petitioner asserts that § 2680(c), like the clauses at issue in *Keffeler* and *Dolan*, " 'presents a textbook ejusdem generis scenario.' " * * * We disagree. The structure of the phrase "any officer of customs or excise or any other law enforcement officer" does not lend itself to application of the canon. The phrase is disjunctive, with one specific and one general category, not—like the clauses at issue in *Keffeler* and *Dolan*—a list of specific items separated by commas and followed by a general or collective term. The absence of a list of specific items undercuts the inference embodied in ejusdem generis that Congress remained focused on the common attribute when it used the catchall phrase.

Moreover, it is not apparent what common attribute connects the specific items in § 2680(c). Were we to use the canon to limit the meaning of "any other law enforcement officer," we would be required to determine the relevant limiting characteristic of "officer of customs or excise." In *Jarecki v. G.D. Searle Co.*, 367 U.S. 303 (1961), for example, the Court invoked noscitur a sociis in limiting the scope of the term " 'discovery' " to the common characteristic it shared with " 'exploration' " and " 'prospecting.' " The Court noted that all three words in conjunction "describe[d] income-producing activity in the oil and gas and mining industries." Here, by contrast, no relevant common attribute immediately appears from the phrase "officer of customs or excise." Petitioner suggests that the common attribute is that both types of officers are charged with enforcing the customs and excise laws. But we see no reason why that should be the relevant characteristic as opposed to, for example, that officers of that type are commonly involved in the activities enumerated in the statute: the assessment and collection of taxes and customs duties and the detention of property.

Petitioner's appeals to other interpretive principles are also unconvincing. [Justice Thomas rejects petitioner's argument based on the canon noscitur a sociis because] although customs and excise are mentioned twice in § 2680(c), nothing in the overall statutory context suggests that customs and excise officers were the exclusive focus of the provision. The emphasis in subsection (c) on customs and excise is not inconsistent with the conclusion that "any other law enforcement officer" sweeps as broadly as its language suggests.

Similarly, the rule against superfluities lends petitioner sparse support. The construction we adopt today does not necessarily render "any officer of customs or excise" superfluous; Congress may have simply intended to remove any doubt that officers of customs or excise were included in "law enforcement officers." See *Fort Stewart Schs. v. FLRA*, 495 U.S. 641 (1990) (noting that "technically unnecessary" examples may have been "inserted out of an abundance of caution"). Moreover, petitioner's construction threatens to render "any other law enforcement officer" superfluous because it is not clear when, if ever, "other law enforcement officer[s]" act in a customs or excise capacity. In any event, we do not woodenly apply limiting principles every time Congress includes a specific example along with a general phrase.

In the end, we are unpersuaded by petitioner's attempt to create ambiguity where the statute's text and structure suggest none. Had Congress intended to limit § 2680(c)'s reach as petitioner contends, it easily could have written "any other law enforcement officer acting in a customs or excise capacity." Instead, it used the unmodified, all-encompassing phrase "any other law enforcement officer." * * *

JUSTICE KENNEDY, with whom JUSTICE STEVENS, JUSTICE SOUTER, and JUSTICE BREYER join, dissenting.

Statutory interpretation, from beginning to end, requires respect for the text. The respect is not enhanced, however, by decisions that foreclose consideration of the text within the whole context of the statute as a guide to determining a legislature's intent. To prevent textual analysis from becoming so rarefied that it departs from how a legislator most likely understood the words when he or she voted for the law, courts use certain interpretative rules to consider text within the statutory design. These canons do not demand wooden reliance and are not by themselves dispositive, but they do function as helpful guides in construing ambiguous statutory provisions. Two of these accepted rules are ejusdem generis and noscitur a sociis, which together instruct that words in a series should be interpreted in relation to one another.

Today the Court holds, if my understanding of its opinion is correct, that there is only one possible way to read the statute. Placing implicit reliance upon a comma at the beginning of a clause, the Court says that the two maxims noted, and indeed other helpful and recognized principles of statutory analysis, are not useful as interpretative aids in this case because the clause cannot be understood by what went before. In my respectful submission the Court's approach is incorrect as a general rule and as applied to the statute now before us. * * *

[Justice Kennedy addressed the background of the FTCA, noting that the statute allowed those harmed by the government to seek damages for tortious conduct, with certain exceptions, and he warned that overly generous interpretations of those exceptions could defeat the central purpose of the statute.]

Both on first reading and upon further, close consideration, the plain words of the statute indicate that the exception is concerned only with customs and taxes. The provision begins with a clause dealing exclusively with customs and tax duties. And the provision as a whole contains four express references to customs and tax, making revenue duties and customs and excise officers its most salient features.

This is not to suggest that the Court's reading is wholly impermissible or without some grammatical support. After all, detention of goods is not stated until the outset of the second clause and at the end of the same clause the words "any other law enforcement officer" appear; so it can be argued that the first and second clauses of the provision are so separate that all detentions by all law enforcement officers in whatever capacity they might act are covered. Still, this ought not be the preferred reading; for between the beginning of the second clause and its closing reference to "any other law enforcement officer" appears another reference to "officer[s] of customs or excise," this time in the context of property detention. This is quite sufficient, in my view, to continue the limited scope of the exception. At the very least, the Court errs by adopting a rule which simply bars all consideration of the canons of ejusdem generis and noscitur a sociis. And when those canons are consulted, together with other common principles of interpretation, the case for limiting the exception to customs and tax more than overcomes the position maintained by the Government and adopted by the Court.

The ejusdem generis canon provides that, where a seemingly broad clause constitutes a residual phrase, it must be controlled by, and defined with reference to, the "enumerated categories . . . which are recited just before it," so that the clause encompasses only objects similar in nature.* * * The words "any other law enforcement officer" immediately follow the statute's reference to "officer[s] of customs or excise," as well as the first clause's reference to the assessment of tax and customs duties. 28 U.S.C. § 2680(c).

The Court counters that § 2680(c) "is disjunctive, with one specific and one general category," rendering ejusdem generis inapplicable. The canon's applicability, however, is not limited to those statutes that include a laundry list of items. * * * A proper reading of § 2680(c) thus attributes to the last phrase ("any other law enforcement officer") the discrete characteristic shared by the preceding phrases ("officer[s] of customs or excise" and "assessment or collection of any tax or customs duty"). Had Congress intended otherwise, in all likelihood it would have drafted the section to apply to "any law enforcement officer, including officers of customs and excise," rather than tacking "any other law enforcement officer" on the end of the enumerated categories as it did here.

The common attribute of officers of customs and excise and other law enforcement officers is the performance of functions most often assigned to revenue officers, including, *inter alia*, the enforcement of the United States' revenue laws and the conduct of border searches. Although officers of customs and officers of excise are in most instances the only full-time staff charged with this duty, officers of other federal agencies and general law enforcement officers often will be called upon to act in the traditional capacity of a revenue officer. For example, Drug Enforcement Administration or Federal Bureau of Investigation agents frequently assist customs officials in the execution of border searches. To the extent they detain goods whose possession violates customs laws, the Coast Guard officers—while not "officer[s] of customs or excise," 28 U.S.C. § 2680(c)—are without doubt engaging in the enforcement of the United States' revenue laws.* * *

The Court reaches its contrary conclusion by concentrating on the word "any" before the phrase "other law enforcement officer." 28 U.S.C. § 2680(c). It takes this single last phrase to extend the statute so that it covers all detentions of property by any law enforcement officer in whatever capacity he or she acts. There are fundamental problems with this approach, in addition to the ones already mentioned.

First, the Court's analysis cannot be squared with the longstanding recognition that a single word must not be read in isolation but instead defined by reference to its statutory context. As already mentioned, the context of § 2680(c) suggests that, in accordance with these precedents, the statutory provision should be interpreted narrowly to apply only to customs and revenue duties.* * *

Second, the Court's construction of the phrase "any other law enforcement officer" * * * renders "officer[s] of customs or excise" mere surplusage, as there would have been no need for Congress to have specified that officers of customs and officers of excise were immune if they indeed were subsumed within the allegedly all-encompassing "any" officer clause. * * *

[Third, Justice Kennedy pointed to the lack of any reference within the legislative history to a Congressional desire to limit liability to officers beyond customs and excise agents as indicative that Congress did not believe the exception to the waiver applied to officers outside of the customs and excise context. Kennedy maintained that if Congress had meant for the exception to sweep so broadly, it would have spoken more clearly when undermining the Act's general purpose.]

If Congress had intended to give sweeping immunity to all federal law enforcement officials from liability for the detention of property, it would not have dropped this phrase onto the end of the statutory clause so as to appear there as something of an afterthought. The seizure of property by an officer raises serious concerns for the liberty of our people and the Act should not be read to permit appropriation of property without a remedy in tort by language so obscure and indirect.

JUSTICE BREYER, with whom JUSTICE STEVENS joins, dissenting.

* * * I write separately to emphasize, as Justice Kennedy's dissent itself makes clear, that the relevant context extends well beyond Latin canons and other such purely textual devices. * * * As with many questions of statutory interpretation, the issue here is not the meaning of the words. The dictionary meaning of each word is well known. Rather, the issue is the statute's scope. What boundaries did Congress intend to set? To what circumstances did Congress intend the phrase, as used in this statutory provision, to apply? * * *

The word "any" is of no help because all speakers (including writers and legislators) who use general words such as "all," "any," "never," and "none" normally rely upon context to indicate the limits of time and place within which they intend those words to do their linguistic work. And with the possible exception of the assertion of a universal truth, say by a mathematician, scientist, philosopher, or theologian, such limits almost always exist. When I call out to my wife, "There isn't any butter," I do not mean, "There isn't any butter in town." The context makes clear to her that I am talking about the contents of our refrigerator. That is to say, it is context, not a dictionary, that sets the boundaries of time, place, and circumstance within which words such as "any" will apply.

Context, of course, includes the words immediately surrounding the phrase in question. And canons such as ejusdem generis and noscitur a sociis offer help in evaluating the significance of those surrounding words. Yet that help is limited. That is because other contextual features can show that Congress intended a phrase to apply more broadly than the immediately surrounding words by themselves suggest. * * * It is because canons of construction are not "conclusive" and "are often countered . . . by some maxim pointing in a different direction." * * * And it is because these particular canons simply crystallize what English speakers already know, namely, that lists often (but not always) group together items with similar characteristics. * * * In this case, not only the immediately surrounding words but also every other contextual feature supports Justice Kennedy's conclusion. The textual context includes the location of the phrase within a provision that otherwise exclusively concerns customs and revenue duties. And the nontextual context includes several features that, taken together, indicate that Congress intended a narrow tort-liability exception related to customs and excise.

[Justice Breyer relied on the FTCA drafting history to argue that a limited exception made more sense based on what tort remedies were available to those harmed by the government at the time of the statute's drafting, and also on Congress's silence as to any intent that the waiver provision apply more broadly than the customs and excise setting.] [T]he law's history contains much that indicates the provision's scope is limited to customs and excise, [but] it contains nothing at all suggesting an intent to apply the provision more broadly, indeed, to multiply the number of officers to whom it applies by what is likely one or more orders of magnitude. It is thus not the Latin canons, ejusdem generis and noscitur a sociis, that shed light on the application of the statutory phrase but Justice Scalia's more pertinent and easily remembered English-language observation that Congress "does not . . . hide elephants in mouseholes." * * *

NOTES ON ALI AND EJUSDEM GENERIS

1.   *What Constitutes the "Common Attribute" of "Words in a Series?"* For Justice Thomas, the meaning of "any" is so clear that ejusdem generis doesn't come into play. But even if it did, Thomas insists the canon would be improperly applied here. In Justice Kennedy's dissent, the fact that "officer[s] of customs or excise" are mentioned immediately before "any other law enforcement officer" narrows the scope of the "law enforcement officer" exception to the waiver of sovereign immunity. Justice Thomas counters by arguing that "customs" and "excise" have no common attribute that would constrain the broad general meaning of "any other law enforcement officer." For the majority, the fact that "any officer of customs or excise" and "any other law enforcement officer" are disjunctive phrases indicates that *ejusdem*—and also *noscitur*—do not apply at all.

If § 2680(6) were phrased "any officer of customs, excise, or any other law enforcement officer," would this change Justice Thomas's position on *ejusdem's* applicability? What if the phrase read "any officer of customs or excise or border searches or any other law enforcement officer"? How many specific common attributes should be listed before applying the canon to the phrase "any other law enforcement officer"? Should the answer to these questions change depending on other tools used in statutory interpretation, such as the rule against surplusage, the provision's legislative history, or the practical implications of different readings?

Justice Breyer has yet another perspective: both the majority and Justice Kennedy's dissent focus too intensely on close textual readings and textual canons while giving short-shrift to the drafting history and overriding purpose of the Federal Tort Claims Act. Is it appropriate to infer from Congress's failure to discuss a broad reading of the phrase "any other law enforcement officer" that the words were not meant to have that broad an application? The FTCA is itself a statutory waiver of the underlying principle of sovereign immunity: thus one could view § 2680(c) as a specific exception to a more general statutory exception. In this setting, what exactly are the "elephants" and the "mouseholes"? In the end, which approach to construing the contested language do you find most persuasive: The literalist approach taken by Justice Thomas? The canonical position espoused by Justice Kennedy? The purposivist approach utilized by Justice Breyer?

2. *Textual Canons as Constraints on Judicial Activism?* Advocates for the textual canons regularly argue that this canonical approach constrains judges from the tendency "to imbue authoritative texts with their own policy preferences." Antonin Scalia & Bryan A. Garner, *Reading Law: The Interpretation of Legal Texts* xxviii (2012). In Justice Scalia's view, a canons-based textual approach "will provide greater certainty in the law, and hence greater predictability and greater respect for the rule of law." *Id.* at xxix. More pessimistic observers, from both the academy and the judiciary, suggest that canons tend to disguise the creative elements of statutory construction by presenting the interpretive process as essentially mechanical, and that judges often use the textual canons strategically to justify their own policy preferences or to frustrate clear legislative intent.[5] One of us has argued that far from constraining the imposition of value preferences, these textual canons effectively require judges to engage in normative evaluations—as when textualist judges enforce their understanding of "normal" English-speaking usage on Congress, or decide that the commonality of terms in a list should be specified without regard to the statutory purpose that gave rise to the list itself. See William Eskridge, *The New Textualism and Normative* Canons, 113 Colum. L. Rev. 531, 557–60 (2013) (reviewing *Reading Law*).

Scalia and Garner devote fifteen pages to ejusdem generis, recounting the canon's origins and justifications, and concluding that "it does not always predominate, but neither is it a mere tiebreaker." *Id.* at 213. They assert that ejusdem is generally triggered by the presence of two or more words to establish a genus before the general phrase that follows. Yet they argue that the majority in *Ali* correctly found the canon inapplicable because of the "unexamined but probably correct" premise that the phrase 'officer of customs or excise' reflects a traditional pairing of the two terms as a single type of officer (they cite to Great Britain's Bureau of Customs and Excise) which is not equivalent to 'customs officer or excise officer.' See *id.* at 206–07. Given that in *Ali*, Justices Thomas and Kennedy draw opposing inferences from the presence of two specific words before a general phrase, and that Justice Scalia justifies Justice Thomas's inference based on a premise never articulated in the opinion for the Court,

---

[5] See Richard Posner, The Federal Courts: Crisis and Reform, 285–86 (1985); T. Alexander Aleinikoff & Theodore Shaw, *The Costs of Incoherence: A Comment on Plain Meaning*, West Virginia Univ. Hospitals, Inc. v. Casey, *and Due Process of Statutory Interpretation*, 45 Vand. L. Rev. 687, 688–89, 696–97 (1992); Stephen Ross, *Where Have You Gone, Karl Llewellyn? Should Congress Turn Its Lonely Eyes to You?*, 45 Vand. L. Rev. 561, 562 (1992).

does this case perhaps illustrate how textual canons are unlikely to constrain judicial discretion?

3.   *Congressional Drafters' Use of Textual Canons and Dictionaries.* A recent study by Abbe Gluck and Lisa Schultz Bressman surveyed 137 congressional staffers—drawn from both parties and both chambers—on their knowledge and use of the various interpretive tools in drafting legislation. The study found that the assumptions underlying the ejusdem and noscitur canons were widely used by legislative drafters, although not recognized by their Latin cognates. Over 70 percent of respondents stated that terms in a statutory list often or always relate to one another (when asked by name, two-thirds did not know ejusdem and 85 percent did not know noscitur). Gluck and Bressman found that the 70 percent level of usage was considerably higher than the reliance levels for two other textual canons, discussed below: expressio unius (33 percent) and the rule against superfluities (30 percent). Abbe Gluck & Lisa Schultz Bressman, *Statutory Interpretation From the Inside—An Empirical Study of Congressional Drafting, Delegation, and the Canons: Part I,* 65 Stan. L. Rev. 901, 930–34 (2013). The drafters' reliance on dictionaries was even lower: 15 percent said they often or always used them when drafting whereas more than 50 percent said dictionaries are never or rarely used. The latter finding contrasts starkly with the Court's burgeoning increase in dictionary usage.

How relevant is the Gluck and Bressman study when considering what constitutes an appropriate interpretive approach? Their findings on ejusdem and noscitur suggest that textual canons may ultimately be ornate labels describing certain ways in which we process language through context. Should special weight be given to ejusdem and noscitur because the concepts underlying both are readily understood and incorporated by congressional drafters?

Conversely, does it matter whether some textual canons—as well as dictionary definitions—that Justice Scalia and fellow textualists extol as common sense resources are in fact discounted or ignored by those who draft statutory text? Should judges be concerned only with how a "reasonable person" would understand the language that has been enacted? Should those drafting and negotiating the language of the statutes be deemed part of any reasonable person construct? Why might they even be regarded as especially important reference points when deciding which interpretive sources to consult?

Expressio unius. Words omitted may be just as significant as words set forth. The maxim "expressio [or inclusio] unius est exclusio alterius" means "expression (or inclusion) of one thing indicates exclusion of the other." The notion is one of negative implication: the enumeration of certain things in a statute suggests that the legislature had no intent of including things not listed or embraced. See *Tate v. Ogg,* 195 S.E. 496 (Va. 1938) (statute covering "any horse, mule, cattle, hog, sheep or goat" did not cover turkeys); 2A Sutherland § 47.25 (discussing the limitations of the canon); *Maxwell,* 293–97; *Sullivan,* 243–52.

As *Holy Trinity Church* (Chapter 6, § 1) exemplifies, courts feel free to refuse to apply the maxim when they believe it would lead to a result Congress did not intend.[6]

---

[6]   In that case, the statute that prohibited bringing into the United States an alien for employment exempted certain persons such as lecturers and domestic servants. Had the Court followed expressio unius, it would have held that the listed exceptions were the only ones not covered by the prohibition, and therefore that the church had violated the statute.

One basic problem is that this canon, like many of the others, assumes that the legislature thinks through statutory language carefully, considering every possible variation. This is clearly not true, for the legislature often omits things because no one thinks about them or everyone assumes that courts will fill in gaps. See Richard Posner, *The Federal Courts: Crisis and Reform* 282 (1985). Some judges have reflected this concern, suggesting that the maxim is unreliable because "it stands on the faulty premise that all possible alternative or supplemental provisions were necessarily considered and rejected by the [legislature]." *Nat'l Petroleum Refiners Ass'n v. FTC*, 482 F.2d 672, 676 (D.C. Cir. 1973).

Another way of looking at this issue is to consider context, including normative context. If Mother tells Sally, "Don't hit, kick, or bite your sister Anne," Sally is *not* authorized by expressio unius to "pinch" her little sister. The reason is that the normative baseline (discerned from prior practice or just family culture) is "no harming sister," and the directive was an expression of that baseline that ought not be narrowly limited. Contrariwise, where the directive in question is a departure from the normative baseline, the canon ought to apply. For example, if Mother tells Sally, "You may have a cookie and a scoop of ice cream," Sally has implicitly been forbidden to snap up that candy bar lying on the kitchen table. For cases where normative statutory baselines augured against application of expressio unius, see, *e.g.*, *Marrama v. Citizens Bank of Mass.*, 549 U.S. 365, 373–76 (2007) (Stevens, J.); *Christensen v. Harris Cnty.*, 529 U.S. 576, 583–84 (2000) (Thomas, J.).

But consider *Chan v. Korean Air Lines*, 490 U.S. 122 (1989), where the Supreme Court held that international air carriers do not lose their Warsaw Convention limitation on damages arising out of passenger injury or death when they fail to provide the passenger with the requisite notice of limitation on her ticket. Article 3(1) of the Convention requires such notice, and article 3(2) provides that if the carrier fails to deliver a ticket to the passenger it cannot avail itself of the Convention's liability limits. Although many lower courts had interpreted article 3(2) to include situations where the passenger received a ticket, but without the requisite notice, the Court, in an opinion by Justice Scalia, held to the contrary. Justice Scalia's key argument was that other sections of the Convention provide parallel rules for limiting carrier liability and providing notice thereof, for baggage checks (article 4) and cargo waybills (article 9). The various sections are identical in their notice requirements, but not in their remedies. Article 3 (passenger injury) provides no remedy explicitly covering insufficient notice, while articles 4 and 9 explicitly waive liability limits for the carrier's failure to include the required notice in the documents given to the consumer. By negative implication, Scalia construed article 3 not to have the remedy that had been clearly provided in the other articles.

The dissenting opinion argued from the Convention's negotiating history that the lack of a similar remedy in article 3(2) was probably inadvertent. Justice Scalia considered such evidence inadmissible. If such evidence were admissible, would it persuade you that Justice Scalia's invocation of expressio unius was too hasty? Note that fellow textualist Judge Easterbrook considers expressio unius arguments question-begging and unreliable. See *In re Am. Reserve Corp.*, 840 F.2d 487, 492 (7th Cir. 1988) ("Why should we infer from the list of ways to do something that there are no others? * * * A list of four ways may imply only that Congress has yet to consider whether there should be others. The history and structure of a statute may show that a list is exhaustive, * * * but also may show that Congress has not grappled with the problem.") At the Supreme Court level, though, arguments drawn from the expressio unius concept have had an enduring appeal.[7]

2. Grammar Canons

Although "justice should not be the hand maiden of grammar," *Value Oil Co. v. Irvington*, 377 A.2d 1225, 1231 (N.J. Super. Ct. Law Div. 1977), the legislature is presumed to know and follow basic conventions of grammar and syntax. *Maxwell* 28. Like the canons discussed above, the following are more rules of thumb than commands.

(a) *Punctuation Rules.* "The punctuation canon in America * * * has assumed at least three forms: (1) adhering to the strict English rule that punctuation forms no part of the statute; (2) allowing punctuation as an aid in statutory construction; and (3) looking on punctuation as a less-than-desirable, last-ditch alternative aid in statutory construction. The last approach * * * seems to have prevailed as the majority rule." Ray Marcin, *Punctuation and the Interpretation of Statutes*, 9 Conn. L. Rev. 227, 240 (1977). The English rule noted by Marcin was adopted because "[a]t one time * * * punctuation [was] inserted by a clerk after the statute had been enacted by Parliament." U.S. legislatures (at both state and federal levels) generally consider and pass bills whose punctuation is not changed after enactment. 2A Sutherland § 47.15, argues that "an act should be read as punctuated unless there is some reason to do otherwise," such as an indication that such a reading would defeat the apparent intent of the legislature. "This is especially true where a statute has been repeatedly reenacted with the same punctuation, or has been the subject of numerous amendments without alteration of punctuation." See also *Sullivan* 400–02; Pa. Stat. Constr. Act § 1923(b): "In no case shall the punctuation of a statute control or affect the intention of the General Assembly in the enactment thereof but punctuation may be used in aid in the construction thereof. * * * "

The punctuation canon has *not* played a major role in the legisprudence of the U.S. Supreme Court. The Court found the punctuation rule decisive in *United States v. Ron Pair Enterprises, Inc.*, 489 U.S. 235, 241–42 (1989), but otherwise this canon is rarely controlling. In *United States National Bank v. Independent Insurance Agents*, 508 U.S. 439, 453–62 (1993), the Court in effect repunctuated a statute after concluding that a scrivener's error had occurred.

(b) *Referential and Qualifying Words: The Last Antecedent Rule.* Referential and qualifying words or phrases refer only to the last antecedent, unless contrary to the apparent legislative intent derived from the sense of the entire enactment. E.g., *Jama v. Immigration & Customs Enforcement*, 543 U.S. 345 (2005). For example, in a statute providing that "the limitation of an action will not be extended beyond six

---

[7]   See, e.g., *Hinck v. United States*, 550 U.S. 501, 506 (2007) (Roberts, C.J.); *TRW, Inc. v. Andrews*, 534 U.S. 19 (2001) (Ginsburg, J.); *Solid Waste Agency v. Army Corps of Eng'rs*, 531 U.S. 159 (2001) (Rehnquist, C.J.); *City of Chicago v. Envtl. Def. Fund*, 511 U.S. 328 (1994) (Scalia, J.,); *Key Tronic Corp. v. United States*, 511 U.S. 809, 818–19 (1994) (Stevens, J.); *United States v. Smith*, 499 U.S. 160 (1991) (Marshall, J.); *Mississippi Band of Choctaw Indians v. Holyfield*, 490 U.S. 30, 46–47 & n.22 (1989) (Brennan, J., who wrote the dissenting opinion in *Chan*).

years of the act or omission of alleged malpractice by a nondiscovery thereof," the "thereof" refers to the "act or omission of alleged malpractice." *Anderson v. Shook*, 333 N.W.2d 708 (N.D. 1983). Similarly, a proviso applies only to the provision, clause, or word immediately preceding it.

Consider this recent example. The Social Security Act's disability benefits program is available to a worker whose "physical or mental impairment or impairments are of such severity that he is not only unable to do his previous work but cannot, considering his age, education, and work experience, engage in any other kind of substantial gainful work which exists in the national economy." 42 U.S.C. § 423(d)(2)(A). Pauline Thomas was an elevator operator until that job was eliminated from the economy; she claimed to be disabled from other jobs in the economy. The Third Circuit ruled that she was disabled, rejecting the agency's argument that she could still do "[her] previous work." Then-Judge Alito reasoned that "previous work" (like "any other kind of substantial gainful work") had to exist "in the national economy," but the Supreme Court unanimously reversed, based upon the rule of the last antecedent. Only the "other kind" of work—and *not* the "previous work"—had to exist in the national economy. *Barnhart v. Thomas*, 540 U.S. 20, 26 (2003).[8]

The last antecedent rule can be trumped by the punctuation rule. "Evidence that a qualifying phrase is supposed to apply to all antecedents instead of only to the immediately preceding one may be found in the fact that it is separated from the antecedents by a comma." 2A Sutherland § 47.33. Thus, if the statutory definition in *Thomas* had included a comma before "exists in the national economy," Pauline Thomas would have had a better chance of success at a textually oriented Supreme Court.

The last antecedent rule can also be negated by other statutory context. Some courts have developed an "across the board rule" which is a special exception to the last antecedent rule: "[W]hen a clause follows several words in a statute and is applicable as much to the first word as to the others in the list, the clause should be applied to all of the words which preceded it." *Bd. of Trustees v. Judge*, 123 Cal. Rptr. 830, 834 (Cal. App. 1975).

(c) *Conjunctive Versus Disjunctive Connectors: The "And" Versus "Or" Rule.* The nature of the conjunctions connecting different words or phrases may be significant. Terms connected by the disjunctive "or" are often read to have separate meanings and significance. For instance, 18 U.S.C. § 2114 (1988),[9] prohibits assault with intent to rob "any person having lawful charge, control, or custody of any mail

---

[8] Judge Alito did not dispute that "which exists in the national economy" modified "any other kind of substantial gainful work," the last antecedent point. Alito's argument was that by using "*any other* kind of work," Congress was demanding a parallelism between these other jobs which exist in the national economy and the applicant's "previous work." The Supreme Court responded: "Consider, for example, the case of parents who, before leaving their teenage son alone in the house for the weekend, warn him, 'You will be punished if you throw a party or engage in any other activity that damages the house.' If the son nevertheless throws a party and is caught, he should hardly be able to avoid punishment by arguing that the house was not damaged. The parents proscribed (1) a party, and (2) any other activity that damages the house." Is this a persuasive answer to Judge Alito?

[9] Similarly, as *Chisom v. Roemer* (Chapter 6, § 3) indicates, the use of "and" usually is held to create a conjunctive rather than disjunctive meaning.

[handwritten marginalia at top: "person control, custody Mail matter (or) of any money (or) other property — only mail carriers"]

matter or of any money or other property of the United States." The issue in *Garcia v. United States*, 469 U.S. 70 (1984), was whether § 2114 applies to robbery of a Secret Service agent of his "flash money" (to be used to buy counterfeit currency from perpetrators). Petitioners argued that § 2114 only covered robbery of mail carriers, and that may have been the original focus of the statute. But the Court found the plain meaning clear: by separating "mail matter," "money," and "other property" with "or" (rather than "and"), Congress meant to include each of the three as an object of the statute and *not* to limit the statute to robbery of money and property in the custody of postal carriers. Why doesn't the ejusdem generis rule dictate the opposite result in *Garcia*? See *Schreiber v. Burlington Northern, Inc.*, 472 U.S. 1, 7–8 (1985) (interpreting "fraudulent, deceptive, or manipulative" language of Securities Act § 14(e) as all aimed at same thing: failures to disclose).

Linguists complicate the matter with these further observations: (1) The word "or" technically means "and/or" (a locution gaining in popularity). When I say "I want this or that," I might be saying I want either one item or the other, but I might also be saying I want both items. (2) In ordinary usage, people often use the two conjunctions interchangeably. "I want this and that" might signify that I want both items, or that I want only one. (3) De Morgan's Rules state that when preceded by a negative the logic is as follows:

Not (A *and* B) means Not A *or* Not B.

Not (A *or* B) means Not A *and* Not B.

See Solan, *Language of Judges*, 45–49. Professor Solan observes that courts do not always follow this logic, and typically for good reason.

[handwritten marginalia: "or and AND"]

The Comprehensive Crime Control Act of 1984 permits the United States to seize property used to commit crimes related to drug dealing. Under § 881(a)(7) such "real property" cannot be seized if the owner can establish (as an affirmative defense) that the criminal activity was "committed or omitted without the knowledge *or* consent of that owner." Can an owner prevail if he can only show lack of consent? Or does the owner also have to show lack of knowledge? If "without" has a negative connotation (which Solan and we think it does), De Morgan's Rules suggest that the defense requires both lack of knowledge (Not A) *and* lack of consent (Not B). But the Second Circuit held that the property owner could defend if he or she could show lack of consent, but only if the owner had taken reasonable steps to prevent illicit use of the property once the owner knew of such use. *United States v. 141st Street Corp.*, 911 F.2d 870, 878 (2d Cir. 1990). Solan says that this is an appropriate interpretation, notwithstanding De Morgan's Rules. Do you agree?

[handwritten marginalia: "Do"]

(d) *Mandatory Versus Discretionary Language: The "May" Versus "Shall" Rule.* When a statute uses mandatory language ("shall" rather than "may"), courts often interpret the statute to exclude discretion to take account of equitable or policy factors. See *Escondido Mut. Water Co. v. LaJolla Indians*, 466 U.S. 765 (1984); *Dunlop v. Bachowski*, 421 U.S. 560 (1975). On the other hand, ordinary usage does sometimes consider "may" and "shall" interchangeable. "You may help Mother" may be either permissive or directive, depending upon the circumstances.

The statute in *In re Cartmell's Estate*, 138 A.2d 588 (Vt. 1958), provided that probate matters of law are to be tried by a court, and "if a question of fact is to be decided, issue *may* be joined thereon under the direction of the court and a trial had by jury unless waived * * *." The trial court had denied a jury trial, over objections. The appeals court reversed: "The word 'may' can be construed as 'shall' or 'must' when such was the legislative intention." The court, correctly, assumed that "may" applied both to the phrase "be joined * * * court" and to "trial had by jury." Solan, *Language of Judges*, supra, at 46–48. Compare *Lopez v. Davis*, 531 U.S. 230 (2001) (a law providing that the sentence of a nonviolent offender "may be reduced" by the Bureau of Prisons vested discretion with the Bureau not only to deny or grant this benefit to specific nonviolent offenders, but also to create a new category of nonviolent offenders (those whose crime involved a firearm) who could not receive the benefit of its discretion).

(e) *Singular and Plural Numbers, Male and Female Pronouns.* One grammar rule that is *not* often followed by statutory interpreters is the difference between singular and plural nouns. "In determining the meaning of any act or resolution of Congress, unless the context otherwise indicates, words importing the singular include and apply to several persons, parties, or things; words importing the plural include the singular * * *." 1 U.S.C. § 1; accord, Interpretation Act of 1889, § 1(1)(b) (U.K.). Many states have analogous provisions.

A grammar rule even less often followed is the pronoun gender rule: He means a male referent, she a female referent. Because most statutes were drafted in eras when the main legal actors who counted were men, the male pronoun includes the female, and vice-versa. 1 U.S.C. § 2; Interpretation Act § 1(1)(a). Most states and the District of Columbia have a similar rule.

(f) *The Golden Rule (Against Absurdity)—and the Nietzsche Rule.* English-speaking jurisdictions have a few catch-all rules providing a mental check for the technical process of word-parsing and grammar-crunching. The *golden rule* is that interpreters should "adhere to the ordinary meaning of the words used, and to the grammatical construction, unless that * * * leads to any manifest absurdity or repugnance, in which case the language may be varied or modified, so as to avoid such inconvenience, but no further." *Becke v. Smith*, 150 Eng. Rep. 724, 726 (U.K. Exch. 1836). See also Hart & Sacks' excerpts from old British cases in Chapter 6, § 1. For example, an early admiralty statute required purchasers of a vessel to register it immediately and barred them from receiving favorable duty treatment until they did so. In *Willing v. United States*, 8 U.S. (4 Cranch) 48, Chief Justice Marshall allowed favorable duty treatment for purchasers who had bought the vessel at sea and therefore could not have registered the purchase until their return. A strict application of the statute under those circumstances would have been manifestly unreasonable, the Chief Justice reasoned.

The golden rule is, in short, an *absurd results* exception to the plain meaning rule. In *Barnhart v. Thomas*, supra, Judge Alito thought it absurd for the government to consider the applicant not disabled from working her previous job when it no longer existed. Writing for the Supreme Court, Justice Scalia disagreed. A claimant who is concededly able to do her previous job is *probably* able to perform a job *somewhere* in the national economy. Hence, the agency's position was at most stingy, but by no means an absurd proof rule for a program with limited resources.

Relatedly, courts should be willing to revise *scrivener's errors*—obvious mistakes in the transcription of statutes into the law books. See, e.g., *Lamie v. U.S. Trustee*, 540 U.S. 526, 530–31 (2004) (Court rewrites Bankruptcy Act to fix drafting error); *Green v. Bock Laundry* (Chapter 6, § 3A) (all Justices agreeing to rewrite statute to correct an absurd provision that must have been the result of a scrivener's error); *Schooner Paulina's Cargo v. United States*, 11 U.S. (7 Cranch) 52, 67–68 (1812) (Marshall, C.J., revising statute to clean up scrivener's error).

The golden rule and its corollaries are now subject to academic debate. Although Justice Scalia recognized an absurd results exception to the plain meaning rule in *Bock Laundry* (concurring opinion), scholars of various persuasions maintain that an absurd results exception to plain meaning is inconsistent with the premises of the new textualism.[10] In *Zuni Public School District v. Department of Education*, 550 U.S. 81, 104–07 (2007), Justice Stevens's concurring opinion rests the absurd result exception upon notions of probable legislative intent: if a plain meaning interpretation is truly absurd, that is prima facie reason to think Congress did not intend it (absent evidence to the contrary, of course). Justice Scalia roundly denounced this approach, in absolute language suggesting that he now agrees with his critics that there should be no absurd result exception to the plain meaning rule. *Id.* at 116–22 (Scalia, J., dissenting).

Friedrich Nietzsche admonished in *Mixed Opinions and Maxims* No. 137 (1879): "The worst readers are those who proceed like plundering soldiers: they pick up a few things they can use, soil and confuse the rest, and blaspheme the whole."[11] All the Justices would agree with this sentiment; indeed, both Stevens and Scalia invoke it in their *Zuni* debate. We read Nietzsche's lesson for the statutory interpreter to include the following: Be humble. Consider how other people use language. Be helpful to the project rather than hypertechnical.

C. THE WHOLE ACT RULE AND ITS COROLLARIES

Some textually-grounded rules or maxims of statutory interpretation derive not from the association of words or the principles of grammar but instead from the particular language's relationship to the larger structural context of a statute. The Sutherland treatise identifies different approaches that have been used: interpretation of each section in isolation from the others; interpretation of all sections within each part of a statute together; resolution of ambiguities based upon the purposes and goals set forth in the preamble to the statute; and interpretation of each section in the context of the whole enactment. The treatise endorses the "whole act rule" as "the most realistic in view of the fact that a

---

[10] E.g., William Eskridge Jr., *Textualism, The Unknown Ideal?*, 96 Mich. L. Rev. 1509 (1998) (criticizing the new textualism for this inconsistency); John Manning, *The Absurdity Doctrine*, 116 Harv. L. Rev. 2387 (2003) (agreeing with Eskridge and urging textualists to abandon the absurd results canon); John Nagle, *Textualism's Exceptions*, Issues in Legal Scholarship (Nov. 2002), www.bepress.com/ils/iss3/art5 (same).

[11] Friedrich Nietzsche, *On the Genealogy of Morals (and Other Works)* 175 (Walter Kaufman trans. and ed. 1967). David Krentel, Georgetown University Law Center, Class of 1995, brought this maxim to our attention.

legislature passes judgment upon the act as an entity, not giving one portion of the act any greater authority than another. Thus any attempt to segregate any portion or exclude any other portion from consideration is almost certain to distort the legislative intent." 2A Sutherland § 47.02. See *Maxwell* 47–64 (English background and current application of the whole act rule); *Sullivan* 325–409 (Canadian cases).

1. The Whole Act Rule

From its earliest cases, the U.S. Supreme Court has followed the whole act rule in construing statutes. E.g., *United States v. Fisher*, 6 U.S. (2 Cranch) 358 (1805); *United States v. Priestman*, 4 U.S. (4 Dall.) 29 (1800) (per curiam). "Statutory interpretation * * * is a holistic endeavor. A provision that may seem ambiguous in isolation is often clarified by the remainder of the statutory scheme—because the same terminology is used elsewhere in a context that makes its meaning clear, or because only one of the permissible meanings produces a substantive effect that is compatible with the rest of the law." *United Savings Ass'n of Texas v. Timbers of* *Inwood Forest Assocs.*, 484 U.S. 365, 371 (1988). "When 'interpreting a statute, the court will not look merely to a particular clause in which general words may be used, but will take in connection with it the whole statute * * * and the objects and policy of the law, as indicated by its various provisions, and give to it such a construction as will carry into execution the will of the legislature.' " *Kokoszka v. Belford*, 417 U.S. 642, 650 (1974); see also *Doe v. Chao*, 540 U.S. 614 (2004) (considering uncodified parts of the "whole act"). A critical assumption of the whole act approach is *coherence*: the interpreter presumes that the legislature drafted the statute as a document that is internally consistent in its use of language and in the way its provisions work together.[12] Note similarities to interpretation of contracts and sacred texts like the Bible.

Consider some corollaries to the whole act rule.

(a) *Titles.* Because Parliament's clerks, rather than Parliament, provided the titles of acts, the traditional English rule has been that the title could not be used for interpretive purposes. Thus, if the statute in Problem 8–1 had the title, "An Act to Prohibit Motorized Vehicles from the Park," English courts would have ignored this evidence of the statute's ambit. (The foregoing, by the way, is the *long title* of the statute; a *short title* would be something like the "The Motor Vehicles in the Park Act.") This is no longer the practice in most English-speaking jurisdictions, for the long title, and often a short title as well, are part of the legislative bill from the very beginning. In the United States, most state constitutions require the legislated enactment to have a title that gives accurate notice of the contents of the law. See also 2A Sutherland § 47.03 (the "title cannot control the plain words of the statute" but "[i]n case of ambiguity the court may consider the title to resolve uncertainty in the purview [the body] of the act or for the correction of obvious errors."); *Maxwell*

---

[12] See, e.g., *Ledbetter v. Goodyear Tire & Rubber Co.*, 550 U.S. 618 (2007); *Gonzales v. Oregon*, 546 U.S. 243 (2006); *Conroy v. Aniskoff*, 507 U.S. 511 (1993); *King v. St. Vincent's Hosp.*, 502 U.S. 215 (1991). See also *Canada Sugar Refining Co. v. Regina*, [1898] A.C. 735, 741 (U.K. House of Lords) (Davey, J.) (every clause of a law should be "construed with reference to the context and other clauses of the Act, so as, so far as possible, to make a consistent enactment of the whole statute"); *Greenshields v. Regina*, [1958] S.C.R. 216, 225 (Can. Sup. Ct.) ("a section or enactment must be construed as a whole, each portion throwing light, if need be, on the rest").

3–6 (long title but probably not short title may be used to resolve ambiguities); *Sullivan* 376–81.

The U.S. Supreme Court in *Holy Trinity Church* (Chapter 6, § 1) considered the statute's long title as cogent evidence of its purpose and indeed reworked the statutory provision to be consistent with it. However, today's Supreme Court generally does not rely on statutory titles as important evidence of statutory meaning, although Justices will sometimes quote the title as marginally relevant context. E.g., *Porter v. Nussle*, 534 U.S. 516, 524 (2002).

(b) *Preambles and Purpose Clauses.*[13] The traditional English rule gave great weight to statutory preambles because they were considered the best source for determining statutory purpose. American courts, following the whole act approach, have declined to give the preamble any greater weight than other parts of the statute (the title, purview, individual sections). "[T]he settled principle of law is that the preamble cannot control the enacting part of the statute in cases where the enacting part is expressed in clear, unambiguous terms" but "may be resorted to help discover the intention of the law maker." 2A Sutherland § 47.04. On the other hand, to the extent that the interpreter is able to find ambiguity and follows the Hart and Sacks purpose/context approach to statutory interpretation (Chapter 6, § 2), the preamble will be a particularly valuable contribution to the interpretive task. The Canadian Supreme Court, for example, vigorously relies on statutory preambles for this reason. See *Rawluk v. Rawluk*, [1990] 1 S.C.R. 70 (Can. Sup. Ct.) (concluding that because the preamble of Ontario's Family Law Act spoke of marriage as a "form of partnership," the common law remedy of "constructive trust" was authorized under the Act).

A preamble played a key interpretive role in *Sutton v. United Airlines, Inc.*, 527 U.S. 471 (1999). The Americans with Disabilities Act (ADA) prohibits job discrimination against people with disabilities. The airline had refused to consider hiring two pilots (they were twin sisters) whose eyesight was severely myopic. The airline argued that because poor eyesight could be completely corrected by eyeglasses, the pilots and other myopics did not have a "physical or mental impairment that substantially limits one or more . . . major life activities." 42 U.S.C. § 12102(2)(C). This was an ironic construction of the ADA, for it would allow the airline to refuse to hire the sisters because of an impairment that the airline conceded was correctable. Yet the Supreme Court agreed, in part because the ADA's preamble found that 43 million people in the U.S. had disabilities, 42 U.S.C. § 12101(a)(1)—a far smaller number than people with poor enough vision to justify eyeglasses. *Id.* at 484–86; see *id.* at 494–95 (Ginsburg, J., concurring especially for this reason).

(c) *Provisos.* Provisos restrict the effect of statutory provisions or create exceptions to general statutory rules. They typically follow the provision being restricted or excepted, and start with: " * * * *Provided that* * * *." If there is doubt about the interpretation of a proviso, it is supposed to be strictly (narrowly)

---

[13] A *preamble* sets out the important facts or considerations that gave rise to the legislation. A *purpose clause* sets out the objectives the legislation seeks to achieve or the problems it tries to solve. In text, we shall refer to both as preambles.

construed. "The reason for this is that the legislative purpose set forth in the purview of an enactment is assumed to express the legislative policy, and only those subjects expressly exempted by the proviso should be freed from the operation of the statute." 2A Sutherland § 47.08. We do not detect much interest in the proviso rule among recent Supreme Court Justices.

2. The Rule to Avoid Redundancy (Rule Against Surplusage)

Under the whole act rule, the presumption is that every word and phrase adds something to the statutory command. Accordingly, it is a "cardinal rule of statutory interpretation that no provision should be construed to be entirely redundant." *Kungys v. United States*, 485 U.S. 759, 778 (1988) (plurality opinion by Scalia, J.); see, e.g., *Circuit City Stores, Inc. v. Adams*, 532 U.S. 105 (2001); *United States v. Alaska*, 521 U.S. 1 (1997); *Walters v. Metro. Educ. Enters., Inc.*, 519 U.S. 202 (1997); *Rake v. Wade*, 508 U.S. 464 (1993); *Colautti v. Franklin*, 439 U.S. 379, 392 (1979). "A construction which would leave without effect any part of the language of a statute will normally be rejected." *Maxwell* 36.

For example, the issue in *Western Union Telegraph Co. v. Lenroot*, 323 U.S. 490 (1945), was whether the Fair Labor Standards Act prohibition against child labor applied to telegraph messengers. The prohibition reached any shipment of "goods" in interstate commerce, and "goods" were defined as "wares, products, commodities, merchandise, and articles or subjects of commerce of any character." The telegraph company argued that its service was intangible and therefore not a "good." Both Judge Learned Hand for the Court of Appeals and Justice Jackson for the Supreme Court held that telegraph services were "subjects of commerce." Hand suggested that if the definition were read to include only tangible things, the term "subjects," which had been added by a special Senate amendment to "articles of commerce of any character," would add nothing to the statute.

The rule against redundancy is more at odds with the legislative drafting process than most of the other whole act rules, as words and phrases are added to important legislation right up to the last minute. Nonetheless, the rule against redundancy plays a more important role in Supreme Court opinions in the new millennium than it did in the old. *Circuit City* is but one example. Responding to Justice Souter's textual argument that "seamen, railroad employees, or any other class of workers engaged in foreign or interstate commerce" included all contract employees, Justice Kennedy's *Circuit City* opinion fell back on the rule against surplusage: "there would be no need for Congress to use the phrases 'seamen' and 'railroad employees' if these same classes of workers were subsumed within the meaning of the 'engaged in . . . commerce' residual clause." 532 U.S. 105, 114 (2001).

3. Presumptions of Consistent Usage, and Meaningful Variation

(a) *Consistent Usage*. Under the holistic assumptions of the whole act rule, it is "reasonable to presume that the same meaning is implied by the use of the same expression in every part of the Act." *Maxwell* 278. Similarly, where a statutory word has been used in other statutes dealing with the same subject matter and has a settled meaning in those statutes, interpreters will presumptively follow the settled meaning. See Section 2.C.1 Although this is viewed as a weak presumption in most English-speaking countries, it has emerged as a stronger one in the United States, where it is presumed that "identical words used in different parts of the same act are intended to have the same meaning." *Sullivan v. Stroop*, 496 U.S. 478, 484 (1990), followed in, e.g., *Powerex Corp. v. Reliant Energy Servs., Inc.*, 551 U.S. 224 (2007); *Gustafson v. Alloyd Co.*, 513 U.S. 561, 570 (1995). But see *Dewsnup v. Timm*, 502 U.S. 410, 417 & n.3 (1992) (finding such argument unilluminating).

(b) *Meaningful Variation.* Additionally, "[f]rom the general presumption that the same expression is presumed to be used in the same sense throughout an Act or a series of cognate Acts, there follows the further presumption that a change of wording denotes a change in meaning." *Maxwell* 282; cf. *id.* at 286 (but this is a weak presumption). The leading American case for this presumption of meaningful variation is Chief Justice Marshall's opinion in *United States v. Fisher*, 6 U.S. (2 Cranch) 358, 388–97 (1805). A statute whose first four sections regulated the relationship between the United States and "receivers of public monies" had a fifth section which said that "where any revenue officer, or other person[,] hereafter becoming indebted to the United States . . . shall become insolvent, . . . the debt due to the United States shall be first satisfied." A competing creditor argued that § 5 should have been limited to receivers of public moneys, like §§ 1–4 and the title of the law, but Marshall found no reason to think that Congress intended a narrower ambit for § 5 and so read it without the limitation. Accord, *Lawrence v. Florida*, 549 U.S. 327, 333–34 (2007); *Hamdan v. Rumsfeld*, 548 U.S. 557, 577–79 (2006).

Variation in terminology ought to have less force when one statute is adopted at a different time than another. E.g., *Gutierrez v. Ada*, 528 U.S. 250 (2000) (declining to apply a rule of meaningful variation when a later amendment used different terminology from the provision at issue). But if Congress changes a statute when reenacting it, the rule has renewed bite, as in *Osborn v. Bank of the United States*, 22 U.S. (9 Wheat.) 738, 817–18 (1824) (construing a provision to allow for federal jurisdiction because Congress had expanded the provision's language after a previous Supreme Court decision had denied such jurisdiction under the earlier statutory wording).

A wedding of *expressio unius* and consistent usage is the rule that "[w]here Congress includes particular language in one section of a statute but omits it in another . . ., it is generally presumed that Congress acts intentionally and purposely in the disparate inclusion or exclusion." *Keene Corp. v. United States*, 508 U.S. 200, 208 (1993); accord, *Arlington Cent. Sch. Dist. Bd. of Educ. v. Murphy*, 548 U.S. 291, 299–304 (2006); *Gozlon-Peretz v. United States*, 498 U.S. 395, 404–05 (1991). The Court refined this canon in *Field v. Mans*, 516 U.S. 59, 67–76 (1995), where it held this negative implication rule was inapplicable when there was a reasonable explanation for the variation. "The more apparently deliberate the contrast, the stronger the inference, as applied, for example, to contrasting statutory sections originally enacted simultaneously in relevant respects. * * * The rule is weakest when it suggests results strangely at odds with other textual pointers, like the common-law language at work in the [bankruptcy] statute here." *Id.* at 75–76. See also *Lindh v. Murphy*, 521 U.S. 320 (1997) (Court vigorously debates use of the canon in interpreting Antiterrorism and Effective Death Penalty Act).

(c) *Rule Against Interpreting a Provision in Derogation of Other Provisions.* An important corollary of the whole act rule is that one provision of a statute should not be interpreted in such a way as to derogate from other provisions of the statute (to the extent this is possible). An interpretation of provision 1 might derogate from other parts of the statute in one or more of the following ways:

- operational conflict. As interpreted, provision 1's operation conflicts with that of provision 2. For example, a citizen cannot obey provision 1 without violating provision 2.

- philosophical tension. As interpreted, provision 1 is in tension with an assumption of provision 2. For example, provision 2 might reflect a legislative compromise inconsistent with a broad reading of provision 1.

- structural derogation. Sharing elements of both operational conflict and philosophical tension, provision 1's interpretation might be at odds with the overall structure of the statute. Thus, provisions 2 and 3 might reflect a legislative policy that certain kinds of violations be handled administratively rather than judicially, which a broad view of judicially enforceable provision 1 might undermine.

For an example of cross-cutting derogations, see *Robinson v. Shell Oil Co.*, 519 U.S. 337, 345–46 (1997).

WEST VIRGINIA UNIVERSITY HOSPITALS V. CASEY
Supreme Court of the United States, 1991.
499 U.S. 83, 111 S.Ct. 1138, 113 L.Ed.2d 68.

JUSTICE SCALIA delivered the opinion of the Court.

This case presents the question whether fees for [expert] services in civil rights litigation may be shifted to the losing party pursuant to 42 U.S.C. § 1988, which permits the award of "a reasonable attorney's fee."[1]

[I. Petitioner (WVUH) filed suit against the governor of Pennsylvania and other state officials under 42 U.S.C. § 1983, challenging changes made by Pennsylvania to the reimbursement schedule for Medicaid patients. The District Court ruled in favor of petitioner and awarded fees under § 1983, including over $100,000 in fees for expert services. The Court of Appeals affirmed on the merits, but reversed as to the expert fees, disallowing them except to the extent that they fell within the $30-per-day fees for witnesses prescribed by 28 U.S.C. § 1821(b).]

[II] Title 28 U.S.C. § 1920 provides:

---

[1]   Title 42 U.S.C. § 1988 provides in relevant part: "In any action or proceeding to enforce a provision of sections 1981, 1982, 1983, 1985, and 1986 of this title, title IX of Public Law 92–318 . . ., or title VI of the Civil Rights Act of 1964 . . ., the court, in its discretion, may allow the prevailing party, other than the United States, a reasonable attorney's fee as part of the costs."

"A judge or clerk of any court of the United States may tax as costs the following:

"(1) Fees of the clerk and marshal;

"(2) Fees of the court reporter for all or any part of the stenographic transcript necessarily obtained for use in the case;

"(3) Fees and disbursements for printing and witnesses;

"(4) Fees for exemplification and copies of papers necessarily obtained for use in the case;

"(5) Docket fees under section 1923 of this title;

"(6) Compensation of court appointed experts, compensation of interpreters, and salaries, fees, expenses, and costs of special interpretation services under section 1828 of this title."

Title 28 U.S.C. § 1821(b) limits the witness fees authorized by § 1920(3) as follows: "A witness shall be paid an attendance fee of $30 per day for each day's attendance. A witness shall also be paid the attendance fee for the time necessarily occupied in going to and returning from the place of attendance. . . ." In *Crawford Fitting Co. v. J.T. Gibbons, Inc.*, 482 U.S. 437 (1987), we held that these provisions define the full extent of a federal court's power to shift litigation costs absent express statutory authority to go further. * * * The question before us, then, is—with regard to both testimonial and nontestimonial expert fees—whether the term "attorney's fee" in § 1988 provides the "explicit statutory authority" required by *Crawford Fitting*.

[III] The record of statutory usage demonstrates convincingly that attorney's fees and expert fees are regarded as separate elements of litigation cost. While some fee-shifting provisions, like § 1988, refer only to "attorney's fees," see, *e.g.*, Civil Rights Act of 1964, 42 U.S.C. § 2000e–5(k), many others explicitly shift expert witness fees *as well as* attorney's fees. In 1976, just over a week prior to the enactment of § 1988, Congress passed those provisions of the Toxic Substances Control Act, 15 U.S.C. §§ 2618(d), 2619(c)(2), which provide that a prevailing party may recover "the costs of suit and reasonable fees for attorneys *and expert witnesses.*" (Emphasis added.) Also in 1976, Congress amended the Consumer Product Safety Act, 15 U.S.C. §§ 2060(c), 2072(a), 2073, which as originally enacted in 1972 shifted to the losing party "cost[s] of suit, including a reasonable attorney's fee," see 86 Stat. 1226. In the 1976 amendment, Congress altered the fee-shifting provisions to their present form by adding a phrase shifting expert witness fees *in addition to* attorney's fees. See Pub. L. 94–284, § 10, 90 Stat. 506, 507. Two other significant Acts passed in 1976 contain similar phrasing: the Resource Conservation and Recovery Act of 1976, 42 U.S.C. § 6972(e) ("costs of litigation (including reasonable attorney and expert witness fees)"), and the Natural Gas Pipeline Safety Act Amendments of 1976, 49 U.S.C.A. § 1686(e) ("costs of suit, including reasonable attorney's fees and reasonable expert witnesses fees").

Congress enacted similarly phrased fee-shifting provisions in numerous statutes both before 1976, see, *e.g.*, Endangered Species Act of 1973, 16 U.S.C.

§ 1540(g)(4) ("costs of litigation (including reasonable attorney and expert witness fees)"), and afterwards, see, e.g., Public Utility Regulatory Policies Act of 1978, 16 U.S.C. § 2632(a)(1) ("reasonable attorneys' fees, expert witness fees, and other reasonable costs incurred in preparation and advocacy of [the litigant's] position"). These statutes encompass diverse categories of legislation, including tax, administrative procedure, environmental protection, consumer protection, admiralty and navigation, utilities regulation, and, significantly, civil rights: The Equal Access to Justice Act (EAJA), the counterpart to § 1988 for violation of federal rights by federal employees, states that " 'fees and other expenses' [as shifted by § 2412(d)(1)(A)] includes the reasonable expenses of expert witnesses . . . and reasonable attorney fees." 28 U.S.C. § 2412(d)(2)(A). At least 34 statutes in 10 different titles of the United States Code explicitly shift attorney's fees *and* expert witness fees.

The laws that refer to fees for nontestimonial expert services are less common, but they establish a similar usage both before and after 1976: Such fees are referred to *in addition to* attorney's fees when a shift is intended [under a] provision of the Criminal Justice Act of 1964, 18 U.S.C. § 3006A(e). * * *

To the same effect is the 1980 EAJA, which provides: " 'fees and other expenses' [as shifted by § 2412(d)(1)(A)] includes the reasonable expenses of expert witnesses, *the reasonable cost of any study, analysis, engineering report, test, or project* which is found by the court to be necessary for the preparation of the party's case, and reasonable attorney fees." 28 U.S.C. § 2412(d)(2)(A) (emphasis added). If the reasonable cost of a "study" or "analysis"—which is but another way of describing nontestimonial expert services—is by common usage already included in the "attorney fees," again a significant and highly detailed part of the statute becomes redundant. The Administrative Procedure Act, 5 U.S.C. § 504(b)(1)(A) (added 1980), and the Tax Equity and Fiscal Responsibility Act of 1982, 26 U.S.C. § 7430(c)(1), contain similar language. Also reflecting the same usage are two railroad regulation statutes, the Regional Rail Reorganization Act of 1973, 45 U.S.C. §§ 726(f)(9) ("costs and expenses (including reasonable fees of accountants, experts, and attorneys) actually incurred"), and the Railroad Revitalization and Regulatory Reform Act of 1976, 45 U.S.C. § 854(g) ("costs and expenses (including fees of accountants, experts, and attorneys) actually and reasonably incurred").[5]

We think this statutory usage shows beyond question that attorney's fees and expert fees are distinct items of expense. If, as WVUH argues, the one includes the other, dozens of statutes referring to the two separately become an inexplicable exercise in redundancy.

[IV] WVUH argues that at least in pre-1976 *judicial* usage the phrase "attorney's fees" included the fees of experts. To support this proposition, it relies

⁵ WVUH cites a House Conference Committee Report from a statute passed in 1986, stating: "The conferees intend that the term 'attorneys' fees as part of the costs' include reasonable expenses and fees of expert witnesses and the reasonable costs of any test or evaluation which is found to be necessary for the preparation of the . . . case." H.R. Conf. Rep. No. 99–687, p. 5 (1986) (discussing the Handicapped Children's Protection Act of 1986, 20 U.S.C. § 1415(e)(4)(B)). In our view this undercuts rather than supports WVUH's position: The specification would have been quite unnecessary if the ordinary meaning of the term included those elements. The statement is an apparent effort to depart from ordinary meaning and to define a term of art.

upon two historical assertions: first, that pre-1976 courts, when exercising traditional equitable discretion in shifting attorney's fees, taxed as an element of such fees the expenses related to expert services; and second, that pre-1976 courts shifting attorney's fees pursuant to statutes identical in phrasing to § 1988 allowed the recovery of expert fees. We disagree with these assertions. The judicial background against which Congress enacted § 1988 mirrored the statutory background: expert fees were regarded not as a subset of attorney's fees, but as a distinct category of litigation expense. * * *

[V] WVUH suggests that a distinctive meaning of "attorney's fees" should be adopted with respect to § 1988 because this statute was meant to overrule our decision in *Alyeska Pipeline Service Co. v. Wilderness Society*, 421 U.S 240 (1975). [P]rior to 1975 many courts awarded expert fees and attorney's fees in certain circumstances pursuant to their equitable discretion. In *Alyeska*, we held that this discretion did not extend beyond a few exceptional circumstances long recognized by common law. [Justice Scalia argued that the text of § 1988 is both broader and narrower than the pre-*Aleyska* regime, notwithstanding statements by the bill's drafters suggesting a goal of repealing the *Aleyska* decision. Accordingly, Justice Scalia saw no reason to depart from the "normal import of the text" by inferring that a repeal of the whole decision was part of the statute.]

WVUH further argues that the congressional purpose in enacting § 1988 must prevail over the ordinary meaning of the statutory terms. It quotes, for example, the House Committee Report to the effect that "the judicial remedy [must be] full and complete," H.R. Rep. No. 94–1558, at 1 (1976), and the Senate Committee Report to the effect that "[c]itizens must have the opportunity to recover what it costs them to vindicate [civil] rights in court," S. Rep. No. 94–1011, *supra*, at 2. As we have observed before, however, the purpose of a statute includes not only what it sets out to change, but also what it resolves to leave alone. The best evidence of that purpose is the statutory text adopted by both Houses of Congress and submitted to the President. Where that contains a phrase that is unambiguous— that has a clearly accepted meaning in both legislative and judicial practice—we do not permit it to be expanded or contracted by the statements of individual legislators or committees during the course of the enactment process. Congress could easily have shifted "attorney's fees and expert witness fees," or "reasonable litigation expenses," as it did in contemporaneous statutes; it chose instead to enact more restrictive language, and we are bound by that restriction.

[Justice Scalia addressed two final arguments of WVUH. First, WVUH argued that the Court's previous decision in *Missouri v. Jenkins*, 491 U.S. 274, 285 (1989), should control. In *Jenkins*, the Court concluded that § 1988 permitted separately billed paralegal and law clerk time to be charged to the losing party. Justice Scalia rebutted WVUH's argument that paralegal fees were analogous to expert fees. He noted that paralegal fees were traditionally included in attorney's fees and only recently had that billing practice been changing. By contrast, the lengthy record in this case illustrated that expert fees and attorneys fees are frequently distinguished within various statutes. Second, WVUH argued that, even if Congress did not expressly include expert fees in the fee-shifting provisions, it would have done so if it had thought about it. Justice Scalia rejected this argument, insisting that to expand unambiguous language to cover what was inadvertently omitted transcends and misunderstands the role of the judiciary.]

JUSTICE STEVENS, with whom JUSTICE MARSHALL and JUSTICE BLACKMUN join, dissenting.

[Justice Stevens began by contending that the Court should look to how this statute, § 1988, has been interpreted in the past, and to its legislative history, instead of analyzing the many other statutes that contain express provisions shifting expert fees.]

[I]   Under either the broad view of "costs" typically assumed in the fee-shifting context or the broad view of "a reasonable attorney's fee" articulated by this Court, expert witness fees are a proper component of an award under § 1988. Because we are not interpreting these words for the first time, they should be evaluated in the context that this and other courts have already created.

The term "costs" has a different and broader meaning in fee-shifting statutes than it has in the cost statutes that apply to ordinary litigation. [Justice Stevens explained that in *Missouri v. Jenkins*, Chief Justice Rehnquist, in a lone dissent, espoused the view that the majority holds in this case, but that the rest of the Court all agreed that fees for the services of paralegals and law clerks, as part of the final work product of the attorneys, were compensable as attorneys fees under the statute. In Justice Stevens' view, this reasoning should apply with equal force to expert fees.] To allow reimbursement of these other categories of expenses, and yet not to include expert witness fees, is both arbitrary and contrary to the broad remedial purpose that inspired the fee-shifting provision of § 1988.

[II]   The Senate Report on the Civil Rights Attorney's Fees Awards Act of 1976 explained that the purpose of the proposed amendment to 42 U.S.C. § 1988 was "to remedy anomalous gaps in our civil rights laws created by the United States Supreme Court's recent decision in *Alyeska Pipeline Service Co. v. Wilderness Society*, 421 U.S. 240 (1975), and to achieve consistency in our civil rights laws." S. Rep. No. 94–1011, at 1 (1976), 1976 U.S. Code Cong. & Admin. News 5909. The Senate Committee on the Judiciary wanted to level the playing field so that private citizens, who might have little or no money, could still serve as "private attorneys general" and afford to bring actions, even against state or local bodies, to enforce the civil rights laws. The Committee acknowledged that "[i]f private citizens are to be able to assert their civil rights, and if those who violate the Nation's fundamental laws are not to proceed with impunity, then citizens must have the opportunity to recover *what it costs them* to vindicate these rights in court." *Id.* at 2 (emphasis added). According to the Committee, the bill would create "no startling new remedy," but would simply provide "the technical requirements" requested by the Supreme Court in *Alyeska,* so that courts could "continue the practice of awarding attorneys' fees which had been going on for years prior to the Court's May decision." *Id.* at 6.

To underscore its intention to return the courts to their pre-*Alyeska* practice of shifting fees in civil rights cases, the Senate Committee's Report cited with approval not only several cases in which fees had been shifted, but also all of the cases contained in Legal Fees, Hearings before the Subcommittee on Representation of Citizen Interests of the Senate Committee on the Judiciary, 93d Cong., 1st Sess., pt. 3, pp. 888–1024, 1060–1062 (1973) (hereinafter Senate Hearings). See S. Rep. No. 94–1011, at 4, n.3. The cases collected in the 1973 Senate Hearings included many in which courts had permitted the shifting of costs, including expert witness fees. At the time when the Committee referred to these cases, though several were later reversed, it used them to make the point that prior to *Alyeska*, courts awarded attorney's fees and costs, including expert witness fees, in civil rights cases, and that they did so in order to encourage private citizens to bring such suits. It was to this pre-*Alyeska* regime, in which courts could award expert witness fees along with attorney's fees, that the Senate Committee intended to return through the passage of the fee-shifting amendment to § 1988. [Justice Stevens explained that the House Report raised similar concerns about providing access to the courts, and alleviating hardships to civil rights litigants after the *Aleyska* decision.] * * *

The case before us today is precisely the type of public interest litigation that Congress intended to encourage by amending § 1988 to provide for fee shifting of a "reasonable attorney's fee as part of the costs." Petitioner, a tertiary medical center in West Virginia near the Pennsylvania border, provides services to a large number of Medicaid recipients throughout Pennsylvania. In January 1986, when the Pennsylvania Department of Public Welfare notified petitioner of its new Medicaid payment rates for Pennsylvania Medicaid recipients, petitioner believed them to be below the minimum standards for reimbursement specified by the Social Security Act. Petitioner successfully challenged the adequacy of the State's payment system under 42 U.S.C. § 1983. This Court's determination today that petitioner must assume the cost of $104,133 in expert witness fees is at war with the congressional purpose of making the prevailing party whole. * * *

[III] In recent years the Court has vacillated between a purely literal approach to the task of statutory interpretation and an approach that seeks guidance from historical context, legislative history, and prior cases identifying the purpose that motivated the legislation. Thus, for example, in *Christiansburg Garment Co. v. EEOC*, 434 U.S. 412 (1978), we rejected a "mechanical construction," *id.* at 418, of the fee-shifting provision in § 706(k) of Title VII of the Civil Rights Act of 1964 that the prevailing defendant had urged upon us. Although the text of the statute drew no distinction between different kinds of "prevailing parties," we held that awards to prevailing plaintiffs are governed by a more liberal standard than awards to prevailing defendants. That holding rested entirely on our evaluation of the relevant congressional policy and found no support within the four corners of the statutory text. Nevertheless, the holding was unanimous and, to the best of my knowledge, evoked no adverse criticism or response in Congress.

On those occasions, however, when the Court has put on its thick grammarian's spectacles and ignored the available evidence of congressional purpose and the teaching of prior cases construing a statute, the congressional response has been dramatically different. It is no coincidence that the Court's literal reading of Title VII, which led to the conclusion that disparate treatment of pregnant and nonpregnant persons was not discrimination on the basis of sex, see

General Electric Co. v. Gilbert, 429 U.S. 125 (1976), was repudiated by the 95th Congress; that its literal reading of the "continuous physical presence" requirement in § 244(a)(1) of the Immigration and Nationality Act, which led to the view that the statute did not permit even temporary or inadvertent absences from this country, see *INS v. Phinpathya*, 464 U.S. 183 (1984), was rebuffed by the 99th Congress; that its literal reading of the word "program" in Title IX of the Education Amendments of 1972, which led to the Court's gratuitous limit on the scope of the antidiscrimination provisions of Title IX, see *Grove City College v. Bell*, 465 U.S. 555 (1984), was rejected by the 100th Congress; or that its refusal to accept the teaching of earlier decisions in *Wards Cove Packing Co. v. Atonio*, 490 U.S. 642 (1989) (reformulating order of proof and weight of parties' burdens in disparate-impact cases), and *Patterson v. McLean Credit Union*, 491 U.S. 164 (1989) (limiting scope of 42 U.S.C. § 1981 to the making and enforcement of contracts), was overwhelmingly rejected by the 101st Congress, and its refusal to accept the widely held view of lower courts about the scope of fraud, see *McNally v. United States*, 483 U.S. 350 (1987) (limiting mail fraud to protection of property), was quickly corrected by the 100th Congress.

In the domain of statutory interpretation, Congress is the master. It obviously has the power to correct our mistakes, but we do the country a disservice when we needlessly ignore persuasive evidence of Congress' actual purpose and require it "to take the time to revisit the matter" and to restate its purpose in more precise English whenever its work product suffers from an omission or inadvertent error.
* * *

The fact that Congress has consistently provided for the inclusion of expert witness fees in fee-shifting statutes when it considered the matter is a weak reed on which to rest the conclusion that the omission of such a provision represents a deliberate decision to forbid such awards. Only time will tell whether the Court, with its literal reading of § 1988, has correctly interpreted the will of Congress with respect to the issue it has resolved today.

NOTES ON CASEY AND THE WHOLE ACT RULE

1.   *Immediate Override.* When the Supreme Court decided *Casey* in March 1991, Congress was holding hearings on the proposed Civil Rights Act of 1991, which was an effort to modify the vetoed 1990 version enough to secure final enactment. See Chapter 1, § 3C. The negotiated compromise between a Democratic Congress and President Bush senior focused on whether the language overriding the *Wards Cove* decision would encourage employers to adopt racial quotas. Adding a new provision to override *Casey* was not controversial; it easily became part of the bill that eventually passed by overwhelming margins in both chambers and was signed by the President in November 1991. Does this result vindicate Justice Stevens' position? Read more before you settle on your answer.

The Senate Committee report accompanying § 1988 states that "citizens must have the opportunity to recover what it costs them to vindicate these [civil] rights in court." Assume the report had added that this includes recovering all costs that go into the attorney's preparation and presentation of the case, including the use of paralegals, expert witnesses, and all reasonable non-attorney costs associated with trial preparation. Would that addition change Justice Scalia's analysis or conclusion? Should it?

Justice Stevens in dissent concludes that "we [the Court] do the country a disservice when we needlessly ignore persuasive evidence of Congress' actual purpose and require it 'to take time to revisit the matter.'" What is the disservice to which Stevens refers? Is Congress's override of *Casey* a mere eight months after it was decided an example of such a disservice? Or is it more like an exception that proves the rule? What costs are really involved in requiring Congress to "take time to revisit" a judicial construction of statutory meaning?

2. *Inferences from Text of Other Statutes: Whole Code Rule.* Justice Scalia's majority opinion relies heavily on Congress' use of the terms "attorney's fees" and "expert fees" in other federal statutes. He concludes that "[i]f, as WVUH argues, the one [attorney's fees] includes the other [expert fees], dozens of statutes referring to the two separately become an inexplicable exercise in redundancy." Consider the four statutes with which Justice Scalia begins, all approved by the same Congress that enacted § 1988. Does it matter that these other statutes were drafted and reported to the floor by different committees than the ones that produced the Civil Rights Attorney's Fees Awards Act? Are differences in subject matter among these statutes relevant to Justice Scalia's argument?

In looking to these other statutes, Justice Scalia implicitly invokes another corollary to the whole act rule, the "whole code" rule. The whole code approach looks beyond the statute in question to various additional enactments addressing an identical or comparable issue, including some laws that may have been enacted decades before or after the text under review. The Court has relied on the whole code approach in a number of decisions since *Casey*. See, e.g., *FDA v. Brown & Williamson Tobacco Corp.*, 529 U.S. 120 (2000) (Justice O'Connor for majority); *Amoco Production Co. v. S. Ute Indian Tribe*, 526 U.S. 865 (1999) (Justice Kennedy for majority); *Bennett v. Spear*, 520 U.S. 154 (1997) (Justice Scalia for majority). This reliance on inter-statutory references has been criticized as prone to judicial manipulation and also likely to unsettle bodies of federal law not before the court. See William W. Buzbee, *The One-Congress Fiction in Statutory Interpretation*, 149 U. Pa. L. Rev. 171, 234–40 (2000). Moreover, a recent study of congressional overrides documents that decisions like *Casey*, relying heavily on the whole code rule, are disproportionately likely to be overridden by Congress, as indeed are Court decisions that rely heavily on the whole act rule.[14]

Although the whole act and whole code rules operate under a similar presumption of coherence, there are instances where the two rules conflict. In *Robinson v. Shell Oil Co.*, 519 U.S. 337 (1997), a unanimous Court (per Justice Thomas) determined that the word "employees" in § 704(a) of Title VII, was ambiguous on its face as to whether it encompassed former as well as current employees. Justice Thomas noted that a number of other federal statutes differentiated between "former employees" and "employees," but he viewed this practice in other statutes as simply illustrating that "Congress *can* use the unqualified term 'employees' to refer only to current employees, not that it did

---

[14] See Matthew Christiansen & William Eskridge Jr., *Congressional Overrides of Supreme Court Statutory Interpretation Decisions, 1967–2011*, 92 Tex. L. Rev. 1317, 1405–06 (2014)(reporting that 8 percent of statutory decisions rely heavily on whole code rule yet this rule is a central factor in just under one-fourth of Court decisions that are overridden. Similarly, 10 percent of statutory decisions rely heavily on the whole act rule, but more than four in ten overridden decisions rely centrally on [this] canon.).

so in this particular statute." *Id.* at 341–42. Thomas then focused on a number of other provisions within Title VII to conclude that the term "employees" plainly did encompass former employees.

Dissenting in *Casey*, Justice Stevens argued that the legislative history of "*this statute*" and the previous interpretations of "*this statute*" were the proper interpretive tools for determining whether attorney's fees included experts fees. The majority, however (including Justice Thomas, the author of *Robinson v. Shell Oil*) found the argument based on inter-statutory textual references persuasive. Can these two decisions, each interpreting provisions of Title VII, be reconciled?

3. *The Dubious Presumption of Coherence.* Both *Casey* and *Robinson* suggest that the presumption of overarching coherence may be an unrealistic one. Congress does not usually approach statutory drafting the way God is thought to have dictated the Bible. Instead, statutes are often assembled the way Christmas trees are decorated, with ornaments being added or subtracted willy nilly, and at the last minute, just to satisfy enough interest groups and legislators to gain majorities needed to get through various legislative vetogates (recall Chapter 1 and the history of the 1964 Civil Rights Act). Staff and drafting offices are supposed to clean up legislation to make it appropriate for inclusion in the code, but even the best drafters cannot always meld all the negotiated deals into a coherent whole.

Among the textual canons, the whole act rule and its corollaries have come in for especially harsh criticism from scholars and also some judges—for mistakenly imputing omniscience to the legislature and for assuming that a statute is written as a whole, internally coherent document, like a short story. See Richard Posner, *The Federal Courts: Crisis and Reform* 281 (1985) ("The conditions under which legislators work are not conducive to careful, farsighted, and parsimonious drafting. Nor does great care guarantee economy of language; a statute that is the product of compromise may contain redundant language as a by-product of the strains of the negotiating process").

In recent years, empirical examinations of Congress's approach to legislative drafting have found that the key players from both chambers do not view the whole act rule or its corollaries as important elements when statutory language is being drafted, debated, and enacted. Victoria Nourse and Jane Schacter interviewed a bipartisan group of Senate Judiciary Committee staff as well as lawyers from the Senate Legislative Counsel's office. Those interviewed described drafting as a highly contextual and intensely pressured process, focused on securing collective action through negotiated agreement, often involving a shifting coalition of both invited and late-arriving players. The drafters were generally aware of the whole act rule (and other textual canons), but the promotion of structural coherence and the avoidance of surplus words or phrases were not valued nearly as highly as they are by courts. For those interviewed, successful lawmaking negotiations required achieving sufficient consensus about language, and this tended to result in a fair amount of verbal repetitions, linguistic residues, and incomplete redactions. See Victoria Nourse & Jane Schacter, *The Politics of Legislative Drafting: A Congressional Case Study*, 77 N.Y.U. L. Rev. 575, 590–600, 614–16 (2002).

The results from the Gluck & Bressman study (*Statutory Interpretation From The Inside*, appearing in the Stanford Law Review; see § 1B1 above) reinforce and expand upon these findings. The authors' 137 congressional staff respondents were aware of the rule against surplusage but over three-fifths stated that it applies either rarely or only sometimes in the drafting process. Gluck and Bressman reported respondents' practical justifications for redundancy, based on a desire "to ensure that the statute covers the intended terrain," and their frequent political preference for redundant wording in order to secure a compromise: "that constituent, that senator, that lobbyist wants to see that word." 65 Stan. L. Rev. at 934. The authors found that the whole act and whole code rules face even greater institutional barriers based on the way Congress is organized. Major statutes are generally amalgamations of work by multiple committees that draft different parts without any focus on internal consistency. Lengthy multidrafter statutes and bundled legislative deals make it highly unlikely that drafters will review a product for consistent word usage even though drafters believe that this should be a goal. And the whole code rule fares worse: it was dismissed as irrelevant to how Congress drafts or even how it attempts to draft. Less than ten percent of respondents indicated that drafters often or always intend to apply terms consistently across statutes that are unrelated by subject matter. *Id.* at 936–37.

In spite of these criticisms, courts around the world continue to operate under the coherence presumption. One common justification, articulated by Justice Scalia in his recent book, is that the presumption will encourage Congress to draft with greater care:

> The canons . . . promote better drafting. When it is widely understood in the legal community that, for example, a word used repeatedly in a document will be taken to have the same meaning throughout . . . you can expect those who prepare legal documents competently to draft accordingly. Antonin Scalia & Bryan Garner, *Reading Law: The Interpretation of Legal Texts* 51 (2012)

Do you find this justification persuasive? Gluck and Bressman concluded that, given the range of practical, political, and institutional barriers to drafting coherent and cohesive statutes, Congress is very unlikely to alter its drafting methods in response to the whole act family of canons. Can you think of other justifications for continuing to apply the presumption in favor of coherence? Should courts rely less on the whole act and its corollaries than they do at present?

Although the Supreme Court regularly invokes the whole act rule, several Justices have recognized that the arrangement and phraseology of different statutory provisions is often "the consequence of a legislative *accident*, perhaps caused by nothing more than the unfortunate fact that Congress is too busy to do all of its work as carefully as it should." *Delaware Tribal Business Comm. v. Weeks*, 430 U.S. 73, 97 (1977) (Stevens, J., dissenting) (emphasis in original), quoted in *Mountain States Tel. & Tel. v. Pueblo of Santa Ana*, 472 U.S. 237, 255 (1985) (Brennan, J., dissenting). Note that this latter point is a critique of the textual canons in general. Still, even if Judge Posner, Justice Stevens, and the studies summarized above are descriptively accurate, the whole act rule might be prescriptively correct. Perhaps the virtues of clarity and predictability promoted by the judiciary warrant discounting if not disregarding the realities of the legislative process. Think about both descriptive and prescriptive issues in connection with the case described in the next paragraph.

4. *A Case of Haphazard Drafting. Sorenson v. Secretary of the Treasury*, 475 U.S. 851 (1986), involved interpretation of the Omnibus Budget Reconciliation Act of 1981 (OBRA), Pub. L. No. 97–35, § 2331, 95 Stat. 860. The Act added provisions to the Social Security Act and the Internal Revenue Code to provide for "interception" of tax refunds for the benefit of state agencies that had been assigned child-support rights. Thus when a taxpayer is in arrears for his or her child support payments, and when the former

spouse assigns them to a state (welfare) agency as a condition of receiving public assistance, the state can notify the IRS. The IRS will then give the state's recoupment claim priority over the taxpayer's claim for refunds of overpayment of federal income taxes. The issue in *Sorenson* was whether the "overpayment" which is subject to the recoupment claim includes refunds resulting from an earned-income credit. The Supreme Court held that it does. Section 6402(c), added by OBRA, provides that "*any* overpayment to be refunded * * * shall be reduced by the amount of any past-due support" (emphasis added). Section 6402(b), which was already in the Code, provides that if an earned-income credit exceeds taxpayer's tax liability, the excess amount is "considered an overpayment." Given the whole act rule that terms used in different parts of the statute should presumptively have the same meaning, the result follows.

But Justice Stevens' dissenting opinion pointed out the policy anomalies of the Court's result. The Earned Income Credit Program was created by Congress in 1975 to help keep low-income families off welfare: (1) social security taxes were assessed against earned income but not against welfare payments; (2) as a result, $500 a month in welfare meant more money in the pocket than $500 a month in earned income; (3) to redress this disincentive to work, Congress created a fully refundable credit for low income workers. Applying the OBRA recoupment scheme (one of the obscure goodies given to states in the 1981 reconciliation bill) to penalize low-income families is an accidental consequence of the statute's drafting; nothing in the legislative history supports any legislative desire to curtail the Earned Income Credit Program.

The Court's response to Justice Stevens was that "it defies belief that Congress was unaware" of the impact of the Intercept Program on the Earned Income Credit Program. Justice Stevens riposted: "With all due respect to the Court and to our hard working neighbors in the Congress, I think it 'defies belief' to assume that a substantial number of legislators were sufficiently familiar with OBRA to realize that somewhere in that vast piece of hurriedly enacted legislation there was a provision that changed the 6-year-old Earned Income Credit Program." In footnote 2, Justice Stevens quoted the following passage from N.Y. Times, July 1, 1981, p. A16, col. 1:

> Smoking a big cigar, the Speaker [of the House of Representatives] got angry again over the slap-dash quality of the bill [that became OBRA], with parts of it photocopied from memorandums, other parts handwritten at the last minute, and some final sections hastily crossed out in whorls of pencil marks. * * *

> But then he smiled, too, noting such cryptic and accidental entries in the bill as a name and phone number—"Ruth Seymour, 225–4844"—standing alone as if it were a special appropriation item.

There is a larger point to be drawn from Justice Stevens' criticisms. In the last generation, Congress has done an increasing amount of its work through gigantic and complex omnibus proposals, as identified in the Gluck and Bressman study. Doesn't the majority's approach in *Sorenson* ignore the realities of drafting and enacting a budget reconciliation bill—often in the days or even hours before congressional recess, with provisions added and dropped at the last minute in the conference room? In light of this new operation of the legislative process, should federal courts rethink the whole act rule and perhaps some other canons of construction? Should there be special canons, or at least practices, for construing omnibus reconciliation legislation like that in *Sorenson*? For a proposal that such omnibus bills be approached cautiously, see Seth Grossman,

Tricameral Legislating: Statutory Interpretation in an Era of Conference Committee Ascendancy, 9 N.Y.U. J. Leg. & Pub. Pol'y 251 (2006).

2. SUBSTANTIVE POLICY CANONS

The canons discussed in Section 1 are linguistic or syntactic guidelines that are policy-neutral on their face. Other canons represent substantive decisions, and hence their application is not policy-neutral. Traditionally, the main substantive canons were directives to interpret different types of statutes "liberally" or "strictly." The old Anglo-American rule was that "remedial" statutes were to be liberally interpreted, while statutes in derogation of the common law were to be strictly interpreted. (But what remedial statute is not in derogation of the common law?)

More modern typologies of the liberal-versus-strict construction canons have emerged. Certain statutes (such as civil rights, securities, and antitrust statutes) are supposed to be liberally construed—in other words, applied expansively to new situations.[15] Appendix B, reporting the Court's deployment of canons from the 1986 through the 2012 Terms, reflects that these liberal construction canons have not been often invoked by the Rehnquist and Roberts Courts. Other statutes are to be strictly construed—in other words, applied stingily. The rule of lenity, requiring strict construction of penal statutes, is the best example and is explored in Part A below. Strict construction of statutes, especially for quasi-constitutional reasons, has been highly popular in the Rehnquist and Roberts Courts.

Consider other canons reflecting substantive judgments about how broadly to read the statute's text:

• *Strict Construction of Statutes in Derogation of Sovereignty.* If a statute is written in general language, it is presumed that it only applies to private parties; governments and their agencies are presumptively not included unless the statute clearly says so. See *Nevada Dep't Human Res. v. Hibbs*, 538 U.S. 721 (2003) (finding such clarity). This canon is based upon the old idea of sovereign immunity: the state cannot be sued or otherwise regulated without its consent. See 3A Sutherland § 62.01.[16]

---

[15] The Supreme Court has invoked the liberal-construction maxim when interpreting civil rights legislation such as § 1983, see *Dennis v. Higgins*, 498 U.S. 439 (1991); statutes providing benefits to seamen, *Cox v. Roth*, 348 U.S. 207 (1955), and to veterans, *King v. St. Vincent's Hosp.*, 502 U.S. 215, 221 n.9 (1991); and safety legislation such as the Occupational Safety and Health Act, *Whirlpool Corp. v. Marshall*, 445 U.S. 1 (1980). See generally William Eskridge Jr. & John Ferejohn, *Super-Statutes*, 50 Duke L.J. 1215, 1234–35, 1239, 1244 (2001) (super-statutes whose policy or principle comes to be entrenched in the public culture over time will be interpreted liberally to advance their policies or principles, and expansively vis-a-vis more ordinary statutes; examples include the Sherman Act of 1890, the Civil Rights Act of 1964, the Endangered Species Act of 1973).

[16] Since the absolute immunity of the state has eroded substantially in the last thirty years, this presumption has lost much of its original justification. A better rationale for the rule may be that the sovereign needs few constraints upon its freedom of activity as it decides how best to serve the public interest (though this explanation may be a naive view of the way government works). In the United States this rule has quasi-constitutional dimensions, since the states retained their basic immunities when they joined the union, see U.S. Const. amends. X–XI, and the federal government enjoys supremacy over states and their regulation. *Id.* art. VI. In any event, many states have statutes rejecting this rule of strict construction. 3A Sutherland § 62.04. For example: "The term 'person' may be construed to include the United States, this state, or any state or territory or any public or private corporation, as well as an individual." Wash. Rev. Code

• *Strict Construction of Public Grants.* Similarly, public grants by the government to private parties are to be construed narrowly, that is, in favor of the government. Sometimes, this precept has been justified on the grounds that such grants were gratuitous or solicited by the grantee, but the canon has been invoked in the whole range of cases—from leases and contracts with the government, to statutes allowing compromise settlements with the government, to pension and compensation laws for public officials.[17]

• *Strict Construction of (Some) Revenue Provisions.* 3 Sutherland § 66.01, announces that "it is a settled rule that tax laws are to be strictly construed against the state and in favor of the taxpayer. Where there is reasonable doubt as to the meaning of a revenue statute, the doubt is resolved in favor of those taxed." See *Gould v. Gould*, 245 U.S. 151 (1917). Generations of taxpayers who have lost lawsuits against the Internal Revenue Service over fine points of statutory interpretation would dispute that generalization. See *United States v. Fior D'Italia*, 536 U.S. 238, 242–43 (2002) (presuming that IRS-generated tax assessments are correct). Courts are turning to more liberal construction because of the necessary public purpose implicated in the system of taxation, "and it is the duty of the courts to see that no one, by mere technicalities which do not affect his substantial rights, shall escape his fair proportion of the public expenses." *Atlantic City Transp. Co. v. Walsh*, 55 A.2d 652 (1947); see 3A Sutherland § 66.02. Under this new thinking, the *tax-imposing* provisions would not be strictly construed—but the *tax-exempting* provisions ought to be. See *United States v. Burke*, 504 U.S. 229, 248 (1992) (Souter, J., concurring in judgment).[18]

One way of formulating substantive canons is as presumptions or rules of thumb that cut across different types of statutes and statutory schemes. These represent policies that the Court will "presume" Congress intends to incorporate into statutes, but such presumptions are rebuttable ones. Presumptions will generally not trump a contrary statutory text, legislative history, or purpose. See *Astoria Fed. Savings & Loan Ass'n v. Solimino*, 501 U.S. 104, 108 (1991). A presumption or rule of thumb can be treated as a starting point for discussion, a tiebreaker at the end of discussion, or just a balancing factor. The policies underlying interpretive presumptions are derived by courts from the Constitution, federal statutes, and the common law. Some examples of substantive presumptions:

• Presumption against congressional diminishment of American Indian rights. See *Hagen v. Utah*, 510 U.S. 399 (1994); *Montana v. Blackfeet Tribe*, 471 U.S. 759 (1985).

Ann. § 1.16.080 (West 1961). . These state rules, of course, are subject to the Supremacy Clause and may be invalid as regards the United States. E.g., *McCulloch v. Maryland*, 17 U.S. (4 Wheat.) 316 (1819).

[17] 3A Sutherland § 63.04, posits that the main reason for this canon is a general tendency "to regard all such grants with extreme distrust, so that in all its dealings the government will not suffer loss." Yet the rule has not generally been applied when the grant is for a great public purpose, such as the land grants to railroads in return for their building the transcontinental railroad in the 1860s. E.g., *Leo Sheep v. United States*, 440 U.S. 668, 682 (1979); *Platt v. Union Pac. R.*, 99 U.S. (9 Otto) 48 (1878).

[18] Public choice theory (Chapter 1, § 2B) lends support to this suggestion. Rent-seeking interest groups can be expected to extract from the legislature special exemptions from the broad taxing provisions. Not only do these exemptions undermine the public fisc, but they tend to do so for already-advantaged groups, thereby making the income tax system much less progressive than it is advertised as being.

• Presumption that Congress does not intend to pass statutes that violate international law. See *Sosa v. Alvarez-Machain*, 542 U.S. 692 (2004); *Murray v. The Schooner Charming Betsy*, 6 U.S. (2 Cranch) 64, 118 (1804).

• Presumption that Congress does not intend to pass statutes that violate treaty obligations. See *Hamdan v. Rumsfeld*, 548 U.S. 557 (2006).

• Presumption that Congress does not intend that statutes have extraterritorial application. See *Foley Brothers v. Filardo*, 336 U.S. 281 (1949).

• Presumption that Congress does not intend that substantive statutes be applied retroactively. See *Landgraf* (Chapter 5, § 3C).

• Presumption that Congress does not intend that federal regulation unnecessarily intrude into traditional state responsibilities (more than is necessary to subserve national objectives). See *Rush Prudential HMO v. Moran*, 536 U.S. 355 (2002); *Cipollone v. Liggett Group, Inc.*, 505 U.S. 504 (1992).

• Presumption that Congress will not withdraw the courts' traditional equitable discretion. See *Weinberger v. Romero-Barcelo*, 456 U.S. 305, 320 (1982); *Hecht Co. v. Bowles*, 321 U.S. 321, 330 (1944).

• Presumption that Congress will not withdraw all remedies or judicial avenues of relief when it recognizes a statutory right. See *South Carolina v. Regan*, 465 U.S. 367 (1984).

• Presumption of judicial review. See *Demore v. Kim*, 538 U.S. 510 (2003); *Dunlop v. Bachowski*, 421 U.S. 560 (1975); *Abbott Laboratories v. Gardner*, 387 U.S. 136 (1967).

• Presumption against derogation of the President's traditional powers. See *Dep't of Navy v. Egan*, 484 U.S. 518, 527 (1988); *Haig v. Agee*, 453 U.S. 280 (1981).

Another way of formulating substantive canons is as *clear statement rules*, which are presumptions that can be rebutted only by clear language in the text of the statute. See *Solimino*, 501 U.S. at 108–09 (contrasting presumptions and clear statement rules). Clear statement rules have been developed by the Supreme Court as expressions of quasi-constitutional values. For example, Congress cannot impose liability and process directly against the states unless the statutory text clearly says so (Section 2C below).

There is some mobility in the Court's articulation of these substantive canons. For example, in *EEOC v. Arabian American Oil Co.*, 499 U.S. 244, 258–59 (1991), a majority of the Court transformed the old *Foley Brothers* presumption against extraterritorial application into a clear statement rule (applied to Title VII in that case), requiring explicit statutory language in order for a law to apply outside the United States. Justice Marshall's dissenting opinion strongly objected to the Court's transformation; he criticized the majority's clear statement approach for sidestepping legislative history evidence reflecting Congress's clear understanding that U.S. employers who operated in foreign lands were within the purview of Title VII. *Id.* at 260–63, 268–69. Note here how the general rule that civil rights laws, like Title VII, should be liberally construed was itself trumped by the more specific (and now fortified) canon against extraterritorial regulation.

As suggested above, substantive canons may vary in their impact upon interpretation, and it is critical to identify how a court is using a canon. By way of review, consider three possibilities alluded to above. First, sometimes courts will treat a substantive canon as merely a *tiebreaker* that affects the outcome only if, at the end of the basic interpretive process, the court is left unable to choose between the two competing interpretations put forward by the parties. Second, courts might treat substantive canons as *presumptions* that, at the beginning of the interpretive process, set up a presumptive outcome, which can be overcome by persuasive support for the contrary interpretation. Typically, the party attempting to overcome the presumption may use any potential evidence of statutory meaning (e.g., statutory text, legislative history, statutory purposes, policy arguments, and so on) to rebut the presumption. On this understanding, a presumption simply adds weight to one side of the balancing process captured by eclectic statutory interpretation. Third, courts may treat substantive canons as *clear statement rules*, which purport to compel a particular interpretive outcome unless there is a clear statement to the contrary. We shall call those canons "clear statement rules" when they may be overcome by clear statutory language and those canons "super-strong clear statement rules" when they may be overcome only by extremely clear statutory text (where the "clear statement" is, in effect, a targeted statement of textual meaning). Keep a sharp eye on which of these approaches is used to implement the canons that are discussed in the remainder of this part.

A. THE RULE OF LENITY IN CRIMINAL CASES

One of the hoariest canons of statutory interpretation states that laws whose purpose is to punish (usually by fine or imprisonment) must be construed strictly. This is called the "rule of lenity" in construing penal statutes: If the punitive statute does not clearly outlaw private conduct, the private actor cannot be penalized. While criminal statutes are the most obvious and common type of penal law, many civil statutes have been so classified by at least some jurisdictions.[19]

What is the purpose of the rule of lenity?[20] In England, courts have long used this canon vigorously for humanitarian reasons "when the number of capital offences was still very large, when it was still punishable with death to cut down a cherry-tree." *Maxwell* 238.[21] Early practice in this country was ambivalent about the rule of lenity: state and federal courts sometimes invoked it, but in early prosecutions for public insurrections and seditious libel, federal judges in particular showed no lenity; the Marshall Court, however, firmly established the rule of lenity

---

[19] Among the statutes to which this canon has been applied are (i) statutes whose penalties include forfeiture; (ii) statutes providing for "extra" damages beyond those needed to make the complainant whole, including punitive damages, treble damages, attorneys' fees, penalty interest (often part of the remedy under usury laws); (iii) statutes permitting revocation of a professional license or disbarment of lawyers; (iv) statutes against extortion or discrimination; (v) statutes declaring certain acts to be per se negligence; and (vi) others. See 3A Sutherland § 59.02.

[20] For a comprehensive treatment, see Lawrence Solan, *Law, Language, and Lenity*, 40 Wm. & Mary L. Rev. 57 (1998).

[21] The main line of cases are those construing Parliament's attempted narrowing of the "benefit of clergy" in ways that preserved it as a defense to the death penalty. See J.M. Beattie, *Crime and the Courts in England, 1600–1800* (1986); Livingston Hall, *Strict or Liberal Construction of Penal Statutes*, 48 Harv. L. Rev. 748 (1935).

in American legisprudence.[22] Especially as penalties have been ameliorated, other kinds of reasons have been invoked to justify the rule of lenity.

For years, the leading justification has been *fair notice.* The state may not impose penalties upon people without clearly warning them about unlawful conduct and its consequences. A classic reference for this rationalization is *McBoyle v. United States*, 283 U.S. 25 (1931). A 1919 federal statute prohibited the transportation of stolen *motor vehicles* in interstate commerce. The law defined motor vehicle to "include an automobile, automobile truck, automobile wagon, motor cycle, or any other self-propelled vehicle not designed for running on rails." The issue in the case was whether defendant's transportation of a stolen airplane fell within the statute. Because *airplane* was not within the popular (or what linguists today call the prototypical) meaning of *motor vehicle*, Justice Holmes' opinion for the Court held that it did not. He justified lenity on grounds of notice:

> Although it is not likely that a criminal will carefully consider the text of the law before he murders or steals, it is reasonable that a fair warning should be given to the world in language that the common world will understand, of what the law intends to do if a certain line is passed. To make the warning fair, so far as possible the line should be clear. When a rule of conduct is laid down in words that evoke in the common mind only the picture of the vehicles moving on land, the statute should not be extended to aircraft, simply because it may seem to us that a similar policy applies, or upon the speculation that if the legislature had thought of it, very likely broader words would have been used.

Accord, *United States v. Lanier*, 520 U.S. 259, 265–66 (1997) (excellent elaboration of *McBoyle* and the various fair warning doctrines).

Under a fair warning rationalization, the rule of lenity is most appropriately applied to criminal statutes that create offenses that are *malum prohibitum* (bad only because they are prohibited) rather than *malum in se* (bad by their very nature).[23] Thus, a law criminalizing homicide doesn't have to be as clear in all respects as a law criminalizing hunting and fishing without a license from the state. But can this precept explain *McBoyle*? Or *Regina v. Harris*, 173 Eng. Rep. 198 (Cent. Crim. Ct. 1836), in which an English court held that one who bit off the end of the nose of another was not guilty of violating a statute punishing anyone "who shall unlawfully and maliciously stab, cut, or wound any person" because the statute reached only wounds inflicted by an instrument. In both those cases—and many others—defendants engaging in unquestionably squalid behavior got the benefit of the rule.

A justification related to fair notice might be the Anglo-American emphasis on *mens rea as a presumptive requirement* for criminal penalties. Although ignorance of the law is no defense to a crime, the inability of the reasonable defendant to

---

[22] See William Eskridge Jr., *All About Words: Early Understandings of the "Judicial Power" in Statutory Interpretation, 1776–1806*, 101 Colum. L. Rev. 990 (2001).

[23] Oliver Wendell Holmes, Jr., *The Common Law* 50 (1881) (positing the *malum in se/prohibitum* distinction). See also J. Willard Hurst, *Dealing with Statutes* 64–65 (1982); John Calvin Jeffries, Jr., *Legality, Vagueness, and the Construction of Penal Statutes*, 71 Va. L. Rev. 189 (1985).

know that his actions are criminal undermines the justice of inferring a criminal intent in some cases. It also suggests a corollary of the rule of lenity, namely, the presumption that criminal statutes carry with them a mens rea, or intentionality, requirement.

A dramatic illustration of the rule of lenity and its corollary is *Ratzlaf v. United States*, 510 U.S. 135 (1994), which construed the Money Laundering Control Act of 1986. Prior law required banks to report cash transactions in excess of $10,000; to prevent people from "structuring" their transactions to avoid the reports, the 1986 law made it illegal to make lower deposits for the purpose of evading the reporting requirements. The Court interpreted the statute to require *double scienter*: not only must the government prove that defendants Waldemar and Loretta Ratzlaf intended to evade the bank reporting law, but also that they knew about and intended to evade the anti-structuring law as well.[24] Justice Ginsburg's opinion for the Court emphasized that there were many benign reasons people would want to structure their transactions to avoid bank reporting requirements, including fear of burglary and a desire to secrete assets from a spouse or tax inspectors. According to Justice Ginsburg, "structuring is not inevitably nefarious." *Id.* at 144. Four dissenting Justices argued that a double scienter requirement was not justified by the statutory language, would render the statute a nullity, and focused on unduly extreme cases.

A third justification for the rule of lenity was originally suggested by Chief Justice Marshall in *United States v. Wiltberger*, 18 U.S. (5 Wheat.) 76, 92 (1820): *separation of powers.* After much debate, the Marshall Court adopted the proposition that Congress cannot delegate to judges and prosecutors power to make common law crimes, because the moral condemnation inherent in crimes ought only to be delivered by the popularly elected legislature. If the legislature alone has the authority to define crimes, it is inappropriate for judges to elaborate on criminal statutes so as to expand them beyond the clear import of their directive words adopted by the legislature. There is also a separation of powers concern that judicial expansion of criminal statutes, common law style, risks expanding prosecutorial discretion beyond that contemplated by the legislature. See Herbert Packer, *The Limits of the Criminal Sanction* 79–96 (1968).

Notwithstanding the antiquity of and multiple rationales for the rule of lenity, it has fallen into decline since the New Deal. See generally Francis Allen, *The Erosion of Legality in American Criminal Justice: Some Latter-Day Adventures of the* Nulla Poena *Principle*, 29 Ariz. L. Rev. 385 (1987). As of 2013, twenty-eight of the thirty-six states that had codified the rule of lenity have abolished or reversed the rule by statute. Typical is Arizona Penal Code § 13–104, added in 1977: "The general rule that a penal statute is to be strictly construed does not apply to this title, but the provisions herein must be construed according to the fair meaning of

---

[24] The Supreme Court similarly read special scienter requirements into a statute making it a crime to possess a "machine gun," *Staples v. United States*, 511 U.S. 600 (1994) (government must prove defendant knew the gun was a machine gun), or to distribute images of minors engaged in sexually explicit conduct, *United States v. X-Citement Video, Inc.*, 513 U.S. 64 (1994) (government must prove defendant knew the performer was actually a minor). See also *Cheek v. United States*, 498 U.S. 192 (1991) (taxpayer's honest but unreasonable belief that he did not have to pay taxes was a valid defense to a charge of willful failure to pay taxes).

their terms to promote justice and effect the objects of the law." The primary explanation for these anti-lenity statutes is that state legislatures in the late twentieth century were prone to invoke the criminal sanction liberally and did not want judges obstructing such an expansion. If this rationale holds up, does that provide a reason *favoring* the rule of lenity? Do the rule's constitutional overtones trump such statutes under some circumstances? See *State v. Pena*, 683 P.2d 744, 748–49 (Ariz. App.), aff'd, 683 P.2d 743 (Ariz. 1984) (applying rule of lenity notwithstanding the legislative abrogation).

Criticism of the rule of lenity has not been limited to legislators, however. Professor Dan Kahan, *Lenity and Federal Common Law Crimes*, 1994 Sup. Ct. Rev. 345, maintains that the nondelegation reason is the only coherent justification for the rule of lenity, at least for federal criminal statutes, but further argues that the rule of lenity should be abolished as a canon of construction. The polity would be better off without the rule of lenity. Accord, John Calvin Jeffries, Jr., *Legality, Vagueness, and the Construction of Penal Statutes*, 71 Va. L. Rev. 189, 189 (1985). Normal interpretation of criminal statutes, without a judicial thumb on either side of the scale, would promote a more orderly and less costly development of criminal law (common law style, the way commercial law has developed, for example), without much in the way of unfairness, especially if the Department of Justice cleared up ambiguities by authoritative interpretations of federal criminal statutes. Consider this thesis in light of the following cases. Is there a coherent rationale for the rule of lenity? Does it serve useful purposes? Or does it impose needless costs on the system?

STATUTORY PREFACE TO THE MUSCARELLO CASE

Gun Control Act of 1968, Pub. L. 90–618, 82 Stat. 1213 (as codified in chapter 44 of 18 U.S.C. as of March 1998).

Section 924. * * *

(b) Whoever, with intent to commit therewith an offense punishable by imprisonment for a term exceeding one year, or with knowledge or reasonable cause to believe that an offense punishable by imprisonment for a term exceeding one year is to be committed therewith, ships, transports, or receives a firearm or any ammunition in interstate or foreign commerce shall be fined under this title, or imprisoned not more than ten years, or both.

(c)(1) Whoever, during and in relation to any crime of violence or drug trafficking crime * * * for which the person may be prosecuted in a court of the United States, uses or carries a firearm, shall, in addition to the punishment provided for such crime of violence or drug trafficking crime, be sentenced to imprisonment for five years * * *.

Section 925. * * *

(a)(2) The provisions of this chapter * * * shall not apply with respect to **(A)** the shipment or receipt of firearms or ammunition when sold or issued by the Secretary of the Army pursuant to section 4308 of title 10 before the repeal of such section by section 1624(a) of the Corporation for the Promotion of Rifle Practice and Firearms

Safety Act, and **(B)** the transportation of any such firearm or ammunition carried out to enable a person, who lawfully received such firearm or ammunition from the Secretary of the Army, to engage in military training or in competitions.

Section 926A.

Notwithstanding any other provision of any law or any rule or regulation of a State or any political subdivision thereof, any person who is not otherwise prohibited by this chapter from transporting, shipping, or receiving a firearm shall be entitled to transport a firearm for any lawful purpose from any place where he may lawfully possess and carry such firearm to any other place where he may lawfully possess and carry such firearm if, during such transportation the firearm is unloaded, and neither the firearm nor any ammunition being transported is readily accessible or is directly accessible from the passenger compartment of such transporting vehicle: *Provided,* That in the case of a vehicle without a compartment separate from the driver's compartment the firearm or ammunition shall be contained in a locked container other than the glove compartment or console.

MUSCARELLO V. UNITED STATES

Supreme Court of the United States, 1998.
524 U.S. 125, 118 S.Ct. 1911, 141 L.Ed.2d 111.

JUSTICE BREYER delivered the opinion of the Court.

[Section 924(c)(1) of 18 U.S.C. provides that "[w]hoever, during and in relation to any crime of violence or drug trafficking crime * * * uses or carries a firearm, shall, in addition to the punishment provided for such crime of violence or drug trafficking crime, be sentenced to imprisonment for five years[.]" The practical consequence of this provision is that someone who possessed a gun at the time of a drug offense gets a mandatory additional five-year sentence if § 924(c)(1) was violated; if that provision was not violated, the possession of the gun would be taken into account under the federal sentencing guidelines and would add some time to the sentence (perhaps a 30–40% enhancement) unless the gun was clearly not involved in the drug offense. Apparently it is almost always in the interest of the defendant to be subjected to the sentencing guidelines in this way rather than receive the mandatory additional sentence provided by § 924(c)(1). Accordingly, there has been much litigation concerning what the government must show beyond the mere possession of a gun during a drug offense to satisfy § 924(c)(1).

[In *Smith v. United States*, 508 U.S. 223 (1993), the Court held that, when a person traded a gun for drugs, he "used" the gun in violation of § 924(c)(1). Justice Scalia's dissenting opinion contended that the ordinary meaning of § 924(c)(1), read in context, is that "uses a firearm" means "uses the firearm as a weapon," and that in any event the issue was sufficiently doubtful for the rule of lenity to control the outcome in favor of the defendant. In *Bailey v. United States*, 516 U.S. 137 (1995), a unanimous Court held that the "use" element requires active employment of the firearm by the defendant, such that it did not apply to a defendant who had a gun in the trunk of his car in which illegal drugs were found or to a defendant who had a gun locked in a trunk in a closet in a bedroom where illegal drugs were stored.

[Muscarello unlawfully sold marijuana from his truck and confessed that he "carried" a gun in the truck's locked glove compartment " 'for protection in relation' to the drug offense." In a companion case, Donald Cleveland and Enrique Gray-Santana were arrested for stealing and dealing drugs; they had bags of guns in the locked trunk of their car at the scene. The issue was whether these defendants had "carrie[d]" a firearm within the meaning of § 924(c)(1).]

We begin with the statute's language. The parties vigorously contest the ordinary English meaning of the phrase "carries a firearm." Because they essentially agree that Congress intended the phrase to convey its ordinary, and not some special legal, meaning, and because they argue the linguistic point at length, we too have looked into the matter in more than usual depth. Although the word "carry" has many different meanings, only two are relevant here. When one uses the word in the first, or primary, meaning, one can, as a matter of ordinary English, "carry firearms" in a wagon, car, truck, or other vehicle that one accompanies. When one uses the word in a different, rather special, way, to mean, for example, "bearing" or (in slang) "packing" (as in "packing a gun"), the matter is less clear. But, for reasons we shall set out below, we believe Congress intended to use the word in its primary sense and not in this latter, special way.

Consider first the word's primary meaning. The Oxford English Dictionary gives as its *first* definition "convey, originally by cart or wagon, hence in any vehicle, by ship, on horseback, etc." 2 Oxford English Dictionary 919 (2d ed. 1989); see also Webster's Third New International Dictionary 343 (1986) (*first* definition: "move while supporting (*as in a vehicle* or in one's hands or arms)"); The Random House Dictionary of the English Language Unabridged 319 (2d ed. 1987) (*first* definition: "to take or support from one place to another; convey; transport").

The origin of the word "carries" explains why the first, or basic, meaning of the word "carry" includes conveyance in a vehicle. See The Barnhart Dictionary of Etymology 146 (1988) (tracing the word from Latin "carum," which means "car" or "cart"); 2 Oxford English Dictionary, *supra*, at 919 (tracing the word from Old French "carier" and the late Latin "carricare," which meant to "convey in a car") * * *.

The greatest of writers have used the word with this meaning. See, e.g., the King James Bible, 2 Kings 9:28 ("[H]is servants carried him in a chariot to Jerusalem"); *id.*, Isaiah 30:6 ("[T]hey will carry their riches upon the shoulders of young asses"). Robinson Crusoe says, "[w]ith my boat, I carry'd away every Thing." D. Defoe, Robinson Crusoe 174 (J. Crowley ed. 1972). And the owners of Queequeg's ship, Melville writes, "had lent him a [wheelbarrow], in which to carry his heavy chest to his boardinghouse." H. Melville, Moby Dick 43 (U. Chicago 1952). This Court, too, has spoken of the "carrying" of drugs in a car or in its "trunk." [Citations omitted.]

These examples do not speak directly about carrying guns. But there is nothing linguistically special about the fact that weapons, rather than drugs, are being carried. * * * And, to make certain that there is no special ordinary English restriction (unmentioned in dictionaries) upon the use of "carry" in respect to guns, we have surveyed modern press usage, albeit crudely, by searching computerized newspaper databases—both the New York Times data base in Lexis/Nexis, and the "US News" data base in Westlaw. We looked for sentences in which the words "carry," "vehicle," and "weapon" (or variations thereof) all appear. We found thousands of such sentences, and random sampling suggests that many, perhaps more than one third, are sentences used to convey the meaning at issue here, *i.e.*, the carrying of guns in a car. [Justice Breyer gave several examples of such newspaper stories.]

Now consider a different, somewhat special meaning of the word "carry"—a meaning upon which the linguistic arguments of petitioners and the dissent must rest. The Oxford English Dictionary's *twenty-sixth* definition of "carry" is "bear, wear, hold up, or sustain, as one moves about; habitually to bear about with one." Webster's [Third New International Dictionary] defines "carry" as "to move while supporting," not just in a vehicle, but also "in one's hands or arms." And Black's Law Dictionary defines the entire phrase "carry arms or weapons" as "[t]o wear, bear or carry them upon the person or in the clothing or in a pocket, for the purpose of use, or for the purpose of being armed and ready for offensive or defensive action in case of a conflict with another person."

These special definitions, however, do not purport to *limit* the "carrying of arms" to the circumstances they describe. No one doubts that one who bears arms on his person "carries a weapon." But to say that is not to deny that one may also "carry a weapon" tied to the saddle of a horse or placed in a bag in a car.

Nor is there any linguistic reason to think that Congress intended to limit the word "carries" in the statute to any of these special definitions. To the contrary, all these special definitions embody a form of an important, but secondary, meaning of "carry," a meaning that suggests support rather than movement or transportation, as when, for example, a column "carries" the weight of an arch. 2 Oxford English Dictionary, *supra*, at 919, 921. In this sense a gangster might "carry" a gun (in colloquial language, he might "pack a gun") even though he does not move from his chair. It is difficult to believe, however, that Congress intended to limit the statutory word to this definition—imposing special punishment upon the comatose gangster while ignoring drug lords who drive to a sale carrying an arsenal of weapons in their van.

We recognize, as the dissent emphasizes, that the word "carry" has other meanings as well. But those other meanings, (e.g., "carry all he knew," "carries no colours") are not relevant here. And the fact that speakers often do *not* add to the phrase "carry a gun" the words "in a car" is of no greater relevance here than the fact that millions of Americans did *not* see Muscarello carry a gun in his car. The relevant linguistic facts are that the word "carry" in its ordinary sense includes carrying in a car and that the word, used in its ordinary sense, keeps the same meaning whether one carries a gun, a suitcase, or a banana. * * *

We now explore more deeply the purely legal question of whether Congress intended to use the word "carry" in its ordinary sense, or whether it intended to limit the scope of the phrase to instances in which a gun is carried "on the person." We conclude that neither the statute's basic purpose nor its legislative history

support circumscribing the scope of the word "carry" by applying an "on the person" limitation.

This Court has described the statute's basic purpose broadly, as an effort to combat the "dangerous combination" of "drugs and guns." *Smith v. United States*, 508 U.S. 223, 240 (1993). And the provision's chief legislative sponsor has said that the provision seeks "to persuade the man who is tempted to commit a Federal felony to leave his gun at home." 114 Cong. Rec. 22231 (1968) (Rep. Poff); see *Busic v. United States*, 446 U.S. 398, 405 (1980) (describing Poff's comments as "crucial material" in interpreting the purpose of § 924(c)); *Simpson v. United States*, 435 U.S. 6, 13–14 (1978) (concluding that Poff's comments are "clearly probative" and "certainly entitled to weight"); see also 114 Cong. Rec. 22243–44 (statutes would apply to "the man who goes out taking a gun to commit a crime") (Rep. Hunt); *id.* at 22244 ("Of course, what we are trying to do by these penalties is to persuade the criminal to leave his gun at home") (Rep. Randall); *id.* at 22236 ("We are concerned . . . with having the criminal leave his gun at home") (Rep. Meskill).

From the perspective of any such purpose (persuading a criminal "to leave his gun at home") what sense would it make for this statute to penalize one who walks with a gun in a bag to the site of a drug sale, but to ignore a similar individual who, like defendant Gray-Santana, travels to a similar site with a similar gun in a similar bag, but instead of walking, drives there with the gun in his car? How persuasive is a punishment that is without effect until a drug dealer who has brought his gun to a sale (indeed has it available for use) actually takes it from the trunk (or unlocks the glove compartment) of his car? It is difficult to say that, considered as a class, those who prepare, say, to sell drugs by placing guns in their cars are less dangerous, or less deserving of punishment, than those who carry handguns on their person.

We have found no significant indication elsewhere in the legislative history of any more narrowly focused relevant purpose. * * * One legislator indicates that the statute responds in part to the concerns of law enforcement personnel, who had urged that "carrying short firearms in motor vehicles be classified as carrying such weapons concealed." *Id.* at 22242 (Rep. May). Another criticizes a version of the proposed statute by suggesting it might apply to drunken driving, and gives as an example a drunken driver who has a "gun in his car." *Id.* at 21792 (Rep. Yates). Others describe the statute as criminalizing gun "possession"—a term that could stretch beyond both the "use" of a gun and the carrying of a gun on the person. See *id.* at 21793 (Rep. Casey); *id.* at 22236 (Rep. Meskill); *id.* at 30584 (Rep. Collier); *id.* at 30585 (Rep. Skubitz).

We are not convinced by petitioners' remaining arguments[.] First, they say that our definition of "carry" makes it the equivalent of "transport." Yet, Congress elsewhere in related statutes used the word "transport" deliberately to signify a different, and broader, statutory coverage. The immediately preceding statutory subsection, for example, imposes a different set of penalties on one who, with an intent to commit a crime, "ships, transports, or receives a firearm" in interstate commerce. 18 U.S.C. § 924(b). Moreover, § 926A specifically "entitle[s]" a person "not otherwise prohibited . . . from transporting, shipping, or receiving a firearm" to "transport a firearm . . . from any place where he may lawfully possess and carry" it to "any other place" where he may do so. Why, petitioners ask, would Congress have used the word "transport," or used both "carry" and "transport" in the same provision, if it had intended to obliterate the distinction between the two?

The short answer is that our definition does not equate "carry" and "transport." "Carry" implies personal agency and some degree of possession, whereas "transport" does not have such a limited connotation and, in addition, implies the movement of goods in bulk over great distances. See Webster's Third New International Dictionary 343 (noting that "carry" means "moving to a location some distance away while supporting or maintaining off the ground" and "is a natural word to use in ref. to cargoes and loads on trucks, wagons, planes, ships, or even beasts of burden," while "transport refers to carriage in bulk or number over an appreciable distance and, typically, by a customary or usual carrier agency"); see also Webster's Dictionary of Synonyms 141 (1942). If Smith, for example, calls a parcel delivery service, which sends a truck to Smith's house to pick up Smith's package and take it to Los Angeles, one might say that Smith has shipped the package and the parcel delivery service has transported the package. But only the truck driver has "carried" the package in the sense of "carry" that we believe Congress intended. Therefore, "transport" is a broader category that includes "carry" but also encompasses other activity.

The dissent refers to § 926A and to another statute where Congress used the word "transport" rather than "carry" to describe the movement of firearms. 18 U.S.C. § 925(a)(2)(B). According to the dissent, had Congress intended "carry" to have the meaning we give it, Congress would not have needed to use a different word in these provisions. But as we have discussed above, we believe the word "transport" is broader than the word "carry."

And, if Congress intended "carry" to have the limited definition the dissent contends, it would have been quite unnecessary to add the proviso in § 926A requiring a person, to be exempt from penalties, to store her firearm in a locked container not immediately accessible. See § 926A (exempting from criminal penalties one who transports a firearm from a place where "he may lawfully possess and carry such firearm" but not exempting the "transportation" of a firearm if it is "readily accessible or is directly accessible from the passenger compartment of transporting vehicle"). The statute simply could have said that such a person may not "carry" a firearm. But, of course, Congress did not say this because that is not what "carry" means.

As we interpret the statutory scheme, it makes sense. Congress has imposed a variable penalty with no mandatory minimum sentence upon a person who "transports" (or "ships" or "receives") a firearm knowing it will be used to commit any "offense punishable by imprisonment for [more than] . . . one year," § 924(b), and it has imposed a 5–year mandatory minimum sentence upon one who "carries" a firearm "during and in relation to" a "drug trafficking crime," § 924(c). The first subsection imposes a less strict sentencing regime upon one who, say, ships firearms by mail for use in a crime elsewhere; the latter subsection imposes a mandatory sentence upon one who, say, brings a weapon with him (on his person or in his car) to the site of a drug sale.

Second, petitioners point out that, in *Bailey v. United States*, we considered the related phrase "uses . . . a firearm" found in the same statutory provision now before us. We construed the term "use" narrowly, limiting its application to the "active employment" of a firearm. Petitioners argue that it would be anomalous to construe broadly the word "carries," its statutory next-door neighbor.

In *Bailey*, however, we limited "use" of a firearm to "active employment" in part because we assumed "that Congress . . . intended each term to have a particular, non-superfluous meaning." A broader interpretation of "use," we said, would have swallowed up the term "carry." But "carry" as we interpret that word does not swallow up the term "use." "Use" retains the same independent meaning we found for it in *Bailey*, where we provided examples involving the displaying or the bartering of a gun. "Carry" also retains an independent meaning, for, under *Bailey*, carrying a gun in a car does not necessarily involve the gun's "active employment." More importantly, having construed "use" narrowly in *Bailey*, we cannot also construe "carry" narrowly without undercutting the statute's basic objective. For the narrow interpretation would remove the act of carrying a gun in a car entirely from the statute's reach, leaving a gap in coverage that we do not believe Congress intended.

Third, petitioners say that our reading of the statute would extend its coverage to passengers on buses, trains, or ships, who have placed a firearm, say, in checked luggage. To extend this statute so far, they argue, is unfair, going well beyond what Congress likely would have thought possible. They add that some lower courts, thinking approximately the same, have limited the scope of "carries" to instances where a gun in a car is immediately accessible, thereby most likely excluding from coverage a gun carried in a car's trunk or locked glove compartment. * * *

In our view, this argument does not take adequate account of other limiting words in the statute—words that make the statute applicable only where a defendant "carries" a gun *both* "during *and* in relation to" a drug crime. § 924(c)(1) (emphasis added). Congress added these words in part to prevent prosecution where guns "played" no part in the crime. See S. Rep. No. 98–225, at 314, n.10.

Once one takes account of the words "during" and "in relation to," it no longer seems beyond Congress' likely intent, or otherwise unfair, to interpret the statute as we have done. If one carries a gun in a car "during" and "in relation to" a drug sale, for example, the fact that the gun is carried in the car's trunk or locked glove compartment seems not only logically difficult to distinguish from the immediately accessible gun, but also beside the point.

At the same time, the narrow interpretation creates its own anomalies. The statute, for example, defines "firearm" to include a "bomb," "grenade," "rocket having a propellant charge of more than four ounces," or "missile having an explosive or incendiary charge of more than one-quarter ounce," where such device is "explosive," "incendiary," or delivers "poison gas." 18 U.S.C. § 921(a)(4)(A). On petitioners' reading, the "carry" provision would not apply to instances where drug lords, engaged in a major transaction, took with them "firearms" such as these, which most likely could not be carried on the person.

Fourth, petitioners argue that we should construe the word "carry" to mean "immediately accessible." * * * That interpretation, however, is difficult to square with the statute's language, for one "carries" a gun in the glove compartment whether or not that glove compartment is locked. Nothing in the statute's history suggests that Congress intended that limitation. And, for reasons pointed out above, we believe that the words "during" and "in relation to" will limit the statute's application to the harms that Congress foresaw.

Finally, petitioners and the dissent invoke the "rule of lenity." The simple existence of some statutory ambiguity, however, is not sufficient to warrant application of that rule, for most statutes are ambiguous to some degree. "The rule of lenity applies only if, 'after seizing everything from which aid can be derived,' . . . we can make 'no more than a guess as to what Congress intended.' " *United States v. Wells*, 519 U.S. 482, 499 (1997) [quoting earlier cases]. To invoke the rule, we must conclude that there is a " 'grievous ambiguity or uncertainty' in the statute." *Staples v. United States*, 511 U.S. 600, 619 n.17 (1994) (quoting *Chapman v. United States* [Chapter 7, § 3B]. Certainly, our decision today is based on much more than a "guess as to what Congress intended," and there is no "grievous ambiguity" here. The problem of statutory interpretation [in this case] is indeed no different from that in many of the criminal cases that confront us. Yet, this Court has never held that the rule of lenity automatically permits a defendant to win. [Affirmed.]

JUSTICE GINSBURG, with whom THE CHIEF JUSTICE [REHNQUIST], JUSTICE SCALIA, and JUSTICE SOUTER join, dissenting.

[Justice Ginsburg explained that defendants' gun possession would have adverse consequences even if § 924(c)(1) were held to be inapplicable. For example, the federal sentencing guidelines provided Muscarello a 6–12 month presumptive sentence for his involvement in the distribution of 3.6 kilograms of marijuana. The "two-level enhancement" under the guidelines for possession of a gun would increase the sentencing range to 10–16 months. If, instead, as the majority held, Muscarello violated § 924(c)(1), his sentence would reflect the underlying drug offense (6–12 months) *plus* the five-year mandatory additional sentence provided by § 924(c)(1).]

* * * Unlike the Court, I do not think dictionaries, surveys of press reports,[3] or the Bible[4] tell us, dispositively, what "carries" means embedded in § 924(c)(1). On definitions, "carry" in legal formulations could mean, *inter alia*, transport, possess,

---

[3] Many newspapers, the New York Times among them, have published stories using "transport," rather than "carry," to describe gun placements resembling petitioners'. [Quoting stories.]

[4] The translator of the Good Book, it appears, bore responsibility for determining whether the servants of Ahaziah "carried" his corpse to Jerusalem. Compare [majority opinion] with, e.g., The New English Bible, 2 Kings 9:28 ("His servants *conveyed* his body to Jerusalem."); Saint Joseph Edition of the New American Bible ("His servants *brought* him in a chariot to Jerusalem."); Tanakh: The Holy Scriptures ("His servants *conveyed* him in a chariot to Jerusalem."); see also *id.*, Isaiah 30:6 ("They *convey* their wealth on the backs of asses."); The New Jerusalem Bible ("[T]hey *bear* their riches on donkeys' backs.") (emphasis added in all quotations).

have in stock, prolong (carry over), be infectious, or wear or bear on one's person.[5] At issue here is not "carries" at large but "carries a firearm." The Court's computer search of newspapers is revealing in this light. Carrying guns in a car showed up as the meaning "perhaps more than one third" of the time. One is left to wonder what meaning showed up some two thirds of the time. Surely a most familiar meaning is, as the Constitution's Second Amendment ("keep and *bear* Arms") (emphasis added) and Black's Law Dictionary, at 214, indicate: "wear, bear, or carry . . . upon the person or in the clothing or in a pocket, for the purpose . . . of being armed and ready for offensive or defensive action in a case of conflict with another person."

On lessons from literature, a scan of Bartlett's and other quotation collections shows how highly selective the Court's choices are. If "[t]he greatest of writers" have used "carry" to mean convey or transport in a vehicle, so have they used the hydra-headed word to mean, *inter alia*, carry in one's hand, arms, head, heart, or soul, sans vehicle. [Justice Ginsburg quoted Isaiah 40:11, poems by Oliver Goldsmith and Rudyard Kipling, and Theodore Roosevelt's famous advice to "[s]peak softly and carry a big stick."][6]

These and the Court's lexicological sources demonstrate vividly that "carry" is a word commonly used to convey various messages. Such references, given their variety, are not reliable indicators of what Congress meant, in § 924(c)(1), by "carries a firearm."

Noting the paradoxical statement, " 'I *use* a gun to protect my house, but I've never had to *use* it,' " the Court in *Bailey* emphasized the importance of context—the statutory context. Just as "uses" was read to mean not simply "possession," but "active employment," so "carries," correspondingly, is properly read to signal the most dangerous cases—the gun at hand, ready for use as a weapon. It is reasonable to comprehend Congress as having provided mandatory minimums for the most life-jeopardizing gun-connection cases (guns in or at the defendant's hand when committing an offense), leaving other, less imminently threatening, situations for the more flexible guidelines regime. As the Ninth Circuit suggested, it is not apparent why possession of a gun in a drug dealer's moving vehicle would be thought more dangerous than gun possession on premises where drugs are sold: "A drug dealer who packs heat is more likely to hurt someone or provoke someone else to violence. A gun in a bag under a tarp in a truck bed [or in a bedroom closet] poses substantially less risk." *United States v. Foster*, 133 F.3d 704, 707 (1998) (en banc).

For indicators from Congress itself, it is appropriate to consider word usage in other provisions of Title 18's chapter on "Firearms." The Court, however, does not derive from the statutory complex at issue its thesis that " '[c]arry' implies personal agency and some degree of possession, whereas 'transport' does not have such a

---

[5] The dictionary to which this Court referred in *Bailey v. United States* contains 32 discrete definitions of "carry," including "[t]o make good or valid," "to bear the aspect of," and even "[t]o bear (a hawk) on the fist." See Webster's New International Dictionary of English Language 412 (2d ed. 1949).

[6] Popular films and television productions provide corroborative illustrations. * * * [I]n the television series "M*A*S*H," Hawkeye Pierce (played by Alan Alda) presciently proclaims: "I will not carry a gun. . . . I'll carry your books, I'll carry a torch, I'll carry a tune, I'll carry on, carry over, carry forward, Cary Grant, cash and carry, carry me back to Old Virginia, I'll even 'hari-kari' if you show me how, but I will not carry a gun!" See http://www.geocities.com/Hollywood/8915/mashquotes.html.

limited connotation and, in addition, implies the movement of goods in bulk over great distances." [Quoting majority opinion.] Looking to provisions Congress enacted, one finds that the Legislature did not acknowledge or routinely adhere to the distinction the Court advances today; instead, Congress sometimes employed "transports" when, according to the Court, "carries" was the right word to use.

Section 925(a)(2)(B), for example, provides that no criminal sanction shall attend "the transportation of [a] firearm or ammunition carried out to enable a person, who lawfully received such firearm or ammunition from the Secretary of the Army, to engage in military training or in competitions." The full text of § 926A, rather than the truncated version the Court presents, is also telling [Justice Ginsburg quoted the text of 18 U.S.C. § 926A, which is reproduced in the Statutory Preface].

In describing when and how a person may travel in a vehicle that contains his firearm without violating the law, §§ 925(a)(2)(B) and 926A use "transport," not "carry," to "impl[y] personal agency and some degree of possession." [Again quoting majority opinion.][10]

Reading "carries" in § 924(c)(1) to mean "on or about [one's] person" is fully compatible with these and other "Firearms" statutes.[11] For example, under § 925(a)(2)(B), one could carry his gun to a car, transport it to the shooting competition, and use it to shoot targets. Under the conditions of § 926A, one could transport her gun in a car, but under no circumstances could the gun be readily accessible while she travels in the car. "[C]ourts normally try to read language in different, but related, statutes, so as best to reconcile those statutes, in light of their purposes and of common sense." [*United States v. McFadden*, 13 F.3d 463, 467 (1st Cir. 1994) (Breyer, C.J., dissenting).] So reading the "Firearms" statutes, I would not extend the word "carries" in § 924(c)(1) to mean transports out of hand's reach in a vehicle.[12]

---

[10] The Court asserts that "'transport' is a broader category that includes 'carry' but encompasses other activity." "Carry," however, is not merely a subset of "transport." A person seated at a desk with a gun in hand or pocket is carrying the gun, but is not transporting it. Yes, the words "carry" and "transport" often can be employed interchangeably, as can the words "carry" and "use." But in *Bailey*, this Court settled on constructions that gave "carry" and "use" independent meanings. Without doubt, Congress is alert to the discrete meanings of "transport" and "carry" in the context of vehicles, as the Legislature's placement of each word in § 926A illustrates. The narrower reading of "carry" preserves discrete meanings for the two words, while in the context of vehicles the Court's interpretation of "carry" is altogether synonymous with "transport." Tellingly, when referring to firearms traveling in vehicles, the "Firearms" statutes routinely use a form of "transport"; they never use a form of "carry."

[11] The Government points to numerous federal statutes that authorize law enforcement officers to "carry firearms" and notes that, in those authorizing provisions, "carry" of course means "both on the person and in a vehicle." Brief for United States 31–32, and n. 18. Quite right. But as viewers of "Sesame Street" will quickly recognize, "one of these things [a statute *authorizing* conduct] is not like the other [a statute *criminalizing* conduct]." The authorizing statutes in question are properly accorded a construction compatible with the clear purpose of the legislation to aid federal law enforcers in the performance of their official duties. It is fundamental, however, that a penal statute is not to be construed generously in the Government's favor. See, *e.g.*, *United States v. Bass*, 404 U.S. 336, 348 (1971).

[12] The Court places undue reliance on Representative Poff's statement that § 924(c)(1) seeks " 'to persuade the man who is tempted to commit a Federal felony to leave his gun at home.' " See [majority opinion] (quoting 114 Cong. Rec. 22231 (1968)). As the Government argued in its brief to this Court in Bailey:

> In making that statement, Representative Poff was not referring to the "carries" prong of the original Section 924(c). As originally enacted, the "carries" prong of the statute prohibited only the "unlawful" carrying of a firearm while committing an offense. The statute would thus not have applied to an

Section 924(c)(1), as the foregoing discussion details, is not decisively clear one way or another. The sharp division in the Court on the proper reading of the measure confirms, "[a]t the very least, . . . that the issue is subject to some doubt. Under these circumstances, we adhere to the familiar rule that, 'where there is ambiguity in a criminal statute, doubts are resolved in favor of the defendant.' " *Adamo Wrecking Co. v. United States*, 434 U.S. 275, 284–285 (1978); see *United States v. Granderson*, 511 U.S. 39, 54 (1994) ("[W]here text, structure, and history fail to establish that the Government's position is unambiguously correct—we apply the rule of lenity and resolve the ambiguity in [the defendant's] favor."). "Carry" bears many meanings, as the Court and the "Firearms" statutes demonstrate.[13] The narrower "on or about [one's] person" interpretation is hardly implausible nor at odds with an accepted meaning of "carries a firearm."

Overlooking that there will be an enhanced sentence for the gun-possessing drug dealer in any event, the Court asks rhetorically: "How persuasive is a punishment that is without effect until a drug dealer who has brought his gun to a sale (indeed has it available for use) actually takes it from the trunk (or unlocks the glove compartment) of his car?" Correspondingly, the Court defines "carries a firearm" to cover "a person who knowingly possesses and conveys firearms [anyplace] in a vehicle . . . which the person accompanies." Congress, however, hardly lacks competence to select the words "possesses" or "conveys" when that is what the Legislature means.[14] Notably in view of the Legislature's capacity to speak plainly, and of overriding concern, the Court's inquiry pays scant attention to a core reason for the rule of lenity: "[B]ecause of the seriousness of criminal penalties, and because criminal punishment usually represents the moral condemnation of the community, legislatures and not courts should define criminal activity. This policy embodies 'the instinctive distaste against men languishing in prison unless the lawmaker has clearly said they should.' " *United States v. Bass* (quoting H. Friendly, Mr. Justice Frankfurter and the Reading of Statutes, in Benchmarks 196, 209 (1967)). * * *

---

individual who, for instance, had a permit for carrying a gun and carried it with him when committing an offense, and it would have had no force in "persuading" such an individual "to leave his gun at home." Instead, Representative Poff was referring to the "uses" prong of the original Section 924(c). [Quoting U.S. Brief in *Bailey*.]

Representative Poff's next sentence confirms that he was speaking of "uses," not "carries": "Any person should understand that if he *uses* his gun and is caught and convicted, he is going to jail." 114 Cong. Rec., at 22231 (emphasis added).

[13] Any doubt on that score is dispelled by examining the provisions in the "Firearms" chapter, in addition to § 924(c)(1), that include a form of the word "carry": 18 U.S.C. § 922(a)(5) ("*carry out* a bequest"); §§ 922(s)(6)(B)(ii), (iii) ("*carry out* this subsection"); § 922(u) ("*carry away* [a firearm]"); 18 U.S.C.A. § 924(a)(6)(B)(ii) (Supp.1998) ("*carry* or otherwise possess or discharge or otherwise use [a] handgun"); 18 U.S.C. § 924(e)(2)(B) ("*carrying* of a firearm"); § 925(a)(2) ("*carried out* to enable a person"); § 926(a) ("*carry out* the provisions of this chapter"); § 926A ("lawfully possess and *carry* such firearm to any other place where he may lawfully possess and *carry* such firearm"); § 929(a)(1) ("uses or *carries* a firearm and is in possession of armor piercing ammunition"); § 930(d)(3) ("lawful *carrying* of firearms . . . in a Federal facility incident to hunting or other lawful purposes") (emphasis added in all quotations).

[14] See, e.g., 18 U.S.C.A. § 924(a)(6)(B)(ii) (Supp.1998) ("if the person sold . . . a handgun . . . to a juvenile knowing . . . that the juvenile intended to *carry or otherwise possess* . . . the handgun . . . in the commission of a crime of violence"); 18 U.S.C. § 926A ("may lawfully *possess and carry* such firearm to any other place where he may lawfully *possess and carry* such firearm"); § 929(a)(1) ("uses or *carries a firearm and is in possession* of armor piercing ammunition"); § 2277 ("brings, *carries, or possesses* any dangerous weapon") (emphasis added in all quotations).

Postscript: Soon after the Court's opinion in *Muscarello*, Congress overrode *Bailey* in Pub. L. No. 105–386, 112 Stat. 3469 (1998). The new law amended 18 U.S.C. § 924(c)(1), to trigger the sentence-enhancement provisions where the defendant possesses a firearm "in furtherance of" one of the predicate offenses. An additional enhancement is triggered if the firearm is "brandished," and a yet-higher one if it is "discharged." Brandish is defined in new § 924(c)(4): "to display all or part of the firearm, or otherwise to make the presence of the firearm known to another person, regardless of whether the firearm is directly visible to that person." Does this new statute lend support to the majority's approach in *Muscarello*?

McNally v. United States
483 U.S. 350 (1987).

The federal mail fraud statute, 18 U.S.C. § 1341, provides that "[w]hoever, having devised or intending to devise any scheme or artifice to defraud, or for obtaining money or property by means of false or fraudulent pretenses, representations, or promises, * * * for the purpose of executing such scheme or artifice or attempting to do so [uses the mails or causes them to be used,] shall be fined not more than $1,000 or imprisoned not more than five years, or both." The lower courts upheld the convictions of several public officials and one private party activist who made a deal with an insurance company, whereby the state would send business to the company, which in turn would send some of the commissions to other companies designated by the conspirators, including one company they owned. The record apparently did not demonstrate that the state had lost any money by virtue of this kickback scheme. The Court, in an opinion by **Justice White**, reversed the lower courts' interpretation of § 1341, concluding that the statute outlawed only those "frauds on the public" that result in a tangible loss to the public.

"As first enacted in 1872, as part of a recodification of the postal laws, the statute contained a general proscription against using the mails to initiate correspondence in furtherance of 'any scheme or artifice to defraud.' The sponsor of the recodification stated, in apparent reference to the antifraud provision, that measures were needed 'to prevent the frauds which are mostly gotten up in the large cities . . . by thieves, forgers, and rapscallions generally, for the purpose of deceiving and fleecing the innocent people in the country.' Insofar as the sparse legislative history reveals anything, it indicates that the original impetus behind the mail fraud statute was to protect the people from schemes to deprive them of their money or property. * * *

"As the Court long ago stated, * * * the words 'to defraud' commonly refer 'to wronging one in his property rights by dishonest methods or schemes,' and 'usually signify the deprivation of something of value by trick, deceit, chicane or overreaching.' *Hammerschmidt v. United States*, 265 U.S. 182, 188 (1924). [Congress' adding the phrase "or for obtaining money or property" in] 1909 does not indicate that Congress was departing from this common understanding. As we see it, adding the second phrase simply made it unmistakable that the statute reached false promises and misrepresentations as to the future as well as other frauds involving money or property.

"We believe that Congress' intent in passing the mail fraud statute was to prevent the use of the mails in furtherance of such schemes. The Court has often stated that when there are two rational readings of a criminal statute, one harsher than the other, we are to choose the harsher only when Congress has spoken in clear and definite language. * * * Rather than construe the statute in a manner that leaves its outer boundaries ambiguous and involves the Federal Government in setting standards of disclosure and good government for local and state officials, we read § 1341 as limited in scope to the protection of property rights. If Congress desires to go further, it must speak more clearly than it has."

Justice Stevens, in dissent, relied on the plain meaning of the statute, which prohibits the use of the United States mails for the purpose of executing "[1] *any* scheme or artifice to defraud, [2] *or* for obtaining money or property by means of false or fraudulent pretenses, representations, or promises, [3] *or* to sell, dispose of, loan, exchange, alter, give away, distribute, supply, or furnish or procure for unlawful use any counterfeit or spurious coin, obligation, security, or other article, or anything represented to be or intimated or held out to be such counterfeit or spurious article . . ." 18 U.S.C. § 1341 (emphasis and brackets added).

"As the language makes clear, each of these restrictions is independent. One can violate the second clause—obtaining money or property by false pretenses—even though one does not violate the third clause—counterfeiting. Similarly, one can violate the first clause—devising a scheme or artifice to defraud—without violating the counterfeiting provision. Until today it was also obvious that one could violate the first clause by devising a scheme or artifice to defraud, even though one did not violate the second clause by seeking to obtain money or property from his victim through false pretenses. Every court to consider the matter had so held. Yet, today, the Court, for all practical purposes, rejects this longstanding construction of the statute by imposing a requirement that a scheme or artifice to defraud does not violate the statute unless its purpose is to defraud someone of money or property. I am at a loss to understand the source or justification for this holding. Certainly no canon of statutory construction requires us to ignore the plain language of the provision.

"In considering the scope of the mail fraud statute it is essential to remember Congress's purpose in enacting it. Congress sought to protect the integrity of the United States mails by not allowing them to be used as 'instruments of crime.' *United States v. Brewer*, 528 F.2d 492, 498 (4th Cir. 1975). 'The focus of the statute is upon the misuse of the Postal Service, not the regulation of state affairs, and Congress clearly has the authority to regulate such misuse of the mails.' *United States v. States*, 488 F.2d 761, 767 (8th Cir. 1973). Once this purpose is considered, it becomes clear that the construction the Court adopts today is senseless. Can it be that Congress sought to purge the mails of schemes to defraud citizens of money but was willing to tolerate schemes to defraud citizens of their right to an honest government, or to unbiased public officials? Is it at all rational to assume that Congress wanted to ensure that the mails not be used for petty crimes, but did not prohibit election fraud accomplished through mailing fictitious ballots? Given Congress' 'broad purpose,' I 'find it difficult to believe, absent some indication in the statute itself or the legislative history, that Congress would have undercut sharply that purpose by hobbling federal prosecutors in their effort to combat' use of the mails for fraudulent schemes."

Postscript: Justice White's memorandum to the Conference, in which he circulated his opinion, expressed reservations about the broad holding but concluded: "But it is not rare that Opinions of the Court are no more persuasive than an opinion on the other side would have been. Of course, the saving grace in Statutory Construction cases is that Congress may have its way if it does not like the product of our work."[25] In 1988, Congress adopted 18 U.S.C. § 1346, which provides that for purposes of the mail fraud statute " 'scheme or artifice to defraud' includes a scheme or artifice to deprive another of the intangible right of honest services." The statute's legislative history indicates that it was meant to override *McNally* and reinstate the "intangible rights" theory. But see *Skilling v. United States*, 561 U.S. 358 (2010) below, revisiting the meaning of § 1346.

NOTES ON MUSCARELLO, MCNALLY, AND THE SUPREME COURT'S APPROACH TO CRIMINAL STATUTES

1. *The Rule of Lenity Cuts Across Political Lines.* Note the peculiar—perhaps unprecedented—lineup of Justices on both sides of the issue in *Muscarello*. The lineup in *McNally* is almost as odd, with Justices Scalia and Brennan in the majority and Stevens and O'Connor in dissent. The reason for the odd lineups is that the rule of lenity appeals to both civil libertarians (like Brennan, Marshall, Ginsburg) and high formalists who are fans of the nondelegation argument (like Scalia and perhaps Ginsburg), while a more expansive application of criminal statutes appeals to both pragmatists who are willing to apply common-law reasoning to statutory cases (like Stevens, O'Connor, Breyer) and hard-liners against criminals (Thomas perhaps). This heterogeneity also makes the rule of lenity cases hard to predict. We were surprised to find Scalia with the nontextualist majority in *McNally* and Rehnquist (usually a hard-liner in criminal cases) with the lenient *Muscarello* dissent.[26]

2. *The Supreme Court's Inconsistency in Applying the Rule of Lenity?* Can *McNally*, where the Court invoked lenity, and *Muscarello*, where it did not, be reconciled? The cases are similar: each involved broadly phrased federal statutes being applied to antisocial conduct. Some possible bases for distinction: (a) the statute was clearer in the firearms case; (b) Supreme Court precedent supported lenity in the mail fraud case but not the firearm case, where *Smith* had already construed "carry" in a broad way; or (c) the mail fraud case involved federal prosecution of state officials and so trenched on federalism values more deeply if broadly construed (as lower courts had been doing).[27] Even if those distinctions work to distinguish *Muscarello* from *McNally*, they do not distinguish it from *Ratzlaf*, where a clear statute that had not been construed by the Court and was not being applied to state officials was nonetheless

[25] The Thurgood Marshall Papers, Library of Congress (Madison Building), Box 423, Folder 3 (Court memoranda regarding *McNally*, Nos. 86–234 & 86–286). Indeed, Congress does often override the Court's statutory decisions, and when the Court applies the rule of lenity to protect federal criminal defendants, the Department of Justice has an especially strong record for obtaining overrides. See generally Matthew Christiansen & William Eskridge Jr., Congressional Overrides of Supreme Court Statutory Interpretation Decisions, 1967–2011, 92 Tex. L. Rev. 1317, 1357, 1360–61 (2014). Is this a good justification for writing a weak opinion, though?

[26] The lineup in *Ratzlaf* was also substantially explicable along lines noted in text. The majority opinion, invoking lenity, was written by Ginsburg, a civil libertarian, and joined by libertarians Souter and Kennedy and by the formalist Scalia, while the dissent was written by the pragmatic Blackmun and joined by Rehnquist and Thomas, both tough on criminals, and by the highly pragmatic O'Connor. An oddity was that the pragmatic Stevens (no fan of the rule of lenity and surely not sympathetic to the Ratzlafs) provided the critical fifth vote for the majority.

[27] In *McCormick v. United States*, 500 U.S. 257 (1991), the Court overturned a Hobbs Act prosecution of a state official who allegedly "extorted" campaign contributions from private parties.

applied leniently—indeed, in a way that rendered the statute unenforceable.[28] However one resolves the distinction between *Muscarello* and *McNally*, there are plenty of Supreme Court cases going one way or the other.

Although the Supreme Court in *McNally* invoked the rule of lenity, *Muscarello* better reflects Supreme Court practice. Since 1984, the Court has cited the rule of lenity in just over one-fourth of its cases interpreting criminal statutes. In more than 60 percent of the cases, the Court has agreed with the government's interpretation.[29] Although there are still cases where the Court applies the rule of lenity, e.g., *Arthur Andersen LLP v. United States*, 544 U.S. 696 (2005); *Cleveland v. United States*, 531 U.S. 12 (2000), it remains unclear whether the rule has a systematic effect.

3. *Recent Rule of Lenity Developments: Sentencing, Legislative History, Civil Statutes.* For most of American history, the rule of lenity was applied only in the context of substantive criminal law, because sentencing was largely a matter of judicial discretion within well-defined statutory confines. *McNally* is an example. In the last 20 years, the law of sentencing has become more complex and less discretionary with judges—and the Supreme Court applied the rule of lenity to criminal sentencing in *United States v. R.L.C.*, 503 U.S. 291 (1992). See Phillip Spector, *The Sentencing Rule of Lenity*, 33 U. Toledo L. Rev. 511 (2002), who argues against application of the rule to sentencing statutes, on the ground that the notice, prosecutorial discretion, and nondelegation rationales do not apply nearly as strongly to sentencing laws as to those defining substantive crimes.

As in substantive criminal law cases, the Court will not invoke the rule of lenity in sentencing cases where the statutory directive is clear. See *Chapman v. United States*, 500 U.S. 453 (1991) (affirming the Easterbrook decision in *Marshall*, Chapter 6, § 3); *Gozlon-Peretz v. United States*, 498 U.S. 395 (1991). To the extent § 924, an enhancement statute, is viewed as a sentencing law, *Muscarello* illustrates the difficulty of figuring out when sentencing statutes are clear. (*Muscarello* and *Chapman* are also consistent with Spector's argument that the rule of lenity ought not be applied to sentencing statutes.)

As to this point, there is debate within the Court whether legislative history can be considered. In *R.L.C.*, a plurality of Justices stated that the application of the rule of lenity is reserved "for those situations in which a reasonable doubt persists about the statute's intended scope even *after* resort to the language and structure, legislative history, and motivating policies of the statute." 503 U.S. at 305–06. See also *Moskal v. United States*, 498 U.S. 103, 108 (1990). Justice Scalia, joined by Justices Kennedy and Thomas, objected in *R.L.C.* to the presence of legislative history and statutory policies in this inquiry. Note that Kennedy and Thomas joined the Court's opinion in *Muscarello*, which relied on legislative history.

The Court has sometimes ruled that the rule of lenity also applies when a civil-type remedy is applied to a defendant for conduct violating a criminal-type statute. Thus, in *Hughey v. United States*, 495 U.S. 411 (1990), the Court applied the rule of lenity to a statute requiring a criminal defendant to provide restitution. And in *Crandon v. United*

---

[28] For students tough on crime, don't worry about the lenity in cases like *Ratzlaf*, for it was immediately overridden by Congress. See Pub. L. No. 103–325, § 411, 108 Stat. 2253 (1994). The most frequent legislative overrides come where the government loses criminal law cases. See Christiansen & Eskridge, *supra*.

[29] See William Eskridge Jr. & Lauren Baer, *The Continuum of Deference: Supreme Court Treatment of Agency Statutory Interpretations from Chevron to Hamdan*, 96 Geo. L. J. 1083 (2008).

States, 494 U.S. 152 (1990), the Court invoked the rule of lenity to protect a civil defendant, where the applicable standard of conduct was found in a criminal statute.

Skilling v. United States
561 U.S. 358 (2010).

Founded in 1985, Enron Corporation swiftly became the seventh highest-revenue-grossing company in America. Jeffrey Skilling was a longtime Enron officer, its chief executive officer for most of 2001. Less than four months after he resigned, Enron crashed into bankruptcy, and its stock plummeted in value. After an investigation uncovered a conspiracy to prop up Enron's stock prices by overstating the company's financial well-being, the federal government prosecuted dozens of Enron employees, culminating in prosecutions of Skilling and two other top executives. The indictment charged that these three defendants violated several federal criminal statutes when they allegedly engaged in a scheme to deceive investors about Enron's true financial performance by manipulating its publicly reported financial results and making false and misleading statements. Count 1 of the indictment charged Skilling with conspiracy to commit "honest-services" wire fraud, 18 U.S.C. §§ 371, 1343, 1346, by depriving Enron and its shareholders of the intangible right of his honest services. Skilling was convicted of these and other charges, and his conviction was upheld on appeal to the Fifth Circuit.

The Supreme Court reversed Skilling's § 1346 conviction. **Justice Ginsburg's** opinion for the Court on this issue (joined by **Chief Justice Roberts** and **Justices Stevens, Breyer, Alito**, and **Sotomayor**) interpreted § 1346 to be limited to schemes to defraud of honest services only where there have been bribes and kickbacks. Justice Ginsburg started with a review of pre-1987 mail and wire fraud prosecutions under §§ 1341 and 1343 that expanded "scheme to defraud" crimes to include "honest services" and not just tangible property losses. The leading case was *Shushan* v. *United States*, 117 F.2d 110 (5th Cir. 1941), which upheld the mail-fraud prosecution of a public official who allegedly accepted bribes from entrepreneurs in exchange for urging city action beneficial to the bribe payers. "A scheme to get a public contract on more favorable terms than would likely be got otherwise by bribing a public official," the court observed, "would not only be a plan to commit the crime of bribery, but would also be a scheme to defraud the public." By 1987, every federal court of appeals had accepted the "honest services" interpretation of the wire (§ 1341) and mail (§ 1343) fraud statutes, usually in cases that involved bribes or kickbacks.

In *McNally*, the Supreme Court stopped the lower court development of the intangible rights doctrine "in its tracks"—and Congress "responded swiftly" with new § 1346. Skilling argued that the swift response was too vague to satisfy the Due Process Clause, however. "To satisfy due process, 'a penal statute [must] define the criminal offense [1] with sufficient definiteness that ordinary people can understand what conduct is prohibited and [2] in a manner that does not encourage arbitrary and discriminatory enforcement.' *Kolender* v. *Lawson*, 461 U. S. 352, 357 (1983)." Skilling claimed that § 1346 does not clearly define what behavior it prohibits, and its "standardless sweep allows policemen, prosecutors, and juries to pursue their personal predilections" and sought a judgment invalidating the statute.

"In urging invalidation of § 1346, Skilling swims against our case law's current, which requires us, if we can, to construe, not condemn, Congress' enactments." No court of appeals had ruled that § 1346 was void for vagueness, and the Supreme Court agreed that the better path was a narrowing construction. "First, we look to the doctrine developed in pre-*McNally* cases in an endeavor to ascertain the meaning of the phrase 'the intangible right of honest services.' Second, to preserve what Congress certainly intended the statute to cover, we pare that body of precedent down to its core: In the main, the pre-*McNally* cases involved fraudulent schemes to deprive another of honest services through bribes or kickbacks supplied by a third party who had not been deceived. Confined to these paramount applications, § 1346 presents no vagueness problem."

Based upon constitutional vagueness concerns and the rule of lenity in criminal cases, Justice Ginsburg rejected the government's suggestion that § 1346 also include cases where there is "undisclosed self-dealing by a public official or private employee—*i.e.*, the taking of official action by the employee that furthers his own undisclosed financial interests while purporting to act in the interests of those to whom he owes a fiduciary duty." Because Skilling's alleged misbehavior did not include charges that he received bribes or kickbacks, Justice Ginsburg reversed his § 1346 conviction and remanded to the lower courts to determine whether the other convictions could stand.

Justice Scalia (joined by **Justices Thomas** and **Kennedy**) concurred in the Court's judgment but would have declared § 1346 void for vagueness. He viewed the Court's surgery on § 1346 to be "not interpretation but invention," the equivalent of judicial crafting of a common law crime, which our nation's constitutional culture has long abjured. *E.g., United States v. Hudson*, 11 U.S. (7 Cranch) 32, 34 (1812). Additionally, Justice Scalia wondered what rewritten/narrowed § 1346 now covered: Does it apply to private officials, such as Skilling, at all? What would constitute a "bribe" or "kickback" (terms that do not appear in the statute but that are now interpolated into it by the majority) in future cases?

PROBLEM ON RULE OF LENITY

Problem 7–2. The Case of the Fraudulent Insurance Schemers. Alice Adams, the state Commissioner of Insurance, decides which insurance companies will receive contracts to insure certain state activities and buildings. Barbara Bashford heads the Squalid Insurance Company, which wants to secure contracting rights to insure all state buildings associated with public education. Carl Cox is a leader of the Cut-Taxes Party, which has won control of the state legislature and just elected a governor in the state. Adams switches parties to become a Cut-Taxer. In the process, Adams, Bashford, and Cox enter into an agreement whereby Adams would funnel all state education insurance contracts to Squalid Insurance, which would then pay $100,000 per year to a company partly owned by Adams and would contribute $500,000 a year to the Cut-Taxes Party.

Federal prosecutors uncover this scheme and indict Adams, Bashford, and Cox for violating § 1346. Each defendant argues that the statute does not apply to him or her after *Skilling*. Should any of the defendants prevail? Which one(s)?

B. THE RULE OF CONSTITUTIONAL AVOIDANCE

One justification for the rule of lenity arises from the constitutional notion that a legislature cannot penalize people who are wholly passive and unaware of any wrongdoing, based upon a vague criminal prohibition. See *Lambert v. California*, 355 U.S. 225 (1957); *Papachristou v. Jacksonville*, 405 U.S. 156 (1972). Assuming that the legislature is loathe to come close to enacting unconstitutional criminal statutes, courts will construe criminal penalties narrowly enough so that there is no question of the statute's constitutionality, as construed. Penal statutes, of course, are not the only ones that may venture close to the precipice beyond which a statute will run afoul of the Constitution, and the Supreme Court from time to time interprets non-penal statutes restrictively to avoid constitutional problems. Like the rule of lenity, this canon of construction has both defenders and detractors. Consider the following cases and the notes that follow.

STATUTORY PREFACE TO THE CATHOLIC BISHOP CASE

National Labor Relations Act of 1935, as amended in 1947, 1959, 1974 (codified in chapter 7 of 29 U.S.C.).

§ 152. Definitions

(2) The term "employer" includes any person acting as an agent of an employer, directly or indirectly, but shall not include the United States or any wholly owned Government corporation, or any Federal Reserve Bank, or any State or political subdivision thereof, or any person subject to the Railway Labor Act, * * * or any labor organization (other than when acting as an employer), or anyone acting in the capacity of officer or agent of such labor organization.

§ 169. Employees with religious convictions; payment of dues and fees

Any employee of a health care institution who is a member of and adheres to established and traditional tenets or teachings of a bona fide religion, body, or sect which has historically held conscientious objections to joining or financially supporting labor organizations shall not be required to join or financially support any labor organization as a condition of employment; except that such employee may be required, in lieu of periodic dues and initiation fees, to pay sums equal to such dues and initiation fees to a nonreligious charitable fund exempt from taxation * * * chosen by such employee from a list of at least three such funds, designated in a contract between such institution and a labor organization, or if the contract fails to designate such funds, then to any such fund chosen by the employee. * * *

NATIONAL LABOR RELATIONS BOARD V. CATHOLIC BISHOP OF CHICAGO

Supreme Court of the United States, 1979.
440 U.S. 490, 99 S.Ct. 1313, 59 L.Ed.2d 533.

THE CHIEF JUSTICE [BURGER] delivered the opinion for the Court.

[The National Labor Relations Board (NLRB) exercised jurisdiction over lay faculty members at two groups of Roman Catholic high schools, certified unions as bargaining agents for the teachers, and ordered the schools to cease and desist their refusals to bargain with these unions. The NLRB asserted jurisdiction based on its policy of declining jurisdiction only when schools are "completely religious," not "religiously associated." The NLRB found that the schools in the instant case were in the latter category, since secular as well as religious topics were taught in the schools.

[The Court of Appeals denied enforcement of the NLRB order, and the Supreme Court affirmed. The Court first held that the NLRB distinction between schools that were "completely religious" and those that were "religiously associated" was not a workable guide for the exercise of the NLRB's discretionary jurisdiction. Recognizing that rejection of this distinction meant that the Board could extend its jurisdiction to all church-operated schools, the Court stated that the Free Exercise and Establishment Clauses of the First Amendment might preclude such an exercise of jurisdiction.]

Although the respondents press their claims under the Religion Clauses, the question we consider first is whether Congress intended the Board to have jurisdiction over teachers in church-operated schools. In a number of cases the Court has heeded the essence of Mr. Chief Justice Marshall's admonition in *Murray v. The Schooner Charming Betsy*, 6 U.S. (2 Cranch) 64, 118 (1804), by holding that an Act of Congress ought not to be construed to violate the Constitution if any other possible construction remains available. Moreover, the Court has followed this policy in the interpretation of the Act now before us and related statutes.

In *Machinists v. Street*, 367 U.S. 740 (1961), for example, the Court considered claims that serious First Amendment questions would arise if the Railway Labor Act were construed to allow compulsory union dues to be used to support political candidates or causes not approved by some members. The Court looked to the language of the Act and the legislative history and concluded that they did not permit union dues to be used for such political purposes, thus avoiding "serious doubt of [the Act's] constitutionality." * * *

The values enshrined in the First Amendment plainly rank high "in the scale of our national values." In keeping with the Court's prudential policy it is incumbent on us to determine whether the Board's exercise of its jurisdiction here would give rise to serious constitutional questions. If so, we must first identify "the affirmative intention of the Congress clearly expressed" before concluding that the Act grants jurisdiction. [Quoting *McCulloch v. Sociedad Nacional de Marineros de Honduras*, 372 U.S. 10 (1963).]

In recent decisions involving aid to parochial schools we have recognized the critical and unique role of the teacher in fulfilling the mission of a church-operated school. What was said of the schools in *Lemon v. Kurtzman*, 403 U.S. 602, 617 (1971), is true of the schools in this case: "Religious authority necessarily pervades the school system." The key role played by teachers in such a school system has been the predicate for our conclusions that governmental aid channeled through teachers creates an impermissible risk of excessive governmental entanglement in the affairs of the church-operated schools. * * *

Only recently we again noted the importance of the teacher's function in a church school: "Whether the subject is 'remedial reading,' 'advanced reading,' or simply 'reading,' a teacher remains a teacher, and the danger that religious doctrine will become intertwined with secular instruction persists." *Meek v. Pittenger*, 421 U.S. 349, 370 (1975). Good intentions by government—or third parties—can surely no more avoid entanglement with the religious mission of the school in the setting of mandatory collective bargaining than in the well-motivated legislative efforts consented to by the church-operated schools which we found unacceptable in *Lemon* [and *Meek*.]

The Board argues that it can avoid excessive entanglement since it will resolve only factual issues such as whether an anti-union animus motivated an employer's action. But at this stage of our consideration we are not compelled to determine whether the entanglement is excessive as we would were we considering the constitutional issue. Rather, we make a narrow inquiry whether the exercise of the Board's jurisdiction presents a significant risk that the First Amendment will be infringed.

Moreover, it is already clear that the Board's actions will go beyond resolving factual issues. The Court of Appeals' opinion refers to charges of unfair labor practices filed against religious schools. The court observed that in those cases the schools had responded that their challenged actions were mandated by their religious creeds. The resolution of such charges by the Board, in many instances, will necessarily involve inquiry into the good faith of the position asserted by the clergy-administrators and its relationship to the school's religious mission. It is not only the conclusions that may be reached by the Board which may impinge on rights guaranteed by the Religion Clauses, but also the very process of inquiry leading to findings and conclusions.

The Board's exercise of jurisdiction will have at least one other impact on church-operated schools. The Board will be called upon to decide what are "terms and conditions of employment" and therefore mandatory subjects of bargaining. See 29 U.S.C. § 158(d). Although the Board has not interpreted that phrase as it relates to educational institutions, similar state provisions provide insight into the effect of mandatory bargaining. The Oregon Court of Appeals noted that "nearly everything that goes on in the schools affects teachers and is therefore arguably a 'condition of employment.' " *Springfield Educ. Ass'n. v. Springfield Sch. Dist. No. 19*, 547 P.2d 647, 650 (Or. App. 1976). [The introduction of the mandatory bargaining process itself represents an encroachment by the government into the autonomy of the school's management, which in these cases is pursuing religious purposes that will be compromised.]

The church-teacher relationship in a church-operated school differs from the employment relationship in a public or other nonreligious school. We see no escape from conflicts flowing from the Board's exercise of jurisdiction over teachers in church-operated schools and the consequent serious First Amendment questions that would follow. We therefore turn to an examination of the National Labor Relations Act to decide whether it must be read to confer jurisdiction that would in turn require a decision on the constitutional claims raised by respondents.

There is no clear expression of an affirmative intention of Congress that teachers in church-operated schools should be covered by the Act. Admittedly,

Congress defined the Board's jurisdiction in very broad terms; we must therefore examine the legislative history of the Act to determine whether Congress contemplated that the grant of jurisdiction would include teachers in such schools.

In enacting the National Labor Relations Act in 1935, Congress sought to protect the right of American workers to bargain collectively. The concern that was repeated throughout the debates was the need to assure workers the right to organize to counterbalance the collective activities of employers which had been authorized by the National Industrial Recovery Act. But congressional attention focused on employment in private industry and on industrial recovery. See, *e.g.*, 79 Cong. Rec. 7573 (1935) (remarks of Sen. Wagner).

Our examination of the statute and its legislative history indicates that Congress simply gave no consideration to church-operated schools. It is not without significance, however, that the Senate Committee on Education and Labor chose a college professor's dispute with the college as an example of employer-employee relations *not* covered by the Act. S. Rep. No. 573, 74th Cong., 1st Sess., 7 (1935).

Congress' next major consideration of the jurisdiction of the Board came during the passage of the Labor Management Relations Act of 1947—the Taft-Hartley Act. In that Act Congress amended the definition of "employer" in § 2 of the original Act to exclude nonprofit hospitals. 61 Stat. 137, 29 U.S.C. § 152(2) (1970 ed.). There was some discussion of the scope of the Board's jurisdiction but the consensus was that nonprofit institutions in general did not fall within the Board's jurisdiction because they did not affect commerce. [Citing various portions of legislative history.]

The most recent significant amendment to the Act was passed in 1974, removing the exemption of nonprofit hospitals. Pub. L. No. 93–360, 88 Stat. 395. The Board relies upon that amendment as showing that Congress approved the Board's exercise of jurisdiction over church-operated schools. A close examination of that legislative history, however, reveals nothing to indicate an affirmative intention that such schools be within the Board's jurisdiction. Since the Board did not assert jurisdiction over teachers in a church-operated school until after the 1974 amendment, nothing in the history of the amendment can be read as reflecting Congress' tacit approval of the Board's action.

During the debate there were expressions of concern about the effect of the bill on employees of religious hospitals whose religious beliefs would not permit them to join a union. 120 Cong. Rec. 12946, 16914 (1974). The result of those concerns was an amendment which reflects congressional sensitivity to First Amendment guarantees. [Chief Justice Burger quoted the text of 29 U.S.C. § 169, which is reproduced in the Statutory Preface].

The absence of an "affirmative intention of the Congress clearly expressed" fortifies our conclusion that Congress did not contemplate that the Board would require church-operated schools to grant recognition to unions as bargaining agents for their teachers.

The Board relies heavily upon *Associated Press v. NLRB*, 301 U.S. 103 (1937). There the Court held that the First Amendment was no bar to the application of the

Act to the Associated Press, an organization engaged in collecting information and news throughout the world and distributing it to its members. Perceiving nothing to suggest that application of the Act would infringe First Amendment guarantees of press freedoms, the Court sustained Board jurisdiction. Here, on the contrary, the record affords abundant evidence that the Board's exercise of jurisdiction over teachers in church-operated schools would implicate the guarantees of the Religion Clauses.

Accordingly, in the absence of a clear expression of Congress' intent to bring teachers in church-operated schools within the jurisdiction of the Board, we decline to construe the Act in a manner that could in turn call upon the Court to resolve difficult and sensitive questions arising out of the guarantees of the First Amendment Religion Clauses. [*Affirmed.*]

MR. JUSTICE BRENNAN, with whom MR. JUSTICE WHITE, MR. JUSTICE MARSHALL, and MR. JUSTICE BLACKMUN join, dissenting.

* * * The general principle of construing statutes to avoid unnecessary constitutional decisions is a well-settled and salutary one. The governing canon, however, is *not* that expressed by the Court today. The Court requires that there be a "clear expression of an affirmative intention of Congress" before it will bring within the coverage of a broadly worded regulatory statute certain persons whose coverage might raise constitutional questions. But those familiar with the legislative process know that explicit expressions of congressional intent in such broadly inclusive statutes are not commonplace. Thus, by strictly or loosely applying its requirement, the Court can virtually remake congressional enactments. * * *

The settled canon for construing statutes wherein constitutional questions may lurk was stated in *Machinists v. Street*, 367 U.S. 740 (1961), cited by the Court, *ante*:

> " 'When the validity of an act of the Congress is drawn in question, and even if a serious doubt of constitutionality is raised, it is a cardinal principle that this Court will first ascertain whether a construction of the statute is *fairly possible* by which the question may be avoided.' *Crowell v. Benson*, 285 U.S. 22, 62." *Id.*, at 749–750 (emphasis added).

This limitation to constructions that are "fairly possible" and "reasonable" acts as a brake against wholesale judicial dismemberment of congressional enactments. It confines the judiciary to its proper role in construing statutes, which is to interpret them so as to give effect to congressional intention. The Court's new "affirmative expression" rule releases that brake.

The interpretation of the National Labor Relations Act announced by the Court today is not "fairly possible." The Act's wording, its legislative history, and the Court's own precedents leave "the intention of the Congress * * * revealed too distinctly to permit us to ignore it because of mere misgivings as to power." Section 2(2) of the Act, 29 U.S.C. § 152(2), defines "employer" as:

> " * * * any person acting as an agent of an employer, directly or indirectly, *but shall not include* the United States or any wholly owned Government

corporation, or any Federal Reserve Bank, or any State or political subdivision thereof, or any person subject to the Railway Labor Act, as amended from time to time, or any labor organization (other than when acting as an employer), or anyone acting in the capacity of officer or agent of such labor organization." (Emphasis added.)

Thus, the Act covers all employers not within the eight express exceptions. The Court today substitutes amendment for construction to insert one more exception—for church-operated schools. This is a particularly transparent violation of the judicial role: The legislative history reveals that Congress itself considered and rejected a very similar amendment.

[The 1935 Act could not have been written more broadly, and the NLRB rejected efforts to except nonprofit employers from its reach.] The Hartley bill, which passed the House of Representatives in 1947, would have provided the exception the Court today writes into the statute:

"The term 'employer' * * * shall not include * * * any corporation, community chest, fund, or foundation organized and operated exclusively for *religious*, charitable, scientific, literary, or *educational* purposes, * * * no part of the net earnings of which inures to the benefit of any private shareholder or individual * * *." (Emphasis added.) H.R. 3020, 80th Cong., 1st Sess., § 2(2) (Apr. 18, 1947).

But the proposed exception was not enacted. The bill reported by the Senate Committee on Labor and Public Welfare did not contain the Hartley exception. Instead, the Senate proposed an exception limited to nonprofit hospitals, and passed the bill in that form. The Senate version was accepted by the House in conference, thus limiting the exception for nonprofit employers to nonprofit hospitals.

Even that limited exemption was ultimately repealed in 1974. In doing so, Congress confirmed the view of the Act expressed here: that it was intended to cover all employers—including nonprofit employers—unless expressly excluded, and that the 1947 amendment excluded only nonprofit hospitals. See H.R. Rep. No. 93–1051, p. 4 (1974); 120 Cong. Rec. 12938 (1974) (Senator Williams); 120 Cong. Rec. 16900 (1974) (Rep. Ashbrook). Moreover, it is significant that in considering the 1974 amendments, the Senate expressly rejected an amendment proposed by Senator Ervin that was analogous to the one the Court today creates—an amendment to exempt nonprofit hospitals operated by religious groups. Senator Cranston, floor manager of the Senate Committee bill and primary opponent of the proposed religious exception, explained:

"[S]uch an exception for religiously affiliated hospitals would seriously erode *the existing national policy which holds religiously affiliated institutions generally such as* proprietary nursing homes, residential communities, and *educational facilities to the same standards as their nonsectarian counterparts*." 120 Cong. Rec. 12957 (1974) (emphasis added).

See also *ibid.* (Sen. Javits); 120 Cong. Rec. 12957 (1974) (Sen. Williams).

In construing the Board's jurisdiction to exclude church-operated schools, therefore, the Court today is faithful to neither the statute's language nor its history. Moreover, it is also untrue to its own precedents. "This Court has consistently declared that in passing the National Labor Relations Act, Congress intended to and did vest in the Board the fullest *jurisdictional* breadth constitutionally permissible under the Commerce Clause." *NLRB v. Reliance Fuel Oil Corp.*, 371 U.S. 224, 226 (1963) (emphasis in original). As long as an employer is within the reach of Congress' power under the Commerce Clause—and no one doubts that respondents are—the Court has held him to be covered by the Act regardless of the nature of his activity. Indeed, *Associated Press v. NLRB*, 301 U.S. 103 (1937), construed the Act to cover editorial employees of a nonprofit news-gathering organization despite a claim—precisely parallel to that made here—that their inclusion rendered the Act in violation of the First Amendment. Today's opinion is simply unable to explain the grounds that distinguish that case from this one.

Thus, the available authority indicates that Congress intended to include—not exclude—lay teachers of church-operated schools. The Court does not counter this with evidence that Congress *did* intend an exception it never stated. Instead, despite the legislative history to the contrary, it construes the Act as excluding lay teachers only because Congress did not state explicitly that they were covered. In Mr. Justice Cardozo's words, this presses "avoidance of a difficulty * * * to the point of disingenuous evasion." *Moore Ice Cream Co. v. Rose*, 289 U.S. at 379.[11]

FAIR HOUSING AUTHORITY OF SAN FERNANDO VALLEY V. ROOMMATE.COM, LLC

United States Court of Appeals for the Ninth Circuit, 2012.
666 F.3d 1216.

KOZINSKI, CHIEF CIRCUIT COURT JUDGE:

There's no place like home. In the privacy of your own home, you can take off your coat, kick off your shoes, let your guard down and be completely yourself. While we usually share our homes only with friends and family, sometimes we need to take in a stranger to help pay the rent. When that happens, can the government limit whom we choose? Specifically, do the anti-discrimination provisions of the Fair Housing Act ("FHA") extend to the selection of roommates?

---

[11] Not even the Court's redrafting of the statute causes all First Amendment problems to disappear. The Court's opinion implies limitation of its exception to church-operated schools. That limitation is doubtless necessary since this Court has already rejected a more general exception for nonprofit organizations. See *Polish National Alliance v. NLRB*, 322 U.S. 643 (1944). But such an exemption, available only to church-operated schools, generates a possible Establishment Clause *question* of its own. *Walz v. Tax Comm'n*, 397 U.S. 664 (1970), does not put that question to rest, for in upholding the property tax exemption for churches there at issue, we emphasized that New York had "not singled out * * * churches as such; rather, it has granted exemption to all houses of religious worship within a broad class of property owned by nonprofit, quasi-public corporations * * *." Like the Court, "at this stage of [my] consideration [I am] not compelled to determine whether the [Establishment Clause problem] is [as significant] as [I] would were [I] considering the constitutional issue." It is enough to observe that no matter which way the Court turns in interpreting the Act, it cannot avoid constitutional questions.

Roommate.com, LLC ("Roommate") operates an internet-based business that helps roommates find each other. Roommate's website receives over 40,000 visits a day and roughly a million new postings for roommates are created each year. When users sign up, they must create a profile by answering a series of questions about their sex, sexual orientation and whether children will be living with them. An open-ended "Additional Comments" section lets users include information not prompted by the questionnaire. Users are asked to list their preferences for roommate characteristics, including sex, sexual orientation and familial status. Based on the profiles and preferences, Roommate matches users and provides them a list of housing-seekers or available rooms meeting their criteria. Users can also search available listings based on roommate characteristics, including sex, sexual orientation and familial status.

The Fair Housing Councils of San Fernando Valley and San Diego ("FHCs") sued Roommate in federal court, alleging that the website's questions requiring disclosure of sex, sexual orientation and familial status, and its sorting, steering and matching of users based on those characteristics, violate the Fair Housing Act ("FHA"), 42 U.S.C. § 3601 et seq., and the California Fair Employment and Housing Act ("FEHA"), Cal. Gov't Code § 12955. * * *

If the FHA extends to shared living situations, it's quite clear that what Roommate does amounts to a violation. The pivotal question is whether the FHA applies to roommates.

[I]   The FHA prohibits discrimination on the basis of "race, color, religion, sex, familial status, or national origin" in the "sale or rental *of a dwelling*." 42 U.S.C. § 3604(b) (emphasis added). The FHA also makes it illegal to

> make, print, or publish, or cause to be made, printed, or published any notice, statement, or advertisement, with respect to the sale or rental *of a dwelling* that indicates any preference, limitation, or discrimination based on race, color, religion, sex, handicap, familial status, or national origin, or an intention to make any such preference, limitation, or discrimination.

Id. § 3604(c) (emphasis added). The reach of the statute turns on the meaning of "dwelling."

The FHA defines "dwelling" as "any building, structure, or portion thereof which is occupied as, or designed or intended for occupancy as, a residence by one or more families." *Id.* § 3602(b). A dwelling is thus a living unit designed or intended for occupancy by a family, meaning that it ordinarily has the elements generally associated with a family residence: sleeping spaces, bathroom and kitchen facilities, and common areas, such as living rooms, dens and hallways.

It would be difficult, though not impossible, to divide a single-family house or apartment into separate "dwellings" for purposes of the statute. Is a "dwelling" a bedroom plus a right to access common areas? What if roommates share a bedroom? Could a "dwelling" be a bottom bunk and half an armoire? It makes practical sense to interpret "dwelling" as an independent living unit and stop the FHA at the front door.

There's no indication that Congress intended to interfere with personal relationships *inside* the home. Congress wanted to address the problem of landlords discriminating in the sale and rental of housing, which deprived protected classes of housing opportunities. But a business transaction between a tenant and landlord is quite different from an arrangement between two people sharing the same living space. We seriously doubt Congress meant the FHA to apply to the latter. Consider, for example, the FHA's prohibition against sex discrimination. Could Congress, in the 1960s, really have meant that women must accept men as roommates? Telling women they may not lawfully exclude men from the list of acceptable roommates would be controversial today; it would have been scandalous in the 1960s.

While it's possible to read dwelling to mean sub-parts of a home or an apartment, doing so leads to awkward results. And applying the FHA to the selection of roommates almost certainly leads to results that defy mores prevalent when the statute was passed. Nonetheless, this interpretation is not wholly implausible and we would normally consider adopting it, given that the FHA is a remedial statute that we construe broadly. Therefore, we turn to constitutional concerns, which provide strong countervailing considerations.

[II] The Supreme Court has recognized that "the freedom to enter into and carry on certain intimate or private relationships is a fundamental element of liberty protected by the Bill of Rights." *Bd. of Dirs. of Rotary Int'l v. Rotary Club of Duarte*, 481 U.S. 537, 545 (1987). "[C]hoices to enter into and maintain certain intimate human relationships must be secured against undue intrusion by the State because of the role of such relationships in safeguarding the individual freedom that is central to our constitutional scheme." *Roberts v. U.S. Jaycees*, 468 U.S. 609, 617–18 (1984). Courts have extended the right of intimate association to marriage, child bearing, child rearing and cohabitation with relatives. *Id.* While the right protects only "highly personal relationships," *IDK, Inc. v. Clark Cnty.*, 836 F.2d 1185, 1193 (9th Cir. 1988) (quoting *Roberts*, 468 U.S. at 618), the right isn't restricted exclusively to family, *Bd. of Dirs. of Rotary Int'l*, 481 U.S. at 545. The right to association also implies a right *not* to associate. *Roberts*, 468 U.S. at 623.

To determine whether a particular relationship is protected by the right to intimate association we look to "size, purpose, selectivity, and whether others are excluded from critical aspects of the relationship." *Bd. of Dirs. of Rotary Int'l*, 481 U.S. at 546. The roommate relationship easily qualifies: People generally have very few roommates; they are selective in choosing roommates; and non-roommates are excluded from the critical aspects of the relationship, such as using the living spaces. Aside from immediate family or a romantic partner, it's hard to imagine a relationship more intimate than that between roommates, who share living rooms, dining rooms, kitchens, bathrooms, even bedrooms.

Because of a roommate's unfettered access to the home, choosing a roommate implicates significant privacy and safety considerations. The home is the center of our private lives. Roommates note our comings and goings, observe whom we bring back at night, hear what songs we sing in the shower, see us in various stages of undress and learn intimate details most of us prefer to keep private. Roommates also have access to our physical belongings and to our person. As the Supreme

Court recognized, "[w]e are at our most vulnerable when we are asleep because we cannot monitor our own safety or the security of our belongings." *Minnesota v. Olson*, 495 U.S. 91, 99 (1990). Taking on a roommate means giving him full access to the space where we are most vulnerable.

Equally important, we are fully exposed to a roommate's belongings, activities, habits, proclivities and way of life. This could include matter we find offensive (pornography, religious materials, political propaganda); dangerous (tobacco, drugs, firearms); annoying (jazz, perfume, frequent overnight visitors, furry pets); habits that are incompatible with our lifestyle (early risers, messy cooks, bathroom hogs, clothing borrowers). When you invite others to share your living quarters, you risk becoming a suspect in whatever illegal activities they engage in. Government regulation of an individual's ability to pick a roommate thus intrudes into the home, which "is entitled to special protection as the center of the private lives of our people." *Minnesota v. Carter*, 525 U.S. 83, 99 (1998) (Kennedy, J., concurring). "Liberty protects the person from unwarranted government intrusions into a dwelling or other private places. In our tradition the State is not omnipresent in the home." *Lawrence v. Texas*, 539 U.S. 558, 562 (2003). Holding that the FHA applies inside a home or apartment would allow the government to restrict our ability to choose roommates compatible with our lifestyles. This would be a serious invasion of privacy, autonomy and security.

For example, women will often look for female roommates because of modesty or security concerns. As roommates often share bathrooms and common areas, a girl may not want to walk around in her towel in front of a boy. She might also worry about unwanted sexual advances or becoming romantically involved with someone she must count on to pay the rent.

An orthodox Jew may want a roommate with similar beliefs and dietary restrictions, so he won't have to worry about finding honey-baked ham in the refrigerator next to the potato latkes. Non-Jewish roommates may not understand or faithfully follow all of the culinary rules, like the use of different silverware for dairy and meat products, or the prohibition against warming non-kosher food in a kosher microwave. Taking away the ability to choose roommates with similar dietary restrictions and religious convictions will substantially burden the observant Jew's ability to live his life and practice his religion faithfully. The same is true of individuals of other faiths that call for dietary restrictions or rituals inside the home.

The U.S. Department of Housing and Urban Development recently dismissed a complaint against a young woman for advertising, "I am looking for a female christian roommate," on her church bulletin board. In its Determination of No Reasonable Cause, HUD explained that "in light of the facts provided and after assessing the unique context of the advertisement and the roommate relationship involved . . . the Department defers to Constitutional considerations in reaching its conclusions." *Fair Hous. Ctr. of W. Mich. v. Tricia*, No. 05–10–1738–8 (Oct. 28, 2010) (Determination of No Reasonable Cause).

It's a "well-established principle that statutes will be interpreted to avoid constitutional difficulties." *Frisby v. Schultz*, 487 U.S. 474, 483 (1988). "[W]here an otherwise acceptable construction of a statute would raise serious constitutional problems, the Court will construe the statute to avoid such problems unless such construction is plainly contrary to the intent of Congress." *Pub. Citizen v. U.S. Dep't of Justice*, 491 U.S. 440, 466 (1989) (internal quotation marks omitted). Because the FHA can reasonably be read either to include or exclude shared living arrangements, we can and must choose the construction that avoids raising constitutional concerns. See *INS v. St. Cyr*, 533 U.S. 289, 299–300 (2001) ("[I]f an otherwise acceptable construction of a statute would raise serious constitutional problems, and where an alternative interpretation of the statute is fairly possible, we are obligated to construe the statute to avoid such problems.") (internal citation and quotations marks omitted). Reading "dwelling" to mean an independent housing unit is a fair interpretation of the text and consistent with congressional intent. Because the construction of "dwelling" to include shared living units raises substantial constitutional concerns, we adopt the narrower construction that excludes roommate selection from the reach of the FHA. * * *

[IV] The same constitutional concerns over the right to intimate association would arise if the California Fair Employment and Housing Act ("FEHA") were applied to roommates. Accordingly, we interpret "housing accommodation" in section 12955(c) of the FEHA to exclude the sharing of living units. Similarly to how the FHA defines "dwelling," the FEHA defines "housing accommodation" as "any building, structure, or portion thereof that is occupied as, or intended for occupancy as, a residence by one or more families." Cal. Gov't Code § 12927(d). This ambiguous definition allows us to apply the canon of constitutional avoidance to find that the FEHA does not reach the selection of roommates.

In a 1995 amendment, the FEHA carved out from the definition of discrimination "the use of words stating or tending to imply that the housing being advertised is available only to persons of one sex," "[w]here the sharing of living areas in a single dwelling unit is involved." Cal. Gov. Code § 12927(c)(2)(B). The concurrence infers from this 1995 exemption that the statute as passed in 1974 must have covered roommates. But the acts of a subsequent legislature tell us nothing definitive about the meaning of laws adopted by an earlier legislature. See *Pension Benefit Guar. Corp. v. LTV Corp.*, 496 U.S. 633, 650 (1990) ("[S]ubsequent legislative history is a hazardous basis for inferring the intent of an earlier Congress." (internal quotation marks omitted)); see also *Sullivan v. Finkelstein*, 496 U.S. 617, 632 (1990) (Scalia, J., concurring) ("Arguments based on subsequent legislative history . . . should not be taken seriously, not even in a footnote."). The 1995 legislature may have been uncertain about whether the statute, as passed decades earlier, covered roommates, and wanted to remove any doubt that roommates could select each other by sex. But the amendment can shed no light on the meaning of "housing accommodation" in the FEHA, a statutory phrase it does not modify or reference.

Nothing in the language of the statute provides that a "housing accommodation" includes shared living quarters. Under the canon of constitutional avoidance, the interpretation of the statute need not be the best reading, so long as it's "fairly possible." *St. Cyr*, 533 U.S. at 299–300. It is "fairly possible" that the statute does not apply to roommates. Interpreting it as excluding roommates avoids a ruling on a difficult and unexplored constitutional issue.

The concurrence also relies on a FEHC decision, but the FEHC had no authority to address the underlying constitutional problems raised by the FEHA, and thus had no reason to consider the constitutional avoidance canon: "Whether it is sound policy to ban discrimination in the selection of roommates, and whether such a policy implicates constitutional rights of privacy or association, are not questions for this decision to resolve. Those are issues for the Legislature and the courts, respectively, to decide." *Dep't of Fair Emp't & Hous. v. Larrick*, FEHC Dec. No. 98–12, (July 22, 1998). We, on the other hand, have a duty to consider constitutional concerns and to adopt an interpretation that avoids ruling on the constitutionality of a statute, if we can fairly do so. * * *

Because precluding individuals from selecting roommates based on their sex, sexual orientation and familial status raises substantial constitutional concerns, we interpret the FHA and FEHA as not applying to the sharing of living units. Therefore, we hold that Roommate's prompting, sorting and publishing of information to facilitate roommate selection is not forbidden by the FHA or FEHA. * * *

IKUTA, CIRCUIT JUDGE, concurring and dissenting:

* * * I must respectfully dissent from the majority's decision to "apply the canon of constitutional avoidance to find that FEHA does not reach the selection of roommates." The interpretive canon of constitutional avoidance directs that "where an otherwise acceptable construction of a statute would raise serious constitutional problems, the Court will construe the statute to avoid such problems." *Edward J. DeBartolo Corp. v. Fl. Gulf Coast Bldg. & Constr. Trades Council*, 485 U.S. 568, 575 (1988). But this interpretive tool can be used only when a statute is ambiguous. It does not give federal courts the power to "rewrite a state law to conform it to constitutional requirements." *Virginia v. Am. Booksellers Ass'n, Inc.*, 484 U.S. 383, 397 (1988).

In this case, FEHA's language and its application by the California agency tasked with interpreting it suggest that FEHA is "unambiguous on the point under consideration here." See *Salinas v. United States*, 522 U.S. 52, 60 (1997). FEHA expressly defines "discrimination" as not including "the use of words stating or tending to imply that the housing being advertised is available only to persons of one sex," in a situation "[w]here the sharing of living areas in a single dwelling unit is involved." Cal. Gov't. Code § 12927(c)(2)(B). This language is not in the FHA. Because a statute's "mention of [one example] implies the exclusion of others not mentioned," *United Dominion Indus., Inc. v. United States*, 532 U.S. 822, 836 (2001), FEHA's definition of "discrimination" in § 12927(c)(2)(B) expresses the state legislature's intent to exempt sex-specific advertisements for shared living units in a single dwelling from the restrictions of FEHA, but not exempt advertisements that discriminate on the basis of other protected characteristics, such as race or religion.

This plain-language reading of § 12927(c)(2)(B) is confirmed by the decision of the California Fair Employment and Housing Commission in *Dep't of Fair Emp't and Housing v. Larrick*, FEHC Dec. No. 98–12, (July 22, 1998). *Larrick* involved two roommates who decided not to rent to a potential third roommate because she was black. The Commission held that the "plain language" of FEHA applied to this shared living situation and prohibited the two roommates "from rejecting an applicant on the basis of race and color." In arriving at this conclusion, the Commission stated that none of FEHA's exceptions were applicable, specifically noting that § 12927(c)(2)(B) "allow[s] sex-specific (but not race-specific) advertisements for single dwellings with shared living areas."

Because FEHA (unlike the FHA) is unambiguous regarding its applicability to shared living arrangements, the majority cannot interpret FEHA in a way to avoid the constitutional problems that may arise if the act is applied to bar advertisements for shared living arrangements that discriminate on the basis of protected characteristics such as race or religion. The constitutionality of FEHA's applicability to such shared living arrangements is both novel and difficult. Given that neither the Fair Housing Councils nor Roommate addressed this issue in their briefs, I would remand this issue to allow the district court to hear from the parties and rule on this issue in the first instance. * * *

NOTES ON THE "AVOIDANCE CANON"

1. *Different Ways of Framing the Avoidance Canon.* As the debate in *Catholic Bishop* indicates, there are several ways to express this canon:[30] When one interpretation of an ambiguous statute would be unconstitutional, choose another one that would pass constitutional muster. *Murray v. The Schooner Charming Betsy*, 6 U.S. (2 Cranch) 64 (1804). When one interpretation would raise serious constitutional problems, choose the one that would not. *United States ex rel. Attorney General v. Delaware & Hudson Co.*, 213 U.S. 366 (1909); cf. *Ex parte Bollman*, 8 U.S. (4 Cranch) 75 (1807). When one interpretation presents constitutional difficulties, do not impose it unless there has been an affirmative indication from Congress that it is required. *McCulloch v. Sociedad Nacional de Marineros de Honduras*, 372 U.S. 10 (1963).

The most aggressive way of framing the avoidance canon is *McCulloch*, which Chief Justice Burger invokes in *Catholic Bishop*. The dissenters assail the Chief Justice for this, and the *McCulloch* language is rarely applied today. But neither is the *Charming Betsy* language. Generally, the avoidance canon today follows the *Delaware & Hudson* language.

2. *What Is a "Serious" or "Substantial" Constitutional Problem?* The Ninth Circuit in *Roommate.com* follows the *Delaware & Hudson* approach, requiring courts to interpret a statute in a manner that avoids serious or substantial constitutional problems. How does a court know when a constitutional question is serious or substantial? Does it depend on the fundamental nature of the constitutional provision in question? The First Amendment is implicated in both *Catholic Bishops* and

---

[30] For useful introductions, see Trevor Morrison, *Constitutional Avoidance in the Executive Branch*, 106 Colum. L. Rev. 1189 (2006); John Copeland Nagle, Delaware & Hudson *Revisited*, 72 Notre Dame L. Rev. 1495 (1997); Adrian Vermeule, *Saving Constructions*, 85 Geo. L.J. 1945 (1997).

Roommate.com; would the avoidance canon be presumptively less applicable if a statute implicated the excessive bail provision of the Eighth Amendment?

Alternatively, does the seriousness of a constitutional problem depend on the likelihood that there has been a constitutional violation? The court in *Roommate.com* appears quite confident that interpreting "dwelling" to include roommates would violate privacy-based constitutional rights. What if a court believes a certain interpretation would raise constitutional questions but this interpretation would nonetheless be constitutional? Should a court invoke constitutional avoidance even if it would uphold the challenged interpretation as constitutional anyway?

3.   *Values Underlying the Avoidance Canon.* There are a number of values the avoidance doctrine might serve, such as avoiding unnecessary constitutional holdings or advisory opinions by the Court. Consider three potentially important values. First, it may be a *rule of thumb for ascertaining legislative intent.* The avoidance interpreter assumes that the legislature would *not* have wanted to press constitutional limits. Fred Schauer, Ashwander *Revisited*, 1995 Sup. Ct. Rev. 71, finds such an implicit legislative intent theory most implausible. The assumption rests upon no evidence of actual legislative intent. In the average case, why shouldn't the enacting legislature prefer that its work product be given full force—and if it's unconstitutional the Court should say so openly so that there can be a full-blown constitutional controversy? See Jerry Mashaw, *Greed, Chaos, and Governance: Using Public Choice Theory to Improve Public Law* 105 (1997). Consider *Catholic Bishop*: Is it plausible that Congress would have wanted the Court to trim back the statute in the way that it did?

A second value of the avoidance canon is that it might provide a low-salience mechanism for giving effect to what Larry Sager calls "*underenforced constitutional norms.*"[31] For instance, judges are loathe to strike down immigration statutes, because of either the plenary powers idea or institutional competence concerns. But as Hiroshi Motomura has identified, while judges may be unwilling to close off congressional options through constitutional review, they will give effect to due process and free speech norms through narrowing constructions.[32] And so the norm is vindicated—but Congress can (re)assert a broader result after deliberation and debate over a statutory amendment that clearly overrides the norm-adhering interpretation.

Consider ways in which this idea might apply to *Catholic Bishop*. Labor law has been another area where the avoidance canon has been especially active in the Supreme Court's jurisprudence. See the cases discussed in *Catholic Bishop*, as well as more recent cases such as *Edward J. DeBartolo Corp. v. Fla. Gulf Coast Building & Constr. Trades Council*, 485 U.S. 568, 575 (1988).

---

[31] William Eskridge Jr. & Philip Frickey, *Quasi-Constitutional Law: Clear Statement Rules as Constitutional Lawmaking*, 45 Vand. L. Rev. 593 (1992), drawing from Lawrence Sager, *Fair Measure: The Legal Status of Underenforced Constitutional Norms*, 91 Harv. L. Rev. 1212 (1978). See also Neal Katyal, *Judges as Advicegivers*, 50 Stan. L. Rev. 1709 (1998); Ronald Krotoszynski, Jr., *Constitutional Flares: On Judges, Legislatures, And Dialogue*, 83 Minn. L. Rev. 1 (1998); Ernest Young, *Constitutional Avoidance, Resistance Norms, and the Preservation of Judicial Review*, 78 Tex. L. Rev. 1549, 1585–87 (2000).

[32] Hiroshi Motomura, *Immigration Law After a Century of Plenary Power: Phantom Constitutional Norms and Statutory Interpretation*, 100 Yale L.J. 545, 561–75 (1990). There are good recent examples of Professor Motomura's thesis, such as *Zadvydas v. Davis*, 533 U.S. 678, 696–99 (2001); *INS v. St. Cyr*, 533 U.S. 289 (2001).

A third value for the avoidance canon is suggested by Professor Bickel's theory of the *passive virtues*.[33] One way that courts conserve their institutional capital is by techniques of avoidance. Standard techniques are for the Court to divest itself of constitutional cases whose resolution is premature by dismissing the complaint on procedural grounds such as standing, ripeness, etc. The avoidance canon represents a middle ground between pure passive virtues and constitutional invalidation. That middle ground allows the Court to slow down a political process that is moving too hastily and overriding human rights, but without incurring the full wrath of a political process that doesn't like to be thwarted. As Philip Frickey has argued, this theory best explains several cases where the Warren Court impeded McCarthy-era initiatives, but without creating a full-blown constitutional crisis.[34] How might this theory apply to *Catholic Bishop*, which was handed down a generation later, and by a more conservative majority?

Which of these three values, if any, is operative in *Roommate.com*? The presumption that the California legislature intends to enact constitutional legislation? Giving effect to the underenforced constitutional norm of privacy? Avoiding conflict with other branches of government?

4. *Constitutional Avoidance and Administrative Agencies.* Judge Ikuta's opinion in *Roommate.com* (concurring and dissenting) relies on an administrative interpretation of the FEHA in determining that the statute is not ambiguous and therefore the canon of constitutional avoidance is inapplicable. Judge Kozinski rejects this line of reasoning by arguing that the California administrative agency "had no authority to address the underlying constitutional problems raised by the FEHA, and thus had no reason to consider the constitutional avoidance canon." Do administrative agencies have no duty to consider constitutional implications when interpreting a statute? If a statute can be interpreted in more than one way, why shouldn't an agency adopt the least constitutionally problematic interpretation?

5. *Criticisms of the Avoidance Canon.* Perhaps the leading critique of the avoidance canon remains Judge Henry Friendly, *Mr. Justice Frankfurter and the Reading of Statutes*, in *Benchmarks* 211–12 (1967):

> Although questioning the doctrine of construction to avoid constitutional doubts is rather like challenging Holy Writ, the rule has always seemed to me to have almost as many dangers as advantages. For one thing, it is one of those rules that courts apply when they want and conveniently forget when they don't—some, perhaps, would consider that to be a virtue. * * * Some considerations advanced in its favor, such as the awesome consequences of "a decree of unconstitutionality," overlook that if the Court finds the more likely construction to be unconstitutional, another means of rescue—the principle of construing to avoid unconstitutionality—will be at hand. The strongest basis for the rule is thus that the Supreme Court ought not to indulge in what, if adverse, is likely to be only a constitutional advisory opinion. While there is force in this, the rule of "construing" to avoid constitutional doubts should, in

---

[33] Alexander Bickel, *The Least Dangerous Branch: The Supreme Court at the Bar of Politics* 156–69 (1962). Bickel's ideas about statutory interpretation are set forth in Alexander Bickel & Harry Wellington, *Legislative Purpose and the Judicial Process: The* Lincoln Mills *Case*, 71 Harv. L. Rev. 1 (1957).

[34] Philip Frickey, *Getting from Joe to Gene (McCarthy): The Avoidance Canon, Legal Process Theory, and Narrowing Statutory Interpretation in the Early Warren Court*, 93 Cal. L. Rev. 397 (2005).

my view, be confined to cases where the doubt is exceedingly real. Otherwise this rule, whether it be denominated one of statutory interpretation or, more accurately, of constitutional adjudication—still more accurately, of constitutional nonadjudication—is likely to become one of evisceration and tergiversation.

Judge Friendly's charge is that the avoidance canon will be an occasion for *stealth judicial activism*, which is both anti-democratic and unhealthy for the judiciary. Accord, Judge Richard Posner, *The Federal Courts: Crisis and Reform* 285 (1985); Lisa Kloppenberg, *Avoiding Constitutional Questions*, 35 B.C. L. Rev. 1003 (1994); John Manning, *The Nondelegation Doctrine as a Canon of Avoidance*, 2000 Sup. Ct. Rev. 223; John Nagle, Delaware & Hudson *Revisited*, 72 Notre Dame L. Rev. 1495 (1997).

A corollary to Judge Friendly's charge is that the avoidance canon will be applied unpredictably. Even in the immigration area, where it has made regular appearances in Supreme Court opinions, this charge has much weight. For an example of a case where there were strong constitutional doubts and less than clear statutory language, yet the Court refused to apply this canon (or the rule of lenity, which was also applicable), see *Almendarez-Torres v. United States*, 523 U.S. 224 (1998). See also *Rust v. Sullivan*, 500 U.S. 173 (1991).

6. *Avoiding Avoidance When Presented with Two Distinct Constitutional Rationales.* In *National Federation of Independent Business v. Sebelius*, 132 S.Ct. 2566 (2012), the Supreme Court reviewed constitutional challenges to the Patient Protection and Affordable Care Act. Chief Justice Roberts authored the pivotal opinion upholding the Act's individual mandate, which requires most Americans to maintain minimum essential health care coverage or else make a "shared responsibility" payment to the federal government that is assessed and collected by the Internal Revenue Service.

The Obama Administration sought to sustain the constitutionality of this provision on several different grounds. The Chief Justice concluded first, writing for himself, that the individual mandate was not a valid exercise of Congress's powers under the Commerce Clause or the Necessary and Proper Clause. He then delivered the opinion of the Court upholding the individual mandate as within Congress's power under the Taxing Clause. The Chief Justice concluded, for himself and Justices Ginsburg, Breyer, Sotomayor, and Kagan, that construing the provision as a tax was "fairly possible" even if this was not the "most natural interpretation" of the mandate.

Why was it necessary for Chief Justice Roberts to analyze and reject the Government's commerce power argument—and in doing so add his voice to the conclusion reached by dissenting Justices Scalia, Kennedy, Thomas, and Alito—given that the Court ultimately sustained the individual mandate as constitutional on an independently sufficient ground? The Chief Justice explained his position as follows: "[T]he statute reads more naturally as a command to buy insurance than as a tax, and I would uphold it as a command if the Constitution allowed it. It is only because the Commerce Clause does not authorize such a command that it is necessary to reach the taxing power question. And it is only because we have a duty to construe a statute to save it, if fairly possible, that [the individual mandate] can be interpreted as a tax. Without deciding the Commerce Clause question, I would find no basis for such a saving construction."

Has Chief Justice Roberts added a new dimension to the canon of constitutional avoidance? The Court typically applies the avoidance canon in order to *avoid* expressing a position on the meaning of the Constitution except insofar as is necessary to determine the outcome of the case. That is how the Supreme Court applied the canon in *Catholic Bishop* and how the Ninth Circuit applied it in *Roommate.com.* Is the traditional approach now qualified when a party offers two or more rationales for sustaining a law against constitutional challenge? Or only when one of the rationales is plainly the most natural one, triggering an "unavoidable" constitutional analysis? Should the parties be asked specifically to address the question of what qualifies as the most natural construction? How much weight should a reviewing court accord to the government's position on this question, as explained in its brief or at oral argument?

PROBLEM ON THE AVOIDANCE CANON

Problem 7–3. Use of Sampling as Part of the Census. Article I, § 2, cl. 3 of the Constitution apportions Representatives among the states "according to their respective Numbers" and requires that there be an "Enumeration" of the "Numbers" of people in the various states every ten years, "in such Manner as they [Congress] shall by Law direct." The Census Act, 13 U.S.C. § 1 et seq., delegates the responsibility for this endeavor to the Commerce Department. Prior to 1976, the Census Bureau's practice, required by statute before that date, was never to use sampling techniques for apportionment purposes.

Congress revised the Census Act in 1976, adding two relevant provisions. Section 141(a), as rewritten in 1976, states: "The Secretary shall * * * take a decennial census of the population * * * in such form and content as he may determine, including the use of sampling procedures and special surveys." Section 195 says: "Except for the determination of population for purposes of apportionment of Representatives in Congress among the several States, the Secretary shall, if he considers it feasible, authorize the use of the statistical method known as 'sampling' in carrying out the provisions of this title." For the 2000 Census, the Commerce Department proposed to supplement its survey with statistical sampling techniques to cure what had been documented as an "undercount" of the population, especially of racial minorities and poor people.

The Department's proposed use of sampling is challenged as unlawful under the 1976 Census Act and the Census Clause of Article I. You are the district court judge deciding the case. Should you (or can you) avoid the constitutional question through a construction of the Census Act? Is there a serious and substantial problem as to whether the "Enumeration" requirement would be satisfied if the Department used statistical sampling as a supplement—not a substitute—for actual counting? See *Dep't of Commerce v. U.S. House of Representatives*, 525 U.S. 316 (1999).

NOTE ON SEVERABILITY

When a provision in a statute is unconstitutional, should the court treat the remainder of the statute as good law, or declare the entire statute invalid? This is a question of *severability.* When the statute contains an express severability clause (instructing courts to save the remainder of the statute) or an express nonseverability clause, the issue would appear to be easy. Nonetheless, because such clauses are sometimes inserted as boilerplate in bills without much thought given to their effects, courts sometimes struggle with whether the clause should be given its full textual meaning if that seems inconsistent with the probable legislative intent concerning the particular severability issue.[35]

Often the statute is silent on the question. In that circumstance, "[u]nless it is evident that the Legislature would not have enacted those provisions which are within its power, independently of that which is not, the invalid part may be dropped if what is left is fully operative as a law." *Alaska Airlines, Inc. v. Brock*, 480 U.S. 678, 684 (1987).

C. THE NEW FEDERALISM CANONS

The Supreme Court in the 1980s and early 1990s created or clarified "clear statement rules" that reflect constitutional norms of federalism.[36] See *Pennhurst State Sch. & Hosp. v. Halderman*, 451 U.S. 1 (1981) (conditions attached to federal funding for state programs must be clear); *Atascadero State Hosp. v. Scanlon*, 473 U.S. 234 (1985) (super-strong clear statement rule against congressional abrogation of state Eleventh Amendment immunity from suit in federal courts).[37] The following case is the most dramatic example to date of the Court's activity in protecting state sovereignty through the use of canons.

As background, note that in *Maryland v. Wirtz*, 392 U.S. 183 (1968), the Court upheld the application of the Fair Labor Standards Act's minimum wage provisions to state hospital and school employees, rejecting the claim that the Constitution forbids such direct federal regulation of important state functions. Then, in *National League of Cities v. Usery*, 426 U.S. 833 (1976), by a 5–4 vote, the Court overruled *Wirtz* and refused to apply the FLSA's minimum wage and maximum hours provisions to many state and municipal employees. *National League of Cities* then met its own apparent demise in *Garcia v. San Antonio Metropolitan Transit Authority*, 469 U.S. 528 (1985), another 5–4 case, which explicitly overruled the nine-year-old precedent. As the next case demonstrates, what the Court taketh away as constitutional protection it can revive as canonical interpretive protection.

GREGORY V. ASHCROFT
Supreme Court of the United States, 1991.
501 U.S. 452, 111 S.Ct. 2395, 115 L.Ed.2d 410.

JUSTICE O'CONNOR delivered the opinion of the Court.

[It is a prima facie violation of the federal Age Discrimination in Employment Act (ADEA), 29 U.S.C. §§ 621–34, for an "employer" covered by the Act to specify a mandatory retirement age for "employees" over forty years of age who are covered by the Act. State and local governments are "employers" covered by the ADEA. In

---

[35] For excellent critical analyses of the Court's severability jurisprudence, see Michael Shumsky, *Severability, Inseverability, and the Rule of Law*, 41 Harv. J. Leg. 227 (2004); Comment, Israel Friedman, *Inseverability Clauses in Statutes*, 64 U. Chi. L. Rev. 903 (1997)

[36] Recall our terminology: a "clear statement rule" requires that a statute be interpreted a certain way unless the contrary interpretation is clearly required by statutory text; a "super-strong clear statement rule" requires that the statutory text targets the issue unmistakably, especially through specific language.

[37] See generally William Eskridge Jr. & Philip Frickey, *Quasi-Constitutional Law: Clear Statement Rules as Constitutional Lawmaking*, 45 Vand. L. Rev. 593 (1992), surveying and analyzing the Court's aggressive deployment of these federalism-inspired super-strong clear statement rules.

this case, the Missouri Constitution provided a mandatory retirement age of seventy for most state judges. Petitioners were state judges seeking to obtain a declaration that the mandatory retirement age violates the ADEA. The district court dismissed the action, concluding that the judges were "appointees on the policymaking level," a category of state officials excluded from the definition of "employees" covered by the Act. The Court of Appeals affirmed. What follows is Part II of Justice O'Connor's opinion.]

[IIA]   As every schoolchild learns, our Constitution establishes a system of dual sovereignty between the States and the Federal Government. This Court also has recognized this fundamental principle. In *Tafflin v. Levitt*, 493 U.S. 455, 458 (1990), "[w]e beg[a]n with the axiom that, under our federal system, the States possess sovereignty concurrent with that of the Federal Government, subject only to limitations imposed by the Supremacy Clause." Over 120 years ago, the Court described the constitutional scheme of dual sovereigns:

> " '[T]he people of each State compose a State, having its own government, and endowed with all the functions essential to separate and independent existence,' . . . '[W]ithout the States in union, there could be no such political body as the United States.' Not only, therefore, can there be no loss of separate and independent autonomy to the States, through their union under the Constitution, but it may be not unreasonably said that the preservation of the States, and the maintenance of their governments, are as much within the design and care of the Constitution as the preservation of the Union and the maintenance of the National government. The Constitution, in all its provisions, looks to an indestructible Union, composed of indestructible States." *Texas v. White*, 74 U.S. (7 Wall.) 700, 725 (1869), quoting *Lane County v. Oregon*, 74 U.S. (7 Wall.) 71, 76 (1869).

The Constitution created a Federal Government of limited powers. "The powers not delegated to the United States by the Constitution, nor prohibited by it to the States, are reserved to the States respectively, or to the people." U.S. Const. amend. X. The States thus retain substantial sovereign authority under our constitutional system. As James Madison put it:

> "The powers delegated by the proposed Constitution to the federal government are few and defined. Those which are to remain in the State governments are numerous and indefinite. . . . The powers reserved to the several States will extend to all the objects which, in the ordinary course of affairs, concern the lives, liberties, and properties of the people, and the internal order, improvement, and prosperity of the State." The Federalist No. 45, 292–293 (C. Rossiter ed. 1961).

This federalist structure of joint sovereigns preserves to the people numerous advantages. It assures a decentralized government that will be more sensitive to the diverse needs of a heterogenous society; it increases opportunity for citizen involvement in democratic processes; it allows for more innovation and experimentation in government; and it makes government more responsive by putting the States in competition for a mobile citizenry.

Perhaps the principal benefit of the federalist system is a check on abuses of government power. "The 'constitutionally mandated balance of power' between the States and the Federal Government was adopted by the Framers to ensure the protection of 'our fundamental liberties.'" *Atascadero State Hosp. v. Scanlon*, 473 U.S. 234, 242 (1985), quoting *Garcia v. San Antonio Metro. Transit Auth.*, 469 U.S. 528, 572 (1985) (Powell, J., dissenting). Just as the separation and independence of the coordinate Branches of the Federal Government serves to prevent the accumulation of excessive power in any one Branch, a healthy balance of power between the States and the Federal Government will reduce the risk of tyranny and abuse from either front. Alexander Hamilton explained to the people of New York, perhaps optimistically, that the new federalist system would suppress completely "the attempts of the government to establish a tyranny":

> "[I]n a confederacy the people, without exaggeration, may be said to be entirely the masters of their own fate. Power being almost always the rival of power, the general government will at all times stand ready to check usurpations of the state governments, and these will have the same disposition towards the general government. The people, by throwing themselves into either scale, will infallibly make it preponderate. If their rights are invaded by either, they can make use of the other as the instrument of redress." The Federalist No. 28, 180–181 (C. Rossiter ed. 1961).

James Madison made much the same point:

> "In a single republic, all the power surrendered by the people is submitted to the administration of a single government; and the usurpations are guarded against by a division of the government into distinct and separate departments. In the compound republic of America, the power surrendered by the people is first divided between two distinct governments, and then the portion allotted to each subdivided among distinct and separate departments. Hence a double security arises to the rights of the people. The different governments will control each other, at the same time that each will be controlled by itself." The Federalist No. 51, 323.

One fairly can dispute whether our federalist system has been quite as successful in checking government abuse as Hamilton promised, but there is no doubt about the design. If this "double security" is to be effective, there must be a proper balance between the States and the Federal Government. These twin powers will act as mutual restraints only if both are credible. In the tension between federal and state power lies the promise of liberty.

The Federal Government holds a decided advantage in this delicate balance: the Supremacy Clause. U.S. Const. Art. VI, cl. 2. As long as it is acting within the powers granted it under the Constitution, Congress may impose its will on the States. Congress may legislate in areas traditionally regulated by the States. This is an extraordinary power in a federalist system. It is a power that we must assume Congress does not exercise lightly.

The present case concerns a state constitutional provision through which the people of Missouri establish a qualification for those who sit as their judges. This provision goes beyond an area traditionally regulated by the States; it is a decision of the most fundamental sort for a sovereign entity. Through the structure of its government, and the character of those who exercise government authority, a State defines itself as a sovereign. * * *

Congressional interference with this decision of the people of Missouri, defining their constitutional officers, would upset the usual constitutional balance of federal and state powers. For this reason, "it is incumbent upon the federal courts to be certain of Congress' intent before finding that federal law overrides" this balance. *Atascadero*. We explained recently:

> "[I]f Congress intends to alter the 'usual constitutional balance between the States and the Federal Government,' it must make its intention to do so 'unmistakably clear in the language of the statute.' *Atascadero*; see also *Pennhurst State School and Hosp. v. Halderman*, 465 U.S. 89, 99 (1984). *Atascadero* was an Eleventh Amendment case, but a similar approach is applied in other contexts. Congress should make its intention 'clear and manifest' if it intends to pre-empt the historic powers of the States. . . . 'In traditionally sensitive areas, such as legislation affecting the federal balance, the requirement of clear statement assures that the legislature has in fact faced, and intended to bring into issue, the critical matters involved in the judicial decision.' " *Will v. Mich. Dep't. of State Police*, 491 U.S. 58, 65 (1989).

This plain statement rule is nothing more than an acknowledgment that the States retain substantial sovereign powers under our constitutional scheme, powers with which Congress does not readily interfere.

In a recent line of authority, we have acknowledged the unique nature of state decisions that "go to the heart of representative government." [Here Justice O'Connor referred to cases holding that, although state exclusion of aliens from public employment generally raises serious equal protection questions, the Court has created a "political function" exception and upheld state programs limiting to citizens employment in positions that are "intimately related to the process of democratic self-government."]

These cases stand in recognition of the authority of the people of the States to determine the qualifications of their most important government officials. It is an authority that lies at " 'the heart of representative government.' " It is a power reserved to the States under the Tenth Amendment and guaranteed them by that provision of the Constitution under which the United States "guarantee[s] to every State in this Union a Republican Form of Government." U.S. Const. Art. IV, § 4.

The authority of the people of the States to determine the qualifications of their government officials is, of course, not without limit. Other constitutional provisions, most notably the Fourteenth Amendment, proscribe certain qualifications; our review of citizenship requirements under the political-function exception is less exacting, but it is not absent. Here, we must decide what Congress did in extending the ADEA to the States, pursuant to its powers under the Commerce Clause. See *EEOC v. Wyoming*, 460 U.S. 226 (1983) (the extension of the ADEA to employment by state and local governments was a valid exercise of Congress' powers under the Commerce Clause). As against Congress' powers "[t]o regulate Commerce . . . among the several States," U.S. Const. Art. I, § 8, cl. 3, the authority of the people of the States to determine the qualifications of their government officials may be inviolate.

We are constrained in our ability to consider the limits that the state-federal balance places on Congress' powers under the Commerce Clause. See *Garcia v. San Antonio Metro. Transit Auth.* (declining to review limitations placed on Congress' Commerce Clause powers by our federal system). But there is no need to do so if we hold that the ADEA does not apply to state judges. Application of the plain statement rule thus may avoid a potential constitutional problem. Indeed, inasmuch as this Court in *Garcia* has left primarily to the political process the protection of the States against intrusive exercises of Congress' Commerce Clause powers, we must be absolutely certain that Congress intended such an exercise. "[T]o give the state-displacing weight of federal law to mere congressional *ambiguity* would evade the very procedure for lawmaking on which *Garcia* relied to protect states' interests." Lawrence Tribe, American Constitutional Law § 6–25, 480 (2d ed. 1988).

[IIB]   In 1974, Congress extended the substantive provisions of the ADEA to include the States as employers. At the same time, Congress amended the definition of "employee" to exclude all elected and most high-ranking government officials. Under the Act, as amended:

> "The term 'employee' means an individual employed by any employer except that the term 'employee' shall not include any person elected to public office in any State or political subdivision of any State by the qualified voters thereof, or any person chosen by such officer to be on such officer's personal staff, or an appointee on the policymaking level or an immediate adviser with respect to the exercise of the constitutional or legal powers of the office." 29 U.S.C. § 630(f).

Governor Ashcroft contends that the § 630(f) exclusion of certain public officials also excludes judges, like petitioners, who are appointed to office by the Governor and are then subject to retention election. The Governor points to two passages in § 630(f). First, he argues, these judges are selected by an elected official and, because they make policy, are "appointee[s] on the policymaking level."

Petitioners counter that judges merely resolve factual disputes and decide questions of law; they do not make policy. Moreover, petitioners point out that the policymaking-level exception is part of a trilogy, tied closely to the elected-official exception. Thus, the Act excepts elected officials and: (1) "any person chosen by such officer to be on such officer's personal staff"; (2) "an appointee on the policymaking level"; and (3) "an immediate advisor with respect to the constitutional or legal powers of the office." Applying the maxim of statutory construction *noscitur a sociis*—that a word is known by the company it keeps—petitioners argue that since (1) and (3) refer only to those in close working relationships with elected officials, so too must (2). Even if it can be said that judges may make policy, petitioners contend, they do not do so at the behest of an elected official.

Governor Ashcroft relies on the plain language of the statute: It exempts persons appointed "at the policymaking level." [The Governor argued that state judges make policy in making common law decisions and exercising supervisory authority over the state bar. Moreover, state appellate judges have additional policymaking responsibilities: supervising inferior courts, establishing rules of procedure for the state courts, and developing disciplinary rules for the bar.]

The Governor stresses judges' policymaking responsibilities, but it is far from plain that the statutory exception requires that judges actually make policy. The statute refers to appointees "on the policymaking level," not to appointees "who make policy." It may be sufficient that the appointee is in a position requiring the exercise of discretion concerning issues of public importance. This certainly describes the bench, regardless of whether judges might be considered policymakers in the same sense as the executive or legislature.

Nonetheless, "appointee at the policymaking level," particularly in the context of the other exceptions that surround it, is an odd way for Congress to exclude judges; a plain statement that judges are not "employees" would seem the most efficient phrasing. But in this case we are not looking for a plain statement that judges are excluded. We will not read the ADEA to cover state judges unless Congress has made it clear that judges are *included*. This does not mean that the Act must mention judges explicitly, though it does not. Rather, it must be plain to anyone reading the Act that it covers judges. In the context of a statute that plainly excludes most important state public officials, "appointee on the policymaking level" is sufficiently broad that we cannot conclude that the statute plainly covers appointed state judges. Therefore, it does not.

The ADEA plainly covers all state employees except those excluded by one of the exceptions. Where it is unambiguous that an employee does not fall within one of the exceptions, the Act states plainly and unequivocally that the employee is included. It is at least ambiguous whether a state judge is an "appointee on the policymaking level." * * *

[IIC]   The extension of the ADEA to employment by state and local governments was a valid exercise of Congress' powers under the Commerce Clause. *EEOC v. Wyoming*. In *Wyoming*, we reserved the questions whether Congress might also have passed the ADEA extension pursuant to its powers under § 5 of the Fourteenth Amendment, and whether the extension would have been a valid exercise of that power. We noted, however, that the principles of federalism that constrain Congress' exercise of its Commerce Clause powers are attenuated when Congress acts pursuant to its powers to enforce the Civil War Amendments. This is because those "Amendments were specifically designed as an expansion of federal power and an intrusion on state sovereignty." One might argue, therefore, that if Congress passed the ADEA extension under its § 5 powers, the concerns about federal intrusion into state government that compel the result in this case might carry less weight.

By its terms, the Fourteenth Amendment contemplates interference with state authority: "No State shall . . . deny to any person within its jurisdiction the equal protection of the laws." But this Court has never held that the Amendment may be applied in complete disregard for a State's constitutional powers. Rather, the Court has recognized that the States' power to define the qualifications of their officeholders has force even as against the proscriptions of the Fourteenth Amendment.

We return to the political-function cases. In *Sugarman* [*v. Dougall*, 413 U.S. 634 (1973)], the Court noted that "aliens as a class 'are a prime example of a "discrete and insular" minority,' * * * and that classifications based on alienage are 'subject to close judicial scrutiny.' " The *Sugarman* Court held that New York City had insufficient interest in preventing aliens from holding a broad category of public jobs to justify the blanket prohibition. At the same time, the Court established the rule that scrutiny under the Equal Protection Clause "will not be so demanding where we deal with matters resting firmly within a State's constitutional prerogatives." Later cases have reaffirmed this practice. See [cases concerning the "political-function" exception from strict scrutiny of state classifications disadvantaging aliens]. These cases demonstrate that the Fourteenth Amendment does not override all principles of federalism.

Of particular relevance here is *Pennhurst State School and Hospital v. Halderman*, 451 U.S. 1 (1981). The question in that case was whether Congress, in passing a section of the Developmentally Disabled Assistance and Bill of Rights Act, 42 U.S.C. § 6010 (1982 ed.), intended to place an obligation on the States to provide certain kinds of treatment to the disabled. Respondent Halderman argued that Congress passed § 6010 pursuant to § 5 of the Fourteenth Amendment, and therefore that it was mandatory on the States, regardless of whether they received federal funds. Petitioner and the United States, as respondent, argued that, in passing § 6010, Congress acted pursuant to its spending power alone. Consequently, § 6010 applied only to States accepting federal funds under the Act.

The Court was required to consider the "appropriate test for determining when Congress intends to enforce" the guarantees of the Fourteenth Amendment. We adopted a rule fully cognizant of the traditional power of the States: "Because such legislation imposes congressional policy on a State involuntarily, and because it often intrudes on traditional state authority, we should not quickly attribute to Congress an unstated intent to act under its authority to enforce the Fourteenth Amendment." Because Congress nowhere stated its intent to impose mandatory obligations on the States under its § 5 powers, we concluded that Congress did not do so.

The *Pennhurst* rule looks much like the plain statement rule we apply today. In *EEOC v. Wyoming*, the Court explained that *Pennhurst* established a rule of statutory construction to be applied where statutory intent is ambiguous. In light of the ADEA's clear exclusion of most important public officials, it is at least ambiguous whether Congress intended that appointed judges nonetheless be included. In the face of such ambiguity, we will not attribute to Congress an intent to intrude on state governmental functions regardless of whether Congress acted pursuant to its Commerce Clause powers or § 5 of the Fourteenth Amendment.

[The Court also held that the mandatory retirement requirement for judges did not violate the Equal Protection Clause of the Fourteenth Amendment, rejecting arguments that it was irrational to distinguish between judges who have reached age 70 and younger judges, and between judges 70 and over and other state employees of the same age who are not subject to mandatory retirement.]

JUSTICE WHITE, with whom JUSTICE STEVENS joins, concurring in part, dissenting in part, and concurring in the judgment.

[I]   While acknowledging [the] principle of federal legislative supremacy, the majority nevertheless imposes upon Congress a "plain statement" requirement. The majority claims to derive this requirement from the plain statement approach developed in our Eleventh Amendment cases, see, *e.g.*, *Atascadero*, and applied two Terms ago in *Will*. The issue in those cases, however, was whether Congress intended a particular statute to extend to the States *at all*. In *Atascadero*, for example, the issue was whether States could be sued under § 504 of the Rehabilitation Act of 1973, 29 U.S.C. § 794. Similarly, the issue in *Will* was whether States could be sued under 42 U.S.C. § 1983. In the present case, by contrast, Congress has expressly extended the coverage of the ADEA to the States and their employees. Its intention to regulate age discrimination by States is thus "unmistakably clear in the language of the statute." *Atascadero*. The only dispute is over the precise details of the statute's application. We have never extended the plain statement approach that far, and the majority offers no compelling reason for doing so.

The majority also relies heavily on our cases addressing the constitutionality of state exclusion of aliens from public employment. In those cases, we held that although restrictions based on alienage ordinarily are subject to strict scrutiny under the Equal Protection Clause, the scrutiny will be less demanding for exclusion of aliens "from positions intimately related to the process of democratic self-government." This narrow "political function" exception to the strict scrutiny standard is based on the "State's historical power to exclude aliens from participation in its democratic political institutions." *Sugarman*.

It is difficult to see how the "political function" exception supports the majority's plain statement rule. First, the exception merely reflects a determination of the scope of the rights of aliens under the Equal Protection Clause. Reduced scrutiny is appropriate for certain political functions because "the right to govern is reserved to citizens." This conclusion in no way establishes a method for interpreting rights that are statutorily created by Congress, such as the protection from age discrimination in the ADEA. Second, it is one thing to limit *judicially-created* scrutiny, and it is quite another to fashion a restraint on *Congress'* legislative authority, as does the majority; the latter is both counter-majoritarian and an intrusion on a co-equal branch of the Federal Government. Finally, the majority does not explicitly restrict its rule to "functions that go to the heart of representative government," and may in fact be extending it much further to all "state governmental functions."

The majority's plain statement rule is not only unprecedented, it directly contravenes our decisions in *Garcia v. San Antonio Metropolitan Transit Authority* and *South Carolina v. Baker*, 485 U.S. 505 (1988). In those cases we made it clear "that States must find their protection from congressional regulation through the national political process, not through judicially defined spheres of unregulable state activity." We also rejected as "unsound in principle and unworkable in practice" any test for state immunity that requires a judicial determination of which state activities are "traditional," "integral," or "necessary." The majority disregards those decisions in its attempt to carve out areas of state activity that will receive special protection from federal legislation.

The majority's approach is also unsound because it will serve only to confuse the law. First, the majority fails to explain the scope of its rule. Is the rule limited to federal regulation of the qualifications of state officials? Or does it apply more broadly to the regulation of any "state governmental functions"? [Quoting majority opinion.] Second, the majority does not explain its requirement that Congress' intent to regulate a particular state activity be "plain to anyone reading [the federal statute]." Does that mean that it is now improper to look to the purpose or history of a federal statute in determining the scope of the statute's limitations on state activities? If so, the majority's rule is completely inconsistent with our pre-emption jurisprudence. See, *e.g.*, *Hillsborough County v. Automated Medical Laboratories, Inc.*, 471 U.S. 707, 715 (1985) (pre-emption will be found where there is a "clear and manifest *purpose*" to displace state law) (emphasis added). The vagueness of the majority's rule undoubtedly will lead States to assert that various federal statutes no longer apply to a wide variety of State activities if Congress has not expressly referred to those activities in the statute. Congress, in turn, will be forced to draft long and detailed lists of which particular state functions it meant to regulate.

The imposition of such a burden on Congress is particularly out of place in the context of the ADEA. Congress already has stated that all "individual[s] employed by any employer" are protected by the ADEA unless they are expressly excluded by one of the exceptions in the definition of "employee." See 29 U.S.C. § 630(f). The majority, however, turns the statute on its head, holding that state judges are not protected by the ADEA because "Congress has [not] made it clear that judges are *included*." * * *

The majority asserts that its plain statement rule is helpful in avoiding a "potential constitutional problem." It is far from clear, however, why there would be a constitutional problem if the ADEA applied to state judges, in light of our decisions in *Garcia* and *Baker*, discussed above. As long as "the national political *process* did not operate in a defective manner, the Tenth Amendment is not implicated." *Baker*. There is no claim in this case that the political process by which the ADEA was extended to state employees was inadequate to protect the States from being "unduly burden[ed]" by the Federal Government. In any event, as discussed below, a straightforward analysis of the ADEA's definition of "employee" reveals that the ADEA does not apply here. Thus, even if there were potential constitutional problems in extending the ADEA to state judges, the majority's proposed plain statement rule would not be necessary to avoid them in this case. Indeed, because this case can be decided purely on the basis of statutory interpretation, the majority's announcement of its plain statement rule, which purportedly is derived from constitutional principles, *violates* our general practice of avoiding the unnecessary resolution of constitutional issues.

My disagreement with the majority does not end with its unwarranted announcement of the plain statement rule. Even more disturbing is its treatment of Congress' power under § 5 of the Fourteenth Amendment. Section 5 provides that "[t]he Congress shall have power to enforce, by appropriate legislation, the provisions of this article." Despite that sweeping constitutional delegation of authority to Congress, the majority holds that its plain statement rule will apply with full force to legislation enacted to enforce the Fourteenth Amendment. The majority states: "In the face of . . . ambiguity, we will not attribute to Congress an intent to intrude on state governmental functions *regardless of whether Congress acted pursuant to its Commerce Clause powers or § 5 of the Fourteenth Amendment.*" (Emphasis added).

The majority's failure to recognize the special status of legislation enacted pursuant to § 5 ignores that, unlike Congress' Commerce Clause power, "[w]hen Congress acts pursuant to § 5, not only is it exercising legislative authority that is plenary within the terms of the constitutional grant, it is exercising that authority under one section of a constitutional Amendment whose other sections by their own terms embody limitations on state authority." *Fitzpatrick v. Bitzer*, 427 U.S. 445, 456 (1976). Indeed, we have held that "principles of federalism that might otherwise be an obstacle to congressional authority are necessarily overridden by the power to enforce the Civil War Amendments 'by appropriate legislation.' Those Amendments were specifically designed as an expansion of federal power and an intrusion on state sovereignty."

The majority relies upon *Pennhurst State School and Hospital v. Halderman*, but that case does not support its approach. There, the Court merely stated that "we should not quickly attribute to Congress an unstated intent to act under its authority to enforce the Fourteenth Amendment." In other words, the *Pennhurst* presumption was designed only to answer the question whether a particular piece of legislation was enacted pursuant to § 5. That is very different from the majority's apparent holding that even when Congress *is* acting pursuant to § 5, it nevertheless must specify the precise details of its enactment.

The majority's departures from established precedent are even more disturbing when it is realized, as discussed below, that this case can be affirmed based on simple statutory construction.

[II] The statute at issue in this case is the ADEA's definition of "employee," which provides:

> "The term 'employee' means an individual employed by any employer except that the term 'employee' shall not include any person elected to public office in any State or political subdivision of any State by the qualified voters thereof, or any person chosen by such officer to be on such officer's personal staff, or an appointee on the policymaking level or an immediate adviser with respect to the exercise of the constitutional or

legal powers of the office. The exemption set forth in the preceding sentence shall not include employees subject to the civil service laws of a State government, governmental agency, or political subdivision." 29 U.S.C. § 630(f).

A parsing of that definition reveals that it excludes from the definition of "employee" (and thus the coverage of the ADEA) four types of (non-civil service) state and local employees: (1) persons elected to public office; (2) the personal staff of elected officials; (3) persons appointed by elected officials to be on the policymaking level; and (4) the immediate advisers of elected officials with respect to the constitutional or legal powers of the officials' offices.

The question before us is whether petitioners fall within the third exception. * * * [I] conclude that petitioners are "on the policymaking level."

"Policy" is defined as "a definite course or method of action selected (as by a government, institution, group, or individual) from among alternatives and in the light of given conditions to guide and usu[ally] determine present and future decisions." Webster's Third New International Dictionary 1754 (1976). Applying that definition, it is clear that the decisionmaking engaged in by common-law judges, such as petitioners, places them "on the policymaking level." In resolving disputes, although judges do not operate with unconstrained discretion, they do choose "from among alternatives" and elaborate their choices in order "to guide and . . . determine present and future decisions." * * *

Moreover, it should be remembered that the statutory exception refers to appointees "on the policymaking level," not "policymaking employees." Thus, whether or not judges actually *make* policy, they certainly are on the same *level* as policymaking officials in other branches of government and therefore are covered by the exception. * * *

Petitioners argue that the "appointee[s] on the policymaking level" exception should be construed to apply "only to persons who advise or work closely with the elected official that chose the appointee." In support of that claim, petitioners point out that the exception is "sandwiched" between the "personal staff" and "immediate adviser" exceptions in § 630(f), and thus should be read as covering only similar employees.

Petitioners' premise, however, does not prove their conclusion. It is true that the placement of the "appointee" exception between the "personal staff" and "immediate adviser" exceptions suggests a similarity among the three. But the most obvious similarity is simply that each of the three sets of employees are connected in some way with elected officials: the first and third sets have a certain working relationship with elected officials, while the second is *appointed* by elected officials. There is no textual support for concluding that the second set must *also* have a close working relationship with elected officials. Indeed, such a reading would tend to make the "appointee" exception superfluous since the "personal staff" and "immediate adviser" exceptions would seem to cover most appointees who are in a close working relationship with elected officials.

Petitioners seek to rely on legislative history, but it does not help their position. There is little legislative history discussing the definition of "employee" in the ADEA, so petitioners point to the legislative history of the identical definition in Title VII, 42 U.S.C. § 2000e(f). If anything, that history tends to confirm that the "appointee[s] on the policymaking level" exception was designed to exclude from the coverage of the ADEA all high-level appointments throughout state government structures, including judicial appointments. * * *

[The dissenting opinion of JUSTICE BLACKMUN, joined by JUSTICE MARSHALL, is omitted.]

NOTES ON GREGORY AND CLEAR STATEMENT RULES

1. *Contrasting Approaches.* As Justice O'Connor noted, there is a respectable textual argument that the ADEA exceptions do not apply to appointed judges, in part because of the *noscitur a sociis* canon. But note that every other potential source of statutory meaning points in the other direction. See Philip Frickey, *Lawnet: The Case of the Missing (Tenth) Amendment*, 75 Minn. L. Rev. 755 (1991).

Consider first the absurd-result exception to the plain meaning approach, which even textualists will sometimes apply.[38] On the face of it, the exceptions provision to the ADEA seems to take elected judges completely out of the statute (and thus they can be required to step down at age 70), but protects appointed judges against any retirement requirement. This seems absolutely backwards from any public-policy perspective: if superannuated judges are to remain in authority, presumably that judgment should be made by the voters on a judge-by-judge basis, not as a categorical decision made by Congress. Why would Congress want to hogtie states in this manner? On the other hand, does the "absurdity" here rise to the level called for by Justice Kennedy in his separate opinion in *Public Citizen* (Chapter 6, § 2B)? Is the apparent distinction between elected and appointed judges so irrational as to raise a serious constitutional question that should be avoided through statutory interpretation (cf. *Catholic Bishop of Chicago*)?

Sources of statutory meaning available to nontextualists strongly cut against the apparent plain meaning of the ADEA exceptions provision as well. The legislative history, irrelevant to Justice O'Connor because of her application of a super-strong clear statement rule, supports excepting these judges from the statute, as explained in a portion of Justice White's separate opinion that we have deleted. The statutory purpose, again irrelevant to Justice O'Connor's approach, seems narrower than the plain meaning of the exception; at least as originally conceived, the ADEA was designed to protect workers from being replaced by younger employees who would accept lower pay, and had little to do with persons who possess guaranteed tenure and who would be replaced by persons receiving the same salary. From the standpoint of public values, as Justice O'Connor suggests, the people of the state ought to be able to choose how to structure important governmental positions. But this need not lead to the creation of a super-strong clear statement rule: any kind of canon (a presumption at the outset, a tiebreaker at the end, a factor to be weighed in the interpretive process) based on federalism would surely be sufficient to tip the case to the conclusion Justice O'Connor

---

[38] See Justice Kennedy's separate opinion in *Public Citizen* (Chapter 6, § 2B) and Justice Scalia's separate opinion in *Bock Laundry* (Chapter 6, § 3A).

desired. Why create the canonical equivalent of a nuclear weapon when a fly swatter would have been sufficient?

For a more recent debate among the Justices as to the application of the federalism canons in the context of the ADEA, compare *Kimel v. Florida Bd. of Regents*, 528 U.S. 62 (2000) (O'Connor, J., for the Court, finding that the ADEA does make it "unmistakably clear" that its remedial provision abrogates the states' Eleventh Amendment immunity from suit, but finding the abrogation unconstitutional), with *id.* at 654–59 (Thomas, J., dissenting in part) (arguing that the ADEA is not sufficiently clear in abrogating state Eleventh Amendment immunity). Does it matter which approach is taken? (Four dissenting Justices found statutory abrogation and believed it constitutional.)

2.   *When Does the Canon Apply? What Does It Require?* As Justice White stressed, it is by no means clear what Congress must do to comply with the *Gregory* canon. Must Congress rely upon its legislative authority under section 5 of the Fourteenth Amendment, or may it rely upon its commerce power as well? To what kinds of state governmental operations does the canon apply? Note that in *Garcia* one justification for overruling *National League of Cities* was that the standard identified there for state immunity from federal regulation—the federal government could not "directly displace the States' freedom to structure integral operations in areas of traditional government functions"—proved too vague for any consistent application in the lower courts. Is the *Gregory* canon any clearer?

One would think that, at a minimum, the canon applies with full force to federal regulation of state judges. One would be wrong. In *Chisom v. Roemer* (Chapter 6, § 3A), the majority of the Court applied section 2 of the Voting Rights Act to the election of state judges without any mention of the *Gregory* canon. *Chisom* and *Gregory* were decided *the same day*, and Justice O'Connor was in the majority in *Chisom* (and, of course, the author of *Gregory*). Justice Scalia, dissenting in *Chisom*, began with his textualist approach, concluded that the key statutory term "representatives" did not include judges, and then asked whether any canon suggested a deviation from the textualist answer. He then had this to say:

> If the [*Gregory*] principle were applied here, we would have double reason to give "representatives" its ordinary meaning. It is true, however, that in *Gregory* interpreting the statute to include judges would have made them the only high-level state officials affected, whereas here the question is whether judges were excluded from a general imposition upon state elections that unquestionably exists; and in *Gregory* it was questionable whether Congress was invoking its powers under the Fourteenth Amendment (rather than merely the Commerce Clause), whereas here it is obvious. Perhaps those factors suffice to distinguish the two cases. Moreover, we tacitly rejected a "plain statement" rule as applied to unamended § 2 in *City of Rome v. United States*, 446 U.S. 156 (1980), though arguably that was before the rule had developed the significance it currently has. I am content to dispense with the "plain statement" rule in the present case[,] but it says something about the Court's approach to today's decision that the possibility of applying that rule never crossed its mind.

Fairly read, is *Gregory* susceptible to the potential distinctions between it and *Chisom* that Justice Scalia suggests? If not, are the two cases simply irreconcilable?

3.   *The Relationship of Textualism and Super-Strong Clear Statement Rules.* Under Justice Scalia's formula for textualism set forth in his dissenting opinion in *Chisom*, it is critical to know what the "established canons" are and how they operate. How can the *Gregory* canon be an "established" one, when in fact the case took what was at most a presumption in prior cases and transformed it into a super-strong clear statement rule? What is Justice Scalia doing in the *Gregory* majority? Why didn't he join Justice White's more textualist concurring opinion?

Critics could suggest that cases like *Gregory* demonstrate that textualism fails to live up to its promise of providing objective interpretive methods in the face of outcomes judges cannot tolerate. In other words, every human interpretive technique, including textualism, needs a "safety valve" of some sort. For liberals, the *Holy Trinity Church* "purpose trumps plain meaning" approach sometimes serves this purpose, as in *Weber*. For conservative textualists who care about federalism, the safety valve when textualism gets them boxed in, as in *Gregory*, is the creation of a super-strong clear statement rule that trumps the result suggested by ordinary meaning. Is it fair to say that *Gregory* undercuts the textualist principle of constraining judicial discretion in interpretation? Is it fair to go even further and suggest that *Gregory* and *Chisom*, when read together, undermine the very notion of predictability and coherence in interpretation?

Another concern about *Gregory* is whether the notion of deference to ultimate congressional determination is more illusion than reality. The congressional agenda is limited, access to it is skewed in a variety of ways (toward more powerful interests, toward the interests of the federal, state, and local governments, and so on), and it is far easier to kill a bill than to pass a bill. Thus, in many circumstances at least, the use of a super-strong clear statement rule may be as "countermajoritarian" as invalidating the statute outright.

Yet another concern is whether the use of such rules may actually encourage judicial activism because it seems far easier to use them than to do constitutional decisionmaking. Because a decision like *Gregory* is made at the interpretive rather than the constitutional level, the visibility of the decision is lower and the attention paid to it even inside the Court may be less. Contrast the reaction to *Gregory* (except in limited academic and states' rights circles, virtually nothing) to the reaction to a hypothetical overruling of *Garcia* and a return to *National League of Cities* (where the Court's disrespect for stare decisis and return to a regime already arguably demonstrated to be unworkable would surely cause considerable controversy).

Ultimately, probably the most important question about the new super-strong clear statement rules is normative. In *Gregory*, for example, should the Court be promoting the value of federalism so strongly, or should it defer more to the political process (Congress and the President) to protect the states? Can textualists provide any objective grounding for the values promoted by their super-strong clear statement rules?

4.   *The Need for Super-Strong Rules Once the Court Gives Teeth to Previously Underenforced Constitutional Norms?* Does the *Gregory* rule add anything to the rule to avoid constitutional questions? Perhaps as a special application of the avoidance canon, *Gregory* might be defended on the ground that the Tenth Amendment was underenforced by the Supreme Court, which had rarely invalidated federal laws

because they intruded into core state functions.[39] (The Court in *National League of Cities* in 1976 had invalidated such a law, but *Garcia* overruled it.) After *Gregory*, the Court has invalidated several federal statutory provisions on the ground that they commandeered state officials in violation of the Tenth Amendment. See *Printz v. United States*, 521 U.S. 898 (1997); *New York v. United States*, 505 U.S. 144 (1992). If these cases augur an overruling or narrowing of *Garcia*, should the Court trim back its use of the *Gregory* rule? See also *Kimel v. Fla. Bd. of Regents*, 528 U.S. 62 (2000) (Court finds clear statement in ADEA abrogating states' Eleventh Amendment immunity and then rules the abrogation unconstitutional).

The parallel to the avoidance canon suggests a further criticism of the *Gregory* rule: it is a kind of stealth constitutionalism.[40] If the Supreme Court had struck down the ADEA provisions as violations of the Tenth Amendment, you can be sure that the *New York Times* would have given the cases front-page treatment; probably, a certain amount of controversy would have ensued. By announcing these results in statutory, rather than constitutional decisions, the Court avoided any serious public scrutiny or controversy.

5.   *The Problem of Congressional Reliance. Bait and Switch?* In Chapter 6, § 3C, we suggested that one important factor in assessing any theory of statutory interpretation is whether it is compatible with the assumptions about law held by other legal actors (the Congress, the President, attorneys, citizens). One way of criticizing the Court's creation of new super-strong clear statement rules is, then, to focus on the ways in which our political system has relied upon understandings that the Court is now unraveling through the use of these rules.[41] The use of reliance arguments in statutory interpretation appeals not just to the traditional conservative idea of legislative supremacy, but also answers the Court's frequent riposte that legislative supremacy is not implicated unless something is clear on the face of the statute. Consider the following example.

The Education of the Handicapped Act (EHA) is a comprehensive statutory scheme to assure that disabled children may receive a free public education appropriate to their needs. The Act guarantees parental rights to participate in state planning of their children's educational needs and to challenge state plans they don't like. The statute imposes pervasive obligations on state and local governments, and it provides that "[a]ny party aggrieved by the findings and decision [made in the state or local administrative process] shall have the right to bring a civil action . . . in any State court of competent jurisdiction or in a district court of the United States without regard to the amount in controversy." 20 U.S.C. § 1415(e)(2). EHA's sponsor made it clear "that a parent or guardian may present a complaint alleging that a State or local educational agency has refused to provide services to which a child may be entitled" and may sue state and local governments in state or federal court. 121 Cong. Rec. 37415 (1975).

---

[39] This was the defense provided *Gregory* in William Eskridge Jr. & Philip Frickey, *Quasi-Constitutional Law: Clear Statement Rules as Constitutional Lawmaking*, 45 Vand. L. Rev. 593 (1992).

[40] William Eskridge Jr. & Philip Frickey, *The Supreme Court, 1993 Term—Foreword: Law as Equilibrium*, 108 Harv. L. Rev. 4, 81–87 (1994) (criticizing *Gregory* and *BFP v. Resolution Trust Corp.*, 511 U.S. 531 (1994) as examples of stealth constitutionalism).

[41] See Ruth Colker and James Brudney, *Dissing Congress,*100 Mich. L. Rev. 80, 105–15 (2001) (describing how the Court in *Kimel* and related decisions created "crystal ball" problems for a coequal branch, because the enacting Congress failed to create a legislative record that could satisfy a legal standard announced years or decades later).

When the EHA was enacted in 1975, the above-noted evidence would probably have sufficed to abrogate the states' Eleventh Amendment immunity from suit in federal court, pursuant to *Employees v. Missouri Department of Public Health & Welfare*, 411 U.S. 279 (1973) (general jurisdictional grant plus explicit legislative history would be sufficient to abrogate Eleventh Amendment immunity). In *Atascadero State Hospital v. Scanlon*, 473 U.S. 234 (1985), however, the Court changed the rule for congressional abrogation of Eleventh Amendment immunity: "Congress may abrogate the States' constitutionally secured immunity from suit in federal court only by making its intention unmistakably clear in the language of the statute." The Court held that the Rehabilitation Act of 1973, another statute protecting the disabled, did not abrogate states' immunity, because there was no clear textual indication of such abrogation.

Sensing that the rules had changed, and reacting to the Court's restrictive interpretation of the Rehabilitation Act, Congress in 1986 enacted the following: "A State shall not be immune under the Eleventh Amendment * * * from suit in Federal Court for a violation of [enumerated provisions of the Rehabilitation Act], or the provisions of any other Federal statute prohibiting discrimination by recipients of Federal financial assistance." The latter clause clearly covers the EHA. Then, in *Dellmuth v. Muth*, 491 U.S. 223 (1989), a case that arose before the 1986 amendment, the Court held that the EHA did not abrogate state immunity. The Court pointed to the 1986 statute as a good example of the drafting clarity needed to abrogate immunity, and held that there was no abrogation before 1986.

Poor Congress. It thought it had abrogated state immunity in 1975, and given precedent in 1975 it probably had done so. Then it reiterated its intent in 1986, but the new statute was used by the Court to confirm Congress' failure to abrogate in 1975. This might be amusing if important rights were not involved.[42] The matter might become even worse for Congress. Following *Kimel*, the Supreme Court in *Board of Trustees, University of Alabama v. Garrett*, 531 U.S. 356 (2001), ruled that Congress had no power under the Fourteenth Amendment to abrogate the states' Eleventh Amendment immunity in the Americans with Disabilities Act. The Court reasoned that Congress had not found enough of a "history and pattern" of intentional discrimination against people with disabilities by the states themselves to justify the exercise of its enforcement power under the Fourteenth Amendment. Under *Garrett*, Congress' repeated efforts to render the states liable for violations of the EHA might ultimately fail on constitutional grounds.

In assessing the statutory interpretation developments, be certain first that you understand the force of the *Atascadero* clear statement rule: Not only does it require abrogation of state immunity in the statute's text, without regard to legislative history, but the abrogation must be explicit and really clear. E.g., *Hoffman v. Conn. Dep't of Income Maintenance*, 492 U.S. 96 (1989); *Will v. Mich. Dep't of State Police*, 491 U.S. 58 (1989). Thus *Atascadero*, like *Gregory*, fits our definition of a "super-strong clear statement rule." Others that the Court has created include the toughened rule against waivers of federal sovereign immunity, *United States v. Nordic Village*, 503 U.S. 30 (1992); the toughened rule against extraterritorial application of federal statutes, *EEOC v. Arabian Am. Oil Co.*, 499 U.S. 244 (1991); the rule against congressional

---

[42] Congress immediately overrode *Dellmuth* in the Education of the Handicapped Act of 1990, Pub. L. No. 101–476, § 103, 104 Stat. 1103, 1106, again with complaints that its expectations had been thwarted. It took Congress three statutes to effectuate a policy it thought had been effectuated in 1975.

derogation of traditional presidential powers, *Japan Whaling Ass'n v. Am. Cetacean Soc'y*, 478 U.S. 221 (1986); and the rule created in 1981 that congressional conditions of grants to the states be explicit and clear, *Pennhurst State Sch. and Hosp. v. Halderman*, 451 U.S. 1 (1981).

A more recent bait-and-switch debate occurred under the *Pennhurst* rule. Congress in a 1986 statute provided for "reasonable attorneys' fees as part of the costs" to prevailing litigants (usually parents) in cases arising under the Individuals with Disabilities Education Act. In *Arlington Central School District Board of Education v. Murphy*, 548 U.S. 291 (2006), the Court invoked *Pennhurst* to require a more targeted statement in order to justify recovery of expert fees as part of an attorney's fees award. Dissenting Justices accused the Court of bait-and-switch: when Congress added the fees provision in 1986, it had every reason to believe—and the relevant committees expressed a belief—that the enacted language was sufficient to justify the award of expert witness fees. Such belief was undone by Supreme Court decisions handed down in 1987 and 1991 (*Casey*, digested in Chapter 7, § 3A)—decisions which Congress immediately overrode in the Civil Rights Act of 1991. The *Murphy* Court not only ignored the 1991 override, but cited the earlier decisions as confirming evidence that there was a plain meaning that trumped Congress's expectations. (Congress's override only extended to job discrimination cases, and not IDEA cases.)

The *Murphy* dissenters had another argument the *Dellmuth* dissenters did not have. It was undisputed that the 1986 statute not only added a provision giving attorneys' fees and other costs to prevailing parents, but also charged the GAO with collecting fee data and analyzing "the range of such *fees, costs and expenses* awarded in the actions and proceedings under such section, * * * and * * * *the number of hours spent by personnel, including attorneys and consultants.*" (Emphasis added.) The legislative history confirmed that this section was written under Congress's assumption that the 1986 authorization included expert witness fees. Thus, the parents had an argument grounded in the whole act, as well as the legislative history. The Court found this whole act evidence insufficient to refute the conventional text-based evidence. The dissenters expressed astonishment that the majority did not concede there was at least ambiguity in the statute, given this dramatic evidence.

NOTE ON SUBSTANTIVE VERSUS TEXTUAL CANONS

In his Tanner Lectures at Princeton University (excerpted in chapter 6, § 3A), Justice Scalia extolled the common-sense and content-neutral virtues of the textual canons while questioning the legitimacy of more substantive canons, which he referred to as "dice-loading rules." *A Matter of Interpretation: Federal Courts and the Law* 28 (1997). Perhaps relatedly, of the 27 majority opinions Justice Scalia authored construing federal workplace law statutes between 1986 and 2002, he invoked textual canons one-third of the time as part of his reasoning but never invoked substantive canons.[43] In his more recent book, excerpted in Section 1C of this chapter, Justice Scalia is more ecumenical: he endorses certain substantive canons (including constitutional avoidance, the presumption against extraterritoriality, and lenity—the latter only as a

---

[43] See James Brudney and Corey Ditslear, *Canons of Construction and the Elusive Quest for Neutral Reasoning*, 58 Vand. L. Rev. 1, 50–51 (2005). Justice Scalia did regularly join majority opinions that relied on substantive canons, and he did not distance himself from such reasoning in separate concurrences as he has done when the majority relies on legislative history.

tiebreaker) although he and his coauthor devote more attention to the textually grounded canons. See Antonin Scalia & Bryan Garner, *Reading Law: The Interpretation of Legal Texts* (2012). Is Justice Scalia's initial concern about substantive canons warranted? Are canons grounded in policy norms more susceptible to judicial misuse than canons based on considerations of semantics or textual structure? In thinking about these questions, consider the following state court decision.

Marion Energy, Inc. v. KFJ Ranch Partnership
267 P.3d 863 (Utah 2011).

The Supreme Court of Utah held that a statute authorizing the use of eminent domain for the construction of "roads . . . to facilitate . . . the working of . . . mineral deposits" did not allow the state to condemn land containing oil and gas deposits.

After considering the plain text of the statute, and noting that "other sections of the Utah Code define the phrase "mineral deposits" as both including or excluding oil and gas," **Associate Chief Justice Durant**, writing for the court, concluded that the phrase "does not have a single fixed meaning." Given this ambiguity, the court resorted to a substantive canon to dispose of the case. "[B]ecause the exercise of eminent domain results in the derogation of a property owner's right to use and enjoy his land, we strictly construe any ambiguity in statutory language purporting to grant the power of eminent domain in favor of the property owner and against the condemning party. Strictly construing the ambiguity at issue in this case in favor of KFJ compels us to conclude that section 78B–6–501(6) (a) of the Utah Code does not provide Marion authority to condemn KFJ's land to build a road to access its leased oil and gas deposits.

"In reaching this conclusion, we recognize that Marion and the Trust have advanced public policy arguments in support of their interpretation of section 501(6)(a). But given our rules of statutory construction in the context of eminent domain statutes, we feel these arguments should be directed to the Legislature rather than to this court. Thus, without considering these policy concerns, and relying solely on our eminent domain canon of interpretation, we resolve section 501(6)(a)'s ambiguity against Marion and conclude that the section does not provide Marion with the authority it seeks to exercise."

In dissent, **Justice Lee** strongly criticized the court's reliance on the substantive canon, arguing that "[w]hen courts resort too hastily to substantive canons, they run the risk of substituting their own policy views for the balance struck by the legislature." Justice Lee distinguished substantive canons from language canons. "As the majority indicates, this court and others have sometimes indicated an inclination to read eminent domain statutes narrowly. Although this principle often flies under the banner of a 'canon,' it is not the kind of canon we ordinarily employ in ascertaining statutory meaning. By 'canon,' we usually have reference to the kinds of 'tools that guide our construction of statutes in accordance with common, ordinary usage and understanding of language.' Such linguistic canons are often uncontroversial, since they aid in the judicial attempt to assign meaning to statutory terms in a predictable fashion that respects reasonable reliance interests of the parties regulated by statute and likewise validates legislators' expectations of the import of their legislative text.

"The 'canon' embraced by the majority is not of this ilk. There is no reason to expect that the common, ordinary usage of language regarding the eminent domain power is typically exaggerated, necessitating a 'narrow' construction to determine its true meaning. Presumably, the legislature meant what it said when it prescribed the terms of the eminent domain authority to build roads to access 'mineral deposits.' If so, we undermine the reasonable reliance interests of the parties regulated by the statute if we read it narrowly, just as we also invalidate legislative intent on the matter.

"I recognize that this and other courts have sometimes 'canonized' other principles of construction that have nothing to do with identifying ordinary usage or meaning. Such canons are *substantive*, in that they seek to advance values or principles exogenous to the goal of identifying legislative intent. Courts ought to tread lightly in canonizing these sorts of principles, as they threaten to impinge on the policymaking domain of the legislature.

"I do not mean to suggest that all substantive canons are inappropriate. Such canons are least problematic when they advance policies that emanate from some other source of positive law like the Constitution. When courts narrowly construe federal statutes that impinge on traditional state functions, for example, they protect values inherent in constitutional principles of federalism. In such cases, courts are advancing the values or principles canonized in the Constitution, not in the mind or heart of the judiciary. Courts are also on solid ground when they embrace substantive canons that claim a long, unbroken pedigree. When we construe statutes to avoid constitutional doubts or to favor criminal defendants, for example, we are embracing substantive canons embraced long and wide by courts everywhere. Such canons may be justified on the ground that the legislature acts in full knowledge of them, so we may properly assume that it took these canons into account in adopting the statutory language it chose."

After examining a "counter-canon" in Utah precedent regarding eminent domain, Justice Lee concluded that "[t]his canon, like so many other so-called 'substantive canons,' is nothing but policy. Absent any legislative or constitutional directive, we have concluded that we will resolve cases in favor of a particular party based exclusively on *our own* policy rationale." In light of the policy-based motivations for the eminent domain canon, the dissent argued that it was inappropriate for the majority to refuse to consider the parties' public policy arguments: "It seems to me that the court is telling the parties that we won't listen to *their* policy concerns because we favor our own."

Consider Justice Lee's distinction between language canons and substantive canons, contending it is only the latter group of canons that "seek to advance values or principles exogenous to the goal of identifying legislative intent." Do canons that purport to reveal ordinary meaning or conventional usage effectively constrain judges' ability to make pragmatic or normative choices? In what ways, if any, are language canons more content-neutral than substantive canons?

Consider as well the dissent's distinction between substantive canons that implicate constitutional considerations and those that do not. After reading *Catholic Bishop, Roommates.com,* and *Gregory,* do you agree with the dissent that substantive canons are "least problematic" when they advance policies emanating from the Constitution?

D. DEBUNKING AND DEFENDING THE CANONS

KARL LLEWELLYN, *REMARKS ON THE THEORY OF APPELLATE
DECISION AND THE RULES OR CANONS ABOUT HOW
STATUTES ARE TO BE CONSTRUED*
3 Vand. L. Rev. 395, 401–06 (1950).
Reprinted by permission.

When it comes to presenting a proposed construction in court, there is an accepted conventional vocabulary. As in argument over points of case-law, the accepted convention still, unhappily, requires discussion as if only one single correct meaning could exist. Hence there are two opposing canons on almost every point. An arranged selection is appended. Every lawyer must be familiar with them all: they are still needed tools of argument. At least as early as Fortescue the general picture was clear, on this, to any eye which would see.

Plainly, to make any canon take hold in a particular instance, the construction contended for must be sold, essentially, by means other than the use of the canon: The good sense of the situation and a *simple* construction of the available language to achieve that sense, *by tenable means, out of the statutory language.*

Canons of Construction

Statutory interpretation still speaks a diplomatic tongue. Here is some of the technical framework for maneuver.

Thrust	But	Parry
1. A statute cannot go beyond its text.		1. To effect its purpose a statute may be implemented beyond its text.
2. Statutes in derogation of the common law will not be extended by construction.		2. Such acts will be liberally construed if their nature is remedial.
3. Statutes are to be read in the light of the common law and a statute affirming a common law rule is to be construed in accordance with the common law.		3. The common law gives way to a statute which is inconsistent with it and when a statute is designed as a revision of a whole body of law applicable to a given subject it supersedes the common law.
4. Where a foreign statute which has received construction has been adopted, previous construction is adopted too.		4. It may be rejected where there is conflict with the obvious meaning of the statute or where the foreign decisions are unsatisfactory in reasoning or where the foreign interpretation is not in harmony with the spirit or policy of the laws of the adopting state.

Thrust	**But**	**Parry**
5. Where various states have already adopted the statute, the parent state is followed.		5. Where interpretations of other states are inharmonious, there is no such restraint.
6. Statutes in pari materia must be construed together.		6. A statute is not in pari materia if its scope and aim are distinct or where a legislative design to depart from the general purpose or policy of previous enactments may be apparent.
7. A statute imposing a new penalty or forfeiture, or a new liability or disability, or creating a new right of action will not be construed as having a retroactive effect.		7. Remedial statutes are to be liberally construed and if a retroactive interpretation will promote the ends of justice, they should receive such construction.
8. Where design has been distinctly stated no place is left for construction.		8. Courts have the power to inquire into real—as distinct from ostensible—purpose.
9. Definitions and rules of construction contained in an interpretation clause are part of the law and binding.		9. Definitions and rules of construction in a statute will not be extended beyond their necessary import nor allowed to defeat intention otherwise manifested.
10. A statutory provision requiring liberal construction does not mean disregard of unequivocal requirements of the statute.		10. Where a rule of construction is provided within the statute itself the rule should be applied.
11. Titles do not control meaning; preambles do not expand scope; section headings do not change language.		11. The title may be consulted as a guide when there is doubt or obscurity in the body; preambles may be consulted to determine rationale, and thus the true construction of terms; section headings may be looked upon as part of the statute itself.
12. If language is plain and unambiguous it must be given effect.		12. Not when literal interpretation would lead to absurd or mischievous consequences or thwart manifest purpose.
13. Words and phrases which have received judicial		13. Not if the statute clearly requires them to have a different

Thrust	**But**	**Parry**
construction before enactment are to be understood according to that construction.		meaning.
14. After enactment, judicial decision upon interpretation of particular terms and phrases controls.		14. Practical construction by executive officers is strong evidence of true meaning.
15. Words are to be taken in their ordinary meaning unless they are technical terms or words of art.		15. Popular words may bear a technical meaning and technical words may have a popular signification and they should be so construed as to agree with evident intention or to make the statute operative.
16. Every word and clause must be given effect.		16. If inadvertently inserted or if repugnant to the rest of the statute, they may be rejected as surplusage.
17. The same language used repeatedly in the same connection is presumed to bear the same meaning throughout the statute.		17. This presumption will be disregarded where it is necessary to assign different meanings to make the statute consistent.
18. Words are to be interpreted according to the proper grammatical effect of their arrangement within the statute.		18. Rules of grammar will be disregarded where strict adherence would defeat purpose.
19. Exceptions not made cannot be read.		19. The letter is only the "bark." Whatever is within the reason of the law is within the law itself.
20. Expression of one thing excludes another.		20. The language may fairly comprehend many different cases where some only are expressly mentioned by way of example.
21. General terms are to receive a general construction.		21. They may be limited by specific terms with which they are associated or by the scope and purpose of the statute.
22. It is a general rule of construction that where general words follow an enumeration they are to be held as applying		22. General words must operate on something. Further, ejusdem generis is only an aid in getting the meaning and does not warrant

Thrust	But	Parry
only to persons and things of the same general kind or class specifically mentioned (*ejusdem generis*).		confining the operations of a statute within narrower limits than were intended.
23. Qualifying or limiting words or clauses are to be referred to the next preceding antecedent.		23. Not when evident sense and meaning require a different construction.
24. Punctuation will govern when a statute is open to two constructions.		24. Punctuation marks will not control the plain and evident meaning of language.
25. It must be assumed that language has been chosen with due regard to grammatical propriety and is not interchangeable on mere conjecture.		25. "And" and "or" may be read interchangeably whenever the change is necessary to give the statute sense and effect.
26. There is a distinction between words of permission and mandatory words.		26. Words imparting permission may be read as mandatory and words imparting command may be read as permissive when such construction is made necessary by evident intention or by the rights of the public.
27. A proviso qualifies the provision immediately preceding.		27. It may clearly be intended to have a wider scope.
28. When the enacting clause is general, a proviso is construed strictly.		28. Not when it is necessary to extend the proviso to persons or cases which come within its equity.

NOTES ON THE INTELLECTUAL WARFARE OVER CANONS OF STATUTORY INTERPRETATION

1. *Assault on the Citadel by Legal Realists and Critical Scholars.* Llewellyn's wonderful *tour de farce* is a justly celebrated exposure of the many faces of the canons of statutory construction, and it is representative of the legal realists' tendency to debunk legal formalisms. Their view was that nothing turned on them. Canons of construction, for example, "are useful only as facades, which for an occasional judge may add luster to an argument persuasive for other reasons." Frank Newman & Stanley Surrey, *Legislation—Cases and Materials* 654 (1955). Critical scholars of the 1970s and 1980s did not focus on the canons, but the perspective of many of them (intellectual heirs to the most skeptical realists) would go one step further. The canons are just part of the mystifying game that is played with legal logic, which is ultimately indeterminate. Critical scholars argue that legal reasoning can be oppressive by denying its own

contingency, i.e., denying that there are other ways of looking at the situation. Perhaps the canons of construction might be deemed similarly oppressive, for they are part of the linguistic and logical pretense that the legislature goes about its work in a methodical, rational way and that judicial interpreters can scientifically discern the proper meaning through simple rules.

2.   *Legal Process Defense of the Canons.* Conventional legal process thinkers have tended to defend at least some of the canons against the mockery of the realists. For example, Henry Hart, Jr. & Albert Sacks, *The Legal Process* 1191 (Eskridge & Frickey eds. 1994) (tent. ed. 1958), responded to Llewellyn as follows:

> All this [skepticism], it is ventured, involves a misunderstanding of the function of the canons, and at bottom of the problem of interpretation itself. Of course, there are pairs of maxims susceptible of being invoked for opposing conclusions. Once it is understood that meaning depends upon context and that contexts vary, how could it be otherwise? Maxims should not be treated, any more than a dictionary, as saying what meaning a word or group of words *must* have in a given context. They simply answer the question whether a particular meaning is linguistically permissible, if the context warrants it. Is this not a useful function?

Professor Dickerson suggests that some of the canons "reflect the probabilities generated by normal usage or legislative behavior. These represent either (1) lexicographical judgments of how legislatures tend to use language and its syntactical patterns, or (2) descriptions of how legislatures tend to behave. They serve as useful presumptions of supposed actual legislative intent and are, therefore, modestly useful in carrying [out] legislative meaning." Reed Dickerson, *The Interpretation and Application of Statutes* 228 (1975).

3.   *The Law & Economics Debate over the Canons.* The canons were subjected to sharp criticism by Judge Richard Posner in *Statutory Interpretation—In the Classroom and in the Courtroom*, 50 U. Chi. L. Rev. 800, 806–07 (1983). Judge Posner complains that "most of the canons are just wrong" in that (1) they do not reflect a code by which legislatures draft statutes, (2) they are not even common-sense guides to interpretation, (3) they do not operate to constrain the discretion of judges, and (4) they do not force legislatures to draft statutes with care. Judge Posner blasts one canon after another— from the plain meaning rule to expressio unius to the whole act rule—by showing that the canons erroneously assume legislative omniscience and rest on wholly unrealistic conceptions of the legislative process. For a contrary position, Einer Elhauge, *Statutory Default Rules: How to Interpret Unclear Legislation* (2008), argues that many of the canons reflect preference-eliciting default rules that actually minimize political dissatisfaction with statutory results. These default rules need not correspond either to likely legislative preferences or to sound policy. Their justification is that "the default result is more likely to be corrected [when] it burdens some politically powerful group with ready access to the legislative agenda." *Id.* at 152. Congress, Elhauge suggests, is perfectly happy that the Court smooths over statutory potholes, integrates statutes with the larger legal terrain, and sends some sensitive issues back for more work. Which is the more credible understanding of Congress? Can both be right?

From an economic point of view, it may be better to view the canons ex ante rather than ex post. Under an ex ante perspective, it may not matter whether a canon reflects legislative realities. Instead, the question is this: Does the legal process, including the lawmaking process, work *better* with this set of rules than with another set or with no rules at all? The canons might also be defended from an economic point of view as an *interpretive regime* that affords greater predictability for statutory interpreters. See William Eskridge Jr. & John Ferejohn, *Politics, Interpretation, and the Rule of Law*, in *The Rule of Law* 265, 282–85 (Ian Shapiro ed. 1994), as well as Appendix B to this Casebook (a complex array of more than two hundred canons followed by the Rehnquist-Roberts Court), and Adrian Vermeule, *Interpretive Choice*, 75 NYU L. Rev. 74, 140–43 (2000), who argues that the Court should just pick a set of canons and stick with them. The problem with the canons as an interpretive regime is that the canons are not deployed in a completely predictable manner. (See the Brudney and Ditslear article, excerpted below).

Also from an ex ante point of view, some of the canons can be understood as institutional default rules. The best example is the rule of lenity: when the Court interprets criminal statutes narrowly, Congress typically returns to the issue and often overrides the Court with a better-specified statutory crime. See William Eskridge Jr., *Overriding Supreme Court Statutory Interpretation Decisions*, 101 Yale L.J. 331 (1991), as well as our notes after *Muscarello* and *McNally*. This dovetails perfectly with the best justification for the rule of lenity, the nondelegation idea. Eskridge and Frickey, *Quasi-Constitutional Law, supra,* argue that the avoidance canon, the federalism canons, and separation of powers canons can also be understood as requiring Congress—and not agencies or judges—to deliberate and decide to press constitutional envelopes. Accord, Elhauge, *Statutory Default Rules, supra.*

4. *Pragmatic Defenses of the Canons.* Geoffrey Miller, *Pragmatics and the Maxims of Interpretation*, 1990 Wis. L. Rev. 1179, presents a defense of many of the linguistic canons, showing them to be consistent with the teachings of (Gricean) philosophical linguistics. Gricean theory understands communication as a purposive, cooperative endeavor, and communicative precepts are means by which cooperation is facilitated. Thus, the canons might be understood as essential to the communicative process and therefore inevitable.

Perhaps the least ambitious defense of the canons is to posit that they are just a checklist of things to think about when approaching a statute. If context will guide interpretation of statutes whose language is ambiguous (and some whose language is not), then the canons may at least be a catalogue of contextual factors which might be investigated. Expressio unius, in this way, will stimulate an investigation into why the legislators did include only one thing and not the other. The rule of lenity will remind interpreters that penal laws require greater clarity and justification in their prohibitions, and that one should be aware of fairness problems in particular. The whole act maxim will suggest that other parts of the statute, including definitional provisions, be read for clues about how the drafters used certain words, phrases, and concepts. And so on.

Professor Mermin says that the canons of construction are similar to folksayings. Samuel Mermin, *Law and the Legal System: An Introduction* 264 (2d ed. 1982). Does "haste make waste" have any validity as a suggestion on how to live? What about "the early bird catches the worm," one obvious "parry" to this "thrust"? Or "nothing ventured, nothing gained" versus "discretion is the better part of valor"? Don't all of those sayings have some truth in them, depending upon the context? Do any of these sayings provide guidance in decisionmaking, or do they simply provide a *post hoc* explanation of why we made a certain decision? Judge Posner believes that the canons never contribute to judicial decisionmaking. Is this a decisive objection to them?

5.   *Openly Normative Visions of the Canons.* David Shapiro, in *Continuity and Change in Statutory Interpretation*, 67 N.Y.U. L. Rev. 921, 925 (1992), has provided a different justification for the canons: they promote legal stability, in that they assume "that close questions of statutory interpretation should be resolved in favor of continuity and against change."[44] A difficulty in assessing this claim is figuring out the relevant status quo: Does it consist of longstanding general assumptions in the legal community (embodied in many canons, particularly the substantive ones), or the specific legislative assumptions surrounding a particular statute, which may be undone if a canon controls statutory meaning? As the next note indicates, these competing definitions may create widely divergent conclusions about the dynamic or static impact of canons in interpretation. Shapiro concludes that promoting continuity rather than change is more often than not consistent with legislative purposes.

6.   *Dynamic Canons and the Problem of Legislative Supremacy. Catholic Bishop* illustrates the way in which the canons can contribute to the dynamic evolution of statutes. The dissenters may have more accurately discerned the expectations of Congress, but the Court majority found that evidence insufficient to require the result that they found constitutionally questionable. The Court's creation of a series of new or strengthened clear statement rules in the last few decades has generated results in case after case that would have surprised the enacting Congresses. Recall *Dellmuth* and *Gregory*. Also compare *EEOC v. Arabian Am. Oil Co. (Aramco)*, 499 U.S. 244 (1991) (Court invokes a clear statement rule as basis for holding that Title VII does not apply extraterritorially, to U.S. company allegedly discriminating against U.S. employees in its foreign offices), with *id.* at 263–64 (Marshall, J., dissenting) (arguing that the Court's clear statement rule was much tougher than the traditional presumption against extraterritoriality).

7.   *An Empirical Perspective.* One of us has taken a more systematic approach to the canons, collecting 630 Supreme Court workplace-law decisions between 1969 and 2003 and coding them by result (pro-employee or pro-union liberal and pro-employer conservative) and mode of reasoning. James Brudney and Corey Ditslear, *Canons of Construction and the Elusive Quest for Neutral Reasoning*, 58 Vand. L. Rev. 1 (2005). Using multiple regression analyses that control for other variables, Brudney and Ditslear found that the Rehnquist Court relied on the canons (both textual and substantive canons) much more, and legislative history much less, than the Burger Court had done. *Circuit City, Inc. v. Adams*, 532 U.S. 105 (2001) (analyzed in § 1B of this chapter) and *EEOC v. Arabian American Oil Co.*, 499 U.S. 244 (1991) (discussed at the start of § 2), exemplify the Rehnquist Court's (and now the Roberts Court's) approach to workplace law cases.

A troubling though perhaps unsurprising finding was that this methodological development is serving ideological purposes (58 Vand. L. Rev. at 53–69). As summarized at the beginning of the lengthy article:

"[C]anon usage by justices identified as liberals tends to be linked to liberal outcomes, and canon reliance by conservative justices to be associated with

---

[44]   For an extended elaboration of this thesis, see Amanda Tyler, *Continuity, Coherence, and the Canons*, 99 Nw. U. L. Rev. 1389 (2005).

conservative outcomes. We also found that canons are often invoked to justify conservative results in close cases—*i.e.*, those decided by a one-vote or two-vote margin. Indeed, closely divided cases in which the majority relies on substantive canons are more likely to reach conservative results than close cases where those canons are not invoked.

"In addition, we identified a subset of cases in which the majority relies on canons while the dissent invokes legislative history: these cases, almost all decided since 1988, have yielded overwhelmingly conservative results. Doctrinal analysis of illustrative decisions indicates that conservative members of the Rehnquist Court are using the canons in such contested cases to ignore—and thereby undermine—the demonstrable legislative preferences of Congress. Taken together, the association between canon reliance and outcomes among both conservative and liberal justices, the distinctly conservative influence associated with substantive canon reliance in close cases, and the recent tensions in contested cases between conservative majority opinions that rely on canons and liberal dissents that invoke legislative history, suggest that the canons are regularly used in an instrumental if not ideologically conscious manner." *Id.* at 6.

Brudney and Ditslear apply their empirical findings to the theoretical debate over the utility of the canons. Their conclusions are as follows. First, the authors are skeptical that the canons form an interpretive regime which can provide an ordering mechanism for legislators and lawyers to make statutory interpretation more predictable. Aside from the fact that legislators do not rely on the canons when drafting statutes (see studies by Nourse & Schacter, and more recently Gluck & Bressman, summarized in § 1C), the canons are unreliable predictors for how statutes will be applied because they are deployed in such an ideological way by both liberal and conservative judges. A neutral observer who just read the statute and the legislative history in *Circuit City*, for example, would have expected the Court to construe the employment-contract exemption to the Arbitration Act much more expansively than the five-Justice majority in fact did. Brudney and Ditslear offer almost two dozen equally dramatic canon surprises from their dataset.

Second, and relatedly, the study lends empirical support to relatively cynical accounts of the canons. Stephen Ross, *Where Have You Gone Karl Llewellyn? Should Congress Turn Its Lonely Eyes to You?*, 45 Vand. L. Rev. 561 (1992), and Edward Rubin, *Modern Canons, Loose Canons, and the Limits of Practical Reason*, 45 Vand. L. Rev. 579 (1992), maintain that Supreme Court Justices, and perhaps other judges, use the canons strategically, to justify judicial policy preferences or to frustrate legislative intent. The malleability noted by Professor Llewellyn not only undermines canonical predictability, but allows the canons to be manipulated by result-oriented jurists. Brudney and Ditslear say their evidence is consistent with, though does not conclusively prove, this claim.

Third, the study found some support for the hypothesis, first advanced by Jonathan Macey and Geoffrey Miller, *The Canons of Construction and Judicial Preferences*, 45 Vand. L. Rev. 647 (1992), that the canons are substitutes for judicial expertise and can reduce error costs in areas (such as ERISA and some procedural complexities of Title VII) where judicial knowledge and preferences are low. E.g., *Adams Fruit Co. v. Barrett*, 494 U.S. 638 (1990) (expressio unius provides the ground for a conservative Court to allow, without dissent, a private right of action under a technical migrant workers' law). Brudney and Ditslear add that such cases may be more strongly influenced by legislative purpose analysis and, most important, agency views than by canon reliance. In short, there is a correlation between canon invocation and certain technical issues but not necessarily any causal link.

These conclusions raise the possibility that in the most technical and nonpartisan areas of law—such as bankruptcy, energy regulation, patents, or taxation—canon usage would be more important and less ideologically slanted than in workplace law. In less technical or more normatively charged areas—such as civil rights, criminal law, and environmental law—canon usage would be less frequent and more ideologically slanted.

8. *Recent Normative Exchanges.* In *Reading Law*, Justice Scalia and Professor Garner acknowledge that statutory interpretation "is a human enterprise, which cannot be carried out algorithmically by an expert system on a computer." Accepting the inevitability of some judicial discretion, the authors promote the elevation of their 57 "valid canons" or "sound principles of interpretation" as a systematic approach that would minimize or at least reduce problems of unpredictability and judicial policymaking. They argue that their regime of primarily textually-based presumptions and guidelines will constrain judicial discretion because judges will understand they must follow these rules or else risk exposure as willful abusers of power.

One of us has expressed admiration for what Scalia and Garner are attempting to accomplish while concluding that their proposed canons-based regime is plagued by several substantial problems (by now perhaps familiar to readers). See William Eskridge Jr., *The New Textualism and Normative Canons*, 113 Colum. L. Rev. 531 (2013). First, the Scalia and Garner list of 57 approved canons (which they concede may include only one-third of all valid canons), reveals *enormous scope for judicial cherry-picking.* This is due both to the challenge of competing canons (see Llewellyn critique) and to the challenge of deciding what makes a canon canonical in the first instance. The absence of any authoritative hierarchy of canons, along with empirical evidence that their use by judges is ideologically linked (Brudney and Ditslear) deepens this cherry-picking problem. Second, Eskridge discusses the related *norms problem.* Even discounting the risks of cherry-picking, many of Scalia and Garner's valid canons are open-ended and normative. Some reflect non-constitutional values of continuity, fixed-meaning, and presumptions against change; others reflect constitutional values of libertarianism (lenity, respect for property) or federalism (presumptions against federal preemption, against abrogating state sovereign immunity, for respecting state sovereign functions). Judges will have plenty of canons to choose from (subconsciously or otherwise) to support imposing their policy preferences on a contested statutory provision. This is especially troubling because Scalia and Garner disparage a range of purposive guidelines grounded in examination of what Congress communicated during the lawmaking process itself.

This disparagement relates to the final challenge, which Eskridge identifies as a *democracy problem.* Scalia and Garner's canons-based regime enshrines textual canons that legislative drafters tend to dismiss (Gluck and Bressman; Nourse and Schacter). At the same time, Scalia and Garner reject legislative history (exposed in a series of "false notions") as unworthy of interpretive consideration (see § 3B of this chapter). Their posture ignores the reality, reported dramatically by Gluck and Bressman, that "legislative history was emphatically viewed by almost all of our respondents—

Republican and Democrat alike—as the most important drafting and interpretive tool apart from text." In opting for a set of valid canons that isolate them from the legislative (and often legislative-executive) deliberations preceding a statute's enactment, Scalia and Garner exacerbate the countermajoritarian difficulty with judicial interpretation of statutes.

As we turn to section 3, addressing extrinsic sources for statutory interpretation, you should keep in mind the tensions between Justice Scalia's canons-based regime and a more purposive approach which is embraced by some of his judicial colleagues. In particular, consider how we should assess the comparative advantages of these two approaches—from the standpoint of predictability, stability, and legitimacy.

NOTE ON LEGISLATED CANONS OF STATUTORY INTERPRETATION

Sometimes the legislature attempts to direct the court in how to approach interpreting a particular statute. For example, a provision of the federal Racketeer Influenced and Corrupt Organizations Act (RICO), 18 U.S.C. § 1961, which contains criminal sanctions, provides that "[t]he provisions of this title shall be liberally construed to effectuate its remedial purposes." There could conceivably be some constitutional objections to such a provision—the most straightforward would be that it violates the separation of powers because it invades the court's power to say what the law is—but leaving that problem aside, what should a court do with it? In *Russello v. United States*, 464 U.S. 16, 26–27 (1983), the Court cited the RICO provision as well as legislative history to support a broad construction of the statute. In contrast, in *Reves v. Ernst & Young*, 507 U.S. 170, 183–84 (1993), the Court said the following about the RICO clause:

> This clause obviously seeks to ensure that Congress' intent is not frustrated by an overly narrow reading of the statute, but it is not an invitation to apply RICO to new purposes that Congress never intended. Nor does the clause help us to determine what purposes Congress had in mind. Those must be gleaned from the statute through the normal means of interpretation. The clause " 'only serves as an aid for resolving an ambiguity; it is not to be used to beget one.' "

Does this approach leave any role for the interpretive clause at all?

Congress has also adopted the Dictionary Act, which codifies a few generic canons of statutory construction, such as the rules that singular terms include the plural, and male pronouns also include females. See 1 U.S.C. § 1 et seq. All fifty states and the District of Columbia have adopted more ambitious model interpretation acts providing legislated canons to guide judicial interpretation for all statutes. Chapter 645 of the Minnesota Statutes, for example, contains the following provisions:

645.16. LEGISLATIVE INTENT CONTROLS

The object of all interpretation and construction of laws is to ascertain and effectuate the intention of the legislature. Every law shall be construed, if possible, to give effect to all its provisions.

When the words of a law in their application to an existing situation are clear and free from all ambiguity, the letter of the law shall not be disregarded under the pretext of pursuing the spirit.

When the words of a law are not explicit, the intention of the legislature may be ascertained by considering, among other matters:

(1)   The occasion and necessity for the law;

(2)   The circumstances under which it was enacted;

(3)   The mischief to be remedied;

(4)   The object to be attained;

(5)   The former law, if any, including other laws upon the same or similar subjects;

(6)   The consequences of a particular interpretation;

(7)   The contemporaneous legislative history; and

(8)   Legislative and administrative interpretations of the statute.

645.17.   PRESUMPTIONS IN ASCERTAINING LEGISLATIVE INTENT

In ascertaining the intention of the legislature the courts may be guided by the following presumptions:

(1)   The legislature does not intend a result that is absurd, impossible of execution, or unreasonable;

(2)   The legislature intends the entire statute to be effective and certain;

(3)   The legislature does not intend to violate the constitution of the United States or of this state;

(4)   When a court of last resort has construed the language of a law, the legislature in subsequent laws on the same subject matter intends the same construction to be placed upon such language; and

(5)   The legislature intends to favor the public interest as against any private interest.

Notice that Minnesota's legislated canons provide (1) a general theory of statutory interpretation, (2) an indication of the sources judges should consult and when they might consult them, and (3) specific presumptions of statutory meaning.

In an important recent study, Jacob Scott, *Codified Canons and the Common Law of Interpretation*, 98 Geo. L.J. 341 (2010), collected and categorized the statutory canons for all fifty states and the District of Columbia. Scott then analyzed the patterns he found across the nationwide sample. Among the patterns he reported are the following:

• **Plain Meaning.** Fifteen legislatures, including Minnesota's, have codified the plain meaning rule, but with explicit inclusion of exceptions for "absurd results" and/or "scrivener's errors" (Table 1). Thirty-four legislatures have codified the dictionary canon and the canon that "ordinary usage" should normally be applied (Table 1). No legislature has codified *expressio unius*, and only two have codified *ejusdem generis* or *noscitur a sociis*.

• **Whole Act.** Thirty legislatures (including Minnesota's) have codified the whole act rule *and* the presumption of consistent usage of terms within a statute (Table 3). Thirty-one have codified the rule against interpreting one provision in a way that is inconsistent with the structure of the statute (Table

3). Ten states (including Minnesota) have codified the rule against surplusage (Table 3).

• **Consistency Across Statutes.** Twenty-six states (including Minnesota) have codified the presumption that the same term should be interpreted consistently across different statutes (Table 6). Fifteen states have codified the canon against implied repeals (Table 10).

• **Legislative History.** Eleven states (including Minnesota) have codified the rule that legislative history "may" be considered under various circumstances; no state has legislated against consideration of legislative history (Table 7). Like Minnesota's codification, most of these codifications require the statute to be ambiguous, but a few states (such as Texas) say legislative history can be consulted under any circumstances.

• **Constitutional Canons.** Minnesota is unusual in not codifying any of the constitutional canons. Five states have codified the avoidance canon, though none has rejected it either (Table 8). Thirty-five states have codified the presumption of severability (Table 8). Twenty-four states have codified the presumption against statutory retroactivity (Table 9).

• **Purposive Canons.** Like Minnesota, twenty-one other states have codified the canon that ambiguous statutes should be interpreted to carry out the legislative purpose (Table 10). Nineteen state legislatures say that remedial statutes should be liberally construed, and seventeen states say that all statutes should be liberally construed (Table 11). Eleven states have codified the presumption that the legislature intends "reasonable" results (Table 11).

Scott argues from this exhaustive survey that there is a "common law" of canons of statutory construction—a common law to which legislatures and not just courts are contributing. He suggests that judges ought to be chary of deploying canons, such as *expressio unius*, that legislatures have uniformly failed to embrace. If statutory interpretation is supposed to be attentive to legislative intent, as most state legislatures and courts claim, is it not relevant that legislated canons never include *expressio unius* or *ejusdem generis* and overwhelmingly endorse the absurd results exception to plain meaning and the importance of legislative purpose in resolving statutory ambiguities?

Moreover, this survey might have some traction for general theories of statutory interpretation. Scott concludes that state legislatures are not friendly to the new textualism's methodology: although legislatures endorse the plain meaning rule, they do so with allowance for an absurd result exception and tend to favor consultation of legislative history and statutory purpose. Conversely, Scott suggests that the pattern of legislative codification lends legislative, and perhaps democratic, support and legitimacy to the pragmatic approach laid out in William Eskridge Jr. and Philip Frickey, *Statutory Interpretation as Practical Reasoning*, 42 Stan. L. Rev. 321 (1990) (Chapter 6, § 3C). How would a new textualist respond to this?

For an argument that Congress has and should exercise the authority to enact more ambitious federal rules of statutory interpretation (more like those of Minnesota and other states), see Nicholas Rosenkranz, *Federal Rules of Statutory Interpretation*, 115 Harv. L. Rev. 2085 (2002). For a critique and modification of this approach, see Adam Kiracofe, Note, *The Codified Canons of Statutory Construction: A Response and Proposal to Nicholas Rosenkranz's* Federal Rules of Statutory Interpretation, 84 B.U. L.

Rev. 571 (2004). For a critique and counter-proposal suggesting that an organization like the American Law Institute formulate a restatement of statutory interpretation, see Gary O'Connor, *Restatement (First) of Statutory Interpretation*, 7 N.Y.U. J. Legis. & Pub. Pol'y 333 (2003–04). But see Lawrence Solan, *Is it Time for a Restatement of Statutory Interpretation?*, 79 Brooklyn L. Rev. 733 (2014) (arguing that it would be misleading to suggest that consensus about statutory interpretation is sufficient to justify a restatement).

3. EXTRINSIC SOURCES FOR STATUTORY INTERPRETATION

Extrinsic aids for statutory interpretation are sources outside the text of the statute being interpreted. Such sources include the common law (examined in Part A of this Section), the legislative background of the statute (Part B), and other statutes and their interpretation (Part C). The traditional rule was that extrinsic aids should not be considered if the statute had a "plain meaning." But how can we be sure that the statute really has a plain meaning, without considering context? For example, if the legislature uses a term such as "fraud," which had an established common law meaning at the time, we should have to consult extrinsic evidence just to figure out what the plain meaning might be. Or if legislative discussions reveal a specialized use of the term "fraud," shouldn't they be relevant?

The new textualists introduced in Chapter 6, § 3A believe that the common law and other statutes are usually admissible extrinsic evidence, but legislative background or history is not. This position is examined more closely in Parts B(1) and (2). It has had some influence on the Supreme Court and the lower federal courts. Ironically, state courts have in the last several decades become more likely to consider legislative history, because documentary legislative materials are more readily available.[45]

A. THE COMMON LAW

The traditional rule in Anglo-American law was that statutes in derogation of the common law should be narrowly construed. This was the philosophy of Blackstone's *Commentaries*, which were pervasively influential at the founding of our constitutional republic, and in the early Supreme Court, especially in admiralty cases.[46] As the Supreme Court later articulated the principle, "[n]o statute is to be construed as altering the common law, farther than its words import." *Shaw v. Railroad Co.*, 101 U.S. (11 Otto) 557, 565 (1879). This canon reflected the

---

[45] For a comprehensive overview, see Jos Torres & Steve Windsor, *State Legislative Histories: A Select, Annotated Bibliography*, 85 Law Libr. J. 545 (1993). For an in-depth examination of developments in five states, see Abbe Gluck, *The States as Laboratories of Statutory Interpretation: Methodological Consensus and the New Modified Textualism*, 119 Yale L.J. 1750 (2010).

[46] For early history, see William Eskridge Jr., *All About Words: The Original Understandings of the "Judicial Power" in Statutory Interpretation, 1776–1806*, 101 Colum. L. Rev. 990 (2001). The best historical source for eighteenth century English thinking is David Lieberman, *The Province of Legislation Determined* 16–20, 28, 52–72 (1989) (discussing the proliferation of mangled statutes in eighteenth-century England and Blackstone's disdainful attitude toward them, with judges being the main salvation by protecting the common law against bad statutes).

foundational character of the common law as a regulatory regime. Any deviation from common-law rules needed special justification.

Such a rule has eroded in the modern regulatory statute, where statutes are the rule and common law the exception. For example, in *Isbrandtsen Co. v. Johnson*, 343 U.S. 779, 783 (1952), the Supreme Court held, in an admiralty proceeding by a seaman for wages earned, that the employer's common-law right to set off damages resulting from the seaman's dereliction of duty had been preempted by federal statute. The Court stated:

> Statutes which invade the common law or the general maritime law are to be read with a presumption favoring the retention of long-established and familiar principles, except when a statutory purpose to the contrary is evident. No rule of construction precludes giving a natural meaning to legislation like this that obviously is of a remedial, beneficial and amendatory character. It should be interpreted so as to effect its purpose. Marine legislation, at least since the Shipping Commissioners Act of June 7, 1872, 17 Stat. 262, should be construed to make effective its design to change the general maritime law so as to improve the lot of seamen.

Isbrandtsen noted, further, that federal statutes regulated virtually every aspect of a seaman's rights and duties, hence negating the force of the common law argument. This suggests another reason for the demise of the common law canon: statutes substantially occupy the field to regulate many areas of human activity, whereas in the nineteenth century (the heyday of the common law canon) statutory regulation was the exception.[47]

Nonetheless, the common law remains an important extrinsic source for interpreting many statutes. As noted above, when the legislature deploys words with established common law meanings, courts will presume that those meanings are adopted by Congress. E.g., *Wallace v. Kato*, 549 U.S. 384, 388–89 (2007) (§ 1983); *Cmty. for Creative Non-Violence v. Reid*, 490 U.S. 730, 739 (1989). Especially for older, more generally phrased statutes, the common law serves a broader "gap-filling" role: For issues entirely unaddressed by the statute, the interpreter might presume that the legislature intended to adopt the established common law rule. Consider the following problem, and then a leading case, to see how important the common law still is for filling in gaps.

INTRODUCTORY PROBLEM:
THE COMMON LAW AS EXTRINSIC EVIDENCE

Problem 7–4. The Civil Rights Act of 1871, 17 Stat. 13, codified as amended at 42 U.S.C. § 1983, provides as follows:

> Every person who, under color of any statute, ordinance, regulation, custom, or usage, of any State or Territory or the District of Columbia, subjects, or causes to be subjected, any citizen of the United States or other

---

[47] Compare *United States v. Texas*, 507 U.S. 529 (1993) (applying *Isbrandsten* standard but concluding that federal common law principle was not abrogated by federal statute).

person within the jurisdiction thereof to the deprivation of any rights, privileges, or immunities secured by the Constitution and laws, shall be liable to the party injured in an action at law, suit in equity, or other proper proceeding for redress.

This statute was passed in 1871, as part of the Reconstruction effort to ensure newly freed slaves their rights as citizens.

Carl Doe, an official of the NAACP, organizes a boycott of stores in Tylertown, Mississippi, because the stores follow segregated practices. He also organizes a sit-in. The sheriff arrests Doe for breach of the peace, and state Judge Joyce Judicious orders Doe to cease any and all activity meant to disrupt Tylertown businesses. Doe points out that a long line of Supreme Court First Amendment precedents render such an order "lawless," and Judge Judicious holds Doe in contempt and sentences him to a day in jail. When Judge Judicious' order is overturned, Doe sues the sheriff and the judge under § 1983 for violating his First Amendment rights. The sheriff settles the case with Doe, but Judge Judicious argues judicial immunity.

Judge Judicious demonstrates that at common law judges were immune from lawsuits arising out of their judicial duties. The Supreme Court in *Bradley v. Fisher*, 80 U.S. (13 Wall.) 335 (1871), endorsed absolute judicial immunity in order to protect the integrity of judicial decisionmaking, which would be compromised if the judge were worried about being sued by the losers of lawsuits. Because Congress may be assumed not to disturb such a long-established rule of immunity, § 1983 should be interpreted to include this immunity, argues Judicious.

Doe disagrees and cites to the legislative background of § 1983. During Reconstruction, the South was marked by disorder and violence, especially against the newly emancipated black citizens. Often this violence was accomplished under color of state law—through lynchings, rigged trials, and official harassment of freed slaves. The Reconstruction Congress enacted the Civil Rights Act of 1866, 14 Stat. 27, to abate the violence. Section 2 of the 1866 Act provided criminal liability for any person who, under color of any law, deprived another of federal rights by reason of race. Most of the discussion of § 2 recognized that it would apply to state judges, for much of the oppression was conducted through state tribunals. A proposed amendment to exempt state judges from criminal liability failed. President Johnson vetoed the 1866 bill, in part because it would allow prosecution of state court judges. Members of Congress objected to President Johnson's reason. "I answer it is better to invade the judicial power of the State than permit it to invade, strike down, and destroy the civil rights of citizens. A judicial power perverted to such uses should be speedily invaded," argued Representative Lawrence. Congress passed the bill over the President's veto.

Another amendment not adopted in 1866 was Representative Bingham's proposal to substitute a civil action for the criminal penalties of § 2. (The bill's sponsor said the law's beneficiaries could not afford civil suits.) Violence against African Americans continued in the South, and this proposal was renewed in 1871. After President Grant informed Congress of the urgency of attacking the violence of Southern racists against blacks, Congress passed the Civil Rights Act of 1871, § 1 of which is the predecessor of § 1983. Representative Shellabarger, the main House sponsor of the 1871 bill, said on the floor of the House that § 2 of the 1866 Act was "the model" for § 1 of the 1871 bill. "[Section 2] provides a criminal proceeding in identically the same case as [§ 1] provides a civil remedy for, except that the deprivation under color of State law must, under the

[1866 Act], have been on account of race, color, or former slavery." The Senate sponsor, Senator Edmunds, stated that § 1 was intended to carry out the principles of the 1866 Act. No one in Congress disputed the analogy.

There was little discussion of § 1 in Congress (most of the discussion focused on the criminal conspiracy provision of the 1871 bill). Opponents of § 1 stressed its invasion of judicial independence and cited to criminal prosecutions of judges under the 1866 Act. "By the first section, in certain cases, the judge of a State court, though acting under oath of office, is made liable to a suit in Federal court and subject to damages for his decision against a suitor," exclaimed Representative Lewis (an opponent of the 1871 bill). Although Representative Shellabarger often corrected opponents' mischaracterizations of his bill, he never disputed opponents' allegations that § 1 would render judges civilly liable. Supporters of the 1871 bill argued that in the South "courts are in many instances under the control of those who are wholly inimical to the impartial administration of law and equity" and that the criminal liability of the 1866 Act was not enough to stop those abuses of justice. The 1871 bill was passed overwhelmingly. This legislative background, argues Doe, shows that the 1871 Congress did *not* expect that § 1 would include the common law's judicial immunity doctrine.

Would the Supreme Court accept Judicious' argument that she is immune from § 1983 in this setting? Is this a case where the Court should follow long-established and familiar common law principles? Alternatively, is there a plainly evident statutory purpose that Congress meant to depart from or abolish common law immunities? Compare *Pierson v. Ray*, 386 U.S. 547 (1967).

Now that you know something about § 1983, evaluate a different kind of issue: For officials who can be sued for damages, what damages might be allowed? Under what circumstances can punitive damages be awarded, for example? Consider the following case.

STATUTORY PREFACE TO *SMITH V. WADE*

42 U.S.C. 1983.   *Civil action for deprivation of rights.*

Every person who, under color of any statute, ordinance, regulation, custom, or usage, of any State or Territory or the District of Columbia, subjects, or causes to be subjected, any citizen of the United States or other person within the jurisdiction thereof to the deprivation of any rights, privileges, or immunities secured by the Constitution and laws, shall be liable to the party injured in an action at law, suit in equity, or other proper proceeding for redress, * * *

SMITH V. WADE
Supreme Court of the United States, 1983.
461 U.S. 30, 103 S.Ct. 1625, 75 L.Ed.2d 632.

JUSTICE BRENNAN delivered the opinion of the Court.

[Wade, an inmate of a Missouri state prison, brought a § 1983 suit against Smith and four guards and correction officials. Wade alleged that he was assaulted by cellmates and that defendants did nothing even though they knew or ought to have known that such an assault was likely to occur. The trial judge instructed the jury that Wade could obtain punitive damages if defendants' conduct was in reckless disregard of, or indifferent to, Wade's safety. The jury found Smith liable for both compensatory and punitive damages, and the circuit court affirmed. The issue before the Court was whether punitive damages may be awarded in a § 1983 action based upon a finding of reckless or callous disregard of, or indifference to, plaintiff's rights, or, as Smith contended, only upon a finding that the defendant acted with "actual malicious intent."]

Section 1983 is derived from § 1 of the Civil Rights Act of 1871, 17 Stat. 13. It was intended to create "a species of tort liability" in favor of persons deprived of federally secured rights. *Carey v. Piphus*, 435 U.S. 247, 253 (1978); *Imbler v. Pachtman*, 424 U.S. 409, 417 (1976). We noted in *Carey* that there was little in the section's legislative history concerning the damages recoverable for this tort liability. In the absence of more specific guidance, we looked first to the common law of torts (both modern and as of 1871), with such modification or adaptation as might be necessary to carry out the purpose and policy of the statute. We have done the same in other contexts arising under § 1983, especially the recurring problem of common-law immunities.[2]

[Smith conceded that punitive damages are available in a "proper" § 1983 action.] Smith argues, nonetheless, that this was not a "proper" case in which to award punitive damages. More particularly, he attacks the instruction that punitive damages could be awarded on a finding of reckless or callous disregard of or indifference to Wade's rights or safety. Instead, he contends that the proper test is one of actual malicious intent—"ill will, spite, or intent to injure." He offers two arguments for this position: first, that actual intent is the proper standard for punitive damages in all cases under § 1983; and second, that even if intent is not always required, it should be required here because the threshold for punitive damages should always be higher than that for liability in the first instance. We address these in turn.

[III] Smith does not argue that the common law, either in 1871 or now, required or requires a showing of actual malicious intent for recovery of punitive damages.

---

[2] [Citing cases, including *Pierson* (See Problem 7–4).]

Justice Rehnquist's dissent faults us for referring to modern tort decisions in construing § 1983. Its argument rests on the unstated and unsupported premise that Congress necessarily intended to freeze into permanent law whatever principles were current in 1871, rather than to incorporate applicable general legal principles as they evolve. [citing Justice O'Connor's dissent as well]. The dissents are correct, of course, that when the language of the section and its legislative history provide no clear answer, we have found useful guidance in the law prevailing at the time when § 1983 was enacted; but it does not follow that that law is absolutely controlling or that current law is irrelevant. On the contrary, if the prevailing view on some point of general tort law had changed substantially in the intervening century (which is not the case here), we might be highly reluctant to assume that Congress intended to perpetuate a now-obsolete doctrine. See *Carey v. Piphus* ("[O]ver the centuries the common law of torts has developed a set of rules to implement the principle that a person should be compensated fairly for injuries caused by the violation of his legal rights. These rules, defining the elements of damages and the prerequisites for their recovery, provide the appropriate starting point for the inquiry under § 1983 as well.") (footnote omitted). Indeed, in *Imbler* we recognized a common-law immunity that first came into existence 25 years after § 1983 was enacted. Under the dissents' view, *Imbler* was wrongly decided.

Perhaps not surprisingly, there was significant variation (both terminological and substantive) among American jurisdictions in the latter nineteenth century on the precise standard to be applied in awarding punitive damages—variation that was exacerbated by the ambiguity and slipperiness of such common terms as "malice" and "gross negligence."[8] Most of the confusion, however, seems to have been over the degree of negligence, recklessness, carelessness, or culpable indifference that should be required—not over whether actual intent was essential. On the contrary, the rule in a large majority of jurisdictions was that punitive damages (also called exemplary damages, vindictive damages, or smart money) could be awarded without a showing of actual ill will, spite, or intent to injure.

This Court so stated on several occasions, before and shortly after 1871. In *Philadelphia, W. & B.R. Co. v. Quigley*, 62 U.S. (21 How.) 202 (1859), a diversity libel suit, the Court held erroneous an instruction that authorized the jury to return a punitive award but gave the jury virtually no substantive guidance as to the proper threshold. We described the standard thus:

> "Whenever the injury complained of has been inflicted maliciously or wantonly, and with circumstances of contumely or indignity, the jury are not limited to the ascertainment of a simple compensation for the wrong committed against the aggrieved person. But the malice spoken of in this rule is not merely the doing of an unlawful or injurious act. The word implies that the act complained of was conceived in the spirit of mischief, *or of criminal indifference to civil obligations.*" *Id.* at 214. * * *

The large majority of state and lower federal courts were in agreement that punitive damages awards did not require a showing of actual malicious intent; they permitted punitive awards on variously stated standards of negligence, recklessness, or other culpable conduct short of actual malicious intent.[12]

The same rule applies today. The Restatement (Second) of Torts (1977), for example, states: "Punitive damages may be awarded for conduct that is outrageous, because of the defendant's evil motive *or his reckless indifference to the rights of others.*" *Id.*, § 908(2) (emphasis added); see also *id.*, Comment *b.* Most cases under

---

[8] [Footnote 8 is 76 lines of the U.S. Reports, attacking Justice Rehnquist's assumption that in 1871 "malice," "wantonness," and "willfulness" all denoted ill will. Justice Brennan asserted that "[w]ith regard to 'malice' the assumption is dubious at best; with regard to 'wantonness' and 'willfulness,' it is just plain wrong."]

[12] * * * *Maysville & L.R. Co. v. Herrick*, 76 Ky. 122 (1877), held that the trial court correctly refused to instruct the jury that "willful or intentional wrong" was required to award punitive damages in a railroad accident case, remarking: "The absence of slight care in the management of a railroad station, or in keeping a railroad track in repair, is gross negligence; and to enable a passenger to recover punitive damages, in a case like this, it is not necessary to show the absence of all care, or 'reckless indifference to the safety of * * * passengers,' or 'intentional misconduct' on the part of the agents and officers of the company." *Id.* at 127 (ellipsis in original). [Justice Brennan cited 30 cases in accord with this proposition.]

Justice Rehnquist's assertion that a "solid majority of jurisdictions" required actual malicious intent is simply untrue. In fact, there were fairly few jurisdictions that imposed such a requirement, and fewer yet that adhered to it consistently. Justice Rehnquist's attempt to establish this proposition with case citations does not offer him substantial support. Because the point is not of controlling significance, we will not tarry here to analyze his citations case-by-case or state-by-state, but will only summarize the main themes. [According to Justice Brennan, some of the dissenters' cases support the availability of punitive damages for recklessness, others are too equivocal to categorize, and others support the dissenters' interpretation only if one assumes that terms like "malice," "wantonness," and "criminal" always meant actual intent to injure.]

state common law, although varying in their precise terminology, have adopted more or less the same rule, recognizing that punitive damages in tort cases may be awarded not only for actual intent to injure or evil motive, but also for recklessness, serious indifference to or disregard for the rights of others, or even gross negligence.[13]

The remaining question is whether the policies and purposes of § 1983 itself require a departure from the rules of tort common law. As a general matter, we discern no reason why a person whose federally guaranteed rights have been violated should be granted a more restrictive remedy than a person asserting an ordinary tort cause of action. Smith offers us no persuasive reason to the contrary.

Smith's argument, which he offers in several forms, is that an actual-intent standard is preferable to a recklessness standard because it is less vague. He points out that punitive damages, by their very nature, are not awarded to compensate the injured party. He concedes, of course, that deterrence of future egregious conduct is a primary purpose of both § 1983 and of punitive damages, see * * * Restatement (Second) of Torts § 908(1) (1979). But deterrence, he contends, cannot be achieved unless the standard of conduct sought to be deterred is stated with sufficient clarity to enable potential defendants to conform to the law and to avoid the proposed sanction. Recklessness or callous indifference, he argues, is too uncertain a standard to achieve deterrence rationally and fairly. A prison guard, for example, can be expected to know whether he is acting with actual ill will or intent to injure, but not whether he is being reckless or callously indifferent.

Smith's argument, if valid, would apply to ordinary tort cases as easily as to § 1983 suits; hence, it hardly presents an argument for adopting a different rule under § 1983. In any event, the argument is unpersuasive. While, *arguendo*, an intent standard may be easier to understand and apply to particular situations than a recklessness standard, we are not persuaded that a recklessness standard is too vague to be fair or useful. In [*Milwaukee & St. Paul R. Co. v. Arms*, 91 U.S. (1 Otto) 489 (1876),] we adopted a recklessness standard rather than a gross negligence standard precisely because recklessness would better serve the need for adequate clarity and fair application. Almost a century later, in the First Amendment context, we held that punitive damages cannot be assessed for defamation in the absence of proof of "knowledge of falsity or reckless disregard for the truth." [*Gertz v. Robert Welch, Inc.*, 418 U.S. 323, 349 (1974).] Our concern in *Gertz* was that the threat of punitive damages, if not limited to especially egregious cases, might "inhibit the vigorous exercise of First Amendment freedoms"—a concern at least as pressing as any urged by Smith in this case. Yet we did not find it necessary to impose an actual-intent standard there. Just as Smith has not shown why § 1983 should give higher protection from punitive damages than ordinary tort law, he has not explained why it gives higher protection than we have demanded under the First Amendment.

More fundamentally, Smith's argument for certainty in the interest of deterrence overlooks the distinction between a standard for punitive damages and a

---

[13] [Justice Brennan cited 33 recent state cases to support the proposition in text.]

standard of liability in the first instance. Smith seems to assume that prison guards and other state officials look mainly to the standard for punitive damages in shaping their conduct. We question the premise; we assume, and hope, that most officials are guided primarily by the underlying standards of federal substantive law—both out of devotion to duty, and in the interest of avoiding liability for compensatory damages. At any rate, the conscientious officer who desires clear guidance on how to do his job and avoid lawsuits can and should look to the standard for actionability in the first instance. The need for exceptional clarity in the standard for punitive damages arises only if one assumes that there are substantial numbers of officers who will not be deterred by compensatory damages; only such officers will seek to guide their conduct by the punitive damages standard. The presence of such officers constitutes a powerful argument *against* raising the threshold for punitive damages.

In this case, the jury was instructed to apply a high standard of constitutional right ("physical abuse of such base, inhumane and barbaric proportions as to shock the sensibilities"). It was also instructed, under the principle of qualified immunity, that Smith could not be held liable at all unless he was guilty of "a callous indifference or a thoughtless disregard for the consequences of [his] act or failure to act," or of "a flagrant or remarkably bad failure to protect" Wade. These instructions are not challenged in this Court, nor were they challenged on grounds of vagueness in the lower courts. Smith's contention that this recklessness standard is too vague to provide clear guidance and reasonable deterrence might more properly be reserved for a challenge seeking different standards of liability in the first instance. As for punitive damages, however, in the absence of any persuasive argument to the contrary based on the policies of § 1983, we are content to adopt the policy judgment of the common law—that reckless or callous disregard for the plaintiff's rights, as well as intentional violations of federal law, should be sufficient to trigger a jury's consideration of the appropriateness of punitive damages.

[Justice Brennan, finally, rejected Smith's last argument, that it was error for the court to describe the standard of punitive damages in terms similar to those of the basic liability under § 1983 (indifference to Wade's rights). Primary reliance was placed on the Restatement (Second) of Torts and the modern common law, which generally provide that where the standard for compensatory liability is as high or higher than the usual threshold for punitive damages, such damages may be given without requiring any extra showing.]

JUSTICE REHNQUIST, with whom THE CHIEF JUSTICE [BURGER] and JUSTICE POWELL join, dissenting.

The Court rejects a "wrongful intent" standard, instead requiring a plaintiff to show merely "reckless * * * indifference to the federally protected rights of others." The following justifications are offered by the Court for this result: first, the rule in "[m]ost cases [decided in the last 15 years] under state common law" is "more or less" equivalent to a recklessness standard; second, the Court asserts that a similar rule "prevail[ed] at the time when § 1983 was enacted"; and finally, there is an "absence of any persuasive argument" for not applying existing state tort rules to the federal statutory remedies available against state and local officials under

§ 1983. In my opinion none of these justifications, taken singly or together, supports the Court's result. First, the decisions of state courts in the last decade or so are all but irrelevant in determining the intent of the 42d Congress, and thus, the meaning of § 1983. Second, the Court's characterization of the common law rules prevailing when § 1983 was enacted is both oversimplified and misleading; in fact, the majority rule in 1871 seems to have been that some sort of "evil intent"— and not mere recklessness—was necessary to justify an award of punitive damages. Third, the Court's inability to distinguish a *state* court's award of punitive damages against a state officer from a *federal* court's analogous action under §§ 1983 and 1988 precludes it from adequately assessing the public policies implicated by its decision. Finally, the Court fails utterly to grapple with the cogent and persuasive criticisms that have been offered of punitive damages generally.

[Part I of Justice Rehnquist's dissenting opinion is a brief consideration of criticism of punitive damages. In light of this criticism, some states do not allow punitive damage awards, and others have required some sort of evil motive to justify punitive awards. This latter proposition is supported by footnote 3, which spends more than 120 lines analyzing nineteenth-century use of the terms "malice," "willfulness," and "wantonness." His overall point is that nineteenth-century thinkers reserved punitive awards for those who "subjectively" visited evil on others, not those whose conduct was deemed to have failed an "objective" or recklessness standard.]

[II] At bottom, this case requires the Court to decide when a particular remedy is available under § 1983. Until today, the Court has adhered, with some fidelity, to the scarcely controversial principle that its proper role in interpreting § 1983 is determining what the 42d Congress intended. That § 1983 is to be interpreted according to this basic principle of statutory construction is clearly demonstrated by our many decisions relying upon the plain language of the section. The Court's opinion purports to pursue an inquiry into legislative intent, yet relies heavily upon state court decisions decided well after the 42d Congress adjourned. I find these cases unilluminating, at least in part because I am unprepared to attribute to the 42d Congress the truly extraordinary foresight that the Court seems to think it had. The reason our earlier decisions interpreting § 1983 have relied upon common law decisions is simple: members of the 42d Congress were lawyers, familiar with the law of their time. In resolving ambiguities in the enactments of that Congress, as with other Congresses, it is useful to consider the legal principles and rules that shaped the thinking of its Members. The decisions of state courts decided well after 1871, while of some academic interest, are largely irrelevant to what Members of the 42d Congress intended by way of a standard for punitive damages.

In an apparent attempt to justify its novel approach to discerning the intent of a body that deliberated more than a century ago, the Court makes passing reference to our decisions relating to common law immunities under § 1983. These decisions provide no support for the Court's analysis, since they all plainly evidence an attempt to discern the intent of the 42d Congress, albeit indirectly, by reference to the common law principles known to members of that body. * * * More recently, in *City of Newport v. Fact Concerts, Inc.*, 453 U.S. 247, 258 (1981), we said:

It is by now well settled that the tort liability created by § 1983 cannot be understood in a historical vacuum. * * * One important assumption underlying the Court's decisions in this area is that members of the 42d Congress were familiar with common-law principles, including defenses previously recognized in ordinary tort litigation, and that they likely intended these common-law principles to obtain, absent specific provisions to the contrary.

Likewise, our other decisions with respect to common law immunities under § 1983 clearly reveal that our consideration of state common law rules is only a device to facilitate determination of Congressional intent. Decisions from the 1970s, relied on by the Court, are almost completely irrelevant to this inquiry into legislative intent.

[III] The Court also purports to rely on decisions, handed down in the second half of the last century by this Court, in drawing up its rule that mere recklessness will support an award of punitive damages. In fact, these decisions unambiguously support an actual malice standard. The Court rests primarily on *Philadelphia, W. & B.R. Co. v. Quigley*, 62 U.S. (21 How.) 202 (1859), a diversity tort action against a railroad. There, we initially observed that in "certain actions of tort," punitive damages might be awarded, and then described those actions as "[w]henever the injury complained of has been inflicted maliciously or wantonly, and with circumstances of contumely or indignity." *Id.* at 214. * * * [I]t was relatively clear at the time that "malice" required a showing of actual ill will or intent to injure. Perhaps foreseeing future efforts to expand the rule, however, we hastened to specify the type of malice that would warrant punitive damages: "the malice spoken of in this rule is not merely the doing of an unlawful or injurious act. The word implies that the act complained of *was conceived in the spirit of mischief, or of criminal indifference to civil obligations*." It would have been difficult to have more clearly expressed the "actual malice" standard. We explicitly rejected an "implied malice" formulation, and then mandated inquiry into the "spirit" in which a defendant's act was "conceived."

[Justice Rehnquist analyzed other nineteenth century Supreme Court decisions consistent with his reading of *Quigley*.] In *Lake Shore & Michigan Southern Railway Co. v. Prentice*, 147 U.S. 101 (1893), the Court considered whether punitive damages were properly awarded against a railroad in a diversity action. The Court noted that the law on the subject was "well-settled," and paraphrased the *Quigley* standard: The jury may award punitive damages "if the defendant has acted wantonly, or oppressively, or with such malice as implies a spirit of mischief or criminal indifference to civil obligations." Then, * * * the Court explained this formulation, observing that a "*guilty intention* on the part of the defendant is *required* in order to charge him with exemplary or punitive damages." *Ibid.* (emphasis added). * * *

In addition, the decisions rendered by state courts in the years preceding and immediately following the enactment of § 1983 attest to the fact that a solid majority of jurisdictions took the view that the standard for an award of punitive damages included a requirement of ill will. To be sure, a few jurisdictions followed a broader standard; a careful review of the decisions at the time uncovers a number of decisions that contain some reference to "recklessness." And equally clearly, in more recent years many courts have adopted a standard including "recklessness" as the minimal degree of culpability warranting punitive damages.

Most clear of all, however, is the fact that at about the time § 1983 was enacted a considerable number of the 37 States then belonging to the Union required some showing of wrongful intent before punitive damages could be awarded.[12] As the cases set out in the margin reveal, it is but a statement of the obvious that "evil motive" was the general standard for punitive damages in many states at the time of the 42d Congress. * * *

[IV] Even apart from this historical background, I am persuaded by a variety of additional factors that the 42d Congress intended a "wrongful intent" requirement. As mentioned above, punitive damages are not, and never have been, a favored remedy. In determining whether Congress, not bound by *stare decisis*, would have embraced this often-condemned doctrine, it is worth considering the judgment of one of the most respected commentators in the field regarding the desirability of a legislatively enacted punitive damages remedy: "It is probable that, in the framing of a model code of damages today for use in a country unhampered by legal tradition, the doctrine of exemplary damages would find no place." C. McCormick, *Damages* 276 (1935).

In deciding whether Congress heeded such advice, it is useful to consider the language of § 1983 itself—which should, of course, be the starting point for any inquiry into legislative intent. Section 1983 provides:

> "Every person who, under color of any statute, ordinance, regulation, custom, or usage of any State * * * subjects, or causes to be subjected, any citizen of the United States or other person within the jurisdiction thereof to the deprivation of any rights, privileges, or immunities secured by the Constitution and laws, shall be liable to the party *injured* in an action at law, suit in equity, or other proper proceeding *for redress*." (emphasis added).

Plainly, the statutory language itself provides absolutely no support for the cause of action for punitive damages that the Court reads into the provision.

---

[12] See, *e.g., Roberts v. Hiem,* 27 Ala. 678, 683 (1855) ("the law allows [punitive damages] whenever the trespass is committed in a rude, aggravating, or insulting manner, as malice may be inferred from these circumstances"); [citations to 76 state cases followed, most with quotations to illustrate Justice Rehnquist's position]

The Court's treatment of the law prevailing in 1871 relies principally upon state-court decisions from the 1880's and 1890's. These cases are admittedly somewhat more relevant to what the 42d Congress intended than the 20th-century cases cited by the Court; particularly if they explain prior decisions, these cases may reflect a well-settled understanding in a particular jurisdiction of the law regarding punitive damages. Yet, decisions handed down well after 1871 are considerably *less* probative of legislative intent than decisions rendered before or shortly subsequent to the enactment of § 1983: it requires no detailed discussion to demonstrate that a member of the 42d Congress would have been more influenced by a decision from 1870 than by one from the 1890's. Accordingly, the bulk of the cases cited by the Court must be ignored; they simply illustrate the historical shift in legal doctrine, pointed out in text, from an actual-intent standard to a recklessness standard. If the Court is serious in its attention to 19th-century law, analysis must focus on the common law as it stood at the time of the 42d Congress. Here, notwithstanding the Court's numerous attempts to explain why decisions do not mean what they plainly say, it remains clear that in a majority of jurisdictions, actual malice was required in order to recover punitive damages.

Indeed, it merely creates "liab[ility] to the party injured * * * for redress." "Redress" means "[r]eparation of, satisfaction or compensation for, a wrong sustained or the loss resulting from this." 8 Oxford English Dictionary 310 (1933). And, as the Court concedes, punitive damages are not "reparation" or "compensation"; their very purpose is to punish, not to compensate. If Congress meant to create a right to recover punitive damages, then it chose singularly inappropriate words: both the reference to injured parties and to redress suggests compensation, and not punishment.

Other statutes roughly contemporaneous with § 1983 illustrate that if Congress wanted to subject persons to a punitive damages remedy, it did so explicitly. For example, in § 59, 16 Stat. 207, Congress created express punitive damage remedies for various types of commercial misconduct. Likewise, the False Claims Act, § 15, 12 Stat. 698, provided a civil remedy of double damages and a $2,000 civil forfeiture penalty for certain misstatements to the Government. As one Court of Appeals has remarked, "Where Congress has intended [to create a right to punitive damages] it has found no difficulty in using language appropriate to that end." *United Mine Workers v. Patton*, 211 F.2d 742, 749 (4th Cir. 1954). And yet, in § 1983 one searches in vain for some hint of such a remedy.

In the light of the foregoing indications, it is accurate to say that the foundation upon which the right to punitive damages under § 1983 rests is precarious, at the best. * * *

JUSTICE O'CONNOR, dissenting.

Although I agree with the result reached in Justice Rehnquist's dissent, I write separately because I cannot agree with the approach taken by either the Court or Justice Rehnquist. Both opinions engage in exhaustive, but ultimately unilluminating, exegesis of the common law of the availability of punitive damages in 1871. Although both the Court and Justice Rehnquist display admirable skills in legal research and analysis of great numbers of musty cases, the results do not significantly further the goal of the inquiry: to establish the intent of the 42d Congress. In interpreting § 1983, we have often looked to the common law as it existed in 1871, in the belief that, when Congress was silent on a point, it intended to adopt the principles of the common law with which it was familiar. This approach makes sense when there was a generally prevailing rule of common law, for then it is reasonable to assume that congressmen were familiar with that rule and imagined that it would cover the cause of action that they were creating. But when a significant split in authority existed, it strains credulity to argue that Congress simply assumed that one view rather than the other would govern. Particularly in a case like this one, in which those interpreting the common law of 1871 must resort to dictionaries in an attempt to translate the language of the late nineteenth century into terms that judges of the late twentieth century can understand, and in an area in which the courts of the earlier period frequently used inexact and contradictory language, we cannot safely infer anything about congressional intent from the divided contemporaneous judicial opinions. The battle of the string citations can have no winner.

Once it is established that the common law of 1871 provides us with no real guidance on this question, we should turn to the policies underlying § 1983 to determine which rule best accords with those policies. In *Fact Concerts*, we identified the purposes of § 1983 as preeminently to compensate victims of constitutional violations and to deter further violations. The conceded availability of compensatory damages, particularly when coupled with the availability of attorney's fees under § 1988, completely fulfills the goal of compensation, leaving only deterrence to be served by awards of punitive damages. We must then confront the close question whether a standard permitting an award of unlimited punitive damages on the basis of recklessness will chill public officials in the performance of their duties more than it will deter violations of the Constitution, and whether the availability of punitive damages for reckless violations of the Constitution in addition to attorney's fees will create an incentive to bring an ever-increasing flood of § 1983 claims, threatening the ability of the federal courts to handle those that are meritorious. Although I cannot concur in Justice Rehnquist's wholesale condemnation of awards of punitive damages in any context or with the suggestion that punitive damages should not be available even for intentional or malicious violations of constitutional rights, I do agree with the discussion in * * * his opinion of the special problems of permitting awards of punitive damages for the recklessness of public officials. Since awards of compensatory damages and attorney's fees already provide significant deterrence, I am persuaded that the policies counseling against awarding punitive damages for the recklessness of public officials outweigh the desirability of any incremental deterrent effect that such awards may have. Consequently, I dissent.

NOTES ON THE EVOLVING COMMON LAW AS A SOURCE FOR CONSTRUING STATUTES

1.   *Interpretation and the Common Law.* Justice Brennan's opinion for the Court argues that the common law in 1871 supports punitive damages for reckless misconduct. Perhaps, but would the common law have permitted a prisoner to obtain such damages from his or her jailer in the circumstances of *Smith v. Wade*? Certainly not! See, e.g., *Moxley v. Roberts*, 43 S.W. 482 (Ky. 1897) (jailer not liable for beating of one prisoner by another unless he actually knew of the beating and failed to stop it); *Williams v. Adams*, 85 Mass. (3 Allen) 171 (1861). Why didn't Justice Brennan just rely on the modern common law, which does support his position?

Contrary to Justice Rehnquist's dissent, the Supreme Court sometimes looks to modern common law to fill in the gaps of § 1983. See *Imbler v. Pachtman*, 424 U.S. 409, 421–22 (1976) (rule of prosecutorial immunity, which was first recognized 25 years after § 1983 was enacted); *Carey v. Piphus*, 435 U.S. 247, 257–58 (1978) (modern law is the starting point for determining which injuries are to be compensated under § 1983). Do you suppose the Congress that adopted § 1983 in 1871 intended that the common law of that era was to supply binding answers to questions left open by the statute? Do you think that the Congress intended courts to develop § 1983 law over time by reference to contemporary developments, and thus that § 1983 might mean one thing in 1871 and quite another thing today?

Note this puzzle: Justices Brennan and Rehnquist looked at the same historical evidence yet came up with diametrically opposed conclusions about what the "common law" was in 1871. The initial, and cynical, impulse is to think that they were just manipulating the evidence to support the result each wanted. A less cynical view is that, in this case, each Justice was an amateur historian, but like professional historians the Justices had to figure out which evidence was important, what to make of conflicting signals, and how to assimilate the evidence into an account. In this complicated task, isn't the perspective of the interpreter going to make a difference? Professional historians recognize this. Shouldn't the Justices? Indeed, this is a point suggested by Justice O'Connor's dissent.

2. *Common Law Statutes.* Going one step beyond Justice Brennan's approach, Judge Richard Posner has argued in *The Federal Courts: Crisis and Reform* (1985) that some statutes, such as § 1983 and the Sherman Act, are essentially "common law statutes." That is, briefly phrased statutes addressing an important societal problem may be the occasion for judicial evolution in the common law tradition, especially if the legislature does not amend the statutes. In legal process argot, courts are institutionally competent to fill in the gaps to a statutory scheme when Congress essentially leaves the statute to judicial elaboration. Does this suggest a defense of Justice Brennan's majority opinion?

Classic instances in which the Supreme Court has interpreted a simple and vague federal statute as evidencing a congressional intent that the federal courts are to resolve open questions by use of an essentially common law method include the antitrust prohibitions of the Sherman Act and § 301 of the Taft-Hartley Act, which gives federal district courts jurisdiction to hear suits for violation of collective bargaining agreements. See, e.g., *Textile Workers Union v. Lincoln Mills*, 353 U.S. 448 (1957) ("federal common law" under § 301). More recently, the Foreign Sovereign Immunities Act of 1976 (FSIA), 28 U.S.C. §§ 1331, 1602–1611 et al., sets forth guidelines for federal and state court treatment of the sovereign immunity defense by foreign states. The main exception to immunity is the "commercial activity" exception, *id.* § 1605(a)(2), but the Act gives no precise definition of commercial activity. "The courts would have a great deal of latitude in determining what is a 'commercial activity' for purposes of this bill," said the House Report, and courts have taken that as a charter to apply the most current common law approaches to the issue. For a recent example applying common law property concepts to fill out the details of the FSIA, see *Permanent Mission of India to the United Nations v. City of New York*, 551 U.S. 193 (2007).

One corollary of the common law statute idea is that Supreme Court precedents interpreting them ought to have the normal stare decisis effect of common law precedents—and not the super-strong presumption of correctness that accompanies other statutory precedents (Chapter 5, Section 2B). See *Leegin Creative Leather Prods., Inc. v. PSKS, Inc.*, 551 U.S. 877 (2007) (precisely this justification for overruling a Sherman Act precedent); *State Oil Co. v. Khan*, 522 U.S. 3 (1997) (same); William Eskridge Jr., *Overruling Statutory Precedents*, 76 Geo. L.J. 1361 (1988). A number of Supreme Court decisions have overruled previous constructions of Section 1983, essentially for common law reasons. E.g., *Monell v. Dep't of Soc. Servs.*, 436 U.S. 658 (1978). It is very likely that a Roberts Court majority would disagree with the *Smith v.*

Wade approach to punitive damages. Should the Court feel free to overrule *Smith*? Are there reasons to exercise caution? Jot down your thoughts and read the next note.

3.   *Recent Statutory Treatment of Punitive Damages in Civil Rights Cases.* The Civil Rights Act of 1991 amended Title VII to permit awards of punitive damages in cases of intentional discrimination. New 42 U.S.C. § 1981a(b)(1) allows such an award if the complainant can show that defendant engaged in such discrimination "with malice or with reckless indifference to the federally protected rights of an aggrieved individual." Carole Kolstad sues her employer for allegedly passing over her for promotion on the basis of her sex. She seeks punitive damages because the decisionmaker not only manipulated the rules to deny her the promotion, but also made repeated derogatory references to women. The lower courts refuse Kolstad a charge to the jury for punitive damages; they rule that, to satisfy § 1981a(b)(1), the complainant must show "egregious" misconduct beyond that which would justify a finding of intentional discrimination.

Following *Smith v. Wade*, the Supreme Court reversed the lower courts and interpreted the 1991 Act to allow punitive damages for reckless as well as egregious conduct. See *Kolstad v. Am. Dental Ass'n*, 527 U.S. 526 (1999). Should *Kolstad* augur against overruling *Smith v. Wade* in section 1983 cases—or does it now provide an *additional reason* to overrule? Under the whole code rule of meaningful variation (*Casey*, § 1C of this chapter), when Congress wants liberal punitive damage awards in civil rights statutes, it explicitly provides for such damages (the 1991 Act). Because § 1983 says nothing about punitive damages, should they be available at all?

How should the Court approach the separate issue of when an employer should be liable in punitive damages for unauthorized conduct on the part of its supervisors? What relevance should the common law of agency have in this inquiry? See *Burlington Indus., Inc. v. Ellerth*, 524 U.S. 642 (1998) (standards for employer liability for hostile work environment and quid pro quo sexual harassment by supervisors).

4.   *The Remedial Canon Versus the Derogation Canon.* In *CSX Transportation, Inc. v. McBride*, 131 S.Ct. 2630 (2011), the Justices divided on whether the tort principle of proximate cause applies to suits brought by railroad employees against their employers for negligence under the Federal Employers Liability Act (FELA). Justice Ginsburg, writing for the Court (joined by Justices Thomas, Breyer, Sotomayor, and Kagan), reasoned that because FELA sought to achieve broad remedial goals, the Court had long applied a relaxed standard of causation under which it would be inappropriate to import the common-law requirement of proximate cause. In dissent, Chief Justice Roberts (joined by Justices Scalia, Kennedy, and Alito) contended that the Court should apply proximate cause to FELA because the statute does not expressly abrogate the common law principle although it does abrogate several other common law rules.

Can the remedial canon be reconciled in some neutral way with the presumption favoring retention of longstanding common law principles? Or do they simply create conflicts that enable judges to cloak their own policy preferences? Should courts rely on either canonical presumption if the text or legislative history indicates that Congress intended a statute to be read broadly or narrowly?

ANOTHER PROBLEM ON THE COMMON LAW AND STATUTES

Problem 7–5. A federal statute prohibits the knowing transportation of "falsely made, forged, altered or counterfeited securities" in interstate commerce. Brook and Crook purchased used cars in Pennsylvania, rolled back the cars' odometers, and fraudulently altered the Pennsylvania titles to reflect the reduced mileage. They then sent the titles to Frook, a Virginia resident. Frook took the titles to Virginia authorities, represented that he owned the cars, and was issued Virginia titles to the cars with the false mileage figures. Frook then sent the Virginia titles to Hook, a Maryland resident, where they were used to sell the cars to unsuspecting buyers. Has Hook violated the statute? Hook says "no," arguing that the Virginia titles he received were not "falsely made" by the Virginia authorities, who had no reason to suspect the accuracy of the information contained in the titles they issued. Hook also argues that, at common law, "falsely made" meant "forgery," and that a document genuinely issued by an appropriate official is therefore not "falsely made." Do you agree? What if a sizable minority of the common law decisions existing at the time the statute was enacted treated such a document as "forged" or "falsely made"? Should the rule of lenity provide an easy way out of this problem? See *Moskal v. United States*, 498 U.S. 103 (1990).

B. LEGISLATIVE BACKGROUND (HISTORY)

Statutory history is, in a broad sense, the entire circumstances of a statute's creation and evolution, a point illustrated by the materials in the first subpart that follows. The formal history of a statute's evolution is widely considered relevant to statutory interpretation, even in jurisdictions whose courts will not examine legislative debates. See, e.g., Donald Gifford, *Statutory Interpretation* 91–95 (1990) (Australia). The same is true for the United States, whose courts do generally examine legislative documents and debates. Thus, the Court in *United States v. Wells*, 519 U.S. 482 (1997), interpreted 18 U.S.C. § 1014, criminalizing false statements to federally insured banks, not to have a materiality requirement. Justice Souter's opinion for the Court relied on the formal history of federal criminal provisions regarding such statements. Section 1014 was a synthesis of thirteen different provisions, at least ten of which had no materiality requirements at the time. This background suggested that Congress did not expect § 1014 to have a materiality requirement.

In this country, the term *legislative history* is mostly used in a narrower sense, to refer to the internal legislative pre-history of a statute—the internal institutional progress of a bill to enactment and the deliberation accompanying that progress.[48] The record of that journey may be quite voluminous and often contains

---

[48] Otto Hetzel, Michael Libonati & Robert Williams, *Legislative Law and Process* 589 (3d ed. 2001), gives an excellent checklist of the materials that will constitute the "legislative history" of a law:

1. Floor debate.
2. Planned colloquy.
3. Prepared statements on submission of a bill, in committee hearings and at the time of floor debates.
4. Revised and amended statements.
5. Statements in committees by the relevant executive branch administrators.
6. Committee reports.
7. Transcripts of discussions at committee hearings.

statements by all sorts of people—legislators, bureaucrats, citizens, experts—which support one or another interpretation of the statute. A preliminary issue is how to carry out legal research that will reveal all the components of a statute's legislative history.[49] Once the material is identified, the question turns to what stuff in this internal legislative history "counts" toward interpreting the statute, and how much weight each relevant component should receive. Four subparts (2–5) will explore judicial use (or misuse) of statements made in committee reports, statements in hearings and floor debates, statements by sponsors, and post-enactment statements by legislators and committees. The last subpart (6) will ask whether interpretive meaning can be derived from things that are *not* said or done in the legislature.

As you read the following materials, consider the suggestion of Judge Patricia Wald, in *Some Observations on the Use of Legislative History in the 1981 Supreme Court Term*, 68 Iowa L. Rev. 195, 214 (1983), that "consistent and uniform rules for statutory construction and use of legislative materials are not being followed today. It sometimes seems that citing legislative history is still, as my late colleague Harold Leventhal once observed, akin to 'looking over a crowd and picking out your friends.' "[50]

1. The Circumstances Surrounding the Introduction and Consideration of Legislation

STATUTORY PREFACE TO THE LEO SHEEP CASE

An Act to aid in the Construction of a Railroad and Telegraph Line from the Missouri River to the Pacific Ocean, and to secure to the Government

---

8. Statements and submissions by interested persons, both local or state government and private parties.

9. Committee debates on "mark-up" of bills.

10. Conference committee reports.

11. Analysis of bills by legislative counsel.

12. Analysis of bills by relevant executive departments.

13. Amendments accepted or rejected.

14. Actions on and discussions about separate bills on the same topic, offered by each house, or in contrast to a similar composite bill.

15. Executive branch messages and proposals whether from the President, cabinet secretaries or from independent agencies.

16. Prior relevant administrative action or judicial decisions, with or without congressional acknowledgment.

17. Other subsequent or prior legislation, especially conflicting acts.

18. Recorded votes.

19. The status of the person speaking, *i.e.*, a sponsor, committee chairman, floor leader, etc.

20. Actions taken and reports, hearings and debates on prior related legislation.

[49] Many law schools offer advanced legal research courses that deal with legislative history and include excellent reference materials.

[50] Judge Leventhal's quip, in somewhat different form, has now made its way into the Supreme Court reports. Justice Scalia has offered it as a justification for his new textualism: "Judge Harold Leventhal used to describe the use of legislative history as the equivalent of entering a crowded cocktail party and looking over the heads of the guests for one's friends." *Conroy v. Aniskoff*, 507 U.S. 511, 519 (1993) (Scalia, J., concurring in the judgment).

the Use of the same for Postal, Military, and Other Purposes (Union Pacific Act) of 1862, § 3, 12 Stat. 489.

Section 3. And be it further enacted, That there be, and is hereby, granted to the said company, for the purpose of aiding in the construction, of said railroad and telegraph line, and to secure the safe and speedy transportation of the mails, troops, munitions of war, and public stores thereon, every alternate section of public land, designated by odd numbers, to the amount of five alternate sections per mile on each side of said railroad, on the line thereof, and within the limits of ten miles on each side of said railroad, not sold, reserved, or otherwise disposed of by the United States, and to which a preemption or homestead claim may not have attached, at the time the line of said road is definitely fixed: Provided, That all mineral lands shall be excepted from the operation of this act; but where the same shall contain timber, the timber thereon is hereby granted to said company. And all such lands, so granted by this section, which shall not be sold or disposed of by said company within three years after the entire road shall have been completed, shall be subject to settlement and preemption, like other lands, at a price not exceeding one dollar and twenty-five cents per acre, to be paid to said company.

LEO SHEEP CO. v. UNITED STATES

Supreme Court of the United States, 1979.
440 U.S. 668, 99 S.Ct. 1403, 59 L.Ed.2d 677.

MR. JUSTICE REHNQUIST delivered the opinion of the Court.

This is one of those rare cases evoking episodes in this country's history that, if not forgotten, are remembered as dry facts and not as adventure. Admittedly the issue is mundane: Whether the Government has an implied easement to build a road across land that was originally granted to the Union Pacific Railroad under the Union Pacific Act of 1862—a grant that was part of a governmental scheme to subsidize the construction of the transcontinental railroad. But that issue is posed against the backdrop of a fascinating chapter in our history. As this Court noted in another case involving the Union Pacific Railroad, "courts, in construing a statute, may with propriety recur to the history of the times when it was passed; and this is frequently necessary, in order to ascertain the reason as well as the meaning of particular provisions in it." *United States v. Union Pac. R. Co.*, 91 U.S. 72, 79 (1875). In this spirit we relate the events underlying passage of the Union Pacific Act of 1862.

[I] The early 19th century—from the Louisiana Purchase in 1803 to the Gadsden Purchase in 1853—saw the acquisition of the territory we now regard as the American West. During those years, however, the area remained a largely untapped resource, for the settlers on the eastern seaboard of the United States did not keep pace with the rapidly expanding western frontier. A vaguely delineated area forbiddingly referred to as the "Great American Desert" can be found on more than one map published before 1850, embracing much of the United States' territory west of the Missouri River. As late as 1860, for example, the entire population of the State of Nebraska was less than 30,000 persons, which represented one person for every five square miles of land area within the State.

With the discovery of gold at Sutter's Mill in California in 1848, the California gold rush began and with it a sharp increase in settlement of the West. Those in the East with visions of instant wealth, however, confronted the unenviable choice among an arduous 4–month overland trek, risking yellow fever on a 35–day voyage via the Isthmus of Panama, and a better than 4–month voyage around Cape Horn. They obviously yearned for another alternative, and interest focused on the transcontinental railroad.

The idea of a transcontinental railroad predated the California gold rush. From the time that Asa Whitney had proposed a relatively practical plan for its construction in 1844, it had, in the words of one of this century's leading historians of the era, "engaged the eager attention of promoters and politicians until dozens of schemes were in the air." The building of the railroad was not to be the unalloyed product of the free-enterprise system. There was indeed the inspiration of men like Thomas Durant and Leland Stanford and the perspiration of a generation of immigrants, but animating it all was the desire of the Federal Government that the West be settled. This desire was intensified by the need to provide a logistical link with California in the heat of the Civil War. That the venture was much too risky and much too expensive for private capital alone was evident in the years of fruitless exhortation; private investors would not move without tangible governmental inducement.

In the mid-19th century there was serious disagreement as to the forms that inducement could take. Mr. Justice Story, in his Commentaries on the Constitution, described one extant school of thought which argued that "internal improvements," such as railroads, were not within the enumerated constitutional powers of Congress. Under such a theory, the direct subsidy of a transcontinental railroad was constitutionally suspect—an uneasiness aggravated by President Andrew Jackson's 1830 veto of a bill appropriating funds to construct a road from Maysville to Lexington within the State of Kentucky.

The response to this constitutional "gray" area, and source of political controversy, was the "checkerboard" land-grant scheme. The Union Pacific Act of 1862 granted public land to the Union Pacific Railroad for each mile of track that it laid. Land surrounding the railway right-of-way was divided into "checkerboard" blocks. Odd-numbered lots were granted to the Union Pacific; even-numbered lots were reserved by the Government. As a result, Union Pacific land in the area of the right-of-way was usually surrounded by public land, and vice versa. The historical explanation for this peculiar disposition is that it was apparently an attempt to disarm the "internal improvement" opponents by establishing a grant scheme with "demonstrable" benefits. As one historian notes in describing an 1827 federal land grant intended to facilitate private construction of a road between Columbus and Sandusky, Ohio:

> "Though awkwardly stated, and not fully developed in the Act of 1827, this was the beginning of a practice to be followed in most future instances of granting land for the construction of specific internal improvements: donating alternate sections or one half of the land within a strip along the line of the project and reserving the other half for sale. . . . In later

donations the price of the reserved sections was doubled so that it could be argued, as the *Congressional Globe* shows *ad infinitum*, that by giving half the land away and thereby making possible construction of the road, canal, or railroad, the government would recover from the reserved sections as much as it would have received from the whole." P. Gates, *History of Public Land Law Development* 345–346 (1968).

In 1850 this technique was first explicitly employed for the subsidization of a railroad when the Illinois delegation in Congress, which included Stephen A. Douglas, secured the enactment of a bill that granted public lands to aid the construction of the Illinois Central Railroad. The Illinois Central and proposed connecting lines to the south were granted nearly three million acres along rights of way through Illinois, Mississippi, and Alabama, and by the end of 1854 the main line of the Illinois Central from Chicago to Cairo, Ill., had been put into operation. Before this line was constructed, public lands had gone begging at the Government's minimum price; within a few years after its completion, the railroad had disposed of more than one million acres and was rapidly selling more at prices far above those at which land had been originally offered by the Government.

The "internal improvements" theory was not the only obstacle to a transcontinental railroad. In 1853 Congress had appropriated moneys and authorized Secretary of War Jefferson Davis to undertake surveys of various proposed routes for a transcontinental railroad. Congress was badly split along sectional lines on the appropriate location of the route—so badly split that Stephen A. Douglas, now a Senator from Illinois, in 1854 suggested the construction of a northern, central, and southern route, each with connecting branches in the East. That proposal, however, did not break the impasse.

The necessary impetus was provided by the Civil War. Senators and Representatives from those States which seceded from the Union were no longer present in Congress, and therefore the sectional overtones of the dispute as to routes largely disappeared. Although there were no major engagements during the Civil War in the area between the Missouri River and the west coast which would be covered by any transcontinental railroad, there were two minor engagements which doubtless made some impression upon Congress of the necessity for being able to transport readily men and materials into that area for military purposes. * * *

These engagements gave some immediacy to the comments of Congressman Edwards of New Hampshire during the debate on the Pacific Railroad bill:

> "If this Union is to be preserved, if we are successfully to combat the difficulties around us, if we are to crush out this rebellion against the lawful authority of the Government, and are to have an entire restoration, it becomes us, with statesmanlike prudence and sagacity, to look carefully into the future, and to guard in advance against all possible considerations which may threaten the dismemberment of the country hereafter." Cong. Globe, 37th Cong., 2d Sess., 1703 (1862).

As is often the case, war spurs technological development, and Congress enacted the Union Pacific Act in May 1862. Perhaps not coincidentally, the Homestead Act was passed the same month.

The Union Pacific Act specified a route west from the 100th meridian, between a site in the Platte River Valley near the cities of Kearney and North Platte, Neb., to California. The original plan was for five eastern terminals located at various points on or near the Missouri River; but in fact Omaha was the only terminal built according to the plan.

The land grants made by the Union Pacific Act included all the odd-numbered lots within 10 miles on either side of the track. When the Union Pacific's original subscription drive for private investment proved a failure, the land grant was doubled by extending the checkerboard grants to 20 miles on either side of the track. Private investment was still sluggish, and construction did not begin until July 1865, three months after the cessation of Civil War hostilities.[13] Thus began a race with the Central Pacific Railroad, which was laying track eastward from Sacramento, for the Government land grants which went with each mile of track laid. The race culminated in the driving of the golden spike at Promontory, Utah, on May 10, 1869.

[II] This case is the modern legacy of these early grants. Petitioners, the Leo Sheep Co. and the Palm Livestock Co., are the Union Pacific Railroad's successors in fee to specific odd-numbered sections of land in Carbon County, Wyo. These sections lie to the east and south of the Seminoe Reservoir, an area that is used by the public for fishing and hunting. Because of the checkerboard configuration, it is physically impossible to enter the Seminoe Reservoir sector from this direction without some minimum physical intrusion upon private land. In the years immediately preceding this litigation, the Government had received complaints that private owners were denying access over their lands to the reservoir area or requiring the payment of access fees. After negotiation with these owners failed, the Government cleared a dirt road extending from a local county road to the reservoir across both public domain lands and fee lands of the Leo Sheep Co. It also erected signs inviting the public to use the road as a route to the reservoir.

Petitioners initiated this action pursuant to 28 U.S.C. § 2409a to quiet title against the United States. The District Court granted petitioners' motion for

---

[13] Construction would not have begun then without the Crédit Mobilier, a limited-liability company that was essentially owned by the promoters and investors of the Union Pacific. One of these investors, Oakes Ames, a wealthy New England shovel maker, was a substantial investor in Crédit Mobilier and also a Member of Congress. Crédit Mobilier contracted with the Union Pacific to build portions of the road, and by 1866 several individuals were large investors in both corporations. Allegations of improper use of funds and bribery of Members of the House of Representatives led to the appointment of a special congressional investigatory committee that during 1872 and 1873 looked into the affairs of Crédit Mobilier. These investigations revealed improprieties on the part of more than one Member of Congress, and the committee recommended that Ames be expelled from Congress. The investigation also touched on the career of a future President. See M. Leech & H. Brown, *The Garfield Orbit* (1978).

In 1872 the House of Representatives enacted a resolution condemning the policy of granting subsidies of public lands to railroads. Cong. Globe, 42d Cong., 2d Sess., 1585 (1872); see *Great N. R. Co. v. United States*, 315 U.S. 262, 273–274 (1942). Of course, the reaction of the public or of Congress a decade after the enactment of the Union Pacific Act to the conduct of those associated with the Union Pacific cannot influence our interpretation of that Act today.

summary judgment, but was reversed on appeal by the Court of Appeals for the Tenth Circuit. The latter court concluded that when Congress granted land to the Union Pacific Railroad, it implicitly reserved an easement to pass over the odd-numbered sections in order to reach the even-numbered sections that were held by the Government. Because this holding affects property rights in 150 million acres of land in the Western United States, we granted certiorari, and now reverse.

The Government does not claim that there is any express reservation of an easement in the Union Pacific Act that would authorize the construction of a public road on the Leo Sheep Co.'s property. Section 3 of the 1862 Act sets out a few specific reservations to the "checkerboard" grant. The grant was not to include land "sold, reserved, or otherwise disposed of by the United States," such as land to which there were homestead claims. Mineral lands were also excepted from the operation of the Act. Given the existence of such explicit exceptions, this Court has in the past refused to add to this list by divining some "implicit" congressional intent. In *Missouri, K. & T.R. Co. v. Kansas Pac. R. Co.*, 97 U.S. 491, 497 (1878), for example, this Court in an opinion by Mr. Justice Field noted that the intent of Congress in making the Union Pacific grants was clear: "It was to aid in the construction of the road by a gift of lands along its route, without reservation of rights, except such as were specifically mentioned * * *." The Court held that, although a railroad right-of-way under the grant may not have been located until years after 1862, by the clear terms of the Act only claims established prior to 1862 overrode the railroad grant; conflicting claims arising after that time could not be given effect. To overcome the lack of support in the Act itself, the Government here argues that the implicit reservation of the asserted easement is established by "settled rules of property law" and by the Unlawful Inclosures of Public Lands Act of 1885.

Where a private landowner conveys to another individual a portion of his lands in a certain area and retains the rest, it is presumed at common law that the grantor has reserved an easement to pass over the granted property if such passage is necessary to reach the retained property. These rights-of-way are referred to as "easements by necessity." There are two problems with the Government's reliance on that notion in this case. First of all, whatever right of passage a private landowner might have, it is not at all clear that it would include the right to construct a road for public access to a recreational area.[15] More importantly, the easement is not actually a matter of necessity in this case because the Government has the power of eminent domain. Jurisdictions have generally seen eminent domain and easements by necessity as alternative ways to effect the same result. For example, the State of Wyoming no longer recognizes the common-law easement

---

[15] It is very unlikely that Congress in 1862 contemplated this type of intrusion, and it could not reasonably be maintained that failure to provide access to the public at large would render the Seminoe Reservoir land useless. Yet these are precisely the considerations that define the scope of easements by necessity. As one commentator relied on by the Government notes: "As the name implies, these easements are the product of situations where the usefulness of land is at stake. The scope of the resultant easement embodies the best judgment of the court as to what is reasonably essential to the land's use. * * * Changes in the dominant parcel's use exert some, but not a great influence, in determining the scope of such easements." 3 [R. Powell, Real Property ¶ 416 (1978).] See, *e.g.*, *Higbee Fishing Club v. Atlantic City Elec. Co.*, 79 A. 326 (1911) (footpath, not roadway, proper scope of easement where use of dominant estate as clubhouse could not have been contemplated by parties to original grant).

by necessity in cases involving landlocked estates. It provides instead for a procedure whereby the landlocked owner can have an access route condemned on his behalf upon payment of the necessary compensation to the owner of the servient estate. For similar reasons other state courts have held that the "easement by necessity" doctrine is not available to the sovereign.

The applicability of the doctrine of easement by necessity in this case is, therefore, somewhat strained, and ultimately of little significance. The pertinent inquiry in this case is the intent of Congress when it granted land to the Union Pacific in 1862. The 1862 Act specifically listed reservations to the grant, and we do not find the tenuous relevance of the common-law doctrine of ways of necessity sufficient to overcome the inference prompted by the omission of any reference to the reserved right asserted by the Government in this case. It is possible that Congress gave the problem of access little thought; but it is at least as likely that the thought which was given focused on negotiation, reciprocity considerations, and the power of eminent domain as obvious devices for ameliorating disputes.[18] So both as matter of common-law doctrine and as a matter of construing congressional intent, we are unwilling to imply rights-of-way, with the substantial impact that such implication would have on property rights granted over 100 years ago, in the absence of a stronger case for their implication than the Government makes here.

The Government would have us decide this case on the basis of the familiar canon of construction that, when grants to federal lands are at issue, any doubts "are resolved for the Government not against it." *Andrus v. Charlestone Stone Prods. Co.*, 436 U.S. 604, 617 (1978). But this Court long ago declined to apply this canon in its full vigor to grants under the railroad Acts. In 1885 this Court observed:

> "The solution of [ownership] questions [involving the railroad grants] depends, of course, upon the construction given to the acts making the grants; and they are to receive such a construction as will carry out the intent of Congress, however difficult it might be to give full effect to the

---

[18] The intimations that can be found in the Congressional Globe are that there was no commonly understood reservation by the Government of the right to enter upon granted lands and construct a public road. Representative Cradlebaugh of Nevada offered an amendment to what became the Union Pacific Act of 1862 that would have reserved the right to the public to enter granted land and prospect for valuable minerals upon the payment of adequate compensation to the owner. The proposed amendment was defeated. The only Representative other than Cradlebaugh who spoke to it, Representative Sargent of California, stated:

"The amendment of the gentleman proposes to allow the public to enter upon the lands of any man, whether they be mineral lands or not, and prospect for gold and silver, and as compensation proposes some loose method of payment for the injuries inflicted. Now, sir, it may turn out that the man who thus commits the injuries may be utterly insolvent, not able to pay a dollar, and how is the owner of the property to be compensated for tearing down his dwellings, rooting up his orchards, and destroying his crops?" Cong. Globe, 37th Cong., 2d Sess., 1910 (1862).

In debates on an earlier Pacific Railroad bill it was explicitly suggested that there be "a reservation in every grant of land that [the Government] shall have a right to go through it, and take it at proper prices to be paid hereafter." The author of this proposal, Senator Simmons of Rhode Island, lamented the lack of such a reservation in the bill under consideration. Cong. Globe, 35th Cong., 2d Sess., 579 (1859). Apparently the intended purpose of this proposed reservation was to permit railroads to obtain rights-of-way through granted property at the Government's behest. Senator Simmons' comments are somewhat confused, but they certainly do not evince any prevailing assumption that the Government implicitly reserved a right-of-way through granted lands.

language used if the grants were by instruments of private conveyance. To ascertain that intent we must look to the condition of the country when the acts were passed, as well as to the purpose declared on their face, and read all parts of them together." *Winona & St. Peter R. Co. v. Barney*, 113 U.S. 618, 625 (1885).

[Justice Rehnquist then discussed the Unlawful Inclosures of Public Lands Act of 1885 and concluded that it was aimed at a different sort of problem: the use of fencing arrangements by cattlemen to deprive sheepherders of access to grazing lands. The Court's opinion concluded with the observation that Congress in 1862 did not anticipate these problems:] The order of the day was the open range—barbed wire had not made its presence felt—and the type of incursions on private property necessary to reach public land was not such an interference that litigation would serve any motive other than spite. Congress obviously believed that when development came, it would occur in a parallel fashion on adjoining public and private lands and that the process of subdivision, organization of a polity, and the ordinary pressures of commercial and social intercourse would work itself into a pattern of access roads. * * * It is some testament to common sense that the present case is virtually unprecedented, and that in the 117 years since the grants were made, litigation over access questions generally has been rare.

Nonetheless, the present times are litigious ones and the 37th Congress did not anticipate our plight. Generations of land patents have issued without any express reservation of the right now claimed by the Government. Nor has a similar right been asserted before. When the Secretary of the Interior has discussed access rights, his discussion has been colored by the assumption that those rights had to be purchased. This Court has traditionally recognized the special need for certainty and predictability where land titles are concerned, and we are unwilling to upset settled expectations to accommodate some ill-defined power to construct public thoroughfares without compensation. * * *

Mr. Justice White took no part in the consideration or decision of this case.

Notes on *Leo Sheep* and *Legislative Context*

1. *The Sweep Versus the Reality of History.* Reading Justice Rehnquist's opinion, you can almost feel the wagon train moving you West. The first part of the opinion, the historical saga of the railroad project, strikes us as cogent and useful. The next part, the legal reasoning, strikes us as less so. The unanimous Court is obviously following the "imaginative reconstruction" approach of Judge Hand and Dean Pound—putting oneself in the mindset of the 1862 Congress (see Chapter 6, § 1). But the Court's assertion that "[i]t is possible that Congress gave the problem of access little thought" strikes us as an understatement. Is there any evidence adduced by the Court that the 1862 Congress gave *any* thought to the access issue? And if Congress had given some thought, surely it would have wanted the government to have a reasonable right of access. Is the Court's assumption credible that "the thought which was given focused on negotiation, reciprocity considerations, and the power of eminent domain" as ways of obtaining access? Congress in 1866, for example, enacted a statute giving any person free and unrestricted access over the public domain. Right of Way Act, 14 Stat. 251 (1866). If the 1862 Congress had "assumed" that it could negotiate a trade of railroad access through

public lands in return for state access through the railroad's lands, why would Congress have given away that bargaining chip in 1866? Why would Congress in 1862 want to use eminent domain—paying money—for access rights that it could retain by simple statutory fiat? Would the venture capitalists (or robber barons, if you prefer) not have built the transcontinental railroad otherwise?

2.   *The Flip Side of* Leo Sheep. Does the private grantee or its successor have an easement by necessity through the government's checkerboard squares? The leading discussion on this question argued that it does. Comment, *Easements by Way of Necessity Across Federal Lands*, 35 Wash. L. Rev. 105, 113–17 (1960). This remarkable student comment correctly anticipated the *Leo Sheep* result and reasoning but argued that the same result (no easement by necessity) should not occur for the converse situation. The common law objections in *Leo Sheep*—that easements by necessity are not created for recreational uses or for government entities which may obtain access through eminent domain—have no force when a private developer demands an easement through the government lands. Nor does the legislative policy argument work against the private grantee's easement, since private access would subserve the Congressional goal of developing the granted land as quickly as possible. Cf. *Utah v. Andrus*, 486 F. Supp. 995, 1002 (D. Utah 1979), *appeal dismissed per stip.*, Nos. 79–2307 & 79–2308 (10th Cir. Jan. 28 & Mar. 28, 1980) (Congress conveyed permanent rights of access to Utah when it granted school trust lands to the State as a means of generating revenue). A contrary position was taken in an Opinion by Attorney General Civiletti. 43 Op. Att'y Gen. 26 (1980). The opinion determined that easements by necessity did not run against the government, unless that was an implied term of the granting statute. "[L]and grants generally are to be strictly construed. This rule must be balanced against the conflicting rule that in some situations certain types of land grants may deserve a more liberal construction because of the circumstances surrounding passage of the statutes in question. [*Leo Sheep*.] Absent express language to the contrary, however, a grant should not be construed to include broad rights to use retained Government property, particularly in the case of gratuitous grants."

Consider this policy argument: not to infer an easement by necessity in the original grant would impel the United States and private grantees holding alternate checkerboard squares to cooperate. That is, if neither holder has an easement, each has an incentive to work out a reasonable deal with the other, or neither will be able to have meaningful access to its land. On the other hand, if the United States has no easement but the grantee does, the grantee has little incentive to reach a "fair" bargain with the United States, forcing the United States to pay a high price or go to the trouble and expense of condemning the easement through eminent domain. Once the Supreme Court has decided that the government does not have an easement, doesn't it make sense then to deny the easement for the private holders as well? (One might argue that the rule which would minimize transactions costs would be to give *both* the government and the private holders an easement, or give them both eminent domain power.)

3.   *Subsequent Developments*. In any event, the context in which the *Leo Sheep* problem arose was vastly different from that in which the law was passed. A shift in statutory policy came in the late nineteenth century, to protect the nation's natural resources from the results of what was then perceived as excessively generous land grants earlier. See Roy Robbins, *Our Landed Heritage: The Public Domain, 1776–1970*, at 301–24 (1976). Thus after giving away more than 125 million acres of public land to

the railroads, Congress discontinued the land grant policy in the 1890s. See Paul Gates, *History of Public Land Law Development* (1968). And in 1891, Congress passed a law authorizing the President to reserve forest lands from the public domain (thus taking them out of the coverage of the 1866 access law), Act of March 3, 1891, ch. 561, § 24, 26 Stat. 1103 (the Forest Reserve Act), and 20 million acres were thereby reserved by Presidential proclamation in 1897. Further reservations were made throughout the twentieth century, as federal policy decisively turned toward conserving what was becoming perceived as a scarce resource. The Wilderness Act of 1964, 78 Stat. 890, codified at 16 U.S.C. §§ 1131–1136 (1988), placed even greater restrictions on certain federal lands, and this leading Act was followed in the 1970s and 1980s by more wilderness designations by Congress. In 1976, Congress repealed the access law of 1866 and replaced it with Title V of the Federal Land Policy & Management Act of 1976, 90 Stat. 2744, 2776, codified at 43 U.S.C. §§ 1761–1770 (1988), which authorizes the Department of the Interior to grant rights of access through a discretionary system. Are these subsequent statutes and federal policies relevant to the issue whether private grantees have an absolute right of access across federal checkerboard lands?

2. Committee Reports (and an Introduction to the Great Legislative History Debate)

Most judges and scholars agree that committee reports should be considered as authoritative legislative history and should be given great weight (i.e., a statement in a committee report will usually count more than a statement by a single legislator). Justice Jackson, concurring in *Schwegmann Bros. v. Calvert Distillers Corp.*, 341 U.S. 384, 395 (1951), objected to the use of legislative materials to interpret statutes, but excepted committee reports from his quarrel. Jorge Carro & Andrew Brann, *The U.S. Supreme Court and the Use of Legislative Histories: A Statistical Analysis*, 22 Jurimeterics J. 294, 304 (1982), report that over a 40–year period, over 60% of the Supreme Court's citations to legislative history were references to committee reports. A more recent study indicates that the qualitative dominance of committee reports continues: when the Court invoked legislative history in its workplace law and tax law decisions between 1969 and 2008, it relied on House and Senate committee reports from over half the time (workplace law cases) to over two-thirds of the time (tax law cases). See James Brudney and Corey Ditslear, *The Warp and Woof of Statutory Interpretation: Comparing Supreme Court Approaches in Tax Law and Workplace Law*, 58 Duke L.J. 1231, 1262 (2009).

Committee reports appear particularly well-suited for the authoritative role they have played. Most legislation is essentially written in committee or subcommittee, and any collective statement by the members of that subgroup will represent the best-informed thought about what the proposed legislation is doing. Committee reports are also accessible documents, both in the sense of being easily located through legal research and of being easy to comprehend once found. They usually set forth the problem(s) calling forth the proposed legislation, the general solution(s) posited by the bill, and a section-by-section summary of the provisions of the bill. The report of a conference committee (where the two legislative chambers have passed different forms of the same bill and must resolve their differences in conference) typically sets forth, for each provision, the version passed by each chamber and what the conference committee did with the provision (and sometimes also an explanation why it took the action it did).

There are, on the other hand, limitations on the usefulness of committee reports in giving meaning to ambiguous statutes. First, there is sometimes *no* committee report for a particular bill or an important provision in the bill, because it has been added as part of the floor debate. This is especially true of many of the civil rights bills. Recall from Chapter 1, § 1, that the sex discrimination provision in Title VII was added as a floor amendment in the House (and as something of a surprise to the bill's sponsors); hence, there is no discussion of that critical amendment in the House Judiciary Committee report. There was no committee report for the Act in the Senate, because the sponsors avoided sending the House bill to committee, which was Senator Eastland's preserve. Compare *Hishon v. King & Spalding*, 467 U.S. 69, 75 & n.7 (1984) (relying on Senate report for civil rights bill that was similar but never enacted). And there was no conference committee report, because the House rapidly acceded to the Senate's revisions, the sponsors knowing that further delays in the bill's enactment might prove fatal. See also *Local 82, Furniture & Piano Moving Union v. Crowley*, 467 U.S. 526 (1984) (interpreting Landrum-Griffin Act, much of which was written on the House and Senate floor).

Second, the committee report is often as ambiguous as the statute. As a shorter, more compressed form of the statute, the committee report may even be misleading, as it leaves out important qualifications in its discussion of the proposed legislation or particular provisions. (The committee report is probably most useful as a statement of the goals and their relative importance in the statutory scheme, since most statutes do not carry with them statements of purpose.) Indeed, a striking feature of the committee report is that it is the end-product of the committee's consideration, and therefore comes at a stage of consensus. In many instances, the key point in the process is "mark-up" of the bill in committee or subcommittee, for it is there that the legislators make the critical choices and compromises and specifically reject proposed alternatives. See John Kernochan, *The Legislative Process* 25 (1981). Traditionally, there was no official record of mark-up sessions, a practice that has been opened up to the public somewhat in the last two decades. As a consequence, what is often the most revealing collection of statements was often not available, or admissible, in the process of statutory interpretation. See Wald, *Legislative History in the 1981 Term*, at 202. In the last twenty years, however, committee mark-ups, especially of tax bills, have increasingly been made available, either through quasi-official transcripts or unofficial reports in tax journals or online. One might therefore expect to see more references to these sources by judges willing to consider legislative history. E.g., *Regan v. Wald*, 468 U.S. 222 (1984) (both majority and dissenting opinions relying on explanation accompanying House committee mark-up).

Third, when there is a committee report and the report contains relevant statements, one might be suspicious of the usefulness of those statements under some circumstances. Lobbyists and lawyers maneuver endlessly to persuade staff members (who write the committee reports) or their legislative bosses to throw in helpful language in the reports when insertion of similar language would be inappropriate or infeasible for the statute itself. "Smuggling in" helpful language through the legislative history is a time-tested practice.

In state legislatures, committee reports can take a variety of forms, not all of which are published or are readily available to the public: (1) regular reports of standing committees or conference committees, like those produced in the U.S. Congress; (2) staff analysis of a pending bill, which is in many states the main document which is actually distributed to legislators; and (3) reports of special committees created to investigate and to resolve important problems expeditiously or to investigate problems, as well as reports of collections of experts (often "law revision commissions") who have drafted legislation adopted in the state. As *Li v. Yellow Cab Co.* (Chapter 6, § 2B) suggests, committee reports and similar documents are often used to interpret ambiguous statutes at the state level.

BLANCHARD V. BERGERON
Supreme Court of the United States, 1989.
489 U.S. 87, 109 S.Ct. 939, 105 L.Ed.2d 181.

JUSTICE WHITE delivered the opinion of the Court.

[A jury awarded Blanchard $5,000 in compensatory damages and $5,000 in punitive damages on his civil rights claim, under 42 U.S.C. § 1983, that he had been beaten by a sheriff's deputy. He sought attorney's fees under the 1976 Civil Rights Attorney's Fee Award Act, codified at 42 U.S.C. § 1988. The district court awarded $7,500 in fees. The Fifth Circuit, however, held that under its decision in *Johnson v. Georgia Highway Express, Inc.*, 488 F.2d 714 (5th Cir. 1974), the 40% contingency fee agreement Blanchard had entered into with his attorney set a ceiling on recoverable fees. Thus, the Fifth Circuit limited the fee award to $4,000 (40% of the $10,000 damages awarded).]

Section 1988 provides that the court, "in its discretion, may allow . . . a reasonable attorney's fee. . . ." The section does not provide a specific definition of "reasonable" fee, and the question is whether the award must be limited to the amount provided in a contingent fee agreement. The legislative history of the Act is instructive insofar as it tells us: "In computing the fee, counsel for prevailing parties should be paid, as is traditional with attorneys compensated by a fee-paying client, 'for all time reasonably expended on a matter.' " S. Rep. No. 94–1011, at 6 (1976) (citing *Davis v. County of Los Angeles*, 1974 WL 180 (C.D. Cal. 1974); and *Stanford Daily v. Zurcher*, 64 F.R.D. 680, 684 (N.D. Cal. 1974)).

In many past cases considering the award of attorney's fees under § 1988, we have turned our attention to *Johnson v. Georgia Highway Express, Inc.*, a case decided before the enactment of the Civil Rights Attorney's Fee Award Act of 1976. As we stated in *Hensley v. Eckerhart*, 461 U.S. 424, 429–431 (1983), *Johnson* provides guidance to Congress' intent because both the House and Senate Reports refer to the 12 factors set forth in *Johnson* for assessing the reasonableness of an attorney's fee award. The Senate Report, in particular, refers to three District Court decisions that "correctly applied" the 12 factors laid out in *Johnson*.

In the course of its discussion of the factors to be considered by a court in awarding attorney's fees, the *Johnson* court dealt with fee arrangements:

> " 'Whether or not [a litigant] agreed to pay a fee and in what amount is not decisive. Conceivably, a litigant might agree to pay his counsel a fixed dollar fee. This might be even more than the fee eventually allowed by the court. Or he might agree to pay his lawyer a percentage contingent fee that would be greater than the fee the court might ultimately set. Such arrangements should not determine the court's decision. The criterion for the court is not what the parties agree but what is reasonable.' "

Yet in the next sentence, *Johnson* says "In no event, however, should the litigant be awarded a fee greater than he is contractually bound to pay, if indeed the attorneys have contracted as to amount." This latter statement, never disowned in the Circuit, was the basis for the decision below. But we doubt that Congress embraced this aspect of *Johnson*, for it pointed to the three District Court cases in which the factors are "correctly applied." Those cases clarify that the fee arrangement is but a single factor and not determinative. In *Stanford Daily v. Zurcher*, [*supra*,] for example, the District Court considered a contingent-fee arrangement to be a factor, but not dispositive, in the calculation of a fee award. In *Davis v. County of Los Angeles*, *supra*, the court permitted a fee award to counsel in a public interest firm which otherwise would have been entitled to no fee. Finally, in *Swann v. Charlotte-Mecklenburg Board of Education*, 66 F.R.D. 483 (W.D. N.C. 1975), the court stated that reasonable fees should be granted regardless of the individual plaintiff's fee obligations. *Johnson*'s "List of 12" thus provides a useful catalog of the many factors to be considered in assessing the reasonableness of an award of attorney's fees; but the one factor at issue here, the attorney's private fee arrangement, standing alone, is not dispositive.

The *Johnson* contingency-fee factor is simply that, a factor. The presence of a pre-existing fee agreement may aid in determining reasonableness. " 'The fee quoted to the client or the percentage of the recovery agreed to is helpful in demonstrating that attorney's fee expectations when he accepted the case.' " *Pennsylvania v. Del. Valley Citizens' Council for Clean Air*, 483 U.S. 711 (1987), quoting *Johnson*. But as we see it, a contingent-fee contract does not impose an automatic ceiling on an award of attorney's fees and to hold otherwise would be inconsistent with the statute and its policy and purpose.

As we understand § 1988's provision for allowing a "reasonable attorney's fee," it contemplates reasonable compensation, in light of all of the circumstances, for the time and effort expended by the attorney for the prevailing plaintiff, no more and no less. Should a fee agreement provide less than a reasonable fee calculated in this manner, the defendant should nevertheless be required to pay the higher amount. The defendant is not, however, required to pay the amount called for in a contingent-fee contract if it is more than a reasonable fee calculated in the usual way. It is true that the purpose of § 1988 was to make sure that competent counsel was available to civil rights plaintiffs, and it is of course arguable that if a plaintiff is able to secure an attorney on the basis of a contingent or other fee agreement, the purpose of the statute is served if the plaintiff is bound by his contract. On that basis, however, the plaintiff should recover nothing from the defendant, which would be plainly contrary to the statute. And Congress implemented its purpose by broadly requiring all defendants to pay a reasonable fee to all prevailing plaintiffs, if ordered to do so by the court. Thus it is that a plaintiff's recovery will not be reduced by what he must pay his counsel. Plaintiffs who can afford to hire their own lawyers, as well as impecunious litigants, may take advantage of this provision. And where there are lawyers or organizations that will take a plaintiff's case without compensation, that fact does not bar the award of a reasonable fee. All of this is consistent with and reflects our decisions in cases involving court-awarded attorney's fees.

Hensley v. Eckerhart, [*supra*,] directed lower courts to make an initial estimate of reasonable attorney's fees by applying prevailing billing rates to the hours reasonably expended on successful claims. And we have said repeatedly that "[t]he initial estimate of a reasonable attorney's fee is properly calculated by multiplying the number of hours reasonably expended on the litigation times a reasonable hourly rate." The courts may then adjust this lodestar calculation by other factors. We have never suggested that a different approach is to be followed in cases where the prevailing party and his (or her) attorney have executed a contingent-fee agreement. To the contrary, * * * we have adopted the lodestar approach as the centerpiece of attorney's fee awards. The *Johnson* factors may be relevant in adjusting the lodestar amount but no one factor is a substitute for multiplying reasonable billing rates by a reasonable estimation of the number of hours expended on the litigation. * * *

If a contingent-fee agreement were to govern as a strict limitation on the award of attorney's fees, an undesirable emphasis might be placed on the importance of the recovery of damages in civil rights litigation. The intention of Congress was to encourage successful civil rights litigation, not to create a special incentive to prove damages and shortchange efforts to seek effective injunctive or declaratory relief. Affirming the decision below would create an artificial disincentive for an attorney who enters into a contingent fee agreement, unsure of whether his client's claim sounded in state tort law or in federal civil rights, from fully exploring all possible avenues of relief. Section 1988 makes no distinction between actions for damages and suits for equitable relief. Congress has elected to encourage meritorious civil rights claims because of the benefits of such litigation for the named plaintiff and for society at large, irrespective of whether the action seeks monetary damages.

It should also be noted that we have not accepted the contention that fee awards in § 1983 damages cases should be modeled upon the contingent-fee arrangements used in personal injury litigation. "[W]e reject the notion that a civil rights action for damages constitutes nothing more than a private tort suit benefiting only the individual plaintiffs whose rights were violated. Unlike most private tort litigants, a civil rights plaintiff seeks to vindicate important civil and constitutional rights that cannot be valued solely in monetary terms."

Respondent cautions us that refusing to limit recovery to the amount of the contingency agreement will result in a "windfall" to attorneys who accept § 1983 actions. Yet the very nature of recovery under § 1988 is designed to prevent any such "windfall." Fee awards are to be reasonable, reasonable as to billing rates and reasonable as to the number of hours spent in advancing the successful claims. Accordingly, fee awards, properly calculated, by definition will represent the reasonable worth of the services rendered in vindication of a plaintiff's civil rights claim. It is central to the awarding of attorney's fees under § 1988 that the district court judge, in his or her good judgment, make the assessment of what is a reasonable fee under the circumstances of the case. The trial judge should not be limited by the contractual fee agreement between plaintiff and counsel. * * *

JUSTICE SCALIA, concurring in part and concurring in the judgment.

I * * * join the opinion of the Court except that portion which rests upon detailed analysis of the Fifth Circuit's opinion in *Johnson* and the District Court decisions in *Swann, Stanford Daily,* and *Davis.* The Court carefully examines those opinions, separating holding from dictum, much as a lower court would study our opinions in order to be faithful to our guidance. The justification for this role reversal is that the Senate and House Committee Reports on the Civil Rights Attorney's Fees Awards Act of 1976 referred approvingly to *Johnson,* and the Senate Report alone referred to the three District Court opinions as having "correctly applied" *Johnson.* The Court resolves the difficulty that *Johnson* contradicts the three District Court opinions on the precise point at issue here by concluding in effect that the analysis in *Johnson* was dictum, whereas in the three District Court opinions it was a holding. Despite the fact that the House Report referred *only* to *Johnson,* and made no mention of the District Court cases, the Court "doubt[s] that Congress embraced this aspect of *Johnson,* for it pointed to the three District Court cases in which the factors are 'correctly applied.'"

In my view Congress did no such thing. Congress is elected to enact statutes, rather than point to cases, and its Members have better uses for their time than poring over District Court opinions. That the Court should refer to the citation of three District Court cases in a document issued by a single committee of a single house as the action *of Congress* displays the level of unreality that our unrestrained use of legislative history has attained. I am confident that only a small proportion of the Members of Congress read either one of the Committee Reports in question, even if (as is not always the case) the Reports happened to have been published before the vote; that very few of those who did read them set off for the nearest law library to check out what was actually said in the four cases at issue (or in the more than 50 other cases cited by the House and Senate Reports); and that *no* Member of Congress came to the judgment that the District Court cases would trump *Johnson* on the point at issue here because the latter was dictum. As anyone familiar with modern-day drafting of congressional committee reports is well aware, the references to the cases were inserted, at best by a committee staff member on his or her own initiative, and at worst by a committee staff member at the suggestion of a lawyer-lobbyist; and the purpose of those references was not primarily to inform the Members of Congress what the bill meant (for that end *Johnson* would not merely have been cited, but its 12 factors would have been described, which they were not), but rather to influence judicial construction. What a heady feeling it must be for a young staffer, to know that his or her citation of obscure district court cases can transform them into the law of the land, thereafter dutifully to be observed by the Supreme Court itself.

I decline to participate in this process. It is neither compatible with our judicial responsibility of assuring reasoned, consistent, and effective application of the statutes of the United States, nor conducive to a genuine effectuation of congressional intent, to give legislative force to each snippet of analysis, and even every case citation, in committee reports that are increasingly unreliable evidence of what the voting Members of Congress actually had in mind. By treating *Johnson* and the District Court trilogy as fully authoritative, the Court today expands what I regard as our cases' excessive preoccupation with them—and with the 12–factor *Johnson* analysis in particular. * * * Except for the few passages to which I object, today's opinion admirably follows our more recent approach of seeking to develop an interpretation of the statute that is reasonable, consistent, and faithful to its apparent purpose, rather than to achieve obedient adherence to cases cited in the committee reports. I therefore join the balance of the opinion.

NOTES ON THE NEW TEXTUALIST CRITIQUE OF COMMITTEE REPORTS

1. *Judge Scalia's Attack on Committee Reports.* Justice Scalia believes that committee reports, in particular, are untrustworthy legislative history. His first effort to explain his position systematically, an unpublished speech delivered at various law schools while he was a judge on the D.C. Circuit, is summarized, quoted, and criticized in Daniel Farber & Philip Frickey, *Legislative Intent and Public Choice*, 74 Va. L. Rev. 423 (1988). Judge Scalia also set forth his doubts in a concurring opinion in *Hirschey v. FERC*, 777 F.2d 1, 7–8 (D.C. Cir. 1985):

> I frankly doubt that it is ever reasonable to assume that the details, as opposed to the broad outlines of purpose, set forth in a committee report come to the attention of, much less are approved by, the house which enacts the committee's bill. And I think it time for courts to become concerned about the fact that routine deference to the detail of committee reports, and the predictable expansion in that detail which routine deference has produced, are converting a system of judicial construction into a system of committee-staff prescription.

Note the similarity to his reason for not joining the Court's opinion in *Bergeron*. In a footnote at the end of the first sentence of the above quotation, Judge Scalia reported the following "illuminating exchange" in the Senate; *id.* at 7–8 n.1. After joining the Supreme Court, Justice Scalia has reproduced the identical exchange in his two books addressing statutory interpretation; see Scalia, *A Matter of Interpretation*, 32–34; Scalia & Garner, *Reading Law*, 384–85. We have inserted *in bracketed italics a portion of Senator Dole's explanation that Judge Scalia chose to omit from this exchange*:

> Mr. ARMSTRONG. * * * My question, which may take [the Chairman of the Committee on Finance] by surprise, is this: Is it the intention of the chairman that the Internal Revenue Service and the Tax Court and other courts take guidance as to the intention of Congress from the committee report which accompanies this bill?

> Mr. DOLE. I would certainly hope so. * * *

Mr. ARMSTRONG. Mr. President, will the Senator tell me whether or not he wrote the committee report?

Mr. DOLE. Did I write the committee report?

Mr. ARMSTRONG. Yes.

Mr. DOLE. No; the Senator from Kansas did not write the committee report.

Mr. ARMSTRONG. Did any Senator write the committee report?

Mr. DOLE. I have to check.

Mr. ARMSTRONG. Does the Senator know of any Senator who wrote the committee report?

Mr. DOLE. I might be able to identify one, but I would have to search. I was here all during the time it was written, I might say, and worked carefully with the staff as they worked. * * * [As I recall, during the July 4 recess week, there were about five different working groups of staff from both parties, the Joint Committee, and the Treasury working on different provisions.]

Mr. ARMSTRONG. Mr. President, has the Senator from Kansas, the chairman of the Finance Committee, read the committee report in its entirety?

Mr. DOLE. I am working on it. It is not a bestseller, but I am working on it.

Mr. ARMSTRONG. Mr. President, did members of the Finance Committee vote on the committee report?

Mr. DOLE. No.

Mr. ARMSTRONG. Mr. President, the reason I raise the issue is not perhaps apparent on the surface, and let me just state it: * * * The report itself is not considered by the Committee on Finance. It was not subject to amendment by the Committee on Finance. It is not subject to amendment now by the Senate. * * *

* * * If there were matter within this report which was disagreed to by the Senator from Colorado or even by a majority of all Senators, there would be no way for us to change the report. I could not offer an amendment tonight to amend the committee report.

* * * [F]or any jurist, administrator, bureaucrat, tax practitioner, or others who might chance upon the written record of this proceeding, let me just make the point that this is not the law, it was not voted on, it is not subject to amendment, and we should discipline ourselves to the task of expressing congressional intent in the statute.

Consider the different ways in which this Dole-Armstrong colloquy might constitute an "illuminating exchange." For Justice Scalia, focused on what he regards as the systematic flaws of legislative history, Senator Armstrong (then a first-term Republican from Colorado) has emphasized the fact that members rarely if ever draft committee reports, and they also do not vote on these reports. But members of Congress rarely draft text either—should this matter? To be sure, committee reports (unlike text) are not voted on by committee members, and in this important respect they should not be confused with "the law." On the other hand, there is plenty of anecdotal evidence that legislators facing a vote often pay more attention to the report than to the language of the bill. Senator Arlen Specter, who represented Pennsylvania from 1980 to 2010 and served for decades on the Judiciary Committee, opined that "[M]embers of Congress are more likely to read a committee report than the bill itself. The prose of a report is easier to understand, and, because a bill usually amends an existing statute, it is impossible to follow without referring to the U.S. Code." Joan Biskupic, *Scalia Takes a Narrow View in Seeking Congress' Will*, 48 Cong. Q. 913, 917 (1990) (summarizing Specter's views).[51]

And what about the omitted excerpts from Senator Dole, Chair of the Finance Committee? Dole, who spent over a decade as a chief architect of federal tax legislation, regarded legislative history in this setting as providing valuable guidance to the IRS and the federal courts. The omitted language seems to suggest that Senator Dole was attempting to educate his freshman colleague about how tax legislative history was produced—in deliberative bipartisan fashion and with the cooperative participation of the executive branch. Taken as a whole, does this colloquy indicate that legislative history should be excluded from judicial consideration as a matter of principle? Or that review of such history by courts should be a question of relative weight rather than threshold admissibility?

The co-parent of the new textualism has been Judge Frank Easterbrook of the Seventh Circuit, the author of the textualist en banc opinion in *Marshall* (Chapter 6, § 3B1). Another of his opinions, *In re Sinclair*, is the next case in this chapter.

2. *Justice Scalia Updates His Critique of Committee Reports.* Since he has been elevated to the Supreme Court, Justice Scalia has developed a more systematic critique of the Court's traditional use of legislative history. See Antonin Scalia, *A Matter of Interpretation* (1997); *Bock Laundry* (Scalia, J., concurring in the judgment) (both excerpted in Chapter 6, § 3A).[52] Justice Scalia's more systematic critique goes well beyond the cynicism of *Bergeron* and rests upon a constitutional interpretation of Article I, § 7. Statutory text is the alpha and the omega of statutory interpretation because it is the only matter that is enacted as authoritative *law* under our constitutional rule of recognition (Article I, § 7).[53] Even if there were a coherent legislative "intent" (a matter Scalia disputes), it would have no authority as law under the Constitution. Like Judge Easterbrook, who developed the structural constitutional features of the new textualism at an earlier stage, Justice Scalia would be willing to

[51] See also Abner Mikva, *Reading and Writing Statutes*, 28 S. Tex. L. Rev. 181, 184 (1986) (Mikva, a House member for five terms who then served on the D.C. Circuit for fifteen years, described the committee report as the "bone structure of the legislation. It is the road map that explains why things are in and things are out of the statute").

[52] Some of Justice Scalia's classic criticisms are found in *Zuni Public School District No. 89 v. Department of Education*, 550 U.S. 81, 116–211 (2007) (Scalia, J., dissenting); *Hamdan v. Rumsfeld*, 548 U.S. 557, 665–68 (2006) (Scalia, J., dissenting); *Koons Buick Pontiac GMC, Inc. v. Nigh*, 543 U.S. 50, 70–76 (2004) (Scalia, J., dissenting); *Crosby v. National Foreign Trade Council*, 530 U.S. 363 388–91 (2000) (Scalia, J., concurring in the judgment); *Thunder Basin Coal Co. v. Reich*, 510 U.S. 200, 219 (1994) (Scalia, J., concurring in part and in the judgment); *Conroy v. Aniskoff*, 507 U.S. 511, 519 (1993) (Scalia, J., concurring in the judgment); *United States v. Thompson/Center Arms Co.*, 504 U.S. 505, 521 (1992) (Scalia, J., concurring in the judgment); *Union Bank v. Wolas*, 502 U.S. 151, 163 (1991) (Scalia, J., concurring); *Wisconsin Public Intervenor v. Mortier*, 501 U.S. 597, 617–23 (1991) (Scalia, J., concurring in the judgment); *Sullivan v. Finkelstein*, 496 U.S. 617, 631–32 (1990) (Scalia, J., concurring in all of the Court's opinion except footnote 8); *Begier v. IRS*, 496 U.S. 53, 67–71 (1990) (Scalia, J., concurring in the judgment).

[53] William Eskridge Jr., *The New Textualism*, 37 UCLA L. Rev. 621 (1990); John Manning, *Textualism as a Nondelegation Doctrine*, 97 Colum. L. Rev. 673 (1997); Jonathan Molot, *The Rise and Fall of Textualism*, 106 Colum. L. Rev. 1, 23–29 (2006).

examine legislative materials as evidence of how statutory language was used at the time.

3.   *Committee Reports and the Constitution.* Notwithstanding Justice Scalia's argument that the Constitution prohibits reliance on legislative history, some scholars have contended that the provisions of Article I, § 5, requiring each chamber to "keep a Journal of its Proceedings, and from time to time publish the same," and authorizing each chamber to "determine the Rules of its Proceedings," create a constitutional framework that allows for the use of legislative history. See generally Adrian Vermeule, *The Constitutional Law of Congressional Procedure*, 71 U. Chi. L. Rev. 361, 411 (2004). One of us has pushed this argument further, maintaining that the Journal Clause and the Rules Clause gave rise to distinctively American legislative design features in the early years of the Republic that effectively invite courts to invoke legislative history in suitable settings. James Brudney, *Canon Shortfalls and the Virtues of Political Branch Interpretive Assets*, 98 Cal. L. Rev. 1199 (2010). The Constitution's insistence on publication under the Journal Clause departed from traditions of secrecy that had prevailed for centuries in the British Parliament and had operated in both the Continental Congress and the Constitutional Convention. As early as 1792, Representative Elbridge Gerry (a signer of the Declaration of Independence and later Vice President under James Madison) argued that the publication of floor debates would "aid the Executive in administering the Government [and] the Judiciary in expounding the laws." *Id.* at 1220 (quoting from Gerry's proposal for the House to appoint official stenographers who would transcribe and publish its debates).

The Rules Clause allowed the House and Senate to create permanent standing committees between 1789 and 1820, in order to shape the priorities and agenda of each chamber. These standing committees—reviewing and reporting bills prior to full chamber consideration—differed dramatically from the temporary select committees relied on by the British Parliament at the time and by Congress during its first few sessions. By the early nineteenth century, first oral and then written committee reports were invoked by members during floor debates and deliberations. Given these foundational developments, Brudney argues that the existence of such constitutionally linked origins "confers upon legislative history an element of authoritative legitimacy that enhances its stature as an interpretive asset." *Id.* at 1224.

4.   *The Impact of the New Textualism in the Supreme Court.* Justice Scalia's critique has had an impact upon the Court's practice, which is now more cautious in its use of legislative history. The new textualism has had even more of an impact upon the arguments made by the Supreme Court Bar (especially the Solicitor General and others regularly arguing before the Court), who now emphasize and usually lead with their textual arguments and use legislative history to back up these contentions rather than as the touchstone of statutory meaning. The Rehnquist and Roberts Courts (1986 onward) have been less likely to rely heavily upon legislative history today than did the Burger Court (1969–1986). There are more decisions like *Circuit City* (where the majority refused to examine legislative materials) than there have been since the pre-New Deal era.[54]

---

[54] E.g., David Law & David Zaring, *Law versus Ideology: The Supreme Court and the Use of Legislative History*, 51 Wm. & Mary L. Rev. 1653 (2010); James Brudney & Corey Ditslear, *The Decline and Fall of Legislative History? Patterns of Supreme Court Reliance in the Burger and Rehnquist Eras*, 89 Judicature 220 (2006); Michael Koby, *The Supreme Court's Declining Reliance on Legislative History: The Impact of Justice Scalia's Critique*, 36 Harv. J. Legis. 369 (1999). Because Justices Scalia and Thomas routinely refuse to join

Nonetheless, the new textualism has not swept the field, and the debate within the Supreme Court continues. Although Justice Scalia has picked up a good deal of academic support,[55] the majority of the commentators are unpersuaded.[56] The Supreme Court still relies on committee reports (even if less than before). Moreover, in *Wisconsin Public Intervenor v. Mortier*, 501 U.S. 597, 610 n.4 (1991), all of the other justices joined in a footnote explicitly rejecting Justice Scalia's general position that legislative history is irrelevant to proper statutory interpretation. See also *Bank One Chi. N.A. v. Midwest Bank & Trust*, 516 U.S. 264, 276–79 (1996) (Justice Stevens in concurring opinion, joined by Justice Breyer, objecting strenuously to Justice Scalia's general critique of legislative history). Especially after the appointment of Justice Breyer (a big fan of legislative history), the Supreme Court relied on legislative materials more often in the late 1990s and the early part of the new century.[57] It is too early to be confident whether the Roberts Court will continue or reverse this trend.

IN RE SINCLAIR

United States Court of Appeals for the Seventh Circuit, 1989.
870 F.2d 1340.

EASTERBROOK, CIRCUIT JUDGE.

This case presents a conflict between a statute and its legislative history. The Sinclairs, who have a family farm, filed a bankruptcy petition in April 1985 under Chapter 11 of the Bankruptcy Act of 1978. In October 1986 Congress added Chapter 12, providing benefits for farmers, and the Sinclairs asked the bankruptcy court to convert their case from Chapter 11 to Chapter 12. The bankruptcy judge declined, and the district court affirmed. Each relied on § 302(c)(1) of the

---

any majority opinion that relies upon legislative history, in any case in which their votes might be necessary to form a majority the Justice drafting the opinion may strategically avoid reliance upon legislative history. James Brudney and Corey Ditslear, *Liberal Justices' Reliance on Legislative History: Principle, Strategy, and the Scalia Effect*, 29 Berkeley J. Emp. & Lab. L. 117, 160–67 (2008); Thomas Merrill, *Textualism and the Future of the* Chevron *Doctrine*, 72 Wash. U. L.Q. 351 (1994).

[55] E.g. John Manning, *What Divides Textualists from Purposivists?*, 106 Colum. L. Rev. 70 (2006); John Manning, *Justice Scalia and the Legislative Process*, 62 N.Y.U. Ann. Surv. Am. L. 33 (2006); Frank Easterbrook, *Text, History, and Structure in Statutory Interpretation*, 17 Harv. J.L. & Pub. Poly 61 (1994); Kenneth Starr, *Observations About the Use of Legislative History*, 1987 Duke L.J. 371.

[56] Skeptical treatments include Stephen Breyer, *Making Our Democracy Work: A Judge's View* (2010); Stephen Breyer, *On the Uses of Legislative History in Interpreting Statutes*, 65 S. Cal. L. Rev. 845 (1992); George Costello, *Average Voting Members and Other "Benign Fictions": The Relative Reliability of Committee Reports, Floor Debates, and Other Sources of Legislative History*, 1990 Duke L.J. 39; William Eskridge Jr., *Textualism, The Unknown Ideal?*, 96 Mich. L. Rev. 1509 (1998); Daniel Farber & Philip Frickey, *Legislative Intent and Public Choice*, 74 Va. L. Rev. 423 (1988); Philip Frickey, *Revisiting the Revival of Theory in Statutory Interpretation: A Lecture in Honor of Irving Younger*, 84 Minn. L. Rev. 199 (1999); Paul McGreal, *A Constitutional Defense of Legislative History*, 13 Wm. & Mary Bill Rts. J. 1267 (2005); Abner Mikva & Eric Lane, *The Muzak of Justice Scalia's Revolutionary Call To Read Unclear Statutes Narrowly*, 53 SMU L. Rev. 121 (2000); Stephen Ross & Daniel Tranen, *The Modern Parol Evidence Rule and Its Implications for New Textualist Statutory Interpretation*, 87 Geo. L.J. 195 (1998); Peter Strauss, *The Common Law and Statutes*, 70 U. Colo. L. Rev. 225 (1999); Patricia Wald, *The Sizzling Sleeper: The Use of Legislative History in Construing Statutes in the 1988–89 Term of the United States Supreme Court*, 39 Am. U.L. Rev. 277 (1990); Nicholas Zeppos, *Justice Scalia's Textualism: The "New" New Legal Process*, 12 Cardozo L. Rev. 1597 (1991).

[57] See Jane Schacter, *The Confounding Common Law Originalism in Recent Supreme Court Statutory Interpretation: Implications for the Legislative History Debate and Beyond*, 51 Stan. L. Rev. 1 (1998); Charles Tiefer, *The Reconceptualization of Legislative History in the Supreme Court*, 2000 Wis. L. Rev. 205. For a fairly recent example, featuring a lavish deployment of legislative history by a majority opinion (written by O'Connor but joined without cavil by Scalia and Thomas), see *FDA v. Brown & Williamson Tobacco Co.* (Chapter 6, § 3B3).

Bankruptcy Judges, United States Trustees, and Family Farmer Bankruptcy Act of 1986, Pub. L. 99–554, 100 Stat. 3088:

> The amendments made by subtitle B of title II shall not apply with respect to cases commenced under title 11 of the United States Code before the effective date of this Act.

The Sinclairs rely on the report of the Conference Committee, which inserted § 302(c)(1) into the bill:

> It is not intended that there be routine conversion of Chapter 11 and 13 cases, pending at the time of enactment, to Chapter 12. Instead, it is expected that courts will exercise their sound discretion in each case, in allowing conversions only where it is equitable to do so.
>
> Chief among the factors the court should consider is whether there is a substantial likelihood of successful reorganization under Chapter 12.
>
> Courts should also carefully scrutinize the actions already taken in pending cases in deciding whether, in their equitable discretion, to allow conversion. For example, the court may consider whether the petition was recently filed in another chapter with no further action taken. Such a case may warrant conversion to the new chapter. On the other hand, there may be cases where a reorganization plan has already been filed or confirmed. In cases where the parties have substantially relied on current law, availability [sic] to convert to the new chapter should be limited.

The statute says conversion is impossible; the report says that conversion is possible and describes the circumstances under which it should occur.

Which prevails in the event of conflict, the statute or its legislative history? The statute was enacted, the report just the staff's explanation. Congress votes on the text of the bill, and the President signed that text. Committee reports help courts understand the law, but this report contradicts rather than explains the text. So the statute must prevail. * * *

Yet the advice from the Supreme Court about how to deal with our situation seems scarcely more harmonious than the advice from the legislature. The reports teem with statements such as: "When we find the terms of a statute unambiguous, judicial inquiry is complete," *Rubin v. United States*, 449 U.S. 424, 430 (1981). See also, e.g., *United States v. Ron Pair Enters., Inc.*, 489 U.S. 235 (1989) ("where, as here, the statute's language is plain, 'the sole function of the courts is to enforce it according to its terms.'"); [Judge Easterbrook cited several other cases, including *Locke* (Chapter 6, § 2B) and *TVA v. Hill* (Chapter 6, § 2C)]. Less frequently, yet with equal conviction, the Court writes: "When aid to the construction of the meaning of words, as used in the statute, is available, there certainly can be no 'rule of law' which forbids its use, however clear the words may appear on 'superficial examination.'" *United States v. Am. Trucking Assoc., Inc.*, 310 U.S. 534, 543–44 (1940) (footnotes omitted), repeated in *Train v. Colo. Public Interest Research Grp., Inc.*, 426 U.S. 1, 10 (1976). See also, e.g., * * * *Holy Trinity Church* [Chapter 6, § 1]. Some cases boldly stake out a middle ground, saying, for example: "only the most extraordinary showing of contrary intentions from [the legislative history] would justify a limitation on the 'plain meaning' of the statutory language." *Garcia v. United States*, 469 U.S. 70, 75 (1984). See also, e.g., *Griffin* [Chapter 6, § 2C] * * *. This implies that once in a blue moon the legislative history trumps the statute (as opposed to affording a basis for its interpretation) but does not help locate such strange astronomical phenomena. These lines of cases have coexisted for a century, and many cases contain statements associated with two or even all three of them, not recognizing the tension.

What's a court to do? The answer lies in distinguishing among uses of legislative history. An unadorned "plain meaning" approach to interpretation supposes that words have meanings divorced from their contexts—linguistic, structural, functional, social, historical. Language is a process of communication that works only when authors and readers share a set of rules and meanings. What "clearly" means one thing to a reader unacquainted with the circumstances of the utterance—including social conventions prevailing at the time of drafting—may mean something else to a reader with a different background. Legislation speaks across the decades, during which legal institutions and linguistic conventions change. To decode words one must frequently reconstruct the legal and political culture of the drafters. Legislative history may be invaluable in revealing the setting of the enactment and the assumptions its authors entertained about how their words would be understood. It may show, too, that words with a denotation "clear" to an outsider are terms of art, with an equally "clear" but different meaning to an insider. It may show too that the words leave gaps, for short phrases cannot address all human experience; understood in context, the words may leave to the executive and judicial branches the task of adding flesh to bones. These we take to be the points of cases such as *American Trucking* holding that judges may learn from the legislative history even when the text is "clear". Clarity depends on context, which legislative history may illuminate. The process is objective; the search is not for the contents of the authors' heads but for the rules of language they used.

Quite different is the claim that legislative intent is *the* basis of interpretation, that the text of the law is simply evidence of the real rule. In such a regimen legislative history is not a way to understand the text but is a more authentic, because more proximate, expression of legislators' will. One may say in reply that legislative history is a poor guide to legislators' intent because it is written by the staff rather than by members of Congress, because it is often losers' history ("If you can't get your proposal into the bill, at least write the legislative history to make it look as if you'd prevailed"), because it becomes a crutch ("There's no need for us to vote on the amendment if we can write a little legislative history"), because it complicates the task of execution and obedience (neither judges nor those whose conduct is supposed to be influenced by the law can know what to do without delving into legislative recesses, a costly and uncertain process). Often there is so much legislative history that a court can manipulate the meaning of a law by choosing which snippets to emphasize and by putting hypothetical questions—questions to be answered by inferences from speeches rather than by reference to the text, so that great discretion devolves on the (judicial) questioner. Sponsors of opinion polls know that a small change in the text of a question can lead to large differences in the answer. Legislative history offers willful judges an opportunity to pose questions and devise answers, with predictable divergence in results. These and related concerns have lead to skepticism about using legislative history to find legislative intent. E.g., *Blanchard v. Bergeron* (Scalia, J., concurring); [Judge Easterbrook cited several lower court opinions, including Judge Scalia's separate opinion in *Hirschey*]. These cautionary notes are well taken, but even if none were salient there would still be a hurdle to the sort of argument pressed in our case.

Statutes are law, not evidence of law. References to "intent" in judicial opinions do not imply that legislators' motives and beliefs, as opposed to their public acts, establish the norms to which all others must conform. "Original meaning" rather than "intent" frequently captures the interpretive task more precisely, reminding us that it is the work of the political branches (the "meaning") rather than of the courts that matters, and that their work acquires its meaning when enacted ("originally"). Revisionist history may be revelatory; revisionist judging is simply unfaithful to the enterprise. Justice Holmes made the point when denouncing a claim that judges should give weight to the intent of a document's authors:

> [A statute] does not disclose one meaning conclusively according to the laws of language. Thereupon we ask, not what this man meant, but what those words would mean in the mouth of a normal speaker of English, using them in the circumstances in which they were used. . . . But the normal speaker of English is merely a special variety, a literary form, so to speak, of our old friend the prudent man. He is external to the particular writer, and a reference to him as the criterion is simply another instance of the externality of the law. . . . We do not inquire what the legislature meant; we ask only what the statute means.

Oliver Wendell Holmes, *The Theory of Legal Interpretation*, 12 Harv. L. Rev. 417, 417–19 (1899), reprinted in Collected Legal Papers 204, 207 (1920). Or as Judge Friendly put things in a variation on Holmes's theme, a court must search for "what Congress meant by what it said, rather than for what it meant *simpliciter*." Henry J. Friendly, *Mr. Justice Frankfurter and the Reading of Statutes*, in Benchmarks 218–19 (1967).

An opinion poll revealing the wishes of Congress would not translate to legal rules. Desires become rules only after clearing procedural hurdles, designed to encourage deliberation and expose proposals (and arguments) to public view and recorded vote. Resort to "intent" as a device to short-circuit these has no more force than the opinion poll—less, because the legislative history is written by the staff of a single committee and not subject to a vote or veto. The Constitution establishes a complex of procedures, including presidential approval (or support by two-thirds of each house). It would demean the constitutionally prescribed method of legislating to suppose that its elaborate apparatus for deliberation on, amending, and approving a text is just a way to create some *evidence* about the law, while the *real* source of legal rules is the mental processes of legislators. We know from *INS v. Chadha*, 462 U.S. 919 (1983) [Chapter 8, § 2C], that the express disapproval of one house of Congress cannot change the law, largely because it removes the President from the process; it would therefore be surprising if "intents" subject to neither vote nor veto could be sources of law.

* * * If Congress were to reduce the rate of taxation on capital gains, "intending" that this stimulate economic growth and so yield more in tax revenue, the meaning of the law would be only that rates go down, not that revenue go up—a judge could not later rearrange rates to achieve the "intent" with respect to federal coffers. On the other hand, doubt about the meaning of a term found in the statute could well be resolved by harmonizing that provision with the structure of the rest of the law, understood in light of a contemporaneous explanation. In this sense legislative intent is a vital source of meaning even though it does not trump the text.

Concern about the source of law—is the statute law, or is it just evidence of the law?—lies behind statements such as: "[T]he language being plain, and not leading to absurd or wholly impracticable consequences, it is the sole evidence of the ultimate legislative intent." *Caminetti* [v. *United States*, 242 U.S. 470 (1917)]. [Chapter 6, § 1] To treat the text as conclusive evidence of law is to treat it *as* law—which under the constitutional structure it is. Legislative history then may help a court discover but may not change the original meaning. *Pierce v. Underwood*, 487 U.S. 552 (1988). The "plain meaning" rule of *Caminetti* rests not on a silly belief that texts have timeless meanings divorced from their many contexts, not on the assumption that what is plain to one reader must be clear to any other (and identical to the plan of the writer), but on the constitutional allocation of powers. The political branches adopt texts through prescribed procedures; what ensues is the law. Legislative history may show the meaning of the texts—may show, indeed, that a text "plain" at first reading has a strikingly different meaning—but may not be used to show an "intent" at variance with the meaning of the text. *Caminetti* and *American Trucking* can comfortably coexist when so understood. This approach also supplies the underpinning for the belief that legislative history is "only admissible to solve doubt and not to create it," which punctuates the U.S. Reports. Legislative history helps us learn what Congress meant by what it said, but it is not a source of legal rules competing with those found in the U.S. Code.

Ours is now an easy case. Section 302(c)(1) of the statute has an ascertainable meaning, a meaning not absurd or inconsistent with the structure of the remaining provisions. It says that Chapter 11 cases pending on the date the law went into force may not be converted to Chapter 12. No legislative history suggests any other meaning. The committee report suggests, at best, a different intent. Perhaps a reader could infer that the committee planned to allow conversion but mistakenly voted for a different text. So two members of the committee have said since, calling § 302(c)(1) an oversight. See 133 Cong. Rec. S2273–76 (daily ed. Feb. 19, 1987) (Sen. Grassley), E544 (daily ed. Feb. 19, 1987) (Rep. Coelho). Not only the committee's remarks on conversion but also the omission of § 302(c)(1) from the section-by-section description of the bill suggest that whoever wrote the report (a staffer, not a Member of Congress) wanted § 302(c)(1) deleted and may have thought that had been accomplished. Still another possibility is that the Conference Committee meant to distinguish Chapter 11 from Chapter 13: to ban conversions from Chapter 11 (covered by § 302(c)(1)) but allow them from Chapter 13. On this reading the gaffe is the failure to delete the reference to Chapter 11 from the report, which could still stand as a treatment of conversions from Chapter 13.

Congress has done nothing to change § 302(c)(1), implying that the statement in the committee report may have been the error. It is easy to imagine opposing forces arriving at the conference armed with their own texts and legislative histories, and in the scramble at the end of session one version slipping into the bill and the other into the report. Whichever was the blunder, we know which one was enacted. What came out of conference, what was voted for by House and Senate, what was signed by the President, says that pending Chapter 11 cases may not be converted. Accordingly, pending Chapter 11 cases may not be converted.

NOTES ON SINCLAIR AND THE SEARCH FOR OBJECTIVITY IN STATUTORY INTERPRETATION

1.   *Textual Evidence Judge Easterbrook Missed.* Judge Easterbrook cites § 302 of the 1986 statute, which seems to prevent conversion of the *Sinclair* proceeding. But the legislative history he cites is the Conference Committee language not of § 302, but of § 256(1), which amended 11 U.S.C. § 1112(d). Section 1112 is the provision of Chapter 11 that deals with conversions. As amended, it now reads:

> (d)   The Court may convert a case under this chapter to a case under chapter 12 or 13 of this title only if—
>
>> (1)   the debtor requests such conversion;
>>
>> (2)   the debtor has not been discharged under section 1141(d) of this title; and
>>
>> (3)   if the debtor requests conversion to chapter 12 of this title, such conversion is equitable.

Is the statutory text 100% clear against conversion? It is only if § 256(1) is interpreted not to apply to pending proceedings (see Chapter 5, § 3C).

In light of this evidence, construct an argument that *In re Sinclair* is wrongly decided.[58] We have brought this evidence to Judge Easterbrook's attention, and he responded that it would not change his thinking about this case, because the new textual evidence was not briefed by the parties and in any event he was not persuaded that this new evidence created any statutory ambiguity. Does this additional information demonstrate ambiguity?

2.   *Judicial Fears of the Mischievous Staffer.* An enduring image from Justice Scalia's *Bergeron* concurring opinion (and a standard trope in Scalia's speeches deriding legislative history) is the possibility that mischievous staffers will smuggle stuff into committee reports and thereby "trick" judges into bad interpretations that Congress did not "intend." Notice how staffers bent on mischief can do the same thing to statutory text. In *Sinclair*, Judge Easterbrook notes that several Members of Congress later said that a mistake somehow arose with respect to § 302(c)(1), the effective date provision, and that the Congress intended to allow conversion of pending farmer bankruptcy proceedings. There are at least three reasons to believe that this is accurate.

---

[58]   For an extraordinary discussion concerning broader jurisprudential issues lingering in the *Sinclair* case, see Paul Campos, *The Chaotic Pseudotext*, 94 Mich. L. Rev. 2178 (1996).

First, it is fishy that the Conference Report has no mention of § 302(c)(1). That the "dog didn't bark" in the Conference Report is odd in light of a second factor, the emergency nature of this law. The 1986 act creating Chapter 12 was adopted during the most serious farm economic depression since the 1930s. Farmers had been going under left and right, and Congress decided to ameliorate their debt situation somewhat by adopting Chapter 12, which is more favorable to farmers than is the bankruptcy scheme of Chapter 11, which is available to all debtors. This "help the farmers during this emergency" purpose of the 1986 statute seems in stark conflict with the notion that only future cases could be converted to new Chapter 12. Moreover, § 1112(d) as amended allows conversion only in cases in which it would be equitable, thereby providing some measure of protection to creditors in pending proceedings. Finally, according to prevalent rumors in one segment of the bankruptcy bar, at the behest of lending interests a Senate staff member put § 302 into the bill, contrary to the apparent wishes of the sponsors and supporters of the 1986 statute. It appears that sponsors and supporters of the statute did not even notice § 302 until well after the statute had been adopted. This may shed new light on why § 302 was not discussed in the section-by-section description of the bill in the conference committee report. This rumor seems to turn on its head the complaint by new textualists that *legislative history* is unreliable stuff because of potential shenanigans by legislative staff.[59]

3. *Objectivity in Statutory Interpretation: Empirical Evidence from the Supreme Court's Labor and Employment Cases.* Complementing the image of the mischievous staffer in Justice Scalia's pitch for the new textualism is the result-oriented judge who will look out over the legislative history crowd and pick out his friends. You might review the *big cases* in this Casebook, such as *Weber*, the affirmative action case in Chapter 1; *Holy Trinity* and the FDA Tobacco Case in Chapter 6; and *Sweet Home* at the end of this chapter. In all these cases, Justices (including Scalia, in *Sweet Home*) invoke legislative history to support results that match those Justices' apparent ideologies—but in all the cases except *Holy Trinity* the Justices also invoke textual plain meaning in the same way.

Properly phrased, the inquiry demanded by the new textualism's appeal to objectivity in judging is that a judge who looks at legislative history as well as text is *more likely* to read his or her ideological presuppositions into a statute than a judge who just looks at the text alone. There is no empirical evidence that this is the case—and now some evidence to the contrary. See James Brudney and Corey Ditslear, *Liberal Justices' Reliance on Legislative History: Principle, Strategy, and the Scalia Effect*, 29 Berkeley J. Emp. & Lab. L. 117 (2008). In conducting a deeper empirical analysis of the 578 Supreme Court decisions interpreting basically pro-employee labor and employment statutes (1969–2006), the authors analyzed the voting records of the eight Justices conventionally considered "liberal" and reached the following conclusions:

> [F]or the eight liberals, the relationship between pro-employee outcomes and legislative history usage is not significant. If anything, these Justices' legislative history reliance is associated more often with outcomes to which they would likely be ideologically opposed. When liberal Justices use legislative history as part of their majority reasoning, they do so to help justify

---

[59] On end-of-the-game strategic moves in the legislative process, see William Rodgers, Jr., *The Lesson of the Red Squirrel: Consensus and Betrayal in the Environmental Statutes*, 5 J. Contemp. Health L. & Pol. 161 (1989).

more than half of their *pro-employer* opinions for the Court but just under one-half of their *pro-employee* outcomes. Further evidence of this moderating association is that majority opinions authored by liberal Justices reach liberal outcomes 30 percent more often than conservative results when *not* relying on legislative history, but the liberal-conservative outcome differential declines to 21 percent when the majority opinion's reasoning includes legislative history. *Id.* at 121.

For the Justices considered "conservative," Brudney and Ditslear found that reliance on legislative history also was correlated with slightly more conservative voting. As for what types of legislative history from pro-employee federal statutes supported so many pro-employer outcomes, the authors identified three distinct categories: (1) legislative history that amplified or unpacked the meaning of employer defenses or exemptions built into the statutes; (2) history that established the existence or details of a compromise on the issue under review; (3) history demonstrating that the legal position identified with employees and their supporters had overreached in its claims. An example of the second category outside of labor law is *Muscarello* in § 2A of this chapter, where liberal Justice Breyer relied on legislative history to interpret ambiguous statutory language and impose a harsh sentence on gun-"carrying" defendants. This is preliminary evidence *against* the judicial objectivity argument for textualism.

On the other hand, Brudney and Ditslear also found that this moderating association has waned among the cohort of liberal Justices since Justice Scalia's appointment to the Court. The authors' provisional explanation is that Justice Scalia's hard-hitting style has polarized the Court, leading liberal Justices who wish to secure Scalia's unqualified support for their pro-employer majorities to abandon legislative history even when the prevailing parties have relied heavily on that history in their briefs. See *id.* at 160–67. Has Judge Leventhal's quip become a self-fulfilling prophesy?

Carr v. United States
560 U.S. 438 (2010).

The Sex Offender Registration and Notification Act of 2006 (SORNA) makes it a federal crime for any person (1) who "is required to register under [SORNA]," and (2) who "travels in interstate or foreign commerce," to (3) "knowingly fai[l] to register or update a registration." 18 U.S.C. § 2250(a). Before SORNA's enactment, Thomas Carr, a registered sex offender in Alabama, relocated to Indiana without complying with Indiana's registration requirements. The federal government charged Carr with violating SORNA. After the trial court rejected his constitutional (ex post facto) challenge to this indictment, Carr pleaded guilty. On appeal, he argued that the statute requires that the interstate travel (as well as the failure to register or update a registration) be accomplished *after* SORNA went into effect. The government argued that only the failure to register or update needs to be after the effective date.

Reversing the Seventh Circuit, **Justice Sotomayor's** opinion for the Court interpreted SORNA to apply only if both the travel and the failure to register/update occurred after the statute went into effect. "By its terms, the first element of § 2250(a) can only be satisfied when a person 'is required to register *under the Sex Offender Registration and Notification Act.*' § 2250(a)(1) (emphasis added)." The implication of this requirement is that SORNA is applicable to the defendant when he engages in travel and failure to register/update.

Justice Sotomayor found this reading consistent with the second requirement, that the defendant "travels" in commerce. "That § 2250 sets forth the travel requirement in the present tense ('travels') rather than in the past or present perfect ('traveled' or 'has traveled') reinforces the conclusion that pre-enactment travel falls outside the statute's compass. Consistent with normal usage, we have frequently looked to Congress' choice of verb tense to ascertain a statute's temporal reach. [E.g.,] *Gwaltney of Smithfield, Ltd.* v. *Chesapeake Bay Found., Inc.*, 484 U.S. 49, 57 (1987) ('Congress could have phrased its requirement in language that looked to the past . . ., but it did not choose this readily available option'). The Dictionary Act also ascribes significance to verb tense. It provides that, '[i]n determining the meaning of any Act of Congress, unless the context indicates otherwise[,] . . . words used in the present tense include the future as well as the present.' 1 U.S.C. § 1. By implication, then, the Dictionary Act instructs that the present tense generally does not include the past. Accordingly, a statute that regulates a person who 'travels' is not readily understood to encompass a person whose only travel occurred before the statute took effect. Indeed, neither the Government nor the dissent identifies any instance in which this Court has construed a present-tense verb in a criminal law to reach pre-enactment conduct."

"The Government accepts that th[e] last element—a knowing failure to register or update a registration—must postdate SORNA's enactment. Had Congress intended pre-enactment conduct to satisfy the first two requirements of § 2250 but not the third, it presumably would have varied the verb tenses to convey this meaning. Indeed, numerous federal statutes use the past-perfect tense to describe one or more elements of a criminal offense when coverage of pre-enactment events is intended. See, *e.g.*, 18 U.S.C. § 249(a)(2)(B)(iii) (Supp. 2010) (proscribing hate crimes in which 'the defendant employs a firearm, dangerous weapon, explosive or incendiary device, or other weapon that *has traveled* in interstate or foreign commerce' (emphasis added)); 18 U.S.C. § 922(g)(9) (2006 ed.) (proscribing firearm possession or transport by any person 'who *has been convicted*' of a felony or a misdemeanor crime of domestic violence (emphasis added). The absence of similar phrasing here provides powerful evidence that§ 2250 targets only post-enactment travel."

"In a final effort to justify its position, the Government invokes one of SORNA's underlying purposes: to locate sex offenders who had failed to abide by their registration obligations. SORNA, the Government observes, was motivated at least in part by Congress' concern about these 'missing' sex offenders—a problem the House Committee on the Judiciary expressly linked to interstate travel: 'The most significant enforcement issue in the sex offender program is that over 100,000 sex offenders, or nearly one-fifth in the Nation[,] are 'missing,' meaning they have not complied with sex offender registration requirements. This typically occurs when the sex offender moves from one State to another." H.R. Rep. No. 109–218, pt. 1, at 26 (2005). The goal of tracking down missing sex offenders, the Government maintains, 'is surely better served by making Section 2250 applicable to them in their new States of residence immediately than by waiting for them to travel in interstate commerce and fail to register yet again.' Brief for United States 23–24."

"The Government's argument confuses a general goal of SORNA with the specific purpose of § 2250. Section 2250 is not a stand-alone response to the problem of missing sex offenders; it is embedded in a broader statutory scheme enacted to address the deficiencies in prior law that had enabled sex offenders to slip through the cracks. Among its many provisions, SORNA instructs States to maintain sex-offender registries that compile an array of information about sex offenders, § 16914; to make this information publicly available online, § 16918; to share the information with other jurisdictions and with the Attorney General for inclusion in a comprehensive national sex-offender registry, §§ 16919–16921; and to 'provide a criminal penalty that includes a maximum term of imprisonment that is greater than 1 year for the failure of a sex offender to comply with the requirements of this subchapter,' § 16913(e). Sex offenders, in turn, are required to 'register, and keep the registration current, in each jurisdiction where the offender resides, where the offender is an employee, and where the offender is a student,' § 16913(a), and to appear in person periodically to 'allow the jurisdiction to take a current photograph, and verify the information in each registry in which that offender is required to be registered,' § 16916. By facilitating the collection of sex-offender information and its dissemination among jurisdictions, these provisions, not § 2250, stand at the center of Congress' effort to account for missing sex offenders.

"Knowing that Congress aimed to reduce the number of noncompliant sex offenders thus tells us little about the specific policy choice Congress made in enacting § 2250. While subjecting pre-SORNA travelers to punishment under § 2250 may well be consistent with the aim of finding missing sex offenders, a contrary construction in no way frustrates that broad goal."

"None of the legislative materials the Government cites as evidence of SORNA's purpose calls this reading into question. To the contrary, the report of the House Judiciary Committee suggests not only that a prohibition on post-enactment travel is consonant with Congress' goals, but also that it is the rule Congress in fact chose to adopt. As the Government acknowledges, the bill under consideration by the Committee contained a version of § 2250 that 'would not have reached pre-enactment interstate travel.' Brief for United States 24, n.9. This earlier version imposed federal criminal penalties on any person who 'receives a notice from an official that such person is required to register under [SORNA] and . . . thereafter travels in interstate or foreign commerce, or enters or leaves Indian country.' H.R. Rep. No. 109–218, pt. 1, at 9. Yet this did not stop the Committee from describing its legislation as a solution to the problem of missing sex offenders. The Government identifies nothing in the legislative record to suggest that, in modifying this language during the course of the legislative process, Congress intended to alter the statute's temporal sweep."

Justice Scalia concurred in all but this last portion of the Court's opinion, discussing SORNA's legislative history. "I do not join that part because only the text Congress voted on, and not unapproved statements made or comments written during its drafting and enactment process, is an authoritative indicator of the law. But even if those pre-enactment materials were relevant, it would be unnecessary to address them here. The Court's thorough discussion of text, context, and structure demonstrates that the meaning of 18 U.S.C. § 2250(a) is plain."

Justice Alito (joined by **Justices Thomas** and **Ginsburg**) dissented. "A man convicted in State A for sexual abuse is released from custody in that State and then, after the enactment of SORNA, moves to State B and fails to register as required by State B law. Section 2250(a) makes this offender's failure to register in State B a federal crime because his interstate movement frustrates SORNA's registration requirements. Because this offender is convicted and then released from custody in State A, the State A authorities know of his presence in their State and are thus in a position to try to ensure that he remains registered. At the time of his release, they can ascertain where he intends to live, and they can make sure that he registers as required by state law. Thereafter, they can periodically check the address at which he is registered to confirm that he still resides there. And even if he moves without warning to some other address in the State, they can try to track him down. Once this offender leaves State A, however, the authorities in that State are severely limited in their ability to monitor his movements. And because the State B authorities have no notice of his entry into their State, they are at a great disadvantage in trying to enforce State B's registration law. Congress enacted § 2250(a) in order to punish and deter interstate movement that seriously undermines the enforcement of sex-offender-registration laws.

"The second case is the same as the first in all respects except that the sex offender travels from State A to State B before SORNA's enactment. In other words, the sex offender is convicted and later released in State A; prior to SORNA's enactment, he moves to State B; and then, after SORNA takes effects, he fails to register in State B, as SORNA requires.

"Is there any reason why Congress might have wanted to treat the second case any differently from the first?" Justice Alito thought not—nor did he think that the statutory text required or even supported what he considered an absurd result. The Court's argument, that § 2250(a) uses the present tense and that the "present" is the date the law was enacted, "flies in the face of the widely accepted modern legislative drafting convention that a law should *not* be read to speak as of the date of enactment. The United States Senate Legislative Drafting Manual directly addresses this point: 'A legislative provision speaks as of any date on which it is read (*rather than as of when drafted, enacted, or put into effect*).' Senate Office of the Legislative Counsel, Legislative Drafting Manual § 103(a), at 4 (1997) (emphasis added). The House Manual makes the same point: 'Your draft should be a movable feast—that is, it speaks as of whatever time it is being read (*rather than as of when drafted, enacted, or put into effect*).' House Legislative Counsel's Manual on Drafting Style, HLC No. 104–1, § 102(c), at 2 (1995).

"In accordance with this convention, modern legislative drafting manuals teach that, except in unusual circumstances, all laws, including penal statutes, should be written in the present tense. The Senate Manual, *supra*, § 103(a), at 4, states: '[A]lways use the present tense unless the provision addresses only the past, the future, or a sequence of events that requires use of a different tense.' Similarly, the House Manual, *supra*, § 102(c), at 2, advises: 'STAY IN THE PRESENT.—Whenever possible, use the present tense (rather than the past or future).' Numerous state legislative drafting manuals and other similar handbooks hammer home this same point. [Justice Alito cited the drafting manuals used by nine different states.]

"Once it is recognized that § 2250(a) should not be read as speaking as of the date when SORNA went into effect, petitioner's argument about the use of the present tense collapses. In accordance with current drafting conventions, § 2250(a) speaks, not as of the time when the law went into effect, but as of the time when the first act necessary for conviction is committed. In the case of § 2250(a), that occurs when an individual is convicted of a qualifying sex offense, for it is that act that triggers the requirement to register under SORNA." Justice Alito challenged the majority Justices to "double check" their too-confident textual analysis against the legislative history and purpose of the law.

"SORNA was a response to a dangerous gap in the then existing sex-offender-registration laws. In the years prior to SORNA's enactment, the Nation had been shocked by cases in which children had been raped and murdered by persons who, unbeknownst to their neighbors or the police, were convicted sex offenders. In response, Congress and state legislatures passed laws requiring the registration of sex offenders. See *Smith* v. *Doe*, 538 U.S. 84, 89–90 (2003); Jacob Wetterling Crimes Against Children and Sexually Violent Offender Registration Act, Tit. 17, 108 Stat. 2038; Megan's Law, 110 Stat. 1345. Despite those efforts, by 2006 an estimated 100,000 convicted sex offenders—nearly one-fifth of the Nation's total sex-offender population—remained unregistered. H.R. Rep. No. 109–218, pt. 1, at 26 (2005). The principal problem, a House Report determined, was that sex offenders commonly moved from one State to another and then failed to register in their new State of residence. *Ibid.* In other words, interstate travel was dangerously undermining the effectiveness of state sex-offender-registration laws.

"Interpreting § 2250(a)(2)(B) to reach only post-enactment travel severely impairs § 2250(a)'s effectiveness. As interpreted by the Court, § 2250(a) applies to a pre-SORNA sex offender only if that offender traveled in interstate commerce at some point *after* SORNA's enactment. As the examples discussed at the beginning of this opinion illustrate, however, there is no apparent reason why Congress would have wanted to impose such a requirement. To the contrary, under the Court's interpretation, the many sex offenders who had managed to avoid pre-existing registration regimes, mainly by moving from one State to another before SORNA's enactment, are placed beyond the reach of the federal criminal laws. It surely better serves the enforcement of SORNA's registration requirements to apply § 2250(a) to all pre-SORNA sex offenders, regardless of whether their interstate travel occurred before or after the statute's enactment.

"The Court provides only a weak defense of the result its analysis produces. The Court suggests that enhanced information collection and sharing and state enforcement of registration laws were the sole weapons that Congress chose to wield in order to deal with those convicted sex offenders whose whereabouts were unknown when SORNA was passed. I see no basis for this conclusion. There can be no dispute that the enactment of § 2250(a) shows that Congress did not think these measures were sufficient to deal with persons who have qualifying sex-offense convictions and who move from State to State after SORNA's enactment. And in light of that congressional judgment, is there any plausible reason to think that Congress concluded that these same measures would be adequate for those with qualifying sex offense convictions who had already disappeared at the time of SORNA's enactment?"

NOTES ON THE SEX OFFENDER REGISTRATION CASE AND NEW DIRECTIONS IN THE LEGISLATIVE HISTORY DEBATE

1.   *The Court Continues to Discuss and Analyze Legislative History.* The Justices' debate in *Carr* provides a current snapshot of the Great Committee Report Debate within the Court, as of 2010. Since 2005, four new Justices have been confirmed (Roberts, Alito, Sotomayor, and Kagan), and *Carr* indicates that legislative history remains alive and well at the Supreme Court level—over the continued (indeed, renewed) objections of Justice Scalia.

The dissenting Justices (Thomas, Ginsburg, and Alito), spanning the political spectrum, rely centrally on legislative history to make their case against the Court's narrow construction of SORNA. It is significant that Justice Alito's dissent does not stop after it has made its logical and textual arguments—and that Justice Sotomayor's majority opinion (for an equally heterogeneous cluster of Roberts, Stevens, Kennedy, and Breyer) responds with her own sharp-eyed analysis of the legislative history.

Justice Scalia remains alone in his objections to the admissibility of legislative history. Why does he persist? What is the purpose of his solo concurring opinions objecting to legislative history arguments in majority opinions? Jot down your thoughts, and then consider the next note.

2. *But Legislative History Is Rarely Decisive at the Supreme Court.* If the Justices continue to discuss and analyze legislative history, they do not often give it decisive effect in their opinions. Speaking for the Court (and for Justice Scalia), Justice Sotomayor's opinion says that there is a plain meaning—and the legislative history materials are discussed mainly in response to Justice Alito's dissenting opinion. But Justice Alito himself starts with a textual argument and seems to deploy legislative history mainly to confirm what he thinks the statute's plain meaning is.

Does Justice Scalia not have a point, that the Court's (and, for that matter, Justice Alito's) legal analysis would not change significantly if legislative history were discarded? Because the Justices cite and discuss legislative history, lawyers in federal court cases and even advising clients must research legislative history, which generates enormous social expense. Is that expense worth the value added by legislative history? How would Justice Sotomayor respond to these concerns?

3. *Confirmatory Legislative History.* In *Samantar v. Yousuf*, 560 U.S. 305 (2010), a case decided on the same day as *Carr*, Justice Scalia reiterated his particular distaste for legislative history when used simply to confirm a clear statutory text:

> The Court's admirably careful textual analysis demonstrates that the term "foreign state" in the provision "a foreign state shall be immune from the jurisdiction of the courts of the United States and of the States," 28 U.S.C. § 1604, does not include foreign officials. Yet the Court insists on adding legislative history to its analysis. I could understand that (though not agree with it) if, in the absence of supposed legislative-history support, the Court would reach a different result. Or even if there was something in the legislative history that clearly contradicted the Court's result, and had to be explained away. That is not the situation here (or at least the Court's opinion does not think it to be so) * * *

> The Court's introduction of legislative history serves no purpose except needlessly to inject into the opinion a mode of analysis that not all of the Justices consider valid. And it does so, to boot, in a fashion that does not isolate the superfluous legislative history in a section that those of us who disagree categorically with its use, or at least disagree with its superfluous use, can decline to join. * * * It should be no cause for wonder that, upon careful examination, all of the opinion's excerpts from legislative history turn out to be, at best, nonprobative or entirely duplicative of text. After all, legislative history is almost never the real reason for the Court's decision— and make-weights do not deserve a lot of the Court's time.

In his *Samantar* concurrence, Justice Scalia complains that the Court's use of confirmatory legislative history precludes him from joining majority opinions in full. Perhaps in response, the Court has very recently been including qualifying language before its discussions of legislative history. *Hall v. United States*, 132 S.Ct. 1882, 1888 n.3 (2012) (Sotomayor) ("For those of us for whom it is relevant, the legislative history confirms. . . ."); *Microsoft Corp. v. i4i Ltd. P'ship*, 131 S.Ct. 2238, 2249 n.8 (2011) (Sotomayor) ("For those of us for whom it is relevant, the legislative history of § 282 provides additional evidence . . ."); *United States v. Tinklenberg*, 131 S.Ct. 2007, 2015 (2011) (Breyer) ("Fifth, for those who find legislative history useful. . . ."). How should one characterize this development? As a strategic or collegial effort to minimize the number of vehement separate opinions from Justice Scalia? As a retreat from institutional support for an interpretive resource that seven other justices (all except Justice Thomas) find relevant and useful at times?

Is Justice Scalia correct that the use of legislative history is particularly troubling and unnecessary when the statutory text is clear? In *Confirmatory Legislative History*, 76 Brooklyn L. Rev. 901 (2011), Brudney notes that confirmatory legislative history has a long historical pedigree motivated by a concern for judicial completeness:

> From the early days of the Supreme Court, justices have observed that when "labour[ing] to discover the design of the legislature, [a judge] seizes everything from which aid can be derived." *United States v. Fisher*, 6 U.S. (2 Cranch) 358, 386 (1805) (Marshall, C.J.). More recently, the Court has explained that in a confirmatory setting 'common sense suggests that inquiry benefits from reviewing additional information rather than ignoring it." *Wis. Pub. Intervenor v. Mortier*, 501 U.S. 597, 611–12 n.4 (1991) (White, J.). This judicial instinct to explore all potentially relevant information is crosscultural if not universal. In Britain, even when the House of Lords prohibited courts from consulting legislative history at all to aid in construing enacted laws, there were distinguished jurists who confessed—in their opinions and on the floor of Parliament—to peeking at the legislative record evidence in search of further enlightenment.

Brudney contends that this quest for completeness when interpreting presumptively clear text reflects in part a desire to avoid error or injustice. Beyond the search for reassurance, confirmatory discussion in judicial opinions may promote other important values. One is judicial accountability: courts considering legislative history arguments in their decisions demonstrate respect for attorneys' efforts in presenting the arguments and thereby attest to the procedural neutrality of our judicial system. Another is transparency: by illuminating all plausible arguments as an essential aspect of their reasoned decision-making, judges avoid succumbing to more conclusory and less deliberative thinking on contested statutory matters. Finally, there is guidance to repeat litigants, especially the executive branch that must construe and apply statutes featuring varying degrees of semantic detail, technical complexity, ideological compromise, and potential for constitutional controversy.

4. *A New Source of Textual Analysis: Legislative Drafting Manuals?* Justice Alito's textualist argument drawn from legislative drafting manuals caught *everyone* by surprise—the lawyers and law students working for Mr. Carr, the lawyers for the government (which had not briefed this issue), and legal academics (who had neglected

this source of textual understanding). Why did his argument not garner more than three votes? Why did Justice Scalia not find it persuasive?

Perhaps the element of surprise worked against Justice Alito: Just as the majority Justices may have been concerned with the retroactive application of a major penal statute to Mr. Carr, so they might have been worried that he should not lose the case based upon novel, unbriefed and uncontested evidence of legislative practice.[60] If this was a concern in *Carr*, however, it should *not* be a concern in future cases. The word is now out, that both the House and the Senate have drafting manuals that may provide important insights into how legislators understand, as a conventional matter, the textualist rules of the game. Moreover, both manuals are available on-line and so are easily available to lawyers and judges.

A recent student comment argues that textualists ought to pay attention to legislative drafting manuals. See B.J. Ard, Comment, *Legislative Drafting Manuals as a Guide to Statutory Interpretation*, 120 Yale L.J. 185 (2010). Mr. Ard points out that one critique of the new textualism is that it represents a judicial bait-and-switch game on Congress: Legislators enact statutes under conventional assumptions that text-loving judges later ignore and even thwart. If these legislative assumptions are well-documented rules for drafting statutory *texts*, then the new textualism seems theoretically mistaken, and the good faith of its users might be questioned. Should Justice Scalia incorporate legislative drafting manuals into his arsenal? (Ard believes that drafting manuals are not the textualist treasure trove that dictionaries are, but he does claim that new textualists need to consider them as well.)

On the other hand, if *Carr* stimulates a new cottage industry surveying legislative drafting manuals, doesn't that add further complexity to textualist analysis? The more sources textualists draw into their net, the more judges will be tempted to look out over the crowd and pick out their friends. Cf. Adrian Vermeule, *Judging Under Uncertainty* (2006) (worrying that the new textualism is already subject to this problem).

More importantly, do drafting manuals really reflect widely-followed rules for drafting statutory texts? The recent exhaustive study by Gluck and Bressman casts serious doubt on this score. Of the 137 congressional staff interviewed by the authors, 28 were counsels for the nonpartisan Offices of House and Senate Legislative Counsel. Gluck and Bressman report that even inside these nonpartisan offices, the House and Senate manuals differ from one another and each diverges from drafting checklists and style manuals used in the House and Senate Legislative Counsel offices.[61] In addition, these two legislative counsel offices cannot coordinate the process of drafting text because much if not most drafting takes place after office hours or simply without consulting Legislative Counsel, and it is very often done by the major committees that effectively operate as "drafting silos."[62] Finally, the primary users of these manuals believe strongly in the relevance of legislative history to the drafting process: over two-thirds of Legislative Counsel respondents consider legislative history to be valuable both for statutory drafters and for courts seeking to determine what Congress

---

[60] This is not the only recent instance where the Court relied on drafting manuals prepared by the House and Senate Legislative Counsel offices. See *Koons Buick Pontiac GMC, Inc. v. Nigh*, 543 U.S. 50, 60–61 (2004) (Justice Ginsburg, majority opinion).

[61] See Abbe Gluck and Lisa Schultz Bressman, *Statutory Interpretation From the Inside—An Empirical Study of Congressional Drafting, Delegation, and the Canons*, Part II, 66 Stan. L. Rev. 725, 750–52 (2014).

[62] See *id.* at 746–47.

intended.[63] In light of this evidence, should the Court abandon its recent forays into the world of Drafting Manuals?

PEREZ V. WYETH LABORATORIES, INC.
New Jersey Supreme Court, 1999.
734 A.2d 1245.

[Excerpted in Chapter 6, § 3B2]

NOTE ON THE NORPLANT CASE AND STATE COURT RELIANCE ON COMMITTEE AND OTHER LEGISLATIVE REPORTS

The Norplant Case (*Perez*) is an unusually apt one for consideration of legislative history, as the statute itself contained a reference to the committee report.[64] Moreover, **New Jersey** is one of about a dozen states that have regular reports from standing committees to accompany legislation, and it is one of eight states to make committee reports for recent legislation available on-line. See Brian Barnes, "The Transformation of State Statutory Interpretation," at 7 (Yale Law School Seminar Paper, May 4, 2010). Traditionally, New Jersey state judges are among the most willing to rely on legislative history to construe statutes; judges in that state sometimes consider committee reports whether or not the statute's text is ambiguous. See, *e.g., State v. Fleischman*, 917 A.2d 722, 730 n.4 (N.J. 2007) (committee report and whole act creating textual ambiguity, triggering rule of lenity); *State v. Froland*, 936 A.2d 947, 951 (N.J. 2007); *Bosland v. Warnock Dodge, Inc.*, 964 A.2d 741, 747 (2009). But compare *State v. Lyons*, 260, 9 A.3d 596, 601 (N.J. App. Div. 2010) ("[i]f the statute is clear and unambiguous on its face and admits of only one interpretation, we need delve no deeper than the act's literal terms to divine the Legislature's intent").

As in other states, the methodological lay-of-the-land in New Jersey is subject to challenge and possible change; Governor Chris Christie, elected in 2009, theoretically will have a chance to appoint four new justices, a majority of the court, and has vowed to appoint strict textualists in the mold of Justice Scalia.[65] Should Governor Christie cite the Norplant Case as an example of contextualist interpretation gone awry? Or should he consider Justice Pollock's dissent (relying on the committee report and other legislative materials) to be the best approach to the issues in the Norplant Case?

For recent examples of state appellate courts' reliance on committee reports, see *People v. Gonzalez*, 184 P.3d 702 (**California** 2008); *Aiken v. United States*, 956 A.2d 33, 43–44 (**District of Columbia** 2008); *State v. Woodfall*, 206 P.3d 841, 847–50 (**Hawaii** 2009); *State v. Dohlman*, 725 N.W.2d 428, 432 (**Iowa** 2006); *Risdall v. Brown-*

---

[63] See *Statutory Interpretation From the Inside, Part I*, 65 Stan. L. Rev. at 967 & n.218.

[64] Compare *Landgraf* (Chapter 5, § 3), where the statute contained a provision limiting judicial reference to legislative history. Should a strict textualist honor a statutory text requiring judges to consult legislative history? Compare Jonathan Siegel, *The Use of Legislative History in a System of Separated Powers*, 53 Vand. L. Rev. 1457 (2000) (statutory incorporation by reference of legislative history removes separation-of-powers objection) with John Manning, *Putting Legislative History to a Vote: A Response to Professor Siegel*, 53 Vand. L. Rev. 1529 (2000) (taking contrary position).

[65] We learned this bit of political intelligence, as well as confirmation of New Jersey's highly contextual approach to statutory interpretation, from Adam Yoffie, "Statutory Interpretation at the State Level: A Case Study of the New Jersey Supreme Court, 2000–2010" (Yale Law School, May 28, 2010).

Wilbert, Inc., 753 N.W.2d 723, 730 & n.6 (**Minnesota** 2008); *State v. Neesley*, 239 S.W.3d 780, 785–86 (**Texas** Crim. App. 2007).

In many other states a "bill report" is prepared by the committee staff after a bill is voted out of committee, but it is not necessarily reviewed by the committee or even its chair. The bill report typically contains a background statement, a summary of the bill's provisions, changes made by the committee, a list of the proponents and opponents who testified before the committee, and the pro and con arguments. Courts will sometimes discount such sources. In *Gates v. Jensen*, 595 P.2d 919 (**Washington** 1979), for example, the court failed to mention a bill report which explained the ambit of a statutory override of the Court's prior decisions imposing a rather strict standard of care in medical malpractice actions. Dissenting justices argued from the bill report that the override went further than the majority was willing to take it. The current trend among the states is to consider bill reports as weak but admissible evidence of legislative intent. The Supreme Court of **Florida** has deemed bill reports "one touchstone of the legislative will." *White v. State*, 714 So. 2d. 440, 443 n.5 (1998), see also *GTC, Inc. v. Edgar*, 967 So. 2d 781, 789 (**Florida** 2007); accord, *People v. Ramirez*, 201 P.3d 466, 470 (**California** 2009) and *In re Derrick B.*, 139 P.3d 485 (**California** 2006); *Kramer v. Liberty Prop. Trust*, 968 A.2d 120 (**Maryland** 2009); *Fournier v. Elliott*, 966 A.2d 410 (**Maine** 2009); *Mayor of City of Lansing v. Mich. Pub. Serv. Comm'n*, 680 N.W.2d 840, 849 (**Michigan** 2004); *Krupa v. State*, 286 S.W.3d 74 (**Texas** Crim. App. 2009); *Cosmopolitan Engr'g Group, Inc. v. Ondeo Degremont, Inc.*, 149 P.3d 666, 672–73 (**Washington** 2006).

In **New York**, the governor's staff compiles a "bill jacket" (the New York term) to assist the governor in her or his decision whether to veto a bill the legislature has passed. Containing analyses from legislative sponsors as well as interested agencies and private parties, bill jackets are often treasure troves of legislative background materials and legal arguments. Similar reports, called "governor's bills files," can be found in public archives for California, Massachusetts, Oregon, Utah, Washington, and perhaps other states. E.g., *Ramirez*, 201 P.3d at 471–72 (relying on sponsor's letter to file compiled for governor in **California**).

In addition to committee reports and bill reports, state legislative history can include a number of other reports compiled by official sources before statutes are enacted. In her dissenting opinion in *State ex rel. Kalal v. Circuit Ct., Dane Cnty.*, 681 N.W.2d 110, 125–26 (**Wisconsin** 2004), Chief Justice Shirley Abrahamson listed other sources her court had traditionally considered, including not just legislative committee reports, but also legislative reference bureau drafting files and prefatory notes for bills, governor's study commission reports, judicial council notes, joint legislative council notes, and governor's veto messages. Wisconsin's Supreme Court still routinely relies on such materials. E.g., *State v. Duchow*, 749 N.W.2d 913 (**Wisconsin** 2008) (legislative reference bureau's drafting file); *State v. Grunke*, 738 N.W.2d 137, 142 (**Wisconsin** 2007) (same). See also *Price v. Tens Built Buses, Inc.*, 260 S.W.3d 300, 305–06 (**Arkansas** 2007) (resolving ambiguity by reference to legislative council report); *Jones v. Lodge*, 177 P.3d 232, 240–43 (**California** 2008) (relying on legislative counsel's digest summarizing bills, as well as committee report and agency bill analysis); *People v. Garson*, 848 N.E.2d 1264 (**New York** 2006) (commission staff notes relied on); *McKinney v. Richetelli*, 586 S.E.2d 258, 263 (**North Carolina** 2003) (report of general statutes commission).

In at least one state, there has been serious debate as to what kinds of legislative materials might be admissible. An important decision is *People v. Gardner*, 753 N.W.2d 78, 89 (**Michigan** 2008), where a divided Michigan Supreme Court ruled that legislative materials could only be considered when the statute is ambiguous *and* that only certain legislative materials should be admissible. *Admissible* materials included the statutory history and evidence of proposals rejected by one chamber or the other. *Inadmissible* materials, even when the statute is ambiguous, included committee reports, staff analyses of bills, and floor speeches by sponsors and other legislators. In 2008, the textualist chief justice was turned out of office by the voters, and the Michigan Supreme Court may not remain committed to such a stingy view in subsequent cases.

Consideration of committee and bill reports is hardly a monopoly of large-population states. Practices similar to those in the previous paragraphs can be found in **Alaska**, see, e.g., *Municipality of Anchorage v. Adamson*, 301 P.3d 569, 576–77 (Alaska 2013); **Arizona**, see, e.g., *Haag v. Steinle*, 255 P.3d 1016, 1018 (Ariz. Ct. App. 2011); **Connecticut**, see, e.g., *Biafore v. Bozeman*, 2005 WL 469177 at *6 (Conn. Super. Ct. 2005); **Oregon**, e.g., *A.G. v. Guitron*, 268 P.3d 589, 597–99 (2011).

Some states have no high-court authorization for considering committee reports but they may be open to the practice in cases yet to be decided. Although its judges will discuss "statutory history" (the formal evolution of the statute, as amended over time), appellate courts in **Missouri, Virginia**, and **Georgia** generally do not cite to legislative history. E.g., *State v. Ware*, 653 S.E.2d 21, 23 (Ga. 2007); *State v. Premium Standard Farms, Inc.*, 100 S.W.3d 157 (Mo. Ct. App. 2003). Many smaller states have no readily available legislative history, and there are too few reported decisions to discern a hard-and-fast rule for lawyer use of legislative history. E.g., **Rhode Island**, *Such v. State*, 950 A.2d 1150, 1158–59 (R.I. 2008); **Wyoming**, *Kennedy Oil v. Dep't of Revenue*, 205 P.3d 999, 1006 (Wyo. 2008). Finally, legislative history at the state level is more accessible than it was a generation ago. See William Manz, *Guide to State Legislative and Administrative Materials* (7th ed. 2008); Barnes, "Transformation of State Statutory Interpretation" (documenting how every category of legislative history is much more widely available in 2010 than it was in 1980, and much of the recent materials are available on-line). Indeed, judges are sometimes even encouraging counsel to research it. In *Dilleley v. State*, 815 S.W.2d 623 (**Texas** Crim. App. 1991), the appeals court not only relied on legislative history but, in an appendix to the court's opinion, provided counsel in future cases with a roadmap for researching legislative history in Texas. Increasingly, state legislative history is online. Some state supreme courts provide guides to researching legislative history on their websites.[66]

3. Statements by Sponsors or Drafters of Legislation

Next to committee reports, the most persuasive legislative materials are explanations of statutory meanings, and compromises reached to achieve enactment, by the sponsors and floor managers of the legislation. Recall that Senator Humphrey and the other primary sponsors of the Civil Rights Act of 1964 were primary sources of legislative history on both sides of the affirmative action debate in *United Steelworkers v. Weber* (Chapter 1, § 3). Because there was no

---

[66] See, e.g., the Washington Supreme Court's website, www.courts.wa.gov/library/legis.cfm (viewed July 30, 2014).

Senate Report for that legislation, the sponsors' statements were most reliable. Even Justice Scalia relied on a sponsor's explanation as key evidence for his dissent in *Sweet Home*, excerpted at the end of this chapter.

As the availability of legislative history for state statutes has dramatically increased, state courts, too, are relying on statements of sponsors to interpret statutes. See, e.g., *Commonwealth v. Ahlborn*, 626 A.2d 1265 (Pa. 1993) (relying on explanation of clarifying amendment, acquiesced in by the committee chair, as useful evidence of legislative intent); *Dillehey v. State*, 815 S.W.2d 623 (Tex. Crim. App. 1991) (relying on colloquy and providing counsel with roadmap for researching legislative history in Texas). On the other hand, statements by ordinary legislators are rarely given much, if any, weight. See *Murphy v. Kenneth Cole Prods., Inc.*, 40 Cal. 4th 1094 (2007) ("we do not consider the motives or understandings of individual legislators, including the bill's author"); *Quelimane Co. v. Stewart Title Guar. Co.*, 960 P.2d 513 (Cal. 1998).

The statements by sponsors are given such deference in part because the sponsors are the most knowledgeable legislators about the proposed bill and in part because their representations about the purposes and effects of the proposal are relied upon by other legislators. This approach is not without its detractors, however. Sponsors or their friends might have incentives to distort the legislative history through "planned colloquies." Congressman William Moorhead, in *A Congressman Looks at the Planned Colloquy and Its Effect in the Interpretation of Statutes*, 45 A.B.A.J. 1314, 1314 (1959), observed that Members of Congress are aware that courts will look to the record of floor debates, especially statements by sponsors of legislation, and that "by the use of the 'friendly colloquy', two [legislators] may be able to legislate more effectively than all of Congress." He continued:

> Many if not most bills are controversial to some degree, and often it may be desirable when drafting a bill to couch provisions in innocuous language in order to minimize possible objections during committee consideration. Naturally, however, the proponents of a particular viewpoint would like to insure that their interpretation be the accepted one. The friendly colloquy on the floor during debate can serve well in this situation. Acquiescence by the committee [chair] in a stated intent will very likely be relied upon by the courts in the absence of objection or other reliable evidence of an opposite intent.

Note the similarity between this bit of realism about colloquies and the Armstrong-Dole exchange about committee reports (Note 1 after *Bergeron*).

Political scientists tend to discount this kind of evidence, because sponsors who distort the deals reached to achieve statutory enactments will not be trusted in future legislative deals. Moreover, judges have shown themselves increasingly sophisticated in handling such evidence. For a recent example, Justice Stevens interpreted the Detainee Treatment Act of 2005 to be not retroactive in *Hamdan v. Rumsfeld*, 548 U.S. 557 (2006) (excerpted in Chapter 8, § 3B6). He relied on the statement of Senator Levin, one of the sponsors, and discounted statements by two other sponsors (Senators Kyl and Graham) whose remarks were apparently inserted into the Congressional Record *after the fact. Id.* at 580 n.10. Characteristically, Justice Scalia objected that the majority's editing of the legislative history was not only selective, but illustrated the general unreliability of such materials. *Id.* at 665–68 (Scalia, J., dissenting). See also *Landgraf v. USI Film Prods.* (Chapter 5, § 3).

Speaking of Justice Scalia, when he was a judge on the D.C. Circuit, one of his arguments against judicial use of legislative history was that the United Kingdom's House of Lords had long excluded its use.[67] He lost that argument in the case that follows—where the House of Lords found the statutory explication by the parliamentary floor manager not only decisive evidence, but evidence that flipped everyone's reading of the statute's "plain meaning."

PEPPER V. HART
House of Lords for the United Kingdom, 1992.
[1993] 1 All E.R. 42, [1992] 3 W.L.R. 1032.

[Malvern College allowed employees to send their children to the school for 20% of the fees paid by other parents. The employees and the tax collector agreed that this kind of fringe benefit was subject to income taxation, but disagreed on how to measure the benefit. The statute in question, § 63 of the Finance Act of 1976, defined "cash equivalent of the benefit," which was the measure of taxable benefit, as follows:

> (1) The cash equivalent of any benefit chargeable to tax under section 61 above is an amount equal to the cost of the benefit, less so much (if any) of it as is made good by the employee to those providing the benefit.

> (2) Subject to the following subsections, the cost of a benefit is the amount of any expense incurred in or in connection with its provision, and (here and in those subsections) includes a proper proportion of any expense relating partly to the benefit and partly to other matters.

Because the school in question had not been able to fill all its seats, its marginal costs in providing education to these children were minimal (involving a few items of equipment and food) and amounted to less than the fees paid by the employees. Accordingly, the employees argued that they had received no actual income at all, because the fringe benefit they received, measured as the (marginal) expense incurred by their employer, was less than the fees they had paid. The tax collector disagreed, arguing that the "expense incurred" should be average cost per pupil incurred by the school. When this case made its way to the Law Lords on appeal, they initially voted 4–1 in favor of the tax collector. On rehearing, when they were urged to consider the legislative history, the Law Lords expanded the appellate panel, which then reached the opposite result. In a landmark ruling under English

---

[67] This argument was made in then-Judge Scalia's standard speech against legislative history, a copy of which was obtained and distributed by the *Virginia Law Review* and is analyzed in Daniel Farber & Philip Frickey, *Legislative Intent and Public Choice*, 74 Va. L. Rev. 423, 440–43 (1988).

law, the expanded panel abandoned the rule that British courts may not consult legislative history.]

LORD MACKAY OF CLASHFERN [LORD CHANCELLOR].

* * * The benefit which the taxpayers in this case received was the placing of their children in surplus places at the college, if as a matter of discretion the college agreed to do so. * * * They were in a similar position to the person coming along on a standby basis for an airline seat as against the passenger paying a full fare, and without the full rights of a standby passenger, in the sense that the decision whether or not to accommodate them in the college was entirely discretionary. If one regards the benefit in this light I cannot see that the cost incurred in, or in connection with, the provision of the benefit, can properly be held to include the cost incurred, in any event, in providing education to fee-paying pupils at the school who were there as a right in return for the fees paid in respect of them. * * * Although the later words of section 63(2) * * * provide that the expense incurred in, or in connection with, the provision of a benefit includes a proper proportion of any expense relating partly to the benefit and partly to other matters, I consider that the expenses incurred in provision of places for fee-paying pupils were wholly incurred in order to provide those places. * * * I conclude that looking at the matter from the point of view of expense incurred and not from the point of view of loss to the employer no expense could be regarded as having been incurred as a result of the decision of the authorities of the college to provide this particular benefit to the taxpayer.

Notwithstanding the views that have found favour with others I consider this to be a reasonable construction of the statutory provisions and I am comforted in the fact that, apart from an attempt to tax airline employees, which was taken to the Special Commissioners who decided in favour of the taxpayer, this has been the practice of the Inland Revenue in applying the relevant words where they have occurred in the Income Tax Acts for so long as they have been in force, until they initiated the present cases.

At the very least it appears to me that the manner in which I have construed the relevant provisions in their application to the facts in this appeal is a possible construction and that any ambiguity there should be resolved in favour of the taxpayer.

For these reasons I would allow these appeals. I should perhaps add that I was not a member of the committee who heard these appeals in the first hearing * * *.

But much wider issues than the construction of the Finance Act 1976 have been raised in these appeals and for the first time this House has been asked to consider a detailed argument on the extent to which reference can properly be made before a court of law in the United Kingdom to proceedings in Parliament recorded in Hansard.

For the appellant [taxpayers] Mr. Lester submits that it should now be appropriate for the courts to look at Hansard in order to ascertain the intention of the legislators as expressed in the proceedings on the Bill which has then been enacted in the statutory words requiring to be construed. This submission appears to me to suggest a way of making more effective proceedings in Parliament by allowing the court to consider what has been said in Parliament as an aid to resolving an ambiguity which may well have become apparent only as a result of the attempt to apply the enacted words to a particular case. * * *

The principal difficulty I have on this aspect of the case is that in Mr. Lester's submission reference to Parliamentary material as an aid to interpretation of a statutory provision should be allowed only with leave of the court and where the court is satisfied that such a reference is justifiable:

> (a) to confirm the meaning of a provision as conveyed by the text, its object and purpose;

> (b) to determine a meaning where the provision is ambiguous or obscure; or

> (c) to determine the meaning where the ordinary meaning is manifestly absurd or unreasonable.

I believe that practically every question of *statutory* construction that comes before the courts will involve an argument that the case falls under one or more of these three heads. It follows that the parties' legal advisors will require to study Hansard [the official collection of parliamentary debates] in practically every such case to see whether or not there is any help to be gained from it. I believe this is an objection of real substance. It is a practical objection not one of principle * * *. Such an approach appears to me to involve the possibility at least of an immense increase in the cost of litigation in which statutory construction is involved. * * * [T]he Law Commission and the Scottish Law Commission, in their joint report on *The Interpretation of Statutes* (1969) (Law Com. no. 21) (Scot. Law Com. no. 11) and the Renton Committee Report on *The Preparation of Legislation* ((1975) Cmnd. 6053), advised against a relaxation on the practical grounds to which I have referred. * * *

[We omit the separate opinions of LORD BRIDGE OF HARWICH, LORD GRIFFITHS, LORD OLIVER OF AYLMERTON, LORD KEITH OF KINKEL, and LORD ACKNER. With varying degrees of enthusiasm, all five agreed with the following opinion by LORD BROWNE-WILKINSON. Lords Bridge and Oliver had voted in the first hearing to dismiss the appeal, but the Hansard materials impelled them to change their votes. Finding the statute ambiguous, Lord Griffiths had voted with the taxpayer in the first hearing.]

LORD BROWNE-WILKINSON.

* * * [I]t is necessary first to refer to the legislation affecting the taxation of benefits in kind before 1975. Under the Finance Act 1948, section 39(1), directors and employees of bodies corporate earning more than £2,000 per annum were taxed under Schedule E on certain benefits in kind. The amount charged was the expense incurred by the body corporate "in or in connection with the provision" of the benefit in kind. By section 39(6) it was provided that references to expenses "incurred in or in connection with any matter includes a reference to a proper proportion of any expense incurred partly in or in connection with that matter." Employment by a school or charitable organisation was expressly excluded from the

charge: sections 41(5) and 44. These provisions were re-enacted in the Income and Corporation Taxes Act 1970.

Those provisions covered in-house benefits as well as external benefits. We were told that after 1948 the Revenue sought to tax at least two categories of employees in receipt of in-house benefits. Higher-paid employees of the railways enjoy free or concessionary travel on the railways. The Revenue reached an agreement that such employees should be taxed on 20% (later 25%) of the full fare. Airline employees also enjoy concessionary travel. We were told that in the 1960s the Revenue sought to tax such employees on that benefit on the basis of the average cost to the airline of providing a seat, not merely on the marginal cost. The tax commissioners rejected such claim: the Revenue did not appeal. Therefore in practice from 1948 to 1975 the Revenue did not seek to extract tax on the basis of the average cost to the employer of providing in-house benefits. * * *

The Finance Bill 1976 sought to make a general revision of the taxation of benefits in kind. The existing legislation on fringe benefits was to be repealed. Clause 52 of the Bill as introduced eventually became section 61 of the Act of 1976 and imposed a charge to tax on benefits in kind for higher-paid employees, i.e., those paid more than £5,000 per annum. Clause 54 of the Bill eventually became section 63 of the Act of 1976. As introduced, clause 54(1) provided that the cash equivalent of any benefit was to be an amount equal to "the cost of the benefit." Clause 54(2) provided that, except as provided in later subsections "the cost of a benefit is the amount of any expense incurred in or in connection with its provision." Crucially, clause 54(4) of the Bill sought to tax in-house benefits on a different basis from that applicable to external benefits. It provided that the cost of a benefit consisting of the provision of any service or facility which was also provided to the public (i.e., in-house benefits) should be the price which the public paid for such facility or service. Employees of schools were not excluded from the new charge.

Thus if the 1976 Bill had gone through as introduced, railway and airline employees would have been treated as receiving benefits in kind from concessionary travel equal to the open market cost of tickets and schoolmasters would have been taxed for concessionary education on the amount of the normal school fees.

After second reading, clause 52 of the Bill was committed to a committee of the whole House and clause 54 to Standing Committee E. On 17 May 1976, the House considered clause 52 and strong representations were made about the impact of clause 52 on airline and railway employees. At the start of the meeting of Standing Committee E on 17 June 1976 (before clause 54 was being discussed) the Financial Secretary to the Treasury, Mr. Robert Sheldon, made an announcement (Hansard, columns 893–895) in the following terms:

> "The next point I wish to make concerns services and deals with the position of employees of organisations, bodies, or firms which provide services, where the employee is in receipt of those services free or at a reduced rate. Under Clause 54(4) the taxable benefit is to be based on the arm's length price of the benefit received. At present the benefit is valued on the cost to the employer. Representations have been made concerning

airline travel and railway employees. . . . It was never intended that the benefit received by the airline employee would be the fare paid by the ordinary passenger. The benefit to him would never be as high as that, because of certain disadvantages that the employee has. Similar considerations, although of a different kind, apply to railway employees. I have had many interviews, discussions and meetings on this matter and I have decided to withdraw Clause 54(4). I thought I would mention this at the outset because so many details, which would normally be left until we reached that particular stage, will be discussed with earlier parts of the legislation. I shall give some reasons which weigh heavily in favour of the withdrawal of this provision. The first is the large difference between the cost of providing some services and the amount of benefit which under the Bill would be held to be received. There are a number of cases of this kind, and I would point out that air and rail journeys are only two of a number of service benefits which have a number of problems attached to them. But there is a large difference between the cost of the benefit to the employer and the value of that benefit as assessed. It could lead to unjustifiable situations resulting in a great number of injustices and I do not think we should continue with it. . . .

"The second reason for withdrawing Clause 54(4) is that these services would tend to be much less used. The problem would then arise for those who had advocated the continuation of this legislation that neither the employer nor the employee nor the Revenue would benefit from the lesser use of these services. This factor also weighed with me. The third reason is the difficulty of enforcement and administration which both give rise to certain problems. Finally, it was possible to withdraw this part of the legislation as the services cover not only a more difficult area, but a quite distinct area of these provisions, without having repercussions on some of the other areas. . . .

[His Lordship quoted several further references where the Financial Secretary insisted that the government's intent was not to change the tax treatment previously afforded to railway and airline employees; they would and should be allowed to receive free travel and be assessed only for the extra cost to the employer.]

Simultaneously with the announcement to the standing committee, a press release was issued announcing the withdrawal of clause 54(4). It referred to the same matters as the Financial Secretary had stated to the Committee and concluded:

"The effect of deleting this subclause will be to continue the present basis of taxation of services, namely the cost to the employer of providing the service."

The point was further debated in committee on 22 June 1976. A member is reported as saying, at column 1013, that

"Like many others, I welcome the concession that has been made to leave out the airline staff and the railway employees and all the others that are left out by the dropping of clause 54(4)." * * *

The very question which is the subject matter of the present appeal was also raised. A member said, at columns 1091–1092:

"I should be grateful for the Financial Secretary's guidance on these two points. . . . The second matter applies particularly to private sector, fee-paying schools where, as the Financial Secretary knows, there is often an arrangement for the children of staff in these schools to be taught at less than the commercial fee in other schools. I take it that because of the deletion of Clause 54(4) that is not now caught. Perhaps these examples will help to clarify the extent to which the Government amendment goes."

The Financial Secretary responded to this question as follows:

"He mentioned the children of teachers. The removal of clause 54(4) will affect the position of a child of one of the teachers at the child's school, because now the benefit will be assessed on the cost to the employer, which would be very small indeed in this case." (Column 1098.)

Thereafter, clause 54 was not the subject of further debate and passed into law as it now stands as section 63 of the Act. * * *

Under present law, there is a general rule that reference to Parliamentary material as an aid to statutory construction is not permissible ("the exclusionary rule") * * *. The exclusionary rule was probably first stated by Willes J. in *Millar v. Taylor* [1769] 4 Burr. 2303, 2332. [Lord Browne-Wilkinson provided a brief history of the exclusionary rule and possible loopholes as well as criticisms that developed over time.]

My Lords, I have come to the conclusion that, as a matter of law, there are sound reasons for making a limited modification to the existing rule (subject to strict safeguards) unless there are constitutional or practical reasons which outweigh them. In my judgment, subject to the questions of the privileges of the House of Commons, reference to Parliamentary material should be permitted as an aid to the construction of legislation which is ambiguous or obscure or the literal meaning of which leads to an absurdity. Even in such cases references in court to Parliamentary material should only be permitted where such material clearly discloses the mischief aimed at or the legislative intention lying behind the ambiguous or obscure words. In the case of statements made in Parliament, as at present advised I cannot foresee that any statement other than the statement of the minister or other promoter of the Bill is likely to meet these criteria.

I accept Mr. Lester's submissions [for the taxpayers], but my main reason for reaching this conclusion is based on principle. Statute law consists of the words that Parliament has enacted. It is for the courts to construe those words and it is the court's duty in so doing to give effect to the intention of Parliament in using those words. It is an inescapable fact that, despite all the care taken in passing legislation, some statutory provisions when applied to the circumstances under consideration in any specific case are found to be ambiguous. One of the reasons for such ambiguity is that the members of the legislature in enacting the statutory provision may have been told what result those words are intended to achieve. Faced with a given set of words which are capable of conveying that meaning it is not surprising if the words are accepted as having that meaning. Parliament never intends to enact an ambiguity. Contrast with that the position of the courts. The courts are faced simply with a set of words which are in fact capable of bearing two meanings. The courts are ignorant of the underlying Parliamentary purpose. Unless something in other parts of the legislation discloses such purpose, the courts are forced to adopt one of the two possible meanings using highly technical rules of construction. In many, I suspect most, cases references to Parliamentary materials will not throw any light on the matter. But in a few cases it may emerge that the very question was considered by Parliament in passing the legislation. Why in such a case should the courts blind themselves to a clear indication of what Parliament intended in using those words? The court cannot attach a meaning to words which they cannot bear, but if the words are capable of bearing more than one meaning why should not Parliament's true intention be enforced rather than thwarted?

A number of other factors support this view. As I have said, the courts can now look at white papers and official reports for the purpose of finding the "mischief" sought to be corrected, although not at draft clauses or proposals for the remedying of such mischief. A ministerial statement made in Parliament is an equally authoritative source of such information: why should the courts be cut off from this source of information as to the mischief aimed at? In any event, the distinction between looking at reports to identify the mischief aimed at but not to find the intention of Parliament in enacting the legislation is highly artificial. Take the normal Law Commission Report which analyses the problem and then annexes a draft Bill to remedy it. It is now permissible to look at the report to find the mischief and at the draft Bill to see that a provision in the draft was *not* included in the legislation enacted. There can be no logical distinction between that case and looking at the draft Bill to see that the statute as enacted reproduced, often in the same words, the provision in the Law Commission's draft. Given the purposive approach to construction now adopted by the courts in order to give effect to the true intentions of the legislature, the fine distinctions between looking for the mischief and looking for the intention in using words to provide the remedy are technical and inappropriate. Clear and unambiguous statements made by ministers in Parliament are as much the background to the enactment of legislation as white papers and Parliamentary reports.

The decision in *Pickstone v. Freemans Plc.* [1989] A.C. 66 which authorises the court to look at ministerial statements made in introducing regulations which could not be amended by Parliament is logically indistinguishable from such statements made in introducing a statutory provision which, though capable of amendment, was not in fact amended. * * *

Text books often include reference to explanations of legislation given by a minister in Parliament, as a result of which lawyers advise their clients taking account of such statements and judges when construing the legislation come to know of them. In addition, a number of distinguished judges have admitted to breaching the exclusionary rule and looking at Hansard in order to seek the intention of Parliament. When this happens, the parties do not know and have no opportunity to address the judge on the matter. A vivid example of this occurred in the *Hadmor* case [1983] 1 A.C. 191 where Lord Denning in the Court of Appeal relied on his own researches into Hansard in reaching his conclusions: in the House of Lords, counsel protested that there were other passages to which he would have wished to draw the court's attention had he known that Lord Denning was looking at Hansard: see the *Hadmor* case at 233. It cannot be right for such information to be available, by a sidewind, for the court but the parties be prevented from presenting their arguments on such material. * * *

It is said that Parliamentary materials are not readily available to, and understandable by, the citizen and his lawyers who should be entitled to rely on the words of Parliament alone to discover his position. It is undoubtedly true that Hansard and particularly records of Committee debates are not widely held by libraries outside London and that the lack of satisfactory indexing of Committee stages makes it difficult to trace the passage of a clause after it is redrafted or renumbered. But such practical difficulties can easily be overstated. It is possible to obtain Parliamentary materials and it is possible to trace the history. The problem is one of expense and effort in doing so, not the availability of the material. In considering the right of the individual to know the law by simply looking at legislation, it is a fallacy to start from the position that all legislation is available in a readily understandable form in any event: the very large number of statutory instruments made every year are not available in an indexed form for well over a year after they have been passed. Yet, the practitioner manages to deal with the problem albeit at considerable expense. Moreover, experience in New Zealand and Australia (where the strict rule has been relaxed for some years) has not shown that the non-availability of materials has raised these practical problems.

Next, it is said that lawyers and judges are not familiar with Parliamentary procedures and will therefore have difficulty in giving proper weight to the Parliamentary materials. Although, of course, lawyers do not have the same experience of these matters as members of the legislature, they are not wholly ignorant of them. If, as I think, significance should only be attached to the clear statements made by a minister or other promoter of the Bill, the difficulty of knowing what weight to attach to such statements is not overwhelming. In the present case, there were numerous statements of view by members in the course of the debate which plainly do not throw any light on the true construction of section 63. What is persuasive in this case is a consistent series of answers given by the minister, after opportunities for taking advice from his officials, all of which point the same way and which were not withdrawn or varied prior to the enactment of the Bill.

Then it is said that court time will be taken up by considering a mass of Parliamentary material and long arguments about its significance, thereby increasing the expense of litigation. In my judgment, though the introduction of further admissible material will inevitably involve some increase in the use of time, this will not be significant as long as courts insist that Parliamentary material should only be introduced in the limited cases I have mentioned and where such material contains a clear indication from the minister of the mischief aimed at, or the nature of the cure intended, by the legislation. Attempts to introduce material which does not satisfy those tests should be met by orders for costs made against those who have improperly introduced the material. Experience in the United States of America, where legislative history has for many years been much more generally admissible than I am now suggesting, shows how important it is to maintain strict control over the use of such material. That position is to be contrasted with what has happened in New Zealand and Australia (which have relaxed the rule to approximately the extent that I favour): there is no evidence of any complaints of this nature coming from those countries.

There is one further practical objection which, in my view, has real substance. If the rule is relaxed legal advisers faced with an ambiguous statutory provision may feel that they have to research the materials to see whether they yield the crock of gold, i.e., a clear indication of Parliament's intentions. In very many cases the crock of gold will not be discovered and the expenditure on the research wasted. This is a real objection to changing the rule. However, again it is easy to overestimate the cost of such research: if a reading of Hansard shows that there is nothing of significance said by the minister in relation to the clause in question, further research will become pointless.

In sum, I do not think that the practical difficulties arising from a limited relaxation of the rule are sufficient to outweigh the basic need for the courts to give effect to the words enacted by Parliament in the sense that they were intended by Parliament to bear. Courts are frequently criticised for their failure to do that. This failure is due not to cussedness but to ignorance of what Parliament intended by the obscure words of the legislation. The courts should not deny themselves the light which Parliamentary materials may shed on the meaning of the words Parliament has used and thereby risk subjecting the individual to a law which Parliament never intended to enact.

[The last section of his Lordship's opinion discussed the "constitutional" issue whether adverting to Hansard is a "questioning" of the freedom of parliamentary speech and debate that is prohibited by article 9 of the Bill of Rights of 1688. His Lordship interpreted article 9 much like the U.S. Constitution's Speech and Debate Clause (see Chapter 3, § 2) and found it inapplicable.]

The Attorney General raised a further constitutional point, namely, that for the court to use Parliamentary material in construing legislation would be to confuse the respective roles of Parliament as the maker of law and the courts as the interpreter. I am not impressed by this argument. The law, as I have said, is to be found in the words in which Parliament has enacted. It is for the courts to interpret those words so as to give effect to that purpose. The question is whether, in addition to other aids to the construction of statutory words, the courts should have regard to a further source. Recourse is already had to white papers and official reports not because they determine the meaning of the statutory words but because they assist the court to make its own determination. I can see no constitutional impropriety in this. * * *

I therefore reach the conclusion, subject to any question of Parliamentary privilege, that the exclusionary rule should be relaxed so as to permit reference to Parliamentary materials where:

> (a) legislation is ambiguous or obscure, or leads to an absurdity;
>
> (b) the material relied on consists of one or more statements by a minister or other promoter of the Bill together if necessary with such other Parliamentary material as is necessary to understand such statements and their effect;
>
> (c) the statements relied on are clear.

[In the present case, the statute was ambiguous and the Hansard materials clearly resolved the ambiguity in favor of the taxpayers.]

The question then arises whether it is right to attribute to Parliament as a whole the same intention as that repeatedly voiced by the Financial Secretary. In my judgment it is. It is clear from reading Hansard that the committee was repeatedly asking for guidance as to the effect of the legislation once subclause (4) of clause 54 was abandoned. That Parliament relied on the ministerial statements is shown by the fact that the matter was never raised again after the discussions in committee, that amendments were consequentially withdrawn and that no relevant amendment was made which could affect the correctness of the minister's statement. * * *

NOTES ON PEPPER AND THE DEMISE OF THE EXCLUSIONARY RULE

1. *The Abandonment of the Exclusionary Rule in English-Speaking Countries.* In the United Kingdom, *Pepper v. Hart* created quite a stir, and unleashed a fair amount of interest in legislative history by lower courts and the House of Lords. See James Brudney, *Below the Surface: Comparative Legislative History Usage by the House of Lords and the Supreme Court*, 85 Wash. U.L. Rev. 1 (2007) (demonstrating that much of the Hansard reliance is to minister (floor manager) explanations and *not* to committee reports, which are not routinely generated in Parliament). On the other hand, Brudney found that during the post-*Pepper* period, the Lords have greatly increased their references to government white papers and commission reports, background documents with some similarity to our committee reports. In short, the Lords are explicitly considering a lot more background materials than they did twenty years ago.

Although the Law Lords remain divided over the wisdom of *Pepper*, a majority of them are committed to this new course of action, within limits that have yet to be determined once and for all.[68] In *Regina (Jackson) v. Attorney General*, [2005] All Eng. Law Rep. 1253, for example, the Lords unanimously upheld the famous Hunting Act, which deployed a 1911 statute to override House of Lords opposition to a popular

---

[68] For example, Lord Millett, *Construing Statutes*, 20 Stat. L. Rev. 107 (1999), maintained that *Pepper* was a mistake and that the Lords should return to their previous practice of relying exclusively on statutory text. Lord Hoffman praised *Pepper* for opening up probative evidence of legislative intent (and for discouraging government ministers from making promises to Parliament that they might later renounce) but was skeptical that the costs of extra research were worth these benefits. Hon. Lord Hoffman, *The Intolerable Wrestle With Words and Meanings*, 114 S. Afr. L. J. 656, 669 (1997); see also *Robinson v. Sec'y of State for Northern Ireland*, [2002] N. Ir. L. Rep. 390, 405 (Lord Hoffman, repeating his lament that *Pepper* generated large research costs, with scant benefit).

measure. Lord Bingham's lead opinion rejected the relevance of Hansard as authoritative evidence of parliamentary "intent" but relied on the debates (including eight rejected proposals) to confirm the meaning of words Parliament used in the 1911 statute. Lord Nicholls's speech relied even more extensively on Hansard, as confirmation of what he and the other Lords considered the apparent meaning of the text. Lord Steyn objected to any use of Hansard in these circumstances.

The House of Lords' decision has had echoes throughout the Commonwealth countries. The leading Canadian treatise states: "Since the 1980s the [exclusionary] rule has been eroding. Some courts have ignored it while others have carved out significant exceptions and qualifications." *Sullivan* 595. See also David Duff, *Interpreting the Income Tax Act*, 47 Can. Tax. J. 471 & 741 (1999) (two-part article on use of legislative history in tax cases). The exclusionary rule had previously been abandoned in the United States, see *Holy Trinity* (Chapter 7, § 1); Australia, see Commonwealth Acts Interpretation Act § 15ab, discussed in Gifford, *supra*, at 126–29; and other Commonwealth countries. Many civil-law countries still follow such a rule or practice, however.

2.   *When Should Legislative Materials Be Admissible? The Potato Chip Problem.* The key opinion is that of Lord Browne-Wilkinson, who admits legislative materials, but only in limited circumstances. But how should we characterize the holding of the case? This is more difficult than appears on first glance.

(a)   *Sponsor Statements May Be Consulted When the Statute Is Ambiguous.* This appears to be the holding as articulated by Lord Browne-Wilkinson, and the U.S. Supreme Court sometimes says it follows a like rule. See, e.g., *Director, OWCP v. Greenwich Collieries*, 512 U.S. 267 (1994). But does this precept explain the decision in this case? The first committee of Law Lords found the statute unambiguous against the taxpayer; on the original panel, only Lord Griffith found ambiguity. Lord Chancellor Mackay found ambiguity on rehearing and voted for the taxpayer on that ground, but only Lord Griffith agreed with him. Other Lords, including Browne-Wilkinson, *found ambiguity only after they consulted the Hansard materials.*

(b)   *Hansard Materials May Be Consulted to Confirm Statutory Plain Meaning.* The narrowest interpretation of *Pepper*, embraced by Lord Steyn and others, is that Hansard materials can only be introduced for textualist reasons, namely, to suggest or confirm standard usage of statutory terms and the plain meaning they have to reasonable speakers of the English language.

(c)   *Hansard May Be Invoked to Clear Up Any Statutory Matters.* In the aftermath of *Pepper*, some Law Lords used the decision as a Magna Carta for browsing parliamentary debates for what they were worth, essentially ignoring Lord Browne-Wilkinson's suggested limits. See David Miers, *Taxing Perks and Interpreting Statutes: Pepper v. Hart*, 56 Mod. L. Rev. 695, 705–06 (1993). Few Lords in the new millennium openly endorse this position, and there are procedural hurdles in place,[69] but there is some indication that some lower court judges are running wild with legislative materials. Should this have been expected?

---

[69]   The Lords directed that financial sanctions would be visited upon a party who relied on Hansard in a case that did not meet the three requirements of Lord Browne-Wilkinson's opinion. Also, the Lords issued a Practice Directive in 1994 (reaffirmed in 1999 and 2002) which required parties intending to invoke Hansard to give prior notice, including copies of the pages in Hansard and the argument to be made from it. Brudney, *Below the Surface.*

Aside from the precise limits suggested in this case, consider a *potato chip theory*, suggested by the U.S. history after *Holy Trinity*: once a court starts looking at the "best" legislative history, like committee reports and sponsor statements, other kinds of history will get smuggled in, on the ground that they provide "context" for understanding the committee reports (which of course provide "context" for understanding the text). Before long, everything becomes relevant and might be considered "for what it is worth" (the trend in modern evidence law, by the way). Just as you can never eat just one potato chip, you can never admit just one bit of legislative history. It might take decades for the potato chip process to develop, but the theory is that Hansard reliance will grow by fits and starts until there is some kind of crisis that pushes in the other direction.

3. *Relevance for the U.S. Debate?* Should *Pepper* suggest to the new textualists that they should adopt a more moderate skepticism about legislative materials?[70] If you were Justice Scalia, how would you have voted in *Pepper*? (Hint: Consider the *evolution* of the treatment of in-house benefits, from 1948 to 1993, nicely laid out in Lord Browne-Wilkinson's opinion. You can be a textualist and consider the formal evolution of the statutory scheme, as the U.S. Supreme Court did in *Leo Sheep*. What argument might a textualist draw from that?)

Brudney, *Below the Surface*, argues that the U.S. Supreme Court should conclude from the Mother Country's post-*Pepper* practice that the most fruitful debates focus not on the tired admissibility debate, but rather on the circumstances under which legislative history would be useful. "[S]hould legislative history be regarded as presumptively more valuable to help resolve textual ambiguities that stem from lack of foresight rather than lack of political consensus? Is legislative history accompanying omnibus bills generally less suitable for judicial use because congressional deals on such a grand scale are simply indecipherable? Should legislative history in certain subject areas be presumed to have less weight where the law is administered primarily by a federal agency rather than private parties, or where the statutory text tends to be detailed and technical rather than open-ended and of more general public interest?"

NOTE ON STATE COURT RELIANCE ON SPONSOR'S STATEMENTS

Like the U.K. House of Lords (and now the Supreme Court of the United Kingdom), and unlike the U.S. Supreme Court, state supreme courts in this country rely perhaps more heavily on the statements of legislative sponsors than on committee or bill reports as the sources for illumination about legislative expectations. A large majority of states make available to the public transcripts of legislative floor debates and of committee hearings. See Brian Barnes, "The Transformation of State Statutory Interpretation," at 10–11 (Yale Law School Seminar Paper, May 4, 2010) (33 states offer transcripts or tapes of current legislative floor debates, with 17 offering them on-line as of 2010); *id.* at 12–13 (37 states offer transcripts or tapes of current committee hearings, with 16 offering them on-line as of 2010). Much of the floor debate consists of statements by the sponsor or floor manager presenting the case for the proposed

---

[70] See, e.g., John Manning, *Textualism as a Nondelegation Doctrine*, 97 Colum. L. Rev. 673 (1997), which presents a constitutional justification for refusing to consider committee reports "authoritative" (in the way the statute is) but admitting them as evidence of what the statutory words might mean. On *Pepper* and American practice, see Michael Healy, *Legislative Intent and Statutory Interpretation in England and the United States: An Assessment of the Impact of* Pepper v. Hart, 35 Stan. J. Int'l L. 231 (1999).

legislation, responding to objections made by opponents, and answering questions posed by colleagues.

Committee chairs (who are usually later the floor managers) play a large role in committee hearings, making speeches, questioning witnesses, and explaining proposed legislation. Because the sponsor/floor manager is usually the most knowledgeable legislator on topics relating to the proposed legislation and usually represents the coalition pushing for the legislation, his or her statements are much more probative than those of other legislators. Recall, for example, the Oregon Court of Appeals decision in *PGE* (Chapter 6, § 3C), where the dissenting judges relied on the explanation by the committee chair.

For examples of recent state supreme court decisions relying on statements by legislative sponsors or floor managers, see *State v. Batts*, 195 P.3d 144, 151–52 (**Alaska** 2008) (sponsor's explanation critical evidence of statutory meaning); *Carter v. Cal. Dep't of Veterans Affairs*, 135 P.3d 637, 646–47 (**California** 2006) (treating sponsor's memo as authoritative but finding that it does not answer the issue before the court); *CLPF-Parkridge One, L.P. v. Harwell Invs., Inc.*, 105 P.3d 658, 664–65 (**Colorado** 2005) (relying entirely on legislative history to interpret law); *People v. Collins*, 824 N.E.2d 262, 267 (**Illinois** 2005); *State v. Allen*, 708 N.W.2d 361, 366–67 (**Iowa** 2006); *Rural Water Dist. #2 v. City of Louisburg*, 207 P.3d 1055 (**Kansas** 2009) (post-enactment letter from sponsor invoked to support plain meaning); *Ky. Pub. Serv. Comm'n v. Commonwealth ex rel. Stumbo*, 2008 WL 4822263 (**Kentucky** Ct. App. 2008); *Stockman Bank of Mont. v. Mon-Kota, Inc.*, 180 P.3d 1125 (**Montana** 2008); *Chanos v. Nevada Tax Comm'n*, 181 P.3d 675, 680 & n.17 (**Nevada** 2008); *State v. Mayer*, 186 P.3d 293, 297–98 (**Oregon** App. 2008) (relying on evidence from drafter as well as sponsor); *Stewart Title Guar. Co. v. State Tax Assessor*, 963 A.2d 169, 178–79 (**Maine** 2009) (ambiguity resolved by reference to statutory history as explained by sponsor); *Kramer v. Liberty Prop. Trust*, 968 A.2d 120 (**Maryland** 2009) (sponsor's statement confirms plain meaning); *Milton S. Hershey Med. Ctr. of Pa. State Univ. v. Commonwealth Med. Professional Liab. Catastrophe Loss Fund*, 821 A.2d 1205, 1211 (**Pennsylvania** 2003); *Lawrence Cnty. Educ. Ass'n v. Lawrence Cnty. Bd. of Educ.*, 244 S.W.3d 302, 312 (**Tennessee** 2007); *Dep't of Corr. v. Human Rights Comm'n*, 917 A.2d 451, 453 (**Vermont** 2007).

Like the U.S. Supreme Court, state supreme courts will not credit stray statements by legislators who are probably not speaking for the enacting coalition. See, e.g., *Wright v. Home Depot U.S.A., Inc.*, 142 P.3d 265, 275 n.8 (**Hawaii** 2006). Likewise, state supreme courts (like federal courts) will not credit post-hoc affidavits by the sponsors or floor managers of enacted bills, because the post-hoc nature of such evidence deprives it of reliability. Efforts to invoke after-the-fact legislator affidavits often occur (and are usually rebuffed) in states where there is not (at the time) much publicly available legislative material. See, e.g., *Tomei v. Sharp*, 902 A.2d 757, 769 n.41 (**Delaware** Super. 2006); *Utility Ctr., Inc. v. City of Fort Wayne*, 868 N.E.2d 453, 459–60 (**Indiana** 2007); *Direct TV, Inc. v. Levin*, 907 N.E.2d 1242, 1253 (**Ohio** App. 2009); *Lynch v. Norwood Autoplex*, 2006 WL 2243018, at *5 (**Rhode Island** Super. Ct. 2006); *Catawba Indian Tribe of S.C. v. State*, 642 S.E.2d 751, 754 n.5 (**South Carolina** 2007); *Phillips v. Larry's Drive-In Pharmacy, Inc.*, 647 S.E.2d 920, 924–26 (**West Virginia** 2007).

NOTES ON VIEWS OF NONLEGISLATOR DRAFTERS

1. *Statements of Nonlegislative Drafters*. In *Kosak v. United States*, 465 U.S. 848 (1984), the Court construed the Federal Tort Claims Act (FTCA) to reject a serviceman's claim for liability after his personal art objects, being shipped from Guam to Philadelphia, were damaged while detained in the custody of the Customs Service. Writing for the majority, Justice Marshall relied in part on an explanation of the contested FTCA text (§ 2680(c), the same exemption at issue in *Ali v. Federal Bureau of Prisons*, see Section 1B) that had been offered by Judge Alexander Holtzoff, a major figure in developing the FTCA and the likely author of the precise language in dispute. The Holtzoff Report on the proposed FTCA, prepared while Judge Holtzoff was a Special Assistant to the Attorney General, was submitted to the Justice Department and the GAO in 1931, fifteen years before Congress enacted the law. Justice Marshall agreed with the dissent that, "because the report was never introduced into the public record, the ideas expressed therein should not be given great weight in determining the intent of the legislature. But, in the absence of any direct evidence regarding how members of Congress understood the provision that became § 2680(c), it seems to us senseless to ignore entirely the views of its draftsman." *Id*. at 857, n.13.

The majority opinion in *Kosak* realistically recognized that much legislation is drafted by nonlegislators—mainly executive officials and interest groups. But why should the views of a nonlegislator count—especially if the Court deems its inquiry as a search for the "intent" of *Congress*? Moreover, Holtzoff's memorandum was not "public." Distinguish between the testimony at congressional hearings by Holtzoff, in which Members of Congress could disagree with him (either then or during subsequent floor debate),[71] and his Department of Justice memorandum, which was written before the bill was acted upon even by a committee and which may have represented only his (and not even the Department's) point of view. Why should the latter be entitled to any consideration at all? Are there other ways of thinking about statutory interpretation which make Judge Holtzoff's statement relevant? (Hint: maybe, like a good commentary in a treatise or a law review article, it makes the most sense of the legislation.) See generally Alison Giles, Note, *The Value of Nonlegislators' Contributions to Legislative History*, 79 Geo. L.J. 359 (1991).

Notwithstanding these objections, the Supreme Court or individual Justices have occasionally relied on statements by public, nonlegislative officials who draft or promote statutes. See, e.g., *Circuit City Stores, Inc. v. Adams*, 532 U.S. 105, 128–29 (2001) (Stevens, J., dissenting) (dissenters relying on defense of statute by Secretary of Commerce; majority does not address this argument because of plain meaning rule); *Negonsott v. Samuels*, 507 U.S. 99, 106–09 (1993); *Gollust v. Mendell*, 501 U.S. 115, 125 & n.7 (1991); *Howe v. Smith*, 452 U.S. 473, 485 (1981); *Monroe v. Standard Oil Co.*, 452 U.S. 549, 558–59 (1981). Note, however, that (as in *Kosak*) the Court will not rely on these statements as the most probative—and certainly not the *only*—evidence of statutory meaning. There are very few state cases; almost all of them either reject or denigrate such evidence. E.g., *Hayes v. Continental Ins. Co.*, 872 P.2d 668 (Ariz. 1994).

2. *Statements of Private Drafters*. At least Holtzoff was a public servant. Should the Court consider authoritative the statements of interest groups which draft and

---

[71] Ironically, when Holtzoff's public testimony was relevant to an issue of interpretation, the Court ignored it. Compare *Sheridan v. United States*, 487 U.S. 392 (1988) (opinion of the Court), with *id*. at 410 (O'Connor, J., dissenting).

press for legislation? In some instances the Court or some Justices have considered testimony about legislation by private groups or individuals who drafted or commented on the legislation. See, e.g., *Circuit City Stores*, 532 U.S. at 127 (Stevens, J., dissenting) (relying on explanation by ABA committee that originated the statute); *Gustafson v. Alloyd Co.*, 513 U.S. 561 (1995) (relying on statement by Professor Landis, submitted as part of legislative deliberations, as support for Court's text-based interpretation); *Jefferson Cnty. Pharm. Assoc. v. Abbott Labs*, 460 U.S. 150, 159–62 (1983) (relying upon explanation of lobbyist who was principal drafter of the statute in question); *NLRB v. Robbins Tire & Rubber Co.*, 437 U.S. 214, 230–32 (1978) (relying on explanation of ABA Administrative Law Division, which had originally proposed the statutory amendment in question during Senate hearings). See also *Grp. Life & Health Inc. Co. v. Royal Drug Co.*, 440 U.S. 205 (1979); *Southland Corp. v. Keating*, 465 U.S. 1, 26–29 (1984) (O'Connor, J., dissenting).

4. Legislative Deliberation: Hearings, Floor Debate, Rejected Proposals, and Dogs That Didn't Bark

Compared to statements in committee reports, statements made during committee hearings and floor debates have traditionally received less weight in evaluating legislative intent. If the statement was made by a sponsor or informed supporter of the bill, courts might credit it as a reliable indication of legislative intent—as did the Supreme Court majority and dissenting opinions in *Weber* or as the House of Lords did in *Pepper v. Hart*. The conventional wisdom is that what is said in hearings and floor debates is usually of little value, except for confirmatory purposes. Reed Dickerson, *Statutory Interpretation: Dipping into Legislative History*, 11 Hofstra L. Rev. 1125, 1131–32 (1983).

Reflecting on the Burger Court's practice, Judge Patricia Wald, *Legislative History in the 1981 Term*, *supra*, 68 Iowa L. Rev. at 202, opined that "[t]he hornbook rule that hearings are relevant only as background to show the purpose of the statute no longer holds. In many cases, the best explanation of what the legislation is about comes from the executive department or outside witnesses at the hearings." Indeed, since proposed legislation is frequently drafted by the executive department or by private interest groups, their statements and explanations at hearings might be the only truly informed explanation of the structure and operation of the statute. E.g., *Gustafson v. Alloyd Co.*, 513 U.S. 561 (1995) (testimony of academic expert commenting on interest group arguments made during congressional deliberations); *Lowe v. SEC*, 472 U.S. 181, 195–99 (1985) (testimony of industry witnesses at hearings); *Trbovich v. United Mine Workers of America*, 404 U.S. 528 (1972) (Senate hearing testimony by Senator John Kennedy, the sponsor, and Professor Archibald Cox, primary drafter of the proposed legislation). Now that many states record committee hearings, and still others provide staff summaries of statements made in them, state courts are coming to rely on statements made in those hearings.[72]

---

[72] For state cases relying on statements in hearings, see, e.g., *Pac. Bell v. Cal. State and Consumer Servs. Agency*, 275 Cal. Rptr. 62, 67–68 (Cal. App. 1990) (testimony in committee hearings); *People v. Luciano*, 662 P.2d 480, 482 n.4 (Colo. 1983) (recordings of Senate and House committee hearings); *In re Sheldon G.*, 583 A.2d 112, 116 & n.6 (Conn. 1990) (testimony in committee hearings); *Jackson v. Kansas City*, 235 Kan. 278 (1984) (statements in committee hearings); *First Nat'l Bank of Deerwood v. Gregg*, 556 N.W.2d 214 (Minn.

Potentially relevant for similar reasons are presidential statements initiating or issued during congressional deliberations, especially when the President has been a prime mover behind a piece of legislation, as he was with the Civil Rights Act of 1964 and the Voting Rights Act of 1965. Thus, presidential transmittal letters or speeches advocating legislation have sometimes been considered useful legislative history, e.g., *NLRB v. Local 103, Int'l Ass'n of Bridge Workers*, 434 U.S. 335, 347 n.9 (1978); *Connell Constr. Co. v. Plumbers & Steamfitters Local 100*, 421 U.S. 616, 629 n.8 (1975); *W. Union Tel. Co. v. Lenroot*, 323 U.S. 490, 492 (1945). See generally Kathryn Dessayer, Note, *The First Word: The President's Place in "Legislative History,"* 89 Mich. L. Rev. 399 (1990).

In a like spirit, Justices sometimes rely on floor debates, including exchanges between supporters and opponents. Although statements by legislators about bills they oppose are not reliable, see *NLRB v. Fruit & Vegetable Packers*, 377 U.S. 58, 66 (1964), exchanges with supporters may sharpen the precise deals that have been reached. An interesting illustration is *BankAmerica v. United States*, 462 U.S. 122 (1983), where the Court interpreted the Clayton Act's general bar to interlocking corporate directorates to be inapplicable to bank-nonbank interlocks.[73] Chief Justice Burger's opinion for the Court relied on the plain meaning of the statutory provision, the structure of the statute, the longstanding interpretation by the relevant regulatory agencies and subcommittees, and the legislative history. The theme of the legislative history was that many progressives wanted to prohibit bank-nonbank interlocks, and at various points in the process criticized the general provision in the proposed legislation for not barring them.

The clinching evidence in *BankAmerica* was a colloquy among two supporters and an opponent at the close of the House debate. The opponent, Representative Mann, raised a point of order, that the House conferees had improperly agreed to a conference bill that cut back both Senate and House bills, which he construed as having regulated *all* bank interlocks. The supporters, Representatives Sherley and Webb, admonished Mann and asserted that the general catch-all bar never applied to banks, and the final version of the bill only regulated bank-bank interlocks in a special provision. The Chief Justice believed that these representations by supporters of the legislation were persuasive—and their cogency was confirmed when the Speaker overruled Mann's point of order, apparently on the ground that the House conferees had not betrayed the earlier deal.

BankAmerica is perhaps an unusual case, because the key colloquy occurred at the very end of the legislative debate and spoke directly, and dramatically, to the

---

1996) (tape-recorded hearings); *Wiseman v. Keller*, 358 N.W.2d 768 (Neb. 1984) (judiciary committee hearing); *Linlee Enters., Inc. v. State*, 445 A.2d 1130, 1131 (N.H. 1982) (House committee hearing and subcommittee report); *Dickinson v. Fund for Support of Free Pub. Schs.*, 469 A.2d 1 (N.J. 1983) (statements made in subcommittee and committee hearings); *Golden v. Koch*, 415 N.Y.S.2d 330 (Sup. Ct. 1979) (committee hearings and report); *Sager v. McClenden*, 672 P.2d 697 (Or. 1983) (minutes of committee hearings). A number of states have ruled that legislator statements during committee hearings cannot be the basis for the court's finding of legislative intent. See *State v. Miranda*, 715 A.2d 680 (Conn. 1998).

[73] The fourth paragraph of the Clayton Act § 8, 15 U.S.C. § 19, reads: "No person at the same time shall be a director in *any two or more corporations*, any one of which has capital, surplus, and undivided profits aggregating more than $1,000,000, engaged in whole or in part in commerce, *other than banks, banking associations, trust companies, and common carriers* subject to the Act to regulate commerce * * *." The second paragraph prohibits bank-bank interlocks.

issue before the Court. In *Weber*, by way of contrast, Justice Brennan's majority opinion responded that all of Justice Rehnquist's parade of quotes critical of racial quotas were uttered before Title VII achieved its final form, laden with compromises, including § 703(j) (which Brennan found critical to his judgment that Congress was tolerant of *voluntary* affirmative action). "To permit what we regard as clear statutory language to be materially altered by such colloquies, which often take place before the bill has achieved its final form, would open the door to the inadvertent, or perhaps even planned, undermining of the language actually voted on by Congress * * *." *Regan v. Wald*, 468 U.S. 222, 237–42 (1984).

Because legislative history has become much more controversial, among federal judges at least, one might expect that references to congressional hearings and floor debates would dry up at the Supreme Court level. This has *not* been the case, as the following opinions and notes will reflect. The first two cases present a recurring issue: what to make of the *rejection* of legislative proposals in committee, on the floor of either chamber, in conference committee, and so forth. The third case brings together a host of legislative sources and the famous "dog that doesn't bark" canon.

FDA v. BROWN & WILLIAMSON TOBACCO CORP.

Supreme Court of the United States, 2000.
529 U.S. 120, 120 S.Ct. 1291, 146 L.Ed.2d 121.

[Excerpted in Chapter 6, § 3B3]

NOTE ON REJECTED PROPOSALS

Justice O'Connor's opinion in the *FDA Tobacco* Case is the most lavish deployment in the Court's history of what might be called the *rejected proposal rule*, that interpreters should be reluctant to read statutes broadly when a committee, a chamber, or a conference committee rejected language explicitly encoding that broad policy. *United States v. Riverside Bayview Homes, Inc.*, 474 U.S. 121, 137 (1985) reflects this presumption as well. See also, e.g., *Hamdan v. Rumsfeld*, 548 U.S. 557 (2006); *United States v. Yermian*, 468 U.S. 63 (1984) (relying on congressional adoption of broadening language of false swearing statute, 18 U.S.C. § 1001, after earlier bill was vetoed by President). Yet similar rejected proposal arguments were not persuasive to Court majorities in *Rapanos v. United States*, 547 U.S. 715 (2006) and *Solid Waste Agency of Northern Cook County v. U.S. Army Corps of Engineers*, 531 U.S. 159 (2001). How would you distinguish those cases? Or should they be signals that the Supreme Court should no longer follow a rejected proposal rule?

Commentators have been wary, because the range of reasons for rejecting a proposed amendment varies so widely. "It may be rejected by some legislators because they disagree with its substance (but not necessarily the same substance). On the other hand, those who agree with the substance may nevertheless vote against it as a spurious or unnecessary attempt to clarify. Simple non-action, being consistent with many explanations in circumstances not calling for consensus, has no probative value for any purpose." Dickerson, *supra*, at 1133; accord *Solid Waste* (majority opinion's response to the dissenters); *Pattern Makers' League of N. Am. v. NLRB*, 473 U.S. 95 (1985); William Eskridge Jr., *Interpreting Legislative Inaction*, 87 Mich. L. Rev. 67

(1988) (collecting cases using and declining to use the rejected proposal rule); Wald, *supra*, at 202.

A broader point links Justice O'Connor's opinion for the Court in *FDA Tobacco* and Justice Stevens's dissenting opinions in *Solid Waste* and *Rapanos*. Both Justices find in the legislative deliberations evidence that Congress has both accepted and relied upon well-grounded agency policy stances as regards their regulatory mandate. In *FDA Tobacco*, there seems to have been a political consensus that the FDA did not have jurisdiction over tobacco products, and in the Wetlands Cases there seems to have been a similar consensus that the Corps has broad jurisdiction to protect hydrological ecosystems. Why did one consensus fail to move the Court while the other did move the Court? Consider not only the political preferences of the Justices, but also the Court's traditional role as braking or slowing down political actors.

MONTANA WILDERNESS ASSOCIATION V. UNITED STATES FOREST SERVICE

United States Court of Appeals for the Ninth Circuit, May 14, 1981.
Docket No. 80–3374.

NORRIS, CIRCUIT JUDGE:

This appeal raises fundamental questions concerning the conflict between the ability of the executive branch of the federal government to manage public lands and the access rights of persons whose property is surrounded by those lands. Environmentalists and a neighboring property owner seek to block construction by Burlington Northern of roads over parts of the Gallatin National Forest. They appeal from a partial summary judgment in the district court granting Burlington Northern a right of access to its totally enclosed timber lands. The district court held that Burlington Northern has an easement by necessity or, alternatively, an implied easement under the Northern Pacific Land Grant of 1864. The defendants argue that the Alaska National Interest Lands Act of 1980, passed subsequent to the district court's decision, also grants Burlington Northern assured access to its land. The appellants contend that the doctrine of easement by necessity does not apply to the sovereign, that there was no implied easement conveyed by the 1864 land grant, and that the access provisions of the Alaska Lands Act do not apply to land outside the state of Alaska. We conclude that the appellants are correct on all three issues. We therefore reverse the partial summary judgment and remand the case for further proceedings.

Defendant-appellee Burlington Northern, Inc. owns timber land located within the Gallatin National Forest southwest of Bozeman, Montana. This land was originally acquired by its predecessor, the Northern Pacific Railroad, under the Northern Pacific Land Grant Act of 1864, 13 Stat. 365. The Act granted odd-numbered square sections of land to the railroad, which, with the even-numbered sections retained by the United States, formed a checkerboard pattern.

To harvest its timber, Burlington Northern in 1979 acquired a permit from defendant-appellee United States Forest Service, allowing it to construct an access road across national forest land. The proposed roads would cross the Buck Creek and Yellow Mules drainages, which are protected by the Montana Wilderness

Study Act of 1977, Pub. L. 95–150, 91 Stat. 1243, as potential wilderness areas. The proposed logging and road-building will arguably disqualify the areas as wilderness under the Act. * * *

Appellees contend that the recently enacted Alaska National Interest Lands Conservation Act (Alaska Lands Act), Pub. L. No. 96–487, 94 Stat. 2371 (1980), establishes an independent basis for affirming the judgment of the district court. They argue that § 1323(a) of the Act requires that the Secretary of Agriculture provide access to Burlington Northern for its enclosed land. Upon examination of the statute and the legislative history, we do not find this interpretation of the Alaska Lands Act convincing.

Section 1323 is a part of the administrative provisions, Title XIII, of the Alaska Lands Act. Appellees argue that it is the only section of the Act which applies to the entire country; appellants argue that, like the rest of the Act, it applies only to Alaska. Section 1323 reads as follows:

> Sec. 1323.   (a) Notwithstanding any other provision of law, and subject to such terms and conditions as the Secretary of Agriculture may prescribe, the Secretary shall provide such access to nonfederally owned land within the boundaries of the National Forest System as the Secretary deems adequate to secure to the owner the reasonable use and enjoyment thereof: *Provided*, That such owner comply with rules and regulations applicable to ingress and egress to or from the National Forest System.
>
> (b)   Notwithstanding any other provision of law, and subject to such terms and conditions as the Secretary of the Interior may prescribe, the Secretary shall provide such access to nonfederally owned land surrounded by public lands managed by the Secretary under the Federal Land Policy and Management Act of 1976 (43 U.S.C. 1701–82) as the Secretary deems adequate to secure to the owner the responsible use and enjoyment thereof: *Provided*, That such owner comply with rules and regulations applicable to access across public lands.

This section provides for access to nonfederally-owned lands surrounded by certain kinds of federal lands. Subsection (b) deals with access to nonfederal lands "surrounded by public lands managed by the Secretary [of the Interior]." Section 102(3) of the Act defines "public lands" as certain lands "situated in Alaska." Subsection (b) is therefore limited by its terms to Alaska.

Subsection (a) deals with access to nonfederally-owned lands "within the boundaries of the National Forest System." The term "National Forest System" as used in § 1323(a) is to be interpreted as being limited to national forests in Alaska or as including the entire United States.

The parties have not directed us to, nor has our research disclosed, an established or generally accepted meaning for the term "National Forest System." The United States Code contains no statutory definitions for it. We find no record of Congressional use of the term prior to the enactment of the Federal Land Policy and Management Act of 1976. The term "National Forest System" appears in that Act but is nowhere defined; from the context, however, it is apparent that it is used there to refer to national forests anywhere in the United States. See 43 U.S.C. §§ 1701, *et seq.* The same Act also uses the term "public lands" and defines it as meaning lands "owned by the United States within the several States," clearly a definition different from that given the same term in the Alaska Lands Act.

We therefore perceive no basis for assuming that Congress necessarily used the term "National Forest System" in the Alaska Lands Act to refer to national forests in the United States generally. We think that in this context the meaning of the term is ambiguous and therefore look to other indicia.

The Act itself provides some help. Title V of the Act is entitled "National Forest System." Section 501(a) states: "The following units of the National Forest System are hereby expanded * * *." This language shows that Congress used the term "National Forest System" in this Act in a context which refers to and deals with national forests in Alaska. It is not unreasonable to read Section 1323(a) as referring to the "National Forest System" in the context in which it is used in Title V of the Act, rather than to all national forests in the United States.

As the parties agreed at oral argument, moreover, § 1323(b) is *in pari materia* with § 1323(a). The two subsections are placed together in the same section, and use not only a parallel structure but many of the same words and phrases. The natural interpretation is that they were meant to have the same effect, one on lands controlled by the Secretary of Agriculture, the other on lands controlled by the Secretary of the Interior. Since § 1323(b), by the definition of public lands in § 102(3), applies only to Alaskan land, a strong presumption arises that § 1323(a) was meant to apply only to Alaska as well.

That interpretation is confirmed by a review of the entire Act which discloses no other provision having nation-wide application.[4] To attach such a sweeping effect to this obscure and seemingly minor provision of the Act would seem incongruous under the circumstances. We therefore conclude that the language of the Act supports the interpretation that § 1323(a) applies only to national forests in Alaska. Bearing in mind that "[a]bsent a clearly expressed legislative intent to the contrary, [the statutory] language must ordinarily be regarded as conclusive," *Consumer Prod. Safety Comm'n. v. GTE Sylvania*, 447 U.S. 102, 108 (1980), we turn to the legislative history.

Section 1323 was added to the Alaska Lands Bill by the Senate Committee on Energy and Natural Resources in its amendment to H.R. 39, originally passed by

---

[4] The appellees concede that no other section of the Act applies nationwide. They argue, however, that because another provision of the Act, § 1110(b), gives access rights to all Alaskan inholders, § 1323(a) is superfluous unless it is interpreted to apply to the entire country. Section 1110(b), they argue, like § 1323(b), applies only to Alaska because it uses terms, "public lands" and "conservation system unit," which are defined to include only Alaskan land.

The flaw in appellee's argument is that however § 1323(a) is interpreted, § 1110(b) essentially duplicates the protection given Alaskan lands by § 1323 as a whole. Section 1110(b) overlaps § 1323(b) just as much as it overlaps § 1323(a). If, as appellees claim, § 1110(b) gives access to all Alaskan inholders and § 1323(a) gives access to holders of land surrounded by land administered by the Secretary of Agriculture, the inclusion of § 1323(b) in the Act makes no sense at all. Section 1323(b), after all, gives access to holders of Alaskan land surrounded by land administered by the Secretary of the Interior. Under this view, not only is § 1323(b) superfluous in light of § 1110(b), it is paired with a provision, § 1323(a), of parallel structure but widely different scope. We do not see how the existence of § 1110(b) gives much support to the appellees' position.

the House. S. Rep. No. 96–413, 96th Cong. 1st Sess. (1979). It was incorporated in the Tsongas substitute bill which replaced by amendment the Energy Committee's proposed bill, 126 Cong. Rec. S11099, S11140 (daily ed. Aug. 18, 1980). The Tsongas substitute bill was passed by the Senate, 126 Cong. Rec. S11193 (daily ed. Aug. 19, 1980), and House, 126 Cong. Rec. H10552 (daily ed. Nov. 12, 1980), and became law on December 1, 1980, 94 Stat. 2371.

Section 1323 is mentioned only twice in the Senate materials. The Energy Committee report discussed it in its section-by-section analysis, S. Rep. No. 96–413 at 310, and Senator Melcher, the author of the section, discussed it on the floor of the Senate, 126 Cong. Rec. S14770–71 (daily ed. Nov. 20, 1980). The remarks of Senator Melcher, however, were made on November 20th, eight days after Congress passed H.R. 39. His remarks clearly demonstrate that his personal understanding of the section is that it applies nationwide, but because they are the remarks of but one senator made subsequent to the passage of the bill they do not provide a reliable indication of the understanding of the Senate as a whole.

Although the appellees contend that the language of the Energy Committee report makes perfectly clear the Committee's intent that § 1323 apply nationwide, we do not find their interpretation of the report's language persuasive:

> This section is designed to remove the uncertainties surrounding the status of the rights of the owners of non-Federal lands to gain access to such lands across Federal lands. It has been the Committee's understanding that such owners had the right of access to their lands subject to reasonable regulation by either, the Secretary of Agriculture in the case of national forests, or by the Secretary of the Interior in the case of public lands managed by the Bureau of Land Management under the Federal Land Policy and Management Act of 1976. However, a recent District Court decision in Utah (*Utah v. Andrus et al.*, C79–0037, October 1, 1979, D.C. Utah) has cast some doubt over the status of these rights. Furthermore, the Attorney General is currently reviewing the issue because of differing interpretations of the law by the Departments of Agriculture and the Interior. * * *
>
> The Committee amendment is designed to resolve any lingering legal questions by making it clear that non-Federal landowners have a right of access [across] National Forests and public land, subject, of course, to reasonable rules and regulations.

S. Rep. No. 96–413 at 310.

While the Committee's intent to guarantee access is clear, it is less than clear whether this provision was meant to guarantee access outside of Alaska. The problem raised in the first paragraph—the differing interpretations of the law of access—is not confined to Alaska, but the scope of the remedy as set forth in the last paragraph could be so confined. As with § 1323 itself, the report uses indiscriminately terms defined in the Act as applying only to Alaskan land ("public land") and terms not so defined ("National Forests").

The absence of any reference to Alaska is not of much import. The report's discussion of other access provisions such as § 1110 and § 1111, which all parties agree apply only to Alaska, fails to mention Alaska and is as ambiguous about whether § 1110 and § 1111 apply nationwide as is the discussion of § 1323. S. Rep. No. 96–413, at 299–300.

What we find most significant in the legislative history in the Senate is the same thing that Sherlock Holmes found to be crucial in solving the case of the Hound of the Baskervilles—the failure of the dog to bark. The Alaska Lands bill was discussed endlessly on the Senate floor. There are numerous occasions when one would expect a change in current laws of access of the magnitude of the appellees' proposed interpretation of § 1323 to be discussed, mentioned or at least alluded to. Yet we have not found in the Senate debates, and appellees have not called to our attention, one single suggestion that anything in the Alaska Land Bill would affect access rights in the rest of the country. In Senator Tsongas' long, detailed comparison of his substitute bill with the Energy Committee bill, § 1323 is not mentioned. 126 Cong. Rec. S11193 (daily ed. Aug. 19, 1980).[6] In discussion about the adequacy of the substitute bill's access provisions (which include § 1323) no mention is made of a change in the law of access for the rest of the country. 126 Cong. Rec. S11061–62 (daily ed. Aug. 18, 1980). We find it difficult to believe that the Senate would have contemplated and effected a profound change in the law of access across government land for the entire country without ever mentioning it.

The legislative history in the House, which considered and passed the Tsongas substitute bill after it was passed by the Senate, also presents an ambiguous picture of § 1323. On October 2, 1980, Representative Udall, chairman of the Committee on Interior and Insular Affairs which had joint responsibility for the bill, introduced an amendment one section of which was to "make clear that [the bill] applies only to Alaska." 127 Cong. Rec. 10376 (daily ed. Oct. 2, 1980). This amendment was never adopted. Representative Udall subsequently declared in prepared remarks inserted into the Congressional Record that although the final version of the bill was "ambiguously drafted and not expressly limited to Alaskan lands, the House believes that, as with all the other provisions of the bill, the language of the section applies only to lands within the State of Alaska." 126 Cong. Rec. H10549 (daily ed. Nov. 12, 1980). Representative Weaver stated that the section granting access rights to inholders on national forest and BLM lands "apparently applies not only to Alaska but also to the entire United States." 126 Cong. Rec. H8638 (daily ed. Sept. 9, 1980). Representative Sieberling inserted into the record a summary of proposed amendments, which refers to Section 1323 as the "nationwide access amendment." 126 Cong. Rec. H10350 (daily ed. Oct. 2, 1980). Representative AuCoin stated that one of the flaws of the final bill is that it "grants private inholders carte blanche access across national forest and public lands nationwide." 126 Cong. Rec. H10529–30 (daily ed. Nov. 12, 1980).

---

[6] Neither did Senator Tsongas remark on § 1323 when it was first proposed in the Energy Committee bill, even though in his statement in the Committee report he spends several pages criticizing the bill's overbroad provisions on access. [Citing Senate Report, additional views of Senators Metzenbaum and Tsongas.] Yet the extension of § 1323(a) to the entire country would certainly have a greater impact than the other measures he discusses.

Appellees rely heavily upon an exchange of letters between Representatives Sieberling and Weaver, chairmen of the subcommittees responsible for the bill (Public Lands of the Committee on Interior and Insular Affairs and Forest of the Committee on Agriculture), and the Attorney General's office. In their letter, the representatives express concern over § 1323, which they state applies nationwide, and ask for a clarification of how different the § 1323 access language is from existing access provisions. It is indeed clear from their letter that they believed that § 1323 applies nationwide.

Appellees argue, on the basis of the September 5, 1980 return letter from Assistant Attorney General Alan Parker, that the Department of Justice confirmed this interpretation of § 1323. We interpret the letter differently. As we read the letter, the Assistant Attorney General assumed without analysis that the representatives' interpretation of § 1323 was correct, and proceeded to discuss in detail the effect of such a change in the law.

The exchanged letters are entitled to little weight. In general, off-the-record views of congressmen are not attributed to Congress as a whole. See *T.V.A. v. Hill*, 437 U.S. 153, 190–91 (1978). This is particularly true where, as here, there is no indication that the House as a whole was aware of the correspondence. *Id.* at 191–92.

In summary, the legislative history concerning § 1323 is surprisingly sparse. The report of the Senate committee which drafted the section is ambiguous. At times when the Senate could have been expected to comment on its intention to make a major change in current law, it did not. The only expression of intent that § 1323 apply nationwide came from a single senator eight days after the Alaska Lands Act was passed by Congress. In the House debates, three representatives suggested that § 1323 did apply nationwide, but the chairman of one of the responsible committees said it did not. Two chairmen of House subcommittees responsible for the bill did state in a letter to the Attorney General that they believed that § 1323 applied nationwide, but there is no indication that the contents of this letter were generally known by members of the House, and so the letter carries little weight in our analysis. We conclude that the ambiguous legislative history gives only slight support at best to the appellees' interpretation that § 1323 applies nationwide. It is not nearly sufficient to overcome the actual language of the statute, which we believe is more naturally read as applying only to Alaska.

Moreover, § 1323 as interpreted by the appellees would repeal by implication a portion of § 5(a) of the Wilderness Act, 16 U.S.C. § 1134(a).[7] "It is, of course, a cardinal principle of statutory construction that repeals by implication are not favored," *Radzanower v. Touche Ross & Co.*, 426 U.S. 148, 154 (1976), and that "the intention of the legislature to repeal must be clear and manifest." *Posadas v. Nat'l. City Bank*, 296 U.S. 497, 503 (1936). Here it is far from clear that the legislature intended that § 1323 apply nationwide. We hold that § 1323 of the Alaska National

---

[7] 16 U.S.C. § 1134(a) gives the Secretary of Agriculture the choice between granting access to state or privately-owned land surrounded by wilderness land and permitting the exchange of the in-held land for federally-owned land of equal value. Section 1323(a), by making access mandatory, renders nugatory the land exchange provision. See generally Op. Att'y Gen. slip at 1, 23–30 (June 23, 1980).

Interest Lands Conservation Act is limited in its application to the state of Alaska, and so has no relevance to this case. * * *

NOTES ON THE "CHECKERBOARD CASE" AND STATEMENTS DURING LEGISLATIVE DELIBERATION

1. *The Ninth Circuit's Use of Legislative History.* A textualist would likely agree with Judge Norris' analysis of the statutory text, and then would stop. Why should the judge proceed any further? When Judge Norris does, he causes himself some trouble. Note his strategy: Even though the opinion adduces no affirmative support in the legislative history for its view that § 1323(a) only applies to Alaska, Judge Norris isolates all the evidence to the contrary and seeks to neuter each piece of evidence in isolation, either by demonstrating ambiguity or by denigrating the authority of the evidence. This technique—the "piecemeal critique"—is effective advocacy in response to a showing of a variety of evidence to the contrary, but shouldn't that evidence be allowed to have cumulative weight in assessing overall legislative intent? As you evaluate the following, consider whether an "intentionalist" interpreter would disagree with Judge Norris' outcome.

(a) *Committee Reports.* On first reading, the Senate Report in the Checkerboard Case is ambiguous. But reread the quoted language of the Report. The Senate wants to avoid the problems raised by a federal district court decision in Utah and the Attorney General's consideration (described in Note 2 after *Leo Sheep*). The Utah case (in the Tenth Circuit) is not controlling law in Alaska (in the Ninth Circuit). The Senate Report wants "to resolve *any* lingering legal questions by *making it clear* that non-Federal landowners have a right of access [across] National Forests" (emphasis added). While this Report is not 100% clear that § 1323(a) was meant to apply nationwide, isn't the more probable reading of the Report that it was?

(b) *Statements of Sponsors and Committee Chairs.* Senator Melcher, the sponsor of the amendment adding § 1323(a), explicitly said that it applied nationwide. Judge Norris denigrates this clear evidence by saying that it was uttered after the bill was passed by Congress (but before it had been signed by the President). But he doesn't say that Representative Udall's statements, upon which he relies, were inserted into the Congressional Record *after* the bill was passed. (Udall's remarks are reported in the *Record* for the day the bill was passed, but they are proceeded by a "bullet" [•], which signifies that they were not spoken on the floor of the House but were inserted later.) Indeed, look at the dates of the Udall and Melcher statements. Why might Udall have abandoned any attempt to amend the statute to make it clearly apply only to Alaska and instead simply uttered a comment that the unamended version had the same impact? Why might Melcher have made his comment? Which is the more reliable?

Leaving strategic considerations aside, consider the roles of the key players. Melcher, the sponsor of § 1323(a), and Representatives Seiberling and Weaver, chairs of the relevant House subcommittees, interpreted § 1323(a) to apply nationwide, in statements made to their respective chambers. Udall, chair of the House Committee, interpreted it otherwise, in a statement inserted after the fact. Yet Judge Norris treats Udall's statements as roughly equal to those of Melcher, Seiberling, and Weaver in combination. Isn't this wrong, especially in light of the common view that greater weight should be accorded statements of *supporters* of a provision over statements of *opponents*? See also *Ernst & Ernst v. Hochfelder*, 425 U.S. 185, 204 n.24 (1976).

(c) *Dialogue with Bureaucrats.* The exchange of letters between Seiberling/Weaver and the Justice Department concerning the effect of the Melcher amendment is not unusual in Congress. It is quite common in state legislatures, where assistants to state attorneys general typically advise legislative committees about the probable legal effects of bills. Since Seiberling and Weaver were key House negotiators, and the House accepted the Melcher amendment in negotiations, isn't this exchange of letters more significant than Judge Norris was willing to admit? Compare *Lindahl v. Office of Personnel Management*, 470 U.S. 768, 785 n.17 (1985), where the Supreme Court relied heavily on letters from the OPM Director to the Chairs of the Senate and House Committees to interpret amendments to the Civil Service Retirement Act. Judge Wald, *supra*, at 202–03, noted in the early 1980s an increasing tendency of lawyers to use, and judges to cite, unpublished portions of the legislative history to support their interpretations of statutes. See *Borrell v. U.S. Int'l Commc'n Agency*, 682 F.2d 981, 988 (D.C. Cir. 1982).

2. *Evidence Judge Norris (and Everybody Else) Missed.* Judge Norris makes much of the fact that Senator Melcher's statement that § 1323 applies nationwide was made on the floor of the Senate after the bill was passed. But on July 29, 1980 (well before the bill passed the Senate), Senator Melcher sent a letter to every Senator, explaining that he was opposed to a portion of one of the amendments that would be offered when the Alaska Lands bill came before the Senate. The letter explained that Melcher's amendment was in response to the recent Department of Justice opinion (described in Note 2 following *Leo Sheep, supra*) indicating that private checkerboard landowners did not have an automatic right of access across government land; Melcher considered the Department of Justice view an innovation that disrupted prior understandings among property owners and federal lands administrators. The letter then said:

> In the Alaskan Lands Bill, for Alaska only, specific access to state or private lands was explicitly guaranteed. In order to avoid any change in federal policy on this question, last October [1979] I introduced an amendment to that bill for continuing the historic policy of granting access to property inholders in all the rest of the Bureau of Land Management and National Forest lands. My amendment was accepted by the committee without objection and *it applies to landowners within federal lands (either in national forests or in public lands administered by the Bureau of Land Management) in all the rest of the states where such lands are located.* * * *

The letter warned that Amendment No. 1783, offered by Senators Tsongas and McGovern, would strike this committee amendment, and Melcher urged the other Senators to support his effort to preserve this national right of access provision.[74] Was Judge Norris wrong about the "deal" in Congress?

---

[74] The letter is reproduced in *Oversight on The Montana Wilderness Study Act: Hearing Before the Subcomm. on Public Lands and Reserved Water of the Senate Comm. on Energy and Natural Resources*, 97th Cong., 1st Sess. 53 (May 28, 1981). Senator Melcher represents that the letter was sent to every Senator. *Id.* at 12. One of our students in the Georgetown University Law Center, Class of 1990 came up with this "smoking gun" during class discussion. (Imagine our embarrassment that we didn't find this smoking gun when we worked on the case in private practice. This is one of the cases two of us plundered from our experience as attorneys at the old Washington, D.C. law firm of Shea & Gardner (now absorbed into another law firm). Apparently, it did not occur to us that anything relevant to the Alaska Act would be found in the legislative history of another act, the Montana Wilderness Study Act. *Should* that have occurred to us? Keep this question in mind when you read the next case.)

3. *The Dog That Didn't Bark Canon.* Although Judge Norris cited the wrong Sherlock Holmes story,[75] he is correct to say that the Supreme Court sometimes follows the *dog didn't bark* canon. That is, it may be significant that an intense congressional debate does not even mention an issue—suggesting that the statute contained no unusual departure from the status quo against which Congress was legislating. Thus, in a bill whose title and subject matter are all about Alaska, one would expect some special mention of a provision that adjusted important legal rights in the lower 49 states as well.

We have seen examples of it in *Zuni Public School District No. 89 v. Department of Education*, *Bock Laundry*, and *Chisom v. Roemer* (all in Chapter 6, § 3A). In *Chisom*, recall that Justice Scalia lustily assailed this canon on the grounds that it is highly subjective and unreliable (how one characterizes the "status quo" drives the operation of the canon, and that is quite subjective), as well as contrary to Justice Scalia's view (e.g., *Rapanos*) that Congress can proceed *only* through positive legislation adopted under Article I, § 7, and *never* through inaction, etc.

5. Post-Enactment Legislative History ("Subsequent Legislative History")

Statutes are often enacted and forgotten by the legislature. Sometimes, though, the legislature—or at least its members and committees—will continue to talk about the statute after enactment. Circumstances for post-enactment discussion include (1) proposals to amend the statute or to enact a new and related statute, including debate and hearings and committee reports on such proposals; (2) oversight hearings in response to agency and/or judicial implementation of the statute; and (3) efforts to "bend" interpretation of the statute. The statutory interpreter is torn between considering relevant evidence and avoiding strategic trickery. One way to set this balance would be to consider only "subsequent legislative history" that is tied to a subsequent statute enacted by the legislature. (The Supreme Court has not always limited itself in this way, as you will see in the notes after the following case.)

In the immediately preceding case, Judge Norris dismissed Senator Melcher's comment as mere subsequent legislative history. The following case is a later opinion on rehearing in the Checkerboard Case. Notice how Judge Norris' interpretation changed when he was confronted with different subsequent legislative history. Should he have changed his mind?

MONTANA WILDERNESS ASSOCIATION V. UNITED STATES FOREST SERVICE

United States Court of Appeals for the Ninth Circuit, 1981.
655 F.2d 951, cert. denied, 455 U.S. 989.

[After the May 1981 opinion, *supra*, which held that there was no easement created by the railroad land grant act of 1864 or the Alaska Lands Act of 1980, an

---

[75] In *Silver Blaze*, Sherlock Holmes solves the case of a missing racehorse by observing that the dog guarding the barn had not barked the night before when an intruder entered to get the horse; the deduction (elementary!) was that the culprit was someone the dog knew well. In *The Hound of the Baskervilles*, which Judge Norris cites, the dog barked quite a lot and did not contribute to Holmes's solution of the mystery.

intervening party defendant moved for reconsideration based upon yet another new statute, shedding light on the Alaska lands statute construed in the earlier opinion. In light of the new statute, the panel withdrew the May opinion and issued the instant opinion. Judge Norris, the author of the original panel opinion, also wrote the new one.]

The sole issue on appeal is whether Burlington Northern has a right of access across federal land to its inholdings of timberland. Appellees contend that the recently enacted Alaska National Interest Lands Conservation Act (Alaska Lands Act), Pub. L. No. 96–487, 94 Stat. 2371 (1980), establishes an independent basis for affirming the judgment of the district court. They argue that § 1323(a) of the Act requires that the Secretary of Agriculture provide access to Burlington Northern for its enclosed land.

Section 1323 is a part of the administrative provisions, Title XIII, of the Alaska Lands Act. Appellees argue that it is the only section of the Act which applies to the entire country; appellants argue that, like the rest of the Act, it applies only to Alaska. Section 1323 reads as follows:

> Sec. 1323.(a) Notwithstanding any other provision of law, and subject to such terms and conditions as the Secretary of Agriculture may prescribe, the Secretary shall provide such access to nonfederally owned land within the boundaries of the National Forest System as the Secretary deems adequate to secure to the owner the reasonable use and enjoyment thereof: *Provided*, That such owner comply with rules and regulations applicable to ingress and egress to or from the National Forest System.

> (b) Notwithstanding any other provision of law, and subject to such terms and conditions as the Secretary of the Interior may prescribe, the Secretary shall provide such access to nonfederally owned land surrounded by public lands managed by the Secretary under the Federal Land Policy and Management Act of 1976 (43 U.S.C. 1701–82) as the Secretary deems adequate to secure to the owner the responsible use and enjoyment thereof: *Provided*, That such owner comply with rules and regulations applicable to access across public lands.

This section provides for access to nonfederally-owned lands surrounded by certain kinds of federal lands. Subsection (b) deals with access to nonfederal lands "surrounded by public lands managed by the Secretary [of the Interior]." Section 102(3) of the Act defines "public lands" as certain lands "situated in Alaska." Subsection (b), therefore, is arguably limited by its terms to Alaska, though we do not find it necessary to settle that issue here. Our consideration of the scope of § 1323(a) proceeds under the assumption that § 1323(b) is limited to Alaska.

Subsection (a) deals with access to nonfederally-owned lands "within the boundaries of the National Forest System." The term "National Forest System" is not specifically defined in the Act.

The question before the court is whether the term "National Forest System" as used in § 1323(a) is to be interpreted as being limited to national forests in Alaska or as including the entire United States. We note at the outset that the bare language of § 1323(a) does not, when considered by itself, limit the provision of access to Alaskan land. We must look, however, to the context of the section to determine its meaning.

Elsewhere in the Act, Congress used the term "National Forest System" in a context which refers to and deals with national forests in Alaska. Title V of the Act is entitled "National Forest System." Section 501(a) states: "The following units of the National Forest System are hereby expanded * * *." It is not unreasonable to read Section 1323(a) as referring to the "National Forest System" in the context in which it is used in Title V of the Act, rather than to all national forests in the United States.

Congress did, however, supply us with a general definition of the term in another statute. Pub. Law 93–378, 88 Stat. 480 (1974). 16 U.S.C. § 1609(a) states *inter alia* that:

> Congress declares that the National Forest System consists of units of federally owned forest, range, and related lands throughout the United States and its territories, united into a nationally significant system dedicated to the long-term benefit for present and future generations, and that it is the purpose of their section to include all such areas into one integral system. The 'National Forest System' shall include all national forest lands reserved or withdrawn from the public domain of the United States * * *.

Application of this definition to § 1323(a) would necessarily yield the conclusion that the section was intended to have nation-wide effect. This seems especially so when Congress uses the term "National Forest System" in § 1323(a) without limitation or qualification.

As the parties agreed at oral argument, however, § 1323(b) is *in pari materia* with § 1323(a). The two subsections are placed together in the same section, and use not only a parallel structure but many of the same words and phrases. The natural interpretation is that they were meant to have the same effect, one on lands controlled by the Secretary of Agriculture, the other on lands controlled by the Secretary of the Interior. Since we assume that § 1323(b), by definition of public lands in § 102(3), applies only to Alaskan land, we face a presumption that § 1323(a) was meant to apply to Alaska as well.

That interpretation is supported by a review of the entire Act which discloses no other provision having nation-wide application. We therefore conclude that the language of the Act provides tentative support for the view that § 1323(a) applies only to national forests in Alaska. Bearing in mind that "[a]bsent a clearly expressed legislative intent to the contrary, [the statutory] language must ordinarily be regarded as conclusive," *Consumer Prod. Safety Comm'n v. GTE Sylvania*, 447 U.S. 102, 108 (1980), we turn to the legislative history.

The legislative history concerning § 1323 is surprisingly sparse. The report of the Senate committee which drafted the section is ambiguous.[7] At times when the

---

[7] The Energy Committee report discussed it in its section-by-section analysis, S.Rep. No. 96–413 at 310. (The Committee analysis mixes up §§ 1323 and 1324. Thus, the analysis entitled § 1324 is really concerned

Senate could have been expected to comment on its intention to make a major change in current law, it did not. The only expression of intent that § 1323 apply nation-wide came from a single senator eight days after the Alaska Lands Act was passed by Congress.[8] In the House debates, three representatives suggested that § 1323 did apply nation-wide, but the chairman of one of the responsible committees said it did not.[9] Two chairmen of House subcommittees responsible for the bill did state in a letter to the Attorney General that they believed that § 1323 applied nation-wide, but there is no indication that the contents of this letter were generally known by members of the House, and so the letter carries little weight in our analysis. All this gives only slight support at best to the appellees' interpretation that § 1323 applies nation-wide.

The appellees, however, have uncovered subsequent legislative history that, given the closeness of the issue, is decisive. Three weeks after Congress passed the

---

with § 1323 and vice versa.) Although the appellees contend that the language of the Energy Committee report makes perfectly clear the Committee's intent that § 1323 apply nationwide, we do not find their interpretation of the report's language persuasive:

> This section is designed to remove the uncertainties surrounding the status of the rights of the owners of non-Federal lands to gain access to such lands across Federal lands. It has been the Committee's understanding that such owners had the right of access to their lands subject to reasonable regulation by either, the Secretary of Agriculture in the case of national forests, or by the Secretary of the Interior in the case of public lands managed by the Bureau of Land Management under the Federal Land Policy and Management Act of 1976. However, a recent District Court decision in Utah (*Utah v. Andrus et al.*, C79-0037, October 1, 1979, D.C. Utah) has cast some doubt over the status of these rights. Furthermore, the Attorney General is currently reviewing the issue because of differing interpretations of the law by the Departments of Agriculture and the Interior.
> * * *
> The Committee amendment is designed to resolve any lingering legal questions by making it clear that non-Federal landowners have a right of access [across] National Forests and public land, subject, of course, to reasonable rules and regulations.

S. Rep. No. 96–413, at 310.

While the Committee's intent to guarantee access is clear, it is less than clear whether this provision was meant to guarantee access outside of Alaska. The problem raised in the first paragraph—the differing interpretations of the law of access—is not confined to Alaska, but the scope of the remedy as set forth in the last paragraph could be so confined. As with § 1323 itself, the report uses indiscriminately terms defined in the Act as applying only to Alaskan land ("public land") and terms not so defined ("National Forests").

[8] Senator Melcher, the author of the section, discussed it on the floor of the Senate, 126 Cong. Rec. S14770-71 (daily ed. Nov. 20, 1980). The remarks of Senator Melcher, however, were made on November 20th, eight days after Congress passed H.R. 39. His remarks clearly demonstrate that his personal understanding of the section is that it applies nation-wide, but because they are the remarks of but one senator made subsequent to the passage of the bill they do not provide a reliable indication of the understanding of the Senate as a whole.

[9] On October 2, 1980, Representative Udall, chairman of the Committee on Interior and Insular Affairs which had joint responsibility for the bill, introduced an amendment one section of which was to "make clear that [the bill] applies only to Alaska." 127 Cong. Rec. 10376 (daily ed. Oct. 2, 1980). This amendment was never adopted. Representative Udall subsequently declared in prepared remarks inserted into the Congressional Record that although the final version of the bill was "ambiguously drafted and not expressly limited to Alaskan lands, the House believes that, as with all the other provisions of the bill, the language of the section applies only to lands within the State of Alaska." 126 Cong. Rec. H10549 (daily ed. Nov. 12, 1980). Representative Weaver stated that the section granting access rights to inholders on national forest and BLM lands "apparently applies not only to Alaska but also to the entire United States." 126 Cong. Rec. H8638 (daily ed. Sept. 9, 1980). Representative Sieberling inserted into the record a summary of proposed amendments, which refers to Section 1323 as the "nationwide access amendment." 126 Cong. Rec. H10350 (daily ed. Oct. 2, 1980). Representative AuCoin stated that one of the flaws of the final bill is that it "grants private inholders carte blanche access across national forest and public lands nationwide." 126 Cong. Rec. H10529-30 (daily ed. Nov. 12, 1980).

Alaska Lands Act, a House-Senate Conference Committee considering the Colorado Wilderness Act interpreted § 1323 of the Alaska Lands Act as applying nation-wide:

> Section 7 of the Senate amendment contains a provision pertaining to access to non-Federally owned lands within national forest wilderness areas in Colorado. The House bill has no such provision.
>
> *The conferees agreed to delete the section because similar language has already passed Congress in Section 1323 of the Alaska National Interest Lands Conservation Act.*

H.R. Rep. No. 1521, 96th Cong., 2d Sess., 126 Cong. Rec. H11687 (daily ed. Dec. 3, 1980) (emphasis supplied).

This action was explained to both Houses during discussion of the Conference Report. See 126 Cong. Rec. S15571 (daily ed. Dec. 4, 1980) (remarks of Sen. Hart); *id.* at S15573 (remarks of Sen. Armstrong); *id.* at H11705 (daily ed. Dec. 3, 1980) (remarks of Rep. Johnson). Both houses then passed the Colorado Wilderness bill as it was reported by the Conference Committee.

Although a subsequent conference report is not entitled to the great weight given subsequent legislation, *Consumer Prod. Safety Comm'n v. GTE Sylvania*, 477 U.S. 102, 118 n.13 (1980), it is still entitled to significant weight, *Seatrain Shipbuilding Corp. v. Shell Oil Co.*, 444 U.S. 572 (1980), particularly where it is clear that the conferees had carefully considered the issue. The conferees, including Representatives Udall and Sieberling and Senator Melcher, had an intimate knowledge of the Alaska Lands Act.[11] Moreover, the Conference Committee's interpretation of § 1323 was the basis for their decision to leave out an access provision passed by one house. In these circumstances, the Conference Committee's interpretation is very persuasive. We conclude that it tips the balance decidedly in favor of the broader interpretation of § 1323.[12] We therefore hold that Burlington Northern has an assured right of access to its land pursuant to the nation-wide grant of access in § 1323. * * *

---

[11] The participation of Representative Udall is particularly noteworthy since he was the one congressman to proclaim in the legislative history of the Alaska Lands Act that Section 1323 applied only to Alaska.

[12] We recognize a facial problem or tension between § 1323(a) and a portion of § 5(a) of the Wilderness Act, 16 U.S.C. § 1134(a). We need not decide in this case whether there is repeal by implication. In passing, we note only that it is arguable that the two can stand together. § 1134(a) deals specifically with right of access "[i]n any case where State-owned or privately-owned land is completely surrounded by national forest lands *within areas designated by this chapter as wilderness* * * *." (emphasis added). Section 1323(a), on the other hand, deals with "* * * access to non-federally owned land within the boundaries of the National Forest System * * *." Section 1134(a) is addressed specifically to an area designated as "wilderness," while § 1323(a) is addressed to National Forest System lands in general. In cases involving wilderness areas, the Secretary has the option of exchanging land of equal value so that the wilderness area may be preserved. Thus, § 1134(a) could be construed to apply in the specific case of a wilderness area, and § 1323(a) could be construed to apply in all other cases.

Whether or not they are in fact irreconcilable we leave to another case when the issue is squarely presented for review.

NOTES ON THE SECOND CHECKERBOARD OPINION
AND THE USE OF POST-ENACTMENT STATEMENTS

1. *The Burger Court's Use of Subsequent Legislative History.* Is Judge Norris' reliance on subsequent legislative history persuasive? While the Supreme Court has said that subsequent statutes should inform interpretation of an earlier one, the Court has professed some skepticism about reliance on subsequent legislative statements. For example, in *Consumer Product Safety Comm'n v. GTE Sylvania*, 447 U.S. 102, 117–18 (1980), petitioners relied upon statements in a conference committee report concerning the 1976 amendments to the Consumer Product Safety Act that purported to interpret a section of the Act enacted in 1972 and not amended in 1976. The Court noted "the oft-repeated warning that 'the views of a subsequent Congress form a hazardous basis for inferring the intent of an earlier one.' " In a footnote, the Court further explained:

> Petitioners invoke the maxim that states: "Subsequent legislation declaring the intent of an earlier statute is entitled to great weight in statutory construction." With respect to subsequent *legislation*, however, Congress has proceeded formally through the legislative process. A mere statement in a conference report of such legislation as to what the Committee believes an earlier statute meant is obviously less weighty.

> The less formal types of subsequent legislative history provide an extremely hazardous basis for inferring the meaning of a congressional enactment.

In *Andrus v. Shell Oil Co.*, 446 U.S. 657 (1980), a case decided the same Term as *GTE Sylvania*, the Court stated: "While arguments predicated upon subsequent congressional actions may be weighed with extreme care, they should not be rejected out of hand as a source that a court may consider in the search for legislative intent." *Id.* at 666 n.8. In a third case decided the same Term, the Court adopted the interpretation of a 1936 statute set forth in a 1971 House committee report based on the theory that, "while the views of subsequent Congresses cannot override the unmistakable intent of the enacting one, * * * such views are entitled to significant weight, * * * and particularly so when the precise intent of the enacting Congress is obscure." *Seatrain Shipbuilding Corp. v. Shell Oil Co.*, 444 U.S. 572, 596 (1980). Later, in *South Carolina v. Regan*, 465 U.S. 367, 378 n.17 (1984), the Court once again "rejected" any suggestion that statutory interpretation can be informed by "the committee reports that accompany subsequent legislation."

2. *The Checkerboard Problem, Subsequent Legislative History, and the New Textualism.* The policy consequences of Judge Norris' new opinion seem quite malign. The fairest rule for checkerboard cases would be to give a right of reasonable access to both the government and the private holder, but this is precluded by *Leo Sheep, supra.* The second best rule, then, might be to deny rights of access to both parties, for their mutual dependence would probably lead to a deal approximating the best rule (but with more transactions costs). The worst rule is one in which one party has a right of access (*Montana Wilderness*) and the other does not (*Leo Sheep*). This does not create incentives to bargain and may force the government to pay extra money and high transactions costs to take the right of access through eminent domain.

Is this seemingly dysfunctional result compelled by § 1323(a)? Has Judge Norris persuaded you that Congress "intended" to deprive the public fisc of this money, and impair wilderness lands as well? Has Judge Norris even persuaded himself that his first opinion was wrong? Perhaps Judge Norris lost heart when Representative Udall—his bulwark in the first opinion—abandoned his earlier view of § 1323(a). So what? Wasn't Udall posturing in the first place? If Congress is going to create such a dysfunctional rule, shouldn't courts require explicit *statutory* language? If your instinct is "yes," then you need to bring a canon of interpretation into play. Could any established substantive canon apply here?

Subsequent legislative history is surely of no use to the new textualists. If ordinary legislative history is, as Justice Scalia argues, often cooked up by congressional staff and lobbyists to try to slant interpretation after the fact, the possibility for abuse is worse with subsequent legislative history, because there is less congressional monitoring and correction of misleading statements after the statute has been passed. One effect of the new textualism has been to push the current Court toward greater skepticism about the value of subsequent legislative history than the Court had shown in the 1970s and early 1980s. *Rapanos* and *Solid Waste* illustrate this reluctance, as the Court in both cases was extremely reluctant to read the 1972 Water Act in light of proposals rejected by Congress in 1977.[76] But even the skeptical decisions say that the Court will consider subsequent legislative history if it is very persuasive and/or accompanied by an amendment to the statute. See *Solid Waste*; *Mackey v. Lanier Collections Agency & Serv.*, 486 U.S. 825, 839–40 (1988).

The Court in *Gozlon-Peretz v. United States*, 498 U.S. 395 (1991), accepted a "public reliance" type of argument similar to the one accepted by Judge Norris in the Second Checkerboard opinion: When a subsequent Congress assumes one interpretation of an earlier statute and acts upon that assumption in enacting a new statute, the Court will consider that as evidence in favor of the assumed interpretation. See also Justice Scalia's opinion concurring in the judgment in *Franklin v. Gwinnett County Public Schools*, 503 U.S. 60 (1992), arguing that the Court should generally be reluctant to imply causes of action to enforce federal statutes, but not when Congress has relied on that understanding in subsequent legislation. Compare *Pub. Emps. Ret. Sys. of Ohio v. Betts*, 492 U.S. 158, 167–68 (1989) (refusing to credit subsequent conference report's understanding of statutory meaning when Congress amended statute). See also the extensive use of such history, including references to discussions pertaining to bills never enacted into law, in *FDA v. Brown & Williamson Tobacco Corp.*

3. *Post-Enactment Testimony and* Amicus *Briefs by Legislators.* The second Checkerboard Opinion is just one example of how the battle to create legislative meaning can continue after the statute is enacted. Two other techniques have been used. One is the use of affidavits and depositions by legislators, especially at the state level (where legislative history is not always readily available or elaborate enough to

---

[76] See *Massachusetts v. EPA*, 549 U.S. 497, 529–30 (2007); *Doe v. Chao*, 540 U.S. 614 (2004) (rejecting Privacy Act plaintiff's reliance on statutes in pari materia, when such statutes were enacted after the Privacy Act); *Cent. Bank of Denver N.A. v. First Interstate Bank of Denver N.A.*, 511 U.S. 164, 185–86 (1994) (ignoring congressional interpretations in 1983 and 1988 committee reports in interpreting 1934 statute); *Chapman v. United States*, 500 U.S. 453, 464 n.4 (1991), *aff'g Marshall v. United States* (Chapter 7, § 3B1) (refusing even to consider subsequent legislative discussion as evidence of statutory ambiguity in criminal sentencing case); *Sullivan v. Finkelstein*, 496 U.S. 617, 628 n.8 (1990) (rejecting arguments based upon subsequent committee print and report; in this case, Scalia, J., concurred but refused to join note 8, because he thought it inappropriate even to discuss subsequent legislative history); *United States v. Monsanto*, 491 U.S. 600, 609–10 (1989) (disregarding postenactment statements of several legislators).

provide much guidance). Some states consider such testimony "inadmissible evidence" of "legislative intent" but are, nonetheless, sometimes moved by it. For example, the Washington Supreme Court in *City of Spokane v. State*, 89 P.2d 826 (Wash. 1939), refused to admit affidavits or depositions of the Governor, Speaker of the House, chairs of the relevant committees, 33 Senators and 68 Representatives in one legislature and 33 Senators and 70 Representatives in the next legislature. Nonetheless, the Court overruled its prior interpretation of the statute, effectively conforming to the views pressed in the affidavits and depositions. Compare *Western Air Lines v. Bd. of Equalization*, 480 U.S. 123, 130 n.* (1987) (refusing to consider affidavit from lobbyist involved in the enactment of the law in question).

Another method is a legislator *amicus* brief. The Supreme Court in *Blanchette v. Connecticut General Ins. Corp.*, 419 U.S. 102 (1974), relied on the statements made at oral argument by Representative Brock Adams (D–Wash.), representing 36 Members of Congress, as evidence that the Act did not withdraw a Tucker Act remedy for just compensation. The *Gingles* case, discussed in Chapter 2, § 1B2, reached a result consistent with, and perhaps influenced by, an *amicus* brief filed by a dozen key Members of Congress, opposing the Administration's interpretation of the Voting Rights Act Amendments of 1982.

Nine key legislators (six Democrats, then the majority party in Congress, and three key Republicans) involved in the controlling legislation filed an *amicus* brief in *Rapanos*.[77] Their brief provided a comprehensive examination of the evolution of wetlands regulation, from the Federal Water Pollution Control Act of 1948, through the transformational amendments in 1972 and concluding with the Clean Water Act of 1977. The theme of their brief was that the 1972 law "articulated one of the broadest ecosystem restoration and protection aspirations in all of environmental law." The mandate of the statute was for the EPA and the Army Corps to view the country as a collection of integrated hydrological ecosystems whose integrity was threatened, a threat that had dire consequences for flood control, safe drinking water, and damage to animal populations. The aggressive and comprehensive Corps regulations were affirmatively ratified by the 1977 statute. Although the *Rapanos* plurality rejected this analysis, it was adopted by the four dissenters and may have had an impact on Justice Kennedy, who followed its key points.

4.   *Post-Enactment History from Related Funding Legislation.* In *Bruesewitz v. Wyeth LLC*, 131 S.Ct. 1068 (2011), the Court considered whether the National Childhood Vaccine Injury Act of 1986 (NCVIA) preempted state-law design-defect claims against vaccine manufacturers. The statute states that "No vaccine manufacturer shall be liable in a civil action for damages arising from a vaccine-related injury or death associated with the administration of a vaccine after October 1, 1988, if the injury or death resulted from side effects that were unavoidable even though the vaccine was properly prepared and was accompanied by proper directions and warnings." The majority opinion written by Justice Scalia (joined by Chief Justice Roberts and Justices Kennedy, Thomas, Breyer, and Alito), focused on the text of the statute and held that the statute preempted design-defect claims.

---

[77]   Brief of the Honorable John Dingell, John Conyers, Jr., Robert Drinan, Gary Hart, Kenneth Hechler, Charles Mathias, Jr., Paul McCloskey, Jr., Charles Rangel, and Richard Schultz Schweiker, as *Amici Curiae* in Support of the Respondent, *Rapanos v. United States*, 547 U.S. 715 (2006).

In a dissenting opinion, Justice Sotomayor (joined by Justice Ginsburg) invoked post-enactment legislative history to support her position that Congress intended to incorporate the definition of "unavoidable" found in comment k of the Restatement (Second) of Torts and cases expounding upon this comment. (If the statute incorporated comment k it would not preempt certain design-defect claims.) Justice Sotomayor referred to a committee report accompanying legislation enacted in 1987 that provided funding for the no-fault compensation program established by the NCVIA in 1986. The 1987 committee report clearly stated that the NCVIA codified comment k. Justice Sotomayor argued:

> To be sure, postenactment legislative history created by a subsequent Congress is ordinarily a hazardous basis from which to infer the intent of the enacting Congress. But unlike ordinary postenactment legislative history, which is justifiably given little or no weight, the 1987 Report reflects the intent of the Congress that enacted the funding legislation necessary to give operative effect to the principal provisions of the Vaccine Act * * * Because the tort reforms in the 1986 Act * * * had no operative legal effect unless and until Congress provided funding for the compensation program, the views of the Congress that enacted that funding legislation are a proper and, indeed, authoritative guide to the meaning of [the NCVIA].

Responding to Justice Sotomayor's argument, Justice Scalia rejected her proposed exception to the general rule against post-enactment legislative history:

> Post-enactment legislative history (a contradiction in terms) is not a legitimate tool of statutory interpretation. * * * Real (pre-enactment) legislative history is persuasive to some because it is thought to shed light on what legislators understood an ambiguous statutory text to mean when they voted to enact it into law. * * * But post-enactment legislative history by definition "could have had no effect on the congressional vote." * * *. Those who voted on the relevant statutory language were not necessarily the same persons who crafted the statements in the later Committee Report; or if they were did not necessarily have the same views at that earlier time; and no one voting at that earlier time could possibly have been informed by those later statements. Permitting the legislative history of subsequent funding legislation to alter the meaning of a statute would set a dangerous precedent. Many provisions of federal law depend on appropriations or include sunset provisions; they cannot be made the device for unenacted statutory revision.

NOTES ON PRESIDENTIAL SIGNING OR VETO STATEMENTS

1. *Presidents' Use of Signing Statements.* Throughout history, Presidents have made statements about the bills they sign into law, and sometimes those statements have addressed important policy-related issues of statutory meaning, along one of at least three dimensions: (1) discussions highlighting important features of legislation; (2) objections to the constitutionality of some part of a law, usually with an indication that the administration would apply the law more narrowly than it was written; or (3) an intention to apply a law in a particular way, based upon the executive department's interpretation of that statute. See Curtis Bradley & Eric Posner, *Presidential Signing Statements and Executive Power*, 23 Const. Comm. 307 (2006).

The Reagan Administration used the presidential signing statement more aggressively for reasons (2) and (3) than prior administrations had done. In some statements, President Reagan took positions that were apparently inconsistent with congressional deals made in the enactment process. For example, Congress rebuffed Administration attempts to dilute the Safe Drinking Water Act of 1986 by giving the EPA discretion whether to compel local governments to maintain safe water. The bill said EPA "shall" (not "may") issue the safe-water orders. Yet in his signing statement, President Reagan declared that the new law did not "require" EPA to take any enforcement action. Also, the Administration gained wider publication for its signing statements. Such statements ordinarily appear in the Weekly Compilation of Presidential Documents, but beginning in 1986 the West Publishing Company has regularly included signing statements in its *United States Code Congressional and Administrative News* (USCCAN), which is the most readily accessible reference work for legislative history. Legal advisers to the President took the position that the President's statements are authoritative on issues of "legislative intent," perhaps trumping contrary statements of Senators and Representatives themselves.[78]

The Bush 41 Administration was similarly aggressive in its use of signing statements, with the Clinton Administration being moderately aggressive. Most aggressive of all was the Bush 43 Administration. In his first five years, President George W. Bush challenged or sought to alter more than 800 statutory provisions, apparently more than the total number of provisions reinterpreted by all three of his immediate predecessors in their 20 years of combined service as Presidents. Bradley & Posner, *Presidential Signing Statements*, 324–25.

The Bush 43 signing statements received more publicity, in part because they often rested upon a controversial understanding of the President's Article II powers. For example, the Detainee Treatment Act of 2005 banned cruel, inhuman, or degrading treatment of detainees, such as those at Guantanamo Bay, Cuba. When signing this bill (which his allies had resisted) into law, President Bush 43 stated that the executive branch would construe the ban "in a manner consistent with the constitutional authority of the President to supervise the unitary executive branch and as Commander in Chief and consistent with the constitutional limitations on the judicial power." This language was reminiscent of the language in the controversial memorandum of Bush 43 Administration Justice Department official John Yoo that argued that presidential agents are immune from prosecution for torture of suspects.

Like his predecessors, President Obama has regularly issued presidential signing statements. Shortly after taking office, President Obama published a memorandum explaining his approach to signing statements. He noted that "[f]or nearly two centuries, Presidents have issued statements addressing constitutional or other legal questions upon signing bills into law" but "[i]n recent years, there has been considerable public discussion and criticism of the use of signing statements to raise constitutional objections to statutory provisions."

Recognizing the potential for abuse, President Obama articulated four principles to guide his use of signing statements. First, the President will make every effort to

---

[78] *The New Republic*, 3 Nov. 1986, at 13–14. See also Memorandum from Samuel Alito, Jr., Deputy Assistant Attorney Gen., Office of Legal Counsel, to the Litigation Strategy Working Group (Feb. 5, 1986), available at http://www.archives.gov/news/samuel-alito/accession–060–89–269/Acc060–89–269–box6–SG–LSWG–AlitotoLSWG–Feb1986.pdf.

communicate his concerns to Congress before enactment of legislation. Second, the President will adopt a presumption of constitutionality and will only conclude that a portion of a bill is unconstitutional if it violates well-founded constitutional principles. Third, the President will articulate his constitutional objections with specificity in order to promote transparency and accountability. Finally, when construing a provision in a manner that is meant to avoid a constitutional problem, the President will only apply legitimate constructions of legislative language. See Memorandum, Presidential Signing Statements, 74 Fed. Reg. 10,669 (Mar. 9, 2009)

Two days after publishing this memorandum, President Obama issued a lengthy signing statement for the Omnibus Appropriations Act of 2009, Pub. L. No. 111–8, 123 Stat. 524, in which he explained that he would refuse to be bound by provisions the White House perceived as congressional encroachments on his constitutional authority in multiple areas, including foreign affairs ("effectively directing the Executive on how to proceed or not proceed in negotiations or discussions with international organizations and foreign governments"), and the Art. II, § 3 Recommendations Clause ("effectively purport[ing] to require me and other executive officers to submit budget requests to the Congress in particular forms").

A recent student comment argues that the enduring presence of signing statements results from "an inefficient equilibrium" between Congress and the President. Recent Signing Statement, *Omnibus Appropriations Act of 2009*, *President Obama Issues First Constitutional Signing Statement*, *Declares Appropriations Bill Provisions Unenforceable.—Statement on Signing the Omnibus Appropriations Act, 2009, Daily Comp. Pres. Doc. No. DCPD200900145 (Mar. 11, 2009)*, 123 Harv. L. Rev. 1051 (2010):

> For Congress, the costs of including self-aggrandizing bill provisions are de minimis. The executive, in contrast, must internalize the high costs of an overt, defensive response because the interbranch dialogue occupies two planes: one political, one constitutional. Small political issues, like obscure omnibus provisions, implicate larger constitutional questions. For example, President Obama's objection to budget reporting provisions may seem insignificant, but it reflects a broader concern that Congress might aggrandize its constitutional powers. The executive, it follows, continually fears that the Court and Congress might interpret a political compromise as a constitutional concession in the absence of a signal to the contrary. Concession, it is feared, might foreclose for present and future administrations the ability to invoke executive prerogative when needed. To minimize this risk, the executive adopted a positive system of denial, which, across administrations, entrenched itself as the default practice. But having established this pattern of denial, the executive cannot go back. In this system, silence no longer constitutes an objection; courts and Congress may construe silence as a concession. In effect, executive practice engendered an inefficient equilibrium in which a skewed incentive structure precipitated—and later solidified—Pavlovian signaling practices. Signaling costs might change, but the risk-averse and forward-thinking executive will continue to signal—not because it is efficient, but because the executive has delegitimized silence as an alternative.

Justice Breyer's dissent in *Free Enterprise Fund v. Public Company Accounting Oversight Board*, 130 S.Ct. 3138, 3169 (2010) (see Chapter 8, § 1C) indicates how a president's failure to object to certain provisions of a bill in a signing statement may be construed as tacit approval. The Court struck down statutory provisions that restricted the President in his ability to remove members of the Oversight Board. Justice Breyer contended that the Court should decline to create a separation-of-powers issue when there was apparently no disagreement between Congress and the President at the time of enactment: "The President signed the Act. And, when he did so, he issued a signing statement that critiqued multiple provisions of the Act but did not express any separation-of-powers concerns."

2.   *Should Presidential Signing Statements Be Considered Persuasive of Statutory Meaning?* Reagan Administration Attorney General Edward Meese and some subsequent commentators maintain that presidential signing statements should "count" as evidence of statutory meaning, for the same reasons a committee report or a congressional sponsor's explanation might count. Academic commentators and the ABA have been reluctant to accept the argument that signing statements are authoritative, for the same reasons they are dubious about "subsequent legislative history"—it is unreliable evidence of the expectations of the enacting coalition, and there is too much opportunity for manipulation.[79] If an interpreter is a textualist, she would be suspicious of or uninterested in any such background material, whether originating in the Capitol or the White House. For more contextualist interpreters, problems of reliability are troubling: Congress cannot respond officially to the President's signing statement, whereas a misleading statement by a legislative sponsor can trigger all sorts of counterattacks (amendments to the bill, contrary statements by other Members, and so on). It is probably for these kinds of reasons that federal judges rarely mention presidential signing statements and almost never give them dispositive weight.[80]

On the other hand, for the same reasons that interpreters are usually interested in the views of the congressional sponsors, they might be interested in the views of the President, who effectively sponsors much major legislation and whose veto power (not to mention his status as chief of one of the two major political parties) gives him an important bargaining role in virtually all major legislation.[81] Such views provide useful policy or even linguistic context for understanding the statute, and they can be good evidence of where the political equilibrium lies. While the President might be tempted to negate deals made in Congress, the fact remains that Members can publicly denounce any such interpretation, as they have been doing, with increasing vigor, from the Reagan Administration through the Bush 43 Administration. Because the President

---

[79]   American Bar Association, Task Force on Presidential Signing Statements and the Separation of Powers Doctrine, Report with Recommendations (2006) (rejecting the Bush 43 Administration's aggressive use of signing statements); Marc Garber & Kurt Wimmer, *Presidential Signing Statements as Interpretations of Legislative Intent: An Executive Aggrandizement of Power*, 24 Harv. J. Legis. 363 (1987); William Popkin, *Judicial Use of Presidential Legislative History: A Critique*, 66 Ind. L.J. 699 (1991). See also Trevor Morrison, *Constitutional Avoidance in the Executive Branch*, 106 Colum. L. Rev. 1189 (2006), who argues against executive department reliance on the avoidance canon, which has been a mainstay of controversial presidential signing statements since the Reagan Administration.

[80]   Among the few court of appeals decisions giving weight to signing statements, consider *United States v. Perlaza*, 439 F.3d 1149, 1163 (9th Cir. 2006) (Clinton signing statement confirms suggestion in conference report); *United States v. Gonzales*, 311 F.3d 440, 443 & n.2 (1st Cir. 2002) (similar); *United States v. Story*, 891 F.2d 988, 994 (2d Cir. 1989) (relying on a Reagan signing statement, among other factors, to resolve conflicting interpretations in the House and Senate legislative history).

[81]   Charles Cameron, *Veto Bargaining: Presidents and the Politics of Negative Power* (2000); William Eskridge Jr. & John Ferejohn, *The Article I, Section 7 Game*, 80 Geo. L.J. 523 (1992).

is a repeat player on Capitol Hill, he or she has some incentive not to lie about what deals were made.

Finally, from a more formal perspective, in assessing presidential signing statements it may be useful to retreat to a fundamental issue, whether the bill is ambiguous. If it is, and if the congressional history does not clear up the problem, there may be good reason for the President to state that he or she is signing it based on a certain interpretation of it, at least so long as that interpretation is reasonable. In this circumstance, the President is not violating the text or legislative intent, and the President's good-faith interpretation may be a useful guide to courts and administrative agencies.[82] On the other hand, if the bill, as supplemented by the legislative history, is pretty clear on a point, our constitutional system seems to give the President only two options—to acquiesce (by signing it or by allowing it to go into law without presidential signature) or to veto it—and not the option of attempting to skew it in some other direction. Although Congress may formally override a veto, it has no authoritative way to reject a signing statement (if the statute is already clear).

3.   *Veto Statements.* Courts will sometimes rely on the President's veto statement. If Congress overrides the President's veto, then an interpreter might infer that Congress rejected the President's preferences. See *McDonald v. Santa Fe Trail Transportation Co.*, 427 U.S. 273, 295 & n.26 (1976); *Kennedy v. Mendoza-Martinez*, 372 U.S. 144, 178 & n.33 (1963); *United States v. CIO*, 335 U.S. 106, 138–39 (1948) (Rutledge, J., concurring in the result). If, instead, the bill is modified and enacted with the President's signature, the veto statement may provide a good understanding of the nature of the new bill. See *United States v. Yermian*, 468 U.S. 63, 72–75 (1984). In assessing whether the 1991 Civil Rights Act was retroactive, the Court in *Landgraf* (*Chapter* 6, § 3) considered President Bush's veto of the 1990 version of that legislation as relevant background.

PROBLEM ON PRESIDENTIAL SIGNING STATEMENTS

Problem 7–6. Congressional outrage at media accounts of torture of non-American prisoners by American guards and interrogators led to the enactment, by large margins, of the Detainee Treatment Act of 2005, Pub. L. No. 109–148, Div. A, tit. X (2005). As noted above, the Act sets limits on torture that President Bush resisted on grounds that they interfered with his executive authority to conduct the war on terror. For war-on-terror prisoners held at Guantanamo Bay, the Act also substitutes for habeas corpus a special summary appeals process to the D.C. Circuit. When the Act was passed, in 2005, numerous Guantanamo detainees were already pursuing habeas relief in the federal courts. The question arose whether the Act applied to (and therefore required dismissal of) habeas cases filed by those detainees and pending on the date of enactment.

Section 1005(e) of the DTA amended 28 U.S.C. § 2241 (the federal habeas law) by adding at the end the following:

(e)   Except as provided in section 1005 of the Detainee Treatment Act of 2005, no court, justice, or judge shall have jurisdiction to hear or consider—

(1)   an application for a writ of habeas corpus filed by or on behalf of an alien detained by the Department of Defense at Guantanamo Bay, Cuba; or

---

[82] For a vigorous defense of presidential signing statements as improving the transparency of law enforcement and interpretational debates, see Bradley & Posner, *Presidential Signing Statements.*

(2) any other action against the United States or its agents relating to any aspect of the detention by the Department of Defense of an alien at Guantanamo Bay, Cuba, who—

(A) is currently in military custody; or

(B) has been determined by the United States Court of Appeals for the District of Columbia Circuit in accordance with the procedures set forth in section 1005(e) of the Detainee Treatment Act of 2005 to have been properly detained as an enemy combatant.

Section 1005(h)(1) provides that "this section shall take effect upon the date of the enactment of this Act." Section 1005(h)(2) says: "Paragraphs (2) and (3) of subsection (e) shall apply with respect to any claim whose review is governed by one of such paragraphs and that is pending on or after the date of the enactment of this Act."

The government invoked the canon in favor of applying statutes conferring or ousting jurisdiction immediately, *Landgraf v. USI Film Prods.*, 511 U.S. 244, 274 (1994) (Chapter 5, § 3), while the habeas claimants relied on the presumption against retroactive application of new statutes. *Id.* at 280. The claimants relied on statements by Senator Levin, a sponsor, that the DTA would not apply to pending cases and objected to a proposal by Senator Graham, another sponsor, that would have made § 1005(e)(1) applicable to pending cases. The government responded with statements by Senators Graham and Kyl, a third sponsor, that the Act as passed applied to pending Guantanamo cases.

The government also invoked President Bush's signing statement, which said this: "[T]he executive branch shall construe section 1005 to preclude the Federal courts from exercising subject matter jurisdiction over any existing or future action, including applications for writs of habeas corpus, described in section 1005." See Statement on Signing the Department of Defense, Emergency Supplemental Appropriations to Address Hurricanes in the Gulf of Mexico, and Pandemic Influenza Act, 2006, 41 Weekly Comp. Pres. Doc. 1918 (Dec. 30, 2005).

This issue reached the Supreme Court, where the government argued that federal judges no longer had jurisdiction to adjudicate the Guantanamo habeas claims. What role, if any, should the President's signing statement have played in the Court's interpretation? (How should textualist Justices Scalia and Thomas treat the signing statement? Justices Breyer and Stevens?) In your view, what is the right interpretation? Compare *Hamdan v. Rumsfeld*, 548 U.S. 575–84 (2006), with *id.* at 656–68 (dissenting opinion).

6. Legislative Inaction

What the legislature doesn't do may be as significant as what it does. Recall the dog didn't bark canon: When no one in the legislative discussions says that an important policy is being changed, a court should presume that no big changes are intended. This canon is related to the *canon of continuity* defended by David Shapiro, *Continuity and Change in Statutory Interpretation*, 67 N.Y.U. L. Rev. 921 (1992). Shapiro maintains that the structure of American government suggests a constitutional bias against discontinuity in legal obligations and rights. Thus, in the absence of clear indications to the contrary, statutes should be construed to maintain established rules and practices.

You have already seen plenty of examples of judicial inferences (or not) from legislative inaction, especially in Chapter 7 and this chapter. There are three specific doctrines that relate to Congress's failure to do something, and it is useful to separate them out.[83]

(a) *The Acquiescence Rule.* If Congress is aware of an authoritative agency or judicial interpretation of a statute and doesn't amend the statute, the Court has sometimes presumed that Congress has "acquiesced" in the interpretation's correctness. The acquiescence rule was followed by the Court to reaffirm its own prior interpretations of statutes in *Johnson v. Transportation Agency* (Chapter 1, § 3B) and in *Flood v. Kuhn* (Chapter 6, § 2B). But the acquiescence rule can also support implicit congressional ratification of a uniform line of federal appellate interpretations or in a longstanding agency interpretation. E.g., *Zuni Pub. Sch. Dist. No. 89 v. Dep't of Educ.* (excerpted in Chapter 7, § 3A).

This rule is one that the new textualists find particularly abhorrent. E.g., *Johnson* (Scalia, J., dissenting). Absent "overwhelming evidence of acquiescence," the *Solid Waste* Court announced it is "loathe to replace the plain text and original understanding of a statute" with a new construction. Nonetheless, this doctrine is still invoked if there is concrete evidence Congress was aware of the longstanding interpretation and paid attention to the issue, as in the *FDA Tobacco* Case, where Justice Scalia himself signed onto dozens of pages of legislative history discussion. See also *Zuni Pub. Sch. District.*[84]

(b) *The Reenactment Rule.* If Congress reenacts a statute without making any material changes in its wording, the Court will often presume that Congress intends to incorporate authoritative agency and judicial interpretations of that language into the reenacted statute. The leading Supreme Court statement of this rule is found in *Lorillard v. Pons* (Part C1 of this section), which stated: "Congress is presumed to be aware of an administrative or judicial interpretation of a statute and to adopt that interpretation when it reenacts a statute without change." Like the acquiescence rule, the reenactment rule is much more likely to be invoked if the interpretation is a foundational one—that is, the interpretation is authoritative (namely, a leading Supreme Court case or the decision of the chief agency enforcing the law), settled, and likely to have yielded private and public reliance. See *Jama v. Immigration & Customs Enforcement*, 543 U.S. 345 (2005) (application of reenactment rule inappropriate because prior state of the law not well settled); *Fogerty v. Fantasy, Inc.*, 510 U.S. 517, 527–33 (1994) (same, and contrasting the

---

[83] This account is drawn from James Brudney, *Congressional Commentary on Judicial Interpretations of Statutes: Idle Chatter or Telling Response?*, 93 Mich. L. Rev. 1 (1994); and William Eskridge Jr., *Interpreting Legislative Inaction*, 87 Mich. L. Rev. 67 (1988), which also contains appendices listing cases following or declining to follow these doctrines.

[84] See also *Evans v. United States*, 504 U.S. 255, 269 (1992) (assuming Congress had acquiesced in longstanding and highly visible interpretation of statute in lower courts); *Riverside Bayview* (Conference Committee killed House effort to overrule Corps of Engineers' jurisdiction over "wetlands"); *Heckler v. Day*, 467 U.S. 104 (1984) (congressional hearings on disability benefit delays did not produce legislation to hurry agency along); *Guardians Ass'n v. Civil Serv. Comm'n*, 463 U.S. 582, 593 & n.14 (1983) (opinion of White, J.) (acquiescence in Title VI regulations).

well-settled stature of Creedence Clearwater Revival "as one of the greatest American rock and roll bands of all time").

A dramatic invocation of the reenactment rule came in *Faragher v. City of Boca Raton*, 524 U.S. 775 (1998). The Court ruled that employers can be vicariously liable under Title VII for hostile work environments created or tolerated by supervisors, subject to a reasonableness defense. Justice Souter's opinion for the Court relied on the holding and reasoning in *Meritor Savings Bank FSB v. Vinson*, 477 U.S. 57 (1986), which had greatly elaborated upon the spare language in Title VII that employers cannot "discriminate" because of sex by holding that "hostile environment sexual harassment" was prohibited. Dissenting Justices Thomas and Scalia objected that the Court's opinions were no more than "willful policymaking" in violation of the statute. Justice Souter responded that the holding and reasoning of *Meritor* was binding on the Court not only as a matter of stare decisis, but also because it had been ratified by Congress when it amended Title VII in 1991. See 524 U.S. at 792. Although the 1991 Act overrode a number of Supreme Court interpretations of Title VII, it left *Meritor* intact, which Justice Souter deemed "conspicuous. We thus have to assume that in expanding employers' potential liability under Title VII, Congress relied on our statements in *Meritor* about the limits of employer liability. To disregard those statements now * * * would be not only to disregard *stare decisis* in statutory interpretation, but to substitute our revised judgment about the proper allocation of the costs of harassment for Congress's considered decision on the subject." *Id.* at 804 n.4.

(c) *The Rejected Proposal Rule.* If Congress (in conference committee) or one chamber (on the floor) considers and rejects specific statutory language, the Court has often been reluctant to interpret the statute along lines of the rejected language. The leading case is *Runyon v. McCrary*, 427 U.S. 160 (1976), where the Court reaffirmed a debatable precedent interpreting the Civil Rights Act of 1866, based in large part upon its perception that the Senate in 1971 had rejected attempts to override that interpretation. See also the FDA Tobacco Case.

The *Solid Waste* Court expressed a more skeptical view of this kind of evidence.

" '[F]ailed legislative proposals are "a particularly dangerous ground on which to rest an interpretation of a prior statute.' *Cent. Bank of Denver N.A. v. First Interstate Bank of Denver N.A.*, 511 U.S. 164, 187 (1994). A bill can be proposed for any number of reasons, and it can be rejected for just as many others. The relationship between the actions and inactions of the 95th Congress and the intent of the 92d Congress in passing § 404(a) is also considerably attenuated. Because 'subsequent history is less illuminating than the contemporaneous evidence,' *Hagen v. Utah*, 510 U.S. 399, 420 (1994), respondents face a difficult task in overcoming the plain text and import of § 404(a)."

Consider these various doctrines in connection with the following case, which is excerpted at length in Chapter 6.

BOB JONES UNIVERSITY V. UNITED STATES
Supreme Court of the United States, 1983.
461 U.S. 574, 103 S.Ct. 2017, 76 L.Ed.2d 157.

[Excerpted in Chapter 6, § 2B3]

NOTES ON POST-ENACTMENT ACQUIESCENCE AND "LAW AS EQUILIBRIUM"

1.   *Criticisms of the Acquiescence Doctrine. Bob Jones* is now a leading citation for the acquiescence rule. That rule has, however, long been subject to criticism, see, e.g., Henry Hart, Jr. & Albert Sacks, *The Legal Process* 1313–70 (Eskridge & Frickey eds. 1994) (tent. ed. 1958); John Grabow, *Congressional Silence and the Search for Legislative Intent: A Venture into "Speculative Unrealities,"* 64 B.U. L. Rev. 737 (1984), and several current Justices strongly object to it. Dissenting from the Court's reaffirmation of *Weber* in *Johnson* (see Chapter 1, § 3B), Justice Scalia rejected the majority's invocation of legislative acquiescence. For him, "vindication by congressional inaction is a canard," because congressional inaction has no formal significance under Article I as interpreted in *INS v. Chadha* (see Chapter 8, § 3A), and no functional significance given difficulties in figuring out why Congress did nothing. More recently, the Supreme Court has become much more reluctant to accept legislative acquiescence arguments. See, e.g., *Patterson v. McLean Credit Union* (Chapter 5, § 2), which rejected the dissenting opinion's reliance on legislative inaction (not only the acquiescence rule but also the reenactment and rejected proposal rules) as reason to reaffirm and expand the Court's decision in *Runyon v. McCrary*. Is there any special reason for a skeptic such as Justice Scalia to apply the acquiescence rule in a case like *Bob Jones*, or is this just another "canard"?

Note *Bob Jones'* inconsistent use of congressional inaction. The Court relies on the failure of Congress to overrule the 1971 revenue ruling: Congress, by doing nothing, acquiesced in the agency's action. The Court ignores the failure of Congress to overrule the IRS policy before 1971: that doesn't count, the Court seems to be saying. The Court ignores the repeated failure of Congress to enact statutes penalizing private education discrimination: Congress, by passing statutes which did not cover private schools, nonetheless disapproved of the private action. Is there any good reason to interpret congressional inaction as the Court does?

Justice Rehnquist is critical of the Court's reliance on legislative inaction in *Bob Jones* and, later when he was Chief Justice, in *Solid Waste*. Yet Justice Rehnquist has himself relied upon congressional inaction. See, e.g., *Weinberger v. Rossi*, 456 U.S. 25, 33 (1982) (Rehnquist, J.) (unless Congress says otherwise, Court will presume that it acquiesces in executive agreements). See also *Haig v. Agee*, 453 U.S. 280 (1981) (Burger, C.J.) (absent intent to repudiate executive interpretation of the Passport Act, Congress is presumed to acquiesce in it). Are these foreign-affairs cases more appropriate occasions for relying on legislative inaction than *Bob Jones* is?

2.   *Law as Equilibrium.* In Chapter 6, § 3B3, we suggested that one way to think about law is that it is the result of the equilibrium of institutional forces, rather than the result of formal deduction from first premises. From this perspective, an important issue in *Bob Jones* was how clear the practical equilibrium was in the early 1980s on the question whether the federal government should indirectly support racially

segregated schools through tax preferences. Even if the IRS had taken a bold step a decade earlier, the lower courts had ratified it; if by 1980 the Congress and the executive branch were also settled in their support of that policy as well, then that policy is "law" in a very practical way (none of the three federal branches of government would change it) that should be apparent to such schools. When the Reagan Administration switched positions from that taken by the Nixon, Ford, and Carter Administrations, it was, under this perspective, changing the law, not returning the law to its "true" state, and therefore should have been allowed to do that only with the approval of Congress. The Court in *Bob Jones* recognized this practical reality and stabilized the law around its equilibrium point, leaving the Reagan Administration the option of seeking congressional authorization for reviving tax preferences for segregated schools. Is this a persuasive way to justify *Bob Jones*? You might want to apply a similar idea to the *FDA Tobacco* Case and the Court's recent cutbacks on the Army Corps' wetlands regulations in *Solid Waste* and *Rapanos*.[85]

Even if this explains *Bob Jones*, and even if you find it a good justification for the decision, this perspective leaves the Court a lot of room in which to affect the political balance, especially during periods of divided government when it is particularly hard for Congress to override the Court. An example is *Central Bank of Denver N.A. v. First Interstate Bank of Denver N.A.*, 511 U.S. 164 (1994). Justice Kennedy's majority opinion held that an action could not be brought alleging that defendant aided and abetted a violation of § 10(b) of the Securities Exchange Act of 1934, which prohibits securities fraud. In our judgment, this outcome upset a longstanding equilibrium to the contrary. *All* eleven federal courts of appeals that had considered the question had recognized a cause of action against aiders and abettors. Petitioner had asked the Court to address questions, such as the *mens rea* standard for aider and abettor liability, that also assumed that such a private right of action existed.

The Court *sua sponte* requested the parties to address the question whether the aiding and abetting action existed at all. Justice Kennedy's opinion stressed the plain meaning of § 10(b), which does not mention aiding and abetting liability. In dissent, Justice Stevens argued (1) that the majority had, in effect, engaged in "bait and switch" tactics (our term, not his) by applying the textualist interpretative approach to an old statute adopted by Congress in an era in which courts routinely elaborated upon rights of action, (2) that the majority had rejected a settled interpretation of law in terms of both judicial and administrative construction, which should be the province of Congress, not the Court, and (3) that actions of Congress since 1934 indicated congressional knowledge and approval of the implied right of action. One might add that, in light of this consensus, had a lawyer in the mid-to late–1980s informed Central Bank that it could *not* have been sued as an aider and abettor under § 10(b), that lawyer would have committed malpractice. (Recall that the certiorari petition filed by the lawyers for Central Bank did not even raise the question Justice Kennedy ultimately decided in Central Bank's favor.)

---

[85] *Solid Waste* (2001) and *Rapanos* (2006) were both handed down when the Republican Party controlled the Presidency, the House, and the Senate. After *Rapanos*, the Army Corps, under strong pressure from farmers, ranchers, mining companies, and the like, issued new wetlands regulations that cut back on the prior protections.

PROBLEM ON LEGISLATIVE INACTION AND LAW AS EQUILIBRIUM

Problem 7–7. The Age Discrimination Act of 1967 (ADEA) prohibits age discrimination by employers in language that is identical to the core antidiscrimination provision of Title VII enacted in the 1964 Civil Rights Act. Each makes it unlawful for an employer "to fail or refuse to hire or to discharge any individual, or otherwise to discriminate against any individual with regard to his compensation, terms, conditions, or privileges of employment, because of such individual's" *age* (ADEA) or *race, color, religion, sex, or national origin* (Title VII). For decades, the Court recognized that its interpretations of this Title VII language applied with equal force in the context of age discrimination. See, e.g., *Trans World Airlines, Inc. v. Thurston*, 469 U.S. 111, 121 (1985) (quoting *Lorillard v. Pons*, 434 U.S. 575, 584 (1978)).

In *Price Waterhouse v. Hopkins*, 490 U.S. 228 (1989), the Court construed the Title VII language above to mean that once a plaintiff proves her membership in the protected class played a motivating part in an employment decision, the defendant may avoid liability if it proves by a preponderance of the evidence that it would have made the same decision even without this factor. Justice Kennedy in dissent argued the proper standard was that a member of the Title VII protected class must prove by a preponderance of the evidence that age was the "but-for" cause of the challenged adverse employment action, and that no burden shifts to the employer simply because the plaintiff showed that race or sex was a motivating factor in that decision.

As part of its 1991 Civil Rights Act, Congress overrode a portion of *Price Waterhouse* by adding two provisions to Title VII. One provides that when a plaintiff establishes that membership in the protected class was a motivating factor for any adverse employment practice, this practice is unlawful even though other lawful factors also motivated the practice. The second provision states that if the employer demonstrates it would have made the same decision anyway, the plaintiff may be entitled to declaratory and injunctive relief and attorney's fees but not to reinstatement or back pay. In other words, the 1991 Act changed the "motivating factor" test into an issue of remedy rather than one of liability. Congress made no similar change to the ADEA in the 1991 Civil Rights Act. Indeed Congress did not address the ADEA in substantive terms at all in its 1991 statute amending Title VII in numerous places (see discussion of 1991 Act in Chapter 1, § 3C).

In 2004, Jack Gross filed an ADEA claim in federal district court alleging that he was demoted by his financial services company employer because of his age. The trial court jury instruction applied the *Price Waterhouse* standard: Gross should prevail if he proved that age was a motivating factor, but the employer should prevail if it proved that it would have demoted him regardless of age.

The case comes to the Supreme Court and there are three options for the applicable standard of proof: (1) *apply Price-Waterhouse as the trial court did*; the ADEA language being construed is the same language the Court construed in 1989 and Congress has not changed it; (2) *apply the 1991 Civil Rights Act standard*; Congress clarified the substantive meaning of the contested Title VII language to assure that proof of "a motivating factor" establishes liability, and Congress's clarification should extend to the exact parallel language of the ADEA; (3) *start afresh with the ADEA*; by amending Title VII in 1991 without making similar changes to the ADEA (then or in the ensuing 13 years), Congress uncoupled the two laws. The Court is free to reinstate the *Price-Waterhouse* majority reasoning, and is also free or to adopt Justice Kennedy's "but-for cause" dissenting position if it believes the ADEA should be construed this way.

How would you rule? See *Gross v. FBL Fin. Servs.*, 557 U.S. 167 (2009).

C. INTERPRETATION IN LIGHT OF OTHER STATUTES

"Statutory interpretation is a holistic endeavor," so that a provision "that may seem ambiguous in isolation is often clarified by" the greater consistency of one interpretation with "the rest of the law." *United Sav. Ass'n of Tex. v. Timbers of Inwood Forest Assocs.*, 484 U.S. 365, 371 (1988). See also *W. Va. Univ. Hosp. v. Casey* (Chapter 7, § 1C), (interpreting one statute that authorized prevailing parties to recover attorney's fees by examining the text of many other such statutes.) There are several reasons an interpreter might consider other statutes, and each is associated with a statutory interpretation canon or doctrine:

• *the in pari materia rule:* other statutes might use the same terminology or address the same issue as the statute being interpreted (Subpart 1);

• *modeled or borrowed statute rule*: another statute might have been the template from which the statute in issue was designed (Subpart 2),

• *presumption against implied repeals*: there might be a later statute possibly changing the implications of the statute being interpreted (Subpart 3).

Note that the first two precepts are weaker versions of the rule that a word used several times in a statute is strongly presumed to have the same meaning every time it is used. See § 1C3 of this chapter and the cases discussed therein. The third precept is more complex, for it raises the possibility that statutes enacted at different times will be inconsistent with one another. How should interpreters figure out what law to apply when different statutes press in different directions? This conundrum vexed Judge Norris's two opinions in *Montana Wilderness, supra*. Subpart 3 will explore several different ways to reconcile apparently clashing statutes.

1.   Similar Statutes (The *In Pari Materia* Rule)

STATUTORY PREFACE TO ADEA JURY TRIAL CASE

Age Discrimination in Employment Act of 1967, 29 U.S.C. § 621 *et seq.* (as of 1978)

Section 626. * * *

(b) The provisions of this Act shall be enforced in accordance with the powers, remedies, and procedures provided in sections 11(b), 16 (except for subsection (a) thereof), and 17 of the Fair Labor Standards Act of 1938, as amended (28 U.S.C. § 211(b), 216, 217), and subsection (c) of this section. * * * Amounts owing to a person as a result of a violation of this Act shall be deemed to be unpaid minimum wages or unpaid overtime compensation for purposes of sections 16 and 17 of the Fair Labor Standards Act of 1938, as amended (28 U.S.C. § 216, 217): *Provided,* That liquidated damages shall be payable only in cases of willful violations of this

Act. In any action brought to enforce this Act the court shall have jurisdiction to grant such legal or equitable relief as may be appropriate to effectuate the purposes of this Act, including without limitation judgments compelling employment, reinstatement or promotion, or enforcing the liability for amounts deemed to be unpaid minimum wages or unpaid overtime compensation under this section.

(c) Any person aggrieved may bring a civil action in any court of competent jurisdiction for such legal or equitable relief as will effectuate the purposes of this Act: *Provided*, That the right of any person to bring such action shall terminate upon the commencement of an action by the Secretary to enforce the right of such employee under this Act.

Title VII of the Civil Rights Act of 1964, 42 U.S.C. § 2000e *et seq.* (as of 1978)

Section 2000e–5.

(g) If the court finds that the respondent has intentionally engaged in or is intentionally engaging in an unlawful employment practice charged in the complaint, the court may enjoin the respondent from engaging in such unlawful employment practice, and order such affirmative action as may be appropriate, which may include, but is not limited to, reinstatement or hiring of employees, with or without back pay (payable by the employer, employment agency, or labor organization, as the case may be, responsible for the unlawful employment practice), or any other equitable relief as the court deems appropriate. * * *

LORILLARD V. PONS

Supreme Court of the United States, 1978.
434 U.S. 575, 98 S.Ct. 868, 55 L.Ed.2d 40.

MR. JUSTICE MARSHALL delivered the opinion of the Court.

This case presents the question whether there is a right to a jury trial in private civil actions for lost wages under the Age Discrimination in Employment Act of 1967 (ADEA or Act), 81 Stat. 602, as amended, 88 Stat. 74, 29 U.S.C. § 621 *et seq.* (1970 ed. and Supp. V). * * *

[I] The ADEA broadly prohibits arbitrary discrimination in the workplace based on age. Although the ADEA contains no provision expressly granting a right to jury trial, respondent nonetheless contends that the structure of the Act demonstrates a congressional intent to grant such a right. Alternatively, she argues that the Seventh Amendment requires that in a private action for lost wages under the ADEA, the parties must be given the option of having the case heard by a jury. We turn first to the statutory question since " 'it is a cardinal principle that this Court will first ascertain whether a construction of the statute is fairly possible by which the [constitutional] question may be avoided.' " Because we find the statutory issue dispositive, we need not address the constitutional issue.

The enforcement scheme for the statute is complex—the product of considerable attention during the legislative debates preceding passage of the Act. Several alternative proposals were considered by Congress. The Administration submitted a bill, modeled after §§ 10(c), (e) of the National Labor Relations Act, 29

U.S.C. §§ 160(c), (e), which would have granted power to the Secretary of Labor to issue cease-and-desist orders enforceable in the courts of appeals, but would not have granted a private right of action to aggrieved individuals, S. 830, H.R. 4221, 90th Cong., 1st Sess. (1967). Senator Javits introduced an alternative proposal to make discrimination based on age unlawful under the Fair Labor Standards Act (FLSA), 29 U.S.C. § 201 *et seq.*; the normal enforcement provisions of the FLSA, 29 U.S.C. § 216 *et seq.*, (1970 ed. and Supp. V), then would have been applicable, permitting suits by either the Secretary of Labor or the injured individual, S. 788, 90th Cong., 1st Sess. (1967). A third alternative that was considered would have adopted the statutory pattern of Title VII of the Civil Rights Act of 1964 and utilized the Equal Employment Opportunity Commission.

The bill that was ultimately enacted is something of a hybrid, reflecting, on the one hand, Congress' desire to use an existing statutory scheme and a bureaucracy with which employers and employees would be familiar and, on the other hand, its dissatisfaction with some elements of each of the preexisting schemes. Pursuant to § 7(b) of the Act, 29 U.S.C. § 626(b), violations of the ADEA generally are to be treated as violations of the FLSA. "Amounts owing * * * as a result of a violation" of the ADEA are to be treated as "unpaid minimum wages or unpaid overtime compensation" under the FLSA and the rights created by the ADEA are to be "enforced in accordance with the powers, remedies and procedures" of specified sections of the FLSA.

Following the model of the FLSA, the ADEA establishes two primary enforcement mechanisms. Under the FLSA provisions incorporated in § 7(b) of the ADEA, 29 U.S.C. § 626(b), the Secretary of Labor may bring suit on behalf of an aggrieved individual for injunctive and monetary relief. 29 U.S.C. §§ 216(c), 217 (1970 ed. and Supp. V). The incorporated FLSA provisions together with § 7(c) of the ADEA, 29 U.S.C. § 626(c), in addition, authorize private civil actions for "such legal or equitable relief as will effectuate the purposes of" the ADEA. Although not required by the FLSA, prior to the initiation of any ADEA action, an individual must give notice to the Secretary of Labor of his intention to sue in order that the Secretary can attempt to eliminate the alleged unlawful practice through informal methods. § 7(d), 29 U.S.C. § 626(d). After allowing the Secretary 60 days to conciliate the alleged unlawful practice, the individual may file suit. The right of the individual to sue on his own terminates, however, if the Secretary commences an action on his behalf. § 7(c), 29 U.S.C. § 626(c).

[II] Looking first to the procedural provisions of the statute, we find a significant indication of Congress' intent in its directive that the ADEA be enforced in accordance with the "powers, remedies, and *procedures*" of the FLSA. § 7(b), 29 U.S.C. § 626(b) (emphasis added). Long before Congress enacted the ADEA, it was well established that there was a right to a jury trial in private actions pursuant to the FLSA. Indeed, every court to consider the issue had so held. Congress is presumed to be aware of an administrative or judicial interpretation of a statute and to adopt that interpretation when it reenacts a statute without change. So too, where, as here, Congress adopts a new law incorporating sections of a prior law, Congress normally can be presumed to have had knowledge of the interpretation given to the incorporated law, at least insofar as it affects the new statute.

That presumption is particularly appropriate here since, in enacting the ADEA, Congress exhibited both a detailed knowledge of the FLSA provisions and their judicial interpretation and a willingness to depart from those provisions regarded as undesirable or inappropriate for incorporation. For example, in construing the enforcement sections of the FLSA, the courts had consistently declared that injunctive relief was not available in suits by private individuals but only in suits by the Secretary. Congress made plain its decision to follow a different course in the ADEA by expressly permitting "such * * * equitable relief as may be appropriate to effectuate the purposes of [the ADEA] including without limitation judgments compelling employment, reinstatement or promotion" "in *any* action brought to enforce" the Act. § 7(b), 29 U.S.C. § 626(b) (emphasis added). Similarly, while incorporating into the ADEA the FLSA provisions authorizing awards of liquidated damages, Congress altered the circumstances under which such awards would be available in ADEA actions by mandating that such damages be awarded only where the violation of the ADEA is willful.[8] Finally, Congress expressly declined to incorporate into the ADEA the criminal penalties established for violations of the FLSA.

This selectivity that Congress exhibited in incorporating provisions and in modifying certain FLSA practices strongly suggests that but for those changes Congress expressly made, it intended to incorporate fully the remedies and procedures of the FLSA. Senator Javits, one of the floor managers of the bill, so indicated in describing the enforcement section which became part of the Act: "The enforcement techniques provided by [the ADEA] are directly analogous to those available under the Fair Labor Standards Act; in fact [the ADEA] incorporates by reference, to the greatest extent possible, the provisions of the [FLSA]." 113 Cong. Rec. 31254 (1967).[10] And by directing that actions for lost wages under the ADEA be treated as actions for unpaid minimum wages or overtime compensation under the FLSA, § 7(b), 29 U.S.C. § 626(b), Congress dictated that the jury trial right then available to enforce that FLSA liability would also be available in private actions under the ADEA.

This inference is buttressed by an examination of the language Congress chose to describe the available remedies under the ADEA. Section 7(b), 29 U.S.C. § 626(b), empowers a court to grant "*legal* or equitable relief" and § 7(c), 29 U.S.C.

[8] By its terms, 29 U.S.C. § 216(b) requires that liquidated damages be awarded as a matter of right for violations of the FLSA. However, in response to its dissatisfaction with that judicial interpretation of the provision, Congress enacted the Portal-to-Portal Pay Act of 1947, 61 Stat. 84, which, *inter alia*, grants courts authority to deny or limit liquidated damages where the "employer shows to the satisfaction of the court that the act or omission giving rise to such action was in good faith and that he had reasonable grounds for believing that his act or omission was not a violation of" the FLSA, § 11, 29 U.S.C. § 260 (1970 ed., Supp. V). Although § 7(e) of the ADEA, 29 U.S.C. § 626(e), expressly incorporates §§ 6 and 10 of the Portal-to-Portal Pay Act, 29 U.S.C. §§ 255 and 259 (1970 ed. and Supp. V), the ADEA does not make any reference to § 11, 29 U.S.C. § 260 (1970 ed., Supp. V).

[10] Senator Javits made the only specific reference in the legislative history to a jury trial. He said:

"The whole test is somewhat like the test in an accident case—did the person use reasonable care. A jury will answer yes or no. The question here is: Was the individual discriminated against solely because of his age? The alleged discrimination must be proved and the burden of proof is upon the one who would assert that that was actually the case." 113 Cong. Rec. 31255 (1967).

It is difficult to tell whether Senator Javits was referring to the issue in ADEA cases or in accident cases when he said the jury will say yes or no.

§ 626(c), authorizes individuals to bring actions for "*legal* or equitable relief" (emphases added). The word "legal" is a term of art: In cases in which legal relief is available and legal rights are determined, the Seventh Amendment provides a right to jury trial. "[W]here words are employed in a statute which had at the time a well-known meaning at common law or in the law of this country they are presumed to have been used in that sense unless the context compels to the contrary." We can infer, therefore, that by providing specifically for "legal" relief, Congress knew the significance of the term "legal," and intended that there would be a jury trial on demand to "enforc[e] * * * liability for amounts deemed to be unpaid minimum wages or unpaid overtime compensation." § 7(b), 29 U.S.C. § 626(b).

Petitioner strives to find a contrary congressional intent by comparing the ADEA with Title VII of the Civil Rights Act of 1964, 42 U.S.C. § 2000e *et seq.* (1970 ed. and Supp. V), which petitioner maintains does not provide for jury trials. We, of course, intimate no view as to whether a jury trial is available under Title VII as a matter of either statutory or constitutional right. However, after examining the provisions of Title VII, we find petitioner's argument by analogy to Title VII unavailing. There are important similarities between the two statutes, to be sure, both in their aims—the elimination of discrimination from the workplace—and in their substantive prohibitions. In fact, the prohibitions of the ADEA were derived *in haec verba* from Title VII.[12] But in deciding whether a statutory right to jury trial exists, it is the remedial and procedural provisions of the two laws that are crucial and there we find significant differences.

Looking first to the statutory language defining the relief available, we note that Congress specifically provided for both "legal or equitable relief" in the ADEA, but did not authorize "legal" relief in so many words under Title VII. Compare § 7(b), 29 U.S.C. § 626(b), with 42 U.S.C. § 2000e–5(g) (1970 ed., Supp. V). Similarly, the ADEA incorporates the FLSA provision that employers "shall be liable" for amounts deemed unpaid minimum wages or overtime compensation, while under Title VII, the availability of backpay is a matter of equitable discretion. Finally, rather than adopting the procedures of Title VII for ADEA actions, Congress rejected that course in favor of incorporating the FLSA procedures even while adopting Title VII's substantive prohibitions. Thus, even if petitioner is correct that Congress did not intend there to be jury trials under Title VII, that fact sheds no light on congressional intent under the ADEA. Petitioner's reliance on Title VII, therefore, is misplaced. * * * [*Affirmed.*]

NOTES ON LORILLARD *AND* REASONING *FROM STATUTES* IN PARI MATERIA

1. *Reasoning from One Statute to Another: What If There Are Several Statutory Analogies?* Justice Marshall in *Lorillard* relies on the interpretational structure of previously enacted statutes to justify his interpretation. Why does he consider this

---

[12] Title VII with respect to race, color, religion, sex, or national origin, and the ADEA with respect to age make it unlawful for an employer "to fail or refuse to hire or to discharge any individual," or otherwise to "discriminate against any individual with respect to his compensation, terms, conditions, or privileges of employment," on any of those bases. [Citing provisions of each statute.]

persuasive? Because Congress really and truly "intended" to incorporate all prior interpretations of similarly worded provisions into the newer statute? Because the other interpretations somehow represent "wise" public policy? Because the interpretational history of these other statutes represents a reasoned policy context which ought to affect the application of a related statute, so as to give greater coherence to the law? See *Moragne v. States Marine Lines* (Chapter 5, § 1B).

Even if justified in general, this approach has its limitations. One is that there may be more than one statute in pari materia, and the statutes may have been interpreted differently. E.g., *Ledbetter v. Goodyear Tire & Rubber Corp.*, 550 U.S. 618 (2007), discussed in Note 2. Or there may be several "similar" statutes, but none quite the same as the statute being interpreted. Thus, in *Lorillard*, the Supreme Court rejected the proposed analogy with Title VII. Are the Court's reasons persuasive? Why should an alleged victim of age discrimination get a jury trial (ADEA), when an alleged victim of race discrimination (Title VII) apparently does not get one? Is there an underlying purposive explanation for why Congress in the 1960s may have intended age discrimination lawsuits to be tried to juries but not race or sex discrimination actions?[86]

In 1974, Congress amended the ADEA to permit age discrimination lawsuits against the federal government. The enforcement provision says: "Any person aggrieved may bring a civil action in any Federal district court of competent jurisdiction for such legal or equitable relief as will effectuate the purposes of this Act." ADEA § 15(c), 29 U.S.C. § 633a(c). The Supreme Court held that § 15(c), unlike § 7, affords no jury trial right, finding the analogy to Title VII closer than the analogy to the FLSA. *Lehman v. Nakshian*, 453 U.S. 156 (1981). Is this consistent with *Lorillard*, upon which the four dissenting Justices relied? The majority responded that *Lorillard* is distinguishable (how?), the federal government is subject to jury trials only if it explicitly permits them (why?), and Congress in 1978 amended § 7(c) explicitly to allow ADEA jury trials but made no comparable amendment to § 15(c) (so what?).

2.   *Different Statutes, Different Policies.* A second limitation on reasoning from one statute to another is that the new statute may embody policies or compromises subtly different from those in the similar statutes—if for no other reason than the different political context of the later statute. For example, the Supreme Court has interpreted Title VI of the Civil Rights Act of 1964 (prohibiting discrimination "under any program or activity receiving Federal financial assistance") to reach only instances of intentional discrimination. See *Guardians Ass'n v. Civ. Serv. Comm'n of NYC*, 463 U.S. 582 (1983). Yet the Court in *Alexander v. Choate*, 469 U.S. 287, 294–99 (1985), was unwilling to limit § 504 of the Rehabilitation Act of 1973 (prohibiting discrimination or exclusion of any "qualified handicapped individual" "under any program or activity receiving Federal financial assistance") to instances of intentional discrimination. In dictum, the Court suggested that by 1973 national policy was more concerned with "disparate impact" discrimination than with the "intentional" discrimination that had been a focal point in 1964. *Id.* at 294–95 n.11. Ergo, the Court's interpretation of Title VI was not a helpful guide in its interpretation of § 504. Does this temporal dimension (evolving policy) help explain the result in *Lorillard*? See also *Webb v. Bd. of Ed. of Dyer Cnty.*, 471 U.S. 234 (1985) (rejecting analogy of Title VII attorney's fees provision as guide for interpreting 42 U.S.C. § 1988, because of different statutory schemes).

---

[86] Congress eliminated this disparity when it provided for jury trials in Title VII cases in the Civil Rights Act of 1991. See *Landgraf v. USI Film* (Chapter 5, § 3).

In *Ledbetter v. Goodyear Tire & Rubber Co.*, 550 U.S. 618 (2007), the Supreme Court strictly enforced the limitations period imposed by Title VII on plaintiffs bringing pay discrimination complaints to the EEOC. Under the Court's approach, an employee subjected to intentional race or sex discrimination in pay has to file a complaint with the EEOC soon after the illegal pay differential first shows up (and before many plaintiffs are even aware of the discrimination, because they do not know how much everyone else is paid). Ledbetter argued that the Court has allowed equitable tolling of Equal Pay Act claims, a statutory analogy the Court rejected because EPA claims do not have to be brought before the EEOC first. The different statutory schemes required different interpretations of the limitations provisions. Indeed, the Court found a better analogy in the NLRA, also enforced by an agency. The Court had previously enforced that policy with similar strictness as it applied in *Ledbetter*.

3.   *The Possibility of Compromise.* A third limitation on reasoning from one statute to another is that it may undermine deliberative legislative compromises. Consider *Ridgway v. Ridgway*, 454 U.S. 46 (1981). Richard Ridgway, a career sergeant in the U.S. Army, was granted a divorce from his wife April in 1977. The state divorce decree required Richard to keep in force then-existing life insurance policies for the benefit of the three children. Richard remarried and changed the beneficiary to his second wife, Donna, contrary to the divorce decree. When he died, both April and Donna claimed the proceeds to the life insurance—April relying on state law and Donna relying on the Servicemen's Group Life Insurance Act of 1965, 79 Stat. 880, codified as amended at 38 U.S.C. § 765 *et seq.* (1982). The Act provides comprehensive life insurance for members of the armed services, including Richard, and stipulates that the service person can designate the beneficiary, *id.* § 770(a), and that payment of insurance proceeds is not subject to attachment or "any legal or equitable process whatever." *Id.* § 770(g). The Supreme Court held that § 770(a) & (g) preempts state property decrees for support and alimony pursuant to a divorce. The Act's policy that the statutory benefits actually reach the designated beneficiary and that the insurance be operated on a national level clashes with state family law and supersedes it. See also *Hisquierdo v. Hisquierdo*, 439 U.S. 572, 584 (1979).

Three Justices dissented. Justice Stevens' dissenting opinion relied heavily on the equitable argument that Richard's designation of Donna as his beneficiary violated his moral duty to support his children. Surely Congress would not have intended such a scandalous result, argued the dissenters. (What canine metaphor is apt here?) The majority in *Ridgway* responded that "[a] result of this kind, of course, may be avoided if Congress chooses to avoid it," but Congress has not so chosen. Compare *Rose v. Rose*, 481 U.S. 619 (1987).

See also *Cartledge v. Miller*, 457 F. Supp. 1146 (S.D.N.Y. 1978), in which the district court construed the broad and seemingly unambiguous anti-assignment provision of ERISA (the Employee Retirement Income Security Act of 1974) to create an implied exception for family support orders issued pursuant to state law. Judge Weinfeld invoked "an overall congressional purpose not to interfere with the States' power to enforce family support obligations, [which] may be gleaned from judicial interpretation of exemption provisions in other federal statutes" including the Social Security Act, the Veterans Benefits Act, and the Railway Retirement Act. In 1984, Congress amended ERISA to add an explicit statutory exception to the anti-assignment provisions for "qualified domestic orders." Does this codification support or undermine

Judge Weinfeld's position? If such an issue arose today, would a more textualist court reason that judges should simply apply the anti-assignment provision as written and leave it to Congress to create exceptions?

    4. *The Challenge of Interpreting Legislative Overrides.* When Congress overrides a Supreme Court interpretation, how should the Court apply the override text to other similarly worded provisions in analogous statutes that have not been amended? If the analogous provisions have been construed *in pari materia* in past decisions, does Congress's failure to amend all such provisions justify departure from that approach, on the theory that there is now a meaningful variation between texts? Deborah Widiss criticizes the Court's determination, in *Gross v. FBL Financial Services, Inc.*, 557 U.S. 167 (2009), to reject *in pari materia* considerations in an employment discrimination setting where these considerations had been regularly applied in the past. Deborah Widiss, *Undermining Congressional Overrides: The Hydra Problem in Statutory Interpretation*, 90 Tex. L. Rev. 859 (2012). Widiss argues in favor of applying the *in pari materia* canon to similar employment statutes:

> [T]he practice of interpreting identical or similar language in statutes *in pari materia* to bear consistent meanings will often have the independent virtue of advancing the values served by precedent in a true common law context. That is, it will often promote fairness—in the sense of treating similar issues alike—to interpret distinct statutes that address related subjects (e.g., age discrimination and race discrimination) consistently. The practice will also typically promote efficiency and predictability. This is particularly essential because the Supreme Court and state supreme courts rule on any given statute relatively infrequently. For example, it has been almost fifty years since Title VII was enacted, and many other federal and state statutes have since been enacted that use similar language to prohibit discrimination in employment. In that half century, the Supreme Court has directly addressed the standard of causation that should be applied to claims alleging a mix of legitimate and illegitimate motives just twice: *Price Waterhouse* (interpreting Title VII) and *Gross* (interpreting the ADEA). If lower courts lack an authoritative construction of the statute actually at issue in a given case, they naturally rely on authoritative interpretations of analogous language in related statutes.

Widiss contends that the 1991 Amendments to Title VII should have been interpreted to apply to similar statutes, including the Age Discrimination in Employment Act text at issue in *Gross*. She argues that there should be "a rebuttable presumption that enactment of an override calls for the (re)interpretation of the preexisting language in the statute amended—and analogous provisions in related statutes—consistent with the meaning endorsed by Congress, so long as the preexisting text can reasonably bear that meaning."

2.   The Borrowed Statute Rule

    Reasoning from statutes in pari materia (similar statutes) generally has greater force when the statutes are all in the same jurisdiction. Indeed, sometimes, as *Lorillard* indicates (though *Gross* does not), such statutes have a familial relationship because the drafting of a newer statute (e.g., the ADEA) was modeled on existing statutes in the same jurisdiction (e.g., the FLSA, Title VII). As *Lorillard* exemplifies, courts routinely assume that, unless there are strong indications to the contrary, the newer statute should be interpreted consistently with the older statutes upon which it was modeled.

Borrowed statutes are those adapted by one jurisdiction from another jurisdiction. For example, if West Virginia were to enact a pension regulation statute, it might "borrow" the language used in ERISA's anti-alienation and assignment provision or that used in a similar statute of another state. See Frank Horack, Jr., *The Common Law of Legislation*, 23 Iowa L. Rev. 41 (1937) (one legislature will copy a successful prior statute from another jurisdiction, following a process Horack calls "stare de statute"). The issues of interpretation for borrowed statutes are subtly different from those concerning modeled statutes, in large part because the policies followed in one jurisdiction may be different from those followed in the original jurisdiction.

Smith v. Bayer Corp.
131 S.Ct. 2368 (2011).

The Supreme Court held that a federal court could not enjoin a plaintiff from litigating a putative class action in state court after a federal district court rejected a previous attempt to certify the class in federal court. Although West Virginia's rule on class certification was nearly textually identical to Federal Rule of Civil Procedure 23, the Court held that it was improper to enjoin the West Virginia lawsuit because West Virginia courts interpreted the state's class certification rule differently from federal courts and thus the state court lawsuit presented a different legal issue. **Justice Kagan** wrote for the unanimous Court.

"The Court of Appeals and Smith offer us two competing ways of deciding whether the West Virginia and Federal Rules differ, but we think the right path lies somewhere in the middle. The Eighth Circuit relied almost exclusively on the near-identity of the two Rules' texts. That was the right place to start, but not to end. Federal and state courts, after all, can and do apply identically worded procedural provisions in widely varying ways. If a State's procedural provision tracks the language of a Federal Rule, but a state court interprets that provision in a manner federal courts have not, then the state court is using a different standard and thus deciding a different issue. See 18 Wright & Miller § 4417, at 454 (stating that preclusion is 'inappropriate' when 'different legal standards . . . masquerad[e] behind similar legal labels'). At the other extreme, Smith contends that the source of law is all that matters: a different sovereign must in each and every case 'have the opportunity, if it chooses, to construe its procedural rule differently.' Brief for Petitioners 22 (quoting ALI, Principles of the Law, Aggregate Litigation § 2.11, Reporters' Notes, *cmt. b*, p. 181 (2010)). But if state courts have made crystal clear that they follow the same approach as the federal court applied, we see no need to ignore that determination; in that event, the issues in the two cases would indeed be the same. So a federal court considering whether the relitigation exception applies should examine whether state law parallels its federal counterpart. But as suggested earlier, * * * the federal court must resolve any uncertainty on that score by leaving the question of preclusion to the state courts.

"Under this approach, the West Virginia Supreme Court has gone some way toward resolving the matter before us by declaring its independence from federal courts' interpretation of the Federal Rules—and particularly of Rule 23. In *In re West Virginia*

Rezulin Litigation, 585 S.E.2d 52 (2003) *(In re Rezulin)*, the West Virginia high court considered a plaintiff's motion to certify a class—coincidentally enough, in a suit about an allegedly defective pharmaceutical product. The court made a point of complaining about the parties' and lower court's near-exclusive reliance on federal cases about Federal Rule 23 to decide the certification question. Such cases, the court cautioned, 'may be persuasive, but [they are] not binding or controlling.' *Id.* at 61. And lest anyone mistake the import of this message, the court went on: The aim of this rule is to avoid having our legal analysis of our Rules 'amount to nothing more than Pavlovian responses to federal decisional law.' *Ibid.* (italics omitted). Of course, the state courts might still have adopted an approach to their Rule 23 that tracked the analysis the federal court used in McCollins' case. But absent clear evidence that the state courts had done so, we could not conclude that they would interpret their Rule in the same way. And if that is so, we could not tell whether the certification issues in the state and federal courts were the same. That uncertainty would preclude an injunction."

The Court concluded that federal courts should be influenced "if state courts have made crystal clear that they follow the same approach as the federal court applied." What should constitute a "crystal clear" statement from a state court that it follows federal precedent when interpreting an identical state statute? In *In Re Rezulin*, the West Virginia Supreme Court had clearly indicated that it *does not* necessarily follow federal precedent. What if, instead, a state court has consistently followed federal precedent when interpreting its state statute but never affirmatively declared that it would always do so?

3.   Statutory Clashes—The Rule Against Implied Repeals

Not only similar statutes in the same jurisdiction and statutes copied from other jurisdictions, but also subsequent statutes in the same jurisdiction may be sources of guidance concerning the appropriate interpretation of a statute. The second opinion in *Montana Wilderness* (§ 3B5 of this chapter) is an example of how a similar, subsequently enacted statute may sometimes shed light on a prior statutory provision. In *Babbitt v. Sweet Home* (at end of this chapter), the Court was persuaded to read a provision of the Endangered Species Act of 1973 broadly, in part to assure its consistency with a 1982 amendment to the law.

Both opinions in *Montana Wilderness* point to a clash between the Alaska Lands Act (as applied nationwide in the second opinion) and the Wilderness Act. How do judges resolve apparently conflicting statutes? Obviously, if the more recent statute expressly provides that it controls, the issue is easy. Similarly, if the newer statute contains a savings clause, which states that it does not alter existing law, the older statute controls. Unfortunately, most of the time the more recent statute says nothing on this question. Typically, courts do their best to reconcile the statutes, based on the presumption of whole-code coherence. As the next case demonstrates, there is a longstanding canon in this area, which disfavors *implied repeals*.[87]

---

[87]   For an excellent analysis of this canon, see Karen Petroski, Comment, *Retheorizing the Presumption Against Implied Repeals*, 92 Cal. L. Rev. 487 (2004).

MORTON V. MANCARI

Supreme Court of the United States, 1974.
417 U.S. 535, 94 S.Ct. 2474, 41 L.Ed.2d 290.

MR. JUSTICE BLACKMUN delivered the opinion of the Court.

The Indian Reorganization Act of 1934, also known as the Wheeler-Howard Act, 48 Stat. 984, 25 U.S.C. § 461 *et seq.*, accords an employment preference for qualified Indians in the Bureau of Indian Affairs (BIA or Bureau). Appellees, non-Indian BIA employees, challenged this preference as contrary to the anti-discrimination provisions of the Equal Employment Opportunity Act of 1972, 86 Stat. 103, 42 U.S.C. § 2000e *et seq.* (1970 ed., Supp. II), and as violative of the Due Process Clause of the Fifth Amendment. * * *

[I]   Section 12 of the Indian Reorganization Act, 48 Stat. 986, 25 U.S.C. § 472, provides:

> "The Secretary of the Interior is directed to establish standards of health, age, character, experience, knowledge, and ability for Indians who may be appointed, without regard to civil-service laws, to the various positions maintained, now or hereafter, by the Indian Office, in the administration of functions or services affecting any Indian tribe. Such qualified Indians shall hereafter have the preference to appointment to vacancies in any such positions."

In June 1972, pursuant to this provision, the Commissioner of Indian Affairs, with the approval of the Secretary of the Interior, issued a directive (Personnel Management Letter No. 72–12) stating that the BIA's policy would be to grant a preference to qualified Indians not only, as before, in the initial hiring stage, but also in the situation where an Indian and a non-Indian, both already employed by the BIA, were competing for a promotion within the Bureau. The record indicates that this policy was implemented immediately.

Shortly thereafter, appellees, who are non-Indian employees of the BIA at Albuquerque, instituted this class action, on behalf of themselves and other non-Indian employees similarly situated, in the United States District Court for the District of New Mexico, claiming that the "so-called 'Indian Preference Statutes'" were repealed by the 1972 Equal Employment Opportunity Act and deprived them of rights to property without due process of law, in violation of the Fifth Amendment. * * *

After a short trial focusing primarily on how the new policy, in fact, has been implemented, the District Court concluded that the Indian preference was implicitly repealed by § 11 of the Equal Employment Opportunity Act of 1972, Pub. L. 92–261, 86 Stat. 111, 42 U.S.C. § 2000e–16(a) (1970 ed., Supp. II), proscribing discrimination in most federal employment on the basis of race.[6] Having found that

---

[6] Section 2000e–16(a) reads:

"All personnel actions affecting employees or applicants for employment (except with regard to aliens employed outside the limits of the United States) in military departments as defined in section 102 of Title 5, in executive agencies (other than the General Accounting Office) as defined in section 105 of Title 5 (including employees and applicants for employment who are paid from nonappropriated funds), in the United States Postal Service and the Postal Rate Commission, in

Congress repealed the preference, it was unnecessary for the District Court to pass on its constitutionality. The court permanently enjoined appellants "from implementing any policy in the Bureau of Indian Affairs which would hire, promote, or reassign any person in preference to another solely for the reason that such person is an Indian." * * *

[II] The federal policy of according some hiring preference to Indians in the Indian service dates at least as far back as 1834. Since that time, Congress repeatedly has enacted various preferences of the general type here at issue.[8] The purpose of these preferences, as variously expressed in the legislative history, has been to give Indians a greater participation in their own self-government; to further the Government's trust obligation toward the Indian tribes;[9] and to reduce the negative effect of having non-Indians administer matters that affect Indian tribal life.

The preference directly at issue here was enacted as an important part of the sweeping Indian Reorganization Act of 1934. The overriding purpose of that particular Act was to establish machinery whereby Indian tribes would be able to assume a greater degree of self-government, both politically and economically. Congress was seeking to modify the then-existing situation whereby the primarily non-Indian-staffed BIA had plenary control, for all practical purposes, over the lives and destinies of the federally recognized Indian tribes. Initial congressional proposals would have diminished substantially the role of the BIA by turning over to federally chartered self-governing Indian communities many of the functions normally performed by the Bureau.[13] Committee sentiment, however, ran against such a radical change in the role of the BIA. The solution ultimately adopted was to strengthen tribal government while continuing the active role of the BIA, with the understanding that the Bureau would be more responsive to the interests of the people it was created to serve.

One of the primary means by which self-government would be fostered and the Bureau made more responsive was to increase the participation of tribal Indians in the BIA operations. In order to achieve this end, it was recognized that some kind

---

those units of the Government of the District of Columbia having positions in the competitive service, and in those units of the legislative and judicial branches of the Federal Government having positions in the competitive service, and in the Library of Congress shall be made free from any discrimination based on race, color, religion, sex, or national origin."

[8] Act of May 17, 1882, § 6, 22 Stat. 88, and Act of July 4, 1884, § 6, 23 Stat. 97, 25 U.S.C. § 46 (employment of clerical, mechanical, and other help on reservations and about agencies); Act of Aug. 15, 1894, § 10, 28 Stat. 313, 25 U.S.C. § 44 (employment of herders, teamsters, and laborers, "and where practicable in all other employments" in the Indian service); Act of June 7, 1897, § 1, 30 Stat. 83, 25 U.S.C. § 274 (employment as matrons, farmers, and industrial teachers in Indian schools); Act of June 25, 1910, § 23, 36 Stat. 861, 25 U.S.C. § 47 (general preference as to Indian labor and products of Indian industry).

[9] A letter, contained in the House Report to the 1934 Act, from President F. D. Roosevelt to Congressman Howard states:

"We can and should, without further delay, extend to the Indian the fundamental rights of political liberty and local self-government and the opportunities of education and economic assistance that they require in order to attain a wholesome American life. This is but the obligation of honor of a powerful nation toward a people living among us and dependent upon our protection." H.R. Rep. No. 1804, 73d Cong., 2d Sess., 8 (1934).

[13] Hearings on H.R. 7902, Readjustment of Indian Affairs, 73d Cong., 2d Sess., 1–7 (1934) (hereafter House Hearings).

of preference and exemption from otherwise prevailing civil service requirements was necessary.[16] Congressman Howard, the House sponsor, expressed the need for the preference:

> "The Indians have not only been thus deprived of civic rights and powers, but they have been largely deprived of the opportunity to enter the more important positions in the service of the very bureau which manages their affairs. Theoretically, the Indians have the right to qualify for the Federal civil service. In actual practice there has been no adequate program of training to qualify Indians to compete in these examinations, especially for technical and higher positions; and even if there were such training, the Indians would have to compete under existing law, on equal terms with multitudes of white applicants. * * * The various services on the Indian reservations are actually local rather than Federal services and are comparable to local municipal and county services, since they are dealing with purely local Indian problems. It should be possible for Indians with the requisite vocational and professional training to enter the service of their own people without the necessity of competing with white applicants for these positions. This bill permits them to do so." 78 Cong. Rec. 11729 (1934).

Congress was well aware that the proposed preference would result in employment disadvantages within the BIA for non-Indians.[17] Not only was this displacement unavoidable if room were to be made for Indians, but it was explicitly determined that gradual replacement of non-Indians with Indians within the Bureau was a desirable feature of the entire program for self-government.[18] Since 1934, the BIA has implemented the preference with a fair degree of success. The percentage of Indians employed in the Bureau rose from 34% in 1934 to 57% in 1972. This reversed the former downward trend, see n.16, *supra*, and was due, clearly, to the presence of the 1934 Act. The Commissioner's extension of the preference in 1972 to promotions within the BIA was designed to bring more Indians into positions of responsibility and, in that regard, appears to be a logical extension of the congressional intent.

[III] It is against this background that we encounter the first issue in the present case: whether the Indian preference was repealed by the Equal

---

[16] "The bill admits qualified Indians to the position [*sic*] in their own service.

"Thirty-four years ago, in 1900, the number of Indians holding regular positions in the Indian Service, in proportion to the total of positions, was greater than it is today."The reason primarily is found in the application of the generalized civil service to the Indian Service, and the consequent exclusion of Indians from their own jobs." House Hearings 19 (memorandum dated Feb. 19, 1934, submitted by Commissioner Collier to the Senate and House Committees on Indian Affairs).

[17] Congressman Carter, an opponent of the bill, placed in the Congressional Record the following observation by Commissioner Collier at the Committee hearings:

"[W]e must not blind ourselves to the fact that the effect of this bill if worked out would unquestionably be to replace white employees by Indian employees. I do not know how fast, but ultimately it ought to go very far indeed." 78 Cong. Rec. 11737 (1934).

[18] "It should be possible for Indians to enter the service of their own people without running the gauntlet of competition with whites for these positions. Indian progress and ambition will be enormously strengthened as soon as we adopt the principle that the Indian Service shall gradually become, in fact as well as in name, an Indian service predominantly in the hands of educated and competent Indians." *Id.* at 11731 (remarks of Cong. Howard).

Employment Opportunity Act of 1972. Title VII of the Civil Rights Act of 1964 was the first major piece of federal legislation prohibiting discrimination in *private* employment on the basis of "race, color, religion, sex, or national origin." 42 U.S.C. § 2000e–2(a). Significantly, §§ 701(b) and 703(i) of that Act explicitly exempted from its coverage the preferential employment of Indians by Indian tribes or by industries located on or near Indian reservations. 42 U.S.C. §§ 2000e(b) and 2000e–2(i).[19] This exemption reveals a clear congressional recognition, within the framework of Title VII, of the unique legal status of tribal and reservation-based activities. The Senate sponsor, Senator Humphrey, stated on the floor by way of explanation:

> "This exemption is consistent with the Federal Government's policy of encouraging Indian employment and with the special legal position of Indians." 110 Cong. Rec. 12723 (1964).[20]

The 1964 Act did not specifically outlaw employment discrimination by the Federal Government. Yet the mechanism for enforcing longstanding Executive Orders forbidding Government discrimination had proved ineffective for the most part. In order to remedy this, Congress, by the 1972 Act, amended the 1964 Act and proscribed discrimination in most areas of federal employment. See n.6, *supra*. In general, it may be said that the substantive anti-discrimination law embraced in Title VII was carried over and applied to the Federal Government. As stated in the House Report:

> "To correct this entrenched discrimination in the Federal service, it is necessary to insure the effective application of uniform, fair and strongly enforced policies. The present law and the proposed statute do not permit industry and labor organizations to be the judges of their own conduct in the area of employment discrimination. There is no reason why government agencies should not be treated similarly. * * * " H.R. Rep. No. 92–238, on H.R. 1746, at 24–25 (1971).

Nowhere in the legislative history of the 1972 Act, however, is there any mention of Indian preference.

Appellees assert * * * that since the 1972 Act proscribed racial discrimination in Government employment, the Act necessarily, albeit *sub silentio*, repealed the provision of the 1934 Act that called for the preference in the BIA of one racial group, Indians, over non-Indians:

> "When a conflict such as in this case, is present, the most recent law or Act should apply and the conflicting Preferences passed some 39 years earlier should be impliedly repealed." Brief for Appellees 7.

---

[19] Section 701(b) excludes "an Indian Tribe" from the Act's definition of "employer." Section 703(i) states:

"Nothing contained in this subchapter shall apply to any business or enterprise on or near an Indian reservation with respect to any publicly announced employment practice of such business or enterprise under which a preferential treatment is given to any individual because he is an Indian living on or near a reservation."

[20] Senator Mundt supported these exemptions on the Senate floor by claiming that they would allow Indians "to benefit from Indian preference programs now in operation or later to be instituted." 110 Cong. Rec. 13702 (1964).

We disagree. For several reasons we conclude that Congress did not intend to repeal the Indian preference and that the District Court erred in holding that it was repealed.

First: There are the above-mentioned affirmative provisions in the 1964 Act excluding coverage of tribal employment and of preferential treatment by a business or enterprise on or near a reservation. These 1964 exemptions as to private employment indicate Congress' recognition of the longstanding federal policy of providing a unique legal status to Indians in matters concerning tribal or "on or near" reservation employment. The exemptions reveal a clear congressional sentiment that an Indian preference in the narrow context of tribal or reservation-related employment did not constitute racial discrimination of the type otherwise proscribed. In extending the general anti-discrimination machinery to federal employment in 1972, Congress in no way modified these private employment preferences built into the 1964 Act, and they are still in effect. It would be anomalous to conclude that Congress intended to eliminate the longstanding statutory preferences in BIA employment, as being racially discriminatory, at the very same time it was reaffirming the right of tribal and reservation-related private employers to provide Indian preference. Appellees' assertion that Congress implicitly repealed the preference as racially discriminatory, while retaining the 1964 preferences, attributes to Congress irrationality and arbitrariness, an attribution we do not share.

Second: Three months after Congress passed the 1972 amendments, it enacted two *new* Indian preference laws. These were part of the Education Amendments of 1972, 86 Stat. 235, 20 U.S.C. §§ 887c(a) and (d), and § 1119a (1970 ed., Supp. II). The new laws explicitly require that Indians be given preference in Government programs for training teachers of Indian children. It is improbable, to say the least, that the same Congress which affirmatively approved and enacted these additional and similar Indian preferences was, at the same time, condemning the BIA preference as racially discriminatory. In the total absence of any manifestation of supportive intent, we are loathe to imply this improbable result.

Third: Indian preferences, for many years, have been treated as exceptions to Executive Orders forbidding Government employment discrimination. The 1972 extension of the Civil Rights Act to Government employment is in large part merely a codification of prior anti-discrimination Executive Orders that had proved ineffective because of inadequate enforcement machinery. There certainly was no indication that the substantive proscription against discrimination was intended to be any broader than that which previously existed. By codifying the existing anti-discrimination provisions, and by providing enforcement machinery for them, there is no reason to presume that Congress affirmatively intended to erase the preferences that previously had co-existed with broad anti-discrimination provisions in Executive Orders.

Fourth: Appellees encounter head-on the "cardinal rule * * * that repeals by implication are not favored." *Posadas v. Nat'l City Bank*, 296 U.S. 497, 503 (1936). They and the District Court read the congressional silence as effectuating a repeal by implication. There is nothing in the legislative history, however, that indicates affirmatively any congressional intent to repeal the 1934 preference. Indeed, as explained above, there is ample independent evidence that the legislative intent was to the contrary.

This is a prototypical case where an adjudication of repeal by implication is not appropriate. The preference is a longstanding, important component of the Government's Indian program. The anti-discrimination provision, aimed at alleviating minority discrimination in employment, obviously is designed to deal with an entirely different and, indeed, opposite problem. Any perceived conflict is thus more apparent than real.

In the absence of some affirmative showing of an intention to repeal, the only permissible justification for a repeal by implication is when the earlier and later statutes are irreconcilable. *Georgia v. Pennsylvania R. Co.*, 324 U.S. 439, 456–457 (1945). Clearly, this is not the case here. A provision aimed at furthering Indian self-government by according an employment preference within the BIA for qualified members of the governed group can readily coexist with a general rule prohibiting employment discrimination on the basis of race. Any other conclusion can be reached only by formalistic reasoning that ignores both the history and purposes of the preference and the unique legal relationship between the Federal Government and tribal Indians.

Furthermore, the Indian preference statute is a specific provision applying to a very specific situation. The 1972 Act, on the other hand, is of general application. Where there is no clear intention otherwise, a specific statute will not be controlled or nullified by a general one, regardless of the priority of enactment. See, *e.g.*, *Bulova Watch Co. v. United States*, 365 U.S. 753, 758 (1961); *Rodgers v. United States*, 185 U.S. 83, 87–89 (1902).

The courts are not at liberty to pick and choose among congressional enactments, and when two statutes are capable of co-existence, it is the duty of the courts, absent a clearly expressed congressional intention to the contrary, to regard each as effective. "When there are two acts upon the same subject, the rule is to give effect to both if possible * * *. The intention of the legislature to repeal 'must be clear and manifest.'" *United States v. Borden Co.*, 308 U.S. 188, 198 (1939). In light of the factors indicating no repeal, we simply cannot conclude that Congress consciously abandoned its policy of furthering Indian self-government when it passed the 1972 amendments.

We therefore hold that the District Court erred in ruling that the Indian preference was repealed by the 1972 Act. * * *

NOTES ON MANCARI AND INTERPRETATION IN LIGHT OF SUBSEQUENT STATUTES

1. *Repeals by Implication. Mancari* introduces you to a canon of statutory interpretation not mentioned in § 1 of this chapter: repeals by implication are not favored.[88] This canon is subject to the criticism that it naively assumes legislative

---

[88] See also *Hamdan v. Rumsfeld*, 548 U.S. 557, 594–95 (2006); *Granholm v. Heald*, 544 U.S. 460 (2005); *Cnty. of Yakima v. Confederated Tribes & Bands of Yakima Indian Nation*, 502 U.S. 251 (1992); *St. Martin*

omniscience—legislators and their staff members do not search the statute books to ensure that new legislation will interfere minimally with established legislation. And why should they? Shouldn't new legislative policy be applied to full effect, liberally supplanting outdated prior statutes? On the other hand, the canon against implied repeals might be defended, "not only to avoid misconstruction of the law effecting the putative repeal, but also to preserve the intent of later Congresses that have already enacted laws that are dependent on the continued applicability of the law whose implicit repeal is in question." *Smith v. Robinson*, 468 U.S. 992, 1026 (1984) (Brennan, J., dissenting).

As Judge Norris recognized, *Mancari* is in tension with the Ninth Circuit's ultimate position in the Checkerboard Case: the Alaska Lands Act's access provision was found to repeal huge chunks of wilderness protection acts passed by Congress in the 1960s and 1970s. Why isn't the Checkerboard Case a much better case for *refusing* to allow repeals by implication?

2.   *Applying the Canon in* Mancari. Figure out the best arguments against Justice Blackmun's reasons why no repeal by implication occurred in *Mancari*. (Hint: As to the first, Congress showed itself able to exempt Indians from the operation of antidiscrimination laws in 1964; the absence of any express exemption in the 1972 Act, then, gives a strong *expressio unius* argument to plaintiffs. In addition, sticking to the first argument made by Justice Blackmun, isn't it quite different to exempt an Indian tribe or a private employer from the coverage of an employment discrimination statute, on the one hand, and to exempt the federal government, on the other?) We think that the best arguments against Justice Blackmun's first three points are strong ones. If we are right, then the "repeal by implication" canon is crucial to the outcome of the case. As note 1 above suggests, that canon has some theoretical problems when it is stated broadly, as saying that repeals of *statutes* by implication are disfavored. Can the Blackmun result be saved by narrowing the canon to "repeals of *longstanding policies* are disfavored, especially where there is no collateral evidence (in other statutes, regulations, executive orders, authoritative committee reports, and the like) supporting the notion that the longstanding policy has been repudiated"? Does narrowing the canon in this way alleviate the general objections to it suggested in note 1 as well?

3.   *Policy Behind Overcoming the Presumption.* Unlike the presumption against federal preemption of state law, the *Mancari* presumption against implied repeals is one that is rarely overcome. The presumption has usually been litigated, and occasionally rebutted, in antitrust cases. Antitrust defendants often argue that post-1890 regulatory statutes create implicit exceptions to the Sherman Act. They generally lose with such arguments but have at times prevailed. E.g., *United States v. Nat'l Ass'n of Sec. Dealers*, 422 U.S. 694 (1975). Outside of the antitrust context, it is almost unheard of for federal judges to declare that a recent federal law has implicitly repealed a previous one. One reason why courts may overcome the presumption involves a perceived duty to harmonize the law when two statutes are capable of co-existence; judges will usually strain to reconcile federal statutes seemingly at odds. Should we be concerned that such efforts at reconciliation amount to "judicial legislation"? Compare Judge Norris's effort to reconcile his interpretation of the Alaska Lands Act with the Wilderness Act in the published opinion in the Checkerboard Case.

Evangelical Lutheran Church v. South Dakota, 451 U.S. 772, 788 (1981); *Watt v. Alaska*, 451 U.S. 259 (1981); *Radzanower v. Touche Ross & Co.*, 426 U.S. 148, 154 (1976).

4. *Repeal of Treaties by Implication.* Treaties, like statutes, are the law of the land under the Supremacy Clause, U.S. Const. Art. VI, and the Supreme Court has stated that "[a] treaty," like a statute, "will not be deemed to have been abrogated or modified by a later statute unless such purpose on the part of Congress has been clearly expressed." *Cook v. United States*, 288 U.S. 102, 120 (1933); see *Weinberger v. Rossi*, 456 U.S. 25 (1982). Consider the following problem. The United States in 1934 ratified the Warsaw Convention, which sets forth uniform rules governing air transportation. Article 22 sets a limit on carrier liability for lost cargo; the liability is expressed in terms of gold, a uniform international standard of value when the Convention was drafted in the 1920s. The United States suspended convertibility of the dollar for gold in 1971 and in 1978 passed a statute implementing an international agreement creating a new regime for international monetary cooperation. The CAB, charged with implementing the Warsaw Convention in the U.S., set the liability limits in 1978 at $9.07 per pound of lost cargo—the last figure it had used under the gold conversion approach before the 1978 statute. The Supreme Court in *TWA v. Franklin Mint Corp.*, 466 U.S. 243 (1984), rejected the Second Circuit's determination that the Warsaw Convention's liability limits were unenforceable as implicitly nullified by the 1978 statute, based upon the presumption against implied repeals. The Court noted that the presumption is potentially stronger in the case of treaties, because they usually have provisions requiring the U.S. to notify the other country (or countries) party to the treaty if the U.S. is withdrawing from it.

PROBLEM ON THE RULE AGAINST IMPLIED REPEALS

Problem 7–8. The 2000 census caused Mississippi to lose one congressional seat. The state legislature failed to pass a new redistricting plan after the decennial census results were published in 2001. A number of state residents filed suit in Mississippi state court, seeking a redistricting plan for the 2002 congressional elections. Article I, § 4, cl. 1, of the Constitution provides that the "Times, Places and Manner of holding Elections for Senators and Representatives, shall be prescribed in each State by the Legislature thereof. . . ." It reserves to Congress, however, the power "at any time by Law [to] make or alter such Regulations, except as to the Places of chusing Senators." Pursuant to this authority, Congress in 1929 enacted the current statutory scheme governing apportionment of the House of Representatives. 2 U.S.C. §§ 2a(a), (b). In 1941, Congress added to those provisions a subsection addressing what is to be done pending redistricting:

> "Until a State is redistricted in the manner provided by the law thereof after any apportionment, the Representatives to which such State is entitled under such apportionment shall be elected in the following manner: * * * (5) if there is a decrease in the number of Representatives and the number of districts in such State exceeds such decreased number of Representatives, they shall be elected from the State at large." § 2a(c).

In 1967, 26 years after § 2a(c) was enacted, Congress adopted § 2c, which provides, as relevant here:

> "In each State entitled in the Ninety-first Congress or in any subsequent Congress thereafter to more than one Representative under an apportionment made pursuant to the provisions of section 2a(a) of this title, there shall be established by law a number of districts equal to the number of

Representatives to which such State is so entitled, and Representatives shall be elected only from districts so established, no district to elect more than one Representative. . . ."

There is a clear tension between these two provisions. Section 2c apparently requires States entitled to more than one Representative to elect their Representatives from single-member districts, rather than from the State at large. Section 2a(c)(5) seems to require at-large elections in certain situations, such as where Mississippi, by reason of the 2000 census, lost a congressional seat.

One way to reconcile the two provisions is by interpreting the introductory phrase of § 2a(c) ("Until a State is redistricted in the manner provided by the law thereof after any apportionment"), and the phrase "established by law" in § 2c to refer exclusively to *legislative* redistricting—so that § 2c tells the legislatures what to do (single-member districting) and § 2a(c) provides what will happen *absent* legislative action—in the present cases, the mandating of at-large elections.

The clause in § 2c "there shall be established by law a number of districts equal to the number of Representatives to which such State is so entitled" could be construed so that the phrase "by law" refers only to legislative action. But its more common meaning encompasses judicial decisions as well. In addition, the limited role that a narrow construction would assign to § 2c (governing legislative apportionment but not judicial apportionment) is contradicted by the historical context of § 2c's enactment. When Congress adopted § 2c in 1967, the immediate issue was precisely the involvement of the courts in fashioning electoral plans. The Voting Rights Act of 1965 had recently been enacted, assigning to the federal courts jurisdiction to involve themselves in elections. In addition, the Court's decisions in a series of one-person, one-vote cases had ushered in a new era in which federal courts were overseeing efforts by badly malapportioned States to conform their congressional electoral districts to the constitutionally required one-person, one-vote standards. In a world in which the role of federal courts in redistricting disputes had been transformed from spectating to directing, there was a risk that judges forced to fashion remedies would simply order at-large elections.

Assuming that in enacting 2 U.S.C. § 2c, Congress mandated that States are to provide for the election of their Representatives from single-member districts, and that this mandate applies equally to courts remedying a state legislature's failure to redistrict constitutionally, the key remaining question is what to make of § 2a(c)? Representatives cannot be "elected only from districts," § 2c, while being elected "at large," § 2a(c). Some lower courts confronted with this conflict have concluded that § 2c repeals § 2a(c) by implication. Yet the Supreme Court has repeatedly stated that absent "a clearly expressed congressional intention," *Morton v. Mancari*, "repeals by implication are not favored." An implied repeal will only be found where provisions in two statutes are in "irreconcilable conflict," or where the latter act covers the whole subject of the earlier one and "is clearly intended as a substitute." What is the better answer: that § 2c was a substitute for § 2a(c), or that § 2a(c) continues to apply in this setting? See *Branch v. Smith*, 538 U.S. 254 (2003).

REVIEW CASE FOR DOCTRINES OF INTERPRETATION

Now that you have studied a full range of interpretive resources, we offer the case below as an unusually rich example of how those resources can be marshaled by two Justices operating at the top of their respective games. *Sweet Home* involves judicial review of an agency rule interpreting a statutory provision, and federal courts typically approach review of agency interpretations with a certain degree of deference (the topic of agency deference is addressed at length in chapter 9). In this instance, however, Justice Stevens for the majority and Justice Scalia in dissent engage in what effectively amounts to de novo review; each invokes a range of arguments based on word meaning, various canons, and appeals to legislative history and purpose. For this reason, we believe the decision provides an excellent opportunity for you to review many of the issues raised in this long chapter.

STATUTORY PREFACE TO THE SWEET HOME CASE

Endangered Species Act of 1973, 16 U.S.C. § 1531 *et seq.*

Section 1532.   Definitions.

(19) The term "take" means to harass, harm, pursue, hunt, shoot, wound, kill, trap, capture, or collect, or to attempt to engage in any such conduct.

Section 1536.   Interagency Cooperation

(a) * * * **(2)** Each Federal agency shall, in consultation with and with the assistance of the Secretary, insure that any action authorized, funded, or carried out by such agency * * * is not likely to jeopardize the continued existence of any endangered species or threatened species or result in the destruction or adverse modification of habitat of such species which is determined by the Secretary * * * to be critical, * * *. In fulfilling the requirements of this paragraph each agency shall use the best scientific and commercial data available.

Section 1538.   Prohibited Acts

(a) Generally

(1) Except as provided in sections 1535(g)(2) and 1529 of this title, with respect to any endangered species of fish or wildlife listed pursuant to section 1533 of this title it is unlawful for any person subject to the jurisdiction of the United States to—* * *

(B) take any such species within the United States or the territorial sea of the United States;

Section 1539.   Exceptions

(a) Permits.

(1) The Secretary may permit, under such terms and conditions as he shall prescribe—* * *

(B) any taking otherwise prohibited by section 1538(a)(1)(B) of this title if such taking is incidental to, and not the purpose of, the carrying out of an otherwise lawful activity.

(2)(A)   No permit may be issued by the Secretary authorizing any taking referred to in paragraph (1)(B) unless the applicant therefor submits to the Secretary a conservation plan that specifies—

(i) the impact which will likely result from such taking;

(ii) what steps the applicant will take to minimize and mitigate such impacts, and the funding that will be available to implement such steps;

(iii) what alternative actions to such taking the applicant considered and the reasons why such alternatives are not being utilized; and

(iv) such other measures that the Secretary may require as being necessary or appropriate for purposes of the plan. * * *

Section 1540.   Penalties and Enforcement

(b) Criminal violations

(1) Any person who knowingly violates any provision of this chapter, of any permit or certificate issued hereunder, or of any regulation issued in order to implement * * * shall, upon conviction, be fined not more than $50,000 or imprisoned for not more than one year, or both. * * *

(e) enforcement

* * * (4)

(B) All guns, traps, nets, and other equipment, vessels, vehicles, aircraft, and other means of transportation used to aid the taking, possessing, selling, purchasing, offering for sale or purchase, transporting, delivering, receiving, carrying, shipping, exporting, or importing of any fish or wildlife or plants in violation of this chapter, any regulation made pursuant thereto, or any permit or certificate issued thereunder shall be subject to forfeiture to the United States upon conviction of a criminal violation pursuant to subsection (b)(1) of this section.

BABBITT V. SWEET HOME CHAPTER OF COMMUNITIES FOR A GREAT OREGON

Supreme Court of the United States, 1995.
515 U.S. 687, 115 S.Ct. 2407, 132 L.Ed.2d 597.

JUSTICE STEVENS delivered the opinion of the Court.

The Endangered Species Act of 1973 (ESA or Act), 87 Stat. 884, 16 U.S.C. § 1531 (1988 ed. and Supp. V), contains a variety of protections designed to save from extinction species that the Secretary of the Interior designates as endangered or threatened. Section 9 of the Act makes it unlawful for any person to "take" any endangered or threatened species. The Secretary has promulgated a regulation that defines the statute's prohibition on takings to include "significant habitat modification or degradation where it actually kills or injures wildlife." This case presents the question whether the Secretary exceeded his authority under the Act by promulgating that regulation.

Section 9(a)(1) of the Act provides the following protection for endangered species:

> Except as provided in sections 1535(g)(2) and 1539 of this title, with respect to any endangered species of fish or wildlife listed pursuant to section 1533 of this title it is unlawful for any person subject to the jurisdiction of the United States to—
>
> . . .
>
> (B) take any such species within the United States or the territorial sea of the United States. [16 U.S.C. § 1538(a)(1).]

Section 3(19) of the Act defines the statutory term "take":

> The term "take" means to harass, harm, pursue, hunt, shoot, wound, kill, trap, capture, or collect, or to attempt to engage in any such conduct. [16 U.S.C. § 1532(19).]

The Act does not further define the terms it uses to define "take." The Interior Department regulations that implement the statute, however, define the statutory term "harm":

> *Harm* in the definition of "take" in the Act means an act which actually kills or injures wildlife. Such act may include significant habitat modification or degradation where it actually kills or injures wildlife by significantly impairing essential behavioral patterns, including breeding, feeding, or sheltering. [50 CFR § 17.3 (1994).]

This regulation has been in place since 1975.

A limitation on the § 9 "take" prohibition appears in § 10(a)(1)(B) of the Act, which Congress added by amendment in 1982. That section authorizes the Secretary to grant a permit for any taking otherwise prohibited by § 9(a)(1)(B) "if such taking is incidental to, and not the purpose of, the carrying out of an otherwise lawful activity." 16 U.S.C. § 1539(a)(1)(B).

In addition to the prohibition on takings, the Act provides several other protections for endangered species. Section 4, 16 U.S.C. § 1533, commands the Secretary to identify species of fish or wildlife that are in danger of extinction and to publish from time to time lists of all species he determines to be endangered or threatened. Section 5, 16 U.S.C. § 1534, authorizes the Secretary, in cooperation with the States, see § 1535, to acquire land to aid in preserving such species. Section 7 requires federal agencies to ensure that none of their activities, including the granting of licenses and permits, will jeopardize the continued existence of endangered species "or result in the destruction or adverse modification of habitat of such species which is determined by the Secretary . . . to be critical." 16 U.S.C. § 1536(a)(2).

[A group of small landowners, logging companies, and families dependent on the forest products industries and organizations that represent their interests brought this action to challenge the Secretary's definition of *harm* to include habitat modification and degradation. They specifically objected to the application of the regulation to protect the red-cockaded woodpecker and the spotted owl by prohibiting changes in their natural habitat that would have the effect of injuring or killing those animals. The court of appeals agreed with respondents' challenge, but the Supreme Court reversed.]

The text of the Act provides three reasons for concluding that the Secretary's interpretation is reasonable. First, an ordinary understanding of the word "harm" supports it. The dictionary definition of the verb form of "harm" is "to cause hurt or damage to: injure." Webster's Third New International Dictionary 1034 (1966). In the context of the ESA, that definition naturally encompasses habitat modification that results in actual injury or death to members of an endangered or threatened species.

Respondents argue that the Secretary should have limited the purview of "harm" to direct applications of force against protected species, but the dictionary definition does not include the word "directly" or suggest in any way that only direct or willful action that leads to injury constitutes "harm." Moreover, unless the statutory term "harm" encompasses indirect as well as direct injuries, the word has no meaning that does not duplicate the meaning of other words that § 3 uses to define "take." A reluctance to treat statutory terms as surplusage supports the reasonableness of the Secretary's interpretation.

Second, the broad purpose of the ESA supports the Secretary's decision to extend protection against activities that cause the precise harms Congress enacted the statute to avoid. In *TVA v. Hill*, 437 U.S. 153 (1978) [Chapter 7, § 2C], we described the Act as "the most comprehensive legislation for the preservation of endangered species ever enacted by any nation." Whereas predecessor statutes enacted in 1966 and 1969 had not contained any sweeping prohibition against the taking of endangered species except on federal lands, the 1973 Act applied to all land in the United States and to the Nation's territorial seas. As stated in § 2 of the Act, among its central purposes is "to provide a means whereby the ecosystems upon which endangered species and threatened species depend may be conserved. . . ."

In *Hill*, we construed § 7 as precluding the completion of the Tellico Dam because of its predicted impact on the survival of the snail darter. Both our holding and the language in our opinion stressed the importance of the statutory policy. "The plain intent of Congress in enacting this statute," we recognized, "was to halt and reverse the trend toward species extinction, whatever the cost. This is reflected not only in the stated policies of the Act, but in literally every section of the statute." Although the § 9 "take" prohibition was not at issue in *Hill*, we took note of that prohibition, placing particular emphasis on the Secretary's inclusion of habitat modification in his definition of "harm." In light of that provision for habitat protection, we could "not understand how TVA intends to operate Tellico Dam without 'harming' the snail darter." Congress' intent to provide comprehensive protection for endangered and threatened species supports the permissibility of the Secretary's "harm" regulation. * * *

Third, the fact that Congress in 1982 authorized the Secretary to issue permits for takings that § 9(a)(1)(B) would otherwise prohibit, "if such taking is incidental to, and not the purpose of, the carrying out of an otherwise lawful activity," 16 U.S.C. § 1539(a)(1)(B), strongly suggests that Congress understood § 9(a)(1)(B) to prohibit indirect as well as deliberate takings. The permit process requires the applicant to prepare a "conservation plan" that specifies how he intends to "minimize and mitigate" the "impact" of his activity on endangered and threatened species, 16 U.S.C. § 1539(a)(2)(A), making clear that Congress had in mind foreseeable rather than merely accidental effects on listed species. No one could seriously request an "incidental" take permit to avert § 9 liability for direct, deliberate action against a member of an endangered or threatened species, but respondents would read "harm" so narrowly that the permit procedure would have little more than that absurd purpose. "When Congress acts to amend a statute, we presume it intends its amendment to have real and substantial effect." Congress' addition of the § 10 permit provision supports the Secretary's conclusion that activities not intended to harm an endangered species, such as habitat modification, may constitute unlawful takings under the ESA unless the Secretary permits them.

[The court of appeals had come to a contrary conclusion on the basis of the *noscitur a sociis* canon: the surrounding words—such as pursue, hunt, shoot—connoted application of force directed at a particular animal. But other words, such as harass, do not so connote, and the lower court's construction would effectively write *harm* out of the statute entirely.]

We need not decide whether the statutory definition of "take" compels the Secretary's interpretation of "harm," because our conclusions that Congress did not unambiguously manifest its intent to adopt respondents' view and that the Secretary's interpretation is reasonable suffice to decide this case. See generally *Chevron, U.S.A., Inc. v. Nat. Res. Defense Council* [Chapter 9, § 1]. The latitude the ESA gives the Secretary in enforcing the statute, together with the degree of regulatory expertise necessary to its enforcement, establishes that we owe some degree of deference to the Secretary's reasonable interpretation. See Breyer, *Judicial Review of Questions of Law and Policy*, 38 Admin. L. Rev. 363, 373 (1986). [Justice Stevens also rejected application of the rule of lenity. Although there is a separate criminal sanction for "knowing" violations of the ESA, the Court has never applied the rule of lenity to review agency rules implementing a civil statute that has parallel criminal sanctions.]

Our conclusion that the Secretary's definition of "harm" rests on a permissible construction of the ESA gains further support from the legislative history of the statute. The Committee Reports accompanying the bills that became the ESA do not specifically discuss the meaning of "harm," but they make clear that Congress intended "take" to apply broadly to cover indirect as well as purposeful actions. The Senate Report stressed that " "[t]ake' is defined . . . in the broadest possible manner to include every conceivable way in which a person can 'take' or attempt to 'take' any fish or wildlife." S. Rep. No. 93–307, at 7 (1973). The House Report stated that "the broadest possible terms" were used to define restrictions on takings. H.R. Rep. No. 93–412, at 15 (1973). The House Report underscored the breadth of the "take" definition by noting that it included "harassment, *whether intentional or not.*" *Id.* at 11 (emphasis added). The Report explained that the definition "would allow, for example, the Secretary to regulate or prohibit the activities of birdwatchers where the effect of those activities might disturb the birds and make it difficult for them to hatch or raise their young." *Ibid.* * * *

The definition of "take" that originally appeared in S. 1983 differed from the definition as ultimately enacted in [this] significant respect: It included "the destruction, modification, or curtailment of [the] habitat or range" of fish and wildlife. Respondents make much of the fact that the Commerce Committee removed this phrase from the "take" definition before S. 1983 went to the floor. See 119 Cong. Rec. 25663 (1973). We do not find that fact especially significant. The legislative materials contain no indication why the habitat protection provision was deleted. That provision differed greatly from the regulation at issue today. Most notably, the habitat protection in S. 1983 would have applied far more broadly than the regulation does because it made adverse habitat modification a categorical violation of the "take" prohibition, unbounded by the regulation's limitation to habitat modifications that actually kill or injure wildlife. The S. 1983 language also failed to qualify "modification" with the regulation's limiting adjective "significant." We do not believe the Senate's unelaborated disavowal of the provision in S. 1983 undermines the reasonableness of the more moderate habitat protection in the Secretary's "harm" regulation. [In footnote 19, Justice Stevens rejected the argument that statements by Senate and House sponsors supported the idea that the § 5 land acquisition provision and not § 9 was expected to be the ESA's remedy for habitat modification.]

The history of the 1982 amendment that gave the Secretary authority to grant permits for "incidental" takings provides further support for his reading of the Act. The House Report expressly states that "[b]y use of the word 'incidental' the Committee intends to cover situations in which it is known that a taking will occur if the other activity is engaged in but such taking is incidental to, and not the purpose of, the activity." H.R. Rep. No. 97–567, p. 31 (1982). This reference to the foreseeability of incidental takings undermines respondents' argument that the 1982 amendment covered only accidental killings of endangered and threatened animals that might occur in the course of hunting or trapping other animals. Indeed, Congress had habitat modification directly in mind: Both the Senate Report and the House Conference Report identified as the model for the permit process a cooperative state-federal response to a case in California where a development project threatened incidental harm to a species of endangered butterfly by modification of its habitat. See S. Rep. No. 97–418, at 10 (1982); H.R. Conf. Rep. No. 97–835, at 30–32 (1982). Thus, Congress in 1982 focused squarely on the aspect of the "harm" regulation at issue in this litigation. Congress' implementation of a permit program is consistent with the Secretary's interpretation of the term "harm." * * *

JUSTICE SCALIA, with whom THE CHIEF JUSTICE [REHNQUIST] and JUSTICE THOMAS join, dissenting.

I think it unmistakably clear that the legislation at issue here (1) forbade the hunting and killing of endangered animals, and (2) provided federal lands and federal funds for the acquisition of private lands, to preserve the habitat of endangered animals. The Court's holding that the hunting and killing prohibition incidentally preserves habitat on private lands imposes unfairness to the point of financial ruin—not just upon the rich, but upon the simplest farmer who finds his land conscripted to national zoological use. I respectfully dissent.

[Justice Scalia objected to three features of the regulation, which, as he saw it, (1) failed to consider whether death or injury to wildlife is an intentional or even foreseeable effect of a habitat modification; (2) covered omissions as well as acts; and (3) considered injuries to future as well as present animal populations, and not just specific animals.] *None* of these three features of the regulation can be found in the statutory provisions supposed to authorize it. The term "harm" in § 1532(19) has no legal force of its own. An indictment or civil complaint that charged the defendant with "harming" an animal protected under the Act would be dismissed as defective, for the only *operative* term in the statute is to "take." If "take" were not elsewhere defined in the Act, none could dispute what it means, for the term is as old as the law itself. To "take," when applied to wild animals, means to reduce those animals, by killing or capturing, to human control. [Citing dictionaries, cases, and Blackstone.] This is just the sense in which "take" is used elsewhere in federal legislation and treaty. See, e.g., Migratory Bird Treaty Act, 16 U.S.C. § 703 (1988 ed., Supp. V) (no person may "pursue, hunt, take, capture, kill, [or] attempt to take, capture, or kill" any migratory bird); Agreement on the Conservation of Polar Bears, Nov. 15, 1973, Art. I, 27 U.S.T. 3918, 3921, T.I.A.S. No. 8409 (defining "taking" as "hunting, killing and capturing"). And that meaning fits neatly with the rest of § 1538(a)(1), which makes it unlawful not only to take protected species, but also to import or export them (§ 1538(a)(1)(A)); to possess, sell, deliver, carry, transport, or ship any taken species (§ 1538(a)(1)(D)); and to transport, sell, or offer to sell them in interstate or foreign commerce (§§ 1538(a)(1)(E), (F)). The taking prohibition, in other words, is only part of the regulatory plan of § 1538(a)(1), which covers all the stages of the process by which protected wildlife is reduced to man's dominion and made the object of profit. It is obvious that "take" in this sense—a term of art deeply embedded in the statutory and common law concerning wildlife—describes a class of acts (not omissions) done directly and intentionally (not indirectly and by accident) to particular animals (not populations of animals).

[Although "harm" has a range of meaning, the most likely in this statutory context is one that focuses on specific and intentional harming.] "Harm" is merely one of 10 prohibitory words in § 1532(19), and the other 9 fit the ordinary meaning of "take" perfectly. To "harass, pursue, hunt, shoot, wound, kill, trap, capture, or collect" are all affirmative acts (the provision itself describes them as "conduct," see § 1532(19)) which are directed immediately and intentionally against a particular animal—not acts or omissions that indirectly and accidentally cause injury to a population of animals. * * * What the nine other words in § 1532(19) have in common—and share with the narrower meaning of "harm" described above, but not with the Secretary's ruthless dilation of the word—is the sense of affirmative conduct intentionally directed against a particular animal or animals.

I am not the first to notice this fact, or to draw the conclusion that it compels. In 1981 the Solicitor of the Fish and Wildlife Service delivered a legal opinion on § 1532(19) that is in complete agreement with my reading:

> The Act's definition of "take" contains a list of actions that illustrate the intended scope of the term. . . . With the possible exception of "harm," these terms all represent forms of conduct that are directed against and likely to injure or kill *individual* wildlife. Under the principle of statutory construction, *ejusdem generis*, . . . the term "harm" should be interpreted to include only those actions that are directed against, and likely to injure or kill, individual wildlife. [Memorandum of April 17, 1981 (emphasis in original).]

I would call it *noscitur a sociis*, but the principle is much the same: The fact that "several items in a list share an attribute counsels in favor of interpreting the other items as possessing that attribute as well." * * * [Moreover,] the Court's contention that "harm" in the narrow sense adds nothing to the other words underestimates the ingenuity of our own species in a way that Congress did not. To feed an animal poison, to spray it with mace, to chop down the very tree in which it is nesting, or even to destroy its entire habitat in order to take it (as by draining a pond to get at a turtle), might neither wound nor kill, but would directly and intentionally harm.

The penalty provisions of the Act counsel this interpretation as well. Any person who "knowingly" violates § 1538(a)(1)(B) is subject to criminal penalties under § 1540(b)(1) and civil penalties under § 1540(a)(1); moreover, under the latter section, any person "who otherwise violates" the taking prohibition (i.e., violates it unknowingly) may be assessed a civil penalty of $500 for each violation, with the stricture that "[e]ach such violation shall be a separate offense." This last provision should be clear warning that the regulation is in error, for when combined with the regulation it produces a result that no legislature could reasonably be thought to have intended: A large number of routine private activities—for example, farming, ranching, roadbuilding, construction and logging—are subjected to strict-liability penalties when they fortuitously injure protected wildlife, no matter how remote the chain of causation and no matter how difficult to foresee (or to disprove) the "injury" may be (e.g., an "impairment" of breeding). * * *

So far I have discussed only the immediate statutory text bearing on the regulation. But the definition of "take" in § 1532(19) applies "[f]or the purposes of this chapter," that is, it governs the meaning of the word *as used everywhere in the Act*. Thus, the Secretary's interpretation of "harm" is wrong if it does not fit with the use of "take" throughout the Act. And it does not. In § 1540(e)(4)(B), for example, Congress provided for the forfeiture of "[a]ll guns, traps, nets, and other equipment . . . used to aid the taking, possessing, selling, [etc.]" of protected animals. This listing plainly relates to "taking" in the ordinary sense. If environmental modification were part (and necessarily a major part) of taking, as the Secretary maintains, one would have expected the list to include "plows, bulldozers, and backhoes." * * * The Act is full of like examples. See, e.g.,

§ 1538(a)(1)(D) (prohibiting possession, sale, and transport of "species taken in violation" of the Act). "[I]f the Act is to be interpreted as a symmetrical and coherent regulatory scheme, one in which the operative words have a consistent meaning throughout," *Gustafson v. Alloyd Co.*, 513 U.S. 561, 569 (1995), the regulation must fall.

The broader structure of the Act confirms the unreasonableness of the regulation. Section 1536 provides:

> Each Federal agency shall . . . insure that any action authorized, funded, or carried out by such agency . . . is not likely to jeopardize the continued existence of any endangered species or threatened species or *result in the destruction or adverse modification of habitat* of such species which is determined by the Secretary . . . to be critical. [16 U.S.C. § 1536(a)(2) (emphasis added).]

The Act defines "critical habitat" as habitat that is "essential to the conservation of the species," §§ 1532(5)(A)(i), (A)(ii), with "conservation" in turn defined as the use of methods necessary to bring listed species "to the point at which the measures provided pursuant to this chapter are no longer necessary." § 1532(3).

These provisions have a double significance. Even if §§ 1536(a)(2) and 1538(a)(1)(B) were totally independent prohibitions—the former applying only to federal agencies and their licensees, the latter only to private parties—Congress's explicit prohibition of habitat modification in the one section would bar the inference of an implicit prohibition of habitat modification in the other section. "[W]here Congress includes particular language in one section of a statute but omits it in another . . ., it is generally presumed that Congress acts intentionally and purposely in the disparate inclusion or exclusion." *Keene Corp. v. United States*, 508 U.S. 200, 208 (1993). And that presumption against implicit prohibition would be even stronger where the one section which uses the language carefully defines and limits its application. That is to say, it would be passing strange for Congress carefully to define "critical habitat" as used in § 1536(a)(2), but leave it to the Secretary to evaluate, willynilly, impermissible "habitat modification" (under the guise of "harm") in § 1538(a)(1)(B).

In fact, however, §§ 1536(a)(2) and 1538(a)(1)(B) do *not* operate in separate realms; federal agencies are subject to *both*, because the "person[s]" forbidden to take protected species under § 1538 include agencies and departments of the Federal Government. See § 1532(13). This means that the "harm" regulation also contradicts another principle of interpretation: that statutes should be read so far as possible to give independent effect to all their provisions. See *Ratzlaf v. United States*, 510 U.S. 135, 140–41 (1994). By defining "harm" in the definition of "take" in § 1538(a)(1)(B) to include significant habitat modification that injures populations of wildlife, the regulation makes the habitat-modification restriction in § 1536(a)(2) almost wholly superfluous. As "critical habitat" is habitat "essential to the conservation of the species," adverse modification of "critical" habitat by a federal agency would also constitute habitat modification that injures a population of wildlife.

The Court makes * * * other arguments. First, "the broad purpose of the [Act] supports the Secretary's decision to extend protection against activities that cause the precise harms Congress enacted the statute to avoid." I thought we had renounced the vice of "simplistically . . . assum[ing] that *whatever* furthers the statute's primary objective must be the law." *Rodriguez v. United States*, 480 U.S. 522, 526 (1987) (*per curiam*) (emphasis in original). Deduction from the "broad purpose" of a statute begs the question if it is used to decide by what *means* (and hence to what *length*) Congress pursued that purpose; to get the right answer to that question there is no substitute for the hard job (or in this case, the quite simple one) of reading the whole text. "The Act must do everything necessary to achieve its broad purpose" is the slogan of the enthusiast, not the analytical tool of the arbiter.

Second, the Court maintains that the legislative history of the 1973 Act supports the Secretary's definition. Even if legislative history were a legitimate and reliable tool of interpretation (which I shall assume in order to rebut the Court's claim); and even if it could appropriately be resorted to when the enacted text is as clear as this, but see *Chicago v. Environmental Defense Fund*, 511 U.S. 328, 337 (1994); here it shows quite the opposite of what the Court says. I shall not pause to discuss the Court's reliance on such statements in the Committee Reports as " '[t]ake' is defined . . . in the broadest possible manner to include every conceivable way in which a person can 'take' or attempt to 'take' any fish or wildlife." [S. Rep. No. 93–307, at 7 (1973)]. This sort of empty flourish—to the effect that "this statute means what it means all the way"—counts for little even when enacted into the law itself. See *Reves v. Ernst & Young*, 507 U.S. 170, 183–84 (1993).

Much of the Court's discussion of legislative history is devoted to two items: first, the Senate floor manager's introduction of an amendment that added the word "harm" to the definition of "take," with the observation that (along with other amendments) it would " 'help to achieve the purposes of the bill' "; second, the relevant Committee's removal from the definition of a provision stating that "take" includes " 'the destruction, modification or curtailment of [the] habitat or range' " of fish and wildlife. The Court inflates the first and belittles the second, even though the second is on its face far more pertinent. But this elaborate inference from various pre-enactment actions and inactions is quite unnecessary, since we have direct evidence of what those who brought the legislation to the floor thought it meant—evidence as solid as any ever to be found in legislative history, but which the Court banishes to a footnote.

Both the Senate and House floor managers of the bill explained it in terms which leave no doubt that the problem of habitat destruction on private lands was to be solved principally by the land acquisition program of § 1534, while § 1538 solved a different problem altogether—the problem of takings. Senator Tunney stated:

> *Through [the] land acquisition provisions, we will be able to conserve habitats necessary to protect fish and wildlife from further destruction.*

> Although most endangered species are threatened primarily by the destruction of their natural habitats, a significant portion of these animals

are subject to *predation by man for commercial, sport, consumption, or other purposes.* The provisions of [the bill] would prohibit the commerce in or the importation, exportation, or taking of endangered species. . . . [119 Cong. Rec. 25669 (1973) (emphasis added).]

The House floor manager, Representative Sullivan, put the same thought in this way:

> [T]he principal threat to animals stems from destruction of their habitat. . . . *[The bill] will meet this problem by providing funds for acquisition of critical habitat. . . .* It will also enable the Department of Agriculture to cooperate with willing landowners who desire to assist in the protection of endangered species, *but who are understandably unwilling to do so at excessive cost to themselves.* Another hazard to endangered species arises from those who would *capture or kill them for pleasure or profit.* There is no way that the Congress can make it less pleasurable for a person to take an animal, but we can certainly make it less profitable for them to do so. [*Id.* at 30162 (emphasis added).]

Habitat modification and takings, in other words, were viewed as different problems, addressed by different provisions of the Act. [Justice Scalia argued that these statements destroy the Court's legislative history case and that the Court has no response.]

Third, the Court seeks support from a provision that was added to the Act in 1982, the year after the Secretary promulgated the current regulation. The provision states:

> [T]he Secretary may permit, under such terms and conditions as he shall prescribe—
>
> . . .
>
> any taking otherwise prohibited by section 1538(a)(1)(B) . . . if such taking is incidental to, and not the purpose of, the carrying out of an otherwise lawful activity. [16 U.S.C. § 1539(a)(1)(B).]

This provision does not, of course, implicate our doctrine that reenactment of a statutory provision ratifies an extant judicial or administrative interpretation, for neither the taking prohibition in § 1538(a)(1)(B) nor the definition in § 1532(19) was reenacted. The Court claims, however, that the provision "strongly suggests that Congress understood [§ 1538(a)(1)(B)] to prohibit indirect as well as deliberate takings." That would be a valid inference if habitat modification were the only substantial "otherwise lawful activity" that might incidentally and nonpurposefully cause a prohibited "taking." Of course it is not. This provision applies to the many otherwise lawful takings that incidentally take a protected species—as when fishing for unprotected salmon also takes an endangered species of salmon. * * *

This is enough to show, in my view, that the 1982 permit provision does not support the regulation. I must acknowledge that the Senate Committee Report on this provision, and the House Conference Committee Report, clearly contemplate that it will enable the Secretary to permit environmental modification. But the *text* of the amendment cannot possibly bear that asserted meaning, when placed within the context of an Act that must be interpreted (as we have seen) not to prohibit private environmental modification. The neutral language of the amendment cannot possibly alter that interpretation, nor can its legislative history be summoned forth to contradict, rather than clarify, what is in its totality an unambiguous statutory text. There is little fear, of course, that giving no effect to the relevant portions of the Committee Reports will frustrate the real-life expectations of a majority of the Members of Congress. If they read and relied on such tedious detail on such an obscure point (it was not, after all, presented as a revision of the statute's prohibitory scope, but as a discretionary-waiver provision) the Republic would be in grave peril. * * *

[JUSTICE O'CONNOR wrote a separate concurring opinion, responding to some of Justice Scalia's concerns. "[T]he regulation's application is limited by ordinary principles of proximate causation, which introduce notions of foreseeability." For example, she disapproved of an application of the statute where the grazing of sheep was found to be a "taking" of palila birds, as the sheep destroyed seedlings which would have grown into trees needed by the bird for nesting. The chain of causation is simply too attenuated, Justice O'Connor concluded. Justice Scalia responded that this was Justice O'Connor's gloss on the statute, not the agency's. He chided his colleague for trying to have it both ways—deferring to the agency under *Chevron* (see Chapter 9, § 1) but then rewriting the regulation to suit her fancy. Justice Scalia concluded: "We defer to reasonable agency interpretations of ambiguous statutes precisely in order that agencies, rather than courts, may exercise policymaking discretion in the interstices of statutes. See *Chevron*, 467 U.S. at 843–45. Just as courts may not exercise an agency's power to adjudicate, and so may not affirm an agency order on discretionary grounds the agency has not advanced, so also this Court may not exercise the Secretary's power to regulate, and so may not uphold a regulation by adding to it even the most reasonable of elements it does not contain."]

NOTES ON SWEET HOME

1.   *The Canons Debate.* Notice, first, how many of the canons are relevant to the Justices' deliberations about the plain meaning of the text in this case: the ordinary meaning rule, and its corollaries regarding dictionaries and technical meaning; noscitur a sociis and (possibly) ejusdem generis; expressio (or inclusio) unius and other rules of negative implication; the rule against redundancy; the rule of consistent usage and of significant variation; and the anti-derogation rule. Notice also how the anti-derogation rule figures centrally in both majority and dissenting opinions. Justice Scalia emphasizes the structural conflict between Congress' asserted allocation of responsibilities in §§ 5 and 7 and the majority's broad interpretation of § 9; Justice Stevens emphasizes the philosophical and structural conflict between a narrow reading of § 9 and the statutory scheme established in § 10.

A problem sharply illustrated by *Sweet Home* is that different canons cut in different directions. How can one resolve conflicting canonical signals? One way to resolve the conflict is resort to the statutory purpose, but that may only generalize the disagreement. The dissenters' sarcasm suggests the possibility that they were not sympathetic to the statutory goals of biodiversity: note their alarm that the "simplest farmer" finds his land "conscripted to national zoological use." Does this reflect a neutral interpretation of the law? Is the Nietzsche rule possibly applicable here?

2. *Bringing in Legislative History.* In assessing the relative strengths of the majority and dissent, consider too their deployment of non-canonical resources. If the canons skirmish is a wash (or maybe even if it favors one side but not conclusively?), do the legislative history arguments cut clearly in favor of the majority or dissent? Is your response the same for the 1973 history and the 1982 history?

The verb "harm" was added to the text on the Senate floor by Senator Tunney (Dem., California), the Senate manager of the 1973 Act. Tunney added "harm" to the nine-verb definition of "take" that appeared in the text of the bill reported by the Senate committee. The change was part of a series of "technical and clarifying" amendments approved unanimously by the Senate. See 119 Cong. Rec. 25682–83. Senator Tunney referred to the amendments as "technical in nature" but also "important." Does this addition clarify the Senate committee report explanation of "take" that appears in the Court's decision? In what way is the addition "important"?

According to Justice Scalia, Rep. Sullivan's floor statement signifies that the law addresses habitat destruction through its land acquisition program rather than through its prohibition on takings. Is this the only inference one can draw from Rep. Sullivan's statement? Can you offer any alternative reading?

3. *The Bottom Line.* Which side is able to create a more complete—or more elegant—case for its interpretation? We are particularly impressed with the dissenters' ability to weave together a wide array of canons to support their position. Should this assure their triumph? If so, why did their usual ally, Justice O'Connor, jump ship? She might have been influenced by the fact that the *political equilibrium* favored the agency (remember that she authored the Court's opinion in the *FDA Tobacco* Case, Chapter 6, § 3B). Indeed, the agency itself reflected the prevailing political consensus in this case, perhaps justifying the Court's deferring to its rule. (See Chapter 9).

CHAPTER 8

IMPLEMENTATION OF STATUTES IN THE ADMINISTRATIVE STATE

∎ ∎ ∎

Under the system of mutually encroaching government powers described in *Federalist* #51 (Madison), the legislature shares lawmaking power with the executive and the judiciary. By now, it should be clear that statutes are not the end of lawmaking; indeed they are often only the beginning. Earlier chapters have explored how courts may construe statutory text narrowly while discounting evidence of legislative history or purpose; expand statutes beyond their literal terms by reference to that same historical and purposive evidence; and update statutes in appropriate circumstances. In the next two chapters, we focus on the parallel and often primary role played by agencies in the implementation and interpretation of statutes. This chapter considers implementation issues; chapter 9 addresses the methods courts apply when reviewing agency interpretation of statutory provisions—methods that may involve varying levels of judicial deference.

There are several implementation choices available to the legislature. First, the legislature can authorize public enforcers to prosecute violators of the statute and exact some penalty from them (e.g., criminal laws). Second, the legislature can authorize victims of conduct violating the statute to sue the violators for damages and/or injunctive relief (e.g., the Uniform Commercial Code and most tort statutes). In these first two implementation choices, the legislature is authorizing courts to adjudicate the enforcement lawsuits and to develop the standards and rules of the statute. Third, the legislature can delegate the development of standards, the adjudication of violations, and the promulgation of guidance to a public administrative agency or a private group (e.g., the federal securities laws, state licensing regulations). This last choice has been increasingly characteristic of the modern administrative state, at both the federal and state levels.

Section 1 traces the history of the modern federal administrative state during the twentieth century. It then presents a Case Study addressing commercial airplane safety in the modern age of terrorism that introduces some of the challenges agencies face when seeking to fulfill their mission. Section 1 also considers two core constitutional issues related to implementation choices: the limits on agency authority and the tenure of agency officials. First, is it legitimate for Congress to delegate so much of its authority to agencies? At what point does delegation of *law implementing* power essentially become abdication of *lawmaking* power? Second, does the President's authority to appoint inferior officers include *unlimited power to remove them from office*? To what extent does Congress's authority to restrict presidential removal powers differ based on the two types of agencies created by Congress—executive branch agencies and independent agencies? Assuming Congress may exercise greater control over the tenure of certain agency officials, are there constitutional limits on this ability to restrict presidential power?

Section 2 explores agency implementation under the Administrative Procedure Act (APA), the statute that has shaped agency procedural approaches since 1946. It begins with an overview of the APA, including a look at its extensive legislative history and some core definitional issues. Section 2 then examines the major procedures by which agencies exercise their statutorily assigned policymaking responsibilities pursuant to the APA: (1) *rulemaking*—both formal rulemaking "on the record after opportunity for an agency hearing," and the more prevalent informal or notice-and-comment rulemaking; (2) *adjudication*; and (3) *interpretive rules* and *policy statements*. Congress and the courts help determine which options agencies may pursue in a given set of circumstances, although agencies retain a degree of flexibility in this regard. Under rulemaking and adjudication, agencies must conform to certain APA procedural requirements, subject to judicial review that can be searching.

Section 3 addresses efforts by all three branches to monitor and control day-to-day aspects of agency implementation. It examines congressional monitoring mechanisms, including legislative oversight and investigation of agency enforcement, and the appropriations power. These mechanisms are somewhat indirect and often not terribly effective means of congressional control. Two other congressional monitoring approaches—the legislative veto and the use of Senate confirmation authority—raise troubling constitutional questions which we discuss. Section 3 next explores efforts by the President to monitor and influence agency policymaking conduct. It focuses on the formal role played by the Office of Management and Budget, including the Office of Information and Regulatory Affairs (OIRA), as well as informal influence exerted from inside the White House. These monitoring approaches tend to be less headline-grabbing than many congressional efforts, but they may also be more effective. Finally, Section 3 examines judicial review of agency action under the APA. Like congressional oversight and investigation (and unlike cost-benefit analysis and OIRA review), litigation typically comes into play only after an agency has engaged in some form of implementation. Consider in this setting whether judicial review is more effective than Congress's ex post approaches, and perhaps also more influential than the ex ante approaches that characterize executive branch monitoring efforts.

1.   IMPLEMENTATION CHOICES AND THE SEPARATION OF POWERS

State and federal criminal laws are typically enforced exclusively by official prosecution of offenders. Many other statutes provide for both civil and criminal penalties that may be enforced by official actions filed in court. For example, the Justice Department may bring a civil lawsuit for an injunction under the Sherman Act to prevent or terminate violations of the Act, or it may refer discovered violations to a U.S. Attorney's Office for criminal prosecution, or both.

Since 1875, however, public enforcement has gradually been transformed from such a *prosecutorial model*, in which a government agency or department brings lawsuits against statutory violators and the adjudication and development of rules is accomplished by courts, to a *bureaucratic model.* Under the bureaucratic model, the government agency or department itself adjudicates the individual prosecutions or makes the rules, and the only role for courts is limited judicial review of what the administrators have done. In this section, we present a short history of the modern administrative state, and the main constitutional problems that it presents.

A. A BRIEF HISTORY OF THE MODERN ADMINISTRATIVE STATE[1]

1.   *Origins: Regulatory Police.* Wherever there is government there is bureaucracy, but through most of the nineteenth century very little policy creation was done through bureaucracy in the United States. Most administrative activity was on the state level, in the form of rate regulation of natural monopolies, such as grain elevators, utilities, and railroads. There were 25 state railroad commissions in 1886, for example. The Supreme Court invalidated state railroad regulation under the Commerce Clause in *Wabash, St. Louis and Pacific Railway v. Illinois*, 118 U.S. 557 (1886), which stimulated Congress to create the first major federal regulatory agency, the Interstate Commerce Commission (ICC), in 1887. 24 Stat. 379.[2] Congress established the Federal Trade Commission (FTC) in 1914 to enforce some of the antitrust laws and regulate unfair competition, the United States Shipping Board in 1916, the Federal Power Commission in 1920, and the Federal Radio Commission (predecessor to the Federal Communications Commission) in 1927. These commissions and the ICC were the first modern *independent federal agencies,* bureaucracies set up outside of the formal departments of the Executive Branch and with their own adjudicatory and rulemaking responsibilities.[3] See generally Geoffrey Miller, *Independent Agencies*, 1986 Sup. Ct. Rev. 41.

The philosophy behind the establishment of these agencies and bureaus by Populist reformers in the 1880s and 1890s and Progressives in the 1900s and 1910s was to police the excesses of businesses. Many laws were responses to scandals exposed during the Progressive Era. For example, the Pure Food and Drug Act of 1906 and the Meat Inspection Act of 1906–07 were triggered by the publication of Upton Sinclair's *The Jungle*, which exposed horrid meat processing practices. Both the Populists, who favored draconian measures against the enemies of the farmer (especially railroads), and the Progressives, who favored marginal change,

---

[1]   This history is drawn, in substantial part, from Robert Rabin, *Federal Regulation in Historical Perspective*, 38 Stan. L. Rev. 1189 (1986). See also Joseph Kearney & Thomas Merrill, *The Great Transformation of Regulated Industries Law*, 98 Colum. L. Rev. 1323 (1998).

[2]   Ironically, or perhaps appropriately, the ICC was also one of the first major regulatory agencies to be abolished by the Republican Congresses in the late 1990s that sought to reduce the federal bureaucracy. See also Jerry Mashaw, *Federal Administration and Administrative Law in the Gilded Age*, 119 Yale L.J. 1362 (2010) (demonstrating, *contra* the more familiar narrative, that Congress created multiple departments, bureaus, and programs in the post-Reconstruction period, and federal civilian employment grew more rapidly than the population as a whole).

[3]   At the same time Congress was creating independent agencies, it gave bureaus or divisions within the existing executive departments similar duties. The Patent Office had existed within the executive department since 1790, and the Secretary of Agriculture accumulated a great amount of adjudicatory responsibility as a result of the Pure Food and Drug Act of 1906, 34 Stat. 768; the Meat Inspection Act of 1906–07, 34 Stat. 674, 1260; the Cotton Futures Act and the Warehouse Act of 1916, 39 Stat. 453 & 486; and later statutes.

generally accepted the existing market mechanisms as the norm. They envisioned the work of the ICC and FTC and the Bureau of Chemistry (which administered the Pure Food and Drug Act) as merely facilitating the "natural" operation of the competitive market by preventing the intrusion of "unnatural" practices—fraud, price-fixing, and discrimination.[4]

The reformist approach in this early policing period was, therefore, ambivalent. The judiciary's attitude was often openly hostile, as judges treated determinations by the ICC and FTC with little deference and refused to enforce well-justified agency requests. On the other hand, the ICC managed to increase its statutory power in 1906 and 1910, when Congress granted the agency authority to regulate rates. Courts gradually came to defer to the agency, though they also required it to follow essential procedural safeguards (a trial-type hearing) in order to develop an administrative record that could be the basis for meaningful judicial review. See, e.g., *ICC v. Louisville & Nashville Ry. Co.*, 227 U.S. 88, 93 (1913).

The evolution of the ICC brought to light a problem with viewing agencies merely as policing institutions. World War I was to underscore the problem, as lawmakers and the public began to perceive government boards as necessary to compel the private sector to meet the needs of the war effort. An immediate result of the war effort was the Transportation Act of 1920, 41 Stat. 456, which greatly expanded the powers of the ICC beyond the policing of price discrimination against shippers. During the war, the government ran the railroads, and the Act gave the ICC authority to do the same—by regulating rates, mergers and consolidations, and service schedules comprehensively (and, presumably, efficiently).

2.   *The New Deal: Regulatory Planning and Market Management.* The Great Depression suggested to many that the "natural" operation of the market was not necessarily a good thing at all, and that much more government direction was needed. FDR's New Deal was a cluster of experiments proceeding in many different directions—from the aspirations of comprehensive industrial planning in the National Industrial Recovery Act to the ambitious subsidy program of the Agricultural Adjustment Act. Most of these regulatory initiatives rejected the policing approach of the Populists and Progressives. The New Deal measures were more comprehensive and affirmative (and sometimes managerial) approaches to a market that was seen to be structurally unfair and unreliable. The distinction between public and private spheres of American life became more blurred.

The New Deal created an unprecedented array of new independent agencies and departmental bureaus. Some of them had brief lives. The National Industrial Recovery Act (NIRA), representing the New Deal's most ambitious effort at economic planning, did little to help the economy and was declared unconstitutional by the Supreme Court in *A.L.A. Schechter Poultry Corp. v. United States*, 295 U.S. 495 (1935). Other New Deal agencies have become part of our federal governance. The National Labor Relations Board (NLRB) was established as an independent

---

    [4]   See 3 Robert Himmelberg, *Growth of the Regulatory State, 1900–1917: State and Federal Regulation of Railroads and Other Enterprises* (1994). For an argument that most of these early statutes represented rent-seeking by regulated interests, see Gabriel Kolko, *The Triumph of Conservatism: A Reinterpretation of American History* (1963).

agency outside the Labor Department to alleviate inequality in the labor market and to head off labor strife by adjudicating the existence of "unfair labor practices" by management and labor unions. It had the authority to enforce its determinations through "cease-and-desist" orders. The Securities and Exchange Commission (SEC) was established to prevent unstable capital markets by registering and regulating securities offerings according to the commands provided in the applicable statutes and SEC rules. The Federal Deposit Insurance Corporation (FDIC) was a response to the disastrous bank runs of the Great Depression and sought to improve confidence in the system by insuring small depositors. By 1941, there were, by one count, 19 separate lawmaking bureaus within the executive branch and 22 independent agencies. *Final Report of the Attorney General's Committee on Administrative Procedure* (1941).

As administrative agencies and bureaus proliferated, so did criticisms of them. But given the New Deal's transformation of attitudes about across-the-board federal structural intervention in the market, most criticisms did not focus on the appropriate field of administrative activity. Instead, critics targeted the inadequacies of agency procedure and judicial review: important property rights were being stripped away without proper procedural safeguards, such as trial-type hearing procedures and/or meaningful judicial review of the bureaucratic decision. In 1945, the Attorney General endorsed legislation standardizing administrative procedure, and the Administrative Procedure Act (APA), 60 Stat. 237, codified as amended at 5 U.S.C. §§ 551–559, 701–706 *et al.*, was enacted in 1946. The APA legislative history and purpose are addressed in detail in Section 2 below.

The APA compromise was essentially designed to recognize the legislative and adjudicative roles of independent agencies and departmental bureaus (both of which are included in the APA definition of "agency," *Id.* § 551(1)), but also to "rein in" the bureaucratic state with procedural safeguards and judicial review to prevent arbitrary or unlawful action. The APA's enactment broadly validated the bureaucratic revolution of the New Deal and ushered in a period of relative consensus in favor of agency lawmaking in the 1950s.

3.   *The Public Interest Era: New Kinds of Regulation.* As early as the 1950s, some scholars raised concerns that bureaucratic regulation of the economy is subject to bias and debilitation over time. Marver Bernstein, *Regulating Business by Independent Commission* (1955), for example, argued that agencies, like human beings, typically go through a "life cycle." The agency's *youth* is characterized by a crusading spirit engendered by its statutory mandate, but also by the agency's struggle to devise a regulatory strategy to deal with the better organized and often savvy industry to be regulated. The agency's *maturity* comes after it has lost much of the political support and enthusiasm that spawned its enabling statute, but in this period the agency "understands" the industry better and takes a less aggressive approach to regulating it, often becoming a "captive" of the regulated industry and even a pawn in the industry's own plans. *Senescence* comes when the agency grows not only less vital but also inflexible, a condition that may lead to some form of euthanasia. Later public choice scholars have been even less charitable in thinking about the typical agency biography than Bernstein was, characterizing agencies as captured from childhood by rent-seeking special

interests.[5] The 1950s also saw the true beginnings of noneconomic regulatory activities stimulated first by the civil rights revolution, followed in the 1960s by the environmental movement.

These two developments inspired a new period of administrative law development in the 1960s and the 1970s. Bureaucracy became both more distrusted and better integrated into the great public interest movements of those decades. The regulatory emphasis has shifted from comprehensive direction of the economy to *command-and-control* statutes aimed at specific problems not traditionally thought of in market terms.

The Great Society was the linchpin of this shift. The Civil Rights Act of 1964, 78 Stat. 241, established an impressive range of bureaucratic sanctions for civil rights violations. For example, Titles III and IV of the Act authorized the Attorney General to file public lawsuits to desegregate public facilities and public education. Title VI provided for nondiscrimination in federally assisted programs. It was to be implemented by rules that made federal grants, loans, or other financial assistance contingent upon the recipient following nondiscriminatory policies.

Chapter 1 describes Title VII of the 1964 Act, which established the Equal Employment Opportunity Commission (EEOC) and charged it with rulemaking and adjudication of the very broad prohibition of employment discrimination. Although troubled with administrative problems over time, the EEOC served as a model for a new bureaucracy of conscience. Its intrusion into the affairs of corporations and state and local institutions helped broaden the concept of regulation. The Government's agenda extended beyond the economic marketplace and toward concern for the creation of a "great society" in which racial, sexual, and ethnic equality would be recognized. Even many of the economic initiatives of the 1960s— the War on Poverty, Medicare, the Food Stamp Program—were aimed at different targets from traditional New Deal regulation. These programs, like Title VII, sought to help the poor and the disadvantaged, often without any attempted justification based on systemic or isolated market failure.

The 1970s saw the societal transformation approach to regulation expand to include consumer rights, public health and safety, and environmental purity as important agenda items. Just as the regulatory *agenda* was changing, so was the regulatory *mechanism*. Both authorized and encouraged by the new generation of regulatory statutes, United States agencies in the 1970s showed unprecedented interest in *rulemaking* rather than adjudication and less formal mechanisms.

The National Traffic and Motor Vehicle Safety Act of 1966 exemplified the new approach. The Vehicle Safety Act and other regulatory statutes of this period tended to have more specific mandates, to focus authority in a single administrator (rather than a multi-member commission), to open up agencies to public input, and to focus agency action on the establishment of mandatory policy through general

---

[5] See, e.g., Anthony Downs, *Inside Bureaucracy* (1967); William Niskanen, *Bureaucracy and Representative Government* (1971); Sam Peltzman, *Toward a More General Theory of Regulation*, 19 J.L. & Econ. 211 (1976); George Stigler, *The Theory of Economic Regulation*, 2 Bell J. Econ. & Mgmt. Sci. 3 (1971).

rules.[6] The agency rules themselves were different from what came before: rather than command-and-control models, agencies emphasized goals and limits, and left regulated institutions with choices about how to reach those goals and limits.

Closely following this new model was a wave of pollution control legislation, mainly the Clean Air Act Amendments of 1970 (CAA), 84 Stat. 1676, and the Federal Water Pollution Control Act Amendments of 1972 (FWPCA), 86 Stat. 816. Congress established ambitious mandates to clean up our environment. Most of the directives were very general, with the details filled in by the Environmental Protection Agency (EPA). The National Environmental Policy Act of 1969 (NEPA), 83 Stat. 852, and other statutes directed all federal departments and agencies to consider environmental effects when decisions are made. The Occupational Health and Safety Act of 1970, 84 Stat. 1590, created the Occupational Health and Safety Administration and directed it to enforce more stringent standards of safety in the workplace. Several pieces of landmark legislation worked to redistribute resources to the less well-off in society; Congress enacted the Food Stamp Act, 1 U.S.C. § 2011 et seq., Head Start programs, Medicare, and Medicaid, and it expanded welfare programs substantially.

These statutes marked a significant change in economic regulation as well. First, they redefined market imperfection. The New Deal approach defined costs rather mechanically in terms of lost output and distorted flows of resources. Things like pollution and injuries were treated as *externalities* borne for the most part by those receiving them. Regulation in the 1970s compelled businesses to consider these social costs and to do something about them. Second, the public interest legislation of the 1970s at least implicitly recognized and built upon perceived biases in the federal bureaucracy. Many reformers argued that even the few agencies and bureaus that were not essentially captured by their regulated interests were limited by their statutory mandate to consider only a few policy concerns, usually of a material and tangible nature. The regulatory structures created in the 1970s insisted that quality of life concerns be factored into the bureaucratic calculus (NEPA) and often provided very specific substantive guidelines and time deadlines for agencies to accomplish their regulatory goals (CAA).

Other developments have sought to open up agency decisionmaking. For example, the Freedom of Information Act, 5 U.S.C. § 552, was passed in 1966, 80 Stat. 250, and significantly amended in 1974, 88 Stat. 1561, to require federal agencies and departments to disclose documents and information to persons requesting them, subject to specific exemptions in the Act. The purpose of the Act was to encourage citizens to monitor government performance and publicize problems. See also Privacy Act of 1974, 88 Stat. 1896, codified at 5 U.S.C. § 552a (protecting personal information from disclosure). The Government in the Sunshine Act of 1976, 90 Stat. 1241, codified at 5 U.S.C. § 552b, requires agencies headed by collegial bodies (e.g., FTC, SEC) to conduct their official business in public

---

[6]   Jerry Mashaw, *The Story of Motor Vehicle Manufacturers Association etc: Law, Science, and Politics in the Administrative State*, in *Administrative Law Stories* 334, 339–42 (Peter Strauss ed., 2006); David Shapiro, *The Choice of Rulemaking or Adjudication in the Development of Administrative Policy*, 78 Harv. L. Rev. 921 (1965).

meetings, again subject to specific exemptions. Like the APA, these statutes were enacted to assure structures of agency decisionmaking that are responsive to the reasoned public interest. Indeed, this statutory liberalization in the 1970s was accompanied by more aggressive APA judicial review of agency decisions and procedures in the 1970s and 1980s, a phenomenon explored in Section 3.

4. *1980 to the Present: Deregulation Revived, and Criticized.* During the 1970s, the American economy experienced an extended period of slow economic growth and high inflation (stagflation) combined with rising unemployment, leading many politicians and scholars to argue for diminished regulation of the economy.[7] The real sea change for the American administrative state came with the election of President Reagan in 1980. Reagan and the conservative wing of the Republican Party made "supply-side economics" a household phrase during the 1980 campaign. Sometimes cynically labeled "trickle-down economics," supply-side economics argues that lower barriers to the production or supply of goods and services are the most effective path to economic growth. The Reagan Administration implemented the supply-side approach, advocating successfully for reductions in income tax and capital gains tax rates and for rolling back regulatory controls on various industries. During the 1980s, extensive deregulation was implemented by means of Executive Order,[8] separate agency efforts,[9] and legislative change.[10]

In the 1990s, President Clinton, a member of the same Democratic Party that enacted New Deal and Great Society legislation, continued this deregulatory movement. Clinton famously declared in his 1996 State of the Union address that "the era of big government is over." The Clinton Administration oversaw deregulation of credit-default swaps through the Commodity Futures Modernization Act of 2000, loosening of housing rules through the Community Reinvestment Act of 1995, and—most notably—repeal of the Glass-Steagall Act, a central component in New Deal regulation of the banking industry that had restricted the securities-related activities of commercial banks. Many economists and commentators have argued that the erosion and repeal of these banking restrictions contributed in important ways to the financial crisis that began in 2007.[11]

In the new millennium, some of this deregulatory spirit has remained evident, as with President George W. Bush's public campaign, following his 2004 re-election,

---

[7]   Major legislative responses during the Carter Administration included the Airline Deregulation Act of 1978 (deregulating the commercial airline industry) and the Motor Carrier Reform Act of 1980 (deregulating the trucking industry).

[8]   See, e.g., Exec. Order 12,287, 46 Fed. Reg. 9909 (Jan. 28, 1981) (removing controls on crude oil and refined petroleum products).

[9]   See, e.g., *In re Deregulation of Radio*, 84 F.C.C. 2d 968 (1981) (deregulating controls on radio); *Syracuse Peace Council*, 2 FCC Rcd. 5043 (1987) (eliminating fairness doctrine).

[10]   See, e.g., 1982 Bus Regulatory Reform Act; 1982 Garn-St. Germain Depository Institutions Act (deregulating savings and loan associations); 1984 Cable Television Deregulation Act; 1989 Natural Gas Wellhead Decontrol Act. For an overview of deregulatory efforts from the 1970s through the 1990s, see John E. Kwoka, *Twenty-Five Years of Deregulation: Lessons for Electric Power*, 33 Loy. U. Chi. L.J. 885 (2001–02).

[11]   See, e.g., Joseph E. Stiglitz, *Capitalist Fools*, Vanity Fair, January 2009 at 52; Robert Kuttner, *The Alarming Parallels Between 1929 and 2007*, (testimony before House Committee on Financial Services, available at The American Prospect, October 2, 2007).

to privatize Social Security.[12] However, a growing chorus of deregulation critics contended that some regulation is important in allowing companies to remain competitive, to create level playing fields, to maintain quality control over the provision of services (through licensing and other qualification requirements), and to protect the public from risks like environmental degradation and excessive risk-taking by banks.

Moreover, since 2001 there has been a surge of renewed regulatory interest on the part of Congress and the President. In response to the attacks of September 11 on the World Trade Center and the Pentagon, Congress passed the Homeland Security Act of 2002, 116 Stat. 2135, conferring vast regulatory powers on a new Department of Homeland Security. Also in response to 9/11, Congress enacted the Aviation and Transportation Security Act, which is discussed in the Case Study that follows this history. Then, following the financial crisis that began in 2007, Congress enacted the Dodd-Frank Wall Street Reform and Consumer Protection Act of 2010, 124 Stat. 1376–2223. Dodd-Frank imposed additional regulatory controls on the finance industry and created the Consumer Financial Protection Bureau (CFPB), an agency designed to protect the interests of consumers with respect to financial products and services. Finally, Congress enacted, with President Obama's crucial support, the Patient Protection and Affordable Care Act (PPACA) of 2010, 124 Stat. 119–1025. Unlike the Dodd-Frank and Homeland Security legislation, the PPACA was not a response to a particular crisis of the moment. Also unlike those two other laws, the PPACA carved out a sizable role for private industry as part of its regulatory efforts. Although there was debate over the possibility of including a public option or single-payer health insurance, Congress enacted legislation mandating that individuals purchase health insurance from private companies on regulated exchanges. Indeed, without the support of the private insurance industry, the PPACA might never have become law at all.

Partisan debates continue to rage over whether the administrative state is having an intrusive and stultifying impact on the American economy, or instead has been seriously weakened by decades of deregulatory efforts, to the detriment of consumers, the public, and our environment. It remains to be seen if developments such as the three major statutes described above augur the beginning of a new regulatory era of agency strength, or simply a pause in the ongoing deregulatory movement.

A PRELIMINARY TAXONOMY OF FEDERAL AGENCIES

As this brief history illustrates, federal agencies are units of government, created by Congress through statutes and given considerable powers to implement public policy that Congress has set forth in legislation—policy often expressed in general or expansive terms. The chart below presents the fifteen cabinet departments and when they began operating at cabinet-level status, as well as a sample of other important federal agencies.[13] The total number of agencies listed

---

[12] See Jeanne Sahadi, *Bush's Plan for Social Security*, CNN Money, March 4, 2005, available at http://money.cnn.com/2005/02/02/retirement/stofunion_socsec/.

[13] We are indebted for the excellent idea to include such a chart to the work of Lisa Schultz Bressman, Edward Rubin, and Kevin Stack, *The Regulatory State*, 3–4 (2010).

(42) is less than half the number that exist today. See, e.g. listing at end of § 1A, excerpted from Kirti Datla & Richard Revesz, *Deconstructing Independent Agencies (and Executive Agencies)*, 98 Cornell L. Rev. 769, 825 (2013). Even our abbreviated list conveys a sense of how federal agencies affect so many aspects of everyday life—for all of us as individuals and as a nation. Notice too how Congress has created agencies in response to evolving perceptions of national policy priorities. When did Congress first mandate cabinet-level attention on issues of war and peace? On matters of workplace protection? On the need to respond to the energy crisis? On the threat of global terrorism?

Cabinet Departments*

Department of State (1789)	Department of the Treasury (1789)	Department of Defense (1789)†
Department of the Interior (1849)	Department of Justice (1870)	Department of Agriculture (1889)
Department of Commerce (1903)	Department of Labor (1913)	Department of Health and Human Services (1953)+
Department of Housing and Urban Development (1966)	Dept. of Transportation (1967) (Fed. Aviation Admin. located within DOT)	Department of Energy (1977)
Department of Education (1979)	Department of Veterans Affairs (1989)	Department of Homeland Security (2002)

* Dates of initial operation in parentheses

† 1789 War Department, 1798 Navy Department, 1949 Unified Defense Department

+ began as Department of Health, Education and Welfare

Some Prominent Other Agencies*

Central Intelligence Agency	Commodity Futures Trading Commission	Consumer Product Safety Commission
Environmental Protection Agency	Equal Employment Opportunity Commission	**Export-Import Bank of the United States**
Federal Communications Commission	**Federal Deposit Insurance Corporation**	Federal Election Commission
Federal Maritime Commission	**Federal Reserve System**	**Federal Trade Commission**

General Services Administration	National Aeronautics and Space Administration	National Archives and Records Administration
National Labor Relations Board	National Transportation Safety Board	Nuclear Regulatory Commission
Occupational Safety and Health Review Commission	Office of Personnel Management	Pension Benefit Guaranty Corporation
Railroad Retirement Board	**Securities and Exchange Commission**	**Social Security Administration**
Small Business Administration	United States International Trade Commission	**United States Postal Service**

* Agencies in bold were established before 1960

A CASE STUDY: THE FEDERAL AVIATION ADMINISTRATION AND AIRPLANE COCKPIT SECURITY

The Administrator of the Federal Aviation Administration (FAA) has long had authority for aviation safety under laws codified at title 49. Section 44701(a) confers on the FAA authority to "prescribe minimum standards required in the interest of safety * * * for the design, material, construction, quality of work, and performance of aircraft." From the mid-1970s through late 2001, the FAA issued several rules and notices of proposed rulemaking and undertook assessments pursuant to this authority in response to the presence of terrorist acts abroad.

Starting in the 1960s and continuing into the late 1980s, commercial airplanes around the world experienced a series of bombings and also hijackings in which planes were diverted to different locations.[14] The International Civil Aviation Organization (ICAO), a non-government organization under the United Nations comprised of 189 member countries, began considering proposals to incorporate security safeguards into the design of new airplanes. On December 21, 1988, a terrorist placed a bomb on an airplane, causing the plane to explode over Lockerbie, Scotland, killing all 259 people on board and 11 people on the ground. As a result, ICAO intensified its efforts. Within several months, ICAO formed the Incorporation of Security into Aircraft Design study group, with representatives from the airworthiness authorities of the United States, the United Kingdom, France, Germany, Brazil, and Russia, as well as various trade association members. The study group was charged with reviewing the existing proposals and recommending standards for security in airplane design. The study group considered, among other things, the "protection of [the] pilot compartment from penetration by small arms fire or shrapnel."

---

[14] This history is drawn principally from two sources produced after the 9/11 attacks. *Security Related Considerations in the Design and Operation of Transport Category Airplanes*, 72 Fed. Reg. 630–01, 631–33 (proposed Jan. 5, 2007); National Commission on Terrorist Attacks Upon the United States, *The 9/11 Commission Report* 82–85 (2004).

On March 12, 1997, ICAO adopted new standards with respect to many safety concerns, including protection of pilot compartments from penetration by small arms fire or shrapnel, standards that the member countries subsequently approved. Normally, ICAO standards do not apply directly to the design of an airplane; they are implemented by adoption into the airworthiness codes of ICAO member countries. The 1997 standard sought compliance within three years. Once implemented, airplane certification by a member country implies compliance with the standard. As a signatory, the United States was required to implement ICAO's standards into its aviation regulations and statutes to the extent practicable. However, a signatory may file differences with ICAO if it is unable to implement the ICAO standards in the timeframe adopted, an action the United States took (along with all other signatories of manufacture). The United States did not disagree with the ICAO standards or believe a permanent difference was warranted or required, but the FAA needed time to promulgate rulemaking and implement the ICAO standards into its own airworthiness standards (at Title 14 of the Code of Federal Regulations). Accordingly, the U.S. filed a temporary difference with the ICAO standards while the FAA tasked certain working groups with proposing ways to incorporate the ICAO standards.

In 1991, during the period when the U.S. was working on international standards with ICAO, the FAA chartered the creation of the Aviation Rulemaking Advisory Committee (ARAC), in order to maintain harmonized security standards between the United States and Europe. Composed of 76 member organizations reflecting a range of interests in the aviation community, ARAC provided the FAA with firsthand information regarding proposed rules. On October 27, 1999, the FAA tasked ARAC to propose harmonized regulations incorporating security measures into airplane design, including "Pilot Compartment—Penetration Resistance." 64 Fed. Reg. 57,921–02. The FAA specifically asked ARAC to develop regulations incorporating the ICAO security design provisions that had been adopted on March 12, 1997, and that would have been effective on March 12, 2000. The task was assigned to the Design for Security Harmonization Working Group (DSHWG), which included members from the aviation industry and the governments of Europe, the United States, Brazil, and Canada. ARAC was given until February 1, 2000, to submit the first part of its report and until the end of 2001 to submit the second part. *Id.*

As subsequently described in the 9/11 Commission Report, the FAA's efforts took place in the context of its "sometimes conflicting mandate [from Congress] of regulating the safety and security of U.S. civil aviation while also promoting the aviation industry." National Commission on Terrorist Attacks Upon the United States, *The 9/11 Commission Report* 82 (2004). In the late 1990s, the FAA perceived sabotage as posing a higher safety risk than hijacking, given that no domestic hijacking had occurred in a decade and the commercial aviation system was viewed as more vulnerable to explosives than to weapons such as firearms. *Id.* Further, the air carriers played a major role in the pre-9/11 security system. The Inspector General for the Department of Transportation emphasized the pressures these carriers exerted to control security costs, and to "limit the impact of security requirements on aviation operations, so that the industry could concentrate on its primary mission of moving passengers and aircraft." *Id.* at 85.

It is perhaps not surprising that security efforts on board commercial aircraft were not designed to counter suicide hijackings.

"The FAA-approved 'Common Strategy' had been elaborated over decades of experience with scores of hijackings, beginning in the 1960s. It taught flight crews that the best way to deal with hijackers was to accommodate their demands, get the plane to land safely, and then let law enforcement or the military handle the situation. * * * The strategy operated on the fundamental assumption that hijackers issue negotiable demands (most often for asylum or the release of prisoners), and that, as one FAA official put it, 'suicide wasn't in the game plan of hijackers.' FAA training material provided no guidance for flight crews should violence occur.'" *Id.*

On June 11, 2001, after several airlines reported incidents of flightdeck intrusion by aggressive passengers, the FAA further tasked the DSHWG to propose harmonized regulations to improve the intrusion resistance of the flightdeck. 66 Fed. Reg. 31,273–01. FAA regulations already mandated that the cockpit door remain closed and locked in flight, but this requirement was not always observed or vigorously enforced. Indeed, some interested parties responded skeptically to the proposed rulemaking to install reinforced cockpit doors. A pilots association representative observed that "even if you make a vault out of the door, if they have a noose around my flight attendant's neck, I'm going to open the door." The June 11, 2001 Notice of New Task Assignment indicated completion was due no later than December 31, 2001.

On September 11, 2001, nineteen hijackers gained access to the flightdeck of four commercial airplanes, crashing two of the airplanes into the North and South Towers of the World Trade Center and crashing a third into the Pentagon. The fourth plane crashed outside of Shanksville, Pennsylvania.

Following these terrorist acts, Congress moved to pass legislation. On October 11, 2001, the Senate passed a version of an aviation security bill; on November 1, 2001, the House passed a significantly different bill. After a conference, President Bush signed the Aviation and Transportation Security Act (ATSA) on November 19, 2001. Pub. L. 107–71, 115 Stat. 597 (codified as amended in scattered sections of 49 U.S.C.). ATSA directed the FAA to take action to improve airplane security both immediately and in the long-term, giving the FAA the authority to carry out the ATSA's directives. As soon as possible, ATSA required that the FAA prohibit unauthorized access to the airplane cockpit, control authorized access to the cockpit, require strengthening of the cockpit door and door locks to ensure that the door cannot be forced open from the passenger cabin, require that flight deck doors remain locked during flight, and prohibit the possession of a key to the cockpit door by anyone not assigned to the cockpit. Section 104 of ATSA directed the FAA to issue final rules, without seeking public comment prior to adoption, normally a requirement for any rulemaking, in order to accomplish the goals of cockpit door reinforcement.

In response to this law, and to President Bush's call for increased aircraft security during a speech at Chicago O'Hare International Airport, the FAA issued a series of Special Federal Aviation Regulations (SFARs) and four final rules without notice. On October 9, 2001, the FAA published the first SFAR, which expedited the immediate modification of cockpit doors in the U.S. as a first phase short-term fix. 66 Fed. Reg. 51,546. The major U.S. airlines voluntarily modified the cockpit doors on 4,000 airplanes within the first 45 days of the SFAR. By January 2002, 98 percent of the airlines had voluntarily installed this fix. By March 1, 2002, the major U.S. airlines completed installation of cockpit door modifications on all U.S. airplanes. *FAA Fact Sheet on Aircraft Security Accomplishments Since Sept. 11*, released September 5, 2002.

On January 15, 2002, as a permanent measure, the FAA published an amendment requiring the flightdeck door to be strengthened to resist forcible intrusion by unauthorized persons or penetration by small arms fire and fragmentation devices. This amendment required compliance by April 9, 2003, for all U.S. operators. 67 Fed. Reg. 2,118. This measure was published without prior notice or prior comment. On June 21, 2002, the FAA published a final rule requiring foreign airlines to install reinforced cockpit doors on aircrafts serving the United States by April 9, 2003, the same deadline as U.S. carriers. This measure also was published without prior notice or prior comment.

In both its January 15, 2002 and June 21, 2002 measures, the FAA noted that federal regulations must undergo several economic analyses. First, and most importantly, agencies must conduct a cost-benefit analysis pursuant to Executive Order 12,866, which directs each federal agency proposing or adopting a regulation to show that the benefits of the intended regulation justify its costs. (see Appendix D of the Casebook) With respect to the domestically affected aircraft, the January 15, 2002 rule estimated that the retrofitted cockpit door costs would range between $79.6 million and $112.7 million (the cost of the new doors would range between $12,000 and $17,000 and over 6,600 airplanes were affected). In addition, the FAA estimated that the additional 50 pounds resulting from a heavier door would result in additional fuel requirement costs of $27.5 million over ten years. Therefore, the FAA determined that the total cost was expected to range from a base of $107.1 million to $140.2 million over the ten-year period.

With respect to foreign aircraft affected by the June 21, 2002 rule, the FAA estimated that the retrofitted cockpit door costs would be approximately $32.7 million; the costs of the doors was about $17,000 each and the number of affected aircraft was 1,921. The FAA noted that because the air carriers might have to have their doors installed by the original manufacturer, the cost would increase to about $27,500 per door for narrowbody aircraft and $39,900 for widebody aircraft. Accordingly, the cost to foreign air carriers to purchase and install the compliant doors could be as high as $72.0 million. The FAA also estimated that the additional 50 pounds would result in an additional $11.2 million fuel requirement cost over the next decade. In explaining both rules, the FAA determined that the benefits—to ensure the safety and security of the flying public; to prevent the reoccurrence of an event like September 11, 2001, in terms of averted loss of life and property; and to avoid damage to the economy—justified the costs. Although the FAA could not provide a reasonable quantitative estimate of benefits, the agency noted that the benefit would most likely be in the tens of billions of dollars, clearly justifying any cost associated with the rules.[15]

---

[15] The second means of economic analysis the FAA undertook was pursuant to the Regulatory Flexibility Act of 1980, requiring agencies to analyze the economic impact of regulatory changes on small entities. The FAA determined that both rules would not have a significant impact on a substantial number of small entities. Third, the Trade Agreements Act prohibits agencies from setting standards that create unnecessary obstacles to the foreign commerce of the United States. The FAA determined that both rules would have no effect on trade-sensitive activity. Finally, the Unfunded Mandates Act of 1995 requires agencies to prepare a written assessment of the costs and benefits, and other effects of proposed and final rules, where the rule imposes on state, local, or tribal governments, or on the private sector, a mandate likely to result in a total expenditure of $100 million or more in any one year. The FAA determined that these rules did not impose an unfunded mandate on state, local, or tribal governments, or on the private sector.

On September 28, 2001, the President had already announced an FAA federal grant program to help U.S. airlines finance reinforced cockpit doors, and Congress appropriated $100 million to fund the initiatives. The FAA distributed approximately $97 million to air carriers to strengthen their cockpit doors, leaving $3 million to fund other pilot programs aimed at cabin surveillance and alert systems.

Although the January 15, 2002 and June 21, 2002 measures were final rules, the FAA also requested comments, inviting interested parties to submit written data, views, or arguments. While expressing general support for the requirements of the rulemaking, the trade association representing U.S. domestic carriers commented that the agency had significantly underestimated the cost of replacement doors. The association attached a letter indicating that one major domestic airline was spending $49,000 per flight deck door ($39,000 for the door plus $10,000 for installation), not the $17,000 upper bound identified by the FAA on January 15, 2002. The trade association requested that "the rule be modified as necessary" to take account of this issue.

ATSA also established a new agency, the Transportation Security Administration (TSA), to assume responsibility for most civil aviation security functions from the FAA. However, the statute gave FAA immediate authority to change airplane design, and that continues to be an FAA responsibility. 115 Stat. 597, § 104.

In addition to enacting ATSA, Congress addressed the issue of liability in the aftermath of the September 11 attacks. On September 22, 2001, after two hours of debate and less than two days of hearings, both the House and the Senate passed the Air Transportation Safety and System Stabilization Act (ATSSSA), Pub. L. 107–42, 115 Stat. 230 (2001) (codified at 49 U.S.C. § 40101 note). This was an attempt to stabilize the airline industry, which had lost billions of dollars as a result of the attacks and faced even greater losses in litigation that threatened to bankrupt the entire industry.[16] ATSSSA capped "liability for all claims . . . arising from . . . September 11, 2001 against any air carrier" not to exceed "the limits of the liability coverage maintained by the air carrier." Pub. L. No. 107–42, at § 408(a). The Act provided for a federally-funded Victim Compensation Fund (VCF), offering victims a no-fault alternative to tort litigation by compensating "any individual (or relatives of a deceased individual) who was physically injured or killed as a result of the terrorist-related aircraft crashes of September 11, 2001." *Id.* § 405.

The Attorney General was to administer the VCF, acting through a Special Master charged with promulgating all procedural and substantive rules for the administration of the statute. On November 26, 2001, Attorney General John Ashcroft appointed mediator Kenneth Feinberg as Special Master of the VCF. About 97 percent of those eligible chose to opt for recovery through the VCF, not through the court system. Six billion dollars was distributed to the families of the 2,880 deceased victims and one billion dollars was distributed to 2,680 injury victims. *See* Kenneth Feinberg et al., U.S. Dept. of Justice, *Final Report of the Special Master for the September 11th Victim Compensation Fund of 2001.*

In order to receive compensation from the VCF, victims or their representatives were required to waive all rights to file a civil suit for damages against the aviation industry. For those victims that did not opt in to the VCF, ATSSSA created an exclusive cause of action for all claims "arising out of the hijacking and subsequent crashes" of

---

[16] United Airlines, American Airlines, and U.S. Airways subsequently filed for Chapter 11 bankruptcy.

September 11, 2001, providing for federal jurisdiction in the United States District Court for the Southern District of New York. *Id.* at § 408(b)(3). Further, the United States had not waived its sovereign immunity under the Federal Tort Claims Act, 18 U.S.C. § 2671 et seq., with respect to being sued for damages arising from the attacks.

Some ninety-five of the injured and representatives of those who died plus twenty-one entities that sustained property damage chose to file lawsuits against defendants they claimed were legally responsible to compensate them: the airlines, the airport security companies, the airport operators, the airplane manufacturer, and the operators and owners of the World Trade Center. Early on, the defendants moved to dismiss the claims, and the judge held each of the defendants owed a duty of care to the plaintiffs who sued. *In re September 11 Litig.*, 280 F. Supp. 2d 279, 286–87 (S.D.N.Y. 2003); see also *In re September 11 Litig.*, 600 F. Supp. 2d 549, 550 (S.D.N.Y. 2009). When this edition went to print, all ninety-five personal injury or wrongful death claims and nineteen of the twenty-one property damage claims had settled. See Docket, *In re September 11 Litig.*, No. 21 MC 101 (AKH) (S.D.N.Y); *Cantor Fitzgerald Settles 9/11 Suit Against American Airlines for $135 Million*, N.Y. Times, Dec. 18, 2013, at A1.

As we consider various aspects of agency implementation procedures and agency oversight by all three branches, you should keep this Case Study in mind. Did the agency initiate and proceed with rulemaking in a responsible and diligent fashion prior to the 9/11 attacks?

PROBLEMS ON THE FAA CASE STUDY

Problem 8–1. Assume you are the FAA policymaker responsible for coordinating the agency's anti-hijacking flight deck security measures as of June 10, 2001. In addition to the facts presented in the Case Study, you are aware that there were a handful of hijackings on Europe-originating flights during the 1990s, all of which ended without casualties. You also know that on December 24, 1994, an Air France flight destined for Paris was hijacked at its originating point of Algiers, Algeria by four hijackers, armed with Kalashnikov assault rifles, Uzi submachine guns, pistols, homemade hand grenades, and two 10–stick dynamite packs. The hijackers planned to crash the plane into the Eiffel Tower in Paris. They murdered three passengers before departing Algiers, but when they were forced to land in Marseilles to refuel, French law enforcement stormed the plane, killing all hijackers and freeing the remaining passengers.

What actions (rulemakings, policy statements, studies) would you recommend the agency undertake to strengthen flight deck security, *other than* requesting—as the Case Study shows FAA did at the time—that the Design for Security Harmonization Working Group (DSHWG) propose harmonized regulations? Is your proposed action something the agency is authorized to initiate under 49 U.S.C. § 44701(a)? Assuming there is some action you deem worth taking, with whom would you consult before proposing it: The White House? Relevant congressional committee chairs? Federal law enforcement officials? Foreign governments? The domestic airlines or their trade association? The airline pilots union?

Problem 8–2. It is still June 10, 2001 and the same additional facts as in Problem 8–1 are known to you, but now you are the FAA General Counsel heading an agency task force to coordinate passenger safety for all domestic flights. How foreseeable is the risk of suicide hijackings on U.S. domestic flights in June 2001? Is the risk substantially greater than it was in 1988 before Lockerbie? In 1994 before Air France? How should you determine the foreseeable risk of such hijackings in this setting? Is the idea of foreseeable risk even something the agency should be thinking about or acting on? If your answer is yes, is weighing costs associated with new security measures a relevant consideration? Why or why not?

The data on hijackings establish that almost all attempts involve the use of firearms or explosives. Assume it would cost $300 million for the domestic airlines to install reinforced cockpit doors on all their planes, and would cost $900 million to install and staff metal detectors and x-ray machines for passenger and luggage security screening at every major U.S. airport. Would these costs lead you to prefer one approach to the other? What if the airlines bring you a valid scientific study indicating that the public will take 15 percent fewer airplane trips annually if they are required to go through the metal detector/x-ray machine screening process (they will take buses, trains, or cars, or else not travel as much); would this affect the safety measures you recommend in June 2001?

B. THE NONDELEGATION DOCTRINE

The nondelegation doctrine posits that the legislature may not delegate its inherent lawmaking powers to agencies without providing specific standards for the bureaucracy to apply in administering the delegation—in the Supreme Court's words, laying down "an intelligible principle" to which administrators must conform. *J.W. Hampton, Jr. & Co. v. United States*, 276 U.S. 394, 409 (1928). The doctrine was highly controversial during the New Deal when it was used by the Supreme Court to strike down major provisions of the National Industrial Recovery Act. See *Panama Refining v. Ryan*, 293 U.S. 388 (1935); *A.L.A. Schechter Poultry Corp. v. United States*, 295 U.S. 495 (1935).

After President Franklin Roosevelt made several new appointments to the Supreme Court and the administrative state became an accepted part of our democracy, the nondelegation doctrine fell into constitutional disuse. In *Yakus v. United States*, 321 U.S. 414 (1944), the Court upheld a broad delegation of price control authority to the Office of Price Administration during World War II. The only "intelligible principle" in the statute was that prices be "fair and equitable" but the court sustained the delegation. "Only if we could say that there is an absence of standards for the guidance of the Administrator's action, so that it would be impossible in a proper proceeding to ascertain whether the will of Congress has been obeyed, would we be justified in overriding its choice of means for effecting its declared purpose of preventing inflation."

The Economic Stabilization Act of 1970, 84 Stat. 799, codified at 12 U.S.C. § 1904 note, did not even have a "fair and equitable" standard when it authorized the President "to issue such orders and regulations as he may deem appropriate to stabilize prices, rents, wages, and salaries at levels not less than those prevailing on May 25, 1970." Nonetheless, when President Nixon exercised that power to freeze prices and wages in Executive Order 11,615, 36 Fed. Reg. 15,727 (1971), a special three-judge court rejected a nondelegation doctrine challenge. See *Amalgamated Meat Cutters and Butcher Workmen of N. Am. v. Connolly*, 337 F.

Supp. 737 (D.D.C. 1971) (three-judge court). Judge Leventhal constructed standards to guide presidential implementation of the Act from (1) its legislative history, which revealed the purposes of the law; (2) prior price control statutes, such as the one upheld in *Yakus;* and (3) judicial power to elaborate on implicit statutory terms, such as a "fairness and equitable" standard, enforceable through judicial review of the executive implementation decisions. In addition, the court found that the agency's ability to act arbitrarily was blunted by a requirement that it promulgate additional standards to guide its actions taken under the statute. "This requirement, inherent in the Rule of Law and implicit in the Act, means that however broad the discretion of the Executive at the outset, the standard once developed limits the latitude of subsequent Executive action." *Id.* at 759. This period was the nadir of the nondelegation doctrine. Cf. *Mistretta v. United States,* 488 U.S. 361 (1989) (Court unanimously rejects nondelegation challenge to Sentencing Commission; majority opinion suggests that doctrine might be limited to "giving narrow constructions to statutory delegations that might otherwise be thought to be unconstitutional").

WHITMAN V. AMERICAN TRUCKING ASSOCIATIONS, INC.
Supreme Court of the United States, 2001.
531 U.S. 457, 121 S.Ct. 903, 149 L.Ed.2d 1.

JUSTICE SCALIA delivered the opinion of the Court.

These cases present the following questions: (1) Whether § 109(b)(1) of the Clean Air Act (CAA) delegates legislative power to the Administrator of the Environmental Protection Agency (EPA) * * *

[I]   Section 109(a) of the CAA, as added, 84 Stat. 1679, and amended, 42 U.S.C. § 7409(a), requires the Administrator of the EPA to promulgate [National Ambient Air Quality Standards] NAAQS for each air pollutant for which "air quality criteria" have been issued under § 108, 42 U.S.C. § 7408. Once a NAAQS has been promulgated, the Administrator must review the standard (and the criteria on which it is based) "at five-year intervals" and make "such revisions . . . as may be appropriate." CAA § 109(d)(1), 42 U.S.C. § 7409(d)(1). These cases arose when, on July 18, 1997, the Administrator revised the NAAQS for particulate matter and ozone. American Trucking Associations, Inc., and its co-respondents * * * challenged the new standards in the Court of Appeals for the District of Columbia Circuit, pursuant to 42 U.S.C. § 7607(b)(1).

The District of Columbia Circuit accepted some of the challenges and rejected others. It agreed with the respondents that § 109(b)(1) delegated legislative power to the Administrator in contravention of the United States Constitution, Art. I, § 1, because it found that the EPA had interpreted the statute to provide no "intelligible principle" to guide the agency's exercise of authority. The court thought, however, that the EPA could perhaps avoid the unconstitutional delegation by adopting a restrictive construction of § 109(b)(1), so instead of declaring the section unconstitutional the court remanded the NAAQS to the agency. * * *

[III] Section 109(b)(1) of the CAA instructs the EPA to set "ambient air quality standards the attainment and maintenance of which in the judgment of the Administrator, based on [the] criteria [documents of § 108] and allowing an adequate margin of safety, are requisite to protect the public health." 42 U.S.C. § 7409(b)(1). The Court of Appeals held that this section as interpreted by the Administrator did not provide an "intelligible principle" to guide the EPA's exercise of authority in setting NAAQS. "[The] EPA," it said, "lack[ed] any determinate criteria for drawing lines. It has failed to state intelligibly how much is too much." The court hence found that the EPA's interpretation (but not the statute itself) violated the nondelegation doctrine. We disagree.

In a delegation challenge, the constitutional question is whether the statute has delegated legislative power to the agency. Article I, § 1, of the Constitution vests "[a]ll legislative Powers herein granted . . . in a Congress of the United States." This text permits no delegation of those powers, and so we repeatedly have said that when Congress confers decisionmaking authority upon agencies *Congress* must "lay down by legislative act an intelligible principle to which the person or body authorized to [act] is directed to conform." *J.W. Hampton, Jr., & Co. v. United States*, 276 U.S. 394, 409 (1928). We have never suggested that an agency can cure an unlawful delegation of legislative power by adopting in its discretion a limiting construction of the statute. Both *Fahey v. Mallonee*, 332 U.S. 245, 252–253 (1947), and *Lichter v. United States*, 334 U.S. 742, 783 (1948), mention agency regulations in the course of their nondelegation discussions, but *Lichter* did so because a subsequent Congress had incorporated the regulations into a revised version of the statute, *ibid.*, and *Fahey* because the customary practices in the area, implicitly incorporated into the statute, were reflected in the regulations, 332 U.S. at 250. The idea that an agency can cure an unconstitutionally standardless delegation of power by declining to exercise some of that power seems to us internally contradictory. The very choice of which portion of the power to exercise—that is to say, the prescription of the standard that Congress had omitted—would *itself* be an exercise of the forbidden legislative authority. Whether the statute delegates legislative power is a question for the courts, and an agency's voluntary self-denial has no bearing upon the answer.

We agree with the Solicitor General that the text of § 109(b)(1) of the CAA at a minimum requires that "[f]or a discrete set of pollutants and based on published air quality criteria that reflect the latest scientific knowledge, [the] EPA must establish uniform national standards at a level that is requisite to protect public health from the adverse effects of the pollutant in the ambient air." Tr. of Oral Arg. in No. 99–1257, p. 5. Requisite, in turn, "mean[s] sufficient, but not more than necessary." *Id.*, at 7. These limits on the EPA's discretion are strikingly similar to the ones we approved in *Touby v. United States*, 500 U.S. 160 (1991), which permitted the Attorney General to designate a drug as a controlled substance for purposes of criminal drug enforcement if doing so was " 'necessary to avoid an imminent hazard to the public safety.' " *Id.* at 163. They also resemble the Occupational Safety and Health Act of 1970 provision requiring the agency to " 'set the standard which most adequately assures, to the extent feasible, on the basis of the best available evidence, that no employee will suffer any impairment of health' "—which the Court upheld in *Indust. Union Dep't., AFL-CIO v. Am. Petroleum Inst.*, 448 U.S. 607, 646 (1980), and which even then-Justice Rehnquist, who alone in that case thought the statute violated the nondelegation doctrine, see *Id.* at 671 (opinion concurring in judgment), would have upheld if, like the statute here, it did not permit economic costs to be considered. See *Am. Textile Mfrs. Inst., Inc. v. Donovan*, 452 U.S. 490, 545 (1981) (Rehnquist, J., dissenting).

The scope of discretion § 109(b)(1) allows is in fact well within the outer limits of our nondelegation precedents. In the history of the Court we have found the requisite "intelligible principle" lacking in only two statutes, one of which provided literally no guidance for the exercise of discretion, and the other of which conferred authority to regulate the entire economy on the basis of no more precise a standard than stimulating the economy by assuring "fair competition." See *Panama Refining Co. v. Ryan*, 293 U.S. 388 (1935); *A.L.A. Schechter Poultry Corp. v. United States*, 295 U.S. 495 (1935). We have, on the other hand, upheld the validity of § 11(b)(2) of the Public Utility Holding Company Act of 1935, 49 Stat. 821, which gave the Securities and Exchange Commission authority to modify the structure of holding company systems so as to ensure that they are not "unduly or unnecessarily complicate[d]" and do not "unfairly or inequitably distribute voting power among security holders." *Am. Power & Light Co. v. SEC*, 329 U.S. 90, 104 (1946). We have approved the wartime conferral of agency power to fix the prices of commodities at a level that " 'will be generally fair and equitable and will effectuate the [in some respects conflicting] purposes of th[e] Act.' " *Yakus v. United States*, 321 U.S. 414, 420, 423–426 (1944). And we have found an "intelligible principle" in various statutes authorizing regulation in the "public interest." See, e.g., *Nat'l Broad. Co. v. United States*, 319 U.S. 190, 225–226 (1943) (Federal Communications Commission's power to regulate airwaves); *N.Y. Cent. Sec. Corp. v. United States*, 287 U.S. 12, 24–25 (1932) (Interstate Commerce Commission's power to approve railroad consolidations). In short, we have "almost never felt qualified to second-guess Congress regarding the permissible degree of policy judgment that can be left to those executing or applying the law." *Mistretta v. United States*, 488 U.S. 361, 416 (1989) (Scalia, J., dissenting); see *id.* at 373 (majority opinion).

It is true enough that the degree of agency discretion that is acceptable varies according to the scope of the power congressionally conferred. While Congress need not provide any direction to the EPA regarding the manner in which it is to define "country elevators," which are to be exempt from new-stationary-source regulations governing grain elevators, see 42 U.S.C. § 7411(i), it must provide substantial guidance on setting air standards that affect the entire national economy. But even in sweeping regulatory schemes we have never demanded, as the Court of Appeals did here, that statutes provide a "determinate criterion" for saying "how much [of the regulated harm] is too much." In *Touby*, for example, we did not require the statute to decree how "imminent" was too imminent, or how "necessary" was necessary enough, or even—most relevant here—how "hazardous" was too hazardous. Similarly, the statute at issue in *Lichter* authorized agencies to recoup "excess profits" paid under wartime Government contracts, yet we did not insist that Congress specify how much profit was too much. It is therefore not conclusive for delegation purposes that, as respondents argue, ozone and particulate matter are "nonthreshold" pollutants that inflict a continuum of adverse health effects at any airborne concentration greater than zero, and hence require the EPA to make judgments of degree. "[A] certain degree of discretion, and thus of lawmaking, inheres in most executive or judicial action." *Mistretta v. United States, supra,* at 417 (Scalia, J., dissenting) (emphasis deleted); see 488 U.S. at 378–379 (majority opinion). Section 109(b)(1) of the CAA, which to repeat we interpret as requiring the EPA to set air quality standards at the level that is "requisite"—that is, not lower or higher than is necessary—to protect the public health with an adequate margin of safety, fits comfortably within the scope of discretion permitted by our precedent.

We therefore reverse the judgment of the Court of Appeals remanding for reinterpretation that would avoid a supposed delegation of legislative power. It will remain for the Court of Appeals—on the remand that we direct for other reasons—to dispose of any other preserved challenge to the NAAQS under the judicial-review provisions contained in 42 U.S.C. § 7607(d)(9).

[The concurring opinion of JUSTICE THOMAS is omitted.]

JUSTICE STEVENS, with whom JUSTICE SOUTER joins, concurring in part and concurring in the judgment.

Section 109(b)(1) delegates to the Administrator of the Environmental Protection Agency (EPA) the authority to promulgate national ambient air quality standards (NAAQS). In Part III of its opinion, the Court convincingly explains why the Court of Appeals erred when it concluded that § 109 effected "an unconstitutional delegation of legislative power." I wholeheartedly endorse the Court's result and endorse its explanation of its reasons, albeit with the following caveat.

The Court has two choices. We could choose to articulate our ultimate disposition of this issue by frankly acknowledging that the power delegated to the EPA is "legislative" but nevertheless conclude that the delegation is constitutional because adequately limited by the terms of the authorizing statute. Alternatively, we could pretend, as the Court does, that the authority delegated to the EPA is somehow not "legislative power." Despite the fact that there is language in our opinions that supports the Court's articulation of our holding, I am persuaded that it would be both wiser and more faithful to what we have actually done in delegation cases to admit that agency rulemaking authority is "legislative power."[2]

The proper characterization of governmental power should generally depend on the nature of the power, not on the identity of the person exercising it. See Black's Law Dictionary 899 (6th ed. 1990) (defining "legislation" as, *inter alia*, "[f]ormulation of rule[s] for the future"); 1 K. Davis & R. Pierce, Administrative Law Treatise § 2.3, p. 37 (3d ed. 1994) ("If legislative power means the power to

---

[2]   See *Mistretta v. United States,* 488 U.S. 361, 372 (1989) ("[O]ur jurisprudence has been driven by a practical understanding that in our increasingly complex society . . . Congress simply cannot do its job absent an ability to delegate power . . ."). See also *Loving v. United States,* 517 U.S. 748, 758 (1996) ("[The nondelegation] principle does not mean . . . that only Congress can make a rule of prospective force"); 1 K. Davis & R. Pierce, *Administrative Law Treatise* § 2.6, at 66 (3d ed. 1994) ("Except for two 1935 cases, the Court has never enforced its frequently announced prohibition on congressional delegation of legislative power").

make rules of conduct that bind everyone based on resolution of major policy issues, scores of agencies exercise legislative power routinely by promulgating what are candidly called 'legislative rules' "). If the NAAQS that the EPA promulgated had been prescribed by Congress, everyone would agree that those rules would be the product of an exercise of "legislative power." The same characterization is appropriate when an agency exercises rulemaking authority pursuant to a permissible delegation from Congress.

My view is not only more faithful to normal English usage, but is also fully consistent with the text of the Constitution. In Article I, the Framers vested "All legislative Powers" in the Congress, Art. I, § 1, just as in Article II they vested the "executive Power" in the President, Art. II, § 1. Those provisions do not purport to limit the authority of either recipient of power to delegate authority to others. See *Bowsher v. Synar*, 478 U.S. 714, 752 (1986) (Stevens, J., concurring in judgment) ("Despite the statement in Article I of the Constitution that 'All legislative powers herein granted shall be vested in a Congress of the United States,' it is far from novel to acknowledge that independent agencies do indeed exercise legislative powers"); *INS v. Chadha*, 462 U.S. 919, 985–986 (1983) (White, J., dissenting) ("[L]egislative power can be exercised by independent agencies and Executive departments . . ."); 1 Davis & Pierce, Administrative Law Treatise § 2.6, at 66 ("The Court was probably mistaken from the outset in interpreting Article I's grant of power to Congress as an implicit limit on Congress' authority to delegate legislative power"). Surely the authority granted to members of the Cabinet and federal law enforcement agents is properly characterized as "Executive" even though not exercised by the President. Cf. *Morrison v. Olson*, 487 U.S. 654, 705–706 (1988) (Scalia, J., dissenting) (arguing that the independent counsel exercised "executive power" unconstrained by the President).

It seems clear that an executive agency's exercise of rulemaking authority pursuant to a valid delegation from Congress is "legislative." As long as the delegation provides a sufficiently intelligible principle, there is nothing inherently unconstitutional about it. Accordingly, while I join Parts I, II, and IV of the Court's opinion, and agree with almost everything said in Part III, I would hold that when Congress enacted § 109, it effected a constitutional delegation of legislative power to the EPA.

[The opinion of JUSTICE BREYER, who concurred in part and concurred in the judgment, is omitted.]

NOTES ON THE NONDELEGATION DOCTRINE

1.   *Judicial Manageability.* Justice Scalia reiterates a statement he made twelve years earlier (dissenting in *Mistretta*) that the Court "has almost never felt qualified to second guess Congress" regarding how much policy discretion may be left in the hands of agency officials. Is this prudential consideration related simply to the Court's sense of its own competence? Is the Court perhaps worried, as Cass Sunstein has suggested, that given the vagueness of the "intelligible principle" standard, any delegation the Court invalidates is "likely to suffer from the appearance, and perhaps the reality, of judicial hostility to the particular program at issue"? See Cass Sunstein, *Nondelegation*

Canons, 67 U. Chi. L. Rev. 315, 327 (2000). Should the Court's concerns about its own perceived legitimacy justify a virtual abandonment of the nondelegation doctrine?

2.   *Continuing Vitality?* Although no federal statute has been invalidated by the Supreme Court pursuant to the nondelegation doctrine since the 1930s, individual Justices have occasionally invoked the doctrine. See, e.g., *Zemel v. Rusk*, 381 U.S. 1, 20 (1965) (Black, J., dissenting); *Indus. Union Dep't, AFL-CIO v. Am. Petroleum Inst.*, 448 U.S. 607, 685–86 (1980) (Rehnquist, J., dissenting); *American Textile Mfrs. Inst., Inc. v. Donovan*, 452 U.S. 490, 543 (1981) (Rehnquist, J., dissenting). Moreover, some state courts still enforce a nondelegation doctrine.[17]

Notwithstanding the apparent demise of the nondelegation doctrine after *Schechter Poultry*, some scholars find the doctrine to be a useful concept and argue for its resurrection. Political scientist Theodore Lowi, in *The End of Liberalism: The Second Republic of the United States* (2d ed. 1979), argues that legislatures tend to avoid hard political choices by delegating virtually blanket authority to bureaucrats. Public choice theory, discussed in Chapter 1, § 2, reinforces Lowi's point. Public choice theorists posit that legislators' chief motivation is to achieve reelection. One effective method for achieving reelection is for legislators to spend most of their time doing things which their constituents find uncontroversial, such as casework helping constituents wind their way through the bureaucracy and pork barrel projects benefitting their districts. As to substantive legislation, the best strategy is usually to avoid positions that offend important electoral groups in the legislator's district. This can be done through ducking the issue entirely or, if that is impossible, delegating resolution of the most divisive issues to agencies. With Lowi, one can argue from a public choice perspective that the temptation to pass the substantive buck to agencies is as tempting as it is undemocratic (bureaucrats rather than legislators are making important policy choices) and counterproductive (the choices may be biased if the agency is captured and timid if the agency is not). See David Schoenbrod, *Power Without Responsibility: How Congress Abuses the People Through Delegation* (1993).

Jerry Mashaw disputes the pessimistic public choice perspective on the nondelegation doctrine, and he argues instead that broad delegations to administrative agencies can sometimes ensure better policymaking. *Greed, Chaos, and Governance: Using Public Choice to Improve Public Law* (1997). He demonstrates that broad delegations may actually reduce rent-seeking by interest groups because they inhibit vote-trading and deal-making. Once power has been delegated to an agency, lawmakers find it more difficult to offer bargains in that issue arena, and administrators cannot make tradeoffs on issues outside their jurisdiction. In fact, some laws that result from the most questionable interest group activity are often very specifically worded to guarantee that bargainers get the deals they struck. Mashaw also argues that voters can often hold members of Congress accountable for broad delegations more easily than they can learn of specific deals found in the details of omnibus legislation. "No one has been able to demonstrate any systematic relationship between improving accountability, or enhancing the public welfare, or respecting the rule of law, and the specificity of legislation." Mashaw goes on to make the affirmative case for broad delegations, arguing that they take advantage of administrative expertise and

---

[17]   E.g., *Hampton v. Haley*, 743 S.E.2d 258 (S.C. 2013); *Cobb v. State Canvassing Bd.*, 140 P.3d 498 (N.M. 2006); *Thygesen v. Callahan*, 385 N.E.2d 699 (Ill. 1979). See Hans Linde, George Bunn, Fredericka Paff & W. Lawrence Church, *Legislative and Administrative Processes* 478 (2d ed. 1981).

flexibility. Furthermore, agencies may be more responsive to public desires, because they can often act more quickly than Congress can enact legislation, and they benefit from the President's accountability to a national electorate.[18]

In recent years, the nondelegation doctrine has also enjoyed an indirect revival at the Supreme Court level. As two of us noted in 1992, although "the Court has not invalidated a statute on [nondelegation] grounds since the 1930s," the Court now "refers to the nondelegation idea as a canon of statutory interpretation rather than as an enforceable constitutional doctrine."[19] When agencies aggressively assert a broad jurisdiction not supported by a congressional authorization, clearly expressed in the statute, the Court ought to overrule the agency and insist on a more targeted statutory authorization.[20] This thesis is supported by the Court's decision in *Whitman*, which rejected a constitutional nondelegation challenge to the Clean Air Act but construed the Act narrowly in light of the apparent limiting principle, and in *MCI v. AT&T* (Chapter 9), which narrowly construed a telecommunications law on the ground that the broad revisionary authority claimed by the FCC had to be more clearly stated on the face of the statute for the Court to give it effect. See also *FDA v. Brown & Williamson Tobacco Co.* (Chapter 6, § 3B3). If a court is faced with an extremely broad delegation that might implicate constitutional concerns, it uses the canon to adopt a narrow interpretation that would restrain agency discretion. This approach is similar to the one used in *Yakus* or *Amalgamated Meat Cutters*, discussed above, where the courts poured meaning into general statutory language to find intelligible guidelines and procedural requirements to limit agency discretion.

On the other hand, the Court in *Whitman* rejected the D.C. Circuit's reasoning that an agency can avoid an unlawful delegation by adopting in its discretion a limiting construction of the statute. What is the justification for allowing *courts*, but not *agencies*, to invoke this form of the avoidance canon? From a pragmatic standpoint, is it that the Court trusts the judiciary to constrain the powers exercised by an agency but does not trust agencies to narrow their own powers? Alternatively, from an institutional perspective, perhaps courts are authorized under Article III to help Congress act constitutionally but agencies—as subordinate extensions of Congress—lack this authority?

3. *Nondelegation and the FAA Case Study.* Review the language of 49 U.S.C. § 44701(a), conferring certain safety-related authority on the FAA. Also consider section 104(a) of the Aviation and Transportation Security Act of 2001 (115 Stat. 597), which directs the FAA Administrator to strengthen flight deck doors and locks, and "take such

---

[18] See also Edward Rubin, *Law and Legislation in the Administrative State*, 89 Colum. L. Rev. 369 (1989) (offering a pragmatic justification for broad delegations); David Spence & Frank Cross, *A Public Choice Case for the Administrative State*, 89 Geo. L.J. 97 (2000) (using public choice theory to defend broad delegations). See generally *Symposium: The Phoenix Rises Again: The Nondelegation Doctrine from Constitutional and Policy Perspectives*, 20 Cardozo L. Rev. 731–1018 (1999) (providing various scholarly perspectives on the nondelegation doctrine).

[19] William Eskridge Jr. & Philip Frickey, *Quasi-Constitutional Law: Clear Statement Rules as Constitutional Lawmaking*, 45 Vand. L. Rev. 593, 607 (1992). See also Lisa Schultz Bressman, *Schechter Poultry at the Millennium: A Delegation Doctrine for the Administrative State*, 109 Yale L.J. 1399 (2000) (making a similar argument that the doctrine survives in the judicial requirement that an agency rule include standards limiting its own discretion). For support in the cases, see, e.g., *Mistretta*, 488 U.S. at 373 n.7; *Indust.Union Dep't, AFL-CIO v. Am Petroleum Inst.*, 448 U.S. 607 (1980).

[20] See William Eskridge Jr. & John Ferejohn, *The Article I, Section 7 Game*, 80 Geo. L.J. 523, 561–62 (1992).

other action, including modification of safety and security procedures and flight deck redesign, as may be necessary to ensure the safety and security of the aircraft."

El Al Israel Airlines, which has long been a prime target for terrorists, requires that all cockpits have locked double doors to prevent access by unauthorized persons. Each door has a separate access code, and the second door can be opened only after the first has been closed and the person seeking entry has been identified by the captain or first officer. In addition, undercover agents carrying concealed firearms sit among the passengers on every international El Al flight. Would one or both of the two statutory provisions cited above authorize the FAA to require double doors with coded access on every U.S. passenger plane? To direct that federal sky marshals with concealed firearms travel on all international flights to and from the U.S.?

C. APPOINTMENT AND REMOVAL OF AGENCY OFFICIALS

In order to understand the constitutional basis for administrative agencies, it is worth reviewing the language of Article II, section 2, found in Appendix A of the Casebook. Several references indicate that the Framers anticipated the national government would need departments or agencies in order to function. The President is authorized to require written opinions from *"the principal Officer in each of the executive Departments"*; he is further authorized to appoint "Ambassadors, other public Ministers and Consuls, Judges of the supreme Court, and *all other [impliedly inferior] Officers* of the United States, whose Appointments are not herein otherwise provided for"; finally, Congress is authorized to "vest the Appointment *of such inferior Officers* in the President alone, in the Courts of Law, or *in the Heads of Departments.*" (emphases added). The Constitution does not elaborate further as to the structure or organization of departments, or the distinction between principal and inferior officers within those departments. The Framers evidently decided to leave determinations about how agencies would be created, what powers they would exercise, and what procedures they would follow, to the new national government.

As for what qualifies as an "agency," Congress has developed more than one statutory definition. In the Paperwork Reduction Act of 1980, which imposed various procedural requirements on agencies seeking to collect information from the public, the term 'agency' means:

> "any executive department, military department, Government corporation, Government controlled corporation, or other establishment in the executive branch of the Government (including the Executive Office of the President), or any independent regulatory agency,"

but excluding two specifically named government entities and also excluding governments of the District of Columbia and U.S. territories as well as facilities that are government-owned and contractor-operated. 44 U.S.C. § 3502(1). Compare this definition with an earlier one from the APA, enacted in 1946 and set forth in Appendix B, 5 U.S.C. § 551(1). Are there any important differences? Is the President an agency under the APA? Is the military treated identically under the two statutes?

The Paperwork Reduction Act also defines the term "independent regulatory agency" as encompassing 19 specific agencies plus "any other similar agency designated by statute as a Federal independent regulatory agency or commission." 44 U.S.C. § 3502(5). If an independent regulatory agency is not within the executive branch, where precisely does it reside? Does it occupy a different constitutional status from executive branch agencies? Consider these questions as you read the next two cases.

MYERS V. UNITED STATES

Supreme Court of the United States 1926.
272 U.S. 52, 47 S.Ct. 21, 71 L.Ed. 160.

MR. CHIEF JUSTICE TAFT delivered the opinion of the Court.

This case presents the question whether under the Constitution the President has the exclusive power of removing executive officers of the United States whom he has appointed by and with the advice and consent of the Senate.

Myers, appellant's intestate, was on July 21, 1917, appointed by the President, by and with the advice and consent of the Senate, to be a postmaster of the first class at Portland, Oregon, for a term of four years. On January 20, 1920, Myers' resignation was demanded. He refused the demand. On February 2, 1920, he was removed from office by order of the Postmaster General, acting by direction of the President. February 10th, Myers sent a petition to the President and another to the Senate Committee on Post Offices, asking to be heard, if any charges were filed. He protested to the department against his removal, and continued to do so until the end of his term. He pursued no other occupation and drew compensation for no other service during the interval. On April 21, 1921, he brought this suit in the Court of Claims for his salary from the date of his removal. * * *

By the sixth section of the Act of Congress of July 12, 1876, 19 Stat. 80, 81, c. 179 (Comp. St. § 7190), under which Myers was appointed with the advice and consent of the Senate as a first-class postmaster, it is provided that: "Postmasters of the first, second, and third classes shall be appointed and may be removed by the President by and with the advice and consent of the Senate, and shall hold their offices for four years unless sooner removed or suspended according to law."

The Senate did not consent to the President's removal of Myers during his term. If this statute in its requirement that his term should be four years unless sooner removed by the President by and with the consent of the Senate is valid, the appellant, Myers' administratrix, is entitled to recover his unpaid salary for his full term. * * * The government maintains that the requirement is invalid, for the reason that under article 2 of the Constitution the President's power of removal of executive officers appointed by him with the advice and consent of the Senate is full and complete without consent of the Senate. If this view is sound, the removal of Myers by the President without the Senate's consent was legal.* * *

The question where the power of removal of executive officers appointed by the President by and with the advice and consent of the Senate was vested, was presented early in the first session of the First Congress. There is no express provision respecting removals in the Constitution, except as section 4 of article 2, above quoted, provides for removal from office by impeachment. The subject was not discussed in the Constitutional Convention. Under the Articles of Confederation, Congress was given the power of appointing certain executive officers of the Confederation, and during the Revolution and while the articles were given effect, Congress exercised the power of removal.

[The Court reviewed the Constitutional Convention's consideration of the shape and scope of executive power, and the First Congress's establishment of a Department of Foreign Affairs whose Secretary was to be appointed by the President with the advice and consent of the Senate, and removable by the President.]

The debates in the Constitutional Convention indicated an intention to create a strong executive, and after a controversial discussion the executive power of the government was vested in one person and many of his important functions were specified so as to avoid the humiliating weakness of the Congress during the Revolution and under the Articles of Confederation. Mr. Madison and his associates in the discussion in the House dwelt at length upon the necessity there was for construing article 2 to give the President the sole power of removal in his responsibility for the conduct of the executive branch, and enforced this by emphasizing his duty expressly declared in the third section of the article to "take care that the laws be faithfully executed."

The vesting of the executive power in the President was essentially a grant of the power to execute the laws. But the President alone and unaided could not execute the laws. He must execute them by the assistance of subordinates. This view has since been repeatedly affirmed by this court. As he is charged specifically to take care that they be faithfully executed, the reasonable implication, even in the absence of express words, was that as part of his executive power he should select those who were to act for him under his direction in the execution of the laws. The further implication must be, in the absence of any express limitation respecting removals, that as his selection of administrative officers is essential to the execution of the laws by him, so must be his power of removing those for whom he cannot continue to be responsible. It was urged that the natural meaning of the term "executive power" granted the President included the appointment and removal of executive subordinates. If such appointments and removals were not an exercise of the executive power, what were they? They certainly were not the exercise of legislative or judicial power in government as usually understood. * * *

The power to prevent the removal of an officer who has served under the President is different from the authority to consent to or reject his appointment. When a nomination is made, it may be presumed that the Senate is, or may become, as well advised as to the fitness of the nominee as the President, but in the nature of things the defects in ability or intelligence or loyalty in the administration of the laws of one who has served as an officer under the President are facts as to which the President, or his trusted subordinates, must be better informed than the Senate, and the power to remove him may therefor be regarded as confined for very sound and practical reasons, to the governmental authority which has administrative control. The power of removal is incident to the power of appointment, not to the power of advising and consenting to appointment, and when the grant of the executive power is enforced by the express mandate to take care that the laws be faithfully executed, it emphasizes the necessity for including within the executive power as conferred the exclusive power of removal.* * *

The constitutional construction that excludes Congress from legislative power to provide for the removal of superior officers finds support in the second section of article 2. By it the appointment of all officers, whether superior or inferior, by the President is declared to be subject to the advice and consent of the Senate. In the absence of any specific provision to the contrary, the power of appointment to executive office carries with it, as a necessary incident, the power of removal. Whether the Senate must concur in the removal is aside from the point we now are considering. That point is that by the specific constitutional provision for appointment of executive officers with its necessary incident of removal, the power of appointment and removal is clearly provided for by the Constitution, and the legislative power of Congress in respect to both is excluded save by the specific exception as to inferior offices in the clause that follows. This is "but the Congress may by law vest the appointment of such inferior officers, as they think proper, in the President alone, in the Courts of Law, or in the Heads of Departments." * * *

It is reasonable to suppose also that had it been intended to give to Congress power to regulate or control removals in the manner suggested, it would have been included among the specifically enumerated legislative powers in article 1, or in the specified limitations on the executive power in article 2. The difference between the grant of legislative power under article 1 to Congress which is limited to powers therein enumerated, and the more general grant of the executive power to the President under article 2 is significant. The fact that the executive power is given in general terms strengthened by specific terms where emphasis is appropriate, and limited by direct expressions where limitation is needed, and that no express limit is placed on the power of removal by the executive is a convincing indication that none was intended. * * *

Mr. Madison and his associates pointed out with great force the unreasonable character of the view that the convention intended, without express provision, to give to Congress or the Senate, in case of political or other differences, the means of thwarting the executive in the exercise of his great powers and in the bearing of his great responsibility by fastening upon him, as subordinate executive officers, men who by their inefficient service under him, by their lack of loyalty to the service, or by their different views of policy might make his taking care that the laws be faithfully executed most difficult or impossible. As Mr. Madison said in the debate in the First Congress: "Vest this power in the Senate jointly with the President, and you abolish at once the great principle of unity and responsibility in the executive department, which was intended for the security of liberty and the public good. If the President should possess alone the power of removal from office, those who are employed in the execution of the law will be in their proper situation, and the chain of dependence will be preserved: the lowest officers, the middle grade, and the highest will depend, as they ought, on the President, and the President on the community." * * *

Made responsible under the Constitution for the effective enforcement of the law, the President needs as an indispensable aid to meet it the disciplinary influence upon those who act under him of a reserve power of removal. But it is contended that executive officers appointed by the President with the consent of the Senate are bound by the statutory law, and are not his servants to do his will, and that his obligation to care for the faithful execution of the laws does not authorize him to treat them as such. The degree of guidance in the discharge of their duties that the President may exercise over executive officers varies with the character of their service as prescribed in the law under which they act. The highest and most important duties which his subordinates perform are those in which they act for him. In such cases they are exercising not their own but his discretion. This field is a very large one. It is sometimes described as political. Each head of a department is and must be the President's alter ego in the matters of that department where the President is required by law to exercise authority. * * *

The ordinary duties of officers prescribed by statute come under the general administrative control of the President by virtue of the general grant to him of the executive power, and he may properly supervise and guide their construction of the statutes under which they act in order to secure that unitary and uniform execution of the laws which article 2 of the Constitution evidently contemplated in vesting general executive power in the President alone. Laws are often passed with specific provision for adoption of regulations by a department or bureau head to make the law workable and effective. The ability and judgment manifested by the official thus empowered, as well as his energy and stimulation of his subordinates, are subjects which the President must consider and supervise in his administrative control. Finding such officers to be negligent and inefficient, the President should have the power to remove them. Of course there may be duties so peculiarly and specifically committed to the discretion of a particular officer as to raise a question whether the President may overrule or revise the officer's interpretation of his statutory duty in a particular instance. Then there may be duties of a quasi-judicial character imposed on executive officers and members of executive tribunals whose decisions after hearing affect interests of individuals, the discharge of which the President cannot in a particular case properly influence or control. But even in such a case he may consider the decision after its rendition as a reason for removing the officer, on the ground that the discretion regularly entrusted to that officer by statute has not been on the whole intelligently or wisely exercised. Otherwise he does not discharge his own constitutional duty of seeing that the laws be faithfully executed.

We have devoted much space to this discussion and decision of the question of the presidential power of removal in the First Congress, not because a congressional conclusion on the constitutional issue is conclusive, but first because of our agreement with the reasons upon which it was avowedly based, second because this was the decision of the First Congress on a question of primary importance in the organization of the government made within two years after the Constitutional Convention and within a much shorter time after its ratification, and third because that Congress numbered among its leaders those who had been members of the convention. * * *

[The Court reviewed in detail legislation enacted through the Civil War and concluded that Congress had consistently supported its initial understanding as to the President's power of removal. The Court then recounted how Congress's position changed when the 1867 Tenure of Office Act, enacted over President Johnson's veto, specified that executive officers appointed with the advice and consent of the Senate could only be removed with the Senate's concurrence. The Court added that in the nearly sixty years since the Tenure of Office Act, several presidents had stated that Congress lacked constitutional authority to limit their removal powers, and the Court had not resolved the issue.]

What, then, are the elements that enter into our decision of this case? We have, first, a construction of the Constitution made by a Congress * * * whose constitutional decisions have always been regarded, as they should be regarded, as of the greatest weight in the interpretation of that fundamental instrument. This construction was followed by the legislative department and the executive department continuously for 73 years. * * * This court has repeatedly laid down the principle that a contemporaneous legislative exposition of the Constitution, when the founders of our government and framers of our Constitution were actively participating in public affairs, acquiesced in for a long term of years, fixes the construction to be given its provisions.

We are now asked to set aside this construction thus buttressed and adopt an adverse view, because the Congress of the United States did so during a heated political difference of opinion between the then President and the majority leaders of Congress over the reconstruction measures adopted as a means of restoring to their proper status the states which attempted to withdraw from the Union at the time of the Civil War. The extremes to which the majority in both Houses carried legislative measures in that matter are now recognized by all who calmly review the history of that episode in our government leading to articles of impeachment against President Johnson and his acquittal. Without animadverting on the character of the measures taken, we are certainly justified in saying that they should not be given the weight affecting proper constitutional construction to be accorded to that reached by the First Congress of the United States during a political calm and acquiesced in by the whole government for three-quarters of a century, especially when the new construction contended for has never been acquiesced in by either the executive or the judicial departments. * * *

For the reasons given, we must therefore hold that the provision of the law of 1876 by which the unrestricted power of removal of first-class postmasters is denied to the President is in violation of the Constitution and invalid.

The dissenting opinions of MR. JUSTICE MCREYNOLDS and MR. JUSTICE HOLMES are omitted.

MR. JUSTICE BRANDEIS, dissenting.

[Brandeis began by quoting from Justice Story's *Commentaries on the Constitution* (1833) concerning the President's power of removal; Story stated that "in regard to 'inferior officers' (which appellation probably includes ninety-nine out of a hundred of the lucrative offices in the government), the remedy for any permanent abuse is still within the power of Congress, by the simple expedient of requiring the consent of the Senate to removals in such cases." Brandeis noted that postmasters first class are inferior officers, although Congress vested their appointment in the President rather than the head of the department.]

The contention that Congress is powerless to make consent of the Senate a condition of removal by the President from an executive office rests mainly upon the clause in section 1 of article 2 which declares that "the executive Power shall be vested in a President." The argument is that appointment and removal of officials are executive prerogatives; that the grant to the President of "the executive power" confers upon him, as inherent in the office, the power to exercise these two functions without restriction by Congress, except in so far as the power to restrict his exercise of them is expressly conferred upon Congress by the Constitution; that in respect to appointment certain restrictions of the executive power are so provided for; but that in respect to removal there is no express grant to Congress of any power to limit the President's prerogative. The simple answer to the argument is this: The ability to remove a subordinate executive officer, being an essential of effective government, will, in the absence of express constitutional provision to the contrary, be deemed to have been vested in some person or body. But it is not a power inherent in a chief executive. The President's power of removal from statutory civil inferior offices, like the power of appointment to them, comes immediately from the Congress. It is true that the exercise of the power of removal is said to be an executive act, and that when the Senate grants or withholds consent to a removal by the President, it participates in an executive act. But the Constitution has confessedly granted to Congress the legislative power to create offices, and to prescribe the tenure thereof; and it has not in terms denied to Congress the power to control removals. To prescribe the tenure involves prescribing the conditions under which incumbency shall cease. For the possibility of removal is a condition or qualification of the tenure. When Congress provides that the incumbent shall hold office for four years unless sooner removed with the consent of the Senate, it prescribes the term of the tenure.* * *

The end to which the President's efforts are to be directed is not the most efficient civil service conceivable, but the faithful execution of the laws consistent with the provisions therefor made by Congress. * * * Power to remove, as well as to suspend, a high political officer, might conceivably be deemed indispensable to democratic government and, hence, inherent in the President. But power to remove an inferior administrative officer appointed for a fixed term cannot conceivably be deemed an essential of government. To imply a grant to the President of the uncontrollable power of removal from statutory inferior executive offices involves an unnecessary and indefensible limitation upon the constitutional power of Congress to fix the tenure of the inferior statutory offices. That such a limitation cannot be justified on the ground of necessity is demonstrated by the practice of our governments, state and national. In none of the original 13 states did the chief executive possess such power at the time of the adoption of the federal Constitution. In none of the 48 states has such power been conferred at any time since by a state Constitution, with a single possible exception. * * * The practice of the federal government will be set forth in detail. * * *

The practice of Congress to control the exercise of the executive power of removal from inferior offices is evidenced by many statutes which restrict it in many ways besides the removal clause here in question. Each of these restrictive statutes became law with the approval of the President. Every President who has held office since 1861, except President Garfield, approved one or more of such statutes. Some of these statutes, prescribing a fixed term, provide that removal shall be made only for one of several specified causes. Some provide a fixed term, subject generally to removal for cause. Some provide for removal only after a hearing. Some provide a fixed term, subject to removal for reasons to be communicated by the President to the Senate. Some impose the restriction in still other ways.

The practical disadvantage to the public service of denying to the President the uncontrollable power of removal from inferior civil offices would seem to have been exaggerated. Upon the service, the immediate effect would ordinarily be the same, whether the President, acting alone, has or has not the power of removal. For he can, at any time, exercise his constitutional right to suspend an officer and designate some other person to act temporarily in his stead; and he cannot while the Senate is in session, appoint a successor without its consent. On the other hand, to the individual in the public service, and to the maintenance of its morale, the existence of a power in Congress to impose upon the Senate a duty to share in the responsibility for a removal is of paramount importance. The Senate's consideration of a proposed removal may be necessary to protect reputation and emoluments of office from arbitrary executive action. Equivalent protection is afforded to other inferior officers whom Congress has placed in the classified civil service and which it authorized the heads of departments to appoint and to remove without the consent of the Senate. The existence of some such provision is a common incident of free governments. In the United States, where executive responsibility is not safeguarded by the practice of parliamentary interpellation, such means of protection to persons appointed to office by the President with the consent of the Senate is of special value.* * *

The historical data submitted present a legislative practice, established by concurrent affirmative action of Congress and the President, to make consent of the Senate a condition of removal from statutory inferior, civil, executive offices to which appointment is made for a fixed term by the President with such consent. They show that the practice has existed, without interruption, continuously for the last 58 years; that throughout this period it has governed a great majority of all such offices; that the legislation applying the removal clause specifically to the office of the postmaster was enacted more than half a century ago; and that recently the practice has, with the President's approval, been extended to several newly created offices. * * * A persistent legislative practice which involves a delimitation of the respective powers of Congress and the President, and which has been so established and maintained, should be tantamount to judicial construction, in the absence of any decision by the court to the contrary. * * *

The action taken by Congress in 1789 * * * does not present an instance [of recognizing uncontrollable executive power to remove an inferior civil officer]. The vote then taken * * * involved merely the decision that the Senate does not, in the absence of legislative grant thereof, have the right to share in the removal of an officer appointed with its consent, and that the President has, in the absence of restrictive legislation, the constitutional power of removal without such consent. Moreover * * * the debate and the decision related to a high political office, not to inferior ones. Nor does the [congressional] debate show that the majority of those then in Congress thought that the President had the uncontrollable power of removal. The Senators divided equally in their votes. As to their individual views we lack knowledge; for the debate was secret. In the House only 24 of the 54 members voting took part in the debate. Of the 24, only 6 appear to have held the opinion that the President possessed the uncontrollable power of removal. * * *

The separation of the powers of government did not make each branch completely autonomous. It left each in some measure, dependent upon the others, as it left to each power to exercise, in some respects, functions in their nature executive, legislative and judicial. Obviously the President cannot secure full execution of the laws, if Congress denies to him adequate means of doing so. Full execution may be defeated because Congress declines to create offices indispensable for that purpose; or because Congress, having created the office, declines to make the indispensable appropriation; or because Congress, having both created the office and made the appropriation, prevents, by restrictions which it imposes, the appointment of officials who in quality and character are indispensable to the efficient execution of the law. If, in any such way, adequate means are denied to the President, the fault will lie with Congress. The President performs his full constitutional duty, if, with the means and instruments provided by Congress and within the limitations prescribed by it, he uses his best endeavors to secure the faithful execution of the laws enacted.

Checks and balances were established in order that this should be "a government of laws and not of men." * * * The doctrine of the separation of powers was adopted by the convention of 1787 not to promote efficiency but to preclude the exercise of arbitrary power. The purpose was not to avoid friction, but, by means of the inevitable friction incident to the distribution of the governmental powers among three departments, to save the people from autocracy. In order to prevent arbitrary executive action, the Constitution provided in terms that presidential appointments be made with the consent of the Senate, unless Congress should otherwise provide; and this clause was construed by Alexander Hamilton in The Federalist, No. 77, as requiring like consent to removals. Limiting further executive prerogatives customary in monarchies, the Constitution empowered Congress to vest the appointment of inferior officers, "as we think proper, in the President alone, in the Courts of Law, or in the Heads of Departments." Nothing in support of the claim of uncontrollable power can be inferred from the silence of the convention of 1787 on the subject of removal. For the outstanding fact remains that every specific proposal to confer such uncontrollable power upon the President was rejected. In America, as in England, the conviction prevailed then that the people must look to representative assemblies for the protection of their liberties. And protection of the individual, even if he be an official, from the arbitrary or capricious exercise of power was then believed to be an essential of free government.

NOTES ON MYERS

1. *Original Congressional Intent Versus Consistent Congressional Practice.* In interpreting the President's removal powers under Article II, Chief Justice Taft relied heavily on the discussion and decision by the First Congress, emphasizing that congressional leaders, who had been members of the Constitutional Convention, were deciding a key question of government organization less than two years after the Convention. By contrast, Justice Brandeis invoked a continuous practice of nearly sixty years, in place since 1876 and continued through concurrent action of Congress and every President except Garfield since that time. Assuming arguendo that each argument is historically accurate, is one interpretive foundation more legitimate or convincing than the other with respect to the tenure of inferior officers such as Myers? Would your answer be different if Article II were a legislative provision rather than a constitutional one?

2. *The Meaning of Silence.* The Chief Justice ascribes conclusive weight to the President's constitutional duty to take care that the laws be faithfully executed, noting that unlike the appointment power, there is no express limitation on this general duty with respect to removal of administrative officers. Justice Brandeis responds that the ability to remove such inferior officers is not an inherent executive power; rather, absent an express constitutional provision to the contrary, removal power like appointment power comes immediately from Congress. Which inference from constitutional silence do you find more persuasive? Is Taft correct that in this context, "[t]he difference between the grant of legislative power under article 1 to Congress which is limited to powers therein enumerated, and the more general grant of the executive power to the President under article 2 is significant"? Does Congress have any general or unenumerated powers under Article I? If so, are they relevant here?

3. *Policy Considerations.* What substantive reasons does the Chief Justice offer to explain why the President alone is in the right position to evaluate the performance of his subordinates? What substantive concerns does Justice Brandeis express regarding the consequences if the President alone retains removal power over administrative officers? Who has the better of this policy-based disagreement? Can you argue that the disagreement should be resolved differently for high political officers as opposed to inferior officials?

HUMPHREY'S EXECUTOR v. UNITED STATES

Supreme Court of the United States, 1935.
295 U.S. 602, 55 S.Ct. 869, 79 L.Ed. 1611.

MR. JUSTICE SUTHERLAND delivered the opinion of the Court.

Plaintiff brought suit in the Court of Claims against the United States to recover a sum of money alleged to be due the deceased for salary as a Federal Trade Commissioner from October 8, 1933, when the President undertook to remove him from office, to the time of his death on February 14, 1934. * * *

William E. Humphrey, the decedent, on December 10, 1931, was nominated by President Hoover to succeed himself as a member of the Federal Trade Commission, and was confirmed by the United States Senate. He was duly commissioned for a term of seven years, expiring September 25, 1938; and, after taking the required oath of office, entered upon his duties. On July 25, 1933, President Roosevelt addressed a letter to the commissioner asking for his resignation, on the ground "that the aims and purposes of the Administration with respect to the work of the Commission can be carried out most effectively with personnel of my own selection," but disclaiming any reflection upon the commissioner personally or upon his services. The commissioner replied, asking time to consult his friends. After some further correspondence upon the subject, the President on August 31, 1933, wrote the commissioner expressing the hope that the resignation would be forthcoming, and saying: "You will, I know, realize that I do not feel that your mind and my mind go along together on either the policies or the administering of the Federal Trade Commission, and, frankly, I think it is best for the people of this country that I should have a full confidence." The commissioner declined to resign; and on October 7, 1933, the President wrote him: "Effective as of this date you are hereby removed from the office of Commissioner of the Federal Trade Commission."

Humphrey never acquiesced in this action, but continued thereafter to insist that he was still a member of the commission, entitled to perform its duties and receive the compensation provided by law at the rate of $10,000 per annum. Upon these and other facts set forth in the certificate, which we deem it unnecessary to recite, the following questions are certified:

1.   Do the provisions of section 1 of the Federal Trade Commission Act, stating that 'any commissioner may be removed by the President for inefficiency, neglect of duty, or malfeasance in office', restrict or limit the power of the President to remove a commissioner except upon one or more of the causes named?

If the foregoing question is answered in the affirmative, then—

2.   If the power of the President to remove a commissioner is restricted or limited as shown by the foregoing interrogatory and the answer made thereto, is such a restriction or limitation valid under the Constitution of the United States?

The Federal Trade Commission Act, §§ 1, 2, 15 U.S.C. §§ 41, 42, creates a commission of five members to be appointed by the President by and with the advice and consent of the Senate, and section 1 provides:

"Not more than three of the commissioners shall be members of the same political party. The first commissioners appointed shall continue in office for terms of three, four, five, six, and seven years, respectively, from the date of the taking effect of this Act (September 26, 1914), the term of each to be designated by the President, but their successors shall be appointed for terms of seven years, except that any person chosen to fill a vacancy shall be appointed only for the unexpired term of the commissioner whom he shall succeed. The commission shall choose a chairman from its own membership. No commissioner shall engage in any other business, vocation, or employment. Any commissioner may be removed by the President for inefficiency. neglect of duty, or malfeasance in office. * * * "

Section 5 of the act (15 U.S.C. § 45) in part provides that: "Unfair methods of competition in commerce are declared unlawful. The commission is empowered and directed to prevent persons, partnerships, or corporations, except banks, and common carriers subject to the Acts to regulate commerce, from using unfair methods of competition in commerce." * * *

Section 6 (15 U.S.C. § 46), among other things, gives the commission wide powers of investigation in respect of certain corporations subject to the act, and in respect of other matters, upon which it must report to Congress with recommendations. Many such investigations have been made, and some have served as the basis of congressional legislation.

Section 7 (15 U.S.C. § 47), provides that:

"In any suit in equity brought by or under the direction of the Attorney General as provided in the antitrust Acts, the court may, upon the conclusion of the testimony therein, if it shall be then of opinion that the complainant is entitled to relief, refer said suit to the commission, as a master in chancery, to ascertain and report an appropriate form of decree therein. The commission shall proceed upon such notice to the parties and under such rules of procedure as the court may prescribe, and upon the coming in of such report such exceptions may be filed and such proceedings had in relation thereto as upon the report of a master in other equity causes, but the court may adopt or reject such report, in whole or in part, and enter such decree as the nature of the case may in its judgment require."

First. The question first to be considered is whether, by the provisions of section 1 of the Federal Trade Commission Act already quoted, the President's power is limited to removal for the specific causes enumerated therein. * * *

[T]he language of the act, the legislative reports, and the general purposes of the legislation as reflected by the debates, all combine to demonstrate the congressional intent to create a body of experts who shall gain experience by length of service; a body which shall be independent of executive authority, except in its selection, and free to exercise its judgment without the leave or hindrance of any other official or any department of the government. To the accomplishment of these purposes, it is clear that Congress was of opinion that length and certainty of tenure would vitally contribute. And to hold that, nevertheless, the members of the commission continue in office at the mere will of the President, might be to thwart, in large measure, the very ends which Congress sought to realize by definitely fixing the term of office. We conclude that the intent of the act is to limit the executive power of removal to the causes enumerated, the existence of none of which is claimed here; and we pass to the second question.

Second. To support its contention that the removal provision of section 1, as we have just construed it, is an unconstitutional interference with the executive power of the President, the government's chief reliance is *Myers v. United States*. That case has been so recently decided, and the prevailing and dissenting opinions so fully review the general subject of the power of executive removal, that further discussion would add little of value to the wealth of material there collected. These opinions examine at length the historical, legislative, and judicial data bearing upon the question, beginning with what is called 'the decision of 1789' in the first Congress and coming down almost to the day when the opinions were delivered. They occupy 243 pages of the volume in which they are printed. Nevertheless, the narrow point actually decided was only that the President had power to remove a postmaster of the first class, without the advice and consent of the Senate as required by act of Congress. In the course of the opinion of the court, expressions occur which tend to sustain the government's contention, but these are beyond the point involved and, therefore, do not come within the rule of stare decisis. In so far as they are out of harmony with the views here set forth, these expressions are disapproved.* * *

The office of a postmaster is so essentially unlike the office now involved that the decision in the *Myers* Case cannot be accepted as controlling our decision here. A postmaster is an executive officer restricted to the performance of executive functions. He is charged with no duty at all related to either the legislative or judicial power. The actual decision in the Myers Case finds support in the theory that such an officer is merely one of the units in the executive department and, hence, inherently subject to the exclusive and illimitable power of removal by the Chief Executive, whose subordinate and aid he is. Putting aside dicta, which may be followed if sufficiently persuasive but which are not controlling, the necessary reach of the decision goes far enough to include all purely executive officers. It goes no farther; much less does it include an officer who occupies no part in the executive department and who exercises no part of the executive power vested by the Constitution in the President.

The Federal Trade Commission is an administrative body created by Congress to carry into effect legislative policies embodied in the statute in accordance with the legislative standard therein prescribed, and to perform other specified duties as a legislative or as a judicial aid. Such a body cannot in any proper sense be characterized as an arm or an eye of the executive. Its duties are performed without executive leave and, in the contemplation of the statute, must be free from executive control. In administering the provisions of the statute in respect of "unfair methods of competition," that is to say, in filling in and administering the details embodied by that general standard, the commission acts in part quasi-legislatively and in part quasi-judicially. In making investigations and reports thereon for the information of Congress under section 6, in aid of the legislative power, it acts as a legislative agency. Under section 7, which authorizes the commission to act as a master in chancery under rules prescribed by the court, it acts as an agency of the judiciary. To the extent that it exercises any executive function, as distinguished from executive power in the constitutional sense, it does so in the discharge and effectuation of its quasi-legislative or quasi-judicial powers, or as an agency of the legislative or judicial departments of the government.

If Congress is without authority to prescribe causes for removal of members of the trade commission and limit executive power of removal accordingly, that power at once becomes practically all-inclusive in respect of civil officers with the exception of the judiciary provided for by the Constitution. * * * We are thus confronted with the serious question whether not only the members of these quasi-legislative and quasi-judicial bodies, but the judges of the legislative Court of Claims, exercising judicial power, continue in office only at the pleasure of the President.

We think it plain under the Constitution that illimitable power of removal is not possessed by the President in respect of officers of the character of those just named. The authority of Congress, in creating quasi-legislative or quasi-judicial agencies, to require them to act in discharge of their duties independently of executive control cannot well be doubted; and that authority includes, as an appropriate incident, power to fix the period during which they shall continue, and to forbid their removal except for cause in the meantime. For it is quite evident that one who holds his office only during the pleasure of another cannot be depended upon to maintain an attitude of independence against the latter's will.

The fundamental necessity of maintaining each of the three general departments of government entirely free from the control or coercive influence, direct or indirect, of either of the others, has often been stressed and is hardly open to serious question. So much is implied in the very fact of the separation of powers of these departments by the Constitution; and in the rule which recognizes their essential coequality. * * * The power of removal here claimed for the President falls within this principle, since its coercive influence threatens the independence of a commission, which is not only wholly disconnected from the executive department, but which, as already fully appears, was created by Congress as a means of carrying into operation legislative and judicial powers, and as an agency of the legislative and judicial departments.

* * * The result of what we now have said is this: Whether the power of the President to remove an officer shall prevail over the authority of Congress to condition the power by fixing a definite term and precluding a removal except for cause will depend upon the character of the office; the *Myers* decision, affirming the power of the President alone to make the removal, is confined to purely executive officers; and as to officers of the kind here under consideration, we hold that no removal can be made during the prescribed term for which the officer is appointed, except for one or more of the causes named in the applicable statute.

To the extent that, between the decision in the *Myers* Case, which sustains the unrestrictable power of the President to remove purely executive officers, and our present decision that such power does not extend to an office such as that here involved, there shall remain a field of doubt, we leave such cases as may fall within it for future consideration and determination as they may arise.

NOTES ON THE TENSION BETWEEN MYERS AND HUMPHREY'S EXECUTOR

1. *Two Kinds of Agencies.* The decision in *Myers* seems to suggest that Congress may not place any limits on the President's Article II power to remove executive officers. By contrast, *Humphrey's Executor* makes clear that Congress has the Article I

power to create federal offices, charge them with implementing congressional statutes, and assure their independence by specifying that occupants of these offices may not be dismissed except for cause. The Court in *Humphrey's* insists that *Myers* decided only a "narrow point" about the power to remove a postmaster of the first class, although Chief Justice Taft's in-depth historical analysis in *Myers* (occupying 117 pages in the U.S. Reports) suggests otherwise. Is the *Humphrey's* Court persuasive in reconciling these two holdings by reference to whether an officer (and presumably the agency she helps direct) performs purely executive functions versus effectuating legislative policies? The FTC has congressional authority to investigate and report to Congress in aid of legislative power, and to issue adjudicative orders. But what about an executive-branch agency like the Department of Labor (DOL), created by Congress in 1913? Over the past century, Congress has given various DOL offices authority to investigate and report as a means of legislative assistance, and to dispense statutory benefits or penalties through the application of adjudicative processes. Yet the Secretary of Labor, as well as DOL bureau chiefs appointed by the President, are subject to removal at the President's whim. Are there really two different types of agencies, as Justice Sutherland concluded in *Humphrey's Executor*?

2.   *Brandeis Vindicated?* Another possibility is that Brandeis was right all along. There is only one kind of agency, created by Congress pursuant to its powers under Article I, § 8, with agency offices structured by Congress pursuant to its "necessary and proper" authority under Article I, § 10. The President controls many (perhaps most) aspects of agencies' operations, and he can remove appointed federal officials. But Congress retains authority to define and constrain the conditions for removal, just as Congress defines other features of these agency offices such as single versus multimember heads, the length of terms to be served, and any requirements for partisan balance among multi-member agency heads. Are you persuaded by this argument? Does it help explain the Court's decision in *Morrison v. Olson*, discussed below in "More Recent Separation of Powers Developments"? Might it help support the idea from the recent Datla and Revesz article (see below) that the executive-independent agency distinction is fundamentally misguided?

MORE RECENT SEPARATION OF POWERS DEVELOPMENTS

In *Humphrey's Executor*, the Supreme Court characterized the FTC as performing both adjudicative and quasi-legislative duties, and reasoned that Congress could restrict presidential removal power in such agencies in ways it could not do with respect to officials in purely executive agencies. *Humphrey's Executor* suggested that Congress might have some room within the constitutional scheme to exercise direct control over officials implementing quasi-legislative duties. This hypothesis was tested in a series of decisions beginning 50 years later.

Bowsher v. Synar
478 U.S. 714 (1986).

The litigation arose out of the 1985 balanced budget law. The Graham-Rudman-Hollings Act (GRH), 99 Stat. 1038, codified at 2 U.S.C. § 901 et seq. was designed to eliminate the budget deficit through adherence to a set of deficit targets. If Congress failed to make spending and taxing changes in any year sufficient to meet the target, then a sequester would take place to implement pro rata spending reductions in all eligible programs. The key to accomplishing these automatic reductions was the

Comptroller General (CG) of the General Accounting Office (GAO), who is an agent of Congress (appointed by the President but removable by Congress). The CG reviewed deficit projections and possible program spending reductions calculated and reported to him by the executive Office of Management and Budget (OMB) and the legislative Congressional Budget Office (CBO), and then made his own report to the President. The Act required the President to issue a "sequestration order" to implement the spending reductions specified by the CG. Congress had an opportunity to alter or implement the reductions by legislation, but if nothing were done the sequestration order automatically became effective.

The Supreme Court invalidated the enforcement provision of GRH. **Chief Justice Burger's** opinion for the Court accepted Congress's characterization of sequestration as executive in nature; in other words, the CG was merely implementing a congressional policy decision. Executive actions can be delegated to executive branch entities or to independent agencies without raising constitutional concerns. Further, the GRH sequestration provisions constrained the CG's discretion in numerous ways—specifying which programs were eligible for cuts and which were exempt; demanding uniformity; and requiring pro rata cuts at the program, project, and activity level. Nonetheless, the Chief Justice concluded that the GRH "usurped" executive power by giving an officer of Congress the authority to execute the laws. Such power can be unproblematically delegated to an executive entity; it cannot be retained by a direct agent of Congress.

Burger's analysis is subject to several objections. **Justices White** and **Blackmun** (dissenting) and **Justices Marshall** and **Stevens** (concurring in the judgment) found unrealistic the Court's suggestion that the CG would be "subservient" to Congress. The CG enjoys a 15–year term and may only be removed by Congress for (i) permanent disability; (ii) inefficiency; (iii) neglect of duty; (iv) malfeasance; or (v) felony or conduct involving moral turpitude. 31 U.S.C. § 703(e)(1)(B). A Comptroller General has never been removed for policy reasons. Is there *any* reason to believe that official might kowtow to Congress under GRH, especially given that the CG's duties under the Act are substantially limited by the OMB and CBO projections? Justices Marshall and Stevens also argued that if the Court's opinion were taken literally—that Congress may not "control" an official who performs "executive" rather than "legislative" powers—it would be an absurdity. The Capitol Police who arrest lawbreakers, the Sergeant-at-Arms who manages the congressional payroll, and the Capitol Architect who maintains the grounds are all agents of Congress who "execute" laws. Do these positions violate the Constitution?

One might read *Bowsher* as suggesting a broad principle against *excessive* congressional control over statutory implementation. The vice in *Bowsher* was handing over statutory implementation to a congressional agent, but what if Congress hands over statutory implementation to an "independent" agency that Congress bullies into policy shifts because of *ex parte* pressure by Members of Congress, threats of funding cutoffs, or brutal accusations during oversight hearings? As discussed in Section 3, none of these mechanisms of congressional control is per se unconstitutional. Still, perhaps there is a *Bowsher* line that Congress would cross if it went "too far." How might you define that line?

Since *Bowsher*, the Court has addressed two other federal statutes that creatively insulated the tenure of agency officials—including purely executive officials—from presidential control. The Ethics in Government Act of 1978, codified at 28 U.S.C.

§§ 591–599 (EGA), established a special court and empowered the Attorney General to recommend to that court the appointment of an independent counsel to investigate, and, if necessary, prosecute government officials for certain violations of federal criminal laws. In 1986, Alexia Morrison was appointed to investigate charges that former Assistant Attorney General Theodore Olson and two other DOJ officials had obstructed a House Judiciary Committee investigation into alleged mismanagement of the "Superfund Law" by the Environmental Protection Agency. Olson challenged the constitutionality of the independent counsel provision, arguing that it deprived the President of executive powers and created a hybrid fourth branch of government ultimately not answerable to anyone.

Morrison v. Olson
487 U.S. 654 (1988).

Chief Justice Rehnquist, writing for seven of the eight sitting justices (**Justice Kennedy** took no part), held that the EGA did not violate the Appointments Clause or the separation of powers doctrine. With respect to the Appointments Clause, Morrison possessed some independent discretion to exercise the powers delegated to her, but the statute authorized her removal by the Attorney General for misconduct, indicating her "inferior" rank and authority. The Court pointed to further evidence of inferior office status: the independent counsel was empowered to perform only limited duties (investigation and prosecution but not administration or policy formulation); the counsel could act only within the scope of jurisdiction granted by the Attorney General; and the position was "temporary" in that appointment was to perform only a single task.

With respect to separation of powers, the Court acknowledged that its earlier decisions had distinguished between limits on presidential removal authority for "purely executive" officers and "quasi-legislative" or "quasi-judicial" officials. It concluded, however, that Congress may in appropriate circumstances create good-cause type protections even for independent agencies that exercise purely executive powers because "faithful execution of the laws" under Article II does not require at-will removability. In this instance, Congress had properly walked the line between respecting the President's removal authority and establishing the necessary independence of the office. Importantly, the EGA did not include any attempt by Congress to increase its own powers at the expense of the Executive Branch. Congress' role was limited to receiving reports or other information and to overseeing the independent counsel's activities—both functions that are incidental to the legislative power of Congress. Although the independent counsel was free from Executive Branch supervision to a greater degree than other federal prosecutors, the EGA gave the Executive sufficient control to ensure that the President was able to perform his constitutionally assigned duties. (The Court further held that the EGA did not violate Article III; that article does not prevent Congress from vesting certain miscellaneous powers in a special court, and the special court's powers were not inherently "executive," but rather analogous to functions that federal judges perform in other contexts)

Justice Scalia, the lone dissenter, argued that criminal law enforcement is a "quintessentially executive activity" under the Constitution, and the EGA deprived the President of exclusive control over that activity. In doing so, the statute substantially altered the balance of power between the two political branches. Scalia further predicted that the law would be abused in practice: "If Congress is controlled by the party other than the one to which the President belongs, it has little incentive to repeal [the EGA]; if [Congress] is controlled by the same party, it dare not. By its shortsighted action today, I fear the Court has permanently encumbered the Republic with an institution that will do it great harm."

Republicans began to echo Scalia's pragmatic concern when, shortly before the 1992 Presidential election, independent counsel Lawrence Walsh announced the re-indictment of former Reagan Administration defense secretary Caspar Weinberger on charges related to the Iran-Contra affair. Democrats in turn became concerned when independent counsel Kenneth Starr spent four years in the mid 1990s investigating President Clinton's land deals and extramarital affairs. With legislators on both sides of the aisle believing that these investigations had become intensely partisan, Congress allowed the independent counsel provision to expire in 1999.

The Sarbanes-Oxley Act of 2002, 116 Stat. 745, created the Public Company Accounting Oversight Board (PCAOB), codified at 15 U.S.C. §§ 7211 et seq.). The Board was composed of five members serving for staggered five-year terms; it was appointed by the SEC and modeled on private self-regulatory organizations in the securities industry such as the New York Stock Exchange. Sarbanes-Oxley gave the PCAOB expansive powers to govern the accounting industry: every accounting firm that audits public companies under the securities laws must register with the PCAOB, pay it an annual fee, and comply with its rules and oversight. While the SEC had oversight of the PCAOB, it could not remove Board members at will, but only "for good cause shown" and in accordance with specified procedures. An accounting firm being investigated by the PCAOB challenged the Board's constitutional status.

Free Enterprise Fund v. Public Co. Accounting Oversight Board
561 U.S. 477 (2010).

The Court by a 5–4 vote held that the dual for-cause limitations on the removal of Board members contravened the separation of powers doctrine. **Chief Justice Roberts** for the majority reasoned that because the Act vested removal power in SEC Commissioners, who are not subject to the President's direct control, and because the SEC could not remove a PCAOB member at will, the President was unable to hold the SEC fully accountable for the PCAOB's conduct. The President's power was limited to reviewing SEC determinations, and where the President disagreed, he was unable to intervene. The Court concluded that the Board's lack of accountability to the President violated Article II, which gives the President ultimate responsibility for the actions of the executive branch. The Chief Justice observed that the Act "shelter[s] the bureaucracy behind two layers of good-cause tenure," and he warned that this would allow Congress to create agencies with three or even five layers of insulation. "The officers of such an agency—safely encased within a Matryoshka doll of tenure protections—would be immune from Presidential oversight, even as they exercised power in the people's name."

In dissent, **Justice Breyer** emphasized the intersection of two constitutional principles: separation of powers and the Necessary and Proper Clause, which gives Congress broad authority to create and structure government offices "as it chooses." He argued that neither principle is absolute when applied to removal cases. "The Necessary and Proper Clause does not grant Congress power to free *all* Executive

Branch officials from dismissal at the will of the President. Nor does the separation-of-powers principle grant the President an absolute authority to remove *any and all* Executive Branch officials at will." Absent clear constitutional guidance on the removal issue, the Court should resolve the constitutional issue based on considerations of function and context while taking account of the judicial branch's comparative lack of expertise. Breyer noted that Board members perform complex technical roles as well as adjudicative functions, adding that the subject matter of financial regulation "historically . . . has been thought to exhibit a particular need for independence." The dissent concluded that Congress and the President "could reasonably have thought it prudent to insulate . . . Board members from fear of purely politically based removal" and that the Court should defer to the "two comparatively more expert branches" that had supported the Act's removal provisions.

Executive Versus Independent Agencies in Practice. Myers and *Humphrey's Executor* establish a constitutional distinction involving the leadership status of executive and independent agencies. But in an important article examining agencies from a functional standpoint, Peter Strauss argues that executive branch agencies and independent commissions are more similar than different when viewed below the highest levels. See Peter Strauss, *The Place of Agencies in Government: Separation of Powers and the Fourth Branch*, 84 Colum. L. Rev. 573, 584–90 (1984). Strauss discusses how the two types of agencies follow the same principles of bureaucratic organization; they have the same reliance on civil service-protected staff; they perform the same basic functions of legislating (rules), investigating (compliance) and adjudicating (complaints); and they use the same public procedures for rules and adjudications that are governed by the APA. Strauss recognizes that bipartisan membership requirements for independent agencies may help lower the political temperature, and that independent agencies have somewhat more control when making budget submissions to Congress or conducting litigation, but he views these differences as relatively modest.

Is there any basis to push back against Strauss's argument for overriding functional similarity? To what extent does the deeper reach of presidential appointments in executive agencies—not just the Secretary but deputy and assistant secretaries, who in turn control some appointments themselves—encourage or even assure greater political influence over daily operations? Can the President and his "minions" influence mid-level bureaucrats at the Department of Labor more easily than at the National Labor Relations Board? At the Justice Department more readily than the SEC? Further, with respect to the *Free Enterprise Fund* decision, isn't the President's influence over SEC Commissioners greater than over the PCOAB?

Even when comparing independent agencies, certain differences may have functional consequences. Some independent agencies serve a relatively dispersed and unorganized public—think of the SEC, which has a basic mission to protect investors who depend on accurate information and the integrity of securities markets. Other independent agencies perform more as a traffic cop—think of the National Labor Relations Board, which historically has overseen relations between unions and management in the private sector. How might this difference in mission affect the likelihood of agency capture? How might it affect the risk of agency ossification?

One apparent lesson of *Myers* and *Humphrey's Executor* is that for-cause tenure protection is the crucial element when determining agency independence. But Adrian Vermeule has recently argued that such protection from presidential removal does not capture the observable practices shaping agency independence in the administrative state. See *Conventions of Agency Independence*, 113 Colum. L. Rev. 1163, 1165–81 (2013). A number of features—including staggered terms, multimember boards at the top level, bipartisan composition, and independent budgetary or litigating authority—distinguish many independent agencies, but for-cause tenure protection is typically viewed as necessary for independence, even if not sufficient. Vermeule agrees that judicial doctrine accords a crucial role to for-cause protections against removal, citing the Supreme Court's post-*Humphrey's Executor* decisions in *Bowsher*, *Morrison*, and *Free Enterprise Fund* (discussed above).

Despite these Supreme Court holdings, Vermeule maintains that as a practical matter, executive and legislative officials, agency personnel, administrative law commentators and practitioners, and regulated parties create and follow observable norms of agency independence—unwritten conventions—that are not derived from the judicial doctrine and in some cases cannot be squared with it. Thus, for instance, *for-cause tenure protection is not necessary to agency independence*. Commissioners of the Securities and Exchange Commission (SEC), the Federal Communications Commission (FCC), and the Federal Election Commission (FEC), as well as the Chair and two Vice Chairs of the Federal Reserve, are conventionally considered "independent." Indeed, Congress included the SEC and FCC in a list of independent agencies under the Paperwork Reduction Act although these officials do *not* have for-cause tenure protections written into their statutes. *Nor is for-cause protection sufficient to create an independent agency.* The National Labor Relations Board (NLRB) statute expressly provides the reasons for removal of Board members, and the NLRB itself was designed to be independent, but, Vermeule argues that the NLRB is one of the "most politicized agencies" and that Board members vote reliably in accordance with the party of the appointing President and their own partisan affiliation.

The Agency Continuum. Another recent law review article questions the binary view of agencies as either executive or independent. The authors contend instead that agencies are best understood from a continuum perspective: all agencies should be regarded as executive but seen as falling on a spectrum from more independent to less independent. Kirti Datla & Richard Revesz, *Deconstructing Independent Agencies (and Executive Agencies)*, 98 Cornell L. Rev. 769 (2013). Datla and Revesz identify seven indicia of independence: (1) for-cause removal protection, (2) set term tenure, (3) multimember structure, (4) partisan balance requirements, (5) budget and congressional communication authority, (6) litigation authority, and (7) adjudication authority. Using these seven factors, Datla and Revesz create the following continuum of agency independence, with the "more independent" agencies possessing a higher number of indicia. *Id.* at 825 (reprinted by permission).

Agencies by Number of Indicia of Independence

Number of Indicia	Agencies
7	Consumer Product Safety Commission; Federal Energy Regulatory Commission; Surface Transportation Board; U.S. Postal Service
6	Commodity Futures Trading Commission; Federal Election Commission; Securities & Exchange Commission; Federal Reserve; Federal Labor Relations Authority; Federal Maritime Commission; Federal Trade Commission; Merit Systems Protection Board; National Transportation Safety Board; Postal Regulatory Commission
5	Consumer Financial Protection Bureau; Federal Housing Finance Authority; National Labor Relations Board; Nuclear Regulatory Commission; Defense Nuclear Facilities Safety Board; Equal Employment Opportunity Commission; Farm Credit Administration; Federal Deposit Insurance Corporation; U.S. International Trade Commission; National Credit Union Administration
4	National Mediation Board; Chemical Safety and Hazard Investigation Board; Commission on Civil Rights; Independent Payment Advisory Board; Mine Safety and Health Review Commission; Occupational Safety & Health Review Commission; Social Security Administration; Advisory Council on Historic Preservation; Department of Transportation; Election Assistance Commission; Export-Import Bank; Federal Communications Commission
3	Office of Special Counsel; African Development Foundation; Federal Retirement Thrift Investment Board; Millennium Challenge Corporation; Overseas Private Investment Corporation; Railroad Retirement Board; Small Business Administration; Tennessee Valley Authority
2	Administrative Conference of the United States; Corporation for National and Community Service; Department of Labor; Department of Defense; Department of Education; Department of Justice; Environmental Protection Agency; National Capital Planning Commission; National Council on Disability; Department of Veterans Affairs
1	Department of Agriculture; Department of State; Department of the Interior; Department of the Treasury; Department of Homeland Security; Department of Health and Human Services; Nuclear Energy Agency; National Endowment for the Humanities; National Science Foundation; Office of

Government Ethics; Office of Personnel Management; Panama Canal Commission; Pension Benefit Guaranty Corporation; Selective Service

0   Central Intelligence Agency; Department of Commerce; Department of Education; Federal Mediation and Conciliation Service; General Services Administration; Department of Housing and Urban Development; International Broadcasting Bureau; National Archives and Record Administration; National Aeronautics and Space Administration; Office of the Director of National Intelligence; Peace Corps; U. S. Trade and Development Agency; U.S. Agency for International Development

Datla and Revesz classify the NLRB as more independent than the FCC, a conclusion disputed under Vermeule's less formally doctrinal analysis and presumably questioned under Strauss's functional approach as well. Do you think one of these approaches best captures the reality of agency operations? Should they be considered together? Are there any agencies traditionally regarded as "independent" that Datla and Revesz list towards the less-independent end of the spectrum? Conversely, are there any traditionally "executive" agencies that appear toward the more-independent end of the spectrum? Although SEC Commissioners do not have for-cause removal protection, they still appear toward the more-independent end of the table because they possess six of the seven indicia. Does this seven-factor continuum approach reflect the genuine status of agencies more accurately than the constitutional distinctions identified and developed by the Supreme Court?

2. AGENCY IMPLEMENTATION UNDER THE ADMINISTRATIVE PROCEDURE ACT

Federal bureaucrats have existed since the dawn of the Republic, when Congress in 1789 established agencies charged with collecting import duties and providing military pensions to wounded veterans. There are sound policy reasons why Congress regularly opts for administrative processes to complement both statutory and judicial decisionmaking. When addressing scientific or technical subjects such as pollution, broadcast licensing, or taxes, neither Congress nor the federal courts can acquire the same *expertise* as civil servants trained in these areas. Moreover, from an *efficiency* standpoint, Congress lacks the time to resolve innumerable first-order implementation questions, like what qualifies as a valid job-specific performance criterion under an anti-discrimination provision, or how many portable toilets should be available for seasonal farmworkers under an occupational health and safety law. And in terms of *flexibility*, statutes create rules and standards that are meant to apply over many decades; agencies may be in the best position to update these policies in modest yet important respects by taking account of post-enactment changes in technological, scientific, or social circumstances.

On the other hand, the proliferation of administrative processes, particularly when developed separately for each agency, carries attendant risks—the public may not understand how laws are being implemented; agencies may be captured by the interests they are meant to regulate; agencies may become rigidly self-serving and unresponsive to new developments; or agencies may simply engage in arbitrary decisionmaking. A partial antidote to these risks is for Congress to develop a framework of fair procedures and to insist that agencies adhere to them. The APA, the end-product of more than a decade of legislative consideration, is a framework statute. It sets forth an array of process-related steps agencies must follow, and related determinations they must make, when acting to implement their statutory directives.

A. ORIGINS AND BASIC PROVISIONS OF THE APA

1. Legislative Origins

As noted in Section 1A, federal agencies were created long before the passage of the Administrative Procedure Act of 1946. But with the enormous expansion of executive branch and independent agencies during the New Deal, some private sector observers voiced increasing alarm about the bureaucracy's authority and influence over the actions of individuals and entities. The American Bar Association (ABA) was an early and persistent critic. In 1933, the ABA appointed a special committee on administrative law, which in turn began issuing annual reports. In 1938, the ABA committee, chaired by former Dean Roscoe Pound of Harvard Law School, scathingly denounced the new bureaucracy for malign "tendencies" to decide without a hearing, to consider matters not in the record, and to conflate the legislative, prosecutorial, and adjudicative functions—all to the detriment of hapless regulated interests. Between 1938 and 1945, the ABA had legislation introduced in every session of Congress that urged the adoption of a "Code of Standards of Fair Procedure." The ABA's efforts met with regular opposition from administrative agencies.

In 1939, the Walter-Logan administrative procedure bill, intended to limit the burgeoning power of the agencies, was favorably reported to the Senate. A passage from the Senate Judiciary Committee report, included in the House committee report accompanying the APA seven years later, captures the mischief at which that bill was aimed:

> "Unfortunately, the statutes providing for hearings before the so-called independent agencies of the Federal Government as well as those providing for the conduct of the affairs of the single-headed agencies, *do not provide for uniform procedure for * * * hearings or for a uniform method and scope of judicial review.* * * * The results of the lack of uniform procedure * * * have been at least threefold: (1) The respective administrative agencies give little heed to, and are little assisted by, the decisions of other administrative agencies or by the decisions of the courts applicable to such agencies; (2) the courts are placed at considerable disadvantage because they must verify the basic statutes of all decisions relating to other administrative agencies which are cited to them * * *; (3) individuals and their attorneys are at a disadvantage in the presentation

of their administrative appeals.* * * " H.R. Rep. No. 79–1980, at 9 (1946) (emphasis added).

Congress passed the Walter-Logan bill in 1940, but President Roosevelt vetoed it, noting his desire to await recommendations from the Attorney General's Committee on Administrative Procedure before approving any administrative law measure. In 1941, the committee issued its final report along with 27 separate studies of 33 administrative agencies. Subsequently, the United States' entry into World War II interrupted the process.

In early 1945, the chairmen of the two Judiciary Committees introduced revised bills and requested that the administrative agencies submit their further views and suggestions in writing. In October 1945, the Attorney General favorably recommended enactment. In November 1945 and May 1946, the Judiciary Committees of both Houses unanimously reported the bill. After further changes, the bill was approved by both House and Senate in May 1946. President Truman signed the APA into law on June 11, 1946, and it became effective on September 11, 1946.

The following excerpts from the House Judiciary Committee report convey a sense of what Congress expected from its new legislation:

"The present bill must be distinguished from the Walter-Logan bill in several essential respects. Unlike that bill it differentiates the several types of rules. It requires no agency hearings in connection with either regulations or adjudications unless statutes already do so in particular cases. Where statutory hearings are already provided, it fills in some of the essential requirements; and it provides for a special class of semi-independent hearing officers. * * * The bill is an outline of minimum essential rights and procedures. Agencies may fill in details so long as they publish them. It affords private parties a means of knowing what their rights are and how they may protect them, while administrators are given a simple framework upon which to base such operations as are subject to the provisions of the bill. What the bill does in substance may be summarized under four headings: 1. It provides that agencies must issue as rules certain specified information as to their organization and procedure, and also make available other materials of administrative law. 2. It states the essentials of the several forms of administrative proceedings and the general limitations on administrative powers. 3. It provides in more detail the requirements for administrative hearing and decisions in cases in which statutes require such hearings. 4. It sets forth a simplified statement of judicial review designed to afford a remedy for every legal wrong." H.R. Rep. No. 79–1980, at 10, 16–17 (1946).

Over the years, scholars have identified the APA's goals variously as (1) the codification of administrative procedure, (2) the achievement of uniformity, standardization, and simplification, (3) the curbing of arbitrary administrative excesses, and (4) the publicizing of administrative acts. But while Congress acted to limit the arbitrary exercise of power by agencies and to provide for judicial review by affected individuals and entities, the APA did not reduce the number of agencies or prevent their growth. In examining the APA text and the ways it has been construed and applied in judicial decisions, consider the meaning of this "compromise" statute. Does the Act subject agencies to uniformity of procedures as recommended by the ABA and the earlier Walter-Logan bill? To what extent does the statute standardize agencies' procedural choices with regard to implementation of policy? More broadly, do the cases in this Section suggest that the APA has succeeded in balancing agency accountability and discretion while providing for public participation that is both procedurally inclusive and substantively meaningful?

2. Basic Statutory Requirements and Definitions

The key provisions of the APA are reproduced in Appendix C. On its face, the Act divides administrative decisions according to a *bipolar model*, to use Dean Ronald Cass's term. Administrative decisions are treated as either *rules* or *orders*. Rules are like statutes, for they are agency statements "of general or particular applicability and future effect [that are] designed to implement, interpret, or prescribe law or policy." 5 U.S.C. § 551(4). Most rules are *informal*, but the procedure generating most informal rules is the more formal-sounding *notice-and-comment rulemaking*. In this process, the agency must publish notice of proposed rules in the Federal Register, followed by the opportunity for interested persons to submit comments, usually written, on the proposed rules. *Id.* § 553. See Cornelius Kerwin, *Rulemaking: How Government Agencies Write Law and Policy* (2d ed. 1999) (comprehensive description and analysis of notice-and-comment rulemaking); Peter Strauss, *The Rulemaking Continuum*, 41 Duke L.J. 1463 (1992) (the variety of rulemaking options).

Orders are like judicial decisions in that they constitute the "final disposition" of a controversy involving the statutory or agency rules. 5 U.S.C. § 551(6). The typical procedure for formal adjudicative orders is similar to trial in a court. If the enabling statute calls for decision "on the record after opportunity for an agency hearing," *Id.* §§ 554(a) and 556(a), the agency must not only provide particularized notice to the affected person, but it must also allow him or her "to present his [or her] case or defense by oral or documentary evidence, to submit rebuttal evidence, and to conduct such cross-examination as may be required for a full and true disclosure of the facts." *Id.* § 556(d). The agency's decision must be based on the trial-type record and supported by reliable, probative, and substantial evidence. *Id.* § 557.[21] Sections 554 and 556–557 mandate at least a partial separation of functions between the prosecutorial staff and agency decisionmakers, particularly in formal adjudications. For example, formal adjudications are usually handled by *administrative law judges* (§ 3105), who have their own staff and are monitored and rewarded by the Civil Service Commission and not by the agency itself.

Agency communications may require a less conventional structure than either notice-and-comment rules or orders that result from formal adjudications. The APA

---

[21] The text sets forth the typical procedures for formal rulemaking, informal rulemaking, and adjudication. The APA has alternate procedures in each instance. See *United States v. Fla. E. Coast Ry.*, 410 U.S. 224 (1973) (presented and discussed below). The vast amount of agency work is done through informal initiatives or communications, covering actions that do not fall into one of the other three categories.

recognizes *interpretive rules* and *general policy statements* as more flexible modes of agency transmission; the Act exempts them from notice-and-comment requirements (§ 553(b)(A)) but requires that they be separately published in the Federal Register when they are of "general applicability" (§ 552(a)(1)(D)). In addition, agencies may merely "make available" (without publication in the Federal Register) guidance documents that are not of general applicability. (§552(a)(2)).

Sections 701–706 provide for judicial review of agency rules and orders. "A[ny] person suffering legal wrong because of agency action, or adversely affected or aggrieved by agency action within the meaning of a relevant statute, is entitled to judicial review thereof," *id.* § 702, unless "(1) statutes preclude judicial review; or (2) agency action is committed to agency discretion by law." *Id.* § 701(a). In an action for judicial review, the court "shall" under § 706:

(1) compel agency action unlawfully withheld or unreasonably delayed; and

(2) hold unlawful and set aside agency action, findings, and conclusions found to be—

(A) arbitrary, capricious, an abuse of discretion, or otherwise not in accordance with law;

(B) contrary to constitutional right, power, privilege, or immunity;

(C) in excess of statutory jurisdiction, authority, or limitations, or short of statutory right;

(D) without observance of procedure required by law;

(E) unsupported by substantial evidence in a case subject to sections 556 and 557 of this title or otherwise reviewed on the record of an agency hearing provided by statute; or

(F) unwarranted by the facts to the extent that the facts are subject to trial de novo by the reviewing court.

3. Formal Rulemaking

Before enactment of the APA, federal agencies that engaged in rulemaking proceeded largely as they saw fit. Statutes enabling an agency to issue rules may have specified that a "hearing" be provided as part of rulemaking procedures. The Court, however, often construed such "hearing" requirements to mean not trial-type adversarial proceedings but something more akin to public meetings where arguments take place. See *Norwegian Nitrogen Prods. Co. v. United States*, 288 U.S. 294, 299–301, 306–08 (1933).

The APA in section 553(c) set forth procedures to be followed in notice-and-comment rulemaking, and prescribed more formal trial-type procedures "when rules are required by statute to be made on the record after opportunity for an agency hearing." The scope of this provision for trial-type formal rulemaking was initially considered and narrowly construed by the Supreme Court in *United States v. Allegheny-Ludlum Steel Corp.*, 406 U.S. 742 (1972). The *Florida East Coast* decision, elaborating on the narrowness of the exception, came down the following Term.

UNITED STATES V. FLORIDA EAST COAST RAILWAY CO.

United States Supreme Court, 1973.
410 U.S. 224, 93 S.Ct. 810, 35 L.Ed.2d 223.

MR. JUSTICE REHNQUIST delivered the opinion of the Court.

[Appellees, two railroad companies, brought this action to set aside incentive per diem rates established by the Interstate Commerce Commission in a rulemaking proceeding. The District Court concluded that the Commission had failed to comply with applicable provisions of the APA. The Court held that the language of § 1(14)(a)[1] of the Interstate Commerce Act, 24 Stat. 379, as amended, 49 U.S.C. § 1(14)(a), required the Commission in a proceeding such as this to act in accordance with section 556(d) of the APA; and that the Commission's determination to receive submissions from the railroads only in written form violated the companies' presumptive right to a trial-type hearing because it left them 'prejudiced' within the meaning of that APA section].

[I] Congressional concern for the problem [of chronic freight car shortages] was manifested in the enactment in 1966 of an amendment to § 1(14)(a) of the Interstate Commerce Act, enlarging the Commission's authority to prescribe per diem charges for the use by one railroad of freight cars owned by another. The Senate Committee on Commerce stated in its report accompanying this legislation: "Car shortages, which once were confined to the Midwest during harvest seasons, have become increasingly more frequent, more severe, and nationwide in scope as the national freight car supply has plummeted." S. Rep. No. 386, 89th Cong., 1st Sess., 1–2.

The Commission in 1966 commenced an investigation "to determine whether information presently available warranted the establishment of an incentive element increase, on an interim basis, to apply pending further study and investigation." 332 I.C.C. 11, 12 (1967).

* * * In December 1967, the Commission initiated the rulemaking procedure giving rise to the order that appellees here challenge. It directed Class I and Class II line-haul railroads to compile and report detailed information with respect to freight-car demand and supply at numerous sample stations for selected days of the week during 12 four-week periods, beginning January 29, 1968.

Some of the affected railroads voiced questions about the proposed study or requested modification in the study procedures outlined by the Commission in its notice of proposed rulemaking. In response to petitions setting forth these carriers'

---

[1] Section 1(14)(a) provides:
"The Commission may, after hearing, on a complaint or upon its own initiative without complaint, establish reasonable rules, regulations, and practices with respect to car service by common carriers by railroad subject to this chapter, including the compensation to be paid and other terms of any contract, agreement, or arrangement for the use of any locomotive, car, or other vehicle not owned by the carrier using it (and whether or not owned by another carrier), and the penalties or other sanctions for nonobservance of such rules, regulations, or practices. * * * "

views, the Commission staff held an informal conference in April 1968, at which the objections and proposed modifications were discussed. * * *

The results of the information thus collected were analyzed and presented to Congress by the Commission during a hearing before the Subcommittee on Surface Transportation of the Senate Committee on Commerce in May 1969. Members of the Subcommittee expressed dissatisfaction with the Commission's slow pace in exercising the authority that had been conferred upon it by the 1966 Amendments to the Interstate Commerce Act. Judge Simpson in his opinion for the District Court said:

> "Members of the Senate Subcommittee on Surface Transportation expressed considerable dissatisfaction with the Commission's apparent inability to take effective steps toward eliminating the national shortage of freight cars. Comments were general that the Commission was conducting too many hearings and taking too little action. Senators pressed for more action and less talk, but Commission counsel expressed doubt respecting the Commission's statutory power to act without additional hearings."

* * * The Commission, now apparently imbued with a new sense of mission, issued in December 1969 an interim report announcing its tentative decision to adopt incentive per diem charges on standard boxcars based on the information compiled by the railroads. The substantive decision reached by the Commission was that so-called 'incentive' per diem charges should be paid by any railroad using on its lines a standard boxcar owned by another railroad. Before the enactment of the 1966 amendment to the Interstate Commerce Act, it was generally thought that the Commission's authority to fix per diem payments for freight car use was limited to setting an amount that reflected fair return on investment for the owning railroad, without any regard being had for the desirability of prompt return to the owning line or for the encouragement of additional purchases of freight cars by the railroads as a method of investing capital. The Commission concluded, however, that in view of the 1966 amendment it could impose additional "incentive" per diem charges to spur prompt return of existing cars and to make acquisition of new cars financially attractive to the railroads. It did so by means of a proposed schedule that established such charges on an across-the-board basis for all common carriers by railroads subject to the Interstate Commerce Act. Embodied in the report was a proposed rule adopting the Commission's tentative conclusions and a notice to the railroads to file statements of position within 60 days, couched in the following language:

> "That verified statements of facts, briefs, and statements of position respecting the tentative conclusions reached in the said interim report, the rules and regulations proposed in the appendix to this order, and any other pertinent matter, are hereby invited to be submitted pursuant to the filing schedule set forth below by an interested person whether or not such person is already a party to this proceeding.

> "That any party requesting oral hearing shall set forth with specificity the need therefor and the evidence to be adduced." 337 I.C.C. 183, 213.

Both appellee railroads filed statements objecting to the Commission's proposal and requesting an oral hearing, as did numerous other railroads. In April 1970, the Commission, without having held further 'hearings,' issued a supplemental report making some modifications in the tentative conclusions earlier reached, but overruling in toto the requests of appellees.

The District Court held that in so doing the Commission violated § 556(d) of the Administrative Procedure Act, and it was on this basis that it set aside the order of the Commission.

[II] In *United States v. Allegheny-Ludlum Steel Corp.*, *supra*, we held that the language of § 1(14)(a) of the Interstate Commerce Act authorizing the Commission to act "after hearing" was not the equivalent of a requirement that a rule be made "on the record after opportunity for an agency hearing" as the latter term is used in § 553(c) of the Administrative Procedure Act. Since the 1966 amendment to § 1(14)(a), under which the Commission was here proceeding, does not by its terms add to the hearing requirement contained in the earlier language, the same result should obtain here unless that amendment contains language that is tantamount to such a requirement. Appellees contend that such language is found in the provisions of that Act requiring that:

'(T)he Commission shall give consideration to the national level of ownership of such type of freight car and to other factors affecting the adequacy of the national freight car supply, and shall, on the basis of such consideration, determine whether compensation should be computed. . . .'

While this language is undoubtedly a mandate to the Commission to consider the factors there set forth in reaching any conclusion as to imposition of per diem incentive charges, it adds to the hearing requirements of the section neither expressly nor by implication. We know of no reason to think that an administrative agency in reaching a decision cannot accord consideration to factors such as those set forth in the 1966 amendment by means other than a trial-type hearing or the presentation of oral argument by the affected parties. Congress by that amendment specified necessary components of the ultimate decision, but it did not specify the method by which the Commission should acquire information about those components.

Both of the district courts that reviewed this order of the Commission concluded that its proceedings were governed by the stricter requirements of §§ 556 and 557 of the Administrative Procedure Act, rather than by the provisions of § 553 alone.[6] The conclusion of the District Court for the Middle District of Florida, which we here review, was based on the assumption that the language in § 1(14)(a) of the Interstate Commerce Act requiring rulemaking under that section to be done 'after hearing' was the equivalent of a statutory requirement that the rule 'be made on the record after opportunity for an agency hearing.' Such an assumption is inconsistent with our decision in *Allegheny-Ludlum*, *supra*.

---

[6]   Both district court opinions were handed down before our decision in *United States v. Allegheny-Ludlum Steel Corp.*, 406 U.S. 742 (1972), and it appears from the record before us that the Government in those courts did not really contest the proposition that the Commission's proceedings were governed by the stricter standards of §§ 556 and 557.* * *

The District Court for the Eastern District of New York * * * observed that it was "rather hard to believe that the last sentence of § 553(c) was directed only to the few legislative spots where the words 'on the record' or their equivalent had found their way into the statute book." This is, however, the language which Congress used, and since there are statutes on the books that do use these very words, See, e.g., the Fulbright Amendment to the Walsh-Healey Act, 41 U.S.C. § 43a, and 21 U.S.C. § 371(e)(3), the regulations provision of the Food and Drug Act, adherence to that language cannot be said to render the provision nugatory or ineffectual. We recognized in *Allegheny-Ludlum* that the actual words 'on the record' and 'after . . . hearing' used in § 553 were not words of art, and that other statutory language having the same meaning could trigger the provisions of §§ 556 and 557 in rulemaking proceedings. But we adhere to our conclusion, expressed in that case, that the phrase "after hearing" in § 1(14)(a) of the Interstate Commerce Act does not have such an effect.

[III] Inextricably intertwined with the hearing requirement of the Administrative Procedure Act in this case is the meaning to be given to the language "after hearing" in § 1(14)(a) of the Interstate Commerce Act. Appellees, both here and in the court below, contend that the Commission procedure here fell short of that mandated by the 'hearing' requirement of § 1(14)(a), even though it may have satisfied § 553 of the Administrative Procedure Act. The Administrative Procedure Act states that none of its provisions "limit or repeal additional requirements imposed by statute or otherwise recognized by law." 5 U.S.C. § 559. Thus, even though the Commission was not required to comply with §§ 556 and 557 of that Act, it was required to accord the "hearing" specified in § 1(14)(a) of the Interstate Commerce Act. Though the District Court did not pass on this contention, it is so closely related to the claim based on the Administrative Procedure Act that we proceed to decide it now. * * *

The term "hearing" in its legal context undoubtedly has a host of meanings. Its meaning undoubtedly will vary, depending on whether it is used in the context of a rulemaking-type proceeding or in the context of a proceeding devoted to the adjudication of particular disputed facts. It is by no means apparent what the drafters of the Esch Car Service Act of 1917, 40 Stat. 101, which became the first part of § 1(14)(a) of the Interstate Commerce Act, meant by the term. * * *

Under these circumstances, confronted with a grant of substantive authority made [by the 1966 amendment to § 1(14)(a)] after the Administrative Procedure Act was enacted, we think that reference to that Act, in which Congress devoted itself exclusively to questions such as the nature and scope of hearings, is a satisfactory basis for determining what is meant by the term 'hearing' used in another statute. Turning to that Act, we are convinced that the term 'hearing' as used therein does not necessarily embrace either the right to present evidence orally and to cross-examine opposing witnesses, or the right to present oral argument to the agency's decisionmaker.

Section 553 excepts from its requirements rulemaking devoted to "interpretative rules, general statements of policy, or rules of agency organization, procedure, or practice," and rulemaking "when the agency for good cause finds . . .

that notice and public procedure thereon are impracticable, unnecessary, or contrary to the public interest." This exception does not apply, however, 'when notice or hearing is required by statute'; in those cases, even though interpretative rulemaking be involved, the requirements of § 553 apply. But since these requirements themselves do not mandate any oral presentation, see *Allegheny-Ludlum, supra,* it cannot be doubted that a statute that requires a "hearing" prior to rulemaking may in some circumstances be satisfied by procedures that meet only the standards of § 553. * * *

Appellee railroads cite a number of our previous decisions dealing in some manner with the right to a hearing in an administrative proceeding. Although appellees have asserted no claim of constitutional deprivation in this proceeding, some of the cases they rely upon expressly speak in constitutional terms, while others are less than clear as to whether they depend upon the Due Process Clause of the Fifth and Fourteenth Amendments to the Constitution, or upon generalized principles of administrative law formulated prior to the adoption of the Administrative Procedure Act. * * *

The basic distinction between rulemaking and adjudication is illustrated by this Court's treatment of two related cases under the Due Process Clause of the Fourteenth Amendment. In *Londoner v. Denver,* 210 U.S. 373 (1908), the Court held that due process had not been accorded a landowner who objected to the amount assessed against his land as its share of the benefit resulting from the paving of a street. Local procedure had accorded him the right to file a written complaint and objection, but not to be heard orally. This Court held that due process of law required that he "have the right to support his allegations by argument, however brief; and, if need be, by proof, however informal." But in the later case of *Bi-Metallic Investment Co. v. State Board of Equalization,* 239 U.S. 441 (1915), the Court held that no hearing at all was constitutionally required prior to a decision by state tax officers in Colorado to increase the valuation of all taxable property in Denver by a substantial percentage. The Court distinguished *Londoner* by stating that there a small number of persons 'were exceptionally affected, in each case upon individual grounds.'

Later decisions have continued to observe the distinction adverted to in *BiMetallic Investment Co.* * * * While the line dividing them may not always be a bright one, these decisions represent a recognized distinction in administrative law between proceedings for the purpose of promulgating policy-type rules or standards, on the one hand, and proceedings designed to adjudicate disputed facts in particular cases on the other.

Here, the incentive payments proposed by the Commission in its tentative order, and later adopted in its final order, were applicable across the board to all of the common carriers by railroad subject to the Interstate Commerce Act. No effort was made to single out any particular railroad for special consideration based on its own peculiar circumstances. Indeed, one of the objections of appellee Florida East Coast was that it and other terminating carriers should have been treated differently from the generality of the railroads. But the fact that the order may in its effects have been thought more disadvantageous by some railroads than by others does not change its generalized nature. Though the Commission obviously relied on factual inferences as a basis for its order, the source of these factual inferences was apparent to anyone who read the order of December 1969. The factual inferences were used in the formulation of a basically legislative-type judgment, for prospective application only, rather than in adjudicating a particular set of disputed facts.

The Commission's procedure satisfied both the provisions of § 1(14)(a) of the Interstate Commerce Act and of the Administrative Procedure Act, and were not inconsistent with prior decisions of this Court. * * *

MR. JUSTICE POWELL took no part in the consideration or decision of this case.

MR. JUSTICE DOUGLAS with whom MR. JUSTICE STEWART concurs, dissenting.

The present decision makes a sharp break with traditional concepts of procedural due process. The Commission order under attack is tantamount to a rate order. Charges are fixed that nonowning railroads must pay owning railroads for boxcars of the latter that are on the tracks of the former. * * * I do not believe it is within our traditional concepts of due process to allow an administrative agency to saddle anyone with a new rate, charge, or fee without a full hearing that includes the right to present oral testimony, cross-examine witnesses, and present oral argument. That is required by the Administrative Procedure Act, 5 U.S.C. § 556(d); § 556(a) states that § 556 applies to hearings required by § 553. Section 553(c) provides that § 556 applies "(w)hen rules are required by statute to be made on the record after opportunity for an agency hearing." A hearing under § 1(14) (a) of the Interstate Commerce Act fixing rates, charges, or fees is certainly adjudicatory, not legislative in the customary sense. * * *

Accordingly, I would hold that appellees were not afforded the hearing guaranteed by § 1(14)(a) of the Interstate Commerce Act and 5 U.S.C. §§ 553, 556, and 557, and would affirm the decision of the District Court.

NOTES ON FLORIDA EAST COAST RAILWAY

1.   *The Demise of Formal Rulemaking?* In Judge Friendly's words, *Florida East Coast* "seems to say that 'hearing' provisions in regulatory statutes, which had long been regarded as requiring trial-type hearings, have been modified by the Administrative Procedure Act so that nothing more than notice and written comment is required if the action falls within the APA's expansive definition of rulemaking." Henry J. Friendly, *"Some Kind of Hearing"*, 123 U. Pa. L. Rev. 1267, 1308 (1975). Does anything in the APA text allow it to preempt earlier statutes that agencies previously determined to require formal rulemaking? Does *Florida East Coast* foreclose Congress from mandating trial-type hearings as part of rulemaking in future statutes? Congress has enacted very few provisions since 1974 requiring rules to be made "on the record after opportunity for a hearing."[22] Perhaps this reflects Congress's belief that "too much process" will simply paralyze agency rulemaking. On the other hand, perhaps regulated

---

[22]   We identified one such post-1974 enacted provision, the Deep Seabed Hard Mineral Resources Act, 94 Stat. 553 (1980) (codified at 30 U.S.C. §§ 1401–1473); Congress there required *amendments to a regulation* to be "on the record after opportunity for an agency hearing." Other introduced bills have included this phrase or some permutation of it, but we found none that have become law.

entities and the public are left with inadequate procedural protections under section 553. Should we expect lower courts reviewing agency rulemaking to strengthen the meaning of notice-and-comment procedures once the Supreme Court has made clear that trial-type procedures are truly exceptional? In that regard, consider the Second Circuit's decision that follows in *United States v. Nova Scotia Food Products Corp.*

     2.   *Constitutional Aspects of the Hearing Requirement.* The Court in *Florida East Coast* relied on two early twentieth century decisions, each involving taxes levied by Colorado authorities, to explain why agency action requires a "hearing" under the Due Process Clause for adjudication but not rulemaking. In *Londoner v. Denver*, 210 U.S. 373 (1908), the city of Denver imposed a special assessment on a small group of property-owners based on their individual circumstances, without allowing them an opportunity to be heard in person and present evidence. The Court held that the failure to provide an oral hearing violated the Due Process Clause of the Fourteenth Amendment. But in *Bi-Metallic Investment Co. v. State Board of Equalization*, 239 U.S. 441 (1915), the Court rejected a similar due process challenge to a general increase in property taxes. Writing for the Court, Justice Holmes distinguished *Londoner*, where a relatively small number of persons "were exceptionally affected, in each case upon individual grounds," from *Bi-Metallic*, where the taxpayers of Denver were affected equally and in large numbers. Holmes then famously observed: "Where a rule of conduct applies to more than a few people, it is impracticable that everyone should have a direct voice in its adoption. * * *There must be a limit to individual argument in such matters if government is to go on." *Id.* at 445. Should the due process distinction between rulemaking and adjudication depend more on the small number of persons affected or on whether there has been an individualized fact-bound agency determination?

     Even for adjudicative orders that require a "hearing" under the Due Process clause, the nature and timing of the hearing may vary depending on the interests at stake. In *Mathews v. Eldridge*, 424 U.S. 319, 335 (1976), the Court stated that

> "identification of the specific dictates of due process generally requires consideration of three distinct factors: First, the private interest that will be affected by the official action; second, the risk of an erroneous deprivation of such interest through the procedures used, and the probable value, if any, of additional or substitute procedural safeguards; and finally, the Government's interest, including the function involved and the fiscal and administrative burdens that the additional or substitute procedural requirement would entail."

     Establishing a proper balance among these three factors may determine the timing of a hearing as well as the extent of trial-type rights accorded to the private interest affected by government action. For example, should an untenured university professor be entitled to an oral hearing before a state university may terminate her employment? Should a middle school student be entitled to an oral hearing before the school implements his planned three-day suspension? In either instance, should any such hearing include the right to present evidence on one's own behalf? To cross-examine university or school administrators? Is the case for a pre-deprivation hearing stronger in one instance than the other? Compare *Board of Regents v. Roth*, 408 U.S. 564 (1972) with *Goss v. Lopez*, 419 U.S. 565 (1975).

B. NOTICE AND COMMENT RULEMAKING

The Supreme Court's *Florida East Coast* decision signaled the ascendancy of the notice and comment approach for rulemaking. At the same time, the comparative "informality" of notice and comment does not mean an absence of predictable procedures. Consider for a moment the analogy to Congress, which enacts laws based on sequential consideration within each chamber—notice to the public and members through bill introduction and referral; development and explanation of the proposal through standing committee hearings and reports; full chamber consideration through floor debate including amendments; and final resolution through conference and presentment to the President.

Notice and comment rulemaking follows a comparably predictable process. An agency typically issues a notice in the Federal Register, proposing to take certain action, providing background data and information, and establishing a period in which interested members of the public may respond with comments. The agency's final published rule includes discussion of the comments received and how they have been treated, including identification of revisions made by the agency, and also an explanation of the basis for the most salient policy decisions embedded in the rule itself. Within these broad stages of notice and comment rulemaking, procedural issues arise regarding the adequacy of the record, the treatment of public comments, and the agency's justification for its final work product. The leading case addressing these issues is *Nova Scotia*.

UNITED STATES v. NOVA SCOTIA FOOD PRODUCTS CORP.

United States Court of Appeals for the Second Circuit, 1977.
568 F.2d 240.

GURFEIN, CIRCUIT JUDGE:

This appeal involving a regulation of the Food and Drug Administration is not here upon a direct review of agency action. It is an appeal from a judgment of the District Court for the Eastern District of New York enjoining the appellants, after a hearing, from processing hot smoked whitefish except in accordance with time-temperature-salinity (T-T-S) regulations contained in 21 C.F.R. Part 122 (1977). * * * The injunction was sought and granted on the ground that smoked whitefish which has been processed in violation of the T-T-S regulation is "adulterated." Food, Drug and Cosmetics Act ("the Act") §§ 302(a) and 301(k), 21 U.S.C. §§ 332(a), 331(k).

Appellant Nova Scotia receives frozen or iced whitefish in interstate commerce which it processes by brining, smoking and cooking. The fish are then sold as smoked whitefish.

The regulations cited above require that hot-process smoked fish be heated by a controlled heat process that provides a monitoring system positioned in as many strategic locations in the oven as necessary to assure a continuous temperature through each fish of not less than 180° F. for a minimum of 30 minutes for fish which have been brined to contain 3.5% Water phase salt or at 150° F. for a minimum of 30 minutes if the salinity was at 5% Water phase. Since each fish must meet these requirements, it is necessary to heat an entire batch of fish to even higher temperatures so that the lowest temperature for any fish will meet the minimum requirements.

Government inspection of appellants' plant established without question that the minimum T-T-S requirements were not being met. There is no substantial claim that the plant was processing whitefish under "insanitary conditions" in any other material respect. Appellants, on their part, do not defend on the ground that they were in compliance, but rather that the requirements could not be met if a marketable whitefish was to be produced. They defend upon the grounds that the regulation is invalid (1) because it is beyond the authority delegated by the statute; (2) because the FDA improperly relied upon undisclosed evidence in promulgating the regulation and because it is not supported by the administrative record; and (3) because there was no adequate statement setting forth the basis of the regulation. We reject the contention that the regulation is beyond the authority delegated by the statute, but we find serious inadequacies in the procedure followed in the promulgation of the regulation and hold it to be invalid as applied to the appellants herein.

The hazard which the FDA sought to minimize was the outgrowth and toxin formation of Clostridium botulinum Type E spores of the bacteria which sometimes inhabit fish. There had been an occurrence of several cases of botulism traced to consumption of fish from inland waters in 1960 and 1963 which stimulated considerable bacteriological research. These bacteria can be present in the soil and water of various regions. They can invade fish in their natural habitat and can be further disseminated in the course of evisceration and preparation of the fish for cooking. A failure to destroy such spores through an adequate brining, thermal, and refrigeration process was found to be dangerous to public health.

The Commissioner of Food and Drugs ("Commissioner"), employing informal "notice-and-comment" procedures under 21 U.S.C. § 371(a), issued a proposal for the control of C. botulinum bacteria Type E in fish. 34 Fed. Reg. 17,176 (Oct. 23, 1969). For his statutory authority to promulgate the regulations, the Commissioner specifically relied only upon § 342(a)(4) of the Act which provides:

"A food shall be deemed to be adulterated

"(4) if it has been prepared, packed, or held under insanitary conditions whereby it may have become contaminated with filth, or whereby it may have been rendered injurious to health;"

* * * Responding to the Commissioner's invitation in the notice of proposed rulemaking, members of the industry, including appellants and the intervenor-appellant, submitted comments on the proposed regulation.

The Commissioner thereafter issued the final regulations in which he adopted certain suggestions made in the comments, including a suggestion by the National Fisheries Institute, Inc. ("the Institute"), the intervenor herein. 35 Fed. Reg. 17,401 (Nov. 13, 1970). The original proposal provided that the fish would have to be cooked to a temperature of 180° F. for at least 30 minutes, if the fish have been brined to contain 3.5% Water phase salt, with no alternative. In the final regulation, an alternative suggested by the intervenor "that the parameter of 150° F. for 30 minutes and 5% Salt in the water phase be established as an alternate procedure to that stated in the proposed regulation for an interim period until specific parameters can be established" was accepted, but as a permanent part of the regulation rather than for an interim period.

The intervenor suggested that "specific parameters" be established. This referred to particular processing parameters for different species of fish on a "species by species" basis. Such "species by species" determination was proposed not only by the intervenor but also by the Bureau of Commercial Fisheries of the Department of the Interior. That Bureau objected to the general application of the T-T-S requirement proposed by the FDA on the ground that application of the regulation to all species of fish being smoked was not commercially feasible, and that the regulation should therefore specify time-temperature-salinity requirements, as developed by research and study, on a species-by-species basis. The Bureau suggested that "wholesomeness considerations could be more practically and adequately realized by reducing processing temperature and using suitable concentrations of nitrite and salt." The Commissioner took cognizance of the suggestion, but decided, nevertheless, to impose the T-T-S requirement on all species of fish (except chub, which were regulated by 21 C.F.R. 172.177 (1977) (dealing with food additives)).

He did acknowledge, however, in his "basis and purpose" statement required by the Administrative Procedure Act ("APA"), 5 U.S.C. § 553(c), that "adequate times, temperatures and salt concentrations have not been demonstrated for each individual species of fish presently smoked". 35 Fed. Reg. 17,401 (Nov. 13, 1970). The Commissioner concluded, nevertheless, that "the processing requirements of the proposed regulations are the safest now known to prevent the outgrowth and toxin formation of C. botulinum Type E". He determined that "the conditions of current good manufacturing practice for this industry should be established without further delay." *Id.*

The Commissioner did not answer the suggestion by the Bureau of Fisheries that nitrite and salt as additives could safely lower the high temperature otherwise required, a solution which the FDA had accepted in the case of chub. Nor did the Commissioner respond to the claim of Nova Scotia through its trade association, the Association of Smoked Fish Processors, Inc., Technical Center that "(t)he proposed process requirements suggested by the FDA for hot processed smoked fish are neither commercially feasible nor based on sound scientific evidence obtained with the variety of smoked fish products to be included under this regulation."

Nova Scotia, in its own comment, wrote to the Commissioner that "the heating of certain types of fish to high temperatures will completely destroy the product". * * * We have noted above that the response given by the Commissioner was in general terms. He did not specifically aver that the T-T-S requirements as applied to whitefish were, in fact, commercially feasible.

When, after several inspections and warnings, Nova Scotia failed to comply with the regulation, an action by the United States Attorney for injunctive relief was filed on April 7, 1976, six years later, and resulted in the judgment here on appeal. * * *

[I]   [The court rejected Nova Scotia's contention that the FDA lacked statutory authority to promulgate the challenged T-T-S regulation]

[II] Appellants contend that there is an inadequate administrative record upon which to predicate judicial review, and that the failure to disclose to interested persons the factual material upon which the agency was relying vitiates the element of fairness which is essential to any kind of administrative action. Moreover, they argue that the "concise general statement of . . . basis and purpose" by the Commissioner was inadequate.

The question of what is an adequate "record" in informal rulemaking has engaged the attention of commentators for several years. The extent of the administrative record required for judicial review of informal rulemaking is largely a function of the scope of judicial review. Even when the standard of review is whether the promulgation of the rule was "arbitrary, capricious, an abuse of discretion, or otherwise not in accordance with law," as specified in 5 U.S.C. § 706(2)(A), judicial review must nevertheless, be based on the "whole record" (*Id.*). Adequate review of a determination requires an adequate record, if the review is to be meaningful. What will constitute an adequate record for meaningful review may vary with the nature of the administrative action to be reviewed. Review must be based on the whole record even when the judgment is one of policy, except that findings of fact such as would be required in an adjudicatory proceeding or in a formal "on the record" hearing for rulemaking need not be made. Though the action was informal, without an evidentiary record, the review must be "thorough, probing, [and] in depth".

This raises several questions regarding the informal rulemaking procedure followed here: (1) What record does a reviewing court look to? (2) How much of what the agency relied on should have been disclosed to interested persons? (3) To what extent must the agency respond to criticism that is material?

[A]   With respect to the content of the administrative "record," the Supreme Court has told us that in informal rulemaking, "the focal point for judicial review should be the administrative record already in existence, not some new record made initially in the reviewing court." See *Camp v. Pitts*, 411 U.S. 138 (1973).

No contemporaneous record was made or certified.[12] When, during the enforcement action, the basis for the regulation was sought through pretrial discovery, the record was created by searching the files of the FDA and the memories of those who participated in the process of rulemaking. This resulted in what became Exhibit D at the trial of the injunction action. Exhibit D consists of (1)

---

[12] A practice developed in the early years of the APA of not making a formal contemporaneous record, but rather, when challenged, to put together a historical record of what had been available for agency consideration at the time the regulation was promulgated. "One can conclude that 'record' now means whatever the agency produces on review." Verkuil, *supra*, 60 Va. L. Rev. at 204. Professor Davis in a balanced review, has stated: "When the facts are of central importance and might be challenged, parties adversely affected by them should have a chance to respond to them. Clearly, whatever "factual information the agency has considered should be a part of the record for judicial review." K. Davis, *supra*, § 29.01–6, pp. 672–73.

Tab A containing the comments received from outside parties during the administrative "notice-and-comment" proceeding and (2) Tabs B through L consisting of scientific data and the like upon which the Commissioner now says he relied but which were not made known to the interested parties.

Appellants object to the exclusion of evidence in the District Court "aimed directly at showing that the scientific evidence relied upon by the FDA was inaccurate and not based upon a realistic appraisal of the true facts. Appellants attempted to introduce scientific evidence to demonstrate that in fixing the processing parameters FDA relied upon tests in which ground fish were injected with many millions of botulism (sic) spores and then tested for outgrowth at various processing levels whereas the spore levels in nature are far less and outgrowth would have been prevented by far less stringent processing parameters." The District Court properly excluded the evidence.

In an enforcement action, we must rely exclusively on the record made before the agency to determine the validity of the regulation. The exception to the exclusivity of that record is that "there may be independent judicial fact-finding when issues that were not before the agency are raised in a proceeding to *enforce* non-adjudicatory agency action." *Overton Park*, 401 U.S. at 415, (1971). (Emphasis added.)

Though this is an enforcement proceeding and the question is close, we think that the "issues" were fairly before the agency and hence that de novo evidence was properly excluded. *Camp v. Pitts.* Our concern is, rather, with the manner in which the agency treated the issues tendered.

[B] The key issues were (1) whether, in the light of the rather scant history of botulism in whitefish, that species should have been considered separately rather than included in a general regulation which failed to distinguish species from species; (2) whether the application of the proposed T-T-S requirements to smoked whitefish made the whitefish commercially unsaleable; and (3) whether the agency recognized that prospect, but nevertheless decided that the public health needs should prevail even if that meant commercial death for the whitefish industry. The procedural issues were whether, in the light of these key questions, the agency procedure was inadequate because (i) it failed to disclose to interested parties the scientific data and the methodology upon which it relied; and (ii) because it failed utterly to address itself to the pertinent question of commercial feasibility.

The history of botulism occurrence in whitefish, as established in the trial record, which we must assume was available to the FDA in 1970, is as follows. Between 1899 and 1964 there were only eight cases of botulism reported as attributable to hot-smoked whitefish. In all eight instances, vacuum-packed whitefish was involved. All of the eight cases occurred in 1960 and 1963. The industry has abandoned vacuum-packing, and there has not been a single case of botulism associated with commercially prepared whitefish since 1963, though 2,750,000 pounds of whitefish are processed annually. Thus, in the seven-year period from 1964 through 1970, 17.25 million pounds of whitefish have been commercially processed in the United States without a single reported case of botulism. The evidence also disclosed that defendant Nova Scotia has been in business some 56 years, and that there has never been a case of botulism illness from the whitefish processed by it.

Interested parties were not informed of the scientific data, or at least of a selection of such data deemed important by the agency, so that comments could be addressed to the data. Appellants argue that unless the scientific data relied upon by the agency are spread upon the public records, criticism of the methodology used or the meaning to be inferred from the data is rendered impossible.

We agree with appellants in this case, for although we recognize that an agency may resort to its own expertise outside the record in an informal rulemaking procedure, we do not believe that when the pertinent research material is readily available and the agency has no special expertise on the precise parameters involved, there is any reason to conceal the scientific data relied upon from the interested parties. As Judge Leventhal said in *Portland Cement Ass'n v. Ruckelshaus*, 486 F.2d 375, 393 (1973): "It is not consonant with the purpose of a rulemaking proceeding to promulgate rules on the basis of inadequate data, or on data that (in) critical degree, is known only to the agency." This is not a case where the agency methodology was based on material supplied by the interested parties themselves. Cf. *Int'l Harvester Co. v. Ruckelshaus*, 478 F.2d 615, 632 (1973). Here all the scientific research was collected by the agency, and none of it was disclosed to interested parties as the material upon which the proposed rule would be fashioned.[14] Nor was an articulate effort made to connect the scientific requirements to available technology that would make commercial survival possible, though the burden of proof was on the agency. This required it to "bear a burden of adducing a reasoned presentation supporting the reliability of its methodology." *Int'l Harvester*, 478 F.2d at 643.

Though a reviewing court will not match submission against counter-submission to decide whether the agency was correct in its conclusion on scientific matters (unless that conclusion is arbitrary), it will consider whether the agency has taken account of all "relevant factors and whether there has been a clear error of judgment." *Overton Park, supra*, 401 U.S. at 415–16. * * *

If the failure to notify interested persons of the scientific research upon which the agency was relying actually prevented the presentation of relevant comment, the agency may be held not to have considered all "the relevant factors." We can think of no sound reasons for secrecy or reluctance to expose to public view (with an exception for trade secrets or national security) the ingredients of the deliberative process. Indeed, the FDA's own regulations now specifically require that every notice of proposed rulemaking contain "references to all data and information on which the Commissioner relies for the proposal (copies or a full list of which shall be a part of the administrative file on the matter . . .)." 21 C.F.R. § 10.40(b) (1) (1977). And this is, undoubtedly, the trend.[15]

---

[14] We recognize the problem posed by Judge Leventhal in *International Harvester*, that a proceeding might never end if such submission required a reply ad infinitum, *ibid*. Here the exposure of the scientific research relied on simply would have required a single round of comment addressed thereto.

[15] And see Judge Friendly's discussion of recent developments in rulemaking and judicial review in Friendly, "*Some Kind of Hearing*," 123 U. Pa. L. Rev. 1267, 1305–15 (1975).

We think that the scientific data should have been disclosed to focus on the proper interpretation of "insanitary conditions." When the basis for a proposed rule is a scientific decision, the scientific material which is believed to support the rule should be exposed to the view of interested parties for their comment. One cannot ask for comment on a scientific paper without allowing the participants to read the paper. Scientific research is sometimes rejected for diverse inadequacies of methodology; and statistical results are sometimes rebutted because of a lack of adequate gathering technique or of supportable extrapolation. Such is the stuff of scientific debate. To suppress meaningful comment by failure to disclose the basic data relied upon is akin to rejecting comment altogether. For unless there is common ground, the comments are unlikely to be of a quality that might impress a careful agency. The inadequacy of comment in turn leads in the direction of arbitrary decision-making. We do not speak of findings of fact, for such are not technically required in the informal rulemaking procedures. We speak rather of what the agency should make known so as to elicit comments that probe the fundamentals. Informal rulemaking does not lend itself to a rigid pattern. Especially, in the circumstance of our broad reading of statutory authority in support of the agency, we conclude that the failure to disclose to interested persons the scientific data upon which the FDA relied was procedurally erroneous. Moreover, the burden was upon the agency to articulate rationally why the rule should apply to a large and diverse class, with the same T-T-S parameters made applicable to all species.

[C] Appellants additionally attack the "concise general statement" required by APA, 5 U.S.C. § 553, as inadequate. We think that, in the circumstances, it was less than adequate. It is not in keeping with the rational process to leave vital questions, raised by comments which are of cogent materiality, completely unanswered. The agencies certainly have a good deal of discretion in expressing the basis of a rule, but the agencies do not have quite the prerogative of obscurantism reserved to legislatures. "Congress did not purport to transfer its legislative power to the unbounded discretion of the regulatory body." *F.C.C. v. RCA Commc'ns, Inc.*, 346 U.S. 86, 90 (1953) (Frankfurter, J.). * * *

The test of adequacy of the "concise general statement" was expressed by Judge McGowan in the following terms:

"We do not expect the agency to discuss every item of fact or opinion included in the submissions made to it in informal rulemaking. We do expect that, if the judicial review which Congress has thought it important to provide is to be meaningful, the 'concise general statement of . . . basis and purpose' mandated by Section 4 will enable us to see what major issues of policy were ventilated by the informal proceedings and why the agency reacted to them as it did." *Auto. Parts & Accessories Ass'n v. Boyd*, 407 F.2d 330, 338 (1968).

* * * The Secretary was squarely faced with the question whether it was necessary to formulate a rule with specific parameters that applied to all species of fish, and particularly whether lower temperatures with the addition of nitrite and

salt would not be sufficient. Though this alternative was suggested by an agency of the federal government, its suggestion, though acknowledged, was never answered.

Moreover, the comment that to apply the proposed T-T-S requirements to whitefish would destroy the commercial product was neither discussed nor answered. We think that to sanction silence in the face of such vital questions would be to make the statutory requirement of a "concise general statement" less than an adequate safeguard against arbitrary decision-making.

We cannot improve on the statement of the District of Columbia Circuit in *Industrial Union Dep't, AFL-CIO v. Hodgson*, 499 F.2d 467, 475 (1974).

> "What we are entitled to at all events is a careful identification by the Secretary, when his proposed standards are challenged, of the reasons why he chooses to follow one course rather than another. Where that choice purports to be based on the existence of certain determinable facts, the Secretary must, in form as well as in substance, find those facts from evidence in the record. By the same token, when the Secretary is obliged to make policy judgments where no factual certainties exist or where facts alone do not provide the answer, he should so state and go on to identify the considerations he found to be persuasive."

One may recognize that even commercial infeasibility cannot stand in the way of an overwhelming public interest. Yet the administrative process should disclose, at least, whether the proposed regulation is considered to be commercially feasible, or whether other considerations prevail even if commercial infeasibility is acknowledged. This kind of forthright disclosure and basic statement was lacking in the formulation of the T-T-S standard made applicable to whitefish. It is easy enough for an administrator to ban everything. In the regulation of food processing, the worldwide need for food also must be taken into account in formulating measures taken for the protection of health. In the light of the history of smoked whitefish to which we have referred, we find no articulate balancing here sufficient to make the procedure followed less than arbitrary.

After seven years of relative inaction, the FDA has apparently not reviewed the T-T-S regulations in the light of present scientific knowledge and experience. In the absence of a new statutory directive by Congress regarding control of micro-organisms, which we hope will be worthy of its consideration, we think that the T-T-S standards should be reviewed again by the FDA.

We cannot, on this appeal, remand to the agency to allow further comments by interested parties, addressed to the scientific data now disclosed at the trial below. We hold in this enforcement proceeding, therefore, that the regulation, as it affects non-vacuum-packed hot-smoked whitefish, was promulgated in an arbitrary manner and is invalid. * * *

NOTES ON NOVA SCOTIA *AND THE*
NOTICE-AND-COMMENT RULEMAKING PROCESS

1.   *Contents of the Nova Scotia Administrative Record.* The "record" in *Nova Scotia* was constructed after the fact by searching agency files and the memories of

agency participants. As Judge Gurfein observes, agencies no longer rely on such informal post-hoc techniques; instead, notices of proposed rulemaking typically include references to all data and information on which the agency is relying for its proposal. The court criticizes the FDA for failing to disclose in its original notice the scientific studies on which it based its proposed T-T-S regulation. At the time it issued its notice, did the agency need to disclose every scientific study of which it was aware regarding the risks of botulism and methods of preventing it? Or only those on which it actually relied when formulating its proposal? On what basis did the Second Circuit decide that certain scientific evidence was properly excluded by the district court?

2.   *The Record as Described in the APA.* The APA text is not terribly precise with respect to what should be part of the rulemaking record. Under section 553(b)(3), the notice of proposed rulemaking that appears in the Federal Register "shall include . . . either the terms or substance of the proposed rule or a description of the subjects and issues involved." After this notice, section 553(c) accords interested persons "an opportunity to participate in the rule making through submission of written data, views, or arguments. . . ." Notwithstanding the statute's failure to require inclusion of an evidentiary basis for proposed rules, reviewing courts have devoted considerable attention to the adequacy of informal rulemaking records pursuant to the Supreme Court's holding that under section 706, judicial review of agency action must be based on the "whole record" compiled by the agency. *Citizens to Preserve Overton Park v. Volpe*, 401 U.S. 402, 419 (1971).

Richard McMillan Jr. and Todd Peterson argue that courts have created five guidelines for determining the proper scope of what constitutes a whole or complete record: (1) the record should include all documents the agency considers, not just those on which the agency relies; (2) the record should include all documents considered or relied on by agency personnel whose work and recommendations reached the agency decisionmaker; (3) bona fide confidential business information ordinarily need not be included in the record; (4) deliberative intra-agency memoranda and staff reports should ordinarily be excluded from the record, although a court may require their inclusion to supply a contemporaneous explanation for the decision if the agency has made no findings to explain its decision or its findings are incomplete; (5) materials that provide factual support for materials in the record need not be part of the record unless they were reviewed or considered by the agency personnel involved in the decision. Richard McMillan, Jr. and Todd Peterson, *The Permissible Scope of Hearings, Discovery, and Additional Factfinding During Judicial Review of Informal Agency Action*, 1982 Duke L.J. 333, 341–43 (1982). To what extent do these five guidelines reflect the concerns Judge Gurfein raises in his opinion? Why do courts want the record to include documents *considered*, rather than simply *relied on*, by the agency? How onerous might it be for a record to include all documents considered by agency employees whose work contributed to the final decision? What about the guidelines that presumptively exclude certain materials—what is the basis for such limitations?

3.   *Scope and Timing of Disclosure Requirement.* Quoting Judge Harold Leventhal, Judge Gurfein emphasized that "it is not consonant with the purpose of a rulemaking proceeding to promulgate rules [based on] data that [in] critical degree is known only to the agency." We have discussed whether this disclosure requirement covers only information or data the agency relied on, or also information the agency considered or even information of which it was aware. Another aspect of scope involves

what constitutes *publicly available information*. Suppose the agency has relied on an enormous number of well-settled scientific studies, information that is clearly *not* "known only to the agency"? Do agency officials need to list hundreds of studies and explain how each study contributes to their proposal? Isn't it likely that some publicly available information will be so plainly relevant that it would neither promote fairness to interested parties nor improve the quality of judicial review to have it listed as part of the record? Alternatively, should such exclusions be limited to studies that are truly background sources rather than any information on which the agency relies as central to its proposal? See *Chamber of Commerce v. SEC*, 443 F.3d 890, 906 (D.C. Cir. 2006).

Then there is the matter of the *timing of the disclosure requirement*. In *Nova Scotia*, the agency's failure occurred during the period before the FDA began soliciting comments. What are the agency's disclosure obligations with respect to information or data received during the comment period or after the period ends? If the APA requires the agency to disclose all new material by issuing an amended notice of proposed rulemaking setting a further period for comments, what problems might result? On the other hand, if the agency is permitted to issue a final rule relying primarily or exclusively on material received once the comment period began, is such discretion consistent with the language and purposes of the APA? In responding to these questions, is it relevant whether the after-acquired information was generated by the agency itself or by a potentially affected party? If the latter, does it matter whether the information was produced at the party's initiative or in response to an agency request or invitation? Should it make a difference whether the information contributes genuinely new evidence as opposed to supporting or confirming data already in the record?

Consider two decisions from the Ninth Circuit that address an agency's obligations to disclose material after the close of the comment period. In *Rybachek v. EPA*, 904 F.2d 1276 (9th Cir. 1990), plaintiffs alleged that the EPA's addition of over 6,000 pages to the administrative record following the comment period on a proposed Clean Water Act regulation had deprived them of their rights as interested parties to comment on the record. The court held that no right to meaningful public participation was violated:

> "The additional material was the EPA's response to comments made during a public-comment period. Nothing prohibits the Agency from adding supporting documentation for a final rule in response to public comments. In fact, adherence to the [plaintiffs'] view might result in the EPA's never being able to issue a final rule capable of standing up to review: every time the Agency responded to public comments, such as those in this rulemaking, it would trigger a new comment period. Thus, either the comment period would continue in a never-ending circle, or, if the EPA chose not to respond to the last set of public comments, any final rule could be struck down for lack of support in the record. The [plaintiffs'] unviolated right was to comment on the proposed regulations, not to comment in a never-ending way on the EPA's responses to their comments." *Id.* at 1286.

In *Ober v. EPA*, 84 F.3d 304 (9th Cir. 1996), plaintiffs complained that the EPA had violated their rights to notice and an opportunity to comment on pending air quality standards when the agency requested additional material from the state of Arizona after the time period for comments had closed and then relied on this additional information in its final plan. This time the court reached a different result, and in doing so limited the reach of *Rybachek*:

> "In *Rybachek*, the added materials were the EPA's *own* responses to comments received during the public comment period. Here, in contrast, the additional documentation was submitted by the State in response to the EPA's request for further information. * * * Thus, the additional materials in *Rybachek* involved the EPA's internal assessment of comments from the public; whereas, here, the new information was solicited by the EPA from an interested party. Furthermore, in *Rybachek*, * * * [t]he additional information was not relied on or critical to the EPA's decision. Instead, the EPA decided not to alter the regulation based on the additional information it developed in response to the comments. Here, on the other hand, the added material related to the Implementation Plan's compliance with a critical statutory provision. * * * Although there is merit to EPA's argument that agencies are not required to review an endless cycle of comments from interested parties, the nature and extent of the additional information in this case required another round of comment and review." *Id.* at 314–15.

Is the court in *Ober* persuasive in distinguishing its *Rybachek* holding? Why should it matter whether EPA solicited new information from an interested party? Assuming that the new information was merely confirmatory and not "related to . . . compliance with a critical statutory provision," would the court even have invoked this factor? If the different results really hinge on the importance of the after-acquired information, what is the risk that courts will wield undue discretion in making such judgments?

4. *Agency Responses to Criticism.* Judge McGowan in the D.C. Circuit's *Automotive Parts* decision (quoted by Judge Gurfein) explained that an agency is not "expect[ed] to discuss every item of fact or opinion included in the submissions made to it in informal rulemaking," but at the same time the statement should "enable [courts] to see what major issues of policy were ventilated by the informal proceedings and why the agency reacted to them as it did." *Auto. Parts & Accessories Ass'n v. Boyd*, 404 F.2d 330, 338 (1968). In Judge Gurfein's words, "[i]t is not in keeping with the rational process to leave vital questions, raised by comments which are of cogent materiality, completely unanswered."

The court in *Nova Scotia* views the general statement requirement as a critical safeguard against arbitrary decisionmaking. But how does an agency determine which questions raised by the comments are "vital," thus requiring a response? Does vital encompass every non-frivolous comment or is the universe more limited? If an agency receives hundreds of non-frivolous comments, should it anticipate having to respond to a substantial number in order to establish its bona fides for a reviewing court? For example, assume the Federal Aviation Administration issues a notice and proposed rule to close air traffic control towers at 150 regional airports across the country. All 150 airports respond with comments explaining why their tower should not be closed—for reasons of safety, fairness, or convenience. Is every comment vital? Judge Gurfein's quote mentions responding to comments of "cogent materiality" but this seems rather open-ended: is there any reason to view safety as more cogent than fairness, or fairness as more material than convenience? Alternatively, should the meaning of vitality relate to some more quantifiable factor, such as the number of parties affected? The extent to which scientific data is implicated? Whether a comment is predominantly or substantially repetitive of points raised by others? Is the test for vitality likely to differ between agencies?

Once it has determined which questions are vital, how expansive must an agency be in discussing each question? Should the agency be obligated to dispel the criticism in full or simply say enough to show that it considered the comment? Many questions may raise complex factual issues related to cost, safety, or efficiency; must the agency always provide individualized responses or may it rely in part on boilerplate approaches? One can imagine a menu of agency responses: some aimed at establishing the correctness of the agency's position, others indicating that reasonable minds can disagree on the issue raised, and still others suggesting that the question is best addressed with more information collected in some subsequent notice and comment proceeding. Won't agencies inevitably consider a version of this blended response as they anticipate how to survive judicial review? Does this type of strategic thinking serve the goals underlying the concise general statement requirement?

Should the standard of judicial review be influenced at all by whether an agency receives little or no public input, as opposed to responding to hundreds or thousands of individualized comments and suggestions? David Fontana proposes that the APA require agencies to include as part of their general statement a "democratic participation statement (DPS) . . . indicat[ing] the number of relevant and non-repetitive comments received during rulemaking, and break[ing] down by category and by individual or institutional interest who precisely submitted these comments." Comments that are unresponsive or that duplicate other comments would not be counted. Courts would have jurisdiction to review the DPS (under a flexible standard) to make sure it is truthful. Fontana contends that the number of relevant and non-repetitive comments submitted should form the basis for determining whether the agency rule is entitled to special deference from a reviewing court. He recognizes various criticisms, but argues that individual counting of comments would be relatively objective while screening out repetitive comments would minimize the risks of agency capture from organized interest group campaigns. David Fontana, *Reforming the Administrative Procedure Act: Democracy Index Rulemaking*, 74 Fordham L. Rev. 81, 89–90, 99, 120–21 (2005). Does Fontana's proposal seem like an improvement on the current judicial review process? Does it adequately account for considerations of equality or for public choice-related concerns?

5.   *Agency Versus Legislative Rulemaking.* With respect to the "concise general statement of basis and purpose" required under section 553(c), Judge Gurfein observed that "agencies do not have quite the prerogative of obscurantism reserved to legislatures." Why not? What explains the fact that an agency must respond to material questions or concerns about its proposed rule when Congress need not do so as part of its lawmaking process? More generally, the language of section 553(c) does not require that agencies compile a complete documentary record, or furnish rational explanations in writing for their final rules that include responses to significant critical comments. Yet Judge Gurfein, Judge McGowan, and other circuit court judges have essentially read these requirements into the APA. To what extent have reviewing courts undermined the idea of agencies as experts in the subject matter delegated to them by Congress? Or have they simply replaced the expertise model of agency decisionmaking with a different one? See Lisa Schultz Bressman, *Beyond Accountability: Arbitrariness and Legitimacy in the Administrative State*, 78 N.Y.U. L. Rev. 461, 473–74 (2003).

Assume that concerns about botulism and smoked fish had been taken up by Congress instead of the FDA, and that following committee consideration and floor debate, Congress had adopted the same approach in statutory form—a single provision applicable to all forms of smoked or salted fish without reference to the particular species. What procedural objections could Nova Scotia raise before a reviewing court? Would you expect Nova Scotia to prevail in challenging such a statute? If not, how can you justify the company's success in contesting the FDA rulemaking effort under the APA? Is the different result due to considerations of political accountability? To differences in the level of generality between laws and regulations? Are there other reasons?

C. ADJUDICATION

The APA provides for rulemaking and adjudication as the two main procedural channels for agencies implementing statutory policies. From APA enactment in 1946 until the late 1960s, most agencies relied on case-by-case adjudication to develop policies. See M. Elizabeth Magill, *Agency Choice of Policymaking Form*, 71 U. Chi. L. Rev. 1383, 1398 (2004) (citing sources). In the course of adjudicating a particular controversy, an agency may develop detailed rules to which it subsequently ascribes precedential status. These adjudicatory rules will affect if not control the resolution of future cases presenting identical or comparable issues. The agency may, for example, amplify the meaning of crucial yet ambiguous statutory terms (see *Town & Country Elec. Co.*, 309 N.L.R.B. 1250 (1992)), or it may set forth burdens of proof with respect to certain statutorily protected activities (see *Levitz Furniture Co.*, 333 N.L.R.B. 717 (2001)). These types of adjudicatory rules effectively make policy, facilitating resolution of similar issues in later cases.

Between the late 1960s and late 1970s, many agencies shifted from adjudication to rulemaking as their primary policymaking approach. Multiple factors contributed to this shift. An important element was Congress, which created new health and safety agencies such as EPA, OSHA, and the National Highway Traffic Safety Administration, and required that these agencies pursue rulemaking in specified contexts. In addition, existing agencies acted from efficiency considerations, responding to increasingly onerous caseloads and to being criticized for lack of predictability or rationality in explaining their policies. See Reuel Schiller, *Rulemaking's Promise: Administrative Law and Legal Culture in the 1960s and 1970s*, 53 Admin. L. Rev. 1139, 1148–51 (2001). Not all agencies followed this trend: the NLRB and the FTC, among others, continued to rely heavily on adjudication as a mode of policy implementation. And Magill observes that we may now be experiencing another sea change in agency behavior: "making policy through [strategic agency-initiated] litigation, negotiated settlements, or the waiver of rules in individual contexts can be seen as a shift back" to the case-by-case approach. 71 U. Chi. L. Rev. at 1399.

In reading the two cases that follow, consider the benefits and costs of adjudication versus rulemaking from the standpoint of agencies and also regulated entities. Does one approach offer a better prospect for developing and implementing policies that are predictable? Consistent? Flexible? What role does Congress play in shaping agency choice of procedural approach? What about the role of reviewing courts: does the extent of judicial scrutiny, and an agency's related ability to survive judicial challenge, exert influence in a particular direction?

SECURITIES AND EXCHANGE COMMISSION V. CHENERY CORPORATION

Supreme Court of the United States, 1947.
332 U.S. 194, 67 S.Ct. 1575, 91 L.Ed. 1995.

MR. JUSTICE MURPHY delivered the opinion of the Court.

This case is here for the second time. In *S.E.C. v. Chenery Corporation*, 318 U.S. 80, we held that an order of the Securities and Exchange Commission could not be sustained on the grounds upon which that agency acted. We therefore directed that the case be remanded to the Commission for such further proceedings as might be appropriate. On remand, the Commission reexamined the problem, recast its rationale and reached the same result. The issue now is whether the Commission's action is proper in light of the principles established in our prior decision.

When the case was first here, we emphasized a simple but fundamental rule of administrative law. That rule is to the effect that a reviewing court, in dealing with a determination or judgment which an administrative agency alone is authorized to make, must judge the propriety of such action solely by the grounds invoked by the agency. If those grounds are inadequate or improper, the court is powerless to affirm the administrative action by substituting what it considers to be a more adequate or proper basis. To do so would propel the court into the domain which Congress has set aside exclusively for the administrative agency.

We also emphasized in our prior decision an important corollary of the foregoing rule. If the administrative action is to be tested by the basis upon which it purports to rest, that basis must be set forth with such clarity as to be understandable. It will not do for a court to be compelled to guess at the theory underlying the agency's action; nor can a court be expected to chisel that which must be precise from what the agency has left vague and indecisive. In other words, "We must know what a decision means before the duty becomes ours to say whether it is right or wrong."

Applying this rule and its corollary, the Court was unable to sustain the Commission's original action.

[The case involved a complicated reorganization of the Federal Water Service Corporation (Federal), a holding company registered under the Public Utility Holding Company Act of 1935. Company shareholders with "preferred" stock lacked voting rights to elect corporate directors. Chenery and his group (respondents) owned a controlling block of "common" stock that gave them the power to select corporate management. In rejecting numerous consecutive reorganization plans submitted by Federal, the SEC insisted initially that an acceptable plan must convert the non-voting preferred stock into common stock in order to insure adequate distribution of shareholder voting power; and subsequently that respondents' purchases of preferred shares in contemplation of this conversion (although fully disclosed and at a fair market price) improperly conferred the same voting rights as were given to other converted preferred shares. In the end, the agency amended Federal's plan, over respondents' objections, to provide that respondents' preferred stock was to be surrendered at cost plus any accumulated dividends.

The SEC justified its decision based on its understanding of judicial precedent, which was that corporate management occupied a fiduciary position toward all shareholders during a reorganization, and that pursuant to applicable judge-made equitable principles, management's "duty of fair dealing" would be violated if it traded in the corporation's stock during this period, even at a fair price and without fraud. The Supreme Court held against the SEC, concluding that the agency's decision was based on a misreading of principles of equity derived from judicial decisions; the courts had not imposed upon corporate officers and directors any fiduciary duty to stockholders that precluded them from buying and selling the corporation's stock simply because they were officers and directors.]

The latest order of the Commission definitely avoids the fatal error of relying on judicial precedents which do not sustain it. This time, after a thorough reexamination of the problem in light of the purposes and standards of the Holding Company Act, the Commission has concluded that the proposed transaction is inconsistent with the standards of §§ 7 and 11 of the Act. It has drawn heavily upon its accumulated experience in dealing with utility reorganizations. And it has expressed its reasons with a clarity and thoroughness that admit of no doubt as to the underlying basis of its order.

The argument is pressed upon us, however, that the Commission was foreclosed from taking such a step following our prior decision. It is said that, in the absence of findings of conscious wrongdoing on the part of Federal's management, the Commission could not determine by an order in this particular case that it was inconsistent with the statutory standards to permit Federal's management to realize a profit through the reorganization purchases. All that it could do was to enter an order allowing an amendment to the plan so that the proposed transaction could be consummated. Under this view, the Commission would be free only to promulgate a general rule outlawing such profits in future utility reorganizations; but such a rule would have to be prospective in nature and have no retroactive effect upon the instant situation.

We reject this contention, for it grows out of a misapprehension of our prior decision and of the Commission's statutory duties. We held no more and no less than that the Commission's first order was unsupportable for the reasons supplied by that agency. * * * Still unsettled, however, was the answer the Commission might give were it to bring to bear on the facts the proper administrative and statutory considerations, a function which belongs exclusively to the Commission in the first instance. The administrative process had taken an erroneous rather than a final turn. Hence we carefully refrained from expressing any views as to the propriety of an order rooted in the proper and relevant considerations. * * * After the remand was made, therefore, the Commission was bound to deal with the problem afresh, performing the function delegated to it by Congress. It was again charged with the duty of measuring the proposed treatment of the management's preferred stock holdings by relevant and proper standards. Only in that way could the legislative policies embodied in the Act be effectuated.

The absence of a general rule or regulation governing management trading during reorganization did not affect the Commission's duties in relation to the particular proposal before it. The Commission was asked to grant or deny effectiveness to a proposed amendment to Federal's reorganization plan whereby the management would be accorded parity treatment on its holdings. It could do that only in the form of an order, entered after a due consideration of the particular facts in light of the relevant and proper standards. That was true regardless of whether those standards previously had been spelled out in a general rule or regulation. Indeed, if the Commission rightly felt that the proposed amendment was inconsistent with those standards, an order giving effect to the amendment merely because there was no general rule or regulation covering the matter would be unjustified.

It is true that our prior decision explicitly recognized the possibility that the Commission might have promulgated a general rule dealing with this problem under its statutory rule-making powers, in which case the issue for our consideration would have been entirely different from that which did confront us. But we did not mean to imply thereby that the failure of the Commission to anticipate this problem and to promulgate a general rule withdrew all power from that agency to perform its statutory duty in this case. To hold that the Commission had no alternative in this proceeding but to approve the proposed transaction, while formulating any general rules it might desire for use in future cases of this nature, would be to stultify the administrative process. That we refuse to do.

Since the Commission, unlike a court, does have the ability to make new law prospectively through the exercise of its rule-making powers, it has less reason to rely upon ad hoc adjudication to formulate new standards of conduct within the framework of the Holding Company Act. The function of filling in the interstices of the Act should be performed, as much as possible, through this quasi-legislative promulgation of rules to be applied in the future. But any rigid requirement to that effect would make the administrative process inflexible and incapable of dealing with many of the specialized problems which arise. See Report of the Attorney General's Committee on Administrative Procedure in Government Agencies, S. Doc. No. 8, 77th Cong., 1st Sess., at 29. Not every principle essential to the effective administration of a statute can or should be cast immediately into the mold of a general rule. Some principles must await their own development, while others must be adjusted to meet particular, unforeseeable situations. In performing its important functions in these respects, therefore, an administrative agency must be equipped to act either by general rule or by individual order. To insist upon one form of action to the exclusion of the other is to exalt form over necessity.

In other words, problems may arise in a case which the administrative agency could not reasonably foresee, problems which must be solved despite the absence of a relevant general rule. Or the agency may not have had sufficient experience with a particular problem to warrant rigidifying its tentative judgment into a hard and fast rule. Or the problem may be so specialized and varying in nature as to be impossible of capture within the boundaries of a general rule. In those situations, the agency must retain power to deal with the problems on a case-to-case basis if the administrative process is to be effective. There is thus a very definite place for the case-by-case evolution of statutory standards. And the choice made between proceeding by general rule or by individual, ad hoc litigation is one that lies primarily in the informed discretion of the administrative agency.

Hence we refuse to say that the Commission, which had not previously been confronted with the problem of management trading during reorganization, was forbidden from utilizing this particular proceeding for announcing and applying a new standard of conduct. That such action might have a retroactive effect was not necessarily fatal to its validity. Every case of first impression has a retroactive effect, whether the new principle is announced by a court or by an administrative agency. But such retroactivity must be balanced against the mischief of producing a result which is contrary to a statutory design or to legal and equitable principles. If that mischief is greater than the ill effect of the retroactive application of a new standard, it is not the type of retroactivity which is condemned by law. * * *

The Commission concluded that it could not find that the reorganization plan, if amended as proposed, would be "fair and equitable to the persons affected (thereby)" within the meaning of § 11(e) of the Act, under which the reorganization was taking place. Its view was that the amended plan would involve the issuance of securities on terms 'detrimental to the public interest or the interest of investors' contrary to §§ 7(d)(6) and 7(e), and would result in an 'unfair or inequitable distribution of voting power' among the Federal security holders within the meaning of § 7(e). It was led to this result "not by proof that the interveners (Federal's management) committed acts of conscious wrongdoing but by the character of the conflicting interests created by the interveners program of stock purchases carried out while plans for reorganization were under consideration."

* * * Drawing upon its experience, the Commission indicated that [the broad range of] normal and special powers [wielded by] holding company management during the course of a § 11(e) reorganization placed in the management's command "a formidable battery of devices that would enable it, if it should choose to use them selfishly, to affect in material degree the ultimate allocation of new securities among the various existing classes, to influence the market for its own gain and to manipulate or obstruct the reorganization required by the mandate of the statute." In that setting, the Commission felt that a management program of stock purchase would give rise to the temptation and the opportunity to shape the reorganization proceeding so as to encourage public selling on the market at low prices. No management could engage in such a program without raising serious questions as to whether its personal interests had not opposed its duties "to exercise disinterested judgment in matters pertaining to subsidiaries' accounting, budgetary and dividend policies, to present publicly an unprejudiced financial picture of the enterprise, and to effectuate a fair and feasible plan expeditiously." * * *

Turning to the facts in this case, the Commission noted the salient fact that the primary object of Federal's management in buying the preferred stock was admittedly to obtain the voting power that was accruing to that stock through the reorganization and to profit from the investment therein. That stock had been purchased in the market at prices that were depressed in relation to what the management anticipated would be, and what in fact was, the earning and asset value of its reorganization equivalent. The Commission admitted that the good faith and personal integrity of this management were not in question; but as to the management's justification of its motives, the Commission concluded that it was merely trying to "deny that they made selfish use of their powers during the period when their conflict of interest, vis-a-vis public investors was in existence owing to their purchase program." Federal's management had thus placed itself in a position where it was 'peculiarly susceptible to temptation to conduct the reorganization for personal gain rather than the public good' and where its desire to make advantageous purchases of stock could have an important influence, even though subconsciously, upon many of the decisions to be made in the course of the reorganization. Accordingly, the Commission felt that all of its general considerations of the problem were applicable to this case.

The scope of our review of an administrative order wherein a new principle is announced and applied is no different from that which pertains to ordinary administrative action. The wisdom of the principle adopted is none of our concern. Our duty is at an end when it becomes evident that the Commission's action is based upon substantial evidence and is consistent with the authority granted by Congress. We are unable to say in this case that the Commission erred in reaching the result it did. The facts being undisputed, we are free to disturb the Commission's conclusion only if it lacks any rational and statutory foundation. In that connection, the Commission has made a thorough examination of the problem, utilizing statutory standards and its own accumulated experience with reorganization matters. In essence, it has made what we indicated in our prior opinion would be an informed, expert judgment on the problem. * * *

The "fair and equitable" rule of § 11(e) and the standard of what is "detrimental to the public interest or the interest of investors or consumers" under § 7(d)(6) and § 7(e) were inserted by the framers of the Act in order that the Commission might have broad powers to protect the various interests at stake. The application of those criteria, whether in the form of a particular order or a general regulation, necessarily requires the use of informal discretion by the Commission. The very breath of the statutory language precludes a reversal of the Commission's judgment save where it has plainly abused its discretion in these matters. Such an abuse is not present in this case.

The purchase by a holding company management of that company's securities during the course of a reorganization may well be thought to be so fraught with danger as to warrant a denial of the benefits and profits accruing to the management. The possibility that such a stock purchase program will result in detriment to the public investors is not a fanciful one. The influence that program may have upon the important decisions to be made by the management during reorganization is not inconsequential. Since the officers and directors occupy fiduciary positions during this period, their actions are to be held to a higher standard than that imposed upon the general investing public. There is thus a reasonable basis for a value judgment that the benefits and profits accruing to the management from the stock purchases should be prohibited, regardless of the good faith involved. And it is a judgment that can justifiably be reached in terms of fairness and equitableness, to the end that the interests of the public, the investors and the consumers might be protected. But it is a judgment based upon public policy, a judgment which Congress has indicated is of the type for the Commission to make.

The Commission's conclusion here rests squarely in that area where administrative judgments are entitled to the greatest amount of weight by appellate courts. It is the product of administrative experience, appreciation of the complexities of the problem, realization of the statutory policies, and responsible treatment of the uncontested facts. It is the type of judgment which administrative agencies are best equipped to make and which justifies the use of the administrative process. Whether we agree or disagree with the result reached, it is an allowable judgment which we cannot disturb.

MR. JUSTICE BURTON concurs in the result.

The CHIEF JUSTICE and MR. JUSTICE DOUGLAS took no part in the consideration or decision of this case.

MR. JUSTICE JACKSON, dissenting.

* * * The difference between the first and the latest decision of the Court is simply the difference between holding that administrative orders must have a basis in law and a holding that absence of a legal basis is no ground on which courts may annul them.

* * * The Court's reasoning adds up to this: The Commission must be sustained because of its accumulated experience in solving a problem which it had never before confronted! Of course, thus to uphold the Commission by professing to find that it has enunciated a "new standard of conduct" brings the Court squarely against the invalidity of retroactive law-making. But the Court does not falter: "That such action might have a retroactive effect was not necessarily fatal to its validity." "But such retroactivity must be balanced against the mischief of producing a result which is contrary to a statutory design or to legal or equitable principles." Of course, if what these parties did really was condemned by "statutory design" or "legal and equitable principles," it could be stopped without resort to a new rule and there would be no retroactivity to condone. * * * I give up. Now I realize what Mark Twain meant when he said, "The more you explain it, the more I don't understand it."

* * * This administrative authoritarianism, this power to decide without law, is what the Court seems to approve in so many words. "The absence of a general rule or regulation governing management trading during reorganization did not affect the Commission's duties * * * " This seems to me to undervalue and to belittle the place of law, even in the system of administrative justice. * * *

MR. JUSTICE FRANKFURTER joins in this opinion.

NOTES ON CHENERY II

1. *Post-Hoc Justifications.* Justice Murphy explains that the Court's first *Chenery* decision announced a fundamental rule of administrative law. Agency action can be upheld by a court solely on the grounds invoked by the agency when taking the action under review, not based on some "more adequate or proper" rationale offered after the fact by the agency or a reviewing court. From the standpoint of administrative law, what justifies a ban on making use of post-hoc rationalizations? Does it derive from the non-delegation doctrine, in that agencies as politically accountable actors must state the grounds for their exercise of delegated authority? See Kevin Stack, *The Constitutional Foundations of Chenery*, 116 Yale L.J. 952, 958–59 (2007). Alternatively, perhaps separation of powers is not implicated; rather, the agency's legal authority to act is conceded but the ban on post-hoc justifications stems from the core nature of reasoned decisionmaking. See Elizabeth Magill and Adrian Vermeule, *Allocating Power Within Agencies*, 120 Yale L.J. 1032, 1043 (2011). However it is justified, one practical effect of the ban may be to allocate power horizontally within agencies. The argument is that allowing post-hoc rationalizations would elevate the role of lawyers within an agency, especially appellate lawyers, whereas the ban on such rationalizations privileges agency personnel who formulate policy before it is challenged in court. These policy-formulators may include lawyers but they will also include other agency professionals—notably scientists, technical experts, civil servants, and political appointees. See Magill and Vermeule, 120 Yale L.J. at 1043–44.

2. *The Adjudication "Exceptions"?* Justice Murphy opines that "filling in the interstices of the Act should be performed, as much as possible, through" rulemaking. He then sets forth three settings in which case-by-case adjudication is more likely to be warranted. Are these three settings genuinely limiting exceptions? To what extent do lack of reasonably foreseeable circumstances, insufficient agency experience, and specialized problems invite the exercise of broad agency discretion? Justice Jackson in dissent contends that the Court has approved "administrative authoritarianism, th[e] power to decide without law." Do you find his argument persuasive?

Is it the Court's position that an agency is permitted to proceed by adjudication only in one of the three specified settings identified in the opinion? If not, are there *any* limits on the agency's choice of implementation options? What sources of institutional authority besides reviewing courts might create such limits? *See* Magill, *supra*, 71 U. Chi. L. Rev. at 1409.

NATIONAL LABOR RELATIONS BOARD V. BELL AEROSPACE COMPANY

Supreme Court of the United States, 1974.
416 U.S. 267, 94 S.Ct. 1757, 40 L.Ed.2d 134.

MR. JUSTICE POWELL delivered the opinion of the Court.

This case presents two questions: first, whether the National Labor Relations Board properly determined that all "managerial employees," except those whose participation in a labor organization would create a conflict of interest with their job responsibilities, are covered by the National Labor Relations Act; and second, whether the Board must proceed by rulemaking rather than by adjudication in determining whether certain buyers are "managerial employees." We answer both questions in the negative. * * *

[In answering the first question, the Court rejected the Board's recent re-interpretation of the NLRA to establish protections for some managerial employees. The majority held that the Board's early decisions on this issue, the purpose and legislative history of the Act's 1947 amendments, subsequent and consistent agency interpretations over two decades, and the decisions of the courts of appeals, "all point unmistakably to the conclusion that 'managerial employees' are not covered by the Act." The Court observed that "the Board is not now free to read a new and more restrictive meaning into the Act, and added that "in view of our conclusion, the case must be remanded to permit the Board to apply the proper legal standard in determining the status of these buyers. *SEC v. Chenery Corp.*, 318 U.S. 80, 85 (1943)."]

The Court of Appeals also held that, although the Board was not precluded from determining that buyers or some types of buyers were not 'managerial employees,' it could do so only by invoking its rulemaking procedures under § 6 of the Act, 29 U.S.C. § 156. We disagree.

At the outset, the precise nature of the present issue must be noted. The question is not whether the Board should have resorted to rulemaking, or in fact improperly promulgated a 'rule,' when in the context of the prior representation proceeding it held that the Act covers all 'managerial employees' except those meeting the new 'conflict of interest in labor relations' touchstone. Our conclusion that the Board applied the wrong legal standard makes consideration of that issue unnecessary. Rather, the present question is whether on remand the Board must invoke its rulemaking procedures if it determines, in light of our opinion, that these buyers are not 'managerial employees' under the Act. The Court of Appeals thought that rulemaking was required because any Board finding that the company's buyers are not 'managerial' would be contrary to its prior decisions and would presumably be in the nature of a general rule designed 'to fit all cases at all times.'

A similar issue was presented to this Court in its second decision in *SEC v. Chenery Corp.*, 332 U.S. 194 (1947) (*Chenery II*). There, the respondent corporation argued that in an adjudicative proceeding the Commission could not apply a general standard that it had formulated for the first time in that proceeding. Rather, the Commission was required to resort instead to its rulemaking procedures if it desired to promulgate a new standard that would govern future conduct. In rejecting this contention, the Court first noted that the Commission had a statutory duty to decide the issue at hand in light of the proper standards and that this duty remained 'regardless of whether those standards previously had been spelled out in a general rule or regulation.' *Id.* at 201. The Court continued:

> "The function of filling in the interstices of the (Securities) Act should be performed, as much as possible, through this quasi-legislative promulgation of rules to be applied in the future. But any rigid requirement to that effect would make the administrative process inflexible and incapable of dealing with many of the specialized problems which arise. . . . Not every principle essential to the effective

administration of a statute can or should be cast immediately into the mold of a general rule. Some principles must await their own development, while others must be adjusted to meet particular, unforeseeable situations. *In performing its important functions in these respects, therefore, an administrative agency must be equipped to act either by general rule or by individual order. To insist upon one form of action to the exclusion of the other is to exalt form over necessity.*"

(Emphasis added.)

The Court concluded that 'the choice made between proceeding by general rule or by individual, ad hoc litigation is one that lies primarily in the informed discretion of the administrative agency.' *Id.* at 203.

And in *NLRB v. Wyman-Gordon Co.*, 394 U.S. 759 (1969), the Court upheld a Board order enforcing an election list requirement first promulgated in an earlier adjudicative proceeding in *Excelsior Underwear Inc.*, 156 N.L.R.B. 1236 (1966). The plurality opinion of Mr. Justice Fortas, joined by The Chief Justice, Mr. Justice Stewart, and Mr. Justice White, recognized that "(a)djudicated cases may and do . . . serve as vehicles for the formulation of agency policies, which are applied and announced therein," and that such cases "generally provide a guide to action that the agency may be expected to take in future cases." *NLRB v. Wyman-Gordon Co.*, at 765–766. The concurring opinion of Mr. Justice Black, joined by Mr. Justice Brennan and Mr. Justice Marshall, also noted that the Board had both adjudicative and rulemaking powers and that the choice between the two was "within its informed discretion." *Id.* at 772.

The views expressed in *Chenery II* and *Wyman-Gordon* make plain that the Board is not precluded from announcing new principles in an adjudicative proceeding and that the choice between rulemaking and adjudication lies in the first instance within the Board's discretion. Although there may be situations where the Board's reliance on adjudication would amount to an abuse of discretion or a violation of the Act, nothing in the present case would justify such a conclusion. Indeed, there is ample indication that adjudication is especially appropriate in the instant context. As the Court of Appeals noted, "(t)here must be tens of thousands of manufacturing, wholesale and retail units which employ buyers, and hundreds of thousands of the latter." 475 F.2d at 496. Moreover, duties of buyers vary widely depending on the company or industry. It is doubtful whether any generalized standard could be framed which would have more than marginal utility. The Board thus has reason to proceed with caution, developing its standards in a case-by-case manner with attention to the specific character of the buyers' authority and duties in each company. The Board's judgment that adjudication best serves this purpose is entitled to great weight.

The possible reliance of industry on the Board's past decisions with respect to buyers does not require a different result. It has not been shown that the adverse consequences ensuing from such reliance are so substantial that the Board should be precluded from reconsidering the issue in an adjudicative proceeding. Furthermore, this is not a case in which some new liability is sought to be imposed on individuals for past actions which were taken in good-faith reliance on Board pronouncements. Nor are fines or damages involved here. In any event, concern about such consequences is largely speculative, for the Board has not yet finally determined whether these buyers are "managerial."

It is true, of course, that rulemaking would provide the Board with a forum for soliciting the informed views of those affected in industry and labor before embarking on a new course. But surely the Board has discretion to decide that the adjudicative procedures in this case may also produce the relevant information necessary to mature and fair consideration of the issues. Those most immediately affected, the buyers and the company in the particular case, are accorded a full opportunity to be heard before the Board makes its determination.

Judgment of the Court of Appeals affirmed in part and reversed in part, and cause remanded.

[The opinion of MR. JUSTICE WHITE, with whom MR. JUSTICE BRENNAN, MR. JUSTICE STEWART, and MR. JUSTICE MARSHALL join, dissenting in part, is omitted.]

NOTES ON RULEMAKING V. ADJUDICATION

1.   *Adjudication to Revise a Longstanding Policy?* Justice Powell near the end of his opinion in *Bell Aerospace* dismisses as unpersuasive the fact that the NLRB had changed its position from prior orders in which it had determined that similar buyers were not entitled to the Act's protections for collective bargaining. Is there a salient difference between adjudicatory policymaking in the first instance and adjudicatory policymaking reversing a prior agency adjudication? Judge Friendly, who authored the Second Circuit opinion reversed by the Supreme Court, suggested that "the argument for rulemaking is especially strong when the Board is proposing to reverse a long-standing and oft-repeated policy on which industry and labor have relied." *Bell Aerospace Co. v. NLRB*, 475 F.2d 485, 496–97 (2d Cir. 1973). Justice Powell concedes that "there may be situations where the Board's reliance on adjudication would amount to an abuse of discretion." When, if ever, might it be an "abuse of discretion" under section 706(2) of the APA for the NLRB to reverse a heavily-relied-upon adjudicatory ruling without going through notice-and-comment rulemaking? Courts reverse longstanding statutory precedents from time to time, because the precedent is deemed irreconcilable with competing legal doctrines or even inconsistent with the sense of justice or social welfare. See *Patterson v. McLean Credit Union*, 491 U.S. 164, 173–74 (1989) (discussed in Chapter 5, § 2). Is there any reason why an agency's policy precedents should not be similarly revisited? Why regard reliance interests differently in agency adjudicatory settings? See Problem 8–1 following these Notes.

2.   *The Advantages of Rulemaking?* In his classic article, *The Choice of Rulemaking or Adjudication in the Development of Administrative Policy*, 78 Harv. L. Rev. 921, 929–42 (1965), David Shapiro sets forth a number of potential advantages to rulemaking over adjudication in the development of administrative policies: (a) *fairness:* the requirement for notice and comment facilitates general participation in the deliberative process by all parties who may be affected; (b) *advance planning:* an agency is better able to allocate its limited resources in a rational manner, as opposed to litigating a possibly voluminous number of fact-specific cases; (c) *prospectivity:* rulemaking is more likely to be limited to determining the status of future conduct and

therefore less likely to defeat justifiable expectations based on prior agency policy; (d) *uniformity:* rulemaking's uniform application to all regulated entities minimizes the chance that competitors will pursue or gain an unfair advantage; (e) *flexibility:* rulemaking leaves agencies relatively free to consult experts on their staffs, to receive far-ranging submissions of data, and to pursue information unconstrained by rules of evidence or other formalities of a trial-type proceeding; (f) *accessibility and clarity of formulation:* rulemaking requires the development and articulation of policies over time and through processes that are both formal and relatively transparent, making it likely that the rules or standards finally enunciated are easier to locate, decipher and understand; and (g) *judicial review:* rulemaking allows affected parties to test agency positions in the courts on a readily available and timely basis when compared to post-hoc review of adjudications or even to the deterrent effect of threatened agency sanctions that secure changes in private conduct without an adjudicatory decision.

Shapiro is nuanced and judicious in presenting these advantages, but there are counterarguments. Indeed, agencies as well as regulated entities often prefer adjudication to rulemaking, although perhaps for different reasons. In what ways are the advantages for rulemaking overstated? For each of the benefits set forth above, can you think of possible rebuttals in defense of adjudication as a policymaking option?

3. *Judicial Review of Agency Choice of Procedures.* Under section 706(2)(A) of the APA, courts may review agency adjudicatory and rulemaking decisions under the arbitrary and capricious standard. But what about the predicate agency decision to choose between rulemaking and adjudication? Magill contends that this predicate agency choice has been regarded as essentially unreviewable by courts: "an agency does not feel obligated to explain, much less defend, why it chose a particular policymaking tool; and the agency is not asked to do so by parties or courts. An agency's choice of procedure is not in doctrinal terms "unreviewable," but it might as well be." 71 U. Chi. L. Rev. at 1414. Magill is critical of the absence of any reason-giving requirement; she contends that the arbitrary and capricious standard can and should apply to the review of an agency's choice between rulemaking and adjudication. Specifically, she maintains that the agency should be required to provide an explanation for its choice and that the agency's rationale should be sufficient to persuade the court that the agency exercised its discretion in a reasoned way, i.e. that the agency considered the important alternatives and settled on its course of action for sensible reasons.

What factors might have lead courts not to review an agency's choice between rulemaking and adjudication? Based on the text and plain meaning of the APA, should courts be conducting reviews of these agency determinations? If the courts were to undertake such reviews, should they be based on the arbitrary and capricious standard as Magill suggests? Or is there a third option, other than arbitrary-and-capricious and non-review?

4. *Adjudication and Presidential Review.* Jennifer Nou suggests that agencies may prefer adjudication to rulemaking as a means of insulating themselves from presidential review. Jennifer Nou, *Agency Self-Insulation Under Presidential Review,* 126 Harv. L. Rev. 1755 (2013). Under the current structure of presidential oversight (discussed in section 3B of this chapter), review generally focuses on actions that are "economically significant" and that are expected to lead to the promulgation of a rule or regulation. Accordingly, agencies can choose adjudication (as well as other strategies like guidance documents, non-significant rules or simple inaction) as an instrument

that is likely to escape presidential review. Agencies issue thousands of adjudications annually, and "[b]ecause adjudication, unlike rulemaking, proceeds on a case-by-case basis, each adjudication's policy impacts are limited and aggregate policy change is developed only incrementally." *Id.* at 1783–84 (2013). Should insulation from presidential review through adjudication be added to Shapiro's list of reasons why rulemaking is more advantageous? Or are there certain benefits to this insulation through the use of adjudication?

5. *Power Allocation and the Choice Between Adjudication and Rulemaking.* In *Allocating Power Within Agencies*, 120 Yale L.J. 1032 (2011), Elizabeth Magill and Adrian Vermeule hypothesize that allocation of power within an agency can influence the choice between rulemaking and adjudication. Lawyer-dominated agencies will tend to prefer adjudication whereas agencies more dominated by scientists, or other non-lawyer professionals will tend to favor rulemaking. This is in part because empowering particular types of professionals within agencies can have spillover effects: "Once lawyers, scientists, or economists—or any other professionals—are employed to cope with a particular issue, they become major stakeholders within agencies, and their influence can seep out laterally to encompass issues other than the one for which they were originally conscripted." The authors concede, however, that their hypothesis, "is fragile because it depends upon the proposition that lawyers, qua lawyers, are more likely to favor case-specific modes of agency policymaking." *Id.* at 1080–81.

Magill and Vermeule then provide the following example, based on a previous account by Jerry Mashaw and David Harfst.[23] In the early 1970s, safety engineers dominated the National Highway Transportation Safety Administration's (NHTSA's) culture, and the agency made extensive use of ex ante rulemaking. When the courts rejected these standards in a series of 1972 decisions, this resulted in the engineers' efforts being delegitimized. The medium-term impact was to bend agency strategy toward litigation, specifically a large number of ex post recalls that were successful in the courts. This shift led to increased power being allocated to lawyers and economists over engineers in the NHTSA; a further result was "to bias systematically the agency's choice of policymaking away from rulemaking and toward adjudication." *Id.* at 1083. What lessons, if any, might other agencies draw from this episode? Assuming that the judges reviewing NHTSA rules did not anticipate the reshaping of internal agency decisionmaking, should courts today be more sensitive to such possibly dynamic effects of judicial review?

PROBLEM ON AGENCY CHOICE OF PROCEDURES

Problem 8–3. In *Excelsior Underwear Inc.*, 156 N.L.R.B. 1236 (1966), employees asked their employer for a list of names and addresses of all employees eligible to vote in an upcoming union representation election. The employer refused to provide the list, the union lost the election, and employees then filed a charge with the agency alleging unlawful conduct under the National Labor Relations Act (NLRA). The National Labor Relations Board (Board), which usually resolves such adjudicatory disputes based on written submission from the parties, took the unusual step of inviting interested groups to submit amicus briefs and make oral arguments. The Board's subsequent decision included its so-called "Excelsior Rule": within one week after a union representation

---

[23] See Jerry Mashaw & David Harfst, *Inside the National Highway Traffic Safety Administration: Legal Determinants of Bureaucratic Organization and Performance*, 57 U. Chi. L. Rev. 443 (1990).

election has been ordered or agreed upon, the employer is required to submit to the Board, for transmittal to the union, the names and addresses of all employees eligible to vote. In reaching this decision, the Board considered and rejected employer arguments that sharing addresses would raise important problems of employee privacy. The *Excelsior* decision was not appealed and remains the relevant legal standard under the NLRA.

Recently, another dispute has arisen in which employees seek the phone numbers and email addresses of all employees eligible to vote in an upcoming union election. The employees contend that mailing addresses no longer provide timely or even adequate access to contact voters given the typically short time period (21–30 days) for an election campaign and the fact that employees often live great distances from their workplace. The employer refuses to provide this information; she maintains that requiring disclosure of employee phone numbers and email addresses raises a novel set of privacy issues, and that disclosure of company-issued email addresses is also highly problematic. The employees have filed a charge with the Board alleging unlawful employer conduct.

You are a Board attorney in the General Counsel's office; your boss wants your advice as to *how the Board should handle this dispute as a procedural matter.* Some colleagues have recommended the dispute be treated as a garden-variety adjudicatory matter, to be resolved based on written submissions from the parties. Others argue that the dispute calls for *Excelsior*-type treatment: the Board should invite amicus submissions and oral argument. A third group contends that any change from the *Excelsior* standard should be implemented only through notice-and-comment rulemaking. What is your recommendation on the appropriate process to follow, and why? Regardless of which process you propose the agency should follow, what weight should be given to the reliance interests of the parties—or of any regulated entities that will be affected by a change in the Board's substantive approach?

D. INTERPRETIVE RULES AND POLICY STATEMENTS

Agencies often implement statutory provisions through processes that are less prescribed or conventional than formal rulemaking, notice-and-comment rulemaking, and adjudication. Indeed, most federal agencies issue hundreds of communications each year that never appear in the Federal Register yet are designed to guide the conduct of private parties as well as agency employees. Examples include benefit or eligibility forms and instructions for completing them; inspection reports; staff training manuals; press releases; responses to frequently asked questions (FAQs); and speeches given by bureaucrats at varying levels of authority.

Two additional types of less conventional agency communication specifically addressed in the APA are interpretive rules and general statements of policy. Although section 553(b)(A) exempts them from notice-and-comment requirements, section 552(a)(1)(D) requires that they be "separately state[d] and currently publish[ed] in the Federal Register for the guidance of the public" when they are "of general applicability." Interpretive rules and policy statements may be thought of as "rule-like" in applying broadly to potentially affected individuals and entities, but as "non-legislative" in that they do not express new substantive rights or responsibilities.

Interpretive rules and policy statements also differ from one another. The Attorney General's Manual on the APA, drafted in 1947, describes *interpretive rules* as "rules or statements issued by an agency to advise the public of the agency's construction of the statutes and rules which it administers," and *general statements of policy* as "statements issued by an agency to advise the public prospectively of the manner in which the agency proposes to exercise a discretionary power." This distinction may be difficult to apply when considering ways in which an agency exercises its interpretive discretion to address ambiguous statutory or regulatory language. Think about the difference between interpretive rules and policy statements as you consider the cases in this subsection.

1. Interpretive Rules

AMERICAN MINING CONGRESS V. MINE SAFETY & HEALTH ADMINISTRATION

United States Court of Appeals for the District of Columbia Circuit, 1993.
995 F.2d 1106.

STEPHEN F. WILLIAMS, CIRCUIT JUDGE:

This case presents a single issue: whether Program Policy Letters of the Mine Safety and Health Administration, stating the agency's position that certain x-ray readings qualify as "diagnose[s]" of lung disease within the meaning of agency reporting regulations, are interpretive rules under the Administrative Procedure Act. We hold that they are.

The Federal Mine Safety and Health Act, 30 U.S.C. § 801 *et seq.*, extensively regulates health and safety conditions in the nation's mines and empowers the Secretary of Labor to enforce the statute and relevant regulations. See *Id.* at §§ 811, 813–14. In addition, the Act requires "every operator of a . . . mine . . . [to] establish and maintain such records, make such reports, and provide such information, as the Secretary . . . may reasonably require from time to time to enable him to perform his functions." *Id.* at § 813(h). The Act makes a general grant of authority to the Secretary to issue "such regulations as . . . [he] deems appropriate to carry out" any of its provisions. *Id.* at § 957.

Pursuant to its statutory authority, the Mine Safety and Health Administration (acting on behalf of the Secretary of Labor) maintains regulations known as "Part 50" regulations, which cover the "Notification, Investigation, Reports and Records of Accidents, Injuries, Illnesses, Employment, and Coal Production in Mines." See 30 CFR Part 50. These were adopted via notice-and-comment rulemaking. See 42 Fed. Reg. 55,568 (1977) (notice of proposed rulemaking); 42 Fed. Reg. 65,534 (1977) (adopted rules). Subpart C deals with the "Reporting of Accidents, Injuries, and Illnesses" and requires mine operators to report to the MSHA within ten days "each accident, occupational injury, or occupational illness" that occurs at a mine. See 30 CFR § 50.20(a). Of central importance here, the regulation also says that whenever any of certain occupational illnesses are *"diagnosed,"* the operator must similarly report the diagnosis within ten days. *Id.* (emphasis added). Among the occupational illnesses covered are "[s]ilicosis, asbestosis, coal worker's pneumoconiosis, and other pneumoconioses." *Id.* at § 50.20–6(b)(7)(ii). An operator's failure to report may lead to citation and penalty. See 30 U.S.C. §§ 814(a), 815(a) & (d), 816(a).

As the statute and formal regulations contain ambiguities, the MSHA from time to time issues Program Policy Letters ("PPLs") intended to coordinate and convey agency policies, guidelines, and interpretations to agency employees and interested members of the public. See *MSHA Administrative Policy and Procedures Manual*, Volume II, paragraph 112 (July 17, 1990); *MSHA Program Information Bulletin No. 88–03* (August 19, 1988). One subject on which it has done so— apparently in response to inquiries from mine operators about whether certain x-ray results needed to be reported as "diagnos[es]"—has been the meaning of the term diagnosis for purposes of Part 50.

The first of the PPLs at issue here, PPL No. 91–III–2 (effective September 6, 1991), stated that any chest x-ray of a miner who had a history of exposure to pneumonoconiosis-causing dust that rated 1/0 or higher on the International Labor Office (ILO) classification system would be considered a "diagnosis that the x-rayed miner has silicosis or one of the other pneumonoconioses" for the purposes of the Part 50 reporting requirements. (The ILO classification system uses a 12–step scale to measure the concentration of opacities (i.e., areas of darkness or shading) on chest x-rays. A 1/0 rating is the fourth most severe of the ratings.) The 1991 PPL also set up a procedure whereby, if a mine operator had a chest x-ray initially evaluated by a relatively unskilled reader, the operator could seek a reading by a more skilled one; if the latter rated the x-ray below 1/0, the MSHA would delete the "diagnosis" from its files. We explain the multiple-reader rules further in the context of the third PPL, where they took their final form (so far).

The second letter, PPL No. P92–III–2 (effective May 6, 1992), superseded the 1991 PPL but largely repeated its view about a Part 50 diagnosis. In addition, the May 1992 PPL stated the MSHA's position that mere diagnosis of an occupational disease or illness within the meaning of Part 50 did not automatically entitle a miner to benefits for disability or impairment under a workers' compensation scheme. The PPL also said that the MSHA did not intend for an operator's mandatory reporting of an x-ray reading to be equated with an admission of liability for the reported disease.

The final PPL under dispute, PPL No. P92–III–2 (effective August 1, 1992), replaced the May 1992 PPL and again restated the MSHA's basic view that a chest x-ray rating above 1/0 on the ILO scale constituted a "diagnosis" of silicosis or some other pneumoconiosis. The August 1992 PPL also modified the MSHA's position on additional readings. Specifically, when the first reader is not a "B" reader (i.e., one certified by the National Institute of Occupational Safety and Health to perform ILO ratings), and the operator seeks a reading from a "B" reader, the MSHA will stay enforcement for failure to report the first reading. If the "B" reader concurs with the initial determination that the x-ray should be scored a 1/0 or higher, the mine operator must report the "diagnosis". If the "B" reader scores the x-ray below

1/0, the MSHA will continue to stay enforcement if the operator gets a third reading, again from a "B" reader; the MSHA then will accept the majority opinion of the three readers.

The MSHA did not follow the notice and comment requirements of 5 U.S.C. § 553 in issuing any of the three PPLs. In defending its omission of notice and comment, the agency relies solely on the interpretive rule exemption of § 553(b)(3)(A). * * *

The distinction between those agency pronouncements subject to APA notice-and-comment requirements and those that are exempt has been aptly described as "enshrouded in considerable smog." Given the confusion, it makes some sense to go back to the origins of the distinction in the legislative history of the Administrative Procedure Act. Here the key document is the *Attorney General's Manual on the Administrative Procedure Act* (1947), which offers "the following working definitions":

> *Substantive rules*—rules, other than organizational or procedural under section 3(a)(1) and (2), issued by an agency pursuant to statutory authority and which implement the statute, as, for example, the proxy rules issued by the Securities and Exchange Commission pursuant to section 14 of the Securities Exchange Act of 1934 (15 U.S.C. § 78n). Such rules have the force and effect of law.
>
> *Interpretative rules*—rules or statements issued by an agency to advise the public of the agency's construction of the statutes and rules which it administers. . . .
>
> *General statements of policy*—statements issued by an agency to advise the public prospectively of the manner in which the agency proposes to exercise a discretionary power.

* * * Our own decisions have often used similar language, inquiring whether the disputed rule has "the force of law". We have said that a rule has such force only if Congress has delegated legislative power to the agency and if the agency intended to exercise that power in promulgating the rule.

On its face, the "intent to exercise" language may seem to lead only to more smog, but in fact there are a substantial number of instances where such "intent" can be found with some confidence. The first and clearest case is where, in the absence of a legislative rule by the agency, the legislative basis for agency enforcement would be inadequate. The example used by the Attorney General's Manual fits exactly—the SEC's proxy authority under § 14 of the Securities Exchange Act of 1934, 15 U.S.C. § 78n. Section 14(b), for example, forbids certain persons, "to give, or to refrain from giving a proxy" "in contravention of such rules and regulations as the Commission may prescribe." 15 U.S.C. § 78n(b). The statute itself forbids *nothing* except acts or omissions to be spelled out by the Commission in "rules or regulations." The present case is similar, as to Part 50 itself, in that § 813(h) merely requires an operator to maintain "such records . . . as the Secretary . . . may reasonably require from time to time." 30 U.S.C. § 813(h). Although the Secretary might conceivably create some "require[ments]" ad hoc, clearly some agency creation of a duty is a necessary predicate to any enforcement against an operator for failure to keep records. Analogous cases may exist in which an agency may offer a government benefit only after it formalizes the prerequisites.

Second, an agency seems likely to have intended a rule to be legislative if it has the rule published in the Code of Federal Regulations; 44 U.S.C. § 1510 limits publication in that code to rules "having general applicability and legal effect." Third, " '[i]f a second rule repudiates or is irreconcilable with [a prior legislative rule], the second rule must be an amendment of the first; and, of course, an amendment to a legislative rule must itself be legislative.' " * * *

In *United States v. Picciotto*, 875 F.2d 345 (D.C. Cir. 1989), the Park Service had issued an indisputably legislative rule containing an "open-ended" provision stating that a "permit may contain additional reasonable conditions". Then, in a rule issued without notice and comment, it established some such conditions. We struck down the disputed condition, as it was not an interpretation of the prior regulation but an exercise of the legislative authority reserved by the prior legislative rule.

Th[e] focus on whether the agency *needs* to exercise legislative power (to provide a basis for enforcement actions or agency decisions conferring benefits) helps explain some distinctions that may, out of context, appear rather metaphysical. For example, * * * we drew a distinction between instances where an agency merely "declare[s] its understanding of what a statute requires" (interpretive), and ones where an agency "go[es] beyond the text of a statute" (legislative). The difficulty with the distinction is that almost every rule may seem to do both. But if the dividing line is the necessity for agency legislative action, then a rule supplying that action will be legislative no matter how grounded in the agency's "understanding of what the statute requires," and an interpretation that spells out the scope of an agency's or regulated entity's pre-existing duty will be interpretive, even if * * * it widens that duty even beyond the scope allowed to the agency under *Chevron U.S.A., Inc. v. NRDC*, 467 U.S. 837 (1984).

Similarly, we have distinguished between cases where a rule is "based on specific statutory provisions" (interpretive), and where one is instead "based on an agency's power to exercise its judgment as to how best to implement a general statutory mandate" (legislative). A statute or legislative rule that actually establishes a duty or a right is likely to be relatively specific (and the agency's refinement will be interpretive), whereas an agency's authority to create rights and duties will typically be relatively broad (and the agency's actual establishment of rights and duties will be legislative). But the legislative or interpretive status of the agency rules turns not in some general sense on the narrowness or breadth of the statutory (or regulatory) term in question, but on the prior existence or non-existence of legal duties and rights.

* * * Nor is there much explanatory power in any distinction that looks to the use of mandatory as opposed to permissive language. While an agency's decision to use "will" instead of "may" may be of use when drawing a line between *policy statements* and legislative rules, the endeavor miscarries in the interpretive/legislative rule context. Interpretation is a chameleon that takes its

color from its context; therefore, an interpretation will use imperative language—or at least have imperative meaning—if the interpreted term is part of a command; it will use permissive language—or at least have a permissive meaning—if the interpreted term is in a permissive provision.

A non-legislative rule's capacity to have a binding effect is limited in practice by the fact that agency personnel at every level act under the shadow of judicial review. If they believe that courts may fault them for brushing aside the arguments of persons who contest the rule or statement, they are obviously far more likely to entertain those arguments. And, as failure to provide notice-and-comment rulemaking will usually mean that affected parties have had no prior formal opportunity to present their contentions, judicial review for want of reasoned decisionmaking is likely, in effect, to take place in review of specific agency actions implementing the rule. * * * Because the threat of judicial review provides a spur to the agency to pay attention to facts and arguments submitted in derogation of any rule not supported by notice and comment, even as late as the enforcement stage, *any* agency statement not subjected to notice-and-comment rulemaking will be more vulnerable to attack not only in court but also within the agency itself.

Not only does an agency have an incentive to entertain objections to an interpretive rule, but the ability to promulgate such rules, without notice and comment, does not appear more hazardous to affected parties than the likely alternative. Where a statute or legislative rule has created a legal basis for enforcement, an agency can simply let its interpretation evolve ad hoc in the process of enforcement or other applications (e.g., grants). The protection that Congress sought to secure by requiring notice and comment for legislative rules is not advanced by reading the exemption for "interpretive rule" so narrowly as to drive agencies into pure ad hocery—an ad hocery, moreover, that affords less notice, or less convenient notice, to affected parties.

Accordingly, insofar as our cases can be reconciled at all, we think it almost exclusively on the basis of whether the purported interpretive rule has "legal effect", which in turn is best ascertained by asking (1) whether in the absence of the rule there would not be an adequate legislative basis for enforcement action or other agency action to confer benefits or ensure the performance of duties, (2) whether the agency has published the rule in the Code of Federal Regulations, (3) whether the agency has explicitly invoked its general legislative authority, or (4) whether the rule effectively amends a prior legislative rule. If the answer to any of these questions is affirmative, we have a legislative, not an interpretive rule.

Here we conclude that the August 1992 PPL is an interpretive rule. The Part 50 regulations themselves require the reporting of diagnoses of the specified diseases, so there is no legislative gap that required the PPL as a predicate to enforcement action. Nor did the agency purport to act legislatively, either by including the letter in the Code of Federal Regulations, or by invoking its general legislative authority under 30 U.S.C. § 811(a). See *MSHA Program Information Bulletin No. 88–03* (August 19, 1988) (characterizing PPLs generally as "[i]nterpretation"). The remaining possibility therefore is that the August 1992 PPL is a de facto amendment of prior legislative rules, namely the Part 50 regulations.

A rule does not, in this inquiry, become an amendment merely because it supplies crisper and more detailed lines than the authority being interpreted. If that were so, no rule could pass as an interpretation of a legislative rule unless it were confined to parroting the rule or replacing the original vagueness with another. * * *

Although petitioners cite some definitions of "diagnosis" suggesting that with pneumoconiosis and silicosis, a diagnosis requires more than a chest x-ray—specifically, additional diagnostic tools as tissue examination or at least an occupational history, * * * MSHA points to some administrative rules that make x-rays at the level specified here the basis for a finding of pneumoconiosis. * * * A finding of a disease is surely equivalent, in normal terminology, to a diagnosis, and thus the PPLs certainly offer no interpretation that repudiates or is irreconcilable with an existing legislative rule.

We stress that deciding whether an interpretation is an amendment of a legislative rule is different from deciding the substantive validity of that interpretation. An interpretive rule may be sufficiently within the language of a legislative rule to be a genuine interpretation and not an amendment, while at the same time being an incorrect interpretation of the agency's statutory authority. Here, petitioners have made no attack on the PPLs' substantive validity. Nothing that we say upholding the agency's decision to act without notice and comment bars any such substantive claims.

NEW YORK CITY EMPLOYEES' RETIREMENT SYS. V. SEC

United States Court of Appeals for the Second Circuit, 1995.
45 F.3d 7.

MCLAUGHLIN, CIRCUIT JUDGE:

The plaintiffs, New York City Employees' Retirement System ("NYCERS") and two other institutional investors, sued the Securities and Exchange Commission ("SEC") in the United States District Court for the Southern District of New York, to enjoin the SEC from violating section 553(b) of the Administrative Procedure Act ("APA"). The lawsuit stemmed from an SEC "no-action" letter, in which the SEC announced that it was changing its interpretation of SEC Rule 14a–8(c)(7). * * *

[After investing in a company, the plaintiffs, who are major institutional shareholders, regularly use their shareholder status as a bully pulpit to promote non-discriminatory policies in the workplace. When the plaintiffs want to change a company policy, they put their idea up for a shareholder vote by submitting a shareholder proposal to the board of directors. Then, the plaintiffs ask the board to include the proposal in the proxy materials that are sent to all shareholders before meetings.

In 1991, Cracker Barrel Old Country Store, Inc. attracted the plaintiffs' ire when the restaurant chain issued a press release stating that it "is founded upon a concept of traditional American values," and that it "is inconsistent with our concept and values, and is perceived to be inconsistent with those of our customer base, to continue to employ individuals ... whose sexual preferences fail to demonstrate normal heterosexual values which have been the foundation of families in our society." Upon the heels of this release, Cracker Barrel fired several gay employees, triggering public protests, boycotts, and negative media coverage. To defuse the furor, Cracker Barrel rescinded the anti-gay policy but it did not rehire the former employees. It also did not include "sexual orientation" among the inappropriate criteria for employment decisions in its published anti-discrimination policy.]

In November 1991, plaintiff NYCERS, a Cracker Barrel shareholder, proposed to Cracker Barrel's board of directors that the company expressly prohibit discrimination on the basis of sexual orientation. NYCERS called for a shareholder vote and asked Cracker Barrel to include the proposal in the proxy materials for the 1992 annual shareholder meeting. Cracker Barrel wanted no part of this proposal, and did not even want to include it in the proxy materials. Under Rule 14a–8, however, Cracker Barrel had to include the proposal in the proxy materials unless the proposal dealt with "ordinary business operations." See Rule 14a–8(c)(7). The construction of that term lies at the heart of the controversy. * * *

In 1976, the SEC proposed to revise various parts of Rule 14a–8. It wanted to tighten the exception for "ordinary business operations" so that only proposals regarding "routine, day to day matters relating to the conduct of the ordinary business operations" could be excluded from proxy materials. This way, the SEC believed, corporations could not exclude proposals regarding policies important to shareholders just because they also happened to concern "ordinary business operations." [In its 1976 Adoption, the SEC decided not to change the subsection in any material way, but indicated that] the SEC staff would thereafter interpret it so that corporations could not exclude proposals regarding "matters which have significant policy, economic or other implications inherent in them."

Befuddled by the 1976 Adoption, Cracker Barrel wrote to the SEC's Corporation Finance Division (the "Division") in 1991, to find out whether the SEC would bring an enforcement action if Cracker Barrel left NYCERS's proposal out of the proxy materials for the 1992 meeting. * * * In October 1992, the Division issued a no-action letter, stating that the SEC would not bring an enforcement action against Cracker Barrel. The letter conceded that the Division's staff had already experienced difficulty trying to discern when a proposal involved significant policy issues. [Based on the staff's experience and concerns, the letter stated that] "The Division has reconsidered the application of Rule 14a–8(c)(7) to employment related proposals [and * * *] has determined that the fact that a shareholder proposal concerning a company's employment policies and practices for the general workforce is tied to a social issue will no longer be viewed as removing the proposal from the realm of ordinary business operations of the registrant. * * * "

[NYCERS unsuccessfully petitioned the SEC to reverse the *Cracker Barrel* no-action letter. NYCERS and two other institutional investors then sued the SEC in the Southern District of New York. The district court, on plaintiffs' motion for summary judgment, determined that the SEC's no-action letter announced a "legislative rule," as that term is used in the APA. The court therefore enjoined the SEC from issuing any no-action letter inconsistent with the SEC's previous understanding of Rule 14a–8(c)(7) without first submitting the rule for notice and comment. The SEC appealed to the Second Circuit.] * * *

Not all agency issuances are subject to notice and comment requirements. Notice and comment are required only if the statement is (1) a rule, and (2) legislative, as opposed to interpretive. A "rule," under the APA, is statutorily defined as "the whole or a part of an agency statement of general or particular applicability and future effect designed to implement, interpret, or prescribe law or policy." Under this sweeping definition, the *Cracker Barrel* no-action letter's statement that the SEC would no longer follow the "significant policy implications" exception was a rule: it stated generally that the Division staff was making a sea change and that it was abandoning its former policy regarding proxy inclusion requirements.

There are two types of rules, legislative and interpretive. Legislative rules are those that create new law, rights, or duties, in what amounts to a legislative act. Legislative rules have the force of law. Interpretive rules, on the other hand, do not create rights, but merely clarify an existing statute or regulation. Since they only clarify existing law, interpretive rules need not go through notice and comment. These rules do not have force of law, though they are entitled to deference from the courts. * * *

The no-action process works as follows: Whenever a corporation decides to exclude a shareholder proposal from its proxy materials, it "shall file" a letter with the Division explaining the legal basis for its decision. If the Division staff agrees that the proposal is excludable, it may issue a no-action letter, stating that, based on the facts presented by the corporation, the staff will not recommend that the SEC sue the corporation for violating Rule 14a–8. The no-action letter, however, is an informal response, and does not amount to an official statement of the SEC's views. See 17 C.F.R. § 202.1(d).

No-action letters are deemed interpretive because they do not impose or fix a legal relationship upon any of the parties. * * * The *casus belli* of the *Cracker Barrel* letter is the statement that the SEC staff would no longer distinguish shareholder proposals concerning employment-related social issues from those involving ordinary business operations. But this interpretation binds no one: The SEC may still bring an enforcement action against Cracker Barrel (or any other company) based on its failure to include a proposal regarding an employment-related social issue. As the SEC has noted, "no-action . . . responses by the staff are subject to reconsideration and should not be regarded as precedents binding on the [SEC]."

The *Cracker Barrel* no-action letter certainly does not bind the parties. * * * And, as the SEC itself has explained, the SEC "and its staff do not purport in any way to issue 'rulings' or 'decisions' on shareholder proposals management indicates it intends to omit, and they do not adjudicate the merits of management's posture concerning such a proposal." *Statement of Informal Procedures for the Rendering of Staff Advice with Respect to Shareholder Proposals*, Exchange Act Rel. No. 12,599 (July 7, 1976). Thus, a no-action letter does not affect a shareholder's right "to institute a private action with respect to the management's intention to omit the proposal from its proxy materials." *Id.*

Finally, the *Cracker Barrel* no-action letter does not bind the courts. Should NYCERS bring a federal suit against Cracker Barrel under Rule 14a–8, the court may find a violation despite the no-action letter. While the court would treat the no-action letter as persuasive, the court need not give it the same high level of deference that is accorded formal policy statements or rule-making orders. Indeed, at least one district court has found a Rule 14a–8 violation and then issued a preliminary injunction in the face of an SEC no-action letter opining to the contrary. Even when district courts have ruled in accord with no-action letters, they almost always have analyzed the issues independently of the letters. * * *

As the district court noted, however, this is not a garden variety no-action letter. While most no-action letters merely state that the Division staff will not recommend an enforcement action, the *Cracker Barrel* no-action letter went further: it expressly abandoned a previous SEC rule. The district court, relying chiefly on *American Mining Congress v. Mine Safety & Health Adm'n.*, 995 F.2d 1106 (D.C. Cir 1993), concluded that renouncing the former SEC rule transubstantiated the no-action letter from interpretive to legislative. We do not agree.

American Mining Congress addressed whether an agency's policy position letters are legislative or interpretive. In finding these letters interpretive, *American Mining Congress* stated that a rule is legislative if it has "legal effect," and suggested that a rule has legal effect if: (1) in the absence of the rule, no legislative basis would exist for an enforcement action; (2) "the agency has published the rule in the Code of Federal Regulations"; (3) the agency "explicitly invoked its general legislative authority" to pass the rule; or (4) "the rule effectively amends a prior legislative rule."

The rule enunciated in the *Cracker Barrel* no-action letter manifestly does not fit in any of the first three *American Mining Congress* categories. * * * The fourth factor—whether the rule effectively amends a prior legislative rule—requires deeper analysis. True, the *Cracker Barrel* no-action letter abandoned the understanding of "ordinary business operations" espoused in the 1976 Adoption. And, since the "significant policy implications" rule announced in the 1976 Adoption provides a basis for SEC enforcement actions, this part of the 1976 Adoption was a legislative rule.

The district court surmised from these facts that the *Cracker Barrel* no-action letter "effectively amended" a legislative rule (*viz.*, the legislative portion of the 1976 Adoption), and was thus itself legislative. [But] no-action letters are nonbinding statements of the SEC's intent not to prosecute a potential rule violation; they do not oblige or prevent action by the SEC, the parties, or the courts. A necessary corollary of this proposition is that rules announced in no-action letters also have no binding authority. Thus, the *Cracker Barrel* no-action letter did not effectively amend the 1976 Adoption within the meaning of *American Mining Congress*, and did not contain a legislative rule. Rather, the letter merely expressed the view of the Division's staff that it lacks the necessary expertise in identifying issues as having "significant policy implications," and that the staff does not expect to allocate its limited resources to making such subjective determinations.

In so holding, we are mindful of the plaintiffs' warning that the SEC might be able to skirt the entire notice and comment process by using no-action letters to amend legislative rules. We are not persuaded by their prophecy of doom. As *American Mining Congress* wisely observed, "[a] non-legislative rule's capacity to have a binding effect is limited in practice by the fact that agency personnel at every level act under the shadow of judicial review." Agency rules that have not undergone notice and comment receive much closer scrutiny from the courts than do those that have cleared the procedural hurdles. And, since no-action letters are informal, they receive even less deference than other interpretive rules. Consequently, because the *Cracker Barrel* no-action letter did not go through notice and comment, and was only an informal statement by the SEC, courts will not accord great deference to it. * * *

In light of the foregoing, we vacate the injunction and reverse the order of summary judgment.

NOTES ON INTERPRETIVE RULES

1. *Legislative Versus Interpretive.* Interpretive rules clarify an agency's interpretation of an existing legislative rule or statute without imposing substantive changes. Although they do not carry the force of law, interpretive rules may, nonetheless, have the effect of altering conduct. In *American Mining Congress*, couldn't you argue that the rule in question—defining "diagnosis" based on a certain x-ray rating—does more than simply interpret the legislative rule requiring mine operators to report diagnosed instances of occupational disease? MSHA relied on the fourth most severe rating out of twelve under the ILO classification system. What if the agency's definition of diagnosis relied on the least severe of the twelve ILO ratings? What if MSHA devised its own rating system for measuring the concentration of opacities on chest x-rays? Is there some point at which the agency's x-ray rating approach would constitute a distinctly stronger (or weaker) safety standard, requiring notice-and-comment?

Courts have employed different approaches to determine whether a rule is legislative or interpretive. Prominent among them is Judge Williams' four-part test, set forth in *American Mining Congress* and relied upon in *NYCERS*. For many decisions invoking this test, the final factor—whether the rule effectively amends a prior rule—receives particular emphasis. See e.g. *Hemp. Indus. Ass'n v. DEA*, 333 F.3d 1082, 1088–91 (9th Cir. 2003). Why do you think the fourth factor has received greater attention from reviewing courts? If the first three factors suggest that a rule is interpretive but the fourth factor suggests legislative, how should a court resolve the matter?

2. *SEC No-Action Letter Subsequent History.* When a publicly traded corporation wishes to exclude a particular shareholder proposal from its own proxy statements, it may request a "no-action" letter from the SEC to shed light on whether the exclusion would violate the securities law based on the facts and representations described in the request. These "no action" letters declare the contested proposal either excludable or non-excludable under one of thirteen grounds set forth in Rule 14a–8—including the "ordinary business" exclusion. The no-action letter is limited to the requester and the

specific facts set forth in the request and has no binding or precedential effect on other similarly situated parties or even the same requester in different circumstances. Why are no-action letters traditionally considered interpretive and not legislative? Could a no-action letter ever be legislative?

In 1998 (three years after the Second Circuit decision), the SEC revisited its 1992 position on whether a corporation may exclude employment-related shareholder proposals under Rule 14a–8(c)(7)—the "ordinary business" exclusion. Returning to a case-by-case analysis, the agency explained that "the relative importance of certain social issues relating to employment matters has reemerged as a consistent topic of widespread public debate. In addition, as a result of the extensive policy discussions that the *Cracker Barrel* position engendered, and through the rulemaking notice and comment process, we have gained a better understanding of the depth of interest among shareholders in having an opportunity to express their views to company management on employment-related proposals that raise sufficiently significant social policy issues." See 63 Fed. Reg. 29,106, 29,108 (1998) (codified at 17 C.F.R. § 240.14a–8). The agency further observed, however, that a proposal on a significant social policy issue could still be excluded depending on "the degree to which [it] seeks to 'micro-manage' the company." *Id.*

The SEC has issued hundreds of no-action letters addressed to corporate social responsibility since 1998. The agency's revised position arguably protects shareholder democracy more than the precedent set by *NYCERS*. At the same time, it seems likely to result in more inconsistency and unpredictability based on how the SEC applies the ordinary business" exception in particular instances. Why might unpredictability be a shortcoming? Don't we want an agency to determine the application of the exception on a case-by-case basis so that each corporation receives specialized treatment? On the other hand, if we think that consistency and predictability are desirable objectives, can a reviewing court remedy this situation? What about Congress?

3.   *First Interpretations and Later Interpretations.* In *Paralyzed Veterans of America v. D.C. Arena L.P.*, 117 F.3d 579 (D.C. Cir. 1997) and *Alaska Professional Hunters Ass'n v. FAA*, 177 F.3d 1030 (D.C. Cir. 1999), the D.C. Circuit confronted claims that an agency may not change its own authoritative interpretation of its regulation except through notice and comment rulemaking. In *Paralyzed Veterans*, a veterans association filed suit under the Americans with Disabilities Act (ADA) to require that an athletic arena provide certain lines of sight for wheelchair seating. The appellate court held that the Department of Justice's 1994 interpretation of its own ADA regulation was not sufficiently distinct from or additive to the regulation to require notice and comment, and that a mid-level agency official's 1992 speech suggesting a different interpretation did not qualify as an authoritative department position. By contrast, in *Alaska Professional Hunters*, Alaskan hunting and fishing guides and guide organizations challenged a 1998 FAA Notice that altered advice given by the agency since 1963 with respect to its pilot licensing regulations. Resolving the case in favor of the plaintiffs, the court held that "[t]hose regulated by an administrative agency are entitled to 'know the rules by which the game will be played,'" and that the FAA could not change its longstanding and definitive interpretation, on which parties had relied, without notice-and-comment rulemaking. The *Alaskan Professional Hunters* doctrine has been cited with approval in several circuits while other circuits have rejected it. See Brian Shearer, *Outfoxing Alaska*

Hunters: How Arbitrary and Capricious Review of Changing Regulatory Interpretations Can More Efficiently Police Agency Discretion, 62 Am. U. L. Rev. 167, 180–81 (2012).

Why should a reviewing court impose notice-and-comment limitations on an agency's authority to change regulatory interpretations if both its initial and subsequent efforts constitute interpretive rules? Shouldn't an agency be free to update its interpretations of its own regulations, taking account of intervening legal and factual circumstances? Perhaps reliance on the initial interpretation by the regulated parties should be an important or even decisive factor. Yet the D.C. Circuit recently held that a regulated party was not required to demonstrate any reliance at all when invoking the *Alaskan Hunters* doctrine. See *Mortgage Bankers Ass'n v. Harris*, 720 F.3d 966 (2013). If a court considers the duration or definitiveness of the previous regulation, how should these factors be measured? Did the court in *Alaska Hunters* faithfully apply the APA, or did it effectively write a new requirement into the statute? You should keep these questions in mind when considering the Supreme Court's decision in *FCC v. Fox Television Stations, Inc.*, 556 U.S. 502 (2009), discussed in section 3C below.

2. Policy Statements

PASSENGER CAPACITY INCREASES AND COMPLIANCE WITH TYPE CERTIFICATION REQUIREMENTS FOR TRANSPORT AIRPLANE EMERGENCY EVACUATION

* * *

Policy Statement No. ANM–98–2; March 17, 1998

Federal Aviation Administration, DOT.

Notice of policy statement and request for comments.

[The full-scale evacuation demonstration requirement was introduced into the Federal Aviation Regulations (FAR) in 1965 by a change to the operating rules following a Notice of Proposed Rulemaking and a public hearing. The primary basis was the identification of deficiencies in "equipment, procedures, and training" discovered during evacuation testing. The rule applied to all passenger-carrying airplanes with more than 44 passengers, and any subsequent increase in passenger capacity of those airplanes of more than five percent. The time limit for evacuation demonstrations was two minutes. In 1967, as part of additional rule changes, that time limit was reduced to 90 seconds. In 1978, the requirements were amended again to allow the use of analysis and tests to substantiate the evacuation performance of an airplane; this change also removed the previous explicit five percent limit on passenger increase. In July 1986, the FAA Administrator established policy limiting the use of analysis to passenger capacity increases of five percent or less. In 1989, the FAA issued Advisory Circular (AC) 25.803–1, Emergency Evacuation Demonstrations, to provide specific demonstration test criteria, and discuss the use of analysis.]

The Performance Standards Working Group, under the auspices of the Aviation Rulemaking Advisory Committee (ARAC) on emergency evacuation issues, was tasked to develop a standardized protocol to determine when an analysis is appropriate. One of the primary objectives of this effort was to reduce the number and severity of injuries that can occur in full-scale evacuation demonstrations * * *

The FAA has now determined that standardized methodologies have been developed and there are sufficient data now available, such that a limitation on the use of analysis based only on an increase in passenger capacity is no longer necessary. This position is supported by the aviation industry. * * * Analytical techniques are used to substantiate various certification requirements, including those with safety of flight ramifications, and in all cases the key element in their use is the underlying data to support the analysis. The FAA has determined that evacuation demonstrations should be treated no differently and, where sufficient data are available, analysis is an option. Since the existing advisory circular has been interpreted by the public as effectively prohibiting the use of a combination of analysis and test in cases where the passenger capacity is increased by greater than five percent, the FAA is issuing a formal notice that analysis in such cases may be acceptable. Full-scale demonstrations will still be required when sufficient data are not available to support a combination of analysis and test.

While the FAA is seeking public comment on this policy, it is the FAA intention to immediately apply this policy to two specific certification programs in progress during the period of public comment and disposition of comments. It is the FAA position that for the Boeing 777–300 and the Airbus A330/340, there are currently sufficient full-scale evaluation data available to support analysis. The Boeing 777–300 involves a fuselage stretch and the addition of a pair of exits with an increase in demonstrated passenger capacity from 440 to 550. * * * The FAA intends to publish a revised proposed advisory circular that reflects this policy. Resolution of the public comment will be considered in determining whether the policy should be refined for future projects, and so reflected in the advisory circular.

HUDSON V. FEDERAL AVIATION ADMINISTRATION

United States Court of Appeals for the District of Columbia Circuit, 1999.
192 F.3d 1031.

SILBERMAN, CIRCUIT JUDGE:

Petitioners claim that respondent Federal Aviation Administration violated the Administrative Procedure Act by issuing a purported policy statement without notice and comment rulemaking and that the FAA's issuance of a "type certificate" for the Boeing 777–300 pursuant to the newly adopted policy was an abuse of discretion. We conclude that notice and comment rulemaking was not required nor was the issuance of the type certificate illegal.

The administrator of the FAA is responsible for prescribing the minimum standards required in the interest of safety for the design of aircraft, and may establish tests to ensure compliance with the standards. *See* 49 U.S.C. § 44701 *et seq.* If the administrator is satisfied that the design of an aircraft meets these standards, the FAA issues the manufacturer a so-called type certificate allowing it to begin production of such aircraft.

The FAA has promulgated a rule with respect to emergency evacuation of aircraft that requires manufacturers to demonstrate that:

> For airplanes having a seating capacity of more than 44 passengers . . . the maximum seating capacity, including the number of crewmembers required . . . can be evacuated from the airplane to the ground under simulated emergency conditions within ninety seconds. Compliance with this requirement must be shown by actual demonstration . . . *unless* the Administrator finds that a combination of analysis and testing will provide data equivalent to that which would be obtained by actual demonstration.

14 C.F.R. § 25.803(c) (emphasis added).

The regulation as originally promulgated in 1967 required an actual demonstration when the design of an aircraft was altered to allow a passenger capacity increase of greater than five percent. In 1978, the regulation was amended to eliminate the five-percent provision, so that it assumed its current, discretionary, form. Then in 1989, the FAA released an "advisory circular" that again called for demonstrations if the five-percent benchmark was reached. But the circular cautioned that it "provides guidance on a means, but not the only means, of compliance with the Federal Aviation Regulations" concerning emergency evacuations, and it stated only that "a full-scale demonstration *should* be conducted when . . . [t]he proposed passenger seating configuration is an increase of more than five percent above that which has been previously demonstrated on an airplane . . . with an identical . . . exit configuration." (emphasis added).

This case arises from the FAA's change in its position in 1998, following a reconsideration of the use of full-scale demonstrations sparked by injuries among demonstration participants. On March 17 of that year, the FAA issued a new policy statement—ANM–98–2—which announced that: "The FAA has now determined that standardized methodologies have been developed and there are sufficient data now available, such that a limitation on the use of analysis based only on an increase in passenger capacity is no longer necessary, and therefore, the "FAA has determined that . . . where sufficient data are available, analysis is an option. . . . Full-scale demonstrations will still be required when sufficient data are not available to support a combination of analysis and test [sic]."

Besides altering the agency's general policy by allowing manufacturers to demonstrate compliance with the regulation through analysis *whatever* the percentage increase in seating capacity, the statement also foreshadowed the FAA's decision to act in accordance with this policy in two pending certification applications [for the Boeing 777–300 and the Airbus A330/340 because] "there are currently sufficient evacuation data available to support analysis." * * *

In a rather unorthodox manner the policy statement also invited public comment, stating that "[r]esolution of the public comment will be considered in determining whether the policy should be refined for future projects, and so reflected in [a new] advisory circular." The FAA received 23 responses prior to May, several of which were critical of the FAA's decision to allow analysis in lieu of full-scale demonstrations.

Boeing transmitted to the FAA its evacuation analysis for the 777–300, and the FAA informed Boeing that the analysis demonstrated compliance with 14 C.F.R. § 25.803. The FAA consequently on May 4, 1998, issued Boeing a type certificate for the 777–300. It simply states that "[t]his certificate . . . certifies that the type design . . . meets the airworthiness requirements of Part 25 of the Federal Aviation Regulations."

Petitioners, who represent an international group of air travelers, airline pilots, and flight attendants, filed this petition for review. They allege that policy statement ANM–98–2 could not be adopted by the FAA without the agency undertaking notice and comment rulemaking, and, in any event, issuance of the 777–300 type certificate was an abuse of discretion because the FAA failed to explain both its underlying change in policy and the reasons 777–300 type certification complied with regulatory standards. The FAA counters that petitioners cannot challenge the policy statement since it was issued more than 60 days before petitioners filed their petition, see 49 U.S.C. § 46110(a), and defends its substantive decision to issue Boeing a type certificate for the 777–300.

[The court first rejected the FAA's contention that the APA procedural claim had to be raised within sixty days of the issuance of the policy statement.]

Turning then to petitioners' procedural challenge, we do not agree that the FAA was obliged to follow APA notice and comment procedures prior to issuance of ANM–98–2. It appears on its face to be just a policy statement. It limits itself to situations "where sufficient data *are* available," states only that "analysis in such cases *may* be acceptable," and cautions that "[f]ull-scale demonstrations *will still* be required when sufficient data *are not* available to support a combination of analysis and test [sic]." (emphasis added). Moreover, as noted, it calls for public comments on the policy, and indicates that there will be a determination of whether "the policy should be refined for future projects." With respect to the 777–300, it states that the type certificate will be approved only "if a satisfactory analysis is produced." Since the statement does not cabin agency discretion, even as to the 777–300, it has the characteristics of a policy statement. To be sure, the government relies on the reasoning expressed in the policy statement to support its subsequent administrative decision, but that is not surprising because the policy statement, as we noted, came only a short time before the decision and explicitly contemplated the decision. Furthermore, although the statement purported to abandon the prior practice whereby the agency invariably required a demonstration if the five-percent threshold was reached, nothing prevented the agency from changing its enforcement policy again without notice, or requiring a full demonstration for the 777–300.

Petitioners argue that notice and comment rulemaking was nonetheless required because ANM–98–2 is actually an interpretation of the governing regulation that is at variance with the FAA's prior "interpretation" embodied in the 1989 advisory circular. They rely on *Alaska Professional Hunters Ass'n, Inc. v. FAA*, 177 F.3d 1030 (D.C. Cir. 1999), and *Paralyzed Veterans of Am. v. D.C. Arena L.P.*,

117 F.3d 579 (D.C. Cir. 1997). In these cases, we said that "[o]nce an agency gives its regulation an interpretation, it can only change that interpretation as it would formally modify the regulation itself: through the process of notice and comment rulemaking." The instant case, however, does not fit within the *Paralyzed Veterans/Alaska Professional Hunters* line for the simple reason that it does not involve an *interpretation* of a regulation. As we stated in *Syncor Int'l Corp. v. Shalala*, 127 F.3d 90, 94 (D.C. Cir. 1997), "[I]nterpretative rules and policy statements are quite different agency instruments. An agency policy statement does not seek to impose or elaborate or interpret a legal norm. It merely represents an agency position with respect to how it will treat—typically enforce—the governing legal norm." * * *

In the instant case there is no dispute as to the regulation's meaning. The regulation states that where the Administrator finds that a combination of analysis and testing provides data equivalent to an actual evacuation, the former may be used in place of the latter. Whether this test is met requires a factual determination by the FAA, and clearly, as methods of analysis and other considerations develop over time, the FAA's response to the test can also. In 1989, the FAA did not believe that analysis would provide equivalent data when seating capacity changed by over five percent, but in 1998, spurred on by injuries to demonstration participants, it reviewed its policy and concluded that the situation had changed such that analysis and testing were now sufficient. This is not a different interpretation of the regulation, just an application of the regulation to a changed situation which calls for a different policy.

Petitioners alternatively argue that the FAA was at least obliged to give a fuller explanation for the switch of position that led to the issuance of the certificate—one that took into account the adverse comments submitted in response to the policy statement. The agency was not, however, required to seek comments on its policy statement nor its pending certification decision. The APA includes no such requirement and we are not at liberty to create one. A policy statement can be issued at any time without a comment period and the certificate is merely an administrative action, a so-called informal adjudication, for which an agency is only obliged to provide an explanation adequate to give a reviewing court a basic understanding—and not a very detailed one—of its action. In this case the policy statement—and the explanation provided in the government's brief combined with Boeing's submission—easily meets that standard. The agency decided that a full-scale demonstration created too great a risk of injury to the demonstrators and this spurred an examination of the use of analysis. The administrator concluded that, in particular cases, testing and analysis would provide equivalent data to an actual demonstration even if the capacity increase were greater than five percent, and also found that such was the case for the 777–300. That some "commentators"—whether or not their views should be considered part of the record—disagreed with the FAA's policy shift is of no moment.

Petitioners do not really claim that the FAA's position was arbitrary and capricious, only that its failure to respond to the comments and give a fuller explanation is illegal. For the reasons we have given, we think petitioners are wrong. The petition for review is denied.

NOTES ON POLICY STATEMENTS AND AGENCY CHOICES

1.   *An Overview of Policy Guidance Materials.* Policy Guidance may be found in an array of agency communications, including advice documents, manuals, circulars, memoranda, and bulletins. All are aimed at providing the public with a sense of how the agency intends to implement a particular statutory or regulatory provision pursuant to a relatively broad grant of authority. As previously noted, section 552(a)(1)(D) of the APA requires agencies to publish interpretive rules and policy statements of general applicability in the Federal Register. (Other guidance materials are exempt from this publication requirement, although § 552(a)(2)(B) requires that additional guidance materials be made available to the general public). Failure to publish documents that are required to appear in the Federal Register precludes the agency from using the documents in a way that adversely affects any parties, § 552(a)(1). Policy statements are nonbinding on both private parties and the issuing agency. Nonetheless, determining if an agency has exceeded the limits of what it may advise in a policy statement, straying into legislative rule territory, can raise difficult questions. Robert Anthony contends that some nonlegislative rules "have the purpose or effect of binding the public *as a practical matter*" because they "are intended to impose mandatory standards or obligations, or [that] as a practical matter are given that effect." Robert Anthony, *Interpretive Rules, Policy Statements, Guidances, Manuals, and the Like—Should Federal Agencies Use Them to Bind the Public?*, 41 Duke L.J. 1311, 1328 (1992) (emphasis in original). How can it be determined whether a policy statement is meant to bind the public? In *Hudson*, the FAA's 1998 Policy Statement altered a long-term agency practice that had arguably constituted an application of the relevant regulation. Would a reasonable member of the public consider herself bound under these circumstances?

2.   *Legal Effect of Policy Statements.* The courts generally agree that policy statements are nonbinding and that they are meant to inform rather than to control. In *Colwell v. Department of Health and Human Services*, 558 F.3d 1112, 1124 (9th Cir. 2009), the Ninth Circuit reiterated that the "critical factor" in determining whether "a directive announcing a new policy constitutes a rule or a general statement of policy is the extent to which the challenged [directive] leaves the agency, or its implementing official free to exercise discretion to follow, or not to follow, the [announced] policy in an individual case." What factors must a reviewing court consider when deciding if a challenged policy statement is meant to bind the public, as opposed to "merely provid[ing] guidance to agency officials in exercising their discretionary power while preserving their flexibility and their opportunity to make individualized determinations"? *Id.* Judge Williams in *American Mining Congress* suggested in passing that an agency's use of permissive instead of mandatory language may aid in linedrawing between policy statements and legislative rules. Should judicial inquiry focus primarily on such language? How important are non-mandatory terms, as when a Policy Guidance describes conduct that *may* constitute a violation of law, or identifies practices that are *encouraged*, or lists steps that *may be helpful* in attaining compliance, or *clarifies* that failure to act in a certain way does not necessarily amount to non-compliance? See *Colwell, supra,* at 1125–26. Is this permissive language sufficient, or must courts look to more contextual factors to determine whether a policy statement is meant to bind? Conversely, what if the agency announces that it will *refrain* from instituting enforcement proceedings based on criteria set forth in a policy statement?

Does the presence of such safe harbors in a policy statement establish or imply that there are certain obligations for which compliance is mandatory. See *id.* at 1126–27.

Should courts distinguish between policy statements meant to bind the public and those meant to bind agency employees? Agencies often use policy guidance to control the conduct of their employees. Is this type of guidance material permissible without notice-and-comment if it effectively controls how an agency conducts policy-related business? Consider, for example, a policy statement that determines aspects of how agency employees must evaluate eligibility for benefits? What sort of problems, if any, do such policy statements raise?

3. *Interpretive Rules and Policy Statements Versus Rulemaking.* Agencies may have both practical and strategic reasons to opt for interpretive rules or policy statements rather than notice-and-comment rulemaking. As Nina Mendelson explains, issuing a guidance document is inexpensive compared to the costs of rulemaking; the agency retains flexibility to modify the guidance cheaply and quickly; avoiding notice-and-comment publication in the Federal Register means that guidance documents are less likely to attract media attention or congressional oversight; and these documents also are less likely to provoke costly and time-consuming litigation on substantive or procedural grounds. "In short, by issuing a guidance document, an agency can obtain a rule-like effect while minimizing political oversight and avoiding the procedural discipline, public participation, and judicial accountability required by the APA." *Regulatory Beneficiaries and Informal Agency Policymaking*, 92 Cornell L. Rev. 397, 408 (2007). Does Mendelson's analysis suggest that courts are the only potentially effective means of oversight with respect to agency guidance? Concerned that agencies were using guidance documents to formulate policy outside the rulemaking process, the Bush Administration in 2007 issued an executive order that subjected these documents to a standardized review process focused especially on "significant guidance documents" that may reasonably be expected to have a material budgetary impact or a sizable effect on the economy, to interfere with actions by other agencies, or to raise novel legal or policy issues. See Executive Order No. 13,422, 72 Fed. Reg. 2763.

In *Strategic or Sincere? Analyzing Agency Use of Guidance Documents*, 119 Yale L.J. 782 (2010), Connor Raso recognized the concerns expressed by the Bush Administration and others regarding agency preferences for guidance documents over legislative rules. But based on his empirical study of agency behavior, Raso concluded that agencies rarely abuse guidance documents to avoid issuing legislative rules. In testing for possible strategic use by agencies, Raso found that (i) agency leaders do not use guidance to implement a flurry of policies at the end of their terms of office, nor do they revise guidance to reflect the ideological preferences of a new president; (ii) agencies issue guidance slightly more often under divided government but the difference was not statistically significant; (iii) agencies do not rely more heavily on guidance documents in the face of congressional disapproval (measured by the number of oversight hearings); (iv) agencies do not use significant guidance documents on a wide scale relative to significant legislative rules (see chart below); and (v) agencies that issue guidance documents at a substantially high rate do so when acting under a mandated time constraint (Homeland Security) or primarily to clarify technical details (EPA, OSHA, and Transportation). Raso concludes that while there are instances of egregious abuse, agencies overall are not using guidance documents to circumvent APA processes. Absent a strong empirical case for change, Raso warns that restrictions on the use of these documents could increase the cost to agencies of clarifying their legislative rules (thus encouraging agencies to substitute adjudication for rulemaking) and undermine ability of agency leaders to manage their own organizations.

Use of Guidance Documents by Agency

AGENCY	NUMBER OF SIGNIFICANT GUIDANCE DOCUMENTS IN EFFECT IN AUGUST 2008	NUMBER OF SIGNIFICANT LEGISLATIVE RULES ISSUED, 1993–2008	RATIO OF SIGNIFICANT GUIDANCE DOCUMENTS TO LEGISLATIVE RULES
Agriculture	25	1327	0.02
Defense	0	199	0.00
Education	127	405	0.31
Energy	1	108	0.01
Environmental Protection Agency	204	1095	0.19
Health and Human Services	46	1792	0.03
Homeland Security	67	170	0.39
Housing and Urban Development	2	607	0.00
Interior	2	570	0.00
Justice	43	432	0.10
Labor	80	405	0.20
State	0	61	0.00
Transportation	124	853	0.15
Treasury	2	853	0.00
Veterans Affairs	0	461	0.00
TOTAL:	723	9338	0.08

Raso, 119 Yale L.J. at 813 table 3.

Why do you think the empirical evidence contradicts the traditional hypothesis regarding agencies' preference for guidance documents? What factors might explain why presidents do not engage in the revision of previous administrations' guidance? If agencies have more latitude to issue agency guidance and are subject to less oversight through this channel, why would agencies so overwhelmingly choose to issue legislative rules? What makes agency guidance less appealing to agencies as a policymaking option?

PROBLEMS ON POLICY STATEMENTS

Problem 8–4. Judicial Enforcement of NASD Fines. The SEC issued a press release in 2000, announcing that it would begin enforcing in federal court fines imposed by the National Association of Securities Dealers (NASD) and sustained by the Commission. The agency's declared aim was to prevent persons sanctioned by the NASD from escaping payment of fines or restitution orders. The relevant federal law provided that the SEC has the power to apply to the U.S. district courts for relief in commanding "any person to comply with the provisions of this chapter, the rules, regulations, and orders thereunder, the rules of a national securities exchange or registered securities association of which such person is a member." Although this language had been part of the Exchange Act for 20 years, the SEC had never sought judicial enforcement prior to its press release. Some two years before issuance of the 2000 press release, the NASD adjudicatory counsel found that Michael and Joseph had violated NASD rules and federal securities laws, and imposed disciplinary sanctions in the amount of $300,000 and $250,000 plus costs, respectively. In 2005, the SEC applied to the district court to enforce the sanctions. Michael and Joseph argued that the SEC's program of seeking judicial enforcement was a new rule that required notice and comment under the APA. The SEC responded that it was not following a new rule, but relying on the plain language of the statute, which it had always had the power to do. Is the press release a statement of policy or a rule change? See *SEC v. Markowksi*, 277 F. App'x 903 (11th Cir. 2008).

Problem 8–5. Broadcast Indecency.[24] In 2001, the FCC issued a 22–page Policy Statement intended "to provide guidance to the broadcast industry regarding our case law * * * and enforcement policies with respect to broadcast indecency." The Commission's administrative enforcement responsibility (conferred by statute) authorizes it to revoke a station license, impose a monetary forfeiture, or issue a warning for broadcast of indecent material. The Policy Statement reviewed and discussed the Commission's analytical approach when making indecency determinations pursuant to 18 U.S.C. § 1464, which prohibits the utterance of "any obscene, indecent, or profane language by means of radio communication."

The Statement explained that under the agency's enforcement policy, shaped by a number of Supreme Court and congressional decisions, obscene speech may not be broadcast at any time; *indecent speech*, which enjoys some First Amendment protection, may be prohibited between 6am and 10pm based on concern for the welfare of children and support for parental supervision of children. The Commission's definition of "indecency" had been upheld against constitutional challenge in the D.C. Circuit and quoted "with apparent approval" by the Supreme Court in 1978; it was substantially unchanged since the late 1970s: "language or material that, in context, depicts or describes, in terms *patently offensive* as measured by contemporary community

---

[24] In addition to the agency's 2001 Policy Statement and its 2004 Memorandum Opinion and Order, this problem draws on Michael Botein & Darius Adamski, *The FCC's New Indecency Enforcement Policy and its European Counterparts: A Cautionary Tale*, 15 Media L. & Pol'y 7 (Fall 2005), and Clay Calvert, *Bono, The Culture Wars, and a Profane Decision: The FCC's Reversal of Course on Decency Determinations and its New Path on Profanity*, 28 Seattle U. L. Rev. 61 (2004).

standards for the broadcast medium, sexual or excretory activities or organs."
(emphasis added).

Elaborating on the meaning of "patently offensive" (as exemplified in over 30
Commission determinations cited and described), the Policy Statement emphasized the
importance of full context. When reviewing for indecency, the Commission had
considered whether the broadcast material dwells on or repeats at length descriptions
of sexual organs or activities, and whether the material is used to titillate or for shock
value. Finally, the Policy Statement cited various examples to demonstrate that
"fleeting and isolated references" to sexual organs or activities had regularly been found
not to be indecent.

In November 2003, NBC broadcast the Golden Globes Awards program during
evening prime time, prior to 10pm. The artist Bono won an award for "Best Original
Song"; in receiving his award on stage, he said "This is really, really fucking brilliant.
Really really great." The Commission received hundreds of complaints from individuals
associated with the Parents Television Council (PTC), a public interest group with a
strong anti-indecency agenda. The FTC Enforcement Bureau concluded that the
material was not indecent, because Bono's utterance was fleeting and isolated, and it
did not describe sexual activity in any context.

The full Commission reversed the Bureau in March 2004, making a number of
changes in the settled law summarized in its 2001 Policy Statement. First, the
Commission rejected the string of cases holding that isolated, fleeting, and otherwise
unanticipated uses of "fuck" were not indecent. Second, the FCC ruling relied for the
first time on technological advances as a factor in indecency determinations, specifically
the ease with which broadcasters today can bleep out even fleeting words during a live
broadcast. Third, the ruling deemed it irrelevant whether broadcast or use of the word
"fuck" was unintentional. [Finally, the Commission held that use of the F-word was also
unlawfully profane under § 1464, departing from FCC and judicial precedent that had
long understood "profane" as focused on blasphemy or divine imprecation.]

The Commission's abandonment of its Policy Statement position occurred in the
midst of intense congressional pressure and apparent public outcry. The agency's
recorded complaints alleging "indecent" broadcasting had grown from 111 in 2000 to
346 in 2002, 13,922 in 2003, and 1,068,802 in 2004. And in March 2004, one week
before the FCC released its *Golden Globe* ruling, the House had passed (by 391–22) an
anti-indecency bill that *inter alia* raised the cap on fines for indecent broadcasts from
$32,500 to $500,000, and authorized the FCC to fine performers who utter indecencies,
not just broadcast station licensees.[25]

The FCC Policy Statement is a reasoned in-depth review of decades of agency
practice, taking account of constitutional as well as policy factors. If you are a reviewing
court, what weight would you give this Statement in considering the agency's decision
to adopt a wholly new indecency policy? Assuming that NBC appeals the *Golden Globe*
decision, should the Policy Statement be any more persuasive or probative to a
reviewing court than the sum total of the 30–plus agency precedents it analyzes? Is
there any problem with the Commission abandoning a policy guidance that is based on
20 years of settled analysis by means of a single adjudicatory order? Is abandonment

---

[25]   The bill did not pass the Senate before Congress adjourned.

based on consideration of a heretofore unexamined factor (technology) particularly troubling? Or is it perhaps especially justifiable?

Assume that virtually all of the one million indecency complaints filed in 2004 were orchestrated by the PTC and other "family values" interest groups. How seriously should the agency take this showing of public concern? How seriously should it take the passage of House legislation, imposing severe new penalties for indecency in broadcasting, while the case is *sub judice*?

Assume the FCC in *Golden Globe* ruled that although its reasoning on indecency was a departure from precedent, the agency was levying a $30,000 fine against NBC and each affiliate that broadcast the Awards show, because these stations should be held to know the F-word is both inherently indecent and prohibited profanity. Should the Policy Statement be relevant to a reviewing court in determining whether the agency may impose such fines?

3. OVERSIGHT BY THE THREE BRANCHES

You should appreciate by this point why administrative agencies are routinely called the fourth branch of government. Although Article I vests lawmaking powers in Congress, much of the federal "law" that affects our daily lives is enacted not as statutes but as agency regulations and orders. Article II empowers the President to hold federal officers accountable, but in practice the federal bureaucracy operates with considerable independence when engaged in regulatory activity. Article III authorizes the judiciary to resolve cases or controversies arising under federal law, but today "a citizen is ten times more likely to be tried by an agency than by an actual court."[26]

Given the accumulation by agencies of what Chief Justice Roberts has referred to, with regret, as "a potent brew of executive, legislative, and judicial power,"[27] it is not surprising that the three other branches devote considerable attention to oversight of agency performance. *Congress* invests in the oversight function to determine whether its laws are being properly applied, its funds well-spent, and its powers respected. The *President* exerts a measure of control in an effort to assure that agencies minimize overlapping jurisdictions and conflicting missions, weigh costs as well as benefits before taking action, and defer to the White House as necessary for faithful execution of the laws. Finally, *Federal Courts* review administrative decision-making in an attempt to monitor whether agencies are adhering to Congress's original substantive directives, and whether agencies are complying with the APA's procedural requirements—to consider all relevant evidence, provide well-reasoned explanations for their decisions, and avoid acting (or refusing to act) in an arbitrary fashion.

In this Section, we present and analyze principal methods of oversight employed by each branch. In doing so, we emphasize the practical and

---

[26] See Jonathan Turley, *The Rise of the Fourth Branch of Government*, Washington Post, May 24, 2013, at B–01 (reporting that federal judges conduct 95,000 adjudicatory proceedings, including trials, in a given year, whereas federal agencies complete more than 939,000.

[27] *City of Arlington, Texas v. FCC*, 133 S.Ct. 1863, 1886 (2013) (Roberts, C.J., dissenting).

constitutional questions raised by these efforts to control or even monitor the growing federal bureaucracy.

A. CONGRESSIONAL MONITORING

1. Oversight Hearings and Investigations

A Congress that has delegated much of its lawmaking authority to agencies would rationally seek to monitor those agencies to assure their continued adherence to the original legislative delegation. Before 1933, there were few agencies to oversee, and Congress devoted little effort to monitoring. Agencies proliferated during the New Deal. Congress responded with the Legislative Reorganization Act of 1946, 60 Stat. 812, codified at 2 U.S.C. § 31 *et al.*, which signaled a new commitment to oversight and started a process by which Congress and its committees added legislative staff to accomplish this goal. The conventional wisdom of the 1950s was that oversight could effectively assure majoritarian control of policy.

Some political scientists suggest that the conventional wisdom was too optimistic because structural problems impede effective legislative oversight.[28] Thus, legislative oversight committees may become captured by the same forces that capture agencies—interested persons and firms, who provide information, ideas, and encouragement. Also, motivations of legislators are more important in determining oversight activity than is the availability of resources. "Unless [oversight] reveals a scandalous situation with possibilities for favorable publicity for the legislators, the work is considered dull and potentially troublesome."[29] There are opportunity costs for oversight; time spent monitoring agencies is time away from fundraising, casework, and enacting new programs to benefit constituents. The latter are activities that often mean more to a legislator's reelection chances than tedious oversight. Finally, and most important, partisan politics can eviscerate oversight: in periods where Congress is controlled by the same political party as the President (1993–95, 2003–07, 2009–11), one would expect little critical oversight. On the other hand, when at least one branch of Congress and the President are controlled by different parties, as has been the recent norm (1981–93, 1995–2001, May 2001–03, 2007–09, 2011–14), one would expect to see more aggressive oversight.

Whatever the partisan make-up of the federal government, positive political theorists argue that Congress can be expected to protect its institutional interests relatively vigorously. It is helpful to distinguish among the various forms of oversight because some actions that occur steadily are less public and thus may be overlooked. We tend to think first of formal committee hearings as the main mechanism to monitor agencies, but in fact, much of the oversight done by

---

[28] For leading surveys of congressional oversight, and its problems, see, e.g., Martin James, *Congressional Oversight* (2002); Kathleen Bawn, *Choosing Strategies to Control* the *Bureaucracy: Statutory Constraints, Oversight, and the Committee System*, 13 J.L. Econ. & Org. 101 (1997); Morris Ogul, *Congressional Oversight: Structures and Incentives*, in Congress Reconsidered 317 (Lawrence Dodd & Bruce Oppenheimer eds. 2d ed. 1981); Charles Shipan, *Regulatory Regimes, Agency Actions, and the Conditional Nature of Congressional Influence*, 98 Am. Pol. Sci. Rev. 467 (2004).

[29] Bernard Rosen, *Holding Government Bureaucracies Accountable* 21 (1982).

legislators is informal. Lawmakers jawbone agency officials as policy is formulated, or they intervene on behalf of constituents to present arguments and perspectives. Although rules prohibit some forms of *ex parte* communications, particularly during formal adjudication, there are numerous ways for members of Congress to communicate with bureaucrats as rules are being considered. Mark Moran and Barry Weingast, for example, argue that the FTC is strongly influenced by subtle messages sent outside the formal oversight process and that this influence is statistically significant for both enforcement and policymaking initiatives by the FTC.[30] See also Joel Auerbach, *Keeping A Watchful Eye: The Politics of Congressional Oversight* (1990), arguing that vigorous congressional oversight is responsive to public demands for greater government accountability.

Various mechanisms exist to provide members of Congress with information that alerts them to the need for aggressive oversight or that supports them as they engage in monitoring. Mathew McCubbins and Thomas Schwartz describe two kinds of monitoring strategies. *Congressional Oversight Overlooked: Police Patrols Versus Fire Alarms*, 28 Am. J. Pol. Sci. 165 (1984). A *police patrol* strategy is time-consuming as legislators and their staffs regularly monitor to discover bureaucratic drift. In contrast, employing *a fire alarm* strategy saves congressional resources as members wait to hear the alarm raised by interested parties upset about agency policy. Once the alarm has been sounded, members can begin aggressive oversight, and they can ignore areas where no discontent is evident. In this way, lawmakers externalize some of the costs of oversight, perhaps engaging in police patrols only in arenas without much interest group activity and thus with less possibility of alarms. After they sound the alarm, lobbyists and interest groups continue to provide supporters with information and expertise to further reduce legislative monitoring costs.

Congress engages in more oversight than it once did. Unfortunately, there is evidence that oversight has many problems.

Regulatory Priorities and Efficacy. Oversight hearings, controlled by a congressional subgroup, may push agencies away from their public-regarding agendas. With their scarce resources, committed agencies have their hands full devising workable strategies and fighting off industry attacks. If an oversight committee is controlled or even influenced by the regulated industry, it can thwart agency regulation by pressuring the agency toward less intrusive (and often less efficacious) modes of regulation. Even well-intended oversight might undermine agency efficacy if it adds more to the agency's plate, as illustrated in the auto safety area.[31] A major regulatory initiative undertaken by the National Highway Traffic Safety Administration (NHTSA) was Standard 208, which required automakers to

---

[30] Barry Weingast & Mark Moran, *Bureaucratic Discretion or Congressional Control? Regulatory Policymaker at the Federal Trade Commission*, 91 J. Pol. Econ. 765 (1983); Weingast & Moran, *The Myth of the Runaway Bureaucracy; The Case of the FTC*, Regulation, May/June 1982, at 33. To the same effect is John Ferejohn's study of communications policy. See John Ferejohn & Charles Shipan, *Congressional Influence on Bureaucracy*, 6 J. L. Econ. & Org. 1 (1990) (special issue).

[31] See Jerry Mashaw, *The Story of* Motor Vehicle Manufacturers Association etc: *Law, Science, and Politics in the Administrative State*, in *Administrative Law Stories* 334, 357–67 Peter Strauss ed., 2006) See also Steven Balla & John Wright, *Interest Groups, Advisory Committees, and Congressional Control of the Bureaucracy*, 45 Am. J. Pol. Sci. 799 (2001).

produce cars that would protect passengers against injury under specified performance criteria. Manufacturers could meet the standard with airbags, automatic seatbelts, and other mechanisms. For various institutional reasons, after 1971, the only way to comply with the standard was an "ignition interlock" system, whereby the car would not start until all passengers engaged their seatbelts. The public was not pleased. Drivers disengaged their interlocks (which were mandatory for the 1974 auto market) and wrote their members of Congress against this intrusion into their "freedom to drive."

Responding to public outrage, Congress held several oversight hearings, and the result was a massive disruption in the agency's regulatory program. On the one hand, the auto industry and elected representatives alike had a field day deriding the interlock system. Senator Norris Cotton joked, to great laughter, that his car would not start when he placed groceries in the passenger's seat. Instead of placing them on the floor (duh!), the New Hampshire legislator belted "a pound of cheese and a loaf of bread" to satisfy the system. Although the experts maintained that ignition interlocks saved lives, popular resentment about inconveniences and infringements on their freedom to drive overwhelmed the theoretical safety gains.

On the other hand, oversight focused on a decidedly minor problem: schoolbus design. Of the 54,000+ annual death toll as a result of auto accidents, the agency found only a few dozen where an expensive schoolbus redesign might have saved the lives of schoolchildren. (As many as 80% of child deaths from schoolbus accidents occur *outside* of the bus.) Even sympathetic Members of Congress were appalled by the agency's failure to focus on *children's deaths* because of schoolbus accidents. Representative Les Aspin, a liberal, berated the agency for "misusing the concept of cost-benefit analysis" (Mashaw, *Law, Science, and Politics*, 363–65).

The upshot of all this oversight was the Motor Vehicle and Schoolbus Safety Amendments of 1974. These amendments forbade imposition of the ignition interlock (which saved hundreds and probably thousands of lives each year) and required the agency to impose stringent new design requirements on schoolbuses (which might save a life or three each year, at much greater expense). As Jerry Mashaw wearily concludes, "[i]f Congress had wanted to protect the lives of children, it would have done better to re-energize NHTSA's lagging standard-setting enterprise as it applied to the passenger car" (*Id.* at 367).

Congressional Oversight and Individual Rights. When Congress or its committees exercise vigorous oversight power, there may be problems involving overreaching or violation of individual rights. In the 1950s, several congressional committees engaged in what many regard as a "witch hunt" for Communists and "homosexuals" in American government and society. The legislative investigations often seemed bent on ruining peoples' reputations rather than on serving valid legislative goals, and courts through the 1950s and 1960s sometimes overturned contempt citations against uncooperative witnesses.[32]

---

[32] Witnesses refusing to answer questions posed by these committees or to produce documents requested by the committees were subject to criminal prosecution under 2 U.S.C. § 192.

The leading case was *Watkins v. United States*, 354 U.S. 178 (1957), in which the Supreme Court overturned a contempt conviction based upon its finding that the House Un-American Activities Committee had ventured far beyond its House-authorized arena of investigation. See also Judge Weinfeld's earlier decision in *United States v. Lamont*, 18 F.R.D. 27 (S.D.N.Y. 1955), *aff'd*, 236 F.2d 312 (2d Cir. 1956), which made similar findings for the Senate's Permanent Subcommittee on Investigations (chaired by Joseph McCarthy (R–Wis.)). Chief Justice Warren's opinion in *Watkins* suggested, moreover, that legislative investigations are limited to building a factual record for proposed legislation and providing information for the exercise of legislative insight. "We have no doubt that there is no congressional power to expose for the sake of exposure," concluded Warren. 354 U.S. at 200.

The holding in *Watkins* was based on lack of "pertinency" of the questions asked to the mission Congress had delegated to its committee, see *Barenblatt v. United States*, 360 U.S. 109 (1959) (upholding contempt and distinguishing *Watkins*), but Chief Justice Warren's concerns included the process's threat to First Amendment freedoms (354 U.S. at 197):

> Abuses of the investigative process may imperceptibly lead to abridgment of protected freedoms. The mere summoning of a witness and compelling him to testify, against his will, about his beliefs, expressions or associations is a measure of governmental interference. And when those forced revelations concern matters that are unorthodox, unpopular, or even hateful to the general public, the reaction in the life of the witness may be disastrous. This effect is even more harsh when it is past beliefs, expressions or associations that are disclosed and judged by current standards rather than those contemporary with the matters exposed. * * *

Interference with Agency Adjudication of Pending Cases. Effective legislative oversight often requires congressional committees to challenge executive branch officials in ways that are tough and even intimidating. Relatively recent examples include committee hearings on Watergate (1973–74), the Iran-Contra affair (1987), China's acquisition of U.S. nuclear weapon secrets (1998–2000), and the administration of TARP, the Troubled Assets Relief Program (2009–11). Recognizing Congress's constitutional responsibility to monitor what the Executive Branch is doing right or wrong, courts traditionally give Congress broad leeway to engage in aggressive oversight activity.

This oversight power may be subject to certain limitations, however, when Congress investigates an ongoing adjudicatory proceeding. Agency officials acting in the midst of an adjudicatory dispute are analogous to prosecutors or judges, and appellate courts have held that extreme political pressures might influence—or appear to influence—the agency's decisions, undermining basic notions of fairness or due process. The leading case is *Pillsbury Co. v. Federal Trade Commission*, 354 F.2d 952 (5th Cir. 1966), where Senator Kefauver and other members of a Senate Judiciary subcommittee interrogated the FTC Chair and several of his staff with respect to a pending injunctive proceeding that involved Pillsbury. The senators expressed strong views on how the case should be decided, and the FTC subsequently ruled as the senators had wanted. The Fifth Circuit reversed on the ground that the agency's decisionmaking process was impermissibly biased by congressional pressure. Chief Judge Tuttle explained:

> "when [a congressional] investigation focuses directly and substantially upon the mental decisional processes of a Commission in a case which is pending before it, Congress is no longer intervening in the agency's legislative function, but rather, in its judicial function. At this latter point, we become concerned with the right of private litigants to a fair trial and, equally important, with their right to the appearance of impartiality, which cannot be maintained unless those who exercise the judicial function are free from powerful external influences." *Id.* at 964.[33]

A PROBLEM ON OVERSIGHT AND ADJUDICATION

Problem 8–6. On April 20, 2011, the Acting General Counsel (GC) of the National Labor Relations Board, Lafe Solomon, who had been nominated by the President for the permanent position, issued a complaint against the Boeing Company. The complaint alleged that top managers and executives from Boeing had repeatedly announced that the company was moving the manufacture of its second 737–Dreamliner airplane from the state of Washington to South Carolina because of past lawful strikes engaged in by the Machinists Union. Acting GC Solomon's complaint asserted that Boeing was relocating work for illegal discriminatory reasons. Boeing responded that the move was based on a lawful business judgment to avoid future disruptions in the production process. The complaint was scheduled to be heard by an Administrative Law Judge (ALJ) in Seattle on June 14.

In early May, ten Republican Senators wrote to Solomon expressing dismay over the Boeing complaint and suggesting that his prospects for confirmation were linked to his position on the Boeing case. The next day, 19 Republican senators wrote to President Obama urging that he immediately withdraw Solomon's nomination to become GC, due to the Boeing case. On May 12, a number of Republican Senators introduced a bill amending the NLRA to immunize the conduct that was allegedly unlawful as set forth in the Boeing complaint.

In mid-May, the chairmen of the House committees on Education and Workforce, and Oversight and Government Reform sent separate letters to Acting GC Solomon demanding that he turn over all internal Board documents addressing the Boeing complaint and all documents relating in any way to the GC Office's investigation of Boeing, and do so in advance of the June 14 ALJ hearing. Solomon declined to provide these documents in an explanatory letter, citing the pending litigation. House Oversight Committee chair Darrell Issa then announced that his committee would hold a hearing in South Carolina to address the Boeing complaint on June 17, three days after the ALJ hearing. Issa requested that Solomon attend his committee hearing. Solomon declined Chair Issa's invitation on the ground that his appearance could threaten the rights of the parties to a fair trial. Chair Issa wrote to Solomon asking him to reconsider or else face a subpoena compelling his attendance. Solomon responded on June 10, offering as alternatives either to submit written testimony or to provide the

---

[33] See also *Koniag v. Kleppe*, 405 F. Supp. 1360 (D.D.C. 1975), *modified sub nom Koniag v. Andrus*, 580 F.2d 601 (D.C. Cir 1978) (setting aside adjudicatory decisions of Secretary of Interior under Alaska Native Claims Settlement Act based at least partially on improper congressional subcommittee pressure during oversight hearings).

Associate General Counsel, who did not have a direct role in the case. Chair Issa rejected those offers and insisted on Solomon's presence at the oversight hearing. Ultimately, Solomon attended the June 17 hearing.

Assume that the ALJ hearing took place as scheduled on June 14, and the ALJ subsequently ruled in favor of Boeing, dismissing the Labor Board complaint. Did any actions taken by members of Congress impermissibly taint the ALJ proceeding? Would you evaluate the oversight actions of the Senators differently from the actions taken in the House? If so, on what basis?

Agency Defiance and Executive Privilege. A final concern about legislative oversight is that even when it is vigorous and public-seeking—and respectful of individual rights—it may face frustrating obstacles to obtaining information from the agency, particularly one located in the executive branch. Some of the recent oversight hearings during the Clinton and Bush 43 Administrations demonstrate that difficulty, as well as the political aspects of oversight.

A CASE STUDY: THE DISMISSAL OF U.S. ATTORNEYS DURING THE GEORGE W. BUSH ADMINISTRATION

1.   *Background.* In late 2006, the Justice Department under President George W. Bush dismissed eight United States Attorneys. United States Attorneys are federal prosecutors appointed to four-year terms by the President with the advice and consent of the Senate. Although the nature of the position is non-partisan, the Bush Administration allegedly dismissed several U.S. Attorneys for investigating or prosecuting Republican politicians and declining to investigate or prosecute Democratic politicians. At least one U.S. Attorney was terminated because the White House wanted to fill the position with a Bush loyalist who had political ambitions.

During the months preceding the dismissals, Bush Administration officials considered removing all ninety-three U.S. Attorneys but ultimately decided to replace about one-fifth. As Administration officials planned the removals, the Senate Judiciary Committee, at the request of the Department of Justice, inserted language into the 2005 Patriot Act reauthorization allowing the Attorney General to appoint new U.S. Attorneys in the event of a vacancy for an indefinite term and without the advice and consent of the Senate. Thus the dismissals potentially gave the Attorney General unchecked authority to install the Administration's cronies as U.S. Attorneys.

2.   *Congressional Oversight of the Justice Department.* In January 2007, Senators Patrick Leahy and Dianne Feinstein of the Senate Judiciary Committee responded to the firings and the newly enacted appointment procedures. On January 18, Attorney General Alberto Gonzales testified before the Senate Judiciary Committee:

> **Senator FEINSTEIN.** You and I talked on Tuesday about what is happening with U.S. Attorneys. It spurred me to do a little research, and let me begin. Title 28, Section 541 states, "Each U.S. Attorney shall be appointed for a term of 4 years. On the expiration of his term, a U.S. Attorney shall continue to perform the duties of his office until his successor is appointed and qualified." Now, I understand that there is a pleasure aspect to it, but I also understand what practice has been in the past. We have 13 vacancies. Yesterday you sent up two nominees for the 13 existing vacancies.

Attorney General GONZALES. There have been 11 vacancies created since the law was changed, 11 vacancies in the U.S. Attorney's offices. The President has now nominated as to six of those. As to the remaining five, we are in discussion with home-State Senators. So let me publicly sort of preempt, perhaps, a question you are going to ask me. That is, I am fully committed, as the administration is fully committed, to ensure that with respect to every U.S. Attorney position in this country, we will have a Presidentially appointed, Senate-confirmed U.S. Attorney. I think a U.S. Attorney, who I view as the leader, law enforcement leader, my representative in the community, has greater imprimatur of authority if in fact that person has been confirmed by the Senate.

Senator FEINSTEIN. All right.

Now, let me get at where I am going. How many U.S. Attorneys have been asked to resign in the past year?

Attorney General GONZALES. Senator, you are asking me to get into a public discussion about personnel.

Senator FEINSTEIN. No. I am just asking you to give me a number, that is all.

Attorney General GONZALES. I do not know the answer.

Senator FEINSTEIN. I am just asking you to give me a number.

Attorney General GONZALES. I do not know the answer to that question. But we have been very forthcoming—

Senator FEINSTEIN. You did not know it on Tuesday when I spoke with you. You said you would find out and tell me.

Attorney General GONZALES. I am not sure I said that.

Senator FEINSTEIN. Yes, you did, Mr. Attorney General.

Attorney General GONZALES. Well, if that is what I said, that is what I will do. But we did provide to you a letter where we gave you a lot of information about—

Senator FEINSTEIN. I read the letter.

Attorney General GONZALES. All right.

Senator FEINSTEIN. It does not answer the questions that I have. I know of at least six that have been asked to resign. I know that we amended the law in the Patriot Act and we amended it because if there were a national security problem the Attorney General would have the ability to move into the gap. We did not amend it to prevent the confirmation process from taking place. I am very concerned. I have had two of them ask[ed] to resign in my State from major jurisdictions with major cases ongoing, with substantially good records as prosecutors. I am very concerned because, technically, under the Patriot Act, you can appoint someone without confirmation for the remainder of the President's term. I do not believe you should do that. We are going to try to change the law back.

Attorney General GONZALES. Senator, may I just say that I do not think there is any evidence that that is what I am trying to do? In fact, to the contrary. The evidence is quite clear that what we are trying to do is ensure that, for the people in each of these respective districts, we have the very best possible representative for the Department of Justice and that we are working to nominate people, and that we are working with home-State Senators to get U.S. Attorneys nominated. So the evidence is just quite contrary to what you are possibly suggesting. Let me just say—

Senator FEINSTEIN. Do you deny that you have asked, your office has asked, U.S. Attorneys to resign in the past year, yes or no?

Attorney General GONZALES. Yes. No, I do not deny that. What I am saying is, that happens during every administration, during different periods for different reasons. So the fact that that has happened, quite frankly, some people should view that as a sign of good management.

What we do, is we make an evaluation about the performance of individuals. I have a responsibility to the people in your district that we have the best possible people in these positions. That is the reason why changes sometimes have to be made, although there are a number of reasons why changes get made and why people leave on their own.

I think I would never, ever make a change in a U.S. Attorney position for political reasons or if it would in any way jeopardize an ongoing serious investigation. I just would not do it.

Senator FEINSTEIN. Well, let me just say one thing. I believe very strongly that these positions should come to this committee for confirmation.

Attorney General GONZALES. They are, Senator.

Senator FEINSTEIN. I believe very strongly we should have the opportunity to answer questions about it.

Attorney General GONZALES. I agree with you.

In February 2007, Deputy Attorney General Paul McNulty testified that the dismissals were performance related, in spite of the fact that all but one of the fired U.S. Attorneys had positive performance reviews. McNulty's claim prompted the dismissed U.S. Attorneys to testify on March 6, 2007 where they claimed that they had favorable performance reviews and that the Justice Department never expressed concerns about their performance. In spite of this testimony, Gonzales penned an op-ed in USA Today on March 6, in which he insisted that "To be clear, it was for reasons related to policy, priorities and management—what have been referred to broadly as 'performance-related' reasons—that seven U.S. attorneys were asked to resign last December." He further stated that "While I am grateful for the public service of these seven U.S. attorneys, they simply lost my confidence. I hope that this episode ultimately will be recognized for what it is: an overblown personnel matter."[34]

In the following weeks, the Justice Department released documents showing extensive communications between the White House and Justice Department officials relating to the removal of U.S. Attorneys. These revelations led Gonzales to

---

[34] Alberto Gonzales, *They Lost My Confidence*, USA TODAY, Mar. 6, 2007.

acknowledge that "mistakes were made. I accept the responsibility." Nonetheless, he stood by the decision to dismiss the U.S. Attorneys, contending that "it was a right decision."[35]

On April 19, 2007, Attorney General Gonzales appeared again before the Senate Judiciary Committee where he continued to express regret for "mistakes" at the Department of Justice but insisted that the dismissals were appropriate.

> **Attorney General GONZALES.** I acknowledge the mistakes that I have made here. I've identified the mistakes. I know what I would do differently. I think it was still a good idea.

> **Senator GRAHAM.** What kind of damage do you believe needs to be repaired on your part with the Congress or the Senate in particular?

> **Attorney General GONZALES.** Senator, I think I need to continue to have dialog with the Congress, to try to be as forthcoming as I can be to reassure the Congress. I've tried to inform the Congress that I don't have anything to hide. I didn't say no, to the document request. I didn't say "no, you can't interview" to my internal staff.

> You know, I asked OPR [Office of Professional Responsibility] to get involved. I've done—everything I've done has been consistent with the principle of pursuing truth and accountability.

> **Senator GRAHAM**. Finally, you are situationally aware that you have a tremendous credibility problem with many Members of the Congress, and you are intent on trying to fix that. Today is a start, right?

> **Attorney General GONZALES**. Absolutely, Senator.

Although Gonzales expressed a willingness to mend relations with Congress, his inability to recall various meetings and conversations frustrated the senators, a growing number of whom called for his resignation. Senator Leahy and Senator Arlen Specter (the ranking Republican on the Senate Judiciary Committee) wrote to Gonzales, requesting that he supplement his testimony:

> You spent weeks preparing for the April 19th hearing. Yet during your testimony, in response to questions from Senators on both sides of the aisle, you often responded that you could not recall. By some counts you failed to answer more than 100 questions, by other counts more than 70, but the most conservative count had you failing to provide answers well over 60 times. As a result, the Committee's efforts to learn the truth of why and how these dismissals took place, and the role you and other Department and White House officials had in them, has been hampered.

> The questions asked by Senators should not have been a surprise. You were alerted in letters to you well in advance of last Thursday's hearing. By letter sent April 4, you were asked to include in your written testimony a "full and complete account of the development of the plan to replace Untied States Attorneys, and all the specifics of your role in connection with that matter." That account was not included in your written testimony nor in your answers to questions at the hearing. You were also alerted in advance of the hearing,

---

[35] Dan Eggen & Paul Kane, *Gonzales: 'Mistakes Were Made'*, WASH. POST, Mar. 14, 2007.

by a letter sent on April 13, that you would be asked about information derived from the staff interviews of your senior aides. You were, nevertheless, unprepared to answer those questions.[36]

During the following months Gonzales testified again before the Senate Judiciary Committee as well as before the House Judiciary Committee but calls for his resignation only intensified. On August 27, 2007, Gonzales announced his resignation.

3. *Congressional Oversight of the White House.* As House and Senate Committees wrote letters, issued subpoenas, and held hearings to learn about the Justice Department officials' involvement in the dismissals, they also sought documents and testimony from White House officials. On March 20, **White House Counsel Fred Fielding** responded to congressional requests with an offer to provide documents and testimony subject to certain conditions:

> In keeping with the President's commitment to ensure that Congress and the American people understand the resignations of the U.S. Attorneys, the Department of Justice has produced more than 3,000 pages of documents relating to this matter. These documents do not reflect that any U.S. Attorney was replaced to interfere with a pending or future criminal investigation or for any other improper reason. These documents, together with the interviews to be provided by Department officials, will provide extensive background on the decisions in question, including an account of communications between the Department and senior White House officials. Congress, in short, is receiving a virtually unprecedented window into personnel decision-making within the Executive Branch.

> In the midst of this current debate, the President must remain faithful to the fundamental interests of the Presidency and the requirements of the constitutional separation of powers. We wish to reach a reasonable accommodation so as to provide your Committees the information they are seeking in a way that will allow this President, and future Presidents, to continue to discharge their constitutional responsibilities effectively.

> In response to the invitations for interviews extended by the Committees, I am prepared to make available for interviews the President's former Counsel [Harriet Miers]; current Deputy Chief of Staff and Senior Advisor [Karl Rove]; Deputy Counsel [William Kelley]; and a Special Assistant in the Office of Political Affairs [Scott Jennings]. We are prepared to agree to the following terms, which, considering applicable constitutional principles relating to the Presidency and your Committee's interests, we believe are fair, reasonable, and respectful. We believe that such interviews should be a last resort, and should be conducted, if needed, only after Congress has heard from Department of Justice officials about the decision to request the resignations of the U.S. Attorneys.

> Such interviews may cover, and would be limited to, the subject of a) communications between the White House and persons outside the White House concerning the request for resignations of the U.S. Attorneys in question; and b) communications between the White House and Members of Congress concerning those requests. Those interviews should be conducted by

---

[36] Letter from Sens. Leahy & Specter to Attorney General Alberto Gonzales (Apr. 25, 2007)

both Committees jointly. Questioning of White House officials would be conducted by a Member or limited number of Members, who would be accompanied by committee staff. Such interviews would be private and conducted without the need for an oath, transcript, subsequent testimony, or the subsequent issuance of subpoenas. A representative of the Office of the Counsel to the President would attend these interviews and personal counsel to the invited officials may be present at their election.

As an additional accommodation, and as part of this proposal, we are prepared to provide to your Committee copies of two categories of documents: a) communications between the White House and the Department of Justice concerning the request for resignation of the U.S. Attorneys in question; and b) communications on the same subject between White House staff and third parties, including Members of Congress or their staffs on the subject.

We trust and believe that the accommodation we offer here, in addition to what the Department of Justice has provided, should satisfy the Committee's interests.[37]

Senator Patrick Leahy, Chairman of the Senate Judiciary Committee and **Representative John Conyers,** Chairman of the House Judiciary Committee, responded by insisting that the White House make available internal communications. They also suggested that a compromise might be possible.

We do believe your willingness to provide documents is worth pursuing. We hope that you will reconsider your "all or nothing" approach with respect to documents you identified that you would be willing to provide. We urge you to provide all relevant documents without delay. The White House documents to and from the Department of Justice and with third parties, such as Republican state party officials, should be provided without delay. You have acknowledged your willingness to provide those to us previously.

That would narrow the dispute over White House documents to those you refer to as "internal". We believe that these are important to our investigation, as well. For example, if there is a memorandum or an e-mail from Karl Rove to Harriet Miers initiating consideration of firing some United States attorneys in order to impede an investigation, that would be very important for the Committees to know. Thus, while we do not agree with you that what you describe as "internal" White House documents should be off limits, we recognize that you view them as a separate category and you disagree whether those should be shared with the Committees. Recognizing we have a dispute over those documents should not delay the Committees receiving the other documents that you indicate you are willing to provide.

If we can narrow our dispute, we may then be able to work through it by agreeing, for example, that we initially designate as "Committee Confidential" what you refer to as "internal" White House documents. We could then consider a process by which we would consult with you prior to making them public.[38]

---

[37] Letter from Fred Fielding, Counsel to the President, to Sen. Leahy, Rep. Conyers, Sen. Specter, Rep. Smith & Rep. Sánchez (Mar. 20, 2007).

[38] Letter from Sen. Leahy and Rep. Conyers to Fred Fielding (Mar. 28, 2007).

Fielding rejected this proposal and stated that the White House's initial offer of interviews and documents already "reflect[ed] a series of balanced compromises designed to respect and accommodate your interests in obtaining information while also protecting the institution of the Presidency."[39]

Unable to negotiate a mutually agreeable arrangement, the House and Senate Judiciary Committees issued subpoenas on June 13, 2007 to several White House officials including President Bush's Chief of Staff Joshua Bolten (for documents) and former White House Counsel Harriet Miers (for testimony and documents). On June 28, after receiving legal advice from Solicitor General and Acting Attorney General Paul Clement, Fielding informed Chairmen Conyers and Leahy that "the President has decided to assert Executive Privilege and therefore the White House will not be making any production in response to these subpoenas for documents."[40] The House and Senate Committees rejected the White House's basis for executive privilege and on July 25, 2007 the House Judiciary Committee recommended that the full House cite Miers and Bolten for contempt of Congress. On February 14, 2008, after further fruitless attempts to negotiate a settlement, the full House of Representatives voted to hold Miers and Bolten in contempt by a vote of 223–32.

The House's contempt citation consisted of two resolutions. The first called on the Attorney General and the U.S. Attorney for the District of Columbia to prosecute Miers and Bolten for criminal contempt. This approach was unsuccessful because the Attorney General determined that Miers and Bolten had properly invoked executive privilege and thus no prosecution was authorized. The House's second resolution authorized the Chairman of the House Judiciary Committee to bring a declaratory action against Miers and Bolten in federal court requiring them to comply with the subpoenas. The D.C. district court held that the House Judiciary Committee had standing to bring a civil action to enforce congressional subpoenas issued to senior presidential aides. It further held that the judiciary was the "ultimate arbiter" of executive privilege and concluded that Miers and Bolten lacked absolute executive privilege, although they could make specific claims when appearing before the Committee to provide testimony.[41]

The parties eventually reached a settlement in March 2009 whereby the Bush White House agreed to provide internal documents, and Miers and former Bush senior advisor Karl Rove agreed to testify under oath in a closed-door hearing. For further discussion of the U.S. Attorneys controversy see, e.g., John McKay, *Train Wreck at the Justice Department: An Eyewitness Account*, 31 Seattle U. L. Rev. 265 (2008); David C. Weiss, Note, *Nothing Improper? Examining Constitutional Limits, Congressional Action, Partisan Motivation, and Pretextual Justification in the U.S. Attorney Removals*, 107 Mich. L. Rev. 317 (2008). For the Department of Justice report on the matter see U.S. DEPARTMENT OF JUSTICE, AN INVESTIGATION INTO THE REMOVAL OF NINE U.S. ATTORNEYS IN 2006 (Sept. 2008).

---

[39] Letter from Fred Fielding to Sen. Leahy and Rep. Conyers (Apr. 12, 2007).

[40] Letter from Fred Fielding to Sen. Leahy and Rep. Conyers (June 28, 2007).

[41] *Committee on the Judiciary, U.S. House of Representatives v. Miers*, 558 F. Supp. 2d 53 (2008).

NOTES ON THE U.S. ATTORNEYS DISMISSAL CAPER

1.   *Antiseptic Sunbeams.* Justice Brandeis famously remarked that "sunlight is said to be the best of disinfectants." By shedding substantial light on the controversial new appointment procedures for U.S. Attorneys, the Senate Judiciary Committee was able to force Attorney General Gonzales to promise to submit future appointments to the Senate for confirmation. This congressional ability to draw attention to controversial executive department practices may be viewed as similar to the role of the press. Unlike the press, however, Congress has the power to compel executive officials to answer questions and offer justifications for controversial policies. Should the Senate interrogation of Attorney General Gonzales, eventually leading to his resignation, be understood as an example of effective investigatory oversight? Or is it better viewed as an instance of the Senate redressing its own earlier mistake in the 2005 Patriot Act reauthorization?

2.   *Removal Power Under* Myers. Aren't U.S. Attorneys executive branch officials who serve at the President's pleasure? Under *Myers v. United States* (§1C above), could President Bush have removed all 93 sitting U.S. Attorneys without regard to Congress conferring appointment authority on the Attorney General in the 2005 Patriot Act reauthorization? If so, why do you think Bush did not pursue this course? Is this, perhaps, an instance when informal norms trumped constitutionally permissible options?

3.   *Executive Agencies Versus the White House.* Congress obtained considerable access to Justice Department documents and testimony from the Attorney General and several lower-level officials. The White House was also willing to provide documents related to communications between the White House and the Department of Justice, but not internal White House communications. Are there constitutional justifications for drawing a distinction between Congress's oversight power over White House officials and Justice Department officials? In a letter of June 28, 2007, White House Counsel Fielding contended that congressional discovery of internal White House communications would unconstitutionally encroach upon presidential authority. Should White House officials be considered agents of the President or should they instead be treated like officials in executive agencies such as the Department of Justice or Department of State? Does it matter that, unlike the Attorney General, the President's Chief of Staff and White House Counsel are appointed without the advice and consent of the Senate?

4.   *Congressional Contempt.* Josh Chafetz has noted that the Miers-Bolten episode constituted "only the second time in the nation's history [that] a house of Congress sued high-ranking executive branch officials in an attempt to enforce a subpoena for their testimony in the face of the officials' claims of executive privilege," adding that "[u]nlike the previous suit, in which the defendant was none other than the president of the United States, the 2008 suit was successful." Josh Chafetz, *Executive Branch Contempt of Congress*, 76 U. Chi. L. Rev. 1083 (2009). Chafetz argues that in the Miers-Bolten contempt proceedings "all three branches—including, and perhaps most significantly, Congress itself—have acted improperly in this case so as to diminish Congress's constitutional powers." After reviewing the history of the English parliament, pre-Revolutionary colonial legislatures, and earlier congresses Chafetz concludes that Congress has an independent authority to punish executive officials for contempt of Congress without the cooperation of the executive (through a prosecution)

or the judiciary (through a court order). Is it troubling that in the Miers-Bolten affair, Congress could not vindicate its authority without the assistance of other branches of government? Is this predicament any different from that of the executive which must rely on Congress for the laws it enforces, or the judiciary which cannot pass judgment on a criminal matter unless the executive initiates a prosecution? As summarized above, the D.C. district court insisted that the judiciary was the "ultimate arbiter" of privilege claims. Does the Constitution require this role for the courts or is it simply motivated by a desire to subject disputes between Congress and the Executive to an ostensibly neutral arbiter?

2.   Budget and Appropriations

Under Article I, § 8, clauses 1 and 18 and § 9, clause 7, Congress has virtually plenary power to determine how the United States' money will be spent. This power of the purse gives Congress an ongoing substantive power as well—notably, Congress's power of the purse and legislative oversight activities are related. Much oversight occurs when programs are reauthorized or receive appropriations, not only in primary-purpose oversight hearings. Auerbach, *Keeping a Watchful Eye*, 130–33. The use of spending control to influence executive branch actions works in several different ways.

The statute establishing a program or agency typically does not also appropriate money to fund its activities. With regard to discretionary spending programs, the authorization process is separate from the appropriations process. What one Congress establishes as a statutory scheme can be negated entirely by a subsequent Congress's failure to fund that scheme or the agency administering it. More commonly, Congress will fund a statutory scheme and the agency, but the level of funding will depend upon Congress's attitude toward the scheme and the agency. An agency might have a strong incentive to move statutory policy close to the House or Senate position even though the agency's preferred policy would be protected by a presidential veto, if the agency fears that Congress will fail to fund it adequately in retaliation for the agency's policy position. This reveals the great advantage the appropriations power gives Congress: because the agency needs each Congress to act affirmatively to give it money, Congress has something of a backdoor "legislative veto" if it chooses to exercise it through the appropriations process. Moreover, because most appropriations of discretionary money must be renewed annually, the process provides Congress continuing influence.

It is impossible to tell how important the appropriations power is in this respect. The main limitation involves a coordination problem: the oversight (sub)committee cannot routinely pressure the agency to adopt new substantive policies by threatening to cut off funds, because separate appropriations subcommittees control funding. Unless the two different congressional entities share the same political preferences *and* can coordinate their activities, the funding weapon will be hard to deploy. Moreover, the preferences of the two (sub)committees can be expected to diverge most of the time. Because of the requirements of the congressional budget process, the appropriations committees are usually required to operate under a zero-sum mentality more often than the corresponding substantive committees: the primary goal of the former is to meet certain budget needs, while the primary goal of the latter is to solve social or economic problems. The NHTSA was caught in this bind. It received ample funding in the 1960s but suffered budget cuts as a consequence of general belt-tightening during the Nixon Administration and beyond. Even though the substantive committees were still quite keen on auto safety, the President and the appropriations committees were much more concerned with other budgetary priorities. Moreover, when Congress does bestir itself to focus on auto safety concerns, as during the interlock controversy in 1973–74, it may well make the agency's job more difficult (with diminishing funds) by curtailing unpopular regulatory options and adding low priority issues (school-bus safety) to the already-crowded agency agenda.

Congress's spending power can be used as a mechanism of control in less direct ways than not funding or underfunding a particular agency. For example, committee reports accompanying appropriations bills include directives to agencies about how the money should be spent. Reports contain line items with specific instructions to fund particular projects, usually in the districts of key congressional players. Although language in committee reports is not legally binding, agencies usually follow the mandates in order to retain the good will of the appropriators whom they will face again next year. Not infrequently, Congress will include substantive restrictions in appropriations measures, which are legally binding because they meet the constitutional requirements for laws. This occurs even though congressional rules often forbid riders or other substantive legislation on an appropriations bill. Although such provisions obviously subject the appropriations bill to a possible veto, the President will sometimes swallow them because of the need to fund the government.

The Supreme Court has taken a balanced approach to substantive provisions in appropriations measures. On the one hand, repeals by implication are especially disfavored in the appropriations context. E.g., *TVA v. Hill*, 437 U.S. 153, 190 (1978), where the Court refused to credit continued congressional funding of the Tellico Dam as an amendment to the Endangered Species Act (ESA). On the other hand, Congress may amend substantive law in an appropriations statute, as long as it does so clearly. E.g., *Robertson v. Seattle Audubon Society*, 503 U.S. 429 (1992), where the Court applied an appropriations rider to allow timber-cutting that threatened the habitat of an endangered species (the spotted owl), which would otherwise have been a violation of the ESA.

3. The Legislative Veto of Agency Rules

Another response to the tension between administrative lawmaking and majoritarian government has been the development of the *legislative veto*. The legislative veto is generally any statutory mechanism that renders the implementation of agency decisions or actions subject to some further form of legislative review or control, usually for a specified time period. The purpose of the legislative veto is to provide a quick mechanism to slow down or overturn administrative actions that are unresponsive to the legislature's aims in the original authorizing statute, without going through the obstacle course of the full legislative process. Hence, the power to nullify an administrative decision has been vested in joint action of both chambers of the legislature, action by only one house, or action by a legislative committee. (At the state level, there have been mechanisms for suspension, rather than veto, of agency decisions by joint legislative committees.) Any of these procedures is more streamlined than the normal legislative process; even a two-house legislative veto avoids the presentment clause. Getting around the President is important because he would presumably veto most legislative nullifications of regulations passed by agencies in his government, thereby requiring a supermajority in each house to implement congressional preferences.

The form of the veto can be either negative or positive. A *negative veto provision* (the typical one) stipulates that administrative decisions will be effective, unless the legislature or its designated subgroup actually disapproves the decisions. A *positive veto provision* requires legislative approval of the administrative decision before it becomes effective.

The legislative veto idea was used sporadically in the early part of the previous century, but it was only in the 1970s that it became a popular mechanism for legislative oversight of the administrative process. A Library of Congress study for the period 1932 to 1975 found 295 congressional review provisions in 196 federal statutes; for the year 1975 alone, there were 58 provisions in 21 statutes.[42] Legislative veto provisions were attached to important legislation involving defense and foreign policy (e.g., the War Powers Resolution, 87 Stat. 555); energy and environmental policy (e.g., the Energy Policy and Conservation Act, 89 Stat. 871); consumer welfare policy (e.g., the Employee Retirement Income Security Act of 1974, 88 Stat. 829); and transportation policy (e.g., the Regional Rail Reorganization Act of 1973, 87 Stat. 985).[43] When Congress revisited the Motor Vehicle Safety Act in 1974, it required that any future regulation of passive restraints be subject to a two-house legislative veto. State legislatures in the 1970s adopted a variety of legislative veto devices as well. The tendency at the state level was to create a committee, consisting either of legislators or bureaucrats or experts, to advise the legislature and, in some cases, to suspend operation of agency rules until the legislature could study them.

The concept of the legislative veto drew criticisms from political scientists, who argued that they created as many problems for popular government as they solved, and from legal scholars, who argued that they were hard to reconcile with the concept of separation of powers. These constitutional and political concerns generated a series of challenges to legislative vetoes at both the state and federal level.

Immigration & Naturalization Service v. Chadha
462 U.S. 919 (1983).

Section 244(c)(2) of the Immigration and Nationality Act (8 U.S.C. § 1254(c)(2)) authorized one chamber of Congress, by resolution, to invalidate a decision by the

---

[42] Clark Norton, *Congressional Review, Deferral and Disapproval of Executive Actions: A Summary and Inventory of Statutory Authority* 8–12 (1976).

[43] See Louis Fisher, *Constitutional Conflicts Between Congress and the President* 134–143 (3d rev. ed. 1991).

executive to allow a deportable alien to remain in the United States. Chadha, an East Indian born in Kenya and holding a British passport, was able to obtain a suspension of his deportation pursuant to the Act. He had been deportable because he remained in the United States after the expiration of his nonimmigrant student visa. At the behest of Representative Eilberg, Chair of the Judiciary Committee Subcommittee on Immigration, the House overrode the suspension of Chadha's deportation. After the House action, the immigration judge reopened Chadha's case and ordered him deported. Chadha appealed the order through the Department of Justice, and then to the federal courts. The Ninth Circuit declared § 244(c)(2) unconstitutional. The Supreme Court affirmed.

Chief Justice Burger's opinion for the Court relied on Article I, § 7, the bicameralism and presentment requirements for congressional statutes and resolutions having the force of law. "The decision to provide the President with a limited and qualified power to nullify proposed legislation by veto was based on the profound conviction of the Framers that the powers conferred on Congress were the powers to be most carefully circumscribed. It is beyond doubt that lawmaking was a power to be shared by both Houses and the President."

The Court's opinion relied extensively on statements from the Federalist Papers, the Constitutional Convention debates, and Story's Commentaries on the Constitution. Chief Justice Burger concluded that the Court must strictly enforce both the presentment and the bicameralism requirements whenever Congress was seeking to exercise its *legislative* power. The House resolution abrogating the suspension of Chadha's deportation was such an action, because it "had the purpose and effect of altering the legal rights, duties and relations of persons, including the Attorney General, Executive Branch officials and Chadha, all outside the legislative branch. Section 244(c)(2) purports to authorize one House of Congress to require the Attorney General to deport an individual alien whose deportation otherwise would be cancelled under § 244. The one-House veto operated in this case to overrule the Attorney General and mandate Chadha's deportation; absent the House action, Chadha would remain in the United States. Congress has *acted* and its action has altered Chadha's status."

The Chief Justice recognized that "[t]he veto authorized by § 244(c)(2) doubtless has been in many respects a convenient shortcut; the 'sharing' with the Executive by Congress of its authority over aliens in this manner is, on its face, an appealing compromise. In purely practical terms, it is obviously easier for action to be taken by one House without submission to the President; but it is crystal clear from the records of the Convention, contemporaneous writings and debates, that the Framers ranked other values higher than efficiency."

Justice Powell concurred only in the Court's judgment. He was unwilling to strike down the hundreds of legislative veto provisions that Congress had included in laws since the New Deal. "One reasonably may disagree with Congress' assessment of the veto's utility, but the respect due its judgment as a coordinate branch of Government cautions that our holding should be no more extensive than necessary to decide those cases. In my view, the case may be decided on a narrower ground. When Congress finds that a particular person does not satisfy the statutory criteria for permanent residence in this country it has assumed a judicial function in violation of the principle of separation of powers."

Justice White was the only dissenter. He characterized the legislative veto as "an important if not indispensable political invention that allows the President and Congress to resolve major constitutional and policy differences, assures the accountability of independent regulatory agencies, and preserves Congress' control over lawmaking. Perhaps there are other means of accommodation and accountability, but the increasing reliance of Congress upon the legislative veto suggests that the alternatives to which Congress must now turn are not entirely satisfactory.

"The history of the legislative veto also makes clear that it has not been a sword with which Congress has struck out to aggrandize itself at the expense of the other branches—the concerns of Madison and Hamilton. Rather, the veto has been a means of defense, a reservation of ultimate authority necessary if Congress is to fulfill its designated role under Article I as the Nation's lawmaker."

Justice White also emphasized the tensions between the Court's holding and the realities of agency rulemaking. "The Court's holding today that all legislative-type action must be enacted through the lawmaking process ignores that legislative authority is routinely delegated to the Executive Branch, to the independent regulatory agencies, and to private individuals and groups. * * * There is no question but that agency rulemaking is lawmaking in any functional or realistic sense of the term. The Administrative Procedure Act, 5 U.S.C. § 551(4) provides that a 'rule' is an agency statement 'designed to implement, interpret, or prescribe law or policy.' When agencies are authorized to prescribe law through substantive rulemaking, the administrator's regulation is not only due deference, but is accorded 'legislative effect.' These regulations bind courts and officers of the federal government, may pre-empt state law, and grant rights to and impose obligations on the public. In sum, they have the force of law.

"If Congress may delegate lawmaking power to independent and executive agencies, it is most difficult to understand Article I as prohibiting Congress from also reserving a check on legislative power for itself. Absent the veto, the agencies receiving delegations of legislative or quasi-legislative power may issue regulations having the force of law without bicameral approval and without the President's signature. It is thus not apparent why the reservation of a veto over the exercise of that legislative power must be subject to a more exacting test. In both cases, it is enough that the initial statutory authorizations comply with the Article I requirements."

NOTES ON CHADHA

1.   *Different Visions of the Structure of the Constitution.* The three *Chadha* opinions offer strikingly different visions of the structures of constitutional law. The opinions of Justices Powell and White (who would allow legislative vetoes in many instances) take a functional approach to the separation of powers concept. Their main concern is that Congress should not usurp duties given to the executive (Justice White) or judicial (Justice Powell) powers. See Articles I–III of the Constitution.[44]

The Chief Justice's opinion seems to focus on a distinct but related issue of the circumstances under which Congress can legislate, under Article I, § 7. Because the

---

[44] See Martin Redish, *The Constitution as Political Structure* 113–125 (1995) (arguing in favor of a pragmatic formalism in this area); E. Donald Elliott, INS v. Chadha: *The Administrative Constitution, the Constitution, and the Legislative Veto*, 1983 Sup. Ct. Rev. 125 (distinguishing between formalist and functionalist approaches to separation of powers issues).

Framers considered the lawmaking branch the most dangerous arm of government, they limited the instances in which Congress could act decisively by erecting anti-majoritarian barriers within the legislative process—bicameralism and presentment to the President. If Congress can make "law" without going through both Houses of Congress and the President, then there is a greater danger of abuse of legislative power, Chief Justice Burger contends. Is the Chief Justice right in focusing on this feature of the Constitution, and treating it so strictly? His approach has been termed a formalist one, in contrast to the more functional approach reflected in the other opinions. How do Justices Powell and White justify their different focus?

2.   *Policy Arguments.* Underlying the different constitutional visions of the various opinions in *Chadha* are probably different attitudes about the necessity or usefulness of the legislative veto. See generally Stanley Brubaker, *Slouching Toward Constitutional Duty: The Legislative Veto and the Delegation of Authority*, 1 Const. Comm. 81 (1984).

The chief argument for the legislative veto is that once the Court has allowed Congress to delegate enormous lawmaking power to agencies, with virtually no enforceable guidelines, Congress ought to be allowed to attach "strings" to that delegation, especially strings that allow the democratic process (Congress) to provide agencies with feedback having greater bite than oversight hearings. Moreover, the legislative veto provides flexibility in the conduct of public affairs in situations that could not have been foreseen by the Framers. Congress does not have the capacity to oversee the complicated regulatory state, and if it attempted to do so, the machinery of government would grind to a halt. "By delegating a qualified authority, Congress can maintain the system's energy, while by reserving authority to review proposed rules and acts, it can restore balance and accountability." *Id.* at 85.

Brubaker surveys several policy arguments against the legislative veto. First, the legislative veto distorts the legislative process. Legislation that would otherwise fail will pass if key legislators know that later they will have the opportunity to block offending provisions through the use of the legislative veto. This allows Congress to appear to be addressing hard questions, when in fact the legislative veto will thwart any substantial action by an administrative agency to address those questions.

Second, the legislative veto makes agencies vitally concerned with the views of entities other than the enacting Congress, which may be problematic. For example, because interest in the legislation will be lower when, months or years after its passage, the agency proposes implementing regulations, the task of reviewing those regulations will fall upon the congressional committees and subcommittees. "Thus a likely and apparently common occurrence is a significant skewing of the original legislative intent towards the interest of the congressmen on the overseeing committee or subcommittee and the groups and people most responsible for their re-election." *Id.* at 92. If committees are comprised of members with preferences more extreme than that of the body, a one-committee legislative veto may produce regulations far away from the preferences of the median legislator. In addition, the legislative veto allows subsequent Congresses a great deal of influence over the implementation of statutes enacted in the past. This may allow for substantial shifts from the original intent of the enactors. Consider how a committee in a conservative Republican Congress might influence policies enacted by more liberal Democratic Congresses with very different ideological commitments. Is that legitimate?[45]

Third, the legislative veto may have encouraged very broad delegations because Congress could exert continuing and effective control over the agencies as they exercised their delegated authority. In other words, the incentive to constrain agency discretion *ex ante* by enacting detailed and precise statutes is less compelling if Congress has *ex post* tools to constrain agencies. For those who object to broad delegations, perhaps on the ground that they reduce political accountability, this possibility is disturbing. An excellent empirical study of the legislative veto suggests that it had some effect on the breadth of congressional delegations. See Jessica Korn, *The Power of Separation: American Constitutionalism and the Myth of the Legislative Veto* (1996). For example, after *Chadha* invalidated the legislative veto, members of Congress rescinded broad authority given the Secretary of Education with respect to Pell Grants and enacted their policy preferences more precisely. But other forces, practical and political, continue to discourage legislators from using specific and detailed statutory directives to reduce agency discretion, so the effect of *Chadha* in this area has not been substantial.

3.   *Constitutionality of State Legislative Vetoes.* As an interpretation of Article I of the U.S. Constitution, *Chadha* does not control the validity of state legislative vetoes. Most states have followed *Chadha*, e.g., *Blank v. Department of Corrections*, 564 N.W.2d 130 (Mich. 1997), but there are some interesting variations.

In *Opinion of the Justices*, 431 A.2d 783 (N.H. 1981), the Court advised the legislature that a legislative committee veto is not valid under the New Hampshire Constitution but that other legislative veto arrangements were valid. "The objectives of the proposed legislation could be met and the constitutional objections minimized, if the statute were to provide for approval or rejection of the rules to be determined by a majority of a quorum of both houses, possibly acting pursuant to the recommendations of significantly representative committees, and then presented to the Governor for his approval. In such an instance, if any rule was rejected by either house or the Governor, its resubmission as a law would have to await enactment by the General Court and would be subject to a veto as with bills."

The Idaho Supreme Court in *Mead v. Arnell*, 791 P.2d 410 (Idaho 1990), upheld a statute allowing the legislature to override agency rules by a concurrent resolution passed by both chambers but not submitted to the governor for veto. The court explicitly relied on Justice White's dissenting opinion in *Chadha*. Iowa's voters added a new article III, § 40 to that state's constitution in 1984: "The general assembly may nullify an adopted administrative rule of a state agency by the passage of a resolution by a majority of all the members of each house of the general assembly." New Jersey similarly amended its constitution in 1992.

Would these state developments violate the U.S. Constitution's requirement, Art. IV, § 4, that states have a "Republican form of Government"? See *Van Sickle v. Shanahan*, 511 P.2d 223 (Kan. 1973) (provision in state constitution authorizing

---

[45] See Michael Herz, *The Legislative Veto in Times of Political Reversal:* Chadha *and the 104th Congress,* 14 Const. Comm. 319 (1997) (using game theory to demonstrate how legislative vetoes could radically shift regulatory outcomes when the partisan makeup of Congress changes). See also Eskridge & Ferejohn, *The Article I, Section 7 Game, supra.*

governor to reorganize state legislature, subject to one-house veto, does not violate Article IV, § 4).

4.   *The Impact of* Chadha. Law professors tend to read great import into constitutional decisions; political scientists tend to see them gobbled up by larger structural features of American governance. So it has been with *Chadha.* Several scholars maintain that this decision had relatively little effect on congressional practice or on Congress-agency relations. On the one hand, congressional scholar Louis Fisher reports that many statutes enacted after *Chadha* continue to include legislative vetoes, and administrative agencies regularly attend to them as though they were the "law," seeking committee permission for certain decisions. See Louis Fisher, *The Legislative Veto: Invalidated, It Survives,* 56 Law & Contemp. Probs. 273 (1993).

On the other hand, Jessica Korn argues that other mechanisms, constitutional under *Chadha,* can and do work just as well as the legislative veto. Korn's comprehensive study leads her to conclude that the practice was never a particularly important weapon in the arsenal of congressional oversight. "Members did not need the legislative shortcut to force executive branch officials to attend to congressional concerns, because the most useful sources of congressional oversight power—the power to make laws, and the power to require that executive branch and independent agency officials report [to committees] proposed actions before implementation—are well nestled in the authorities granted to members by Article I of the Constitution." Korn, *Power of Separation,* at 116. Of fourteen potential oversight mechanisms, some of which we discuss in this section, the legislative veto ranked last in terms of frequency of use and ninth in terms of effectiveness, according to Joel Auerbach, *Keeping a Watchful Eye: The Politics of Congressional Oversight* 132 (Table 6–1), 135 (Table 6–2) (1990).

Does it make sense to think that *Chadha* has had *no* effect, as these scholars seem to maintain? Doesn't the *threat* of a one-House veto change the bargaining game between Congress and the President or an agency?

5.   *The Line Item Veto Case.* In 1995, Congress enacted the Line Item Veto Act, 110 Stat. 1200, which authorized the President to "cancel" statutory items relating to discretionary spending or tax benefits. See Chapter 3, § 2B, discussing the Act and its invalidation in *Clinton v. City of New York,* 524 U.S. 417 (1997). *Query:* If Congress really wants the President to have something like a line item veto authority, as a way of restraining Congress's tendency to undertax and overspend, is there a way to do that after *Clinton?*

4.   Congressional Design of Agency Structure and Procedures

Oversight, appropriations pressure, and the legislative veto are all *ex post* methods for Congress to control the agencies to which it has delegated power. That is, these methods are after-the-fact: the agency does something Congress doesn't like, and Congress responds. Another way to control agency policy is *ex ante:* by careful design of the agency's procedure, jurisdiction, and composition, the enacting coalition can press agency policy in desired directions. McNollgast[46] have called this "hardwiring" the agency.

---

[46]   Matthew McCubbins, Roger Noll, and Barry Weingast have combined their names and efforts to create McNollgast. The hardwiring concept is developed in McNollgast, *Administrative Procedures as*

By the design of the agency's procedures and jurisdiction, the enacting Congress can create a powerful or a weak agency. We saw an example of the latter in Chapter 1. When Congress created the EEOC in the Civil Rights Act of 1964, it created procedural complexities and denied substantive rulemaking authority to the agency as part of the deal with conservative Senator Dirksen, who wanted to protect small businesses against too much federal meddling in their affairs.[47] Dirksen correctly believed that the agency would be captive of pro-civil rights super-regulatory activists, although the EEOC has been a more successful policy entrepreneur than Dirksen probably would have wanted.

Congressional Restrictions Apart from the APA. One mechanism Congress has deployed in the last generation has been to impose statutory restrictions on agency rulemaking beyond what is provided for under the APA. These statutes have been systematically examined in Connor Raso, *Procedural Constraints on Agency Rulemaking* (Ph. D. Diss., Stanford University, Political Science Dep't, 2010). Raso explores the many ways that Congress tries to build *ex ante* controls on the administrative process by imposing various requirements on agency rulemaking. Among the statutes following such a strategy are the following:

National Environmental Policy Act, 1969, 42 U.S.C. § 4321 et seq., which requires environmental impact statements before federal projects can proceed;

Consumer Products Safety Act Amendments, 1981, 15 U.S.C. § 2058, which imposes new requirements before the Consumer Product Safety Commission (CPSC) issues new regulations, including a major curtailment in the role of consumer groups and the accountability of the CPSC to such groups;

Regulatory Flexibility Act, 1980, 5 U.S.C. § 601 et seq., which requires a "regulatory flexibility" analysis for agency action imposing significant costs on small businesses;

Congressional Review Act, 1995, 5 U.S.C. § 801, which requires agencies to report new rules to Congress and prevents their taking effect for 60 days so that Congress can overturn them, through a resolution that must be adopted by both chambers and presented to the President but is not subject to the Senate filibuster;

Unfunded Mandates Reform Act, 1995, 2 U.S.C. § 658 et al., which requires agencies to disclose new costs its rules will impose on private parties or state/local governments and to consider alternatives to those "unfunded" costs.

Raso evaluates the efficacy of these structural restrictions, determining whether agencies actually follow the new rules and whether the restrictions have

---

Instruments of Political Control, 3 J.L. Econ. & Org. 243 (1987). See also Jonathan Macey, *Separated Powers and Positive Political Theory: The Tug of War Over Administrative Agencies*, 80 Geo. L.J. 671 (1992).

[47] For one in depth perspective on the complex "deal" with Dirksen, see Daniel Rodriguez & Barry Weingast, *The Positive Political Theory of Legislative History: New Perspectives on the 1964 Civil Rights Act and Its Interpretation*, 151 U. Pa. L. Rev. 1417 (2003).

had the effect desired by their sponsors. The evidence is clear that the first two statutes have been reasonably effective, while the latter three have had no discernible effect on agency rulemaking.

NEPA has been a model of effectiveness because (1) the statute sets forth a broad and easily understood directive, with few exemptions; (2) empowers environmental groups to participate early in the process of creating and responding to environmental impact statements; and assures compliance through (3) judicial review and (4) executive branch monitoring (NEPA created a Council on Environmental Quality within the White House). In contrast, the Regulatory Flexibility Act (RFA), even as strengthened in 1996, has been ineffective because the statute (1) contains big loopholes that can easily be exploited by agencies; (2) does not empower interested groups to have much influence early in the process; and (3) has no effective monitoring (the 1996 amendment added limited judicial review, but to little effect).

The Consumer Financial Protection Bureau. In response to the financial crisis of 2008, rooted in the default of subprime mortgages, Congress passed the Consumer Financial Protection Act as part of the Dodd-Frank Wall Street Reform and Consumer Protection Act of 2010 (the "Act"). The Act created the Consumer Financial Protection Bureau (CFPB) with the mandate of regulating "the offering and provision of consumer financial products or services under the federal consumer financial laws."

The CFPB has a number of features that give it unusual power and independence. First, the CFPB is granted exclusive authority to promulgate regulations and orders administering federal consumer financial laws. This includes exclusive authority over all existing consumer protection laws such as the Fair Debt Collection Practices Act, the Equal Credit Opportunity Act, and the Home Mortgage Disclosure Act. Second, unlike other independent agencies such as the SEC and FEC that have multi-member boards, the CFPB has a single director who serves a term of five years and is appointed by the President with the advice and consent of the Senate. Third, the CFPB is insulated from the executive branch because the President may only remove the director for cause. Finally, and perhaps most uniquely, the CFPB is insulated from congressional budgetary control. The CPFB relies for its funding not on Congress but, rather, on the Federal Reserve within which it is technically housed. At the same time, the Federal Reserve does not control the CFPB budget. The CFPB is entitled to request each year, and the Federal Reserve must transfer, an amount "reasonably necessary" from the earnings of the Federal Reserve, up to a statutory cap.

Does this structure raise constitutional concerns? Does *Free Enterprise Fund* (discussed in §1C), suggest that the Supreme Court might be willing to intervene in this kind of case? What could be the doctrinal basis for a Supreme Court intervention?

5. The Confirmation Process[48]

Policy Debates and Political Pressures. Presidents traditionally use their appointment authority to help control the administrative state by creating a bureaucracy that is supportive of the presidential agenda. The Constitution's formal barrier to unlimited presidential control over appointments is the Senate's advice and consent role under Article II. Through its confirmation power, the Senate may conduct a serious review of nominees' professional, ethical, or personal qualifications and prevent unqualified nominees from taking office. Senators may also use confirmation hearings to raise questions about administration policies linked to the nominee's agency, or to develop a record against which nominees can later be measured. During the 1983 confirmation hearings for Reagan nominee Kenneth Adelman to head the Arms Control and Development Agency, Senate Democrats used the process to stimulate a high-profile debate on arms control while also "hoping to obtain answers that affect future actions," noting that nominees "with extreme views often come in and soften them." See Steven V. Roberts, *A Lesson in Advising and Consenting*, N.Y. Times, Apr. 14, 1983.

For most of our history, the Senate's role in confirming appointments has been fairly deferential. Political scientists Nolan McCarty and Rose Razaghian reviewed more than 3500 executive branch nominations from 1885 to 1996, and found a nominations failure rate (Senate rejections or presidential withdrawals) of only 4.4%. The rate was somewhat higher (7%) during periods of divided party control of White House and Senate than in periods of same-party control (3%). Still, although "the conventional wisdom [was] that when it [came] to appointees to the executive branch the confirmation process [was] little more than a technicality, formality, or perhaps nuisance," McCarty and Razaghian determined that successful confirmations often take substantially longer during periods of divided government and in periods when the Senate is ideologically polarized. They also found that the average duration of confirmation processes had been climbing since the 1970s, which coincided with the growth in other types of Senate obstruction such as filibusters.

Starting in the 1990s, the confirmation process has grown far more contentious as levels of partisan polarization intensified and both parties have perceived increased policy stakes associated with executive appointments. In the past decade, the Senate has blocked up-or-down votes for "qualified" candidates based on their ideological beliefs.[49] More recently, the Senate has prevented up-or-down votes as a bargaining chip to modify agency authority or even to frustrate agency operations. From July 2011 to July 2013, Senate Republicans refused to allow an up-or-down vote on President Obama's nomination of Richard Cordray to head the Consumer Financial Protection Bureau (CFPB) unless the President agreed to weaken the

---

[48] Background is drawn in large part from Nolan McCarty and Rose Razaghian, *Advice and Consent: Senate Responses to Executive Branch Nominations 1885–1996*, 43 Am. J. Pol. Sci. 122–43 (1999) and *Developments in the Law—Presidential Authority: Executive Appointments*, 125 Harv. L. Rev. 2135–55 (2012).

[49] Among well-qualified candidates (in professional terms) who never received an up-or-down-vote are Obama nominee Dawn Johnsen to head the Office of Legal Counsel in the Justice Department and George W. Bush nominee John Bolton to serve as U.S. Ambassador to the United Nations.

agency's statutory powers.[50] And between April 2009 and July 2013, Republicans similarly blocked up-or-down votes on four Obama nominees to the National Labor Relations Board (NLRB), knowing that failure to confirm at least three individuals to the five-member Board would have meant the agency lacked a quorum to function.

The *internal* response to these Senate tactics was for majority party senators to threaten the obstructionist minority with the so-called "nuclear option," a Senate rule change allowing a simple majority—rather than the current supermajority of 60 Senators—to invoke cloture and vote to confirm executive branch nominees. Democrat Majority Leader Harry Reid was on the brink of imposing the nuclear option in July 2013, following years of delay on Cordray and various NLRB nominees. Instead, Reid and the Democrats secured an agreement from a group of more moderate Republicans to allow up or down votes on these nominees and several others; all were confirmed prior to the Senate's August 2013 recess. In assessing their own conduct, Republican Senator Lindsey Graham, who helped negotiate the agreement after vigorously opposing Cordray, stated, "Cordray was being filibustered because we don't like the law [that created the CPFB]. That's not a reason to deny someone their appointment. We were wrong." Jonathan Weisman & Jennifer Steinhauer, *Senators Reach Agreement to Avert Fight Over Filibuster*, N.Y. Times, July 17, 2013. Was it wrong for Senator Graham and his Republican colleagues to withhold their consent power in order to extract policy concessions from the President? Is there some principled or pragmatic basis for limiting the consent power in this regard?

Constitutional Considerations—Recess Appointments. The response of Presidents George W. Bush and Barack Obama to the Senate's obstructionism was to begin using their recess appointment powers to bypass the Senate. The Recess Appointments Clause grants the President "Power to fill up all Vacancies that *may happen during the Recess* of the Senate, by granting Commissions which shall expire at the End of their next Session." Art. II, § 2, cl. 3 (emphasis added). In 2006 President Bush made 40 appointments of executive officials during Senate recesses.[51] The Senate in turn began conducting pro forma sessions to prevent recess appointments. In 2007, Democrat Senate Majority Leader Reid enlisted senators to return to the empty Senate chamber every few days during the Thanksgiving holiday to conduct pro forma sessions, typically lasting under one minute. This tactic prevented Bush from making any recess appointments in his final twenty-one months as President.[52] In late 2010, Republican Senators deployed the pro forma sessions to prevent President Obama from using his recess appointment power.

President Bush did not challenge the opposition party's pro forma tactic, but President Obama did. On January 4, 2012, during a pro forma session, Obama announced the recess appointments of three NLRB members and Richard Cordray.

---

[50] The Republicans hoped to force an amendment that would alter the CFPB's budgetary insulation from congressional accountability and also convert the agency into a multi-member commission.

[51] Henry Hogue & Maureen Bearden, Cong. Research Serv., RL33310, *Recess Appointments Made by President George W. Bush, January 20, 2001–October 31, 2008*, at 2 (2008).

[52] *Id.* at 15, 19.

President Obama relied on advice from the Justice Department Office of Legal Counsel (OLC) that the pro forma sessions do not sufficiently interrupt a recess for purposes of the Recess Appointments Clause. The OLC's January 2012 memorandum invoked a 1921 Attorney General opinion prepared for President Harding, which in turn had relied on a 1905 Senate committee report.[53] The Senate committee report asserted "The word 'recess' is one of ordinary, not technical signification, and it is evidently used in the constitutional provision in its common and popular sense"; the report described the Senate as being in recess when "its members have no duty of attendance; when its Chamber is empty; when, because of its absence, it cannot receive communications from the president or participate as a body in making appointments." The Justice Department memorandum observed that the Senate's 2011 and 2012 pro forma sessions were conducted pursuant to a unanimous consent resolution providing that there would be "no business conducted" during those sessions.

Subsequently, Noel Canning (a Pepsi-Cola bottling firm in Yakima, Wash.) appealed from an adverse ruling by the NLRB, alleging that the three recess appointments were invalid and the Board therefore lacked a three-member quorum. In January 2013, a D.C. Circuit panel agreed. The court reasoned that the phrase "the recess" in the Recess Appointments Clause would have been understood by the Framers to refer only to the period of adjournment between two sessions of Congress, and the challenged appointments were made after the second session of the 112th Congress had commenced on January 3, 2013. Two members of the D.C. Circuit panel went further, concluding that the original meaning of "happen" in the Clause requires the vacancies to occur during a recess between sessions of Congress as well as being filled during that period. Few if any of the more than 1300 presidential recess appointments made since 1933 would satisfy this latter requirement.

The Supreme Court, interpreting the Recess Clause for the very first time, affirmed the D.C. Circuit's holding but not its reasoning. In *NLRB v. Noel Canning*, 134 S.Ct. 2550 (2014), Justice Breyer (joined by Justices Kennedy, Ginsburg, Sotomayor, and Kagan) relied on the purpose of the Clause and the long historical practice of recess appointments by Presidents of both parties, rather than a close reading of the text. The Court observed that Presidents for two centuries had made recess appointments during breaks that occur both between sessions of Congress and within those sessions, and it held they may constitutionally do so provided the break is of sufficient length. At times, a congressional recess can be too short to make a recess appointment necessary. Noting that under Art. I, § 5, the House must consent to any Senate recess of more than three days, Justice Breyer concluded that a recess of three days or less is automatically too short. A recess of four to nine days will ordinarily be too short except for "some very unusual circumstance—a national catastrophe, for instance, that renders the Senate unavailable but calls for an urgent response."

---

[53] This legal background is set forth by Peter Shane in *The Future of Recess Appointments in Light of Noel Canning v. NLRB*, 27 Lab. Relations Week 1078–85 (June 5, 2013)

The Court further held that the President may fill any vacancies that happen to exist during a recess, as opposed to only vacancies created during that recess. Justice Breyer invoked the Clause's purpose: the President, who is always acting to execute the law, must be able to obtain the assistance of subordinate officers while the Senate is unavailable to confirm those officers. A narrower reading would prevent Presidents from filling vacancies that arise before a recess, "no matter who the official, * * * how dire the need, * * * how uncontroversial the appointment, and * * * how late in the session the office fell vacant." Justice Breyer also again pointed to historical practice: presidents had made recess appointments to preexisting vacancies for 200 years and the Senate as a body had not objected for at least three-quarters of a century.

Finally, however, the Court held that the Senate can prevent the President from making recess appointments by conducting "pro forma" sessions every three days, even in the midst of longer recesses. The Court rejected the Justice Department's argument that these pro forma sessions are simply a sham to thwart the President's appointment powers. All that matters, said Justice Breyer, is whether the Senate says it is in session and "under its own rules, it retains the capacity to transact Senate business"; the latter is possible even if unlikely during pro forma sessions.

Applying its newly articulated standard, the Court held the Senate was in session during the pro forma sessions scheduled intermittently in December 2011 and early January 2012. The challenged NLRB appointments were made during a three day recess between two such pro forma sessions in early January, and three days was too short a time to bring a recess within the scope of the Clause. Justice Scalia (joined by the Chief Justice and Justices Thomas and Alito) concurred in the judgment, substantially following the D.C. Circuit's text-based analysis, and insisting that the Clause applies only during the single recess between two formal congressional sessions and only for offices that become vacant during that intermission.

Practical Implications? The majority decision in *Noel Canning* may be viewed as a victory for the Senate, as both parties (at different times since 2007) have pursued the strategy of enlisting members to help conduct pro forma sessions that prevent a recess from taking place. But consider whether political actors will now seek creative ways to prevent a recess the Senate wants, or to impose a recess the Senate resists. On the one hand, because the House under Art. I, § 5 can prevent a recess of more than three days, it may be able to undermine the President's recess appointments power when both the White House and the Senate are controlled by the opposite party. What if the Senate votes to adjourn, initiating a recess period, but the House disagrees and objects? Under Art. II, § 3, "in Case of Disagreement between the [chambers], with Respect to the Time of Adjournment, [the President] may adjourn them to such a time as he shall think proper." This power has never been exercised. Could a President order a recess in the setting described here?

On the other hand, Justice Breyer's conclusion about the validity of pro forma sessions presumes that the Senate retains power to conduct business in such sessions even when it passes a resolution that it will not do so. The Senate's capacity to conduct business during a pro forma session rests in turn on its ability to act by unanimous consent agreement, because Senate rules presume the existence of a quorum for action unless a Senator who is present questions the quorum. See *Noel Canning*, 134 S.Ct. at 2575. Given that any Senator can suggest the absence of a quorum under Senate rules, what if a Senator from the President's party comes to the floor and repeatedly makes this suggestion during a pro forma session? Would the Senator's stance activate the Recess Clause by establishing that in this particular pro forma session the Senate is, in Justice Breyer's terms, "[without] the capacity to transact Senate business"?

B. PRESIDENTIAL MONITORING AND OVERSIGHT

1. OMB and Cost-Benefit Analysis

Historical Development of OMB Involvement. Although the Constitution does not expressly provide for presidential involvement in agency decision-making, the president has come to exercise considerable influence through monitoring and oversight of agency actions. The legal authority for presidential involvement may be located in Article II of the Constitution, which directs the President to "take Care that the Laws be faithfully executed." In pragmatic terms, the president is "uniquely capable of assuming a role that is distinct from other forms of oversight." Harold Bruff, *Presidential Power and Administrative Rulemaking*, 88 Yale L.J. 451, 461–63 (1979). Bruff identifies certain features of the Presidency that create special oversight advantages. One is the President's national constituency, a characteristic not shared by individual legislators or the congressional committees that oversee federal agencies. Even more important is the President's "unique responsibility to superintend the execution of many statutes at once." Bruff invokes Chief Justice Vinson's observation in a 1952 dissenting opinion that "[u]nlike an administrative commission confined to the enforcement of the statute under which it was created, or the head of a department when administering a particular statute, the President is a constitutional officer charged with taking care that a 'mass of legislation' be executed," *Youngstown Sheet & Tube Co. v. Sawyer*, 343 U.S. 579, 702 (1952) (Vinson, C.J., dissenting). Bruff argues for the President's implied authority "to harmonize the welter of statutes, or to act interstitially at times," because "legislation necessarily distributes power in a somewhat fragmented fashion" to agencies, and it "cannot resolve all the future problems of coordinating policy under separate statutes." Thus, the President "has a unique vantage point from which he can focus on a vital issue that falls within the jurisdiction of a variety of executive and independent agencies, each having power to deal with only part of the problem." 88 Yale L.J. at 462.

Notwithstanding arguments based on Article II, the absence of explicit constitutional delegation led presidents to defer to agency decisionmaking through much of the last century.[54] President Nixon became more involved in agency policymaking. He created the Office of Management and Budget (OMB) from the existing Bureau of the Budget, see Executive Order 11,541, and directed OMB to

---

[54] The account of historical developments through the Clinton Administration is drawn substantially from Elena Kagan, *Presidential Administration*, 114 Harv. L. Rev. 2245, 2275–2300 (2001).

perform "Quality of Life" review, which involved circulating an agency's proposed rules related to environmental quality, consumer protection, and certain matters of public health to other agencies for comment and subsequent feedback. This coordinated review rarely involved OMB exerting substantive influence, but the review process initiated an enhanced presidential role in agency decisionmaking. While Presidents Ford and Carter added incrementally to the centralizing process, there was a general belief that decisionmaking authority remained with the agency. And because agencies viewed the presidential representatives' roles as primarily consultative, they tended to regard these initiatives as more of a paperwork obligation than a meaningful constraint.

President Reagan altered the playing field in substantial ways. He signed Executive Order 12,291 (46 Fed. Reg. 13,193, Feb.17, 1981), which required executive—but not independent—agencies to submit "major rules" to the *Office of Information and Regulatory Affairs (OIRA)*, an office within OMB that had been created initially in 1980 by the Paperwork Reduction Act, Pub. L. No. 96–511, 94 Stat. 2812 (1980) (codified as amended at 44 U.S.C. §§ 3501–21). Major rules were basically regulations likely to have an annual effect on the economy of at least $100 million, or to result in a "major increase" in costs or prices or in "significant adverse effects" on competition, employment, or productivity. The agency submissions to OMB were for the purpose of prepublication review, and agencies were required to accompany their submissions with "regulatory impact analyses" and cost-benefit analyses "to the extent permitted by law." The Reagan Executive Order further charged OMB with responsibility to review and approve, or decline to approve, federal rules from executive agencies. Agencies could regulate only if "the potential benefits to society outweigh the potential costs to society," and the choice among alternatives "involv[ed] the least net cost to society. This Order effectively gave OMB a form of substantive control over executive agencies, because OMB's authority to determine the adequacy of agency impact analyses allowed it to delay or even prevent the publication of a rule. During the Reagan era, an average of 85 rules per year were either withdrawn by agencies in the course of OMB review or returned to the agencies for reconsideration.

President Clinton increased presidential involvement in several respects. Clinton signed Executive Order 12,866 (58 Fed. Reg. 51,735, Sept. 30, 1993), modifying the Reagan approach; major excerpts from the Clinton Executive Order are reproduced in Appendix D. The Order required that OMB review for "significant regulatory action" (comparable to Reagan's "major rule") take place during a specified window of time; it increased the number of factors that agencies should consider in their mandatory cost-benefit analyses; and it required OIRA to disclose its communications with the agency and with persons outside of the executive branch. Should these changes be viewed as expansions of OIRA authority or as constraints on that authority? With respect to cost-benefit analysis, the Executive Order directed that "[e]ach agency shall assess both the costs and the benefits of the intended regulation and, recognizing that some costs and benefits are difficult to quantify, propose or adopt a regulation only upon a reasoned determination that the *benefits of the intended regulation justify its costs*." Does this formulation differ meaningfully from the Reagan Executive Order requirement that the benefits to society must *outweigh* the costs?

The Executive Order reiterated that OMB was to carry out the regulatory review function, and that within OMB, OIRA was the repository of expertise concerning regulatory issues, including methodologies and procedures that affect more than one agency and more broadly the President's regulatory policies. President Clinton expanded the role of OIRA by (1) requiring executive agencies to designate Regulatory Policy Officers (RPOs) to serve as OIRA point-persons, (2) subjecting independent agencies to the regulatory planning process administered by OMB and overseen by the Vice President, although not requiring them to submit individual rules for review, and (3) stipulating that the President would resolve agency-OMB disputes "to the extent permitted by law."

President George W. Bush further increased the level of presidential involvement by issuing an executive order requiring that agency RPOs be presidential appointees and that "unless specifically authorized by the head of the agency," no rulemaking may commence without RPO consent. This effectively meant that an RPO need not report to an agency head and may not even have to be Senate-confirmed. See Peter Strauss, *Overseer, or "The Decider"? The President in Administrative Law*, 75 Geo. Wash. L. Rev. 696, 701 (2007). Upon taking office, President Obama revoked the Bush era changes and returned to the original Clinton executive order. See Executive Order 13,497 (74 Fed. Reg. 6,113, Jan. 30, 2009). The current cost-benefit analysis requirements for agencies basically reflect the Clinton directive with some clarifications from President Obama, who introduced some additional principles and requirements involving public participation, integration and coordination, flexibility, and scientific integrity to the cost-benefit analysis. See Executive Order 13,563 (76 Fed. Reg. 3,821, Jan. 18, 2011), reproduced in Appendix D.

Cost-Benefit Analysis; Economic Issues.[55] Cost-benefit analysis requires agencies to assign a monetary value to both the benefits and costs associated with their proposed regulation. With respect to benefits, one key challenge is determining how much a human life is worth in dollars. As explained by the OIRA Administrator for the second President Bush, "administrative law saves lives by reducing small probabilities of premature death, injury, or illness among large numbers of anonymous workers, consumers, travelers, and residents. The names of those whose lives will be saved are unknown when the rule is adopted and may never be known. They are sometimes called 'statistical lives.'" John Graham, *Saving Lives Through Administrative Law and Economics*, 157 U. Pa. L. Rev. 395, 398 (2008). The valuation methodology for statistical lives—based on amounts we are willing to pay (to secure a benefit) or willing to accept (to bear a risk)—can seem straightforward. Viscusi analogizes establishing the value of risk reduction to assessing benefits in other contexts. Just as we measure benefits from construction of a new public parking garage by estimating the sum of community residents'

---

[55] What follows on the economics of cost-benefit analysis is drawn substantially from W. Kip Viscusi, *Fatal Tradeoffs* (1972); Cass Sunstein, *The Real World of Cost-Benefit Analysis: Thirty-Six Questions (and Almost as Many Answers)*, 114 Colum. L. Rev. 167 (2014), and Cass Sunstein, *Cost-Benefit Default Principles*, 99 Mich. L. Rev. 1651 (2001).

willingness to pay, so when assessing the benefits of reducing the risk of death or disease, we estimate the amount of tax dollars we are willing to spend to reduce incrementally the probability of an adverse health outcome that might otherwise affect one or more random members of the community. *Fatal Tradeoffs* at 19. For example, suppose a regulation is expected to prevent fifty premature deaths. If the agency uses $7 million as the value of a statistical life (VSL), the estimated benefits would be $350 million.[56]

The approach an agency takes to VSL raises a number of issues. In terms of valuation methodology, agencies vary considerably in the dollar amount they assign to a statistical life; OMB has recommended a range of between $1 million and $10 million. Agencies also may adjust their VSL over time. In 2008, EPA lowered its VSL by almost $1 million (11%) although EPA's valuation was still higher than all other federal agencies, including the Department of Transportation which had twice raised its VSL in the same time period.[57] And in 2002, EPA decided the VSL for elderly persons was 38 percent less than that of persons under age 70; the agency reversed itself after the move became public.[58] It is not surprising that skeptics claim the valuation process is heavily tainted by political considerations.

Another valuation issue involves how an agency should discount future gains and losses. Assuming that a certain adjustment in permissible exposure levels to a hazardous substance would reduce the risk of a fatal disease occurring in 50 years time, how should the agency value that reduced risk in today's dollars? Sunstein observes that if an agency values human life at $8 million and selects a 10% discount rate, a life saved 100 years from now is worth only $581. OMB guidelines, which suggest a 7% discount rate (departing from its 10% rate in the 1980s), are not mandatory. Even within a single agency, discount rates vary widely: EPA at one point chose a 3% rate for regulation of lead-based paint, a 7% rate for regulation of drinking water, and a 10% rate for regulating emissions from locomotives. *Cost-Benefit Default Principles* at 1711–12.

Further, Viscusi notes that "economic valuations of risk tend to be distorted by underlying misweighting of risks." For example, we tolerate voluntarily assumed risks more than environmental hazards over which we have no control; we tend to regulate new technologies more strictly than familiar risks; and we scrutinize man-made carcinogens while often accepting much higher levels of natural carcinogens. *Fatal Tradeoffs* at 151–52. The weighting of risks also can have serious equity consequences. With respect to locating an environmental hazard like a toxic dump site or a landfill facility, wealthy communities may be seen as willing to pay far more than poor communities can afford to pay for the benefit of avoidance. The "net

---

[56] In Sunstein's words, "the government is not actually "valuing life" [but instead] valuing the reduction of mortality risks—typically by eliminating low-level risks, for example risks of 1 in 100,000. When it is said that a life is "worth" $7 million in such cases, what is really meant is that people are willing to pay, or ask to be paid, $70, on average, to eliminate a risk of 1 in 100,000." *Thirty-Six Questions (and Almost as Many Answers)*, 114 Colum. L. Rev. at 182.

[57] See Seth Borenstein, *American Life Worth Less Today*, Huffington Post, July 10, 2008.

[58] See *id.*

benefit" to society as a whole is therefore maximized by putting the facility in a low-income area.[59]

When assessing an agency's estimates of both costs and benefits, OIRA must assure that there has been consideration of alternative options in order to evaluate whether the agency has chosen the approach that maximizes net benefits. This requirement too raises various questions, for the agencies and OIRA. How many alternative options must an agency consider? How serious and detailed must this consideration be? Do the alternatives considered have to meet some benchmark of reasonableness? What if the agency concludes there are no reasonable alternatives?

When the benefits do not appear to justify the costs, OIRA will raise questions about whether the agency should proceed with the rule at all. In practical terms, the monetized benefits exceed the monetized costs for the great majority of recent, economically significant rules where the agency submitted monetized costs and benefits. (If an agency determines that the monetized costs are larger than the monetized benefits, the agency may simply choose not to submit a draft rule to OIRA.) In addition, there are certain situations where an agency cannot provide monetized benefits but the agency may be able to show the kinds and breadth of benefits a certain rule will achieve. For example, a regulation limiting workers' exposure to a carcinogenic substance may prevent only a small number of cancers but also prevent a much larger number of painful non-fatal illnesses that are not as readily quantified. A regulation that would increase water quality may have no quantifiable beneficial effects on human health yet produce various aesthetic or recreational benefits. In the latter instance, OIRA would focus on questions like: how many water bodies will experience improved quality? What kind of improvements, and what would they actually achieve? Would there be any benefits for humans and if so, what kind? Would there be other kinds of beneficiaries, such as fish and wildlife, or the environment? Is the number of such beneficiaries large? Is it large relative to the total number? How much would they be helped—in a substantial or a marginal way? *Thirty-Six Questions* at 196–97. By addressing such questions, the agency is seeking to justify the monetized costs with information relating to the breadth of the benefits rather than to monetized figures, which it cannot provide.

Suppose that a proposed rule's monetized benefits are outweighed by the monetized costs or that the analysis yields no net monetized benefit. Would OIRA decline to approve it? The answer is not necessarily for two reasons. First, if Congress through a statute requires the agency to proceed with a certain task, the rule may still proceed even if the monetized benefits are lower than the costs. A well-known illustration is the 1958 Delaney Clause amendment to the Food, Drugs, and Cosmetic Act, which effectively banned consideration of costs by prohibiting the use in food of any chemical additives that had been found to induce cancer in man or animals. Second, the current cost-benefit analysis framework requires agencies to show that the benefits *justify* the costs, not that they *outweigh* the costs. This

---

[59] See Frank Ackerman & Lisa Heinzerling, *Pricing the Priceless: Cost-Benefit Analysis of Environmental Protection*, 150 U. Pa. L. Rev. 1553, 1574 (2002) (discussing *inter alia* the 1991 memo from Larry Summers, then chief economist at World Bank, that explained the economic logic behind migration of "dirty industries" to developing countries).

distinction clearly recognizes that hard numbers are not the only determinative factor. Executive Order 13,563 expressly states that "each agency may consider (and discuss qualitatively) values that are difficult or impossible to quantify, including equity, human dignity, fairness, and distributive impacts."

One recent example involves a 2010 Justice Department regulation increasing building access for disabled persons, which included a requirement that new bathrooms contain sufficient space for wheelchair users to transfer onto toilets from the side. The Department acknowledged that the monetized costs (which were relatively high) substantially exceeded the monetized benefits, but the Department offered several non-monetary counterarguments: "the additional benefits that persons with disabilities will derive from greater safety, enhanced independence, and the avoidance of stigma and humiliation" were also likely to be quite high. Returning war veterans confined to wheelchairs are taught to use side-transfers because they are safe, efficient, and independence-producing; and the Americans With Disabilities Act "is intended to provide important benefits [such as these water closet clearance provisions] that are distributional and equitable in character."[60]

Cost-benefit analyses are not simple undertakings. Agencies may spend hundreds of thousands of dollars collecting data, conducting studies surveying consumer preferences, and analyzing all relevant information. Think back to the FAA's cost-benefit analysis in the Case Study at the start of this chapter. In its January 15, 2002 final rule, the FAA estimated that the cost per fortified cockpit door ranged from $12,000 to $17,000. At the time, the fleet of American airplanes numbered just under 7,000. A letter from a major domestic air carrier responded that the FAA's estimation was low, and that the actual cost per fortified door was $49,000. Is a substantial change in cost, from $84 million to $343 million, justified? Would other options—such as modestly improving the current intense airport security screening of passengers—yield the same or comparable benefits at far less additional cost? If not, how would you quantify the distinct benefits of reinforced cockpit doors? Are the benefits the same for a small regional airline flying 10–passenger planes as for an international airline flying planes that carry 200 or more passengers?

PROBLEM ON COST-BENEFIT ANALYSIS

Problem 8–7. Pursuant to the Safe Drinking Water Act of 1970 (SDWA), the EPA proposed regulations that sought to establish standards regarding the maximum contaminant level goal (MCLG) and the maximum contaminant level (MCL) for naturally occurring uranium in public water systems. The SDWA provides that when proposing any national clean water regulation that includes an MCL, the agency must "publish a determination as to whether the benefits of the [MCL] justify or do not justify the costs. . . ." The Act also directs that the EPA first establish an MCLG which is "the level at which no known or anticipated adverse effects on the health of persons occur and which allows an adequate margin of safety," and then the EPA is to set an MCL "as close to the [MCLG] as is feasible." With respect to cost-benefit analysis, the

---

[60] *Nondiscrimination on the Basis of Disability in State and Local Government Services,* 75 Fed. Reg. 56,164, 56,170 (Sept. 15, 2010).

SDWA requires the EPA to analyze "[q]uantifiable and nonquantifiable costs for which there is a factual basis in the rulemaking record to conclude that such costs are likely to occur solely as a result of compliance with the maximum contaminant level, including monitoring, treatment, and other costs and excluding costs resulting from compliance with other proposed or promulgated regulations."

Based on the risks of carcinogenicity and toxicity of uranium to the human kidney, EPA first set the MCLG for uranium. The EPA concluded that the lowest feasible level for controlling the risks of cancer and protecting the human kidney from natural uranium in drinking water was 20 µg/L (microgram per liter). EPA added that 30 µg/L would be expected to protect against the effects of kidney toxicity, but that any higher level substantially increased the risk of serious adverse effects on human kidneys. The EPA issued a final rule, including the following cost-benefit chart, and determining that (1) the relatively modest annual cancer risk reductions between 30 µg/L and 20 µg/L (the benefits) do not justify the high annual compliance costs for an MCL of 20 µg/L (note that the monetized benefits focus on the cancer benefits because those could be readily monetized whereas the kidney benefits could not be), and (2) therefore the uranium MCL would be set at 30 µvg/L. Focusing on the MCL change from 30 µg/L to 20 µg/L, one can see that in terms of incremental cancer cases, the estimated number of cancer cases avoided for an MCL of 30 µg/L is 0.8 annually, while lowering the MCL to 20 µg/L would result in an additional 0.2 cases avoided annually (25% reduction) at an additional incremental cost of $39 million annually (75% increase from $54 million). And the incremental monetized cancer benefits, again excluding the difficult-to-quantify kidney benefits, received for this additional $39 million cost is limited to $1 million.

Incremental Costs and Benefits for Uranium MCLs of 30 µg/L, and 20 µg/L				
Uranium MCL	Exposure change	Incremental annual cancer cases avoided	Incremental annual compliance costs (millions)	Incremental annual monetized cancer benefits (kidney benefits not monetized) (millions)
3 µg/L	∞ -30 µg/L	0.8	54	3
20 µg/L	30–20 µg/L	0.2	39	1

Has the EPA conducted a judicially reviewable cost-benefit analysis under applicable Executive Order requirements? Has EPA made a reasonable or non-arbitrary determination in choosing to set the MCL at 30 µg/L? The agency's cost-benefit analysis focuses on the quantitative and does not discuss the fairness or distributive impacts of the added exposure. Should this cost-benefit analysis include consideration of such qualitative factors? In a case like this, where the monetized costs from a lower exposure level are 39 times more than the monetized benefits, is such consideration necessary? Would it be necessary where the costs were ten times the monetized benefits? Five times? *See City of Waukesha v. EPA*, 320 F.3d 228, 251–55 (D.C. Cir. 2003); *National Primary Drinking Water Regulations; Radionuclides; Final Rule*, 65 Fed. Reg. 76,708–01, at 76,714.

Cost-Benefit Analysis; Legal Issues. OMB is not the only institutional player shaping the cost-benefit approach. Congress plays an important *ex ante* role, in that cost-benefit analysis may be prohibited, permitted, or required under approaches set forth in statutes that regulate health, safety, and the environment. Thus, for example, the Clean Air Act provisions defining national ambient air quality standards as those "requisite to protect public health" have been recognized as requiring a cost-blind judgment based on "public health" alone. See *Whitman v. Am. Trucking Associations*, 531 U.S. 457 (2001), in § 1B of this chapter. And the Occupational Safety and Health Act (OSHA) provisions authorizing promulgation of workplace health and safety standards have been understood as requiring the agency to make a threshold finding that "significant risks" are present and can be reduced by a change in practices. See *Indus. Union Dep't, AFL-CIO v. Am. Petroleum Inst.*, 448 U.S. 607, 642–43 (1980). This approach suggests that OSHA regulation is permissible once risk-reduction benefits rise above the threshold, regardless of what costs accompany the benefits. At the same time, the fact that an agency is not *required* to engage in cost-benefit analysis may not mean the agency isn't *permitted* to do so. See *Entergy Corp. v. Riverkeeper, Inc.*, 556 U.S. 208, 223 (2009). What if a statute prohibits an executive branch agency from engaging in cost-benefit analysis when promulgating its health and safety rules, but a proposed rule constitutes a "significant regulatory action" under Executive Order 12,866. May OIRA require the agency to assess the proposed rule's costs and benefits? Is the agency justified in refusing to do so based on its congressional directive? How is this situation likely to be resolved?

Assume instead that Congress requires an agency to undertake safety or health regulation "to the extent feasible"? Does this refer to technical feasibility: regulation should proceed as long as the relevant control technology exists? Is it better understood to mean economic feasibility: regulation should go forward unless the regulated entities cannot bear the cost without experiencing business failures across significant portions of the industry? What if the two feasibility concepts inevitably overlap—does this suggest that feasibility requirements in a statute implicate only analysis of the cost-side of the equation? Or is cost-benefit analysis also permitted?

In addition to Congress's input, courts can play an influential *ex post* role when asked to review agency cost-benefit analyses. Consider whether the economic concerns raised in this part (valuation of statistical lives, discount rates, misweighting of risks, equity, politicization) might be exacerbated by judicial review of an agency's cost-benefit determinations. Should we assume that federal judges have levels of expertise comparable to agency regulators when applying highly technical economic models and assumptions? If a reviewing court concludes that the agency chose wrongly from among complex conflicting studies about economic costs or benefits, what are the chances the court is simply aligning with the opposite side of a politically charged debate? Is close judicial oversight of an agency's cost-benefit analysis especially suspect when the statute that authorized the regulation reflects strongly pro-regulatory intent? For a recent example of aggressive judicial review on cost-benefit matters, see *Business Roundtable v. SEC*, 647 F.3d 1144 (D.C. Cir. 2011) (striking down an SEC regulation promulgated under the Dodd-Frank Wall Street Reform and Consumer Protection Act of 2010, on the grounds that the agency's failure adequately to consider the economic consequences of its expanded proxy ballot access rule made its decision arbitrary and capricious). For sharp criticism of the decision, see *Recent Cases: D.C. Circuit Finds*

SEC Proxy Access Rule Arbitrary and Capricious for Inadequate Economic Analysis, 125 Harv. L. Rev. 1088 (2011).

2. OIRA: Aggregating Information and Coordinating Among Agencies

Created by Congress in 1980, OIRA has in a short time become a central actor in the agency review process. Executive Order 12,866 (1993) describes OIRA as "the repository of expertise concerning regulatory issues, including methodologies and procedures that affect more than one agency, this Executive Order, and the President's regulatory policies." President Clinton's Order adds that the OIRA Administrator initiates centralized review of all planned "significant regulatory actions,"[61] and has the power to investigate—and if necessary reject—agency actions that he believes "may be inconsistent with the President's priorities or the principles set forth in this Executive Order or may be in conflict with any policy or action taken or planned by another agency." Between January 21, 2009 and August 10, 2012, OIRA reviewed just over 2300 regulatory actions. During this period, it approved 320 actions (14%) without change, and approved 1758 actions (76%) "consistent with change" meaning that the published rule differed from the submitted version in either minor or substantial respects. An additional 161 regulatory actions (7%) were withdrawn following OIRA intervention.[62]

The OIRA Administrator is appointed by the President, subject to being confirmed by the Senate. Under Executive Order 12866, he is a "regulatory policy advisor" to the President; in this respect he shares status with the Director of OMB (also a Senate-confirmed position) as well as various other Assistants to the President who are lodged within the White House but are not subject to confirmation (see §3B3 below).

From September 2009 to August 2012, Harvard law professor Cass Sunstein served as the Administrator of OIRA. Sunstein's *Commentary*, published in 2013 in the Harvard Law Review, provides a unique insider's perspective on OIRA's operations, priorities, and challenges. In an effort to dispel misunderstandings about how OIRA functions, Sunstein highlights four central propositions:

(1) *Oversight of a genuinely interagency process.* Sunstein emphasizes that OIRA often functions as a conveyer and convener, identifying and sharing interagency views and striving to develop a reasonable consensus, rather than insisting on its own positions.

(2) *Delays in OIRA review.* Often, a rule is delayed even though there is consensus that it should ultimately be promulgated, because matters such as legal complexity or language precision deserve more attention to avoid publishing anything that could generate needless confusion or apprehension. Even a proposed rule containing such technical issues may well alter behavior, and thus create

---

[61] As referenced in section 3B1, a "significant regulatory action" is a broad category, encompassing actions that have an annual effect on the economy of at least $100 million; have a material adverse effect on the economy, the environment, or public health or safety; create a serious inconsistency with action by another agency; or raise novel legal or policy issues arising out of legal mandates or presidential priorities. See Exec. Order 12,866, § 3(f).

[62] See Cass Sunstein, *Commentary, The Office of Information and Regulatory Affairs: Myths and Realities*, 126 Harv. L. Rev. 1838, 1847 (2013).

difficulties, if the public or regulated entities believe that it is likely to be finalized in the same form.

(3) *Cost-benefit analysis important but not usually dominant.* For economically significant rules, the cost-benefit analysis required under the applicable executive orders receives careful attention. But most of OIRA's day-to-day work involves addressing interagency concerns, ensuring adequate discussion of alternatives, and promoting the receipt and consideration of public comments.

(4) *OIRA review process often highly technical.* This relates to point (2) above. OIRA may seek the Justice Department's position on a legal issue, or the U.S. Trade Representative's input on an issue involving international trade, or the Energy Department's views as to a rule's effects on the energy supply. Because career officials with technical expertise are frequently the central actors, delays result as these technical specialists work through the technical questions to arrive at solid answers. 126 Harv. L. Rev. at 1841–43.

Sunstein's emphasis on the OIRA role as a convenor and facilitator between agencies and an aggregator of information, and his downplaying of cost-benefit analysis, are somewhat at odds with popular conceptions of how OIRA operates to monitor executive agencies. Later in his *Commentary*, Sunstein identifies the two chief criticisms directed at OIRA: (a) meddling beyond its competence with agencies that are more specialized and expert about the relevant facts and law; and (b) unduly politicizing the regulatory review process because of its intimate ties to a White House staffed by political actors. Sunstein responds by reiterating that most of the OIRA process is technical, not political. This technical focus is appropriately coordinated in that it combines OIRA's own expertise with a convening of outside agency officials who bring scientific, economic, and legal expertise to the table. And politics—in the sense of electoral factors and broader public reactions—is not a significant part of OIRA's role although it may be important for other offices within the White House. *Id.* at 1871–73.

The concerns that OIRA may be overly meddlesome and unduly politicized deserve some separate attention.

OIRA and Meddling. Sunstein notes the existence of litigation about whether agencies have used interpretive rules and guidance documents to reach decisions that are the functional equivalent of rules (see related discussion in § 2D above). Even if such agency documents fall within proper legal bounds, they may still have substantial effects on the private sector—whether or not they amount to significant regulatory actions. Sunstein contends that OIRA is interested in promoting public comment in such situations, "not because such comment is required as a matter of law, * * * but because when the stakes are high and the issues novel, obtaining public comment is good practice as a way of avoiding mistakes." *Id.* at 1854.

Sunstein concedes that the APA exempts interpretive rules and guidance documents from notice and comment requirements. Does OIRA's promotion of public comment on such proposed agency actions undermine Congress's explicit understanding of a limited public role? Does it improperly interfere with an agency's internal choices on what procedural strategies or tactics to follow? Will the mere threat of OIRA mandating a public comment period for policy guidances issued by the SEC or FAA make those agencies less willing to pursue more efficient and flexible approaches? Alternatively, is it proper for OIRA to insist that agencies invite public input and response whenever they might be engaged in regulatory conduct that involves "high stakes" or "novel issues"?

OIRA and Politicization. In elaborating on his four core propositions, Sunstein discusses OIRA's open-door policy of meeting upon their request with representatives of affected companies, public interest groups, state and local governments, and congressional staffs. He acknowledges that businesses and others subject to regulation arrange the great majority of these meetings, in which they seek to scale back or oppose planned agency actions. But while recognizing the attendant risk of "epistemic capture"—that OIRA or others within the President's Office "will ultimately form a view that matches what those around them are telling them"—Sunstein discounts this risk. He contends that meetings are only one aspect of a complex OIRA review process and their sheer numbers reveal little of value, given that often the meeting initiators present no new information or repeat well-known arguments or speak in unhelpfully general terms. For these and other reasons, Sunstein argues that the role of meetings tends to be greatly exaggerated; the review process relies more on interagency comments and written comments from the public. *Id.* at 1860–62.

Some others are less convinced. Based on its detailed 2011 study of OIRA operations, the Center for Progressive Reform (CPF) claimed that "[n]early three years into the Obama Administration, * * * the regulatory process is every bit as political as it was during the Bush years, while being no more transparent; and vigorous enforcement of the nation's health, safety, and environmental laws has suffered as a result."[63] The CPF study, covering OIRA meetings from October 2001 to June 2011, concluded *inter alia* that not only does industry dominate the meetings process (on this point Sunstein agrees), but (1) rules that were the subject of OIRA meetings were 29% more likely to be changed than those that were not; and (2) EPA is a special OIRA target—its rules made up only 11% of all OIRA reviews but 41% of OIRA meetings, and EPA rules were changed at a significantly higher rate (84%) than those of other agencies (65%) during the ten-year period.[64] Do you find persuasive Sunstein's view that the risk of capture in these settings is largely illusory? Assuming the accuracy of the CPF findings on OIRA meeting participation—65% of attendees represented industry groups while 12% represented public interest groups—is this pattern likely to have only minimal or cosmetic effects?

A high-profile illustration of CPF's concerns involved OIRA deliberations in the summer of 2011, ending with White House refusal to approve the draft final rule on ozone pollution submitted by President Obama's EPA Administrator, Lisa

---

[63] *Politicizing the Regulatory Process*, available at http://www.progressivereform.org/OIRASpecInterests. cfm.

[64] Center for Progressive Reform, *Behind Closed Doors at the White House: How Politics Trumps Protection of Public Health, Worker Safety, and the Environment*, available at http://www.progressivereform. org/articles/OIRA_Meetings_1111.pdf.

Jackson.[65] The ozone standard had been set in 2008 by the Bush Administration at a level of 75 parts per billion (ppb); this was above the range of 60 to 70 ppb recommended by the EPA scientific advisory panel at the time. Environmental and public health groups challenged the Bush standard in court, arguing that it would endanger human health and had been tainted by political interference. Administrator Jackson asked the groups to hold their lawsuit in abeyance while she reconsidered the ozone standard, a reconsideration she expected would be complete by summer 2010.

After several delays that carried into spring 2011, EPA determined the standard should be set at 65 ppb to meet Clean Air Act requirements; the agency calculated this new level would avoid up to 7,200 deaths, 11,000 emergency room visits, and 38,000 acute cases of asthma each year. Jackson understood that the costs of compliance with this new standard would be highly controversial with businesses and local governments. Before submitting the draft final rule to OIRA, she met several times with White House chief of staff William M. Daley, listened to his sharp questioning about costs, burdens, and timing, and eventually offered Daley a somewhat weaker standard as well as measures to allow for substantial flexibility in compliance. In early July, Jackson was convinced she and Daley had a deal, and she sent the White House a 500–page package that included a detailed cost-benefit analysis.

The business community, however, remained adamantly opposed to the proposal, as did Republicans in Congress. In a campaign that featured intense lobbying, letter-writing, and advertising, business representatives claimed the rule would cost $90 billion a year—far more than EPA cost estimates—and would result in massive economic retrenchment in the Midwest. Local and state government officials weighed in, complaining to the White House that they lacked the resources to enforce the new rule. And some Democratic lawmakers warned the White House that the regulation would damage their re-election prospects. Listening closely to these concerns was Daley, whose mission as recently appointed chief of staff was in part to help repair relations with the business community and Congress. Business executives met with Jackson at EPA in mid-July to argue their case. They emphasized that the rule would result in massive local government non-compliance with the Clean Air Act, and they urged that she wait until the next review in 2013. Jackson listened politely and demurred; the business executives left the meeting frustrated.

OIRA Administrator Sunstein was not overly enthused about the proposed ozone rule. He knew the rule was subject to revision again in 2013 and was also aware that nearly half the EPA's own case studies found the cost of the new rule outweighed its benefits. Sunstein and Daley agreed to meet with the business lobbyists on August 16, the same day they were meeting with the environmental and public health groups. Business representatives brought a map showing how many midwestern and east coast states that Obama had won in 2008 would be out of compliance with the proposed regulation. Several governors also attended this

---

[65] The following account is drawn from John M. Broder, *Re-election Strategy is Tied to a Shift on Smog*, New York Times, Nov. 16, 2011, at A1.

meeting; North Carolina governor Bev Perdue (a Democrat) argued against the new rule and her air quality director sent a letter to EPA pleading for a delay and citing the health effects to North Carolina citizens from lack of employment and loss of health care. Several hours after meeting with business interests, Sunstein and Daley met with the environmental and public health groups. These groups explained why the proposed standard would reduce smog levels, and the consequent impact in terms of fewer deaths and incidents of lung disease including for children. Daley listened and then asked "What are the health impacts of unemployment?"

Following two weeks of silence, the President met with Jackson on September 1, and informed her of his decision to return the ozone rule to EPA for reconsideration. The next day, Sunstein sent a letter to Jackson offering three related reasons for the President's decision: (1) the Clean Air Act's current five-year cycle for review of this air quality standard began in 2008 and was to end in 2013; accordingly, issuing a final rule in late 2011 right before having to develop a new assessment and potentially a new standard would not promote predictability and reduce uncertainty, as called for in Executive Order 13,563; (2) the agency had relied on its review of scientific literature as of 2006; this scientific assessment was no longer current, raising concerns in light of the Executive Order's requirement that rules must be based on the best available science; (3) the EPA under Jackson had already promulgated groundbreaking air quality standards (addressed to heavy-duty trucks and cross-state air pollution) projected to reduce ozone pollution as well as other toxic pollutants; reconsideration would enable the agency to assess operation of these rules and in doing so avoid duplicative or inconsistent efforts.

When the White House publicly announced the decision on September 3, environmental and public health advocates were furious. The New York Times reported their characterization of the OIRA action as "a bald surrender to business pressure, an act of political pandering and, most galling, a cold-blooded betrayal of a loyal constituency." Interviewed by the Times, Sunstein said "the decision was made on the merits and not on politics. There isn't an agreement to do things until the process runs its course. There is sometimes a surprise."

The Center for Progressive Reform study described OIRA's actions on the ozone standard as disturbingly secretive and politically motivated. Sunstein rejected that position, insisting the decision was based on judgments about the merits. *What do you think?* To what extent does Chief of Staff Daley's direct continuing involvement compromise the integrity of the OIRA review process? In his *Commentary*, Sunstein emphasized that "the Office of the Chief of Staff has an important role insofar as it works to advise on and help coordinate executive branch activity with close reference to the President's own commitments." 126 Harv. L. Rev. at 1874. In instances where congressional lawmakers and governors have expressed strong views to the White House, shouldn't politics have some role? At this elevated level, does politics become part of "the merits"? On the other hand, should an agency's scientific conclusions, reached after years of public dialogue and deliberations, be overridden by considerations of presidential politics? Or is this simply a rare instance where politics plays an influential or determining part in the OIRA review process?

Postscript on Ozone. In July 2013, the D.C. Circuit issued a decision in the lawsuit challenging the 2008 standard, which earlier had been held in abeyance pursuant to EPA Administrator Jackson's request. The appellate court concluded that although the ozone standard of 75 ppb was weaker than recommended unanimously by EPA's science advisors, the agency had not acted arbitrarily in 2008 when it determined to adopt this weaker standard.

Meanwhile, the five-year cycle for review of the 2008 standard ended in 2013, with no new notice of proposed rulemaking. In February 2014, the EPA released a draft policy statement that contained an EPA staff suggestion of lowering the current ozone standard to 60 ppb based on the available scientific evidence, as well as two draft risk and exposure documents. The EPA made the documents available for public comment. On April 30, 2014, a federal judge in the Northern District of California ordered the EPA to finish its ozone review and update the national standards, directing the agency to issue a proposal by December 1, 2014, and a final rule by October 1, 2015. *Sierra Club v. EPA*, 13-CV-2809-YGR, slip opinion (N.D. Cal. Apr. 30, 2014).

3. Presidential Czars

The federal government includes more than 80 executive branch departments and agencies[66] and well over two million employees. Apart from the formal monitoring mechanisms developed through OMB and OIRA, Presidents depend on an array of personal advisors and deputies within the White House in their efforts to coordinate and control this vast bureaucracy. In recent decades, there has been a proliferation of high-level advisors charged with overseeing parts of the presidential agenda. They are often referred to by appointing presidents and the media as "czars."

Although no advisor has been given the official title of czar, it has become a familiar and increasingly pejorative moniker—as when Senator John McCain remarked that President Obama has "more czars than the Romanovs." See Aaron J. Saiger, *Obama's "Czars" for Domestic Policy and the Law of the White House Staff*, 79 Fordham L. Rev. 2577 (2011).[67] Obama and his predecessor, George W. Bush, have been especially active in making use of advisors appointed by the president, accountable only to him, and assigned a particular subject matter portfolio. During the first term of the Obama Administration, Carol Browner was appointed director of a newly created White House Office of Energy and Climate Change Policy, Nancy-Ann De Parle was named to head a new Office of Health Reform, and two other White House offices, addressed to Urban Affairs and Domestic Violence, were

---

[66] See Kirti Datla & Richard Revesz, *Deconstructing Independent Agencies (and Executive Agencies)*, 98 Cornell L. Rev. 769, 825 (2013) (listing 80 separate agencies). We discuss this article in Section 1C.

[67] The McCain quote appears in Steve Holland, *Obama Fashions a Government of Many Czars*, Reuters, May 29, 2009. The full electronic citation is available in Professor Saiger's article, 79 Fordham L. Rev. at 2578. The discussion in this part also draws on Lanora Pettit, *Cincinnatus or Caesar: American Czars and the Appointments Clause*, 26 J. of Law and Politics 81 (2010), and Kevin Sholette, *The American Czars*, 20 Cornell J. of L. & Pub. Pol'y 219 (2010).

headed by "czars."[68] Additionally, the Obama Administration named a number of czars with subject matter responsibilities who were nominally accountable to confirmed executive branch officers. Prominent examples in the first Obama administration include Steven Rattner, the "car czar," who helped orchestrate the multi-billion dollar bailout of General Motors and Chrysler (Rattner reported to the Treasury Secretary and the head of the National Economic Council), and Kenneth Feinberg, the "pay czar," who reviewed and approved—and in some instances strikingly reduced—compensation for executives at large financial firms that received federal funding under TARP, the Troubled Asset Relief Program (Feinberg was appointed by and reported to the Treasury Secretary).

From the President's standpoint, relying on these czars to define or structure administration policies in a particular field offers a range of benefits. Unlike agency heads, senior advisors are not confirmed by the Senate and they are not required to justify their actions to Congress through committee inquiries or hearings. Moreover, Congress cannot exercise oversight through its budgetary powers the way it does for agencies, because a czar's budget comes through the Executive Office of the President. Another benefit is that as a White House official, a czar may invoke executive privilege to the extent that it is available (but this may be contested and litigated—see the saga of White House advisors involved in the U.S. Attorney dismissals, discussed in Section 3A).

Finally, policy advice or guidance from White House czars is not subject to APA judicial review in the same way that agency guidance is. Although the APA defines "agency" to include any "authority of the Government of the United States" and does not specifically exclude the President (it does exclude a long list of actors including Congress and federal courts, see 5 U.S.C. § 551(1)), the Supreme Court has held that the President himself is not an agency under the APA. The Court excluded the President "[o]ut of respect for the separation of powers and [his] unique constitutional position." *Franklin v. Massachusetts*, 505 U.S. 788, 800–01 (1993). Thus the President's actions may not be reviewed for abuse of discretion under the APA (although they may still be reviewed for constitutionality; *Id.* at 801). What about the declarations, statements, or guidance documents issued by the director of the White House Office of Energy and Climate Change Policy—should these actions be reviewable for abuse of discretion under the APA? On what statutory basis could that Office be deemed subject to the public information and procedural requirements of APA sections 552 to 554?

In constitutional terms, consider the case of pay czar Kenneth Feinberg. In October 2009, Feinberg slashed compensation for executives in seven large financial firms by an average of 50%. Professor and former federal judge Michael McConnell argues that the nature of Feinberg's duties, setting compensation levels for certain large American businesses, made him an inferior officer within the Treasury Department, exercising significant authority pursuant to federal law. Because Feinberg was not confirmed by the Senate and the Secretary was not authorized by statute to appoint him absent Senate confirmation, McConnell

[68] See *Examining the History and Legality of Executive Branch Czars, Hearing Before the Senate Committee on the Judiciary*, 111th Cong., 96–98 (2011) (letter to Sen. Russell Feingold from White House Counsel Gregory Craig).

contends that Feinberg functioned in violation of the Appointments Clause. Are you convinced? Assume the Special Master position is not a continuing one (it is set to expire in three to six months); is its occupant a mere employee rather than any kind of officer? Alternatively, Congress long ago gave the Treasury Secretary authority to "delegate duties and powers . . . to another officer or employee of the Department of the Treasury." 31 U.S.C. § 321(b)(2). Is this language sufficient to vest in the Secretary Article II authority to appoint Feinberg as an inferior officer? See Federalist Society, *The Pay Czar and the Appointments Clause—A Forum*, November 19, 2009, available at http://www.fed-soc.org/debates/detail/the-pay-czar-the-appointments-clause-a-forum.

Suppose that Treasury Secretary Geitner had received Feinberg's recommended pay cuts and then issued them as orders under his own name? Wouldn't this remove the constitutional concerns? Why do you think President Obama and Secretary Geitner chose not to follow this course? To retain greater influence over how the TARP compensation review process was handled ex ante? To avoid the risk of reversal ex post by captured agency bureaucrats? Some other reason?

More broadly, to what extent does a White House focus on czars pursuing their field-specific mandates conflict with OIRA's efforts at coordination across agency domains? With OIRA's interest in receiving public input as part of the decision-making process? Former Administrator Sunstein lauded OIRA's efforts at information-aggregation as furthering the possibilities for transparency in the administration of government. Is this support for transparency at odds with the way policy czars seek to operate at the President's behest, free from congressional accountability or judicial review? Can these two relatively recent forms of presidential oversight be reconciled?

Barely a month into the new Obama Administration, Democrat Senator Robert Byrd sent the President a letter expressing his concerns about the establishment of various new White House policy offices. Byrd, whose illustrious Senate career included service with 11 Presidents, warned that "[t]he rapid and easy accumulation of power by White House staff can threaten the Constitutional system of checks and balances," and that in the past "White House staff have taken direction and control of programmatic areas that are the statutory responsibility of Senate-confirmed officials." In September 2009, Republican Senator Susan Collins and five other Republican senators sent a similar letter of concern to President Obama. In October, Democrat Russell Feingold and Independent Joseph Lieberman held separate Senate hearings addressing the constitutionality of the various czar appointments. Sparked by similar concerns, legislators introduced bills in both chambers during the 111th Congress proposing to curb or sunset the appointment of czars.

In early 2011, the White House announced that it was abolishing both the Office of Health Reform and the Office of Energy and Climate Change Policy, and that the work of these offices was now the responsibility of the Domestic Policy Council.

C. JUDICIAL REVIEW OF AGENCY RULES AND ORDERS

Section 2 of this chapter approached agency-court relations under the APA from the standpoint of how agencies implement legislative policy. We examined the requirements agencies face and the procedural strategies and tactics they adopt to regulate or guide the conduct of private parties and the general public. We now focus on court-agency relations under the APA as a primary form of judicial monitoring and oversight.

Judicial review of *agency action* under the APA is separate from judicial review of whether *agency statutory interpretation* is persuasive or reasonable. See chapter 9 § 3E (Notes to *Brand X*). Although both forms of review seek to assure that an agency's decision is sufficiently attentive to applicable congressional text and purposes, APA review focuses more on whether the agency's action includes an adequate response in *procedural terms* to material questions raised by commenters, and whether that response has a plausible *factual basis*. In short, courts reviewing agency action face a distinct set of challenges as they seek to assure that agencies have followed through on legislative policies, complied with procedural requirements, and adequately protected the interests of the affected public.

If the federal courts can use their review powers under the APA to enforce Congress's original directives upon the agency, then Congress presumably could feel more comfortable about delegating lawmaking authority to those agencies. Consistent with this idea and with the further idea that judicial review can counteract "capture" of the agency by "special interests," appellate judges in the 1960s and 1970s grew more aggressive, especially in the Court of Appeals for the District of Columbia Circuit. The main developments were (1) the establishment of a strong presumption in favor of judicial review of agency action or inaction, and the enlargement of the class of interests which can invoke judicial review; (2) more searching judicial review based upon a detailed agency justification for its decision, including an indication that reasonable alternatives were considered; and (3) judicial policing of informal lobbying of agency officials by special interests. See Richard Stewart, *The Reformation of American Administrative Law*, 88 Harv. L. Rev. 1669, 1716 (1975). As you examine these developments, consider the drawbacks of expanded judicial review.

1. *Expanding Judicial Review: The "Hard Look Doctrine."* The APA explicitly provides for judicial review of discretionary agency action under §§ 702–06. Formal adjudication and rulemaking must be supported by "substantial evidence"; informal action, including notice and comment rulemaking, must not be "arbitrary and capricious." In *Citizens to Preserve Overton Park, Inc. v. Volpe*, 401 U.S. 402 (1971), the Supreme Court applied the arbitrary and capricious standard in the context of an informal adjudication, where there was a written record and only a few public hearings, none of which rose to the level of a judicial proceeding. The Department of Transportation Act of 1966, 80 Stat. 931, codified at 49 U.S.C. § 1653(f) (1964, Supp. V, 1969), and the Federal-Aid Highway Act of 1966, 80 Stat. 771, codified at 23 U.S.C. § 138 (1964, Supp. V, 1969), prohibited the Secretary of Transportation from authorizing the use of federal funds to finance construction of highways through public parks if a "feasible and prudent" alternative route existed. Proposed

Interstate 40 would have cut across Overton Park, a 342–acre park in Memphis, Tennessee. Pursuant to the above statutes, the Secretary approved the highway project in 1968; concerned citizens and a national environmental group sued the Secretary, on the ground that it would be "feasible and prudent" to route I–40 around Overton Park.

The lower courts dismissed the lawsuit because of the Secretary's broad discretion to approve highway routes. The Supreme Court, in an opinion by Justice Marshall, reversed. The Court made short shrift of the Government's argument that informal, discretionary decisions are not reviewable. The Court saw nothing to meet the Court's standard of " 'clear and convincing evidence' of a * * * legislative intent" to restrict access to judicial review. *Abbott Laboratories v. Gardner*, 387 U.S. 136, 141 (1967). "Similarly, the Secretary's decision here does not fall within the exception for action 'committed to agency discretion.' This is a very narrow exception. * * * The legislative history of the Administrative Procedure Act indicates that it is applicable in those rare instances where 'statutes are drawn in such broad terms that in a given case there is no law to apply.' S. Rep. No. 752, 79th Cong., 1st Sess., 26 (1945)." Both relevant statutes provided that the Secretary "shall not approve any program or project" that requires the use of any public parkland "unless (1) there is no feasible and prudent alternative to the use of such land, and (2) such program includes all possible planning to minimize harm to such park. * * * " Such language was sufficiently directive to foreclose a finding that these determinations were committed to agency discretion.

The Court determined that review should be limited, however, to whether the Secretary's action was "arbitrary or capricious" under APA § 706(2)(A). The reviewing court should conduct a review that is "thorough, probing, in-depth" and "must consider whether the [agency] decision was based on a consideration of the relevant factors and whether there has been a clear error of judgment. * * * Although this inquiry into the facts is to be searching and careful, the ultimate standard of review is a narrow one. The court is not empowered to substitute its judgment for that of the agency." In *Overton Park*, the Court remanded the case to the district court to obtain from the Secretary a statement of reasons that might be reviewed. The Secretary on remand was ultimately unable to justify his decision and so declined to approve the parkland route. See *Citizens to Preserve Overton Park, Inc. v. Brinegar*, 494 F.2d 1212 (6th Cir. 1974), cert. denied, 421 U.S. 991 (1975). After more back-and-forth between local authorities and the Nixon, Ford, and Carter Administrations, the whole idea of an east-west expressway through Memphis was abandoned. The park and its protectors won. Had the public?

Peter Strauss has reassessed *Overton Park*.[69] Strauss found the statutory directive much less clear than Justice Marshall did and credited legislative history which assumed that the Secretary would consider the importance of the parkland, along with cost, community disruption, and other factors. The Secretary did consider park values, and plans were changed several times in response to park

---

[69] See Peter Strauss, *Revisiting* Overton Park: *Political and Judicial Controls over Administrative Actions Affecting the Community*, 39 U.C.L.A. L. Rev. 1251 (1992), deepened in Strauss, *Citizens to Preserve Overton Park v. Volpe—Of Politics and Law, Young Lawyers and the Highway Goliath*, in *Administrative Law Stories* 258–332 (Peter Strauss ed., 2006).

concerns. By requiring that parklands be given paramount rather than ordinary consideration, the Court was imposing values by judicial dictate on the Secretary that were not clearly those Congress had put into the statute. Strauss maintains that the political balance between park values and efficient roadbuilding values was disrupted by the Court's hurried, blunderbuss decision.

The Supreme Court struck a different balance in *Heckler v. Chaney*, 470 U.S. 821 (1985), which upheld the refusal by the Food and Drug Administration (FDA) to investigate the applicability of the federal food and drug standards to the use of lethal injections in some states as their means of imposing the death penalty. Justice Rehnquist's opinion for the Court stated that an agency's decision not to prosecute or enforce, whether through civil or criminal process, is a decision generally committed to an agency's absolute discretion. "[A]n agency decision not to enforce often involves a complicated balancing of a number of factors which are peculiarly within its expertise. Thus, the agency must not only assess whether a violation has occurred, but whether agency resources are best spent on this violation or another, whether the agency is likely to succeed if it acts, whether the particular enforcement action requested best fits the agency's overall policies, and indeed, whether the agency has enough resources to undertake the action at all." Additionally, when an agency refuses to prosecute, "it generally does not exercise its *coercive* power over an individual's liberty or property rights, and thus does not infringe upon areas that courts often are called upon to protect."

The *Overton Park* litigation was a signal not just that a presumption of reviewability under the APA was to be enthusiastically applied, but also that judicial scrutiny should have teeth. Such review has become known as the *hard look doctrine*, because courts scrutinize agency rationales and justifications so closely. See Harold Leventhal, *Environmental Decisionmaking and the Role of the Courts*, 122 U. Pa. L. Rev. 509 (1973); *Ethyl Corp. v. EPA*, 541 F.2d 1, 68–69 (D.C. Cir. 1976) (Leventhal, J., concurring). Hard-look review requires that the agency examine all relevant evidence, explain its decisions in detail, justify departures from past practices, and consider all reasonable alternatives before reaching a final policy decision. Hard look requires a well-reasoned explanation of agency policy; courts in most cases do not pass on the merits of the decision, merely the support the agency provides. Thus, in some cases, a rule that is remanded to the agency for further consideration is adopted again in similar form, but the agency provides a better explanation.

2. *Softening "Hard Look."* Critics of aggressive review of agency policy (*Overton Park*) worried that it led to agency *ossification* because second-guessing by nonexpert courts undermined agencies' ability to act decisively on important national policies.[70] And over time, judges have backed away from the hard-look

---

[70] See, e.g., R. Shep Melnick, *Administrative Law and Bureaucratic Reality*, 44 Admin. L. Rev. 245, 246 (1992) ("Judicial review has subjected agencies to debilitating delay and uncertainty. Courts have heaped new tasks on agencies while decreasing their ability to perform any of them. They have forced agencies to substitute trivial pursuits for important ones."). But see William Jordan, III, *Ossification Revisited: Does Arbitrary and Capricious Review Significantly Interfere with Agency Ability to Achieve Regulatory Goals Through Informal Rulemaking?*, 94 Nw. U. L. Rev. 393 (2000) (arguing that arbitrary and capricious review has not significantly impeded agencies in pursuit of policy goals). See also Mark Seidenfeld, *Demystifying*

doctrine. In *Syracuse Peace Council v. FCC*, 867 F.2d 654 (D.C. Cir. 1989), Judge Stephen Williams accepted the FCC's decision to reject the "fairness doctrine" that it had applied in the past to require broadcast media licensees to provide coverage of issues of public interest and to provide opportunities for the airing of contrasting viewpoints. The FCC claimed, *inter alia*, that the requirements of the fairness doctrine actually discouraged broadcasters from covering controversial issues. The study that "proved" a chilling effect on speech was based primarily on the representations of broadcasters in a survey. At its height, the hard look doctrine would have been applied to call into question this sort of evidence from arguably self-interested parties. Judge Williams' opinion seems more willing to give the benefit of the doubt to the expert regulatory commission, however. Furthermore, although Williams explicitly found that the FCC rule was based on a misunderstanding of the law, he did not remand it to the agency for a reconsideration. Rather, the correct understanding "appear[s] so obvious and compelling that a remand to extract the magic words from the Commission would be pure waste."

In a similar use of a soft-glance rather than a hard-look analysis, Judge Posner upheld regulations adopted by OSHA regulating occupational exposure to blood-borne pathogens, a rule designed to protect health care workers from hepatitis and AIDS. *Am. Dental Ass'n v. Martin*, 984 F.2d 823 (7th Cir. 1993), cert. denied, 510 U.S. 859 (1993). The opinion has a much more deferential tone than *Overton Park* and its progeny. Much regulation occurs under conditions of uncertainty, Posner argues, and in such cases, the conclusions of experts on technical issues "are entitled to respect by the nonspecialist, biomedically unsophisticated Article III judiciary, at least in the absence of a more systematic showing of harms" by the challengers. Whether these cases represent a trend away from hard look review, at least in the context of notice-and-comment rulemaking and other informal decisions, remains to be seen.

3. *Procedural Requirements in Rulemaking Proceedings.* When an agency engages in informal rulemaking, it is acting like a legislature (APA § 553) and so does not have to follow the formal procedures of adjudication (APA § 554), where the agency is acting like a court. Under a benign view of agency decisionmaking, this makes perfect sense. But if one fears that the agency has been captured by special interests, one fears that the informal rulemaking process might easily be "corrupted." A few decades ago, the D.C. Circuit considered procedural ways to open up such rulemaking, a process ostensibly halted by the Supreme Court. See Gillian Metzger, *The Story of Vermont Yankee: A Cautionary Tale of Judicial Review and Nuclear Waste*, in *Administrative Law Stories* 124–67 (Peter Strauss ed., 2006).

The D.C. Circuit in *Home Box Office, Inc. v. FCC*, 567 F.2d 9 (D.C. Cir. 1977), overturned rules easing limitations on cable and pay television programming in part because of evidence that the public docket for the proposed rules was "a sham" and the "real" deliberations had been conducted privately between the Commissioners and industry representatives. The Court read *Overton Park* to

---

Deossification: Rethinking Recent Proposals to Modify Judicial Review of Notice and Comment Rulemaking, 75 Tex. L. Rev. 483 (1997) (surveying and analyzing arguments and reform proposals).

require that agency decisions be rendered upon a record that discloses all relevant evidence and argumentation that the agency considered. Hence, a decision in which there were undisclosed *ex parte* communications was invalid.

Home Box Office generated great criticism. The introduction of this feature into informal rulemaking threatened a valuable flow of information. Not only do members of the industry have detailed, first-hand information that is intrinsically useful, but it could be a check on the information developed by agency staffs. The dialogue between administrators and the private sector is a necessary part of regulation. Retreating from *Home Box Office*, the D.C. Circuit in *Sierra Club v. Costle*, 657 F.2d 298, 402–04 (D.C. Cir. 1981), only required the EPA to docket descriptions of oral communications which are of "central relevance" to the rulemaking proceedings. The Court in *Sierra Club* also faced objections that the EPA's rule was invalid because of undisclosed contacts between agency decisionmakers and the White House and one Member of Congress, Senator Byrd (D–W.Va.). Judge Wald's opinion exempted most such contacts from the rule that *ex parte* communications be docketed, based upon principles of separation of powers.

Home Box Office was something of a judicial disaster, but its core idea—that agencies should observe judicial norms of openness when they affect private parties and the public interest—did not die. In the 1970s, the D.C. Circuit in some instances required some form of oral hearings, with cross-examination, in § 553 informal rulemaking. For example, in *Mobil Oil Corp. v. Federal Power Commission*, 483 F.2d 1238 (D.C. Cir. 1973), a suit to review the FPC's order setting minimum rates charged by natural gas pipelines for transporting liquid hydrocarbons, Judge Wilkey agreed that even when an agency is not statutorily required to engage in formal rulemaking, it must in some circumstances afford interested persons an opportunity to test the evidence upon which the agency intends to rely. The Court held that "the rule that the 'whole record' be considered—both evidence for and against—means that procedures must provide some mechanism for interested parties to introduce adverse evidence and criticize evidence introduced by others" (*Id.* at 1258). See also *International Harvester Co. v. Ruckelshaus*, 478 F.2d 615 (D.C. Cir. 1973) (Leventhal, J.), analyzed in Stephen Williams, *"Hybrid Rulemaking" Under the Administrative Procedure Act: A Legal and Empirical Analysis*, 42 U. Chi. L. Rev. 401 (1975).

The Supreme Court, however, was hostile to "judicializing" rulemaking proceedings. See, for example, *United States v. Fla. E. Coast Ry. Co.*, 410 U.S. 224 (1973), discussed at length in Section 2A3. And the Court's decision in *Vermont Yankee Nuclear Power Co. v. Natural Resources Defense Council, Inc.*, 435 U.S. 519 (1978), is a milestone for the administrative state because the Court passed on the legitimacy of judicially imposed hybrid procedures. See Metzger, *The Story of Vermont Yankee*, for a comprehensive analysis.

In 1971, Vermont Yankee applied to the Atomic Energy Commission for a license to operate a nuclear plant in Vernon, Vermont. NRDC opposed the application, in part because of alleged environmental effects of operations to reprocess fuel or to dispose of wastes resulting from the reprocessing operations. The environmental issue was excluded from consideration by the Licensing Board which conducted the adjudicatory hearing, but in 1972 the Commission itself began rulemaking proceedings on the issue of what consideration should be given by the Licensing Board to the environmental effects of the uranium fuel cycle. The Commission's notice set forth two possible rules. In 1973, the Commission scheduled a hearing on the alternative rules and made available to the public an Environmental Survey prepared by its staff. Both written and oral comments were received, and the Commission in 1974 issued a rule requiring consideration of such environmental impact. Although that rule was inconsistent with the practice of the Licensing Board in the Vermont Yankee proceeding, the Commission affirmed the grant of an operating license to Vermont Yankee. On appeal, the D.C. Circuit found that although the Commission had followed all the § 553 procedures for informal rulemaking, and more, the procedures were inadequate overall; the court remanded for the agency to follow procedures permitting greater public scrutiny of information upon which the Commission relied.

The Supreme Court, in an opinion by Justice Rehnquist, pointedly criticized the D.C. Circuit's "Monday morning quarterbacking" of the agency's procedures. Rehnquist cited *Florida East Coast Railway* for the proposition that § 553 of the APA "established the maximum procedural requirements which Congress was willing to have the courts impose upon agencies in conducting rulemaking procedures." While "[t]his is not to say necessarily that there are no circumstances which would ever justify a court in overturning agency action because of a failure to employ procedures beyond those required by statute * * * such circumstances, if they exist, are extremely rare." Moreover, apart from the APA, "this Court has for more than four decades emphasized that the formulation of procedures was basically to be left within the discretion of the agencies to which Congress had confided the responsibility for substantive judgments." The Court reversed the D.C. Circuit's invalidation of the procedures used in the agency's informal rulemaking and remanded to the D.C. Circuit to review the rule on the merits.

Does *Vermont Yankee* implicitly overrule *Home Box Office? Mobil Oil?* Is there any way to distinguish those cases?[71] Notwithstanding *Vermont Yankee*, federal courts of appeals have continued to impose procedural requirements on "informal" rulemaking—but under cover of liberally "interpreting" the notice-and-comment requirements of § 553, rather than imposing them as a matter of administrative common law. See Gary Lawson, *Federal Administrative Law* 240–83 (4th ed. 2007) (disapproving); Metzger, *Story of Vermont Yankee* (acquiescent).

---

[71] For a fascinating discussion of *Vermont Yankee*, particularly given his prominence as a textualist, see Antonin Scalia, Vermont Yankee: *The APA, The D.C. Circuit, and the Supreme Court*, 1978 Sup. Ct. Rev. 345. For an illuminating debate about the case, see Clark Byse, Vermont Yankee *and the Evolution of Administrative Procedure: A Somewhat Different View*, 91 Harv. L. Rev. 1823 (1978); Richard Stewart, Vermont Yankee *and the Evolution of Administrative Procedure*, 91 Harv. L. Rev. 1805 (1978).

MOTOR VEHICLE MANUFACTURERS ASS'N V. STATE FARM MUTUAL AUTOMOBILE INS. CO.

Supreme Court of the United States, 1983.
463 U.S. 29, 103 S.Ct. 2856, 77 L. Ed. 2d 443.

JUSTICE WHITE delivered the opinion of the Court.

The development of the automobile gave Americans unprecedented freedom to travel, but exacted a high price for enhanced mobility. Since 1929, motor vehicles have been the leading cause of accidental deaths and injuries in the United States. * * * Congress responded by enacting the National Traffic and Motor Vehicle Safety Act of 1966. The Act, created for the purpose of "reduc[ing] traffic accidents and deaths and injuries to persons resulting from traffic accidents," 15 U.S.C. § 1381, directs the Secretary of Transportation or his delegate to issue motor vehicle safety standards that "shall be practicable, shall meet the need for motor vehicle safety, and shall be stated in objective terms." 15 U.S.C. § 1392(a). In issuing these standards, the Secretary is directed to consider "relevant available motor vehicle safety data," whether the proposed standard "is reasonable, practicable and appropriate" for the particular type of motor vehicle, and the "extent to which such standards will contribute to carrying out the purposes" of the Act. 15 U.S.C. § 1392(f)(1),(3), (4).

The Act also authorizes judicial review under the provisions of the Administrative Procedure Act (APA), 5 U.S.C. § 706, of all "orders establishing, amending, or revoking a Federal motor vehicle safety standard," 15 U.S.C. § 1392(b). Under this authority, we review today whether NHTSA acted arbitrarily and capriciously in revoking the requirement in Motor Vehicle Safety Standard 208 that new motor vehicles produced after September 1982 be equipped with passive restraints to protect the safety of the occupants of the vehicle in the event of a collision. Briefly summarized, we hold that the agency failed to present an adequate basis and explanation for rescinding the passive restraint requirement and that the agency must either consider the matter further or adhere to or amend Standard 208 along lines which its analysis supports.

[I] As originally issued by the Department of Transportation in 1967, Standard 208 simply required the installation of seatbelts in all automobiles. 32 Fed. Reg. 2408, 2415 (Feb. 3, 1967). It soon became apparent that the level of seatbelt use was too low to reduce traffic injuries to an acceptable level. The Department therefore began consideration of "passive occupant restraint systems"—devices that do not depend for their effectiveness upon any action taken by the occupant except that necessary to operate the vehicle. Two types of automatic crash protection emerged: automatic seatbelts and airbags. The automatic seatbelt is a traditional safety belt, which when fastened to the interior of the door remains attached without impeding entry or exit from the vehicle, and deploys automatically without any action on the part of the passenger. The airbag is an inflatable device concealed in the dashboard and steering column. It automatically inflates when a sensor indicates that deceleration forces from an accident have exceeded a preset minimum, then rapidly deflates to dissipate those forces. The life-saving potential of these devices was immediately recognized, and in 1977, after substantial on-the-road experience with both devices, it was estimated by NHTSA that passive restraints could prevent approximately 12,000 deaths and over 100,000 serious injuries annually. 42 Fed. Reg. 34,298.

In 1969, the Department formally proposed a standard requiring the installation of passive restraints, 34 Fed. Reg. 11,148 (July 2, 1969), thereby commencing a lengthy series of proceedings. In 1970, the agency revised Standard 208 to include passive protection requirements, 35 Fed. Reg. 16,927 (Nov. 3, 1970), and in 1972, the agency amended the standard to require full passive protection for all front seat occupants of vehicles manufactured after August 15, 1975. 37 Fed. Reg. 3911 (Feb. 24, 1972). In the interim, vehicles built between August 1973 and August 1975 were to carry either passive restraints or lap and shoulder belts coupled with an "ignition interlock" that would prevent starting the vehicle if the belts were not connected. On review, the agency's decision to require passive restraints was found to be supported by "substantial evidence" and upheld. *Chrysler Corp. v. Dep't of Transp.*, 472 F.2d 659 (6th Cir. 1972).

In preparing for the upcoming model year, most car makers chose the "ignition interlock" option, a decision which was highly unpopular, and led Congress to amend the Act to prohibit a motor vehicle safety standard from requiring or permitting compliance by means of an ignition interlock or a continuous buzzer designed to indicate that safety belts were not in use. Motor Vehicle and Schoolbus Safety Amendments of 1974, Pub. L. 93–492, § 109, 88 Stat. 1482, 15 U.S.C. § 1410b(b). The 1974 Amendments also provided that any safety standard that could be satisfied by a system other than seatbelts would have to be submitted to Congress where it could be vetoed by concurrent resolution of both houses. 15 U.S.C. § 1410b(b)(2).

The effective date for mandatory passive restraint systems was extended for a year until August 31, 1976. 40 Fed. Reg. 16,217 (April 10, 1975); *id.* at 33,977 (Aug. 13, 1975). But in June 1976, Secretary of Transportation William T. Coleman, Jr., initiated a new rulemaking on the issue, 41 Fed. Reg. 24,070 (June 9, 1976). After hearing testimony and reviewing written comments, Coleman extended the optional alternatives indefinitely and suspended the passive restraint requirement. Although he found passive restraints technologically and economically feasible, the Secretary based his decision on the expectation that there would be widespread public resistance to the new systems. He instead proposed a demonstration project involving up to 500,000 cars installed with passive restraints, in order to smooth the way for public acceptance of mandatory passive restraints at a later date. Department of Transportation, *The Secretary's Decision Concerning Motor Vehicle Occupant Crash Protection* (December 6, 1976).

Coleman's successor as Secretary of Transportation disagreed. Within months of assuming office, Secretary Brock Adams decided that the demonstration project was unnecessary. He issued a new mandatory passive restraint regulation, known as Modified Standard 208. 42 Fed. Reg. 34,289 (July 5, 1977); 42 CFR § 571.208 (1978). The Modified Standard mandated the phasing in of passive restraints beginning with large cars in model year 1982 and extending to all cars by model year 1984. The two principal systems that would satisfy the Standard were airbags and passive belts; the choice of which system to install was left to the manufacturers. In *Pacific Legal Foundation v. Department of Transportation*, 593 F.2d 1338 (D.C. Cir.), cert. denied, 444 U.S. 830 (1979), the Court of Appeals upheld Modified Standard 208 as a rational, nonarbitrary regulation consistent with the agency's mandate under the Act. The standard also survived scrutiny by Congress, which did not exercise its authority under the legislative veto provision of the 1974 Amendments.

Over the next several years, the automobile industry geared up to comply with Modified Standard 208. As late as July, 1980, NHTSA reported:

> "On the road experience in thousands of vehicles equipped with airbags and automatic safety belts has confirmed agency estimates of the life-saving and injury-preventing benefits of such systems. When all cars are equipped with automatic crash protection systems, each year an estimated 9,000 more lives will be saved and tens of thousands of serious injuries will be prevented."

NHTSA, Automobile Occupant Crash Protection, Progress Report No. 3, p. 4. In February 1981, however, Secretary of Transportation Andrew Lewis reopened the rulemaking due to changed economic circumstances and, in particular, the difficulties of the automobile industry. 46 Fed. Reg. 12,033 (Feb. 12, 1981). Two months later, the agency ordered a one-year delay in the application of the standard to large cars, extending the deadline to September 1982, 46 Fed. Reg. 21,172 (April 9, 1981) and at the same time, proposed the possible rescission of the entire standard. 46 Fed. Reg. 21,205 (April 9, 1981). After receiving written comments and holding public hearings, NHTSA issued a final rule (Notice 25) that rescinded the passive restraint requirement contained in Modified Standard 208.

[II] In a statement explaining the rescission, NHTSA maintained that it was no longer able to find, as it had in 1977, that the automatic restraint requirement would produce significant safety benefits. Notice 25, 46 Fed. Reg. 53,419 (Oct. 29, 1981). This judgment reflected not a change of opinion on the effectiveness of the technology, but a change in plans by the automobile industry. In 1977, the agency had assumed that airbags would be installed in 60% of all new cars and automatic seatbelts in 40%. By 1981 it became apparent that automobile manufacturers planned to install the automatic seatbelts in approximately 99% of the new cars. For this reason, the life-saving potential of airbags would not be realized. Moreover, it now appeared that the overwhelming majority of passive belts planned to be installed by manufacturers could be detached easily and left that way permanently. Passive belts, once detached, then required "the same type of affirmative action that is the stumbling block to obtaining high usage levels of manual belts." 46 Fed. Reg., at 53,421. For this reason, the agency concluded that there was no longer a basis for reliably predicting that the standard would lead to any significant increased usage of restraints at all.

In view of the possibly minimal safety benefits, the automatic restraint requirement no longer was reasonable or practicable in the agency's view. The requirement would require approximately $1 billion to implement and the agency did not believe it would be reasonable to impose such substantial costs on manufacturers and consumers without more adequate assurance that sufficient safety benefits would accrue. In addition, NHTSA concluded that automatic restraints might have an adverse effect on the public's attitude toward safety. Given the high expense and limited benefits of detachable belts, NHTSA feared that many consumers would regard the standard as an instance of ineffective regulation, adversely affecting the public's view of safety regulation and, in particular, "poisoning . . . popular sentiment toward efforts to improve occupant restraint systems in the future." 46 Fed. Reg., at 53424.

[The United States Court of Appeals for the District of Columbia Circuit invalidated the agency's rule rescinding the passive restraint requirement, on the ground that it was arbitrary and capricious and therefore in violation of the APA. 680 F.2d 206 (1982).]

[III. The Court held that the APA fully applied to NHTSA's rulemaking proceeding, and that a reviewing court has an obligation to set aside any rule found to be "arbitrary, capricious, an abuse of discretion, or otherwise not in accordance with law." 5 U.S.C. § 706(2)(A); see *Overton Park*. The Court rejected Motor Vehicle's argument that an agency's rescission of a rule should be governed by the same narrow standard as the agency's refusal to issue a rule in the first place.]

[Justice White explained the "arbitrary and capricious" standard of review.] [T]he agency must examine the relevant data and articulate a satisfactory explanation for its action including a "rational connection between the facts found and the choice made." *Burlington Truck Lines Inc. v. United States*, 371 U.S. 156, 168 (1962). In reviewing that explanation, we must "consider whether the decision was based on a consideration of the relevant factors and whether there has been a clear error of judgment." *Bowman Transp. Inc. v. Arkansas-Best Freight System*, [419 U.S. 281, 285 (1974)]. Normally, an agency rule would be arbitrary and capricious if the agency has relied on factors which Congress has not intended it to consider, entirely failed to consider an important aspect of the problem, offered an explanation for its decision that runs counter to the evidence before the agency, or is so implausible that it could not be ascribed to a difference in view or the product of agency expertise. The reviewing court should not attempt itself to make up for such deficiencies; we may not supply a reasoned basis for the agency's action that the agency itself has not given. * * * For purposes of these cases, it is also relevant that Congress required a record of the rulemaking proceedings to be compiled and submitted to a reviewing court, 15 U.S.C. § 1394, and intended that agency findings under the Motor Vehicle Safety Act would be supported by "substantial evidence on the record considered as a whole." S. Rep. No. 1301, 89th Cong., 2d Sess. 8 (1966); H.R. Rep. No. 1776, 89th Cong., 2d Sess. 21 (1966).

[In Part IV, Justice White rejected the lower court's requirement that NHTSA was obligated to provide "increasingly clear and convincing reasons" for its action. The Court of Appeals relied on post-1974 congressional signals (such as Congress's failure to override the Carter-era NHTSA initiatives) to infer a "congressional commitment to the concept of automatic crash protection devices for vehicle occupants." Justice White found the lower court's reading of the materials misguided. Also, "this Court has never suggested that the *standard* of review is enlarged or diminished by subsequent congressional action. While an agency's interpretation of a statute may be confirmed or ratified by subsequent congressional failure to change that interpretation, *Bob Jones University* [Chapter 6B3], in the cases before us, even an unequivocal ratification—short of statutory incorporation—of the passive restraint standard would not connote approval or disapproval of an agency's later decision to rescind the regulation. That decision remains subject to the arbitrary and capricious standard."]

[V] The ultimate question before us is whether NHTSA's rescission of the passive restraint requirement of Standard 208 was arbitrary and capricious. We conclude, as did the Court of Appeals, that it was. We also conclude, but for somewhat different reasons, that further consideration of the issue by the agency is therefore required. * * *

[A] The first and most obvious reason for finding the rescission arbitrary and capricious is that NHTSA apparently gave no consideration whatever to modifying the Standard to require that airbag technology be utilized. Standard 208 sought to achieve automatic crash protection by requiring automobile manufacturers to install either of two passive restraint devices: airbags or automatic seatbelts. There was no suggestion in the long rulemaking process that led to Standard 208 that if only one of these options were feasible, no passive restraint standard should be promulgated. Indeed, the agency's original proposed Standard contemplated the installation of inflatable restraints in all cars. Automatic belts were added as a means of complying with the standard because they were believed to be as effective as airbags in achieving the goal of occupant crash protection. 36 Fed. Reg. 12,858, 12,859 (July 8, 1971). At that time, the passive belt approved by the agency could not be detached. Only later, at a manufacturer's behest, did the agency approve of the detachability feature—and only after assurances that the feature would not compromise the safety benefits of the restraint. Although it was then foreseen that 60% of the new cars would contain airbags and 40% would have automatic seatbelts, the ratio between the two was not significant as long as the passive belt would also assure greater passenger safety.

The agency has now determined that the detachable automatic belts will not attain anticipated safety benefits because so many individuals will detach the mechanism. Even if this conclusion were acceptable in its entirety, standing alone it would not justify any more than an amendment of Standard 208 to disallow compliance by means of the one technology which will not provide effective passenger protection. It does not cast doubt on the need for a passive restraint standard or upon the efficacy of airbag technology. In its most recent rulemaking, the agency again acknowledged the lifesaving potential of the airbag:

> "The agency has no basis at this time for changing its earlier conclusions in 1976 and 1977 that basic airbag technology is sound and has been sufficiently demonstrated to be effective in those vehicles in current use. . . ."

NHTSA Final Regulatory Impact Analysis (RIA) at XI–4 (Oct. 1981). Given the effectiveness ascribed to airbag technology by the agency, the mandate of the Act to achieve traffic safety would suggest that the logical response to the faults of detachable seatbelts would be to require the installation of airbags. At the very least this alternative way of achieving the objectives of the Act should have been addressed and adequate reasons given for its abandonment. But the agency not only did not require compliance through airbags, it also did not even consider the possibility in its 1981 rulemaking. Not one sentence of its rulemaking statement discusses the airbags-only option. * * * [W]hat we said in *Burlington Truck Lines v. United States* is apropos here:

> "There are no findings and no analysis here to justify the choice made, no indication of the basis on which the [agency] exercised its expert discretion. We are not prepared to and the Administrative Procedure Act will not permit us to accept such . . . practice. . . . Expert discretion is the lifeblood of the administrative process, but 'unless we make the requirements for administrative action strict and demanding, *expertise*, the strength of modern government, can become a monster which rules with no practical limits on its discretion."

We have frequently reiterated that an agency must cogently explain why it has exercised its discretion in a given manner, and we reaffirm this principle again today.

The automobile industry has opted for the passive belt over the airbag, but surely it is not enough that the regulated industry has eschewed a given safety device. For nearly a decade, the automobile industry waged the regulatory equivalent of war against the airbag and lost—the inflatable restraint was proved sufficiently effective. Now the automobile industry has decided to employ a seatbelt system which will not meet the safety objectives of Standard 208. This hardly constitutes cause to revoke the Standard itself. Indeed, the Motor Vehicle Safety Act was necessary because the industry was not sufficiently responsive to safety concerns. The Act intended that safety standards not depend on current technology and could be "technology-forcing" in the sense of inducing the development of superior safety design. If, under the statute, the agency should not defer to the industry's failure to develop safer cars, which it surely should not do, *a fortiori* it may not revoke a safety standard which can be satisfied by current technology simply because the industry has opted for an ineffective seatbelt design. * * *

[In Part V—B, Justice White ruled that NHTSA was "too quick to dismiss the safety benefits of automatic seatbelts." Although an agency may decline to issue and may revoke a safety standard on the basis of serious uncertainties about its efficacy, those uncertainties must be supported in the administrative record and reasonably explained. In this case, there was no direct evidence in the record supporting NHTSA's finding that detachable automatic belts cannot be predicted to yield a substantial increase in usage. Evidence in the record revealed more than a doubling of seat belt use under those circumstances. For one example, Volkswagen between 1975 and 1980 sold 350,000 Rabbits equipped with passive seatbelts guarded by an ignition interlock. NHTSA found that seatbelt use in Rabbits averaged 34% where the cars had regular manual belts, and 84% for the detachable passive belts. Although Justice White maintained that the agency had discretion to refuse to generalize from studies of Rabbit drivers to the general population of drivers, the agency was required to consider a fact that it neglected but that critically distinguishes detachable automatic belts and ordinary manual ones: A detachable passive belt requires an affirmative act to detach it, while a manual belt can be safely ignored. "Thus, inertia—a factor which the agency's own studies have found significant in explaining the current low usage rates for seatbelts—works in favor of, not against, use of the protective device." This would suggest that seatbelt use by occasional users would be substantially increased by detachable passive belts. "Whether this is in fact the case is a matter for the agency to decide, but it must bring its expertise to bear on the question."]

The agency is correct to look at the costs as well as the benefits of Standard 208. The agency's conclusion that the incremental costs of the requirements were no longer reasonable was predicated on its prediction that the safety benefits of the regulation might be minimal. Specifically, the agency's fears that the public may resent paying more for the automatic belt systems is expressly dependent on the assumption that detachable automatic belts will not produce more than "negligible safety benefits." 46 Fed. Reg., at 53,424. When the agency reexamines its findings as to the likely increase in seatbelt usage, it must also reconsider its judgment of the reasonableness of the monetary and other costs associated with the Standard. In reaching its judgment, NHTSA should bear in mind that Congress intended safety to be the preeminent factor under the Motor Vehicle Safety Act. [Quoting committee reports for the Safety Act.] * * *

JUSTICE REHNQUIST, with whom THE CHIEF JUSTICE [BURGER], JUSTICE POWELL, and JUSTICE O'CONNOR join, concurring in part and dissenting in part.

I join Parts I, II, III, IV, and V–A of the Court's opinion. In particular, I agree that, since the airbag and continuous spool automatic seatbelt were explicitly approved in the standard the agency was rescinding, the agency should explain why it declined to leave those requirements intact. In this case, the agency gave no explanation at all. Of course, if the agency can provide a rational explanation, it may adhere to its decision to rescind the entire standard.

I do not believe, however, that NHTSA's view of detachable automatic seatbelts was arbitrary and capricious. The agency adequately explained its decision to rescind the standard insofar as it was satisfied by detachable belts.

The statute that requires the Secretary of Transportation to issue motor vehicle safety standards also requires that "[e]ach such ... standard shall be practicable [and] shall meet the need for motor vehicle safety." 15 U.S.C. § 1392(a). The Court rejects the agency's explanation for its conclusion that there is substantial uncertainty whether requiring installation of detachable automatic belts would substantially increase seatbelt usage. The agency chose not to rely on a study showing a substantial increase in seatbelt usage in cars equipped with automatic seatbelts and an ignition interlock to prevent the car from being operated when the belts were not in place *and* which were voluntarily purchased with this equipment by consumers. It is reasonable for the agency to decide that this study does not support any conclusion concerning the effect of automatic seatbelts that are installed in all cars whether the consumer wants them or not and are not linked to an ignition interlock system.

The Court rejects this explanation because "there would seem to be grounds to believe that seatbelt use by occasional users will be substantially increased by the detachable passive belts," and the agency did not adequately explain its rejection of these grounds. It seems to me that the agency's explanation, while by no means a model, is adequate. The agency acknowledged that there would probably be some increase in belt usage, but concluded that the increase would be small and not worth the cost of mandatory detachable automatic belts. 46 Fed. Reg. 53,421–54,323 (1981). The agency's obligation is to articulate a "'rational connection between the facts found and the choice made.'" I believe it has met this standard. * * *

The agency's changed view of the standard seems to be related to the election of a new President of a different political party. It is readily apparent that the responsible members of one administration may consider public resistance and uncertainties to be more important than do their counterparts in a previous administration. A change in administration brought about by the people casting their votes is a perfectly reasonable basis for an executive agency's reappraisal of the costs and benefits of its programs and regulations. As long as the agency remains within the bounds established by Congress, it is entitled to assess administrative records and evaluate priorities in light of the philosophy of the administration.

NOTES ON STATE FARM

1. *Right or Wrong?* Did the Court do the right thing in this case—either from the Court's point of view, or the nation's? Write down your answer in the margin, and read on.

2. *The Proper Role of the Judiciary in the Implementation of Public Policy?* In light of the national experience with implementation of the Safety Act, what do you think the role of the Court should be: (1) Agent of Congress? If so, which Congress—the enacting one, the amending one, or the current one? (2) Independent principal, imposing the Court's own values, thwarting agencies implementing bad policies, and rewarding agencies that protect the Court's conception of the public interest? (3) Independent principal, imposing rule of law values? If so, what does the rule of law require in *State Farm?*

Chapter 11 of Mashaw and Harfst's book asks this question: Does the participation of the judiciary in the statutory implementation game advance the public interest? Their analysis suggests some doubt that the Court performs a useful role. The judiciary is the forum of choice whenever the government tries to upset traditional ways of doing things (ways easily translated into "rights"). Thus, the courts were a forum for the auto industry to harass the agency and delay implementation of its rules. The proceduralization of the rulemaking process rendered it less decisive and more vulnerable to shifts in public opinion and presidential leadership. Recall the wild shifts in Standard 208 from the Johnson Administration to the Nixon-Ford Administration to the Carter Administration to the Reagan Administration.

Adverse judicial decisions in the 1970s (the hard look decade) directly contributed to the interlock debacle and contributed less directly to an increasingly cautious attitude toward regulation. For example, *Chrysler* required "objective" testing

standards that the agency's "dummy" regulations did not meet. This requirement discouraged the agency from imposing rules before it had "objective" scientific evidence well in hand, and thereby prevented the sort of experimentation and technology-forcing rules that the early experts thought were necessary to make genuine advances to reduce auto injuries and fatalities. More generally, the adverse judicial decisions discouraged NHTSA from proceeding by rulemaking, which had been the agency's original mandate and was probably its only hope for regulatory success. Favorable judicial decisions in response to NHTSA's recall campaigns, on the other hand, encouraged the agency to rely more and more heavily on that less effective regulatory mechanism. Like a Pavlovian dog, NHTSA was trained by the judiciary to quail at the thought of rules and salivate at the prospect of recalls.

Mashaw and Harfst are pessimistic about the role of the "legal culture" and of multiple principals in our administrative state of separated powers. "[T]he combination of congressional oversight and appropriations, Executive Office intervention and monitoring, and judicial review, has sharply limited the degree to which NHTSA could translate [its regulatory] aspirations into concrete technological requirements." Jerry Mashaw & David Harfst, *The Struggle for Auto Safety* 228 (1990). Do you find this level of pessimism persuasive? Jot down your initial thoughts in the margin, and then read the next note.

3. *The Aftermath of* State Farm. Transportation Secretary Elizabeth Dole initiated rulemaking to answer the Court's inquiries, and 7,800 comments were filed. On July 17, 1984, Dole issued the final rule, which (1) dropped mandatory airbags like a lead balloon and (2) required phasing in "automatic occupant restraints" (including airbags as an option for the manufacturer) between 1986 and 1989, unless (3) before April 1, 1989, two-thirds of the U.S. population are covered by state mandatory seat belt use laws meeting NHTSA's conditions. 49 Fed. Reg. 28,962–63 (1984).

With the support of the auto industry as well as new groups such as Mothers Against Drunk Driving (MADD), almost all the states adopted mandatory seatbelt laws—although most were careful *not to* satisfy the requirements of the Dole rule. "As a consequence, the American public got both airbags and mandatory use laws." Mashaw, *Law, Science, and Politics*, in *Administrative Law Stories* 385. Most surprisingly, *both* kinds of regulations captured the imagination of Americans. We the People started buckling up in record numbers *and* demanded more airbags from manufacturers than the law required. Professor Mashaw reports these results with no dimming of his customary pessimism, but do they suggest that the judiciary might play a productive role in the evolution of statutory policy?

Presumably in response (at least partly) to the public's persisting appetite, Congress and NHTSA have remained active on both airbags and seatbelts. The Intermodal Surface Transportation Efficiency Act of 1991 (ISTEA) ordered NHTSA to require both driver's side and passenger air-bags in all new vehicles by 1998 while subsequent legislation also ordered NHTSA to issue a rule that would minimize the risks to children and other occupants from injuries or deaths caused by airbags. NHTSA's 2000 regulation specified a range of design requirements to diminish the risk of serious airbag-induced injuries.

On seatbelts, ISTEA required equipping the driver and passenger side front seats with a lap/shoulder seat belt. In its 2002 Conference Report accompanying the DOT Appropriations Act, Congress requested that NHTSA study seat belt reminder technologies with a goal of further increasing seat belt use. Current federal standards require all new vehicles to be equipped with a "basic" seat belt reminder system, consisting of an audible signal and warning light that are activated immediately after the vehicle is started: the signal continues for four to eight seconds and the light for at least 60 seconds if the driver is not belted. Studies conducted by NHTSA in 2013 indicate that most vehicle manufacturers equip their vehicles with enhanced safety belt reminder systems.

Contrast all this congressional and agency involvement with McDonald's more skeptical account. Looking back on decades of expensive federal regulation of auto safety, he argues that NHTSA's focus on passive standards has reduced occupant fatality risk by only 15–20%, not an impressive amount given the tens of billions of dollars in cost and the much greater traffic safety achieved in Canada, Europe, and Australia, which focus on seat belts and driver error. Kevin McDonald, *Shifting Out of Park: Moving Auto Safety from Recalls to Reason*, 18–19 (2006); Leonard Evans, *Traffic Safety* 117 (2004). Indeed, in the United States, reducing the speed limit has had greater safety effects than all the design changes posed by NHTSA. McDonald, 42 n.65.

FCC v. Fox Television Stations, Inc.
556 U.S. 502 (2009).

Federal law prohibits the broadcasting of "any . . . indecent . . . language," 18 U.S.C. § 1464, which includes expletives referring to sexual or excretory activity or organs, see *FCC v. Pacifica Foundation*, 438 U.S. 726 (1978). For many years, the FCC followed an announced regulatory approach that banned sexual or excretory "expletives" only if their use was "deliberate and repetitive"; mere "fleeting" expletives would generally be allowed. Even as the FCC expanded its indecency standard to encompass ever more words and phrases, it preserved this approach—until a 2006 FCC ruling against Fox. In that ruling, the FCC rejected its longstanding distinction between "expletive" and "literal" uses of terms like "fuck" as "artificial." Also, the FCC ended its tolerance for "fleeting" expletives, finding that they have the power to offend parents and children and that permitting them gives broadcasters too much freedom to be offensive.

Invoking the Supreme Court's decision in *State Farm*, the Second Circuit overturned the agency's order against Fox, on the ground that the FCC had not adequately explained why it was jettisoning its longstanding rule The Supreme Court reversed in a 5–4 vote, in an opinion by **Justice Scalia**. "We find no basis in the Administrative Procedure Act or in our opinions for a requirement that all agency [action that changes prior policy] be subjected to more searching review. The Act mentions no such heightened standard. And our opinion in *State Farm* neither held nor implied that every agency action representing a policy change must be justified by reasons more substantial than those required to adopt a policy in the first instance. That case, which involved the rescission of a prior regulation, said only that such action requires 'a reasoned analysis for the change beyond that which may be required when an agency *does not act* in the first instance.' ([E]mphasis added). Treating failures to act and rescissions of prior action differently for purposes of the standard of review makes good sense, and has basis in the text of the [APA], which likewise treats the two separately. It instructs a reviewing court to 'compel agency action unlawfully withheld or unreasonably delayed,' 5 U.S.C. § 706(1), and to 'hold unlawful and set aside agency action, findings, and conclusions found to be [among other things] . . . arbitrary [or] capricious,' § 706(2)(A). The statute makes no distinction, however, between initial agency action and subsequent agency action undoing or revising that action.

"To be sure, the requirement that an agency provide reasoned explanation for its action would ordinarily demand that it display awareness that it *is* changing position. An agency may not, for example, depart from a prior policy *sub silentio* or simply disregard rules that are still on the books. And of course the agency must show that there are good reasons for the new policy. But it need not demonstrate to a court's satisfaction that the reasons for the new policy are *better* than the reasons for the old one; it suffices that the new policy is permissible under the statute, that there are good reasons for it, and that the agency *believes* it to be better, which the conscious change of course adequately indicates. This means that the agency need not always provide a more detailed justification than what would suffice for a new policy created on a blank slate. Sometimes it must—when, for example, its new policy rests upon factual findings that contradict those which underlay its prior policy; or when its prior policy has engendered serious reliance interests that must be taken into account. It would be arbitrary or capricious to ignore such matters. In such cases it is not that further justification is demanded by the mere fact of policy change; but that a reasoned explanation is needed for disregarding facts and circumstances that underlay or were engendered by the prior policy."

Under this understanding of the law, Justice Scalia ruled that the FCC's order was not "arbitrary and capricious." The FCC had "forthrightly acknowledged" that it was creating new policy and repudiating inconsistent prior actions taken by the Commission and staff. Also, the FCC's reasons for its decision were "entirely rational." It was reasonable for the FCC to conclude that the literal-expletive distinction was nonsensical given that both kinds of uses could cause offense and subject children to a harmful "first blow" of indecency; given technological advances, it was reasonable for the FCC to expect broadcasters to "bleep out" even fleeting expletives.

Justice Kennedy, whose vote was needed to obtain a majority, joined Justice Scalia's opinion as to all of the foregoing matters but issued a concurring opinion that adopted a more situation-specific approach. "Where there is a policy change the record may be much more developed because the agency based its prior policy on factual findings. In that instance, an agency's decision to change course may be arbitrary and capricious if the agency ignores or countermands its earlier factual findings without reasoned explanation for doing so. An agency cannot simply disregard contrary or inconvenient factual determinations that it made in the past, any more than it can ignore inconvenient facts when it writes on a blank slate." This is the lesson Justice Kennedy drew from *State Farm*. "The present case does not raise the concerns addressed in *State Farm*" because the FCC had based its prior policy not on factual findings, but on its interpretation of the Court's *Pacifica* ruling, and had given appropriate reasons for changing its policy.

Justice Stevens dissented in an opinion emphasizing the FCC's status as an independent agency, which, he believed, should be relatively free from political influence. He referred to "a strong presumption that the FCC's initial views, reflecting the informed judgment of independent commissioners with expertise in the regulated area, also reflect the views of the Congress that delegated the Commission authority to flesh out details not fully defined in the enacting statute." Justice Stevens also pointed to that fact that the rules adopted after *Pacifica* had been in effect for decades.

"[B]roadcasters have a substantial interest in regulatory stability; the threat of crippling financial penalties looms large over these entities. The FCC's shifting and impermissibly vague indecency policy only imperils these broadcasters and muddles the regulatory landscape. It therefore makes eminent sense to require the Commission to justify why its prior policy is no longer sound before allowing it to change course."

Justice Breyer (joined by **Justices Stevens, Souter,** and **Ginsburg**) dissented. He started with the premise that, as an independent agency, the FCC was relatively insulated from political oversight. "That insulation helps to secure important governmental objectives, such as the constitutionally related objective of maintaining broadcast regulation that does not bend too readily before the political winds. But that agency's comparative freedom from ballot-box control makes it all the more important that courts review its decisionmaking to assure compliance with applicable provisions of the law—including law requiring that major policy decisions be based upon articulable reasons." Additionally, the agency must act consistently, and when it changes its own rules the agency must focus on the fact of change and explain the basis for that change.

"To explain a change requires more than setting forth reasons why the new policy is a good one. It also requires the agency to answer the question, 'Why did you change?' And a rational answer to this question typically requires a more complete explanation than would prove satisfactory were change itself not at issue." *State Farm* "requires the agency here to focus upon the reasons that led the agency to adopt the initial policy, and to explain why it now comes to a new judgment.

"I recognize that *sometimes* the ultimate explanation for a change may have to be, 'We now weigh the relevant considerations differently.' But at other times, an agency can and should say more. Where, for example, the agency rested its previous policy on particular factual findings; or where an agency rested its prior policy on its view of the governing law; or where an agency rested its previous policy on, say, a special need to coordinate with another agency, one would normally expect the agency to focus upon those earlier views of fact, of law, or of policy and explain why they are no longer controlling. Regardless, to say that the agency here must answer the question 'why change' is not to require the agency to provide a justification that is '*better* than the reasons for the old [policy].' It is only to recognize the obvious fact that *change* is sometimes (not always) a relevant background feature that sometimes (not always) requires focus (upon prior justifications) and explanation lest the adoption of the new policy (in that circumstance) be 'arbitrary, capricious, an abuse of discretion.' "

Like the Second Circuit, Justice Breyer concluded that the FCC's decision violated the *State Farm* requirement that an agency making a policy change "consider . . . important aspect[s] of the problem." In particular, he faulted the FCC for failing adequately to consider its new policy's First Amendment implications and potential impact on local broadcasters, many of whom might not be able to afford the technology necessary to "bleep out" fleeting expletives. Justice Breyer dismissed as inadequate the various reasons the FCC had adduced for its policy change—in particular, the claim that the literal-expletive distinction was nonsensical and the claim that the new policy better protects children against "the first blow" of broadcast indecency. Neither of these claims, Justice Breyer argued, could justify the FCC's policy *change* since both claims remained conclusory, failing to address the rationales underlying the prior policy.

NOTES ON STATE FARM v. FOX TELEVISION:
WHEN ARE AGENCY POLICY SHIFTS "ARBITRARY"?

State Farm can be read as trying to strike a balance between two kinds of risks attending judicial review of agency policy changes. On the one hand, if courts are too deferential, there is the "yo-yo" risk that agency policies will fluctuate too frequently. On the other hand, if courts are too scrutinizing, there is the "ossification" risk that agencies will become too loath to change their policies. While the *State Farm* Court and the *Fox* dissenters seem to be more troubled by the yo-yo risk than the ossification risk, the *Fox* Court seems to have the opposite concern. Is *Fox* therefore inconsistent with *State Farm*? If so, can the inconsistency be justified?

1. *Independent Versus Executive Agencies?* The agency in *State Farm* was an executive department directly accountable to the President, while the agency in *Fox* was an independent agency. The dissenters, of course, argue that, because of the relative insulation of independent agencies from political pressures, policy changes made by independent agencies should be subject to *more* stringent judicial scrutiny than those made by executive agencies and, consequently, that *State Farm* applies a fortiori to *Fox*. But might the opposite be true? Might the relative insulation of independent agencies from political pressures lead one to expect their decisions to be generally *more* reasoned than the decisions of executive agencies and thus to merit *more* deference from courts?

Writing for a plurality of Justices (Part III—E of his opinion, which Justice Kennedy did not join), Justice Scalia argues that independent agencies like the FCC are subject to significant political pressures exerted by Congress through its oversight authority. Thus, "independent" agencies are not necessarily free from politics; the political pressure just comes from different branches of government. (In fact, Justice Scalia argues that the FCC's new policy in *Fox Television* was a direct consequence of congressional complaints that families were being subjected to inappropriate language during prime-time television.) But once again, might the opposite be true? Might the political accountability of independent agencies lead one to expect their decisions to be *as poorly* reasoned as those of executive agencies and thus to merit *as much* scrutiny from courts?

Should APA judicial review distinguish between the kinds of agency promulgating the evolving policy that is being reviewed?

2. *Facts Versus Law.* Rather than trying to distinguish *State Farm* and *Fox* based on the different kinds of *agencies* involved in each, one might try to distinguish them based on the different kinds of *policies* involved in each: whereas the policy in *State Farm* seemed to be based on a relatively technical cost-benefit factual analysis, the policy in *Fox* seemed to be based more on a social or moral judgment.

This difference might help to explain Justice Scalia's observation about the difficulty of obtaining data about the harmfulness of fleeting expletives in broadcasts and the comparative ease of obtaining data about the benefits of passive restraints in automobiles. Perhaps the FCC's policy change rested on the judgment that, whatever the tangible harm caused by fleeting expletives, it was simply *wrong or immoral* to expose the public—and especially children—to such indecency. If this was in fact the nature of the FCC's judgment, should courts be more willing to defer to it than they would be to defer to a more technical cost-benefit analysis?

Consider the historical analysis developed in Thomas Merrill, *Article III, Agency Adjudication, and the Origins of the Appellate Review Model in Administrative Law*, 111 Colum. L. Rev. 939 (2011). Professor Merrill demonstrates that the Supreme Court's twentieth century doctrines of administrative law were grounded in the model of judge-jury interaction: judges declared the law, and agencies (like juries) found facts, subject to lenient rational basis review. Under this model, which is the conceptual foundation for the APA, *Fox Television* might be a better candidate for hard-look judicial review, because the key issues did not rest upon factual findings by the agency. As Professor Merrill notes, judicial review of informal rulemaking fits uneasily in the Supreme Court's classic model of administrative law. Perhaps *State Farm* might be defended on the ground that the Court was not "finding" facts but was merely sending the factfinders back to explain why they had rejected obvious alternatives.

Note also that the moral judgment represented in *Fox* raises important First Amendment concerns not present in the cost-benefit judgment represented in *State Farm*: Isn't a "fleeting expletive" a classic example of free expression? Cf. *Cohen v. California*, 403 U.S. 15 (1971) (invalidating state censorship of a young man with "Fuck the Draft" on his jacket). As *Pacifica* held, Congress has greater leeway to regulate indecent speech on the radio and television than in newspapers and the print media—but the regulatory authority is not unlimited. Shouldn't there be more specific guidance from Congress as to such important matters—or is Justice Scalia probably right, that Congress was behind the FCC's tighter rule? (1996).

Postscript. On remand, the Second Circuit ruled that the FCC's fleeting expletive policy, no longer confined to the earlier seven dirty words, violated the First Amendment. *Fox Television Stations, Inc. v. FCC*, 613 F.3d 317 (2d Cir. 2010). The Supreme Court reviewed the Second Circuit's decision and held, more narrowly, that the Commission's standards as applied were impermissibly vague, because it had failed to give Fox fair notice prior to the broadcasts that fleeting expletives and momentary nudity could be found actionably indecent. *FCC v. Fox Television Stations, Inc.*, 132 S.Ct. 2307 (2012). The Court therefore did not reach the First Amendment implications of the indecency policy or reconsider its ruling in *Pacifica*.

3. *The Difference Process Might Make?* Should process distinguish *State Farm* from *Fox Television*? The obvious process difference is that the former was a rulemaking proceeding, while the latter was an agency adjudication—but that difference might just as easily cut the other way. That is, a shift in agency policy might be more legitimate in the kind of rulemaking that *State Farm* overturned than in an adjudication that *Fox Television* sanctioned. In notice-and-comment rulemaking, for example, a greater variety of interests will submit formal analyses, and the agency must consider them—in contrast to adjudication, where the agency must only respond to the parties' presentations.

Another possible process distinction is that the DOT's auto safety policy had been a political football through several administrations, and the *State Farm* Court might have felt that the agency needed to buckle down and take its law work more seriously. In contrast, perhaps, the FCC's policy was more stable over several administrations. Although the FCC was moving policy toward greater regulation in *Fox Television*, it was making a small step (expanding the longstanding policy to include "fleeting" expletives), and a step that was arguably justified by proliferation of fleeting expletives during prime time (when more children are watching TV) and by technology allowing networks to bleep out fleeting expletives.

Are any of these distinctions persuasive—or is *Fox Television* simply a precedent-narrowing reading of *State Farm*? Should *State Farm* be reframed, or even overruled?

MASSACHUSETTS V. ENVIRONMENTAL PROTECTION AGENCY

Supreme Court of the United States, 2007.
549 U.S. 497, 127 S.Ct. 1438, 167 L.Ed.2d 248.

JUSTICE STEVENS delivered the opinion of the Court.

[In 1999, a group of private organizations filed a rulemaking petition asking the Environmental Protection Agency (EPA) to regulate the emissions of four greenhouse gases, including carbon dioxide, pursuant to its responsibility under the Clean Air Act. EPA denied the petition in 2003. Petitioners were joined by Massachusetts and other state and local governments seeking review in the D.C. Circuit. The appeals court ruled that the agency's denial was a proper exercise of its discretion. The Supreme Court agreed to review that decision. In a part of its decision omitted here, the Court held that Massachusetts and other governments had standing to challenge EPA's denial, because the agency's decision not to regulate greenhouse gases "contributes" to Massachusetts' injuries related to global warming]

[I]   Section 202(a)(1) of the Clean Air Act, as added by Pub. L. 89–272, § 101(8), 79 Stat. 992, and as amended by, *inter alia*, 84 Stat. 1690 and 91 Stat. 791, 42 U.S.C. § 7521(a)(1), provides:

> "The [EPA] Administrator shall by regulation prescribe (and from time to time revise) in accordance with the provisions of this section, standards applicable to the emission of any air pollutant from any class or classes of new motor vehicles or new motor vehicle engines, which in his judgment cause, or contribute to, air pollution which may reasonably be anticipated to endanger public health or welfare. . . ."

The Act defines "air pollutant" to include "any air pollution agent or combination of such agents, including any physical, chemical, biological, radioactive . . . substance or matter which is emitted into or otherwise enters the ambient air." § 7602(g). "Welfare" is also defined broadly: among other things, it includes "effects on . . . weather . . . and climate." § 7602(h).

When Congress enacted these provisions, the study of climate change was in its infancy. [By the time Congress enacted § 202(a)(1) in 1970, carbon dioxide levels had reached 325 parts per million, up from a recorded mean level of 316 parts per million in 1959. In 1978, Congress enacted the National Climate Program Act, requiring the President to establish a program to "assist the Nation and the world to understand and respond to natural and man-induced climate processes and their implications." President Carter asked the National Research Council, the working arm of the National Academy of Sciences, to investigate the subject. Congress in 1987 enacted the Global Climate Protection Act, directing EPA to propose to Congress a "coordinated national policy on global climate change," and ordering the

Secretary of State to work "through the channels of multilateral diplomacy" and coordinate diplomatic efforts to combat global warming.

In 1990, the Intergovernmental Panel on Climate Change (IPCC), a multinational scientific body organized under the United Nations, published its first comprehensive report on the topic, concluding that greenhouse gases will increase the warming of the Earth's surface. In response, the United Nations convened the "Earth Summit" in 1992 in Rio de Janeiro, and the first President Bush attended and signed the United Nations Framework Convention on Climate Change (UNFCCC), a nonbinding agreement among 154 nations to reduce atmospheric concentrations of carbon dioxide and other greenhouse gases, which the Senate unanimously ratified. In 1997, after the IPCC's second comprehensive report concluded that there was a discernible human influence on global climate, the UNFCCC signatories adopted the Kyoto protocol assigning mandatory targets for industrialized nations to reduce greenhouse gas emissions. Because those targets did not apply to China, India, and other developing countries that were heavy polluters, the Senate passed a resolution expressing its sense that the United States should not enter into the protocol. President Clinton did not submit the protocol to the Senate for ratification.]

[II] On October 20, 1999, a group of 19 private organizations filed a rulemaking petition asking EPA to regulate "greenhouse gas emissions from new motor vehicles under § 202 of the Clean Air Act." Petitioners maintained that 1998 was the "warmest year on record"; that carbon dioxide, methane, nitrous oxide, and hydrofluorocarbons are "heat trapping greenhouse gases"; that greenhouse gas emissions have significantly accelerated climate change; and that the IPCC's 1995 report warned that "carbon dioxide remains the most important contributor to [manmade] forcing of climate change." The petition further alleged that climate change will have serious adverse effects on human health and the environment. As to EPA's statutory authority, the petition observed that the Agency itself had already confirmed that it had the power to regulate carbon dioxide. In 1998, Jonathan Z. Cannon, then EPA's general counsel, prepared a legal opinion concluding that "CO_2 emissions are within the scope of EPA's authority to regulate," even as he recognized that EPA had so far declined to exercise that authority. Cannon's successor, Gary S. Guzy, reiterated that opinion before a congressional committee just two weeks before the rulemaking petition was filed.

Fifteen months after the petition's submission, EPA requested public comment on "all the issues raised in [the] petition," adding a "particular" request for comments on "any scientific, technical, legal, economic or other aspect of these issues that may be relevant to EPA's consideration of this petition." 66 Fed. Reg. 7,486, 7,487 (2001). EPA received more than 50,000 comments over the next five months.

Before the close of the comment period, the White House sought "assistance in identifying the areas in the science of climate change where there are the greatest certainties and uncertainties" from the National Research Council, asking for a response "as soon as possible." The result was a 2001 report titled Climate Change Science: An Analysis of Some Key Questions (NRC Report), which, drawing heavily on the 1995 IPCC report, concluded that "[g]reenhouse gases are accumulating in Earth's atmosphere as a result of human activities, causing surface air temperatures and subsurface ocean temperatures to rise. Temperatures are, in fact, rising."

On September 8, 2003, EPA entered an order denying the rulemaking petition. The Agency gave two reasons for its decision: (1) that contrary to the opinions of its former general counsels, the Clean Air Act does not authorize EPA to issue mandatory regulations to address global climate change; and (2) that even if the Agency had the authority to set greenhouse gas emission standards, it would be unwise to do so at this time.

In concluding that it lacked statutory authority over greenhouse gases, EPA observed that Congress was well aware of the global climate change issue when it last comprehensively amended the Clean Air Act in 1990, yet it declined to adopt a proposed amendment establishing binding emissions limitations. Congress instead chose to authorize further investigation into climate change. EPA further reasoned that Congress' specially tailored solutions to global atmospheric issues—in particular, its 1990 enactment of a comprehensive scheme to regulate pollutants that depleted the ozone layer, see 42 U.S.C. §§ 7671–7671q—counseled against reading the general authorization of § 202(a)(1) to confer regulatory authority over greenhouse gases.

EPA stated that it was urged on in this view by this Court's decision in *FDA v. Brown & Williamson Tobacco Corp.*, 529 U.S. 120 (2000). In that case, relying on "tobacco['s] unique political history," we invalidated the Food and Drug Administration's reliance on its general authority to regulate drugs as a basis for asserting jurisdiction over an "industry constituting a significant portion of the American economy." *Id.* at 159.

EPA reasoned that climate change had its own "political history": Congress designed the original Clean Air Act to address *local* air pollutants rather than a substance that "is fairly consistent in its concentration throughout the *world's* atmosphere"; declined in 1990 to enact proposed amendments to force EPA to set carbon dioxide emission standards for motor vehicles; and addressed global climate change in other legislation. Because of this political history, and because imposing emission limitations on greenhouse gases would have even greater economic and political repercussions than regulating tobacco, EPA was persuaded that it lacked the power to do so. In essence, EPA concluded that climate change was so important that unless Congress spoke with exacting specificity, it could not have meant the Agency to address it.

Having reached that conclusion, EPA believed it followed that greenhouse gases cannot be "air pollutants" within the meaning of the Act. . . . The Agency bolstered this conclusion by explaining that if carbon dioxide were an air pollutant, the only feasible method of reducing tailpipe emissions would be to improve fuel economy. But because Congress has already created detailed mandatory fuel economy standards subject to Department of Transportation (DOT) administration, the Agency concluded that EPA regulation would either conflict with those standards or be superfluous.

Even assuming that it had authority over greenhouse gases, EPA explained in detail why it would refuse to exercise that authority. The Agency began by recognizing that the concentration of greenhouse gases has dramatically increased as a result of human activities, and acknowledged the attendant increase in global surface air temperatures. EPA nevertheless gave controlling importance to the NRC Report's statement that a causal link between the two cannot be unequivocally established. Given that residual uncertainty, EPA concluded that regulating greenhouse gas emissions would be unwise.

The Agency furthermore characterized any EPA regulation of motor-vehicle emissions as a "piecemeal approach" to climate change, and stated that such regulation would conflict with the President's "comprehensive approach" to the problem. That approach involves additional support for technological innovation, the creation of nonregulatory programs to encourage voluntary private-sector reductions in greenhouse gas emissions, and further research on climate change—not actual regulation. According to EPA, unilateral EPA regulation of motor-vehicle greenhouse gas emissions might also hamper the President's ability to persuade key developing countries to reduce greenhouse gas emissions.

[III] Petitioners, now joined by intervenor States and local governments, sought review of EPA's order in the United States Court of Appeals for the District of Columbia Circuit. Although each of the three judges on the panel wrote a separate opinion, two judges agreed that the EPA Administrator properly exercised his discretion under § 202(a)(1) in denying the petition for rule making. The court therefore denied the petition for review. . . . [The Supreme Court granted certiorari regarding the following two questions concerning the meaning of § 202(a)(1) of the Act: whether EPA has the statutory authority to regulate greenhouse gas emissions from new motor vehicles; and if so, whether its stated reasons for refusing to do so are consistent with the statute.]

[In Part IV, The EPA argued that the Supreme Court should not address the questions raised unless at least one petitioner has standing to invoke jurisdiction under Article III of the Constitution. The majority found that it had jurisdiction, emphasizing Massachusetts' status as a sovereign with the ability to litigate as *parens patriae* to protect quasi-sovereign interests as distinct from private litigants.]

[V] The scope of our review of the merits of the statutory issues is narrow. As we have repeated time and again, an agency has broad discretion to choose how best to marshal its limited resources and personnel to carry out its delegated responsibilities. See *Chevron U.S.A. Inc. v. Natural Resources Defense Council, Inc.*, 467 U.S. 837, 842–845 (1984). That discretion is at its height when the agency decides not to bring an enforcement action. Therefore, in *Heckler v. Chaney*, 470 U.S. 821 (1985), we held that an agency's refusal to initiate enforcement proceedings is not ordinarily subject to judicial review. Some debate remains, however, as to the rigor with which we review an agency's denial of a petition for rulemaking.

There are key differences between a denial of a petition for rulemaking and an agency's decision not to initiate an enforcement action. See *Am. Horse Protection*

Ass'n., Inc. v. Lyng, 812 F.2d 1, 3–4 (D.C. Cir. 1987). In contrast to nonenforcement decisions, agency refusals to initiate rulemaking "are less frequent, more apt to involve legal as opposed to factual analysis, and subject to special formalities, including a public explanation." *Id.* at 4; see also 5 U.S.C. § 555(e). They moreover arise out of denials of petitions for rulemaking which (at least in the circumstances here) the affected party had an undoubted procedural right to file in the first instance. Refusals to promulgate rules are thus susceptible to judicial review, though such review is "extremely limited" and "highly deferential." *Nat'l Customs Brokers & Forwarders Ass'n. of America, Inc. v. United States*, 883 F.2d 93, 96 (D.C. Cir. 1989).

EPA concluded in its denial of the petition for rulemaking that it lacked authority under 42 U.S.C. § 7521(a)(1) to regulate new vehicle emissions because carbon dioxide is not an "air pollutant" as that term is defined in § 7602. In the alternative, it concluded that even if it possessed authority, it would decline to do so because regulation would conflict with other administration priorities. As discussed earlier, the Clean Air Act expressly permits review of such an action. § 7607(b)(1). We therefore "may reverse any such action found to be . . . arbitrary, capricious, an abuse of discretion, or otherwise not in accordance with law." § 7607(d)(9).

[VI] On the merits, the first question is whether § 202(a)(1) of the Clean Air Act authorizes EPA to regulate greenhouse gas emissions from new motor vehicles in the event that it forms a "judgment" that such emissions contribute to climate change. We have little trouble concluding that it does. In relevant part, § 202(a)(1) provides that EPA "shall by regulation prescribe . . . standards applicable to the emission of any air pollutant from any class or classes of new motor vehicles or new motor vehicle engines, which in [the Administrator's] judgment cause, or contribute to, air pollution which may reasonably be anticipated to endanger public health or welfare." 42 U.S.C. § 7521(a)(1). Because EPA believes that Congress did not intend it to regulate substances that contribute to climate change, the agency maintains that carbon dioxide is not an "air pollutant" within the meaning of the provision.

The statutory text forecloses EPA's reading. The Clean Air Act's sweeping definition of "air pollutant" includes "any air pollution agent or combination of such agents, including any physical, chemical . . . substance or matter which is emitted into or otherwise enters the ambient air. . . ." § 7602(g) (emphasis added). On its face, the definition embraces all airborne compounds of whatever stripe, and underscores that intent through the repeated use of the word "any." Carbon dioxide, methane, nitrous oxide, and hydrofluorocarbons are without a doubt "physical [and] chemical . . . substance [s] which [are] emitted into . . . the ambient air." The statute is unambiguous.

Rather than relying on statutory text, EPA invokes postenactment congressional actions and deliberations it views as tantamount to a congressional command to refrain from regulating greenhouse gas emissions. Even if such postenactment legislative history could shed light on the meaning of an otherwise-unambiguous statute, EPA never identifies any action remotely suggesting that Congress meant to curtail its power to treat greenhouse gases as air pollutants. That subsequent Congresses have eschewed enacting binding emissions limitations to combat global warming tells us nothing about what Congress meant when it amended § 202(a)(1) in 1970 and 1977. And unlike EPA, we have no difficulty reconciling Congress' various efforts to promote interagency collaboration and research to better understand climate change with the Agency's pre-existing mandate to regulate "any air pollutant" that may endanger the public welfare. Collaboration and research do not conflict with any thoughtful regulatory effort; they complement it.

EPA's reliance on *Brown & Williamson Tobacco Corp.*, is similarly misplaced. In holding that tobacco products are not "drugs" or "devices" subject to Food and Drug Administration (FDA) regulation pursuant to the Food, Drug and Cosmetic Act (FDCA), we found critical at least two considerations that have no counterpart in this case.

First, we thought it unlikely that Congress meant to ban tobacco products, which the FDCA would have required had such products been classified as "drugs" or "devices." *Id.* at 135–137. Here, in contrast, EPA jurisdiction would lead to no such extreme measures. EPA would only *regulate emissions,* and even then, it would have to delay any action "to permit the development and application of the requisite technology, giving appropriate consideration to the cost of compliance," § 7521(a)(2). However much a ban on tobacco products clashed with the "common sense" intuition that Congress never meant to remove those products from circulation, *Brown & Williamson*, 529 U.S. at 133, there is nothing counterintuitive to the notion that EPA can curtail the emission of substances that are putting the global climate out of kilter.

Second, in *Brown & Williamson*, we pointed to an unbroken series of congressional enactments that made sense only if adopted "against the backdrop of the FDA's consistent and repeated statements that it lacked authority under the FDCA to regulate tobacco." *Id.* at 144. We can point to no such enactments here: EPA has not identified any congressional action that conflicts in any way with the regulation of greenhouse gases from new motor vehicles. Even if it had, Congress could not have acted against a regulatory "backdrop" of disclaimers of regulatory authority. Prior to the order that provoked this litigation, EPA had never disavowed the authority to regulate greenhouse gases, and in 1998 it in fact affirmed that it *had* such authority. There is no reason, much less a compelling reason, to accept EPA's invitation to read ambiguity into a clear statute.

EPA finally argues that it cannot regulate carbon dioxide emissions from motor vehicles because doing so would require it to tighten mileage standards, a job (according to EPA) that Congress has assigned to DOT. But that DOT sets mileage standards in no way licenses EPA to shirk its environmental responsibilities. EPA has been charged with protecting the public's "health" and "welfare," 42 U.S.C. § 7521(a)(1), a statutory obligation wholly independent of DOT's mandate to promote energy efficiency. See Energy Policy and Conservation Act, § 2(5), 89 Stat. 874, 42 U.S.C. § 6201(5). The two obligations may overlap, but there is no reason to think the two agencies cannot both administer their obligations and yet avoid inconsistency.

While the Congresses that drafted § 202(a)(1) might not have appreciated the possibility that burning fossil fuels could lead to global warming, they did understand that without regulatory flexibility, changing circumstances and scientific developments would soon render the Clean Air Act obsolete. The broad language of § 202(a)(1) reflects an intentional effort to confer the flexibility necessary to forestall such obsolescence. See *Pa. Dep't. of Corr. v. Yeskey*, 524 U.S. 206, 212 (1998) ("[T]he fact that a statute can be applied in situations not expressly anticipated by Congress does not demonstrate ambiguity. It demonstrates breadth" (internal quotation marks omitted)). Because greenhouse gases fit well within the Clean Air Act's capacious definition of "air pollutant," we hold that EPA has the statutory authority to regulate the emission of such gases from new motor vehicles.

[VII]   The alternative basis for EPA's decision—that even if it does have statutory authority to regulate greenhouse gases, it would be unwise to do so at this time—rests on reasoning divorced from the statutory text. While the statute does condition the exercise of EPA's authority on its formation of a "judgment," 42 U.S.C. § 7521(a)(1), that judgment must relate to whether an air pollutant "cause[s], or contribute[s] to, air pollution which may reasonably be anticipated to endanger public health or welfare," *ibid.* Put another way, the use of the word "judgment" is not a roving license to ignore the statutory text. It is but a direction to exercise discretion within defined statutory limits.

If EPA makes a finding of endangerment, the Clean Air Act requires the Agency to regulate emissions of the deleterious pollutant from new motor vehicles. *Ibid* (stating that "[EPA] shall by regulation prescribe . . . standards applicable to the emission of any air pollutant from any class or classes of new motor vehicles"). EPA no doubt has significant latitude as to the manner, timing, content, and coordination of its regulations with those of other agencies. But once EPA has responded to a petition for rulemaking, its reasons for action or inaction must conform to the authorizing statute. Under the clear terms of the Clean Air Act, EPA can avoid taking further action only if it determines that greenhouse gases do not contribute to climate change or if it provides some reasonable explanation as to why it cannot or will not exercise its discretion to determine whether they do. *Ibid.* To the extent that this constrains agency discretion to pursue other priorities of the Administrator or the President, this is the congressional design.

EPA has refused to comply with this clear statutory command. Instead, it has offered a laundry list of reasons not to regulate. For example, EPA said that a number of voluntary Executive Branch programs already provide an effective response to the threat of global warming, that regulating greenhouse gases might impair the President's ability to negotiate with "key developing nations" to reduce emissions, and that curtailing motor-vehicle emissions would reflect "an inefficient, piecemeal approach to address the climate change issue."

Although we have neither the expertise nor the authority to evaluate these policy judgments, it is evident they have nothing to do with whether greenhouse gas emissions contribute to climate change. Still less do they amount to a reasoned justification for declining to form a scientific judgment. * * *

Nor can EPA avoid its statutory obligation by noting the uncertainty surrounding various features of climate change and concluding that it would therefore be better not to regulate at this time. If the scientific uncertainty is so profound that it precludes EPA from making a reasoned judgment as to whether greenhouse gases contribute to global warming, EPA must say so. That EPA would prefer not to regulate greenhouse gases because of some residual uncertainty—which, contrary to Justice Scalia's apparent belief, is in fact all that it said—is irrelevant. The statutory question is whether sufficient information exists to make an endangerment finding.

In short, EPA has offered no reasoned explanation for its refusal to decide whether greenhouse gases cause or contribute to climate change. Its action was therefore "arbitrary, capricious, . . . or otherwise not in accordance with law." 42 U.S.C. § 7607(d)(9)(A). We need not and do not reach the question whether on remand EPA must make an endangerment finding, or whether policy concerns can inform EPA's actions in the event that it makes such a finding. Cf. Chevron, 467 U.S. at 843–844. We hold only that EPA must ground its reasons for action or inaction in the statute. * * *

[CHIEF JUSTICE ROBERTS' dissenting opinion, joined by JUSTICES SCALIA, THOMAS, and ALITO, is omitted. The Chief Justice argued that the Court lacked jurisdiction because none of the petitioners had standing under Article III]

JUSTICE SCALIA, with whom the CHIEF JUSTICE, JUSTICE THOMAS, and JUSTICE ALITO join, dissenting.

I join the Chief Justice's opinion in full, and would hold that this Court has no jurisdiction to decide this case because petitioners lack standing. The Court having decided otherwise, it is appropriate for me to note my dissent on the merits.

[I—A]   The provision of law at the heart of this case is § 202(a)(1) of the Clean Air Act (CAA or Act), which provides that the Administrator of the Environmental Protection Agency (EPA) "shall by regulation prescribe . . . standards applicable to the emission of any air pollutant from any class or classes of new motor vehicles or new motor vehicle engines, which *in his judgment* cause, or contribute to, air pollution which may reasonably be anticipated to endanger public health or welfare." 42 U.S.C. § 7521(a)(1) (emphasis added). As the Court recognizes, the statute "condition[s] the exercise of EPA's authority on its formation of a 'judgment.'" There is no dispute that the Administrator has made no such judgment in this case.

The question thus arises: Does anything *require* the Administrator to make a "judgment" whenever a petition for rulemaking is filed? Without citation of the statute or any other authority, the Court says yes. Why is that so? When Congress wishes to make private action force an agency's hand, it knows how to do so. See, e.g., *Brock v. Pierce County*, 476 U.S. 253, 254–255 (1986) (discussing the Comprehensive Employment and Training Act (CETA), 92 Stat. 1926, 29 U.S.C. § 816(b) (1976 ed., Supp. V), which "provide[d] that the Secretary of Labor 'shall' issue a final determination as to the misuse of CETA funds by a grant recipient within 120 days after receiving a complaint alleging such misuse"). Where does the

CAA say that the EPA Administrator is required to come to a decision on this question whenever a rulemaking petition is filed? The Court points to no such provision because none exists.

Instead, the Court invents a multiple-choice question that the EPA Administrator must answer when a petition for rulemaking is filed. The Administrator must exercise his judgment in one of three ways: (a) by concluding that the pollutant *does* cause, or contribute to, air pollution that endangers public welfare (in which case EPA is required to regulate); (b) by concluding that the pollutant *does not* cause, or contribute to, air pollution that endangers public welfare (in which case EPA is *not* required to regulate); or (c) by "provid[ing] some reasonable explanation as to why it cannot or will not exercise its discretion to determine whether" greenhouse gases endanger public welfare, (in which case EPA is *not* required to regulate). * * *

The Court, with no basis in text or precedent, rejects all of EPA's stated "policy judgments" as not "amount[ing] to a reasoned justification," effectively narrowing the universe of potential reasonable bases to a single one: Judgment can be delayed *only* if the Administrator concludes that "the scientific uncertainty is [too] profound." The Administrator is precluded from concluding *for other reasons* "that it would . . . be better not to regulate at this time."[9] Such other reasons—perfectly valid reasons—were set forth in the Agency's statement.

The Court dismisses this analysis as "rest[ing] on reasoning divorced from the statutory text." "While the statute does condition the exercise of EPA's authority on its formation of a 'judgment,' . . . that judgment must relate to whether an air pollutant 'cause[s], or contribute[s] to, air pollution which may reasonably be anticipated to endanger public health or welfare.'" True but irrelevant. When the Administrator *makes* a judgment whether to regulate greenhouse gases, that judgment must relate to whether they are air pollutants that "cause, or contribute to, air pollution which may reasonably be anticipated to endanger public health or welfare." 42 U.S.C. § 7521(a)(1). But the statute says *nothing at all* about the reasons for which the Administrator may *defer* making a judgment—the permissible reasons for deciding not to grapple with the issue at the present time. Thus, the various "policy" rationales that the Court criticizes are not "divorced from the statutory text," except in the sense that the statutory text is silent, as texts are often silent about permissible reasons for the exercise of agency discretion. The reasons EPA gave are surely considerations executive agencies *regularly* take into account (and *ought* to take into account) when deciding whether to consider entering a new field: the impact such entry would have on other Executive Branch programs and on foreign policy. There is no basis in law for the Court's imposed limitation.* * * As the Administrator acted within the law in declining to make a "judgment" for the policy reasons above set forth, I would uphold the decision to deny the rulemaking petition on that ground alone.

---

[9]   The Court's way of putting it is, of course, not quite accurate. The issue is whether it would be better *to defer the decision about whether to exercise judgment.* This has the *effect* of deferring regulation but is quite a different determination.

[I—B]   Even on the Court's own terms, however, the same conclusion follows. As mentioned above, the Court gives EPA the option of determining that the science is too uncertain to allow it to form a "judgment" as to whether greenhouse gases endanger public welfare. Attached to this option (on what basis is unclear) is an essay requirement: "If," the Court says, "the scientific uncertainty is so profound that it precludes EPA from making a reasoned judgment as to whether greenhouse gases contribute to global warming, EPA must say so." But EPA *has* said precisely that—and at great length, based on information contained in a 2001 report by the National Research Council (NRC) entitled Climate Change Science: An Analysis of Some Key Questions [Justice Scalia notes several excerpts from the report that highlighted the complexity of climate change, the continued evolution of the scientific study, the substantial scientific uncertainties that limit NRC's ability to assess climate change, and NRC's infant study of the relationships between climate and human health.]

[II—A]   Even before reaching its discussion of the word "judgment," the Court makes another significant error when it concludes that "§ 202(a)(1) of the Clean Air Act *authorizes* EPA to regulate greenhouse gas emissions from new motor vehicles in the event that it forms a 'judgment' that such emissions contribute to climate change." * * * The Court's analysis faithfully follows the argument advanced by petitioners, which focuses on the word "including" in the statutory definition of "air pollutant." As that argument goes, anything that *follows* the word "including" must necessarily be a subset of whatever *precedes* it. * * *

That is certainly one possible interpretation of the statutory definition. The word "including" can indeed indicate that what follows will be an "illustrative" sampling of the general category that precedes the word. [But] the word "including" does not require the Court's (or the petitioners') result. It is perfectly reasonable to view the definition of "air pollutant" in its entirety: An air pollutant *can* be "any physical, chemical, . . . substance or matter which is emitted into or otherwise enters the ambient air," but only if it retains the general characteristic of being an "air pollution agent or combination of such agents." This is precisely the conclusion EPA reached: "[A] substance does not meet the CAA definition of 'air pollutant' simply because it is a 'physical, chemical, . . . substance or matter which is emitted into or otherwise enters the ambient air.' It must also be an 'air pollution agent.' * * * Evidently, the Court defers only to those reasonable interpretations that it favors. * * *

The Court's alarm over global warming may or may not be justified, but it ought not distort the outcome of this litigation. This is a straightforward administrative-law case, in which Congress has passed a malleable statute giving broad discretion, not to us but to an executive agency. No matter how important the underlying policy issues at stake, this Court has no business substituting its own desired outcome for the reasoned judgment of the responsible agency.

NOTES ON MASS. V. EPA AND AGENCY REFUSALS TO ACT

1.   *Perverse Incentives.* In *Massachusetts v. EPA: Breaking New Ground on Issues Other Than Global Warming*, 102 Nw. U. L. Rev. Colloquy 1, 16 (2007), Kathryn Watts

and Amy Wildermuth suggest that the Court's rigorous standard for review of agency inaction "will create perverse incentives for agencies." Although the Court made clear that EPA was not required to act on the rulemaking petition within a certain time frame, once the agency decided to act it effectively invited a challenge to its reasons for denying the petition, reasons that had to conform to the authorizing statute. Accordingly, the authors continue, a key lesson that agencies may well take away from *Massachusetts* is that "whatever discretion [exists] prior to taking action on a rulemaking petition may well disappear once [the agency] affirmatively rules on a petition." *Id.* What recourse, if any, does a private party have when an agency has simply ignored a petition for rulemaking? How should a court assess agency discretion not to respond at all in light of the Court's reasoning?

2. *Reasonableness.* Relatedly, what will qualify as a reasonable explanation when an agency denies a rulemaking petition? The Court's opinion dismisses policy-driven considerations as divorced from the statutory text but "does not even hint at a general line between permissible and impermissible reasons to regulate." *Id.* at 15. If policy considerations will not be a basis, what else may an agency invoke for exercising its discretion to deny a petition? Will courts only entertain reliance on scientific or technical data? If so, what options will agencies like the Securities & Exchange Commission, whose rulemaking is necessarily tethered to policy considerations, offer as reasonable explanations?

3. *Aftermath of* Massachusetts v. EPA. Following the Supreme Court decision, the Bush EPA announced that it would promulgate greenhouse gas (GHG) regulations for cars and trucks. Before the agency could act, however, Congress in 2007 passed the Energy Independence and Security Act, 121 Stat. 1492, amending the Clean Air Act to require that EPA and the Department of Transportation (DOT) jointly establish fuel economy and GHG vehicle emission standards.

Between 2009 and 2010, the Obama EPA promulgated a series of GHG-related rules. An Endangerment Finding concluded that GHGs may reasonably be anticipated to endanger public health or welfare and that emissions from motor vehicles contribute to this pollution. 74 Fed. Reg. 66,496 (Dec. 15, 2009). A Tailpipe Rule, promulgated with DOT, set GHG emission standards for cars and light trucks. 75 Fed. Reg. 25,324 (May 7, 2010). Finally, Timing and Tailoring Rules required *major stationary sources of greenhouse gases* to obtain construction and operating permits but limited initial permitting requirements to the largest GHG emitters. 75 Fed. Reg. 31,514 (June 3, 2010). More than 35 petitioners filed some 80 lawsuits challenging these agency actions. In July 2012, the D.C. Circuit ruled on the consolidated lawsuits, upholding the agency's positions—EPA's Endangerment Finding and Tailpipe Rules were not arbitrary or capricious, and EPA's determination to extend permitting programs to major emitters was an unambiguously correct interpretation of the applicable CAA provisions.

In *Utility Air Regulatory Group v. EPA*, 134 S.Ct. 2427 (2014), the Supreme Court affirmed in part and reversed in part. Writing for the Court, Justice Scalia ruled that the CAA does not *compel* EPA to adopt an interpretation requiring a source to obtain a permit on the sole basis of its potential greenhouse-gas emissions. The majority reasoned that while the Court in *Massachusetts v. EPA* had held the Act-wide definition of "air pollutant" includes greenhouse gases, the agency has routinely given that term a narrower context-appropriate meaning in the Act's specific operative provisions governing permitting requirements. In addition, Justice Scalia concluded that the statute does not *permit* the EPA's "Tailoring Rule" interpretation focusing on the largest GHG emitters. Because the CAA specifies particular threshold amounts of greenhouse gas pollution that EPA may regulate, the agency has no power to rewrite those limits, even though it was doing so to make regulation more manageable by precluding agency efforts to control GHG emissions beyond major sources like power plants. If the text as written cannot be implemented without bringing "millions of small sources" such as schools or apartment buildings under EPA supervision, then it falls on Congress, not the agency, to narrow the statutory terms.

Justice Scalia also concluded, though, that the EPA had reasonably interpreted the CAA to allow for the regulation of greenhouse-gas emissions from sources already emitting other kinds of pollution and thus subject to regulation pursuant to established CAA permitting programs. And the Court held the agency may require those sources to use the best available technology to control greenhouse gases.

In announcing his majority opinion from the bench, Justice Scalia stated that the result of the Court's decision was to leave the agency with authority to cut back on greenhouse-gas pollution at eighty-three percent of sources across the country while denying it that authority for an additional three percent. What are we to make of this ongoing saga of rulemaking, resistance, and litigation? Do you regard the decision in *Utility Air Regulatory Group* as a "win" for EPA? What are the future implications of the Court's analysis, largely vindicating the agency's bottom line position while sharply criticizing much of its regulatory approach? Is seven years (and counting) since *Massachusetts v. EPA* an appropriate period of time for national debate and disagreement over regulatory action of this magnitude?

4. *Failure to Act.* The APA authorizes suit by "[a] person suffering legal wrong because of agency action, or adversely affected or aggrieved by agency action within the meaning of a relevant statute," 5 U.S.C. § 702, where an " 'agency action' " includes "the whole or a part of an agency rule, order, license, sanction, relief, or the equivalent or denial thereof, or failure to act," § 551(13). Under § 706(1), the APA provides the following relief: "The reviewing court shall . . . compel agency action unlawfully withheld or unreasonably delayed." At first blush, this appears to provide an answer to the question of how a court can compel an agency to respond to a petition for rulemaking rather than indefinitely ignore the petition. However, the Supreme Court in 2004 handed down a unanimous opinion in *Norton v. Southern Utah Wilderness Alliance*, 542 U.S. 55, that limited a "failure to act" claim under § 706(1) to proceedings where plaintiff can assert that an agency failed to take a discrete agency action that it is required to take. The opinion, authored by *Massachusetts* dissenter Justice Scalia, stated that "a failure to act" was "properly understood to be limited, as are the other items in § 551(13), to a discrete action." 542 U.S. at 63. Justice Scalia wrote that the phrase, "or the equivalent or denial thereof," which appears after the list of examples of specific affirmative agency actions, "must also be discrete (or it would not be equivalent)," so a "denial thereof" must be the denial of a discrete agency action. *Id.* Next, he moved to the final term in the definition in § 551(13), "failure to act," which the Court understood as a failure to take an agency action; and moreover, the canon of ejusdem generis would attribute to the last item, "failure to act," the same characteristic of discreteness shared by all the preceding items even if the Court did not tether "act" to "agency action." *Id.* at 64. Is responding to a petition for rulemaking a

discrete agency action under *Norton*? By reading § 706(1)'s authorization for courts to "compel agency action *unlawfully* withheld," the opinion holds that only agency action that can be compelled under the APA is action legally required. Is an agency required to take action in response to a petition for rulemaking? Where would a potential litigant look to find out whether a particular agency must respond to petitions?

In *The Federal Inaction Commission*, 59 Emory L.J. 369 (2009), Glen Staszewski proposes the establishment of a new, independent federal administrative agency that would be charged with "(1) identifying policy areas in which Executive Branch agencies have declined to exercise their delegated statutory authority; (2) directing agencies to adopt sensible enforcement guidelines for implementing their existing programs; (3) investigating and resolving complaints regarding particular non-enforcement decisions; (4) securing reasoned explanations from Executive Branch agencies for any perceived deficiencies in the foregoing areas; (5) reporting to elected officials and the public on the nature and scope of regulatory inaction by Executive Branch agencies; and (6) making recommendations regarding budgetary matters and substantive legislation that could alleviate perceived deficiencies." In light of *Massachusetts*, *Norton*, and *Heckler v. Chaney*, 470 U.S. 821 (1985) (discussed at start of this part; Court held that agency non-enforcement decisions are presumptively nonreviewable), would such an agency serve a useful purpose? Or is adding to the alphabet soup of American national bureaucracy only likely to create further problems? If a Federal Inaction Commission were to assume oversight of other agencies, what entity would be responsible for oversight of this Commission?

CHAPTER 9

JUDICIAL DEFERENCE TO AGENCY INTERPRETATIONS

■ ■ ■

1. INTRODUCTION

This chapter builds from the basic issues of statutory interpretation covered in chapters 6 and 7. The earlier chapters focused on rules and guidelines followed by courts, especially the Supreme Court, when construing statutes. Yet we know that most authoritative constructions of federal statutes are promulgated by agencies.

Jerry Mashaw argues that agencies will and *ought to* follow different approaches to statutory interpretation, because of their different institutional competences and responsibilities. The table below encapsulates his normative suggestions.

Mashaw Table of Canons for Agency and Court Statutory Interpretation

Canon for Statutory Interpretation	Appropriate for Agencies?	Appropriate for Courts?
1. *Follow presidential directives unless clearly outside your authority*	Yes	No
2. *Interpret to avoid raising constitutional questions*	No	Yes
3. *Use legislative history as a primary interpretive guide*	Yes	No
4. *Interpret to give energy and breadth to all legislative programs within your jurisdiction*	Yes	No
5. *Engage in activist lawmaking*	Yes	No
6. *Respect all judicial precedent*	No	Yes
7. *Interpret to lend coherence to the overall legal order*	No	Yes
8. *Pay particular attention to the strategic parameters of interpretive efficiency*	Yes	No
9. *Interpret to secure hierarchical control over subordinates*	Yes	No
10. *Pay constant attention to your contemporary political milieu*	Yes	No
* Source: Jerry Mashaw, *Agency Statutory Interpretation*, Issues in Legal Scholarship, Issue 3: Dynamic Statutory Interpretation (2002): Article 9, *available at* www.bepress.com/ils/iss3/art9.		

Some items in Mashaw's table might be questioned. For example, item 5 strikes us as meaningless without a careful definition of "activist." Trevor Morrison, *Constitutional Avoidance in the Executive Branch*, 106 Colum. L. Rev. 1189 (2006), argues, contra Mashaw, that agencies should consider the avoidance canon when they interpret statutes. Overall, we should add that agencies are more instrumental, or purposive, in their application of statutes than courts tend to be. Kevin Stack, *Interpreting Regulations,* 111 Mich. L. Rev. 355 (2012) (explaining how agencies justify their regulations with an overwhelming focus on statutory purpose).

Consider a dramatic example of statutory interpretation "outside the courts," in the following problem.

INTRODUCTORY PROBLEM ON AGENCY INTERPRETATION

Problem 9–1. In the wake of the al Qaeda-organized attacks on the World Trade Center and the Pentagon on 9/11/01, President Bush authorized the National Security Agency (NSA) to intercept international communications into and out of the United States of persons linked to al Qaeda or related terrorist organizations. The President's purpose was to "establish an early warning system to detect and prevent another catastrophic terrorist attack on the United States." Presidential Press Conference, December 19, 2005. "[A] two-minute phone conversation between somebody linked to al Qaeda here and an operative overseas could lead directly to the loss of thousands of lives." Because terrorists pose such a significant threat and move quickly from place to place, the President maintains that protocols Congress set in place in 1978 for long-term electronic communications monitoring must be supplemented with shorter-term measures. NSA activities are "carefully reviewed every 45 days to ensure that [they are] being used properly." The Attorney General monitors for legality, and NSA officials themselves monitor to assure protection of civil liberties.

Members of Congress express concern. You are the General Counsel to the Senate Judiciary Committee, chaired in 2005–06 by Senator Arlen Specter (R–PA). Senator Specter wonders whether the NSA program is legal. It might violate the Fourth Amendment, which the Supreme Court has construed to require warrants and probable cause for wiretaps, e.g., *Katz v. United States*, 389 U.S. 347 (1967), but the Court has never ruled on the Fourth Amendment validity of surveillance to investigate foreign-sponsored terrorist activities. See *United States v. United States District Court*, 407 U.S. 297 (1972) (reserving this issue). Set the Fourth Amendment questions aside. Instead, Senator Specter asks you to tell him whether the NSA program is a legitimate exercise of the President's authority, in light of prior legislation. The following materials will help you frame an answer to Senator Specter.[1]

January 9, 2006 Letter from Scholars and Former Government Officials [Curtis A. Bradley et al.] to Congressional Leadership in Response to Justice Department Letter of December 22, 2005.[2] In 1978, Congress enacted the Foreign Intelligence Surveillance Act (FISA). "With minor exceptions, FISA authorizes

---

[1]   These materials are taken from the appendices to David Cole & Martin Lederman, *The National Security Agency's Domestic Spying Program: Framing the Debate*, 81 Ind. L.J. 1363–1424 (2006).

[2]   This Letter, 81 Ind. L.J. at 1364–72, was a response to the December 22, 2005 Letter from the Department of Justice to the Leadership of the Senate Select Committee on Intelligence and House Permanent Select Committee on Intelligence." *Id.* at 1360–63.

electronic surveillance only upon certain specified showings, and only if approved by a court. The statute specifically allows for warrantless *wartime* domestic electronic surveillance—but only for the first fifteen days of a war. 50 U.S.C. § 1811. It makes criminal any electronic surveillance not authorized by statute, *id.* § 1809; and it expressly establishes FISA and specified provisions of the federal criminal code (which govern wiretaps for criminal investigation) as the 'exclusive means by which electronic surveillance . . . may be conducted.' 18 U.S.C. § 2511(2)(f) (emphasis added)."

The Department of Justice (DOJ) conceded that FISA did not authorize the NSA program, but argued that the Authorization for the Use of Military Force (AUMF) did. Signed on September 18, 2001, the AUMF empowers the President to use "all necessary and appropriate force against" al Qaeda. According to the DOJ, collecting "signals intelligence" on the enemy, including U.S. phone tapping, is a "fundamental incident of war" authorized by the AUMF.

The scholars argued that the President was wrong about that conclusion: (1) The statute specifically addressing the matter of wiretaps (FISA) governs the more generally phrased law (AUMF). (2) Repeals by implication, the effect of the DOJ's broad AUMF interpretation, are disfavored in the law. (3) While "foreign battlefield capture of enemy combatants is an incident of waging war that Congress intended to authorize," it is "another matter entirely to treat unchecked warrantless *domestic* spying as included in that authorization, especially where an existing statute specifies that other laws are the 'exclusive means' by which electronic surveillance may be conducted and provides that even a declaration of war authorizes such spying only for a fifteen-day emergency period."

" * * * [T]he [old] federal law involving wiretapping specifically provided that '[n]othing contained in this chapter or in section 605 of the Communications Act of 1934 shall limit the constitutional power of the President . . . to obtain foreign intelligence information deemed essential to the security of the United States.' 18 U.S.C. § 2511(3) (1976).

"But FISA specifically repealed that provision, FISA § 201(c), 92 Stat. 1797, and replaced it with language dictating that FISA and the criminal code are the 'exclusive means' of conducting electronic surveillance. In doing so, Congress did not deny that the President has constitutional power to conduct electronic surveillance for national security purposes; rather, Congress properly concluded that 'even if the President has the inherent authority in the absence of legislation to authorize warrantless electronic surveillance for foreign intelligence purposes, Congress has the power to regulate the conduct of such surveillance by legislating a reasonable procedure, which then becomes the exclusive means by which such surveillance may be conducted.' H.R. Rep. No. 95–1283 (1978). * * *

U.S. Department of Justice, "Legal Authorities Supporting the Activities of the National Security Agency Described by the President," January 19, 2006.[3] "As Congress expressly recognized in the AUMF, 'the President has authority under the Constitution to take action to deter and prevent acts of international terrorism against the United States,' AUMF pmbl., especially in the context of the current conflict. Article II of the Constitution vests in the President all executive

---

[3]   This Letter, 81 Ind. L.J. at 1374–1414, was a response to the Scholars' Letter of January 9 and a detailed elaboration of arguments suggested in the Department's Letter of December 22.

powers of the United States, including the power to act as Commander in Chief of the Armed Forces, *see* U.S. Const. Art. II, § 2, and authority over the conduct of the Nation's foreign affairs. As the Supreme Court has explained, '[t]he President is the sole organ of the nation in its external relations, and its sole representative with foreign nations.' *United States v. Curtiss-Wright Export Corp.*, 299 U.S. 304 (1936). In this way, the Constitution grants the President inherent power to protect the Nation from foreign attack, *see, e.g., The Prize Cases*, 67 U.S. 635, 668 (1863), and to protect national security information, *see, e.g., Department of Navy v. Egan*, 484 U.S. 518, 527 (1988).

"To carry out these responsibilities, the President must have authority to gather information necessary for the execution of his office. The Founders, after all, intended the federal Government to be clothed with all authority necessary to protect the Nation. *See, e.g., The Federalist* * * * No. 41 (James Madison) ('Security against foreign danger is one of the primitive objects of civil society. . . . The powers requisite for attaining it must be effectually confided to the federal councils.'). Because of the structural advantages of the Executive Branch, the Founders also intended that the President would have the primary responsibility and necessary authority as Commander in Chief and Chief Executive to protect the Nation and to conduct the Nation's foreign affairs. See, e.g., *The Federalist* No.70, at 471–72 (Hamilton). * * *

"In reliance on these principles, a consistent understanding has developed that the President has inherent constitutional authority to conduct warrantless searches and surveillance within the United States for foreign intelligence purposes. Wiretaps for such purposes thus have been authorized by Presidents at least since the administration of Franklin Roosevelt in 1940. *See, e.g., United States v. United States District Court*, 444 F.2d 651, 669–71 (6th Cir. 1971) (reproducing as an appendix memoranda from Presidents Roosevelt, Truman, and Johnson). In a Memorandum to Attorney General Jackson, President Roosevelt wrote on May 21, 1940:

> You are, therefore, authorized and directed in such cases as you may approve, after investigation of the need in each case, to authorize the necessary investigation agents that they are at liberty to secure information by listening devices directed to the conversation or other communications of persons suspected of subversive activities against the Government of the United States, including suspected spies. You are requested furthermore to limit these investigations so conducted to a minimum and limit them insofar as possible to aliens. *Id.* at 670 (appendix A).

President Truman approved a memorandum drafted by Attorney General Tom Clark in which the Attorney General advised that 'it is as necessary as it was in 1940 to take the investigative measures' authorized by President Roosevelt to conduct electronic surveillance 'in cases vitally affecting the domestic security.' *Id.* * * *.

"The AUMF passed by Congress on September 14, 2001 [in the wake of 9/11] * * * authorizes the President 'to use all *necessary* and *appropriate force* against those nations, organizations, or persons *he determines* planned, authorized, committed, or aided the terrorist attacks that occurred on September 11, 2001.' AUMF § 2(a) (emphasis added). In the field of foreign affairs, and particularly that of war powers and national security, congressional enactments are to be broadly construed where they indicate support for authority long asserted and exercised by the Executive Branch. * * * This authorization transforms the struggle against al Qaeda and related terrorist organizations from what Justice Jackson called 'a zone of twilight,' in which the

President and Congress may have concurrent powers whose 'distribution is uncertain,' *Youngstown* (Jackson, J., concurring), into a situation in which the President's authority it at its maximum because 'it includes all that he possesses in his own right plus all that Congress can delegate,' *id.* With regard to these fundamental tools of warfare—and, as demonstrated below, warrantless electronic surveillance against the declared enemy is one such tool—the AUMF places the President's authority at its zenith under *Youngstown.* * * *

"The Supreme Court's interpretation of the scope of the AUMF in *Hamdi v. Rumsfeld*, 542 U.S. 507 (2004), strongly supports this reading of the AUMF. In *Hamdi*, five members of the Court found that the AUMF authorized the detention of an American within the United States, notwithstanding a statute that prohibits the detention of U.S. citizens 'except pursuant to an Act of Congress.' 18 U.S.C. § 4001(a). Drawing on historical materials and 'longstanding law-of-war principles,' a plurality of the Court concluded that detention of combatants who fought against the United States as part of an organization 'known to have supported' al Qaeda 'is so fundamental and accepted an incident to war as to be an exercise of the "necessary and appropriate force" Congress has authorized the President to use.' *Id.* at 518; *see also id.* at 587 (Thomas, J., dissenting) (agreeing with the plurality that the joint resolution authorized the President to 'detain those arrayed against our troops'). Thus, even though the AUMF does not say anything expressly about detention, the Court nevertheless found that it satisfied section 4001(a)'s requirement that detention be congressionally authorized. * * *

"The history of warfare—including the consistent practice of Presidents since the earliest days of the Republic—demonstrates that warrantless intelligence surveillance against the enemy is a fundamental incident of the use of military force, and this history confirms the statutory authority provided by the AUMF. Electronic surveillance is a fundamental tool of war that must be included in any natural reading of the AUMF's authorization to use 'all necessary and appropriate force.' " The DOJ argued that, from General Washington onward, American leaders have "intercepted communications for wartime intelligence purposes and, if necessary, ha[ve] done so within [American] borders." This practice continued during World War II and, according to one historian, "helped shorten the war by perhaps two years."

FISA § 109 prohibits anyone from "engag[ing] . . . in electronic surveillance under color of law *except as authorized by statute.*" 50 U.S.C. § 1809(a)(1) (emphasis added). "The AUMF qualifies as a 'statute' authorizing electronic surveillance within the meaning of section 109 of FISA. * * * Just as a majority of the Court concluded in *Hamdi* that the AUMF authorizes detention of U.S. citizens who are enemy combatants without expressly mentioning the President's long-recognized power to detain, so too does it authorize the use of electronic surveillance without specifically mentioning the President's equally long-recognized power to engage in communications intelligence targeted at the enemy. And just as the AUMF satisfies the requirement in 18 U.S.C. § 4001(a) that no U.S. citizen be detained 'except pursuant to an Act of Congress,' so too does it satisfy section 109's requirement for statutory authorization of electronic surveillance. * * * "

Even if the foregoing provisions were ambiguous, the DOJ argued that any doubt should be resolved in favor of presidential authority here. "It is well established that the first task of any interpreter faced with a statute that may present an unconstitutional infringement on the powers of the President is to determine whether the statute may be construed to avoid the constitutional difficulty. '[I]f an otherwise acceptable construction of a statute would raise serious constitutional problems, and where an alternative interpretation of the statute is "fairly possible," then we are obligated to construe the statute to avoid such problems.' *INS v. St. Cyr*, 533 U.S. 289, 299–300 (2001); *Ashwander v. TVA*, 297 U.S. 288, 345–48 (1936) (Brandeis, J., concurring). Moreover, the canon of constitutional avoidance has particular importance in the realm of national security, where the President's constitutional authority is at its highest. See *Department of the Navy v. Egan*, 484 U.S. 518, 530 (1988); William N. Eskridge Jr., *Dynamic Statutory Interpretation* 325 (1994) (describing '[s]uper-strong rule against congressional interference with the President's authority over foreign affairs and national security')." The AUMF should be interpreted broadly, and FISA narrowly, to avoid constructions where FISA would unconstitutionally obstruct the President's commander-in-chief powers.

February 2, 2006 Letter from Scholars and Former Government Officials to Congressional Leadership in Response to Justice Department White Paper of January 19, 2006. The Scholars found no authorization for illegal wiretapping in the AUMF, especially in light of section 111. "An amendment to FISA of the sort that would presumably be required to authorize the NSA program here would be a momentous statutory development, undoubtedly subject to serious legislative debate. It is decidedly *not* the sort of thing that Congress would enact *inadvertently.* As the Supreme Court recently noted, ' "Congress does not alter the fundamental details of a regulatory scheme in vague terms or ancillary provisions—it does not, one might say, hide elephants in mouseholes." ' *Gonzales v. Oregon*, 126 S.Ct. 904, 921 (2006) (quoting *Whitman v. American Trucking Ass'ns*, 531 U.S. 457, 468 (2001))."

Section 111 also distinguishes this situation from that in *Hamdi*. The detention statute in *Hamdi* did not mention detention of citizens in wartime. "Had there been a statute on the books providing that when Congress declares war, the President may detain Americans as 'enemy combatants' *only* for the first fifteen days of the conflict, the Court could not reasonably have read the AUMF to authorize silently what Congress had specifically sought to limit. Yet that is what the DOJ's argument would require here. [See also 18 U.S.C. § 2511(2)(f), which specifies that FISA and the criminal code are the 'exclusive means' by which electronic surveillance can be conducted. The Department of Justice concedes that its interpretation requires an implicit repeal of § 2511, which is strongly disfavored in the law.]

"The argument that conduct undertaken by the Commander in Chief that has some relevance to 'engaging the enemy' is immune from congressional regulation finds no support in, and is directly contradicted by, both case law and historical precedent. *Every* time the Supreme Court has confronted a statute limiting the Commander-in-Chief's authority, it has upheld the statute. No precedent holds that the President, when acting as Commander in Chief, is free to disregard an Act of Congress, much less a *criminal statute* enacted by Congress, that was designed specifically to restrain the President as such. [See, e.g., *Little v. Barreme*, 6 U.S. 170 (1804), holding unlawful a presidential seizure of a ship coming *from* France during the Quasi-War with France, when Congress authorized seizure only of ships going *to* France.]

"In fact, as cases such as *Hamdi* and *Rasul* demonstrate, Congress has routinely enacted statutes regulating the Commander-in-Chief's 'means and methods of engaging the enemy.' It has subjected the Armed Forces to the Uniform Code of Military Justice, which expressly restricts the means they use in 'engaging the enemy.' It has enacted statutes setting forth the rules for governing occupied territory. And, most recently, it has enacted statutes prohibiting torture under all circumstances, 18 U.S.C. §§ 2340–2340A, and prohibiting the use of cruel, inhuman, and degrading treatment. Pub. L. No. 109–148, Div. A, tit X, § 1003, 119 Stat. 2739–40 (2005). These limitations make ample sense in light of the overall constitutional structure. Congress has the explicit power 'To make Rules for the Government and Regulation of the land and naval Forces.' U.S. Const., art. I, § 8, cl. 14. The President has the explicit constitutional obligation to 'take Care that the Laws be faithfully executed,' U.S. Const., art. II, § 3—including FISA. And Congress has the explicit power to 'make all Laws which shall be necessary and proper for carrying into Execution . . . all . . . Powers vested by this Constitution in the Government of the United States, or in any Department or Officer thereof.' U.S. Const., art. I, [§ 8, cl. 18].

"If the DOJ were correct that Congress cannot interfere with the Commander in Chief's discretion in 'engaging the enemy,' all of these statutes would be unconstitutional. Yet the President recently conceded that Congress may constitutionally bar him from engaging in torture."

Queries: This exchange illustrates most of the Mashaw-endorsed canons for agencies and the executive to interpret statutes. Is this a model that seems attractive to you? If not, can you come up with one that would work better? Relevant to the Mashaw-Morrison debate, do you think the executive branch handled the constitutional arguments productively? If an American subject to the President's wiretapping brought a justiciable claim in federal court, challenging the President's authority under FISA, should the Supreme Court "defer" to the executive interpretation of FISA and AUMF?

2. THE BASIC FRAMEWORK: *SKIDMORE* AND *CHEVRON*

The New Deal approach to deference was founded on the comparative expertise of courts and agencies: the former should defer to the experts who worked with the statute day-in and day-out and developed wisdom about what worked and what did not. The leading case was *Skidmore v. Swift & Co.*, 323 U.S. 134 (1944). The case arose out of claims by Jim Skidmore and six other employees to recover overtime pay withheld allegedly in violation of the Fair Labor Standards Act of 1938 (FLSA). The men worked at the Fort Worth, Texas packing plant of Swift & Co. Two were engaged in general fire hall duties and maintenance of fire-fighting equipment of the plant. The others operated elevators or acted as relief men in fire duties. They worked from 7:00 a.m. to 3:30 p.m., with a half-hour lunch period, five days a week. Under an agreement with Swift, however, the workers agreed to stay in the fire hall on the company premises, or within hailing distance, three to four nights a week. This involved no task except to answer alarms, either because of fire or because the sprinkler was set off for some other reason. The employees claimed overtime pay under the FLSA. Swift refused, on the ground that the evening "on-call time" did not constitute "hours worked" for purposes of the statute.

Skidmore and his colleagues lost in the lower courts—but on appeal the Administrator of the Wage and Hour Division of the Department of Labor filed an *amicus* brief with the Supreme Court that described the flexible approach he had taken to the issue in a bulletin issued soon after the law was enacted. The Administrator distinguished situations where the employee carries on his normal life activities, subject to being called to solve a problem (such as a mechanic on-call to address problems with a company pump when they arise), from situations where the employee must stay in the office or close by (such as a company chauffeur). In the first situation, the employer was not required to pay workers for time spent sleeping and eating, but was required to pay for their "waiting around" time; in the second situation, the employer would usually be required to pay for "on call" time.

In the Administrator's view, the on-call time Skidmore spent sleeping and eating should not have been included in "hours worked," but the remainder of the on-call time should have been included. Justice Jackson's opinion for the *Skidmore* Court observed that the Administrator's practices and his recommendation in this case did not constitute a "binding" interpretation of the statute, but they were entitled to "respect," because they "constituted a body of experience and informed judgment" regarding workplace practices. "The weight of such a judgment in a particular case will depend upon the thoroughness evident in its consideration, the validity of its reasoning, its consistency with earlier and later pronouncements, and all those factors which give it power to persuade, if lacking power to control." The Court followed the Administrator's judgment and reversed the court below upon this point of law.

Soon after the adoption of the Administrative Procedure Act of 1946 (APA), Louis Jaffe explained how the modern administrative state fit into the traditional statutory interpretation framework, while at the same time altering it subtly. Louis Jaffe, *Judicial Review: Question of Law*, 69 Harv. L. Rev. 239 (1955). Consistent with *Marbury* and APA § 706, the Supreme Court remained the expositor of what the law is, but in carrying out that duty the Court was and ought to be open to agency inputs. Sometimes the Court found that the statute was relatively clear, but other times statutory vagueness suggested a range of possible meanings and the Court was willing to accept the agency's interpretation if it were within that range, as in *Skidmore* and later decisions such as *Udall v. Tallman*, 380 U.S. 1, 16 (1965).

Jaffe also maintained that the New Deal had regularized a different kind of agency role. In many statutes, Congress had delegated to agencies the authority to create enforceable "law," usually through binding adjudications and legislative rules. Under those circumstances, Jaffe argued that the role of the Court was more like the deferential judicial review that the New Deal Court applied to social and economic legislation. Likewise, when reviewing agency *lawmaking*, the Court should give the agency's rule the benefit of the doubt and overturn it only if it was *unreasonable,* in light of the statutory text and purposes. Jaffe, *Judicial Review,* 243–44. This idea was the germ for what would become the famous "*Chevron* Doctrine," below.

Title VII was an important situs for debates about how deferential federal courts should be to agency interpretations of statutes Congress had charged them with implementing. Recall, from Chapter 1, the EEOC's aggressive interpretation of Title VII to prohibit employer policies having a disparate impact on racial minorities (unless the policy was required by business necessity). One of the reasons the Supreme Court gave for following that interpretation was strong deference to the EEOC's views. *Griggs v. Duke Power Co.*, 401 U.S. 424, 433–34 (1971).

Contrast the Supreme Court's attitude in *General Electric Co. v. Gilbert*, 429 U.S. 125 (1976). General Electric Co. provided for all of its employees a disability plan which paid weekly nonoccupational sickness and accident benefits. Excluded from the plan's coverage were disabilities arising from pregnancy. Female employees challenged this plan as sex discrimination in violation of Title VII. The Supreme Court, in an opinion by Justice Rehnquist, held that the exclusion of pregnancy was, technically, not sex discrimination, as the exclusion did not affect most female employees. More important, because there was "no proof that the package is in fact worth more to men than to women, it is impossible to find any gender-based discrimination in the scheme simply because women disabled as a result of pregnancy do not receive benefits * * *."

The employees relied on a 1972 guideline issued by the EEOC and urged the Court to defer to it. Because Congress did not give the EEOC authority to promulgate legislative rules to implement Title VII, Justice Rehnquist evaluated the agency's views under the *Skidmore* standard. Unlike the Administrator's bulletin in *Skidmore,* the EEOC's guideline in *Gilbert* was promulgated almost a decade after the statute was enacted, was at odds with advice the agency had been giving companies before 1972, and was inconsistent with the Department of Labor's interpretation of the Equal Pay Act of 1963. (Section 703(h) of Title VII explicitly permits practices allowed under § 6 of the Equal Pay Act.)

The dissenting Justices argued that the EEOC moved slowly and deliberatively toward a policy on pregnancy and maternity, because the agency needed more information and study of this difficult issue. "Therefore, while some eight years had elapsed prior to the issuance of the 1972 guideline, and earlier opinion letters had refused to impose liability on employers during this period of deliberation, no one can or does deny that the final EEOC determination followed thorough and well-informed consideration. Indeed, realistically viewed, this extended evaluation of an admittedly complex problem and an unwillingness to impose additional, potentially premature costs on employers during the decision making stages ought to be perceived as a practice to be commended. It is bitter irony that the care that preceded promulgation of the 1972 guideline is today condemned by the Court as tardy indecisiveness, its unwillingness irresponsibly to challenge employers' practices during the formative period is labeled as evidence of inconsistency, and this indecisiveness and inconsistency are bootstrapped into reasons for denying the Commission's interpretation its due deference." (Congress agreed with the dissenters, overriding *Gilbert* in the Pregnancy Discrimination Act of 1978, Pub. L. No. 95–555, 92 Stat. 2076, codified at § 2000e(k).)

The Supreme Court's *Skidmore* jurisprudence had become quite complicated by the time *Gilbert* was decided. The level of deference the Court accorded an agency interpretation depended on whether Congress had delegated the agency lawmaking authority, whether the agency interpretation was contemporaneous with the statute, whether the agency had consistently interpreted the statute, whether

public or private institutions had relied on the agency's interpretation, and so forth. See Colin Diver, *Statutory Interpretation in the Administrative State*, 133 U. Pa. L. Rev. 549, 562 n.95 (1985). The Court generally followed agency views, as in *Skidmore* (but not *Gilbert*), but lacked a general doctrinal approach to the meta-issue of when judges must defer to agency views.

**CHEVRON, U.S.A., INC. V.
NATURAL RESOURCES DEFENSE COUNCIL**
Supreme Court of the United States, 1984.
467 U.S. 837, 104 S.Ct. 2778, 81 L.Ed.2d 694.

JUSTICE STEVENS delivered the opinion of the Court.

In the Clean Air Act Amendments of 1977, Pub. L. 95–95, 91 Stat. 685, Congress enacted certain requirements applicable to States that had not achieved the national air quality standards established by the Environmental Protection Agency (EPA) pursuant to earlier legislation. The amended Clean Air Act required these "nonattainment" States to establish a permit program regulating "new or modified major stationary sources" of air pollution. Generally, a permit may not be issued for a new or modified major stationary source unless several stringent conditions are met.[1] The EPA regulation promulgated to implement this permit requirement allows a State to adopt a plantwide definition of the term "stationary source."[2] Under this definition, an existing plant that contains several pollution-emitting devices may install or modify one piece of equipment without meeting the permit conditions if the alteration will not increase the total emissions from the plant. The question presented by these cases is whether EPA's decision to allow States to treat all of the pollution-emitting devices within the same industrial grouping as though they were encased within a single "bubble" is based on a reasonable construction of the statutory term "stationary source." * * *

[II] When a court reviews an agency's construction of the statute which it administers, it is confronted with two questions. First, always, is the question whether Congress has directly spoken to the precise question at issue. If the intent of Congress is clear, that is the end of the matter, for the court, as well as the agency, must give effect to the unambiguously expressed intent of Congress.[9] If, however, the court determines Congress has not directly addressed the precise question at issue, the court does not simply impose its own construction on the

---

[1]   Section 172(b)(6), 42 U.S.C. §7502(b)(6), provides:

"The plan provisions required by subsection (a) shall— * * *

"(6) require permits for the construction and operation of new or modified major stationary sources in accordance with section 173 (relating to permit requirements)." 91 Stat. 747.

[2]   "(i) 'Stationary source' means any building, structure, facility, or installation which emits or may emit any air pollutant subject to regulation under the Act.

"(ii) 'Building, structure, facility, or installation' means all of the pollutant-emitting activities which belong to the same industrial grouping, are located on one or more contiguous or adjacent properties, and are under the control of the same person (or persons under common control) except the activities of any vessel." 40 CFR §§ 51.18(j)(1)(i) and (ii) (1983).

[9]   The judiciary is the final authority on issues of statutory construction and must reject administrative constructions which are contrary to clear congressional intent. If a court, employing traditional tools of statutory construction, ascertains that Congress had an intention on the precise question at issue, that intention is the law and must be given effect.

statute, as would be necessary in the absence of an administrative interpretation. Rather, if the statute is silent or ambiguous with respect to the specific issue, the question for the court is whether the agency's answer is based on a permissible construction of the statute.[11]

"The power of an administrative agency to administer a congressionally created . . . program necessarily requires the formulation of policy and the making of rules to fill any gap left, implicitly or explicitly, by Congress." If Congress has explicitly left a gap for the agency to fill, there is an express delegation of authority to the agency to elucidate a specific provision of the statute by regulation. Such legislative regulations are given controlling weight unless they are arbitrary, capricious, or manifestly contrary to the statute. Sometimes the legislative delegation to an agency on a particular question is implicit rather than explicit. In such a case, a court may not substitute its own construction of a statutory provision for a reasonable interpretation made by the administrator of an agency.

We have long recognized that considerable weight should be accorded to an executive department's construction of a statutory scheme it is entrusted to administer, and the principle of deference to administrative interpretations

> "has been consistently followed by this Court whenever decision as to the meaning or reach of a statute has involved reconciling conflicting policies, and a full understanding of the force of the statutory policy in the given situation has depended upon more than ordinary knowledge respecting the matters subjected to agency regulations.

> ". . . If this choice represents a reasonable accommodation of conflicting policies that were committed to the agency's care by the statute, we should not disturb it unless it appears from the statute or its legislative history that the accommodation is not one that Congress would have sanctioned."

United States v. Shimer, 367 U.S. 374, 382, 383 (1961).

In light of these well-settled principles it is clear that the Court of Appeals misconceived the nature of its role in reviewing the regulations at issue. Once it determined, after its own examination of the legislation, that Congress did not actually have an intent regarding the applicability of the bubble concept to the permit program, the question before it was not whether in its view the concept is "inappropriate" in the general context of a program designed to improve air quality, but whether the Administrator's view that it is appropriate in the context of this particular program is a reasonable one. Based on the examination of the legislation and its history which follows, we agree with the Court of Appeals that Congress did not have a specific intention on the applicability of the bubble concept in these cases, and conclude that the EPA's use of that concept here is a reasonable policy choice for the agency to make.

[The 1977 Amendments added a definition of "major stationary source," as "any stationary facility or source of air pollutants which directly emits, or has the

---

[11] The court need not conclude that the agency construction was the only one it permissibly could have adopted to uphold the construction, or even the reading the court would have reached if the question initially had arisen in a judicial proceeding. * * *

potential to emit, one hundred tons per year or more of any air pollutant." Justice Stevens found this definition ambiguous. Examining the legislative history, he found only that Congress sought to accommodate both the "economic interest in permitting capital improvements to continue and the environmental interest in improving air quality." There was no clear evidence as to how Congress expected this balance to be carried out with regard to stationary sources.]

In these cases the Administrator's interpretation represents a reasonable accommodation of manifestly competing interests and is entitled to deference: the regulatory scheme is technical and complex, the agency considered the matter in a detailed and reasoned fashion, and the decision involves reconciling conflicting policies. Congress intended to accommodate both interests, but did not do so itself on the level of specificity presented by these cases. Perhaps that body consciously desired the Administrator to strike the balance at this level, thinking that those with great expertise and charged with responsibility for administering the provision would be in a better position to do so; perhaps it simply did not consider the question at this level; and perhaps Congress was unable to forge a coalition on either side of the question, and those on each side decided to take their chances with the scheme devised by the agency. For judicial purposes, it matters not which of these things occurred.

Judges are not experts in the field, and are not part of either political branch of the Government. Courts must, in some cases, reconcile competing political interests, but not on the basis of the judges' personal policy preferences. In contrast, an agency to which Congress has delegated policymaking responsibilities may, within the limits of that delegation, properly rely upon the incumbent administration's views of wise policy to inform its judgments. While agencies are not directly accountable to the people, the Chief Executive is, and it is entirely appropriate for this political branch of the Government to make such policy choices—resolving the competing interests which Congress itself either inadvertently did not resolve, or intentionally left to be resolved by the agency charged with the administration of the statute in light of everyday realities.

When a challenge to an agency construction of a statutory provision, fairly conceptualized, really centers on the wisdom of the agency's policy, rather than whether it is a reasonable choice within a gap left open by Congress, the challenge must fail. In such a case, federal judges—who have no constituency—have a duty to respect legitimate policy choices made by those who do. The responsibilities for assessing the wisdom of such policy choices and resolving the struggle between competing views of the public interest are not judicial ones: "Our Constitution vests such responsibilities in the political branches." *TVA v. Hill*, 437 U.S. 153, 195 (1978). * * *

JUSTICE MARSHALL and JUSTICE REHNQUIST did not participate in the consideration or decision of these cases.

JUSTICE O'CONNOR did not participate in the decision of these cases.

NOTES ON CHEVRON DEFERENCE
TO ADMINISTRATIVE INTERPRETATIONS

1. *The Accidental Birth of a New Regime.* The "bubble concept" adopted by the EPA was twice rebuffed in the D.C. Circuit, but the Department of Justice pressed it before the Supreme Court in an effort to reduce judicial interference with its deregulatory agency initiatives. Representing the EPA, Deputy Solicitor General Paul Bator argued that Congress's purpose was complex—to clean up the nation's air (the lower court's focus), but at a reasonable cost to industry (the EPA's focus). Because the statute was fairly open-ended, the EPA had considerable discretion in setting this policy balance, and federal judges should not upset that balance unless the EPA's view was clearly contrary to the statute.[4]

Penned by the first "political" deputy within the SG's Office, Bator's brief was a roadmap for relief from excessive regulatory burdens that was a hallmark of the Reagan Administration (1981–89). Liberal Justice William Brennan was suspicious of Bator's framework, but the Administration caught some lucky breaks as Justices dropped out of the case like flies in a hailstorm.[5] Their biggest break, though, was that the legality of the bubble concept was impossibly complicated for the Court. Apparently the shakiest voice in the original 4–3 conference vote to reverse the D.C. Circuit, Justice Stevens explained his tentative willingness to side with the EPA: "When I am so confused, I go with the agency." (Conference Notes by Justice Blackmun.) Encouraged by Justice White, the assigning Justice in the case, Justice Stevens not only accepted Bator's argument from complex statutory purpose, but went further to write an opinion that was analytically quite innovative.

2. *The Different Approach of* Chevron. *Chevron* reflects a different analytical approach to deference issues than *Gilbert* or *Skidmore* does. To begin with, the new approach is more formal and much simplified: Step One asks whether Congress specifically addressed the interpretive question. Justice Stevens's opinion says this is an issue Congress fudged. In that event, the Court moved to Step Two, which asks whether the agency's interpretation is "reasonable." If so, the Court has an obligation to defer. "Where an agency acts pursuant to delegated legislative authority, the task of interpretation is merely to define the boundaries" of what Peter Strauss calls the "zone of indeterminacy" within which Congress has authorized the agency to act.[6]

Chevron is also an important recognition of dynamic statutory interpretation in the modern administrative state, because it recognizes that first-order statutory interpretation will usually be accomplished by politically accountable—and therefore

---

[4] On the Bator brief and its background, see Thomas Merrill, *The Story of* Chevron USA Inc. v. Natural Resources Defense Council, Inc.: *Sometimes Great Cases Are Made, Not Born,* in *Statutory Interpretation Stories* 164, 177–80 (Eskridge, Frickey & Garrett eds., 2011).

[5] Although liberal Justice Brennan voted to affirm the D.C. Circuit, his liberal colleague Thurgood Marshall was absent due to illness. After voting with Brennan to affirm, Justice O'Connor also dropped out of the case because of a potential conflict of interest after her father died. See Memorandum from O'Connor to the Conference, June 14, 1984, in the Papers of Harry A. Blackmun, Library of Congress, Madison Building, Box 397, Folder 7. Also out of the case was Justice Rehnquist, who would probably have been a voice for deference.

[6] Peter Strauss, *One Hundred and Fifty Cases Per Year: Some Implications of the Supreme Court's Limited Resources for Judicial Review of Agency Action,* 87 Colum. L. Rev. 1093, 1124 (1987); see also Michael E. Herz, *Deference Running Riot: Separating Interpretation and Lawmaking under* Chevron, 6 Admin. L.J. Am. U. 187, 199 (1992); Peter Strauss, *"Deference" Is too Confusing—Let's Call Them "Chevron Space" and "Skidmore Weight,"* 112 Colum. L. Rev. 1143 (2012).

politically protean—agencies; because it further recognizes that under general statutory language that does not target the interpretive issue (Step One) there may be several "reasonable" agency interpretations, any of which must be upheld (Step Two); and because it recognizes that agency interpretations may themselves change over time. "An initial agency interpretation is not carved in stone. On the contrary, the agency, to engage in informal rulemaking, must consider varying interpretations and the wisdom of its policy on a continuing basis." *Chevron,* 467 U.S. at 863–64.

Finally, *Chevron* rests the idea of deference, at least in part, on the greater democratic legitimacy that agencies enjoy over courts in making policy choices that have been left open by Congress. This reflects the legal realist insight that the law will often be indeterminate, susceptible of more than one reading, but reconciles the realist insight with democratic accountability by insisting that unelected judges ratify the "reasonable" alternative adopted by the agency. Note that agencies may be accountable to Congress as well as the President, which gives them a double dose of greater policymaking legitimacy than federal courts have.

3. *Critical Reception. Chevron* was controversial from the very beginning. Then-Judge Breyer objected that a broad reading of *Chevron* is inconsistent with the judicial role articulated in both *Marbury* and in the APA. Both require courts to exercise independent judgment to declare what the law of the land is. Stephen Breyer, *Judicial Review of Questions of Law and Policy,* 38 Admin. L. Rev. 363, 370 (1986); see Cynthia Farina, *Statutory Interpretation and the Balance of Power in the Administrative State,* 89 Colum. L. Rev. 452 (1989) (developing this objection in detail). "[T]he present law of judicial review of administrative decisionmaking, the heart of administrative law, contains an important anomaly," Breyer said. "The law (1) requires courts to defer to agency judgments about *matters of law,* but (2) it also suggests that courts conduct independent, 'in-depth' reviews of agency judgments about *matters of policy.* Is this not the exact opposite of a rational system? Would one not expect courts to conduct a stricter review of matters of law, where courts are more expert, but more lenient review of matters of policy, where agencies are more expert?" Breyer, *Judicial Review,* 397.

John Duffy suggested that the APA and *Chevron* can be reconciled only by understanding that regulatory statutes delegate to agencies the power to interpret ambiguous statutory commands, so long as the agencies' decisions do not conflict with other provisions of law. "Thus, *Chevron* is primarily a case about delegation, not deference." Duffy, *Administrative Common Law in Judicial Review,* 77 Tex. L. Rev. 113, 202 (1998). How consistent is Duffy's conclusion with the reasoning in *Chevron*? Or with the actual ruling of the case (upholding the agency)?

4. *Was There a* Chevron *Revolution? Preliminary Soundings.* The conventional wisdom in administrative law has been that *Chevron* was a revolutionary decision ushering in a new period of greater deference to agency interpretations of statutes agencies are charged with enforcing. This might be questioned or qualified. On the one hand, deference to agencies was a trend long preceding *Chevron.* Peter Schuck & E. Donald Elliott, *To the* Chevron *Station: An Empirical Study of Federal Administrative Law,* 1990 Duke L.J. 984, conclude from a lengthy historical study of federal appellate review of agency determinations that long before *Chevron* agency affirmance rates were on the rise in the federal courts—especially during the 1970s, even though that was the heyday of hard look review in the D.C. Circuit (which supposedly subjected administrative decisions to a greater degree of review).

On the other hand, it is not clear how much *Chevron* changed the prevailing Supreme Court practice. Since the New Deal, the Court has been deferential to agency decisions, sometimes with language presaging *Chevron*. In *Batterton v. Francis*, 432 U.S. 416 (1977), the Court held that when Congress delegates lawmaking authority to an agency, "Congress entrusts to the [agency], rather than to the courts, the primary responsibility for interpreting the statutory term." Once the agency has authoritatively construed the statute through legislative rules, the reviewing court "is not free to set aside the [agency] regulation simply because it would have interpreted the statute in a different manner."

Just as the Court was often highly deferential before *Chevron*, it was often pretty scrutinizing after *Chevron*. For example, in *INS v. Cardoza-Fonseca*, 480 U.S. 421 (1987), the Court not only rejected the INS's interpretation of its obligations not to deport noncitizens who have a "well-founded fear" of political persecution, 8 U.S.C. § 1158(a), but laid out a detailed legal regime for the INS to follow. Moreover, the Court in *Christensen v. Harris County*, 529 U.S. 576, 586–88 (2000), *id.* at 596–97 (Breyer, J., dissenting on other grounds), reaffirmed the *Skidmore* standard for weighing the views of an agency when expressed through informal opinions and letters. In both cases, Justice Scalia objected that the *Chevron* theory for deference (the superior legitimacy agencies had in filling in genuine statutory gaps) should apply to the EEOC and to informal but public rulings by the agency, but agreed that the EEOC's interpretations should be set aside because they were inconsistent with the statute.

Many well-informed judges and scholars believe that *Chevron* has had a bigger impact among federal courts of appeals than at the Supreme Court itself.[7] This is a plausible (albeit not empirically demonstrated) phenomenon, because of the Supreme Court's discretionary jurisdiction. Courts of appeals must rule on all legitimate appeals, and *Chevron* gives them an easy way to dispatch many routine regulatory issues. The Supreme Court, in contrast, usually takes only the hardest issues that divide the lower courts, and the Justices may be reluctant just to go along with agency constructions that raise complicated normative as well as doctrinal issues.

MCI TELECOMMUNICATIONS CORP. V. AT&T

Supreme Court of the United States, 1994.
512 U.S. 218, 114 S.Ct. 2223, 129 L.Ed.2d 182.

JUSTICE SCALIA delivered the opinion for the Court.

Section 203(a) of Title 47 of the United States Code requires communications common carriers to file tariffs with the Federal Communications Commission, and § 203(b) authorizes the Commission to "modify" any requirement of § 203. These cases present the question whether the Commission's decision to make tariff filing optional for all nondominant long-distance carriers is a valid exercise of its modification authority.

---

[7]   Schuck & Elliott, Chevron *Station*, found that the D.C. Circuit's agency agreement rates went up significantly in the years immediately after *Chevron*. Other scholars have found an ongoing *Chevron* effect at the lower court level, e.g., Thomas Miles & Cass Sunstein, *Do Judges Make Regulatory Policy? An Empirical Investigation of* Chevron, 73 U. Chi. L. Rev. 823 (2006) (examining court of appeals decisions reviewing EPA and NLRB decisions). See also Kristin Hickman & Mathew Krueger, *In Search of the Modern* Skidmore *Standard,* 107 Colum. L. Rev. 1235 (2007), finding a statistically significant amount of *Skidmore* deference among the courts of appeals.

[The Communications Act of 1934, 48 Stat. 1064, as amended, authorized the FCC to regulate the rates charged for communication services to ensure that they were reasonable and nondiscriminatory. The requirements of § 203 that common carriers file their rates with the Commission and charge only the filed rate were the centerpiece of the Act's regulatory scheme. For the next 40 years, AT&T had a virtual monopoly over the nation's telephone service, but in the 1970s new competitors emerged. During the 1980s, the Commission allowed, and briefly required, nondominant carriers an exemption from the tariff requirements. The Supreme Court accepted AT&T's challenge to the agency rule.]

The dispute between the parties turns on the meaning of the phrase "modify any requirement" in § 203(b)(2). Petitioners [MCI and the FCC] argue that it gives the Commission authority to make even basic and fundamental changes in the scheme created by that section. We disagree. The word "modify"—like a number of other English words employing the root "mod-" (deriving from the Latin word for "measure"), such as "moderate," "modulate," "modest," and "modicum"—has a connotation of increment or limitation. Virtually every dictionary we are aware of says that "to modify" means to change moderately or in minor fashion. See, e.g., Random House Dictionary of the English Language 1236 (2d ed. 1987) ("to change somewhat the form or qualities of; alter partially; amend"); [similar references from Webster's Third New International Dictionary, Oxford English Dictionary, and Black's Law Dictionary].

In support of their position, petitioners cite dictionary definitions contained in, or derived from, a single source, Webster's Third New International Dictionary 1452 (1981) (Webster's Third), which includes among the meanings of "modify," "to make a basic or important change in." Petitioners contend that this establishes sufficient ambiguity to entitle the Commission to deference in its acceptance of the broader meaning, which in turn requires approval of its permissive detariffing policy. See *Chevron*. In short, they contend that the courts must defer to the agency's choice among available dictionary definitions. * * *

Most cases of verbal ambiguity in statutes involve * * * a selection between accepted alternative meanings shown as such by many dictionaries. One can envision (though a court case does not immediately come to mind) having to choose between accepted alternative meanings, one of which is so newly accepted that it has only been recorded by a single lexicographer. (Some dictionary must have been the very first to record the widespread use of "projection," for example, to mean "forecast.") But what petitioners demand that we accept as creating an ambiguity here is a rarity even rarer than that: a meaning set forth in a single dictionary (and, as we say, its progeny) which not only *supplements* the meaning contained in all other dictionaries, but *contradicts* one of the meanings contained in virtually all other dictionaries. Indeed, contradicts one of the alternative meanings contained in the out-of-step dictionary itself—for * * * Webster's Third itself defines "modify" to connote *both* (specifically) major change *and* (specifically) minor change. It is hard to see how that can be. When the word "modify" has come to mean *both* "to change in some respects" *and* "to change fundamentally" it will in fact mean *neither* of those things. It will simply mean "to change," and some adverb will have to be called into service to indicate the great or small degree of the change.

If that is what the peculiar Webster's Third definition means to suggest has happened—and what petitioners suggest by appealing to Webster's Third—we simply disagree. "Modify," in our view, connotes moderate change. It might be good English to say that the French Revolution "modified" the status of the French nobility—but only because there is a figure of speech called understatement and a literary device known as sarcasm. And it might be unsurprising to discover a 1972 White House press release saying that "the Administration is modifying its position with regard to prosecution of the war in Vietnam"—but only because press agents tend to impart what is nowadays called "spin." Such intentional distortions, or simply careless or ignorant misuse, must have formed the basis for the usage that Webster's Third, and Webster's Third alone, reported.[3] It is perhaps gilding the lily to add this: In 1934, when the Communications Act became law—the most relevant time for determining a statutory term's meaning, see *Perrin v. United States*, 444 U.S. 37, 42–45 (1979)—Webster's Third was not yet even contemplated. To our knowledge *all* English dictionaries provided the narrow definition of "modify," including those published by G. & C. Merriam Company. We have not the slightest doubt that is the meaning the statute intended. * * *

Since an agency's interpretation of a statute is not entitled to deference when it goes beyond the meaning that the statute can bear, *Chevron*, the Commission's permissive detariffing policy can be justified only if it makes a less than radical or fundamental change in the Act's tariff-filing requirement. The Commission's attempt to establish that no more than that is involved greatly understates the extent to which its policy deviates from the filing requirement, and greatly undervalues the importance of the filing requirement itself. [Tariff-filing is at the heart of the regulatory scheme, because it provides the data by which the FCC can police rate-discrimination and unreasonableness in charges.]

Bearing in mind, then, the enormous importance to the statutory scheme of the tariff-filing provision, we turn to whether what has occurred here can be considered a mere "modification." The Commission stresses that its detariffing policy applies only to nondominant carriers, so that the rates charged to over half of all consumers in the long-distance market are on file with the Commission. It is not clear to us that the proportion of customers affected, rather than the proportion of carriers affected, is the proper measure of the extent of the exemption (of course *all* carriers in the long-distance market are exempted, except AT&T). But even assuming it is, we think an elimination of the crucial provision of the statute for 40% of a major sector of the industry is much too extensive to be considered a "modification." What we have here, in reality, is a fundamental revision of the statute, changing it from a scheme of rate regulation in long-distance common-carrier communications to a scheme of rate regulation only where effective competition does not exist. That may be a good idea, but it was not the idea Congress enacted into law in 1934. * * *

---

[3]   That is not an unlikely hypothesis. Upon its long-awaited appearance in 1961, Webster's Third was widely criticized for its portrayal of common error as proper usage. See, e.g., Follett, Sabotage in Springfield, 209 Atlantic 73 (Jan. 1962); Barzun, What is a Dictionary? 32 The American Scholar 176, 181 (spring 1963); Macdonald, The String Unwound, 38 The New Yorker 130, 156–157 (Mar. 1962). An example is its approval (without qualification) of the use of "infer" to mean "imply". * * *

[JUSTICE O'CONNOR took no part in the consideration or decision of these cases.]

JUSTICE STEVENS, with whom JUSTICE BLACKMUN and JUSTICE SOUTER join, dissenting. * * *

Although the majority observes that further relaxation of tariff-filing requirements might more effectively enhance competition, it does not take issue with the Commission's conclusions that mandatory filing of tariff schedules serves no useful purpose and is actually counterproductive in the case of carriers who lack market power. As the Commission had noted in its prior detariffing orders, if a nondominant carrier sought to charge inflated rates, "customers would simply move to other carriers." Moreover, an absence of market power will ordinarily preclude firms of any kind from engaging in price discrimination. The Commission plausibly concluded that any slight enforcement benefits a tariff-filing requirement might offer were outweighed by the burdens it would put on new entrants and consumers. Thus, the sole question for us is whether the FCC's policy, however sensible, is nonetheless inconsistent with the Act.

In my view, each of the Commission's detariffing orders was squarely within its power to "modify any requirement" of § 203. Section 203(b)(2) plainly confers at least some discretion to modify the general rule that carriers file tariffs, for it speaks of "*any* requirement." Section 203(c) of the Act, ignored by the Court, squarely supports the FCC's position; it prohibits carriers from providing service without a tariff "*unless otherwise provided by or under authority of this Act.*" Section 203(b)(2) is plainly one provision that "otherwise provides," and thereby authorizes, service without a filed schedule. The FCC's authority to modify § 203's requirements in "particular instances" or by "general order applicable to special circumstances or conditions" emphasizes the expansive character of the Commission's authority: modifications may be narrow or broad, depending upon the Commission's appraisal of current conditions. From the vantage of a Congress seeking to regulate an almost completely monopolized industry, the advent of competition is surely a "special circumstance or condition" that might legitimately call for different regulatory treatment. * * *

According to the Court, the term "modify," as explicated in all but the most unreliable dictionaries, rules out the Commission's claimed authority to relieve nondominant carriers of the basic obligation to file tariffs. Dictionaries can be useful aids in statutory interpretation, but they are no substitute for close analysis of what words mean as used in a particular statutory context. Even if the sole possible meaning of "modify" were to make "minor" changes,[3] further elaboration is needed to show why the detariffing policy should fail. The Commission came to its present policy through a series of rulings that gradually relaxed the filing requirements for nondominant carriers. Whether the current policy should count as a cataclysmic or merely an incremental departure from the § 203(a) baseline depends on whether one focuses on particular carriers' obligations to file (in which

---

[3]   As petitioner MCI points out, the revolutionary consent decree providing for the breakup of the Bell System was, per AT&T's own proposal, entitled "Modification of Final Judgment." See *United States v. American Telephone & Telegraph Co.*, 552 F. Supp. 131 (D.C. 1982), aff'd, 460 U.S. 1001 (1983).

case the Commission's policy arguably works a major shift) or on the statutory policies behind the tariff-filing requirement (which remain satisfied because market constraints on nondominant carriers obviate the need for rate filing). When § 203 is viewed as part of a statute whose aim is to constrain monopoly power, the Commission's decision to exempt nondominant carriers is a rational and "measured" adjustment to novel circumstances—one that remains faithful to the core purpose of the tariff-filing section. See Black's Law Dictionary 1198 (3d ed. 1933) (defining "modification" as "A change; an alteration which introduces new elements into the details, or cancels some of them, but leaves *the general purpose and effect of the subject-matter* intact").

The Court seizes upon a particular sense of the word "modify" at the expense of another, long-established meaning that fully supports the Commission's position. That word is first defined in Webster's Collegiate Dictionary 628 (4th ed. 1934) as meaning "to limit or reduce in extent or degree." The Commission's permissive detariffing policy fits comfortably within this common understanding of the term. The FCC has in effect adopted a general rule stating that "if you are dominant you must file, but if you are nondominant you need not." The Commission's partial detariffing policy—which excuses nondominant carriers from filing *on condition that* they remain nondominant—is simply a relaxation of a costly regulatory requirement that recent developments had rendered pointless and counterproductive in a certain class of cases.

A modification pursuant to § 203(b)(1), like any other order issued under the Act, must of course be consistent with the purposes of the statute. On this point, the Court asserts that the Act's prohibition against unreasonable and discriminatory rates "would not be susceptible of effective enforcement if rates were not publicly filed." That determination, of course, is for the Commission to make in the first instance. But the Commission has repeatedly explained that (1) a carrier that lacks market power is entirely unlikely to charge unreasonable or discriminatory rates, (2) the statutory bans on unreasonable charges and price discrimination apply with full force regardless of whether carriers have to file tariffs, (3) any suspected violations by nondominant carriers can be addressed on the Commission's own motion or on a damages complaint filed pursuant to § 206, and (4) the FCC can reimpose a tariff requirement should violations occur. The Court does not adequately respond to the FCC's explanations, and gives no reason whatsoever to doubt the Commission's considered judgment that tariff filing is altogether unnecessary in the case of competitive carriers; the majority's ineffective enforcement argument lacks any evidentiary or historical support. * * *

The filed tariff provisions of the Communications Act are not ends in themselves, but are merely one of several procedural *means* for the Commission to ensure that carriers do not charge unreasonable or discriminatory rates. The Commission has reasonably concluded that this particular means of enforcing the statute's substantive mandates will prove counterproductive in the case of nondominant long-distance carriers. Even if the 1934 Congress did not define the scope of the Commission's modification authority with perfect scholarly precision, this is surely a paradigm case for judicial deference to the agency's interpretation, particularly in a statutory regime so obviously meant to maximize administrative flexibility. Whatever the best reading of § 203(b)(2), the Commission's reading cannot in my view be termed unreasonable. It is informed (as ours is not) by a practical understanding of the role (or lack thereof) that filed tariffs play in the modern regulatory climate and in the telecommunications industry. Since 1979, the FCC has sought to adapt measures originally designed to control monopoly power to new market conditions. It has carefully and consistently explained that mandatory tariff-filing rules frustrate the core statutory interest in rate reasonableness. The Commission's use of the "discretion" expressly conferred by § 203(b)(2) reflects "a reasonable accommodation of manifestly competing interests and is entitled to deference: the regulatory scheme is technical and complex, the agency considered the matter in a detailed and reasoned fashion, and the decision involves reconciling conflicting policies." *Chevron.* The FCC has permissibly interpreted its § 203(b)(2) authority in service of the goals Congress set forth in the Act. We should sustain its eminently sound, experience-tested, and uncommonly well-explained judgment.

NOTES ON MCI, THE NEW TEXTUALISM, AND "EXCESSIVE" LEGISLATIVE DELEGATIONS TO AGENCIES

1. *The New Textualism and* Chevron: *Should the Court Consider Legislative History?* In *INS v. Cardoza-Fonseca*, 480 U.S. 421 (1987), Justice Scalia alone adhered to the view that *Chevron* permits overturning agency action only when the agency view clashes with a clear statutory text. All other Justices consulted the legislative history to determine the validity of the agency view under *Chevron.* Justice Scalia has continued to press his view that statutory text and structure are the only relevant inquiries in Step One of the *Chevron* analysis (has Congress specifically addressed the issue?). Justice Stevens's approach, that other traditional tools such as legislative history and purpose are also relevant in Step One, seemed to lose ground on the Court after *Cardoza-Fonseca.* E.g., *Sutton v. United Air Lines, Inc.*, 527 U.S. 471, 482 (1999); *City of Chicago v. Environmental Defense Fund*, 511 U.S. 328 (1994).[8]

However, there have also been many post-*MCI* decisions in which the Court considered legislative history and other nontextual arguments when doing a *Chevron* analysis. E.g., *FDA v. Brown & Williamson Tobacco Corp.* (Chapter 6, § 3B); *Babbitt v. Sweet Home* (the last case in Chapter 7). In *Wisconsin Public Intervenor v. Mortier*, 501 U.S. 597, 610 n.4 (1991), the Court *Chevron*-deferred to an agency interpretation that the federal pesticide law did not preempt state law. In determining whether Congress had directly addressed this question (*Chevron* Step One), the Court examined the legislative history as well as the statutory text. Justice White's opinion marshaling legislative history won over the votes of Chief Justice Rehnquist and Justice O'Connor, who had originally thought that the statutory scheme "occupied the field" and therefore preempted state law (according to Justice Blackmun's conference notes). In dissent, Justice Scalia mounted a full-scale assault on the Court's reliance on legislative history—an assault that drew no support from any other Justice. See also William Eskridge Jr. & Lauren Baer, *The Continuum of Deference: Supreme Court Treatment of Agency Statutory Interpretations from* Chevron *to* Hamdan, 96 Geo. L.J. 1083, 1135–36

---

[8] See the excellent discussion in Richard Lazarus & Claudia Newman, City of Chicago v. Environmental Defense Fund: *Searching for Plain Meaning in Unambiguous Ambiguity*, 4 N.Y.U. Envtl. L.J. 1 (1995).

(2008) (finding that the Court relies on legislative history *more* often in *Chevron* cases than in other statutory interpretation cases).

Consider a suggestion made by the Seventh Circuit in *Bankers Life & Cas. Co. v. United States*, 142 F.3d 973 (1998). "While this circuit has examined legislative history during the first step of *Chevron*, we now seem to lean toward reserving consideration of legislative history and other appropriate factors until the second *Chevron* step." This approach would focus on statutory text and structure to determine whether the law is ambiguous (Step One) and, if so, would consider legislative history and the statutory purpose while evaluating the reasonableness of the agency's construction (Step Two). One might evaluate *Sweet Home* (the spotted owl case) along these lines. The statutory text was ambiguous as to whether destruction of habitat constituted a taking of endangered animals, and so the Justices should have evaluated the agency's position under Step Two of *Chevron*. The legislative discussions surrounding the 1973 statute (relied on by dissenting Justice Scalia) and its 1982 amendment (relied on by Justice Stevens's opinion for the Court) would then have been relevant to the reasonableness of the agency's choice.

2. *The Implications of the New Textualism for Deference, More Generally.* If Justice Scalia's position on *Chevron* were adopted by the Court, agency rules might be *more* prone to reversal than under Justice Stevens's position. Justice Scalia explains why this might be so in *Judicial Deference to Administrative Interpretation of Law*, 1989 Duke L.J. 511, 521:

> * * * One who finds *more* often (as I do) that the meaning of a statute is apparent from its text and from its relationship with other laws, thereby finds *less* often that the triggering requirement for *Chevron* deference exists. It is thus relatively rare that *Chevron* will require me to accept an interpretation which, though reasonable, I would not personally adopt. Contrariwise, one who abhors a "plain meaning" rule, and is willing to permit the apparent meaning of a statute to be impeached by legislative history, will more frequently find agency-liberating ambiguity. * * *

Accord, Thomas Merrill, *Textualism and the Future of the* Chevron *Doctrine*, 72 Wash. U.L.Q. 351, 372 (1994).[9]

---

[9]   Professor Merrill speculates that textualism may lead to a "permanent subordination of the *Chevron* doctrine." 72 Wash. U.L.Q. at 372. He explains:

> This has to do with the style of judging associated with textualism. Intentionalism mandates an "archeological" excavation of the past, producing opinions written in the style of the dry archivist sifting through countless documents in search of the tell-tale smoking gun of congressional intent. Textualism, in contrast, seems to transform statutory interpretation into a kind of exercise in judicial ingenuity. The textualist judge treats questions of interpretation like a puzzle to which it is assumed there is one right answer. The task is to assemble the various pieces of linguistic data, dictionary definitions, and canons into the best (most coherent, most explanatory) account of the meaning of the statute. This exercise places a great premium on cleverness. In one case the outcome turns on the place of a comma, in another on the inconsistency between a comma and rules of grammar, in a third on the conflict between quotation marks and the language of the text. One day arguments must be advanced in support of broad dictionary definitions; the next day in support of narrow dictionary definitions. New canons of construction and clear statement rules must be invented and old ones reinterpreted.

This active, creative approach to interpretation is subtly incompatible with an attitude of deference toward other institutions—whether the other institution is Congress or an administrative agency. In effect, the textualist interpreter does not *find* the meaning of the statute so much as *construct* the meaning. Such a person will very likely experience some difficulty in deferring to the meanings that other institutions have developed.

A milder conclusion suggested by Justice Scalia's law review article would be that the new textualism is more likely to resolve cases at Step One of *Chevron* (the agency is either right or wrong) and is less likely to get to Step Two, which is where deference really kicks in (the law is unclear, so the agency can make a choice the judges would not have otherwise made). Others are skeptical that methodology per se is decisive. See Eskridge & Baer, *Continuum of Deference*, 96 Geo. L.J. at 1153–56 (reporting relatively low agency agreement rates for textualist Justices Scalia and Thomas, but even lower rates for Justice Stevens, who relies on legislative history). Indeed, there are plenty of cases where Justice Scalia's textualism is more lenient toward agency interpretations than it was in *MCI* or *Sweet Home*. E.g., *Massachusetts v. EPA*, 549 U.S. 497 (2007) (Scalia, J., dissenting) (deferring to EPA interpretation narrowly construing its broad statutory authority over greenhouse gases allegedly contributing to global warming).

3.   MCI, *Dictionaries, and Excessive Delegations. MCI* is a leading case for the Court's well-honed deployment of dictionaries. See Chapter 7, § 1A; James Brudney & Lawrence Baum, *Oasis or Mirage: The Supreme Court's Thirst for Dictionaries in the Rehnquist and Roberts Eras*, 55 Wm & Mary L. Rev. 483 (2013). The Court faults *Webster's Third* for too readily incorporating ordinary usage—which would seem to be most desirable for discerning the meaning an ordinary reader would draw from the statute. One might argue, however, that legislative drafters use language more formally, and thus more consistently with the prescriptive approach of *Webster's Second. MCI* also involves a methodological debate over the extent to which policy context matters.

One reading of *MCI* is that it supports a rule or presumption against excessive delegations. The Supreme Court will not enforce the nondelegation doctrine anymore—it will not strike down, as a constitutional violation, even extremely broad legislative delegations of lawmaking authority to administrative agencies. The Court can still give this "underenforced constitutional norm" some teeth, however, by "canonizing" it. Thus, the Court will be reluctant to read statutory delegations broadly, for fear that this will encourage the legislature to make excessive delegations. Does this reading make *MCI* a more persuasive opinion? How can this be reconciled with *Chevron*?

This reading of *MCI* reappeared in *FDA v. Brown & Williamson* (Chapter 6, § 3B), where the Court said: "Deference under *Chevron* to an agency's construction of a statute that it administers is premised on the theory that a statute's ambiguity constitutes an implicit delegation from Congress to the agency to fill in the statutory gaps. In extraordinary cases, however, there may be reason to hesitate before concluding that Congress has intended such an implicit delegation." The Court then noted the "unique place" tobacco has in American history and the "distinct regulatory scheme" Congress created for tobacco products. "Given this history and the breadth of the authority that the FDA has asserted, we are obliged to defer not to the agency's expansive construction of the statute, but to Congress' consistent judgment to deny the FDA this power. * * * As in *MCI*, we are confident that Congress could not have intended to delegate a decision of such economic and political significance to an agency in so cryptic a fashion." *Brown & Williamson*, 529 U.S. at 159–60. Is this a persuasive deployment of *MCI*? Should this precept have counseled a different result in some of the other cases where the Court has deferred to agencies, such as *Sweet Home* (end of Chapter 7)? *Bob Jones* (Chapter 6, § 2)?

UNITED STATES V. MEAD CORP.

Supreme Court of the United States, 2001.
533 U.S. 218, 121 S.Ct. 2164, 150 L.Ed.2d 292.

JUSTICE SOUTER delivered the opinion of the Court.

The question is whether a tariff classification ruling by the United States Customs Service deserves judicial deference. The Federal Circuit rejected Customs's invocation of *Chevron* in support of such a ruling, to which it gave no deference. We agree that a tariff classification has no claim to judicial deference under *Chevron*; there being no indication that Congress intended such a ruling to carry the force of law, but we hold that under *Skidmore*, the ruling is eligible to claim respect according to its persuasiveness. * * *

[II.A]   When Congress has "explicitly left a gap for an agency to fill, there is an express delegation of authority to the agency to elucidate a specific provision of the statute by regulation," *Chevron*, and any ensuing regulation is binding in the courts unless procedurally defective, arbitrary or capricious in substance, or manifestly contrary to the statute. See APA, 5 U.S.C. § 706(2)(A), (D). But whether or not they enjoy any express delegation of authority on a particular question, agencies charged with applying a statute necessarily make all sorts of interpretive choices, and while not all of those choices bind judges to follow them, they certainly may influence courts facing questions the agencies have already answered. "[T]he well-reasoned views of the agencies implementing a statute 'constitute a body of experience and informed judgment to which courts and litigants may properly resort for guidance,'" *Bragdon v. Abbott*, 524 U.S. 624, 642 (1998) (quoting *Skidmore*), and "[w]e have long recognized that considerable weight should be accorded to an executive department's construction of a statutory scheme it is entrusted to administer. . . ." *Chevron* (footnote omitted).

The fair measure of deference to an agency administering its own statute has been understood to vary with circumstances, and courts have looked to the degree of the agency's care, its consistency, formality, and relative expertness, and to the persuasiveness of the agency's position, see *Skidmore*. * * * Justice Jackson summed things up in *Skidmore*:

> "The weight [accorded to an administrative] judgment in a particular case will depend upon the thoroughness evident in its consideration, the validity of its reasoning, its consistency with earlier and later pronouncements, and all those factors which give it power to persuade, if lacking power to control."

Since 1984, we have identified a category of interpretive choices distinguished by an additional reason for judicial deference. This Court in *Chevron* recognized that Congress not only engages in express delegation of specific interpretive authority, but that "[s]ometimes the legislative delegation to an agency on a particular question is implicit." Congress, that is, may not have expressly delegated authority or responsibility to implement a particular provision or fill a particular gap. Yet it can still be apparent from the agency's generally conferred authority and other statutory circumstances that Congress would expect the agency to be able to

speak with the force of law when it addresses ambiguity in the statute or fills a space in the enacted law, even one about which "Congress did not actually have an intent" as to a particular result. When circumstances implying such an expectation exist, a reviewing court has no business rejecting an agency's exercise of its generally conferred authority to resolve a particular statutory ambiguity simply because the agency's chosen resolution seems unwise, but is obliged to accept the agency's position if Congress has not previously spoken to the point at issue and the agency's interpretation is reasonable; *cf.* 5 U.S.C. § § 706(2) (a reviewing court shall set aside agency action, findings, and conclusions found to be "arbitrary, capricious, an abuse of discretion, or otherwise not in accordance with law").

We have recognized a very good indicator of delegation meriting *Chevron* treatment in express congressional authorizations to engage in the process of rulemaking or adjudication that produces regulations or rulings for which deference is claimed. [Citing cases, including *Gilbert*, that apply only *Skidmore* deference to EEOC interpretations.] It is fair to assume generally that Congress contemplates administrative action with the effect of law when it provides for a relatively formal administrative procedure tending to foster the fairness and deliberation that should underlie a pronouncement of such force. Thus, the overwhelming number of our cases applying *Chevron* deference have reviewed the fruits of notice-and-comment rulemaking or formal adjudication. That said, and as significant as notice-and-comment is in pointing to *Chevron* authority, the want of that procedure here does not decide the case, for we have sometimes found reasons for *Chevron* deference even when no such administrative formality was required and none was afforded, see, *e.g.*, *NationsBank of N.C., N.A.* v. *Variable Annuity Life Ins. Co.*, 513 U.S. 251, 256–257, 263 (1995). The fact that the tariff classification here was not a product of such formal process does not alone, therefore, bar the application of *Chevron*.

There are, nonetheless, ample reasons to deny *Chevron* deference here. The authorization for classification rulings, and Customs's practice in making them, present a case far removed not only from notice-and-comment process, but from any other circumstances reasonably suggesting that Congress ever thought of classification rulings as deserving the deference claimed for them here.

[II.B]   No matter which angle we choose for viewing the Customs ruling letter in this case, it fails to qualify under *Chevron*. On the face of the statute, to begin with, the terms of the congressional delegation give no indication that Congress meant to delegate authority to Customs to issue classification rulings with the force of law. We are not, of course, here making any global statement about Customs's authority, for it is true that the general rulemaking power conferred on Customs authorizes some regulation with the force of law, or "legal norms" * * *. It is true as well that Congress had classification rulings in mind when it explicitly authorized, in a parenthetical, the issuance of "regulations establishing procedures for the issuance of binding rulings prior to the entry of the merchandise concerned," 19 U.S.C. § 1502(a). The reference to binding classifications does not, however, bespeak the legislative type of activity that would naturally bind more than the parties to the ruling, once the goods classified are admitted into this country. And though the statute's direction to disseminate "information" necessary to "secure" uniformity, *ibid.*, seems to assume that a ruling may be precedent in later transactions, precedential value alone does not add up to *Chevron* entitlement; interpretive rules may sometimes function as precedents, see Strauss, *The Rulemaking Continuum*, 41 Duke L.J. 1463, 1472–1473 (1992), and they enjoy no *Chevron* status as a class. In any event, any precedential claim of a classification ruling is counterbalanced by the provision for independent review of Customs classifications by the CIT [Court of International Trade]; the scheme for CIT review includes a provision that treats classification rulings on par with the Secretary's rulings on "valuation, rate of duty, marking, restricted merchandise, entry requirements, drawbacks, vessel repairs, or similar matters," § 1581(h). It is hard to imagine a congressional understanding more at odds with the *Chevron* regime. [Indeed, the Customs Service itself did not act as though its letter rulings were lawmaking. The agency did not even follow the notice-and-comment process when issuing such documents—10,000 to 15,000 letter rulings a year churned out by 46 different Customs offices. Hence, the Court treated them the same way it treats agency guidances or policy documents, as "beyond the *Chevron* pale."]

[II.C]   To agree with the Court of Appeals that Customs ruling letters do not fall within *Chevron* is not, however, to place them outside the pale of any deference whatever. *Chevron* did nothing to eliminate *Skidmore*'s holding that an agency's interpretation may merit some deference whatever its form, given the "specialized experience and broader investigations and information" available to the agency, and given the value of uniformity in its administrative and judicial understandings of what a national law requires.

There is room at least to raise a *Skidmore* claim here, where the regulatory scheme is highly detailed, and Customs can bring the benefit of specialized experience to bear on the subtle questions in this case: whether the daily planner with room for brief daily entries falls under "diaries," when diaries are grouped with "notebooks and address books, bound; memorandum pads, letter pads and similar articles"; and whether a planner with a ring binding should qualify as "bound," when a binding may be typified by a book, but also may have "reinforcements or fittings of metal, plastics, etc." A classification ruling in this situation may therefore at least seek a respect proportional to its "power to persuade," *Skidmore*. Such a ruling may surely claim the merit of its writer's thoroughness, logic and expertness, its fit with prior interpretations, and any other sources of weight.

[II.D]   Underlying the position we take here, like the position expressed by Justice Scalia in dissent, is a choice about the best way to deal with an inescapable feature of the body of congressional legislation authorizing administrative action. That feature is the great variety of ways in which the laws invest the Government's administrative arms with discretion, and with procedures for exercising it, in giving meaning to Acts of Congress. Implementation of a statute may occur in formal adjudication or the choice to defend against judicial challenge; it may occur in a central board or office or in dozens of enforcement agencies dotted across the country; its institutional lawmaking may be confined to the resolution of minute detail or extend to legislative rulemaking on matters intentionally left by Congress to be worked out at the agency level.

Although we all accept the position that the Judiciary should defer to at least some of this multifarious administrative action, we have to decide how to take account of the great range of its variety. If the primary objective is to simplify the judicial process of giving or withholding deference, then the diversity of statutes authorizing discretionary administrative action must be declared irrelevant or minimized. If, on the other hand, it is simply implausible that Congress intended such a broad range of statutory authority to produce only two varieties of administrative action, demanding either *Chevron* deference or none at all, then the breadth of the spectrum of possible agency action must be taken into account. Justice Scalia's first priority over the years has been to limit and simplify. The Court's choice has been to tailor deference to variety. This acceptance of the range of statutory variation has led the Court to recognize more than one variety of judicial deference, just as the Court has recognized a variety of indicators that Congress would expect *Chevron* deference. * * *

Since the *Skidmore* assessment called for here ought to be made in the first instance by the Court of Appeals for the Federal Circuit or the CIT, we go no further than to vacate the judgment and remand the case for further proceedings consistent with this opinion.

JUSTICE SCALIA, dissenting.

Today's opinion makes an avulsive change in judicial review of federal administrative action. Whereas previously a reasonable agency application of an ambiguous statutory provision had to be sustained so long as it represented the agency's authoritative interpretation, henceforth such an application can be set aside unless "it appears that Congress delegated authority to the agency generally to make rules carrying the force of law," as by giving an agency "power to engage in adjudication or notice-and-comment rulemaking, or . . . some other [procedure] indicati[ng] comparable congressional intent," and "the agency interpretation claiming deference was promulgated in the exercise of that authority." What was previously a general presumption of authority in agencies to resolve ambiguity in the statutes they have been authorized to enforce has been changed to a presumption of no such authority, which must be overcome by affirmative legislative intent to the contrary. And whereas previously, when agency authority to resolve ambiguity did not exist the court was free to give the statute what it considered the best interpretation, henceforth the court must supposedly give the agency view some indeterminate amount of so-called *Skidmore* deference. We will be sorting out the consequences of the *Mead* doctrine, which has today replaced the *Chevron* doctrine, for years to come. I would adhere to our established jurisprudence, defer to the reasonable interpretation the Customs Service has given to the statute it is charged with enforcing, and reverse the judgment of the Court of Appeals.

[I.A]   As to principle: The doctrine of *Chevron*—that all *authoritative* agency interpretations of statutes they are charged with administering deserve deference—was rooted in a legal presumption of congressional intent, important to the division of powers between the Second and Third Branches. When, *Chevron* said, Congress leaves an ambiguity in a statute that is to be administered by an executive agency, it is presumed that Congress meant to give the agency discretion, within the limits of reasonable interpretation, as to how the ambiguity is to be resolved. By committing enforcement of the statute to an agency rather than the courts, Congress committed its initial and primary interpretation to that branch as well.

There is some question whether *Chevron* was faithful to the text of the Administrative Procedure Act (APA), which it did not even bother to cite. But it was in accord with the origins of federal-court judicial review. Judicial control of federal executive officers was principally exercised through the prerogative writ of mandamus. That writ generally would not issue unless the executive officer was acting plainly beyond the scope of his authority. [Quoting *Wilbur v. United States ex rel. Kadrie*, 281 U.S. 206, 221–222 (1930).] Statutory ambiguities, in other words, were left to reasonable resolution by the Executive.

The basis in principle for today's new doctrine can be described as follows: The background rule is that ambiguity in legislative instructions to agencies is to be resolved not by the agencies but by the judges. Specific congressional intent to depart from this rule must be found—and while there is no single touchstone for such intent it can generally be found when Congress has authorized the agency to act through (what the Court says is) relatively formal procedures such as informal rulemaking and formal (and informal?) adjudication, and when the agency in fact employs such procedures. The Court's background rule is contradicted by the origins of judicial review of administrative action. But in addition, the Court's principal criterion of congressional intent to supplant its background rule seems to me quite implausible. There is no necessary connection between the formality of procedure and the power of the entity administering the procedure to resolve authoritatively questions of law. The most formal of the procedures the Court refers to—formal adjudication—is modeled after the process used in trial courts, which of course are not generally accorded deference on questions of law. The purpose of such a procedure is to produce a closed record for determination and review of the facts—which implies nothing about the power of the agency subjected to the procedure to resolve authoritatively questions of law. * * *

[In Part II.B, Justice Scalia lamented the terrible "practical effects" of the Court's new rule.] (1) The principal effect will be protracted confusion. As noted above, the one test for *Chevron* deference that the Court enunciates is wonderfully imprecise: whether "Congress delegated authority to the agency generally to make rules carrying the force of law, . . . as by . . . adjudication[,] notice-and-comment rulemaking, or . . . some other [procedure] indicati[ng] comparable congressional intent." But even this description does not do justice to the utter flabbiness of the Court's criterion, since, in order to maintain the fiction that the new test is really just the old one, applied consistently throughout our case law, the Court must make a virtually open-ended exception to its already imprecise guidance: In the present case, it tells us, the absence of notice-and-comment rulemaking (and "[who knows?] [of] some other [procedure] indicati[ng] comparable congressional intent") is not enough to decide the question of *Chevron* deference, "for we have sometimes found reasons for *Chevron* deference even when no such administrative formality was required and none was afforded." The opinion then goes on to consider a grab bag of other factors—including the factor that used to be the sole criterion for *Chevron* deference: whether the interpretation represented the *authoritative* position of the agency. It is hard to know what the lower courts are to make of today's guidance.

(2) Another practical effect of today's opinion will be an artificially induced increase in informal rulemaking. Buy stock in the GPO. Since informal rulemaking and formal adjudication are the only more-or-less safe harbors from the storm that the Court has unleashed; and since formal adjudication is not an option but must be mandated by statute or constitutional command; informal rulemaking—which the Court was once careful to make voluntary unless required by statute—will now become a virtual necessity. As I have described, the Court's safe harbor requires not merely that the agency have been given rulemaking authority, but also that the agency have *employed* rulemaking as the means of resolving the statutory ambiguity. (It is hard to understand why that should be so. Surely the mere *conferral* of rulemaking authority demonstrates—if one accepts the Court's logic—a congressional intent to allow the agency to resolve ambiguities. And given that intent, what difference does it make that the agency chooses instead to use another perfectly permissible means for that purpose?) Moreover, the majority's approach will have a perverse effect on the rules that do emerge, given the principle (which the Court leaves untouched today) that judges must defer to reasonable agency interpretations of their own regulations. Agencies will now have high incentive to rush out barebones, ambiguous rules construing statutory ambiguities, which they can then in turn further clarify through informal rulings entitled to judicial respect.

(3) Worst of all, the majority's approach will lead to the ossification of large portions of our statutory law. Where *Chevron* applies, statutory ambiguities remain ambiguities subject to the agency's ongoing clarification. They create a space, so to speak, for the exercise of continuing agency discretion. As *Chevron* itself held, the Environmental Protection Agency can interpret "stationary source" to mean a single smokestack, can later replace that interpretation with the "bubble concept" embracing an entire plant, and if that proves undesirable can return again to the original interpretation. For the indeterminately large number of statutes taken out of *Chevron* by today's decision, however, ambiguity (and hence flexibility) will cease with the first judicial resolution. *Skidmore* deference gives the agency's current position some vague and uncertain amount of respect, but it does not, like *Chevron*, *leave* the matter within the control of the Executive Branch for the future. Once the court has spoken, it becomes *unlawful* for the agency to take a contradictory position; the statute now *says* what the court has prescribed. It will be bad enough when this ossification occurs as a result of judicial determination (under today's new principles) that there is no affirmative indication of congressional intent to "delegate"; but it will be positively bizarre when it occurs simply because of an agency's failure to act by rulemaking (rather than informal adjudication) before the issue is presented to the courts.

One might respond that such ossification would not result if the agency were simply to readopt its interpretation, after a court reviewing it under *Skidmore* had rejected it, by repromulgating it through one of the *Chevron*-eligible procedural formats approved by the Court today. Approving this procedure would be a landmark abdication of judicial power. It is worlds apart from *Chevron* proper, where the court does not *purport* to give the statute a judicial interpretation—except in identifying the scope of the statutory ambiguity, as to which the court's judgment is final and irreversible. (Under *Chevron* proper, when the agency's authoritative interpretation comes within the scope of that ambiguity—and the court therefore approves it—the agency will not be "overruling" the court's decision when it later decides that a different interpretation (still within the scope of the ambiguity) is preferable.) By contrast, under this view, the reviewing court will not be holding the agency's authoritative interpretation within the scope of the ambiguity; but will be holding that the agency has not used the "delegation-conferring" procedures, and that the court must therefore *interpret the statute on its own*—but subject to reversal if and when the agency uses the proper procedures.

* * * I know of no case, in the entire history of the federal courts, in which we have allowed a judicial interpretation of a statute to be set aside by an agency—or have allowed a lower court to render an interpretation of a statute subject to correction by an agency. As recently as 1996, we rejected an attempt to do *precisely* that. In *Chapman* v. *United States*, 500 U.S. 453 (1991) [affirming *Marshall v. United States*, excerpted and discussed in Chapter 7, § 3], we had held that the weight of the blotter paper bearing the lysergic acid diethylamide (LSD) must be counted for purposes of determining whether the quantity crossed the 10–gram threshold of 21 U.S.C. § 841(b)(1)(A)(v) imposing a minimum sentence of 10 years. At that time the United States Sentencing Commission applied a similar approach under the Sentencing Guidelines, but had taken no position regarding the meaning of the statutory provision. The Commission later changed its Guidelines approach, and, according to the petitioner in *Neal* v. *United States*, 516 U.S. 284 (1996), made clear its view that the statute bore that meaning as well. The petitioner argued that we should defer to that new approach. We would have none of it.

> "Were we, for argument's sake, to adopt petitioner's view that the Commission intended the commentary as an interpretation of § § 841(b)(1), and that the last sentence of the commentary states the Commission's view that the dose-based method is consistent with the term 'mixture or substance' in the statute, he still would not prevail. The Commission's dose-based method cannot be squared with *Chapman*. . . . In these circumstances, we need not decide what, if any, deference is owed the Commission in order to reject its alleged contrary interpretation. Once we have determined a statute's meaning, we adhere to our ruling under the doctrine of *stare decisis*, and we assess an agency's later interpretation of the statute against that settled law."

There is, in short, no way to avoid the ossification of federal law that today's opinion sets in motion. What a court says is the law after according *Skidmore* deference will be the law forever, beyond the power of the agency to change even through rulemaking.

(4) And finally, the majority's approach compounds the confusion it creates by breathing new life into the anachronism of *Skidmore*, which sets forth a sliding scale of deference owed an agency's interpretation of a statute that is dependent "upon the thoroughness evident in [the agency's] consideration, the validity of its

reasoning, its consistency with earlier and later pronouncements, and all those factors which give it power to persuade, if lacking power to control"; in this way, the appropriate measure of deference will be accorded the "body of experience and informed judgment" that such interpretations often embody. Justice Jackson's eloquence notwithstanding, the rule of *Skidmore* deference is an empty truism and a trifling statement of the obvious: A judge should take into account the well-considered views of expert observers.

It was possible to live with the indeterminacy of *Skidmore* deference in earlier times. But in an era when federal statutory law administered by federal agencies is pervasive, and when the ambiguities (intended or unintended) that those statutes contain are innumerable, totality-of-the-circumstances *Skidmore* deference is a recipe for uncertainty, unpredictability, and endless litigation. To condemn a vast body of agency action to that regime (all except rulemaking, formal (and informal?) adjudication, and whatever else might now and then be included within today's intentionally vague formulation of affirmative congressional intent to "delegate") is irresponsible.

[In Part II of his dissenting opinion, Justice Scalia criticized the majority's approach as an important departure from the Court's post-*Chevron* precedents as well as *Chevron* itself. In Part III, Justice Scalia explained why *Chevron*, properly understood, required deference to the Customs Service. "*Chevron* sets forth an across-the-board presumption, which operates as a background rule of law against which Congress legislates: Ambiguity means Congress intended agency discretion. Any resolution of the ambiguity by the administering agency that is authoritative— that represents the official position of the agency—must be accepted by the courts if it is reasonable." Given that precept as his starting point, Justice Scalia found nothing in the customs statute to rebut the presumptive discretion Congress gave the Service to draw lines as to tariff categories. In Part IV, Justice Scalia maintained that deference was required by *Nations Bank of N. C., N. A.* v. *Variable Annuity Life Ins. Co.*, 513 U. S. 251 (1995), which the Court acknowledged as an instance in which *Chevron* deference was warranted notwithstanding the absence of formal adjudication, notice-and-comment rulemaking, or comparable administrative formality.]

NOTES ON MEAD AND RECENT REPORTS ON THE "CHEVRON REVOLUTION"

1. *The Grounding of* Chevron *on the Notion of Delegated Authority to Issue Orders or Rules Having the Force of Law.* The Court's decision in *Mead* makes clear that the normative basis for *Chevron*'s deference-plus regime is congressional intent to delegate *lawmaking* authority to agencies. See Thomas Merrill & Kristin Hickman, Chevron's *Domain*, 89 Geo. L.J. 833 (2001), as well as Thomas Merrill, *Rethinking Article I, Section 1: From Nondelegation to Exclusive Delegation*, 104 Colum. L. Rev. 2097 (2004). Again over the dissents of Justice Scalia, the Court reaffirmed this understanding in *National Cable & Telecommunications Ass'n v. Brand X Internet Services*, 545 U.S. 967 (2005), and *Gonzales v. Oregon*, 546 U.S. 243 (2006) (both excerpted below).

Although this is the Court's official test, it is one that the post-*Chevron* Court has applied unevenly. On the one hand, the Court does not seem to have a clear idea of when Congress has vested agencies with authority to create rules or orders having the "force of law." Thus, the Court often treats NLRB orders as having the force of law, even though that is clearly incorrect as a technical or historical matter: The NLRA says that the agency's orders should *not* have legal effect unless the agency or a party goes to court and obtains an order to that effect. See Thomas Merrill & Kathryn Tongue Watts, *Agency Rules with the Force of Law: The Original Convention*, 116 Harv. L. Rev. 467 (2002). Indeed, the EPA rule in *Chevron* was not, in 1984, a rule having the force of law. *Id.* at 587. The Court's approach is further complicated in *Mead*, where the Court says that Congress might implicitly delegate lawmaking authority to an agency. See also *Barnhart v. Walton*, 535 U.S. 212 (2002) (providing an even more functional *Skidmore*-like approach to *Chevron* than *Mead*). It is far from clear what kinds of statutory schemes would amount to an "implicit" delegation, and the lower courts have shown evidence of increased confusion since *Mead*.[10]

On the other hand, the Court's deployment of *Chevron* has been underwhelming in those cases where there has been an explicit grant of lawmaking authority. The Eskridge and Baer study surveyed 1014 post-*Chevron* Supreme Court decisions between 1984 and 2006 where an agency statutory interpretation was presented to the Court. In 8.3% of those cases, the Court majority applied the *Chevron* framework—but almost 27% of the cases involved agency decisions pursuant to grants of adjudicatory or legislative rulemaking authority. About 10% of the *Chevron* cases involved very informal agency action clearly not derived from lawmaking grants—agency letters, interpretive guidances, and even opinions voiced in *amicus* briefs. See William Eskridge Jr. & Lauren Baer, *The Continuum of Deference: Supreme Court Treatment of Agency Statutory Interpretations from* Chevron *to* Hamdan, 96 Geo. L.J. 1083, 1125 (2008) (Table 4).

The Eskridge and Baer study also found that, for the period 1984–2006, the Court followed pre-*Chevron* deference-plus (i.e., non-*Skidmore*) regimes in 4.8% of its cases. *Id.* at 1099–1100 (Table 1). Most of these involved deference to NLRB, IRS, HHS, and FDA interpretations. The conceptual basis for these cases falls somewhere between *Chevron* and *Skidmore*: Congress has vested such-and-such agency with authority to carry out the statutory purpose; to carry out the congressional purpose, the agency needs interpretational breathing room; hence, courts ought to defer to reasonable agency readings of the statute. E.g., *Beth Israel Hospital v. NLRB*, 437 U.S. 483 (1978), applied in *Auciello Iron Works v. NLRB*, 517 U.S. 781 (1996) (NLRB); *National Muffler Dealers v. United States*, 440 U.S. 472 (1979), overruled in *Mayo Foundation v. United States*, 131 S.Ct. 704 (2011) (requiring that *Chevron* replace *National Muffler* as the deference standard in tax cases where there has been a delegation of lawmaking authority to the IRS).

2. *The Survival—Indeed, Flourishing—of* Skidmore. *Mead* confirmed the survival of *Skidmore* as the default deference regime. The Eskridge and Baer study identified 6.7% of the cases in their database as ones where the Court explicitly applied *Skidmore* deference, almost as many cases as where the Court applied *Chevron* during

---

[10] See Lisa Schultz Bressman, *How* Mead *Has Muddled Judicial Review of Agency Action*, 58 Vand. L. Rev. 1443 (2005) (yes, *Mead* has muddled judicial review of agency action); Adrian Vermeule, *Introduction:* Mead *in the Trenches*, 71 Geo. Wash. L. Rev. 347 (2003) (*Mead* has created very muddled trenches).

their time period (1984–2006). See Eskridge & Baer, *Continuum of Deference,* 96 Geo. L.J. at 1099–1100 (Table 1). Moreover, in 17.8% of the cases Eskridge and Baer collected, the Court relied on or was clearly influenced by an agency rule or *amicus* brief (the format followed by the agency in *Skidmore*), but without citation of *Skidmore* or an announcement that the Court was "deferring." The authors call this last group of cases *Skidmore*-Lite. *Id.* (Table 1). Not only has *Skidmore* not been overruled, but it has perhaps been the dominant deference regime within the Supreme Court.

Even this summary illustrates the authors' argument that the primary mechanism for agency success at the Supreme Court level is neither formal lawmaking delegation nor *Chevron* deference, but some combination of institutional acquiescence and statutory subject matter. For all statutes, the Solicitor General usually persuades the Court that the government's construction of the statute is correct, even in cases (like civil rights) where the Justices have strong opinions themselves. For statutes that are technical and instrumental to some routine economic or foreign affairs goal, the Justices have less strong opinions and are cognizant that they do not have full command of the technical considerations important to these cases; hence, the Justices are super-deferential in those cases.

3.   *Evidence of Ideological Voting by the Justices in Agency Deference Cases.* In the wake of *Mead,* a number of academic studies found evidence of ideological voting in agency deference cases. For example, consider the pattern of voting found in the Eskridge and Baer study of 1014 cases in which agency interpretations were in play:

Agreement with Agency Interpretations, by Justice (*Chevron* to *Hamdan*)

Supreme Court Justice (Tenure)	Agreement with Agency Overall	Agreement with Liberal Agency Interpretations	Agreement with Conservative Agency Interpretations
Warren Burger (1969–86)	82.3%	75.9%	87.0%
Byron White (1962–93)	74.0%	71.9%	76.3%
Lewis Powell (1971–87)	72.7%	73.9%	73.0%
Stephen Breyer (1994–)	72.0%	79.5%	64.9%
William Rehnquist (1971–2006)	70.6%	59.4%	79.1%
Ruth Bader Ginsburg (1993–)	69.5%	77.1%	61.9%
Anthony Kennedy (1986–)	69.3%	61.8%	74.0%
David Souter (1990–2009)	68.7%	75.6%	62.5%
Sandra Day O'Connor (1981–2007)	68.6%	61.5%	73.7%
Harry Blackmun (1970–1993)	65.1%	80.6%	55.3%
Antonin Scalia (1986–)	64.5%	53.8%	71.6%

Clarence Thomas (1991–)	63.1%	46.8%	75.8%
John Paul Stevens (1975–2010)	60.9%	79.2%	49.6%
Thurgood Marshall (1967–91)	55.6%	84.8%	38.8%
William Brennan (1956–90)	52.6%	81.6%	36.7%
Source: Eskridge & Baer, *Continuum of Deference,* 96 Geo. L.J. at 1154 (Table 20).			

These data reveal a wide variance of judicial willingness to go along with agency interpretations: Warren Burger, Byron White, and Lewis Powell were quite deferential, while William Brennan and Thurgood Marshall went against agency views most of the time. Surprisingly, John Paul Stevens, the author of *Chevron,* is one of the less deferential in practice, as is Antonin Scalia.

Eskridge and Baer found pretty much the same pattern when they limited their analysis to the *Chevron* cases in their database or to the 267 cases involving agency interpretations pursuant to delegated lawmaking authority. The Justices had slightly higher deference rates, but the ideological pattern remained the same. Accord, Thomas Miles & Cass Sunstein, *Do Judges Make Regulatory Policy? An Empirical Investigation of* Chevron, 73 U. Chi. L. Rev. 823 (2006).

PROBLEM INVOLVING AN AGENCY'S DYNAMIC INTERPRETATION OF AN OLD STATUTE

Problem 9–2. Section 30 of the National Bank Act of 1864, Rev. Stat. § 5197, as amended, 12 U.S.C. § 85, provides that a national bank may charge its loan customers "interest at the rate allowed by the laws of the State * * * where the bank is located." In *Marquette Nat. Bank of Minneapolis v. First of Omaha Service Corp.,* 439 U.S. 299 (1978), the Supreme Court held that this provision authorizes a national bank to charge out-of-state credit-card customers an interest rate allowed by the bank's home state, even when that rate is higher than what is permitted by the states in which the cardholders reside. Citibank is a national bank, and it starts to charge late-payment fees that are lawful in its home state but prohibited in many states where cardholders reside. Can Citibank lawfully charge the late-payment fees? Are such fees "interest" authorized by the Bank Act, as Citibank claims?

(a) How would a judge decide this issue? A judge would start with the statutory language and the Supreme Court's *Marquette National Bank* precedent. Is a late-payment fee "interest" as that term is used in ordinary or regulatory parlance? You might consult modern dictionaries as well as dictionaries of the era in which the statute was enacted. For example, 1 J. Bouvier, *A Law Dictionary* 652 (6th ed. 1856), defined "interest" as "compensation which is paid by the borrower to the lender or by the debtor to the creditor for * * * use [of money]." The Supreme Court said this in *Brown v. Hiatts,* 15 Wall. 177, 185 (1873): "Interest is the compensation allowed by law, or fixed by the parties, for the use or forbearance of money or as damages for its detention." More recently, *Webster's Ninth New Collegiate* defines interest as "a charge for borrowed money, generally a percentage of the amount borrowed." And the Oxford

English Dictionary (2d edition) defined it this way in 1989: "Money paid for the use of money lent (the principal), or for forbearance of a debt, according to a fixed ratio."

Is there a statutory plain meaning here? If you were a lower court judge obligated to follow the Supreme Court's guidance, would you also consult legislative history and the purpose of the National Bank Act? If you think you should, read the Court's decision in *Marquette National Bank*, which has an excellent discussion of the legislative history and goals of the 1864 Act. Is it relevant that the Federal Reserve Board does not consider late-payment fees to be "finance charges" that must be disclosed to mortgage borrowers as an annual percentage interest rate under the Truth in Lending Act of 1967? Federal Reserve Board, Regulation Z, § 226.4(c)(2).

Ultimately, how would you rule on the late-payments issue: Interest? Or not?

(b) Does an agency interpretation make a difference? The issue of late-payment fees was not a salient one in 1864, when the statute was enacted. But once late-payment fees became an important consumer issue and many states prohibited the practice, the Comptroller of the Currency started to address the issue. "The Comptroller of the Currency is charged with the enforcement of banking laws to an extent that warrants the invocation of [judicial deference] with respect to his deliberative conclusions as to the meaning of these laws." *NationsBank of N.C., N.A. v. Variable Annuity Life Ins. Co.,* 513 U.S. 251, 256–257 (1995).

In 1996, more than a century after the statute's enactment, the Comptroller, after notice-and-comment, adopted the following rule:

> The term "interest" as used in 12 U.S.C. § 85 includes any payment compensating a creditor or prospective creditor for an extension of credit, making available of a line of credit, or any default or breach by a borrower of a condition upon which credit was extended. It includes, among other things, the following fees connected with credit extension or availability: numerical periodic rates, late fees, not sufficient funds (NSF) fees, overlimit fees, annual fees, cash advance fees, and membership fees. It does not ordinarily include appraisal fees, premiums and commissions attributable to insurance guaranteeing repayment of any extension of credit, finders' fees, fees for document preparation or notarization, or fees incurred to obtain credit reports."

61 Fed. Reg. 4862 (codified in 12 CFR § 7.4001(a)). Is this regulation entitled to *Chevron* deference, even though it was adopted more than a century after the statute was enacted? Does this regulation change the answer you gave to Problem 9–2(A)?

(c) Does the agency's change of position make a difference? Consider, further, that the 1996 regulation was not the first occasion for the Comptroller's Office to address the issue of late-payment fees. In June 1964, the Comptroller wrote a letter to the President's Committee on Consumer Interests, which states that "[c]harges for late payments, credit life insurance, recording fees, documentary stamp are illustrations of charges which are made by some banks which would not properly be characterized as interest." In a 1988 opinion letter, the Deputy Chief Counsel of the OCC stated that "it is my position that [under § 85] the laws of the states where the banks are located * * * determine whether or not the banks can impose the foregoing fees and charges [including late fees] on Iowa residents," OCC Interpretive Letter No.

452, reprinted in 1988–1989 Transfer Binder, CCH Fed. Banking L. Rep. ¶ 85,676, p. 78,064 (1988).

Do these earlier interpretations change your answer to Problem 9–2(B)? In other words, do they undermine the deference you might otherwise accord the 1996 rule? Cf. *Gilbert v. General Electric Co.*, above. Is *Gilbert* distinguishable? Should the Court treat an agency interpretation modified from one opinion letter to the next differently from a changed interpretation that is expressed through notice and comment rulemaking?

For the U.S. Supreme Court's analysis of the foregoing issues, see *Smiley v. Citibank (South Dakota), N.A.*, 517 U.S. 735 (1996). Would a similar issue (namely, the meaning of a statutory term) be handled the same by a state supreme court. Do state courts follow something like the *Chevron* regime? If so, would they handle issues like this the same way the U.S. Supreme Court does? Consider the following case and the Note following it.

Seeton v. Pennsylvania Game Commission
594 Pa. 563, 937 A.2d 1028 (2007).

Johnna Seeton sued to require the Pennsylvania Game Commission to assume authority over the Tioga Boar Hunt Preserve's alleged violations of the Pennsylvania Game and Wildlife Code, 34 Pa.C.S. §§ 101, *et seq.* Tioga was in the business of selling "canned hunts," in which customers paid a fee to shoot and kill an animal in an enclosed area which limited the ability of the animal to escape and the amount of pursuit in which the customer might engage. Seeton alleged that "[a]nimals used in canned hunts are often drugged, tied to stakes or lured to feeding stations in order to further assure that the 'hunter' will get the guaranteed kill that has been promised by the hunting preserve's proprietor." Complaint in Mandamus ¶ 6.

The Commission's Chief Counsel rejected Seeton's contention that the animals hunted at the Preserve, including wild boar (as well as elk, rams, and buffalo), were "protected mammals" pursuant to the Commission's regulations promulgated under the Game and Wildlife Code. *See* 58 Pa. Code § 133.1. Among the mammals protected under the Commission's regulations were "wild mammals," but that term was defined nowhere in the Game and Wildlife Code or in the Commission's regulations. Relying on a dictionary, the Chief Counsel opined that "wild mammals" must apply only to "mammals that are currently living in a state of nature," thus excluding "mammals that are currently living in a state of captivity, either in pens or within enclosures." Because the animals at the Preserve were kept within enclosures, the Commission concluded that they are not "wild" for purposes of the Game and Wildlife Code and regulations issued thereunder; rather, they are "the personal property of their owners." *Id.*

The Declaration of Policy in the Game & Wildlife Code referred to the Commission's "proprietary ownership, jurisdiction and control of game or wildlife living free in nature," which the same provision identifies as "a renewable natural resource of this Commonwealth." 34 Pa.C.S. § 2161(a). The Code empowered and directed the Commission "to protect, propagate, manage, and preserve the game or wildlife of this Commonwealth and to enforce, by proper actions and proceedings, the laws of this Commonwealth relating thereto." 34 Pa.C.S. § 322(a). The Code also conferred discretion upon the Commission to regulate hunting, *id.* §§ 322(c)(1)–(7), classify wild birds and animals, *id.* § 322(c)(8), manage and develop game lands, *id.* § 322(c)(10); and to promulgate necessary and appropriate regulations concerning hunting and fur-taking in the Commonwealth, *id.* § 2102(a).

The Commission's main argument on appeal was that the Court should defer to its interpretation, so long as it was a reasonable one, even if not the only reasonable reading of the Game & Wildlife Code. Writing for the majority, **Justice Baer** agreed that judges should defer to agency interpretations of statutes it is charged with implementing, but not when the General Assembly has directly addressed the issue.

"While an agency's interpretation of an ambiguous statute it is charged with enforcing is entitled to deference, courts' deference never comes into play when the statute is clear. Notably, the United States Supreme Court, in its extensive precedent concerning judicial deference to administrative interpretations of ambiguous enabling statutes, *see, e.g., Chevron*, has recognized the dangers of deferring to interpretations developed in anticipation of litigation. *See Bowen v. Georgetown Univ. Hosp.*, 488 U.S. 204 (1988) (declining to defer to agency interpretations forwarded for the first time in connection with litigation)." In footnote 12, Justice Baer said this: "[W]e appear never to have explicitly adopted even *Chevron*'s general rule in the context of state administrative law. The *Chevron* approach to such cases at the federal level, however, is indistinguishable from our own approach to agency interpretations of Commonwealth statutes."

The Court decided the case at what the U.S. Supreme Court would consider *Chevron* Step One. "Wildlife," the Justice Baer noted, "is defined by the Game and Wildlife Code as, *inter alia,* 'wild birds' and 'wild mammals.' 34 Pa.C.S. § 102. Thus, while the Commission is correct that the term 'wild mammals' is not itself defined by either the Game and Wildlife Code or the Commission's regulations, it is not wholly undetermined within the statutory scheme. Rather, 'wild mammals' plainly are a subset of the term 'wildlife.' Thus, whatever is true of 'wildlife' must also be true of 'wild mammals,' barring an explicit statutory exception. Interestingly, 34 Pa.C.S. § 2163(b) prohibits, *inter alia,* the release within the Commonwealth of 'imported game or wildlife *or game or wildlife reared in captivity*' (emphasis added). This provision undermines the Commission's claims regarding the meaning of the word 'wild' in at least two dimensions. First, insofar as 'wildlife' is defined to include 'wild animals' and 'wild mammals,' as explained above, the notion of 'wildlife reared in captivity' (which posits the prospect of 'wild animals' and 'wild mammals' reared in captivity), is wholly antithetical to the Commission's attempt to tie the word 'wild' to the degree of freedom enjoyed by a given animal. Similarly, it is impossible to 'release' 'wildlife' (and hence 'wild animals' and 'wild mammals'), the activity proscribed in the abovementioned section, if the animal's liberty is a necessary condition to its status as 'wild,' since one cannot release an animal from a non-captive state.

"Notably, the Commission does not dispute [Seeton's] assertion that Tioga drugs or otherwise disables wild boar to facilitate easier kills, nor does it argue that, were it bound to enforce the law against Tioga, the alleged conduct would be permissible. The Game and Wildlife Code makes it illegal to hunt through use of poison or chemical of any kind. 34 Pa.C.S. § 2308(9). Thus, the Commission effectively argues that the hunting of captive animals on fenced, private property may be undertaken by means such as drugs or restraint that violate, at a minimum, the spirit of the Game and Wildlife Code. This is an untenably narrow interpretation of its statutory mandate.

"Interestingly, the Commission does not in all instances espouse such a restrained view of its authority. In *Commonwealth v. Gosselin,* 861 A.2d 996 (Pa. Super. 2004), appellants rescued and effectively domesticated an injured squirrel, [they named] Nutkin, while residing in South Carolina, where to do so was legal. Later, however, appellants moved to Pennsylvania, where they had some dealings with the Commission. Specifically, a Wildlife Officer, while investigating an unrelated tip lodged by appellants, observed Nutkin in the house, explained that appellants were barred by Pennsylvania law from housing a squirrel, and cited them for a violation when they refused to surrender custody of Nutkin to the officer. In resolving the case, the Commission agreed that Nutkin was a 'wild animal' under the Game and Wildlife Code."

The Court ruled that mandamus should have been granted to require the Commission to accept authority over Tioga. Retiring **Justices Nigro** (turned out in a retention election) and **Newman** (winning her retention election but then retiring voluntarily) did not participate in the case.

Dissenting, **Justice Eakin** maintained that Seeton did not have standing to bring suit, because she was not directly affected by the alleged violations; that mandamus was not a proper remedy in light of the Commission's discretionary authority; and that the Court should have deferred to the Commission's interpretation. "The majority does not afford due deference to [the Commission's] determination that boars are not protected wild animals under the Game Code. An administrative interpretation receives controlling weight unless the interpretation is plainly erroneous or inconsistent with the agency's regulation. *Department of Public Welfare v. Forbes Health System,* 492 Pa. 77, 422 A.2d 480, 482 (1980). [Seeton] argues the term wild animals is defined as all non-domestic mammals; therefore, wild animals and wild mammals are the same. Although the Game Code defines wild animals as all non-domestic mammals, it does not formally define the term wild mammal or the term wild. The boars at Tioga Boar Hunt Preserve (Preserve) are living in a state of captivity; thus, they are not living in a state of nature. The Game Code's policy declaration regarding actions for damages to game or wildlife provides:

> The Commonwealth has sufficient interest in *game or wildlife living in a free state* to give it standing, through its authorized agents, to recover compensatory and punitive damages in a civil action against any person who kills any game or wildlife or who damages any game or wildlife habitat. The proprietary ownership, jurisdiction and control of *game or wildlife living free in nature* is vested in the Commonwealth by virtue of the continued expenditure of its funds and its efforts to protect, propagate, manage and preserve the game or wildlife population as a renewable natural resource of this Commonwealth.

34 Pa.C.S. § 2161(a) (emphasis added). Considering the legislative expression of Pennsylvania's inherent interest in preserving wildlife living free in nature, the Commission's interpretation that the Preserves boars are not wild animals is not plainly erroneous or inconsistent with the Game Code."

NOTE ON THE PENNSYLVANIA WILD BOARS CASE AND DEFERENCE TO AGENCY INTERPRETATIONS BY STATE COURTS

Chevron has received a mixed reception in the state courts. The dominant view, as of 2014, is to give strong deference (akin to *Chevron* Step Two) to agency interpretations only in limited circumstances, such as where the interpretation is longstanding or is the product of the agency's particular expertise. Otherwise, state courts cling to their traditional prerogative to review questions of law de novo, which allows them to substitute their judgment for that of the agency where they believe the agency has incorrectly construed the statute. See Eric Lane, *How to Read a Statute in New York: A Response to Judge Kaye and Some More*, 28 Hofstra L. Rev. 85, 123–24 (1999). A growing number of states have adopted the *Chevron* deference regime (or something akin to it), while a smaller and shrinking group goes to the opposite extreme, affording agencies little or no respect on question of statutory construction. See Michael Asimow et al., *State and Federal Administrative Law* § 9.2 (1998).

States that have adopted a *Chevron*-like posture include **Colorado**, see *North Colorado Medical Center, Inc. v. Committee on Anticompetitive Conduct*, 914 P.2d 902, 907 (Colo. 1996) (citing *Chevron* for the proposition that the "interpretation of a statute by the agency charged with enforcement of that statute is generally entitled to deference"); **Florida**, see *Donato v. AT&T*, 767 So.2d 1146, 1153 (Fla. 2000) (adopting a two-step, *Chevron*-style analysis); and **Massachusetts**, see *Protective Life Ins. Co. v. Sullivan*, 682 N.E.2d 624, 627–28 (Mass. 1997). States that have explicitly adopted *Chevron* itself for reviewing points of law announced in legislative rulemaking and adjudications by agencies include **Kentucky,** see *Board of Trustees of Judicial Form Retirement System v. Attorney General of the Commonwealth,* 132 S.W.3d 770, 786–87 (Ky. 2003); **Montana,** see *Thompson v. J.C. Billion, Inc.,* 294 P.3d 397 (Mont. 2013); and **West Virginia,** see *Shroyer v. Harrison County Bd. of Educ.,* 564 S.E.2d 425 (W.Va. 2002); *Maikotter v. University of West Virginia Bd. of Trustees,* 527 S.E.2d 802 (W.Va. 1999). As the Montana Supreme Court's decision in *Billion* suggests, the modest trend in the state cases is in the direction of *Chevron* or its equivalent, at least when agency interpretations are generated by legislative rulemaking or agency adjudications.

As reflected in *Seeton,* **Pennsylvania** follows something like the *Chevron* approach, but without the elaborate doctrinal trappings that the U.S. Supreme Court has associated with *Chevron.* As *Seeton* also reflects, it is not clear that the Pennsylvania Supreme Court is actually more deferential to agency interpretations than other state high courts. While Justice Baer makes out a very good case for Seeton's view, doesn't Justice Eakins make out an equally good case for the Commission's view? Were the Pennsylvania Justices deferential? Was there really a plain meaning that defeated the agency's views? How would the U.S. Supreme Court have decided the Case of the Wild Boars?

Some states, such as **Washington**, have articulated a formal *Chevron* approach, but have not applied it with regularity. Compare *Waste Management of Seattle, Inc. v. Utilities and Transp. Comm'n*, 869 P.2d 1034, 1038 (Wash. 1994) ("Where an agency is charged with the administration and enforcement of a statute, the agency's interpretation of an ambiguous statute is accorded great weight in determining legislative intent."), with *Sebastian v. Department of Labor and Industries*, 12 P.3d 594 (Wash. 2000) (finding that the text of the statute at issue was ambiguous, but refusing to defer to the agency construction and instead applying a different interpretive canon, namely, the rule that coverage provisions of remedial statutes are to be construed broadly, and the limitations on coverage narrowly). Of course, the Eskridge and Baer study found that the U.S. Supreme Court did not apply *Chevron* with regularity either.

Such inconsistency also characterizes the situation in **California**. The state supreme court's basic approach is deferential to administrative agencies. E.g., *People ex rel. Lungren v. Superior Court*, 926 P.2d 1042, 1051 (Cal. 1996). However, in certain circumstances, California state courts have departed significantly from the *Chevron* principle. E.g., *Henning v. Industrial Welfare Comm'n*, 762 P.2d 442, 451 (Cal. 1988) (holding that while "in the abstract, a current administrative interpretation would ordinarily be entitled to great weight," a non-contemporaneous interpretation that "flatly contradicts the position which the agency had enunciated at an earlier date, closer to the enactment of the statute" cannot command significant deference). In *Henning*, Justice Broussard, concurring, went even further, arguing that because statutory interpretation is an act of judicial power, once the court has endorsed "a particular interpretation of a statute, an administrative agency lacks authority to interpret the statute differently." *Id.* at 455; see also *City of Long Beach v. Department of Industrial Relations*, 102 P.3d 904, 910 (Cal. 2004).

As of 2014, most state supreme courts have not adopted the *Chevron* deference regime and defer to agency interpretations only in a limited range of cases. The majority position is illustrated by *Connecticut State Medical Society v. Connecticut Board of Examiners in Podiatry*, 546 A.2d 830 (Conn. 1988). There, the state's podiatry board had interpreted the statutory term "foot" to include the ankle. The **Connecticut** Supreme Court overturned this construction, holding that the dictionary definition of the word, rather than the agency's understanding of the legislature's intent, provided the proper resolution of the interpretation question. The court's approach to the *Chevron* issue was instructive. First, the court described statutory interpretation as "purely a question of law," requiring less deference to the agency than would normally be shown in judicial review of administrative action. The court then suggested that only when the statute has previously been subjected to judicial scrutiny or to "time-tested agency interpretations" should a court afford the agency's interpretation any "special deference." Here, the court held that because "neither the board nor the courts have previously ruled on the issue presented . . . such deference is not due."

Also representative of such a narrower deference approach are **Michigan**, see *West Bloomfield Hospital. v. Certificate of Need Bd.*, 550 N.W.2d 223, 227 (Mich. 1996); **New Jersey**, see *In re Distribution of Liquid Assets*, 773 A.2d 6 (N.J. 2001) (citing *Chevron*, but nonetheless concluding that courts are "in no way bound" by agency interpretations and do not sit simply to "rubber stamp" agency determinations); *James v. Board of Trustees of Public Employees' Retirement System*, 753 A.2d 1061, 1066 (N.J. 2000); **New York**, see *Lorillard Tobacco Co. v. Roth*, 786 N.E.2d 7, 10 (N.Y. 2003); and **Ohio**, see *State ex rel. Celebrezze v. Natl. Lime & Stone Co.*, 627 N.E.2d 538 (Ohio 1994) (rejecting a *Chevron*-style rule in favor of a canon presuming that any uncertainty about the scope of an environmental law should be resolved "in favor of the person or entity (manufacturer or otherwise) affected by the law," regardless of how the agency has construed the statute).

An example of a no-deference state is **Delaware**, which has explicitly declined to adopt *Chevron*. See *Public Water Supply Co. v. DiPasquale*, 735 A.2d 378, 382–83 (Del. 1999) ("A reviewing court may accord due weight, but not defer, to an agency interpretation of a statute administered by it. A reviewing court will not defer to such an interpretation as correct merely because it is rational or not clearly erroneous.")

3. IMPORTANT *CHEVRON* DOCTRINAL ISSUES

So long as the Supreme Court sticks with the *Mead* understanding of *Chevron*, the linchpin is whether the agency interpretation is pursuant to a congressional delegation of authority to issue orders or rules having the force of law. Many of the implications of this conceptual basis for *Chevron* are spelled out in Thomas Merrill & Kristin Hickman, Chevron's *Domain*, 89 Geo. L.J. 833 (2001), which the Court cited and drew from in *Mead*. Consider some of these issues as the Supreme Court has wrestled with them.

A. IS THE AGENCY ACTING WITHIN ITS DELEGATED AUTHORITY?

If the *Chevron* deference boost rests upon congressional delegation of lawmaking authority, then the Court should make sure that Congress has delegated such authority to the agency in general *and* as applied to the issue in suit. Merrill & Hickman, Chevron's *Domain*, 89 Geo. L.J. at 873, call this Step Zero of *Chevron*. Although written as a Step One opinion, *MCI v. AT&T* may be read as an early example of Step Zero. Consider the following case, which is clearly Step Zero and illustrates the complexity that Step Zero inquiries might have.

GONZALES V. OREGON
Supreme Court of the United States, 2006.
546 U.S. 243, 126 S.Ct. 904, 163 L.Ed.2d 748.

JUSTICE KENNEDY delivered the opinion of the Court.

In 1994, Oregon became the first State to legalize assisted suicide when voters approved a ballot measure enacting the Oregon Death With Dignity Act (ODWDA). ODWDA, which survived a 1997 ballot measure seeking its repeal, exempts from civil or criminal liability state-licensed physicians who, in compliance with the specific safeguards in ODWDA, dispense or prescribe a lethal dose of drugs upon the request of a terminally ill patient.

The drugs Oregon physicians prescribe under ODWDA are regulated under a federal statute, the Controlled Substances Act (CSA or Act). 84 Stat. 1242, as amended, 21 U.S.C. § 801 et seq. The CSA allows these particular drugs to be available only by a written prescription from a registered physician. In the ordinary course the same drugs are prescribed in smaller doses for pain alleviation.

A November 9, 2001 Interpretive Rule issued by the Attorney General addresses the implementation and enforcement of the CSA with respect to ODWDA. It determines that using controlled substances to assist suicide is not a legitimate medical practice and that dispensing or prescribing them for this purpose is unlawful under the CSA. The Interpretive Rule's validity under the CSA is the issue before us.

[I] We turn first to the text and structure of the CSA. Enacted in 1970 with the main objectives of combating drug abuse and controlling the legitimate and illegitimate traffic in controlled substances, the CSA creates a comprehensive, closed regulatory regime criminalizing the unauthorized manufacture, distribution, dispensing, and possession of substances classified in any of the Act's five schedules. 21 U.S.C. § 841; 21 U.S.C. § 844. The Act places substances in one of five schedules based on their potential for abuse or dependence, their accepted medical use, and their accepted safety for use under medical supervision. Schedule I contains the most severe restrictions on access and use, and Schedule V the least. 21 U.S.C. § 812. Congress classified a host of substances when it enacted the CSA, but the statute permits the Attorney General to add, remove, or reschedule substances. He may do so, however, only after making particular findings, and on scientific and medical matters he is required to accept the findings of the Secretary of Health and Human Services (Secretary). These proceedings must be on the record after an opportunity for comment. See 21 U.S.C. § 811.

The present dispute involves controlled substances listed in Schedule II, substances generally available only pursuant to a written, nonrefillable prescription by a physician. 21 U.S.C. § 829(a). A 1971 regulation promulgated by the Attorney General requires that every prescription for a controlled substance "be issued for a legitimate medical purpose by an individual practitioner acting in the usual course of his professional practice." 21 CFR § 1306.04(a) (2005).

To prevent diversion of controlled substances with medical uses, the CSA regulates the activity of physicians. To issue lawful prescriptions of Schedule II drugs, physicians must "obtain from the Attorney General a registration issued in accordance with the rules and regulations promulgated by him." 21 U.S.C. § 822(a)(2). The Attorney General may deny, suspend, or revoke this registration if, as relevant here, the physician's registration would be "inconsistent with the public interest." § 824(a)(4); § 822(a)(2). When deciding whether a practitioner's registration is in the public interest, the Attorney General "shall" consider:

"(1) The recommendation of the appropriate State licensing board or professional disciplinary authority.

"(2) The applicant's experience in dispensing, or conducting research with respect to controlled substances.

"(3) The applicant's conviction record under Federal or State laws relating to the manufacture, distribution, or dispensing of controlled substances.

"(4) Compliance with applicable State, Federal, or local laws relating to controlled substances.

"(5) Such other conduct which may threaten the public health and safety." § 823(f).

The CSA explicitly contemplates a role for the States in regulating controlled substances, as evidenced by its pre-emption provision.

"No provision of this subchapter shall be construed as indicating an intent on the part of the Congress to occupy the field in which that provision operates . . . to the exclusion of any State law on the same subject matter which would otherwise be within the authority of the State, unless there is a positive conflict between that provision . . . and that State law so that the two cannot consistently stand together." § 903.

[After Oregon voters adopted that state's DWDCA in 1994 and reaffirmed it in a 1997 referendum, several senators, including John Ashcroft of Missouri, petitioned Attorney General Janet Reno to override the Oregon law through an interpretation of the CSA declaring that use of controlled substances for "assisted suicide" was a federal crime. Reno declined, but when Ashcroft himself became Attorney General, he issued the Directive. The Ninth Circuit rejected his interpretation, and the Attorney General appealed. He argued that his Interpretive Rule was entitled to *Chevron* deference. Because Congress had not directly addressed the issue of "assisted suicide," the Court should defer to his interpretation. (The government also argued that he was entitled to super-deference because he was interpreting the 1971 regulation.)]

[II. After rejecting the Attorney General's argument for super-deference because he was construing a Department rule, the Court considered his *Chevron* deference argument and posed the *Mead* question: Has Congress delegated lawmaking authority to the Attorney General to preempt this kind of state law?] The Attorney General has rulemaking power to fulfill his duties under the CSA. The specific respects in which he is authorized to make rules, however, instruct us that he is not authorized to make a rule declaring illegitimate a medical standard for care and treatment of patients that is specifically authorized under state law. * * *

The CSA gives the Attorney General limited powers, to be exercised in specific ways. His rulemaking authority under the CSA is described in two provisions: (1) "The Attorney General is authorized to promulgate rules and regulations and to charge reasonable fees relating to the registration and control of the manufacture, distribution, and dispensing of controlled substances and to listed chemicals," 21 U.S.C. § 821; and (2) "The Attorney General may promulgate and enforce any rules, regulations, and procedures which he may deem necessary and appropriate for the efficient execution of his functions under this subchapter," 21 U.S.C. § 871(b). As is evident from these sections, Congress did not delegate to the Attorney General authority to carry out or effect all provisions of the CSA. Rather, he can promulgate rules relating only to "registration" and "control," and "for the efficient execution of his functions" under the statute.

Turning first to the Attorney General's authority to make regulations for the "control" of drugs, this delegation cannot sustain the Interpretive Rule's attempt to define standards of medical practice. Control is a term of art in the CSA. "As used in this subchapter," § 802—the subchapter that includes § 821—

"The term 'control' means to add a drug or other substance, or immediate precursor, to a schedule under part B of this subchapter, whether by transfer from another schedule or otherwise." § 802(5).

To exercise his scheduling power, the Attorney General must follow a detailed set of procedures, including requesting a scientific and medical evaluation from the Secretary. See 21 U.S.C. §§ 811, 812. The statute is also specific as to the manner in which the Attorney General must exercise this authority: "Rules of the Attorney General under this subsection [regarding scheduling] shall be made on the record after opportunity for a hearing pursuant to the rulemaking procedures prescribed by [the Administrative Procedure Act, 5 U.S.C. § 553]." 21 U.S.C. § 811(a). The Interpretive Rule now under consideration does not concern the scheduling of substances and was not issued after the required procedures for rules regarding scheduling, so it cannot fall under the Attorney General's "control" authority. * * *

We turn, next, to the registration provisions of the CSA. Before 1984, the Attorney General was required to register any physician who was authorized by his State. The Attorney General could only deregister a physician who falsified his application, was convicted of a felony relating to controlled substances, or had his state license or registration revoked. The CSA was amended in 1984 to allow the Attorney General to deny registration to an applicant "if he determines that the issuance of such registration would be inconsistent with the public interest." 21 U.S.C. § 823(f). Registration may also be revoked or suspended by the Attorney General on the same grounds. § 824(a)(4). In determining consistency with the public interest, the Attorney General must * * * consider five factors, including: the State's recommendation; compliance with state, federal, and local laws regarding controlled substances; and public health and safety. § 823(f).

The Interpretive Rule cannot be justified under this part of the statute. It does not undertake the five-factor analysis and concerns much more than registration. Nor does the Interpretive Rule on its face purport to be an application of the registration provision in § 823(f). It is, instead, an interpretation of the substantive federal law requirements (under 21 CFR § 1306.04 (2005)) for a valid prescription. It begins by announcing that assisting suicide is not a "legitimate medical purpose" under § 1306.04, and that dispensing controlled substances to assist a suicide violates the CSA. 66 Fed. Reg. 56608 (2001). Violation is a criminal offense, and often a felony, under 21 U.S.C. § 841. The Interpretive Rule thus purports to declare that using controlled substances for physician-assisted suicide is a crime, an authority that goes well beyond the Attorney General's statutory power to register or deregister.

The Attorney General's deregistration power, of course, may carry implications for criminal enforcement because if a physician dispenses a controlled substance after he is deregistered, he violates § 841. The Interpretive Rule works in the opposite direction, however: it declares certain conduct criminal, placing in jeopardy the registration of any physician who engages in that conduct. To the extent the Interpretive Rule concerns registration, it simply states the obvious because one of the five factors the Attorney General must consider in deciding the "public interest" is "[c]ompliance with applicable State, Federal, or local laws relating to controlled substances." 21 U.S.C. § 823(f)(4). The problem with the design of the Interpretive Rule is that it cannot, and does not, explain why the Attorney General has the authority to decide what constitutes an underlying violation of the CSA in the first place. The explanation the Government seems to advance is that the Attorney General's authority to decide whether a physician's actions are inconsistent with the "public interest" provides the basis for the Interpretive Rule.

By this logic, however, the Attorney General claims extraordinary authority. If the Attorney General's argument were correct, his power to deregister necessarily would include the greater power to criminalize even the actions of registered physicians, whenever they engage in conduct he deems illegitimate. This power to criminalize—unlike his power over registration, which must be exercised only after considering five express statutory factors—would be unrestrained. It would be anomalous for Congress to have so painstakingly described the Attorney General's limited authority to deregister a single physician or schedule a single drug, but to have given him, just by implication, authority to declare an entire class of activity outside "the course of professional practice," and therefore a criminal violation of the CSA. * * * See also *Adams Fruit Co. v. Barrett,* 494 U.S. 638, 649–50 (1990) (holding that a delegation of authority to promulgate motor vehicle safety "*standards*" did not include the authority to decide the pre-emptive scope of the federal statute because "[n]o such delegation regarding [the statute's] enforcement provisions is evident in the statute").

The same principle controls here. It is not enough that the terms "public interest," "public health and safety," and "Federal law" are used in the part of the statute over which the Attorney General has authority. The statutory terms "public interest" and "public health" do not call on the Attorney General, or any other Executive official, to make an independent assessment of the meaning of federal law. The Attorney General did not base the Interpretive Rule on an application of the five-factor test generally, or the "public health and safety" factor specifically. Even if he had, it is doubtful the Attorney General could cite the "public interest" or "public health" to deregister a physician simply because he deemed a controversial practice permitted by state law to have an illegitimate medical purpose. * * *

The authority desired by the Government is inconsistent with the design of the statute in other fundamental respects. The Attorney General does not have the sole delegated authority under the CSA. He must instead share it with, and in some respects defer to, the Secretary [of the Department of Health and Human Services], whose functions are likewise delineated and confined by the statute. The CSA allocates decisionmaking powers among statutory actors so that medical judgments, if they are to be decided at the federal level and for the limited objects of the statute, are placed in the hands of the Secretary. In the scheduling context, for example, the Secretary's recommendations on scientific and medical matters bind the Attorney General. The Attorney General cannot control a substance if the Secretary disagrees. 21 U.S.C. § 811(b). See H.R. Rep. No. 91–1444, pt. 1, p. 33 (1970) (the section "is not intended to authorize the Attorney General to undertake or support medical and scientific research [for the purpose of scheduling], which is within the competence of the Department of Health, Education, and Welfare").

In a similar vein the 1970 Act's regulation of medical practice with respect to drug rehabilitation gives the Attorney General a limited role; for it is the Secretary who, after consultation with the Attorney General and national medical groups, "determine[s] the appropriate methods of professional practice in the medical treatment of . . . narcotic addiction." 42 U.S.C. § 290bb–2a; see 21 U.S.C. § 823(g) (2000 ed. and Supp. II) (stating that the Attorney General shall register practitioners who dispense drugs for narcotics treatment when the Secretary has determined the applicant is qualified to treat addicts and the Attorney General has concluded the applicant will comply with record keeping and security regulations); H.R. Rep. No. 93–884, p 6 (1974) ("This section preserves the distinctions found in the [CSA] between the functions of the Attorney General and the Secretary. . . . All decisions of a medical nature are to be made by the Secretary. . . . Law enforcement decisions respecting the security of stocks of narcotics drugs and the maintenance of records on such drugs are to be made by the Attorney General"). * * *

The structure of the CSA, then, conveys unwillingness to cede medical judgments to an Executive official who lacks medical expertise. In interpreting statutes that divide authority, the Court has recognized: "Because historical familiarity and policymaking expertise account in the first instance for the presumption that Congress delegates interpretive lawmaking power to the agency rather than to the reviewing court, we presume here that Congress intended to invest interpretive power in the administrative actor in the best position to develop these attributes." *Martin v. OSHRC*, 499 U.S. 144, 153 (1991). This presumption works against a conclusion that the Attorney General has authority to make quintessentially medical judgments. * * *

The idea that Congress gave the Attorney General such broad and unusual authority through an implicit delegation in the CSA's registration provision is not sustainable. "Congress, we have held, does not alter the fundamental details of a regulatory scheme in vague terms or ancillary provisions—it does not, one might say, hide elephants in mouseholes." *Whitman v. American Trucking Assns., Inc.*, 531 U.S. 457, 468 (2001); see *FDA v. Brown & Williamson* ("[W]e are confident that Congress could not have intended to delegate a decision of such economic and political significance to an agency in so cryptic a fashion").

The importance of the issue of physician-assisted suicide, which has been the subject of an "earnest and profound debate" across the country, [*Washington v. Glucksberg*, 521 U.S., 702, 735 (1997), which upheld a state prohibition on physician-assisted suicide, in part on the argument that the states should have discretion to decide such issues for themselves], makes the oblique form of the claimed delegation all the more suspect. Under the Government's theory, moreover, the medical judgments the Attorney General could make are not limited to physician-assisted suicide. Were this argument accepted, he could decide whether any particular drug may be used for any particular purpose, or indeed whether a physician who administers any controversial treatment could be deregistered. This would occur, under the Government's view, despite the statute's express limitation of the Attorney General's authority to registration and control, with attendant restrictions on each of those functions, and despite the statutory purposes to combat drug abuse and prevent illicit drug trafficking.

[III. Finding no delegation, and therefore no *Chevron* deference, the Court considered the Attorney General's facts and arguments à la *Skidmore* as it interpreted the CSA to determine whether Congress meant to preempt laws like the ODWDA.] The statute and our case law amply support the conclusion that Congress regulates medical practice insofar as it bars doctors from using their prescription-writing powers as a means to engage in illicit drug dealing and trafficking as conventionally understood. Beyond this, however, the statute manifests no intent to regulate the practice of medicine generally. The silence is understandable given the structure and limitations of federalism, which allow the States " 'great latitude under their police powers to legislate as to the protection of the lives, limbs, health, comfort, and quiet of all persons.' " *Medtronic, Inc. v. Lohr*, 518 U.S. 470, 475 (1996).

* * * [W]e find only one area in which Congress set general, uniform standards of medical practice. Title I of the Comprehensive Drug Abuse Prevention and Control Act of 1970, of which the CSA was Title II, provides that

> "[The Secretary], after consultation with the Attorney General and with national organizations representative of persons with knowledge and experience in the treatment of narcotic addicts, shall determine the appropriate methods of professional practice in the medical treatment of the narcotic addiction of various classes of narcotic addicts, and shall report thereon from time to time to the Congress." § 4, 84 Stat. 1241, codified at 42 U.S.C. § 290bb–2a.

This provision strengthens the understanding of the CSA as a statute combating recreational drug abuse, and also indicates that when Congress wants to regulate medical practice in the given scheme, it does so by explicit language in the statute [and with consultation involving the medical experts in HHS]. * * *

JUSTICE SCALIA, joined by CHIEF JUSTICE ROBERTS and JUSTICE THOMAS, dissenting. * * *

Even if the Directive were entitled to no deference whatever, the most reasonable interpretation of the Regulation and of the statute would produce the same result. Virtually every relevant source of authoritative meaning confirms that the phrase "legitimate medical purpose" does not include intentionally assisting suicide. "Medicine" refers to "[t]he science and art dealing with the prevention, cure, or alleviation of disease." Webster's Second 1527. The use of the word "legitimate" connotes an *objective* standard of "medicine," and our presumption that the CSA creates a uniform federal law regulating the dispensation of controlled substances means that this objective standard must be a federal one. As recounted in detail in the memorandum for the Attorney General that is attached as an appendix to the Directive (OLC Memo), virtually every medical authority from Hippocrates to the current American Medical Association (AMA) confirms that assisting suicide has seldom or never been viewed as a form of "prevention, cure, or alleviation of disease," and (even more so) that assisting suicide is not a "legitimate" branch of that "science and art." Indeed, the AMA has determined that " '[p]hysician-assisted suicide is fundamentally incompatible with the physician's role as a healer.' " *Glucksberg.* "[T]he overwhelming weight of authority in judicial decisions, the past and present policies of nearly all of the States and of the Federal Government, and the clear, firm and unequivocal views of the leading associations within the American medical and nursing professions, establish that assisting in suicide . . . is not a legitimate medical purpose." OLC Memo. See also *Glucksberg* (prohibitions or condemnations of assisted suicide in 50 jurisdictions, including 47 States, the District of Columbia, and 2 Territories). * * *

Even if the Regulation did not exist and "prescription" in § 829 could not be interpreted to require a "legitimate medical purpose," the Directive's conclusion that "prescribing, dispensing, or administering federally controlled substances . . . by a physician . . . may 'render his registration . . . inconsistent with the public interest' and therefore subject to possible suspension or revocation under 21 U.S.C. [§] 824(a)(4)," 66 Fed. Reg. 56608, would nevertheless be unassailable in this Court.

Sections 823(f) and 824(a) explicitly grant the Attorney General the authority to register and deregister physicians, and his discretion in exercising that authority is spelled out in very broad terms. He may refuse to register or deregister if he determines that registration is "inconsistent with the public interest," 21 U.S.C. § 823(f), after considering five factors, the fifth of which is "[s]uch other conduct which may threaten the public health and safety," § 823(f)(5). As the Court points out, these broad standards were enacted in the 1984 amendments for the specific purpose of *freeing* the Attorney General's discretion over registration from the decisions of state authorities.

The fact that assisted-suicide prescriptions are issued in violation of § 829 is of course sufficient to support the Directive's conclusion that issuing them may be cause for deregistration: such prescriptions would violate the fourth factor of § 823(f), namely "[c]ompliance with applicable . . . Federal . . . laws relating to controlled substances," 21 U.S.C. § 823(f)(4). But the Attorney General did not rely solely on subsection (f)(4) in reaching his conclusion that registration would be "inconsistent with the public interest"; nothing in the text of the Directive indicates that. Subsection (f)(5) ("[s]uch other conduct which may threaten the public health and safety") provides an independent, alternative basis for the Directive's conclusion regarding deregistration—provided that the Attorney General has authority to interpret "public interest" and "public health and safety" in § 823(f) to exclude assisted suicide.

Three considerations make it perfectly clear that the statute confers authority to interpret these phrases upon the Attorney General. First, the Attorney General is solely and explicitly charged with administering the registration and deregistration provisions. See §§ 823(f), 824(a). By making the criteria for such registration and deregistration such obviously ambiguous factors as "public interest" and "public health and safety," Congress implicitly (but clearly) gave the Attorney General authority to interpret those criteria—*whether or not* there is any explicit delegation provision in the statute. "Sometimes the legislative delegation to an agency on a particular question is implicit rather than explicit. In such a case, a court may not substitute its own construction of a statutory provision for a reasonable interpretation made by the administrator of an agency." *Chevron*. The Court's exclusive focus on the *explicit* delegation provisions is, at best, a fossil of our pre-*Chevron* era; at least since *Chevron*, we have not conditioned our deferral to agency interpretations upon the existence of explicit delegation provisions. *Mead* left this principle of implicit delegation intact.

Second, even if explicit delegation were required, Congress provided it in § 821, which authorizes the Attorney General to "promulgate rules and regulations . . . relating to the *registration and control* of the manufacture, distribution, and dispensing of controlled substances. . . ." (Emphasis added.) Because "dispensing" refers to the delivery of a controlled substance "pursuant to the lawful order of a practitioner," 21 U.S.C. § 802(10), the deregistration of such practitioners for writing impermissible orders "relat[es] to the registration . . . of the . . . dispensing" of controlled substances, 21 U.S.C.A. § 821 (Supp. 2005).

Third, § 821 also gives the Attorney General authority to promulgate rules and regulations "relating to the . . . control of the . . . dispensing of controlled substances." As discussed earlier, it is plain that the *ordinary* meaning of "control" must apply to § 821, so that the plain import of the provision is to grant the Attorney General rulemaking authority over all the provisions of part C of the CSA, 21 U.S.C. §§ 821–830. Registering and deregistering the practitioners who issue the prescriptions necessary for lawful dispensation of controlled substances plainly "relat[es] to the . . . control of the . . . dispensing of controlled substances." § 821.

The Attorney General is thus authorized to promulgate regulations interpreting §§ 823(f) and 824(a), both by implicit delegation in § 823(f) and by two grounds of explicit delegation in § 821. The Court nevertheless holds that this triply unambiguous delegation cannot be given full effect because "the design of the statute" evinces the intent to grant the Secretary of Health and Human Services exclusive authority over scientific and medical determinations. This proposition is not remotely plausible. The Court cites as authority for the Secretary's exclusive authority two specific areas in which his medical determinations are said to be binding on the Attorney General—with regard to the "scientific and medical evaluation" of a drug's effects that precedes its scheduling, § 811(b), and with regard to "the appropriate methods of professional practice in the medical treatment of the narcotic addiction of various classes of narcotic addicts," 42 U.S.C. § 290bb–2a. Far from establishing a general principle of Secretary supremacy with regard to all scientific and medical determinations, the fact that Congress granted the Secretary specifically defined authority in the areas of scheduling and addiction treatment, *without otherwise mentioning him* in the registration provisions, suggests, to the contrary, that Congress envisioned *no* role for the Secretary in that area—where, as we have said, interpretive authority was both implicitly and explicitly conferred upon the Attorney General.

Even if we could rewrite statutes to accord with sensible "design," it is far from a certainty that the Secretary, rather than the Attorney General, ought to control the registration of physicians. Though registration decisions sometimes require judgments about the legitimacy of medical practices, the Department of Justice has seemingly had no difficulty making them. But unlike decisions about whether a substance should be scheduled or whether a narcotics addiction treatment is legitimate, registration decisions are not exclusively, or even primarily, concerned with "medical [and] scientific" factors. See 21 U.S.C. § 823(f). Rather, the decision

to register, or to bring an action to deregister, an individual *physician* implicates all the policy goals and competing enforcement priorities that attend any exercise of prosecutorial discretion. It is entirely reasonable to think (as Congress evidently did) that it would be easier for the Attorney General occasionally to make judgments about the legitimacy of medical practices than it would be for the Secretary to get into the business of law enforcement. It is, in other words, perfectly consistent with an intelligent "design of the statute" to give the Nation's chief law enforcement official, not its chief health official, broad discretion over the substantive standards that govern registration and deregistration. That is *especially* true where the contested "scientific and medical" judgment at issue has to do with the legitimacy of physician-assisted suicide, which ultimately rests, not on "science" or "medicine," but on a naked value judgment. It no more depends upon a "quintessentially medical judgmen[t]" than does the legitimacy of polygamy or eugenic infanticide. And it requires no particular *medical* training to undertake the objective inquiry into how the continuing traditions of Western medicine have consistently treated this subject. The Secretary's supposedly superior "medical expertise" to make "medical judgments" is strikingly irrelevant to the case at hand.
* * *

It follows from what we have said that the Attorney General's authoritative interpretations of "public interest" and "public health and safety" in § 823(f) are subject to *Chevron* deference. As noted earlier, the Court does not [contend] that the absence of notice-and-comment procedures for the Directive renders *Chevron* inapplicable. And there is no serious argument that "Congress has directly spoken to the precise question at issue," or that the Directive's interpretations of "public health and safety" and "inconsistent with the public interest" are not "permissible." *Chevron*. On the latter point, in fact, the condemnation of assisted suicide by 50 American jurisdictions supports the Attorney General's view. The Attorney General may therefore weigh a physician's participation in assisted suicide as a factor counseling against his registration, or in favor of deregistration, under § 823(f).
* * *

NOTES ON THE OREGON AID-IN-DYING CASE AND DEFERENCE FOR ISSUES OF AGENCY AUTHORITY

1.   *The Debate over Textual Authorization for the Attorney General.* The take-no-prisoners debate between Justices Kennedy and Scalia provides an occasion for students to practice their skills with the statutory interpretation rules and practices covered in this casebook. Note especially the skillful combination of dictionary meanings, grammatical analyses, and structural points made in the dissent. Justice Scalia has excellent arguments for the proposition that the Ashcroft Directive is literally within at least one of the CSA delegations, maybe several of them. Such a reading may also fit with the CSA's purpose, which was to create a federal regulatory regime for the dispensation of drugs by doctors. Yet this deft wedding of Reagan Era textualism and New Deal purposivism was not persuasive to Justices Kennedy and O'Connor, Reagan conservatives who were probably not great friends to the death-with-dignity movement. Why are they not persuaded?

Here's one way of understanding why some pretty conservative jurists rejected Justice Scalia's legal arguments. Consider this: Parents A and B retain babysitter C to look after their beloved child while they attend the opera. Their instructions to C: "You are in charge; we delegate you all decisions regarding his care while we are gone." In a tragic twist of fate, the baby has a terrible accident, and C rushes him to the hospital. The hospital asks C who has authority to make decisions about treatment options, risk assessment, and even possible termination of life support. Can C legitimately respond that she is "authorized" to make those decisions? A strict reading of the instructions might suggest "yes," but common sense makes us sure the answer is "no."

This is probably the point of the Court's invocation of the idea that Congress does not hide elephants in mouseholes. Assuming this point, however, why would Justices O'Connor and Kennedy consider the "assisted suicide" rule an "elephant" and not a "mouse"? If the CSA represented a federalization of drug regulation, why isn't the Ashcroft Directive simply the routine agency decision suggested by the dissenters? Does a negative answer to that question rest upon a reservation of a special judicial role for aid-in-dying issues?

2.   *Deference to the Agency's View of Its Own Jurisdiction or Delegated Authority?* Justice Scalia has long argued that the Court should defer to agency interpretations of its own authority or jurisdiction. His reason is that there is "no discernible line between an agency's exceeding its own authority and an agency's exceeding authorized application of its authority." *Mississippi Power & Light v. Mississippi ex rel. Moore*, 487 U.S. 354, 381–82 (1988) (Scalia, J., concurring in the judgment). He does not press this point in *Oregon*, presumably because he believes his plain meaning arguments are unanswerable. Is there a cogent response to this concern? Keep this issue in mind when you read the next case, following these notes.

By the way, if *Chevron* deference does not apply to the agency's interpretation of its own delegated authority, should *Skidmore* deference apply to that issue? Would *Skidmore* have made a difference to the *Oregon* Court on the delegation issue? Assume that the Court applies *Skidmore* deference to the application of the CSA to the Oregon law, but *not* to the issue of delegation of lawmaking authority to the Attorney General.

3.   *Deference When Congress Has Delegated Responsibilities to More Than One Agency.* The Oregon Aid-in-Dying Case is an example of a growing range of controversies involving several possibly relevant agencies. Recall that one reason the *Gilbert* Court rejected the EEOC's understanding of pregnancy exclusions as being sex discrimination was that another body had reached a different interpretation. In addition to inter-agency *conflict* is the problem of *primacy* among agencies. As Justice Kennedy was in *Oregon*, the Court is usually pretty particular about matching the most apparently authorized agency with an award of deference. E.g., *Martin v. OSHRC*, 499 U.S. 144 (1991), where the Court ruled that in OSHA cases deference was owed to the Department of Labor, which issues substantive rules, rather than the Commission which adjudicates controversies by applying rules to facts.

Sometimes, the Court has been very picky about this matching game. For example, in *Sutton v. United Air Lines, Inc.*, 527 U.S. 471 (1999), the Court interpreted the ADA's definition of "disability" to exclude conditions easily corrected for. (The plaintiffs lost their jobs as airline pilots because they had poor vision; the Court held that this was not a disability, because it could be corrected by eyeglasses. The employer's policy was that corrected vision was still disqualifying. Catch–22.) Although the EEOC had been given rulemaking authority for implementing the jobs title of the Act, which was the basis for Sutton's claims, the Court ruled that the EEOC was *not* delegated authority to determine the scope of the ADA's coverage of "disability," which was defined in a different title to the Act (as to which there was no agency with delegated lawmaking authority).

4.   *Deference in Matters of Criminal Law.* The *Oregon* majority was troubled that Ashcroft was expansively interpreting a statute imposing serious criminal liability. Recall from Chapter 3, § 2A that the rule of lenity theoretically requires anti-deference—presumptive rejection of the agency's interpretation—when a criminal statute is ambiguous. Indeed, Justice Scalia is one of the few Justices who seems to apply the rule of lenity with rigor and even enthusiasm—but not in *Oregon.* Why not? Apparently, Justice Scalia views the notice and nondelegation policies underlying the rule of lenity to be satisfied by an open rule promulgated by the Attorney General pursuant to congressional authorization. Accord, Dan Kahan, *Is* Chevron *Relevant to Federal Criminal Law?*, 110 Harv. L. Rev. 469 (1996) (arguing that criminal law should move in precisely this direction).

Note that *Chevron* might apply in federal criminal sentencing law. Congress has vested the Sentencing Commission with substantive rulemaking authority as regards sentencing, and the Court sometimes gave *Chevron* deference to the Sentencing Guidelines before they were partially nullified. See *Stinson v. United States*, 508 U.S. 36 (1993). Should *Stinson* make us more willing to defer in cases like *Oregon*?

5.   *Ideological Voting in* Chevron *Cases.* Commentators are finding that ideology is a better predictor than doctrine with respect to the Justices' voting patterns in agency deference cases. The Oregon Aid-in-Dying Case helps us see how this works. Notice the completely different linguistic as well as normative attitudes in the majority and chief dissenting opinions. Thus, the majority cites *Glucksberg* (the constitutional "right to die" case) and its treatment of aid-in-dying as a matter for serious national debate. These and other bits of textual evidence suggest that the majority understands the matter as a possible privacy right of persons to choose "death with dignity." Is it for this *normative* reason that the majority thinks that aid-in-dying is an "elephant" that cannot hide in a normative "mousehole"? Consider, in addition, the federalism argument that Oregon ought to have authority to decide the question of aid in dying without federal intervention.

The dissenters, in contrast, rhetorically agree with Ashcroft that this is "assisted suicide," a half step away from murder. Because the matter has long been settled by religious doctrine, state law, and national policy, this is no "elephant," but is instead a mouse hiding in the mousehole. It is for this *normative* reason that the dissenters believe it outrageous for the majority to treat Oregon's law as a great matter for state experimentation and deviance from settled national policy.

The process by which the Justices are voting their norms more than their dictionaries is probably unconscious. Social scientists would explain this phenomenon as an example of framing effects and cognitive dissonance: the way an interpreter frames the issue drives her thinking, and indeed she will filter evidence through the lens of this frame. Philosophers would cite this as an example of how interpretation is an activity by which we come to be who we are.

6. *Process Matters: Deliberative Agency Actions May Trigger More Deference.* Another way to read the Oregon Aid-in-Dying Case emphasizes the agency's public process and justifications. One of us argues that the Court was reluctant to defer in the case because the agency had tackled a big normative issue without the public process of information-gathering and deliberation that usually accompanies agency rulemaking. See William Eskridge Jr., *The Story of* Gonzales v. Oregon: *Death, Deference, Deliberation,* in *Statutory Interpretation Stories* 366–98 (Eskridge, Frickey & Garrett eds., 2011). Eskridge endorses "deliberation-rewarding" canons of statutory interpretation, such as the Oregon Case, where the Court rewards public deliberation with greater deference. Is this a sensible canon? Does such a canon create too much complexity in an already complicated regime of rules and principles?

City of Arlington, Texas v. FCC
133 S.Ct. 1863 (2013).

The Communications Act of 1934 is the super-statute regulating electronic communications; § 201(b) of the 1934 Act empowers the Federal Communications Commission (FCC) to "prescribe such rules and regulations as may be necessary in the public interest to carry out [its] provisions." One substantive provision, added to the law in 1996, requires state or local governments to act on wireless siting applications "within a reasonable period of time after the request is duly filed." 47 U.S.C. § 332(c)(7)(B)(ii). In 2009, the FCC issued a rule providing that a "reasonable period of time" for purposes of § 332(c)(7)(B)(ii) is presumptively (and therefore rebuttably) 90 days to process an application to place a new antenna on an existing tower and 150 days to process all other applications.

State and local governments challenged the rule as inconsistent with the statute. They maintained that the FCC has no authority to narrow § 332(c)(7)(B)(ii). Section 332(c)(7)(A) provides that nothing in § 332 "shall limit or affect the authority of a State or local government" over siting decisions. Section 332(c)(7)(B)(v), moreover, authorizes a person who believes a state or local government's wireless-siting decision to be inconsistent with any of the limitations in § 332(c)(7)(B) to "commence an action in any court of competent jurisdiction." Rejecting the challenge, the Ninth Circuit held that the FCC was acting pursuant to delegated lawmaking authority and therefore was entitled to *Chevron* deference, given the reasonableness of its rule and the vagueness of § 332(c)(7)(B)(ii).

Affirming the Ninth Circuit, **Justice Scalia** wrote a majority opinion joined by Justices Thomas, Ginsburg, Sotomayor, and Kagan (an unusual majority coalition). The key issue, as the majority framed it, was whether *Chevron* applied to agency interpretations of its own "jurisdiction." Justice Scalia said yes, in large part because there is no way to separate jurisdictional issues and merits issues. For agencies, unlike for courts, "[b]oth their power to act and how they are to act is authoritatively prescribed by Congress, so that when they act improperly, no less than when they act beyond their jurisdiction, what they do is ultra vires. Because the question—whether framed as an incorrect application of agency authority or an assertion of authority not conferred—is always whether the agency has gone beyond what Congress has permitted it to do, there is no principled basis for carving out some arbitrary subset of such claims as 'jurisdictional.' "

Justice Scalia provided a hypothetical pair of statutes to illustrate his point. The first "Common Carrier Act" read this way:

Section 1.   The Agency shall have jurisdiction to prohibit any common carrier from imposing an unreasonable condition upon access to its facilities.

An interpretation of § 1's terms is "jurisdictional." But the statute could just as easily have been drafted in another way:

Section 1.   No common carrier shall impose an unreasonable condition upon access to its facilities.

Section 2.   The Agency may prescribe rules and regulations necessary in the public interest to effectuate Section 1 of this Act.

Justice Scalia continued: "Now imagine that the Agency, invoking its Section 2 authority, promulgates this Rule: '(1) The term 'common carrier' in Section 1 includes Internet Service Providers. (2) The term 'unreasonable condition' in Section 1 includes unreasonably high prices. (3) A monthly fee greater than $25 is an unreasonable condition on access to Internet service.' By this Rule, the Agency has claimed for itself jurisdiction that is doubly questionable: Does its authority extend to Internet Service Providers? And does it extend to setting prices? Yet Section 2 makes clear that Congress, in petitioners' words, 'conferred interpretive power on the agency' with respect to Section 1. Even under petitioners' theory, then, a court should defer to the Agency's interpretation of the terms 'common carrier' and 'unreasonable condition'— that is to say, its assertion that its 'jurisdiction' extends to regulating Internet Service Providers and setting prices.

"In the first case, by contrast, petitioners' theory would accord the agency no deference. The trouble with this is that in both cases, the underlying question is *exactly the same*: Does the statute give the agency authority to regulate Internet Service Providers and cap prices, or not? The reality, laid bare, is that there is *no difference,* insofar as the validity of agency action is concerned, between an agency's exceeding the scope of its authority (its 'jurisdiction') and its exceeding authorized application of authority that it unquestionably has. 'To exceed authorized application is to exceed authority. Virtually any administrative action can be characterized as either the one or the other, depending on how generally one wishes to describe the authority.' *Mississippi Power & Light Co. v. Mississippi ex rel. Moore,* 487 U.S. 354, 381 (1988) (Scalia, J., concurring in judgment).

"In sum, judges should not waste their time in the mental acrobatics needed to decide whether an agency's interpretation of a statutory provision is 'jurisdictional' or 'nonjurisdictional.' Once those labels are sheared away, it becomes clear that the question in every case is, simply, whether the statutory text forecloses the agency's assertion of authority, or not. The federal judge as haruspex, sifting the entrails of vast statutory schemes to divine whether a particular agency interpretation qualifies as 'jurisdictional,' is not engaged in reasoned decisionmaking."

Justice Scalia said that the Court has "consistently" held that *Chevron* applies to agency interpretations of their own jurisdiction. His "prime example" was *Commodity Futures Trading Comm'n v. Schor,* 478 U.S. 833 (1986). The CFTC interpreted 7 U.S.C. § 18(c), which provides that before the Commission takes action on a complaint, the complainant must file a bond to cover "any reparation award that may be issued by the

Commission against the complainant *on any counterclaim* by respondent." (Emphasis added.) Pursuant to rulemaking authority, the CFTC claimed "the power to take jurisdiction over" not just federal-law counterclaims, but state-law counterclaims as well. The Court deferred under *Chevron* to the Commission's "eminently reasonable . . . interpretation of the statute it is entrusted to administer," and also chided the Court of Appeals for declining to afford deference because of the putatively " 'statutory interpretation-jurisdictional' nature of the question at issue." Justice Scalia also invoked the FDA Tobacco Case and *MCI v. AT&T*. Although the agency was rebuked in both cases, the Court applied the *Chevron* framework to issues that were allegedly "jurisdictional."

Under *Chevron*, the agency's interpretation of the vague statutory provision was eminently reasonable, and so the Court sustained it. Concurring in part and in the judgment, **Justice Breyer** rejected any special rule for "jurisdictional" questions but also applied a more contextual *Mead*-like approach to the question whether Congress intended the agency to fill in the details of § 332(c)(7)(B)(ii). He felt there was no good reason not to defer to the general rulemaking authority the FCC had been given over the entire statute, even as amended.

Writing also for Justices Kennedy and Alito, **Chief Justice Roberts** dissented. "A court should not defer to an agency until the court decides, on its own, that the agency is entitled to deference. Courts defer to an agency's interpretation of law when and because Congress has conferred on the agency interpretive authority over the question at issue. An agency cannot exercise interpretive authority until it has it; the question whether an agency enjoys that authority must be decided by a court, without deference to the agency." Because *Mead* held that *Chevron* rests upon Congress's delegation of lawmaking authority to the agency, courts ought to take care that there actually *has been such a delegation.* For this reason, the Chief Justice rejected the Court's articulation of the issue. The issue is *not* whether an agency enjoys *Chevron* deference to its assertion of "jurisdiction." Instead, the issue is whether an agency's interpretation has been issued pursuant to a congressional authorization to make rules with the force of law (the *Mead* inquiry).

Indeed, the Chief Justice maintained, the judicial role under *Marbury* demands that a court, before it abdicates its authority to declare the law, be certain that *Congress* has authorized an agency to create rules with the force of law for this kind of issue. Indeed, this was the precise holding of *Chevron*. Recall that *Chevron* rested upon the notion that, because Congress had not answered the specific question at issue, judges had no business providing their own resolution on the basis of their "personal policy preferences." Instead, the "agency to which Congress ha[d] delegated policymaking responsibilities" was the appropriate political actor to resolve the competing interests at stake, "within the limits of that delegation." As the Chief Justice emphasized, "the Court did not ask simply whether Congress had delegated to the EPA the authority to administer the Clean Air Act generally. We asked whether Congress had 'delegat[ed] authority to the agency to elucidate a *specific provision* of the statute by regulation.' *Chevron* (emphasis added); see *id.* (discussing 'the legislative delegation to an agency on a *particular question*' (emphasis added)). We deferred to the EPA's interpretation of 'stationary sources' based on our conclusion that the agency had been 'charged with responsibility for administering *the provision.*' *Id.* (emphasis added)."

The Chief Justice claimed that the Court had "never faltered" in refusing deference on the question of lawmaking authorization. In *Adams Fruit Co. v. Barrett*, 494 U.S. 638 (1990), for example, the Court did not defer to the Department of Labor's interpretation of the scope of the private right of action provided by the Migrant and Seasonal Agriculture Worker Protection Act, 29 U.S.C. § 1854, against employers who intentionally violated the Act's motor vehicle safety provisions. "A precondition to deference under *Chevron* is a congressional delegation of administrative authority." Although "Congress clearly envisioned, indeed expressly mandated, a role for the Department of Labor in administering the statute by requiring the Secretary to promulgate *standards* implementing AWPA's motor vehicle provisions," the Court found "[n]o such delegation regarding AWPA's enforcement provisions."

The dissenters concluded: "*Adams Fruit, Mead,* and *Gonzales* thus confirm that *Chevron* deference is based on, and finds legitimacy as, a congressional delegation of interpretive authority. An agency interpretation warrants such deference only if Congress has delegated authority to definitively interpret a particular ambiguity in a particular manner. Whether Congress has done so must be determined by the court on its own before *Chevron* can apply."

NOTE ON CHEVRON *DEFERENCE TO AGENCY ASSERTIONS OF JURISDICTIONAL AUTHORITY*

City of Arlington seems to settle the thorny issue whether *Chevron* applies to an agency's interpretation of its own authority or jurisdiction. Most scholars seem to have agreed with the Chief Justice on this point,[11] but six Justices embracing different theories about *Chevron* have rejected the point. It is especially notable that Justice Breyer, an early critic of *Chevron* as inconsistent with *Marbury* (the key point made by the Chief Justice), agreed with Justice Scalia's critique (though Breyer went his own way to decide the case). Consider how *City of Arlington* plays into the Court's ongoing debate about how to apply *Chevron*.

For example, can *Gonzales v. Oregon* be reconciled with *City of Arlington*? Notice that Justice Kennedy, the author of *Oregon*, was in dissent for *City of Arlington*. And Justice Scalia, dissenting in *Oregon*, wrote a very different opinion for the Court in *City of Arlington*. Justice Ginsburg was in the majority for both *Oregon* and *City of Arlington*. How might she reconcile the two opinions? Also, do not think that Justice Scalia has given up on his *Kulturkampf* against *Mead*. The Chief Justice's dissent and Justice Breyer's concurring opinion were carefully tied to *Mead*, and the majority opinion somewhat less so. Perhaps *Oregon* is not the decision in peril after *City of Arlington*: Should the Court revisit *Mead*?

---

[11] See Ernest Gellhorn & Paul Verkuil, *Controlling Chevron-Based Delegations*, 20 Cardozo L. Rev. 989, 1006–17 (1999); Merrill & Hickman, Chevron's *Domain*, 89 Geo. L.J. 833; see also Bressman, *Has* Mead *Muddled*, 1469–74 (after *Mead,* lower courts have tended to avoid applying *Chevron* deference to issues of agency jurisdiction or authority); Eskridge & Baer, *Continuum of Deference*, 96 Geo. L.J. at 1131–32 (Tables 8–9) (finding lower agency win rates for issues where the agency was interpreting its own jurisdiction or authority). But see Kevin M. Stack, *The Statutory President*, 90 Iowa L. Rev. 539, 594–95 (2005) (agreeing with the Scalia position).

B. DOES THE AGENCY HAVE BROADER FREEDOM TO INTERPRET ITS OWN RULES AND REGULATIONS?

Since the New Deal, the Supreme Court has sometimes given special deference to agency interpretations of their own regulations. Such interpretations are "controlling unless plainly erroneous or inconsistent with the regulation." *Bowles v. Seminole Rock & Sand Co.*, 325 U.S. 410, 414 (1945). The *Seminole Rock* rule survives *Chevron*, as illustrated by *Auer v. Robbins*, 519 U.S. 452 (1997).

This very issue was the first claim by the Attorney General in *Gonzales v. Oregon,* 546 U.S. 243 (2006). Under the Controlled Substances Act (CSA), Schedule II substances are generally available only pursuant to a written, nonrefillable prescription by a physician. 21 U.S.C. § 829(a). A 1971 regulation promulgated by the Department of Justice requires that every prescription for a controlled substance "be issued for a legitimate medical purpose by an individual practitioner acting in the usual course of his professional practice." 21 C.F.R. § 1306.04(a). Attorney General Ashcroft presented his Directive preempting the Oregon Death With Dignity Act, as an interpretation of the Department's 1971 regulation and therefore entitled to *Seminole Rock-Auer* deference.

The Court rejected this assertion of deference. "In *Auer,* the underlying regulations gave specificity to a statutory scheme the Secretary was charged with enforcing and reflected the considerable experience and expertise the Department of Labor had acquired over time with respect to the complexities of the Fair Labor Standards Act. Here, on the other hand, the underlying regulation does little more than restate the terms of the statute itself. The language the Interpretive Rule addresses comes from Congress, not the Attorney General, and the near-equivalence of the statute and regulation belies the Government's argument for *Auer* deference. [21 U.S.C. §§ 812(b), 830(b)(3)(A)(ii).]"

In dissent, Justice Scalia questioned whether there was any authority creating a "parroting" exception to *Auer* and insisted that the regulation did more than "parrot" the statute. Indeed, the regulation used the term "prescription," which the Ashcroft Directive interpreted to provide guidance to doctors regulated by the statute. That the Attorney General opted for a narrow understanding of "prescription" (issued for a legitimate medical purpose, as determined by the Attorney General), poses no problem whatsoever under the deferential scrutiny required by *Auer.*

NOTE ON AN AGENCY'S INTERPRETATIONS OF ITS OWN REGULATIONS

An agency's interpretation of its own rules can come in a variety of formats—*amicus* briefs (as in *Auer*), directives or interpretive rules/guidances (as in *Oregon*), opinion letters (SEC and IRS especially), and so forth. Generally, agency interpretations in these formats are entitled to *Skidmore* deference, as in the Oregon Aid-in-Dying Case—but if the agency can relate them somehow to an existing *Chevron*-eligible rule, then it can not only jump *Skidmore,* but also jump *Chevron,* all the way to *Seminole-Auer.* This concern with "agency bootstrapping" is probably what worried Justice Kennedy, and it has certainly worried other Justices, e.g., *Thomas Jefferson Univ. v. Shalala,* 512 U.S. 504, 525 (1994) (Thomas, J., dissenting), and commentators, e.g., John Manning, *Constitutional Structure and Judicial Deference to Agency Interpretations of Agency Rules*, 96 Colum. L. Rev. 612 (1996).

The Eskridge and Baer survey of 1014 Supreme Court cases between *Chevron* and *Hamdan* identified 155 cases where an agency said it was interpreting its own prior rules—yet the Court applied *Seminole-Auer* deference in only 12 of those cases, a surprisingly low number unless the bootstrapping concern is at work. See Eskridge & Baer, *Continuum of Deference,* 96 Geo. L.J. at 1104–05 (Table 2). Perhaps *Seminole Rock* is most relevant under the circumstances identified in *Auer:* The regulatory concept in play is one that the agency itself created (pursuant to a valid congressional delegation) and is now interpreting.

State supreme courts have been reluctant to create a special rule for agency interpretations of its own regulations. Recall the Pennsylvania Supreme Court's decision in *Seeton v. Pennsylvania Game Commission.* That Court's deference jurisprudence parallels *Chevron*, but none of the Justices in *Seeton* mentioned that the agency was interpreting its own regulations. The majority was, if anything, not very deferential to the agency—nor did dissenting Justice Eakins rely on anything like *Auer* as a reason for going along with the agency. Notice that Justice Kennedy's "parroting exception" to *Auer* could have applied in *Seeton.*

Another issue, closely related to the deference issue, is how judges as well as administrators should interpret agency regulations. Agencies tend to construe them purposively, sometimes with a political edge (as was the case with the Ashcroft Directive)—and Kevin Stack argues that judges should *also* construe agency regulations in a purposive manner, using regulatory statements of basis and purpose as privileged sources of interpretation. See Kevin Stack, *Interpreting Regulations,* 111 Mich. L. Rev. 355 (2012). Because regulations typically contain explicit discussions of statutory purpose and why the agency thinks particular rules and standards are the best mechanism for carrying out those purposes, judges have more to work with, as a legal matter, than they often do in ordinary statutory interpretation. Stack argues that interpretations of a regulation should pass muster under *Chevron* only if the interpretations are permitted by the text of the regulation and also consistent with the regulatory purposes as set forth in the statement of basis and purpose as well as the regulation's text. In the Oregon Aid-in-Dying Case, it is Justice Scalia who reads the 1971 Department of Justice regulation purposively. Would Stack join that dissent? How would his analysis apply in the following case?

Coeur Alaska, Inc. v. Southeast Alaska Conservation Council

557 U.S. 261 (2009).

Coeur Alaska proposed to reopen a defunct gold mine in Alaska. To extract the gold, it planned to use a technique known as "froth flotation" in which crushed rock from the mine would be churned in tanks of chemical-laden, frothing water. Gold-bearing minerals would float to the surface, where they would be skimmed off. Coeur Alaska sought permission to discharge the remaining mixture of crushed rock and water, known as slurry, into Lower Slate Lake, a navigable waterway of the United States subject to the Clear Water Act (CWA or Act). The discharge would eventually raise the lakebed to the current surface, significantly expanding the lake's area.

Respondents, a coalition of three environmental groups known as SEACC, challenged the decision of the Army Corps of Engineers to grant Coeur Alaska a permit for the discharge on two grounds: (1) that only the EPA, not the Corps, had authority under the CWA to grant the permit and (2) that even if the Corps had permitting authority, it could not grant the permit without violating an EPA regulation, known as a "new source performance standard," promulgated under the CWA. Section 402 gives the EPA authority to issue "permit[s] for the discharge of any pollutant," with one important exception: The EPA may not issue permits for fill material that fall under the Corps' § 404 permitting authority. Section 402(a) states:

> "*Except as provided in* . . . *[CWA § 404, 33 U.S.C. § 1344]*, the Administrator may . . . issue a permit for the discharge of any pollutant, . . . notwithstanding [CWA § 301(a), 33 U.S.C. § 1311(a)], upon condition that such discharge will meet either (A) all applicable requirements under [CWA § 301, 33 U.S.C. § 1311(a), and other enumerated provisions], or (B) prior to the taking of necessary implementing actions relating to all such requirements, such conditions as the Administrator determines are necessary to carry out the provisions of this chapter." 33 U.S.C. § 1342(a)(1) (emphasis added). * * *

Justice Kennedy's opinion for the Court sided with the company, holding that the CWA "is best understood to provide that if the Corps has authority to issue a permit for a discharge under § 404, then the EPA lacks authority to do so under § 402."

"Even if there were ambiguity on this point, the EPA's own regulations would resolve it. Those regulations provide that '[d]ischarges of dredged or fill material into waters of the United States which are regulated under section 404 of CWA' 'do not require [§ 402] permits' from the EPA. 40 CFR § 122.3. * * * Before us, the EPA confirms this reading of the regulation. Brief for Federal Respondents 27. The agency's interpretation is not 'plainly erroneous or inconsistent with the regulation'; and so we accept it as correct. *Auer*."

Justice Kennedy then found that the Corps of Engineers had authority under § 404 to regulate the slurry discharge. Section 404(a) gives the Corps power to "issue permits . . . for the discharge of dredged or fill material." 33 U.S.C. § 1344(a). The slurry met the definition of fill material agreed upon by the EPA and the Corps in a joint regulation promulgated in 2002. That regulation defined "fill material" to mean any "material [that] has the effect of . . . [c]hanging the bottom elevation" of water—a definition that includes "slurry, or tailings or similar mining-related materials." 40 CFR § 232.2. Justice Kennedy rejected the challengers' effort to read an "implicit exception" into § 404 that material is subject to an EPA new source performance standard. Not only did the statutory text not support an exception, but the EPA's own guidelines, adopted pursuant to § 404(b), do not purport to strip the Corps of authority to issue permits for fill in cases where the fill is also subject to an EPA new source performance standard. 40 CFR pt. 230.

The environmental challengers had one more line of argument. When a performance standard applies to a point source, § 306(e) makes it "unlawful" for that point source to violate it: "[I]t shall be unlawful for any owner or operator of any new source to operate such source in violation of any standard of performance applicable to such source." CWA § 306(e), 33 U.S.C. § 1316(e). The challengers argued that § 306(e), forbids the mine from discharging slurry into Lower Slate Lake—and therefore the Corps cannot authorize an activity that is contrary to law, i.e., § 306(e). Alaska and the agencies responded that CWA § 404 clearly authorizes the activity and that § 306(e) ought not be read to nullify § 404 here.

"The CWA is ambiguous on the question whether § 306 applies to discharges of fill material regulated under § 404. On the one hand, § 306 provides that a discharge that violates an EPA new source performance standard is 'unlawful'—without any exception for fill material. On the other hand, § 404 grants the Corps blanket authority to permit the discharge of fill material—without any mention of § 306. This tension indicates that Congress has not 'directly spoken' to the 'precise question' of whether § 306 applies to discharges of fill material. *Chevron*."

Unfortunately, there were no agency regulations dispositive on this key issue. "The regulations, like the statutes, do not address the question whether § 306, and the EPA new source performance standards promulgated under it, apply to § 404 permits and the discharges they authorize." But Justice Kennedy found "that agency interpretation and agency application of the regulations are instructive and to the point. *Auer*. The question is addressed and resolved in a reasonable and coherent way by the practice and policy of the two agencies, all as recited in a memorandum written in May 2004 by Diane Regas, then the Director of the EPA's Office of Wetlands, Oceans and Watersheds, to Randy Smith, the Director of the EPA's regional Office of Water with responsibility over the mine. (Regas Memorandum). The Memorandum, though not subject to sufficiently formal procedures to merit *Chevron* deference, see *Mead*, is entitled to a measure of deference because it interprets the agencies' own regulatory scheme. See *Auer*.

"The Regas Memorandum explains:

As a result [of the fact that the discharge is regulated under section 404], the regulatory regime applicable to discharges under section 402, including effluent limitations guidelines and standards, such as those applicable to gold ore mining . . . do not apply to the placement of tailings into the proposed impoundment [of Lower Slate Lake]. See 40 CFR § 122.3(b).

To be sure, the regulation cited in the Memorandum (40 CFR § 122.3) was ambiguous. But because the Memorandum offered "a reasonable interpretation of the regulatory regime," the Court deferred to its interpretation as not "plainly erroneous or inconsistent with the regulation[s]." *Auer*. Among its features that supported this finding were that "the Memorandum preserve[d] a role for the EPA's performance standard"; acknowledged that this is not an instance in which the discharger was trying to evade the requirements of the EPA's performance standard; preserved the Corps' authority to determine whether a discharge is in the public interest; provided some protection against allowing toxic pollutants (as distinguished from other, less dangerous pollutants, such as slurry) to enter the navigable waters; and was, in the words of the Court, "a sensible and rational construction that reconciles §§ 306, 402, and 404, and the regulations implementing them, which the alternatives put forward by the parties do not."

Justice Breyer concurred, on the ground that the statute itself created a legal zone within which the regulating agencies might reasonably classify material either as "dredged or fill material" subject to § 404, or as a "pollutant," subject to §§ 402 and 306. "Within this zone, the law authorizes the environmental agencies to classify material as the one or the other, so long as they act within the bounds of relevant regulations, and provided that the classification, considered in terms of the purposes of the statutes and relevant regulations, is reasonable." Agreeing with the dissenters that the Court ought to guard against a huge regulatory gap, Justice Breyer was persuaded that the

EPA/Corps understanding of the statute, ratified by the Court, protected against this possibility.

Justice Scalia concurred in part and in the judgment. Justice Scalia claimed that what the Court was doing, in effect, was affording *Chevron* deference to an informal agency document. "It is quite impossible to achieve predictable (and relatively litigation-free) administration of the vast body of complex laws committed to the charge of executive agencies without the assurance that reviewing courts will accept reasonable and authoritative agency interpretation of ambiguous provisions. If we must not call that practice *Chevron* deference, then we have to rechristen the rose. Of course the only reason a new name is required is our misguided opinion in *Mead*, whose incomprehensible criteria for *Chevron* deference have produced so much confusion in the lower courts that there has now appeared the phenomenon of *Chevron* avoidance—the practice of declining to opine whether *Chevron* applies or not. I favor overruling *Mead*. Failing that, I am pleased to join an opinion that effectively ignores it."

Writing also for Justices Stevens and Souter, **Justice Ginsburg** dissented. The purpose of the Clean Water Act of 1972 was "to restore and maintain the chemical, physical, and biological integrity" of the waters of the United States. 33 U.S.C. § 1251(a). "The use of any river, lake, stream or ocean as a waste treatment system is unacceptable." S. Rep. No. 92–414, p. 7 (1971). The overall objective was to eliminate, by 1985, the discharge of all pollutants into America's navigable waters. 33 U.S.C. § 1251(a).

"The Act instructs EPA to establish various technology-based, increasingly stringent effluent limitations for categories of point sources. *E.g.,* §§ 1311, 1314. * * * Of key importance, new sources must meet stringent 'standards of performance' adopted by EPA under § 306. That section makes it 'unlawful for *any* . . . new source to operate . . . in violation of' an applicable performance standard. 33 U.S.C. § 1316(e) (emphasis added). * * *

"In 1982, EPA promulgated new source performance standards for facilities engaged in mining, including those using a froth-flotation milling process. Existing mills, the Agency found, were already achieving zero discharge; it was therefore practicable, EPA concluded, for new mills to do as well. Accordingly, under 40 CFR § 440.104(b)(1), new mines using the froth-flotation method, as Coeur Alaska proposes to do, may not discharge wastewater directly into waters of the United States."

In light of these broad purposes and rules, Justice Ginsburg objected to the Court's willingness to create an exception to the plain and broad rule of § 306(e) based upon the Corps' permission under § 404. "The Act can be home to both provisions, with no words added or omitted, so long as the category of 'dredged or fill material' eligible for a § 404 permit is read in harmony with § 306. Doing so yields a simple rule: Discharges governed by EPA performance standards are subject to EPA's administration and receive permits under [§ 402], not § 404.

"This reading accords with the Act's structure and objectives. It retains, through [§ 402], uniform application of the Act's core pollution-control requirements, and it respects Congress' special concern for new sources. Leaving pollution-related decisions to EPA, moreover, is consistent with Congress' delegation to that agency of primary responsibility to administer the Act. Most fundamental, adhering to § 306(e)'s instruction honors the overriding statutory goal of eliminating water pollution, and Congress' particular rejection of the use of navigable waters as waste disposal sites.

"The Court's reading, in contrast, strains [credibility]. A discharge of a pollutant, otherwise prohibited by firm statutory command, becomes lawful if it contains sufficient solid matter to raise the bottom of a water body, transformed into a waste disposal facility. Whole categories of regulated industries can thereby gain immunity from a variety of pollution-control standards. * * *

"Congress, we have recognized, does not 'alter the fundamental details of a regulatory scheme in vague terms or ancillary provisions—it does not, one might say, hide elephants in mouseholes.' *Whitman v. American Trucking Assns., Inc.,* 531 U.S. 457, 467–468 (2001). Yet an alteration of that kind is just what today's decision imagines. Congress, as the Court reads the Act, silently upended, in an ancillary permitting provision, its painstaking pollution-control scheme. Congress did so, the Court holds, notwithstanding the lawmakers' stated effort "to restore and maintain the chemical, physical, and biological integrity" of the waters of the United States, 33 U.S.C. § 1251(a); their assignment to EPA of the Herculean task of setting strict effluent limitations for many categories of industrial sources; and their insistence that new sources meet even more ambitious standards, not subject to exception or variance. Would a rational legislature order exacting pollution limits, yet call all bets off if the pollutant, discharged into a lake, will raise the water body's elevation? To say the least, I am persuaded, that is not how Congress intended the Clean Water Act to operate."

NOTES ON COEUR ALASKA: SHOULD AUER DEFERENCE BE FOLDED INTO CHEVRON?

1. *The Bootstrapping Concern with* Auer *Deference.* Justice Kennedy depicted the Regas Memorandum as an interpretation of the "regulatory scheme" and the "regulatory regime." Was the memorandum interpreting only the ambiguous EPA regulation, or was it construing the relevant provisions of the CWA as well? If Justice Kennedy was treating the memorandum as an interpretation not only of the regulation, but also, by extension, of the statute, then he seems to have countenanced the kind of "bootstrapping" that concerned him in *Gonzales v. Oregon.* Here, the EPA promulgated an ambiguous regulation to implement an ambiguous statute. It then interpreted the regulation in an internal memorandum. As an interpretation of the regulation, the memorandum should be assessed under *Auer* and should receive deference so long as that interpretation is not "plainly erroneous or inconsistent with the regulation." But insofar as the interpretation of the regulation also resolves an ambiguity in the statute, the memorandum should be assessed under *Chevron* and should receive deference only if its resolution of the statutory ambiguity is "reasonable." To assess the agency's *statutory* interpretation under *Auer,* simply because it is embedded in an interpretation of a regulation, would be to permit the agency to bootstrap that interpretation from *Chevron* to the (possibly) more deferential *Auer* regime.

Justice Kennedy failed—at least explicitly—to assess the memorandum under the *Chevron* standard. Instead, he concluded his analysis by asserting that the memorandum satisfied the *Auer* standard. Insofar as the memorandum also interpreted the statute, Justice Kennedy should have taken the further step of ensuring that, per *Chevron,* there had been a delegation of lawmaking authority and that the agency lawmaking was "reasonable." See *Mead.*

This amounts to both substantive and procedural bootstrapping. It is *substantive*, as it enables an agency to shift its statutory interpretation from one regime of judicial review (*Chevron*) to a (possibly) more deferential one (*Auer*). It is *procedural,* as it enables the agency to reap the advantages of lawmaking without considering whether Congress has delegated that kind of authority (*Mead*). It does not appear that the Regas Memorandum was issued under a delegation of lawmaking authority, however. Thus, if the majority was tacitly treating the memorandum as a *statutory* interpretation, then it is allowing the agency to circumvent *Mead*. (Justice Kennedy ignored this point, but Justice Scalia waved it like a bloody flag.)

Justice Ginsburg's dissenting opinion made the bootstrapping charge in another way: under cover of *Auer*, the agency radically amended the statutory scheme, creating a huge loophole for "fill" material to elbow out the strict no-tolerance EPA policy toward mining slurry. Her elephants-not-in-mouseholes argument is very similar to the one that Justice Kennedy found cogent in *Oregon*. (What *did* distinguish *Oregon* from *Coeur Alaska* for Justice Kennedy?)

2.   *The Difference Between* Chevron *and* Auer*, and the Closeted Role of* Skidmore. Justice Scalia suggested that the majority was actually applying *Chevron* deference to the Regas Memorandum, despite its claim to be applying *Auer* deference. Is there any practical difference between the two regimes? That is, will judges be any more deferential under a "clearly erroneous" standard than under a "reasonableness" one? Or will judges simply make independent, policy-based judgments about the merits of deference in cases they adjudicate, regardless of the particular deference regime they ultimately announce? This might be an implication of Justice Breyer's concurring opinion here, as well as his opinions in earlier cases. From Breyer's perspective, there is in reality just one deference regime: *Skidmore*, with its various factors for assessing whether deference is warranted.

Bring these two points together and relate them to the majority opinion. Justice Kennedy accorded the Regas Memorandum "a measure of deference"—a phrase that appears to equivocate between *Chevron* and *Auer* deference. Note also that the factors he adduced for deferring to the memorandum sit comfortably within the *Skidmore* framework.

3.   *Should* Seminole Rock-Auer *Deference Be Retired as an Independent Category?* Justice Scalia's concurring opinion suggested that the Court's *Auer* analysis boiled down to a *Chevron* analysis without the *Mead* requirement of lawmaking delegation. In *Decker v. Northwest Environmental Defense Center,* 133 S.Ct. 1326, 1339 (2013), Justice Scalia wrote a separate opinion urging the Court to jettison *Auer* as a special category of deference. "*Auer* deference encourages agencies to be 'vague in framing regulations, with the plan of issuing "interpretations" to create the intended new law without observance of notice and comment procedures.' Anthony, The Supreme Court and the APA: Sometimes They Just Don't Get It, 10 Admin. L.J. Am. U. 1, 11–12 (1996). *Auer* is not a logical corollary to *Chevron* but a dangerous permission slip for the arrogation of power."

Ironically, Justice Scalia wrote *Auer* and strongly relied on it in his dissenting opinion in the Oregon Aid-in-Dying Case. Why the change of heart? Surely important is the influential criticism of *Auer* deference by his former law clerk, John Manning. See Manning, *Constitutional Structure and Judicial Deference to Agency Interpretations of Agency Rules,* 96 Colum. L. Rev. 612 (1996). Perhaps also relevant is Justice Scalia's strong commitment to overturning *Mead*. His chief argument for that is a simple but powerful *Chevron* doctrine, where statutory text is the anchor and agency interpretations of all sorts are given deference only if there is textual ambiguity or vagueness.

Thus far, Scalia is the only Justice to call for a jettisoning of *Auer* as a separate category for deference, and the Court explicitly applied *Auer* in *Decker* and in *Chase Bank USA, N.A. v. McCoy*, 131 S.Ct. 871, 880 (2011) (the latter, with no separate statement from Justice Scalia). Chief Justice Roberts, joined by Justice Alito, wrote a separate opinion in *Decker* rebuking Justice Scalia for his reconsideration of *Auer* in that case. Should the Court reconsider *Auer* in an appropriate case (i.e., where *Auer* is briefed)? Recall that state courts have not followed the Supreme Court here, in contrast to their interest in the *Chevron* regime. E.g., *Seeton v. Pennsylvania Game Comm'n*, 937 A.2d 1028 (Pa. 2007).

C. SHOULD COURTS DEFER WHEN THE AGENCY INTERPRETATION PRESENTS SERIOUS CONSTITUTIONAL DIFFICULTIES?

Yet another way to read the Oregon Aid-in-Dying Case is through a constitutional lens. Five Justices (O'Connor, Stevens, Souter, Ginsburg, Breyer), all in the *Oregon* majority, had opined in *Washington v. Glucksberg* that they were open to recognizing a "constitutionally cognizable interest in controlling the circumstances of his or her imminent death," in at least some instances. Without any constitutional nuance or case-by-case reservation, the Ashcroft Directive made aid-in-dying a crime under any and all circumstances. Justice Kennedy's opinion mentioned the "earnest and profound debate" over the constitutionality of state efforts to ban all forms of euthanasia as one reason the Court was reluctant to find a congressional delegation to the Attorney General on this issue. Most and perhaps all of the majority Justices found the Ashcroft Directive constitutionally problematic in the breadth of its intrusion into private decisionmaking and state policymaking. It is likely that none of the dissenting Justices had these constitutional problems. See Eskridge, *Story of* Gonzales v. Oregon, 366–75, 384–94.

Does the existence of potential constitutional problems make a difference in the Court's overall willingness to defer? What would be the theoretical basis for that? One might presume that Congress does not normally delegate to agencies the authority to press constitutional limits, and so constitutional concerns would show up at Step Zero, as in the *Oregon* case. Or one might invoke the avoidance canon in Step One: when there are two possible meanings of statutory language, the Court should for institutional process reasons follow the one that does not raise constitutional problems. (In that event, the avoidance canon would trump *Chevron*. The Court has in fact gone that route in some *Chevron*-eligible cases. E.g., *Department of Commerce v. U.S. House of Representatives* (Chapter 5, § 3).) One can even imagine the constitutional analysis coming in *Chevron* Step Two: an agency interpretation is not "reasonable" if it raises constitutional concerns when a more cautious interpretation would just as easily serve congressional goals.

Do these arguments lose their cogency when fewer than five Justices flag constitutional problems? Perhaps surprisingly, the Eskridge and Baer study suggests not. In the 75 cases where at least one Justice flagged a constitutional concern with the agency's interpretation, the agency view prevailed only 45.3 percent of the time, while the agency view won in 70.7 percent of the cases where no Justice raised constitutional concerns. Eskridge & Baer, *Continuum of Deference*. This is the most dramatic differential in their study and strongly suggests that agencies do *not* get nearly as much deference when there are constitutional concerns with their interpretations.

PROBLEM WHEN AGENCY INTERPRETATIONS RAISE CONSTITUTIONAL CONCERNS

Problem 9–3. In 1970, Congress enacted Title X of the Public Health Service Act, 84 Stat. 1499, 1504, which provides federal funding for family-planning services. The purposes of the Act expressed in § 2 are:

(1) to assist in making comprehensive voluntary family planning services readily available to all persons desiring such services; * * *

(5) to develop and make readily available information (including educational materials) on family planning and population growth to all persons desiring such information.

The Act authorizes the provision of federal funds to support the establishment and operation of voluntary family planning projects and empowers the Secretary of Health and Human Services to promulgate regulations imposing conditions on grant recipients to ensure that "grants will be effectively utilized for the purposes for which made."

Section 1 of the Act authorizes the Secretary to "make grants to and enter into contracts with public or nonprofit private entities to assist in the establishment and operation of voluntary family planning projects which shall offer a broad range of acceptable and effective family planning methods and services." Section 1008 provides: "None of the funds appropriated under this Act shall be used in programs where abortion is a method of family planning." According to the conference report for the Act, the § 1008 restriction was to ensure that Title X funds would "be used only to support preventive family planning services, population research, infertility services, and other related medical, informational, and educational opportunities."

The Secretary's 1971 regulations implementing the Act described the kind of services that grant recipients had to provide in order to be eligible for federal funding. Pursuant to § 1008, the regulations stipulated that "the project will not provide abortions as a method of family planning." The 1971 regulations, even as revised in 1986, did not regulate the form of counseling or the distribution of information at federally funded projects.

In 1988, the Secretary promulgated new regulations to clarify the "family planning" services that Title X funds may be used to assist. Section 59.2 of the new regulations limits Title X services to "preconceptual counseling, education, and general reproductive health care (including obstetric or prenatal care)." Section 59.8(a)(1) specifies that henceforth a "Title X project may not provide counseling concerning the use of abortion as a method of family planning or provide referral for abortion as a method of family planning." Section 59.8(a)(2)–(3) makes clear that Title X programs have to refer pregnant women to other services, but doctors in the program cannot "steer" expectant mothers to health care providers who perform abortions. Even if the client specifically requests referral to an abortion provider, the Title X program cannot do so, nor can doctors associated with the program. According to § 59.8(b)(5), the appropriate response is that "the project does not consider abortion an appropriate method of family planning and therefore does not counsel or refer for abortion."

Grantees and doctors immediately challenge the new regulations. What arguments can they invoke against the Secretary's interpretation of § 1008? What arguments should the Secretary make in response? How would the Supreme Court analyze and decide this issue? Compare *Rust v. Sullivan*, 500 U.S. 173 (1991).

PALM BEACH COUNTY CANVASSING BOARD V. HARRIS

Supreme Court of Florida, 2000.
772 So.2d 1220 *Vacated and remanded sub nom.*
Bush v. Palm Beach Canvassing Bd., 531 U.S. 70 (2000).

[On November 8, 2000, the Florida Division of Elections reported that George W. Bush had received 2,909,135 votes for President in that state, narrowly winning Florida over Albert Gore, Jr., who received 2,907,351 votes. An automatic recount narrowed the gap between the candidates, with Bush still in the lead. On November 9, the Florida Democratic Party Executive Committee requested that manual recounts be conducted in Broward, Palm Beach, and Volusia Counties. The Florida Division of Elections determined, however, in Advisory Opinion DE 00–10, that absent unforeseen circumstances, returns from all counties must be received by 5:00 p.m., November 14, 2000, in order to comply with Fla. Stat. § 101.111(1). Based on this advisory opinion, the Florida Secretary of State announced that she would ignore returns submitted after that cut-off time.

[Volusia County, joined by Palm Beach County, went to court for an injunction barring the Secretary from ignoring returns after that time. The trial court ruled on November 14 that the deadline was mandatory but that the Secretary had discretion to accept amended returns filed after that date. The Secretary announced on November 15 that she would not exercise her discretion to accept amended returns from Volusia and Palm Beach Counties; Gore and the Democratic Party filed suit to compel the Secretary to accept the amended returns. The trial court denied relief, and the Florida Supreme Court accepted an expedited appeal to consider, first, the circumstances authorizing an elections board to require a county-wide manual recount under § 102.166(5) and, second, whether the Secretary could accept the recounts submitted after the passing of the § 101.111(1) deadline.]

[II] Twenty-five years ago, this Court commented that the will of the people, not a hyper-technical reliance upon statutory provisions, should be our guiding principle in election cases:

> [T]he real parties in interest here, not in the legal sense but in realistic terms, are the voters. They are possessed of the ultimate interest and it is they whom we must give primary consideration. * * * Our federal and state constitutions guarantee the right of the people to take an active part

in the process of that government, which for most of our citizens means participation via the election process. *The right to vote is the right to participate; it is also the right to speak, but more importantly the right to be heard.* We must tread carefully on that right or we risk the unnecessary and unjustified muting of the public voice. By refusing to recognize an otherwise valid exercise of the right of a citizen to vote for the sake of sacred, unyielding adherence to statutory scripture, we would in effect nullify that right.

Boardman v. Esteva, 323 So. 2d 259, 263 (Fla. 1975) (emphasis added). We consistently have adhered to the principle that the will of the people is the paramount consideration. Our goal today remains the same as it was a quarter of a century ago, i.e., to reach the result that reflects the will of the voters, whatever that might be. This fundamental principle, and our traditional rules of statutory construction, guide our decision today. * * *

[IV] The first issue this Court must resolve is whether a County Board may conduct a countywide manual recount where it determines there is an error in vote tabulation that could affect the outcome of the election. Here, the Division issued opinion DE 00–13, which construed the language "error in vote tabulation" to exclude the situation where a discrepancy between the original machine return and sample manual recount is due to the manner in which a ballot has been marked or punched.

Florida courts generally will defer to an agency's interpretation of statutes and rules the agency is charged with implementing and enforcing. Florida courts, however, will not defer to an agency's opinion that is contrary to law. We conclude that the Division's advisory opinion regarding vote tabulation is contrary to law because it contravenes the plain meaning of section 102.166(5). [The court observed that the Legislature used broad language not suggesting the agency's limitation; also the Legislature required the administrators to make sure that "[n]o vote shall be declared invalid or void if there is a clear indication of the intent of the voter as determined by the canvassing board." § 101.5614(5). This and other provisions indicated that the statute targeted much more than system failures and surely included miscounted votes.]

Having concluded that the county canvassing boards have the authority to order countywide manual recounts, we must now determine whether the Commission [i.e., the Secretary of State, the Director of the Division of Elections, and the Governor] must accept a return after the seven-day deadline set forth in sections 102.111 and 102.112 under the circumstances presented. * * *

[VI] The provisions of the Code are ambiguous in two significant areas. First, the time frame for conducting a manual recount under section 102.166(4) is in conflict with the time frame for submitting county returns under sections 102.111 and 102.112. Second, the mandatory language in section 102.111 conflicts with the permissive language in 102.112.

[*A. The Recount Conflict.*] Section 102.166(1) states that "[a]ny candidate for nomination or election, or any elector qualified to vote in the election related to such candidacy, shall have the right to protest the returns of the election as being erroneous by filing with the appropriate canvassing board a sworn written protest." The time period for filing a protest is "prior to the time the canvassing board certifies the results for the office being protested or within 5 days after midnight of the date the election is held, whichever occurs later."

Section 102.166(4)(a), the operative subsection in this case, further provides that, in addition to any protest, "any candidate whose name appeared on the ballot . . . or any political party whose candidates' names appeared on the ballot may file a written request with the county canvassing board for a manual recount" accompanied by the "reason that the manual recount is being requested." Section 102.166(4)(b) further provides that the written request may be made prior to the time the Board certifies the returns or within seventy-two hours after the election, whichever occurs later:

> (4)(a)   Any candidate whose name appeared on the ballot, any political committee that supports or opposes an issue which appeared on the ballot, or any political party whose candidates' names appeared on the ballot may file a written request with the county canvassing board for a manual recount. The written request shall contain a statement of the reason the manual recount is being requested.
>
> (b) *Such request must be filed with the canvassing board prior to the time the canvassing board certifies the results for the office being protested or within 72 hours after midnight of the date the election was held, whichever occurs later.* § 102.166, Fla. Stat. (2000) (emphasis added).

[The Board "may" then authorize a recount, including at least three precincts and 1% of the total votes for the protesting candidate. If the manual recount then indicates an error in the vote tabulation which could affect the election, the Board "shall" either "(a) [c]orrect the error and recount the remaining precincts * * *; (b) [r]equest the Secretary of State to verify the tabulation software; or (c) [m]anually recount all ballots." § 102.166(5).]

Under this scheme, a candidate can request a manual recount at any point prior to certification by the Board and such action can lead to a full recount of all the votes in the county. Although the Code sets no specific deadline by which a manual recount must be completed, logic dictates that the period of time required to complete a full manual recount may be substantial, particularly in a populous county, and may require several days. The protest provision thus conflicts with section 102.111 and 102.112, which state that the Boards "must" submit their returns to the Elections Canvassing Commission by 5:00 p.m. of the seventh day following the election or face penalties. For instance, if a party files a pre-certification protest on the sixth day following the election and requests a manual recount and the initial manual recount indicates that a full countywide recount is necessary, the recount procedure in most cases could not be completed by the deadline in sections 102.111 and 102.112, i.e., by 5:00 p.m. of the seventh day following the election.

[B. *The "Shall" and "May" Conflict.*] In addition to the conflict in the above statutes, sections 102.111 and 102.112 contain a dichotomy. Section 102.111, which sets forth general criteria governing the State Canvassing Commission, was enacted in 1951 as part of the Code and provides as follows:

> (1) * * * The Elections Canvassing Commission shall, as soon as the official results are compiled from all counties, certify the returns of the election and determine and declare who has been elected for each office. * * * *If the county returns are not received by the Department of State by 5 p.m. of the seventh day following an election, all missing counties shall be ignored*, and the results shown by the returns on file shall be certified. § 102.111, Fla. Stat. (2000) (emphasis added).

The Legislature in 1989 revised chapter 102 to include section 102.112, which provides that returns not received after a certain date "may" be ignored and that members of the County Board "shall" be fined:

> (1) The county canvassing board or a majority thereof shall file the county returns for the election of a federal or state officer with the Department of State immediately after the certification of the election returns. Returns must be filed by 5 p.m. on the 7th day following the first primary and general election and by 3 p.m. on the 3rd day following the second primary. *If the returns are not received by the department by the time specified, such returns may be ignored* and the results on file at that time may be certified by the department. * * *

> [Subsection (2) sets forth fines against board members "for each day such returns are late," and (3) establishes a procedure for board members to appeal such fines.] § 102.112, Fla. Stat. (2000) (emphasis added).

The above statutes conflict. Whereas section 102.111 is mandatory, section 102.112 is permissive. While it is clear that the Boards must submit returns by 5 p.m. of the seventh day following the election or face penalties, the circumstances under which penalties may be assessed are unclear.

[VII] Legislative intent—as always—is the polestar that guides a court's inquiry into the provisions of the Florida Election Code. Where the language of the code is clear and amenable to a reasonable and logical interpretation, courts are without power to diverge from the intent of the Legislature as expressed in the plain language of the Code. As noted above, however, chapter 102 is unclear concerning both the time limits for submitting the results of a manual recount and the penalties that may be assessed by the Secretary. In light of this ambiguity, the Court must resort to traditional rules of statutory construction in an effort to determine legislative intent.

[The Court concluded that § 102.112 should control, for a variety of reasons: it was the more specific provision and was enacted more recently than § 102.111. Most important, however, a preference for the mandatory rule of § 102.112 must be rendered because it makes the best sense of the statutory scheme.]

Section 102.166 states that a candidate, political committee, or political party may request a manual recount any time before the County Canvassing Board certifies the results to the Department and, if the initial manual recount indicates a significant error, the Board "shall" conduct a countywide manual recount in certain cases. Thus, if a protest is filed on the sixth day following an election and a full manual recount is required, the Board, through no fault of its own, will be unable to submit its returns to the Department by 5:00 p.m. on the seventh day following the election. In such a case, if the mandatory provision in section 102.111 were given effect, the votes of the county would be ignored for the simple reason that the Board was following the dictates of a different section of the Code. The Legislature could not have intended to penalize County Canvassing Boards for following the dictates of the Code.

And finally, when the Legislature enacted the Code in 1951, it envisioned that all votes cast during a particular election, including absentee ballots, would be submitted to the Department at one time and would be treated in a uniform fashion. Section 97.012(1) states that it is the Secretary's responsibility to "[o]btain and maintain uniformity in the application, operation, and interpretation of the election laws." Chapter 101 provides that all votes, including absentee ballots, must be received by the Supervisor no later than 7 p.m. on the day of the election. Section 101.68(2)(d) expressly states that "[t]he votes on absentee ballots shall be included in the total vote of the county." Chapter 102 requires that the Board submit the returns by 5 p.m. on the seventh day following the election.

The Legislature thus envisioned that when returns are submitted to the Department, the returns "shall" embrace all the votes in the county, including absentee ballots. This, of course, is not possible because our state statutory scheme has been superseded by federal law governing overseas voters; overseas ballots must be counted if received no later than ten days following the election (i.e., the ballots do *not* have to be received by 7 p.m. of the day of the election, as provided by state law). In light of the fact that overseas ballots cannot be counted after until the seven day deadline has expired, the mandatory language in section 102.111 has been supplanted by the permissive language of section 102.112.

Further, although county returns must be received by 5 p.m. on the seventh day following an election, the "official results" that are to be compiled in order to certify the returns and declare who has been elected must be construed in pari materia with section 101.5614(8), which specifies that "write-in, absentee *and manually counted results* shall constitute the official return of the election." (Emphasis added).

Under this statutory scheme, the County Canvassing Boards are required to submit their returns to the Department by 5 p.m. of the seventh day following the election. The statutes make no provision for exceptions following a manual recount. If a Board fails to meet the deadline, the Secretary is not required to ignore the county's returns but rather is permitted to ignore the returns within the parameters of this statutory scheme. To determine the circumstances under which the Secretary may lawfully ignore returns filed pursuant to the provisions of section 102.166 for a manual recount, it is necessary to examine the interplay between our statutory and constitutional law at both the state and federal levels.

[VIII]   * * * To the extent that the Legislature may enact laws regulating the electoral process, those laws are valid only if they impose no "unreasonable or unnecessary" restraints on the right of suffrage:

> The declaration of rights expressly states that "all political power is inherent in the people." Article I, Section 1, Florida Constitution. The right of the people to select their own officers is their sovereign right, and the rule is against imposing unnecessary and unreasonable [restraints on that right]. . . . *Unreasonable or unnecessary* restraints on the elective process are prohibited.

Treiman v. Malmquist, 342 So. 2d 972, 975 (Fla. 1977) (emphasis added).

Because election laws are intended to facilitate the right of suffrage, such laws must be liberally construed in favor of the citizens' right to vote:

> Generally, the courts, in construing statutes relating to elections, hold that the same should receive a liberal construction in favor of the citizen whose right to vote they tend to restrict and in so doing to prevent disfranchisement of legal voters and the intention of the voters should prevail when counting ballots. . . . It is the intention of the law to obtain an honest expression of the will or desire of the voter.

State ex rel. Carpenter v. Barber, 198 So. 49, 51 (Fla. 1940). Courts must not lose sight of the fundamental purpose of election laws: The laws are intended to facilitate and safeguard the right of each voter to express his or her will in the context of our representative democracy. Technical statutory requirements must not be exalted over the substance of this right.

Based on the foregoing, we conclude that the authority of the Florida Secretary of State to ignore amended returns submitted by a County Canvassing Board may be lawfully exercised only under limited circumstances as we set forth in this opinion. The clear import of the penalty provision of section 102.112 is to deter Boards from engaging in dilatory conduct contrary to statutory authority that results in the late certification of a county's returns. This deterrent purpose is achieved by the fines in section 102.112, which are substantial and personal and are levied on each member of a Board. The alternative penalty, i.e., ignoring the county's returns, punishes not the Board members themselves but rather the county's electors, for it in effect disenfranchises them.

Ignoring the county's returns is a drastic measure and is appropriate only if the returns are submitted to the Department so late that their inclusion will compromise the integrity of the electoral process in either of two ways: (1) by precluding a candidate, elector, or taxpayer from contesting the certification of an election pursuant to section 102.168; or (2) by precluding Florida voters from participating fully in the federal electoral process. In either case, the Secretary must explain to the Board her reason for ignoring the returns and her action must be adequately supported by the law. To disenfranchise electors in an effort to deter Board members, as the Secretary in the present case proposes, is unreasonable, unnecessary, and violates longstanding law. [The Secretary made no such claim in this case.] * * *

Because of the unique circumstances and extraordinary importance of the present case, wherein the Florida Attorney General and the Florida Secretary of State have issued conflicting advisory opinions concerning the propriety of conducting manual recounts, and because of our reluctance to rewrite the Florida Election Code, we conclude that we must invoke the equitable powers of this Court to fashion a remedy that will allow a fair and expeditious resolution of the questions presented here.

Accordingly, in order to allow maximum time for contests pursuant to section 102.168, amended certifications must be filed with the Elections Canvassing Commission by 5 p.m. on Sunday, November 26, 2000 and the Secretary of State and the Elections Canvassing Commission shall accept any such amended certifications received by 5 p.m. on Sunday, November 26, 2000, provided that the office of the Secretary of State, Division of Elections is open in order to allow receipt thereof. If the office is not open for this special purpose on Sunday, November 26, 2000, then any amended certifications shall be accepted until 9 a.m. on Monday, November 27, 2000. The stay order entered on November 17, 2000, by this Court shall remain in effect until the expiration of the time for accepting amended certifications set forth in this opinion. The certificates made and signed by the Elections Canvassing Commission pursuant to section 102.121 shall include the amended returns accepted through the dates set forth in this opinion.

NOTES ON PALM BEACH CANVASSING BOARD AND THE ROLE OF CANONS IN JUDICIAL EVALUATION OF AGENCY INTERPRETATIONS

1.   *The Subsequent History of* Palm Beach Canvassing Bd. v. Harris. The U.S. Supreme Court unanimously vacated the foregoing opinion, on the ground that the Florida court's interpretation of the statutes may have been influenced by their view of the state constitution. *Bush v. Palm Beach County Canvassing Bd.*, 531 U.S. 70 (2000) (per curiam). The Court's reasoning was as follows: In normal cases, the Supreme Court would not second-guess a state court in this way. Article II of the U.S. Constitution,[12] as well as a federal statute, 3 U.S.C. § 5,[13] vest the state "Legislature," alone, with the authority to determine the procedures by which the state chooses its electors for President. Thus, the Constitution has delegated an important federal role to the state legislature, not to the legislature-cum-court. The state court's only role is to determine what procedures the legislature has *actually* chosen, not what procedures the state constitution—superseded on this point by federal law—would require the legislature to choose in state elections. The Supreme Court remanded the case to the state courts. (On remand, the Florida Supreme Court reaffirmed its prior interpretation.) For a

---

[12]   "Each state shall appoint, in such Manner as the Legislature thereof may direct, a Number of Electors, equal to the whole Number of Senators and Representatives to which the State may be entitled in the Congress * * *." U.S. Const., art. I, § 1, cl. 2.

[13]   "If any State shall have provided, by laws enacted prior to the day fixed for the appointment of the electors, for its final determination of any controversy or contest concerning the appointment of all or any of the electors of such State, by judicial or other methods or procedures, and such determination shall have been made at least six days before the time fixed for the meeting of the electors, such determination made pursuant to such law so existing on said day, and made at least six days prior to said time of meeting of the electors, shall be conclusive, and shall govern in the counting of the electoral votes as provided in the Constitution, and as hereinafter regulated, so far as the ascertainment of the electors appointed by such State is concerned." 3 U.S.C. § 5.

discussion of the Article II issue, see Samuel Issacharoff, Pamela Karlan & Richard Pildes, *When Elections Go Bad* (2001).

On November 26, the Florida Elections Canvassing Commission certified the Bush electors for that state. Vice President Gore immediately challenged the certification under the state contest law, Fla. Stat. § 102.168, which allows a contest if there is "[r]eceipt of a number of illegal votes or rejection of a number of legal votes sufficient to change or place in doubt the result of the election." Reversing the trial court in several respects, a divided Florida Supreme Court in *Gore v. Harris*, 772 So. 2d 1243 (Dec. 8, 2000), ruled that Miami-Dade and other counties must conduct manual recounts of "undervotes," those ballots the machines did not count but where the intent of the voter might be discerned through examination of "chads" created by a partial punch-through in the ballot and even of "dimples," or indentations not amounting to punch-throughs. The court ruled that the "intent of the voter" was the standard each county must follow. The recounts were to be completed by December 12, the federal safe-harbor date under 3 U.S.C. § 5 (if a state has chosen electors by that date, they cannot be challenged). The recounts began but were stayed by the U.S. Supreme Court on December 9. *Bush v. Gore*, 531 U.S. 1046 (2000). The Supreme Court reversed the second Florida Supreme Court decision on December 12, on the ground that the state recount procedures violated the Equal Protection Clause. *Bush v. Gore*, 531 U.S. 98 (2000) (per curiam). Florida certified its Bush electors, and the next day candidate Gore conceded the election to Governor Bush.

2. *Was the Florida Supreme Court's Statutory Interpretation Beyond the Pale? Should the Court Have Deferred?* A concurring opinion in *Bush v. Gore* maintained that the state court constructions of the state statutes violated Article II on the ground that they rewrote the Legislature's directives. *Bush v. Gore,* 531 U.S. at 113 (Rehnquist, C.J., joined by Scalia and Thomas, JJ., concurring). The Chief Justice maintained that the state court's interpretation misread the legislature's election-contest law, in its view that a fraction of "undervote" ballots were "legal votes" that needed to be counted and in its remedy of new manual recounts, which threatened Florida's compliance with the safe-harbor December 12 deadline. These were criticisms of the Florida court's December 8 opinion, not its November 21 opinion, but other criticisms applied to the earlier opinion as well. The Chief Justice would have ruled that "[n]o reasonable person would call [an undervote, where the voter did not completely punch through] 'an error in the vote tabulation,'" within the meaning of § 102.166(5). (Hint: look up *tabulate* in the dictionary.) The Chief Justice also criticized the Florida court for failing to defer to the "reasonable interpretation" offered by the administrative official (Secretary of State Katharine Harris, the Bush campaign chief in the state) and insisting instead on its "peculiar one." *Id.* at 537.

The dissenting opinions in *Bush v. Gore* took the position that the Florida court made a reasonable interpretation of its own state law and, therefore, should receive the deference the Chief reserved for the administrators. *Id.* at 542 (Stevens, J., dissenting); *id.* at 544 (Souter, J., dissenting); *id.* at 546–52 (Ginsburg, J., dissenting). In short, while the Florida justices would have appreciated more deference to their efforts to make sense of the statutory scheme and construct a fair but expeditious recount procedure, the Florida election administrators would have appreciated more deference to their efforts to bring the factious election to a close. Even under the Florida Supreme Court's opinion, the Secretary of State had discretion in receiving late vote tallies because of manual recounts. Why was it that the Secretary was found to have abused her discretion? Was there no room for deference—at least as to that?

The answer in *Palm Beach Canvassing Board* seems to have been, in part, that the Secretary was not giving proper weight to the state constitutional right to vote. The U.S. Supreme Court's first opinion rejected reliance on the state constitution—but the state court could then have relied on the federal constitutional right to vote. But under federal precedents, it appears doubtful that a decision by a state election board to call a halt to manual recounts in order to meet a statutory deadline would violate anyone's federal right to vote. (It's hard to imagine a different result under the Florida Constitution, but there are fewer precedents to guide prediction.) If that's right, then the interpretive principle seems to have no traction. This recalls the quandary we raised in connection with *Catholic Bishop* in Chapter 5: Should a court go out of its way to avoid a constitutional difficulty if it's clear that both statutory approaches actually are constitutional? So should the state court have deferred to the Secretary in the exercise of her discretion? Is there good reason for a court not to defer in matters of voting law?

Another angle, unexamined in the various opinions, is that agency *litigating positions* are not entitled to *Chevron* deference under federal law. See *Bowen v. Georgetown Univ. Hosp.*, 488 U.S. 204 (1988); *United States v. Western Elec. Co.*, 900 F.2d 283, 297 (D.C. Cir. 1990). For example, in the rule of lenity cases, courts do not defer to Department of Justice guidelines for implementing criminal laws, in part because they are developed for purposes of litigation. To the extent that the administrative interpretations in *Palm Beach Canvassing Board* were "litigating positions," they are probably not entitled to deference. But were they litigating positions?

3. *Deference and Canons of Construction.* Deference to administrative interpretations is, among other things, one of the canons of statutory construction. But under the *Chevron* framework, that canon has no application if the statute is otherwise clear. One way to determine whether the statute is clear is to examine it through the lens of the various canons—precisely as the Florida Supreme Court did (and it found the statute clear, so deference was unwarranted). The debate rehearsed in our note about legislative history after *Chevron* can be understood in this light.

All judges agree that determination of statutory clarity under *Chevron* Step One requires consideration of the textual canons or the principles embedded in them. Thus, U.S. Supreme Court Justices have refused to defer to agency interpretations when their Step One inquiry has found a statutory plain meaning based on such canonical chestnuts as the rule against surplusage, e.g., *National Credit Union Admin. v. First Nat'l Bank & Trust Co.*, 522 U.S. 479, 500, 502 (1998); *noscitur a sociis*, e.g., *Sweet Home* (Chapter 3, § 1C) (Scalia, J., dissenting); *inclusio unius*, e.g., *City of Chicago*; the dictionary rule, e.g., *MCI*; and so forth.

The role of substantive canons in the *Chevron* analysis is even murkier. Like the Florida Supreme Court, the U.S. Supreme Court seems to consider such canons highly relevant in determining whether there is a statutory plain meaning that terminates the inquiry with Step One. See Elizabeth Garrett, *Legal Scholarship in the Age of Legislation*, 34 Tulsa L.J. 679, 695–96 (1999) (discussing the relationship between substantive canons and textualism). Note the irony, therefore, in the U.S. Supreme Court's first and second decisions reviewing the Florida court. The kind of substantive canon the Florida court invoked in *Palm Beach Canvassing Board* is, according to the U.S. Supreme Court in other cases, a part of the plain meaning inquiry. The message of the earlier U.S. Supreme Court cases is that the interpretive process itself requires a court to consider substantive canons—a message in some tension with the first opinion in the Bush and Gore election mess. Moreover, the concurring Justices in the second Supreme Court opinion (Rehnquist, Scalia, Thomas) are aggressive users of constitutional clear statement rules—yet they faulted the Florida court for a milder invocation of the kinds of rules that they regularly deploy.

D. DO COURTS DEFER TO AGENCIES ON WHETHER FEDERAL LAW PREEMPTS STATE REGULATION?

The Supremacy Clause of Article VI requires that federal statutes be the supreme law of the land and that state courts enforce them rather than state law when they are inconsistent, or "preempted." There are three different circumstances when state law, such as the Oregon Death With Dignity Act, might be preempted by federal law. First, a valid federal statute can stipulate that it preempts state law, and the Court will follow that statutory directive (unless there is a constitutional problem). E.g., *Shaw v. Delta Airlines*, 463 U.S. 85 (1983). Of course, Congress can also write a "non-preemption" *saving clause* into legislation, which will direct courts not to read the legislation to preempt state law.

Second, a federal statute will preempt state law whose operation is inconsistent with that of the federal statutory scheme. This applies not only "where compliance with both federal and state regulations is a physical impossibility," *Florida Lime & Avocado Growers, Inc. v. Paul*, 373 U.S. 132, 142–43 (1963), but also where the state law "stands as an obstacle to the accomplishment and execution of the full purposes and objectives of Congress." *Hines v. Davidowitz*, 312 U.S. 52, 67 (1941).

Third is "field" preemption. "The scheme of federal regulations may be so pervasive as to make reasonable the inference that Congress left no room for the States to supplement it. Or the Act of Congress may touch a field in which the federal interest is so dominant that the federal system will be assumed to preclude enforcement of state laws of the same subject." *Rice v. Santa Fe Elevator Corp.*, 331 U.S. 218, 230 (1947). Areas such as immigration, naturalization, and regulation of noncitizens are examples of fields where federal legislation is likely to be preemptive. E.g., *Toll v. Moreno*, 458 U.S. 1 (1982).

Assume you have a federal statute, such as the Motor Vehicle Safety Act of 1966, which delegates lawmaking and other authority to an agency such as the NHTSA. The agency might have important input into a court's determination of the scope of federal preemption. First, Congress might give the agency direct authority to preempt state law through notice-and-comment rulemaking. Such rules would be subject to *Chevron* deference. Second, Congress might delegate to the agency the authority to adopt substantive rules which could then be the basis for federal preemption the same as explicit statutory rules would. The validity of such rules would be evaluated under *Chevron*, but the agency's understanding of their preemptive force would probably entail only *Skidmore* deference. Third, the agency might, on its own, present its views, usually through interpretive guidances or in *amicus* briefs. What level of deference should that entail?

As you ponder that question, recall that the Supreme Court has recognized a substantive canon that is relevant: "The historic police powers of the States [are] not to be superseded by . . . Federal Act unless that [is] the clear and manifest purpose of Congress." *Cipollone v. Liggett Group, Inc.*, 505 U.S. 504, 516 (1992). How does this canon relate to the three different kinds of preemption *and* to the three kinds of agency inputs? Consider the following case.

GEIER V. AMERICAN HONDA MOTOR CO., INC.

United States Supreme Court, 2000.
529 U.S. 861, 120 S.Ct. 1913, 146 L.Ed.2d 914.

JUSTICE BREYER delivered the opinion of the Court.

[In 1992, petitioner Alexis Geier, driving a 1987 Honda Accord, collided with a tree and was seriously injured. The car was equipped with manual shoulder and lap belts which Geier had buckled up at the time. The car was not equipped with airbags or other passive restraint devices. Geier and her parents, also petitioners, sued the car's manufacturer, American Honda, under District of Columbia tort law. They claimed that American Honda had designed its car negligently and defectively because it lacked a driver's side airbag. The District Court dismissed the lawsuit on grounds of preemption. Because Geier's lawsuit sought to establish a stricter safety standard (an airbag requirement) than FMVSS 208 (which then permitted choice between airbags and passive restraints), the asserted tort claim was pre-empted by a provision of the Safety Act of 1966 which pre-empts "any safety standard" that is not identical to a federal safety standard applicable to the same aspect of performance, 15 U.S.C. § 1392(d).

[Disagreeing, the Supreme Court held that the preemption provision was inapplicable because of a saving provision, which says that "compliance with" a federal safety standard "does not exempt any person from any liability under common law." 15 U.S.C. § 1397(k). The saving clause assumes that there are some significant number of common-law liability cases to save. Justice Breyer did not, however, agree that the saving clause precluded the Court's application of ordinary pre-emption principles. See *Freightliner Corp. v. Myrick*, 514 U.S. 280 (1995).]

The basic question, then, is whether a common-law "no airbag" action like the one before us actually conflicts with FMVSS 208. We hold that it does.

In petitioners' and the dissent's view, FMVSS 208 sets a minimum airbag standard. As far as FMVSS 208 is concerned, the more airbags, and the sooner, the better. But that was not the Secretary's view. DOT's comments, which accompanied the promulgation of FMVSS 208, make clear that the standard deliberately provided the manufacturer with a range of choices among different passive restraint devices. Those choices would bring about a mix of different devices introduced gradually over time; and FMVSS 208 would thereby lower costs, overcome technical safety problems, encourage technological development, and win widespread consumer acceptance—all of which would promote FMVSS 208's safety objectives. See generally 49 Fed. Reg. 28962 (1984).

* * * Read in light of this history, DOT's own contemporaneous explanation of FMVSS 208 makes clear that the 1984 version of FMVSS 208 reflected the following significant considerations. First, buckled up seatbelts are a vital ingredient of automobile safety. Second, despite the enormous and unnecessary risks that a passenger runs by not buckling up manual lap and shoulder belts, more than 80% of front seat passengers would leave their manual seatbelts unbuckled. Third, airbags could make up for the dangers caused by unbuckled manual belts, but they could not make up for them entirely.

Fourth, passive restraint systems had their own disadvantages, for example, the dangers associated with, intrusiveness of, and corresponding public dislike for, nondetachable automatic belts. Fifth, airbags brought with them their own special risks to safety, such as the risk of danger to out-of-position occupants (usually children) in small cars.

Sixth, airbags were expected to be significantly more expensive than other passive restraint devices, raising the average cost of a vehicle price $320 for full frontal airbags over the cost of a car with manual lap and shoulder seatbelts (and potentially much more if production volumes were low). And the agency worried that the high replacement cost—estimated to be $800—could lead car owners to refuse to replace them after deployment. Seventh, the public, for reasons of cost, fear, or physical intrusiveness, might resist installation or use of any of the then-available passive restraint devices—a particular concern with respect to airbags.

FMVSS 208 reflected these considerations in several ways. Most importantly, that standard deliberately sought variety—a mix of several different passive restraint systems. It did so by setting a performance requirement for passive restraint devices and allowing manufacturers to choose among different passive restraint mechanisms, such as airbags, automatic belts, or other passive restraint technologies to satisfy that requirement. And DOT explained why FMVSS 208 sought the mix of devices that it expected its performance standard to produce. DOT wrote that it had *rejected* a proposed FMVSS 208 "all airbag" standard because of safety concerns (perceived or real) associated with airbags, which concerns threatened a "backlash" more easily overcome "if airbags" were "not the only way of complying." It added that a mix of devices would help develop data on comparative effectiveness, would allow the industry time to overcome the safety problems and the high production costs associated with airbags, and would facilitate the development of alternative, cheaper, and safer passive restraint systems. And it would thereby build public confidence necessary to avoid another interlock-type fiasco.

The 1984 FMVSS 208 standard also deliberately sought a *gradual* phase-in of passive restraints. It required the manufacturers to equip only 10% of their car fleet manufactured after September 1, 1986, with passive restraints. It then increased the percentage in three annual stages, up to 100% of the new car fleet for cars manufactured after September 1, 1989. And it explained that the phased-in requirement would allow more time for manufacturers to develop airbags or other, better, safer passive restraint systems. It would help develop information about the comparative effectiveness of different systems, would lead to a mix in which airbags and other nonseatbelt passive restraint systems played a more prominent role than would otherwise result, and would promote public acceptance. * * *

In effect, petitioners' tort action depends upon its claim that manufacturers had a duty to install an airbag when they manufactured the 1987 Honda Accord. Such a state law—*i.e.*, a rule of state tort law imposing such a duty—by its terms would have required manufacturers of all similar cars to install airbags rather than other passive restraint systems, such as automatic belts or passive interiors. It thereby would have presented an obstacle to the variety and mix of devices that the federal regulation sought. It would have required all manufacturers to have installed airbags in respect to the entire District-of-Columbia-related portion of their 1987 new car fleet, even though FMVSS 208 at that time required only that 10% of a manufacturer's nationwide fleet be equipped with any passive restraint device at all. It thereby also would have stood as an obstacle to the gradual passive restraint phase-in that the federal regulation deliberately imposed. In addition, it could have made less likely the adoption of a state mandatory buckle-up law. Because the rule of law for which petitioners contend would have stood "as an obstacle to the accomplishment and execution of" the important means-related federal objectives that we have just discussed, it is pre-empted. * * *

One final point: We place some weight upon DOT's interpretation of FMVSS 208's objectives and its conclusion, as set forth in the Government's brief, that a tort suit such as this one would " 'stand as an obstacle to the accomplishment and execution' " of those objectives. Brief for United States as *Amicus Curiae* 25–26 (quoting *Hines v. Davidowitz*, 312 U.S. 52, 67 (1941)). Congress has delegated to DOT authority to implement the statute; the subject matter is technical; and the relevant history and background are complex and extensive. The agency is likely to have a thorough understanding of its own regulation and its objectives and is "uniquely qualified" to comprehend the likely impact of state requirements. And DOT has explained FMVSS 208's objectives, and the interference that "no airbag" suits pose thereto, consistently over time. In these circumstances, the agency's own views should make a difference. * * *

[We omit the dissenting opinion of JUSTICE STEVENS, joined by JUSTICES SOUTER, THOMAS, and GINSBURG. Most of the dissenters' arguments are mentioned in the notes following the decision.]

NOTES ON GEIER AND FEDERAL PREEMPTION OF STATE LAW

1.   *The Debate Among the Justices.* Key to Justice Breyer's opinion is the Court's belief that allowing state courts to find that airbags are sometimes required to satisfy the manufacturer's duty of care would undermine the federal statute's compromise, whereby manufacturers would have choices. Justice Stevens's dissent objected that case-by-case adjudications would not establish a hard-and-fast rule that airbags were required; not only could different juries reach different results, but manufacturers could win all the cases if they showed airbags to be ineffective or other methods just as effective. See Peter Strauss, *The Story of* Geier v. American Honda Motor Co.: *Statutes,*

Regulation, and the Common Law, in *Statutory Interpretation Stories* 294, 320–32 (Eskridge, Frickey & Garrett eds., 2011).

The dissenters also argued that the Court ignored the *Cipollone* presumption and was too willing to preempt the state tort suit. Was it clear that preemption was required by the "clear and manifest purpose of Congress"? Justice Stevens also insisted that the majority's holding was in tension with the saving clause: "The saving clause in the Safety Act unambiguously expresses a decision by Congress that compliance with a federal safety standard does not exempt a manufacturer from *any* common-law liability. In light of this reference to common-law liability in the saving clause, Congress surely would have included a similar reference in § 1392(d) if it had intended to pre-empt such liability. Cf. *Chicago v. Environmental Defense Fund,* 511 U.S. 328, 338 (1994) (noting presumption that Congress acts intentionally when it includes particular language in one section of a statute but omits it in another)." Should the Court be especially chary of preempting state common law under "inconsistent application" preemption when there is a saving clause?

Note, finally, that state law is essentially preempted by an agency rule and not by a statutory provision. Although the agency had authority to issue the rule, the Court ought to think twice before giving the rule preemptive authority to displace state law, especially in light of the federalism presumption of *Cipollone.* Should the Court allow agency opinions to venture too far into constitutionally murky territory or should the Justices essentially remand the issue for Congress, not just the agency, to make such constitutionally sensitive policy choices? Should this argument have had some weight in *Geier?*

2. *Titanic Concerns: Underenforcement Versus Overenforcement of Safety Norms?* Addressing this issue, Ralph Nader and Joe Page had argued in *Automobile-Design Liability and Compliance with Federal Standards,* 64 Geo. Wash. L. Rev. 415, 419 (1996), that the statutory minimum should not preclude state regulation that raised the floor. In addition to the saving clause, which seemed to embody this philosophy, Nader and Page invoked the *Titanic* precedent. That famous vessel had fully "complied with British governmental regulations setting minimum requirements for lifeboats when it left port on its final, fateful voyage with boats capable of carrying only about [half] of the people on board," W. Wade, The *Titanic*: End of a Dream 68 (1986), yet one might reasonably conclude that the *Titanic* had not satisfied its duty of care to the other half of the passengers who lost their lives when the ship sunk in ice-cold waters. Because people's lives are at stake just as much in auto safety regulation, Nader and Page maintained that states ought to be able to raise the floor. The dissenting Justices agreed and cited their article and its *Titanic* analogy. Their position was that the majority was standing in the way of permissible enforcement of the safety norm. The Court may have even been seen as pandering to the auto industry's determination to *underenforce* safety norms.

The majority did not respond but might have said that the regulatory scheme sought a balance of safety and cost. To be blunt, NHTSA was willing to trade off human lives (more people would die in accidents each year) for cost savings by manufacturers. This may seem terrible, but don't forget that the nation's decision to allow automobiles on the road and to travel 65 miles per hour has predictable costs in human lives each year—lives that could be saved if all of us suffered the inconvenience of not being able to drive (or drive so fast) on the open road. The majority's view was that Congress had authorized the agency to make these kinds of trade-offs (recall Justice White's opinion in *State Farm*, not to mention Justice Stevens's opinion in *Chevron*). Hence, the dissenters' position would have *overenforced* safety norms.

3.   *Should the Court Defer to the Agency in Preemption Cases?* How should *Chevron/Skidmore* interact with *Cipollone* in these cases? Justice Thomas has reconciled the different authorities with the suggestion that the Court should be *less* deferential if the federal agency is pushing for preemption and *more* deferential when the agency is arguing against preemption, especially in conflict or field preemption cases. *Pharmacological Res. & Mfrs. v. Walsh*, 538 U.S. 644, 675–83 (2003) (Thomas, J., concurring in the judgment). This is consistent with his dissenting vote in *Geier*, but not his dissenting vote in the Oregon Aid-in-Dying Case. And, of course, the *Geier* majority gives significant credit to the Department's views.

Nina Mendelson, Chevron *and Preemption*, 102 Mich. L. Rev. 737 (2004), argues against *Chevron* deference for agency views regarding preemption. Although she demonstrates that agencies are more accountable to state interests than the Court or (surprisingly) Congress, she cautions against *Chevron* deference because courts continue to have some comparative advantages in evaluating preemption claims and because agencies will often tend to expand their own authority at the expense of the states. Mendelson believes that agencies often have useful contributions and so favors *Skidmore* deference as appropriate—the same accommodation reached by Justice Breyer in *Geier* and Justice Kennedy in *Oregon*.

Wyeth v. Levine
555 U.S. 555 (2009).

Directly injecting the drug Phenergan into a patient's vein creates a significant risk of catastrophic consequences. A Vermont jury found that Wyeth, the manufacturer of the drug, had failed to provide an adequate warning of that risk and awarded damages to Diana Levine to compensate her for the amputation of her arm. Because the warnings on Phenergan's label had been deemed sufficient by the federal Food and Drug Administration (FDA) when it approved Wyeth's new drug application in 1955 and when it later approved changes in the drug's labeling, Wyeth challenged the state tort verdict on the ground that it was preempted by the Food, Drug & Cosmetic Act of 1938 (FDCA), which bars unsafe drugs.

Justice Stevens's opinion for the Court (joined by Justices Kennedy, Souter, Ginsburg, and Breyer) ruled that the FDCA did not preempt these state tort claims. Justice Stevens started with this presumption: "[i]n all pre-emption cases, and particularly in those in which Congress has 'legislated . . . in a field which the States have traditionally occupied,' . . . we 'start with the assumption that the historic police powers of the States were not to be superseded by the Federal Act unless that was the clear and manifest purpose of Congress.' " ([Q]uoting *Medtronic, Inc. v. Lohr*, 518 U.S. 470, 485 (1996).)

Wyeth's main argument rested upon a 2007 amendment to the FDCA that required FDA approval of drug labels. Because the FDA had okayed the warning that was the basis for the state tort suit, Wyeth argued that state tort law was implicitly preempted, because it would be impossible for Wyeth to comply with both its federal duty to use the approved label and its state duty to provide more detailed warnings (the doctrine of "impossibility preemption"). In an *amicus* brief, the FDA agreed and urged the Court to find preemption here. Justice Stevens rejected that argument, in part because federal law allowed Wyeth to amend its label without FDA approval based on safety concerns of the sort raised by the state tort suit. Thus, it was *not* impossible for Wyeth to comply with both federal law and state law. More generally, Justice Stevens ruled that the federal statute vests primary responsibility for labeling with drug companies, not the FDA, which is merely a monitor.

Wyeth and the FDA also argued that state tort liability undermined the purposes of federal law (the doctrine of "obstacle preemption"). In a preface to a 2006 rule, the FDA had opined that drug standards in the statute represented *both* a floor *and* a ceiling for manufacturers; hence, state tort liability was preempted when the manufacturer was following the label requirements of the federal law.

"In prior cases, we have given 'some weight' to an agency's views about the impact of tort law on federal objectives when 'the subject matter is technica[l] and the relevant history and background are complex and extensive.' *Geier*. Even in such cases, however, we have not deferred to an agency's *conclusion* that state law is pre-empted. Rather, we have attended to an agency's explanation of how state law affects the regulatory scheme. While agencies have no special authority to pronounce on pre-emption absent delegation by Congress, they do have a unique understanding of the statutes they administer and an attendant ability to make informed determinations about how state requirements may pose an 'obstacle to the accomplishment and execution of the full purposes and objectives of Congress.' [See *Geier*.] The weight we accord the agency's explanation of state law's impact on the federal scheme depends on its thoroughness, consistency, and persuasiveness. Cf. *Mead*; *Skidmore*.

"Under this standard, the FDA's 2006 preamble does not merit deference. When the FDA issued its notice of proposed rulemaking in December 2000, it explained that the rule would 'not contain policies that have federalism implications or that preempt State law.' In 2006, the agency finalized the rule and, without offering States or other interested parties notice or opportunity for comment, articulated a sweeping position on the FDCA's pre-emptive effect in the regulatory preamble. The agency's views on state law are inherently suspect in light of this procedural failure.

"Further, the preamble is at odds with what evidence we have of Congress' purposes, and it reverses the FDA's own longstanding position without providing a reasoned explanation, including any discussion of how state law has interfered with the FDA's regulation of drug labeling during decades of coexistence. The FDA's 2006 position plainly does not reflect the agency's own view at all times relevant to this litigation. Not once prior to Levine's injury did the FDA suggest that state tort law stood as an obstacle to its statutory mission. To the contrary, it cast federal labeling standards as a floor upon which States could build and repeatedly disclaimed any attempt to pre-empt failure-to-warn claims. For instance, in 1998, the FDA stated that it did 'not believe that the evolution of state tort law [would] cause the development of standards that would be at odds with the agency's regulations.' It further noted that, in establishing 'minimal standards' for drug labels, it did not intend 'to preclude the states from imposing additional labeling requirements.' "

Justice Breyer (the author of *Geier*) wrote a concurring opinion, reserving judgment on the possibility that the FDA could in the future adopt a rule having preemptive force (as in *Geier*) if the agency found a specific clash between federal policy and state tort lawsuits.

Justice Thomas concurred in the judgment. "I have become increasingly skeptical of this Court's 'purposes and objectives' pre-emption jurisprudence. Under this approach, the Court routinely invalidates state laws based on perceived conflicts with broad federal policy objectives, legislative history, or generalized notions of congressional purposes that are not embodied within the text of federal law." Drawing from the Tenth Amendment, the Constitution's federal structure, and Article I, Section 7, Justice Thomas argued that, as a matter of constitutional principle, state law remains the default law for citizens unless there is a *federal statutory text* that preempts it under Article VI (the Supremacy Clause). Hence, he was skeptical of obstacle preemption doctrine entirely and would apply impossibility preemption doctrine very cautiously—and was unwilling to apply either doctrine to the Levine case.

Justice Alito (joined by Chief Justice Roberts and Justice Scalia) dissented. Justice Alito relied on the notion that the FDA is responsible for determining drug safety and, hence, that its determinations are both a floor and a ceiling for a manufacturer's legal responsibility. Cf. *Riegel v. Medtronic, Inc.*, 552 U.S. 312 (2008) (ruling that federal regulation preempts state tort suits for warning defects for medical devices, also regulated by the FDA). Indeed, Justice Alito believed the case was controlled by *Geier*.

"Notwithstanding the statute's saving clause, and notwithstanding the fact that Congress gave the Secretary authority to set only 'minimum' safety standards, we held Geier's state tort suit pre-empted. In reaching that result, we relied heavily on the view of the Secretary of Transportation—expressed in an *amicus* brief—that Standard 208 "'embodies the Secretary's policy judgment that safety would best be promoted if manufacturers installed *alternative* protection systems in their fleets rather than one particular system in every car.'" Because the Secretary determined that a menu of alternative technologies was 'safe,' the doctrine of conflict pre-emption barred Geier's efforts to deem some of those federally approved alternatives 'unsafe' under state tort law.

"The same rationale applies here. Through Phenergan's label, the FDA offered medical professionals a menu of federally approved, 'safe' and 'effective' alternatives—including IV push—for administering the drug. Through a state tort suit, respondent attempted to deem IV push 'unsafe' and 'ineffective.' To be sure, federal law does not prohibit Wyeth from contraindicating IV push, just as federal law did not prohibit Honda from installing airbags in all its cars. But just as we held that States may not compel the latter, so, too, are States precluded from compelling the former. If anything, a finding of pre-emption is even more appropriate here because the FDCA—unlike the National Traffic and Motor Safety Vehicle Act—contains no evidence that Congress intended the FDA to set only 'minimum standards,' and the FDCA does not contain a saving clause."

NOTE ON WYETH AND AGENCY VIEWS IN PREEMPTION CASES

Recall that Nina Mendelson argued in Chevron *and Preemption*, 102 Mich. L. Rev. 737 (2004), that *Chevron* deference should presumptively not be available for agency interpretations preempting state law. *Wyeth* seems consistent with her position and reasoning—though Justice Breyer suggests that the FDA might be given greater deference if it developed a preemption rule through notice-and-comment rulemaking.

Consider other patterns we have discerned from reading and categorizing all Supreme Court preemption decisions between 1984 and 2006:

• The Court was more skeptical of agency interpretations that expanded national power than of those that respected the regulatory authority of the states. When an agency argued against preemption (39 cases, 1984–2006) the Court agreed with its assessment 84.6% of the time, an astounding rate of agreement. So *Wyeth* was squarely in the mainstream of Supreme Court practice in this regard.

• For technical areas of law, as in *Geier,* the Court was super-deferential: For the 31 cases involving transportation, energy, and communications, the Court agreed with agency recommendations (usually favoring preemption) a whopping 87.1% of the time. Health law cases, such as *Wyeth* and *Riegel,* had lower but still impressive agreement rates. Normative areas such as civil rights and criminal law saw much less impressive agency performances.

• There was no significant difference between agency win rates for express preemption cases (97 cases, with 72.2% agreement rate) and for conflict or obstacle preemption cases (29 cases, with 72.4% agreement rate), perhaps surprising in light of the Article I, § 7 and the federalism concerns raised by Justice Thomas against conflict or obstacle preemption in *Wyeth* and other cases.

See William Eskridge Jr., *Vetogates,* Chevron, *Preemption*, 83 Notre Dame L. Rev. 1441 (2008) (reporting and analyzing these data).

Note that federalism-loving Justice Scalia dissented in *Wyeth* and is probably unsympathetic to the Mendelson position. Why would a strong federalist favor an agency-driven preemption of traditional state law? Justice Thomas's position, also from a strong federalist orientation, is very different from Justice Scalia's. Accord, Bradford Clark, *Separation of Powers as a Safeguard of Federalism*, 79 Tex. L. Rev. 1321 (2001). Is there any principled reason a federalist should follow Justice Scalia over Justice Thomas as to this issue?

Pliva, Inc. v. Mensing
131 S.Ct. 2567 (2011).

In an opinion by **Justice Thomas**, a closely divided Court ruled that state tort-law claims based on certain drug manufacturers' alleged failure to provide adequate warning labels for generic metoclopramide were preempted by the federal statute. It was undisputed that the drug had bad side effects that were not disclosed in its warning; the plaintiffs claimed that the manufacturer should have known of those side effects and should have disclosed them. The manufacturer responded that the FDCA governed its labeling responsibilities, and that it had complied with the new rules established by the Hatch-Waxman Amendments of 1984 for generic drugs (i.e., that their labels simply have to follow the precise disclosures required for the patented drugs that they copy). The plaintiffs argued that the manufacturers had a state tort obligation to disclose the deadly side effects.

The FDA agreed with the manufacturer that it was required under the 1984 Amendments to follow the disclosures required for the manufacturer of the patented drug—but the FDA also maintained that the manufacturer had an obligation to request from the FDA authority to change the drug labeling once it knew about the deadly side effects. Citing *Auer,* Justice Thomas deferred to the FDA's interpretation of its own regulations, including those implementing the 1984 Amendments.

Notwithstanding his caution in *Wyeth,* Justice Thomas ruled that compliance with both state tort law (requiring disclosure) and federal law (not requiring that disclosure) was impossible, and therefore state law was preempted even though there was no congressional rule indicating preemption. "The federal duty to ask the FDA for help in strengthening the corresponding brand-name label, assuming such a duty exists, does not change this analysis. Although requesting FDA assistance would have satisfied the Manufacturers' federal duty, it would not have satisfied their state tort-law duty to provide adequate labeling. State law demanded a safer label; it did not instruct the Manufacturers to communicate with the FDA about the possibility of a safer label. Indeed, Mensing and Demahy deny that their state tort claims are based on the Manufacturers' alleged failure to ask the FDA for assistance in changing the labels."

Justice Thomas recognized the injustice, from plaintiffs' point of view, of the Court's disposition. If they had taken Reglan, the non-generic version of the drug, they would have had a valid tort suit under *Wyeth,* because the non-generic manufacturer could have complied with both state and federal law by a more detailed disclosure. But because they took a generic version of Reglan, the manufacturer's disclosure obligations were governed by the 1984 Amendments, which made the manufacturer's impossibility claim much stronger.

Dissenting, **Justice Sotomayor** (joined by Justices Ginsburg, Breyer, and Kagan) noted the irony created by the Court's disposition. Three-quarters of the drugs sold in the United States are generic, and the 1984 Amendments were enacted to make their availability easier for consumers—with the wholly unintended consequence of denying consumers the needed protections of state tort law.

PROBLEM REVISITING THE COURT'S DECISION IN GEIER

Problem 9–4. Some lower courts interpreted *Geier* to allow preemption of state tort law when claims arose out of choices auto manufacturers were allowed to make under Standard 208. One case arose out of an accident where Thanh Williamson, a passenger in the middle back row of a Mazda van, died. Williamson's estate claimed that she would have survived if she had been wearing a seatbelt that covered both her lap and shoulder—but the NHSTA's Standard 208 allowed auto manufacturers to use just lap belts for the inner seat belts for the back seats of automobiles, a less expensive choice that manufacturers overwhelmingly used in their recent models.

The Williamson case reaches the Supreme Court, which decides whether Standard 208 preempts the state tort lawsuit. Unless it overrules *Geier,* the Court would rule that the express preemption clause of the statute would apply to the lawsuit—but that the savings clause takes "common law" tort lawsuits out of the preemption clause (as the Court ruled in *Geier*). Hence, the key issue would be whether ordinary principles of conflict/obstacle preemption would suggest negation of state law in this case.

In several respects, this case was just like *Geier*: The manufacturer had a choice between two design features, one of which tort plaintiff complained was unsafe. There is one big difference between the cases. In *Geier,* the Solicitor General told the Court that the Department of Transportation (where the NHSTA is located) wanted manufacturers to have a choice of airbags or passive seatbelts, in order to see how the different safety devices would work and how they would be received by consumers. The SG told the Court that state law liability for not using airbags would disrupt this valuable experiment and stand as an obstacle to the agency's mission.

In contrast, in Williamson's case, the SG told the Court that the agency left manufacturers this limited choice of regular seatbelts and lap-and-shoulder seatbelts primarily for cost-benefit reasons, but expected the costs and the benefits to evolve over time. Hence, the SG told the Court that the NHSTA and the Department did not believe that state common law actions such as Williamson's stood as an obstacle to the agency's achievement of its statutory mission.

How should the Court decide Williamson's case? Should the Court overrule *Geier*? Consider Justice Thomas's position in *Wyeth*. State law can be preempted in one of three ways: (1) Congress explicitly preempts state law or delegates such power to an agency, which issues a regulation preempting state law (*Geier,* if there had not been a savings clause). (2) The Supreme Court decides that regulated entities would find it impossible to comply with both the federal rule and a different state rule (*Pliva*). (3) The Supreme Court, often assisted by the agency, decides that differing state rules would pose obstacles to the agency's pursuit of the federal statutory mission (*Geier*). Justice Thomas suggests that this third mechanism for preempting state law might be retired, on the ground that it is inconsistent with our federalist system. Is this a cogent position?

If the Court declines to revisit *Geier,* is the different posture of the agency sufficient to decide the case differently? See *Williamson v. Mazda Motor of America, Inc.,* 131 S.Ct. 1131 (2011).

E.   DEFERENCE AND *STARE DECISIS*

National Cable & Telecommunications Association v. Brand X Internet Services
545 U.S. 967 (2005).

Title II of the Communications Act of 1934, 48 Stat. 1064, as amended, 47 U.S.C. § 151 *et seq.,* subjects all providers of "telecommunications servic[e]" to mandatory common-carrier regulation. An FCC order concluded that cable companies selling broadband Internet service do not provide "telecommunications servic[e]" as the 1934 Act defined the term, and hence were exempt from mandatory common-carrier regulation under Title II.

The traditional means by which consumers in the United States access the network of interconnected computers that make up the Internet had been through "dial-up" connections provided over local telephone facilities. These "narrow-band" connections were relatively slow by modern standards and have been superseded by "broadband" Internet service, which transmits data at much higher speeds. There are two principal kinds of broadband Internet service: cable modem service and Digital Subscriber Line (DSL) service. Cable modem service transmits data between the Internet and users' computers via the network of television cable lines owned by cable companies. DSL service provides high-speed access using the local telephone wires owned by local telephone companies. Cable companies and telephone companies can either provide Internet access directly to consumers, thus acting as [Information

Service Providers, or ISPs] themselves, or can lease their transmission facilities to independent ISPs that then use the facilities to provide consumers with Internet access.

As amended in 1996, the Communications Act of 1934 distinguishes between telecommunications carriers and information-service providers. The Act regulates telecommunications carriers, but not information-service providers, as common carriers that must charge just and reasonable, nondiscriminatory rates to their customers, 47 U.S.C. §§ 201–209, and must design their systems so that other carriers can interconnect with their communications networks, § 251(a)(1). These provisions are mandatory, but the FCC must forbear from applying them if it determines that the public interest requires it. §§ 160(a), (b). Information-service providers, by contrast, are not subject to mandatory common-carrier regulation under Title II, though the FCC has jurisdiction to impose additional regulatory obligations under its Title I ancillary jurisdiction to regulate interstate and foreign communications, see §§ 151–161.

These two statutory classifications originated in the late 1970s, in FCC rules that were essentially adopted by Congress in the 1996 Amendments. "Telecommunications service" is "the offering of telecommunications for a fee directly to the public . . . regardless of the facilities used." 47 U.S.C. § 153(46). "Telecommunications" is "the transmission, between or among points specified by the user, of information of the user's choosing, without change in the form or content of the information as sent and received." § 153(43). "Telecommunications carrier[s]"—those subjected to mandatory Title II common-carrier regulation—are defined as "provider[s] of telecommunications services." § 153(44). And "information service" is "the offering of a capability for generating, acquiring, storing, transforming, processing, retrieving, utilizing, or making available information via telecommunications." § 153(20).

In 2002, after notice-and-comment rulemaking, the FCC concluded that broadband Internet service provided by cable companies is an "information service" but not a "telecommunications service" under the Act, and therefore not subject to mandatory Title II common-carrier regulation. On appeal, the Ninth Circuit vacated the ruling and held that the FCC could not construe the Communications Act to exempt cable companies providing Internet service from Title II regulation. The Court of Appeals grounded its holding in the *stare decisis* effect of *AT&T Corp. v. Portland,* 216 F.3d 871 (9th Cir. 2000), where a panel of the Ninth Circuit held that cable modem service was a "telecommunications service," though the FCC was not a party to the case. In an opinion by **Justice Thomas,** the Supreme Court reversed the Ninth Circuit and upheld the FCC's order.

Justice Thomas rebuked the lower court for applying its precedent rather than *Chevron*-deferring to the FCC: "A court's prior judicial construction of a statute trumps an agency construction otherwise entitled to *Chevron* deference only if the prior court decision holds that its construction follows from the unambiguous terms of the statute and thus leaves no room for agency discretion. This principle follows from *Chevron* itself. *Chevron* established a 'presumption that Congress, when it left ambiguity in a statute meant for implementation by an agency, understood that the ambiguity would be resolved, first and foremost, by the agency, and desired the agency (rather than the courts) to possess whatever degree of discretion the ambiguity allows.' Yet allowing a judicial precedent to foreclose an agency from interpreting an ambiguous statute, as the Court of Appeals assumed it could, would allow a court's interpretation to override an agency's *Chevron's* premise is that it is for agencies, not courts, to fill statutory gaps.

The better rule is to hold judicial interpretations contained in precedents to the same demanding *Chevron* step one standard that applies if the court is reviewing the agency's construction on a blank slate: Only a judicial precedent holding that the statute unambiguously forecloses the agency's interpretation, and therefore contains no gap for the agency to fill, displaces a conflicting agency construction.

"A contrary rule would produce anomalous results. It would mean that whether an agency's interpretation of an ambiguous statute is entitled to *Chevron* deference would turn on the order in which the interpretations issue: If the court's construction came first, its construction would prevail, whereas if the agency's came first, the agency's construction would command *Chevron* deference. Yet whether Congress has delegated to an agency the authority to interpret a statute does not depend on the order in which the judicial and administrative constructions occur. The Court of Appeals' rule, moreover, would 'lead to the ossification of large portions of our statutory law,' *Mead* (Scalia, J., dissenting), by precluding agencies from revising unwise judicial constructions of ambiguous statutes. Neither *Chevron* nor the doctrine of *stare decisis* requires these haphazard results." Compare *Neal v. United States*, 516 U.S. 284 (1996) (trumping an agency interpretation with a precedent recognizing the unambiguous plain meaning of a criminal statute).

Was the statute unambiguous? Is a cable modem service a "telecommunications service"? Recall that "telecommunications" is defined as "the transmission, between or among points specified by the user, of information of the user's choosing, without change in the form or content of the information as sent and received." § 153(43). The FCC conceded that, like all information-service providers, cable companies use "telecommunications" to provide consumers with Internet service; cable companies provide such service via the high-speed wire that transmits signals to and from an end user's computer. For the Commission, however, the question whether cable broadband Internet providers "offer" telecommunications involved more than whether telecommunications was one necessary component of cable modem service. Instead, whether that service also includes a telecommunications offering "turn[ed] on the nature of the functions the *end user* is offered," for the statutory definition of "telecommunications service" does not "res[t] on the particular types of facilities used." See § 153(46) (definition of "telecommunications service" applies "regardless of the facilities used").

Understood from the consumer's point of view, the Commission concluded, cable modem service is not a telecommunications offering, because the consumer uses the high-speed wire always in connection with the information-processing capabilities provided by Internet access, and because the transmission is a necessary component of Internet access: "As provided to the end user the telecommunications is part and parcel of cable modem service and is integral to its other capabilities." The wire is used, in other words, to access the World Wide Web, newsgroups, and so forth, rather than "transparently" to transmit and receive ordinary-language messages without computer processing or storage of the message. The integrated character of this offering led the Commission to conclude that cable modem service is not a "stand-alone," transparent offering of telecommunications.

Justice Thomas ruled that the FCC's reading was a plausible understanding of the statutory text. "Cable companies in the broadband Internet service business 'offe[r]' consumers an information service in the form of Internet access and they do so 'via telecommunications,' § 153(20), but it does not inexorably follow as a matter of ordinary language that they also 'offe[r]' consumers the high-speed data transmission (telecommunications) that is an input used to provide this service, § 153(46). * * * It is common usage to describe what a company 'offers' to a consumer as what the consumer perceives to be the integrated finished product, even to the exclusion of discrete components that compose the product, as the dissent concedes. One might well say that a car dealership 'offers' cars, but does not 'offer' the integrated major inputs that make purchasing the car valuable, such as the engine or the chassis. It would, in fact, be odd to describe a car dealership as 'offering' consumers the car's components in addition to the car itself. Even if it is linguistically permissible to say that the car dealership 'offers' engines when it offers cars, that shows, at most, that the term 'offer,' when applied to a commercial transaction, is ambiguous about whether it describes only the offered finished product, or the product's discrete components as well. It does not show that no other usage is permitted. * * *

"The question, then, is whether the transmission component of cable modem service is sufficiently integrated with the finished service to make it reasonable to describe the two as a single, integrated offering. We think that they are sufficiently integrated, because '[a] consumer uses the high-speed wire always in connection with the information-processing capabilities provided by Internet access, and because the transmission is a necessary component of Internet access.' In the telecommunications context, it is at least reasonable to describe companies as not 'offering' to consumers each discrete input that is necessary to providing, and is always used in connection with, a finished service."

Justice Thomas also ruled that the FCC's interpretation was "reasonable," the *Chevron* Step Two inquiry. The challengers argued that the FCC's rule was unreasonable because it allowed communications providers to "evade" mandatory Title II (common-carrier) regulation by bundling information services with telecommunications. The Court was not persuaded that companies could easily escape regulation in this way, however. For example, a local telephone company could not escape Title II by bundling its service with voice mail, because the information transmission is not integrated with the voice mail, and hence subject to FCC regulation under the 2002 rule. "Equally, were a telephone company to add a time-of-day announcement that played every time the user picked up his telephone, the 'transparent' information transmitted in the ensuing call would be only trivially dependent on the information service the announcement provides. By contrast, the high-speed transmission used to provide cable modem service is a functionally integrated component of that service because it transmits data only in connection with the further processing of information and is necessary to provide Internet service. The Commission's construction therefore was more limited than respondents assume."

Finally, Justice Thomas ruled that the FCC's rule was not "arbitrary and capricious" in violation of APA § 706(2)(A). MCI claimed that the FCC's treatment of cable modem service was inconsistent with its treatment of DSL service and therefore was an arbitrary and capricious deviation from agency policy. When local telephone companies began to offer Internet access through DSL technology in addition to telephone service, the FCC invoked Title II to require them to make the telephone lines used to transmit DSL service available to competing ISPs on nondiscriminatory, common-carrier terms. The Court rejected that claim, on the ground that the agency had a reasonable explanation for the different treatment. The FCC's treatment of DSL providers was dictated by its earlier ruling that applied Title II to regulate any Internet providers where a telephone network was the primary or exclusive means through which information service providers can gain access to their customers.

The 2002 rule, in contrast, addressed new market conditions, with a range of competitive substitutes. The Commission concluded that "broadband services should exist in a minimal regulatory environment that promotes investment and innovation in a competitive market." This, the Commission reasoned, warranted treating cable companies unlike the facilities-based enhanced-service providers of the past. "We find nothing arbitrary about the Commission's providing a fresh analysis of the problem as applied to the cable industry, which it has never subjected to these rules," concluded Justice Thomas. "This is adequate rational justification for the Commission's conclusions."

"The questions the Commission resolved in the order under review involve a 'subject matter [that] is technical, complex, and dynamic.' The Commission is in a far better position to address these questions than we are. Nothing in the Communications Act or the Administrative Procedure Act makes unlawful the Commission's use of its expert policy judgment to resolve these difficult questions."

Dissenting **Justice Scalia** (joined by Justices Souter and Ginsburg) objected that the FCC was doing the same thing in this case that the Court rejected in *MCI,* namely, substantially deregulating an industry without proper statutory authority. He maintained that the statute was clear: DSL providers "offer * * * telecommunications for a fee directly to the public," and hence the FCC must regulate such companies under Title II.

"The Court concludes that the word 'offer' is ambiguous in the sense that it has 'alternative dictionary definitions' that might be relevant. It seems to me, however, that the analytic problem pertains not really to the meaning of 'offer,' but to the identity of what is offered. The relevant question is whether the individual components in a package being offered still possess sufficient identity to be described as separate objects of the offer, or whether they have been so changed by their combination with the other components that it is no longer reasonable to describe them in that way.

"Thus, I agree (to adapt the Court's example) that it would be odd to say that a car dealer is in the business of selling steel or carpets because the cars he sells include both steel frames and carpeting. Nor does the water company sell hydrogen, nor the pet store water (though dogs and cats are largely water at the molecular level). But what is sometimes true is not, as the Court seems to assume, *always* true. There are instances in which it is ridiculous to deny that one part of a joint offering is being offered merely because it is not offered on a 'stand-alone' basis.

"If, for example, I call up a pizzeria and ask whether they offer delivery, both common sense and common 'usage,' would prevent them from answering: 'No, we do not offer delivery—but if you order a pizza from us, we'll bake it for you and then bring it to your house.' The logical response to this would be something on the order of, 'so, you *do* offer delivery.' But our pizza-man may continue to deny the obvious and explain, paraphrasing the FCC and the Court: 'No, even though we bring the pizza to your house, we are not actually 'offering' you delivery, because the delivery that we provide to our end users is 'part and parcel' of our pizzeria-pizza-at-home service and is 'integral to its other capabilities.' Any reasonable customer would conclude at that point that his interlocutor was either crazy or following some too-clever-by-half legal advice."

From the consumer's point of view, Justice Scalia argued, the question is what other products a cable-modem service substitutes for in the marketplace. For dial-up and DSL access, the two competing products, the physical transmission pathway to the Internet is sold separately from the Internet functionality. (The pathway is a regulated telecommunications service but the enhanced Internet functionality is not.) The typical consumer will view cable-modem service in the same way, as offering both computing functionality (the pizza) *and* the physical pathway (pizza delivery).

Finally, Justice Scalia observed that the FCC might, in the future, require cable companies to offer other ISPs access to their facilities on common-carrier terms, based upon the FCC's Title I discretionary authority. "In other words, what the Commission hath given, the Commission may well take away—unless it doesn't. This is a wonderful illustration of how an experienced agency can (with some assistance from credulous courts) turn statutory constraints into bureaucratic discretions. The main source of the Commission's regulatory authority over common carriers is Title II, but the Commission has rendered that inapplicable in this instance by concluding that the definition of 'telecommunications service' is ambiguous and does not (in its current view) apply to cable-modem service. It contemplates, however, altering that (unnecessary) outcome, not by changing the law (*i.e.,* its construction of the Title II definitions), but by reserving the right to change the facts. Under its undefined and sparingly used 'ancillary' powers, the Commission might conclude that it can order cable companies to 'unbundle' the telecommunications component of cable-modem service. And presto, Title II will then apply to them, because they will finally be 'offering' telecommunications service! Of course, the Commission will still have the statutory power to forbear from regulating them under § 160 (which it has already tentatively concluded it would do). Such Möbius-strip reasoning mocks the principle that the statute constrains the agency in any meaningful way."

In a portion of his dissent not joined by Justices Souter and Ginsburg, Justice Scalia continued his *Kulturkampf* against *Mead.* As he characterized it, *Brand X* is the Court's response to his own objection in *Mead* that agency law would be "ossified" by incessant judicial review; under *Brand X,* that would not be a problem, because agencies would not be bound by precedents giving them discretion under *Chevron-Mead.* Indeed, according to Justice Scalia, *Brand X* violates Article III by allowing agencies to disregard judicial precedent.

Justice Thomas responded: "Since *Chevron* teaches that a court's opinion as to the best reading of an ambiguous statute an agency is charged with administering is not authoritative, the agency's decision to construe that statute differently from a court does not say that the court's holding was legally wrong. Instead, the agency may, consistent with the court's holding, choose a different construction, since the agency remains the authoritative interpreter (within the limits of reason) of such statutes. In all other respects, the court's prior ruling remains binding law (for example, as to agency interpretations to which *Chevron* is inapplicable). The precedent has not been 'reversed' by the agency, any more than a federal court's interpretation of a State's law can be said to have been 'reversed' by a state court that adopts a conflicting (yet authoritative) interpretation of state law."

NOTES ON BRAND X

1. *What Does It Mean to "Defer" to an Agency Interpretation?* The debate in *Brand X* raises a deeper question about what, exactly, it means for the Court to "defer" to an agency. *Chevron* suggests a spatial metaphor: the Court sets the goalposts, the statutory parameters within which the agency sets policy, subject to a "reasonableness" requirement:

Court	Agency	Court

Skidmore suggests a gravity metaphor: in figuring out how to interpret statutory language, judges weigh the views and policy reasons advanced by the agency having greater experience with the statutory area. See Peter Strauss, *"Deference" Is too Confusing—Let's Call Them "Chevron Space" and "Skidmore Weight,"* 112 Colum. L. Rev. 1143 (2012).

Brand X is a case where the majority Justices not only "defer" to the FCC's decision within the policy "space" not occupied by a congressional judgment, but also seem to "defer" to the FCC's views about how to define the parameters of the statute (i.e., what is a "telecommunications service"). Even in *Chevron* cases, shouldn't judges give *Skidmore* deference to an agency's views about whether Congress has answered the interpretive question in the statute itself? If that is the case, the diagram might look something like this:

Court, With Agency Inputs	Agency, With Court Check	Court, With Agency Inputs

Ever a critic of *Mead*, Justice Scalia would have none of this in his *Brand X* dissent. Even as he insists that agencies have great discretion within the parameters set by Congress, Justice Scalia jealously guards the Court's primacy in determining precisely what those parameters are. In *Brand X*, he accuses the FCC of pulling a "fast one" on the gullible ("credulous") majority.

2. *The Relationship Between* Chevron *Step Two and* State Farm *Arbitrariness Review.* Although it is hard for the layperson (or your casebook editors) to figure out whether the Court is right to accept the FCC's flexible understanding of "telecommunications service," Justice Thomas's opinion does an excellent job setting forth the different analytical hurdles the FCC must surmount:

> *Chevron* Step One: Did Congress decide this issue? No. Hence, the agency's interpretation falls with the agency's reasoned discretion.

> *Chevron* Step Two: Was the agency's interpretation "reasonable"? Yes. Hence, the agency's interpretation passes *Chevron*.

> *State Farm*: Was the agency's rule arbitrary or capricious? No. Hence, the rule passes APA § 706(2)(A) review as well.

So the larger doctrinal question is this: What is the difference between *Chevron* Step Two and APA § 706(2)(A), as applied in *State Farm*?

On the one hand, the two standards both assume a range of agency choices and great discretion as to which choice the agency must make. Additionally, both standards ask whether the agency's decision is supported by reasons that are cognizant of and attentive to the congressional purpose(s). On the other hand, the *State Farm* inquiry is more fact-based and procedural. It is procedural in the sense that the agency needs to respond to material questions and problems raised by commenters; it is factual in the sense that the agency's responses need a plausible basis in fact.

3. *The Role of* Stare Decisis *and Deference.* Another bone of contention between the majority and the dissent is what role judicial precedent plays in the *Chevron* inquiry. As a precedent, *Chevron* itself allows the agency to shift environmental policy within the parameters set by the statute. But the Ninth Circuit thought its decision fixed a statutory parameter that the agency traversed. What did the majority believe was wrong with that? Was the Ninth Circuit's parameter decision wrong? Or was it not a parameter-setting decision?

Consider this question: After *Brand X*, under what circumstances is an agency bound by a much earlier (pre-*Chevron*) Supreme Court decision interpreting a statute? Jot down your thoughts and then read the next case.

United States v. Home Concrete & Supply, LLC
132 S.Ct. 1836 (2012).

Ordinarily, the IRS must assess a deficiency against a taxpayer within "3 years after the return was filed." 26 U.S.C. § 6501(a). The three-year period is extended to six years, however, when a taxpayer "*omits from gross income an amount properly includible therein* which is in excess of 25 percent of the amount of gross income stated in the return." § 6501(e)(1)(A) (emphasis added). The question before the Court was whether this latter provision applies (and extends the ordinary three-year limitations period) when the taxpayer *overstates his basis* in property that he has sold, thereby *understating the gain* that he received from its sale.

The IRS had issued a regulation explicitly confirming its practice, that an overstatement of a property's basis is, functionally, the same as understating income, because the taxpayer's income is the difference between the sale price and the basis. Overruling earlier cases that had recognized a special deference regime for Treasury regulations, the Supreme Court had in *Mayo Found. v. United States,* 131 S.Ct. 704 (2011), ruled that *Chevron* is now the appropriate framework for judicial consideration of the legality of IRS regulations such as this one.

Although the statute was susceptible to the IRS's interpretation, usually a finding that requires deference under *Chevron*, the Court still rejected the agency's regulation. In *Colony, Inc. v. Commissioner,* 357 U.S. 28 (1958), the Court had held that a virtually identical provision in the 1939 Revenue Code did not apply to an overstatement of basis and, hence, left the taxpayer free from review after three years (rather than six). **Justice Breyer**'s opinion for the Court conceded that *Colony* recognized that the statute was "not unambiguous" and that the IRS interpretation was plausible, even if ultimately not persuasive to the Court in 1958.

"In our view, *Colony* determines the outcome in this case. The provision before us is a 1954 reenactment of the 1939 provision that *Colony* interpreted. The operative language is identical. It would be difficult, perhaps impossible, to give the same language here a different interpretation without effectively overruling *Colony*, a course of action that basic principles of *stare decisis* wisely counsel us not to take." The surrounding statutory text was changed in the 1954 Code, but Justice Breyer found the changes were too slight to justify a different result.

Should the new Treasury regulation have changed the result? "As the Government points out, the Court in *Colony* stated that the statutory language at issue is not 'unambiguous.' But the Court decided that case nearly 30 years before it decided *Chevron*. There is no reason to believe that the linguistic ambiguity noted by *Colony* reflects a post-*Chevron* conclusion that Congress had delegated gap-filling power to the agency. At the same time, there is every reason to believe that the Court thought that Congress had 'directly spoken to the question at hand,' and thus left '[no] gap for the agency to fill.' *Chevron*.

"For one thing, the Court said that the taxpayer had the better side of the textual argument. *Colony*. For another, its examination of legislative history led it to believe that Congress had decided the question definitively, leaving no room for the agency to reach a contrary result. It found in that history 'persuasive indications' that Congress intended overstatements of basis to fall outside the statute's scope, and it said that it was satisfied that Congress 'intended an exception * * * only in the restricted type of situation' it had already described. Further, it thought that the Commissioner's interpretation (the interpretation once again advanced here) would 'create a patent incongruity in the tax law.' And it reached this conclusion despite the fact that, in the years leading up to *Colony,* the Commissioner had consistently advocated the opposite in the circuit courts. Thus, the Court was aware it was rejecting the expert opinion of the Commissioner of Internal Revenue. And finally, after completing its analysis, *Colony* found its interpretation of the 1939 Code 'in harmony with the [now] unambiguous language' of the 1954 Code, which at a minimum suggests that the Court saw nothing in the 1954 Code as inconsistent with its conclusion."

Justice Scalia concurred in most of the Court's analysis and in its judgment, but also criticized *Brand X*, which exacerbated the indeterminacy of *Chevron*'s domain that the Court had racheted up in *Mead*.

Justice Kennedy (joined by Justices Ginsburg, Sotomayor, and Kagan) dissented. He believed the statutory changes made in the 1954 Code created some ambiguity that allowed the IRS to reach a different result, by regulation, than *Colony* had reached by judicial decision. Justice Kennedy was willing to look at the statutory text through the agency's eyes—much as the *Brand X* Court had been willing to do. But the majority, including Justice Thomas (who authored the Court's opinion in *Brand X*), were not persuaded by that.

NOTE ON ADMINISTRATIVE OVERRIDES OF SUPREME COURT STATUTORY INTERPRETATION DECISIONS

In this casebook, you have seen a number of examples of congressional overrides of Supreme Court statutory interpretation decisions. E.g., *Flood v. Kuhn* (Chapter 5, § 2), overridden by the Curt Flood Act of 1998, Pub. L. No. 105–297; *TVA v. Hill* (Chapter 6, § 3A), overridden by the Energy and Water Development Appropriations Act of 1980, Pub. L. No. 96–69, tit. 4, as well as the Endangered Species Act Amendments of 1978, Pub. L. No. 95–632, § 7; and *FDA v. Brown & Williamson* (Chapter 6, § 3B), overridden by the Family Smoking Prevention and Tobacco Control Act of 2009, Pub. L. No. 111–

31. Most scholars believe that the process whereby Congress overrides the Court periodically is both democratically legitimate and necessary for the orderly evolution of statutory policy. See Matthew Christiansen & William Eskridge Jr., *Congressional Overrides of Supreme Court Statutory Interpretation Decisions, 1967–2011*, 92 Tex. L. Rev. 1317 (2014).

Since 1998, however, congressional overrides have fallen off substantially, see Christiansen & Eskridge, *Congressional Overrides*; Richard Hasen, *End of the Dialogue? Political Polarization, the Supreme Court, and Congress*, 86 S. Cal. L. Rev. 205 (2013), and the 113th Congress (2013–14) is proving to be one of the most unproductive in American history. The falloff of congressional overrides, however, has brought to light the policy punch line of *Brand X*—namely, the new significance of *administrative overrides* of Supreme Court statutory interpretation decisions.

Brand X can be understood to vest the executive branch with formal override authority for a limited subset of cases. This is most commonly understood in the context *Brand X* presented, namely, where a court upholds one interpretation as reasonable under *Chevron* Step Two. Subsequently, the agency (often after a change in presidential administration) decides to change its interpretation. *Brand X* thus gives administrators the authority to make such changes when the rule is made pursuant to an ambiguous statute. By itself, that is a significant power. And it might be even broader. In an earlier decision, the Court had suggested that even when an agency prevails under *Chevron* Step One, there might be some room for agency updating within the statutory scheme. See *Edelman v. Lynchburg College*, 535 U.S. 106, 114 & n.8 (2002). In other words, even where the text compels one option rather than another, the agency may nonetheless retain some flexibility to reinterpret the margins of the statutorily compelled policy. As Justice Scalia's *Brand X* dissent demonstrated, the Communications Act and other regulatory statutes create a huge policy space for agencies to update statutes in ways that are the functional equivalent to policy-updating overrides by Congress.

Because many cases are resolved at *Chevron* Step Two, *Brand X* has the potential to counteract statutory ossification in a number of important areas. The treatment of the Internet as an information service in *Brand X* is perhaps the best example. In 2014, the D.C. Circuit struck down the FCC's "net neutrality" regulations, because they effectively imposed common carrier status on regulated cable companies, a status prohibited by the Communications Act. *Verizon v. FCC*, 740 F.3d 623, 628 (D.C. Cir. 2014). This case could be considered a candidate for a second administrative override— undoing the rule at issue in *Brand X*. The FCC has indicated that it will not appeal the decision, instead focusing on rewriting its rules and potentially reclassifying Internet providers. *See* Statement of Tom Wheeler, FCC Chairman, on the FCC's Open Internet Rules (Feb. 19, 2014).

As *Home Concrete* indicates, the Supreme Court reserves final authority to determine when it will be permissible for agencies to "override" the Court administratively. One might suspect that highly technical issues, such as those in the 1996 Telecommunications Act, are more likely to get a pass from the Justices than more normative issues, such as those raised by Title VII and other antidiscrimination laws. Consider, now, the special case of statutes that relate to the armed forces, national security, and foreign affairs

F. DEFERENCE IN NATIONAL SECURITY AND FOREIGN AFFAIRS

In *United States v. Curtiss-Wright Export Co.*, 299 U.S. 304 (1936), the Court opined that "congressional legislation * * * within the international field must often accord to the President a degree of discretion and freedom from statutory restriction which would not be admissible were domestic affairs alone involved." The source of this discretion in statutory enforcement was Article II, namely, the inherent powers of the President to represent the nation in foreign matters and to protect America's security interests.

Curtiss-Wright deference is theoretically distinguishable from *Chevron* deference. Because it rests upon the President's Article II powers, rather than Congress's Article I authority, *Curtiss-Wright* deference does not necessarily depend upon a statutory delegation of lawmaking responsibilities, although the power of its presumption might be augmented by such delegation. Moreover, the *Curtiss-Wright* rule is a more deferential standard than *Chevron*: the executive department interpretation prevails not only in cases of statutory ambiguity, but also in cases where Congress has not clearly trumped the agency or presidential construction.

For example, the Court in *Department of Navy v. Egan*, 484 U.S. 518 (1988), ruled against judicial review of presidential revocation of security clearances. Given the President's broad powers to protect national security and conduct foreign policy, the Court reasoned that, "unless Congress specifically has provided otherwise, courts traditionally [should be] * * * reluctant to intrude upon the authority of the Executive in military and national security affairs." *Egan* is a strong post-*Chevron* statement of *Curtiss-Wright* deference, but is a rare instance where the Court actually discusses such deference. See Eskridge & Baer, *Deference Continuum*, 96 Geo. L.J. at 1100–02 (reporting that the Court invoked *Curtiss-Wright* deference in fewer than 10% of its foreign affairs and national security docket). For a recent debate over this doctrine, consider the following case.

Hamdan v. Rumsfeld
548 U.S. 557 (2006).

The Supreme Court ruled that presidential military commissions dispensing summary justice could not legally try Salim Ahmed Hamdan, a Yemeni national apprehended by American allies in Afghanistan and turned over to American authorities; since 2002, he had been detained at the American naval base in Guantanamo. The Government claimed that Hamdan was the chauffeur of terrorist Osama bin Laden and had engaged in various activities supporting al Qaeda. In 2003, President George W. Bush deemed Hamdan triable by a military commission as defined in the Military Order of November 13, 2001. In 2004, the United States charged him with "conspiracy to commit crimes triable by military commission" and ruled that the commissions would not follow the procedures provided for court martials in the Uniform Code of Military Justice (UCMJ) or for prisoners of war stipulated in the Geneva Conventions.

In a petition for habeas corpus, Hamdan challenged the legality of such a trial. Reversing the D.C. Circuit, the Supreme Court, in an opinion by Justice Stevens, agreed with Hamdan. Justice Kennedy concurred in most of the Stevens opinion and wrote a lengthy separate statement. Three Justices (Scalia, Thomas, Alito) dissented; Chief Justice Roberts did not participate (as he had joined the lower court opinion the Court was reviewing, and reversing).

Justice Stevens's opinion provided the following background which was not disputed among the Justices: "The common law governing military commissions may be gleaned from past practice and what sparse legal precedent exists. Commissions historically have been used in three situations. First, they have substituted for civilian courts at times and in places where martial law has been declared. Their use in these circumstances has raised constitutional questions, see *Duncan v. Kahanamoku*, 327 U.S. 304 (1946); [*Ex parte*] *Milligan*, 4 Wall. 2, 121–122 [1866], but is well recognized. Second, commissions have been established to try civilians 'as part of a temporary military government over occupied enemy territory or territory regained from an enemy where civilian government cannot and does not function.' *Duncan*, 327 U. S., at 314 see *Milligan*, 4 Wall., at 141–142 (Chase, C.J., concurring in judgment) (distinguishing '*martial law proper*' from '*military government*' in occupied territory). Illustrative of this second kind of commission is the one that was established, with jurisdiction to apply the German Criminal Code, in occupied Germany following the end of World War II. See *Madsen v. Kinsella*, 343 U.S. 341, 356 (1952).

"The third type of commission, convened as an 'incident to the conduct of war' when there is a need 'to seize and subject to disciplinary measures those enemies who in their attempt to thwart or impede our military effort have violated the law of war,' [*Ex parte Quirin*, 317 U.S. 1, 28–29 (1942)], has been described as 'utterly different' from the other two. Not only is its jurisdiction limited to offenses cognizable during time of war, but its role is primarily a factfinding one—to determine, typically on the battlefield itself, whether the defendant has violated the law of war. The last time the U.S. Armed Forces used the law-of-war military commission was during World War II. In *Quirin*, this Court sanctioned President Roosevelt's use of such a tribunal to try Nazi saboteurs captured on American soil during the War. And in *Yamashita*, we held that a military commission had jurisdiction to try a Japanese commander for failing to prevent troops under his command from committing atrocities in the Philippines. 327 U.S. 1 [1946]."

The Administration's military commissions were of the third type. The main issue was whether the President had the authority to deploy these military commissions to impose sanctions (including death) on suspected enemy combatants. The Justices disagreed over the precise level of deference the Court ought to accord the President's interpretation of his own statutory and constitutional authority to command the nation's armed forces. **Justice Stevens** emphasized the primacy of Congress in setting rules for military engagement. "Exigency alone, of course, will not justify the establishment and use of penal tribunals not contemplated by Article I, § 8 and Article III, § 1 of the Constitution unless some other part of that document authorizes a response to the felt need. See *Ex parte Milligan* ('Certainly no part of the judicial power of the country was conferred on [military commissions]'). And that authority, if it exists, can derive only from the powers granted jointly to the President and Congress in time of war. *Yamashita*.

"The Constitution makes the President the 'Commander in Chief of the Armed Forces, Art. II, § 2, cl. 1, but vests in Congress the powers to 'declare War . . . and make

Rules concerning Captures on Land and Water,' Art. I, § 8, cl. 11, to 'raise and support Armies,' id., cl. 12, to 'define and punish . . . Offences against the Law of Nations,' id., cl. 10, and 'To make Rules for the Government and Regulation of the land and naval Forces,' id., cl. 14.

"The interplay between these powers was described by Chief Justice Chase in the seminal case of *Ex parte Milligan*:

> 'The power to make the necessary laws is in Congress; the power to execute in the President. Both powers imply many subordinate and auxiliary powers. Each includes all authorities essential to its due exercise. But neither can the President, in war more than in peace, intrude upon the proper authority of Congress, nor Congress upon the proper authority of the President. . . . Congress cannot direct the conduct of campaigns, nor can the President, or any commander under him, without the sanction of Congress, institute tribunals for the trial and punishment of offences, either of soldiers or civilians, unless in cases of a controlling necessity, which justifies what it compels, or at least insures acts of indemnity from the justice of the legislature.' 4 Wall., at 139–140.

Whether Chief Justice Chase was correct in suggesting that the President may constitutionally convene military commissions 'without the sanction of Congress' in cases of 'controlling necessity' is a question this Court has not answered definitively, and need not answer today."

Writing for the three dissenters, **Justice Thomas** emphasized that "the structural advantages attendant to the Executive Branch—namely, the decisiveness, 'activity, secrecy, and dispatch' that flow from the Executive's 'unity' (quoting The Federalist No. 70, p. 472 (J. Cooke ed. 1961) (A. Hamilton))—led the Founders to conclude that the 'President ha[s] primary responsibility—along with the necessary power—to protect the national security and to conduct the Nation's foreign relations.' Consistent with this conclusion, the Constitution vests in the President '[t]he executive Power,' Art. II, § 1, provides that he 'shall be Commander in Chief' of the Armed Forces, § 2, and places in him the power to recognize foreign governments[.] This Court has observed that these provisions confer upon the President broad constitutional authority to protect the Nation's security in the manner he deems fit. See, e.g., *Prize Cases*, 2 Black 635, 668 (1863) ('If a war be made by invasion of a foreign nation, the President is not only authorized but bound to resist force by force . . . without waiting for any special legislative authority').

"Congress, to be sure, has a substantial and essential role in both foreign affairs and national security. But 'Congress cannot anticipate and legislate with regard to every possible action the President may find it necessary to take or every possible situation in which he might act,' and '[s]uch failure of Congress . . . does not, "especially . . . in the areas of foreign policy and national security," imply "congressional disapproval" of action taken by the Executive.' *Dames & Moore v. Regan*, 453 U.S. 654, 678 (1981). Rather, in these domains, the fact that Congress has provided the President with broad authorities does not imply—and the Judicial Branch should not infer—that Congress intended to deprive him of particular powers not specifically enumerated. See *Dames & Moore* ('[T]he enactment of legislation closely related to the question of the President's authority in a particular case which evinces legislative intent to accord the President broad discretion may be considered to invite measures on independent presidential responsibility.').'" Following a *Curtiss-Wright* approach strongly deferential to presidential authority, Justice Thomas argued that application of that framework in military matters required *expansive* interpretation of congressional authorizations to meet the unpredictable demands of war.

On the merits of the statutory arguments, the Court ruled that UCMJ Article 21, adopted in 1950, did *not* authorize the Bush Administration military commissions. **Justice Stevens** offered three reasons: (1) Article 21 authorizes military commissions to try "offenders or offenses" that "by statute or by the law of war may be tried by" such commissions. The government could point to no statute, and conspiracy to commit war crimes is not a recognized violation of the law of war. In contrast, the sabotage in *Quirin* was an accepted violation of the law of war. This reason commanded only a plurality of the eight-Justice Court (Stevens, Souter, Ginsburg, Breyer), but the other two commanded a majority. (2) The military commissions did not comport with UCMJ Article 36(b), which requires uniformity in procedural rules under the UCMJ unless "impracticable." The Court ruled that Article 36(b) creates a baseline whereby the court-martial procedures presumptively apply to military commissions; the Bush Administration's commission's relaxed evidentiary rules and its failure to give the defendant access to all the evidence against him were important departures from the court-martial rules that the Administration could not justify. (3) Until Hamdan is judged to be an enemy combatant, the 1949 Geneva Conventions require that he be subject to punishment only by a "regularly constituted court affording all the judicial guarantees which are recognized as indispensable by civilized peoples."

Justice Kennedy's concurring opinion emphasized the following procedural differences between the Bush Administration military commissions and court-martials and reasoned from those differences that the military commissions were not justified: (a) quasi-independent military judges preside over court-martials, while any military lawyer can preside over a military commission; (b) the Appointing Authority controls the number of judges and various procedural appeals for military commissions, but not for court-martials; (c) military commissions follow relaxed evidentiary rules and consider evidence without the accused even being present.

Writing for the three dissenters, **Justice Thomas** sharply disagreed. He argued that (a) UCMJ Article 21 constituted an explicit congressional authorization for the military commission in Hamdan's case, and Article 36 constituted virtually a blank check for the President to devise special procedures for those tribunals; (b) the Iraq War Authorization for Use of Military Force was a separate congressional authorization; and (c) the Geneva Conventions create no judicially enforceable rights for unlawful combatants in Hamdan's position. Speaking for the same three dissenters, **Justice Alito** argued that the military commissions satisfied the Geneva Conventions and the requirements of UCMJ Articles 21 and 36.

In his extensive analysis, Justice Thomas approached the same statutory materials that the Court analyzed, but did so with a more expansive eye. Specifically, he deferred to the President's judgment about what was needed to fight terrorism effectively and his interpretation of the relevant statutes and treaties, considered past practice relevant and read it expansively, and stressed the process that the President's Military Order and the DTA afforded accused terrorists like Hamdan.

As to the last point, consider the Government's Brief, page 4: "Petitioner is entitled to appointed military legal counsel, 32 C.F.R. 9.4(c)(2), and may retain a civilian attorney (which he has done), 32 C.F.R. 9.4(c)(2)(iii)(B). Petitioner is entitled to the presumption of innocence, 32 C.F.R. 9.5(b), proof beyond a reasonable doubt, 32 C.F.R. 9.5(c), and the right to remain silent, 32 C.F.R. 9.5(f). He may confront witnesses against him, 32 C.F.R. 9.5(i), and may subpoena his own witnesses, if reasonably available, 32 C.F.R. 9.5(h). Petitioner may personally be present at every stage of the trial unless he engages in disruptive conduct or the prosecution introduces classified or otherwise protected information for which no adequate substitute is available and whose admission will not deprive him of a full and fair trial, 32 C.F.R. 9.5(k); Military Commission Order No. 1 (Dep't of Defense Aug. 31, 2005) § 6(B)(3) and (D)(5)(b). If petitioner is found guilty, the judgment will be reviewed by a review panel, the Secretary of Defense, and the President, if he does not designate the Secretary as the final decisionmaker. 32 C.F.R. 9.6(h). The final judgment is subject to review in the Court of Appeals for the District of Columbia Circuit and ultimately in this Court. See DTA § 1005(e)(3), 119 Stat. 2743; 28 U.S.C. 1254(1)."

NOTE ON CURTISS-WRIGHT *DEFERENCE*

In evaluating the cogency of Justice Thomas's dissenting opinion, consider the President's "inherent powers" under Article II. (This was the conceptual basis for *Curtiss-Wright* itself.) If there were no statute, the President as Commander-in-Chief would have inherent authority to deal with prisoners of war and enemy combatants. This would include the authority to establish tribunals for the summary trial of enemy agents, prisoners, etc. The UCMJ (1950) channels and perhaps cabins that authority, but the issue in *Hamdan* was what limits the UCMJ actually placed on the President. Article II might require, as *Curtiss-Wright* suggests, that the UCMJ be read to displace the President's inherent authority only when it has clearly done so. See *Egan*. Is there any flaw in this argument?

The issues of military justice and the conduct of the war on terror would seem even more centrally implicated by *Curtiss-Wright* than those adjudicated in *Egan*, yet the *Hamdan* Court applied neither *Curtiss-Wright* nor *Chevron* deference. Is there a sufficient distinction between the two cases? Why were the majority Justices so undeferential in *Hamdan*? For an illuminating analysis, see Oona Hathaway, Hamdan v. Rumsfeld: *Domestic Enforcement of International Law*, in *International Law Stories* 229–60 (John Noyes et al. eds., 2007).

4. QUO VADIS THE *"CHEVRON* REVOLUTION"?

Commentators and judges agree there has been a "*Chevron* Revolution" of some sort, but its contours remain unclear, especially after *Mead*. *Chevron* had an immediate impact in the D.C. Circuit; most judges and commentators believe that the *Chevron* framework has transformed federal judicial treatment of agency interpretations among district and circuit courts. *Chevron* is now the most cited Supreme Court decision in our history, because lower courts are citing *Chevron* so extensively.[14] There is also anecdotal evidence that agencies themselves have internalized the new *Chevron* regime as freeing them up to make more decisions on

---

[14] E.g., Orin Kerr, *Shedding Light on* Chevron: *An Empirical Study of the* Chevron *Doctrine in the U.S. Courts of Appeals*, 15 Yale J. on Reg. 1 (1998). Moreover, lower court judges have not only applied *Skidmore* deference in many non-*Chevron* cases, but have applied it with serious attention to agency inputs. See Kristin Hickman & Mathew Krueger, *In Search of the Modern* Skidmore *Standard*, 107 Colum. L. Rev. 1235 (2007).

policy or political lines rather than legal ones. E.g., E. Donald Elliot, *Chevron Matters: How the* Chevron *Doctrine Redefined the Roles of Congress, Courts, and Agencies in Environmental Law*, 16 Vill. Envtl. L.J. 1, 11–12 (2005).

Ironically, the effect of *Chevron* is most equivocal at the Supreme Court itself. The Court was highly deferential to agency rules and interpretations before *Chevron* and has continued to be deferential after *Chevron*. It remains unclear whether *Chevron* has had *any* influence at the Supreme Court level—beyond creating the increasingly complicated legisprudence that we have presented in this chapter. Consider matters concretely. Is there any reason to believe that the Court would have decided the leading cases in this chapter any differently in the pre-*Chevron* era? Except for Justice Breyer's opinion in *Geier*, the opinions for the Court were *reasoned* differently under the *Chevron* criteria, but the fundamental role of agency views, the key precepts, and the results in the cases are not affected at all in our view.

Also, the Supreme Court follows a more elaborate *deference continuum* than is captured by the simple *Chevron-Skidmore* dichotomy. The Eskridge and Baer study gives us a complete lay of the land in cases between *Chevron* and *Hamdan* where there was an agency interpretation.

Supreme Court Deference Regimes, 1984–2006, *Chevron* **to** *Hamdan*

Deference Regime (% Cases)	Deference Accorded	Basis for Deference	Subject Areas
Curtiss-Wright (0.9%)	Super-strong deference in national security cases	Article II + Congressional Delegation	Foreign Affairs; Immigration; National Security
Seminole Rock/Auer (1.1%)	Strong deference for agency interpretations of own regulations	Congressional Delegation + Agency Expertise	Entitlements; Tax; Telecommunications
Chevron (8.3%)	Defer to reasonable interpretations unless Congress has directly addressed the issue	Congressional Delegation	Energy; Envir'l; Entitlements; Immigration; Labor; Securities; Transportation; Taxation (after 2011)
Diaz/Beth Israel (4.8%)	Defer to reasonable interpretations if consistent with statute	Congressional Purposes	Health; Immigration; Labor; Taxation (until 2011)
Skidmore (6.7%)	Consider agency views for persuasive value (e.g., policy goals and reliance interests)	Agency Expertise and Experience	Civil Rights; Education; Energy; Environmental; Transportation

Skidmore-Lite (17.8%)	Consider agency-generated factual materials + background rules	Agency Expertise and Experience	Antitrust; Bankruptcy; Civil Rights; Energy; Intellectual Property; Indian Law; Pensions
No Deference (53.6%)	Court follows ordinary, ad hoc judicial reasoning	No basis for deference	All areas of Supreme Court practice are dominated by this category
Anti-Deference (6.8%)	Presumption *against* agency interpretation	Constitutional Values	Criminal Law; Immigration

Source: William Eskridge Jr. & Lauren Baer, *The Continuum of Deference: Supreme Court Treatment of Agency Statutory Interpretations from* Chevron *to* Hamdan, 96 Geo. L.J. 1083, 1100 (2008) (Table 1).

Assume that this chart accurately reflects the Court's practice since *Chevron*. Eskridge and Baer also report that when the Court applies the *Chevron* framework the agency wins 76.2% of the time, a very high agreement rate. But the agency win rate is also very high when the Court invokes other deference regimes: 80.6% when the Court follows a *Skidmore*-Lite approach; 73.5% when the Court invokes *Skidmore*; 73.5% when it invokes *Beth Israel*; 90.9% when it invokes *Seminole Rock*; and 100.0% when it invokes *Curtiss-Wright* deference. Eskridge & Baer, *Continuum of Deference*, 96 Geo. L.J. at 1100 (Table 1). All these figures are inflated by the fact that the Court probably cites these deference regimes primarily when it is inclined to decide in favor of the agency. Recall Eskridge and Baer's finding that the Court follows *Chevron* in only one-third of the cases where it is potentially applicable (and in some cases where it is not, under *Mead*). The same is even truer of the other regimes: they are rarely applied even when theoretically applicable.

What a mess.

Surely this elaborate continuum can be simplified, and if simplified maybe the Justices would follow it more faithfully. But how should the continuum be simplified? Different Justices and commentators have come up with a dizzying array of proposed simplifications—which cut in all sorts of different directions. In concluding this chapter, we offer you several clusters of theories, and you are responsible for developing the approach that makes the best legal sense. You might want to apply these theories to some of the harder cases presented in this and the previous chapters, such as *Weber*, where the Court followed the EEOC (Chapter 1, § 3); *Brown & Williamson*, where the Court rejected an FDA rule (Chapter 6, § 3B); *Sweet Home*, where the Court followed a Department of Interior rule (end of Chapter 7); the FISA debate between President George W. Bush and Congress (the problem opening this chapter); and *Gonzales v. Oregon*, where the Court rejected a Department of Justice Directive (the case opening § 2 of this chapter).

A. SHARPEN *CHEVRON* AND *SKIDMORE* WITHIN THE *MEAD* FRAMEWORK

The dominant impulse among judges and law professors has been to work within the assumptions of *Mead* and to formulate and consistently apply *Chevron* and *Skidmore* accordingly. Most of these commentators would be happy to absorb *Beth Israel* and *Seminole Rock* into *Chevron*, and to jettison or deemphasize *Curtiss-Wright* deference. See Kristin Hickman, *The Need for* Mead: *Rejecting Tax Exceptionalism in Judicial Deference*, 90 Minn. L. Rev. 1537 (2006), proposing that the Supreme Court jettison the special deference regime the Court long applied to IRS revenue rulings and just apply *Chevron*, a proposal the Court unanimously adopted in *Mayo Foundation v. United States*, 131 S.Ct. 704 (2011).

Many commentators would reject *Mead*'s notion that Congress can delegate lawmaking authority *implicitly*. This notion has created confusion among lower courts. E.g., Lisa Schultz Bressman, *How* Mead *Has Muddled Judicial Review of Agency Action*, 58 Vand. L. Rev. 1443 (2005). Different authors, of course, have come up with somewhat different prescriptions. More important, different authors have emphasized different normative underpinnings of *Mead*.

1. ***Legislative Supremacy.*** Probably the most important normative assumption of *Mead* is legislative supremacy: both judges and administrators are faithful agents of congressional directives embodied in statutes. Congress's intent as to who decides is just as important as its intent as to what the decision ought to be.[15]

Thomas Merrill and Kristin Hickman anticipated *Mead*'s holding that an agency interpretation is entitled to *Chevron* deference *only* when it is pursuant to congressional delegation of lawmaking authority to the agency. See Merrill & Hickman, Chevron's *Domain*, 89 Geo. L.J. 833 (2001). They lay out the doctrinal consequences for this foundation, including the notion that courts should *not* *Chevron*-defer to an agency's interpretation of its own jurisdiction or authority, a precept the Court recently rejected in *City of Arlington v. FCC*. Thus, for them, *Chevron* Step Zero is critical, and the Oregon Aid-in-Dying Case exemplifies the kind of inquiry the Court should be making.

Thomas Merrill and Kathryn Tongue Watts complicate the implications of *Mead* in *Agency Rules with the Force of Law: The Original Convention*, 116 Harv. L. Rev. 467 (2002). They demonstrate that the longstanding legislative tradition for delegating "lawmaking" authority required an expression of direct sanctions for violation of an agency rule or order. Many of the cases where the Court has applied *Chevron* deference—including *Chevron* itself—did not meet this conventional test. Because they require a court order to be enforceable, NLRB orders are not properly considered "lawmaking" delegations for this reason. The authors discuss various ways their discoveries could push the *Chevron* line of cases but come to no firm conclusions.

---

[15] For an excellent constitutional analysis of Congress's power to delegate lawmaking authority to agencies, see Thomas Merrill, *Rethinking Article I, Section 1: From Nondelegation to Exclusive Delegation*, 104 Colum. L. Rev. 2097 (2004).

2. *Democratic Legitimacy.* In our democracy, the legitimacy of legislation (the moral reason we accept and obey its commands) rests in part on popular participation or, at least, the accountability of elected representatives to We the People for the laws they adopt. In the modern administrative state, most of the actual rules are developed by unelected agencies, and so there is a potential democracy deficit.

Henry Richardson, *Democratic Autonomy: Public Reasoning About the Ends of Policy* (2003), argues that agencies can contribute to rather than derogate from democratic decisionmaking when they engage in notice-and-comment rulemaking which replicates the legislative process (proposal, popular feedback, deliberated decision, with opportunity for people to object). Richardson's focus, therefore, would not be the fact of legislative *delegation,* but instead the manner in which delegated *lawmaking* is accomplished. Thus, the agency decisions in *Mead, Oregon,* and *Hamdan* (administrative or presidential fiat) do not deserve as much deference as the decision in *Chevron* itself (notice-and-comment rulemaking) does.

Complementing Richardson's analysis, Lisa Schultz Bressman, *Beyond Accountability: Arbitrariness and Legitimacy in the Administrative State*, 78 N.Y.U. L. Rev. 461 (2003), argues that we ought to be even more concerned about administrative arbitrariness than political accountability. Bressman's prescription is that notice-and-comment rulemaking is most likely to produce decisions that reflect reasoned judgment and not arbitrary fiat.[16]

In a recent study, Abbe Gluck & Lisa Schultz Bressman, *Statutory Interpretation from the Inside—An Empirical Study of Congressional Drafting, Delegation, and the Canons: Part I,* 65 Stan. L. Rev. 901 (2013), engaged a huge sample of congressional drafting and committee staff to determine how much they knew about the Supreme Court's statutory interpretation rules, practices, and doctrine. Gluck and Bressman found that an overwhelming majority of congressional drafters were aware of and understood *Chevron,* more than any other doctrine apart from the plain meaning rule. *Id.* at 995–96. Although the drafters did not know all the ins and outs of the Court's *Chevron* legisprudence, they did draft statutes with *Chevron* in mind and believed that congressional enacting coalitions routinely expected judicial deference to agency interpretations when the drafters did not nail down points of law through specific statutory text. *Id.* at 996; see *id.* at 997–1006 (detailed discussion of other fascinating findings along these lines). The Gluck and Bressman study is the best, and perhaps the only rigorous, evidence that *Chrevron* is a doctrine that implements presumed legislative preferences.

3. *Institutional Competence.* Few scholars have focused on *Skidmore,* which is not only the default regime under the *Chevron* jurisprudence, but is a default regime that both dominates *Chevron* and generates high agency win rates. In recent empirical articles, one focusing on the Supreme Court and the other on lower courts, scholars have sought to clarify *Skidmore* with a focus on *institutional*

---

[16] Accord, William Eskridge Jr. & John Ferejohn, *A Republic of Statutes: Our New American Constitution* ch. 6 (2010); Mark Seidenfeld, *A Syncopated* Chevron: *Emphasizing Reasoned Decisionmaking in Reviewing Agency Interpretations of Statutes,* 73 Tex. L. Rev. 83 (1994).

competence. Competence is the old New Deal theme: agencies are better qualified than judges to make certain kinds of policies. William Eskridge and Lauren Baer found that the Justices' inability to handle technical issues in the fields of intellectual property, telecommunications, taxation, pensions, and bankruptcy generated high levels of deference to agency interpretations, whatever the deference regime the Court invoked. In contrast, more normative arenas such as criminal, Indian affairs, civil rights, and labor law found the Justices agreeing less often, again regardless of the deference regime invoked or applicable. Eskridge & Baer, *Continuum of Deference*, 96 Geo. L.J. at 1144 (Table 16). An implication of their empirical study, which Eskridge and Baer endorse normatively, is that *Skidmore* factors like institutional competence show up in *Chevron* cases as well.

Focusing on *Skidmore* as the critical regime even before *Mead*, Eskridge and Baer urge the Court to focus on three factors: (1) the rule of law, including agency consistency and public reliance on agency interpretations; (2) comparative institutional competence, with technical issues, matters of regulatory tradeoffs, and uncertainty better handled by agencies and bigger normative issues as those where courts should be more scrutinizing; and (3) legitimacy, with open processes and public participation being pluses for the agency. *Id.* at 1180–83. The Gluck and Bressman study found that congressional drafters were alert to these kind of functional criteria as well. See Gluck & Bressman, *Statutory Interpretation from the Inside: Part I,* 65 Stan. L. Rev. at 998–1004 (also announcing that *Mead* best reflected the assumptions in the congressional drafting process).

B. REJECT *MEAD* IN FAVOR OF GREATER DEFERENCE TO AGENCY INTERPRETATIONS

A number of other commentators reject or would go beyond *Mead* and would read *Chevron* much more expansively than the Supreme Court has thus far been willing to do. These scholars are broadly critical of judicial "interference" in the ongoing administration of statutory schemes and urge that agency monitoring is better left to the political than the judicial process. Most of these scholars favor an expanded reading of *Chevron*, a vigorous revival of *Curtiss-Wright*, and/or a diminished role for *Skidmore* (which they tend to reject as exemplifying what is wrong with the Court's deference jurisprudence). As before, there are several theoretical ways to reach this conclusion.

1. *Agencies Rather Than Courts as the Preferred Congressional Agents.* A respected administrative law scholar before his appointment as a judge, Justice Scalia finds no inconsistency between congressional supremacy and a broad reading of *Chevron* that defers to any interpretation adopted by the head of an agency that is not a litigating position. His argument is that any ambiguity or gap that Congress leaves in a statute is an implicit delegation of lawmaking authority to the agency Congress has charged with enforcing the statute. *Mead,* 533 U.S. at 256–57 (Scalia, J., dissenting); Antonin Scalia, *Judicial Deference to Administrative Interpretations of Law,* 1989 Duke L.J. 511, 516.

John Duffy responds that such a broad reading of *Chevron* is inconsistent with the text, structure, and original meaning of the Administrative Procedure Act, especially 5 U.S.C. §§ 558(b) (limits on agency sanctions) and 706(2) (judicial review of agency action), which Duffy believes codify a *Marbury* model of judicial review for agency decisions (under which it is the responsibility of the judiciary to say what the law is). Duffy, *Administrative Common Law in Judicial Review*, 77 Tex. L. Rev. 113, 193–99 (1998). Scalia does not read the APA so restrictively, and scholars are now thinking about deeper responses he might have to Duffy's critique.

Jack Goldsmith and John Manning argue for a "completion power" in Article II, namely "the President's authority to prescribe incidental details needed to carry into execution a legislative scheme, even in the absence of any congressional authorization to complete that scheme." Goldsmith & Manning, *The President's Completion Power*, 115 Yale L.J. 2280 (2006). The authors rely on historical practice, where the President has exercised such a "completion power" with the acquiescence of both Congress and the Court. E.g., *Dames & Moore v. Regan*, 453 U.S. 654 (1981); Proposed Executive Order Entitled "Federal Regulation," 5 Op. O.L.C. 59 (1981) (defending presidential cost-benefit review of proposed agency rules).

Goldsmith and Manning justify a broad reading of *Chevron* in light of the completion power: "[W]hile Congress can legitimately give either courts or agencies ultimate authority to resolve statutory ambiguities or fill up statutory interstices, it is more consistent with the background premises of our constitutional democracy to embrace a default rule that Congress prefers to leave such completion power in the hands of the more accountable executive." *Completion Power*, 115 Yale L.J. at 2299. This constitutional default rule would inform one's reading of the APA as well as *Chevron* and would provide Scalia with an argument for his notion that statutory ambiguities represent an implicit delegation of lawmaking authority to agencies, not courts. Interestingly, Goldsmith and Manning do not maintain that *Mead* was wrongly decided, but do argue for a narrow reading of *Mead* that leaves plenty of room for a broad reading of *Chevron*.

2.   *Democratic Legitimacy.* Recall that *Chevron* emphasized the relatively greater accountability of agencies (responsible to the nationally elected President) compared with federal courts (responsible to the unelected Supreme Court). Elena Kagan, *Presidential Administration*, 114 Harv. L. Rev. 2245 (2001), takes this normative point one step further to support something like the Scalia position. When the President has taken a role in an agency interpretation *or* an interpretation has been adopted by the President's appointee (the agency head), see David Barron & Elena Kagan, Chevron's *Nondelegation Doctrine*, 2001 Sup. Ct. Rev. 201, 234–57 (amending the suggestions of the earlier article), then federal judges ought to *Chevron*-defer. According to Kagan, the main advantage of this approach would be *national transparency*. The buck stops with the President, and any policy option he or she chooses will be subject to national examination and critique—much more legitimate checks than those offered by judicial review. Kagan, *Presidential Administration,* 114 Harv. L. Rev. at 2332–33.

How would Kagan's proposal work as a practical matter? Pointing to numerous examples, Lisa Schultz Bressman questions whether presidential interventions are either transparent or public-regarding. Bressman, *Beyond Accountability,* 78

N.Y.U. L. Rev. at 503–13. A lot of presidential interventions are either behind-the-scenes or below the media radar, but can easily be trumpeted by the Solicitor General if needed to give an agency interpretation a boost. Moreover, many presidential interventions represent the worst sort of rent-seeking politics. It is not clear that the balance of rent-seeking and public-regarding presidential interventions weighs in favor of the latter.[17]

A more modest proposal is that made in Kevin Stack, *The Statutory President*, 90 Iowa L. Rev. 539 (2005). Stack argues that *Chevron* deference ought to apply to congressionally authorized lawmaking by the President. Other scholars would go much further in situations where the President is acting to protect national security or engage in matters touching foreign affairs. For example, Curtis Bradley & Jack Goldsmith, *Congressional Authorization and the War on Terrorism*, 118 Harv. L. Rev. 2047, 2100–06 (2005), argue that congressional authorizations for the President's use of force against foreign enemies should be interpreted to include previous presidential practices *and* should be interpreted not to interfere with the President's inherent powers to respond to international emergencies and threats.

　　3.　*Comparative Institutional Competence.* Neil Komesar argues in *Imperfect Alternatives: Choosing Institutions in Law, Economics, and Public Policy* (1997), that lawmakers and commentators must consider the institutional costs as well as the benefits of having judges involved in public policy decisions. His book points out that the structural limitations of the judiciary create significant costs for statutory as well as constitutional judicial review. Although he does not address *Chevron*, Komesar's analytical framework is playing an important role in the *Chevron* debate, with some of the most judge-critical voices explicitly invoking his framework. Under a Komesarian analysis, the theorist must ask which institution is the most institutionally capable of creating optimal default interpretations. Because agencies are more both more knowledgeable about statutory policy (*Skidmore*) and more democratically legitimate policymakers (*Chevron*), most commentators applying institutional cost-benefit analysis have concluded that agency interpretations should be the baseline, with courts in a monitoring role, whether or not Congress has delegated lawmaking authority.[18] Unsurprisingly, scholars are divided as to how aggressively courts ought to engage in "monitoring."

　　Less ambitious institutional criticisms have been made by other commentators. They maintain that judicial review of agency rulemaking has been counterproductive because judges are not sufficiently knowledgeable, because judicial interventions tend to be legalistic and thereby derogate from the agency's purposive activities, and because even well-considered judicial interventions may have counterproductive side effects. These problems are illustrated by Jerry

---

　　17　See also Jide Nzelibe, *The Fable of the Nationalist President and the Parochial Congress*, 53 UCLA L. Rev. 1217 (2006), arguing that the President does not necessarily represent a national majoritarian constituency any better than Congress does.

　　18　Accord, Adrian Vermeule, *Judging Under Uncertainty* (2006) (following Komesar's comparative institutional analysis to argue for a marginal role for judges and much greater role for agencies in statutory interpretation); William Eskridge Jr., *Expanding* Chevron's *Domain: A Comparative Institutional Analysis of the Relative Competence of Courts and Agencies to Interpret Statutes*, 2013 Wis. L. Rev. 411 (applying Komesar's analysis to argue for an expanded *Chevron*, along Scalia-Kagan lines); David Spence & Frank Cross, *A Public Choice Case for the Administrative State*, 89 Geo. L.J. 97 (2000).

Mashaw & David Harfst, *The Struggle for Auto Safety* (1990). Mashaw, in general, has urged courts to be more deferential in the sense that judges need to leave agencies alone so that they can do the jobs Congress has given them. For this reason, he supports a broad reading of *Chevron*. See Jerry Mashaw, *Prodelegation: Why Administrators Should Make Political Decisions*, 1 J.L. Econ. & Org. 81, 91–99 (1985). Mashaw would probably be even more deferential in practice than Scalia has been, because he would allow agencies a wide berth in construing statutory language that Scalia would often consider clear and therefore confining.

C. SYNTHESIZE *CHEVRON* AND *SKIDMORE*

Justice Breyer has long been a critic of *Chevron* deference as inconsistent with the judicial role.[19] Yet he has not urged the overruling of *Chevron* or the abandonment of its two-step framework. Instead, Breyer seems to apply *Chevron* as a special case of general *Skidmore* (Article III) deference, and the *Mead* notion of congressionally delegated lawmaking authority as a big "plus" in the *Skidmore* scale.

For example, in *Barnhart v. Walton*, 535 U.S. 212 (2002), decided soon after *Mead*, Justice Breyer wrote for the Court in affirming a recent rule adopted by the Social Security Administration. His opinion cheerfully announced that *Chevron* was applicable, because Congress had delegated lawmaking authority to the agency. But the opinion continued the threshold analysis with the further observations that *Chevron*'s applicability was confirmed by the agency's expertise and its longstanding adherence to that interpretation for years before the rule was adopted—classic *Skidmore* considerations. *Id.* at 219–22.

The upshot of Breyer's point of view would be that *Skidmore* is the rule, with pluses awarded for congressional delegation (as in *Chevron*), agency expertise (as in *Chevron*) or foreign affairs subject matter (as in *Curtiss-Wright*), and minuses subtracted for agency wishy-washiness, secret processes, or lack of obvious expertise (all exemplified in *Gonzales v. Oregon*). By the way, Breyer is the Justice on the current Court who is most willing to go along with agency interpretations, including those at odds with his overall political philosophy, according to the Eskridge and Baer study.

Although Breyer's approach sounds kind of radical after almost a quarter century of *Chevron*, it is not so dissimilar from what the Supreme Court has actually been doing. According to Eskridge & Baer, *Continuum of Deference*, 96 Geo. L.J. at 1142–51, agency success rates have no correlation with announced deference regimes and strong correlation with perceived agency expertise and consistency of the agency's position over time (the same *Skidmore* factors Breyer emphasized in *Barnhart*). Moreover, Congress seems to be operating under the kinds of assumptions reflected in *Barnhart*, a point documented by Gluck & Bressman, *Statutory Interpretation from the Inside: Part I*, 65 Stan. L. Rev. at 1000–03.

---

[19] E.g., Stephen Breyer, *Judicial Review of Questions of Law and Policy*, 38 Admin. L. Rev. 363 (1986); accord. Cynthia Farina, *Statutory Interpretation and the Balance of Power in the Administrative State*, 89 Colum. L. Rev. 452 (1989).

APPENDIX A

THE CONSTITUTION OF THE UNITED STATES

. . .

We the People of the United States, in Order to form a more perfect Union, establish Justice, insure domestic Tranquility, provide for the common defence, promote the general Welfare, and secure the Blessings of Liberty to ourselves and our Posterity, do ordain and establish this Constitution for the United States of America.

ARTICLE I

Section 1. All legislative Powers herein granted shall be vested in a Congress of the United States, which shall consist of a Senate and House of Representatives.

Section 2. [1] The House of Representatives shall be composed of Members chosen every second Year by the People of the several States, and the Electors in each State shall have the Qualifications requisite for Electors of the most numerous Branch of the State Legislature.

[2] No Person shall be a Representative who shall not have attained to the Age of twenty five Years, and been seven Years a Citizen of the United States, and who shall not, when elected, be an Inhabitant of that State in which he shall be chosen.

[3] Representatives and direct Taxes shall be apportioned among the several States which may be included within this Union, according to their respective Numbers, which shall be determined by adding to the whole Number of free Persons, including those bound to Service for a Term of Years, and excluding Indians not taxed, three fifths of all other Persons. The actual Enumeration shall be made within three Years after the first Meeting of the Congress of the United States, and within every subsequent Term of ten Years, in such Manner as they shall by Law direct. The Number of Representatives shall not exceed one for every thirty Thousand, but each State shall have at Least one Representative; and until such enumeration shall be made, the State of New Hampshire shall be entitled to chuse three, Massachusetts eight, Rhode Island and Providence Plantations one, Connecticut five, New York six, New Jersey four, Pennsylvania eight, Delaware one, Maryland six, Virginia ten, North Carolina five, South Carolina five, and Georgia three.

[4] When vacancies happen in the Representation from any State, the Executive Authority thereof shall issue Writs of Election to fill such Vacancies.

[5] The House of Representatives shall chuse their Speaker and other Officers; and shall have the sole Power of impeachment.

Section 3. [1] The Senate of the United States shall be composed of two Senators from each State, chosen by the Legislature thereof, for six Years; and each Senator shall have one Vote.

[2] Immediately after they shall be assembled in Consequence of the first Election, they shall be divided as equally as may be into three Classes. The Seats of the Senators of the first Class shall be vacated at the Expiration of the second Year, of the second Class at the Expiration of the fourth Year, and of the third Class at the Expiration of the sixth Year, so that one third may be chosen every second Year; and if Vacancies happen by Resignation, or otherwise, during the Recess of the Legislature of any State, the Executive thereof may make temporary Appointments until the next Meeting of the Legislature, which shall then fill such Vacancies.

[3] No Person shall be a Senator who shall not have attained to the Age of thirty Years, and been nine Years a Citizen of the United States, and who shall not, when elected, be an Inhabitant of that State for which he shall be chosen.

[4] The Vice President of the United States shall be President of the Senate, but shall have no Vote, unless they be equally divided.

[5] The Senate shall chuse their other Officers, and also a President pro tempore, in the Absence of the Vice President, or when he shall exercise the Office of President of the United States.

[6] The Senate shall have the sole Power to try all Impeachments. When sitting for that Purpose, they shall be on Oath or Affirmation. When the President of the United States is tried, the Chief Justice shall preside: And no Person shall be convicted without the Concurrence of two thirds of the Members present.

[7] Judgment in Cases of Impeachment shall not extend further than to removal from Office, and disqualification to hold and enjoy any Office of honor, Trust, or Profit under the United States: but the Party convicted shall nevertheless be liable and subject to Indictment, Trial, Judgment, and Punishment, according to Law.

Section 4. [1] The Times, Places and Manner of holding Elections for Senators and Representatives, shall be prescribed in each State by the Legislature thereof; but the Congress may at any time by Law make or alter such Regulations, except as to the Places of chusing Senators.

[2] The Congress shall assemble at least once in every Year, and such Meeting shall be on the first Monday in December, unless they shall by Law appoint a different Day.

Section 5. [1] Each House shall be the Judge of the Elections, Returns, and Qualifications of its own Members, and a Majority of each shall constitute a Quorum to do Business; but a smaller Number may adjourn from day to day, and may be authorized to compel the Attendance of absent Members, in such Manner, and under such Penalties as each House may provide.

[2] Each House may determine the Rules of its Proceedings, punish its Members for disorderly Behaviour, and, with the Concurrence of two thirds, expel a Member.

[3] Each House shall keep a Journal of its Proceedings, and from time to time publish the same, excepting such Parts as may in their Judgment require Secrecy;

and the Yeas and Nays of the Members of either House on any question shall, at the Desire of one fifth of those Present, be entered on the Journal.

[4] Neither House, during the Session of Congress, shall without the Consent of the other, adjourn for more than three days, nor to any other Place than that in which the two Houses shall be sitting.

Section 6. [1] The Senators and Representatives shall receive a Compensation for their Services, to be ascertained by Law, and paid out of the Treasury of the United States. They shall in all Cases, except Treason, Felony, and Breach of the Peace, be privileged from Arrest during their Attendance at the Session of their respective Houses, and in going to and returning from the same; and for any Speech or Debate in either House, they shall not be questioned in any other Place.

[2] No Senator or Representative shall, during the Time for which he was elected, be appointed to any civil Office under the Authority of the United States, which shall have been created, or the Emoluments whereof shall have been encreased during such time; and no Person holding any Office under the United States, shall be a Member of either House during his Continuance in Office.

Section 7. [1] All Bills for raising Revenue shall originate in the House of Representatives; but the Senate may propose or concur with Amendments as on other Bills.

[2] Every Bill which shall have passed the House of Representatives and the Senate, shall, before it become a Law, be presented to the President of the United States; If he approve he shall sign it, but if not he shall return it, with his Objections to that House in which it shall have originated, who shall enter the Objections at large on their Journal, and proceed to reconsider it. If after such Reconsideration two thirds of that House shall agree to pass the Bill, it shall be sent, together with the Objections, to the other House, by which it shall likewise be reconsidered, and if approved by two thirds of that House, it shall become a Law. But in all such Cases the Votes of both Houses shall be determined by Yeas and Nays, and the Names of the Persons voting for and against the Bill shall be entered on the Journal of each House respectively. If any Bill shall not be returned by the President within ten Days (Sundays excepted) after it shall have been presented to him, the Same shall be a Law, in like Manner as if he had signed it, unless the Congress by their Adjournment prevent its Return, in which Case it shall not be a Law.

[3] Every Order, Resolution, or Vote to which the Concurrence of the Senate and House of Representatives may be necessary (except on a question of Adjournment) shall be presented to the President of the United States; and before the Same shall take Effect, shall be approved by him, or being disapproved by him, shall be repassed by two thirds of the Senate and House of Representatives, according to the Rules and Limitations prescribed in the Case of a Bill.

Section 8. [1] The Congress shall have Power To lay and collect Taxes, Duties, Imposts and Excises, to pay the Debts and provide for the common Defence and general Welfare of the United States; but all Duties, Imposts and Excises shall be uniform throughout the United States;

[2] To borrow Money on the credit of the United States;

[3] To regulate Commerce with foreign Nations, and among the several States, and with the Indian Tribes;

[4] To establish an uniform Rule of Naturalization, and uniform Laws on the subject of Bankruptcies throughout the United States;

[5] To coin Money, regulate the Value thereof, and of foreign Coin, and fix the Standard of Weights and Measures;

[6] To provide for the Punishment of counterfeiting the Securities and current Coin of the United States;

[7] To establish Post Offices and Post Roads;

[8] To promote the Progress of Science and useful Arts, by securing for limited Times to Authors and Inventors the exclusive Right to their respective Writings and Discoveries;

[9] To constitute Tribunals inferior to the supreme Court;

[10] To define and punish Piracies and Felonies committed on the high Seas, and Offences against the Law of Nations;

[11] To declare War, grant Letters of Marque and Reprisal, and make Rules concerning Captures on Land and Water;

[12] To raise and support Armies, but no Appropriation of Money to that Use shall be for a longer Term than two Years;

[13] To provide and maintain a Navy;

[14] To make Rules for the Government and Regulation of the land and naval Forces;

[15] To provide for calling forth the Militia to execute the Laws of the Union, suppress Insurrections and repel Invasions;

[16] To provide for organizing, arming, and disciplining, the Militia, and for governing such Part of them as may be employed in the Service of the United States, reserving to the States respectively, the Appointment of the Officers, and the Authority of training the Militia according to the discipline prescribed by Congress;

[17] To exercise exclusive Legislation in all Cases whatsoever, over such District (not exceeding ten Miles square) as may, by Cession of particular States and the Acceptance of Congress, become the Seat of the Government of the United States, and to exercise like Authority over all Places purchased by the Consent of the Legislature of the State in which the Same shall be, for the Erection of Forts, Magazines, Arsenals, dock-Yards, and other needful Buildings;—And

[18] To make all Laws which shall be necessary and proper for carrying into Execution the foregoing Powers, and all other Powers vested by this Constitution in the Government of the United States, or in any Department or Officer thereof.

Section 9. [1] The Migration or Importation of such Persons as any of the States now existing shall think proper to admit, shall not be prohibited by the Congress prior to the Year one thousand eight hundred and eight, but a Tax or duty may be imposed on such Importation, not exceeding ten dollars for each Person.

[2] The Privilege of the Writ of Habeas Corpus shall not be suspended, unless when in Cases of Rebellion or Invasion the public Safety may require it.

[3] No Bill of Attainder or ex post facto Law shall be passed.

[4] No Capitation, or other direct, Tax shall be laid, unless in Proportion to the Census or Enumeration herein before directed to be taken.

[5] No Tax or Duty shall be laid on Articles exported from any State.

[6] No Preference shall be given by any Regulation of Commerce or Revenue to the Ports of one State over those of another: nor shall Vessels bound to, or from, one State, be obliged to enter, clear, or pay Duties in another.

[7] No Money shall be drawn from the Treasury, but in Consequence of Appropriations made by Law; and a regular Statement and Account of the Receipts and Expenditures of all public Money shall be published from time to time.

[8] No Title of Nobility shall be granted by the United States: And no Person holding any Office of Profit or Trust under them, shall, without the Consent of the Congress, accept of any present, Emolument, Office, or Title, of any kind whatever, from any King, Prince, or foreign State.

Section 10. [1] No State shall enter into any Treaty, Alliance, or Confederation; grant Letters of Marque and Reprisal; coin Money; emit Bills of Credit; make any Thing but gold and silver Coin a Tender in Payment of Debts; pass any Bill of Attainder, ex post facto Law, or Law impairing the Obligation of Contracts, or grant any Title of Nobility.

[2] No State shall, without the Consent of the Congress, lay any Imposts or Duties on Imports or Exports, except what may be absolutely necessary for executing its inspection Laws: and the net Produce of all Duties and Imposts, laid by any State on Imports or Exports, shall be for the Use of the Treasury of the United States; and all such Laws shall be subject to the Revision and Controul of the Congress.

[3] No State shall, without the Consent of Congress, lay any Duty of Tonnage, keep Troops, or Ships of War in time of Peace, enter into any Agreement or Compact with another State, or with a foreign Power, or engage in War, unless actually invaded, or in such imminent Danger as will not admit of delay.

ARTICLE II

Section 1. [1] The executive Power shall be vested in a President of the United States of America. He shall hold his Office during the Term of four Years, and, together with the Vice President, chosen for the same Term, be elected, as follows:

[2] Each State shall appoint, in such Manner as the Legislature thereof may direct, a Number of Electors, equal to the whole Number of Senators and Representatives to which the State may be entitled in the Congress: but no Senator

or Representative, or Person holding an Office of Trust or Profit under the United States, shall be appointed an Elector.

[3] The electors shall meet in their respective States, and vote by ballot for two Persons, of whom one at least shall not be an Inhabitant of the same State with themselves. And they shall make a List of all the Persons voted for, and of the Number of Votes for each; which List they shall sign and certify, and transmit sealed to the Seat of the Government of the United States, directed to the President of the Senate. The President of the Senate shall, in the Presence of the Senate and House of Representatives, open all the Certificates, and the Votes shall then be counted. The Person having the greatest Number of Votes shall be the President, if such Number be a Majority of the whole Number of Electors appointed; and if there be more than one who have such Majority, and have an equal Number of Votes, then the House of Representatives shall immediately chuse by Ballot one of them for President; and if no Person have a Majority, then from the five highest on the List the said House shall in like Manner chuse the President. But in chusing the President, the Votes shall be taken by States, the Representation from each State having one Vote; A quorum for this Purpose shall consist of a Member or Members from two thirds of the States, and a Majority of all the States shall be necessary to a Choice. In every Case, after the Choice of the President, the Person having the greatest Number of Votes of the Electors shall be the Vice President. But if there should remain two or more who have equal Votes, the Senate shall chuse from them by Ballot the Vice-President.

[4] The Congress may determine the Time of chusing the Electors, and the Day on which they shall give their Votes; which Day shall be the same throughout the United States.

[5] No Person except a natural born Citizen, or a Citizen of the United States, at the time of the Adoption of this Constitution, shall be eligible to the Office of President; neither shall any Person be eligible to that Office who shall not have attained to the Age of thirty five Years, and been fourteen Years a Resident within the United States.

[6] In Case of the Removal of the President from Office, or of his Death, Resignation, or Inability to discharge the Powers and Duties of the said Office, the Same shall devolve on the Vice President, and the Congress may by Law provide for the Case of Removal, Death, Resignation or Inability, both of the President and Vice President, declaring what Officer shall then act as President, and such Officer shall act accordingly, until the Disability be removed, or a President shall be elected.

[7] The President shall, at stated Times, receive for his Services, a Compensation, which shall neither be encreased nor diminished during the Period for which he shall have been elected, and he shall not receive within that Period any other Emolument from the United States, or any of them. [8] Before he enter on the Execution of his Office, he shall take the following Oath or Affirmation: "I do solemnly swear (or affirm) that I will faithfully execute the Office of President of the United States, and will to the best of my Ability, preserve, protect and defend the Constitution of the United States."

Section 2. [1] The President shall be Commander in Chief of the Army and Navy of the United States, and of the Militia of the several States, when called into the actual Service of the United States; he may require the Opinion, in writing, of the principal Officer in each of the executive Departments, upon any Subject relating to the Duties of their respective Offices, and he shall have Power to grant Reprieves and Pardons for Offenses against the United States, except in Cases of Impeachment.

[2] He shall have Power, by and with the Advice and Consent of the Senate, to make Treaties, provided two thirds of the Senators present concur; and he shall nominate, and by and with the Advice and Consent of the Senate, shall appoint Ambassadors, other public Ministers and Consuls, Judges of the supreme Court, and all other Officers of the United States, whose Appointments are not herein otherwise provided for, and which shall be established by Law: but the Congress may by Law vest the Appointment of such inferior Officers, as they think proper, in the President alone, in the Courts of Law, or in the Heads of Departments.

[3] The President shall have Power to fill up all Vacancies that may happen during the Recess of the Senate, by granting Commissions which shall expire at the End of their next Session.

Section 3. He shall from time to time give to the Congress Information of the State of the Union, and recommend to their Consideration such Measures as he shall judge necessary and expedient; he may, on extraordinary Occasions, convene both Houses, or either of them, and in Case of Disagreement between them, with Respect to the Time of Adjournment, he may adjourn them to such Time as he shall think proper; he shall receive Ambassadors and other public Ministers; he shall take Care that the Laws be faithfully executed, and shall Commission. all the Officers of the United States.

Section 4. The President, Vice President and all civil Officers of the United States, shall be removed from Office on Impeachment for, and Conviction of, Treason, Bribery, or other high Crimes and Misdemeanors.

ARTICLE III

Section 1. The judicial Power of the United States, shall be vested in one supreme Court, and in such inferior Courts as the Congress may from time to time ordain and establish. The Judges, both of the supreme and inferior Courts, shall hold their Offices during good Behaviour, and shall, at stated Times, receive for their Services, a Compensation, which shall not be diminished during their Continuance in Office.

Section 2. [1] The judicial Power shall extend to all Cases, in Law and Equity, arising under this Constitution, the Laws of the United States, and Treaties made, or which shall be made, under their Authority;—to all Cases affecting Ambassadors, other public Ministers and Consuls;—to all Cases of admiralty and maritime Jurisdiction;—to Controversies to which the United States shall be a Party;—to Controversies between two or more States;—between a State and Citizens of another State;—between Citizens of different States;—between Citizens of the same State claiming Lands under Grants of different States, and between a State, or the Citizens thereof, and foreign States, Citizens or Subjects.

[2] In all Cases affecting Ambassadors, other public Ministers and Consuls, and those in which a State shall be Party, the supreme Court shall have original Jurisdiction. In all the other Cases before mentioned, the supreme Court shall have appellate Jurisdiction, both as to Law and Fact, with such Exceptions, and under such Regulations as the Congress shall make.

[3] The Trial of all Crimes, except in Cases of impeachment, shall be by Jury; and such Trial shall be held in the State where the said Crimes shall have been committed; but when not committed within any State, the Trial shall be at such Place or Places as the Congress may by Law have directed.

Section 3. [1] Treason against the United States, shall consist only in levying War against them, or in adhering to their Enemies, giving them Aid and Comfort. No Person shall be convicted of Treason unless on the Testimony of two Witnesses to the same overt Act, or on Confession in open Court.

[2] The Congress shall have Power to declare the Punishment of Treason, but no Attainder of Treason shall work Corruption of Blood, or Forfeiture except during the Life of the Person attainted.

ARTICLE IV

Section 1. Full Faith and Credit shall be given in each State to the public Acts, Records, and judicial Proceedings of every other State. And the Congress may by general Laws prescribe the Manner in which such Acts, Records and Proceedings shall be proved, and the Effect thereof.

Section 2. [1] The Citizens of each State shall be entitled to all Privileges and Immunities of Citizens in the several States.

[2] A person charged in any State with Treason, Felony, or other Crime, who shall flee from Justice, and be found in another State, shall on Demand of the executive Authority of the State from which he fled, be delivered up, to be removed to the State having Jurisdiction of the Crime.

[3] No Person held to Service or Labour in one State, under the Laws thereof, escaping into another, shall, in Consequence of any Law or Regulation therein, be discharged from such Service or Labour, but shall be delivered up on Claim of the Party; to whom such Service or Labour may be due.

Section 3. [1] New States may be admitted by the Congress into this Union; but no new State shall be formed or erected within the Jurisdiction of any other State; nor any State be formed by the Junction of two or more States, or Parts of States, without the Consent of the Legislatures of the States concerned as well as of the Congress.

[2] The Congress shall have Power to dispose of and make all needful Rules and Regulations respecting the Territory or other Property belonging to the United States; and nothing in this Constitution shall be so construed as to Prejudice any Claims of the United States, or of any particular State.

Section 4. The United States shall guarantee to every State in this Union a Republican Form of Government, and shall protect each of them against Invasion; and on Application of the Legislature, or of the Executive (when the Legislature cannot be convened) against domestic Violence.

ARTICLE V

The Congress, whenever two thirds of both Houses shall deem it necessary, shall propose Amendments to this Constitution, or on the Application of the Legislatures of two thirds of the several States, shall call a Convention for proposing Amendments, which, in either Case, shall be valid to all Intents and Purposes, as Part of this Constitution, when ratified by the Legislatures of three fourths of the several States, or by Conventions in three fourths thereof, as the one or the other Mode of Ratification may be proposed by the Congress; Provided that no Amendment which may be made prior to the Year One thousand eight hundred and eight shall in any Manner affect the first and fourth Clauses in the Ninth Section of the first Article; and that no State, without its Consent, shall be deprived of its equal Suffrage in the Senate.

ARTICLE VI

[1] All Debts contracted and Engagements entered into, before the Adoption of this Constitution, shall be as valid against the United States under this Constitution, as under the Confederation.

[2] This Constitution, and the Laws of the United States which shall be made in Pursuance thereof; and all Treaties made, or which shall be made, under the Authority of the United States, shall be the supreme Law of the Land; and the Judges in every State shall be bound thereby, any Thing in the Constitution or Laws of any State to the Contrary notwithstanding.

[3] The Senators and Representatives before mentioned, and the Members of the several State Legislatures, and all executive and judicial Officers, both of the United States and of the several States, shall be bound by Oath or Affirmation, to support this Constitution; but no religious Test shall ever be required as a Qualification to any Office or public Trust under the United States.

ARTICLE VII

The Ratification of the Conventions of nine States, shall be sufficient for the Establishment of this Constitution between the States so ratifying the Same.

ARTICLES IN ADDITION TO, AND AMENDMENT OF, THE CONSTITUTION OF THE UNITED STATES OF AMERICA, PROPOSED BY CONGRESS, AND RATIFIED BY THE LEGISLATURES OF THE SEVERAL STATES, PURSUANT TO THE FIFTH ARTICLE OF THE ORIGINAL CONSTITUTION.

AMENDMENT I [1791]

Congress shall make no law respecting an establishment of religion, or prohibiting the free exercise thereof; or abridging the freedom of speech, or of the press; or the right of the people peaceably to assemble, and to petition the Government for a redress of grievances.

AMENDMENT II [1791]

A well regulated Militia, being necessary to the security of a free State, the right of the people to keep and bear Arms, shall not be infringed.

AMENDMENT III [1791]

No Soldier shall, in time of peace be quartered in any house, without the consent of the Owner, nor in time of war, but in a manner to be prescribed by law.

AMENDMENT IV [1791]

The right of the people to be secure in their persons, houses, papers, and effects, against unreasonable searches and seizures, shall not be violated, and no Warrants shall issue, but upon probable cause, supported by Oath or affirmation, and particularly describing the place to be searched, and the persons or things to be seized.

AMENDMENT V [1791]

No person shall be held to answer for a capital, or otherwise infamous crime, unless on a presentment or indictment of a Grand Jury, except in cases arising in the land or naval forces, or in the Militia, when in actual service in time of War or public danger; nor shall any person be subject for the same offence to be twice put in jeopardy of life or limb; nor shall be compelled in any criminal case to be a witness against himself, nor be deprived of life, liberty, or property, without due process of law; nor shall private property be taken for public use, without just compensation.

AMENDMENT VI [1791]

In all criminal prosecutions, the accused shall enjoy the right to a speedy and public trial, by an impartial jury of the State and district wherein the crime shall have been committed, which district shall have been previously ascertained by law, and to be informed of the nature and cause of the accusation; to be confronted with the witnesses against him; to have compulsory process for obtaining witnesses in his favor, and to have the Assistance of Counsel for his defence.

AMENDMENT VII [1791]

In Suits at common law, where the value in controversy shall exceed twenty dollars, the right of trial by jury shall be preserved, and no fact tried by a jury, shall be otherwise re-examined in any Court of the United States, than according to the rules of the common law.

AMENDMENT VIII [1791]

Excessive bail shall not be required, nor excessive fines imposed, nor cruel and unusual punishments inflicted.

AMENDMENT IX [1791]

The enumeration in the Constitution, of certain rights, shall not be construed to deny or disparage others retained by the people.

AMENDMENT X [1791]

The powers not delegated to the United States by the Constitution, nor prohibited by it to the States, are reserved to the States respectively, or to the people.

AMENDMENT XI [1798]

The Judicial power of the United States shall not be construed to extend to any suit in law or equity, commenced or prosecuted against one of the United States by Citizens of another State, or by Citizens or Subjects of any Foreign State.

AMENDMENT XII [1804]

The Electors shall meet in their respective states and vote by ballot for President and Vice-President, one of whom, at least, shall not be an inhabitant of the same state with themselves; they shall name in their ballots the person voted for as President, and in distinct ballots the person voted for as Vice-President, and they shall make distinct lists of all persons voted for as President, and of all persons voted for as Vice-President, and of the number of votes for each, which lists they shall sign and certify, and transmit sealed to the seat of the government of the United States, directed to the President of the Senate;-The President of the Senate shall, in the presence of the Senate and House of Representatives, open all the certificates and the votes shall then be counted;-The person having the greatest number of votes for President, shall be the President, if such number be a majority of the whole number of Electors appointed; and if no person have such majority, then from the persons having the highest numbers not exceeding three on the list of those voted for as President, the House of Representatives shall choose immediately, by ballot, the President. But in choosing the President, the votes shall be taken by states, the representation from each state having one vote; a quorum for this purpose shall consist of a member or members from two-thirds of the states, and a majority of all the states shall be necessary to a choice. And if the House of Representatives shall not choose a President whenever the right of choice shall devolve upon them, before the fourth day of March next following, then the Vice-President shall act as President, as in the case of the death or other constitutional disability of the President. The person having the greatest number of votes as Vice-President, shall be the Vice-President, if such number be a majority of the whole number of Electors appointed, and if no person have a majority, then from the two highest numbers on the list, the Senate shall choose the Vice-President; a quorum for the purpose shall consist of two-thirds of the whole number of Senators, and a majority of the whole number shall be necessary to a choice. But no person constitutionally ineligible to the office of President shall be eligible to that of Vice-President of the United States.

AMENDMENT XIII [1865]

Section 1. Neither slavery nor involuntary servitude, except as a punishment for crime whereof the party shall have been duly convicted, shall exist within the United States, or any place subject to their jurisdiction.

Section 2. Congress shall have power to enforce this article by appropriate legislation.

AMENDMENT XIV [1868]

Section 1. All persons born or naturalized in the United States, and subject to the jurisdiction thereof, are citizens of the United States and of the State wherein they reside. No State shall make or enforce any law which shall abridge the privileges or immunities of citizens of the United States; nor shall any State deprive any person of life, liberty, or property, without due process of law; nor deny to any person within its jurisdiction the equal protection of the laws.

Section 2. Representatives shall be apportioned among the several States according to their respective numbers, counting the whole number of persons in each State, excluding Indians not taxed. But when the right to vote at any election for the choice of electors for President and Vice President of the United States, Representatives in Congress, the Executive and Judicial officers of a State, or the members of the Legislature thereof, is denied to any of the male inhabitants of such State, being twenty-one years of age, and citizens of the United States, or in any way abridged, except for participation in rebellion, or other crime, the basis of representation therein shall be reduced in the proportion which the number of such male citizens shall bear to the whole number of male citizens twenty-one years of age in such State.

Section 3. No person shall be a Senator or Representative in Congress, or elector of President and Vice President, or hold any office, civil or military, under the United States, or under any State, who, having previously taken an oath, as a member of Congress, or as an officer of the United States, or as a member of any State legislature, or as an executive or judicial officer of any State, to support the Constitution of the United States, shall have engaged in insurrection or rebellion against the same, or given aid or comfort to the enemies thereof. But Congress may by a vote of two-thirds of each House, remove such disability.

Section 4. The validity of the public debt of the United States, authorized by law, including debts incurred for payment of pensions and bounties for services in suppressing insurrection or rebellion, shall not be questioned. But neither the United States nor any State shall assume or pay any debt or obligation incurred in aid of insurrection or rebellion against the United States, or any claim for the loss or emancipation of any slave; but all such debts, obligations and claims shall be held illegal and void.

Section 5. The Congress shall have power to enforce, by appropriate legislation, the provisions of this article.

AMENDMENT XV [1870]

Section 1. The right of citizens of the United States to vote shall not be denied or abridged by the United States or by any State on account of race, color, or previous condition of servitude.

Section 2. The Congress shall have power to enforce this article by appropriate legislation.

AMENDMENT XVI [1913]

The Congress shall have power to lay and collect taxes on incomes, from whatever source derived, without apportionment among the several States, and without regard to any census or enumeration.

AMENDMENT XVII [1913]

[1] The Senate of the United States shall be composed of two Senators from each State, elected by the people thereof, for six years; and each Senator shall have one vote. The electors in each State shall have the qualifications requisite for electors of the most numerous branch of the State legislatures.

[2] When vacancies happen in the representation of any State in the Senate, the executive authority of such State shall issue writs of election to fill such vacancies: *Provided,* That the legislature of any State may empower the executive thereof to make temporary appointments until the people fill the vacancies by election as the legislature may direct.

[3] This amendment shall not be so construed as to affect the election or term of any Senator chosen before it becomes valid as part of the Constitution.

AMENDMENT XVIII [1919]

Section 1. After one year from the ratification of this article the manufacture, sale, or transportation of intoxicating liquors within, the importation thereof into, or the exportation thereof from the United States and all territory subject to the jurisdiction thereof for beverage purposes is hereby prohibited.

Section 2. The Congress and the several States shall have concurrent power to enforce this article by appropriate legislation.

Section 3. This article shall be inoperative unless it shall have been ratified as an amendment to the Constitution by the legislatures of the several States, as provided in the Constitution, within seven years from the date of the submission hereof to the States by the Congress.

AMENDMENT XIX [1920]

[1] The right of citizens of the United States to vote shall not be denied or abridged by the United States or by any State on account of sex.

[2] Congress shall have power to enforce this article by appropriate legislation.

AMENDMENT XX [1933]

Section 1. The terms of the President and Vice President shall end at noon on the 20th day of January, and the terms of Senators and Representatives at noon on the 3d day of January, of the years in which such terms would have ended if this article had not been ratified; and the terms of their successors shall then begin.

Section 2. The Congress shall assemble at least once in every year, and such meeting shall begin at noon on the 3d day of January, unless they shall by law appoint a different day.

Section 3. If, at the time fixed for the beginning of the term of the President, the President elect shall have died, the Vice President elect shall become President. If a President shall not have been chosen before the time fixed for the beginning of his term, or if the President elect shall have failed to qualify, then the Vice President elect shall act as President until a President shall have qualified; and the Congress may by law provide for the case wherein neither a President elect nor a Vice President elect shall have qualified, declaring who shall then act as President, or the manner in which one who is to act shall be selected, and such person shall act accordingly until a President or Vice President shall have qualified.

Section 4. The Congress may by law provide for the case of the death of any of the persons from whom the House of Representatives may choose a President whenever the right of choice shall have devolved upon them, and for the case of the death of any of the persons from whom the Senate may choose a Vice President whenever the right of choice shall have devolved upon them.

Section 5. Sections I and 2 shall take effect on the 15th day of October following the ratification of this article.

Section 6. This article shall be inoperative unless it shall have been ratified as an amendment to the Constitution by the legislatures of three-fourths of the several States within seven years from the date of its submission.

AMENDMENT XXI [1933]

Section 1. The eighteenth article of amendment to the Constitution of the United States is hereby repealed.

Section 2. The transportation or importation into any State, Territory, or possession of the United States for delivery or use therein of intoxicating liquors, in violation of the laws thereof, is hereby prohibited.

Section 3. This article shall be inoperative unless it shall have been ratified as an amendment to the Constitution by conventions in the several States, as provided in the Constitution, within seven years from the date of the submission hereof to the States by the Congress.

AMENDMENT XXII [1951]

Section 1. No person shall be elected to the office of the President more than twice, and no person who has held the office of President, or acted as President, for more than two years of a term to which some other person was elected President shall be elected to the office of the President more than once. But this Article shall not apply to any person holding the office of President when this Article was proposed by the Congress, and shall not prevent any person who may be holding the office of President, or acting as President, during the term within which this Article becomes operative from holding the office of President or acting as President during the remainder of such term.

Section 2. This article shall be inoperative unless it shall have been ratified as an amendment to the Constitution by the legislatures of three-fourths of the several States within seven years from the date of its submission to the States by the Congress.

AMENDMENT XXIII [1961]

Section 1. The District constituting the seat of Government of the United States shall appoint in such manner as the Congress may direct:

A number of electors of President and Vice President equal to the whole number of Senators and Representatives in Congress to which the District would be entitled if it were a State, but in no event more than the least populous State; they shall be in addition to those appointed by the States, but they shall be considered, for the purposes of the election of President and Vice President, to be electors appointed by a State; and they shall meet in the District and perform such duties as provided by the twelfth article of amendment.

Section 2. The Congress shall have power to enforce this article by appropriate legislation.

AMENDMENT XXIV [1964]

Section 1. The right of citizens of the United States to vote in any primary or other election for President or Vice President, for electors for President or Vice President, or for Senator or Representative in Congress, shall not be denied or abridged by the United States or any State by reason of failure to pay any poll tax or other tax.

Section 2. The Congress shall have power to enforce this article by appropriate legislation.

AMENDMENT XXV [1967]

Section 1. In case of the removal of the President from office or of his death or resignation, the Vice President shall become President.

Section 2. Whenever there is a vacancy in the office of the Vice President, the President shall nominate a Vice President who shall take office upon confirmation by a majority vote of both Houses of Congress.

Section 3. Whenever the President transmits to the President pro tempore of the Senate and the Speaker of the House of Representatives his written declaration that he is unable to discharge the powers and duties of his office, and until he transmits to them a written declaration to the contrary, such powers and duties shall be discharged by the Vice President as Acting President.

Section 4. Whenever the Vice President and a majority of either the principal officers of the executive departments or of such other body as Congress may by law provide, transmit to the President pro tempore of the Senate and the Speaker of the House of Representatives their written declaration that the President is unable to discharge the powers and duties of his office, the Vice President shall immediately assume the powers and duties of the office as Acting President.

Thereafter, when the President transmits to the President pro temp ore of the Senate and the Speaker of the House of Representatives his written declaration that no inability exists, he shall resume the powers and duties of his office unless the Vice President and a majority of either the principal officers of the executive department or of such other body as Congress may by law provide, transmit within four days to the President pro tempore of the Senate and the Speaker of the House of Representatives their written declaration that the President is unable to discharge the powers and duties of his office. Thereupon Congress shall decide the issue, assembling within forty-eight hours for that purpose if not in session. If the Congress, within twenty-one days after receipt of the latter written declaration, or, if Congress is not in session, within twenty-one days after Congress is required to assemble, determines by two-thirds vote of both Houses that the President is unable to discharge the powers and duties of his office, the Vice President shall continue to discharge the same as Acting President; otherwise, the President shall resume the powers and duties of his office.

AMENDMENT XXVI [1971]

Section 1. The right of citizens of the United States, who are eighteen years of age or older, to vote shall not be denied or abridged by the United States or by any State on account of age.

Section 2. The Congress shall have power to enforce this article by appropriate legislation.

AMENDMENT XXVII [1992]

No law, varying the compensation for the services of the Senators and Representatives, shall take effect, until an election of Representatives shall have intervened.

APPENDIX B

THE SUPREME COURT'S CANONS OF STATUTORY INTERPRETATION

■ ■ ■

This is a collection of canons invoked by the Rehnquist and Roberts Courts (1986–2014) and divided into categories that parallel the typology provided in Chapters 6 and 7.[*]

TEXTUAL CANONS

- Plain meaning rule: follow the plain meaning of the statutory text,[1] except when textual plain meaning requires an absurd result[2] or suggests a scrivener's error.[3]

LINGUISTIC INFERENCES

- *Expressio* (or *inclusio*) *unius*: expression of one thing suggests the exclusion of others.[4] Inapplicable if context suggests listing is not comprehensive.[5]

- *Noscitur a sociis*: interpret a general term to be similar to more specific terms in a series.[6] *Noscitur* is often not helpful when applied to a technical statute whose details were hammered out through a complex process.[7]

- *Ejusdem generis*: interpret a general term to reflect the class of objects reflected in more specific terms accompanying it.[8] *Ejusdem* might be trumped by other canons, such as the rule against redundancy.[9]

---

[*] Diana Rusk, Yale Law School Class of 2009, provided invaluable assistance in the preparation of this appendix.

[1] Mohamad v. Palestinian Auth., 132 S.Ct. 1702 (2012); Pacific Operators Offshire, LLC v. Valladolid, 132 S.Ct. 680 (2012); Massachusetts v. EPA, 549 U.S. 497 (2007); Arlington Cent. Sch. Dist. Bd. of Educ. v. Murphy, 548 U.S. 291, 296 (2006); Barnhart v. Thomas, 540 U.S. 20, 26–29 (2003); West Virginia Univ. Hosps. v. Casey, 499 U.S. 83 (1991); United States v. Providence Journal Co., 485 U.S. 693, 700–01 (1988).

[2] Utility Air Regulatory Group v. EPA, 134 S.Ct. 2427 (2014) (plurality and concurring opinions); Brown v. Plata, 131 S.Ct. 1910, 1950-51 (2011) (Scalia, J., dissenting); Zuni Pub. Sch. Dist. No. 89 v. Department of Educ., 550 U.S. 81, 104–07 (2007) (Stevens, J., concurring); United States v. Wilson, 503 U.S. 329, 334 (1992); Green v. Bock Laundry Mach. Co., 490 U.S. 504, 509–11 (1989).

[3] Lamie v. United States Trustee, 540 U.S. 526, 530–31 (2004); United States Nat'l Bank v. Independent Ins. Agents, 508 U.S. 439, 462 (1993).

[4] POM Wonderful LLC v. Coca-Cola Co., 134 S.Ct. 2228, 2237-38 (2014); Hinck v. United States, 550 U.S. 501 (2007); TRW, Inc. v. Andrews, 534 U.S. 19 (2001); City of Chicago v. Environmental Def. Fund, 511 U.S. 328 (1994); United States v. Smith, 499 U.S. 160 (1991); Mississippi Band of Choctaw Indians v. Holyfield, 490 U.S. 30, 46–47 & n.22 (1989); Chan v. Korean Air Lines, Ltd., 490 U.S. 122, 133–34 (1989).

[5] Marrama v. Citizens Bank of Mass., 549 U.S. 365 (2007); Christensen v. Harris County, 529 U.S. 576, 583–84 (2000); Burns v. United States, 501 U.S. 129, 136 (1991); Sullivan v. Hudson, 490 U.S. 877, 891–92 (1989).

[6] Entergy Corp. v. Riverkeeper, Inc., 556 U.S. 208, 222 (2009); Circuit City Stores, Inc. v. Adams, 532 U.S. 105 (2001); Gustafson v. Alloyd Co., 513 U.S. 561, 575 (1995); Dole v. United Steelworkers of Am., 494 U.S. 26, 36 (1990); Massachusetts v. Morash, 490 U.S. 107, 114–15 (1989).

[7] Bilski v. Kappos, 561 U.S. 593 (2010); S.D. Warren Co. v. Maine Bd. of Envtl. Prot., 547 U.S. 370 (2006).

- Follow ordinary usage of terms, unless Congress gives them a specified or technical meaning.[10]

- Where Congress uses terms that have settled meaning, either by common usage or through the common law, interpreters should apply that settled meaning.[11]

- Defer to experts, including agencies, regarding the meaning of technical terminology.[12]

- Follow dictionary definitions of terms,[13] unless Congress has provided a specific definition.[14] Consider dictionaries of the era in which the statute was enacted.[15] For technical terms, consult specialized dictionaries.[16] Do not credit nonstandard, "idiosyncratic" dictionary definitions.[17]

- Rules of Construction Act (Dictionary Act), 1 U.S.C. § 1 et seq., contains default definitions that apply if Congress fails to define a particular term.[18]

- A statute has a plain meaning if you'd use its terminology at a cocktail party, and "no one would look at you funny."[19]

GRAMMAR AND SYNTAX

- Punctuation rule: Congress is presumed to follow accepted punctuation standards, so that placements of commas and other punctuation are assumed to be meaningful.[20]

---

[8] James v. United States, 550 U.S. 192 (2007); Circuit City Stores, Inc. v. Adams, 532 U.S. 105 (2001); Hughey v. United States, 495 U.S. 411, 419 (1990); Norfolk & Western Ry. Co. v. American Train Dispatchers' Ass'n, 499 U.S. 117, 129 (1991).

[9] Ali v. Federal Bur. of Prisons, 552 U.S. 214 (2008); Babbitt v. Sweet Home Chapter of Communities for a Great Oregon, 515 U.S. 687 (1995).

[10] Octane Fitness, LLC v. Icon Health & Fitness, Inc., 134 S.Ct. 1749 (2014); Lopez v. Gonzales, 549 U.S. 47 (2006); Pasquantino v. United States, 544 U.S. 349, 355 (2005); Will v. Michigan Dep't of State Police, 491 U.S. 58, 64 (1989).

[11] CTS Corp. v. Waldburger, 134 S.Ct. 2175 (2014); Merck & Co. v. Reynolds, 559 U.S. 633 (2010); Stewart v. Dutra Constr. Co., 543 U.S. 481, 487 (2005); Scheidler v. NOW, Inc., 537 U.S. 393, 402 (2003); United States v. Wells, 519 U.S. 482, 491 (1997); Community for Creative Non-Violence v. Reid, 490 U.S. 730, 739 (1989).

[12] Zuni Pub. Sch. Dist. No. 89 v. Department of Educ., 550 U.S. 81 (2007).

[13] CTS Corp. v. Waldburger, 134 S.Ct. 2175 (2014) (Black's); Taniguchi v. Kan Pacific Saipan, Ltd., 132 S.Ct. 1997 (2012) (many dictionaries); Rapanos v. United States, 547 U.S. 715 (2006) (plurality opinion.) (Webster's Second); Muscarello v. United States, 524 U.S. 125 (1998) (Oxford English); Pittston Coal Group v. Sebben, 488 U.S. 105, 113 (1988) (Webster's Third).

[14] Burwell v. Hobby Lobby Stores, Inc., 134 S.Ct. 2751 (June 30, 2014); Babbitt v. Sweet Home Chapter of Communities for a Great Oregon, 515 U.S. 687 (1995).

[15] Bilski v. Kappos, 561 U.S. 593 (2010); Permanent Mission of India to the United Nations v. City of New York, 551 U.S. 193 (2007); Cook County v. United States ex rel. Chandler, 538 U.S. 119, 125–27 (2003); St. Francis College v. Al-Khazraji, 481 U.S. 604 (1987).

[16] Zuni Pub. Sch. Dist. No. 89 v. Department of Educ., 550 U.S. 81 (2007).

[17] MCI v. AT&T, 512 U.S. 218 (1994) (disrespecting Webster's Third for including colloquial as well as standard definitions).

[18] Burwell v. Hobby Lobby Stores, Inc., 134 S.Ct. 2751 (June 30, 2014) (definition of "person" presumptively includes corporations); Stewart v. Dutra Constr. Co., 543 U.S. 481 (2005).

[19] Johnson v. United States, 529 U.S. 694, 718 (2000) (Scalia, J., dissenting).

[20] Jama v. Immigration & Customs Enforcement, 543 U.S. 335, 344 (2005) (significance of periods); United States v. Ron Pair Enters., 489 U.S. 235, 241–42 (1989) (comma placement); San Francisco Arts & Athletics, Inc. v. United States Olympic Comm'n, 483 U.S. 522, 528–29 (1987).

- Grammar rule: Congress is presumed to follow accepted standards of grammar.[21]

- Rule of the last antecedent: referential and qualifying words or phrases refer only to the last antecedent, unless contrary to the apparent legislative intent derived from the sense of the entire enactment.[22] Do not have to apply this rule if not practical.[23]

- "May" is usually precatory and connotes decisionmaking discretion,[24] while "shall" is usually mandatory and suggests less discretion.[25]

- "Or" means in the alternative.[26]

TEXTUAL INTEGRITY (WHOLE ACT RULE)

- Each statutory provision should be read by reference to the whole act.[27] Statutory interpretation is a "holistic" endeavor.[28]

- The statute's preamble may provide clues to statutory meaning,[29] as may the title.[30]

- Presumption against redundancy: avoid interpreting a provision in a way that would render other provisions of the statute superfluous or unnecessary.[31] This presumption must give way when offset by other evidence of statutory meaning, however.[32]

---

[21] Carr v. United States, 560 U.S. 438 (2010); Limtiaco v. Camacho, 549 U.S. 483 (2007); Rapanos v. United States, 547 U.S. 715 (2006) (plurality opinion); Jama v. Immigration & Customs Enforcement, 543 U.S. 335. (2005).

[22] Jama v. Immigration & Customs Enforcement, 543 U.S. 335 (2005); Barnhart v. Thomas, 540 U.S. 20, 26 (2003); Nobelman v. American Savs. Bank, 508 U.S. 324, 330 (1993).

[23] Nobelman v. American Sav. Bank, 508 U.S. 324, 330–31 (1993).

[24] Jama v. Immigration & Customs Enforcement, 543 U.S. 335 (2005); Lopez v. Davis, 531 U.S. 230 (2001) ("may" vests wide discretion in agency).

[25] Mallard v. United States Dist. Ct., 490 U.S. 296, 302 (1989).

[26] Loughrin v. United States, 134 S.Ct. 2384, 2389–90 (2014); Hawaiian Airlines v. Norris, 512 U.S. 246, 253–54 (1994).

[27] Samantar v. Yousuf, 560 U.S. 305 (2010); Ricci v. DeStefano, 557 U.S. 557 (2009); Ledbetter v. Goodyear Tire & Rubber Co., 550 U.S. 618 (2007); Gonzales v. Oregon, 546 U.S. 243, 273–74 (2006); Doe v. Chao, 540 U.S. 614 (2004) (considering uncodified parts of the "whole act"); Clark v. Martinez, 543 U.S. 371 (2005); Babbitt v. Sweet Home Chapter of Communities for a Great Oregon, 515 U.S. 687 (1995); Pavelic & Leflore v. Marvel Entm't Group, 493 U.S. 120, 123–24 (1989); Massachusetts v. Morash, 490 U.S. 107, 114–15 (1989).

[28] Burwell v. Hobby Lobby Stores, Inc., 134 S.Ct. 2751 (2014); United Sav. Ass'n v. Timbers of Inwood Forest Assocs., Ltd., 484 U.S. 365, 371 (1988).

[29] Sutton v. United Airlines, Inc., 527 U.S. 471 (1999) (majority and concurring opinions)).

[30] Almendarez-Torres v. United States, 523 U.S. 224, 234 (1998).

[31] Fifth Third Bancorp v. Didenhoeffer, 134 S.Ct. 2459 (2014); Ricci v. DeStefano, 557 U.S. 557 (2009); Circuit City Stores, Inc. v. Adams, 532 U.S. 105 (2001); United States v. Alaska, 521 U.S. 1 (1997); Walters v. Metropolitan Educ. Enters., Inc., 519 U.S. 202 (1997); Rake v. Wade, 508 U.S. 464 (1993); Kungys v. United States, 485 U.S. 759, 778 (1988) (plurality opinion by Scalia, J.).

[32] United States v. Home Concrete & Supply LLC, 132 S.Ct. 1836 (2012); Gutierrez v. Ada, 528 U.S. 250 (2000); Landgraf v. USI Film Prods., 511 U.S. 240, 259–60 (1994).

- Presumption of statutory consistency: interpret the same or similar terms in a statute the same way.[33] Presumption rebutted when other evidence suggests Congress was using the same term in different ways.[34]

- Presumption of meaningful variation: different statutory wording suggests different statutory meaning,[35] especially when Congress considered and rejected the alternate wording.[36] Presumption inapplicable when there is a reasonable explanation for variation (e.g., different provisions are enacted at different times).[37]

- Avoid interpreting a provision in a way that is inconsistent with the overall structure of the statute[38] *or* with another provision[39] *or* with a subsequent amendment to the statute[40] *or* with another statute enacted by a Congress relying on a particular interpretation.[41]

- Presumption of purposive amendment: statutory amendments are meant to have real and substantial effect.[42]

- Avoid the implication of broad congressional delegation of agency authority when statute carefully limits agency authority in particular matters.[43]

- Avoid broad readings of statutory provisions if Congress has specifically provided for the broader policy in more specific language elsewhere.[44]

- Broad term is presumptively ambiguous if Congress has elsewhere used more targeted terminology.[45]

---

[33] Robers v. United States, 134 S.Ct. 1854 (2014); Powerex Corp. v. Reliant Energy Servs., Inc., 551 U.S. 224 (2007); IBP, Inc. v. Alvarez, 546 U.S. 21, 34 (2005); Commissioner v. Lundy, 516 U.S. 235, 249–50 (1996); Gustafson v. Alloyd Co., 513 U.S. 561, 570 (1995); Sullivan v. Stroop, 496 U.S. 478, 484 (1990); United Sav. Ass'n v. Timbers of Inwood Forest Assocs., Ltd., 484 U.S. 365, 371 (1988).

[34] Utility Air Regulatory Group v. EPA, 134 S.Ct. 2427 (2014); Environmental Defense v. Duke Energy Corp., 549 U.S. 561 (2007); Robinson v. Shell Oil Co., 519 U.S. 337, 343–44 (1997); Dewsnup v. Timm, 502 U.S. 410, 417 & n.3 (1992).

[35] Burwell v. Hobby Lobby Stores, Inc., 134 S.Ct. 2751, 2772–74 (2014); Loughrin v. United States, 134 S.Ct. 2384, 2390–92 (2014); Lawrence v. Florida, 549 U.S. 327 (2007); Lopez v. Gonzales, 549 U.S. 47 (2006); Lindh v. Murphy, 521 U.S. 320 (1997); Keene Corp. v. United States, 508 U.S. 200, 208 (1993); Gozlon-Peretz v. United States, 498 U.S. 395, 404–05 (1991). The leading case is Russello v. United States, 464 U.S. 16, 23 (1983).

[36] Hamdan v. Rumsfeld, 548 U.S. 557 (2006).

[37] Gutierrez v. Ada, 528 U.S. 250 (2000); Field v. Mans, 516 U.S. 59, 67–69 (1995).

[38] Abramski v. United States, 134 S.Ct. 2259 (2014); Samantar v. Yousuf, 560 U.S. 305 (2010); Ledbetter v. Goodyear Tire & Rubber Co., 550 U.S. 618 (2007); Beck v. PACE Int'l Union, 551 U.S. 96 (2007).

[39] Petrella v. MGM, Inc., 134 S.Ct. 1962 (2014); Ricci v. DeStefano, 557 U.S. 557 (2009); Babbitt v. Sweet Home Chapter of Communities for a Great Oregon, 515 U.S. 687 (1995); Gade v. National Solid Waste Management Ass'n, 505 U.S. 88, 100–01 (1992); United Sav. Ass'n v. Timbers of Inwood Forest Assocs., Ltd., 484 U.S. 365, 371 (1988).

[40] Gonzales v. Oregon, 546 U.S. 243, 257–58 (2006).

[41] FDA v. Brown & Williamson Tobacco Corp., 529 U.S. 120, 144 (2000).

[42] Rumsfeld v. Forum for Academic & Institutional Rights, Inc., 547 U.S. 47 (2006); Babbitt v. Sweet Home Chapter of Communities for a Great Oregon, 515 U.S. 687 (1995).

[43] Gonzales v. Oregon, 547 U.S. 243, 262–63 (2006).

[44] Arlington Cent. Sch. Dist. Bd. of Educ. v. Murphy, 548 U.S. 291 (2006); Jama v. Immigration & Customs Enforcement, 543 U.S. 335 (2005); Custis v. United States, 511 U.S. 485, 491 (1994); West Virginia Univ. Hosps. v. Casey, 499 U.S. 83, 99 (1991).

[45] Zuni Pub. Sch. Dist. No. 89 v. Department of Educ., 550 U.S. 81 (2007).

- Specific provisions targeting a particular issue apply instead of provisions more generally covering the issue.[46]

- Provisos and statutory exceptions should be read narrowly.[47]

- Do not create exceptions in addition to those specified by Congress.[48]

EXTRINSIC SOURCE CANONS

AGENCY INTERPRETATIONS

- *Skidmore* deference. Agency interpretations are entitled to respect to the extent that they have "power to persuade" based upon consistency, factual basis, and expertise.[49] Contrariwise, agency views that are shifting or insufficiently developed have little or no persuasive value.[50]

- Even informal and unsettled agency interpretations (such as those embodied in handbooks or litigation briefs) may be useful confirmations for the interpreter's interpretation of statutory language.[51]

- *Chevron* deference. "Reasonable" agency interpretations pursuant to congressional delegation of lawmaking authority are binding on courts unless Congress has directly addressed the issue.[52] *Chevron* might also apply to notice-and-comment rules filling statutory gaps that the agency reasonably treats as binding on itself and the public.[53] The agency's discretion is at its height when the agency decides not to enforce a statute.[54]

- For *Chevron* purposes, whether Congress has delegated the agency lawmaking authority is itself a matter of statutory interpretation.[55] Presumption against congressional delegation of authority for agency to make fundamental changes

---

[46] Green v. Bock Laundry Mach. Co., 490 U.S. 504, 524–26 (1989); Crawford Fitting Co. v. J.T. Gibbons, Inc., 482 U.S. 437, 444–45 (1987).

[47] Maracich v. Spears, 133 S.Ct. 2191, 2200 (2013); Cherokee Nation of Oklahoma v. Leavitt, 543 U.S. 631 (2005); City of Edmonds v. Oxford House, Inc., 514 U.S. 725, 732 (1995). The leading case is Commissioner v. Clark, 489 U.S. 726, 739-40 (1989). But see Republic of Iraq v. Beaty, 556 U.S. 848, 857-58 (2009) (relaxing this presumption in foreign affairs context).

[48] Argentina v. NML Capital, Ltd., 134 S.Ct. 2250 (2014); United States v. Smith, 499 U.S. 160, 166–67 (1991).

[49] Beck v. PACE Int'l Union, 551 U.S. 96 (2007); Gonzales v. Oregon, 546 U.S. 243, 255–56 (2006); United States v. Mead Corp., 533 U.S. 218, 226–27 (2001); EEOC v. Arabian Am. Oil Co., 499 U.S. 244 (1991). The leading case is Skidmore v. Swift & Co., 323 U.S. 134, 140 (1944).

[50] Burlington Northern & Santa Fe Ry. v. White, 548 U.S. 53 (2006).

[51] S.D. Warren Co. v. Maine Bd. of Envtl. Prot., 547 U.S. 370 (2006).

[52] Utility Air Regulatory Group v. EPA, 134 S.Ct. 2427 (2014) (plurality and concurring opinions); Scialabba v. Cuellar de Osorio, 134 S.Ct. 2191 (2014) (plurality and concurring opinions); Zuni Pub. Sch. Dist. No. 89 v. Department of Educ., 550 U.S. 81 (2007) (majority and concurring opinions); National Cable & Telecommunications Ass'n v. Brand X Internet Servs., 545 U.S. 967 (2005); ABF Freight Sys., Inc. v. NLRB, 510 U.S. 317, 324 (1994); Sullivan v. Everhart, 494 U.S. 83, 88–89 (1990); K Mart Corp. v. Cartier, Inc., 486 U.S. 281, 291–92 (1988). The leading case is Chevron U.S.A., Inc. v. Natural Resources Defense Council, 467 U.S. 837 (1984).

[53] Long Island Care at Home, Ltd. v. Coke, 551 U.S. 158 (2007).

[54] Massachusetts v. EPA, 549 U.S. 497 (2007).

[55] City of Arlington, Texas v. FCC, 133 S.Ct. 1863 (2013) (deferential on this issue); Gonzales v. Oregon, 546 U.S. 243 (2006) (not so deferential).

in the statute.[56] The Court demands a clear statement authorizing agency constructions that press the envelope of constitutional validity.[57]

- *Seminole Rock* deference. Agency interpretation of its own regulations is controlling unless "plainly erroneous or inconsistent with the regulation."[58] Rule does not apply when agency rule merely "parrots" the statute,[59] or where agency interpretation has been unstable over time.[60]

- *Curtiss-Wright* deference. In matters of foreign affairs and national security, presidential or executive statutory interpretations enjoy a super-strong presumption of correctness.[61] (The executive is still bound by statutory and treaty directives.[62]) Similar deference for executive branch views of federal jurisdiction over foreign states.[63]

- Courts accord great weight to executive department interpretation of treaties.[64]

CONTINUITY IN LAW

- Super-strong presumption of correctness for statutory precedents,[65] sometimes including statutory precedents whose narrow holding has been overridden by Congress.[66] The super-strong rule against overruling statutory precedents is less applicable to the Sherman Act, which is a common law statute.[67]

---

[56] Utility Air Regulatory Group v. EPA, 134 S.Ct. 2427 (2104) (plurality and concurring opinions); Gonzales v. Oregon, 546 U.S. 243 (2006); FDA v. Brown & Williamson Tobacco Corp., 529 U.S. 120 (2000); MCI v. AT&T, 512 U.S. 218 (1994).

[57] Bond v. United States, 134 S.Ct. 2077 (2014); Wyeth v. Levine, 555 U.S. 555, 576 (2009); Rapanos v. United States, 547 U.S. 715 (2006) (plurality opinion); Edward J. DeBartolo Corp. v. Florida Gulf Coast Building & Constr. Trades Council, 485 U.S. 568, 575 (1988).

[58] Pliva, Inc. v. Mensing, 131 S.Ct. 2567, 2575-76 (2011); Chase Bank NA v. McCoy, 131 S.Ct. 871, 880 (2011); Coeur Alaska, Inc. v. Southeastern Alaska Conserv. Coun., 557 U.S. 261 (2009); Auer v. Robbins, 519 U.S. 452, 461–63 (1997); Thomas Jefferson Univ. v. Shalala, 512 U.S. 504, 512 (1994); Mullins Coal Co. v. Director, Office of Workers' Compensation Programs, 484 U.S. 135, 159 (1987). The leading case is Bowles v. Seminole Rock & Sand Co., 325 U.S. 410, 414 (1945). This canon has been questioned in Decker v. Northwest Envir. Def. Center, 133 S.Ct. 1326, 1339 (2013) (Scalia, J., concurring).

[59] Gonzales v. Oregon, 546 U.S. 243, 257 (2006).

[60] Commissioner v. Schleier, 515 U.S. 323 (1995); Bowen v. Georgetown Univ. Hosp., 488 U.S. 204 (1988).

[61] Hamdi v. Rumsfeld, 542 U.S. 507, 518 (2004) (plurality opinion of O'Connor, J.); id. at 580–81 (Thomas, J., concurring in part); Cheney v. U.S. Dist. Court, 542 U.S. 367 (2004); Crosby v. National Foreign Trade Council, 530 U.S. 363 (2000); Department of Navy v. Egan, 484 U.S. 518 (1988). The leading case is United States v. Curtiss-Wright Export Corp., 299 U.S. 304 (1936).

[62] Hamdan v. Rumsfeld, 548 U.S. 557 (2006).

[63] Republic of Austria v. Altmann, 541 U.S. 677, 689–90 (2004). But see Argentina v. NML Capital, 134 S.Ct. 2250 (2014) (ignoring this canon).

[64] Medellin v. Texas, 552 U.S. 491 (2008); Sanchez-Llamas v. Oregon, 548 U.S. 331 (2006); El Al Israel Airlines v. Tsui Yuan Tseng, 525 U.S. 155 (1999).

[65] Halliburton Co. v. Erica P. John Fund, Inc., 134 S.Ct. 2398 (2014); Michigan v. Bay Mills Indian Community, 134 S.Ct. 2024 (2014); CSX Transp., Inc. v. McBride, 131 S.Ct. 2630, 2641 (2011); John R. Sand & Gravel Co. v. United States, 552 U.S. 130 (2007); Hohn v. United States, 524 U.S. 236, 251 (1998); Neal v. United States, 516 U.S. 284 (1996); California v. FERC, 495 U.S. 490, 498–99 (1990); Patterson v. McLean Credit Union, 491 U.S. 164 (1989).

[66] Ledbetter v. Goodyear Tire & Rubber Co., 550 U.S. 618 (2007); Arlington Cent. Sch. Dist. Bd. of Educ. v. Murphy, 548 U.S. 291 (2006); Public Emp. Ret. Sys. of Ohio v. Betts, 492 U.S. 158 (1989). This canon is controversial within the Court, see *Ledbetter,* 550 U.S. at 652–54 (Ginsburg, J., dissenting), and, even more, within Congress, which angrily overrode both *Betts* and *Ledbetter.*

[67] Leegin Creative Leather Prods. v. PSKS, Inc., 551 U.S. 877 (2007); State Oil Co. v. Khan, 522 U.S. 3 (1997).

- Wrongly decided precedents that are also inconsistent with recent legal developments can be overruled.[68]

- Where a court decision follows an agency interpretation filling a gap in the law left by Congress *(Chevron),* a revised agency interpretation through rulemaking is not barred by *stare decisis.*[69]

- Presumption of continuity: Congress does not create discontinuities in legal rights and obligations without some clear statement.[70]

- Presumption against repeals by implication.[71] But where there is a clear repugnancy between a more recent statutory scheme and an earlier one, partial repeal will be inferred.[72]

- Presumption against hiding elephants in mouseholes: Congress usually does not alter the fundamental details of a regulatory scheme in vague or ancillary provisions.[73]

- Presumption that Congress uses same term consistently in different statutes.[74]

- Presumption that statutes be interpreted consistent with international law and treaties.[75] But international agreements do not trump the plain meaning of federal statutes.[76]

- Borrowed statute rule: when Congress borrows a statute, it adopts by implication interpretations placed on that statute,[77] absent indication to the contrary.[78]

- *In pari materia* rule: when similar statutory provisions are found in comparable statutory schemes, interpreters should presumptively apply them the same way.[79]

---

[68] Leegin Creative Leather Prods. v. PSKS, Inc., 551 U.S. 877 (2007); Bowles v. Russell, 127 S.Ct. 2360 (2007); Rodriguez de Quijas v. Shearson/American Express, Inc., 490 U.S. 477, 480–81 (1989).

[69] National Cable & Telecomm. Serv. v. Brand X Internet Servs., 545 U.S. 967 (2005); Christensen v. Harris County, 529 U.S. 576, 589 (2000) (Souter, J., concurring); United States v. Watts, 519 U.S. 148 (1997) (Breyer, J., concurring). This canon does not apply when it appears that a court has closed off agency discretion. United States v. Home Concrete & Supply, LLC, 132 S.Ct. 1836 (2012)

[70] POM Wonderful LLC v. Coca-Cola Co., 134 S.Ct. 2228 (2014); Pacific Operators Offshire, LLC v. Valladolid, 132 S.Ct. 680 (2012) (concurring opinion); Green v. Bock Laundry Mach. Co., 490 U.S. 504, 521–22 (1989); Finley v. United States, 490 U.S. 545, 554 (1989).

[71] POM Wonderful LLC v. Coca-Cola Co., 134 S.Ct. 2228 (2014); Hamdan v. Rumsfeld, 548 U.S. 557 (2006); Granholm v. Heald, 544 U.S. 460 (2005); Branch v. Smith, 538 U.S. 254, 273 (2003); Pittsburgh & Lake Erie R.R. v. Railway Labor Executives' Ass'n, 491 U.S. 490, 509 (1989); Traynor v. Turnage, 485 U.S. 535, 547–48 (1988). The leading case is Morton v. Mancari, 417 U.S. 535 (1974).

[72] Credit Suisse Securities (USA) LLC v. Billing, 551 U.S. 264 (2007).

[73] Gonzales v. Oregon, 546 U.S. 243, 267 (2006); Whitman v. American Trucking Ass'ns, Inc., 531 U.S. 457, 468 (2001); FDA v. Brown & Williamson Tobacco Corp., 529 U.S. 120, 160 (2000).

[74] Hawaiian Airlines v. Norris, 512 U.S. 246, 254 (1994); Smith v. United States, 508 U.S. 223, 234–35 (1993); Pierce v. Underwood, 487 U.S. 552 (1988).

[75] Spector v. Norwegian Cruise Line Ltd., 545 U.S. 119 (2005) (majority and concurring opinions); Hamdi v. Rumsfeld, 542 U.S. 507 (2004) (plurality opinion); INS v. Cardoza-Fonseca, 480 U.S. 421 (1987) (strong presumption when statute is implementing an international agreement).

[76] Société Nationale Industrielle Aerospatiale v. U.S. Dist. Ct., 482 U.S. 522, 538–39 (1987).

[77] Molzof v. United States, 502 U.S. 301, 307 (1992); Metropolitan Life Ins. Co. v. Taylor, 481 U.S. 58, 65–66 (1987).

[78] Shannon v. United States, 512 U.S. 573, 581 (1994).

- Re-enactment rule: when Congress re-enacts a statute, it incorporates settled interpretations of the re-enacted statute.[80] The rule is inapplicable when there is no settled standard Congress could have known.[81]

- Acquiescence rules: consistent agency or Supreme Court interpretation known to Congress is presumed correct.[82] Also, consider unbroken line of lower court decisions interpreting statute, but do not give them decisive weight.[83]

EXTRINSIC LEGISLATIVE SOURCES

- Statutory history (the formal evolution of a statute, as Congress amends it over the years) is always potentially relevant.[84]

- Consider legislative history (the internal evolution of a statute before enactment) if the statute is ambiguous.[85] Legislative history may also be useful to confirm statutory plain meaning.[86]

- Committee reports (especially conference committee reports reflecting the understanding of both House and Senate) are the most authoritative legislative history,[87] but cannot trump a textual plain meaning,[88] and should not be relied on if they are themselves ambiguous or imprecise.[89]

---

[79] Hardt v. Reliance Standard Life Ins. Co., 560 U.S. 242 (2010); Ledbetter v. Goodyear Tire & Rubber Co., 550 U.S. 618 (2007) (finding NLRA but not EPA analogous to Title VII for limitations purposes).

[80] Merck & Co. v. Reynolds, 559 U.S. 633 (2010); Davis v. United States, 495 U.S. 472, 482 (1990); Pierce v. Underwood, 487 U.S. 552 (1988).

[81] Jama v. Immigration & Customs Enforcement, 543 U.S. 335 (2005).

[82] Michigan v. Bay Mills Indian Community, 134 S.Ct. 2024 (2014); Zuni Pub. Sch. Dist. No. 89 v. Department of Educ., 550 U.S. 81 (2007) (agency interpretation); FDA v. Brown & Williamson Tobacco Corp., 529 U.S. 120 (2000) (agency).

[83] Gonzalez v. Crosby, 545 U.S. 524 (2005); General Dynamics Land Sys., Inc. v. Cline, 540 U.S. 581 (2004); National Archives & Records Admin. v. Favish, 541 U.S. 157 (2004); Monessen Sw. Ry. Co. v. Morgan, 486 U.S. 330, 338–39 (1988).

[84] Burwell v. Hobby Lobby Stores, Inc., 134 S.Ct. 2751 (2014); Powerex Corp. v. Reliant Energy Servs., Inc., 551 U.S. 224 (2007); Ballard v. Commissioner, 544 U.S. 40 (2005). Unlike reference to internal legislative materials, this canon is *not* controversial within the Court.

[85] Bond v. United States, 134 S.Ct. 2077 (2014); Safeco Ins. Co. of Am. v. Burr, 551 U.S. 47 (2007); Zuni Pub. Sch. Dist. No. 89 v. Department of Educ., 550 U.S. 81 (2007); Gonzales v. Oregon, 546 U.S. 243, 257–58 (2006); Rumsfeld v. Forum for Academic & Institutional Rights, 547 U.S. 47 (2006); Koons Buick Pontiac GMC, Inc. v. Nigh, 543 U.S. 50, 62–64 (2004); id. at 65–66 (Stevens, J., concurring); FDA v. Brown & Williamson Tobacco Corp., 529 U.S. 120 (2000); Babbitt v. Sweet Home Chapter of Communities for a Great Oregon, 515 U.S. 687 (1995); Wisconsin Pub. Intervenor v. Mortier, 501 U.S. 597, 610 n.4 (1991). This canon is controversial within the Court. See id. at 616–17 (Scalia, J., concurring in the judgment). Cf. James v. United States, 127 S.Ct. 1586, 1593 (2007) (legislative history not useful if provision is obsolete).

[86] Loughrin v. United States, 134 S.Ct. 2384 (2014); Carr v. United States, 560 U.S. 438 (2010); Samantar v. Yousuf, 560 U.S. 305 (2010); Shinseki v. Sanders, 556 U.S. 396, 406-07 (2009); United States v. Ressam, 553 U.S. 272, 275-76 (2008).

[87] Brown v. Plata, 131 S.Ct. 1910, 1937 (2011); Tellabs, Inc. v. Makor Issues & Rights, Ltd., 551 U.S. 308 (2007); Rumsfeld v. Forum for Academic & Institutional Rights, 547 U.S. 47 (2006); Cherokee Nation of Oklahoma v. Leavitt, 543 U.S. 631 (2005); Intel Corp. v. Advanced Micro Devices, Inc., 542 U.S. 241 (2004); Jones v. R.R. Donnelley & Sons Co., 541 U.S. 369 (2004); Boeing Co. v. United States, 537 U.S. 437 (2003); Johnson v. DeGrandy, 512 U.S. 997, 1010–11 & n.9 (1994).

[88] Arlington Cent. Sch. Dist. Bd. of Educ. v. Murphy, 548 U.S. 291 (2006) (majority and concurring opinions); City of Chicago v. Environmental Def. Fund, 511 U.S. 328, 337 (1994); American Hosp. Ass'n v. NLRB, 499 U.S. 606, 613 (1991). This canon is controversial within the Court. See *Murphy,* 126 S.Ct. at 2466–68 (Breyer, J., dissenting).

[89] Marrama v. Citizens Bank of Mass., 549 U.S. 365 (2007); Small v. United States, 544 U.S. 385 (2005).

- Committee report language that cannot be tied to a specific statutory provision cannot be credited.[90] House and Senate reports inconsistent with one another should be discounted.[91]

- Caution against interpretation considered and rejected by floor vote of a chamber of Congress or committee.[92] Cautionary principle inapplicable when it is not clear why Congress rejected the proposal.[93]

- Floor statements, especially by statutory sponsors, can be used to confirm apparent meaning.[94]

- Public give-and-take between Members of Congress and executive department drafters or sponsors during committee hearings are relevant if they illuminate a shared meaning of statutory language by the participants closest to the process.[95]

- The "dog didn't bark" canon: presumption that prior legal rule should be retained if no one in legislative deliberations even mentioned the rule or discussed any changes in the rule.[96]

- Views of a subsequent Congress are a hazardous basis for inferring the intent of an earlier one,[97] but are sometimes relevant.[98] Subsequent legislation clearly incorporating these views is relevant and persuasive.[99]

SUBSTANTIVE POLICY CANONS

CONSTITUTION-BASED CANONS

- Avoidance canon: avoid interpretations that would render a statute unconstitutional *or* that would raise serious constitutional difficulties.[100]

---

[90]   Shannon v. United States, 512 U.S. 573, 583 (1994).

[91]   Moreau v. Klevenhagen, 508 U.S. 22, 26 (1993).

[92]   Mohamad v. Palestinian Auth., 132 S.Ct. 1702 (2012); Hamdan v. Rumsfeld, 548 U.S. 557 (2006); Doe v. Chao, 540 U.S. 614 (2004); F. Hoffmann-LaRoche, Ltd. v. Empagran S.A., 540 U.S. 1088 (2004); FDA v. Brown & Williamson Tobacco Corp., 529 U.S. 120, 144 (2000); Department of Revenue v. ACF Indus., 510 U.S. 332, 345–36 (1994).

[93]   Safeco Ins. Co. of Am. v. Burr, 551 U.S. 47 (2007); Rapanos v. United States, 547 U.S. 715 (2006) (plurality opinion); Solid Waste Agency v. Army Corps of Eng'rs, 531 U.S. 159, 169 (2001).

[94]   Entergy Corp. v. Riverkeeper, Inc., 556 U.S. 208, 230-35 (2009) (Breyer, J., concurring); Hamdan v. Rumsfeld, 548 U.S. 557 (2006); Department of Revenue v. ACF Indus., Inc., 510 U.S. 332, 345–46 (1994).

[95]   General Dynamics Land Sys., Inc. v. Cline, 540 U.S. 581 (2004); FDA v. Brown & Williamson Tobacco Corp., 529 U.S. 120 (2000); Hagen v. Utah, 510 U.S. 399, 418 (1994); Darby v. Cisneros, 509 U.S. 137, 147–51 (1993).

[96]   Zuni Pub. Sch. Dist. No. 89 v. Department of Educ., 550 U.S. 81 (2007); Chisom v. Roemer, 501 U.S. 380, 396 & n.23 (1991).

[97]   Bruesewitz v. Wyeth LLC, 131 S.Ct. 1068, 1081-82 (2011); Massachusetts v. EPA, 549 U.S. 497 (2007); Doe v. Chao, 540 U.S. 614 (2004); Solid Waste Agency v. Army Corps of Eng'rs, 531 U.S. 159, 170 (2001); Sullivan v. Finkelstein, 496 U.S. 617, 628 n.8 (1990).

[98]   Musick, Peeler & Garrett v. Employers Ins. of Wassau, 508 U.S. 286, 293 (1993). This canon is controversial within the Court. Sullivan v. Finkelstein, 496 U.S. 617, 631–32 (1990) (Scalia, J., concurring in part).

[99]   FDA v. Brown & Williamson Tobacco Corp., 529 U.S. 120, 144 (2000); Babbitt v. Sweet Home Chapter of Communities for a Great Oregon, 515 U.S. 687 (1995); Franklin v. Gwinnett County Pub. Sch., 503 U.S. 60 (1990); id. at 77–78 (Scalia, J., concurring in the judgment); Bowen v. Yuckert, 482 U.S. 137, 149–51 (1987).

[100] Bond v. United States, 134 S.Ct. 2077 (2014); Brown v. Plata, 131 S.Ct. 1910, 1928-29, 1937 (2011); Northwest Austin Mun. Utility Dist. No. 1 v. Holder, 557 U.S. 193 (2010); Rapanos v. United States, 547 U.S. 715 (2006) (plurality opinion); Cherokee Nation of Oklahoma v. Leavitt, 543 U.S. 631 (2005); Zadvydas v.

Inapplicable if statute would clearly survive constitutional attack, or if statutory text is clear.[101]

1.   *Separation of Powers*

- Super-strong rule against congressional interference with President's inherent powers, his executive authority.[102] Avoid interpretations whereby judges would interfere with foreign affairs.[103]

- Rule against review of President's core executive actions for "abuse of discretion. "[104]

- Where Congress appropriates money without specific textual restrictions, the executive has leeway as to its expenditure, unlimited by more informal signals.[105]

- Rule of special treatment of President and Vice-President as litigants, affording them special privileges so as not to interfere with their official duties.[106]

- Rule against congressional curtailment of the judiciary' s "inherent powers" or its· "equity" powers.[107]

- Rule against congressional expansion of Article III injury in fact to include intangible and procedural injuries.[108]

- Presumption that Congress does not delegate authority without sufficient guidelines.[109]

- Presumption against "implying" causes of action into federal statutes.[110]

- Presumption that U.S. law conforms to U.S. international obligations.[111] Presumption that Congress takes account of the legitimate sovereign interests of other nations when it writes American laws.[112]

Davis, 533 U.S. 678, 696–99 (2001); Public Citizen v. United States Dep't of Justice, 491 U.S. 440, 465–66 (1989); Edward J. Debartolo Corp. v. Florida Gulf Coast Building & Constr. Trades Council, 485 U.S. 568, 575 (1988).

[101] Stern v. Marshall, 131 S.Ct. 2594, 2607-08 (2011); Peretz v. United States, 501 U.S. 923, 932 (1991); Rust v. Sullivan, 500 U.S. 173, 182 (1991).

[102] Department of Navy v. Egan, 484 U.S. 518, 527 (1988); Morrison v. Olson, 487 U.S. 654, 682–83 (1988); Carlucci v. Doe, 488 U.S. 93, 99 (1988); United States v. Johnson, 481 U.S. 681, 690–91 (1987).

[103] Sosa v. Alvarez-Machain, 542 U.S. 692 (2004).

[104] Franklin v. Massachusetts, 505 U.S. 788, 800–01 (1991).

[105] Cherokee Nation of Oklahoma v. Leavitt, 543 U.S. 631 (2005); Lincoln v. Vigil, 508 U.S. 182, 191 (1993).

[106] Cheney v. U.S. Dist. Court, 542 U.S. 367 (2004).

[107] Brown v. Plata, 131 S.Ct. 1910, 1928-29, 1936-37 (2011); Chambers v. Nasco, Inc., 501 U.S. 32, 43–44 (1991).

[108] Lujan v. Defenders of Wildlife, 504 U.S. 555, 557–61 (1992); id. at 579–80 (Kennedy, J., concurring in part).

[109] Mistretta v. United States, 488 U.S. 361, 373 n.7 (1989).

[110] Virginia Bancshares, Inc. v. Sandberg, 501 U.S. 1083, 1102–05 (1991); Thompson v. Thompson, 484 U.S. 174, 179 (1988).

[111] Hamdan v. Rumsfeld, 548 U.S. 557 (2006) (majority and concurring opinions); Sale v. Haitian Centers Council, 509 U.S. 155, 173–74 (1993).

[112] Samantar v. Yousuf, 560 U.S. 305 (2010); Microsoft Corp. v. AT&T, 550 U.S. 437 (2007); F. Hoffmann-LaRoche, Ltd. v. Empagran S.A., 542 U.S. 155, 164 (2004).

- Rule against congressional abrogation of Indian treaty rights.[113]

- Presumption favoring severability of unconstitutional provisions.[114]

2. *Federalism*

- Super-strong rule against federal invasion of "core state functions."[115] Strong presumption against statutory interpretations that would alter the federal-state balance.[116]

- Super-strong rule against federal abrogation of states' Eleventh Amendment immunity from lawsuits in federal courts.[117] Eleventh Amendment rules does not apply to municipalities and counties[118]

- Super-strong rule against inferring conditions on federal grants to the states under the Spending Clause; conditions must be expressed clearly and unambiguously.[119] Sometimes the Court will require less than targeted statutory language, so long as states are reasonably on notice of conditions, as through agency guidances to that effect.[120]

- Presumption against federal preemption of traditional state regulation.[121]

- Presumption trumped if clear statutory language or the statutory purpose requires preemption.[122]

---

[113] Michigan v. Bay Mills Indian Community, 134 S.Ct. 2024 (2014); South Dakota v. Bourland, 508 U.S. 679, 687 (1993).

[114] Executive Benefits Ins. Agency v. Arkison, 134 S.Ct. 2165 (2014); National Fed. Indep. Business v. Sebelius, 132 S.Ct. 2566 (2012) (plurality and concurring opinions). The leading case is Alaska Airlines, Inc. v. Brock, 480 U.S. 678, 684 (1987).

[115] Rapanos v. United States, 548 U.S. 715 (2006) (plurality opinion); Nixon v. Missouri Municipal League, 541 U.S. 125 (2004); BFP v. Resolution Trust Corp., 511 U.S. 531, 544 (1994); Gregory v. Ashcroft, 501 U.S. 452, 461–64 (1991).

[116] Bond v. United States, 134 S.Ct. 2077 (2014); Gonzales v. Oregon, 546 U.S. 243 (2006); Owasso Indep. Sch. Dist. v. Falvo, 534 U.S. 426 (2002); Raygor v. Regents of the Univ. of Minn., 534 U.S. 533 (2002); BFP v. Resolution Trust Corp., 511 U.S. 531, 544 (1994); Gregory v. Ashcroft, 501 U.S. 452, 461–64 (1991); Will v. Michigan Dep't of State Police, 491 U.S. 58, 65 (1989).

[117] Nevada Dep't of Human Resources v. Hibbs, 538 U.S. 721 (2003) (finding abrogation); Raygor v. Regents of the Univ. of Minn., 534 U.S. 533 (2001); Blatchford v. Native Village of Noatak, 501 U.S. 775, 779 (1991); Dellmuth v. Muth, 491 U.S. 223, 227–28 (1989); Pennsylvania v. Union Gas, 491 U.S. 1, 7 (1989) (finding abrogation). The leading case is Atascadero State Hosp. v. Scanlon, 473 U.S. 234, 241 (1985).

[118] Jinks v. Richland County, 538 U.S. 456 (2003).

[119] Arlington Cent. Sch. Dist. Bd. of Educ. v. Murphy, 548 U.S. 291 (2006); Barnes v. Gorman, 536 U.S. 181 (2002); Gonzaga Univ. v. Doe, 536 U.S. 273 (2002); Blessing v. Freestone, 520 U.S. 329 (1997); Suter v. Artist M., 503 U.S. 347 (1991). The leading case is Pennhurst State Sch. & Hosp. v. Halderman, 451 U.S. 1 (1981).

[120] Davis v. Monroe County Bd. of Educ., 526 U.S. 629 (1999); Franklin v. Gwinnett County Pub. Sch., 503 U.S. 60 (1992).

[121] CTS Corp. v. Waldburger, 134 S.Ct. 2175, 2188-89 (2014); Wyeth v. Levine, 555 U.S. 555 (2008); Altria Group, Inc. v. Good, 555 U.S. 70, 77 (2008); Bates v. Dow Agrosciences LLC, 544 U.S. 431 (2005); Rush Prudential HMO v. Moran, 536 U.S. 355 (2002); Medtronic, Inc. v. Lohr, 518 U.S. 470 (1996); Hawaiian Airlines v. Norris, 512 U.S. 246, 252 (1994); BFP v. Resolution Trust Corp., 511 U.S. 531, 544 (1994); Cipollone v. Liggett Group, Inc., 505 U.S. 504 (1992); California v. ARC Am. Corp., 490 U.S. 93, 100–01 (1989); Rose v. Rose, 481 U.S. 619, 635–36 (1987) (O'Connor, J., concurring in part).

[122] FTC v. Phoebe Putney Health Sys., Inc., 133 S.Ct. 1003 (2013); National Meat Ass'n v. Harris, 132 S.Ct. 965 (2012); Riegel v. Medtronic, Inc., 552 U.S. 312 (2008); Geier v. Honda Motor Co., 529 U.S. 861 (2000).

- Presumption against federal regulation of intergovernmental taxation by the states.[123]

- Presumption against application of federal statutes to state and local political processes,[124] except when statutory plain meaning or other factors counsel in favor of such application.[125]

- Presumption against congressional derogation from state's land claims based upon its entry into Union on an "equal footing" with all other states.[126] Presumption that upon statehood, the new state acquires title to the land under navigable rivers.[127]

- Rule against federal habeas review of state criminal convictions unless prisoner has properly exhausted state remedies.[128] Rule against federal habeas review of state criminal convictions supported by independent state ground.[129] Presumption of finality of state convictions for purposes of habeas review.[130]

- Narrow construction of federal court jurisdictional grants that would siphon cases away from state courts.[131]

- Rule against reading an ambiguous federal statute to authorize states to engage in activities that would violate the dormant commerce clause.[132]

- Rule favoring concurrent state and federal court jurisdiction over federal claims.[133]

- Super-strong rule that Indian tribes retain their sovereign immunity, unless Congress has unequivocally negated it.[134]

- Presumption that states can tax activities within their borders, including Indian tribal activities,[135] but also presumption that states cannot tax on Indian lands.[136]

---

[123] Davis v. Michigan Dep't of Treasury, 489 U.S. 803, 810 (1989).

[124] City of Columbia v. Omni Outdoor Advertising, Inc., 499 U.S. 365, 373 (1991); McCormick v. United States, 500 U.S. 257, 269 n.6 (1988); McNally v. United States, 483 U.S. 350, 361 n.9 (1987).

[125] Evans v. United States, 504 U.S. 255, 270–71 (1992).

[126] Utah Div'n of State Lands v. United States, 482 U.S. 193, 196 (1987).

[127] Idaho v. United States, 533 U.S. 262 (2001).

[128] O'Sullivan v. Boerckel, 526 U.S. 838, 845 (1999).

[129] Sanchez-Llamas v. Oregon, 548 U.S. 331 (2006); Massaro v. United States, 538 U.S. 500, 504 (2003); Wright v. West, 505 U.S. 277, 289 (1992); Coleman v. Thompson, 501 U.S. 722, 729 (1991).

[130] Felkner v. Jackson, 132 S.Ct. 1305 (2011); Hardy v. Cross, 132 S.Ct. 490 (2011); Brecht v. Abrahamson, 507 U.S. 619, 635–38 (1993).

[131] Smith v. Bayer Corp., 131 S.Ct. 2368 (2011); Kokkonen v. Guardian Life Ins. Co. of Am., 511 U.S. 375, 377 (1994); Finely v. United States, 490 U.S. 545, 552–54 (1989).

[132] Granholm v. Heald, 544 U.S. 460 (2005); Wyoming v. Oklahoma, 502 U.S. 437, 458 (1992).

[133] Mims v. Arrow Financial Serv., LLC, 132 S.Ct. 740 (2012); Tafflin v. Levitt, 493 U.S. 455, 458 (1990); Yellow Freight Sys., Inc. v. Donnelly, 494 U.S. 820, 823 (1990).

[134] Michigan v. Bay Mills Indian Community, 134 S.Ct. 2024 (2014); Kiowa Tribe of Oklahoma v. Manufacturing Technologies, Inc., 523 U.S. 751 (1998).

[135] Atkinson Trading Co. v. Shirley, 532 U.S. 645 (2001); Cotton Petroleum Corp. v. New Mexico, 490 U.S. 163, 174 (1989).

[136] Oklahoma Tax Comm'n v. Sac and Fox Nation, 508 U.S. 114 (1993); County of Yakima v. Confederated Tribes & Bands of the Yakima Indian Nation, 502 U.S. 251, 268 (1992).

- Principle that federal equitable remedies must consider interests of state and local authorities.[137]

- Presumption that Congress borrows state statutes of limitations for federal statutory schemes.[138]

3. Due Process

- Rule of lenity: rule against applying punitive sanctions if there is ambiguity as to underlying criminal liability or criminal penalty.[139] Rule is trumped when Congress clearly intended to criminalize the conduct in question.[140]

- Rule of lenity may apply to civil sanction that is punitive or when underlying liability is criminal.[141]

- Rule against criminal penalties imposed without showing of specific intent.[142] But willfulness requirement in civil sanction cases typically includes to reckless conduct as well.[143]

- Super-strong rule against implied congressional abrogation or repeal of habeas corpus.[144]

- Rule against interpreting statutes to be retroactive,[145] even if statute is curative or restorative.[146]

- Rule against interpreting statutes to deny a right to jury trial.[147]

- Presumption in favor of judicial review.[148]

- Presumption against pre-enforcement challenges to implementation.[149]

---

[137] Raygor v. Regents of the Univ. of Minn., 534 U.S. 533 (2002); Spallone v. United States, 493 U.S. 265, 276 (1990).

[138] Wallace v. Kato, 549 U.S. 384 (2007); Lampf, Pleva, Lipkind, Prupis & Petigrow v. Gilbertson, 501 U.S. 350, 355–56 (1991).

[139] Burrage v. United States, 134 S.Ct. 881 (2014) (majority and concurring opinions); Skilling v. United States, 561 U.S. 358 (2010); Arthur Andersen LLP v. United States, 544 U.S. 696 (2005); Cleveland v. United States, 531 U.S. 12 (2000) (explaining both notice and nondelegation rationales); United States v. Aguilar, 515 U.S. 593 (1995); United States v. Granderson, 511 U.S. 39 (1994); United States v. Kozminski, 487 U.S. 931, 939 (1988). The leading case is United States v. Bass, 404 U.S. 336, 347-49 (1971).

[140] Abramski v. United States, 134 S.Ct. 2259 (2014); Robers v. United States, 134 S.Ct. 1854 (2014); Muscarello v. United States, 524 U.S. 125 (1998); Chapman v. United States, 500 U.S. 453, 463–64 (1991).

[141] Crandon v. United States, 494 U.S. 152, 158 (1990). The Court applies this canon very unevenly. E.g., Babbitt v. Sweet Home Chapter of Communities for a Great Oregon, 515 U.S. 687 (1995).

[142] Arthur Andersen LLP v. United States, 544 U.S. 696 (2005); Bryan v. United States, 524 U.S. 184, 191–92 (1998); Ratzlaf v. United States, 510 U.S. 135, 137 (1994); Cheek v. United States, 498 U.S. 192, 200–01 (1991).

[143] Safeco Ins. Co. of Am. v. Burr, 551 U.S. 47 (2007); McLaughlin v. Richland Shoe Co., 486 U.S. 128, 132–33 (1988).

[144] Demore v. Kim, 538 U.S. 510 (2003); INS v. St. Cyr, 533 U.S. 289 (2001).

[145] Vartelas v. Holder, 132 S.Ct. 1479 (2012); Fernandez-Vargas v. Gonzales, 548 U.S. 30 (2006). The leading case is Landgraf v. USI Film Prods., 51 I.U.S. 244 (1994).

[146] Rivers v. Roadway Express, 511 U.S. 298 (1994).

[147] Gomez v. United States, 490 U.S. 858, 863 (1989).

[148] Sackett v. EPA, 132 S.Ct. 1367 (2012); Demore v. Kim, 538 U.S. 510 (2003); Webster v. Doe, 486 U.S. 592 (1988).

[149] Thunder Basin Coal Co. v. Reich, 510 U.S. 200, 208–10 (1994).

- Presumption against exhaustion of remedies requirement for lawsuit to enforce constitutional rights.[150]

- Presumption that judgments will not be binding upon persons not party to adjudication.[151]

- Presumption against national service of process unless authorized by Congress.[152]

- Presumption against foreclosure of private enforcement of important federal rights.[153]

- Presumption that preponderance of the evidence standard applies in civil cases.[154]

COMMON LAW-BASED CANONS

- Presumption in favor of following common law usage and rules where Congress has employed words or concepts with well-settled common law traditions.[155] Presumption inapplicable when Congress has directly addressed the issue[156] or when common law usage is inconsistent with statutory purpose.[157]

- Rule against extraterritorial application of U.S. law.[158] Presumption that Congress legislates with domestic concerns in mind.[159]

- American laws apply to foreign-flag ships in U.S. territory and affecting Americans, but will not apply to the "internal affairs" of a foreign-flag ship unless there is a clear statutory statement to that effect.[160]

---

[150] McCarthy. v. Madigan, 503 U.S. 140, 146–49 (1992).

[151] Martin v. Wilks, 490 U.S. 755, 761–62 (1989).

[152] Omni Capital Int'l v. Rudolf Wolff & Co., 484 U.S. 97, 107–08 (1987).

[153] Wilder v. Virginia Hosp. Ass'n, 496 U.S. 498, 520–21 (1990). This presumption is probably no longer viable. See Gonzaga Univ. v. Doe, 536 U.S. 273 (2002).

[154] Grogan v. Garner, 498 U.S. 279, 286 (1991).

[155] CTS Corp. v. Waldburger, 134 S.Ct. 2175 (2014) (CERCLA); Wal-Mart Stores v. Dukes, 131 S.Ct. 2541, 2557-58 (2011) (FRCP); Permanent Mission of India to the United Nations v. City of New York, 551 U.S. 193 (2007) (FSIA); Wallace v. Kato, 549 U.S. 384 (2007) (§ 1983); Dura Pharmaceuticals, Inc. v. Broudo, 544 U.S. 336 (2005) (§ 10(b)); Stewart v. Dutra Constr. Co., 543 U.S. 481, 487 (2005) (LWHCA); United States v. Texas, 507 U.S. 529, 534 (1993) (Debt Collection Act); Nationwide Mut. Ins. Co. v. Darden, 503 U.S. 318 (1992) (ERISA); Kamen v. Kemper Fin. Servs., Inc., 500 U.S. 90, 98–99 (1991) (Investment Company Act); Community for Creative Nonviolence v. Reid, 490 U.S. 730, 739–40 (1989) (Copyright Act). See also Pacific Operators Offshore, LLC v. Valladolid, 132 S.Ct. 680, 691-94 (2012) (Scalia, J., concurring in the judgment) (presuming that Congress intended an easy-to-apply common law standard rather than a novel standard that would be harder to administer).

[156] Pasquantino v. United States, 544 U.S. 349, 356 (2005).

[157] CSX Transp., Inc. v. McBride, 131 S.Ct. 2630 (2011); Taylor v. United States, 495 U.S. 575, 593–95 (1990).

[158] Morrison v. National Australia National Bank Ltd., 561 U.S. 247 (2010); Microsoft Corp. v. AT&T, 550 U.S. 437 (2007); F. Hoffman-LaRoche, Ltd. v. Empangran S.A., 540 U.S. 1088 (2004); Sale v. Haitian Centers Council, 509 U.S. 155 (1993); EEOC v. Arabian Am. Oil Co., 499 U.S. 244, 248 (1991); Argentine Republic v. Amerada Hess Shipping Corp., 488 U.S. 428, 440 (1989).

[159] Morrison v. National Australia National Bank Ltd., 561 U.S. 247 (2010); Small v. United States, 544 U.S. 385 (2005); Smith v. United States, 507 U.S. 197, 204 n.5 (1993).

[160] Spector v. Norwegian Cruise Line Ltd., 545 U.S. 119 (2005).

- Super-strong rule against waivers of United States sovereign immunity.[161] Even if there is a waiver of immunity from suit, the scope of the immunity will be narrowly read.[162]

- Super-strong rule against congressional abrogation of state immunity from suit.[163] Common law rule does not apply to counties and other subdivisions created by the states.[164]

- Rule that debts to the United States shall bear interest.[165]

- Presumption against conveyance of U.S. public lands to private parties.[166]

- Rule presuming against attorney fee-shifting in federal courts and federal statutes,[167] and narrow construction of fee-shifting statutes to exclude costs that are not explicitly identified.[168]

- Presumption that jury finds facts, judge declares law.[169]

- Rule presuming that law takes effect on date of enactment.[170]

- Presumption that public (government) interest not be prejudiced by negligence of federal officials.[171]

- Presumption that federal agencies launched into commercial world with power to "sue and be sued" are not entitled to sovereign immunity.[172] Presumption favoring enforcement of forum selection clauses.[173] Presumption that federal judgment has preclusive effect in state administrative proceedings.[174]

- Presumption importing common law immunities into federal civil rights statutes.[175]

---

[161] Richlin Security Serv. Co. v. Chertoff, 553 U.S. 571, 589 (2008); United States v. White Mt. Apache Tribe, 537 U.S. 465, 472–73 (2003); United States v. Nordic Village; Inc., 503 U.S. 30 (1992); Ardestani v. INS, 502 U.S. 129 (1991); United States v. Dalm, 494 U.S. 596, 608 (1990).

[162] FAA v. Cooper, 132 S.Ct. 1441 (2012).

[163] Alden v. Maine, 527 U.S. 706, 713 (1999) (announcing that state immunity from suit was based on common law, not just Eleventh Amendment). This canon is controversial within the Court. See id. at 760 (Souter, J., dissenting).

[164] Northern Ins. Co. of N.Y. v. Chatham County, 547 U.S. 189 (2006).

[165] United States v. Texas, 507 U.S. 529 (1993).

[166] Utah Div. of State Lands v. United States, 482 U.S. 193, 197–98 (1987).

[167] Key Tronic Corp. v. United States, 511 U.S. 809 (1994). The leading case is Alyeska Pipeline Serv. Co. v. Wilderness Society, 421 U.S. 240 (1975).

[168] Arlington Cent. Sch. Dist. Bd. of Educ. v. Murphy, 548 U.S. 291 (2006); West Virginia Univ. Hosps., Inc. v. Casey, 499 U.S. 83 (1991). But cf. Octane Fitness, LLC v. Icon Health & Fitness, Inc., 134 S.Ct. 1749 (2014) (presuming that fee-shifting statutes reach beyond common law bases for fee shifting, such as bad faith or contempt).

[169] Shannon v. United States, 512 U.S. 573 (1994).

[170] Gozlon-Peretz v. United States, 498 U.S. 395 (1991).

[171] United States v. Montalvo-Murillo, 495 U.S. 711, 717–18 (1990).

[172] Loeffler v. Frank, 486 U.S. 549, 554–55 (1988).

[173] Carnival Cruise Lines v. Shute, 499 U.S. 585, 589 (1991); Stewart Org. v. Ricoh Corp., 487 U.S. 22, 33 (1988) (Kennedy, J., concurring).

[174] Astoria Fed. Sav. & Loan Ass'n v. Solimino, 501 U.S. 104, 108 (1991).

[175] Rehberg v. Paulk, 132 S.Ct. 1497 (2012); Burns v. Reed, 500 U.S. 478, 484–85 (1991); Forrester v. White, 484 U.S. 219, 225–26 (1988).

STATUTE-BASED CANONS

- Purposive construction: interpret ambiguous statutes so as best to carry out their statutory purposes.[176] Caution: no law pursues its purpose at all costs, and text-based limits on a law's scope are part of its "purpose.[177]

- Anti-Messiness Rule: avoid interpretations that create "messy" (vague, obscure, muddy) rules of law that will be hard to implement.[178]

1. *General canons*

- Presumption against repeals by implication.[179] But where there is a clear repugnancy between a more recent statutory scheme and an earlier one, partial repeal will be inferred.[180]

- *In pari materia:* similar statutes should be interpreted similarly,[181] unless legislative history or purpose suggests material differences.[182]

- Presumption *against* private right of action unless statute expressly provides one,[183] [183] but once recognized a private right of action carries with it all traditional remedies.[184] Regulations cannot create a private cause of action not authorized by the statute.[185]

- A precisely drawn, detailed statute preempts or governs a more general statute or remedies.[186]

- When Congress enacts a specific remedy when no remedy was clearly recognized previously, the new remedy is regarded as exclusive.[187]

---

[176] ABC, Inc. v. Aereo, Inc., 134 S.Ct. 2498 (2014); Clark v. Rameker, 134 S.Ct. 2242 (2014); Abramski, v. United States, 134 S.Ct. 2259 (2014); CSX Transp., Inc. v. McBride, 131 S.Ct. 2630, 2641 (2011); Zuni Pub. Sch. Dist. No. 89 v. Department of Educ., 550 U.S. 81 (2007); Burlington Northern & Santa Fe Ry. v. White, 126 S.Ct. 2405, 2412–14 (2006); Jones v. R.R. Donnelley & Sons Co., 541 U.S. 369 (2004); PGA Tour, Inc. v. Martin, 532 U.S. 661 (2001); Reves v. Ernst & Young, 494 U.S. 56, 60–61 (1990). See also POM Wonderful LLC v. Coca-Cola Co., 134 S.Ct. 2228 (2014) (applying different statutory schemes so that each carries out its mission).

[177] Utility Air Regulatory Group v. EPA, 134 S.Ct. 2427 (June 23, 2014) (plurality opinion); Rapanos v. United States, 547 U.S. 715 (2006) (plurality opinion).

[178] Limelight Networks Inc. v. Akamai Technologies, Inc., 134 S.Ct. 2111 (2014); Robers v. United States, 134 S.Ct. 1854 (2014).

[179] See sources in note 71, *supra.*

[180] Credit Suisse Securities (USA) LLC v. Billing, 551 U.S. 264 (2007).

[181] Powerex Corp. v. Reliant Energy Servs., Inc., 551 U.S. 224 (2007); Ledbetter v. Goodyear Tire & Rubber Co., 550 U.S. 618 (2007); John Hancock Mut. Life Ins. Co. v. Harris Trust & Sav. Bank, 510 U.S. 86, 101–06 (1993); Morales v. TWA, Inc., 504 U.S. 374 (1992); Communications Workers v. Beck, 487 U.S. 735, 750–52 (1988); Wimberly v. Labor & Indus. Relations Comm'n, 479 U.S. 511, 517 (1987).

[182] Ledbetter v. Goodyear Tire & Rubber Co., 550 U.S. 618 (2007); Fogerty v. Fantasy, Inc., 510 U.S. 517 (1994).

[183] Gonzaga Univ. v. Doe, 536 U.S. 273 (2002); Blessing v. Freestone, 520 U.S. 329 (1997); Suter v. Artist M., 503 U.S. 347 (1992).

[184] Franklin v. Gwinnett County Pub. Sch., 503 U.S. 60 (1992).

[185] Alexander v. Sandoval, 532 U.S. 275 (2001).

[186] Credit Suisse Securities (USA) LLC v. Billing, 551 U.S. 264 (2007); EC Term of Years Trust v. United States, 550 U.S. 429 (2007). The leading case is Brown v. General Serv. Admin., 425 U.S. 820, 834 (1976).

[187] Hinck v. United States, 550 U.S. 501 (2007).

- Presumption against creating exemptions in a statute that has none.[188] Narrow interpretation of explicit exemptions.[189]

- Allow *de minimis* exceptions to statutory rules, so long as they do not undermine statutory policy.[190]

2. *Process Canons*

- Presumption that adjudicative bodies are vested with inherent authority to sanction abusive litigation practices.[191] Judges presumptively have discretion to raise procedural errors sua sponte.[192]

- Presumption that statutory exhaustion requirements entail implicit requirements that the petitioner follow the proper procedures; failing that, the petitioner has not met statutory exhaustion requirements.[193]

- Strict construction of statutes authorizing appeals.[194] Rule that Court of Claims is proper forum for Tucker Act claims against federal government.[195]

- Rule that "sue and be sued" clauses waive sovereign immunity and should be liberally construed.[196] Presumption that statute creating agency and authorizing it to "sue and be sued" also creates federal subject matter jurisdiction for lawsuits by and against the agency.[197]

- American rule: strong presumption that each side bears its own costs in adjudications.[198] Super-strong rule against finding statutory authorization of witness fees as costs unless the statute refers explicitly to witness fees.[199]

- Rule that the burden of proof is on the party requesting benefits or entitlements from the state.[200]

- Rule that nonjurisdictional process objections (e.g., exhaustion of remedies, venue) are waived if not timely raised.[201]

---

[188] Burwell v. Hobby Lobby Stores, Inc., 134 S.Ct. 2751 (June 30, 2014); City of Chicago v. Environmental Def. Fund, 511 U.S. 328, 33 7 (1994).

[189] John Hancock Mut. Life Ins. Co. v. Harris Trust & Sav. Bank, 510 U.S. 86, 96–97 (1994); United States Dep't of Justice v. Landano, 508 U.S. 165 (1993); Citicorp Indus. Credit, Inc. v. Brock, 483 U.S. 27, 33–35 (1987).

[190] Wisconsin Dep't of Revenue v. William Wrigley, Jr., Co., 505 U.S. 214 (1992).

[191] Marrama v. Citizens Bank of Mass., 549 U.S. 365 (2007).

[192] Day v. McDonough, 547 U.S. 198 (2006).

[193] Woodford v. Ngo, 548 U.S. 181 (2006); see also O'Sullivan v. Boerckel, 526 U.S. 838, 845 (1999) (similar rule in habeas corpus law).

[194] Bowles v. Russell, 551 U.S. 205 (2007); Hohn v. United States, 524 U.S. 236, 24 7 (1998); California Coastal Comm'n v. Granite Rock Co., 480 U.S. 572, 579 (1987).

[195] Preseault v. ICC, 494 U.S. 1, 11–12 (1990).

[196] FDIC v. Meyer, 510 U.S. 471 (1994).

[197] American Nat'l Red Cross v. S.G., 505 U.S. 247 (1992).

[198] Buckhannon Bd. & Care Home, Inc. v. West Virginia Dep't Health & Human Resources, 532 U.S. 598 (2001). The leading case is Alyeska Pipeline Serv. Co. v. Wilderness Soc'y, 421 U.S. 240 (1975).

[199] Arlington Cent. Sch. Dist. Bd. of Educ. v. Murphy, 548 U.S. 291 (2006); Crawford Fitting Co. v. J.T. Gibbons, Inc., 482 U.S. 437, 445 (1987).

[200] NLRB v. Kentucky River Community Care, Inc., 532 U.S. 706 (2001).

[201] Kontrick v. Ryan, 540 U.S. 443 (2004).

3. *Specific statutory subject areas*

- **Antitrust.** Sherman Act should be applied in light of its overall purpose of benefitting consumers.[202]

- Presumption against application of Sherman Act to activities authorized by states.[203]

- Exemption from antitrust liability should not be lightly inferred.[204] Principle that statutes should not be interpreted to create anti-competitive effects.[205]

- **Arbitration.** Federal court deference to arbitral awards, even where the Federal Arbitration Act is not by its terms applicable.[206]

- Strong presumption in favor of arbitration and of enforcing labor arbitration agreements.[207]

- Rule favoring arbitration of federal statutory claims.[208]

- **Banking.** National Bank Act (NBA) policy shielding national banks from "burdensome" state regulation.[209] But national banks are subject to state laws not conflicting with the NBA's purposes.[210]

- **Bankruptcy.** Bankruptcy Act of 1978 (BRA) should be construed in light of its overall purpose, to give a fresh start to the class of "honest but unfortunate debtors."[211]

- Presumption that the BRA preserved prior bankruptcy doctrines.[212]

- Where statute is ambiguous, courts should create gapfilling rules that are familiar, objective, and less expensive to administer.[213]

- **Civil Procedure & Jurisdiction.** Subject-matter jurisdictional rules will be strictly enforced and applied.[214]

---

[202] Weyerhauser v. Ross-Simmons Hardwood Lumber, 549 U.S. 312 (2007).

[203] City of Columbia v. Omni Outdoor Advertising, Inc., 499 U.S. 365, 370 (1991).

[204] Credit Suisse Securities (USA) LLC v. Billing, 551 U.S. 264 (2007).

[205] Nautilus, Inc. v. Biosig Instruments, Inc., 134 S.Ct. 2120 (2014); Two Pesos, Inc. v. Taco Cabana, Inc., 505 U.S. 763 (1992).

[206] United Paperworkers Int'l Union v. Misco, Inc., 484 U.S. 29, 36–37 (1987).

[207] Howsam v. Dean Witter Reynolds, Inc., 537 U.S. 79, 83 (2002); Groves v. Ring Screw Works, Ferndale Fastener Div'n, 498 U.S. 168, 173 (1990).

[208] CompuCredit Corp. v. Greenwood, 132 S.Ct. 665 (2012); Circuit City Stores, Inc. v. Adams, 532 U.S. 105 (2001); Gilmer v. Interstate/Johnson Lane Corp., 500 U.S. 20, 26 (1991); Shearson/American Express, Inc. v. McMahon, 482 U.S. 220, 226–27 (1987).

[209] Watters v. Wachovia Bank, 550 U.S. 1 (2007); Beneficial Nat'l Bank v. Anderson, 539 U.S. 1, 10 (2003); Barnett Bank of Marion County, N.A. v. Nelson, 517 U.S. 25, 32–34 (1996).

[210] Atherton v. FDIC, 519 U.S. 213, 221–22 (1997).

[211] Marrama v. Citizens Bank of Mass., 549 U.S. 365 (2007).

[212] Dewsnup v. Timm, 502 U.S. 410 (1992).

[213] Till v. CSC Credit Corp., 541 U.S. 465 (2004) (plurality opinion of Stevens, J.).

[214] Bowles v. Russell, 551 U.S. 205 (2007). Relatedly, courts will interpret even long-established jurisdictional exceptions narrowly. Marshall v. Marshall, 547 U.S. 293 (2006) (narrow interpretation of "probate exception"); Ankenbrandt v. Richards, 504 U.S. 689 (1992) (narrow interpretation of "domestic relations exception").

- Jurisdictional provisions will not be inferred.[215] Article III baseline is that litigation involves claims by individuals (and not groups of people) aggrieved by a defendant's actions and presenting enough facts to warrant a plausible claim for legal relief.[216]

- Federal Rules of Civil Procedure apply in habeas cases, except to the extent they are inconsistent with the Habeas Corpus Rules.[217]

- Presumption that time-limitation periods, venue, and other nonjurisdictional requirements are waivable.[218]

- **Civil Rights.** Aspects of section 1983 not governed by state law are governed by federal rules conforming to common law tort principles.[219]

- Title VII of the Civil Rights Act should be interpreted to effectuate its goal of a workplace where individuals are not discriminated against because of their racial, ethnic, religious, or gender-based status.[220] But Title VII does not set forth a general code of workplace civility.[221]

- Voting Rights Act should be interpreted in light of its core purpose of preventing race discrimination in voting and fostering a transformation of America into a society no longer fixated on race.[222]

- **Criminal Law and Sentencing.** Rule of lenity: ambiguities in criminal statutes shall be decided in favor of the accused.[223] Likewise, ambiguous sentencing provisions should be interpreted against the government.[224]

- Failure of U.S. Attorneys to initiate criminal prosecutions in the past is evidence that the Attorney General's current reading of the statute is too broad.[225]

- Even when courts are not bound by Sentencing Commission interpretations, such interpretations may be considered.[226]

- **Environmental Law.** Environmental laws should be applied in light of their overall purpose of cleaning up the environment at a reasonable cost.[227]

---

[215] Stern v. Marshall, 131 S.Ct. 2594, 2606-07 (2011); Henderson v. Shinseki, 131 S.Ct. 1197 (2011); Arbaugh v. Y&H Corp., 546 U.S. 500, 516 (2006).

[216] Wal-Mart Stores, Inc. v. Dukes, 131 S.Ct. 2541, 2550 (2011); Ashcroft v. Iqbal, 556 U.S. 662 (2009). Compare the majority and dissenting opinions in Brown v. Plata, 131 S.Ct. 1910 (2011).

[217] Woofard v. Garceau, 538 U.S. 202, 208 (2003).

[218] Eberhart v. United States, 546 U.S. 12, 17–18 (2006) (per curiam).

[219] Wallace v. Kato, 549 U.S. 381 (2007).

[220] Burlington Northern & Santa Fe Ry. v. White, 548 U.S. 53 (2006).

[221] Oncale v. Sundowner Offshore Servs., Inc., 523 U.S. 75, 80 (1998); Faragher v. Boca Raton, 524 U.S. 775, 788 (1998).

[222] League of United Latin Am. Citizens v. Perry, 548 U.S. 399 (2006); Georgia v. Ashcroft, 539 U.S. 461, 490 (2003).

[223] See sources in note 138, supra.

[224] United States v. R.L.C., 503 U.S. 291 (1992).

[225] Lopez v. Gonzales, 549 U.S. 47 (2006).

[226] James v. United States, 550 U.S. 192 (2007).

[227] Massachusetts v. EPA, 549 U.S. 497 (2007).

- NEPA contains an implicit "rule of reason," relieving agencies of filing environmental impact statements that would serve no statutory purpose.[228]

- **Immigration.** Construe ambiguities in deportation statutes in favor of aliens.[229]

- **Indian Law.** Rule against state taxation of Indian tribes and reservation activities.[230]

- Presumption against national "diminishment" of Indian lands.[231]

- Longstanding assertion of state jurisdiction over Indian lands creates justifiable expectations of sovereign authority.[232]

- Presumption against criminal jurisdiction by an Indian tribe over a nonmember.[233]

- Presumption that party cannot invoke federal jurisdiction until she has exhausted her remedies in Indian tribal courts.[234]

- **Labor Law.** Rule against statutory interference in labor-management discipline disputes.[235]

- **Patent Law.** Practice and precedent of Patent Office are particularly persuasive evidence of statutory meaning in this area, given the much greater competence of that Office.[236]

- Strong presumption that abstract ideas and laws of nature are not patentable.[237]

- **Taxation.** Presumption that IRS tax assessments are correct.[238]

- Narrow interpretation of exemptions from federal taxation.[239] Presumption against taxpayer claiming income tax deduction.[240]

---

[228] Department of Transportation v. Public Citizen, 541 U.S. 752 (2004); Marsh v. Oregon Natural Resources Council, 490 U.S. 360, 373–74 (1989).

[229] INS v. St. Cyr, 533 U.S. 289, 320 (2001); INS v. Cardoza-Fonseca, 480 U.S. 421, 449 (1987). This canon is applied with an unusual level of unpredictability. Compare, e.g., INS v. Elias-Zacarias, 502 U.S. 478 (1992).

[230] California v. Cabazon Band of Mission Indians, 480 U.S. 202, 208 (1987).

[231] Hagen v. Utah, 510 U.S. 399 (1994).

[232] City of Sherrill v. Oneida Indian Nation of N.Y., 544 U.S. 197 (2005); Hagen v. Utah, 510 U.S. 399, 421 (1994).

[233] Duro v. Reina, 495 U.S. 676, 693–94 (1990).

[234] Iowa Mut. Ins. Co. v. LaPlante, 480 U.S. 9, 15–17 (1987).

[235] Eastern Associated Coal Corp. v. UMW Dist. 17, 531 U.S. 57 (2000).

[236] Festo Corp. v. Shoketsu Kinzoku Kogyo Kabushiki Co., 535 U.S. 722 (2002). This canon seems to be exceedingly weak in practice. E.g.,

[237] Alice Corp. Pty. Ltd. v. CLS Bank Int'l, 134 S.Ct. 2347 (2014); Mayo Collaborative Servs. v. Prometheus Labs., Inc., 132 S.Ct. 1289 (2012).

[238] United States v. Fior D'Italia, 536 U.S. 238, 242–43 (2002).

[239] United States v. Burke, 504 U.S. 229 (1992) (Souter, J., concurring in the judgment); United States v. Wells Fargo Bank, 485 U.S. 351, 357 (1988).

[240] INDOPCO, Inc. v. Commissioner, 503 U.S. 79 (1992).

- Presumption that tax valuation statutes follow majority approach, and that departures from the majority approach would be signaled with clear statutory language.[241]

- **Veterans Benefits.** Principle that veterans' benefits statutes be construed liberally for their beneficiaries.[242]

---

[241] Limtiaco v. Camacho, 549 U.S. 483 (2007).

[242] King v. St. Vincent's Hosp., 502 U.S. 215 (1991).

ADMINISTRATIVE PROCEDURE ACT
(SELECTED PROVISIONS)

■ ■ ■

5 U.S.C. § 551. Definitions

For the purpose of this subchapter—

(1) "agency" means each authority of the Government of the United States, whether or not it is within or subject to review by another agency, but does not include—

(A) the Congress;

(B) the courts of the United States;

(C) the governments of the territories or possessions of the United States;

(D) the government of the District of Columbia; or except as to the requirements of section 552 of this title—

(E) agencies composed of representatives of the parties or of representatives of organizations of the parties to the disputes determined by them;

(F) courts martial and military commissions;

(G) military authority exercised in the field in time of war or in occupied territory; or

(H) functions conferred by sections 1738, 1739, 1743, and 1744 of title 12; subchapter II of chapter 471 of title 49; or sections 1884, 1891–1902, and former section 1641(b)(2), of title 50, appendix;

(2) "person" includes an individual, partnership, corporation, association, or public or private organization other than an agency;

(3) "party" includes a person or agency named or admitted as a party, or properly seeking and entitled as of right to be admitted as a party, in an agency proceeding, and a person or agency admitted by an agency as a party for limited purposes;

(4) "rule" means the whole or a part of an agency statement of general or particular applicability and future effect designed to implement, interpret, or prescribe law or policy or describing the organization, procedure, or practice requirements of an agency and includes the approval or prescription for the future of rates, wages, corporate or financial structures or reorganizations thereof, prices, facilities, appliances, services

or allowances therefore or of valuations, costs, or accounting, or practices bearing on any of the foregoing;

(5) "rule making" means agency process for formulating, amending, or repealing a rule;

(6) "order" means the whole or a part of a final disposition, whether affirmative, negative, injunctive, or declaratory in form, of an agency in a matter other than rule making but including licensing;

(7) "adjudication" means agency process for the formulation of an order;

(8) "license" includes the whole or a part of an agency permit, certificate, approval, registration, charter, membership, statutory exemption or other form of permission;

(9) "licensing" includes agency process respecting the grant, renewal, denial, revocation, suspension, annulment, withdrawal, limitation, amendment, modification, or conditioning of a license;

(10) "sanction" includes the whole or a part of an agency—

(A) prohibition, requirement, limitation, or other condition affecting the freedom of a person;

(B) withholding of relief;

(C) imposition of penalty or fine;

(D) destruction, taking, seizure, or withholding of property;

(E) assessment of damages, reimbursement, restitution, compensation, costs, charges, or fees;

(F) requirement, revocation, or suspension of a license; or

(G) taking other compulsory or restrictive action;

(11) "relief" includes the whole or a part of an agency—

(A) grant of money, assistance, license, authority, exemption, exception, privilege, or remedy;

(B) recognition of a claim, right, immunity, privilege, exemption, or exception; or

(C) taking of other action on the application or petition of, and beneficial to, a person;

(12) "agency proceeding" means an agency process as defined by paragraphs (5), (7), and (9) of this section;

(13) "agency action" includes the whole or a part of an agency rule, order, license, sanction, relief, or the equivalent or denial thereof, or failure to act; and

(14) "ex parte communication" means an oral or written communication not on the public record with respect to which reasonable prior notice to all

parties is not given, but it shall not include requests for status reports on any matter or proceeding covered by this subchapter.

5 U.S.C. § 552. Public information; agency rules, opinions, orders, records, and proceedings

(a) Each agency shall make available to the public information as follows:

(1) Each agency shall separately state and currently publish in the Federal Register for the guidance of the public—

(A) descriptions of its central and field organization and the established places at which, the employees (and in the case of a uniformed service, the members) from whom, and the methods whereby, the public may obtain information, make submittals or requests, or obtain decisions;

(B) statements of the general course and method by which its functions are channeled and determined, including the nature and requirements of all formal and informal procedures available;

(C) rules of procedure, descriptions of forms available or the places at which forms may be obtained, and instructions as to the scope and contents of all papers, reports, or examinations;

(D) substantive rules of general applicability adopted as authorized by law, and statements of general policy or interpretations of general applicability formulated and adopted by the agency; and

(E) each amendment, revision, or repeal of the foregoing.

Except to the extent that a person has actual and timely notice of the terms thereof, a person may not in any manner be required to resort to, or be adversely affected by, a matter required to be published in the Federal Register and not so published. For the purpose of this paragraph, matter reasonably available to the class of persons affected thereby is deemed published in the Federal Register when incorporated by reference therein with the approval of the Director of the Federal Register.

(2) Each agency, in accordance with published rules, shall make available for public inspection and copying—

(A) final opinions, including concurring and dissenting opinions, as well as orders, made in the adjudication of cases;

(B) those statements of policy and interpretations which have been adopted by the agency and are not published in the Federal Register;

(C) administrative staff manuals and instructions to staff that affect a member of the public;

(D) copies of all records, regardless of form or format, which have been released to any person under paragraph (3) and which, because of the nature of their subject matter, the agency determines have become or are likely to become the subject of subsequent requests for substantially the same records; and

(E) a general index of the records referred to under subparagraph (D);

unless the materials are promptly published and copies offered for sale. * * * To the extent required to prevent a clearly unwarranted invasion of personal privacy, an agency may delete identifying details when it makes available or publishes an opinion, statement of policy, interpretation, staff manual, instruction, or copies of records referred to in subparagraph (D). However, in each case the justification for the deletion shall be explained fully in writing, and the extent of such deletion shall be indicated on the portion of the record which is made available or published, unless including that indication would harm an interest protected by the exemption in subsection (b) under which the deletion is made. If technically feasible, the extent of the deletion shall be indicated at the place in the record where the deletion was made. Each agency shall also maintain and make available for public inspection and copying current indexes providing identifying information for the public as to any matter issued, adopted, or promulgated after July 4, 1967, and required by this paragraph to be made available or published. Each agency shall promptly publish, quarterly or more frequently, and distribute (by sale or otherwise) copies of each index or supplements thereto unless it determines by order published in the Federal Register that the publication would be unnecessary and impracticable, in which case the agency shall nonetheless provide copies of such index on request at a cost not to exceed the direct cost of duplication. Each agency shall make the index referred to in subparagraph (E) available by computer telecommunications by December 31, 1999. A final order, opinion, statement of policy, interpretation, or staff manual or instruction that affects a member of the public may be relied on, used, or cited as precedent by an agency against a party other than an agency only if—

(i) it has been indexed and either made available or published as provided by this paragraph; or

(ii) the party has actual and timely notice of the terms thereof.

(3)(A) Except with respect to the records made available under paragraphs (1) and (2) of this subsection, and except as provided in subparagraph (E), each agency, upon any request for records which (i) reasonably describes such records and (ii) is made in accordance with published rules stating the time, place, fees (if any), and procedures to be followed, shall make the records promptly available to any person.

(B) In making any record available to a person under this paragraph, an agency shall provide the record in any form or format requested by the person if the record is readily reproducible by the agency in that form or format. Each agency shall make reasonable efforts to maintain its records in forms or formats that are reproducible for purposes of this section.

(C) In responding under this paragraph to a request for records, an agency shall make reasonable efforts to search for the records in electronic form or format, except when such efforts would significantly interfere with the operation of the agency's automated information system.

(D) For purposes of this paragraph, the term "search" means to review, manually or by automated means, agency records for the purpose of locating those records which are responsive to a request.
* * *

(4)(A)(i) In order to carry out the provisions of this section, each agency shall promulgate regulations, pursuant to notice and receipt of public comment, specifying the schedule of fees applicable to the processing of requests under this section and establishing procedures and guidelines for determining when such fees should be waived or reduced. Such schedule shall conform to the guidelines which shall be promulgated, pursuant to notice and receipt of public comment, by the Director of the Office of Management and Budget and which shall provide for a uniform schedule of fees for all agencies.

(ii) Such agency regulations shall provide that—

(I) fees shall be limited to reasonable standard charges for document search, duplication, and review, when records are requested for commercial use;

(II) fees shall be limited to reasonable standard charges for document duplication when records are not sought for commercial use and the request is made by an educational or noncommercial scientific institution, whose purpose is scholarly or scientific research; or a representative of the news media; and

(III) for any request not described in (I) or (II), fees shall be limited to reasonable standard charges for document search and duplication.

* * *

(iii) Documents shall be furnished without any charge or at a charge reduced below the fees established under clause (ii) if disclosure of the information is in the public interest because it is likely to contribute significantly to public understanding of the operations or activities of the government and is not primarily in the commercial interest of the requester. * * *

(b) This section does not apply to matters that are—

(1) (A) specifically authorized under criteria established by an Executive order to be kept secret in the interest of national defense or foreign policy and (B) are in fact properly classified pursuant to such Executive order;

(2) related solely to the internal personnel rules and practices of an agency;

(3) specifically exempted from disclosure by statute (other than section 552b of this title), if that statute—

(A)(i) requires that the matters be withheld from the public in such a manner as to leave no discretion on the issue; or

(ii) establishes particular criteria for withholding or refers to particular types of matters to be withheld; and

(B) if enacted after the date of enactment of the OPEN FOIA Act of 2009, specifically cites to this paragraph.

(4) trade secrets and commercial or financial information obtained from a person and privileged or confidential;

(5) inter-agency or intra-agency memorandums or letters which would not be available by law to a party other than an agency in litigation with the agency;

(6) personnel and medical files and similar files the disclosure of which would constitute a clearly unwarranted invasion of personal privacy;

(7) records or information compiled for law enforcement purposes, but only to the extent that the production of such law enforcement records or information (A) could reasonably be expected to interfere with enforcement proceedings, (B) would deprive a person of a right to a fair trial or an impartial adjudication, (C) could reasonably be expected to constitute an unwarranted invasion of personal privacy, (D) could reasonably be expected to disclose the identity of a confidential source,

* * *

5 U.S.C. § 553. Rule making

(a) This section applies, according to the provisions thereof, except to the extent that there is involved—

(1) a military or foreign affairs function of the United States; or

(2) a matter relating to agency management or personnel or to public property, loans, grants, benefits, or contracts.

(b) General notice of proposed rule making shall be published in the Federal Register, unless persons subject thereto are named and either personally served or otherwise have actual notice thereof in accordance with law. The notice shall include—

(1) a statement of the time, place, and nature of public rule making proceedings;

(2) reference to the legal authority under which the rule is proposed; and

(3) either the terms or substance of the proposed rule or a description of the subjects and issues involved.

Except when notice or hearing is required by statute, this subsection does not apply—

> (A) to interpretative rules, general statements of policy, or rules of agency organization, procedure, or practice; or

> (B) when the agency for good cause finds (and incorporates the finding and a brief statement of reasons therefor in the rules issued) that notice and public procedure thereon are impracticable, unnecessary, or contrary to the public interest.

(c) After notice required by this section, the agency shall give interested persons an opportunity to participate in the rule making through submission of written data, views, or arguments with or without opportunity for oral presentation. After consideration of the relevant matter presented, the agency shall incorporate in the rules adopted a concise general statement of their basis and purpose. When rules are required by statute to be made on the record after opportunity for an agency hearing, sections 556 and 557 of this title apply instead of this subsection.

(d) The required publication or service of a substantive rule shall be made not less than 30 days before its effective date, except—

> (1) a substantive rule which grants or recognizes an exemption or relieves a restriction;

> (2) interpretative rules and statements of policy; or

> (3) as otherwise provided by the agency for good cause found and published with the rule.

(e) Each agency shall give an interested person the right to petition for the issuance, amendment, or repeal of a rule.

5 U.S.C. § 554. Adjudications

(a) This section applies, according to the provisions thereof, in every case of adjudication required by statute to be determined on the record after opportunity for an agency hearing, except to the extent that there is involved—

> (1) a matter subject to a subsequent trial of the law and the facts de novo in a court;

> (2) the selection or tenure of an employee, except a[n] administrative law judge appointed under section 3105 of this title;

> (3) proceedings in which decisions rest solely on inspections, tests, or elections;

> (4) the conduct of military or foreign affairs functions;

> (5) cases in which an agency is acting as an agent for a court; or

> (6) the certification of worker representatives.

(b) Persons entitled to notice of an agency hearing shall be timely informed of—

> (1) the time, place, and nature of the hearing;

(2) the legal authority and jurisdiction under which the hearing is to be held; and

(3) the matters of fact and law asserted.

When private persons are the moving parties, other parties to the proceeding shall give prompt notice of issues controverted in fact or law; and in other instances agencies may by rule require responsive pleading. In fixing the time and place for hearings, due regard shall be had for the convenience and necessity of the parties or their representatives.

(c) The agency shall give all interested parties opportunity for—

(1) the submission and consideration of facts, arguments, offers of settlement, or proposals of adjustment when time, the nature of the proceeding, and the public interest permit; and

(2) to the extent that the parties are unable so to determine a controversy by consent, hearing and decision on notice and in accordance with sections 556 and 557 of this title.

(d) The employee who presides at the reception of evidence pursuant to section 556 of this title shall make the recommended decision or initial decision required by section 557 of this title, unless he becomes unavailable to the agency. Except to the extent required for the disposition of ex parte matters as authorized by law, such an employee may not—

(1) consult a person or party on a fact in issue, unless on notice and opportunity for all parties to participate; or

(2) be responsible to or subject to the supervision or direction of an employee or agent engaged in the performance of investigative or prosecuting functions for an agency.

An employee or agent engaged in the performance of investigative or prosecuting functions for an agency in a case may not, in that or a factually related case, participate or advise in the decision, recommended decision, or agency review pursuant to section 557 of this title, except as witness or counsel in public proceedings. This subsection does not apply—

(A) in determining applications for initial licenses;

(B) to proceedings involving the validity or application of rates, facilities, or practices of public utilities or carriers; or

(C) to the agency or a member or members of the body comprising the agency.

(e) The agency, with like effect as in the case of other orders, and in its sound discretion, may issue a declaratory order to terminate a controversy or remove uncertainty.

5 U.S.C. § 555.   Ancillary matters

(a) This section applies, according to the provisions thereof, except as otherwise provided by this subchapter.

(b) A person compelled to appear in person before an agency or representative thereof is entitled to be accompanied, represented, and advised by counsel or, if permitted by the agency, by other qualified representative. A party is entitled to appear in person or by or with counsel or other duly qualified representative in an agency proceeding. So far as the orderly conduct of public business permits, an interested person may appear before an agency or its responsible employees for the presentation, adjustment, or determination of an issue, request, or controversy in a proceeding, whether interlocutory, summary, or otherwise, or in connection with an agency function. With due regard for the convenience and necessity of the parties or their representatives and within a reasonable time, each agency shall proceed to conclude a matter presented to it. This subsection does not grant or deny a person who is not a lawyer the right to appear for or represent others before an agency or in an agency proceeding.

(c) Process, requirement of a report, inspection, or other investigative act or demand may not be issued, made, or enforced except as authorized by law. A person compelled to submit data or evidence is entitled to retain or, on payment of lawfully prescribed costs, procure a copy or transcript thereof, except that in a nonpublic investigatory proceeding the witness may for good cause be limited to inspection of the official transcript of his testimony.

(d) Agency subpoenas authorized by law shall be issued to a party on request and, when required by rules of procedure, on a statement or showing of general relevance and reasonable scope of the evidence sought. On contest, the court shall sustain the subpoena or similar process or demand to the extent that it is found to be in accordance with law. In a proceeding for enforcement, the court shall issue an order requiring the appearance of the witness or the production of the evidence or data within a reasonable time under penalty of punishment for contempt in case of contumacious failure to comply.

(e) Prompt notice shall be given of the denial in whole or in part of a written application, petition, or other request of an interested person made in connection with any agency proceeding. Except in affirming a prior denial or when the denial is self-explanatory, the notice shall be accompanied by a brief statement of the grounds for denial.

5 U.S.C. § 556.   Hearings; presiding employees; powers and duties; burden of proof; evidence; record as basis of decision

(a) This section applies, according to the provisions thereof, to hearings required by section 553 or 554 of this title to be conducted in accordance with this section.

(b) There shall preside at the taking of evidence—

   (1) the agency;

   (2) one or more members of the body which comprises the agency; or

   (3) one or more administrative law judges appointed under section 3105 of this title.

This subchapter does not supersede the conduct of specified classes of proceedings, in whole or in part, by or before boards or other employees specially provided for by or designated under statute. The functions of presiding employees and of employees participating in decisions in accordance with section 557 of this title shall be conducted in an impartial manner. A presiding or participating employee may at any time disqualify himself. On the filing in good faith of a timely and sufficient affidavit of personal bias or other disqualification of a presiding or participating employee, the agency shall determine the matter as a part of the record and decision in the case.

(c) Subject to published rules of the agency and within its powers, employees presiding at hearings may—

(1) administer oaths and affirmations;

(2) issue subpoenas authorized by law;

(3) rule on offers of proof and receive relevant evidence;

(4) take depositions or have depositions taken when the ends of justice would be served;

(5) regulate the course of the hearing;

(6) hold conferences for the settlement or simplification of the issues by consent of the parties or by the use of alternative means of dispute resolution as provided in subchapter IV of this chapter;

(7) inform the parties as to the availability of one or more alternative means of dispute resolution, and encourage use of such methods;

(8) require the attendance at any conference held pursuant to paragraph (6) of at least one representative of each party who has authority to negotiate concerning resolution of issues in controversy;

(9) dispose of procedural requests or similar matters;

(10) make or recommend decisions in accordance with section 557 of this title; and

(11) take other action authorized by agency rule consistent with this subchapter.

(d) Except as otherwise provided by statute, the proponent of a rule or order has the burden of proof. Any oral or documentary evidence may be received, but the agency as a matter of policy shall provide for the exclusion of irrelevant, immaterial, or unduly repetitious evidence. A sanction may not be imposed or rule or order issued except on consideration of the whole record or those parts thereof cited by a party and supported by and in accordance with the reliable, probative, and substantial evidence. The agency may, to the extent consistent with the interests of justice and the policy of the underlying statutes administered by the agency, consider a violation of section 557(d) of this title sufficient grounds for a decision adverse to a party who has knowingly committed such violation or knowingly caused such violation to occur. A party is entitled to present his case or defense by oral or documentary evidence, to submit rebuttal evidence, and to conduct such cross-examination as may be required for a full and true disclosure of the facts. In rule making or determining claims for money or benefits or applications for initial licenses an agency may, when a party will not be prejudiced thereby, adopt procedures for the submission of all or part of the evidence in written form.

(e)   The transcript of testimony and exhibits, together with all papers and requests filed in the proceeding, constitutes the exclusive record for decision in accordance with section 557 of this title and, on payment of lawfully prescribed costs, shall be made available to the parties. When an agency decision rests on official notice of a material fact not appearing in the evidence in the record, a party is entitled, on timely request, to an opportunity to show the contrary.

5 U.S.C. § 557.   Initial decisions; conclusiveness; review by agency; submissions by parties; contents of decisions; record

(a)   This section applies, according to the provisions thereof, when a hearing is required to be conducted in accordance with section 556 of this title.

(b)   When the agency did not preside at the reception of the evidence, the presiding employee or, in cases not subject to section 554(d) of this title, an employee qualified to preside at hearings pursuant to section 556 of this title, shall initially decide the case unless the agency requires, either in specific cases or by general rule, the entire record to be certified to it for decision. When the presiding employee makes an initial decision, that decision then becomes the decision of the agency without further proceedings unless there is an appeal to, or review on motion of, the agency within time provided by rule. On appeal from or review of the initial decision, the agency has all the powers which it would have in making the initial decision except as it may limit the issues on notice or by rule. When the agency makes the decision without having presided at the reception of the evidence, the presiding employee or an employee qualified to preside at hearings pursuant to section 556 of this title shall first recommend a decision, except that in rule making or determining applications for initial licenses—

(1)   instead thereof the agency may issue a tentative decision or one of its responsible employees may recommend a decision; or

(2)   this procedure may be omitted in a case in which the agency finds on the record that due and timely execution of its functions imperatively and unavoidably so requires.

(c)   Before a recommended, initial, or tentative decision, or a decision on agency review of the decision of subordinate employees, the parties are entitled to a reasonable opportunity to submit for the consideration of the employees participating in the decisions—

(1)   proposed findings and conclusions; or

(2)   exceptions to the decisions or recommended decisions of subordinate employees or to tentative agency decisions; and

(3)   supporting reasons for the exceptions or proposed findings or conclusions.

The record shall show the ruling on each finding, conclusion, or exception presented. All decisions, including initial, recommended, and tentative decisions, are a part of the record and shall include a statement of—

(A) findings and conclusions, and the reasons or basis therefor, on all the material issues of fact, law, or discretion presented on the record; and

(B) the appropriate rule, order, sanction, relief, or denial thereof.

(d)(1)   In any agency proceeding which is subject to subsection (a) of this section, except to the extent required for the disposition of ex parte matters as authorized by law—

(A) no interested person outside the agency shall make or knowingly cause to be made to any member of the body comprising the agency, administrative law judge, or other employee who is or may reasonably be expected to be involved in the decisional process of the proceeding, an ex parte communication relevant to the merits of the proceeding;

(B) no member of the body comprising the agency, administrative law judge, or other employee who is or may reasonably be expected to be involved in the decisional process of the proceeding, shall make or knowingly cause to be made to any interested person outside the agency an ex parte communication relevant to the merits of the proceeding;

(C) a member of the body comprising the agency, administrative law judge, or other employee who is or may reasonably be expected to be involved in the decisional process of such proceeding who receives, or who makes or knowingly causes to be made, a communication prohibited by this subsection shall place on the public record of the proceeding:

(i)   all such written communications;

(ii) memoranda stating the substance of all such oral communications; and

(iii) all written responses, and memoranda stating the substance of all oral responses, to the materials described in clauses (i) and (ii) of this subparagraph;

(D) upon receipt of a communication knowingly made or knowingly caused to be made by a party in violation of this subsection, the agency, administrative law judge, or other employee presiding at the hearing may, to the extent consistent with the interests of justice and the policy of the underlying statutes, require the party to show cause why his claim or interest in the proceeding should not be dismissed, denied, disregarded, or otherwise adversely affected on account of such violation; and

(E) the prohibitions of this subsection shall apply beginning at such time as the agency may designate, but in no case shall they begin to apply later than the time at which a proceeding is noticed for hearing unless the person responsible for the communication has knowledge that it will be noticed, in which case the prohibitions shall apply beginning at the time of his acquisition of such knowledge.

(2) This subsection does not constitute authority to withhold information from Congress.

5 U.S.C. § 558.   Imposition of sanctions; determination of applications for licenses; suspension, revocation, and expiration of licenses

(a) This section applies, according to the provisions thereof, to the exercise of a power or authority.

(b) A sanction may not be imposed or a substantive rule or order issued except within jurisdiction delegated to the agency and as authorized by law.

(c) When application is made for a license required by law, the agency, with due regard for the rights and privileges of all the interested parties or adversely affected persons and within a reasonable time, shall set and complete proceedings required to be conducted in accordance with sections 556 and 557 of this title or other proceedings required by law and shall make its decision. Except in cases of willfulness or those in which public health, interest, or safety requires otherwise, the withdrawal, suspension, revocation, or annulment of a license is lawful only if, before the institution of agency proceedings therefor, the licensee has been given—

(1) notice by the agency in writing of the facts or conduct which may warrant the action; and

(2) opportunity to demonstrate or achieve compliance with all lawful requirements. When the licensee has made timely and sufficient application for a renewal or a new license in accordance with agency rules, a license with reference to an activity of a continuing nature does not expire until the application has been finally determined by the agency.

* * *

5 U.S.C. § 701.   Application; Definitions

(a) This chapter applies, according to the provisions thereof, except to the extent that—

(1) statutes preclude judicial review; or

(2) agency action is committed to agency discretion by law.

(b) For the purpose of this chapter—

(1) "agency" means each authority of the Government of the United States, whether or not it is within or subject to review by another agency, but does not include—

(A) the Congress;

(B) the courts of the United States;

(C) the governments of the territories or possessions of the United States;

(D) the government of the District of Columbia;

(E) agencies composed of representatives of the parties or of representatives of organizations of the parties to the disputes determined by them;

(F) courts martial and military commissions;

(G) military authority exercised in the field in time of war or in occupied territory; or

(H) functions conferred by sections 1738, 1739, 1743, and 1744 of title 12; subchapter II of chapter 471 of title 49; or sections 1884, 1891–1902, and former section 1641(b)(2), of title 50, appendix; and

(2) "person", "rule", "order", "license", "sanction", "relief", and "agency action" have the meanings given them by section 551 of this title.

5 U.S.C. § 702.   Right of review

A person suffering legal wrong because of agency action, or adversely affected or aggrieved by agency action within the meaning of a relevant statute, is entitled to judicial review thereof. An action in a court of the United States seeking relief other than money damages and stating a claim that an agency or an officer or employee thereof acted or failed to act in an official capacity or under color of legal authority shall not be dismissed nor relief therein be denied on the ground that it is against the United States or that the United States is an indispensable party. The United States may be named as a defendant in any such action, and a judgment or decree may be entered against the United States: *Provided,* That any mandatory or injunctive decree shall specify the Federal officer or officers (by name or by title), and their successors in office, personally responsible for compliance. Nothing herein (1) affects other limitations on judicial review or the power or duty of the court to dismiss any action or deny relief on any other appropriate legal or equitable ground; or (2) confers authority to grant relief if any other statute that grants consent to suit expressly or impliedly forbids the relief which is sought.

5 U.S.C. § 703.   Form and venue of proceeding

The form of proceeding for judicial review is the special statutory review proceeding relevant to the subject matter in a court specified by statute or, in the absence or inadequacy thereof, any applicable form of legal action, including actions for declaratory judgments or writs of prohibitory or mandatory injunction or habeas corpus, in a court of competent jurisdiction. If no special statutory review proceeding is applicable, the action for judicial review may be brought against the United States, the agency by its official title, or the appropriate officer. Except to the extent that prior, adequate, and exclusive opportunity for judicial review is provided by law, agency action is subject to judicial review in civil or criminal proceedings for judicial enforcement.

5 U.S.C. § 704.   Actions reviewable

Agency action made reviewable by statute and final agency action for which there is no other adequate remedy in a court are subject to judicial review. A preliminary, procedural, or intermediate agency action or ruling not directly reviewable is subject to review on the review of the final agency action. Except as otherwise expressly required by statute, agency action otherwise final is final for the purposes of this section whether or not there has been presented or determined an application for a declaratory order, for any form of reconsideration, or, unless the agency otherwise requires by rule and provides that the action meanwhile is inoperative, for an appeal to superior agency authority.

5 U.S.C. § 705.   Relief pending review

When an agency finds that justice so requires, it may postpone the effective date of action taken by it, pending judicial review. On such conditions as may be required and to the extent necessary to prevent irreparable injury, the reviewing court, including the court to which a case may be taken on appeal from or on application for certiorari or other writ to a reviewing court, may issue all necessary and appropriate process to postpone the effective date of an agency action or to preserve status or rights pending conclusion of the review proceedings.

5 U.S.C. § 706.   Scope of review

To the extent necessary to decision and when presented, the reviewing court shall decide all relevant questions of law, interpret constitutional and statutory provisions, and determine the meaning or applicability of the terms of an agency action. The reviewing court shall—

(1) compel agency action unlawfully withheld or unreasonably delayed; and

(2) hold unlawful and set aside agency action, findings, and conclusions found to be—

    (A) arbitrary, capricious, an abuse of discretion, or otherwise not in accordance with law;

    (B) contrary to constitutional right, power, privilege, or immunity;

    (C) in excess of statutory jurisdiction, authority, or limitations, or short of statutory right;

    (D) without observance of procedure required by law;

    (E) unsupported by substantial evidence in a case subject to sections 556 and 557 of this title or otherwise reviewed on the record of an agency hearing provided by statute; or

    (F) unwarranted by the facts to the extent that the facts are subject to trial de novo by the reviewing court.

In making the foregoing determinations, the court shall review the whole record or those parts of it cited by a party, and due account shall be taken of the rule of prejudicial error.

* * *

5 U.S.C. § 3105. Appointment of administrative law judges

Each agency shall appoint as many administrative law judges as are necessary for proceedings required to be conducted in accordance with sections 556 and 557 of this title. Administrative law judges shall be assigned to cases in rotation so far as practicable, and may not perform duties inconsistent with their duties and responsibilities as administrative law judges.

APPENDIX D

EXECUTIVE ORDERS ADDRESSING REGULATORY PLANNING AND REVIEW

■ ■ ■

Executive Order 12866; 58 Fed. Reg. 51735, October 4, 1993

The American people deserve a regulatory system that works for them, not against them: a regulatory system that protects and improves their health, safety, environment, and well-being and improves the performance of the economy without imposing unacceptable or unreasonable costs on society; regulatory policies that recognize that the private sector and private markets are the best engine for economic growth; regulatory approaches that respect the role of State, local, and tribal governments; and regulations that are effective, consistent, sensible, and understandable. We do not have such a regulatory system today.

With this Executive order, the Federal Government begins a program to reform and make more efficient the regulatory process. The objectives of this Executive order are to enhance planning and coordination with respect to both new and existing regulations; to reaffirm the primacy of Federal agencies in the regulatory decision-making process; to restore the integrity and legitimacy of regulatory review and oversight; and to make the process more accessible and open to the public. In pursuing these objectives, the regulatory process shall be conducted so as to meet applicable statutory requirements and with due regard to the discretion that has been entrusted to the Federal agencies.

Accordingly, by the authority vested in me as President by the Constitution and the laws of the United States of America, it is hereby ordered as follows:

Section 1. *Statement of Regulatory Philosophy and Principles.*

(a) *The Regulatory Philosophy.* Federal agencies should promulgate only such regulations as are required by law, are necessary to interpret the law, or are made necessary by compelling public need, such as material failures of private markets to protect or improve the health and safety of the public, the environment, or the well-being of the American people. In deciding whether and how to regulate, agencies should assess all costs and benefits of available regulatory alternatives, including the alternative of not regulating. Costs and benefits shall be understood to include both quantifiable measures (to the fullest extent that these can be usefully estimated) and qualitative measures of costs and benefits that are difficult to quantify, but nevertheless essential to consider. Further, in choosing among alternative regulatory approaches, agencies should select those approaches that maximize net benefits (including potential economic, environmental, public health and safety, and other advantages; distributive impacts; and equity), unless a statute requires another regulatory approach.

(b) *The Principles of Regulation.* To ensure that the agencies' regulatory programs are consistent with the philosophy set forth above, agencies should adhere to the following principles, to the extent permitted by law and where applicable:

(1) Each agency shall identify the problem that it intends to address (including, where applicable, the failures of private markets or public institutions that warrant new agency action) as well as assess the significance of that problem.

(2) Each agency shall examine whether existing regulations (or other law) have created, or contributed to, the problem that a new regulation is intended to correct and whether those regulations (or other law) should be modified to achieve the intended goal of regulation more effectively.

(3) Each agency shall identify and assess available alternatives to direct regulation, including providing economic incentives to encourage the desired behavior, such as user fees or marketable permits, or providing information upon which choices can be made by the public.

(4) In setting regulatory priorities, each agency shall consider, to the extent reasonable, the degree and nature of the risks posed by various substances or activities within its jurisdiction.

(5) When an agency determines that a regulation is the best available method of achieving the regulatory objective, it shall design its regulations in the most cost-effective manner to achieve the regulatory objective. In doing so, each agency shall consider incentives for innovation, consistency, predictability, the costs of enforcement and compliance (to the government, regulated entities, and the public), flexibility, distributive impacts, and equity.

(6) Each agency shall assess both the costs and the benefits of the intended regulation and, recognizing that some costs and benefits are difficult to quantify, propose or adopt a regulation only upon a reasoned determination that the benefits of the intended regulation justify its costs.

(7) Each agency shall base its decisions on the best reasonably obtainable scientific, technical, economic, and other information concerning the need for, and consequences of, the intended regulation.

(8) Each agency shall identify and assess alternative forms of regulation and shall, to the extent feasible, specify performance objectives, rather than specifying the behavior or manner of compliance that regulated entities must adopt.

(9) Wherever feasible, agencies shall seek views of appropriate State, local, and tribal officials before imposing regulatory requirements that might significantly or uniquely affect those governmental entities. Each agency shall assess the effects of Federal regulations on State, local, and tribal governments, including specifically the availability of resources to carry out those mandates, and seek to minimize those burdens that uniquely or significantly affect such governmental entities, consistent with

achieving regulatory objectives. In addition, as appropriate, agencies shall seek to harmonize Federal regulatory actions with related State, local, and tribal regulatory and other governmental functions.

(10) Each agency shall avoid regulations that are inconsistent, incompatible, or duplicative with its other regulations or those of other Federal agencies.

(11) Each agency shall tailor its regulations to impose the least burden on society, including individuals, businesses of differing sizes, and other entities (including small communities and governmental entities), consistent with obtaining the regulatory objectives, taking into account, among other things, and to the extent practicable, the costs of cumulative regulations.

(12) Each agency shall draft its regulations to be simple and easy to understand, with the goal of minimizing the potential for uncertainty and litigation arising from such uncertainty.

Section 2. *Organization.* An efficient regulatory planning and review process is vital to ensure that the Federal Government's regulatory system best serves the American people.

(a) *The Agencies.* Because Federal agencies are the repositories of significant substantive expertise and experience, they are responsible for developing regulations and assuring that the regulations are consistent with applicable law, the President's priorities, and the principles set forth in this Executive order.

(b) *The Office of Management and Budget.* Coordinated review of agency rulemaking is necessary to ensure that regulations are consistent with applicable law, the President's priorities, and the principles set forth in this Executive order, and that decisions made by one agency do not conflict with the policies or actions taken or planned by another agency. The Office of Management and Budget (OMB) shall carry out that review function. Within OMB, the Office of Information and Regulatory Affairs (OIRA) is the repository of expertise concerning regulatory issues, including methodologies and procedures that affect more than one agency, this Executive order, and the President's regulatory policies. To the extent permitted by law, OMB shall provide guidance to agencies and assist the President, the Vice President, and other regulatory policy advisors to the President in regulatory planning and shall be the entity that reviews individual regulations, as provided by this Executive order.

(c) *The Vice President.* The Vice President is the principal advisor to the President on, and shall coordinate the development and presentation of recommendations concerning, regulatory policy, planning, and review, as set forth in this Executive order. In fulfilling their responsibilities under this Executive order, the President and the Vice President shall be assisted by the regulatory policy advisors within the Executive Office of the President and by such agency officials and personnel as the President and the Vice President may, from time to time, consult.

Section 3. *Definitions.* For purposes of this Executive order:

(a) "Advisors" refers to such regulatory policy advisors to the President as the President and Vice President may from time to time consult, including, among others: (1) the Director of OMB; (2) the Chair (or another member) of the Council of Economic Advisers; (3) the Assistant to the President for Economic Policy; (4) the Assistant to the President for Domestic Policy; (5) the Assistant to the President for National Security Affairs; (6) the Assistant to the President for Science and Technology; (7) the Assistant to the President for Intergovernmental Affairs; (8) the Assistant to the President and Staff Secretary; (9) the Assistant to the President and Chief of Staff to the Vice President; (10) the Assistant to the President and Counsel to the President; (11) the Deputy Assistant to the President and Director of the White House Office on Environmental Policy; and (12) the Administrator of OIRA, who also shall coordinate communications relating to this Executive order among the agencies, OMB, the other Advisors, and the Office of the Vice President.

(b) "Agency," unless otherwise indicated, means any authority of the United States that is an "agency" under 44 U.S.C. 3502(1), other than those considered to be independent regulatory agencies, as defined in 44 U.S.C. 3502(10).

(c) "Director" means the Director of OMB.

(d) "Regulation" or "rule" means an agency statement of general applicability and future effect, which the agency intends to have the force and effect of law, that is designed to implement, interpret, or prescribe law or policy or to describe the procedure or practice requirements of an agency. It does not, however, include:

   (1) Regulations or rules issued in accordance with the formal rulemaking provisions of 5 U.S.C. 556, 557;

   (2) Regulations or rules that pertain to a military or foreign affairs function of the United States, other than procurement regulations and regulations involving the import or export of non-defense articles and services;

   (3) Regulations or rules that are limited to agency organization, management, or personnel matters; or

   (4) Any other category of regulations exempted by the Administrator of OIRA.

(e) "Regulatory action" means any substantive action by an agency (normally published in the Federal Register) that promulgates or is expected to lead to the promulgation of a final rule or regulation, including notices of inquiry, advance notices of proposed rulemaking, and notices of proposed rulemaking.

(f) "Significant regulatory action" means any regulatory action that is likely to result in a rule that may:

   (1) Have an annual effect on the economy of $100 million or more or adversely affect in a material way the economy, a sector of the economy, productivity, competition, jobs, the environment, public health or safety, or State, local, or tribal governments or communities;

(2) Create a serious inconsistency or otherwise interfere with an action taken or planned by another agency;

(3) Materially alter the budgetary impact of entitlements, grants, user fees, or loan programs or the rights and obligations of recipients thereof; or

(4) Raise novel legal or policy issues arising out of legal mandates, the President's priorities, or the principles set forth in this Executive order.

Section 4. *Planning Mechanism.* In order to have an effective regulatory program, to provide for coordination of regulations, to maximize consultation and the resolution of potential conflicts at an early stage, to involve the public and its State, local, and tribal officials in regulatory planning, and to ensure that new or revised regulations promote the President's priorities and the principles set forth in this Executive order, these procedures shall be followed, to the extent permitted by law:

(a) *Agencies' Policy Meeting.* Early in each year's planning cycle, the Vice President shall convene a meeting of the Advisors and the heads of agencies to seek a common understanding of priorities and to coordinate regulatory efforts to be accomplished in the upcoming year.

(b) *Unified Regulatory Agenda.* For purposes of this subsection, the term "agency" or "agencies" shall also include those considered to be independent regulatory agencies, as defined in 44 U.S.C. 3502(10). Each agency shall prepare an agenda of all regulations under development or review, at a time and in a manner specified by the Administrator of OIRA. The description of each regulatory action shall contain, at a minimum, a regulation identifier number, a brief summary of the action, the legal authority for the action, any legal deadline for the action, and the name and telephone number of a knowledgeable agency official. Agencies may incorporate the information required under 5 U.S.C. 602 and 41 U.S.C. 402 into these agendas.

(c) *The Regulatory Plan.* For purposes of this subsection, the term "agency" or "agencies" shall also include those considered to be independent regulatory agencies, as defined in 44 U.S.C. 3502(10).

(1) As part of the Unified Regulatory Agenda, beginning in 1994, each agency shall prepare a Regulatory Plan (Plan) of the most important significant regulatory actions that the agency reasonably expects to issue in proposed or final form in that fiscal year or thereafter. The Plan shall be approved personally by the agency head and shall contain at a minimum:

(A) A statement of the agency's regulatory objectives and priorities and how they relate to the President's priorities;

(B) A summary of each planned significant regulatory action including, to the extent possible, alternatives to be considered and preliminary estimates of the anticipated costs and benefits;

(C) A summary of the legal basis for each such action, including whether any aspect of the action is required by statute or court order;

(D) A statement of the need for each such action and, if applicable, how the action will reduce risks to public health, safety, or the environment, as well as how the magnitude of the risk addressed by the action relates to other risks within the jurisdiction of the agency;

(E) The agency's schedule for action, including a statement of any applicable statutory or judicial deadlines; and

(F) The name, address, and telephone number of a person the public may contact for additional information about the planned regulatory action.

(2) Each agency shall forward its Plan to OIRA by June 1st of each year.

(3) Within 10 calendar days after OIRA has received an agency's Plan, OIRA shall circulate it to other affected agencies, the Advisors, and the Vice President.

(4) An agency head who believes that a planned regulatory action of another agency may conflict with its own policy or action taken or planned shall promptly notify, in writing, the Administrator of OIRA, who shall forward that communication to the issuing agency, the Advisors, and the Vice President.

(5) If the Administrator of OIRA believes that a planned regulatory action of an agency may be inconsistent with the President's priorities or the principles set forth in this Executive order or may be in conflict with any policy or action taken or planned by another agency, the Administrator of OIRA shall promptly notify, in writing, the affected agencies, the Advisors, and the Vice President.

(6) The Vice President, with the Advisors' assistance, may consult with the heads of agencies with respect to their Plans and, in appropriate instances, request further consideration or inter-agency coordination.

(7) The Plans developed by the issuing agency shall be published annually in the October publication of the Unified Regulatory Agenda. This publication shall be made available to the Congress; State, local, and tribal governments; and the public. Any views on any aspect of any agency Plan, including whether any planned regulatory action might conflict with any other planned or existing regulation, impose any unintended consequences on the public, or confer any unclaimed benefits on the public, should be directed to the issuing agency, with a copy to OIRA.

(d) *Regulatory Working Group.* Within 30 days of the date of this Executive order, the Administrator of OIRA shall convene a Regulatory Working Group ("Working Group"), which shall consist of representatives of the heads of each agency that the Administrator determines to have significant domestic regulatory responsibility, the Advisors, and the Vice President. The Administrator of OIRA shall chair the Working Group and shall periodically advise the Vice President on the activities of the Working Group. The Working Group shall serve as a forum to assist agencies in identifying and analyzing important regulatory issues (including, among others (1) the development of innovative regulatory techniques, (2) the methods, efficacy, and utility of comparative risk assessment in regulatory decision-making, and (3) the development of short forms and other streamlined regulatory approaches for small businesses and other entities). The Working Group shall meet at least quarterly and may meet as a whole or in subgroups of agencies with an interest in particular issues or subject areas. To inform its discussions, the Working Group may commission analytical studies and reports by OIRA, the Administrative Conference of the United States, or any other agency.

(e) *Conferences.* The Administrator of OIRA shall meet quarterly with representatives of State, local, and tribal governments to identify both existing and proposed regulations that may uniquely or significantly affect those governmental entities. The Administrator of OIRA shall also convene, from time to time, conferences with representatives of businesses, nongovernmental organizations, and the public to discuss regulatory issues of common concern.

Section 5. *Existing Regulations.* * * *

Section 6. *Centralized Review of Regulations.* The guidelines set forth below shall apply to all regulatory actions, for both new and existing regulations, by agencies other than those agencies specifically exempted by the Administrator of OIRA:

(a) *Agency Responsibilities.* (1) Each agency shall (consistent with its own rules, regulations, or procedures) provide the public with meaningful participation in the regulatory process. In particular, before issuing a notice of proposed rulemaking, each agency should, where appropriate, seek the involvement of those who are intended to benefit from and those expected to be burdened by any regulation (including, specifically, State, local, and tribal officials). In addition, each agency should afford the public a meaningful opportunity to comment on any proposed regulation, which in most cases should include a comment period of not less than 60 days. Each agency also is directed to explore and, where appropriate, use consensual mechanisms for developing regulations, including negotiated rulemaking.

(2) Within 60 days of the date of this Executive order, each agency head shall designate a Regulatory Policy Officer who shall report to the agency head. The Regulatory Policy Officer shall be involved at each stage of the regulatory process to foster the development of effective, innovative, and least burdensome regulations and to further the principles set forth in this Executive order.

(3) In addition to adhering to its own rules and procedures and to the requirements of the Administrative Procedure Act, the Regulatory Flexibility Act, the Paperwork Reduction Act, and other applicable law, each agency shall develop its regulatory actions in a timely fashion and adhere to the following procedures with respect to a regulatory action:

(A) Each agency shall provide OIRA, at such times and in the manner specified by the Administrator of OIRA, with a list of its planned regulatory actions, indicating those which the agency believes are significant regulatory actions within the meaning of this Executive order. Absent a material change in the development of the planned regulatory action, those not designated as significant will not be subject to review under this section unless, within 10 working days of receipt of the list, the Administrator of OIRA notifies the agency that OIRA has determined that a planned regulation is a significant regulatory action within the meaning of this Executive order. The Administrator of OIRA may waive review of any planned regulatory action designated by the agency as significant, in which case the agency need not further comply with subsection (a)(3)(B) or subsection (a)(3)(C) of this section.

(B) For each matter identified as, or determined by the Administrator of OIRA to be, a significant regulatory action, the issuing agency shall provide to OIRA:

(i) The text of the draft regulatory action, together with a reasonably detailed description of the need for the regulatory action and an explanation of how the regulatory action will meet that need; and

(ii) An assessment of the potential costs and benefits of the regulatory action, including an explanation of the manner in which the regulatory action is consistent with a statutory mandate and, to the extent permitted by law, promotes the President's priorities and avoids undue interference with State, local, and tribal governments in the exercise of their governmental functions.

(C) For those matters identified as, or determined by the Administrator of OIRA to be, a significant regulatory action within the scope of section 3(f)(1), the agency shall also provide to OIRA the following additional information developed as part of the agency's decision-making process (unless prohibited by law):

(i) An assessment, including the underlying analysis, of benefits anticipated from the regulatory action (such as, but not limited to, the promotion of the efficient functioning of the economy and private markets, the enhancement of health and safety, the protection of the natural environment, and the elimination or reduction of discrimination or bias) together with, to the extent feasible, a quantification of those benefits;

(ii) An assessment, including the underlying analysis, of costs anticipated from the regulatory action (such as, but not limited to, the direct cost both to the government in administering the regulation and to businesses and others in complying with the regulation, and any adverse effects on the efficient functioning of the economy, private markets (including productivity, employment, and competitiveness), health, safety, and the natural environment), together with, to the extent feasible, a quantification of those costs; and

(iii) An assessment, including the underlying analysis, of costs and benefits of potentially effective and reasonably feasible alternatives to the planned regulation, identified by the agencies or the public (including improving the current regulation and reasonably viable nonregulatory actions), and an explanation why the planned regulatory action is preferable to the identified potential alternatives.

(D) In emergency situations or when an agency is obligated by law to act more quickly than normal review procedures allow, the agency shall notify OIRA as soon as possible and, to the extent practicable, comply with subsections (a)(3)(B) and (C) of this section. For those regulatory actions that are governed by a statutory or court-imposed deadline, the agency shall, to the extent practicable, schedule rulemaking proceedings so as to permit sufficient time for OIRA to conduct its review, as set forth below in subsection (b)(2) through (4) of this section.

(E) After the regulatory action has been published in the **Federal Register** or otherwise issued to the public, the agency shall:

(i) Make available to the public the information set forth in subsections (a)(3)(B) and (C);

(ii) Identify for the public, in a complete, clear, and simple manner, the substantive changes between the draft submitted to OIRA for review and the action subsequently announced; and

(iii) Identify for the public those changes in the regulatory action that were made at the suggestion or recommendation of OIRA.

(F) All information provided to the public by the agency shall be in plain, understandable language.

(b) *OIRA Responsibilities.* The Administrator of OIRA shall provide meaningful guidance and oversight so that each agency's regulatory actions are consistent with applicable law, the President's priorities, and the principles set forth in this Executive order and do not conflict with the policies or actions of another agency. OIRA shall, to the extent permitted by law, adhere to the following guidelines:

(1) OIRA may review only actions identified by the agency or by OIRA as significant regulatory actions under subsection (a)(3)(A) of this section.

(2) OIRA shall waive review or notify the agency in writing of the results of its review within the following time periods:

(A) For any notices of inquiry, advance notices of proposed rulemaking, or other preliminary regulatory actions prior to a Notice of Proposed Rulemaking, within 10 working days after the date of submission of the draft action to OIRA;

(B) For all other regulatory actions, within 90 calendar days after the date of submission of the information set forth in subsections (a)(3)(B) and (C) of this section, unless OIRA has previously reviewed this information and, since that review, there has been no material change in the facts and circumstances upon which the regulatory action is based, in which case, OIRA shall complete its review within 45 days; and

(C) The review process may be extended (1) once by no more than 30 calendar days upon the written approval of the Director and (2) at the request of the agency head.

(3) For each regulatory action that the Administrator of OIRA returns to an agency for further consideration of some or all of its provisions, the Administrator of OIRA shall provide the issuing agency a written explanation for such return, setting forth the pertinent provision of this Executive order on which OIRA is relying. If the agency head disagrees with some or all of the bases for the return, the agency head shall so inform the Administrator of OIRA in writing.

(4) Except as otherwise provided by law or required by a Court, in order to ensure greater openness, accessibility, and accountability in the regulatory review process, OIRA shall be governed by the following disclosure requirements:

(A) Only the Administrator of OIRA (or a particular designee) shall receive oral communications initiated by persons not employed by the executive branch of the Federal Government regarding the substance of a regulatory action under OIRA review;

(B) All substantive communications between OIRA personnel and persons not employed by the executive branch of the Federal Government regarding a regulatory action under review shall be governed by the following guidelines:

(i) A representative from the issuing agency shall be invited to any meeting between OIRA personnel and such person(s);

(ii) OIRA shall forward to the issuing agency, within 10 working days of receipt of the communication(s), all written communications, regardless of format, between OIRA personnel and any person who is not employed by the executive branch of the Federal Government, and the dates and names of individuals involved in all substantive oral communications (including meetings to which an agency representative was invited, but did not attend, and telephone conversations between OIRA personnel and any such persons); and

(iii) OIRA shall publicly disclose relevant information about such communication(s), as set forth below in subsection (b)(4)(C) of this section.

(C) OIRA shall maintain a publicly available log that shall contain, at a minimum, the following information pertinent to regulatory actions under review:

(i) The status of all regulatory actions, including if (and if so, when and by whom) Vice Presidential and Presidential consideration was requested;

(ii) A notation of all written communications forwarded to an issuing agency under subsection (b)(4)(B)(ii) of this section; and

(iii) The dates and names of individuals involved in all substantive oral communications, including meetings and telephone conversations, between OIRA personnel and any person not employed by the executive branch of the Federal Government, and the subject matter discussed during such communications

(D) After the regulatory action has been published in the **Federal Register** or otherwise issued to the public, or after the agency has announced its decision not to publish or issue the regulatory action, OIRA shall make available to the public all documents exchanged between OIRA and the agency during the review by OIRA under this section.

(5) All information provided to the public by OIRA shall be in plain, understandable language.

Section 7. *Resolution of Conflicts.* To the extent permitted by law, disagreements or conflicts between or among agency heads or between OMB and any agency that cannot be resolved by the Administrator of OIRA shall be resolved by the President, or by the Vice President acting at the request of the President, with the relevant agency head (and, as appropriate, other interested government officials). Vice Presidential and Presidential consideration of such disagreements may be initiated only by the Director, by the head of the issuing agency, or by the head of an agency that has a significant interest in the regulatory action at issue. Such review will not be undertaken at the request of other persons, entities, or their agents.

Resolution of such conflicts shall be informed by recommendations developed by the Vice President, after consultation with the Advisors (and other executive branch officials or personnel whose responsibilities to the President include the subject matter at issue). The development of these recommendations shall be concluded within 60 days after review has been requested.

During the Vice Presidential and Presidential review period, communications with any person not employed by the Federal Government relating to the substance of the regulatory action under review and directed to the Advisors or their staffs or to the staff of the Vice President shall be in writing and shall be forwarded by the recipient to the affected agency(ies) for inclusion in the public docket(s). When the communication is not in writing, such Advisors or staff members shall inform the outside party that the matter is under review and that any comments should be submitted in writing.

At the end of this review process, the President, or the Vice President acting at the request of the President, shall notify the affected agency and the Administrator of OIRA of the President's decision with respect to the matter.

Section 8. *Publication.* * * *

Section 9. *Agency Authority.* Nothing in this order shall be construed as displacing the agencies' authority or responsibilities, as authorized by law.

Section 10. *Judicial Review.* Nothing in this Executive order shall affect any otherwise available judicial review of agency action. This Executive order is intended only to improve the internal management of the Federal Government and does not create any right or benefit, substantive or procedural, enforceable at law or equity by a party against the United States, its agencies or instrumentalities, its officers or employees, or any other person.

Section 11. *Revocations.* Executive Orders Nos. 12291 and 12498; all amendments to those Executive orders; all guidelines issued under those orders; and any exemptions from those orders heretofore granted for any category of rule are revoked.

> WILLIAM CLINTON
>
> THE WHITE HOUSE
>
> SEPTEMBER 30, 1993.

Executive Order 13563; 76 Fed. Reg. 3821, January 21, 2011

By the authority vested in me as President by the Constitution and the laws of the United States of America, and in order to improve regulation and regulatory review, it is hereby ordered as follows:

Section 1. *General Principles of Regulation.* (a) Our regulatory system must protect public health, welfare, safety, and our environment while promoting economic growth, innovation, competitiveness, and job creation. It must be based on the best available science. It must allow for public participation and an open exchange of ideas. It must promote predictability and reduce uncertainty. It must identify and use the best, most innovative, and least burdensome tools for achieving regulatory ends. It must take into account benefits and costs, both quantitative and qualitative. It must ensure that regulations are accessible, consistent, written in plain language, and easy to understand. It must measure, and seek to improve, the actual results of regulatory requirements.

(b) This order is supplemental to and reaffirms the principles, structures, and definitions governing contemporary regulatory review that were established in Executive Order 12866 of September 30, 1993. As stated in that Executive Order and to the extent permitted by law, each agency must, among other things: (1) propose or adopt a regulation only upon a reasoned determination that its benefits justify its costs (recognizing that some benefits and costs are difficult to quantify); (2) tailor its regulations to impose the least burden on society, consistent with obtaining regulatory objectives, taking into account, among other things, and to the extent practicable, the costs of cumulative regulations; (3) select, in choosing among alternative regulatory approaches, those approaches that maximize net benefits (including potential economic, environmental, public health and safety, and other advantages; distributive impacts; and equity); (4) to the extent feasible, specify performance objectives, rather than specifying the behavior or manner of compliance that regulated entities must adopt; and (5) identify and assess available alternatives to direct regulation, including providing economic incentives to encourage the desired behavior, such as user fees or marketable permits, or providing information upon which choices can be made by the public.

(c)   In applying these principles, each agency is directed to use the best available techniques to quantify anticipated present and future benefits and costs as accurately as possible. Where appropriate and permitted by law, each agency may consider (and discuss qualitatively) values that are difficult or impossible to quantify, including equity, human dignity, fairness, and distributive impacts.

Section 2. *Public Participation.* (a) Regulations shall be adopted through a process that involves public participation. To that end, regulations shall be based, to the extent feasible and consistent with law, on the open exchange of information and perspectives among State, local, and tribal officials, experts in relevant disciplines, affected stakeholders in the private sector, and the public as a whole.

(b)   To promote that open exchange, each agency, consistent with Executive Order 12866 and other applicable legal requirements, shall endeavor to provide the public with an opportunity to participate in the regulatory process. To the extent feasible and permitted by law, each agency shall afford the public a meaningful opportunity to comment through the Internet on any proposed regulation, with a comment period that should generally be at least 60 days. To the extent feasible and permitted by law, each agency shall also provide, for both proposed and final rules, timely online access to the rulemaking docket on regulations.gov, including relevant scientific and technical findings, in an open format that can be easily searched and downloaded. For proposed rules, such access shall include, to the extent feasible and permitted by law, an opportunity for public comment on all pertinent parts of the rulemaking docket, including relevant scientific and technical findings.

(c)   Before issuing a notice of proposed rulemaking, each agency, where feasible and appropriate, shall seek the views of those who are likely to be affected, including those who are likely to benefit from and those who are potentially subject to such rulemaking.

Section 3. *Integration and Innovation.* Some sectors and industries face a significant number of regulatory requirements, some of which may be redundant, inconsistent, or overlapping. Greater coordination across agencies could reduce these requirements, thus reducing costs and simplifying and harmonizing rules. In developing regulatory actions and identifying appropriate approaches, each agency shall attempt to promote such coordination, simplification, and harmonization. Each agency shall also seek to identify, as appropriate, means to achieve regulatory goals that are designed to promote innovation.

Section 4. *Flexible Approaches.* Where relevant, feasible, and consistent with regulatory objectives, and to the extent permitted by law, each agency shall identify and consider regulatory approaches that reduce burdens and maintain flexibility and freedom of choice for the public. These approaches include warnings, appropriate default rules, and disclosure requirements as well as provision of information to the public in a form that is clear and intelligible.

Section 5. *Science.* Consistent with the President's Memorandum for the Heads of Executive Departments and Agencies, "Scientific Integrity" (March 9, 2009), and its implementing guidance, each agency shall ensure the objectivity of any scientific and technological information and processes used to support the agency's regulatory actions.

Section 6. *Retrospective Analyses of Existing Rules.* (a) To facilitate the periodic review of existing significant regulations, agencies shall consider how best to promote retrospective analysis of rules that may be outmoded, ineffective, insufficient, or excessively burdensome, and to modify, streamline, expand, or repeal them in accordance with what has been learned. Such retrospective analyses, including supporting data, should be released online whenever possible.

(b) Within 120 days of the date of this order, each agency shall develop and submit to the Office of Information and Regulatory Affairs a preliminary plan, consistent with law and its resources and regulatory priorities, under which the agency will periodically review its existing significant regulations to determine whether any such regulations should be modified, streamlined, expanded, or repealed so as to make the agency's regulatory program more effective or less burdensome in achieving the regulatory objectives.

Section 7. *General Provisions.* (a) For purposes of this order, "agency" shall have the meaning set forth in section 3(b) of Executive Order 12866.

(b) Nothing in this order shall be construed to impair or otherwise affect:

    (i)   authority granted by law to a department or agency, or the head thereof; or

    (ii) functions of the Director of the Office of Management and Budget relating to budgetary, administrative, or legislative proposals.

(c) This order shall be implemented consistent with applicable law and subject to the availability of appropriations.

(d) This order is not intended to, and does not, create any right or benefit, substantive or procedural, enforceable at law or in equity by any party against the United States, its departments, agencies, or entities, its officers, employees, or agents, or any other person.

BARACK OBAMA

THE WHITE HOUSE

JANUARY 18, 2011.

INDEX

References are to Pages